b

The accepted name for money in Latin America.

When you take **Thomas Cook** travellers cheques, you can be assured of a travellers cheque service second to none. **Thomas Cook** travellers cheques are available in a wide range of currencies at your local **Thomas Cook** office or bank. In Latin America, we recommend US$ cheques as the most acceptable currency in the area. Our cheques are encashable at most banks and Casas de Cambio.

If your travellers cheques should be lost or stolen, please contact Emergency Assistance Points, listed at end of book, located in most cities on the Continent.

Thomas Cook
Travellers Cheques
A member of Midland Bank Group

c

The 1979
South American
Handbook

(A traveller's guide to
Latin America and the Caribbean)

*"When I was but thirteen or so
I went into a golden land;
Chimborazo, Cotopaxi
Took me by the hand."*
— W. J. Turner

The 1979 South American Handbook

FIFTY-FIFTH ANNUAL EDITION

Editor　　　　　JOHN BROOKS
Associate Editor　JOYCE CANDY

Trade & Travel Publications, Bath

TRADE & TRAVEL PUBLICATIONS LTD
THE MENDIP PRESS, PARSONAGE LANE
BATH BA1 1EN, ENGLAND
TEL. 0225 64156   TELEX 44600 SOWPAL G

© Trade & Travel Publications Ltd., 1978

55th Annual Edition, published December 1978

ISBN 0 900751 088

United States and Canada distribution by
Rand McNally & Company,
Chicago, New York, San Francisco

Front Cover: Folk-dancers in the Zócalo, Mexico City

Printed in Great Britain by
Richard Clay (The Chaucer Press) Ltd, Bungay, Suffolk

CONTENTS

Lloyds Bank International.

LBI is the international bank of the Lloyds Bank Group and has 187 offices in 42 countries across 5 continents.

Through its subsidiary, the Bank of London & South America, LBI is the only British bank with a branch network covering virtually the whole of Latin America.

Our special knowledge of the people, the markets and local conditions make us uniquely well-equipped to help international companies in import and export arrangements, introducing capital, securing local finance, etc.

Please contact us if you believe we could assist or advise you.

LLOYDS BANK INTERNATIONAL

40/66 Queen Victoria St., London EC4P 4EL. Tel: 01-248 9822
A member of the Lloyds Bank Group

LBI, the Bank of London & South America and their subsidiaries have offices in:
Argentina, Australia, Bahamas, Bahrain, Belgium, Brazil, Canada, Cayman Islands, Colombia, Costa Rica, Ecuador, Egypt, El Salvador, France, Federal Republic of Germany, Guatemala, Guernsey, Honduras, Hong Kong, Iran, Japan, Jersey, Lebanon, Malaysia, Mexico, Monaco, Netherlands, New Zealand, Nicaragua, Panama, Paraguay, Peru, Philippines, Portugal, Singapore, Spain, Switzerland, United Kingdom, U.S.A., U.S.S.R., Uruguay, Venezuela.

PREFACE

THIS YEAR THE MOST NOTICEABLE INNOVATIONS in the *Handbook* are in presentation, rather than in content. Firstly, the book has been reset using the latest electronic photo-typesetting equipment; this is particularly useful for an annual publication because it greatly simplifies the handling of the updating process. Secondly, in the interest of reducing bulk, we have increased the number of abbreviations used in hotel lists: s = single, d = double, p.p. = per person, p.r. = per room.

Early in 1978 the Editor visited Mexico for the first time, and enjoyed short stays in the Dominican Republic, Puerto Rico and Trinidad, so he has been able to make some amendments from first-hand. He would here like to express his warmest thanks to the Mexican Consejo Nacional de Turismo, and particularly to Sres. Javier Rivas and René Ruiz Escalante in Mexico City, and Miss Mona King and her staff in London (who also most kindly provided the cover photograph), for all the assistance so kindly given and all the facilities so generously made available for the trip.

Improvements in content in this issue include a revised map for Buenos Aires and new ones for Cuzco, Easter Island and Santo Domingo, drawn by Valerie Millington; an account by the explorer and writer Christopher Portway of a surviving stretch of the royal Inca road in central Peru; an expansion by Susan Pierres of the sections on Curaçao, Aruba and Bonaire; and additional information on Guyana by Elizabeth Allen. We are most grateful to them, to the Editor's colleagues in LBI Economics Department for doing the sub-editing, to our regular correspondents, and finally to our army of voluntary contributors, who find time during their fascinating journeys to write and bring us up to date; names will be found at the end of each country section.

Two further points, in conclusion. Firstly, we have been asked to stress the growth of "overland" travel, by four-wheel-drive vehicles in places where ordinary cars and buses cannot go, and of specialized companies in this field. These companies tended to concentrate until recently on the Middle East, Africa and Asia; they are now giving much more attention to Latin America. Three London-based overland companies are as follows: Encounter Overland, 280 Old Brompton Road, SW5; Penn Overland Tours, 122 Knightsbridge, SW1; Aardvaark Expeditions, 14 Coleridge Road, N8. Similar companies are established in most important cities round the world.

Secondly, the problem of malaria. It used to be thought that this disease had been virtually conquered in Latin America, except for the remotest jungle areas. However, every year more travellers seem to be contracting it, and the British Department of Health has warned that it may be caught in virtually any jungle or swampy region in the tropics. This means that apart from Argentina, Chile and Uruguay, the low-lying regions of any Latin American country—outside the big cities and the more arid areas—could be malarious, and the use of one of the recognized prophylactic regimes is most urgently advised for anyone visiting those regions.

THE EDITOR

ACKNOWLEDGEMENTS

WE HAVE RESUMED our previous practice (up to 1975), bowing to popular demand, of acknowledging the great help received from travellers' letters at the end of the country sections concerned, instead of in one alphabetical list as in 1976-78. We would however like to thank here the following: John Lewis, for a wealth of hotel information; and Fergus Flynn, Dean Frank Macgregor and Richard and Ela Salvage.

(Incidentally, contrary to what some correspondents imagine, we do receive letters from British travellers. The reason why we don't follow their names in the lists by "(UK)" is that their Britishness is assumed in the absence of any specific label; this is, after all, a British publication.)

Those who use this book should know . . .

. . . that it is being revised continuously, right up to the day when it streams off the presses in the early autumn of each year. Facts no longer true are deleted, new facts are added, maps are changed for the better, whole passages and sometimes whole chapters are rewritten. You may very well hand this book on to a friend about to visit Latin America.

On second thoughts, make him a present of the current edition—yours may be out of date

INTRODUCTION
AND GENERAL HINTS

THIS BOOK tells the visitor whether sightseer or businessman, what he most needs to know. Each chapter on each country runs more or less to a pattern. It opens with a physical description of the country, its people, its history and its present form of government. This section is designed to show the reader how the inhabitants, by their history, racial admixture and employment dictated by natural resources, soil and climate, have come to be what they are. This is important in Latin America where, despite superficial similarities, countries are as different from one another as in Europe. There follows a survey of the towns, in separate areas where the areas within a country (as in Argentina and Brazil) are different in kind, but always, within the country or region, along lines of travel by road or railway or both. Under each town particulars are given of what is worth seeing, and what services there are in the way of banks, chambers of commerce, cable offices, hotels, restaurants, entertainments, etc., likely to be of use to the visitor. There follows an account of the country's economy, and each chapter ends with "Information for Visitors", giving details about the best time for visiting a country and how it can be visited by sea or land or air, what documents are necessary, what clothes should be worn, what the food is like, what health precautions should be taken, what the currency regulations are (at the time of going to press), and much else.

Travel to and in Latin America Under "Information for Visitors" you are told the best way of reaching each country by air, by sea, or by land from neighbouring countries. All the main airline and shipping companies plying to and from Latin America are given in separate sections at the end of the book, and are given again in "Information for Visitors". Air companies will only allow a certain weight of luggage without a surcharge; this is normally 30 kg. for first class and 20 kg. for economy class, but these limits are often not strictly enforced when it is known that the plane is not going to be full. On the other hand, weight limits for internal flights are often lower; best to enquire beforehand. These sections also tell you how many cigarettes, how much tobacco or drink you can take free into each country, and we also say what the taxi fare should be between the airport you arrive at and the city you are going to. (This is often a racket, but there is always a local bus between airport and city, if you are travelling fairly light.) Some airports have a very high tax on leaving. Within each country there are fairly cheap air services to any place where there is an airstrip. If you buy internal airline tickets in South American countries you may find cash refunds difficult to get if you change your plans. Better to change your ticket for a different one.

There is as yet no easy, cheap way of flying directly to Latin America from Europe. Part-charters are strongly resisted by the local airlines, which at present lack the spare capacity to attract their share of this traffic. There are, however, various ways of getting there more cheaply than by 45-day excursion flight:

(i) From Luxembourg to Barbados by International Caribbean Airways, and then on to Caracas (cheaper *via* Trinidad and Maturín than direct), or from

Luxembourg to Bahamas by Air Bahama for about US$220 s. A Laker ABC flight London (Gatwick)—Barbados, operated by Caribbean Airways, costs from £189 return.

(ii) Advance Booking Charter by British Airways, or a full charter flight to Trinidad. Book 3 months in advance. Then flights to Maturín, Caracas or Curaçao. KLM flies direct from the Netherlands to Curaçao.

(iii) From London to New York by cheap charter flight (about US$250 return), then to Miami (US$60), then to Barranquilla by Aero-cóndor (US$180 s); these flights go on to Bogotá. There will no doubt be cheap charter flights direct to Miami in the near future; check on this. Trailfinders, 48 Earl's Court Road, London W.8. (Tel.: 01-937 9631) are helpful.

(iv) Loftleidir Icelandic Airways still fly (rather slowly) between London and New York at prices well below the normal jet flights. There is also the Laker Airways "Skytrain" between London (Gatwick) and New York (US$118 s), and Gatwick, San Francisco and Los Angeles. British Caledonian fly between London and Houston (Texas) for about US$260 return. From New York, if you have unlimited time, you can take a Greyhound bus all the way to Mexico City.

(v) There are several cheap French charters to Mexico, Guatemala, Colombia, Ecuador, Peru, Bolivia and the southern countries; the flights to Lima are exceptionally cheap. Try: Le Point, 4 rue des Orphelins, 68200 Mulhouse; or Uniclam-Voyages, 63 rue Monsieur-le Prince, 75006 Paris.

Pay as you go along   We advise those people who travel the cheap way in Latin America to pay for all transport as they go along, and not in advance. Wait until you are inside a country before you buy transport. This applies to buses, trains, and flights. As a general rule international flights are very much dearer than flights over the same distance within one country, and in some countries are dearer still because of taxes on air passages.

The one exception to this general principle is in transatlantic flights; here money is saved by booking as far as possible in one operation. We are told, for example, that London-Foz do Iguaçu is cheaper by US$20 than London-São Paulo and São Paulo-Foz do Iguaçu.

The national airlines of Argentina, Colombia and Venezuela operate schemes for unlimited travel within those countries at a set price. See the respective country sections.

There is also an "Amerailpass", giving unlimited travel on the railways of Argentina, Bolivia, Brazil, Chile, Paraguay and Uruguay, which can be bought for one (US$80) two (US$110) or three (US$140) months. Payment must be in U.S. dollars.

Warning   Many countries in Latin America are reluctant to let travellers enter their territory if they do not already have outward tickets. (Look under "Information for Visitors" sections for the countries you intend to visit.) This burdensome condition can sometimes be got over by applying to their respective Consuls for notes stating that you have the necessary money to buy the tickets. Other travellers have told us that the purchase of a Miscellaneous Charges Order (open ticket) from an IATA airline for (say) US$100 will satisfy this requirement in almost all countries; it can be exchanged for a ticket or cashed at the airline offices in the country of issue.

Money can be carried in the form of U.S. dollar travellers' cheques or letters of credit. Other currencies are not recommended. Travellers' cheques are very convenient but they have two disadvantages: they attract thieves (though refunds can of course be arranged) and you will find that they are sometimes discounted, and may be difficult to change in small towns. Some places in Brazil do not honour them, nor will the hydrofoil company between Buenos Aires and Montevideo. Letters of credit are less convenient—fewer banks are now issuing them and they cannot be changed outside banks so the black market is closed to you—but they are of no use to a thief. Though the risk of loss is greater, many travellers take part of their funds in U.S. dollar notes, for which better rates can usually be obtained than for travellers' cheques. Small U.S. dollar bills are very useful for shopping: shopkeepers and exchange shops (*Casas de Cambio*) tend to give better exchange rates than hotels or banks. The better hotels will normally change travellers' cheques for their guests, but if you're travelling on the cheap it is essential to keep in funds; watch weekends and public holidays carefully and never run out of local currency. Mr. John Wiseman suggests that if one is desperate at 0100 in the morning, sailors' bars are good places to change foreign currency—as long as one isn't too well dressed and can "sink into the background". Take plenty of local currency when making trips into the interior. We are told that in Argentina, outside Buenos Aires, only the foreign banks will readily negotiate travellers' cheques.

Take your credit cards to Latin America; there are many outlets for their use. American Express, Carte Blanche and Diners' Club are very useful, and so are cards affiliated to the Visa system (in Britain, Barclaycard) and (somewhat less so) the Master Charge group (in Britain, Access). If you take them, however, make sure you know the correct procedures to follow if they are lost or stolen.

A list of American Express agents will be found at the end of each chapter, and one of Diners' Club agents at the end of the book. These can change at short notice, however.

American Express offices in the main cities (except in Brazil) will provide, on demand, up to US$500 in travellers' cheques, or the equivalent in local currency, on the basis of a cheque drawn on a U.S. bank account.

We recommend in general the use of American Express travellers' cheques, but should point out that less commission is often charged on Citibank or Bank of America travellers' cheques, if they are cashed at Latin American branches of those banks. These cheques are certainly generally accepted, even though they may not be as well known outside banks as those of American Express.

In those countries where there is a black market, find out how much of their currency you are allowed to take in, *and buy before you enter,* preferably at a big city where banks are unlikely to make a charge on the transaction. (In small places the bank may charge up to 50 cents on a 10-dollar travellers' cheque.) There is always an active (but illegal) black market in local currency in all those countries that have no free exchange; it is, however, not illegal to buy currency outside the country you are about to enter, up to any limit that may be imposed.

N.B.   If you are having additional sums of money sent out during a tour of Latin America, try to have it sent to one of the countries with the fewest exchange controls, where you can exchange dollar travellers' cheques for dollars cash; at present these are Bolivia, Ecuador, Panama, Uruguay and Venezuela. These countries, and Paraguay, are also good for buying other Latin American currencies at favourable rates.

Whenever you leave a country, sell what money you have in its currency before leaving, because the further away you get, the less the value of a country's money. In general this is true of all Latin American countries.

Americans (we are told) should know that if they run out of funds they can expect no help from the U.S. Embassy or Consul other than a referral to some welfare organization.

Costs   It seems, from travellers' accounts, that it is still possible to travel through Latin America (or at least Mexico, Central America and the Andean countries) spending no more for basic outgoings (travel, food and shelter) than US$12-15 p.p. per week. This presupposes hitch-hiking and free camping; if putting up in hotels and travelling by bus you would need to raise it to at least US$20-25.

Passports   Remember that Latin Americans, especially officials, are very document-minded. You should always carry your passport in a safe place about your person; you never know when you might need to prove your identity.

Identity and Membership Cards   Membership cards of British, European and US motoring organizations have been found useful for discounts off maps, towing charges, etc. Student cards must carry a photograph if they are to be of any use in Latin America.

Law Enforcement   Whereas in Europe and North America we are accustomed to law enforcement on a systematic basis, in general, enforcement in Latin America is achieved by periodic campaigns. The most typical is a round-up of criminals in the cities just before Christmas. In December, therefore, you may well be asked for identification at any time, and if you cannot produce it, you will be jailed. Similarly you might drive through red lights for years with impunity, but on the day they have a campaign, you will be jailed on the spot and the car will be impounded. At first sight, on arrival, it may seem that you can flout the law with impunity, because everybody else is obviously doing so. Nevertheless, to be jailed is a serious matter, and is not to be taken lightly. If a visitor is jailed his friends should take him food every day. Even if the officials say the prisoner is well fed, food should still be taken to him, because they may have said he is being well fed just to comfort the visitor, when, in fact, the prisoner is receiving nothing at all. This is especially important for people on a diet, such as diabetics. It must also be borne in mind that in the event of a vehicle accident in which anyone is injured, all drivers involved are automatically detained until blame has been established, and this does not usually take less than two weeks. Sometimes these problems can be avoided by offering a bribe, but this, naturally, is illegal and is therefore extremely dangerous. Never offer a bribe, unless you are fully conversant and up-to-date with the customs of the country. Wait until the official makes the suggestion, or offer money in some form which is apparently not bribery, e.g. "In our country we have a system of on-the-spot fines. Is there a similar system here?" Do not assume that an official who accepts a bribe is prepared to do anything else which is illegal. You bribe him to persuade him to do his job, or to persuade him not to do it, or to do it more quickly, or more slowly. You do not bribe him to do something which is against the law. The mere suggestion would make him very upset.

Assaults   Assaults on travellers are becoming depressingly frequent, usually with robbery as a motive. Try and look as little like a tourist as possible, especially in poor areas of cities; hide your main cash supply under your clothes; keep cameras in bags or briefcases; take spare spectacles (eyeglasses); distribute your cash and cheques between several different hiding places, etc., don't wear wrist-watches or jewellery. If attacked, remember your assailants will almost certainly be armed, and don't resist. Certain cities—Panama City, Cartagena, Bogotá, Cali, Buenaventura, Medellín, Callao, Cuzco, Guayaquil—are particularly notorious. When you have all your luggage with you, be especially careful and don't get into arguments—or even conversations—with any locals if you can help it. They may be trying just to distract your attention.

Hotels We give information about all kinds of hotels: the luxurious, the good, and the cheap. We do the same for restaurants. We give information about what taxis cost, what road services and night-clubs and entertainments there are. For those who want them we give cheap hotels, cheap eating places and cheap buses to take them from place to place.The cheap hotels will probably lack hot water, but if they do not, we say so. A cheap but not bad hotel might run to US$5 a night in Mexico or Brazil, but is less in Argentina (US$3) and the Andean countries (US$1.50-2). For the indigent, it is a good idea to ask for a boarding house—*casa de huéspedes, hospedaje, pensión, casa familial* or *residencial,* according to country—rather than a hotel. A useful tip: ask the Hertz employee at the airport when you arrive—as long as he's not busy renting cars!

We should warn readers here that hotel prices in most countries have been seriously affected by inflation—even in the US-dollar terms we adopt. Many of our prices will therefore be seriously out-of-date by the time this edition is published.

Youth Hostels Organizations affiliated to the Youth Hostels movement exist in Argentina, Brazil, Chile and Uruguay. Further information in the country sections.

Meals In all republics breakfast usually means coffee or tea with rolls and butter, but hotels will give something more substantial if it is asked for. Lunch *(almuerzo)* is served from 1200 to 1400 or sometimes 1500; dinner *(comida* or *cena)* is rarely before 1900, sometimes (as in Peru and Bolivia) not until 2000 and is then served until about 2200. Dinner tends to be late because shows rarely start before 2100. Afternoon tea (called "lunch" in Brazil and Peru) can be got in all the main cities. There is a paragraph on each nation's food under "Information for Visitors". For reliable cheap meals, look in and near the markets.

Travelling with Children We are grateful to Tim and Arlene Frost, of New Zealand, for the following notes:

People contemplating overland travel in South America with children should take into account the fact that a lot of time can be spent waiting for buses, trains, and especially for aeroplanes (which seldom, if ever, leave on time). On buses, journeys are generally long; if the children are good at amusing themselves, or can readily sleep while travelling, the problems can be considerably lessened. Travel on trains, while not as fast or at times as comfortable as buses, allows more scope for moving about. Some trains, notably in Peru, provide tables between pairs of seats, so that games, cards, etc. can be played.

Food can be a problem if the children are not adaptable. It is easier to take biscuits, drinks, bread etc. with you on longer trips than to rely on meal stops where the food may not be to taste. A small immersion heater and jug for making hot drinks is invaluable, but remember that electric current varies. A 220v heater can work on 110v (slowly), but not vice versa.

Fares On all long-distance buses you pay for each seat, and there are no half-fares if all children occupy a seat each. For shorter trips it is cheaper, if less comfort-able, to sit small children on your knee. Often there are spare seats which children can occupy after tickets have been collected, though this is rare in Peru, where buses are more crowded. In city and local excursion buses, small children generally do not pay a fare, but are not entitled to a seat when paying customers are standing. On sightseeing tours you should *always* bargain for a family rate—often children can go free.

Trains have half-fares for children in all countries—up to 10 years in some, up to 12 in others. Exception is service from Cuzco to Machu Picchu. In Bolivia children pay 75% fare on *ferrobuses*.

All civil airlines charge half for children under 12, but some military services don't have ½-fares, or have younger age limits. Again in Bolivia, children's fares on Lloyd Aéreo Boliviano are considerably more than half, and there is only a 7kg. baggage allowance. (Lloyd also checks children's ages on passports.)

Hotels In all hotels, bargain for rates. If charges are per person, always insist that two children will occupy one bed only, therefore counting as one tariff. If rates are per bed, the same applies. In either case you can almost always get a reduced rate at cheaper hotels.

Generally, travel with children presents no special problems—in fact the path is often smoother for family groups. Officials at borders and in government offices tend to be more amenable where children are concerned. Moreover, even thieves and pickpockets in South America seem to have some of the traditional respect for families, and may leave you alone because of it!

Camping Becoming more and more common throughout Latin America with new sites (campgrounds) opening every year. Peter Ford and Sally Wilson tell us that they camped everywhere, from Mexico down to Bolivia (except Panama and Colombia), anywhere from idyllic meadows to rubbish tips to main plazas, and never had any trouble or anything stolen. Gas cylinders and bottles may not be exchangeable, but can be recharged; specify whether you have butane or propane.

Souvenirs Remember that these can almost invariably be bought more cheaply away from the capital, though on the other hand the choice may be less wide. Bargaining seems to be the general rule in most countries' street markets, but don't try it in supermarkets. Americans should remember that souvenirs made from, for example, sea-turtle shells may not be imported into the US, under the Endangered Species Act of 1973, and are advised to ask the US Fish and Wildlife Service (Department of the Interior), Washington D.C. 20240, for a complete list of the endangered species concerned.

Mail Some travellers recommend that mail should be sent to one's Embassy (or, if a client, American Express agent, though make sure your address list is up-to-date) rather than to the Poste Restante (Lista de Correos) department of a country's Post Office. If there seems to be no mail at the Lista under the initial letter of your surname, ask them to look under the initial of your forename—or even your middle name. You may be surprised—and gratified—at the result!

Travellers' Appearance It is regrettable, but none the less true, that a prejudice has grown up among the authorities of several Latin American countries against young male travellers with long hair, beards, and hippy-style clothes. Travellers of this description are therefore strongly recommended, in their own interests, to moderate their hair and dress styles. There is also a prejudice against rucksacks or back-packs; suitcases may be more cumbersome but are certainly more acceptable to officialdom. A combination back-pack/suitcase, which sounds like the ideal arrangement, is now available, at least in North America; apparently not in Europe. One tip we have received; young people of informal dress and life-style may find it advantageous to procure a letter from someone in an official position—JP, MP, Senator, Congressman, police chief—testifying to their good character, on official-looking notepaper!

Some countries have laws (*e.g.* Venezuela) or prejudices (*e.g.* Argentina) against the wearing by civilians of khaki army-surplus clothing.

Drugs Users of drugs, even of soft ones, without medical prescription should be particularly careful, as some countries impose heavy penalties—up to ten years' imprisonment—for even the simple possession of such substances. "Hippies" are often automatically suspect in this connection; another reason for moderating hair and dress styles.

Clothing Study the temperature charts near the end of this book, and remember that in the high Andes it can be bitterly cold at night. A warm woollen garment and preferably also a blanket is required.

Toilets (apologies in advance to the sensitive). Many of the cheap hotels have poor water supplies. This may mean that used toilet paper should not be flushed down the pan, but thrown in the receptacle provided. This is not very sanitary, of course, but a blocked pan or drain is infinitely more of a health risk.

Cockroaches These are ubiquitous and unpleasant, but not dangerous. Take some insecticide powder if staying in cheap hotels; Baylon (Bayer) has been recommended.

Language "Without a good knowledge of Spanish you can become very frustrated and feel helpless in many situations. But sometimes knowing none at all is an even greater help"—Mr. and Mrs. Clive Foot.

The basic Spanish of Latin America is that of south-western Spain, with soft "c's" and "z's" pronounced as "s", and not as "th" as in the other parts of Spain. There are several regional variations in pronunciation, particularly in the River Plate countries, which are noted in the Argentine section "Information for Visitors". However, Castilian Spanish is readily understood. Differences in vocabulary also exist, but they are no more numerous than those between English and American English. Always remember that it is possible to speak Spanish in Brazil if you first apologize for not being able to speak Portuguese; you will be understood but you may not be able (because Portuguese uses on the whole fewer syllables than Spanish, and pronounciation is different) to understand the answers!

Courtesy Remember that politeness—even a little ceremoniousness—is much appreciated in Latin America, and is certainly useful when dealing with officials of any description. Michael Davison makes the following suggestions: men should always remove their headgear when entering offices, and be prepared to shake hands (this is much commoner in Latin America than in Europe or North America); always say "Buenos días" or "Buenos tardes" and wait for a reply before proceeding further; always remember that the traveller from abroad has enjoyed greater advantages in life than most Latin American minor officials, and should be kindly and tolerant in consequence.

Explorers The South American Explorers' Club has been established at Avenida Portugal 146 (Casilla 3714), Lima, Peru (Telephone: 31-44-80.) For further details see page 566.

Photography Take as much film in from Europe and the USA as you can; it is expensive everywhere except Panama, where all luxuries are cheap, and Argentina, where it is made locally (Ferrania). When walking through poor districts, remember that a camera is the badge of the rich tourist; hide it in a case or bag. Camera-snatching is common: a carrying chain instead of a strap could be helpful. Photographers are warned that the ordinary ultra-violet filter will not cut down the ever-present tropical haze; especially in the highlands, you may need a neutral density filter. A polarizing lens has also been recommended for heightening the colour.

Surface Transport The continent has a growing road system for motor traffic. The roads are given in the text. There are frequent bus services on most of them. Accommodation is often more than adequately comfortable; Argentina, Brazil, Chile and Venezuela are the best; the other Andean countries are a long way behind, because of difficulties of terrain. Some services in Mexico and Central America are excellent. In montainous country, however, do not expect buses to get to their destination, after long journeys, anywhere near on time. When the journey takes more than 3 or 4 hours, meal stops at country inns, good and bad, are the rule. See what the locals are eating—and buy likewise. For drinks, stick to beer, coke, minerals or coffee (black). The stuff sold by vendors at bus stops cannot be trusted, though unpeeled fruit is of course reliable.

In most countries trains are slower than buses, and also less secure for luggage. They do tend, however, to provide finer scenery, and from them you can normally see much more wildlife than from the road—it is much less disturbed by one or two trains a day than by the more frequent road traffic.

When choosing a seat on a bus, remember that the window seat gives you views and rather more security for your valuables; the aisle seat gives you more leg-room.

Beware of Central American bus companies who claim to be in a position to sell tickets for travel in South American countries, which they don't themselves serve. In most cases they can't do this, and even if they can, the tickets will be much more expensive than if bought in the normal way.

Hitchhiking This custom is increasing in Latin America, and travellers have reported considerable success in virtually all countries. Argentina seems the easiest, and the northern Andean countries the most difficult. In Bolivia and the interior of Peru the budget traveller might try the paying cattletrucks if unsuccessful with "autostop". Half the price of buses.

Motoring The normal saloon car reaches most destinations of interest to the tourist. High ground clearance is useful for badly surfaced or unsurfaced roads. In some places, service is not available for sophisticated items like automatic transmission and fuel injection, so the simpler the car the better. It's an advantage if you can sleep comfortably in it; hence the liking for minibuses such as the VW. Four-wheel-drive vehicles are useful for the back country; on the other hand, luggage cannot be hidden, as in the boot of a car, so the contents are more susceptible to theft. Consider installing a large trunk to put your bags in.

Theft of all vehicles is common. Apply at least two anti-theft devices when parked, even in car parks, and remove easily detachable items such as hub-caps, mirrors and windscreen wipers. A policy of insurance may not satisfactorily solve the problem of a car stolen outside its country of origin. There will be a delay of at least a month in paying the claim, and the sum insured may be inadequate if the theft occurs in a country where cars are more expensive than in the country of origin. Import duty becomes payable on the stolen car, and again on any car bought for the return trip home. If, on the other hand, a cash settlement is made, there may be difficulties with exchange control. The same is largely true if a vehicle becomes a total loss in an accident.

Spare fuel should be in steel, not plastic, cans. You won't have travelled far before the plastic can will spring a leak, and there is danger of a spark from static electricity igniting the petrol when pouring. Furthermore, if you empty a plastic can at a high altitude and then replace the cap, it will implode on descent to sea level. (In Venezuela, it is illegal to carry petrol from a garage in a can without a permit from the police, and this can only be obtained after paying a fine of Bs 500 for running out of fuel.) In remote areas, gas stations are unmarked. Look for a building with empty oil drums outside or ask. In this connection, it is wise to carry a funnel and/or hose to help fill the tank; often in rural areas there are no pumps and fuel must be taken from a drum. If the motor fails after refuelling, the probability is that the petrol has been adulterated with a cheap substitute such as kerosene, or that there is water or dirt in the fuel. An in-line fuel filter is an advantage.

If the motor is not to fail at high altitudes, the spark must be advanced and cold spark plugs changed for hot. You can reduce the risk of a broken windscreen on gravel roads by reducing speed when other cars are passing. A reversing light is needed for driving on narrow mountain roads at night or in narrow unlit tunnels built on curves. Landslides are frequent in the mountains in the rainy season. Keep enough reserve of fuel to be able to turn back and take warm clothes and food in case you are delayed a day or so. The car is liable to be searched for arms and drugs with some frequency in certain areas.

In addition to the normal spares carried, fan belt, spark plugs etc. the more adventurous driver needs a spade, tow cable, planks for placing under the wheels when stuck in dust or sand, spare parts for the suspension and steering, and either an extra spare wheel or repair patches, air pump and valve screw. Help to repair a tyre is sometimes only available if you can provide these items yourself. An emergency fan belt which can be fitted without the use of tools is available from Flexicom Ltd, North Wing Mills, Bradford BD1 4EP, England.

If you are not a mechanic, or don't have one with you, try to get to know the general look of your engine so that at least you'll know after a repair if anything looks unfamiliar, and always get on chatty terms with the mechanics when you're having anything done to the car.

Make a check list to ensure you have everything before you start each journey. The list is also useful for establishing what it is essential to replace after the theft of a car's contents. If carrying a cooler for food and drink, any official on the highway who spots it is likely to ask for refreshments, so take plenty or you may end up with none for yourself.

The car freely crosses international frontiers without payment of customs duties provided it is eventually returned to its country of origin. In Central America, this is controlled by an entry made in your passport. In South America, it is controlled by a separate document, the Carnet de Passages en Douanes or Libreta de Pasos por Aduana, which must be stamped at both sides of each frontier. Failure to obtain a stamp will result in being turned back, perhaps after driving as much as 200 km, so it is important to find the Customs Offfice (Aduana) in order to avoid this inconvenience; it may be at the border or in the town nearest the border. Most countries have special (and cheaper) arrangements for motorists visiting neighbouring countries only.

A separate insurance policy has to be issued in each country if a claim is to be legally payable in the country where an accident occurs. Companies with the necessary international connections include American International Underwriters, Guardian Royal Exchange Assurance, AFIA and Saint Paul. Give them at least four months' notice of your requirements. Remember that in many countries third-party insurance for drivers may not be compulsory, or if compulsory, not enforced; you may have no claim on the other driver after an accident, except through the courts—a time-consuming exercise!

Finally, overland motorists would be very well advised to read *Overland and Beyond,* by Theresa and Jonathan Hewat, a young couple who motored round the world in 3½ years in a VW minibus. This little 80-page book, sold only by the authors from 106 West Street, Corfe Castle, Dorset BH20 5HE, England, contains a wealth of good sense on all aspects of overland motoring; cost £1.80, plus postage 20p (UK), 50p (Europe), 80p (outside Europe).

Gasoline prices vary considerably. Approximate prices per U.S. gallon are US$0.40-0.50 in the Andean countries, US$1.20-1.50 in Argentina and Uruguay, and US$2.00-2.50 in Brazil. In Peru it is now very expensive; the price rose in 1976 by over 400 per cent and again in 1978 by 50 per cent.

If driving and camping, the purchase of a 12-volt low-consumption neon light will add greatly to convenience.

If travelling from Europe with a car, do not go to Panama if you are going south. You will still have the Darien Gap to negotiate. Much better to take the ship to Curaçao, where there is a thrice-weekly car ferry to Venezuela for about US$50.

Motorcycling   Captain D. J. H. Collins, of the Royal Marines, who motorcycled from Buenos Aires to Barranquilla with three companions in 1974, has very kindly sent us some notes based on his experience:

Requirements for machine: Very strong frame and forks, low compression (poor-quality fuel), simple carburettor (frequent adjustment needed for altitude changes), high handlebars (easier for back), windscreen (protection from flying stones as well as cold), big seat, very efficient air filter (much dust) and oil cooler (there are hills!). The party used three Triumphs and a BSA.

Spares Needed: pistons and rings etc., valve springs etc., carburettor, coil, chains, tyres, tubes, wire, battery, points—in fact just about everything! Good spares backup at Devimead Ltd., Tamworth, Staffs.

Clothing and Equipment: Helmet, balaclava-type face scarf, goggles, visor, thick trousers, gauntlets and under-gloves, boots, anorak, jerseys, money-belt, sleeping-bag, spare food, lockable panniers for kit, first-aid kit, tools.

Repair Facilities: Hundreds of "bush" repair shops. But motorcycles are rare in Latin America outside cities. Best to do it yourself when you can.

Accommodation: What you can afford. Always bring bike inside at night and chain it up.

Principles: Let nothing and no-one deter you from getting there. Make sure you know some Spanish. Don't worry when lorries force you off the road three or four times a day, and if you fall off, just get on again. (Everyone does it.) Never think of carrying a firearm (this advice is confirmed by the Hewats in their book—see above). Never get angry.

Slight Difficulties: Hole in piston—lift in lorry to engineering shop—weld hole—fit car piston rings—push on! Robbery—remedy is never to travel alone; bikes should always be within sight or chained up under cover. Police at checkpoints expecting money—pretend ignorance of the language (in a friendly way).

Documentation: Carnet de Passages, international licence, passport, vaccination certificate, registration certificate, Hoja de Ruta in Bolivia.

Final Comment: You will be cold, sore, tired, wet, hot and fed up. You will also have the best time of your life!

Travelling between South America and Africa

Mr. Bill Roberts informs us that there is no regular passenger-ship service between South Africa and South America, though cruise ships do operate, mainly in December-February; Chandris Line has been mentioned in this connection.

There are direct air services linking South Africa and South America; six flights a week each way are operated by Varig, Pan Am and South African Airways between Johannesburg and Rio and two per week each way, Cape Town-Buenos Aires, by South African Airways and Aerolíneas. Air Maroc flies twice weekly between Casablanca and Rio-São Paulo.

(We have been informed that there is a US guide to Africa: "The Travellers' Africa", by P. M. Allen and A. Segal, published by Dutton. It appears not to be readily available in Europe, but the "Hitchhiker's Guide to Africa", published in Denmark in English and available from the Youth Hostels Association in John Adam Street, London WC2, has been recommended.)

Travelling between South America, Australia and New Zealand

There is one flight a week each way between Tahiti-Easter Island-Santiago operated by LAN Chile. The flight Tahiti-Lima operated by Air France is temporarily withdrawn, in spite of high demand on this route. Services on this route may be re-commenced by 1979; check with Air France offices. There are several air services from both countries to Tahiti. It is dearer to fly Australia-South Africa-South America, than Australia-Tahiti-Santiago. There are several air services from both countries to Tahiti. Various freighters ply between Australia/New Zealand and Europe *via* Panama, and take a few passengers. If taking a car, it is probably best to take a ship to Curaçao, where there is a thrice-weekly car ferry to Venezuela for US$50. Far cheaper than any way of crossing the Darien Gap from Panama.

Travel to the USA

Remember that all foreigners need visas to enter the USA. If you are thinking of visiting the USA after Latin America, you are strongly advised to get your visa while still in your own country, not while travelling.

Final Hints

After a long tour of South America by train and bus, Mrs. G. M. Walker, of Farncombe, wrote to us that the most useful thing she and her husband had taken was a small petrol stove (to which we would add: a combination canteen to go with it). The most useful things they wished they had taken (but did not) were air cushions for slatted seats, and heavy shoes or boots for muddy and uneven streets and country walking (and remember that footwear over 9½—English size (or 42—European size) is difficult to obtain in Latin America—except Argentina and Brazil). Other travellers have recommended taking a small 220v electric immersion heater for making hot drinks, fully waterproof top clothing (cape, hat, leggings), a plastic sheet 2 × 1 metres to cover possibly infested beds and shelter your luggage, a sheet, sleeping-bag, a mosquito net (or a hammock with fitted net), a clothes line, a nailbrush (useful for scubbing dirt off clothes as well as oneself), a vacuum flask, a light nylon waterproof shopping bag, a universal bath- and basin-plug (of the flanged type that will fit any waste-pipe), a ball of string, large penknife (preferably with tin and bottle openers and corkscrew—the famous Swiss Army knife has been repeatedly recommended, alarm clock and torch, also a padlock for the doors of the cheapest and most casual hotels. Useful medicaments are given at the end of the "Health Information" section (page 27); to these might be added some lip salve ("Lypsil" has been recommended). Always carry toilet paper with you; it can often be embarrassingly absent. Women travelling alone may find it useful to wear a wedding ring. You can always pretend to be on the point of meeting your husband, as a way of getting rid of a particularly adhesive admirer.

Be careful when asking directions. Many Latin Americans will give you the wrong answer rather than admit they do not know; this may be partly because they fear losing face, but is also because they like to please.

And the last word from Miss Charmian Bramwood, of Olivos, Argentina: "All women visiting South America should know how to cry. It is *very* useful at times!"

HEALTH INFORMATION

The following information has been very kindly compiled for us by Dr. David C. Snashall, M.B., Ch.B.(Ed.), M.R.C.P.(U.K.), who has confirmed his information with the Gorgas Hospital, Panama, and has since revised it thoroughly from experience gained from working in Peru. The vaccination schedule is that of the World Health Organization. The publishers have every confidence that the following information is correct, but cannot assume any direct responsibility in this connection.

THE TRAVELLER to Latin America is inevitably exposed to health risks not encountered in Britain or the U.S.A., especially if he spends time in the tropical regions. Epidemic diseases have been largely brought under control by vaccination programmes and public sanitation but, in rural areas, the latter is rudimentary and the chances of contracting infections of various sorts are much higher than at home.

There are English-speaking doctors in most major cities, If you fall ill the best plan is to attend the out-patient department of a local hospital or contact your Embassy representative for the name of a reputable doctor. Their practices vary from those at home but remember they have particular experience in dealing with locally-occurring diseases.

Self-medication is undesirable except for minor complaints but may be forced on you by circumstances. Whatever the circumstances, never let pharmacists prescribe medicines for you; many are poorly trained and unscrupulous enough to sell you potentially dangerous drugs or old stock they want to get rid of. The large number of pharmacies throughout Latin America is a considerable surprise to most people, as is the range of medicines you can purchase over the counter. Polypharmacy is a minor religion. Many drugs are manufactured under licence from American or European companies so the trade names may be familiar to you. This means that you do not need to carry a whole chest of medicines, but remember that the shelf-life of some items, especially vaccines and antibiotics, is markedly reduced in tropical conditions. Buy your necessary supplies at the better outlets where they have refrigerators, even though it is more expensive. Check the expiry date of all drugs you buy.

Immigration officials sometimes confiscate scheduled drugs (Lomotil is an example) if they are not accompanied by a doctor's signed prescription.

With the following precautions and advice, you should keep as healthy as usual. Make local enquiries about health risks if you are apprehensive and take the general advice of European and North American families who have lived or are living in the country.

Before you go take out medical insurance! You should have a dental check-up, obtain a spare glasses prescription and, if you suffer from a chronic illness (such as diabetes, high blood pressure, ear or sinus troubles, cardiopulmonary disease or a nervous disorder) arrange for a check-up with your doctor, who can at the same time provide you with a letter explaining the details of your disability, if possible in English and Spanish. Such a letter is extremely helpful.

Inoculations The following is the ideal programme for maximum immunity; it takes a long time and can be modified according to your particular circumstances. You may, for example, only need one booster dose of tetanus or polio vaccine. International certificates of vaccination are issued only for smallpox, yellow fever, and cholera, and immigration officials can insist they be produced. In the case of cholera this would happen only during an epidemic.

Week

1. *Yellow Fever* Advisable for anyone anticipating tropical conditions. Not to be given under 9 months of age. The inoculation is available at special centres only. Immunity lasts 10 years.
4. *Smallpox* Primary or re-vaccination. If contra-indicated, such as in persons with eczema, an exemption certificate can be obtained from your doctor and stamped by the Local Authority. The international certificate is valid for 3 years.
7. *Typhoid* (monovalent) (first). Paratyphoid inoculation (T.A.B.) is unreliable and no longer recommended. To maintain protection, a booster is required every year although immunity conferred by some of the newer vaccines lasts longer.
   Tetanus toxoid (first).
10. *Poliomyelitis* (oral trivalent) (first).
13. *Typhoid* (monovalent) (second).
   Tetanus toxoid (second).
16. *Poliomyelitis* (oral trivalent) (second).
22. *Poliomyelitis* (oral trivalent) (third).
39. *Tetanus* toxoid (third).

Children should, in addition, be inoculated against diphtheria and against whooping cough and measles, both of which can exist in a more virulent form than at home. Consult your doctor for advice on tuberculosis inoculation (BCG); the disease is widespread.

Infectious Hepatitis (jaundice) is endemic throughout Latin America and seems frequently to be caught by travellers. The best prevention is the careful preparation of food, avoidance of contaminated drinking water and scrupulous attention to toilet hygiene. But some additional measure of protection can be given by the injection of human immunoglobulin (gammaglobulin). The dose is: under 10 years of age, 250 mg.; 11 years and over, 500 mg. Relative protection lasts 4-6 months. A specific vaccine is being developed.

If at special risk or in the case of epidemics, vaccines are available against cholera, plague, typhus, influenza, anthrax and rabies.

Common Problems, some of which will almost certainly be encountered, are:

Heat Full acclimatization to high temperatures takes about two weeks and during this period it is normal to feel relatively apathetic, especially if the relative humidity is high. Drink plenty of water, use extra salt on your food and avoid extreme exertion. Tepid showers are more cooling than hot or cold ones. Remember that, especially in the highlands, there can be a large and sudden drop in temperature between sun and shade and between night and day, so dress accordingly.

Altitude Acute mountain sickness or *soroche* can strike from 2,200 metres upwards, although it is uncommon under 3,000 metres. Predisposing conditions are rapid ascent, overexertion, and poor physical shape, in that order of importance. Those persons who have experienced it before are likely to experience it again and should make the ascent to high altitude in easy stages, as should those with heart or lung conditions. The symptoms can come on quite rapidly within a few hours and include headache, dizziness, anorexia, flatulence, nausea and vomiting. Relative breathlessness and heart pounding are normal due to the low pressure of oxygen and are not part of the syndrome. Insomnia is common and, over 4,000 metres, so is periodic breathing during sleep—a distressing but harmless symptom. The treatment is rest, simple pain-killers (preferably not aspirin-based) for headache and anti-emetics for vomiting. Oxygen gives relief and is available on most trains and on some buses. Various local panaceas such as "Coramina Glucosada" or "Effortil" are not worth the while but *mate de coca* (a tea made from coca leaves), if you can get it, certainly alleviates some of the symptoms. On arrival at places over 3,000 metres, a few hours lying down in bed and abstinence from alcohol and greasy food will go a long way towards preventing *soroche*. If the symptoms are severe and prolonged it is wise to descend to a lower altitude and re-ascend slowly, Recurrent sufferers from severe *soroche* can consider the prophylactic use of the drug Acetazoleamide under a doctor's guidance. (Heavy smokers are reported to be particularly vulnerable to *soroche*—Ed.)

Other general problems of altitude relate to sunburn, intense cold at night and excessive dryness of the air causing sore eyes and nasal stuffiness. There is some evidence that rapid ascent can provoke miscarriage and cause peptic ulcers to bleed. True acclimatization takes over six months and during this period it is normal to feel relatively breathless on exertion.

Occasionally, a person living at high altitude who descends to sea level and then returns to the high sierra develop a condition known as acute pulmonary oedema, characterised by cough, severe breathlessness and blueness of the lips. Andean natives, children, and mountaineers are commonly affected. Medical help must be sought and oxygen given as soon as possible. Despite these various hazards, many people find living at high altitude healthier and more invigorating than at sea level.

Rapid descent from high places will aggravate sinus and middle ear conditions and may cause carious teeth to ache as well as discharging ink from your pen over your shirt, so check with your doctor or dentist for advice on prevention.

Intestinal upsets Practically nobody escapes this one, so be prepared for it. Ninety per cent of the time it is due to the insanitary preparation of food, so if you want to minimize your chances of succumbing, cook it yourself or eat in decent restaurants. Don't eat uncooked vegetables, unpeeled fruit, food that is exposed to flies or salads that may have been washed in contaminated water. Tap water is rarely safe outside the major cities, especially in the rainy season, and stream water is often contaminated by communities living surprisingly high in the mountains. Filtered or bottled water is usually available and safe. Ice for drinks should be made from boiled water but rarely is. Filthy water should first be strained through a filter bag (available from camping shops) and then boiled or treated. Water in general can be rendered safe in the **following ways: boil for 5 minutes at sea level, longer at higher altitudes;** add three drops of household bleach to 1 pint of water and leave for 15 minutes; or add 1 drop of tincture of iodine to 1 pint of water and leave for 3 minutes. Commercial water-sterilizing tablets are available.

Milk, apart from tinned varieties, is rarely pasteurized and, therefore, a source of tuberculosis, brucellosis and food-poisoning germs. This applies equally to ice cream, yoghurt and cheese. Fresh milk can be rendered safe by heating it to 62°C for 30 minutes followed by rapid cooling, or by boiling it. Matured or processed cheeses are safer than fresh varieties.

The most effective drugs against diarrhoea are: Diphenoxylate with Atropine (Lomotil, Searle; up to 16 tablets in 24 hours), Kaolin and Morphine, Paregoric and Codeine Phosphate. They are all potentially addictive.

For vomiting use Metoclopramide (Maxolon, Beechams, Primperan, Berk) 10 mg. every 8 hours (tablets or injection). Travel sickness pills are also a useful standby.

The vast majority of cases of diarrhoea and/or vomiting are due to microbial infections of the bowel plus an effect from strange food and drink. They represent no more than a temporary inconvenience which you learn to live with and need no special treatment with antibiotics, diets, vaccines or "re-establishment of the intestinal flora". Fortunately, as you get accustomed to Latin American germs, the attacks become less frequent and you can be more daring in your eating habits.

If, in addition, to cramps and diarrhoea, you pass blood in the bowel motion, have severe abdominal pain, fever and feel really terrible, you may well have dysentery and a doctor should be consulted at once. If this is not possible, the recommended treatment for bacillary dysentery is Tetracycline or Ampicillin 500 mg. every 6 hours plus replacement of water and salts. You should not try to cure yourself of amoebic dysentery; the treatment can be complex and self-medication may just damp down the symptoms with the risk of serious liver involvement later on.

Enterovioform (Ciba) gives some protection against amoebic dysentery but is useless in the general prevention of diarrhoea and can have serious side effects (nerve damage) if taken prophylactically over a long period. If dysentery, of any type, is practically unavoidable (such as on Amazonian river trips) it is justifiable to take Furamide (diloxanide furoate) 500 mg. daily plus a sulphonamide 500 mg. twice daily, for a short period only, when relative protection is afforded.

Editorial Note   Some travellers have recently recommended Imodium, a diarrhoea remedy with a different action to most others, and Streptotriads have also been praised. These suggestions do not, of course, bear Dr. Snashall's authority.

Paradoxically, constipation is also common, probably induced by dietary change, inadequate fluid intake in hot places and long bus journeys. Simple laxatives are useful in the short term.

Insects   These can be a great nuisance, especially in the tropics and some, of course, are carriers of serious diseases. The best way of keeping them away at night is to sleep off the ground with a mosquito net and to burn mosquito coils containing pyrethrum. Aerosol sprays have only a temporary effect. The best repellants contain di-ethyl-meta-toluamide or di-methyl phthalate—sold as "Deet", "Six-Twelve Plus", "Off", "Boots' Liquid Insect Repellant", "Flypel". Liquid is best for arms and face (care around eyes) and aerosol spray for clothes and ankles to deter chiggers, mites and ticks.

If you are bitten, itching may be relieved by baking-soda baths, anti-histamine tablets (care with alcohol or driving), corticosteroid creams (great care—never use if any hint of sepsis) or by judicious scratching. Calamine lotion and cream have limited effectiveness and antihistamine creams have a tendency to cause skin allergies and are, therefore, not recommended.

Bites which become infected (commonly in the tropics) should be treated with a local antiseptic or antibiotic cream, such as Cetrimide BP (Savlon, ICI) as should infected scratches.

Skin infestations with body lice (crabs) and scabies are, unfortunately, easy to pick up. DDT powder is now unacceptable for ecological reasons, so use gamma benzene hexachloride for lice and benzene benzoate solution for scabies. Crotamiton cream (Eurax, Geigy) alleviates itching and also kills a number of skin parasites.

Malaria and Chagas' Disease are carried by insects, so protection against being bitten has an importance beyond that of just avoiding discomfort.

Malaria in South America is confined to coastal and jungle zones and is in part resistant to some of the usual drugs. Make local enquiries if you intend to visit possibly infective zones and use one of the following prophylactic regimes. Start taking the tablets one week before exposure and continue taking them for six weeks after leaving the malarious area.

Low risk: Chloroquine 500 mg. wekly, or Chloroguanide 100-200 mg. daily.

High risk: (especially of drug-resistant falciparum malaria):
  Pyrimethamine (Daraprim, Wellcome) 12.5 mg. and Dapsone 100 mg., combined as Maloprim (Wellcome): 1 tablet per week; *or* Pyrimethamine 25 mg. plus Sulfadoxine (Fanasil) 500 mg.: 1 dose per week.

If, despite taking antimalarial tablets, you develop malarial symptoms, seek medical advice immediately.

Editorial Note The UK health authorities hold that malaria is on the increase throughout the world; prophylaxis should be used if travelling outside major cities in any humid tropical areas, particularly forest and coastal zones.

Chagas' Disease (South American Trypanosomiasis) is a chronic illness, incurable, transmitted by the "barber bug", which lives in rural districts on dirt floors frequented by opossums. It bites at night so avoid sleeping in such conditions.

Sunburn The burning power of the tropical sun, especially at high altitude, is phenomenal and can quickly cause very severe sunburn. Always wear a wide-brimmed hat and use some form of suncream lotion on untanned skin. Regular suntan lotions are no good; you need to use the types designed for mountaineers or skiers, Glacier Cream (Savory & Moore), Skreen (Pacific Labs., Vancouver), Spectraban (Stiefel), Piz Buin Extrem Cream (Sonnen Schutzfaktor 6) (Greiter Cosmetic). These are not available in South America; a reasonable substitute is zinc oxide ointment. Glare from the sun can cause conjunctivitis, so wear sunglasses. (Screening cream is also advisable for the noses, cheeks and chins of sunbathers on tropical beaches.—Ed.)

Snakebite If you are unlucky enough to be bitten by a venomous snake, spider, scorpion or sea creature, always try (within limits) to catch the animal for identification. The reactions to be expected are: swelling, pain and bruising around the bite, soreness of the regional lymph glands, nausea, vomiting and fever. If any of the following symptoms supervene, get the victim to a doctor without delay: numbness and tingling of the face, muscular spasms, convulsion, shortness of breath and haemorrhage.

Commercial snakebite kits are available, but only useful if you use them for the specific type of snake for which they are designed. If the bite is on a limb, immobilize the limb and apply a tourniquet proximally, not so tight that the pulse is obliterated, and release for 90 seconds every fifteen minutes. Reassurance is very important. Do not slash the bite area and try to suck out the poison unless you are experienced in this technique.

Other Afflictions   Remember that rabies is endemic in Mexico and South America so avoid crazy-looking dogs. If you are bitten, try to have the dog captured for observation and see a doctor at once.

Hookworm can be contracted from walking barefoot on infested earth or beaches. Schistosomiasis (Bilharzia) is present in lakes and some rivers. In others lurk the unmentionable piranha (or caribe) fish, so ask someone before you go for a dip in a river in Brazil.

When you return home, remember to keep taking your antimalarial tablets; remember that malaria and amoebic dysentery can still occur; if you have had severe diarrhoea, a bacteriological test on a specimen of bowel motion is a good idea.

Basic supplies   The following items you may find useful to take with you from home:

Sunglasses.

Ear plugs ("Muffles") to be used when swimming to prevent outer ear infections, and when sleeping in noisy hotels.

Suntan cream.

Insect repellant, mosquito net and coils.

Water-sterilizing tablets, *e.g.* Sterotabs (Boots), Puritabs (Kirby & Co. Ltd.), Globaline.

Antimalarials.

Anti-infective ointment, *e.g.* Savlon (ICI).

Dusting powder for feet, *e.g.* Tinaderm (Glaxo), Desenex.

Travel-sickness pills, *e.g.* Dramamine (Searle), Gravol (Carter-Wallace).

Antacids, *e.g.* Maalox.

Antidiarrheals, *e.g.* Lomotil (Searle).

The following organizations give information regarding well-trained, English-speaking physicians in South America:

International Associations for Medical Assistance to Travellers, 745 Fifth Avenue, New York 10022.

Intermedic, 777 Third Avenue, New York 10017.

Information regarding country-by-country malaria risk can be obtained from the World Health Organization (WHO), or The Ross Institute, London School of Hygiene and Tropical Medicine, Keppel Street, London W.C.1.

HISTORY
AND THE PEOPLE

IT IS impossible to understand the great diversity of peoples in Latin America without a digression into the history of the land they occupy. Columbus, first of the European navigators to reach Latin America, discovered Watling Island, Cuba, and Haiti in 1492. On his third voyage, in 1498, he reached the mouth of the Orinoco. In the next ten years the coast was explored by others as far as the River Plate. Balboa discovered the Pacific at the Gulf of Panama in 1513, and in 1520 Magellan passed into the Pacific through the Magellan Strait. A year earlier Cortés had begun his conquest of Mexico from his base at Veracruz. By 1531 Pizarro was conquering Peru, and in 1536 Jiménez was conquering the Chibchas of Colombia. Spurred in about equal proportions by religious zeal and lust for gold, these men and their followers were not to be daunted by heat, by cold, by jungle, by disease, or by an almost equally fanatical opposition.

When the Europeans arrived, the greater part of Latin America was inhabited, very thinly, by nomadic hunters, fishers, and farmers, but four groups of Indians had developed elaborate civilizations: the Incas, in the highlands of Peru, Bolivia, Ecuador, and northern Chile; the Chibchas, in the highlands of Colombia; the Mayas, of Guatemala and Yucatán; and the Aztecs of Mexico. In these areas a prosperous population based their agriculture on maize, the potato and sweet potato, mandioca (or cassava), beans, tomato, tobacco and cacao. Maize, developed by the early Mayas, was known to them all. They worked gold and silver, and were organized in forms of government which can be described as totalitarian and collectivist. It was once thought that these cultures had risen independently, but it is now known that at least the Mexican and Peruvian cultures had not only a common origin but that they remained more or less connected with each other. In the short interval between the conquest of Mexico and that of Peru, a Spanish caravel met at sea a Peruvian raft laden deep with pottery and metal goods and bound for the markets of the north.

The European conquerors "first fell upon their knees and then upon the Indians." The pattern of their conquest was, indeed, determined by the Indian settlements, for it was in them only that they could find souls to save, and gold and silver to take. In a comparatively short time the collected stores of precious metal were exhausted. None, indeed, had been found by the Portuguese when they colonized Brazil (the Treaty of Tordesillas between Spain and Portugal had given all lands to the E of 50 degrees W longitude to the Portuguese), and they, like the Spaniards, had to turn their attention to the soil. The Portuguese were the first to grow a cash crop for overseas markets, but the Indians were too few to work their sugar estates and slaves were imported from Africa. The Spaniards, too, in time, turned their attention to sugar, and wherever cane was grown, the African slave was imported to work it.

The Spanish and Portuguese at first rarely brought their women with them and cohabited freely with the natives. The present racial constitution is the result of the intermarriage between the earlier settlers and their black slaves with the indigenous peoples. The African element is strongest in Brazil, where ordinary people are conscious of race (who isn't?), but this natural awareness has never escalated into the problem it is elsewhere. The peoples of Argentina and Uruguay are almost totally white, for they have been settled in the main during the past 150 years by immigrants from Europe. In some parts of Latin America the indigenous Indian has survived and may yet take a decisive part in shaping the fortunes of the country in which he lives. This is more particularly the case in the Andean uplands of Peru, Bolivia, and Ecuador, in Paraguay, and in Mexico and Guatemala.

For 300 years, from the arrival of the Spaniards and Portuguese early in the 16th century to the wars of independence in the early years of the 19th century, Latin America was held as colonies of the two Iberian powers. Both Spanish and Portuguese sovereigns owned in person all land and water in their respective colonies; the grant or refusal of territory was in their hands, and they could claim all or portions of the produce of both land and water. They could control all trade, determine what crops should or should not be grown, which metals mined, collect all revenue and spend it as they pleased. They decided the appointment of church officers, could veto papal decrees aimed at the Colonies, and control education, printing and literature. The sovereigns could and did make all colonial laws and try the colonists under those laws. Public and even private life and all amusements were subject to their regulation, and the indigenous natives could be enslaved or freed as they saw fit. Power, after a while, was delegated by both sovereigns to Viceroys, who lived in great state. There was much corruption in both colonies, for in both the sale of office was permitted by law. Complete economic control lapsed after a while into the retention by the sovereign of the Royal Fifth, or *Quinto*, of certain products, mainly minerals. Both crowns expected, to the end, a personal and state revenue from their colonies. As affairs degenerated at home, both required more and more funds and revenues from overseas. Taxes not only grew larger, but they proliferated until there were more than forty kinds in the Spanish colonies and nearly as many in Brazil. Collection was often exigent and unfair, and embezzlement and corruption the rule.

Under these paternalist controls there was slowly emerging a social pattern: at the top of the scale the whites born in the Iberian Peninsula; below them the Creoles, or Criollos, the whites born in Latin America, often educated, intelligent, and dissatisfied with their complete lack of power in their homeland; below them again, the vast mass of mestizos, sometimes throwing up leaders of note; and at the bottom of the scale, often slaves or little better, were the indigenous races and the imported blacks.

Rough estimates have been made of the population of Latin America in 1800, before the struggle for independence began. It totalled, apart from Brazil, about 15,000,000 of whom 30,000 were Peninsulars, 3,000,000 Creoles, 6,000,000 mestizos, or half-castes, and 6,000,000 or so indigenous natives and Africans. The largest cities were: Lima, with 80,000 inhabitants; Quito, with 70,000; Buenos Aires with 60,000; and Santiago, with 36,000. There were, in Brazil, about 2,500,000 of whom 400,000 were white, 1,500,000 were black, and 600,000 were Indians. Rio de Janeiro had then a population of 30,000.

Independence High taxation, severe control of trade, local discontents fomented by secret study of the forbidden eighteenth century philosophers, and the accidents of European history, led at first sporadically, and then with growing momentum, to a movement for independence from Spain and Portugal. The American revolution and the support of Great Britain, then suffering from Napoleon's European blockade, had profound effects upon the struggle. On May 25, 1810, the people of Argentina overthrew the viceregal government. Under José de San Martín they marched in January, 1817, to the relief of Chile, which was already struggling for independence under Bernardo O'Higgins. By the end of 1818, Chile was free. In August, 1820, San Martín landed his forces in Peru. After entering Lima, he proclaimed the independence of Peru on July 28, 1821. On July 26, 1822, San Martín was at Guayaquil, meeting the great Bolívar, who had already freed Venezuela, Colombia, and Ecuador, and was soon to liberate Bolivia. Paraguay became independent in 1811, but Uruguay, a bone of contention between Argentina and Brazil, was not able to free itself till 1828.

The independence of Brazil came about somewhat differently. When Napoleon attacked Portugal in 1807, the British Navy took the Regent João to Brazil, where he stayed until his return to Europe in 1821. His son, Pedro, was left there as Vice-Regent for his father, but on September 7th, 1822, he declared Brazil an independent empire. He himself was deposed in 1831 but his son was to reign in Brazil until that country became a republic in 1889.

Great Britain took a notable, if in the main an unofficial part, in the liberation movement. A large number of British soldiers under their own English officers served with Bolívar in the war which freed Venezuela, Colombia, Ecuador and Bolivia. Others took part in the Chilean struggle, which is associated in particular with the name of Lord Cochrane, under whose command the Argentine and Chilean forces were shipped north to fight in Peru. Cochrane was later to defeat the Portuguese navy when it was contesting Brazil's claim to independence. Canning's intervention was responsible for the creation of a separate republic in Uruguay. British diplomacy, bent upon calling a "new world into existence to redress the balance of the old", was a powerful influence both in creating freedom and in maintaining it. The fact has not been forgotten in Latin America and colours the relationship between it and Britain to this day.

Later History The revolution was no less economic than political in that it freed trade and permitted, for the first time, immigration, but it made little difference to the social stratification. For a century after emancipation the general picture (as it still is in some republics) was of landowner, priest and soldier in alliance to maintain the ancient social structure of privilege on the one hand, and the illiterate peasant, poorly paid and under-nourished, on the other. Personality has always counted for more than principle in Latin America, and there was a spate of dictators, often ruthless and cruel, but it seemed at the time that the only alternative to them was chaos. (Bolivia had 60 revolutions in the first 100 years of its independence and Colombia 10 civil wars). But the circle was not a closed one: immigrants were pouring in to people a semi-empty land; railways and roads and ports were being built; there was an inflow of capital from Britain and the United States—capital very often looked upon as a new form of exploitation by Latin Americans; and most important of all, there was slowly being created an informed middle class whose affiliations were with world as much as local ideas. Some countries, more particularly Argentina, Brazil, Chile and Uruguay, were more or less stabilized by the end of the 19th century. To quote R. A. Humphreys: "the development of industry, immigration, and the growth of populations, the rise of the cities, the improvement of communications, all these have resulted in the advent of a new commercial and industrial governing class, a middle class, an artisan class and of organized labour." The cruder forms of militarism have gone, but for all that the military have intervened directly in politics in every Latin American country except Colombia, Venezuela, Costa Rica and Mexico during the last ten years.

The two world wars had a profound effect in shaping the emergence of Latin America. Both had the effect of severing it from the customary inflow of imports, and there has been an increasing attempt at autonomy. Crops have been diversified; manufacturing industries have been developed, mostly in Argentina, Brazil, Chile, Mexico, Peru, Venezuela and Colombia; there has been an attack on illiteracy and in some places on foreign investment and foreign enterprises. This attempt to gain economic independence will no doubt continue, but may not succeed, even in the long run. Some degree of international economic specialization is surely desirable; the rest of the world is in great need of what Latin America has to offer, and Latin America, with its standards of living rising to a reasonable level, will always clamour for what the rest of the world has to offer it.

Don't leave home without us.

With your American Express Card you can travel easily throughout South America. Our Travel Service Representatives are at your service for Emergency Check Cashing facilities, emergency replacement of stolen or lost cards, Travelers Cheques refunds, and travel and sightseeing arrangements.

CONTACT US AT

ARGENTINA - City Service Travel Agency
Florida, 890 - 4th floor - Buenos Aires - Argentina - Phone: 32.8416/18
BOLIVIA - Crillon Tours Ltda.
Avenida Camacho, 1223 - P. O. Box 4785 - La Paz - Bolivia -
Phone: 40402 - 20222
BRAZIL - Kontik Franstur S. A.
Av. Atlântica, 2316A - Rio de Janeiro - RJ — Phone: 235.1396 - 237.7797
Rua Marconi, 71 - 2º andar - São Paulo - S. P. - Phone: 36.6301
COLOMBIA - Tierra Mar Aire ltda.
Edif. Bavaria Torre B. Local 126 - Carrerra 10 nº 27-91 - Apartado Aéreo
5371 - Bogotá - Colombia - Phone: 83.2955
CHILE - Turismo Cocha
Agustinas, 1122 - P. O. Box. 1001 - Santiago - Chile - Phone:
83.487-72.3923-72.6528
ECUADOR - Ecuadorian Tours S. A.
Amazonas 339 - P. O. Box 2605 - Quito - Ecuador - Phone: 52.8177 -
52.0777
Ecuadorian Tours S. A.
313 Ballen St. - P. O. Box 3862 - Guayaquil - Ecuador - Phone:
51.1525-51.2980-51.2805
PARAGUAY - Inter-Express, S. R. L.
Nuestra Sra. Asunción, 588 - Asunción - Paraguay - Phone: 48.888
PERU - Lima Tours S. A.
Ocoña, 160 - P. O. Box 4340 - Lima - Peru - Phone: 27.6624
SURINAM - Travelbureau C. Kersten & Co., N. V.
C/O Hotel Krasnapolsky - Domineestraat 39 - Surinam - Paramaribo
- Phone: 74.448 - 77.148
URUGUAY - Turisport Limitada
Bartolomé Mitre, 1318 - Montevideo - Uruguay -
Phone: 90.6300
VENEZUELA - TMC Consolidado C. A.
Lobby Tamanaco Hotel - Urb. Las Mercedes -
Caracas 105 - Venezuela - P. O. Box 68459 -
Phone: 91.4224-91.4308-92.3219

ARGENTINA

ARGENTINA is the eighth largest country in the world, the fourth largest in the Americas and the second largest in area and population in South America. It covers an area of 2,807,560 square km., or 29% of the area of Europe; it is 3,460 km. long from N to S and is, in places, 1,580 km. wide. Apart from the estuary of the Río de la Plata its coast line is 2,575 km. long. Its western frontier runs along the crest of the high Andes, a formidable barrier between it and Chile. Its neighbours to the N are Bolivia and Paraguay and (in the NE) Brazil. To the E is Uruguay. Its far southern limit is the Beagle Channel.

Argentina is enormously variable both in its types of land and its climates, which range from the great heat of the Chaco through the pleasant climate of its central pampas to the sub-antarctic cold of the Patagonian S. Geographers usually recognise four main physical areas: the Andes, the North and Mesopotamia, the Pampas, and Patagonia.

The first division, the Andes, includes the whole length of the Cordilleras, low and deeply glaciated in the Patagonian S, high and dry in the prolongation into NW Argentina of the Bolivian Altiplano, the high plateau. S of this is the very parched desert and mountain region S of Tucumán and W of Córdoba. The oases in this area strung along the eastern foot of the Andes—Jujuy, Salta, Tucumán, Catamarca, La Rioja, San Juan, Mendoza and San Rafael—were the first places to be colonised by the Spaniards.

The second division, the North and Mesopotamia, contains the vast, forested plains of the Chaco and the floodplain and gently rolling land known as the Argentine Mesopotamia lying between the rivers Paraná and Uruguay. In the far NE a comparatively small area is actually on the great Paraná Plateau. The plains cover 582,750 square km.

The third division, the flat rich pampa, takes up the heart of the land. These vast plains lie S of the Chaco, E of the Andes, W of the Río Paraná and N of the Río Colorado. The eastern part, which receives more rain, is usually called the Humid Pampa, and the western part the Dry Pampa. They stretch for hundreds of km. in almost unrelieved flatness and cover some 650,000 square km.

The final division is Patagonia, the area S of the Río Colorado—a land of arid, wind-swept plateaux cut across by ravines. In the deep S the wind is wilder and more continuous. There is no summer, but to compensate for this the winters are rarely severe. Patagonia is about 780,000 square km.

Three-quarters of Argentina's territory cannot be cultivated without irrigation but only 400,000 hectares are artificially watered.

History of settlement and economic growth   When, in the early 16th century, the first white men came to Argentina, the native Indians had already halted the Inca drive southwards from Peru through Bolivia into northern Argentina. The Spaniard, Juan de Solís, landed on the shores of the Plata estuary in 1516, but he was killed and the expedition failed. Magellan touched at the estuary four years later, but turned southwards to make his way into the Pacific. In 1527 both Sebastian Cabot and his rival Diego García sailed into the Estuary and up the Paraná and the Paraguay. They formed a small settlement, Sancti Spiritus, at the junction of the Caraña and Coronda rivers near their confluence with the Paraná, but it was wiped out by the Indians about two years later and Cabot and García returned to Spain. Ten years later, in 1536, Pedro de Mendoza, with a large force well supplied with equipment and horses, founded a settlement at Buenos Aires. The natives soon made it too hot for him; the settlement was abandoned, and Mendoza returned home, but not before sending Juan de Ayolas, and a small force up the Paraná. Ayolas set off for Peru, already conquered by Pizarro, leaving Irala in charge. It is not known for certain what happened to Ayolas. In 1537, Irala and his men settled at Asunción, in Paraguay, where the natives were friendly. This was the first settlement in the interior of South America. There were no further expeditions from Spain to colonise what is now called Argentina, and it was not until 1573 that the settlement at Asunción sent forces S to establish Santa Fe and not until June 11, 1580 that Juan de Garay refounded the settlement at Buenos Aires. It was only under his successor, Hernando Arias de Saavedra (1592-1614), that the new colony became secure.

In the meantime there had been successful expeditions into Argentina both from Peru and Chile—the first, from Peru, as early as 1543. These expeditions led, in the latter half of the 16th century, to the foundation at the eastern foot of the Andes of the oldest towns in Argentina: Santiago del Estero, Tucumán, Córdoba, Salta, La Rioja and Jujuy by the Peruvians following the old Inca road, and San Juan, Mendoza, and San Luis by the Chileans from across the Andes. Peru was given the viceroyalty over all the Spanish possessions in South America in 1543. Under the dependency of this Viceroy a Gobernación of Paraguay and Río de la Plata was formed in 1544, with Asunción as capital. A Gobernación of Tucumán was likewise created in 1563, but in 1617 the first was split into two: the Gobernación del Paraguay (capital, Asunción) and the Gobernación del Río de la Plata (capital, Buenos Aires). The Viceroyalty of Río de la Plata, to rule over Argentina, Bolivia, Paraguay and Uruguay, was created in 1776.

For 270 years after its foundation Buenos Aires was of little

importance. Spanish stress was upon Lima, and Lima did not send its treasures home by way of Buenos Aires but through Panama and the Caribbean. Buenos Aires was not allowed by Spain to take part in any overseas trade until 1778; its population then was only 24,203. It was merely a military outpost for Spain to confront the Portuguese outpost at Colonia, across the estuary, and lived, in the main, by smuggling. Even when (in 1776) a Viceroyalty of Río de la Plata was formed, it made little difference to Buenos Aires as a capital, for its control of the cabildos (town councils) in distant towns was very tenuous. When the British, following Spain's alliance with Napoleon, held Buenos Aires for a few months in 1806, and marched against it again in 1807, there was no inkling of its future potential. But the attacks had one important result: a large increase in the confidence of the Porteños (the name given to those born in Buenos Aires) to deal with all comers, including the mother-country, whose restrictions were increasingly unpopular. On May 25, 1810, the cabildo of Buenos Aires deposed the viceroy and governed on behalf of King Ferdinand VII, then a captive of Napoleon. Six years later, when Buenos Aires was threatened by invasion from Peru and blockaded by a Spanish fleet in the River Plate, a national congress held at Tucumán on July 9 declared independence. The declaration was given reality by the selfless devotion of José de San Martín, who boldly marched an Argentine army across the Andes to free Chile, and (with the help of Lord Cochrane, commander of the Chilean Navy), embarked his forces for Peru, where he captured Lima, the first step in the freedom of Peru.

When San Martín returned home, it was to find the country rent by conflict between the central government and the provinces. Disillusioned, he retired to France. The internal conflict was to last a long time. On the one hand stood the Unitarist party, bent on central control; on the other the Federalist party, insisting on local autonomy. The latter had for members the great caudillos, the large landowners backed by the gauchos, suspicious of the cities. One of their leaders, Juan Manuel de Rosas, took control of the country in 1829. During his second term as Governor of Buenos Aires he asked for and was given extraordinary powers. The result was a 17-year reign of terror. His rule was an international scandal; and when he began a blockade of Asunción in 1845, Britain and France promptly countered with a three-year blockade of Buenos Aires. But in 1951 Justo José de Urquiza, Governor of Entre Ríos, one of his old henchmen, organised a triple entente of Brazil, Uruguay, and the Argentine opposition to overthrow him. He was crushed in 1852 at Caseros (a few miles from Buenos Aires), and fled to England, where he farmed quietly for 25 years, dying at Southampton.

Rosas had started his career as a Federalist; once in power he was a Unitarist. His downfall meant the triumph of federalism. In 1853 a federal system was finally incorporated in the constitution, but the old quarrel had not been solved. In 1859, when the constitution was ratified, the capital was moved to Paraná, the province of Buenos Aires seceded, and Buenos Aires, under Bartolomé Mitre, was defeated by the federal forces under Urquiza. Two years later Buenos Aires again fought the country, and this time it won. Once again it became the seat of the federal government, with Bartolomé Mitre as its first constitutional president. (It was during his office that the Triple Alliance of Argentina, Brazil, and Uruguay defeated Francisco Solano López of Paraguay). There was another political flare-up of the old quarrel in 1880, ending in the humiliation of Buenos Aires, which then ceased to be the capital of its province; a new provincial capital was founded at La Plata, 48 km. to the SE. At that time a young colonel, Julio A. Roca, was finally subduing all the Indian tribes of the pampas and the S. This was an event which was to make possible the final supremacy of Buenos Aires over all rivals.

Politically Argentina was a constitutional republic with a very restricted suffrage up to the passage in 1912 of the Sáenz Peña law, which established universal manhood suffrage. From 1916 to 1930 the Unión Cívica Radical (founded in 1890) held power, under the leadership of Hipólito Yrigoyen and Marcelo T. de Alvear, but lost it to the military uprising of 1930. Though seriously affected by the world depression of the 1930's, Argentina's rich soil and educated population had made it one of the ten wealthiest countries in the world, but this wealth was most unevenly distributed, and the political methods followed by the conservatives and their military associates in the 1930's seemed to deny the middle and working classes any effective share in their own country's wealth and government. In 1943 came another military coup, which had a distinctly fascist tinge; in 1946 emerged, as President, Gen. Juan Domingo Perón (see also page 41), who based his power on an alliance between the army and labour; his contacts with labour were greatly assisted by his charismatic wife Eva (recently immortalized in the rock-opera "Evita") and the living conditions of the workers were greatly improved—but at the expense of the economic state of the country. By the time a military coup unseated Perón in 1955 serious harm had been done; ever since, Argentina has been struggling to recover its lost political and economic health.

The transformation of the pampas   The pampas, the economic heart of the country, extend fanwise from Buenos Aires for a distance of between 550 and 650 km. Apart from three groups of sierras or low hills—the Sierras de Córdoba (1,500 metres), the Sierras del Tandil (500 metres), and the Sierra de la Ventana, N of Bahía Blanca (1,200 metres)—the surface seems an endless flat monotony, relieved occasionally, in the SW, by sand dunes. There are few rivers. One, the Río Salado, flows sluggishly through swamps from Junín south-eastwards to its Atlantic mouth, 160 km. S of the capital. Of the five streams which rise in the Córdoba Hills two only are unabsorbed by the land: the Tercero and the Cuarto, which unite into the Río Carcaraná to join the Paraná above Rosario. Drinking water is pumped to the surface from a depth of from 30 to 150 metres by the windpumps which are such a prominent feature of the landscape. There are no trees other than those that have been planted, except in the monte of the W. But there is, in most years, ample rainfall. It is greatest at Rosario, where it is about 1,020 mm., and evenly distributed throughout the year. The further S from Rosario, the less the rain. At Buenos Aires it is about 940 mm.; it drops to 535 at Bahía Blanca, and is only 400 along the boundary of the Humid Pampa. The further from Rosario, too, the more the rainfall is concentrated during the summer. Over the whole of the pampa the summers are hot, the winters mild, but there is a large climatic difference between various regions: at Rosario the growing season between frosts is about 300 days; at Bahía Blanca it falls to 145 days.

When the Spanish arrived in Argentina the pampas were an area of tall coarse grasses. The cattle and horses they brought with them were soon to roam wild and in time transformed the Indian's way of life. The only part of the pampa occupied by the settlers was the Pampa Rim, between the Río Salado and the Paraná-Plata rivers. Here, in large estancias, cattle, horses and mules in great herds roamed the open range. There was a line of forts along the Río Salado: a not very effective protection against marauding Indians. The Spaniards had also brought European grasses with them; these soon supplanted the coarse native grasses, and formed a green carpet surface which stopped abruptly at the Río Salado.

The estancia owners and their dependent gauchos were in no sense an agricultural people, but towards the end of the 18th century, tenants—to the great contempt of both estanciero and gaucho—began to plant wheat in the valleys along the Paraná-Plata shore. This was the situation as late as the fifties of the nineteenth century. The fall of Rosas in 1852, and the constitution of 1853, made it possible for Argentina to take a leap forward. But it must be remembered that its white population at that time was only 1,200,000. Preston James, in his book *Latin America*, lists four attributes of Argentina at that date: (1) the sparse population—Buenos Aires had less than 90,000; (2) a people almost exclusively interested in horses, cattle and sheep and not at all in agriculture; (3) an abundance of free first-rate land for grazing and grain farming; and (4), a tradition of large private estates.

The modern period   The rapidly rising population of Europe during the latter half of the 19th century and the consequent clamour for cheap food was the spur that impelled Argentina (as it did the United States and Canada) to occupy its grasslands and take to agriculture. This was made possible by the new techniques already developed; agricultural machinery to till the soil and reap the crops, barbed wire to delimit pasture and tillage, well-drilling machines and windpumps to raise water to the surface, roads and railways to carry produce from farm to port, and steamships to bear it to distant markets. (The first Royal Mail Steam Packet ship reached Buenos Aires in 1851). Roads were, and are, a difficulty in the Argentine pampa; the soil lacks gravel or stones to surface the roads, and dirt roads become a quagmire in wet weather and a fume of dust in the dry. Railways, on the other hand, were simple and cheap to build. The first—a short stretch running SW from Buenos Aires—was built in 1857. Soon after another was built along the old Colonial road from Rosario to Córdoba and Tucumán. The system grew as need arose and capital (mostly from Britain) became available. The lines in the pampa radiate out fanwise (with intricate inter-communication) from the ports of Buenos Aires, Rosario, Santa Fe and Bahía Blanca. Argentina, unlike most other countries, had extensive railways before a road system was built.

The occupation of the pampa was made finally possible by a war against the Indians in 1878-83 which virtually exterminated them. Many of the officers in that campaign were given gifts of land of more than 40,000 hectares each. The pampa had passed into private hands on the old traditional pattern of large estates.

Cattle products—hides, tallow, and salt beef—had been the mainstay of Argentine overseas trade during the whole of the Colonial period. (In the early 19th century wool challenged the supremacy of cattle). The occupation of the grass lands did not, at first, alter the complexion of the foreign trade; it merely increased its volume. In 1877, however, the first ship with refrigeration chambers made it possible to send frozen beef to England. But the meat of the scrub cattle was too strong for English taste. As a result, pedigree bulls were imported from England and the upgrading of the herds began. The same process was applied to sheep. But the improved herds could only flourish where there were no ticks—ticks are prevalent in the N—and thrived best where forage crops were available. Argentina adopted as its main forage crop alfalfa (lucerne), a plant like clover which proved extremely suitable on the pampa. The cultivation of alfalfa for fodder necessitated more immigrant labour. It has since been supplemented with barley, oats, rye and particularly maize and sorghums.

During the earlier periods of immigration the landowners were only interested in beef cattle and the forage for them. They rented plots of land for four years or so to the immigrants, on the understanding that they moved on to fresh plots at the expiration of their lease and when the ground had been planted in the final year with alfalfa. And for a share in the profits, they permitted the tenants to sow wheat for the first three years. Alfalfa, in this rotation, was cuttable five or six times a year for as long as six or ten years, when new tenants were leased the land again. It was in this way that wheat—a profitable crop, grown more and more for its own sake—became popular in Argentina. To-day the pampa in most places combines the growing of wheat, maize, linseed, and sorghums with the basic stress still upon the rearing of beef cattle, now strongly in demand for the feeding of urban millions as well as for export. In no part of the pampa is less than 40% of the land given over to pasture. In some places, and more particularly in the bulge S of Buenos Aires, farming is still confined to cattle and sheep rearing and the provision of suitable forage. In a few places, notably around Buenos Aires, the land has been devoted to truck and dairy farming and fruit growing.

The country given over to arable and pastoral farming is monotonously flat except in the undulating country of Entre Ríos. It is astonishing to drive hour after hour and see no brook or river. Nor are there ponds or pools save in times of unusual rain, when shallow pools appear. Tall windpumps stand in the fields, and from them radiate long lines of galvanised iron troughs for the cattle and sheep. Fields are fenced into very large potreros, or pastures, of from 40 to 2,000 hectares each. Cattle, sheep and horses usually graze in the same pasture. The fences are wire and were built at great cost, for all wood has to be brought from the northern forests.

In the villages the roads are wide and commonly treeless, though now and then there are estancias where trees have been planted with care. The chinaberry tree is the favourite, for it is not devoured by locusts; next comes the Eucalyptus globulus.

A striking thing about the Pampas is the bird life. Flamingoes rise in a pink and white cloud as the train passes, heron egrets gleam white against the blue sky, pink spoonbills dig in the mud and ostriches stalk in the distance. Most facinating are the oven birds, called *horneros,* which build enormous nests six times as big as themselves, with one entrance into an interior which contains two communicating chambers, on the top of telegraph and fence posts.

To sum up, the transformation of the pampa has had two profound effects. Because its newly-created riches flowed out and its needs flowed in mainly through Buenos Aires, that port grew from comparative insignificance into one of the greatest cities in the world. The whole of Argentina now turns to the capital for leadership. And the transformation of the Humid Pampa led, through immigration, to a vast predominance of the European strain.

Immigration The first immigrants settled NW of Santa Fe in 1856. Between 1857 and 1930, total immigration was over six million, and almost all of them from Europe. The process has gone on of late years, with interruptions during the 1930 economic crisis and the second world war. During the 1947-51 period 629,685 immigrants settled in Argentina, but by 1961 the net influx was only 2,500. Italians were by far the most numerous, followed by Spaniards, and then, far behind, Portuguese, Germans, Dutch and limited numbers of Yugoslavs, Syrians, Austrians, French and Latin Americans. British and North Americans are contracted technicians and business executives. During the last decade many Bolivians, Uruguayans, Paraguayans and Chileans have settled in Argentina.

The British in Argentina We must allow ourselves an appendix on the part played by the British in the transformation of Argentina into a modern state. The introduction of the British horse was followed in 1826 by the all-British "Racing Club". In 1827 John Miller imported the first shorthorn—Miller's Estancia is still British owned. In 1844 Richard Newton set up the first wire-fence. The first steamship to arrive at Buenos Aires was the Royal Mail *Esk* in 1851. In 1874 a British estancia saw the first sheep-dip and the first game of polo. The first Aberdeen-Angus was imported in 1876. All the following were started by British capital and engineers: gas, electric light, the meat packing industry, tea planting, agricultural and industrial machinery, insurance, banks, tramways, telephones, telegraphs, wireless; and so, incidentally, were football, rugby, rowing, tennis, golf, polo, and boxing. And most important of all, the railways. When the 53,000 km. of railway were taken over by the State, 32,000 km. were British owned. As late as 1954, when most of the British enterprises had passed into Argentine hands, there were 11,425 British residents in Argentina, and its British community is still the largest, save for South Africa's, outside the Commonwealth.

The Argentine People are predominantly white; in the Federal Capital and Province of Buenos Aires, where nearly half the population lives, the people are almost exclusively of European origin. But settlements in the W along the foot of the Andes were colonised from Chile, those in the NW from Peru, and those in the N and NE from Paraguay. In these places at least half the people are mestizos though they form less than 2% of the population of the whole country. In the highlands of the NW, in the Chaco, and in southern Patagonia there are small remnants of pure bred Indians.

A curious sidelight of the racial composition is that up till 1850 about 40% of the population of Buenos Aires was black. This element has completely disappeared.

In 1914 the population was 7.9 million. In 1960 it was 20.0 million, and by 1976 had risen to about 25.0 million. Some 65% are urban and 40% live in cities of 100,000 or more. Population growth: 1.6%; urban growth, 2.8%. Death rate per thousand: 8.0; infantile mortality, 60; birth rate, 22.0. It is estimated that 12.8% are foreign born and generally of European origin. From 90 to 95% can read and write.

Political System The form of government has traditionally been a representative, republican federal system. By the 1853 Constitution (amended in 1880) the country is now divided into a Federal Capital district (the City of Buenos Aires), 22 Provinces and the National Territory of Tierra del Fuego, Antarctica and South Atlantic Islands. The Central Government deals with such matters as affect the State as a whole, but the provinces have extensive powers in internal matters. Each Province has its own Senate and Chamber of Deputies. The national Congress is empowered, when a Provincial Government breaks down, to vote for an "Interventor" to take over from the suspended Governor and legislature and govern by decree. The municipal government of the capital is exercised by a Mayor appointed by the President with the approval of the Senate. On June 28, 1966, the army deposed the constitutional president, taking over the government and suspending the sittings of Congress and the provincial legislatures. Elections for a new constitutional government were held in March 1973 and the Peronista candidate, Dr. Héctor Cámpora, was elected President, taking office on May 25. He resigned in July, and after a further election, Gen. Juan Domingo Perón became President in October 1973. President Perón died on July 1, 1974, leaving the Presidency to his widow, Vice-President María Estela Martínez de Perón. A highly complex political situation, of which a high level of violence (including kidnapping and assassination) is a regrettable feature, followed his death; by early 1976 conditions in the country, both of violence and of economic crisis, had deteriorated to the point when the military felt itself again obliged to intervene. Sra. de Perón was deposed from the Presidency and replaced by a military junta, led by Gen. Jorge Videla, on 24th March 1976. Congress and the provincial legislatures have been closed, and new elections are not expected until the 1980's.

Communications Argentina has only four good sea ports: Buenos Aires, La Plata, Rosario and Bahía Blanca. The two great rivers flowing southward into the Plate, the Paraná and the Uruguay, are not very satisfactory routes. The Colorado and the Negro rivers in northern Patagonia are navigable by small vessels only.

Roads Most of Argentina is served by 140,000 km. of road, but only 25% are metalled and a further 25% improved. Even so, the network carries 80% of freight tonnage and 82% of medium and long-distance passengers. The 43,100 km. of railway line carry only 8% of freight and 15% of the passenger traffic, and are subsidised to an outrageous extent. Services, which declined in the 1950s, have improved in recent years, but profitability is very low.

The Cities of the Pampas

The pampa is little more than a fifth of the total area of the country, but 35% of the people live in Greater Buenos Aires and 32% in the Pampas. Some 67% of the people, that is, live in the Pampa area, which has 70% of all the railways, 86% of the land used for cereals and linseed, 65% of the cattle, 40% of the sheep, 77% of the pigs, and nearly 90% of the industrial production.

The River Plate, or Río de la Plata, the main seaward entrance on which Buenos Aires lies, is not a river but an estuary or great basin into which flow the Rivers Paraná and Uruguay and their tributaries.

Buenos   Aires (CENTRE)

N

7/78

Measured from Punta Piedras, Argentina, to Punta Brava, Uruguay, it has a width of about 90 km., and where the Rivers Paraná and Uruguay branch off (say from Martín Chico to San Fernando) the width is 37 km. The Río de la Plata is 160 km. long, and mud and sand give it a thick, brownish colour. It is shallow and the passage of ocean vessels is only made possible by continuous dredging. The tides are of little importance, for there is only a 1.2 metre rise and fall at spring tides. The depth of water is influenced mainly by the direction of the wind and the state of the Paraná and Uruguay rivers.

Buenos Aires, the capital, which spreads over some 200 square km., is the second largest city in the S hemisphere and the eighth largest in the world. It is an imposing city with a character all its own, and has some fine buildings and attractively laid out parks and gardens. Its municipal population is about 3,323,000, but the population of greater Buenos Aires is already estimated at 8.7 millions: more than a third of the country's inhabitants.

Buenos Aires has been virtually rebuilt since the beginning of this century and very few of the old buildings are left. The main streets have been built on a grid system with two diagonals across the rectangular pattern. (See street map.) In the centre, which has maintained the original lay-out since its foundation, the streets and pavements are often very narrow. They are mostly one-way. Some traffic lights have now been installed, an innovation which had long been resisted.

The heart of the City, now as in Colonial days, is the Plaza de Mayo, with the historic Cabildo, the Town Hall, where the movement for independence from Spain was first planned; the pink Casa Rosada (Presidential Palace); the City Hall; the Cathedral, where San Martín, one of the liberators of S. America, is buried; the Ministry of Social Welfare, with the Banco Hipotecario Nacional and the Banco de la Nación. Within a few blocks are the fashionable church of Nuestra Señora de la Merced, the National Library and the main banks and business houses.

Running W from the Plaza, the Avenida de Mayo leads 1½ km. to the Congress building in the Plaza del Congreso. Halfway it crosses the wide Avenida Nueve de Julio. A tall obelisk commemorating the 400th anniversary of the city's founding stands at its centre in the Plaza de la República, surrounded by sloping lawns. Beneath it is an underground car park. The Av. Nueve de Julio itself, one of the widest in the world, consists of three traffic arteries separated by wide grass borders.

N of the Plaza de Mayo is the shopping, theatre and commercial area. The city's traditional shopping centre, Calle Florida, is in this district. This is the fashionable down-town meeting place, particularly in the late afternoon. It is now reserved for pedestrians only. Another shopping street is Avenida Santa Fe, which meets the Florida at the Plaza San Martín. Avenida Corrientes is the entertainment centre, a street of theatres, restaurants, cafes and night life; good for leather work between numbers 2200 and 2400 (Pasteur station on 'B' line of underground). Close by, in Calle Lavalle and in nearby streets, there are numerous cinemas and many good and relatively reasonable restaurants; Calle Lavalle is reserved to pedestrians each evening. (Many cinemas reduce their prices on Mondays, Tuesdays and Wednesdays.)

A broad avenue, Paseo Colón, runs S to the waterfront and the

picturesque old port district known as the Boca, where the Riachuelo
flows into the Plata. It was here, near Parque Lezama, that Pedro de
Mendoza founded the first Buenos Aires. The Boca, mostly Italian, has
its own distinctive life. At its restaurants and cafés, frequented by sailors
and working people, you can eat Italian dishes and a variety of sea foods.
It has everything from sleazy dance halls and cabarets to bars, the haunts
of Bohemians and singing waiters. Cobblestoned streets wind in and out
amongst quaint and gaily painted houses. In one of these streets one side
has been sealed off and a theatre, Caminito, set up. The huge Avellaneda
Bridge crosses the Riachuelo, giving splendid views of the port.

Typical Boca restaurant: *Spadavecchia,* Necochea 1180. Well-known, seats some 500
people, loud band, and now rather expensive, but there are several other good
restaurants nearby. *Torna Sorrento,* Lamadrid 701/09 is Italian run, and has Chilean
folk music. Try a small family restaurant at corner of Necochea and Aristóbulo del
Valle; complete meal with wine under US$3, excellent, about 4 blocks from
commercial centre. At Pedro de Mendoza 1835 there is an art gallery of modern
Argentine artists in a school. Well worth seeing, entrance free.

Calle Brasil leads from this area to the far side of the docks and the
splendid Avenida Costanera which runs along the river front. Here are
bathing places (Balneario Municipal), gardens, many restaurants and
public concerts: a pleasant place on a hot summer's day but overcrowded
on Sundays and holidays. (Care should be taken in what one eats at the
stalls selling food.) The Avenida stretches along the seawall from the S
port to the northern boundary of the city. (Note: the municipal
promenade has been closed to the public in the vicinity of Dock No. 4
since the military coup.) Bathing is no longer allowed; the water is highly
contaminated.

There are lovely parks, large and small, wherever you go. The city has
more than 150 of them, some of which you pass as you traverse streets
lined with jacaranda trees—they blossom for 10 days about mid-
November—and flanked by balconied apartment houses and rambling
mansions.

One of the few places which still have late Colonial and Rosista
buildings is the barrio of San Telmo, S of Plaza de Mayo, centred on
Calle Independencia along the slope which marks the old beach of the
River Plate. It is becoming an artistic centre, and there is a regular Sunday
antiques market at the Plaza Dorrego (see page 47).

Union Bar, Paseo Colón e Independencia, is famous for tango music.

The theatre retains its hold on the people of Buenos Aires. About 20
commercial theatres play the year round. There is a large number of
amateur theatres. There is never an empty seat at a concert, ballet, or
opera; the season at the Colón (April—early December) is probably the
finest in Latin America. Some of the daily papers rank with the best in the
world. There are many publishing houses, numerous bookshops, and
active scientific, cultural, and welfare centres.

A good way of seeing Buenos Aires and its surroundings is by using the
excellent day and night services of Autobuses Sudamericanos, Bernardo
de Irigoyen 1370, Local 19, Phone: 26-8061 & 67-8994. They take you to
Tigre and the delta of the Paraná, to La Plata and Luján, on an estancia
tour, and show you the city by day and by night, including the Boca area.
English-speaking guides. Similar tours are offered, at somewhat lower
prices, by Teletours, on Cerrito corner with Av. Córdoba. Meliá operates
from the *Sheraton Hotel.*

Local Steamships The following services, among others, are by the Flota Fluvial del Estado with sailings from Buenos Aires, South Basin.

Rosario (Paraná River), 2 weekly sailings.

Corrientes (Paraná and Paraguay Rivers), 2 weekly sailings.

South Coast. Down to Punta Arenas and intermediate Patagonian ports, served by the Imp. & Exp. de la Patagonia and State Steamship Lines. Very irregular sailings. For connexions with Uruguay, see page 57.

To Antarctica with the Jefatura de Servicio de Transportes Navales in February, once-only sailing (in 1978, 10th Feb.) for 30 days on Transporte ARA, Bahía Buen Suceso, stopping between 2-5 days at each port of call, including Puerto Belgrano, Antarctica (6 days), Ushuaia, Port Stanley, Puerto Madryn. Excursions to Lapataia and Lake Fagnano from Ushuaia and to sea-elephants at Puetro Madryn. 2-4 berth cabins US$1,350-1,950, includes meals. Information from: Jefatura del Servicio de Transportes Navales, Reconquista 385, 7° Piso, Tel. 45-0034 and 45-1116, 0900-1200 and 1300-1700.

Airports Ezeiza, 35 km. by road from the centre. The highway to the airport is a fairly good divided lane highway, now well marked, which links with the General Paz circular highway round the city. Woods are planted on both sides. The airport is up-to-date and its hotel, the *Internacional*, is very good. Ezeiza is used by international servces but Jorge Newbery airport (normally known as Aeroparque), on the N side river front at the end of the New Port, 4 km. from the centre, is the airport mainly used for internal services and smaller aircraft, and also flights to Asunción, Santiago and Montevideo. At Ezeiza and at all Argentine airports the exit tax is US$5 for international flights, US$1.60 to neighbouring countries, and US$0.40 for internal flights. (Try not to exchange travellers' cheques at airport; charge is an extra US$2 on top of commission.)

Taxis to and from Ezeiza airport operate at a fixed price (US$7, but one must queue for a slip against payment of this amount and hand it to the driver) to the centre. Passengers at Buenos Aires can book in their luggage at Plaza Once, corner of Bartolomé Mitre, 3 hours prior to departure, from which buses run them to Ezeiza at a fixed price. On arrival in Ezeiza, buy tickets for city centre at the kiosk in the terminal building, before boarding the bus. No. 86 bus can also be caught at corner of Perú and Av. de Mayo (500), cheap, but no good if you have much luggage. Make sure bus has sign "Aeropuerto" inside; many 86's stop short of the airport. Journeys to and from Jorge Newbery (Aeroparque) are charged according to meter, or you can catch the local No. 56 bus from outside the airport to the Retiro railway station; again, decisions should depend on luggage.

Local Airline Offices Aerolíneas Argentinas, Calle Florida 1 (30-8551). Austral Lineas Aéreas, Av. R. S. Peña 701 (46-8841). Lineas Aéreas del Estado LADE), Calle Perú 710 (34-7071).

Railways Terminals (good snacks available at Retiro and Constitución at all hours).

Retiro: Ferrocarril Nacional General Bartolomé Mitre (Central).

    Ferrocarril Nacional General San Martín (Pacific).

    Ferrocarril Nacional General Belgrano (North-Western).

Constitución: Ferrocarril Nacional General Roca (Southern).

Once: Ferrocarril Nacional Domingo F. Sarmiento (Western).

F. Lacroze: Ferrocarril Nacional General Urquiza (North-Eastern).

Puente Alsina: Ferrocarril Nacional Provincia de Buenos Aires.

Vélez Sarsfield: Ferrocarril Nacional General Belgrano (North-Western).

NB The railways maintain a most helpful information centre in Galerías Pacífico, Florida 753. There is a good left-luggage facility at Retiro station. Book tickets well in advance wherever possible, also for connecting services, especially those going south of Buenos Aires. In December and January, all seats may be taken two weeks in advance in any direction due to local holidays. Pullman services are usually air conditioned; there is not a very great distinction between 1st and 2nd class. Buffet cars usually offer coffee and drinks; sandwiches and refreshments are usually touted down the train during journeys.

Underground Railways Five lines link the outer parts of the City to the centre. "A" line runs under Calle Rivadavia, from Plaza de Mayo up to Primera Junta. "B" line from central Post Office, Avenida L. N. Alem, under Av. Corrientes to the Chacarita Cemetery. "C" line links Plaza Constitución with the Retiro railway station, and provides connections with all the other lines. "D" line runs from Plaza de Mayo, under the North Diagonal, Córdoba and Santa Fe to Palermo. "E" line runs from Plaza de Mayo through San Juan to Avs. Directorio and José María Moreno. The fare is about US$0.10, the same for any direct trip or combination between lines; tokens must be bought at booking offices *(boleterías)*; buy a few in advance to save time. Stations closed between 0100 and 0500. The local name for the system is the "Subte". Most stations have some very fine tile-work. Backpacks and luggage allowed.

National Tourist Information Office Santa Fe 883. Extremely friendly and helpful, with masses of maps and literature. Open 0800-2000, Mon.-Fri.; Tel.: 31-2300; 31-2089; 31-6800; 32-2232; 32-5550. National Parks Information Service, Santa Fe 680, very helpful. There are also helpful *Casas de Turismo* for most provinces (open Mon.-Fri., 1200-1900, closed 1st March onwards during winter period), including Buenos Aires, La Rioja, Mendoza, Catamarca, Río Negro, Córdoba and Chaco (all on Callao); Chubut, Paraguay 876; Corrientes, Bmé. Mitre 1685; Entre Ríos, Cangallo 451; Formosa, Bdo. de Irigoyen 188; Jujuy, Santa Fe 967; Misiones, Av. Santa Fe 989 ; Neuquén, Cangallo 685; Salta, Maipú 663; Tucumán, Avda. Roque Sáenz Peña 550. Information service for Bariloche in the Royal Bank of Canada building on Florida and Cangallo; also hotel, flat and bungalow service at Florida and Lavalle. A useful local booklet is *What's on in Argentina,* printed in Spanish, English, and Portuguese, with local information on festivals, etc.

Tourist Agents Exprinter, San Martín 176, Galería Güemes; Thos. Cook & Son, Av. Córdoba 746; Fairways, Viamonte 640, 3° piso (392-1716); City Service Travel Agency, Florida 890 (32-8416), which is the American Express agent; E.V.E.S., Tucumán 702; Star Travel Service, Florida 556 (392-2744); Tennant's, Bartolomé Mitre 559 (33-7645); Furlong's; Mitchell's, Av. Córdoba 657. *Schenker Argentina,* Lavalle 530, German, helpful for sending home presents or unwanted luggage (Tel.: 46-2074/2192) by boat, 4 kg. US$25, 4-8 kg. US$28. Gleizer Travel, on the ground floor of the *Sheraton Hotel,* has information about flights to New York.

Taxis are painted yellow and black,¹ and carry red number plates, and *Taxi* flags. Present rates are several times the price shown on the meter, e.g.—0.05 on the meter on 1.1.78 meant 200 pesos; there should be a list on the back of the front seat. A charge is made for each piece of hand baggage. Tips not necessary. Beware of overcharging late at night.

Car Hire Cars for hire, relatively expensive, can be got through hotel reception clerks. Use of Avis Car Credit card with central billing in one's home country is possible. Traffic drives on the right. Driving in Buenos Aires is recommended to only the most intrepid foreigner! Avis agency in the *Sheraton Hotel;* Godfrey Davis Rent-A-Car, M.T. de Alvear (ex Charcas) 680. Tel.: 32-9475/76.

Local bus services *(colectivos)* cover a very wide radius. The basic fare is about US$0.10. Give street destination and number to driver, who will charge accordingly.

Buses Long-distance buses leave from the bus stations at Plaza Constitución, and Once station. Some bus companies charge extra for luggage.

Cables State CyT on Calle Corrientes, near corner of Calle Maipú, public telex in basement; alternatively in Central Post Office, Leandro N. Alem 300, also telex. Another office is in Calle San Martín 322. Encotel, the state agency, has a monopoly.

Banks Bank of London & South America Ltd., corner of Reconquista and Bartolomé Mitre. It has 12 other branches in the city, and 6 others in Greater Buenos Aires.

Royal Bank of Canada, corner of Florida and Cangallo; Branch: Av. Callao 291. Citibank, B. Mitre 502. Branch: Florida 746. First National Bank of Boston, Florida 99. Bank of America, Cangallo and San Martín, Branch: Florida 999; Banco Holandés Unido, Florida 359. Banco Alemán Transatlántico, Bmé. Mitre and Reconquista. Open 1000-1600 (exchange operations up to 1300 only), Mon.-Fri.

A good exchange shop is Viatur, Reconquista 511; also Exprinter, San Martín 170; there are various good ones on San Martín, including Baires (215), Mercurio (229),

Baupesa (363), Piano (347) and Velox (298). Open from 0900 to 1630, Mon.-Fri. and on Sats., 0900-1200, in rotation. Buenos Aires is a good place to exchange money, also into other L.A. currencies.

The Markets Cattle auctions are among the sights and may be seen at Mercado de Liniers, in Liniers, for cows and pigs; Mercado Municipal at Mataderos, slaughtering and market place; and Mercado Nacional de Hacienda at Avellaneda, reached by 155 bus from Calle Tucumán (50 mins.). Said to be the largest cattle market in the world. Sale at 0730 on weekdays. Proper herding by riders on horseback. Helpful public relations staff. Mercado Central de Frutos, in Avellaneda, for wool and hides. The wholesale fish market is in Calle Algarrobo 1053 (Barracas). The largest vegetable market is the Mercado de Abasto, Calle Corrientes 3247. Sunday markets for souvenirs, antiques, etc.: Plaza Dorrego (San Telmo), Sunday 1000-1700, on Humberto 1° and Defensa. Also Fería de Las Artes (Fri., 1400-1700) on Defensa and Alsina. Plaza Francia (in front of La Recoleta cemetery, and Plaza San Martín, Sunday afternoons. Auction sales: some bargains at weekday auctions, Edificio de Ventas, Banco de la Ciudad de Buenos Aires, Esmeralda 660.

Hotels
The Dirección de Turismo fixes maximum and minimum rates for 1, 2 and 3-star hotels, guest houses and inns. Four and five-star hotels are free to apply any rate they wish.

| Name | Address | Price per day, US$ | | Grading |
		Single	Double	
Sheraton	San Martín 1225	34	40	****
Libertador	Córdoba y Maipú	35	40	****
Plaza	Florida 1005	34	41	****
Alvear Palace	Av. Alvear 1891	25	30	****
Claridge	Tucumán 535	40	50	****
Presidente	Cerrito 850	22	25	****
Eldorado	Av. Córdoba 622	18	21	****
City Hotel	Bolívar 160	11	19	***
Buenos Aires	M.T. de Alvear 767	20	24	***
Eibar	Florida 328	12	14	***
Savoy	Av. Callao 181	9	14	***
Crillón	Av. Santa Fe 796	11	17	***
Carlton	Libertad 1180	17	20	***
Lancaster	Av. Córdoba 405	19	27	***
Regidor	Tucumán 451	17	20	***
Nogaro	Av. J. A. Roca 562	9	15	***
Adriático	Reconquista 730	8	10	***
Carsson	Viamonte 650	12	17	***
Gran Hotel Dora	Maipú 963	13	15	***
Salles	Cerrito 208	18	22	***
Sussex	Tucumán 572	12	13	**
Liberty	Av. Corrientes 626	13	20	**
Italia Romanelli	Reconquista 647	12	17	**
Transocean	Lavalle 538	13	15	**
República	Cerrito 370	13	15	**
Rochester	Esmeralda 542	15	20	**
Los Dos Chinos	Brasil 764	7	9	**
Regis	Lavalle 813	9	14	*
King's	Av. Corrientes 623	7	10	*

Hotel Ocean, Maipú 907, clean, comfortable and reasonable, US$3 single, US$3.50 double; *Hotel Comercial,* Tucumán 664, between Florida and Maipú, is also cheap at US$4 single; some rooms have private bath. *Constitución Hotel,* about US$5 for room only, is good, clean; above bus terminus and convenient for railway station. *Mobal,* Tucumán 512, opposite Claridge, newly-furnished and converted old mansion, single US$4 with hot shower. *Florida House,* Florida 527, clean, comfortable, US$8 double, hot shower, recommended; *Hotel Jockey Club,* Florida 586, US$5 for double room, quiet and clean; *Hotel Florida Palace,* Florida 629,

US$5 single with shower, very friendly; *Central Argentino,* next to Retiro stations, US$2.30; *Splendide,* Calle Bouchard (by Luna Park), US$1.50; *Petit Hotel Goya,* Suipacha 748, very central, room with shower and toilet, US$1.75 single; *Hotel Gran Vía,* Sarmiento 1450, clean and friendly; *Sheltown,* M.T. de Alvear 742, US$16 double; *Gran Hotel Roi,* Avda. Corrientes y Esmeralda, US$2.50-3 per person; *Odeon Hotel,* near the Roi; *Jousten,* Corrientes 260, US$4 with bath; *Tres Sargentos,* Tres Sargentos 345, clean, pleasant and helpful, US$11.50 double; *Fénix,* San Martín 780, US$3 single, private bath, clean, recommended; *Castelar,* US$11 double, central, clean, friendly; *Cambridge,* Suipacha, between Lavalle and Corrientes, US$3.50 double, excellent and friendly; *Silver Home,* Suipacha 778, about US$7.65 double, recommended; *Gran Orly,* Paraguay 474, US$8.80 double, good position, helpful; *Hotel Varela,* Estados Unidos 342 (San Telmo), US$1.50 double, pleasant; *Hotel Florencia,* Florida, US$2.50 double, clean, hot water. Real bargain is *Hotel Viena,* Lavalle 368, US$1.50 single, with reasonable restaurant downstairs, friendly, English spoken, popular with Americans. Other cheap hotels are *Internacional,* México 950, US$0.70 double; *Iris,* Av. de Mayo 1277, piso 5; *Hotel Familiar San Martín* (not to be confused with *Residencial Familiar San Martín* in same building), San Martín 523, corner with Lavalle (no signs on street); *Parada,* Rivadavia 1291, US$1.20 with hot showers, central, very friendly; *Hotel Carlos,* Azcuénaga 1268, 10 minutes from centre, good, reasonably priced family hotel. *Residencial de Olga González,* Av. Callao 260; *San Martín,* Marcelo T. de Alvear, US$1 single; *Uruguay* 39 (pensión), US$1; *Once de Setiembre,* Cangallo y Castelli, US$1.50 single, English and French spoken, near Plaza Miserere; *Patagonia,* Suipacha 119, central, cheap; *Victoria,* Chacabuco 726, US$1 per person, use of kitchens. There are many economy-class hotels along Florida and east of it, towards Calle 25 de Mayo. Cheap hotels (US$1 per person) also near Plaza Constitución, *e.g.* the *Micromar,* English-owned, in Calle Dr. Finochetti, US$2.25 a day, serves three meals. *Hotel Gloria,* cheap, hot water and cooking facilities available. *Hotel Torino,* 25 de Mayo 724, simple but clean, US$1.30 per person; 2 mins. from Florida, *Aguila,* Cangallo 1554, US$2.80, clean. *Hotel Gran Mitre,* in Bartolomé Mitre, near Callao, US$3 double, old and airy, friendly. *Hotel Novus,* Sarmiento 631 (near Plaza de Mayo), US$3 each, recommended. Many hotels around Plaza Miserere, *Hotel Once,* good value; *Richmond,* Cerrito 286, US$14.70 double; *Embajador,* Carlos Pellegrin 1185, US$15.50 double; *Tucumán Palace,* Tucumán 384, US$13.35 double; *Wilton Palace,* Av. Callao 1162, US$13 double; *Diplomat,* San Martín 918, US$11.70 double; *King's,* Av. Corrientes 623, US$10 double; *Waldorf,* Paraguay 450, US$8.70 double; *Gran Royal,* Lavalle 450, US$6.70 double.

We have no report yet on the new *Hotel Continental,* Diagonal Norte 750, US$20 double, nor an up-to-date one on the *Internacional,* US$22 double, at Ezeiza airport.

One can rent flats on a daily basis in *Edificios Esmeralda,* Marcelo T. de Alvear 842, Tel. 31-3929, US$16.60 a day, cleaning included.

NB Additional service charges at both hotels and restaurants are about 24% *(laudo)*; VAT is also charged *(IVA)* at 16%. All the rates quoted are subject to alteration and it should be noted that for the most part they are the basic or minimum rates.

Tips In spite of the high service charge it is customary to tip 10% of the total bill; porters at hotels expect a tip—about US$0.50 per day of stay or service rendered. Hairdressers expect 10% of the bill, cinema ushers about US$0.20.

Electric Current 220 volts, 50 cycles, A.C., European Continental-type plugs in old buildings, American 3-pin flat-type in the new.

Restaurants *La Emiliana,* Av. Corrientes 1431; *London Grill,* Reconquista 435; chop-house style popular with British, US$7 per head with wine; *El Recodo,* Lavalle 130, recommended; *Pedemonte,* Av. de Mayo 676; *Lo Prete,* Luis S. Pena 749; *Hotel Español,* Av. de Mayo 1202 and *El Imparcial,* H. Irigoyen 1201, first-class service (Spanish); *La Tabla* and *El Muñdo,* Maipú 550, are recommended, reasonably priced. Another good cheap restaurant is *Pippo's,* near corner of Corrientes and Montevideo, with branches elsewhere. For roast chicken try *Pepito,* on Uruguay, between Corrientes and Sarmiento. Many excellent cheap restaurants on Lavalle and Maipú: *Las Deliciosas Papas Fritas,* 3-course meal with wine, Maipú

527, US$1.50; *El Imperio de las Papas Soufflée,* Maipú 558, first-class meals, US$2.50-3, good service; *El Palacio de La Pizza,* Corrientes 750, excellent, cheap; popular and cheap is *Oriente,* corner of Av. de Mayo and Av. 9 de Julio; *Pizzeria Americana* on Av. Callao, is cheap and excellent; *Corneta del Cazador,* 300 block of Cerrito, typical, excellent service, reasonable; *El Ceibal,* food from the NE, at Pueyrredón, corner Las Heras, distinguished, expensive; *Irish Pub-Downton Matias,* San Martín 979, lunch only.

Alejandra (English, cheaper than the *London Grill*), Calle San Martín 780. Typical Argentine restaurants: *La Cabaña,* Entre Ríos 436, old tavern style with local atmosphere, very good, under US$5 per head with wine; *Yapeyú,* Calle Maipú 389, recommended as good value and friendly; *El Fogón de Martín Fierro,* Palermo, good barbecue; *La Estancia,* Lavalle 941, barbecued meat and local dishes in typical surroundings, moderate prices; *Corrientes* 11, Av. Corrientes 135; *El Tropezón,* Callao 248; and *Mesón Español,* Av. Caseros 1750, good food and very good show of folk music. The typical parrilla is a speciality of *Tranquera,* in Palermo Park. *Cluquín,* on Cangallo 920 is a well-known traditional restaurant. *Rocinante,* Carlos Pellegrini 715, near Teatro Colón, recommended as delicious and not expensive. Other restaurants near the Colón are *Hamburgo,* Carlos Pellegrini 581; *El Quijote,* on No. 663; *Don Luis,* Viamonte 1169; and *Zum Edelweiss,* Libertad 431. Good Italian restaurant at Juncal called *Ligure,* US$8 for two. *Pichín No 1* or *No 2* on corner of Paraná and Sarmiento for gigantic "asado de tira"; *La Auténtica Banderita,* Moreno 1100, excellent meat dishes; *El Pulpo,* corner of Tucumán and Reconquista, Spanish sea-food; *La Casserolla,* Carlos Calvo 2000, best French food in town. Nearly all restaurants in the Boca area offer fixed price meals with "community" entertainment, from 2100 to 0400. *El Pescadito,* P. de Mendoza 1483, recommended for pasta and sea-food. *Los Immortales,* pizza-chain restaurants. For high international standards, with the best view of Buenos Aires and the river, try the *Sheraton's* rooftop restaurant. *Giulio,* Tucumán 732, *the* Italian restaurant in Buenos Aires. *Hispano,* Rivadavia 1200, reasonable, good sea-food. *El Repecho de San Telmo,* Carlos Calvo 242, excellent, reserve in advance. *La Veda,* on Florida 1 is new and expensive. Well-known and sophisticated are *La Biela, Don Juan* and *Clark's,* near the *Recoleta.*

Au Bec Fin, Calle Arenales and Libertad, is first class, expensive and French. The *Claridge Hotel* has an excellent restaurant. There are good restaurants all along Calle Lavalle, parallel to Corrientes, one block N serving 4 to 5 course meals at very reasonable table d'hôte prices. Others, like *El Palacio de la Papa Frita,* serve à la carte dishes which are very reasonably priced and plentiful, and are open from 1500-2000 when most other restaurants are closed. There are also several economical restaurants along Florida, e.g. *Santa Generosa, Cheburger.* The Costanera along the river front is lined with little cafés: a popular eating place, *El Rancho Inn,* is best. Good snacks all day and night at Retiro and Constitución railway termini, also at *La Escalerita,* Lavalle 717. *La Cautiva,* Sucre 1546, typical local game dishes.

Tea Rooms and Bars *Ideal,* Suipacha 384; *Richmond,* Florida 468; *London Grill,* Reconquista 435; *La Estrella* and *El Reloj,* Lavalle and Maipú; *Queen Bess,* Santa Fe 868; well-known are the *Confitería Suiza,* Tucumán 753, and the *Florida Garden* at Florida and Paraguay. *Exedra* on Carlos Pellegrini and Av. Córdoba and many on the Avda. Libertador in the Palermo area, such as *Round Point, Café Tabac* are fashionable. The more bohemian side of the city's intellectual life is centred on Avenida Corrientes, between Cerrito and Callao, where there are many bars and coffee shops, such as *La Paz* and *Politeama.* On Lavalle there are "whiskerías" and "cervecerías" where one can have either coffee or exotic drinks, the latter for some US$1 with small snacks. *Bar-baro,* cosmopolitan, Reconquista and Córdoba. *Barila,* Santa Fe 2375, has excellent confectionery.

Clubs and Social Centres Del Progreso, Sarmiento 1334; Círculo Militar, Florida 770; Centro Naval, Florida and Córdoba; Círculo de la Prensa, Rodríguez Peña 80; English, 25 de Mayo 586; Strangers, "Club de Residentes Extranjeros" (founded in 1841, and so the oldest in South America), Sarmiento 1334; English, 25 de Mayo 581; American, Viamonte 1133; French, R. Peña 1832; Spanish, B. de Irigoyen 172; Uruguayan, Tucumán 844; Automóvil Club, Av. Libertador 1850; Gimnasia and Esgrima, Bmé. Mitre 1154; Rotary Club, Suipacha 552, 3rd floor, Oficina 1;

International "SKAL" club, Viamonte 867; Lions; Swedish, Tacuari 147. Lastly, and most important, the Jockey Club (founded 1882), Av. Alvear 1345.

Sports Clubs Tennis, football, rugby, hockey, and basketball clubs are many, for these games are played by all nationalities. Cricket is played by the British community and baseball by the American. Hurling is played by the Irish-Argentines. Polo of a very high standard is also played. The Tigre Boat Club, founded in 1888, is the only British rowing club. It is open to British or American visitors for a small fee and a limited period.

Golf Clubs The leading clubs are the Hurlingham, Ranelagh, Ituzaingó, Lomas, San Andrés, San Isidro, Sáenz Peña, Olivos, Jockey, Campos Argentinos and Hindú Country Club.

Gambling Weekly lotteries. Totalisator betting at Palermo and San Isidro horse races. Football pools, known as *Prode*.

Night Clubs *Gong,* Córdoba 630, very fashionable; *Cabaret,* on M.T. de Alvear 628 facing *Plaza Hotel; Michelangelo,* impressive setting, restaurant and nightclub in an old reconverted monastery US$5 each, including cover charges and drink, in Balcarce; *Karina,* US$5 with cover charge and drink, good tango show at 0100, next door to *Liberty Hotel;* more locally coloured are *Mi Rincón,* Cerrito 1050; *La Querencia,* Av. de Mayo 870; *Achalay Huasi,* Esmeralda 1040; and many others. *Union Bar,* a very old inn, Paseo Colon e Independencia (San Telmo), excellent for tango music. Also at *El Viejo Almacén* and *Caño 14.*

Cinemas Many, centred on Lavalle. The selection of films is as good as anywhere else in the world; cost per ticket, some US$1.30. Reductions on Mon., Tues. and Wed. to US$1 unless they are holidays. When buying a cinema ticket in B.A. one has bought also a lottery ticket; this can be sent to the lotteries office to take part in a draw for a car. Tickets free of lottery charge, 25% cheaper, from ticket agencies *(cartelerías).* All foreign films are shown with subtitles.

Bookshops, English books and periodicals
Acme Agency, Suipacha 245; Mackern's English Bookstore, Sarmiento 525, Tel.: 49-4202; Pigmalion Bookstores (English and German), Corrientes 515 (books only, including secondhand paperbacks); Rodriguez, Sarmiento 871; ABC, Florida 725, Av. Córdoba 685 and Av. Libertador 13777 in Martínez suburb.

Libraries Biblioteca Lincoln, Florida 935; Harrods (2nd floor), on Florida, US$3 a month; Cultura Inglesa, Suipacha 1333 (for members only).

Useful Addresses
Argentine Association of English Culture, Suipacha 1333.
American Club, Viamonte 1133, facing Colón Theatre.
American Society of the River Plate, Viamonte 1133.
American Women's Club, Av. Córdoba 632, 11° piso.
Australian Embassy and Trade Mission, Av. Santa Fe 846 (Swissair Building). Tel.: 32-6841.
British Caledonian Airways, Córdoba 369. Tel.: 392-8203/8043.
British Chamber of Commerce, 25 de Mayo 444, 5° piso. Tel.: 32-6773.
British Community Council, Reconquista 314.
British Council, Marcelo T. de Alvear 590, 4° piso. Tel.: 31-4480.
British Embassy and Consulate-General, Luis Agote 2412/52 (Near corner Pueyrredón & Guido), Casilla de Correos 2050. Tel.: 80-7071.
British Embassy Residence, Gelly y Obés 2301.
British Hospital, Calle Perdriel 74. Tel.: 23-1081. Cheap dental treatment at Av. Caseros y Perdriel 76.
Canadian Embassy, Suipacha 1111.
Centre of British Engineering & Transport Institute, Bmé. Mitre 441.
English Club, 25 de Mayo 581. Tel.: 31-9121. Temporary membership available to British business visitors.
Salvation Army, Rivadavia 3255.
St. Andrew's Society, Perú 352.
South African Embassy, Marcelo T. de Alvear 590-8° piso. Tel.; 35-5050.
U.S.A. Chamber of Commerce, Roque Sáenz Peña 567.

U.S. Embassy and Consulate General, Colombia 4300, Palermo. Tel.: 744-8811.
U.S. Embassy Residence, Av. Liberatador General San Martín 3502.
U.S. Information Library (Biblioteca Lincoln), Florida 935.
Youth Hostel Association—information for all South America but no hostel in
B.A.—Av. Corrientes 1373, 1° piso.
Y.M.C.A. (Central), Reconquista 439.
Y.W.C.A., Tucumán 844.
Municipality offices, Av. de Mayo 525, facing Plaza de Mayo.
Central Police Station, Moreno 1550. Tel.: 38-8041. (Emergency, Tel.: 101).
Urgent medical service (day and night)   Tel.: 34-4001/4.

Inoculations   Free, without appointment, from Centro de Inmunización. Address
and hours from Tourist Office.

Camera Repairs   Casa del Flash, Av. de Mayo 839, 24-hour service for small
repairs.

General Post Office (Correo Central), corner of Sarmiento and L.N. Alem. State
Railways Building, Av. Maipú 4, in the New Port District; open 0800-2000 except on
Sundays and national holidays. Parcels from post office near port (Dock 2) at end of
Av. Chile, about US$1 for 5 kilos.

Principal Public Buildings

Casa de Gobierno   On the E side of the Plaza Mayo, and called because of its pink
colour the Casa Rosada, is where the President of the Republic conducts his official
business, holds Cabinet meetings, etc. Within the building there are several
Government departments of minor importance. (The President's official residence is
at Olivos, a northern suburb. The Foreign Minister's offices are at San Martín
Palace, Plaza San Martín). The interior can be seen by tourists if they apply to the
National Tourist Information Office. With a little persistence they can see a great
deal of it. The Casa Rosada is notable for its statuary, the rich furnishing of its halls
and for its libraries. The Museo de la Casa de Gobierno on the lower floors has
interesting historical exhibits. Open Tues., Wed., Fri.: 0900-1600: Thur.: 0900-1900;
Sun. 1500-1800.

The **Cabildo** on the W side of the same Plaza, formerly a seat of government used by
the councillors of the Viceroy, was put up in 1711 but has been rebuilt several times.
Its original structure, fittings and furniture were replaced in 1940 and it was declared
a national monument; it is guarded by soldiers in the red and blue uniform of San
Martín's grenadiers. See under "Museums".

Old Congress Hall on the S of the Square, built 1863, is a National Monument. It has
been encircled and built over by a palatial bank building. Open Thursday.

Congress Hall (Palacio del Congreso) to the SW and at the end of Avenida de Mayo,
of great size and in Greco-Roman architecture, is the seat of the legislature. It
contains the Senate and the Chamber of Deputies. There is limited accommodation
for the public at the sittings of either. The normal Parliamentary session, May 1 to
September 30, is often prolonged for extraordinary sessions. (Congress has held no
sessions since March 1976.)

Teatro Colón, one of the world's great opera houses, has its own National
Symphony Orchestra, opera and ballet companies. The cultural life of the capital
centres around the Colón Theatre, the National Museum of Fine Arts, and the
University of Buenos Aires. The theatre overlooks Avenida 9 de Julio, with its main
entrance on Libertad, between Tucumán and Viamonte. Like a huge jewel box, the
Colón's interior is resplendent with red plush and gilt; its vast stage is almost a block
long. Salons, dressing rooms and banquet halls are equally sumptuous. Open daily to
visitors (but not always in summer, so check). Male visitors are advised to wear
jacket and tie to performances. (Cheapest tickets, US$0.50).

Law Courts   The main entrance faces Calle Talcahuano 550. There are four large
central buildings, some 130 ft. high, built in Neo-Greek style.

The **Mint** (Casa de Moneda) in Avenida Wilson, New Port District, was opened in
1881 but at an old building in Calle Defensa.

The **Banco Central,** Calle Reconquista 258, is the seat of the gold reserve and of the Board which controls and issues the paper currency.

The **Bolsa de Comercio,** built in 1916, a handsome building in Calle 25 de Mayo, corner Sarmiento, is the meeting place of Buenos Aires brokers. It is at once a stock exchange, a grain market, a foreign exchange, and a general produce market. There is a very large membership. A new Stock Exchange was opened in 1929.

Banco de la Nación occupies a whole block in front of Plaza de Mayo, and is a most sumptuous building.

Churches

All historical churches are open 1630-1900; some at 0900-1100 also.

Note Very severe damage to some of the churches listed below was caused on the night of June 16, 1955, during anti-Catholic riots.

The **Cathedral** on the N of Plaza de Mayo is flanked by the former residence of the Archbishop. On this site was built the first church in Buenos Aires, a building which was under repair in 1618. After reconstruction in 1677 the edifice collapsed in 1753 and the rebuilding was not completed until 1823. The eighteenth century towers were never rebuilt, so that the architectural proportions have suffered. A frieze upon the Greek façade represents Joseph and his brethren. The tomb (1878) of the Liberator, General José de San Martín, is imposing. There are large and elegant marble carvings and mural paintings of interest in the central nave. Some destruction took place: the valuable collection of precious vestments dating from the earliest part of the colonial epoch was completely burnt, and the contents of the vestry set on fire. The Archbishop's Palace (Curia) was set on fire and has now been rebuilt. The valuable library, containing historical records of the River Plate since 1600, was destroyed.

The **Church of San Ignacio de Loyola,** at Calles Alsina and Bolívar, founded in 1710, is the oldest Colonial building in Buenos Aires. It has two lofty towers. All the religious ornaments were smashed beyond repair. The vestry and adjoining dependencies were reduced to cinders. The **San Francisco,** Calles Alsina and Defensa, controlled by the Franciscan Order, was inaugurated in 1754 and given a new façade in 1808. Completely gutted, all treasures burnt, as also in the adjoining Chapel of San Roque (1750), but the buildings are now completely restored.

La Merced, Calles Cangallo and Reconquista, was founded 1604 and rebuilt 1732. One of the altars has a seated figure of the Lord of Humility and Patience carved in wood during the 18th century by an Indian in Misiones. The vicarage library and all the adjoining dependencies with their valuable colonial ornaments were smashed and burnt. It has one of the best organs in the country, and one of the few fine carillons of bells in Buenos Aires.

Santo Domingo, Calles Defensa and Belgrano, was founded in 1756. During the British attack on Buenos Aires in 1806 some of Whitelocke's soldiers took refuge in the Church. The local forces shelled it (some of the hits can still be seen on one of the towers); the British capitulated and their regimental colours were captured and preserved at the church. On the night of June 16, 1955, the flags were saved from the fire, but all but one chapel was destroyed. Restoration is now complete. The adjoining Salón Belgraniano (with many relics of General Belgrano and much Colonial furniture) was heavily damaged. There are summer evening concerts in the church; check times.

San Miguel Arcangel at Suipacha and Bmé. Mitre. This fine church, which contained most valuable treasures dating from 1751, was set on fire and all the ornaments smashed. The vestry, library, archives, etc., were all gutted.

El Pilar, Calle Junín 1904, is attended by Porteño society. It is a jewel of Colonial architecture dating from 1717, in a delightful setting of public gardens. An exceptionally fine wooden image of San Pedro de Alcántara, attributed to the famous 17th century Spanish sculptor Alonso Cano, is preserved in a side chapel on the left.

English speaking Churches

The **Holy Cross,** Calle Estados Unidos 3150, established by the Passionists, a modern Gothic building in granite, is a monument to Irish piety.

St. John's Cathedral (Anglican), 25 de Mayo 282, was built one-half at the expense of the British Government and decicated in 1831. **St. Paul's, St. Peter's, St. Michael and All Angels** and **St. Saviour's** are Anglican places of worship in the suburbs.

St. Andrew's, Calle Belgrano 579, is one of the 8 Scottish Presbyterian churches.

The **American Church,** Corrientes 718, is Methodist, and the first of its kind to be established in South America. It was built in 1863. Service at 1100.

First Methodist (American) Church, Av. Santa Fe 839, Acassuso.

American Community Church, built in a suburb where Americans mostly live.

Christian Science First Church of Christ, Scientist, Ayacucho 349; Second Church of Christ, Scientist, Sargento Cabral 841-7; Christian Science Society, Chacabuco 863.

The **Cemetery of Recoleta,** near Palermo Park, is one of the sights of Buenos Aires. "A Doric portico gives on to the main, paved, cypress-lined avenue of a little city of the dead. At the end of the avenue there is a great bronze statue of the resurrected Saviour; on either side, hard up against each other, like houses in a street, there are the family vaults of the Argentine patricians. Every possible style of architecture is represented; there are little pyramids, little banks, little war memorials; sometimes you can see a coffin through a side door; other vaults are arranged like sets of pigeon holes, with the coffins slipped in, their ends either visible, or concealed by a hinged votive tablet." G. S. Fraser, in *News from Latin America.*

Museums, Libraries, Arts, Exhibitions, etc.
Note: Most museums closed on Monday, and in January, and most of February for summer holidays.

Museo de la Casa de Gobierno (basement of Government House), Hipólito Irigoyen 218. Historical memorabilia, particularly of former Presidents. See p. 51.

Museo de Bellas Artes (National Gallery), Avenida Libertador Gral. San Martín 1473. In addition to modern Argentine, American and European works, there are paintings attributed rightly or wrongly to old masters; paintings representing the conquest of Mexico, executed 300 or 400 years ago, and wooden carvings from the Argentine hinterland. Open 1000-1300, 1530-1900; closed Wednesdays.

The National Museum of the Decorative Arts is at Av. Libertador Gral. San Martin 1902. The building is shared with the **Museo Nacional de Arte Oriental;** both are open Wed.-Mon., 1500-1900.

Biblioteca Nacional (The National Library). Calle México 566, founded in 1810, moved here in 1902. About 500,000 volumes and 10,000 manuscripts.

Museo Histórico Nacional (The National Historical Museum). Defensa 1600. It has 6 salons and a gallery. Trophies and mementoes of historical events are displayed in large numbers. Here are San Martín's uniforms, a replica of his famous curved sabre, and the original furniture and door of the house in which he died at Boulogne. Open Thursday to Sunday, 1400-1800.

Museo de La Ciudad, Alsina 412, open 1000-1900. Permanent exhibition of architectural and urban development exhibits.

Museo Mitre y Biblioteca (The Mitre Museum and Library). San Martín 336, preserves intact the household of President Bartolomé Mitre. The manuscripts, documents and printed works constitute a unique record of Argentine political development. Open 1500-1700.

Museo de Ciencias Naturales (The Natural Science Museum) at Avenida Angel Gallardo 470, facing Parque Centenario. It houses palaeontological, zoological, mineralogical, botanical, archaeological and marine sections. Open Tue., Thurs., Sun. 1400-1800. Library, Mon.-Fri., 1100-1700.

Museo Municipal (The Municipal Museum), Quinta Saavedra, Av. Gral. Paz y Republiquetas. It contains coins, utensils hammered from precious metals, old watches, fans, hair-combs, furniture and pictures.

Museo Municipal de Arte Moderno (Tues.-Sun. 1600-2200) and **Museo Municipal de**

Artes Plásticas Eduardo Sivori (Tues.-Sun. 1600-2000) are at Avenida Corrientes 1530, where there are also a cinema and a theatre.

Museo de Artes Visuales, Av. Corrientes 1530, Tue.-Fri. 1600-2000. Free entry on Wed. 19th century and contemporary Argentine painting.

Museo de Motivos Populares Argentinos José Hernández, Av. del Libertador 2373, Gaucho collection, open Tues.-Sun., 1400-1800.

Museo del Instituto Nacional Sanmartino, Sánchez de Bustamente and Av. A. M. de Aguado; Mon.-Fri. 0900-1200 and 1400-1700; Sat., Sun. 1400-1700.

Museo de Arte Español Enrique Larreta, Juramento 2291, in Belgrano. 1500-1945. Closed Thurs. The home of the writer Larreta. Also **Biblioteca Alfonso El Sabio,** Mon.-Fri., 1300-1930.

Museo de Cabildo y Revolución de Mayo (Cabildo and May 1810 Revolution Museum),Bolívar 65, is the old Cabildo building, converted into a museum in 1940. It contains paintings, documents, furniture, etc., recording the May 1810 revolution. Open Wed., Thurs. and Sun. 1600-2000; Fri. and Sat. 1800-2200. Library, Mon.-Fri., 1100-1900.

Museo de Arte Hispano-Americano Isaac Fernández Blanco, (the Isaac Fernández Museum of Hispanic-American Art), Suipacha 1422. Contains a most interesting and valuable collection of Colonial art, especially silver, in a beautiful Colonial mansion. Open Thursday to Sunday, 1400-1800. Latin American art and history library at Suipacha 1444, 0900-1900, Mon.-Fri.

Museo y Biblioteca Ricardo Rojas, Charcas 2837, open Wednesays and Fridays 1500-1800, free. Rojas, "Prince of Argentine Letters" for more than two generations, lived in this beautiful Colonial house for several decades. It contains his library, souvenirs of his travels, and many intriguing literary and historical curios. House is often used as a meeting place for scholars and literary men.

Numismatic Museum; fascinating, well kept, little known, at the Banco Central.

"Presidente Sarmiento", Dársena Norte, a sailing ship built 70 years ago and long used as a naval training ship; now a museum. Open on weekend afternoons. Small charge. Another sailing ship nearby, the **"Uruguay",** is also due to become a museum.

Bank of London and South America, corner of Bartolomé Mitre and Reconquista, has a miniature museum on its fifth floor: old notes, scales, ledgers, pictures and mementoes of its history since it was founded in 1862. Open during banking hours.

Museo Nacional Ferroviario, Av. Libertador 405, next to Retiro station. Mon.-Fri., 0800-1800, free. For railway fans.

Museo Botánico, Las Heras 4102 and Malabia 2690. Open 0800-1200 and 1400-1800, Mon.-Fri. Herbarium.

Museo de La Dirección Nacional del Antártico, Angel Gallardo 470, Tue., Thurs. and Sun., 1400-1800. Dioramas.

Museo del Teatro Colón, Tucumán 1161. Mon.-Fri. 1200-1800. Documents and objects related to the theatre.

Museo Histórico Saavedra, Republiquetas 6309. Wed.-Fri., 1400-1800; Sat., 1800-2200; Sun., 1500-1900. City history from the eighteenth century. Free on Wed.

Parks and Squares

Parque Lezama, Calles Defensa and Brasil, originally one of the most beautiful in the city, has been somewhat vandalised. It has old trees, shady paths, rose gardens, terraces, a bandstand, and an imposing statue of Pedro de Mendoza, the founder of the original city in 1535. The tradition is that the first founding took place on this spot.

The **Municipal Botanical Gardens,** Santa Fe 2951, entrance from Plaza Italia (take "subte", line E), contain characteristic specimens of the world's vegetation. The trees proper to the several provinces of Argentina are brought together in one section.

The **Zoo** is next to the Botanical Gardens; it is attractive because several of the animals, such as the Patagonian Mara (a local short-eared hare), are permitted to roam where they will.

Planetarium is worth a visit. There is a ½ hour display for US$0.10. Best on Sunday afternoons. Architecture distinctive.

The **Palermo Parks** with their magnificent avenues are the city's Bois de Boulogne. They are famous for their rose garden, Andalusian Patio, and the Hipódromo Argentino, the internationally-known Palermo racetrack. Opposite the parks are the Botanical and Zoological Gardens. Nearby are the Municipal Golf Club, Buenos Aires Lawn Tennis Club, riding clubs and polo field, and the popular Club de Gimnasia y Esgrima (Athletic and Fencing Club), given over to all types of sports.

The **Show Grounds** of the Argentine Rural Society, on a site next to Palermo Park, are the finest in the world. The Annual Livestock Exhibition, usually held in July, is the main agricultural show of the year. The finest Argentine specimens of pedigree cattle, horses, sheep, and pigs can be seen there.

The **Racecourse** or Hipódromo Argentino, in Palermo Park, seats about 45,000.

There is an equally large and modern racecourse (one of the best of its kind) with grass track at San Isidro, 25 minutes by train or road. The meetings alternate with those at Palermo. There are Saturday and Sunday races throughout the year, and upon all holidays other than May 25 and July 9. Betting is by totalisator only.

There are many other important and large parks, such as 3 de Febrero, Centenario, Saavedra, Avellaneda, Retiro, Chacabuco, etc., which are beautifully laid out.

Plazas The most interesting are the Plaza de Mayo, containing so many public buildings: the Plaza San Martín, with a monument to San Martín in the centre; the Plaza Británica, with the clock tower presented by British and Anglo-Argentine residents: "a florid Victorian sentinel, royal crest upon its bosom"; the Plaza Lavalle; the Plaza del Congreso, the largest in the city; the Plaza Rodríguez Peña, with its statue to the Chilean General O'Higgins; the Plaza Italia, with its Garibaldi statue; the Plaza Miserere, outside the Sarmiento Railway terminus; the Plaza Constitución, with the Roca Railway terminus station. There are also the Plazas Independencia, Libertad, Francia, Moreno, Las Heras, Alvear, Colón and the great Plaza de la República, with a 67-metre Obelisk at the junction between the Northern Diagonal and the widened Avenida Corrientes.

Travel into Neighbouring Countries

NB *Foreign tourists must pay fares for international journeys in foreign currency.*

By Road
Four branches of the Pan American Highway run from Buenos Aires to the borders of Chile, Bolivia, Paraguay and Brazil. The roads are paved except when otherwise stated. (Distances in kilometres.)

Road to Chile Buenos Aires to Pergamino, 224 km.; Venado Tuerto, 146; Río Cuarto, 238; Mercedes, 128; San Luis, 98; Mendoza, 264; Luján de Cuyo, 18; Potrerillos, 40; Uspallata, 53; Polveradas, 45; Punta de Vacas, 11; international tunnel into Chile, 43. Total: 1,310 km. Paved as far as Potrerillos (though section between Río Cuarto and Mercedes is poor) and from Uspallata to Polveradas.

To Bolivia Buenos Aires to General Pacheco 35; San Nicolás, 212; Rosario, 61; Villa María, 271; Córdoba, 713; Río Pisco; Huasi, 134; Rayo Cortado, 31; Villa de María, 18; boundary of Córdoba Province, 27; Villa Ojo de Agua, 16; Loreto, 151; Santiago del Estero, 56; Tucumán, 163; Tapia, 32; Ruiz de los Llanos, 56; Rosario de la Frontera, 47; Metán, 35; Cabeza de Buey, 95; Salta, 27; Caldera, 16; El Carmen, 51; Jujuy, 26; Yala, 16; Huacalera, 92; Humahuaca, 29; Azul Pampa, 42; La Quiaca, on Bolivian border, 121. Total; 1,994 km.

To Paraguay To Rosario (as for Bolivia), 309 km.; Santa Fe, 166; Jobson, 258; Reconquista, 66; Resistencia, 220; Puerto Vélez, 127; Formosa, 74; Puerto Pilcomayo, 135. Total: 1,353 km. (all paved). Cross the Río Paraguay by ferry to Itá Enramada, in Paraguay, and on 10 km. to Asunción. The bus service from Buenos Aires to Asunción leaves 0900 Tue., Thur., Sat., with *común* service, 23 hours, US$13; or 1400 Wed., Fri., Sun., with *diferencia*, 19 hours, US$25. The journey may be done more cheaply by catching an Empresa Godoy bus to Pilcomayo, Argentine terminal of the ferry to Asunción. (Bus from Santa Fe to Asunción US$18.)

Those who wish to drive to Misiones to visit San Ignacio Mini or the Iguazú Falls should cross the river by the bridge between Santa Fe and Paraná, or the one between Resistencia and Corrientes. From there Route 12 leads NE through Posadas to the Iguazú Falls. From Corrientes to Esperanza is paved, and the last 15 km. to Iguazú are now in process of paving. (Daily bus to Puerto Iguazú, except Sunday, US$15, 24 hrs.) From Posadas you can cross the river to Encarnación (ferry takes cars) and take a good 370-km. road to Asunción (see Paraguayan chapter).

To Brazil   To the Iguazú Falls, take the road given above to Asunción, Paraguay, and then a paved 326-km. road to Puerto Stroessner and cross by bridge to Brazil—or go by the ferry (which takes cars), from Puerto Iguazú. A second road to Iguazú, rather shorter, is Route 12, as given above for Paraguay. A second road to the border with Brazil at Paso de los Libres goes from Buenos Aires to Rosario, 309; Santa Fe, 166; cross by bridge and tunnel to Paraná; Villa Federal, 200 (98 paved); Junction with Route No. 14 (unpaved, and from here on), 126; Curuzú Cuatiá, 243; Bonpland, 68; Paso de los Libres, 42, opposite Uruguaiana (Brazil), across the Río Uruguay. Total: 960 km. For the roads from Colonia and Montevideo to the Brazilian frontier, see the Uruguay section. Direct bus from Buenos Aires to São Paulo and Rio de Janeiro, about US$56 (takes 50 hrs. to Rio, pay in US$ cash) with Expreso Americano; buy tickets at Agencia Buen Viaje, Córdoba 415, Tel.: 31-2953. Bus terminal at Catamarca 47, Plaza Once (Chevallier), Tel.: 87-4569. Leaves at 1230 on Thurs., Fri., and Sat. Super Pullman buses. Brazilian company Pluma, Córdoba 461 daily buses to São Paulo at 0900 and 1600, US$50, and to Rio at 1500.

To Uruguay   Direct road connections have been established by means of two new bridges over the River Uruguay between Puerto Colón and Paysandú and between Puerto Unzué and Fray Bentos.

Air, River and Railway Services

Brazil   Daily services to São Paulo, Rio de Janeiro and other Brazilian cities by air. Steamship service between Buenos Aires and Brazilian ports by various transatlantic lines.

Chile   Trains leave from Retiro Station (San Martín Railway) with Libertador train (Sun. and Thurs.) and Sanjuanino (Mon. and Fri.) at 1825, arrive next day in Mendoza at 0830. Return connecting journey from Mendoza at 2145, arrive next day 1105, US$32 with Pullman, US$51.60 with sleeper. Connections to Santiago (Mapocho). Bed as far as Mendoza only. At Los Andes passengers change to Chilean trains to Santiago and Valparaíso. Both Santiago (Mapocho) and Valparaíso can be reached with de luxe buses from Los Andes; there is a connecting direct route, better than railway *via* Llay-Llay. Return trains from Santiago go to B.A. on Mon., Wed., Fri., and Sat. from Mendoza at 2045. Free baggage allowance is 30 kg., and excess is charged. During the winter, May to November, the line is sometimes blocked by snow. Train services are then reduced to Tue. and Thurs. (sleeping car) 1815 from Buenos Aires; arr. Mendoza 0830 Wed. and Fri., respectively, change and leave Mendoza at 0945 and 0905, arrives Santiago 1930. Santiago-Buenos Aires leave Mon. (sleeping cars) and Sat. at 0900, arrive at Mendoza 1935 and 2000, leave 2045, arrive 1045. There is also a train service to Antofagasta, *via* Salta and Socompa. Train leaves Retiro, Belgrano Railway, on Mon. at 2000, arriving on Thurs. 2210, staying over at Salta from 0945 to 2315 Fridays. Fare US$19.50 single with bed.

Foreign and national lines fly daily between Buenos Aires and Santiago. Time taken: 1 to 2 hours. There are 2 or 3 flights weekly by Aerolíneas Argentinas to Punta Arenas on the S coast of Chile, *via* Comodoro Rivadavia and Río Gallegos.

Bolivia   Trains leave from Retiro Station (US$24.70, US$58.35 with sleeping accommodation), Mitre Railway 1800 Sun. and Thurs., arr. Tucumán 1240 Mon. and Fri. respectively and leave at 1515, arriving at La Paz at 1615 on Wed. and Sun. Alternatively, Belgrano Railway trains leave at 2005 Wednesday, sleeping car between Buenos Aires and Jujuy (arr. 0820 Fri.). Journeys can be delayed in rainy season. Return 1130 Mon., Thurs., Fri., from La Paz, arriving 1255 Thurs., 1105 Sun. and 1255 Mon. Free baggage allowance 30 kg., and excess is charged. A weekly train to Santa Cruz de la Sierra from Retiro Station *via* Güemes, Pocitos and

Yacuiba takes 3 days. Leaves Buenos Aires 2205 Sat., arrives Santa Cruz 1603 Tues. From Santa Cruz, dep. 0915 Thurs., arrival 1105 at Retiro.

There are also regular air services 5 or 6 times a week to La Paz by Braniff, Aerolíneas and Lloyd Aéreo Boliviano.

Paraguay Two trains a week to Asunción from Lacroze Station, on Mon. and Wed. (no sleeper) at 0710 and arrives at 1430 Wed. and Fri., arriving 1950 Wed. and Sun. in Buenos Aires. Friday service has sleeper from Posadas 1325. Fare about US$18 first class and Us$14 second. Dusty journey. Three additional trips each way between Buenos Aires and Posadas for that route, with sleeping-car service twice a week. There is a daily air service to Asunción by various companies. Time taken: 2 to 6 hours. The regular steamship service (April-November only) to Asunción leaves Buenos Aires fortnightly, a 4½-day trip at 1400 on Mon. Very comfortable, with excellent food. Boats sail up the Río Paraná and Río Paraguay calling at Rosario, Paraná, Corrientes and Formosa. Fare to Asunción, US$90. By bus with Empresa La Internacional from Plaza Once daily at 1400 exc. Sun., US$33.35, to Asunción.

Uruguay A river-boat service to Montevideo leaves most nights at 2100, arrives at Montevideo the following morning at 0700, and starts back same day at 2100 (cost is US$16 for 1st class and US$12 for 2nd class single. Tickets at Flota Fluvial, Av. Corrientes 389). Take the train to Tigre (Mitre suburban line), 35 mins. (US$0.20), leaves at 10 min. intervals from Retiro, for a daily boat (tickets at Cacciola S.A., Suipacha 465, which leaves at 0800 for Carmelo (the journey takes 4½ hours, US$12, where a connecting bus is caught for Montevideo. It gets there in the afternoon. There is also a fast *aliscafo* (hydrofoil) service from Dársena "D", taking one hour, four times a day (0815, 1115, 1430, 1715) to Colonia and Montevideo 2 and 5 hrs. respective journeys, US$27.30 return, US$14.30 single (not recommended in bad weather), by Alimar, Marcelo T. de Alvear 1199. Each morning (except Sunday) there is also a plane service to Colonia. Air service to Montevideo, mornings or afternoon, daily except Sunday, about US$25. Flight takes 1 hour. The cheapest way of crossing the River Plate is by daily motor launch from Tigre to Carmelo,(necessary to book day before at ONDA bus company near Florida, corner of Lavalle). From Dársena Sur ferry to Colonia with car, US$29.90 up to 800 kg., US$40.15 to 1,200 kg., US$49.50 over 1,200 kg. There are many buses between Colonia and Montevideo. For northern Uruguay, take the Urquiza train to Concordia, then the ferry to Salto.

Guest rooms in Tigre at Montes de Oca 142, US$2.30 a night (Antonio J. Pissini).

Note On the night ferry to Montevideo rush to the dining room if you want to spare yourself a supperless night.

Suburbs of Buenos Aires

Avellaneda, a separate municipality of over 650,000 people. It is one of the most important industrial centres in the country; the handling of hides, wool and animal produce is concentrated here. It is 5 km. from P. Constitución station and is served by up-to-date buses which cross the Riachuelo river.

Bank of London and South America, Av. Gral. Mitre 553. First National Bank of Boston. 1000-1600.

Belgrano, about 15 minutes by train and 25 by road, is a favourite suburb for British residents. The Av. Cabildo is a popular shopping street.

Bank of London and South America, Avenida Cabildo 1939. 1000-1600.

Hurlingham, on the San Martín railway (27 km., 45 minutes), has a fine club run on English lines, possibly the country's best. The principal sports are polo, cricket, golf, and tennis. Many residents are British. Pop.: about 60,000.

Lomas, 14½ km. on the Roca Railway. There is a large British community in this popular residential suburb. Population: 90,000.

Bank of London and South America, Boedo 99. 1000-1600.

Temperley, an important junction on the Roca Railway, 18 km. from Plaza Constitución and also served by minibuses. It has many British residents, Pop.: 105,000.

Olivos, on the River Plate coast, 20 minutes by the Bartolomé Mitre Railway, is a favourite residential district. It has quays for small trading vessels, the presidential residence is there, many British and American residents. Population, about 160,000. Nearby, at La Lucila, there are many American families.

San Isidro, just beyond Olivos, a resort for golf, yachting, swimming, and athletics, is one of the most picturesque places on the coast. There is a magnificent turf racecourse, an attractive central plaza and fine colonial buildings. Pop.: 80,000.

Bank of London and South America, Chacabuco 328. 1000-1600.

Quilmes has one of the world's largest breweries. It is an important industrial centre where textiles, ironware and glass are manufactured. Population about 150,000. There are some British residents and St. George's College, an English boarding school. Bathing is now both dangerous and prohibited; in one day 19 lives were lost. It is served by the Roca Railway and buses.

The naturalist, W. H. Hudson (1841-1922) was born at Florencia Varela, near Quilmes, about 32 km. from Buenos Aires. His birthplace is now a national monument. A railway station in the Quilmes district is named after him.

Bank of London and South America, Hipólito Yrigoyen 616. 1000-1600.

Ranelagh, on the General Roca railway, another purely residential district patronised by the British and Americans, is 15 minutes by train from Quilmes. It has one of the best golf courses in the country.

Tigre, on Bartolomé Mitre Railway, amidst rivers and streams, is about 29 km. (35 minutes) from Buenos Aires. It is a pleasant place, with yachting, rowing, and other clubs. Regattas are held in November and March on the River Luján. There are numerous "Recreos" and restaurants on the river front, but sleeping accommodation is not good. Inland from Tigre is the Delta of the Paraná, with innumerable canals and rivulets, a profitable fruit growing centre and an attraction for holiday makers. The fishing is excellent and there is peace on the waterways, apart from motor-boats at week-ends. Regular launch services for all parts of the Delta, including taxi launches—watch prices for these!—leave from wharf opposite railway station. Population: 40,000. Delta Youth Hostel at Colón y Río Luján, San Fernando, ask at Corrientes 1373, 1st floor, Buenos Aires. Direct ferry to Carmelo, Uruguay daily at 0800, from opposite railway station. (If you miss the boat, Antonio J. Pissini has guest rooms for US$2.30 a night at Montes de Oca 142, Tigre.)

The Naval Museum is worth a visit. It contains models, old and new, navigation instruments, flags and banners and paintings of naval battles. The Reconquista Museum was opened on Aug. 12, 1956, on the 150th anniversary of the reconquest of Buenos Aires from the British; much of the story is told in the relics preserved.

There is one town which belongs to Argentina as a whole rather than to any province or area, though it is actually in the province of Buenos Aires and only 71 km. W of the capital by Sarmiento railway from Once station (1½ hours, US$1) or by road. This is

Luján, a place of pilgrimage for all devout Catholics in Argentina. An image of the Virgin was being taken from church to church in the area in 1630 by ox cart. At a certain spot the cart got stuck, in spite of strenuous efforts by men and oxen to move it. This was taken as a sign that the Virgin willed she should stay there. A chapel was built for the image, and around it grew Luján. The chapel has long since been superseded by a magnificent neo-Gothic basilica and the Virgin now stands on the High Altar. May 8 is her day. Each arch of the church is dedicated to an Argentine province, and two of the transepts to Uruguay and Paraguay. Population: 30,000. Reached by infrequent train (US$1.50 return) or bus (Plaza Miserere) from Once station. The bus does tend to get caught at weekends in traffic.

Museo Colonial e Histórico (The Colonial and Historical Museum) is in the old Cabildo building. Exhibits illustrate the historical and political development of the country. One of the most interesting museums. Open daily, except Monday and Tuesday, 1200-1800. General Beresford, the leader of an attempt to capture Buenos

Aires, was a prisoner here, and so, in later days, were Generals Mitre, Paz, and Belgrano. There are also two transport and one art museum. The river Luján is picturesque at this point, and is a favourite spot for picnic parties.

Hotels *España, La Paz.* There are numerous **restaurants**: an excellent one is *L'Eau Vive* on the road to Buenos Aires on Constitución 2112; it is run by nuns, expensive, pleasant surroundings, 3-course meal with wine US$10.

Other Towns in the Pampas

There are dozens of small, prosperous towns scattered throughout the vast area of the pampas. They serve as clearing centres for the cattle and grain and supply the rural population, which is much denser in the Humid Pampa than elsewhere in Argentina. They are built in the Spanish style around a central plaza which usually contains the church, the administrative offices of the area and the hotels. There is, invariably, a railway station, one or more cinemas, a market and, quite often, an airstrip nearby. Only the larger towns and resorts are dealt with here.

La Plata, capital of Buenos Aires Province by the River Plate and only 56 km. SE of Buenos Aires, is reached by Roca railway or by many buses. This modern city, founded in 1882, has a population of about 406,000. The streets and diagonals are wide and there are imposing public buildings. It has most successfully fused its dual role of great port and cultural centre. Its port, one of the best in the Republic and accessible to ships of the largest tonnage, makes it a main outlet for the produce of the pampas. Its major industrial interest is in refrigerated meat products and the YPF petroleum refinery; a 72-km. pipeline runs to the South Dock at Buenos Aires. It is also the seat of an archbishopric; its university, colleges and secondary schools, and technical schools for women rank high in Argentina. Its Museum of Natural History is one of the best in the world and has several unique exhibits (open 1300-1800).

Points of Interest The Museum at La Plata, famous for its collection of extinct animals, is open daily except in January and on public holidays. Its treasures are largely ethnological and include human skulls, mummies, and prehistoric implements. There are zoological, botanical, geological, mineralogical, palaeontological and archaeological sections with cases interesting both to the curious and the scientific. Well laid-out Zoological Gardens; fine racecourse, run under similar rules to the Palermo course, and Observatory. The Museum, Zoological Gardens, and Observatory are all in the public park; The town has a Garden of Peace, each country in the world represented by one flower, with a plaque in front of it; on October 12 flags are put up there. The Town Hall and Cathedral are in the Plaza Moreno. Ten minutes in the train takes one to the Islas de Rio Santiago and to the Yacht Club, Arsenal, and Naval Academy. Nearby is an interesting children's village with scaled-down public buildings, built under the first Perón administration.

Local Holiday Foundation of the City, November 19.

Hotels *City; Marini; Provincial,* on Calle 8 between 50 and 52, US$5 double.

British Vice-Consul, Calle 49, No. 709. (Tel.: 28090.)

Buses To Buenos Aires, Rápido, 1½ hrs. Fare US$0.40. A motorway is being built to Buenos Aires.

Tourist Office Pasaje Dardo Rocha, Calle 49, between Calle 6 and 7.

Buenos Aires to Mar del Plata Along the same shore, on the coast 400 km. S from Buenos Aires, lies Mar del Plata, the celebrated Argentine seaside resort. There are Roca line trains from Constitución Station, a day and night bus service and an air service. The road and rail routes S are through Chascomus and Dolores.

Chascomus, 126 km. from Buenos Aires, is in a wide plain on the shores of Lake Chascomus, which covers 3,000 hectares and swells greatly in size during the rains. Its slightly brackish water is an important breeding place for pejerrey fish; up to 1,000 kg. have been caught in one day during the winter season, when amateur fishing competitions are held. There is a gaucho museum, and also a Regatta Club and bathing beaches and camping grounds at Monte Brown, on the far side of the lake.

Hotels   *Del Lago; Riviera; Americano; Santa Maria.*

Camping Sites   *Estancia El Carmen* and *Casa Amarilla.*

Dolores, 204 km. from Buenos Aires, has a district population of 30,000; it was founded in 1818, destroyed by Indians three years later, and rebuilt. It is a grain and cattle farming centre.

Hotel   *Argentina.*

About 130 km. N of Mar del Plata a new seaside resort, **Villa Gesell,** has sprung up, very popular with young people and families. The town offers dunes, pine forests and sandy beaches, over a dozen pleasant, intimate hotels *(Tejas Rojas, Aloha, Capri,* etc.), and villas to let. Direct bus service to Buenos Aires by Empresas Antón and Río de la Plata.

Camping Sites   *Del Sol, El Faro,* hot water. The first is open all year round.

Pinamar, 22 km. N of Villa Gesell, is a new and growing resort, with a casino.

Hotels   *Playa* and *Libertador.* **Youth hostel** at Ostende.

Mar del Plata is 4½ hours by train, 7 by Pullman bus, 45 minutes by air from the capital, 400 km. away. The normal population is 350,000, but during the summer about two million visitors stay there for an average of 14 to 20 days, for it is a popular resort with all classes. There are luxurious hotels and several hundred catering for families and the lower income groups, as well as a host of boarding houses and lodgings. The season, from November to Easter, is preceded by the sporting events of the annual "Spring Week". During January and February leaders in most spheres of Argentine life make Mar del Plata their temporary home. It is famous for its spacious and luxurious casino, which is said to take US$200,000 a night, on average. Profits go to the Welfare Ministry. The upper floor is open to the public, for a small admission charge (men must wear jackets and ties). Palatial apartment buildings have been built near the beaches. In the centre are the shops, markets, banks, exchange bureaux, tea-rooms, restaurants, cinemas and nightclubs.

There are fine squares, especially Plaza Luro, planted with trees and flowers. There are eight km. of beaches. They include fashionable Playa Grande, with its private clubs and the summer estates of wealthy *porteños*; Bristol Beach, where the casino is; and Playa Perla, with moderately priced hotel accommodations. At Punta Iglesia there is a large rock carving of Florentino Ameghino, the palaeontologist who collected most of the fossils in the museum at La Plata. On other beaches are the municipal swimming pool, the pier of the Fishing Club, a Yacht Club, the Club Náutico, and the port, with the golf links behind it. (There is another golf club in the grounds of the Club Mar del Plata, 7 km. S of the Mogotes lighthouse, on the way to Miramar). The wooded municipally owned Parque Camet is 8 km. to the N. It has polo grounds and playing fields. For those who do not care for surf bathing, there are salt water pools. Fishing is good all along the coast and pejerrey, corvina and merluza (hake) abound; it is possible to charter a private launch for shark fishing.

The port can be reached by bus, 15 mins. from bus terminal. There is a large fishing fleet, excursion boats, seafood restaurants.

Visits can be paid to the rocky promontory of Cabo Corrientes to watch the breakers; to Punta Mogotes lighthouse (open Thursdays 1330-1700); to the Gruta de Lourdes, and the Bosque Peralta Ramos.

Trains and buses leave Buenos Aires from Constitución, 10 minutes from the centre by any bus marked "Constitución". The best trains (a/c) take 4½ hours (US$7), against 7 hours by bus (US$4).

Hotels First class hotels include *Provincial,* 500 rooms, many overlooking ocean; *Hermitage,* 150 rooms; *Chateau Frontenac; Gran Nogaró;* and the *Astor,* all luxury with tariffs of US$15 to $20 single and double and more during season (January to March 15), plus 5% tourist tax and from 20-23% service charge. There are scores of good hotels at reasonable rates with the *Hotel Doré* facing casino and sea, *e.g.* *Residencia Don Quixote,* 1 block from bus station, good, quiet, U.S.$4 double. *Little Hotel,* Lamadrid 2461, nr. bus station, nice and cheap. During summer months it is essential to book in advance.

Casino Open December to end-April, 1600-0330; 1600-0400 on Sats. Entrance US$1.20.

Camping *Pinar de la Serena* and other sites, reasonable prices.

Bank of London & South America, Ltd., Av. Luro 3201. Open 1000-1600.

Local Holidays Feb. 10 (Foundation of City); Nov. 10 (Day of Tradition); Nov. 22 (St. Cecilia).

Outside the town the country is undulating. To the N (34 km.) is a lagoon—the Mar Chiquita—joined to the sea by a narrow channel. There is good fishing, yachting, boating and bathing here. Picturesque spots reached from the road to Balcarce are (19 km.) Laguna de los Padres, and Sierra de los Padres and (32 km. beyond) the Laguna la Brava, at the foot of the Balcarce hills. In these hills, 68 km. by paved road from Mar del Plata, is the town of **Balcarce,** a centre for hill visits to La Brava, above Ruca-Lauquén, and the Cinco Cerros, five hills most strangely shaped. Balcarce is the birthplace of world famous racing driver Juan Fangio; it has a racing circuit.

Hotel *Balcarce,* good, US$8 a room, double or single.

Beyond Balcarce a paved road runs 103 km. to Tandil, also reached from Mar del Plata (254 km.) by rail.

Tandil, at the northern end of the Sierra del Tandil, a ridge of hills which run W from the sea into the pampa for 250 km. Tandil is 390 km. by road from Buenos Aires *via* Azul. It is a health and pleasure resort with fine views of sierra scenery. The air is splendidly clear and refreshing. There are golf links and a race track. The Holy Week festivities are outstanding. Excursions to the Sierra La Aurora. Population: 70,000.

From the Plaza Moreno an avenue leads to the foot of a hill; here is an arch erected by Italians. Beyond, in Parque Independencia, stairs lead to a terrace above which stands a statue of General Martín Rodríguez, who took an active part in the wars against the Indians. There is a wide and splendid view from the top of the hill. On a cliff overlooking a reservoir and dam near the town is a statue of Juan Fugl, a Danish pioneer, some of whose compatriots settled here.

1½ km. W of Tandil stood the famous balancing stone called the Piedra Movediza; it fell of its own accord in 1912. Whilst it stood the huge mass of granite was so exquisitely balanced that light puffs of wind would set it swaying. Indians in the last century believed the stone would fall as a sign of God's approbation if white men were driven out of the country. General Rosas ordered the stone to be pulled down, but a number of men hauling away with ox teams failed to dislodge it. A somewhat similar phenomenon, the Sentinel Stone, is on top of Cerro Américo Rossi.

Hotels *Continental; Palace; Roma; Eden; California; Manantial.* Others near railway station.

From Mar del Plata, along the rocky sea-front to the SW, there is a road (53 km.) to Miramar.

Miramar, like Mar del Plata, is a summer bathing resort, but the cliffs backing the beach are higher, the surrounding hills more picturesque, and it is a good deal cheaper to stay at. There is a fine golf course at *Hotel Golf Roca* and a Casino for roulette, etc. Fourteen km. by road or railway to the S, amongst dunes and black rocks, is Mar del Sur *(Atlantic Hotel)* with good fishing in a lagoon and bathing on the beach.

Hotels *Atlántico,* somewhat run down; *Normandie; Ideal; Putamar; Gran Rex; Royal; Palace.*

Camping *Escargot, El Fortía, Miramar.* Many sites, reasonably priced.

About 109 km. further by road along the shore to the SW is another famous bathing resort,

Necochea, 500 km. from Buenos Aires, is reached by Roca Railway in 12½ hours. It stands next to Mar del Plata in repute. The surroundings are picturesque. Visits can be paid to the Paseo del Puente, Punta Negra, the Cascada (or waterfalls) 16 km. up the Río Quequén Grande, Los Manantiales, and the Laguna de los Padres. Grain is exported from the port. Urban population: 50,000. About 100,000 tourists visit during the season, for the 24-km. long beach is one of the best in the country. A new municipal recreation complex, boasting a large modern casino and various sports facilities has recently been opened; entry charge is nominal. The Casino is open in summer. Airport.

Hotels *Royal; Atlántico; San Miguel; Trocadero; Marino.*

Camping Doble-J campsite; follow sign from 3 km. N of wharves. Excellent, US$0.40 per person.

Restaurants *La Vieja Taberna,* Calle 85, reasonable, good chicken and beef dishes; *Caviar,* by fishing wharf, good steak, chicken, seafood.

About 3¼ km. across the mouth of the river from Necochea is

Quequén, with an excellent beach, good bathing, and pleasant scenery. The channel to the port has to be dredged daily.

Hotels *Quequén; Faro; Costa Azul.*

Camping *Monte Pasuvio* and *Doble J* sites.

Over 320 km. westwards from Necochea by paved road through the coastal area is the port of Bahía Blanca.

Buenos Aires to Bahía Blanca This port can be reached by sea, by rail (900 km.), by air, or by a 688-km. paved road (Route 3) through Las Flores, Azul, Juárez and Tres Arroyos.

Azul, 264 km. from Buenos Aires, is a cattle centre with an attractive plaza and a stream flowing through picturesque sierras and the town. Population: about 45,000.

Hotels *Gran Hotel Azul; Argentino; Roma; Torino.* **Restaurant** *Mitre,* Avda. Mitre.

Bank of London and South America Ltd., San Martín 518. Open 0800-1400.

Tres Arroyos, about 195 km. from Bahía Blanca, is a cattle and wheat growing centre of 40,000 people encircled by 3 streams. A 68-km. paved road runs S to the sea at the pleasant little resort of **Claromecó,** with a beautiful beach of dark sand backed by high dunes.

Hotels at Tres Arroyos *Alfil, Parque* (restaurant) and *Andrea* are best. *City, París, Plaza and Tres Arroyos* (friendly), all modest.

Hotels at Claromecó *Claromecó* (only open in summer; restaurant); *Residencial La Perla.*

Camping at Claromecó Good campsite at "Dunamar", hot showers, fire pits and laundering basins, US$1 a day; also ACA campsite.

Bahía Blanca, population 200,000, the most important centre S of Buenos Aires, stands at the head of a large bay where the river Naposta runs into it. The region has over a million people. Bahía Blanca consists of the city itself, built back from the river front, and five ports at various distances from the city strung along the N bank of the Naposta: Arroya Pareja and the naval base of Puerto Belgrano at the mouth of the estuary; Puerto Ingeniero White, 23 km. inland, Puerto Galván, 3¼ km. beyond, and Cuatreros, 8 km. upstream.

The city has some fine modern buildings and two parks. In the Parque de Mayo are some lakes fed by the River Naposta and, interesting statuary. There is a Zoological Garden in Parque Independencia, on the outskirts.

To the E of Bahía Blanca is an enormous stretch of almost unoccupied sandy beaches, scarcely developed for visitors. Pehuén-Có, 70 km. away, is an example of the beaches with camping places, well shaded by pine trees. Signs to it on the main road 24 km. from Bahía Blanca. Another fine beach, with hotels and camping places, is Monte Hermoso, 2 hours by bus (106 km.) from Bahía Blanca.

Bahía Blanca Hotels Category A: *Austral* and *Del Sur* (with restaurants), *City Hotel.* Category B: *Italia, Belgrano, Central Muñiz.* Category C: *Atlántico, Argentino* (restaurant), *Ocean, Res. Palace, Barre.* Cheap: *Hotel Hogar,* Rodríguez 64, behind bus station, US$2 double. *Gunther,* US$2 double, basic.

Restaurants *Hué-Telén, Vieja Esquina, Taberna, Baska, Lavalle, Viena, Palichué Golf Club, Italia.*

Airport 11 km. from centre. Flights to Buenos Aires, the coastal cities, and the Lake District.

Local Holidays Sept. 24 (Our Lady of Mercy); Nov. 10 (Day of Tradition).

Bank of London and South America, Calle Chiclana 102. Citibank. Open 0800-1400.

Roads Apart from Route 3 to Buenos Aires, there are Route 33 to Guaminí and the N, and Route 35 NW to Neuquén and Mendoza.

Some 100 km. to the N is the Sierra de la Ventana, a favourite area for excursions from Bahía Blanca. The small town **Sierra de la Ventana,** with hotels *(Golf,* near station, is OK) and the excellent Don Diego campsite (hot water, open all year round) is a good centre for exploring them. Tres Picos, rising bare and barren from the rich farmlands to 1,070 metres, is only 6¼ km. away. There is a 9-hole golf course and good trout fishing in the Río Sauce Grande.

193 km. N of Bahía Blanca by road/rail through Saavedra is

Carhué, in the district of Adolfo Alsina, served by three railways, one of which, *via* Bolívar, runs to (603 km.) Buenos Aires. Five km. away is a sheet of water, Lake Epecuén, which covers over 40,000 hectares and is so strongly mineralised that it is over twenty times saltier than the sea. No fish can live in it. These waters are very helpful for chronic rheumatism and skin diseases, and thousands of visitors bathe in them. There are many hotels and residenciales at the lake side. A fort used in the wars against the Indians is now a museum of those wars. Pop.: 18,000.

Hotels at Lake Epecuén With restaurant: *Gran Parque Patera, Plage, Elkie, Victoria, Rambla, Cuatro Hermanos, Villa Marta, Italia, Espanola, Las Familias, Gran Rose.* Also: *El Lago, Castello.*

Hotels at Carhué With Restaurant: *Buenos Aires, Marconi.* Without: *Volpe, Bristol.*

About 38 km. by road NE of Carhué, on the Ferrocarril Nacional General Roca, which runs to the capital, is

Guaminí (Hotels: *La Aragonesa, Roma),* a small but pleasant summer hill resort of 3,500 inhabitants on the shore of Laguna del Monte, not as salty as Lake Epecuén; pejerrey fishing is one of the attractions.

Santa Rosa (Hotel: *Calfacura),* capital of the Province of La Pampa, is 332 km. NW of Bahía Blanca by road, and can be reached (619 km.) by Route 5, *via* Chivilcoy and Pehuajó, from Buenos Aires.

The North West and the Andean Country

If the reader will consult the first few pages of the chapter on Bolivia, he will find that the pattern of the land, from the crest of the Andes in the W to the river Paraguay in the E, consists of a high, dry Altiplano rising to a Puna cut into on its eastern face by rivers which flow into the Lowlands. This configuration of the land is carried southwards into all the north-western provinces of Argentina as far S as Tucumán, but the altitudes in Argentina are not so great as in Bolivia, and the whole area not so large. Altiplano and Puna together are not more than 400 km. wide; the former is about 3,350 metres and the latter about 4,000 metres above sea level. As in Bolivia, higher ranges stand out of the Puna; in some cases they reach a height of over 5,800 metres. It is into the Chaco that the E running rivers born of the Puna flow; their broad valleys, or quebradas, make access to the heights comparatively easy. Between the base of the Puna and the Chaco lie a series of front range hogback hills running roughly from N to S; the lowlands between them are known in Argentina as the valles. As in Bolivia, the Puna is sparsely covered with shrubs, its eastern face and many of the front ranges are forested, though the scrub forest of the Chaco is also found in the valles. Tucumán is the southern boundary of this kind of land. N of Tucumán crops can be grown without irrigation (though there is irrigation where the soil is absorbent) but S of Tucumán is droughty land, with long N-S ranges of low hills such as the Sierras de Córdoba, set in plains which have salt flats and swamps in the depressions.

Settlement and Economy The Incas were unable to push further S than Tucumán. The stone-paved Camino de los Incas—it has long since disappeared—ran along the eastern slopes of the Andes through uplands of the Puna de Atacama, and descended into the plains W of Tucumán. The Puna is bleak and desolate, windswept, stony and treeless: the only growth is a low, blackish shrub ("tola"), and an occasional cactus. The first Spanish expedition from Bolivia came down this road in 1542. A little later a better and lower route was discovered—the main route used today—descending from La Quiaca to Jujuy through the Quebrada de Humahuaca, with rugged and colourful mountain ranges closing in on both sides. Over a distance of 290 km. the altitude falls from 3,450 metres to 1,270. Along this new route the Spaniards pressed S and founded a group of towns in the north-west: Santiago del Estero (the first) in 1551, Tucumán in 1565, Córdoba in 1573, Salta in 1582, La Rioja in 1591, and Jujuy in 1592. Mendoza (1561), San Juan (1562), and San Luis (1598),

NORTH-WEST ARGENTINA

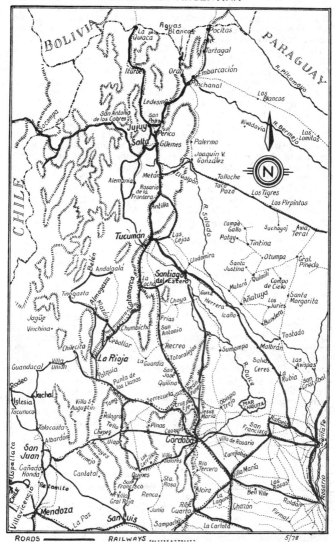

ROADS —— RAILWAYS 5/78

ROUGH SKETCH

were all colonised by people who crossed the passes from Chile. All these colonies were hemmed in by the warlike tribes of the Pampas, and until the war of extermination in 1880 the route from Buenos Aires to Córdoba was often unsafe. The Indians raided frequently for cattle, which they drove S and over the Andes for sale in Chile.

During the whole of the Colonial era the trade of the area was with Bolivia and Peru rather than with Buenos Aires, which was little more than a garrison and smuggling port, and trade was almost entirely in mules for the mining areas of the N. The mules were bred mainly in the plains between Rosario, Santa Fe, and Córdoba. These were driven finally into the town of Salta for the great fair in February and March at which they were traded for silver or for imports through Lima. At the end of the summer rains they were driven into the mountains and the Argentine muleteers trekked home. Salta traded in as many as 60,000 mules a year, and was the north-wests greatest commercial centre until the beginning of the nineteenth century. It was then reduced to trading the maize and wheat of the valles for the wool and salt of the uplands, but tourism has brought it to life again.

It is cattle, not mules, that are grazed in the valles of the front ranges to-day during the summer; during the dry winter they are driven into the mountains for fodder; an ancient case of transhumance. As in the pampas, alfalfa and maize are grown as feed and food crops; there is also some sugar.

The large sugar production of Tucumán, Jujuy and Salta, and the fruits of the Cuyo Provinces (Mendoza and San Juan) have temporarily eclipsed all other products. Historically, Tucumán was always important, for the two river routes of the Salado and the Dulce across the dry belt forced the mule traffic to pass through Tucumán on the way to Salta. The waggons and the harness of Tucumán were important for the trade. But Tucumán, unlike Salta, did not sink into insignificance with the ending of the mule trade: it was saved from that by the advent of sugar, for the area is singularly well placed for the growing of cane. A little to the S, a little to the E, and frosts make cane impossible; frost would make cane impossible at Tucumán too if it were not for a happy chance. The front ranges come to an end N of Tucumán, so there is nothing to deflect the impact of the warm, wet winds from the E against the high Sierra de Aconquija to the W of the town. This has two effects: several streams rise in the Sierra (they join the Río Dulce), and there is ample water for irrigation; more important still, the cloudbanks close to the mountain prevent frost within a distance of about 56 km from its base. On the lower slopes of the mountain even irrigation is not necessary. Three-fifths of the land possible for cane is planted to cane, and the rest mostly to maize. When sugar growing got into its stride there was, naturally, a great inflow of immigrants, but nearly all of them came from neighbouring towns and lands, and not from overseas. That is why Tucumán to-day is still different from the towns of the Humid Pampa. It produced 62% of Argentina's sugar before the late crisis. Tobacco is becoming important in the area, and a new and important factor in the North West is the growth of tourism.

Main Towns of the North-West

Córdoba and the resorts in the hills of Córdoba, and the towns to the north—Tucumán, Salta and Jujuy—will be dealt with first, followed later by the towns at the base of the Andes—Catamarca, La Rioja, San Juan, Mendoza and San Rafael. Note that in nearly all the provincial towns everything shuts between mid-day and 1600 except restaurants, hotels and post offices. There is nothing to do or see. We suggest that this is a good time for travelling; buses are generally preferable to trains, being faster, though dearer.

From Buenos Aires to Córdoba   Approaches: By air, in 1 hour, US$23. By Mitre railway through Rosario, Bell Ville and Villa María, 724 km., takes about 12 hours. By bus, 13 hours, US$9. Several companies. If hitch-hiking, take the train from Retiro (San Martín line) to Pilar to reach main highway. There are two main road routes. The first, 713 km., follows the line of this railway and is given under "Road to Bolivia" on page 55.

The second, 835 km., is the same as the "Road to Chile" (page 55), as far as Río Cuarto.

It goes through **San Antonio de Areco**—also on the Mitre Railway—113 km. NW of Buenos Aires. Here is the Museo ˋGauchesco Ricardo Güiraldes, a typical estancia of the late 19th century with manor house, mill, tavern, open Wed.-Sun., 1000-1200, 1500-1800 in summer; in winter 1000-1200 and 1400-1700. Check if it is open in Jan.-Feb. Güiraldes was a writer who described Gaucho life. Día de la Tradición is a gaucho festival with traditional parades, games, events on horseback, music and dance, celebrated on Nov. 10, 11 and 12 each year. Camping near the centre of town; 12 km. from centre, auto-camping *La Porteña* on the Güiraldes estancia, good access roads. Six hotels. Many handicrafts, mainly gaucho objects, ceramics, silver, leather, colonial furniture. The Argentine artist Gasparini has a museum-school where he sells his drawings of gauchos to tourists; Calle de los Martínez, between Bolívar and Rivadavia. There is also a local natural history museum, Parque Metri, on Matheu and Hernández. For tourist information go to the Sub-Dirección de Turismo at Alsina and Lavalle. Tel.: 2101. Restaurant *El Fogón del Chaco,* very good.

Beyond Pergamino, 146 km., is **Venado Tuerto,** a pleasant town of 17,000 people with a fine Country Club at which race meetings and tournaments are held twice a year. At **Río Cuarto,** 70,000 people, there is a golf club and a fine old Municipal building with an outlook tower worth seeing. (*Gran,* new, 1st class; *City Hotel,* good, about US$3.50 per person. Restaurant: *Cantina Italiana "Sorrento",* fair.) Córdoba is 225 km. N of Río Cuarto across flatlands and rolling hills. About half-way along the road runs on the containing wall of the great Río Tercero dam; the artificial lake here has been turned into a delightful playground for tourists.

Villa María, at a vital crossroads on the main Buenos Aires-Córdoba road, where it meets the most convenient highway route linking central Chile with Paraguay, Uruguay and Brazil, is a prosperous agricultural town with a great future. Hotel: *City,* US$10 double. Restaurant: *La Churrasquita.*

Córdoba, capital of Córdoba Province and Argentina's third city, has about a million inhabitants; it stands at an altitude of 440 metres. The district is renowned for its beauty and the city for its buildings, for Córdoba was founded as early as 1573; the plan of Córdoba is a grid, as are all Spanish plans of the sixteenth century. Its university, founded in

1613, was the first in the country. Picturesque in itself, the city faces eastward towards the pampas with sierras of exceptional beauty rising in three chains to the N, S, and W. The heart of the city is Plaza San Martín (the Liberator's statue is there). On the western side is the ancient Cabildo, now the police headquarters. Next to it stands the Cathedral, started in 1697 and finished 1787. The neo-gothic Church of the Sacred Heart, built in 1933 (Sagrado Corazón), at Buenos Aires e Yrigoyen, is worth a visit.

On Calle Independencia, leading S from the Plaza San Martín, is the Church and Convent of Santa Teresa (beautiful doorway, 1770). An old colonial building, the Viceroy's House (Casa del Virrey), is on Calle Rosario, E of the central plaza; it houses the Historical and Colonial Museum, open Tues.-Fri. 0830-1300, 1530-1930, Sat.-Sun. 0900-1200. N of Plaza San Martín, on Calle Rivadavia, is the Church of La Merced, whose old colonial pulpit is well worth seeing. The Church of La Compañía, on Calles Trejo y Sanabria, with a simple façade, dates from about 1650 and is a far better building than the Cathedral; its façade was rebuilt in the 20th century. The barrel vault and cupola, built entirely of Paraguayan cedar, are unique. There are some exciting but small 18th century churches with striking bell gables and undulating pediments. An astonishing building is the Palacio Ferreyra, built 1910-14, with a central hall measuring 30 metres square. It is now used by a firm and is not open to the public. The Natural History Museum, previously in the Cabildo, has moved to Av. Yrigoyen 115.

The Academy of Fine Arts, the theatre and the Olmos School are near the Plaza Vélez Sarsfield (there is a statue to this jurist, who gave Argentina its civil code). A diagonal, Avenida Yrigoyen, runs to the round Plaza España, where the Museum of Fine Arts is housed in a pillared building. E from this plaza is Parque Sarmiento, where there is a Zoological Garden with a serpentarium, a small waterfall, and excellent views of the many-towered town. Argentina's main observatory is at the S end of Calle General Artigas. The city has grown rapidly during the last twenty years. The centre now has many modern buildings, and blocks of flats and offices surround the old churches and other historical buildings, and there are numerous suburbs with homes built in Californian and other modern styles. Córdoba is a good shopping city; it has a large area of pedestrian streets, but prices tend to be higher than in Buenos Aires. Pajas Blancas airport is close to the city.

The great San Roque dam defends the city from avalanches of water, regulates the flow of the Río Primero, provides drinking water and electrical power, feeds two large systems of irrigation, and forms a blue lake ringed by hills which has become a tourist resort.

Buses   Excellent bus station with Tourist Office, shops, bank, post office, restaurants, and showers in bathrooms. Buenos Aires-Córdoba by bus takes about 13 hours, and on from Córdoba to Salta, about 15 hours. Many buses on both routes. Bus to Mendoza (10 hours), book early, US$17. Bus Córdoba-Asunción (Paraguay) direct, Sun. and Tues., US$14. In general, it is best to travel from Córdoba if you are going N, as at stations in between it may be hard to get a seat; a seat is only guaranteed if one pays US$1 extra.

Railways   The "Rayo del Sol" night train takes 12 hours to Buenos Aires, US$9. The Alta Córdoba railway station for long-distance journeys is a good 2 km. from the city centre.

Rent-a-Car   (Godfrey Davis), Entre Rios 70. Tel.: 420-30-32.

Industries The State Aeronautical and Mechanical Industries produce motor cars and tractors; and amongst other industrial plants are the Fiat and Renault works.

Hotels Best are: *Dorá,* US$7.50 single, US$13 double; *Alexander,* US$7.50 single, US$9 double; *Mediterráneo,* US$9 single, US$13 double; all these have garages. Also *Crillón,* US$9.50 single, US$12.50 double, very friendly; *Nogaró,* US$9 single, US$12.50 double; *Sussex,* US$8 single, US$10 double; *Windsor,* US$7.50 single, US$10 double. More economical: *Plaza; Palace.* US$4.50 single; *Ritz,* US$5.50 per person, helpful; *City,* US$2 each; *Dallas,* US$6 double, recommended; *Argentina; Astoria; Viña de Italia; Waldorf; Claridge,* recently redecorated, US$2.50 single. For "economy", *Emperador,* US$1.50 room with bath; *Pensión Susy,* Entre Ríos, US$2.50 double; *Hotel Los Alpes,* near railway station; *Hotel Sportsman,* San Jerónimo, near bus and Railway station, US$1.50 double; *Residencial Plaza,* 150 metres from bus station, US$3 double, clean, friendly and quiet; *Gran Terminal,* Pasaje Corrientes 64, a/c, next to new bus station, US$6.50 double; *Hotel Lady, also* near bus station, US$3 double with shower, friendly and good value. *Hotel Central,* US$2.50 double, hot water, 100 m. from bus station, good; restaurant, cheap and good. *Hotel Entre Ríos,* close to bus terminal on Entre Ríos, reasonably clean, hot water, US$1 single.

Restaurants Good but not cheap: *Crillón Hotel* and *Ludovico.* Good food and moderate prices: *San Martín, Buono, Don Emiliano, Dixie.* There are also numerous grills of all categories on the outskirts of the city, especially in the Cerro de las Rosas district, for meals out-of-doors when the weather is suitable. *Mendel,* and the restaurant in *Hotel Familiar,* S. Jerónimo, near railway station, cheap and good, recommended; *Munich,* good food, not cheap; *El Tabero,* fair; *Palacio de Pasta,* good cheap food. Two useful budget restaurants: *Romagnolo,* opposite the Mitre railway station and *Comedor Albéniz,* opposite Alto Córdoba station, a bit noisy. Try also at bus station.

Bank of London and South America, Buenos Aires 23. Citibank. Summer, 0730-1230; Winter, 0745-1345. Exchange at banks and following travel agencies: Exprinter, Viacor, Avincor, Epoca and Barujel. If travelling N it is advisable to change money in Córdoba; not easy further N.

Tourist Office Dirección Provincial de Turismo, near bus station.

British Council Boul. San Juan 137, has a good library.

Casino Recently opened nearby, at Alta Gracia.

Local Holidays July 6 (Foundation of the City); September 30 (St. Jerome).

The Sierras of Córdoba, rising in undulating hills from the pampas, their lower slopes often wooded, particularly in the S, attract each year a large number of visitors. The highest peak, Champaqui (2,575 metres) has a small lake on top. The hills run, roughly, for 500 km. from N to S; west of Córdoba they are 150 km. wide. There are three ranges of them: the Sierra Grande, the longest, in the middle, with Sierra Chica to the E and Sierra de Guisapampa and its continuation, the Sierra de Pocho, to the W. Swimming, riding, walking, climbing and golf are the main recreations of a holiday in these hills. The irregular contour of the region gives a considerable choice of altitudes and of surroundings. A network of good roads gives panoramic drives and dramatic contrasts of scenery: quiet valleys, deep gorges, high mountain passes and plateaux. The region's climate is dry, sunny and exhilarating throughout the year.

At the foot of the Sierra Chica are three large dams to contain the waters of Río Primero, Río Molinos, and Río Tercero. There are two other large dams in the hills, at Cruz del Eje and La Viña. They provide power and irrigation for farms and orchards and the lakes are in themselves exceptionally beautiful. The Government keeps them stocked with fish. Sailing draws a number of visitors.

Information can be obtained at travel agencies, at the Dirrección Provincial de Turismo near the bus station, or at Casa de Córdoba at Callao 332, Buenos Aires.

Note There are innumerable good hotels and pension houses in the Córdoba mountain region; names are therefore not always given.

A road running NW from Córdoba through the Punilla Valley leads to the following string of resorts shadowed by the Sierra Chica:

Carlos Paz, on lovely Lake San Roque, a pleasant resort in the Punilla Valley and the nearest to Córdoba. Much frequented by the British community in Argentina. Sports: tennis, fishing, boating, golf. Its cuckoo clock is the biggest in the world. A ski-lift runs up the slopes to a tearoom and night club overlooking the valley. Plenty of hotels, big and small. Best buy at cheap prices: leather mats, bags, pottery. Tourist office at bus station. Recommended cheap hotel is *Chalet Suizo,* near bus station, US$1.20 single. Camping at A.C.A. campground, and associated sites at *Las Tolderías* and *El Mirador Lago San Roque;* there is a municipal campground with swimming at Bialet Massé, N of Carlos Paz.

Cosquín, 63 km. by Route 38 from Córdoba, on the banks of a river. Altitude, 720 metres. Beautiful surroundings, with a dry healing air. Good camping on south bank of river; swimming. 19 km. on is **Valle Hermoso,** near La Falda. Altitude, 850 metres. Old restored chapel of San Antonio, a little gem. Riding, motoring. Excellent youth hostel, river swimming, address "Steinhaus". A famous folklore festival is held in the last half of January.

La Falda, 82 km from Córdoba. Altitude, 933 metres. Pleasant at all seasons. Golf, swimming. Students of all nations welcome at Córdoba University holiday centre at Vaquerías, 2 km. from La Falda. Camping near small river. Excursions to Quebrada Chica, Cascada del Molino, Alto San Pedro. 3½ km. on by Route 38 is **Huerta Grande,** at 971 metres, a bathing resort with good fishing and medicinal waters. Eleven km. further on is:

Candonga, altitude 810 metres, is in the hilly district of Alpatanca in the Sierra Chica. The road from Córdoba city (55 km.) goes through Argüello, Villa Allende, Río Ceballos, and Salsipuedes to El Manzano, where it branches off to the left leading to La Cumbre. The historic and beautiful Colonial church at Candonga, now a National Monument, was built in 1730 as an oratory of the Jesuit Estancia of Santa Gertrudis. The arch protrudes to form a porch which covers the entrance.

La Cumbre, 97 km. from Córdoba. Bus, US$1.30. Altitude, 1,141 metres. Trout streams with good fishing from November to April. Swimming, golf, tennis. Has an airport.

Cruz Chica, altitude, 1,067 metres. Swimming, tennis, climbing, motoring, riding, walking; most attractive. Has one of the best English boys' schools in S. America.

Los Cocos, just N of Cruz Chica, is a delightful, extremely popular mountain resort with 3 first rate hotels and many holiday houses. Lovely walks, horses for hire. A famous orphanage, the Allen Gardiner Homes for British-descended orphans, is here. The *Hotel Gran Mansión El Descanso* has a very popular park and museum with (imitation) Roman statuary, a Spanish garden, patriotic and "historic" exhibits—an excellent example of what the Germans call "Kitsch". Argentines flock to it.

Capilla del Monte, 106 km. from Córdoba, in the heart of the Sierras. Altitude, 914 metres. Medicinal waters, rocks and waterfalls and wide views; see particularly El Zapato rock, despite its graffiti. Tennis, golf, target shooting, and horseback excursions in the hills, particularly to Cerro Uritorco (2,060 metres). Excellent trout fishing at Tío Mayo, an hour away by car.

A road runs N from Córdoba to Asochinga and Jesús María.

Asochinga, 63 km. N of Córdoba by road *via* such pleasant little townships as Villa Allende, Unquillo, and La Granja. Altitude, 700 metres. Picturesque, dating from colonial days. Good winter fishing. Fine golf links. Nearby is Santa Catalina, originally a Jesuit mission founded in 1622 and the most elaborate Jesuit establishment in the hills around Córdoba. (See the church, begun in 1754, workshops and stone conduits.)

Jesús María, 51 km. N or Córdoba. Altitude, 533 metres. Good 18th century Jesuit church and the remains of its once famous winery; in the cloister is an excellent Museo Jesuítico, said to be one of the best on the continent (closed Mon.). Good trout, dorado, and carp fishing in winter. Road to Córdoba paved but rough. Some 4 km. N of Jesús María is Sinsacate with an interesting church. There is also a fine colonial posting inn, with long, deep verandah and chapel attached. Beyond Jesús María the paved road runs another 132 km. to Villa de María, the birthplace of Leopoldo Lugones, a poet of country life. His house is a museum.

South-west of Córdoba a scenic road climbs through the Sierra Grande to another chain of resorts, Mina Clavero, Villa Dolores and Yacanto.

Mina Clavero, 140 km. from Córdoba by bus through grand lake and hill scenery. A charming town, and good centre for exploring the high sierra, especially Champaquí, the highest peak in the Sierras. Altitude, 915 metres. Usual sports.

Villa Dolores, 187 km. from Córdoba, 48 km. from Mina Clavero. Altitude, 529 metres. Population; 10,000. The road from Córdoba crosses the two mountain ranges to reach finally the Pampa de Achala, a huge desert plateau of grey granite. Rail from Buenos Aires *via* Villa Mercedes. Swimming. The district of San Javier, to the SE, is Argentina's biggest supplier of herbs for flavouring, garnishing and perfuming food, and for homeopathic medicine.

Yacanto, near Villa Dolores, at the foot of Mount Champaquí, in a region of woods and waterfalls. Reached by road from Villa Dolores station (San Martín Railway). Curative waters. Tennis, golf, fishing, bathing, riding, climbing.

A road S from Córdoba runs to Alta Gracia and to the Río Tercero dam.

Alta Gracia, altitude, 580 metres, 48 km. SW of Córdoba. Interesting colonial church, finished c.1762, and buildings beside Lake Trajamar. Recreations: motoring, walks, riding, tennis, golf, swimming and fishing. *Hotel Sierras* (with 9-hole golf course and also croquet; not modern, but almost Edwardian comfort, attractive service, good, plentiful food but expensive when bill is made up due to 40% taxes *et al.*). New casino. To the Río Tercero dam is 79 km.; on the lake is a model holiday colony for Argentine workers and a "Tourist Unit".

The Belgrano railway runs N to Tucumán, 522 km. away. From Recreo a branch runs W to Chumbicha, where it connects with a line N to Catamarca and S to La Rioja; they will be described later. The city is reached from Buenos Aires (1,149 km., 19 hours) by the Mitre line running through Rosario and La Banda; the daily *Estrella del Norte* train leaves Retiro station, Buenos Aires, at 1800, returns daily at 1815; costs US$34 single, including pullman fee, US$46 with sleeper. Beyond Tucumán the line runs N *via* Rosario de La Frontera and Jujuy to La Quiaca, on the Bolivian border, 644 km. from Tucumán. There are also roads to all these places and their use seems preferable; the trains N of Tucumán have been described to us as slow, crowded and in general not recommended.

Trains from Buenos Aires   Express train, Mon., Wed., Fri., leaves at 1630, arrives 0940. Slightly more expensive; returns Sun., Tues., Thurs. at 1700. About half price are *Cinta de Plata*, leaves Mon. and Thurs. at 2055, arrives 2248 next day; returns Wed. and Sat. at 0711. Also *El Norteno*, leaves Wed. and Sat. at 0955, arrives 0902 next day; returns 2101 Mon. and Thurs. Express train and *Estrella del Norte* can combine with bus La Veloz del Norte to Salta, for about US$10 more, also to Jujuy (express only).

Tucumán, capital of its province and with a population of 340,000, is the busiest and the most populous city in the N. Its natural beauties are great. The city itself is on a plain, at 450 metres, but to the W towers the Sierra de Aconquija. Over 400,000 hectares irrigated by streams flowing from the mountain were once planted to sugar cane. The city was founded by Spaniards coming S from Peru in 1565. There are still many colonial buildings left, and amongst rows of elaborately stuccoed, spacious, one-storey houses (many of them sadly dilapidated) rise three or four handsome churches with blue, yellow and white tiled domes. Much less sugar is now produced.

Tucumán's main square is Plaza Independencia, beautified with palm and orange trees planted round a statue of Liberty. On its W side is the ornate Government Palace, next is the Church of San Francisco, with a picturesque façade. On the S side is the Cathedral, with a rough rustic cross, kept near the baptismal font, used when founding the city.

To the S, on Calle Congreso, is the Casa Histórica where, in 1816, the Congress of the United Provinces of Río de la Plata met to draft and proclaim Argentina's Declaration of Independence. The simple room in which it was proclaimed survived the destruction of the original house in 1908 and has now been enclosed in a modern museum. The room contains the chair used by the President of the Congress, a few other pieces of furniture, and portraits. A bas-relief on the museum walls shows the delegates proclaiming independence. Some distance to the W is Plaza Belgrano, with a statue to General Belgrano, who won a decisive battle against the royalists here in 1812. Two blocks E is the University, with a grand view from the vivero. Nightly "son et lumière" programme at Casa Histórica.

The Benjamín Matienza airport (frequent flights to other cities) is close to the town.

There are two beautiful parks in the city: Nueve de Julio and Avellaneda. There are an interesting menhir stone and an artificial lake in the former as well as Bishop Colombres' house; it was he who introduced sugar cane to Tucumán in the early 19th century, and in the house is his first crude attempt at a pressing machine. In the back garden is a gigantic steam press imported from France in 1883. Villa Nougués, an hour up the mountain side (one of the most interesting spots), is the summer residence of the well-to-do at Tucumán; it has an excellent private hotel; Aconquija park, with glorious trees, is at the foot of the mountains. The Quebrada de Lules, not far from the town, is worth visiting. Other possible excursions are to San Javier, (hotel), and to Tafí del Valle, where there are a Provincial Hostería and two dams.

El Cadillal dam, in the gorge of the Río Sali, 30 km. N of Tucumán, supplies electricity and water for the city and permanent irrigation for 80,000 hectares of parched land. There are restaurants, a good ACA campsite and a small museum at the dam.

An area SW of Tucumán, El Mollar, has many carved standing stones.

Local holiday Sept. 24 (Battle of Tucumán).

Museums Casa Histórica, see above; Anthropological Museum, 25 de Mayo 492, open Mon.-Fri.; Folklore Museum; the Instituto Miguel Lillo, associated with the natural history department of the University, and one of the world's major institutions for natural history, has a large collection of animals, insects, and a herbarium, with the display greatly improved. One of the library's treasures is one of eight copies of the original edition of von Humboldt's travels in Spanish America, another is a sixteenth -century Pliny. All these four museums have been described as "quite exceptional". Next to *Hotel Colonia* on Av. Entre Ríos is Museo Iremain, a very interesting memorial to the sculptor. Open 0830 to 1200 and 1500-1800, Mon.-Fri.

Casinos The Winter Casino is in an elegant 19th century building on the outskirts. It is open all year except January. The Summer Casino at the top of Aconquija is now closed.

Hotels *Metropol*, 24 de Setiembre 524, expensive but good service—worth it; *Claridge*, new, expensive; also good—*Viena; Francia; Premier; Coventry*, US$5 per person, not a/c. *Hotel Plaza*, US$12.50 double. Tucumán can be almost unbearably hot and sticky in summer. Best stay at *Hotel St. James*, on top of Sierra de Aconquija, expensive, comfortable, good food, swimming pool, good views, and fine walking. *Hotel Minia* and *Munich* (not recommended) and *Hotel Alcázar*,

US$1.80 double, are cheap, and there are other cheap hotels near the bus station. *Palace Hotel,* 24 de Setiembre, US$4 double with bath, recommended. *Hotel Colonia,* Av. Entre Ríos 31, US$1.70 per person, clean, friendly, near the bus station. *Hotel Colonial,* San Martín 35, 5 mins. from bus station. *Hotel Estrella,* cheap and basic.

Restaurants *Mi Abuela,* opposite casino, self-service, US$2 meal (3-course), cheap and good; *El Lago,* Parque 9 de Julio, fully recommended; *Palacio de las Empanadas,* also recommended. Snacks at *El Buen Gusto,* 9 de Julio 29; *Nueva Italia,* Calle Congreso; *El Puerto Viejo,* near *Hotel Metropol;* *La Cantina,* San Martín 750, good; also good, cheap meals at *Champaquí,* Av. Sarmiento, corner with Catamarca, opp. bus station.

Shopping An active centre, but no cheaper than Buenos Aires.

Camping Free at Parque 9 de Julio; two roadside camp sites a few km. N of city.

Bank of London and South America, San Martín 622. Open 0700-1300.

Tourist Office In main plaza.

Library North American Centre, on 800 block of Calle Junín.

For the roads and railways N from Tucumán to Salta and Jujuy, see the map on page 79. The Inter-American Highway goes to Jujuy (with a 43-km. spur W from Güemes to Salta), and on through the Quebrada de Humahuaca to Bolivia; it is now largely paved.

For travellers to Salta from Tucumán the road *via* Santa María and Cafayate is longer but more interesting than the direct road. Bus to Salta, 5½ hours, several daily. Train to Salta (2nd class, US$2), 9 hours.

For those who wish to travel direct from N Argentina to Central Chile, there is a daily bus from Tucumán to Mendoza, leaving 1300 (19 hours), *via* Catamarca, La Rioja, Patquía, Chepes and San Juan, through interesting and little-toured arid country. Bus to Córdoba, 10-11 hours, US$6, leaves 0630, 1430 and at night. Train to Córdoba, 1915, arrives 0700, US$2.50. Bus to La Rioja, 7 hours, US$4.40.

A railway runs N to (145 km.) **Rosario de la Frontera,** a popular resort from June to September. Altitude: 760 metres. Eight km. away there are sulphur springs, famous for their curative properties. Golf course; casino. From Buenos Aires, by Belgrano Railway: 1,296 km.

Hotel *Termas,* well run, good food but many rooms without private bath.

Excursions To **El Naranjo** (19 km.) a Jesuit colonial town; a church contains images and carvings made by Indians. About 80 km. N of Rosario de la Frontera, at Lumbreras, a road branches off the Inter-American Highway and runs 80 km. NE to the Parque Nacional Finca El Rey, a 4,500-hectare forest and wildlife preserve set among 900-1,500 metre hills with clear streams (good fishing). A *National Tourist Hotel* open. The access road is still poor and fords the river half a dozen times.

From Güemes, 148 km. N of Rosario de la Frontera, a branch line and road run W through the mountains for 43 km. to

Salta, at 1,190 metres, 568,552 people, on the Río Arias, in the Lerma Valley, in a hilly and strikingly beautiful district. Salta, capital of its province, is itself a handsome city founded in 1582, with fine Colonial buildings. The Cathedral, on the N side of the central Plaza 9 de Julio, was built 1858-1878; it contains the much venerated images of the Cristo del Milagro and of the Virgin Mary, the first sent from Spain in 1592, and has a rich interior mainly in red and gold, as well as a huge late baroque altar. The miracle was the sudden cessation of a terrifying earthquake when the images were paraded through the streets on September 13, 1692. They still are, each September, when 80,000 people visit the town. Another curious story is that when the statues were sent over from Spain the ship carrying them over sank, but both statues were washed onto the Peruvian shore together, undamaged. The Cabildo, on Calle Caseros, was built 1783, but the Convent of San Bernardo was built in Colonial style in the mid-19th century; it has a famous wooden portal of 1762. San Francisco church, built around 1880, is said to have the tallest tower in South America. Salta, 1,600 km. from Buenos Aires by rail or paved road, is now a great tourist and handicraft centre (visit Mercado de Artesanía and shops—closed midday to 1600) and the best starting place for tours of the NW.

The most attractive excursion is a walk uphill, or drive by motor road, to the Cerro San Bernardo (1,250 metres). Very beautifully set at the foot of the hill is an impressive statue by Victor Cariño, 1931, to General Güemes who, with gaucho help, repelled seven powerful attacks by the Spaniards between 1814 and 1821. A steep path behind it with Stations of the Cross leads to the top of the hill, where there is an old wooden cross. This is a good place from which to ponder the magnificent view of Salta, its main avenue lined with ceiba trees.

Bus Services Bus companies: La Veloz del Norte, Av. Tavella; Atahualpa SRL, Lerma 161; Coop. Gen. Güemes, Acevedo 188; Expreso Panamericano, bus terminal, and El Indio. Salta provides the most useful cheap land connection between Bolivia and Paraguay. Four buses a week to Resistencia, 0500, US$11.25, 16½ hrs. (up to 150 hrs. in the rainy season), for crossing into Paraguay. There is a direct bus from Salta to Asunción on Saturdays and indirect links on Mondays and Thursdays by Autobuses Atahualpa to Formosa, where there is a connection to Asunción. Bus Salta-Formosa, US$10, leaves 0500, arrives 0400 next morning. First bus from Formosa to Asunción 0430. Bus, Salta-Córdoba leaves 0700, 1600, 2030, arrives 2130, 0645 and 1030, respectively. Three buses daily (US$6 or 7.50) to La Quiaca, on Bolivian frontier. Buses also NE to Orán (US$4), six hours, for connection with Tarija, Bolivia; and to Yacuiba, for Santa Cruz, Bolivia. Buses to Pocitos (Bolivian frontier) US$3, comfortable. Bus to Jujuy, 2 hours. Bus to Calama and Antofagasta (Chile) leaves Sat. at 1600, US$17. Tickets *only* from Residencial Balcarce on Av. Balcarce 460. The bus station is quite a way out of town.

Airport General Belgrano. Regular Aerolíneas Argentinas connections. Two Aerolíneas flights to Santa Cruz (Bolivia) a week, and also Lloyd Boliviano. One flight a week to La Paz, Bolivia (US$88), and Asunción. Aerochaco flies Mon., Wed., Fri. to Resistencia, US$11. Special bus service between airport and Plaza 9 de Julio, US$0.75.

Railways Apart from services to Buenos Aires, Chile and Bolivia, there is a line to Resistencia (Chaco), 3 trains a week (Tues., Thurs. and Sat. at 0825), 36 hours; you may on some days have to change at Güemes and Metán, (6 hour wait) or at Roque Sáenz Peña (same wait) so probably better to get bus from Salta to Metán if this is the case; alternatively go by bus to Metán, train to Roque Sáenz Peña, and then frequent bus to Resistencia, 2½ hours. Train is dusty, no 1st class. There is a train from Güemes to La Quiaca, 16 hrs., but it is reported very crowded. Service to Formosa (for Asunción) twice weekly, Mon. and Thurs. at 0705 *via* Embarcación, on Belgrano Railway, on Paraguayan frontier, arr. 1930 Tue. and Fri., with sleeping cars and restaurant. There is one train a week (indirect connection) between Salta and Posadas (Misiones). One train daily to Córdoba, leaves 2315, due to arrive 2140 next day but sometimes at least 4 hrs. late. From Salta to Mendoza, one takes a train to Dean Funes, near Córdoba, and after a 3-hr. wait gets another to Mendoza, takes 2 nights and one and a half days. Slow but pleasant. Avoid during rainy periods as the track can get washed out. Ordinary train to Tucumán, Tue, Thurs. and Sat., 0835, 11½ hours (very slow). To Bolivian border there are four local trains (at 0600 on Mon., Thurs., Sat., Sun.) a week, 15 hours, US$4 first class; two international trains (1750 on Mon. and Fri.) same fares, very dusty, 6-hr. wait at Metán. To Antofagasta, Chile, there is one train a week (Wed. 1640), often late, US$4 to border and US$4 more to Antofagasta; it does not operate in winter. Tickets booked only at Villalonga Furlong in Calle Alvarado, any time up to 1000 on Wednesday you wish to travel. Second class US$4.20, no apparent difference between 1st and 2nd class. No seats guaranteed. Train full by 1600; board with food, by 1430 at latest. Restaurant car, reasonably priced food, but avoid on Chilean side. No heating, very cold at night. No water for washing. (See page 77 for description of line, and page 77 for road taking similar route.)

Rent-a-Car (Godfrey Davis) at Caseros 225, Tel.: 12069. Salta in advance from Buenos Aires or abroad and meet you at the airport; mainly Renault 4, 12 and Ford, US$0.10 per km.

Consulates Bolivia, Urquiza 583, 1st floor; Chile, Zuviría 118; Spain, Las Heras 1329; Italy, Zuviría 380; France, Balcarce 521; Germany, Del Milagro 218.

Hotels *Hotel de Turismo,* in main plaza, excellent food; *Victoria Plaza,* US$6.50 per person, Zuviría 16, porter has all information about travel, etc.; *Salta* and *California,* both 1st class in main plaza. *Hotel Club,* a commercial hotel, bed and use of bath. *Continental,* new, 2 blocks from bus station, Hipólito Yrigoyen 295, US$8 double, with bath, is recommended. *Hotel Daguerre,* US$12 double, water off and on, nr. bus station. *Hotel Colonial,* US$12 double, with bath, Zuviría 6. *Hotel Colón,* old fashioned, central, US$6 double. Hotels, 1st class—*Provincial,* Caseros 786; *Premier,* San Martín and Jujuy; *Plaza,* España 505; *General Güemes,* España 446; *Motel Huaico,* Campo Castanares; *Residencial Misoroj,* San Luis 190, and *Cañoto,* 20 de Febrero 56. *Residencial Güemes,* Av. Buenos Aires, near central plaza, US$5, double, basic; US$2.50 single, clean, private bath. *Residencial Familiar,* Calle Santiago del Estero, US$4 double; *Residencias Sandra, Provincial, Crillón* (near main plaza), good; *Hotel Lido,* Calle Buenos Aires, US$8 double. *Residencial España,* corner Balcarce and Necochea, US$3.20 double. *Savoy* and *Internacional* (near railway station), US$2-3 double, basic. *Residencial Elena,* US$6 double, clean, friendly and quiet, on Calle Buenos Aires; *Residencias Richard,* US$5 double, good value; *Residencial Oriental,* on Ituzaingo, same price. *Residencial Hispano,* Calle San Juan 619, good, US$2 (3rd class) per person, US$1 for a meal. *Pensión Madrid,* B. Mitre, US$3.50 double; *Residenciales Siena, Florida,* Calle Florida y Urquiza and *Mendoza,* US$4 single, US$6 double, with shower, very clean; *Residencial Royal,* US$3.50 double, with bath, 5 blocks from bus station; *Residencial Cepmer,* Yrigoyen 1195, US$3 double, good. *Residencial Artur,* Rivadavia 752, single, US$1.25, no hot water. *Residencial Rapsodia* on Buenos Aires is US$4.50 double; *Residencial Cayetano,* Balcarce 747, clean, good meals at US$1.50 each, hot water. *Hotel Centro,* Belgrano 657, friendly, reasonable; *Hotel Palermo,* cheap, clean, comfortable, close to railway station; also *Hospedaje Gómez.* Many other cheap hotels near railway station.

Tourist Office Buenos Aires 93 (two blocks from main square). Very helpful, and offers slide shows some evenings. Ask for the Tourist Market here, excellent leather goods. The **Mercado de Artesanías** is just out of town.

Restaurants *San Francisco,* good grills; *Carlitos, Balcarce* and *Güemes,* good; *Las Flores,* Calle España; *La Posta,* good meals for US$2.50. *Los Dos Chinos,* Alberdi 187, cheap and very good. *Taberna del Jockey,* Calle Zuviría 84, excellent food; try puchero de gallina. *La Castiza, La Madrileña,* C. España, good value; *La Pergola,* Belgrano 472, very friendly, local dishes; *El Rey del Bife,* very good. Pleasant outdoor restaurants in Parque San Martín, at foot of Cerro San Bernardo. *Restaurant Pinocho,* cheap, friendly. *Gauchos de Güemes,* 10 blocks from centre for hearty food and music, Uruguay 750; *Restaurant Ezevra,* San Martín 1044, gives a good 4-course lunch for US$0.80. Empanadas—*La Casa de las Empanadas,* O'Higgins 575.

Camping Casino Provincial grounds, by river. There is no signposting. In front of the Casino turn left, go to the *balneario* administration (see below) office, US$0.30 each, car US$0.40. Free hot showers available if there is gas. Permission from the Policía Municipal de Tránsito, Santa Fe 545 (Tel.: 10744). At *Motel Huaico,* Campo Castanares and *Residencial Hispano,* San Juan 619. Camping also allowed in a park near centre, and near bus stations.

Museums Cabildo Histórico, Caseros 549, fascinating historical museum, the best in the provinces, open Wed.-Sun., 1500-2000. Museo Colonial Histórico y de Bellas Artes, Caseros 575, open every day 1600-1900 and Wed.-Sun. 0900-1200. Casa Uriburu, Caseros 421, has relics of a distinguished Salteño family. There is also a new archaeological museum.

Festival Sept. 24, commemorating the battles of Tucumán and Salta. On June 16, folk music playing by youngsters in the evening and gaucho parade in the morning around the Güemes statue at the foot of the S. Bernardo hill. Salta celebrates Mardi Gras (Shrove Tuesday) with a procession of decorated floats and of dancers with intricate masks of feathers and mirrors. It is the custom to squirt water at passers-by and *bombas atómicas de agua* (small balloons to be filled with water) are on sale for dropping from balconies on to unwary pedestrians below. Wear a light waterproof!

Bathing Balneario Municipal on outskirts, reached by bus No. 4 from Calle Ituzaingó, entry US$0.04.

A magnificent round trip of about 520 km. can be taken going SW from Salta to Cafayate, then through the Valles Calchaquíes and Cachi, and back E to Salta. About a day is needed for the trip from Cafayate to Cachi. The roads are mainly gravel (half paved from Salta to Cafayate, but dusty and mostly single carriageway from Cafayate to Cachi) and can be very difficult after rain but the views of the Andean-foothill desert country are endlessly varied, and fascinating for those to whom strange rock formations and unexpected colours have an appeal. The population is largely Indian, and regional costumes abound. (Buses only up to Molinos, irregular services.)

Another suggested route is through the Lerma Valley connecting Salta and Cafayate (paved road as far as Alemania and then very good earth road) with wild and semi-arid landscapes.

Cafayate A quiet, clean, small town, lying between two ranges of Andean foothills and surrounded by vineyards (try Bodega El Recreo's dry white wine, known as Nuevo Retiro). About 18 km. S is Tolombón, where there are reported Indian ruins among giant cacti and other scrub plants. (The ruins are vestigial; the cacti are far more interesting.) See Sr. Rodolfo Bravo's private museum of Calchaquí archaeology, full of Indian artefacts dug up nearby. Excursions to bodegas (e.g. La Rosa) and vineyards possible.

Hotels *Hostería Cafayate* (A.C.A.), modern, quiet, colonial-style, US$10 double, good food; *Gran Reál, Asturias, Melchor,* new; *Güemes, Colonial,* basic and cheap; *Parador,* colonial style; *Briones,* nr. church, US$1.50 double; *Savoy,* off main square, with nice restaurant. Municipal campsite at Cafayate.

Restaurants *Miguelito's,* simple, but clean; *El Rancho,* parrilla.

Continuing S from Cafayate, the road goes to **Santa María** *(Plaza Hotel,* US$5 single, and others), and ultimately to Tucumán.

About 24 km. N of Cafayate is San Carlos (altitude 1,660 m), a small settlement destroyed four times by Indians. It has a pleasant white church completed 1854, and another A.C.A. hostería, as well as a municipal campsite.

Entering the Calchaquí river valley, one comes N into a hillier region centred on Angastaco, another small town, expanding rapidly, surrounded again by vineyards. At **Molinos,** further N again, the church (a national monument, built *c.* 1720), contains the mummified body of the last royal governor, Colonel Severo Siqueira de Isasmendi y Echalar, who died in 1837. This relic can be seen by arrangement with the priest.

After **Cachi** (Quechua for "salt", a beautiful little town) (*Hostería Rumi Huasi,* with good food, and *Hotel Nevado de Cachi,* very cheap and friendly) good *ACA Hostería Cachi,* US$10, the road to Salta climbs over the Cuesta del Obispo (summit 3,620 metres). This road, including a dead-straight stretch of 14 km. known as Recto Tin-Tin, gives magnificent views of high moorland country (páramo), then after the summit plunges down to Salta through luxuriously-wooded steep valley picturesquely populated by Indians in local costumes.

If one wishes to make a round trip to just Cachi, take a bus at 0630 from Salta (4 hrs.) stay the night and return the next morning at 1000. The Church at Cachi has its floor, roof and confessional made of cactus wood.

Ask also at tour agencies about excursions to Quebrada del Toro, rugged and striking countryside (see below).

In the intermont basin of which Salta is the centre, sugar cane is grown and there is much livestock ranching with agriculture: the meat is sent over the mountains to North Chile and to Bolivia. The growing of tobacco and the wine grape are important industries. There is lumbering in the mountain forests. Salta is rich in minerals: petroleum, iron, silver, lead, copper, gold, and marble, but only oil and iron are much exploited. The oil is piped from the Campo Durán to San Lorenzo on the Paraná.

Communications were greatly improved in 1948 by building the Huaytiquina railway from Salta through the little town of San Antonio de los Cobres to Antofagasta, in north Chile. It is 900 km. long—571 km. lie in Argentina—and reaches an altitude of 4,453 metres as it passes over the Chorillos Pass. From Salta to San Antonio de los Cobres (3,750 m.) it passes through the Quebrada del Toro, even more picturesque and impressive than the Humahuaca valley. Muñano, in the Muñano gorge (4,165 metres), is the highest railway station in Argentina, 3,936 metres. (The gorge is peculiar in that there is no pass over the mountains. The line is hewn out of the wall closing the end of the valley, zig-zags up and then across the top of the ridge). The Argentine country the railway runs through is a barren, rocky plateau 2,150-3,350 metres above sea level and inhabited by Coya Indians whose racial character and economy bear a far closer resemblance to their cousins in Bolivia than to the Salteño lowlander. Antofagasta is now within some hours' contact with Argentina instead of having 6,450 km. of ocean between. Meat, fresh vegetables and dairy products are taken to Chile, zinc to Japan. The road from Salta to San Antonio de los Cobres (6 hours, bus four times a week, US$3) follows much the same route as the railway (day trip from Salta by minibus US$6, stop at Santa Rosa de Tastil to see Indian ruins).

There is a road from San Antonio de los Cobres over the pass of Huaytiquina to San Pedro de Atacama. It is a very beautiful trip: you cross salt lakes with flamingoes and really impressive deserts. The road on the Argentine side is very good, but on the Chilean side there are very steep gradients. There are no petrol stations between San Antonio de los Cobres and Calama, or in San Pedro. Due to snow, this route is available only part of the year. A car must be in very good condition to cope with the heights. A bus service also runs from San Antonio to San Pedro on Saturdays; return journey on Wednesdays. Weekly bus, Salta-Antofagasta, US$17 (see page 74).

The direct road from Salta to Jujuy is picturesque with its winding 92-km. stretch through the mountains, now finally paved, known as *la cornisa*. The buses use the longer road, *via* Güemes.

Jujuy, or San Salvador de Jujuy, the capital of Jujuy province, is 66 km. by rail N of the Güemes junction on the Tucumán-Bolivia railway. It was founded in 1593. Most of the town is on the southern side of the Río Grande. The Government House is in a fine square, Plaza Belgrano, in the eastern part of the city. The first Argentine insignia, designed by General Belgrano, is shown here. On the western side of this plaza is a colonial Cathedral with very fine 18th century images, pulpits, walls and paintings finished about 1746. It has been almost ruined by restoration, but in the nave is a superb wooden pulpit, carved and painted by Indians, a colonial treasure without its equal in Argentina. The townspeople show the doorway on Calle Lavalle through which General Lavalle, the enemy of Rosas, was killed by a bullet in 1848, but the door is a copy; the original was taken to Buenos Aires. In the western part of the city are the Parque San Martín and an open space, La Tablada. See the Palacio de Tribunales near the river, one of the best new buildings in Argentina. Jujuy stands at 1,260 metres, completely surrounded by wooded mountains. Streets are lined with orange trees. Pop.: 120,000; The scenery is as varied as it is splendid.

Airport 40 km. out of town or 45 mins. by bus. Daily service to Buenos Aires by Aerolíneas Argentinas, at 10.30. Aerochaco flies on Mondays and Wednesdays to Resistencia, Posadas and Puerto Iguazú.

Train Train to Bolivia takes some 11 hrs. for the 350 km. ride; make sure you arrive early to get a seat, as the ordinary service only runs three times a week. It climbs from 1,260 metres in Jujuy to 3,442 metres at La Quiaca; it's chilly after sunset. The direct train to La Paz is usually late, and you can only book sleepers once the train has arrived.

Buses Jujuy-Tucumán, at 0600, 1300, 1900, 6 hours, US$2.25. Jujuy-Salta, many, 2¼ hours, US$1.80.

Hotels Just outside, and above the town, is excellent *Hotel Provincial de Turismo,* with good views and food. *Alto la Viña,* attractive, on hill 6 km. away. *Augustus,* US$10 double, modern, comfortable. *Internacional* (on main square), US$6 double; cheap alojamientos (nameless) nearby, US$1 per person. *Avenida,* on riverside, with good restaurant. *Bristol,* US$4 double, hot water, opposite railway station; *Paris,* 1st class, but a bit noisy from traffic. *Plaza* and *Ritz,* 2nd class. *Motel Huaico* (good), just outside on road to Humahuaca. *Residencial Belgrano,* US$6 double, old but clean. *Cleveland,* Alvear 782, US$2 single, clean. *Residencial San Remo,* US$4 double, recommended, 6 blocks from bus station towards town. *Residencial San Marcos,* US$2.50 per person, friendly. *Residencial Lavalle,* recommended, US$4 double. *Hotel del Norte,* US$2 per person, clean and friendly, near railway station. *Savoy,* opposite railway station, good value. *Motel Posta de Lazano,* just N of Jujuy, US$5 single.

Camping 14 km. N of Jujuy on Humahuaca road.

Restaurants *La Rueda,* Lavalle 320; *Internacional,* Av. Belgrano. *Restaurant Belgrano,* good.

Tourist Office Güemes 1632 and shop in Av. Belgrano (the main street), very helpful.

Public Holiday August 23-24.

The main problem of Jujuy Province, which has little industry apart from the small iron and steel works at Zapla and small industrial areas in the capital and Ledesma, is controlling the influx of labourers from Bolivia—10,000 a year—and the 40,000 seasonal sugar workers.

Some 24 km. from Jujuy is **Termas de Reyes,** where there are hot springs. This resort, with the very nice *Gran Hotel Termas de Reyes,* is set amongst magnificent mountains 45 mins. by bus from Jujuy. it is possible to camp below the hotel free of charge.

Anyone who has an itch for old churches, an eye for scenery and the hardihood to rough it will find Salta and Jujuy excellent centres for getting what he wants. Mr. Paul Dony, a well known writer on the religious architecture of Latin America, wrote an article on these Andean churches in the *Architectural Review* of December, 1959, and has since supplied a sketch from which the accompanying map has been drawn. Franciscan and Dominican friars arrived in the area from Bolivia as early as 1550. The Jesuits followed about 1585. Along both the old Camino de

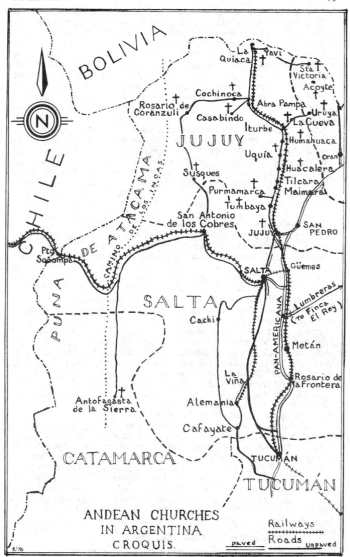

BOLIVIA

CHILE

JUJUY

SALTA

CATAMARCA

TUCUMÁN

PUNA DE ATACAMA

CAMINO DE LOS INCAS

PAN-AMERICANA

La Quiaca · Yavi
Sta Victoria
Acoyte
Cochinoca · Abra Pampa
Rosario de Coranzuli
Casabindo
Iturbe
Uruya
La Cueva
Humahuaca
Oran
Uquía
Huacalera
Susques
Tilcara
Maimará
Purmamarca
Tumbaya
San Antonio de los Cobres
JUJUY
SAN PEDRO
Pto. Socompa
SALTA · Güemes
Cachi
Lumbreras (To Finca El Rey)
Metán
La Viña
Rosario de la Frontera
Antofagasta de la Sierra
Alemania
Cafayate
TUCUMÁN

ANDEAN CHURCHES
IN ARGENTINA
CROQUIS.

Railways
Roads
paved unpaved

ROUGH SKETCH

los Incas and the new route through the Quebrada de Humahuaca the padres, in the course of two centuries, built simple but beautiful churches. In an area three times the size of Wales about 20 of these old chapels and oratories still exist. A few of them were built in the second half of the 17th century; the rest of them date from the 18th century. They are marked by a cross in the map. All of them can be visited by car from Salta, though some of the roads are very rough. About half of them can be visited more easily from Jujuy, *via* the Pan American Highway. A spare fuel can should be carried because service stations are far apart. (There are A.C.A. stations at Jujuy, Humahuaca and La Quiaca, and a YPF station at Tilcara).

One group, in the Puna de Atacama, on the old Camino de los Incas (which has completely disappeared), can be reached by the road which runs W from Salta through the picturesque Quebrada del Toro to San Antonio de los Cobres at 3,132 metres (196 km.; basic hotel). There is a fine piece of engineering 20 km. W of San Antonio: the "Viaducto de la Polvorilla", 213 metres long, and 62 high. The road S from San Antonio to Antofagasta de la Sierra is pretty severe going. The road N to Susques (105 km.), is comparatively comfortable, but runs through utter desert. There is no lodging at Susques, but a rustic meal can be got by telegraphing in time. The road on to Rosario de Coranzuli is a mule track.

The second group is either on the road N from Jujuy to La Quiaca through the Quebrada de Humahuaca or can be reached from it. The Quebrada de Humahuaca is itself extremely beautiful, with spectacular and dramatic rock colours and giant cacti in the higher, drier parts; the Pan-American Highway through it has been reconstructed and partly paved. Beyond Tumbaya, where there is an old church originally built in 1796 and rebuilt in 1873 a road runs 5 km. to **Purmamarca,** a very poor but picturesque village surrounded by hills of colourful rock strata; there is no hotel, but lodging can be obtained by asking at the ceramic shop opposite the church (mid-17th century). Not far N of the turn, on the main road, is Maimará (*Albergue Maimará,* also camping, 5 km. from Maimará, US$1.20 a day). **Tilcara,** a short distance N in the quebrada, has a folk museum run by Buenos Aires University (closed in June) and the new *Hotel Tilcara* (US$5 per person, swimming pool); cheaper are *El Viejo Rincón,* pleasant and traditional, U.S.$2 per person, and *Hotel Edén,* Av. Rivadavia, one block from plaza, clean, US$5 double. (The plaza has now been ploughed up, and will take many years to restore), *Restaurante Plaza,* recommended. Within walking distance is a Pucará, or Inca village, incorrectly reconstructed, closed in June. The churches of Huacalera (in bad condition), Uquía, and Humahuaca are on the main road. At Huacalera is the comfortable *Hotel Monterrey.* Two km. S of Huacalera, a small obelisk gives the exact latitude of the Tropic of Capricorn; it is easy to reach the monument if one stays on the main road, because the site is well signposted and only 20 metres W of the road. At Uquía (church built 1691) and Casabindo, the walls of the naves are hung with 17th century paintings of winged angels dressed as musketeers: the so called "ángeles caballeros". Cactus-wood decoration is found in many local churches. Road from Tilcara to Humahuaca about half paved.

Humahuaca (alt. 2,940 metres), 126 km. from Jujuy, is a small traditional town with an attractive church (originally begun 1631, but totally reconstructed in 1873-80), and a large independence monument flanked by huge cacti. See the Estudio Museo Ramoneda, combined studio and museum, entrance US$0.20. Hotels: *Provincial de Turismo,* US$7.50 per person, swimming pool; *Hotel Humahuaca,* US$5 double, basic but clean, with hot water, and offering excellent local food. Several residenciales at US$2 per person. Pleasant attraction: Museo de Carnaval. Eat at *La Cacharpaya,* near church. On October 17 and 24 the "Manca Fiesta", or the festival of the pots, is held here, and Indians from Jujuy and the Bolivian altiplano come, carrying all sorts of pots; local dishes are eaten. Near Humahuaca is the Santa Bárbara Tower, now in utter neglect; you can see Indian artistic remains nearby at Hornaditas and Incacueva, and an Indian mine at Rinconada. Also near Humahuaca, at Estación Iturbe, a road leads right to La Cueva (6 km.). Roads to Cochinoca (25 km.) and Casabindo (62 km.) branch off left at a point 4 km. N of Abra Pampa. Road from Humahuaca to La Quiaca unpaved.

Yavi, with the fine church of San Francisco, which has magnificent gold decoration and windows of onyx, is easily reached by a bad road (16 km.) from La Quiaca. Only a mule track leads on to the three churches of Santa Victoria, Acoyte and Uruya.

The ordinary tourist should be warned that a passion for old churches alone would justify the arduous quest for them in this area. There is little accommodation away from the main road, and no help can be expected in a breakdown.

Twenty-four km. beyond Jujuy the railway and road ascend into the dry uplands. For about 110 km. glimpses are caught of pockets of cultivated land in the valleys, but beyond Humahuaca (see above) the puna is bleak and barren all the way to **La Quiaca,** on the Bolivian border and 292 km. from Jujuy. It has a couple of paved streets and looks infinitely pleasanter and neater than its Bolivian neighbour, Villazón, to which it is joined by a concrete international bridge. Altitude, 3,442 metres. The cool climate calls for overcoats the year round. If going on into Bolivia, buy your basic rations, medicaments etc. in La Quiaca, where prices are lower. (Border on Argentine side closed 1200-1500.) When travelling by car from Jujuy to La Quiaca or vice versa and it rains, wait, or you may find yourself on flooded roads.

Hotels *Cristal,* best, 1 km. from railway station, US$7 per person, US$8.50 double, clean and comfortable; *Residencia Argentina,* clean; *Grand,* opp. railway station, clean, US$3.50 double; *Hotel Gran Victoria,* US$4 double; *Residencial El Turista,* very good, but expensive; has garages and swimming pool; *Club Social; Alojamiento Cruz del Sur,* cheap; *Hotel International,* cheap, good value meals. *Residencial Victoria,* nr. railway station, US$1.20 single, no hot water.

There is only one **restaurant** in La Quiaca, opposite the Atahualpa bus office on the main shopping street; recommended.

Transport Bus to Jujuy, about US$5 for an 8-hour trip over a partly-paved road. Atahualpa and Panamericana bus companies have 4 services each to Jujuy, at 1000, 1230, 1500, 1900 and 2130. Buses may be stopped and searched on the way. The train is cheaper but always arrive early to make sure of a seat: Coche motor, US$1.80, 6 hours, very comfortable, daily, but irritating delays may occur. Train from Jujuy to La Quiaca, US$1.70, one class, daily 2015, arrives 0800. On Saturday, it leaves at 1045, arrives 2130. The train does not run very fast, so you can admire the scenery. It stops at many local stations, where Indians sell you food and woollen goods. The railway goes up to 3,692 metres at Tres Cruces. Take warm sweaters, as temperature drops sharply after sunset. Bus to Salta, US$7, at 1000, 1500 and 2130 from outside *Hotel Cristal*, 8-9 hours.

The Belgrano railway's terminus is here, over a km. from the Bolivian railway station of Villazón, where connection can be made with the Bolivian system to La Paz. There are taxis at the Argentine station, or hire a porter with a luggage barrow to take you through the immigration office opposite the Automóvil Club, and customs and final control on the frontier. There is still the Bolivian immigration office at Villazón to visit after he has left you. (At the border post there is a notice that "all hippies" must carry at least US$50.) There are no exchange facilities on the Argentine side, but you can tell the policeman at the border where you are going and say you'll be back. Change (unofficially) travellers cheques at Casa León next to *Hotel Cristal* at La Quiaca, 10% discounted. If shop is shut, young man on duty from 1600 at *Cristal* will find him for you. Travellers' cheques can be cashed at the Turismo building, or at a better rate at the Banco del Estado in Villazón; only dollar bills and Argentine pesos are accepted at the exchange shops. Going into Argentina, change your Bolivian pesos at Villazón; you can also buy Argentine pesos there for US notes, but not for travellers' cheques. There are sleeping cars with plenty of rugs and a dining car on the train to La Paz. The Argentine sleeper is the best. Food is good and cheap. Tip conductor at start and end of trip for service. See also "Information for Visitors", Bolivian chapter. Motorists should visit the Argentine Automóvil Club just off the international bridge for maps, gasoline, etc., and information; and in Villazón, the Servicio Nacional de Turismo to obtain the Hoja de Ruta, which permits travel. It is not restrictive in any practical sense; just a nuisance! If the Bolivian Immigration Officer at Villazón is not in his office, you can ask for him at *Hotel Panamericano,* just up from the Post Office—on your own from there! Taxis are available from the frontier to the Bolivian stations; quite a distance.

Entering Argentina from Bolivia, Argentine border is open 0730-1230, 1430-1800; Sats., Suns., and holidays 0800-1100. Entry tax payable at Argentine frontier US$1.20; exit tax same. Porters US$0.50 from Villazón bus depot to border another US$0.50 from border to Argentine depot.

Hotels in Villazón *Savoy,* just possible; *Gran; Residencial El Cortijo,* clean, US$3.30, hot water. *Panamericano,* basic but clean.

N.B. Bolivian time is one hour earlier than Argentine.

Bolivia can also be reached by road from **Orán,** an ugly place (hotels expensive, US$10 at *Hotel Centro,* dirty room at *Hotel Crillon,* US$8 double) where there are bus services to Agua Blanca (1 hour), on the frontier they are generally very crowded and there is nowhere to stay at Agua Blanca. Buses run from Bermejo, across the river, to Tarija (6 hours, US$2). Another way into Bolivia is by road from Salta to Yacuiba and then on to Santa Cruz. There is also a direct bus (Mon. 1300) from Orán to Asunción, Paraguay.

The Andean Towns
Mendoza and the Vineyard Areas. In the W there is little rain and nothing can be grown except under irrigation. On the irrigated lands grapes and fruit are possible, and alfalfa takes the place of the maize grown in the N. Three of the more important oases in this area of slight rainfall are Mendoza itself, with two rivers from the Andes, the Mendoza and the

Tunuyán; San Rafael, 160 km. to the S, with two rivers, the Diamante and the Atuel; and San Juan, whose oasis is fed by the Río San Juan. The rivers do not flow far; they run into swamps and are swallowed by the land.

Of the 15 million hectares in Mendoza Province, only 2% are cultivated. Of the cultivated area 40% is given over to vines, 25% is under alfalfa grown for cattle, and the rest under olive groves and fruit trees; peaches, apples, pears, plums, quinces, apricots, and cherries. In the other oases there is a little more alfalfa than there is vineyard or fruit orchard. Petroleum is produced in the Province, and there are important uranium deposits.

Individual owners do not always produce their own wine, as in France. Wine making is expensive, and the grapes are sold for pressing to central bodegas. Generally speaking, the wine is less good than the imported French or even Chilean wines, but good types are produced when proper maturity is given.

"The rural landscape of the vineyard oases is distinctive", says Preston E. James in *Latin America*. "Always in the background are the naked, rocky slopes of the easternmost ranges which shut out the view of the higher peaks, such as Aconcagua. In the foreground on irrigated land are straight rows of vines, some festooned on trellises, some pruned low on wires, but all threaded with the little irrigation ditches. . . . Between the fields, and along the sides of the dusty roads are long rows of tall slender poplars; and here and there groups of houses are to be seen, low, one-storey structures with whitewashed adobe walls and red-tiled roofs."

The Transandine Route Mendoza, at the foot of the Andes, 1,060 km. from Buenos Aires, is linked to it by air, the San Martín railway which runs through the great flat Pampa *via* Mercedes, Junín, San Luis and La Paz, and a paved road along which modern buses ply. The road and railway continue from Mendoza across the Andes to Chile, to complete a journey from Buenos Aires of over 1,450 km.

The places along the route can be very cold at night and also expensive to stay at; it is best to stay overnight in Mendoza.

The monotony of the cattle breeding and grain-growing plains is broken only by clusters of trees surrounding the farm buildings of the estancias. Brightly coloured flamingoes rise from an occasional lake, such as the Laguna La Picaza, between Junín and Ruino. The train is comfortable, with sleeping berths. Ninety-seven km. from Buenos Aires is **Mercedes,** in Buenos Aires Province, an old but progressive city with a population of 40,000. It has many fine buildings, both public and private, and is a railway junction of some commercial importance. (There is another Mercedes in San Luis Province.)

Hotels *Paris; Comercio.*

The workshops of the San Martín railway are at **Junín,** 256 km. from Buenos Aires. Also served by Mitre railway, the town is close to lagoons from which quantities of freshwater fish are taken to the capital. Population, about 60,000.

Hotels *Junín; Central.*

At Mercedes (San Luis Province), 693 km. from Buenos Aires, a line runs NE to (122 km.) Río Cuarto. About 65 km. beyond Villa Mercedes we begin to run into the rolling hills of San Luis; beyond there are stretches of woodland. **San Luis,** 98 km. from Villa Mercedes, is the capital of the Province of San Luis. It stands at 765 metres at the southern end of the Punta de los Venados hills. It was founded by Martín de Loyola, the governor of Chile, in 1596, and is still faintly colonial. The grain and cattle country here is varied by an occasional vineyard. The area is rich in minerals and an onyx quarry is worked. Population: 38,000. San Luis to Mendoza is 264 km.

A "Via Crucis" sculptured in white marble skirts the mountainside. Beyond Salto Grande, Salto Colorado and the Gruta de la Virgen de las Flores (Grotto of the Virgin of the Flowers) is El Volcán, in whose neighbourhood is Cruz de Piedra dam (drives, fishing), and Cañada Honda (placer gold mining, riding and fishing). Hotels and inns along the road.

Hotels *Nacional de Turismo,* well kept, basic service; *España; Royal; Venados,* modern.

Restaurant *Pizzería Munich,* recommended for cheap food.

Beyond San Luis (27 km.) the line climbs to a height of 460 metres and descends again along the valley of the Río Desaguadero. From the small junction of Las Catitas, 92 km. from Mendoza, a branch line runs S to (183 km.) San Rafael, through country which is typical of the land E of the Andes, sometimes aridly dry, sometimes marshy, and sometimes cultivated. At San Rafael itself, at the foot of the Andes, irrigation makes it possible to grow fruit in large quantities. The town—there are some oil wells near—has a population of 46,000. A new road runs W over the El Pehuenche Pass to Talca (Chile).

San Rafael "Before you go over the Andes to Chile, a visit to San Rafael might be recommended. It is about 2-3 hours by bus from Mendoza along a good paved road, and is another pleasant oasis city with tree-lined streets; it is a little more brash and modern than Mendoza, with a slight aspect of the frontier (this was the frontier against the Indians until about 1870). Above the town, up the Río Atuel valley, there is beautiful scenery (it is called Valle Hermoso, or Beautiful Valley) up to the dams of El Nihuil which provide irrigation water and much hydroelectric power to Mendoza. There is fishing in the reservoir above the highest dam,"—Dr. Arthur Morris.

Hotels *Rex; España,* corner of San Martín and España, single, with bath, US$7, clean but shabby, no restaurant.

Campsite at Tunuyán, 77 km. before Mendoza from San Rafael; there are three more campsites on the road from Luján outside Mendoza to Potrerillos (52 km.).

Bank Banco de Mendoza.

Roads Between San Martín de Los Andes (see page 135) and San Rafael is a treeless landscape, with a few small towns. The only place where fields can be seen extensively cultivated on this route is Malargüe, situated in a vast, flat plain shaded by tall trees against a backdrop of the Andes peaks. The town is in the middle of an oilfield.

As we approach Mendoza in the early morning we see the foothills of the Cordillera on the sky line. At 756 metres, lies

Mendoza, capital of its province, is an expanding and very pleasant city. Rainfall is slight, but irrigation has turned the area into a green oasis covered with fruit trees and vineyards. The city was first colonised from Chile. It was founded in 1561 by a Spanish captain who named the new town in honour of his master, the then governor of Chile. It was from here that the Liberator José de San Martín set out with his Army of the

Andes to cross the mountains, first to help in the liberation of Chile, and then to move N by sea to capture Lima and liberate Peru. The city was completely destroyed by fire and earthquake in 1861, so Mendoza to-day is essentially a modern city of low dwellings (as a precaution against earthquakes), but thickly planted with trees and gardens. Population of city and suburbs: 500,000.

The best thing in it, from a tourist's point of view, is the Cerro de la Gloria (depicted on the 500 peso note), a hill in the great Parque San Martín, crowned by an astonishing monument to San Martín. There is a big rectangular stone block with bas-reliefs depicting various episodes in the equipping of the army of the Andes—the women offering their jewels to San Martín—and the actual crossing. In front of the block, San Martín bestrides his charger. The monument is surmounted by a great bronze condor and the Goddess of Liberty. The statue is surrounded by groves of eucalyptus trees. Steep and twisting paths in the park run to the Zoological Gardens, good and very well laid out. There are watercourses and a lake in the park too, and views of the backcloth of the Andes rising in a blue-black perpendicular wall, topped off with dazzling snow, into a china-blue sky.

The entrance to the Parque San Martín is ten blocks W of the Plaza Independencia; there is a bus that will take you to the top of the hill.

The Palacio de Gobierno is about 5 blocks S of Plaza Independencia between Pedro Molina and Santa Cruz, almost bordering on the suburb of Godoy Cruz. It is a 7-8 storey building, magnificent in a simple 18th century colonial style. It faces N and the square in front of it is flanked on the NE side by the Law Courts, equally magnificent in classical style. The San Martín Museum is housed in a school building on Av. General San Martín some 8 blocks N of the town's centre. The Museum of Natural History is on Plaza Independencia, lodged underground; this, too, has some colonial exhibits but is best known for its collection of Argentine plants and animals. The Palacio Municipal has a rooftop observation platform, no charge. The Municipal Aquarium is underground at Calle Buenos Aires and Pedro Palacios, very interesting, free admission. Worth seeing, also, are the ruins of the San Francisco church near Plaza Pedro de Castillo. The Historical Museum, on Calle Montevideo near Calle Chile, beautifully furnished, has a collection on San Martín and history of Mendoza. The best shopping centre is Avenida Las Heras. The grape harvest festival, ''Fiesta de la Vendimia'', is in March.

A ''traditional'' dangerous nuisance is the system of drainage gutters lining nearly all streets, but covered over at intersections and house entrances. A minor nuisance is the insects living in the trees lining virtually all the main streets, which have hearty appetites for passers-by.

Airport Plumerillo, 9 km. from centre; ''remise'' taxis (US$1.50) and buses run. Flying time from Buenos Aires: 3 hours. LAN Chile to Santiago, US$33, 3-4 times a week. Aerolineas twice a week. Aerolineas Argentinas to and from Bariloche, 3 times a week. Daily jets Buenos Aires to Mendoza, US$30 (25% discount for accompanied wives). Several flights to Córdoba and Buenos Aires with Aerolineas and Austral.

Trains to Santiago depart at 0905, arrival at Mapocho at 1930. Cheapest one-way fare is US$12 (1st class), 10 hours. Passengers to Santiago may have to change at Los Andes, bus 1¼ hours with same ticket. Passengers can go to Valparaíso from Los Andes by bus also.

The Pullman train is excellent, reclining seats, steward service, good bar and food and airconditioned. Leaves 0945 Wed., arrives 1930 at Mapocho. US$22.50, Express US$24.

Buses to Santiago, daily at 0600-1000, taking about 8 hours. Buses stop for passengers to take photographs of Cristo Redentor. Road somewhat rough. Several companies. Passengers are normally collected from their hotels. Fare about US$9; if returning, buy a return ticket in Mendoza as the Chilean fare is just about double! Book early as many Chileans visit Mendoza for shopping. Be prepared to wait a long time at the border for the customs check. For direct bus to Tucumán, see page 73. Buses also run to Bariloche, leave 0830 Sun., Tues., Thurs., US$24, about 27 hours; to Córdoba, daily 11 hrs., US$5; to San Juan every 2 hours, to San Luis 4-6 a day; to San Rafael; to Buenos Aires, daily, 19 hrs., at 1315 and 2030, US$14. Hitch-hiking from Mendoza to Buenos Aires is not recommended; few lifts are offered.

Industries at Mendoza   Wine bodegas and fruit preserving; Bodega de Arizú, one of the biggest, 10 minutes by bus from central bus station, direction Godoy Cruz, routes no. 8, 9, 10, 11, 12, is open to inspection any time; so are many of the others, and they are generous with wine after the visit. Mendoza is also one of Argentina's main oil producing provinces.

Local holidays   January 18 (Crossing of the Andes); July 25 (St. James); September 8 (Virgin of Carmen de Cuyo). Annual wine festival in mid-February.

Hotels *Sussex,* good; *Ritz; Plaza,* considered leading hotel locally; *Ariosto/ Nutibara,* on Bartolomé Mitre, US$10 d, modern swimming pool, recommended. Without dining room—*Balbi,* modern; *Palace* (English spoken), US$4, helpful; *San Martín; Cervantes,* restaurant. Lower ratings: *Imperial; Los Andes,* San Juan 1135; *El Descanso,* Gral. Paz 463, US$2.50 d, highly recommended; *Rincón Vasco,* US$8 d, with private bath, Las Heras 590; *La Gran Vía,* US$4 d, with bath, good cheap breakfast, very friendly; *Residencial Espejo,* central, US$5.50 d with bath; *Namuncua,* Chile 829, US$4 d, with bath; *Derby,* Calle Patricias Mendocinas, bath; *Margat,* Juan B. Justo 75, clean, US$2; *Ideal,* US$4 d, English spoken, transport to bus station; *Zamora,* Perú 1156, reasonable and friendly, converted house, US$5 d; *Madrid,* US$3.80 d with shower, friendly, good value. Try *Pension Janni,* junction 9 de Julio and Infanta Mercedes San Martín, *Motel Demo* (not one in the American sense); *Motel Chacras de Coria,* S of town, for stays of over 4 days. *Residencial Ceferín,* very cheap, friendly owner speaks English; *Residencial Verona,* Julio L. Aguirre 413, very friendly, run by Uruguayan woman, cheap; *Residencial Unión,* Plaza España, US$1 with bath and breakfast, clean, hot water; *Santiago,* nr. train station; *Turismo,* 2 blocks from railway station, US$1.40 d, with hot water; *Residencial 9 de Julio,* US$0.80 d, hot water; *Hotel Maxius,* Lavalle, US$0.75 s, hot shower; *Pensión Cuatro Ríos,* single rooms, US$3, dormitories US$1, hot water; *Residencial Valente,* San Juan de Dios, corner Laprida, 5 min. from bus station, clean, modern, US$1.75 s; *Residencial Copahué,* between Rioja and Entre Ríos, US$2.50 d, hot water.

Camping   Free in Parque Gral. San Martín; also about 1 mile past the university—hot showers if you provide kerosene. Three campsites at Challao, about 8 km. from the town centre, reached by colectivos leaving every hour. *Camping Suizo* best value. About 13 km. from Mendoza, two sites near the turn-off for Barballón.

Restaurants   *Hotel Sussex* and *Trevi* restaurants de luxe. Good ones are the *Automobile Club,* Italian restaurants *Montecatini* and *Marchigiani,* Restaurant and Bar *San Marco,* on Las Heras, and the *Mendoza Regatta Club.* Expensive tearooms in Galeria Tonsa. *Vecchia Roma,* recommended for good food, atmosphere and service. *Piccolini,* Sarmiento 234, Italian, cheap, good and friendly. *El Rey de la Milanesa,* cheap and good. *Fritz y Franz,* Ave Gral. San Martín 1901.

Tourist Offices on 11th block of Avda. San Martín and in Museum of Modern Art. Most helpful. There is a Chilean tourist office at 9 de Julio 1022.

Casino   Recently opened.

Mountain Climbing   Information from Club Andinista Mendoza, Calle Pardo y Rubén Lemos. Tel.: 24-1840.

Bank of London and South America, Av. San Martín 1498; Citibank. Open 0715-1315.

Cables Westec (British), Mercury House, Calle Rivadavia 1030, Godoy Cruz.

Excursions Buses run to pleasant places nearby. The thermal springs of **Villavicencio**, 45 km. N, are at 1,800 metres. The climate is delightful and the scenery beautiful. The curative waters vary between 37°C and 48°C, and are expecially valueable for long cures where a weak alkaline treatment is indicated. Bus leaves 0600, US$1.60. Buses also run to the hot springs at **Cacheuta** (thermal baths for those with doctors' certificates only), 45 km. to the SW (hotels not recommended); the charming resort of **Potrerillos** is 13 km. from Cacheuta, with ski slopes not far away *(Gran Hotel)*; the skiing, however, is reported less good than at Portillo, on the Chilean side of the Andes. Two other popular resorts within a few km. of the city are Barballón, to the NE, and Challao, to the NW. On the road to Luján de Cuyo (buses go every 15 mins. from near bus terminal) is a fine arts museum dedicated to Argentine artists, surrounded by sculpture in gardens, admission free.

Hotel *Termas* at Villavicencio is well worth visiting, about US$15 per person including breakfast and 2 enormous good meals. Unfortunately open only during short summer season., Many tourists come to visit the springs, which are all set in concrete. Pleasant walks around the area.

N.B. For people not travelling to Chile, there are frequent trips from Mendoza (at least two bus companies every day) to the statue of Christ the Redeemer and back in the day, when weather permits. These are usually small buses for 24 passengers, but quite comfortable and show you as much country as the railway which goes through at a lower level in the Mendoza river valley. The trip takes all day and starts between 0500 and 0800, but drivers will stop near your hotel or lodgings to pick you up. Most bus agencies are in Av. Las Heras. The trip is often crowded.

The fare for these trips is about US$6. A stop is made for lunch at Las Cuevas near the summit, on the way back (or you can take your own), but beware the altitude and eat and drink (alcohol) sparingly.

Over the Andes to Chile

By road there are 2 alternates of Route 7, which meet at the town of Uspallata *(Hotel Uspallata,* US$18 d, dinner at 2100; payment for meals and drinks in cash, bowling alley. Quite good, but vast herds of people get driven through it. Also *Los Cóndores)*, the only sizeable town between Mendoza and the Chilean frontier; the road is unpaved from Uspallata to the border. (Prices are usually much higher at frontier, temperatures much lower. Frontier closes early.) The southern branch, *via* Cacheuta and Potrerillos, parallels the railway through the Mendoza river valley except for a brief distance where the road rises very steeply over a mountain while the railway tunnels through. It is wider and better than the northern branch, which goes *via* Villavicencio with a stretch of one-way traffic just beyond the resort, where the road leads up spectacularly to the 3,050 metres high Cruz del Paramillo. (The return loop a little longer and less steep, is through the picturesque Quebrada del Toro.) This northern branch is still unpaved. (Remember to put your watch back an hour when travelling into Chile from Argentina.)

Camping There is a pleasant municipal site at Uspallata, US$0.30 per head, full washing facilities but no hot water.

Beyond Las Cuevas the road divides. The easier route goes through the railway tunnel (charge for car, US$3); the other—negotiable on the Argentine side; in good condition on the Chilean side—goes over La Cumbre Pass, and should be taken if at all possible. Pass closed in winter.

Turismo cars—ordinary cars carrying 4 to 5 passengers—and microbuses do the trip to Santiago in 8 hours (US$9) daily. The ride is rather dusty but spectacular. Excursions go only as far as Las Cuevas.

If travelling by bus from Mendoza to Santiago take a direct bus as it is difficult to walk across the border. Several companies do the trip, US$8.40, children under 8 60%, but no seat; 8-10 hrs., book two days ahead. Two-hour wait at Customs.

People travelling by car over the Andes in winter are advised to enquire about road conditions from A.C.A. (San Martín y Amigorena). The road from Punta de Vacas to Las Cuevas is not surfaced and difficult when snow is melting. Buy ticket for journey through international railway tunnel, if motoring privately, at Las Cuevas, otherwise you may risk being turned back (2 km.); tickets at railway station near customs shed. Cristo Redentor is 2 km. beyond the frontier.

Customs at the frontier are closed 1200-1400. Pay the dollar per passport and vehicle and push on, or you may be held up interminably at this post. Good food at frontier hotel, and there is an excellent motel on the Chilean side about an hour down. US$3 toll per vehicle for using the rail tunnel.

By rail from Mendoza to Santiago is pleasant and easy. Meals from the pantry-buffet are dear: better take sandwiches and fruit, but eat the fruit before you reach the frontier. Services usually run from September onwards, depending on snow-fall. Journey lasts about 10 hours.

It is possible to cross the frontier from Las Cuevas to Chile with the afternoon goods train, in the guard's van, after clearing Argentine immigration. Fare paid in Chile at Portillo; beware overcharging, ask for fare list.

Breakfast is served at Mendoza, but the through passenger has no time to see more of the place than can be viewed from the railway. Passengers for Chile take to the narrow gauge line which runs into the mountains and through Cumbre tunnel to Los Andes. Restaurant cars are attached on this section as far as Puente del Inca. The route is along the green fruitful valley of the Mendoza river to the foot of the Andes, 20 km. away. Here the limit of irrigation is marked by scrub and stunted trees on the lower slopes.

The engine begins to labour up the gradients. A curve reveals the crevice out of which the Mendoza river debouches on to the plain. Past Cacheuta, with its mineral baths, the line curves right and left following the river, crossing lattice work bridges and rushing through short tunnels. This is the old mountain trail the Spaniards named the Camino de los

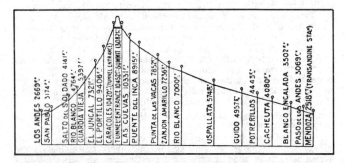

The Climb and the Descent. Wayside Stations and their Altitudes (in feet)

Andes. The river is still close. Beyond Uspallata is a vast, open, undulating plain, wild and bare, with dried bushes and cactus as the only vegetation. On all sides stand the grey, gaunt, barren mountains. On the far side of this plain the valley narrows till Río Blanco is reached, and there the mountain torrents rush and froth into the river. Soon we look up the Tupungato Valley at the majestic cone of Tupungato, one of the giants of the Andes, rising 6,797 metres. An equally majestic mass of pinnacled rocks, Los Penitentes, is passed. In the clear air it is difficult to realise that they are 65 km. away. The climber to their base (an easy task from Puente del Inca with a guide) sees a remarkable sight. The higher rocks look very like a cathedral, and the smaller, sharper rocks below give the impression of a number of cowled monks climbing upwards. On the other side of the valley we get a good view of the bright white Aconcagua (6,964 metres), one of the two loftiest mountains in the western hemisphere, sharply silhouetted against the blue sky. (Best time for climbing it is from mid-January to mid-February.)

In a short time we are at **Puente del Inca,** 160 km. from Mendoza, and 2,718 metres above sea level. It is a sports resort set amongst mountains of great grandeur, most often visited between November and May. The old hotel was destroyed by an earthquake; visitors now stay at the guest house on the army base. The natural bridge after which it is named is one of the marvels of South America; it crosses over the river Mendoza at a height of 19 metres, has a span of 21 metres, and is 27 metres wide, and seems to have been formed by sulphur-bearing hot springs. Puente del Inca is the best point for excursions into the higher Andean valleys or for a visit to the base of Aconcagua, which was first climbed by Vines and Zurbriggen of the Fitzgerald Expedition in 1897. Visits can be paid on horseback from Puente del Inca to Los Penitentes; or on foot to the green lake of Laguna de los Horcones; or by car (only with a well regulated engine) or on horseback to the statue of Christ the Redeemer set above La Cumbre (or Uspallata) Pass on the frontier at an altitude of 3,855 metres. It cannot be seen from the train, and is somewhat disappointing from the road, for it is completely dwarfed by the landscape. It was put up by the workers of Argentina.

Leaving Puente del Inca the train climbs the Paramillo de los Horcones, passing over the high-level bridge that spans the Horcones river. The Paramillo is the moraine of an ancient glacier on the flanks of Aconcagua. After a comparatively level stretch of valley, the train climbs by rack rail through the narrow gorge of the Paramillo de las Cuevas and enters the tunnel.

The tunnel is 3,137 metres long, or 48 metres short of its altitude (3,185 metres). The Transandine Railway has been electrified between Uspallata and the Chilean frontier at **Las Cuevas,** a neat, modern settlement now being developed as a ski-ing resort though there is no ski-lift as yet. It has the Argentine customs station. Pullman passengers change at Las Cuevas, but not those in the slower Friday train. It usually means a long cold wait but there is a fire in the hotel.

Hotel *Hostería Las Cuevas,* only one, poor food, no heating in annexe.

From the tunnel on the Chilean side at Caracoles, the descent, at first winding and gentle, suddenly becomes very steep. Between Caracoles and Portillo lies some of the grandest rock scenery in the world; prodigious, snow-clad, towering, sharp-pointed peaks, standing in relief against the blue of the sky. At intervals on the downward course are passed small, squat refuge-huts. The River Aconcagua is now at hand. Bare rock gives place to grass, sparse at first but growing thicker as we descend. Golden-yellow blossom blazes out. Flowers of many colours mingle with the cactus. The mountain barrier causes the clouds from the Pacific Ocean to discharge upon this side; that is why the Pacific slope is green and why the Argentine side of the mountains is so barren. At Portillo, a Chilean centre for ski-ing and winter sports, are the *Gran Hotel Portillo* with swimming pool and two *alojamientos*. The line traverses the Salto by short tunnels and follows the S bank of the river. The valley widens out and cultivation spreads rapidly until, at Los Andes, we reach the head of a wide and cultivated valley running to the sea. Los Andes—the terminus of the Chilean Transandine Railway—is beautifully set and its roads are lined with poplar trees. There is no meal at Los Andes (where we change to the broad-gauge Chilean State Railway for Santiago and Valparaíso, a run of 2 hours 43 minutes) nor is there a diner on the inward train. The junction for both places is Llay-Llay, but there are through coaches for international passengers, so there is no change at the junction. There are also services between Los Andes and both Santiago and Valparaíso by Pullman buses.

North of Mendoza

NB North of Mendoza pumps often run out of fuel so it pays to keep your petrol tank topped up.

There are three other oases standing between the plains and the mountains to the N of Mendoza, in much the same way as San Rafael to the S. Three streams from the Andes have made irrigation possible and the growing of fruit and vines and alfalfa. The three oases are San Juan, La Rioja, and Cata marca. La Rioja does fairly well with its wines and olive oil, but Catamarca is virtually unproductive and has always lived on the brink of economic disaster. The first oasis, 177 km. from Mendoza by paved road or railway, is

San Juan, 400,000 people, the capital of the Province of San Juan, established in 1562 by Don Juan Jufre de Loaysa y Montese, at 650 metres. An earthquake in 1944 practically destroyed the place but the centre, including the Cathedral, has been rebuilt. Sarmiento, the historian and educationist, and President from 1868 to 1874, was born in a one-storey building here; his house contains the Sarmiento Museum, with a signed portrait of Lincoln. There is an Archaeological Museum, which has a number of fascinating mummies. The ruins of the Santo Domingo Convent are worth seeing. Much of the local trade is with Chile. The surrounding country is picturesque.

A new road runs W over Agua Negra pass and down the Elqui valley to La Serena (Chile). The Argentine side is quite good (spot the condors in the sky), but the Chilean side is deplorable; the road may be closed from May onwards for the winter season. The scenery is superb. The road from San Juan to La Rioja is also poor, but passable; look out for the picturesque ponies and carts *Surquis.*).

Hotels *Estornell* (modern, good, no dining room), Mitre 31; *Sussex,* has night club and casino attached, Av. Libertador and Las Heras; *Nogaró,* Ignacio de La Roza and Gral. Acha; *Jardin Petit Hotel,* 25 de Mayo 345; *Selby,* Av. Rioja 183; *Plaza,* Sarmiento 344; *Bristol,* Entre Ríos 368; *Brescia,* Av. España 336; *Austria,* Sarmiento 246, opp. railway station; *Provincial Tourist Hotel.* Others are 2nd class, including

Lido, 9 de Julio 429; *Lara,* Rivadavia 213; *Hispano Argentino,* and *San Francisco,* on España 410 and 284; *Oller,* Jujuy 45; *Rex,* Gral. Acha 187; *Central,* Mitre 131; *Roy,* Entre Ríos 180.

Restaurants 1st class: *Diego,* Entre Ríos 142; *La Tablada,* Sarmiento 444; *Fogón Sanjuanino,* Laprida 207. Grills at: *Las Palmeras,* Gen. Acha and Juan Jufré; *Don Zoilo,* Mendoza 347; *Los Paraísos,* San Martín 1101; *La Tranquera,* Rivadavia 225; *Restaurant El Mendocino,* quite good, opp. railway station.

"Camping permitted" signs along road from Mendoza to San Juan. Campsite in olive grove, 7 km. S of San José de Jachal on the road to San Juan, and 23 km. after Jachal, Villa Unión road.

Tourist Office, opposite Sarmiento Museum, arranges tours.

The route from San Juan to Salta is *via* San José de Jáchal, Villa Unión, Famatima, Tinogasta, Sta. María, Cafayate, Cachi and El Carrila. Leaving San Juan, the route follows the railwaý as far as San José de Jáchal with barren mountains on the Chilean side and bush in the valley. From Jáchal (84 km. paved) alternating desert scenes, vineyards, orchards and olive groves. 251 km. on, at **Chilecito** (20,000 people), are good views of Sierra de Famatima. Chilecito is a pleasant town, with fine and difficult mountain drives nearby, including the Cuesta de Miranda, which runs along a cornice through a deep narrow canyon in a series of hairpin bends; only small vehicles should venture up the Cuesta de Zapata. *Motel ACA* at sleepy village of Salicas, 152 km. on, and nearby is *Hostería Termas de Santa Teresita.* Carry on *via* Alpasinche (7 km. unpaved from Salicas), 71 km. to Tinogasta (poor road), 83 km. to Belén (unpaved) and 177 km. to Santa María (only 16 km. paved); 22 km. beyond Santa María is Amaicha del Valle (partly paved) with good *Hostería ACA;* on 14 km. (paved) to Río Santa María and then 52 km. unpaved to Cafayate (see page 76). See Londres, 21 km. S of Belén, the 2nd oldest village in Argentina, founded in 1558 and named in honour of the marriage of Mary Tudor and Philip II in 1554. At the town hall one can see a glass coat of arms of the City of London and a copy of the marriage proposal.

Hotels at Chilecito: *ACA,* good, US$6.60 s on T. Cordillo and 8 de Julio; *Hotel Provincial de Turismo,* José Hernández 62; *Riviera,* Castro Barros 133. B category: *Americano,* Libertad 60 and *Hotel Bellia,* El Maestro and A. Marasso.

Camping 15 km. from Chilecito on the road to Guauchía, near a Jesuit estancia established in 1652; also 6 km. along Calle de La Plata, at Santa Florentina; and 2 km. further at Los Tabas.

Tourist Office on 19 de Febrero and La Plata; Post Office on J. V. González and Mitre, Chilecito.

Excursion One can visit the colourful Valle de La Luna by taking a bus to **San Agustín del Valle Fértil** and hiring a jeep from the ACA (not cheap). Entrance US$1.50; there is an ACA camping and an hostería in San Agustín (also *Pensión Doña Zoilia* and *Anda Collo*). Information from San Juan tourist office.

The Valle de La Luna is 330 km. from San Juan and 60 km. from San Agustín, and is interesting to geologists and paleontologists for its relics of the Mesozoic Age. Fossils found are exhibited in the Museo Bernardino Rivadavia in Buenos Aires.

It takes 6½ hours by road through San Agustín del Valle Fértil to get to the second oasis, **La Rioja**, at 500 metres, 45,000 people, the capital of La Rioja province. It has some colonial buildings and a folk museum (Sunday open 0900-1300); regional costumes are sometimes seen, and its peculiarly flavoured dry wine is worth trying. Worth a visit is the solid adobe ruin of the Jesuit church (now encased in another building for protection) in which Francisco Solano baptised the local Indians. A remarkable image of the Child Jesus can be seen in the Church of San Francisco. Inca Huasi museum (Sundays open at 0900-1300) has Indian skulls, a fine collection of funerary urns, and "pregnant pots" or jars thought to belong to the Florescent Era: 300 B.C./A.D. 400.

In the town are plenty of the amusing *palo borracho* trees, usually a bottle-shaped thorn-studded trunk at a drunken angle hung with pods like

Avocado pears which, when ripe, open to disclose large brown seeds in a kapok-like substance. The tree is also found in several parks and promenades in Buenos Aires.

How reached From Córdoba or San Juan by San Martín railway or road. From Buenos Aires, 2,092 km., by train, 39 hours. From Mendoza by road (see above). Bus to Mendoza only by night, two companies: Borio, 12 hrs., US$7.65, very comfortable.

Hotels *Nacional de Turismo,* well set up but poorly run; *Savoy; El Centro; Progreso,* small rooms, overpriced but almost clean. No hot water. Better value from *Hotel La Rioja, Libertador, Parlamento, Central* and *Residencial Aparicia.*

Excursions To Nonogasta, Samay Huasi, and the Chacho caves.

Tourist Office at P.B. Lona 650, near Plaza, maps, information.

A paved road and a railway run NE to the third oasis, Catamarca.

From Cebollar, on this line, a railway runs NW into parched mountains, rising in hard, pink forms as preludes to distant steel blue peaks. The line rises 760 metres through Copacabana to Tinogasta *(Hotel Provincial de Turismo),* a half-Indian copper-mining township. Both lie cradled, by virtue of rare water, in deep green valleys lush with vineyards and olive groves and rows of poplar trees. A track threads through the towering mountains to Copiapó, in Chile.

Catamarca, capital of its small province, lies on a river between two of the southern slopes of the Sierra de Aconquija, about 130 km. S of Tucumán. This old colonial city is set amongst hills at an altitude of 490 metres. Cotton growing is added here to the cattle, fruit and grapes of the oasis. It is also famous for the hand-weaving of ponchos and for its preserves; an especially excellent one is from the fruit of a cactus (try Casa Vásquez, on Sarmiento). Pilgrimages are made to the Virgin of the Valley in her church. The thermal springs of Catamarca are curative. Population: about 29,000. Road to Tucumán.

A pleasant excursion is to El Dique Las Pirquitas, 3 hrs. with local bus 1A from bus station, with terminus at Isla Larga, pleasant hills and woods.

A road runs NE to Lavalle (on the way to Santiago del Estero). This 116-km. run over the Cuesta del Portezuelo Pass (1,980 metres), with its 20 km. of steep gradients and numerous hairpin bends—small hairpins—is one of the toughest in the country. There is a bus service.

Museum The "Esquiú" Cultural Institute, Sarmiento 450. (Archaeology, colonial history, iconography, mineralogy.) There are traces of the "Belén" civilization elsewhere in the province, at Hualfín and Punta de Balasto.

Hotels *Nacional de Turismo* (much as at La Rioja); *Ancasti.* More reasonable, clean and well run, is *Hotel Suma Huasi. Centro,* Juan M. de Rosas, esq. 9 de Julio, basic.

The Chaco

Between the north-western highlands already described and the Río Paraná to the E lies the Argentine Chaco, the southern end of that Gran Chaco which stretches also into Bolivia and Paraguay. The Argentine Chaco is a huge area containing the Provinces of Formosa and Chaco, Santiago del Estero, and northern Santa Fe. Its southern limit is the Río Dulce valley, running for nearly 320 km. from Santiago del Estero to the lake of Mar Chiquita. This great lowland and swamp in the N, formed by the alluvium carried down from the Andes, is covered with thorn scrub and grassy savannah, the thorn bushes sometimes impenetrable and sometimes set widely apart on grassland. The highest summer temperatures in all South America have been recorded in the Argentine Chaco; the winters are mild with an occasional touch of frost in the S. Rain falls mostly during the winter. A vertical line drawn down the centre of the Chaco will roughly delimit an eastern area of sufficient rainfall from a western area of deficient rainfall. The further W, the less the rain. Resistencia, in the E on the Río Paraná, gets an average of over 1,220 mm. a year; Santiago del Estero, in the W, gets about 510 mm., and this, where evaporation is so rapid, will not permit agriculture without irrigation. Only four main streams run through these lowlands: the Pilcomayo, 2,000 km. long, the boundary between Argentina and Paraguay in the N; the Bermejo, about the same length as the Pilcomayo; the Salado (not the Río Salado of the Pampas); and the Dulce, running 800 km. from the Sierra de Aconquija W of Tucumán to the Mar Chiquita, "the little sea", which has no outflow. During the summer rains these sluggish and unnavigable tributaries of the Paraná swamp great areas of the land, particularly in the E, and often change their courses.

Communications The last few years have seen a significant spread in the communications of the region. Before the recent building of highways, the only all weather routes were provided by the Belgrano Railway. There are two main north/south lines from Buenos Aires: the international route to La Paz, which passes along the western boundary of the region, and the line through Rosario and Santa Fe which has its terminus at Resistencia. There are two east/west connections, from Resistencia to Métan and Salta and from Formosa to Embarcación. A third line runs SW from Roque Sáenz Peña to Anatuya in the province of Santiago del Estero. There are three short branch lines in Chaco province. Roads are given in the text and air services link the major towns.

Tannin and cotton are the two great industries of the Chaco. The iron-hard quebracho tree (quebracho is Spanish for axe-breaker) grows only in the Chaco of northern Argentina and Paraguay; it is the purest known source of tannin, extracted by grinding the tree down to a coarse sawdust which, when boiled, exudes a sticky residue. There are two varieties: the white quebracho from the sparsely populated scrubland of the western provinces of Santiago del Estero, Salta, west Chaco and Formosa, with a low tannin yield which limits its use to fence posts, railway sleepers and firewood; and the red quebracho, at the turn of the century the world's major source of tannin. Led by the Forestal Land Company, the forest was opened up, first in northern Santa Fe and then in the Chaco; The Company built towns round its plants and its own railway lines. After the second world war it moved N to the towns of Fontana and Puerto Tirol, 16 km. W of Resistencia, in search of unexploited forest. The industry, still very important, is failing slowly against competition from synthetic tannin and Forestal's huge mimosa plantations in S. Africa: mimosa tannin is cheaper but not so good. The most accessible forest is worked out; most of the cutting is now in the N and W of the province and logs are brought in by road and rail. Higher wages have put up costs and town life is attracting the hacheros, the men who do the cutting in the hot, mosquito-infested forests.

Cotton growing, centred on Roque Sáenz Peña in Chaco Province, is now more important. The area round this cotton capital now grows 75% of Argentina's cotton; the rest is grown in Formosa. Since the first boom years in the twenties and thirties, there has been an increasing struggle to keep up production in the face of soil exhaustion and bad husbandry:

small scale tenant farmers have neither the money nor the will to experiment in low cost production. Crops in the fifties averaged around half a million tons of raw cotton and the seed from which oil is extracted. Bad harvests and floods in the sixties forced many of the smaller units to give up. But the total crop has, surprisingly, been almost maintained by the more efficient units. Sunflower is the chief crop replacing cotton, and there is also some maize and sorghum.

Roque Sáenz Peña can be reached by excellent road from Puerto Pilcomayo. *Residencial Sáenz Peña*, near bus station, is cheap, clean and friendly.

The rest of the Chaco is cattle country but there are few animals to the square km. Large estancias are the rule, some growing cotton, linseed and other crops by irrigation. There is a fair amount of industry now round Resistencia, but unemployment is still very high. There are jobs in plenty from January to April during the cotton harvest, but little for the rest of the year. It is not as bad as when the migrant Golondrinas used to come from Paraguay to pick the cotton. Only a quota is now allowed in by law. But all the towns are ringed by large areas of squatters' huts—villas miseria—which are the great social problem of the region. But Santiago del Estero is an old and stable settlement, placed where the Río Dulce, confined by banks during its course from Tucumán, debouches on the plain.

The birds of the area are described in *The Review of the River Plate:* "First there are the flamingos, hundreds of them, those awkward, pinky white objects when standing fishing, that change as if by magic as they rise into the air, transformed in flight into creatures of elegance, flaming coral and black. Then there are the swans that look as if they had just thrust their necks down to the base into the black mud. Singly come the heron egrets, gleaming white in the sunlight; they will stand on one leg for hours, staring, unlearned as to the value of their plumes. Waterfowl of many kinds, some with brilliant green legs, paddle and quack and fuss, hardly noticing the presence of man; they are inedible, and know it—all except the duck who seems to have been born wary. Storks stand like cricketers fielding in a slow game; grey sparrow hawks dart about at ground level, vultures and great eagles higher up, and then, as far as the binoculars can see, a very occasional condor, a speck in the blue."

Towns of the Chaco   The more important ones—Resistencia and its port Barranqueras, and Formosa—are all on the W bank of the Paraná and Paraguay and will be described, for convenience's sake, under "Up the Paraná River" when dealing with Argentine Mesopotamia. Apart from Roque Sáenz Peña (the cotton centre), the only other town of any importance, Santiago del Estero, is on the western boundary of the Chaco, 167 km. SE of Tucumán.

Santiago del Estero, the oldest Argentine town, was founded in 1553 by settlers pushing S from Peru. It is near the bank of the Río Dulce where that river, coming from Tucumán, flows into the plains of the Chaco; a 1½-km. steel bridge across the river carries the railway from La Banda (6½ km.) on the Buenos Aires-Rosario-Tucumán route. There is a branch line *via* Forres to Córdoba. Population, 92,000. The main square, Plaza Libertad, contains the Casa de Gobierno, and the Cathedral (the 5th on the site) stands next to it. On Plaza Lugones is the pleasant old church of San Francisco; this, the City's first church, was founded in

1590 by San Francisco de Solano, patron saint of Tucumán. His cell is in the near-by convent; his festival, celebrated with folk-music (he was himself a violinist), is on July 24. Beyond the church is the comely Parque Aguirre, with a good zoo. Airport.

In the convent of Santo Domingo is a "Holy Sheet", one of the three copies of the sheet which covered the sacred body of Our Lord given by Philip II to his "beloved colonies of America". The Provincial Museum of Archaeology (Calle Avellaneda) founded by Emil and Duncan Wagner, has over 10,000 samples of Indian pottery. There is also a provincial history museum, previously known as the Museo Gancedo.

Hotels *Palace, Savoy,* simple, well run, good and very ample food. *Residencial San Antonio,* Belgrano 485, US$3 d.

The arid north can be vividly experienced by a bus journey S from Santiago de Estero to Córdoba over paved roads, through enlessly varying semi-desert.

The **Río Hondo** hot springs, reached by road, 65 km., are halfway betwen Santiago del Estero and Tucumán, at 264 metres. Their only attraction is the sparkling crystal-clear thermal water which wells up out of the earth already conveniently heated to bath temperature. This is good for blood pressure and rheumatism. Good to drink, too, and used for the local soda water. A casino (roulette and card games) is open during the winter season. The huge Río Hondo dam on the Río Dulce is close by; it forms a lake of 33,000 hectares, good for sailing and fishing.

Hotels *Grand* (with Casino); *Los Pinos,* the most pleasant; *Panamericano; Palace; Ambassador.*

Some 320 km. SE of Santiago del Estero the Río Dulce, flowing in places through salt flats, runs into the shallow Mar Chiquita on the southern margin of the Chaco. People who live in the valley of the Río Dulce are so used to the taste of its water that they often add a pinch of salt to the water they drink when away from home, "to make it drinkable". Mar Chiquita, 80 by 25 km., is naturally salty, and the water is warm. No river drains it, though two other rivers flow into it from the Sierras de Córdoba in the flood season. There are several islands in the lake. On its southern shore is the small town of **Miramar.** Mar Chiquita is a very popular resort during the summer months for its salt waters are helpful in the treatment of rheumatic ailments and skin diseases. It is best reached by a railway W from Santa Fe to Dean Funes; it runs within a few miles of the southern shore. The lake is reached from Córdoba by car or bus: 200 km;

Hotels *Gran Copacabana, Gran España, Miramar, Marchetti.*

(**Note** This Mar Chiquita and its town, Miramar, must not be confused with the other Mar Chiquita to the N of Mar del Plata and the seaside resort of Miramar, S of Mar del Plata.)

Mesopotamia

The north-eastern part of Argentina is very different from the NW. Here, between the rivers Paraná and Uruguay lies Argentine Mesopotamia: the provinces of Corrientes, Entre Ríos, and Misiones. The distance between the rivers is 390 km. in northern Corrientes, but narrows to about 210 km. in the latitude of Santa Fe. From the Alto Paraná, the northern boundary, to the junction of the Paraná and the Uruguay in the S is about 1,130 km.

The province of Corrientes, in the N, is marshy and deeply-wooded, with low grass-covered hills rising from the marshes. The normal rainfall is about 2,000 mm, but the rains are not spread uniformly and drain off so quickly through the sandy soil that a rainfall of 1,500 mm., which is

NORTH-EASTERN ARGENTINA

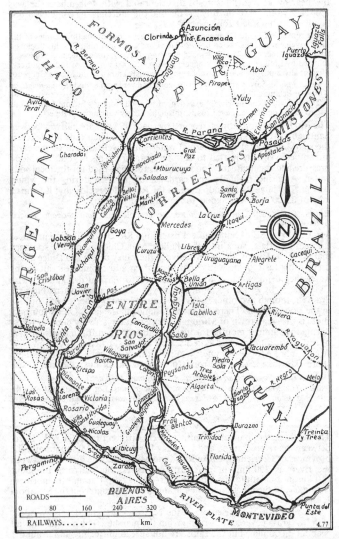

ROUGH SKETCH

not unusual, may be insufficient to prevent drought. Entre Ríos, to the S, has undulating plains of rich pasture land not unlike those of Uruguay. Winters in Mesopotamia are mild; the summers are hot and much rain falls in short, sharp storms, though both Entre Ríos and Corrientes often suffer from summer drought.

Much of Entre Ríos and Corrientes is still now pastoral, a land of large estancias raising 4½ million improved cattle and 4 million sheep. The rough pastures are burnt off in the spring to rid them of the unpalatable grasses the cattle will not eat. But in the "tick free" S, in Entre Ríos, where the grass is better, there are over 3 million improved cattle and over 4 million sheep producing important quantities of meat and wool for the Buenos Aires market. Maize (a gamble in the N) is largely grown in southern Entre Ríos, which is also the most important producer of linseed, citrus fruit and poultry in Argentina. In Corrientes, along the banks of the Paraná between the cities of Corrientes and Posadas, a good deal of rice is grown. Corrientes also grows excellent oranges.

Thrusting into the far NE is a strip of land between the Alto Paraná and the Uruguay rivers, 80-100 km. wide and about 400 km. long. This is Misiones province, and its capital is the river port of Posadas. Its boundary to the N is the river Iguazú, which here tumbles over the great Iguazú Falls. Misiones is on the Paraná Plateau, and over 80% of it is covered with forests of pine and cedar and broad-leaved trees, for here too the rainfall is heavy: twice as heavy as in Entre Ríos. The days are hot, and the nights cool. It is a sub-tropical land, the forests tangled with brilliant flowers; in the woods are multitudes of wild monkeys, parrots and toucans, and the fauna includes tapirs, jaguars, pumas and water hogs. About 25% of the people are foreign born, mostly Paraguayans.

Mesopotamia was first colonised by Spaniards pushing S from Asunción to re-occupy Buenos Aires; both Corrientes and Paraná were founded as early as 1588. But Misiones was first occupied by the Jesuit Fathers fleeing from the Brazilian Alto-Paraná with their devoted Indian followers before the slave-hunting Bandeirantes. These missions and their history are described under Posadas (see page 103).

It was the Jesuits who first grew yerba maté in plantations, and Misiones from its first settlement until to-day has been largely dependent on this leaf. After the Jesuit expulsion the collection of yerba was entirely from the wild forest, but to-day the plantation system has been reintroduced with great success E of Posadas. The province has of late years attracted immigrants from Europe and from Mesopotamia. Nearly all the nation's tung oil comes from Misiones, which has also a large area under tobacco and citrus fruit. Timber is an important industry. There is good fishing in many of the small towns. In NE Corrientes and in Misiones, more Indian tea is now grown than can be absorbed by the internal market.

The Indian-tea industry was started by a member of the British community in Argentina. Believing that tea could be grown in the country, the late Sir Herbert Gibson sent for seed from Assam in 1929; it was sown in Playadito, Corrientes province. Six seeds developed into sturdy trees. Year after year their seed was given to anyone interested. All Argentina's tea plantations today have their origin in Sir Herbert Gibson's enterprise.

Communications in the area are by road (now greatly improved), by railway, and by the two rivers which bound it to E and W. Both rivers leave much to be desired. The Paraná floods disastrously, shifts its

channel frequently, and that channel is both shallow and often clogged
with sandbars, but it is the only exit by water from the land-locked
Republic of Paraguay. The Río Uruguay, eastern limit of Mesopotamia
and the boundary with Uruguay, is navigable by large vessels as far as
Concepción del Uruguay, but above that city it runs between high banks
and has many rapids, so that only small boats can ply on it. Bridges
between Fray Bentos (Uruguay) and Puerto Unzué, near Gualeguaychú,
and between Paysandú (Uruguay) and Colón were opened in 1976.

The area is served by the Urquiza railway, the only standard gauge line in the
country; the most important line, the international one from Buenos Aires to
Posadas and Asunción, the capital of Paraguay, with a branch at Monte Caseros for
Corrientes. The Province of Entre Ríos is served by two trains a day from Buenos
Aires to Concordia, with communications to almost all the province.

Up the Paraná River

Most of the important towns of Mesopotamia and Misiones lie on the E
bank of the Paraná or the S bank of the Alto Paraná. A journey up these
rivers is given here; the towns on both banks are described, but it must be
remembered that those on the W bank as far as Santa Fe are in the
pampas; beyound Santa Fe those on the W bank are in the Chaco.

River Shipping Line River boats of the Flota Fluvial del Estado
(Av.,Corrientes 389, Buenos Aires), usually leave the Argentine capital
twice a week for Corrientes, and fortnightly for Asunción. According to
the tide, they enter the Paraná river by either the Las Palmas reach of the
delta, on which is Zárate, or the Paraná-Guazú reach, on which is Ibicuy.
The fare Buenos Aires-Asunción (2nd class) is US$60; the journey takes 3
days, and the cost includes meals. Services are often suspended in the
summer.

Zárate, with 52,000 inhabitants, is industrially important, with large
frigoríficos and paper works. It is served from Buenos Aires (90 km.) by
two railways: the Bartolomé Mitre and the General Urquiza. Urquiza
trains used to be ferried 84 km. across the river to **Ibicuy** on their way N
to Corrientes, Posadas and Asunción. The crossing took 4 to 5 hours, but
a bridge-tunnel complex has been built between Zárate and Brazo Largo,
accelerating rail and road journeys alike; this complex will be completely
operational at end-1978. The picturesque Ibicuy Islands can be visited by
steamer.

On the way upstream to Rosario, on the western bank, are two ports
which export grain: **San Nicolás** (55,000 people), 80 km. below Rosario,
and **Villa Constitución**, 37 km. below Rosario. Both are served by a
railway from the capital. At San Nicolás is the General Savio steel plant.
Pergamino, an important road/rail junction in the pampas, is 72 km. S
by road or rail.

About 108 km. N from Ibicuy by rail is **Gualeguay,** with a population
of 26,000. It is the centre of one of the richest cattle and sheep ranching
regions in Entre Ríos. The house from whose ridgepole Garibaldi was
hung by one hand and tortured by the local chief of police in 1837, in the
time of Rosas, still exists. Eight km. S is its river port—Puerto Ruiz—on
the Gualeguay river, which flows into an eastern channel of the Paraná
almost due E of San Nicolás. The road from Gualeguay northwards along
the E bank of the Paraná is paved all the way to Posadas.

Hotels *Ferrechio; Diez.*

Rosario, chief city of the province of Santa Fe, is the second city of the republic, with a population of about 1 million. It is a great industrial centre, but is primarily concerned with the shipment overseas of produce brought from the central and northern provinces and a convenient base for the inland distribution of general supplies. On the top of the Minetti building, 11 storeys high, stand two bronze female figures, one with a stalk of wheat, and the other with a head of maize, in their hands—symbols of the great grain lands of the neighbouring pampas.

The river bank is high at this point. The streets are wider than those of Buenos Aires, and there are fine boulevards and handsome open spaces. From October to early March it is warm, and from December to the end of February uncomfortably hot. Changes of temperature are sudden.

Rosario is 320 km. N of Buenos Aires. Ships of 10,000 tons can reach it.

Points of Interest Monument of the Flag, a new memorial on the river bank in honour of General Belgrano, designer of the Argentine flag, who raised it on this spot for the first time; Parque Independencia (Rose Garden); Boulevard Oroño; Cathedral (Roman Catholic) in Calle 25 de Mayo; S. Batholomew's Church (English), Calle Paraguay; racecourse, law courts, university, hospitals, the Frigorifico Swift, grain elevators, petrol installations, the Alberdi and Arroyito boat clubs, and Saladillo (salt water springs). Golf Club (Station Parada Links, Mitre line). The Aero Club is at the fashionable suburb of Fisherton, headquarters of the British community. The Juan B. Castagnino Municipal Museum and the provincial Historical Museum (open Thurs. and Sat. 15-18, and Sun. 10-12, 15-18) are in Parque Independencia. Swimming at sandy Florida beach, about 8 km. N of Rosario. The boat *Ciudad de Rosario* does a short trip round the nearby river islands at weekends and holidays. It leaves from the Estación Fluvial near the monument of the Flag.

British Consulate, Rosario (Santa Fe, 939). British Consul's telephone number: 25593.

Hotels *Riviera,* new, air conditioned, but expensive; *Italia,* old, a little musty; *Bailboa,* medium priced, satisfactory.

Restaurant *El Paco,* Plaza de Mayo, nr. Cathedral, specialises in parrilladas; *Doña María* in Calle Santa Fe does good Italian food.

Airport at Fisherton, 14 km. from centre. Taxi charges vary.

Markets Mercado Central, Calle San Martín; also Mercados Norte, Sud, and Abasto. Best time, 0600-0800.

Local holiday October 7 (Foundation of the City).

Rail Rosario is 5 hours from Buenos Aires (320 km.) on the Bartolomé Mitre Railway and Belgrano Railway by express train, and is served also by the general Belgrano (narrow gauge), and the Mitre and Roca railways to Puerto Belgrano.

Road Transport There are regular bus services to Arroyo Seco, Casilda, Cañada de Gómez, San Lorenzo and other important centres up to 80 km. from the city. Also to Buenos Aires, by paved roads *via* San Nicolás and General Pacheco or *via* Pergamino, 309 km. (bus, US$3.50), and *via* Bell Ville NW to Córdoba (bus, US$3.50) and Tucumán. Local bus fare—US$0.07.

Rosario can also be reached from Buenos Aires by Route 8 (marked Córdoba) to Pergamino, and then, following signs, by Route 188, and then 178 to Rosario. This is a better way than lorry-packed Route 9.

Ferries between the ports of Rosario and Victoria, in Entre Ríos.

Bank of London and South America, Calle San Martín 843, and at Córdoba 2301 (Orono); Citibank, Santa Fe 1101. (Its bronze doorway is a copy of Ghiberti's Door of Paradise in the Baptistry at Florence); First National Bank of Boston, Córdoba esq. Mitre. Open 1000-1600.

Above Rosario the river is very braided and islanded. Some 23 km. N of Rosario is **San Lorenzo,** where an associate company of ICI has one of the largest chemical works in Argentina. See the restored San Carlos monastery on the river bank, where in 1813 San Martín won his first battle in the War of Independence. Visitors are shown a pine tree grown from a cutting of the tree under which the Liberator rested after the battle. Some 180 km. beyond Rosario, on the E bank, is

Paraná, capital of Entre Ríos (pop.; 200,000) and the port for the grain, cattle and sheep area to the E. From 1853 to 1862 the city was the capital of the Republic; it is still one of the most handsome cities in the country, with a fine centre, the Plaza San Martín, where there are fountains and a statue of the Liberator. The Cathedral, E of the plaza, is notable for its portico and its interior; opposite it is the tourist information office. A modern building on Plaza Alvear houses the Bazán Museum of Fine Arts and the local history museum, open 0900-1200 and 1500-1800 except Mon. The Government Palace (Casa de Gobierno), in another plaza, has a grand façade. But the city's glory is the Urquiza Park, to the NW, where Paseo Rivadavia ends. It has an enormous statue to General Urquiza, and a bas-relief showing the battle of Caseros, at which the tyrant Rosas was brought low. There are excellent views of the country and of Santa Fe on the other side of the river. Roads fan out into the province, and one (paved) leads to Paso de los Libres, 483 km.

Hotels *Mayorazgo,* new, with fine view of park and river, has casino and swimming pool, US$15 d; *Alvear,* also new, in centre; *Gran Hotel Paraná,* US$8 d; *Plaza* (only fair); *Atenas,* central.

Restaurants *Molino Rojo,* down by river; *La Posta del Olivo,* just off Plaza San Martín; both good.

Santa Fe and Paraná do not face one another. At present it takes 20 mins. to get from one to the other by car, and 1 hr. by bus, US$0.50, every half-hour. You cross a bridge close to Santa Fe, travel for some km. over an uninhabited island, cross another bridge, run over another uninhabited island to dive into the 2-km. Hernandarias tunnel, which leads to a hill running up to Paraná city.

Santa Fe, a larger city of some 300,000 inhabitants, has two large docks for ocean-going steamers. It is the capital of its Province and the centre of a very fertile region. It was founded by settlers from Asunción in 1573, though its present site was not occupied until 1651. It was in its Cabildo (town hall) that the Constitution of 1853 was adopted. The oath of allegiance was taken before the crucifix in the sacristy of the remarkable church of San Francisco, built in 1680 from materials floated down the river from Paraguay. This old colonial church has been tampered with but is still fine.

Santa Fe is a university city, with theatres and a racecourse. Most of its best buildings are grouped round Plaza Mayo and Plaza San Martín in the eastern end of the city. Plaza Mayo, on Calle General López, has the small Jesuit church of La Merced (1660-1754), next to the majestic Casa de Gobierno, and (on the N side) a church begun in 1741 (see an old painting from Cuzco and the interesting archives). A block SE of the Plaza has the famous Church of San Francisco (see above). Opposite it is the Museo Histórico Provincial. The buildings on Plaza San Martín are modern. In Calle General López is the Rosa Galisteo de Rodríguez Museum of Fine Arts, where local painters hold their exhibitions. Twice weekly boats from Buenos Aires, 483 km. to the south; regular only in winter.

Industries Flour milling, cereals, dairy, quebracho extract, zinc and copper smelting. **Export** Grain.

Railways Mitre and Belgrano railways to Buenos Aires, 483 km., 10 hours, also up N to Resistencia. Santa Fe is the H.Q. of the Belgrano railway.

Roads Fully paved to Rosario, 160 km.; to Formosa, 894 km.; to Roque Sáenz Peña, with spurs S to Villa Angela and General Pinedo and N to San Martín. Bus for Asunción (Paraguay) leaves daily at 1640, US$18, arrives 0930.

Airport at Sauce Viejo, 14 km. from the City.

Hotels *Hostal de Santa Fe de La Vera Cruz,* best, US$15 d; *Castellar,* small rooms, helpful staff, US$7 d, with bath; *El Conquistador,* new, US$6 d, with bath; *Río Grande; Hernandarias,* central, US$5 d; *Residencial Corrientes,* near Palacio del Gobierno and shops; *España; Plaza; Hospedaje Nueva Tripolitania,* Vera 2230, US$1.50 p.p., friendly, good restaurant; *Royal,* clean, modern, opposite bus station, US$3.20 d.

Restaurants Many good ones, offering excellent meals with good wine for US$4.

Bank of London & South America, Calle 25 de Mayo 2501, open 0715-1315.

Local holidays Sept. 30 (St. Jerome); Nov. 15 (Foundation of City).

Swimming On river at Guadalupe beach; local bus.

Upriver from Santa Fe the Paraná rapidly loses depth and is navigable only by river boats and small coastal vessels.

Between Santa Fe and Corrientes the boat calls at several river ports, including Goya and Empedrado. **Goya,** on the E bank, the second town of the Province of Corrientes, is near the junction of the Paraná with the Santa Lucia river. It is a large tobacco centre on the Urquiza railway, with a population of 40,000. There is a motor-ferry service across the river to **Reconquista.** The road N from Goya to Empedrado and Corrientes is paved.

Empedrado, further up the river on the E bank, has a population of 21,000. It is on the railway line between Buenos Aires (1,014 km.) and Corrientes. Oranges and rice are grown in the neighbourhood.

Hotel at Goya *Hotel de Turismo,* modern, recommended.

Hotels at Reconquista *Magui,* on main street, excellent restaurant. *Hotel Olessio,* opposite bus terminal, US$1.50 d. *Residencial San Martín ,* US$6 d, with bath, on B. Mitre and Bolívar. *Motel Hostal del Rey,* located on the edge of town, clean, new, US$6 d, with bath. Many around bus station.

Hotel at Empedrado *Hotel de Turismo,* with swimming pool and fine views.

About 600 km. upstream from Santa Fe, on the W bank, is the little port of **Barranqueras,** served also from Santa Fe by railway (17 hours). It is on a steep bluff overlooking the Paraná. A paved road connects it with **Resistencia,** the bustling and energetic capital of the Province of Chaco, 6½ km. up the Barranqueras stream. Pop.: 94,000. The road N from Resistencia to Formosa (200 km.) and on to Puerto Pilcomayo (137 km.) is paved. There are 2 bridges over the Río Bermejo. The planning department of the Universidad del Nordeste, near railway station, is very active in the area. International airport.

Hotels *Sahara,* new and central, now best, US$15 d; *Oasis; Covadonga,* US$11 d, friendly; *Colón,* good, US$8 d; *España; Aragón,* basic. Several cheap ones near bus station at US$1.50 p.p., e.g. *Paraná; Hotel Comedor; Hotel Arrayanes,* not recommended. *Residencia Chaco,* US$2.50; *San José,* US$2.50 d, with bath, recommended; *Hotel El Oriente,* Av. 25 de Mayo 554, US$8 d, with bath.

Restaurant *Tú y Yo,* good value, *Café Mecca,* good breakfast and coffee. *Santafecinos,* tasty meals at family style restaurant, US$0.80 for large meal.

Camping Parque 2 de Febrero. *Parque Mitre,* showers and toilets.

Fogón de los Arrieros, a famous house-and-club-full of local art and "objets" from abroad. No fee. Anyone can drink at the bar.

Air Resistencia-Salta, flights by Aerochaco, Mon., Wed., Fri., 0730, US$25, avoids tedious bus journey.

Rail   S to Santa Fe, leaves 1900 on Tue., Thurs. and Sat. (Belgrano Railway); W to Metán and spa of Rosario de la Frontera, 145 km. N of Tucumán; this has connections to both La Paz and Santa Cruz, Bolivia. Train to Salta, 30 hours, no restaurant car, 1st and 2nd classes identical except for price (US$9.60 or US$6.50).

Buses   3 a day to Buenos Aires *via* Santa Fe, 10 hours. 3 a day to Formosa and Pto. Pilcomayo, 6-7 hours, US$2. To Posadas, 6/7 hours, dull, hot journey. Four buses a week direct to Salta (Mon., Wed., Fri., Sun.) (US$11.25) at 1700, 17½ hours; one daily to Tucumán. Also to Formosa and Asunción.

Roads between Resistencia and Salta: there is a dirt road Río Muerto-Macapillo (180 km., passable only when dry), but a paved road is under construction. No petrol stations along most of the route.

Area Products   Cotton, quebracho, cattle.

Industries   Lead smelter; cotton gins.

Across the river from Resistencia is Corrientes. The 2¾-km. General Belgrano bridge across the river, completed in 1973, is bringing enormous benefits to both banks; the best view of it is from the Corrientes side.

Corrientes, capital of Corrientes Province. The Urquiza railway journey to Buenos Aires is 1,046 km. (0705 Sun., Tue., Wed. and Fri., arrives 1148 the next day; trains carry sleeping car and restaurant car). Population, 104,000. The city was founded in 1588. Tourists will be most interested in the Government Palace, on Plaza 25 de Mayo; the Church of La Cruz (1808), which houses a miraculous cross placed there by the founder of the city, Alonzo de Vera—Indians who tried to burn it were killed by lightning from a cloudless sky—and the Cathedral, in the renaissance style. Plaza Sargento Cabral has a statue to the sergeant who saved San Martín's life at the battle of San Lorenzo. On the river bank, NE of the city, is a park with good views of the river. There is a Colonial, Historical and Fine Arts Museum. The pre-Lenten Carnival is said to be the most interesting in Argentina; reserve hotel in advance. Road to Posadas, 320 km., now well paved.

Hotels   *Nacional de Turismo,* adequate; *Paraná; Colón,* near river, 15 minutes' walk to centre, comfortable, US$4 d, with bath; *Buenos Aires.*

Shipping   Flota Fluvial del Estado steamers up the Río Paraguay to Asunción, the capital of Paraguay; down the Paraná to Buenos Aires. Regular services only in winter (April-November).

Airport   Camba Punta, close to city.

Tourist Office, Quintana 940, very friendly, has maps.

To the N of Corrientes is the small town of **Paso de la Patria,** a paradise for dorado fishing, with plenty of bungalows to stay at.
   A tiny port on the Alto Paraná—**Itatí**—is reached by bus. Here, on July 16, is held a gala festival which celebrates jointly the crowning of the Virgin of Itatí (housed in a sanctuary built 1638), and St. Louis of France. Thousands of pilgrims arrive on the 16th (when the religious ceremonies begin) from San Luis del Palmar in picturesque procession.

Corrientes is 40 km. below the confluence of the Paraguay and Alto Paraná rivers. Up the former is Asunción; up the latter are Posadas and Iguazú. Passengers change at Corrientes to boats of a shallower draught.
   The only Argentine port of any note on the Paraguay river is **Formosa,** 240 km. above Corrientes. It is the capital of Formosa Province, and has a population of 40,000. There are many Indians in the area. The surroundings are flat and swampy, the climate and vegetation tropical. By road from Buenos Aires: 1,365 km. Airport.

Hotels   *Turismo,* best; *Ideal, Palace, España.*

Restaurant *Sen San,* near bus terminal, cheap and good.

Shipping Bolivian Lloyd River Shipping Co.'s vessels (cargo and passenger) to Puerto Suárez (Bolivia), with call at Asunción. Irregular.

Roads S to Resistencia (200 km.); N to Clorinda and Puerto Pilcomayo (now surfaced; 137 km.) and the ferry across the Río Paraguay to Itá Enramada near Asunción.

Railway across the Chaco to Embarcación (Sr. Sarmiento's Hotel), N of Jujuy, in NW Argentina and Salta. Passenger trains leave 0725 Wed. and Sat. (carrying sleeping and dining cars), arr. at Embarcación at 0930 Thurs. and Sun. and at Salta at 2100 same day. Additional journeys to Embarcación only, 1830 Mon. and Thurs., arriving at 0750 Wed. and Sat.

About 137 km. N of Formosa, almost opposite Asunción (Paraguay), are **Clorinda** and **Puerto Pilcomayo,** whence a ferry crosses to Itá Enramada (Paraguay), US$3.75.Clorinda has a well-known Banana Festival in early October.

At the confluence of the two rivers above Corrientes the Paraguay river comes in from the N, the Alto Paraná from the E. The Alto Paraná is difficult to navigate; it is, in parts, shallow; there are several rapids, and sometimes the stream is braided, its various channels embracing mid-stream islands. Much rice is grown on its banks. The main Argentine port, on the S bank, is

Posadas, capital of the province of Misiones, 377 km. above Corrientes. A ferry plies the 2½ km. of river between Posadas and the Paraguayan town of Encarnación opposite (US$0.15); it takes cars (US$2) and links the railway from Buenos Aires (1,070 km.; 31 hours), with the line to Asunción (440 km.; 14 hours), several times a day. Population, 44,000. Yerba mate (there is even a mate museum in the Palacio del Mate), tea and tobacco are grown in the area. There is a head shrinker's museum on Dos de Mayo, near Posadas. The 320-km. road to Corrientes is paved. Bus from Buenos Aires, US$17, 28 hours; some go *via* Resistencia, some *via* Concordia. There is a road from Posadas to Iguazú, paved and passing through jungle, yerba mate, tea and tung plantations, also pine forests for a cellulose plant. Bus to Asunción, US$7.

Train from Buenos Aires (Lacroze Station), Pullman, US$14, leaves Buenos Aires at 0710, five times a week, 30-35-hour journey. One advantage over the buses is that the wild life in woods and swamps may be seen more easily from the railway (because it is less often disturbed) than from the road. Train leaves for Buenos Aires daily at 1325 except Mon. and Wed., arrives 1950 next day, US$6 1st class, US$5 2nd class. Meals on board, US$1.75. Sleeping coaches weekdays only. To Concordia by rail, 1st class, US$2.50. Train to Asunción leaves Posadas 1450 Tues. and Thurs., arrives 1430 next day.

Airport General San Martín, reached from Posadas by Bus No. 8 in 20 mins., US$0.15. Daily flights to Buenos Aires.

Hotels Prices in the Province of Misiones are on the whole significantly higher than elsewhere. *Continental,* Bolívar 314, US$9 d, comfortable, but noisy and poor breakfast; *Grand Hotel,* swimming pool, central, reasonable; *City; Hotel de Turismo,* US$12 d, with bath; *Ideal,* clean and reasonable, US$4; *Majestic,* Calles Santa Fe and 3 de Febrero, hot showers, good meals available, US$4, clean and cheap; *Residencial Nagel,* US$2.50 d, very clean bathroom; *San Ignacio,* US$2 p.p., hot shower, good; *Asunción,* comfortable, breakfast next door, 15 mins. from centre; *Italia,* one block from plaza; *Eldorado,* near bus station, Av. Mitre 84, basic, US$1.50 p.p.; *Argentina,* with fan, corner of Colón and Sarmiento, US$1 p.p.; *Kiri-Motel,* reasonable; *Casa Doña Rosa,* near bus terminal, basic but cheap; *Savoy Hotel,* nr. central plaza, US$2.50 d, bathroom, clean, pleasant, excellent restaurant adjoining. *Residencial Tupi,* US$1 with bath, near bus terminal, Calle San Luis.

Avoid *Hospedaje Familiar*. *Hotel Tía Julia,* US$4 d, hot shower, nr. bus terminal. Many adequate residenciales in the centre.

Restaurants   *Hotel de Turismo. Bar Itá* for good coffee and sandwiches, on San Martín.

Tourist Office next to *Hotel de Turismo,* Av. Bolívar, helpful, maps and brochures in English of Formosa and Iguazú Falls.

Bank   Only Banco de La Nación changes travellers' cheques. Opens very early.

Camping   Municipal camping ground on the river, off the road to San Ignacio Miní.

Posadas is in red-earth country; when dry it blows into everything, so wear old clothes. The Paraguayan market has leatherwork and other crafts but prices are high and some of the goods show bad commercially-oriented workmanship. During the yerba mate harvest celebrations chosen beauties from the regions parade Posadas in allegorically decorated coaches until one of them is chosen queen. Local arts and crafts and industries are on show. There are a great many Polish and Ukrainian settlers throughout Misiones.

From Posadas a visit should be paid to the impressive ruins of Jesuit settlements and to the picturesque Falls of Iguazú. It is possible, by leaving Posadas at 0700, to see the Jesuit ruins and continue on by bus or colectivo to Iguazú the same day, arriving 2130: a most interesting but dusty journey over a good road through virgin jungle and recent settlements; at one of these, Puerto Rico, there is an excellent restaurant, *Osvin.* The express bus takes 7 hours (US$5), and leaves at 0200 and 0400, but will not stop at San Ignacio Miní; the ordinary buses, which will, take 11-12 hours for the journey and there are hourly departures from Posadas; these buses make 35 stops in all. The Posadas-Iguazú road is paved.

Not far from Posadas are 30 ruins of the old Jesuit missions among the Guaraní Indians, from which the province of Misiones derives its name. Tourists should not fail to see those at San Ignacio Miní, (free entry), reached by paved road in an hour (bus, hourly, US$0.55).

At **San Ignacio Miní** the grass-covered plaza, a hundred metres square, is flanked north, east and west by 30 parallel blocks of stone buildings with ten small, one-room dwellings to the block. The roofs have gone, but the massive metre-thick walls are still standing except where they have been torn down by the ibapoi trees; it looks as if there had been an arcade in front of each block., The public buildings, some of them still 10 metres high, are on the south side. In the centre are the ruins of a large church finished about 1724. To the right is the old cemetery, to the left the school and the cloisters of the priests. Beyond are other buildings which were no doubt the workshops, refectory and storerooms. The masonry, a red or yellow sandstone from the Paraná River, was held together by a sandy mud. There is much bas relief sculpture, mostly of floral designs. Now maintained as a National Monument.

The Jesuits set up their first missions amongst the Guaraní Indians about 1609. These were in the region of Guaíra, now in Brazil. One mission near the confluence of the Pirapo and Paranapanema rivers was named San Ignacio Miní. The missions flourished, and by 1614 there were 2,000 Indians living there. Cotton had been introduced, the Indians wove their own clothes, dressed like Europeans, bred cattle, and built and sculpted and painted their own churches. But in 1627 they were heavily attacked by the slave-seeking Bandeirantes from São Paulo in Brazil. By 1632 the position of the mission had beome impossible, and 12,000 converts, led by the priests, floated on 700 rafts down the Paranapanema into the Paraná, only to find their route made impassable by the Guaíra Falls. They pushed for eight days through impenetrable forests on both sides of the river, then built new boats and continued their journey; 725 km. from their old homes they founded new missions, some in Paraguay, some in Argentine Misiones, and some in what is to-day Brazil. San Ignacio Miní was re-established on the banks of the small Yabebiri river, but moved 64 years later, in 1696, to the present site of its ruins. By the early 18th century there were, on both sides of the river, 30 mission villages with a combined population of over 100,000 souls. Only four of these show any signs of their former splendour: San Ignacio Miní (Argentina), São Miguel (Brazil), and Jesús and Trinidad (Paraguay). San Ignacio Miní is the only one that is easily accessible. At the height of its prosperity in 1731 it contained 4,356 people. In 1767, Charles III of Spain expelled the Jesuits from Spanish territory; the Franciscans and Dominicans then took over control. After the Jesuits had gone, there was a rapid decline in prosperity. By 1784 there were only 176 Indians at San Ignacio Miní; by 1810, there was none. By order of the Paraguayan dictator Francia, all the settlements were evacuated in 1817, and San Ignacio was set on fire. The village was lost in the jungle until it was discovered again in 1897. In 1943 the Historical Monuments Section of the Argentine Agricultural Directorate took control of the village. Some of the craft work turned out at the settlement can be seen at two museums in Buenos Aires: the Museo Colonial Isaac Fernández Blanco and the municipal Museo de Arte Colonial. Small Museo Jesuítico on site, close to ruins on main avenida. The caretaker will show you a 350-mm. statue of Moses, said to be by Michelangelo, held at the museum.

Accommodation There are A.C.A. hotels (US$5.20 d; lunches at US$1.40 each) both at San Ignacio Miní and at Monte Carlo, half-way between San Ignacio and Iguazú. The *Residencial San Martín,* US$2 p.p., friendly, is near the police station at San Ignacio; nearby is *Hotel Ideal,* US$3 d, hot water. Festival July 30-31. Interesting local crafts sold opposite ruins. Wooden carvings are especially worthwhile.

The Hungarian caretaker at the Museo Jesuítico can tell you the address of a young German, Michael Apel, who owns a farmhouse about ½ hr. walk from the village. He will lodge clean-shaven (due to terrorist controls) travellers in exchange for a bit of housework or help in the fields. You only pay for things he has had to pay for; fruit and farm produce free.

Camping outside the ruins is permitted.

The Iguazú Falls

The Iguazú Falls are the most overwhelming falls in South America. They surpass in grandeur both Niagara and the Victoria Falls. They lie about 350 km. upstream from Posadas where, 19 km. above the confluence of a tributary, the Iguazú, the waters fall thunderously in virgin forest bright with orchids and serpentine creepers festooning the branches. Above the impact of water on basalt rock hovers a perpetual 30-metre high cloud of mist in which the sun creates blazing rainbows. The Iguazú (Guaraní for great waters) rises in the Brazilian hills near Curitiba and receives some 30 streams on its course across the plateau. Above the main falls the river, sown with wooded islets, opens out to a width of 4 km. There are cataracts for 3½ km. above the 60-metre precipice over which the water plunges in 275 falls over a frontage of 2,470 metres, at a rate of 1,750 cubic metres a second. Its height is greater than Niagara's by 20 metres or so and its width by one half, but many of the falls are broken midway by ledges of rock. The best season for seeing them is from August to November, not from May to July when the river is usually in flood, though the tumbling water in its setting of begonias, orchids, fern and palms with myriads of magnificent butterflies is always majestically beautiful.

The several falls have distinctive names. Of those on the Argentine side the San Martín Falls are glorious; the Bossetti, the most turbulent and picturesque, is usually crowned by a rainbow; the Two Sisters are smaller. Mitre, the Three Musketeers, and the Devil's Throat are best seen from an island reached by canoe; a motor-canoe goes to the latter from Puerto Canoa, 0900-1700 daily. Below the falls the Igúaza runs swiftly for some km. through a deep canyon, the Garganta del Diablo (The Devil's Throat), before it joins the Alto Paraná.

On the Argentine side Iguazú Park (or National Park of the North) embraces a large area. The fauna is rich and various but hunting is not allowed. Fishing is permitted—and The Devil's Throat teems with salmon, pia-pirá, dorado and manguruyú. The best months are October and November. Information and permits can be got from the Park Superintendent in the park's headquarters at Puerto Iguazú: a colonial style building which also houses an interesting regional museum. Horses can be hired for riding. Take swimming gear.

There is a US$0.10 charge which allows 5-day entry and camping for the same period. The kiosk at the park gate has a good Spanish book on the local flora (US$0.50).

Entrance (US$0.20) to the falls is good for 3 consecutive days so hold your tickets for re-entry.

Frontier crossing to see both sides is easy. If you are coming from Brazil and you just want to see the Argentine side tell officials, and they won't stamp your passport.

There is an Argentine domestic airport near the Falls, and a Brazilian international airport, about half-way between Foz do Iguaçu and the falls. On the Argentine side buses take passengers (or it is 10 minutes' walk uphill) from boat and plane to **Puerto Iguazú**, splendidly set 60 metres above the stream. It is recommended that when flying from Buenos Aires one should land on the Argentine side even if intending to stay on the Brazilian side. Travel by domestic flights avoids a long journey to the international airport in B.A. and is much cheaper than international flights. The air fare is about US$100 cheaper from Buenos Aires than from Río. Most hotels on the Argentine side are cheaper and include meals.

Hotels   *Hotel Cataratas* at the falls (see page 108). There is a water shortage in late November and December so check before you take a room. The *Iguazú Hotel* in the town (no swimming pool), is being used to offer rest accommodation to the elderly, but transients are still welcome, US$14 without food. A new hotel, the *Paraná*, is clean and friendly and much cheaper. *La Cabaña* (US$7.25 d, with shower and breakfast, with fan, good clean and friendly) is a nice but decaying hotel with swimming pool. Two luxury hotels have recently been opened at Puerto Iguazú: the *Libertador* (US$20 single) and the *Esturión*. Cheap places include *Residenciales Segovia* (US$1.50 p.p.), *Alvaro Núñez* (US$1.80), and *Vivi* (US$1.80). *Misiones*, new, good, moderate, US$3.20 d; *El Pilincho de Don Antonio*, clean, hot shower. Small primitive pensión just at entrance to National Park, near falls; *Hostería del Polaco*, run by a Pole and his 15 children, 1 km. from Falls and near Pto. Iguazú,

FRIENDSHIP BRIDGE
BRASIL
TO ASUNCION 202 miles
HOTEL ICARAÍ & CASINO AIRSTRIP
Pto.Pte. Stroessner
AIRSTRIP
TO CURITIBA
FOZ DO IGUAÇU
PTO. PTE. FRANCO
PTO. MEIRA
FERRY
20 miles
AIRPORT
PTO. IGUAZÚ
N
14 miles
PARAGUAY
HOTEL CATARATAS
HOTEL DAS CATARATAS
HOTEL RIO IGUAÇU
AIRPORT
PUERTO CANOAS
ARGENTINA
RIO ALTO PARANA
RIO IGUAÇU
TO POSADAS 232 miles
4/78

ROUGH SKETCH

basic but very cheap. Camping allowed in grounds, but there is no water and there
are no safety precautions. Bus to Falls passes *Residencial Pagnita,* very clean, just
like a home, only 2 rooms, US$2.50 d, opposite bus station. *Hotel Turista,*
inexpensive, charmingly old fashioned, spectacularly set above river. *Pensión Krivo,*
cheap, friendly, highly recommended. *Hotel San Jorge,* opp. bus station, US$5 p.p.
with breakfast.

Restaurants Restaurant (nameless), ½ block from *Hotel Sol de Iguazú,* Brazilian
food, all you can eat for US$1.40. *Restaurant Guayaca,* opp. *Hotel Libertador,*
US$1 for very good steak. *Restaurante Don Nicola,* good, large meals for about
US$2. Good small, cheap restaurant behind the bus terminal; you can sit outside in
the evening and listen to a harp and guitar duo while you eat.

Camping Parque Nacional "Opé" camping ground by river, 2 km. from falls;
Camping Parque Nandú on Argentine side, ½ km. from the Devil's Throat, but
4 km. by road. Take food and drink with you; cheap wine available on site and
barbecues permitted. Take good supply of insect repellant. Camping Pindó at edge
of Town, US$0.35, good facilities.

Buses Puerto Iguazú to Posadas, 8 hrs., US$4.25, one almost every hour. Pto.
Iguazú-Córdoba, every day except Tue. and Sat. at 0630, 26 hrs. To Resistencia daily
0900, 12 hrs., US$9. To Buenos Aires two buses daily, 23 hrs. *via* Zárate bridge.

Ferry There is a direct ferry to Paraguay, 0800 to 1600 every ½ hour daily, for
passengers on foot, which connects with bus to Puerto Stroessner and avoids
Brazilian customs.

On the Brazilian side arrivals by air are taken to the hotel at the falls or to
Foz do Iguaçu. The falls can be seen from either the Argentine or the
Brazilian side. (The concensus seems to be that though you can see the
whole falls from Brazil only, the partial views from Argentina are more
spectacular.)

On the Argentine side there are buses, mostly in the morning (10
minutes from centre, US$0.50) and taxis (US$3) from Puerto Iguazú to
the Falls, a distance of 22½ km. There are fixed rates for taxis. From the
river brink you can penetrate right into the falls by a series of cat walks
over the river all the way to the Garganta del Diablo: an extraordinary
experience; by boat, the trip costs US$1 (0900-1800). There is also a trip
by boat to San Martín island, in mid-stream, US$2.50 (1100-1800). Or
you can take a boat (US$1.40) from a launch point 2 km. in on a dirt road
that branches off the park entrance road, just before the control toll
house; pay toll and take ticket out to launch, otherwise you can't board.
Waterproof coats are advisable but not absolutely necessary; they can be
hired for US$0.40. Wear good shoes when walking around, e.g. tennis
shoes, as the rocks are very slippery in places. Put your camera in a plastic
bag.

There is a strong prejudice in favour of the Brazilian side. It stems probably from the
well-known luxury hotel there. But the *Hotel Cataratas* on the Argentine side
(US28.50 p.p. including meals), though simpler and older, has excellent food and
many people think the surroundings are more spectacular. The catwalks into the
river, rock formations, birds, butterflies, vegetation, views, and the paths through
the woods around are spellbinding. About 4 hrs. walking required. If you want to see
both sides within a day, an early start about 0730 is required from bus station at Foz
do Iguaçu to reach Argentine side and return by the time border is closed at 1800 (in
winter). In general, it is best to exchange currency in Argentina.

The Brazilian **Foz do Iguaçu** is reached from Puerto Iguazú by frequent
motor boat or a ferry to Porto Meira (takes cars and buses, US$2.70
round trip, double on weekends and holidays, from 0800 to 1800) and on
by road again (buses every hour, US$0.36, between Porto Meira and Foz
do Iguaçu, US$2; taxi to *Hotel das Cataratas,* US$3-4. Beware of
overcharging!) Note that the ferry does not function during the lunch
break (1200-1400—Brazilian time) or at high water times for cars (about
February). Foz do Iguacu is a rather ugly and dirty town of 25,000
people. Buses run the 32 km. to the falls in summer from 0700, last at
1700 and 2315, every hour from bus station, past airport (Empresa
Sgarioni, to *Hotel das Cataratas).* Buses return 0730, 0830, 0900-1900
hourly, and 2400, return fare of about US$2.30. Entry to park US$0.50.
(In winter buses run every two hours.) (The taxi fare is US$7, plus US$2
for each hour of waiting.) On a height directly overlooking the falls is the
luxurious *Hotel das Cataratas,* an attractive colonial-style building with
nice gardens and a swimming pool not without mosquitoes. Rates start
from US$40 a day without food. A 1½ km. paved walk runs part of the
way down the cliff near the rim of the falls, giving a stupendous view of
the Devil's Throat. It ends up near the powerful Floriano Falls, but an
elevator hoists the visitor to a path leading to Porto Canoa, where

boats—if the conditions are right—ply along the upper levels of the river and into the water which is about to plunge into the Devil's Throat. If on a day trip, an electric lift in the jungle takes coach passengers to the road above where a jeep runs people back from the lift to the *Hotel das Cataratas.* Helicopter flight over falls—US$25 per head lasts 8 minutes; the boat trip is probably better value at US$1.50.

The Brazilian immigration office is on the Brazilian side of the bridge into Paraguay; there is also one at Porto Meira, but none at the Falls. Warning: Customs on Brazil-Argentina border close at 1800, and Brazilian border police said to be hard on rucksack-carriers with long hair. Be sure to get a stamp on your passport if going on into Brazil. Brazilian currency can be bought more cheaply in Puerto Iguazú.

Hotels at Foz do Iguaçu *Salvatti,* US$20 d, all a/c (with restaurant and cinema); *Foz do Iguaçu* (US20 d, with breakfast); *Carima, Apolo Palace, Belvedere, San Martín, Naipi, Colonial Palace, Mona Lisa, Alvorada Inn, Estoril, Diplomata* (some a/c), US$15 d, with shower, breakfast, excl. service, expensive, but value for money. *Hotel Lord,* US$12 with breakfast; *Bogari,* US$17.50 with breakfast; *Hotel Luz,* US$6.50 s, US$7.50 with a/c. Recommended: *Pinheirão,* US$4 d, with breakfast; *Itamaraty,* 1 block SW of bus station, off Av. Brasil, US$4 s, US$6.50 d, including good breakfast; *Cisne Hotel,* Av. Brasil, US$10 d, with breakfast, good; *Hotel Brasil,* clean, US$3 s, nr. bus station; *Hotel Santos,* US$3.65 each, on Av. Brasil; *Hotel Americano,* on Av. Brasil, 3 blocks from bus station, US$3.50 s, with breakfast; recommended, hot showers; *Hotel Comercial,* US$1.80 s. Be sure to leave hotels punctually, or you will be charged an extra day.

Restaurants *Rafain,* with Paraguayan harp trio, expensive, but good, opp. *Hotel Cisne; Viena,* 1½ blocks off road to falls, ½ km. from centre of Foz.

N.B. Sra Murro, at Estrada Velha das Cataratas, Tel.: 72-1808, rents rooms at her house, US$5, with fine breakfast, lovely atmosphere; it is in the country about 10 minutes' drive from Foz. Leave town on road to falls, drive 1 km. then on to road to Porto Meira for 1 km., then turn left for 3.4 km. at School of Agriculture; house is on left, painted red.

Hotels between Foz and Falls *Hotel Bourbon,* excellent new hotel, US$22 incl. large breakfast, swimming pool. Several miles from falls, but plenty of buses connect it. There are half a dozen luxury motels with all facilities on the road out to the falls themselves.

Travel Agents Transatlântica Turismo, Av. Brasil 99, and others.

Camping 8 km. from Foz, on road to falls. Camping Club do Brasil, US1.60 a night (half with International Camping Card). Not permitted by hotel and falls.

How to get there The Falls can be reached by plane or paved road from Asunción (Paraguay); by plane or paved road from São Paulo or Curitiba (Brazil) (Brazil: see "Trips to the Far west"). Foz is reached by many buses from Curitiba (13 hours), and from São Paulo (18 hours, about US$14 with Pluma) and also from Asunción (7½ hours, about US$6.15); there are direct buses from Rio (US$18), Asunción (Pluma, US$6, 7 hours) and Curitiba to the falls, but many more to Foz do Iguaçu. It is also possible to stay in Puerto Presidente Stroessner (Paraguay) visiting both sides of the falls without immigration stamps; documents must be carried at all times, however. Take the Foz do Iguaçu bus (US$0.50) or walk over the Friendship Bridge past Brazilian Customs and take Ponte-Cidade bus (US$0.20) to Rodoviária, where buses go every hour (0700-1600) to the Falls (US$0.50) or to Porto Meira for Argentina (US$0.25). There are also buses to the airport. Conversely, Ortega exchange at the bus station arranges evening taxi trips to Puerto Presidente Stroessner to enable tourists to visit the street markets and the casino. (Avoid *Restaurante Guarania* at all costs.) The falls may be reached in 3 ways from Buenos Aires.

By Rail and Road is comfortable, cheap, and picturesque. There are sleeping and restaurant cars, good meals and wines. Passengers take a train from Lacroze Station in Buenos Aires at 1730 (Urquiza Railway), *via* the Zárate-Ibicuy bridge-tunnel to Concordia (some 450 km., 4 hours). Here it is divided into two sections: one goes to Corrientes by way of Federal and Curuzú Cuatía; the other runs close by the river through Monte Caseros, Paso de los Libres, Guaviraví (station for Yapeyú, the birthplace of General San Martín), Santo Tomé and Apóstoles to Posadas, reached by this route is 32 hours (US$11.50 first class, 3 days a week). There is a road, now paved, from Posadas to Puerto Iguazú (bus, US$6, 7 hours).

By Road from Buenos Aires. N to Puerto Pilcomayo, ferry across Río Paraguay to near Asunción, and on by paved Rutas 2 and 7 to Foz do Iguacu, 2,021 km. Fill up with petrol before entering Paraguay—it costs twice as much there. Agencies in B.A. sell bus tours to Iguazú. Ordinary bus lines do the B.A.-Iguazú run in 28-34 hours (US$25). Direct buses take some 24 hours. Trains B.A.-Posadas are met at the station by a special express bus (6 hrs.) for Puerto Iguazú. Service runs both ways, reliable. The bus will often stop in San Ignacio Miní for 10 minutes, giving time for a look round.

Those who do not wish to visit Paraguay should cross the Paraná at Santa Fe or Resistencia and take the paved road to Posadas. There is a good road, with bus services, from Posadas to the Iguazú Falls. The most successful colonisation in Argentina of late years has been at **Eldorado,** on this route. This prosperous small town is surrounded by flourishing mate, tung, citrus, eucalyptus and tobacco plantations. There are tung oil factories, sawmills, plywood factories, mate drying installations and a citrus packing plant.

Hotels at Eldorado *La Colina* and *Buddenberg,* both good; *Castellar,* clean, recommended, US$4.50 d, with bath. Restaurant: *Copetinal Paso,* excellent, reasonable for price, but doesn't cook every day.

Camping Camping site with showers and toilets; take the road toward the river from the main highway, for 2 km. There is a bus which takes you to within 1 km. of Eldorado, where food can be bought. The ACA office is very helpful and has a large illuminated map of Eldorado and its surroundings.

By Air from Buenos Aires Two hours by Boeing 737 (Aerolíneas Argentinas) from Buenos Aires, *via* Corrientes or Posadas, direct to improved Iguazú airport, 5 days a week. For best view on landing, sit on left side of aircraft. Flights back to Buenos Aires are very crowded. There are also Aerochaco flights 4 days a week in "Twin Otter" 16-seat planes, from Resistencia *via* Posadas and Eldorado.

Up the Río Uruguay (1,510 km.)

The Río Uruguay is the eastern boundary of Mesopotamia: the Cía. de Navegación Fluvial Argentina once operated services on the river as far as Concepción del Uruguay, but passenger services have now been discontinued because of improved air and road transport.

Boats leaving Buenos Aires go past Martín García island, and enter the wide estaury of the Uruguay river. At 193 km. from B.A., the Uruguayan town of Fray Bentos is to the right; a bridge has now been built to link Fray Bentos with the Argentine town of Puerto Unzué, near Gualeguaychú. The river now becomes braided into channels and islands. Opposite Fray Bentos, on the left, is the mouth of the Río Gualeguay; 19 km. up is **Gualeguaychú.** It has frigoríficos and tanneries, and can be reached by rail from Buenos Aires (370 km.) and Concordia. Garibaldi captured the city for one day in 1845. Population, 43,000. Airport.

Hotels Comercio, Paris.

Concepción del Uruguay, the first Argentine port of any significance on the river, was founded in 1778 and was the scene of a sharp revolutionary engagement in 1870, the year in which Urquiza was assassinated in the San José Palace. There are train services to all parts of Mesopotamia. A large trade is done with Uruguay. Population, 40,000. Paved roads to Paraná and Colón.

Hotels *Grand, Concordia, Paris.*
Local Steamers Daily to Paysandú (Uruguay).

Some 37 km. above Concepción del Uruguay, past the Uruguayan port of Paysandú, is **Colón.** The river is more picturesque here with cliffs visible from a considerable distance; a road bridge now links Colón and Paysandú. (Toll for cars US$1.40. All border formalities, including stamping of vehicle carnets, are conducted at both ends of the bridge.) About 105 km. above Colón, a little downriver from the Uruguayan city of Salto, is

Concordia, doing a considerable business with Uruguay, Brazil and Paraguay. This prosperous city, with a population of 56,000, has some quite splendid public buildings, a racecourse, rowing clubs, and a 9-hole golf club. Five km. out is Rivadavia Park, with a circular road used occasionally as a motor-racing track; there are pleasant views here of the river and an old ruined French palace. Paved road to Paraná.

The river is impassable for large steamers beyond the rapids of Salto Chico ("small waterfall") near the town, and Salto Grande ("big waterfall") 32 km. up-river, where a large international hydro-electric plant is being built. They can be visited by motor car. Beyond them the river is generally known as the Alto Uruguay.

Hotels *Imperial, Argentino* (US$1.60 s, 2.50 d), *Central.*
Restaurants *Lion d'Or; Don Juan,* 1° de Mayo 21, near main plaza, excellent and cheap.
Tourist Office, Plaza 25 de Mayo, helpful.
Transport Four day trains a week from Buenos Aires (Chacarita Station), 530 km., by Urquiza line. The line runs *via* Santo Tomé to Posadas, 598 km. Bus services also.

About 153 km. upstream from Concordia lies the small port of **Monte Caseros,** with the Uruguayan town of Bella Unión, on the Brazilian border, almost opposite. Above Bella Unión, the Alto Uruguay is the boundary between Argentina and Brazil. Ninety-six km. above Monte Caseros is **Paso de los Libres,** with the Brazilian cattle town of Uruguaiana opposite: a road and rail bridge join the two. The railway from Buenos Aires to Posadas runs through the town (there is a train from Buenos Aires to Paso de los Libres, leaves B.A. 1950, arrives 1450); from Uruguaiana there is a line eastwards through Rio Grande do Sul to Porto Alegre. Paso de los Libres was founded in 1843 by General Madariaga; it was here that the Argentine refugee general crossed the river from Brazil with his hundred men and annexed Corrientes province for Argentina. Road (paved) to Paraná.

There are several small river ports in the next 320 km. of river. From one of them, Santo Tomé, the railway from Buenos Aires strikes N across Misiones Territory through Apóstoles for Posadas. For generations there has been a good deal of cattle rustling and smuggling between Argentina and Brazil across the river.

Patagonia

South of the Río Colorado is the vast plateau known generally as Patagonia. The area is sub-divided into the provinces of Neuquén, Río Negro, Chubut, Santa Cruz and the Territory of Tierra del Fuego. The name comes from "Patacones", or big feet, apparently the Spanish explorers' nickname for the aborigines of the extreme S. The area covers 780,000 square km.: 28% of the national territory, but has a population of only 600,000, little over 2.7% of the total population; and 57% of it is urban. Wide areas have less than one person to the square km., and there are virtually no trees except in the north.

Patagonia is bordered to the W by the Andes, which decrease in height to the S, where they are heavily glaciated. At the foot of these mountains lies a series of lakes in a long trough or depression which reaches, with some obstruction, from the southern seas as far as Lake Nahuel Huapí. Over the whole land there blows a boisterous, cloud-laden strong wind which raises a haze of dust in summer, but in winter the dust can turn into thick mud. Temperatures, considering the latitude, are moderated by the proximity of the sea and are singularly mild, neither rising high during the summer nor falling low during the winter. Even in Tierra del Fuego, where the warmest summer months average 10½°C., the winter days average can reach a high of about 2°C. Make sure you have plenty of warm clothing and anti-freeze in your car, available locally. Northwards the summer temperatures rise: it is 15°C at Santa Cruz, 18°C at Colonia Sarmiento, and as high as 24°C in the valley of the Río Negro. Rain falls mostly in the winter, but not more than 200-250 mm. a year. The whole eastern part of the area suffers from a lack of rainfall and the land is more or less desert. The desert is sharply cliffed as it falls to the sea, and the tidal range is so great (except at Madryn and Punta Arenas, Chile), that it is difficult for ships to tie up at the ports. Deep crevices or canyons intersect the land from E to W. Few of them contain permanent water, but ground water is easily pumped to the surface. The great sheep estancias are along these canyons, sheltered from the wind, and in the depression running N from the Strait of Magellan to Lakes Argentino and Buenos Aires and beyond. During a brief period in spring, after the melting of the snows, there is grass on the plateau. Most of the land is devoted to sheep raising. Sheep are clipped for wool or slaughtered at the mainland frigoríficos of Puerto Deseado, San Julián, Santa Cruz, and Río Gallegos, or at Río Grande in Tierra del Fuego. The wool is carried to port by waggon and lorry and railway and shipped N to Buenos Aires. It is mostly the fine and fine-crossbred wool used by the Argentine mills, but is often heavy with sand. There are 15 million sheep in the area, 5 million less than a few years ago. Over-grazing is an alarming phenomenon leading to much erosion. Wild dogs and the red fox are the sole enemies.

Because of the high winds and insufficient rainfall there is little or no agriculture except in the N, in the valleys of the Colorado and Negro rivers. Some cattle are raised in both valleys where irrigation permits the growing of alfalfa. A large area has been irrigated from the Río Negro dam near Neuquén and here, as a supplement to cattle raising, fruit growing has been highly successful: apples and pears are the chief crops, and many are exported.

Patagonia is rich in extractive resources: the oil of Comodoro Rivadavia and Tierra del Fuego, the hardly-exploited iron ore of Sierra Grande, the coal of Río Turbio, the hydro-electric potential of El Chocón, plentiful deposits of minerals (particularly bauxite) and undeveloped fisheries. But their exploitation has been slow. Tourism is opening up too. There is now a steady, but still small flow of visitors who travel by road to the tip of the Continent. (The road network is far from perfect but is being improved.) Visitors find the wildlife attractive. Guanacos and ostriches are a common sight: ostrich families of 8 to 10 young ones shepherded by the father make an endearing picture. On parts of the coast, particularly the Valdés peninsula, seals, sea-elephants, walruses and other aquatic mammals may be seen, as well as penguins, although these seem to have suffered recently from oil slicks, and many affected penguins leave the colony to die alone at Punta Norte. Further S, particularly in Tierra del Fuego, the antarctic wild goose (quequén) is the most commonly seen of the 152 species of birds. "In spite of the eternal wind, the dusty roads and the inadequate accommodation" write Mr. and Mrs. Richard G. Pohl, "Patagonia is perhaps our favourite area in Argentina. It has a certain pioneer freshness which is reflected in the attitudes of its people and which compensates for the many inconveniences."

N.B. We are informed that in summer there are insufficient hotel beds to meet the demand. Camping is increasingly popular, and estancias seem hospitable to travellers who are stuck for a bed.

Discovery and Colonisation. The coast of Patagonia was first visited by a European late in 1519, when the Portuguese Ferdinand Magellan, then in the service of Spain, was on his voyage round the world. Early in 1520 he turned W into the strait which now bears his name and there struggled with fierce headwinds until he reached that Sea of Peace he named the Pacific. All later European expeditions which attempted to land on the coast were repelled by the peculiarly dour and aggressive native Indians, but these were almost entirely wiped out in the wars of 1879-1883 against them, generally known as the "Campaign of the Desert". But before this there had been a long established colony at Carmen de Patagones; it shipped salt to Buenos Aires during the colonial period. There had also been a settlement of Welsh people at Puerto Madryn since 1865. After the wars colonisation was rapid, the Welsh, Scots and English taking a great part. Immigrants followed the coast southwards from Bahía Blanca, and moved inland up the canyons. Chilean sheep farmers from Punta Arenas moved northwards along the Depression at the foot of the Andes, eastwards into Tierra del Fuego, and northwards to Santa Cruz: about 40% of the population is still Chilean. Other European nationals have arrived in the area since.

Ports and Towns of Patagonia

In all Patagonia there is only one town—Comodoro Rivadavia—with a population of over 50,000. Most of them are small ports, "dead" towns except during the few months when the wool clip is being shipped N. They lie at the mouths of the few rivers in the area, but the high tidal range makes it impossible in most of them for ships to tie up at the docks. The few railways inland from the ports have a little traffic except during the sheep-shearing season.

N.B. Travellers are warned that prices tend to climb higher in Patagonia, the further S you go, even though the region is a free zone for Argentine-made goods. Also, during Argentine summer holidays (Jan., Feb., March) getting a hotel room in Ushuaia, Río Grande, Río Gallegos and Calafate is practically impossible.

Communications Calls at the chief ports by passenger/cargo ships of the Flota Carbonera del Estado. Vessels of the Ministry of the Navy go as far as Ushuaia (Tierra del Fuego) once a month and carry 60 passengers; a nine-day trip for US$32.

Information Obtainable in Buenos Aires about Santa Cruz and Tierra del Fuego at Casa de la Pcia. de Santa Cruz, 25 de Mayo 35, 2nd floor (Tel.: 32-4620). For Chubut at Paraguay 876; Tel.: 32-2262.

Air Services Aerolíneas Argentinas from Buenos Aires either direct to Río Gallegos or calling at Bahía Blanca, Viedma, Trelew and Comodoro Rivadavia on the way. Cía. Argentina de Transportes Aéreos from Buenos Aires to Bahía Blanca, Trelew, Comodoro Rivadavia and Río Gallegos. Beware delays for bad weather. Flight Travel Agency of Buenos Aires arranges visits to Tierra del Fuego; US$180 for 6 days, US$390 for a grand tour of the area; air fares extra.

We are informed that the air force LADE flights in the region S of Bariloche are almost as cheap as the buses—Río Gallegos to Bariloche US$44, to Ushuaia US$13, to Perito Moreno US$15, to Calafate US$7—must be booked in advance from departure point of flght. The planes are small and fly low; passengers miss little of what there is to be seen. The baggage allowance is 15 kg. Travellers are warned that the flights are often heavily booked ahead, but always check again on the day of the flight if you are told beforehand that it is sold out.

Bus Service   There is now a fast daily bus service taking about 50 hours from Buenos Aires *via* most of the Patagonian coastal towns to Río Gallegos. The company's Buenos Aires office is at Gral. Hornos 255, near Constitución station. The main road, Route 3, is paved from Buenos Aires to Fitz Roy, near Comodoro Rivadavia. From Comodoro Rivadavia to Piedra Buena the road has a very well maintained all-weather surface. The last 230 km. to Río Gallegos are paved. S of this town to Ushuaia is a combination of fair all-weather road and pavement in a bad state of repair.

Roads   Many of the roads in Southern Argentina are gravelled; it is in your interest to buy a windscreen protector, costing US$25 in Bariloche or US$15 in Comodoro Rivadavia. The best type to buy is the grid-type (available in Buenos Aires) or inflatable plastic ones which are made for some standard-type vehicles (in Buenos Aires) the only disadvantage being a loss of visibility.

The upper course of the Río Colorado is the northern limit of Patagonia. 160 km. S of where it reaches the sea (250 km. S of Bahía Blanca), about 27 km. from the mouth of the Río Negro, is

Carmen de Patagones, standing on high ground on the northern bank, with **Viedma** (7,000 people) the capital of Río Negro Province, across the river, which is spanned by a connecting rail and road bridge. There is a good view of both from the Cerro de la Caballada, behind Carmen de Patagones. On this hill a monument commemorates an attack on the twin towns by a Brazilian squadron in 1827. There are daily air services to Viedma, 966 km. from Buenos Aires.

Hotels at Carmen de Patagones: *Percaz; Gran Argentino.* At Viedma: *Roma* (recommended; convenient for buses and ferry); *Viedma; Austral,* modern.

Almost due W and 180 km. along the coast, in the Gulf of San Matías, is **Puerto San Antonio Oeste** (4,000 people), served by Transportes Patagónicos, whose buses ply from Bahía Blanca S through the coastal ports to Punta Arenas, 1,930 km. (Also the "La Puntual" company, which is about 25% cheaper.) Near San Antonio Oeste (17 km. N) is a seaside resort, **Las Grutas,** developed in the 60's with good safe beach. ACA has a *Unidad Turística,* with 6-bed rooms, no restaurant. *Tour du Golfe,* friendly, 3-bed rooms, US$5, provide cooking facilities. There is also a camping ground. *Restaurant Rambla* recommended. Between San Antonio and Puerto Madryn is Sierra Grande, which is being rapidly developed as the local iron-ore deposits are exploited. The ore is piped in solution to an ocean terminal 32 km. E.

Hotels   *Vasquito,* just acceptable, US$1.60 per person; *Albatros,* and *Americana,* US$2.50 per person, not recommended. Good beach 7 km. away.

Railway *via* Viedma to Bahía Blanca and Buenos Aires and westwards to Bariloche (630 km.), on Lake Nahuel Huapi.

Route to Bariloche: *via* (17 km.) Las Grutas, paved road. Continue 201 km. through bush country providing fodder for a few cattle, with a view to the S of the salt flats called Salina del Gualicho. The road then meets the Zapala-Buenos Aires highway at Choelle Choel. Then 223 km. to Neuquén through an unbroken series of groves of tall trees sheltering vineyards and orchards. On (424 km.) to Bariloche along fast road, skirting the entire length of the Ezequiel Ramos Mejía dam. Then it drops over an escarpment to cross the Collon Curá river. Continue through valley of the river

Limay to Confluencia and the Enchanted Valley. The journey can be completed in 11 hours.

About 250 km. to the S, in Chubut, is

Puerto Madryn, a small port on a good bay, Golfo Nuevo. It was founded by the Welsh colonist, Parry Madryn, in 1865. Population, 20,000. A large aluminium plant is now operating, and the town is becoming a popular tourist centre, with a casino, skin-diving and nature reserves. Museo de Ciencias Naturales y Oceanografía on J. García and J. Menéndez. Airport. No Youth Hostel. People with more than a couple of days' stay should stay in Puerto Madryn or Puerto Pirámides (see below) to visit the area, otherwise Trelew is a better base.

There are nature reserves nearby at Punta Loma on Golfo Nuevo (seals and sea-lions), only 15 km. from Puerto Madryn; Punta Pirámides (sea-lions) and Isla de los Pájaros (sea birds) on Golfo San Jorge; and Punta Norte, on the Valdés Peninsula (see below). The natural history of the region is most interesting, with other seal and penguin colonies, whales in Golfo Nuevo, fossils in the cliffs, and guanacos, rheas and armadillos in the countryside. Scuba diving is popular (lessons from Turismo Subacuático) as one can swim with the sea-lions—avoiding the killer whales, or *orcas*—and explore the kelp forests along the coast. It is feared that a project to develop electricity from tidal waters will affect the breeding ground of the whales at the neck of the peninsula. Past the lighthouse and Naval Zone at Punta Delgada on the other side of the Valdés peninsula is Salina Grande, Argentina's lowest point, 35 metres below sea level.

Bus runs to Punta Norte (176 km.; camping ground) to see sea-elephants (colony now fenced in to avoid excessive disturbance), late spring and summer (Nov.-March), once a day, US$7, 0800 hours. Hired car (Auto Remise) charges US$12-18 to each of group of four for whole-day trip. Out of season, ask Centro Nacional Patagónico for visits to the sites. (Taxi US$25.) James K. Bock recommends Jorge Caro's microbus service (up to 16 people) which is fairly priced and will make the complete trip round the Valdés Peninsula *via* Punta Delgada, where most wildlife is (475 km. in all) except the penguins, which have moved away. The peninsula is private property. One third belongs to one man, who grazes 40,000 sheep.

Tourist Agencies Tur-Mar, M.A. Zar 113; Pu-Ma, J. A. Roca 1100; Sur Turismo, J. A. Roca 39, and Turismo Submarino, J. A. Roca 755.

Hotels *Gran Hotel* (best); *Yanco,* Av. Julio Roca 610, on beach, US$7.50 s; *Playa,* J. Roca 189; *Siguero: Gran Madryn I,* Leopoldo Lugones 40; *Pu-Ma,* Av. J. Roca 1045; *Hostal del Rey,* B. A. Brown; *Tolosa,* Saénz Peña 260; *Suyai,* 9 de Julio 57; *La Posta Federal,* Av. J. Roca 53; *Anclamar,* 25 de Mayo, 874; *Atalaya,* Domec García 149; *Ruca-Hué,* Rivera Marítima Sur; *Paris,* Roque Sáenz Peña and 25 de Mayo, US$2 d (beware of overcharging); *Aguila,* Peña and Mazar; *Vasconia,* 25 de Mayo 43, US$1.50 s, hot water; *El Cid,* 25 de Mayo 854; *Mora,* J. B. Justo 645; *España; Argentino; Petit Residencial,* US$3 d, meals US$1.50 each; *Gran Palace,* 28 de Julio 400, near centre, modern, US$2.60 d, with bath; *ACA Motel,* cheap, clean, Rivera Marítima Norte.

Restaurants *Don Alberto,* Av. 9 de Julio 451, good, cheap, fixed-price menus; *Cantina El Náutico,* Julio Roca and Lugones; *Rancho Grande* (excellent sea food); *Comedor ACA,* Costanera Norte; *Cantina Club Náutico,* Costanera Norte; *Pizzería Cruz del Sur* and *Palace Hotel,* on 28 de Julio and *Palace Hotel; Pizzería Quine,* J. A. Roca and R. S. Peña; *La Cueva de Pepe,* San Martín 123; *La Cueva de Singarella,* 28 de Julio and M. A. Zar. **Tea Rooms:** *Camwy,* San Martín 149; *Centenario,* on Belgrano and Paraguay, and *Fraser,* on bank of River Chubut.

Camping At far end of bay, 6 km. from town, is a site, but many people camp on beach. Also ACA at S of town. Camping out can be interesting as one can watch foxes, armadillos, skunks and ñandúes roaming around in the evening.

Transport Daily buses to Buenos Aires, 24 hours. To Río Gallegos, also 24 hours, four times a week. Bus to Bahía Blanca 0700 daily, 12 hours, about US3.75.
  Bus four times a week from Puerto Madryn in summer to **Puerto Pirámides,** from

which excursions can be made by bus to Punta Norte. Tourist excursions there are organized by Coyun-Co. Turismo, 37 Av. Roca, US$3.20. The peninsula is virtually inaccessible in winter.

Restaurants *Comedor Motel ACA* and *Parrilla El Salmón* on Rivera Marítima; *Café El Médano* makes huge sandwiches; ACA hostería and municipal camping; sleeping facilities at Almacén Torino.

The road from Puerto Madryn to Puerto Pirámides (94 km.) is only paved for 9 km., Puerto Pirámides to San Antonio Oeste (328 km.) has 72 km. paved.

On July 28, 1865, one hundred and fifty Welsh immigrants landed at Puerto Madryn, then a deserted beach deep in Indian country, for the only settlement between it and the Río Salado, which reaches the Atlantic 160 km. S of Buenos Aires, was at Patagones, at the mouth of the Río Negro, 320 km. N of Madryn. After three weeks they pushed, on foot, across the parched pampa and into the Chubut river valley, where there is flat cultivable land, from 6 to 16 km. wide, along the riverside for a distance of 80 km. upstream. Here, maintained in part by the Argentine Government, they settled, but it was three years before they realised the land was barren unless watered. They drew water from the river, which is higher than the surrounding flats, and later built a fine system of irrigation canals. The Colony, reinforced later by immigrants from Wales and from the United States, prospered, but in 1899 a great flood drowned the valley and some of the immigrants left for Canada. The last Welsh contingent arrived in 1911. The object of the colony had been to create a "Little Wales beyond Wales", and for four generations they kept the Welsh language alive through their schools and newspapers and chapels. The language is, however, dying out in the fifth generation. Only 7,000 out of a population of 75,000 at Chubut and Treflen can speak Welsh. The centenary monument to the pioneers at Puerto Madryn is topped by the figure of a Welshwoman. There is an offshoot of the colony of Chubut at Treflen (Trevelin), at the foot of the Andes nearly 650 km. to the west. It was settled in 1888. One of the more curious facts of history is that this distant land gave to the Welsh language one of its most endearing and well-written classics: *Dringo'r Andes* (Climbing the Andes), written in Patagonia by a woman, one of the early settlers.

Trevelin Museo Histórico in the Municipalidad Restaurant: *Che Ferrada,* grills. Tea houses: *El Adobe, La Pantera Rosa, Preeman.*

The Florentino Ameghino dam, 110 km. inland on the River Chubut, covers 7,000 hectares with water and irrigates 28,000 hectares in the lower Chubut Valley, as well as producing 129 million kWh a year of electric power.

Along the Río Chubut are several small townships. **Rawson** (2,500 people), the capital of Chubut Province, is a small, derelict river port 7 km. from the sea (*Hotel Provincial,* on Mitre). It has law courts, port installations for fisheries, and a beach. A 70-km. road runs S to the Chubut Valley, where the Welshmen settled in 1865. Some 20 km. up the river is **Trelew** (18,000 people), a prosperous town served by Aerolíneas Argentinas. A paved road runs from Rawson through Trelew (63 km.) Gaiman and Dolavon, all on the river, to Las Plumas (mind the bridge if driving) and the Upper Chubut Valley, all the way to Esquel (see page 132) and Trevelin. **Gaiman,** 18 km. from Trelew, a pretty place, is now the most Welsh and has a museum of the colony. (The museum and the only restaurant often seem to be closed, but tea rooms opposite the square, *Plass y Coed* and *Tee Gwnyn,* and *Elma,* Tello 571 are open; interesting local agriculture.) There is also a railway tunnel marked: "Tunel; Primer Ferrocarril Galés". (Tunnel, first Welsh railway.)

Trelew Hotels *Tourist; Galicia,* Rivadavia 215; *Pirámides; Argentino,* new, clean, US$4 s; *España,* US$3 d, clean, pleasant; *Plaza,* US$4 d; *Residencial Avenida,* Av. Jones 44, very clean and pleasant, US$150 p.p.; *Hotel Central,* 25 de Mayo 102, US$3.65 d; *Hotel Touring Club,* Av. Fontana 240, US$2 d; *Centenario,* San Martín 150; *City,* Rivadavia 254, very friendly; *Rayentray,* Belgrano and San Martín;

Cheltum, Av. Irigoyen 1485, modern, US$3.50 s; *Parque,* Irigoyen and Cangallo, good; *Grand Residencial,* Rawson and Pecoraro; *Rivadavia,* Rivadavia 55; *Sarmiento,* Sarmiento 260; *Amancay,* Paraguay 961. Camping possible south of the town on the road to Rawson and Comodoro Rivadavia, on right about 200 metres beyond the bridge over River Chubut; turn off at the sign Frasers Tea Room.

Restaurants *San Martín,* good meal US$1; *Luque,* H. Yrigoyen and Chile; *Parrilla Don Pedro,* intersection of Routes 3 and 25; *El Quijote,* 25 de Mayo 86; *El Mesón,* Rivadavia 540; *El Progreso,* San Martín 140; *El Galicia,* Rivadavia and 9 de Julio; *Cantina Acapulco,* Belgrano and San Martín.

Bank of London and South America, Av. 9 de Julio esq. Belgrano, Trelew. Open 0700-1300.

Local holidays At Trelew, July 28 (Founding of Chubut Colony); Dec. 13 (Petroleum Day).

Transport LADE flight, Trelew-Río Gallegos, US$20, 1-3 flights daily. Daily flights to Buenos Aires (Aerolíneas, Austral), Río Grande (*via* R. Gallegos), 1-3 flights a week; to Comodor Rivadavia/Esquel/Bariloche with LADE; crowded, book pref. in Buenos Aires in advance; 2-3 times a week, to Esquel with A.A. Bus, Trelew-Esquel, 14 hours, US$6, Mon. (0600), Wed. (2000), Sat. (2000) with Empresa Chubut. Buses to Rawson every 20 min.; 6 a day to Gaimán; 8 a day to Puerto Madryn (last at 1800); long-distance to Comodor Rivadavia. Transportes Patagónicos Belgrano and J. Roca; Transp. Chubut, 25 de Mayo 660; Cooperativa, 28 de Julio; and Empresa Rawson on Av. Fontana and 9 de Julio. Rent-a-Car (Godfrey Davis) at Citrolew, 25 de Mayo and Entre Ríos. Tourist agencies: Chubut Turismo, Av. Fontana 478; and Sur Turismo on No. 280, organise a few excursions.

Petrol at Garayalde, 193 km. from Trelew.

Wild life may also be seen at Camarones and Punta Tomba, (130 km. S of Trelew on a dirt road branching off 4 km. S of Trelew, near the refuse tip; 6-7 hrs. by taxi), between Rawson and Comodoro Rivadavia.

Camarones is less crowded than Punta Tomba; there is a large penguin colony 30 km. away along a dirt road in fair condition; free camping possible there and in the town itself. In summer there is a sealion nursery nearby. At **Punta Tomba** the wildlife is very varied: penguins, guanacos etc. You can take a taxi and share it from Trelew to Punta Tomba (season Sept.-Oct. to Feb.-March) to see the penguins. Taxis available from J. A. Roca 200, More no. 291, Av. Fontana and L. Jones, San Martín 470 and 751. All tourist agencies provide trips; also to the bird reserve at Isla de los Pájaros, where flamingoes flourish. Example of tour operator: Estrella del Sur, 25 de Mayo 601, Trelew, which does a day tour for US$7, and a longer day tour for US$9 to the Valdés peninsula. Local buses very scarce: only once a week from Trelew; book at Uruguay 590, Trelew. Bus leaves Mon. 0730 from San Martín and Belgrano. In Camarones take a taxi to the penguin colony and return to Trelew Tues. (Taxi: US$10 return). Hotel at Camarones, *Kau-i-Keuken,* US$4 d, and *Torino.*

396 km. S is **Comodoro Rivadavia,** in the Province of Chubut. About 28% of all Argentina's oil production comes from wells up to 40-65 km. to the W and the same distance to the S. A 1,770-km. pipeline carries the natural gas to Buenos Aires, and a petrochemical plant has been built. There is a regional Patagonian Museum at the ex-Hotel de Turismo, on the 2nd floor. Population: 70,000.

Local holidays July 28 (Founding of Chubut); Dec. 13 (Petroleum Day).

Hotels *Austral,* Rivadavia 190, US$6 p.p.; *Luso Argentino,* US$3 d, friendly; *Comodoro,* Rivadavia and 9 de Julio (11 floors, large rooms, unreliable water system); *Colón* (US$5 d); *España,* US$3 d, clean, pleasant; *Gran; Hospedaje Hamburgo,* US$1.30 p.p., with good restaurant on B. Mitre; *Residencial Azul,* good service, Sarmiento 724; cheaper hotels near bus station; *Comercio,* Rivadavia 341, US$2.50 p.p., good meals, US$1.80; *Hospedaje Belgrano,* Belgrano 546, US$4 d; *Hotel Central,* San Martín 611, US$1.50 p.p., has good restaurant; *Residencial Comodoro,* España 919; *Residencial del Sur,* Maipú 1083, *El Patagón Motel,* Access (S) of Route 3. Camping 5 km. S at Rada Tilly, and at 20 km. N signposted "Bar y Camping"; not as inviting.

Restaurants Excellent value at *Restaurant Mundial,* Belgrano and Rawson, Portuguese run; also *Restaurant Bon Fife,* España 832; *Austral,* US$6 d, fair; *El Ancla de Oro,* Caleta Córdoba (18 km. from Comodoro); *Las Papas Fritas,* Belgrano 851; La Estancia, Urquiza 863; *La Minuta,* Alem 35; *Los Troncos,* Av. Costanera and Rada Tilly; *El Náutico,* Playa Costanera.

Bank of London and South America, Av. Rivadavia 264. Summer 0700-1300; winter 1200-1800.

British Vice-Consul Estancia Cameron, Las Heras. Tel.: 2627. Belgian Vice-Consul, Rivadavia 283; Chilean Consul, Sarmiento 940; Italian Vice-Consul, Belgrano 1053.

Tourist Office Av. 25 de Mayo, on Esplanada, in the same building as the local museum. Travel Agencies: *Puelche EVT,* Rivadavia 527; *Richard Pentreath,* Mitre 952; *San Gabriel, Atlas, Monitur* and *Ceferino,* on San Martín 488, 263, 811 and 372.

Transport Bus service to Buenos Aires daily, 32 hrs., US$30. 3 buses a week to Bariloche (Don Otto leaves 2230, stops at Esquel 0825, arrives 1758 at Bariloche, US$7) and 4 to Río Gallegos (US$18), but LADE aircraft little dearer (Comodoro Rivadavia is its operational centre); 1-3 flights to Buenos Aires a day with Aerolíneas or Austral; offices on San Martín 421 and 291; flight to Bariloche 3 times a week, US$16. LADE also flies weekly to Islas Malvinas (Falkland Is.), US$42 return, on Mondays, and to Ushuaia, 5 hours, *via* Lago Argentino, Río Gallegos and Río Grande, US$24. Buy tickets in advance in Buenos Aires, at LADE office, Perú 714; *remises* are dearer; taxi to airport,US$3.

A paved road (buses 0700, 1300 and 1700) runs inland from Comodoro Rivadavia to (193 km.) **Colonia Sarmiento** (Archaeological Museum next to Cathedral), on Lake Musters, near the large Lake Colhué Huapí. S of Colonia Sarmiento there is a large petrified forest (see p. 119). There is a road westwards from Colonia Sarmiento *via* Paso Río Mayo (which has three hotels, the *Covadonga, La Ruta* and *San Martín,* C category), to Puerto Aysén in Chile. A branch from this road goes 130 km. S to Perito Moreno, by Lake Buenos Aires. From Colonia Sarmiento you can reach Esquel, at the southern edge of the Lake District. The first 210 km. from Sarmiento are paved, then it is mostly a dirt or all-weather road, though short stretches have been paved.

Hotels *Lago Musters,* P. Moreno and Ing. Coronel; *Hostería Los Lagos,* Roca and Alberdi, has restaurant. Food at *Hotel Colón,* P. Moreno 645, and *El Gaucho,* Route 20, access Sarmiento. *Americano,* basic, US$1 each.

Transport Airport reached by local bus or railcar (faster).

Travel Agency at Sarmiento: Julio Lew, Roca and Alberdi.

Perito Moreno (population 1,700), with an airport, is close to Lake Buenos Aires, which continues into Chile as Lake General Carrera. Twice-weekly buses (US$2) to Los Antiguos on lake. The famous Cuevas de las Manos, 10,000-years-old paintings of human hands and of animals, are very impressive—red, orange, black, white and green colours. Difficult to reach; 57 km. S of Perito Moreno on Ruta Nacional 40, turn left at sign to Estancia Elisa, 8 km. from main road. Ask curator, Sr. Antonio Barrío, for permission to continue 15 km. further to Cañón, 1½ hrs. crossing, after which caves are reached. No buses, but try hitching.

Hotels at Perito Moreno *Belgrano,* US$5 with shower, very good, clean, with good restaurant; *Austral,* US$4 p.p., open Dec. to Feb.; *Fénix,* US$1.50 p.p.; *Argentina y Chile,* US$2.50 s.

Camping Parque Laguna in town, and 33 km. out of town on the S shore of Lake Buenos Aires, beside a very small hostería on the road to Los Antiguos and Chile Chico.

The road to Fitz Roy, 110 km. S of Comodoro Rivadavia, is paved, and a major short-cut now by-passes Puerto Deseado. Fitz Roy to Piedra Buena is unpaved, but paving is complete from Piedra Buena to Río Gallegos (231 km.). Fitz Roy is a tiny town, only two small hosterías, very primitive, not recommended. Better stay 22 km. N at Caleta Olivia. New hotel there, *Residencial Robert*.

About halfway between Comodoro Rivadavia and Puerto Deseado, some 5 km. S of Fitz Roy, where the new short-cut starts, a road first goes S then SW 106 km. across bleak estancia country to a national park area called Bosque Petrificado, where there is a petrified forest, 70,000 years old, of fallen Araucaria trees, nearly 3 metres round and 15-20 metres long: a remarkable sight. Taxi, Sarmiento to forests US$5-10. It is best to do the trip this way or in groups, as tyre punctures are a menace.

There are in fact three sites you can visit: The Bosque Petrificado José Ormachea, due W of Comodoro Rivadavia, about 140 km. by road (116 km. paved) towards Sarmiento, in Chubut; the Víctor Szlapelis, some 40 km. further SW along the same road; and Monumento Natural Bosques Petrificados, W of Puerto Deseado in Santa Cruz, surrounding the Laguna Grande on a road SW from Fitz Roy, 113 km. away, the road is marked "Huella o camino no relevado".

South of Comodoro Rivadavia (254 km.), at Tres Cerros, is a new ACA hotel—US$3 p.p., quite attractive. At Piedra Negra, the previous turn-off, for Puerto Deseado, there is a cheap hotel, *Florida Negra*. The only other building is a police post.

About 300 km. S of Comodoro Rivadavia is **Puerto Deseado** (airport), at the mouth of a river which drains Lake Buenos Aires, far to the W, reached by road in 7 hours: 280 km. to Las Heras, on to Perito Moreno, on the lake, 177 km., and a further 72 km. to the Chilean border at Chile Chico.

It was at Puerto Deseado that a Welshman in Cavendish's expedition of 1586 gave the name of pengwyn (white head) to a certain strange-looking bird. With a slight alteration, to penguin, the bird has gone by that name ever since. It is only fair to relate the opposing theory that the name is derived from a Spanish word, pingüe, meaning fat.

Local holidays   Jan. 31 (St. John Bosco); Oct. 9 (Coat of Arms day).

From Puerto Deseado to Santa Cruz by the old road is about 470 km. Some 156 km. short of Santa Cruz it reaches **San Julián**, the best place for breaking the 925 km. run from Comodoro Rivadavia to Río Gallegos. The first Christian mass in Argentina was held here after Magellan had executed a crew member. Francis Drake also put in here to hang Thomas Doughty, after amiably taking breakfast with him.

Hotels   New hotel *Residencial Sada*, nice; *Residencial, 9 de Julio,* and *Hotel Colonial,* both US$2 p.p.; *Hotel Londres,* US$1.50 p.p., 3-course meal for US$1.50, clean, recommended. Also older *Hotel Colón.* Campsite at town entrance.

Santa Cruz, one of the best of the coastal harbours (airport), is near the mouth of the Santa Cruz river which drains Lake Argentino. Population 3,000.

An unpaved road runs NW from San Julián to Route 40 along the foothills of the Andes. About halfway is Gobernador Gregores (*Hotel San Francisco,* acceptable), with petrol pump.

At Piedra Buena, 35 km. W (paved road to Río Gallegos) of Santa Cruz, is *Hotel Argentina,* old but clean, US$0.90 p.p. ACA motel, simple, functional but good, warm and nice (US$5 s for members, non-members US$6), 1 km. outside Santa Cruz on Route 3. Campsite nearby; also campsites at Piedra Buena N of town on Route 3. Police tend to ask motorists for petrol or cigarettes in this town. Saves you from 2 hr.-long car search. The *Select* restaurant is very dear for what it offers. Route 1603 (unpaved, no petrol) Piedra Buena to Calafate, runs along the edge of a plateau with occasional panoramic views across the valley of the River Cruz below.

Then at about 170 km. it drops down into the valley itself to follow the river into the hills and Lake Argentino. A pleasant run, without being spectacular.

Río Gallegos, not a very attractive or friendly town, at the mouth of the Río Gallegos, the capital of Santa Cruz Province, is 265 km. S of Santa Cruz. The tidal range here during spring tides may be as high as 16 metres. A frigorífico is operated by Swifts, and there is a large trade in wool and sheepskins. The scenery around is not interesting. (The cave paintings and Laguna Azul, 60 km. from Río Gallegos, are now reported not available for visiting.) Population: 35,400. Foundation Day: Dec. 19. Prices are high. Good museum on Tucumán and Belgrano.

Communications Good road to Punta Arenas, 303 km.; Taxi US$40-60; Punta Arenas *via* Puerto Williams will cost some US$120, with boat trip, one night at the port and a flight to Punta Arenas; buses (US$8), at least one daily at 0900 (booking office near *Hotel Comercio,* 0900-1230 and 1500-1930), take 8-10 hours depending on border-crossing process, and if you are leaving Argentina you must present permission from the police before you buy the ticket (only from Río Gallegos and Punta Arenas). Four buses a week to Río Turbio (2 companies); one bus on Tue. to Puerto Natales. A weekly steamer, but no air service. Route 40, which goes to Calafate, and a provincial road that goes west from Route 3 to Calafate are both rough; Route 40 is all-weather, the other is dirt. A better alternative is Route 1603, which branches off Route 3 some 43 km. from Piedra Buena. Occasional steamers, frequent flights (2-6 a day with Austral and Aerolíneas stopping mostly in ComodoroRivadavia) and buses (US$50) at four times a week (48 hours), to Buenos Aires, 2,575 km. Jet airport. Numerous flights to Ushuaia (Tierra del Fuego), direct or *via* Río Grande (US$14 single). Buses also to Comodoro Rivadavia, Calafate (Fridays, very fully booked), Esquel and Bariloche, but LADE flights are little dearer (e.g. US$7 to Calafate), LADE flights also to Bariloche *via* Santa Cruz, San Julián, Puerto Deseado, Comodor Rivadavia, Trelew and Esquel, 3 times a week, US$44. Personal controls and luggage search at Río Gallegos, delays of 30 min. to 2 hrs. Book seats in Buenos Aires to avoid difficulties with departures. Taxi to town, US$2-3.

Hotels *Comercio,* US$16 s, good, with restaurant; *Gran Paris,* US$7 d; *Argentino* and *Gran España,* very expensive. Strongly recommended: *Hotel Alonso,* simple, not cheap, very clean and comfortable; no meals but tea or coffee and toast morning and evening. *Plaza,* US$2 p.p.; *Colón,* US$2 p.p.; *Internacional,* US$1.50 p.p., hot water; *Victoria,* at far end of main street, basic but friendly, US$2 p.p.; *Covadonga,* fairly good, US$3.50 p.p.; *Punta Arenas,* cheaper, US$2.50 d; *Residencial Mariol,* Calle Avellaneda, US$2.50, clean, recommended. *Hotel Maddalena,* good value, friendly and often has rooms when all else is full; *Pensión Belgrano,* Calle Belgrano 119, very cheap, clean, has good restaurant; *Hotel Convenio,* adequate, US$4 s. *Hotel Tehuelche,* 16 km. from ferry at Primera Angostura on junction of Punta Arenas-Río Gallegos Route, US$1 s, old fashioned, bar. In the summer a Catholic school in the centre of town allows "backpackers" to sleep in classrooms, without charge.

Eating Places Plenty and good, some specializing in sea food. *Armonía,* Roca 1112, fast service, good.

Bank of London and South America, Sarmiento 47. Open 1000-1600. Amex cheques easily accepted, others need some persuasion. Change travellers' cheques in Río Gallegos if going to Calafate, where it can't be done; good rates at Expreso Pingüin bus office and at back of Rotisería next to Post Office.

British Vice-Consul Casilla de Correo 65.   Tel.: 176.

British Club

Tourist Office 9 de Julio, between Alberdi and Avellaneda. Obtain documents here if you intend to cross the Chilean part of Tierra del Fuego; also visit the police and customs officials to complete your complicated paperwork; this way you need not make the trip to the border at Aymont (65 km.) twice.

From Río Gallegos a railway runs 260 km. to Río Turbio (6,000 people) where is found Argentina's largest coalfield (*Hotel Gato Negro*, expensive and poor, so is pensión nearby). Also four buses a week to and from Río Gallegos.

Calafate, on Lake Argentino, 320 km. NW of Río Gallegos, is the southern gateway to the Parque Nacional de los Glaciares (the northern end is at Lake Viedma). At the far end of the lake the Ventisquero Moreno (Moreno glacier, named after the founder of the park), the only glacier in the world that is growing larger, descends to the surface of the water over a one-km. frontage and a height of about 50 metres. It has virtually cut the lake in two, blocking the outlets and forming an ice barrier to the water's outflow. Pieces break off and float away as icebergs. From Calafate there are daily microbus trips in the morning, Nov.-Feb. only, to the glaciers edge (US$5), returning the next morning; you have to pay return fare to go there and single to come back. Better travel from "Burbuja Loca" general store in pick-up truck for 8, spend day at glacier for set, cheaper price than tourist bus. The owner is an ardent glacier-lover, very friendly. Taxis US$25-30 per vehicle, round trip. The Parque Nacional truck leaves Calafate each morning at 0900 and may give lifts. The distance to the glacier is about 80 km. Colourful but not very exciting cave paintings some 5 km. from Calafate. The Lake Argentino area is very popular, booking in advance of all transport is a *must.*

N.B. Only possibility for changing US$ in Calafate is at the administration of the ACA motel.

A worthwhile trip is by motor-boat (US$7) from Punta Bandera to the Upsala glacier at the end of Lake Argentino. The boat passes by the 30-metre high glacier; it is reported however that the captain often decides the weather is too rough and does not go to Upsala. Tourist Office is not always helpful about complaints. Put inshore and cross a little forest to reach the small Lake Onelli, quiet and very impressive, beech trees on one side, and ice-covered mountains on the other. Small icebergs in the lake. The boats do not run in winter, and not always in summer, because of the danger of the glaciers "calving". At other times the boats are reserved by groups or have broken down. Book tickets at Intendencia del Parque wherever possible; if you can't get tickets try to catch the boat in Punta Bandera with tickets from a travel agency, your own car or a taxi.

Another worthwhile excursion is to the N end of the Glaciares National Park to Cerro Fitzroy and Cerro Torres; it is difficult to get there without one's own transport as the road is appalling, but well worth a day's trip. There is a base camp at Cerro Fitzroy.

Camping and fishing permits from the Parque Nacional rangers in Calafate. Although the mountains are snow capped, you can camp out in the pleasant woods around the lake in summer and even swim in it on warm days. One camp site is 8 km. from the glacier and the other near the park entrance; they are warmly recommended; free. There is utter stillness apart from squawking flocks of parakeets and an occasional roar as ice falls off the glacier and thunders into the lake. Patagonians flock to the February rural show and camp out with much revelry: dances and *"asados"* (barbecued sides of sheep).

How Reached Planes from Río Gallegos (US$7) and Comodoro Rivadavia, US$6, most days, also Ushuaia, US$8. There are about six flights a week (LADE) between Río Gallegos and Calafate (but not in winter. By a rough but interesting road from Santa Cruz, Route 1603 (Route 288 not recommended, 100 km. longer and 2 ferry crossings), 5 or 6 hours by car, but not always possible after rain. From Esquel go *via* Perito Moreno, good accommodation; then *via* Gobernador Gregores (*Hotel San Francisco,* C category, better divert to Piedra Buena and stay at ACA motel, only making journey 50 km. longer but avoids possible delay at ferry crossings near Lake Viedma). Very lonely road, occasional guanacos, flamingos and armadillos, but mostly sheep. Few shrubs or trees. Sparse population. Taxi to Río Gallegos, 4 hours, US$50 irrespective of number of passengers; buses also available, but only once a week (US$6). There are no buses to Chile. The Río Gallegos-Calafate road trip is worth while, for the number of animals and birds one sees. It is reported the road trip from Calafate to Puntas Arenas is very interesting: from Calafate take Route 507 (although route 40 is shorter when passable), unpaved (209 km.) to La Esperanza, where there is a petrol pump and modest hotel; 126 km. to Cancha Carrera (border point Dec.-April), 63 km. to La Laurita, pay US$0.50 at control, 4 km. to Chilean control, then paved road (14 km.) to Puerto Natales and 245 km. to Punta Arenas, 42 km. paved.

Hotels *ACA Motel Calafate* (US$6.50 s, bungalows with good restaurant); next to this is *Hostería El Calafate*, built by Government, very good value; *Hotel Carlitos,* US$3 p.p. or US$9 full board, very friendly; *Amado,* US$2 p.p.; *Residencial Avenida; El Quijote,* motel type accommodation; *Hotel Tehuel Aike,* good meals; *Michelangelo,* US$2.50 each, new, modern, clean, excellent, open from November; *Hostería Kau-Yatún,* US$4 d, with bath, many facilities, horses for hire. Several cheaper hotels, US$2-3 a night. Calafate has a tourist office from which caravans, tents (US$0.75, sleep 4) and 4-berth cabanas (US$0.75 p.p.) may be hired, showers extra.

Restaurant *Richards.* At Moreno Glacier, Unidad Turística has a restaurant and a bar (no accommodation).

Travel Agents, Intralagos, do excursions and car-rentals. Cost of car hire for trip to Cerro Fitzroy about US$50.

Camping Near ACA service station in Calafate, and at Parque Nacional camping ground 5 km. outside town. A permit is required from the *guardaparques* hut at the park entrance. A municipal camp site, US$0.30, and US$0.15 for hot showers, also tents for rent. Park "refugio" is free, with firing for cooking and heating supplied free, suitable for 3. Permission obtainable from the Intendencia in Calafate, some 77 km. away. There is no water at the refugio. Key from warden at the site. ACA has cabins beside Moreno glacier (4-berth, US$2.50-3 p.p.). It is somewhat noisy, due to the glacier rumbling. Also two free camp sites by lake—the lower one sometimes floods.

Tierra del Fuego is the name given to the island at the extreme south of South America. It is surrounded by the Magellan Strait to the north, the Atlantic Ocean to the east, the Beagle Channel to the south—which separates it from the southern islands—and by the Whiteside, Gabriel, Magdalena and Cockburn Channels etc.—which divide it from the islands situated to the west. The western side belongs to Chile and the eastern to Argentina. Part of this country is a new National Parks Reserve: trout and salmon in nearly all the lakes and rivers, and in summer wild geese, ducks, 152 different species of birds, and imported musk rats and beaver. Book: *Tierra del Fuego* (2nd edition), in English, by Rae Natalie Presser de Goodall.

There are two ways of crossing the Straits of Magellan to Tierra del Fuego. Coming S from Río Gallegos (where you should buy some Chilean currency as ferry-operators accept only their own currencies) an unpaved road turns left for Punta Delgada. A 30-minute crossing can be made (US$1 for car and driver) by the ENAP oil boats from Primera Angostura terminal to Punta Espora. The boats, which take 4 lorries and 2 vans, run every day, with schedule determined by tides and a 1200-1400 lunch hour rest. Under normal conditions they run from 0800 to 2100 daily, with tidal breaks lasting 4 hrs. (autumn and winter timetable). If going by car, do not go before 1000, as first crossings are taken by buses, etc. From Punta Espora (Balúa Aril is ferry terminal) a road runs through Chilean territory to San Sebastián (Chile) and 14 km. further to San Sebastián (Argentina) (usually 15 min. each delay in crossing borders), Río Grande and Ushuaia. There is an Esso petrol pump 38 km. from Punta Espora. If Esso has no petrol, try ENAP at Cerro Sombrero, although normally they only sell to employees. Accommodation only at Porvenir in the Chilean part, and it is not always possible to cross it in one day because of the irregularity of the ferry. It is sometimes possible, coming and going, to spend the night at the guest house of

ENAP at Sombrero (petrol there for employees only, but if you are running out, they may help), but do not count on it. Try *Hostería Karu-Kinka*. The ferry charge for a passenger is US$2, and for a car US$9-12 (Dec. 1977).

Hitch-hiking is not recommended in Tierra del Fuego, as sometimes you may have to wait 2-3 days before you even see a vehicle.

The road from Río Gallegos goes on to Punta Arenas, from where there are two regular crossings a day to Porvenir (passenger US$1.10, motor car US$2.50), at 0800 and 1400 (Sun. 0900), from Porvenir at 1100 and 1700 (Sun. 1700). A 225-km. road runs from Porvenir E to Río Grande (6 hours) *via* San Sebastián; or on alternative route at Cerro Sombrero (see previous paragraph) (on Chilean side of Tierra del Fuego, petrol available only at Porvenir). Reservations must be made at the hi-fi shop at Bulnes 637, Punta Arenas. The Argentine Consul in Punta Arenas is at Calle Valdivia 961 (Tel.: 22887).

The largest town in the Argentine part is

Ushuaia, the most southerly town in the world; its steep streets overlook the green waters of the Beagle Channel, named after the ship in which Darwin sailed the Channel in 1832. It is reached from Buenos Aires by ship (monthly, US$32, 9 days) or plane (5 hours). There are impressive views of the snow-clad peaks, rivers, waterfalls and dense woods. It has a naval station whose barracks used to be a prison which attracted sightseers from Buenos Aires in years gone by. Also, the town is a home port for the US scientific research vessel *The Hero,* whose crew will gladly show members around. Its friendly inhabitants (6,000) are engaged in sheep raising for the Río Grande cold storage plant, timber cutting, fishing, and trapping. Trade is mostly with Magallanes (Chile). Buses run a few times a week in summer between Ushuaia and Río Grande (US$4, at 0600, from *Albatros Hotel*); the LADE (air force) 'plane serving Río Gallegos, Ushuaia and Río Grande is US$10.50 single between Río Gallegos and Ushuaia; return exactly double, daily or twice a day. There is a microbus (essential to book in advance during Jan.-March) between Río Grande (see p. 124) and Porvenir in the Chilean part of the island (242 km., 6-8 hours) but no air connection. It is sometimes difficult to get a flight out in the tourist season.

N.B. Cheap cigarettes available, due to local tax exemptions.

Hotels *Mafalda,* San Martín 5, no food, US$10 d, with bath, excellent; *Hotel Mustapic,* Piedrabuena and Deloqui, new, friendly multi-lingual owner, US$7 d; *Albatros,* Lasserre and Maipú (ACA) with restaurant, new, US$10 s; *ACA Albergue* (Youth Hostel), US$1.30, 15 minutes' walk out of town; *Antártida,* also new, San Martín 1600, US$4.50 s; *Castelar,* San Martín 845 (US$3 s), reasonable restaurant; *Hispano, Residencial Capri,* San Martín 700, US$8 p.p., but dirty. Good pensión, US$1.50 per head, at San Martín 1058; for food, try the king crabs. For cheap, basic but kindly accommodation see Sra. de Asora, *Residencial Ushuaia (Fernández),* 3rd house on the left side of Onachanga and A. Lope, very cheap and friendly; *Hotel María Rosa,* cheap, friendly, on the waterfront (near *Hotel Ona,* US$5.50 d, not recommended). *Hotel Aeropuerto* at airport; *Hotel Atlántida,* US$15 d. Lodging in Ushuaia has recently become rather a problem. You can ask permission to stay at government office in town, four to a room.

Restaurant *Tante Nina,* best fish, but expensive, on Calle San Martín. Also *Charzasan.* Best king crab *(centella)* restaurant is *Don Pepe.*

Airport Only LADE flights. Try alternative: Bus to Río Grande, US$3 at 0600, breakfast at Lake Fagnano, board the 1130 Aerolíneas plane to Río Gallegos-Comodoro Rivadavia-Buenos Aires.

Excursions There are excursions to a glacier behind the town (or you can walk, breathtaking views, 2½ hours through woods, log-cabin half way); to the so-called Indian Cemetery, 5 km. W of town (archaeologists on site only too pleased to tell of Indian history), to Lendegaia and Lapataia bays, the falls of the Olivia river. In winter the temperature drops to as low as − 12°C, in summer it goes up to 25°C. In summer, boat trips may be taken to see sea lions at the Isla de los Lobos. Beavers may be seen in the Parque Nacional by the Chilean border; ask ranger. Hosterías at Lapataia (*Alakush,* US$4 d, 20 km. W of Ushuaia, on Route 3, in the Parque Nacional Tierra del Fuego, open for summer season from Dec. 1st to March); at Lake Fagnano (*El Kaiken Inn,* also bungalows, wonderful site, well-run facilities, on a promontory 93 km. from Ushuaia), and at Lake Escondido (*El Petrel Inn,* 54 km. from Ushuaia), after a spectacular climb through Garibaldi Pass, on the road to Río Grande; all three are good. Facilities at Kaiken are open all year round, but at Petrel only from Dec. to March. All are run by the ACA (US$9-11 d). Even in summer the climate can often be cold, damp and unpredictable. It is possible to hitch-hike as far as Lapataia; bus there US$1;

Travellers' Cheques can be changed at Banco de La Nación, but high commission for any amount charged. Banks in Ushuaia only open in the afternoon.

Rumbo Sur, at San Martín 342 (behind *Hotel Albatros*) runs good excursions: 2½-hour trip to Tierra del Fuego Parque Nacional, US$2.50 p.p. Tours also arranged to Lake Fagnano and aerial excursions over the Beagle Channel, Lake Fagnano, Lapataia and Ushuaia Bay. To Lago Estondida/Fagnano US$10. It is usually cheaper to hire a car than to go by taxi.

A tourist bureau at *Hotel Albatros* arranges very enjoyable excursions. The unpaved 240 km. road N to Río Grande passes through spectacular scenery.

Camping At Lapataia, by forested shore of Lake Roca in Parque Nacional, with facilities, including gas (18 km. from Ushuaia; weather can be bad). There is a free site by restaurant, with no facilities, on road to Parque Nacional about 4 km. from Ushuaia. Camping at Río Pipo, 5 km. W of town on Lapataia road, Monte Susana, 10 km. W, Ensenada, 14 km. W, and Río Olivia, 12 km. E of Ushuaia.

Taxi to airport US$1, or 15 min. walk. Rent-a-Car (Godfrey Davis) at Galvarini Automotores, Avda. San Martín 513, Tel.: 9185. US$4 per car (max. 5 people).

Río Grande (5,000 people) is a port in windy, monotonous sheep grazing and oil-bearing plains; the oil is refined at San Sebastián (partly paved but bad road) in the smallest and most southerly refinery in the world. Río Grande is also a free port: cheap films. At the Salesian school there is cheap accommodation for travellers, Dec.-Feb.; accommodation is very troublesome in Jan.-March. The British Vice-Consul can be contacted easily through the telephone exchange. Change travellers cheques at Banco de la Nación. Fill up with petrol here.

Hotels *Villa,* US$10 per double; *Antártida,* similar; *Yaganes,* on Avda. San Martín, has a restaurant; *Argentino,* US$1 p.p., friendly, on Belgrano and Ameghino; *Atlántida/ ACA Albergue,* near Gymnasium, 4-bed rooms, very comfortable, US$0.60 p.p., central heating, hot showers, restaurant, US$1.80 a meal, on Luis Piedrabuena; *Hotel Miramar* on Belgrano and Mackinlay; nearby *Hotel La Verde Casona,* on Piedrabuena and Mackinlay; *Hotel Shelkham; La Candela.* Rivadavia 637, no food but clean and friendly, US$8.

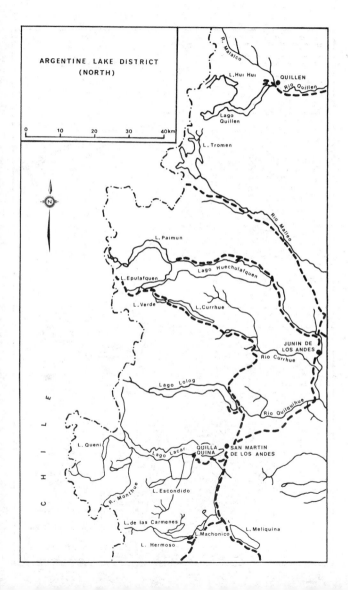

ARGENTINE LAKE DISTRICT
(NORTH)

0   10   20   30   40km

N

CHILE

R. Malalco
L. Hui Hui
QUILLEN
Rio Quillen
Lago Quillen
L. Tromen
Rio Malleo
L. Paimun
Lago Huechulafquen
L. Epulafquen
L. Verde
L. Currhue
JUNIN DE LOS ANDES
Rio Currhue
Lago Lolog
Rio Quilquihue
L. Queni
Lago Lacar
QUILLA QUINA
SAN MARTIN DE LOS ANDES
R. Monthue
L. Escondido
L. de las Carmenes
L. Meliquina
L. Machonico
L. Hermoso

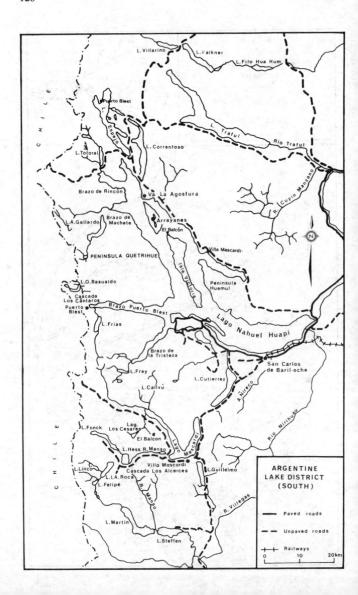

ARGENTINE
LAKE DISTRICT
(SOUTH)

——— Paved roads

- - - - Unpaved roads

+-+-+ Railways

0   10   20km

Restaurants   *Club Social; Río Grande; Comedor Porteño; Cantina Restaurant; Bottiche Felix; Fiori, Yaganes, Atlántida, Miramar, Villa, La Verde Casona.* Supermarket SADOS on San Martín, near 25 de Mayo.

Airport   Río Grande-Buenos Aires flight US$80, 5 hrs., stops at Río Gallegos and Comodoro Rivadavia. LADE flight Río Grande to Ushuaia, US$23 return, heavily booked. Telephone LADE office, 308. Conversely, travel with navy aircraft, mostly Hercules transports, for half the price.

Buses leave at 0600 Mon., Tue. and Thurs., US$10 each, for Porvenir, then connect with ferry to Punta Arenas. Transportes Turicisne go to Porvenir, very crowded. Rent-a-Car at Galvarin Automotores, Av. San Martín 381, Tel. 307. Daily bus service to Ushuaia, US$10, 6 hrs, stopping at Lake Fagnano for a drink.

The Lake District

Northern Patagonia has 4 routes of travel: the rivers Colorado and Negro, and two railway lines. The more northern runs from Bahía Blanca across the Río Colorado and along the valley of the Negro to Neuquén and Zapala; the southern line runs from Bahía Blanca southwards across the Colorado and Negro and then westwards through San Antonio Oeste to Bariloche and the Lake District, which can also be easily reached from Zapala. The roads and airlines are in the text.

The **Lake District** contains a series of great lakes strung along the foot of the Andes from above Lat. 40° South to below Lat. 50° in the Los Glaciares National Park area. In the N they are some 650 km. from the Atlantic Ocean, but the far southern ones are only some 200 km. from the southern Atlantic port of Santa Cruz. In the N the western ends of these lakes cut deeply into the mountains, their water lapping the forested skirts of high snow-and-ice capped mountains that are among the most spectacular peaks in the world; their eastern ends are contained by the old frontal moraines deposited there by the ancient glaciers which melted to form these huge fjord-like lakes. The water is a deep blue, sometimes lashed into white froth by the region's high winds, sometimes so still that the mountains are deeply mirrored in them.

On the far side of the Andes, in Chile, lies another system of lakes: these are easily visited through the low pass at Puerto Blest near Bariloche on Lake Nahuel Huapí, weather conditions permitting. The route is given on pages 133-4, with an alternative in the Chilean section.

National Park   Lake Nahuel Huapí and its surroundings, an area of 7,850 square km., was set aside in 1903 as a National Park. It contains the most diverse and spectacular natural phenomena: lakes, rivers, glaciers, waterfalls, torrents, rapids, valleys, forest, bare mountains and snow-clad peaks. The whole park is covered with abundant vegetation. Age-old trees, some of which reach a height of 50 metres or more, form vast forests, and alternate with flower-decked prairies and clumps of wild berry-laden shrubs. From December to April lake shores, roads and woodland trails are bordered by foxgloves, lupins and fuchsias; patches of primroses, lilies and daisies dot the fields. Wild animals of a wide variety of species live in the region, but they are extremely shy and seldom glimpsed by the explorer. Bird life, on the other hand, is so extremely rich—particularly the aquatic species: swans, geese and ducks—that it is seen at any time and everywhere in large flocks. In the far N of this region, near the town of Zapala, all these species and many others can be seen in their hundreds in the nature reserve of Laguna Blanca (see page 124).

Lake Nahuel Huapí   But the outstanding feature of this national park is the splendour of the lakes. The largest of these is Nahuel Huapí, 531 square km. and over 300 metres deep in places. It is 767 metres above sea level, in full view of the now-covered peaks of the Cordillera and of the forests covering the lower slopes. Towering over the scene is Mount Tronador. The blue waters of the lake, the mountains, and the loneliness give it a haunting charm. Some 65 km. long, and not more than 10 km. wide, it is very irregular in shape; long arms of water, or brazos, which look like fjords, stretch far into the land. There are many islands. The largest is the **Isla Victoria,** on which is the forest research station where the Directorate of National Parks carries out its work of acclimatising new species of vegetation. A visit to this island is a "must" for nature lovers but it takes a day (US$3) and don't go if you can help it by the larger steamers—they are too crowded. There is a small hotel. A Zoological Board is adding to the indigenous fauna; the trout and salmon of the lakes, for instance, have been introduced from abroad. Lake Nahuel Huapí is drained eastwards by the Río Limay; beyond its junction with the Río Neuquén it becomes the Río Negro. The Limay has good trout fishing but the rivers farther N—the Quilquihue, Malleu, Chimehuín, Collon-Curá, Hermoso, Meliquina and Caleufú—are much less fished and better, They are all in the neighbourhood of San Martín de los Andes (see page 135, and map on page 125). The season is from early November to the end of March.

A half-day excursion (1300-1830) may be taken from Bariloche to Puerto Panuelo, then by boat to Isla Victoria. The full-day excursion (0900-1730) includes the Arrayán forest and 3 hours on Isla Victoria, picnic lunch advised. From Puerto Panuelo, opposite the *Hotel Llao-Llao,* boats also leave for Puerto Blest.

A mere sand bar in one of the northern brazos separates the lake of Nahuel Huapí from Lake Correntoso, which is quite close to Lake Espejo. Lake Traful is a short distance to the NE. It can be reached by a road which follows the Limay River through the Valle Encantado (Enchanted Valley), with its fantastic rock formations. S of Nahuel Huapí there are other lakes. The three main ones are Mascardi, Guillelmo, and Gutiérrez. On the shores of Lake Gutiérrez, in a grotto, is the Virgen de las Nieves (Virgin of the Snows). There is a road to these lakes from Bariloche.

Summer is cool and the winters comparatively mild. June is the rainy month. During January to May, the summer winds are sometimes calmed and there are magical mirrorings in the lakes.

The lakes, and particularly Nahuel Huapí, are well served by boats of all kinds. On Nahuel Huapí the National Parks Board has a 300-ton steamer, the *Modesta Victoria,* which carries 150 passengers in great comfort (though the pop music is sometimes loud!). It is also able to embark two motor cars for the convenience of passengers touring the lake district.

Fishing The lakes are full of fish, and the best time for fishing is at the beginning of the season, that is, in November and December. Amongst the best are: Lakes Traful, Gutiérrez, Mascardi, Futulafquen (in the Los Alerces National Park), Meliquina, Falkner, Villarino, Nuevo, Lacar, Log-Log, Curruhué, Chico, Huechuafquen, Paimun, Epulafquen, Tromen (all in the Lanín National Park), and, in the far N, Quillén. In the far S, the fishing in Lake Argentino is also good.

Bariloche (San Carlos de), on the southern shore of Lake Nahuel Huapí, is without doubt the best centre for exploring the National Park. It is a town of steep streets, its wooden chalets perched Swiss fashion upon an old moraine at the foot of Cerro Otto. To the S lie the heights of the Ventana and the Cerro Colorado (2,135 metres). The place is full of hotels and cheap hosterías. There are some fine buildings and main streets are paved. The main church, built in 1946, dominates the town; interior unfinished, but good multivision slide-shows three times a week at 2200, US$2.50. The roads into Bariloche are paved and in good condition. Unhappily, because of its phenomenal growth, it has become overcrowded, and the best time to visit it is out of season either in the spring or autumn. When twelve strikes, four 2½ metre effigies pop out of the clock on the town hall's tower. There is a belvedere at the top of Cerro Otto with wide views of lake and mountain. Population, over 25,000. Lido swimming pool on the lake shore, is beautifully sited but somewhat run down.

Museum The "Perito Francisco Moreno" Nahuel Huapi Museum, well worth seeing for collection of Indian artefacts. Open 1400-1800, Mon.-Fri. The Museo de la Patagonia in the Civic Centre has a nice collection of stuffed animals. Free and heated.

Hotels To check local hotel rates, the most complete listing with map is published by the Oficina Municipal de Turismo in the Centro Civico, open 24 hrs. a day. The best are: *Bella Vista*, Rolando 351; *Huemul* (road to Llao-Llao, 1½ km.); *El Casco* (same road, 11 km.); *Tunquelén* (same road, 24 km.) and the *Llao-Llao* (casino) are on a peninsula between Lakes Nahuel Huapí and Moreno, 1½ km. from one another on a paved road. Also at Llao-Llao, 26 km. from Bariloche, is *Hostería Aunancay*, US$11 p.p., including 2 meals, friendly and delightful setting. Golf links, belonging to the *Gran Hotel*, on this peninsula. Other luxury class hotels: *Catedral Ski*, on Cerro Catedral; *El Monasterio* (5 km. out on Faldeo route); *Tres Reyes*, on 12 de Octubre 135. Comparable but better value is *Motel Chamonix*, right on Lake Nahuel Huapí, nice views from most rooms, excellent service and meals. *Hotel Austral*, US$20 d, with bath, small room, has restaurant. First class: *Cristal*, Mitre 335; *Roma*, San Martín 102. *Hotel Bariloche Center* (casino), new and well located, caters to charter tours at economic rates, and runs buses to the ski slopes of Cerro Catedral, July to August. *King's Hotel*, very nice, clean, warm, US$10 d, with bath and breakfast; *Residencial Portofino*, two blocks from plaza, US$7 d, small but spotless. Nameless guest house across the road. *Residencial Flamingo*, on Mitre, US$4 p.p., breakfast and view of lake; *Los Andes*, US$3.50 d, with shared bath; *Hostería Blancas Nieves*, room and breakfast only, expensive. Cheap pensións: *Hotel Feltre*, US$2.50, bed and breakfast; *Residencial Candeago*, just up hill from main square, US$3.50 d, excellent; *Residencial La Fontana*, Saavedra 689, Plaza Belgrano, clean, friendly; *Residencial Riviera*, US$3.75 s, with breakfast; *Residencial Angelina*, US$4.20 d, with bath and breakfast in bed; *Residencial Las Dos Rosas*, US$4; *Gran Luz*, US$3.50 for bed and breakfast; *Residencial Matterhorn*, Swiss-run, Pasaje Gutiérrez 1122; *Residencial Villa Elfrida*, US$2. *Residencial Los Brothers*, Albarracín 427, US$3 d; *Hostería Rex*, on Elflein above church, very friendly, US$1.50 including light breakfast; *Residencial Andrea*, Libertad 121, top of hill, US$3.50 d, with bath; *Hotel Ideal*, behind police station, pleasant, clean, quiet, away from the commercial centre, US$3 s, with restaurant, some doubles have lake view; *Hostería Nahuel*, Calle Gallardo 454, US$0.90 s; *Residencial Panorámico*, F.P. Moreno 646, private shower, US$4 d, highly recommended; *Residencial Sur*, opposite church, excellent value; *Residencial El Retalito*, US$1 p.p. Residenciales on main street: *Colón*, US$2; *Victoria*, US$2.50; *Las Tres Rosas*. Others: *Hotel El Mirador*, Moreno 500, US$3.50. d, with breakfast, hot water; *Residencial Bambi*, US$6.50 d, with bath, breakfast, Mitre 458, lovely view; *Residencial El Nire* (Tel.: 2-3041), hot showers, clean, very pleasant, breakfast. *Residencial Comodoro Rivadavia*, US$3.60 p.p., bath and breakfast. Hotels may be much cheaper off-season.

The *Llao-Llao* is large and impersonal. *Hotel Tunquelén* is high priced for what it offers. At both: meals of 6 or 7 courses and service charge of 26%. *El Casco*, German-run, opened in 1970, has won golden opinions for service and cuisine, and is only 10 minutes from the ski-lifts. Try one of the hosterías near the lakes for intimacy and charm (e.g. *Hostería Arrayán* at San Martín de los Andes, on Lake

Lacar, particularly good, or one at Lake Meliquina, both English-run; also *Pájaro Azul*, at Puerto Moreno, on Km. 10 on the Llao-Llao road, US$12 with two meals).*Refugio Challhuaco* is 16 km; outside town.

Restaurants Most restaurants have a cover charge *and* 20-25% service charge; read small print on menu well. *Casita Suiza* (fine steaks), *La Vizcacha, La Huella, El Molinito, Miguelito, El Tronador,* and *El Fortín,* which throws in folk-singing entertainment with a good dinner for US$1; *Parrilla La Vizcacha* and *Lazo,* barbecues; *Viejo Munich,* cheap and good; *Nikola* and *Eiflein,* very good value; *Pizzería Girafe; La Costa,* excellent; 4 km. towards Llao-Llao, *Parrilla de Tío Luis,* excellent. Superb coffee and cakes at *Chocolate Casero del Turista* at Mitre 239. Many good delicatessens in the area with take-away food, including chicken pizzas and cheeses, for picnics. *La Cosa Nostra,* B. Mitre 357, good cheap take-away pizzas.

Tourist Agency *Patagonia Travel,* efficient, recommended. *Varastur* organizes trips to Puerto Montt (Chile) from Bariloche, which are recommended in summer and are spectacular. *Alunco Turismo,* friendly.

Camping Most sites W of town and around lake, but good site E of Bariloche, about 1½ km. on Bariloche side of ski-lifts, with hot showers, US$0.50 per person. Also Selva Negra, 2½ km. out of town, hot water, excellent (US$0.80) and sites along Llao-Llao road, at Cascada Los Alerces and elsewhere. Cost about US$1 per person. Also site within few hundred metres of railway station and a hostel for US$0.50 a night. Good sites nr. Lake Gutiérrez, *Auto Camping W* and *Lago Gutiérrez, Los Rápidos,* Lake Mascardi. Police permit needed for camping outside sites.

Best Buy Sweaters, any amount of beautiful ones. An obvious bargain. The products of the local chocolate industry are worth trying.

Air Services Frequent to Buenos Aires (US$40, 2 hrs.) but poor for international connexions; flights to Puerto Montt (US$27) and Santiago on Sats. only (LAN Chile). Reservations slow and difficult. Flights, 3-4 times a week, with Aerolíneas and LADE to Esquel. Small tax at airport on leaving. Taxi to or from airport, US$4; bus US$1 from Aerolíneas office.

Road and Rail Bus service, to Buenos Aires, 1st class, with hostess, US$28, 27-28 hrs. Chevalier line leaves at 1 p.m. daily, La Estrella, at 2 p.m. Light snacks and drinks included in price. Trains take 40 hrs., and reservations can be made at the Bariloche Center as well as at the station. The "Los Arrayanes" train runs once a week from Buenos Aires to Bariloche and back; it is airconditioned, has pullman seats and a cinema, US$21, 29 hrs.; book at least 48 hrs. in advance, daily at 1100. Bus to Mendoza, 27 hrs., mainly on an unpaved road *via* Zapala, Buta Ranquil and San Rafael. Buses to El Bolsón and Esquel daily, with a thrice weekly extension to Comodoro Rivadavia. Buses also to Puyehue (Chile), San Martín de Los Andes and Neuquén. Rent-a-Car (Godfrey Davis), San Martín 120. Many other firms, mainly at airport.

Activities Apart from sailing and boating, there is golf, mountaineering, walking, ski-ing, and fishing. The climbing may mean a ride on horseback or a skilled ascent of the slopes of the Tronador mountain (excursion by bus US$5, full day, including walk to black glacier) which looms over the area. The Club Andino Bariloche arranges for guides; ask for Sr. Ricardo, the Secretary, who organises easy weekend climbs and walks with friendly visitors. The Government has convenient rest lodges at from 1,040 to 2,040 metres on the mountains. Firing, light and food are provided at these points. There is grand ski-ing during the winter season (July to end-August), supervised by the Club Andino at Bariloche. The favourite ski-ing slopes are on Cerro Catedral (*Catedral Ski Hotel,* excellent night club and Refugio Frey US0.60 a night, 3½ hours from cable-car base). There are a cable car and a chair lift from the foot of Cerro Catedral to points high on the ridge. The cable car, with a chair lift from its upper terminus, takes one higher than the main (2-stage) chair lift. Bus tours from Bariloche to the foot of Cerro Catedral (US$3 including lift ticket) gave time for less than 2 hours on top of the mountain. The only disadvantage at Bariloche is that the snow is unreliable except at the top. There are other ski-ing slopes on Cerro Otto (cable car, US$5.50), which can be reached in ½ day's walk from the town, or in a minibus which goes every ½ hour from a car park near the National Park headquarters, US$4 round trip (local bus US$0.90 return); also on López (try a car trip to this one, rough road, US$5), Dormilón and La Ventana. Whole-day trip to Lakes Gutiérrez, Mascardi, Hess, the Cascada Los Alerces and Cerro Tronador, US$10. If one is staying only 1-2 days in the area the best excursions are to go to Cerro Tronador the 1st day and on the 2nd to Cerro Catedral in the morning and Isla Victoria in the afternoon. Camping is freely allowed.

"The camping facilities in the National Park are generally good and uncrowded and should be recommended, even for those travelling generally from hotel to hotel. Firewood and water generally to hand, as well as food supplies."—Dr. Arthur Morris.

Mountain Climbing In the area there is everything for every kind of mountaineer, from the adventurous specialist to the enthusiastic amateur. National Park mountain guides are available but can be expensive. Information from Club Andino Bariloche, E.B. Morales y Elflein (1 block behind Civic Centre).

Swimming in some of the very big lakes such as Nahuel Huapí and Huechulafquen is not recommended, for the water is cold. But swimming in such lakes as Log-Log, Lacar, Curruhué Chico, Hermoso, Meliquina, Espejo, Hess and Fonck (all smaller lakes) is very pleasant and the water—especially where the bottom shelves to a shingly beach—can be positively warm.

Currency There are no exchange houses; the Bancos de la Nacion and de la Provincia operate facilities, but only for US dollars. Only American Express cheques cashed at Banco de la Nación, at high cost and inconvenience.

Excursions There is good motoring on the 500 km. of highways which run through the park. There are numerous excursions; prices vary very widely, and it is best to buy tours on the spot rather than in advance. The road to El Bolsón and Esquel (a new, faster, but less interesting road is being built between Bariloche and Esquel) is paved for the first 30 km. and goes past the beautiful lakes of Gutiérrez, Mascardi and Guillelmo and over fine mountain passes.

Río Villegas, about 80 km. S of Bariloche on the road to El Bolsón, is very beautiful. Cheap but picturesque hostería just outside the gates of the National Park, by the river.

Villa La Angostura is extremely picturesque, 80 km. from Bariloche on the way to Chile, US$3 by excursion bus (day trip) or local bus (US$1) which requires staying overnight; hotels a little dearer than Bariloche. The port, 3 km. from town, is spectacular in summer. **Hotels** *Correntoso, Motel Lomas de Correntoso.* **Camping** *El Cruce* and *ACA, Osa Mayor.*

Excellent *Hostería Los Peraltoches* on Lake Gutiérrez, 116 km. from Bariloche, US$10 with meals; magnificent views, English spoken, very homelike, open Nov.-March and June-Aug.

El Bolsón (full-day tour from Bariloche, about US$5, Empresa Don Otto, very crowded and difficult to get on in high season) is 130 km. to the S, on the road to Esquel (about 260 km. S of Bariloche). It is a most attractive small town in beautiful country, with many mountain walks and waterfalls nearby. Good fishing. Within half an hour's drive are Lakes Puelo and Epuyen (shops and petrol available). The valley, set between high mountains, is most attractive. The farms and the orchards sell their produce at Bariloche, which can be reached in about 4 hours by car. Famous local fruit preserves can be bought at the factories in town.

Accommodation at El Bolsón *Hostería Steiner,* clean and pleasant, on the Lake Puelo route; *Hotel Piltriquitrón,* San Martín; *Hostería Amancay,* San Martín and Cervantes; *Alojamientos El Bolsón* and *Villa Turismo* (Route 258); *Motel La Posta* (Route 258). Up to 2 days' stay possible at the Franciscan school, but get recommendation from tourist agent (opposite the bus stop at *Hotel Piltriquitrón*). *Hotel Salinas,* in private house (everyone knows it), US$0.80 per person, friendly, clean, hot water. Several residencias and camping sites nearby. Very difficult to find accommodation in the high season.

Restaurants   *San Diego,* good and cheap; four or five others. Welsh tea room. *Casa del Té Galés.*

Tourist Office   The agent, Sr. Sigfrido Janett, is most helpful, and a great authority on the area. Office open 0900-2000, on main plaza.

On the way from Epuyen to Esquel is Cholilla, with superb views of Lake Cholilla, crowned by the Matterhorn-like mountains of Cerros Dos and Tres Picos. There is a bus service between Bariloche, El Bolsón, and Esquel, and there is a direct thrice-weekly bus service between Comodoro Rivadavia and Esquel. A recommended journey for motorists is to spend the night at El Bolsón, enter the Los Alerces park *via* Cholilla and drive right through it to Esquel, driving the whole length of Lakes Rivadavia and Futalaufquen.

Camping   Parque Nacional camping ground at Lake Puelo, with hot showers and small store on lake-shore.

Esquel, about 260 km. S of Bariloche, was originally an offshoot of the Welsh colony at Chubut, nearly 650 km. away; Trevelin (see page 116) is only 15 km. SW from Esquel. It is now a modern town with reasonable amenities (population 15,600). Good tourist office at bus station. Major skiing location at La Hoya, ski-lift, 15 km. north of Esquel. Restaurant. Bariloche-Esquel bus (lovely route) Mon. to Sat. 0730, arrives 1630; Esquel-Bariloche 0825, arrives 1800 three times a week from Comodoro Rivadavia. It is best to take the daily bus which leaves at 0900. Stop for lunch at El Bolsón. Esquel-Trelew bus Wed. 2010, Fri. 0730 and Mon. 0730, 14 hrs., US$6 (La Estrella); the LADE flight is no dearer.

Hotels at Esquel   *Vascongada,* comfortable. *Residencial Argentina,* US$5· d, pleasant. Hotel *Ski Residencial,* room with bath, US$5.50 d, San Martín 963. No youth hostel although it is still in the YHA handbook. Hostería nr. Italian consulate, nice, friendly, US$1.50 each, meals. *Tour d'Argent,* US$8, excellent restaurant; *Residencial Esquel* on San Martín 1402; *Atalaya,* 9 de Julio 1036; *Maika,* 25 de Mayo 507; *Huemul,* Alvear 1015; *Los Alerces,* Rivadavia and Argentina; *San Antonio,* US$1.50 p.p., basic; *Hotel Tehuelche,* modern, corner Belgrano and 9 de Julio, US$2.50 s. *Residencial Las Mutisias,* Av. Alvear 1021, 2 blocks S of bus station, US$1 s, with bath. *Hostería Arroyán,* Av. Argentina 767; *Casa de Esquel,* Sarmiento 120; *Al Sol,* Chacabuco 762. *Zacharias,* adequate, US$4 d, as is *Nuevo. Motel La Hoya,* Ameglino 2296, clean and reasonable, on road to airport, 1 km. Also *Hostería La Hoya* at the Centro Depostíco de Ski (under construction) at La Hoya itself. *La Cabaña,* restaurant is good; so is *Las Nieves.* Restaurant *Mary-Mary,* very popular, excellent meal for 2, US$1.50, on Roca 647; *Chicken King,* restaurant, good and cheap; *Jockey Club,* Alvear 947; *La Terrazza,* 25 de Mayo, 1st Floor; *La Casa de Tucumán,* Alvear and Sarmiento; *Tour d'Argent,* San Martín 1063. Tea Room: *Casa Esquel,* Sarmiento 120.

Sixty km. W of Esquel, which can also be reached by road from Rawson (q.v.), is the Los Alerces National Park, with centuries-old larch trees. (An interesting part of the park can be reached from a separate entrance through Trevelin (paved road) following the Río Futaleufú and along Lake Situación. One can only go a short distance into the park this way, because the Futaleufú hydroelectric dam is to be built there.) There is no public transport, but Turicord or Mencué in Esquel go there. Turicord charges US$10 p.p. for a trip to the *Motel Pucon-Pai* and collect passengers 2 days later. (Other hotels on Route 258, on E side of Lake Futulafquen are, *Quimai-Quipan* and *Cume-Hué*). It has much the same natural attractions as the Nahuel Huapí and Lanín parks, but is much less developed for tourism; barbecues and tables are scattered all over the park. Its great Lake Futulafquen has some of the best fishing in this huge area, begins Nov. 25. The *Hostería Los Tepúes,* on the E side, is simpler, more rustic, and frequented by teenagers. (Both *hosterías* are closed in winter.) Recommended for fishermen are the *Quime Quipán* and *Pucón Pai* inns (room for 4 with bath and full board, US$4 each, plentiful meals). Regular launch trips to the end of the lake, to Lake Menéndez, and (a sheer delight) through Arrayanes river to windless Lake Verde; the boat leaves at 0900 but book the day before, as it will not leave if there are not enough passengers. There are local guides with outboard motor boats for fishermen. Tours arranged at Esquel. Other excursion tours offered are less interesting, because they only involve short stops in front of points of interest. A road connecting all the lakes is nearly completed.

Post Office and Bank Banco de La Nación on Güemes and San Martín. Post Office at Roca 445.

Camping Parque Nacional camping ground in the Park, by lakeside, by Lake Futulafquen, 6 km.; hot showers and small store. Permit needed from Intendencia, who also provide fishing permits. Camping facilities closed in winter; also on the way to El Bolsón. Camping at *Cabaínas Tejas Negras,* by *Pucon Pai Motel,* good facilities. Those with sleeping bags can go to the Salesian school and sleep in the school classrooms, Dec. to March, get recommendation from tourist office.

Airport 20 km. E of Esquel, by paved road, US$4 by taxi. US$2 by bus. Four flights a week to Buenos Aires *via* Bariloche; 3 a week *via* Trelew, Bahía Blanca.

Buses Transportes Patagónicos (Don Otto) go to Comodoro Rivadavia, Bariloche, El Bolsón; Giobbi SA operate two routes to Comodoro Rivadavia; other bus companies on Av. Fontana and Alvear (bus terminal) Empresa Don Otto, Chubut, Denis and Turicord. Bus terminal Tel.: 2233, also for taxis.

Tourist agencies Turicord, Mencué, Lago Verde, Vía Sur, all near Sarmiento.

From Esquel one can also drive to Perito Moreno (see p. 118) *via* Teckia (95 km. paved), Gobernador Costa (84 km. unpaved), La Laurita (last 61 km. paved, ACA petrol station, breakdown truck and snack bar), 65 paved km. to join route 22 (60 km.) which is being paved, and on to Río Mayo, with 121-km. unpaved road to Perito Moreno.

The Route to Chile from Bariloche Permission may be required to go to Chile. Check. "The preferred route is now that over Puyehue Pass, a good modern highway which is now paved on the Chilean side but not yet on the Argentine. Road from Bariloche goes around east end of Lake Nahuel Huapí, then follows north side of lake through resort town of Villa Angostura to junction with 'Ruta de Siete Lagos' for San Martín at Km. 94, Argentine customs at Km. 109 and pass at Km. 125 at elevation of about 1,280 metres. Chilean customs (checks made for fruit and literature) at Km. 146 in midst of a temperate zone rain forest. *Hotel Termas de Puyehue* is at Km. 168. New and very pleasant *Motel Nilque* on Lake Puyehue is at Km. 174. An easy five-hour drive which is the best of all those between the two countries."

Visión Turismo runs a thrice-weekly (Mon., Wed. and Fri.) day-trip from Bariloche to Puerto Montt and back, beginning 0830; sit on left side for best views. In winter, under normal weather conditions, the service runs 3 times a week, on Tuesdays, Thursdays and Sundays. To save money, take food with you. There is also an ordinary daily bus in summer *via* Osorno, US$14.70. Patagonia Tours in Bariloche runs a one-day crossing to Puerto Montt, *via* the lake. No cars taken on ferry on Lake Todos Los Santos. Try going to Puerto Montt *via* the Pérez Rosales Pass, a beautiful all-day trip, but check weather first. **N.B.** If you pay fares as you go along you can save up to 30%. Request information and get your first ticket at Turisur. (This agency also runs trips to Puerto Montt, includes lunch at Puerto Blest, US$18.) The most satisfactory way of doing the trip full-circle is by car from Bariloche, going first *via* Puyehue to Pto. Montt, returning *via* Tromen Pass (see the Villarrica volcano, good road), then Junín and San Martín de los Andes. There are steam locomotives in operation at Puerto Montt, and if you ask the driver you can get a ride with him.

"The Tromen (Chileans call it Mamuil Malal) pass route between Argentina and Chile is much less developed than the Puyehue route, and definitely not usable during heavy rain or snow, although during summer both Argentine and Chilean bus services use it. (As a border crossing it is more expedient than the Puyehue Pass.) Parts are narrow and steep. Argentine customs are at the pass. The Chilean *aduana* is at Puesco, 58 km. SE of Pucón. Ferry at Lake Quilleihue has been eliminated by road blasted across cliffs. Interesting araucaria pine forest at boundary at foot of Lanín Volcano. New paved highway under construction from 10 km. north to Junín through San Martín to Nahuel Huapí national park boundary, along with jet airport for San Martín. Big tourist hotel in San Martín."—Mr. Jim Halsema.

Nancy and Greg Schirm from Havertown, Pa., have made the following suggestions: "Leave Puerto Pañuelo Mon., Wed., Fri., at 1030 by launch across Lake Nahuel Huapí to Pto. Blest, which is just a customs post (2 hrs.). Lunch (US$5 for one with wine). Bus (10 min.) to Pto. Alegre on Lake Frías. Launch on Lake Frías, to Pto. Frías, a wharf for boats, go through Argentine customs but keep Chilean maps and magazines on you or they may be confiscated. Sometimes there is a long wait; take bus (45 mins., US$12) to Peulla *(Hotel Peulla, US$9 d with supper and breakfast),* pass Chilean customs; board launch (2½ hrs., US$7) on Lake Todos Los Santos to Petrohué *(Hostelería Petrohué, US$13 d, very comfortable, log fire in lounge and trout and salmon fishing)."*

Further information on border crossings in the Lake District will be found in the Chilean section.

From Buenos Aires to the Lakes

(1) **By air** to Bariloche, 5 hours by ordinary air services, 2 by jet aircraft. Daily flights by Aerolíneas Argentinas to Neuquén, and on next day to San Martín de los Andes by TAN, in one hour, arriving at 0900. Also from Mendoza by Aerolíneas Argentinas, with short stop at Neuquén.

(2) **By rail** to Bariloche. Trains leave Constitución Station, B.A. daily during the summer for Bariloche direct, crossing fertile B.A. Province and the bleak Río Negro Province: 1,770 km., about 40 hours. There are restaurant and sleeping cars (US$50). New train, Los Arrayanes, runs weekly, 29 hrs. B.A.—Bariloche US$39 1st class; only about US$1 dearer than 2nd and very much better. Winter timetable for ordinary trains is Tues. and Thurs. at 1800, 40 hrs.; Sundays, 30 hours. Journey daily 27 hrs. with Estrella del Valle, with full sleeping facilities.

There are trains also to Zapala, 1,367 km., 35 hours, using the same route as far as Bahía Blanca. From there to Zapala is 746 km. (19 hrs.). Trains are daily at 1340, one class, fare US$10.40, 24 hrs. From Zapala take bus to La Rinconada (US$1.50), and from there bus to Bariloche (US$2.20). The line follows the Río Colorado for some distance, then crosses it and turns into the valley of the Río Negro where large fruit growing areas at (343 km.) Choele-Choel (*ACA* motel on edge of town, US$12.65 for four, with bath, and fine modern hotel *Choele Choel*) and at (472 km.) Villa Regina are irrigated from the Río Negro dam. To Zapala *via* Neuquén, 1350 daily, US$8.50 first class, 23 hours. El Petróleo bus leaves Zapala 1315 daily for San Martín de Los Andres (5 hours) *via* Junín de los Andes, US$4.20. In winter the direct route from San Martín de Los Andes *via* the lakes may be impassable, so a bus must be taken back from San Martín to La Rinconada and then round to Bariloche, US$3.50, 4 hrs.

(3) **By road,** 1,930 km., takes about 32 hours. There are 2 or 3 coach services from Buenos Aires to Bariloche. One leaves at 0500 daily (24-26 hrs.), fast, comfortable and cheap; about US$14, very good refreshments en route. Another leaves at 1200 and includes supper and hostess snack service. The road is paved (beautiful views of Lanín Volcano and local wildlife) throughout from B.A. to Neuquén, and also the branch S to Bariloche (523 km.). Another branch goes W from Neuquén to **Zapala** (247 km.) through the oil zone at Challacó and Plaza Huincul. A Pullman bus, with hostess service, plies between Bahía Blanca and Zapala (15 hours). There are direct

bus services connecting Mendoza with Bariloche, US$24, 26 hours, and Córdoba with Bariloche, US$21, 25 hours, Mon., Wed., Fri. and Sun. at 1200.

Camping   There is an excellent free municipal camp site at Choele-Choel; shady, beside the Río Negro.

Neuquén (500 km.), capital of Neuquén Province, is near the confluence of the Limay and Neuquén rivers. Airport.

Hotels at Neuquén   *Apollo,* US$4.50 p.p., very good; *Cristal,* same price, adequate; *Europa,* good and clean, restaurant, opposite bus station, US$5, private bath. *Gran Confluencia. ACA Cipolletti,* just outside Neuquén. *Residencial Imperio,* US$4 d. Some 50 km. W from Neuquén there is a motel at Arroyitos. Municipal camping site at Neuquén and various camping sites mostly by the river. Site at Piedra Buena, 211 km. from Bariloche on Route 237.

Restaurant   *Bariloche,* good food but poor service.

Hotels at Zapala   *Huincul,* US$3.50 d; *Costa Rica,* US$2.50 d; *Zapala,* opposite railway station, US$0.75 p.p.

Hotels N of Zapala include those at Churriaca (131 km.), Chos Malal (202 km.) and Río Barrancas (at 340 km.). Road mostly unpaved.

North of Zapala on the Chilean border is Copahué National Reservation, best-known for its thermal baths and volcano of the same name. At 1,980 metres above sea-level in a volcanic region, Copahué Termas is enclosed in a gigantic amphitheatre formed by mountain walls, with an opening to the E. There is a bus service from Zapala to Copahué, which may also be reached by road from Mendoza. The Laguna Blanca National Park (to the W of Zapala) is famous for its animal and bird life, but has not yet become a tourist centre.

Bariloche is 418 km. S of Zapala by a road through Junín de los Andes and San Martín de los Andes, which takes 5 hours by bus. A short detour from Junín leads to the very beautiful lake of Huechulafquen; from Junín, too, a motor boat runs W over the Tromen Pass through glorious scenery to Pucón (135 km.) on Lake Villarrica, in Chile; on the way there are splendid views of Lanín volcano, extinct and 3,975 metres high, one of the world's most beautiful mountains. At **Junín de los Andes**—a famous spot for salmon and rainbow trout—is the *Chimehuín,* a very small fishing hostelry. Some 30 km. N of Junín are the *ACA La Rinconadas* facilities; paved road. There is an airport between Junín and San Martín, but it is mainly used by the military.

San Martín de los Andes, 40 km. S. of Junín (paved road), and 196 km. from Zapala, is a lovely little town at the eastern end of Lake Lacar; it is the best centre for exploring Lanín National Park, with its sparkling lakes, wooded mountain valleys and the snow-capped Lanín Volcano. The numerous deer in the park are the red deer of temperate Europe and Asia. There is excellent ski-ing on Cerro Chapelco, to which there is a road. The most popular trips by car are to Lakes Log-Log, Alumine and Huechulafquen, to Villarrica Pass and Lanín Volcano. Shorter excursions can be made on horseback or by launch; recommended day excursion by El Valle on Lake Lacar for US$4. The road goes on *via* Lake Hermoso and Villa Angostura to Bariloche, a beautiful drive of 220 km., 10 hours by bus, which stops for views and an hour for lunch at Angostura—an excellent, well organised bus route, but not in winter. Many buses, however, use a rather less scenic route following Río Traful, then Lake Lanín and joining the paved Bariloche highway at Confluencia (ACA station and a hotel, also motel *El Rancho* just before Confluencia). For several km. S of this point there are spectacular rock formations. Camping along this "Seven Lake Drive" route is freely allowed to

National Park permit-holders. No buses from Seven Lakes to San Martín de los Andes. Two buses a day San Martín-Bariloche, 5 hours.

Ski-ing   There is now a chair-lift on Cerro Chapelco and a ski-tow higher up. Very good slopes and snow conditions for the beginner, the practised, and the expert. As yet uncrowded and much cheaper than at Bariloche. Atmosphere friendly, casual and unsophisticated.

Restaurant   *Parrilla La Tranquera,* good value; *Los Ciervos* (opposite roundabout, with deer statues) and *Parrilla del Esquiador* on Belgrano 885, reasonable home-cooked food. It is difficult to get dinner before 2200, but there are various good restaurants in the area.

Hotels   New modern motel, *El Sol de los Andes,* very expensive and nice, set above the town; *Lacar,* old but central and good value for US$3.20 d, good meals; the *Hostería Arrayán,* one of 2 English guest lodges in the Lake District, is 3 km. from San Martín. (Self-contained cabins for 14 guests; superb view over Lake Lacar; US$3.50 a day, all in.) At San Martín is *Los Pinos,* German-run, and at least 2 other excellent ones; *Hotel Turismo* is recommended, US$4 d, shared bathroom. Also good, *Casa Alba,* US$2; *Residencial Peumayen,* Ave. San Martín, new and very clean, US$6 d, with bath and breakfast. At 24 km. from Villa La Angostura is *Hotel Ruca Malen;* at 53 km. *Hotel Pichi Traful,* and at 75 km. *Hostería Lago Hermoso.*

Camping   ACA camping and Autocamping S. Martín de los Andes, both with hot water and laundering facilities. Not open all year round.

The Economy

Argentina has the second highest standard of living in Latin America, is one of the most highly developed countries of the region and is potentially one of the richest farming countries in the world. The importance of agriculture and livestock production is shown by the fact that this sector still provides about 80% of foreign exchange earnings. A high proportion of livestock rearing and farming generally is concentrated in an area with a radius of about 600 km. from Buenos Aires. The Province of Buenos Aires alone accounts for about 40% of the cattle and about 30% of the sheep reared in the country. Although Argentina has lost its dominant world position as an exporter of cereals and beef, it has great resources in relation to its population and therefore has the potential to increase its total output. Argentina's population growth rate is only 1.5% a year, and its gross national product per head is estimated at US$1,400.

When the Peronist movement returned to power in May 1973, economic growth initially picked up, with an increase of 7% in the gdp recorded in 1974, but in 1975, with increasing inflation and a downturn in investment, the rate fell to 0.5%; there was a further fall of 2.9% in 1976, but there was a substantial rise of 4.4% in 1977.

The external sector strengthened in 1977, with exports and imports at record levels of US$5,686m. and 3,900m. respectively. A trade surplus of US$1,780m. was recorded in 1977, thanks to sales of bumper grain crops in rising markets. Official balance-of-payments estimates show a surplus of US$2,250m. in 1977 against one of US$1,192m. in 1976.

Official estimates place total foreign indebtedness at just under US$10,000m. at end-1977. The gross official reserves improved strongly in 1977, to US$4,200m at the end of the year from US$2,205m. at end-1976.

The outlook for 1978 is a little less rosy as exports are expected to fall because of rather smaller crops, and imports to rise with some lowering of tariffs; a trade surplus of about US$700m. is forecast for 1978.

The world energy crisis is not affecting Argentina badly, and the Government is implementing its long-term plans to increase the use of power from hydroelectric, solid-fuel and nuclear sources. Argentina produces about 85% of its domestic requirements for petroleum.

Despite the initial success of the Government's price control policy introduced in April 1976, inflation is still Argentina's main economic problem. Following the removal of price controls in April 1976 by the new military government, the rise in the cost of living was reduced somewhat; the annual figure was 566% at end-March 1976 and stabilised due to the effect of market forces, reaching 347.5% for the year, and was more than halved to 160.4% for 1977. Prospects for holding down the level of inflation are somewhat uncertain; the trade unions have been pressuring the Government to re-establish real wage levels, which have fallen by some 50% since 1976. Another main cause of inflation has been the Government's budget deficits, which had grown out of control up to 1976. In 1977 the budget deficit was held down to 3% of gdp; in 1978 it is hoped to contain it to 1% of gdp, which will be financed without significantly increasing the total of currency in circulation.

The Government's ambitious development plans for the rest of the decade include expansion of the iron-and-steel, petrochemical, energy, mining and livestock sectors. Work has already started on various important infrastructure developments, including two nuclear plants in the Province of Córdoba, a new petrochemical terminal at San Sebastián, road and bridge construction, several railway developments and the Salto Grande hydroelectric complex (in conjunction with Uruguay). Studies are being carried out for other hydroelectric plants, including the Yacyretá-Apipé and Corpus schemes (both in conjunction with Paraguay) and other complexes, some with the cooperation of the governments of Bolivia, Brazil, Paraguay and Uruguay.

Foreign Trade (US$m.)

Year			Exports (f.o.b.)	Imports (c. & f.)
1972	..	..	1,941	1,905
1973	..	..	3,266	2,235
1974	..	..	4,005	3,570
1975	..	..	2,961	3,947
1976	..	..	3,916	3,032
1977*	..	..	5,680	3,900

*Provisional

Information for Visitors

How to reach Argentina

By Air   Britain to B.A.: British Caledonian Airways and Aerolíneas Argentinas have direct flights from London twice a week. Varig Airlines runs a weekly service. British Caledonian's flight from Gatwick takes 18 hours. Several international airlines such as Air France, KLM, Lufthansa, Iberia, Alitalia, Swissair and TAP have frequent flights to Argentina from most European countries.

N.B. Since air travel prices are worked out in mileage bands, check what the maximum for your price is. It is possible, for instance, to travel for the price of a Buenos Aires-London ticket (7,051 miles) up to 8,434 miles, enabling a Buenos Aires, Rio, Recife, Lisbon, London, Paris, Nice, Rome, Milan, Zürich trip for that price!

From New York there are services by Pan American World Airways (New York to Buenos Aires by non-stop jet, 10¼ hours); by Pan American and Braniff (no change of plane and stops at Santiago and

Lima only), 14 hours; by Aerolíneas Argentinas, Varig, and from Miami by LAN-Chile and Braniff (two non-stop Services). From Canada the Canadian Pacific Airlines fly to B.A. *via* Mexico.

By Sea from U.K.   Cargo ships carrying up to 12 passengers are run by the Lamport and Holt Line, the Blue Star Line and the Argentine Lines (Empresa Líneas Marítimas Argentinas-Elma). Houlder Bros. carry a few passengers in cargo ships from Southampton.The normal time for the voyage is 17 to 21 days. Luggage should be kept to a minimum and insured.

From the Continent of Europe   Apart from the sailings from Britain already given, Messagéries Maritimes run passenger liners, and the "Italia" Line sails from Mediterranean ports and the Johnson Line from Swedish and Baltic ports.

From the U.S.A.   There are sailings from New York to Buenos Aires by the American Republics Line, operated by Moore-McCormack Lines; sailings from San Francisco and Los Angeles by Pacific Republics Line, by the same operators; and from New Orleans by the Delta Line. The Argentine Lines (Elma), also run a passenger service between New York and Buenos Aires. Buenos Aires is 19 days by ship from New York or New Orleans.

Internal Air Services are run by Aerolíneas Argentinas, Austral, and the army airline LADE (in Patagonia, highly recommended). There are frequent flights to all neighbouring republics. Aerolíneas flies to Ushuaía and Lake Argentino only in summer. LADE flights are cheaper than the others, and there is a good extended schedule with brand new Fokker F-28 jets. (Even though sometimes offices in various towns may tell you the flights are full, it is usually worth a try out at the airport.) The naval air passenger service, Aeronaval, carries paying civilian passengers, ⅓ cheaper than LADE. No firm schedule though; 2 flights a week between Ushuaia, Río Grande and Río Gallegos; once a week between Ushuaia and Buenos Aires.

Visit Argentina Fare   Those visiting Argentina should note the following excellent bargain. For US$180, or the peso equivalent, one can buy from Aerolíneas Argentinas *or* Austral, in Buenos Aires, a voucher for this scheme, available to non-Argentines not resident in Argentina. The system permits travel anywhere on the domestic network of Aerolíneas or Austral for a period of 30 days, provided that no point is visited twice except to make an immediate or first available connection. The voucher is surrendered for a complete set of tickets which are not refundable (i.e. the whole tour must be planned before it is begun). Domestic timetables are not available to the public, but a friendly approach to an airline office is likely to yield enough information about the days of week and times of flights to enable reasonable plans to be laid. It is unwise to set up too tight a schedule because of delays which may be caused by bad weather; however, if your itinerary changes, it is possible to trade off unused sections for others. Flights between Buenos Aires and Río Gallegos are often fully booked 2 to 3 weeks ahead, and there may be similar difficulties on the routes to Bariloche and Iguazú. Reconfirmation at least 24 hours ahead of a flight is important and it is essential to make it at the point of departure. Extra charges are made for reconfirming LADE flights (useful in Santa Cruz and Tierra del Fuego) but these are not very costly.

Airport Tax   US$5 for international flights, US$0.60 for international flights of less than 300 km., US$0.40 for internal flights.

N.B.   International air fares bought in Argentina may not be paid for in pesos; foreign currency is obligatory, except for flights to the Falkland Islands.

Do not send unaccompanied luggage to Argentina, if necessary pay overweight; it can take up to 3 days of form-filling to retrieve it from the airport.

Railways A permit to travel anywhere by the Argentine railways costs US$65 a month, and US$111 for two months. There is no connected railway system south of Bariloche. A "Pase Americano" which enables you to travel on Pullman coaches through Uruguay, Argentina, Brazil, Chile, Bolivia, Paraguay, without mileage limit is US$100 for a month (US$180 for 3) free carriage, 30 kg. (children ½ price) and obtainable at the Centro de Información de Ferrocarriles Argentinos in Galerías Pacifico Florida 53, Buenos Aires, open office hours and Sat. mornings. **N.B.** Once out of Buenos Aires, train information is hard to come by. Stations have wall time-tables of complete schedules for their own line (e.g. Belgrano Railway) but no information for other systems. To avoid disappointments, make long-distance call to nearest station on line you require—although this requires fluency in Spanish. There are no general time-tables in circulation at present.

Motoring For entering Argentina by automobile the *Carnet de passages en douanes (Libreta de aduana),* issued by a recognised automobile club, is required. Tourists can now bring their cars into Argentina temporarily under international documentation. Petrol (gasoline) is from about 30 US cents a litre. A British international driving licence is only valid if it is endorsed by the Automóvil Club Argentino (ACA). Most main roads are paved, if rather narrow, and roadside services are good; road surface conditions vary once one leaves main towns, though the dirt and gravel roads are well maintained. High speeds are quite possible on them, as long as you have the essential guard for the windscreen. You may not export fuel from Argentina, so empty spare jerry cans while you are in the country. Do fill up with petrol when you can in less developed areas like Chaco and Formosa as petrol stations are infrequent. Diesel fuel prices are about 20-30% of those for gasoline; it is known as *gas-oil*. Octane rating is as follows: regular gasoline 83; super 93; gasoline is called "nafta".

To obtain documents for a resident to take a car out of Argentina, you can go to ACA in Buenos Aires, which may take up to 4 working days, or you can ask for a list of other ACA offices that can undertake the work; take forms with you from Buenos Aires, and papers may be ready in 24 hours. You will need at least 1 passport sized photo, which you can have taken at ACA at a fair cost. If the car is not your own, you require a special form signed by the owner and witnessed by a notary public.

Sometimes one may not be allowed to reach a border if one does not intend to cross it, stopping one e.g. 20 km. from the border.

Automóvil Club Argentino, Av. Libertador General San Martín 1850, has a travel document service, complete car service facilities, road information, road charts *(hojas de ruta)* (about US$1 each to members, if available) and maps, a hotel list, camping information, and a tourist guide book sold at a discount to its members and members of other recognised automobile clubs upon presentation of a membership card). Members of other recognized automobile clubs can also, on presentation of membership cards, benefit from lower prices for their rooms and meals at ACA hosterías. The Club has service stations, some with a parking garage, all over the country. The organization is efficient, but the maps are undated.

ACA accommodation comes in 4 basic types: Motel, Hostería, Hotel, and the somewhat unpredictable Unidades Turísticas. A motel may have as few as 3 rooms. Hosterías have very attractive buildings and are very friendly. Hotels are smarter, more distant and more impersonal. Unidades Turísticas may have a restaurant. The other three have meal facilities. All can get in touch by phone or radio with the organisation to find put about accommodation or road conditions.

Touring Club Argentino, Esmeralda & Tucumán, has similar travel services but no service stations at all. The exceptionally high-standard Fiat map it sells in 8 sheets covers the whole country with gratifying accuracy.

Camping is now very popular in Argentina and sites with services are being installed, as well as in municipal and private campsites in most tourist centres. Camping is now allowed at the side of major highways, at no cost. References to sites will be found in the text. There are few Youth Hostels, but some towns offer free accommodation to young travellers in the holiday season, on floors of schools or church halls. Regular (blue bottle) Camping Gas International is available in Buenos Aires only, at Longvie, Libertad 731, Tel.: 42-0014/19.

Hitch-hiking Argentina is one of the countries in South America where this can be practicable. Note, however, that recent problems with terrorists as well as robberies have made hitch-hiking more difficult. Carry little foreign cash on you, especially loose dollars, because of frequent stoppages along the road. If you can, avoid backpacking; look clean, and for men, hair should be short: it helps to look like a tourist rather than a local ! Don't rely on it absolutely, though; traffic can be sparse, especially in Patagonia.

Films Buying and developing are cheaper in Argentina than elsewhere in Latin America.

Documents Passports are not required by citizens of neighbouring countries who hold identity cards issued by their own Governments. A passport visa from an Argentine consulate is necessary, except for nationals of Western Hemisphere countries (excluding Cuba), Western European countries (excluding Portugal), and Japan, who may stay for 3 months, a period which can be renewed for another 3 months at the National Directorate of Migration. For all others there are three forms of visa: a business "temporary" visa, a tourist visa, and a transit visa. We are informed that U.S. citizens have been known to need visas for border crossings by land, e.g. at Yacuiba. Australians, New Zealanders and South Africans need visas. Tourist visas are usually valid for one year in Argentina and for any number of exits and entrances during that period. Visitors should carry passports at all times, as there are frequent security checks. All visitors must have an International Certificate of Vaccination against smallpox.

Vaccinations Centro Médico Rivadavia, S. de Bustamante 2531, Mon.-Fri. 0730-1900 or Guardia de Sanidad del Puerto de Buenos Aires, Ing. Huergo 1497, Mon.-Fri. 0730-1900 and Sat.-Sun. 0800-1200.

British Businessmen are strongly advised to read "Hints to Business Men visiting Argentina", free on application to Export Services Division, Department of Trade, Export House, 50 Ludgate Hill, London EC4M 7HU. Similar information is provided for U.S. citizens by the U.S. Department of Commerce.

Customs No duties are charged on clothing, personal effects, toilet necessities, etc. Cameras, typewriters, binoculars, radios and other things which a tourist normally carries are duty free if they have been used and only one of each article is carried. This is also true of scientific and professional instruments for the personal use of the traveller. New personal goods of up to a value of US$150 may also be introduced duty-free by tourists.

   Two litres of alcoholic drinks, 400 cigarettes, 50 cigars and 5 kg. of foodstuffs are also allowed in duty free; for tourists originating from neighbouring countries the quantities allowed are about half of these.

Climate ranges from sub-tropical in the N to sub-Antarctic in Tierra del Fuego but is temperate and quite healthy in the densely populated central zone. From mid-December to the end of February Buenos Aires can be oppressively hot and humid, with temperatures ranging from 27°C (80°F) to 35°C (95°F) and an average humidity of 70%. The winter months of June, July and August are best for a business visit, though spring weather in Buenos Aires is often very pleasant indeed. The last two weeks in July are not recommended for Buenos Aires, because of the inflow for the Palermo Livestock Show. The skiing season in Bariloche ends by 30th August.

Clothing In summer, December to March, lightweight but not light coloured suits for men, and summer dresses (and cocktail dresses in the evening) for women. In winter, June to August, both men and women need woollens and a topcoat. What is worn in Europe will do for the spring and autumn. Shorts are not worn.

Hours of Business Banks, government offices, insurance offices and business houses are not open on Saturdays. *Government offices:* 12.30-1930 in the winter and 0730-1300 in summer. *Banks:* generally 1200-1600 but time varies according to the city, and sometimes according to the season. (See under names of cities in text.) *Post Offices:* 0800 to midnight for telegrams. Stamps on sale during working days 0800-2000 but 0800-1400 on Saturdays. Registered letters are accepted also on Saturdays between 0800 and 1400. *Shops* are open from about 0900 to 1900, though many close at midday on Saturdays. In the north many close for the daily afternoon siesta, reopening at about 1700. At the beginning of 1978, the Government passed a decree allowing 24-hour opening.

Language Spanish, with variant words and pronunciation. English comes second; French or Italian may be useful. Interpreters—who advertise in the *Buenos Aires Herald*—can be obtained at a reasonable fee. Technical terms are often of local invention and peculiar. Documents for official use have to be translated by authorised public translators who charge heavily. The telephone directory lists them under *Traducciones.*

The chief variant pronunciations are the replacement of the "ll" and "y" sounds by a soft "j" sound, as in English "azure" (though note that this is not done in Mendoza), the omission of the "d" sound in words ending in "-ado", the omission of final "s" sounds, the pronunciation of "s" before a consonant as a Scottish or German "ch", and the substitution in the north and west of the normal rolled "r" sound by a hybrid "rj".

For those who are staying some time, courses in Spanish at the Instituto Orly, Rivadavia 764, 1° 17, Buenos Aires, have been recommended. Tel.: 34 3321. Reasonable prices, private or group tuition.

Cost of Living Inflation is again serious. After an average price rise for 1971-74 of about 50% a year, the 1975 increase was 335%, 347% in 1976, mostly in the first three months of the year, and 174% in 1977. An increase of 80% is forecast for 1978.

A cheap meal is available for about US$2.

Standard Time is 3 hours behind GMT.

Holidays No work may be done on the national holidays (May 1, May 25, June 20, July 9, August 17 and December 25) with the exceptions specifically established in the legislation in force. On the non-working days (January 1, Holy Thursday and Good Friday, and December 8) employers are left free to decide whether their employees should work, but banks and public offices are closed. Banks are also closed on December 31. On January 1 there is a ticker-tape tradition in downtown Buenos Aires: it snows paper and the crowds stuff passing cars and buses with long streamers. November 11 is a holiday in Buenos Aires.

Food National dishes are based in the main upon plentiful supplies of beef. Many are distinctive and excellent; the *asado,* a roast made on an open fire or grill; *puchero,* a pot-au-feu, very good indeed if all the ingredients are correct; *bife a caballo,* steak topped with a fried egg; the *carbonada* (onions, tomatoes, minced beef), particularly good in Buenos Aires; *churrasco,* a thick grilled beef steak; *parrillada,* a mixed grill, mainly roast meat, sausages (including *morcilla,* or blood sausage) and offal; and *humitas,* made with sweet corn, tasty but not so strictly national. *Arroz con pollo* is a delicious complex of rice, chicken, eggs, vegetables and strong sauce. *Puchero de gallina* is chicken, sausage, maize, potatoes and squash cooked together. *Empanada* is a tasty meat pie, and *chorizo,* a highly spiced sausage, though do not confuse this with *bife de chorizo,* which is a rump steak *(bife de lomo* is fillet steak). Try also local *milanesas* (Wiener Schnitzel), *mollejas* (sweetbreads) and *Mayonesa de ave*, poultry mayonnaise. *Locro* is a thick soup made of maize, white beans, beef, sausages, pumpkin and herbs. Almost uniquely in Latin America, salads are quite safe. A popular dessert is *dulce de leche* (especially from Chascomús), milk and sugar evaporated to a pale, soft fudge; best eaten with cheese *(queso fresco)* to offset the sweetness. Other popular desserts are *dulce de batata* (sweet potato preserve), *dulce de membrillo* (quince preserve), *dulce de zapallo* (pumpkin in syrup) with cream and *queso fresco*, and *postre Balcarce*, a cream and meringue cake. *Alfajores,* maize-flour biscuit filled with *dulce de leche* or apricot jam, are also very popular. Sweets: the Havana brands have been particularly recommended. Excellent Italian-style ice-cream with exotic flavours. For local recipes (in Spanish) *Las Comidas de Mi Pueblo*, by Margarita Palacios, recommended.

Rolls and coffee and perhaps fruit for breakfast. A small immersion heater (US$5) may be purchased locally to make hot drinks for very early risers. Offices close for 2 to 2½ hours for lunch between 1200 and 1400. Around 1700, many people go to a confitería—a cross between tea-room and cocktail lounge—for tea, sandwiches and cakes. The cocktail hour is 1900-2100. No one eats before 2100, and dinner often begins at 2200 or 2230; it is, in the main, a repetition of lunch. The service charge is 23%, but you still tip, if you want good service. Some restaurants do not charge the 23% and state "no cobramos laudo" on the menu.

Drink Argentine wines are good throughout the price range, though probably the best are not as good as the best Chilean. The local beers, mainly lager-type, are quite acceptable, available in small bottles *(porrón)* or disposables. Hard liquor is relatively expensive. Tap water in the main cities is safe, but often heavily chlorinated; it is usual to drink soda or mineral water at restaurants, and many Argentines mix it with their wine, as a refreshing drink in summer. Coffee and milk are expensive.

Best Buys Local leather goods, although prices have shot up: men's leather coats, US$100; suede, US$150-200 on Florida; handbags and shoes, US$20-30. A gourd for drinking *yerba maté* and the silver *bombilla* which goes with it, perhaps a pair of gaucho trousers, the *"bombachas"*. Ponchos (red and black for men, all colours for women). Articles of onyx, specially in Salta. Silver handicrafts. Knitted woollens, especially in Bariloche. Almost everything you see in Calle Florida, Buenos Aires, may be bought more cheaply in the Once district, or in Calle Cabildo (Belgrano district).

Currency Banknotes of 5, 10, 50, 100, 500, 1,000, 5,000 and 10,000 pesos. Coins of 1, 5, 10, 20, 25 and 50 centavos and one peso. Travellers are warned that many people still figure in terms of the old currency, called "peso viejo"; the "peso nuevo" is called *Peso Ley* 18.188 and is worth 100 times more than the old peso. The free-market rate of exchange is not quoted here because it changes so often (the previous black market no longer operates). See "Latest Exchange and Inflation Rates" at the end of book. Travellers can take into or out of Argentina any amount of foreign or Argentine currency. It is sometimes difficult to change travellers' cheques in the smaller towns, except at branches of Bank of London and South America, known locally as "Banco de Londres"; commissions can be as high as 6% and in general it takes a long time and many forms to transact these cheques. Remember money remitted to Argentina from abroad is invariably paid out in pesos.

Note that shops and *casas de cambio* (exchange shops) will often give a better rate than the banks, especially for dollar notes. This is true also of travel agents.

Weights and Measures The metric system is used.

Postage Rates It would be misleading to give these because inflation changes them so often; the same is true of cable and 'phone rates. Letters from Argentina take up to a week to get to the UK, and about 5 days to the USA.

Encomiendas Internacionales, at Calle Chile 16, Buenos Aires, has an efficient international parcel service, including wrapping for a modest fee.

American Express Agents Buenos Aires: City Service Travel Agency, Florida 890, Tel.; 32-8416. Bariloche: Alun-Co. Turismo (City Service Travel), Bartolomé Mitre 5, Tel.: 2283/4.

Press Buenos Aires dailies: "La Nación", "La Prensa", "Clarín", a tabloid "La Opinión". Evening papers: "La Razón" and "Crónica". English language daily: "Buenos Aires Herald"; French: "Le Quotidien"; German: "Argentinisches Tageblatt", "Freie Presse". Magazines: "Siete Días", "Gente", "Panorama", "Primera Plana", "Confirmado", "Mercado", "Análisis", "Camping" (tourism), "El Gráfico" (sports): English language magazines: "The Review of the River Plate" (commercial, agricultural, and intelligent comment), and "The Southern Cross" (Irish community).

This section has been revised by Barbara Wijngaard, of LBI Economics Department, with the very welcome help of José A. Buchmann, Bank of London & South America, Buenos Aires, and the following travellers: Ulrich von Aswegen (Osnabruck), Diana Birkbeck and Nicholas Davies, James K. Bock (Mexico City), Dr. Klaus Busch (Osnabruck), Markus Casanova (Fribourg), Andrew Cox, Johan P. Dahl and Ulla R. Hoyna (Sweden), Michael Davison, Ben Fawcett, Vittorio Ferretti (São Paulo), Astrid Fickinser (Bernkastel), Tim and Arlene Frost (Hamilton, N.Z.), Mary Goodykoontz and Ken Scarlett (Woodlands, Calif.), Robert Hertzig (New York City), Gerhard Keilbach (Stuttgart), Leslie Kent (Pretoria), Paul and Theresa Legare (Ottawa), Rolf Maag (Caracas), James N. Maas, Klaus Matzka (Perchtoldsdorf, Austria), Dr. Terry McCarthy (Singapore), George Meegan, Phoebe Mayer (Peru), Dr. Patrik von zur Mühlen (Bonn), Dr. G. B. Mulkern (Fargo, N. Dakota), Alexander Nemeth and Janette Roberts (Australia), Patricio van Nievelt (Chile), Dirk Partridge (Washington, D.C.), Dr. Margaret Peil, Thomas Pensler (Benediktbeuern, W. Germany), Fredy Peter (Kloten, Switzerland), Carole Peirce (USA), E. C. Pindes, Judith Rattenbury and Nicole Visart, Rosalind and Stuart Read (N.Z.), Michael Reeve, Henri van Rooy (Rosendaal, Netherlands), Wendy Sarsby (Port Credit, Ontario), André Schepens (Brussels), Helga and Herbert Schmidt (W. Germany), Chris Sharpe (Mullewa, W. Australia), Barbara Singleton (USA), Lothar Springer (Münster), Ken and Judy Stevenson (Ottawa), Margaret Thoms and Neil Duncan (Australia), Andreas Weber (Wohlen, Switzerland), Nicholas Westwood and Julia Amies, and Dr. R. Clive Willis.

FALKLAND ISLANDS
(ISLAS MALVINAS)

The Falkland Islands lie 300 miles east and slightly to the north of the entrance to the Straits of Magellan. They form a land surface of 4,618 square miles. Their conformation, with fjord-like inlets and evidences of glacial action, shows some resemblance to Eastern Tierra del Fuego.

East Falkland, with its adjacent islands, has an area of 2,580 square miles; West Falkland, with its islands, 2,038 square miles. These two groups constitute the "Colony", as distinct from the Dependencies, far to the southward, which form part of Antarctica. They lie between lat. S 51° and 53° and between long. W 57° and 62°; approximately 1,000 miles due south of Montevideo and 480 miles north-east of Cape Horn. Mount Adam, the highest point of West Falkland, is 2,315 ft. high. Mount Usborne, the tallest peak of the Wickham Heights, on East Falkland, is 2,245 ft.

The 1,957 inhabitants (census, December 1972) are almost exclusively of pure British descent, and descendants of the early pioneers own the greatest part of the land. They are hard-working and thrifty. Half of them work and live on the sheep farms. The general health is good, despite inbreeding.

Early History

The Falklands were visited in 1592 by the English navigator Captain John Davis and in 1594 by Sir Richard Hawkins, who first described them in detail. Captain Strong landed upon them in 1690 and gave them their present name. During the first half of the 17th century adventurers from St. Malo visited the islands, and called them Iles Malouines in French, and Islas Malvinas in Spanish.

In 1764 they were taken by France and Bougainville planted a small colony at Port Louis. Two years later France admitted Spain's prior claim and ceded its rights. In 1767 England asserted its dominion, and a post was established in the West Falklands to survey the group. This was closed by the Spaniards in 1770 and restored in the following year, after threat of war. The post was abandoned in 1774, and there was no further formal occupation until 1820, when the "United Provinces of South America" hoisted their flag at Port Louis. This settlement was broken up in 1831 by an American warship owing to the illegal imprisonment, by a German in charge of the settlement, of some American sealers. In 1832 British warships were sent to reassert Britain's claim. Argentina refused to leave; its flag was struck, the British flag raised, and the Argentine garrison expelled. There has been no change of ownership since. But Argentina still claims the Malvinas, as it calls the Islands, and does not recognise British occupation.

Administration

The Falkland Islands Constitution provides for a Governor, an Executive Council, and a Legislative Council. The Legislative Council consists of the Governor (President), two ex-officio members, the Chief Secretary and the Financial Secretary; four Elected Members; and two Nominated Independent Members.

The Dependencies, with the exception of South Georgia and the South Sandwich Islands, now form a separate area known as the British Antarctic Territory. The Governor and Commander-in-Chief of the Falkland Islands (together with the Dependencies of South Georgia and the South Sandwich Islands) is also the High Commissioner for the British Antarctic Territory.

Justice and Courts There is a Supreme Court with the Chief Secretary acting as Judge at Stanley. The Falkland Islands Court of Appeal sits in London. A number of farm managers are Justices of the Peace and have power to deal with minor offences. In the Dependencies the Administrative Officer, who is stationed in South Georgia, is the Magistrate and sits at King Edward Point.

Education, which is free, is provided in Stanley by Government. A school owned by the Falkland Islands Company has been established at Darwin on the East Falkland. In other places education is carried on either in settlement schools or by itinerant teachers.

The Colony's annual total revenue is about £500,000.

Climate The islands are in the same latitude South as London is North but there is little similarity in climate apart from the hours of sunshine, which are almost identical. Mean monthly temperatures are uniformly lower than in London but London has both higher and lower extremes. There are no warm spells, such as occur in a good English summer; there may be cold outbreaks at almost any time of the year and the weather is generally changeable. The Islands are exposed and persistent strong winds spoil many otherwise pleasant days in the summer, though calm days are far from unknown. (The wind reaches gale force one day in five.) The annual rainfall is rather higher than in London. Some people find the strong winds trying though somewhat similar conditions are found in the exposed coastal districts of Scotland. Spring, autumn and winter clothing, as used in the United Kingdom, is suitable. There is no need for extra-heavy underclothes, and wind-proof outer clothing is much warmer.

The annual extreme range of temperature is from 13°F to 77°F (records for 30 years), but the normal range is from 20°F to 70°F, with a mean annual temperature of 42°F. The mean wind speed is 15 knots (17 m.p.h.) and the annual rainfall is about 28 inches.

Stanley, on East Falkland, in the north-east group, the only place of importance, has a fine inner and outer harbour. The population is about 1,100 and the houses are mostly of wood and iron. The bay, surrounded by low-lying hills covered with a brownish vegetation, looks somewhat like home to the native of Northern Scotland. It is very difficult to rent a house at Stanley, but there is one hotel, the *Upland Goose* (which has recently been modernized and enlarged—£12 a day full board), a good small guesthouse, *Byron House* (Mr. and Mrs. Dave Ryan), and the Tourist Office in Stanley (very friendly and helpful) can find private accommodation for visitors, if asked in advance, at £4-£7 a day, full board. Better not to arrive without prior arrangements for accommodation.

A good evening meal may be had at *Emma's Restaurant*, close to the public jetty.

The town has a small police force dressed in British uniforms; it has little more to do than see that drinking and traffic regulations are obeyed. There is a fully equipped hospital, a town hall and library and even a prison. *Upland Goose Hotel* has rooms, bars, and a fine trade in the short drinking hours available. The few shops sell everything from peanuts to penguin eggs. The roads are electrically lit but not all are paved. There is a race course. Government House and the little Cathedral are worth looking at, and so is the monument commemorating the battle of 1914. There is a small but interesting museum of the early settlers in the Falkland Islands Company Building; it is under the control of John Smith, who is extremely knowledgeable about the history of the Islands.

Tourists find the abundant wild-life of the Islands interesting. Cruise liners anchor in Port William, outside Stanley inner harbour, and landing is by motor launch: the vessels usually have their own fast launches which take about 15 minutes to reach the Public Jetty at Stanley. Several Land-Rover owners will drive visitors to the penguin rookeries and fine white beaches at Gypsy Cove and near Port Harriet. The more energetic may fancy climbing the local hills; they are not high but have considerable charm, in a rugged sort of way. Those who stay for some time can travel further afield: the Islands off the West Falklands are particularly attractive.

Travel Agent Outward Bound Tours, P.O. Box 178, Stanley (Cables: Boundbooks).

The normal method of travelling between the Islands these days is by Beaver seaplane, which costs £4.50 for take-off plus 10p a mile. It is often heavily booked in advance. Land-Rover and boats more readily available at weekends.

Points of Interest Sparrow Cove, where Brunel's great iron ship, the *Great Britain* lay beached for 33 years, is now the home of sealion and the Jackass penguin, which will on occasion fearlessly attack human beings, waving its small wings and crying out loud. Its eggs make excellent omelettes. Seals lie like hulks of timber on the smooth white beaches, twitching their noses, opening their large black eyes and scratching themselves before heaving into the sea, where they suddenly flash into supple questers for fish.

Bird-lovers should visit the small tussac-covered Kidney Island, just outside Stanley, and one of the wildlife sanctuaries. Rockhopper and Macaroni penguins, short-eared owls and numerous other birds may be seen. The Tourist Office in Stanley will inform you on transport; cost of boat is normally £15 irrespective of number of passengers. The tameness of most birds and animals in the Falklands is very noticeable. The shanty on the island has four bunks and is free, but no bedding is supplied. Take your own food, water, and cooking utensils. Between December and January is the nesting time. The most interesting wild-life reserve is at New Island (cost £10 a day to stay, including guide and Land-Rover). At Volunteer Point there is another fine nature reserve, including sea elephants and King Gentoo and Jackass penguins; permission to visit must be sought from owner, Mr. Osmond Smith, at Johnson's Harbour, who allows people to stay in a house at Volunteer Point for £2 per head, excluding food, but including fuel.

Communication with the outside world was maintained by the R.M.S. *Darwin* until December 1971, when she was withdrawn. On July 1, 1971, regular air and sea communications between Argentina and the Falkland Islands were agreed between British and Argentine representatives. Argentina provides a weekly (Monday) air link with Comodoro Rivadavia (operated by the Argentine airline LADE) for passengers, mails and freight and Britain is responsible for a shipping service. An airport is being built at Cape Pembroke, near Stanley.

Passengers travelling from Argentina will need a smallpox vaccination certificate and a Certificado Provisorio ("white card") from the Foreign Ministry, Arroyo 1034, Buenos Aires before they can buy an air ticket from LADE. Two passport photos are required. The ticket may be paid for in pesos because the Argentine authorities regard the flight as an internal one; buy return ticket in Argentina because it is much more expensive in the Falklands. Argentines and Falklanders travelling between each other's countries need the "white card".

There are no buses or taxis at the airstrip. The hotel collects expected guests; others will have no trouble getting a lift!

Landing   Two jetties for vessels drawing up to 14 ft.; landing by launch for larger vessels. All visitors need a passport and a smallpox vaccination certificate; the TB certificate previously required is not now necessary. No visa required for British Commonwealth and U.S. citizens.

Economy   In East Falkland the country is wild moorland, interspersed with rocks and stones. Building-stone of Devonian and Gondwana formations is found in different parts of the island. The soil, mostly soft peat, makes travel difficult. There are no proper roads except in Stanley, and communication is by horse, boat, seaplane and Land-Rovers or motor cycles. The islands are so well adapted for sheep-farming that the whole acreage has been devoted to that industry. The tussac, which grows to the height of 7 ft., yields fattening food for cattle; it has disappeared from the main East and West Falklands, but abounds on the smaller islands. There are only a few trees.

The poverty of the soil, isolation, and the intemperate climate make progress difficult. Re-grassing schemes are in progress. The islands carried only 10,063 cattle, 3,094 horses, and 31 head of swine in 1971-72. Sheep-farming is the only important activity, and there are some 634,160 sheep, yielding about 4.4 million lb. of wool for sale, chiefly on the London market.

Wool is the only important export: £1,095,448 in 1972. Sheepskin exports were 115,494 kg., valued at £18,206.

A single company farms almost one-third of the area and one-third of the sheep. The larger of the 23 remaining farms are owned by companies and farmed by resident managers. Small quantities of oats and potatoes are grown.

Cost of living is rather higher than it is in Britain. Freight necessarily adds to the prices of groceries, all imported. There is, however, no purchase tax, and only tobacco, wines, spirits and beer pay import duty. Small luxury goods on which the freight is correspondingly low are therefore much cheaper than in the U.K. A farm labourer's wages are about £120 a month.

Overseas Trade

	1969	1970	1971	1972
	£	£	£	£
Exports	908,751	803,105	676,967	1,118,379
Imports	508,977	610,435	606,973	651,579

The principal imports are hardware, groceries, timber, drapery and wearing material. The exports consist of wool, hides and sheepskins.

Mails   Following the Communications Agreement with Argentina, there is now a weekly air-mail service *via* Buenos Aires. Heavy parcel mails come direct from the U.K. four or five times a year. The inter-island service for mails is carried out by the inter-island vessel *Monsunen* and by the local Government Air Service, which uses "Beaver" float planes that can carry up to five passengers.

Currency   Local government notes and British and local coins. The local Treasury will change Argentine pesos and dollars, but sterling much preferred.

Wireless communication is now maintained with London and Argentina. There is a Government local broadcasting and relay system, and a telephone link with Buenos Aires operates between 1400 and 1700 (local time).

(We are grateful to Christine Czajkowski for some additional information. She tells us that it is not difficult to get a job on a farm in the shearing season (Nov.-Feb.), even though in general work permits are hard to get.)

Dependencies

The Falkland Islands Dependencies now cover only the island groups of South Georgia and South Sandwich.

South Georgia, in latitude 54½° S and longitude 36° to 38°W, has an area of about 1,450 square miles, and a small population composed entirely of scientists of the British Antarctic Survey, who man the scientific station. The commander of the station is the resident magistrate, who also acts as postmaster. Communications are supported entirely by the Survey.

South Georgia is a mass of high mountains covered with snow where not too precipitous. Observations extending over three years point to snowfall upon 124 days per annum. The valleys are filled with glaciers which descend in many cases to the sea. The coastal region is free from snow in summer when it is partially covered by vegetation.

British Antarctic Territory

The Territory was constituted on 3rd March, 1962, and includes that part of the Antarctic continent lying between 20°W and 80°W longitude and stretching south of 60°S to the South Pole, together with a number of islands. Of these, the South Shetland Islands and the South Orkney Islands are the chief groups. These territories were formerly part of the Falkland Islands Dependencies.

The total area of about 3 million square miles includes about 1 million square miles of sea, fairly accessible for whaling, sealing and fishing. The Weddell Sea, with its floes and icebergs, forms part of the area.

A chain of stations at which work on surveying, geology, meteorology, etc., is done, is maintained in the Territory. This work is carried out by the British Antarctic Survey. At each of the British Antarctic Survey Bases a member of the Survey Party acts as Magistrate.

The South Shetlands, about 400 miles SE of Cape Horn, have good summer harbours, including one at Port Foster on Deception Island, a place notable for its hot springs. On Deception Island there were British, Chilean and Argentine scientific bases.

BOLIVIA

BOLIVIA, straddling the Andes, is a land of gaunt mountains, cold desolate plains and now slowly developing semi-tropical and fertile lowlands. Its area of about 1,098,580 square kilometres makes it twice the size of Spain. It is one of two land-locked countries in Latin America, with Chile and Peru to the W, Brazil bordering it to N and E, and Argentina and Paraguay to the S. Of the population of 5,790,000 people some 70% are Indians, 25% mestizo and 5% European, a white minority which until 1952 owned most of the good land and the mines.

The Andean range, is at its widest—some 650 km.—in Bolivia. The Western Cordillera, the formidable barrier which separates Bolivia from Chile, has high peaks of between 5,800 and 6,500 metres and a number of active volcanoes along its crest. The passes across it are above 4,000 metres. The great rainless belt which stretches southwards over the continent along the northern coasts of Peru and Chile runs diagonally across this Western Cordillera and southern Bolivia.

To the E of this range lies a lofty plateau, the bleak, treeless, windswept Altiplano, much of it 4,000 metres above sea-level. It has a mean width of 140 km., is 840 km. long, and covers an area (in Bolivia) of 102,300 square km., or nearly 10% of the country. Its surface is by no means flat, for the Western Cordillera sends spurs into it which tends to partition it into basins. The northern part is the more inhabited; the southern part is parched desert and almost unoccupied, save for a mining town here and there. Nearly 75% of the population lives on it, for it contains most of the major cites. Lake Titicaca, at the northern end of the Altiplano, is an inland sea of 8,965 square km. at 3,810 metres: the highest navigable water in the world. Its maximum length and breadth are 171 and 64 km., and the greatest known depth is 280 metres. There are large annual variations between high and low water levels; 95% of the water flowing into it is lost by evaporation, making it more salty than most freshwater lakes.

There is enough rain for crops; the immense depth of the water keeps the lake at an even all-the-year-around temperature of 10°C, and modifies the extremes of winter and night temperatures on the surrounding land. There is therefore a large and prosperous farming population of Indians in this basin, tilling the fields and the hill terraces and tending their sheep and llamas. They grow barley, oca, potatoes and quinoa, and have entered the national economy more actively since the agrarian revolution of 1952. They are no longer forced to sell or give their surplus produce to absentee landlords, but have their own markets and new villages and towns along the main roads.

The Altiplano is a harsh, strange land, a dreary grey solitude except for the bursts of green after rain. But rain comes seldom, mostly in the storms of December and January, and when it does come, it is rapidly absorbed by the sandy soil, which soon reverts to its customary parched and arid state. The air is unbelievably clear—the whole Altiplano is a bowl of luminous light. A cold wind blows frequently in the afternoons causing dust storms. During the winter temperatures fall below freezing-point; there is frost every night in July and August, but during the day the bright sun raises temperatures over 20°C.

Tourists are fascinated by the animals of the Altiplano, not the small flocks of ill-kept sheep (though chalona, or dried and salted mutton, is considered a great delicacy), but the magnificent llamas, the alpacas, and the fur-bearing animals. Llamas serve as pack animals—they carry up to 22 kg. loads up to 20 km. a day and yield about 2½ kg. of wool when sheared at intervals of from two to five years. The alpaca, bred not for work but for wool, belongs to the same group; the two may be distinguished by differences in the texture of their coats and shape of their tails. Alpaca wool is traded at Charaña, on the Arica-La Paz railway, and at Puerto Acosta, on Lake Titicaca.

The vicuña, chinchilla and the red fox are the main wild animals. The vicuña, an untamed member of the family to which the llama and the alpaca belong, is found though in diminishing numbers, on the bleak pampas. It cannot be hunted, but its wool can be sold. It is smaller than the alpaca, and has a fine silky, tawny coloured wool.

Agriculture in the area is unrewarding: the potato and the oca (a vegetable tuber), eaten in the dehydrated form of chuño and tunta, are the main crops. Quinoa, a kind of millet, and cañava, a smaller and darker grain, are the main cereals; both are extremely nutritious. Chicha, the national intoxicant, is brewed from maize (corn). Edible fish (small boga, large white-fleshed pejerrey and rainbow and salmon trout) are widely sold in the towns of the Altiplano.

But far more important to the economy of the Altiplano than agriculture is mining. Just S of the railway from La Paz to Arica is Corocoro (4,500 inhabitants), which supplies most of Bolivia's copper, found here in its "native" form and long used by the Indians. And 210 km. S of La Paz along the passageway at the base of the Eastern Cordillera is Oruro (110,000 inhabitants), where a low belt of hills supplies tin, copper, silver and tungsten. Oruro is important also as a rail centre: the main line sends out two branches here, one to the tin mines of Uncia in the Eastern Cordillera, and one to the basin of Cochabamba on the far eastern slops of the Puna.

From this plateau rises, to the E, the sharp façade of the Eastern Cordillera. As luck would have it there is a gently graded passageway along the plateau at the foot of the Eastern Cordillera from Lake Titicaca, in the N, to the Argentine frontier, in the S. From Viacha, near La Paz, the main trunk-line of the Bolivian railways runs along this passageway to Villazón, with connections to Salta and Buenos Aires.

The giant masses of the northern parts of the Eastern Cordillera rise to very great heights in the Cordillera Real to the east of Lake Titicaca: four

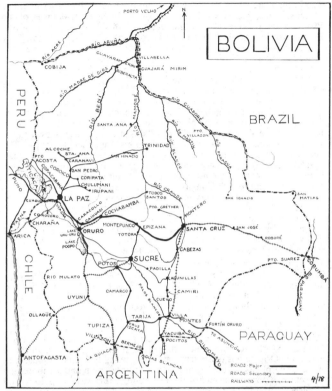

peaks soar to above 6,000 metres. This magnificent sight can be seen on a clear day from the top of a ridge on the Titicaca-La Paz highway. Their far sides fall away to the NE, very sharply, towards the Amazon basin. These heavily forested north-eastern slops are deeply indented by the fertile valleys of the Nor Yungas and Sud Yungas.

In these rich tropical valleys, drained by the Río Beni and its tributaries, cacao, coffee, sugar, coca and a wealth of tropical fruits are grown. But the problem of transport to the consuming centre of La Paz is formidable: the connecting all-weather road, hair-raising in places, climbs 3,430 metres in 80 km. to surmount La Cumbre pass standing at 4,650 metres within 24 km. of La Paz.

But from a point just N of Cochabamba to the S the Eastern Cordillera is tilted, not to the NE, but to the E. This part of the Eastern Cordillera rises abruptly in sharp escarpments from the Altiplano, and then flattens out to an easy slope eastwards to the plains: an area known as the Puna.

The Puna is, however, itself the pediment of an occasional soaring range of peaks. The streams which flow across the Puna are tributaries of the Río Grande flowing NE to the basin of the Amazon, and of the Pilcomayo flowing SE through the Chaco to the River Plate system. They cut increasingly deep incisions as they gather volume until, to the E, the Puna is eroded to little more than a high remnant between the river valleys. These valleys deeply incising the surface of the eastern-sloping Puna are densely inhabited; in the flat lands ribboning along them, or in occasional more open basins, agriculture is intensively practised and a variety of grain crops and fruits grown. All these semi-tropical mountain valleys are known as Yungas: the generic name is not confined to the valleys of the Provinces of Nor and Sud Yungas to the E of La Paz. Rainfall in the Yungas is from 700 to 800 mm. a year, as opposed to the 400 to 700 mm. of the northern Altiplano and much less further S. The heaviest rain is during December, January and February. The mean average temperture is between 16° and 18°C, but in spite of a high humidity the Yungas are not unhealthy. Chulumani in the Sud Yungas and Coroico in the Nor Yungas are popular resorts.

Typical valleys are the very fertile basins in which Cochabamba, Sucre, and Tarija lie. These send food and cattle to the towns of the Altiplano, but the valleys have often no way of doing so. The inhabitants of this area are 'mostly either mestizos or whites, but the basins and long ribbons of valley farmland are isolated, and transport to the areas where they might sell their produce is only now being developed.

The Lowland Tropics, streching from the foothills of the Eastern Cordillera to the frontiers with Brazil to the NE and E and with Paraguay and Argentina to the SE and S, take up 70% of the total area of Bolivia, but contain only a very thin sprinkling of its population. The land slopes gradually from about 450 metres at the foothills to 200 metres or less at the frontiers. Rainfall is high but seasonal, and large stretches suffer from alternate flooding and drought. The climate is hot, ranging from 23° to 25°C in the S and to 27°C in the N. Occasional cold dust-laden winds from the S—the *surazos*—lower the temperature considerably. In the N and E the Oriente has dense tropical forest, possibly 500,000 square km. of it. Open plains covered with rough pasture, swamp and scrub occupy the centre. Towards the end of the 18th century this was a populous land of plenty; for 150 years Jesuit missionaries had controlled the area and guided it into a prosperous security. A symbol of their great effort is the Cathedral at San José de Chiquitos: a gem of elegance and dignity. But the Jesuits were expelled; 250 years of maladministration, despoilation and corruption reduced the area to lethargy.

This once rich land, drained by the Madre de Dios, Beni and Mamoré rivers into the Madeira, a tributary of the Amazon, was isolated from the rest of the country. It is as difficult to get at from the E as from the W, for there are rapids and falls in the Madeira which limit navigation. In its heart lie the seasonally inundated tropical Llanos de Mojos, ringed in by rain forest or semi-deciduous tropical forest—230,000 square km. with only 120,000 people. Roads and river connections are now being improved; a road from Cochabamba to Todos Santos was opened in 1976, and one from La Paz to Trinidad—a great event—in 1977. Meat is already flown from Trinidad, capital of Beni Department, and from air strips in the area, to the consuming centres at La Paz, Oruro, and Cochabamba.

Much the same could be said of the forests and plains beyond the Eastern Cordillera as they sweep S towards the Pilcomayo River, getting progressively less rain and merging into a comparatively dry southern land of scrub forest and arid savannah. The main city of this area is Santa Cruz de la Sierra, founded in the 16th century, now becoming the centre of a growing farming area. Here conditions favour the growing of sugar-cane, rice, oil plants and citrus fruit. The plains to the E are mainly grazing lands with small areas under cultivation. But in this area are extensive oil, gas, and iron-ore deposits, possibly Bolivia's greatest asset when developed.

Mining in the Eastern Cordillera The Spaniards of Peru discovered the Cerro Rico in 1545. It is a mountain rising out of the Puna to a height of 4,780 metres, and is almost a solid mass of ore containing tin, silver, bismuth and tungsten. The Spaniards, interested only in silver, built Potosí at its base, 4,065 metres above sea level. The city grew till it had a population of 150,000, but rapidly dwindled after silver had been found in Peru and Mexico. It remained a dead town till a demand for tin arose early this century.

Tin also accounts for the busy mining communities in the Cordillera to the SE of Oruro: the ex-Patiño mines at Catavi, to which there is a branch railway from Oruro, produce nearly half the tin of Bolivia. Silver is still mined or extracted from the tailings left by past generations, and variable amounts of lead, bismuth, antimony, tungsten and zinc from pockets in the Cordillera are exported. Large deposits of silver have been found south of the Altiplano, near Lípez, and mines are being reopened two centuries after the Spaniards abandoned them.

Communications After centuries of isolation new roads are now integrating the food-producing eastern zones with the bulk of the population living in the towns of the Altiplano or the westward-facing slopes of the Eastern Cordillera. The communications between the mining towns and the coast have always been better. Under Spanish rule there were four great trails in use within the country: three of them led through passes in the Western Cordillera to the Pacific; the fourth led from La towns and the coast have always been better. Under Spanish rule there were four great trails in use within the country: three of them led through passes in the Western Cordillera to the Pacific; the fourth led from La Paz along the passage-way at the foot of the Eastern Cordillera southwards into Argentina: it was along this trail that the silver from Potosí was taken to Buenos Aires for shipment. At the turn of the century, railways replaced the llamas and mules which carried the minerals to the ports. By far the shortest is the one from La Paz to Arica (Chile), completed in 1913. Arica is now an international port, with a Bolivian custom-house; it ships a large part of the exports together with Antofagasta (Chile) and Matarani (Peru).

Bolivia has 3,524 km. of railway, all of it Government owned. All is of one-metre gauge. The national highway system at the end of 1974 totalled 37,523 km., of which only 3.1% were paved and 17.5% gravel-surfaced.

The People The racial composition varies from place to place: pure Indian around Lake Titicaca; more than half Indian at La Paz; 3 out of 4 mestizo or European in the Yungas, Cochabamba, Santa Cruz and Tarija, the most European of all. Only 50% of children of school age are attending school. There are State universities at La Paz, Sucre,

Cochabamba, Santa Cruz, Oruro, Potosí and Tarija, and a Catholic university at La Paz.

Most of the population lives in adobe huts and medical services are almost confined to the towns and mining camps; birth rate, 45, general death rate, 20 per 1,000, but infantile mortality is 333 per 1,000 during the first year. Epidemics are comparatively rare on the Altiplano; malaria and yellow fever have been conquered in the Oriente. About 32% is urban. Annual population growth = 2.8%; urban growth = 3.1%. Life expectancy at birth: 45.7 years for men, 47.9 years for women.

The Indians are mainly composed of two groups: those in the north of the Altiplano who speak the guttural Aymará, and those elsewhere, who speak Quechua, the Inča tongue. Outside the big cities few of them speak much Spanish, but knowledge of Spanish is increasing. They have become adapted to the scarcity of oxygen by an amazing lung development; they have more red corpuscles in their blood than those who live at sea-level.

The most obdurate of Bolivian ploblems has always been that the main mass of population is, from a strictly economic viewpoint, in the wrong place, the poor Altiplano and not the potentially rich Oriente, and that the Indians lived largely outside the monetary system on a self-sufficient basis. But the land reform of 1952 has brought about dramatic changes. Isolated communities continue the old life but in the agricultural area around Lake Titicaca, the valleys of Cochabamba, the Yungas and the irrigated areas of the south, most peasants now own their own land, however small the plot may be; in most areas they sell far more produce than before, though land productivity has increased only in those areas where new techniques or improved seeds have been used. Their increased income is reflected in corrugated iron roofs for their homes instead of thatch, in the widespread use of bicycles and transistor radio sets. Traditional social structures are being rapidly modified.

The Indian women retain their traditional costume, with petticoats of bright, uncommon hues and in the highlands wear, apparently from birth, a flattish brown or grey bowler. This they take off on entering a church just like a man. In Cochabamba they wear a white top hat of ripolined straw. Many Indians chew the coca leaf, which makes them feel as if they had had something to eat and gives a measure of oblivion. On feast days they drink with considerable application, wear the most sensational masks and dance till they drop.

N.B.   Remember to refer to rural Indians not as "Indios" (an insult) but as "campesinos" (peasants).

History

At Tiahuanaco (Tiwanaku), near Lake Titicaca, stands a gateway and some shattered terraces and roofless walls; the remains of a pre-Incaic civilization which the archaeologists are trying to piece together. The primative Aymará-speaking Indians in this area seem to have been subjected, around A.D. 600, to influences from the coast of Peru and to have emerged into a second phase of civilization characterized by massive stone buildings and monuments, exquisite textiles, pottery and metalwork. This phase seems to have been ended abruptly by some unexplained calamity around A.D. 900. When the Quechua-speaking Incas of Cuzco conquered the area around A.D. 1200, they found the Aymarás at Tiahuanaco living amongst ruins they could no longer explain. The Aymarás resisted obstinately and were not finally conquered until the latter part of the 15th century under the reign of Inca Túpac Yupangi (1471-93). Even so, they kept most of their traditional social structures and language, and fought for the Incas under their own officers. Only religion was formally imposed by the Incas.

Francisco Pizarro landed in Peru in 1532. Six years later Spain conquered Bolivia, and the next year Sucre (then Charcas), still the official capital, was founded. By 1559 Bolivia had become the *audiencia* of Charcas, in the Vice-Royalty of Peru, for it had become extremely important for the Spaniards after the discovery of the silver mountain at Potosí in 1545.

The excellent Inca communications and economic organization fell into ruin. Revolutionary movements against the colonial rule of the Spaniards began earlier in Bolivia than anywhere else; there were revolts by the mestizos at La Paz in 1661, and at Cochabamba in 1730; by Indians at Sucre, Cochabamba, Oruro and La Paz from 1776 to 1780, when they were defeated when besieging Sucre. La Paz was in their hands in 1780 for a few days. In 1809 the University of San Francisco Xavier, at Sucre, called for the liberty of all the Latin American colonies from Spain. Several attempts were made to liberate Bolivia in the next few years, but they failed. Finally, on December 9, 1824, Bolívar's general, Sucre, with the help of a large British contingent, won the decisive battle of Ayacucho and invaded what is now Bolivia.

But the Spanish general Olañeta still resisted. Sucre defeated him finally at the battle of Tumusla on April 2, 1825. On February 9, when he had entered La Paz, Sucre had already promulgated the famous decree of independence, convoking a deliberative assembly to discuss the political future of the country. Sucre was for independence from both Peru and La Plata; his second in command, Santa Cruz, was for the traditional union with Peru; Bolívar was in two minds. But finally Sucre had his way and Bolivia was declared independent. On August 25, 1825, Bolívar named the new country after himself. In 1828, when Sucre left the country, Santa Cruz became President; pursuing his dream of amalgamation he proclaimed a Peruvian-Bolivian confederation in 1836, but Chile and Argentina intervened; there was a revolution in Bolivia, and in 1839 Santa Cruz was overthrown and the confederation dissolved.

In a century and a half of unsettled history since, Bolivia has suffered a grievous contraction of its territory. It had never very actively worked its nitrate fields in the Atacama desert. In the War of the Pacific (1879-1883) Bolivia in alliance with Peru fought the Chileans for the right to hold this wealthy desert. After a year the Bolivians withdrew, but, all the same, Chile took over the desert and the port of Antofagasta, though it later compensated by building Bolivia the railway between Arica and La Paz. Railways traded for valuable territory has been Bolivia's fate. A railway for Bolivia was Argentina's return for annexing some of the Chaco. When Brazil annexed the rich Acre Territory in 1903, Bolivia was compensated by yet another railway, but the Madeira-Mamoré line never reached its destination, Riberalta, and proved of little use; the line was closed in 1972. A fouth railway, completed in the 1950s connects Santa Cruz in East-Central Bolivia with Corumbá in Brazil.

There was not even an unbuilt railway to compensate Bolivia for its next loss. Constant disputes between Bolivia and Paraguay over the Chaco led to open warfare between 1928 and 1930, and again between

1933 and 1935. In 1938, by arbitration, Bolivia lost to Paraguay three-quarters of the Chaco, but obtained a doubtfully valuable outlet to the Río Paraguay. Bolivia's failure to occupy its empty spaces is the explanation for these losses.

The moral results of this last defeat had revolutionary consequences. As a culmination to over a decade of disorder, President Villaroel was shot and hanged in La Paz in 1946 and Víctor Paz Estenssoro, his minister of finance, fled to Buenos Aires. His party, the Movimento Nacionalista Revolucionario (MNR) was outlawed, but it was actually voted into power again in the presidential election of 1951. A military junta, however, intervened, and the new president, Paz Estenssoro, was not allowed to return from exile. In April, 1952, a popular revolution overthrew the military junta: Paz Estenssoro returned as president. His government, a coalition of MNR and the Labour Party, committed itself to a profound social revolution, announcing three decrees which altered fundamentally the social structure of the country: (1) the expropriation and the nationalisation of the tin mines; (2) universal suffrage without literacy or income qualifications; and (3) a policy of land reform and redistribution of the large estates. This Revolution was the 179th Bolivian rising, and almost the only one with far-reaching results. Hernán Siles Zuazo, a revolutionary leader and vice president under Paz from 1952-56, was president from 1956-60. During his term the economy was stabilized. Paz Estenssoro was again elected president from 1960-64, but shortly after beginning his third term was overthrown in 1964 by General Barrientos, killed in an air crash in 1969. An army coup replaced his successor, President Siles Salinas, with General Ovando Candia, who was overthrown in October 1970 by left-wing General Torres. This latter was ousted in turn in August 1971 by right-wing General Hugo Banzer Suárez, the present President, who has said that there will be elections in July 1978, for a new President, Vice-President and constituent assembly.

The Constitution of 1967 vests executive power in the President, elected by popular vote for a term of 4 years; he cannot be re-elected. He nominates the Cabinet. The Congress of two chambers—Senate and Chamber of Deputies—meets at La Paz on August 6. Senators, three for each Department, are elected for 6 years, one-third retiring every two years. Deputies are elected for 4 years, one-half retiring every two years. There are nine departments; each is in charge of a Delegate appointed by the President. Supreme political, administrative, and military authority in each Department is vested in a prefect appointed by the President. The Constitution has been suspended since 1969.

There is universal suffrage. Foreigners may be naturalised after a residence period of three years. The State no longer supports the Roman Catholic religion. The death penalty is abolished.

Bolivia has, in effect, two capitals. Although Sucre is the legal capital, La Paz is in almost all respects the actual capital. It is there the President and his official advisers live; the national Congress meets there, and it is the residence of the foreign diplomats accredited to the Bolivian Government. On the other hand, the Supreme Court still holds its sessions in Sucre.

La Paz, the highest capital in the world, lies at 3,600 metres in a natural basin or canyon; it is sunk about 370 metres below the level of the Altiplano in its north-eastern corner. The Spaniards chose this odd place for a city on October 20, 1548, to avoid the chill winds of the plateau, and because they had found gold in the Choqueyapu River which runs through the canyon. The mean average temperature is 10°C, but it varies greatly during each day, and the nights are cold. It rains almost every day from December to February, but the sun usually shines for several hours. The rest of the year the weather is mostly clear and sunny. Snow is rare. At first the visitor will probably feel some discomfort, known as *soroche* (altitude sickness), from the rarified air; a few hours in bed when you arrive will put that right. Tea made from coca leaves (mate de coca) is also recommended; if the discomfort persists many people take 'Micoren' tablets, a respiratory stimulant (though visitors with heart problems should probably consult a physician). According to the recent census, the population of La Paz is over 650,000, half of it Indian.

Mount Illimani, with its snow-covered peaks, towers over the city. The La Paz river (Río Choqueyapu), whose headwaters have cut across the Eastern Cordillera and now collect streams which once flowed into Lakes Titicaca and Poopó, runs through the city. The streets along the canyon slope gently, but those which rise from them towards the heights are often steep and slippery. Most of the Indians live in the higher terraces. Below is the business quarter, the government offices, the restaurants and the university. The wealthier residential district is lower still: strung from Sopocachi to the bed of the valley at Obrajes, 5 km. from the centre and 500 metres lower than Plaza Murillo. Beyond Obrajes are the elegant districts of Calacoto and La Florida. The main sport and social clubs have moved to these districts.

There is some Colonial building left, but much of La Paz—and there are many skyscrapers—is modern, with a variety of corrugated iron and red tiles on the roofs, Plaza Murillo, on the north-eastern side of the river, is the traditional centre; facing its formal gardens are the huge Cathedral (modern but very graceful); the Presidential Palace in Italian renaissance style, usually known as the Palacio Quemado—burnt palace—twice gutted by fire in its stormy 125-year history; and on the E side the Congreso Nacional where the Senate and House of Representatives meet. In the square is the lamp-post from which President Villarroel was hanged after being lynched by a mob in 1946. Across from the Cathedral on Calle Socabaya is the Palace of the Condes de Arana, now the Museo Nacional del Arte. Calle Comercio, running cross-wise past the Plaza, has most of the stores and shops. On Av. Bolívar (to which Mount Illimani provides a backdrop), continuing the Av. Camacho, is the Central Market (called "Mercado Camacho"), a picturesque medley of Indian victuals and vendors presiding raucously over stalls, their black braids topped by hard-brimmed bowler hats. Av. Camacho leads to the residential district of Miraflores.

The Prado (Avenida 16 de Julio is its proper name), runs from Plaza Venezuela, with a statue of Bolívar, to the Plaza del Estudiante, which is half a block from University), with a statue of Sucre. Some distance beyond the Plaza del Estudiante is a small park, the Montículo, on the height called the Montículo de Sopocachi, with a fine view of the city and its surrounding mountains.

The Prado, main artery of La Paz, is a wide, double roadway on either side of a grassed promenade beautified with shrubs and flower beds. People stroll along it at sunset each day, and around 1100 on Sunday it is very full, with a band usually playing.

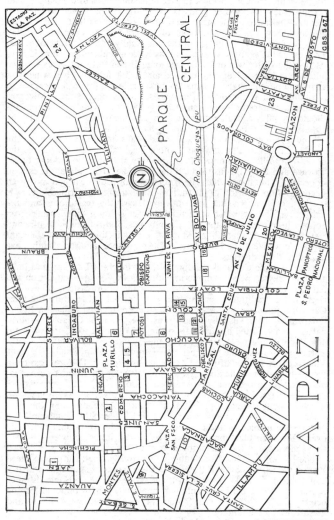

ROUGH SKETCH

Key to map: page 161

From the Plaza Venezuela, Avenida Mariscal Santa Cruz leads to the Plaza San Francisco and to the church and monastery of San Francisco, well worth seeing (a church of the colonial period, richly decorated around native and religious themes, where Indian weddings can be seen on Sats. 1000-1200). SW from Plaza San Francisco runs Calle Sagárnaga, with rows of small shops which specialise in handicrafts (ponchos, alpaca rugs, wall hangings, devil masks, wood carvings, etc.) for visitors. Going higher still up Sagárnaga is a local market and, turning right on Max Paredes heading west one reaches Avenida Buenos Aires, one of the liveliest streets in the Indian quarter.

Museo Nacional de Arte, across from the Cathedral on Calle Socabaya, housed in an 18th century baroque palace of the Condes de Arana, with beauitiful exterior and patio. It has a fine collection of Colonial paintings and also exhibits the works of comtemporary local artist. Open 1030-1830 weekdays; but 1030-1300 on Saturdays, closed Sundays. Admission US$0.25. There are other exhibits at the Galería Municipal, on Colón, and at Galería Naira, on Sagárnaga.

Museo Tiahuanaco (Tiwanaku), or National Museum of Archaeology, easily reached by the flight of stairs by María Auxili church on the Prado. This modern building, simulating the Tiahuanaco style, contains splendid collections of the arts and crafts of ancient Tiahuanaco and items from the eastern jungles. Open Monday to Friday 1030-1830, Saturdays 0900-1200, Sundays 1030-1230. Admission US$0.15.

Museo Semisubterráneo, in front of National Stadium, with restored statues and other artefacts from Tiahuanaco. It's in a sunken garden out of doors, and much may be seen from street level.

Museo Murillo, on Calle Jaén, was originally the home of Pedro Domingo Murillo, one of the leaders of the abortive La Paz revolution for independence from Spain of July 16, 1809; he was later hanged, uttering these prophetic words on his way to the gallows 'No one will be able to extinguish the torch which I have lit.' This colonial house has been carefully restored and has a good collection of paintings, furniture and national costumes of the period; there is also a special room dedicated to herbal medicine and magic. Open 0930-1230, 1400-1800 on weekdays; Saturdays 1000-1300, 1500-1800, closed Sundays and Mondays. Admission US$0.25. Callle Jaén, a picturesque colonial street with many craft shops, is well worth seeing for itself.

Museo Nacional de Etnografía y Folklore, on Calle Ingavi 916, is housed in the palace of the Marqueses de Villaverde and is currently under restoration.

Mineral Museum Banco Minero, Comercio 1290, 3rd floor. Open Mon.-Fri. 0900-1300, 1400-1630.

Hotels

Hotel			Address	Telephone	Single US$	Double US$
Sheraton	..	..	Av. Arce	n.a.	32.00	38.00
Crillón		..	Plaza Isabel La Católica	52121	24.15	33.00
Copacabana	..		Av. 16 de Julio 1802	52244	22.85	27.80
El Dorado	..	..	Av. Villazón	26952	22.85	27.95
Sucre	..	..	Av. 16 de Julio 1787	55080	19.95	24.45
Gloria	..		Av. Genaro Sanjines	n.a.	20.00	25.00
La Paz	..	..	Av. Camacho 1277	55292	22.85	27.15
La Hostería	..	..	Calle Bueno 138	22925	17.55	23.40
Libertador	..	..	Calle Obispo Cárdenas 1421	43360	25.15	31.75

Key to Map

1. House of Murillo (Museum); 2. Villaverde Palace; 3. Museo Nacional del Arte; 4. Cathedral; 5. Government Palace; 6. Legislative Palace; 7. General Post Office; 8. Banco Central; 9. Mercado Lanza; 10. San Francisco Church; 11. Braniff; 12. *Hotel La Paz*; 13. Municipality; 14. United States Embassy; 15. Citibank; 16. Dirección Nacional de Turismo; 18. Lloyd Aéreo Boliviano; 19. Mercado Camacho; 20. *Sucre Palace Hotel*; 21. Tiahuanaco Museum; 22. Municipal Library; 23. University; 24. Parque Prehistórico Tiahuanaco (Museo Semisubterráneo).

The new *Sheraton,* opened in 1977, is reported to be excellent, with a good restaurant. This aside, the *Libertador* and the *La Paz* are nearest the business section and are reported to be the best; the *El Dorado,* across from the University, and the *Gloria* are also brand new. The *Sucre* gives good value and the *Hostería* is small but also good value. A Holiday Inn is under construction. Rates are without meals but include taxes and service charges which run up to 27% in total. For people staying several weeks, often looking for permanent residences, boarding houses (*pensiones*) are popular. Several can be recommended; *Pensión Sopocachi,* Francisco Bedregal 2941; *Pensión Crespo,* Av. 6 de Agosto; *Pensión Colonial,* Av. Arce, and *Pensión Bedoya* (more expensive) also on Av. Arce, 2047. For those wanting to stay in the suburbs at a lower altitude there is the *Hotel Calacoto,* Calle 13 on the corner of Bustamente, in Calacoto, US$15 s, US$18 d. A recommended medium-priced hotel is the *Panamericano,* Manco Kapac 454, clean, US$10.50 d.

Economy: *City Hotel,* on the Prado, No. 1598, US$3 s, US$6.50 d; *Hotel Newman,* Loayza 442, US$2 p.p; *Hotel Austria,* Yanacocha 531, US$3 p.p. is a favourite. *Hotel Torino,* Socabaya 457, friendly, central, US$2; *Hotel Búlgaro,* Colón 570, US$1.80, good value, clean; *Alojamiento Ideal,* Av. Mcal Santa Cruz 1058, US$2; *Hotel España,* Av. 6 de Agosto 2047, US$2.75, clean, opposite University. Cheap hotels located more in the Indian quarter include: *Hotel Grand,* Evaristo Valle 127, friendly, US$2.60 with shower; *Hotel Andes,* Av. Manco Kapac 364, US$2 p.p., good; *Hotel Oruro,* Plaza Alonso de Mendoza, US$7.50 d; *Hotel Tumusla,* Tumusla 580, near Indian market, new, US$2.25 p.p.; *Hotel Avenida,* Av. Montes 862, US$3.25 with shared bath; *Hotel Italia,* Av. Manco Kapac 303, US$2 p.p., hot shower; *Alojamiento Central,* Av. Manco Kapac 384, US$1.25 p.p., good value; *Residencial Universo,* Inca 175, US$2 p.p., clean, friendly, recommended; *Hotel Illimani,* Av, Illimani 1817, US$1.50 p.p., cheap; *Alojamiento Buenos Aires,* Passaje Tumusla 651, US$3.50, hot showers; trucks to all parts of Bolivia leave from its yard.

Motel   Kori-Tambo, Achocalla, Tel. 27078.

Restaurants in La Paz can be roughly divided into two categories: either they serve international cuisine and are expensive or they serve local dishes and are fairly cheap. There are no really outstanding international-type restaurants though many can be recommended. The restaurants with international cooking are to be found mainly on three streets, the Av. 16 de Julio (the Prado), Av. 6 de Agosto and Av. 20 de Octubre. Service charges of up to 10% are usually included on the bill but it is customary to leave a few pesos anyway as a tip. (Street numbers given in brackets.)

Av. 16 de Julio; there is the *Hotel Sucre* restaurant, which possibly serves the best food in town and has a pleasant view of the Prado, a favourite for lunch (fixed 4-course lunch for US$3.50 excluding taxes); there is also a good snack bar downstairs (all the other large hotels also have fairly good restaurants). In the expensive range on the Prado is the *Las Vegas* (1616 top floor), with good view of the city; the *Restaurant España* (1698) serves good paellas; *Maxim's* (1577), good international cooking; the *City Hotel Restaurant* expensive, with shows Friday and

Saturday nights. Slightly cheaper restaurants include the German restaurant *Bavaria* (1732); the *Daiquiri* (1695), excellent value, fine grills (parrilladas) and local dishes; the *China* (1549), good Chinese food.

There are many snack bars: there is the *Confitería Pick* on the 2nd floor of the Alameda Building, tallest building in La Paz, and a good pizzeria, *El Mesón de la Pizza,* on the ground floor; the *Scaramouch,* next to the *Daiquiri,* offers good value; the *Tokio* (1832), good for salteñas; *Snack El Prado* (1468) has cheap snacks; *Confitería Elis* (1497), with good plate lunches, breakfasts and pastries. The open air café next door to the *Hotel Copacabana* is popular with the Paceños at noon to sip beer and watch the people go by.

Off the Prado, on Calle Campero, one can recommend the *Club de la Prensa,* set in a pleasant garden, especially for Saturday lunch when there are guitarists; the food is typical Bolivian and moderately priced and the company is boisterous. The *Club Alemán,* off Calle Reyes Ortiz, is expensive but good; may need a member to get in. The *Carreta,* an Argentine-type restaurant at Batallón Colorados 32, serves very good steaks, a favourite of businessmen for lunch. Off the latter street at Capital Ravelo 2070 (Edificio Venezuela, 2nd floor), is *El Tropero* which serves very good grills, very expensive.

On the continuation of the Prado going west, on Av. Mariscal Santa Cruz, is *Los Escudos,* Munich-type bierkeller with fixed 4-course lunch for US$2, food and shows Friday and Saturday nights. *Restaurant Parrillada Las Tablitas,* at Mariscal Santa Cruz 1283, excellent steaks and cheap. At Av. Ayacucho 206 is the *Restaurant Internacional,* expensive, a lunch-time favourite of local businessmen and has good shows Friday and Saturday nights.

At the other end of the Prado, on Plaza del Estudiante, is a Chinese restaurant, the *Hongkong* (1916), and at Av. Villazón 1936 is *Julio,* where lunch or supper costs only around US$0.75.

Av. 6 de Agosto: starting at the top end and heading southeast, there is the *Snack Shop* (2012), good hamburgers, doughnuts and milkshakes; *La Créperie* (2048), French-owned, wide variety of pancakes and good pizzas, stays open late; *Oriental* (2179), good moderately-priced Chinese food; *Chifa Casa Lin* (2420), *Casa Argentina* (2535), good parrilladas; and the *Círculo Italiano* (2595), good Italian meals.

Av. 20 de Octubre: there is *Zlato's* (1824), regular international cooking; *Max Bieber's Restaurant and Tea-Room,* food very good, including good pastries, moderate prices (2080); *Chifa Gran Muralla* (2172); *Chifa Pletora* on corner of Rosendo Justiniano; *Churrasquería* (2344), good steaks; the Chinese restaurant *Patito Pekin* (2463), good, not cheap. *In the shopping and business district:* there are numerous snack bars and cheap restaurants, one can recommend *Marilyn,* corner of Potosí and Socabaya, good salteñas and 3-course lunches for US$1; *Rayito de Luna,* Comercio 1072, is also good; *Daiyo,* Comercio 801; *Caravelle,* Mercado 1136, very clean, very good salteñas and snacks; *Los Pinos,* on Potosí between Colón and Ayacucho, rather dingy but gives good meals for US$1; next door is *Paulo,* new; *Salón de Té Rosedal,* Socabaya 311, offers 3-course lunches for US$0.75 and snacks; *Confitería Club La Paz,* at the junction of the Prado and Comercio, offers good teas; on Calle Loayza is the basement *Pizzería Verona,* good pizzas, fixed 3 course lunches for US$1.50. The restaurant *Club Hogar Austríaco* on Yanacocha is fairly cheap and recommended for local dishes. *Lasky,* on Plaza Venezuela, offers huge helpings and varied meals for less than US$2. *Restaurant Huari,* corner of Manco Kapac and Tumusla, offers good value. Vegetarian restaurant at *Hotel Torino.* Rather attractive, but out of the way, is the *Naira,* on Calle Sagárnaga 161, French-run 'fondue' restaurant, expensive, do not be put off by dingy entrance.

Comedor Popular for the strictly limited budgets, cheap but filling local meals around US$0.30, available at Camacho and Loayza markets. Bread from street vendors.

N.B. Bolivian highland cooking is usually very tasty and often *picante,* which means highly spiced with chilli peppers. Local specialities, which visitors should try, include *salteñas* (hot tasty meat or chicken pies served only in the mornings), *empanadas* (cheese pies) and *humintas* (corn pies); *pukacapas* are piquant cheese pies. Recommended main dishes include *sajta de pollo* hot spicy chicken with *chuño* (dehydrated potatoes), *parrillada* (a Bolivian kind of mixed grill), *fricase* (juicy pork dish served with chuño), *silpancho* (fried breaded meat with eggs, rice and bananas). The soups are also good, especially a *chairo* soup made of meat, vegetables, chuño and ají (hot pepper) to which the locals like to add *llajua* or *halpahuayca* (hot sauces always set on restaurant tables) to make it even more *picante*.

Entertainment   Best entertainment for visitors are the folk shows, only on Fridays and Saturday nights. Tourists should visit the *Kori-Thika* folk club, Juan de la Riva 1435 (Tel.: 52151); entrance around US$1.50, charge for drinks US$1.50 each; very good, make reservations, shows start around 2200. Folk show at *Pena Naira*, on Sagárnaga next door to restaurant, also on Fri. and Sat. evenings. The restaurants mentioned above which have shows are also worth seeing. At these folk shows, visitors will be able to listen to the wide variety of local musical instruments, the different types of flutes, including the *queña*, and the *charango*, a small guitar with five strings, the back often being made from the hide of an armadillo. There are a few discotheques of which the best are *Michelangelo's*, Av. 20 de Octubre 1832, and the *Viejoteca*, in Obrajes, which also has shows at week-ends. For drinks, there is *Giorgissimo* on Loayza, which is very popular and also serves meals, *Charlie's Bar* on Av. 6 de Agosto, and *St. George's Pub* at Av. 20 de Octubre 2019. There is a jazz club, *La Cueva del Jazz*, Calle Jáuregui 2280. There are some good cinemas, films being mainly in English. La Paz has a resident ballet and symphony orchestra but no theatre company. The Coloseo Cerrado stages folk events on Sunday afternoons.

Camping   No organized site, but the river gorge below the suburb of La Florida has been recommended; also Chinguihue, 10 km from the city.

Air Services   Lloyd Aéreo Boliviano (LAB) and TAM (the air force and not recommended) fly to the main cities and towns, fares being comparatively low. LAB, who are non-IATA members, also have international flights which are slightly cheaper than the IATA flights, e.g. US$151 to São Paulo and US$299 to Miami.

Dirección Nacional de Turismo   Office on the central island of the Prado (Plaza Venezuela end). Most helpful.

Travel Agents   Crillon Tours, Av. Camacho 1223 (Tel.: 20222), expensive and reputation slipping; Tur-Bol, Mercado 1385 (Tel.: 24873); Turismo Balsa, Av. 16 de Julio 1787 (Tel.: 53927, 27844); Pacific Tours; and Martin (Travel). Taveline Tours, English-speaking at Av. Camacho 1404, will cater for the unusual request. See also names and addresses under "Exchange Houses", page 166.

Airport   El Alto, on plain above La Paz, the highest commercial airport in the world, about ½ hour by taxi (US$2) from centre. A motorway is being built to link city and airport. International airport tax US$5, internal US$1.

Taxis   US$0.15 per person, US$0.25 for two, for short trips within city limits. Between city and airport, up to US$4, including luggage. Between city and Obrajes, US$0.70 for up to 4. Between city and Calacoto US$1 for up to 4. Taxi drivers are not tipped; tip for porters—US$0.10 for each large piece of luggage. LAB runs a free bus service from their office to connect with all their flights. Sharing of taxis is common.

Taxi-like vehicles flying variously coloured flags are *Trufis*, following routes on a standard charge, e.g., city centre to Obrajes or Calacoto US$0.20.

Car Hire   Cars may be hired direct from Hertz Rent-a-Car, Gen. Bernardo Trigo 429, Tel.: 25592-22654, or through a travel agent. Charges from US$11-13 a day, plus 10 cents a km.

Local Buses   Fares: US$0.02 in town; US$0.04 to Obrajes; US$0.12 to Calacoto. Microbuses are dearer than buses, but much less crowded.

Bus Services to Copacabana (5 hours, US$4), Oruro (3½ hours, US$1.75, Flota Oruro or Kjirkincho), Potosí (12 hours, US$4.25), Sucre (24 hours, US$6-7.50), Cochabamba (all overnight except one line, 12 hours, US$4), Santa Cruz (23 hours, US$8), Tarija (26 hours, US$10), Puno (see below), Coroico (1 hr. US$1.50), Villazón (US$6.50), Tiahuanaco (US$0.60). Lima (48 hours, US$20) and Cuzco, Flota Morales, US$15.50 (poor reputation but cheap). There are also services to towns in the Yungas. As only the Oruro road is paved (so far), train is preferable to bus when there is a "ferrobus" service (see below).

A luxury service to Puno (US$20) and Cuzco (US$30) has been started by Transturin, Av. 16 de Julio 1656 (Edificio Alameda), Mon., Wed., and Fri., 19 hours to Cuzco, 10 to Puno.

Bus to Buenos Aires 4 days a week at 1830, Expresos Panamericanos.

Bus to Puno Sun., Tues., Thurs. and Sat., US$10 single, 9-12 hours. Flota Morales (very poor reputation) or US$20 by Transturin and other lines. Private car to Puno can be arranged with travel agencies—US$80-100.

Trains There are excellent daily "ferrobus" (railcar) services between La Paz and Oruro (4¾ hours, US$3.45, 1st) and Cochabamba (8½ hours, US$6.70, 1st). Mondays and Thursdays, to Potosí (11½ hours US$8.95, 1st) and Sucre (16 hours, US$12.05, 1st).

Acceptable food is served. Book well ahead. There are two stations: one for the Guaqui trains (Tel.: 52510) and one for all the others. There is also a booking office at Bolívar 724. See also pages 166-168.

Electric Current 110 volts, 50 cycles A.C. in La Paz, 220 volts 50 cycles A.C. elsewhere. U.S.-type plugs can be used in most hotels.

Books Foreign language books at Los Amigos del Libro, opposite U.S. Embassy on Calle Mercado, and El Alto airport. Los Amigos del Libro sell tourist maps of the region from Puno to the Yungas. Treat the details with caution. USIS has lending library and 2nd-hand paper-backs.

Films Kodak, Casa Kavlin, Calle Potosí 1130; Foto Linares, Colón 248, will develop both Ansco and Agfa colour film as well as black-and-white—1-day service on black-and-white, and repair cameras. Kodak colour in 24 hours by Foteco, 1557 Av. 16 de Julio.

Hospital Efficient and well run nursing homes such as Clínica Americana, Clínica Sta. Isabel opposite Hotel Crillón, Clínica Alemana, etc. Red Cross opposite Mercado Camacho, will give innoculations if required. The Methodist Hospital runs clinic at US$3.50, telephone for appointment.

Clubs Anglo-American (no sleeping accommodation). Círculo de la Unión Alemán; Alliance Française; de la Paz; Sucre Tennis; La Paz Tennis; de Caza y Pesca; Automóvil; Malasilla & Pinos Golf Clubs; Rotary; Freemasonary; Junior Chamber International; British Commonwealth Society; Los Sargentos Riding Club; Yacht Club (on Lake Titicaca, boats and fishing). Lions Club; Illimani Bridge Club; Club Andino Boliviano, Av. 6 de Julio 1473, P.O. Box 1346, for mountain-climbing information.

Church Protestant Community Church (inter-denominational), with services on Sunday (9.30 a.m.) in English, American Co-operative School, Calle 10 Calacoto (Tel.: 8.2052). The former Pastor and his wife (The Rev. & Mrs. Charles F. King) have written an excellent large cyclostyled guide to "Life in La Paz" which can be got on Sunday at the Community Church. It tells you, amongst other things, about where to buy what. We have used several items from it. Anglican-Episcopalian services are held at the Community Church on the third Sunday of each month.

Synagogues Polish and German, the latter with a Hebrew school.

Sport Ninety minutes by car from La Paz (36 km.) is Chacaltaya, the highest ski run in the world. Season: December to March. Ski-ing equipment may be hired, and a rope-tow reaches 5,570 metres. A half-day trip to the top by rented car costs about US$20; no visitor should miss the experience and the views. Also on Saturdays and Sundays in season, the Club Andino runs its own buses; the day trip, beginning at 0800 and returning at 1700, comes to about US$7 (lunch extra, US$1.50). Ski equipment can be hired (if you're not very large!) for the day at the Club in La Paz at US$2.50, and the lift pass costs US$2.50. Balsatours also does a day trip, at US$9. Club Andino also occasionally arrange trips to Mount Illimani.

Freight Transamericana, Calle Loayza 250, will ship goods to US and Europe; 9 kg costs US$17.50.

There are 2 golf clubs (one of them, at Malasilla, is the world's highest), two tennis clubs, and two riding clubs. Football is popular and played on Sunday at the Siles Stadium in Miraflores; there are reserved seats. Fishing and duck-shooting on Lake

Titicaca and other lakes and rivers. There is a yacht club at Huatajata on Lake Titicaca; sail and motor boats can be hired there and at Cúa for fishing and duck-shooting.

Souvenirs There is inexpensive silver and jewellery in the little cabinets outside Lanza Market on Av. Santa Cruz. Up Sagárnaga, by the side of San Francisco Church, are booths and small stores with interesting local items of all sorts. At Sagárnaga 177 is Artesanía Nacional Tiwanaku, very good for paintings, silver jewellery and woven goods. Many Indian objects are sold near Av. Buenos Aires, and Indian musical instruments at Colombiano Potosí 1276, and on Calle Granier, near the General Cemetery. There are good jewellery stores throughout the city, but visit the gold factories for lower prices and special orders. Visit "kunturi, a fine vocational workshop for girls at Avenida Arce 2847 for handicraft items. "Artesanías Bolivianas", near Hotel La Paz, a government-run store, sells very high quality handicrafts and will pack and ship them home for you. Puma Punku, Av. 16 de Julio, for weaving. Artesanías Titicaca, Av. Sánchez Lima 2320, retail and wholesale weaving. The Bolivia, Av. 16 de Julio 1591, best for alpaca. Curerex has four shops in la Paz, recommended for leather goods. Also weavers' co-operative in central plaza. Alpaca goods are more varied and cheaper than in Peru. In a patio on Calle Mercado, opposite the Amigos del Libro Bookstore, is the Anticuario, with interesting, usually genuine antiques. There is also an antique store on the Prado next to the Restaurant China and another on Calle Goitia. The Indian market is a good place for ponchos and local handicrafts. See also the "witchcraft market" along Max Paredes and Linares.

Maps Servicio Nacional de Camiones, Av. 20 de Octobre, US$0.75 each.

Addresses
Dirección Nacional de Turismo, kiosk on central island of the Prado. (Av. 16 de Julio, 1440). **No longer necessary to obtain an exit stamp here.** The stamp is normally put on your passport by Immigration when you enter Bolivia; check, it is triangular in shape. Also ask for lists of museum opening times, hotels, bus timetables, etc., which are published in a small booklet.
British Embassy and Consulate, Av. Arce, No. 2732-2734. Tel.: 51400.
United States Embassy on Calle Colón, Consulate on Av. Potosí.
West German Embassy, Av. Arce 2395.

Cables West Coast (British), Calle Mercado between Ayacucho and Socabaya. Tel.:53921. Public Telex booths at CWC offices. Cables All America, Calle Socabaya 326, Tel.: 53030.

Telephone service to the U.S.A. is now fairly good, though less so to the U.K. 'Collect' telephone calls out of the country can only be made to the U.S.A.

Banks Citibank, Bank of America, Bank of Boston, Banco do Brasil, Banco Popular del Perú, Banco de la Nación Argentina; Banco Mercantil, Banco de Santa Cruz de la Sierra and other local banks. Open 0900-1200, 1400-1630. Closed Saturday. Money is changed in hotels or *casas de cambio* rather than in banks.

Exchange Houses *(Casas de Cambio):* American Traders, Loayza 118; América Ltda., Ayacucho 224; Exprinter, Mariscal Santa Cruz y Loayza; Incatur, Av. Camacho 1476; La Paz, Calle Ayacucho; Sudamer, Colón 256; Titikaka Tours, Loayza 203; Tony Tours, Yanacocha y Asbún. Airport exchange booth will only change up to US$10 in travellers cheques.

Railways from the Coast (1) By the Southern Railway of Peru from Arequipa (bus from Mollendo) to Puna, on Lake Titicaca. There are two ways of getting to La Paz from Puno: by road (several lines, 10-hour journey), or by lake steamer to Guaqui (Bolivia), and on by the Guaqui-La Paz Railway, 98 km. There is a baggage allowance of 70 kg. Time taken, Puno-La Paz: 16 hours. Sufferers from soroche, or height sickness, rest at Arequipa. Only one lake crossing a week, on Thursdays, returning Friday. Crillon Tours run a daily hydrofoil service; interesting, but noisy and expensive (0600 from Puno; 0830 bus departure from La Paz).

The route through Peru is described in the Peruvian chapter. Lake Titicaca is described on pages 171 and 172. It is crossed by steamers built in England and carried up in sections from the coast. The service was started in 1872. The staterooms are comfortable, but the crossing may feel cold to some. The two boats kept in service—the *Inca* and *Ollanta*—have first and second-class accommodation; they both carry cars and motorcycles at reasonable rates. It is first come, first served for the bunks in each cabin. They cannot be reserved, so pay no money to anyone who says he can reserve one. Sanitation is now much improved. Dinner, served late in two shifts, is not good. Coffee and rolls are served at 0800, long before arrival at Bolivian Customs in Guaqui about 0930. It is light by six in the morning so early risers have three hours or so to see the lake before they get to port.

From Guaqui, where there are only a few scattered buildings, to El Alto, above La Paz, the railway follows the broad plateau on an almost level gradient, rising only about 300 metres to El Alto. The journey is done in about 2 hours by modern diesel railcar, but usually only half the people on the steamer can get on it. It stops for 20-40 minutes at Tiahuanaco to give passengers a quick look at the ruins. The rest have to go on by bus—rather rough (3½ hours, US$0.40) or colectivo (2 hours), or by the ordinary train (4 hours). It is only after the twisting corkscrew descent has begun that La Paz comes into view, nearly 400 metres below. By a series of circles and loops over a distance of only 8 km. the train arrives at the station near the centre of town.

Travelling from Bolivia to Peru, the train leaves the Guaqui station in La Paz on Fridays at 1400. Travellers are recommended to buy soles in La Paz, up to the limit of 5,000 soles permitted.

Fare Puno-La Paz, boat and train, 1st class, about US$11 including bunk and meals (poor); 2nd class US$6.75.

Of the ordinary Guaqui-La Paz train, Nicholas Humphrey writes: "It drooled down to La Paz so slowly that the fireman on our train stepped off at one point, walked into a field, picked up a lamb from a flock, and trotted back to catch the train, which had not decelerated to help him in his larceny."

(2) **Arica-La Paz International Railway**, 447 km.; 8-10 hours by diesel railcar express service leaving Arica at 0900 on Tuesdays and Fridays (sometimes also Wednesdays); returning from La Paz Wednesdays and Saturdays (sometimes also Thursdays) at 0820. Accommodation limited, tickets may be booked up to 2 weeks ahead in La Paz and Arica only. The twice-a-week slow train takes 22 hours (there is no longer a change at the frontier during the night); it is common to tip seat reservers up to US$1, seats being safer than the floor from the danger of pickpockets. The line from Arica skirts the coast for 10 km. and passes into the Lluta Valley, whose vegatation is in striking contrast with the barrenness of the surrounding hills.

From Kilometre 70 there is a sharp rise of 2,241 metres, in 42 km. The line is racked for 48 km., and the Andean massif has been cut through and tunnelled in many places. At Puquíos Station, Kilometre 112, the plateau is reached. The altitude here is 4,168 metres. The line runs along the plateau, interrupted only by the Huaylas quebrada, to the bottom of which it descends to rise again rapidly to plateau level. In the distance can be seen the snowcapped heights of Tacora, Putre, Sajama, and their fellows. At Kilometre 155 (altitude 4,046 metres), are the famous sulphur deposits. The greatest altitude is reached at General Lagos (4,247 metres).

The frontier station of Visviri is at Kilometre 205, with a custom house. Beyond, the train enters Bolivia and the station of Charaña, usually blacked-out after dark by smugglers.

In the Bolivian section the line skirts the Mauri, Desaguadero, and Colorado rivers, and leads *via* Corocoro, the copper mining town to Viacha, the junction of the several railways running to Antofagasta, Guaqui, and Buenos Aires. The mountain peaks visible include Illimani, Sorata, Huayna—Potosí, Mururata, and many others.

An hour and a half later the train reaches La Paz, at the bottom of a gigantic amphitheatre formed by the surrounding mountains.

Fares La Paz-Arica on ferrobus, US$20 including lunch and tea; 1st class slow train US$10; 2nd class US$8. Tickets to Arica from La Paz are sold at Calle Potosí 1007.

(3) Antofagasta-La Paz, by Antofagasta and Bolivia Railway, 1,173 km.; 33 hrs. This, the most southerly of three railway routes connecting La Paz with the Pacific coast, passes through magnificent scenery. As the passenger climbs over the huge Pacific shelf, where no rain falls and nothing grows, among dead volcanoes and livid lake beds, he cannot help thinking that he is being transported across the deserts of the moon. There is one train a week, rarely on time, leaving Antofagasta 0645 on Wednesday, arriving La Paz 1957 on Thursday. Leaves La Paz on Friday at 1100 arriving Antofagasta 2120 Saturday. Fares: 1st, US$11.50; 2nd US$6; sleeping car about US$15 (recommended), but book both ticket and sleepers early.

N.B. If going from Bolivia into Chile, buy Chilean currency before journey. The train arrives in Antofagasta Saturday evening and you could have a money-less Sunday. Also best to use Chilean pesos in dining-car.

The line starts at Antofagasta (950 km. N of Valparaíso), well served by ocean steamers. The railway is of metre gauge, its coaches are roomy and smooth running, and there is no change of carriage during the journey. But the heating system may not work and the temperature may fall below zero in the cold season. At an early stage the traveller gets covered by fine desert dust and there is no hot water.

The line reaches an altitude of 3,960 metres in 366 km., and negotiates gradients as steep as one in thirty. It crosses the principal Chilean nitrate district in the Atacama Desert (between El Buitre and Sierra Gorda stations). At Calama (240 km.) there is a large and fertile oasis. Standing 2,255 metres above the sea, it is a useful point at which to stay for a day or two to get used to the altitude before going higher. (The train leaves Calama at 1300; some travellers prefer to board it there rather than in Antofagasta, as you thus avoid the dusty part of the journey, but you also find all the sleepers are taken.) The line crosses another wide desert before it reaches another oasis at (317 km.) San Pedro. Large reservoirs here supply fresh snow water to the nitrate fields and ports. Near this point the line skirts the base of two volcanoes: San Pedro (still smoking) and San Pablo.

The summit is reached at Ascotán (3,960 metres), and the line desends to 3,735 metres at Cebollar, where it skirts a great borax lake, 39 km long. The Bolivian frontier is crossed a short distance beyond (444 km.) Ollagüe station, from which there is a 77 km. spur to the copper mines of Collahuasi. For the next 174 km. to Uyuni the line maintains an almost uniform level of 3,660 metres.

Uyuni is the junction with the Bolivia Railway Company's branch line of 90 km. to Atocha. From Uyuni there is rail access, *via* Villazón on the

Argentine border, to Buenos Aires, a route which is not interrupted by snowstorms. After crossing the Bolivian border there are direct coaches for Potosí on the train.

Note that after crossing the Bolivian border you have to have Bolivian pesos to buy food on the train. Money can be changed at Ollagüe and Oruro. **Watch baggage** at Oruro; the thieves are notorious.

From Río Mulato (716 km.) a branch line runs to Potosí and Sucre. Near Huari (801 km.) Lake Poopó comes into sight. Beyond Oruro (925 km.) the scenery is uninteresting until near Viacha, where the majestic Illimani comes into view; then El Alto station is reached with its fascinating view of La Paz in the basin below.

In March 1962 the main line from the frontier to La Paz and the branches to Atocha, Potosí and Cochabamba passed into the possession of the Bolivian State.

(4) Buenos Aires-La Paz: This railway journey of about 2,400 km. takes 71 hours. There are 3 or 4 trains a week from both La Paz and Buenos Aires. The route goes through immensely varied scenery; northbound the plains of the pampa are succeeded by the sugar fields of Tucumán with the mountains in their rear. The line, ascending to the frontier through bare hillsides clad with cacti, passes to the high plateau with vistas of distant peaks and occasional fertile valleys. It skirts rugged crags and precipices, we see flocks of llamas and the colourful journey across the roof of the world is succeeded by the joy of surviving it. First class passengers don't change coaches; others do. If you wish to vary the train journey from La Paz to Buenos Aires, get off the train at La Quiaca, take a bus to Jujuy or on to Salta, and fly from either to Buenos Aires.

From La Paz you reach Villazón at 1145 next day (26 hours). Only one of the 3 sleeping cars—the Argentine one—goes on to Buenos Aires. Through 1st-class La Paz-Buenos Aires fare is US$51 with sleeper and US$28 without; 2nd-class fare without sleeper is US$22.

Note that many travellers from La Paz on the Buenos Aires and Antofagasta lines take a bus to Oruro (more comfortable and quicker than the train) and board the train there. Again, you may have trouble getting a sleeper if you do this.

Excursions from La Paz   By agency tours, but bargaining for a taxi is cheaper and a colectivo is cheaper still. There is trout fishing in the many glacier lakes and streams near La Paz.

The best near-by excursion is to Río Abajo and Malasilla golf course: through suburb of Calacoto and La Florida follow the river road past lovely picnic spots and through some of the weirdest rock formations on earth (this is the "Moon Valley"). About 3 km. from bridge at Calacoto the road forks; sharp right leads to the Rod & Gun Club and lovely Malasilla Golf Course. Small entrance fee at weekends and holidays. Moon Valley can also be reached by bus No.1 to Florida, walking 1 km. to Ancillo Arce cactus gardens (free) and a further 1 km. uphill to road fork. You get puffed walking uphill though, and taxis are not dear, especially if shared! Near the cactus gardens is the Balneario Los Lobos, popular for lunch at weekends and puts on a folklore show (peña) on Friday nights. To Zongo Valley: a steep but scenic ride down past several of La Paz's electric power plants. In 32 km. the altitude drops from 4,265 to 1,830 metres. To Devil's Tooth Mountain, yellow microbus to San Miguel, then bus to Cotacota.

Urmiri   Take road S towards Oruro across the Altiplano, turn left at

Urmiri sign at Km. 75. A steep scenic descent leads to pool filled by mineral springs and a pleasant primitive inn. Worth visiting. A 2½-hour trip one way.

Sorata,   105 km. from La Paz, at 2,695 metres, giving appreciable relief. A 5-6 hour trip each way. It is in a valley at the foot of Illampu, second highest peak in Bolivia. Area has lovely views, mountain climbing, cave exploring (with lake inside). Sunday market. Also Sunday market festival, including bull market, at village of **Achacachi,** on the road. Not far from Sorata, along E shore of Lake Titicaca, is a tremendous slough giving the best duck shooting in Bolivia. Typical fiestas, both at Sorata and Achachi, on Sept. 14.

Sorata Hotel   *Prefectural,* good, US$4 with meals. *Residencia Sorata* above Casa Gunther, US$4.50 with good meals.

Tiahuanaco (Tiwanaku)   The ruins of Tiahuanaco are near the southern end of Lake Titicaca, by rail through Viacha or by road through the village of Laja (solid silver altar in church; entrance US$0.50), the first site of La Paz. There are now two pensions, both called *Ingavi,* one in Calle Bolívar and the other near plaza, in Tiahuanaco village; also simple meals at US$0.40. There is a restaurant near the ruins. The 72-km. journey from La Paz by Guaqui bus takes 2-3 hours. Flag a colectivo or bus to return or catch one in the main plaza of the village, whose church is in striking contrast with the pre-Incaic statuary in front of it. The ruins, which are believed to date from 800 A.D. and are being reconstructed, comprise four main structures: the Kalasasaya compound, the Acapana pyramid, the underground temple, and lastly the great Gate of the Sun, with carved stone blocks weighing many tons. There is a private museum near the ruins, but it is closed for repairs; in any event, most of the best statues are in the Museo Tiahuanaco or the Museo Semisubterráneo in La Paz. Indians trade arrowheads and bronze figures.

Guidebook in English   *Tiwanaku,* by Mariano Baptista (a former Bolivian Minister of Education), Plata Publishing Ltd., Chur, Switzerland. It is obtainable from Los Amigos del Libro.

The bus terminus for Tiahuanaco and Guaqui is at corner of Av. Buenos Aires (an Indian market street) and Calle Tumusla. Buses can also be caught outside the main railway station, but may be full already! Fare to Tiahuanaco is about US$0.40 by ordinary bus. Transportes Ingavi, Calle Manco Kapac, US$0.70 (1½ hrs.) leaving 0900. Some buses go on from Tiahuanaco to Desguadero, US$0.30.

Road and railway go on 20 km. to **Guaqui,** the port for the Titicaca passenger ships (*Hotel Guaqui,* US$1.30 per person, good value). The road crosses the Bolivian border at Desaguadero into Peru and runs along the western shores to the Peruvian port of Puno, at the northern end. Desaguadero is noted for its lack of accommodation and mercenary officals; during markets on Tuesday and Friday police are busy, a good time to cross border. At Yunguyo a side road to the right re-enters Bolivian territory and leads to Copacabana. (Occasional buses, taking 45 minutes.)

Copacabana, 158 km. from La Paz, is an attractive little red-roofed town on Lake Titicaca. Festivals are held in August. It has a heavily restored church containing a famous 16th century miracle-working Dark Virgin of the Lake, also known as the Virgin of Candelaria. Candlelight procession on Good Friday; many come from La Paz to attend. The church itself is notable for its spacious atrium with four small chapels; the main chapel has one of the finest altars in Bolivia. There are 17th and 18th century paintings and statues in the sanctuary and monastery. Good food and drink at the hotels and in the market; money-changing facilities at pharmacy in plaza. Banks only open Wednesday-Sunday, and hotels and shops give poor rates, so buy Bolivian money in Yunguyo before crossing frontier, if coming from Peru. There is a fiesta, every Saturday, followed by penance on following Sunday climbing up the hill to the Church.

Hotels at Copacabana: *Playa Azul,* US$10 full board, good food, no hot water, bookable through Riveros bus company, Av. Montes, La Paz; *Ambassador,* US$10 full board only (bookings through the Copacabana bus company in Av. Montes, La Paz); *Hotel Patria,* in main square, US$1.25 p.p.; cold water, good food; *Tumulán,* US$1 s; *Prefectural,* new US$1.50 s, no hot water, only hotel with view of lake; *Residencial La Porteñita,* off main plaza, US$2.50 d, hot water; *Alojamiento Santa Rosa,* US$1.25 s, US$1.50 d; *Hotel Tunari,* US$0.50 p.p., clean and friendly. Electricity only 1900-2200. *Alojamiento Copacabana,* corner of main plaza, US$0.75 p.p.; *Residencial San Silvestre,* cheap and clean, also *Alojamiento Bolívar.* Good value is *Residencial Copacabana,* US$1 p.p.

By car from La Paz to Copacabana (direct), 4 hours. Bus (Flota Copacabana, slightly dearer, or book at office by *Hotel Tumusla*), 5 hrs., 0630, 0730 and 1300, US$1.45-1.75. Bus, Copacabana-Yunguyo (for Peruvian frontier), hourly, US$0.15. Trucks from Yunguyo to Puno. To reach Copacabana (or Tiquina) you cross the lovely straits of Tiquina. Vehicles are loaded on to a barge equipped with outboard motors. The official charge for a car is US$1.60, though they ask for more and there is a US$0.50 car toll to enter Copacabana. A plane seat from La Paz to Copacabana costs US$17 single, US$0.50 airport tax.

Lake Titicaca Sailing boats and motor-boats can be hired in Copacabana to visit the Island of the Sun, to see two sets of Inca ruins and the views of the lake. This takes almost a day. The Island of the Moon may be closed; there are ruins of an Inca settlement. Boats (not tackle) are hired at reasonable rates for fishing. Dawns and sunsets are spectacular. At Chúa, on the lake, there is shooting, fishing, sailing and at Huatajata a yacht club (*Hotel Chúa,* situated on lake between Huatajata and Tiquina, good). From Huatajata boats may be taken to Suriqui, where the reed boats are made (US$5 return).

Boats on Lake 6 hours to Island of Sun, US$30 for boat taking 10, best ruins on N side, but difficult to persuade boatowners to go there. (Sailing boats, which take five and cost US$9, often suffer from lack of wind in the morning.) Rowing boat, US$50 an hour. Danger of sunburn on lake.

Crillón Tours, Avenida Camacho 1223, run a hydrofoil service on Lake Titicaca with a bilingual guide. Leaving La Paz at 0600 (except Sunday), you get to Huatajata on Lake Titicaca for breakfast by 0800. The hydrofoil sets off at 0830, moves past the reed balsa fishing boats, and stops in the Straits of Tiquina for a few minutes to watch the wooden ferry boats crossing. The Island of the Sun is visited to see the ruins. You arrive at Copacabana for sightseeing and a trout lunch, with local folk music. The short tour returns to La Paz from Copacabana; the longer one continues to Puno by taxis, which stop at Pomata and Juli to see the fine Colonial churches. Charge: US$52 from La Paz to Copacabana; US$101.50 for the La Paz-Cuzco or Arequipa trip. The hydrofoil seems expensive, but the trip is certainly fascinating, not least for the magnificent views of the Cordillera.

Tristan Jones, who has been crossing South America in his sailing cutter *Sea Dart,* writes as follows: "During my crossing I have spent over eight months cruising Lake Titicaca and probably know it better than anyone, including the Indians, as they are not people who like to be away from home much, and rarely visit parts of the Lake other than their own area.

"On the Bolivian side, in Lake Huanamarca, i.e. from Straits of Tiquina south, the best way to visit the Lake from La Paz is to take a bus from Avenida Buenos Aires to Huatajata and there ask for Nicolás Catari. He is a great boatbuilder and knows the Lake well. Avoid Suriqui Island, which has become very commercialized. The best islands to visit are **Pariti**, where the weaving is very good indeed and the school-master *(maestro)* speaks Spanish and is very civilised; and, only a mile or so away, **Quebraya**, where there are pre-Inca *chulpas,* or tombs, stretching along the shore. This was the ancient port for Tiahuanaco, when the lake fell back from that city. No-one lives there, and it is best always to go with an Aymará guide, for the locals are very jealous of the place. Another good island to visit, with very friendly and cordial inhabitants, is **Taquire**, where the local customs are retained in their ancient purity. Cost of a launch from Catari: about US$6 per trip.

"Trout is very scarce. The chances of catching one are about 100-1 against in an average fishing trip. The best places are off the river mouths.

"Guaqui has the cheapest cost of living on all Lake Titicaca and one can get a *sajta* for the equivalent of US$0.08.

"The only hotel on Lake Huanamarca, at Chúa, is now expensive, but the trout is good. Nicolás Catari will also, if he likes you, arrange sleeping accommodation but it is very rough and you would have to take your own sleeping gear.

"**Note** The Titicaca Indians' most interesting music, and quite rare, is at masses held for the dead. On Pariti Island they will arrange a dance for a US$5 donation to the school."

Crossing the Peruvian Frontier

Many tourists still prefer the water route (see page 167) to the journey by road we give below. In this connection it is said that the crossing into Peru *via* Tiquina, Copacabana and Yunguyo can be pleasanter than the Desguadero route, though it requires more vehicles and time and the road is no better or worse than through Desaguadero, in that the Peruvian customs officials are more friendly. Also, the Bolivian navy may be seen at Tiquina.

No hotel at Tiquina, but ask for the Casa Verde, where you can stay for US$0.25 p.p. Two cheap eating places at Yunguyo.

More interesting than the water route is the bus journey from Puno along the western side of the lake *via* Juli (short stop), Pomata (short stop), Yunguyo, where exit stamp may be obtained if travelling in opposite direction (hour for lunch bur no decent place to eat it), then back almost to Pomata to take the main road on to Desaguadero at the border. Puno-Desaguadero takes 5 hours by taxi and 6 hours by bus. La Paz is reached any time between 1800 and 2100. This is a colourful trip, with wonderful views of the brilliantly blue lake dotted with occasional sailing balsas against a background of snow-capped Bolivian peaks. The road on the Peruvian side is pretty bad, but you really see the Indian life of the Altiplano. There are Morales buses from La Paz to Puno most days (also Transturin), tickets at Exprinter, La Paz, US$10, 9-12 hours.

A colectivo from Puno to Desaguadero costs US$25. For a party of 5, this is cheaper and much more interesting. A colectivo from Puno to La Paz costs US$15 a passenger (8 hours). A bus can be caught at Desaguadero for La Paz, 114 km., but this route is not really recommended because there is sometimes a shortage of buses leaving Desaguadero for La Paz (fare US$0.75). At the risk of another change it may be better to catch buses Puno-Yunguyo (get exit stamp), Yunguyo-

Copacabana-and Copacabana-La Paz, *via* Tiquina. This is possible in one day in the reverse direction. Ferry at Tiquina, US$0.10.

If you are leaving Copacabana for Peru, get exit stamp at Bolivian immigration office (open 0800-1800) in Square.

N.B. Remember that if you wish to enter Peru from Bolivia you must have an onward ticket (or return ticket) out of Peru. Bolivia is also demanding outward tickets, but they don't seem to check.

The Yungas

NE of La Paz an all-weather road runs to the **Yungas**; it is along this road that produce comes to market. It circles cloudwards over La Cumbre Pass at 4,725 metres; the highest point is reached in an hour; all around stand titanic snowcapped peaks and snowfields glinting in the sun. Then it drops over 3,400 metres to the luxuriant green Alto Beni in 80 km. The little town of **Coroico** is perched on a hill at 1,525 metres; the scenery is beautiful.

Buses from La Paz to Coroico (US$1.50) leave at 0830 daily (except Sunday) and take 4 hours each way; the return bus leaves at 0730 (except Saturday). Flota Yungueña, Av. Coroico 1577, La Paz. *Hotel Prefectural* runs a 14-seater bus to La Paz now and then, taking 3½ hours for the 96 km. Transport and accommodation can be problems on holiday weekends. Trucks leave from Villa Fátima in La Paz.

The best places to stay at in Coroico are the *Hotel Prefectural,* in a pleasant situation with decent food (US$5.50 daily) and the *Lluvia de Oro,* US$1.50 s., US$3.50 full board, swimming pool, friendly. *Pensión Pijoán* is very basic, US$1.50 d. Better still is the hotel near the junction of the La Paz-Chulumani and Coripata-Chulumani roads. Somewhat surprisingly there is another very good place to stay at, with beautiful views: a few kilometres from Chulumani is the *Motel San Antonio,* a good resort-type motel with pleasant cabins (US$18 per night). A camping site will be found by the small church on the hill overlooking the town—a stiff climb though.

"The roads to Coroico and to Coripata or Chulumani divide at Unduavi at a height of about 3,000 metres on the East side of La Cumbre. If the road to Coruico is blocked by landslide the news will probably be heard at Unduavi. Those who hire their own taxi in La Paz to go to Coroico should start from La Paz with a clear understanding with the driver about where they will go if Coroico cannot be reached. It should be noted that there is no good place for lunch at Unduavi, or at Santa Rosa on the road to Coripata, or Chulumani." (J. S. Rollett)

Chulumani, the capital of Sud Yungas, is an hour away from Puente Villa and is the main regional centre. Citrus fruits are the main products from this area as well as some coffee. Along the road from Puente Villa to Coripata you enter the main coca growing area of northern Bolivia and the countryside is quite different from that near Coroico, where coffee, as well as coca and fruits, is the main crop.

Hotels *Motel San Bartolomé* and *Motel San Antonio,* both new and expensive, with swimming pools. *Hotel Bolívar,* cheap, clean and friendly.

Bus La Paz-Chulumani, run by Yungueña, 120 km., 5 hours, US$1.50.

From below Coroico the road forks, the lower fork following the river NE to **Caranavi,** 166 km. from La Paz, at times along a picturesque gorge towards the settled area of the Alto Beni, and Santa Ana. *Hotel Esplendido* and *Hotel Universo* (US$1 per person) in Caranavi are bearable.

Bus Yungueña buses leave La Paz for Caranavi at 0900 each day; the 164-km. journey (US$2) takes 6-7 hours. Direct bus Coroico-Caranavi on Sundays.

Oruro is built on the slopes of a hill at an altitude of 3,700 metres. The population, mostly Indian, is 110,000. Oruro is important as a railway centre and for its tin, silver, and tungsten. A 20,000 tons-a-year tin smelter has been built, and a pesticides plant is being built, with Argentina. It has a university with a strong bias towards engineering. There is excellent pejerrey fishing on a large nearby lake. Excellent market, near railway station, Wednesdays. Airport. Rail travellers from Antofagasta can change at Oruro and continue to La Paz by bus.

Hotels *Repostero,* German-run, good by local standards, US$5 s with bath, US$3.50 s without bath; *Prefectural-Oruro,* near station, but not so good; *Plaza,* best and most modern, US$5 d, good food; *Hotel Residencial,* good and clean, US$2, Chinese restaurant attached; *Residencial Pagador,* Calle Ayacucho, US$0.90 s; *Alojamiento La Paz,* near railway station, US$1.50 d; *Alojamiento Porvenir,* near bus station, US$0.70; *Residencial Ideal,* Bolivar 392, US$1.50 s, new and clean but noisy. *Hispanoamericano,* opposite station, US$2, hot showers. *Hotel Derby,* US$1, good value, 2 blocks above market.

Restaurants The *Club Español,* 3 or 4 blocks up the hill off the main square, open to non-members, has the best food in town. *Restaurant Edén,* 6 de Octubre 1599; *Confitería Chic,* Bolivar (500 block); *Restaurant Richy,* lunch US$0.80.
   There are hot springs at **Obrajes,** where you have the choice of private baths or swimming pool, both hot. Bus leaves Oruro daily at 1000 and waits at baths for several hours. Bring picnic lunch.

Cables Cables All America, Calle Adolf Mier 581. Cables can be filed at the Empresa Nacional Office with the routing *via:* Cable West Coast.

La Diablada There is little in Oruro for the tourist, but at carnival on the Saturday before Ash Wednesday, there is a remarkable ceremony. Two figures, a "bear" and a "condor", clear the way for a procession of masked dancers, led by two luxuriously costumed masqueraders representing Satan and Lucifer. Alternating with them in the lead are St. Michael the Archangel and China Supay, the Devil's wife, who plays the role of carnal temptress. Behind them come hundreds of dancers in ferocious diabolical costumes, leaping, shouting, and pirouetting. The parade ends in the crowded football stadium. Here to the music of a band, the masqueraders perform various mass and solo dances. These are followed by two masques: in one—a tragic re-enactment of the Conquest—the helmeted and breast-plated Pizarro and his Spanish soldiers defeat the sad, noble and resplendent Inca and his retinue; in the second the golden-haired Archangel commands Lucifer and the seven cardinal sins to battle. Satan and his retinue join in; China Supay coquettishly tempts St. Michael. In defeat the rout of devils confess their evil doing and are banished from human company.
   In the contest between good and evil, the result in favour of the good is pronounced by the Virgen del Socavón, the patroness of miners. And after the performance the dancers all enter her chapel, bend the knee, take off their heavy masks, chant a hymn in Quechua and pray for pardon. The ceremony dates from Colonial times. The Diablada was traditionally performed by Indian miners, but three other guilds have taken up the custom and there are in all four Diabladas in Oruro.
   The costume always features the heavy, gruesome mask modelled in plaster over a special fabric, with a toad or snake on top; huge glass eyes; triangular-looking glass teeth; a horsehair wig; and pointed, vibrating ears. Tied around the neck a large silk shawl embroidered with dragons or other figures enhances the elegance of the dancer, who also has a jewelled, fringed breastplate. Over his white shirt and tights he wears a dark, broad sash trimmed with coins, and from it hang the four flaps of the native skirt, embroidered in gold and silver thread and loaded with precious stones. Special boots equipped with spurs complete the elaborate outfit. Satan and Lucifer wear expensive cloaks of scarlet plush, a serpent twisted around one arm, and a trident. The working-class Oruro district known as La Ranchería is particularly famous for the excellence of the costumes and masks made there. One of the most famous folklore groups is the stately Morenada. Carnival lasts 8 days with displays

of dancing by day and night often superior to those given on the opening Saturday. Seats can be booked at the town hall. Take raincoats as protection against water pistols and *bombas de agua* (water-filled balloons).

Guide Carnival de Oruro. Dance costumes and masks, Calle La Paz, 400 block.

From Machacamarca, 24 km. S of Oruro, a branch line runs to Uncia (108 km.) and the ex-Patiño tin mines, which are open to visitors.

Excursion West Anthropologists or tough tourists with a Land Rover might explore the country W of Oruro towards the Chilean frontier. It's a day's drive to the western mountains following tracks rather than roads. There are no hotels in any of the towns, such as Escara or Sabava, but lodging could be found by asking a school-teacher or local mayor. From Escara it is only an hour S to **Chipaya,** the main settlement of the most interesting Indians of the Altiplano. They speak a language closely related to the almost extinct Uru, but many speak Spanish learnt when temporary migrants to Chile. Their dress is distinctive and their houses unique. (See warning on page 190.)

This is a very difficult trip without your own transport. Truck (no bus) to Escara, 12 hours, then 25-km. walk to Chipaya, where you are welcomed by a US$5 tourist tax imposed by the Mayor! Bring your own food; shelter for US$0.25 per head in adobe "alojamiento". Bicycles may be hired in Chipaya to visit lake 2 hours away with great variety of bird life.

From Oruro a branch line runs eastwards to Cochabamba (204 km.). As the line cuts across the Puna, through wild scenery, it reaches a height of 4,140 metres at Cuesta Colorada before it begins to descend to the fertile basin in which Cochabamba lies, a basin of 260 square km. It is 394 km. from La Paz to Cochabamba by road now paved to Oruro and from there paved except for 50 km. midway, where the going is very rough; about 8 hours by private car. A new high road is being built to Cochabamba, *via* Quillacollo. On the present road, a short cut from Caracollo to Colhuasi avoids Oruro and saves 65 km.

Trains from Oruro About 7 hours to La Paz and 8 to Cochabamba. To Villazón twice a week, 12 hours, exhausting but exhilarating to hardy traveller, US$7.35 (1st). Antofagasta (Chile), 29½ hours, US$5.75, train from La Paz connects here, very crowded and dusty for first few stops. Ferrobus to La Paz 4¾ hours; to Cochabamba 4½ hours; to Potosí 12 hours (US$7.50).

Buses from Oruro To La Paz, 3½ hours, US$1.45 to 1.65 according to grade; to Potosí, 8 hours, US$2.75. Road S to Río Mulato and Uyuni is very bad.

Cochabamba, Bolivia's second-largest city, founded in 1542, less than an hour by air from La Paz. Population: 180,000; altitude 2,560 metres; average temperature: 18°C. It is by far the most agreeable city in Bolivia to live in, so far as climate goes. It has fine buildings, a University, many Spanish houses with overhanging eaves, and much for the tourist: a grand view from San Sebastián, a hill on the edge of the city; a visit to El Cortijo (tennis and swimming pool); to the Golf Club on Lake Alalay, and (Mon.-Fri. 1700-1800) to Los Portales, the Patiño mansion in the outskirts, set in beautiful grounds; built 1910 but never occupied (open 1700-1800 and Saturdays 1000-1100 and Sundays 1100-1200). (President de Gaulle slept there in 1964 in an extra long bed.) The Cathedral is in the main plaza. It is pleasantly decorated; panels painted to look like marble. Just off the plaza is La Compañía, whose whitewashed interior is completely free from the usual riot of late Baroque decoration. The municipal market and the Cancha, a retail market (Wednesday and Saturday), also are full of local colour. Fiestas are frequent and fascinating. Cochabamba is set in a bowl of rolling green hills and is an important agricultural centre. To the N, in a high fault-block range of mountains, is Cerro Tunari, 5,180 metres. A road runs to within 300 metres of the top, usually sprinkled with a little snow.

An imposing monument overlooks the town from La Coronilla, part of the same hill as San Sebastián. It commemorates the heroic defence of Cochabamba by its womenfolk during the War of Independence. It has fine views and just below it is a charming little ancient bull ring, little used. The University has a small but interesting collection of prehistoric pieces and of Indian hieroglyphic scripts (Mon.-Fri. only). A very good bookshop is Los Amigos del Libro, with branches in La Paz and Santa Cruz. There are thermal baths near the city. Small zoo, free, on banks of river. The Palacio de Cultura, Perú y 25 de Mayo, has a group of local museums under one roof.

There are day and night ferrobuses leaving La Paz at 0800 and 2200, and Cochabamba at 0730 and 2150, both taking about nine hours; fares US$6.70 (1st), US$5.60 (2nd). On Sunday the ferrobus leaves at 07.30, arriving La Paz 16.30. Cochabamba-Oruro ferrobus, US$3, "Especial" leaves 0715, 4½ hours. Meals and refreshments.

Swimming *Club Hawaii,* outside city, includes sauna. Cheaper is *El Paraíso,* halfway to Quillacollo, sauna and pool, US$0.50 entrance, accessible by bus or train. Pools at *El Cortijo,* outside town, and at *Gran Hotel Cochabamba* are open to the public.

Fishing Excellent trout fishing on lake formed by the Corani dam, 48 km. N of Cochabamba.

Air Service Jorge Wilstermann airport. Daily by LAB to and from La Paz (½ hour), one way, US$14.20 (15 kg baggage allowance).

Bus Services Buses and colectivos have day and night services to Santa Cruz, taking 12 to 16 hours (US$4), a beautiful trip; to La Paz *via* Oruro (terrifying road) or Caracollo, by night or by day, 10-12 hours (US$4.10). Daily to Sucre, 12 hours (US$3.50, Flota Oruro is a good line) but last 2 hours are very bad. Two weekly, 1000 Wed. and Sat., from Calle Lanza to Puerto Villaroel, US$1.50, but lorries run daily from Calle Uruguay for US$1. Most buses start from Calle Aroma, at foot of San Sebastián and Coronilla hills, about 1 km. S of main square. Trucks to Sucre leave from Av. Aguirre (US$2).

Hotels *Capitol,* in town, US$15 d; *Gran Hotel Cochabamba,* beautifully set on the outskirts of the town, with garden, swimming pool (US$0.50) and tennis courts, good food, US$20 d, US$11 s. In the town: motel-type *Berkeley* (French run, solarium with each room, swimming pool); *Ambassador,* Calle España, approaching luxury: private bath, hot water, telephone, modern, central and reasonable (US$10 d, including tax). *Bolívar,* Av. San Martín, near central plaza (US$1.25 s), cheap; and *Colón,* US$5 s, hot water, breakfast inc. *Hotel Cortijo* (good food), behind *Hotel Cochabamba,* US$6.50 s, peaceful and luxurious, with swimming pool. *Hotel Boston,* 25 de Mayo, 2928, US$9 d, US$5.25 s. *Hotel Metropole,* 25 de Mayo, new, clean, US$5.50 d (with bath). *Residencial Copacabana,* Calle Esteban Arze, new, basic, clean US$4 d. *Hotel Commercio,* US$1.50 s, good, cheap, central. *Residencial Santa Cruz,* 25 de Mayo, US$1.75 s. *Residencial Familiar,* Calle Sucre, hot water, very clean, recommended, US$6 p.p., with breakfast. *City Hotel,* Calle Jordán, near centre, about US$2.50, without breakfast, noisy but modern. *Hotel Plaza,* near plaza, US$0.75, hot water, but noisy. *Residencial Agustín López,* near bus station, US$1.60 d, clean, comfortable, hot water. *Residencial Oriente,* Calle Aroma, US$1 s; *Residencial Pullman,* Calle Aroma, very clean, US$2.50 p.p. *Residencial Madrid,* off Aroma, next to Flota Continental bus depot, US$2.50 d, clean. *Alojamiento Sudamericano,* Calle Esteban Arze 6882, US$2.50, attractive; *Hotel Liberty,* Calle Sucre, US$1.50 (meals not recommended); *Flecha Azul,* basic with meals. *Residencial Escobar,* US$2.50, very clean and comfortable. *Residencial La Paz,* near station, US$1.75 (dusty), p.p.; *Hotel Espinoza,* US$1.50, near market, hot water. *Residencial Gutiérrez,* US$1. *Hotel Sucre,* Calle Aroma, US$1.25 s. *Gran Hotel Las Vegas,* US$5 p.p., bath plus breakfast, ½ block from main plaza; *Alojamiento Cochabamba,* US$3 d, clean, is our latest recommendation, Calle Nataniel Aguirre; *Hotel La Coruña,* US$5.30 per room.

Restaurants *Guadalquivir* (N of town); good Spanish-type food out of doors; (nice garden), and *Victor* (on Prado), same ownership and quality. **Don Gerardo,** good and cheap, traditional Bolivian food. *El Horno,* main square, good food at about US$1.60 excl. drinks. Good food at *Hotel Bolívar; Restaurant-Confitería Continental,* on main plaza; *Napoli,* Calle Sucre, just off main plaza, meals at US$1-1.25; excellent pastries and ice cream at the *Zurich Tea Room,* Av. San Martín 5980, but expensive; medium-price *Restaurant China* nearby, on Calle San Martín, good meal US$2; *Café Paula,* 25 de Mayo y Bolívar, good cheap snacks, lunch US$1. *La Candela,* Calle San Martín, pleasant; *Snack 6 de Agosto* serves beautiful trout (US$1.25); *Moulin Rouge,* US$1.50, meal; *Restaurant 6 de Agosto* on the street of the same name; *California Doncito* has been highly praised; *La Quinta Bar Taquiña,* at brewery 12 km. from city, roast duck lunches Saturday and Sunday.

Tourist Office Plaza 10 de Noviembre.

Shopping Large market near railway station. On sale in the market are superbly woven woollen blankets, women's skirts and runners, and exquisite examples of folk art: figurines in wood painted in polychrome colours, llamas and horses of many shapes and sizes, carved gourds, and murals in miniature of carnivals, religious processions or harvest festivals. However, expensive compared with La Paz. Come early to weaver market on Wednesday and Saturday as they often leave by 0830. "Fotrama" for alpaca sweater, stoles, rugs, etc. (expensive); or Madam Eleska's "Andea" shop, now run by her son; or "Amerindia", San Martín 6064, for good rugs and lengths of alpaca material, as well as ponchos and jumpers; or picturesque Indian market and nearby shops. Market fruit and vegetables excellent and very cheap. Try local hot drink, *api,* made from maize. Main markets Wed. and Sat.; beware pickpockets and thieves.

Cables can be filed at Empresa Nacional office with the routing *via* Cable West Coast.

British Consul, Obispo Anaya, Casilla 496. Telephone: 4627.

Industries Oil refining, shoes, furniture, fruit canning, rubber tyre factory, a milk plant.

Language School Spanish/Aymará/Quechua, at Instituto de Idioma, Casilla 550, run by Maryknoll Fathers.

Festivals Fiesta de Cochabamba August 15, folk music, and September 14, dancing.

The Cochabamba basin, dotted with several small townships, is the greatest grain and fruit producing area in Bolivia. **Quillacollo,** a 45 minute bus ride (good Sunday market), is the most interesting of these little towns; 7 km. from there are Balneario Liriuni (thermal baths). A railway line runs from Cochabamba through the Punata Valley as far as

Arani (60 km.). Another runs to Vila-Vila (132 km.). Two seldom visited Inca ruins might interest the scholar: Inca-Rakay, a small outpost about 45 minutes' drive from Cochabamba and a 2-hour hike up a mountain; and Incallacta (now being restored), just beyond Montepunco (see below) on a 24 km. branch road to Pocona. This is now being "restored". The Samaipata ruins, on the road to Santa Cruz (see below) are worth seeing. There is a large Sunday market at **Clisa,** accessible by bus from Calle Aroma, Cochabamba.

The 500-km. road to Santa Cruz was paved completely at the end of 1971. At the top of the pass at Siberia about one-third of the way along, clouds roll over the top of the mountain range and across the road: an impressive sight. Before the pass, 5 km. beyond Montepunco, the 20-km. road to Incallacta (unpaved and very bad) turns off at Km. 120. The ruins, on a flat spur of land at the mouth of a steep valley, are extensive and the temple is of special interest. At Km. 386 are the ruins of Samaipata, worth a stop. At Epizana, 13 km. beyond Montepunco (Km. 128), with hotels and service stations, a branch road, right—dusty, stony, and narrow in parts, but very scenic—goes 233 km. to Sucre, 7-8 hours drive. Another road has been built to link Cochabamba with the Beni area (see page 187).

S of Oruro the railway from La Paz skirts Lake Poopó, over 90 km. long and 32 km. wide. From **Río Mulato** a branch line runs eastwards to Potosí (174 km.) and Sucre. It takes 9½ hours to Potosí along one of the highest metre gauge railways in the world, by ordinary train—pretty horrible—but far less by the new excellent "ferrobus" service. The track, a difficult engineering feat, reaches the height of 4,786 metres at Cóndor: one of the highest points in the world's railway lines.

Potosí, with a population of over 100,000, stands at 3,900 metres, higher than La Paz, that is. The climate is often bitterly cold. It was founded by the Spaniards on April 10, 1545, after they had discovered old Indian workings at Cerro Rico, the hill at whose foot it stands.

Immense amounts of silver were once extracted from this hill. In Spain "éste es un Potosí" (it's a Potosí) is still used for anything superlatively rich. The 17th century house of wealthy mine-owner José de Quiroz is shown to visitors. Early in the 17th century Potosí had a population of 150,000, but two centuries later, as its lodes began to deteriorate and silver had been found in Peru and Mexico, Potosí became little more than a ghost town. It is the demand for tin—a metal Spaniards ignored—which has lifted the town to comparative prosperity again. Silver, copper and lead are also mined.

Large parts of Potosí are colonial, with twisting, narrow streets and an occasional great mansion with its coat of arms over the door-ways. Some of the best buildings are grouped round the Plaza 10 de Noviembre, the main square. The Convent of Santa Teresa has a collection of colonial and religious art here, organized by theme. Entrance US$1. The old Cabildo and the Royal Treasury—Las Cajas Reales—are both here, but converted to other uses. The Cathedral faces the square, and near-by is the Mint—the Casa Real de Moneda (founded 1542, rebuilt 1759)—one of the chief monuments of civilian building in all South America. Amongst Potosí's baroque churches, typical of the Andean or "mestizo" architecture of the 18th century, is the Compañía (Jesuit) Church, with an impressive bell-gable (1700), San Francisco, with a fine organ, and San Lorenzo, with a rich portal (1728-1744).

Hotels *El IV Centenario,* deteriorated recently, heated and very spacious rooms, hot water, dining room cold, expensive at US$12.50 d. More central: *Hotel Turista,* Calle Lanza, US$9 d, now remodelled, heating, hot shower, breakfast only. *Hotel Royal* and *Hotel San Antonio,* US$3, d. *Residencial América,* Calle Cochabamba, US$4.50 d (private bath, breakfast); *Hotel Municipal,* US$12.20 d; *Gran Hotel,* US$7.20 d; *Hotel Central,* Calle Bustillos 1230, US$2; *Residencial Vera Cruz,* US$1.50 d; *Residencial 10 de Novembre,* US$1.25 s; *Alojamiento Ferrocarril,* Av. Villazón 159, US$0.90, hot showers; best cheap lodgings (for which Potosí has a bad reputation) between Av. Oruro and Av. Serrudo, clean but rarely with hot water. *Residencial Copacabana,* Av. Serrudo, US$1.25 shared room, restaurant;

Alojamiento San Cristóbal and *Residencial Tarija,* the same; *Hotel Villa Imperial,* dirty, noisy, US$1 p.p., US$0.20 for hot shower. *Residencial Rosario,* Calle Oruro 526, US$1.25 p.p. *Residencia Bolivia,* Calle San Alberto, US$2 p.p. *Hotel San José,* US$1.25 p.p., hot shower; *Alojamiento Barquito,* Calle Oruro, 7, US$1 p.p., clean.

Restaurants *Sumacoreko, AS,* Calle Padilla; *Petit Restaurant Criollo,* Calle Bolívar, excellent food, good value; *Escudo,* Calle Oruro, pleasant; *El Crillón,* opp. cinema, good. *Confitería Americana,* Calle España (US$1.50); *Las Vegas,* three blocks above main plaza, three course meal, US$1.25. *Pensión Florida,* US$0.50 each meal; *Scaramuch,* Calle Bolívar 814. Salteñas (meat pies) from Calle Linares 41 at US$0.15 each are "delectable".

Transport To La Paz by rail, 625 km., US$8 1st class; Ferrobus, Wednesdays and Saturdays, US$9 (1st), US$7.50 (2nd), by road, 12 hours, US$4.25. To Sucre, by train US$1.75 (2nd), 5½ hours; by private car, about 5 hours; Expreso La Plata bus US$1.50, about 7 hours. Road poor; may be impassable after rain. To Oruro, 8 hours (bus, US$2.75, road slow, all-weather. Bus to Villazón, US$4, 12-16 hours), rough trip requiring warm clothing; train Monday and Friday 1540 (24 hours), US$5 (2nd), take food; to Uyuní on Tuesdays, 1st class (US$4). Daily bus to Tarija, Flota Tarija, Calle Chayanta, often booked, US$5, 10-12 hours, full range of scenery. New bus station out of town. Trucks for Tarabuco leave from Plaza San Francisco.

The Moneda (entrance US$0.25) has a museum in many sections. The main art gallery is in a glorious salon on the first floor: the salon better than the paintings. Elsewhere are coin dies and huge wooden presses which made the silver strip from which coins were cut. You are advised to wear warm clothes, as it is cold inside. The smelting houses have carved altar pieces from Potosí's ruined churches. Open every day 0900-1200 and Mon.-Sat. 1400-1700, but can only view with a guide at opening times (admission US$1.25). Energetic visitors can see over the Pailaviri tin mine; visits can be arranged through hotels. Taxi up the hill to mine entrance before 0900, US$0.75, or go by bus, Línea B or up with miners in truck from Plaza 10 de Novembre or 25 de Mayo, leaving at 0730. Entrance fee about US$1 for up to 3-hour tour, special clothing provided, hot in mine though cold in access tunnels. Watch out for electrified cable at head level.

Shopping Silver (sometimes containing nickel) and native cloth; there are stalls in Calle Bustillos. Silver coins, jewellery and coca leaves in market.

Tourist Office On 2nd Floor, Cámara de Minería, Calle Aniceto Arce 99; good town maps, information, helpful.

Thermal Baths at lake below city. Laguna de Tarapaya, Miraflores, Chaqui and Tora.

Banks Change at Banco del Estado, Calle España esq. San Alberto, though high commission charged.

Tourist Agents Candería Tours, Bolívar 634, Tel.: 2458 and Tursul Ltda, Calle San Alberto, 24, Tel.: 1360.

Sucre, the official capital of Bolivia, is reached from Potosí (175 km.) by daily train or "ferrobus" (a grand trip) or by road (bad). A branch road runs to it from the Cochabamba-Santa Cruz highway. The altitude is 2,790 metres, and the climate is mild (mean temperature 12°C, but sometimes 24°C in November-December and 7°C in June). The population is about 90,000. The road from Oruro to Sucre runs E to the oil centre of Camiri.

Sucre was founded in 1538. Its long isolation has helped the city to maintain a certain courtly charm; local law now requires all buildings to be painted original colonial white. Public buildings are impressive. Amongst these are the Legislative Palace, where the country's

Declaration of Independence was signed; the modern Santo Domingo (Palace of Justice), the seat of Bolivia's judiciary; the modern Government Palace; the beautiful 17th century Cathedral and museum, open 1000-1200, 1500-1700 (worth seeing are the Chapel of the famous jewel-encrusted Virgin of Guadalupe (fiesta 8th September), and the monstance and other church jewels by appointment with the Padre Tesorero); the Consistorial building; the Teato Gran Mariscal Sucre, and Junín College. Sucre University was founded in 1624. Early 17th century wooden ceilings ("alfarjes") with intricate patterns of Moorish origin are found in San Miguel and San Francisco. Churches tend to be closed after 1000.

Behind the town a road flanked by Stations of the Cross ascends a gracious hill, Cerro Churuquilla, with slim eucalyptus trees on its flank, to a statue of Christ at the top and views of Sucre and the countryside, though an unobstructed view is obtained from the adjacent barren Cerro Sicasica.

Museums These include the University's anthropological and colonial collections at the Charcas Museum (Bolívar 401), its presidential and modern-art galleries, and its Princesa de la Glorieta collection. There are also the Museo de Santa Clara (Calle Calvo 204) and the Museo de la Recoleta (Calle Pedro de Anzures). The Casa de la Independencia, main plaza, is a museum; it has the Bolivian Declaration of Independence. The Recoleta monastery on a hill above the town is notable for the beauty of its cloisters and gardens; the carved wooden choirstalls in the chapel (upstairs) are especially beautiful. The Glorieta mansion outside the city on the road to Potosí is now a military school and museum.

San Miguel must be seen. It is the oldest church in use in S. America. Shut for 120 years, it is now being lovingly restored and is quite exquisitely beautiful with carved and painted ceilings, pure-white walls and lovely gold and silver altar. In the Baptistry the font (very old) is made of silver and carved alabaster and there is a painting by Viti, the first great painter of the New World, who studied under Raphael. In the Sacristy is another of his paintings and some early sculpture. It was from San Miguel that Jesuit missionaries went south to convert Argentina, Uruguay and Paraguay. (Open 1000-1200, 1500-1700).

During pre-Lenten holidays there is a parade in which tons of treasured family silver are carried on burros to the Cathedral to be blessed.

Train Service There is a "ferrobus" service to Potosí (US$3.50, 1st class, 4½ hours); ordinary train ("carril") US$1.70. Also to Oruro and La Paz by "ferrobus", US$12.50 second, on Wednesday and Saturday. The ordinary train to La Paz, distinctly basic, takes 36 hours.

Air Service By LAB there is a direct La Paz-Sucre air service Mondays, Wednesdays and Fridays (US$23), from Cochabamba on Tuesdays, Thursdays and Saturdays (US$12) and Santa Cruz on Tuesdays and Thursdays (US$16). There are also LAB-F27 flights to Tarija (US$18) and Yacuiba (US$25).

Bus daily to La Paz *via* Cochabamba (24 hours, US$7.40), very rough but worthwhile *via* Potosí, US$7.50 (18 hours); to Cochabamba US$3.30; also daily bus to Potosí (7 hours, US$1.75). Bus to Santa Cruz, Flota La Plata (US$8, 18 hours). All leave early in the morning.

Hotels *Municipal,* US$6.50 d; *Gran,* food good; *Londres,* Av. Venezuela 6, 3 blocks uphill from station, US$6 d, good value, bed and breakfast, has restaurant; *Paris,* rather basic, US$1.75 p.p.; *Potosí.* US$1.25 s; *Residencial Bolivia,* near plaza in Calle San Alberto, US$2.25 p.p., good with hot water; *La Plata,* US$1, and *Alojamiento San José,* very cheap; *Residencial Oriental,* Calle San Alberto, US$3 d, clean, friendly, hot water; *Hotel Municipal,* good food; *Residencial El Turista.* San Ravelo, US$1.50 s, good; *Residencial San Francisco,* clean, cheap with shower US$2.50 d; *Residencial Copacabana,* 4 blocks up from station, US$1; *Residencial Bolívar,* US$1.20, clean and *Residencial Bustillo,* San Ravelo, US$2 s, clean and modern.

Restaurants *El Sol,* Colón 423, for good local food, cheap and strongly recommended, lunches only; *Confitería-Restaurant El Rosedal,* just off plaza by University, reasonable. Salteñas from *Grisby,* Estudiantes 20, and from *Convento de la Imaculada. Pizzería* in main square. *Confitería Florida,* Americana (US$1 chicken or steak dinner) and *Palet* on plaza area, together with *Restaurant China* (expensive). Restaurant next door to *Hotel Londres. Confitería Potosí,* Calle Oruro (cheap).

Tourist Office   Calle Aniceto Arce 99. Helpful. Check church and museum opening hours.

Shopping   Antique woven items must be sought. Small shops opposite Church of San Francisco for handicrafts. On Arenales, opposite Casa Schütt, try at university women's hostel for alpaca clothes woven at Yotala, a nearby town. Also Centro de Entrenamiento Juvenil, Arenales 214.

Night Clubs   La Cabaña El Quyote, Barrio Universitario; Night Club Municipal, Av. Venezuela, El Iterraje Aniceto Arce 11.

Doctor   Dr. Julio Gutiérrez, San Alberto 306, English-speaking.

Industry   Oil refining; cement factory. There will be further expansion following completion in 1974 of a gas pipeline from Monteagudo.

On Sunday visit **Tarabuco,** ferrobus, US$1.70 return, leaves Sucre on Sunday at 0700, 2 hours, or lorry (US$0.50)—4 hours—from open space at top of Calle Calvo, bus (US$1, return at 1800) or taxi, for uniquely colourful market, particularly good for ponchos and other typical garments. Indians are catching on to tourism idea; come early. There is a fairly basic hotel, and two alojamientos in plaza, US$0.75 (*Bar California,* basic). Festival with fair: Virgen de Rosario, 1st Sunday in October and 12th March.

"Surely this is one of the most colourful Indian markets in S America. The costume of these Indians is unique and fantastic, and the men wander around playing the 'charango', a stringed instrument with an armadilo shell as a sound-box. Women do most of the work. The woven skirts and belts of the women are some of the finest to be found in Bolivia, and good weaving may be bought."—Mrs. Hilary Bradt.

A main road runs SE from Sucre through Tarabuco and **Monteagudo** (pretty town, *Hotel Salamanca,* US$1 bed and breakfast) for 216 km. to **Villa Serrano,** where the musician Mauro Nuñez lived. A music festival is held on 28th-29th December. (The journey is beautiful through wild mountains.) 460 km. from Sucre is **Camiri,** growing rapidly because of nearby oilfields—the oil refinery may be visited. As a garrison town (Régis Debray was in prison there) it has lots of hotels (*Hotel Ortuño,* US$1.50), restaurants, bars and has flights to La Paz and Santa Cruz, 180 km. Permission may be required to pass through. There are bus services to Sucre and to Santa Cruz. S along a very bad road is **Villa Montes,** more easily reached from Tarija (260 km.), famous for the highest temperatures in Bolivia. It is on the edge of the Gran Chaco and has a road and railway S to Yacuiba and Argentina and another dry-season road E to Paraguay. *Hotel Pilcomayo,* US$1.20, community bath. The bus trip *via* Tarabuco and Camiri to Argentina is very rough; poor road and little comfort. Just from Sucre to Camiri takes nearly 24 hours.

It is possible to drive from Camiri into Paraguay direct in a truck or 4-wheel-drive vehicle, carrying food and water for a week. No help can be relied on in case of a breakdown. Mr. J. I. Kelly, a traveller from New Zealand with a ¾-ton truck, has written as follows:

"From Camiri, a journey of 64 km. over a poor road, with deep sand and rough sections, bring you in 2-3 hours to the last town in Bolivia. Boyuibe. There are some rivers to ford and although they are dry in the dry season they could be impassable if there was any rain in the area. At Boyuibe you must attend to customs and immigration. Gas and water are available. A few km. out of Boyuibe the road forks. Take the left fork—no signs as usual. 24 km. from Boyuibe take the right fork on to little more than a track.

"From here to the border the road (track) becomes increasingly difficult to keep to as there are numerous forks, no signpost and very few people to ask. You need a lot of patience and a compass. The track becomes narrower and a high-axle vehicle is a must—a winch would be an advantage. Ask truck drivers at Boyuibe about the condition of the road before you attempt it. For the 154 km. from Boyuibe to the border allow 11-12 hours driving time, plus time for bogging down. No gas or water on route. The track has a sandy surface with increasingly frequent patches of swamp, some of which are bypassed. There is little traffic (we saw 3 trucks in 2 days) and no houses for the last 80 km. The border is marked by a large patch of swamp and a steel signpost. 20 km. on is the Paraguayan post of Fortín Garay (water only available) where passports are processed. The 240 km. to Mariscal (another military post) is over a fair dirt road and takes 6 hours—passable if dry. At Mariscal gas can be obtained from the mission of Santa Teresia. There are no shops or money changes here, but a good *pensión* which accepts Bolivian currency. For the 90 km. to the Mennonite colony of Filadelfia allow about 2 hours. The town is 1 km. off the main road. There are plenty of gas stations and money can be changed at the Co-operative building. From the Filadelfia turnoff to Asunción is 450 km. The trip should take 7-8 hours, but the road is often closed for days at a time whenever there is rain. The stretches of swamp on either side of the road are inhabited by large numbers of swamp birds and they provide an endless and varied spectacle as you drive through the Chaco.''

There are no buses beyond Camiri on this road. Petrol tankers and other lorries go through to Paraguay; they will sometimes take one passenger, as regulations forbid more, from Camiri to Filadelfia for US$5—possibly less. There are hotels and exchange houses at Yacuiba and Pocitos.

The railway line S from Río Mulato goes through **Uyuni** (3,660 metres), the junction for the line to Antofagasta. (The road down from Oruro is very bad.) It lies bitterly cold and unprotected on the plain at the edge of the vast salt lake, the Salar of Uyuni. ''When it still has water in it (up to 4 or possibly 6 inches), being in the middle is like being an ant on a gigantic mirror. The blue sky merges into the blue water, the islands are perfectly reflected and since there is no horizon they appear suspended in space. Some areas may be dry, in which case the salt crust is as blinding-white and featureless as the most perfect snowfield.''—Stephen Saker, who endorses our warning on the Ollagüe-Uyuni track (see page 190). Uyuni's 5,000 inhabitants are mostly Indian. Its market is the only point of interest.

Hotel   *Avenida,* basic fairly clean, US$1.25 p.p.

S of Uyuni, 200 km., is **Tupiza** (2,990 metres), a centre of the silver, tin lead, and bismuth mining industries (*Hotel Mitru,* US$1.75 p.p., private shower and bath; *Hotel Americano,* US$0.90, opposite railway station). Six trains to border every week. Fair road from Potosí which goes on S to Villazón; often closed in rainy season because there is no bridge over the Río Suipacha.

From **Villazón** (good local market), on the border with Argentina, there is a poor road to Tarija, 965 km. by road from La Paz. The road linking Potosí with Villazón *via* Camargo is in poor condition and about 100 km. longer than the better road *via* Tupiza. For information on border crossing with Argentina see page 181. Little to see in Villazón; border area should not be photographed.

Hotels at Villazón   *Panamericano,* US$1.50 p.p., breakfast and lunch; *Savoy,* just possible; *Gran; Residencial El Cortyo,* clean, US$3.30, hot water. Restaurant opposite bus station. Money-changing at Cambio Porvenir.

Buses from Villazón   To Potosí at 1600 and 1700, 15 hours, US$4; to Tarija at 0900, US$1.75, 6 hours. Bus passengers for La Paz must cross from Argentina the previous day.

Trains from Villazón   To La Paz, Sunday at 1330, express arriving 1120 on Monday.

At **Camargo**, on road from Potosí to Tarija, is an excellent restaurant, *Media Luz*. Guest rooms are being built for overnight stop.

Tarija, at 1,900 metres (population, about 50,000), one of the oldest settlements in Bolivia (founded July 4, 1574), in the rich valley of the Guadalquivir river. The road from Villazón, 183 difficult km., is the shortest one from Argentina, threading its way through multi-coloured mountains and descending the last 50 km. into the basin; there is also a road to Potosí *via* Camargo. Wind erosion is a notable feature of the area. Journey by bus is 13 hours. The alternative route from Bermejo, 269 km., runs at a fairly low altitude and in a mild climate. There is no railway. Tarija had a tumultuous struggle against Spain, declaring itself independent—a little Republic—in 1807, and has a strong cultural heritage. Its own university was founded in 1946. Maize, vegetables, wheat, potatoes and splendid grapes thrive in the basin, but all are for local consumption: there is no profitable way of getting them out. Its people are markedly religious and strongly individualistic: they even look more like southern Europeans or Levantines than Bolivians. The modern Avenida Costanera gracefully flanks the curves of the river. Air service by LAB to Cochabamba (US$35), La Paz, Santa Cruz, Trinidad, Yacuibá (US$13) and Sucre (US$20).

The city is famous for its niño (child) processions: colourful and charming. During processions of San Roque on the first 3 Sundays in September the richly dressed saint's statue is paraded through the streets; wearing lively colours, cloth turbans and cloth veils, the Chunchos dance before it as goes, and women throw flowers from the balconies. Dogs are decorated with ribbons for the day. On the second Sunday in October the flower festival commemorates the Virgen del Rosario.

Buses   Six days a week on 935-km. route Potosí-Oruro-La Paz, leaving 0430 (26 hours, US$8); (check which company runs the route the day you want to go, and which operates the best buses). To Potosí (386 km.), takes 12 hours (US$4), the last hour cold. To and from Villazón 7 days a week in summer, taking 6 hours, leaving in mornings (US$1.75); otherwise you need to take a local truck. Daily buses to Bermejo, (6 hours, US$2.10) leave in morning; at Bermejo cross river by ferry to Agua Blanca, Argentina. Road E to Villa Montes; bus US$2.50, 12 hours, thrice-weekly.

Hotels   *Hotel Prefectural,* US$7.50 s US$12 d with bath; *Internacional* US$5 p.p. with bath; *Club Social,* on main plaza; *Hotel América,* hot showers, good at US$6.50 d; *Hotel España,* US$0.50 s, hot shower. *Hotel Asturias,* clean and well furnished, US$3 d. *Residencial Sucre,* Sucre 771, US$2, quite good. *Residencial Bolívar,* US$3 d, clean, comfortable, hot water. *El Hí gar,* US$1 p.p. *Turista,* US$0.75 p.p. *Residencial Londres,* US$1.25 shared room and bath, hot water; *Hotel Familiar* US$1 d, friendly, good food; *Hotel Central,* US$2.50 d, *Residencial Ocho Hermosos,* near main plaza, US$2 s, clean.

Restaurants   *Domingo,* Paz 641, simple and good. *La Paz,* "a pleasant surprise in this little town". Excellent food in market, but get there before 1300. After, go to Calle Carrero.

Shopping   Fine craft goods in market and in co-operative shop in plaza; ceramics at Frial Susy, Sucre 776.

Santa Cruz (at 433 metres) is the only other city of note, capital of the Department of Santa Cruz, Bolivia's largest and richest in natural resources, lying in the vast and largely undeveloped plains to the E of the Eastern Cordillera, 552 km. by air from La Paz. This hot, windswept boom town, whose population has doubled since 1968 and is now more than 130,000, was founded in 1561 by Spaniards who had come from

Paraguay. Its isolation is now over: there is a 500 km. paved road across the mountains to Cochabamba; airlines call on regular schedules; a railway (and now a dirt road) runs E for 648 km. to Corumbá on the Paraguay River, where it connects with the Brazilian system to São Paulo and Santos; a Bolivian railway runs 530 km. S to Yacuiba, where it links with the Argentine system; this line is now being extended W of Santa Cruz, to Cochabamba.

Santa Cruz town centre with its roofed-over sidewalks and pillars is reminiscent of a Hollywood set for a western. It is only in the last few years that the streets have been paved (with hexagonal interlocking cement blocks for easy repair because of subsiding sandy soil). Santa Cruz is usually a hot and dusty town, although when the cold *surazo* blows from the Argentine pampas, the temperature drops sharply; the rainy season is December-February. The Plaza 24 de Setiembre is the town's social centre with the Cathedral (intersting hand-wrought Colonial silver), the University and prefecture set around it. People stroll around the Plaza in the cool of the evening. Pleasant residential areas are being developed on the outskirts of town. The water supply is quite good, though typhoid and hepatitis are endemic to the area.

Cruceños are famous for their gaiety—their music, the carnavalitos, can be heard all over South America. Of the various festivals, the merriest one is Carnival, celebrated for the 15 days before Lent: fife, flute, drum, violin and guitar music in the streets, dancing, fancy dress and the coronation of a queen.

Until recently Santa Cruz was fairly isolated, with little inter-marriage between the mostly white *cambas* (peoples of the tropical lowland, descendants of Spaniards and jungle Indians) and the highland Indians. However, new rail and road links in the 1950s ended this isolation and now there is an ever-increasiing flow of immigrants from the highlands (*collas*) as well as Mennonites from other Latin American countries and Japanese settlers, such as the Okinawan colony near Montero, to grow cotton, sugar, rice, coffee and other crops, which yield profusely. Cattle breeding and timber projects are also becoming important. A trip out of Santa Cruz to see these newly-settled areas carved out of the jungle is interesting, especially towards the Río Grande or Yapacaní (beautiful birds and butterflies; the fish are highly recommended). Very close to town are the Botanical Gardens, somewhat disappointing but there is an interesting collection of cacti (bus 4 from centre, or taxi, US$1). The exploitation of oil in the Department of Santa Cruz since early 1960s has greatly contributed to the town's rapid development. There are several oil fields: at Caranda, 50 km. to the NW, at Colpa, 32 km. to the N and a large gas field at Río Grande, 40 km. to the SE. YPFB has an oil refinery at Santa Cruz. One of the world's largest iron ore and magnesium deposits has been discovered in the south-east of the Department of Santa Cruz, at El Mutún, near the border with Brazil.

A road is being driven into fertile lowland to the NW of Santa Cruz. It goes N to Montero (37 km.), where there are a sugar refinery and various cotton gins, and on to Puerto Grether, high on the River Ichilo, a tributary of the Mamoré. It will later connect at Todos Santos with the 200-km. road to Cochabamba.

Hotels The new *Hotel Los Tajibos* (Holiday Inn) is best, US$20 s, US$35 d, has swimming pool. The *Hotel Cortez* (Poza del Bato) on the outskirts of town, Av.

Mendoza, is very good, with swimming pool and good food, US$9.50 s, US$13 d; *Hotel Santa Cruz,* Pari 59, also good with pool and restaurant, US$6 s, US$ 12 d; *Motel Asturias,* Moldes 154, (pool) US$7.50 s, US$11 d; *Hotel Bolivia,* Libertad 365, a good new hotel, US$8 s, US$11 d; *Hotel Premier,* René Moreno 552, small new hotel, US$10 s; US$12 d; *Hotel Florida,* centrally heated, noisy, US$6 s, US$10 d with breakfast; *Hotel Orion,* US$3.35 shared room and bath; *Hotel La Siesta,* Vallegrande 17, US$7.50 s, US$11 d; *Hotel Jenecheru,* España 40, US$5 s, US$10 d; *Hotel Litoral,* Ayacucho 276, US$5 s with bath, US$3 without; *Hotel Brasilia,* Junín 163, US$3 p.p.; *Hotel Guaraní,* Independencia 83, US$3 p.p. with breakfast; *Hotel Londres,* Ayacucho 263, US$1.50 p.p., good clothes-washing facilities; *Residencial Bolívar,* Sucre 131, US$2.50 with breakfast (hot showers); *Residencial Central,* Junín 190, US$1.50 p.p. (basic but clean); *Residencial Oriente,* Junín 362, US$2 p.p., clean, hot water; *Residencial Copacabana,* Junín 217, near centre, US$1.50 p.p.; *Residencial Ferrocarril,* opp. station, US$3 d, washing facilities suspect; Pension at Calle Villaroel 188, US$1 p.p.; *Alojamiento 24 de Septiembre,* US$2 each; *Residencial Astoria,* cheapest at US$0.75 p.p., adequate. The better hotels have some air-conditioned rooms but there is usually an extra charge. All prices include taxes.

Restaurants The best restaurants are the *Floresca,* which has a good discotheque upstairs; the "85" on Calle Bolívar 85; and the *Ambassador* (all air-conditioned). The *Skorpio* also serves international cuisine and has a discotheque. *La Empalizada* has very good *parrilladas* (grills) in a very pleasant outdoor setting with discotheque. *Don Miguel,* on Av. Uruguay, has good *parrilladas* and the *Lido,* Ingavi 71, serves good Italian food and good meat at reasonable prices. Chinese restaurants include *Restaurante China,* Sucre 209; *China Law,* Velasco 64; *Dragón de Oro,* 21 de Mayo 209; *Patito Pekin,* 24 de Setiembre 307. Japanese *Restaurant Kiku,* near Loposo market. For good pizzas try the *Playboy* just off the Plaza on Independencia; the *Viena* a few doors down (Indendencia 42) serves good cheap meals. The *Madrid,* René Moreno 10, is also good value with cheap meals and snacks. Two quite good duck restaurants are located on Km.2 and Km.8 on the road to Cochabamba. *La Pascana* on the Plaza is a favourite of tourists and locals alike for ice-cream and snacks and to watch the beautiful cruceñas. Cheap, good *parrilladas* at *Gauchito Moya.* The bakeries on Junín, Los Manzanos and España look scruffy but sell the local specialities: *empanadas de queso* (cheese pies), *cuñapés* (yuca buns), rice bread and *humintas* (maize pies).

Entertainment Discotheques: Floresca; Skorpio; Dino's, Sucre 23; Acuario; Jumbo; Passe-Pateur; El Caballito Blanco (popular with the young on Saturday night for open air dancing); El Mau-Mau, open only during Carnival.

Museum Casa de la Cultura, with occasional exhibitions and also an archaeological display.

Clubs Tennis Club; Club Las Palmas, 2½ km. on road to Cochabamba, has 9-hole golf course and pool; Club Hípico, riding club, nearby.

Books Los Amigos del Libro, René Moreno 26, sells foreign language books and *Newsweek,* and a useful guide 'Con Usted La Señorial Santa Cruz de la Sierra' for US$0.25 (list of cheap boarding houses); Cruz del Sur, 21 de Mayo, 62, sells *Time.*

Shopping Leather goods, baskets, hammocks. Carvings and other objects made from beautiful guayacán and jacarandá wood (though reported these crack in drier climates). The market Los Pozos is rather dirty but worth going to in summer for its exotic fruits: *ambaiba* (looks like a glove and the fruit is sucked out of the "fingers"), *guaypurú* (like a cherry), *ocoro* (like a prickly mandarin), *achachayrú* (mandarin-like with hard skin), *pitón* (like sour grapes) as well as better-known tropical fruits such as papayas and pineapples. There are plenty of smuggled Brazilian goods on sale, exchanged for Bolivian coca (made into cocaine).

Banks Bank of America, Velasco 19; Banco do Brasil, Ayacucho 168; Banco Popular del Perú, 24 de Setiembre 156; Banco de la Nación Argentina, Sucre 31; Banco del Estado and Banco Mercantil, both on the Plaza; Banco de Santa Cruz, Juín 214; Banco Hipotecario Nacional, René Moreno 136. Open 0730 to 1300.

Cables can be sent from ENTEL just off the Plaza on Independencia; Cable West Coast, 24 de Setiembre 238, only sends telexes.

Tourist Agents Exprinter, Santa Cruz Tur and Orientur are all on the Plaza; Camba Tur, Sucre 8; and Turismo Balas, Bolívar 16. Bolivian Tours holds an allotment of Ferrobus tickets for Corumbá and Yacuiba.

Air Service LAB flies daily to La Paz (US$40) and Cochabamba (US$20). LAB and Líneas Aéreas Paraguayas (LAP) fly once a week Asunción-Santa Cruz (US$60). Cruzerio do Sul has weekly flight to Campo Grande, São Paulo and Rio de Janeiro. LAB and Aerolíneas Argentinas also fly to Salta and Buenos Aires (US$109), four times a week. There are also three flights by LAB to São Paulo (US$111) a week. LAB flies to some of the outlying towns in the Dept. of Santa Cruz as also to Trinidad, Camiri, Sucre, Tarija and Yacuiba. Trompillo Airport is 5 minutes from town centre, taxi US$1. A new international airport is being built at Viru-Viru, about 16 km. from the town.

Buses Daily buses to Cochabamba (US$3, 12hours) leave around 0600 and in the evening with connections to Sucre, Oruro and La Paz (23 hours, US$7.75). Bus companies on Junín.

Railways The Santa Cruz-Corumbá railway is still rather primitive, but has recently been improved; toilets are still dirty but there is an adequate dining car (built in Belgium in 1925!) and sleeping car. Ordinary slow trains run once a day each way (Monday and Saturday, 0700); they leave Santa Cruz at 1800 and arrive at Puerto Suárez, near the frontier, 19 hours later. From there travellers must go by bus (US$0.40) or Land-Rover (US$1) to Corubmá in Brazil; these meet the slow trains as they arrive in Puerto Suárez. Before departing passengers must obtain an "Interpol" passport stamp. Trains leave Puerto Suárez for Santa Cruz on Tuesdays and Saturdays at 1815. The "ferrobus" train service is much faster and better and goes directly to Corumbá; it leaves Santa Cruz at 0600 (often booked) except Friday and Sunday (12 hour trip), returning from Corumbá the following days at 0730 (meals served at seats). Fares: for ordinary trains, "Pullman", US$8, first class US$7, second class US$4.10; ferrobus, "Pullman", US$9, "especial", US$7.50. Book in advance at Brasileña station. It is a monotonous journey except for the first half hour through the mountain. A rail flat-car can be hired to transport cars to Santa Cruz, US$185; you may have to wait several days for a flat-car, however. Food is available on the train or at frequent stops. There is now an unpaved road between Santa Cruz and the Brazilian border, but not recommended. The ticket office at the station is not open for 0700 to Corumbá and 0730 to Yacuiba; purchase the night before, or at Bolivia Tours in town.

Puerto Suárez Beware thieves. *Residencial Sucre* on main plaza, US$2, is good, but most people prefer to go to Corumbá where hotels are better (see page 327).

To Rio or São Paulo take the Noroeste do Brasil from Corumbá to Campo Grande, 9 hours (morning—0900—and evening trains). There fast overnight buses meet the train and get to São Paulo 14 hours later and Rio 22 hours later. Book seats for Mato Grosso bus lines at Corumbá. You can, of course, stay on the train, which goes to São Paulo *via* Bauru, It's slower, but comfortable and probably cheaper than the buses. To enter Brazil, need to get passport stamped by Federal Police in Corumbá station.

To Buenos Aires by the weekly train *via* Yacuiba takes 3 days and is a long and tiring trip. Train leaves Santa Cruz Thursday at 0900 and gets to Retiro Station at 1105 on Sunday. First class (US$26) and second class (US$19) passengers must disembark at Yacuiba (1800-2000 hours), taking taxi (US$0.25) to Pocitos on the border and walking across to Argentine side before boarding train for Buenos Aires. However, passengers in sleeper (US$50) go straight through from Santa Cruz to Buenos Aires.

Tickets should be purchased from Incatur travel agents in Santa Cruz who can book you directly to Buenos Aires; at the Argentine station you can only buy a ticket as far as Yacuiba. Return train leaves Retiro Station on Saturday at 2030 and arrives in Santa Cruz Tuesday 1650. A more comfortable alternative is to take the "ferrobus" trains which leave Santa Cruz Thursdays and Saturdays at 0730 to Yacuiba (9-10 hour journey) and then to take a bus from Pocitos on the Argentine side of the border to Güemes (2 buses daily with connections to Salta and Buenos Aires). The ferrobus returns from Yacuiba to Santa Cruz on Mondays and Fridays at 1715 and costs US$7 Pullman, US$6 "especial".

The Beni Lowlands

A road to open the underinhabited Beni Department runs from Cochabamba NE for 200 km. to Todos Santos, on the Chaparé river, a tributary of the Mamoré (the previous narrow road has now been much improved and partly paved). From **Villa Tunari** (daily buses from Cochabamba, *Hotel Las Vegas,* basic but clean, US$2 s, and others) a road goes through (bus twice a week but plenty of lorries) to the new **Puerto Villaroel** (*Hotel Rivera*) from where cargo boats ply irregularly to Trinidad in about 4-10 days (US$10, meals included). Take a mosquito net, plenty of reading matter, water-sterilizing tablets and any interesting food you can find before hand. You get to Guayaramerín in 10-15 days (fare US$8), depending on the depth of the river. The Cochabamba-Villa Tuuari run is highly recommended for scenery. In 1976 the extension of the road was completed to Trinidad.

Trinidad   The capital of the lowlands Beni Department, founded 1686, population 26,000 (236 metres), reached by air from La Paz, Cochabamba or Santa Cruz, or by river from Todos Santos (if water not too low) or Puerto Villaroel. Sleeping-bag and mosquito-net essential on boats; passengers sleep on the deck. Food quite varied. Trinidad is very expensive. Excursions interesting for wildlife, as is the river trip. A through road has been built to link Cochabamba with Trinidad, and a fleet of over 200 air taxis also provide local transport.

Hotels   *Beni,* US$7 d, *Magdelena* US$3 s. Many cheaper alternatives.

Guayaramerín   A primitive small town on the bank of the Mamoré river. N of Trinidad, opposite the Brazilian town of Guajará-Mirim. Passage between the two towns is unrestricted, but if intending to continue into Bolivia you need your passport stamped by the Bolivian consul in Guajará-Mirim before leaving Brazil, and by the Bolivian immigration office. Boat trip, US$0.20 during day, US$2.50 at night. No hotel. Restaurant: *La Querencia,* set meal for US$1.

Buses to Riberalta   2½ hrs., 0930 and 1600 daily.

Air Transport   Daily flights to Trinidad (US$18.50) weekly flight to La Paz (US$40).

Riberalta   Another poor town, which with the whole region attained temporary importance during the natural-rubber boom of the late 19th century. It is at the confluence of the Madre de Dios and Beni rivers, which together flow into the Mamoré a few km. N of Guayaramerím. Hotels: *Riberalta, Cochabamba, Residencia, Santa Rita,* all US$1.20 a night without breakfast. Restaurants: *Club Social Bom Progresso,* US$1 a mean; *Restaurant Popular Cochabamba,* US$0.50. Flight, Riberalta-

Cochabamba, US$52. A motorcycle can be hired for US$5 a day for visits to jungle—taxi drivers can give you the address.

N.B. Food in the Beni tends to be expensive, but the steaks are good.

Cobija, capital of lowland Department of Pando, N of La Paz population, 6,000 (280 metres), only connections by air and river transport. It is close to the Brazilian and Peruvian frontiers and the area has many Brazilian residents.

The Economy

The economy performed less well in 1977, growing at about 5% compared with the record 7.6% in 1976, as a result of declines in petroleum and gas production and a bad year for agriculture, following flooding early in 1977 and a drought during sowing time in 1978. Though not yet at the stage of self-sustained growth (income per head is estimated at only US$729), the country appears to have reached a new level of maturity, with relative political stability fostering a high level of foreign interest, reflected in increasing capital inflows.

An unofficial estimate for the balance of payments for a current account deficit in 1977 was US$200m, compared with US$180m the year before; capital inflows, however, led to a large overall surplus. This change was expected, largely because of changes in the trade balance; following the boom conditions of 1974 world prices for Bolivia's primary exports fell in the first half of 1975 but improved through 1976 and 1977, though at the same time import prices were raised by inflation in industrial countries. Preliminary figures suggest that exports in 1977 reached US$670m., with imports about the same. In the case of tin, the chief mineral export, the rise in price led to the removal of export quotas by the International Tin Council.

The improvement in the payments position was reflected in the increase of gross monetary reserves during the year from US$172m. to US$212m., equivalent to over three months' exports. However, foreign confidence in Bolivia is now at a high level and credits of US$379 m. were forthcoming in 1977; many of these came from international agencies and represented funding of the Government's massive investment programme in basic infrastructure. The authorities hope to contract loans of US$400m. in 1978. In consequence of these large inflows, the foreign debt is increasing, to a reported level of US$1,418m. by the end of 1977, of which some US$524m. are yet to be drawn.

The rate of inflation was kept down to 10-12% in 1977, thanks to the use of prices-and-incomes, monetary, fiscal and import-control policies. Inflation has had a disproportionate effect on the poorest sectors of society and unemployment too remains a problem. Thus despite a creditable growth record in recent years, Bolivia remains a poor country.

The Ministry of Agriculture has estimated a decline of 3% in the agricultural sector in 1977, due to drought and flooding earlier in the year. The main development of commercial agriculture continues to be in the eastern lowlands where an increasing number of food-processing industries—vegetable-oil plants, a maize mill, sugar and by-products plants—are being established. Major projects include dams and irrigation projects to help control the floods and droughts which have affected production in recent years.

Mining, together with petroleum production, provides the mainstay of the Bolivian economy. Government plans call for the development of mineral processing for export, so as to increase value-added and revenue earned. This has led to the expansion and establishment in the Altiplano of tin smelters and an antimony smelter (at Vinto) a zinc refinery, a bismuth refinery, tungsten plants and plans for copper, silver and lead refineries.

In the petroleum sector a considerable exploration effort has been launched by the YPFB and foreign oil companies in the Altiplano as well as in the traditional Oriente areas, and the Government has forecast crude oil exports of 200,000 barrels a day by 1980 compared with 37,700 in 1977. Though exports of crude oil and petroleum products declined in 1976 and 1977, internal consumption continued to increase rapidly, by an estimated 16% a year; however, local gas consumption is very low. Completion of the YPFB's US$125m. refinery expansion projects at Santa Cruz and Cochabamba and a lubricants plant at Cochabamba is expected in 1978. Natural gas exports to Argentina benefited from substantial price increases in 1977, but final details of the gas export deal with Brazil, of 1,500 tons per month, have yet to be settled.

The embryonic industrial sector has received some impetus from the Andean Pact agreements. A substanial petrochemical sector has been assigned to Bolivia under Andean Pact Decision 91, which will require an investment of US$640m. by 1980. Most development is directed to mineral and agricultural product-processing, but expansion is also due to take place in the cement industry and the number of textile, and engineering plants, partly under the stimulus of the Andean Pact decisions, is growing, though difficulties in making sales have been reported.

Information for Visitors

To Bolivia by Air

i. From Europe: Lufthansa, twice weekly from Frankfurt to La Paz, *via* New York and Lima. From other places, quickest to fly to Lima (British Caledonian, Air France, etc.), whence 13 flights a week to La Paz; or *via* São Paulo or Buenos Aires.

ii. From North America: Braniff, 6 flights weekly from New York to La Paz, *via* Washington, Miami and Panama. Lufthansa (see above). LAB (non-IATA cheaper, but slower and timekeeping poor), from Miami to La Paz *via* Panama, Santa Cruz and Cochabamba. From California, connections *via* Lima.

iii. Within South America: From Caracas and Bogotá, each weekly, by Iberia. From Guayaquil, 3 a week, by Braniff or Iberia. From Lima, 13 a week by Braniff, Iberia, Lufthansa, LAB (cheaper) or Aerolíneas Argentinas. From Arica, twice weekly by LAB. From Santiago, daily by Iberia, Braniff, LAN-Chile or Lufthansa. From Buenos Aires, daily by LAB, Aerolíneas Argentinas or Braniff. From Asunción, 6 a week by LAB, Braniff or Líneas Aéreas Paraguayas. From Rio, twice weekly by Cruzeiro do Sul. From São Paulo, 4 a week by Cruzeiro or LAB. LAB also fly to Caracas. *Note:* LAB flights to and from points E of La Paz tend also to call at Santa Cruz or Cochabamba, or both.

Tax on airline tickets 5%.

Airport tax of US$5 (only US$0.25 on flights to Arica and internal flights) is levied on leaving. No tax if leaving overland, or if you stay in Bolivia less than 24 hours.

By Sea To Mollendo, Callao, Arica or Antofagasta (see pages 166-169).

By Road　From Cuzco or Puno, several services. Peruvian road bad, Bolivian fair, neither is paved. (See pages 172-173.)

Motoring (1) From Puno (Peru) *via* border stations at Desaguadero (for Guaqui and La Paz) or Yunguyo (for Copacabana, the straits of Tiquina, and La Paz). Unpaved but all-weather. Peruvian customs at Desaguadero do not work after 1730 unless you are prepared to seek out the officials and pay them "overtime". Bolivian customs now operate to 1900. Peruvian time is an hour behind Bolivian time.

(2) From Salta-Jujuy-Laa Quiaca (Argentina) to Potosí or Tarija. Road fords many rivers in Bolivia and is impassable in wet weather (Argentine section is now rebuilt and completely paved). Bolivian border controls work mornings and 1400-1800 only.

(3) Alternative routes lead from the Argentine province of Salta *via* Bermejo or Yacuiba into Tarija. Dry weather only.

Motorists must buy an Hoja de Ruta (driving permit) from local offices of the Servicio Nacional de Tránsito for every road journey, specifying cities to be reached and date. These are checked and tolls charged outside each city. Cost of toll is about US$0.25 per 100 km.

Motorists must be warned against a road from Río Mulato into Chile by way of Ollagüe. "Between Río Mulato and Uyuni it is deep soft sand and possible only for 4-wheel drive vehicles and trucks. Beyond there is the danger of getting lost on the many tracks leading over the deserted salt lakes, no petrol between Uyuni and San Pedro de Conchi (Chile), and little hope of help with a breakdown on the Bolivian side unless you don't mind waiting for perhaps a week. After rain the route is impassable. Where the road has been built up, NEVER forsake it for the appealing soft salt beside it. The salt takes a man's weight but a vehicle breaks through the crust into unfathomable depths of plasticine mud below."—Mr. Andrew Parkin.

Petrol (gasoline) is very bad. "Corriente" (60 octane, costs US$0.28 per U.S. gallon. "Extra", a bit better at 80 octane, is US$0.34 per gallon but difficult to get outside the major towns. "Super Extra" is sold in La Paz at US$0.40 per U.S. gallon.

Buses ply on most of the roads. Reporting time for all Bolivia and Peru is half an hour before the bus leaves, but you may have to reserve a seat a few days in advance.

Trucks congregate at all town markets, with destinations chalked on the sides, to carry passengers on all Bolivian roads; they are cheaper than buses or ordinary trains and not much less comfortable!

Interconnecting roads　La Paz-Oruro, completely paved; La Paz-Guaqui and Oruro-Cochabamba, all-weather; Cochabamba-Santa Cruz, again paved; Cochabamba-Sucre and on to Potosí, S of paved road, now all-weather road. Oruro-Potosí, all-weather. La Paz-Beni-Trinidad which was opened in late 1977, on which we have no reports, so far. Nearly all Bolivian road surfaces, except for the paved sections, are bad.

Travel to Paraguay　Apart from the adventurous journey described on pages 181-182, a cheap way of getting to Paraguay is to travel by bus to Salta or Orán (Argentina), then on to Asunción *via* Resistencia (Argentina), by road or rail.

Travel by Train　Not recommended, except for the "ferrobus" services; the ordinary trains are dirty, slow and unheated, though the food in dining cars and at stations is acceptable.

Exchange rates　Those going to Peru can buy up to 5,000 soles in Bolivia to get a better rate of exchange. (But for the Peruvian regulations see under Peru.)

Documents　A passport only is needed for citizens of the Western European countries, the USA, Canada and Israel; all others need visas unless they have tourist cards, which can be obtained free from the Consuls and travel agencies; they are good for 90 days and can be renewed for 90 more. Tourist cards are not available for nationals of communist countries or Rhodesia. The exit-visa stamp, triangular in shape, which one used to have to get separately in La Paz, is now stamped in one's passport when entering Bolivia. One also needs an exit stamp at the border town.

N.B. When state-of-siege regulations are in force, you need a safe-conduct (*salvo-conducto*) from the DIN branch of the police in Plaza Murillo, La Paz, in order to leave the city. You may need a seperate *salvo-conducto* for each trip, without which bus and train tickets may be unobtainable. These may be obtained from the Interpol offices outside La Paz.

Travellers may be asked to produce an exit ticket, or the money to pay for it, and to show equivalent of US$10 a day for the amount of time they intend to stay in the country. No check, however, at the land frontiers. Visitors have also been required to prove that they have the equivalent of US$500 before being let in. All visitors must have a valid smallpox vaccination certificate.

Duty-free Imports 200 cigarettes, 50 cigars and 1 lb. tobacco; one opened bottle of alcoholic drink.

Camping Chet and Jeri Wade, of Sacramento, California, tell us that one can camp almost anywhere in safety. Warm sleeping gear essential. Beware sandstorms S of Oruro.

British Businessmen are strongly advised to consult "Hints to Business Men visiting Bolivia", which can be obtained free from Room CO7, Export Services Division, Dept. of Trade, Export House, 50 Ludgate Hill, London EC4M 7HU. Similar publications for U.S. businessmen may be obtained from the Government Printing Office, Washington.

The best time for a visit is May to November, the dry season. May, June, and July are the coldest months.

Festivals January (last week), La Paz, "Alacitas", on Av. Montes. Feb. 2, Aug. 25: Virgin Copacabana. May 3: Fiesta de la Invención de la Santa Cruz, various parts, in La Paz at the "Calvario". June 23: San Juan, all Bolivia. June 29: San Pedro y San Pablo, at Tiquina. July 28: Fiesta de Santiago (St. James), Altiplano and lake region; Achocalla a convenient place to go to. Nov. 1 and 2; All Saints and All Souls, any native cemetery. For other festivals on the Altiplano enquire at hotels or tourist office in La Paz. Remember that the cities are very closed up on national holidays, but colourful celebrations will be going on in the villages.

Particularly impressive is the Alacítas Fair held at La Paz in January. "It is dedicated to Ekeko, an Indian household god. You can buy plaster images of him at many of the booths. He is a red nosed cheerfully grinning little personage laden with an assortment of miniature cooking utensils, coins, balls of wool, tiny sacks of sugar, coffee, salt, rice and flour; a kind of Bolivian Santa Claus. Ekeko is said to bring prosperity and to grant wishes. If you buy a toy house, or a cow, or a sheep at the Alacitas, you will get a real one before the year is out. There are also model motor-cars and planes, for the extreme optimists." (Christopher Isherwood, "The Condor and the Cows.")

Climate There are four distinct climatic zones: (1) The tropical departments of Santa Cruz and Beni, drained by the Amazon; altitude between 150 and 750 metres; average temperature, 29°C. (2) The Yungas, or low valleys, north of La Paz and Cochabamba, among the spurs of the Cordillera; altitude, 750-1,500 metres; average temperature, 24°C. (3) The Valles, or high valleys and basins gouged out by the rivers of the Puna; average temperature, 19°C. (4) The Puna, and Altiplano; average temperature, 10°C. Little rain falls upon the western plateaux between May and November, but the rest of the year is wet. There is rain at all seasons in the eastern part of the country, and heavy rains from November to March.

Clothing suitable for Great Britain, with a raincoat or light overcoat, should be worn by visitors to the Altiplano and the Puna, where it is particularly cold at night. The climate in the Eastern Lowlands is tropical. Oruro and Potosí are colder than La Paz; Cochabamba can be very warm.

Health Whatever his age, the traveller arriving in La Paz by air (too quickly, that is, for a progressive adaptation to the altitude) should lie down for half a day, taking very little food and drink. Micoren or Coramina Glucosa tablets can be taken to help adjustment. He will be up and doing the next morning. In Bolivia, do as the Bolivians do: above 3,000 metres, walk slowly, very slowly uphill. Never go out for the whole day without taking an overcoat: the temperature drops sharply at sunset. Inoculate against typhoid and paratyphoid (also have yellow fever inoculation and anti-malaria tablets if visiting the lowlands) and stock up on necessary medicines; they are dear in Bolivia. We have also been asked to mention that hepatitis is very common; the gamma-globulin injection is recommended. Be very careful of salads; they can carry a multitude of vile green bacteria.

Cost of Living Rents, appliances, and some clothing, and especially toilet goods and medicines, are high priced but transport, most foods, and services are low. Hotels, meals, silver, gold, alpaca and llama items are now cheaper than in Lima. After years of monetary stability, the cost of living rose steeply in 1973-74, was reduced to 8% in 1975, and to 5.4% in 1976 but increased again by between 10 and 12% in 1977.

Best Buys Llama- and alpaca-wool knitted and woven items: ponchos, mantas, bags, chultos (bonnets). Gold and silverware. Musical instruments such as the charango (mandolin with armadillo-shell sound-box) and the queña (Inca flute).

Food and Drink The normal international cuisine is found at most good hotels and restaurants. Some local dishes are interesting: *sajta de pollo* contains chicken, onion, fresh potato, frozen-and-dried potato (known as *tunta*) and chilis; *ají de lengua* is basically ox-tongue with chilis, potatoes and *tuntas*. The local beer (Pilsener), lager-type, is the best to be found in Latin America, according to some conoscenti; the local hot maize drink, *api,* should be tried (usually US$0.12). Bottled water cannot always be found; the local tap water should not be drunk without first being sterilized. We have been told that the prepared food found in Indian markets can be relied upon, but we do not recommend this except to the desperate and, of course, to those accustomed to South American food. Avoid salads.

In the pensiones and cheaper restaurants a basic lunch (*almuerzo*) and dinner (*cena*) are normally available, at 9-12 pesos (US$0.45-US$0.60).

Salteñas are meat stew baked in a wrapping of dough, eaten regularly by Bolivians up to midday. Some are extremely picante (hot) with red chili peppers. They come in lessening grades of heat as muy picante, medio picante, and poco picante. For clean milk, try sachets of Leche Pil (plain, chocolate or Strawberry-flavoured), at US$0.05 each.

Currency The unit of currency is the peso boliviano ($b), divided into 100 centavos. Bank notes are for 1, 5, 10, 20, 50 and 100 pesos; coins of 5, 10, 20, 25 and 50 centavos and one peso circulate. Rate of exchange; $b20 to US$1. It is almost impossible to buy dollars at points of exit when leaving. Better unofficial rates can sometimes be obtained, especially for

US dollar notes, in exchange shops, and outside Bolivia. No restrictions on export or import of Bolivian pesos.

Measures The metric system is compulsory, but these Spanish measures are used, chiefly in the retail trade:

Capacity.—Dry: 1 arroba = 6.70 gallons. Liquid: 1 gallon = 0.74 gallon.
Weight.—1 libra = 16 onzas = 1.0147 lb. 1 arroba = 25 libras = 25.36 lb.
1 quintal = 100 libras = 101.47 lb.

Post, telegraph, and telephone Post offices use the post box (casilla) system; there is normally no delivery of letters or packages and recipients have to collect them from the boxes. Items sent by post should therefore bear, not the street address, but the casilla number and town.

There are air-mail and surface postal services both internally and to all parts of the world. Air-mail letters to and from Britain take between 5 and 10 days; surface mails take between one and three months and parcels much longer. West Coast Cables and All America have offices in La Paz for foreign telegrams. Radio telephone services run by the Serval Company serve Cochabamba and other parts of the interior. There is a telephone service to the U.K. between 1700 and 2000 local time *via* Argentina and a satellite call costs only \$b 162 for 3 minutes. Seven-word (minimum length) telegram \$b 77.

Air-mail letters to U.K. and other European countries cost \$b 6.50. Air-mail letters to North and Central American countries cost \$b 4.50. To other S. American countries \$b 1.20. La Paz post office is open Mon.-Sat. 0800-2000, and until 1800 Sunday and holidays.

Hours of Business are normally from 0900-1200, and from 1400-1800. Saturday is a half day. Opening and closing in the afternoon are several hours later in the provinces. Government offices are closed on Saturday. Banks 0900-1200, 1400-1630, but closed on Saturday. Local time is 4 hours behind GMT.

The Press At La Paz: morning papers—"Presencia", modern format (offset), largely Catholic mouthpiece but good coverage of world events; "Hoy" and "El Diario". Evenings: "Ultima Hora", and "Jornada". At Cochabamba—"Prensa Libre"; "Los Tiempos", "Extra". At Oruro—"La Patria". Sucre, Santa Cruz and Trinidad have weekly papers. La Paz papers are on sale in other cities. The "Miami Herald" is available in La Paz.

Internal Air Services are run by Lloyd Aéreo Boliviano between the main towns. Its service to Santa Cruz and Puerto Suárez connects, across the river at Corumbá (Brazil), with services to various parts of Brazil.

Public Holidays

January 1—New Year's Day.
Carnival Week—Mondays, Shrove Tuesday, Ash Wednesday.
Holy Week—Thursday, Friday and Saturday.
May 1—Labour Day.
June 1.

Corpus Christi (movable).
July 16—La Paz Municipal Holiday.

August 5, 7—Independence.
Oct. 12—Columbus Day.
November 2—Day of the Dead.
Christmas Day.

There are local holidays at Tarija, on April 15; at Sucre on May 25; at Cochabamba, Sept. 14; at Santa Cruz and Pando, Sept. 24; at Potosí, Nov. 10; at Beni, Nov. 18, and at Oruro, Feb. 22.

British and U.S. Representatives in Bolivia There are British and American Embassies at La Paz and Consulates at La Paz and Cochabamba. The British Embassy is at Avenida Arce 2740. Letters to First Secretary (Commercial) to: Casilla 694, La Paz. Tel.: 51400 and 29404.

American Express Agents La Paz: Crillon Tours Ltda, Avda. Camacho 1223. Tel.: 40102.

Our grateful thanks for help in revising this section go to Michael Wooller, of LBI Economics Department; to Madeleine Champion, resident in La Paz; to the Paris office of Lloyd Aéreo Boliviano; and to the following travellers: Philip Allen (São Paulo), Diana Birkbeck and Nicholas Davies, James K. Bock (Mexico City), Markus

Casanova (Fribourg, Switzerland), Andrew Cox, Christine Czajkowski, Michael Davison, Peter Ford and Sally Wilson, Tim and Arlene Frost (Hamilton N.Z.), Peter Fürst and Hakon Hegnar (Norway), Helen J. Glover, Mary Goodykoontz and Ken Scarlett (Woodland, Calif.), Ucky Hamilton (N.Z.), Gerhard Keilbach (Stuttgart), Leslie E. Kent (Pretoria), Cornelio Lindenburg and Marieke van der Ploeg (Amersfoort, Netherlands), Rolf Maag (Caracas), Ian Macdonell, Phoebe Mayer (USA-Peru), Bernd Morgeneyer (Berlin), Alexander Nemeth and Janette Roberts (Australia), Jenny Owen, Dirk Partridge (Washington, USA), Dr. Margaret Peil, Thomas Pensler (Benediktbauern, W. Germany), Joni Perkins (Canada), Carole Peirce (USA), E. C. Pineles, Andrew Radclyffe, Judith Rattenbury (Durham) and Nicole Visart (Paris), Rosalind and Stuart Read (N.Z.), Wendy Sarsby (Port Credit, Ontario), Helga Schmidt-Frank and Herbert Schmidt (W. Germany), Chris Sharpe (Mullewa, W. Australia), David Gaddis Smith (USA), Lothar Springer (Münster), Ken and Judy Stevenson (Ottawa), Peter Varey, Andreas Weber (Wohlen, Switzerland), Nicholas Westwood and Julia Amies, Tim Williams and Elizabeth Young.

195

This publication was
Phototypeset by

DAWSON & GOODALL
LIMITED

THE MENDIP PRESS
BATH · ENGLAND

Tel : 0225 64156
Telex : 44600 SOWPAL G

Established in 1770, we are
specialists in the production of fine
colour work in litho and letterpress

BRAZIL

BRAZIL, the fifth largest country in the world, has the eighth largest population. It is almost as large as the United States of America. Its 8,511,965 square km. is nearly half that of the South American sub-continent. For neighbours it has all the South American countries save Chile and Ecuador. Distances are enormous: 4,320 km. from north to south, 4,328 km; from east to west, a land frontier of 15,719 km. and an Atlantic coast line of 7,408 km. Its population of over 115,000,000 is half that of South America, and one in every two is under 25 years of age.

Brazil's topography varies greatly, but may be divided roughly into four main zones: the Amazon Basin, a vast lowland drained by the world's largest river and its tributaries; the River Plate Basin; the Guiana Highlands, north of the Amazon; and the Brazilian Highlands south of the Amazon. The two great river basins account for about three-fifths of Brazil's area.

The Amazon Basin, in northern and western Brazil, takes up more than a third of the whole country. Some of this basin is plain, broadly based on the Andes and funnelling narrowly to the sea; most of the drained area has an elevation of less than 250 metres. The rainfall is heavy, for the winds from the north-east and south-east lose their moisture as they approach the Andes. Some few places receive from 3,750 to 5,000 mm. a year, though over most of the area it is no more than from 1,500 to 2,500 mm. Much of the basin suffers from annual floods. The region is covered by evergreen forest, with little undergrowth except along the streams. The climate is hot and the humidity high throughout the year.

The River Plate Basin, in the southern part of Brazil, has a more varied surface and is less heavily forested than the Amazon Basin. The land is higher and the climate cooler.

Most of the Brazilian territory is in fact highland, and awkwardly placed highland at that, in terms of communication with the sea. The Guiana Highlands, north of the Amazon, are partly forested, partly hot stony desert. Those that face the north-west winds get heavy rainfall, but the southern slopes are arid. The rainfall, which comes during the hot season, is about 1,250 mm a year. The summers are hot and the winters cool.

The Brazilian Highlands lying between the Amazon and the River Plate Basin form a tableland of from 300 to 900 metres high, but here and there, mostly in South-Eastern Brazil, mountain ranges rise from it. The second highest peak in Brazil, the Pico da Bandeira, north-east of Rio de Janeiro, is 2,898 metres; the highest peak, the recently-discovered Pico da Neblina on the Venezuelan border, is 3,014 metres.

For the most part the Highlands cascade sharply to the sea. It is only north of Salvador that there is any appreciable cultivable land between the Highlands and the Atlantic; south of Salvador as far as Porto Alegre the coast rises steeply to a protective barrier, the Great Escarpment. In only two places is this Escarpment breached by deeply cut river beds—where the Rio Doce and the Rio Paraíba find their outlets; and only in two places, between Santos and São Paulo and between Paranaguá and Curitiba, does the land rise in a single slope making for comparatively easy communication with the interior. Along most of its course, the Great Escarpment falls to the sea in parallel steps, each step separated by the trough of a valley.

The few rivers born on the Escarpment which flow direct into the Atlantic do so precipitously and are not navigable. Most of the rivers flow deep into the interior. Those in southern Brazil rise almost within sight of the sea, run through the vast interior, first north-westwards to join the Paraná, and then southwards to its exit as the River Plate. In the central area the Escarpment rivers run away from the sea to join the São Francisco river, which flows northwards parallel to the coast for 2,900 km., to tumble over the Paulo Afonso Falls on its eastward course to the Atlantic.

The Great Escarpment denies to most of Brazil the natural valley outflows and lines of travel from the interior to the sea. Of its rivers the Amazon alone is directly navigable for a great distance inland.

The coastal strip, though on an average only 100 km. wide, is nevertheless extremely important. It contains only 7.7% of the total area of Brazil, but in the strip live 37% of the population. The states of Rio de Janeiro and Espírito Santo are almost completely within it.

Climate The average annual temperature increases steadily from south to north, and the difference in temperature between the coldest and warmest month decreases. But even on the Equator, in the Amazon Basin, the average temperature is not more than 27°C, and the highest recorded has not been more than 36°C. Six degrees more have been recorded in the dry north-eastern states. From the latitude of Recife south to Rio de Janeiro, the mean temperature is from 23° to 27°C along the coast, and from 18° to 21°C in the Highlands, where it is always cooler. From a few degrees south of Rio de Janeiro to the boundary with Uruguay the mean temperature is from 17° to 19°C. Humidity is relatively high in Brazil, particularly along the coast. It is 78% in Rio de Janeiro, which is high enough for discomfort when the wind drops.

It is only in rare cases that the rainfall can be described as either excessive or deficient: few places get more than 2,000 mm.—the coast north of Belém, some of the Amazon Basin, and a small area of the Serra do Mar between Santos and São Paulo, where the downpour has been

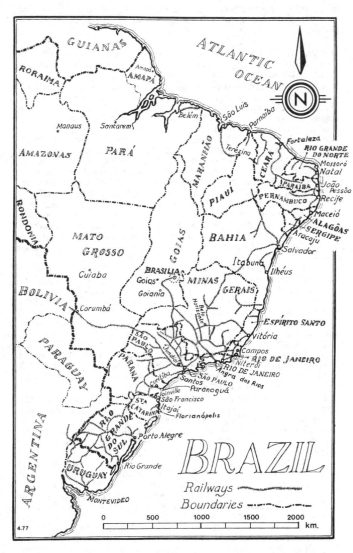

ROUGH SKETCH

harnessed to generate electricity. The north-eastern droughts are caused not by lack of rainfall, but by irregular rainfall; the area is also subject to floods.

Distribution of the Population. One would expect, after centuries of colonisation, a very large population. This is not so. Brazil, considering its size and potential, is very meagerly populated indeed.

By mid-1977 the population of Brazil had reached at least 110 millions, which represents an average density of 11.7 people per square kilometre over the whole country; but this population is heavily concentrated in a comparatively small area—chiefly along the coastal strip where the original Portuguese settlers exploited the agricultural wealth, and further inland in the states of Minas Gerais and São Paulo where more recent development has been centred. Much of the interior of Pará, Amazonas, Goiás and Mato Grosso has densities of one person per square km. or less, and is still far from the frontiers of settlement, which push forward into their more accessible border areas with road-building programmes and associated development projects. Brazil's attention is officially focused on these relatively under-populated regions as a means of syphoning off some of the population growth which is already saturating the urban centres—the industrialised South-East contains more than 50% of the total urban population and two cities, São Paulo and Rio de Janeiro, which both have over six million people in their metropolitan areas.

The deep interior (Sertão) has been relatively unaffected by European and Far Eastern immigration, which has gone to the big cities and the more intensely cultivated lands of the South-East and the South. Its inhabitants are people of Portuguese or Indian origin, or a mixture of the two (mestiço); most live off a primitive, but ecologically effective method of cultivation known as "slash and burn", which involves cutting down and burning the forest for a small patch of ground which is cultivated for a few years and then allowed to return to forest, while the people move on to another patch; some herd unimproved cattle, whereas others live off hunting, fishing and the collection of forest products; their contact is almost solely with traders who take their meagre surplus in exchange for guns, knives and other essentials.

The urban population of Brazil has been increasing at rates more than double the overall average rate, and much of this growth is concentrated in the larger cities—those over 100,000, which numbered 70 in 1970. Internal migration is the major cause of these phenomenal growth rates, bringing to the cities problems of unemployment, housing shortage, and pressure on services which are already stretched to breaking point; shanty towns—or favelas, mocambos, alagados, according to the region—are an integral part of the urban landscape and a constant reminder of the poverty of some of the rural areas from whence these people come. Neither Brasílias nor colonisation schemes in Amazonia can provide sufficiently attractive large scale alternatives to stem the flow of hopeful migrants to urban opportunities.

The decision to found a new federal capital, Brasília, deep in the interior, was a symbolic act of faith in the future of the Sertão: a bold attempt to deflect population from the coastal regions to the under-developed central and western plateaux of the country.

Bank of London & South America in Brazil.

The Bank of London & South America, a subsidiary of Lloyds Bank International, maintains a network of branches throughout Brazil which offer a full range of financial services.

Central Office and São Paulo Branch: Rua 15 de Novembro 143-165, São Paulo Telephone: 239-0322 and 239-5122

Political and Social History. The first system of government adopted by the settlers was a Capitânia, a kind of feudal principality—there were thirteen of them, but these were replaced in 1572 by a Viceroy. In the same year an experiment was tried of dividing the colony into two, north and south, with capitals at Salvador and Rio de Janeiro, a division which corresponded in the main with the tendency of settlers from southern Portugal to settle in northern Brazil, and those from northern Portugal in southern Brazil. It was not until 1763 that Rio became the sole capital.

In quite early days colonial society formed itself into a hierarchy—the white Peninsulars and the whites born in Brazil at the top, with the Mestiços or Mamelucos (the result of intermarriage with the Indian) and Mulattos (the result of intermarriage with the Africans) well below. There was also the Cafuso, the element resulting from the marriage between black and Indian.

The Colonial set-up, which lasted to the early years of the nineteenth century, was complicated. The Indians, contrary to the law, were virtually slaves; the blacks were actually slaves.

The economic structure was, in the main, that of huge estates run by slave labour, with an aristocratically-minded white element that played the absentee landlord and did no manual work. The Portuguese crown expected both a personal and a state revenue from its colony. This was raised partly by payment of a tenth of the produce from grants of land made to colonists, and partly by some forty kinds of taxes levied on the inhabitants. The judicial system was lax, and there was great corruption by sale of office. But in Brazil, unlike the Spanish Colonies, there was a saving laxity in tax collection, in slavery, and in the general regimentation of the colonists.

With two exceptions, the bulk of the colonists, right up to the early 19th century, lived mostly along the coastal belt. The exceptions were the settlers in the states of São Paulo and Minas Gerais, the Paulistas and Mineiros, who had thrust far into the interior.

Three hundred years of easy going colonial life under the paternal eye of Portugal had ill-prepared the colonists for independent existence, but towards the end of the 18th century the infiltration of European thought and, between 1808 and 1815, the machinations of Napoleon in Europe, forced the colonists to decide whether they preferred tutelage or independence. When the troops of Napoleon caused the Portuguese Royal Family to sail in British ships to Brazil in 1808, the fate of the colony was decided. King João VI returned to the mother country in 1821, leaving his son, the handsome young Pedro, as Regent. The Portuguese Parliament (the Cortes) mistrusted this arrangement, and called on Pedro to return, but the Brazilians called upon him to stay. On May 13 he assumed the title of "Perpetual Defender and Protector of Brazil". On September 7 he was challenging Portugal with the cry "Independence or Death" by the Ipiranga River; on October 12, he was being proclaimed constitutional emperor of Brazil, and on December 1 he was being crowned in Rio de Janeiro. Brazil was an independent Empire.

Dom Pedro the First had the bad luck to be faced by a secession movement in the north, to lose the Banda Oriental (today Uruguay) and to get somewhat involved in his marital relations. In sum, he abdicated as the result of a military revolt in 1831, leaving his five-year-old son, Dom Pedro the Second, in the hands of a regent, as ruler. On July 23, 1840, the lad, though only 15, was proclaimed of age and the regency discontinued. And now began a golden time for Brazil, for Dom Pedro the Second, a liberal democrat at heart, was one of the wisest rulers this earth has known. He promoted education, vastly increased communications, encouraged agriculture, and stamped on corruption. It was under him, too, that immigrants began to fill the land. And it was he—no small title to fame—who brought down the tyrant Rosas at Buenos Aires by a sharp and well-conducted war. The war with the dictator López of Paraguay lasted longer, but led to the same salutary end. Above all, it was he who finally declared that he would rather lose his crown than allow slavery to continue, and on May 13, 1888, it was finally abolished.

There is little doubt but that it was this measure which, in fact, lost him his crown. Many plantation owners, who had been given no compensation, were ruined, and turned against the Emperor. On November 15, 1889, the Republic was proclaimed. On November 17, he sailed for Europe. Two years later he died in a second-rate hotel in Paris. after steadfastly refusing a pension from the conscience-stricken revolutionaries. During the first centenary of independence in 1922 the imperial family was allowed to return to Brazil, and the body of Dom Pedro was brought back and buried in the cathedral at Petrópolis. Brazilians, essentially a tender-hearted people, heaved a sigh of relief.

The history of the "Old Republic" (1889-1930) was comparatively eventless, a time of expansion and increasing prosperity. Brazil declared war on Germany during both wars and Brazilian troops fought in the Italian campaign in 1944-45. 1930 is a cardinal point in Brazilian history: a revolution, headed by Getúlio Vargas, Governor of Rio Grande do Sul, who was to become known as "the Father of the Poor" for the social measures he introduced, deposed the then president and Vargas assumed executive power as dictator. He was forced to resign in October 1945. In 1946 a liberal republic was restored and the following 18 years saw considerable economic development and social advance. There was, however, increasing government instability and corruption leading to growing military intervention in civil affairs; this culminated in the military movement of March 1964, which has ruled ever since.

Settlement and Economic History   Preston E. James, in his book *Latin America,* finds little attachment to the land in Brazil. With one exception—the three southern states—he sees in the pattern of Brazilian economy a continuous desire for quick wealth, an ideal, as the Brazilian writer Holanda puts it, "of collecting the fruit without planting the tree". This attitude developed from the traditions of the early Portuguese settlers; its distinguishing marks are swift opportunist changes from one speculative product to another according to world prices and a failure to cultivate intensively to reduce costs: the invariable result is that other parts of the world, after a time, are able to produce more cheaply and overtake Brazil's initial advantage. It is a picture of destructive, rather than of constructive exploitation, played against the curse of a great area and seemingly limitless opportunity, "the ever-present possibility of moving on to new lands and of exploiting new resources . . . and the lack of any compelling reason for the intensification and stabilization of economic life in any one region".

A brief account of the settlement and of the ensuing economic history will make this clear.

Brazil was discovered for the Portuguese by Pedro Alvares Cabral in

1500. The original inhabitants were the Tupi-Guarani Indians, whose males hunted and fished and left the tilling of the soil to the women. The first settlement was at Salvador da Bahia. These wealthy settlers came mainly from southern Portugal, with its feudal traditions of great estates. For the first few years Portugal, then much concerned with the east, paid little attention to Brazil. But about 1507 a second colony was settled at São Vicente, near Santos, and in 1537 a third at Olinda, near Recife. The settlers at São Vicente, who made the first settlement in the highlands at São Paulo in 1534, were unlike those at Salvador and Recife: they came from the poorer and more energetic north of Portugal. All of them were attracted less by the prospect of earning their living by persistent toil than by opportunities of speculative profit. To do the work they impressed the native Indians, a large number of whom died from European diseases. They inter-married freely with them and, later, with slaves imported from Africa.

Sugar cane had been introduced at São Vicente in 1532, but it was the wealthy settlers of the north-east who had the necessary capital to exploit the crop and to buy African slaves to work it; the Indian, with his own tradition of leisure, was a disappointment as a labourer. In the matter of sugar, Salvador and Recife had the advantages over São Vicente of being very much nearer home, and of having better ports and easier access to the interior. During the latter half of the 16th and the whole of the 17th centuries, the states of Bahia, Pernambuco, and Paraíba were the world's prime source of sugar.

The settlers at São Paulo, galled by poverty and envious of the more fortunate north-east, sent out expeditions to explore the interior in a search for gold, which had already been found in small quantities in their own streams. These hardy Bandeirantes pushed as far south as Colonia, opposite Buenos Aires, as far west as the River Paraguay, and north into the area west of the sugar plantations of the north-east. In 1698 they struck gold in the gravels of central Minas Gerais. More was found soon after in central Mato Grosso, and in 1725 in Goiás. Diamonds were discovered in 1729 north of the goldfields of Minas Gerais.

There was a great gold and diamond rush in which the sugar planters participated. Sugar by that time was on the decline; there was competition from other countries; profits had fallen, and the Brazilians had made no attempt to lower costs by ploughing back profits: that was not in their nature or tradition. The gold boom started early in the 18th century, lasted a hundred years, and then petered out. Minas Gerais was transformed from a wilderness into a well populated agricultural, pastoral, and mining region. It was as an outlet for this area that Rio de Janeiro was developed. Some of the wealth went to create the extraordinarily beautiful city of Ouro Preto, to-day a somewhat depopulated national monument of superb building, painting and sculpture, and the similarly attractive cities of São João del Rei, Mariana, Congonhas do Campo, Diamantina and others.

Brazil was ready for the next speculation: coffee. Coffee planting began near Rio de Janeiro and at many places round the coast as far as the Amazon, but by 1825 it had mainly been concentrated in the Paraíba valley, west of the Capital. From there it spread into São Paulo, where its cultivation attracted a large number of immigrants after 1850. About a third of the total production normally still comes from São Paulo state.

There have been many other typical Brazilian booms and recessions.

The best known is the famous rubber boom in the Amazon valley; foreign competition wiped it out after 1912. Cotton, oranges, cocoa, and even maté tea have been the subject of booms, declines, and rehabilitations. In each case Brazil has been challenged by other sources of supply, where more intensive methods of production were applied. The result, in Brazil has been a lack of stability of settlement.

This boom tradition still holds, but it is shifting from agriculture to industry. Agricultural products have accounted for the bulk of Brazil's exports for many years and some 40% of the people are still rural, but Brazilians today resent the description of their country as essentially agricultural: they prefer to think of themselves as a rising industrial people. Industrial production has increased greatly and in 1977 two-fifths of exports were defined as "of manufactures". Nevertheless, Brazil still remains a country where oases of prosperity are edged by deserts of poverty and wilderness.

One interesting aspect of the various booms is the large internal migration which has accompanied them: each product, as its popularity grows, has proved a magnet for the rest of Brazil. Because of its poverty, the North-East has lost a very large number of workers to the industries of the South-East.

Immigration Modern immigration did not begin effectively until after 1850. Over five million have come in since, most of them during this century. Between 1884 and 1954 Brazil received 4,611,024 immigrants from Europe. Of these, 32% were Italians, who make ideal colonists in Brazil, 30% were Portuguese, 14% Spanish, 4% German, and the rest of various nationalities. Since 1954 immigrants have averaged 50,000 a year. There are some 500,000 Japanese in Brazil; so successful are they that they grow a fifth of the coffee, 30% of the cotton, all the tea, and are deeply involved in the market garden industry.

Most of the German immigrants have settled in Santa Catarina, Rio Grande do Sul, and Paraná. It is interesting to see what a different tradition can do. The Germans (and the Italians and Poles and other Slavs who followed them) did not in the main go as wage earners on the big estates, but as cultivators of their own small farms. Possibly because there is no speculative product in the region they occupy, the populations in these three southern states have begun to expand, and without loss of population at the centre: a rare phenomenon in Latin America. Here at last is a settled agricultural population cultivating the soil intensively. It is only by such methods and by such an expansion that the wastes of the Sertão could be put to effective use.

The People The Portuguese colonists inter-married freely with the Indians and the blacks. At first the new colony grew slowly. From 1580 to 1640 the population was only about 50,000 apart from the million or so indigenous Indians. By 1650 it was 70,000. In 1700 there were some 750,000 civilized people in Brazil. Early in the 19th century Humboldt computed there were about 920,000 whites, 1,960,000 Africans, and 1,120,000 Indians and mestiços: after three centuries of occupation a total of only four millions, and over twice as many blacks as there were whites.

The immigrations of the 19th and 20th centuries changed the picture vastly. Today the whites and near-whites are about 60% of the population, people of mixed race about 21%, and blacks 15%; the rest are either aboriginal Indians or Asians. There are large regional variations in the distribution of the races: the whites predominate greatly in the south, which received the largest flood of European immigrants, and decrease more or less progressively towards the north.

The six censuses of the present century show the growth of the population:

1900	..	..	..	17,318,558	1950	..	..	..	51,955,397
1920	..	..	..	30,635,606	1960	..	..	..	70,976,185
1940	..	..	..	41,236,315	1970	..	..	..	93,244,279

Since 1960 the population has grown by over 2 million a year, and this is natural growth in the main and not due to immigration. The population in the cities is rising very rapidly: but ten largest cities now hold 15% of the whole population, and Brazil has 60 other towns with more than 100,000 inhabitants. The average life span has increased from 39 years in 1939 to 56 years today. The population grows by about 2.8% each year.

About one fifth of the people are illiterate. Of the 13 million children between 7 and 14, 2 million have no school to go to. Of those who go to school, only 60% stay long enough to learn how to read and write. Adult literacy campaigns have, however, recently improved the picture.

But there are important facts about a people which no census can reveal. One of these is that there is no legal discrimination against the coloured peoples, but the economic and educational disparity—by default rather than intent of the Government—is such that successful non-white (particularly Afro) Brazilians are active almost exclusively in the worlds of sport, entertainment and art. Another is that the Brazilians are an exceptionally courteous and hospitable people, with an aristocracy to whom blood and tradition is more important than wealth. Religion enters deeply into the communal life, and provides much of its colour in a variety of festivals. There is deep local patriotism: a Brazilian has bonds with his state and often with his native town, as much as with his country.

This table gives the census returns for 1950 to 1970. The capital of each state is given in brackets.

States				1950	1960	1970
North:	Acre (Rio Branco)	..	..	—	160	218
	Amazonas (Manaus)..	..	..	514	721	961
	Pará (Belém)	..	..	1,123	1,551	2,197
North-east:	Maranhão (S. Luís)	..	..	1,583	2,492	3,037
	Piauí (Teresina)	..	..	1,046	1,263	1,735
	Ceará (Fortaleza)	..	..	2,695	3,338	4,492
	Rio Grande do Norte (Natal)		..	968	1,157	1,612
	Paraíba (João Pessoa)		..	1,713	2,018	2,445
	Pernambuco (Recife)		..	3,395	4,137	5,253
	Alagoas (Maceió)		..	1,093	1,271	1,606
East:	Sergipe (Aracaju)	..	..	644	760	911
	Bahia (Salvador)		..	4,835	5,991	7,583
	Minas Gerais (Belo Horizonte)		..	7,718	9,799	11,645
	Espírito Santo (Vitória)		..	862	1,189	1,618
	*Rio de Janeiro (Niterói)		..	2,297	3,403	4,795
	*Guanabara (Rio de Janeiro)		..	2,377	3,307	4,316
South:	São Paulo (São Paulo)		..	9,134	12,975	17,959
	Paraná (Curitiba)		..	2,116	4,278	6,998
	Santa Catarina (Florianópolis)		..	1,561	2,147	2,930
	Rio Grande do Sul (Porto Alegre)			4,165	5,449	6,755
Centre-west:	†Mato Grosso (Cuiabá)		..	522	910	1,624
	Goiás (Goiânia)	..	..	1,215	1,955	2,998
	Federal District	..	..	—	142	546
	Territories (4)	..	..	—	177	275
	Total	..	..	51,944	70,976	93,244

*From March 15, 1975, the State of Guanabara has been incorporated with the State of Rio de Janeiro, of which the city of Rio de Janeiro is now the capital.
†In 1977 Mato Grosso was divided in two, the southern portion forming the new state of Mato Grosso do Sul, with its capital at Campo Grande.

Communications Inadequate communications are a formidable handicap. Transport problems are those of a continent rather than of a country, yet 85% of the railways, 60% of the roads, 85% of the population and 90% of the cultivated land are contained in a coastal belt 480 km. wide.

Railways, of which there are about 30,500 km.—originally built to supply export markets—have divided this belt into economic "islands". To join them effectively by rail, however, means—besides 3,200 km. of new construction—the unifying of Brazil's five existing gauges. This sounds more alarming than in reality it is: 90% of the track is one metre gauge, 7% one metre sixty, and only 3%, mostly of unimportant lines, is of less than one metre gauge. About 2,450 km; have now been electrified, and virtually all the others have adopted diesel traction. A railway-improvement plan is now in operation, as a means towards the more economical use of fossil fuels.

Roads Though the best paved highways are still heavily concentrated in the South-East, those serving the interior are now being improved to all-weather status and many are being paved. Brazil has over one million kilometres of highways, of which in 1975 over 75,000 km. were paved, and the recent road-building programmes have emphasized inter-regional connections and the opening up of the Centre, North and West of the country.

Air Services   The first commercial flight in Brazil was in 1927. Because of the lack (until recently) of railways and roads and the great distances, aircraft have eased the traveller's lot more spectacularly in Brazil than in any other country. The larger cities are now linked with each other several times a day by air, and even the more remote points in the country can now be reached by light aircraft.

Government

The **Constitution** is based on that of the United States of America. There is a federal form of government and legislative power is exercised by a Chamber of Deputies and a Federal Senate. The Federal Senate consists of two representatives from each of the States elected by direct suffrage for a term of eight years and a third elected by an electoral college. The Chamber of Deputies has 280 representatives elected for four years on the proportional system. The Federal District is not represented in either. The President and Vice-President are elected for a term of 6 years by an electoral college and not by popular vote. By the constitutional reforms of 1967, the President has residual control over all aspects of federal government, authority to intervene in any of the 21 States without consulting Congress, and the right to declare a state of siege and rule by decree.

There is universal suffrage for all citizens over 18 with the exception of beggars, illiterates, soldiers, and those whose political rights have been suspended.

Capital punishment is allowed in cases of armed rebellion against the State, the subversion of political or social order by violent means or through the help or subsidy of a foreign State or international political organisation.

Since April 1964, when the military leaders overthrew the left-wing government of João Goulart, the army has controlled the country and the political machine. President (1974-79): Gen. Ernesto Geisel. It is expected that Gen. João Batista Figueiredo will be President for the term 1979-85.

Local Administration   Each Federal State has a Governor who exercises the executive power, and a Legislative Assembly which legislates on all matters affecting provincial administration and provides for State expense and needs by levying taxes. It also legislates on civil and criminal affairs affecting its own territory.

Brazilian Cities

Brasília   On April 21, 1960, Rio de Janeiro ceased to be the Federal Capital of Brazil; as required by the Constitution, it was finally replaced by Brasília, 960 km. away in the unpopulated uplands of Goiás, deep in the heart of the undeveloped Sertão. Brasília's population is now about 400,000 (the Federal District as a whole, with an area of 5,814 square km., has about 1 million inhabitants).

The new capital lies 1,150 metres above sea-level on undulating ground. The climate, unlike the climate of the old capital, is mild and the humidity refreshingly low, but trying in dry weather when it falls below Sahara levels. The noonday sun beats hard, but summer brings heavy rains and the air is usually cool by night.

The creation of an inland capital had been urged since the beginning of the last century, but it was the election policy proposals for developing the interior that finally brought it into being after President Kubitschek came into power in 1956, when a competition for the best general plan was announced. It was won by Professor Lúcio Costa, who laid out the city in the shape of a bent bow and arrow, the bent bow following roughly the shores of a large lake, created by damming the Paranoá river. Along the curve of the bow are the residential areas made up of large six-storey apartment blocks, the "Super-Quadras". Four of these Super-Quadras form a neighbourhood unit (Unidade de Vizinhança) each with its shops, playground, club, cinema and primary school. The main shopping area, with more cinemas, restaurants and so on, is situated at the centre near the Teatro Nacional. Several parks—or at least green areas—are now in being; they were bare red earth for years, but the grass-covered areas are now multiplying fast. The private residential areas are W of the Super-Quadras, and on the other side of the lake.

At right angles to these residential areas is the "arrow", the 8-km. long, 250-metre wide Eixo Monumental. At the tip of the arrow, as it were, on high ground, is the Praça dos Tres Poderes (The Square of the Three Powers), with spacious grounds for the Congress buildings, the Palácio do Planalto (the President's office) and the Supreme Court building. The Cathedral, built in the shape of the crown of thorns, and the Ministry buildings line the Esplanada dos Ministérios, W of the Praça. Where the bow and arrow intersect is the main bus station (Rodoviária), with the cultural and recreational centres and commercial areas on either side. There is a sequence of zones westward along the shaft of the arrow; a hotel centre, a radio city, an area for fairs and circuses, a centre for sports, the Praça Municipal (with the municipal offices in the Palácio do Buriti and a great cross marking the spot on which the first mass was said in Brasília, on May 3, 1957), and, lastly (where the string of the bow is) a site for a railway station with the industrial area nearby. The most impressive buildings are all by Oscar Niemeyer, Brazil's leading architect.

The main north-south road (Eixo Rodoviário) in which fast moving traffic is segregated, follows the curve of the bow; the radial road is along the line of the arrow—intersections are avoided by means of underpasses and cloverleafs. Motor and pedestrian traffic are carefully segregated in the residential areas. Buses leaving Brasília make a full-turn on a cloverleaf, giving the passengers a last view of the city, which can be seen from a long distance away on the broad empty plain.

Both the Palácio da Alvorada (the President's residence) and the Brasília Palace Hotel are near the lake. (The 80-km. drive along an asphalt road round it is attractive, and may be enjoyed on a special bus, caught at the bus station. There is a small restaurant at the dam, below which there are spectacular falls in the rainy season). Between the Praça dos Tres Poderes and the lake are sites for various recreations, including golf, fishing and yacht clubs, and an acoustic shell for shows in the open air. The airport, suitable for "jumbos", is on the far side of the lake. Some 250 hectares between the lake and the northern residential area (Asa Norte) are reserved for the University of Brasília, founded in 1962. It has about 8,000 students, and one of the country's best science departments.

South of the university area, the Avenida das Nacoes (Avenue of the Nations) runs from the Palácio da Alvorada along the lake to join the road from the airport to the centre. Along it will be found all the principal embassies.

Sightseeing Brasília is a strange city to visit. Apart from buildings open only during the week the main points of the city can be seen in a day by bus or taxi tour—don't try walking. The city is very quiet at weekends. Congress is open to visitors Mon.-Fri. 0800-1200 and 1400-1800, guides free of charge (in English 1400-1600). The Palácio da Alvorada can sometimes be visited at weekends by those with passes, easily got from reception desk at the Palácio do Planalto in the Praça dos Tres Poderes. The Planalto itself may be visited; admission restricted to men in lounge suits and women in dresses, Mon.-Fri., 0900-1100 and 1500-1700. The building of the Ministry of Foreign Affairs, the Itamarati, has beautiful water gardens and is one of the most rewarding visits (0800-0900 and 1300-1400); a permit must be obtained on the previous day from the desk in the entrance at side. Opposite the Itamarati is the Palácio de Justica, another magnificent building, with artificial cascades between its concrete columns. Visiting on Mon.-Fri. (lounge suits and dresses needed), 0800-1200 and 1400-1600. Those with no cars and in a hurry should take an inclusive tour: expensive, but distances are enormous. A good and cheap way of seeing Brasília is by taking bus rides from the bus station at the centre: the destinations are clearly marked. A one-day visit by air from Río gives 4 hours in Brasília for a minibus tour, starting and ending at airport (US$15-20). A fine view of the city may be had from the television tower, which has a free observation platform at 75 metres up (also restaurant, bar and souvenir shop). About 4 blocks W of the TV tower is the Church of Dom Bosco (the Igrejinha), a most interesting building constructed largely of blue glass. Other religious buildings worth seeing are the Fátima church in the Asa Sul and the chapel (Ermida) of Dom Bosco, on the other side of the lake opposite the Alvorada. Some 15 km. out along the Belo Horizonte road is the small wooden house, known as O Catetinho, in which President Kubitschek stayed in the late 1950s while the original construction work was going on; it is open to visitors and most interesting.

At the base of the TV tower a "hippie fair" is held every Sunday; some of the craftwork is very good and quite reasonable compared with other cities.

Light industry alone is allowed in the city and its population is limited to 500,000; it is now about 400,000 and about a quarter of a million more people live in a number of shanty towns, with minimal services, located well away from the main city. The Supreme Court, the President and Congress have worked there since 1961; the Ministry buildings have been finished only during the past few years and are now operating. In fact, Brasília is becoming more like a capital all the time. Social amenities are greatly improved, with more cinemas and night clubs opening. Two auditoria of the Teatro Nacional, the Sala Villa-Lobos (1,200 seats) and the Sala Martins Pena (550) are now open; the building is in the shape of an Aztec pyramid.

Ceremonies The States of Brazil take it in turn, the first Sunday of each month, to raise the flag in the Praça dos Tres Poderes, accompanied by music and a cultural presentation.

The guard is changed ceremonially at the Palácio do Planalto on Mon. and Thurs., 0900 and 1730. The President attends if he is present.

Sculptures Brasília is famous for its wealth of modern sculpture, ideally set against the fine modern buildings. Examples are: "Culture" (on the University campus), "The Meteorite" (above the Itamarati water-mirror), and "The Warriors" (in front of the Planalto)—all by Bruno Giorgi; "Justice" (in front of Supreme Court building) and "The Water-Nymphs" (above the Alvorada water-mirror)—both by Alfredo Ceschiatti; "The Rite of Rhythms" (Alvorada gardens), by Maria Martins; and the beautiful "Mermaid" in front of the Navy Ministry on the Esplanada dos Ministérios.

Roads There are two excellent paved roads from Brasília, one *via* Belo Horizonte (645 km., 10-11 hours) to Rio de Janeiro, 1,125 km., and one through Anapolis and Goiânia to São Paulo; a more direct road to São Paulo is being built, *via* Uberlândia and Uberaba. Both leave by the exit marked Saída Sul. From Anápolis a road has been driven N to Belém (2,175 km. from Brasília), through jungle in the last quarter of its length; paving has now been completed. Another road runs W to Rio Branco (Acre) *via* Goiânia, Cuiabá and Porto Velho (2,400 km.); it is paved as far as Cuiabá. There is also a road to Salvador, *via* Barreiras *(Hotel Vandelena*—basic, Youth-Hostel-like, US$8 full board, with large meals), which is partly paved and has a bus service.

Buses To Rio de Janeiro, US$12.20, 20 hours, and a "leito" bus at US$21; São Paulo, US$12, 13 hours; to Belém, leito, US$47.50, 36 hours, US$26 ordinary; to Salvador, 36 hours, US$29.20; to Belo Horizonte, US$8.25, 12 hours; to Fortaleza, US$48; to Goiânia, 3 hours, US$2; to Anápolis, 2½ hours, US$1.60; to Cuiabá, 26 hours, US$24. Book well ahead in summer.

Rail A cheap (US$5.50) and interesting way from Brasília to Belo Horizonte is by train, 3 days a week, with sleeping cars. Very slow, but it passes through some interesting country, and it never gets crowded in second class. Cheap meals are served over the two days it takes. There are also regular trains to and from Rio, *via* Belo Horizonte, and São Paulo. The temporary terminus is outside the city, at Núcleo Bandeirante.

Hotels

	Single US$	Double US$	Pool	Class
Nacional, Southern Hotel Sector	32	44	Yes	De luxe
Eron Palace, Northern Hotel Sector	31	40	No	1st class plus
Torre Palace, Northern Hotel Sector	30	36	Yes	1st class plus
Das Américas, Southern Hotel Sector	30	39	No	1st class
Aracoara, Northern Hotel Sector	27	35	No	1st class
Bristol, Southern Hotel Sector	25	31	Yes	1st class
Brasília Palace, Lake Sector	26	27	Yes	Standard
Alvorada, Southern Hotel Sector	26	35	No	Standard
Das Nações, Southern Hotel Sector	25	34	No	Standard
Diplomat, Northern Hotel Sector	15	20	No	Tourist

Itamarati Parque, Planalto and *Imperial,* Southern Hotel Sector, US$20 d. *Hotel Mirage,* Northern Hotel Sector, US$18 d. Prices given are the minimum; they include breakfast but 10% tax must be added to them. The *Petrobrás Motel* at the Saída Sul is far from the centre but clean and cheaper (US$9 d) for motorists. Also at Saída Sul: Shell's *Motel Sabataia,* US$8 d, no breakfast. Cheaper pensions available; enquire at airport information desk. Two are at Centro Cultural Padres Jesuitas Q601 L-2 Norte (Tel.: 23-0803) and Nélson Freire Penteado W/3 Sul Q705 B1 D Casa 48 (Tel.: 42-4568). *Casa do Ceará* offers beds at US$3 a night. However, the hotels outside the city in Taguatinga (½ hour by bus) and Núcleo Bandeirante, though fairly basic, tend to be recommended for cheapness. Núcleo Bandirante: *Hotel Rio de Janeiro,* US$4 d; *Hotel Jurema,* at Av. Central 1390, US$3.75 d; *Hotel São Judas Tadeu,* US$3 s, with good breakfast; *Hotel Ypacarai,* round corner from *Hotel Rio de Janeiro,* US$2.10 s, O.K. for "young and hearty"; *Hotel Avenida,* US$2 p.p.; *Hotel Europa,* US$1.80 p.p., clean; *Hotel Buriti,* US$8 d, with bath; has cheaper rooms. Taguatinga is pleasanter than the Núcleo, which is full of shanties; there are many cheap hotels and restaurants of a reasonable standard, for example,

Hotel Olympus, US$5 d, with breakfast and *Hotel Central,* US$3 s. Take bus "Taguatinga Centro" from Brasília bus station. Tourist offices (see below) will tell travellers about families who provide bed and breakfast at reasonable rates; unfortunately the offices appear to charge 10 cruzeiros for every introduction so may not be that cheap.

Youth Hostel and Municipal Hostel available to YHA members. Bus 127 from bus station to Youth Hostel.

There are many **Restaurants.** Attached to *Hotel Nacional* is the *Tabu,* a clean and moderately priced restaurant. On the arcades around the hotel are several hot dog stand type eating places. Several not so cheap but adequate eating stands at nearby central bus terminal, typical price for meal is US$3.50. Esso garage next to *Hotel Imperial* serves good cheap steaks. *Cachopa,* Commercial Centre (South), Portuguese, excellent; *La Chaumière,* tiny, superb food. Airport restaurant good, especially on Sundays. *Churrascaria Tordilho,* by lake near *Brasília Palace Hotel,* good meat dishes, also samba shows. *Churrascaria do Lago,* also on lakeside near *Brasília Palace Hotel,* good and reasonable. Also recommended are *Bon Appetit,* SQS 203 (French); *Kazebre 13,* Av. W-2, No. 504; *Xadrezinho,* near lake; *Berlin* (German) and *Amarelinho* (Italian) in SHI Sul Centro Comercial; and *Panela de Barro.* There is also a restaurant at the TV tower. For cheap eating, Mon.-Fri., *Kantino do Japonese,* 2nd floor, Ministry of Health building, and the *New Ximbika,* Setor de Diversões Norte.

Camping   The city's main site is 10 km. out, by the Centro Esportivo, Asa Norte, near the motor-racing track, with room for 3,100 campers. US$2 each, average charge for each person though apparently some travellers have stayed free. Agua Mineral Parque, 6 km. NW of city, direct buses only at weekend; US$1 p.p., mineral pool, showers. One site a few km. S on Belo Horizonte road, another out in the country about 70 km. E. Associação Brasileira de Camping has two sites: one at Km.19 on the Belo Horizonte road and one 25 km. NE of Brasília at Sobradinho. There is a Forestry Commission site 10 km. out of Brasília on the BR 041. There are signs to the sites. "Wild" camping is possible.

Club   Night club, "Fina Flor da Samba", Centro Comercial Salomão, HIS QI BI 10, n 10, lively but expensive.

Local Holidays   Jan. 6, Epiphany; Ash Wednesday; Maundy Thursday, half-day; Christmas Eve.

Shopping Centre   Brasília is an extremely expensive city.

Bank of London and South America Ltd., Av. W-3, Qadra 7c-Loja 8. Citibank. Open 0930-1630. Local banks.

Air Services   Pan Am and Varig service to Miami twice a week. Various services to all Brazil. Bus to airport, every 15 minutes, US$0.50, ½ hour. Taxi is US$2.50, worth it. Left luggage facilities at airport. To Rio costs US$77 single, 2½ hours. To Manaus, US$164; to Belém, US$136. Also to São Paulo, Belo Horizonte and Salvador.

British Commonwealth Chamber of Commerce, at the Bank of London and South America.

British Embassy   Avenida das Nações, Lote 8, Caixa Postal 586; Tel.: 24-6710.

United States Embassy, Avenida das Nações, Lote 3. Tel.: 42-5161.

American Library   Casa Thomas Jefferson, W4 61, Tel.: 70-6906.

Australian Embassy, Edif. Venâncio IV, 5° Andar, Setor de Diversões Sul, Tel.: 23-7179.

Canadian Embassy   Super-Quadra 113, Edifício Gávea Apto. 107.

British Council   Cultura Inglesa, Edif. Antônio Venâncio da Silva 2° andar Av. W3, Quadra 3, bloco C, Lojas 1-4.

Post Office   400 metres E of bus station. General delivery: Agência No. 7, Av. W-3, Quadra 508, about 4 km. from bus station (take airport bus).

Tourist Offices at the Palácio do Buriti, Air Terminal, bus station ground level, and *Hotel Nacional,* English spoken, useful, with maps, hotel information, etc. Tours by bus (US$15-20), may be booked at the airport or *Hotel Nacional:* check that you will be taken back to the airport if you have a flight to catch. The office at the bus station will recommend families who provide bed and breakfast at reasonable rates.

Travel Agent   Trips, in arcade of *Hotel Nacional.* English spoken. Presmic Tours, at bus station.

Historical Museum   Praça dos Tres Poderes, really a hollow monument, with displays on the wall.

State of Rio de Janeiro

The present state of Rio de Janeiro came into being on March 15, 1975 when the states of Guanabara (the city of Rio) and Rio de Janeiro were amalgamated. It covers 43,305 sq. km. (the size of Denmark) and in 1977 had an estimated population of 11 m., 88% of whom lived in metropolitan areas. The working population of 3.5 m. is about 15% of Brazil's total labour force, and the State is Brazil's second-largest industrial centre.

Rio de Janeiro, for 125 years the Federal capital, is on the southern shore of a landlocked harbour 24 km. long and from 3 to 16 km. wide. The setting, with its superb colouring, is most admirable. The city sweeps twenty kilometres along the broken water-front of a narrow alluvial strip between the mountains and the sea. The rich green of the hillside contrasts with expanses of grey rock. The beauty of the panoramic tapestry woven by the rare combination of an aquamarine sea, studded with islands etched in white sand, waving palms and the tumbling green mountains which surround the city is matchless. The entry into Rio harbour, whether by day or night, is a spectacle not to be forgotten. Brazilians say: God made the world in six days; the seventh he devoted to Rio.

The best known of these rocky masses are the Pão de Açúcar (Sugar Loaf Mountain, 375 metres), and Corcovado, a jagged peak rising 700 metres from behind the houses of the city. There are other heights, including Tijuca (1,012 metres), the tallest point in the foreground, and 50 km. away rise the weirdly shaped Organ Mountains with the "Finger of God". The Sugar Loaf is actually the highest peak of a low chain of mountains on the fringe of the harbour. Nature with prodigious artistry has shaped these massive crags into a colossal reclining figure known as the "Sleeping Giant", and the Sugar Loaf represents his bent knee.

The city of Rio de Janeiro is worthy of its splendid setting. The promenade facing the sea is 8 km. long. Many of the buildings are palatial; the city squares are of great beauty, with bronze statuary, fountains, and luxuriant greenery. These pleasances are beautifully maintained, and the open-air life of the cafés adds liveliness and gaiety to the scene. Brazilians know how to be happy and noisy.

Rio is one of the healthiest cities in the tropics. Trade winds cool the air. The maximum temperature of about 40°C is in February, and the minimum, 10°C, in August. Sunstroke is uncommon, but humidity is high. It is important, especially for children, to guard against dehydration in summer by drinking as much liquid as possible. November to May is the rainy season, and the annual rainfall is about 1,120 mm. For those not used to the tropics the best time for a visit is from May to the end of September.

The population is over 6,700,000. The urban population within a radius of 160 km. is 11-12 million. Since March 15, 1975, Rio has been capital of

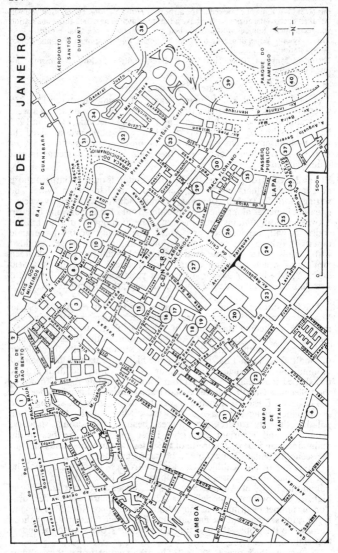

ROUGH SKETCH

the new State of Rio de Janeiro, which includes within its borders the former States of Rio de Janeiro and of Guanabara.

Rio grew from the ill-kempt and fever-stricken port of the early 19th century to its present magnificence and prosperity for two reasons: first, because it lies close to the country's two most economically productive states of São Paulo and Minas Gerais; and secondly, because it lies half-way between the coastal aggregates of people in the north-east and the south.

For the visitor the vast amount of public works (new water, sewerage, power facilities and construction of the metro) presents a hazard in the form of very poor pavement services, diverted bus services and increased noise levels. The opening of the metro in 1979 will lead to a major reorganisation of public transport.

Points of Interest Two of the streets are particularly impressive. The Avenida Rio Branco, nearly 2 km. long and 33 metres wide, is inter-sected by the city's main artery, the Avenida Presidente Vargas, 4½ km. long and over 90 metres wide. From the waterfront it crosses the Rua Primeiro de Março and then divides to embrace the famous Candelária Church. Then the reunited carriage-way sweeps past the Avenida Rio Branco in a magnificent unbroken stretch past the Central do Brasil railway terminal, with its imposing clock tower, until finally it incorporates the palm-lined canal-divided avenue formerly known as the Avenida Mangue. The Avenida Rio Branco is lined with ornate buildings—clubs, banks and steamship offices, shops and public buildings, the School of Art, National Library, Municipal Council Chamber, and Municipal Theatre. The Rua Ouvidor, crossing the Avenida Rio Branco half way along its course, contains the principal shops. Other shopping streets are the Ruas Gonçalves Dias, 7 de Setembro, Uruguaiana, Assembléia, and also the arcade running from Av. Rio Branco to the Rua Gonçalves Dias. The banks are bounded by Av. Rio Branco, Praca Pio X, Rua do Ouvidor and Rua 1° de Marco. The Avenida Beira Mar, with its royal palms, bougainvilleas and handsome buildings, coasting the Botafogo and Flamengo beaches (too polluted for bathing), is one of the most beautiful drives. An urban motorway over

---

Key to Rio de Janeiro Map

1. Touring Clube do Brasil; 2. Monastery and Church of São Bento; 3. Church of Candelária; 4. Palácio do Itamarati (former Foreign Ministry); 5. Dom Pedro II Railway Station; 6. Hospital Sousa Aguiar; 7. Museu de Caça e Pesca; 8. Central Post Office; 9. Church of Santa Cruz dos Militares; 10. Old Cathedral and Church of Carmo; 11. Church of N.S. da Lapa dos Mercadores; 12. Palace of the Viceroys (now Post Office headquarters); 13. Church of São José; 14. Palácio do Tiradentes (former Chamber of Deputies); 15. Flower Market (Praça Olavo Bilac); 16. Church of Rosário; 17. Church of São Francisco de Paula; 18. Gabinete Português de Leitura; 19. Teatro João Caetano; 20. Teatro Carlos Gomes; 21. Library of the State of Rio de Janeiro; 22. National Archive; 23. Teatro Recreio; 24. New Cathedral; 25. Aqueduto da Carioca (Arches, or *Arcos*); 26. Tram Terminus; 27. Monastery of Santo Antônio and Church of São Francisco da Penitência; 28. Teatro Municipal; 29. Museu Nacional de Belas Artes; 30. National Library; 31. Museu da Imagem e do Som; 32. Santa Casa de Misericórdia (convent) and Church of N.S. do Bonsucesso; 33. Church of Santa Luzia; 34. Museu Histórico Nacional; 35. Teatro Mesbla and Teatro Serrador; 36. Church of Carmo da Lapa; 37. Instituto Histórico e Geográfico; 38. Santos Dumont Airport—passenger terminal; 39. Museu do Arte Moderna; 40. Second World War Memorial.

reclaimed land (the Aterro) leads to Botafogo and through three tunnels to Copacabana, described on page 233. There are fine views along the Avenida Niemeyer, beyond Leblon, 40 metres above the sea. Some of the finest modern architecture is to be found along the Avenida Chile, such as the Petrobrás and National Housing Bank buildings, and the new Cathedral, dedicated in November 1976.

Vessels usually berth near the Praça Mauá, leading to Av. Rio Branco, where there are many "cambistas" for changing money. (We are told that the "cambistas" in this area give less than Exprinter, to be found at Av. Rio Branco 57A, near the corner of Av. Presidente Vargas). The Touring Club do Brasil is in a handsome building at the side of Praça Mauá. It has an information bureau for tourists, which among other useful services is prepared to telephone hotels to seek for vacancies.

History   The Portuguese navigator, Gonçalo Coelho, discovered Rio de Janeiro on January 1st, 1502, but it was first settled by the French, who, under the Huguenot Admiral Villegaignon, occupied Lage Island on November 10th, 1555, but later transferred to Sergipe Island (now Villegaignon), where they built the fort of Colligny. The fort has been demolished to make way for the Naval College (Escola Naval), and the island itself, since the narrow channel was filled up, has become a part of the mainland.

In 1557, Villegaignon's nephew, Bois le Comte, arrived with 300 men and took over the whole of the bay. But in March 1560, Mem de Sá, third governor of Brazil, defeated the French in a sea battle and drove them into the interior. But the French, helped by their Tamoyo Indian allies, returned when the victorious fleet sailed away.

In 1565, the Portuguese Government sent Estácio de Sá, with 2 galleons, to help his uncle, Mem de Sá. At the end of February he established a fortified settlement, São Sebastião, near the Sugar Loaf. He failed to oust the French until he was reinforced by his uncle's troops; they defeated the French on January 20, 1567, the anniversary of the town's patron saint. Estácio de Sá was wounded and died a month later.

Mem de Sá transferred the Portuguese settlement to Mount S. Januário—the Esplanada do Castelo covers the site today—and nominated another nephew, Salvador Correa de Sá, as captain of the colony. Though constantly attacked by Indians, the new city grew rapidly, and when King Sebastião divided Brazil into two provinces, Rio was chosen capital of the southern captaincies. Salvador became sole capital again in 1576, but Rio again became the southern capital in 1608 and the seat of a bishopric.

On September 11, 1710, a thousand Frenchmen, under the naval officer François Duclerc, entered the city but were forced to capitulate. Duclerc was assassinated later. But in 1711, the French Admiral, Duguay Trouin, captured the city on September 22; after being sacked, it was ransomed for 1,000 cruzados, 100 cases of sugar and 200 oxen.

Rio de Janeiro was by now becoming the leading city in Brazil. On January 27, 1763, it became the seat of the Governor-General, or Viceroy. After independence, in 1834, Rio de Janeiro was declared capital of the Empire. It remained the capital for 125 years.

Hotels in Rio de Janeiro

Note: All hotels in the following list are either partly or fully air-conditioned. A 10% service charge is usually added to the bill.

	Single US$	*Double* US$	*Grade*

Centre   (Well placed for transport, 30 minutes from the beaches. Most offices and commerce are located here. Rather abandoned at night.)

	Single	Double	Grade
Aeroporto, Av. Beira Mar, 280	21	23	Standard
Ambassador, Senador Dantas, 25	25	30	Standard plus
Ambassador Santos Dumont	30	34	De luxe
Center Hotel, Rio Branco, 33	18	25	Standard
Grande Hotel OK, Senador Dantas, 24	22	31	Standard
Guanabara Palace, Presidente Vargas, 392	20	25	Standard
Itajubá, Alvaro Alvim, 15	18	22	Tourist
Nelba, Senador Dantas, 46	17	23	Tourist
Presidente, Pedro I, 19	13	18	Tourist
São Francisco, Visc. de Inhaúma, 95	20	26	Standard plus

Flamengo   (Residential area midway between centre and Copacabana.)

	Single	Double	Grade
Argentina, Rua Cruz Lima, 30	18	25	Tourist
Empire, Rua da Glória, 46	25	28	Standard
Flamengo Palace, Praia Flamengo, 6	25	28	1st class
Florida, Ferreira Viana, 69	15	19	Tourist
Glória, Rua do Russel, 632	30	36	1st class plus
Novo Mundo, Praia Flamengo, 20	23	27	Standard
Regina, Ferreira Viana, 29	20	25	Standard

Copacabana   (Middle class residential and commercial area.)

	Single	Double	Grade
Apa Hotel, República do Peru, 305	24	32	Standard
Bandeirantes	30	37	1st class
Castro Alves	30	33	1st class
Copacabana Palace, Av. Atlântica, 1720	45	49	De luxe
California, Av. Atlântica, 2616	33	37	1st class
Debret, Av. Atlântica, 3564	30	35	1st class
Excelsior, Av. Atlântica, 1800	40	46	1st class plus
Lancaster, Av. Atlântica, 1470	33	37	1st class
Leme Palace, Av. Atlântica, 656	40	47	1st class plus
Luxor Continental, Gustavo Sampaio, 320	29	33	1st class
Luxor Copacabana, Av. Atlântica, 2554	33	37	1st class plus
Luxor Regente, Av. Atlântica, 3716	36	40	1st class plus
Meridien, Av. Atlântica, 1020	70	80	De luxe
Miramar, Av Atlântica, 3668	33	36	1st class
Olinda, Av. Atlântica, 2233	33	37	1st class
Ouro Verde, Av. Atlântica, 1456	48	56	De luxe
Plaza Copacabana, Av. Princesa Isabel, 263	28	32	Standard
Rio Copa.	38	42	Standard plus
Rio Othon Palace, Av. Atlântica, 3264	45	53	De luxe
Rio Palace. Under construction	—	—	
Rio Ritz. Under construction	—	—	
Savoy Othon, Av. Copacabana, 995	31	37	1st class
Trocadero, Av. Atlântica, 2064	33	37	1st class

Ipanema/Leblon   (Upper class residential and commercial area.)

	Single	Double	Grade
Arpoador Inn, Francisco Otaviano, 177	25	30	Standard plus
Carlton, João Lira 62	27	34	Standard plus
Caesar Park	65	76	De luxe
Everest, Prudente de Morais, 117	47	53	1st class plus
Ipanema Inn, Maria Quitéria, 27	25	30	Standard plus
Marina Rio, Av. Delfim Moreira, 296	40	48	1st class plus
Samambaia. Under construction	—	—	
San Marcos, Visc. de Pirajá, 524	27	31	Standard plus
Sheraton, Av. Niemeyer, 121	45	50	De luxe
Sol Ipanema, Vieira Souto, 320	35	40	1st class plus
Vermont, Visc. de Pirajá, 254	30	36	Standard

São Conrado   (Spectacular setting at Gávea beach, but somewhat isolated.)

	Single	Double	Grade
Nacional, Av. Niemeyer, 569	40	46	De luxe
Intercontinental, Av. Litorânea, 222	40	45	De luxe

Other Hotels in Copacabana *ALL* air-conditioned, double room.

US$20 and up:

Hotel Biarritz, Rua Aires Saldanha 54; *Castro Alves,* Av. Copacabana 552; *Praia Leme,* Av. Atlântica 866 (pleasant, Austrian run, overlooking beach); *Riviera,* Av. Atlântica 4122 (very good, well placed, reasonable). The last two hotels mentioned are the only moderately priced hotels actually facing the beach.

US$10 and up:

Acapulco, Rua Gustavo Sampaio 854; *Cabadá,* Av. Copacabana 687; *Martinique,* Rua Sá Ferreira 30; *Toledo,* Rua Domingos Ferreira 71; *Angarense,* Trav. Angarense, Av. Copacabana 750; *Atlântico,* Rua Santa Clara 116; *Copa Linda,* Av. Copacabana 956, US$19 d (friendly and clean, suits Peace Corps); *Uruguai,* Barata Ribeiro 216 (reportedly used by prostitutes, but nonetheless still recommended for those who don't mind!).

Economy Hotels are found in three districts of Rio: Flamengo/Botafogo, Lapa/Fátima and Saúde/Maúa. All hotel rates are for doubles, and include continental breakfast.

Flamengo/Botafogo (Residential area between centre and Copacabana.): Walking from the centre, you will come across the hotels in this order: Rua Cândido Mendes, off Rua da Glória: *Hotel Alameida,* No. 112 (US$14); *Hotel Cândido Mendes,* No. 117 (US$15); and *Hotel Monte Castelo,* No. 201 (US$9). Across from here, on the hillside is Ladeira da Glória: *Hotel Turístico* (US$5, including breakfast). Continuing on Rua do Catete, opposite the Palácio de Catete is the *Imperial Hotel* (US$16). On Rua do Catete also the *Casa de Hospedagem* (No. 34, men only) US$1.50 and *Pensão Nossa Senhora de Fátima* (No. 128). To the left is Rua Silveira Martins: No. 20, *Hotel Inglês* (US$8 d, reasonable breakfast). *Hospedaje Gloria,* Rua Catete 233, US$2 s. Walking down Praia de Flamengo you will come across the next streets: Ferreira Viana: No. 50, *Hotel Grão Pará* (US$10) and No. 58, *Hotel Ferreira Viana* (US$7). Correia Dutra: No. 19, *Hotel Cambuquirá* (US$10) and No. 81, *Hotel Azteca* (US$8). Rua Paissandú: No. 23, *Hotel Paissandú* (US$21). Beyond Largo de Machado: Rua São Salvador: No. 21, *Hotel Fátima* (US$16) and Rua Gago Coutinho: No. 22, *Hotel Serrano* (US$18), *Hotel Rio Claro,* US$3.50 d, US$2.25 s, recommended; and *Hotel Azteca.*

Lapa/Fátima (Area between Lapa and Praça Tiradentes, lower class residential area, colourful, but a little frowsy.) In Lapa itself, near the Arches just beyond Passeio Público Park is Rua Joaquim Silva: No. 69, *Hotel Americano* (US$6) and No. 99, *Hotel Marajó* (US$7 s, US$8 d, with breakfast). Passing under the Arches you come to Av. Mem de Sá: No. 85, *Hotel Mundo Novo* (US$8-12 d), clean, air-conditioned, and No. 115, *Hotel Bragança* (US$14); *Hotel Casa Blanca* (US$10 d). Walking towards Praça Tiradentes is: Rua Riachuelo, *Hotel Nice* (US$14) and Rua Resende, No. 35, *Hotel Pouso Real* (US$15). Passing Praça Tiradentes is Rua dos Andradas: No. 19, *Hotel Globo* (US$12), No. 25, *Hotel Andradas* (US$9) and No. 129, *Hotel Planalto* (US$10). In Rua Gomes Freire No. 430 is *Hotel Marialva* (US$14). There are a lot of cheap hotels in this area, but many are "hot pillow" establishments.

Saúde/Maúa (Area between the railway station and the docks, a dubious part of town.) *Hotels Bandeirantes,* Rua Bento Ribeiro, 80, not very clean or cheap; *Río Grande,* Rua Senador Pompeu, 220; *Hotel Internacional,* Rua Senador Pompeu 182, US$3-4, clean and friendly; *Cruzeiro Tefé* and *Hotel Vital,* Rua Sacadura Cabral 169a and 107 respectively, US$2 and US$2.75. The very cheapest hotels in town are in this area, but it is not too safe at night.

In the traditional Santa Teresa district, Rua Almirante Alexandrino 660, is the *Santa Teresa Hotel,* US$22, with swimming pool and full board. Take the "Dois Irmãos" tram from Largo da Carioca (see page 235).

The Federal University puts up men during vacations. There is a Youth Hostel on the eleventh floor of the Casa do Estudante, at Praça Ana Amélia 9 (Rua Sta Lúzia), near Santa Lúzia church, open all year (US$1.50 a night—student card required—international youth hostel card is best), in by 2300. Other Youth Hostels at Rua Almte. Gomes Pereira 86, Urca (girls only, Jan.-Feb. and July); Rua Barão Curitiba 93, Glória, US$2; Rua Diomedes Trotta, Ramos (both sexes, Jan-Feb. and July).

If you can't be
a Rio visitor,
we will send
the Rio Visitor to you.

*T**he monthly magazine that provides useful and up-to-date information for thousands of english-speaking visitors each month. Where to go, what to see, the "how-to" of Rio and a little of the rest of Brazil.*

• • •

Mail your subscription today

| Individual copy | £ 1.40 (including postage) |
| Annual rate | £ 13.00 (including postage) |

To:

F.S.R. Participações e Empreendimentos Ltda.
Rua Marquês de São Vicente 52 - Loja 318 - 3.º andar.
Gávea - Rio de Janeiro - 20.000 - RJ - Brasil

The city is extremely noisy. An inside room is cheaper and much quieter. (If you are desperate and it is late, some smaller hotels and hostelries may let you sleep on the floor.)

Apartments If they prefer, tourists can look after themselves at US$12 a day, double, in flatlets (small apartments) in Copacabana. Refrigerator, bath and small cooking area included. Bookings at Rua Barata Ribeiro 90, room 205, Copacabana, and at Rua Barata Ribeiro 87/202, Tel.: 255-2016 or 237-1133. The *Praia Leme Hotel,* Av. Atlântica 866, has apartments, with maid and laundry service at Av. Princesa Isabel 7, close to the beach; these are a little more expensive.

Local Holidays Jan. 20, Foundation of Rio; Ash Wednesday; Christmas Eve; New Year's Eve, half-day.

Electric Current 110-220 volts, 60 cycles, A.C.

Restaurants (centre of Town): *A.B.I.; Aeroporto; Alba Mar* (fish, interesting location overlooking ferry station); *A Minhota; A Cabaça Grande* (Casa das Peixadas, Rua do Ouvidor 12, best for fish, closed Sunday/holidays); *Manon; Tokyo,* in Rua Teófilo Otôni (Japanese); *Vergel* (vegetarian), Rua da Alfândega 176; also *Restaurante Vegetariano,* Rua Alfândega 112—1st floor, good value. There are several Arab restaurants on Av. Senhor dos Passos, also open Saturday and Sunday; *Buksky,* Rua do Rosário 133 (German), recommended for wholesome food and speedy service; *Churrascolândia,* Rua Senador Dantas, quick and simple, "but with character"; *Mesbla* (grand view of harbour and Sugar Loaf); *Museu de Arte Moderno* (excellent view of harbour and Sugar Loaf); *Pensão Guanabara,* Rua Buenos Aires by flower market, excellent meal for less than US$1. *Avis,* Av. Rio Branco 245; *Churrascaria Brasil/Portugal,* Rua do Rosário; *Lanchonette N.S. da Mo,* Rua São Bento 22, recommended; *Lanchonette Brasilândia,* Rua das Marrecas, good value, US$1. Excellent cheap meals obtainable at a private house, Rua Riachuelo 24, in Lapa district; and at *Cantina São Roque,* Evaristo da Veiga 138. **Flamengo:** *Bar KTT,* Rua do Catete, US$1.25 for 2-course meal; *Oklahoma,* Rua Senador Vergueiro, US$1.50; *Restaurante Praia Bar,* Praia do Flamengo 144; *Gaúcha,* Rua das Laranjeiras 114, good and cheap. **Copacabana and Leme:** Hotels *Copacabana Palace, Excelsior, Leme Palace, Miramar Palace, Ouro Verde* (all international food); *Akasaka* (Japanese); *Al Pappagallo* (Italian); *Cantina Sorrento* (Italian); *Doubiansky* (Russian); *Fiorentino* (Italian); *King Wha* (Chinese); *Le Bec Fin* (French); *Rian,* Santa Clara 8 (International); *Le Candelabre* (French); *Le Mazot* (Swiss), first-class; *Nino* (Italian); *Galeto,* Rua Constante Ramos; *Leme,* Rua Rodolfo Dantas 225, good and cheap; *Jardim,* Rua República do Peru; *La Polonesa,* Rua Hilário da Gouveia (Polish); *Chalet Suisse* (Swiss); cheap and good inclusive meal (US$3) at *Frango na Brasa,* Rua Constante Ramos 35; and also at *Cervantes* and *El Cid.* **Ipanema:** *Panorama Palace Hotel* (International); one on top of Morro de Cabritos, good views. **Botafogo:** *Artaca,* Rua Voluntários da Pátria (Amazonian food); *Churrascaria do Sul,* Praia de Botafogo; *Chalé Restaurant,* Rua da Matriz 54 (N and North-eastern Brazilian food) in a Colonial-style house. **Gávea:** *Joá* restaurant. **Largo do Machado:** *Churrascaria Minuano,* and near the Galeria Côndor 2 small Arab bars, cheap and very popular. **Leblon:** *Le Relais* (French); *Les Templiers,* Borges de Medeiros 3207 (also French); *Mandarin* (Chinese). **Lagoa:** *Castelo da Lagoa,* on Av. Epitácio Pessoa. For a meal with a view, try the restaurant and nightclub at the unfinished *Panorama Palace Hotel,* Rua Alberto de Campos 12, quieter than Copacabana.

Grill rooms (Churrascarias) and cheap, clean hamburger stands and lunch counters in the centre and Copacabana. Most less-expensive restaurants in Rio have basically the same type of food (based on steak, fried potatoes and rice) and most restaurants serve large portions. *La Tour,* said to be the first revolving restaurant to be built in South America (it revolves hourly), is now open at the Clube Aeronáutica building, Rua Santa Lúzia 651, 45th floor. Marvellous views! (Reservations, Tel.: 224-2221).

Tea Shops For those who like their teas served English style, the sedate "Belle Epoque" 80-year-old Confeiteria Colombo, 23/6 Rua Gonçalves Dias, is highly recommended, being the only one of its kind in Rio, with the original décor. There is also a branch in Copacabana, Av. Copacabana 890.

Theatres The main theatres in Rio are: *Adolfo Bloch,* Rua do Russel 804, Glória; *Teatro de Bolsa,* Av. Ataulfo de Paiva 269, Leblon; *Carlos Gomes,* Praça Tiradentes; *Casa Grande,* Afrânio de Melo Franco 290, Leblon; *Copacabana,* Av. Copacabana 327; *Dulcina,* R. Alcindo Guanabara 17; *Fonte da Saudade,* Av. Epitácio Pessoa 4866, Lagoa; *Teatro da Galeria,* Rua Senador Vergueiro 93, Flamengo; *Ginástico,* Av. Graça Aranha 187; *Gláucio Gil,* Praça Cardeal Arcoverde, Copacabana; *Glória,* Rua do Russel 632, Glória; *Ipanema,* R. Visconde de Morais 824; *João Caetano,* Praça Tiradentes; *Teatro da Lagoa,* Av. Borges de Medeiros, Lagoa; *Maison de France,* Av. Pres. Antônio Carlos 58; *Mesbla,* Rua do Passeio 42; *Miguel Lemos,* R. Miguel Lemos 51, Copacabana; *Teatro Municipal,* Av. Rio Branco; *Nacional de Comédia,* Av. Rio Branco 179; *Teatro Novo,* R. Gomes Freire 474; *Opinião,* R. Siqueira Campos 143, Copacabana, samba shows Monday evenings; *Teatro da Praia,* R. Francisco Sá 88, Copacabana; *Princesa Isabel,* Av. Princesa Isabel 686, Copacabana; *Sala Cecília Meireles,* Largo da Lapa; *Senac,* Rua Pompeu Loureiro 45, Copacabana; *Teatro Raquel,* R. Siqueira Campos 143, Copacabana.

Night Clubs Of most interest to the visitor will be shows featuring samba dancing. *Hotel Nacional* at São Conrado has the best and most lavish show in town, price for entrance and drink is US$15. Other good samba shows at: *Sambão e Sintrá,* Rua Constante Ramos 140. *Las Brasas,* Rua Humaitá 110. *Katakombe,* Av. Copacabana, 1401. *Oba-Oba,* Visconde de Pirajá 499. For the best Brazilian shows try *Canecão,* Rua Venceslau Bras 215. Other good shows at *Vivará,* Av. Afrânio de Mello Franco 296 and *Sucala,* Av. Borges de Medeiros 1424, both in Leblon. Rio has its share of lively discotheques; amongst the best are *New York City Discotheque,* Av. Visconde de Pirajá 22, Ipanema; *New Jirau,* Rua Siqueira Campos 12-A, Copacabana; *Ye Bateau,* Praça Serzedelo Correia 15-A, Copacabana. For something quieter and more intimate, look in at any of the following piano bars: *Balaio* (Hotel Leme Palace), Av. Atlântica 656. *Franks Bar* and *Crazy Rabbit* next door to each other on Av. Princesa Isabel. *Open,* Maria Quitéria 83 (Ipanema). Two good (and expensive) restaurants with live shows are *Fossa,* Rua Ronaldo de Carvalho 55 and *Flag,* Rua Xavier da Silveira 13, both in Copacabana. *Assyríus,* Av. Rio Branco 277 and *Erotica,* Av. Prado Júnior 63-A, both have good erotic shows at midnight. Around the Praça do Lido in Copacabana, there are innumerable bars for lonely gents. Ladies, if you are also looking for company, take a table at the pavement café of *Castellnho,* Av. Vieira Souto 100. This is where the song "Girl from Ipanema" was written, and is where the young set congregate. Next door is *Barril 1800,* a German-style Bierhalle.

Another good place to see Brazilians at play, and at the same time for the English to feel some "Saudade" (homesickness), is *Lord Jim's Pub,* Paul Redfern 63 (Ipanema), where you will be surprised to find how good the locals are at darts! Out at São Conrado and Joá, on the way to the Barra de Tijuca, there are several small night clubs, often featuring staged macumba (voodoo) rites.

Camping Camping Club do Brasil has beach site at Barra da Tijuca, costing US$2.50 a night for couple with car; nearby bus service to Rio central areas. During January and February this site is often full and sometimes restricted to members of the Camping Club do Brasil. "Wild" camping possible on beaches further out; if trying it nearer centre, beware thieves.

Bookshops For international stock, Livraria Kosmos, Rua do Rosário 137 (in the Centre) is best, but there are many others, especially in Copacabana. *N.B.* Cultura Inglesa, Av. Graça Aranha 327, (subscription US$2, 6 months, US$4 a year) takes *Times, Observer,* magazines: also has lanchonette.

Transport Frequent buses to all parts. Fare normally about US$0.20. Luxurious air-conditioned buses ("Frescões") serve many areas from Rua São José; standard fare about US$0.70. (Hitch-hiking out of Rio is easy. For the motorway entrance north and south take bus 392 or 393 from Praça São Francisco. Make a good sign).

Trams Try the remaining tram service from Largo da Carioca to Dois Irmãos or Santa Teresa—old rickety system, bumpy ride, but historical and most interesting, and currently being refurbished.

Car Hire For self-drive, try Freeway, Ronaldo de Carvalho 154a, Copacabana, tel.

236-4651. US$30 all-in for 24 hours in a VW Beetle. Hertz, Praia do Flamengo 244, tel. 245-7781.

Taxis start at US$0.30 and are quite reasonable. There is 40% surcharge between 2300 and 0600 but there is no extra charge for Sunday and holiday hire. Taxis have red number plates with white numerals (yellow for private cars, with black numerals) and have meters. Smaller ones (mostly Volkswagen) are marked TAXI on windscreen or roof.

Rail (1) Central do Brasil Railway to São Paulo, Belo Horizonte, Santos, the South and the interior. (2) Leopoldina Railway to Vitória and the North. There are day trains to São Paulo (1st class US$8, 6 hours 40 mins) and Belo Horizonte, and night trains with sleepers (9 hours, leaving 2310—highly recommended) to both cities. There are suburban trains to Nova Iguaçu, Nilópolis, Campo Grande and elsewhere; also air-conditioned railcars for commuters. Weekend trains for tourists go to Mangaratiba on Rio's "Green Coast".

Underground Railway The first line, joining Cinelândia in the centre with Tijuca in the North Zone, is under construction, for completion in 1979.

Airports Rio has two airports. The Santos Dumont Airport on Guanabara Bay, right in the city, is used exclusively for Rio-São Paulo shuttle flights (US$36.50), air taxis and private planes. (The shuttle services operate every half hour throughout the day from 0600 to 2050.) The new airport of Galeão, on Governador Island, some 16 km. from the centre of Rio, is divided into two sections, the international and domestic, and was opened in January 1977. An air-conditioned bus runs to Santos Dumont Airport, *via* the city centre, every half hour (US$0.70) and another goes to Copacabana, Ipanema and São Conrado (US$2) every 20 minutes, with space for baggage. Air-conditioned taxis (Cootramo and Transcopass) have fixed rates (US$7 downtown, US$9 Copacabana) and you should buy a ticket at the counter near the arrivals gate before getting into the car. Ordinary taxis also operate with the normal meter reading (about US$4 downtown, US$6 Copacabana). A good policy is to check at the Riotur counter before leaving, for folders, maps and advice. Town buses Nos. 322 and 328 go to Galeão airport, first one with direction Bananal.

Roads The Dutra Highway to São Paulo, 407 km.; to Petrópolis, 58 km.; Juiz de Fora and Belo Horizonte, 420 km.; to Salvador, 1,620 km.; to Brasília; to Porto Alegre. A new road has been built along the coast to Santos; it is not yet paved between São Sebastião and Bertioga (São Paulo).

Buses To Curitiba, 13 hours, US$12; to São Paulo, 6 hours, US$6 (every 10 minutes) for US$10 by leito, a luxury "executive" service was introduced in March 1977 by the Unica company; to Salvador, 27 hours, US$21; to Belo Horizonte, 9 hours, US$6; to Belem, 52-60 hours, 0800 daily, US$43.75; to Vitória, US$9; to Foz do Iguaçu, 22 hours, US$20; to Brasilia, 21 hours, US$16; to Porto Alegre, 25 hours, US$20. International: Asunción, *via* Foz do Iguaçu, 30 hours, US$32; Buenos Aires, *via* Porto Alegre and Santa Fe, 48 hours, 1800, US$50; Montevideo, 37 hours, US$31; the B.A. and M.V. services are fully booked a week in advance. You are allowed to sleep at the bus station, if you don't lie down. The main bus station has an information centre.

Ferry Service From the "barcas" at Praça 15 de Novembro, ferry boats and launches cross every 10 minutes to Niterói (20-30 minutes, US$0.10); to Paquetá Island (70-90 minutes, US$0.30). There are also hydrofoils to Niterói every 10 minutes (about 10 minutes, US$0.40). The Niterói ferry service is still being maintained, despite the competition from the new 14 km. bridge linking the two sides of Guanabara Bay. (The approach to the bridge is *via* Av. Rio de Janeiro, in the Caju district; take the Av. Rodrigues Alves past the docks.) Bus 999 from the Passeio Público crosses the bridge. (For Paquetá, see page 236.)

Public Conveniences There are very few in Rio de Janeiro, but the many bars and restaurants offer conveniences of a sort; just ask for the "banheiro" (banyairoo).

Pickpockets Rio is nowhere near as bad as Bogotá, say, but reasonable precautions are advisable, especially on the famous beaches, where small boys are a real danger to unsuspecting visitors. They work in gangs, some distracting your attention while others go through pockets and bags. So beware of friendly small boys.

Personal Safety   Frequent travellers to Rio and residents there suggest that the problem of personal safety is growing. It is suggested to women that they do not venture out alone at night or visit the cinema alone, and should ensure that they are escorted home.

Sightseeing   Tourist agencies offer tours of the city and of the environs by private car for the day, or for parties by coach, these often save considerable time and therefore may well be worthwhile; the tourist is often picked up from his hotel. Those who do not wish to use these services can go by bus. The main centre for boarding buses is in the Praça Marechal Floriano (Cinelândia), near the far end of the Avenida Rio Branco, for destinations in Zona Sul, other destinations from Praça Quinze de Novembro and Praça Mauá. The centre of Rio is very quiet on Saturdays and Sundays; most shops and restaurants are shut.

See, within the city, Candelária Church, the Monastery of São Bento, the Convent of Santo Antônio, the Glória Church (see under Churches), the Museum of National History, the National Museum of Fine Arts, the Museum of Modern Art, the Municipal Theatre, the National Library, the Ruy Barbosa Museum (see under Public Buildings). Outside the City you should see Copacabana, Ipanema, Leblon and Barra da Tijuca beaches, the Sugar Loaf, Corcovado, Tijuca Forest, Botanical Gardens, Quinta da Boa Vista and Zoological Gardens, the Maracanã Stadium, the "traditional" neighbourhood of Santa Teresa and, if there is time, Niterói and Icaraí, Paquetá Island, Petrópolis and Teresópolis. Descriptions of these places and details of how to reach them are given in the text. There are interesting places to walk in Saúde (the old-style neighbourhood of the Praça Mauá), the Campo da Santana (a large park on Av. Presidente Vargas) and the Rua da Alfândega and neighbouring streets, where there is a bargain shopping district.

One of the most pleasant experiences in Rio is to take bus number 206 from the Largo da Carioca as far as Silvestre. It is attractive because the route is partly up the side of Corcovado Mountain, and the road is narrow and twisty, lined with lovely trees and many picturesque houses, though some of them are coming down. The only remaining open trams (or "bondes") follow the same route, through the "traditional" suburb of Santa Teresa (see page 233); though they do not go as far as the buses, the ride is much more enjoyable. This bus trip can be combined with one to the top of the Corcovado (see page 235). Another magnificently scenic bus ride is that provided by the unnumbered route between Santos Dumont airport and Santa Cruz, right along the coast for 40 minutes.

Travel Agents   Brazilian Holidays, Av. Rio Branco 156 sala 3132 (Martin Crossland); American Express/Kontik, Almirante Barroso 91, 7° andar; Pioneer Turismo, Rua Santa Clara 33, sala 203, for sightseeing tours (see David); Koch Turismo, Rua Miguel Couto 7 (Fred Deakin); Wagon-Lits Cook, Av. Rio Branco 156, basement; Exprinter, Av. Rio Branco, 57a (said to be particularly good for money-changing); Artigas, Av. Presidente Vargas, 466, 14° andar; Agen, Diplomata, Rua Anfilófio de Carvalho, 10th floor; Casa Piano, Av. Rio Branco, 88; Tourservice, Rua Alcindo Guanabara 24, sala 503; Casa Aliança Av. Rio Branco 13a; Brazil Safari Tours, Rua Cosme Velho 103; Bel Air Tours, Av. Rio Branco (Sr. Ambar).

Tourist Information   There are several excellent information centres. Brazilian Tourist Information Centre, Barata Ribeiro 272, Copacabana, Tel.: 257-7069, contains excellent library; and there are several information desks along the Avenida Atlântica. Touring Club do Brasil, Praça Mauá, English speaking staff, highly recommended. Riotur, Rua São José 90, 8th floor, good basic map available. Offical Riotur information stands at Corcovado train station (0800-2000); Pão de Açúcar cablecar station (0800-2000); Petrobrás filling stations on Av. Atlántica at Leme, Posto 3 and Posto 4 (Copacabana) (0900-2100); Galeão International Airport (24 hrs.) and Galeão domestic terminal (0600-2400); Banco do Estado do Rio de Janeiro, 175 Av. Nilo Peçanha (0900-1700), and Ed Cardeal Arcoverde, 8th floor. Secretary of Culture, Sport and Tourism, Rua Real Grandeza 293, Botafogo. Best guide to Rio, with excellent map, "Guia Quatro Rodas do Rio" in Portuguese and English, US$2.50. "Guia Rex" street guide, US$6. "Guia Schaeffer Rio de Janeiro (US$2.50) is an excellent sheet which includes all of Greater Rio de Janeiro down to Jacarepaguá in the west, and its reverse side contains indications for the easy location of any street, Many hotels provide guests with the weekly "Itinerário (Rio This Week)".

Free maps are available from Riotur information desks, Touring Clube do Brasil, touring agencies and hotels, and from H. Stern, the jeweller, at Rio Branco 173. (Visits to H. Stern's workshops to see the transformation of gemstones into jewellery can be easily arranged, without charge, by the better hotels.)

Carnival Carnival in Rio is still one of the most spectacular sights in the world. On Shrove Tuesday and the three preceding days, the city is decorated with fantastic cardboard shapes and coloured lights, and people mill happily about the streets with their children mostly in fancy dress. Special bandstands throughout the city are manned for public street-dancing (see *Brazil Herald* for where and when) and organized carnival groups, the blocos carnavalescos, are very much in evidence, dancing, drumming and singing. Visitors should be sure to get seats in stands—arquibancadas—for the four evenings of carnival to see the dancing groups; the most important is the great procession of the city's main samba clubs, or Escolas da Samba, all through Sunday night and through into Monday afternoon. Each club represents a district, and chooses a theme to illustrate with its own samba; each has its own colour-scheme for costumes and its own percussion section, or bateria. Some clubs are two to three thousand strong and take half an hour to pass the judges' stand—a film-spectacular in real life! There are three leagues of samba clubs; the second and third use the Avenida Rio Branco and Avenida 28 de Setembro respectively, and promotion and relegation take place, as in football leagues. Competition is intense. Make sure you keep your ticket; gatecrashing is a problem on the stands and the police take it very seriously. The main events on the other nights are the parade of "frevo" clubs (the frevo is a rather Cossack-like dance from the North-East) and "rancho" groups (this was the traditional Rio dance before the introduction of the samba in 1917) on Monday, and an amalgam of events on Tuesday, including a huge float parade by the "grandes clubes carnavalescos", and exhibitions by the previous year's champion samba groups, blocos carnavalescos and frevo and rancho groups. (These arrangements change from year to year: check with *Brazil Herald* or tourist bureaux for information.)

Rita Davy writes: For the 1978 Carnival, instead of parades on Av. Presidente Vargas, it was intended to have a permanent new site ready called the "Sambódromo" at Rua Marquês de Sapucaí, Cidade Nova, nor far from the centre, for the four main events of Escolas da Samba and Bloco parades. It has a length of 600 metres, with seats for 60,000 people.

There are also innumerable fancy-dress balls; the main public one is at the Canecão (Saturday night) but there are scores more in hotels and clubs. Remember it will be hot, and wear fancy dress as light as your modesty will allow!

Carnival takes place at a time when Rio is packed with summer visitors, not only for Carnival but also Brazilians from the interior enjoying the beaches. So anyone wishing to attend the Rio Carnival is earnestly advised to make sure of their accommodation well in advance, if at all possible; virtually all hotels raise their prices during Carnival.

Pickpockets and thieves are very active during Carnival. Don't wander into dark corners on your own, and take with you only as much money as you need for fares and refreshments.

If you can't be there at Carnival time, rehearsals are held at various places from November on; e.g. the Portela *escola* at Mourisco, near the Botafogo beach, late Saturday nights. Samba shows are given at the Teatro Opinião, Rua Siqueira Campos 143, Copacabana, on Monday nights.

Less hectic than Carnival, but very beautiful, is the festival of Iemanjá on the night of 31st December, when devotees of the spirit cults brought centuries ago by slaves from Africa gather on Copacabana beach, singing and dancing around open fires and making offerings, and the elected Queen of the Sea is rowed along the seashore. Again, if you go, beware thieves.

Museums and other Public Buildings

The **National Library** (Biblioteca Nacional), in Avenida Rio Branco, was founded in 1810. Its first collection came from the Ajuda Palace in Lisbon, but to-day it houses over 2 million volumes and many rare manuscripts. One of its rarities is a Latin Bible on parchment printed in Mainz in 1469. It has also a first edition of the Lusíadas of Camões, printed in 1572. The library is open Mon.-Fri. 1000-1830, and Sat. 1200-1800.

National Museum of Fine Art (Museu Nacional de Belas Artes), at 199 Avenida Rio Branco. There are some 800 paintings and sculptures, both ancient and modern, and some thousand direct reproductions of the old masters. Exhibitions of modern works by contemporary Brazilian artists are often held here. Open Mon.-Fri. 1300-2000; Sat., Sun. and holidays 1500-1800.

Those interested in contemporary art will also visit the Ministry of Education to see the great murals of Cândido Portinari, whose canvas, "Café", is in the Museum of Fine Art.

Opposite the Art Museum and facing Praça Marechal Floriano, is the handsome **Municipal Theatre** (now completely renovated), a replica of the Paris Opera House to a scale of two to three. Opera and orchestral performances are given here; the small museum exhibit which used to be below the theatre is now housed at 103/105 Rua São João Batista, open 1300-1700 Tues.-Sun.

The **Museum of Modern Art** (Museu de Arte Moderna), is on Avenida Infante Dom Henrique, very near the National War Memorial (see page 229). Open Mon.-Fri, 1200-1900, US$0.20, but there are no permanent exhibitions. It is the work of A. E. Reidy, an outstanding Brazilian architect, who has also built two neighbourhood units, one on the western slope of Pedregulho Hill, one in Gávea. It has works by Picasso, Braque and Matisse (not necessarily on view), and many visiting exhibitions. There is also a non-commercial cinema.

The **Brazilian Academy,** on Av. Presidente Wilson, is a replica of the Petit Trianon at Versailles; it was given to Brazil by the French Government after the Centenary Exhibition of 1922. The Brazilian Academy of Letters was founded in 1897 by the writer Machado de Assis. A millionaire bookseller made the Academy his heir, and the interest on this legacy provides annual prizes for the best Brazilian works in prose, verse, and drama. The Academy is preparing an exhaustive dictionary of the Portuguese language and issues a quarterly; it meets every Thursday at 1700 hours. A new building under construction next door will be the Academy's cultural centre.

The **National Historical Museum** on Praça Marechal Ancora contains a most interesting collection of historical treasures, colonial sculpture and furniture, maps, paintings, arms and armour, silver, and porcelain. The building itself is fascinating; it was once the old War Arsenal of the Empire, part of which was built in 1762. Open Tuesday to Friday, 1200-1700; Saturday, Sunday and holidays 1500-1700. Closed on Monday.

The Historical Museum now houses the **Military Museum and Naval Museum.** There is a particularly large collection of paintings and prints in the Naval Museum, besides the more usual display of weapons and figureheads.

Museum of Image and Sound, also on Praça Marechal Ancora, has many photographs of Brazil and modern Brazilian paintings open Mon.-Fri., 1200-1700; also collections of early Brazilian music and a non-commercial cinema open Friday-Sunday. Close to Praça 15 de Novembro.

The **Museum of the Indian** (Museu do Índio), which was in Rua Mata Machado, is now temporarily closed because the building has been demolished. A new site is being sought.

The **Museum of the City** (Museu da Cidade), near the Gávea bus terminal, at Estrada Santa Marinha, Gávea, in the delightful Parque da Cidade (see page 230), contains an excellent collection of Rio's historical objects, open Tues.-Fri. 1300-1700, Sat. and Sun. 1100-1700. Buses from centre, 106, 176, 178; from Copacabana, 591.

The **National Museum** in the Quinta da Boa Vista is one of the most important museums in South America, or indeed in the world. Up to the proclamation of the Republic the building was the home of the Emperors of Brazil, but only the unfurnished Throne Room and ambassadorial reception room on the 2nd floor reflect past imperial glories. In the entrance hall is the famous "Bendego" meteorite, found in the State of

Bahia in 1888. It is possibly the largest metallic mass ever to fall on earth (though there may be a larger one in Namibia, at Grootfontein); its original weight, before some of it was chipped, was 5,360 kg. Besides several foreign collections of note, the Museum contains Brazilian ethnographic collections of Indian weapons, dresses, utensils, etc., a very rich collection of minerals and a priceless collection of historical documents. There are still other collections of birds, beasts, fishes, and butterflies. Open 1200 to 1700, closed Mondays. Buses: 138, 279 or 299 from centre; 472 from Flamengo; 474 from Copacabana.

The **Fundação Raymundo Ottoni de Castro Maia,** generally known as **Chácara do Céu,** Rua Murtinho Nobre 93, has a wide range of art objects and particularly modern Brazilian painters. Can be reached by taking Santa Teresa tram to Rua Dias de Barros, then follow signposts. (Open Tues.-Sat. 1400-1700, Sun. 1100-1700, US$0.30.) Castro Maia's former residence on the Estrada do Açude in the Tijuca Forest bears the same name and is also a museum, currently under restoration.

Geographic Museum, just off Av. Beira Mar and near the American Consulate, has a very interesting collection of Brazilian products and the artefacts of its peoples. Open Mon.-Fri. 0900-1800.

Museu de Caça e Pesca (Museum of Hunting and Fishing), now at Quinta da Boa Vista, contains a most interesting collection of Brazilian fauna. Open Tues.-Fri. 1200-1700, Sat. and Sun. 1000-1700.

The **São Cristóvão Pavilion,** a permanent exposition hall built in 1961, has the world's largest open floor space without columns or transverse walls. This exciting building is by the Brazilian architect Sérgio Bernardes. Outside on Sundays is the North Eastern Market, although relatively little is from that area: really a large street market with cheap goods, though very colourful, with musical groups from the North East and quack doctors selling their cures. Bus 472 or 474 from Copacabana or centre.

The **National Observatory** is on São Januário hill, in the São Cristóvão district. It was founded as early as 1827.

The **House of Rui Barbosa,** Rua São Clemente 134, Botafogo, former home of this great Brazilian jurist and statesman, whose artistic and cultural relics it contains, is open from 1400-2100 daily, except Mondays. Buses 106, 176, 178 from centre; 571 from Flamengo; 591 from Copacabana.

Itamarati Palace, the former Foreign Ministry on Avenida Marechal Floriano, contains much interesting old furniture, tapestry and other objects of art. Tourists should obtain permission to view.

Museum of the Republic, in Catete Palace (Rua do Catete 179), once the residence of the Barão de Nova Friburgo. When Rio was the Federal Capital it was the official residence of the President for 63 years. It has the nicely furnished bedroom in which President Getúlio Vargas shot himself in 1954. Also contains Folklore Museum. Open Tues.-Fri. 1200-1800; Sat., Sun. and holidays 1500-1800. Bus 571 from Copacabana.

Guanabara Palace, formerly the residence of the Princess Isabel, is now the office of the Governor of the State of Rio de Janeiro.

Churches and Religious Foundations

There are many attractive churches in Rio de Janeiro. Several of them are Colonial, with simple and serene exteriors but with lavishly decorated interiors.

The oldest convent is the **Convent of Carmo,** on Rua Primeiro de Março close to Praça 15 de Novembro, but that is now used as a school. It was built in the first years of the 17th century. Its old church used to be where the old Cathedral now is. Its present church, the Carmo Church in Rua Primeiro de Março, next to the old cathedral, was built in the 1770's and rebuilt between 1797 and 1826. It has strikingly beautiful portals by Mestre Valentim, the son of a Portuguese nobleman and a slave girl. His, too, are the main altar of fine moulded silver, the throne and its chair, and much else.

The second oldest convent is the seventeenth-century **Convent of Santo Antônio,** which is off the Largo da Carioca. It was built between 1608 and 1615. The Church of the Convent contains, in particular, old paintings and a marvellous sacristy adorned with blue tiles. St. Anthony is a particular object of devotion for women who want to find husbands, and many such will be seen in the precincts.

The crypt contains the tomb of a Scottish soldier of fortune known as "Wild Jock of Skelater". He was in the service of the Portuguese Government when it was seated in Brazil during the Napoleonic War, and had the distinction of being appointed the first Commander-in-Chief of the Army in Brazil. The statue of St. Anthony was made a captain in the Portuguese army after his help had been sought to drive out the French in 1710, and his salary paid to the monastery. In 1810 he became a major, in 1814 a lieutenant-colonel, and he was granted the Grand Cross of the Order of Christ. He was retired without pay in 1914.

Separated from this church only by some iron railings is the charming church of St. Francis of the Penitence, built in 1773 with a simple exterior and a lavish interior. The carving and gilding of walls and altar are superb. In the ceiling over the nave is a fine panel painted by José de Oliveira; there is a museum attached to the church, open first and third Sunday of the month, 0700-1000.

The **Monastery of São Bento** (1633); entrance in Rua D. Gerardo, contains much of what is best in the 17th and 18th century art of Brazil. "O Salvador", the masterpiece of Brazil's first painter, Frei Ricardo do Pilar, hangs in the sacristy. The carving in the church is particularly good. The Chapels of the Immaculate Conception and of the Most Holy Sacrament are masterpieces of Colonial art. The Monastery is a few minutes' walk from Praça Mauá, turning left off Av. Rio Branco at the Rua São Bento. The intimate view of the harbour and its shipping from the grounds of the Monastery is in itself worth climbing the hill on which it stands.

The **Old Cathedral** of São Sebastião, in the Rua Primeiro de Março, was built between 1749 and 1770. In the crypt are the bones of many famous men, including those of Pedro Alvares Cabral, the discoverer of Brazil.

The **New Cathedral,** on Avenida República de Chile not far from the Largo da Carioca, was dedicated in November 1976. It is a very modern and exiciting cone-shaped building, and the most striking feature is four enormous stained-glass windows. Though it is in use, completion is not expected until 1978.

The Church of **São Francisco de Paula,** in the square of the same name at the upper end of the Rua do Ouvidor, was build in 1759. It contains some of Mestre Valentim's work—the carvings in the main chapel and the lovely Chapel of Our Lady of Victory. Some of the paintings, and probably the ceiling, are by Manuel da Cunha, who was born a slave. The beautiful fountain at the back plays only at night.

The Church of **Nossa Senhora da Candelária** (1775-1810), on Praça Pio X, at the beginning of Avenida Presidente Vargas, is well worth a visit to see its beautiful interior decorations and paintings. It is on the site of a chapel founded in 1610 by Antônio da Palma after he had survived a shipwreck, an event depicted by paintings inside the present dome.

In the Rua de Santa Lúzia, overwhelmed by the tall modern buildings of Esplanado do Castelo, is one of the nicest little churches in Rio: the double-towered Church of **Santa Lúzia.** When built in 1752 it had only one tower. the other was added late in the 19th century. Inside is a beautiful image of Santa Lúzia; there is also one of the Senhor do Bomfim. Feast day: December 13, when devotees bathe their eyes with holy water, considered miraculous.

In the Rua Primeiro de Março, at the corner of Ouvidor, is the Church of the **Holy Military Cross,** built 1780-1811. It is a large, stately and beautiful temple, with many paintings of the Brotherhood of the Military Cross, founded in 1623.

The famous and graceful church at the Praça Nossa Senhora da Glória 135, on the Glória hill overlooking the Parque do Flamengo, is **Nossa Senhora da Glória do Outeiro** (the Church of Our Lady of Glory on the Hill). It was the favourite church of the imperial family; Dom Pedro II was baptised here. Architecturally, it is very fine indeed. Built in 1791, it contains some excellent examples of blue-faced Brazilian tiling. Its main altar, of wood, was carved by Mestre Valentim. The church, open 0800-1200 (only Sat.-Sun.) and 1400-1700 weekdays, is reached by bus 119 from the centre and 571 from Copacabana. The adjacent museum of religious art is open on application to the priest.

The Church of **Nossa Senhora da Penha,** in the N suburbs, is on a bare rock in which 393 steps are cut. This staircase is ascended by pilgrims on their knees during October, during which a fair is held; there is a funicular for those unable to do this. The church is early 20th century. Bus 497 from Copacabana, 340 and 346 from centre.

When the old Morro do Castelo was razed to make the large new area known as the Esplanada do Castelo, containing the Praça Paris Gardens, the old church of São Sebastião had to be demolished. The Capuchin friars built another temple in the Rua Haddock Lobo, Tijuca suburb, in 1936, and a remarkable modern church it is. It contains the tomb of Estácio de Sá, founder and first Governor of Rio de Janeiro.

Churches where worship is conducted in English:

Christ Church, Rua Real Grandeza 99, Botafogo. (Church of England/American Episcopalian). The foundation stone of the first building in the Rua Evaristo da Veiga, near where the Municipal Theatre is, was laid on August 12, 1819, the 57th birthday of the Prince Regent (later George IV of England). It was dedicated to St. George (after the Prince Regent) and St. John the Baptist (after Dom João VI, then Regent of Portugal) who, in Letters Patent granted by him, stated that subjects of His Britannic Majesty resident in Portugal or its dominions should not be molested by reason of their religion, and granted them permission to build their own churches provided their exteriors resembled private residences and that no bells were installed. A new building was consecrated on its present attractive site in October, 1944. The British School, for children of 5-16, is nearby.

Chapel of Our Lady of Mercy, Rua Visconde de Caravelas 48, Botafogo. (Roman Catholic, with primary school.)

Union Church (Protestant undenominational.) Services held at the Presbyterian Church in Gávea, Rua Oitis 63 (close to the racecourse), until new premises are built in Barra da Tijuca to replace the building in Copacabana, now sold.

First Church of Christ Scientist, Av. 13 de Maio, 13-18th floor, room 1803.

Masonic Temple, in the British School at No. 76, Rua da Matriz, Botafogo. Four English Lodges, all under the U.G.L. of England, use this temple.

Synagogues, General Severiano 170, Botafogo; Rua Barata Ribeiro, Copacabana.

British Cemetery, 181 Rua da Gamboa, was granted to the British Community in perpetuity by Dom João, Regent of Portugal, in 1810. It is the oldest cemetery in Rio. The first recorded burial was on January 15, 1811.

Parks, Squares and Monuments

The city abounds in open spaces and squares, many of which have ornamental gardens and statuary:

On the Glória and Flamengo waterfront, with a view of the Sugar Loaf and Corcovado, is the **Parque do Flamengo,** designed by Burle Marx, a playground for the people of Rio opened in 1965 during the 400th anniversary of the city's founding. It is on 100 hectares reclaimed from the Bay by levelling Santo Antônio hill and bulldozing the spoil into the water.

In the park are many fields for soccer, volleyball and basketball and a botanical garden; for children, there are a sailboat basin, a marionette theatre, a miniature village and a staffed nursery. A tractor-pulled rubber-tyred train makes a trip through the park, allowing 45 minutes for taking in the views. There are night amusements, such as bandstands and areas set apart for dancing and an old DC3 plane, put there by Varig for children to visit. Two divided-lane motorways carry express buses from town to Botafogo non-stop.

The National War Memorial to Brazil's dead in World War II and the Modern Art Museum (see page 225) are where the park begins, opposite Praça Paris. The Memorial takes the form of two slender columns supporting a slightly curved slab, representing two palms outstretched to heaven. The Monument contains the tomb of Brazil's unknown warrior and a fine museum in which there is a plaque presented to Brazilian ex-servicemen by the Guards Brigade. In the crypt are the remains of the Brazilian soldiers killed in Italy in 1944-45. It is well worth a visit; but beach clothes and rubber-thronged sandals will get you ejected—and don't sit on the wall. The crypt and museum are open Tues.-Sun. 1000-1700.

Those who want to see what Rio was like early in the 19th century should go by bus to the **Largo do Boticário,** Rua Cosme Velho 822, a charming small square in pure Colonial style. Buses to Cosme Velho from all parts of the city. The square is close to the terminus for the Corcovado rack railway (see page 235).

Botanical Gardens (Jardim Botânico) founded 1808, open daily, 0800-1800 in summer and 0830-1730 in winter. The most striking features are the transverse avenues of 30-metre Royal Palms. There are over 7,000 varieties of plants, including a famous all-American collection of cacti and 600 types of orchids (which visitors cannot see), a museum, herbarium, aquarium, and library. There are Victoria Regia water-lilies of 6 metres circumference. The Gardens are 8 km. from the centre, between the Gávea and Corcovado hills, 140 hectares in area; take any bus from the centre marked "*via* Jóquei" (Jockey Club). From Copacabana any bus whose number begins with 5 and ends with an even number, except 592.

Parque Laje, near the Jardim Botânico at Rua Jardim Botânico 414, almost jungle-like, has small grottoes, an old tower and lakes. (The Institute of Fine Arts is housed in the mansion.) Open daily, 0800-1730, admittance free.

Quinta da Boa Vista, formerly the Emperor's private park, contains many specimen trees. The Palace now houses the National Museum (see page 225).

Zoological Gardens, which contain good examples of Brazilian and imported wild animals, and a fine collection of birds, are in the Quinta de Boa Vista (admission US$0.20). Open 0800-1800 daily. The Gateway is a perfect replica of Robert Adam's famous gateway to Syon House, near London. Near the Zoological Gardens is the Museum of Natural History.

Parque da Cidade   A pleasant park a short walk beyond the Gávea bus terminus. It was previously the grounds of the home of a very wealthy family, by whom it was presented to the City; the house itself is now the Museu da Cidade (see page 225). Admission to the park is free; open Tues.-Fri. 1300-1700, Sat., Sun. and holidays 1100-1700.

Jockey Club Racecourse, at Praça Santos Dumont, Gávea, meetings on Mon. evenings and Sat. and Sun. afternoons. Take any bus marked "Jóquei". Betting is by totalisator only.

Praça de República and Campo de Santana is an extensive and picturesque public garden close to the Central Railway station. The square contains a monument to Benjamin Constant, one of the founders of the Republic. Praça da República 197 is the old house in which lived Marshal Deodoro da Fonseca, who proclaimed Brazil a republic in 1889 (plaque). The Parque Júlio Furtado in the middle of the square is populated by playful agoutis (or gophers), best seen at dusk; there is also a little artificial grotto, with swans.

Passeio Público (turn right at end of Avenida Rio Branco), is a garden planted by the artist Mestre Valentim, whose bust is near the old former gateway.

Praça Mauá, cross immediately on landing from the steamer; it contains monuments to the Barão de Mauá, the industrialist and Teixeira Soares, famous Brazilian engineer.

Largo de São Francisco has a historic church, and a statue to José Bonifácio, one of the patriarchs of independence.

Praça 15 de Novembro has a statue to the Marquês do Herval, one of the heroes of the Paraguayan War. There is also an ancient fountain from which water for ships was formerly drawn, and statues of General Osório and Buarque de Macedo. To-day the Praça is cut in two and overshadowed by the elevated Avenida Perimetral. It also contains the original royal palace, the Paço, now used by the Department of Posts and Telegraphs; a beautiful Portuguese-style Colonial building begun in 1743.

Esplanada do Castelo, with its monument to the Barão do Rio Branco, is the centre of the district built on ground reclaimed from the Castelo Hill. It is now completely filled up with modern offices.

Praça Tiradentes, old and shady, has a statue to D. Pedro I, first Emperor of Brazil, who proclaimed the independence of the country. Shops in nearby streets specialize in selling goods for umbanda and macumba—African-type religion and magic respectively.

Praça Mahatma Gandhi, at the end of Avenida Rio Branco, is flanked on one side by the cinema amusement centre of the city, known as Cinelândia. The square itself is laid out with ornamental gardens and has a massive statue of Marshal Floriano Peixoto, famous Brazilian soldier, who, as the second President, did much to consolidate the Republic. There is also a bust of Dr. Paulo de Frontin, notable Brazilian engineer, who cut the Avenida Rio Branco and carried out many other notable feats of engineering to modernise the city. The main inhabitants of the square are domestic cats, gone wild. Travellers report a Sunday morning stamp and coin market in the park.

Praça Paris, built on reclaimed ground near the Largo da Glória, and laid out by the famous French town-planner, Professor Agache, is much admired by tourists for the beauty of its formal gardens and illuminated fountains. At the Avenida end of the gardens is a magnificent equestrian statue of Marshal Deodoro da Fonseca, principal founder of the republic and its first president.

Praia do Russell, at the side of the Praia Flamengo, contains a monument to Admiral Barroso, victor of the Battle of Riachuelo, and another commemorates the opening of Brazilian ports to foreign shipping. It also contains a bust of Lord Baden Powell. The most striking statue, however, is that to Saint Sebastian, the city's patron saint.

Largo da Glória, between Praça Paris and Praia do Russell, where there is a very fine monument to Pedro Alvares Cabral, the Portuguese navigator who discovered Brazil in 1500.

Praia do Flamengo has statues of a scout, presented by the Republic of Chile, and the Aztec emperor Cuautéhmoc, presented as a token of esteem to Brazil by the people of Mexico; it has now been moved some 100 metres nearer the sea on the reclaimed land.

At the beginning of the **Praia do Botafogo** there is a monument to Admiral Tamandaré, the Brazilian "Nelson", and another to Francisco Passos, one of the greatest Mayors of Rio de Janeiro, who was largely responsible for making Rio de Janeiro into a modern city. At the farther end of the Praia do Botafogo, just before turning into the Avenida Pasteur, there is a bust of Pasteur.

Martin Crossland writes:

Praia Vermelha Continuing along Av. Pasteur, you pass the Yacht Club (left) and the old buildings of the Federal University, now being transferred to Ilha do Fundão, near Galeão Airport. At the end of the avenue are Praça General Tibúrcio and Praia Vermelha, where the Sugar Loaf cable car station is located (see page 235). The impressive monument in the centre of the square is dedicated to the heroes of Laguna e Dourados, a decisive battle in the war with Paraguay. Their ashes are kept in a crypt below.

Fountains The most popular, Aguadeiro de Dona Maria, is in the Praça 15 de Novembro. The oldest, the Fonte da Glória (1789), has eight bronze spouts. Possibly the finest is at the back of the church of S. Francisco de Paula, at the inland end of the Rua do Ouvidor. These, and eight other old fountains, are illuminated by night.

Clubs Jockey, Av. Presidente Antônio Carlos 501; Naval, Avenida Rio Branco, 180: Militar, Avenida Rio Branco 251; Associação Brasileira da Imprensa, Rua Araújo Porto Alegre, 71; Rotary, Avenida Nilo Peçanha, 26; Automóvel, Rua do Passeio, 90; Cultura Artística, Largo da Carioca, 5; Engenharia, Avenida Rio Branco, 124/6; 40 Club, Rua Alvaro Alvim, 24 (2nd floor); Touring Club do Brasil, Praça Mauá; University Club, Av. Graça Aranha, 182, for students and graduates of U.S. Universities (The American Legion is at the same address); Lions Club, Conde do Bomfim 370. See also "Addresses", below.

Sports Clubs

Paissandu Athletic Club, Leblon (international)—Tennis, bowls, swimming.
Leme Tennis Club (international)—Tennis.
Rio de Janeiro Country Club, Rua Prudente de Morais 1597, Ipanema (international)—Tennis and swimming.
Gávea Golf and Country Club (international)—Golf and polo.

Itanhangá Golf Club, Jacarepaguá (international), visiting cards from Avenida Rio
    Branco 26, 16th floor.
Fluminense Football Club—Football, basketball, swimming, shooting, athletics,
    tennis and water-polo.
Vasco de Gama—Football, basketball, water-polo, rowing, athletics and tennis.
Flamengo—Football, basketball, water-polo, rowing, swimming, tennis, fencing,
    athletics, gymnastics, volley-ball and aviation.
Botafogo—Football, tennis, basketball, volley-ball, athletics and rowing.
Tijuca Tennis Club—Tennis, basketball, volley-ball, swimming, water-polo,
    gymnastics.
América—Football, basketball, volley-ball, tennis, athletics.
São Cristóvão—Football, basketball, tennis.
Guanabara—Rowing, swimming, water-polo, fencing.
Clube Hípico Brasileiro—Riding.
Iate Clube do Rio de Janeiro—Yachting.
Jockey Club—Horse racing on Thurs., Sat. and Sun., pari-mutuel betting.
Sacopan, Lagoa Rodrigo de Freitas—Fishing.

Addresses

Australian Consulate, Rua Barão do Flamengo, 22, Apt. 202.
Canadian Consulate, Avenida Presidente Wilson, 165.
British Consulate, Praia do Flamengo 322.
U.S.A. Consulate General, Avenida Presidente Wilson, 147.
Royal Society of St. George, c/o British Commonwealth Society, Rua da Quitanda
    199, sala 206.
U.S. Peace Corps, Rua Barão de Lucena 81, Botafogo.
Y.M.C.A., Rua da Lapa, 40.
The British Council: Rua Otávio Correa 30, Uria ZC 82, Tel.: 246-8133.
The British School of Rio de Janeiro, Rua da Matriz 76.
The American School of Rio de Janeiro, Estrada da Gávea.
Sociedade Brasileira de Cultura Inglesa, Rua Raúl Pompeia 231, Copacabana.
American Chamber of Commerce for Brazil, and American Club, Avenida Rio
    Branco 123, 21st floor.
Anglican Church, Rua Real Grandeza, 99.
Republic of S. Africa, Consulate, Praia do Flamengo 116.
British Commonwealth Society, Rua da Quitanda 199, sala 206.
St. Andrew's Society, c/o British Commonwealth Society.
Wilson, Sons S.A., shipping agents, Av. Rio Branco 25.
Central Post Office, Rua Primeiro de Março, at corner of Rua do Rosário.

Banks   Banco Internacional (Bank of America and Royal Bank of Canada), Rua do
Ouvidor 90; Banco Holandês Unido, Rua do Ouvidor, corner Tv. Ouvidor;
Citibank, Avenida Rio Branco, 83-85; Bank of London and South America Ltd.,
Praça Pio X, 78 (temporary); The First National Bank of Boston, Av. Rio Branco
110; Banco de Crédito Real de Minas Gerais, S.A., Av. Rio Banco 116; Banco Lar
Brasileiro, Rua do Ouvidor 98; and many others. Banks are open 930 to 1630. Closed
on Saturday.

Exchange Houses (rates tend to be better than banks): American Express, Almirante
Barroso 91, 6th floor, Tel.: 224-7559; at Kontik, São José, Av. Rio Branco 31;
Exprinter, Av. Rio Branco 57A.

Cables   Embratel, Esquina das Ruas Alfândega e Candelária. Telegrams may be
sent through any post office. Larger offices have telex.

Markets   North-eastern market at Campo de São Cristóvão (see page 226) on
Sunday mornings. Flower market at Praça Olavo Bilac, off Rua Buenos Aires in
centre. Sunday open-air handicrafts market at Praça General Osório, Ipanema.
Excellent food and household-goods markets at various places in the city and
suburbs (see newspapers for times and places).

The Suburbs of Rio de Janeiro

Copacabana, built on a narrow strip of land—only a little over 4 square
kilometres—between mountain and sea, has one of the highest densities in

the world: 62,000 people per square kilometre, or 250,000 in all. Its magnificent curved beach backed by skyscraper apartments is an unforgettable "must" for visitors. On all Rio's beaches you should take a towel or mat to protect you against small biting sand insects; in the water stay near groups of other swimmers, bathing is dangerous when the red flag is showing.

The remote stretch of sand which was Copacabana of 80 years ago was transformed when the the Old Tunnel was built and an electric tram service reached it. Week-end villas and bungalows sprang up—a few are still there. In the thirties the Copacabana Palace Hotel was still the only tall building among the houses, but the opening of the New Tunnel in the forties led to an explosion of population which shows no sign of having spent its force. Houses and old buildings are still being torn down ruthlessly and replaced by blocks of high flats.

There is almost everything in this fabulous "city within a city". The shops, mostly in Avenida Copacabana and the Rua Barata Ribeiro, are excellent. There are terrible traffic jams at times but new tunnels have been built to keep the traffic flowing from Copacabana to Ipanema and beyond.

This crammed area has, strangely enough, several fine squares and most of Rio's art galleries. A military fort, mounting 15″ guns, set at the far end of the beach, commands the entrance to Rio Bay and prevents a seashore connection with the Ipanema and Leblon beaches. However, parts of the military area are now being handed over to civilian use, the first being the Parque Garota de Ipanema at Arpoador, at the Copacabana end of the Ipanema beach. Buses to and from the city centre are plentiful and cheap, about US$0.20. If you are going to the centre from Copacabana, look for "Castelo", "Praça 15", "E. Ferro" or "Praça Mauá" on the sign by the front door. "Aterro" means the expressway between Botafogo and downtown Rio. From the centre to Copacabana is easier as all buses on that route are clearly marked; the relevant bus numbers are 120, 121, 123 and 127; the last two leave from the bus station (Rodoviária). Aterro bus does journey in 15 minutes.

Beyond Copacabana are the beautiful seaside suburbs of Ipanema and Leblon; they are less built-up than Copacabana, and still have spacious houses in tree-lined streets and beaches that tend to be cleaner, though no less dangerous, than Copacabana's. Backing Ipanema and Leblon is the spectacular Lagoa Rodrigo de Freitas, a salt-water lagoon on which Rio's rowing and small-boat sailing clubs are active. Too polluted for bathing. Beyond Leblon the coast is rocky; the Avenida Niemeyer skirts the cliffs on the journey past Vidigal, a small beach where the *Sheraton* is situated, to the newest seaside suburbs, of São Conrado and Barra da Tijuca (camp site). At the far end of Barra da Tijuca is the Recreio dos Bandeirantes, a safe bathing beach with a good restaurant.

On New Year's eve the festival of Yemanjá is held by the umbandistas on the beaches of Copacabana, Ipanema and Leblon (see page 224).

Santa Teresa, a very hilly inner suburb SW of the centre, well known as the coolest part of Rio, still has many Colonial and 19th-century buildings, set in narrow, twisting, tree-lined streets. See particularly the Convent (only the outside: the Carmelite nuns do not admit visitors), the Chácara do Céu Museum (see page 226), the Hotel Santa Teresa (the oldest house in the area), Vista Alegre, the Rua Aprazível (Delightful

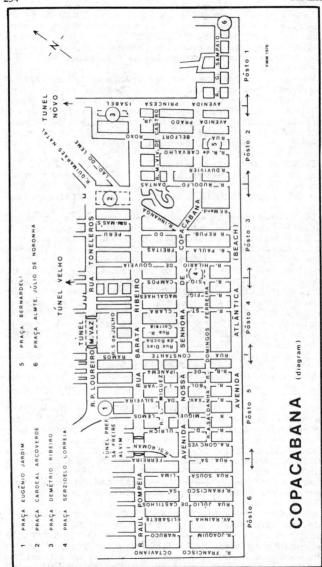

1 PRAÇA EUGÊNIO JARDIM
2 PRAÇA CARDEAL ARCOVERDE
3 PRAÇA DEMÉTRIO RIBEIRO
4 PRAÇA SERZIDELO CORREIA

5 PRAÇA BERNARDELI
6 PRAÇA ALMTE. JÚLIO DE NORONHA

COPACABANA (diagram)

Street), and Largo de Guimarães. Santa Teresa is best visited by the traditional trams, the only ones left in Rio, which leave from near the Largo da Carioca in the centre of the city, for Dois Irmãos, crossing to Santa Teresa via the old 18th-century aqueduct known as the Arcos.

Maracanã Stadium, one of the largest sports arenas in the world. The football ground has seating capacity for 200,000 spectators and most matches are played on Sundays; a smaller covered gymnasium for basketball, boxing and other indoor sports, the Maracanãzinho, can accommodate 50,000 persons. The true name, never used, is the Mário Filho Stadium. Open to visitors Tues.-Sat. (non-match days) at Gate 18, at charge of US$0.70. Buses 455 and 456 from Copacabana; 422, 438 and 442 from Flamengo; 221 and 231 from Castelo; 249 and 269 from Praça Tiradentes; and 254 and 260 from Praça 15 de Novembro.

Corcovado (700 metres), the hunched-backed peak surmounted by a 40-metre high statue of Christ the Redeemer, weighing, with its base, 1,200 tons. There is a superb view from the top, to which a motor road has been opened from the Larangeiras district; both car and cog-train (30 mins. each way) put down their passengers behind the statue—there is a climb of 220 steps to the top, near which there is a café for light refreshments.

Take a Cosme Velho bus (106, 178, 180, 422, 497-8, 583-4) or taxi to the station at Rua Cosme Velho 513. The system is due to be renovated and at the time of writing is operating, or not operating, in a haphazard fashion. Time taken: about 1½ hours for the round trip, exclusive of waiting time, which can be up to 2 hours at weekends and holidays. (Cost: US$2 return; no single tickets.) Alternatively hire a taxi, US$2.80 p.p., or a VW minibus from the Cosme Velho station; taxi waits for an hour at top of Corcovado. Views are possibly better from the road than the railway. Also, a 206 bus does the very attractive run from Praça São Francisco to Silvestre, to one of the stations on the Corcovado cog railway; one can also take a minibus from there. An active walk of one hour will bring one to the top, and the road is shady. (Best done in company; robberies not unknown in this neighbourhood.)

Pão de Açúcar (Sugar Loaf, 395 metres), a massive granite cone at the entrance to Guanabara Bay, ascended by thousands in the cable-car. The bird's eye view of the city and beaches is very beautiful. There is a restaurant and a playground for children on the Morro da Urca, half way up, and there are also shows at night, and refreshments at the top. Buses 107 and 442 (from the centre) and 511-2 (from Copacabana) take you to the station at the foot.

Aerial cableway station is at 520 Avenida Pasteur. The cable car timetable: Praia Vermelha to Urca: first car goes up at 0800, and the last comes down at 2215. From Urca to Sugar Loaf the first connecting cable car goes up at 0815 and the last leaves the summit at 2200; the return trip costs US$2.80; The old cable way has been completely rebuilt. Termini are now ample and efficient and the new Italian cable cars carry many more passengers (about 70) than did the old. Even on the most crowded days, there is little queuing.

Tijuca Forest, for those interested in taking a forest walk through mountain scenery. Martin Crossland writes: An approximately 2½ hour walk will bring you to the summit of the **Pico da Tijuca** (over 1,000 metres), which gives a good idea of the tropical vegetation of the interior and a capital sight of the bay and its shipping. On entering the park at Alto de Boa Vista, follow the signposts to Bom Retiro, a good picnic place, passing by the Cascatinha Taunay, Mayrink Chapel and the restaurant *A Floresta*. At Bom Retiro the road ends and there is another hour's walk along a fair footpath to the summit. The last part consists of steps carved out of the solid rock. The route is shady for almost its entire length, and is not over strenuous.

Take a 221 or 233 bus from the Rodoviária, or from Praça Sáenz Pena, Tijuca (to which, 454 bus from Copacabana) to Alto da Boa Vista, for the forest entrance. Other places of interest not passed on the walk to the peak are the Paul and Virginia Grotto, the Vista do Almirante and the Mesa do Imperador (viewpoints). A good restaurant in Parque Floresta is *Os Esquilos* (squirrels). Allow at least 5 to 6 hours for the excursion. Also, one of the Raymundo Castro Maia museums is nearby (see page 226).

Barra da Tijuca   Martin Crossland writes: This new and very rapidly developing area of Rio can be reached from the Tijuca Forest by continuing on the 233 bus, or from the centre from the bus station at Rua São José (the air-conditioned "Taquara" bus), from Santos Dumont airport (Campo Grande or Santa Cruz bus) and from the end of Leblon beach (bus 554).

This area is planned as an entirely self-supporting metropolitan district of Rio and all new construction is rigidly controlled in order not to create another "concrete jungle". It is also one of the principal recreation areas of Rio, the prime attrtaction being its 20-km. sandy beach. Apart from this, there are innumerable bars and restaurants, campsites, motels and hotels.

A good circular trip is as follows: Take the 221 bus from Rua Erasmo Braga, near the São José bus station, to Praça Afonso Viseu at Alto da Boa Vista. Visit the Tijuca Forest, especially the lovely Taunay waterfall. Continue on by the 233 to Barra de Tijuca. From Barra, take the 554, which will bring you to the end of Leblon beach, where you can find plenty of transport back to the centre of Copacabana.

Viewpoints   Apart from the Pico da Tijuca, Corcovado and Pão de Açúcar, splendid views of different parts of Rio can be seen from the Vista Chinesa (420 m), where from a Chinese-style pavilion one can see the inland lake (the Lagoa), Ipanema and Leblon; the Mesa do Imperador (Emperor's Table) and Vista do Almirante in the Tijuca Forest; and the Mirante de Dona Marta (340 m) off the Corcovado road, with the same direction of view as the Corcovado, but as it is lower the details can be seen more clearly. At Botafogo is the Mirante do Pasmado viewing point, reached from Rua General Severiano. There is yet no public transport to any of these places.

Paquetá Island in Guanabara Bay can be visited by frequent ferry services from Praça 15 de Novembro (fare US$0.30). Paquetá is exceptionally picturesque. It is the traditional meeting place for lovers and is crowded at weekends. Horse drawn carriages hire for US$3 per hour. Tour by "trenzinho", a tractor pulling trailers, US$0.50. Bicycles for hire from US$0.60 to US$1.50 per hour. They even have a bicycle made for four!

Ferry boat departures (one hour's journey) as follows: to Paquetá, 0530 (except Sat. and Sun.), 0710, 1015, 1330, 1500, 1730, 1900 and 2230; to Rio 0530, 0700, 0900,

1200, 1500, 1700, 1900 and 2030. *Hotel Paquetá,* US$8 double with breakfast (US$6.50 double if without bath), *Flamboyant* and *Lido.*

Other boat trips, by *bateau mouche* (air conditioned and restaurant), around Guanabara Bay depart from Av. Néstor Moreira 11, Botafogo, first two trips at 0930, third at 1420, fares from US$17.

The State of Rio de Janeiro: East from Rio

Niterói, founded in 1573, the ex-capital of the State of Rio de Janeiro, across the bay by bridge or ferries, is a city with 335,000 population. Visit the Rio Cricket and Athletic Association and the Rio Sailing Club. Some British and American families live here. Paved roads to Campos, the sugar centre, and other parts of the State of Rio de Janeiro.

Frequent ferry boat and hydrofoil service from Praça 15 de Novembro, Rio. There is a Flumitur tourist information booth to the right of the ferry boat station. Nearby you can take the 33 bus (marked "via Froes") to the quiet bay beaches of Icaraí, São Francisco and Jurujuba, a beautiful ride. Sit on the righthand side. Two minutes' walk from where the bus route ends at Jurujuba are the attractive twin beaches of Adam and Eve, with lovely views of Rio across the bay. From Praça General Gomes Carneiro, near the ferry boats, take a 38 bus to Piratininga, Itaipu and Itacoatiara, fabulous ocean beaches and the best in the area, about 40 minutes ride through picturesque countryside. The beaches inside the bay, though calm, are often overcrowded and polluted, but no more so than those opposite in Rio. The forts on this side of the bay include Santa Cruz (16th century), Barão do Rio Branco (1633), Gragoatá and Nossa Senhora da Boa Viagem.

You should also visit the church of Boa Viagem (1633), built on an island and connected to the mainland by a short causeway, a few minutes' walk from Icaraí beach. Nearby, on Rua Tiradentes, is the interesting Antonio Parreira Museum.

Hotels *Samanguaia,* US$17-20. *Imperial,* US$5-10.

Clubs Rio Cricket, bus No. 9 to Icaraí. Rio Sailing, bus No. 33 marked "via Froes".

The Rio-Niterói bridge was opened on 4th March 1974. Called Ponte Costa e Silva, it has an extension of 14 km. Toll for cars, US$2 weekdays, US$3 weekends. Bus 999 from the corner of Senador Dantas and Av. Beira Mar, Rio, crosses the bridge to Niterói and Icaraí (US$0.40).

Electric Current 110-220 AC 50 cycles

Martin Crossland writes: To the east of Rio and Niterói lie a series of salt-water lagoons, called locally the Lagos Fluminenses. Two small lakes lie behind the beaches of Piratininga and Itaipu, though they are polluted and ringed by mud. The next lakes are much larger, those of Maricá and Saquarema; though they are still muddy, the waters are relatively unpolluted, and wild life abounds in the scrub and bush around the lagoons. At the outlet to the lake of Saquarema (turn right off the main road at Bacaxa) is the holiday village of Saquarema. Of particular interest is the little white church of Nossa Senhora de Nazaré (1675) built atop a green promontory jutting into the ocean. This village is the centre for surfing in Brazil, and the national championships are held here each year in May.

The largest lake is that of Araruama, famous for its medicinal mud. This is so large that it seems more like a bay than a lagoon. The salinity is extremely high, the waters calm, and almost the entire lake is surrounded by sandy beaches, making it very popular with families looking for safe, unpolluted bathing. The major industry of the area is salt, and all around one can see the saltpans and the metal wind pumps (the district's most prominent characteristic) used to carry the water into the pans, where it dries and leaves the salt deposit. At the eastern end of the lake lies the village of **São Pedro de Aldeia,** which, in spite of intensive development, still retains much of it colonial charm, and is known for its lovely Jesuit church built in 1723.

Hotels in the lake district: Saquarema: *Katy Motel,* US$20 d, with meals. Araruama: *Senzala,* on Iguabinha beach, 10 km. from Araruama, US$30 d; *La Gondola,* on the lake beach, US$35 d, with meals: *Lakes Hotel,* over the bus station, US$10 d. São Pedro de Aldeia: *Chapinha do Rei Motel,* on Teresa beach, US$23 d; *Costa do Sol,* on Iguaba Grande beach, 14 km. from São Pedro, US$12 d.

The ocean beaches beside these lagoons, except for the sheltered coves of Ponta Negra and Saquarema, are rough and lonely. The whole area is perfect for camping; there are campsites at Ararauama and São Pedro de Aldeia.

Cabo Frio, 156 km. from Rio, about 2½ hours by bus (US$2.50), is a popular holiday and week-end haunt of Cariocas because of its cool weather, beaches, scenery, sailing and good under-water swimming. (We are told, however, that the beaches have become dirtier in recent years.) The São Mateus Fort nearby was built by the French.

Hotels   *Malibu Palace,* US$30-40, *Cabo Frio Sol* (motel), US$18-40.   15 other hotels with descending prices down to: *Caravela,* US$8-18 and *Colonial,* US$5-10. Youth Hostel, both sexes, open all year.

Camping   Camping Clube do Brasil sites at Estrada dos Passageiros, near town; 4 km. outside town, in Palmeiras; and at Arraial do Cabo on Praia dos Anjos, 10 km. to S. Also site at Cabo Yacht club.

Tourists are also recommended to visit **Búzios,** NE of Cabo Frio, a fishing village now converted into a playground for the rich, with innumerably sandy coves, calm unpolluted waters, beautiful scenery, good but expensive hotels; 45 minutes by bus from Cabo Frio. Camping is allowed. Tourist information office near bus station.

Continuing to the north, one comes to the seaside resorts of Barra de São João, Rio das Ostras (*Hotel Saint Tropez,* US$22 d) and **Macaé** (Hotels *Turismo* and *Panorama* US$5 to 10 d), all containing sheltered coves with good swimming and scuba diving. North of Macaé commences one of the largest sugar-producing areas of Brazil, the centre of which is Campos, 70 km. from Macaé.

From Rio and Niterói a first class motor road (bus, about 4 hours) and a railway (317 km., 7 hours) run NE past Macaé to

Campos, a busy industrial city, some 276 km. from the city of Rio de Janeiro. It stands 56 km. from the mouth of the Paraíba. It was along this river that coffee planting spread to São Paulo state, and coffee is still grown near Campos, though it is now one of the largest sugar-producing zones in Brazil. Important offshore oil discoveries have been made nearby. Town is not uninteresting. Population: 285,000.

Hotels   *Planície,* Rua 13 de Maio 56, US$10 d; *Palace,* Av. 15 de Novembro 143, US$8 d.

Petrópolis (population: 175,000) is a summer hill resort and industrial city at 840 metres, 68 km. from Rio. It is reached by bus along a steep, scenic mountain road, which was due to become a toll road in mid-1978. Until 1962 Petrópolis was the "summer capital" of Brazil, with numbers of picturesque private residences, largely owned by people from Rio de Janeiro. It was founded in 1843 as a summer residence by Dom Pedro II. Now it combines manufacturing industry (particularly textiles, which may be bought cheaply) with floral beauty and hill scenery. Well worth a visit are the Gothic-styled Cathedral, completed in 1925, which contains the tombs of the Emperor and Empress, and the Imperial Museum in the old Imperial Palace. The Museum is open from 1200-1900 every day except Monday, and the Imperial Crown Jewels are on view during the whole time the museum is open. Golf Club. Information office at centre.

Attractions and Excursions   Museu Ferreira da Cunha, Fernandes Vieira 390 (old road to Rio) shows large collection of arms, open Sat. and Sun. 0900-1700. Summer home of air pioneer Santos Dumont, showing early inventions. Crystal Palace in Praça da Conflência, former imperial ballroom and now exhibition centre. Floralia orchid centre in district of Correas has outside exhibitions.

Buses Buses leave from Rio every 10 minutes throughout the day (US$1). Return tickets are not available so that passengers must reserve their places in the return bus as soon as they arrive in Petrópolis. Time occupied on the journey, 90 minutes each way. The ordinary buses leave from the Rodoviaria in Rio; there is a new service of air-conditioned buses, every hour, from Rau Nilo Pecanha, US$1.50. There is a direct overnight bus from Sao Paulo.

Hotels *Margaridas,* Mons. Bacelar 126, chalet-type hotel set in lovely gardens with swimming pool, charming proprietors, US$45 d with meals; *Auto-Tour (Fazenda Inglesa)* at km. 51 on the Petrópolis by-pass, very chic, US$50 d, with meals; *Casablanca Center,* General Osório 28, US$23 d; *Casablanca,* 7 de Setembro beside Imperial Palace, US$20 d; *Casablanca Palace,* 1° de Março 123, US$20 d; *Gran Solar (Pousado do Carmo),* Benjamin Constant 280, US$15 d; *Hotel Comércio,* opp. bus station, US$4 s, with breakfast.

Restaurants *Churrascaria Majórica,* Av. 15 de Novembro 754; *Mirthes Paranhos,* Irmãos d'Angelo 99; *Cantina Italiana,* Paulo Barbosa 48; *Maloca,* Washington Luis 466; *Bauernstube,* João Pessoa 297.

Camping Ass. Brasieira de Camping. Araras district.

Teresópolis (population: 80,000; 910 metres), near the Serra dos Orgãos, is 124 km. from Rio. It was the favourite summer residence of the Empress Teresa Cristina. Now chiefly visited for the beauty of its surroundings and for riding, climbing and walking among them. See the Lago Sloper, the Lago Iaci, the Imbui and Amores waterfalls, the Fonte Judith and the black swans at Granja Comary. Tourist information office near bus station. St. Peter's festival on June 29th is celebrated with fireworks.

About 30,000 hectares of the Serra dos Orgãos, so called because their strange shapes are said to recall organ-pipes, have been turned into a National Park. The main attraction is the precipitous Dedo de Deus (God's Finger) Peak. There is also the rock formation Mulher de Pedra (Stone Woman) 12 km. out on the Nova Friburgo road, and the Von Martinó natural-history museum. The highest point is the Pedra Açu, 2,040 metres. A good way to see the Park is to do the Rio-Teresópolis-Petrópolis-Rio circuit; a long but scenic day trip. The Rio-Teresópolis road is now a toll road (cars US$1, US$1.50 at weekends) from Km. 10.6. Martín Crossland writes: Leave the Rodoviária bus station in Rio on the 0800 bus (Viação Teresópolis, US$1.50) for the two-hour ride around Guanabara Bay and up into the mountains to Teresópolis. Upon arrival at the bus station at 1000, buy another ticket right away for Petrópolis (Viação Teresópolis, US$1) for the 1200 bus in order to get a good seat, as the bus fills rapidly. This gives you two hours to wander around, during which you may visit the lovely landscaped park, or take a bus to "Soberbo" at the entrance to the city, for an impressive view of the Finger of God (Dedo de Deus) peak and the whole of Guanabara Bay. If you feel up to a steep ½ hour climb, try the Colina dos Mirantes for a sweeping view of the city and surroundings. For the less energetic, a taxi is not dear.

The drive from Teresópolis to Petrópolis is extremely beautiful (90 minutes), passing right through the Serra dos Orgãos. The views on either side are spectacular, and in Sept.-Oct. the hortensias are in bloom along the roadside. Again, upon arrival in Petrópolis at 1330, buy your ticket to Rio (Facil or Unica, US$1). Take the 1700 bus "via Quitandinha", and you might catch the sunset over the mountains. This gives you time to visit most of the attractions listed in the city description.

Bus, Rio-Teresópolis Buses leave every half-hour from Rodoviária. As return tickets are not issued, passengers should book for the return journey as soon as they arrive at Teresópolis. Time, 2 hours each way; fare US$1.60.

Hotels *São Moritz,* outside on the Nova Friburgo road, km. 41, US$35 d, US$40 d, with meals; *Clube Caxangá,* resort-type, US$30 d; *Philipp,* Rua Duval Fonseca, US$15 d; *Higino Palace,* Av. Oliveira Botelho 328, US$30 d; *Vila Nova do Paquequer,* Av. Alberto Torres 1149 (by the Guarani waterfall), US$14 d; *Granja Dedo de Deus,* Estrada da Posse, US$18 d.

Camping National Park, entrance to Teresópolis from Rio, no facilities; Quinta de Barra, km. 3 on Petrópolis road; Vale das Choupanas, km. 30 on Rio road.

Restaurants *Taberna Alpina,* Duque de Caxias 131; *Cantina Riviera,* Praça Baltazar de Silveira 112; *La Cremaille,* Av. Feliciano Sodré 1012; *De Stéfano,* Av. Lúcio Meira 695.

Nova Friburgo (850 metres above sea-level), is a popular watering place (around 30 hotels) during summer months, in a beautiful valley with excellent walking and riding possibilities. Founded by Swiss settlers from Fribourg, it can be reached by bus (US$2) from Rio (every half hour) or Niterói in 3 hours, or by car in 1 hr. 45 min. Pop.: 80,000. Cable car from Praça dos Suspiros 650 m. up the Morro da Cruz, for view of rugged country. Road to Teresópolis to be paved by end-1977.

Hotels *Buksky,* 5 km. out on Niterói road, US$50 d, with meals; *Sans-Souci,* 1 km, out, US$40 with meals; *Garlipp,* German-run, in chalets and *Mury Garden,* with swimming pool, at Muri (km. 70 on Niterói road).

Restaurant *Majórica,* traditional churrascaria.

Camping Camping Clube do Brasil has sites on Niterói road, at Cônego (7 km. out) and Muri (15 km. out). Cambrás site also at Cônego, and private site at Fazenda Sanandu, 20 km. out on same road.

The State of Rio de Janeiro: West from Rio

Volta Redonda Brazil's chief steel centre, standing on a broad bend of the Rio Paraíba at an altitude of 565 metres, 113 km. from Rio along the railway to São Paulo. In 1942 it was a little village; today it has the largest steel works in Latin America and a population of 152,000. The mills are on the river bank and the town spreads up the surrounding wooded and gardened slopes, each house different from its neighbour. Here is a model industrial town, "steel mills in a garden".

Hotels *Sider Palace,* Rua 33 No. 10, US$22 d; *Bela Vista,* Alto de Boa Vista, on a hill overlooking town, US$18 d.

Visitors who have a permit from the Companhia Siderúrgica Nacional management at Rio de Janeiro (apply ten days in advance), or locally from the *Bela Vista* hotel are allowed to inspect the mills. Visits start at 0900, and last 2½-3 hours. The town can be reached from Rio by train (Central do Brasil) in about 3 hours, luxury service, or by buses or microbuses in 2½ hours. Some 30 km. W of Volta Redonda, in the town of Resende, is the Military Academy of Agulhas Negras. Grounds, with captured German guns of World War II, are open to the public.

The **Itatiaia National Park,** on the Serra de Itatiaia in the Mantiqueira chain of mountains, is a few km. N of the Dutra Highway from a point 48 km. W of Volta Redonda: 174 km. from Rio. Road to it is paved. The town to Itatiaia is surrounded by picturesque mountain peaks and lovely waterfalls. It has good hotels, and plenty of camping sites.

Hotels *Simon,* km. 13 park road, US$50 d, with meals, lovely views; *Repouso Itatiaia,* km. 10 park road, US$35 d, with meals; *Hotel do Ipé,* km. 13 park road, US$35 d, with meals; *Fazenda da Serra,* Via Dutra km. 151, US$22 d, with meals; *Parque Itatiaia,* entrance to park, US$12 d.

In the same region, 175 km. from Rio, is the small town of **Penedo** which in the 1930s attracted Finnish settlers who brought the first saunas to Brazil. This popular weekend resort also provides horse riding, and swimming in the Portinho river. Some 33 km. beyond Penedo is the small village of Visconde de Mauá. Further along the Dutra Highway (186 km. from Rio) is the small settlement of **Engenheiro Passos** from which a road leads to São Lourenço and Caxamba in Minas Gerais (see page 252), passing Agulhas Negras (2,787 m.) one of the highest peaks in Brazil.

Hotels   Penedo: *Hotel Bertell.* Engenheiro Passos: *Hotel Villa-Forte.*

The new Rio-Santos highway is making the beautiful coastal region SW of Rio more accessible. So far it extends from Rio past Itaguaí, Itacuruçá, Mangaratiba, Angra dos Reis, Parati, Ubatuba and Caraguatatuba to São Sebastião (São Paulo). Several leisure-oriented communities are being built along this coastline. The connecting stretch from São Sebastião to Santos has not yet been modernized. (We are indebted to Rita Davy for the paragraph on Itacuruçá, and to Martin Crossland for the following paragraphs on Angra and Parati.)

Itacuruçá, 91 km. from Rio, is a delightful place to visit if you like beautiful scenery and peace and quiet. The *Hotel Jaguanum,* Ilha de Jaguanum, Itacuruçá, has apartments and chalets with private bathrooms, verandas with panoramic view of the Bay of Sepetiba. There is a private beach, restaurant in original slave quarters, salon for games and recreation bar and beautiful walks around the island. Reservations for the hotel, which include the boat trip to and from the island, cost US$100-120 per day for two with all meals. The only extra is the bus, US$5 return, which picks you up at your hotel. Book by calling 236-3551 or 236-0413, in Rio.

Angra dos Reis founded in 1502, is about 197 km. SW of Rio by bus; it is to be the site of Brazil's first atomic-power stations. A small port with an important fishing and shipbuilding industry, it has a number of small bays with good bathing within easy reach and is situated in an enormous bay full of small and large islands. Of particular interest are the Convent of Our Lady of Carmo, built in 1593, the Parish Church, 1626, the ruins of the Jacuecanga seminary (built 1797, and the Sennor do Bomfim (1780). An unusual fact is that the town jail is located right in the main square. Two hours by ferry boat takes you on a most attractive trip through the bay to **Ilha Grande,** once an infamous pirate lair, and now occupied principally by fishermen and one of Brazil's larger prisons.

Hotel   *Londres,* US$15 d.

Restaurants   *Costa Verde, Verde Mar,* both specializing in sea food.

Bus   Hourly from Rodoviária bus station, Viação Eval (take the "via litoral" bus and sit on the left, US$2.50, 3 hours.

Beyond Angra dos Reis, the road continues along the coast, past the new nuclear-power project at Itaorna, to **Parati**, a small colonial town only accessible these last few years with the opening of the road. It is principally a fishing village and the centre of the town has been declared a national historic monument in its entirety. It was one of the first planned towns in Brazil, with streets ending in a "T" shape as defence from pirates, being the chief port for the export of gold in the 17th century. An interesting point is that the churches were built separately for each race, Indian, black and white. There is a great deal of distinguished Portuguese colonial architecture in delightful settings. Some travellers report that street surfaces in Parati are not suitable for motor vehicles.

Hotels   *Pousada Parieiro* and *Coxixo,* both attractively housed in colonial buildings with lovely gardens, US$12 d, but always full at week-ends. The bus runs every 2 hours from 0600 (Colitur, US$1.50) from Angra and the run is 1½ hours. There is a Camping Club site, but very crowded in January and February.

The road continues from Parati into the State of São Paulo.

It is possible to go from Rio to Parati by bus all along the coast; direct through buses are now running. For a more adventurous journey, take the Santos Dumont-Santa Cruz bus (see page 236) to its terminal, then cross the railway bridge and catch the bus to Itaguaí (on this route a long railway bridge over a wide river has to be crossed on foot, another bus waiting on the other side). On arrival at Itaguaí, change to bus for Mangaratiba, from which there is now a regular bus service on to Angra dos Reis. There are frequent direct buses from Rio's Rodoviária. On Saturdays and Sundays there is a train for Mangaratiba from the Central Station at 0700; on weekdays this train leaves from Santa Cruz at 1000.

Espírito Santo

N of Campos (see page 238) the road and railway run through the State of Espírito Santo to the port of Vitória. The State has a mountainous interior and a hot, damp seaboard. It is an important grower of coffee. In the north there are large forests containing hardwoods. The people are known as "Capixabas", after a former Indian tribe.

Vitória, 644 km. from Rio de Janeiro, is reached by the Leopoldina Railway (2230, 24 hours), irregularly by coastal steamers (24 hours), several times a day by plane (80 minutes), and by bus (7½ hours). Two bridges connect the island on which it stands with the mainland. The country around is picturesque. The town is beautifully set, its entrance second only to Rio's, its beaches quite as attractive, but smaller, and the climate is less humid. Vitória is a growing centre for the sport of sea fishing. Population, about 120,000.

Its growing importance is due to its connection westwards with Belo Horizonte and the iron mines of the Cia. Vale do Rio Doce at Itabira in Minas Gerais by a railway: the E.F. Vitória-Minas, which transports for export millions of tons of iron ore and a large tonnage of coffee and timber. Ships drawing 11 metres and 240 metres in length can enter the port. A supplementary iron ore port has now been built at Ponta do Tubarão, near Vitória, to load ships up to 250,000 tons.

Excursion   To the fortified monastery of Nossa Senhora da Penha (Our Lady of the Rock), on a high hill above the small settlement of Vila Velha. There is a beautiful view of the bay from the monastery, begun 1558, but most of the (unremarkable) structure, now in ruins, is of the 17th and 18th centuries. The Dutch attacked it in 1625 and 1640.

Trains   Daily connections with Rio (24 hours) and Belo Horizonte (18 hours).

Buses   Rio, 7½ hours; Belo Horizonte, 11 hours; also Salvador.

Hotels   *Helal,* Jerônimo Monteiro 935, US$20-25 d; *Cannes Palace,* Jerônimo Monteiro 111, US$30 d; *Estoril,* Praça Pres. Roosevelt 532, US$20 d; *Tabajara,* Jerônimo Monteiro 60, US$14 d. (Av. Jerônimo Monteiro runs along the beautiful Praia da Costa beach and is served by regular buses from the centre).

Restaurants   *Esplanada* and *São Pedro* (fish a speciality).

Banks   Local banks.

Cables   Embratel, Palácio do Café, Praça Costa Pereira 52. Tel.: 30914.

British Vice-Consulate.

Tourist Information   Emcatur, Rua Graciano Neves 165.

The beaches of **Guarapari** (50 km. S of Vitória, 40 mins. by hourly car and bus) attract many people seeking a cure for their ailments (particularly rheumatism and neuritis) from the radioactive monazitic sands. Hotels: *Coronado, Thorium, Atlântico,* US$12 d, recommended.

Minas Gerais

The inland State of Minas Gerais, somewhat larger than France, is mostly on the Brazilian central plateau. The S is mountainous, rising to the 2,560-metre peak of Agulhas Negras, in the Mantiqueira range. From

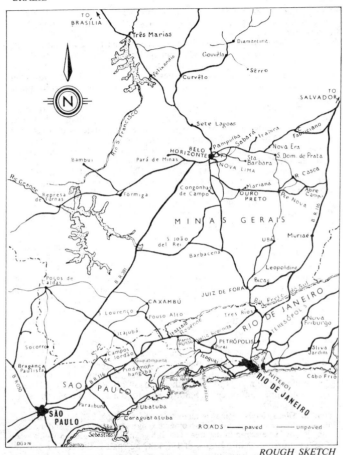

ROUGH SKETCH

ROADS FROM RIO DE JANEIRO,

SAO PAULO & BELO HORIZONTE

Belo Horizonte north are undulating grazing lands, the richest of which are in the extreme W: a broad wedge of country between Goiás in the N and São Paulo in the S—the famous Triângulo Mineiro (Minas Triangle). Most of the upland is also good grazing country and there are some 16 million head of cattle. The best dairy products of Rio de Janeiro come from Minas Gerais. The State is a major producer of beans, maize, garlic, rice, bananas, oranges, tea, coffee, sugar and tobacco, and grows much cotton and grapes besides.

Minas Gerais was once described as having a heart of gold and a breast of iron. Half the mineral production of Brazil comes from the State: nearly all the iron ore, bauxite, cassiterite, graphite, arsenic, and mica, besides large percentages of manganese, amiantus, beryllium, industrial diamonds, chromium and rock crystal. It has the only two gold mines working in Brazil.

It has no port of its own. Its exports move through Rio de Janeiro, Santos, Vitória and Angra dos Reis. There are more than a thousand known waterfalls in the State, with a potential capacity of over two million h.p. The easy availability of power and the local agricultural and mineral production has created a large number of metal-working, textile, mineral water, food processing and timber industries.

The population rose from 7,717,792 in 1950 to 12,550,000 in 1975.

There is much to interest the tourist: the old colonial cities built during the gold rush in the 18th century, and a number of splendid spas and hill resorts. The best way of seeing the charming colonial cities is from Rio or Belo Horizonte; many tourist companies provide short tours, and for those without cars this is perhaps the most efficient way of seeing these monuments.

Exprinter (Av. Rio Branco 57a, Rio de Janeiro), arranges 5-day cultural excursions to Belo Horizonte, Ouro Preto and Congonhas do Campo. Similar tours by Soletur (Rua da Quitanda 11-4°) and others.

The chief glory of the colonial cities is the architecture and, even more, the sculpture of possibly the greatest creative artist ever born in Latin America, the mulatto Antônio Francisco Lisboa (1738-1814), who was the son of a Portuguese architect and a black slave woman. He is known as "O Aleijadinho" (the little cripple) because in later life he developed a maiming disease which compelled him to work in a kneeling (and ultimately a recumbent) position with his hammer and chisel strapped to his wrists. His finest work, which shows a grandeur and power not normally associated with the plastic arts in the 18th century, is probably the statues in the gardens and sanctuary of the great Bom Jesus church in Congonhas de Campo, but the main corpus of his work is in Ouro Preto, with some important pieces in Sabará, São João del Rei and Mariana (see following pages).

Food in Minas Gerais Minas is famous for the roast loin of pork served there, meltingly tender in the mouth and accompanied by a black-bean paste and the crisp, slightly bitter kale grown in the area. The dish is known as "Tutu à Mineira".

129 km. north of Rio by air and 196 km. by road is the city of **Juiz de Fora.** It lies on the Paraibuna river, in a deep valley between the Mar and Mantiqueira mountain chains. This quite pleasant town is at 640 metres. Population: 230,000. The Museum of Mariano Procópio is well worth a visit.

Industries Textiles, brewing, timber sawing, sugar refining. A steel mill is being built, with British assistance, by the Mendes Júnior group.

Hotels *Ritz* (best), Barão do Rio Branco 2000, US$20-25 d; *Imperial,* Batista de Oliveira 605, US$17 d (simple, but well run), and many more, all second class.

From **Barbacena,** a rose-growing town 103 km. on, a paved road runs W to the colonial city of **São João del Rei,** with a grand bridge and two splendid 18th century churches: São Francisco, with exterior and interior sculptures by Áleijadinho, and the Carmo, on the other side of the river, with interior sculptures by him. Population, 50,000. There is also a good museum. See also **Tiradentes**, a few km. away, now hardly more than a village but attractive with goldsmiths, gardens, museum, and a beautiful church.

Barbacena Hotel   *Grogotó,* new, excellent, US$10-20 d.

Tiradentes Hotel   *Solar da Ponte,* atmosphere of country house, US$20-40 d, including breakfast and tea, only ten rooms.

São João del Rei Hotel   *Porto Real,* charming reconstructed colonial building, US$20 d.

Belo Horizonte, the capital of Minas Gerais, is the third largest city in Brazil. It is situated over 800 metres above sea-level, surrounded by mountains, and enjoys an excellent climate all the year round (with the exception of the rainy season during October, November and December). It was Brazil's first modern planned city: wide, tree-lined avenues radiate like the spokes of a wheel from the centre. Information for tourists can be obtained from the Touring Club of Brazil. Sights to be seen are the Palácio da Liberdade, in Praça da Liberdade (every Sunday morning an open-air craft market operates here); the Palácio das Artes (which has a permanent exhibition of Mineiro workmanship and a good souvenir shop, and tourist information); the City Museum; the Museum of Mineralogy, a Gothic building near the park, with interesting exhibits; the Railway Station (the oldest building in Belo Horizonte), the Municipal Park (a large and colourful park right in the centre of the city, not too safe at night). Eight km. from the centre is the picturesque suburb of Pampulha, famous for its modern buildings, and the artificial lake, all designed by the renowned Brazilian architect Oscar Niemeyer (who also designed most of Brasília); in Pampulha the glass and marble Museum of Modern Art may be visited, as well as the Chapel of São Francisco (the interior of which was decorated by the Brazilian painter Cândido Portinari). The best clubs are the Minas Tennis Club (close to the centre), the Morro do Chapeu (25 km. S of the centre, in rugged country), the Serra da Moeda and the Automóvel Club. The airport at Pampulha has a fair volume of traffic and there are frequent daily flights to the other major Brazilian cities. The huge Mineirão stadium is the second largest in Brazil after the Maracanã stadium in Rio. The population of Belo Horizonte is now over the 1,500,000 mark and it is one of the fastest growing of Brazil's main cities.

Belo Horizonte has a fair number of Italian and German settlers and is the capital of the intermediary state dividing the north-east and the south of Brazil, thus accounting for a noticeable mixture of races. Belo Horizonte is an important cultural centre and can boast of having educated some of Brazil's finest poets, writers, musicians, and philosophers. There are two universities, a conservatory of music, a ballet school, a large technical college and an excellent range of secondary and primary schools. Belo Horizonte's Industrial City, about 10 km. from the centre, has now become one of the largest industrial centres of Brazil, and apart from being the traditional centre of important mining and agricultural industries (as well as diamond cutting and precious stones), it is now the centre for huge steelworks and a budding automobile industry. Notwithstanding the upsurge of industrial activity in the last few years, Belo Horizonte still remains relatively pollution-free and many tourists are surprised by the general cleanliness of the city compared with other Brazilian centres.

There are good roads, with frequent buses, connecting Belo Horizonte with São Paulo, Rio de Janeiro, Brasília, and the major cities in the interior of Minas Gerais. The city itself has a good public transport system, and taxis are plentiful, although hard to obtain at peak hours.

Local Holidays Maundy Thursday; Corpus Christi; 15th August (Assumption); 8th December (Immaculate Conception).

Industries Iron, steel, seamless tubes, textiles, cement, electric rolling stock. Fiat has established a vehicle factory nearby, at Betim.

Buses To Rio, 8 hours, US$6; to Brasília, 11 hours, US$12; to Ouro Preto, 2 hours, US$1.50; to Congonhas do Campo, US$1, 1½ hours. To São Paulo, 9 hours, US$11; route passes the great Furnas reservoir.

Train Day (10 hrs.) and night (14 hrs.) trains to Rio de Janeiro, operating problems have made the provision of these services erratic, check carefully; to Brasília 3 times a week at 2100, 33 hours, US$4.50 1st class, US$6 sleeper. São Paulo, 27 hrs., dirty uncomfortable journey, take food, US$8-9.

Airport Pampulha. Internal flights only.

Electric Current 120-220 A.C. 60 cycles.

Addresses

British Vice-Consulate: Rua Antônio Albuquerque 746. Caixa Postal 2755.
American Consulate.
Sociedade Brasileira de Cultura Inglesa: As British Vice-Consulate.

Hotels (Figures in brackets are room prices in US dollars, single/double.) *Del Rey,* Praça Afonso Arinos 60 (34/43); *Normandy,* Rua Tamoios 212 (31/41), excellent grill; *Plaza Palace,* Rua Rio de Janeiro 147 (28/36), own garage; *Excelsior,* Rua Caetés 753 (25/34); *Serrana Palace,* Rua Goitacases 450 (21/28), pleasant restaurant; *Amazonas,* Av. Amazonas 120 (21/25); *Lorman,* Rua Guarani 165 (16/26); *Brazil Palace,* Rua Carijós 269 (Praça Sete de Setembro) (18/25); *Cecília,* Rua Carijós 454 (17/23); *Ambassy,* Rua Caetés 633 (16/21); *Itatiaia,* Praça Rui Barbosa 187 (16/21); *Pampulha Palace,* Rua Tupis 646 (14/21); *Esplanada,* Av. Santos Dumont 304 (12/19), own garage; *Financial,* Av. Afonso Pena 571 (13/18), warmly recommended; *Metrópole,* Rua Bahia 1023 (15/18); *Sul Americano,* Av. Amazonas 50 (8/16); *Bragança,* Av. Paraná 109 (8/15); *Gontigo,* Rua Tupinambás 731 (8/13); *Presidente,* Av. Paraná 437 (8/15); *Minas,* Rua São Paulo 331 (4.50/9.50); *Oeste Palace,* Av. Paraná 39 (7.50/12). Cheaper places are: *Hotel São Cristóvão,* Av. Oiapoque 284 (9/12), near bus station. *Hotel Magnata,* Rua Guarani 124, US$3.75 s, plus breakfast, near bus station, cheap and clean; *Hotel Madrid,* US$6 d; *Hotel São Bento,* Rua Guarani 438, US$3 s; *Pensão Nacional,* US$4 d, clean and very friendly. *Hotel Internacional,* Av. Santos Dumont 260, US$4.50 d, cheap and decent. Near bus station, *Pensão Nova Rodoviária,* US$2, adequate, and many others.

Restaurants Grill at *Hotel Normandie. Tavares,* Rua Sta. Catarina 64 (local dishes). Chinese: *Peking,* Rua Alagoas 1021 and *Yun Ton,* recommended. *Laçador,* churrascaria in garden just up hill from Monjolo railway station. *Martini,* Rua Curitiba, and *Pizzaiolo,* Av. Contorno 8495, good for pizzas. *Casa do Ouvidor,* near central praça, highly recommended but expensive. *Degrau,* Av. Afonso Pena 4221, excellent restaurant and bar, very pleasant; *Favela,* Rua Pouso Alto 720, set high above the city, tremendous views by day or night, can be very busy on Friday and Saturday; *Mangueiras,* at Pampulha, next to Niemeyer chapel of São Francisco, very popular; *Dona Derna,* behind the Palácio de Liberdade, highly recommended; *Torino* (Italian) and *Alpino* (German) in Rua Tupinambás, both good value and popular; good open-air restaurants are *Monjolo,* Av. Assis Chateaubriand 525, and *Minuano,* Rua Prof. Morais 635. Good lanchonete at corner of Av. Afonso Pena and Rua Bahia.

Banks Bank of London and South America, Av. Amazonas 303; Citibank, Rua Espírito Santo 945, and local banks, 1000-1700.

Excursions Within easy motoring distance from Belo Horizonte are several of the 400 caves and grottoes for which Minas Gerais is famous. The best and most famous is the Gruta de Maquiné, 112 km. NW of Belo (well signposted and with restaurants nearby), but the Gruta de Lapinha, almost as good, is only 43 km. N of the city.

John Hale writes: Both caves can be reached by special bus services, however, during winter Lapinha has only one service a day with a gap of 6-7 hours between arrival and departure, though the cave (entrance US$0.35), museum (US$0.25), restaurant and peaceful surrounding countryside do not warrant more than 2-3 hours. However, 10 km. before Lapinha is the small town of **Lagoa Santa**, a weekend resort for Belo Horizonte. The sandy beach on the lake (close to the town centre and bus station) is used for fishing, sun-bathing, swimming (if you don't mind the colour of the water) and boating. Along the beach are bars and restaurants, with more in the nearby main square which also has two small hotels and an interesting modernistic church. The road to Belo Horizonte (hourly bus service) passes the airport of Lagoa Santa, the proposed site for Belo Horizonte's new international airport.

To the NE of the city, a few km. off the BR 262, is the Serra de Piedade, a high peak giving spectacular views over the surrounding countryside. A popular excursion point but only accessible by car or special bus service. There are a small chapel and a churrascaria, serving spiritual and more material needs. From the peak can be seen the small town of **Caeté**, which has one or two interesting churches and the remains of an old ironworks near the railway station.

From Belo Horizonte, excursions can be made to Nova Lima and the picturesque colonial cities of Sabará, Ouro Preto, Mariana and Congonhas do Campo. The road follows the Rio das Velhas in which, at points, one can see the "garimpeiros" waist deep washing for gold. Don't go on Monday; so many things are closed.

Nova Lima, about 27 km. to the south-east by a good road, is set in eucalyptus forests. Its little, square colonial houses, built on uneven ground, are grouped round the gold mine of Morro Velho, opened by a British firm in 1834 but sold to Brazilians in 1959. It is the deepest mine in the Americas. The shaft has followed a rich vein of gold down to 2,591 metres—this is made possible by air cooling. The noise of the ore-crushing machine thunders through the town night and day. There are interesting carvings by Aleijadinho, recovered from elsehwere, in the (modern) Parish Church. Population, 34,000.

A paved road branching off the Belo Horizonte-Brasília Highway leads (30 km., ½ hour) to the ancient gold-mining town of Sabará. Return by the old road over the mountain range of Serra do Curral for fine views. From the crest of the Serra there is a splendid view of Belo Horizonte, left far below, and of the empty purple mountains ahead.

John Hale writes: Alternatively, take the suburban train from Belo Horizonte at 0800, a trip of nearly 1 hour, showing aspects of Belo Horizonte and the countryside rarely seen by the visitor. From the Sabará station it is a short walk across the river to the main square and the bus station (buses every 15 minutes to Belo Horizonte, 40 mins., US$0.20).

Sabará was once very important, and may be so again as the iron of the area is developed. It is its old churches and fountains, its rambling cobbled streets, its simple houses with their carved doors, and its fascinating museum of gold mining in the 18th century in the Intendência de Ouro (built 1732) which draw the visitor to-day. The churches are so spread out that a taxi is virtually necessary to see them all. Population, 42,000.

Passeio a Sabará, by Lúcia Machado de Almeida, with magnificent illustrations by Guignard, is an excellent guide to the place. The main sights are the Prefeitura, in Rua Pedro II; the Theatre in the same street, for its fine interior; the Casa Azul, in the same street, for its portal; the Churches of Nossa Senhora do Carmo, with doorway, pulpits and choir loft by Aleijadinho; Nossa Senhora do Rosário dos Pretos; São Francisco; Nossa Senhora da Conceição; and, last of all, Nossa Senhora do O, built in 1698 and showing unmistakable Chinese influence, 2 km. from the centre of the town. Also the fountains of Kaquende (1757), and Rosário. There is a well stocked souvenir shop next to Nossa Senhora da Conceição, with soapstone carvings and mineral samples. Restaurant: *O Quinto do Curo,* close to the bus station.

At 27 km. S along the Belo Horizonte-Rio de Janeiro highway a 68 km. road, the Rodovia dos Inconfidentes, branches off to

Ouro Preto (black gold), former capital of the State, founded in 1711. Population, 38,000, mostly textile workers and miners of gold, iron and manganese. There is a famous School of Mines, founded in 1876, attended by students from all parts of the country, in the fortress-like Governor's Palace (1742), facing the main square (Praça Tiradentes); it has an interesting museum of minerology and precious stones (for the expert rather than the tourist, US$0.35). Opposite, next to Carmo Church, is the Museu da Inconfidência, a fine historical and art museum which has some drawings by Aleijadinho; the building, begun in the eighteenth century, was a prison and also the local chamber of commerce. See the Casa das Contas, now also a museum.

The city, built on rocky ground 1,065 metres above sea-level, is such a remarkable treasure house of colonial and baroque architecture and painting that it was decreed a national monument in 1933. Its stone-paved streets wind up and down steep hills crowned with 13 glorious churches. Monumental fountains, baroque churches, enchanting vistas of terraced gardens, ruins, towers shining with coloured tiles, all blend together to maintain an exquisite 18th century atmosphere.

Ouro Preto is famous for its Holy Week processions, which in fact begin on the Thursday before Palm Sunday and continue until Easter Sunday. The most famous is that commemorating Christ's removal from the Cross, late on Good Friday. These processions are very dramatic. This is very much a holiday period and many shops are shut—as indeed they are at winter weekends.

Here, as well as at Sabará, can be seen the magnificent Baroque carvings, both in wood and in soapstone, of the sculptor Aleijadinho. The lovely church of São Francisco de Assis and the façade of the Carmo church are his work, and so are the two pulpits in the church of São Francisco, and much else. The charming houses, bridges and wall fountains are well worth seeing. Buy soapstone carvings at roadside stalls and bus stops rather than in the cities; they are much cheaper.

In the Praça de Independência there is a statue of Tiradentes, one of the heroes of independence. The pedestal of the column is the original stone which served as a pillory for the condemned patriot. Another conspirator, the poet Tomás Antônio Gonzaga, was exiled to Africa. (Most Brazilians know his poem based on his forbidden love affair; visitors are shown the bridge and decorative fountain where the impassioned lovers held their trysts.) On June 24 of each year Ouro Preto becomes, for that day only, the capital of the state of Minas Gerais.

An early plane from Rio to Belo Horizonte and a bus gets to Ouro Preto by lunch (2 hours); bus fare, each way, US$1.50. Day trips are run; alternatively take an overnight bus from Rio at 2200 (US$5.50), which arrives in Ouro Preto 0730, return bus to Rio leaves at 2000. Take the earliest bus, for many churches close at mid-day and may not reopen, though the museum and other churches, *e.g.* São Francisco de Assis, N.S. do Pilar and Carmo, only open in the afternoon. At least two days are needed to see them all; the tourist office on Praça Tiradentes and the hotels offer a leaflet showing the opening times. Most of the churches now charge for admission.

Hotels   *Grande,* Rua Sen. Rocha 164, largest hotel in town and the only modern structure, designed by Oscar Niemeyer, US$20 d; *Pouso Chico Rei,* a fascinating old house with Portuguese colonial furnishings, very small and utterly delightful, though extremely difficult to get a reservation, Rua Brig. Mosqueira 90, US$25 d; *Pousada Ouro Preto,* Praça Antônio Dias 10, converted colonial mansion, no twin beds, reservations in Rio, Tel.: 256-2680, US$28 d; *Quinta dos Barões,* Rua Pandiá Calógeras 474, US$28 d; *Pilão,* Praça Tiradentes 57, on main square, US$15 d; *Colonial,* Rua Camilo Veloso 26, US$15 d; *Tófolo,* São José 76, near Contas fountain, US$12 d; *N. S. Aparecida,* US$8 d.

Pensions   *Familiar; Vermelha;* and at Rua Getúlio Vargas 10, US$7 s. In term full of students and difficult to find room.

Students may be able to stay, during holidays and weekends, at the self-governing student hostels, known as "repúblicas". Enquire at the city's tourist office on the main square (Praça Tiradentes 41), which shows filmstrips at 0900, 1200 and 1600 on weekdays, 0900, 1030, 1300, 1500, 1600 at weekends and holidays.

Restaurants   *Calabouço* (in Conde Bobadela, with an antique shop), main hangout of students, noted for their festive beer drinking; *Pilão,* in main square (local painters), and good rooms above. Cheapest is US$1.40 for huge set lunch at *Hotel Tófolo* restaurant. Good feijoada at *Chafariz* restaurant, and *Restaurante Porão.*

Camping   Site of Camping Club do Brasil, 3½ km. N of city; it is quite expensive but very nice. Camping also possible at site of pleasant waterfall. Cachoeira dos Andorinhas, 1½ hrs. walk from city, and at picnic site 4 km. west of Ouro Preto.

Guide Book   Bandeira's *Guia de Ouro Preto* in Portuguese and English, with map, but may be difficult to obtain. You can always find a guide—a schoolboy will do—to take you round.

Henri van Rooy writes that it is possible to reach Vitória (Espírito Santo) from Ouro Preto, by using local bus services *via* Mariana, Ponta Nova and Manhumirim (*Hotel São Luiz,* US$1.75, meal US$1.10, highly recommended). This is good walking country and the Pico da Bandeira is within sight; a climb up and down this mountain can be made in a day. It may also be possible to visit local fazendas, for example Fazenda Modelo, 8 km. from Manhumirim.

Mariana, another old mining city of churches and quaint streets and buildings, is 12 km. E of Ouro Preto on a road which goes on to join the Rio-Salvador highway. See the old prison (Cadeia), the Carmo Church, São Francisco Church (one side-altar by Aleijadinho) and the old Palace of the Governors connected with it, the Museum (formerly the Bishop's Palace) for its church furniture, Aleijadinho statues and ivory cross (open 0900-1100 except Tuesday and 1200-1700; entrance US$0.60), the city hall, the aljube, and the former post office, once the house of a notable. Mariana has the second gold mine in the state: the Brazilian-owned (ex-British) Minas de Passagem. Population; 16,000. Buses every half-hour from behind the town museum, from Ouro Preto, or direct from Belo Horizonte.

Hotels   *Itacolomi,* 6 km. out on Ponte Nova road, US$25 d; Silva, Rua Getúlio

Vargas, US$15 d; *Central,* US$2 s; *Pontes.* The modern service station *(posto)* on the highway above the town offers good clean rooms at US$4 each, with hot showers. **Restaurant**   *Alvorada,* Praça Claudio Mansel 42, US$1-3.

Congonhas do Campo (altitude 866 metres) is a small hill town with a population of 18,000 which is swollen to 250,000 during the September festa at its church. A quite passable earth road through lovely farming country connects with Ouro Preto and a paved 3½-km. road with the Rio-Belo Horizonte Highway. It is also on the Central do Brasil railway between Rio and Belo Horizonte. The town is dominated by its great pilgrimage church of Bom Jesus do Matozinho (1773). There is a wide view of the country from its terrace, below which are six small chapels set in beautifully arranged sloping gardens, recalling the great 18th century religious gardens of Braga in northern Portugal, with life-size Passion figures carved by Aleijadinho (the main figures) and his pupils (the less important ones) in cedar wood. Inside the church is "The Room of Miracles", but the church is mainly famous for its group of prophets sculpted by Aleijadhinho. Standing on the parapets of the terrace, these twelve great dramatic statues come as a shock to the visitor. They are carved in soapstone with a magnificent sense of movement, and surely constitute one of the finest works of art of their period in the world—not only in Latin America.

Congonhas is also celebrated for its Holy Week processions, which centre on the Bom Jesus church. The most celebrated ceremonies are the meeting of Christ and the Virgin Mary on the Tuesday, and the dramatised Deposition from the Cross late on Good Friday.

Hotels   *Colonial,* Praça da Basílica 76, with fascinating restaurant downstairs full of colonial handicrafts and good local food, right next to Bom Jesus, US$13 d; *Freitas,* Rua Marechal Floriano 69, US$10 d, basic.

Bus   From Belo Horizonte, US$1.85, 6 times a day, best to buy a return ticket.

Diamantina, centre of a once active diamond industry, has excellent colonial remains. Its churches are not so grand as those of Ouro Preto, but it is possibly the most interesting and least spoilt of all the colonial mining cities, with fantastically carved overhanging roofs and brackets. It is in the deep interior, 1,120 metres up, and about 25,000 people live there; it is the birthplace of the late President Juscelino Kubitschek, the creator of Brasília.

It is reached from Belo Horizonte by road (buses 5½ hours) but there is no scheduled air-service. Take the asphalted road to Brasília as far as the turnoff for Curvelo; the rest of the road from Curvelo is also paved. Say 4½ hours for the 225 km. but through impressive rocky country. The old railway service has been discontinued. See the Diamond Museum, in house of Padre Rolim, one of the Inconfidentes (plotters for independence in 1789); open (free) every day but Monday. Diamonds are still sought; see traditional methods at Guinda, 7 km. away. *Passeio a Diamantina,* an excellent guide, is written by the author of *Passeio a Sabará.*

The house of Chica da Silva, an eighteenth-century mulatto slave who married a diamond contractor, is at Praça Lobo Mesquita 266; Chica has become something of a folk-heroine among Brazilian blacks.

Hotels   *Tijuco,* Macau do Melo 211, US$22 d, best; *Grande,* Rua da Quitanda 70, and *Dalia,* Praça JK (Jota-Ka) 13, both fairly good at US$13 d.

Restaurants   *Churrascaria Chica da Silva,* on street level of *Dalia Hotel,* is good. Bar-Restaurant *Confinca,* Rua da Quitanda 39, also good.

Serro, near Diamantina and reached by bus from there or from Belo Horizonte, is an unspoilt Colonial town with six fine Baroque churches, a museum and many beautiful squares.

Hotels *Itacolomi,* Praça João Pinheiro 20, US$12 d, fair restaurant; other cheap hotels.

Tres Marias Some 240 km. NW of Belo Horizonte is a lake five times as large as Rio de Janeiro bay formed by the Tres Marias dam in the upper reaches of the São Francisco river. Half a million kilowatts of electricity are generated here and have made possible a number of new industries in Belo. This good stopping place between Belo and Brasília has a motel, and the power company, Cemig, runs a guest house (book in advance through H.Q. at Belo Horizonte). At Barreiro Grande is the Clube Náutico Tres Marias, US$12 d, simple. There are plans to make the Tres Marias area one of the largest tourist developments in Minas Gerais.

Almost the same distance SW of Belo is the even larger lake formed by the Furnas dam. It can be seen from the BR-381 road to São Paulo.

Also north of Belo Horizonte is **Pirapora,** terminus for boat journeys on the **River São Francisco** (see also page 297). The town itself is a tourist attraction because of the falls in the river at this point. The sandy river beaches are used for swimming. The grotesque figureheads of the riverboats, "carrancas", are made in workshops of Lourdes Barroso, Rua Abaeté 390. There are several hotels but they are noted for being rather expensive; *Hotel Carranca* and *Hotel Rex,* Rua Antonio Nascimento 370 and 357 respectively, both US$10 d, have been recommended. Watch the fishermen in their punt-like canoes at work. Those wishing to take the boat trip down the river on wood-burning stern-wheel boats can get information from travel agencies (for example Rua das Andradas 367-loja 4, Belo Horizonte, and Rua Santa Luzia 799-15° andar, Rio, and also the offices of the Companhia de Navegação do São Francisco (CNSF) in Pirapora, Av. São Francisco 1363, and Juazeiro (Bahía), Rua Coronel Aprígio Duarte 3. The service is operated by three boats allegedly built for Mississippi services in the 1860s and imported from the USA in 1922 originally to work on the Amazon; the trip downstream is about seven days, upstream ten days; the distance between the two cities is 1,324 km. Generally speaking the boat stops every day to load wood, but often in the middle of nowhere. The regular stops are at Januária (famous for Brazil's reputed best cachaça), Bom Jesus de Lapa (a pilgrimage centre with a church built in a grotto inside a mountain) and Barra. Between Pirapora and Januária is the colonial town of São Francisco, with many attractive houses and a good handicraft market in the town hall; the boats do not always stop there. The boat leaves early in the morning about 0900 and the cheapest way to arrive there is to take the bus from Belo Horizonte (0730, 9 hours, US$7). The boats are run by CNSF twice a month in each direction, leaving Pirapora on 10th and 25th of each month, and Santana on 3rd and 18th. With the filling of one of the largest man-made lakes in the world behind the new dam at Sobradinho, the terminus point in the North East, which began in late 1977, the journey has been shortened; it now ends at Santana do Sobrado, 47 km. from Juazeiro and Petrolina, which are reached by a free bus for boat passengers. Fares including food are US$216 p.p. in double cabin with bath and US$160 p.p. in double without bath; US$34 2nd class (only for those really on the breadline and with their own hammocks). In 1977 cars can be transported on lighters towed alongside. Food is provided but it is basic fare, so make sure to have some preserved food and sufficient stomach medicines with you. Fruit and other goods can be bought at several stops downstream. The river passes through one of the most backward areas in Brazil, hardly changed for centuries, the landscape itself changes very little and there is a surprising lack of wildlife, though some regard it as more interesting than the Amazon. Because of the vagaries of river travel, one cannot rely on visiting towns such as Barra and Bom Jesus de Lapa during the day. It is possible to do only part of the trip.

Uberaba, in the Minas Gerais "Triangle", is on the Rio da Prata, 718 km. from São Paulo. It is an important rail and road junction, being on the direct highway between São Paulo and Brasília, and serves a wide cattle raising district. At the beginning of May each year the Rural Society of the Minas "Triangle" holds a famous cattle and agricultural exhibition at Uberaba. There are local sugar mills and lime plants. Altitude, 700 metres. Population, 115,000. Hotels: *Palácio; Grande.*

The Spas of southern Minas Gerais, largely visited by the people of the south-east, are easily reached by railway or road and sometimes by air from Rio de Janeiro and São Paulo. The waters of these spas are said to provide cures for rheumatism and skin, liver and stomach complaints. All these places are planned as much for the amusement of the visitor as for his cure; all of them have cinemas and go all out for sports, and many of them are linked together by asphalted roads. The high season is from December through March.

São Lourenço, easily accessible from Rio de Janeiro or São Paulo, stands at 850 metres above sea-level. It attracts two kinds of people, those who want a good holiday and those who seek a cure from its mineral waters. There is a splendid park, tennis, boating, swimming, an aviation field, and fishing from the Ilha dos Amores in a lake ringed by gardens and picturesque forests. There is a grand ride through glorious scenery to the Pico de Buqueré (1,500 metres). Population: 15,000.

Its rich mineral waters are used in the treatment of stomach, liver, kidney and intestinal complaints. There is an up-to-date hydro establishment for douches and for the famous carbo-gaseous baths, unique in South America and comparable with those of Royat and Bad-Nauheim for the treatment of arterial hypertension, arteriosclerosis, tachycardias, etc.

Bus service from Rio de Janeiro, 277 km., 5-6 hours; from São Paulo, 338 km., 6-7 hours. From Rio by train, 9 hours.

Hotels   *Brasil,* nice; *Sul Americano Grande; Ponto Chic,* etc.

Caxambu, N of São Lourenço, at 900 metres, is one of the more sophisticated of these resorts. Its modern thermal establishments treat stomach, kidney and bladder diseases, and are said to restore fertility. (It worked for Princess Isabel, who produced three sons after a visit. The little church of Santa Isabel stands on a hill as a testimony.) Its waters are bottled and sold throughout the country. The mountains and forests around are very beautiful. Population: 12,000. Excellent hotels.

Hotels   *Glória; Palace; Avenida; Caxambu; Bragança,* and 20 others.

Poços de Caldas is reached by rail, road or plane from São Paulo or Rio. It is the most luxurious and fashionable of the resorts. It has complete and up-to-date thermal establishments for the treatment of rheumatic, skin and intestinal diseases. Attractions for visitors include the Country Club and picturesque excursions. Excellent climate. There is now a small industrial estate. Altitude: 1,180 metres; pop.: 45,000.

Hotels *Palace,* old fashioned but well run; *Continental; Capri; Balneário.*

Roads To São Paulo, *via* Campinas and Mogi Mirim, paved, 257 km.; to Rio de Janeiro, about 515 km., paved; to São Lourenço, 228 km.

Lambari, a lesser-known resort, is 56 km. W of Caxambu by road at 900 metres. The smallest and least elegant, it has a very luxurious Casino with oriental decorations and paintings by famous artists on its walls, but it opened and closed on the same night, when Brazil introduced anti-gambling legislation in 1945. Hotels are not luxurious but fairly comfortable.

Hotels *Itaicy,* largest, on lake near Casino. *Glória; Parque,* and others more modest.

Cambuquirá, a little N of Lambari by road or rail at 946 metres, very popular, with uninhibited, cordial atmosphere and lots of trips to picnic sites close by. Biggest hotel is the *Grande Hotel Empresa.*

Araxá, in the Minas Triangle, about 193 km. from Uberaba at 970 metres, is a quiet little place with thorium and radio-active waters and sulphur and mud baths; it has a nice main square. It can be reached from Rio or São Paulo by rail but most easily from Belo Horizonte, 8 hours by bus. Pop.: 30,000; Airport.

Hotels *Grande de Araxá,* luxury, 8 km. away; *Grande Hotel Pinto; Colombo.*

The State of São Paulo

The State of São Paulo, with an area of 247,898 square km. and a population of 21,300,000, is larger than the states of New York and Pennsylvania together and about the same size as Great Britain and Northern Ireland. It has a narrow zone of wet tropical lowland along the coast. Santos, the State's port, lies here. This lowland rises in an unbroken slope to the ridge of the Great Escarpment—the Serra do Mar—at from 800 to 900 metres above sea level. The upland beyond the Great Escarpment is drained westwards by the tributaries of the Rio Paraná. The broad valleys of the uplands are occasionally surmounted by ranges of low mountains; one such range lies between the São Paulo basin and the hinterland of the state. There is a sharp drop between the São Paulo basin and the Paraíba Valley; as it leaves the basin the Central Railway connecting São Paulo with Rio de Janeiro *via* the Paraíba Valley drops 170 metres in 24 km. West of the low mountains between the basin and the rest of the state lie the uplands of the Paraná Plateau, at about 600 metres above the sea. One of the soils in this area is the *terra roxa,* the purple earth in which coffee flourishes. When dry it gives off a red dust which colours everything; when wet it is sticky and slippery and difficult to travel over. There is ample rainfall in São Paulo State; indeed, the highest rainfall in Brazil (3,810 mm.) is over a small area between Santos and São Paulo; at São Paulo itself it is no more than 1,194 mm. Temperatures on the plateau are about 5°C lower than on the coast. Tropical crops (of which coffee is one) cannot be grown where there is much frost; it is only south of the latitude of Sorocaba that frosts occur in

SÃO PAULO
(CENTRE)

ROUGH SKETCH

São Paulo, and then not frequently. Temperatures are too low for coffee in the São Paulo basin itself, but the State produces, on average, about 7.2 million bags a year. It has 11 million head of cattle.

It was in 1847 that the future of São Paulo was settled: a landowner near Limeira introduced a number of German families to work his estate for him as *colonos,* or tenants. This great step was slow in bearing fruit, but between 1885 and the end of the century a boom in coffee and the arrival of large numbers of Europeans transformed the state out of all recognition. Between 1827 and 1873 only 4,182 Italians settled in São Paulo. Between 1887 and 1898 over half a million Italians emigrated to the State. By the end of the thirties there had arrived in São Paulo State a million Italians, half a million each of Portuguese and immigrants from the rest of Brazil, nearly 400,000 Spaniards and nearly 200,000 Japanese. Today the state produces 50% of the country's cotton, 62% of the sugar, a third of its coffee and over 50% of its fruit exports. The state has 62,121 factories employing 1,172,000 workers who turn out 90% of Brazil's motor vehicles, 65% of its paper and cellulose, and 60% of the machinery and tools, being also responsible for 60% of the country's industrial consumption of electric energy. All this comes, in sum, to some 20% of Brazil's agricultural output and over 50% of its industrial production. São Paulo provides 33% of the total exports of Brazil and takes 40% of the total imports: nearly all these pass through the port of Santos.

São Paulo is 407 km. from Rio de Janeiro, and is connected with it by air, an excellent road, and the Central do Brasil railway. It was founded in 1554 by two Jesuit priests from São Vicente, Padre José Anchieta and Padre Manuel Nóbrega, as a mission station; the original settlement, not yet effectively preserved, was at the Pátio do Colégio in the centre of town, where a copy of Anchieta's original church is being built.

São Paulo (altitude 730 metres) is one of the fastest growing cities in the world; people either love it or hate it. It is already the most populous city in South America, and the continent's leading industrial centre. It celebrated the 400th anniversary of its foundation in 1954, but until the 1870s it was a sleepy, shabby little town of 30,000 people. Now, 100 years later, it covers more than 1,500 square km.—three times the size of

---

Key to Map of São Paulo
1. Paulista Academy of Letters; 2. Hotel Vila Rica; 3. Hotel Terminus; 4. Hotel Excelsior; 5. Hotel Normandie; 6. Church of Santa Ifigênia; 7. Central Post Office; 8. Municipal Theatre; 9. Diários Associados Building; 10. Hotel Samambaia; 11. Brazilian Telephone Company; 12. State Secretariat of Health; 13. Edifício Itália; 14. Hotel São Paulo Hilton; 15. Church of Consolação; 16. Grand Hotel Cá' d'Oro; 17. Hotel Jaraguá; 18. Municipal Library; 19. Cambridge Hotel; 20. São Paulo Light Building; 21. Municipal Council Chamber; 22. Hotel Grão Pará; 23. Othon Palace Hotel; 24. Churches of São Francisco and São Francisco das Chagas, and Faculty of Laws; 25. Central State Treasury; 26. State Secretariat of Transport and Public Works; 27. Historical and Geographical Institute; 28. Mauá Palace; 29. Church of São Gonçalo; 30; Cathedral; 31. São Paulo Forum; 32. Palace of Justice; 33. Archbishop's Palace; 34. Federal Savings Bank; 35. Stock Exchange Buildings; 37. State Savings Bank; 38. Banco do Estado de São Paulo; 39. Church and Monastery of São Bento; 40. Municipal Market; 41. Police Station; 42. Pátio do Colégio; 43. Gas Company; 44. Church of Nossa Senhora do Carmo; 45. State Cooperative Building; 46. Church of Boa Morte; 47. Policlinica Hospital; 48. Mauá Engineering School; 49. State Secretariat of Finance; 50. Accounts Tribunal.

Paris—and has a population of over 8m. Today it is a city of shining skyscrapers and extensive parks, a roaring tumult whose population grows at the rate of about 150,000 a year, and whose industrial districts engulf more and more villages and townships as they spread. It bears the impress of an almost vicious energy. In its unsentimental modernity most vestiges of its torpid past have been erased. To all Brazilians it is the city of promise, offering large rewards for initiative and enterprise. Peasant immigrants who arrived only recently, as it were, have created some of the largest industrial empires in the world. The Matarazzo enterprise, founded by an Italian immigrant who arrived in 1893, today controls 300 factories, a bank, a shipping company, farms, and oil refineries. The citizens are intensely proud of its skyscrapers, of its streets lit by high-powered electric lamps (though many are still exceptionally dim), of its efficient water supply, and especially of its underground line, the first in Brazil, which began operating in September 1975, linking Jabaquara in the south with Santana in the north. (Construction of a second line has begun.) The traffic pattern is extremely exasperating: you may have to drive around 10 blocks to reach a point half a block away. Also exasperating is the amount of air pollution; in dry weather eyes and nose are continually troubled.

All this sounds inhuman, and São Paulo is far from that. "The City", to quote the Rio de Janeiro correspondent of *The Times,* "is the cosmopolitan centre of Brazil, and foreigners too, surrounded by manifestations of achievement, tend to feel that the world ends at the city boundaries. São Paulo is not only a place; it is an attitude. While the bustle and the traffic fray the nerves even of visiting New Yorkers, the smell of cooking which seems to hang ever in the air brings a scent of home to Syrians and Italians alike. Your taxi driver may be anything from a Japanese to a Lithuanian. You can take an apéritif on the pavement of a French bar; dine in a Russian restaurant and dance to a Viennese orchestra; or spend the evening in dim, velvety American-style night clubs where the waiter discreetly shines a torch on your bill—presumably to spare your guests the embarrassment of seeing your distress. In the Syrian quarter, old gentlemen sit at the doors of their shops resignedly drawing at their hookahs while inside their grandsons install neon lighting."

Here are some statistics to support the superlatives which the city compels. First, its phenomenal growth. In 1872 the population was 31,385. In 1920 it was 579,033, to Rio de Janeiro's 1,157,873. In 1960 it was 3,825,351 against the capital's 3,307,163. In 1970, it was 5,978,977 to Rio's 4,315,746. The city's population is now estimated at over 8 million; in 1975 the metropolitan area population was estimated at 10,040,000, compared with 8,330,000 for the metropolitan area population of Rio. 11% of all Brazilians live within a radius of 200 km.

The very highest building in São Paulo is the 41-storey Edifício Itália, with a restaurant and sightseeing balcony on the top floor from which the whole city and the country around can be seen. It is on the corner of Av. Ipiranga and Av. São Luís, just by the Praça da República.

São Paulo has 34,000 industrial establishments employing 800,000 workers. It turns out over half of Brazil's textiles, chemicals and pharmaceuticals, over 90% of the motor vehicles, and over 75% of Brazil's electrical materials, rubber goods and machinery. About 40% of the total industrial production for all Brazil is accounted for by São Paulo city.

The two great reasons for the city's development lie in its position at the focus of so much agricultural wealth, and in its climate, which makes the Paulistanos the most hard working and energetic people in Brazil. Visitors, however, find the characteristic sharp changes of temperature troublesome and even Paulistanos seem to catch cold often. (Incidentally, one differentiates between Paulistas—inhabitants of the State—and Paulistanos—inhabitants of the city.) There is another and a most potent factor which explains its industrial growth: the availability of endless power.

Water falling on the plateau on which São Paulo is built forms rivers which flow towards the interior and finally reach the sea at Buenos Aires, 4,000 km. away. Cheap electrical power has been tapped by damming two rivers into two huge artificial lakes—Lake Guarapiranga and the Rio Grande reservoir. Each of these dams backs up about 50 km. of streams which origially flowed inland to the Paraná River but now flow through tunnels in the coastal range, past the turbines, into the sea near Santos. The turbines, at the foot of a 660-metre drop, generate 2 million horse-power. This is the main source of power for São Paulo and Santos, though there are other hydroelectric plants supplying both cities.

The shape of the town is an irregular polygon. The shopping, hotel and restaurant centre embraces the districts of Av. São Luís, the Praça da República, and Rua Barão de Itapetininga. The commercial quarter, containing banks, offices and shops, is centred within a central district known as the Triângulo, comprising Rua Direita, Quinze de Novembro, São Bento and Praça Antônio Prado, but it is already rapidly spreading towards the apartment and shopping district of Praça da República, where several of the most important banks have opened branches. Rua Augusta, near Avenida Paulista, once the home of the wealthier citizens, is now full of boutiques and fashion shops. Avenida Paulista houses most consulates in skyscrapers, many banking head offices, the Assis Chateaubriand Art Museum (opened by Queen Elizabeth in 1968), and still a few of the large mansions built by the coffee barons.

The park in Praça da República is worth going into between 0800 and 1300 on Sunday: birds, trees and Brazilians in all their variety. The place has become a regular handicrafts fair; artists hang their paintings on the fence and collectors bring their stamps, coins, wood carvings, leatherwork, gemstones and oddities for sale.

Close to the viaduct that leads to the smart and busy Praça do Patriarca are the magnificent headquarters of the Serviços de Electricidade, an imposing building in the classic style. It faces across the viaduct the Conde Francisco Matarazzo building, covered entirely with white Carrara marble. Looking over this viaduct to the commercial centre, the landscape is dominated by tall skyscrapers. Av. Paulista is now becoming a new downtown area, more dynamic than the traditional centre, and also Av. Faria Lima, 8 km. from Praça da República.

The Viaduto do Chá, which bridges the central avenue, Anhangabaú, leads to the opera house, a splendid 19th-century edifice; indeed one of the very few distinguished 19th-century survivals that São Paulo can boast. The Av. Paulista and the "jardins" América, Paulista and Paulistano contain mansions of great beauty and interest and are on part of the route to the Butantã Institute or "snake farm". About 10 minutes' walk from the centre of the city is the fine Municipal Market, covering an area of 27,000 square metres, but a new Municipal Market has been built in the outskirts. The Municipal Library, 15 storeys high, surrounded by a pleasant and shady garden, is well worth visiting.

The Cathedral's foundations were laid over 40 years before its inauguration during the 1954 festivities commemorating the 4th century of the city. This massive building in neo-Gothic style, one of the largest cathedrals in South America, with a capacity for 8,000 worshippers, is in the heart of the city. The sumptuous and large underground crypt chapel contains the mortal remains of São Paulo's foremost ecclesiastical figures of the past.

The grandiose Municipal Stadium in the Pacaembu valley, a new and flourishing residential district, is well worth seeing on a Sunday or, preferably, on a Wednesday night when some important football match takes place. Built on Olympic lines in an area of 75,500 square metres, it holds nearly 70,000 spectators. Besides the flood-lit football ground and athletics field and basket-ball court, there are also a covered gymnasium, open-air and covered tennis courts, a magnificent illuminated 50-metre long swimming pool, a youth hostel, and a great hall for receptions and rallies. There is a larger stadium holding 120,000 people in Morumbi, one of the more elegant residential districts.

Typical of modern development are the huge Iguatemi and the recently opened Ibirapuera shopping centres. They both include luxurious cinemas, snack bars and most of the best shops in São Paulo. Parking in each for over 1,000 vehicles. Others have been opened but these two hold the first place. On a rather humbler level are the big supermarkets of El Dorado (Av. Pamplona 1704) and Pão de Açúcar (Praça Roosevelt, near the Hilton); the latter is open 24 hours a day (except Sundays).

The palatial Jockey Club racecourse is in the Cidade Jardim district with easy and plentiful access by bus. Race meetings are held on Saturday, Sunday, and Monday night. The new town premises of the Jockey Club (Rua Boa Vista) are well worth a visit.

Ibirapuera   Take a 620 bus from Anhangabaú to the fine Ibirapuera Park for the architecturally impressive new Legislative Assembly. There is also a planetarium equipped with the most up-to-date machinery (shows at 2000 Tues. and Thurs.; 1600, 1800 and 2000 weekends and holidays); a complete velodrome for cycle and motor-cycle racing; an all-aluminium covered stadium for indoor sports which seats 20,000 people; and the Museum of Contemporary Art, where the Bienal is held. In this park, too, are the Museums of Modern Art, Aeronautics (showing the Santos Dumont plane; US$0.40 entrance), Folklore (interesting) and Sciences. There is also a unique display of nativity scenes and scenes of the life of Christ. At the entrance is a majestic monument to the Bandeirantes, or pioneers. All the Ibirapuera museums are open Tues.-Sun., 1400-1800. (For other museums see page 261.)

Anhembi (Av. Assis Chateaubriand, Santana) is the largest exhibition hall in the world. It was inaugurated in 1970 and all São Paulo's industrial fairs (motor vehicles, industrial products and domestic appliances, as well as fashion and textile shows and industrial fairs of other countries) are now held there. It has a meeting hall seating 3,500 people, three *auditórios,* 24 conference rooms *(salas de reunião)* and two restaurants. Parking space is provided for 3,500 cars. It may be reached by underground (short walk from Tietê station).

Hotels Many new hotels have been opened recently: among the most luxurious are the *Caesar Park,* the *Eldorado* and the *Hilton,* all with swimming pools, American bar, restaurants à la carte, nightclubs and convention halls. Prices for the cheapest room in each category are as follows (incl. continental breakfast), in US dollars:

Hotel and Address	Single	Double	Rooms	Class*
Caesar Park, Rua Augusta 1508	56.00	67.20	200	L
Eldorado, Av. São Luís 234	51.20	59.90	154	L
São Paulo Hilton, Av. Ipiranga 165	50.40	58.80	391	L
Othon Palace, Rua Líbero Badaró 190	35.00	42.00	253	1 +
Brasilton São Paulo, Rua Martins Fontes 330	40.00	46.50		
São Paulo Center, Largo Santa Ifigênia 40	31.50	37.10	111	1 +
Grand Hotel Cá d'Oro, Rua Avanhandava 308	35.00	45.80	240	1 +
Hotel Samambaia, Rua 7 Abril 422	30.80	39.60		
Vila Rica, Av. Vieira de Carvalho 167	31.15	39.50	65	1 +
San Raphael, Av. São joão 1173	32.55	42.00	215	1 +
Jaraguá, Rua Major Quedinho 44	28.00	35.00	197	1 +
Cá d'Oro, Rua Basílio da Gama 101	23.10	30.00	82	
Comodoro, Av. Duque de Caxias 525	24.30	31.00	132	T
Excelsior, Av. Ipiranga 770	23.80	30.00	180	1
Planalto, Cásper Líbero 117	23.00	28.00	268	1
Terminus, Av. Ipiranga 741	19.25	23.45	67	T
Danúbio, Av. Brigadeiro Luís Antônio 1099	21.00	26.25	137	1
Normandie, Ipiranga 1187	25.00	32.70	200	S
Cambridge, Av. 9 de Julho 216	21.60	28.00	120	S
São Paulo, Praça da Bandeira 15	19.60	23.10	178	T +
Solar Paulista, Rua Francisca Miquelina 343	19.00	26.00	60	S

*Class: L — de luxe; 1 + — first class plus; 1 — first class; S + — standard plus; S — standard; T + — tourist plus; T — tourist.

There are scores of cheaper hotels, of which we append a selection (figures in parentheses are for standard rooms, single/double, in US dollars, asterisk * if breakfast included): *Cineasta,* Av. São João 613, 80 rooms (18.50/23*); *Plaza,* Av. São João 407, 42 rooms (14.50/20.10*); *Joamar,* Rua Dom José de Barros 187 (off São João), 50 rooms (9.20/13.75); *Marechal,* Av. Barão de Limeira 339, 67 rooms (8.40/14.30); *Minister,* A. Barão de Piracicaba 105, 27 rooms (8/13.20); *Planeta,* Al. Dino Bueno 54 (5.60/8); *Pontal,* Rua Mauá 248 (5/6.50); *do Comércio,* Rua Mauá 512 (4.80/8*); *Queluz,* Rua Mauá 438 (3.20 p.p.); *Monaco,* Rua Timbiras 143 (4/5.60*); *Noroeste,* Rua Triúnfo 285 (3.20/4.80*); *Senador,* Rua Senador Feijó 106 (5.60/8*).

Also suggested: *S. Sebastião,* 7 de Abril 364, cheap and clean but no rooms with bath; *Hotel Lima,* Rua Santa Ifigênia, has been recommended, US$4.75 p.p. with breakfast; *Hotel São José,* Rua Barão de Piracicaba, US$4.50 s, near bus station; *Hospedaria Familiar,* Rua dos Gusmões 218, US$2 s; *Santa Efigênia,* Rua dos Gusmões, near bus station; *Britânia,* Av. São João 300, US$6 s, US$10 d; *Ouro Fino Hotel Familiar,* Rua General Osório 388, US$8 d, friendly; *Hotel Condeixa,* 145 Rua do Triúnfo, US$3 s, showers; *Eiras,* US$3.50 s, showers.

There are many other hotels near the bus terminal and railway stations with prices ranging from US$3 to over US$20 a night; try Ruas Santa Ifigênia, Mauá, Gusmões and Timbiras. Accommodation of the youth-hostel type is available at the Pacaembu Stadium at a fee of US$2.40 for sheets, etc. plus US$1.20 per night. A letter addressed to the Secretário de Esportes is required; the tourist office at Praça Roosevelt 154 will help tourists to write the letter.

Local Holidays Jan. 25 (Foundation of City).

Electric Current 110-220 volts A.C., 60 cycles.

Camping Cemucam, at Cobia (Rodovia Raposo Tavares, km. 27); Camping Clube do Brasil, Camininha 200, Interlagos.

Restaurants   In a large metropolis such as São Paulo, it is small wonder that the most exigent gourmet of nearly any country in the world should find excellent restaurants where the specialities of his national preference may be found. Apart from the international cuisine in the first-class hotels listed above, here are only a few out of many (**Warning:** most restaurants close at around 2300):

Portuguese   *Abril em Portugal,* Rua Caio Prado 47; *Adega Lisboa Antiga,* Rua Brig. Tobias 280 (subsolo), and others.

Italian   *Tiberio,* Av. Paulista 392; *Pastasciutta,* Rua Barão do Triúnfo 427 (Brooklin Paulista); *Cantina Roma,* Rua Maranhão 512 (Higienópolis); *Trastevere,* Al. Santos 1444; *Bongiovanni,* Av. 9 de Julho 5511; *Don Ciccillo,* Praça Souza Aranha 185; *Giovanni Bruno,* Rua Martinho Prado 165; and many others in Rua 13 de Maio (Bela Vista); *Lazzarella, Roperto, La Fontana di Trevi, La Tavola*—and neighbourhood.

French   *La Cocagne,* Rua Amaral Gurgel 378; *La Casserole,* Largo do Arouche 346; *La Gratinée,* Rua Bento Freitas, 42; *La Maison Basque,* Av. João Dias 239; *Le Bistrot,* Av. Adolfo Pinheiro 510; *Freddy,* Praça Dom Gastão Liberal Pinto 11; *Marcel,* Rua Epitácio Pessoa 98.

German   *Bierhalle,* Av. Lavandisca 263; *Biergarten,* Av. Ibirapuera 3174; *Kobes,* Av. Santo Amaro 5394; *Zillertal,* Av. Brig. Luís Antônio 909.

Swiss   *Chamonix,* Rua Pamplona 1446, very expensive; *Maison Suisse,* Rùa Caio Prado 183; *Chalet Suisse* (Orthon Palace Hotel).

Oriental   *Almanara* (Arab), Rua Basílio da Gama 70; *Sino-Brasileiro,* Rua Alberto Torres 39 (Perdizes); *Golden Dragon,* Av. Rebouças 2371; *Heike* and *Notre Dame,* both Av. Paulista 2064 (Center 3); *Sukiaki,* Rua Conselheiro Furtado (right in the Japanese quarter); *Akasaka,* Rua 13 de Maio 1639. Many other Chinese and Japanese restaurants in Liberdade, the Japanese quarter.

General   *Terraço Itália,* on top of Edifício Itália, 41 floors up; *Mexilhão,* Rua 13 de Maio 626, Bela Vista, very good; *Rubayat,* Av. Vieira de Carvalho 134 and Al. Santos 86; *Dinho's Place,* Largo do Arouche 246, Al. Santos 45 and Av. Morumbi 7976; *Rodeio,* Rua Haddock Lobo 1498; *Paddock,* Av. São Luís 258 (genuine Brazilian, serves feijoada completa, friendly, prices reasonable); *Pandoro,* Av. Cidade Jardim 60; *Bolinha,* Av. Cidade Jardim 53 (for feijoadas on Wednesdays and Saturdays); *Maria Fulô,* Rua São José 563, Santo Amaro, for Bahia dishes—very expensive; *O Profeta,* Al. dos Aicós 40 (for Mineiro food); Airport Restaurant (very good); *Pizza d'Oro,* in Vila Mariana (local painters and sculptors); many snack-bars and pizzerias throughout the city.

Bars   *Scotch Bar,* Rua 24 de Maio 35, cj. 411; *Pepe's Bar,* Edifício Metropole; several outdoor bars in Largo do Arouche and in Moema; all major hotels have bars.

Night Clubs   There are several first-class night-clubs serving excellent meals. Besides very good dance-bands, the majority have floor-shows in which a variety of internationally-famed artists perform. *A. Baiúca,* Praça Roosevelt 256; *Silvio's* and *Plano's,* Oscar Freire 913 and 811 respectively; *Stardust,* Largo do Arouche 336; *Catedral do Samba* (Rua Rui Barbosa 333); *Igrejinha* (Rua Santo Antônio 973) and *O Beco* (Rua Bela Cintra 306), recommended for samba. Also recommended: *O Jogral,* Rua Maceió 66, Higienópolis (reasonable). **Discotheques:** *Hippopotamus* (Av. 9 de Julho 5872); *London Tavern* (São Paulo Hilton Hotel, subsolo); *Ton Ton* (Rua Néstor Pestana 115); *Moustache* (Rua Sergipe 160), amongst others. **Jazz:** *Opus 2004,* at Rua Consolação 2004.

Tourist Offices   Praça Roosevelt 154, Viaduto Jacareí 100, Praça da República 154 (Cedicur).

Tea Rooms   *Vienense, Jaraguá, Cha Mon* (Edifício Metropole); *Chelsea Art Gallery, Hotel Eldorado.*

Golf Courses   About half an hour's drive from the centre there are two 18-hole golf courses, one at Santo Amaro, and another, the São Fernando Golf Club, in beautiful surroundings. There is a sporting 9-hole course at São Francisco club, beyond the Butantã Institute.

Entertainment   The magnificent Opera House, the Teatro Municipal, is for visiting theatrical and operatic troupes but has no resident company. There are several first-class theatres: Aliança Francesa, Teatro Arena, Itália, Maria Della Costa, Paiol, Ruth Escobar, among others. There are also orchestras and choirs, dramatic schools, ballet companies, and the usual multitude of modern and luxurious cinemas.

Local Transport   The metro is clean, cheap and efficient. Combined bus and metro ticket are available, e.g. to **Congonhas** airport. Local buses are normally crowded and rather slow, but not lethal.

Culture and Education   There are three universities: the official university of São Paulo, the Pontifical Catholic University, and the Mackenzie University. The Biological Institute and the Agronomical Institute—the latter in the neighbouring city of Campinas—are outstanding in scientific research. The official University of São Paulo is now situated in the "Cidade Universitária" (buses from main bus station) out of the city beyond Pinheiros. There are a number of architecturally interesting buildings housing different faculties and the four museums of archaeology, ethnology, anthropology and mineralogy. (All keep different hours, but all are open Mon.-Thurs. 1400-1700.)

Galleries and Museums   The Museu de Arte de São Paulo (at Av. Paulista 1578, immediately above the 9 de Julho tunnel) has a large group of French Impressionists, Florentine and Umbrian painters (including Botticelli and Raphael), a magnificent Turner, several Hieronymus Bosch, sculptures by Degas, some interesting work by Brazilian artists, including Portinari. Particularly interesting are the pictures of the North-East done by Dutch artists during the Dutch occupation (1630-54): the exotic tropical landscapes—even the Paulo Afonso falls!—have been made to look incredibly domestic. Temporary exhibitions are held in the basement. Entrance free, 1400-1800 (main collection closes 1700), Tues.-Sun. **The Museum of Brazilian Art** is at Rua Alagoas 903, Higienópolis, entrance free, Tues.-Fri. 1000-2200, Sat.-Sun. 1400-1800. Here there are copies of Brazilian sculptures, including those of Aleijadinho. **The Museum of the Institute of Pre-History** is in the Zoology Pavilion at the University City. Every odd-numbered year the **São Paulo Bienal** at Ibirapuera, has the most important show of modern art in Latin America, open from beginning of Sept. till Nov. For the other museums at Ibirapuera, see page 258, and for the Museu Paulista and Casa do Grito at Ipiranga, see page 263.

There are two museums on Av. Tiradentes, near the Luz Park; a museum of sacred art in the Convento da Luz (open Tues.-Sun. 1300-1700, US$0.20) and the State Art Collection (Pinacoteca do Estado) at No. 141 (open Tues.-Sun. 1400-1800, free).

Not far from the Butantã Institute are the Casa do Bandeirante at Praça Monteiro Lobato, the reconstructed home of a pioneer of 400 years ago (Tues.-Sun. 1200-1730, free); and the Casa do Sertanista, a museum of Indian folklore and handicrafts mounted by the famous expert on the Indians, Orlando Villas Boas, at Av. Francisco Morato 2200, open Tues.-Sun., 1230-1730, entrance free.

The Casa Brasileira, Av. Faria Lima 774, has been established as a museum of Brazilian furniture. Open weekdays 0900-1200 and 1400-1700. The Sound and Image Museum is at Av. Europa 158. The Museum of Lasar Segall, at Rua Alfonso Celso 362, Vila Mariana (near Santa Cruz metro station), shows the works of a German expressionist painter who emigrated to Brazil.

Sport   The most popular is association football. The most important matches are played at Morumbi and Pacaembu grounds. At Interlagos there is a first-class racing track (see page 264). Swimming, horse riding, roller skating, cycling, car racing, hunting and fishing, flying, golf, hockey, tennis, shooting, fencing, boxing, water polo and track and field sports are all very popular. There is yachting, sailing and rowing on the Santo Amaro reservoir, an immense artificial lake.

Railways The Estrada de Ferro Santos a Jundiaí (ex São Paulo Railway) to Santos "down the hill", also to Jundiaí and the interior; Companhia Paulista de Estradas de Ferro, into the coffee, fruit and cattle districts; Central do Brasil Railway to Rio de Janeiro, 9 hours' journey, night sleeper train leaving at 2310 warmly recommended, charges range from around US$6.50 for airline-style seat to US$27.50 for a double cabin. The ordinary train leaves at 0810. Estrada de Ferro Sorocabana to Southern Brazil and Uruguay; Companhia Mogiana to the north-east of the State and southern Minas Gerais; Estrada de Ferro Noroeste do Brasil, from Bauru in São Paulo State across Mato Grosso State to Corumbá (34 hours from São Paulo), and on to Santa Cruz de la Sierra (Bolivia) by the Estrada de Ferro Brasil-Bolivia. There is a railway from São Paulo to Brasília. (The Santos a Jundiaí and Central are now parts of the Federal Railway Network (RFFSA): the Paulista, Mogiana and Sorocabana are components of the Paulista Railways (Fepasa).) There are several railway stations in São Paulo; Julio Poestes for suburban services; Luz for suburban and interior Rio and Santos services; Roosevelt for suburban and slow inter-city trains.

Roads The Presidente Dutra highway, linking São Paulo and Rio de Janeiro, 407 km.; the Anchieta highway to Santos, 63 km.; the new "Immigrants' Highway" to Santos; the Anhanguera highway to Campinas, 88 km.; to Goiás, *via* Ribeirão Preto, 1,230 km.; to Curitiba, Porto Alegre and S to Pelotas, all asphalted; to Belo Horizonte, 580 km.; to Cuiabá (Mato Grosso) *via* Ribeirão Preto; to the north of Paraná, 370 km.; to Bragança Paulista, 85 km. The direct road to Brasília runs *via* Uberaba and Uberlândia (Minas Gerais). The new Castello Branco Motorway gives a quick route to Sorocaba, and is continuing past Marilia, Presidente Prudente and Presidente Epitácio into Mato Grosso.

Road Services, at frequent intervals, of modern and comfortable buses and "limousine" motor-cars run regularly from São Paulo to Santos and its various beaches, and to the majority of the hydro-mineral "spas" throughout the State. Bus to Rio, 6 hours, frequent service, US$6.15; to Curitiba, 7½ hours, US$5.55; to Blumenau, 8½ hours, US$7; to Porto Alegre, 18 hours, US$15.75; to Belo Horizonte, 12 hours, US$8.05; to Salvador, 30 hours, US$26.35; to Recife, 40 hours, US$36.25; to Fortaleza, US$42.75; to Cuiabá, 24 hours, US$23.95; to Campo Grande (Mato Grosso do Sul), 15 hours, US$14.75; to Porto Velho, 60 hours (or more), US$51; to Brasília, 13 hours, US$15.25; to Foz do Iguaçu, 18½-20 hours, US$15.25; to Santos, about 1½ hours, US$1.30 (there is a bus station for Santos near the southern end of the Metro line, at Jabaquara); to Montevideo, US$50.

Visits to coffee fazendas and round trips into the surrounding country are organised by the travel agencies.

Air Services There are air services to all parts of Brazil, Europe, North and South America from the international airport at Viracopos, near Campinas (95 km. from São Paulo (taxi US$45); arrange to be met there if possible), and from the local airport of Congonhas, 14 km. from the city centre (the taxis in the street outside are much cheaper than the airport taxis), (US$4.50) or take a bus (US$0.33) or metro/bus trip to the centre, approx. one hour. There are about four hundred flights per week to Rio de Janeiro. British Caledonian flies to and from Gatwick 3 times a week (Tel.: 257-1245).

Maps of São Paulo in train timetables at news-stands are obtainable free, from the tourist offices, the better hotels and H. Stern, the jeweller, at Praça da República 242, São Paulo.

Emergency Radio patrol police 277 3333.

Addresses

British Consulate General, Av. Paulista 1938, 17th floor; Caixa Postal 846. Tel.: 287-7722.

American Consulate General, Av. Paulista 2023.

Australian Consulate General, Av. Paulista 2433. British Chamber of Commerce of São Paulo, Rua Barão de Itapetininga 257, 7th floor; Caixa Postal 1621 (Telegraphic address: "Britchamb" São Paulo). Tel.: 32-5572.

American Chamber of Commerce for Brazil, Rua Formosa 367, 29th floor.

Canadian Consulate, Av. Paulista 1765, 9th floor.

West German Consulate, Rua Augusta 257.

Samaritan Hospital, Rua Conselheiro Brotero 1486. Tel.: 51-2154.

Sociedade Brasileira de Cultura Inglesa, Avenida Higienópolis 449.

St. Paul's Anglican (Episcopal) Church, Rua Comendador Elias Zarzua 1231, Santo Amaro.

First Church of Christ Scientist, Trav. Brigadeiro Luiz Antônio 2-A.

St. Andrew's Society, the Hon. Sec. c/o British Consulate General.

The Royal Society of St. George, ditto.

American Library, União Cultural Brasil-Estados Unidos, Rua Coronel Oscar Porto 208.

General Post Office, Praça do Correio, corner Av. São João.

Police, Tel.: 239-3333.

First Aid, Tel.: 71-8673, 71-0757.

Banks Times when open vary from bank to bank.

Bank of London & South America, Rua 15 de Novembro 143/165. (Open 0900-1700.)

Banco Internacional, Rua 15 de Novembro 240.

Banco Holandês Unido, Rua 15 de Novembro 150.

Citibank, Av. Ipiranga 855.

First National Bank of Boston, Rua Líbero Baderó 487.

Banco Lar Brasileiro (Chase Manhattan owned), 131 Rua Alvares Penteado, and other national banks.

Shopping Rua Augusta for boutiques. All types of stores at Shopping Center Iguatemi, Av. Brig. Faria Lima, and Shopping Centre, Ibirapuera, Av. Ibirapuera (see page 258). Souvenirs from Mimosa, Joaquim Nabuco 304, Brooklin suburb; Indian handicraft, Rua Conde de Itu 350. São Paulo is cheap for films.

Bookshops Livraria Cultura, Eva Herz e Cia., Av. Paulista 2073, Loja 153. Livraria ABC, Av. São Luís 282, corner of Av. Consolação, including English, German and Spanish books. Ilco, Barão do Triúnfo 371, Brooklyn suburb, books in English. Livraria Kosmos, Praça Dom José Caspar 134, loja 30, international stock.

Cables Embratel, Av. São Luís 50, and Av. Ipiranga 344.

Travel Agents Wilson, Sons S.A., Praça da República 270; Exprinter, Rua Barão de Itapetininga 243; Receptur, same street, 221; Wagon-Lits Cook, Av. São Luís 285; Globe Trotter, Rua 24 de Maio 35; Tunibra, Cons. Crispiniano 69; Itatiaia Publicidade e Turismo, Cons. Crispiniano 69 (for hotel reservations especially); Transatlântica Turismo, Rua Cel. Xavier de Toledo 98 (for domestic excursions); Kontik-Franstur (American Express representative), Rua Marconi 71.

Exchange Many "Câmbios" near Praça da República. Also in travel agencies.

Excursions By making full use of taxis and buses or the "autolotação" (collective taxi), a number of interesting and inexpensive excursions can be made. Three-hour trips around São Paulo in air-conditioned minibuses (ask hotel) are not very expensive.

The Butantã Snake Farm and Museum (Instituto Soroterápico), Av. Dr. Vital Brasil 1500, Pinheiros, is the most popular tourist attraction. The snakes are "milked" for their poison, and though this is normally done between 1000 and 1100 you may see it done at other times (not at weekends); the antidote made from the venom has reduced deaths from snakebite by 80% in Brazil. Open daily from 0800-1700, entrance US$1.60. Restaurant. Informative museum. Bus No. 784 from Praça da República takes about 30 minutes.

The Museu Paulista (Ipiranga), in the suburb of Ipiranga, is a huge palace set in the beautiful Parque da Independência, with coloured fountains and statuary gardens. Here is the famous Ipiranga Monument to commmemorate the declaration of Brazilian independence; beneath the monument is the Imperial Chapel, with the tomb of the first emperor, Dom Pedro I, and Empress Leopoldina (open Tues.-Sun., 1300-1700). The Casa do Grito, the little hut in which Dom Pedro I spent the night before his famous cry of Ipiranga—"Independence or Death"—is preserved in the park (open Tues.-Sun. 1300-1730). The Museum has old maps, traditional furniture, collections of old coins and of religious art and rare documents, and a department of Indian ethnology. Behind the Museum is the Ipiranga Botanical Garden. Open Tues.-Sun. and holidays, 1300-1730. There is a "son et lumière" show, on Brazilian history, in the park on Wed., Fri. and Sat. evenings at 2030.

The Parque do Estado (Jardim Botânico), out at Agua Funda (Av. Jabaquara), is one of the most picturesque spots in São Paulo. There is a vast garden esplanade surrounded by magnificent stone porches, with lakes and trees and places for picnics, and a very fine orchid farm worth seeing during the blossom season, November-December. Over 32,000 different kinds of orchids are cultivated. Open Mon.-Sat., 0900-1700. The astronomical observatory nearby is open to the public Thurs. afternoons. Bus 546 or 548 from near Cathedral.

Zoological Gardens   Near the Jardim Botânico, not more than half an hour's drive from the city centre. Bus 546 or 548 from near Cathedral, marked "Zoológico", takes 1¼ hours, US$0.15. A very large variety of specimens from the three Americas, Africa, Asia and Europe can be seen in an almost natural setting of about 35 hectares of forest: a most interesting site. Open 0900-1800, admission US$0.75. There is a wild-life park, Simba Safari, nearby, admission US$0.75 per pedestrian, US$2 p.p. with a car, open Tues.-Sun. 0900-1800.

Parque Agua Branca (Avenida Agua Branca, 455) has beautiful gardens with specimens of tropical plants, Brazilian birds and wild life. Pavilions house a well stocked aquarium, a zoo, and exhibitions of food produce.

Parque da Cantareira has a beautiful lake surrounded by park land. A museum shows specimens of Brazilian woods and the furniture made from them. In Tremembé, a little beyond Cantareira, half an hour from the down-town area, is the **Horto Florestal**, containing examples of nearly every species of Brazilian woodland flora (admission daily, 0800-1800).

Santo Amaro Dam (Old Lake), is 3 kilometres from the centre of Santo Amaro suburb. This is a popular sailing and motorboat resort with several sailing clubs and many attractive cottages along the shore. There is a bus (30 minutes) from São Paulo to Santo Amaro.

Interlagos, which has a motor-racing circuit with 18 kilometres of track, is São Paulo's lake resort on the Santo Amaro dam. It can be reached from Santo Amaro by bus. Close to the track, where the Fittipaldi brothers began their careers, and where the Brazilian Grand Prix takes place, usually in February, is the 32-km. long Guarapiranga artificial lake with several luxurious sailing and sports clubs. Camping Clube do Brasil site.

Pico de Jaraguá (1,135 metres) the highest peak in the neighbourhood, gives good views of Greater São Paulo on a fine day. This peak is reached from km. 18 on the Campinas highway (Via Anhanguera) by a good road which is approached through Taipas and Pirituba.

Embú, 28 km. from São Paulo, is a Colonial town which has become a centre for artists and craftsmen. Buses from close to the Largo de Pinheiros, São Paulo.

Santos, 320 km. SW of Rio de Janeiro, is the natural gateway for the foreign commerce of the thriving state of São Paulo. (Over 40% by value of all Brazilian imports and about half the total exports pass through Santos, the busiest port in all Brazil, handling 25% of its shipping traffic.) It is reached from Rio by ocean steamers in 12-15 hours, and a direct highway between the two cities is being built (see pages 240 and 267). A railway and the Anchieta and Immigrants' highways run to São Paulo (63 km.). A free-port zone for Paraguay, 1,930 km. by rail or road, has been established at Santos. A few km. outside the city there is an important industrial cluster round the oil refinery and hydroelectric plant at Cubatão. The Cosipa steel works are here, served by a dredged channel which allows ships to reach the plant.

The port is five km. from the open sea and is approached by the winding Santos Channel; at its mouth is a picturesque old fort (1709) complete with its bartizans and a miniature chapel. Winding up the channel there are views of palm-dotted flat shores and irregular hills in the background. (São Paulo City is reached by traversing these hills; there are fine views of Santos during the journey.)

The plain upon which Santos, a city of 450,000 people, stands, is an island which can be circumnavigated by small boats. The extensive wharves are very active. The city has been improved in recent years by modern buildings, wide, tree-lined avenues, and wealthy suburbs—outward signs of the prosperity of its inhabitants. The night-life can best be seen within an area known as Gonzaga, which has the large hotels and several good picture houses. Although best known for its commerce, Santos has a considerable local fame as a holiday resort. Visitors coming from inland towns and neighbouring countries are attracted by the magnificent beaches and views, set in tropical splendour. Santos itself is a seaport, and like most seaports, not very imposing; one must travel into the suburbs to appreciate the beauty it has to offer.

There are fine monuments, including one in Avenida Ana Costa, to commemorate the brothers Andradas, who took a leading part in the movement for independence, attained in 1822. There are others in the Praça Rui Barbosa, Praça da República, and Praça José Bonifácio, the first to Bartholomeu de Gusmão, who has a dubious claim to the world's first airborne ascent, in 1709, the second to Braz Cubas, who founded the city in 1534, and the third to the soldiers of Santos who died in the Revolution of 1932.

Hotels *Universo Palace,* Pres. Wilson, beach front, US$28 d; *Indaia,* Av. Ana Costa 431, US$20 d; *Ritz,* Rua Mar. Deodoro 24, US$18 d; *Maracanã Santos,* Pres. Wilson, beach front, US$20 d; *Avenida Palace,* Pres. Wilson, beach front, US$20 d; *Svea,* Bartolomeu de Gusmão 19, beach area, US$15 d; *Estoril,* Rua Bitencourt 55, US$5 d, with bath, cheap; *Hotel Paris,* US$2.50 s.

Restaurants *Atlântico Bar,* next to *Atlântico Hotel; Cantina Dom Fabrizio,* Av. Ana Costa 482; *Jangadeiro,* Ponta da Praia; *Hong Kong Palace,* Av. Conselheiro Nébias 288 (Chinese food); *Rincón Argentino,* Av. Manuel da Nóbrega 666, at São Vicente (Gaucho food); *Ilha Porchat Grill,* on Ilha Porchat, off São Vicente, at edge of island, overlooking Bays of São Vicente and Santos; first class *Pizzaria Zi Tereza,* Av. Ana Costa 451.

Electric Current   216 A.C. 60 cycles.

Local Holidays (in addition to national): Jan. 26 (Foundation of Santos): Good Friday; Corpus Christi.

Coastal Steamers   Irregular services by Companhia de Navegação Lóide Brasileiro, S to Porto Alegre, N to Belém (Pará) and intermediate ports, and Manaus (Amazon River). Consult their agents, Rua General Câmara 22, 2nd floor, conjunto 34.

Rail   The British-built Santos a Jundiaí up to São Paulo, still in use, is one of the railway wonders of the world, slower though cheaper than buses, it passes through interesting scenery, US$0.80.

Air Services   Passengers who want to travel by air must embark at São Paulo; Santos has no airport.

Car Hire   Cars can be hired on the quay side. All taxis are supplied with meters. The fare is a fixed charge of US$0.12 plus US$0.10 per kilometre.

Consulate   (British) Largo do Senador Vergueiro 2, first floor. Caixa Postal 204. Tel.: 25733, 29608.

All Saints Church, Praça Washington 92, José Menino. Services in English held every Sunday.

Cables   Embratel, Largo Senador Vergueiro 1 and 2.

Banks   Banco Internacional, Rua General Câmara 24; Banco Holandês Unido, Citibank, Banco do Brasil, all in the Rua 15 de Novembro. The First National Bank of Boston, Praça Visc. de Mauá 14. Banks open: 0930-1630.

Clubs   Samambaia and Tortuga, both on heights, commanding the sea. Luxurious and private but occasionally open to non-members at US9 to US$11 entrance fee off season. These fees may be doubled during the season. The Ilha Porchat, a small island reached by a bridge at the far end of Santos/São Vicente bay, has beautiful views from its top over rocky precipices, of the high seas on one side and of the city and bay on the other. At the summit is a splendid night club, the "Top House Restaurante e Discoteca". No entrance fee but there is a minimum charge of US$5.

Exchange Houses   Banco Faro, Rua 15 de Novembro, 80 & 260; Casa Bancária J. Coelho, Praça da República 43; Casa Bancaria Branco & Cia., Praça de República 30.

Bus Services   Comfortable buses run an efficient service between the City and outlying suburbs. These buses start, in the majority of cases, from Praça Mauá, which is in the centre of the city. There are several bus services to São Paulo at intervals of approximately 15 minutes, from the Rodoviária near city centre. This journey is done in 1½ hours and the vehicles used are comfortable, efficient and modern. The single fare each way is US$1.30. Enquire about being picked up or put down outside usual terminal points. Express cars also run to São Paulo at regular intervals, taking 75 minutes. Fare, US$3.50 each way, per passenger.

Excursions   Taxis and buses to Alto da Serra, the coast E of Santos (Guarujá, Bertioga, Ilhabela) and the coast SW (Praia Grande, Itanhaém). Shorter excursions along the Guarujá road to the José Menino suburb for the orchid gardens in the Praça Washington, and to the municipal aquarium at Ponta da Praia. The orchid gardens are particularly attractive (the flowering season is from October to February). There is an open-air cage containing a hundred humming-birds of 20 different species and the park is also a sanctuary for other birds, some brilliantly coloured.

To **Alto da Serra,** the summit of the forest-clad mountain range; magnificent panoramas and views. The return journey can be done in under two hours by car.

Ascent of Monte Serrat   A funicular railway to the summit gives a magnificent view of the city, beaches, river and surrounding countryside (every ½ hour, US$0.80). On the summit is a semaphore station and look-out post which reports the arrival of all ships in Santos harbour. There is also a quaint old church, dedicated to our Lady of

Monte Serrat, said to have performed innumerable miracles. The top can be reached on foot. Seven shrines have been built on the way up. Annual pilgrimages are made by the local people.

Guarujá The route from Santos to the resort of Guarujá is along Conselheiro Nébias to the sea front, continuing along the beach to the Guarujá ferry (every 10 minutes, free) at Ponta da Praia. On the other side proceed as far as Turtle Bay. From the docks tourists should take a taxi but during the season and weekends there is a long delay at the ponta da Praia ferry. To avoid this cross the ferry on foot and take the bus on the Guarujá side. There is more or less dangerous undertow on nearly all the Guarujá beaches; the Jequiti-Mar beach is the safest. Golf club at Guarujá; population, 94,000. (Trolleybus from Praça Mauá in Santos to the ferry, then buses.)

Turn left at centre of Guarujá and drive less than half a mile to reach *Delfin Hotel* and its restaurant *La Popote* at the beginning of the long beach of Praia de Enseada. Close by, at Av. Miguel Estefno 999, is *Casa Grande Hotel,* luxury, in Colonial style. Facing sea is the new luxurious *Ferraretto Hotel* (night club, swimming pool). Camping Clube do Brasil site at Praia do Perequé, near municipal nursery.
Hotel Prices (basic double): *Delfin,* US$35; *Casa Grande,* US$38 (facing pool) or US$45 (facing sea); *Ferraretto,* US$25.

The Jequiti-Mar holiday complex, 8 km. beyond Guarujá on the road to (ferry) Bertioga, is extremely attractive. There are private beaches (excellent swimming and boating) and a very fine fishing ground. Tourists can spend the night or weekend in separate chalets, each with small sitting room and bathroom, at a daily charge, for two, with breakfast, of between US$30 and US$80, depending on the size and placing of the chalet. There is an excellent restaurant and two night clubs; they are open each weekend and every night from December to March, in the holiday season.

There are good sea-food restaurants on the road to Bertioga. Beyond **Bertioga,** an attractive place, the winding coast road (unpaved on this stretch) takes you to **São Sebastião,** where the new paved coast road to Rio starts, and (ferry) to Ilhabela (6 hours by bus from Santos). The São Sebastião beaches are splendid, and foreigners can stay in the Camping Clube do Brasil grounds for US$2 a night.

E. Chafuen-Dougall, of Tigre, Argentina, has most kindly sent us the following description of Ilhabdela:

Ilha de São Sebastião (Ilhabela). The mountainous and luxuriantly tropical island of São Sebastião, known popularly as Ilhabela after its main settlement, is now easily accessible by car or bus from São Paulo and Santos. A bus runs along the only road in the island, on the coastal strip facing the mainland. This newly opened-up resort, which has been colonised for centuries, was once an essential watering place for Spanish and Portuguese sailing vessels on their voyages to the River Plate. Also Cavendish the English pirate, had his secret anchorage in one of the sheltered caves there. Last century it was used as a landing place for illegal slave-traffic.

The island is of volcanic origin, roughly about 390 sq. km. in area, and consists of a central longitudinal mountain range with land sloping towards the sides. Its highest peak, Morro do Papagaio, rises 1,300 metres above sea-level, with its bare peak often obscured by mist; the mountainous slopes are densely wooded. There are many beautiful waterfalls, easily accessible to the enterprising walker. Most of the flatter ground is given over to sugar-cane for the purpose of making *cachaça*. There are several distilleries, which tourists may visit.

The only settled district lies on the coastal strip facing the mainland, the Atlantic side being practically uninhabited except by a few fisherfolk. The place abounds in tropical plants and flowers of the most extraordinary variety, including hibiscus and bougainvillea of all known shades. Many fruits grow wild: mango, mamão or paw-paw, jaca, the tasty but perishable jaboticaba, and the caju (cashew) fruit (whose juice mixed with the local cachaça and sugar makes as delicious a cocktail as can be imagined, but prepare for the after-effects), as well as a host of others of rather dubious flavours.

The authorities have very wisely decided to preserve the character of the frontage of the colourful main township, **Ilhabela;** no structural alterations are allowed. There are several hotels, ranging through the whole price-range. Tourism is still in its initial stages, though visitors abound during week-ends in the summer season. For this reason, motorists are warned to avoid those days as the car-carrying capacity of the ferry is very limited and a prolonged queue may result.

The energetic can climb over the hump of the island down towards the Atlantic, sometimes through dense tropical forest following the old slave trail, but for this a local guide is required. (The round trip can be done in one day if the visitor is exceptionally vigorous.) A visit to the terraced Toca waterfalls amongst dense jungle close to the foot of the 970-metre Baepi peak is also recommended; there is cool freshwater bathing to be had there. To all this there is one serious drawback: in all shady places, especially away from the sea, there abounds a species of gnat or midge known locally as *borrachudos*. A locally sold Aerosol spray keeps them off for some time, however. Those allergic to insect bites should remain on the inhabited coastal strip.

Sightseeing If you prefer it, hire a horse and buggy and drive yourself to the old "Feiticeira" plantation where creepy underground dungeons will give you the shudders. If not, go by car or bus. The road is along the coast, sometimes high above the sea towards the south of the island.

Pedras do Sino (Bell Rocks) These curious seashore boulders, when struck with a piece of iron or stone, emit a loud bell-sounding note. The effect is surprising in the extreme.

Engenho d'Água This is the best laid-out distillery on the island, reputed to produce the best cachaça in all Brazil. It lies quite close to the road, south of Ilhabela.

Praia de Siriuba A coconut-fringed beach, within walking distance, to the north of Ilhabela.

Fishing Interesting catches are made, especially at night. If Japanese tourists arrive watch their special techniques. Squid are so plentiful that they can be had for the asking.

Boating It is possible to hire a launch for a trip to the Atlantic side always providing good weather reigns.

Bathing Bathing is so safe in the warm currentless waters of the mainland side that you can float for hours almost without making a stroke.

Hotels in Ilhabela *Mercedes,* US$20 d, Tel.: 7-0071; *Siriuba,* US$22 d, Tel.: 7-0265; *Ilhabela,* US$28 d, Tel.: 7-0083. There are several other less expensive "pensions".

Transport Ferry every 15 minutes.

In the opposite direction (SW) from Santos, there is a splendid excursion to be made along the 50-km. length of Praia Grande to the picturesque little town of **Itanhaém,** with its pretty Colonial church. There are several

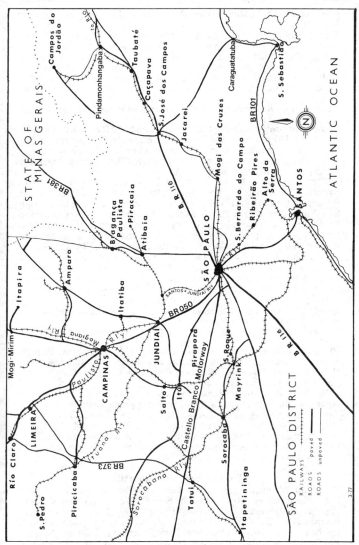

SÃO PAULO DISTRICT

RAILWAYS ┼┼┼┼┼
ROADS paved ──────
ROADS unpaved ──────

ROUGH SKETCH

good sea-food restaurants along the beach, and a Camping Clube do Brasil site.

Serra Negra is a very pleasant small town up in the mountains at 1,080 metres and 145 km. from São Paulo. It is a spa town and a favourite holiday resort for Paulistas and people from all over Brazil who want a rest from the toil and heat of the cities in its pleasant, mild climate. Visitors tour the countryside in horse-drawn carts. The population is about 5,000, and it has many first class hotels, a "balneário" and a small zoo.

Hotels   *Grande Hotel Pavani* (2 swimming pools); *Radio Hotel* (very nice indeed), etc.

Campos do Jordão, between Rio de Janeiro and São Paulo, is a mountain resort at 1,710 metres, in the Serra da Mantiqueira. It is prettily set in a long valley. The climate is cold and dry in winter and cool in summer, a great relief from the coastal heat and humidity. There are many hotels but no airport, as yet. Population: 18,750.

The resort, about 190 km. from São Paulo, is reached by an 87 km. paved road from São José dos Campos, 100 km. from São Paulo, on the Presidente Dutra (BR-116) Highway. By car it takes about 3 hours from São Paulo. 6 to 7 from Rio de Janeiro. Regular bus services from São Paulo. From both it can be reached by the Central Railway to Pindamon-hangaba, changing to a 43-km. electrified line to Campos do Jordão over Alto de Goado at 488 metres, the highest point reached by a railway in Brazil. This is a spectacular and popular journey taking 2 hours. The short road down to "Pinda", starting from the paved road 24 km. SW of Campos do Jordão, should be taken downhill only, for it is very steep and rough and not all-weather. A new and even shorter road should now be open.

Hotels   *Grande; Toriba; Vila Inglesa; Hotel Refúgio Alpino,* at Capivari; and others. *Casa de Juventude* (Youth Hostel).

Transport   Bus from São Paulo, US$2, 4 hours; from Rio, changing at São José dos Campos, US$4.

Places of interest   Pedra do Baú, a rock 2,332 metres high; Pico do Itapeva, a peak 2,050 metres high, commanding a beautiful view of the Paraíba valley; Morro de Elefante; Gruta dos Crioulos. Campos is a popular place for hikers.

Nearer to Rio than the Pindamonhangaba turn, just off the Br-116, is **Aparecida do Norte,** Brazil's chief place of pilgrimage and the seat of its patron saint, Nossa Senhora Aparecida. This small black image of the Virgin was taken by a fisherman from the nearby River Paraíba, and quickly acquired a miraculous reputation. It is now housed in a huge modern cathedral in Romanesque style on top of a hill, with the pleasant clean white-walled, red-roofed town below.

Trips to the Great Waterfalls

In the far W, on the great River Paraná, is the tremendous waterfall known in Brazil as **Sete Quedas** (the Seven Falls), and in Spanish Latin America as the Guaíra Falls. (Some 130 km. S by air or road is Iguaçu, described on page 105.) A train for Presidente Epitácio (Porto Tibiriçá), on the Paraná leaves São Paulo on Sunday evening at 2100, reaching the port at 1700 next day. It has sleepers and a restaurant car. The 900 km. are done in 20 hours. A passenger steamer goes twice weekly upstream to Presidente Epitácio and Tres Lagoas, and a small river boat down stream to **Guaíra,** 400 km. S—a rough and romantic river voyage through tropical forest, if the water is high enough—gets there on Wednesday morning. (Book a passage well in advance.) There is a bus service between Curitiba and Guaíra (US$9, 6½ hours, dusty road). There is also a bus service from Londrina to Guaíra for US$7.50, and from Campo Grande *via* Dourados; 2 days in the dry season. The 6½ km. from Guaíra to the falls are done by bus (US$0.12) or car (US$1.50 one way). Small museum three blocks from Guaíra bus terminal, 0800-1100 and 1400-1700. The great river, nearly 5 km. wide, hurls itself though the rocky gorges of the falls with a tremendous roar. Rocky islands between the falls are connected by wooden suspension bridges; the whole area can warrant a whole day. Many of the falls are from 30 to 40 metres high. This is the most enormous volume of falling water in the world; it is double Niagara's. Paraguay and Brazil are together building, nearby, the 12,000-megawatt Itaipu hydroelectric plant, which will be the largest in the world; it will enter into production in the 1980s. It is sad to note that the Itaipu dam will flood an area of 1,400 sq. km., and as a result Sete Quedas will cease to exist. The dam site can be visited, but first go to the public relations department of the Itaipu Binacional company.

Guaíra Hotels   *Guarujá Motel,* Rua Alvorada 400, US$10 d; *Majestic,* opposite bus station, US$8 d, with breakfast; *Sete Quedas,* Otávio Tosta 385, US$10 d, with breakfast and sandwich lunch, not too clean; *Ypecaraí,* US$1.40 p.p.; and others. Cheap snacks at *Bar São José.*

Take a plane or bus (dry season, 6-7 hours, 4 buses a day, US$4.50) from Guaíra to Foz do Iguaçu. Information on the Iguaçu Falls, together with flights, hotels, transport facilities, etc., in Brazil, Argentina and Paraguay, is set out on pages 105 and 106 in the Argentine chapter.

From Iguaçu the traveller can go to São Paulo or Rio de Janeiro, or to Asunción or Buenos Aires by air or road, or by road only as far as Posadas to take a train for Buenos Aires. Some tours go by road to Posadas, on by train through Argentina to Paso de los Libres on the Río Uruguay, across the river to the Brazilian cattle town of Uruguaiana, then E by air, road or rail (28 hours) to Porto Alegre. The land and river trips are an excellent way of seeing the country, but they require stamina.

Towns in the State of São Paulo

About 11% of Brazil's population lives within 200 km. of São Paulo city, a circle which includes 88 municipalities. (Four of them—the big ABCD towns—share a population of over a million. They are Santo André, São Bernardo, São Caetano and Diadema; they have many of the largest industrial plants, but they are not included here because they are of little interest to the tourist.) There are some 70 cities in the State with populations of over 50,000 and São Paulo is linked with all of them by road, and most of them by railway. One important line, the broad-gauge Santos a Jundiaí, runs from Santos to São Paulo, and across the low mountains which separate São Paulo city from the interior to its terminus at

Jundiaí, 58 km. from São Paulo, to which there is a two-lane road and bus services as well. It has textile factories, Krupp's steel foundry, and other industries. The district grows coffee and grain and there is an annual Grape Festival. Population, 170,000.

Hotel   *Grand Hotel,* Rua do Rosário 605, with good restaurant.

The Paulista Railway, with the same broad gauge, continues from Jundiaí through Campinas, Limeira, and São Carlos do Pinhal—the richest part of the state.

Campinas, 88 km. from São Paulo by a very good super-highway. It is important as a clearing point for coffee, for its Agricultural Institute, and its rapidly growing industries: there are some 15 international companies. The international airport for São Paulo (Viracopos) is 11 km. from Campinas, which also has its own airport. Population, 380,000.

See beautiful cathedral, old market, colonial buildings, and the modern university outside the city.

Hotels *Holiday Inn,* Praça Rotatória 88, US$25 d; *Vila Rica,* Rua Donato Paschoal 100, US$30 d; *Savoy,* Rua Regente Feijó 1064, US$22 d; *Terminus,* Av. Francisco Glicério 1075, US$20 d; *Solar das Andorinhas,* a health farm with pool, sauna, horses, sports, etc. 18 km. outside city on the Mogi-Mirim road, US$30 d, with meals.

Visits can be made to the Agricultural Institute to see all the aspects of coffee raising. São Paulo agents can organize this tour.

Restaurants *Armorial* (French cuisine); *Barão,* and *Churrascaria Gaúcha,* both excellent for Brazilian food.

Banks The First National Bank of Boston, Av. Francisco Glicério 1275, and local banks. Bank of London & South America is to open a branch in mid-1978.

Community Church Services in English at School of Language and Orientation, Rua Eduardo Lane 270.

Besides the super-highway there is a longer, highly picturesque paved motor road from São Paulo *via* the Colonial towns of Pirapora and Itu.

Pirapora de Bom Jesus is a popular place of pilgrimage, in a most attractive setting on both sides of a river. **Itu** was founded by the Bandeirantes in the 17th century. The beautiful falls of Salto de Itu, 8 km. N, are flanked by a park and a textile mill.

Itu Hotels *International,* Rua Barão do Itaím 93, US$12 d; *Sabará,* Praça Padre Miguel 90, US$8 d.

Camping *Casarão de Itu,* km. 95 on the Jundaí road; *Itu,* at km. 89 on the Cabreúva road.

Martin Crossland writes:

Americana 42 km. from Campinas is the interesting town of Americana. This area was settled by Confederate refugees from the south of the U.S.A. after the Civil War. The colony was not a great success, and most of the original settlers soon returned to the States. Nevertheless, many stayed, and even today there are reminders of their occupation here. A visit to the graveyard reveals an unusual number of English surnames. (*Hotel Bradesco,* 12 km. away at km. 118 on the Anhanguera Highway, US$15 d; *Cacique,* Rua Washington Luís 143, US$10 d.)

Limeira, beyond Campinas by rail or road, is a busy town where hats, matches and coffee machinery are manufactured. It is the largest centre of orange cultivation in São Paulo State, and has a large modern American packing house. Population, 91,000.

Hotel *Grande Hotel* and restaurant.

The narrow gauge Mogiana line, connecting with the Paulista at Campinas, serves the north-eastern part of the state. It goes through Riberão Preto and into the Triângulo of Minas Gerais, a great area for fattening beasts which are trucked to the frigoríficos of São Paulo. From Araguari its terminus, there is a line into the state of Goiás.

Ribeirão Preto, the centre of a rich coffee-growing distrtict, also has a steel industry. The town is 422 km. from São Paulo city by rail or paved road. Population 213,000. Altitude, 420 metres. It is a distributing centre for the interior of São Paulo State and certain districts in Minas Gerais, Goiás, and Mato Grosso. Products: coffee, cotton, sugar, grain and rice.

Hotels *Black Stream,* Rua General Osório 830, US$25 d, with T.V.; *Umuarama Recreio,* Praça dos Cafeeiros 140, 6 km. from centre, very pleasant, pool, gardens, US$25 d; *Brasil,* Rua General Osório 20, US$15 d.

All the southern part of the state and most of its western part are served by the metre-gauge Sorocabana railway. The main line runs from São Paulo through Sorocaba to Bauru (428 km.). Here it connects with the Noroeste, which runs across the Paraná river and the state of Mato Grosso to Corumbá, 1,223 km. (A continuation of this line into Bolivia goes on to Santa Cruz, 648 km; from Corumbá.) Of its many branches, one goes from São Paulo to Santos, and one starts off from a junction near Sorocaba and extends (through connections with other lines) across the southern states to the border with Uruguay; from the border there are connections to Montevideo.

Sorocaba, 110 km. west of São Paulo, is an important industrial centre. The altitude is 540 metres, and the climate temperate. The population is 176,000. It has cotton and silk spinning and weaving mills; produces cement, fertilizers, footwear, hats, alcohol, wines; there are railway workshops, extensive orange groves and packing house installations, printing works, and electric power plants. It is an important cotton growing centre. Other products are timber, sugar, cereals, coffee, and minerals. Communications with São Paulo are better by road than by rail; the new Castello Branco motorway passes nearby.

Hotels *Terminus,* Av. General Carneiro 474, US$15 d; *Nova Sorocaba,* Rua Mons. João Soares 158, US$10 d. Cheaper hotels: *Viajantes, Roma, Comércio.*

These railways and the extending roads permit São Paulo city to draw sustenance from and to serve an ever-enlarging area. The Triângulo of Minas Gerais and parts even of the state of Goiás centre naturally by road and rail on São Paulo. The Triângulo has large herds of cattle and, for the sertão, a dense population; Goiás is now cultivating tobacco and cotton, though not as yet in great volume, and produces large quantities of rice. North-western Paraná now grows a good proportion of Brazilian coffee on its frost-free slopes. It grows cotton and soya, too, and has large timber reserves. North-western Paraná's connections by road and Sorocabana railway are more with São Paulo than with the state's capital, Curitiba.

Southern Brazil

This consists, from N to S, of the three states of Paraná, Santa Catarina and Rio Grande do Sul. The conformation of the land is not unlike what it is further north; the Great Escarpment runs down the coastal area as far as Porto Alegre, receding from the coast in a wide curve between Paranaguá and Florianópolis. Beyond it, as in São Paulo, is an inner lowland rising to a vast hilly plateau. But south of Tubarão to the borders of Uruguay the hills of southern Rio Grande do Sul, which never rise higher than 900 to 1,000 metres, are fringed along the coast by sand bars and lagoons. Rio Grande, the largest port in the area, stands at the opening of the largest of the lagoons—the Lagoa dos Patos; Porto Alegre, the greatest city in the area, stands at the head of the same 187-km. long lagoon.

North of the Rio Uruguai the land is deeply forested, but the area of prairie, small in São Paulo, Paraná, and Santa Catarina, grows more extensive than the forest south of the Uruguai valley. In southern Rio

ROUGH SKETCH

Grande do Sul, south and west of the Rio Jacuí (draining into the Lagoa
dos Patos) there are great grasslands stretching as far as Uruguay to the
south and Argentina to the west. This is the distinctive land of the
gaúchos, or cowboys, of bombachas (the baggy trousers worn by the
gaúcho), of the poncho (a blanket with a hole in the middle through
which he thrusts his head to make a cloak of it), and of Ximarão, maté tea
without sugar, the indispensable drink of southern cattlemen. There are

10 million head of cattle, 13.2 million sheep, and some 6.5 million pigs in Rio Grande do Sul. Nearly all the wool exports of Brazil come from this State.

Some 75% of all Brazilian wine comes from Rio Grande do Sul. The state exports rice, timber, wine, meat, hides, wool, animal hair, tobacco and soya beans. Its population is now about 7 million.

There are three sharply contrasted types of colonisation and land owning in Rio Grande do Sul. During the colonial period wars with the Spaniards of Uruguay were frequent. In order to hold Rio Grande do Sul more effectively, the Portuguese government brought into the grasslands of the south a number of militant settlers from the Azores; these soldiers inter-married with the Brazilian herdfolk in the area. The present day gaúchos of the pasture lands are descendants of these two strains. In the Colonial period the Jesuits built several settlements, to acculturate the local Indians; relics of this process include the impressive ruins of the "Sete Povos das Missões Orientais" (São Borja, São Nicolau, São Luiz, São Lourenço, São Miguel (1602), São João, Santo Ângelo). West from Porto Alegre, in the floodlands of the Rio Jacuí and its tributary, the Rio Taquari, rice is cultivated almost exclusively by a large group of Brazilians of European origin in Typical Brazilian fashion: large estates with tenant workers. In spite of the fact that the floods in the rivers occur inopportunely for rice growing, this area is important as a source of supply for the Brazilian home market.

At São Leopoldo, north of Porto Alegre, a group of German peasants and craftsmen were settled in 1824 and all on their own small farms. During the next 25 years over 20,000 Germans were brought into the area by the Brazilian Government. The Germans concentrated on rye, maize, and pigs. Between 1870 and 1890, Italians from northern Italy arrived in numbers and settled north of the Germans at Alfredo Chaves and Caxias. They brought vine culture with them.

Further up the coast, in Santa Catarina, a group of Germans was settled at Lages in 1822. Because of Indian attacks they retreated to Florianópolis but gradually made their way inland again. In 1848 a new German, Austrian and Swiss settlement was made at Blumenau. They spread inland over the mountains to Joinville, inland from the port of São Francisco. The Italians came later. Over northern Rio Grande do Sul and Santa Catarina the vast majority of people to-day can trace their origin from these peoples.

In Santa Catarina, a State of small holdings, the farmer owns the land he tills and the cattle he grazes: the familiar European pattern of mixed farming worked by the family. Sixty-five per cent of the population is rural. A third of all Brazilian wheat comes from the State, where rye, maize, European fruits and grapes, tobacco, beans, rice and much vegetable produce are also grown. Extensive pine forests on the slopes of the Serra do Mar are exploited for timber. There is coal in the S, and flourishing food processing and textile industries. The State has five ports: Itajaí, São Francisco do Sul, Florianópolis, the capital, Joinville and Henrique Laje, but the first two handle 90% of the trade.

The Germans of Santa Catarina pushed north into the state of Paraná, but there are comparatively few of them and they are widely scattered. The Italians were first in Paraná, but to-day most of the settlers are of Slavonic origin—Poles, Russians, Ruthenians and Ukrainians. Paraná has made astonishing progress in the last ten years. It is now the main producer of coffee, beans, maté and timber, the second in cotton, maize and soya, and the third in potatoes and wheat. In a short time the State has become the second largest agricultural producer and the third largest exporter. It has also a large extractive industry, mainly of timber and maté tea. Its population, now 7,000,000, doubles every 10 years—partly as a result of internal migration.

There is one very important difference between these settlers in the south and the settlers in São Paulo. In São Paulo the farm structures in the settlements have a temporary air; the settler has little sentiment of attachment to his land and is ready to uproot himself either to live in a city (his dearest wish) or elsewhere to try his chances with a new boom crop. But in the south the settlements are permanent; the homes are solid; the settlers are attached to their plot of earth in the European sense. It is a good augury for the future of Brazil that the population in the south, with its stable relationship with the land, is increasing rapidly.

Porto Alegre, 274 km. north of the deep sea port of Rio Grande, inside the Lagoa dos Patos, lies at the junction of five rivers which flow into the Rio Guaíba and thence into the lagoon, which is one of South America's largest fresh water lakes. It is the capital of the state of Rio Grande do Sul, and the most important commercial centre south of São Paulo. The Germanic element is still most marked in the city and surrounding districts. Rio Grande do Sul has the highest proportion of literate people in Brazil. Population, 1,250,000 (1976 est.).

Standing on a series of hills and valleys on the banks of the Guaíba, with its business centre jutting out into the water on a kind of promontory, Porto Alegre has rapidly become one of the most up-to-date cities in Brazil, with skyscrapers and new buildings springing up on all sides. The panorama is delightful. The older residential part of the town is on a promontory of fair height dominated (until 1967) by the Governor's Palace, the imposing stone cathedral recently completed, and the two high white towers of the old church of Nossa Senhora das Dores, but Governor and God have now been utterly dwarfed by the new skyscraper of the Legislative Assembly up on the promontory. The streets at the centre are famous for their undulations, and some have extremely steep gradients. The climate is temperate through most of the year, though temperatures at the height of summer often exceed 40°C. The surrounding suburbs, to which there are frequent bus services, are very agreeable.

Do not miss that section of the Rua dos Andradas (Rua da Praia) that is now permanently closed off to traffic. It is the city's principal outdoor meeting place, and by around 1600 it is full of people. Cafezinho sellers and shoeshine boys ply a brisk trade amongst the men. The din is incredible, and at the peak hour of 1900 the street is jammed for about 6 blocks.

Good paved roads radiate from the city, and Highway BR-116 has a paved surface to Curitiba (746 km.), São Paulo, Rio, and Salvador. To the S it is paved to Pelotas (though this stretch is in poor condition), and on from there to Chuy on the Uruguayan frontier. Delightful drives can be taken through the surrounding hills and along the lagoon. The landscape is hilly and picturesque, reminiscent of the less populated parts of central Pennsylvania. The new paved coastal road to Curitiba *via* Itajaí (BR-101), of which the first 100 km. is a four-lane highway, is much better than the Br-116 *via* Caxias and Lajes.

Porto Alegre is a fresh-water port for ocean-going vessels of up to 7,000 tons and 4.87 metres draught. Vessels must come up through Rio Grande and the Lagoa dos Patos, some 275 km. from the open sea. British, American and continental steamship lines maintain regular services of cargo vessels to and from Porto Alegre, in most instances the turn-around port. Large areas of reclaimed land have been used for residential building and to extend the port facilities and quays, now amongst the most up-to-date in Brazil.

Porto Alegre's most important industries are food and farm products, textiles, metallurgy, chemicals and leather products. Chief exports are pinewood, rice, wheat, soya, meat, hides, wool, animal hair, semi-precious stones, wine and tobacco. A visit to Varig's model installations and workshops is well worth while.

Local Holidays Feb. 2 (Our Lady of Sailors).

Tourist Information Secretaria de Turismo (SETUR) main office; Rua dos Andradas 1234, 18th floor. Branch offices: Salgado Filho airport; Interstate bus station; Rua General Câmara 368; Rua Uruguai 317, Av. Salgado Filho 366. CRTUR (Companhia Riograndense de Turismo), Rua dos Andradas 1137, 6th floor. The Secretaria de Turismo maintains information booths at the following frontier towns: Bagé-Aceguá; Chuí; Santana do Livramento; Torres; Porto Mauá; Jaguarão; Uruguaiana; Vacaria. A monthly booklet is available.

Hotels (prices in US dollars, in brackets, are for the lowest-price double room available). *Plaza São Rafael,* Av. Alberto Bins 514 (33); *Alfred Executivo,* Av. Otávio Rocha 270 (18); *Plaza Porto Alegre,* Senhor dos Passos, 154 (18); *City,* Rua José Montaury 20 (20); *Embaixador,* Jerônimo Coelho 354 (17); *Everest Palace,* Rua Duque de Caxias 1357 (24); *Ritter,* in front of Central Bus Station (20); *Umbu,* Av. Farrapos 292 (17); *São Luiz,* Av. Farrapos 45 (19), spotless, good service; *Rishon,* Rua Dr. Flores 27 (20); *Savoy,* Av. Borges de Medeiros 688 (14); *Lido,* R. Andrade Neves 150 (21); *Hermon,* Vigário José Inácio 541 (15); *Motel Clube do Brasil,* Av. Farrapos 4655 (9); *Santa Catarina,* General Vitorino 240 (9); *Açores,* Rua dos Andradas 885 (20); *Motel Charrua,* BR 116, km. 3 (16); *Presidente,* Av. Salgado Filho 140 (14); *Scala,* Av. Júlio Castilhos 30/34 (13); *Henrique,* General Vitorino 182 (7); *Palácio,* Av. Vigário Josè Inácio 644 (7); *Metrópole,* Rua Andrade Neves 59 (12); *Laçador,* Rua Uruguai 330 (10); *La Plata,* Rua Jerônimo Coelho, good and cheap; *Glória* (central, clean, cheap), Trav. Araújo Ribeiro 187; *Hotel Lux,* Av. General João Mendel, just possible; *Casa dos Estudantes* (for those with student cards), corner of Av. Ipiranga and Getúlio Vargas, US$1 a night, with food, if there's room. The bus station is in a dubious part of town; the dubiety almost certainly extends to the cheap hotels nearby.

Camping Do Cocão, 10 km. out on Viamão road; Praia do Guarujá, 16 km. out on Av. Guaíba.

Restaurants (except on the *Everest Roof* and at the *Korote* and *Panarea* (US$5-10), the normal cost of dinner is US$3.50-5).   General: *Everest Roof,* Duque de Caxias 1357; *Le Bon Gourmet,* Hotel Plaza São Rafael; *Mosqueteiro,* Estádio Olímpico; *Martini,* Rua Leopoldo Fróes 126; *Rancho Alegre,* Cristóvão Colombo 2168, good gaúcho music; *Santa Teresa,* Av. Assis Brasil 2750; *Ritter Hotel; Zillerthal,* 24 de Outubro 905; *Panorâmico,* Correia Lima 1949; *Grumete,* 24 de Outubro 905; *Umbu,* Av. Farrapos 292; *Ipanema,* Av. Coronel Marcos 1645; *Korote,* Silva Jardim 16; *Executivo,* Hotel Alfred; *Ratskeller,* Cristóvão Colombo 1654; *City Hotel; Panarea,* Eça de Queirós 819; *Scherazade,* Av. Protásio Alves 3284; *Barranco,* Av. Protásio Alves 1578.

Chinese: *Palácio do Dragão,* Luciana de Albreu 471; *Gold Dragon,* Rua Dr. Valle 479; *Tai Seng Nhe,* Andradas 1097.

German: *Floresta Negra,* 24 de Outubro 905; *Germânia,* 24 de Outubro 945; *Franz,* Av. Protásio Alves 3250.

Portuguese: *Casa de Portugal,* João Pessoa 579; *Galo,* João Alfredo 904.

Italian; *Cantina do Peppe,* Getúlio Vargas 273; *Jardim Itália,* Av. Protásio Alves 3580; *Cantina Vila Romana,* Av. Carlos Gomes 1385.

Night Bars (beer and sandwiches, etc.) *Tivoli,* Av. Protásop Alves 766; *Hubertus,* Rua Professor Annes Dias 116; *Xuvisko,* Cristóvão Colombo 927; *Julius,* José de Alencar 480; *Bartok,* José de Alencar 173; *Barril,* Estádio International; *Bologna,* Av. Coronel Marcos 2359; *Dom Jayme,* Mostardeiro 112.

Discotheques Encoraçado Butekin; Baú; La Locomotive; Espantalho.

Electric Current 110-120 A.C. 50 cycles.

Festivals On February 2 is the festival of Nossa Senhora dos Navegantes, whose image is taken by boat from the central quay in the port to the industrial district of Navegantes.

Points of Interest The Jockey Club at which meets are held on Saturdays and Sundays; the Country Club (picturesque 18-hole golf course); the Parque Farroupilha, a fine park near the city centre; the Zoological Gardens near **São Leopoldo** (bus US$0.50; Hotel: *Rima,* US$12 double, standard) and the Cidade Universitária (University City) are well worth a visit. The 5-km. wide Guaíba River lends itself to every form of boating and there are several sailing clubs which frequently act as host to international sailing events. Porto Alegre is famous for its spectacular sunsets. The Museu Júlio de Castilhos has an interesting historical collection, and there is the Museu do Trem in the old railway station of São Leopoldo, built 1872 with material imported from England. Plays by local and visiting troupes at São Pedro (opposite Government Palace) and Leopoldina (Av. Independência), theatres. Modern cinemas. Pleasant boat ride round the lagoon from the dock on Rua Mauá, US$1. A good view of the city may be had from the Morro de Santa Teresa, approached from Av. Padre Cacique.

Rail The line from Porto Alegre W to (386 km.) Santa Maria (population 57,000) and then southwards to (595 km.) Santana do Livramento (64,000), on the borders of Uruguay, runs through the heart of the little-known cattle country. From Cacequi this line is continued westwards to Uruguaiana (75,000 people), a cattle town on the Argentine frontier 772 km. from Porto Alegre, and south-eastwards to Pelotas and Rio Grande. In December 1977 a tourist train service was inaugurated between Porto Alegre and Montevideo. There is no direct service to São Paulo but Dirk Partridge of Washington D.C. reports that it is possible, with overnight stops, to make the trip by local trains.

Buses Bus to Rio, US$25, 25 hours. Bus to Montevideo, US$18, 14 hours by Expresso Porto Alegre-Montevideo, Praça Rui Barbosa, or US$20, 11 hours, by the Uruguayan Onda service. There is a bus service to Buenos Aires (US$31.25). The new and excellent bus terminal has good facilities, including a post office. The road to Uruguaiana is now entirely paved, and there is a network of paved roads, with bus services, all over the State.

Air Services There are two commercial landing fields and a large modern international airport, Salgado Filho, 8 km. from the City. There are daily flights to Rio, São Paulo, Curitiba, Buenos Aires and Montevideo, and most other Brazilian cities. Vasp flies to Iguaçu and Brasília on Mon., Wed., Fri., and Sun. The airport is served by all Brazilian airlines, Pluna and Aerolíneas Argentinas.

Bookshop Livraria Kosmos, Rua dos Andradas 1644 (international stock); Livraria Lima, Borges de Medeiros 539; Livaria Globo, Andradas 1416; airport bookshop.

Addresses

British Consulate, Edifício Bier & Ulmann, Rua Uruguai, 91, 5th floor. Caixa Postal 737. Tel.: 4-0589.

U.S. Consulate, Rua Uruguai 155, 11th floor.

British Club, Av. Carlos Gomes 534 (Montserrat).

Bank of London and South America Ltd., Rua General Câmara 243 (open 0930-1130 and 1230-1730).

Citibank, Rua 7 de Setembro (open 1300-1700).
Touring Club do Brasil, Av. João Pessoa, 623.
Cables Embratel, Rua Siqueira de Campos 1245. Tel.: 41233.

Excursions from Porto Alegre The best beach resorts of the area are to the north of the city. The towns of **Tramandaí** (126 km.) and **Torres** (209 km.) are the most popular, with lots of luxury (and more reasonable) hotels and motels, bars, restaurants, and other standard requisites associated with seaside resorts. There is no lack of cheap accommodation, but hotels tend to be very full during the summer season. There are fully equipped campsites at both towns, and camping is also allowed on some beaches.

Inland is the lovely Serra Gaúcha, the most beautiful scenery being around the towns of **Gramado** and **Canela.** The scenery is not unlike the Black Forest, and there is a distinctly Bavarian flavour to many of the buildings. In summertime the flowers are a joy to behold, but on the other hand in the winter there are frequently snow showers. This is excellent walking and climbing country among hills, woods, lakes and waterfalls. There are many excellent hotels at all prices in both towns, but it is difficult to get rooms in the summer. Local craftwork includes leather and wickerwork.

Gramado Hotels (prices in US dollars, in brackets, of lowest-price double rooms available): *Hortensias,* Rua Bela Vista 83 (25); *Serrano,* Costa e Silva 1112 (22); *Serra Azul,* Rua Garibaldi 151 (20); *Ritta Hoppner,* Rua Pedro Candiago 305 (14); *Letícia,* Rua Mons. Hipólito Constabili 707 (12); *Planalto,* Rua João Correia 550 (11).

Canela Hotel *Charrua,* Av. das Nações 351, US$23 d.

Camping Camping Clube do Brasil, 8 km. from Canela, near waterfall in Parque de Caracol.

Caxias do Sul, 122 km. from Porto Alegre, connected by regular buses, is the centre of the Brazilian wine industry. The population is principally of Italian descent, and it is an expanding and modern town. One should not miss the opportunity to visit the many "adegas" for free wine-tasting in this town, and the neighbouring towns of Farroupilha, Bento Gonçalves and Garibaldi. Caxias do Sul's festival of grapes is held in February-March every three years; the last was held in 1978. The church of São Pelegrinó has paintings by Aldo Locatelli and sculptured (by Augusto Murer) 5 m. high bronze doors.

Hotels *Alfred Palace,* Rua Sinimbu 2302, US$20 d; *Itália,* Av. Júlio de Castilhos 3076, US$18 d; *Real,* Rua Marquês de Herval 606, US$12 d; *Alfred,* Rua Sinimbu 2266, US$11 d; *Samuara,* 10 km. out on RS-25, US$25 d. Many others.

Camping Municipal campsite, 4 km. out on Rua Cons. Dantas; *Palermo,* 5 km. out on BR 116 at km. 118; *Belvedere Nova Sonda,* 38 km. out in the district of Nova Pádua.

On the road north, 112 km. from Porto Alegre, is **Osório,** a pleasant town near sea and lakes, with a good cheap hotel, *Big Hotel,* US$6 d.

Rio Grande, at the entrance to the Lagoa dos Patos, was founded in 1737 as a fortified port and town by the Portuguese, then skirmishing with the Spaniards of Uruguay. The town lies on a low, sandy peninsula 16 km. from the Atlantic Ocean. To-day it ranks fifth in importance amongst the major ports of Brazil and is the distributing centre for the southern part of Rio Grande do Sul. Its cattle and meat industries, though less impressive than formerly, are still important, and there are also woollen, jute and cotton mills, factories turning out canned goods, fisheries and a large oil refinery. Population, 140,000. Its roads and pavements are very bad.

During the latter half of the 19th century, Rio Grande was also an important social centre. Many rich German and British merchants lived in relative luxury in their large comfortable homes and clubs. But they were lured away to the rising Porto Alegre and today Rio Grande is an active if rather poor town, notable for the charm of its old buildings.

Its main exports—rice, soya beans and other cereals—reflect the agricultural nature of the southern part of the state. There are good shipping services, and numerous tankers call to discharge crude oil.

Hotels *Charrua,* Rua Duque de Caxias 55 (recommended for good value), US$15 d; *Paris,* Rua Mar. Floriano 112, US$9 d.

Restaurants *Haiti* (Italian); *Pescal,* for fish; *Buffet Costa,* good food, with music.

Boat Trip By boat across mouth of Lagoa dos Patos, to pleasant village of São José do Norte.

Cables Embratel, Rua Andrade Neves 94. Tel.: 196.

British Vice-Consul.

Communications by railway to the hinterland. Frequent daily buses to and from Pelotas (56 km.), Bagé (280 km.), Santa Vitória (220 km.), and Porto Alegre (300 km.).

Excursions To **Cassino,** a popular seaside resort on the Atlantic Ocean, 24 km., over a good road. The breakwater, through which all vessels entering and leaving Rio Grande must pass, is a major tourist attraction. Very good fishing.

Hotels *Atlântico,* Av. Rio Grande, US$12 d; *Cassino,* Av. Rio Grande, US$18 d. Private campsite on Avenida 33, on the way out to Rio Grande. Camping Clube do Brasil site near town.

Pelotas, the second largest town in the State of Rio Grande do Sul, is on the left bank of the River São Gonçalo which connects the Lagoa dos Patos with the Lagoa Mirim. Its proximity to the port of Rio Grande (56 km.), to which there is a railway and a road, has hindered the development of its own port. Pelotas is a flat town of traditional one-storey buildings but with a cluster of skyscrapers right in the centre. It is prosperous, with an array of shops and gracious parks. It draws its prosperity from its location between the flatlands of the coast and the fertile hinterland of the Serra de Cangussu. Rice and meat are its mainstays; there are many tanneries, flour mills and other industries linked with agriculture, and the Frigorifico Anglo has a large plant on the river. Like Rio Grande, it is rather damp, but Rio Grande is a better place for the tourist to stay at. Population: 250,000.

Within a radius of 60 km., say an hour's drive, there are numerous excursions into the hilly, pretty and quiet countryside. Simple and clean accommodation and cheap, good and plentiful food can be found on the farms of settlers of German descent.

Hotels *Curi Palace,* Gen. Neto 1279, US$25 d; *Curi,* Gen. Osório 719, US$17 d; *Estoril,* Rua Gen. Osório 718, new, a/c, reasonable at US$16 d; *Tourist Parque,* motel-type, 7 km. south on the BR 116, US$15 d; *Rex,* Praça Pedro Osório 205, US$10 d; *Grande,* Praça Pedro Osório 51, old, some rooms with electric shower, US$7 d; *Germano,* next bus station, owner speaks some German, US$6 d.

Camping 60 km. out at the Arco Iris waterfall, no facilities; *Cascata,* 25 km. out on the Cangussu road.

Restaurant Tyrolean restaurant, opposite *Rex,* excellent, cheap.

Communications Plane a day to Porto Alegre. Frequent daily buses to Porto Alegre (4 hours, paved road); Rio Grande, 75 min. (paved but in poor condition); Jaguarão, on frontier with Uruguay (earth); and inland to Bagé and other towns. The road to the Uruguayan frontier at Chuy (paved), has international bus service. If travelling by car, buy as much gasoline as possible in Uruguay. Bus to Buenos Aires (*via* Uruguaiana), US$13. Railway to Rio Grande, Bagé and Jaguarão (change there for Montevideo).

---

386 km. NE of Porto Alegre is the small fishing port of **Laguna** *(Hotel Imbituba),* in southern Santa Catarina, and another 32 km. to the north is the port of **Imbituba,** well served by both road and railway. Imbituba sends all the coal mined in the area between Araranguá and Tubarão in coastal vessels to Rio de Janeiro, where it is railed to the steel mills at Volta Redonda for coking. There are good beaches (swimming and fishing), and it has bus services to Porto Alegre and Rio de Janeiro.

At Laguna, which is now being developed as a wealthy seaside resort, is the Anita Garibaldi Museum, containing documents, furniture, and the personal effects of the Brazilian wife of the hero who helped to unify Italy. They both fought in the civil wars of Rio Grande do Sul and Uruguay and later in Italy between 1846 and 1849, when Anita died.

Forty-eight km. N of Laguna, on the Island of Santa Catarina, stands **Florianópolis,** capital of the state of Santa Catarina, on an island joined to the mainland by the longest steel suspension bridge in Brazil. It is a port of call for coastal steamers, 725 km. from Rio de Janeiro and 420 from Santos. The natural beauty of the island and bays are making Florianópolis a tourist centre; in this connection is seems a pity that the waterfront, scene of a traditional market, is being filled in and reclaimed. The older parts have narrow streets, and many of the older houses are typically Portuguese: pastel colours with white ornamentation like sugar icing. There are two museums, the Anthropological Museum at the Federal University and the Sambaqui Museum at the Colégio Catarinense, Rua Esteves Júnior. Population: 244,000.

Hotels *Florianópolis Palace,* Rua dos Ilhéus 26, new, best, US$30 d; *Querência,* good, Rua Jerônimo Coelho 1, US$15 d; *Royal,* Trav. João Pinto, US$18 d; *Oscar Palace,* Av. Hercílio Luz 90, US$15 d; *City Hotel,* Rua Emílio Blum 31, near bus station, US$8 d, friendly; *Lux* and *Dimas,* cheaper hotels around US$5 d.

Cables Embratel, Rua João Pinto 26. Tel.: 2014. Radional (interstate and international telephones).

Excursions To the Lagoa da Conceição for beaches, sand dunes, fishing, church of N.S. da Conceição (1730), boat rides on the lake.

Camping Camping Clube do Brasil, São João do Rio Vermelho, near the lake, 21 km. out of town. "Wild" camping allowed on Juremar beach, 18 km. out.

Communications Daily flights by Varig/Cruzeiro and Transbrasil to Porto Alegre and São Paulo. Regular daily buses to Porto Alegre and São Paulo and most other towns in the state. The main north/south highway (BR-116) runs through Lajes (360 km.), and from there are connecting buses to all parts of the country. The coastal highway (BR-101) is now much improved and is preferred as an alternative to the congested inland route.

Excursion Across the island at Barra da Lagoa is a pleasant fishing village and beach which can be reached by bus.

From Florianópolis a poor road runs SW inland *via S*ão Joaquim to **Lajes,** a convenient stopping place on BR-116 between Caxias do Sul and Curitiba. Despite the poor road, however, this journey is perhaps the most interesting in the State. The town is the customary Brazilian combination of a few skyscrapers ringed by somewhat decrepit-looking 50-year-old buildings. (*New Grande Hotel,* good, but no heat). Population, 129,000.

One hundred km. up the coast from Florianópolis by a paved road or by sea is the most important port in Santa Catarina:

Itajaí, at the mouth of the Itajaí river. It is well served by coastal and ocean-going vessels up to 5½ metres draught, and is the centre of an important surrounding and up-country district largely colonised by Germans and Italians. Main exports: lumber, starch, tapioca, sassafras oil, and tobacco. Population, 64,000.

Hotels *Balneário Cabeçudas,* at Cabeçudas beach, best, 6 km. out of town, US$20 d; *Grande,* Rua Felipe Schmidt 44, good value, US$15 d; *Maringá,* N of town, friendly cheap and clean, with Shell service station next door, providing good food, open all night.

Buses to Blumenau, Florianópolis, Joinville and Curitiba.

Airport Daily by Varig, Cruzeiro do Sul to São Paulo.

There is a 61 km. paved road to **Blumenau** (population, 100,000), 47 km. up the Itajaí river. It is an active town in a prosperous agricultural and manufacturing district settled mostly by Germans; important activities include tobacco growing and textile manufacture. See German immigrant museum, Av. Duque de Caxias 78, open every day.

Excursions Boat trips down the Itajaí River, daily in season, Sat. and Sun. out of season. To Pomerode, typical German village, 32 km. on gravel highway.

Hotels *Himmelbleu Palace,* Rua 7 de Setembro 1415, US$20 d; *Garden Terrace,* Rua Pe. Jacobs 45, US$20 d; *Grande Hotel,* Al Rio Branco 21, US$20 d; *Glória,* Rua 7 de Setembro 954, US$18 d (all aforementioned hotels have heating in rooms); *Mering Plaza,* heating and a/c; *Paraíso dos Poneis,* motel 9 km. out of town on the Itajaí road, US$18 d; *Rex,* Rua 7 de Setembro 640, US$18 d; *Geranium,* Rua Uruguai 266, US$15 d; *Hotel Central,* same building as bus station, US$6 d. clean, but noisy. *Rodoviário,* Rua 7 de Setembro, at bus station, German run, delightful, US$18 d. Most hotels and restuarants exceptionally clean.

Camping Municipal campsite, 2 km. out on Rua Pastor Osvaldo Hesse; Paraíso dos Poneis, 9 km. out on the Itajaí road; Refúgio Alpino, 11 km. out on Rua da Glória.

Restaurants Good German food at *Frohsinn* (panoramic view) and *Barril de Ouro;* international eating at *Moinho do Vale.*

To Iguaçu We have received from Gerry Monahan and Gary Rubkin an interesting account of a bus journey from Blumenau to Iguaçu by mostly unpaved roads, through rich and interesting farming country. They stopped at Joaçaba, a town of German immigrants (8 hours by bus), Erechim (6 hours by bus, *Hotel Rex,* US$4 d, strong gaúcho influence), **Iraí** (6 hours by bus, Italian immigrant area, town with thermal springs, *Hotel São Luís,* US$10 d, with full board, town good for semi-precious stones), and Pato Branco (8 hours by bus, immediate connection to Cascavel for Iguaçu).

São Francisco do Sul, 80 km. up the coast (population 15,000) is the port for the town of Joinville, 35 km. inland at the head of the Cachoeira river. It is well worth a visit; it has some attractive colonial architecture around the main square; there are some excellent beaches nearby such as Ubatuba and Cápri. (At weekend trips to Ilha do Farol in port's supply boat.) Petrobrás oil refinery. The *Restaurante Franciscano,* on the Praia dos Coqueiros, is recommended, so is the *Metralhas.*

Joinville, the state's second largest town (population, 220,000), lies 2 km. from the main coastal highway—BR 101—which makes road transport between Joinville and the southern cities a question of one hour (Itajaí, Blumenau) or two hours (Florianópolis); Curitiba is less than two hours away by the same excellent highway. Local trips can be made to the port of São Francisco do Sul (see above). Other beaches are only an hour away by car.

Joinville is a quiet town (hot in summer) with strong German ties; see the Museum of History in the Prince of Joinville's mansion, which has a collection of objects from the original German settlement. The Archaeological Museum has a very interesting pre-Columbian collection of the Sambaquis period.

Joinville no longer concentrates its energies on the export of raw materials. It is the major industrial city in Santa Catarina state, producing automobile parts, refrigerators, plastic goods and textiles, apart from several foundries. The industry does not, however, spoil the considerable charm of this city.

Hotels *Colón Palace,* Rua São Joaquim 80, US$25 d; *Joinville Palace,* Rua do Príncipe 142, US$15 d; *Anthurium Parque,* Rua São José 226, US$20 d, Colonial style, good value; *Ideal,* Rua Jerônimo Coelho 98, US$10 d; *Fiedler,* Rua Jerônimo Coelho 188, US$10 d.

Camping Camping Clube do Brasil, Municipal Park, 1 km. out, Tel.: 5996.

Restaurants *Petisqueira Pinheiro,* Rua 7 de Setembro, is well worth a visit for excellent fish and shrimp dishes for about US$4. For meat or German specialities, *Churrascaria Rex, Familiar, Bierkeller,* Rua 15 de Novembro 497, or the more expensive *Tannenhof* (Rua Visconde de Taunay 340); *Dietrichs,* Rua Princesa Isabel, excellent beer and German food.

Banks Bank of London and South America, Rua Eng. Niemeyer 87; Banco do Brasil. Open 1000-1630.

Air Service Airport 5 km. from city. Daily flights to major cities.

Excursions There is no river passenger boat between Joinville and São Francisco do Sul, but four daily buses go on to Ubatuba beach, a week-end resort.

Curitiba, capital of Paraná state (pop. 800,000), is a modern city with a faint European flavour at 900 metres on the plateau of the Serra do Mar. It still has large remnants of the German, Italian, Polish and Slav settlers who founded it, and into the melting pot, more recently, have come Syrians and Japanese. It has three universities. The commercial centre is busy Rua 15 de Novembro, with its banks, shops, and coffee bars. There is a pedestrian area along the Rua das Flores, where there are Sat. morning painting sessions for children. Art market Sat. morning Praça Zacarias, and on Sun. morning at Praça Garibaldi, beside attractive Rosário church. A striking complex (though not to all tastes) is the Civic Centre at the end of Avenida Dr. Cândido de Abreu, 2 km. from the city centre: a monumental group of five buildings dominated by the Palácio Iguaçu, headquarters of the State and municipal governments. In a patio behind it, is a relief map to scale of Paraná. In contrast is the old municipal government building in French Art Nouveau style, now housing the Museu Paranaense (free, afternoons only, recommended), in Praça Generoso Marques. Nearby, on Praça Tiradentes, is the Cathedral (1894) inspired by the Cathedral of Barcelona, Spain. The most popular public park is the Passeio Público, in the heart of the city; it has a small zoo, a network of canals with small boats, and an aquarium containing many species of tropical fish, all well named and their habitat given. Near the shores of Lake Bacacheri on the northern edge of the city is an unexpected Egyptian temple. There are three modern theatres, the Guaíra for plays and revues, the one for concerts and ballet, and the Teatro Paiol in the old arsenal. Nearby is the Santa Felicidade district, which is mainly Italian, with good eating places. Many of the main streets have been widened and the town is being rapidly transformed.

Highways connect the city with all the most important towns in the S of Brazil, including Londrina and Maringá in the coffee belt in the N of the State.

Transport Passenger trains to São Paulo and Porto Alegre (both direct) and to Paranaguá (see next page). Frequent buses to São Paulo and Rio de Janeiro. By paved (but narrow and twisting) 402 km. BR-116 road to São Paulo takes 7 hours. Buses to Buenos Aires, US$31.25; to Foz do Iguaçu, 6 buses a day, 12 hours, US$7.40. New combined bus and railway station, very efficient; short distance bus services (up to 40 km.), begin at old bus station at Rua João Negrão 340. If travelling by car to Porto Alegre or Montevideo, the new coastal highway (BR-101) is preferable to the inland road (BR-116). Trains can still be taken to Mafra, Ourinhos, Ponta Grossa, Rio Branco do Sul, Roca Nova and Paisauna, though not necessarily every day.

Museums The Museu Paranaense, Praça Generoso Marques, relics from the past, open afternoons, free. Museu David Carneiro, on Rua Brigadeiro Franco, by permission.

Councils Centro Cultural Brasil-Estados Unidos; Sociedade Brasileira de Cultura Inglesa; British Council, Rua General Carneiro 679 (Caixa Postal 505).

Hotels

Name	Address	Single (US$)	Double (US$)	Rooms	Heat	Category*
Caravelle Palace	Rua Cruz Machado 282		30	100	yes	1+
Iguaçu	R. Cândido Lopes 102		30	200	yes	1
Mabu	Praça Santos Andrade 830	18	25	109	yes	S
Colonial	R. Com. Araujo 99		22	95	yes	S
Lancaster	R. Voluntários da Pátria 91		20	106	no	T
Del Rey	Ermelino de Leão 18		25	154	yes	S
Ouro Verde	R. Dr. Murici 419		25	90	yes	S+
Guaíra Palace	Praça Rua Barbosa 537		20	108	yes	T
Eduardo VII	Rua Candido Leão 15		20	163	no	T

*1—first class; S—standard; T—tourist.

Charrua Motel, BR-116, km. 389, exit for São Paulo, pool, heated rooms, US$20 d; *Tourist Universo,* Praça Gen. Osório 63, US$15 d; *Climax,* Rua Dr. Murici 411, good value, popular, US$13 d; *Braz,* Av. Luis Xavier 65, US$13 d; *Regência,* Rua Alfredo Buffern 40, US$10 d; *Cacique,* Rua Tobias Macedo 26, US$10 d. Lots of cheap hotels around new railway/bus station; *Joçoaba,* Rua João Negrão 340, on site of old bus station, US$8 d. *Rheno,* Praça Carlos Gomes, US$9 d. Hotels near railway/bus station are also close to wholesale market, which operates noisily through the night. They include the *Mauá,* US$11 d, good breakfast; *Imperial,* US$10 d.

Camping Official site 7 km. N of city, on São Paulo road, US$1 a night. Camping Clube do Brasil, 16 km. out on same road to São Paulo.

Restaurants at the *Tourist Universo* and *Iguaçu* hotels. Foreign food at the *Emir* (Arab); *Pinheirão* (meat dishes); *Mouraria* (Portuguese); *Ile de France* (French); *Bavaria* and *Frau Leo* (German); *Matterhorn* and *Locanda Suiça* (Swiss); *Lido* (Chinese), near Praça Osório. Lunch at *Nino's,* on 20th floor of a building near Praça Carlos Gomes, for grand views. *Commercial Club,* Rua 15 de Novembro; *TempO,* Rua Mar. Deodoro, good; good feijoada at *Del Rey* on Saturdays. Local food and red wine in nearby Santa Felicidade. Sukiyaki at *Restaurant Vemura,* near Cine Arlequin; on the Rua Vicente Machado, *The Silver Dragon* (Chinese; good). *Paláchio,* Barão Rio Branco, is all-night restaurant, good food and cheap; cheap food also near old railway station. Students can eat at University canteen (student cards required).

Electric Current 110 v. 60 cycles.

Bank of London and South America Limited, Rua 15 de Novembro 317, and national banks. Open: 0900-1700. Best exchange rates at Jade travel agency, Rua des Flores.

Cables Embratel, Galeria Minerva, Rua 15 de Novembro.

Local Holidays Ash Wednesday (half-day); Maundy Thursday (half-day); September 8 (Our Lady of Light).

Excursions   A popular excursion is to the Iguaçu Falls. One Sunday a month the beautiful Ouro Fino estate (34 km.) is open to the public. **Vila Velha,** now a state park, is 97 km. from Curitiba off the road to Ponta Grossa: the sandstone rocks have been weathered into most fantastic shapes. There is a Camping Clube do Brasil site at Vila Velha, where it is possible to stop off on the way to Foz do Iguazu. The Park office is 300 metres from the highway and the park a further 1½ km. Bus, Vila Velha-São Paulo, US$4.50.

The Lagoa Dourada, surrounded by forests, is close by. Popular expeditions during the summer are by paved road or rail (3½ hours) to Paranaguá. Three trains a day (US$2.50) do the journey, the most spectacular in Brazil. The air-conditioned Litorina railcar leaves Curitiba on Sundays and some weekdays at 0810, returning in the afternoon; book well in advance. The slow train, leaving Curitiba at 0700 is cheaper and rarely crowded in 1st class; take seat on left side; unlike the Litorina, you can open the windows to see better. There are numerous tunnels, with sudden views of deep gorges and high peaks and waterfalls as the train rumbles over dizzy bridges and viaducts. You can also visit Antonina and Morrettes, two sleepy colonial towns which can be reached by rail and also by bus on the old Graciosa road, which is almost as scenic as the railway.

The chief port of the state of Paraná is

Paranaguá, one of the main coffee-exporting ports, founded in 1585, 268 km. south of Santos, lying by a lagoon-like harbour. The port is 29 km. from the open sea and is approached *via* the Bay of Paranaguá, dotted with picturesque islands; 28 shipping lines call regularly; steamer passengers go ashore by launch. The fort of Nossa Senhora dos Prazeres was built in 1767 on a nearby island; one hour's boat trip. The former Colêgio dos Jesuitas, a magnificent Baroque building, has been converted into a Museum of Archaeology and Popular Art. Other attractions are a 17th century fountain, the Church of São Benedito, and the shrine of Nossa Senhora do Rocio, 2 km. from town. There is an interesting market near the waterfront. Population, 62,500. Paranaguá is a free port for Paraguay.

The main products of the state, exported through Paranaguá, are coffee, erva-maté, pine, plywood, soya, hides, bananas, and paper. The new paved 116-km. road to Curitiba is picturesque, but less so than the railway, which offers one of the most beautiful journeys in Brazil.

Hotels *Santa Mônica,* Praia de Leste, 30 km. from town, on breach, US$18 d; *Líder,* Rua Julia da Costa 169, US$15 d; *Anexo,* Rua Correira de Freitas 110, US$10 d.

Restaurants *Abud; Bobby's.* Various types of fish, shrimps and oysters are recommended. *Danúbio Azul* is expensive. A very good T-bone steak (without refinements) at *Churrascaria Cacique.*

Air Services Curitiba airport.

Excursions   To Matinhos, Caiobá and Guaratuba, three seaside villages, and to Praia de Leste (hotel and campsite) and popular seaside resorts in the state (30 minutes by road). By special Diesel train, called Litorina, to Curitiba, the capital of Paraná state (see above). Cruises on Paranguá

Bay by launch, daily from Cais do Mercado. Also boat trips to Ilha do Mel.

About 117 km. beyond Curitiba the road and railway from Paranaguá (the road passes Vila Velha—see page 285) reaches

Ponta Grossa, a town of 127,000, at 895 metres. It exports much erva-maté and timber through its ports, Paranguá and Antonina. Other products are tobacco, rice, bananas, and dried beef, and it now calls itself the "World Capital of Soya". A road and a railway run north through Apucarana (Camping Club site) and Londrina to São Paulo, and south to Rio Grande do Sul and the Uruguayan border.

Hotels *Vila Velha Palace,* Rua Balduino Taques 123, US$10 d; *Planalto Palace,* Rua 7 de Setembro 652, plain and clean, US$15 d; *Gravina,* Rua Cor. Bittencourt 92, US$10 d. Cheaper hotels: *Scha Fransky,* US$9 d, very good breakfast; *Luz,* bargain, near railway station.

Camping Camping Clube do Brasil, 26 km. out at the entrance to Vila Velha.

Restaurant *Chopin,* for excellent Churrascos.

In Alto-Paraná in the extreme NW of the state, connexions have traditionally been with São Paulo rather than with Curitiba. Large new centres of populations have risen in a short time. In 1930 four Japanese and two Germans arrived in **Londrina.** Today it is a city with skyscrapers, modern steel and glass cathedral, wide streets and 300,000 people. (*Hotel Coroados,* US$10 d, standard; *Hotel Aliança,* nr. bus station, US$6 d, very clean, good breakfast.) **Maringa,** 80 km. W of it, founded in 1947, already has 80,000 people, half of them Japanese. They are in the heart of the coffee district—Londrina has a large soluble coffee factory—and to them from Curitiba now runs the paved 480-km. 2-lane Coffee Highway. Further to the W again is the important town of **Paranavaí,** where the subsoil is so brittle that the W side of town bids fair to roll gradually down into the river valley.

Best local guide for the south of Brazil is "Quatro Rodas Guia do Sul", in Portuguese and English, at sale by newspaper vendors throughout the country. Includes a first-class map, hotels, restaurants and points of interest.

The North-East

The nine states of the north-eastern bulge of Brazil are best considered as an entity. They cover 2.6 million square km. and contain a third of Brazil's people. The birthrate is the highest in Brazil, but over large areas 60% of the children die before they reach their first birthday. The average life expectancy of its 35 million people is 28: for all Brazil it is 56. Illiteracy is about 50% but reaches 96% in the more feudal backward parts of the interior. The average annual income from subsistence farming is deplorably low. But despite the misery, both regional and state loyalty remain ineradicable. The North-East's able leaders and writers exert a strong influence in Brazil.

There was a brief period of colonization by a northern country in the NE, when the Dutch West India Company, based at Recife, controlled some seven captaincies along the coast. They gained control in 1630, when Portugal was captive to Spain. After 1640, when Portugal freed itself, the Portuguese colonists fought the Dutch and finally expelled them in 1654.

The nine states are Bahia, Sergipe, Alagoas, Pernambuco, Paraíba, Rio Grande do Norte, Ceará, Piauí, and Maranhão. They by no means form a homogenous unity, but may be roughly divided into two contrasting parts. There are the sugar lands of the deep, dark red soil along the coast between Salvador da Bahia and Natal; they are mostly worked by blacks and mulattos for the white plantation owners, and the rainfall can be depended upon. The other north-east is the interior, the sertão, in Rio Grande do Norte, Ceará, Piauí, Paraíba and part of Maranhão. Rainfall here cannot be depended upon; it is irregular and there are periodic droughts and floods; the soil is sandy and hard; only 4% of the rainfall trickles into the soil; there is a little agriculture where water allows it but the herding of cattle is more important. There are few blacks in the interior; the inhabitants are mostly of Portuguese-Indian stock, one of the most distinctive in Brazil. They are known as the *flagelados,* the whipped ones.

When there is rain, food in the zone is plentiful and varied. Manioc is a basic food; in addition, there are goat's milk and cheese, beef, beans, and sweet potatoes; and though the diet lacks fruit, the inhabitants are hardy, capable of prolonged physical effort and able to withstand disease. But in the years of drought, when the hot dry winds from Africa scorch the earth, the effects can be tragic: first, the auxiliaries fail, and eventually there is a shortage of the basic foods. The inhabitants are reduced to sharing with their cattle a cactus-like scrub. The river beds are dusty tracks, the wells dry up, famine stalks the land, and half the children under the age of one die. When their cattle perish and then only, migration towards the coast and the southern towns begins, and they are then exposed to castigation of yet another sort: human exploitation by private labour contractors. But at the first news that there is rain, the exiled north-easterner heads for home. Brazil is his country, any part of it; but the North-East is where his heart is.

The three export crops of the north-east are sugar, cotton and cacao. Sugar has long been in decline, and now São Paulo, Minas Gerais, Rio de Janeiro and the southern states grow two-thirds of the Brazilian total. Cotton, which requires less rain than sugar, is grown on 27% of the total cultivable area inland from the sugar zone and in the sertões and yields 24% of the gross income. In this also the North-East has been successfully challenged by the southern states: São Paulo now produces half the Brazilian crop. But cacao is grown almost entirely in southern Bahia, inland from the port of Ilhéus.

The cultivators of the sugar lands are more or less permanently attached to their land. This is less true of the cotton area. There the great landowners are primarily cattlemen, allowing nomadic tenants to clear their land of brush and to plant cotton, but only so as to turn it into pasture. There is in the North-East, as in southern Rio Grande do Sul, a very great difference between the lives and character of the cattlemen of the interior and the cultivators in the coastal zone. The boundary between them is slowly moving westwards and encroaching upon the sertão.

The less important economic resources of the North-East are carnaúba wax, babaçu, coconuts, oiticica oil, agave (sisal), salt, and goat skins. Brazil's main oilfields are in the State of Bahia; there are also offshore wells in the coastal waters of Alagoas, Sergipe and Rio Grande do Norte.

The abrupt rise of the Great Escarpment from the sea is ended at Salvador, in Bahia; north of Salvador the rise from the coast to the interior is gradual. The highland is from 300 to 450 metres high in northern Bahia, but rises to only about a hundred metres in Ceará.

South of Cape São Roque there is abundant rainfall, but in Pernambuco the zone of ample rain stretches only 80 km. inland, though it deepens southwards. São Luís in Maranhão also gets plenty of rain, but between eastern Maranhão and Pernambuco lies a triangle, with its apex deep inland, where the rainfall is sporadic, and occasionally non-existent for a year. In this "area of calamity",—it suffers from floods as well as drought—the tropical forest gives way to the *caatinga*, or scrub forest bushes which shed their leaves during drought. In this area grows the palm that produces carnaúba wax and the tree which produces oiticica oil.

Cities of the North-East

Salvador is the capital of Bahia state and the fifth city of Brazil. The BR-116 to Rio, 1,659 km., is paved throughout. A new coastal road, the BR-101, reaches Salvador but is not yet paved throughout. From Salvador there are only local train services, though the tracks are continuous to Rio; the nearest inter-city service leaves from Iacu, 260 km. from Salvador (Belo Horizonte train Friday).

Motorists to Rio can do the trip easily (if not comfortably) in 3 days, stopping at Vitória da Conquista (524 km.), *Hotel Bahia,* US\$6.50 d, with huge meals; Teófilo Otôni (946 km.), *Hotel Everest,* US\$8 d, very nice; *Metrópole, Lancaster* and *Beira Rio,* all US\$9 d; or Governador Valadares (1,055 km.), *Hotel São Francisco,* US\$6 d, clean and good value; and Leopoldina (1,402 km.). There are also various motels; two are at km. 1,076, at Vitória da Conquista; and km. 1,470, at Feira de Santana; also between Feira and Salvador. Fairly good hotels are also available in Jequié (*Itajubá, Rex,* and motels), and basic ones in Milagres.

Salvador is a good city to slow down in and relax on the beaches nearby or in Itaparica. The tempo is much slower than in Rio; there is less traffic, confusion, and bustle. Brazilians pour in for their holidays. It rains all the year, but the main rainy season is between April or May and September, when it may drizzle for a week or be absolutely clear, fresh, cool and sparkling.

Salvador's population is about 1,050,000. It was founded in 1549, and was till 1763 the capital of Brazil. Many of its 70 churches, the fortifications, and some other buildings date from the 17th and 18th centuries. The city is divided into two, the Baixa (or lower part), and the Alta (or higher part), on a small plateau some 60-odd metres above the lower city and overlooking the sparkling bay. The commercial quarter, the picturesque market near Praça Cairu, and the old port are in the lower city. The older parts of the upper city, from the Praça Terreiro de Jesus to beyond the Carmo church, are now a National Monument. A new administrative centre is being built on the outskirts.

Salvador is the main centre of the tobacco trade, and is famous for its excellent mild cigars. It also has large exports of castor seed, coffee, hides, waxes, piassava and sisal fibres. There is a small oil refinery at Mataripe, across the bay, serving the nearby oilfields of the Recôncavo area. There is a cement plant and several cigar and cigarette factories. The new industrial centre is at Aratu and at Camaçari nearby a petrochemical centre is under development.

The Government buildings, shopping districts, hotels, and residential quarters are in the upper city, reached from the lower by motor roads and four public lifts close to the Customs House. The Lacerda lift gives passengers à 71-metre lift from Praça Cairu in the lower city to Praça Municipal in the upper. Here are the Government Palace and the Biblioteca Municipal (1811); a steep road runs from the Customs House to Largo dos Aflitos, just behind the Governor's Palace; it has been continued under a viaduct at Campo Grande square and on to the Canela Valley, where the University is. From Praça Municipal runs Rua Chile, with the best shops; the better hotels are in its further extension, Rua 7 de Setembro, which continues along the Atlantic coast as Av. Presidente Vargas.

Steep motor roads ascend to the upper city, where interesting drives can be taken along the Avenida, across Praça Castro Alves, past the São Bento Church (rebuilt after 1624 but with fine 17th century furniture), the Instituto Geográfico e Histórico, São Pedro Fort (1646-1877), and the fine Praça 2 de Julio (also known as Campo Grande), with its column. At Campo Grande square (magnificently lit at night) is the Castro Alves theatre, now reopened after a fire. The route can be continued past the British Club (the sea side of Campo Grande at Rua Banco dos Ingleses 20), the Legislative Assembly, the Vitória and the Graça church (rebuilt 1770), down the Barra hill, past forts and the lighthouse, at the bar, to Avenida Oceânica and along the sea front to the very pleasant residential area of **Rio Vermelho.** On Av. Oceânica, half-way to Rio Vermelho, there is a Zoo in the Botanical Gardens at **Ondina,** and a restaurant at the top of Ondina Hill, overlooking the sea. A road between Rio Vermelho and the airport, 32 km. from the city, runs picturesquely by the sea for 13 km. before turning inland to the airport. (Take bus No. 101 from Praça da Sé to the airport.) Some of the best hotels, including the *Meridien,* the *Othon Palace* and the *Salvador Praia,* are at Ondina and Rio Vermelho, and beyond at Pituba.

Near this turning is the lovely palm-fringed beach of **Itapoan** (primitive restaurants, with good sea food), where the traditional fishing rafts (jangadas) may be seen. There is a Camping Clube do Brasil campsite on the beach, near the lighthouse. Quite near is the dark-green freshwater lake of Abaeté, circled by brilliant white sand dunes.

Many of the old forts are worth looking at, though most are closed to the public. One of them (1723) is next door to the *Hotel da Bahia.* Another is by the beach at Barra, where you can choose between bay and ocean bathing. One of the forts that is open to the public is that of São Marcelo in front of the Mercado Modelo. The best bathing inside the bay that can be easily reached from the city is at Itapagipe, near the Bomfim church, but bathing inside the bay is not really recommended.

Near the older churches are still grouped untouched Colonial mansions and dwellings (especially in the Rua Gregório Mattos), some with heavily carved doors. The early sugar planters of Salvador poured their fortunes into the building of churches. A number of them, built in a Brazilian version of the baroque, are worth seeing; particularly the church of the monastery of São Francisco de Assis for its sculptures in wood, and the cloisters of the monastery for its excellent tiles and its paintings; the church (1701) of the Ordem Terceira (the Franciscan Third Order), next door to São Francisco, for its rich façade and, within, a quite remarkable Chapter House (1430-1730 weekdays, 0830-1130 Saturdays) with striking images of the Order's most celebrated saints; the Cathedral (Terreiro de Jesus, upper city), for its general design, coloured marble and inlaid furniture; Santa Casa de Misericórdia (late 17th century), for its high altar and painted tiles; the Convent of Santa Teresa (for the gate and the tiles in the floor of the kitchen); the 18th century church and monastery of Nossa Senhora do Carmo, for its altar and stalls and statues in the sacristy. A comparison of these churches with a number of simpler and smaller 18th century churches in the city will well repay study. One of them is the Church of Our Lord of Bomfim on the Itapagipe peninsula in the suburbs. It draws an endless number of supplicants (particularly on Fridays and Sundays) offering favours to Our Lord of Bomfim set over the high altar. The small open space in front of it is gay with vendors' booths and good-fortune seekers buying anything from a rosary to a lottery ticket. This festivity reaches its height each year at Epiphany. The processions coming to the church in boats and canoes decorated with flowers are particularly interesting.

Once a year the image of Our Lord of Seafarers sets out from a church on the waterfront at Boa Viagem, on a launch with a winged guardian angel at the prow, and oarsmen in white and blue plying oars row him (followed by an escort of boats and canoes) as far as the Church of Santo Antônio da Barra, where the procession sets out on the return voyage. Upon arrival at the beach of Boa Viagem the statue is then welcomed by the priests in splendid raiment and taken back into the church. Takes place usually on Jan. 1. (See also under Local Holidays, page 292.)

Markets   Mercado Modelo, at Praça Cairu, lower city, very picturesque, tourist items such as wood carvings, silver-plated fruit, local musical instruments. Bands and dancing, especially Sat. afternoons, closed at 1200 Sundays. Largest and most authentic is the Feira de São Joaquim, 5 km. from Mercado Modelo along sea front: barkers, trucks, burros, horses, boats, people, mud, all very smelly, every day except Sunday, busiest on Saturday morning; interesting African-style pottery and basketwork; very cheap. (Car ferry terminal for Itaparica is nearby.) Instituto Mauá, Av. 7 de Setembro 261, also sells handicraft items, but prices are fixed (unlike the markets). There is also a good gift shop at the Convento do Carmo museum.

Museums   The Museum of Contemporary Art, converted from an old church and warehouse off Av. Contorno, is only open for special exhibitions. The good restaurant (Solar do Unhão) is still there, and the buildings are worth seeing for themselves.

There is a remarkable Museum of Sacred Art in the 17th century monastery and church of Santa Teresa, at the bottom of the very attractive, steep Ladeira de Santa Teresa, in the Rua do Sodré 5. Many of the 400 carvings are from the Old World, but a number are local. Among the reliquaries of silver and gold is one of gilded wood by the great Brazilian sculptor Aleijadinho. Open 1000-1200 and 1400-1730, closed Sundays, US$0.40. Many of the treasures which used to be in an old mansion, the Casa de Calmon, Av. Joana Angélica 198, are here now. This important collection is well worth a visit. The Carmo Church has a museum with a collection of icons and Colonial furniture. Next door is a State museum which is architecturally notable and has period furnishings. Museu Costa Pinto, Av. 7 de Setembro 389, US$0.50 (1500-1900 except Tuesday) a magnificently restored house with collections of crystal silver, furniture etc. Museu de Arte da Bahia, Av. Joana Angélica, 189. Tue.-Fri. 0900, 1130 and 1400-1745, Sat.-Sun. 1500-1745. City Museum, Largo do Pelourinho (centre of old upper city), arts and crafts, entrance free, Mon.-Sat. 0800-1200. 1330-1600. Hydrographical Museum, Forte do Farol, free.

The Medical School's museum is now closed and its most famous exhibits, the severed heads of the bandit Lampião, his mistress and 8 of his followers, have been buried in a local cemetery.

On the outskirts of the city is the Museu do Recôncavo, in which one can find artefacts and pictures of three centuries of the economic and social life of this region. The Casa Grande e Senzala (the home of the landowner and the combined dwelling and working area of the slaves) is still intact. It is a peaceful way to spend an afternoon, away from the hectic city life of Salvador, but difficult to get to by public transport. The State Geological Museum is at the new Centro Administrativo.

Folklore Carnival in Salvador is particularly lively, with nearly everyone in fancy dress and dancing in the streets.

The Baianas—black women who dress in all the glory of their traditional costumes—add in particular to the colour of the city's life. Many of them are street vendors who sit behind their trays of delicacies, savoury and seasoned, made from the great variety of local fish, vegetables and fruits. Their cries are a unique feature of the city's quaint streets, especially when heard at the dead of night.

See at all costs the Capoeira, a dance developed from the traditional foot-fighting technique introduced from Angola by black slaves. The music is by drum, tambourine and berimbau; the beat is strong and gets faster and faster. If you want to master Capoeira, and many do, the best schools are in the Teatro Vila Velha behind the Governor's Palace, and in the very picturesque square known as the Largo do Pelourinho. Exhibitions take place in the Largo (cost: US$2). You can also see the experts practising outside the Mercado Modelo on Saturday mornings.

Candomblé, the local Africa-derived religion (counterpart of Rio's macumba) may be seen by tourists—but not photographed—on Sundays and religious holidays. Contact the tourist office, Bahiatursa, in the Mercado Modelo.

Centro Folclórico de Bahia, Praça Castro Alves 356 (at the side and behind the Cinema Guarani) has folklore shows every evening for less than US$1, beginning at 2100. Take your camera. Also Senac restaurant school, Largo do Pelourinho, has folk music every night.

Excursions There are ferries every hour (40-min. journey) from next to the Mercado Modelo (US$0.50) to the island of **Itaparica**, on the other side of the bay from the city; the car ferry leaves from São Joaquim at 1200, 1400 and 1600. It has good beaches, adequate hotels (*Grande Hotel de Itaparica*, by sea, and *Icaraí*, fair food, run by Sam, an expatriate Englishman) and many restaurants and bars, and a fort. From Bom Despacho, on the island, where the car ferry arrives, trips can be made to the picturesque small Colonial port of **Jaguaribe** and to Nazaré, with its market. Jaguribe can be reached by boat from the Mercado Modelo, leaving Thursday and Saturday and returning Friday and Monday.

The Companhia de Navegação Bahiana provides excursions in the ship *Bahia de Todos os Santos,* from near the Mercado Modelo. An excursion along the city front (Tue., Thur., Sat.), taking 3 hours, costs US$4.90; an all-day trip around the bay's islands, including a 3-hour stay at Itaparica, costs US$8 (Wed., Fri., Sun.). Bicycles for hire on Itaparica. Small boats for trips round the bay may be hired privately at the fishing port (Porto dos Saveiros) at the W side of the Mercado Modelo. There is also an excursion to all parts of the city accessible by boat.

Nazaré, inland from Itaparica, and reached over a bridge by bus from Bom Despacho, is a colonial town celebrated for its market, which specializes in the local ceramic figures, or *caxixis*. There is an especially large market in Holy Week, especially on the Thursday and Good Friday.

Mar Grande, which can be reached direct by ferry from the Mercado Modelo, is very unspoilt; "it could easily be in the middle of Africa, and even better are towns a little to the north; to rent a house for one month costs from US$15 to US$25" (Richard Solomons).

Another interesting excursion is to Feira de Santana, the scene of one of Brazil's largest markets (see page 295).

Local Holidays   Jan. 6 (Epiphany); third Sunday in January (Senhor de Bomfim); Ash Wednesday and Maundy Thursday, half-days; July 2 (Independence of Bahia); Oct. 30; Christmas Eve, half-day. An important local holiday is the Festa do Nosso Senhor de Bomfim, on the third Sunday in January, but the colourful washing or *lavagem* of the Bomfim church takes place on the preceding Thursday. The Festa da Ribeira is on the following Monday. The most colourful festival of all is run by the fishermen of the Rio Vermelho district on February 2; gifts for Yemanjá, Goddess of the Sea, are taken out to sea in a procession of sailing boats to the rhythm of Candomblé instruments. The Holy Week processions among the old churches of the Upper City are very colourful and interesting.

Mr. Bobby Benkert of the U.S. Peace Corps writes: "The pre-Carnival festive season begins the first week of December with the Festa da Conceição da Praia, centred on the church of that name at the base of the elevator. (December 8 is the last night—not for those who don't like crowds!) The last week of December is the Festa da Boa Viagem in the lower city; the beach will be packed all night on the 31st. On January 1 is the beautiful boat procession from Conceição da Praia to the church of Boa Viagem, on the beach of that name in the lower city; the leading boat, built in 1892, carries the archbishop and a big Christ image. You can follow in a sailing boat for about US$1; go early (0900) to dock by Mercado Modelo."

Tourist Office   Bahiatursa, Rua Marechal Floriano 1, in the Canela district (Tel.: 5-2150); also at corner of Mercado Modelo, Praça Cairu, lower city, at viewing platform at Praça da Sé, and at bus station. Visitors can obtain itineraries (on foot or by car) planned by the city, well worth doing. Good map for US$0.40. Also details of travel throughout State of Bahia, including boats on River São Francisco (see page 297).

Hotels   There are over 120 in the city and suburbs. Most of those away from the centre have swimming pools;

Name	Address	Price (US$) Single	Double
Meridien	Rua Fonte do Boi 216, Rio Vermelho	23.50	35.00
Bahia Othon Palace	Av. Presidente Vargas 2456, Ondina	27.00	32.50
Salvador Praia	Av. Presidente Vargas 2032, Ondina	21.00	28.00
Farol	Av. Presidente Vargas 68	18.50	22.50
Bahia	Praça Dois de Julho 2, Campo Grande	16.00	24.00
Grande da Barra	Rua Forte de São Diogo 2, Barra	16.50	23.00
Plaza	Av. Sete de Setembro 1839	12.50	18.00
Paulus	Av. Otávio Mangabeira, Pituba	17.50	22.00
Ondina Praia	Av. Presidente Vargas 2275, Ondina	17.50	22.50
Pousada do Carmo	Largo do Carmo 1	21.00	25.00
Praiamar	Av. Sete de Setembro 3577. Vitória	20.00	30.00
Vilha Velha	Av. Sete de Setembro 1971	13.50	17.50
Pelourinho	Rua Alfredo Brito 20	10.00	14.00
Barra Turismo	Av. Sete de Setembro 502	10.00	15.00
Palace	Rua Chile 20 *(recommended)*	8.00	12.00
Bahia de Todos os Santos	Av. Sete de Setembro 106 (Ladeira de São Bento)	11.00	19.00
Vila Romana	Rua Lemos Brito 14	11.50	18.00
Bahia do Sol	Av. Sete de Setembro 2009, Ondina	13.00	24.00

For people who like something out of the ordinary the *Pousada do Convento do Carmo*, in a newly converted monastery dating from 1580, colonial-type furniture and decoration, swimming pool, costs US$25 d.

Paraíso Hotel, Rua Demócrata 45, US$8 d. centre, good views, not too clean. *Hotel Chile*, Rua Chile 7, also with good views (cheap, US$9 d). *Caramuru Hotel*, Av. 7 de Setembro 258, no baths, very clean, US$6 s, US$11 d. *Hotel Benfica*, Rua Monte Alverne 6, near Praça da Sé, US$6 d, includes breakfast. *São José*, Travessa do Rosário 1, from US$4.50 s, US$10 d; *Roma*, 7 de Setembro 1013. Nearby, on Largo São Bento, is *Hotel São Bento*, US$4 s; *Colonial*, US$7.50 s, US$12 d, 7 de Setembro 2726 and *Solar da Vitório*, Largo da Vitória 7, US$7.50 s, US$14 d, near the Church of N.S. da Vitória, and the *Anglo Americana*, Av. Sete de Setembro 1838, across from the *Plaza*. *Hotel Granada*, Rua 7 de Setembro 512, US$4 p.p.; *Hotel Jequié*, Rua Saldanha de Gama, 14, US$4 p.p., with breakfast; *Hotel Miramar*, Rua Artur Catrambi 5 (1st and 2nd floors), near railway station, US$3 d; *Hotel Bella Vista*, Rua Ruy Barbosa, US$4.80 d, friendly and adequate; same street, *Hotel Paris*, US$4.25 s. *Hotel Cintra*, US$3.25 d. *Nova Esperança*, Ladeira das Hortas, friendly, US$3; *Solar São Francisco*, Praia Anchieta 16A, US$2.25, including breakfast, clean and friendly. *Hotel Guadalajara*, Ladeira de Santa Rita 2, across street from bus station, US$7.50 d. *Hotel Bomfim*, nearby, US$2 s. *Pensão* at Rua Independência 63, US$2 s; *Hotel Internacional*, "central, small, simple, clean and cheap", Rua Senador Costa Pinto 88, US$5.50 p.p.; *Pensão Amides*, Rua do Paraíso 330, friendly and clean, US$3 s. Cheap hotels near Terreiro de Jesus, upper city, e.g. *Império*, US$4 d, incl. breakfast. *Belamar*, Rua Tres de Maio 18, off Praça da Sé, US$3.50 d, good and clean. *Pensão Senhor do Bomfim*, Rua Monte Alverne, US$2, friendly. A huge Hilton hotel complex is being built 16 km. from the city, along the road to the airport. Youth Hostel at Barra, US$2.50-5, with breakfast, Av. Sete de Setembro 3513.

Restaurants Upper City: *Palace Hotel*, Rua Chile; *Cacique* (out-door), Praça Castro Alves; *Paris*, Campo Grande; *Pizzaria Guanabara*, Av. Marquês de Leão; *Pérez*, behind Governor's Palace, international food, view over bay; *Ondina Restaurant*, Ondina Hill; *Chez Bouillon*, Barra Hill, next to Yacht Club; *Chez Suzanne*, next to Forte São Diogo; *Taverna Romana*, Italian dishes, at Barra; *Churrascaria Alex*, Boca do Rio (half-way to the airport) on the road by the sea (serves only *churrasco*, or grilled steak). You can get a meal for US$2-3 at 2 restaurants near the *Hotel Bahia*: *Dona Flor*, on Travessa Corneta Lopes, and *La Pergola*, 7 de Setembro 329. *Dona Flor*, *Don Pasquale* (Av. Joana Angélica), and *Bela Nápoli*, nearby, are all Italian and fairly good. *The Mandarin*, on a cross street between Av. 7 de Setembro and Carlos Gomes 3, is Chinese and good, and so is *Tong-Fong*, Av. Joana Angélica 101, slightly dearer, highly recommended. *Solar do Unhão*, in modernized sugar-estate house off Av. do Contorno, right on the side of the bay, is excellent (closed Sundays). *Don Quichoppe*, Av. Carlos Gomes, US$1.50-3, good variety. *Casa de Gamboa*, Rua Newton Prado 51, old colonial home, regional food. *Cantina*, opposite cathedral, wholesome meal for under US$2; *Keutefrio*, Av. Sete de Setembro 379, excellent clean lanchonette, counter service only, closed Sunday. Senac runs a restaurant school at Largo do Pelourinho 19, serving 40 dishes including regional ones, US$4-6, recommended. Every evening at 2030, folk music.

Famous atmosphere and grand food for valiant stomachs at *Maria de São Pedro* and *Canafeu de Oxóssi*, over a shop in the market facing the port. The *Chez Bernard* (French food and grand view), small, on street below the Perce, is one of the city's best. A restaurant so exclusive that it does not advertise is *Casa Culinária*, at Av. Princesa Leopoldina 54, near the Portuguese hospital. Excellent French cuisine, though more expensive than average, at *Le Privé*, Av. 7 de Setembro 554, and *Le Bistroquet*, Rua Santos Dumont 9. Good churrascarias are *Carreta* at Av. Amaral Lins; *Las Palmas*, Rua Manuel Dias da Silva.

Bahian food is spiced and peppery, and some of the most famous cooks in Brazil have come from the region. Typical dishes are those which feature oysters, shrimps and crabs, as well as *Vatapá*, made from fish, rice, cashew-nuts, ginger, mint and parsley cooked in an earthenware dish and garnished with—and this is most important—*dendê* (palm) oil. Try these dishes at *Côco e Dendê*, corner of Av.

Princesa Isabel and Alameda Antunes (Barra district), or at *Novo Continental,* near foot of Lacerda lift in lower city. Good food on the streets from the Bahianas. Another good restaurant serving Bahian food is *O Jangadeiro,* Av. Otávio Mangabeira (at Pituba beach).

Camping Near the lighthouse at Itapoan, take 101 bus from Praça da Sé, about 1 hr., then ¾ hr. walk. Sea bathing is dangerous on seashore near campsite.

Electric Current 120-220 A.C., 60 cycles.

Taxis Taxi meters start at US$0.16 for the "flagdown" and US$0.06 per km. run. They charge US$2.50 per hour within city limits, and "agreed" rates outside.

Road North to Aracaju, 327 km., Maceió, Recife, João Pessoa and Natal (fully paved); to Penedo, 451 km., a 1-day drive if hard pressed. Hitching out of Salvador, take a "Cidade Industrial" bus from the bus station at the port; it goes on to the highway.

Buses to Recife, US$7.50, 12 hours twice daily; plenty to Rio (30 hours, US$18), São Paulo (30 hours), and south, Belo Horizonte at 2300. There is also a road open, with daily bus services to Brasília *via* Barreiras; we are told that this journey is rough; Barreiras-Brasília stretch mostly unpaved. The bus leaves at 2200, 36 hrs., US$18; the journey can be broken at Ibotirama on the River São Francisco; at Barreiras on the River Negro, where the bus stops for 2-3 hrs. *Hotel Vandelena,* US$8 full board; or at Posse (Goiás) to Paulo Alfonso, US$5.50. 10 hrs., leaving 0430, 2000, and 1910 on Sun., Wed. and Fri.

Bus Station 5 km. from city but regular services to centre; bus to Praça da Sé, such as No. 225, is best way to get to the hotel section. Air-conditioned bus service from Praça da Sé to Pituba and airport.

Plane To Brasília, daily, 2 hours; to Rio, about the same. Ipitanga airport is 32 km. from the city; taxis therefore expensive—about US$8. Bus No. 101 goes all the way between airport and city centre, or special taxi (buy ticket at airport desk) US$7.

Steamship Services The Spanish Ybarra from Europe are the only regular transatlantic ships to call. Passengers leave from Rio de Janeiro. National coastal steamers.

British Consulate Willdberger Building, 4th floor, Avenida Estados Unidos 108, Caixa Postal 91 (open 0800-1100).

American Consulate Rua da Grécia 8, 7th floor.

Cables Embratel, Av. Estados Unidos, near Mercado Modelo. Cia. Rádio Internacional do Brasil, Rua Miguel Calmon 41.

Bank of London and South America, Rua Miguel Calmon 22; Citibank, Av. Estados Unidos; Banco Holandês Unido, Praça da Inglaterra; and national banks. Open 0900-1630. Also exchange shops, e.g. next to Citibank.

British Club Campo Grande.

British Chamber of Commerce c/o British Consulate.

Ilhéus, in southern Bahia near the mouth of the Rio Cachoeira, 190 km. south of Salvador, serves a district which produces 65% of all Brazilian cacao, and shipping lines call regularly. A bridge links the Pontal district (where the airport is) to the mainland. Exports are cocoa, cocoa-butter, piassava, and timber. Population, 108,000. The town is the scene of the famous novel by Jorge Amado, "Gabriela, Clove and Cinnamon". The local beaches are splendid and the place is highly recommended for a short stay.

Hotels *Motel Barravento* on Malhado beach, Rua N.S. das Graças, in same street at 574 is *Hotel Panorama; Britânia,* Rua 28 de Junho 16, and at 29 the *San Marino Hotel; Avenida Hotel,* Av. Soares Lopes 508; *Hotel Central,* Araújo Pinho; *Ilhéus Hotel,* Praça Firmino Amaral 150; *Hotel Litorânea,* Rua Antônio Lavigne de Lemos 42; *Motel Cana Brava,* km. 6 on Ilhéus-Olivença road; *Real Hotel,* Rua General Câmara 102.

Buses run every 30 minutes along an asphalt road to **Itabuna** (32 km.; 120,000 people), the trading centre of the rich cacao zone. The town has over 20 hotels; the *Príncipe, Itabuna* and *Itabuna Palace* are probably the best.

Feira de Santana (190,000 people), 113 km. along the Rio road from Salvador, is the centre of a great cattle breeding and trading area; its Monday market, said to be the largest in Brazil, attracts a number of tourists and 20,000 Brazilians to its colourful display of native products. The two roads to Rio, BR-116 (inland) and BR-101 (coastal) diverge here.

Hotels *Luxor Pousada da Feira,* km. 1470 on BR-116; *Vips Hotel Restaurante,* Rua Visconde do Rio Branco 367; *Flecha Motel Feira,* km. 1067 BR-101 (US$10 d); *Hotel da Bahia,* Rua Visconde do Rio Branco, 562; and about 16 others.

There are some interesting old towns such as **Cachoeira** *Pousada do Guerreiro,* Rua 13 de Maio), **São Félix** and **Cruz das Almas** (tobacco centres) etc., S of Feira de Santana, and a new road (BR-101), now paved, has made access by car and bus very easy. When asphalted this road will make an attractive alternative to the main Rio-Bahia highway as far as Vitória da Conquista—it goes through very pretty country and gives one a sight of the older villages in the cacao growing district.

Monte Santo   About 270 km. N of Feira da Santana, *via* the direct BR-116 road to Fortaleza (as yet unpaved), is the famous hill shrine of Monte Santo in the dry Sertão, reached by 3½ km. of steps cut into the rocks of the Serra do Picaraça. This is the scene of pilgrimages and great religious devotion during Holy Week.

Hotel   At Euclides da Cunha, on the BR-116 and 39 km. from Monte Santo, is *Hotel Lua,* simple;

Buses   From Salvador *via* Euclides da Cunha, about 8 hours.

Aracaju, capital of Sergipe, 327 km. N of Salvador by paved road, and the biggest port between that city and Maceió, has a population of 184,000. It stands on the right bank of the Rio Sergipe, about 10 km. from its mouth, and can be reached by steamer from Maceió or Salvador, or from Salvador by road, 5-6 hours driving time, or by rail, very slow, 435 km. The town—unusual for Brazil—is laid out in the grid pattern. A 16-km. road leads to the beach.

Industries   Tanneries, cotton mills, coconut, sugar.

Products   Cotton, sugar, rice, coffee, vegetable oils, salt, and hides.

Hotels   *Palace,* new, in tall building; *Guanabara,* hot water in rooms, 13 de Maio, US$7 d, with breakfast.

Tourist Information   Ensetur, near the Praça Fausto Cardoso.

São Cristóvão, SW of Aracaju, on the road to Salvador, was the old state capital of Sergipe. Its Colonial churches and museum are well worth visiting.

Between Aracaju and the next port to the north—Maceió—is the mouth of the São Francisco river, whose great Paulo Afonso falls upstream (see page 297) can be visited from Maceió or (if travelling from Aracaju to Maceio by bus) from Penedo by river and bus.

Bus passengers from Aracaju to Maceió now ride along the fully-paved BR-101, crossing the São Francisco by bridge between Propriá and Porto Real do Colêgio. At **Penedo,** in Alagoas down the river, a surprisingly charming town, is *Hotel São Francisco* (US$18 d), the only first-class hotel in the NE outside the big cities. Long two-masted sailing vessels with red, yellow or white trapezoidal sails cruise on the river: a pretty sight.

Maceió, capital of Alagoas state, is about 287 km. N of Aracaju by road, and about 270 km. S of Recife, to which there is a railway (not to be recommended, an uncomfortable eight-hour journey) and two roads: the BR-101 federal highway through the interior and the more picturesque state highway partly along the impressively breautiful coastline, and partly through sugar-cane plantations. Bus services are operated on both routes, and the journey in both cases takes about 3¾ hours. It is mainly a sugar port, although there are tobacco exports handled also, with a lighthouse on an eminence built in a residential area of town (Farol), about one km. from the sea. The port is in the Jaraguá district. Population of Maceió is 350,000.

Maceió still has a colonial flavour. Some of its houses are colour-washed and roofed with red tiles. Two of its colonial buildings, the Government Palace and the church of Bom Jesus dos Mártires, are particularly interesting, as is the recently restored Metropolitan Cathedral. There is an enjoyable lagoon (Lagoa do Mundau), 2 km. out of town: excellent shrimp and fish at its small restaurants. It is a ten-minute taxi ride to Pajuçara beach, where there are several good restaurants, from the town centre. The beaches, some of the finest in Brazil (such as Jatiúca, Jacarecica, Guaxuma, Garça Torta, Riacho Doce, Mirante, all within 30 minutes taxi ride from town) have in most cases a protecting coral reef half a mile out. The fishermen and their jangadas (primitive sailing rafts) are interesting.

Hotels   *Luxor,* Av. Orlando Araújo 2076, first class, US$27 d; *Beira Mar,* Av. Duque de Caxias 1994, first class; *Beiriz,* Rua João Pessoa 290, comfortable; *Califórnia,* Rua Barão de Penedo 33, comfortable, US$11 d; *Parque,* Praça Dom Pedro II 73, reasonable; *Atlântico,* Av. Duque de Caxias 1250, reasonable, US$10 d; cheap hotels in Rua Barão de Ataláia, near bus station.

Restaurants   *Gstaad,* Rua Antônio Gouveia, Pajuçara; *Fornace,* Rua Antônio Gouveia, Pajuçara; *Recanto,* Rua Barão de Anadia, Centro; *Alagoas Iate Clube,* Av. Antônio Gouveia, Pajuçara; *Adega do Trapiche,* Av. Siqueira Campos, Prado; *O Dragão,* Av. Antônio Gouveia, Pajuçara; *Bar das Ostras,* Rua Cruzeiro do Sul 487, Vergel do Lago. *Luxor Beiriz* and *Califórnia* hotels also have good restaurants; the *Parque Hotel* is cheap but good.

Camping   There is a site near Jacarecica beach, a 15-minute taxi drive from the town centre. Camping also possible on the Avenida beach, near the *Hotel Atlântico.*

Entertainment   Teatro Deodoro, Praça Marechal Deodoro, in centre; Cinema São Luiz, Rua do Comércio, in centre; the other cinemas tend to be fleapits.

Museum   Instituto Histórico, Rua João Pessoa 382, good small collection of Indian artefacts and Lampião relics. Museu de Arte Sacra, same street.

Bank of London and South America, Praça Dom Pedro II 95, Jaraguá; Banco do Brasil, etc. Open 1230 to 1600.

Cables   Embratel, Rua João Pessoa 57, Praça Dom Pedro II 84. Telegráfico Nacional.

Local Holidays August 27 (Nossa Senhora dos Prazeres); Sept. 16 (Emancipation of Alagoas); December 8 (Nossa Senhora da Conceição); Christmas Eve; New Year's Eve, half-day.

Tourist Information   Ematur, Praça do Centenário 1135, Farol.

Tourist Agencies   Alatur, Rua do Comércio 543; Dreamar Turismo, Rua Dr. Lins Pontes de Miranda 146; Lysturismo, Rua João Pessoa 161.

Excursion   By launch or bus to the Colonial town and former capital of Alagoas, **Marechal Deodoro,** with the fine old church of São Francisco. The trip by launch, leaving from Trapiche on the lagoon, is very pleasant indeed.

The **Falls of Paulo Afonso,** one of the great falls of the world, are 270 km. up the São Francisco river, which drains a valley 3 times the size of Great Britain. There are 2,575 km. of river above the falls to its source in Minas Gerais. The four cascades of the falls themselves are 83 metres high. "Power tremendous, inexorable, irresistible", was Richard Burton's description. Below is a deep gorge clothed with dense tropical vegetation. The lands around are a national park. The power station at the falls supplies current for Salvador, Recife, and other north-eastern cities. The best time to visit the Falls is Jan.-Feb.; only in the rainy season does much water pass over them, as most of the flow now goes through the power plant; virtually all of it will do so by 1985, and the beauty of the spectacle will be past. The best view is from the northern (Alagoas) bank. The Falls are in a security area; no admission for pedestrians, so need to visit by car or taxi (US$4.50 an hour). Guide necessary, and no admission before 1300.

There are the new *Hotel Tropical* and a guest house (apply for room in advance) at the Falls. The township of Paulo Afonso (35,000 people; Hotels *Guadalajara* and *Paulo Afonso,* friendly, cheap; *Hospedagem Lima,* very basic, US$1.50, near *Hotel Guadalajara; Hotel Dormitório,* US$1.15) is a good distance from the Falls, reached by very bad road from Recife, 19 hrs., US$6, from Salvador (475 km., 160 paved, the rest bad), or from Maceió (306 km.) *via* Palmeira dos Indios, partially paved. It is possible, with plenty of time, to go upstream from Penedo (see under Aracaju) to about Pão de Açúcar or Piranhas, but on to the Falls is complicated and involves non-connecting buses.

There are 6 flights from Recife (US$89) and from Salvador (Wednesday and Friday) to Paulo Afonso airport. Buses from Salvador and Recife.

Travel on the River São Francisco (see also page 251). The river is navigable above the Falls from just below the twin towns of **Juazeiro,** in Bahia, and **Petrolina,** in Pernambuco (buses from Salvador, 6 hours, Recife, Fortaleza, Teresina) to Pirapora in Minas Gerais, linked by road to the Belo Horizonte-Brasília highway, and by rail to Belo and the south. While the Sobradinho dam is filling, it is necessary to catch the boat for Pirapora at Santana do Sobrado, 47 km. from Juazeiro (buses).

John Hale writes: Juazeiro and Petrolina are thriving towns compared with many others on the upper São Francisco. Both have cathedrals, that of Petrolina is in the Praça Dom Malan and was consecrated in 1929. Petrolina has its own airport and close to this is the small Museu do Sertão—relics of rural life in the North-East and the age of the "coronéis" and the bandit Lampião. *Hotel Grande Rio* and *Restaurante Rancho Grande.* Juazeiro is perhaps the poorer relation of the two cities. Hotels: *Grande Hotel,* Rua Pititingu, *Vitória,* and *União* (recommended) and *Oliveira,* the last two in Rua Conselheiro Saraiva. Unique restaurant known as the *Vaporzinho* is high and dry on the river front, a side-wheel paddle steamer, the *Saldanha Marinho,* built at Sabará in 1852. A museum for the region of the São Francisco is planned for the old Codevasí building in Juazeiro.

There are quite comfortable boats running between Pirapora and Juazeiro three times a month; from Pirapora (downstream) seven days, from Juazeiro ten days. Malaria pills advisable. The journey, which shows you a part of Brazil that has hardly changed in decades, is broken at a number of small towns along the way.

About 244 km. to the north of Maceió is

Recife (Pernambuco), the capital of Pernambuco state and the most important city in northern Brazil. It consists of three portions: (1) Recife (the Reef), lying on a peninsula (the city is now known by this name); (2) Santo Antônio, on an island between the peninsula and the mainland; (3) Boa Vista on the mainland. The three districts are connected by stone and iron bridges. Waterways run through the city. Wide avenidas have now been cut and high modern buildings have replaced the narrow streets of former times. The population is 1,300,000 and the proportion of blacks is large. There are paved roads into the state and to the neighbouring state capitals—Maceió, João Pessoa, Natal and Fortaleza.

The port is 1,120 nautical miles from Rio de Janeiro, reached in three days by mail steamer. Maceió is 244 km. S by road, and Salvador 835 km.

Purely Local Holidays   Jan. 1 (Universal Brotherhood); June 24 (São João). July 16 (Nossa Senhora do Carmo, patron saint of the city). St. John's Day, though cancelled by the Pope, is still celebrated with bonfires and fireworks all over the State of Pernambuco—and, indeed, throughout Brazil. December 8 (Nossa Senhora da Conceição), a very popular religious holiday since 1904.

Shopping Centres   Rua Nova, Rua da Concórdia, Rua da Palma, Rua Duque de Caxias, Rua Matias de Albuquerque, Avenida Guararapes (Santo Antônio District); Praça do Mercado (São José District); Rua da Imperatriz, Avenida Conde da Boa Vista (Boa Vista District); Rua do Rangel, Rua da Praia; Rua Direita (São José District); Rua Sete de Setembro, Rua do Hospício, Rua do Aragão, Avenida Manoel Borba (Boa Vista District).

Main Manufactures   Sugar, textiles, cement, vegetable oils, phosphate (at Olinda), alcohol, synthetic rubber.   **Main Crops**   Sugar, cotton, castor seed.

Churches   There are many old churches, and most of these are well worth a visit. The best of them are the churches of São Francisco de Assis (1612), on Rua do Imperador; São Pedro dos Clérigos in São José district (1782, for its façade, its fine wood sculpture and a splendid trompe l'oeil ceiling); Santo Antônio (1753), in Praça da Independência, rebuilt in 1864; Conceição dos Militares, in Rua Nova, district of Santo Antônio (1708) grand ceiling and a great 18th century primitive mural of the battle of Guararapes; Nossa Senhora do Carmo, in Praça do Carmo, district of Santo Antônio (1675); the church of Madre de Deus (1706), in the district of Recife, with a splendid high altar, and sacristy; the Pilar Church (1680), in the Rua do Pilar district of Recife; the Igreja do Espírito Santo (1642), the ancient church of the Jesuits, in Santo Antônio district; the Igreja de Santo Antônio do Convento de São Francisco (1606; beautiful Portuguese tiles), in the Rua do Imperador, district of Santo Antônio; the Capela Dourada (Golden Chapel, 1697), in Rua do Imperador, district of Santo Antônio (the finest sight of all, 0800-1100 and 1500-1700: no flash photography); Igreja de S. José do Ribamar (19th century), in São José. There are many others. The best way of seeing them is to buy locally a booklet: *Templos Católicos do Recife*, which has excellent photographs, and let the churches "occur" rather than be sought for during your wanderings. Or join an agency tour.

A few km. S of the city, a little beyond Boa Viagem and the airport, on Guararapes hill, is the historic church of Nossa Senhora das Prazeres. It was here, in 1654, that the Brazilians finally conquered the Dutch after their 30-year occupation of the North-East. It was built by the Brazilian commander to fulfil a vow he made to Our Lady during the course of the battle, which is commemorated at the Church each year.

Other attractions   Visit Fort Brum, built by the Dutch, and the star-shaped fort of Cinco Pontas (only at weekends) built by the Portuguese in 1677. Visit the city markets in the São José and Santa Rita sections. Go fishing on log rafts—*jangadas*—at Boa Viagem with a fisherman who charges US$2. Visit sugar plantations in interior.

Boa Viagem, now a southern suburb, is the newest and most fashionable residential quarter. An imposing promenade runs along the sea shore for a distance of 8 km. This commands a striking view of the Atlantic, whilst the other side is fringed with a belt of coconut palms among which are modern chalets and villas (and apartment blocks). The journey by car or bus from the centre takes about half an hour. Crowded at weekends. Many good restaurants along sea shore.

The artists' and intellectuals' quarter is based on the Pátio de São Pedro, the square round São Pedro dos Clérigos (see under **Churches**). Folk music and poetry shows take place in the square on Friday, Saturday and Sunday evenings and there is a delightful little restaurant, with the friendliest atmosphere imaginable, at No. 46—but don't try the crabs! The square is an excellent shopping centre for typical North-East craftware.

The former municipal prison has now been converted into a cultural centre, the Casa da Cultura, with many cells converted into art or souvenir shops and with areas for exhibitions and shows. most weeks, local dances such as *cirandas* and *bumba-meu-boi* are held as tourist attractions.

The State Museum, in an old house in the Torre district, has excellent paintings by the 19th-century landscape painter, Teles Júnior. The Popular Art Museum contains ceramic figurines, many of them painted—true examples of unsophisticated art. The Museu do Açúcar (sugar museum) is most interesting; it contains models of Colonial mills, devices for torturing slaves, collections of antique sugar bowls and much else. Take the "Dois Irmãos" bus from in front of the Post Office, half-hour ride. The best public buildings are the Pedro II Hospital, the State High School, and the Santa Isabel Theatre. See also the beautiful houses at Av. Rui Barbosa 960, the former home of Joaquim Nabuco at Av. 17 de Agosto 2187, and Av. 17 de Agosto 2223 (afternoons). Also the Museu do Trem, Central Station, Rua Floriano Peixoto, small but interesting. The Law School is one of the most distinguished centres of higher learning in Brazil. The first Brazilian printing press was installed in 1706 and Recife claims to publish the oldest daily newspaper in South America, *Diário de Pernambuco,* founded 1825 by Antônio José de Miranda Falcão.

Carnival time in Recife is altogether remarkable: not a frolic as elsewhere but a colourful expression, by ritual dance and procession, of ancient traditions. There are numerous poverty-ridden hill and mud-flat dwellers round the city. At Carnival time they take Recife by storm, letting their innermost feelings pour forth in a popular eruption. They dance at the doors of all the churches they pass, usually go to the Church of Nossa Senhora do Rosário, patron saint of the slaves, before proceeding in procession into the down-town areas. A small car at the head bears the figure of some animal—a lion or an elephant, perhaps. It is followed by the king and queen under a large, showy umbrella. The *baianas,* who wear snowy-white embroidered skirts, dance in single file on either side of the king and queen. Next comes the Dama do Passo carrying a small doll, or *calunga.* After the Dama comes the *tirador de loas:* he chants to the group which replies in chorus, and last comes a band of local percussion instruments.

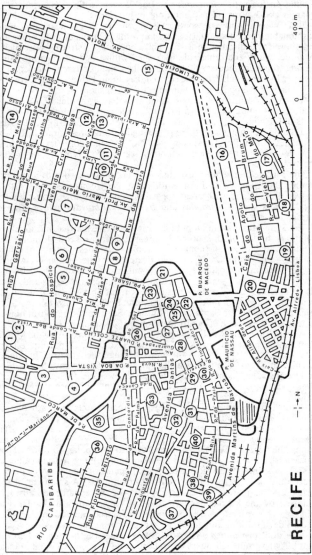

RECIFE

ROUGH SKETCH

Still flourishing is the dance performance of the *caboclinhos*. The groups wear traditional Indian garb: bright feathers round their waists and ankles, colourful cockades, bead and animal-teeth necklaces, a dazzle of medals on their red tunics. The dancers beat out the rhythm with bows and arrows; others of the group play primitive musical instruments, but the dance is the thing: spinning, leaping, and stooping with almost mathematical precision.

Hotels

Name	Address	Price (US$)	
		Single	Double
Miramar (near beach)	Rua dos Navegantes 363 (Boa Viagem)	29.20	35.00
Mar (near beach)	Rua Barão de Souza Leão 451 (Boa Viagem)	24.30	28.40
Vila Rica (beach)	Av. Boa Viagem 4308	23.00	28.50
Jangadeiro (beach)	Av. Boa Viagem 3114	27.50	34.00
Do Sol (beach)	Av. Boa Viagem 978	22.00	26.00
Côte D'Azur (beach)	Av. Boa Viagem 3402	19.00	26.00
Casa Grande e Senzala (near beach)	Av. Conselheiro Aguiar 5000 (Boa Viagem)	18.00	22.70
Boa Viagem (near beach)	Av. Boa Viagem 5000	21.90	25.80
Grande	Av. Martins de Barros 593	22.70	26.80
Guararapes	Av. Guararapes (side street off)	19.50	22.70
São Domingos	Praça Maciel Pinheiro 54/66	20.30	25.20
Central	Av. Manoel Borba 209	8.90	14.60
Avenida	Av. Martins de Barros 292	9.80	13.80
Quatro de Outubro	Rua Floriano Peixoto 141	23.90	27.60
Duzentas Milhas Praia (beach)	Av. Boa Viagem 864	13.00	15.40
Sea View	Rua dos Navegantes 101 (Boa Viagem)	11.40	13.00
Galicia	Rua Jequitinhonha 301	9.80	12.20
Verâncio	Rua Conselheiro Sérgio 150	8.10	12.20
Sete de Setembro	Ria Matias de Albuquerque 318	4.10	6.50
Treze de Maio	Rua do Hospício 659	9.30	14.60
Lido	Rua do Riachuelo 547	10.20	12.20
Solimar (beach)	Av. Boa Viagem 1206	14.60	17.00

There are several other hotels and pensions. *Hotel Pousada Casa Forte,* Av. 17 de Agosto; excellently managed and appointed. A new hotel is *Hotel Nassau,* Travessa do Rosário 253 (breakfast only, served on 7th floor, with a balcony overlooking the city). *Praia,* 5 minutes from bus station, US$4 s, clean and friendly; *Hotel do Parque,* Rua do Hospício 51, good value at US$3 s, US$4.50 d; *Hospedaria São*

Key to Map of Recife

1. Church of Rosário de Boa Vista; 2. Presbyterian Church of Boa Vista; 3. Matriz (Principal Church) de Boa Vista; 4. Presbyterian Church of Recife; 5. Faculty of Law; 6. Municipal Council Chamber; 7. State Institute of Education; 8. State Legislative Assembly; 9. State College of Pernambuco; 10. Church of Piedade; 11-13. TV stations (channels 2 and 6); 14. Central Technical School; 15. University of Pernambuco TV Station; 16. New Municipality Building; 17. Church of Pilar; 18. Moinho Recife SA (Flour Mill); 19. Port Captain's Office; 20. Banco do Brasil; 21. Governor's Palace; 22. State Secretariat of Finance; 23. Santa Isabel Theatre; 24. Palace of Justice; 25. Monastery of Santo Antônio and Church of São Francisco; 26. Central Post Office; 27. Geographical and Statistical Institute (IBGE); 28. Diário de Pernambuco (newspaper); 29. Church of Rosário dos Pretos; 30. Church of Espírito Santo; 31. Church of Nossa Senhora do Livramento; 32. Church of São Pedro dos Clérigos; 33. Basilica of Nossa Senhora do Carmo; 34. (none); 35. Municipal Prison; 36. Central Railway Station; 37. Fort of Cinco Pontas; 38. Church of São José de Ribamar; 39. Central Bus Station; 40. Church of Nossa Senhora da Penha.

Marcos, Rua Padre Muniz 180, US$1.20 s, near São José market. *Hospedaria Rigor,* Praça 17, central, US$5 d, including breakfast. Cheap place near bus station: *Hospedaria Esmeralda,* clean, US$2 s, and many others nearby at similar prices. There are several cheaper hotels in Boa Viagem, e.g. *Hotel Royal* and some listed above.

The sugar cane of Pernambuco and the proximity of such natural ingredients as coconuts, sweet potatoes and nuts, have inspired a host of delicious sweets.

Restaurants   There are many good restaurants, at all prices, in the city, and along beach at Boa Viagem.

City: *Adega da Mouraria,* R. Ulhoa Cintra 40, Centro; *Casa d'Itália,* R. Fernandes Vieira 73, Boa Vista; *Panorâmico AIP,* Av. Dantas Barreto 576 (12°), Centro; *Varanda,* Av. Eng° Abdias de Carvalho (Sport Clube); *Pierre* (French), R. Ulhoa Cintra 102, Centro; *Faia,* R. Ulhoa Cintra 122, Centro; *Rex,* opposite *Hotel do Parque,* plentiful moderate-priced meals; *Leite,* Pe. Joaquim Nabuco 147, Centro; *Bella Trieste,* R. Fernandes Vieira 741, Boa Vista; *Clube de Engenharia,* Av. N.S. do Carmo 110 (4°), Centro; *Buraco da Otília,* Rua da Aurora 1231, Boa Vista.

Boa Viagem: *Aquarius (Hotel Miramar),* R. dos Navegantes 363; *Cote d'Azur,* Av. Boa Viagem 3402; *Casa Grande e Senzala* (Typical), Av. Cons. Aguiar 5000; *Canton* (Chinese), Rua Des. João Paes 123; *Golden Dragon* (Chinese), Rua Barão de Souza Leão 691; *Le Mazot* (French), Av. Boa Viagem 618; *Ouro Preto (Hotel Vila Rica),* Av. Boa Viagem 4308; *Rubayat (Mar Hotel),* Av. Barão de Souza Leão 451; *Veleiro,* Av. Boa Viagem; *Maurício de Nassau,* Av. Boa Viagem 908; *Costa Brava,* Rua Barão de Souza Leão 698; *Mustang Praia,* Av. Boa Viagem 5566; *Coqueiro Verde,* Av. Boa Viagem 5388; *Moenda,* Rua dos Navegantes 1417; *Tio Pepe,* Av. Boa Viagem 5444; *Baiúca,* Praça Boa Viagem 16; *Shangai* (Chinese), Av. Boa Viagem 5262; *Pajuçara,* Rua Tomé Gibson (no number); *Toca do Guiamum,* Av. Herculano Bandeira 865; *Casimiro,* Gamboa do Carmo 104, Portuguese-style food, well recommended. *Bar Restaurante OK,* Av. Marques de Olinda 174; *Restaurante Leite* (lunches only), 147/53 Praça Joaquim Nabuco; *Torres de Londres,* Praça 13 de Maio; *Galo de Ouro,* Gamboa do Carmo 83 (opposite Casimiro). *Dom Pedro,* Rua do Imperador 376, specializes in fish dishes; *O Chocalho,* Av. Barão de Souza Leão 297, Boa Viagem, for local dishes. What is described as authentic colonial food is ceremoniously served by "slave-girls" at *Casa Grande Restaurant* and *Senzala Bar* at Praia de Boa Viagem. Expensive but an experience. (For Olinda restaurants see under Olinda, page 303.)

Electric Current   127-220 AC 50 cycles.

Rail and Road   Recife is the centre of the Rede Ferroviária do Nordeste, with lines south to Maceió, north to Paraíba and Natal, and a central route to Rio Branco. This system is now joined with the Rede de Viação Cearense, serving the port of Fortaleza. Visitors are reminded, however, that buses are normally much quicker than trains (12 hours to Salvador, US$8.50, 11 hours to Fortaleza, US$11.10, and 6 hours to Natal, US$4.50). To Rio, 40 hours, US$32.50; to São Paulo, 48 hours, US$36.80. Hot dusty journey to Teresina (Piauí), 30 hours (US$17), and further to São Luís, 40 hours, US$26.50. To Paulo Afonso, US$7.50, 12 hours.

Conveyances   Buses, taxis, small buses (lotações). Good roads N to João Pessoa, Natal and Fortaleza, W to Arcoverde and Caruaru, SW to Garanhuns and S to Maceió.

Coastal Steamers   Lóide Brasileiro steamers run frequently between Brazilian coastal ports. They have several up-to-date vessels, some luxe.

Air Services   The principal international and national airlines fly to Guararapes Airport, 12 km. from the City. Three direct flights a week from London to Recife *via* Lisbon by Varig and by TAP, and also one by British Caledonian Airways on Thursdays. Bus to airport US$0.33.

British Caledonian Airways, Av. Conde da Boa Vista 1291 (Tel.: 22-4368).

British Consulate   Av. Marquês de Olinda 200, 4th floor. Caixa Postal 184. Tel.: 24-0650.

U.S. Consulate   Gonçalves Maia 163. General Tel.: 21-1412.

Tourist Offices   Empetur, Av. Conselheiro Rosa e Silva 773, in the Aflitos district (Tel.: 22-6907); Rua Matias de Albuquerque, 223, Sala 302; Rua Siqueira Campos,

279, loja 17; Rua da União 27, loja 3; Rua Martins de Barros, 593; Rua Cleto Campelo, 44, loja 16; Av. Conde de Boa Vista, 149, loja 5; Rua Sete de Setembro, 10, loja 1; Pátio de São Pedro, loja 17. Maps available.

Hours of opening of museums, art galleries, churches etc. are published in the daily newspaper Diário de Pernambuco.

Bookshop Second-hand books at Livraria Sedo, Rua da Matriz, and bookstalls on the Rua do Infante Dom Henrique.

Banks Bank of London and South America, Rua do Fogo 22, Santo Antônio district; Banco Internacional; Citibank. Open 0900-1600.

Cables Embratel, Av. Agamenon Magalhães, 1114, Parque Amorim district, Tel.: 214.149; also Praça da Independência-Centro-Telex. Public booth, Av Guararapes, 250-Centro.

Excursions   Olinda, the old capital, founded in 1537, 6 km. to the north, is served by buses and taxis (US$2). This town contains many fine old Colonial churches, monasteries and convents. Particularly interesting are the Prefeitura, once the palace of the viceroys; the monastery of São Bento (paintings, sculpture, furniture); the monastery of São Francisco (splendid woodcarving and paintings); and the Colonial public fountain, the Bica de São Pedro. There are some houses of the 17th century with latticed balconies, heavy doors and pink stucco walls. There is a large colony of artists, and excellent examples of regional art, mainly woodcarving and terra-cotta figurines with a naïve charm, may be bought very cheaply in the beautiful square on top of the hill by the Cathedral. Nearby, in an old jail, is the Museum of Art of Pernambuco; also in the old slave market. The Regional Museum is excellent. A series of low-price motels and restaurants is springing up on the beach N of the town. Population: 200,000.

Restaurants *Mourisco,* Rua João Alfredo 7; *Las Vegas,* Av. Beira Mar 1571; *Zé Pequeno* and *Sambura,* Av. Beira Mar (no number); *La Mer,* Av. Beira Mar 1259; *Agulha Frita, Itapoã* and *Rainha do Mar,* Av. Beira Mar (no numbers); *Las Vegas,* Av. Beira Mar 2619; *Cantinho da Sé,* Ladeira da Se 305; *Ancra Mar,* Av. Getúlio Vargas 1336; *Quebra Mar,* Av. Getúlio Vargas (no number).

Igaraçu, 32 km. N of Recife on the road to João Pessoa, has the first church built in Brazil (SS Cosme e Damião), the Livramento church nearby, and the convent of Santo Antônio with a small museum upstairs. Much of the town (founded in 1535) has been declared a national monument; it is an extremely attractive place, with a number of Colonial houses and Brazil's first Masonic hall. (Pop.: 55,000.)

Excursions The island of **Itamaracá,** near Igaraçu, is an idyllic place with fine, sandy palm-fringed beaches, an old Dutch fort, charming villages and Colonial churches. Buses from Recife and Igaraçu. *(Hotel Caravela,* US$12 d, on beach.)

Another possible excursion is by a slow railway or by a good road to the city of **Garanhuns,** 230 km. to the south-west. It claims to be the best holiday resort in the North-East, partly because of its cool climate—it stands at 890 metres, and has an average temperature of 19°C—and partly because of its mineral waters. Population: normally 74,000, swells to about 100,000 during the summer.

Hotels *Familiar,* Av. Santo Antônio 12; Tel.: 1173. *Grande Hotel Petrópolis,* Praça da Bandeira 129; Tel.: 1097. *Sanatório Hotel,* Av. Rui Barbosa 296; Tel.: 1280-1386. All have hot and cold water.

During Easter Week each year Recife's Department of Information and Culture runs package tours in comfortable buses to the little country town of **Fazenda Nova,** a few km. from Caruaru. Just outside the town is **Nova Jerusalém,** where from the Tuesday before to Easter Sunday an annual passion play, suggested by Oberammergau's, is enacted. The site is one-third the size of the historic quarter of Jerusalem, with 12 permanent stages on which scenes of the Passion are presented; the audience moves from one to the other as the story unfolds, just as the Jerusalem crowds did originally.

Hotels in Fazenda Nova   *Grande,* best; *Mansão Verde; Fazenda Nova.*

Camping   Close to site.

Caruaru, 130 km. W of Recife by paved road (many buses, 2 hours), has a big Wednesday and Saturday market recommended as one of the best and cheapest in Brazil, especially for leather goods, pottery and articles of straw. The little clay figures *(figurinhas de barro)* originated by Mestre Vitalino and very typical of the North-East, are a local speciality. (Population: 149,000.)

Arcoverde, about 126 km. W of Caruaru, a market town in the Sertão, market every Saturday, cool at night. Hotel: *Grande Palace Majestic* (fair), about US$4 s, with breakfast.

Triúnfo, about 200 km. W of Arcoverde *via* Serra Talhada, delightful small town in Serra de Borborema, good climate, with great variety of crops and fruits. Two buses daily to and from Recife (6½ hours). Stay at *Hotel-Orphanage Lar St. Elizabeth,* run by German religious sisters, US$8 a day with private apartment and 3 excellent meals.

Fernando de Noronha is a small archipelago 500 km. off the NE coast, under military control: only one island is inhabited. Total population about 1,000, of whom many are fishermen or civilians working for military. Only hotel, *Pousada Esmeralda* (US$19-25 s, US$30-33.50 d), runs a tour boat for guests. Most food is brought from mainland but prices are reasonable. The islands were discovered 1503, and were for a time a pirate lair. In 1738 the Portuguese built the Forte dos Remédios, of which remains exist as well as a deserted town nearby, and a prison. Sea landing is difficult, but an airstrip has been built; there are flights to Recife. The island, which is dominated by a 300-metre peak, has interesting wildlife; fishing is very good, and so is scuba-diving. Take sufficient cruzeiros: travellers' cheques and dollars are heavily discounted.

It is a bus ride of 2 hours through beautiful scenery and over a good road from Recife to

João Pessoa, capital of the State of Paraíba, on the Paraíba River, with 222,000 inhabitants, port for coasting traffic. Ocean-going steamers load and unload at **Cabedelo** (6,872 population), 18 km. away by rail, where there is a wharf and a rail connection with Recife (105 km.). Ships drawing up to 4¼ metres can enter the River Paraíba and reach the capital. The old monasteries are worth seeing, and the 18th century church of São Francisco is a beauty. Other tourist points include the spectacular Hotel Tambaú; the Cabo Branco lighthouse at Ponta do Seixas, the most easterly point of Brazil; whale fishing from July to December at the Praia de Costinha; the city parks; and trips on the River Paraíba. There is a 126-km. paved road to Recife. Airport for internal services.

Hotels   *Tambaú* and new *Tropicana,* Praia de Tambaú (excellent); *Aurora,* Praça João Pessoa 51; *Miramar; Paraíba Palace,* Praça Vidal de Negreiros; *Globo,* Praça São Pedro Gonçalves 36; *Pedro Américo,* Praça Pedro Américo; *Motel Veraneio* on BR-230; *Motel Fogeama* and *Tropicana,* Rua das Trincheiras (with restaurant);

Pousada do Conde, BR-101 Sul (with churrascaria); cheap hotels near the bus station.

Restaurants   *O Circo,* Av. Ruy Carneiro; *Casino da Lagoa,* Parque Solòn de Lucena; *Cabo Branco Clube* has two restaurants, one in Rua Peregrino de Carvalho and the other in the Miramar district. *Olívio,* Rua Mons. Walfredo 714; *Paraibambu,* Parque Arruda Câmara; *O Elite,* Av. João Maurício, Tambaú; *A caravela,* Quadra 3, Jardim Beiramar; *Badionaldo,* Praia do Poço (20 km. from centre) and also *Bardilucena. Marambaia,* Av. 24 de Maio, Jaguaribe; *Marisco,* Av. Cabo Branco; *Itacoatiara,* near *Hotel Tambaú; Pescador,* near Cabo Branco lighthouse; *O Luzeirinho,* Av. Vasco da Gama, Jaguaribe; *O Boiadeiro,* Av. Coração de Jesus; *A Gameleira,* Av. João Maurício, Tambaú.

Tourist Information   PB Tur, Centro Administrativo 2, 5th floor, Rua João da Mata (Jaguaribe); and *Tambaú Hotel.*

Tourist Agencies   Planetur, Av. Miguel Couto 5, Loja 12, and *Tambaú Hotel;* Agencia de Viagens e Turismo Arnaldo von Sohsten, Rua Gama e Melo 100.

Cables   Embratel, Rua das Trincheiras 398.

Excursions   Twenty minutes by car or taxi to Tambaú, fishing village and seaside resort with lovely beach and excellent bathing. Halfway along is Cabo Branco club, open to visitors: good food, beautiful views; hotels and restaurants also at Tambaú. At Cabedelo are the impressive walls of the 17th-century fortress of Santa Rita.

For the tourist a trip by bus over a good road through fine scenery (2 hours) to **Campina Grande** on market day is a must. Inland about 120 km., Campina is a far more lively and interesting town than João Pessoa. This "Porta do Sertão" is a rapidly growing centre for light industry and an outlet for goods from most of the North-East. The market, which engulfs the city on Saturday, is wonderful, and there is a museum of modern art. *Rique Palace Hotel* (excellent) is on the top floors of the tallest building in town: the restaurant is on the 11th floor. Other hotels: *Ouro Branco,* US$7 s, US$9 d; *Honor Hotel,* cheaper. Most genial climate. Population: 196,000.

W of Campina Grande the main highway, still paved, leads on through **Patos** (*Hotel JK,* US$3 s) to Ipaumirim (Ceará). Here a left turn leads to the twin towns of **Crato** and **Juazeiro do Norte** (Ceará), oases of green in the dry sertão. Mosquitos can be a problem at night.

Hotel in Crato   *Hotel Crato,* US$3 s.

About 180 km. to the north of João Pessoa is

Natal, 350,000 people, capital of Rio Grande do Norte, a short distance from the coast on the right bank of the Rio Potengi. It is served by weekly coastal steamers and there is a railway S through the state of Paraíba to Recife and Maceió. Passable motor roads radiate into the surrounding country. There is a large airport 13 km. from the city. Natal has excellent beaches, some on the far side of the Potengi river, whose mouth is crowded by sailing and motor boats. It is a well-laid-out city, with several attractive streets, centred on the Praça João Maria, with a traditional cathedral at one end and a beautiful new bank building at the other. The Forte dos Reis Magos, a 16th-century fort on the coast, has a small folk museum; it is open 0800-1100, 1400-1700. The Marine Research Institute at the Praia da Areia Prata can be visited. Good local craftware at Mercado do Alecrim. Some 20 km. from Natal is the rocket base of Barreira do Inferno, near Eduardo Gomes, which can be visited with passes obtained from tourist agencies.

Bus to Recife, 5 hours, US$3: to Fortaleza, 9 hours, US$5.

Hotels   *Reis Magos,* Av. Café Filho, Praia do Meio, new, facing sea, fine, US$30 d;

Samburá, Rua Prof. Zuza 263, US$21 d, recommended; *Tirol,* Av. Alexandrino de Alencar 1330; *Pousada do Sul,* BR-101, km. 18; *Motel Tahiti,* Estrada de Ponte Negra, km. 2; *Grande,* cheap, US$6 with meals; *Hotel Natal,* Av. Rio Branco, US$10 d, central, looks clean; *União,* US$9 d, with fan; *7 de Setembro,* near bus station, US$6 d, basic.

Restaurants *Mirante,* Av. Getúlio Vargas; *Casa Grande,* Rua Princesa Isabel 529; *Bosque dos Namorados,* Av. Alexandrino de Alencar; *América,* Av. Rodrigues Alves 950; *Assen,* Av. Prudente de Morais 760; *Marinho,* Rua do Areial 265; *Lira,* Rua Pereira Simões 71; *Pescada da Comadre,* Rua São João 101.

Camping is good on the Praia do Forte beach, near the Forte dos Reis Magos.

Cables Embratel, Av. Duque de Caxias 99. Tel.: 1230.

Tourist Information Emprotur, Av. Hermes da Fonseca 970, Tirol. Seintur, Av. Deodoro, 499.

Tourist Agencies Aertour, Rua João Pessoa 219; Bradesco, Av. Rio Branco 692 1° andar; Aparecida Turismo, Av. Rio Branco, Ed. Barão do Rio Branco.

Electric Current 127-220 A.C., 50 cycles.

The state of Rio Grande do Norte (whose people are called "Potiguares" after a former Indian tribe) has three main paved roads radiating from Natal: S to João Pessoa and Recife, SW to **Caicó** and W to **Mossoró** and Fortaleza. Between Caicó (*Hotel Guanabara,* recommended, US$1.50 p.p.) and Mossoró there is a maze of earth roads leading to some interesting small towns (including **Patu** with its huge basilica on a hillside with views out over the sertão), with passable "hotels", rather primitive.

About 420 km. from Natal, NW along the coast by road (9 hours by bus) is

Fortaleza (Ceará), capital of the state of Ceará, with a population of 950,000. It has a protected roadstead where ships drawing up to 8¼ metres discharge into lighters at Mucuripe Point, 8 km. east of the town. There is also a quay 960 metres long for ships drawing 4¼ to 7¼ metres. Ceará is 980 km. east of Belém and 885 km. from Recife. It is a port of call for European and North American lines and for coastal steamers, who do a large trade. There are fair dirt roads throughout the state, and W to São Luís and SE to Recife; the federal highway S to Salvador and Rio (BR-116) is now almost entirely paved. Fortaleza has a university and attractive residential areas. It is famous for its many magnificent clubs and for being the best place in Brazil to eat lobsters. A beautiful new tourist centre opened in March 1973 in the old prison on the waterfront includes museum, shops and restaurants. A festival takes place on the last Sunday in July, during which the traditional *jangada* (raft) races take place. Also visit Forte Nossa Senhora da Assunção, originally built by the Dutch. The mausoleum of President Castello Branco (1964-67), next to state government building, may also be visited.

Beaches are fine, and you can watch the jangadas, the typical fishing rafts of the NE, coming in at sundown with their catch. The beautiful Serra de Maranguape with thick tropical growth and distant views back to the city is 30 km. inland.

Markets The local specialities are beautiful hand-made lace and embroidered textile goods; also hammocks. Bargaining is O.K. both at the Mercado Central and the Mercado Municipal in the Praça da Sé. Prices are very reasonable.

Local holidays Jan. 6 (Epiphany); Ash Wednesday; March 19 (São José); Christmas Eve; New Year's Eve, half-day.

Hotels *Beira Mar,* on beach, best; *Praia Sol,* Praia do Futuro, US$18 d; *São*

Pedro; Internacional, Rua Barão Rio Branco, US$5 s, with shower, US$7.50 d; *Savanah,* US$16 d; *Excelsior,* US$7 d, with good breakfast; *Globo; Canãa; Itapage; Plaza,* Rua Senador Pompeu, US$5 d; *Premier,* Rua Barão do Rio Branco 829.

Restaurants Several good and cheap fish restaurants at far end of Av. Presidente Kennedy, where the fishing fleet operates. *Sandras,* Av. Presidente Kennedy 3520, has been specially recommended. Good restaurant in Clube Náutico.

Camping possible opposite *Hotel Beira Mar,* on the Praia Meirelles.

Rail South to Baturite, Iguatu and Crato (772 km.; this railway has now been joined to the system serving Recife, in turn connected with the network in Southern Brazil, so that it is possible to travel by rail from Fortaleza to the borders of Argentina, Uruguay and Bolivia, very slowly indeed!). West to Sobral, the junction of a line north to the port of Camocin and south to Crateús.

Air Service Direct flights to Belém, Recife, Rio and other cities in Brazil.

Bus Service The "Expresso de Luxo" runs daily to Recife (11 hours, US$7), also Rio de Janeiro, São Paulo, Crato, Teresina, Parnaíba, and many other cities. Natal, US$4, 7 hours; Teresina, US$6, 10 hours; São Luís, US$9.50, 18 hours, road now paved.

Bank of London and South America, Rua Barão do Rio Branco 862; and national banks. Open 0900-1700.

Tourist Information Emcetur, Rua Senador Pompeu 250.

Tourist Agencies Mundiatur, Turismo Viagens, Itala Viagens Turismo and Intertur.

Cables Embratel, Rua Castro e Silva 286/290.

Excursions 40 km. from Fortaleza, along the coast, one finds **Prainha,** a combination of fishing village and weekend houses. It is possible to see *jangadas* coming in daily in the late afternoon. The beaches are clean and largely empty. There are several small, cheap and good restaurants, where it is possible to see displays of the "carimbó", the main local dance of Ceará.

The Ubajará cave in the Ubajará National Park is regarded by the State as one of its premier tourist attractions; it is just off the road to Teresina, near the Piauí border.

Roads The road to Sobral and Teresina is now paved throughout.

Sobral, the principal town in western Ceará and well-known for straw hats, has *Hotel Municipal,* US$3 s, meals available. South of Sobral is the remote town of **Crateús** (no paved roads there), with the *Crateús Palace Hotel,* very reasonable and clean, US$4 s, with breakfast. Good restaurant, *Churrascaria Pequena Cabana,* at back of hotel. Bus service from Crateús over very bad road to Teresina, every two days.

Between the states of Maranhão and Piauí, which has a coastline of only 27 km., runs the river Parnaíba. Near its mouth is the anchorage of Luís Correia, where ships unload for final delivery by tugs and lighters at Parnaíba, 15 km. up-river.

Parnaíba is the collecting and distributing centre for the trade of Piauí: tropical products and cattle. Population, 79,000. Coastal steamers and vessels of the Booth Line from Europe and New York call at Tutoia Bay (Hotel: *Parnaíba Palace*).

Beaches 18 km. away at Luís. Just off the Parnaíba-Teresina road, Correia and Parnaíba have radioactive sands. 22 km. from Piracuruca is the Parque Nacional de Sete Cidades with its strange eroded rock formations.

About 4354 km. up the river is Teresina, capital of the state of Piauí, reputed to be the poorest in Brazil.

Teresina, 221,000 people, sometimes known as the Green City, is reached by air or paved road from Fortaleza. From the Senador Furtado, across the river, a railway (451 km.) runs N to São Luís, on the coast of

Maranhão; there is also a paved road, with bus service (US$3.50). The town suffers from high temperatures but the heat is dry. There is an interesting open market in one of the main squares and the river is picturesque, with washing laid out to dry along its banks. The market is a good place to buy hammocks, but bargain hard.

Teresina Hotels   *Luxor Hotel do Piauí* and *Teresina Palace,* luxury class; *Grande; Hotel Fortaleza,* basic but expensive; *São João e São Pedro,* US$2 p.p.

Restaurant   *Churrascaria Gaúcha,* ½ km. E of river bridge, on E side of town. All the meat you can eat for US$2.50. Good food in Praça Saraiva.

Buses   No bus station, but different companies located around Praça Saraiva. The bus trip from Fortaleza is wonderfully scenic and takes 10 hours (US$6). Another road, very bad, leads inland to Porto Franco and Imperatriz (Restaurant: *Bar Central,* OK) on the Belém-Brasília highway; daily bus takes 26-40 hours for the trip to Imperatriz (US$10), depending on the state of the road; these buses are very crowded. Another main road runs SE to Petrolina, on the River São Francisco opposite the Bahian town of Juazeiro. Bus, one or two a day, 15 hours, US$6. Buses from Petrolina/Juazeiro (see page 297) SE to Salvador, 6 hours. Bus to Belém, with possible change at Gurupi on Pará border about 16 hours, US$12.

Tourist Information   *Piemtur,* Rua Alvaro Mendes 1364, Caixa Postal 36.

About 560 km. west of Fortaleza (Ceará), 400 km. SE of Belém, is

São Luís, the capital and the port of Maranhão state, founded in 1612, in a region of heavy tropical rains and deep forest. The city stands upon an island between the bays of São Marcos and São José. Its cultural traditions are curiously strong for such an isolated city: some of the greatest Brazilian writers and poets were born here. The heart of the city is only a few minutes' walk from its very old-fashioned port, too shallow for big ships to enter. The old part, on very hilly ground with many steep streets, still has some fine but decayed mansions with elaborately wrought iron balconies, carved doorways, ornamental tiles and stone-flagged courtyards. See the Governor's Palace (open Thursday, 1600-1800) and the old slave market. The best Colonial churches to see—some of them rebuilt and not improved by it—are the Diocesan Church and the churches of Carmo, São João, Rosário, and Santana. The Museu do Estado, Rua Nina Rodrigues, is free. The commercial quarter is still much as it was in the 17th century. Population: 266,000.

São Luís is reached from Fortaleza, Teresina, Belém and Recife by air and road and by steamers of Lóide Brasileiro and Cia. Navegação Costeira. Booth Line steamers serve the port from both Europe and New York.

Folklore festivals   On St. John's Day, June 24, the "Bumba-Meu-Boi", a fantastic bull dance and masque with traditional words; the São Benedito, at the Rosário church in August.

Hotels   *Lord,* US$6 s; *Central,* US$10 s. More basic, but with excellent food, *Hotel Guaraní,* US$6 d; *Aliança,* US$4 s; *Hotel Colonial,* Rua Santana 226, US$3 s, with breakfast. Many cheap hotels in Rua da Palmeira, very central; *Grand,* near market, US$5 d; *Globo,* US$4.50 s, with breakfast; US$8 with full board. Youth Hostel, open all year, Rua 7 de Setembro.

Restaurants   *Atenas,* Humberto de Campos 175, good stew for US$1; *Bem,* 9th floor, Tarquínio Lopes 283.

Cables   Embratel, Avenida Dom Pedro II, 190. Tel.: 2500.

Airport   Internal flights only. 14 km. from centre; buses to city until midnight.

Railway   451 km. S to Teresina, capital of the neighbouring state of Piauí, through the Maranhão towns of Caxias and Senador Furtado, both on the left bank of the Parnaíba.

Road   The Teresina-São Luís road is paved throughout (bus service, US$3.50). Bus to Fortaleza, US$9, 16 hours (road also paved). Also to Recife.

To Belém   Direct road *via* Santa Inês and São José do Gurupi now exists, but is not yet completely paved. There is a bus service (12 hours, US$7), twice daily. There are occasional coastal steamers of the Costeira line, but best to go by air. Sr. Lobato, of Rua Kennedy near the central market, runs a small boat (30 hours) to Bragança, near Belém.

Tourist Offices, Av. dos Franceses and Av. Pedro II; good information on walks in city.

Maranhão state is about the size of Italy; its land is flat and low-lying, with highlands to the S. The Atlantic coastline—a mass of sandbanks and creeks and sandy islands on one of which stands São Luís—is 480 km. long. A quarter of Maranhão is covered with babaçu palms, and by far the most important products are babaçu nuts and kernels and oil. Rice often takes second place, but well behind babaçu; there is raw cotton and cotton seed and some yarn, tucum fibre, hides and skins, manioc flour and maize. There are salt pans along the coast. The huge Boa Esperança hydroelectric station on the Parnaíba river now floods the State with energy, and some petroleum has been discovered. Exports are almost entirely to the rest of Brazil.

Northern Brazil

The North of Brazil is taken up by the states of Pará, Amazonas, and Acre, and the territories of Amapá, Roraima, and Rondônia.

The area is drained by the Amazon, which in size, volume of water—12 times that of the Mississippi—and number of tributaries has no equal in the world. At the base of the Andes, far to the west, the Amazonian plain is 1,300 km. in width between the highlands of the north and the high ground to the south, but east of the confluences of the Madeira and Negro rivers with the Amazon, the highlands close upon it until there is no more than 80 km. of floodplain between them. Towards the river's mouth—about 320 km. wide—the plain widens once more and extends along the coast south-eastwards into the state of Maranhão and northwards into the Guianas.

The whole of Amazonia, most of it covered with tropical forest, is 56% of the national area, equivalent to two-thirds of Canada. The Amazonian jungle is the world's largest and densest rain forest, with more diverse plants, and flowers and trees, birds, serpents, insects and animals than any other jungle in the world. But it has only 6.7% of Brazil's population, and most of this is concentrated around Belém (in Pará), and São Luís (in Maranhão), both not far from the ocean, and in Manaus, 1,600 km. from the sea. The scarcity of population is possibly due to three reasons: there is as yet no pressure of population upon land in Brazil, and other areas are easier to develop; the rainfall is heavy, the humidity high, and the climate hot, though by no means unbearably so; and the soil, as in all tropical forest, is poor.

The Government is now making strenuous efforts to develop Amazonia. Roads have been built parallel to the Amazon to the south (the Transamazônica), from Cuiabá (Mato Grosso) northwards to Santarém (Pará), and NE from Porto Velho to the river bank opposite Manaus. Part of the Perimetral Norte road, paralleling the Amazon to the north, has also been built, but completion is not expected until the mid-1980s. Agricultural settlements are being established along these roads.

The Transamazônica, about 5,000 km. in length, represents the greater part of a direct road connection between Brazil's furthest E and furthest W points. It skirts the southern edge of the Amazonian plain, linking the following places: Estreito (junction with the Belém-Brasilia highway), Santa Isabel and Marabá (on the Araguaia river), Altamira (on the Xingu), Itaituba (on the Tapajòs), Jacareacanga, Humaitá (on the Madeira), Rio Branco, and the Peruvian and Bolivian frontiers. The road was officially opened in December 1973; the road-bed is now complete, paving has started, traffic is operating, and buses will shortly be running along the whole length; there are also services from Santarém to the Belém-Brasília road and to Cuiabá.

Anyone interested in the Amazonian development programme and its ecological, social, economic and political effects, should read Richard Bourne's masterly "Assault on the Amazon" (London, Victor Gollancz, 1978).

Up the Amazon River

Ships of up to 4/5,000 tons regularly negotiate the Amazon for a distance of about 3,200 km. up to Iquitos. Distances up-stream from the river mouth in nautical miles are:

Belém	..	..	..	80	Santarém	..	..	.. 538
Narrows (entrance)	..	..	225	Obidos	..	..	.. 605
Narrows (exit)	..	..	330	Parintins	..	..	.. 694
Garupa	..	..	334	Itacoatiara	..	..	.. 824
Prainha	..	..	452	Manaus	..	..	.. 930

What to wear On board, going up the Amazon, wear trousers or shorts and a shirt (women should wear trousers too). At night put on a sweater or coat, for it gets quite cold. From April to October, when the river is high, the mosquitos at night can be repelled by Super Repelex spray or K13; protective clothing is advisable. Take a hammock; often too hot to lie down in cabin during day.

Health There is a danger of malaria in Amazonia. Take the usual precautions; the local drug is Aralen. On the smaller boats one is almost certain to contract intestinal infections; take plenty of tablets, toilet paper, soap, a container for sterilized (or boiled) water and some plain biscuits. A good idea also to take mineral water, tea bags, seasonings, sauces and jam.

N.B. If going in the smaller boats, be prepared for mechanical breakdowns that prolong the journey. Also remember that little wildlife will be seen unless a foray is made into the jungle, and coming downstream from Manaus boats often keep to the middle of the river leaving little to see but water.

Food in Amazonia Philip Smith writes: Turtle is regarded as a local speciality, though it is apparently a protected animal and such dishes are not commonly sold in restaurants; they are worth the trouble if you have the chance. Inevitably, as Belém is situated on a river, fish dishes are very common, including many fish with Indian names, e.g. *pirarucu, tucunaré,* and *tambaqui,* which are worth trying. Also shrimp and crab dishes (more expensive). Specialities of Pará include duck, often served in a yellow soup made from the juice of the root of the manioc with a green vegetable *(jambo);* this dish is the famous *pato no tucupí,* highly recommended. Also *tacaca* (shrimps served in *tucupí), vatapá* (shrimps served in a thick sauce, highly filling, simpler than the variety found in Salvador), *maniçoba* (a green vegetable mixed with cheaper cuts of meat). Almost all restaurants sell a complete range of meat, poultry and fish dishes for international tastes with regional dishes as a sideline. It is strongly recommended that regional dishes only be tried in good restaurants and never with street vendors, whose standards of hygiene are dubious.

Salinópolis brings the ocean traveller the first glimpse of Brazil and of the waters of the Amazon, which have changed the colour of the sea from deep blue to pale yellow-green. Amazon waters, it is said, make the sea drinkable over 300 km. from the coast. To starboard is Marajó Island, and opposite a dense green wall of the equatorial forest, with its distances veiled in mist. Between the ship and the shore local catamarans, with blue sails, may usually be seen.

This is the Pará River, one of the mouths of the Amazon, with many forest-clad islands. Small settlements of white bungalows and palm-thatch native huts become frequent. Chapéu Virado is passed, then Mosqueiro, both riverside resorts of the people of Belém.

Belem (or Pará), 145 km. from the open sea and slightly S of the equator, is the great port of the Amazon. It is hot (mean temperature, 26°C), but frequent showers freshen the streets. There are some good squares and fine buildings. The largest square is the Praça da República; the main business and shopping area is along the wide Presidente Vargas boulevard leading to the river and the narrow streets which parallel it. The cathedral is eighteenth century, and the Paz Theatre is one of the largest in the country. Belém has a university, 3 newspapers, 8 cinemas, and 3 TV stations with colour transmission. Wide view of town, river, jungle, from terrace on top of Edifício Manuel Pinto, near the Paz Theatre. Population about 700,000.

A good asphalted road leads E out of the city to the coast town of Salinópolis, some 228 km. away, at the extreme end of the eastern part of the Amazon Delta. Various unpaved roads to other towns branch off from this road; 118 km. out of Belém one turns right on to the highway S to Brasília (2,100 km.), which is now completely paved.

Places to visit are the Bosque, a public garden (which is really a preserved area of original flora) with a small animal collection (admission US$0.08), and the Goeldi Museum. Both can be reached by bus (from the Cathedral). The Goeldi Museum, Av. Magalhaes Barata, takes up a city block and consists of the Museum proper (with a fine collection of Marajó Indian pottery), a zoological garden, and botanical exhibits; open Tuesday to Friday, 0900-1200 and 1500-1800, Sunday 0800-1200 and 1400-1800 (afternoons, garden and zoo only).

In the Belém market, known as "Ver-o-Peso" (see the weight) after the large scales on which the fish landed nearby were weighed, there is now little for tourists to buy, being mainly for meat, fish and fruit, though tourists may be interested in the charms on sale for the local African-derived religion, umbanda. Nearby are the shopping centres in the Rua Santo Antônio and João Alfredo. In the old town, too, is the fort built near where the Portuguese explorers first landed, which you can enter on request; the site also contains the *Círculo Militar* restaurant. Near the harbour with its quaint fishing boats can be found the Prefeitura Municipal and the Palace of the State Governor, which you cannot enter. Visit the Cathedral (1748) with several remarkable paintings, and directly opposite the 18th-century Santo Alexandre Church (now Museum of Religious Art) noted for its wood carving. Also the 17th-century Mercês Church, near the market, which is the oldest church in Belém, massive European baroque on to which slight Brazilian baroque towers seem to have been stuck at a later date. The Basilica of Nossa Senhora de Nazaré (1909) is an absolute must for its beautiful marble work and stained glass windows.

Belém's exports are rubber, Brazil nuts, jute, carnauba wax, rice, hardwoods, fish-maws and babaçu nuts.

Tourist Office (Departmento Municipal), Av. Nazaré 231, near Edificio Manuel Pinto. Friendly and helpful.

Post Office   Av. Presidente Vargas.

Travel Agent   Ciatur, Praça da República 645, opposite *Grão Pará Hotel* (Tel.: 22-1995). Very well organized.

Excursions   Travel agents offer short and longer visits to the rivers and jungle. The nearest beach is at **Outeiro** (35 km.) on an island near Icoaraci, about an hour by bus and ferry (the bus may be caught near the Maloca, an Indian-style hut near the docks which serves as a night-club). Further north, about 1½ hours by bus, is the island of **Mosqueiro** (86 km.) now accessible by a recently opened bridge and excellent highway, with many beautiful sandy beaches and jungle inland, many hotels and weekend villas at the villages of Mosqueiro and Vila; recommended *Hotel N.S. de Fátima* (cheap) at latter with good meals (US$8 d) and *Hotel Chapéu Virado* (US$25 d). The traffic is heavy at holiday time, and hotels are full.

Marajó Island is worth visiting for a weekend's buffalo hunting (use a camera, not a gun, or the buffalo won't last long). Trips to the island are arranged by the *Grão Pará Hotel* and travel agents. Alternatively, a light aircraft may be hired to see Marajó from the air (with pilot, about US$80 for 2 hours) e.g. from Kovacs, Av. Dr. Freitas, opposite the airfield of the Aero-Clube do Pará.

Salinópolis (228 km.) about 3½ hours by bus on excellent highway, also worth a visit. Seaside resort with many small places where you can eat and drink at night by the waterfront, and fine sandy beach nearby (buses and cars actually drive onto the beach). Best during holiday month of July.

Bus Services   There are four buses a day to Brasília (US$25), modern and comfortable, and also an additional "leito" bus—US$56 but worth it; the seats are almost fully-reclining, with foot and leg rests, 30 hours. Belém-Imperatriz bus takes 10-12 hours (US$14). There are also direct buses from Belém to Marabá, on the Transamazônica, *via* Porto Franco and Toncantinópolis. The direct road *via* Gurupi and Santa Inês to São Luís and Teresina is now open; there is a bus service, but there is often a change at Gurupi. To Salvador, US$20, 35 hrs.; to Recife, US$19; to São Luís, twice a day, 12 hrs., US$7.50; to Rio, US$39; to Belo Horizonte, US$35.

Local Holidays   Maundy Thursday, half-day; June 9, Corpus Christi; August 15, accession of Pará to the Independence of Brazil; Feast of Our Lady of Nazaré, second Sunday and fourth Monday in October, known as Cirio. Oct. 30, half-day; Nov. 2, All Souls Day; December 8, Immaculate Conception; Christmas Eve, half-day.

Philip Smith writes: Cirio, the Festival of Candles in October, is a remarkable festival based on the legend of the Virgin of Nazaré, a saint whose image is kept in the Basilica, which apparently was found on that site around 1700. A woodcutter (according to one version) found the image and took it home, from whence it disappeared several times, miraculously returning to the place where it was found. To celebrate, on the second Sunday in October, a procession is held to take a copy of the saint from the cathedral to the basilica. The streets are absolutely packed with the faithful and it is deemed an act of devotion to be able to assist in the pulling of the rope towing the carriage in which the saint is placed. On the Monday, two weeks later, a further procession takes place, to return the copy to its usual resting-place. The original, by the way, never leaves the basilica.

Curio shops in Av. Presidente Vargas; also try the Indian handicrafts shop at Praça Kennedy, set in a garden with Amazonian plants and animals.

Camera Repairs   Henri van Ligten, Travessa Cintra 438. Recommended: a Dutchman who speaks English and German.

Cables   Embratel, Tv. Quintino Bocaiúva 1186 (Tel.: 22-9099) or at the Post Office, Av. Presidente Vargas. For phone calls: Telepará, Av. Presidente Vargas.

Banks Bank of London & South America, Rua 15 de Novembro 275 (open 0900-1630, but foreign exchange only until 1300) and Brazilian banks (also foreign exchange mornings only, as this is the result of a local central-bank regulation). Free-market currency at Jake's souvenir shop on Av. Presidente Vargas.

Hotels Expensive: *Selton*, 2 km. from airport (US$30 d), swimming pool; *Excelsior Grão Pará*, Av. Presidente Vargas 718 (US$30 d); *Equatorial*, Av. Braz de Aguiar 612 (US$30 d). Less expensive: *Sagres*, Av. Gov. José Malcher 2927, opp. bus station, recommended (US$27 d); *Regente*, Av. Gov. José Malcher 485 (US$25 d); *Vanja*, Tv. Benjamin Constant 1164 (US$22 d). Medium priced, good reputation: *Terminal*, Av. Gov. José Malcher 2953, near bus station (US$6 d); *Central*, Av. Presidente Vargas 290 (US$12 d), good, reasonable restaurant; *Avenida*, Av. Presidente Vargas 404 (US$10 d); *Transbrasil*, Av. Cipriano Santos 243, behind bus station (US$10 d); *São Geraldo*, R. Padre Prudêncio 54 (US$12 d). Cheaper: *São Braz*, Av. Gov. José Malcher 2979, opp. bus station (US$6 d), friendly and clean; *Hilea*, Av. Gov. José Malcher 312; *Vitória Rêgia*, Frutuoso Guimarães 260; *Transamazônico*, Tv. Indústria 17, waterfront by docks, US$6 d, without breakfast; *King*, R. 28 de Setembro 269, US$13 d, not too clean. Cheap, perhaps dubious: *Hotel Biumenau*. Very shabby: *Palácio das Musas*, Frutuoso Guimarães 275, US$5 d, without breakfast; *Fortaleza*, Frutuoso Guimarães 276, US$4 d, good and cheap restaurant; *Hotel Cayenne*, Rua 28 de Setembro, US$4 s, US8 d; *Itapagé*, Rua 28 de Setembro, US$2.50, recommended; *Belém Palace*, Rua Gaspar Viana, US$3 d; *Terminal*, US$2.50-4.50, near bus terminal. Many cheap hotels close to waterfront, in old part of town; try bargaining for cheaper rate if you have hammock.

Restaurants All the major hotels have good but expensive restaurants. Also *Hotel Central* recommended as more reasonably priced. *Círculo Militar* recommended for its situation in the grounds of the fort with view over river (general price US$5). Also recommended: *Lá em Casa*, Av. Gov. José Malcher 982; *Regatão*, Av. Senador Lemos 3273; *Marisqueira do Luiz*, Av. Senador Lemos 1063; *Casa Portuguesa*, Rua Manoel Barata 897; *Miako*, Rua Caetano Rufino 82 (menu includes pleasant medium-priced Japanese food); *Avenida*, Praça Justo Chermont 1294 (opp. Basilica); *La Romana*, Av. Gentil Bittencourt 574 and *Pizzaria Napolitana*, Praça Justo Chermont 12 (in particular pizzas and Italian dishes); *Pato de Ouro*, Rua Diogo Moia 633 (next to Sorveteria Santa Martha ice-cream parlour) and *Renasci*, Trav. José Pio 322 (in particular regional dishes); *Linda Cap* and *Tucuruví*, both on the highway leading out of Belém, are *churrascarias*, unlimited quantities of meat served on the spit.

Specially recommended for tourists are also some very good *lanchonetes* (cafés, mostly outdoors in Belém) where you can buy anything from a drink or a snack up to a full meal, much cheaper than restaurants: *Onda*, Av. Gentil Bittencourt 663; *Palheta*, bus station; *Pop's*, Av. Conselheiro Furtado 637 (nr. Padre Eutíquio); *Garrafão*, Av. Serzedelo Correa (below Ed. Manuel Pinto); *Tip-Top*, Av. Padre Eutíquio (especially for ice-cream and snacks); *Bug*, near airport; *Bos's*, Av. Gentil Bittencourt/Trav Quintino Bocaiúva (snacks, standing only); *Milano*, Av. Presidente Vargas, next to *Hotel Grão Pará* (especially for cakes and pizzas). There are also many street vendors, who should be viewed with care.

Electric Current 110 A.C., 60 cycles.

Steamship Services Regular communications with Liverpool and New York. Also with West German ports by cargo vessels of the Norddeutsche Lloyd line, with limited passenger accommodation. Occasional services to New Orleans and to Panama Canal and Pacific Coast. Infrequent services to Buenos Aires. Regular coastal services to Southern Brazil. Fairly regular services to Manaus and Porto Velho by the Government's Enasa boats (office: Av. Presidente Vargas), whose schedules are most uncertain but they usually go as far as Manaus 3 times a month, taking 5-6 days. (Fare to Manaus, US$68-110, or US$25 third-class and terribly crowded, moreover, 3rd class tickets may not be available to foreigners unless a written request from the national's consulate is presented.) You must book a week ahead for 1st class to be sure of your passage. Going 3rd a hammock and rope are essential (easily bought for between US$5 and US$25), and you need your own plate, cutlery and mug for coffee; you queue at the cookhouse door. Small river launches for shorter journeys may be found at the old port, *e.g.* to Santarém, US$25-35 with food, but don't drink the water (cargo-boats to Santarém, US$15). There is no regular ferry to Macapá; sporadic boat services; check at docks.

Air Services   Regular flights N to New York and S to Brazilian cities, Montevideo and Buenos Aires; to Brasília and to Santarém and Manaus, the latter with connection for Leticia, Colombia (US$50), with Saturday flight giving connection for Bogotá; S to São Paulo, N to Miami. Twice weekly to Paramaribo and Cayenne; fares US$80 and US$60, respectively. Bus "Perpétuo Socorro" or "Icoaraci", every 15 minutes from Prefeitura to airport, US$0.10; Taxi to airport, US$2.50 (though meter says a little over US$2). Note that there are no money-changing facilities at airport. There are now no flights between Belém and Trinidad and Guyana. To Oiapoque on Cayenne frontier by TABA, US$48, or by Cruzeiro do Sul, US$64. Daily service to Macapá, 1800, US$30.

British Consul   Av. Presidente Vargas 119. Caixa Postal 98. Tel.: 23-5319.

American Consul   Av. Oswaldo Cruz 165. Tel.: 23-0800.

Tour   Herr Volker Filss, a German traveller, has sent us the following suggestion for a one-day sightseeing tour, subsequently revised by Mr. Philip A. Smith, recently of BOLSA, of Belém: "Go to the Ver-o-Peso market early in the morning when the boats are coming in and watch the unloading of the fish and the vendors in the market. Take a bus marked Souza at the market and ask the driver to drop you at the Bosque (open 0800-1100 and 1400-1700). Take the same bus back and get off at the Museu Paraense (Goeldi) in Av. Magalhães Barata (formerly Independência). After visiting museum and gardens, walk down avenue to the Basilica (Nossa Senhora de Nazaré) and then on to the Praça da República (on the way the Tourist Office will be passed on the right). At this end of the Praça da República is the Edifício Manuel Pinto de Silva. From the top (26 floors restaurant and terrace) you have views of the city (entrance free at 2nd door on Av. Serzedelo Correa). From the Edifício you walk to the Teatro da Paz and along Av. Presidente Vargas. Before reaching the docks, turn left along, say, Av. Santo Antônio and Av. João Alfredo, through the shopping and commercial area (interesting narrow streets and open-fronted shops) to reach the harbour with its fishing boats and to the left the Prefeitura Municipal and Palácio do Governo. Beyond stand the Cathedral and the old fort (free entry on request) and *Círculo Militar* restaurant. Depending on your progress, lunch can be taken by the Basilica (*e.g. Avenida* restaurant directly opposite), or on the terrace of Edifício Manuel Pinto, or, say, at *Hotel Central* on Av. Presidente Vargas".

There are sporadic ferries (3 days, US$7) and daily flights from Belém to **Macapá**, an untidy and decaying town on the northern channel of the Amazon Delta. It is the capital of the Territory of Amapá (agriculture, gold, manganese), one-quarter the size of France but with only 115,000 inhabitants, of whom 86,000 live in Macapá. There are interesting old Portuguese fortifications (the Fortaleza de São José do Macapá, built 1764), not much smaller than the Tower of London, and each brick brought from Portugal as ballast. The town is exactly on the equator line, which crosses the jetty outside the *Hotel Macapá*. Gold is sought by washing sand in the river, the criterion being a gallon kerosene can: if you do not find 5 grams of gold in a canful of sand you move on.

Hotels   *Hotel Macapá*, government-owned, on waterfront, small, US$8 s, fair; the *Hotel Excelso*, US$5 s, has been recommended.

Rubber was almost the only other product of the Territory until recently, when manganese was discovered 150 km. NW of Macapá, in the heavily jungled Serra do Navio, near the Rio Amapari, a tributary of the Rio Araguari. A standard-gauge railway, 196 km. long, the only one in Brazil, has been built from the mining camp near the confluence of the two rivers (gravel road from Macapá), to Porto Santana, on the Amazon 34 km. SW of Macapá, from which there is an excellent road. Visitors can

take a taxi to see around the manganese pellet plant. There is a daily air
service from Belém (80 min.). A large power station to supply the north
with electric energy has been built at Cachoeira do Paredão. Malaria is
rampant in Amapá; the illiteracy rate is 85%. Smuggling goes on in a big
way. But the mining area—Icomiland; pop. 4,000—is a startling
exception: swimming pools, football fields, bowling alleys, supermarkets,
dance halls, movies, a healthy oasis in the wilderness hardly matched
elsewhere in Brazil. An unpaved road has been built from Macapá
northward to Oiapoque, on the coast near the French Guiana border, but
there is no regular transport as yet. From Oiapoque a motorized canoe
will take travellers to St. Georges (French Guiana); fare US$0.75 or a
two-passenger canoe can be hired for US$5. Foreigners were not
supposed to enter Brazil *via* Oiapoque, but several have recently done so;
perhaps it is now a recognised crossing point.

There is a monthly boat service between Macapá and Oiapoque, US$6.25, and a
flight from Oiapoque to Cayenne. The boat service on its journey south stops at
Calcoene (24 hrs., US$7, including food) and from there a trip can be made by lorry
(US$4.40) to Macapá.

A few hours up the broad river the region of the thousand islands is
entered. The passage between this maze of islets is known as "The
Narrows". The ship winds through lanes of yellow flood with equatorial
forest within 20 or 30 metres on both sides. In the Furo Grande the vessel
rounds a hairpin bend almost touching the trees, bow and stern. For over
150 km. these lanes of water lead through the jungle. Indians in their
dugout canoes cease paddling to gaze at the huge vessel. Families of
naked children stand on platforms raised above the flood on poles.

When the sun suddenly goes down, troops of monkeys chatter in the
trees. The moon silhouettes the line of palms—ghostly in their
loveliness—and often the indigo vault is ablaze with lightning. These
soundless electric storms, although harmless, are awe-inspiring.

After the Narrows, the first point of special interest is formed by the
curious flat-topped mountains, on one of which stands the little stucco
town of **Monte Alegre** (airport), an oasis in mid-forest.

Santarém, two days up-stream, and on the southern bank, stands at the
confluence of the Tapajós River with the Amazon exactly half-way
between Belém and Manaus, 739 km. from each. It was founded in 1661,
and is the third largest town in Brazilian Amazonia, with 136,000 people.
Colonial buildings faced with Portuguese tiles stand colourfully on the
slope rising from the river, and ships are visited by natives with parrots
and local handicrafts for sale. The yellow Amazon water is mottled with
greenish patches from the Tapajós. By day gorgeous butterflies flit about
the decks, and birds of brilliant plumage, disturbed from their siesta,
cross the river or fly along the banks. At night, immense moths are
attracted by the tiers of lighted decks. The Brazilian army has completed a
road linking Santarém with Cuiabá (Mato Grosso), crossing the Transamazônica at Troncamento.

Hotels in Santarém Varig's new *Hotel Tropical,* de luxe, is now open; *Nova
Olinda,* US$12.50 d for a/c; single room with fan, US$3. *São Luis,* near market,
US$2.20 s, good value; *Nossa Estrella,* brand new, US$10 s, US$15 d, all facilities;
its Italian owner Antonio Piscopo has a boat of the same name going to Belém,
US$19, 43 hrs.

Airport Internal flights only.

River Services Small launches leave for Belém (about US$23) and Manaus 2-5 days (about US$15) most days. Enquire at the waterfront.

Banks Banco do Brasil changes foreign currency and travellers' cheques.

Buses Santarém to Itaituba, 8 hrs. US$7.70, there connecting service to **Marabá** on the River Tocantins, 34 hrs. US$20.40. (Beware of vehicles that offer a lift, which frequently turn out to be taxis.) From Marabá *(Hotel São Félix, Hotel Hilda Palace)* buses leave daily at 0430, 1200 and 1500 for Belém and one for Imperatriz at 1000; buses can be caught going south at Toncantinópolis, opposite Porto Franco on the Belém-Brasília road. Also a bus can be taken to Araguaína, 12½ hrs., US$5.

110 km. up-river from Santarém is **Óbidos,** with a population of 27,000. It is passed during the night. There the river is comparatively narrow, and for many miles little is seen except the wall of the great Amazonian forest. The river shines like molten gold in the noonday sun, changing to silver when the tropical moon rises in the wake of the ship. There is a small airport at Óbidos.

Manaus, the next great city upstream, is quite different from Belém: it is not so much a Brazilian city as a city in Brazil, an urban island in the jungle. This remote "free port" is, in fact, the collecting-point for the produce of a vast area which includes parts of Peru, Bolivia, and Colombia. The products brought into the city for export are mostly Brazil nuts, rubber, hardwoods, cacao and aromatic plants and herbs. A number of paddle-wheeled, wood-burning or diesel converted steamers are tied up to the banks or anchored offshore, along with scores of dilapidated river craft, dugout canoes and launches. There is superb swimming in the natural pools and under falls of clear water in the little streams which rush through the woods, but take locals' advice on swimming in the river; electric eels and various other kinds of unpleasant fish, apart from the notorious piranhas, abound.

Until recently Manaus' only communications were by river and air, but now a road SW to Porto Velho, which is already connected by road with Brasília, has been completed. Another has been built due N to Boa Vista, from where other roads already reach the Venezuelan and Guyanese frontiers; completion was long held up by hostile Indians, who are still a potential danger to travellers.

Manaus, is the capital of the State of Amazonas, the largest in Brazil, with a population of 960,000. About 350,000 live in Manaus, almost the only port of entry and exit in the area. Though 1,600 km. from the sea, it is only 32 metres above sea-level. The average temperature is 27°C. A conglomeration of up-to-date buildings, fine stores, comfortable residences, shacks and thatched huts, the city sprawls over a series of eroded and gently sloping hills divided by numerous streams *(igarapés)*. Dominating the centre is a Cathedral built in simple Jesuit style on a hummock overlooking the dock area: nothing distinguished inside or out. Huge stone steps approach the church from each side. Under it a Funai shop sells souvenirs. To one side and just behind is the main shopping and business area, the tree-lined Avenida Eduardo Ribeiro; crossing it is the wide, attractive Av. 7 de Setembro, bordered by Benjamin Ficus trees. There is a modern air-conditioned theatre. Manaus is building so fast that 20-storey modern buildings are rising above the traditional flat, red-tiled roofs. Manaus was the first city in South America to install trams, but they have now been replaced by rather overcrowded buses.

Other attractions are the Botanic Gardens (with a small zoo), the well stocked Public Library, and the legendary Opera House, the Teatro

Amazonas, completed in 1896 during the fabulous rubber boom and rebuilt in 1929. It is in the city, facing a large square; its back door is opposite the Palace of Justice. Its huge dome of green, yellow, blue and red French tiles can be seen from almost any part of the city. It seats over a thousand people and has many impressive rooms; it reopened in 1974, and restoration is now complete. It is used about once a month for plays; entry to view, US$2.40 (0800-1200 and 1400-1800, Mon.-Fri., 1400-1800 Sat.). It is worthwhile visiting the two markets near the docks; best early in morning. There is a curious little church, the Igreja do Pobre Diabo, in the suburb of Cachoeirinha; it is only 4 metres wide by 5 metres long, and was built by a worker (the "poor devil" of the title).

The Rio Negro has an average annual rise and fall of 14 metres. The Booth Steamship Company have served Manaus ever since 1898, and it was they, through their one-time subsidiary, Manaos Harbour Ltd., who built the remarkable harbour works, a curious feature of which is a floating ramp about 150 metres in length leading from street level to the passenger-ship floating dock. When the water is high, the roadway floats on a series of large iron tanks measuring 7½ metres in diameter. The Alfândega (Customs house) a large yellow building near the harbour, was brought block by block from Scotland. Tourists can visit the docks on Sundays, 0600-1000.

Exports range from timber, rubber, jute products, Brazil nuts, essence of rosewood, lechi caspi, palm oils, fibres, resins, medicinal roots and herbs down to dried fish, dyes and flavourings.

Manaus is a free trade zone. When you leave the city you are required to fill out a customs declaration on all articles you have bought there, which you are requested to pack in your hold luggage; in fact it is a good idea to declare goods of non-Brazilian origin such as cameras, radios, tape-recorders etc. on arrival in order to avoid any problems. If you are travelling elsewhere in Brazil your baggage will be subject to Customs examination on arrival.

Duty-Free Imports   Travellers entering Brazil through Manaus may import from the zone, duty-free, foreign electrical or electronic goods (only one of each type) up to a value of US$150 and food products up to a value of US$25.

Local Holidays   Jan. 6 (Epiphany); Ash Wednesday, half-day; Maundy Thursday; June 24 (St. John); July 14; Sept. 5; Oct. 30; Nov. 1, All Saints Day, half-day; Christmas Eve; New Year's Eve, half-day.

The annual Folklore Festival (dates vary, but about end of June) is well worth seeing for its colour, noise, and pleasure. On Sept. 5 there is a celebration march past between 0800 and 1100, with bands of marchers from all the local schools, clubs, associations, etc.

N.B.   Manaus time is one hour behind Brazilian standard time.

Museu Indígena Salesiano, in Catholic School at end of Av. 7 de Setembro, has most interesting exhibits of Indian culture in Amazonas (entry 0800-1100 and 1400-1700, closed Sundays, US$0.30). Next to it, on Rua Duque de Caxias, is a rubber factory that may be visited free, and a brazil-nut processing plant. The coin museum, Museu Numismática, is at Rua Henrique Martins 458, free.

Zoo   Run by the military; known as Cosac. Ladies should not wear shorts. Bus "São Jorge" or "Ponta Negra" (US$0.10) from centre.

Hotels   *Hotel Tropical,* Varig's hotel 20 km. outside the city, is expensive, cheapest US$55 d, and there are complaints of slow and inefficient service. No problem with reservations; make them through Varig. *Solimões,* very good, US$17 s, with breakfast; *São Francisco,* Av. 7 de Setembro, clean, friendly, swimming pool, US$18 s, US$30 d; *Amazonas, Lord,* and *Lider,* some rooms a/c, expensive for what they offer, US$25 s up, US$40 d up, with breakfast. *Rio Mar,* US$8-12 s; *Itamarati,* US$6 d; *Eusêbios,* US$10 d; *Central,* cheaper, some a/c, US$12-13; *Roraima,* US$3.75 s; *Grande,* US$7 d, but beware mosquitoes; *Palace,* Av. de 7 Setembro 593, old building, now refurbished with a/c—US$13 s, US$23 d; *Topaz,* Av. 7 de Setembro 711, US$8 d, incl. breakfast, central, new, but not recommended; *Lar,* Rua dos Andradas 106, clean, US$10 d, without breakfast; *Fortaleza,* same street, US$3.50 s; *Aurora,* Rua Joaquim Nabuco 130, US$4.75 s, US$7.50 d, bathroom and breakfast, new management, highly recommended; *Hotel Paris,* near Bolivian consulate, US$10 d; *Floriano,* US$9 d, quite good; *Rio Negro,* US$10 d, without bath or air conditioning; *Pensão Buenos Aires,* near Cathedral, US$8 full board; *Pensão Bolivia,* 24 de Maio 542, US$3.50 p.p. without, and US$7 p.p. with, full board; Spanish spoken, all shared rooms; *São Gerardo,* Av. Joaquim Nabuco, US$2 s; *Hospedagem Pensão Pinguim,* Av. Joaquim Nabuco 154, US$3 s, US$4.50 full board; *Formosa,* Rua Leovegildo Coelho 310, US$5 s, only cold water but good breakfast, US$6 d; *Hospedagem Familiar Garrido,* Rua Dr. Moreira 148, US$2.25, quite good; *Pensão Vidal,* cheap and recommended; *Pensão Belo Horizonte,* US$2.50 p.p., hot shower, friendly; *Pensão Tropical,* Av. Joaquim Nabuco 508, US$2, US$1 to sling hammock, basic but recommended if you don't mind the professional ladies.

Restaurants *Canto da Alvorada,* Comendador Clementino 183, and *Manaus* 300, fair; *Chapéu de Palha,* Rua Fortaleza 619, good fish, most atmosphere; *Kavako,* Av. 7 de Setembro; *Suan Lung,* Rua 24 de Maio; *Xodó,* at corner by Opera House, central and recommended; *São Francisco,* Rua Vista Alegre, ½-hour walk from centre, in Educandos suburb, not dear and highly recommended; good Chinese at *Mandarin,* Rua Monsenhor Continho 490; Airport. Food is very expensive in Manaus. Cheap: *"Go-Go",* air-conditioned, a pleasure for U.S. visitors, ask for the "English menu", sandwiches at moderate prices; *Sorveteria Pinguim,* Av. Eduardo Ribeiro, good, medium-priced; *Bar-Restaurante Maranhense,* same street, good; *Central,* Rua José Clemente; *Lanchonete Bali,* Rua Marechal Deodoro 172, US$1.50 for *prato comercial.* On river front at end of Av. Joaquim Nabuco are several floating restaurants serving fish very cheaply—less than US$1. Reasonable, but probably not completely hygienic. Many restaurants close Mondays.

Tours Amazon Explorers' Tour Service, run by Manuel (Bebê) Barros from office in *Hotel Lord;* his day's run up the Rio Negro, US$16 including lunch, has been highly recommended by some users. Boat *Amazon Explorer* available for hire at about US$230 per day. Kurt Gluck, Quintino Bocaiúva 224, Caixa Postal 361, offers a more personal service at US$50 day excl. food; he also does one- or five-day boat trips which need to be booked as far in advance as possible. The better hotels also arrange tours (ask for Joe Sears in *Hotel Tropical*), and so do the Selvatur (office in *Hotel Amazonas)* and Mundial (Av. Pres. Vargas) agencies. Selvatur have a floating hotel on Lake Janari.

The enterprising go to the Capitânia do Porto and find out what boats are making short trips; e.g., Manaus-Itacoatiara, US$6 first-class. It is possible to travel to Ponta Negra beach by Soltur buses for US$0.25. However, Anthony Hellings suggests that the best swimming is at Bolívar Falls; take Taruma bus, getting off at the police checkpoint on the road to Iticoatiara.

About 15 km. from Manaus is the meeting of the Amazon and the Rio Negro, which is itself some 8 km. wide at the confluence. A noteworthy spectacle here is the meeting of the blue-black water of the Rio Negro with the yellow-brown Amazonian flood; such is the force of the water that the two streams run side by side for about 6 km. without their waters mingling. Tourist agencies run boat trips to this spot, or if travelling on a tight budget you can get up about 0330 in Manaus, take the "milk boat" at about 0400 (if it is still operating) and watch the unique way milk is collected from the farms. It returns about 1300, passing through the confluence. Also the "Joanne d'Arc" leaves the dock area around 0730 and returns late afternoon. Alternatively hire a motorized canoe for two hours for about US$10, or take airport bus to ferry. From hill above ferry dock, confluence can be seen. The ferry is free and across the other side of the river can be seen the Victoria Regia water lilies.

(Many people have expressed disappointment with the shorter tours. The trouble is that authentic jungle life, whether human or animal, does not easily co-exist with a large city.)

Souvenirs Indian handicrafts in the Museu do Indio, 7 de Setembro 217, or try Mr. Richard Melnyk's "House of the Hummingbird", Rua Quintinho Bocaiúva (recommended).

Clubs Ideal; Athletic Club of Rio Negro; Bosque (bathing pool, tennis courts). For evening entertainment (including gambling): Vogue Club (jacket and tie obligatory), Boite Inglês, The In Crowd, Danielo's.

Tourist Information Emantur, Av. Taruma 379, and main post office, Rua Marechal Deodoro, airport and floating harbour.

Electric Current 120-240 volt, 60 cycles A.C.

Banks Bank of London and South America Ltd., Rua Guilherme Moreira 147; Banco do Brasil; Banco Nacional Ultramarino. Open 0700-1530. Most offices shut afternoons. Foreign exchange operations 0800-1200 only.

British Consul, Manaus Shopping Center building, 15th floor.

Roads To jute town of Itacoatiara, 285 km. E on the Amazon (bus service); now paved. Through outskirts of city *via* Taruma bathing waterfalls to Ponta Negra bathing beaches on the Rio Negro, 35 km., bus daily. A road has been built to the southern bank of the Amazon, opposite Manaus, from Porto Velho, and another N from Manaus to Boa Vista (see page 321). Bus, Manaus-Porto Velho, 2 a day, US$11.50, 15-22 hrs., need to book 1 week in advance. Bus to Humaitá, on Porto Velho road, leaves at 0600, arrives at 1900, US$8; three buses a day from Humaitá to Porto Velho (3 hrs.). Bus to Boa Vista, 0500 daily, 15 hrs., US$15.50.

Air Services direct from Miami, Paris, Caracas, and from most Brazilian cities. Cruzeiro do Sul flies to Leticia (Colombia) (US$89) and continues to Iquitos (US$120) on Sundays and Wednesdays; return flights are on same days. On Sunday and Wednesday Avianca goes on to Bogotá (US$132). Flights to Benjamin Constant, opposite Leticia (US$50 ferry) 3 times a week, US$80. There are also flights to Boa Vista, Cruzeiro do Sul, US$56, and Tefé and Tabatinga. The taxi fare to or from the airport is US$4 or take bus marked International Airport from Rua Tamandaré near cathedral, US$0.10. Check all connections on arrival.

Shipping Occasional German vessels. There are occasional services on to Iquitos, with many stops, including Leticia (Colombia). Fare to Leticia, US$40, 8 days. Fairly frequent (irregular) river boats to Tefé (3 days, US$15, including food), Santarém, Boa Vista (not good), Benjamin Constant, Leticia and Porto Velho usually half current air fare. Buy a hammock *(rede)* if travelling 3rd class. Other boats to Santarém (Navio Motor Emerson, 2½ days, US$25; also to Santarém, US$12 by "Cidade de Natal", well recommended. Enasa to Belém (4 days, US$65 first class, US$19, third class). The address of the Enasa line is Rua Marechal Deodoro (offices marked Transnave).

N.B. Enasa have in the past insisted on a letter of reference from a consulate for non Latin-Americans travelling 2nd class. Be careful of food on the boats; may be cooked in river-water. You may need a visa to travel to Peru; consulate at Rua Rocha dos Santos. Those arriving from Leticia should go to the police for their immigration entrance stamp. Departures to the less important destinations are not always known at the Capitânia do Porto.

A Canadian correspondent, Brian J. Olding, has sent us the following account of a trip up the upper Amazon from Manaus to Benjamin Constant:

A number of cargo launches ply their trade upriver from the duty-free port of Manaus to Benjamin Constant and Leticia, stopping in for brief business calls at Coari, Tefé and many of the smaller villages along the shores of the Amazon. Limited passenger accommodation on the launches enables travellers to experience a most interesting passage through the Brazilian interior.

The small alleys of Manaus which lead down to the docks where the launches may be boarded are lined with tiny stands in colourful array, crammed with sacks of flour, rice and *farinha*. The docks exude the typically strong odours of exposed, drying fish, uncovered meat and the remains of rotting, discarded fruit, all amidst a flurry of excitement and activity. The launches themselves are from 15 to 25 metres in length and are powered by diesel engines. Most cargo is stored in the hold, while the balance of provisions is stored on the lower deck where the second-class passengers sling their hammocks. These passengers inhabit a dark, crowded and grimy environment, characterized by a pungent blend of exotic odours which will be appreciated by only the more adventurous of travellers. Second-class fare consists of hard, saltless biscuits and coffee in the morning plus two meals of rice, beans, squash and rather unappetizing meat or fish.

First-class passengers enjoy the open airs of the upper deck; while sleeping cabins are available they are hot and stuffy, providing only a modest improvement over slinging a hammock on the deck. Evenings on the river, however, are cool and one is well advised to bring a blanket or a warm jacket. The first-class dining is an improvement over the second-class fare insofar as the soup, spaghetti and salads provide a more balanced diet. The cost of passage from Manaus to Benjamin Constant is approximately US$25 for second-class accommodation, without a hammock, whereas first-class passengers will pay less than US$5 more for the privileges of the upper deck.

Punctuality of service along the river is virtually non-existent. Delays are frequent and are caused by a variety of factors, from fuel shortages (in which case the boat will simply drop anchor until another well-supplied launch passes by) to engine malfunctions. In addition the Amazon is not a particularly easy river to navigate, especially at night when the chances of running into dead logs are increased. Such mishaps are not particularly dangerous, but create further delays nonetheless. It should also be mentioned that unless a ticket is purchased on a launch which is travelling all the way up to Benjamin Constant, a passenger may find it difficult to make convenient connections when he wishes to resume his journey. A direct passage upriver will generally be of 10 to 14 days' duration.

Numerous small homesteads supporting one or two families dot the shores of the Amazon. A few hectares are claimed from the dense jungle growth so as to enable the riverside farmer to grow a small amount of maize and jute, crops which are traded in the nearest village. One may occasionally buy live turtles from these farmers for about US$2; in return for a share of the bounty the crew will generally be co-operative in preparing the turtle, thus providing a most welcome and delicious addition to the launch's menu.

The arrival of a river launch at such towns as Coari and Tefé is a major event which will draw out half of the town's population. The beaches are lined with small river boats whose roofs are stacked with crated chickens and piled high with bananas and vegetables. Smaller dugouts filled with fish are carefully attended to by local villagers. The fish which are not immediately sold are dressed and spread out on wooden racks to dry in the hot, Amazonian sun. (Tefé is a busy town with a population of 10,000 and a flourishing cedarwood trade.—Ed.)

Both Coari and Tefé, which are flanked on three sides by the jungle, are laid out in the typical Portuguese tradition, with a church, a park and shops in the centre, circled by an assortment of stucco houses and small, wooden, thatched huts. The stops at these villages provide passengers with occasion to pick up cigarettes, fruits and rum and any medicaments which may be in short supply. The warm river water allows for excellent swimming and dugouts may be procured for exploration of the jungle's shorelines.

Benjamin Constant and its Colombian neighbour, Leticia, are both large towns where most foods and amenities may be purchased without difficulty. Accommodation ranges from US$12 per night, first-class hotels, to US$0.70 per night, pensions. Regularly scheduled airlines fly direct routes both to Iquitos (Peru) and to Bogotá (Colombia).

Benjamin Constant A small river-town on the frontiers with Colombia and Peru. Several Hotels, including *Pensão Cecília,* US$3 p.p., meals US$1.80 each; also *Hotel São Jorge; Hotel Lanchonete Peruana,* US$4 d, good food. Eat at *Bar-21 de Maio* for less than US$1. Ferry to Leticia twice daily, US$0.50, 1½ hours. Boat services to Manaus, US$36, hammock space and 2½ meals a day, minimum 4½-day trip. Rio Grande Motors have two passenger vessels, cabin US$42 and second class US$35; trip upstream takes 8 days. It is wise to bring food to supplement the rice, beans and salt fish and sterilized water; mosquito spray is a must, all year round.

Entering Brazil from Colombia   Cross frontier between Leticia and Tabatinga; may get Tabatinga-Manaus free army flight. Boats (Recreio) Leticia-Benjamin Constant, or Leticia-Manaus if lucky (US$33 including food), 5-6 days. Passport formalities in Manaus or Tabatinga. Sometimes a long wait for a boat.

Boa Vista (population 25,000), capital of the extreme northern Territory of Roraima, is about 760 km. due N of Manaus, to which there are air services. The connecting road is now completed but should not be used by private motorists after dark; there are still hostile Indians in the area S of Caracaraí. Boa Vista has road connections with the Venezuelan frontier at Santa Helena de Uairen (221 km.) and the Guyanese border at Lethem. Mount Roraima, after which the Territory is named, is the original of Sir Conan Doyle's "Lost World". There is swimming in Rio Branco, 15 minutes from town centre.

Hotels   *Tropical* (Varig), US$22 d, with breakfast, US$14 s; *Eusêbio's,* US$9 s, US$14 d, make sure to demand single if on your own, good restaurant; *Central,* US$2.75, basic; *Hotel Norte* and *Hotel Brasil* (recommended) in Rua Benjamin Constant, US$3 p.p. There are also two missions who offer hospitality to those in need.

Exchange   US$ and Guyanese notes can be changed in Boa Vista; try Ramiro Silva, Rimpex, Av. Jaime Brasil. Travellers' cheques in Banco do Brasil.

Bus   To Manaus, 2400, 15 hours, US$15.50, 6-hr. stop in Caracaraí.

Border Crossing, Guyana   Get exit stamp at police station in Lethem, then take rowing-boat over border river Tacutu. No car ferry, but river can be forded in dry season. Once in Brazil, register at military camp at Bomfim (no hotels). Phone Boa Vista 2290 (for one G$) for car to take you to Boa Vista (US$45), or if lucky, take a colectivo (US$15, 3 hrs.) and Mon., Wed., Fri. bus US$3.50, 2 hrs. From Bomfim to Boa Vista the road is acceptable; bridge under construction over Rio Branco and car ferry operates every two hours. Visit police at Boa Vista for entry stamp.

Border Crossing, Venezuela   Obtain a Venezuelan Tourist Card from the consulate in São Paulo (possibly also Rio or Belém), the Brasília embassy only issues diplomatic visas. The Boa Vista consulate, opposite *Hotel Roraima* in Rua Benjamin Constant, will delay matters by two weeks and charge US$30 for "telegram clearance from Caracas". Border officials may also insist on a visa, ticket out of Venezuela and US$20 a day—however, regulations state that a tourist card is sufficient (reports Edward Everts of Charlotte, Vermont). Trucks leave for Venezuela from outside *Hotel Norte* in Rua Benjamin Constant, drivers officially are not supposed to take passengers. Travellers coming into Brazil may get a ride from timber trucks returning *via* El Dorado, a 20-hr. journey (or by bus US$4). The road is poor but many travellers feel the journey is worthwhile.

Caracaraí   Three hotels, all "just possible".

We have pleasure in publishing the following description of the area, very kindly sent us by Mr. Charles W. Mueller, of Gainesville, Florida:

Boa Vista, capital of Brazil's northernmost territory of Roraima, is a futuristic "cowtown" in a region where cattle outnumber men nearly 10 to 1. Centred in a vast natural grassland, Boa Vista is a blend of the Western cowboy-and-Indian frontier of 19th Century North America and modernistic Brasília. Its wide, paved avenues radiate like the spokes of a wheel from the Praça Roraima, where the government offices, the banks, post office, cathedral, and principal hotel are centred.

The city has an airport (connected by scheduled airline to Manaus, and Georgetown, Guyana), modern water-purification plant, and extensive army post.

New highways radiate north to Venezuela, east to Guyana, and south to the Amazon basin. (Heavy rain and Indian hostility delayed completion of the Boa Vista-Manaus road until 1977. The savage Atroari-Waimiri tribes, who killed 12 roadworkers and an expedition between 1968 and 1973, are being pacified by Brazil's Indian Foundation.)

A dream dating as far back as 1893, when a pathway was cut through the jungle from Manaus to Boa Vista, the new road provides the first overland link for Brazil's far North to the rest of the country. Importantly, it bypasses the treacherous Rio Branco rapids of Bem-Querer, allowing year-round transport of goods to and from the territory.

Europeans first explored the upper Rio Branco in 1670, followed by Carmelite missionaries in 1725. Brazil took possession of the region by erecting a fort, São Joaquim, on the bank of the Rio Tacutu at its confluence with the Rio Uraricoara, in 1765, to guard against frontier incursions by the English, Dutch, and Spanish.

Col. Manoel da Gama Lobo D'Almada, chief of the Portuguese Demarcation Commission delineating boundaries between Portuguese Brazil and Spanish Venezuela between 1782 and 1792, introduced the first cattle into the Roraima savannas in 1787.

The long-disputed Guyana boundary question was settled in 1904 through a decision of the King of Italy, Victor Emanuel III, who had been chosen to arbitrate the dispute between Brazil and Great Britain.

Brazil created the Territory of Rio Branco in 1943 to aid in administering the area, and changed the name to Roraima in 1962 to avoid confusion with the name of the capital of Acre, also Rio Branco.

Road distances: Manaus-Boa Vista (760 km.); Boa Vista-Venezuelan border (210 km.).

Porto Velho (75,000), capital of the Territory of Rondônia with a population of 243,000, is rapidly being developed as the communications hub of west-central Brazil. It is 867 km. from Manaus, 160 km. from the Bolivian border. The town stands on a high bluff overlooking a curve of the River Madeira, and is dominated by the Governor's palace, the modern Cathedral, and the *Hotel Porto Velho*. Porto Velho has little of interest to the tourist, but the railway expert will enjoy the ancient steam engines in the railway station and on a siding 2 km. away. There is still one engine in working order, which runs weekend excursion trains a few km. up the line. Small railway museum at station, open Tues.-Sun., 0800-1130 and 1400-1800. Even dollars can only be changed at a large loss.

Hotels *Seltom,* a/c, US$18 s, US$28.50 d (nice swimming pool), and *Floresta,* US$20 d, a/c, both new. *Fénix Palace,* US$7 d, good steaks and fish. *Hotel Porto Velho, Guaporé Palace,* US$7 s, US$11 d, a/c, restaurant. *Hotel Rodoviária,* US$4 d, with good restaurant. Other hotels on main street, 7 de Setembro; cheap ones *(Amazonas, Posta, Avenida, Kennedy)* near old railway station.

Restaurants At hotels: *Juazeiro, Carretelo, Dejoca, Tókio* (cheap).

Industries Petrochemicals, tiles.

Air Services Airport 8 km. W of town. Daily flights to Manaus (US$52), Brasília, Cuiabá and Rio Branco.

River Services Manaus, 1st class, US$25 with passable food; 2nd class very crowded. Journey takes 3-4 days when river high; as much as 7 days when low. The boat leaves on Wednesdays and Saturdays. 1st class means upper deck, with more hammock-hanging room, or, if lucky, one of two 2-person cabins. Advantages to 1st class: more room, better view, coffee with milk, meals served first. Food is safe to eat, though monotonous; water-purifying tablets or bottles of sterilized water strongly recommended.

Roads to Cuiabá; Rio Branco; Humaitá on the Madeira river, connecting with the Transamazônica Highway, and on to Manaus (867 km.). Bus to Manaus, twice daily 1400 and 1600, US$11.50, 15-22 hours, heavily booked in advance, buses to São Paulo, sixty-plus hours, US$52; to Cuiabá, 40 hours, (or up to four days), US$31.

Travel Agent Rotur, near *Hotel Floresta*.

The Madeira is one of the major tributaries of the Amazon. The four main rivers which form it are the Madre de Dios, rising a short distance from Cuzco (Peru); the Beni, coming from the southern Cordillera bordering Lake Titicaca; the Mamoré, rising near Sucre, Bolivia; and the Guaporé, coming out of Mato Grosso, in Brazil.

Porto Velho was the terminus of the Madeira-Mamoré railway of 367 km. (closed 1971), Brazil's price to Bolivia for annexing the Acre territory during the rubber boom. It cost a life for every hundred sleepers, 6,208 in all, during construction. The line, built 1907-12, by-passed the 19 rapids of the Madeira and Mamoré rivers, and gave Bolivia an outlet of sorts to the Atlantic. It was supposed to go as far as Riberalta, on the Rio Beni, above that river's rapids, but stopped short at Guajará Mirim (12,000 people); *Hotel Comercial,* US$3.50. The railway is now replaced by a fair road, which uses its bridges; the 370-km. bus ride (3 buses a day, US$9, takes 8 hours or more depending on season)—far faster than the train was. The Bolivian town of Guayaramerín is across the Mamoré river (ferry US$0.30); it is connected by road to Riberalta, and there are air connections with Bolivia. An ancient stern wheeler plies down the Guaporé. From Abunã, 220 km. from Porto Velho (*Hotel Ferroviário,* US$6 s, including meals) the road from Porto Velho continues W to **Rio Branco,** the capital of the State of Acre, 90,000 people *(Hotel Chuy).* At Rio Branco the Transamazônica Highway crosses the road from Brasília and will reach Cruzeiro do Sul and the Peruvian frontier further N when completed; it is hoped that it will be continued by the Peruvians to the river port of Iquitos. A road from Rio Branco goes to Brasiléia, opposite the Bolivian town of Cobija on the Acre River, and finally to Assis Brasil at the intersection of the Peruvian, Bolivian and Brazilian frontiers; across the Acre River are Iñapari (Peru) and Bolpebra (Bolivia).

Note If you need a visa to enter Brazil, apply to the Brazilian Consul at Guayaramerín (Bolivia), who lives across the river in Guajarâ Mirim, before crossing the Rio Mamoré into Brazil. Similarly, before crossing into Bolivia you may need a visa from the Bolivian consul in Guajará Mirim (2 photos needed).

The Centre-West

The centre and central west of Brazil is occupied by the states of Goiás, Mato Grosso and Mato Grosso do Sul. Goiás, a tableland with vast forests and pastures, is also one of Brazil's most rapidly developing agricultural areas, producing cattle, coffee and rice.

Goiânia, 214 km. SW of Brasília, the second of Brazil's planned new state capitals, was founded in 1933 and succeeded Goiás Velho as capital of the State of Goiás in 1937. It now has a population of 600,000, three universities, four museums, three theatres, 18 cinemas, four art galleries, five newspapers, three TV stations and eight radio stations. Goiânia is an exceptionally spacious city, with its main avenues excellently lit and ornamented with plants; tourists can enjoy the Parque Mutirama, and the "Educative Park" and zoo in the western sector of the city; there is a racecourse and also a motor-track, which Emerson Fittipaldi has described as one of the safest in the world. Every Sunday morning there is a handicrafts fair in the city's central square, the Praça Cívica.

Hotels *Brasília; Presidente; Regina; Umuarama; Bandeirantes; Augustus* (all first-rate). Many cheap hotels from US$2 d, *e.g. Olimpia,* near bus station; *Santo Antônio,* Av. Anhanguera 6296, US$2 s; *Monte Carlo,* and *J. Alves,* recommended. Restaurants in Goiânia: *Jaó Club; Long Feung.* Goiânia is much cheaper for eating and sleeping than Brasília.

Airport Nearby, with daily flights to main cities.

Roads To Cuiabá (Mato Grosso) paved 1,100 km. 4 buses a day, US$14; continues unpaved to Porto Velho (Rondônia) and Rio Branco (Acre). To Brasília and São Paulo (bus services). To Goiás Velho, 136 km. (see above).

Banks National banks.

Anápolis, 61 km. nearer Brasília, with a population of 105,000, is an important trading centre.

Hotels *Itamarati; Príncipe; Central Palace; Anápolis.*

From **Rondonópolis,** population 60,000 (many cheap hotels, such as *Dormitório Beija Flor,* near bus station, US$4 d) between Goiânia and Cuiabá, a paved road branches southwards to Campo Grande and thence to the western parts of the State of São Paulo.

Buses from Rondonópolis Brasília, US$18, 14½ hours; Goiânia, US$15, 11 hours; Campo Grande, US$7, 6½ hours; Presidente Epitácio, US$6; Presidente Prudente, US$8.50.

Airport, for internal flights.

If you are interested in Indians, there is a tribe, the Bororo, on a reservation three hours by truck from Rondonópolis. To find out how to get there, see Carmelita Cury, a local historian, at Rua 15 de Novembro, 61.

In **Goiás Velho** (25,000 population), the picturesque old gold-mining town that was capital of the State of Goiás until 1937, there is a small, simple *Hotel Municipal* and a new restaurant called the *Pito Aceso* serving grilled meat as the specialty. Pedro's bar is recommended for its cold beer. There is a regular bus service between Goiânia and Goiás Velho.

The Museu da Boa Morte in the colonial church of the same name has a small but interesting collection of old images, paintings, etc. There is also a state-operated museum in the colonial city hall, which is to the right of the centrally-located old colonial water fountain.

José Joaquim da Veiga Valle, who was born in Pirenópolis in 1806, was the "Aleijadinho" of Goiás. Many of his works are in the Boa Morte museum. While they are highly prized as being done by the best local artist, they lack the power of Alejadhinho's images.

Among places of touristic interest in Goiás state is another colonial town, **Pirenópolis** (176 km. from Goiânia, 220 km. from Brasília). There is a regular bus service between Anápolis and Pirenópolis (66 km.).

A medieval Portuguese festival was brought to Pirenópolis in the old days and is still celebrated at Pentecost each year. Called the Festa do Divino Espírito Santo (or simply Festa do Divino), it lasts a week or more. Costumed Moors and Christians compete in a tourney. The Moors' masks resemble bulls' heads and can be bought as souvenirs. A pastoral drama is presented, there are fireworks, bands, early morning Sunday mass, the coronation of the Emperor (who finances the festival), and every other year there is a counterdance performed by men and boys. There is a small hotel which is adequate but full during these celebrations, so many visitors camp out.

The *Pensão do Padre Rosa* is renowned for its menu of dozens of typical dishes and scores of local sweets. The line forms early each morning during the festival to get in for lunch, as capacity is small. Other small towns in the state used to celebrate Pentecost this way, but the programmes have dwindled and Pirenópolis is now the most famous. Another is held at Trindade, only 18 km. from Goiânia.

English artist Robin Macgregor, whose paintings are widely collected throughout Brazil, is a resident of Goiás Velho.

Caldas Novas   187 km. SE of Goiânia (best reached *via* Morrinhos on the BR-153 Goiânia-São Paulo highway) is Caldas Novas (population 10,000) a newly-developed thermal resort with good hotels and camp site. Daily bus from Morrinhos, US$0.50, 1½ hrs. There are three groups of springs within this area, Caldas Novas, Fontes de Pirapetinga (7 km. from the town) and Rio Quente (25 km. from the town).

Hotels   Best known is the *Nacional de Caldas* in the town, and in the country the *Pousada do Rio Quente*, 25 km. away. Also *Motel Aguas Calientes* and *Cabanas do Rio Quente;* camping at Esplanada.

Two other natural attractions in Goiás are the Cachoeira do Salto (160 km. from Brasília) and the thermal waters of the Lagoa de Aporé on the border with Mato Grosso. At Cristalândia (120 km. from Brasília) there is a waterfall; also semi-precious stones for sale. The Araguaia River provides many sandy beaches and good fishing. 1,600 km. of the river are navigable by boat.

A dirt road connects Goiás Velho with Aragarças (on the Goiás side) and Barra dos Garças (on the Mato Grosso side) on the River Araguaia (Barra can also be reached by a more southerly route from Goiânia). These two towns provide a convenient stopping point on the journey between Goiânia and Cuiabá. A road to the north of Barra extends as far as São João do Araguaia; where this road crosses the Rio dos Mortes. is the town of Xavantina (*Hotel Xavantina,* US$2.50 basic, *Churrascaria Arca de Noé,* highly recommended). Anti-malaria precautions are recommended for the Rio Araguaia region.

To the west of Goiás are the states of Mato Grosso and Mato Grosso do Sul, with a combined area of 1,231,549 sq. km. and a population of only about 2.5 million, or just over two persons to the square km. Mato Grosso (meaning the Great Forest), is half covered with forest, with a large area called the Pantanal (roughly west of a line between Campo Grande and Cuiabá), partly flooded in the rainy season. But east of this line the pasture plains begin to appear. The Noroeste Railway and a road run across Mato Grosso do Sul through Campo Grande to Porto Esperança and Corumbá, both on the Upper Paraguay; much of the journey is across swamps, offering many sights of birds and other wildlife. From **Campo Grande,** the capital of the new State of Mato Grosso do Sul, which has a fast growing population of 130,000 people, a road and railway run south to **Ponta Porã** (12,000 people), on the Paraguayan border opposite the town of Pedro Juan Caballero.

Buses from Campo Grande: São Paulo, paved road, US$10, 12 hours; Ponta Porã, 7 hours, US$3.75.

Trains from Campo Grande: Ponta Porã, 5 hours (express), US$2; Porto Esperança, US$2.25. Corumbá, two a day, US$13.50 on night train for double sleeper, or US$2.50 for 2nd class, 12 hours, day train leaves at 0815, meals served at seats US$1.40; São Paulo, 24 hours.

Hotels at Campo Grande: *Campo Grande*, a/c (luxury), US$15 bed and breakfast; *Gaspar*, room and full board, US$5 a day; *Rio; Colombo; Central; Anache; Mônica; Esperança*, near railway station, US$3.50 d; *Estação*, US$2. Hotels near bus station are expensive.

Restaurants at Campo Grande: *Churrascaria Gaúcha, Don Marchitto.*

Hotel at Ponta Porã: *Palace*, US$4-5 s.

The border at Ponta Porã normally closes at 1700; if crossing into Paraguay some nationalities require visa from Paraguayan consul.

N.B. Bus/train travel from Brasilia to Paraguay is much cheaper, and probably quicker, *via* Goiânia and Rondonópolis than *via* São Paulo.

A new area of tourist interest in Mato Grosso do Sul is being established in the municipalities of Bonito and Aquidauana, where cave formations comparable to or better than those found in the Lagoa Santa region of Minas Gerais are encountered. One of the first to be opened is the Lago Azul cave, 320 km. from Campo Grande, within which is a lake 150 metres long and 70 metres wide.

Corumbá, the chief commercial city in Mato Grosso do Sul, has a population of 160,000. It is on the Paraguay river, and river boats go between it and Buenos Aires, carrying hides and skins, jerked beef and ipecac. The town stands on rising ground (altitude 110 metres), and its flat-topped buildings look imposing from the water. In the buttes to the south of it is the world's greatest reserve of manganese, now beginning to be worked. A 650-km. railway is open westwards to the Bolivian town of Santa Cruz de la Sierra, and there is a road of sorts. Corumbá has good air and rail connections with São Paulo. The new Campo Grande-Corumbá road, *via* Aquidauana, crosses the Rio Paraguay by ferry. It is possible to take a boat to Asunción (Paraguay), US$20 including food (but take some extra), 3 days, remember to get exit stamp from Brazil.

The daily train from Corumbá to Bauru leaves at 0800, reaches Bauru at 1250 next day. Very comfortable (1st US$9.50, 2nd US$5.60). Bauru-São Paulo train leaves 1400, arrives 1950, US$3. Buses from Campo Grande, on the railway, to São Paulo are far quicker than the train, but dearer. Bus seat for Campo Grande-São Paulo and Rio can be reserved on the train (Viação Motta) but must be reconfirmed at bus office. Corumbá-São Paulo, US$7.50 (2nd) by rail but food on train high priced. Check rail times before travelling. A second train leaves Corumbá at 2100, arrives Campo Grande 0640 (sleeping cars), reclining seats very comfortable, sleeping cars also available, US$4 2nd class. The Corumbá-São Paulo bus journey takes two days and a night (US$22).

If travelling by train into Bolivia, note that when the train arrives in Corumbá the rail car to Santa Cruz is already waiting in the station, and there is often a rush to get tickets. Customs facilities are at Puerto Suárez; make sure they put your luggage back on the train.

Hotels *Santa Mônica*, a/c, US$10 for bed and breakfast, good restaurant; *Grande Hotel*, US$9 d; *Venizelos*. Cheap: *Ruas*, US$3 p.p.; *Galileu*, on waterfront, US$2 p.p.; *Paraty, Sallette*, US$3 p.p.; *Schabib*, Rua Frei Mariano 1153, US$1.50 a night, basic but clean, owner friendly and helpful. *Espínola*, US$1.75 p.p., and *Internacional*, opposite station which has day and night prices—one night and day US$3; *Mini Corumbá*, US$4.25 cold with breakfast; *Esplanada*, across from railway station, US$6.60 d, US$3.30 s, cold shower. *Pensão Marabo*, Rua 13 de Junho 776, US$1.25 p.p., meals for US$2. *Residencia Perpétuo Socorro*, US$2 s, US$3 d. There are other cheap hotels within sight of railway station; average about US$1.50 a night.

Restaurants *Churrascaria Gaúcha, Katy's; Churrascaria Rodeio.*

For train services between Santa Cruz and Corumbá, see the Bolivian chapter, page 186. (A dirt road runs to Puerto Suárez, across the river, which is best avoided: it offers nothing to man or beast but mosquitoes.) Tourists entering or leaving Brazil at Corumbá should make sure to have their passports stamped at the police station. Normally the immigration people meet the train, collect passports and return them next morning at the passport office on the railway station. If you need a visa to enter Bolivia, the consulate is at Rua 7 de Setembro, 10 mins. from railway station. No regular transport between Corumbá and Puerto Suárez for train, through colectivos are said to be available for US$1 a seat.

Shipping No passenger service.

The capital of Mato Grosso state,

Cuiabá, on Cuiabá river, an upper tributary of the River Paraguay, which can be reached by water from Corumbá, 644 km., is now a modern city with a new imposing government palace and other fine buildings round a green main square. Alt.: 235 metres; pop.: 100,000. The district is pastoral, but a deposit of galena has been found 40 km. from the town, which is a great collecting centre for rubber from northern Mato Grosso and palm nuts for oil extraction at near-by Várzea Grande. There is a road to Campo Grande (885 km.), on the Noroeste railway to São Paulo, and the new 2,400 km. road from Brasília to Porto Velho and Rio Branco passes through Cuiabá; it is paved between Cuiabá and Brasília. A road to connect Cuiabá and Corumbá, across the Pantanal, is under construction and so far has reached Porto Joffre from Cuiabá. A mark in the Praça Moreira Cabral shows the geographical centre of South America. The cost of living is twice that of São Paulo—meat only is cheaper. It is very hot. Coolest months for a visit are June, July, and August, in the dry season. Good fishing in the Cuiabá and smaller Coxipo rivers; hunting trips are arranged, and the Aguas Quentes hot springs, 90 km. *(Hotel Aguas Quentes)* can be visited. The University of Mato Grosso has an attractive museum of Indian objects, and the military post near the University has a small zoo. Embratur, the national tourist authority, has a project for a tourist city at Chapada dos Guimarães, 70 km. to the north of Cuiabá.

Hotels *Santa Rosa Palace; Fenícia,* US$12 with a/c, no restaurant; *Santa Rosa Hotel; Motel Alvorada; Mato Grosso* (small, clean, almost opposite the *Fenícia* and down a side street), rates about US$10 d per day, morning coffee only; *Capri,* US$3 p.p., good food. Cheap, clean hotel near bus station: *Rio Preto,* US$3 s; others in the same area. All hotels cost at least US$6 d.

Restaurants average; try *Novo Mato Grosso,* next *Sayonara Club* on Coxipo river (club is a good place for children). Try also *Tip-Top;* or at Várzea Grande, a short distance away, there is a floating fish-restaurant on the river.

Electric current 110 volts D.C.

Souvenirs Handicrafts in wood, straw, netting, leather, skins, Pequi liquor, crystallized caju fruit, compressed guaraná fruit (for making the drink), Indian objects on sale at airport, bus station, and craft shops in centre; also at Indian museum maintained by the Indian Foundation (Funai).

Excursions Trips into the Pantanal to view the wildlife are arranged by Technik Film Foto Safaris, Caixa Postal 527.

Air, Road, Railway By air to Corumbá, São Paulo, Manaus, Campo Grande, Goiânia, Brasília and Porto Velho. Comfortable buses (toilets) to Campo Grande in 16 hours go on to São Paulo (US$20) and Rio. Sleeper on train to São Paulo from Campo Grande. Buses to Goiânia (18 hours, US$12) and Brasília (26 hours, US$24, change at Goiânia), road now paved. The road through splendid scenery to Porto Velho is at present dusty and bumpy; there are two or three buses a day (US$31), 24 hours in dry season (May-September) and 2 days, or more, during rains; take food and water. The road due N to Santarém on the Amazon has been completed; no details of public transport as yet.

A journey along the Porto Velho road demonstrates the amount of development along Brazil's "Far West" frontier. The various towns along the road—Vilhena, Pimenta Buena and Vila Rondônia, are all brand-new frontier-style places, sprung up during the last few years. Most hotels in Vila Rondônia cost the same—US$5 d. Recommended: *Horizonte,* US$3 s, with reasonable restaurant and *Sol Nascente,* US$2, with churrascaria restaurant.

The Economy

The Brazilian economy made striking progress between 1967 and 1973, and its performance between 1974 and 1977 was moderately good in view of the problems engendered by the downturn in the world economy after 1973. There was a period of retrenchment after the March 1964 *coup d'état,* but from 1967 to early 1976, economic policy was geared to achieving the most rapid rate of development possible; this policy was particularly successful between 1967 and 1973 when there was an annual average growth rate of 10 per cent; at the same time the rate of inflation was reduced from 24 per cent between 1967 and 1969 to 16 per cent in 1972 and 1973. For some time Brazil avoided the consequences of the oil crisis but this together with other factors led to mounting economic problems, though this fact is not revealed in the simple growth-rate figures for 1974-77 (9.6, 4.2, 9.2 and 4.7 per cent). The figures for inflation over this period show the growing problem (34, 29, 46 and 39 per cent). From 1975 the government has gradually introduced a number of deflationary measures aimed at curbing the short- and medium-term problems of inflation, balance-of-payments deficits and the growing foreign debt.

The authorities enjoyed considerable success in strengthening the external accounts position between 1967 and 1973; the balance of payments surpluses attained from 1969 to 1973 were due in the main to the large and sustained influx of foreign capital which has continued since 1967. Deficits were recorded in 1974-75; however, these were principally the result of large adverse current-account balances resulting from increased import costs, especially for petroleum and its products, and increased service payments. Exports have risen at a steady pace since 1967 and a particularly notable feature has been a sharp increase in shipments abroad of industrial goods. Determined action was taken in 1975 to strengthen the balance of payments by reducing the trade deficit, through the fostering of export growth and selective curbs on imports. This was supplemented early in 1976 by a programme designed to reduce oil consumption, and thereby oil imports.

A significant amount of private foreign investment has entered the country in the past years. The latest available figures show that it reached a total of US$9,824m. at 30 June 1977, of which the USA accounted for 31 per cent, Western Germany 12 per cent, Japan 11 per cent and the United Kingdom 5 per cent.

The achievement of annual growth rates between 1967 and 1974 was largely made possible by a sustained rise, averaging 10 per cent a year, in industrial output. There was a spectacular expansion in output of motor vehicles during this period; the increases in 1975 and 1976 however, were below 5 per cent, and production declined in 1977. Solid foundations for the steel and petrochemical industries have been laid since 1967. In this decade cement, shipbuilding and electrical and mechanical equipment emerged as growth sectors. The vast majority of consumer goods are manufactured locally, as well as a wide range of capital goods.

Despite evidence of growing industrialization, Brazil remains one of the world's largest farming countries and in 1970 an estimated 44 per cent of the economically active population was working on the land. It is generally self-sufficient in food production, apart from wheat. The performance of agriculture since 1967 has been uneven; the growth in output in 1974 was 8.7 per cent, mainly as a consequence of a large 1974/75 coffee crop; in 1975 it was only 3.4 per cent because of severe frosts, floods and drought in July and August which caused damage to several crops; these catastrophes were also reflected in the growth of 4.2 per cent in 1976, but in 1977 these were overcome, the sector growing by more than 10 per cent. Agricultural goods, along with mineral ores, still account for the bulk of export earnings. The country remains the world's largest producer of coffee, in normal years, but the proportion which it represents of total annual export receipts fluctuates greatly, having fallen from 50-60 per cent during the late 1950s and early 1960s to a low of 12 per cent in 1975. Other principal export products are soya, cotton, cocoa beans and butter, sugar cane, meat and maize. The cattle population of Brazil, at 97m. in December 1975, is one of the world's largest. About three-fifths of the country is covered by forests, and pinewood is a major export product.

Brazil is generally considered to possess rich mineral resources, which include about a quarter of the estimated world reserves of iron-ore; these are found mainly in the State of Minas Gerais and certain parts of the River Amazon basin. Other metals mined in considerable quantities are manganese, nickel, bauxite, tin, lead and chrome. So far, however, lack of adequate transport and power, or the deposits' geographical location, has often impeded effective development. Iron ore and to a lesser extent manganese are important export products. There are substantial reserves of coal, but these are mostly of poor quality. Four-fifths of crude petroleum consumed locally is imported, despite considerable production centres in the states of Bahia and Sergipe and important discoveries on the continental shelf in recent years; the Garoupa offshore field near Campos (Rio de Janeiro) located late in 1974, is expected to boost local output significantly from 1979 onwards; in October 1975, it was announced that Petrobrás, the state oil agency, would be permitted to sign service contracts with foreign companies to prospect for petroleum in Brazil and several international groups have since signed such contracts.

Since 1968 successive governments have strengthened the infrastructure by improving transport and communications and developing Brazil's vast hydroelectric potential. In 1977 there were 65,000 km. of federal and state roads open to traffic compared with 46,850 km. in 1968. Between 1967 and 1975 a comprehensive network of highways was built throughout the country; the largest of these is the Trans-amazonian highway, the major part of which was opened to traffic in 1974. The country's ports are being extensively modernized from their current poor condition.

A programme was launched in 1975 to raise the proportion of the nation's freight carried by the railways from 16 per cent in 1973 to 32 per cent in 1980, but this has been badly affected by the Government's deflationary policies (see previous page). Telecommunications have been greatly improved by the installation of microwave links between major cities and the telephone services have been made more efficient, particularly in the Centre-South. Substantial investments have also been channelled to building large hydroelectric plants; for example, the Urubupungá complex on the River Paraná is reported to be the third largest in the world and work has begun on another huge project on the Paraná at Itaipu. Total generating capacity has been raised from 8,000 mw. at the end of 1967 to 21,796 mw. in 1976.

The Government is acting with vigour to resolve the serious long-standing problems facing the economy: these include a paucity of employment opportunities for a rapidly-growing population, the relative backwardness of agriculture; widespread poverty, especially in the North-East; and the policy goal of opening up the vast hinterlands of the Amazon basin and Mato Grosso. This determination is demonstrated by the Second (1975-79) Five Year Development Plan, published in September 1974, which provides for massive public and private investment in fostering industrial and agricultural production, cutting imports, increasing exports, and reducing disparities in the levels of living standards.

Foreign Trade (US$m.)

Year			Imports (cif)	Exports (fob)
1971	..	..	3,250	2,900
1972	..	..	4,109	3,991
1973	..	..	6,016	6,198
1974	..	..	12,635	7,951
1975	..	..	12,168	8,655
1976	..	..	12,277	10,126
1977	..	..	11,999	12,139

Information for Visitors

A Brazilian Tourist Office has been opened in London's West End, at 35 Dover Street, W.1.

How to Get to Brazil

By Air Brazil is connected with the principal cities of Europe by the services of British Caledonian, Air France, KLM, Scandinavian Airways, Lufthansa, Alitalia, Iberia, Swissair, Aerolíneas Argentinas, Varig and TAP. The 3 British Caledonian/Varig flights from London to Rio take only 11½ hours. Air France is now flying Concorde to Rio, halving the normal journey time.

Brazil is connected to the U.S.A. by Varig, Pan American, Aerolíneas Argentinas, Braniff, Aeroperú, Avianca and Viasa, though the only direct flights are operated by the first three companies. Braniff and Aeroperú fly *via* Lima, Avianca *via* Bogotá, and Viasa *via* Caracas. Non-stop New York-Rio by Pan-Am or Varig is 9 hours and 20 minutes.

All South American capitals are connected by air services to Rio. Bogotá, Caracas, Santiago four times a week; Lima six times a week; Asunción and Montevideo, daily; Buenos Aires several daily flights. Paramaribo and Cayenne, once a week by Cruzeiro to Belém; Iquitos, Peru, *via* Tabatinga (on the Brazilian border with Colombia, a few miles from Leticia) to Manaus by Cruzeiro on Wed. and Sun. La Paz and Santa Cruz twice weekly to São Paulo.

For many travellers flying to Rio de Janeiro from Europe *via* South Africa, there is little difference in air fares compared to the direct route.

Airport Tax   US$3 is charged for international flights and US$0.80 (or US$0.40 for 2nd-class airports) for local ones. Tax is waived if you stay in Brazil less than 24 hours.

By Sea   Cargo ships carrying up to 12 passengers are run by several European shipping lines including Lamport & Holt and Blue Star lines. The voyage takes about 14 days. The Booth Line serves North Brazil similarly, from Liverpool and New York. For greater detail see under "Steamship Services". Cargo ships, taking a few passengers, ply between Recife and African ports. Cars can be shipped from Genoa, Barcelona, Lisbon and the Canaries to Rio, Santos and Buenos Aires by Linea C.C. Costa; a service highly recommended by Patricio van Nievelt and now the only regular passenger line from Europe. Other cargo lines will transport cars: charges are on a cubic metre basis and usually quoted in Deutsche marks.

Regular steamship services from the United States are: From New York by Moore-McCormack Lines, Booth Line, Lamport & Holt Line and the Argentine State Line; from New Orleans by Delta Line; from San Francisco and Los Angeles (*via* Panama Canal) by Moore-McCormack Line, returning by the Straits of Magellan; from Los Angeles to Rio de Janeiro and Santos and vice-versa by Mitsui O. S. K. Lines; from California *via* Chilean ports, and Straits of Magellan by Grace Line fortnightly. *N.B.* There is an 8% tax on international shipping-line tickets bought in Brazil.

By Car   The *Carnet* issued by the automobile clubs of other countries is not valid in Brazil, though the Touring Club do Brasil does issue carnets for travel in other countries. There are agreements between Brazil and border countries (Uruguay, Paraguay, Argentina and Bolivia) whereby a car can be taken into Brazil for a period of 60 days; an extension of up to 60 days is granted by the Customs Director (Director de Rendas Aduaneiras, Ministério da Fazenda) in Rio de Janeiro on presentation of the paper received at the border though some reports suggest this may be done in most customs posts.

This now applies to cars registered in other countries; the requirements are proof of ownership and/or registration in the home country and valid driving licence (international or from home country). It is better to cross the border into Brazil when it is officially open (from 1300 to 1800 Monday to Friday) because an official who knows all about the entry of cars is then present. The motorist should in any case insist on getting the correct paper "in accordance with Decree No. 53.313/63", or he might find it impossible to get the 60-day extension. You must specify which border station you intend to leave by, but application can be made to the Customs to change this. If you want to leave by ship the Touring Club in Rio (possibly also elsewhere, but this is less definite) will arrange it for about US$60. You can also arrange the paper yourself for taking your car away by ship. It takes about two days and costs about US$15 in port and police charges. The Touring Club provides information on how to go about it. Crossing by a land border is, in any case, easier and probably cheaper. The law allowing for free entry of tourist vehicles applies only to vehicles entering from Argentina, Uruguay, Paraguay and Bolivia. A large deposit is still required if shipped from other countries.

Any foreigner with a passport can purchase a Brazilian car and travel outside Brazil if it is fully paid for or if permission is obtained from the financing body in Brazil. These cars will not necessarily meet safety regulations in N. America and Europe, but they can be easily resold in Brazil.

Stamp for international driving licence can be obtained from "Jaquim Despachante", Praça de Sé 371, sala 115, São Paulo, Tel.: 36-0729.

Most main roads between principal cities are now paved. Some are narrow and therefore dangerous: the BR-116 between São Paulo and Curitiba is notorious. Service stations are rare on some roads, e.g. Belo Horizonte-Brasília, and new regulations introduced in January 1977 provide for stations closing at night and on Sundays and holidays. There is a 80 km. per hour speed limit, to save gasoline.

Warnings Motorists are warned that it is not always possible to buy premium grades of gasoline in the interior; for instance between Anápolis and Belém on the Belém-Brasília road. Motor spirit in Brazil is expensive; about US$3 a US gallon. However, diesel fuel is cheap and can provide fewer maintenance problems for the motoring tourist.

Young tourists crossing the frontier may get "shaken down" by police on both sides for alleged infringements; one way of overcoming this is to refuse to pay and wait to be released—generally an hour or so. (Advisable only for the strong-minded and those with plenty of time!)

Passports Consular visas are not required for stays of up to 90 days by tourists from Western European or American countries, Morocco and the Philippines. Only the following documents are required at the port of disembarkation: valid passport (or *cédula de identidad* for nationals of Argentina, Chile, Paraguay and Uruguay); an international smallpox vaccination certificate and adequate proof that you can pay your way and your return fare, subject to no remuneration being received in Brazil and that no legally binding or contractual documents are signed. Those who cannot meet these obligations *must* get a visa before arrival, and these are usually valid for one entry only.

Exit permits are obtained from the Aliens Office; they are good for more than one departure and allow re-entries without further documentation—provided these fall within the initial stay granted on entry. This may be for 180 days.

Clothing and personal articles are free of import duty. Such articles as cameras, movie cameras, portable radios, tape-recorders, typewriters and binoculars are also admitted free if there is not more than one of each. Tourists may also bring in, duty-free, 2 litres of spirits, 2 litres of champagne, 3 litres of wine, 600 cigarettes, 25 cigars, 280 grams of perfume, and 700 grams of toilet water.

British Businessmen are referred to "Hints to Business Men visiting Brazil", free on application to Dept. of Trade, Export Services Division, Room CO7, Export House, 50 Ludgate Hill, London EC4M 7HU.

Internal Transport Roads and railways are dealt with in the text, under the cities they serve. Surface travel in Brazil is more expensive than in most other Latin American countries.

There is no lack of transport for travelling between the various principal cities of Brazil; though few of them are connected by railway, most are by road. By far the best way to travel, other than by air, is by bus. Brazilian bus services are on the whole fast, though in theory there is now a top speed limit of 80 kph (hence bus journey times in the text may be understated). They are extremely comfortable, stopping fairly frequently for snacks. The bus terminals are usually in the city centres and offer good facilities in the way of snack bars, lavatories, local bus services and information centres. "Leito" buses ply at night between the main centres, offering reclining seats with foot and leg rests, toilets, and sometimes in-board refreshments, at double the normal fare.

We are informed that hitch-hiking ("corona" in Portuguese) is good in Brazil, especially S of São Paulo. Try at the highway-police check points on the main roads, but make sure your documents are in order!

Rail Good train services from Rio to São Paulo and inside the State of São Paulo. The sleeper services between Rio and São Paulo, and Rio and Belo Horizonte, can be recommended, if they are operating. There are trains to S and central Brazil but they are slow, usually require frequent changes and more and more services are being withdrawn; travellers are normally advised to go by air or road. The "Guia Levi", US$2, has a monthly guide to national rail services.

Air Internal air services are highly developed. A monthly magazine "Guia Aeronáutico", gives all the timetables and fares. All four national airlines—Varig, Vasp, Cruzeiro and Transbrasil—offer excellent service on their internal flights. The former air-taxi companies, Nordeste, Rio Sul, Taba, Tam and Votec, have been formed into scheduled domestic airlines by the Government, and now operate Brazilian-built "Bandeirante" 16-seater prop-jets into virtually every city and town with any semblance of an airstrip.

Information Most cities and towns in Brazil have municipal tourist information bureaux, which provide maps, folders and general hints on what to see and do. They are not usually too helpful regarding information on very cheap hotels, tending to imagine that no foreign tourist should consider staying in anything but the best. "Quatro Rodas", a motoring magazine, publishes an exellent series of guides in Portuguese and English. Its Guia do Brasil is a type of Michelin Guide to hotels, restaurants, sights, facilities and general information on hundreds of cities and towns in the country. The same company also publishes guides of Rio, São Paulo, Salvador and the South of Brazil, with other cities and areas in preparation. These guides can be purchased at street newspaper vendors throughout the country.

As part of Brazil's efforts to develop tourism most states have established special bureaux; most of these bodies have established information offices in the capitals and other major cities of their respective states. Many of the more expensive hotels provide locally-produced tourist information magazines for their guests.

Climate and Clothing Conditions during the winter (May to October) are like those of a European summer in Rio de Janeiro, but more like a European autumn in São Paulo and the southern states. Summer-weight woollens can be worn without discomfort in Rio de Janeiro, but further south something heavier is often required. In São Paulo, which is in the Highlands, light-weight clothing is only required in the summer; the climate can be treacherous, however, with large temperature changes in a brief space of time. White dinner jackets can be worn in Rio de Janeiro and São Paulo during the winter, though black is more normal: neither is usually needed by visitors. A dark light-weight lounge suit is useful for the evenings. (Women need light cotton dresses with a stole or wrap for summer evenings, and light woollen clothing for the winter.) At almost every season of the year a light waterproof coat or umbrella comes in handy. The season of heavy rains is from November to March in Rio and São Paulo, January to April in the north, and from April to July around Pernambuco.

Tropical clothing (palm-beach, linen, or drill) is worn throughout the year in the north, and in summer in Rio de Janeiro and the south. Casual clothing is quite cheap to buy. In general, clothing requirements in Brazil are less formal than in the Hispanic countries. It is, however, advisable for men visiting cinemas and restaurants to wear long trousers in Rio, trousers and jackets or pullovers in São Paulo.

Warning Most houses and hotels outside the large cities have electric showers operated by water pressure, delivering a supply of tepid to warm water. Despite electrical earthing, these showers are potentially dangerous especially when operating on 220 volts. Care must be exercised in their use.

Summer conditions all over the country are tropical, but temperatures of 40°C are comparatively rare. In the coastal towns there is a high degree of exhausting humidity. The luminosity is also very high. Sunglasses are dear in Brazil. Bring your own from home.

Best Time for a visit is from April to October, inclusive. Businessmen should avoid from mid-December to the end of February, when it is hot and people are on holiday.

Health Vaccination against smallpox is a legal obligation for visitors, but it is advisable to inoculate against typhoid and paratyphoid as well. If you are going to Amazonia, or to other low-lying forested areas, yellow-fever inoculation and malaria prophylaxis are advised. Water should not be drunk from taps unless there is a porcelain filter attached or unless you have water sterilizing tablets ("Hydrosteril" is a popular local brand); there is mineral water in plenty and excellent light beer, known as "chopp" (pronounced "shoppie"), and soft drinks. Avoid ice in hotels and restaurants; it is likely to be made from unfiltered water. The British will be interested in the fact that good tea is grown and sold in Brazil.

Most vaccinations can be obtained from the Ministério da Saúde, R. C. Pharoux, Rio de Janeiro.

An excellent hospital, supported by the American and British colonies in São Paulo, is Hospital Samaritano, Rua Conselheiro Brotero 1486, São Paulo (Tel.: 51-2154). Good Brazilian medical service is dear.

Hotels Brazilian hotels are, on the whole, dearer than their equivalents in the rest of South America. The best guide to hotels and prices in Brazil is the Guia do Brasil Quatro Rodas. The type known as Hotel Familiar, to be found in the interior—large meals, communal washing, hammocks for children—is much cheaper, but only for the enterprising. The service stations *(postos)* and hostels *(dormitórios)* along the main roads provide excellent value in room and food, akin to lorry driver type accommodation in Europe, for those on a tight budget. In 1978 Embratur, the federal tourist authority, planned to introduce a star rating system for all hotels in Brazil.

NB. Taxi drivers will try to take you to the expensive hotels, who pay them commission for bringing in custom. Beware!

Camping Members of the Camping Clube do Brasil or those with an international campers' card pay only half the rate of a non-member, *i.e.* about US$1 per day. The Club has 43 sites in 13 states and 80,000 members. For enquiries, Camping Clube do Brasil, Divisão de Campings, Rua Senador Dantas 75—29° andar (Tel.: 222 9745), Rio de Janeiro. If without cooking facilities travellers may find the site restaurants a little expensive. For those on a very low budget, petrol stations can be used as camping sites; they have shower facilities and food. There are also various municipal sites; both types are mentioned in the text.

Good camping equipment may be purchased in Brazil and there are several rental companies, Rentalcenter, Av. Brig. Luis Antônio 5088, Rio de Janeiro (Tel.: 852 0081 and 853 5147) and Av. Bernandino de Campos 661, Santos (Tel.: (0132) 41489); Camping Service, Rua Tibiriçá 115, Brooklyn, São Paulo (Tel.: 020 0170). For special jungle equipment, Selva SA Rua do Carmo 65-3° andar, Rio de Janeiro (Tel.: 242 9695); for equipping camping vans, Camp Car, Rua Piauí 375, Todos os Santos (26-16), Rio de Janeiro. It may be difficult to get into some Camping Clube campsites during the high season (January-February). Guia de Camping is produced by Artpress, Rua Araçatuba 487, São Paulo 05058.

Tipping is usual, but less common and less costly than in most other countries, except in the case of porters. Hotels and restaurants, 10% of bill if no service charge but small tip if there is; taxi drivers, none; cloakroom attendants, small tip; cinema usherettes, none; hairdressers, 10-15%; porters, fixed charges but tips as well; airport porters, about US$0.20 per item.

Cost of Living There has been considerable inflation in Brazil for some years, and prices are still rising. The average annual increase in the cost of living over the years 1971-73 was about 16%, but it rose by 34% in 1974, 29% in 1975, 46% in 1976 and 39% in 1977; the increase in 1978 is expected to be 35%. Letters from travellers suggest that Brazil is among the most expensive countries for tourists in South America.

Plenty of clothing should be taken, and as much of it as possible washable. Ready-made men's suits are not expensive if made of Brazilian, but more expensive if made of imported, cloth. In general, food is expensive.

Currency The currency unit is the cruzeiro (Cr$) divided into 100 centavos. Notes are for 1, 5, 10, 50, 100 and 500 cruzeiros; coins of 1, 2, 5, 10, 20 and 50 centavos and 1 cruzeiro. Take care to distinguish the present cruzeiro from its predecessor of the same name; the present cruzeiro is worth 1000 of the previous ones. The old cruzeiro notes are now worthless; they had to be exchanged for new ones by the end of July 1975. Any amount of foreign currency and "a reasonable sum" in cruzeiros can be taken in; residents may only take out the equivalent of US$1,000. In addition, tourists on leaving may change back, from cruzeiros into foreign currency, up to 30% of what they have already changed into cruzeiros if they have kept receipts of their exchange operations. Money sent to Brazil is normally payable only in Brazilian currency, with the 30% limit on subsequent reconversion into dollars, so do not have more money sent to Brazil than you need to spend in the country itself. In mid 1978 the official crueiro rate was about 21 to the US$ or about 37.80 to the £. There is an unofficial market, offering about 20% over the official rate, to be found in travel agencies and exchange shops. Cruzeiros can also be bought very much more cheaply outside Brazil, for instance in Asunción or Buenos Aires, or in Puerto Iguazú (Argentina), but not necessarily in the Paraguayan-Brazilian border towns. Advice given on changing money is only a general guide; make your own thorough investigations as conditions can change rapidly.

Weights and Measures The metric system is used by all.

Cables Cables are listed under cities. Cable facilities are available at all post offices, and the main ones have public telex booths. Post offices are recognizable by the E.C.T. (Empresa de Correios e Telégrafos) signs outside. There is a 40% tax added to the cost of all telegraphic and telephonic communications, which makes international service extremely dear. Local phone calls and telegrams, though, are quite cheap.

Telephone The system has been greatly improved. There is now a trunk-dialling system linking the main cities: for the codes look up DDD in the telephone directory. There are telephone boxes at airports, post offices, railway stations, hotels, most bars, restaurants and cafés, and in the main cities there are telephone kiosks in the shape of large orange shells, for which tokens can be bought from bars, cafés and newsvendors; in Rio they are known as "orelhões" (big ears). Phone calls abroad are costly; US$21 for first 3 minutes to Europe. Note that Brazil is now linked to North America, Japan and most of Europe by trunk dialling (DDI). Codes are listed in the telephone directories. It is useless trying to dial long-distance from hotels or public phone booths, as a blocking device is installed into these lines.

Postal charges are high—about US$0.50 for an air-mail letter to USA or Europe. Air mail takes 4 to 6 days from Britain or the U.S.; surface mail takes some 4 weeks. "Caixa Postal" addresses should be used when possible. Leaflets on postal rates are not issued: consult the hotel head porter or Touring Club. Some post offices will not accept picture postcards unless enclosed in an envelope.

National Holidays are January 1 (New Year); 3 days up to and including Ash Wednesday (Carnival); April 21 (Tiradentes, a Brazilian hero); May 1 (Labour Day); September 7 (Independence Day); November 2 (All Souls' Day); November 15 (Day of the Republic); December 24 (half-day) and December 25 (Christmas). The local holidays in the main cities are given in the text. Four religious or traditional holidays (Good Friday must be one) may be fixed by the municipalities.

Working hours are 0900-1800 Monday to Friday for most businesses, which close for lunch some time between 1130 and 1400. Shops are open on Saturday till 1230 or 1300. Government departments are open from 1100-1800 Monday to Friday. Banks are closed on Saturdays. Early in 1977 the Government instituted a study of the staggering of work hours as a fuel economy measure, and this might lead to considerable changes. The British and American Embassies' hours are 0830-1245 and 1415-1700 Monday to Friday. The Consular Section's hours are 0830-1230; 1330-1630 Monday to Friday.

Language   The language is Portuguese. One gets along fairly well with Spanish, but before trying it, one should first apologize for not being able to speak Portuguese. This is a point on which Brazilians are sometimes a little sensitive; efforts to speak Portuguese are greatly appreciated.

One important point of pronunciation is that words ending in "i" and "u" are accented on the last syllable, though (unlike Spanish) no accent is used there. This is especially important in place names: Parati, Iguaçu.

Time   Brazilian Standard Time is three hours behind G.M.T.; of the major cities, only Manaus is different, with time 4 hours behind G.M.T.

Press in Rio   "Brazil Herald", the only English-language daily in Brazil, Rua do Resende 65, Rio de Janeiro Zc-06. Tel.: 263-7002. Not published Mondays. The main ones are "Jornal do Brasil" in the morning, and "O Globo" in the evening. Weekly magazine: "Manchete".

São Paulo   Morning: "O Estado de São Paulo", "Folha de São Paulo", "Gazeta Mercantil" and "Diário de São Paulo". Evening: "A Gazeta", "Diário do Noite", "Ultima Hora".

There are 1000 radio and many television broadcasting stations.

A monthly publication, "Jornal de Turismo" (Largo do Machado 29, Rio), gives notes on tourism, hotel prices, timetables, etc.

Food The food can be very good indeed. The most common dish is *feijoada,* a combination of black beans and rice, cooked separately. In a variant—*feijoada completa*—one or more meat ingredients (jerked beef, smoked sausage, smoked tongue, salt pork, along with spices, herbs and vegetables) are cooked with the beans. Manioc flour is sprinkled over it at table. Almost all restaurants serve the *feijoada completa* for Saturday lunch. Bahia has some excellent fish dishes; some restaurants in most of the big cities specialise in them. Fish is often served as an entrée with vegetable and rice, or as a thick chowder. Boiled fish is served with shrimp sauce and manioc flour. *Vatapá* is a good dish in the north; it contains shrimp or fish sauced with palm oil, or coconut milk. *Empadinhas de camarão* are worth trying; they are shrimp patties, with the shrimps and various ingredients like olives and heart of palm encased in light pastry. A tender grilled steak served with roasted manioc flour goes under the name of *churrasco* (it came originally from the cattlemen of Rio Grande do Sul). There is plenty of game, most commonly stuffed with manioc flour, boiled eggs, and olives. A white hard cheese is often served for dessert with bananas, or guava or quince paste. Meals are extremely large by European standards; if your appetites are small, you can order, say, one portion and one empty plate, and divide the portion!

There is fruit all the year round, ranging from banana and orange to pineapple *(abacaxi)* and avocado pear *(abacate).* Some people like the mango and the (*fruta do conde* custard apple, which should be taken with fresh guava). Two other fruits, *genipapo* and *jaboticaba,* are very good.

The exotic flavours of Brazilian ice-creams should be experienced. Apart from the humble *baunilha* (vanilla) and *morango* (strawberry), Martin Crossland recommends readers to try *açaí, bacuri, biribá, buruti, cupuaçu, mari-mari, mucajá, murici, pajurá, pariri, patuá, piquiá, pupunha, sorva, tucumá, uxi* and others mentioned below under "drinks".

If travelling on a tight budget, remember to ask in restaurants for the *prato comercial* (sometimes known as *prato feito* or *sortido*), a money-saving table-d'hôte meal for US$2 or so.

Drinks Imported drinks are expensive, but there are some quite fair local wines. The beers are good and there are plenty of local minerals. *Guaraná* is a carbonated fruit drink. There is a surprising range of non-alcoholic fruit drinks, known as *sucos: caju* (cashew), *pitanga, goiaba* (guava), *graviola, maracujá* (passion-fruit), *sapoti* and *tamarindo* are recommended by the Editor personally. Gordons, Gilbeys, and Seagers gin, locally produced, are very good.

Recommended wines are Conde do Foucauld, Château d'Argent, Château Duvalier, Dreher, Preciosa and Bernard Taillan. None is as good as a sound Chilean or Argentine wine. The Brahma and Antárctica beers, on the other hand, are really excellent, of the lighter lager type, and are cheaper by the bottle than on draught.

Scotch whisky essence, imported, then diluted and bottled in Brazil, is becoming very popular because of the high price of Scotch imported in bottle. Locally made vermouth and campari are very good. The local firewater, *aguardente* (known as *cachaça* or *pinga*), made from sugar-cane, is cheap and wholesome, but visitors should seek advice on the best brands; Martin Crossland recommends "São Francisco" and the Editor "praianinha". Mixed with fruit juices of various sorts, sugar and crushed ice, *cachaça* becomes the principal element in a *batida,* a delicious and powerful drink; the special name for a lemon batida is a *caipirinha*.

E. Chafuen-Dougall warns us that when ordering a cachaça at a bar, one should be careful to call it a "pinga" (drop) rather than "cachaça" (booze). *Batidas* should be freshly made, not ready-made commercially.

Best Buys   Jewellery (especially in Minas Gerais), costume jewellery, and articles made of gemstones, such as lamps; ornamented articles of jacaranda and other tropical hardwoods, such as carvings, inlaid boxes, tableware, etc.; clay figurines from the North-East; lace from Ceará; strange pottery from Amazonia; carvings in soapstone and in bone; tiles and other ceramic work, African-type pottery and basketwork from Bahia. Good general shops for those with little time to search are Casa Hugo, Rua Buenos Aires 91, in the centre of Rio, and Antigonovo, at Praça da República 177, São Paulo. Brazilian cigars are excellent for those who like the mild flavours popular in Germany, the Netherlands and Switzerland; in the Editor's opinion, those manufactured by Suerdieck of Bahia are the best of the easily available brands.

Indian artefacts are perhaps best obtained from the Funai shops; Brasília, bus station and airport; Rio de Janeiro, airport and Museu do Indio; São Paulo, Galeria Ouro Velho, Rua Augusta 1371; Cuiabá, Rua Pedro Celestino 305; Manaus, Praça da Matriz; Belém, Galeria do Edf. Assembleia Paraense, Avenida Presidente Vargas.

American Express Agents   *Brasília:* Ciclone Hinterland Turismo Ltda., Av. W-3, Quadra 5, Loja 3-A, Tel.: 2.4004. *Rio de Janeiro:* Kontik Franstur, Av. Almirante Barroso 91, 6th floor, Tel.: 283-3737. *São Paulo:* Kontik Franstur, Rua Marconi 71, 2nd floor, Tel.: 36-6301. *Salvador:* Agencia Kontik de Viagens, Praça da Inglaterra 2, Tel.: 2-4508. With a personal cheque and American Express card, you can get up to US$250 in cash (in cruzeiros), but you may not be able to buy new travellers' cheques against your card.

We wish to offer our grateful thanks for help in revising the Brazilian section to John Hale, late of the LBI Economics Department, and very importantly to Martin Crossland, of Brazilian Holidays, Rio de Janeiro, and to Rita Davy, of the "Brazil Herald". Finally to the following travellers: Philip Allen (São Paulo), Ulrich von Aswegen (Osnabrück), Diana Birkbeck and Nicholas Davies, James K. Bock (Mexico City), Markus Casanova (Fribourg, Switzerland), Andrew Cox, Johan P. Dahl and Ulla R. Hoyna (Sweden), Urcel Daniel (Washington, D.C.), Peter Darrah, Owen Davies, Ben Fawcett, Astrid Fickinser (Bernkastel, W. Germany), Gabriel Foscal-Mella (Longueuil, Québec), Peter Fürst and Hakon Hegnar (Norway), Joe and Gloria Gross (Atlanta), Ucky Hamilton (New Zealand), Robert Hertzig (New York City), Donald Illerman (Brackenbridge, Pennsylvania), Dr. Christopher Jeffree, Gerhard Keilbach (Stuttgart), Leslie E. Kent (Pretoria), Per Leth-Espensen (Herler, Denmark), Rolf Maag (Caracas), Daniel and Jan McAleese (Belfast), Klaus Matzka (Perchtoldsdorf, Austria), Bernd Morgeneyer (Berlin), Dr. Patrik von zur Mühlen (Bonn), Alexander Nemeth and Janette Roberts (Australia), Patricio van Nievelt (Chile), Jenny Owen, Dirk Partridge (Washington, D.C.), Dr. Margaret Peil, Thomas Pensler (Benediktbeuern, W. Germany), E. C. Pineles, Andrew Radclyffe, Judith Rattenbury and Nicole Visart, Ines and Joggi Riedtmann (Basel), Henri van Rooy (Roosendaal, Netherlands), Alan Rosenberg (Los Angeles), F. Rüsberg (Allerod, Denmark), Helga Schmidt-Frank and Herbert Schmidt (W. Germany), Michael Scott, Ross Scott (Camberwell, Australia), Gilles Sicotte (Peru), David Gaddis Smith (USA), Andrew Sortwell (Wallace Expedition to Amazonia 1978), Ken and Judy Stevenson (Ottawa), E. S. Ubing (São Paulo), Nicholas Westwood and Julia Amies, and Dr. Clive Willis.

CHILE

CHILE, with an area of 756,946 square km., is smaller than all other South American republics save Ecuador, Paraguay and Uruguay, but is nonetheless larger than France. Its territory is a ribbon of land lying between the Andes and the Pacific, 4,200 km. long and, on average, no more than 180 km. wide. Of this width the Andes and a coastal range of highland take up from a third to a half. It contains within itself wide variations of soil and vast differences of climate; these are reflected, from area to area, in the density of its population and the occupations of its eleven million people.

In the extreme north Chile has a frontier with Peru running ten km. north of the railway from the port of Arica to the Bolivian capital of La Paz. Its eastern frontier—with Bolivia in the north and with Argentina southwards—is along the crest of the Andes at an altitude of 5,500 metres in the north, 6,000 metres in the centre, and 4,000 metres amongst the active volcanoes further south; the crest then tapers at a steadily diminishing height to the southern seas, where the Strait of Magellan lies, giving access to the Atlantic. Chile's western and southern coastline is 4,500 km long.

A coastal range runs parallel with the Andes from the north to the deep south. In the north and central two-thirds of the land, high and sloping cliffs face the sea: ports are precariously built in small indentations of the cliff face or on shelves of ground lifted slightly above the ocean. All the main ports have now been improved, so the use of lighters is no longer necessary.

Down the whole length of the land, between the towering Andes and the coastal range, there runs a valley depression, though it is not well defined in the north. North of Santiago transverse ranges join the two massifs and impede transport, but for 885 km. south of the capital the great longitudinal valley stetches as far as Puerto Montt. South of Puerto Montt the sea has broken through the coastal range and drowned the valley, and there is a bewildering assortment of archipelagos and channels.

From north to south the country falls into five sharply contrasted zones:
1. The first 960 km. from the Peruvian frontier to Copiapó, is a rainless

hot desert of brown hills and plains devoid of vegetation, with a few oases. Here lies the nitrate deposits and there are large copper mines.

2. From Copiapó to Illapel (650 km.) is semi-desert; there is a slight winter rainfall, but great tracts of land are without vegetation most of the year. Valley bottoms are here cultivated under irrigation.

3. From Illapel to Concepción is Chile's heartland, where the vast majority of its people live. It includes the country's three greatest cities. Here there is abundant rainfall in the winter, but the summers are perfectly dry. The valleys are very fertile and intensively cultivated; great farms and vineyards cover the country, which is exceptionally beautiful.

4. The fourth zone—Forest Chile—between Concepción and Puerto Montt, is a country of huge lakes and many rivers, with heavy rainfall during several months of the year. Cleared and cultivated land alternates with mountains or primeval forests. Here is the tourist's and fisherman's playground.

5. The fifth zone, from Puerto Montt to Cape Horn, stretches for 1,600 km. This is archipelagic Chile, an almost unpopulated region of wild forests and mountains, glaciers, fjords, islands and channels. Rainfall is torrential, and the climate cold and stormy. There is no rail or road connections S of Puerto Montt. A traveller to the south takes the steamer at Puerto Montt, steams for 240 km. between the fertile island of Chiloé and the mainland, and then enters a maze of channels and islands extending for 1,100 km. Chilean Patagonia is in the extreme south of this zone. To make the most of this trip, read Darwin's *Voyage of the Beagle* beforehand.

A subdivision of the fifth zone is Atlantic Chile—that part which lies along the Magellan Strait to the east of the Andes. This is in the rain shadow of the mountains and gets little rain. There is a cluster of population here raising sheep, mining coal and running the only oil wells in Chile.

Later in this chapter each of these regions will be dealt with in greater detail, the occupations of its people discussed, and its ports and cities described.

History   There is much in modern Chile—including its people—which cannot be understood save in relation to its early history.

Native Indians had occupied the country for a very long time before the coming of the Spaniards, but probably not in great numbers. A century before the Spanish conquest the Incas moved south into Chile from Peru, moving across the desert from oasis to oasis at the foot of the Andes. They reached the heartland and conquered it, but were unable to take the forest south of the Río Maule; there the fierce Araucanians held them. In 1530 Pizarro and Almagro began the occupation of Peru. Five years later Almagro, at the head of a hundred Spaniards and some thousands of Indians, took the Inca road south to Salta and across the Andes. Many of the Indians perished, but the heartland was reached; bitterly disappointed at not finding gold they returned to Peru. The next conquistador, who took the desert road, was Pedro de Valdivia; he reached the heartland in 1541 and founded Santiago on February 12. This time the Spaniards had come to stay. Reinforced by fresh colonists from Peru and Spain, Valdivia widened his conquest and pushed S into Araucanian land, but was able to hold only the settlement to which he had given his name. The Araucanians fought desperately—they soon mastered the use of the horse—and in 1554 they captured Valdivia himself and tortured him to death. Nearly a century later the Araucanians entered into a treaty with the Spaniards whereby they were to retain the lands S of the Bío-Bío. But the war continued unchecked, and it was not until 1877 that the Araucanians allowed immigrants to settle in their lands.

Two important things happened during the conquest: first, the land was divided into enormous estates among the officers; and second, the Spanish settlers and soldiers cohabited freely with the Araucanian women they captured. The heartland was until recently subdivided into huge estates, and the cohabitation produced by the end of the Colonial period a singularly homogeneous population of whites and mestizos.

The Colonial period was greatly troubled by constant wars against the Araucanians and by internal dissensions, particularly between the landowners and the priests, who strongly objected to a system of Indian serfdom—the Indians were constantly in revolt. Gradually, during the 17th century, they were freed; serfdom was replaced by a semi-feudal bondage which slowly evolved into the inquilino system. Until quite recently the inquilino, or land worker, found all other estancias closed to him if he left his wretched home and poorly paid job to seek another. Now he is protected by a social security scheme, is free to move, and gets a living wage.

There were, too, natural disasters in the form of earthquakes and tidal waves which wiped out the cities again and again. And from the end of the 16th century British and French pirates frequented the coasts. It was to prevent the French from passing through the Strait of Magellan that a colony was planted in 1842 at Punta Arenas. From the first, Chile formed part of the Viceroyalty of Peru; it was controlled from Lima, and trade was allowed only with Peru. This led to uncontrolled smuggling—piracy and smuggling go together—and by 1715 there were 40 French vessels trading illegally along the coast. It was not till 1778 that trading was allowed between Chile and Spain, but by that time colonial loyalty had been considerably weakened. The powerful Chilean aristocracy was no longer content to remain in tutelage to Lima or to Spain. In 1810 a number of Chilean leaders, including Bernardo O'Higgins—the illegitimate son of a Sligo-born Viceroy of Peru, Ambrosio O'Higgins, and a Chilean mother—revolted against Spain.

This virtual declaration of independence led to seven years of war against the occupying troops of Spain—Lord Cochrane was in charge of the insurrectionist navy—but in 1817 General José de San Martín crossed the Andes with an army from Argentina and helped to gain a decisive victory. O'Higgins became the first head of state: under him the first constitution of 1818 was drafted. But there was one thing which was dangerous to touch in Chile: the interests of the dominant landed aristocracy, and O'Higgins's liberal policies offended them, leading to his downfall in 1823. A period of anarchy followed, but in 1830 conservative forces led by Diego Portales restored order and introduced the authoritarian constitution of 1833. Under this charter, for almost a century, the country was ruled by a small oligarchy of landowners. It was during this period, from 1879 to 1883, that the War of the Pacific was fought against Peru and Bolivia; all three contestants were claiming the new nitrate wealth of the desert in the north. Chile emerged victorious—even Lima was occupied—and for 40 years thereafter it drew great wealth from the nitrate fields. One unsuspected result of this was that the Chilean inquilinos, after a taste of liberty, were unwilling to return to the bondage of the big estates; the ex-service men migrated to the cities, or pushed south into the new lands beyond the Bío-Bío recently opened by pressure on the Araucanians. The free labourer had made his appearance.

The rule of the Right was challenged by the liberal regime of President Alessandri in 1920. Acute economic distress in 1924 led to army intervention—extremely rare in Chile—and reforms were achieved. From 1927 to 1931 Carlos Ibáñez ruled as a semi-dictator but promoted economic development. The world depression of 1931, however, wrecked the economy and brought down Ibáñez. In 1932, when elections were again held, Alessandri was again elected president, but he was prevented from carrying out his programme. A later president, Aguirre Cerda (1938-1941) was the first to come from the ranks of the poor; with his passion for education, health and agrarian reform he was able to achieve something, particularly the foundation of the Development Corporation (Corfo) to organise the republic's economic development. But the outcome of the struggle between left, centre and right for power is as yet in the balance. President Eduardo Frei's policy of "revolution in freedom" (1964-70) was the first concerted attempt at overall radical reform, but it raised hopes it could not satisfy. In 1970 a marxist coalition assumed office under Dr. Salvador Allende; the frantic pace of change under his regime polarized the country into Left- and Right-wing camps, and gradually increasing social and economic chaos, with inflation at over 150% in two successive years, formed the background for Allende's deposition by the army and his death in September 1973. A military junta headed by General Augusto Pinochet now rules the country, and Chile's traditional democratic freedoms are, sadly, in abeyance. However, President Pinochet has assured the people that elections will be held by 1988.

The People   There is less racial diversity in Chile than in most Latin American countries. There are about 150,000 pure blooded indigenous Indians, and closely allied stock; 95% of them live in the forest land between the Bío-Bío and Toltén rivers. A fifth is European; the rest is mestizo, a compound of bloods. The stock has not been much modified by immigration, as in Argentina and Brazil. Immigrants did arrive in the pioneer regions being developed during the 19th and 20th centuries, but always in comparatively small numbers. The German, French, Italian and the Swiss immigrants came mostly between 1846 and 1864 as peasants and small farmers in the forest zone S of the Bío-Bío. Between 1880 and 1900 gold-seeking Yugoslavs settled in Atlantic Chile in the far S, and the British took up sheep rearing and commerce in the same region. The influence throughout Chile of the immigrants is out of proportion to their numbers: their signature on the land is marked in German colonisation of Valdivia, Puerto Montt, Puerto Varas and Osorno, where assimilation is comparatively slight. The British community is believed to number about 5,000, scattered widely over the country. It maintains a church, a benevolent society and several schools in Santiago, and schools in Viña del Mar, Concepción and Punta Arenas.

In the desert north, a third of Chile, there lives only 14% of the population. Middle Chile (from Copiapó to Concepción), 18% of the country's area, contains 77% of the total population. The Metropolitan

Region of Santiago contains, on its own, about 36% of the whole population. The forest zone immediately south of this area has a density of 7.7 to the square km., but is still well below the density of Middle Chile (28 to the square km.). The Archipelago is sparsely populated: it contains only 250,000 people, and 44% of these live in the island of Chiloé—a density for the whole area of 0.6 per square km. Atlantic Chile, 7% of the country, has 1% of the population. The rate of population growth per annum—2.4%—is slightly under the average for Latin America.

The death rate as fallen recently; the birth rate is highest in the cities, particularly of the forest zone. Illegitimacy has fallen from 39% in 1917 to about 16.5% today. The death rate, 8.1%, is highest in the cities. Infant mortality is still 78.7 per thousand live births; it is highest in the rural areas. There are 420 hospital beds per 100,000 population and 1,570 inhabitants per doctor. Life expectancy is low at 59. Illiteracy is 34% in rural areas and 9% in the towns.

Today, there is in process an intense urbanization of the populace. The cities are expanding, partly because internal industries are expanding, and some 74% now live in the towns. Housing in the cities has not often kept pace with the increased population; about 200,000 Chileans live in slum areas called *callampas* (mushrooms) in the outskirts of Santiago and around the factories, but the Corporación de Vivienda is energetically tackling the problem.

The Chilean dilemma is that an increasingly North American and European-style of high living in the cities is based upon under-developed economic capacity. Chilean agricultural exports could and should be capable of earning the foreign exchange needed to buy the capital goods necessary for industrial development. In fact Chile only grows a third of the food it needs; 25% by value of the total imports are food. An inheritance from Colonial days of huge estates (1.1% of the owners held 63.7% of the land) coupled with wretched farming methods was largely reponsible for this. Though several million hectares have been taken from the big landowners and handed to the peasants, many of them now unionised and enjoying vastly improved wages and living conditions, agricultural production is still growing at only 2.0% a year against an annual population increase of 2.4%; in fact, with the institutional chaos on the land that followed the acceleration of agrarian reform under Allende, there was a fall in farm production in 1972, and again in 1976. The effect so far of a more "westernised" style of rural living has been to aggravate the demands on consumer goods and food.

Middle Chile is a beautiful and peaceful land. Great rows of eucalyptus and Lombardy poplar trees and weeping willows criss-cross the landscape. The roads, mile after mile, are lined by high mud walls; alongside them flow the irrigation canals. There is an occasional "quinta" or "chacra", a small fruit or vegetable farm. And amongst groves of eucalptus trees and set in beautiful gardens lie the great rambling hacienda houses of the "fundos", the mediaeval estates, with a huge agglomeration at the back of store-rooms, granaries, wine bodegas, stables, dairies and workshops. At some distance is a single street of "rucas", or huts of the workmen. The land worker is no longer a peon. Most of the estates have now been taken over by the Agrarian Reform Corporation (Cora), and are being worked as co-operatives; some have been sold back to their previous owners.

The small independent farms are mostly in the coastal range and along the foothills of the Andes, generally on poor land. Until modern techniques of farming are widely extended, and more funds spent on irrigation, there is little likelihood that the Chilean people will be able to feed themselves.

Communications   The difficulties of archipelago, forest and desert make communication a formidable problem. It would be much more serious if 90% of the Chilean population did not live in the compact central rectangle between La Serena and Puerto Montt. Its traditional means of communication is the sea. There have been regular services from Europe since 1840: the opening of the Panama Canal made these journeys less arduous. Chilean coastal shipping exceeds international shipping both in tonnage and number of vessels. The three southern provinces can best be reached by sea or air; the only road communications are through Argentina. Only a short distance along one river—the estuary of the Bío-Bío—is navigable.

Railways   Chile was the first country in South America to electrify a section of its railways: that between Santiago and Valparaíso. There are 10,100 km. of line, of which most are state owned. Most of the privately owned 2,130 km. of line are in the desert north, where the northern terminal is Iquique. There are four different gauges in the 2,300 km. of railway from Iquique to Puerto Montt, the southern terminal. From this trunk line branches run westwards to the ports and seaside resorts, or eastwards to mines and spas. From Calera northwards the gauge is 1 metre; on the Valparaíso-Santiago and Southern lines it is 5 ft. 6 in. (1.676 metres). There are also small sections of standard and 3 ft. 6 in. (1.067 metres) gauge.

Five international railways link Chile with its neighbours. There is a local line between Arica and Tacna, linking Chile with Peru. There are two railways to Bolivia: a State line between Arica and La Paz (448 km.), and a British-owned line from Antofagasta through the Calama oasis to Ollagüe; its extension to La Paz has been taken over by the Bolivian government. Nearly all Bolivian imports and exports are carried by these lines. Between Chile and Argentina there are two lines: the railway opened in 1948 from Antofagasta to Salta, in the Argentine north-west, and the Transandine Railway linking Santiago and Valparaíso through Llay-Llay, Los Andes, and Mendoza with Buenos Aires. This line carries very little freight, but is an important link for passengers. The Ferrocarriles del Estado publish annually a *Guía Turística,* available in different languages from the larger stations.

Roads   About one-half of the 56,000 km. of road can be used the year round, though a large proportion of them are unimproved and only about 8,000 km. are first class. The region round the capital and the Central Valley are the best served, but most of the towns, even in the desert zone, have a good network of highway.

The Pan-American Highway runs from Arica to Llay-Llay; from Llay-Llay one branch goes to Los Andes and over the La Cumbre (Uspallata) Pass to Mendoza, in Argentina, and the other to Santiago. Another main international road in the Lake District goes from Osorno or Puerto Varas across the Puyehué pass to Argentina. The Camino Longitudinal, linking Arica in the N with Puerto Montt in the S, vital to the Chilean economy, is paved throughout.

Constitution and Government All Chileans over 18 can vote, and voting is secret. Men and women vote at separate tables. Church and State are separate. Normally the press is free. The parliamentary system is bi-cameral: a Chamber of Deputies, which has 150 seats, is re-elected every 4 years, and a Senate of 50 is elected for 8 years, but half its membership is renewed every 4 years.

The President, who must be over 30, is elected by direct vote for a 6-year period, and cannot be re-elected for the following term. He has wide powers: taxation proposals are his province, and he can also initiate legislation, but a two-thirds majority of both houses can over-ride his proposals.

Executive and judiciary are quite separate; the latter is non-political.

The three paragraphs above are not at present operative, as Chile is now ruled by a military junta with absolute powers. Congress has been dissolved, and the press is subject to censorship; courts-martial have replaced the judiciary for many political offences. The state of siege which existed from September 1973 to March 1978 has been replaced by a state of emergency: the curfew is ended, but vehicles are not allowed to circulate for part of the night, so as to save motor fuel.

President—Gen. Augusto Pinochet Ugarte.

N.B. In 1974 Chile initiated an administrative reform establishing twelve regions and a metropolitan area, to replace the old system of 25 provinces. The twelve regions will be subdivided into 40 new provinces.

THE FIVE ZONES: THEIR CITIES AND PORTS
The Desert North

				Old Provinces					Censuses ('000)	
Regions									1970	1975
I	..	..	..	Tarapacá	..	..	..	..	185	210
II	..	..	..	Antofagasta	..	..	..	..	266	287
III	..	..	..	Atacama	..	..	..	..	161	179
									612	676

Note for the tourist Travel by rail is definitely not advisable N of Santiago; the train takes at least twice as long as a bus, and often more. Few gas stations N of Copiapó. Bus service is excellent. Hitch-hiking is officially prohibited, but it is reported to be tolerated at service stations.

The 965 km. between Arica and Copiapó are desert without vegetation, with little or no rain. Only one river, the Loa, crosses this desert from the Andes to the sea. The inhospitable shore is a pink cliff face rising to a height of from 600 to 900 metres. At the bottom of the cliff are sea-eroded terraces, and on these precarious platforms are built the towns, some of considerable size. The uneasy Pacific often makes it difficult to load and unload ships. The railways and roads into the interior zig-zag up the steep escarpments. Beyond the coastal range are a series of old lake floors, some 80 km. wide and at an elevation of 600 metres. Alluvial fans spread out from the mouths of the Andean valleys into these basins. Sometimes as at Calama, there is an oasis in these valleys as they emerge from the Andes. The nitrate fields exploited in this area lie in the depression between Pisagua and Taltal. Copper, too is mined in the Cordillera; there are two large mines, at Chuquicamata, near Calama, and at El Salvador, inland from Chañaral.

Life in the area is artificial: it subsists on outside help. Water has to be piped for hundreds of km. to the cities and the nitrate fields from the Cordillera; all food and even all building materials have to be brought in from elsewhere. Only the small populations of the oases are self-supporting.

There is some difference of climate between the coast and the interior. The coast is humid and cloudy; in the interior the skies are clear. The temperatures on the coast are fairly uniform; in the interior there is often a great difference in the temperature between day and night; the winter nights are often as cold as −10°C, and there is frequently a cruel wind.

The map on page 347 shows the Inter-American Highway running S through the main towns of Desert Chile to the Aconcagua Valley, where one branch runs SW to Santiago and another over the La Cumbre (Uspallata) pass to Mendoza. The Highway is paved throughout, and most of the desert roads are paved and good, although drivers must beware of high winds and blowing sand.

In the most southern of the Peruvian oases is Tacna; 19 km. S of the border, in Chile, lies its twin,

Arica, with a population of 125,000, built at the foot of the Morro headland and fringed by sand dunes. The Andes can be clearly seen from the anchorage. The Morro, with a good view from the look-out park on top (a 30-minute walk from town), was the scene of a great victory by Chile over Peru on 7th June, 1880. There is a war museum here.

There is no rain, winter or summer. The average winter temperature is 14.9°C, and the average summer temperature 21.8°C. It is frequented for sea-bathing by Bolivian society. The attractive Cathedral church in iron built by Eiffel, and fitted with bright coloured windows, is in the Plaza de Armas. A short 63-km. railway connects the town with Tacna, and another (448 km.) with La Paz, the capital of Bolivia. It is this railway, over which flow about half the imports and exports of Bolivia, that makes the city important; it will become more important when the international highway to Tambo Quemado, Bolivia, is completed, possibly in 1979. LAB flies intermittently to La Paz, 1 hour. An oil pipeline runs from Bolivia. There are large fishmeal plants.

The Free Zone in the Department of Arica now imposes customs duties on all but a few articles. Vessels and aircraft and other transport still enter the Zone without payment of customs dues and other charges. Arica is a free port for Bolivia.

Airport to town cost US$9 for taxi and US$3 for colectivo seat. Flights to La Paz and Santiago.

British Vice-Consul

Shipping The P.S.N.C. vessels call southbound; Grace Line, fortnightly to Valparaiso; Italia, Cía. Sud Americana de Vapores, Johnson Line, Gran Colombiana, once or twice a month. The port is now improved by a breakwater and sheltered berths for sea-going vessels.

Hotels *Hostería Arica* best, US$15, about 2 km. along shore, reached by frequent bus service along front (Nos. 7, 8); *El Paso* (very attractive, bungalow-style with delightful gardens), US$15 d; *El Morro; King,* US$7 s; *International,* US$6, very comfortable, central; *Motel Azapa,* attractive grounds but several km. from beaches and centre, *Timos, Savona, Mora* (US$6 the night); *Hotel Lynch* (US$6 d); *Hotel Osteria,* US$23 d with bath, right on the sea (reportedly those who reserve through Hotelería Nacional, J. Miguel de la Barra 433 (Casilla 4190), Tel.: 391133, or cables Honsa in Santiago, are entitled to a discount); *Hotel San Antonio,* US$2 p.p.; *Residencial Balkys,* US$3 p.p.; *Residencial Mandongo,* US$2 p.p.; *Residencial Madrid,* clean, reasonable, recommended (US$5 d, including hot showers); *Residencial El Cobre,* General Lagos, basic, clean (US$2 a night d); *Residencial Edison,* Maipú 235, cheap; many others in this area, *e.g. Residencial Colón,* US$2.50 d; *Residencial Atenas,* Calle Colón, US$3 d with bath, good value; *Residencial Mogambo,* US$2.50 d; *Residencial Universal,* US$1 s; *Residencial España,* US$2 s.

Casino, the year round.

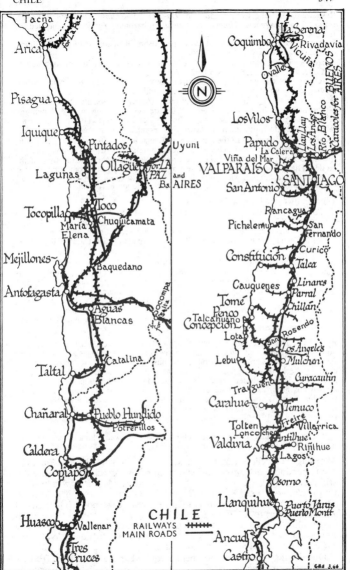

CHILE
RAILWAYS ┼┼┼┼┼┼
MAIN ROADS ━━━━

ROUGH SKETCH

Restaurants At the Casino, *Aduana; Da Aurelio; Chung San; Tourist Ranch; Pollo Siedo; Querencia; Timbao. La Caleta,* on harbour, highly recommended for seafood.

Camping On beach at S end of town, past fishmeal factories. Interesting shoreline; caves, wave blow-holes and birdlife.

Currency Best is Banco de Chile, 21 de Mayo. Also at tourist office on main square and at *Hotel International* when banks closed.

Bathing Nice sandy beach 5 minutes from town by "Balneario" bus from Plaza de Armas. Some good beaches near Chinchorro and others northwards.

Rail To La Paz by Arica-La Paz Railway. No sleeping cars. By Diesal auto-car: Summer, Tues., Fri.; Winter, Wed., 0830, fare US$20 (which includes lunch and afternoon tea, but not breakfast), 10 hours. Tues. and Fri. 1100 ordinary train (US$9.50) gets in following morning at 0700. Food, soft drinks and tea available.

Excursions can be made to the old town of Tacna, in Peru, by road or railway (the railway journey is said to be cheap and entertaining); to the fruitful Azapa valley; to the Lluta valley; and to the wild desert and mountain scenery at the foot of the Andes. The Azapa valley is reached by a bus leaving every hour from same street as Tacna colectivos' depot. Along way there is an interesting museum of stone carvings, information about early settlement and olive production in the valley.

Tourist office 2nd floor of main Post Office.

Colectivo taxis run to and from Tacna for about US$5 and take about an hour for the trip. If there are not enough travellers to fill a taxi, the bus costs only US$1 between Tacna and Arica. Money-changing at frontier, but reported better rates for pesos in Tacna; certainly best to buy Peruvian money in Chile. Local minibus fare is about US$0.10.

Parque Nacional Lauca Yehuda Diner writes: A visit to the Parque Nacional Lauca, some 120 km. E of Arica, is highly recommended. It is in the Altiplano; the scenery shows snowy volcanoes reaching to 6,300 metres, blue cold lakes swarming with waterfowl, and much mammalian life including vicuñas and vizcachas; The Park is maintained by the Corporación Nacional Forestal (Conaf), Caupolicán 1162, Arica, and it is advisable to obtain their advice and approval before making the visit. Conaf has a hut in Putre, a scenic village at Park entrance. The Sajama-Bolivia road to Arica passes through the Park.

Road The Pan-American Highway S is mostly good, fast, 2-lane, concrete with hard shoulders and well signposted and served. Buses to Antofagasta, nightly, Nor-Pacifico, US$7, 10 hrs. *via* Tocopilla, new bus but not a comfortable trip, several customs checks leaving Arica. To Calama and Chuquicamata, daily in evening, 10 hours, US$6. To Iquique, Agencia Norte Sur (Maipú 100, Esquina Prat, locale for several bus lines) daily at 1600 or 1700, US$3.80, 5 hours. 32 hours to Santiago (US$20). There is now a road of sorts into Bolivia; a bus leaves for La Paz at 0900 (about US$12); a better road linking Arica with Tambo Quemado, Bolivia, was due to be opened in 1979. Passports must be stamped at Bolivian Consulate before a ticket may be bought.

If hitch-hiking in a southern direction be prepared to wait a long time; remember hitch-hiking is illegal, though tolerated, in Chile.

Warning Travellers leaving Arica for directions north must obtain a "safe-conduct" or *"salvoconducto militar"*, but check to make sure it is still needed. This is obtained from the *Identificación y Pasaportes* office on the corner of Juan Noé and Baquedaño (take no. 2 or 8 bus). A stamp on the *salvoconducto militar* is then required. Take no. 2 bus (marked *Investigaciones*) to the *Investigaciones* office at the corner of Calle Belén and Calle Chapiquiña (open 0700 to 1100 Monday to Friday). You will not be allowed to travel north without this stamped document. Note, one office issues the safe-conduct, another stamps it.

One driving traveller reports being required at the Chile-Peru frontier to file a form *Relaciones de Pasajeros,* giving details of passengers, obtained from a stationery store in Tacna. In Arica, the driver was required to register at the *Comisaría de Policía*, Av. 18 de Septiembre, in order to drive to Santiago. The first checkpoints outside Arica on the road to Santiago also required the *Relaciones de Pasajeros* from drivers.

Iquique, the capital of the First Region (see page 345) and one of the main northern ports, is 174 km. by sea south of Arica. It was founded in the 16th century on a rocky peninsula sheltered by the headlands of Punta Gruesa and Cavancha. The town was partly destroyed by earthquake in 1877. It has some ancient wooden houses, gaily painted, an outstanding square, Plaza Prat, with a clock tower and bell, and spacious avenues bordered by trees. One, Av. Balmaceda, runs along the coast. The Archaeological Museum of the University of Chile and the Archaeological and Anthropological Museum of the Unversity of the North are here. The latter is small but well displayed and includes a section on minerals; there is an attractive municipal theatre. Population: 90,000. Iquique is a Free Zone area; travellers from the S will meet a customs check. One traveller reports being required to have an exit visa to travel internally from Iquique.

The harbour is well protected and steamers tie up to load at modern docks. A network of good roads and railways runs to the nitrate fields, which are 900 metres above sea level. One road runs SE (80 km.) to the fertile oasis of Pica (2,750 metres), which pipes its water to the port. A road runs NE to the hot mineral springs at Termas de Mamiña, where there is good accommodation for tourists. **Mamiña** is on the Andean slopes, some 130 km. from Iquique.

The Iquique-Mamiña trip by local bus takes about 3 hours. (The police control point just outside Iquique requires registration by foreigners, but the bus waits.) The road is well paved for the first 50 km., but from Pozo Almonte onwards is unpaved. There is a large ravine, Quebrada Duplisa, where no vehicle can pass another, but as it is located slightly on a bend it is easy to look out and cross it. The rainy season is mainly in January, and is called "Invierno Boliviano" (Bolivian winter).

It was at Iquique that the "Esmeralda" and another wooden ship, under Captain Arturo Prat, resisted the attack of the Peruvian ironclad ship "Huáscar" on 21st May 1879, during the war of the Pacific. Fishing used to be good, but the fishmeal factory has altered the marine food chain. The great exports are fishmeal, nitrates, iodine, and salt.

Hotels *Turismo Prat*, in Av. Anibal Pinto, 1 km. from Cavancha Airport; *Phoenix; España*, recommended US$5 d; *Hostería Cavancha*. Plenty of basic but cheaper hotels on Av. Amunátegui (700s); *Hotel Turística*, US$0.80, clean, basic. Reasonably priced *pensiones* include *Residencial España, Residencial Catedral, Residencial Eben-Ezen* and *Motel Primeras Piedras*.

Restaurants *Casablanca; Vina del Mar; Quinta "José Luis"; La Cañada,* near airport, primitive, but food good. Several good, inexpensive seafood restaurants can be found on the second floor of the central market at Playa Cavancha.

Club Casino Español, excellent cheap meals well-served in cool, Moorish decorated 100-year-old rooms; attractive. Club de la Unión; Club Yugoeslavo.

Tourist Information Aníbal Pinto 436.

Banks National banks.

Railway For Santiago, a train leaves on Thursdays at 1035. It is just one coach on the back of a freight train, and the journey takes 6½ days! Check to make sure that it is taking passengers.

Buses To Arica, daily at 1600, US$4, 5 hours, comfortable in spite of 5 or 6 checkpoints. To Antofagasta, daily 0600 and 1400, US$6, a dusty, hot 8-hour drive through the desert, relieved by the occasional oasis. To Calama and Chuquica mata,

US$6, four times a week, at 1400. To Santiago buses leave from Plaza Prat at 0830, (US$18) arriving about 1200 the following day.

Beaches Balneario Cavancha and Huaiquique, excellent November-March. Restaurants at Cavancha.

Shipping P.S.N.C. and coasting steamers. P.S.N.C. agents: Carmona Pahuel, Calle Bolivar 359.

Airlines Cavancha airport. Línea Aérea Nacional (LAN), Tarapacá 320. To Antofagasta, Arica and Santiago daily.

Cables Telégrafo Comercial, Telégrafo del Estado.

Fishing Broadbill sword-fish, striped marlin, yellow fin tuna, oceanic bonito, March till end of August.

N.B. Some travellers in November 1976 were required to obtain stamps on their tourist cards from the Dirección General de Investigaciones.

About 195 km. S of Iquique, and reached by road or from Miraje junction on the north-south longitudinal railway line, is

Tocopilla, which exports nitrate and iodine from two famous nitrate fields—María Elena (76 km.), and Pedro de Valdivia (106 km.). Population: about 26,000.

In the centre is the copper concentrate plant of Cía. Minera de Tocopilla. The electric plant which generates power for the Chuquicamata copper mine, 150 km. to the E, is in the town. There is a sporting 18-hole golf course and fine deep sea fishing if you can find a boat and a guide. There are two paved roads out: a 193-km. coast road S to Antofagasta, and the other E up the narrow valley 72 km. to the Pan American Highway (with a short spur to María Elena and Pedro de Valdivia) and on to Chuquicamata. A dirt road runs N to Iquique, and the final stretch of a coastal road to that city is being built.

There are two sports stadiums and two good beaches: Punta Blanca and Caleta. The place is quite a bathing resort.

Hotels *Hostería Tocopilla* (good); *América* (middling).

Restaurants *Kongton; Leo's.*

Rail Passenger train to María Elena every day except Sunday, connecting with the Longitudinal Railway in Miraje station for Antofagasta, Bolivia, Valparaíso, Santiago and Iquique.

Shipping Regular calls by P.S.N.C. and by coastal steamers.

Cables All America Cables & Radio, Inc., Calle Serrano 1180.

Airport At Barriles, 12 km. from Tocopilla.

From Baquedano junction on the north-south line a branch runs SW to the port of

Antofagasta, some 222 nautical miles S of Iquique and 576N of Valparaíso. It is the capital of the Second Region, and its population of 200,000 makes it the largest town in northern Chile. Vessels anchor in the bay and alongside in Puerto Artificial, which is sheltered by a massive breakwater. It exports the nitrates of the area and the copper of Chuquicamata. A railway runs north-eastwards through the oasis of Calama and over the Andes to Uyuni (Bolivia), from which there are connections by rail to La Paz in the N and Buenos Aires in the S; along this railway nearly half the Bolivian exports and imports are carried. In 1948 a line was opened eastwards over the Andes to Salta, in north-western Argentina. A huge anchor stands high in the mountains, and was used as a navigational aid by ships. The city has little for the tourist, apart from some ruins at its edge, but is lively and attractive, with 3 universities of high standing, quite good parks and public gardens, an interesting waterfront, a clock tower on the main plaza donated by the British community, and very expensive shops. The modern sports stadium is close to the most popular beach (S end of city) where there is also a complete restaurant-pool-discotheque complex. Pavements are bad outside the shopping centre. The delightful climate (apart from the lack of rain) never varies more than a few degrees (18-20°C), but the best time for a visit is from May to September.

LAN has one return service per week from Santiago to Miami *via* Antofagasta. A private Argentine airline, ALA, flies Antofagasta-Salta-Buenos Aires. Ladeco flies Santiago-Antofagasta-Calama.

Industries are mainly beer, mineral drinks, cannery, soap, paint, ice, nails, oxygen, toys, furniture, paving tiles, ready-made clothing, vermicelli, haberdashery, shoemaking, woollen goods, bedding, tubing, printing, parquet flooring, detonators, copper wire, tubes, etc., and sulphuric acid. There are several important foundries, refining plants, a large frigorifico and a shipyard building fishing schooners.

Hotels   *Turismo Antofagasta,* Calle Prat, garage, swimming pool, lovely view of port and city, US$18 s with breakfast, beach and good food; *San Martín,* Calle San Martín 2781, ½ block from main plaza; *Prinz Hotel,* Matta 2321; *Hotel San Marcos,* Avenida La Torre, US$1 d, old, not clean; *Hotel Chile-España,* Condell 2417, US$4 d, friendly, cheap meals; *Hotel San Antonio,* Condell 2235, US$9 d; *Residencial La Riojanita,* Baquedano, cheap and full of young people; *Commercial,* San Martín, friendly, clean; *Residencial Astor,* US$4 d, good value, clothes-washing facilities; *Residencial Calama,* San Martín 2772, and *Residencial Caracoles,* 1½ blocks from railway station, helpful proprietors, both US$2 p.p., shared bathrooms, clean, meals available; *Residencial Lancaster,* cheap and close to railway station; *Residencial Lautaro* in same street; US$2 d; *Residencial Paola,* Prat 766, good value, friendly, clean, US$3 s, US$4 d; *Hotel Chile-Grecia,* US$2 d, Bolivar 455, basic, central; *El Cobre,* US$1 s; *Plaza,* Baquedano 461, US$9 d; *Res. Colón,* Baquedano 329; *Res. O'Higgins,* Sucre 665; *Splendid—Gran,* Baquedano 534 (US$4, warm water at times). *Residencial Crystal,* US$1.50 s; *Hogar Estudiantil,* Calle Sucre; *Hotel Rawaye,* US$4 d, Calle Sucre; *Hotel Takio,* out of old town on the beach, has buses converted into caravans, friendly, beautiful views, US$5 s room or US$3 p.p.

Restaurants   *Climent* Bar-Restaurant, Prat 525; *Helénico,* Sucre 456; *Don Lucho,* Latorre 2356; *Londres,* Sucre/Matta; *Protectora de Empleados,* San Martín 2544; *Italiano,* Prat 732; *Tio Jacinto,* by the central market, friendly, good seafood; *Air Port Station Restaurant; Rancho Coloso* near the Auto Club at the southern end of city; *Arca de Noé,* Mejillones 4835, known for its fish, recommended. The "al fresco" luncheons at the Auto Club are fashionable both in summer and winter. *Club de la Unión,* 470 Calle Prat (quite good). *El Dorado* (music and dancing). *Tatio,* Av. Costanera; *El Arriero,* Condell; *Le Mans,* Prat 488-490; *Delicias de Mar,* Prat 719, good cheap lunch.

Tea Rooms   *La Coquimbana,* Prat 572-582; *La Serenense,* Matta 2383; *Las Mil Delicias,* Prat 677; *Moai,* Prat 461; *Espanol,* Prat 430; *El Gaucho.*

Discotheque   *El Galeón,* transformed from an old fishing boat, 150 metres from *Hotel Turismo Antofagasta,* US$1 entrance fee.

Local Holiday   June 29, day of San Pedro, patron saint of the fishermen: religous procession in which the saint's image is taken out by launch to the breakwater to bless the first catch of the day.

Theatres   In centre: Nacional, Latorre, Imperio, Gran Vía to the S. El Universitario.

Addresses   British Consulate, Baquedano 184; Post Office and State Telegraph, Washington corner Prat; P.S.N.C., Calle O'Higgins 1906; English Club, Calle Washington 2787.

Clubs   English Club, Club de la Unión, Spanish Club, Jugoslav Club, Hellenic Club, Nautical Club, all in (or close to) the main street (Calle Prat); Club de Tennis Antofagasta, in Av. Angamos 906, connected with Av. Brasil, and the Automobile Club, 6½ km. from Antofagasta; Yachting Club, Calle Balmaceda; Italian Club.

Roads To Tocopilla, 193 km.; to Mejillones, 64 km.; to Pedro de Valdivia, 177 km.; to María Elena, 196 km.; to Taltal, 177 km., to Calama, 240 km.; to Chuquicamata, 265 km.

Buses To Santiago, US$15 (dinner and television included) 18 hours, very comfortable. Many buses. On Tuesday at 1800 a less luxurious bus runs, US$10. Bus station at S end of town often has seats left when buses from N terminal are booked. Alternatively, catch a bus to La Serena (US$9) or Ovalle and travel to Santiago from there, US$12. To Arica, US$7. To Chuquicamata, Flecha del Norte leaves at 0700, returns at 1900. To Calama, 0800 US$2.50; leaves later than the train to La Paz but gets to Calama (3 hours) in time to catch the train there, though there may not be many seats left. Frequent buses to Iquique, US$5, 5 hrs., comfortable, checkpoint near Iquique for foreigners. Bus station has a left luggage office.

Coasting Steamers Five companies run services to Valparaíso, Iquique and Arica, and intermediate ports.

Rail Longitudinal railway to Valparaíso twice weekly, Mon., Thurs., at 1835. Take 2 days, 5 hours; sleepers.

Antofagasta (Chile) and Bolivia railway to Oruro and La Paz: train departs Wednesday mornings, at 0645, connecting at Uyuni with the Villazón-La Paz train arriving at La Paz on Thursday at 2000. The frontier is reached about midnight to the accompaniment of considerable palaver. First class fare is US$9, plus US$3 for a sleeper; 2nd class is US$6. For Potosí and Cochabamba change trains at Rio Mulato and Oruro respectively. A down train leaves La Paz on Friday at 1100 and reaches Antofagasta on Saturday at 2120. The desert scenery is spectacular. First-class to La Paz terribly crowded. Note that before leaving you must visit (a) the railway office N end of Calle Washington to make sure there is a seat, (b) the Bolivian consulate for visa (for some nationalities—see Bolivia—not necessary), and (c) the railway station. You must have your passport with you when buying ticket. Meals on train are adequate, but it can be very cold at night; sleeper recommended. The train can be caught at Calama on Wednesdays at 1245; there is a Bolivian consulate there.

Antofagasta-Buenos Aires This train leaves Antofagasta on Thursday at 0015, reaches Salta at 0945 on Friday, leaves at 2315 and reaches Buenos Aires at 1105 on Sunday. The return train leaves B.A. on Mondays at 2005, arrives at Salta at 0830 on Wednesday, leaves at 1640 and arrives in Antofagasta at 2210 on Thursday. Note long stops at Salta (though it's an interesting and fine city). Passengers must change at Socampa. Trains may not run to schedule and journeys may be interrupted by snow between May and October. Fare including sleeper is US$32.

Excursions to nitrate oficinas, over good roads (140 km.) or by train. (Some of the old, deserted nitrate towns are being repopulated as a result of renewed demand for natural nitrates following the 1973 oil price rise.) There are two favourite spots for picnics: near the town of La Chimba, and the fantastic rock scenery at La Portada. A number of bathing beaches, including La Portada, are within easy reach. The port of **Mejillones**, 64 km. N, is reached by road (train only for fiestas); it has a good natural harbour protected from westerly gales by high hills. It exports tin and other metals from Bolivia and its own guano from a nearby mountain largely composed of it. Population: 6,000.

Shipping The P.S.N.C. vessels call on southward and northward voyages; Grace Line.

The desert township of Baquedano is the junction with the North-South Longitudinal line. About 200 km. from Antofagasta is the oasis town of **Calama,** population 72,000, at an altitude of 2,265 metres. The Cía. Sud Americana de Explosivos supplies all Chilean and some Bolivian demand for high explosives. There is a museum which includes a folklore section as well as an archaeological room, closed Mondays. The town is modern and has a developed commercial centre. There is a Bolivian Consulate and a Jugoslav Club.

Hotels *Hostería Calama,* US$2 s, good food; *Hotel Lican Antai; Motel Pukará; Hotel Vivar,* US$1 p.p.; *Hotel Español,* also US$1, hot water, good, US$1.75 s, near main plaza; *Hotel Rolando* (clean and small); *Residencial Vivar,* US$1.50 s, very clean; *Hotel Turismo,* US$10 s; *Residencial Splendid, La Portada, Copacabana, Criollita* and *Angelita,* all cheap.

Restaurants *La Criollita,* on Calle Vivar, *La Florida,* cheap.

Transport Daily bus services to Santiago, Arica, Antofagasta and Iquique.

Consul The Bolivian Consulate is open 1000-1200 and 1400-1600, and will change US dollars for Bolivian pesos.

Excursion Just E of Calama is the village of Chiu Chiu, with a very interesting old church and nearby a unique, perfectly circular, very deep lake. An ancient fortress and rock carvings are to be found in the Río Loa valley.

Some 120 km. SE of Calama—half of road paved, the rest dusty—is **San Pedro de Atacama,** a small town more Spanish-Indian looking than is usual in Chile, is well worth a visit. Both Diego de Almagro and Pedro de Valdivia stopped in this oasis. A most impressive archaelogical museum (0800-1200; 1400-1800) stocked with Indian skulls and artifacts is supervised by Father Le Paige. Graham Greene tells us that "the striking feature of the museum is . . . the mummies of Indian women with their hair and dresses intact dating from before the Conquest, and a collection of paleolithic tools which puts the British Museum in the shade". Along the road are mounds of lava ash and dried-up geysers, making the landscape look rather lunar (see also below) as well as various archaeological remains. Passenger/cargo lorry. from Calama to San Pedro at 0800 (US$0.80, 3 hours) on Mon., Wed., Fri., Sat., returns same day, at 1600. There is also a daily bus service (US$1.75) to Calama, leaving San Pedro de Atacama at 0730 and returning in the afternoon. Extraordinary sunsets. The Valle de la Luna, 18 km. from the town, with fantastic landscapes caused by the erosion of salt mountains, is traversed by a road 13 km. before reaching San Pedro; local residents will drive you there for US$5; driving through the Valle de la Luna at sunset, with the Licanteur volcano in the background, is incredible.

From San Pedro de Atacama one can cross into Argentina over the Pass of Huaytiquina to San Antonio de los Cobres. Travellers by motor car should make careful enquiries into road conditions; petrol must be bought in Calama. (If you are under 21, you may have to show a *permiso del padre* at the border; but any official-looking paper might suffice.

Ulrich von Aswegen, of West Germany, writes: "You have to sign an *acto de compromiso,* which means that you travel at your own risk when crossing the Pass of Huaytiquina. The first village reached is Tocunao, the Atacama desert can be seen in the distance. After a steep climb, you reach the Laguna Legia (4,190 metres), where flamingoes abound. You then pass through the high plains of Huaytiquina (4,200 metres), where only a few herdsmen are found. Before reaching Catua, the first Argentine settlement, you cross the *salares* (salt lakes) and the road winds its way through the Socompa pass (3,880-4,200 metres). The highest altitude reached during the trip was at Chorillos (4,560 metres). The road crosses the Transandean railway, descends into the ghost-like town of Agua Castilla, and after 8 km. reaches San Antonio de los Cobres."

Hotels *Hostería San Pedro,* US$14 s, and two residenciales at US$1.25 per head; *Hotel Licanteur,* reasonable.

Restaurants *Juanita's,* reasonably priced.

At **Chuquicamata,** 21 km. from Calama and at over 3,000 metres, is the world's largest open-cast mine, a state-owned copper mine that used to belong to a U.S. firm. It is an astoundingly large hole. The processes of mining, leaching, electrolysis, smelting and drawing into wire bars can be seen; there are free guided tours with a slide show at 1400 daily, taking 2 hours. Travellers can dine inexpensively beforehand at the works canteen, next to the tourist-reception office. The clean, modern and pleasing town has about 30,000 people. (*Washington* guest house, nice, but book at Santiago or Antofagasta; overnight accommodation may be difficult.) There is a country club with a golf course at Río Loa. Excellent views of the desert and mountain scenery, especially at sunset. Within 30 km. of Chuquicamata there is a series of small towns and villages nestling in remote oases in the Andean massif. Due E of Chuquicamata, 37 km. on the way to Ayquina (see below), are the pre-Incaic ruins of Lasana, a national monument, with explanatory tablets.

Bus from Calama to Chuquicamata, US$0.23, ½ hour, frequent; colectivo to mine, US$0.18.

The old nitrate oficinas working on the Shanks process were closed and many of them have turned into weird ghost towns. (A few have been re-opened.) One of them, Chacabuco, which had 7,000 people in 1938, stands almost untouched near the junction of the Antofagasta-Calama and María Elena road.

Not far from Chuquicamata, in the foothills of the Cordillera, is the little village of **Ayquina,** in whose ancient church is enshrined the statue of the Virgin of Guadalupe. Her feastday is September 8, when pilgrims come to her from far and wide. Processions come from other villages bearing their own Virgins. There is day-long group dancing to the age-old stylised patterns of Indian rhythms on flute and drum. Towards sunset the Virgin is borne on the shoulders of strong men up a steep trail to a small thatched shrine, where she and the people are blessed before the dancing is renewed at the shrine and all the way back to the village. The poor people of the hills gather stones and make toy houses all along the route: pathetic miniatures of the homes they hope to have some day.

Some 440 km. from Antofagasta, at 3,690 metres, on the dry floor of the Salar de Ollagüe near the Bolivian border, is **Ollagüe,** surrounded by a dozen volcanic peaks of over 5,000 metres. Population: 500; one petrol station. A 77-km. spur railroad of metre gauge runs to the copper mines of Collahuasi, and from there a 13-km. aerial tram to the highest mine in the world: the Aucanquilcha, at 6,100 metres. Its sulphur is taken to Aruncha, a town at the foot of the volcano, to be refined. The highest passenger station in this spur is Yuma, at 4,400 metres. A train can be taken from Calama on Tuesdays at 1245, US$1.50. The Collahuasi branch peaks at Punto Alto (4,826 metres), from which there is a magnificent view over 250 km. of the Bolivian Altiplano. Track from Ollagüe into Bolivia.

At this altitude nights are cold, the days warm and sunny. Minimum temperature at Ollagüe is − 20°C, and at the mine, − 37°C. There are only 50 mm of rain a year, and water is very scarce.

The main stock animals are llamas and alpacas, whose principal forage is the ichu bunch-grass covering the lower slopes. There is no timber. Taqui—dried llama dung—and tola heath are used for cooking fires, but the main fuel is yaretal, a resinous moss growing in pillow-like masses in rocky outcrops from 3,500 to 5,000 metres high. Its calorific value is 6,300 Britist Thermal Units per pound—half that of bituminous coal. It apparently is an Ice Age relic, growing very slowly but now worked out in this area. Across the border in Bolivia there is plenty but it is not used. It is claimed, like mineral land, and mined with dynamite to break it into chunks for transport.

From Catalina on the north-south line the Taltal Railway goes W to the port of

Taltal, in the Province of Antofagasta, 300 km. S of that city, connected with it by the Pan American Highway and a poor road along the coast. It is a nitrate and copper ore centre with 7,629 people. Railways run to the oficinas. There is an airport.

Hotels *Plaza; Hostería de la Corfo* (modern; 12 bedrooms, US$12 s). Several boarding houses; one, *La Goyesca,* Martínez 279, has a pleasant cheap restaurant. "The water supply is random, and the Salón de Te has no tea" (J. D. H. Smith).

Buses Three a week to Santiago; several to Antofagasta.

At Pueblo Hundido on the Longitudinal Railway a branch line runs W (64 km.) to the port of

Chañaral, a neglected looking port and town with wooden houses perched on the hillside and beset by water shortages. It is 400 km. S of Antofagasta by sea or rail or Pan-American Highway. Population, including Potrerillos and Caleta Barquito: 50,000. It lies in a rich gold and copper mining area. A short line runs from Chañaral to Caleta Barquito, S of the Bay; this is the headquarters of the state organisation which runs the copper mine of El Salvador, 193 km. to the E. Anchorage is very near jagged rocks which rear out of the sea all round.

Hotels *Hostería El Sarao; Jimènez; La Marina; Hostería Chañaral,* s with evening meal, US$11.

Camping Site at Bahía Inglesa, with small store, laundry, hot showers.

Buses Three leave for Antofagasta between 1100 and 1230.

Steamers Weekly coastal service to Iquique and Valparaíso; service to New York and Valparaíso by Grace Line steamers.

Air Service LAN, daily.

About 240 km. S by rail from Chañaral and 565 km. S of Antofagasta is the inland town of

Copiapó, in a ribbon of farms and orchards about 150 km. long on the river Copiapó, the river generally regarded as the southern limit of the Atacama desert. It is an attractive, well administered copper and iron mining centre with a population of 52,000, and the capital of the Third District; it has an airport. There is a monument to Juan Godoy, a pioneer of the mining industry. The best mineralogical museum in Chile is in the School of Mines. Many ores shown are found only in the Atacama desert.

Copiapó Hotels *Turismo* (good); *Carrera* (small rooms round courtyard, good food, US$3.50 p.p.); *Montán; Inglés,* recommended; *Res. Plaza; Res. Norte,* US$1, recommended.

A branch line of 80 km. runs to the port of **Caldera,** which has a pier of 230 metres; 1½ km. to the S there is a new mechanical pier for the loading of iron ore.

A road runs NE through the pass of San Francisco in the Andes to Tinogasta, in Argentina. South of the pass rises the Ojos del Salado mountain, whose height is given in our map as 7,104 metres. The National Geographic Society makes it 6,874 metres, the Inter-American Geodetic Survey as 6,889, and the American Geographical Society as 6,890. But Captain René Gajardo's Chilean expedition of 1956 calculated its height at 7,087 metres by triangulation and at 7,088 on the altimeters—higher, that is, than Aconcagua's 6,964 metres. Aconcagua has long been held to be the highest peak in the Americas.

Camping Available at Bahía Inglesa.

Thirty-two km. on a railway to the SE, at **Paipote,** is a Chilean Development Corporation smelter for the copper of small producers; gold and silver are also refined.

From Copiapó to Illapel

The second geographical zone, lying between the valleys of the Copiapó and the Aconcagua, contains the southern half of the Third Region and the whole of the Fourth (population at 1970 census, 336,821; 1975 estimate, 385,000). The zone is about 650 km. long.

This is a transition zone between the northern desert and the fruitful heartland. S of Copiapó, the central valley is cut across by transverse spurs of mountain which link the Andes and the coastal cordillera. Between these spurs several rivers flow westwards: the Copiapó, Huasco, Choros, Elqui, Limarí, Choapa, and Aconcagua. Southwards the desert gives way slowly to dry scrub and bush interspersed with sand dunes. Winter rainfall (there is no rain in summer) is still small and lasts only a short time, but it increases from N to S: it is about 115 mm. at Copiapó and 500 mm. at Illapel. In the river valleys under irrigation, fruit, vines, and barley are grown, and some alfalfa for cattle. There are many goats.

These are the main towns and ports in the area:

Vallenar (airport), inland up the Huasco valley, is 174 km. by rail S of Copiapó; it is the second city of Atacama Province, with a population of 42,000. Good wines are produced in the Huasco Valley, in particular a sweet wine known as "Pajarete". A railway runs down the valley to **Huasco** *(Hotel Miramar),* an interesting town and port. 1½ km. S of Huasco is a mechanical pier for the loading of iron ore; it belongs to the Cía. de Acero del Pacífico who work the ore deposits at Algarrobo, inland 32 km. S of Vallenar. The ore deposits blot-out radio at the port. Population: 6,347.

Vallenar Hotels   *Real Hotel Turismo; Hostería Vallenar* (good).

On the coast 200 km. S of Vallenar, 470 km. N of Santiago, is **La Serena** (87,000 people), an attractive old-world town built on a hillside, which has become a tourist resort. It was remodelled in the 1950s and is now one of the pleasantest towns in Chile, with many Colonial-style buildings, pretty gardens and a lot of *azulejos,* or coloured tiles. It has 29 churches, a Cathedral which is the seat of an archbishop, and several old convents. Many rodeos are held, and Chilean independence (first declared here in 1818) is celebrated on September 20 with a huge open-air picinic on the sands at nearby Coquimbo. The most popular nearby beaches are Peñuelas, half way to Coquimbo, and La Herradura. The beach season—and the climate is particularly agreeable—is from early December to late March. A road (about one-third paved) runs 500 km. E over the Paso de Agua Negra (4,775 metres) to San Juan in northern Argentina (closed in winter). At Termas de Socos, 103 km. S on the Pan-American Highway, is a good stopover in arid country at an excellent mineral springs hotel with camping grounds (US$2.50 for 3 persons with vehicle). The climate is often damp and rarely hot. Market on Sundays. La Serena is the capital of the Fourth Region.

History   La Serena was founded by Juan de Bohón, aide to Pedro de Valdivia, in 1544, destroyed by Diaguita Indians in 1546, rebuilt by Francisco de Aguirre in 1552, and sacked by the English pirate Sharpe in 1680. Legends of buried treasure at Guayacán Bay, frequented by Drake, persist.

The Archaeological Museum, in a Colonial-style building, has an interesting collection of Diaguita and Molle Indian exhibits, especially of most attractively decorated pottery, at corner of Calles Córdovez and Cienfuegos. It is closed all day Monday, Sunday afternoon, and from 1300 to 1500 daily.

Hotels   *Alameda,* Av. Francisco de Aguirre, US$12 d, clean and friendly; *Francisco de Aguirre* (Córdovez 210), best, but poor sound insulation; *Berlin; Santiago; La Bahía,* Córdovez 611; *Londres,* Córdovez 566, US$7.50 d; *El Bucanero Hotel* at La Herradura. *Alameda,* US$2 s, clean and comfortable. *Hostería Chile,* basic, fairly

clean, US$1 per head. *Residencial El Loa,* Bernardo O'Higgins 362, US$1.25 s with shower, good inexpensive food available, friendly. *Residencial Petit,* US$1.50, basic.
Motel on Pan-American Highway.

Restaurants *Club Social,* Córdovez 516, unpretentious but excellent; *Oriente,* Balmaceda 677, more expensive but also very good. Cheap one at *Hotel La Bahía.*

Campsite Maki Payi, 153 Vegas Norte, about 5 km. from town, near sea, friendly, recommended, self-contained cabins available.

Transport La Serena is served by a daily automotor (Diesel railcar) from Calera, where connection is made for Santiago and Valparaíso. Bus service (much faster and more comfortable) daily to Calera and Santiago, 7 hours, US$5. By bus to Antofagasta takes 14 hours and to Iquique 20 hours. It takes two days by train to Antofagasta and 3 to Iquique. Bus to Vicuña and Pisco Elqui, 3 hours, US$1.50.

Excursion La Serena is at the mouth of the Elqui river valley, where the Chilean Nobel Prize poet Gabriela Mistral was born. She described the valley as "confined yet lofty, many-sided yet simple, rustic yet a mining area". The road up the valley has been rebuilt and paved as far as Vicuña; "its branches all lead to fertile nooks, to shady vegetation, to dense groves, to gardens fed by the very sap of the hills". Except for Vicuña, most of the tiny towns have but a single street. Of the *elquinos,* the people of the valley, she says that "even the most taciturn of them come out with witty and charming remarks". There are still a few descendants of the Diaguitas, the tribe that inhabited the valley at one time.

The inland motor road and railway to Rivadavia run up this valley, in which there are pisco distilleries, peach and walnut farms and orange groves. **Vicuña** (66 km.; *Hostería,* swimming pool, *Hotel Plaza,* US$4 d with breakfast), capital of the valley, is on the way to Rivadavia at an altitude of 600 metres and has a population of 13,913. There are mines, vineyards and orchards in the district, which produces pisco and dried fruits. The town is picturesque, fairly clean and friendly; it is within reach by car (120 km.) of Termas del Toro in the mountains. A small and disappointing Gabriela Mistral Museum has been opened. Her (unimpressive) grave is at Monte Grande, 20 km. S of Rivadavia. On a peak about 35 km. S of Vicuña is the new **Cerro Tololo** Inter-American Observatory, said to be the largest in the Southern Hemisphere, which has a 400-cm., a 150-cm., a 90-cm. and two 40-cm. reflecting telescopes and a 60-90-cm. Schmidt camera. Permission to visit must be obtained from the AURA office in La Serena. On Cerro La Silla, 100 km. NE, is the European Southern Observatory, with 7 more large telescopes.

Beyond Rivadavia the road runs to the small towns of Paihuano and Pisco Elqui (34 km.), where you can visit old-fashioned pisco distilleries.

Coquimbo, 11 km. S of La Serena and on the same bay, is a port of considerable importance and with several industries. The city has one of the best harbours on the coast, with a mole and pier. There are good beaches to the S near the port of Totoralillo. Population: about 80,000.

Hotels *Hotel Prat; Inglés; El Bucanero* at La Herradura, on Guayacán Bay, 1½ km. from Coquimbo port, listed "de luxe" but is not; *Iberia; Vegmar* and *Coquimbo; Hotel La Valle,* US$1.40, in front of bus station.

Campsites Guanaqueros, at km. 430 on the Pan-American Highway. Camping also available at Morrillos, km. 442 on the Pan-American Highway, and at Socos.

Restaurant *La Barca.*

British Consulate Aldunate 772. Tel.: 445.

Cables Telégrafo del Estado.

Excursions Good beaches to the S at Guanaqueros (29 km.) and Tongoy (56 km.). If motoring, watch the fuel gauge; the nearest service station is at Coquimbo.

A large iron-ore mine operates at El Tofo; the ore is shipped from the port of Cruz Grande. The company also works the iron ore deposits at El Romeral; it is sent by rail to the automatic loading plant at Guayacán Bay.

From here to Santiago, the Pan-American Highway mainly follows the coastline, passing many beautiful coves, alternatively rocky and sandy, with good surf, but the water is very cold, as is the air. The last stretch before Santiago is through green valleys complete with rich blue clover and wild artichokes. Beware, the green caterpillars crossing the road in November bite!

About 248 km. S of Coquimbo along the Pan-American Highway is **Los Vilos,** a small seaside resort with frequent launches to the off-shore Isla de La Reina and a beautiful nearby beach (26 km. S) at **Pichidangui** (*Hotel Kon-Tiki,* state-owned). The *Panamerican Motel* is right on the highway, and is a convenient stopping place between La Serena and Viña del Mar or Santiago; it claims to be American style, which will surprise Americans, but is quite good. Also *Hosteria Arrayán,* clean, US$2 per person. Campsite on Avda. El Bosque.

From La Serena, 51 km. SE by road, is the little town of **Andacollo.** Here, on December 25 and 26, is held one of the most picturesque religious ceremonies in South America. The pilgrimage to the shrine of the miraculous Virgen del Rosario de Andacollo is the occasion for ritual dances dating from a pre-Spanish past. The church is a huge building. Alluvial gold washing and manganese and copper mining in the area. No hotel, but some boarding-houses.

Ovalle, the largest town in the Fourth Region, is in the valley of the Limarí river, and about 50 km. inland from the sea. There is a railway service 3 times a week and a bus service 3 times a day from Coquimbo. It is the centre of a fruit, wool growing, and mining district. Population: 64,300. The thermal springs, Termas de Socos, are 37 km. to the WSW, and 96 km. to the S by rail (or 115 km. by gravel road) is the town of Combarbala, where there is a sanatorium for tuberculous patients. Campsite. A poor 30 km. road runs NW to the small port of Tongoy. The Paloma dam, at the junction of the Grande and Huatulame rivers, SE of Ovalle, is one of the largest in Chile.

Hotels   *Hotel de Turismo; Roxy.*

Airport   6 km. NE.

About 165 km. S of Ovalle by road or rail, and 59 km. by new paved road from Los Vilos, is **Illapel,** in the basin of the river Choapa. Population: about 24,000. Fruit, grains and cattle are raised in the valley.

Hotel   *Illapel* (ex Alemán).

The Heartland

(From the valley of the Aconcagua to the valley of the Bío-Bío.)

Nearly 70% of the people of Chile live in the comparatively small heartland. The nucleus of the nation's social, political, economic and artistic life—the capital, Santiago—is here, and so is its greatest port: Valparaíso. The rural density of population in the area is exceptional for Latin America: it is as high as 48 to the square km. in the Central Valley running S from Santiago to Concepción.

Region				Old Provinces			Population ('000)	
							1970	1975
V ..	..		..	Aconcagua, Valparaíso	..	..	1,028	1,124
Metropolitan	..		..	Santiago	..	..	3,335	3,806
VI ..	..		..	O'Higgins, Colchagua	..	..	500	529
VII	..	..	..	Curicó, Talca, Linares, Maule	..	650	685
VIII	..	..	..	Nuble, Concepción, Arauco,				
				Bío-Bío	..	..	..	1,319	1,406

From 33 to 50% of the width of the area is taken up by the Andes, which are formidably high in the northern sector of the area: at the head of the river Aconcagua, the peak of Aconcagua rises to 6,964 metres. S of Talca,

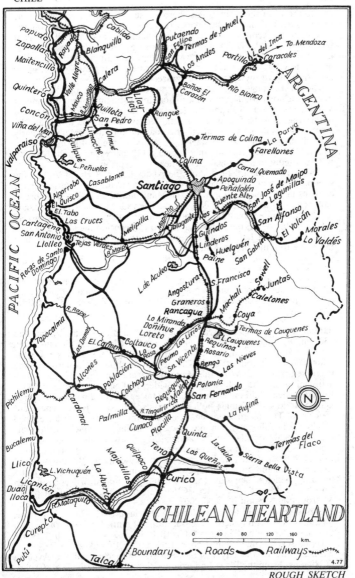

ROUGH SKETCH

and to the W of the main range, there is a series of active volcanoes; the region suffers from earthquakes. There is a mantle of snow on the mountains: at Aconcagua it begins at 4,300 metres; at Curicó at 3,350; at Bío-Bío at 1,980. The lower slopes are covered with dense forests. Between the forest and the snowline there are alpine pastures which narrow towards the S and disappear altogether; during the summer cattle are driven up to these pastures to graze.

The coastal range takes up another third of the width. It is lower here than in the northern desert, but the shoreline is still unbroken; it is only at Valparaíso and at Talcahuano (the port for Concepción) that good harbourage is to be found. The rivers, fed by rains in the winter and by melting snows in the summer, cut this coastal range into great irregularly shaped blocks which are in startling contrast to the gentle slopes of the Central Valley. The coastal range is over 2,130 metres high in the N, but it falls gradually to about 600 metres near Concepción.

Between the coastal range and the Andes lies the Central Valley; the streams cross it at right angles and cut their way to the sea through narrow canyons in the coastal range, but the Maule and the Bío-Bío have broad valleys along the whole of their courses. The valley of the Río Aconcagua is separated by a mountainous spur from the valley of the Mapocho, in which Santiago lies, but from Santiago to Concepción the Central Valley is continuous; the land here is extremely fruitful; it merges gradually into the stony foothills of the Andes.

There is rain during the winter in the heartland, but the summers are dry. The rain increases to the S. On the coast at Viña del Mar it is 483 mm. a year; at Talcahuano it is 1,168 mm., but is somewhat less inland. Temperatures, on the other hand, are higher inland than on the coast. There is frost now and then in the Central Valley, but very little snow falls.

Santiago, the capital and seat of the Government, 187 km. by rail and 130 km. by road from Valparaíso, is the fourth largest city in South America and one of the most beautifully set of any. It stands in a wide plain, 600 metres above the sea. The city covers about 100 square km. and is crossed from E to W by the Mapocho River, which passes through an artificial stone channel, 40 metres wide, spanned by several bridges. Public gardens, laid out with admirable taste, are filled with flowers and kept in good order. Smart policemen control the crowds with courteous efficiency. The magnificent chain of the Andes, with its snow-capped heights, is in full view, rain and smog permitting, for much of the year: there are peaks of 6,000 metres about 100 km. away. More than half the country's manufacturing is done here; it is essentially a modern capital, full of bustle, noise, traffic, smog and skyscrapers. Buildings of 12 storeys are common; the highest, of 22 storeys, is the Diego Portales building, which is being used as the main government offices until such time as La Moneda (see page 363) is repaired. The population of the Metropolitan Region is 3,806,000.

Santiago was founded by Pedro de Valdivia in 1541. His first fort was on Santa Lucía Hill (where there is a statue of him). It became the capital of Chile after the battle of Maipú in 1818. During its history the city has suffered several times from floods, fires and earthquakes.

The centre of the city lies between the Mapocho and the Avenida O'Higgins. From the Plaza Baquedano (Plaza Italia), in the E of the city, the Mapocho flows to the NW and the Avenida O'Higgins runs to the SW, at much the same angle as two widespread fingers. From Plaza Baquedano the Calle Merced runs due W of the Plaza de Armes, the heart of the city; it lies 4 blocks S of Mapocho Station (on Avenida Presidente Balmaceda, on the southern bank of the Mapocho); this is the station for Valparaíso. On the eastern and southern sides of Plaza de Armas there are arcades with shops; on the northern side is the Post Office and the City Hall; and on the western side the Cathedral and the archbishop's palace. The Cathedral, much rebuilt, contains a recumbent statue, in wood, of St. Francis Xavier and the chandelier which lit the first meetings of Congress after the liberation; it also houses an interesting museum of religious art and historical pieces. A block W of the Cathedral is the Congressional Palace; the Chamber of Deputies is worth seeing. Nearby are the Law Courts.

The Avenida O'Higgins (usually known as the Alameda) runs through the heart of the City for over 3 km. It is 100 metres wide, and ornamented with gardens and statuary: the most notable are the equestrian statues of Generals O'Higgins and San Martín (who led the Argentine troops over the Andes to help O'Higgins gain national independence from Spain); the statue of the Chilean historian Benjamín Vicuña Mackenna who, as governor of Santiago, beautified Santa Lucía Hill; and the great monument in honour of the Battle of Concepción in 1879. Under the gardens between the Alameda's twin roadways is the first line of the city's underground railway, which was opened in 1975. A second, connecting the Los Héroes and Franklin districts, has almost been completed.

From the Plaza Baquedano, where there is a statue of General Baquedano and a Tomb of the Unknown Soldier, this magnificent avenue skirts, on the right, Santa Lucía Hill, and on the left, the Catholic University. Santa Lucía Hill, a cone of rock rising steeply to a height of 70 metres, can be scaled from the Caupolicán esplanade, on which, high on a rock, stands a statue of that Araucanian leader, but the ascent from the northern end of the hill, where there is an equestrian statue of Diego de Almagro, is easier and prettier. The hill is a vine-covered, flower-embroidered series of steps, quiet nooks, watch towers, pavilions and small terraces. There are striking views of the city from the top, which is reached by a series of stairs. On this peak is the Observatory and a Colonial fortress, the Hidalgo Castle: at noon each day the report from its cannon reverberates down the city streets. In the basement is an Indian historical museum, often closed. It is best to descend the eastern side, to see the small Plaza Pedro Valdivia with its waterfalls and statue.

Beyond the Hill the Avenida goes past the neo-classical National Library on the right; it is the largest library in South America and contains, among other things, the national archives. In a dignified annex is housed the Museo Histórico. Beyond, on the left, between Calle San Francisco and Calle Londres, is the most ancient church in Santiago: the red-spired Church and Monastery of San Francisco. Inside is a small statue of the Virgin which Valdivia carried on his saddlebow when he rode from Peru to Chile. The church also houses a colonial museum, well worth seeing. On the left, a little further along, is the University of Chile; the Club de la Unión is almost opposite. N of Plaza Bulnes, hemmed in by the skscapers of the Civic Centre, is the gracious Colonial building of the Palacio de la Moneda (1805), containing historic relics, paintings and sculpture, and elaborate "Salón Rojo" used for official and diplomatic

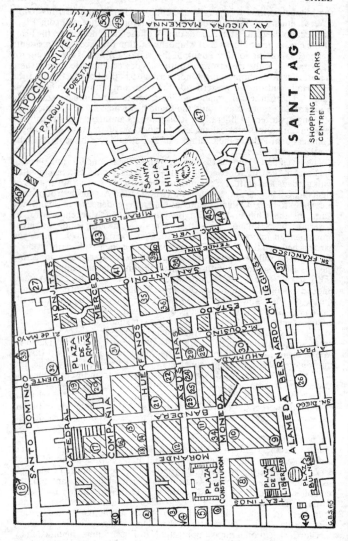

ROUGH SKETCH

receptions. It contains a number of government offices, too. With some insistence, you can see some of the rooms by applying at about 1400 to the building's secretatiat. The Moneda was damaged by air attacks during the military coup of September 11, 1973, and has still not been repaired. President Allende met his death there.

In front of the Palace is the statue of Arturo Alessandri Palma, who was President of the Republic for two terms. The Municipal Theatre is on Calle Agustinas, and nearby on Calle Nueva York is the Bolsa de Comercio. Further along, any of the streets on the left will lead to the great Parque O'Higgins, with a small lake, playing fields, 3 good "typical" restaurants, an open-air stage for local songs and dances, some craft shops and the racecourse of the Club Hípico. The Avenida runs westwards to Plaza Argentina, on the southern side of which is the Alameda (Central) Station for the S. On Avenida Matucana, running N from Plaza Argentina, are the Archaeological Museum (entrance US$0.25) and the Quinta Normal de Agricultura, the latter a large area of ground containing a very popular park. The frozen body of the Inca child found on the summit of El Plomo, 5,398 metres, 40 km. fron Santiago, is in the Museum of Natural History. In the National Museum are pieces of armour worn by Valdivia's men. The Museo Aeronáutico in the Quinta Normal is also worth a visit.

On Calle Dieciocho, some 5 blocks S of the Alameda, is the Palacio Cousiño, a large elaborate mansion amongst crumbling buildings and shanties; it contains some good oriental rugs and second-rate European furniture. It is run by the Municipality as a museum and official guest house. Can be seen by written permission from the Municipalidad.

KEY TO MAP

Steamship Agents and Airlines:
23 Exprinter S.A.
13 Braniff
10 Argentine Airlines
24 Wagons-Lit Cook
21 Canadian Pacific-Air France
12 L.A.N.
4 S.A.S. (Scandinavian)
25 Lufthansa
24 P.S.N.C., General Agent for British Airways and British Caledonian
39 KLM

Miscellaneous:
3 U.S. Consulate
32 Post and Telgr. Office
11 Transradio

Hotels:
5 Carrera Sheraton (1st cl. A)
22 Crillon (1st cl. A)
2 Panamericano (1st cl.)
41 Santa Lucia (1st cl.)
35 Kent (1st cl.)
20 City (2nd cl.)

Night Clubs and Restaurants:
29 Waldorf
9 Escorial
15 Santiago
30 "Ahumada 79"
34 "El Bodegón"
40 Nuria

Night Clubs and Restaurants—cont.:
31 Chez Henry
27 "Taberna Capri"
36 El Pollo Dorado
49 El Parrón

Theatre:
38 Teatro Municipal

Public Bdgs. and Museums:
6 Ministry of Finance
8 La Moneda (Govt. Bdg.)
17 Congress
16 Palace of Justice
44 National Library
45 Prehistoric and Historic Museum
46 Museum of Fine Arts
1 Quinta Normal
47 Catholic University
26 University of Chile

Churches:
19 The Cathedral
37 San Francisco
43 Merced
50 St. Andrew's (Prot.)
33 Sto. Domingo (burnt out)

Railway Stations:
18 Mapocho (to Viña)
7 Alameda (Central Station; to Lakes)

There are several other parks in Santiago, but perhaps the most notable is the Parque Forestal, due N of Santa Lucía Hill and immediately S of the Mapocho. The Palace of Fine Arts is in the wooded grounds; it has a large display of Chilean painting and sculpture, and art exhibitions are held several times a year; the Art School is in the building. The Parque Balmaceda, E of Plaza Baquedano, is perhaps the most beautiful in Santiago, but the sharp, conical hill of San Cristóbal, to the NE of the city, is the largest and most interesting. A funicular railway goes up the 300-metre-high hill every few minutes at the bargain price, both up and down, of US$0.30. The hill has several summits: on one stands a colossal statue of the Virgin, which is floodlit at night; on another is the astronomical observatory of the Catholic University; and on a third a solar observatory (Victoria Castle). The hill is very well laid out with terraces, gardens, and paths; there are three good restaurants with splendid views from the terrace, especially at night, and an Enoteca, or exhibition of Chilean wines (with restaurant and tastery) has been opened. The Zoological Gardens (not very good) are near the foot of the hill (entrance US$0.30). The interesting Central Market is at Puente 21 Mayo.

Ballet is popular. During the summer, free performances are given in the city parks, but seats are sometimes hard to get. The theatre (there are 12 houses) is more active than in most Latin American capitals, but professional standards are below those of Mexico City and Buenos Aires. There are two symphony orchestras, three big universities, two observatories, first-class newspapers and magazines, art galleries, excellent bookshops, the largest library in South America, and a botanical garden. One thing to remember: Santiago's pavements are slippery. Leather-soled shoes are not the thing.

Things to do   Changing of the Guard, ballet, the theatre, golf, horse-racing, churches, visiting Santa Lucía and San Cristóbal hills. Daily list of events in *El Mercurio* should be consulted. During November there is an Art Fair on the banks of the Mapocho River flowing through Forestal Park. This is pleasant, free and lasts a fortnight.

In October or November there is a sumptuous flower show, an awesome display of air devilry at the airport in the spring, and an annual agricultural and industrial show—most popular with town dwellers—in Parque Cerrillos during October or November. Parque O'Higgins has glittering military parades from Sept. 18 to 20. Religious festivals and ceremonies are not confined to Holy Week, when a priest ritually washes the feet of 12 men. The Virgen del Carmen (patron of the Armed Forces) is carried through the streets by cadets on July 16. And there are 14 museums in all.

Climate   In the central region (including Santiago and Valparaiso) the climate is Mediterranean: temperatures average 28°C (82°F) in January, 10°C (50°F) in July. Days are usually hot, the nights cool.

Electric Current   220 volts A.C., 50 cycles.

Shopping   There is a fairly good shopping area on Calle Huérfanos in the centre of the city and, a little further out, a very contemporary shopping centre full of boutiques in Providencia. Best bargains are handicraft articles, black pottery and beautiful wrought copper and bronze. Cocema is a good store for Chilean handicrafts, near the centre,with two branches on Av. Providencia. Good shops for local copper work are Bozzo, at Ahumada 12 in the centre, and at Av. Providencia 2125. Chilean Art, Agustinas 1169, has a good selection of typical wood carvings and copper items. (The pottery is best bought in Pomaire, a tiny settlement about 50 km. towards the coast, where the artists can be observed at work. The area is rich in clay and the traditional town famous for its cider and Chilean dishes.)

Conveyances   There are three kinds of buses: the small fast kind which cost a little more then the regular buses and trolley buses, and the large buses marked Expreso. At present the charge is not more than US$0.07, US$0.09 or US$0.11 (50% higher at night) depending on the class. Taxis are now abundant (black with yellow roofs), and not expensive, US$0.10 for under 1 km. There are also colectivo taxis to the suburbs. Visitors going outside the city should arrange the charge beforehand.

Underground railway   The first line of the new underground railway system runs below the Alameda. The second line, from Los Héroes to Franklin, has almost been completed. The basic ticket costs US$0.15.

Hotels

Name	Address	Price (double) US$	Category
San Cristóbal Sheraton ..	Av. Santa María 1742	35.00	De Luxe
Carrera Sheraton	Teatinos 180	32.00	De Luxe
El Conquistador	Miguel Cruchaga 920	25.00	De Luxe
Panamericano	Teatinos 110	20.00	De Luxe
Tupahué	San Antonio 473	20.00	De Luxe
Las Acacias de Vitacura	El Manantial 1789	30.00	De Luxe
Gran Palace	Huérfanos 1171	16.00	1
City	Compañia 1063	15.00	1
Santa María	S. María 2050	17.00	1
Kent	Huérfanos 878	28.00	1
Ritz	Estado 250	13.00	1
Emperador	Alameda 853	23.00	1
Santa Lucia (garage)	Huérfanos 779	15.00	1
Foresta	V. Subercaseaux 253	16.00	1
Lido	Huérfanos 682	13.00	1
Splendid ..	Estado 360	11.00	1B
Victoria ..	Huérfanos 801	15.00	1B
Cervantes	Morandé 631	9.00	1B
Orly	Pedro de Valdivia 27	12.00	1B
San Paulo	San Antonio 357	12.00	1B
Miami	Dr. Sótero del Río 465	8.00	1B
Canciller ..	Av. Elíodoro Yánez 867	10.00	1B
Windsor ..	Alameda B. O'Higgins 763	6.00	2
Palace	Ahumada 83	7.00	2
Plaza	Ahumada 83	6.50	2
Bristol	Pte. Balmaceda 1114	6.25	2
Albión	Ahumada 95	5.75	2
De France	Puente 530	7.00	2
España	Morandé 511	8.50	2
Mauri	Tarapacá 1112	7.00	2
Bidart	Nueva York 9	11.50	2
Mundial ..	La Bolsa 87	7.25	2

The *Carrera Sheraton* has a popular night club and roof-top swimming pool. The *Miami* is good. The *Foresta* is very comfortable. Hotels *El Conquistador* and *Kent* also very good. *Hotel Victoria* is clean, reasonable, with private bath. The *San Cristóbal Sheraton* is a sumptuous building out on San Cristóbal hill, 6 km. from the centre. The *Hotel del Pasos,* Avda. Noruega 6340, Las Condes, US$9 with bath. Farther out are the *Hotel Santa María,* and *Orly.* The usual charge on hotel bills is 10% for service and 20% for taxes, 30% in all.

More economical are the *Hotel Caribe,* San Martín 851, US$3.10 d, good value, clean, pleasant and quiet, also convenient for centre; *Residencia Alemania,* República 220, excellent food, clean and cheap; note there is no sign; *Hotel Colonial,* Av. General Mackenna 1262, close to Northern bus terminal, US$1.70 s, US$2 with bath; *Residencia Serrano,* US$4 d; *Hotel Mackenna,* General Mackenna 1471, near bus station for journeys South, clean, US$1.50 s; *Valparaíso,* Corner Morandé and San Pablo, US$2.50, hot water, convenient, clean, friendly, excellent value; *Hotel Bristol,* opposite Mapocho station, US$3.50 s, restaurant—4 courses for US$2; *Hotel Montemar,* near bus terminal for South, clean, US$1.20 s; *Hotel Tres Coronas,* Avda Molina 152, US$3; *Residencial Puntarenas,* Avda Compañía, US$1.50 with breakfast in bed, s; *Hotel Larssen,* Nataniel 137-139, US$5.20 d, "grand"; *Residencial Londres,* Londres 54, near San Francisco church, US$6 d, with breakfast, charming former mansion. YMCA rooms at US$2, hot water, heating. *University hostel,* offering bare essentials, at Huérfanos 1681. A little farther from centre (15 min. walk or 5 min. bus) in the embassy district of Providencia two hotels are recommended; *Hotel Canciller,* new (see list) and *Posada del Salvador,* Eliodoro Yáñez 893, slightly more expensive. On the road beyond Santo Domingo are the *Hotel King,* San Pablo 1583, US$2 d, after bargaining; *Hotel Río Claro,* clean, US$2.30 d.

Restaurants In addition to those at the *Carrera Sheraton* and *Crillón* Hotels there are, in the centre of the town, the *Waldorf,* Ahumada 131; *Portada Colonial,* Merced 88 (1st Class); *El Pollo Dorado,* Agustinas 881; *El Escorial,* Morandé 19; *Bellevue (Hotel Kent); Le Due Torri,* San Antonio 258; *Restaurant Auerbach* (German), Calle MacIver 165, US$1.20 for four course lunch; *La Peña, Alameda* and *San Isidro,* folk music, reseasonable prices; *Bar Central,* San Pablo 1063, good chicken and sea food, recommended; *Jacarandá,* recommended; *Mistral* recommended; *Da Carla* excellent Italian; *Naturista* vegetarian; *Nuria,* Agustinas 705-715; *Danubio Azul* (Chinese) Merced 564; *Lung Fun* (Chinese), Agustinas good, but expensive, beware of the high cost of tea; *Chez Henri,* near Plaza de Armas, *Parrillada de mariscos* a speciality; *San Marcos* (Italian) Huérfanos 612; and farther out: *Enoteca,* on San Cristóbal hill, expensive, but excellent views of the city; *Hotel Aport,* Américo Vespucio, has good restaurant; *München,* Providencia 2601; *El Parrón,* Providencia 1188; *Bric-à-Brac* (French), Av. Las Condes 9,100; *La Pirámide,* Av. Américo Vespucio; typical Chilean dishes at *El Pollo Al Coñac,* Lo Barnechea 127. For snacks and excellent ice cream, try *Coppellia.* Drive-in *Charles,* Las Condes; Drive-in *Lo Curro,* Las Condes. Airport meals and snacks are good. If really travelling "economy", do not sit at tables in bars, etc.; the extra service charge for tables is 20%. There are many cheap restaurants around the Municipal Market. Good, cheap snacks can be had from stalls in the arcade of the Plaza de Armas.

Among the first class restaurants in town are *Ex-Emilio, Pimpilinpausha* and *Oriente.* Farther out, *Rendezvous des Gourmets.* New first-class restaurants out of town are *El Alero de los De Ramón,* Av. Las Condes 9889 (Chilean cuisine and music); *Canta Gallo,* Av. Las Condes 12345 (ditto); *La Cascade,* Av. Bilbao 1947 (French, good and dear); and *Los Gordos,* Av. San Enrique 14880 (perhaps the best food of all).

Cafés and Bars *The Old Yellow Book* (pub), *Claeríe Drugstore,* Av. Providencia; *Café di Trevi,* Av. El Bosque 084; *Hollywood* (very good), Av. Irarrázaval 2900. Note that almost all hotel bars are closed Sundays.

Discotheques *Caledonia,* Av. Larrain Parcela 339; *Eve,* Av. Vitacura 3418.

Tea Rooms *Carrera,* Testinos 180; *Waldorf,* Ahumada 131; *Crillón,* Agustinas 1025; *Villa Real,* Compañía 1068; *Nuria,* Agustinas 715; *Oriente,* Plaza Italia; *Paula,* San Antonio 218.

Camping Almost impossible, but try the Farellones road near the river. Or S of Santiago near Puente Alta. Take Avda J Pedro Alessandri S to Las Vizcaches to Puente Alta and La Obra where there is a small park on left side of road. One couple ended up in a picnic spot on top of San Cristóbal hill (not advisable)! For Club Camping Maki, 10 km. from Santiago, see page 369.

Tourist Agencies Wagons-Lits/Cook, "La Universal", "Exprinter", "Turismo Cocha", Gondrand Brothers (Chile), (all in Calle Agustinas). Viajes "Litvak", Cía.

Chilena de Viajes y Turismo, "Civit", Turavion Shipping Express, Turismo Magallanes (all in Calle Bandera). Latour, Hotel Carrera; "Atitur", (Agencia de Viajes Automovil Club de Chile), Moneda 1162, The Pacific Stream Navigation Co. Most of these offer routes in the Lake District. Rapa-Nui, Huérfanos 1160, specialises in trips to Easter Island.

The National Tourist Bureau is at NW corner of Agustinas and Teatinos, next to Hotel Carrera Sheraton. English is spoken and maps, brochures and posters are available. Excellent road maps may also be obtained from the Automóvil Club de Chile, Pedro de Valdivia 195.

Racecourses Club Hipico, racing every Sat. afternoon (at Viña del Mar, January-March); Hipódromo Chile every Sunday morning; pari-mutuel betting.

Tennis Santiago Tennis Club; International; Los Leones; The Prince of Wales Country Club; Stade Française.

Golf Los Leones Golf Club (car from Plaza Italia). The Prince of Wales Country Club. Introduction required to both.

Clubs Unión; Prince of Wales Country Club, Las Aranas, Tel.: 272025; members only (cricket, hockey, swimming, etc.), Club de Setiembre; Ski Club Chile, Calle Bandera 64; Club Andino (winter sports); Lions; Rotary; The French, Spanish and Italian Clubs; Polo y Equitación San Cristóbal; Santiago Paper-chase; Estadio Israelita. Club Andino de Chile, Ahumada 47, Dep. 208, Casilla 1823, for imformation on mountain-climbing.

Night Clubs Boite at *Hotel Carrera*; Waldorf; Tap Room; Charles; Nuria; Night & Day. Outside the city: Las Perdices, Drive-in Charles, Drive-in Lo Curro, La Pirámide. Discotheques: Las Brujas and Caledonia, not far outside centre.

Theatres Spanish plays at Petit Rex, L'Atelier, Antonio Varas, Camilo Henríquez; Maru, Moneda, Talia, La Comedia and Municipal, where the Chilean ballet company performs and concerts are given. Three others, the Opera, Cousiño, and Princesa, show mostly Folies Bergères-type revues.

Addresses British Embassy, British Consulate, La Concepción 177, 4th floor, Providencia 1800, Casilla 72-D; U.S. Embassy, Agustinas 1343; U.S. Consulate, Merced 230; Y.M.C.A.; Compañía 1360-70, British Chamber of Commerce in the Republic of Chile, Calle Bandera 227, Casilla 536. Tel.: 85266. Chilean-British Institute (British Council), Santa Lucía 124. Tel.: 34709. Chilean-North American Cultural Institute, Moneda 1467; P.S.N.C. offices: Agustinas 1066-1070 Casilla 4087. Australian Embassy; Moneda 1123, 9th floor. Canadian Embassy, Ahumada 11. New Zealand Embassy, Avenida Isadora Goyenechea 3516, Las Condes (Tel.: 487071). Laundromat, 494 Merced, Emergency pharmacy, Portugal 155 (Tel.: 382439). Empresa Marítima del Estado, Estado 359, 5th floor.

Bookshops Librería Studio, Providencia 2200, Andrés de Fuenzalida 36 for books in English. Second-hand books in English at Librería La Portada, Compañia 1431. Bookstalls selling second-hand books on Calle San Diego, just off Alameda. Reading rooms at British and U.S. cultural associations (addresses in previous paragraph).

British Community maintains the British Commonwealth Society (old people's home etc.), the interdenominational Santiago Community Church, two masonic lodges, and three schools (The Grange and Redlands—coeducational, and Craighouse and Braemar—girls.

Industries About 54% of all Chilean industries are in the Metropolitan Region, which concentrates mainly on food, textiles, clothes, leather and chemicals.

Airport at Pudahuel, 26 km. from Santiago with a speed limit. Airport taxi, US$7.40, US$0.05 per suitcase. Private taxi to airport expensive, about US$10. Bus runs from Plaza de Bulnes, No. 54, every half-hour, fare, US$0.50 one way; Pullman service by Aerobuses Tour Express from *Hotel Carrera* (US$1 one way), plenty of luggage space; another bus from near Mapocho railway station. Los Cerrillos airport (20 minutes) is used for internal services. Flight to Arica, non-stop US$68; with four stops, US$59. To Mendoza, US$31.

Rail International service to Buenos Aires (tickets to be bought at Alameda 853), see page 83 (Argentina Section). The train to Mendoza tends to be booked up (with

shoppers) weeks in advance. US$10.50 first class, 10 hours, daily at 0830. To
Valparaíso, six expresses daily, besides ordinary and "Flecha" trains on Tues.,
Thurs., and Sat., at 0800, 4 hours, US$1, first class, US$0.80 second class, leaving
from Mapocho station to Concepción daily; to Coquimbo and La Serena, daily; to
Antofagasta, US$13, 2½ days (express at 1400 Tuesdays, locals Thursdays and
Sundays); and Iquique, Thursdays and Sundays; to Valdivia (US$6.50) and Puerto
Montt, one Rápido a day at 1800, about 18 hours, 2nd class fare about US$7 (get
your ticket the morning of the day the train leaves and sit on the train as soon as you
can get on; otherwise you'll stand for the whole journey). Information office in
gallery on Estado, 1¼ blocks from Alameda on the right-hand side; to San Antonio
at 1900 daily. Trains are very cheap, with good meals. Booking offices: for State
Railways, Alameda 853; for Antofagasta-La Paz, Huérfanos 972, oficina 408; for
trains S from Alameda, Alameda 853.

Buses   There are frequent, and good, interurban buses to all parts of Chile. The
longest journey within the country, N to Arica (2,113 km.), costs about US$19-
US$20 (including television), and takes 27 hours. Antofagasta, 22 hours, US$16, an
interesting trip to see the changes in landscape, but cold at night. To Viña del Mar,
Valparaíso, US$1.20, 2 hours; Cóndor and Turbus (US$1.20) or Mapocho or
Alameda (2 hrs.). Buses to Valparaíso and N leave from Terminal de Buses de Norte,
corner of Amunátegui and Gral. Mackenna, one block from Mapocho. Buses leave
from Plaza Diego de Almagro. Via Sur Buses go S to Puerto Montt (1,060 km.),
US$11, 16 hours to Chillán, US$3, to Temuco US$5. Varmontt buses to Puerto
Montt are US$25, including meals and wine, highly recommended. Igi-Llaima runs a
comfortable service to Temuco and points south. There are frequent minibus services
over the Andes to Mendoza, about US$17 (cheaper coming from Argentina (about
US$12)), taking 7 hours, book as far ahead as possible; they do not run in winter.
Transportes Caracoles sell a combination ticket but there are many changes. Bus
offices all along Calle Morandé. Buses to Buenos Aires, US$31, Lima, US$46.
Bogotá (7 days), US$110, Rio de Janeiro, US$96. Bus trip not recommended to
Ecuador.

Cables   West Coast of America Telegraph Co. Ltd. (British), Calle Bandera, 152/6,
Tel.: 82041. Transradio Chilena, Calle Bandera, 168. Entel Chile, Moneda 812.

Banks   Banco Central de Chile, one block from Plaza Constitución, demands the
minimum of formalities. Banco do Brasil, National banks, open from 0900 to 1400,
but closed on Saturday. Warning! It may be difficult to change Chilean pesos into
Peruvian soles.

Excursions from Santiago   Several small resort towns are easily reached
by car from the capital: Colina (915 metres), a spa in the mountains 32
km. to the N; Peñalolén, 16 km., with a very lovely park and a beautiful
view of the city (bus from behind Catholic University); San José de
Maipó, some 80 km. to the SE (return journey by car: 3 hours); just
beyond is the mountain town of Melocotón (*Millahue Hotel*). El Volcán,
in the Andes, 77 km. to the SE (1,400 metres), is a small poor mining
village, uninteresting except for the astounding view. (Hotel: *Lo Valdés*.)
(Bus from behind Catholic University to Puente Alto and then train
through mountains and gorgeous scenery.) From El Volcán the road runs
12 km. E and then N to the ski-ing slopes of Lo Valdés (hut). A splendid
region which deserves the walk or hitch-hike (unless with car!) required to
get there. *Refugio Alemán*, US$5 single with full board, recommended.
The small towns in the Aconcagua Valley to the N—San Felipe, Jahuel,
Los Andes, and Portillo—are described in the section "To Buenos Aires
across the Andes", page 377. Motor-car trips from Santiago to the
Aconcagua Valley and over the Andes to Mendoza (400km.) are arranged
by the travel agencies. The road is excellent except when snowed up in
winter but the last 900 metres of the climb can be avoided by passing
through the Trans-Andean Railway tunnel, 3¼ km. long. The National

Votive Temple of Maipú, 30 min. by car (or about 45 mins. by bus) from Santiago, which commemorates O'Higgins' battle, is interesting, and so is the attached museum, open weekend afternoons. There is also a camping ground with excellent facilities about 70 km. from Santiago at Laguna de Aculeo, called Club Camping Maki. Facilities include electricity, water, swimming pool, boat mooring, restaurant, US$2 daily p.p.

There is an excellent ski centre at **Farellones**, 51 km. to the E of Santiago at 2,470 metres, and reached by car, bus, or truck in 90 minutes: two hotels, one third-class pension and annex. Most skiers stay in the 2 refugios belonging to Santiago's 2 universities. High season: June to September/October, weather depending. An excellent network of 5 ski-lifts. There are excursions for a day from Santiago at US$5, including ski-lifts ticket; enquire, Ski Club Chile, Ahumada 312. Beautiful views for 30 km. across ten Andean peaks. Incredible sunsets. Large restaurants. Five minutes away by car (5 km.) is the village of La Parva with 3 poma lifts and 1 chair lift (good hotel and restaurant), where the runs are a little more difficult. Lift ticket and equipment rental, US$5 each. Another ski-ing area close by is El Colorado. Sunglasses are a must for skiers.

Travellers between Valparaíso and Santiago (187 km. by rail or 130 by road) are well served by express trains with Pullman and dining cars, and by a comfortable bus service.

Valparaíso, the principal port of Chile, is one of the great commercial centres on the W coast of South America. It is built on the shores of a sweeping bay and on a crescent of hills around it. Seen from the ocean, the city presents a majestic panorama: a great circle of hills is backed by the snow-capped peaks of the distant Cordillera. At sunset the city blazes with the illusion of fire reflected in its window-panes. At night, myriads of lights shine out from hill and dale, from point to point of the far outstretching bay, and the cages of the many funiculars move up and down their tracks like fireflies.

There are two completely different cities. The lower part is the seat of banking and commerce, with fine office buildings on narrow, clean, winding streets. Above, in the hills, is a fantastic agglomeration of tattered houses, with corrugated iron shacks beside decaying chalets, public stairways and laundry hanging to the winds. All are scrambled in Oriental confusion along the littered back streets, trodden by pack mules. Ascensores, or funicular railways, and winding roads connect the lower and the upper cities.

Valparaíso is 7,407 miles from England *via* the Panama Canal and 8,854 by Magellan Strait. Population, which has declined from 1960 to 1970, is 252,000 (or about 453,000, including Viña del Mar and nearby suburbs).

The climate is kindly, for the summer heat is tempered by fresh breezes and sunshine mitigates the unkindness of a short winter. (The mean annual temperature is 15°C, with −1°C and 31°C as the extremes.) The city was founded in 1536. Not many antiquities have survived the long roll of pirates, tempests, fires and earthquakes, but a remnant of the old colonial town remains in the hollow known as El Puerto, grouped round the low-built stucco church of La Matriz, hallowed by ten generations of worship. The last devastating earthquake was in 1906, and the palaces, villas, fortifications and churches all date from that time. Until recently, all buildings were low, as a precaution against earthquakes, but during the last few years modern multi-storey blocks of offices and apartments have been constructed. There was another serious earthquake in July 1971.

The main business quarter, with its roads and railways, stands on land reclaimed from the sea. A further large tract has been regained for the port works which, with their large well-equipped warehouses and powerful electric cranes, are partially protected by a sheltering mole; but there is always a high swell, particularly when a northerly blows in from the sea and many ships have to leave the quay. Mail and passenger vessels moor alongside.

The Plaza Sotomayor is opposite the passenger landing pier. It has a fine statue to the "Heroes of Iquique"; the Palace of the Intendente (Government House) is across the way. Near the landing pier is the Port Railway Station (for Santiago and Buenos Aires): the information services of the State Railways and the Empresa Marítima del Estado are here. Certain long distance buses start from the Plaza Sotomayor, the local buses from Aduana, a little further on. The streets of El Puerto (The Port) radiate N and S from Plaza Sotomayor. To the N Calle Cochrane runs for 7 blocks to the Plaza Echaurren, on which stands the old church of La Mariz. A block beyond rises the bold hill of Cerro Artillería, crowned by the huge Naval Academy and a park; there are fine views from this hill. To the W of the Cerro the Avenida Playa Ancha runs to a Stadium, seating 20,000 people, and to Playa Ancha Park. From the western base of the hill the Avenida Altamirano runs by the sea to Las Torpederas, a picturesque bathing beach.

The narrow Calle Prat, the financial centre, runs S from Plaza Sotomayor. After three blocks it becomes Calle Esmeralda; this is the main shopping centre, twisting along the foot of the Cerro Alegre; further along, across Plaza Aníbal Pinto, are Calle Condell, the Plaza Victoria, and the spacious Avenida Pedro Montt with its cafés and theatres and its little Parque Italia leading on to the large Plaza O'Higgins. The Avenidas Brasil and Errázuriz, with trees and many monuments, run parallel until near the Barón district from which Avenida España skirts the shore as far as Viña del Mar.

Leaving Plaza Sotomayor by the Calle Serrano and Plaza Echaurren, the Plaza Aduana is reached, where there is a public lift for the Paseo Veintiuno de Mayo, a terrace, on Cerro Artillería giving views of the bay and the hills. The New Year is celebrated by a fantastic firework display on the bay which can be seen from the many terraces on the hills surrounding the bay.

Local products include textiles, sugar, paints, varnishes, enamels, cottonseed oil, shoes, tanneries, chemicals, pharmaceuticals, cosmetics, and large foundries. The industrial district lies to the E of the city. The oil refinery at Concón is nearby.

Hotels   *Hotel Salcido,* Esmeralda 1107, good, US$6 p.p.; *Herzog,* Blanco 395, Tel.: 4799, 45 beds, US$4; *Prat,* Calle Condell 1443, Tel.: 7634, 220 beds; *Reina Victoria,* Plaza Sotomayor, US$5 d; *Residencial Dinamarca,* Calle Dinamarca, US$2.50 s, excellent value; *Hotel Cecil,* Serrano 591, close to Plaza Sotomayor, good, US$5 d; *Hotel España,* Plaza Victoria, US$5 s with two meals. *Pensión: Sra. Isabel,* Calle Fernando Lesseps, Los Placeres. Many cheap hotels on Cochrane and Blanco Encalda, S of Plaza Sotomayor. Many of the "cheap" hotels in the Chacabuco are for night-time occupation only.

Restaurants   In addition to *Prat Hotel,* El Castillo (Av. Altamirano, on the sea front), *Il Corso* (Condell 1598, Plaza Victoria); *La Terraza,* and *Samoa* are good. Others are *Monico,* Calle Prat; *La Nave,* Calle Serrano, next door to Intendencia;

Port Station Restaurant; Neptuno, Plaza Aníbal Pinto; *Menzel,* Las Heras 563; *Bar-Restaurant Liberty,* try the fish soup; *Café Vienés; Café Riquet* (recommended); *Le Pavillion,* Cura Nurin, Casa Vasca (recommended); *El Rey del Pescado,* Avenida Ecuador; the "cassino" of the Asociación de Clubs de Regata, on the waterfront, is recommended for good seafood. Discotheques: *Topsi-Topsi* and *La Nouvelle Epoque. Bar Roland* is "a classic sailors' dive".

Clubs Español Club Valparaíso, Club Naval (Valparaíso); Valparaíso Sporting Club (Viña del Mar).

Tourist Office Calle Esmeralda.

Tourist Agents Exprinter, Calle Prat 895 (corner of Cochrane); Gondrand Bros., Calle Prat 725; Turismo Forestier, Esmeralda 1069; Turismo Oroco, Esmeralda 960; Servitur, Esmeralda 1028. Agentur, Esmeralda 940.

Addresses The British Consulate, Blanco 737, Tel.: 56117; Y.M.C.A., Blanco 1113; YWCA, Calle Melgarejo 45; Chilean-British Cultural Institute, Calle Blanco 725, Tel.: 2828; Valparaíso Seamen's Institute, Blanco 394, Tel.: 2717; The Pacific Steam Navigation Co., Calle Almirante Senoret 48; Instituto Chileno-Norteamericano (Calle Esmeralda) and Viña del Mar.

Cables Transradio Chilena, Esmeralda 932.

Banks Banco de Talca will change travellers cheques. National banks. Open 0900 to 1400, but closed on Saturday.

Museums Museum of Fine Arts, in fine old house overlooking harbour (recommended), take ascensor from Plaza Sotomayor opposite Law Courts; Severin Library; Museo del Mar Almirante Cochrane, in Lord Cochrane's house overlooking city, take a different ascensor from Plaza Sotomayor.

Rail The main services, subject to changes, are:

To Santiago by State Railway (3 hours), 3 daily expresses, and 7 on certain days. First single, US$1. "Rápido" (automotor) runs Monday-Saturday except feast days. Fare US$1.25.

The Longitudinal Railway is joined at Calera Juncion (88 km.), on the State Railway to Santiago. From this point there are three trains a week to Coquimbo, three trains a week to Antofagasta and one to Iquique.

Trains southward, to Concepción, Valdivia and Puerto Montt, are joined at Santiago.

To Buenos Aires by Transandine Railway: see page 83.

Transport Cars for hire by the hour or day. Taxis; a short run under 1 km. costs US$0.40. Public transport good.

Buses Fares within city limits US$0.20. Excellent and frequent bus service runs between Valparaíso/Viña del Mar (15 min.) and Chorillos; fare US$0.12. No. 20 bus gives fine scenic drive over hills to fishing port. To Santiago, 2 hours, US$1.20; to Concepción, 11 hours, US$5.

Steamship Services One of the great ports of the world, Valparaíso is in touch with all countries. The principal services include, unless suspended:

The Pacific Steam Navigation Company's regular mail services from Liverpool and the Continent, and regular cargo vessels (no passengers), from London, Liverpool, Hull, Swansea and Glasgow *via* Nassau, Bermuda and Panama Canal call at Valparaíso.

New York: frequent service by Grace Line and by C.S.A.V. (Cía. Sud-Americana de Vapores), and *via* Bermuda by P.S.N.C.

Los Angeles, San Francisco, Portland. By P.S.N.C. *via* Balboa. Grace Line.

Frequent local services by Chilean steamer to Guayaquil, Africa, Iquique, Corral, Punta Arenas, and monthly to River Plate and Brazil.

Other lines from Valparaíso are Cie. Générale Transatlantique to French and Continental ports, the Johnston Line to Scandinavian ports and the Italian Line to Mediterranean ports; the German Line.

Lighthouse The orange-and-white-striped Faro de Punta Angeles, on a promontory just beyond the Playa Ancha, was the first on the West Coast; you can get a permit and go up it. On another high point on the other side of the city is El Miradero de O'Higgins, the spot where the Supreme Director exclaimed, on seeing Cochrane's liberating fleet: "On these four craft depends the destiny of America".

Pleasure Resorts near Valparaíso

Laguna Verde, a couple of hours' walk over the hills (or a short road journey) to the W of Valparaíso, is a picturesque bay for picnics. Wayside restaurant.

Viña del Mar, one of the foremost South American social resorts, is the residential area most favoured by well-to-do Chilean and foreign residents. It is 9 km. from the port by electric train or one of the innumerable express buses. They run along a narrow belt between the shore and precipitous cliffs. From the Barón suburb of Valparaíso to the outskirts of Viña takes only a few minutes. Halfway, on the hill of Los Placeres, is the Universidad Técnica. The popular bathing resort of El Recreo is passed, then Caleta Abarca with its crowded beaches and big *Hotel Miramar*.

At the entrance to Viña del Mar a steep bluff rises above the Miramar Station, worth climbing for the views over Viña from its "paseos". Here also is Cerro Castillo, the summer palace of the Presidents of the Republic. Below, to the left, is the lagoon of the Marga Marga, crossed by a bridge which leads direct to the Casino, a most attractive building set in beautiful gardens. Population: 185,000.

From September 15 to March 15, and on Saturdays and Sundays throughout the year, roulette and *chemin de fer* are played at the Casino, which has a good restaurant, an excellent cabaret and jazz orchestra.

One of the sights is the municipally owned Quinta Vergara, set in superb gardens with a famous double avenue of palms; the Palace is picturesque and houses a collection of pictures and an Art School. Part of the grounds have been turned into a children's playground, and there is an outdoor auditorium where concerts and ballet are performed in the summer months, and an international song contest is held every February; quiet walks and terraces lead upwards to considerable heights. The Teatro Municipal, on Plaza Vergara, presents the hit plays of the previous Santiago season. And here is one of Viña's greatest attractions: the Valparaíso Sporting Club with its racecourse and many playing fields. Near it are the Granadilla Golf Club and a large stadium. In the hills behind a large artificial lake, the Tranque, is frequented by picnic parties, and not far away is the Salinas Golf Course.

Viña del Mar is less exposed to wind and storm than Valparaíso. The season is at its height in summer (Dec. to Feb.), when large numbers of tourists arrive from Santiago and Argentina.

There are many discreetly set industries in the town.

Tourist Office   Next to *Hotel O'Higgins,* Plaza Vergara.

Hotels   *San Martín,* 8 Norte, 186 rooms each with bath, radio, and telephone; *O'Higgins,* from US$15 s, Plaza Vergara, 350 rooms each with bath and telephone (very good); *Miramar,* Caleta Abarca, private beach and swimming pool, (not always clean) 101 rooms, US$20 s, US$23 d; *Alcázar,* Alvarez 646, 48 rooms, and 19 modern motel units with parking area, very good; *Hotel Chalet Suisse,* Villanelo 395, lovely gardens, international food; *Residencial Sauce,* US$11.50 d, near railway station; *Residencial Cousina,* US$2.50 s. Many cheap residenciales along Calle Valparaíso and on Av. Libertad.

Motel   *Von Schroeders,* Von Schroeders 392.

Youth Hostel at Sausalito stadium, US$0.20 a night.

Camping 7 km. N of Viña del Mar at Reñaca, US$1; Sausalito.

Restaurants The *Miramar* and *O'Higgins* hotels, the *Petit Trianon, Ciro's, Chez Gerald, Los Lilenes, Las Vegas* and *San Marco* are all good. The *Parrilla Armandita* has Argentine beef. Many smaller ones along the sea front. Discotheque *Topsy Topsy*.

Cultural Associations North American Institute, in fort off Avenida Alvarez; British, Calle 3 Norte.

Museums The Museum of Naval History, in the Castle, good; Institute of Oceanography, in Montemar; worth seeing; Palacio Rioja, built at turn of century by a prominent local family and now used for offical municipal receptions; main floor open to visitors during season; Archaeological Museum on a lower floor. On the coast road between the Naval Museum and Caleta Abarca there is an Easter Island statue.

Schools The British community here maintains two schools: St. Margaret's and Mackay.

Festival El Roto, Jan. 20, a homage to the working men and peasants of Chile.

Excursions El Recreo and Caleta Abarca are the best resorts for bathing and amusements.

There is a very fine drive N of Viña del Mar along the coast (many motels being built) through Las Salinas to Concón, then inland to Quintero. **Las Salinas**, beach between two towering crags, is very popular. **Concón**, on the NE point of Valparaíso Bay, is 16 km. further. Main attractions: tennis, bathing, fishing, shooting and riding. Main eyesore: a national oil refinery (not visible from beach). Near the Concón beach there is a very interesting pelican colony. There is also a new inland road, much faster than the coast road, between Viña del Mar and Concón.

Concón Hotels *Gran Hotel Concón; Astoria.*

Campsite Las Gaviotas.

Another 16 km. to the N of Concón over the new bridge is the resort of **Quintero**, the naval aviation centre. There is a copper smelting plant for the small and medium-sized mines at Las Ventanas, near Quintero, and an electrolytic copper refinery.

Quintero Hotels *Isla de Capri; Hotel Yachting Club.*

From Las Ventanas the road continues N to two fashionable resorts: **Zapallar** and **Papudo**. They can also be reached from Valparaíso by road to Concón, up the Aconcagua valley to Calera, N to just beyond Blanquillo, and thence by a road running SW and then NW to Zapallar and Papudo (2 hours by car); and from Santiago *via* Nogales and Puchuncavi. Excellent bathing, but water is cold. Hotels are 3rd class.

Hotels At Zapallar: *Gran Hotel; César.* At Papudo: *Moderno; Turismo.*

The Chilean Pacific Islands

Juan Fernández Islands are some 650 km. W of Valparaíso. Fernández discovered the group of three islands in 1574. One of them was the home (1704-09) of Alexander Selkirk, whose cave on the beach of Robinson Crusoe island is shown to visitors. Defoe based "Robinson Crusoe" upon Selkirk's adventures. The main island has 550 people housed in log huts, who fish for lobsters which they send to the mainland from the little town of San Juan Bautista. It has a church, schools, post office, and wireless station. The climate is mild, the vegetation rich, and there are plenty of wild goats—and some tourists, for the islands are now easily reached by air and during the summer there is a boat service once a month from Valparaíso (US$25 return). There is an air taxi daily in summer from Santiago (US$130, round trip), by Taxpa, Nueva York 53; also from Valparaíso. The plane lands on an airstrip in the W of the island; at present passengers are taken by boat to San Juan Bautista but a road is being built.

The anvil-shaped peak, El Yunque, is a landmark, and it was upon this mount that Selkirk lit his signal fires. A tablet was set in the rock at Selkirk's look-out by British naval officers in 1858, to commemorate Selkirk's solitary stay on the island for 4 years and 4 months. Since 1966 the islands that make up the Archipelago of Juan Fernández are officially called: Robinson Crusoe (previously Mas a Tierra), Alejandro Selkirk (previously Mas Afuera) and Santa Clara (the smallest island). When it rains heavily, sheets of water drop off the cliff edges in great temporary waterfalls.

Hotels *Hostería Robinson Crusoe,* Tel.: Valparaíso 81573; *Renaldo Green Pensión,* good and cheap. Tourists often stay with villagers.

Easter Island, a Chilean possession, is just S of the Tropic of Capricorn and 3,790 km. W of Chile; its nearest neighbour is Pitcairn Island. It is triangular in shape, 24 km. across, with an inactive volcano at each corner. The population was stable at 4,000 until the 1850s, when Peruvian slavers, smallpox and emigration (encouraged by plantation-owners) to Tahiti reduced the numbers. Now it is about 2,000, of whom about a quarter are from the mainland, mostly living in the village of Hange Roa. Just north of Hanga Roa, there is a reconstructed site with a temple, houses and a ramp leading into the sea. Further along, there is a museum (Monday to Saturday, 0900-1700, Sunday 0900-1500, admission US$0.30). About half the island, of low bare round hills with groves of eucalyptus, is used for sheep, and nearly one-third constitutes a National Park. The islanders, of Polynesian origin, are fine-looking people, innocent, very warm-hearted, with a quick sense of humour. They are great lovers of music, have their own indigenous songs and dances, and are extremely hospitable. Piped water and electrification have radically changed the local life-style, and tourism has grown rapidly since the air service began in 1967. Paid work is now more common, but much carving is still done; the better items are no longer cheap, but are readily bartered for clothing. The airport is the cheapest place to buy carvings, although you may find that they are actually cheaper still in Santiago. The islanders have profited much from the visits of North Americans: a Canadian medical expedition left a mobile hospital on the island in 1966, and when a US missile-tracking station was abandoned in 1971, vehicles, mobile housing and an electricity generator were left behind. Unique features of the island are the Moai—huge stone figures up to 9 metres in height and broad in proportion. There are over 600 of them scattered about, all carved in the same quarry. How they were moved to where they are now is a major mystery. One of them, at Anakena beach, has been restored to its (probable) original state, with a plaque commemorating Thor Heyerdahl's visit. It is recommended to read his book "Aku-Aku" before visiting the island. Most of the statues show elongated ears, and so do many wooden carvings, reminding us of the legend of a long-eared tribe which was annihilated in inter-tribal wars. There is a Trans-Pacific air service operated by LAN-Chile; unfortunately the plane only stops one hour, barely long enough to buy from the local carvers; LAN-Chile also flies twice weekly to and from Tahiti. Tourism to the island has increased in the last few years; January and February are high season, October is more tranquil. Camping requires official permission. The rainy season is from February to the end of August.

Things to See The visitor should see the crater of the volcano Rano Kao; the adjacent ceremonial city of Orongo with its petroglyphs; the volcano Rano Raraku from the cliffs of which the *moai* were carved; the statues at Ahu Tahai; the beaches of Ovahe and Anakena; and the *ahu* (ceremonial raised tombs) and *moai* at Vinapu, Siete Moai, Vaihu and Tahai. Music at the 0800 Sunday mass is "enchanting".

Where to Stay etc. *Hotel Hanga Roa* costs US$45 s, US$65 d, including all meals, belonging to the state hotel agency. Honsa (120 beds); *Residencial Evert House,* Arapiku-Nui-on-Hill, comfortable and homely; *Residencial Apina Nui,* US$18 full board; *Residencial Vaiarepa,* US$11 s, including two meals; *Hotel Hotu Matu'a;* a new hotel is being built at Ahu Tahai. A part of the latter is like a *casa bote,* the oldest form of a house on the island or try *Pensión Pérez,* US$15 s, full board (also known as *Residencial One-One*), rated first-class. Sr. Pérez also provides a tour of the island. Another possibility is to stay with islanders, with whom rates vary from US$10-15, again including meals. Some such recommended homes are Yolanda Ika's, Rosita Cardinale's, Carlos Flores Rosales' or Alonso Rapu's (an ex-mayor). Some families will rent their garden to travellers with a tent, US$7, with meal. Tour guides and guest-house keepers meet arriving air passengers. No restaurant, except in hotel. Wine and beer expensive because of freight charges. There are two discotheques in Hanga Roa. Both are popular, but drinks are expensive. Little in the way of shops—be prepared.

How to Get There LAN-Chile flies in twice a week, Monday at 1130 and Thursday at 1430 from Santiago and on to Tahiti. Return to Santiago on Monday at 1430 and Saturday at 0905. Fare Tahiti-Easter Island-Santiago (1975, November) US$580; Easter Island from Santiago (1976 November) US$165, students studying in Chile eligible for 30% discount. The Monday Santiago-Easter Island-Santiago run is from November to February only. (From Tahiti, connexions can be made *direct* to Santiago, Lima, USA, Japan, Australia/New Zealand, S. Pacific in general.) The airport runway has been improved. There is strict plant quarantine on the island and luggage is searched at arrival and departure. There is an airport (departure) tax of US$0.75. It is advisable to book in advance for all flights to Easter Island.

Transport on Easter Island The state hotel provides tours of the island. Hitch-hiking up main road is possible. Jeep tours of archaeological sights cost US$40 per day (lunch included). It is possible to split the cost up to 6 ways. A horse can be hired for US$4 a day or less (or, we are told, *bought* for US$5!). Scooters can be rented for US$15 a day (petrol included) from Mr Hiatt, an American. Aku-Aku Tours arranges accommodation with islanders and excursions around the island.

Dr. R. H. Webber, to whom we are most grateful for the accompanying sketch map, writes:

"It is possible to walk around the main part of the island in two days, either camping at Anakena or returning to Hanga Roa and setting out again the next day. From Hanga Roa, take the road going past the airport and continue northeast until you come to a right turn at a wireless station. Continue along the south coast, past many Ahus (temple sites) to Rano Raruku. The statues have been pushed over in some places, exposing the hollow chambers where human bones are still to be found. All of the statues in Rano Raruku are carved, some in varying stages of completion. Climb to the summit and look down into the crater lake, where reeds were brought from the mainland to make boats similar to those found on Lake Titicaca (Peru-Bolivia).

"There are also many temple sites in the Hanga Nui area nearby; the road goes past 'The trench of the long-ears' and an excursion can be made to Poike to view the open-mouthed statue that is particularly popular with local carvers. The jeep-track continues to Ovahe, passing many temple sites and conical houses. At Ovahe, there is a very attractive beach with pink sand and some rather recently carved faces and a cave.

"From Ovahe, one can return direct to Hanga Roa or continue to Anakena, site of King Hotu Matua's village. From Anakena the coastal path is variable in quality, but there are interesting remains and beautiful cliff scenery. At Hanga o Teo, there appears to be a large village complex, with several round houses and further on there is a burial place, built like a long ramp with several ditches containing bones.

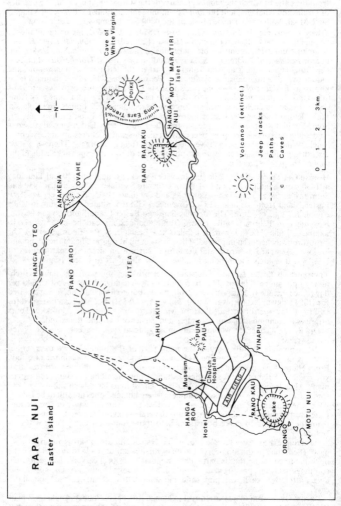

ROUGH SKETCH

"From Hanga o Teo, one can venture inland to Aku Akivi, where there are several other sites and a cave. Near here, there is a trail to Puna Pau, a track near the church leads to the top of the volcano.

"Rano Kau, south of Hanga Roa, is another important site to visit; one finds the curious Orongo ruins here. One final place not to be missed is Vinapu, where the temple platform dates from early times and the masonry work rivals that of the Incas."

To Buenos Aires across the Andes The transandine journey has been described in the Argentine chapter. (See page 83.) By road from Valparaíso to Mendoza along much the same route as the railway is 428 km. On to Buenos Aires is another 1100 km. At Los Andes this Transandine Highway connects with a first-class 88 km. road S to Santiago. Tickets for Buenos Aires are booked at the Transandino office in the Alameda in Santiago. Book well in advance.

Most of the Chilean section of the Transandine Railway runs through the rich Aconcagua Valley, the so-called Vale of Chile. The line from Valparaíso runs through Viña del Mar, climbs out of the bay and goes through (16 km.) **Quilpue**, a mile from El Retiro, a popular inland resort with medicinal springs. It crosses a range of hills and reaches the Aconcagua Valley at **Limache** (40 km. from Valparaíso); (population 22,511). Between Quilpue and Limache is Peñablanca, the town of the white windmills. From Limache interesting drives with grand views can be made. One-day excursions from Valparaíso include visits to Olmue *(Villa Sol)*, Lo Chaparro, and Limache *(Hotel Colegio Alemán)*.

San Pedro, the next station, is the junction for a branch line to Quintero, on the coast.

The line runs NE to **Quillota**, an orchard centre, and to Calera (88 km. from Valparaíso), the junction with the N-S line. Beyond Calera the line swings SE and E for Las Vegas, San Felipe, Los Andes and the pass over the mountains to Mendoza. Llay-Llay is the junction for the railway S to Santiago, which has to climb a spur of mountain, 800 metres high, in crossing from the basin of the Aconcagua to the basin of the Mapocho river in which the capital lies.

Hotel at Quillota *Italiano.*

San Felipe, the capital of Aconcagua Province, is 128 km. from Valparaíso; it is an agricultural and copper and gold mining centre with 42,000 inhabitants. The city is 635 metres above sea level and has an agreeable climate. A paved highway (13 km.) runs N from San Felipe to the old town of Putaendo; there is a road S, 96 km., to Santiago; in 21 km. it leads into the road from Los Andes to Santiago. By rail *via* Llay-Llay to Santiago is 125 km.

Hotel *Hostería San Felipe*, Merced 204.

Termas de Jahuel, or Balneario Jahuel, is high in the Cordillera (1,190 metres) 18 km. by road from San Felipe. The resort is now reported as having seen better days. The hill scenery includes a distant view of Mount Aconcagua. The air is of mountain purity, and the waters are very good for drinking and bathing. Good roads thread the blank stony hills in the neighbourhood.

Hotel *Termas de Jahuel.*

Cuimón, between San Felipe and Los Andes, has an ancient and historical church, with a small museum attached.

Sixteen km. SE of San Felipe is **Los Andes,** in a wealthy agricultural and fruit farming and wine producing area of rich soils and small farms.

There are monuments to José de San Martín and Bernardo O'Higgins in the Plaza de Armas, and a monument to the Clark brothers on Avenida Carlos Díaz: these two engineers, Englishmen by descent, built the Transandine railway. It is 88 km. to Santiago by road. Population: 30,500. Altitude: 730 metres.

Hotels *Continental; Balneario El Corazón, Río Colorado; Español; Plaza,* US$12 d, good.

Beyond Los Andes the line passes in to the Cordillera and begins its climb towards the tunnel through the Andes at 3,175 metres. The railway winds along the Río Aconcagua for 34 km. until it reaches the village of **Río Blanco** (1,370 metres), set at the confluence of two rivers which go to form the Río Aconcagua: the Blanco and the Juncal. There is excellent fishing and good riding and walking in the mountains here; also a fish hatchery with small botanical garden at the entrance of the new Andina copper mine. *Hostería Guardia Vieja,* friendly. Possible to camp. Trains and buses run daily from Los Andes (bus, US$0.65).

(Do not wait around at Los Andes for transport to Argentina as the local buses only go as far as Río Blanco and the train to Mendoza only goes twice a week.)

Portillo, 35 km. further along the rail and road route, is the greatest centre for ski-ing and winter sports in Chile. The weather is ideal, the snow conditions excellent, the runs many and varied; seven lifts carry skiers up the slopes. The season is from June to September/October, weather depending. Cheap package can be arranged at the beginning of the season (US$80 for room, board, lessons and lifts). At this height there are no trees. On three sides the tall rugged mountains soften into snow-clad fields and finally slope gently into the frozen lake which covers nearly all the valley. This is the deep blue glacial Laguna de Inca, 5½ km. long and 1½ km. wide; this lake, at an altitude of 2,835 metres, has no outlet, is frozen over in winter, and its depth is not known.

Portillo is easily reached from Santiago by daily bus services (except in winter). Alternatively, the skier can catch the 1108 train from Los Andes and get to Portillo in the afternoon after one of the most beautiful train journeys on the continent. (The train does not run daily from Portillo to Los Andes, but for a small extra fee, one can ride on the cargo train.) The sun shines all day on the slopes. It was at Portillo that two Americans, Dorworth and Vaughan, created a world speed record of 171.428 km. (106½ miles) an hour on skis.

Hotel *Hotel Portillo,* including a cinema, night club, swimming pool, sauna baths and medical service, on the shores of Laguna de Inca. Rates, meals included, in U.S. dollars: 80 to 100 a day for lake front suites; single room and bath, 30 to 36; double room and bath, 42 to 50; family apts. for 4, 62; bunk room, community bath, 10.50 up; bunk room and private bath US$20. A fabulous view, and parking charges even if you go for a meal; coat and tie must be worn in the dining room. Self-service lunch, US$9 p.p. Lift charges are US$10 per day. Check to make sure the hotel is open in the summer.

There are boats for fishing in the lake; but beware the afternoon winds, which often make the homeward pull 3 or 4 times as long as the outward pull. There are some gentle ski slopes for beginners near the hotel. The major ski-ing events are in August and September. Mules for stupendous expeditions: to Cristo; to the glacier at the head of the valley or of the Cerro Juncal; to the pass in the west side of the valley.

For the mountain scenery between Portillo and the tunnel at Caracoles, see "Transandine Journey" (see page 83). Beyond Caracoles the highway over La Cumbre (Uspallata) Pass rises by steep grades and sharp turns but should be taken if at all possible in preference to the tunnel. The top, at an altitude of 3,856 metres, is reached 8 km. beyond the tunnel. The frontier is crossed at the foot of the statue of Christ the Redeemer, dwarfed by the scenery. The mountain views (including Aconcagua) are stupendous. Heavy snows keep the road over the pass closed from May or June to November or December, but the tunnel is open to road traffic and the journey is 8 km. shorter than over the pass. On the far side of the Andes both road and railway descend 203 km. to Mendoza, where there are rail connections for Buenos Aires. The road from the tunnel to Mendoza is in fair condition, half of it paved and the rest gravelled; all of it should be asphalted in 1978. The gravelled part is a hard drive, narrow and steep.

The Chilean Customs station is some way from the end of the tunnel, at Caracoles; travellers have reported 4 to 5 hour customs delays here.

Lagunillas is a favourite ski-resort only 50 km. from Santiago, 2 hours by bus or car along the beautiful Maipo Valley road to the Ojo de Agua area. Accommodation in the lodges of the Club Andino de Chile.

Several excellent sea beaches are frequented by people who live in the capital: those which lie N of Valparaíso (already described), or those which lie at the mouth of the Río Mapocho, which runs to the sea as the Río Maipo. A road and a railway run to the resorts. The railway runs to the port of **San Antonio**, 113 km. from Santiago and 64 km. by sea south of Valparaíso. Its shipping shows a considerable growth, mostly at the expense of Valparaíso. The port exports copper brought by railway from the large mine at El Teniente, near Rancagua. Population: 60,826. Itself a popular resort, it is also the centre for other resorts to the N and S: **Cartagena**, the terminus of the railway 8 km. to the N, an old town with good hotels, is a great playground for Santiago residents (there are several small resorts—El Tabo, El Quesco, and particularly Algarrobo— to the N of Cartagena); **Llolleo** (a famous resort for those who suffer from heart diseases, on the railway 4 km. to the S), and **Maipo**, at the mouth of the Río Maipo, are other playgrounds. Near Llolleo are many beautiful places, including "La Boca". **Santo Domingo,** with a good hotel, is about 10 minutes by road S of San Antonio. There is a golf course at Santo Domingo, which is by far the most attractive place on this coast.

Hotels At San Antonio: *Jockey Club.* At Cartagena: *Continental; La Bahía; Prince.* At Llolleo: *Oriente; Allhambra.* At Santo Domingo: *Club Hotel.* At El Tabo: *Hotel El Tabol,* quite nice. At Algarrobo: *Pacifico; Aguirrebeña; Internacional; Cantábrico.*

South Through the Central Valley

Road and railway run S through the Central Valley to Concepción (and beyond Concepción to Puerto Montt). They run through the heart of Chile, one of the world's most fruitful and beautiful countrysides, with the snowclad peaks of the Andes delimiting it to the E. It is in this valley that most of Chile's population lives, and here, too, are most of its towns; all can be reached from Santiago by road. The railway has been electrified from Santiago S of Chillán. Along the road from Santiago to Temuco there are several modern motels.

Rancagua, 82 km. S of the capital (1½ hours by train), is an agricultural town with a population of 95,000. Its chief title to fame is a battle fought in its streets in 1814 by O'Higgins against the Royalists. The great El Teniente copper mine is 67 km. to the E, at 2,750 metres; a permit to visit may be obtained at the office in Millán 1040, Rancagua. On this line, 37 km. from Rancagua by rail or car, are the thermal springs of Cauquenes, and nearby is the central hydro-electric plant of Sauzal. Rancagua, which is the capital of the Sixth Region, also has several industries, including a vehicle-assembly plant.

Hotels *Santiago; Ducal; Termas de Cauquenes,* US$15 d, quiet, clean.

San Fernando, capital of Colchagua Province, with 44,500 inhabitants, is 51 km. S of Rancagua. It stands in a broad and fertile valley at a height of

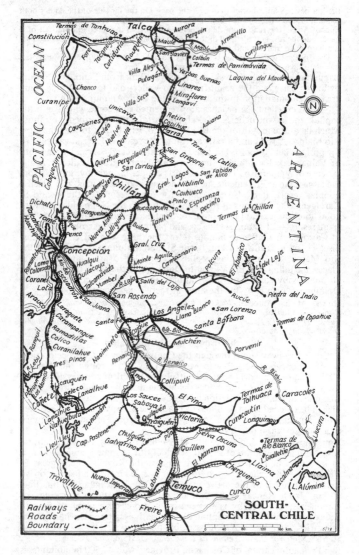

SOUTH-
CENTRAL CHILE

Railways
Roads
Boundary

0   40   80   120   160 km.

ROUGH SKETCH

340 metres. It was founded in 1742, and still has colonial reminders. A branch railway (and road) runs W to the seacoast resort of Pichelemu. A road runs E towards the Cordillera and bifurcates: the northern branch runs to the Termas de Flaco, near the Argentine frontier; the southern branch goes to the resort of Sierra Bella Vista, a private fundo where many Santiago businessmen have holiday houses, but there is also a hostería which caters for about 20 to 25 guests. Cowboy rodeos in October and November.

Hotel *Imperio.*

Curicó, 60 km. S of San Fernando, is in the heart of the wine country; population: 60,000. The surroundings are picturesque and the town's main Plaza de Armas is one of the finest in the country. This prosperous agricultural town is an important centre for the local *huasos* (Chilean cowboys). A branch railroad runs W to Licantén, 26 km. from the popular seacoast beaches of Iloca and Llico.

Hotels *Luis Cruz Marines; Comercio* (recommended); *Curicó; Prat,* near Plaza de Armas, cheap and good value.

Industries Flour milling, alcohol distilling, and wine making.

Talca, 56 km. S of Curicó (250 km. from Santiago) is the most important city between Santiago and Concepción; it is the capital of the Seventh Region, with a population of 103,000. It was founded in 1692, and destroyed by earthquake in 1742 and 1928; Chilean independence was declared in Talca on January 1, 1818. It has been completely rebuilt since 1928, and now has large open parks and well paved streets, a fine stadium with running and cycling tracks, football grounds and an open-air swimming pool. There is a first-class 9-hole golf course. A new road, 175 km. long, runs E through the Pass of Pehuenche (2,490 metres) to San Rafael (Argentina). Near the border is Lake Maule (2,130 metres), where the fishing is good.

The province of Talca, apart from its large wheat and grain production, is the greatest wine producing zone in Chile.

Hotels *Plaza,* good commercial standard, and *Claris. Alcázar* and *Central* are recommended as resonable and clean.

Industries The city is one of the largest manufacturing centres in the country, with the biggest match factory in Chile, 7 shoe factories, 2 biscuit factories, paper mills, 5 flour mills, a tannery, several distilleries, 3 foundries and the principal bed and tube factories in Chile.

Excursions Lake Maule, reached by road (no organised transport) or partly by a railway from Talca, has been stocked with salmon and rainbow trout; the road passes through some of the finest mountain scenery in Chile. Another railway from Talca runs to (90 km.)

Constitución, also reached by a largely unpaved road from San Javier. It is the centre of a wealthy district producing grain and timber, but its main attraction is as a summer resort. The beach, an easy walk from the town, is surrounded by very picturesque rocks, and the nearby scenery is most pleasant. There are plenty of hotels and pensions, but accommodation is difficult from January to March.

Hotels *Hostería Constitución,* new and best; *Gran Hotel; De la Playa; Negri; Plaza. Residencial Mistral,* US$12 d, very friendly.

Chillán, 105 km. S of the road junction of Linares, is an important agricultural centre with a population of 103,000. When the town was destroyed by earthquake in 1833 (it was the birthplace of Bernardo

O'Higgins), the new town was built slightly to the N; that, too, was destroyed by earthquake in 1939 but has been rebuilt. It is a pleasant town with a beautiful plaza and modern buildings. Visit the Municipal Market for handicrafts from Southern Chile. Murals by David Alfaro Siqueiros, the great Mexican artist, in library of Escuela México.

Hotel *Chillán,* US$12 d, good service, very clean; *Gran Hotel,* US$10 s.

Excursion To the thermal baths, Termas de Chillán, 88 km. E, 1,850 metres up in the Cordillera, reached by a motor road all the way. Season: middle December to the end of March. Here the Ski Club de Chile has a tourist centre with hotels and skilifts. There is good ski-ing on the slopes of the Chillán volcano, E of the Termas.

Hotel *Termas de Chillán.*

From Chillán there are 3 road routes to Concepción: (1) from Chillán SW to Penco and S along the coast—there is a scenic railway; (2) along the Pan-American Highway to Bulnes, where a branch road goes SW to Concepción; (3) or along the Highway past the Salto del Laja to Los Angeles, from which a main road and a railway run NW to Concepción. Here both a road and a railway run down the valley of the Bío-Bío to Concepción. The **Salto del Laja** is a spectacular waterfall in which the Laja plunges 47 metres over the rocks. There is a good motel-style hotel with fine restaurant, 2 swimming pools and chalet-type rooms overlooking the falls. Campsite, Los Coyuches. It is 6 hours drive from Santiago.

Concepción, 15 km. up the Bío-Bío river and 580 km. by rail from Santiago, the capital of the Eighth Region, is the most important city in southern Chile and the third city of the Republic. Its port, Talcahuano, on the Bay of Concepción, is 14½ km. away. Population: 250,000.

The climate is very agreeable in summer, but from April to September the rains are heavy; the annual average rainfall, nearly all of which falls in these six months, is from 1,250 to 1,500 mm. Concepción has been outstandingly unfortunate in the matter of earthquakes; it celebrated its fourth centenary during 1950, but its site has been moved more than once during its history.

In the attractive Plaza de Armas at the centre are the Intendencia, the city hall and court house and the Cathedral. The old arcades have given way to a new shopping area. At its centre is a fountain with a statue of Ceres, goddess of corn and of harvest.

In the Alameda is a statue of Don Juan Martínez de Rozas, a hero of Chilean independence. A bas-relief on the pediment shows the people of Chile stretching out their arms to a full rigged ship approaching the shore, heralding free trade with the world and the end of colonial restrictions.

There is a good view of the city from Cerro Caracol. By taking a taxi (quite cheap) to the top of the 90-metre-high hill, SE of the city, you pass through dense woods and come to two viewpoints: first the Mirador Chileno, with a high television aerial on top, from which much of the city can be seen, and then, half a mile away, the Mirador Alemán with a war memorial complete with a statue of Bismarck. Here is a spendid view of Chile's largest river, the Bío-Bío, and its valley running down to the sea. On the far side of the river you see lagoons, the largest of which, San Pedro, is a water-sport playground. On the city side, amongst graceful cypress trees, is the modern Barrio Universitario, much loved by the townfolk because its income is raised by lotteries; the Casa del Arte here contains a fine allegorical mural, 35 by 6 metres, the "Presencia de América Latina", by Jorge González Camerena. There is a golf club on the road to Coronel, "La Posada", by the side of a picturesque lake.

The Bío-Bío flows into the Pacific 15 km. W of Concepción. There are strikingly massive rock formations along the coasts of its estuary. Concepción is linked with Talcahuano, on the bay, by railway and 2 good roads, halfway along one of which is the Club Hípico's racetrack. Races are held on Sundays and holidays. A branch road off leads to good beaches. It passes through a park given to Concepción and Talcahuano by Pedro del Río Zañartu. In it, on a farm, is a small museum containing curious local and Araucanian Indian items. Near-by is the strikingly set beach of Desembocadura del Río. Two other easily reached beaches are Las Escaleras—a flight of natural stairs down a sheer 53-metre sea cliff leads to it—and Ramuntcho, named after a novel by a visitor in 1875: Pierre Loti.

Concepción has now become one of Chile's industrial centres. It has plenty of the most important industrial raw material, water, and good port facilities at Talcahuano and other places in the bay. It is near the coalfields, has ample sources of hydro-electric power, good rail and road communications with the consumming centres of the N, and plenty of room to expand. Its main industries are coal mining, steel (the Huachipato steel works are just outside Talcahuano), textiles (woollen, cotton), paper, glass, cement, cellulose and newsprint; ship repairing; a large petroleum refinery and petrochemical plant are operating.

Hotels *El Araucano* (luxury); *City,* Castellón 510; Bío-Bío, better but smaller, near main square, US$12 s, US$14 d, with private bath; *Concepción,* luxury; *Ritz,* US$6 d, modern and good; *Central,* 1½ blocks from main square, US$8 s, US$10 d, without bath; *El Dorado,* US$15 d; all in Barros Arana; *Panamericano,* new and good; *Res. Turismo,* Calle Caupolicán 67, reasonable; *Hotel King,* US$6.30 d; *Hotel Cecil,* US$10 d; *Hotel Romani,* Barros Arana 790, US$10 s, clean; *Hotel Santiago,* US$1.40, clean, friendly, all across from railway station; *Res. Oriente,* Freire 552, across from the market.

Campsite Santa Sara, at Yumbel.

Restaurants One new recommendation, "acceptable with moderate prices" is the restaurant at Barros Arana 101. Many *fuentes de soda* in centre; *Fuente Alemana,* Av. O'Higgins, recommended. Also, *Restaurante y Pizzería Salvatore,* Av. O'Higgins and *El Estribo,* one block from main plaza.

Clubs Concepción; Alemán; Círculo Francés; Chilean-British Institute, San Martín 573, and Chilean-North American Institute, Caupolicán 81; English Club, O'Higgins 362.

British Consulate San Martín 538. Tel.: 24039.

British School St. John's.

Air In the summer 'planes daily to and from Santiago and connections to Valdivia, Osorno, and Puerto Montt. The new jet airport is by the fast road from Talcahuano and Concepción.

Rail Daily to Temuco at 0710, US$2.10 1st class, US$1.70 2nd class, 7½ hours and Valdivia; to Puerto Montt three times weekly, 18 hours; to Santiago daily and in the summer special fast diesel trains three times weekly, 10 hours.

Buses to and from Santiago, 8½ hours, US$7.60; to Loncoche, 7 hours, US$2; to Puerto Montt *via* Valdivia, US$10.

Talcahuano, on a peninsula jutting out to sea, has the best harbour in Chile. It is Chile's main naval station; its dry docks accommodate vessels of 30,000 tons. Steamers call on both their northward and southward voyages. Population: 152,000.1½ km. away the steel plant at Huachipato has its own wharf to unload the iron ore shipped from the N. There is a new fast road to Concepción.

Shipping   P.S.N.C. and Grace Line vessels call.

The "Huascar", a relic of the War of the Pacific, is in the naval base. On May 21, 1879, at the beginning of the war, the Peruvian Navy's huge warship, the *Huascar,* and a small one arrived at Iquique. Chile sent two small wooden ships under Captain Arturo Prat to challenge them. Prat fought with ferocity. When his broken vessel, the *Esmeralda,* was rammed by the *Huáscar* Prat called upon his men to follow him, boarded the enemy and continued fighting until he was killed. The incident played a large part in inspiring Chile towards final victory (see also Iquique section). The ship is open 1000-1130, 1430-1900 every day, but it seems admittance is sometimes not granted.

The railway to Curanilahue links the coal-producing districts near Concepción. It crosses the Bío-Bío by a 1,885-metre bridge, the longest of its kind in Chile. A new road bridge has been built. The town of **Coronel**, in the heart of the coal area, is 27 km. on. Coronel was the scene of the British naval defeat in 1914, for which vengeance was taken at the Falklands. The coast is very picturesque, the country wooded.

Buses   Buses to Concepción every half hour.

Lota, 8 km. S of Coronel, is a coal-mining centre with 52,000 inhabitants. It is a bunkering port for coastal vessels. In the neighbourhood is the famous Cousiño Park, one of the sights of Chile; it was laid out with views of the sea by an English landscape architect about a century ago and contains many flower gardens, romantic paths, and peafowl and pheasants roaming freely. (Admission US$0.20, no picnicking). The Cousiño mining company runs an excellent ceramic factory. The road is paved beyond Lota as far as the sea-side resort of Laraquete, an hour's run by car from Concepción, where there are mile upon mile of golden sands, and on to Arauco (past the new Celulosa de Arauco wood-pulp plant).

Transport   Rail to Coronel (20 minutes), and Concepción (1½ hours) twice daily. Buses to Concepción every half hour.

Hotel   *Comercio* (25 beds).

The railway goes on to Curanilahue, 96 km. from Concepción. From the terminus a 32 km. road runs to Los Alamos, where a train (26 km.) can be taken W to **Lebu**, a coal port with a population of 17,000. It lies at the mouth of the Río Lebu, and is the capital of Arauco province. The lower river reach and the beach are popular with tourists in summer, and there are daily trains *via* Los Alamos to Puerto Peleco on the highly picturesque Lake Lanalhue, 63 km. S of Lebu. The train continues beyond Peleco along the N shore of Lake Lanalhue. From Lanalhue station a launch service connects with the *Hostería Lanalhue* (adequate, nice location) on the opposite shore of the lake. There is a 16-km. direct road to the hostería from Peleco. (Take the left branch about 3½ km. S of Peleco.) By taking the right branch of this road for about 25 km. and then asking the way to Contulmo, you can reach the south-eastern end of the lake after crossing a high ridge from which you can see both the ocean in the W and the snow-capped Andes to the E. From Contulmo the road goes along the N shore of the lake, parallel with the railway.

Between Puerto Peleco and Los Alamos, 15 km. N, is Cañete, a small town on the site of the ancient Fort Tucapel where Pedro de Valdivia and 52 of his men were killed by Araucanian warriors in 1554.

Hotel   *Gran*.

Rail *Via* Puerto Peleco to Los Sauces, whence there is a line NE to the Longitudinal Railway at Renaico, S of Santa Fe, and another SE to the Longitudinal Railway at Púa.

Travelling on the Longitudinal Railway S from San Rosendo, the junction for Concepción, we come (24 km.) to Santa Fe, from which there is a branch line E to (21 km.) **Los Angeles** (hotel), a town of 90,000 inhabitants in a wine, fruit and timber district. A road runs to the Laguna de Laja past the impressive waterfalls and rapids of the Trubunleo river. A car takes about 3 hours to get to the lake, where there is grand mountain scenery. María Dolores airport at Los Angeles. *Motel Mallorca* (edge of town), US$3.60 p.p., very clean. Campsite: *Los Cabañas,* US$0.25 per tent.

Road and railway are continued from Los Angeles to Santa Bárbara on the Bío-Bío river.

A small town which has hot springs nearby, **Curacautín,** is some 25 km. by railway E of Púa, on the Longitudinal Railway 111 km. S of San Rosendo. The beautiful pine-surrounded Termas de Tolhuaca, with hot springs, are 37 km. to the NE of Curacautín by road. (Good hotel.) SE of Curacautín (32 km. by road) are the hot springs and mud baths of Río Blanco, at 1,046 metres on the slopes of the Sierra Nevada.

Curacautín Hotels *Termas Río Blanco; Turismo; International; Plaza.*

Forest Chile: Temuco to Puerto Montt and Chiloé

Region	Old Provinces	Population ('000)	
		1970	1975
IX	Malleco, Cautín	650	649
X	Valdivia, Osorno, Llanquihue, Chiloé	786	829

South of the Bío-Bío river to the Gulf of Reloncaí the same land formation holds as for the rest of Chile to the N: the Andes to the E, the coastal range to the W, and in between the central valley. But the Andes and passes over them are less high here, and the snowline lower; the coastal range also loses altitude, and the central valley is not as continuous as from Santiago to Concepción. The days are cool and the nights cold; the summer is no longer dry, for rain falls during all the seasons, and more heavily than further N. There is more rain on the coast than inland: some 2,500 mm. on the coast and 1,350 mm. inland. This is enough to maintain heavy forests, mostly beech, but there are large clearings and an active agriculture. The area has been heavily colonised only in the last hundred years; irrigation is not necessary. The farms are mostly medium sized, and no longer the huge haciendas of the N. The characteristic thatched or red tiled houses of the rural N disappear; they are replaced by the shingle roofed frame houses typical of a frontier land. The farms raise livestock and food crops, but there are no Andean pastures on which to graze the cattle in summer. Some 20% of the land is given over to food crops: wheat, potatoes, apples, oats, and hay. The timber industry is being developed.

About 20,000 pure blooded Araucanian Indians live in the area, more particularly around Temuco. There are possibly 150,000 more of slightly mixed blood who speak the Indian tongue, though most of them are bilingual.

The area is important for the tourist because here, between parallels 39 and 42 S, there extends from the Andes one of the most picturesque lake regions in the world. There are some 12 great lakes of varying sizes, some set high on the Cordillera slopes, others in the central valley southwards from Temuco to Puerto Montt. All differ in the colour of their water: some are crystalline and others change from deep blue to an emerald green. Here, too, are imposing waterfalls, large rivers, thermal baths and snowcapped volcanoes. Of the many visitors to the area each year many are anglers revelling in the abundance of fish, the equable climate, and the absence of troublesome insects. The season in the Lake District is from mid-December to mid-March. It is a peaceful area, with fewer tourists than across the border in the Argentine lake district.

The Lake District proper does not begin until we reach Chile's newest city, founded 1881. This is

Temuco, 193 km. S of San Rosendo and 676 km. S of Santiago. This city of 146,500 inhabitants, the capital of the Ninth Region, is now one of the most active centres in the S. Wheat, barley, oats, timber and apples are the principal products of the area. The auctions in the stockyards near the railway on Thursdays and Fridays are interesting; you can see the *huasos* (Chilean cowboys) at work, and the standard of the beef cattle is excellent. The auction begins at 1400 but there is plenty of activity beforehand. Poultry and geese are sold in the market near the railway station, where many Indians may be seen; they make this their market town (you see many of them, particularly women, in their typical costumes). The best places to look for Indian textiles, jewellery etc. are the indoor market in centre of town (corner of Aldunate and Rodríguez), and the shops in the 1100-block of Portales. Temuco is the headquarters of the South American Missionary Society and of the American Baptists, whose public schools are filled from all parts of Chile. There is a grand view of Temuco from Cerro Nielol, where there is bathing pool. Airport.

Hotels *Turismo,* best, good restaurant, *Central, Continental* and *Terraz,* all US$6 d, *Turismo* and *Central* are near main square; *La Frontera,* Manuel Bulnes 733, good, US$23 d; *Residencial Vidal,* between railway station and centre, cheap and good; *Pensión Limache,* nearby, US$4 d, acceptable, Lautaro 1359; *Residencial Prat,* Calle A Prat, US$1.50; *Residencial Varas,* Av. Varas and Calle Las Heras, four blocks from main square, US$4 d, with hot water. Many cheap *residenciales* and *pensiónes* near railway station, in market area.

Restaurants Several—good, clean and popular—in indoor market in centre.

Museum Museo Araucano de Temuco, a good Indian collection. Open Tues.-Sat. 0900-1230, 1430-1830; Sun. 1500-1800.

Rail Twice daily to Talcahuano; daily to Puerto Montt. To Valdivia: once a day in winter, twice a day in summer. To Carahue: daily. To Santiago: twice daily, US$3.50.

Bus to neighbouring towns from market area near railway station. Frequent buses to Villarrica (1¼ hours, US$1) and Pucón (US$1.40). To Junín de los Andes (Argentina) daily. Day and night buses to Santiago. Bus to Concepción (US$4.40).

Excursions A railway runs W through picturesque scenery to (55 km.)

Carahue *(Hotel El Sol),* through Indian country. About 45 km. further, at the mouth of the navigable river Imperial, is Puerto Saavedra, where there is a stretch of beach with black volcanic sand, an easily climbed promontory, but no place to stay at. It is reached from Carahue by car (1 hour), or by river boat (4 hours, or 2 hours on Sunday).

From Puerto Saavedra there are interesting excursions to Nehuentue, on the other side of the river, or to Lakes Budi and Trovolhue, both well worth seeing. Trovolhue is reached by a specially chartered launch which takes 4 hours to go up the Moncul River. Puerto Domínguez, on Lake

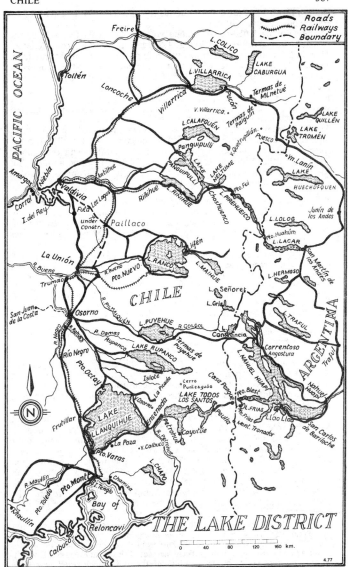

Roads
Railways
Boundary

PACIFIC OCEAN

Freire
L. COLICO
Toltén
LAKE CABURGUA
L. VILLARRICA
Loncoche
Termas de M.netué
Villarrica
Pucón
V. Villarrica
LAKE QUILLÉN
Termas de Paiguín
L. CALAFQUÉN
LAKE TROMÉN
Panguipulli
V. Quetruquillán
Puesco
LAKE NELTUME
Vn. Lanín
Amargos
LAKE PANGUIPULLI
LAKE HUECHUFQUEN
Niebla
Valdivia
Rinihue L. RINIHUE
L. PIREHUEICO
Pto. Fui
Corral
Futa
Choshuenco
Junín de los Andes
I. del Rey
under constr.
Paillaco
L. LOLOG
Pto. Huahúm
San Martín de los Andes
La Unión
R. Bueno
Pto. Nuevo
L. RANCO
Li+én
L. LACAR
Trumao
R. Bueno
L. MAIHUE
L. HERMOSO
CHILE
San Juan de la Costa
L. Señoret
L. Gris
R. Pilmaiquén
Osorno
L. TRAFUL
R. Negro
L. PUYEHUE
R. GOLGOL
Río Negro
R. Damas
Termas de Puyehue
L. Constancia
Pto. Octay
Rupanco
LAKE RUPANCO
Correntoso
Angostura
ARGENTINA
L. NAHUEL HUAPI
Islote
Cerro Puntiagudo
Cosa Pangue
La Picada
Frutillar
LAKE TODOS LOS SANTOS
Pto. Blest
Nahuel Huapí
Osorno
L. FRIAS
Ensenada
Petrohue
Paulla
Mont. Tronador
Llao Llao
San Carlos de Bariloche
La Poza
V. Calbuco
L. Petrohue
Cayutúe
LAKE LLANQUIHUE
R. Maullín
Pto. Varas
L. CHAPO
Pto. Toledo
Pto. Montt
Chamiza
Maullín
I. Tenglo
Bay of Reloncaví
Calbuco

THE LAKE DISTRICT

0   40   80   120   160 km.

4.77

ROUGH SKETCH

Budi, a picturesque little place famous for its good fishing, is reached by road from Carahue (40 km.).

The smoking 3,050-metre Llaima volcano has at its foot one of the prettiest ski-ing resorts in Chile at 1,500 metres, 80 km. from Temuco. The Club Andino de Cautín has two refugios there. It runs a bus from Temuco to the snow-line, where visitors are hauled up to the refugios by tractor-drawn sledges. The *Hotel de la Frontera* will put you in touch with the Club for reservations on the bus and at the refugios.

For details of these excursions visit the State Railways Information Bureau, in a small arcade off Calle Manuel Montt, Temuco. Tours are arranged to lakes, sea beaches, Indian settlements, and salmon and trout streams.

The way from Temuco to Villarrica follows the paved Pan-American highway as far as Freire (24 km.), then runs about 65 km. SE. Another road to Villarrica (48 km.) runs substantially parallel with the railway from Loncoche. Wooded Lake Villarrica, 21 km. long and about 7 km. wide, is the most beautiful in the region, with snow-capped Villarrica Volcano (2,840 metres) for a background.

Villarrica, beautifully set at the extreme SW corner of the lake, is the terminus of a 42-km. branch line which leaves the main line at Loncoche, 80 km. S of Temuco. Villarrica was founded in the 16th century but destroyed by the Indians; the present town (24,000 population) dates from the 1890s.

Hotels *Yachting Club,* pleasant atmosphere, boating and fishing, recommended, US$15 d but cheaper rooms in motel annex; *Hotel El Ciervo,* German-run, also recommended, US$15 d; *Parque Unión,* US$4 d; all on lakefront. *Central,* French-run, clean, good meals, US$3.50 p.p.; *Vista Hermosa,* American-run, recommended, with lovely garden and beautiful views, US$5 d; *Aravena,* US$3.50 s.
Camping *Acapulco.* See also under Pucón *(see below).*
Restaurant *Club Social,* on main street, good; *Restaurant Crillón,* Henrique 475, also good.
Buses To Pucón, US$0.80. To Valdivia *via* Lancoche and Lanco, US$2, 3½ hours, 0700 daily from behind *Municipalidad.*
  Bus, daily, Villarrica-Panguipulli, US$1.80, most attractive ride.

The very attractive small town of **Pucón,** which is on the south-eastern shore of Lake Villarrica, can be reached by bus from Villarrica (26 km.) or Temuco, not by water. Pucón is beautiful, has a good climate, excellent fishing and first class accommodation. The season is from December 15 to March 15.

Excursions from Pucón should be made to Rinconada; to the active Villarrica volcano S of the town for the grand view (bus leaves Pucón at 0900, returns 1300) and good ski-ing slopes (road runs up the lower slopes for 13 km.); to Lake Colico to the N and Lake Caburgua, very pretty, to the NE, both in wild settings; to the thermal baths of Menetue, N of the road to Argentina, and Palguin, S of the same road; to San Martín de los Andes (Argentina), by bus from Villarrica and Pucón. Magnificent scenery, including a monkey-puzzle-tree forest. To Calafquen and Panguipulli (see page 390), on the two lakes of the same names.

Pucón Hotels State-owned *Gran Hotel Pucón* (9-hole golf course), open 2 months of the year, US$16 d, with full board; *Suiza; Maiquillahue; Hotel Antumalal,* luxury class, 30 metres above the shore, 3½ km. from Pucón, very small (18 rooms), picturesque chalet-type, with magnificent views of the lake, but expensive, US$40 d, with meals. Poor beach, but good fishing up the river. *Indian Hotel,* new; *Vista*

Hermosa, a modest residencial; *Hotel Gudenschwager,* classic Bavarian type, moderately expensive, recommended, best sited. *Hotel Central; Residencial Araucarias; Residencial Lincoyán,* Avda. Lincoyán, US$5 d, clean. *Hostería Viena,* clean and pleasant.

Camping   There are several campsites between Villarrica and Pucón: *Huimpalay,* 12 km. from Villarrica; *Lorena,* 10 km. from Villarrica; Acapulco, Playa Linda (Villarrica), *Suyay, Honsa, Millaray,* 7 km. S of Pucón; *Trancura* and *Saltos del Molco.*

Pucón and Villarrica are celebrated fishing centres, where anglers foregather to fish in the lake, and the very beautiful Lincura, Trancura and Toltén rivers. The fishing is now reported to be even better further S, in Lake Ranco (see page 390) for example.

There is a road from Pucón to the Argentine town of Junín de los Andes. The route by car is past the volcanoes of Villarrica and Quetropillán and round Lake Quilleihue, a gem set between mountains at 1,196 metres above sea level. On the border, to the S, is the graceful cone of Lanín Volcano (3,421 metres), and beyond the border is Lake Tromen, much visited by Argentine tourists. The Argentine road from the border to Junín de los Andes is narrow, rough, and not very interesting. The road goes on to San Martín de los Andes, a lovely little town on Lake Lacar, and *via* Lago Hermoso and Villa Angostura (a beautiful drive) to San Carlos de Bariloche. There is a more direct road from San Martín de los Andes to Bariloche but it is not so interesting (see also under Argentina, page 133).

From Antilhue, 148 km. S of Temuco, a branch line and a road run 40 km. W to Valdivia.

The present road runs from Loncoche through Lanco to Valdivia, then cuts SE to Paillaco and S to Osorno. The Longitudinal Highway by-passes all towns except Chillán and Valdivia.

Valdivia, a city standing where two rivers join to form the Río Valdivia, is 18 km. from the port of Coral and the Pacific Ocean. It is the capital of Valdivia Province and has a population of 140,000. It lies 710 km. by sea S of Valparaíso, and is 820 km. by rail (about 16 hours) from Santiago.

The city is set in a rich agricultural area receiving some 2,300 mm. of rain a year; it was founded by Pedro de Valdivia in 1552. From 1850 to 1860 a comparatively small number of German colonists settled in the area; their imprint in terms of architecture and agricultural methods, order, education, social life and custom is still strong. In particular they have created numerous industries, most of them set up on Teja Island (5 kilometres by 2) facing the city. The Universidad Austral de Chile was founded in Valdivia in 1954. Valdivia was badly damaged in the earthquake and tidal wave of May 22, 1960. The river, 2 metres higher since then, has spread over part of the town.

Tourist Office   Av. Gen. Prat, on promenade by river (near market).

Industries   Centre of the metal-processing, food, timber and leather industries based on local raw materials; paper factory, flour mill, rapeseed mill, lumber impregnating plant; presswood and veneer plants, liquor, ceramics.

Hotels   *Pedro de Valdivia,* good, US$15 d; *Schuster,* Calle Maipú; *Palace,* Plaza de la República; *Henriques,* Calle Chacabuco; *Nuria,* Calle Independencia; *Unión,* Av. Prat; *Buxton,* Calle Chacabuco; *Central,* Calle Caupolicán; *Pelz,* Calle Chacabuco, US$9 d; *Regional,* Calle Picarte. The *Schuster* is an old Victorian-type German hotel, a godsend to those who dislike "modern" ones, US$6.50 d; *Hostal Montserrat,* Av. Picarte 849, US$3 p.p., clean and comfortable; *Residencial Los Andes,* clean, friendly. Student *pensiones* include *Juan XXIII,* Gen. Lugos.

Restaurants   *Centro Español,* Calle Henríquez; *Café Cobaña,* Plaza, popular, good nearby food, US$1 for 4-course meal. *Café Haussmann* (good tea and cakes); *Bomba Bar,* Saval on Teja Island.

Campsite   Quillín, between Renco and Valdivia. Also in Parque Saval, Valdivia.

Clubs   Chilean-North American Institute, Calle Beauchef; Santa Elvira Golf Club (9 holes); tennis, sailing, motor, and rowing clubs like Phoenix on Teja Island; also Club Español.

Museum run by University on Teja Island, worthwhile, cartography, archaeology, history of German settlement, ancient musical notes, gramophones, local Indian crafts, etc. Free.

Port Zone of Mulatas in Valdivia: up river, about 16 km. from Corral, a new wharf has been built and vessels can tow alongside and unload direct or to lighters. The wharf, 136 metres long and 31 wide, is used especially by Chilean flag vessels. The navigable channel of the Valdivia river is being dredged to allow vessels up to 8,000 tons to call at the wharf, which is connected with the town by a fair road. Chilean steamers sail frequently for Valparaíso and Punta Arenas and other coastal ports, and Buenos Aires up to Brazil. The P.S.N.C. vessels call when there is sufficient cargo.

Rail   Daily at 0815 ordinary and 1715 express to Santiago; daily to Puerto Montt; 3 times a week the Pullman Express to Santiago leaves 1830. Also night expresses.

Bus to Santiago: Pullman daily, leaving 2100, arriving next morning at 0830. Pullman daily to and from central and southern towns. Hourly buses to Osorno, 2 hours, US$1.30. Twice daily to Llifén. Five buses daily to Panguipulli. Bus terminal at 600's of Av. Picarte.

By air to Santiago from Pichoy airport: five weekly, 2¾ hours by LAN HS748. (Check to make sure service is operating.)

Excursions   The district has much natural beauty with a lovely countryside of woods, beaches, lakes and rivers. The various rivers are navigable and there are pleasant journeys to Futa, Putabla, and San Antonio, behind the Teja Island and through the Tornagaleanes, the "Isla del Rey". Among the waterways are countless little islands, cool and green. Ferryboats (almost every hour in summer) make the beautiful trip down the river to Corral in about two hours (US$2.50), and call at the seaside resorts of Niebla, Cancahual, Mancera and Amargos. There is a "tourist boat" to Corral at midday; the port has two old forts nearby, and the coastal walks are splendid.

The 76-km. road from Valdivia to La Unión goes on to Puerto Nuevo on lovely, island-starred Lake Ranco and to Lake Maihue. A branch of this road curves round the north of the lake to **Llifén,** a picturesque watering place, on the eastern shore. Llifén has an airport and many people fly there direct. From Llifén, visits can be paid to Lakes Maihue and Verde. Another road runs from Valdivia along the river to Los Lagos (61 km.), and on to the beautiful Lake Riñihue (39 km.). Another road runs N from Valdivia into an area from which excursions can be made to Lakes Panguipulli, Calafquén, Neltume and Pirehueico.

From **Panguipulli,** on the W bank, a most attractive town in a beautiful setting (with a train service to Lanco, US$0.35), there is a launch service across Lake Panguipulli to the Choshuenco volcanoes on the eastern bank on Mon., Tues., Thurs., Sat. at 1530, 2½ hours. For fishermen, daily excursions on Lake Panguipulli are recommended (see Donald Nash, a Canadian living in Panguipulli, Martínez de Rozas 646). From Choshuenco there is a road to Puerto Fui, on Lake Pirehueico (bus daily at 1830, 1 hour), a ferry across the lake to Pirehueico (at 2000, 1½ hours) a road thence across the border to Puerto Huahún (good hostería, US$2) on the southern shore of Lake Lacar, in Argentina (bus, a.m., Mon., Wed., and Fri., sometimes Tues. and Sun.). A Launch crosses the Lake to San Martín de Los Andes, on the eastern shore of Lake Lacar, on the same days as the Huahún bus. It is impossible to cross the lake and return in one day.

(We are most grateful to Nancy and Greg Schirm, of Havertown, Pennsylvania, for details of this trip.)

Hotels At Llifén: *Llifén,* US$10 d, and the excellent *Hostería Cholinco,* 3 km. out of town on the road to Lake Mailhue, and also the *Calcarrupe Lodge,* run by English people; *Cumilahue Fishing Lodge,* US$55 p.p., including meals and fishing services. At Niebla: *Miramar.* At Panguipulli: *Hostería Panguipulli; Hostería Riñimapu,* US$30 d, with breakfast, clean, pleasant. At Choshuenco: various hosterías. At Pirehueico: *Hostería Pirehueico* occupied by military, but beds available for US$1 or so in private houses. At the edge of Lake Ranco: *Puerto Nuevo* (very good). At Río Bueno: *Plaza.* At Carboneros: *Villa Lucía.* At La Unión: *Hotels Turismo* and *La Unión.*

The Club Andino Valdivia has ski-slopes on the Mocho and Coshuenco volcanos.

From Cocule, a little S of La Unión (72 km. S of Antilhue, the junction for Valdivia), a branch line runs to the southern shore of Lake Ranco, which offers excellent fishing. A road from La Unión runs to Puerto Nuevo, on the W shore. Lake Ranco has already been mentioned as a possible excursion from Valdivia.

Some 42 km. S of La Unión is another centre for exploring the Lakes. This is

Osorno, 950 km. (15 hours) from Santiago and 122 km. N of Puerto Montt. The city was founded in 1558 on rising ground at the junction of two rivers, the swift Rahue and the quiet Damas. It was destroyed shortly after its foundation, and was later settled by German immigrants, whose descendants are still of great importance in the area. There are local industries of some importance. Good roads radiate into surrounding country, to Valdivia and Puerto Montt and to the Argentine town of San Carlos de Bariloche; it is reached by a road E through Puyehue (bus 2-3 times a week, daily in summer US$10) or *via* the lakes of Todos Los Santos and Laguna Verde, both crossed by ferries. Population: 106,000.

LAN—Chile runs a service to Ceñal Bajo airfield, 8 km. by road from the centre of the city, but this is suspended sometimes in winter. Flying time from Santiago: 2 hours.

Hotels *Gran* (good restaurant), main square, US$14 d; *Waeger,* US$15 d; *Osorno; Heinrich,* Mackenna 736, US$6.25 d, clean, comfortable, friendly; *Astor; Madrid,* Av. Bulnes, US$8 d, a bit overpriced; *Cochrane,* US$12 d; *San Martín,* US$8 d; *Residencial Riga,* US$5 s, highly recommended; *Roma,* near centre, US$3 with breakfast; *Turismo,* US$3 s, rather basic. Student hostel, *Centro Juvenil,* Gen. Mackenna 1731, Casilla 644, Tel.: 3508, US$1 p.p., cooking and bathing facilities included. For other youth hostels, contact Secretaría Provincial de la Juventud, Bilbao 850. Cheap hotels on Av. Bulnes.

Restaurants *Restaurant Plaza* (in the plaza, good German style, usually known as Otto's, closed Sundays, highly recommended); *Don Quixote; German Club; La Playa; Cautín,* Lynch 1591. *Bahía,* Ramírez 1076, recommended for quality and economy. The *Club de Campo* is open to non-members for meals. *Parrillada Argentina,* Calle Lynch; *Café Dino,* a new and expensive restaurant on the plaza; *Hostería Socavi,* 25 km. S on the Panamerican Highway, excellent roast chicken.

Camping *Olegario Mar, Arnoldo Keim.* Official campsite just outside town, US$0.50 for two, plus car; it is clean and there is a restaurant.

Tourist Office At kiosk in the main plaza.

Buses Most leave from next to municipal market. Every ½-hour (from 0700 to 2200) to Puerto Varas and Puerto Montt (to former, 1½ hours, US$1.10). Daily bus to Termas de Puyehue at 1630, US$1, 2 hours. Buses to Valdivia, every hour, 2-hour journey. Instituto Chileno-Norteamericano, Bilbao 934, offers advice to tourists.

Excursions (1) Drive 48 km. SE to **Puerto Octay**, on northern shores of Lake Llanquilhue, a small town in a lovely setting (4 buses daily from Osorno, 1½ hours, US$0.75); follow the road along the lakeside to Ensenada for lunch; a short distance up the road (20 minutes) is Petrohué with the Falls, and Lake Todos los Santos; continue to Puerto Varas for tea, then along the W side of the lake to Octay and back. (2) E to the Pilmaiquen waterfall, and on to Lake Puyehue and the thermal waters at **Termas de Puyehue**; 2 hours by car, bus service. Continue 23 km. to Antillanca (good hostería) through a lovely region of small lakes and fairytale forests. (3) Drive N to Río Bueno, celebrated for its scenery, and to La Unión. (4) Drive to Trumao, a river port on the Río Bueno, whence a steamer may be taken to the sea. (5) Drive to Río Negro and Riachuelo. (6) Drive to beautiful beaches at Pucatrihue on the coast, 65 km. (7) Another excursion can be made to San Juan de la Costa. (8) A further excursion can be made to the S shore of Lake Rupanco (65 km.) taking the road to Puerto Octay and turning E after 33 km. (9) The beach at Maicolpue is worth a visit in the summer (daily bus service from Pandería Pool).

The Club Andino Osorno has two shelters at La Picada (84 km. from Osorno), on the ski slopes at 950 metres, on a road off the main road between Octay and Ensenada; it also has a shelter at the Antillanca ski slopes, where two ski-lifts have been installed; these are only 19 km. by road from the Puyehue Hotel. Apply at the Oficina de Turismo de Osorno, Gran Hotel. A drive from Osorno to Correntoso and San Martín de los Andes, Argentina, is as lovely a trip as across the lakes from Petrohué to Bariloche.

There are hotels at Puerto Octay (*Hotel Haase,* very pleasant, US$5 s; *Posada Gubernatis,* Calle Santiago, lakeside, motorboat, excellent food, clean, comfortable, US$8, including full board). Centinela *(Hotel Centinela).* Puyehue *Gran Hotel Termas de Puyehue* has a hot-springs swimming pool, large and well kept, about US$14-18 a day, main meals US$6 each, breakfast US$2, in beautiful scenery, heavily booked Jan.-Feb.; also near Lake Puyehue, about 4 km. from Termas is *Aguas Calientes,* cheaper and less commercial than the Termas, cabin-type accommodation at US$20 a day per cabin, or good camping, meals available. *Hotel Ensenada* at La Ensenada. 7 km. E of Entrelagos is the *Hostería Tramahuel* (six rooms and two family cabins); *Motel Ñilque,* cabins, US$35 d, half-price April to November; *Hostería Isla Fresia,* located on small island, transport provided; Maicolpue, *Hostería Miller,* on the beach. Pucatrihue, *Hostería Inalear* (summer only).

Campsites Lake Puyehue, Camping Municipal. Entre Lagos, Camping Muelle de Piedra (7 km. east of Entre Lagos); Camping Los Copihues (9 km. east of Entre Lagos).

From Osorno it is 93 km. by rail S to Puerto Varas. The last 25 km. run for the most part along the shore of Lake Llanquihue which, together with Lake Todos los Santos to the E of it, are the most southerly and the best known of all the lakes. Across the great blue sheet of water can be seen two snowcapped volcanoes: the perfect cone of Osorno (2,680 metres) and the shattered cone of Calbuco, and, when the air is clear, the distant Tronador. Lake Llanquihue covers over 540 square km. There is a road, 187 km. long, round it. And between Osorno and Puerto Montt there is a fine paved road running through farmland reminiscent of Scandinavia or Western Canada (2 hours by bus).

Puerto Varas, a beauty spot of about 33,300 inhabitants, is on the edge of Lake Llanquihue. Standard roses are planted along the streets. It is 1,046 km. from Santiago and only 26 by rail or 24 by paved road from Puerto Montt.

Hotels   *Puerto Varas,* luxury class with casino; *Gran Hotel,* Klenner 349, US$25 d; *Motel del Lago,* Klenner y Bellavista, cabins, US$15 p.p.; *Residencial Central,* US$7 d; *Playa Hotel,* lakeside position, clean, comfortable, US$12 d, restaurant is good but comparatively expensive; *Bellavista,* edge of lake, nice gardens, bare but clean, US$3.50 s, good food; *Licardyén,* new, small, US$12 d, highly recommended, book in season; *Grand Hotel Hein* (sometimes known as Grand Hotel Puerto Varas), basic, US$2; *Bella Vista,* on lakeside, US$3 p.p., clean, lovely view; Student hostel, *Centro Juvenil,* San Ignacio 979, Casilla 47, US$1 p.p., including bathing and cooking facilities. Also cheap residenciales opposite bus station and in Plaza de Armas.

Campsite   Playa Venado, apply to Playa Venado Municipal Office. Camping Municipal Puerto Varas (4 km. E), good beach; Camping Playa Niklitschek (8 km. E), full facilities, US$5 per night.

Tourist Office   San José 325, helpful, hotel and restaurant brochures for whole area.

Restaurants   *Club Alemán,* best, dinner, US$3; *Mercado,* next to market, good and reasonable.

Tourist Agent   Graytur.

Excursions   There are motor-boats on the lake; buses run between Puerto Varas and (50 km.) Ensenada, in the south-eastern corner of the lake, and on to Petrohué (for lunch). US$0.50 to Ensenada, US$0.70 to Petrohué, Transporte Esmeralda, 57 Del Salvador. Travellers have warned that these services may be suspended. The two-hour drive around the lake is very picturesque; you go past waterfalls, a waterwheel, small farms and churches. On the northern road between Puerto Varas and Ensenada are Puerto Octay and Centinela (see previous page).

It is not possible to go by private car from Puerto Varas to Bariloche, Argentina, as the ferry on the Argentine side does not take cars; one must go *via* Osorno. The drive takes one through low mountains and past emerald green lakes.

Puerto Varas is within easy reach of many famous beauty spots—Desagüe, Totoral, Frutillar, Los Bajos, Puerto Octay (direct bus only from Osorno), Puerto Chico, Puerto Fonck, Ensenada, La Poza, the Lorelei Island, the Calbuco Volcano, La Fábrica, Puerto Rosales, Playa Venado and Río Pescado.

Bus every half hour from Varas to Alto **Frutillar,** US$0.30, then another half-hourly bus to Bajo Frutillar, 4 km. away and possibly the most attractive town on the lake. Frutillar has *Hostería Alemán* by lakeside, very clean, excellent food, US$1.25 including breakfast.

La Poza is a tiny little lake to the S of the big lake and reached through tortuous channels overhung with vegetation; a concealed channel leads to yet another lake, the Laguna Encantada. On the way back to the first island the launch calls at Isla Lorelei, where there is a small restaurant.

East of Lake Llanquihue is the most beautiful of all the lakes in southern Chile: Lake Todos los Santos, a long irregularly shaped sheet of water with the lake ports of **Petrohué** on its western and **Peulla** on its eastern shores. Trout and salmon fishing at Petrohué are excellent. For anyone who loves mountains Peulla is worth a few days' stay. The waters are emerald green. It is only 18 km. by an enchanting road from **Ensenada,** a lovely spot on Lake Llanquihue (2 buses a day from Varas, 1½ hours,

US$1.30). The bus ride to Ensenada is slightly uncomfortable but is compensated by the scenery, very like that of the blue grass region of Kentucky. The rolling woodland meadows and pastures are delightful. Crops of wheat, oats and potatoes are raised, but the farm implements are often crude. We see cattle herded by riders in their ponchos on the way to some small country town market. Just before midday the bus crosses a bridge and down below is Lake Llanquihue. The driver stops for five minutes so that passengers can enjoy the view. It is very beautiful. Fields of wheat slope down to the water's edge; a great green forest rises on the far side of the purple lake. Away to the left is the snow clad volcano of Osorno. The whole scene is shot through with the most vivid colours. Past the tip of the lake and over another ridge is Ensenada.

Hotels   At Ensenada: *Hotel Ensenada,* US$4 p.p.; two cheaper hotels at about half that price. At Petrohué: *Hostería Petrohué,* US$15 d, small. At Peulla, on the opposite shore: *Hotel Peulla,* US$10 s with full board, big, simple, service sketchy, but cold in winter; *Hospedaje Ensenada,* US$2.80 with breakfast, run by friendly German-Chilean family. Otherwise food hard to find in Peulla, so take your own. Reported that other lodgings may be found, through asking locals; the customs official puts people up for US$4.50 p.p., including two meals.

Campsites   Alcalde Manuel Droquett, Chinquahoe, Playa Maki, and at Petrohué.

This lake has no roads round it, but from Petrohué a rather poor road runs N through mountain land to the ski-ing hut on La Picada; the hut is more usually reached from Ensanada or Osorno.

As for the lake itself, its shores are deeply wooded and several small islands rise from its surface; in its waters are reflected the slopes of Osorno volcano. (A hiker in good condition can climb Osorno and return the same day; there is a shelter for hikers.) Beyond the hilly shores to the E are several graceful snow-capped mountains, with the mighty Tronador in the distance. To the N is the sharp point of Cerro Puntiagudo (2,278 metres), and at the north-eastern end Cerro Techado (1,720 metres) rises cliff-like out of the water. Visitors stay at Peulla (Hotel), for the night when going into or coming out of Argentina. For those who stay longer there are motor launches for excursions on the lake; two good day trips are to Cayutúe and Río Blanco. Boat from Peulla to Petrohue, then bus to Puerto Montt.

Puerto Montt, capital of the Tenth Region, is the terminus of both railway and Longitudinal Highway; the railway twists and winds over the watershed which separates the Bay of Reloncaví from Lake Llanquihue before it descends into the town, built on a patch of flat land at the head of the bay. The first German colonists arrived in 1852. They have remained to this day a small but powerful percentage of the 87,000 inhabitants. The houses are mostly faced with unpainted shingles, very Nordic this; here and there stand structures in the Alpine manner, all high pitched roofs and quaint balconies. Even the big new hotel on the waterfront recalls Bavaria. The handicrafts market by the port merits a visit. See the little fishing port of Angelmó and sample its shellfish or fresh cooked crab; Angelmó is 2 km. from the centre of town and is also noted for its handicrafts. It has become a tourist centre in recent years.

The port is much used by fishing boats and coasting vessels, and it is here that passengers embark for the island of Chiloé, for Puerto Aysén, and for the long haul S to Punta Arenas. A paved road runs 55 km. SW to Ainco, where there is a ferry service to Chiloé. Fare from Puerto Montt to Ancud (Chiloé) is US$2.

Puerto Montt is 1,064 km. from Santiago, 20 hours by train (express train leaves daily at 1700), bus quicker. Empresas "Lit" and "Via Sur" run services in modern buses daily (US$10.50) to Santiago and takes 15 hours, also to Temuco. Also buses daily to and from Bariloche (Argentina), between 9 and 12 hours depending on route, and between US$10 and US$20, on bus. Route passes three lakes: Nahuel Huapi, Frías and Todos los Santos. LAN bus from airport to town, US$0.15, taxi, US$1.50.

Hotels tend to be more expensive than elsewhere. Check Tourist Office. *Vicente Pérez Posales,* Antonio Varas 451, US$15 d, highly recommended, excellent restaurant, seafood; *Colina* and *Portales* (cheapest), all new; *Hotel Stop,* views of bay, US$6 s; *Club Alemán; Hotel Montt,* US$7 s (good restaurant); *Central* (restaurant), US$2.50 d, no toilet; *Hotel Millahue,* US$9 d, next bus station, good food; *Ramwiller,* Quillota 108, near railway station, US$2 each; *Residencial Acapulco,* clean, bargain for price; *Hotel Angelmó,* modern, central heating, centrally located; *Correa,* in Pelluco; *Hotel Sur,* comfortable and quiet, street opposite railway station, US$8 d; *Bahía,* opposite dock gates, US$2 p.p.; *Residencial Porteno,* US$1 a night, basic; *Hospedaje Teresa Felmer,* San Felipe 180, near railway station, very clean and friendly, US$4.50 d, with breakfast; *Residencial Sur* and *Hotel Royal,* both near railway station, US$2 s, very nice. Many private homes give you a bed for US$1; look for signs in windows. Pensión at Anibal Pinto 328, US$1.20 with breakfast, is recommended. Student hostel at 190 Gmo. Gallardo, US$0.50.

Restaurants *Embassy* is recommended for "stunningly cooked", reasonably priced food; *Super Yoco,* Calle Urmaneta, very reasonable and good; *La Scala,* for fish; *Patache* in Angelmó, try Vapor Pecoroco, a local crab-like shellfish; *Diego Rivera,* good food and reasonable; *Restaurant Real,* recommended; fish restaurants in market and along wharves, recommended. Restaurants in market at Angelmó highly recommended for fish.

Camping At Chinquihue, 10 km. W of Puerto Montt (bus service), run by Automóvil Club de Chile, about US$0.75 per person.

Tourist Office New and helpful, Edif. Diego Rivera, Quillota 124, next to Municipal Theatre. Tel.: 3573. Also annexe in railway station.

Museum at Calle O'Higgins 237, interesting.

Shopping Woollen goods. Cheaper at roadside stalls between port and market than at tourist shops in town.

Rail Daily to Osorno, Temuco, and Santiago, 1600, 19-23 hours, US$11.50 Pullman; 2nd class US$7. Direct train to Santiago at 1100.

Bus Service: to Puerto Varas and Osorno every 30 min., US$0.25; to Santiago, express 15 hours, US$10.50. Bus Norte has a service leaving on Tuesdays to Osorno and Punta Arenas.

Air Service Ladeco run regular plane service to Santiago and Balmaceda. LAN direct flight from Puerto Montt to Santiago; also to Punta Arenas (3 a day) and Bariloche, in the Argentine lake district. Flight to Punta Arenas costs US$54 but air force (FACH) flights (military personnel have preference) are half-price. Ask about dates. El Tepual airport is 16 km. from town.

Shipping Service Booking southward only in Puerto Montt, 1-2 weeks before sailing date for first class; third class tickets sold two days prior to departure at Puerto Montt ticket office, but enquiries at Empresa Maritima del Estado, Estado 359, 5th floor, Santiago, or Casilla 37, Puerto Montt. Reservations are very difficult to obtain in advance. If no passages available, go to Castro, on Chiloé island, and get boat from there. Ship "El Navarino" between Puerto Montt and Punta Arenas, first class, US$85, second class US$35, third class US$15, all without food; third class is 6 to a cabin and only 1 blanket each. Food on boat is reasonable, but it is best to bring some; watch for good seafood at Puerto Edén. Four-day trip, "fantastic journey", stopping at Castro, Puerto Edén and Querella. Departure, 15th of month, return 22nd. Cargo boats also ply the route and are recommended for the hardy, US$25 (basic). Four times monthly a cargo boat leaves for Puerto Aysén (US$12, 2½ days; from there a Ladeco plane to Punta Arenas (US$12) or by road through Argentina.

Empresas Marítimas Cochifas also run a service from Puerto Montt to Puerto Aysén and Laguna San Rafael.

Excursions The wooded island of Tenglo, close to Puerto Montt and reached by launch, is a favourite place for picnics. Magnificent view from the summit. The island is famous for its "curantos", a local dish, although some say it is better at Pelluco. *Hostería Miramar,* US$2.40 s, with breakfast, basic, but a nice view overlooking the port of Angelmó. Chamiza, up the River Coihuin, has fine fishing. There is a good bathing beach at Pelluco *(Restaurant Juan Pazos),* a fair walk from Puerto Montt. The (cargo) launch trip up the Reloncaví estuary (8 hours) is very beautiful, fjords, sea lions, local colour, and recommended. The launch leaves 0830 Wednesday and Saturday from Angelmó and returns from Cochamó 0700 Thursday and Sunday, US$2 each way, does not include any meals. (Return from Cochamó can also be made *via* launch up river and thence bus to Puerto Varas but only on Monday, Wednesday and Friday.) Constantino Cochifas organizes a trip to the San Rafael glacier on the cargo ship "Mimi", double staterooms, US$250 for five days including food. At **Cochamó,** at the end of the estuary, there is a small hotel, *Hotel Cochamó,* basic but clean, US$4 s, including dinner and wine. Cochamó itself is pretty but limited; a side trip is to the Termas de Sotomó, but this requires an affinity for mud. The Maullin River, which rises in Lake Llanquihue, has some interesting waterfalls and good fishing (salmon). The little old town of **Maullin,** at the mouth of the Maullin River, is worth a visit. **Calbuso** *(Hotel Francke),* centre of the fishing industry, with good scenery, can be visited direct by steamer or by road. Puerto Montt is a good centre for excursions to the lakes *via* Puerto Varas. From Puerto Montt to Puerto Varas by the "old" (dirt) road is short but strikingly lovely.

From Santiago to Buenos Aires via the Lakes This route between the two capitals is taken by a large number of people every year. It is open the year around but is sometimes disrupted by land-slides from May to July. It is at its very best from December to March. The journey takes five days.

The "Rápido" trains cover the 1,046 km. from Santiago to Puerto Varas in 17 hours, running once a day from Santiago, leaving at 0600. Extra fares are payable on these trains. There is also a daily air service to Concepción, Valdivia and Osorno up to Puerto Montt.

Taking the now more popular bus journey to either Osorno or Puerto Varas, the country becomes more attractive as one leaves Santiago. There are rolling hills, and occasionally there is a glimpse of the sea to the right and snow peaks over to the left. Fundamentally, there are two main routes between Osorno/Puerto Varas/Puerto Montt and Bariloche: the all-road journey *via* Osorno and the Puyehué pass, and the bus-boat-bus-boat-bus journey *via* Ensenada, Petrohué, Lake Todos los Santos, Peulla, the Pérez Rosales pass and Lake Frías. For the former, Bus Norte runs daily from Puerto Montt *via* Osorno to Bariloche at 0730 every day except Tues. and Sun., about 8½ hours, US$15, running beside four lakes; back from Bariloche every day except Mon. and Wed., starting 0800. For the latter Andina del Sur runs a bus/boat combination, about 12 hours, US$35, leaving Puerto Montt at 0800; possible to stop over at Peulla (this route is described below).

The "Esmeralda", a small steamer crosses Lake Todos los Santos in 2-2½ hours. This is a beautiful journey with steep, tree-covered snow-capped slopes on all sides (the trip costs US$4.80 if the traveller has not purchased an inclusive ticket). At Peulla there is a stop for lunch. If your ticket does not include lunch, there is a pleasant walk up beside the stream behind the Peulla hotel. After lunch the traveller may carry on to the customs crossings and to Bariloche, arriving at dinner time. The scenery at Peulla is, however, quite beautiful and worth the overnight stay: *Hotel Peulla,* US$10 including three good meals; accommodation also available in private homes, sleeping bag helpful.

Peulla (where Chilean customs are cleared—travellers have informed us that the frontier is closed at weekends) is left by bus for a run of 18 km. to Casa Pangue. Then the climb is begun over a low pass in the Andes—the Pérez Rosales Pass—with snow peaks left and right. The road is fairly steep, winding and narrow, among big trees and heavy vegetation. The La Cumbre Pass and the Argentine frontier are crossed on a height, but the customs are at the foot, on the edge of Lake Frías, at Puerto Frías. From here this beautiful little lake is crossed by a small motor vessel in 20 minutes to Puerto Alegre. A short bus ride takes us to Puerto Blest for lunch. Puerto Blest—a small hotel (not cheap, but better situation than at Peulla, where the water-level of the lake has receded greatly) and a dock—is on a narrow arm of Lake Nahuel Huapí. A traveller suggests walking from Puerto Blest to Lake Frías through "Lord of the Rings"-type scenery. Another suggests the 28 km. day walk from Peulla to Puerto Frías for the hardy; this is beautiful hiking country. One can also take a local bus (US$0.50) as far as Ensenada and walk the remaining 16 km. to Petrohué.

A small lake boat or the 300-ton "Modesta Victoria" takes us across to Puerto Pañelo on the eastern side of Llao-Llao peninsula. The drive to San Carlos de Bariloche (see p. 133) takes 20 minutes.

Bariloche is left by train at 2035 next day. The line runs E for 11 hours through flat, barren, waste country. In summer the dust and heat are great. A transfer is made at Patagones to a more comfortable Pullman train, but there is still a deal of dust. We arrive at Buenos Aires at 1400 on the second day, after a 40 hour train ride.

Chiloé There are two main towns, Ancud and Castro (airport), and many fishing villages. Typical of the island are substantial wooden houses built on stilts over the water. The hillsides are a patchwork quilt of wheat fields and dark green plots of potatoes. Inland are impenetrable forests. There has recently been appreciable development; in both Ancud and Castro there are several hotels, and power and water shortages and poor sanitation are now things of the past. Though the weather is often cold and foggy, the island is extremely beautiful when the sun is out. Sweaters and woollen caps are good purchases.

From Puerto Montt buses run five times a day to Ainco (55 km.) on the Straits of Chacao; passengers are taken in launches across the Chacao Strait to Chiloé, where buses for Ancud and Castro meet them. The trip passes through beautiful scenery. There are five trips a day between the Continent and Chiloé by the ferryboat. A side trip is to the island (and town) of Achao.

Ancud Beautiful views, Spanish fort and powder magazine restored in 1975-1976. An excellent regional museum on the Plaza de Armas, free; craft shops in same building (speciality is basketwork). **Hotels:** *Hostería Ancud,* de luxe and a most interesting building, US$10 s; *Hotel Caleuche* (ex-*Plaza*), US$3 d; Convent of the Immaculate Conception, Calle Chacabuco 841 offers youth hostel type accommodation for US$0.40; *Residencial Montenegro*, US$3 d, comfortable, hot water. Ferry/bus to Puerto Montt, US$2, to Castro, US$1.25. **Camp site** 5 km. W of town. **Restaurants:** Excellent. Seafoods, especially King crabs (very cheap), almejos and cheese in market area. *Restaurant Cangrejo*, very good; *El Truco*, good seafood.

Castro Capital of the island and a very friendly town. Waterfront market. Large cathedral with excellent wooden interior on the Plaza de Armas. One-room museum contains history, folklore, handicrafts and mythology of Chiloé. An hour's walk from the town is a new park-museum. Several cheap hotels near main plaza (US$1-US$2) and a modern, attractive *hostería* (US$15 d). Many excellent, inexpensive restaurants (sea food) on the water front. Incredible cemetery! *Hotel La Bomba*, US$3.25 d, decent hot water. *Hotelería Nacional*, US$9 s; *Hotel Plaza*, US$6 d. The Punto Arenas-Puerto Montt boats call at Castro. (It is difficult to make bookings from the Castro office of LAN-Chile.) From Castro, a difficult combination of buses and a ferry takes one to **Achao**, 39 km. away (*Hotel Splendid*, US$3.25 d, no heat), a quiet, pretty fishing village with a lovely old wooden church from the 17th century. Many excursions S and W are available. Tourist office on the Plaza de Armas. Also from Castro take local bus (US$0.40) to 0900 Sunday market at picturesque village of **Dalcahue** (2 small cheap pensions), for excellent and cheap woollen goods. Arrive early as the market ends about 1100.

Communications Ferry direct from Puerto Montt or bus (every 2 hours). Puerto Montt-Ancud *via* Straights of Cuacao, US$4.50 including ferry; Ancud-Castro, US$3. Five buses daily on both routes. (We are most grateful to Nancy and Greg Schirm for additional information on Chiloé.)

The islanders of Chiloé were the last supporters of the Spanish Crown. When Chile rebelled the last of the Spanish Governors fled to the island and, in despair, offered it to England. Canning turned the offer down.

Currency Banco de Osorno y la Unión, in Ancud and Castro. If going on south, stock up well with Chilean pesos. It is difficult to change money at the weekend.

Archipelagic Chile   From Puerto Montt and Chiloé to Cape Horn

		Population ('000)	
Region	Old Provinces	1971	1975
XI	Aysén	51	57
XII	Magallanes and Antarctic Territory	95	101

South of Puerto Montt lies a third of Chile, but its land and its climate are such that it can be put to little human use: less than 3% of the country's population lives here. It is one of the rainiest and stormiest regions on earth: over 5,000 mm of rain fall on some of it; 7 days of the year are tempestuous, 25 stormy, 93 squally, and the sun only shines through a blanket of mist and cloud on 51 days of the year. Deep and impenetrable forest covers most of the land. It is only the northern part—a small area round the towns of Puerto Aysén and Coyhaique—and the far S that are inhabited. S of Chiloé, for 1,100 km., there is a maze of islands—the tops of submerged mountains—separated by tortuous fjord-like channels, a veritable topographical hysteria. It is fortunate for shipping that this maze has a more or less connected route through it: down the channel between Chiloé and the mainland, about 290 km. of open sea beyond the southern tip of Chiloé and then down the Moraleda, Mesier, Innocentes and Smyth channels into the Straits of Magellan. In some places along this route the tide levels change by 12 metres. In one particular place two sharp-cut walls, 900 metres high, enclose the constricted channel which leads to Puerto Natales; here the waters are deeper than the cliffs are high and slack water lasts for 30 minutes only. The Smyth Channel enters the Strait of Magellan at Cape Thamar. February is probably the best month for the trip.

LAN has excellent air services to Aysén and Magallanes from Puerto Montt (Tepual Airport). Air force flights half-price.

Aysén The rainy Eleventh Region (Aysén) lies between Chiloé and Magallanes. The administrative capital and commercial centre is **Coyhaique** *(Hotel Honsa),* connected by road to Puerto Aysén, Chile Chico and Balmaceda (airport). Road connections with Argentina (3 buses a week from Coyhaique to Comodoro Rivadavia).

Christian Walter, from Wedel, Germany, writes about Aysén as follows: "LAN and Ladeco fly from Puerto Montt to Balmaceda five times a week for about US$18 one way, US$36 return. From Balmaceda only way to Coyhaique is "taxi-colectivo", about US$2, depends on how many travel in one taxi (1 to 5 persons). Not much to see in Coyhaique; try one of the smaller hotels, you can talk to cattle-merchants and truck-drivers, who will probably take you along into Argentina. I was offered a ride through Argentina *via* Bariloche back into Chile at Puyehué. Roads are bad, persons with a weak stomach should take some pills against travel-sickness when riding a truck! Interesting road from Balmaceda to Coyhaique, but no road is more beautiful than the one from Coyhaique to Puerto Aysén. If you go by bus, sit on the left side; I counted 28 waterfalls of some size along the 67 km. There are several spots where you can have a picnic and watch the wild landscape; buses do not stop, except to take passengers who wait at the side of the road, 4 or 5 buses a day. In Puerto Aysen you can book a passage to Puerto Montt; ships leave from Puerto Chacabuco, 18 km. from Puerto Aysén. Fare for taxi-colectivo is US$2, part with your companions (1 to 4). First-class cabin to Puerto Montt for US$40! One way by boat is more expensive than the return flight with LAN or Ladeco! I would recommend a flight from Puerto Montt to Balmaceda and by boat from Puerto Chacabuco to Chonchi (Chiloé); fare is about US$6, 2nd class (crowded, few seats, but lots of fun and possibity of getting to know people). Arrival at Chonchi after a day and a half, usually in the evening. Stay in one of the *residenciales* and take a bus to Castro the next day. From Castro there are several buses to Ancud, for Puerto Montt. You get there earlier as the boat stops at Chonchi during the night; depends on the freight—mostly cattle.

"If you have plenty of time visit the Laguna San Rafael, some 100 km. south of Puerto Aysén, only way boat or plane."

The Laguna is accessible from the sea *via* Río Témpanos; at the end of it may be seen the San Rafael glacier, 100 metres in height, which calves small icebergs, carried out to sea by wind and tide. The thick vegetation on the shores, with snowy peaks above, is typical of Aysén. The glacier is one of a group of four that flow in all directions from Monte San Valentín. This icefield is part of the Parque Nacional Laguna San Rafael (1.35 m. hectares), one of Aysén's 12 national parks, all set up in 1967 and now regulated by the National Forestry Council (Conaf).

Chilean Patagonia

The Province of Magallanes has 17.5% of Chile's total area, but it is inhabited by only 101,000 people, or under 1% of Chile's population.

The summer months in Patagonia are December, January and February, when rains are frequent, although a spell of several weeks of dry weather is not uncommon during this season. For three months of the year snow covers the country, except those parts near the sea. The country is then more or less impassable, except on horseback, owing to snow and swollen torrents.

Strong, cold, piercing winds blow throughout the year and particularly during the spring, when they reach a velocity of 70 to 80 km. an hour. During the winter they do not blow all that hard, and from May to August a strong wind is almost exceptional. The dry winds parch the ground astonishingly, and prevent the growth of crops, which can only be cultivated in sheltered spots.

The island of Tierra del Fuego has tracts of flat grass lands covering millions of hectares. Forest country backed by mountains rises to a height of over 2,450 metres. The total pastoral area of Magallanes and Tierra del Fuego is reckoned at 4.4 million hectares.

Until the discovery of oil—Tierra del Fuego and N of Magellan Strait produce all Chilean oil—the most important industry was the breeding of sheep: the flocks are estimated at 3.2 millions. The British have always been interested in Chilean Patagonia, and at one time there was a large British colony there; it has been diminishing steadily of late.

The two main towns are Punta Arenas, where 75% of the whole population of the Province live; and Puerto Natales, in Ultima Esperanza, with a population of 14,000; 80% of its males work in the coal mines of Río Turbio across the border in Argentina, to which there is a regular bus service.

Punta Arenas, the most southerly city in Chile, and capital of the Twelfth Region, is in the Straits of Magellan at almost equal distance from the Pacific and Atlantic oceans, 1,432 nautical miles from Valparaíso, and 1,394 from Buenos Aires. The city is laid out in squares, with a population of about 65,000. Most or the smaller and older buildings are of wood, but the town has expanded rapidly, and practically all new building is of brick or concrete. All the main roads are paved and the country roads are of gravel; when driving in Patagonia, some form of windscreen protection is absolutely essential. Punta Arenas is a busy little city somewhat neater looking than the average Chilean town. The cemetery is even more fantastic than the one at Castro (Chiloé).

Punta Arenas is the centre of the sheep farming industry in that part of the world and exports wool, skins, and frozen meat. It is also the port of call for most foreign vessels passing from one ocean to the other, and the home port of the small coasting vessels trading between the southern Chilean ports. Coal has been found in many parts of the territory and a considerable number of small mines are working. Besides the export of oil and gas, there is the regular carriage of crude between the Strait oil terminals and the refineries at the ports of Quinteros and San Vicente. Good roads connect the city with (240 km.) Puerto Natales in Ultima Esperanza and Río Gallegos in Argentina. There are air services to Río Gallegos and Río Grande,Porvenir, Puerto Williams (see page 403), Manantiales and Natales. There are no railways. Punta Arenas has certain free-port facilities.

The summer sports are football, tennis, horse-racing, and there is a nine-hole golf course. In winter there is ice-skating and ski-ing. The glamorous new airport is well worth a visit. There is a quaint museum in the Colegio Salesiano dealing with the Indians, animal and bird life of the region, and other interesting aspects of life in Patagonia and Tierra del Fuego, at the corner of Calles Bulnes and Sarmiento. There is a Patagonian museum on the Plaza de Armas, with good dioramas. The best sight is the Patagonian Institute, at the N end of Av. Bulnes. It has a small zoo with puma, guanaco and deer, and a collection of old local vehicles and machinery. The Cervantes theatre is so ornate it is worth buying a cinema ticket to see it; the films shown are old.

Landing By motor-boat or tug, but one can walk ashore if the ship is moored alongside the long jetty.

Steamers To Valparaíso, by Cía. Chilena de Navegación Interoceánica and Empresa Marítima del Estado. When there is sufficient cargo, direct calls are made at Punta Arenas by P.S.N.C. cargo vessels. Cruise vessels visit this port.

Chilean ships travel the 1,320 km. between Puerto Montt and Punta Arenas and offer passenger accommodation for the 4-day trip. Enquiries to: Empresa Marítima del Estado, at Santiago, Puerto Montt, Punta Arenas, Puerto Natales or Castro. (See page 395, Shipping Services, Puerto Montt.) As an alternative, government supply ships are recommended for the young and hardy, but take sleeping bag and extra food, and travel pills. About US$25. The "Río Baker" takes 7 days and stops at Puerto Aysén and other ports.

Ferries Regular services between Punta Arenas and Puerto Porvenir (Tierra del Fuego) in *Melinka* (tickets at Bovies 647), leaving Tres Puentes (5 km. from Punta Arenas) at 0930 (1400 on Saturdays) (depending on tides), US$1.40 p.p., US$25 per vehicle. It returns from Porvenir (Soto Solas 699) at 1330 (1500 Saturdays). Bus to ferry at either end is US$1. There are two ferries running across the First Narrow between Delgada and Espora Pts., 170 km. NE from Punta Arenas, schedule varying with the tides. Reservations at the ferry. Price US$1 p.p. and US$17, one way. If the ferry is not working, there is a DC-3 air taxi several times a day (enquire at ferry booking office), but remember photographs may not be taken.

Air Services Daily flights to Presidente Ibáñez airport, except Sunday, by LAN Chile's Boeing 727 in 2½ hours between Santiago and Punta Arenas. LAN's service to Sombrero (Tierra del Fuego) daily from Monday to Friday, likewise to Porvenir. On Wed., Sat., Aerolíneas Argentinas fly from Punta Arenas to Buenos Aires and there are also two irregular services with DC-3 super 75 to Tierra del Fuego, Puerto Williams, Río Gallegos, Porvenir and Coyhaique. Propeller service, US$35, to Puerto Montt. Reserve passages in advance in January and February. Bus from airport, US$1.10.

Bus Service To Río Gallegos, at 0900 daily, except Monday (at 1100) (6 hours, including ½ hour lunch). Time should be allowed for visit to customs and police prior to departure from inside dock gates (US$6.50). Puerto Natales, 0900, 1100, 1500 and 1800, US$5. Private cars can be hired.

Hotels *Hotel Cabo de Hornos,* telegraphic address Capotel, Plaza Muñoz G. 1025, US$26.30 d, excellent, recommended. (Warning: hot water switched off for 18 hours a day); *Miramar,* US$8 s, friendly; *Savoy,* Calle Valdivia (Calle Valdivia now called Calle José Menéndez), "gloomy"; *Hotel Turismo Plaza,* excellent value, US$4.25 s, no heat; Posada del Tehvelche, US$7.70s, restaurant; *Cervantes,* Calle Pedro Montt; *Colón,* Avenida Colón; *Hotel Magallanes; Res. La Selecta,* Calle Roca, US$3 s, with breakfast, lunch, dinner, US$1; *Pensión Paris,* US$5.50 s, with breakfast; *Hotel Monte Carlo,* Av. Colón 605, US$6 d, with breakfast, clean; *Residencial Ritz,* 3 blocks from main square toward ocean; *Residencial* at Armando Sanhuesa 965, cheap and pleasant atmosphere; *Residencial Roca,* clean and pleasant, 3 blocks from main square, US$4 p.p., incl. breakfast; *American Service Restaurant,* US$0.60 s; *Hotel Polo Sur,* US$1.20, breakfast included. Cheap floor space for the hardy at the *Salvation Army building,* Calle Bella Vista 377, US$0.50 per head.

Restaurants *Asturias; Hotel Cabo de Hornos.* Good inexpensive food served at *El Lluco* and *Austral* (several travellers recommend the latter, run by a Yugoslavian family); *Union Club* accepts non-members for meals.

Night Club Pullón de Oro, excellent traditional floor show; expensive.

Baths Steam and Turkish, Valdivia 999 esquina O'Higgins, US$0.70.

Ski-ing Transtur buses 0900 and 1400 from in front of *Hotel Cabo de Hornos,* US$2.50, return. Daily lift-ticket, US$4.50; equipment rental, US$6 per adult (not fantastic). Mid-way lodge with food, drink and equipment. Season June to September/November, weather depending.

British Club Not what it used to be but reasonable, drinks and billiards good. A visitor describes it as "resembling a stage set from Victorian melodrama". It is at Roca 858, above the Chamber of Commerce. The Club is sometimes closed in the morning.

Tourist Office Plaza de Armas, kiosk, very helpful.

Tourist Club   Main square, Casilla 127. Correspondence in any European language. Very helpful. Local travel agencies reported unreliable.

Museum on main square; recently renovated, well laid out.

Cables   Calle Pedro Montt 841.

Banks   National banks. Open 0900 to 1400 but closed on Saturday; but the Casa de Cambio Andino is open until 1900 on Friday.

Anglo-Chilean Society.   British School.

British Vice-Consulate   Pedro Montt 842, Casilla 327.

British Chamber of Commerce   Roca 858, Casilla 21-D.

Excursions   Within easy reach are ski-ing slopes, Puerto Hambre and Fuerte Bulnes (old fort, a 56-km. trip). The most interesting excursion is to the Ultima Esperanza region, where the beauty of the scenery can compare with that of the Norwegian fjords. There is fine fishing in the rivers and plenty of game. Ultima Esperanza, 250 km. can be reached by car in 4 to 5 hours in the summer, or by day boat excursions. In summer an interesting trip to the S end of the Patagonian ice cap. On the trip one usually sees dolphins, sea lions, black-neck swans and the quaint steamer ducks. May be cancelled at last moment if weather is bad (6 hours up, 4 back). There is also a boat trip. Magdalena Island in the Straits of Magellan (2 hours from Punta Arenas) is worth seeing for the playful dolphins, thousands of penguins and gulls and many sea-lions on the beaches. Inland are mountains, lakes, waterfall, guanacos and ostriches. It is, however, difficult to arrange transport to the island, outside November-January (Turismo Comapa, Av. Independencia).

Oshirios Turismo, 21 de Mayo 1151, runs 48-hour luxury criuse round Tierra de Fuego in ship "Argonauta". Beautiful scenery and abundant wild life. Cost about US$150 p.p.; ship leaves Punta Arenas twice weekly from spring to autumn.

About 30 km. from **Puerto Natales** the *Patagonia Inn*, at Dos Lagunas, under the management of Hotel Cabo de Hornos, can put up 38 guests (good, but no private bathrooms amongst plenty). Visitors can go by daily bus as far as Puerto Natales; from there the Inn arranges transport. Transport will be greatly eased by the opening of a new road from Puerto Natales through the Paine National Park to Calafate (Argentina). Enap offers week-end excursions to the **Paine National Park**, US$65 p.p., including accommodation and meals. A minibus can be hired for about US$20 at Puerto Natales, to take a party of up to 8 to the refugio in the Paine National Park, which is a "must" for its wildlife and spectacular scenery. From the Inn there is a 110-km. car trip NW to the Torres and Cuernos del Paine; magnificent scenery—oddly shaped peaks surrounded by glaciers which fall from 2,750 metres straight down to sea-level. Along this road it is common to spot the Andean condor and herds of guano. From October to March there is a bus service from Natales to this area: contact Turismo Paine on Calle Eberhardt, or the Conaf (forestry department), Av. Puerto Montt 80, Puerto Natales. *Hostería Paine* is at foot of Torre Paine, US$18 single; 8 hours' walk from the *Hostería* to the foot of the Paine Glacier, with a National Park shelter half-way and another at the glacier. Camping possible. Free huts at Putedo, in charge of friendly national park warden; bring food, sleeping bags and cooking gear. The fjords and glaciers of Tierra del Fuego (70 km. by schooner) are exceptionally beautiful. Once a fortnight there is a 22-hour 320-km. round trip to fjord d'Agostino, 30 km. long, where many glaciers come down to the sea. The Cueva Milondón, a huge cave containing the bones of a prehistoric bear-like mammal, about 28 km. NW from Puerto Natales, can be visited en route or by taxi. Allow 3 days to arrange boat and Port Authority permission. The fjord Ultima Esperanza may be visited by boat if enough tourists, US$5 (take lunch). Finally, a three-day tour to Puerto Natales, the glacier, Balmaceda, Torres del Paine can be arranged from Punta Arenas for US$80, inclusive of pensión.

Puerto Natales *Hotel Colonial,* US$6 d, including breakfast, clean, basic, good dining room; *Hotel Capitán Eberhard,* US$11 s, excellent views, new, good; *Hotel Palace,* US$3 p.p., has new extension, good food; *Residencial Temuco,* friendly, reasonable, good food, US$3 p.p.; *Hostería Kiki,* simple, clean; *Hostería Llanura de Diana,* 40 km. away, on road to Punta Arenas (hidden from the road), highly recommended; *Posada de Cisne de Cuello Negro,* a former guest house for meat-buyers at the *frigorífico,* friendly, clean, reasonable, but inadequate toilet facilities, 5 km. from Puerto Natales at Puerto Bories; *Pensión El Busca,* Calle Valdivia 845, US$0.60 p.p., recommended, good and cheap food available; many mountaineering parties stay here.

Infrequent bus between Natales and Río Gallegos (Argentina), US$5, 6 hours. Also to Río Turbio (Argentina), 2 hours (depending on Customs), US$1. Tourist office in kiosk on main square.

Tierra del Fuego is the name given to the island in the extreme south of America. It is surrounded by the Magellan Strait to the north, the Atlantic Ocean to the east, the Beagle Channel to the south—which separates it from the southern islands—and by the Whiteside, Gabriel, Magdalena and Cockburn Channels etc. which divide it from the islands situated to the west. The western side belongs to Chile and the eastern to Argentina. It produces most of Chile's oil.

In Chilean Tierra del Fuego the only town is **Porvenir,** with a district population of 3,600 largely from Yugoslavia (LAN services from Punta Arenas, two flights per week). TAME-Airlines has a daily flight for US$20, s.

Porvenir Hotels *Tierra del Fuego,* US$6 s, good food; *Turismo,* Soto Salas 698, US$2 s, good value; *Residencial Cameron* (ask at bar called *Somos o no Somos*), US$3 for shared room, "friendly folk", good meals, sleep on dining-room floor for US$0.40! *Hotel Bella Vista,* with restaurant; *Hostería Los Flamencos,* reasonably priced. Many good pensions at US$1.50-US$2 s, with full board. *Yugoslav Club* does wholesome and reasonable lunch.

Buses on Tierra del Fuego Two a week between Porvenir and Río Grande (Argentina), Mon. and Wed., 1300, US$12 from *Hotel Tierra del Fuego,* connection with bus and ferry to Punta Arenas; bus US$1, ferry US$2; trip takes 7-8 hours depending on border crossing. Beware: taxis are not allowed to cross the border.

Puerto Williams is a Chilean naval base on Isla Navarino, S of the Beagle Channel, the most southerly population centre in Chile. It is reached by LAN plane from Punta Arenas (US$10) at least once a week, and can be left (but not reached—the Chileans do not allow it as ownership of the island has been in dispute with Argentina) by a ferry to Ushuaia (Argentina), 3 hours, US$10. The island is totally unspoilt and beautiful, with a chain of rugged snowy peaks, magnificent woods and many animals, including beaver. There is one hotel, open November-April, the *Hostería Wala,* with attractive locally-made furniture and soft furnishings, US$10 p.p. with breakfast (or US$25 full board—good restaurant), run by English-speaking couple, the Neilsons; splendid walks nearby. No other accommodation. LAN will charter a plane, if a sufficiently numerous party is raised, to Cape Horn.

The Economy

Official sources estimate that Chile's national product increased by 8.6% in 1977, against 4.5% in 1976. The economy remains heavily dependent on the exploitation and export of its natural resources, especially minerals and copper in particular, of which Chile is the world's leading exporter. This dependence puts the country's economic well-being at the mercy of world commodity markets and, together with certain structural weaknesses in the economy and problems of inflation and foreign indebtedness, presents the Government with considerable difficulties in economic management and development. The Government, however, has made considerable progress in reducing Chile's dependence on copper by promoting non-traditional exports; copper revenues accounted for only 53% of total export earnings in 1977, compared with 80% in 1973.

Chile currently produces about 16% of the world's copper; in 1977 copper production totalled 1,050,000 tons compared with 1,005,000 tons in 1976. Over 80% of copper production is derived from the large mines of the now state-owned Gran Minería, but current expansion plans are attracting large-scale foreign investment in this sector.

Other major mineral production includes iron ore (1975 10.8m. tons), nitrates (0.73m. tons), coal (1.46m. tons) and iodine (2,278 tons) of which Chile is the world's leading producer. There is also some production of gold, silver, lead, zinc, manganese, molybdenum and mercury. Chile has discovered an offshore petroleum and gas field in the Magellan Straits, and domestic oil production may account for 40% of the country's annual requirements by 1983, compared with an estimated 20% in 1978. Chile has granted a contract for oil exploration and drilling on the Pacific continental shelf to Atlantic Richfield and Amerada Hess, and an extensive drilling programme is currently underway.

Forestry provides Chile's second resource-based export sector. The country has large forested areas, mainly hardwoods of some 60 species; plantations, however, are primarily pine softwoods on which the pulp and paper industry is based. Production in this industry is mainly responsible for most of the forest-products sector's overseas earnings. The favourable internal and external conditions for this sector's development have encouraged the Government to seek rapid expansion, through reafforestation and the attraction of foreign investment. In 1975 a new cellulose plant with an annual capacity of 175,000 tons, virtually all destined for export, was officially opened at La Caleta, Constitución, and the Instituto Forestal is to expand operations at its Nacimiento (Bío-Bío) plant.

Fishery also has great development potential. The annual catch of fish and shellfish is about 1.4m. tons, much of which is anchoveta, the basis of the fish oil and fishmeal industry. The Government is also investigating the possibilities of catching krill an Antarctic crustacean, for export.

Agriculture has provided one of the major problems of Chilean development; although endowed with a diversified environment allowing the production of all temperate and mediterranean products, socio-economic factors have given rise to a generally backward agriculture in terms of techniques and managerial competence. Chile has not been able to attain self-sufficiency in basic foodstuffs; output in the early 1970s fructuated widely, partly as the result of dislocation caused by an accelerated land reform programme and illegal land seizures. The need for food imports, especially wheat, sugar and oilseeds, has been a serious drain on the economy. The cornerstone of the current agricultural policy has been to attain self-sufficiency in foodstuffs by 1985.

Cereal production is dominated by wheat, two-thirds of which is produced in Forest Chile: other grains include barley, oats, rye and rice. Substantial imports are required to meet domestic needs; wheat requirements are estimated at 2m. tons but peak production in the 1970s has only reached 1.4m. tons.

Maize, pulses and a wide variety of root vegetables are grown as well as all temperate and mediterranean fruits. Most grape output is used for wine production for domestic consumption and export. Chilean wines have gained an impressive international reputation. About 20% of fruit production is exported and consists chiefly of apples, pears, peaches, nectarines, plums and prunes. Sugar requirements are met by imports and by domestic beet-sugar production.

Chile has 2.9m. head of cattle, with 1m. in Middle Chile and the rest in Forest Chile. There are 6.7m. sheep, of which the 3.2m. in Patagonia are of the highest quality; and 1.1m. pigs, 60% of which are in Forest Chile.

Much of the impetus for industrialization has come from the Government and in particular from Corfo, the state development corporation. This has included the development of energy resources, including hydroelectricity, petroleum refining and the creation of a steel industry at Concepción which is to be expanded to an annual output of 1m. tons from the current level of 0.6m. tons. Other important developments include chemicals, textiles, electrical and electronic equipment, car assembly and the construction of small vessels. Very nearly a half of all manufacturing is concentrated in the Santiago metropolitan area in spite of the decentralization policy followed by the Government. The full development of manufacturing industry is hindered by the fact that the domestic market is small and dispersed, but the present Government is striving to increase industrial efficiency by its low-tariff policy, which exposes Chilean manufactures to a blast of competition from imported goods.

Foreign Trade (US$m.)

							Exports	Imports
1972	..	..	..	..	..	..	855.4	941.1
1973	..	..	..	..	..	..	1,323.0	1,607.7
1974	..	..	..	..	..	..	2,043.4	2,238.9
1975	..	..	..	..	..	..	1,533.9	1,811.0
1976	..	..	..	..	..	..	2,120.0	1,840.0
1977	..	..	..	..	..	..	2,171.0	2,221.0

Information for Visitors

How to get there: by air

From Europe: Air France (4 per week), British Caledonian (2), Iberia, KLM, LAN-Chile, Lufthansa (4), Sabena, SAS and Swissair fly to Santiago. Some flights go *via* Rio/São Paulo, Montevideo and Buenos Aires; others *via* New York, Lima and/or other points in northern S. America. Also, Varig, Aerolíneas Argentinas and Avianca offer services between Europe and Santiago, with connections *via* Rio, Buenos Aires and Bogotá respectively.

From North America: Braniff have 6 flights per week from Miami, New York and/or Washington; one service is non-stop from Miami, taking 8 hours—others stop at Panama City, Lima or Quito. LAN-Chile have 5 flights per week from New York and Miami. Also from Miami, Aeroperú have 5 flights and Aerolíneas Argentinas 2 per week. Lufthansa have 2 services a week from New York. From California, Braniff have 2 flights per week; also there are good connections *via* Bogotá (by Avianca) or Lima (by several other carriers). CP Air have one flight per week from Montreal and Toronto, and 2 from Vancouver—all *via* Mexico and Lima. LAN-Chile fly once a week between Tahiti (making connections from Japan, Australia and New Zealand) and Santiago, *via* Easter Island.

Within South America: from Buenos Aires (over 30 per week) by LAN-Chile, Aerolíneas Argentinas, Varig, Aeroperú, Avianca, Braniff, CP Air, Air France, Iberia, KLM or Lufthansa; from Rosario, Córdoba or Mendoza (5 per week) by Aerolíneas Argentinas; from Montevideo (5 per week) by LAN-Chile, Iberia, KLM, SAS or Sabena; from Asunción (once a week) by LAN-Chile; from Rio/São Paulo, non-stop by LAN-Chile, Varig, Swissair or British Caledonia (once a week each) or by several other airlines *via* Buenos Aires; from La Paz (5 per week) by Lufthansa, LAB, LAN-Chile or Braniff; from Lima (up to 30 per week) by Aeroperú, LAN-Chile, Braniff, Lufthansa and others; from Bogotá (6 per week) by Avianca, Iberia or Air France (all *via* Lima, and Quito or Guayaquil).

To Arica, from Cochabamba and La Paz (2 per week) by LAB—(fares—one way $35, return $60).

To Puerto Montt from Bariloche, once a week by LAN-Chile.

From the U.S.A. By Sea: By Prudential Line or the Chilean Line from New York *via* Panama Canal. Time taken: 21 days.

From Europe By Sea: The Pacific Steam Navigation Company's steamers from Liverpool no longer carry passengers. By several European steamship lines, including the Swedish Johnson Line and the Italia Line, to Valparaíso.

By Conference Line to New York, then by Prudential Line mail steamers to Chilean ports *via* the Panama Canal. Average, 28 days. Grace Line has a fortnightly passenger cargo service between California and Rio de Janeiro by the Straits of Magellan, calling at Arica, Antofagasta, Valparaíso, Talcahuano, Buenos Aires, Montevideo and Santos.

From Neighbouring Countries By land. There are railways from La Paz (Bolivia) to Antofagasta, and to Arica (see Bolivia section). There are two railways from Argentina: the Transandine from Buenos Aires to Santiago and Valparaíso, and from Salta to Antofagasta. Roads connect Santiago with Mendoza, and Osorno with Bariloche, in Argentina. (The route over the Puyehué pass is faster and slightly cheaper, but the bus-lake-bus crossing is much more scenic and interesting.)

Internal Air Services, provided by LAN-Chile: Daily between Santiago and La Serena, Vallenar, Copiapó, Chañaral, Taltal, Antofagasta, Tocopilla, Calama, Iquique and Arica to the north. Daily between Santiago and Concepción, Temuco, Valdivia, Osorno, Puerto Montt and Punta Arenas to the south. Regional services from Puerto Montt southward. Book well in advance. The private airline Ladeco also serves the main cities.

Transport Reservations are sometimes problematic; trains to Mendoza are often still booked well ahead, queue for 2nd class (unreserved) 4 hours before the train is due to leave. Buses are many and frequent. Trains in Chile are very cheap, and not as slow as in other Andean countries. There is a railway information office on Calle Estado, 1¼ blocks from the Alameda (on the right-hand side), Santiago, for all lines except the Antofagasta-Bolivia (Huérfanos 972). English spoken. Shipping information at Empresa Marítima del Estado, Estado 359, 5th floor.

Taxes There is a tourist tax on single air fares of 2%, and 1% on return fares beginning or ending in Chile. An exit tax of US$6.30 is levied on all passengers going abroad by air, and there is a sales tax of 5% on all transport within Chile.

Travel Documents Passport and tourist card only are required for entry by all foreigners except citizens of Guyana, Haiti, Surinam, Kuwait, African countries and the Communist countries, who require visas. National identity cards are sufficient for entry by citizens of Argentina, Bolivia, Brazil, Ecuador and Uruguay. The tourist card is valid for 90 days and is renewable for 90 more; it is available from Chilean consulates, airline offices and most aircraft bound for Chile; it will be surrendered on departure. If you wish to stay longer than 180 days (as a tourist), it is easier to make a day-trip to Argentina and return with a new tourist card, rather than to apply for a visa, which involves a great deal of paperwork. People travelling N from Arica should read note on page 348.

All foreigners without exception must have valid vaccination certificates against smallpox; general health certificates are required from applicants for visas, and also from nationals of Brazil.

Customs Allowed in free of duty: 500 cigarettes, 100 cigars, 500 grams of tobacco, 3 bottles of liquor, camera, and all articles of personal use. Fruit, vegetables and flowers may not be imported.

Motoring in Chile Car drivers require the usual *"Carnet de Passages en Douanes"* issued by a recognised automobile club. Gasoline (petrol) and oil are sold by the litre; the present price is US$0.20 litre, or US$0.23 for "super". Lock your car. Good maps from Esso petrol stations about US$1. The Carta Caminera from the Dirección de Vialidad is the most detailed road map (series of six). Excellent road maps may also be obtained from the Automóvil Club de Chile, Pedro de Valdivia 195, Santiago. Town maps from the Automóvil Club and Copec service stations.

Car Hire US$4.50 to US$13, plus US$0.10 per km., according to car. National or International driving licences can be used.

Time GMT minus 4 hours; minus 3 hours in summer.

Seasons The best time for a visit is between October and April when fine weather is almost assured but business visits can be made any time during the year; during the holiday season, between January and March, it is sometimes difficult to make appointments.

Clothing Warm sunny days and cool nights are usual during most of the year except in the S where the climate is like that of Scotland. Ordinary European medium-weight clothing can be worn during the winter (June to mid-September), supplemented by a warm overcoat or a light overcoat. Light clothing is best for summer (December to March), but Palm Beach and white tropical suits are not worn. Women wear light cotton or linen dresses in the summer, with a stole or wrap for the evenings.

Health Tap water is safe to drink in the main cities but bottled water is safer on trains and away from the larger centres. Hotels and restaurants are usually clean. Inoculation against typhoid is a wise precaution. Travellers should not eat salads; hepatitis is all too common as the result of the use of sewage for fertilizer.

Hours of Business Banks: 0900-1400, but closed on Saturdays. Government offices: 1000-1230 (the public is admitted for a few hours only). Business houses: 0830-1230, 1400-1800 (Monday to Friday). Shops (Santiago): 1030-1930, but 0930-1330 Saturday.

Taxis are now more plentiful than they used to be. They have meters, but agree beforehand on fare for long journey out of centre or special excursions. Meter readings are (inflation) indexed. A 50% surcharge in applied evenings and Sundays. Taxi drivers rarely know the location of any streets away from the centre—get the hall porter to instruct the driver before setting out. There is no need to tip unless some extra service, like the carrying of luggage, is given.

Language The local pronunciation of Spanish, very quick and lilting, with final syllables cut off, can present difficulties to the foreigner.

Telephones Local telephones use *fichas* costing US$0.10.

Advice It is reported that the police are less exigent about travellers' dress than they were a year or two ago. All the same, travellers are still advised to moderate hair and dress styles, and to keep their tempers.

Living Conditions and Cost Shops throughout Chile are well stocked and there is a seasonal supply of all the usual fruits and vegetables. Milk, in pasteurised, evaporated, or dried form is obtainable. Chilean tinned food is dear. All imported goods (including American films) are relatively cheaper, because of import-tariff reductions, than they used to be. Food is reasonable, though dearer than in Peru or Argentina, but food prices vary tremendously. Buses are excellent but expensive—half as much again as in neighbouring countries. Hotels are relatively cheap, as is postage. Santiago and Valparaíso tend to be the least expensive areas—N and S are much more expensive. Chileans remark that under Allende everything was cheap but unobtainable; now things are available but dear.

The cost of living rose 163% in 1972, 508% in 1973, 376% in 1974 and 340% in 1975, but was reduced to 174.3% in 1976, and 63.5% in 1977. The increase is expected to be less than 30% in 1978.

Hotels On hotel bills service charges are usually 10%, and taxes on bills are 20%. Whether or not the 20% is added to bills in hotel restaurants that are signed and charged to the hotel bill depends on the policy of the establishment. And you tip all the usual people—except cab drivers. When booking in make certain whether meals are included in the price or only breakfast or nothing at all, whether tea is in or out, and don't rely on the posted sheet in the bedroom for any prices.

Camping is easy and cheap, except near Santiago.

Ski-ing Season from June to September/October, weather depending. For information write to: La Federación de Ski de Chile, Casilla 9902, Santiago.

Tipping Standard is 10% in restaurants and 20% in bars and soda fountains. Railway and airport porters: US$0.10 a piece of luggage. Make a deal with dock porters. Cloakroom attendants and cinema usherettes: US$0.05. Hairdressers: 10% of bill.

Currency The unit is the Peso (1 peso = 1,000 escudos), which replaced the Escudo in September 1975; its sign is $. Notes are for 5, 10 and 50 pesos and coins for 5, 10, 20 and 50 centavos and 1 peso. The old escudo notes are no longer acceptable. The peso is being devalued, against the US$ on a "crawling-peg" basis, so as exchange rates change very frequently, it is best to buy pesos in small amounts.

Travellers report difficulty in selling dollars in the far N and S; travellers' cheques must be changed before 1230. Exchange shops (*cambios*) tend to give better rates than banks. Pesos are available at the "brokers' rate" and dollars can be repurchased freely on leaving the country if you keep the exchange slips. Changing travellers' cheques can be time-consuming. There is no black market at present, but pesos may often be bought more cheaply outside Chile, e.g. in Mendoza.

The **metric** system is obligatory but the quintal of 46 kilos (101.4 lb) is not uncommon.

Posts and Telegraphs Airmail takes 3-4 days from the U.K. Seamail takes 8-12 weeks. There is a daily airmail service to Europe with connections to the U.K. Postal rates are not quoted because of inflation, but are not high. Telegrams to Britain: ordinary rate, US$3.40 (minimum 7 words); L.T. rate: US$5.60 (minimum 21 words). A 3-minute telex call to Britain costs US$5.65.

International telephone and telegraph communications are operated by the West Coast of America Telegraph Company Limited; by Transradio Chilena (2 offices);

and by the Cia. Internacional de Radio (2 offices). The main offices are listed under the towns.

Astonishing how throughout Chile one post office official will charge rates different from the next, and they are all "right". Public telex booths are available at the offices of Transradio Chilena in Santiago and Valparaíso.

Public Holidays

Jan. 1—New Year's Day.	Sept. 18, 19—Independence days.
Holy Week (2 days).	Oct. 12—Discovery of America.
May 1—Labour Day.	Nov. 1—All Saints' Day.
May 21—Navy Day.	Dec. 8—The Immaculate Conception.
Aug. 15—Assumption.	Dec. 25—Christmas Day.

The main holiday season is between January and March.

Santiago daily papers "El Merurio", "La Nación", and "El Siglo". "Las Ultimas Noticias", "El Cóndor", weekly in German.

Valparaíso daily papers "El Mercurio", "La Unión", "La Estrella". Monthly: "Caminos y Turismo" (official organ, Automobile Association). "Ercilla" and "Panorama Económico" are best economic journals.

Local Dishes The common denominator of many menus in Peru and Chile is *cazuela de ave*—a nutritious stew containing large piece of chicken, whole potatoes, whole ears of corn, rice, and maybe onions, and green peppers. Another popular Chilean dish is *empanadas de horno,* which are turnovers with a filling made of raisins, stuffed olives, and meat and onions and peppers chopped up together. *Pastel de chocles* has sweet maize as the main ingredient, and is baked in an earthenware bowl. The popular *empanada frita,* a fried meat pasty, is delicious, as is the *empanada de mariscos* (shellfish).

What gives Chilean food its personality is the seafood. The delicious conger eel is a national dish, and *caldillo de congrio* (a soup served with a massive piece of fish, onions and potato balls) is well worth eating. *Paila chonchi* is a kind of bouillabaisse, but has more flavour, more body, more ingredients. *Parrillada de mariscos* is a dish of grilled mixed seafood, brought to the table piping hot on a charcoal brazier. Other excellent local fish are the *cojinoa* and the *corbina*. A delightful entree is the shellfish *loco* (known to Australians as abalone). Avocado pears, or *paltas*, are excellent, and play an important role in recipes. Make sure whether vegetables are included in the price for the main dish; menus often don't make this clear. Always best, if being economical, to stick to fixed-price *table d'hôte* meals or try the local markets.

Lunch is about 1300—the Government has abolished the two- or three-hour lunch break—and dinner not before 2030. Tea is taken at 1700. The cocktail hour starts at 1900. Waiters are known as "garzón"—never as "mozo".

It seems impossible to get real coffee unless you go to expresso bars and specify "café-café, expresso". If you ask for "café", *tout court,* you get soluble coffee! The soluble tea should be avoided.

Drinks Imported whisky and wines are very expensive. The local wines are very good. The best ones (Maipo, Aconcagua, Lontue and Cachapoal) are from the central areas. Itata and Cauquenas in the S produce good wines. The northern wines (Huasco and Elqui) contain more alcohol: the Huasco anejo is a sweet wine almost like sherry. The Editor himself recommends Cousiño Macul, Santa Carolina and Undurraga, while one traveller favours Concha y Toro (also supported by the Editor). The bottled wines are graded, in increasing excellence, as gran vino, vino especial and vino reservado. Beer is quite good and cheap; the best is the draught lager known as Schopp.

Good gin is made in Chile, though tonic water is quite hard to get. Pisco liqueur is also cheap, if somewhat potent. Champagne is cheap and good. Resonably good brandy, anis and creme de menthe are all bottled in Chile. Vaina is worth trying, and so is the traditional Christmas drink, Cola de Mono, a mixture of aguardiente, coffee, milk and vanilla served very cold. Pisco is worth sampling, especially as a "Pisco Sour" or with grapefruit or lemon juice.

Sports The Chilean State Railways and the tourist agencies will give all the necessary information about sport. Ski-ing is popular (see page 408). Horse racing is a popular sport and meetings are held every Sunday and on certain feast days at Viña del Mar and at Santiago throughout the year. Santiago and Valparaiso residents fish at the mountain resort of Rio Blanco, and some of the the world's best fishing is in the Lake District. The licence required can be got from the local police or such angling associations as the Associación de Pesca y Caza, which gives information on local conditions. Other popular sports are Association football and basket ball. Viña del Mar has a cricket ground; on Saturdays there are polo matches at Santiago.

American Express Agents Santiago: Turismo Cocha, Agustinas 1122, Tel.: 82164.

(We are deeply grateful to the following for help with this section: Monique Merriam, of LBI Economics Department ; Terry Schmitz, Patricio van Nievelt and Barbara Rooke, resident in Chile; Aku Aku Tours of Santiago, specializing in Easter Island; and the following travellers: Philip Allen (São Paulo), Ulrich von Aswegen (Osnabrück), Dr. Ing. Klaus Busch (also Osnabrück), Nicholas Carter (BOLSA Belém), Markus Casanova (Fribourg, Switzerland), Michael Davison (São Paulo), Vittorio Ferretti (São Paulo), Peter Ford and Sally Wilson, Gabriel Foscal-Mella (Longueuil, Québec), Tim and Arlene Frost (Hamilton, New Zealand), Mary Goodykoontz and Ken Scarlett (Woodland, Calif.), Ucky Hamilton (New Zealand), Frances Hilton, Gary Horlick (USA), Dieter E. Jungblut (W. Berlin), Gerhard Keilbach (Stuttgart), Leslie E. Kent (Pretoria), Paul and Theresa Legare (Ottawa), Cornelio Lindenburg and Marieke van der Ploeg (Amersfoort, Netherlands), Phoebe Meyer (Peru), Dr. G. B. Mulkern (Fargo, N. Dakota), Alexander Nemeth and Janette Roberts (Australia), Dirk Partridge (Washington, D.C.), Thomas Pensler (Benediktbeuern, W. Germany), Joni Perkins (Canada), Fredy Peter (Kloten, Switzerland), Carole Peirce (USA), Rosalind and Stuart Read (New Zealand), Michael Reeve, André Schepens (Brussels), Michael Scott, Ross Scott (Camberwell, W. Australia, Chris Sharpe (Mullewa, W. Australia), Barbara Singleton (USA), Lothar Springer (Münster), Mati Stein (Ramat-Gan, Israel), Ken and Judy Stevenson (Ottawa), Margaret Thoms and Neil Duncan (Australia), John Turner (Brunswick, Maine), Andreas Weber (Wohlen, Switzerland), and Nicholas Westwood and Julia Amies.

COLOMBIA

COLOMBIA, with 1,138,618 square km., is the fourth largest country in South America and has the third largest population (24.0 millions). It is the only South American republic with coast lines upon both the Atlantic (1,600 km.) and the Pacific (1,306 km.). Nearly 55% of the area is almost uninhabited lowland with only 1.3% of the population; 98.7% of the population is concentrated in the remaining and mostly mountainous 45% of the land, living for the most part in narrow valleys or isolated intermont basins, each with its distinctive soil and climate and pattern of life. Nor is the population homogeneous, as in Chile, but infinitely varied, ranging from pure white, pure Indian, and pure black to blood mixtures of all three.

The 620,000 square km. of almost uninhabited land in Colombia lie E of the Eastern Cordillera, where there are prolongations into the country of the Llanos of the Orinoco, of the Guiana Highlands, and even of the Amazon basin. Near the foot of the Eastern Cordillera the plains are used for cattle ranching, but beyond is jungle. Islands of settlement in it are connected with the rest of the country by air, for there are no railways, and very few roads: communication is by launch and canoe on the rivers: the Putumayo, Caquetá, Guaviare, Vichada, Tomo, Meta and their tributaries, and Colombia's 117 km. of Amazon.

In the western 45% of the country, where nearly all the people live, four ranges of the Andes run from S to N, dipping finally into the lowlands of the Caribbean. Between the ranges run deep longitudinal valleys. Of the 14 main clusters of population in the country, no less than 11 are in the mountain basins or in the longitudinal valleys. The other three are in the lowlands of the Caribbean.

The first 320 km. along the Pacific coast N from the frontier with Ecuador to the port of Buenaventura is a wide, marshy, and sparsely inhabited coastal lowland. But along the coast from just N of Buenaventura to the frontier with Panama there runs a low but extremely rugged chain of mountains: the Serranía de Baudó, whose tallest summit is under 1,830 metres. E of this range the south-western coastal lowlands are prolonged in a low trough of land which runs all the way from Buenaventura to the Caribbean; E of the trough again rise the slopes of the Western Cordillera. The trough—the Department of the Chocó—is

COLOMBIA

Kms.
0   100   200   300   400

CARIBBEAN SEA

Santa Marta
Barranquilla
ATLANTICO
Riohacha
GUAJIRA

Cartagena

PANAMA

MAGDALENA
SUCRE
BOLIVAR
CESAR
Valledupar
NORTE DE SANTANDER

VENEZUELA

Montería
CORDOBA

Cúcuta

ANTIOQUIA
Bucaramanga
SANTANDER
Arauca
ARAUCA

Medellín

Quibdó
CHOCÓ
RISA RALDA
CALDAS
QUINDÍO
CUNDIN AMARCA
Tunja
BOYACA
Pore
CASANARE

Puerto Carreño

Ibagué
Bogotá

VALLE
Cali
TOLIMA
Villavicencio
VICHADA

PACIFIC OCEAN

CAUCA
Popayán
HUILA
Neiva

META

NARIÑO
Pasto
Mocoa
PUTUMAYO
Florencia
CAQUETÁ

VAUPÉS

Mitú

ECUADOR

AMAZONAS

N
W   E
S

PERU

BRAZIL

Leticia

1967
ROUGH SKETCH   4.77

drained southwards into the Pacific by the Río San Juan, navigable for 200 km., and northwards into the Caribbean by the Río Atrato, navigable for 550 km. There have been plans to build a ship canal to connect the two rivers, and thereby the Caribbean and Pacific, but they have come to nothing. About 12% of Colombia's gold and nearly all its platinum is dredged from the two rivers. The climate is hot, torrential rain falls daily, and the land is marshy, pestilential, and heavily forested. The inhabitants are mostly blacks, with a few whites and Indians.

From the borders of Ecuador two ranges of mountain, the Western Cordillera and the Central Cordillera, run N for 800 km. to the Caribbean lowlands. Five peaks in the Western Cordillera are over 3,950 metres; the highest, the volcano of Cumbal, is 4,892 metres, but none reaches the snowline. The Central Cordillera, 50-65 km.; wide, is by much the higher; six of its peaks, snow clad, rise above 4,900 metres and its highest, the volcano cone of Huila, is 5,439 metres. There are no large intermont basins in either, and hardly any level land, but there are narrow ribbons of soil along some of the rivers. In spite of these difficulties, one of the most important population centres—Medellín—is in the heart of the Central Cordillera.

Between the two ranges, as they emerge from Ecuador, lies a valley filled in the S to a height of 2,450 metres by ash from the volcanoes. Not far from the frontier there is a cluster of self-subsisting Indians around Pasto. This highland is drained by the Río Patía, which has broken through the rim of the Western Cordillera to make its way into the Pacific N of the small port of Tumaco. Gold is panned in this river. Further N between these two ranges lies the Cauca Valley. In the northern 190 km. of this valley, roughly from Popayán past Cali to Cartago, there is an important agricultural region based on a deep bed of black alluvial soil which yields as many as five crops a year. This valley, which is at a height of about 900 metres, and up to 50 km. wide, is drained northwards by the Cauca river. Popayán is the historical town of the valley, Cali its business centre, and a road and railway run from Cali over a low pass of less than 1,500 metres in the Western Cordillera to Buenaventura. Sugar cane was the great crop of this valley in Colonial times, and black slaves were imported to work it. Sugar is still one of the main crops, but has now been varied with tobacco, soya, pineapple, cotton, and every other kind of tropical fruit. There is still some cattle raising. Coffee is grown on the Cordillera slopes above 600 metres. A "Tennessee Valley" scheme of development to drain the swamps, control floods, irrigate parched areas, improve farming, and to produce electric power has been applied in the Cauca Valley since 1956.

At Cartago the two Cordilleras close in and the Cauca Valley comes to an end. The river now enters a deep gorge which runs between the Western Cordillera and the Central Cordillera all the way to the Caribbean flatlands. About 200 km. up this gorge is the old colonial gold mining town of Antioquia, built on a narrow lowland along the banks of a tributary of the main stream. There are comparatively unimportant settlements on pockets of land in this area. But to the SE of this small town, in the Cordillera Central and at an altitude of 1,540 metres, is the second largest city and industrial centre in Colombia: Medellín. The valley in which Medellín lies, the valley of the Río Aburrá, is narrow and not more than 20 km. long, but Medellín itself is now a city of over a million people. Much of the coffee and 75% of the gold comes from this area. N of Medellín the Cordillera Central splits into three ranges, separated by streams flowing into the Caribbean.

Near Latitude 2°N, or about 320 km. N of the Ecuadorean border, the Eastern Cordillera, the longest of all, rises and swings N and then NE towards Venezuela. About Latitude 7°N it bifurcates; one branch, the Sierra de Perijá y Motilones, becomes the western rim of the Maracaibo basin. The other branch runs E into Venezuela, to the S of the Maracaibo basin.

Between this Eastern Cordillera and the Central Cordillera runs the 1,600 km. long Magdalena river, with the Caribbean port of Barranquilla at its mouth. There are more intermont basins in the Eastern Cordillera than in the others. Its peaks, like those of the Central Cordillera, rise above the snow line. In the Sierra Nevada del Cocuy (just before the Cordillera bifurcates) there is a group of peaks, all over 5,200 metres; the highest, Alto Ritacova, reaches 5,600 metres. The basins are mostly high; at an altitude of from 2,450 to 2,750 metres. The mountain torrents born in the snow fields run over alluvial fans into these basins and wander sluggishly through the broad valleys, sometimes forming swamps, or lakes, before descending over the lips of the basins—sometimes in cataracts, as in the Falls of Tequendama—towards the Magdalena river.

There are three groups of population in the deep valley of the Magdalena along its upper reaches in the departments of Huila, Tolima, and Cundinamarca. Below Honda the river banks are comparatively unsettled, though there are a few clearings made by the descendants of black slaves who settled along the Magdalena after their emancipation. There are oilfields in the valley, particularly at Barrancabermeja.

The three existing groups on the Upper Magdalena are insignificant compared with the great cluster in a high basin of the Eastern Cordillera, 160 km. E of the Magdalena river. It was here that the Conquistadores found the socially developed Chibchas, the only group of sedentary farmers in Colombia. There was little or no gold or silver, but the Chibchas formed a useful pool of labour, and here, in 1538, the Spaniards founded the city of Bogotá. The great rural activity of this population cluster is the growing of food: cattle, wheat, barley, maize and potatoes, but Bogotá itself, a city of 3,500,000 people, has far outstripped its primary function as a commercial centre: it is now the capital of the whole country.

Roads and railways run N from Bogotá to the basins of Chiquinquirá and Sogamoso, over 160 km. away. Both are in the Department of Boyacá, with Tunja, on a mountain between the two, as capital. Both basins, like the Bogotá basin in Cundinamarca, produce food, and there are emerald mines not far from Chiquinquirá.

There are other basins in the N of the Eastern Cordillera: in the Departments of Santander and Norte de Santander at Bucaramanga and Cúcuta, and a small one at Ocaña. Movement into these basins—by Europeans and mestizos—did not take place until the 19th century, when chinchona bark rose into high demand. By 1885 this trade was dead, but by that time coffee was beginning to be planted. In Bucaramanga coffee is now the main crop, but it has been diversified by cacao, cotton and tobacco, all grown below the zone suitable for coffee, which is also the main crop at both Cúcuta and Ocaña.

There is one more mountain group in Colombia, the Sierra Nevada de Santa Marta, standing isolated from the other ranges on the shores of the

Caribbean. This is the highest range of all, for its snow-capped peaks rise to 5,800 metres within 50 km. of the coast.

To the W of this Sierra, and N of where the Central and Western Cordillera come to an end, lies a great lowland which has three groups of population on its Caribbean shores; at Cartagena (Department of Bolívar), at Barranquilla (Department of Atlántico), and at Santa Marta (Department of Magdalena). This great lowland is peculiar in that the rivers draining it (the Magdalena, the Sinú, the Cauca, the San Jorge and the César) run so slowly that much of the area is a tissue of swamps and lagoons with very little land which can be cultivated. Indeed the whole area E of the channel of the Magdalena is under water at most times of the year. When the floods come, large areas of the land W of the Magdalena—the plains of Bolívar—are covered too, but during the dry season from October to March great herds of cattle are grazed there.

Communications A major problem still facing the country is that of surface transport. Its three Cordilleras, separated by valleys often no more than 1,500 metres above sea-level, make internal communications extremely difficult. The 3,700 km. of narrow gauge railways and the 38,200 km. of roads have eastern and western systems, with inter-communicating laterals (see maps and text). Only about 10% of the road system is paved. Given these difficulties it is natural that Colombia, which ran the first airline in South America, has taken ardently to the air.

History accounts for the present racial variety of the population. Before the coming of the Spaniard the country was occupied by Indians, most of whom were primitive hunters or nomad agriculturists. But one part of the country, the high basins of the Eastern Cordillera, was densely occupied by Chibcha Indians who had become sedentary farmers and had developed a fairly high civilization. Two chiefs ruled over these settled tribes; the Zaque, with his capital near Bogotá, and the Zipa, who had his seat near where Tunja is today. Their staple foods were maize and the potato, and they had no domestic animal save the dog; the use they could make of the land was therefore limited. But they were politically well organised and like the Indians of Peru and Bolivia, held their land in common. Other cultures present in Colombia in the pre-columbian era were the Tairona, Quimbaya, Sinú and Calima. Exhibits of these and the Chibcha (Muisca) Indians' gold-work can be seen at the Gold Museum in Bogotá, the one total "must" for all visitors to the city (see page 423).

The Spaniards sailed along the northern coast as far as Panama as early as 1500. Alonso de Ojeda landed at Cartagena, but the Indians attacked strongly and the settlement was abandoned. The first permanent settlement was by Rodrigo de Bastidas at Santa Marta in 1525. Cartagena was founded in 1533. The interior, however, was not penetrated until 1536, when Gonzalo Jiménez de Quesada (who wrote a full account of his adventures), pushed up the Magdalena river to discover its source. Jiménez, mounting the Eastern Cordillera in 1536, discovered the sedentary Chibchas, conquered them, and founded Santa Fe de Bogotá in 1538. In the meantime other Spanish forces were approaching the same region from two other directions: Pizarro's lieutenant, Sebastián de Benalcázar, had pushed up the Cauca valley from Ecuador and founded Pasto, Popayán and Cali in 1536. Nicolaus de Federmann, on behalf of the German Welsers, who had been granted a colonial concession by Charles V, approached from Venezuela. Benalcázar reached Bogotá in

1538 and Federmann in 1539. A later expedition from Santa Marta brought with it the sugar-cane, barley, wheat, cattle, sheep and horses that made possible a far more extensive use of the land than had been practised by the Indians. Tunja and Neiva were founded in the early stages. As in Peru, the initial period of settlement was one of strife between contending conquistadores. The royal Audiencia de Santa Fe set up in 1550 gave the area a legislative, judicial and administrative entity. In 1564 this was followed by a Presidency of the Kingdom of New Granada controlling the whole country and Panama, except Benalcázar's Province of Popayán. The Presidency was replaced in 1718 by a Viceroyalty at Bogotá which controlled the provinces now known as Venezuela as well; it was independent of the Viceroyalty of Peru, to which this vast area had previously been subject.

The Spaniards found gold in the Antioquia region, and almost as soon as its shipment began the Caribbean ports were pestered by pirates. But the rest of the country was peaceful; it had benefited greatly from Spanish organization, the legal system, the established church, and the agricultural prosperity.

The movement towards independence from Spain was set going in 1794 by a translation into Spanish of the French Declaration of the Rights of Man by the *criollo* Antonio Nariño. In 1796 the Viceroyalty was shaken by a revolt in Venezuela, and in 1806 Francisco Miranda made an abortive attempt to set up a government at Caracas. The movement was given point and force when, in 1808, Napoleon replaced Ferdinand VII of Spain with his brother Joseph. The New World refused to countenance this. There were several revolts in New Granada, culminating in a revolt at Bogotá and the setting up of a junta on July 20, 1810. But the provinces were divided: Cartagena freed itself and bound itself to a junta set up at Tunja, but the junta at Bogotá refused to acknowledge it. Late in 1812 the young Bolívar, driven out of Venezuela, landed at Cartagena. In a brilliant campaign in 1813 he pushed up the Magdalena to Ocaña, and from there to Cúcuta, and obtained permission from the junta at Tunja to advance into Venezuela. In 90 days he marched the 1,200 km. to Caracas over mountain country, fought six battles and destroyed five armies. But he was unable to hold Caracas and withdrew to Cartagena in 1814.

Napoleon fell in 1815, and the Spanish Government immediately set about reconquering, with some success, Venezuela and New Granada. General Pablo Morillo took Cartagena after a bitter siege of 106 days—Bolívar had withdrawn to Jamaica—and was later "pacifying" Bogotá with a "Reign of Terror" by May 1816. The great scientist, José de Caldas, was one of his victims.

Bolívar had by now assembled an army of Llaneros, fortified by a British Legion recruited from ex-servicemen of the Peninsular wars, at Angostura, or Ciudad Bolívar, as it is called today. In the face of incredible difficulties he made a forced march across the Andes in 1819. After joining up with Santander's New Granada army, he defeated the royalists at the Battle of the Swamps of Vargas in July and again at Boyacá on August 7th. He entered Bogotá three days later.

Bolívar reported his success to the revolutionary congress sitting at Angostura, and that body, on December 17, 1819, proclaimed the Republic of Gran Colombia, embracing in one the present republics of Venezuela, Colombia, and Ecuador. A general congress was held at

Cúcuta on January 1, 1821, and here it was that two opposing views which were to sow much dissension in Colombia first became apparent. Bolívar and Nariño were for centralization; Santander, a realist, for a federation of sovereign states. Bolívar succeeded in enforcing his view, for the time being. But Gran Colombia was not to last long; Venezuela broke away in 1829 and Ecuador in 1830. The remaining provinces were named New Granada, and it was not till 1863 that the name Colombia was restored.

Almost from its inception the new country became the scene of much strife between the centralizing Conservatives and the federalizing Liberals, a strife greatly complicated by the still pressing "Question of the Church", which was inveterately Conservative in its attitude. The Conservative president Tomás Cipriano de Mosquera (1845) encouraged education, began building roads, adopted the metric system, and put steamers on the Magdalena. The decentralizing and strongly anti-clerical Liberals were dominant from 1849 for the next 30 years of insurrections and civil wars. From 1879 to 1889 the two parties, each imposing its policy, alternated. In 1885 the Conservatives imposed a highly centralized constitution which has not been modified in this respect to this day. Next year Colombia became, officially, a republic. A Liberal revolt in 1899 turned into a civil war, "the War of the Thousand Days". The Liberals were finally defeated in 1902 after 100,000 men had died. It was in 1903 that Panama declared its independence from Colombia, following U.S. pressure.

The surprisingly stable centralization of government in Colombia—considering its physical diversity—is in the main the creation of this century. It represents, in the words of Preston James, "an astounding victory of man over nature, and of man over man". There was, it is true, a little-publicized but dreadfully bloody war known as "the violence" between Liberals and Conservatives again from 1948 to 1958 (some 200,000 people were killed); but this has now been healed by an amnesty. It was decided by plebiscite in 1957 that the two political parties would support a single presidential candidate, divide all political offices equally between them, and thus maintain political stability for sixteen years. In 1974 the agreement was modified; the two parties nominated their own candidates for the presidency, which was won by the Liberals, but Cabinet posts were divided equally between the Conservatives and the Liberals. From 1978, however, the agreement was abandoned and a winner-take-all system was adopted.

The People of Colombia There are 398 Indian tribes. The clusters vary greatly in their make-up: Antioquia and Caldas are almost entirely of unmixed European blood, Pasto is Indian, the Cauca Valley and the rural area near the Caribbean are African or entirely mestizo. No colour bar is recognised but does exist in certain centres. Colombia has 15 cities with over 100,000 people.

About 50% live in the cities, and 50% are engaged in agriculture, pastoral and forestal pursuits, hunting and fishing. The birth and death rates vary greatly from one area to the other, but for the whole country are 38.6 and 10 per thousand respectively. Infant mortality is very high. Because of housing conditions, the lack of proper water supplies and sanitation, malnutrition and inadequate medical services, health is an acute problem. There are anopheline mosquitoes in the country, but the malaria rate is low. There is much ill-health and mortality from intestinal parasites, especially in rural areas. Leprosy is now on the decline. Venereal diseases are widely spread. Deficiencies in the water supply cause much typhoid: even Medellín has many cases a year. The ordinary diet is ill-balanced: nutritional goitre, scurvy, anaemia, and pellagra are frequent. Nearly 80% of the people in some Departments have goitre. Hospitals and clinics are few in relation to the population. About 66% of the doctors are in the departmental capitals, which contain 12% of the population, though all doctors now have to spend a year in the country before they can get their final diploma. Gastro-enteritis plays havoc with infants and young children. Deplorable barrios clandestinos (shanty-towns) have sprung up around Cali, Barranquilla, Cartagena and Buenaventura. The shacks, put up without permission, lack drinking water, sewers and electricity. The high increase in population is a great problem.

Education   About 35% of the adult population cannot read and write. Schools absorb only about half the youngsters of school age. Education is free, and since 1927 compulsory, but large numbers of children, especially in rural areas, do not attend. Widespread illiteracy is not incompatible with high standards of education at both secondary schools and university, when it is available.

Constitution and Government   Senators and Representatives are elected by popular vote. The Senate has 80 members, and the Chamber of Representatives has 144. When the Representatives are elected the people vote at the same time for the deputies to the Departmental assemblies and the municipal councils. Congress can veto any legislation. In June 1978 a 50-member constituent assembly was to be elected for the first time, coinciding with the presidential elections. The President, who appoints his 13 ministers, is elected by direct vote for a term of four years, but cannot succeed himself in the next term. Every citizen over 18 can vote.

Administratively the country is divided into 22 Departments, 3 Intendencias, 5 Comisarías, and the Special District of Bogotá. Each Department has a Governor appointed by the President; the Departmental Assemblies look after administration and finance, thus enjoying a partial autonomy, but the Intendencias and Comisarías are under direct control.

Liberty of speech and the freedom of the press are in theory absolute but in practice more limited. The language of the country is Spanish. Its religion is Roman Catholicism. There are a Cardinal Archbishop of Bogotá and Archbishops at Cartagena, Medellín and Popayán: the Cardinal Archbishop of Bogotá is Primate of Colombia. There are 13 other Bishops. There is complete freedom for all other creeds which do not contravene Christian morals or the law.

Government

Under the pact which brought the National Front Government on a fifty-fifty Liberal/Conservative basis into being, the President was alternatively Liberal and Conservative until 1974. In April 1974, for the first time since 1950, the Liberal and Conservative parties competed directly in a presidential election, but apart from this the National Front agreement was extended until 1978, when it was abandoned completely and the elected President could nominate a cabinet entirely of his own party members.

President, 1974-78:   Dr. Alfonso López Michelsen (Liberal).

Bogotá

Bogotá, capital of the Republic and a city of over 3,500,000 people, is on a plateau at 2,640 metres. Because of the height visitors may feel some discomfort at first. "The mountains look aloofly down on Bogotá, one crowned with a figure of Christ, one with a white convent, one with a cross. . . . Shrouded often in the clouds of the high plateau, drenched often in rain, cursed with a climate that has no seasons, it is scarcely an exhilarating spot'' (James Morris). The average temperature is 14°C (58°F). It is built on sloping land, and covers 186 square km. The central part of the city is full of character and contrasts. Colonial buildings stand side-by-side with the most modern architecture. For the most part the houses are low, with eaves projecting over the streets, but they are rarely brightly painted.

Visitors should take it easy for the first 24 hours. Some people get dizzy at 2,640 metres above sea-level. Be careful with food and alcoholic drinks for the first day also.

There is a very good view of the city from the top of Montserrate, the lower of the two peaks rising sharply to the E. It is reached by a funicular railway and a cable railway. The ascent requires some nerve, for the gradient is 81°. The new convent at the top is a popular shrine. At the summit, near the church, a platform gives a bird's-eye view of the red-roofed city and of the plains beyond stretching to the rim of the Sabana. Behind the church are popular picnic grounds. The fare up to Montserrate is US$0.60 return; four trips per hour. The funicular works only on Sundays and holidays. The neighbourhood can be dangerous, however; muggings are frequent even in daylight. Take a bus or taxi to the foot of the hill, and don't be tempted to walk down from the top. (This warning cannot be overemphasized.)

At the foot of the hill is the Quinta de Bolívar, a fine old Colonial mansion, with splendid gardens and lawns. There are several cannons captured by the patriots at the Battle of Boyacá from the Spaniards, who had taken them in the Napoleonic Wars. The house, once Bolívar's home, is now a museum showing some of his personal possessions and paintings of events in his career. (Open 1000-1630, except Monday, mornings only on holidays; its address is Calle 20, No. 3-23; charge US$0.30.)

The Plaza Bolívar, with a statue of the Liberator at its centre, is at the heart of the city; around the Plaza are the steep, narrow streets and massive mansions of the old quarter, with their barred windows, carved doorways, brown-tiled roofs and sheltering eaves. Most of the mansions and best colonial buildings are in this district: the Palace of San Carlos, the house of the Marqués de San Jorge, the Municipal Palace, the Capitol, and the Churches of San Ignacio, Santa Clara, San Agustín, San Francisco, and the Cathedral. The old quarter is very congested with traffic.

An important modern street is the extremely long Avenida Caracas, with trees and flower beds along it. Avenida Caracas is Carrera 14. The main shopping areas are at Chapinero, along Carrera 13 between Calles 55 and 63 and Carrera 15 from Calle 72 to the end of Calle Callijo. Other important streets are Carrera 10, and Av. Jiménez de Quesada. (For further details on shopping areas, see page 427.)

The Calles run at right angles across the Carreras. It is easy enough to find a place once the address system is understood. The address Calle 13, No. 12-45 would be the building number 45 on Calle 13 between Carrera 12 and 13. The Avenidas, broad and important streets, may be either Calles (like 19) or Carreras (like 14). Av. Jiménez, one of Bogotá's most important streets, owes its lack of straightness to having been built over a river-bed.

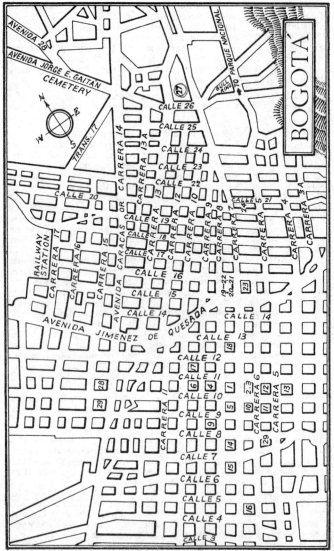

AVENIDA 28

AVENIDA JORGE E. GAITAN

CEMETERY

BOGOTÁ

PARQUE NACIONAL

BULL RING

TO

CALLE 26

CALLE 25

CALLE 24

CALLE 23

CALLE 22

CALLE 20

TRANS. 17

CARRERA 14

CARRERA 13A

CARRERA 13

CARRERA 12

CARRERA 10

CARRERA 9

CALLE 5

CARRERA 8

CARRERA 7

CARRERA 6

CARRERA 5

CARRERA 4

CARRERA 3A

RAILWAY STATION

CARRERA 17

CARRERA 16

CARRERA 15

CARRERA OR CARACAS

CALLE 19

CALLE 18

CALLE 17

CALLE 16

CALLE 15

CALLE 14

AVENIDA

JIMENEZ DE QUESADA

CALLE 14

CALLE 13

CALLE 12

CALLE 11

CALLE 10

CALLE 9

CALLE 8

CALLE 7

CALLE 6

CALLE 5

CALLE 4

CALLE 3

CARRERA 11

AVENIDA CARACAS

CARRERA 6

CARRERA 5

19-22

20·21

23

18

28

29

27

7

4

6

2·3

10

11

12

13

5

9

14

15

16

ROUGH SKETCH

Warning Pickpockets and thieves are notorious in Bogotá. Watch your money and valuables closely; don't wear personal jewellery, earrings or watches, take your glasses off if you can see without them, and *never* walk into a crowd. These precautions seem extreme, but it seems that hardly anyone goes to Bogotá without losing something in this way. Be especially careful of people who describe themselves as plain-clothes police: ask for identification or offer to go to the police station—as long as it isn't dark! Armed attacks on pedestrians are quite common, if the thieves suspect that the pedestrians have something worth stealing. The area around the bus terminals is particularly dangerous; gangs of up to six or eight men armed with knives often attack small groups of tourists and do not hesitate to use their weapons even for small amounts of money or valuables. This warning is one which many travellers have asked us to emphasize and one which *must* be taken seriously. By keeping your eyes open you can avoid a lot of trouble.

Under state-of-siege legislation police may shoot and kill a suspect during any narcotics operation and it will be automatically classified as self-defence. A large number of would-be drug traffickers have been killed in this way.

The street map of Bogotá given here is marked with numerals showing the places of most interest for visitors. Each place will be described under the numeral which stands for it in the map.

1. The Plaza Bolívar, heart of the City, coeval with the City's foundation. On the eastern side rises the Archbishop's Palace, with splendid bronze doors. To one side of it is the colonial Plazuela de Rufino Cuervo. Here is the house of Manuelita Sáenz, the mistress of Bolívar. On the other side is the house in which Antonio Nariño printed in 1794 his translation of "The Rights of Man" which triggered off the movement for independence.

See the Casa del Florero or 20 de Julio museum in a Colonial house on the corner of Plaza Bolívar with Calle 11. It houses the famous flower vase that featured in the 1810 revolution and shows collections from before, during and after the fight for independence. Quite fascinating for those interested in the independence period, especially the documents and engravings. Entry fee US$0.15, free on Wednesdays, open until 1900. Tourist office in Plaza. On the northern side of the Plaza is the spectacular new Palace of Justice.

2. The Cathedral, a beautiful building. Here stood the first simple church built by the colonists, razed in 1572, another built, and rebuilt again in 1807 in a blend of Ionic, Doric and Tuscan. Notable choir loft of carved walnut and wrought silver on altar of Chapel of El Topo. Several treasures and relics; small paintings attributed to Ribera; a turquoise sepulchre inlaid with ivory and silver and gold filigree and set with thousands of precious stones; banner brought by Jiménez to Bogotá, in sacristy, which has also portraits of past Archbishops. In one of the chapels is buried Gregorio Vásquez Arce y Ceballos (1638-1711), by far the best painter in colonial Colombia. Some of his paintings are in the Cathedral.

3. The beautiful Chapel of El Sagrario, built end of the 17th century. Some columns are inlaid with turquoise. Several paintings by Gregario Vásquez Arce.

4. The Municipal Palace.

5. The Capitol, an imposing building with fine colonnades (1847-1925). Congress sits here.

6. La Concepción, colonial church built late 16th century as a chapel for Bogotá's first nunnery. Remarkable ceiling (complicated inlays of wood decorated with Islamic patterns) said to have been saved from a house at Tocaima destroyed by flood in 1581. It is the oldest church in Bogotá.

9. The Church of Santa Clara, another colonial church.

10. San Ignacio, Jesuit church built in 1605. Emeralds from the Muzo mines in Boyacá were used in the monstrance. Paintings by Gregorio Vasquez Arce.

11. The Palace of San Carlos, where Bolívar lived. He is said to have planted the huge walnut tree in the courtyard. On September 25, 1828, there was an attempt on his life. His mistress, Manuela, thrust him out of the window and he was able to hide for two hours under the stone arches of the bridge across the Río San Agustín. Santander, suspected of complicity, was arrested and banished. Now the Presidential

Palace, with a huge banquet hall used for state affairs. The guard is changed—full-dress uniform—every day at 1700.

The Museum of Colonial Art, across from the Palace of San Carlos (Carrera 6, No. 9-77) is one of the finest Colonial buildings in Colombia. It belonged originally to the Society of Jesus, and was once the seat of the most ancient University in Colombia and of the National Library. In this precious architectural legacy from the past there is a splendid collection of Colonial art and paintings by Gregorio Vásquez Arce, all kinds of utensils, and 2 charming patios. Open Tues. to Sat. 1000-1230, 1500-1800. Sun. 0900-1200. Entry fee US$0.60 for adults; free on Saturdays, and every day for students.

12.   Colón Theatre, Calle 11, No. 5-32 (operas, lectures, ballets, plays, orchestras, etc.), late 19th century with lavish decorations. Seating for 1,200, and very ornate. Weekly concerts of high quality.

13.   The Mint (Casa de la Moneda), built in 1720, is at Calle 11, No. 9-77. Open Mon.-Fri. 0830-1200 and 1330-1600 (closed on public holidays). In the same street, at Carrera 4, is the Banco de la República's Angel Arango library, the best endowed and arranged in South America, with 3 reading rooms, research rooms, and a splendid concert hall. There are free concerts and exhibitions. The architecture is impressive and the lavatories are recommended!

14.   The Presidential Palace (1906), but the Presidents no longer live here.

15.   Church of San Agustín, strongly ornamented (1637). Fine paintings by Gregorio Vásquez Arce and the Image of Jesus which was proclaimed Generalisimo of the army in 1812.

16.   Santa Bárbara Church (mid-16th century), one of the most interesting colonial churches. Paintings by Gregorio Vásquez Arce.

17.   Church of San Juan de Dios, a colonial church.

18.   Palace of Communications (postal and telegraph), built on the site of the old colonial church of Santo Domingo.

19.   Government Palace of Cundinamarca Department, almost as imposing as the Capitol. Corinthian style.

20.   San Francisco Church (mid-16th century), with notable paintings of famous Franciscans, choir stalls, and a famous high altar (1622). Remarkable ceiling is in Spanish-Moorish (mudéjar) style. A very good example of Colombian Colonial architecture. This church and 22 below are the best in Bogotá.

21.   Church of La Veracruz, first built five years after the founding of Bogotá, rebuilt in 1731, and again in 1904. In 1910 it became the National Pantheon and Church of the Republic. José de Caldas, famous scientist and botanist, was buried along with many other victims of the "Reign of Terror" under the church. Fashionable weddings.

22.   La Tercera Orden, an old Colonial church famous for its carved woodwork, altars, and confessionals.

23.   The Banco de la República, next to Parque Santander, no longer shows or sells emeralds. Next to the Bank is the wonderful Gold Museum (see next page).

In Parque Santander there is a bronze statue of Santander, who helped Bolívar to free Colombia and was later its President.

24.   Las Nieves, old colonial church, has been demolished and replaced by an ugly modern church.

27.   Tequendama Hotel.

Near by (on Carrera 7 and Calle 26) are the church and monastery of San Diego, a singularly picturesque and lovable old building recently restored. The Franciscan monastery with fine Spanish-Moorish ceiling was built in 1560 and the church in 1607 as its chapel. It is now used as a crafts shop by Artesanías de Colombia. SE of the Tequendama Hotel is the National Library, with an entrance on Calle 24.

28.   Parque Mártires (Park of the Martyrs), on the site of the Plaza in which the Spanish shot many patriots during the struggle for independence. A monument to the Martyrs.

29.   Church of María del Carmen, with excellent stained glass and walls in bands of red and white.

Museums The National Museum, on Carrera 7, No. 28-26, the Panóptico, an old prison converted into a Museum (to the NE of the map), founded by Santander in 1823. In 1977 it was temporarily closed but many of its pre-conquest exhibits have been transferred to the Archaeological Museum at Carrera 6, No. 7-43. See 11 for Museum of Colonial Art, under 1 for Museo 20 de Julio, and under 13 for Biblioteca Luis Angel Arango.

The Museum of Modern Art, the Planetarium and the Museum of Natural History, once in the National Museum building, have been moved to a new building at Carrera 7 and Calle 26. Entry to Modern Art museum US$0.15, to Planetarium and Natural History museum US$0.06 each.

The Museo Mercedes de Pérez, formerly the Hacienda de El Chico, a fine example of Colonial architecture, is on Carrera 7, approximately Calle 100. It contains a world-wide collection of mostly 18th century porcelain, furniture, paintings, etc.

The Museum of Popular Art and Tradition is at Carrera 8, No. 7-21. This museum is in an old monastery and exhibits local arts and crafts. It has a shop and a small, inexpensive but good, restaurant. Open Mon.-Sat. (closed Tues.) 1000-1730. Sundays and holidays 1000-1200. The shop is not open on Sundays and holidays. Entry fee US$0.15.

A fine collection of pre-Columbian pottery has been assembled in the restored mansion of the Marqués de San Jorge, Carrera 6, No. 7-43. The house itself is a beautiful example of 17th century Spanish colonial architecture. US$0.30 entry.

Museum of Urban Development, Calle 10 and Carrera 4, interesting maps and photos of the development of Bogotá in an attractive colonial house near the Palacio San Carlos.

Museo del Oro (the Gold Museum), is now in splendid premises at the Parque de Santander (corner of Calle 16 and Carrera 6-A). This collection is a "must", for it is unique. No less than 18,000 pieces of precolumbian gold work are shown. Open: Tues. to Sat., 0900-1700; Sun. and holidays, 0900-1200. Charge, 10 pesos (or about 30 US cents), a bargain (5 pesos or US$0.15 for children). Do not miss seeing the collections kept in a huge strong-room on the top floor. There are tours in English at 1000 and 1400; several film shows a day; at 1000 and 1430 they are in English.

The ancient gold objects discovered in Colombia were not made by the primitive technique of simple hammering alone, but show the use of virtually every technique known to modern goldsmiths, including the use of moulds employing the "cire perdue" method, in which wax holds the core and outer shell of a mould apart until they are dry; and then is melted out and replaced by molten metal. Objects of great beauty among the exhibits are three magnificent ceremonial vases made by this method, several diadems, and several sceptre-like pins. Galería Cano, Edificio Bavaria, Carrera 7, sells excellent gold reproductions made by the original processes. *Note:* Apart from the Museo del Oro, some of the other museums are closed on Mondays.

The **Universidad Nacional** (about 13,000 students) is off our map, to the NW. The fine buildings are coated with political graffiti, and foreigners are not usually welcome on the campus. The most ancient centres of learning in Bogotá are not however, grouped here. Oldest of all is the Colegio Nacional de San Barolomé (C 10, No. 6-57), in the same block as the Chapel of El Sagrario, founded 1573. Its luminaries include many scholars and writers and statesmen. The second most ancient, founded on December 18, 1653, is the Colegio Mayor de Nuestra Señora del Rosario (C 14, No. 6-25), whose charter is almost a replica of that of the Spanish University of Salamanca; its beautiful colonial building is well worth a look. Other universities are the Universidad Javeriana (law, economics, medicine, architecture and engineering), Universidad de los Andes, Universidad Libre, Universidad Jorge Tadeo Lozano, and others.

Sports Bull fighting on Sats. and Suns. during the season at the municipally owned Plaza de Santamaría, near Parque Independencia. Boxing matches are held here too. Horse races at the Hipódromo del Techo, in the SW, on Sats., Suns. and public holidays. Near-by is the Municipal Stadium, which can hold 50,000 spectators. Football matches are played here. The Country Club has two 18-hole golf courses, several tennis courts, indoor swimming pool and many other facilities. There are two polo clubs.

Industries Vehicle assembly plants, machine tools, cotton and woollen textiles, construction materials, glass, cement, footwear, furniture, tyres, pharmaceuticals, beer, chocolate, cigarettes and soap.

Airport The airport at El Dorado has the world's second largest landing field. "Tourist Guide policemen" with white armbands are a godsend. The taxi fare from airport to city is US$1 plus the meter charge, usually about US$2.30. The airport officials give you a paper, when you leave the airport, confirming this. The taxi driver may try to persuade you to give this to him, but hang on to it—it is a useful protection against overcharging if your Spanish is limited. There are colectivos (about US$0.40, plus luggage p.p.) from airport to centre; also buses, US$0.10. Colectivos back to the airport are not easy to find. The fare is about US$1.75. Airport shops are beautiful.

Hotels One of our correspondents resident in Bogotá has sent us the following selection of hotels:

Name	Address	Single (US$)	Double (US$)	No. of Stars
Hilton	Cra. 7, No. 32-16	30	45	5
Tequendama	Cra. 10, No. 26-21	40	60	5
Bacatá	Calle 19, No. 5-32	16	20	4
Continental	Av. Jiménez, No. 4-16	13	17	3
Dann	Calle 19, No. 5-72	13	16	3
El Presidente	Calle 23, No. 9-48	13	16	3
Tundama	Calle 21, No. 8-81	10	14	2
Cordillera	Cra. 8, No. 16-85	12	16	2
Las Terrazas	Calle 54, No. 3-12	7	9	2
Del Duc	Calle 23, No. 9-38	10	13	2
Cardenal	Av. Jiménez No. 4-38	12	15	2
San Diego	Cra. 13, No. 24-82	8	10	2

There are many others, rather cheaper, some recommended, as follows: *San Francisco,* Av. Jiménez, No. 4-87, US$50 d, recommended; *Regina,* Carrera 5, No. 15-16, US$10 d; *Residencias Steves,* Carrera 10, No. 16-67, US$5 s; *Hotel Comendador,* Carrera 18, No. 38-41, high class, U$8 s, good and in central residential section. Also recommended: *Hotel Santafé de Bogotá,* Calle 14, No. 4-21, with good restaurant and service, US$3.80 s; *Hotel Avenida 19,* Avenida (Calle) 19, No. 5-92, US$6 d, good price considering its central location, very helpful service; *Halifax Private Hotel* (English run), Calle 78, No. 9-58; *Claridge; Manilla; Regis,* Calle 18, No. 6-09 (also known as *Residencias María),* US$4 d, hot water, clean; *Hotel Parque,* Calle 24, No. 4-93,US$12 d; *La Virgen del Camino,* Carrera 14 and Calle 18A, new, extremely clean, hot water, US$3.50 s, US$4.50 d or US$6.50 with bath, US$0.75 breakfast; *Residencia Claudia,* Carrera 8, No. 17-66; *Saratoga,* opposite *Hotel San Francisco,* US$3.35 d, US$2.35 s, good, safe, and clean, hot water; *Kayser,* Carrera 4, No. 13-18, US$3.50 d, safe; *Hotel Residencias* in Calle 14, No. 4-48, US$5.80 d, including breakfast; *Ile de France,* Calle 18, No. 14-56, US$7.50 d, hot water, good food, either breakfast or dinner; nearby *Hotel Gualcalá,* cheap, clean and safe; *Residencias Alemanas,* Carrera 16, No. 16-48, near bus stations, US$3 s, US$2 p.p. for 2 or 3 in a room, laundry service, lots of hot water, very friendly, good breakfasts; *El Buen Amigo,* Carrera 16, No. 14-45, cheap (US$2 s, noisy at night); opposite *Hotel Manizales,* US$1.10 s, US$1.50 d; *Zaratoga,* Sucursal 2, US$3.20 d, hot water; *Motel Tropicana,* Avenida Caracas, cheap, friendly and good food; *Carlos Quinto,* Carrera 7, No. 28-30, US$3 s, English spoken, clean, good food; *Residencial Capri,* Carrera 13, No. 15-89, US$1.20 each; *Residencial Casablanca,* Carrera 15, between Calles 16 and 17, US$3 d, highly recommended; *Hotel Vas,* Calle 15, No. 12-30, US$4.60 d, with bath, safe, clean and friendly; *Residencias Schlief,* Calle 33A, No. 14-38, US$5 per room, with breakfast, hot water, pleasant; *Residencias La Casona,* Calle 14, No. 4-13, old-fashioned, English spoken, US$3 s, with bath, good meals for US$1; *María Luisa,* Carrera 14, between Calles 15 and 16, very reasonable and food is good; *Residencia Aromas,* Calle 15, US$1.50 d; *Picasso,* Calle 17, No. 15-47, safe, clean, US$4.30 d, hot water, but often full, breakfast US$0.40; *Geber,* Carrera 10, No. 22-45, US$4 s, US$8 d;

under same management, *Hotel Quindio,* Calle 17, No. 16-94, US$1.20 s, US$2 d;
Serranía, Calle 17, No. 14-55, very clean and friendly, US$3 d; *Dorado,* Calle 18,
US$7 d, very comfortable; *Aragón,* Carrera 3a, No. 14-13, clean and safe, US$2 s;
Corinto, US$0.70 p.p.; *Residencia Dorantes,* Calle 13, No. 5-07, very clean,
US$4.50 s, reasonable; *Ferlen,* Calle 8a, No. 16-52, basic, US$1.50 d; *Zaddi,* Carrera
13a, No. 12-32, US$2 a night; *Residencias R-B,* next *Hotel San Francisco,* central,
clean, US$3.50 d; *Hotel Niagara,* Carrera 3a, No. 20-35, US$7 d, with turkish bath;
Hotel Palace, Calle 14, No. 12-78, US$2 d; *Italia,* Carrera 7 & Calle 20, US$2 p.p.;
Alcron, Calle 20 & Carrera 5, US$2.30 d, restaurant; *Residencias Ambala,* Carrera
5A, No. 13-46, US$1.60 each, cheap, clean, friendly and central. New, but not 1st
grade, is *Hotel Alexia,* Carrera 9, No. 16-33; *Hotel Volga,* near DAS office in old
town, US$1 each, clean. *Hotel Miami,* Carrera 7, Calle 23, US$5, safe; *Residencias
Reales,* US$4.50 d, ¾ block from Velotax bus terminal; *Residencias Las Vagas,*
Calle 13, Carrera 4, US$1.70, clean, central. We are informed that from Calle 12
southwards is a less salubrious part of town; visitors are therefore advised to pick
hotels in streets NE of Calle 12 with higher numbers. There are certainly many hotels
(and bus companies) between Calles 13 and 17 and Carreras 15 and 17, many of
which are cheap, some of which are clean. *Residencias Españolas,* Calle 13 and
Carrera 16, is one such; it is clean and costs less than US$2 d; *Residencias El Hogar,*
Calle 16, No. 15-87, is another, US$1.25 d.

Restaurants   The restaurant of *Hotel Continental* has been highly recommended.
The *Refugio Alpino,* in the same building as *Hotel Monaco* (an apartment block at
Calle 23, No. 7-49) is an excellent Swiss restaurant: meals cost about US$4.50 and
service is superb. *Gran Vatel,* Calle 24, No. 5-83, French and Belgian food, meals
cost US$4-8, recommended; *Montserrate,* Tel.: 43 65 30, Ext. 05 (Colombian food,
overpriced); *Cyrus,* Carrera 7a, No. 22-48 (French); *La Pampa; El Pollo Dorado,*
Carrera 9, No. 17-38; *Eduardo,* Carrera 11, No. 90-43, international and expensive;
Chesa (speciality Fondue Bourguignonne); *Verners,* Calle 25, No. 12-23, near *Hotel
Tequendama* (very good German food); *Pollo Dorado del Chico; Salinas* (1 in town,
1 in Chico); *Casa Vieja,* Av. Jiménez 3-73 (live music) and *Los Arrayanes* (across
from *Hotel Continental,* in colonial houses, very good local dishes, nice
atmosphere); *El Zaguán de Las Aguas,* Calle 19, No. 5-62, good, but expensive, local
dishes, atmosphere and music; *Henry VIII; Chalet Suizo,* Carrera 7, No. 21-51,
Swiss and international food; *Piazetta; Pizzeria Napolitana,* overpriced; *Salinas;
Chez Dedy* (dine and dance till 0400). The *Donde Canta la Rana,* Carrera 24-C, No.
20-10 Sur, a few km. from centre, is refreshingly local and unspoilt, open 1400-1900.
Also try *La Polla,* Calle 19, No. 1-85. *Doña Bárbara,* Calle 82, corner of Carrera 11,
dinner costs US$2.50-4.25, excellent latino jazz played: *La Barba,* Calle 22, between
Carreras 9 and 10, Spanish atmosphere; *La Piragua,* corner of Av. Jiménez and
Carrera 5, cheap and good; *Temel,* Carrera 19 at Calle 118, good steaks, expensive;
Giuseppe Verdi, Calle 58, No. 5-85, excellent pasta; *Petit Paris,* Carrrera 4 and Calle
74, expensive French food; *Jeno's,* Carrera 15, near Calle 85, serves good, though
not cheap, pizzas; *Chalet Europa,* Carrera 9, No. 16-91, 4-course meals for US$1.20;
Balalaika, Calle 15, No. 32-83; *La Casa en la Esquina,* near Calle 63; *Cafeteria
Romano,* Av. Jiménez, between Carrera 6 and 7, all meals, very clean and
reasonable, well recommended, as is its sister restaurant *Salerno,* at corner of
Carrera 7 and Calle 20; *Café Monterrey,* nearby, cheap, and has good food but is
very dark and has poor service. *Robin Hood,* near *Hotel San Francisco,* very good,
there are also other branches. Also on Avenida Jiménez, *Avenida,* good local food,
meals starting from US$0.80, recommended. *Pío Pío,* on same street, specializes in
roast chicken, and paella on Sundays. For local food, *Teusacán,* Carrera 15, No.
39-16; *Comillas,* in Av. Jiménez; *Tierra Colombiana,* Carrera 10, No. 27-27. There
are two restaurants called *Sandricks,* one on Carrera 16, No. 91-25, the other on
Carrera 15, No. 79-92; they are run by two brothers and are highly recommended,
though not cheap (US$2.50-US$3.85 for a main dish). There is a small chain of
restaurants called *La Sultana:* the best is at Carrera 7, No. 21-14; *El Parrillón,* 1½
blocks from *Hotel Kayser,* serves good steaks and other dishes for less than US$2;
Ranch Burger, Centro El Lago, on Carrera 15, serves hamburgers; *Delphi,* opposite
Teatro Gaitán, on Carrera 7, recommended for cheap meals; *Restaurante Pasapoga*
(near Gold Museum), Calle 12, No. 6-52, full meal for US$0.85; *Trattoria Bistro,*

Calle 59. No. 8-50, with branch at Unicentro (Local 2-45), not cheap, but good food, must book at weekends; *Taverna Alemana,* Avenida Caracas (Carrera 14) with Calle 64; for US$0.50 a two course meal can be had in the cafeteria of the "Leys" and "Tia" supermarkets; *El Vegeteriano,* Calle 22, No. 8-89, set meals for US$0.70, recommended (the restaurant is not easily seen from the street, however, as it is on 3rd floor with only a small sign); there is another branch at Calle 18, No. 5-74; there is another vegetarian restaurant at the yoga centre on Av. Jiménez; *El Dorado,* Carrera 15, No. 16-39, good meal for US$1.20, convenient for bus station. *Monte Blanco,* Carrera 7a, No. 17-31, and other branches, very good. *Diana,* Calle 8 with Carrera 6; Good pizzas are served at branches of *Little John's;* opposite the US embassy, *León's* restaurant for steaks; *La Candelaria,* Calle 11, No. 3-89, 3-course meal for US$0.40; *La Fregata,* Calle 15, No. 9-30 and Calle 77, No. 15-36, expensive but excellent for sea food. Spanish food at *El Mesón de la Paella,* Calle 69, No. 12-14. Typical Colombian food at *Mesón Las Indias.* For Italian food, *Pizzeria Nestore,* and good pizzerias at corner of Calle 19 with Carrera 3. For Chinese food, the *Hong Kong* (overpriced); *Nanking,* Calle 23, between Carreras 6 and 7; and *Pagoda China* on Calle 69, No. 6. Japanese and Korean dishes at *Restaurant Arirang.* For excellent inexpensive Arab food, *Ramses,* Carrera 7 with Calle 19.

Tea Rooms   *Benalcázar,* Plaza Caldas on Carrera 7, excellent pastries and quite all right for women alone; *La Suiza,* Calle 25, No. 9-41, excellent pastries; *William Tell,* Carrera 13, Calle 23; *Cafeteria Romana,* on Calle 15, opposite Banco de la República, very pleasant. A chain of "Cyranos" throughout the city offer good pastries.

Night Clubs   The most fashionable is the Montserrate Room at the Tequendama. Others are Casbach, Candilejas, La Casina delle Rose, Kyreos, As de Copas, Balalaika, La Pampa, Sahara, and La Zambra (Spanish). Unicorn, Calle 94, No. 7-75, now expensive and spectacular; El Padrino, very good.

Clubs   Gun Club, Jockey Club, Anglo-American Club, Country Club (golf, polo, swimming), Magdalena Sports Club (tennis), San Andrés Golf Club, Club de Los Largartos (social; with a pool heated by hot springs, a golf course and tennis courts), Club Campestre Fontanar (tennis), America Sports Club, Lions' Club, Bogotá Sports Club (cricket, football, tennis, squash, rugby and hockey). Both the Lagartos and the Country Club have beautiful gardens designed by Enrique Acosta.

Taxis have meters; insist that they are used. Starting charge, US$0.20, plus US$0.05 for every 90 metres. Additional charge of US$0.10 after 1900 and on public holidays and Sundays. Minimum charge is US$0.30. Large cars can be hired at US$16 a day plus US$0.16 per kilometre. Volkswagens cost US$12 daily plus US$0.12 per kilometre. Car hire firms are *Hertz, Tequendama Hotel; Hernando Zuluaga & Cia.,* Carrera 7, No. 20-80; and *Alaquilautos Ltda.,* Carrera 7, No. 34-81. *Avis* also have an office.

Travel in Bogotá   Bus fares are US$0.03, *busetas* charge US$0.15.

Current   150 volts A.C., 60 cycles, being slowly converted to the 110-120 volts general for the rest of Colombia. Transformer must be 110-150 volt A.C., with flat-prong plugs.

Post Office   Main airmail office and foreign poste restante in basement of Edificio Avianca, Carrera 7, No. 16-36, open 0700-2200 Mon. to Sat. and 0800-1300 Suns., and holidays. Pharmacies and newsagents in Bogotá have an airmail collection.

Tourist Office   Carrera 13A, No. 27-37, floor 16, Edificio Centro de las Américas, Tel.: 839466; Carrera 10, No. 27-27, interior 145; and international airport. Anyone interested in archaeological expeditions (also botanical, ornithological and zoological) should get in touch with: Educational Programmes in Archaeology and the Natural Sciences (EPANS) Ltda., 9 Calle, 4-69, Zona 1, Guatemala City, who run tours of well-known and almost unknown areas of archaeological interest.

Thefts   Most hotels charge US$0.08 a night for insurance against theft. If you have something stolen go to the Corporación Nacional del Turismo for help and collect the insurance; this will probably take a few days of strenuous effort; but it has been known to work.

Shopping Artesanías de Colombia (state-owned) in the old San Diego church, Carrera 7 and Calle 26, and next to the Iglesia de las Aguas, Carrera 3A, No. 18-60, Carrera 10, No. 26-50; and on Av. Jiménez with Carrera 19, has best selection of folk art and crafts, at fair prices. A good place for handicrafts is El Lago, Carrera 15, No. 73-64; some way from centre. There is also a branch at the Avianca building. Another good place is El Balay on Carrera 15, No. 74-38, and, of course, there is the shop in the Museo de Artes y Tradiciones Populares, which is recommended. See H. Stern's jewellery store at *Hilton Hotel*. A good store for ruanas is at "La 19", Calle 19, No. 12-28. A street market on Avenida Jiménez and Carrera 14 (Avenida Caracas) sells cheaper ruanas, blankets, leatherware, etc. New shopping centre at Chapinero, Carrera 13, Calle 55-60, specializes in shoes, and leather. Boutiques are to be found on Carrera 10, Calles 76-100. There is another market, which is good for handicrafts, at Carrera 10, Calle 10. High-quality leather goods on Calle 19, between Carreras 4 and 7; the shops on Carrera 7 are not cheap. Galeria Gano, Edificio Bavaria, Carrera 7, sells gold and gold-plated replicas of some of the jewellery on display in the Gold Museum. Galeria 70, Avenida 13, No. 70-14, exhibition of and shop selling hand-woven textiles and rugs. Nemqueteba, Carrera 13, No. 50-06, produces ruanas etc.: ring for an appointment first: Tel.: 35-50-46. Primitive paintings are interesting; often humorously detailed, as well as brilliantly coloured. They are often on show in the Galería El Callejón, Calle 16, No. 6-34, as well as old maps and prints.

(The pavements and cafés along Av. Jiménez, below Carrera 7, Parque de los Periodistas, Calle 16 and Carrera 3, and El Mosaico restaurant (corner of Calle 14 with Carrera 8) are on weekdays used by dozens and sometimes hundreds of emerald dealers, and have been the scene of some legendary shoot-outs between rivals. A fascinating lunchtime can be spent in El Mosaico, which functions as an emerald stock exchange. Almost every table is filled by dealers with their paper packets of stones, tweezers, scales and lenses and visitors soon find a queue waiting to offer gems. Great care is needed in buying, as bargains are to be had, but synthetics and forgeries abound since the army occupation of the best mines reduced production. Beware of stones that seem too perfect or have a bluish colouring.) Three shops selling good emeralds at reasonable prices are: Joyería Frida, Carrera 7, No. 18-31; Willis F. Bronkie, Edificio Bavaria, Torre A, first floor, Carrera 10, No. 28-49; Jewelry Prado, Carrera 7, No. 16-50. For authentic examples of pre-Columbian art (and there are many fakes on the market) go to Jaime Errázuriz in the *Tequendama Hotel* (a bit expensive) or El Pijao Export, Carrera 7, No. 32-29. Modern Textiles and knitwear (many Rodier products are made in Colombia) can be bought at low prices at Unicentro, a large shopping centre on Carrera 15 at Calle 127A. Técnica, Carrera 7A, No. 16-13 (first floor) will put gold lettering on leather goods quickly and cheaply.

Bookshops Librería Buchholz, Av. Jiménez, at Carrera 8a and Calle 15; useful advice in a number of languages, low prices. Librería Aldina, Carrera 7, Calle 70-80, most helpful on books and Bogotá alike, excellent stock of English-language books, open 0930-1930, Sats. 0930-1700. Librería Central, Calle 16, No. 6-34 (Apartado Aéreo 3484), next Avianca building, also highly recommended, sells pictures, Indian artefacts and records also, but expensive. Books in Colombia are generally more expensive than in the UK, USA, or Canada.

Book Exchange Stalls Calle 19, between Carreras 7 and 10.

Laundry Carrera 7, about ¼ mile beyond *Hilton Hotel; Auto Servicio Burbujas*, Edificio Procoil, Avenida 19, No. 3-A37, open all week 0730-1930.

Rail To Facatativá, Girardot, Ibagué, Ambalema and La Dorada; to Chiquinquirá (154 km. north); to San Miguel (40 km. south-west); to Puerto Salgar and north to Santa Marta (daily, leaving at 1600, US$20, taking 24 hours). At Christmas and Easter the Tayrona Express runs three times a week direct to Cartagena, US$13. To Medellín, de luxe train on Tues., Thurs., Sat. It is no longer possible to go direct to Neiva: train to Girardot, with an auto-ferro connection the next day, or take the bus.

Buses Frequent buses of Exp. Palmira and Magdalena (Calle 13, No. 22), Bolivariano to Cali, 1st class, 10 hours, US$7; 2nd class, 12 hours, US$5. To Manizales, 8 hours, US$14-20. Several lines to Medellín, 18 hours, US$4.70 or 7.50 (Pullman).

To Neiva, also several lines, cost US$3.50. Taxis Verdes for Neiva and San Agustin leave from Calle 18, No. 14-18. To Girardot, US$1.75. To Bucaramanga, up to 10 hours (11 by 2nd-class bus, US$6) and to Cúcuta, 18 hours by Exp. Berlinas and Exp. Copetran, US$8.50, frequent departures p.m. (to Cucúta). It is better not to buy a through ticket (US$15) to Caracas with Exp. Berlinas as this does not guarantee a seat and is only valid for 2 Venezuelan companies; moreover no refunds are possible in Cúcuta. Most long-distance buses leave from streets around Carrera 15-16 and Calle 15. If you want to avoid the Quindio pass, take Avianca plane to Pereira, US$14.90. Small Velotax buses (busetas) to most places; better journey, slightly higher fares. Calle 17, No. 15-07. To San Agustín, 3 buses a day with Coomotor (Carrera 25, No. 15-36), US$6, leaves 0730, takes 2 hours. Bus to Ipiales takes 24 hours and costs US$11.50. Virtually every long-distance bus journey in Colombia offers scenic delights—but keep at least one eye on your luggage!

British Embassy Calle 38, No. 13-35. Tel.: 69 81 00. Postal Address: Apartado Aéreo 4508.

U.S. Embassy Calle 37, No. 8-40. Tel.: 37 91 00.

W. German Embassy Diagonal 34, No. 5-18.

Canadian Embassy Calle 58, No. 10-42, 4th floor.

Venezuelan Embassy Diagonal 68. Visas cost about US$5.

British Council Calle 11, No. 5-16. Tel.: 43 81 81. Has a good library and British newspapers.

Anglo-Colombian School Avenida (Calle) 19, No. 152-48. Tel.: 58 00 65.

Banks Banco Anglo Colombiano (formerly Bank of London and South America), Carrera 8, No. 15-60, and seven local agencies. Banco Royal de Colombia (formerly Royal Bank of Canada); Banco Internacional de Colombia (formerly First National City Bank); Banco Francés e Italiano de Colombia (formerly Banco Francés e Italiano para la América del Sur); Banco Franco Colombiano (formerly Banque Nationale pour le Commerce et l'Industrie), and other Colombian banks. Open 0900-1500 Mondays to Thursdays and 0900-1530 on Fridays. Closed on Saturday; also closed at 1200 on last working day of month.

Currency Exchange house at Edificio Marulanda, Carrera 6a, No. 14-74, office 1104. American Express, Carrera 10, No. 27-91. Also Exprinter on Av. Jiménez and Calle 6.

Cinema Cinemateca Distrital, Carrera 7 with Calle 22. Good films, US$0.25.

Bowling Alleys On Avenida Caracas with Calle 24, and Calle 63 between 13 and 10.

Health Vaccinations free, Carrera 15, No. 58-59; best to go a.m., Cruz Roja Nacional, Carrera 7, No. 34-65, first floor, open 0830-1230, 1400-1530; smallpox vaccinations cost US$0.90. For hepatitis (gamma globulin), Clinica Bogotá, Carrera 17, No. 12-65, US$7.50 a shot. Dr. Biagi, Carrera 13, No. 49-40, office no. 425, Tel.: 32-07-59 recommended as general practitioner. The US Embassy will advise on doctors, dentists, etc. Profamilia, Calle 34, No. 14-46, for contraceptives.

Excursions from Bogotá Many interesting excursions can be made, varying in length from a few hours to as many days. These are arranged, with English-speaking guides, by many tourist agencies. The salt mines of Zipaquirá are described on page 455. Other excursions are to the beautiful artificial lake of Muña, formed by a dam; to **Sopó**, in the Savana (63 km.), where they venerate an image of the Saviour which has appeared in an eroded stone; in Sopó is the *Restaurante Nicolás,* run by a Frenchman, Nicolás Perrée.

For Tunja (2 hours over first-class road), see page 457. Lake Tota, for trout fishing, dam and Lake Neusa (restaurant). On the road to Suba, in the Zafra de Extremadura, a new restaurant which is recommended. To the east of Bogotá is **Choachí**, an attractive village set in a valley, where there are good walks and hot springs. Several buses a day each way, 2 hours. 100 km. from Bogotá is Guatavita Nueva (see page 457).

The Caribbean Ports

The climate is much the same for all three ports: the heat is great—ranging from 26° to 36°C, and there is a difference of only 2° between the hottest and coolest month. The temperature is a little lower by night. From November to March the heat is moderated by trade winds. There is a high proportion of blacks in all three cities.

Character, like climate, seems to change in Colombia with the altitude. The costeños (the people of the coast) are gayer and more light-hearted than the more sober people of the highlands, particularly the Antioquenos of the Cordillera Central. (The contrast is sharply drawn in the great modern Colombian novel, "100 Years of Solitude", by Gabriel García Márquez.) The coastal people talk very fast, slurring their words and dropping the final s's, a characteristic too of the costeños of Venezuela and Cuba.

Barranquilla, with 800,000 people, is the main port. It lies on the western bank of the Magdalena river, about 16 km. from its mouth, which has been deepened and the silted sandbars cleared so that it is now a seaport as well as a river port.

Barranquilla is a modern industrial city. Its chief interest for the tourist is the life of the streets and the river. The principal boulevard is Paseo Bolívar; there is a handsome Cathedral in Plaza Bolívar, the central square, and before it stands a small statue of Columbus. The commercial and shopping districts are round the Plaza. The colourful and vivid market is on a side channel of the Magdalena—the Caño de las Compañías—a few blocks to the E of Plaza Bolívar. The best park in the city is Parque 11 de Noviembre in the northern part. Stretching back into the north-eastern heights overlooking the city is the modern and very well-built suburb of El Prado, where the *El Prado Intercontinental Hotel* is. Not far away is the Country Club. There are three stadiums in the city, a big covered coliseum for sports, and a bull ring.

Airport The new Ernesto Corfisso airport is 10 km. from the city; there is plenty of transport of all types. Taxi to town US$1.70. Bus, from outside the airport, US$0.03. Aerocóndor flies to Miami; ALM to Aruba and Curaçao; to Panama about US$60; Lacsa to Maracaibo and Caracas.

Tourist information at the Library. The main office is in the suburbs on Carrera 52, No. 72-46, Tel.: 57-378.

Festivals Carnival, lasting four days, begins the week before Ash Wednesday: parades, floats, street dancing and beauty contests; Day of San Roque, on August 16.

Main Industries Textile mills, perfumes, vegetable oils, soaps, beer, gaseous drinks, ice, oils and greases, hats, shoes, flour mills, vegetable lard, saw mills, dry docks and shipyard for river craft, paints, plastics, cement, and pharmaceutical products; plywood; insecticide; glass; petrochemical plant.

Hotels *El Prado Intercontinental* (Cables: "Prado Hotel"), swimming pool and tennis courts, US$20 s, US$25 d. good restaurant, some distance from the centre; *Génova,* new, swimming pool, 10 blocks from centre, US$13 s; *Hotel Majestic,* out of city centre, US$8, very good; *Hotel Riviera,* Calle 34, No. 41-81, US7.50 s, very noisy if you have a room on the street; *Central,* US$6 s, US$9 d; *Hotel Spanish-American,* Paseo Bolívar, US$7 d, with bath, clean, meals available at about US$2; *Hotel Victoria,* US$5 s, US$9 d; *Alhambra,* US$5 s; *Majestic,* also new; *Zhivago,* Plaza Bolívar, very good, US$2.40 d, without bath; *Luxor; Santa Sofía,* Calle 38 and Carrera 38B, US$4.50 d, with bath, friendly; *Residencia,* on Carrera 53 with Calle 55, US$2.50, breakfast included, no air conditioning and not very attractive; *California,* US$1.50, basic, but with bath; *Hotel Caribe,* centre, US$11 d, US$7.50

s, coat and tie needed in restaurant; *Hotel San Blas,* Calle 33, No. 4-46, US$1.70 s; *Hotel Colón,* NW of Cathedral, US$0.80 p.p., very simple; *Suiza,* US$5 d, not recommended; *Hotel Roxy,* Plaza Bolívar, US$3.75 d, with bath. At Puerto Colombia (20 mins.), *Hotel Esperia,* and just outside, *Pradomar Hotel. Note:* hotel prices are much higher during carnival.

Restaurants *Metropole; Monserrate* (indifferent service); *Sorrento* (excellent South American food), *El Pelicano,* and *Mesón Español,* all in the residential district of Alto Prado; *La Fonda* (local dishes); *Bar Chicote* (Spanish); *Fogón Gaucho* (meats in the Argentine style); *El Pez que Fuma,* in front of football stadium, sea-food; *Chop Suey Steak House.* Also Chinese: Alto Prado. U.S. and French food at *The Steak House (Chez Ernest),* across from the Prado. New: *Brandes; Don Brisi,* recommended. Local dishes at *José Pazos,* Calle 69F, La Colonia.

Bookshop Librería Nacional has English books and a café which serves excellent fruit juices.

Clubs Country (golf, tennis, swimming pool); Barranquilla; Anglo-American; German; Italian; Centro Israelita.

British Consulate Carrera 44, No. 45-47. Tel.: 19781. Postal address: Apartado Aéreo 706.

Venezuelan Visas may be obtained from the Venezuelan Consulate at a cost of US$5.

Banks Banco Royal de Colombia; Banco Anglo Colombiano, Carrera 44, No. 34-48, with agency at Calle 72; Banco Internacional de Colombia. Open: 0800-1130, 1400-1600; last working day of month 0800-1130.

Royal Mail Agents E. R. Gerlein & Co. S.A., Carrera 44, No. 34-60 (P.O. Box 132).

Roads Regular buses from Plaza Bolívar (one an elongated monster holding 100) to the attractive bathing resort of Puerto Colombia, 19 km. Beach clean and sandy, water a bit muddy. S along the Magdalena to the little town of Palmar de Varela. On this road, 5 km. from the city, is the old colonial town of **Soledad,** with 16,000 inhabitants. The Cathedral and the old narrow streets round it are worth seeing.

Barranquilla-Cartagena, by air or by frequent buses (109 km., 2 hours, US$1.50), or in luxury coaches with hostesses serving "gaseosas" (US$2.10). From Baranoa a branch road runs to Usicurí (72 km. from Barranquilla), well-known for its medicinal waters and for the grave of the popular Colombian poet, Julio Flores. The main road goes on *via* Sabanalarga (50 km. from Barranquilla) to Cartagena. From **Sabanalarga** an all-weather road continues to Puerto Giraldo, a port on the Magdalena River linked by ferry with the small town of Salmina (ferry 0500 to 1800). An all-weather road leads to Fundación, on the Atlántico Railway, and a junction point with the road from Santa Marta to Bucaramanga (bad) and Bogotá.

Buses To Santa Marta, US$0.50, about two hours, also direct to Santa Marta's famous Rodadero beach; to Montería, US$1.65, 8 hours; to Medellín by Pullman, US$9.50, 16 hours; to Bucaramanga, 20 hours; to Bogotá, US$8.50, 28 hours. To Maicao, US$3 (US$5 on a/c buses), 6 hours; to Cartagena, 3 grades of bus, US$2.10 with Brasilia a/c buses, US$1.10-1.40 on ordinary buses.

Warnings Barranquilla is notorious as a place where drugs are "planted" on unsuspecting travellers, who then have to pay a fine to the police. Be very careful. Beware also of people purporting to be ships' officers who say they can arrange a passage if you pay in advance; only buy a passage in a recognized shipping office or agency.

Cartagena, old and steeped in history, is one of the most interesting towns in South America. Its population is 360,000, less than half that of Barranquilla. It is the clearing house for its immediate area and draws a large trade from the hinterland, particularly platinum from the headwaters of the Atrato and San Juan rivers in the Chocó, coffee from the Sierras, and oil products along the 536-km. Andean pipeline from the refineries at Barrancabermeja, far up the Magdalena river. An arm of the river, 145 km. long, canalized in 1650 by Spain from Calamar to

Cartagena—the Canal del Dique—allows free access for steamers from the up-river ports.

But what interests the visitor is a comparatively small part of Cartagena, the old walled city almost completely surrounded by the Caribbean sea on the W, the waters of the Bay of Cartagena on the S, and by lakes and lagoons to the N and E. Because Cartagena was one of the storage points for merchandise sent out from Spain and for treasure collected from the rich Americas to be sent back to Spain, it was highly necessary that it should be able to withstand the attacks of pirates. A series of forts protecting the approaches from the sea, and the formidable walls built around it made it almost impregnable.

Cartagena was founded by Pedro de Heredia on January 13, 1533, but it was not until almost the end of the 16th century that building began. There were then two approaches to it, Bocagrande, at the northern end of Tierra Bomba Island—this was a direct entry from the Caribbean—and Boca Chica. Bocagrande was made unnavigable after Admiral Vernon's attack in 1741, and thereafter the only approach was by the narrow channel of Boca Chica from the S. Boca Chica leads into the great bay of Cartagena, 15 km. long and 5 km. wide. The old walled city lies at the head of it, looking from a distance like a pile of immense castles and cupolas against a clear blue sky.

On our left, as we enter Boca Chica, is the curiously shaped island of Tierra Bomba, but no longer, as explained above, strictly an island. A residential suburb is planned here. At the tip of a jut of land is the fortress of San Fernando (entrance fee, US$0.30); boat trips to it (1 hr.) are worth while. Opposite it, right on the tip of Barú Island, is the fortress of San José. It is said that the two forts were linked by heavy chains to prevent surprise attacks by pirates. The bay widens out before us. The shores of the slightly green, transparent expanse of water are lined with villages and townships. North of Barú Island stretches Manga Island, much larger and now an important suburb. At its northern end a bridge, Puente Román, connects it with the old city. This approach was defended by three forts: San Sebastían del Pastelillo built between 1558 and 1567 (the Club de Pesca has it now) at the north-western tip of Manga Island; the fortress of San Lorenzo near the city itself; and the very powerful fortress of San Felipe inland on a height to the E of the city. Yet another fort, La Tenaza, protected the walled city from a direct attack from the open sea. The huge encircling walls were started in 1634 and finished by 1735. They were on average 12 metres high and 17 metres thick. There were 6 gates, shut at 2200 hours each evening and the keys handed to the Governor. They contained, besides barracks, the old town's water reservoir.

In spite of its daunting outer forts and encircling walls Cartagena was challenged again and again by enemies. The town was sacked in 1544—eleven years after its foundation—by Robert Baal, and a few years later, at the cost of 300 men, by French pirates under Martin Côte. He failed in 1561 and so did the several attacks by John Hawkins. But Sir Francis Drake, with 1,300 men, broke in successfully in 1586. The Frenchmen Baron de Pointis and Ducasse, with 10,000 men, beat down the defences and sacked the city in 1697. But the strongest attack of all, by Sir Edward Vernon with 27,000 men and 3,000 pieces of artillery, failed in 1741 after besieging the city for 56 days; it was defended by the one-eyed, one-armed and lame Blas de Lezo, whose statue is at the entrance to the San Felipe de Barajas fortress. So certain was Vernon of victory that he struck medals to commemorate it in advance. A brother of George Washington was with him; Mount Vernon was so named in the Admiral's honour.

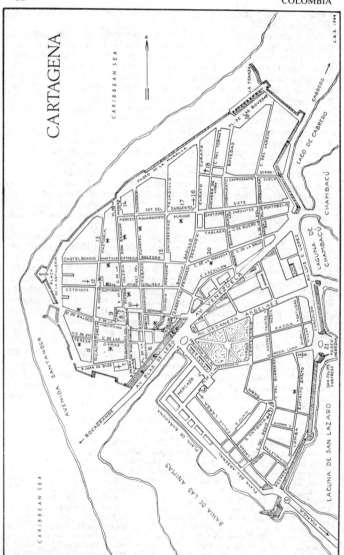

CARTAGENA

ROUGH SKETCH

Cartagena declared its independence from Spain in 1811. A year later Bolívar came to the city and used it as a jumping-off place for his Magdalena campaign. The city, after a heroic resistance which gained it the title of Ciudad Heróica from Bolívar, was retaken by the royalists under Pablo Morillo in 1815. The patriots finally freed it in 1821.

The old walled city was in two sections, inner and outer. Much of the wall between the two was senselessly razed a few years ago. Nearly all the houses are of one or two storeys. There are very few three storey houses and all of them are in two of the streets. The houses in El Centro were occupied by the viceroys, governors, inquisitors, officials and noblemen. San Diego (the northern end of the inner town) was where the middle classes lived: the clerks, artisans, priests and military. The lower classes lived in the one-storey houses of Getsemaní in the outer city.

The architecture is more Spanish than in Spain. To ensure coolness the walls are surprisingly thick and the ceilings very high; the patios contain fountains and gardens and there are many balconies and corridors. The streets are narrow—in the Jimaní neighbourhood both walls can be touched as you walk along—and rarely straight. Each block has a different name, a source of confusion. But who cares? The thing to do is to wander aimlessly, savouring the rich street scenes—the charcoal vendors, the sellers of coconut, the women carrying trays on their heads and selling sweets—and allow the great sights, the "musts", to catch you by surprise. But for the orderly minded there is our map to help. It is marked with numerals where the places of outstanding interest are. The most attractive streets have been given a star (*). All the "great houses" can be visited.

The numbers stand for the following places:

1. The Puente Román, the bridge which leads from the island of Manga into the Getsemaní ward of the outer walled city. This is where the working class lived, in one-storey houses. Visitors should on no account miss those typical examples of Cartagenean architecture: the "casas bajas" or low houses of Getsemaní.

2. The Chapel of San Roque (early 17th century), near the Hospital of Espíritu Santo. Stroll down the colonial Calle Espíritu Santo.

3. The Church of Santísima Trinidad, built 1643 but not consecrated till 1839. The colonial Plaza in which it lies is most interesting. North of the church, at number 10, lived Pedro Romero, the man who set the revolution of 1811 going by coming out into the street shouting "Long Live Liberty".

4. The Monastery and Church of San Francisco. The church was built in 1590 after the pirate Martin Côte had destroyed an earlier church built in 1559. The first Inquisitors lodged at the monastery. From its courtyard a crowd surged into the streets claiming complete independence from Spain on the morning of November 11, 1811. The Church of the Third Order is now the Colón Theatre.

Immediately to the N is Plaza de la Independencia, with the landscaped Parque del Centenario just off it. At right angles to the Plaza runs the Paseo de los Mártires, flanked by the busts of 9 patriots executed in the square by the royalist Morillo when he retook the city in 1815. At its western end is a tall clock tower. There is a riotous fish market in the Plaza. Passing through the tower's arches (the main entrance to the inner walled city) we get to

5. The Plaza de los Coches, which contains the City Hall. Buses leave from this Plaza. Around almost all the plazas of Cartagena arcades offer refuge from the tropical sun. On the W side of this plaza is the famous Portal de los Dulces (arcade of Sweets), a favourite meeting place.

6. Plaza de la Aduana, with a statue of Columbus. Facing old and quaint arcades and overhanging balconies is the modern skyscraper of an oil company.

7. Church of San Pedro Claver and Monastery, built by Jesuits in 1603 and later dedicated to the monk San Pedro Claver who lived in the monastery. He was

canonised 235 years after his death in 1654. He was called the Slave of the Slaves: he used to beg from door to door for money to give to the black slaves brought to the city. His body is in a glass coffin on the high altar. His cell in the monastery and the balcony from which he sighted slave ships are shown to visitors. Entry, US$0.25. Do not be bullied into taking a guide—they charge US$0.90.

8. Plaza Bolívar (the old Plaza Inquisición), beautifully landscaped and with a statue of Bolívar. On its W side is

9. The Palace of the Inquisition, established in 1610, but the building dates from 1706. The stone entrance with its coats of arms and well preserved and ornate wooden door is beautifully designed. Indeed the whole building, with its overhanging balconies, cloisters and patios, is a fine example of colonial baroque. There is a very pleasant and rather elegantly arranged historical museum at the Palace, and a library. Entry charge 10 pesos (US$0.30); good historical books on sale. Closed 1200-1400.

In the NE corner of Plaza Bolívar is

10. The Cathedral, begun in 1575 and probably completed when Francis Drake besieged the city in 1586 and partially destroyed it. Reconstruction was finished by 1612. Great alterations were made between 1912 and 1923. A severe exterior, with a fine doorway, and a simply decorated interior. See the guilded 18th century altar, the Carrara marble pulpit, and the elegant arcades which sustain the central nave. In its historical museum are some of Admiral Vernon's medals struck to commemorate a capture of Cartagena he did not bring off, and a church bell dated 1317.

11. Church and Convent of Santa Teresa, founded 1609, very large and now occupied by the police.

12. The Church and Monastery of Santo Domingo, built 1570 to 1579 and now a seminary. The old monastery was replaced by the present one in the 17th century. Note the spire, said to have been twirled by the devil so that it would not harmonise with the front. Inside, a miracle-making image of Christ, carved towards the end of the 16th century, is set in a baroque 19th century altar. Most interesting neighbourhood, very little changed since the 16th century. In Calle Santo Domingo, No. 33-29, is one of the great patrician houses of Cartagena, the Casa de los Condes de Pestagua, now the Colegio Lourdes. At No. 35-62 is the house where José Fernández de Madrid lived. The Inter-American Museum of Art is also in this street. North of Santo Domingo, at

13. Calle de la Factoría, No. 36-57, is the magnificent Casa del Marqués de Valdehoyos, now owned by the tourist authority and open to visitors, free.

14. The Church and Convent of La Merced, founded 1618. The Convent—a prison during Morillo's reign of terror—is now occupied by the Law Courts and its church by the Municipal Theatre.

15. The Monastery of San Agustín (1580), now the University. From its chapel, now occupied by a printing press, the pirate Baron de Pointis stole a 500-pound silver sepulchre. It was returned by the King of France but the citizens melted it down to pay their troops during the siege by Morillo in 1815.

16. The Church of Santo Torribio de Mongrovejo. Building began in 1729. In 1741, during Admiral Vernon's seige, a cannon ball fell into the church during Mass and lodged in one of the central columns, where it is still. The font of Carrara marble in the Sacristy is a masterpiece. There is a beautiful carved ceiling (mudéjar style) above the main altar.

17. Casa del Consulado (Calle San Agustín, in front of the University) is one of the great houses but has now become the factory of Gaseosas Román.

18. Church and Monastery of Santa Clara of Assisi, built 1617-21, now the Hospital of Santa Clara. Good gold-gilt altar of the period in the church.

19. Plaza de las Bóvedas. The walls of Las Bóvedas, built 1799, are some 12 metres high and from 15 to 18 metres thick. Cars can drive along the rampart, from which there is a grand view of the harbour. At the base of the wall are 23 dungeons used in early days as prisons. Both a lighted underground passage and a drawbridge lead from Las Bóvedas to the fortress of La Tenaza on the sea shore. Shops have been set up in the dungeons and are something of a tourist trap. The exhilarating main

market lies just east of the walls on a rectangle jutting into the bay and bathed on three sides by its water. The city's communications are largely by water; hundreds of sailing boats and motor boats bring in produce from the countryside along the rivers Magdalena, Sinú and Atrato.

Three of the sights of Cartagena are off our map. One of them is the Fortress of San Fernando, already mentioned.

The Fortress of San Felipe, across the Puente Heredía (21), from the outer-walled city, stands on the hill of San Lázaro, 41 metres above sea-level. It was the most powerful of all. Building began in 1639 and it was finished by 1657. Under the huge structure are tunnels lined with living rooms and offices. Some are open and lighted; visitors pass through these and on to the top of the fortress. Baron de Pointis, the French pirate, stormed and took it in 1697, but Admiral Vernon failed to reach it in the abortive attack of 1741. Its mortar, according to fable, was strengthened with the blood of bulls. "Son et lumière" Saturday nights at 2100. Entry US$0.65.

A lovely road leads to the summit of La Popa hill, nearly 150 metres high, from which there is a glorious view of the harbour and the city. Here are the church and monastery of La Santa Cruz and restored ruins of convent dating from 1608. In the church is the beautiful little image of the Virgin of La Candelaría, reputed a deliverer from plague and a protector against pirates. Her day is February 2, Candlemas Day. For nine days before the feast thousands of people go up the hill by car, on foot, or on horseback to visit the ecclesiastical buildings. On the day itself people carry lighted candles as they go up the hill. A visit to the monastery and the views from La Popa should not be missed. The name La Popa was bestowed on the hill because of an imagined likeness to a ship's poop.

Feasts The other great feast is on November 11-14 to celebrate the independence of Cartagena. Men and women in masks and fancy dress roam the streets, dancing to the sound of maracas and drums. There are beauty contests and battles of flowers and general gaiety. This festival tends to be wild and can be dangerous.

Industries Footwear, chemicals, toilet preparations, fats, textile knitting and weaving. At Mamonal an oil refinery, ammonia, chemical fertilizer and caustic soda factories.

Shipping There are modern wharves. The docks can receive six ocean steamers and twelve river boats at the same time. It is possible to ship a car from Cartagena to Panama. The Italian Line is cheapest, but its agent is unreliable; it is better to approach the ships' officers to see if there is a space. Cost about US$300 for a landrover LWB and US$66 for passengers.

Royal Mail Agents E. L. Gerlein & Co. S.A., Calle 34, No. 5-18 (P.O. Box 127).

Hotels On Bocagrande beach, 10 mins, by bus from city: *Capilla del Mar,* US$30 d, excellent French restaurant, first class service, swimming pool on 4th floor, no connection with restaurant of same name ¼ mile away; *Las Velas,* US$15 d; *Hotel del Caribe,* US$15 d, all rooms a/c, swimming pool; *India Castellana,* US$9, new and very good, with a/c; *Bahía,* US$12 d, not very well kept, swimming pool; *Flamingo,* US$10 d, recommended; *Del Lago,* US$15 d; *Park,* US$14.50 d; *El Dorado,* Av. San Martín, No. 4-41, US$14 d, clean, a/c, good service, swimming pool, restaurant, recommended; *Playa,* on Av. San Martín, recommended, US$10 s, US$14 d, all rooms with private bathroom, open air bar, excellent restaurant, private beach, reduced rates Sept.-Nov. and March-June, Av. 2a, No. 4-87; *Avenida,* US$8.15 d; *Residencias Bocagrande,* US$9 d; *Americano,* US$11 d, comfortable; *Residencias Asturias,* US$4.75 s, good, not actually on beach, but nearby; *Residencia Mansiomar,* Carrera 3, No. 4-64, US$3 s; *Residencias Almirante,* US$6.50 s, US$2.10 each extra person. In town: *Bellavista,* US$2 s, on road to airport; *Residencias Stella,* US$1, basic but clean; *Los Corrales,* US$7.50 each; *Hotel Plaza Bolívar,* Plaza Bolívar No. 3-98, located in old city, US$14 d, good; *Santa Cruz,* US$7 d; *Roma,* Tripita y Media 31-29, US$2.10 s, with fan, has good cheap restaurant attached; in same area *Residencias Venezia,* US$1.60 s, clean and secure, and many others; *Hotel Berlín,* US$3.10 s; *Pensión la Presentación* in old city, US$5 each, breakfast US$1; *Hotel Monserrate,* US$1.50 with bath, not well recommended. On the road to the airport are several hotels and pensions, particularly at Marbella beach.

N.B. Hotel prices tend to be up by as much as 25 per cent from December 20 to January 20, and hotels tend to be heavily booked. Either book well in advance yourself, or avoid the city at this time.

Restaurants   *Capilla del Mar,* highly recommended; *Don Boris,* excellent food and service; *El Golpe,* very good food; *Tratoria Pietra,* good Italian food; many good, but expensive, Italian restaurants on Bocagrande; *Rincón Argentino* for good steaks (US$3); *Club de Pesca,* at the Fuerte del Pastelillo: you can dine in the open air in a lovely setting; *Marcel Hostería Sevillana,* Malecón 70, near *Resid, Ligia, Barú* and *El Arabe* (arab dishes), all in Bocagrande; *Candilejas* and *El Candil,* behind the Plaza Aduana. *El Rinconcito,* near Plaza Fernando de Madrid, good cheap meals; also *El Pollo Dorado* on Calle Ricuarte, opposite Banco de Bogotá. *Restaurant Americano,* near central post office, good meals for US$0.60; *La Fragaia,* in old town, two blocks behind *Hotel Bolívar,* good, French maître d'hotel, German cook; *Pargo Roja,* recommended; many restaurants around Plaza Independencia have good meals for about US$0.60; *Heladería Vernón,* a block from San Pedro Claver church towards Plaza Bolívar, has hearty, reasonable meals; *Heladería Cecilia* for good ice-creams. At cafés try the *patacón,* a biscuit made of green banana, mashed and baked.

Camping   People camp on the beach, but may be troubled by thieves—and the police.

Art Gallery   Contemporary Latin American paintings, above Customs House, Plaza de la Aduana. Nearby is the Galería café, opposite the San Pedro Claver church. It is not only a café which serves superb sangría, but also an art gallery and cultural centre.

Market   Exciting and picturesque; good bargains, food and fruit juices.

Shopping   A good selection of artesanías on Plaza Bolívar, but in general shopping is much better in Bogotá.

Banks   Banco Royal; Banco Internacional. Both cash travellers' cheques. There are many "cambios"—try Hiram Preston at 38 Av. de la Inquisición (just behind the Palace). Be sure to count the pesos yourself before handing over your dollars.

Sport   Fishing; yachting; also bullfights and cockfights. The former take place mainly in January and February, the latter throughout the year on Sats., Suns. and holidays. On Saturdays cockfighting takes place at the Teatro Granada and on other days at Ternera, a village 16 km. away.

Swimming   Take bus from Plaza de la Independencia to Bocagrande, which has good beaches. The Boca Chica beach is now reported to be dirty, and the boat service there unreliable. Boats leave from Plaza de la Independencia; the round trip costs about US$2 and takes two hours each way. For about US$0.90 you can take a tour round the fort of San Fernando in a dugout canoe. There are boats from the town; the last return trip is at 1500. Swimming is good. Boats taking in Boca Grande and San Fernando are US$2 return.

Tourist Office   In the Palace of the Inquisition, Plaza Bolívar.

Airport   Crespo, 1½ km. from the city, reached by local buses from Av. Urdaneta Arbeláez. Bus from airport to Plaza San Francisco US$0.06; Taxis to centre US$0.75.

Venezuelan Visas can be obtained from the Consulate in Cartagena, though this takes 2 days and costs US$5.

Warning   Carry your passport with you at all times. Failure to present it on police request can result in imprisonment and fines. Regarding sea passages see warning under Barranquilla (page 430).

Another Warning   The north of Colombia is generally reported to be more dangerous than the centre and south, partly because of the marijuana and cocaine trade. All the dreadful details of the warning in the Bogotá section apply here also.

Taxis   Within the city the minimum fare is about US$0.50. Try to fix price for journey before committing yourself!

Buses   Within the city large buses (with no windows) cost US$0.03, short-wheelbase type (with windows), US$0.06.

Travel from Cartagena   To the picturesque little fishing village of **La Boquilla,** E of Cartagena, about 20 minutes past the airport. On Saturday and Sunday nights people dance the local dances. Go there by taxi (buses are infrequent); can be dangerous for pedestrians. Visit the mangrove swamps nearby to see the birds. To **San Jacinto,** 1½ hours by road S of Cartagena, good place for local craft work. To **Turbaco,** 24 km. SE by road and on S through Sincelejo (193 km., see below), **Planeta Rica** (320 km.) and Yarumal *(Restaurante La Nena)* to Medellín, 665 km. S of Cartagena. About 42 km. beyond Planeta Rica there is a camping site. Five km. further on is **Caucasia,** which makes a good stopping point if you want to break the journey from Cartagena to Medellín. *Hotel Playa Mar,* US$3 s, good food available, friendly, but noisy. Pullman bus from Cartagena to Medellín, US$12, ordinary bus to Medellín US$10. A few km. on from Caucasia towards Medellín is the *Mesón del Gitano,* a hotel with a campsite; camping costs US$2.40. Several buses a day from Cartagena to Medellín, but book early, takes 17 hours, counting stops, does journey in 13 hours. The road is now paved throughout, in good condition. From Cartagena by bus to Santa Marta, US$2, 4 hours. To Barranquilla US$1, or US$3 with Expreso Brasilia pullman, near base of San Felipe fortress. (The Rápidos Ochoa bus station is also here.) Bus to Maicao on Venezuelan frontier, US$5 or 6, depending on type, 10 hours; the road is in good condition, except for 30 km.

Ninety-six km. S of Cartagena along the coast is **Coveñas,** the terminal of the 420-km. crude oil pipeline from the Barco oilfields to the N of Cúcuta, on the Venezuelan frontier. Nearby is Tolú village *(Residencias Manuelito* and *Residencias El Turista,* both US$2.40 d).

Sincelejo, capital of Sucre Department *(Hotel Majestic* and some good basic eating), is a small cattle centre 193 km. S of Cartagena on the main road to Medellín. It is well known for the dangerous bull-ring game, likened to the San Fermín festivities in Pamplona, Spain, in which bulls and men chase each other. The town is hot and dusty and power cuts are a way of life. *Hotel Finzenu,* Carrera 20 and Calle 22, US$9.20 d, with a/c. The beaches of Tolú are 40 minutes away, but it is worth going an extra 20 minutes to those at Coveñas.

Montería, capital of Córdoba Department, on the E bank of the river Sinú, can be reached from Cartagena by air, by river boat, or from the main highway to Medellín. It is the centre of a cattle and agricultural area turning out tobacco, cacao, cotton and sugar. Present population is 126,000. Compared with other Caribbean cities there is little to attract the tourist (apart from a fine church) except for the picturesque street life and the extremely friendly people. Average temperature: 28°C. Road to Planeta Rica (airport). Hotels: *Sinú,* US$9.90 s, a/c and swimming pool; *Santa Rosa,* US$1.50 s, with water, good; *Mocari; Panzenu; Embajador.*

It is to Cartagena that most of the platinum of the Chocó Department comes. Little steamers sail to the Gulf of Urabá (360 km.) and up the Río Atrato another 500 km. to the small jungle town of **Quibdó,** the capital of the Chocó Department (43,000; *Hotel Citará).* There is a good museum at the Normal School. Quibdó can be reached (1) by bus from Medellín; (2) from Buenaventura by river steamer up the Río San Juan to Istmina and on by road; (3) by plane from Cali to Condoto, near Andagoya, from which by river to Istmina and on by bus. There are air services to Quibdó from both Medellín and Cali. Chocó Department is strangely impressive; travel is rough but the rewards are high.

San Andrés and **Providencia,** two small islands in the Caribbean Sea, have belonged to Colombia since 1822. They are 400 km. SW of Jamaica, 180 km. E of Nicaragua, and 480 km. N of the Colombian coast—ferry or plane from Cartagena. Henry Morgan had his headquarters at San Andrés, which has all the charms of a lovely Caribbean island. Sea colours vary entrancingly from ultramarine to light turquoise. A beautiful road circles the island, a coral reef some 11 km. long rising to 104 metres. Providencia, 80 km. back to the NNE, is 7 km. long and rises to 610 metres. The 8,000 natives, mostly black, speak English and are partly Catholic, partly Protestant. San Andrés is a regular stop for Avianca, SAM, Costa Rican and the SAHSA airlines, and Aerocóndor fly in from Barranquilla. Main products: coconuts and vegetable oil. Places to see: the beautiful Keys, like Johnny Key (US$1 return by boat) with a white beach and the so-called Aquarium (US$1.20), off a Key where, using a mask and wearing sandals as protection against sea-urchins, you can see myriads of colourful fish of all shapes and sizes. Snorkelling equipment can be hired on San Andrés for US$0.50-0.80. The Hoyo Soplador is a geyser-like hole through which the sea spouts into the air most surprisingly when the wind is in the right direction. Bicycles are a popular way of getting around on the island and are easy to hire.

The islands are a customs-free zone; this means that they are often very crowded with Colombian shoppers looking for foreign-made bargains. There is an airport tax of US$5 when leaving on international flights and of US$2 for domestic flights. There is a customs tax of about US$2 (rarely enforced) on merchandise exported from the islands. There have been some reports that it is difficult to exchange dollars in the banks and shops, but the manager of the Texaco service station is said to be obliging in this respect.

Note The mistrust which is felt in Colombia towards "hippy types" is also felt here. The police may be helpful, especially to back-packers with long hair and beards. Don't carry drugs; they can get you a 10-year jail sentence.

Cargo boats may be caught at Cartagena but are infrequent, leaving every 10-15 days. The "Johnny Cay" sails from the Muelle de Pegasos and you can find out about other boats for San Andrés at the Marítima San Andrés office. The cost is about US$15, including food for 72-hour journey. Also from Colón (Panama), US$20, 30 hours, at least 2 sailings a week.

Airport Flights to most major Colombian cities: to Bogotá with SAM, US$53 (you can arrange a 72-hour stop-over in Cartagena), with Aerotal (one flight every four days), US$31. Also to Belize, San José, Tegucigalpa, Panama. 15 minutes walk to town.

Hotels at **San Andrés** *Gran Internacional,* US$15 d, a/c, swimming pool; *Bahía Marina,* expensive but has swimming pool and good restaurant; *Gran El Dorado* (casino); *Abacoa,* US$8 s; *Morgan,* US$6 s; *Europa,* US$8.50 d, clean; *Hotel Isleño,* US$8 d; *Casablanca; Las Vegas,* US$7 d; *Mónaco,* US$12 d, with shower, damp, smelly and noisy; *Miramar,* US$16 s, including breakfast, recommended; *Mediterráneo,* US$7 s; *Tropicana,* also US$7 s; *Carib,* US$8 s; *Tiuna; Natania; Residencia Hansa; Residencia Bryan,* US$2.25, with fan, good and reasonably cheap food; *Hotel Cobisco,* US$6 d; *Residencias San Martín,* US$1.75, or US$3.50 with meals, basic; *Residencia Restrepo,* near airport but not noisy, US$2.50 d, meals US$0.80 each, friendly but not very clean; *Hotel Kingston,* US$2.50 p.p.; *Residencias Astor,* next to *Bryan,* is US$2.50 a night; *Residencias Plaza,* about US$3, basic; *Residencial Barú,* US$4.20 d, with fan.

At **Providencia:** *Hotel Aury.* People sleep on the beach.

Restaurants on **San Andrés** *Tortuga; Chez Nous; Oasis* (good); *Lyons* (with bar); *La Parrillada* (Argentine) and *Aldo's* (Italian), good meals US$2-2.50; Comida Corriente at Don Joaco's for US$0.75, good fish. *Mercapollo,* next to *Miramar Hotel,* good value; *San Andrés* also recommended for cheap meals; *Fonda Antioqueña,* on beach, also good value, US$2; *Miami,* special for US$1.50; excellent *jugos* at *Jugolandia,* Calle 20 de Julio; *Mundo Acuático,* snacks of fresh fish and papaya for US$0.50, cheaper beer, soft drinks and mangoes.

Taxis Round the island, US$4.20, to airport, US$1.40: in town, US$0.28; colectivo to airport, US$0.25.

96 km. E of Barranquilla, at the mouth of the Manzanares river, lies the third Caribbean port,

Santa Marta, capital of Magdalena Department. It is best reached from Barranquilla by the paved road along the coast; the Magdalena Bridge (a most interesting design) was opened in April 1974. The road from Barranquilla skirts an extensive and most interesting lagoon, in which all types of swamp birds, plants and animals may be seen. On the E shore of this lagoon, the Ciénaga de Santa Marta, is **Ciénaga,** a town of 75,000 people. Passengers from Barranquilla transfer here to the Atlántico

Railway from Santa Marta to Bogotá. Cotton, bananas, tobacco and cacao are grown in the area. Hotels in Ciénaga: *Tobiexe; Naval.*

Train The express train for Bogotá leaves at 1730 on Tues., Thurs. and Sun., and takes 22-24 hours (fare US$18). One class only; meals at US$1.50 each, quite good. To Medellín, there is an autoferro three times a week. A quicker and cheaper way to Bogotá is by ordinary train at 0450 to La Dorada and from there by bus; total cost US$6, 20 hours. The autoferro from Santa Marta to Barrancabermeja at 1830 is US$7.50, it gets crowded early and is a slow 16 hour journey.

Buses The Copetran bus over a mostly unpaved road to Bucaramanga takes between 16 and 20 hours according to season (US$4.25). There is a good meal stop at Los Límites. From Bucaramanga the buses take 8 hours to Bogotá (11 by 2nd class). (The train is therefore quicker in this case.) Buses to Barranquilla, 2 hours (US$2); to Cartagena, 4 hours. To Riohacha by Pullman, US$2; Pullman to Maicao, US$3. The buses stop at the Venezuelan border on the way to Maracaibo for exit and entry stamps, usually better organised than at Cúcuta. There are three buses a day (Brasilia) direct to Rodadero Beach from Barranquilla, taking 2 hours, and costing US$3.80. They return to Barranquilla at 1300, 1530 and 1730. Santa Marta's bus terminal is on the edge of the town; there are colectivos to the centre.

Santa Marta, with a population of 150,000, lies on a deep bay with high shelving cliffs. There is safe anchorage in the bay (minimum depth of 7½ metres), and vessels come alongside the wharf. Over 9 million banana stems a year are exported from the base of the Sierra Nevada. The climate ranges seasonally from hot and trying to pleasant in February and March, but the heat-stricken townsman has only to lift his eyes to see snow-clad peaks to the E, less than 50 km. away and 5,800 metres high.

Its sandy beaches stretch from the Simón Bolívar airport to Punta Aguja across the Rodadero de Gaira, the little fishing villages of Taganga and Villa Concha, surrounded by meadows and shady trees. A jutting rock—the Punta de Betín—rises from the sea in front of the city and is topped by a lighthouse. Altogether, Santa Marta is the most popular Colombian seaside resort, and its popularity will increase with the imminent completion of the new Caribbean Coast Highway to the Venezuelan border. Rodadero Bay is the most fashionable and tourist-oriented part of Santa Marta, though it lies at some distance from the town. There is a bus service which connects it with Santa Marta, and many of the buses coming from Barranquilla and Cartagena stop at Rodadero on the way to Santa Marta.

Santa Marta was the first town founded (1525) by the conquistadores in Colombia. Founder: Rodrigo de las Bastidas. Most of the famous sea-dogs—the brothers Côte, Drake and Hawkins—sacked the town in spite of the two forts built on a small island at the entrance to the bay, and it was to this city that Simón Bolívar, his dream of a Great Colombia shattered, came to die. Almost penniless he was given hospitality at the hacienda of San Pedro Alejandrino, 5 km. to the SE. He died at one o'clock in the afternoon of December 17, 1830, at the age of 47. He was buried in the Cathedral, but his body was taken to the Panteón at Caracas 12 years later. The simple room in which he died and his few pathetic belongings can be seen today: there is a bus service from Santa Marta to the hacienda. The road goes on for about 32 km. through the forest which covers the lower slopes and past coffee plantations into the Sierra Nevada. There are Indian villages in the mountains, but the trails to them are long and arduous, and intruders are sometimes fiercely resented (see next page).

Hotels In town: *Tairona; Park,* old fashioned but good, on sea front, US$8 d; *Marlindo; Miami; Sierra Nevada; Somballón,* US$5 d, with bath, meals good and cheap; *Corona,* US$4 d, with bath, Italian-owned, food above average but also quite expensive, noisy; *Gran Hotel,* decent service, reasonable; *Bucanero,* Calle 22, US$2 s; *Residencias Medellín,* Calle 23 and Carrera 1, US$7 d, with bath, rooms overlook the sea and there is a cool patio; two blocks from the beach is *Residencia Ile de France,* US$4 each, with private shower, good meals, recommended; *Residencias Aurora,* Carrera 9A, No. 14-08, US$3 d; *Geira,* US$3 d; *Residencias Turísta,* US$5 d, highly recommended; *Yuldama,* US$8 d, clean; *Residencias El Prado,* US$2.25, Carrera 2A, No. 22-60, recommended as very friendly, clean, with showers, meals US$1.50, very good; *Residencia Yarima,* US$2, friendly, close to the beach, clean but no hot water; *Residencias Bugarica,* US$2.50 s, not recommended. At Rodadero Bay: *Tamacá* (best, US$15 s); *Hotel Irotama* (between airport and Rodadero Bay; has bungalows); *Hotel Saratoga; Zulia; Titimar,* Calle 29 and Carrera 1A; *Yarumar,* Carrera 1A, No. 26-61 (serves breakfast, and has parking space), warmly recommended, very quiet, US$5 d, reasonable restaurant nearby; *La Sierra,* US$10 s, good and relatively inexpensive restaurant; *La Riviera,* US$7 s (US$10 with food), US$10 d (US$15); accommodation in *Palacio de las Frutas,* a small café on waterfront, US$1 p.p., clean and safe; *San Francisco* and *Iberia,* US$3 s; *Hotel Valladolid,* US$5 d; *Puerto Galleón; Santa Mar.*

Motels *Rodadero; Taboga* (new); and *Lilium,* secure parking.

Restaurants *Grill Venecia,* in roof garden of Posiheuica building, facing the bay; the *Pan American,* on the beach walk, is pleasant; good food and service; *El Gran Manolo,* excellent, cheap fish restaurant next to *Hotel Yarimar.* At the Rodadero: *La Bella Napolés,* first class; *Cumbeiros,* one block from *Hotel Lilium; Porto Fino,* three blocks from *Tamacá,* good food, not too expensive; *Restaurante Karey,* highly recommended. *El Portón* and *La Brasa,* inexpensive and good for fish. *El Nuevo Chopsuey,* Chinese and sea food, clean and good, reasonable. *Restaurante Pekin,* Calle 22, between Carreras 4 and 5, good value. *Ley* department store on Carrera 5 has cheap cafeteria.

Sightseeing Tours in air-conditioned jeeps run by Airline travel agency at centre. Launches leave Rodadero beach every hour for the Aquarium and the closest safe view you can get of hammerhead sharks, US$1.50.

Airport Simón Bolívar, 20 km. from city.

Port It can take up to 4 working days to get a car out of the port, but it is usually well guarded and it is unlikely that anything will be stolen.

Royal Mail Lines Agents E. L. Gerlein & Co. S.A., Edificio Posiheuica, Calle 11 1-C-29; Aptdo. Aéreo 752.

Bank Change money at the Banco de la República, on Carrera 5; open 0800-1100 and 1400-1530.

Warning Do not stray beyond the railway, as the shanty town on the other side is very dangerous.

The Sierra Nevada, covering a triangular area of 16,000 sq. km., rises abruptly from the sea, as it does on the N side, or from lowlands which nowhere reach over 300 metres above sea-level. "Indeed, the north slope is one of the most striking anywhere, lifting from the Caribbean to 5,800 metres snow peaks in about 45 km., a gradient comparable with the south face of the Himalaya, and unequalled along the world's coasts. The interior is made up of some eight E-W ranges with their intervening valleys. . . . The lower parts of these interior valleys are flanked by forests—the homes of primitive Indians as well as of pumas, jaguars, and a variety of snakes and birds—but for the most part the Sierra is almost lunar in its sterile grandeur, bleak *páramos* leading to naked crag and scree and glacier, where only an occasional questing condor moves. In the rock heart of the area are a large number of small, beautiful lakes, many in cirques."—Frank F. Cunningham, in an excellent illustrated article on exploring the Sierra in *The Geographical Magazine.*

It is difficult to visit the Sierra Nevada and it is advisable to obtain a safe-conduct pass from the Casa Indigena and the police in Valledupar; before doing so. From Valledupar there are jeeps to Puerto Bello (US$0.80). Hans Naeder, who can be found at the "Central de Combustibles" in the centre of Valledupar, drives a jeep to Puerto Bello and on to San Sebastián de Rabago. This is the central village of one of the four tribes of Indians living in the Sierra, the Arhuacos. It is set in beautiful surroundings and is the epitome of an Indian village, as yet unspoilt by tourism. Mr.

Naeder also arranges trips further into the Sierra. The Indians of the Sierra distrust strangers and do not take kindly to being photographed, especially without permission. However they like to be given sea-shells which can be ground into powder and mixed with cocoa leaves and such a gift may improve their reaction to strangers and cameras. Those interested in the Arhuaco culture should seek out Celso Domingo, a dentist in Puerto Bello, himself an Arhuaco. At Puerto Bello there is *El Hogar de Mani* (US$2.20 p.p., full board, very clean).

The Tairona national park, 35 km. from Santa Marta in the Riohacha direction, wild woodland on the coast, is beautiful and unspoilt. Take a Maicao or Riohacha bus to the park entrance (US$0.30), then walk or hitch 5 km. to beach at Cañaveral. Alternatively, there is a bus at 0930 from *Hotel Zulia* in Santa Marta, direct to Cañaveral, US$1.80 return. Bathing not good as the tides are treacherous, and the place is not without thieves, but a most attractive spot for camping. Relics of ancient Tairona culture abound. A taxi there and back from Santa Marta costs US$12. A guided tour round the "Pueblito" archaeological site costs US$6 for the 6 hours involved.

The banana plantations can best be visited from the town of **Sevilla** (56 km. from Santa Marta), on the railway S between Ciénaga and Fundación.

Riohacha, capital of Guajira Department, 160 km. E of Santa Marta, is a small port of 20,000 people at the mouth of the Río César—low white houses, sandy streets, no trees or hills. It was founded in 1545 by Nicolás Federmann, and for some time its pearling industry was large enough to tempt Drake to sack it (1596). Pearling almost ceased during the 18th century and the town was all but abandoned. Its main business today is a tanning factory and the exporting of tagua, dividivi, maguey fibre, fish and contraband. Hotels: *Campestre* (state-owned); *Gimaura,* on beach, US$4 including breakfast, new; *Almirante Padilla* and *Líbano* (neither very good). *Nelly,* US$3 d, basic but convenient for bus stations which are on the edge of town. Many small restaurants along sea-front including *Europa,* German run, good food at moderate prices. There is an airport.

There is a somewhat bad and dusty dirt road from Riohacha to Bucaramanga. At La Paz (Hotel: *Turismo;* Restaurant: *La Fogata*) you join the road that leads through **Valledupar,** capital of César Department (Hotels: *Sicarase,* two-star and the only hotel to have classification; *Ocaña,* US$1.60, basic; bus from Santa Marta, 8½ hours, US$2.10) to Barranquilla and Santa Marta *via* Fundación. On to Codazzi is asphalted, but not beyond until near Bucaramanga. There is a possible overnight stay at Curumaní *(Hotel Himalaya),* or at Aguachica, just off the road. To sum up, this road (which brings you ultimately to Bogotá) is passable, but extremely dusty.

Beyond Riohacha to the E is the arid and sparsely inhabited Guajira Peninsula. The Indians here live primitively, collecting dividivi, tending goats, and fishing. They are a virile race, the only mounted nomads in South America. Anyone interested in the area and in the natives should read Gustaf Bolinder's *Indians on Horseback* (London, Dobson, 1957), or Brian Moser's *The Cocaine Eaters* (London, Longman, 1965). To visit a small part of the Peninsula you can take a pick-up truck from Riohacha (they leave twice a day from the Indian market) to Manaure for US$1.50. It is an uncomfortable 3-hour drive but offers a glimpse of the Indians. Manaure, which is known for its salt flats, has two residencias. From Manaure there are trucks to Uribia and thence to Maicao. Sometimes it is possible to get a lift to Cabo de la Vela, further round the coast, where the lagoons shelter vast flocks of flamingoes, herons and sandpipers. There is a paved road from Riohacha to Maicao near the frontier. Travellers will need a visa or tourist card to enter Venezuela; essential to get it elsewhere because the delays in Riohacha or at the frontier posts can be unconscionable and many are turned back. The Caribbean coastal highway, now mostly paved, runs direct from Santa Marta along the coast to Riohacha, and the Riohacha-Maicao road has been greatly improved. (Hotels in **Maicao:** *Residencia Gallo,* US$4 d, private bath and pool; *El Parador,* but the town has a lawless reputation and travellers are advised to avoid staying there.)

Buses (basic): Maicao-Riohacha, US$0.80; Maicao-Santa Marta, US$3; Maicao-Maracaibo, US$1.70; Maicao-Barranquilla, US$3.05. There are bus services along the new Caribbean coastal highway, and also flights Barranquilla-Maicao for about US$10. Colectivo, Maicao-Maracaibo, US$3.50.

Up The Magdalena River

There are several flights a day from Barranquilla to Bogotá, taking under an hour. Or one can go by taxi or bus to Santa Marta and there take the daily express train to Bogotá (24 hours). (There is also a daily train for Medellín.)

Passenger travel by the lofty and top-heavy paddle boats up river has now come to an end, but the adventurous traveller may still find an occasional passage by cargo paddle boat. But in general the only way of getting from one place to the other along the river is by motor boat, and this is more expensive. Insect repellants should be taken, for mosquitoes are a nuisance.

The Magdalena is wide but shallow and difficult to navigate because of surface eddies, and there are little whirlpools over submerged rocks. Away to the NE, in the morning, one can see the high snow-capped peaks of the Sierra Nevada de Santa Marta. Cargo from Cartagena, taken along the Canal de Dique, is taken aboard at Calamar (population 21,000).

At **Tenerife** Bolívar had his first victory in the Magdalena campaign. At **Zambrano,** a cattle centre 96 km. beyond Calamar, there are tobacco plantations. Population, 4,000. There is a road W to the N-S Cartagena-Medellín road, and a trail E to the oil fields at El Difícil. Near **Pinto** the river divides: the eastern branch, silted and difficult, leads to **Mompós,** an old town of 19,600 people: cattle farming and tobacco, and the scene of another victory for Bolívar: "At Mompós", he said, "my glory was born." Mompós was founded in 1537 and, thanks to its comparative isolation, preserves its colonial character more completely than any other town in Colombia—even Popayán or Tunja. Old buildings are the Casa de Gobierno, once a home of the Jesuits, and the Colegio de Pinillos. There is an oilfield here. The town is well known in Colombia for inexpensive handworked gold jewellery. Airport.

Hotels   *Central; Manjarres; Residencias La Isleña* (fair).

Most vessels go by the western arm of the loop to **Magangué,** a town of 40,800. This is the port for the savannahs of Bolívar, dealing in fruit, coffee, and dairy products. A road runs W to join the N-S Cartagena-Medellín highway. Hotel: *Mardena.*

There are cargo boats which carry passengers from Magangué to Barrancabermeja, but they are slow. To El Banco the charge is US$1.30, and the trip takes 1½ days. By motor boat the distance can be covered in 4 hours at a cost of US$3.30. The boats take 3 days to reach Puerto Berrío, and conditions aboard are basic.

Beyond Magangué, the Río San Jorge, 379 km. long, 240 km. of it navigable, comes in from the Western Cordillera. Later the Río Cauca, 1,020 km. long, comes in from the far S, having threaded its way through the gorge between the Western and Central Cordilleras. Its Caribbean end is navigable for 370 km., and it is navigable again for a distance of 245 km. in the Cauca Valley above the gorge.

At **El Banco**, 420 km. from Barranquilla (airport), the river loops join. This is an old, dirty and beautiful town of 10,000 people. Along the water front are massive stone stairways. The Andes are in the distance, a blue range on either side of the valley. Pink herons here. Blue macaws with streaming tail feathers and orange breasts flit by. There are many sandy islands in the river to complicate navigation. A difficult trail leads N of El Banco to the small town of Chimichagua (5,000 inhabitants), on the shores of the large lake of Zapatosa.

Beyond this are the small towns of Gamarra (3,700 inhabitants) and Puerto Wilches (5,600). Some 30 km. above Puerto Wilches is **Barrancabermeja**, so called because of the reddish-brown oil-stained cliffs on which it stands. With a population of 65,000, the town is an important oil centre; it is a warm, humid place with an interesting indoor market, but the oil refinery is prominent.

Puerto Berrío (airport; 12,500 inhabitants) is on the W bank 100 km. above Barrancabermeja and 756 km. from Barranquilla. The locality is one of lagoons and swamps, but the town itself has been much improved; it is the river port for Medellín and the rich Antioquia Department. A railway from Medellín runs down the slopes of the Cordillera Central and over a low pass to Puerto Berrío, where it connects with a line to Bogotá, a slow, delightful, colourful run.

Hotels at Puerto Berrío: *Hotel Magdalena,* US$3 p.p.; *Residencias El Ganardero,* US$1.50 (air-conditioned—imperative!). **Restaurant:** *Tabrona.*

It is 151 km. up river from Puerto Berrío to **La Dorada** (6,000 people) on the W bank, but only 134 km. by rail (7½ hrs.) along the W bank. (Hotels: *Departamental;* on highway to Honda, *Magdalena Motel*). This railway crosses the Magdalena by a bridge from La Dorada to **Puerto Salgar,** on the E bank, from which the Cundinamarca Railway (198 km.) goes up the slopes of the Eastern Cordillera to Bogotá. (This journey, which takes 10 hours, is described on page 452.) (The train is supposed to leave Puerto Salgar at 0750, but is often late arriving from Santa Marta.) Hotels: *Salgar; Residencia Antioquia,* US$1.20 d, with fan. The Lower Magdalena river navigation stops at La Dorada. There are rapids above, as far as Honda. Cargo is taken by railway to Honda, where it is re-embarked. The Upper Magdalena is navigable as far as Girardot.

Honda (airport) on the W bank of the river, is 32 km. upstream from La Dorada. It is a pleasant old town with many colonial houses. The streets are narrow and picturesque, and the town is surrounded by hills. El Salto de Honda (the rapids which separate the Lower from Upper Magdalena) are just below the city. Population: 21,000. Average temperature: 29°C. Altitude 230 metres. Several bridges span the Magdalena and the Guali rivers, at whose junction the town lies. In February the Magdalena rises and fishing is unusually good. People come from all over the region for the fishing and the festival of the "Subienda" as the season is called.

Hotels *Ondama* (swimming pool), recommended; *Residencias Las Mercedes,* US$4 d, with bath, clean and friendly; *Hotel Moderno,* US$1.50 d. There are about eight hotels in the town.

Restaurant *La Cascada,* overlooking river, good meal for US$1. There is a good *panadería* at the entrance. *Hotel Río Ritz* has a meal for US$1.

Buses from Bogotá by Velotax US$2.20.

From Honda as far as Ibagué there was a road in colonial days. Between the two towns lies one of the three clusters of population in the Upper Magdalena Valley. The great crops here, on the western slopes above the

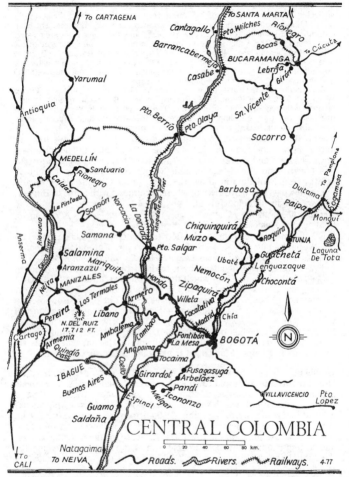

To CARTAGENA

Cantagallo   To SANTA MARTA

Pto Wilches   Rionegro

Barrancabermeja   Bocas

BUCARAMANGA   To Cúcuta

Casabe   Lebrija   Girón

Yarumal

Antioquia

Pto. Berrío   Pto. Olaya   Sn. Vicente

Socorro

MEDELLÍN   Santuario

Rionegro

Caldas

La Pintada   Sonsón   Norcacia   La Dorada   Magdalena River   Barbosa

To Pamplona

Duitama

Paipa   To Cocamaya

Samana   Chiquinquirá   Roquira   Monguí

Salamina   Muzo   TUNJA

Mariquita   Pto. Salgar   Ubaté   Guachetá   Laguna De Tota

Aranzazu   Nemocón   Lenguazaque   Chocontá

MANIZALES   Honda   Zipaquirá

Los Termales   Armero   Villeta   Facatativá

Pereira   Líbano   Madrid   Chía

N. DEL RUIZ 17.712 FT.   Ambalema   Fontibón   La Mesa   BOGOTÁ

Cartago   Armenia   Combao   Anapoima   Tocaima

Quindío Pass   Coello   Girardot   Fusagasugá   Arbeláez   VILLAVICENCIO   Pto Lopez

IBAGUÉ   Buenos Aires   Espinal   Melgar   Icononzo   Pandi

Guamo

Saldaña   **CENTRAL COLOMBIA**

0   20   40   60   80 km.

Natagaima

To CALI   To NEIVA   ~~Roads.~~ ~~Rivers.~~ ~~Railways.~~ 4-77

ROUGH SKETCH

Magdalena Valley, are coffee and cotton. Railway passenger services from Honda have been discontinued.

Excursion from **Honda** A paved road, with buses, goes W 21 km. to **Mariquita** (13,000 people; *Hotel Bocaneme*), the centre of a fruit-growing country—good quality pineapples, mangoes, papayas and coconuts. The road runs through a valley where, to the left, erosion has created an odd fantasy of rocks. On the way is the clean and nicely arranged bathing pool of El Diamante. On again is the Club

Deportivo: private, but visitors are welcome to its swimming pool, a blessing in this climate. There is another, El Virrey, in Mariquita. The town has several old houses and buildings: a mint, a viceroy's house, the parish church. Here José Celestino Mutis lived for 8 years during his famous Botanic Expedition towards the end of the 18th century (when he and his helpers accumulated a herbarium of 20,000 plants, a vast library, and a rich collection of botanical plates and paintings of native fauna), but the house in which he lived has been destroyed. The collection was sent to Madrid, where it still is. Mariquita was founded in 1551, and it was here that the founder of Bogotá, Jiménez de Quesada, died in 1579. From Mariquita a road runs W up the slopes of the Central Cordillera to Manizales.

Motel *Las Acacias.* Outside Mariquita, on the Armero road.

Fresno, in the heart of a big coffee growing area, is 30 km. from Mariquita. Bus to Manizales US$1.50 (Rápido Tolima).

From Honda the road turns S to (32 km.) **Armero** (7,500 inhabitants), a cotton growing centre. (Hotels: *San Lorenzo; Bundima; Astoria*). A branch road runs 35 km. W to **Líbano,** 29,000 inhabitants. (Hotels: *Cumanday; Rex.* Coffee is the great crop here, with potatoes in the uplands. Away to the W looms the snowy peak of Nevado del Ruiz (5,486 metres)—see page 468, the second highest in the Cordillera Central; it can be visited from Líbano by catching the 0500 Libano-Manizales bus and asking to be set down at the right spot—about 3 hours. Bus from Líbano to Ibagué, US$1.30, four hours.

From Armero the railway and a branch road run down to the Magdalena past Cambao to **Ambalema** (Hotels: *Barcelona; Nariño*). (At Cambao the river is crossed for the road to Bogotá.) The railway runs SW about 90 km. to Buenos Aires station, on the Giradot-Ibagué line. The main road from Armero goes direct for 88 km. through some small towns to Ibagué.

Ibagué, capital of Tolima Department, is quite a large town (200,000 inhabitants), lying at the foot of the Quindío mountains at 1,250 metres. It is cooler here (22°C) than in the valley. Parts of the town are old: the Colegio de San Simón is worth seeing, and so is the market. The town specializes in two things; hand-made leather goods (there are many good, cheap shoe shops) and a local drink called mistela. Just outside, on the Armenia road, a dirt road leads to the slopes of the Nevado del Tolima. You can ride or walk to the top from where the road ends.

Tolima is above all a musical province with an excellent Conservatory of Music at Ibagué. The National Folklore Festival is held during the last week of June. The Departments of Tolima and Huila commemorate St. John (June 24) and Sts. Peter and Paul (June 29) with bullfights, fireworks, and local music.

There is a road and a railway to Giradot, 79 km. E on the Magdalena, and both go on to Bogotá on the far side: Bogotá is 224 km. by road from Ibagué. W of Ibagué it runs over the 3,350-metre high Quindío Pass to Armenia, 105 km. from Ibagué across the Cordillera Central. The railway ends at Ibagué. The bus trip to Pereira takes four hours and costs US$1. To Cali, on Flota Magdalena pullman, 7 hours, US$3.50; ordinary buses US$1.80; Velotax US$2.60. To Bogotá, 4½ hours, US$1.50 with Velotax.

Hotels In 1977 hotels in Ibagué were quoted as charging a minimum price of US$1.50. *Ambala,* the best, Calle 1, No. 2-60, US$10.30 s; *Suiza,* US$5.70 d, but not very clean; *Raad; Lusitania; San Luis,* near Expreso Bolivariano bus station, US$1.50 d, good but noisy. *Residencia Puracé* (opposite Tolima bus station), US$1.50; *Residencia La Cordillera,* on Calle 16 between Carreras 2 and 3, US$1.50 d, very clean with good service.

Restaurant *Casino Chamaco,* with excellent, typical tamales at weekend.

Tourist Office Carrera 3, between Calles 10 and 11; helpful.

Girardot (airport) is on the Upper Magdalena. Altitude, 326 metres; population, 50,000. The climate is hot and there are heavy rains. Here the navigation of the Upper Magdalena ends; it is well worth walking across the fine steel bridge to see merchandise being loaded into the boats—coffee and hides are the main items. Large cattle fairs are held in early June and December. There is a two-storey market, at its best in early morning but nevertheless good all day, and another good market on Sunday mornings. Bogotanos come down here at weekends to warm up!

Railways   From Buenos Aires station on this line to Ambalema, Mariquita, and La Dorada. To Bogotá, 142 km., 6 hours (fare US$0.60 one way). Sunday excursions from Bogotá, US$1.50 return.

Roads   To Bogotá, 132 km., bus costs US$1.75, about 5 hours; bus to Neiva, US$1, 3½ hours; to Ibagué, 78 km.

Hotels   *El Peñón,* on site of former hacienda just outside town, fashionable bungalow complex, casino, huge pool, lake, US$22 per bungalow. *Tocarema* (air-conditioned rooms, swimming pool), good and reasonable; *Hotel Bachne,* US$10 d, large pool, excellent; *Hotel Piscina; Hotel Canala,* near bus station, comfortable and reasonable; *Residencias La Paz,* Carrera 1 d, No. 11-33; *Río; Hotel Flamingo,* near market, US$1.50 s.

Banks   Only the Banco de Bogotá in Giradot will change travellers' cheques.

Food   Beware of being overcharged at restaurants specializing in fish.

Cattle Fairs   June 5-10; December 5-10.

The third centre of population—though a small one—in the Magdalena Valley lies upstream from Giradot with Neiva as its capital. Coffee and tobacco are grown on the slopes of the Central and Eastern Cordillera here, and cattle are raised in the valley. The inhabitants are mainly mestizos and Europeans.

The road, and its short branches E and W, runs through a number of small towns of from 5,000 to 25,000. One of these, 35 km. from Giradot, is **Guamo,** with 21,000 inhabitants. The small Tetuán oilfield is 30 km. away. There is a small refinery at Guamo. Eight km. beyond Guamo is **Saldana.** There are vast irrigation works here which have made 15,000 hectares available for rice, sesame and cotton growing.

Hotel at Guamo: *Lemayá* (modern; swimming pool), best in region. At **Saldaña,** *Hotel Saldaña,* not too good.

One of the prettiest spots in Colombia is the reservoir located near **Prado,** Tolima. Turn off the Ibagué-Neiva road at Saldaña for 25 km.; it is well sign-posted. There is a dirt road for the last 12 km. past Purificación. Buses can be caught in Bogotá, Ibagué and all intermediate towns. A luxury government hotel is at the lake (US$9.50 d, US$22.50 cabin for 6-10, free camping on the shoreline, skiing US$2.50, short trip with a boat). The pretty part of the lake is hidden from the end of the road and must be seen from a boat. Swimming is good and the water is warm, but wading is not advisable because of the presence of the fresh-water stingray. Cheap hotels are available in Prado, 4 km. from the lake. There are restaurants of questionable quality in town. Excellent food can be obtained at the end of the road in the boat-dock area, but sanitation leaves something to be desired.

A little beyond the 50 kilometre stone from Neiva you can turn to the left, cross a fence, and see the "Piedra Pintada de Aipe", a stone not in fact painted but carved by Precolumbian Indians with designs akin to the shapes of the gold pieces you see in the Museo del Oro at Bogotá.

Neiva, capital of Huila Department, has a population of 110,000. It was first founded in 1539, when Benalcázar came here in quest of El Dorado across the Cordillera Central from Popayán. It was soon after destroyed by the Indians and re-founded in 1612. There are rich coffee plantations around Neiva, for here the valley bottom is high enough to be in the coffee zone. Panama hats are made in the town. The new cathedral was destroyed by earthquake in 1967. There is a large and colourful market every day. Altitude: 470 metres.

Hotels *Hostería Matamundo,* in old hacienda out of town on road to Garzón and San Agustín, US$6 s, US$10 d, a/c, swimming pool, good meals, US$2.50-7, good service; *Americano* (swimming pool); *Piscina,* US$5 d, swimming pool; *Avirama,* Calle 7, No. 2-40, US$3.65 s, US$4.85 d; *Plaza,* swimming pool, poor service, US$3.90 s, US$5.45 d; *Nader,* US$4 d, very good value; *Imperio; Pacifico; Central,* Cra. 3, No. 7-82, US$4 d, meals US$0.75 each, near market, good value. *Residencias Pacande,* near Taxis Verdes office, US$4.50 d, pleasant and clean. A number of cheap hotels is to be found off the square where the bus companies are centred. *Hospedaje Capri,* US$1.50 s; *Hotel Motorista; Las Damas; Residencias San Jorge,* basic but cheap.

Airport La Marguita, 1½ km. from city. Aeropesca and Satena fly from Bogotá.

Bus from Bogotá (331 km., paved road), US$2.50, 6 hours. Regular bus service with Autobuses Unidos del Sur and Coomotor to San Agustín, US$2.50. To Garzón, US$0.50; to Pitalito, US$1. To Pasto, US$2.60; to Popayán, US$2.30. Long-distance buses leave from Carrera 2, Calles 5 and 6.

Train It is no longer possible to go direct to Bogotá. Instead, take bus to Girardot and train from there to Bogotá. It is difficult to do the journey in a day.

Fiesta from June 18 to 28, when the Bambuco Queen is elected, with folklore, dances and feasting.

Beyond Neiva lie the plains of Huila Department, arid, but still capable of supporting cattle, and dominated by the snow-capped Nevado del Huila to the NW. The road runs S from Neiva; it passes **Garzón** (a pleasant cathedral town set in mountains with roads W across the Cordillera to Popayán and SE to Florencia, capital of the Intendencia of Caquetá, see page 450), and is paved as far as **Pitalito** (1,400 people, airport), 192 km. from Neiva, where horses and mules replace the cattle. If you hitch you'll find it fairly easy to Garzón; slower on to San Agustín, butt plenty of buses. See map of area, page 480.

Hotels at Garzón: *Damasco,* US$4.50 d; *Cecil,* near bus station, US$1.50 d, with private bath; *Arizona,* US$2 d. The *Abeyma,* a new state hotel, is recommended, US$7 d; it is possible to camp in the grounds, US$1. At Pitalito there is a *Hotel de Turismo.* There is a new hotel with swimming pool: the *Calamó,* US$8 s, no hot water; *Pigoanza,* on main square, US$2.50 s; *Hotel Pitalito,* US$0.80. *Restaurant Cando* recommended.

The way to the remarkable Tierradentro underground burials in man-made caves painted with geometrical patterns is given on page 481; they can be reached by Popayán bus from San Agustín, Pitalito or Garzón, with a change at La Plata. The cost is about US$3. The bus from La Plata leaves at 0500.

San Agustín (altitude 1,725 m.) is 40 km. from Pitalito. The first 5 km. of the road are paved, thereafter there is a good unpaved road, which is being improved; it is sometimes flooded after heavy rain. Here, in the Valley of the Statues, are some hundreds of rough hewn stone figures of men, animals and gods. They are very large and odd, with curious affinities—so the archaeologists say—with the carvings of the Tiahuanaco civilization in N Bolivia on the one hand, and the Maya relics of Central America on the other. Nothing is known of the culture which produced them, though traces of small circular bamboo straw-thatched houses have been found. Various crude sculptures found here are exhibited in the National Museum at Bogotá, and there are some life sized copies of San Agustín originals along the highway from Bogotá to its superseded Techo airport, near Fontibón. There are about 20 sites; information can be obtained from the tourist office near the bus station, or from the *Hotel Yalconia*. Free maps to the area can now only be obtained in Bogotá.

The nearest sites are the Parque Arqueológico and the Bosque Arqueológico (open from 0800-1800, entrance to both costs US$0.30), both about 4 km. from San Agustín village, 2 km. from the *Hotel Yalconia*, and less than 1 km. from the *Motel Osoguaico*. It is a steady uphill walk. The statues in the Parque are *in situ,* though they may have been set up on end and fenced in with wire; those in the Bosque (a little wood) have been moved and rearranged, and linked by gravel footpaths. Of particular interest are the carved rocks in and around the stream in the Parque, but the whole site leaves an unforgettable impression, from the strength and strangeness of the statues, and the great beauty of the rolling green landscape.

Transport   San Agustín may be reached directly from Bogotá by taxi (Taxis Verdes have one service a day, leaving at 0300, US$6.20, 10-12 hours or Taxi-Exito, US$6, will pick you up at your hotel in Bogotá, leaves at 0400) or by bus (Coomotor leaves Carrera 25, No. 15-36, three times a day, US$6). Alternatively there are frequent services to Neiva from Bogotá (US$3.50, 6 hours) as well as some to Pitalito. From Neiva there are 6 buses a day to San Agustín, taking 6 hours and costing US$2.75. Colectivo charge is US$3. The journey from Pitalito takes 1½ hours, costs US$0.42. There is an airport at Pitalito. From Popayán there are 2 through buses a day: Autobuses Unidos del Sur have a service leaving Popayán at 0400 and San Agustín at 0630. The journey takes 10 hours and costs US$7.50. A new direct highway is being built between Popayán and San Agustín, but so far only a short section has been paved. Work on the new road, which is still 7 km. short of San Agustín, can cause long delays to traffic, but new buses on this route make the journey more comfortable.

Hotels   *Yalconia,* outside town, government financed, being remodelled, US$5 s, US$8 d, swimming pool, camping allowed in grounds, bookable by phone from *Hotel Monasterio,* Popayán; *Casablanca; Hotel Central,* on Calle 3, near bus station, US$1.75 p.p., US$2.50 d, with bath, good meals, clean and friendly (not to be confused with *Residencias Central,* which is not as good); *Hotel Los Idolos,* US$0.75 a night, US$0.50 breakfast, rather noisy and only hot water in the afternoons. Both these two serve good, cheap meals for about US$0.75. There are also the *Plaza* and *Pasajeros* hotels, among others, and there is accommodation in private houses for about US$2 p.p., which is often preferable. Small boys will meet you off the bus with offers of such accommodation; they are also remarkably competent guides in many languages. Between San Agustín and the Parque Arqueológico is the *Motel Osoguaico,* simple and clean, German-run, US$4 p.p., with food, or US$8 per room (to sleep up to six), without food; sauna now built; camping site nearby, with sheltered tents available (US$1.50 for two); restaurant (good) attached. In town, particularly recommended are *Residencias Náñez,* Calle 5a, No. 14-45, US$1 p.p., hot water, friendly and clean; guests may use the kitchen; also the owners have horses for rent and will act as guides to the archaeological sites; *Residencias Luis Tello,* Calle 4a, No. 15-33, run by a teacher, very pleasant and friendly, US$1 a night, good meals, US$0.60; also *Residencias Cosmopolita,* US$1.60 p.p. and *Familia Torres,* Calle 3A no. 12-25, US$1.50 d, both recommended. *Residencias Eduardo Matto,* Calle 4, No. 15-71, has five rooms, clean, hot water, US$0.75 with coffee for breakfast; *Residencias La Gaitana,* Calle 6A, No. 14-47, clean, friendly management. About 8 km. from San Agustín there is a farm where Mr. and Mrs. René Sorensen offer accommodation for US$3 p.p., including all meals; horses may be hired at an additional charge.

There is splendid riding in the picturesque neighbourhood. The rate for hiring horses is about US$2-3 for 6 hours. (Check the horses carefully before you hire them—they do not all, for instance, have shoes.) It is cheaper to hire a horse yourself than have one brought to your hotel. Do not take a guide if you want to be free to explore the area. Alternatively, jeeps may be hired for about US$17 and about 8 people can fit in one! Jeeps, however, have difficulties on the road to Alto de los Idolos in the rainy season and ordinary vehicles should not even attempt it. The area offers excellent opportunities for hiking, although some trails to remote sites are not well marked.

The best books on the subject are *Exploraciones Arqueológicas en San Agustín,* by Luis Duque Gómez (Bogotá, 1966, 500 pages) or *San Agustín, Reseña Arqueológica,* by the same author (1963, 112 pages); a leaflet in English is obtainable from tourist offices.

The visitor with time to spare should visit Alto de los Idolos, 5 km. as the crow flies, or about 10 km. by horse or on foot, a lovely (if strenuous) walk *via* Puente de la Chaquira, but 27 km. by road *via* San José village (to which a bus can be taken) well signposted. Here on a hill overlooking San Agustín, are more and different statues known as *"vigilantes",* each guarding a burial mound (one is an unusual rat totem). The few excavated have disclosed large stone sarcophagi, some covered by stone slabs bearing a sculpted likeness of the inmate. The whole area, including Alto de los Idolos, is called San Agustín. It needs 1½ days by vehicle and on horseback to see the most important sites, though much can be seen in the Parque and Bosque in three hours. Alto de las Piedras, 5 km. from San José, has a few interesting tombs and monoliths. There is a museum in the Parque (US$0.30) and the director of the Parque (Don Guillermo Guerrero) will arrange transport and guide to outlying sites. Only less remarkable than the statues are the orchids growing nearby. A new government-financed hotel has been built at Alto de los Idolos. From San Agustín the Bordones waterfalls can be visited; best with a car, though from Alto de las Piedras you can catch a bus to Bordones and Pitalito.

Sunday is market day in both San Agustín and San José (Hotel in San José: *Hospedaje Nueva,* US$0.65). There is a fiesta on 18 July, Santa María del Carmen, in San Agustín.

Local food has improved greatly; eggs, meat and vegetables plentiful. Chicken rôtisserie, *La Diosa de Oro,* in middle of San Agustín; *Restaurante Brahama,* good vegetarian meals for US$1 for comida including soup and drink. Bring lots of film. Rainy season June-Sept., but it rains somewhat during most of the year, hence the beautiful green landscape; the driest months are Dec.-Feb. The days are warm but sweaters are needed in the evenings. It has been recommended for travellers to change money before arriving in San Agustín as the exchange rate can vary and is particularly bad for travellers' cheques. Leather goods are beautiful and priced reasonably. Many local shops make boots to your own design for under US$20; *Calzado Líder* has been recommended.

Caquetá

Lying to the E of the Cordillera Oriental is the Intendencia of Caquetá, reached by air, or by road from Neiva or Garzón. This region, although sparsely populated (total pop. about 300,000) is an area of intensive settlement. The population has trebled in the last twelve years; people have been moving down from the highlands since the turn of the century, but especially in the last 12-20 years, to turn the area into a productive agricultural region. The natural forest cover around Florencia, the capital of the Intendencia, has been cleared and for a radius of 10-15 km. lie well-established, undulating pasturelands, dotted with tall palms—the fruits of which are a delicacy for grazing cattle.

The major activity in the region is cattle-farming (mainly Zebu or Zebu-cross cattle) and the vitality and dynamism of life on a new frontier may be seen and felt all over western Caquetá. To the SE, beyond the cleared lands, lie little-touched expanses of tropical forest inhabited by indigenous tribes and wide varieties of Amazonian flora and fauna.

The road Neiva-Florencia is 260 km.—possible in one day, but it is recommended that travellers should try to complete the last 100 km. into Florencia over the mountains by daylight.

From the Garzón-San Agustín road, the only route, for vehicles, into Caquetá branches off at Altamira. Here the surfaced road ends and is replaced by a single-track dirt road which winds up over the Cordillera utilizing all available slopes for a fairly gentle gradient.

The road was originally engineered in 1932 during the Leticia dispute between Colombia and Peru, when the strategic importance of the Amazon lowlands was realized. Then, mules hauled cannon over the route but today cattle trucks come up loaded from Florencia and return either empty or loaded with temperate crops, grains or beer.

The climb up over the mountains passes through a region of small farms (some of their cultivated fields appear to be on almost vertical valley sides), through sugar-cane cultivation and up into cloud at the higher points of the route. Here there is rain-forest, sporadically cleared for farms.

Soon after the summit, and on a clear day, there are extensive views out over Caquetá and then the road winds down through substantial forests—ablaze with the colours of tropical flowers in the dry season (Jan.-March) and into the lowlands. The lower section of the road into the lowlands is prone to frequent landslides (or *derrumbes*) because of weaker geological structures.

The roads in Caquetá run from Florencia along the foothills of the Cordillera; eventually a road is planned to run from Puerto Asís, through Florencia, to Villavicencio, forming a *Carretera Marginal* along the eastern Andes. Other routes are difficult and seasonal (although tracks, or *trochas*, are being laid out as part of the settlement scheme, financed by the World Bank) and the main lines of communication into the lowlands are by boat along the rivers Caquetá and Guayas, and their tributaries.

Florencia (pop. 40,000) is the capital of the region and the centre for settlement in Caquetá. Originally established in 1908 when 37 settlers built their houses according to a plan made by Fray Fidel de Montclar, the town is today spreading out from the central square along the main roads. The square is modern, containing sculptures, fountains and also a large forest tree (saba) and flower beds. In the town jeeps, trucks, mules and carts and horses outnumber cars (when the road to Garzón is obstructed by landslides, petrol supplies are limited).

Hotels   There are a number; those located around the central square are reputed to be more salubrious, and charge about US$1.50 per night.

Cafés, Restaurants   Plenty, but prices tend to be high because much food is brought in by truck from outside the region.

Car parking   Overnight, cars are best left in the care of the fire-station (US$0.20 a night).

Buses   There are regular services from Neiva (US$3, 7 hours), Garzón and Altamira to Florencia and frequent services as far as Puerto Rico and Belén. Bus to Bogotá costs US$5.20.

Air Services Albania or San José airlines—internal flights about 2/3 times a week to Puerto Asís, Leguizano, Neiva and Bogotá.

Fiesta The local Saint's day is on July 16, when there is a candlelight procession in the evening around the town. The statue of the Virgin is held shoulder-high and followed by the Church choir, brass bands, the police force, townspeople and finally a line of taxis, jeeps and trucks all honking their horns.

Travellers Cheques Cash cheques at the Banco de la República.

Excursions From Florencia down the Orteguaza river can be made by taking a morning bus to Puerto Lara and thence by motorized dugout to San Antonio (US$1.25, 4-5 hours) where there is a cheap hotel and from where you can visit Indian villages.

From Florencia the road runs as far as Puerto Rico: it is paved for 34 km. as far as La Montanita and then unsurfaced, passing through:

El Paujil (2,700 pop.) where the residencias are unnamed and are situated alongside the road into the town. A dry-weather road runs from here for 21 km. towards Cartagena before giving way to a mule track.

El Doncello (5,406) a very pleasant town, overlooked by the church which has a brightly painted steeple. The *Residencias Americanas* is highly recommended, and costing only US0.90 per night. On Sundays, people travel into the town for many miles around for the market.

Esmeralda is a small settlement located at a deep ford. The ford is too deep for cars, although trucks and buses may cross, and there is a wooden suspension bridge over the river for which the toll is US$0.20. The hotel there provides a very plain but excellently cooked breakfast.

Puerto Rico (4,853) is at the end of the road—which is interrupted by the River Guayas. It is possible to cross the river by ferry (US$0.08) and travel by bus as far as San Vicente where a mule-track goes over the Cordillera to Algeciras in Huila Department, and carries some produce. Puerto Rico is a river port, and the whole town is based around the junction of road and river. River ferries travel downstream to Río Negro (1½ hours) and Cartagena (4½ hours). Houses built down by the river are raised on stilts above possible flood levels. River boats are made and repaired by the riverside.

Hotels and residencias are full on Saturday nights—book a room early in the day. *El Gran Hotel,* despite its name, provides basic amenities. *Hotel Almacén* is the only place in Puerto Rico serving fresh fruit juices.

The road from Florencia to San José is unsurfaced. At Moralia (709) there is a poor branch road S to the River Pescado, where a ferry will take you upstream and across the river to the town of Valparaíso (1,158), which is quite new and has an electricity supply and lighting until 2200. *Hotel Ceilán* is cheap and friendly; there is also the *Hotel Turista*. From Valparaíso mule tracks go further into the lowlands. If travelling to Valparaíso by car, make sure it is left well away from the river when catching the ferry as, during times of flood, the river may rise rapidly overnight!

Moralia-Belén de los Andes is an unsurfaced road, passing through some very interesting scenery, and crossing very clean, fast-flowing rivers by metal bridges. For some reason prices are higher in **Belén** (2,190) than in other towns in Caquetá. Hotels fill up very quickly, and mosquito nets are not always provided, although they are needed! In the area are a group of co-operative farms, and an oil palm plantation.

From Belén an unsurfaced road runs to Albania (1,056) which is a small, frontier settlement with only one hotel. A semi-surfaced road runs from here for 11 km. further towards the new areas of settlement.

Anyone wanting to look at wildlife in Caquetá is recommended to travel beyond the settlement area. Toucans, monkeys, macaws etc. are kept as pets by settlers, but there is little wild-life. Boats and canoes are easily hired, but horses and mules are more difficult, especially in the dry season when they are needed to transport the harvest.

Routes from the Magdalena to Bogotá

Even at Puerto Salgar, some 970 km. up the river, the altitude is only 150 metres. And Bogotá, only 190 km. or so up the western slopes of the

Eastern Cordillera, is at 2,640 metres. Bogotá, as we have already seen, can be reached from the river in several ways: from Puerto Salgar by railway; from Honda or from Cambao by road; and from Girardot by a railway and three roads. The slopes traversed by these routes are deeply broken and indented. On them, planting coffee and staple crops for the most part, live the people who make up the third cluster of population in the Magdalena valley area.

From Puerto Salgar to Bogotá, by railway, 198 km.; the line is a narrow-gauge and often sharply-curved single track. From the river it passes through wooded ravines, with palm trees growing to the summits, the black Río Negro plunging amongst the rocks below. The climb goes on, through tall woods with glimpses of precipice and gorge, until **Villeta** (84 km.; 9,500 inhabitants), which has become a popular weekend resort for the Bogotanos, is reached. Not far way are the waterfalls of Quebrada Cune. The road from Honda joins the railway route at Villeta. Hotels: *Pacífico* and *Mediterráneo* (both have swimming pools and are expensive).

Beyond, the climb continues. At the stations muffled women sell fruit and cooked chicken wrapped in banana leaf. Above the woods are barren upland meadows, sloping sharply from ridges of naked rock, and suddenly the train is over the top and making a short descent to the flat land of the plateau or Sabana of Bogotá. And over the top, 71 km. beyond Villeta, is **Facatativá,** a town of 22,000 people, 40 km. from Bogotá. Facatativá is the junction of the Cundinamarca railway we have been travelling from Puerto Salgar, and the Girardot railway from Girardot. The road from Cambao joins the railway route just before Facatativá, and a road from Girardot at Facatativá. Some 3 km. from Facatativá, on the road to the W, are the "Piedras de Tunja", a natural rock amphitheatre of enormous stones; it has numerous Indian pictographs, some geometrical, some zoomorphic, and has now been established as a park with an artificial lake.

From Facatativá to Bogotá the flat green plain is dotted with white farms and groves of eucalyptus. The line—and the accompanying Cambao road—pass through two small towns, **Madrid** and **Fontibón,** as they approach Bogotá, built at the far end of the plateau, under encircling mountains, and for that reason, wetter than the rest of the Sabana. Fontibón, 10 km. from Bogotá, has a good colonial church. (Visitors who have no time to visit San Agustín should know that along the road to Bogotá from the old airport at Techo, near Fontibón, are replicas of some of the San Agustín statues.)

The Simón Bolívar Highway also runs from Girardot to Bogotá, coming all the way from distant Ecuador up the Cauca Valley and over the Quindío Pass in the Cordillera Central. The 132-km. stretch between Girardot and Bogotá is extremely picturesque; it runs up the mountains through **Melgar,** a popular weekending place for Bogotanos who like a little warmth. (There are lots of hotels in the area most of which have swimming pools. It is best to try whichever you like the look of and move on to another if it is full. The *Esmeralda* and *Guadaira* have been recommended), the charming town of Fusagasugá, and within 5 km. of the Falls of Tequendama.

Fusagasugá is 16 km. beyond, in a rich wooded valley famous for its fruits. A few miles before we reach it is the *Hotel Catama*. Fusagasugá is noted for its good climate and Sunday market. Population: 22,000, with an admixture of the wealthier families from Bogotá during the summer. A visit should be paid to the Jardín Luxemburgo for its splendid orchids, best flowering Nov.-Feb. There are bathing spots on the Sumapaz river. Altitude: 1,740 metres. Hotels: *La Scala,* US$2 p.p., recommended; *Sabaneta; Manila; Castillo,* US$6 d, recommended. There are many luxury hotels on the road to Melgar.

Another road, not as good as the above, runs from Girardot to Bogotá. It goes through Tocaima, Triunfo, Mesitas del Colegio and Santandercito, and is paved as far as Tocaima; 40 km. beyond Sibate, a 5-km. branch road runs to the **Salto de Tequendama,** where the water of the Río Bogotá or Funza river used to fall 132 metres over the lip of the Sabana; the river is dried up for much of the year, and the water is rather dirty with sewage. The site is 31 km. from Bogotá in an amphitheatre of forest-clad hill sloping to the edge of a rock-walled gorge. There is a good bus service from Bogotá.

The Llanos

A 110-km. road runs from Bogotá to **Villavicencio,** capital of Meta Department in the Llanos at the foot of the eastern slopes of the Eastern Cordillera. Population: 65,000. A good centre for visiting the best Llanos and jungles stretching 800 km. E as far as **Puerto Carreño** (1,461 inhabitants), on the Orinoco, with Venezuela across the river. Cattle raising is the great industry on the plains, sparsely inhabited by a mestizo-cross of warlike Indians and Spaniards. Rice is now grown near Villavicencio and milled there for transport to Bogotá. Most of the foodstuffs grown in the region—rice, maize, plantains, yuca, coffee and beans—are dearer in Villavicencio than in Bogotá. Altitude: 498 metres.

Airport Flights to Miraflores and Mitú for those who want to see "uncommercialized" jungle. Taxi to town, US$1.10.

Buses La Macarena and Bolivariano run from Bogotá, US$1.35, 3½ hours; alternatively there are colectivos (e.g. Velotax) for US$2.30.

Hotels *Los Llanos,* out of town, swimming pool, quite expensive; *Inambú,* central, recommended; *Serranía; Savoy,* clean; *Europa; Residencias Nuevas,* US$1.10 each, adequate. Several cheap restaurants, including one Chinese, in town; others on the road to Puerto López, with swimming pools.

A road has been built E to **Puerto López** (Hotel: *Aves Raris,* clean, each room with bath, no board, excellent, German run), on the Meta river, a port of call for large river steamers, and another S to Acacias and San Juan (airport).

The road S is surfaced as far as San Martín. It runs on to **Granada** (*Hotel Yali; Tio Pepe Motel,* very clean) and from there deteriorates rapidly. **Vistahermosa,** situated near the break-point between the Llanos/savana and the jungle/selva, lies further S along this road (*Residencias Royal* is cheap and comfortable). It is a good place from which to visit the Sierra de la Macarena, a Tertiary outcrop 150 km. long by 35 km. broad. Its vegetation is so remarkable that the Sierra has been designated a national park exclusively for scientific study. The Inderena office in Vistahermosa will advise you on trips to the Sierra. For the energetic, a worthwhile trip is to the Sardinata or Cañones falls. Both can be reached from Maracaibo, which is a day's walk from Vistahermosa.

To the SE of Villavicencio, along the river Vaupés, and near the border with Brazil is **Mutú.** This can be reached by 'plane from Villavicencio and Bagotá. On arrival in the town you must fill in an "entry card" at the police station. Several anthropological studies are being carried out in the Mitú area and from the town trips can be made to Indian villages. The cost of a trip down river to visit an Indian village where you stay overnight is approximately US$10, plus the cost of the petrol used by the boat. Take your own food. The proprietor of Senor León's hotel in Mitú will help you arrange such a trip. The hotel charges US$2 a night, and has the only restaurant in town, meals about US$1 each. Good local buys are baskets and bark paintings.

The following note is to be found on the Esso Colombiana road map: "In the dry season it is possible to drive E and S from Puerto López by good, though unpaved, roads. The Llanos are flat, with solid ground covered by grass; with the help of a guide one can leave the road and drive through vast areas of great beauty." Plenty of reserve gasoline should be carried when travelling in the Llanos, as there are few service stations.

You can get a good away-from-it-all holiday in Llanos. Take food with you, unless you can live by gun and rod. Everybody lets you hang up your hammock or pitch your tent, but mosquito nets are a must. "Roads" are only tracks left by previous vehicles but easy from late December till early April and the very devil during the rest of the year. More information on the Llanos and particularly the Macarena national park can be obtained from the office of the Gobernación del Departmento de Meta, Calle 34 with Carrera 14, Bogotá.

Leticia, 3,200 km. up the Amazon on the frontier with Peru and near the Brazilian border, which has recently grown from a small settlement into a community of some 15,000, is now becoming a clean and progressive town with some small industries and a modern airport. There is also a modern, well equipped hospital. The average tourist could hardly hope to get closer to the jungle than here, though prices have soared as the town has become increasingly important as a tourist centre. A delightfully indiscriminate mixture of Spanish and Portuguese is spoken, and the main occupation is coca smuggling. Anyone adventurous who has the time should make the trip. The best time to visit the area is in July or August, the early months of the dry season. The *Parador Ticuna,* opened in 1969, has 13 apartments (all with bathrooms which have hot and cold running water) which can each sleep up to 6; six more apartments are being built. The hotel has a swimming pool, bar and restaurant and a zoo of local animals. Prices: US$15 s, US$20 d and US$5 for each extra person. In 1975, the owner of the *Ticuna,* Mr. Mike Tsalickis, opened the *Parador Yaguas* in Leticia, and the *Jungle Lodge,* on Monkey Island, an hour's boat ride from Leticia. Cheaper accommodation: *Pensión Caño,* US$4 s, without food; *Residencias Monserrate,* US$1.50 per day without food; *Residencias La Manigua,* comfortable cheap rooms. *Hotel Anaconda,* some a/c, pleasant, helpful, no hot water, US$11 s; there is a restaurant which serves good steaks for US$1.80; swimming pool; *Hotel Alemanas,* US$5 d, German-run, clean; *Residencias Amazonas,* US$3 including 3 good meals; *Residencia Pullman,* US$2 each for a triple room or US$1 to sling your own hammock; *Residencial Quina,* US$2 d; *Tacana,* US$3.50 s, possible to sling your hammock for US$1, not recommended; *Pensión Leticia,* US1.50 s, friendly, clean, good cheap meals, use of kitchen; *Hotel San Francisco,* US$3.50 d, friendly, English spoken. (The only place that boils water is the *Parador Ticuna.*) *La Cabana* restaurant, reasonable food at less than US$2 a meal; *Cafe La Barra* serves beer, wine, and a limited range of mainly Spanish food. *Restaurante Río Grande* serves excellent steaks. The campsite also has a good restaurant. Although there are organized sightseeing tours, they are reported to be a "racket". If you choose to go on one do not accept the first price and check that the supplies and equipment are sufficient for the time you will be away. It is cheaper and better to find yourself a local guide. About 3½ km. upstream from Leticia three lakes open into the river. You can hire a dug-out for about US$3 a day. Motorboats cost much more, of course. Turamazonas, run by Mr. Mike Tsalickis, offers a wide range of tours; provisions and bedding for overnight safaris are supplied by the agency, whose staff are all expert. Turamazonas tours are not cheap, however. For a cheaper, less tourist-oriented excursion, ask for Alberto near the docks. A small airline, ATA, offers flights in a Cessna 'plane at reasonable rates. An interesting walk is to Marcos, in Brazil: walk to the end of the road in which the *Parador Ticuna* is located; where it becomes a dirt track take the first turn left. Leticia is a good place to buy typical products of Amazon Indians. There are good telephone and telegram communications with Bogotá and the rest of the world. The "cambio" next to the *Anaconda Hotel* has good exchange rates for cruzeiros and soles, but the rate for dollars in Leticia generally is not as good as in Bogotá. The town's small zoo and open-air lido are worth visiting.

A cheap, good way of seeing the Amazon and jungle is to seek out Roy Johnson, an American who exports tropical fish. He can arrange a trip upriver with a fisherman for 6 to 8 hours to the house of Sra. Doli. Basic food and lodging are available at reasonable prices. Both river and jungle excursions are possible (sleeping gear, mosquito nets, canned food and Spanish all help, though none is indispensable). When going upstream remember that the slower and dirtier the boat, the more mosquitoes you will get. (You can swim in the Amazon and its tributaries, but do not dive; this disturbs the fish. Also do not swim at sunrise or sunset when the fish are more active, nor when the water is shallow in the dry season, nor if you have a wound, however slight, which might open up and bleed.)

Avianca flies to Leticia from Bogotá on Mon., Wed. and Sat. for US$60; Aerotal has two flights a week, US$29 Bogotá to Leticia, but they try and charge US$34 Leticia to Bogotá from Leticia. Satena has an early flight on Thursdays at 0630 for US$26.50; it is possible to return to Bogotá by freight plane, which is much cheaper but you have to sit with the cargo, often fish. SAM flies to Leticia from Cali. Cruzeiro do Sul flies Manaus-Leticia-Iquitos and back on Wed., Fri. and Sun. (there is a connection on Wed. for Pucallpa from Iquitos): fare from Leticia to Iquitos US$30; Manaus-Leticia, US$70. TANS, the Peruvian military jungle airline, usually offers flights between Iquitos and Ramón Castilla for about US$20, but you must book well in advance and make sure of getting to the airport well ahead of the flight time. These flights are on Fridays and Sundays. It is also possible to get a seat on a Petrobrás (Brazilian oil company) plane to Manaus. This leaves every Friday, and can be arranged with the crew, who stay at the *Anaconda Hotel*. A letter of recommendation helps. The airport tax for international flights is US$10.

The cheapest way to get to Leticia is by bus to Puerto Asís, and then by boat (see **page 485**). There are ferries from Leticia to Benjamín Constant, Brazil (US$2) and boats down to Manaus take passengers for US$36. Departure times are uncertain, and the boats tend to be overcrowded. The trip takes at least 4½ days. Going downstream, try to avoid a long stop at Benjamín Constant; buy everything you will need in Leticia as prices are higher in Brazil. Boats to Ramón Castilla cost US$5. There are irregular sailings for Iquitos on the "Huallacha", cost US$40. Food is provided but is not recommended. Remember to get your passport stamped by the DAS office before you leave.

It is reported that for travellers interested in Amazonian wild life the Putumayo is more accessible than Leticia; it is best reached from Pasto (see page 484).

Chía-Zipaquirá-Chiquinquirá

An interesting trip from Bogotá by road or railway can be made to the salt mine of Zipaquirá and to the large centre of population around Chiquinquirá to the N of Bogotá. Bogotá is left by an autopista, a northern extension of Avenida Caracas and Avenida 13. The autopista ends after 24 km. at an intersection where a road leads off left at a right-angle for Chía and Zipaquirá. Taking this road you soon come to a fork which takes you left to Chía and right to Zipaquirá. At the beginning of the road to Zipaquirá is the Arrieros Restaurant, where Antioqueño food is served by waiters in the appropriate dress and Antioqueño music is sometimes played.

Chía has a gracious Colonial bridge and a typical Sunday market. An autopista is being built direct from Chía to Facatativá, by-passing Bogotá. Near Chía is Terijo, whose metalworks is famous. On the way there you pass through Fonqueta where simple tapestries are made.

From Chía to **Zipaquirá** (29,880 people), centre of a rich cattle farming district, and famous for its rock salt mine, which has enough salt to last the world 100 years, though it has been exploited for centuries. The church in the central plaza is also worth a visit for its stonework.

The immense black galleries of salt gleaming under electric lights are most impressive and a little eerie. A road has been opened into the galleries but because of damage cars are no longer allowed to drive in. You can walk its whole length in 15 minutes. An underground cathedral dedicated in 1954 to Our Lady of the Rosary (patron saint of miners) is about 4 minutes on foot from the entrance and surprisingly impressive. The roof is 23 metres above the floor and the main altar table is a block of salt weighing 18 tons. It took ten years to complete. Entry (adults US$0.15, children US$0.05, more for car) is on a hill, which is a good walk from the Plaza. It closes to the public at 1630. There are free concerts in the cathedral on Sunday mornings. The acoustic effects are striking. Many buses from Avenida Caracas, Bogotá, US$0.80 return, an hour each way. Tours are also arranged by some of the Bogotá hotels and cost about US$6.

The *Hosteria del Libertador,* near the mines, was refurbished in 1975 and now costs US$6.30 s, US$8.70 d, good food.

These salt deposits, mined by the Banco de la República, provide raw material for a large soda plant run by the Instituto de Fomento Industrial at the village of Betania: the salt is taken there in solution by a pipeline. *Pensión Respin.*

Ubaté is 48 km. by road to the N. Here a branch runs E to Lenguazaque (6,000 people). Close by, at Chirbaneque, is a worked-out emerald mine in lovely scenery. A spur from this road branches left to **Guachetá,** 21 km. from Ubaté, and slightly larger than Lenguazaque. Nearby is the Laguna de Fúquene (Devil's Lake, hotel), about 4,000 hectares of water with four cultivated islands.

Chiquinquirá, 30,000 people, 146 km. by rail from Bogotá, is on the W bank of the Suárez river at 2,550 metres. It is a busy commercial centre and the focus of a large coffee and cattle region. In December thousands of pilgrims honour a painting of the Virgin whose fading colours were restored by the prayers of a woman. In 1816, when the town had enjoyed six years of independence and was besieged by the Royalists, this painting was carried through the streets by Dominican priests from the famous monastery, to rally the people. The town fell, all the same.

Hotels *Sarabita; El Escorial,* splendid meals, US$2; El Dorado, US$2.50.

In the shops of Chiquinquirá are displayed the toys made by Indians, pottery horses from Raquirá, some painted in gay colours and others white and porous as they come from the kiln; tops and teetotums of tagua; orange-wood balls to catch on a stick; little boxes lined with rabbit fur; the most durable tambourines in the world; shining, brightly coloured gourds; diminutive nine-stringed guitars on which children try the first measures of the bambuco; accordion-like purses, slung over the shoulder by a strap, half a hand's width but with all the proper fittings and pockets, which delight the children; sets of miniature tagua dishes in which each dish is hardly half a centimetre high; sets of chessmen still more tiny, a miracle of skill; red and black wooden dishes and cups, like Russian toys, for dolls' houses; little glass boxes in which the image of the Virgin disappears under coloured tin foliage like a humble reproduction of the icons cherished by the mujiks; small ivory angels with eyes popping out; rosaries of Job's tears; tiny crosses which, when held to the eye, show the image of the Virgin through an orifice; many scapularies; but, better than anything else, the little horses from Raquirá, or, by the same Indian craftsmen, little birds that whistle, hens with their chicks, and enchanting little couples dancing to an orchestra of guitars and mandolins.

Excursion A road runs 105 km. SW through Caldas to **Muzo,** on the banks of the Río Carare, 600 metres above sea-level. Population: 5,000. Sixteen km. away a famous open cut emerald mine has been worked since 1567, and long before that by the Muzo tribe of Indians. Emeralds were worked by the state mining corporation until robberies and violence forced closure by the army in 1973. Since 1976 private consortia have been mining with some success, though violence is again on the move.

There are roads from Chiquinquirá to Tunja, the capital of the Department, and to Barbosa. Both are on the Bogotá-Cúcuta highway and are described on that route.

On the Tunja road a short branch right at Tinjacá leads to **Raquirá,** where Indians make the pottery described above. There are an old monastery and some waterfalls nearby. The old colonial town of Villa de Leiva is also on this road. Bus from Chiquinquirá takes 1 hour; US$0.50; We describe it under excursions from Tunja (see page 458). Bus to Bogotá, 3 hours, US$1.

Bogotá to Cúcuta

Driving Times Hours: Bogotá-Tunja, 2; Tunja-Barbosa, about 2; Barbosa-San Gil, 4 (one very bad intersection); San Gil-Bucaramanga, 2½; Bucaramanga-Pamplona, 3 to 3½; Pamplona-Cúcuta, 1½. Cheapest bus, Bogotá-Cúcuta, US$7, 1st-class, US$11.50; 20 hours.

There is a 618-km. road running NE from Bogotá to Cúcuta, near the Venezuelan border. It runs through Tunja, Barbosa, Monquirá, Socorro, San Gil, Bucaramanga and Pamplona to Cúcuta and on in Venezuela to Caracas. The road, which runs through some beautiful scenery, is good most of the way except for a stretch between Oiba and Socorro, but this is under repair. The railway *via* Tunja to Duitama and Sogamoso is now for freight only. The road out of Bogotá is the *autopista* to near Chía (see page 455). You turn right at the intersection where the road to the left leads to Chía and after less than a hundred metres you cross the railway by a bridge and join the road which leads to Tunja: a wide and good road over the Sabana, at first.

At Sesquilé you can take a minor road to the right running south to Guatavita.

Guatavita Nueva This modern town, 100 km. from Bogotá, was built in Colonial style when the old town of Guatavita was submerged by a new hydroelectric reservoir. Although the blend of old and new is fascinating, Guatavita Nueva has failed as a social experiment. All the peasants have left and it is now a week-end haunt for Bogotanos and tourists. Cathedral, artisan workshops, museum, and small bull-ring for apprentices to practise Sunday afternoons. Sunday market best in morning, before Bogotanos get there. Bus from Bogotá (Flota Valle de Tenza, Carrera 15A y Calle 9, recommended), US$0.50, three hours. You can walk (or ride) from the town to the Laguna de Guatavita, where the legend of Eldorado originated, but it is a long (2-3 hour) walk. It is easier to approach the lake from a point on the Sesquilé-Guatavita Nueva road (the bus driver will let you off at the right place) where there is a sign offering horses for hire. Here a dirt track runs from the main road to the lake.

Hotels Two in village, US$6 p.p. with food. Bus agency Valle de Tenza has rooms for US0.60.

The town of **Chocontá** (15,000 inhabitants), 88 km. from Bogotá, is famous for its saddles, leather reins, and machete sheaths, all made with Moorish finesse. Beyond Chocontá the route is across the western slopes of the Eastern Cordillera to Tunja, 137 km. from Bogotá.

Tunja, 69,000 inhabitants, capital of Boyacá Department, stands at 2,820 metres in an arid mountainous area. The climate is cold; mean temperature, 13°C. One of the oldest cities in Colombia, it was founded by Gonzalo Suárez Rendón in 1539. It was then the seat of the Zipa, one of the two Chibcha kings. The old city has been compared with Toledo. Certainly its architecture comes direct from Spain: overhanging balconies, patios full of flowers, gracious cloisters and carved columns and doors surmounted by coats of arms. The modern city that has grown up is, however, far less attractive. Of the many colonial buildings the most remarkable is the church of Santo Domingo, a masterpiece begun in 1594; the interior is covered with wood most richly carved; unfortunately it has been closed for restoration for some years and may not reopen until 1979. Another is the Santa Clara Chapel (1580), now the hospital of San Rafael, with some fine wood carving. There are five parks. In Parque Bosque de la República is the adobe wall against which three martyrs of the Independence were shot in 1816. The Tourist Office is helpful. Though Tunja is rather a cold place, it can be quite warm on slopes out of the wind; good for country walks. Bus from Bogotá, 3 hours, US$1.50 (Cotrans). The bus station is some distance from the town centre.

The Casa de Don Juan de Vargas, once the residence of that notable, has been restored as a museum of colonial Tunja. The Church of Santa Bárbara is full of colonial woodwork, and in the nearby parish house are some notable religious objects, including extraordinary silk ornaments said to have been embroidered by Queen Juana la Loca of Spain. Some houses still have colonial portals. There are some fine colonial buildings on the main plaza (Plaza Mayor) opposite the Cathedral, which is of little interest.

The city formed an independent junta in 1811, and Bolívar fought under its aegis during the campaign of the Magdalena in 1812. Six years later he fought the battle of Boyacá, nearby (see below). Mother Francisca Josefa del Castillo wrote *El Libro de su vida* and *Sentimientos espirituales* in her convent at Tunja. Joaquín Ortiz, a writer of epic poetry still considered a model of that genre, also came from Tunja. For the "Piedras de Tunja" see under Facatativá (page 452).

Hotels *Residencias Colonial,* in what used to be the house of Antonio Ruiz Mancipe, by far the best, but only serves breakfast, US$6 s; *Pensión Suárez Rendón,* main plaza (good food, US$6 d, friendly but basic); *Hotel Centenario,* no hot water, but good restaurant, US$6 s; *Residencias El Cid* and *Tunja,* about US$3 each, basic; *Hotel Suiza, Bolívar, Boyacense,* all US$2, near bus stations, 5 minutes from main plaza. A new hotel offering good service is *Hunza,* near the *Colonial;* one of the cheapest is *Hotel Dux,* off the main square, US$1.70 d.

Restaurants Good cheap meal at *Bolo Club* and at a restaurant through an archway leading off the main plaza opposite the cathedral; *La Fonda,* US$0.50 for a big meal.

Tourist Office On main square.

Excursions from Tunja The battle of the Bridge of Boyacá was fought about 16 km. south, on the road to Bogotá. On the bridge at Boyacá is a large monument to Bolívar. Bolívar took Tunja on August 6, 1819, and next day his troops, fortified by a British Legion, the only professional soldiers amongst them, fought the Spaniards on the banks of the swollen Río Boyacá. With the loss of only 13 killed and 53 wounded they captured 1,600 men and 39 officers. Only 50 men escaped, and when these told their tale in Bogotá the Viceroy Samao fled in such haste that he left behind him half a million pesos of the royal funds. There is now a huge modernistic restaurant overlooking the site.

Villa de Leiva is reached from the road to Barbosa by a branch road, left, at Arcabuco. The drive affords some beautiful views. The town, in Colombia's main olive growing region, dates back, like Tunja, to the early days of Spanish rule, but unlike Tunja, has not been spoilt by the construction of modern office and apartment blocks. There are three colonial houses which are worth a visit: the mansion in which the Viceroys lived, the house in which Antonio Nariño lived—he translated the "Rights of Man" into Spanish—and the building in which the first Convention of the United Provinces of New Granada was held. A palaeontological museum has been opened N of the town. The shops in the plaza have an excellent selection of Colombian handicrafts at reasonable prices, while the Saturday market, not yet geared to the tourist trade, still offers many good bargains.

Hotels *El Molino la Mesopotamia,* which used to be a Colonial mill, very good, US$20 s, including all meals, 10% rebate for booking 10 days ahead, a meal costs about US$2.50; *Convento, La Rosita* and *Posada Don Juan de Castellanos* all charge about US$8 s; *San Jorge* is US$6 d; *Hospedaje Los Virreyes,* recommended; *Cabaña Jequenque,* US$5 each, with breakfast, open only on week-ends but recommended; *Edén,* not recommended; *Elvira.* There are rooms for US$2.40 in a house opposite *El Molino;* accommodation also in *Bar Roca,* US$1.80 p.p., very clean and pleasant; cheapest rooms available in bar-cum-bus agency at entrance to town.

Another way of getting to Villa de Leiva is *via* Sáchica, either directly from Tunja or, coming from Bogotá, turning left (W) at the Boyacá monument, *via* Samacá. The houses are closed Monday-Friday out of season, but the trip is worth while just for the views. In any event, the town and surrounding hills are excellent for long, peaceful walks. Buses to Leiva from Tunja, 50 minutes, US$0.50 with Valle de Tenza company. Hard-up travellers should take their own food; it is expensive at Leiva.
N.B. It is better not to visit Leiva on Mondays as the houses and shops are closed.

From Tunja there are two possible routes to Cúcuta; the main road, almost entirely paved, goes *via* Bucaramanga, but the other *via* Duitama and Málaga, rejoining the main road at Pamplona, is also interesting. At Duitama turn right for **Sogamoso,** where a Museum of Archaeology has been opened on the site of the centre of the precolumbian city; open 0900-1200; 1400-1700 (closed Mons.), charge US$0.30. It is possible to camp in the museum grounds if you ask permission. A museum of religious art has recently been opened. On the road from Duitama to Sogamoso is the *Hotel Hacienda Suescun,* US$8 d, in old hacienda, excellent service. E of Sogamoso the churches of Mongui and Topaga are worth a visit, and so is the mountain-ringed Laguna de Tota. NE of Duitama, on the road to Málaga, is the turning at Belén for **Paz de Río,** where Colombia's national steelworks is sited; visitors can see over it. Between Duitama and Paz de Río there is another hotel, also in an old hacienda, the *Hostería San Luis de Ucuenga.*

The main road goes on to **Barbosa** (*Hotel Príncipe,* clean rooms with private bath), 64 km. NW in the Department of Santander. There is also a railway from Bogotá *via* Chiquinquirá. Eleven km. from Barbosa, at Puente Nacional, is *Agua Blanca,* a splendid hotel with a swimming pool.

A road runs NW to the Magdalena at Puerto Oloya, opposite Puerto Berrío. Eighteen km. from Barbosa is **Vélez,** a charming small town where horses and mules are reared. (*Hotel Gales,* US$1.25.)
The road goes NE for 84 km. to

Socorro (23,000 people), with steep streets up a hillside and single storey houses set amongst graceful palms. It has a singularly large and odd stone church. The local museum, La Casa de la Cultura, is worth seeing, as is the market which is open every day.

At Socorro, in 1781, began the revolt of the peasant *comuneros:* not a movement for independence but a protest against poverty. It was led at first by a woman, Manuela Beltrán, and then, when other joined, by Juan Francisco Berbeo. They marched as far as the salt town of Zipaquirá, N of Bogotá; Rebel terms were accepted by the Spaniards, and sworn to by the Bishop of Bogotá, but when they had returned home troops were sent from Cartagena and there were savage reprisals. Another woman from Socorro, Antonia Santos, led guerrillas fighting for independence and was captured and executed by the Spaniards in 1816; her statue is in the main square.
Hotels *Saravita; Venezia,* US$3.80 d, with shower, has dining room, nice old rooms; *Sucre.*
Restaurant *Chanchón.*

About 21 km. beyond Socorro is **San Gil,** which has the tourist attraction of El Gallineral, a riverside spot whose beautiful trees are covered with moss-like tillandsia.

Hotels   *Bella Isla* (swimming pool), a good stopover on the Bogotá-Cúcuta run, US$7.25 d; *Hotel Gales,* US$1.35; *Pensión Elba,* US$2.25 d.

Restaurant   Just outside Pinchote on the road from Socorro to San Gil is the *Mesón del Cuchicote,* which specializes in dishes from the Santander region. Especially good is the barbecued goat meat and the mixed meat plate which includes fried beef mammary glands. A feast for about US$3.

About 24 km. beyond San Gil, a little off the road, is the picturesque village of Aratoca, with a colonial church. Ten km. further on, the descent from the heights along the side of a steep cliff into a thickly wooded valley is one of the most dramatic experiences of the trip to Cúcuta.

Bucaramanga, 203 km. N of Barbosa, is the capital of Santander Department. It stands at 1,018 metres on an uneven plateau sharply delimited by eroded slopes to the N and W, hills to the east and a ravine to the S. A railway runs from Puerto Wilches on the Magdalena River for 117 km. to Palenque, 5 km. from the centre. The city was founded in 1622 but was little more than a village until the latter half of the 19th century, when the area in which it stands was first colonised. The metropolitan area has a population of 324,000, which had expanded rapidly because of the success of coffee, tobacco and staple crops in the area. All traces of its past are gone; it is a clean modern city, well endowed with parks and plazas, a large stadium, a first-class hospital and an Industrial University. Commercially the city is still developing rapidly. Its great problem is space for expansion. Erosion in the lower, western side of the city topples buildings over the edge after heavy rain. The fingers of erosion, deeply ravined between, are spectacular. Its Club Campestre is one of the most beautifully set in Latin America. There is an amusement park in the suburb of Lagos I, SW of the city on the way to Floridablanca.

Average maximum temperature is 28.1°C; average minimum, 19.4°C. Rainfall is about 760 mm., and humidity is high (68% to 90%).

Main Industries   Cigars, cigarettes, forging mill, wine bodega, machine shops.

Excursions   In the neighbourhood are several small towns: **Floridablanca,** 40 km. SW, with famous El Paragüitas gardens, belonging to the national tobacco agency, reputed locally as "a replica of the Garden of Eden"—and known particularly for its pineapples; you can get a free pass to the gardens from the agency's office in town. The gardens are not open at weekends. Lebrija (20,000 people), 17 km. to the W is an attractive plain. Rionegro (36,000 people) is a coffee town 20 km. to the N with, close by, the Laguna de Gálago and waterfalls. **Girón** (27,000 people) a tobacco centre 9 km. SW of Bucaramanga on the Río de Oro, is a quiet and attractive Colonial town with a beautiful church. The buildings are well preserved and the town unspoilt by modernisation. (Hotels: *San Juan de Girón,* outside town on road from Bucaramanga, swimming pool; *Río de Oro,* in centre.) In **Piedecuesta,** 18 km. SE of Bucaramanga, you can see cigars being hand-made, furniture carving and jute weaving—cheap, hand-decorated "figue" rugs can be bought. There are frequent buses to all these places; a taxi costs US$2-3.

Airport   Palo Negro, new, on three flattened hilltops on other side of ravine S of city. Spectacular views on take-off and landing. Taxi, US$2; colectivo, US$0.80.

Roads   To the Magdalena at Barrancabermeja, 174 km. (see page 443); to Cúcuta, 198 km.; to Bogotá, 420 km.; to Medellín, 1,010 km.;to Santa Marta, 732 km; (see under Riohacha, page 441).

Buses   To Bogotá, 8-10 hours, US$5.80 (Pullman); Tunja, 7 hours, US$2.50; Barranquilla, 14 hours (US$7.40); Cúcuta, 6-8 hours, US$2.80; Santa Marta, 14 hours, US$6.90; Barrancabermeja, 3 hours, US$1.80, a scenic ride with one rest stop permitted; this road is now paved. Watch out for pickpockets at the bus station.

Rail to Barrancabermeja 4 hours, daily at 0700 hours, US$1.30. Beautiful scenery; to Santa Marta direct Mon. to Fri., 13 hours, at 1640 hours, US$7.30.

Transport in Town   Taxis do not have meters but the fare within the city is US$0.35 (US$0.42 at night). Buses charge US$0.03.

Hotels at Bucaramanga: *Bucarica,* spacious, on main plaza, US$6 s, US$8 d, good restaurant and snack bar; *Andino,* new, Calle 34, No. 18-44, US$8 d; *Carolina,* next best, US$4.60 d; *Balmoral,* uphill from centre; *El Príncipe* (very good value with superb food—but book ahead); *El Edén,* near main plaza, US$3.50 d; *Tamana,* Carrera 18, No. 30-31, US$4 d, new, clean, friendly. *Tay; Resid. Laura.* A few blocks uphill from the bus terminal are several *residencias;* one is *Resedencias Colonial,* recommended, US$6 d with shower and w.c. Another is *Hotel San Pablo,* US$1.10 d, clean and good; *Hotel El Pilos,* US$4, strongly recommended, friendly service, good food, view from roof; *Residencias Tayrona,* US$3.60 d, with bath, good value; *Hotel los Andes,* US$1 s, basic. Cheap and central, *Residencias El Marqués,* clean. Accommodation at the *Club Campestre* (US$6 d) is good, but you must have an introduction. Try the mayor's office or Chamber of Commerce.

Restaurants   *La Carreta,* excellent and reasonable, music at times; *Mi Bodequín,* also good; good food at *Club del Comercio* (by invitation or introduction). *El Paisa; La Flora* (for lunch, on the road to Cúcuta); *La Puerta del Sol* and *La Fonda* serve typical dishes; *Portofino, Murallas de Cartagena, Cabecera del Llano,* all good; snack bars open at all times, e.g. including *El Tony* and *Gran Gastby* (correct spelling!). Try the hormigas (large black ants), a local delicacy! Service in Bucaramanga's many restaurants is slow, so be warned.

Discotheques   On road to Girón are *El Molino* and *Capricornio.*

Camping   Campo Alegre, about 8 km. out on Bogotá road.

Consulate   There is a Venezuelan Consulate, less crowded than that in Cúcuta, which will supply a Venezuelan tourist card (essential for entry) for US$5.

Banks   Banco Anglo Colombiano, Calle 36, No. 20-04. Open 0800-1130, 1400-1530. Many other banks. Saturdays and last working day of month, 0800-1030.

Our road runs E to Berlín, and then NE (a very scenic run over the Cordillera Oriental) to Pamplona, about 130 km. from Bucaramanga.

Berlin has been recommended to the hardy camper as challenging and rewarding. The village lies in a valley at 3,100 metres, the peaks surrounding it rise to 4,350 metres and the temperature is constantly around 10°C, although on the infrequent sunny days it may seem much warmer. The scenery is awesome. The inhabitants are tolerant of visitors; ask a farmer for permission to camp in his field. Berlín obtained electric power in 1975. There are three crude restaurants providing more than adequate meals and there is a simple hotel with no heat or bath. It has been recommended as an ideal place to feel the power of the Eastern Cordillera and see the hardiness of the people who live on the páramo.

Pamplona, Department of Santander del Norte, lies in a setting of mountains at 2,200 metres, a little lower than Bogotá, 467 km. away. Population, 22,800. The climate is cold and uninviting, but the town is definitely worth seeing. Founded in 1548, it became important as a mining town but is now better known as a university city. Few modern buildings have as yet broken its colonial harmony: low balconied houses and buildings painted in many different colours and gracious old churches. Cathedral in the spacious central plaza. The earthquake of 1875—there had been a severe one in 1644, too—played havoc with the monasteries and some of the churches. There is now a hotel on the site of the former San Agustín monastery, but it may still be possible to visit the ex-monasteries of San Francisco and Santo Domingo. See the Casa Colonial (archaeological) museum.

Hotels   *Cariongo* (new, very good); *Montaña; Sandoval* and *Santander* hotels poor. *Lincoln,* on main square, is new. *Residencias Doran,* US$5 d, basic; *Hotel*

Anzoátequi, US$2.50 for dinner, bed and breakfast. Hotel accommodation may be hard to find at weekends; many Venezuelans visit the town then.

Restaurant   *El Doran,* meals for US$0.80.

Buses   To Bogotá, US$6; to Cúcuta, US$0.75.

Shopping   Pamplona is a good place to buy ruanas.

Warning   DAS can be difficult with "hippies" as the Venezuelan border is close.

It is a run of 72 km. through sparsely populated country, descending to an altitude of only 215 metres, to

Cúcutá, capital of the Department of Santander del Norte, and only 16 km. from the Venezuelan frontier. Founded 1734, destroyed by earthquake 1875, and then rebuilt, elegantly, with wide avenues and pleasant parks, the streets shaded by trees, and they are needed for it is hot: the mean temperature is 27°C. Population: 250,000. Coffee is the great crop in the area, followed by tobacco. There are also large herds of cattle. The coffee is now moved by road to Maracaibo. The city's chief occupation, according to those who know, is contraband.

Cúcuta, because it is the gateway of entry from Venezuela, was a focal point in the history of Colombia during the wars for independence. Bolívar reached it after his lightning Magdalena campaign in 1813, and set out from it for his march to Caracas. On Feb. 28, 1813, after capturing Cúcuta by a typical ruse, he addressed his troops in the plaza: "All America expects liberty and salvation from you, brave soldiers." The Bolívar Column stands now where he stood then. And it was in the old church—destroyed 1875—at El Rosario de Cúcuta, a small town of 8,000 inhabitants 14½ km. from Cúcuta on the road to the frontier, that the First Congress of Gran Colombia opened on May 6, 1821. It was at this Congress that the plan to unite Venezuela, Ecuador, and Colombia was ratified; Bolívar was made President, and Santander (who was against the plan) Vice-President. Santander had been born at a hacienda near El Rosario which is now being developed as a tourist centre. The international bridge between Colombia and Venezuela is only a few miles from El Rosario; just beyond it is San Antonio del Táchira, the first Venezuelan Town, and 55 km. on is San Cristóbal. Taxi, Cúcuta to San Cristóbal, US$5; bus, US$0.70; colectivo (does not stop at frontier), US$1.25; colectivo to San Antonio (will stop at frontier), US$6.30; Expreso Occidente bus on to Caracas, two daily, US$8, 14 hours, or colectivo taxi, US$12. Bus to Bogotá, 17 hours, US$10, with Berlinas del Fonce line (recommended). There are frequent buses, even during the night. To Bucaramanga, US$1.50; from there a connection to Barranquilla can be made. To Tunja, US$2. The road is bad for the first part of the journey.

There are good roads to Caracas, capital of Venezuela (933 km. direct or 1,046 km. *via* Mérida), and to the Venezuelan port of Maracaibo (571 km.).

N.B.   All visitors need a tourist card to enter Venezuela. There is a Venezuelan Consulate at Cúcuta (Av. 5, Calle 15—closed weekends) which supplies tourist cards, but travellers are advised to obtain one in Bogotá. This border is sometimes impassable without a visa as well.   You need evidence of onward transportation outside Venezuela, to obtain a card. It appears that it is no longer necessary to obtain a DAS exit stamp in the town before leaving the country, but it may be best to check first. DAS is open every day, 0800-1200, 1400-1730, except Sunday; Calle 17, No. 2-60. If not, you will need to get exit stamp at border. If going into Venezuela be sure to get an entry stamp at the border or you will be sent back by customs officials further on. (The customs office where vehicle documents for Colombia are checked is on the road to the airport. Venezuelan car documentation is checked at the border post in San Antonio.) Similarly, if arriving from Caracas, make sure bus stops at border for Venezuelan exit formalities.

Hotels   *Tonchalá,* US$18 d, US$13 s, swimming pool, air conditioning; *Residencias Iscalá* (new, reasonable); *Internacional* (swimming pool), not very good. Better are *Tundaya; Rio; San Jorge; Lord; Vasconia; Casa Blanca* (swimming pool), US$7.50 d, good, reasonable meals, recommended; *Nohra,* on main square, US$6 d, friendly; *El Cacique,* new, clean and reasonable. For hard up: *Residencias Gómez,* US$1.50, with bath. Peace Corps recommend *Residencias Los Rosales,* near bus station, Calle 2, 8-39, fan and private bath, US$1 p.p. *Residencia Mary* at bus station, US$5.50 d, with bath, good. Also near the bus station is *Hotel Zulia,* US$4 d, with bath, clean. *Residencias Los Dos Santanderes,* Calle 1 between Av. 9 and 10, US$2.50 d; *Hotel Amaruc,* US$7.90 d, with fan, private bath, no hot water.

Restaurants "M", also called *Chez Esteban,* on highway to San Antonio, very good; *El Aire y Sol; Bahía,* just off main square, pleasant; other good restaurants at reasonable prices are *El Pollo Especial, El Jarrón de Baviera, Cantón* (Chinese), *Auto Lunch El Palacio.*

Shopping A good range of leather goods at possibly the best prices anywhere in Colombia.

Airports At Cúcuta for Colombian services (to Bogotá on Mon., Wed. and Fri., with Avianca, US$25; with Satena, US$18), and at San Antonio, Venezuela (30 minutes) for Venezuelan domestic lines. At latter be sure all baggage is sealed after customs inspection and the paper seals signed and stamped.

Currency A good rate of exchange for pesos is to be had in Cúcuta, or on the border. There are money changers on the street all round the main square and many shops advertise the purchase and sale of bolivares. The price is usually better than at the Banco de la República.

Note Pickpockets are as active here as elsewhere in Colombia. Be careful.

Warning Foreigners entering from Venezuela must have a tourist card (which can be obtained from the Colombian consulate in San Antonio). Unless both Venezuelan and Colombian officials have stamped your passport you will not be allowed to go on.

About 120 km. N of Cúcuta is the Barco oilfield, which lies in a corner of the Maracaibo basin inside Colombia. The oil is taken by pipeline across the 1,800-metre high Andes into the Magdalena valley and then to the coast at Coveñas, 96 km. S of Cartagena. There is a road from Cúcuta N through Petrolea to Tibu, the company's H.Q., where it connects with the disused road W along the pipeline.

The Andes crossed by this oil pipeline is the branch which sweeps north to the Guajira Peninsula after the bifurcation of the Eastern Cordillera near Cúcuta: the other branch sweeps into Venezuela. This western branch is the Sierra de Perijá y Motilones. In this Sierra live the Motilones Indians. A connoisseur of the ironies of history will know that at the Congress of El Rosario one of the items most acclaimed was the admission of aboriginal Indians into citizenship. The Motilones have always turned a blind eye to this, for they are the only Indians in Colombia who have refused to accept the inevitable. Little is known of them, for so far they have persisted in killing many of the missionaries sent to Christianize them, and the anthropologists sent to study them.

The Central Cordillera: Medellín and Manizales

The Central Cordillera lies W of the Magdalena River. In it are two of the most important cities in Colombia: Medellín, the second largest city in the country, and Manizales. There are several ways of reaching them from Bogotá besides going by air. Manizales can be reached by a road (309 km.) passing through Facatativá and Honda; or by road through Girardot to Ibagué, then over the high crest of the Quindío Pass *via* Armenia. (For the road from Manizales to Medellín, see under Manizales, page 468. Medellín, too can be reached from Bogotá by road or railway. The direct road (478 km.) has a 207-km. unpaved stretch from La Dorada to La Unión. The most travelled road is *via* Manizales.

The railway goes to Puerto Salgar, on the Magdalena River, which is crossed by a bridge to La Dorada, on the W bank; from La Dorada the

Atlántico Railway heads N along the western fringes of the river to Puerto Berrío, here to connect with the railway to Medellín. The distance by rail from Bogotá to Medellín is 521 km., or 43 km. longer than by road (express trains on Tuesdays and Saturdays, 1930, 15 hours); by air it is only 238 km.

Puerto Berrío to **Medellín** by rail, 193 km. The route lies, at first, in the hot tropical lowland of the Magdalena, most of it a deep jungle traversed by a maze of muddy streams. Beyond this area are rolling hills and fresh, bright streams. Well over half-way there is a tunnel—La Quiebra—nearly 3 km. long. Beyond the country is different again. We are up in the fertile lands of the temperate zone now. Then we enter into the heart of the mountains, whose many valleys amongst high peaks are sprinkled with russet-red roofs grouped round soaring church towers. The gardens, and even the stations, are bright with flowers. The track, however, leaves much to be desired and always seems to be under repair; the journey by road is much quicker.

Medellín, capital of Antioquia, is a fast growing and remarkable city of 1,500,000 people, at an altitude of 1,540 metres. It could hardly be less advantageously placed, for it faces forbidding mountain barriers in nearly all directions. Its climate alone, that of an English summer day (21°C), is in its favour, despite a certain amount of smog. Yet Medellín is one of the main industrial cities of Colombia, and seethes with energy. The first looms arrived in 1902. Today the city produces more than 80% of the textile output of the country, and textiles account for only half its industrial activity. Excellent views from Cerro Salvador (statue on top), SW of city, and from Cerro Nutibara, S of city, where there is a good restaurant.

One of the city's main exports—as indeed of all Antioquia and Caldas—is talent. Antioqueños hold that nothing worthwhile ever happens in Colombia but that one of them has a hand in it.

Medellín, for an industrial city, is a remarkably clean, well laid out and pleasant town. Even its industrial plants look attractive. It has all the usual facilities for recreation: theatres, picture houses, golf courses, tennis courts, stadiums and football grounds, museums and libraries. Its cultural and technical side is catered for by the University of Antioquia, the Pontifical University, Medellín University, the Latin American University, Pascual Bravo Industrial Institute and other institutions. The old Colonial buildings—the city was founded in 1675—have nearly all disappeared under the flood of modern construction, but there are still some 17th century churches left: the Old Cathedral, on Parque Berrío and the churches of San Benito, La Veracruz, and San José, but none of them is particularly notable. The new Cathedral of Villanueva, one of the largest brick buildings in the world, is on Parque Bolívar, an attractive place. Three churches of the 18th century survive: San Francisco, in Plaza José Felix de Restrepo, San Juan de Dios, and San Antonio. The cattle auctions on Tues. and Thurs., held in specially built cattle yards on the outskirts, are fascinating. The zoo, mainly of South American animals and birds, has been described as "quite charming" and is well worth a visit. Over Christmas the city is decked out with over 600,000 Christmas lights.

Medellín's Main Industries Silk, cotton and woollen textiles, agricultural machinery, leather goods, cigarettes, chinaware, glassware, foodstuffs, cement, chocolate, paint, chemicals, a bar and rod mill, many foundries and machine shops.

Royal Mail Lines Agents E. L. Gerlein & Co. S.A., Apartado Aéreo 797.

Airline Agents Air France has a very helpful office in the new shopping centre.

Hotels *Intercontinental,* the best, but some distance from the centre, US$18 s; *Nutibara* (casino and swimming pool), Carrera 49, No. 52-40, US$15 s; *Gran Hotel,* US$10 s; *Residencias Veracruz,* Carrera 50, No. 54-18, US$10 s, with bath, swimming pool, very good; *Casa Blanca,* Carrera 45 and Calle 70, US$8 d, central but rather a run-down area; *Casa Blanca 70,* Calle 50 and Carrera 47, US$5 s; *Salvatore,* US$6 s; *Residencias Las Mercedes,* Calle 47, No. 43-84, near centre, US$7 d, with bath; *La Montaña,* Calle 48, No. 53-69, US$5 d, with shower, good value, good meals available, safe; *Hotel Bolívar,* new, in centre, good, US$8 s, noisy; *Residencias Los Llanos,* Carrera 51, No. 44-41, quite close to bus station, US$3 d, clean, comfortable, cold showers, inside rooms quieter; *Hotel Lido,* Carrera 49 and Calle 47, US$3.50 d, with bath; *Residencia Hotel Centro,* Carrera 45, No. 50-25, US$2.50 s, with bath; *Residencias Plaza,* Calle 54, US$5 s, US$7 d; *Hotel Da Vinci,* central, US$6 s, recommended; *Pensión Madison,* US$1.50 s, clean and friendly; *Viajes,* US$2.10 d, good cheap meals, friendly, opposite Flota Magdalena terminal; *Normandie,* US$7 s; *Bristol; Don Ramón; Comercial,* Calle 48 (Pichincha y Cúcuta), US$2 s, friendly, clean, hot water available in some rooms, good meals for US$0.65; *Residencial Cordilla,* Calle 46, No. 49-50, US$1 per night for room with bath; *Residencias Gladis,* 1½ blocks from bus station (Carrera 48 and Calle 45), US$3.50 s, US$6 d (modern, clean, friendly and helpful, but rather noisy; all rooms face street). Nearby, *Residencias Caruso,* US$1.50 d (has some rooms away from the street); *Hotel Príncipe,* Bolívar and Carrera 51, US$1 p.p., clean and friendly; *Residencias Medellín,* US$3 s; *Hotel Nuevo* (Calle 48 and Carrera 53, US$4 d, with bathroom, noisy but clean, good meals for US$0.80); *San Francisco,* Carrera 54, No. 48-44 (US$1.60 d, US$1.10 s), good and clean; *Pensión Rumania,* US$3 with food, very nice. Just beyond the police barrier, about 20 km. along road to Manizales, near Caldas, is a rustic type **motel** with swimming pool, *Holiday Motel,* US$4.50 bed and breakfast, US$10.60 all-in. Many cheap hotels near Magdalena bus station. An excellent private house to stay in is on Carrera 58, No. 53A-36, 3rd floor, US$2 a night, very safe.

Restaurants *Salvatore, Lombardo* and *Tonino* (Italian); *Cacique Nutibara,* on Cerro Nutibara, offers excellent views of the city, and good, reasonably-priced food; *Versailles,* Av. Junín, good cheap meals; *Aquarias,* on road past Intercontinental Hotel, first class. Local dishes are served at branches of *La Fonda Antioqueña,* about US$1.40 for a meal, but something of a tourist trap. Roast chicken is provided at the four branches of *Kokariko,* from $1.40; good steaks at *Texas Steak House,* Calle 44 and Carrera 80; good *arroz con pollo* from *Los Alejos* in Centro Comercial Boyacá. *Piemonte* and *La Bella Epoca,* very good and expensive, both on road to El Poblado; *Hostería* (very good); *Don Ramón* (good), *Sebastiano* (fair); *El Boquerón,* on the mountain top; good German restaurant close to University Centre. *Restaurant Fujiyama; Doña María; Aguacatala,* outside off road to Envigado, good, but expensive; *La Postillón; Noche y Día,* Carrera Junín, between Maturín and Amador, good meals for US$0.50; in fact there are several of these round-the-clock cafés in the vicinity which serve cheap meals. *La Margarita,* good local food. *Dino Rojo,* good, cheap food. *Cirus,* Calle 53, meals for US$0.80, good value. Many good, cheap restaurants on Carrera 49.

Clubs Unión; Campestre (good food, rooms, golf, tennis, swimming pool); Medellín; Profesionales; "El Rodeo"; Ejecutivos (lunch club in centre).

Shopping Silver seems cheaper than in Bogotá; there is also a good branch of Artesanías de Colombia (Carrera 50, No. 52-21). Plaza de Flores is worth a visit. Carrera 47 is lined with antique shops. Many of the textile mills have discount clothing departments attached where good bargains can be had. Ask at your hotel. La Piel, at Calle 53, No. 49-131, has an excellent selection of leather goods at very reasonable prices. There is a new shopping centre with many shops, cafés, etc.

Experimental Theatre Pablo Tobón Uribe.

Music Monthly concerts by the Antioquia Symphony Orchestra. Band concerts in the Parque Bolívar every Sunday at 1130.

Museum of Folk Art in the Fábrica Tejicondor; it opens on request. Museo Miguel Angel Builes has an extensive collection of artefacts housed in beautiful new building. The Museum of the Missionary Sisters of Mother Laura has a good collection of indigenous costumes and crafts from Colombia, Ecuador and Guatemala. Museo El Castillo, formerly a landowner's home, has interesting objects and beautiful grounds. Entry US$0.50. The Museo Zea (Carrera Cundinamarca and Diagonal Carabobo) shows contemporary pictures and sculptures. Museo Antropológico at University of Antioquia.

Botanical Gardens Joaquín Antonio Uribe gardens are open daily, US$0.12 entrance, well worth a visit. Also visit El Ranchito, an orchid farm between the towns of Itagüí and La Estrella (entry US$0.30; April to June is the best time to visit) and the aviary at the Franciscan seminary (charge US$0.15) which is only a short uphill walk away from El Ranchito. There is another fine orchid display at Fizebad, 30 minutes by car from the city, an old estate-house restored with original furniture and artefacts.

Bullfights at the bull-ring of La Macarena.

Banks Banco Anglo Colombiano, Carrera 51 (Bolívar), No. 50-19, and agency on Calle 45, No. 55-65; Banco Internacional, Banco Royal, Banco Frances é Italiano de Colombia, and various other Colombian banks. Open: 0830-1130, 1330-1530; last working day of month 0830-1100. Main hotels will cash travellers' cheques when banks are closed.

US Consul Carrera 52, No. 49-21.

Coffee, cattle, gold and silver are the great contributions of the area. The country around is often beautiful, rich in flowers, particularly orchids, and with grand views of the green encircling mountains.

Tourist Office Information on the location of the tourist office differs; however, it seems there is one branch on Calle 55 and Carrera 5, opposite the Teatro Libya. This is helpful and provides lists of buses and bus routes within the city. For a cheap tour of the city take any "Circular" bus, for US$0.03.

Airport Olaya Herrera. International standard. Cheap bus to centre, about 25 minutes. Airport tax is US$1.75.

Rail There is a railway to the Magdalena river and to Bogotá. (Express trains to Bogotá 3 times a week, Tues., Thur., Sat., US$5.50, book well in advance.) There is another S to Cartago and Cali but this was heavily damaged by floods in 1974 (and was still not operating at the end of 1976), and W to Buenaventura, the Pacific port.

Roads A paved road, 665 km. long, goes N to Cartagena (see page 437). A road now paved runs S to Manizales; half an hour along it is Caldas, which has some of the finest scenery in Colombia. There are two other important roads: one, 383 km. long, NW through Antioquia to Turbo, on the Gulf of Urabá; and another, 478 km. long, SE from Medellín through Sonsón and La Dorada and on to Bogotá. The latter is paved as far as Rionegro, but from Rionegro to Sansón is in a bad state of repair. The scenery compensates for this to some extent.

Buses To Bogotá, 14-20 hours ordinary bus US$6, Pullman bus US$8.50. Frequent buses for Cali, Flota Magdalena US$6.35, 10-13 hours. Frequent buses to Manizales, 7 hours, a colectivo costs US$4.75. To Cartagena, US$10 ordinary, 17-20 hours, or US$12, 14 hours, by Pullman bus; road now well paved throughout. To Barraquilla, US$9.50 by Pullman, 16 hours. To Cartago, 8 hours. To Pereira, 8 hours, US$3.35 by Flota Occidental Pullman. To Sincelejo, 9½ hours. To La Dorada, 9 hours.

Excursions A run N along the Cartagena road to (132 km.) **Yarumal**, with 60,000 people, or NW to (80 km.) **Antioquia** (13,000 people) will give a good idea of the very beautiful countryside. Antioquia lies just W of the Cauca river; a bridge of one span, 381 metres long, crosses the Cauca here. It was founded as a gold mining town by the Spaniards in 1541, the first in the area, and still retains its colonial atmosphere. Until 1826 it was the capital of the Department of Antioquia. The fine old Cathedral is worth seeing, as is the church of Santa Bárbara. Hotels: *Mariscal Robledo* (swimming pool); *Turismo*. Bus from Medellín US$0.80 (Flota Urbara or Transporte Sierra), 2½ hours. The road goes on to **Turbo**, on the Gulf of Urabá. Two mountain ranges, each of 600 metres, have to be crossed between Medellín and Turbo (bus, US$4.20), where banana cultivation is now booming (Hotels: *Playa Mar*, US$8.50 d, the best; *Miramar*, about US$1 each; *Rotitom*). A description of an overland journey from Panama to Colombia *via* Turbo will be found in the Panama section; note that if going from Colombia to Panama *via* Turbo you should get an exit stamp from the DAS in Medellín before leaving. We have also been informed that the immigration office at the Panamanian port of Puerto Obaldía can be extremely obstructive.

Another interesting excursion from Medellín is along the Sonsón road SE to (39 km.) the town of **Rionegro**, in a delightful valley of gardens and orchards. Here was born one of Bolívar's generals, José María Córdoba, the hero of the battle of Ayacucho. Bolívar gave a crown to Sucre for winning the battle. Sucre handed it to the man who most deserved it: Córdoba. (It is now in the vault of a bank at Rionegro, where it can be seen when the bank is open.) The Casa de Convención (where the 1863 Convention took place) is now an archive museum, entry US$0.06. The cathedral, with its silver altar, deserves a visit. Many interesting pottery and ceramics factories in Rionegro area, hardly mechanized, as well as leather working; they welcome visitors and explain the process. A day trip can cost US$10, but the Medellín-Rionegro Rápido taxi service is very cheap. Rionegro has become something of a tourist trap, and those thinking of buying leather goods should be warned that prices are high.

La Ceja, also on the Sonsón road, is also said to be well worth a visit. Transportes La Ceja cover the route; the journey takes 1¼ hours. For the energetic, any one of the surrounding hills affords an excellent view of the area. Two delightful hotels have rooms for about US$1-1.50. At Sonsón, there are the *Tahami* (US$1.65 each, very good value) and *Imperio* (US$1 each) hotels.

At Envigado, 10 km. S of Medellín, craftsmen have for generations turned out the traditional Antioqueño pouch called "carriel", carried by the men. Now used for money, its original use was for coffee samples.

At **Bello**, 6½ km. N of Medellín (pop. 150,000), is the hut in which Marcos Fidel Suárez, the distinguished President between 1918 and 1922, was born. This remarkable memorial is completely covered in with glass for its better preservation.

A good trip is by car to **Hatillo**, 32 km. along a road which parallels the railway to Puerto Berrío, and then another 80 km. along a new road to Caldas. There are many restaurants along this road.

The history of the people of Antioquia is remarkable. The town of Antioquia was founded in 1541, but the Spaniards, eager for gold, were not interested in the hinterland, which was then very sparsely inhabited by nomadic Indians who made very poor agricultural labourers. But during the 17th century a new wave of settlers came to Colombia from Spain; many of them were Jewish refugees who were deliberately seeking isolation, and found it in the little valley of the Río Aburrá, where they founded the city of Medellín in 1675. They were peculiar in three ways; they had an extraordinarily high birth rate and even today it is not unusual to find families with from 16 to 20 children; they intermarried very little with either Indian or black, and they divided the land into small farms which they worked themselves. The area could then be reached only by two mule trails: one from Puerto Berrío and one from the Cauca valley, where Spaniards were getting rich by using black slave labour, a thing the new immigrants refused to do. Their exports were small: a little gold and silver from their streams. They lived on the food they themselves produced: maize, beans, sugar-cane, bananas, fruit.

In the early 19th century the settlement began to expand and to push out in all directions, particularly to the S: an all too rare phenomenon in Latin America. They followed the forested slopes on the western side of the Central Cordillera and occupied all the cultivable land. Manizales, 120 km. S, was founded in 1848. In the second half of the century new lands were occupied further S. The settlers have now crossed the Quindío road and spread as far S as Caicedonia and Sevilla, in the Department of Valle.

It was coffee that brought stability to this expansion, but they were slow to adopt it. Coffee appeared in the Magdalena Valley about 1865, but none was being exported from Antioquia before the end of the century. It was the first world war that suddenly gave a fillip to the industry: within 20 years the Departments of Antioquia and Caldas (Caldas was hived off from Antioquia when it became settled) were producing half the coffee of Colombia, and the people of Caldas and Antioquia are by far the most important producers today. The industrialization of Medellín followed the coffee boom. Its mainstay is the textile industry, based on cotton now grown entirely in Colombia. There has been little immigration since the original settlement, but the growth in population has been extraordinary.

Manizales Built on a mountain saddle and dominated by its enormous (still unfinished) concrete Cathedral and the snow-capped mountain Nevado El Ruiz. The city was founded in 1848 by settlers from the Department of Antioquia; it has a population of 400,000 and is the capital of the small Department of Caldas, which originally (until 1965) contained what are now the new Departments of Quindío and Risaralda. The old Department, now known as Viejo Caldas, produces about 30% of all Colombian coffee and picturesque coffee farms abound on the hills and slopes of the surrounding countryside.

Manizales, at 2,150 metres above sea level, rides its mountain saddle uncompromisingly, the houses falling away sharply from the centre of the city into the adjacent valleys. The climate is extremely humid—the annual rainfall is 3,560 mm.—and frequently the city is covered in cloud that descends on the city like a dense fog. The best months of the year are from mid-December through to early March and early in January the traditional Fair and Coffee Festival is held, with good bullfights, beauty parades and folk dancing. The city looks down on the small town of Villa María, "the village of flowers", although with the rapid expansion of Manizales, Villa María is now almost a suburb.

The city has twice been destroyed by fire, and today the architecture is predominantly modern with high-rise office and apartment blocks, although traditional architectural styles still exist in the suburbs and the older sections of the city. The regional government building, "Gobernación", opposite the Cathedral in the Plaza Bolívar, is an imposing example of neo-colonial architecture; the bull-ring built 25 years ago is a copy of the traditional Moorish style and is impressive. Because of the sloping and uneven terrain, many of the houses have five or six floors of which only two are above street level. The suburbs stretch away North and South of the city centre and are reached by the main avenida, a four-lane highway lined with flowers—marguerites—which grow to enormous proportions (as also the geraniums) because of the altitude.

Excursions The scenery is attractive when there is no cloud, with well-wooded hills and mountains against the background of the eternal snows of the Nevado El Ruiz. A 60-km. road—the first 32 km. good, the rest bad—runs through impressive scenery to El Ruiz, skirting some awesome precipices. At the snow-line of the Ruiz is the Refugio, a rest house at 4,700 metres, US$2.80 a night and reported to have heating now and a dining room. Oxygen for those who need it. Skis and toboggans can be hired, but bring your own ski-boots. Ski-lift now dismantled. However, it is exhilarating to see snow so near the Equator and the "Ruiz" is worth the trip. Bring warm clothes, some rations, good sunglasses and take it easy; a guide can be found to take you to the mouth of the crater (hard going about four hours). Round trip to the Ruiz: US$2 by bus, leave Plaza Bolívar Saturdays and Sundays 0900; Jeep can be hired in Las Galerías, Calle 18, for about US$14.

Parque de los Nevados national park includes El Ruiz, Santa Isabel, El Cisne, El Nevado del Tolima—all snow-capped peaks. Contact Inderena (National Conservation Institute) for details. Also La Laguna del Otún where there is trout fishing with permission of Inderena.

Beyond Chinchiná, 15 km. from Manizales, is the National Coffee Federation's experimental station where new strains of coffee, cocoa etc., are produced. Can be visited Monday-Friday by appointment.

Manizales has an airport, La Nubia, which has recently been extended to take modern jet-prop aircraft and the regional airline ACES provides an efficient and punctual service to Bogotá (US$24 return), Medellín, and other cities. However, it is well worth taking a flight to Pereira in the Cauca valley and then driving the 56 km. to Manizales—spectacular scenery and very good road. 15 km. beyond Pereira at Santa Rosa de Cabal a poor 11-km. road branches off to some thermal baths where waters from a hot spring cascade down a mountain into a swimming pool. There are also cold showers fed from a natural spring. Restaurant so-so.

Roads To Medellín direct, 265 km. via La Pintada (*Hostería Los Farallones,* nice pool, meals fair), but further if we go West across the Cauca river via Arauca, Anserma, Riosucio and then on to La Pintada. Buses "Autolegal" via Neira and Aguadas, 9 hours, US$2; "Empresa Arauca" via Anserma, 8 hours, US$3.50 ordinary; colectivo to Medellín, US$4.75. Both routes offer impressive scenery, but the longer route is largely unpaved as far as La Pintada. Bus to Bogotá, 8 hours by "Expreso Bolivariano" Pullman, US$5, Ordinario, US$3.80, 9 hours; 7½ hours by "Flota El Ruiz" buseta, US$3.50—beautiful scenery. Cali by bus "Expreso Palmira", 5½ hours, US$2.60 ordinary; Pullman 5 hours, US$3. Pereira, "Expreso Palmira", 1¼ hours, excellent road, beautiful scenery, US$0.75 ordinary. Armenia, "Expreso Palmira", 3 hours, US$1.

Industry Cement plant, distillery, shoes, agricultural equipment, refrigerators, large textile factory, dry batteries, gelatine, leather goods, furniture ("Preman" quite beautiful), candles, shirts (Arrow).

Hotels *Bonaire,* above "Ley" supermarket, not too noisy, spacious, very clean, hot water, US$6 d, US$2.50 p.p. if room shared, US$4.40 s in own room; *Europa,* Carrera 22, No. 23-17, near the bull-ring, restaurant for breakfast only, comfortable and clean, US$9 d, US$6.50 s; *Las Colinas,* best, three-star, two bars, good restaurant, very comfortable, US$15 d, US$11.50 s; *Rokasol,* Carrera 20, Calle 21, near bus station, hot water, clean but noisy, all rooms have bathrooms, US$3 p.p.; *Pensión Margarita,* Calle 23, No. 22-45 (Plaza Bolívar), fairly noisy, US$3.50 d, with bath, US$2.50 s, breakfast, lunch and supper, US$0.80 per meal; *Villa Kempis,* on road to Pereira, about 2 km. past bullring, old religious retreat house, beautiful view over the valley, very quiet, restaurant and bar, good food at moderate prices, US$10 d, US$8 s. *Tama Internacional,* next to Cathedral, US$4 d, meals US$1, warmly recommended. Cheaper: *San Francisco,* Calle 23, No. 18-50, no hot water, clean but noisy, US$2 p.p.; *Residencias Avenida,* Carrera 18, No. 21-21, hot water, new, very clean, family atmosphere, US$2.50 p.p.; *Residencias Colonial,* Calle 20, No. 17-32, no hot water, US$1.50 to US$2.50 p.p.; *Residencias Monaco,* near bus station, US$2 p.p., adequate, English spoken; *Escorial,* Calle 20 and Carrera 22; *Residencias El Cónsul,* one block from plaza where buses stop, towards Cathedral, US$4 d, US$4.30 with bathroom, US$2 s.

La Rochela hotel in the "hot country" about 30 km. (1 hour) W from Manizales on the road to Arauca, large swimming pool for adults and smaller one for children, US$5 for a room for six; no smaller accommodation, family holiday atmosphere, good food at moderate prices; in process of building separate cabins. *Hotel Termales del Ruiz,* about 30 km. from Manizales on the road to the Nevado, swimming pool, private bathrooms, restaurant.

Restaurants *Los Arrayanes* and *Las Torres,* both beautifully set in the Chipre area of town overlooking valleys: *Los Arrayanes* has plain food at moderate prices; *Las Torres,* Colombian dishes, more expensive. *El Cable,* so-called because it stands beside the remaining tower of a disused cable-car transport system for coffee, good food, two-course meal, US$5.50 without wine; *Las Redes,* predominantly sea food, good but about US$8-10 per head without wine; *Cuezzo,* Argentine restaurant with very good meat—try the *parrillada,* moderate prices but wine expensive; *Vitiani,* Italian and European food, quite smart, food and wine fairly expensive, have good trout *(trucha)* and excellent crab-claws *(muellas de cangrejo); El Dorado Español,* moderate prices, good food, *carne a la parrilla* highly recommended, on road to Chinchiná; *El Pilón,* moderate prices, *plato montañero* and *sopa de mondongo* recommended; *Chung-Mi,* Chinese, does take-away meals; *La Suiza,* good fruit juices and cakes; *La Loboteca,* Calle 21, No. 23-40. Chelsea-style "In" restaurant with interesting decor and good music, definitely the trendy place to eat in Manizales, with pizzas and other Italian food, wine on the expensive side, also exhibits the work of local artists; *Domo,* modern-type hamburger joint and pizzeria, moderate prices; *Picaflor,* very good food at moderate prices.

General food and wine tips: wine is normally about US$3.50-4.50 in restaurants for an acceptable bottle of Chilean or Argentine; don't buy European wines as they don't travel well to South America and are very expensive. Don't eat salads unless you know from experience that you can.

Museums Bellas Artes, anthropology museum with interesting selection of findings from Indian tombs, open in the afternoon after 1400. Banco de la República, gold and anthropology museum open during banking hours (see below). Universidad de Caldas, natural history museum open every day from 0800 to 1200 and 1400 to 1800. La Galería del Arte, Parque de Caldas, exhibitions of work done by local artists, pictures can be bought.

Bank Banco Anglo Colombiano (member of Lloyds Bank Group), Carrera 22, No. 17-10, and other banks. Open 0830-1130, 1350-1600, Monday to Friday only. Last working day of the month 0830-1130.

Tourist Office Plaza de Bolívar, opposite Cathedral.

Teatro de los Fundadores Supposedly has the largest stage in Latin America, a modern cinema-theatre auditorium. Interesting wood-carved mural by local artist, Botero, who also has murals in the entrance hall of the Club Manizales and *Hotel Las Colinas.*

The Cauca Valley

From Manizales a road runs S to Pereira; from Pereira a road and a railway run to Cartago, at the northern end of the rich Cauca Valley, which stretches S for about 240 km. but is little more than 30 km. wide. The road and railway go in company down this valley to Cali and Popayán, at the southern limit of the valley proper. There the railway ends but the road mounts a high plateau between the Western and the Central Cordillera and goes all the way to Ecuador. From Cali there is both a railway and a road W to the Pacific port of Buenaventura. The Valley, which has been described in the introduction to this chapter, is one of the richest in Colombia. From Cartago S the river Cauca is navigable as far as Cali.

Pereira, capital of Risaralda Department, 56 km. SW of Manizales, stands overshadowed by green mountains, at an altitude of 1,460 metres, above the Cauca Valley. Population, 220,000; a considerable centre for coffee and cattle. It is a modern city, founded in 1863, with an undistinguished cathedral and four parks: the best is the Parque del Lago, with an artificial lake; a fountain is illuminated several times a week. Matecaña Airport is 5 km. to the S. Outside it is Colombia's largest zoo, showing the country's animals and birds. A paved road and a railway run SE to Armenia (50 km.). Here the road joins the highway which goes E over the Quindío Pass to Ibagué and through Girardot to Bogotá, and another running SW through Calarcá-Caicedonia-Sevilla to Uribe on the main Medellín-Cali highway. The railway is continued SW to Zarzal, on the railway running S to Cali (plenty of food available).

Industries Coffee mills; biscuits and confectionery; brewery; thread-making; clothing and shirts; mineral waters.

Hotels *Soratama,* main plaza, US$7 s; *Gran,* also US$7 s; *Savoy; Español; Italia,* US$1.80 d, old but clean; *Ansonia; Colonial,* US$3.50 s; *Residencia San Francisco,* near buses, US$4, with bath.

There is a good reasonable restaurant at the service station as you enter Calarcá from Ibagué. Others are *El Pollo Campestre* (near airport), *Bonanza* and *El Manolo,* Calle 20, No. 8-22, which has excellent meals for less than US$2.

Clubs *Club Rialto; Club Campestre,* 5 km. from town.

Banks Banco Anglo Colombiano, Carrera 9, No. 17-48. Banco Internacional. Open 0800-1130, 1400-1530. Saturday and last working day of month, 0800-1030.

Tourist Office Calle 18, No. 8-47.

Transport Bus to Armenia, 1 hour, US$0.25, a beautiful trip. Train no longer carries passengers. SAM flights to and from Bogotá (US$12.50). Bus to Cali, US$1.60; Manizales, US$0.55, 1½ hours; to Bogotá, US$3, 7 hours, rough journey, not recommended for motorbikes.

Armenia, capital of Quindío Department, is in the heart of the Quindío coffee district; population 180,000; altitude 1,550 metres; mean temperature 23°C. This modern city, founded in 1889, is the terminus of the Pacific Railway and the seat of Quindío University. The Bogotá-Armenia-Cali road is fully paved, but slow through the mountains. Fog, reckless drivers and stray animals make the Quindío Pass (3,350 metres) a hazard at night. Colectivo-taxis to Bogotá, 4-6 daily, 8 hours.

Hotels *Zuldemaya,* US$8 s; *Palatino,* new, Calle 21 at Cra. 14, US$5.50 s; *Izcay,* also new, Calle 22 with Cra. 14, US$7 d, restaurant not recommended; *Atlántico,* US$2.50 s; *Embajada,* US$4 s; *Alférez; Mariscal Sucre; Pensión Nueva York,* basic but clean and cheap (US$1.30 for three-bed room); *Hotel Moderno Aristi,* Calle 18, Carrera 20, a block from Palmira bus station, US$1.50 d, with bath, hot water, clean.

Restaurants *La Fogotá,* near university; *La Chalet; El Pollo Campestre,* near Country Club.

Archaeological Museum Calle 21, No. 16-37.

Tourist Office Carrera 14, No. 19-21.

Airport El Edén, 13 km. from city. Fog often makes air services unreliable.

Train to Cali, 0600 and 1430 (first class), 7½ hours; a fascinating journey, though twice as long as the bus.

Cartago, 64,830 people, about 17 km. SW of Pereira, is on a small tributary of the Cauca river before it takes to the gorge separating the two cordilleras. Coffee, tobacco and cattle are the main products. Founded in 1540, it still has some colonial buildings, particularly the very fine House of the Viceroys (Casa de los Virreyes). Visit the cathedral, with the cross set aside from the main building.

Hotels *Mariscal Robledo; Alhambra,* Carrera 5a, No. 9-59, US$2 s; *Villa del Río,* US$2.50 d, recommended. Bus to Cali, 3½ hours, US$2.10.

About 27 km. S of Cartago is **La Victoria** (the Pan-American Highway bypasses it to the east), a pleasant, small colonial town with a shady plaza. There is a *Hotel Turista,* one block from the plaza, and several restaurants. La Victoria is in the centre of a beautiful area where cattle are raised, and cotton, sorghum, maize and soya are grown. You can cross the Cauca River by turning right off the road going to the south (good fishing Jan., Feb. and July) and 10 km. (paved road) further on is **La Unión** at the foot of the mountains on the west side of the valley! Stop at the 4th house on the right before the public swimming pool for excellent pan de yuca straight out of a brick oven. La Unión is a small agricultural town, a centre for grape production. *Residencia Los Arrizos,* Calle 13-26, and *Residencia El Cacique.* The countryside around offers lovely walks.

About 50 km. S of Cartago is Zarzal, with a branch line NE to Armenia. And 71 km. S again is **Buga,** an old colonial city of 75,220 people and a centre for cattle, rice, cotton, tobacco and sugar cane. Founded in 1650, but its modern Cathedral contains a famous image of the Miraculous Christ of Buga to which pilgrimages are made. N of Buga, at Uribe (50 km.), is the junction of the Pan-American Highway coming S from Medellín with the Simón Bolívar Highway from Venezuela.

Hotels *Guadalajara* (swimming pool); *España,* US$4 d; *Real* (not recommended); *Capacari,* US$6 d, with bath, clean (swimming pool).

At La Manuelita, 40 km. S of Buga, is a famous sugar estate: the Riopaila sugar mill grinds 2,000 tons of cane daily; there is a sugar refinery, and a distillery turns out 3.4 million litres of alcohol a year. Before reaching La Manuelita any of 3 roads running E will reach, in 12 km., the fine Colonial hacienda of El Paraíso, where the poet Jorge Isaacs (author of "La María", a Colombian classic) lived and wrote. The hacienda is on a slope overlooking the Cauca valley. The main characters in "La María" are sculptured around the bust of the statue to him in Cali's Parque Jorge Isaacs. To visit the hacienda, take a bus from either Buga or Palmira to El Cerrito, and bargain for taxi to take you on, wait and return. This should be about US$4. On Sundays there are tourist buses from Palmira. The trip is recommended.

If you take the road from Buga to Buenaventura you come to Lake Calima. Taking the southern route round the lake 42 km. from Buga is the *Hotel del Lago Calima* set in very pleasant surroundings on the edge of this 13 km. man-made lake. The hotel (US$8.50) has horses for hire, swings and other amusements for children, table tennis, a launch and tennis courts. There is no swimming pool, but some brave people swim in the lake, which is about 16°C and a kilometre deep.

Five km. S of La Manuelita and 47 from Buga is **Palmira,** in the Department of Valle; population, 160,000. Good tobacco, coffee, sugar, rice and grain are grown, and there is a College of Tropical Agriculture. The town still has horse-drawn carriages which operate as taxis. The paved Pan-American Highway runs direct to Popayán *via* Pradera, but the road through Cali is preferable.

Hotels *La Española; Río Nima; Residencias Benalcázar,* US$1.60 d, with bath, clean, friendly, good value.

Restaurant *Grill Caña de Oro,* nice.

From Palmira the railway and a branch road run direct to Cali (29 km.). In the ultra-modern station at Cali there are frescoes illustrating the story of the Pacific Railway and of the city.

Cali, capital of Valle Department (1,170,166 people), is the third largest city in Colombia, set in an exceptionally rich agricultural area producing sugar, cotton, rice, coffee and cattle. Altitude: 1,000 metres; average temperature: 24°C, hot and humid at mid-day but a strong breeze which blows up about 1600 hours makes the evenings cool and pleasant. It was founded in 1536, and until 1900 was a leisurely and somewhat insanitary Colonial town. Then the railway came, and Cali is now a rapidly expanding industrial complex serving the whole of the Cauca Valley; its population is 4 times what it was in 1950. Very little Colonial building is left. Through it runs the Cali river, a tributary of the Cauca. Green hills into which the residential suburbs and some desperate slums have spread, look down on the city. On one mountain, from which the best views are obtained, there is a statue of Christ visible for 50 km. and there are three large crosses on another mountain. San Fernando, where the Olympic Village is situated, has beautiful views of the city. The statue of

Benalcázar, the city's founder, is worth a view. Two nearby haciendas, the very attractive and renovated "El Paraíso" (see above under Buga) and "Canas Gordas", have important historical and literary associations.

The church and monastery of San Francisco are Cali's best buildings. Inside, the church has been renovated, but the 18th century monastery has a splendidly proportioned domed belltower—an example of the mudéjar unique in South America. The monastery's paintings of former monks and abbots are crude but extremely expressive. The 18th century hermitage of San Antonio on the Colina de San Antonio is worth seeing and there are fine views. The orchid garden along the Río Aguacatal, near the centre, is well worth seeing.

The city's centre is the Plaza de Caicedo, with a statue of one of the independence leaders, Joaquín Caicedo y Cuero. Facing the square are the Cathedral, the Palacio Nacional and large office buildings. See also the Museum of Natural History, Carrera 7 Oeste; has some precolumbian exhibits as well as biological specimens from the area.

Warning Give careful attention to your possessions; Cali's thieves are among the worst.

The city is the Cauca Valley's cultural centre. It has two universities—the Universidad del Valle and the Universidad Santiago de Cali—a Medical School, a School of Arts, an Institute of Popular Culture, a Municipal Theatre, an Open Air Theatre, and a fine Museum of Natural History. Its other great devotion (besides business) is to sport. Within its Villa Olimpica in San Fernando it has three great stadiums: the Pascual Guerrero Stadium, holding 50,000 people; the Olympic Gymnasium (basket ball, boxing, fencing, skating, etc.), holding 7,000 people; and the Piscinas Olímpicas, for water sports, and holding 3,000 people. Another great stadium holding 18,000 spectators, the Monumental de Cali, is 10 minutes from the city on the road to Meléndez. Outside the city also is the new first-class bullring.

Industries include motor vehicles, textiles, footwear, sugar-refining, rubber products, tyres, cardboard and paper, pharmaceuticals, bicycles, paint, soap, tobacco products, veterinary products, shoe polish and cables. Bituminous coal is mined nearby. There is a large number of importing firms. There are some 40 United States concerns.

Hotels *Intercontinental,* recently extended, tennis and pool, from US$25 d; *Americana,* for businessmen, US$17 d, a/c, Carrera 4, No. 8-73; *Menéndez,* Carrera 1 with Calle 10, US$9.50 d, all rooms have own bath, good, reasonably priced meals available, nice old Colonial building, popular with Colombians; *Petecuy,* Cra. 9, No. 15-33, modern, rooftop pool, not-so-good area, US$10 d; *Hotel del Puente,* US$8 d, recommended; *Europa,* US$6 d; *Aristi,* Calle 10 with Carrera 9, large and old by Cali standards, turkish baths, rooftop pool, about US$12 d, good restaurant; *New York,* Calle 12, No. 3-62, US$10.50 d; *Plaza,* Carrera 6, No. 10-29, US$8 d; *Nueva York,* Carrera 19 (bis) No. 18-20, US$1 p.p., clean, hot water, basic, near bus station and market; *María Victoria* (old fashioned), US$6.50 d, good; *Los Angeles; Viena,* Calle 15, No. 8-87, US$3.35 d (US$3.60 with bath); *Hotel Fritman,* Carrera 7, No. 11-22, US$3.25 s, with bath; *Calima,* Calle 15, No. 3-66, US$5 d; *Tayrona,* Calle 16 and Carrera 4, US$2.80 s; *Vigo,* Calle 11, No. 8-55, US$3.15 d, very noisy; *La Merced,* 4 blocks from *Intercontinental,* US$7 d, swim pool, pleasant; *Hotel Residencias Stein,* Av. 4N, No. 3-33, US$10 s, US$18 d, full board only, very good, quiet, excellent food, French, German and English spoken, Swiss-run, swimming pool; *Franco,* Calle 11, No. 6-9, US$1.50 p.p., recommended; *Farallones,* good, agree price first. *Residencias las Américas,* near new bus terminal, Calle 25, 2N-31, US$2 d, good; *Decima Avenida,* US$1.20 d, good; *Hotel Alameda,* Calle 11 and Carrera 3, US$1.20 p.p.; *Bastille,* near centre, is basic but cheap at US$1 a night; *San Francisco* is not recommended; *Hospedaje Bolívar,* Calle 25, Carrera 4N, near bus terminal, US$2.10 d, highly recommended for friendly atmosphere; *Escorial,* Calle 24N, No. 1N-66 and at Carrera 4, No. 15-46, US$1.75 d; *Casa del Viajero,* several, found in converted homes, US$3, many on other side of river round Av. 6. For fabulous views, clean air and good food on the road leading up to the Cristo Rey, at about 500-600 metres up the hills overlooking the Valle, is the *Hostería Los Cristales,* US$8.50 d, TV, pool, own transport, recommended.

Restaurants Cali is a good place for eating, as the attached list attests: *Don Carlos,* Carrera 1, No. 7-53, excellent seafood, elegant and expensive; *Hostería Madrid,* Calle 9, No. 4-50, European specialities, good service, above-average price; *Canarias,* Calle 8, between Carreras 3 and 4, recommended for cheap meals; *Restaurante Suizo,* Calle 5, No. 24A-11, Swiss, excellent fondue bourgignonne, pleasant atmosphere, reasonably priced; *Los Farallones,* at *Hotel Intercontinental* on the 9th floor, is Cali's most atmospheric restaurant, with shows starting at about 2230-2300; try their Chateaubriand for two with drinks and desserts, less than US$20 including tips, a real buy; also their weekday noontime buffet at about US$3 a head is very reasonable, eat all you want; *El Quijote,* Carrera 4, No. 1-64, atmospheric, European dishes, expensive; *Simonetta,* Diagonal 27, No. 27-117, pleasant, reasonable, Italian dishes; *Trattoria di Colavizza,* limited menu, excellent food (Italian), very reasonable; *Pueblito Español,* Spanish foods and wines reasonably priced; *El Cortijo Andaluz,* Carrera 38 and Calle 53, atmospheric (converted residence), Spanish and European foods; *Los Girasoles,* Avda. 6N, Calle 35, steaks, other meat grills, good atmosphere; *Los Gauchos del Sur,* Calle 5 about Carrera 60, Argentine-style grilled meat, dancing, excellent food, very reasonable; *Toy San,* Calle 5, No. 39-46, Chinese food, on expensive side of reasonable; *Restaurante China,* Avda. 6N, No. 24-52, excellent food and service, pleasant atmosphere, large servings for reasonable price; *Restaurante Shanghai,* Avda. 8N, No. 17-33, Chinese, excellent food in utilitarian setting, takeaway, very reasonable; *La Parrillada,* Argentine-style grilled meat, live guitar music, pleasant and very reasonably priced; *Embajada Antioqueña,* Carrera 4, No. 3-25 Oeste, Antioquian regional food, pleasant atmosphere, overlooking city, relatively cheap; *Las Vallas,* Avda. 6N, No. 47-197, "International Tourist Centre", a complex of nightclubs and restaurants, so-so food; *Los Panchos,* Carretera a Meléndez with Autopista Sur, very good Colombian food, a favourite of Caleños; *Embajada Quindiana,* rustic atmosphere, Colombian food, relatively cheap; *Pizzeria Salerno,* two locations, along Calle 5a and on Palmira road, excellent pizza, cheap; *Eduardo VIII,* piano bar, attempt at English pub atmosphere, good food, well-stocked bar; *Mauna Loa,* Centro Comercial del Norte, seafood a speciality, reasonably priced, Lebanese food too; *Great American Disaster,* Avda. 7a N, American bar, youthful atmosphere, rock music, great hamburgers; *Mac Club,* Centro Comercial Imbanaco (Calle 5a and Carrera 39), American-style food, world's biggest hamburgers and hotdogs, excellent, cheap; *Sears Cafeteria,* open 0930-1930, excellent food, rather expensive but large servings. *Kokorico,* places all around town, spit-roasted chicken; *El Galeón,* Calle 8a, No. 1-27, very good seafood and atmosphere, expensive; *Jino's Pizza,* held to be Cali's best pizzas, new and reasonably priced; *Arca de Noé,* on road to Cristo Rey, overlooking city, good food, spectacular views; *Bill's Place* (Rincón Budapest), Calle 15N, No. 6-37, Hungarian Bill is a whiz at fried shrimp (his No. 1 attraction), goulash and other Hungarian specials; huge servings at tiny prices, service individualized and may take hours but surely worth it; one of British colony's favourite places; *Caballo Loco,* in northern sector, excellent, US$3 a meal.

You can find lots of European-style side-walk places along the Avda. 6 at good prices. Try Mexican food at *Mexitaco.* Cheaper are the *fuentes de soda* you'll find all around, mostly with Colombian-style cooking, which is generally plentiful and tasty; a decent meal for between US$1-2. There is also *Masserna* ("your lunch for one dollar") on Carrera 7 between Calles 10 and 11 and *La Sultana* on the corner with *Hotel Aristi.* Try their *buñuelos* (cheesy fritters) and the *pandebono* (cheesy bread buns) next door at *Montecarlo.* Cafés and ice-cream parlours abound in the vicinity of the university, across the river from the main part of town.

Nightclubs Locally known as "Grills". The ones along the Avda. Roosevelt and along Calle 5a are safest and best known. *Arca de Noé, Farallones* at the *Intercontinental* and *El Penol* on the Buenaventura road are probably Cali's best (and most expensive).

Clubs Club Colombia; Club de Tennis de Cali; Club San Fernando, modern and luxurious; Club Campestre, as good as any club anywhere, with a magnificent golf course, tennis courts and swimming pool; Club La Ribera y Náutico.

Fair Held during December; bullfights, masquerade balls, sporting contests. National Art Festival in June (painting, sculpture, theatre, music, etc.).

Rail W to Buenaventura, 169 km.; N to Armenia, Cartago, and Medellín. (At the end of 1977 the line was not in operation, having been damaged by floods in 1974.) There is no through line to Bogotá. Passengers must go by road from Armenia across Quindío Pass to Ibagué, whence there is a railway to the capital. Some sections have a fast passenger service of diesel cars (auto ferros). Trains to Buenaventura 1330 daily, 4½ hours. Train journeys tend to be slower, but more scenic than those by road.

Tourist Office Corporación Nacional de Turismo, Carrera 3 and Calle 11. Maps and general information. Also co-operative for shopping. There is a Thomas Cook office just off the Plaza de Caicedo.

Buses New bus terminal by railway station is now open, but is some distance from the centre. There are plenty of local buses between the bus and railway stations and the centre, which charge US$0.03. Buses to Popayán, US$1.50, 2½-3 hours; to Pasto, US$5.25, 8½ hours; to Ipiales (direct), US$6, 11 hours or by Bolivariano Pullman, US$6.50; to Cartago, 3½ hours, US$2.10; to Ibagué, US$3.50, 7 hours; to Buenaventura, US$1.35, 3 hours; to Manizales, US$3.10, 5 hours; to Medellín, US$5.25, 10 hours; to Bogotá, 10-12 hours, by Magdalena (recommended) and Palmira, US$5.80. "Busetas" (Velotax and others) charge about 50% over bus prices but save time; taxi-colectivos about 2½ times bus prices and save even more.

Road to Bogotá This road is the most important in the country. It passes through the Cauca Valley as far as Armenia (p. 471), then passes over the Quindío Pass to Ibagué (p. 440) and on to Girardot (p. 446).

Banks Banco Anglo Colombiano (formerly BOLSA), Calle 11, No. 4-48 (Plaza de Caicedo), and agency on Avenida Roosevelt; Banco Internacional (ex City Bank); Banco Royal de Colombia (ex Royal of Canada); Banco Francés e Italiano; Banco Colombo Americano (ex Bank of America) and other national banks. Open: 0800-1130. 1400-1600. Last working day of month, 0800-1130. Closed Sats.

Bookshop Librería Nacional, on main square, has English books and a café.

Airport Palmaseca, 20 km. from city. International standard. Minibus seat, US$0.25. Colectivo to city about US$0.50; taxi, US$2. Round trip to Quito with Ecuatoriana (30 days), US$120.

PSNC Agents E. L. Gerlein & Co. S.A., P.O. Box 1594. Same agents for **Royal Mail Lines**.

British Consul Edificio Garcés, office No. 410, Calle 11, No. 1-07. Tel.: 721752-3. Postal address: Apartado Aéreo 1470.

Excursion from Cali to Río Pance, an attractive picnic resort to which the locals go on Sundays. Take the local Blanco y Negro No. 1 buseta to the end of the line; from there a special bus runs to Río Pancé.

169 km. W by railway (4¾ hours) and 145 km. by road (4 hours) over a pass in the Western Cordillera (new highway almost completed) is

Buenaventura, Colombia's only important port on the Pacific, and one of the busiest on the West Coast. It stands on the island of Cascajal, 16 km. inside the Bay of Buenaventura. The entrance has a depth of only 7½ metres, but the tide adds 4 metres and this allows most regular line vessels to discharge alongside. Tankers, the largest to enter, draw around 9½ metres and must always await high tide. Port works are in progress. Beaches such as La Bocana, Juanchaco and Ladrilleras may be reached by motor launch, although these are not very safe.

Buenaventura is 560 km. by sea from Panama, 708 km. by road and rail from Bogotá. Population, 120,000. Mean temperature, 29°C. It rains nearly every day, particularly at night; the average annual rainfall is 6,600 mm. The Rockefeller Foundation's anti-malaria campaign has greatly improved health, although there are still problems with malaria. The main exports are coffee, cotton, sugar and frozen shrimps. The port is congested at times, and so is the railway E to Cali; a single track with no room for a second but an incredibly beautiful journey through luxurious jungle, then a rise to 1,520 metres with tremendous views of the Cauca Valley 600 metres below, and a slow wind down the mountain side. Do the trip from Buenaventura to Cali, starting 0600. The new toll road to Cali is 80% paved; the toll is about US$0.40 for cars and US$0.10 for motorcycles. The ordinary road is not paved. There are plenty of buses. (To Cali US$1.35, 3-4 hours.)

The commercial centre is now entirely paved and has some impressive buildings, but the rest of the town is poor, with steep unpaved streets lined with wooden shacks. Some of it is being rebuilt. The population is largely black. S of the town a swampy coast stretches as far as Tumaco (see page 484); to the N lies the deeply jungled Chocó Department; here are the most important gold and platinum producers.

Shipping Passenger Lines: Grace; French; Gulf & South America; Hamburg-Amerika; Johnson; Knutsen; Nedlloyd; North German Lloyd; Royal Netherlands; Westfal-Larsen, Cargo; Pacific Steam Navigation. The best way of finding out prices (which vary from line to line) is to approach the captain of each ship. Grace Line passenger ships leave roughly every 15 days for Los Angeles; fares from US$735, book well in advance.

Note that it can take a day to clear a vehicle through Customs. The best way to save time is to appoint a customs agent for a fee of US$20 or so; this may get the job done in 2 hours! Helpful to have a *carnet de passages*.

Industry Tanning bark factory; timber yards; four factories (the largest one American) boxing frozen shrimp for export and canning tuna for consumption in the interior of Colombia.

Hotels *The Grand* (US$2.50 p.p.for bed only) is the best of a poor lot. *Hotel Estación*, "well worth seeing for connoisseurs of crumbling tropical hotels"—Robert M. Chipley—US$4.50 per night.

Camping With the permission of the commandant, it is safe to camp in the police compound at the docks while awaiting your ship.

Wireless The Government's Telecomunicaciones now handles all interior and foreign messages, telex and telephone.

American Consular Agency Grace Building.

Air Services Local airport only; flights to Cali.

Warning Thieves are abundant and without scruple.

The paved Pan-American Highway (142 km.) and a railway (169 km.) go S through the Cauca Valley from Cali to Popayán. It takes 2½-3 hours by bus (train services are suspended), through splendid scenery. At first we pass through a land of rich pastures interspersed with sugar-cane plantations. To left and right are the mountain walls of the two Cordilleras. At the stations sellers of fried chicken and fruits press their wares on the passengers. The valley narrows and we begin to climb, with occasional glimpses E of the towering Nevado del Huila (5,750 metres).

Popayán is the garden valley of the Pubenza, at 1,760 metres, in a peaceful landscape of palm, bamboo, and the sharp-leaved agave. Population, 106,000. The early Spaniards, after setting up their rich sugar estates in the hot and wet valley, retreated to Popayán to live, for the city is high enough to give it a delightful climate. From early days Popayán was an aristocratic reserve, lived in mainly by people of pure European descent. It still is so today, and a very attractive town it is. The streets are wide and clean and there is little traffic. They are laid out in regular squares, with buildings of two storeys, in rococo Andalusian style. To N, S, and E the broken green plain is bounded by mountains. To the SE rises the snowcapped cone of the volcano Puracé (3,960 metres); it smokes, but erupts rarely, though there are occasional earthquake shocks.

Popayán was founded by Benalcázar, one of Francisco Pizarro's lieutenants, in 1536. Its early years were clouded by wars against the fierce Pijao Indians, but these were soon conquered and Popayán became the regional seat of government, subject, until 1717, to the Audiencia at Quito, and later to the Audiencia of Bogotá. It is now the capital of the Department of Cauca. The equestrian statue of Benalcázar on the Morro de Tulcán overlooks the city; it is worth climbing up for the sake of the views.

Popayán is to Colombia what Weimar is to Germany, or Burgos is to Spain. There are beautiful old monasteries and cloisters of pure Spanish classic architecture in the city, and nearly all the churches are old, though many of the interiors have been deplorably spoilt by cheap statuary, commercial religious prints, imitation marble, imitation wood, cardboard cherubim and clouds. Popayán was the home of the poet Guillermo Valencia; it has given no less than 7 presidents to the Republic.

The most famous churches are San Francisco and San Agustín; San Francisco (Calle 4 and Carrera 9) is especially famous for its carved pulpit and the bell whose voice can be heard all over the valley. The sacristy has some rich ritual treasures, particularly the gold and enamel monstrance studded with precious stones. There is a most beautiful monstrance, too, at San Agustín (Calle 7 and Carrera 6) and a colonial doorway at Santo Domingo, Calle 4 and Carrera 5. Also splendid is La Encarnación Chapel at Calle 5, Carrera 5: full of carved and gilt wooden altars. Also worth seeing is El Carmen, at Calle 4 and Carrera 3. The Chapel of Belén, Plazuela Belén, on a hill to the E of the city, is worth visiting for the view (but beware of thieves in the area). A typical street of Colonial mansions is Calle Próceres, N of Parque Caldas, the main square.

The versatile Francisco José de Caldas was born here in 1771; it was he who discovered how to determine altitude by variation in the boiling point of water, and it was to him that Mutis (of the famous *Expedición Botánica*) entrusted the directorship of the newly founded Observatory at Bogotá. He was besides an able writer who wrote ardently for the cause of independence, and was executed in 1815 during Morillo's "Reign of Terror".

The University, founded in 1640, is on Calle 4 and Carrera 5. Its main door is next to the entry to Santo Domingo church. It was built in what were the old cloisters of the Dominicans, a block away from the central square.

Hotels *Monasterio,* on Calle 4, in what was the Monastery of San Francisco, US$10 d, very good; *Los Balcones,* Calle 3, new, US$6.50 d; *Tunubala,* US$7 d; *La Casa de San Sebastián,* Calle 4, No. 7-79, US$4.50 s, US$6 d, young, English-speaking owner, has vast knowledge of touristic possibilities of the area. All-day coffee bar in the hotel, clean, with covered patio; *La Casona del Virrey,* Carrera 5a, No. 4-72, US$5 d, with bath, US$4, without bath, very pleasant and safe; *Hotel Gualcalá,* US$1 p.p., with hot shower, pleasant; *Residencial Popayán,* US$0.80; *Colonial,* US$4 d, basic, but central; *Residencia La Viña,* Calle 4, US$3.75 d; *Panamá,* between main plaza and market, cheap, adequate meals; *Viajero,* Calle 8 and Carrera 4, US$1.60 s, with bath, clean, friendly and excellent value; *Victoria* (US$2.25 p.p., with shower, noisy); *Atlanta; Florida; Roosevelt* (rather noisy, at major bus centre, US$1.50 s, US$3 d, without food); other cheap hotels near bus station, quite acceptable, US$1 or US$1.50 d, without private bath. One is *Hotel Huila Internacional,* from US$3 d, friendly, and clean, good meals for US$0.75; *Hospedaje Neiva,* also near the bus station, is not recommended; *Platino,* US$0.60 each, dingy; *Residencias Américas,* US$4 d, with bath; *Santa Fe,* US$1.50 d, clean; *Greco; Residencias Bucareli,* US$1 s, basic, but quieter than some near bus station; *Residencias Bolívar,* US$1.50 p.p., clean and pleasant; *Residencias Turista,* US$1.50 d, noisy.

Note If you enquire at the tourist office, they may be able to find you accommodation in a private house.

Restaurants Many good ones. Try *Herrería* (a good meal costs US$2-3, service is good, pleasant surroundings) at Calle 2, No. 5-88; also *Parma* (Carrera 6 between Calles 3 and 4). *Restaurant Magdalena,* near Magdalena bus office; *La Castellana* is a good, cheap restaurant on Carrera 6 but be careful that they give you the current menu and not an old one with out of date prices which they will then increase; *Mey Chow,* good, but service could be improved; *Restaurant Valencia* inside *Residencias Bolívar,* excellent meal for US$0.65 and breakfast for US$0.55; *Comedores del Mesón,* Calle 4, they have a quick turnover and a good meal costs US$1; *El Faisán,* Calle 4, very good and cheap; *Benalcázar,* Carrera 6, No. 4-65, on main square, good meal for less than US$1. Try also, at the *Heladería Baudilia,* Calle 3, No. 4-85, Salpicón, Guanábana and Curuba ice-cream. Excellent juices and ices at *Lucerna* restaurant. On the road to Cali, about 7 km. outside Popayán, is the Centro Turístico El Bambú, which has a restaurant and a swimming pool.

Banks Banco de la República is the only one that changes foreign currency. (Open 0800-1130; 1400-1530.) However, the *Hotel Monasterio* will accept travellers' cheques when you pay your bill and will give you change in pesos.

Shopping Leather bags are very cheap.

Museums Casa Mosquera, colonial museum, Carrera 5, Calle 3; it has also an ethnological section. Museo Guillermo Valencia, Carrera 6, No. 2-69; Museo de Historia Natural, right opposite the University; enjoyable; Museo de Pintura Efraín Martínez in painter's house, "El Refugio", just outside Popayán on road to Calicanto. Museo de Arte Colonial, Calle 4, interesting, US$0.15 charge.

Tourist Office has recently moved, so you must ask for directions to it when you arrive in Popayán. They will tell you where horses may be hired to explore the surrounding countryside.

Buses To Cali, US$1.50, 2½-3 hours, or "Velotax" microbus, US$2, colectivos leave from the main plaza; to Pasto, US$4, 6 hours, spectacular scenery; Pullman to Pasto, US$3 to Ipiales, US$3.60, 10 hours; to San Agustín (see page 447), US$5.50, 10-12 hours; to San Andrés (see page 481), US$2. (There is an Aeropesca 'plane every day at 0830 for Pasto—only US$9.10.) Watch out for thieves around the bus terminal.

Popayán is famous for its Easter celebrations. A permanent Council for Holy Week directs the preparations. On Palm Sunday a procession brings down two images from the Chapel of Belén, which stands on a hill overlooking the city, to the Cathedral, where they stay between the night processions of Holy Week. The first image is of *El Santo Ecce-Homo,* a near life-size figure of the seated Christ crowned with thorns, brought in the 17th century from Pasto. This image, known as The Master, is patron of the workers and the guardian of the city against lightning, earthquakes and termites. The second image is that of the Fallen Lord, also almost life-size, and depicting Christ fallen on the ground after being whipped.

There are processions throughout the week, and each procession includes eleven, twelve, or thirteen images taking over an hour to pass. Except on Good Friday, each procession is closed with one of the richest, most beautiful, and most venerated of all the images: that of Our Lady of

Sorrows. The Good Friday procession depicts the events between the Crucifixion and the burial of Christ: Death, a grinning skeleton with a scythe; men carrying hammers and instruments to take His body from the Cross; angels bearing the symbols of the Passion and the Holy Sepulchre, showing the body of Jesus lying on a bier decorated with ivory and silver and shell.

In the past few years there has also been a festival of sacred music during Holy Week with some of the best musicians in the hemisphere playing. During Holy Week the streets are filled with Indians and people from the countryside dressed in brilliant skirts and black shawls.

As at Pasto (but less violent), there are the Día de los Negros on Jan. 5 and Día de los Blancos on Jan. 6; as at Carnival, the tourist and his belongings are likely to be drenched in water.

Warnings Thieves and pickpockets, who normally frequent the bus station, also come to Popayán for Easter week during which time extra care should be taken. Muggings often occur at night near the bridge. Police raids on hotels have become quite frequent as part of the nation-wide campaign against drug trafficking, and young people of informal dress and life-style (especially men with long hair and beards) must be especially careful; there are well-authenticated cases of the police planting drugs.

Excursions A favourite is the drive to Silvia, at 2,754 metres, up through Totoró (unpaved) or down by Piendamó (paved) two beautiful routes.

Silvia lies in a high valley. (Hotels: *Hotel de Turismo,* expensive and not recommended. Next door is *Hotel Cali,* an old house, with good craft shop, US$4 a day s, including food. A little primitive, but very pleasant. *La Parrilla,* US$1.20 per night, plus food.) Silvia has become a resort for Cali people seeking a cooler climate. It is no longer an Indian town, but the Guambiano Indian farms nearby may be visited on horseback. Silvia has an interesting Indian market on Tuesday mornings until 1300.

For those who like to go off the beaten track, Sr. Camilo Arroyo (address: Carrera 3, No. 4-65, Popayán) arranges trips into the mountains, and towards the coast, W of Popayán. He charges about US$50 a day p.p., depending on the length of the trip, size of the party, etc.

Road to Neiva (page 447) across the Central Cordillera, which is paved from Puerto Seco to Neiva, has interesting sights off it. Drive 37 km. along it (or take 0400 bus) to the small town of **Puracé,** which has several old buildings. Drive to the Escuela and walk 5 minutes to see Chorrera de las Monjas waterfalls. About 11 km. E of Puracé towards Neiva a road branches S from the main road; 1 km. along this road is another fork; the right branch leads to the Puracé sulphur mines (3,000 metres) 5 km. away; the left fork runs 1½ km. to the office of the Puracé National Park, and hot baths. From here a path leads to the volcano. The volcano is steep; loose ash makes footholds difficult. It takes up to 5 hours to get to the top. The Puracé National Park is one of the regions in Colombia where *páramo,* high altitude vegetation, may be seen at close quarters. Condors are sometimes seen. The 112 geysers are most interesting; according to temperature they produce different coloured algae. The Park's fauna include the spectacled bear and mountain tapir. Accommodation is available. A cabin for 5 persons is US$8. Camping is allowed.

Puracé can also be climbed from the thermal baths at Pisimbalá, where there are US$2-a-bed overnight facilities for tourists—enquire at the Popayán tourist office.

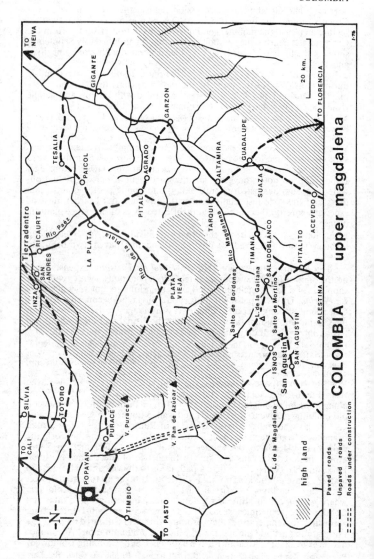

COLOMBIA **upper magdalena**

Take warm clothes (and a sleeping bag) if climbing the volcano; the nights are cold and blankets in the mountain cabins are thin!

Coconuco, at 2,734 metres, has beautiful landscapes. Turn to the right off the Popayán-Neiva road after 21 km. (16 km. *short* of Puracé); then 7 km. along is Coconuco (*Hotel de Turismo* has been closed but is scheduled to reopen by now; *Casa Familiar,* US$0.50, basic). Drive on 12 km. to the impressive scenery of the Paletará highland; a bus to the village of Paletará takes 1 hour and costs US$0.20. Bus to Popayán, US$0.40, 1 hour. There are good thermal baths near the village.

At **La Plata,** 96 km. from Popayán, turn left and drive for 32 km. to Guadualejo, where one road runs left for 12 km. to **San Andrés de Pisimbolá** (a little village near the Archaeological Park) and **Inzá;** another goes straight on for 12 km. to Benalcázar (a dusty drive). An alterative and less-used Popayán-La Plata road (bus, US$0.60) goes *via* Inzá. At San Andrés a unique and beautiful colonial church with a thatched roof was burned down in January 1975, but it has now been reconstructed much as before. Some few km. before reaching San Andrés you pass the Tierradentro Museum.

If you telephone Sr. Francisco Romano in Bogotá you may be able to arrange to be at San Andrés when he takes a group on an archaeological-anthropological visit to the area. He is bilingual and has an extensive knowledge of Tierradentro.

At San Andrés hire horses (US$0.60 an hour)—or you can walk—for visiting the **Tierradentro** man-made burial caves painted with geometric patterns. The three main sites can be visited in a day but it is advisable to start with the furthest, "Aguacate", although this is a very stiff climb, too steep for horses. There are no guards at this site and no illumination. Guards at the other sites have lights, and act as guides. For the other, smaller, caves you must take a torch. The surroundings have spectacular natural beauty.

For people on a one-day visit, go to Segovia, which has over 20 tombs, 4 of which are lit. The site is a 15 minute walk uphill from the administration house. El Duende, close to Segovia, is 25 minutes from the administration house.

At nearby Tablón are huge stone statues; there are several of these in the new plaza at Inzá. Also at Tablón is the only stone representation of an Indian hut to be found in pre-Colombian sites in South America. Monseñor Vallejo will show you the treasures in his museum at Belalcázar. The Páez Indians in the Tierra-dentro region wear special costumes. See them on market days at Inzá (Sat.), San Andrés (Wed.), and Belalcázar (Sat.); all start at 0600. Take bus at 0530 from Tierradentro to Inzá market; best to go into San Andrés and out again to be sure of getting a seat.

Hotels Opposite museum, *State Tourist Hotel,* very clean, US$1 p.p., no food; between San Andrés and museum, rooms in home of Sra. Marta de Angel, US$1 p.p. plus US$0.50 for excellent meals; other cheap accommodation in village and camping is allowed at museum where water is available, US$0.30 p.p. *Albergue San Andrés de Pisimbalá,* US$5.50 s, US$7.50 d, often referred to as *Refugio Pisimbalá* or *Albergue Tierradentro,* dining room, swimming pool. You can camp in the grounds here and at the *State Tourist Hotel.*

Restaurants *Fonda Antioqueña,* reasonably priced, good food. Villagers provide meals—at a price.

Tierradentro may be reached by direct bus from Popayán, or from San Agustín (see p.447) with a change at **La Plata.** (This can be a two-day trip with the bus leaving at 0530 from La Plata.) The road from Popayán is difficult and narrow, but this is compensated by the beautiful scenery. Buses leave Popayán at 0400 (0300 on

Saturdays) and 1300 and cost US$1.50. Take 3½ hours to Cruce San Andrés. Walk (about 20 minutes) from there to the museum. The village is another 20 minutes walk from the museum. There is ample time to visit the caves and San Andrés village before catching the bus at 1600 next day (or the same day if you have left at 0500) to La Plata—3 hours. The last bus to Popayán from San Andrés is at 1300. If you want to go to Silvia, take this bus and change to a colectivo (US$0.45) at Piendamó. There are buses on market day, or trucks (US$0.35).

There is a bus from La Plata to San Agustín at 0800; the road follows the spectacularly beautiful Páez valley. Journey about 7 hours. The bus to San Andrés leaves at 0500, cost US$0.70.

Hotels at La Plata: *Berlin,* US$1 p.p.; *Residencias Tunubalu,* US$0.90 s; others in same price range.

The Pan-American Highway goes S from Popayán to Pasto. Most of the road is now paved, but the 294-km. drive still takes 5-5½ hours. The bus takes 7 hours (US$1.75) in ordinary conditions, though landslides often block the road.

"First", writes Christopher Isherwood in *The Condor and the Cows,* "there is the descent into the hot lowlands around El Bordo. Then the long grinding climb to La Unión, perched on its sheer-sided ridge. From there on the terrain resembles violently crumpled bedclothes. You enter tremendous valleys, and foresee 20 miles of your journey at a glance, for the road is scribbled wildly across them. The tilled fields on the opposite mountain-face look nearly vertical."

Correspondents have told us that Isherwood understates the beauty of this landscape, and the road has been realigned to bypass La Unión and Mercaderes (below). There are three basic hotels at La Union (beware of overcharging at the *Hotel Nevada*).

163 km. south of Popayán is **Mercaderes,** a small town with a pleasant climate. Hotels, about US$1.20 p.p., are good and the *Restaurante Tropical* is recommended.

Pasto, capital of the Department of Narino, stands upon a high plateau (2,600 metres) in the SW, 122 km. from Ecuador. It has a population of 113,000. The city, which has lost its colonial character, was founded in the early days of the conquest. Today it is a centre for the agricultural and cattle industries of the region, which exports little. Pasto varnish is mixed locally, to embellish the strikingly colourful local wooden bowls. There are some gold mines in the area. The smoking volcano, Galeras (4,069 metres), is to the W. A highway traversing all kinds of altitudes and climates has been built round it; the trip along it takes half a day. On it lies the village of Sandoná where Panama hats are made; they can be seen lying in the streets in the process of being finished. The University of Narino was opened at Pasto in 1962. A visit to the Church of Cristo Rey near the centre is recommended.

During the new year's fiesta there is a "Día de los Negros" on Jan. 5 and a "Día de los Blancos" next day. On "black day" people dump their hands in black grease and paint, without exception, each other's faces black. On "white day" they throw talc or flour at each other. Local people wear their oldest clothes. Things can get quite violent. On December 28 and Feb. 5, there is also a "Fiesta de las Aguas" when anything that moves—only tourists because locals know better—gets drenched with water from balconies and even from fire engines' hoses.

During the wars of independence, Pasto was a stronghold of the Royalists and the last town to fall into the hands of the patriots after a long and bitter struggle. This is typical of the character of the men of Narino Department, the most traditional of all the Colombian peoples; they wanted to join Ecuador when that country split off from Gran Colombia in 1830, but were prevented by Colombian troops.

Hotels *Morasurco,* Avenida de los Estudiantes, US$11 d; *Pacifico,* Under German management, US$10 d, good; *Central; Real; Winnipeg* (US$1.60 p.p.); *Niza* (not now recommended); *Residencias América* (hot water); *Residencias Santa Ana; Residencias El Carmen,* near bus station, clean and comfortable, US$4 d; *Res. El Dorado* (hot water, comfortable); the *Hotel Granadero* (US$1 a night); *Embajador* (centre, no food, US$3.50 d); *Residencias Colón.* US$0.65 p.p., clean, hot water; *San Fernando,* US$3 p.p., clean, quiet, next Expreso Bolivariano, good value, hot water; *Hotel Nueva York,* US$1.50 p.p., near Magdalena bus company, the only place in the town where you can put a motorcycle inside; *Miami* (cheap, has restaurant, hot water in the morning, safe); *Zorocán,* near *Miami,* central; *Londres* (US$1.10 s, hot water), *Residencias Suiza* (Calle 19 and Carrera 20, near market, US$4.50 d, with shower, hot water, clean and light, but noisy); *Manhattan,* basic and cheap, has hot water, US$1.20; *Residencias Isa,* clean and new, US$4.80 d, Calle 18. No. 22-23, good; *Residencia Texalia,* Carrera 18, No. 13-39, US$1.60 s; *Residencias Monserrate,* new, clean, near bus station and market (hence extremely noisy), hot showers, US$1.80 p.p., not very safe, but does provide towels and soap; *Residencias Ambala,* Calle 18, US$1.50 s, hot water, clean; *Américas,* US$1.80 d, hot water; *Pensión Pasto,* unsavoury but cheap, US$0.40 p.p.; *Residencias Colonial,* central and cheap; *Residencias Modernas,* behind bus station, US$0.70 per room, clean; *Residencial Marta,* nearby, US$0.80 d. Avoid *Hotel Caribe* unless you like local odour, prostitutes, fleas and police.

Restaurants *Wonderbar,* good meal for US$1; *El Gaucho,* good meal for under US$2; *El Arriero,* Carrera 26, No. 15-58, a popular restaurant; *Metropolitano,* off Carrera 20, good, cheap food; *La Cabana,* next to *Hotel San Francisco,* good meat dishes for US$2. *Erik's* restaurant for a good meal, Erik is German and knows the jungle well, he has got helpful advice; *El Encinar,* Calle 16, No. 13-48, US$0.50. Most restaurants on main street are OK.

Banks Banco Anglo Colombiano (ex-BOLSA), Carrera 25, No. 16-58, and national banks. Open 0830-1130, 1400-1530; Saturdays and last working day of month, 0800-1100. This is the last place before crossing to Ecuador, or going to Tumaco, where travellers' cheques can be cashed. A cambio off the main square will change sucres into pesos, but the Banco de la República will not.

Shopping Artesanías Colombianas have a branch on Carrera 25. See Colegio Artesanías, run by a government institute (sena), 5 km. N on road to Popayán. Visitors welcome. Leather goods are cheaper here than in Bogotá. Most of the shops are on Calle 19. Supermercado Confamiliar de Nariño, Calle 16b, No. 30-53, recommended.

Post Office for air mail, Calle 18 with Carrera 26.

Tourist Office Just off the main square, on Calle 18, near Carrera 25.

Ecuadorean Consulate Carrera 17, No. 26-55, 2nd floor.

Buses To Bogotá (25 hours), US$11 Flota Magdalena, US$13 Expreso Bolivariano. To Ipiales (2 hours), US$1.20 (seat in colectivo, about US$1.50, 1½ hours). To Popayán, ordinary buses take 10-12 hours and cost about US$2.50; expresses take 7-8 hours, cost US$3.50. To Cali, US$5.25, 8½ hours. To Tumaco, US$2.75, 9 hours.

Air Service Daily to Popayán,US$10, 20 minutes, Cali and Bogotá, and to Ipiales by Avianca on Friday. Aerotal, Pasto to Cali, daily at 0800, US$13. The airport is at Cano, 40 km. from Pasto; Colectivo (beautiful drive), US$1, 45 minutes.

Tumaco Region

The 280-km. road W from Pasto to Tumaco is paved 20 km. beyond Túquerres, but is then unsurfaced. After Junín the road runs parallel to the Transandine oil pipeline, which originates in the Putumayo. After El Diviso the very badly-surfaced road follows the line of an old railway; in the villages along the road former stations and booking offices can still be seen, now used as houses and police check-points. The region is very different from highland Colombia, with two-storey Caribbean-style wooden houses and a predominantly black population. Small farms are mixed with cattle ranches, rice farms and oil-palm plantations. Cocoa is grown. The coastal area around Tumaco is mangrove swamp; negotiate with boatmen for a boat-ride into the swamps or to visit the island tourist resort of Boca Grande.

Tumaco is growing rapidly, with a recent influx of people hoping for work in a planned oil refinery or in the growing tourist trade. A natural arch on the main beach, N of the town and port, is reputed to be the hiding place of Henry Morgan's treasure. Swimming is safe and pleasant; stalls provide refreshment on the beach. Hotels are well subscribed and of varying quality—it is advisable to take a place in one early in the day.

Hotels   *Residencias El Dorado,* at US$1-1.25 p.p., is recommended, with a balcony looking out over the sea; *Hotel Sucursal,* US$2.75 each, provides a mosquito net and has a restaurant; (others, e.g. *Residencias California* and *Pensión Ecuador,* are cheaper but only tolerable). **Food:** The main culinary attractions of the town are the fish dishes, in the market and restaurants, fresh from the Pacific.

Buses   There are through buses to Tumaco from Pasto, or else you can catch a bus from Ipiales to Espino (US$0.60) and there change buses for Tumaco (US$2).

Part of the town is built on stilts out over the sea. Visit it during daylight as it is reported to be dangerous at night, and not just because you could fall through the holes in the wooden pavements into the sea! There is an airport, and the area is also noted archaeologically for the finds associated with the Tumaco culture. The town has problems with water and electricity supplies. There are no money exchange facilities.

Barbacoas, 57 km. from Junín, is interesting—a former Spanish gold-producing centre which still retains the remains of an extensive waterfront, a promenade and steps coming down through the town to the river. Gold is still panned from the rivers by part-time prospector-farmers. Hotels (2) are interesting, and very basic. Avoid drinking in the local dance-hall—prices are double the price anywhere else! The road to Barbacoas is limited to one-way traffic in places—enquire at the chain barring the road at Junín and the operator will telephone down the line to see if the route is clear for you to pass.

The Putumayo

One hour E of Pasto, on the road to Mocoa (capital of the Intendencia of Putumayo) is **Lago La Cocha,** the largest lake in S Colombia. By the lake is the Swiss-run *Chalet Guámez,* US$14 d, well recommended. There is also the *Hotel Sindamanoy,* US$2 p.p., clean and comfortable. Rafael Narváez has cheap, basic, rooms to let. The chalet will arrange a US$7 jeep trip to Sibundoy, further along the road. La Cocha may be reached by taking a bus to El Encano and walking the remaining 5 km.

The road from Pasto to the Putumayo deteriorates rapidly after El Encano. It is dangerous between Sibundoy and El Pepino and care should be taken, but there is a magnificent view out over the Putumayo by a large statue of the Virgin, just before the final descent.

Sibundoy   About a quarter of the valley is now reserved for Sibundoy Indian occupation. Craft goods and fashionable striped manas are for sale. Don Manuel, at Calle 18, No. 17-82, should be visited for woven and carved goods. Roasted guinea-pig *(cuy)* may be eaten in the restaurant here. Bus from Pasto (2½ hours, US$0.70). *Hotel Turista,* US$1.20 p.p., clean; *Residencias San Francisco* and *Colón.* You can camp in the hills where there are lovely walks and you can see all kinds of flora and fauna. Peace Corps workers in the remote villages are happy to give information and help.

Mocoa, the administrative capital of the Intendencia of Putumayo, is small, with a number of hotels and residencias. The town has a very modern square, new offices and modern developments. Sugar-cane is grown in the area; milk may be seen alongside the road to the town. The road to Puerto Asís is good—passing through an area cleared mainly in the last 12 years and supporting cattle ranching. *Hotel Viajero,* US$8.80 s.

Puerto Asís is the main town and port of the Putumayo. River traffic is busy and steamers leave each Sunday for Leticia—by far the cheapest way of travel there—with connexions to Manaus. The trip to Leticia costs between US$5 and US$25; see the Jefe de la Marina about a passage. Journey takes 10-15 days. For those interested in flora and fauna it is necessary to travel down river, beyond new areas of settlement.

There are regular flights to and from Puerto Asís three times a week by Satena to Bogotá, *via* Florencia. Flights to Florencia are on Mon., Wed. and Fri. at 1000, cost, US$6.50.

Hotels *Residencias Nevado* is close to the airport on the outskirts of the town—well kept and comfortable, air-conditioning optional and costing US$2-2.50 p.p., without board. *Residencias Nubia,* highly recommended at US$1, especially for the excellent tasty food in the restaurant attached, where river fish are cooked when available. *Residencias Patiño,* US$1, recommended; *Hotel Meri,* US$3 d, with fan; *Residencias Gigante,* clean. There are plenty of cheap hotels in the port.

Buses may be taken to Pasto (a 10 hour journey, mostly on mountainous roads, US$2.20) or locally to San Miguel near the Ecuadorean border where the Sunday market provides a meeting place, and where *canoas* may be hired to visit villages 2-4 hours away on the river.

San Miguel Accommodation is very limited: *Residencias Olga* is the only place available and has only 6 single rooms. Accommodation beyond San Miguel is non-existent, except in **Orita,** W of Puerto Asís, a small town which has grown up on the oilfield.

Leguizamo, upstream from Puerto Asís, can also be reached by air from Florencia (Satena charges US$7). There are boats to Leticia and to Peru. Hotels: *Leguizamo* and *Putumayo* both charge about US$1, basic. Still further upstream are El Encanto and the nearby village of **San Rafael,** which is a good place to visit to see the Huitoto Indians, the most dominant of the many tribes which live along the Putumayo river. At San Rafael there is a mission at which it is possible to stay.

We are informed that travellers interested in Amazonian plants, birds and animals will find Putumayo more accessible, with more abundant wild life, than Leticia. Restaurant food in the Putumayo region is often uninspiring. Take some canned goods for variety. There is also a road of a sort from Mocoa to Puerto Limón, on the Río Caquetá (see Caquetá section, pages 449-450).

South to Ecuador

Passing through deep valleys and a spectacular gorge the Pan-American Highway covers the 80 km. from Pasto to Ipiales in 1½ to 2 hours; this section is paved. A detour *via* Túquerres (later unpaved) and its plain takes over an hour more; it reaches 3,050 metres at Túquerres, dropping to 2,440 at Guachucal, and rising again to 2,740 metres at **Ipiales,** "the city of the three volcanoes", with about 25,000 people and famous for its colourful Saturday morning Indian market and the near-by Sanctuary of the Virgin of Las Lajas, though it is an unattractive town. San Luis airport is 6½ km. out of town.

On days set apart for religion dazzlingly clean Indians come down from the hills in their traditional bright colours. Well worth seeing, especially the women. Seen from afar the Sanctuary is a magnificent architectural conception, set on a bridge over the canyon: close to, it is spoilt by over-ornamentation. There are great pilgrimages to it from Colombia and Ecuador and the Sanctuary must be second only to Lourdes in the number of miracles claimed for it. The Church recognises one only.

Hotels *Mayasquer,* 1½ km. on road to frontier, US$9 d, very good, swings for children, discothèque; *Pasviveros,* bright and clean, US$4 s, with bath and hot water; *Las Lajas* (US$4 s, hot water in the morning, good restaurant); *Buchue,* US$5 d, very good; *New York,* near main square, US$1.60 d, dingy; *Colombia* (US$1.50, hot water); *Residencia Italiana* (US$1.50, hot water); *Residencias El Dorado,* US$1.25 p.p.; *Oasis,* US$1.10, clean; *Rumichaca Internacional,* US$4 s, clean and comfortable with good basic restaurant; *Residencial Valparaíso,* US$2 d, hot water; *Pensión Bolívar,* US$1; *Residencias Victoria,* good; *Residencial Belmonte,* US$1.80 d. hot water; *Residencia Miramar,* US$1.20 d; *Restaurant Vitapán,* comparatively clean; *Restaurant El Dorado,* US$1.75 for two after bargaining. Most young travellers can expect to be questioned and searched by police soon after checking in to a hotel.

Camping possible above the bus parking lot.

Currency It is impossible to cash travellers cheques in Ipiales, and though there are money changers in the streets, better rates are to be had in Quito.

Ipiales is 4 km. from the international Rumichaca bridge across the Carchi river into Ecuador. The frontier post stands on a natural bridge, for the river gorge here is pinched into a bottle neck. The customs and passport examination takes place at this bridge. (It is possible to bathe in the hot springs under the bridge.)

You obtain your Colombian exit stamp from the DAS at the frontier post. You have to get your entry stamp and tourist card for Ecuador at the frontier, or possibly the Edificio Portuario in Tulcán (or at the police station just before Tulcán at weekends). Motorists must have their carnets stamped by the customs post in Ipiales (6 Carrera, 6-19) and at the Edificio Portuario in Tulcán. You may be required by Ecuadorean customs to show that you have enough money for your stay in the country. Colombian customs have the same requirement; US$20 a day is necessary (US$10 for students), though you are not always required to show that you have this amount. There is a duty-free shop about ½ km. from the border.

From Ipiales to Tulcán: taxi, fastest and dear, US$2.50; seat in automobile (waits till all seats are full), US$0.35 to the frontier; sometimes you can get another colectivo on the other side of the border to Tulcán, for US$0.35. Bus, US$0.10 to frontier. Taxis and buses are infrequent and some travellers recommend hitch-hiking from the frontier. Saturday and Sunday are bad days to arrive. From Tulcán's modern bus terminal buses go to Quito throughout the day; a beautiful five-hour Andean trip. If you are lucky you may get a through bus (Flota Imbabura) from Ipiales to Quito.

Pullman bus to Popayán, US$3.60, 10 hours. Rough but beautiful trip. 'Plane to Cali (two flights a day), US$12. Bus to Cali, US$6.50, 11 hours. To Pasto with minibus from main square, US$1.25; Flota Bolivariano buses every hour, US$0.75.

The Economy

Colombia's exceptional geographic conditions and range of climates give it abundant and varied natural resources, and in recent years the country has achieved significant technological progress and planned economic development. The economy showed a growth rate of 5% in 1977 compared with 8% in 1976, but this decline was largely a result of poor agricultural returns after bad weather destroyed many crops.

Colombia is the largest producer and exporter in the world of mild arabica coffee, from which it derives a substantial proportion of its export earnings. Partly as a result of an export-diversification programme introduced in 1967, this proportion was gradually reduced from nearly 90% in 1959 to 45% in 1975. Despite the fact that the volume of coffee exports fell from 8.2m. bags in 1975 to 5.3m. in 1977, soaring prices for the commodity on the world market, coupled with a poor performance by non-traditional exports (everything except coffee), meant that this percentage rose again to 64% in 1977. Although non-traditional exports rose by only 3% in 1977, sales of certain agricultural products included in this category showed significant increases over 1976: cotton, 64%; bananas, 25%; flowers, 45%; beef, 32%; precious and semi-precious stones, 24%; and beans, 220%. Illegal exports of coffee were cut by more than half in 1977 to about 450,000 bags from 1m. in 1976, but it is believed that contraband exports of marihuana and cocaine outstripped total coffee sales by about 200%, although naturally no detailed statistics of this trade are available. Total exports rose by 31% in 1977 to US$2,343m. of which coffee contributed US$1,512m.; there was a trade deficit of US$334m. but the current account was in surplus by approximately US$600m. International reserves rose about US$600m. during the year to stand at over US$1,800m. at end-December.

The principal objective of economic policy in 1977, as in 1976, was to curtail inflation. The workers' cost-of-living index rose by 30% compared with 26% in 1976, but this would have been higher if the Government had not imposed monetary restrictions to curb the growth of the money supply, which had expanded rapidly as the country received record earnings for its coffee exports. In the first half of the year the index rose by 28.9%, but thereafter the rate slowed sharply as the Government's policy of exchange controls and credit restrictions took effect. During the first three months of 1978 the cumulative rise in the cost of living was 6.3%, compared with 10.7% in the first quarter of 1977.

One of Colombia's principal problems is to meet demand for energy, which is currently growing at about 7% a year. Oil constitutes over half of total energy consumption, but national production is falling fast and average daily production declined from 145,700 barrels in 1976 to 137,880 in 1977. Imports of petroleum are expected to reach US$273m. in 1978, an increase of US$87m. over 1977, and the country has had to reduce oil exports to only a few refined products after having been a net exporter for most of the 20th century. An energy programme produced to prevent a possible deficit in the 1980s calls for investments of nearly US$4,000m. in oil exploration and development, US$4,000m. in electricity, and US$500m. each in natural gas and coal by 1985. The outlook for natural gas and coal is good; a gas pipeline from the Guajira fields to Barranquilla and Cartagena came into operation in August 1977 with an initial daily capacity of 200m. cubic feet, which will be gradually increased to 900m. when the gas fields are operating fully. Production from the Guajira is expected to offset the decline in output from the Magdalena Valley, which had dropped to less than 120m. cubic feet a day, and it is estimated that about US$90m. a year will be saved on imports of fuel oil. Coal production at present amounts to about 4m. tons a year from Boyacá and Cundinamarca but this is expected to be doubled in the 1980s when the Cerrejón area in the Guajira is developed; Colombia's coal deposits are estimated to be the largest in Latin America.

Development of Colombia's other mineral resources, other than gold and emeralds, has been relatively neglected, but there is now a growing interest in copper and nickel deposits. It was planned to begin operation in 1978 of a nickel mining project at Cerro Matoso where reserves are estimated at 35m. tons; the project will include a smelter with an annual capacity of 50m. lb., and will make Colombia one of the largest producers in the world. Deposits of uranium are also being explored with the help of French and Spanish companies and planned expenditure for the project is about US$750m. to cover exploration, development and production costs. By 1980 Colombia expects to be producing about 1,000 tons of uranium concentrate a year, but generation of electricity from nuclear power stations is not envisaged until at least the year 2000.

Foreign Trade (US$m.)

	1972	1973	1974	1975	1976	1977*
Exports (f.o.b.)	841	1,008	1,214	1,443	1,774	2,343
Imports (c.i.f.)	655	744	1,050	1,503	1,991	2,009

*Provisional

Information for Visitors

Travel by Air   The quickest way from the United Kingdom (16 hours) is by British Caledonian Airways from London to Bogotá. Other airlines with services between Europe and Bogotá are Air France from Paris, Viasa from Rome, Iberia from Madrid, and Lufthansa from Frankfurt. Avianca, the Colombian national airline, flies from Paris, Madrid and Frankfurt. Copa flies cheaply from Panama to Barranquilla and Medellín.

Frequent services to and from the U.S. by Avianca, Braniff, Aerocóndor (all of them serving Bogotá); and Braniff and Ecuatoriana (serving Cali). Varig and Avianca fly from Bogotá to the U.S. West Coast. Some flights are very cheap; by Aerocóndor from Miami to Barranquilla, weekly, only costs US$275 (round trip, US$378). Miami-Bogotá and back by Aerocóndor (50-day excursion ticket) US$299. San Andrés-Honduras, Sahsa, 4 times a week, US$52, Guatemala, US$75, Costa Rica, US$44. SAM offers cheaper flights than most other airlines: Bogotá-Panamá, US$51 plus 11% tax; to San José, US$78 plus tax, on Tues., Wed., Sat.; to Managua, US$85 plus tax, Thurs. and Sun.; to San Salvador, US$98 plus tax, Thurs. and Sun.; to Guatemala, US$116 plus tax; San Andrés-San Salvador, US$55; San Andrés-Guatemala, US$90; Panamá-Cali, US$70. Flights from Panamá to Medellín cost US$52 plus US$4 tax. Motorcycles may be taken as luggage; remove oil, petrol, battery and anything breakable. Insist on supervising loading and unloading. Medellín customs take more than a day and you have to go from the airport to the *aduana interior,* in town. The cheapest way to fly to Quito is to fly to Pasto or Ipiales, cross the border by road and take another 'plane at Tulcán.

From Neighbouring Republics   Pan-American Airways and Braniff connect Colombia with republics to N and S. Colombia and Venezuela are reciprocally served by the Colombian Avianca and the Venezuelan Viasa, and Avianca flies to Quito and Lima. Turismo Aero flies from Panama to Colombia. British Caledonian, Avianca, Lufthansa, Air France and Ecuatoriana go S from Colombia. The route Bogotá-San Andrés-Tegucigalpa by SAM or Aerocóndor (in the latter case change to Sahsa, Honduran airlines in San Andrés) is cheaper than a direct flight, but the fact that you have to spend a night on expensive San Andrés must be taken into account when deciding your itinerary. SAM can also be picked up in San Salvador.

N.B.   An airport tax of US$10 is charged for all international flights, and there is an 11% tax on all international air tickets bought in Colombia for flights out of the country (5% for other international air tickets). Unfortunately it is no longer possible to avoid the purchase tax by buying tickets outside the country as the charge is included automatically.

Note also that if travelling with Aerocóndor bookings should be confirmed twice, as the company tends to overbook, and you should arrive for Aerocóndor flights well before time, in case the pilot decides to leave early.

Internal Air Services are flown by Avianca, SAM and Aerocóndor, and 15 other, smaller companies. Avianca offers a US$110 round ticket (Conozca a Colombia) giving unlimited domestic travel for 30 days; conditions are that it must be bought outside Colombia, one may not pass through each city more than once, and a proposed itinerary (not firm) must be submitted when buying the ticket; extra must be paid if proposing to visit San Andrés and/or Leticia. For single flights, however, the army airline Satena and SAM tend to be cheaper than Avianca. SAM offers a 25% reduction for students but is said to be somewhat unhelpful in making reservations. There is an airport tax of US$2 on all internal flights, including those to and from San Andrés.

Travel by Sea The Central America Line's fast cargo vessels operated jointly by Royal Mail Lines and Holland America Lines are the only ones which serve the Atlantic ports of Santa Marta, Barranquilla and Cartagena direct from the United Kingdom, but no passengers are carried. The Pacific Steam Navigation Company's cargo vessels are likewise the only ones serving Buenaventura direct from the United Kingdom but they carry no passengers. Elder & Fyffes vessels sail from Avonmouth to Kingston (Jamaica); from here one can fly to Barranquilla. The Grace Line has sailings to Buenaventura *via* the Panama Canal, taking about 7 days, and sailings from New York to Barranquilla by way of La Guaira and Puerto Cabello (Venezuela) to Curaçao, taking about 8 days.

Several European (other than British) shipping companies have services either to Barranquilla and Cartagena or to Buenaventura.

Note If shipping a car from Panama to Colombia it is wise to employ an "agente" who will help you with the documents etc. on arrival. This will speed up the process, but will cost you about US$50.

Travel (in General) Most of our correspondents recommend bus rather than train; train may be preferable, however, if the competing road links are not paved (e.g. Bogotá-Santa Marta) or if there is a railcar autoferro service. The buses are generally very comfortable; they usually stop for about half an hour at lunch time in front of the bus company's office. The luggage compartment is normally locked, but it is wise to keep an eye on your bags. If driving yourself, avoid night journeys; the roads are often in poor condition, lorry- and bus-drivers tend to be reckless, and stray animals are often encountered. Hitch-hiking (autostop) seems to be quite easy in Colombia, especially if you can enlist the co-operation of the highway police checkpoints outside each town. Truck-drivers are often very friendly, but be careful of private cars with more than one person inside, especially if you are travelling on your own. Always insist on taxi-drivers using their meters if they have them, or arrange a price before the journey if they do not have meters.

For travel overland from Panama, see note at end of Panama section.

Motoring Roads are given in the text. Motor fuel is cheap: "super" (only in large cities), US$0.60 per US gallon; "corriente", US$0.50 per US gallon. Roads are not always signposted. If you are planning to sleep in your car, it is better to stop in a "parquedero"; you will be charged a little extra, but the lots are guarded.

Buses Travel in Colombia is far from dull. You may be sitting next to dogs, cats, hens, cockerels or parrots. Breakdowns are many. It is not for weak hearts, queasy stomachs, or long legs. The best bus lines are said to be the Flota Magdalena and especially Expreso Palmira. Note that meal stops tend to be few and far between; bring your own food. A full colectivo, such as a "Taxi Verde" costs only twice as much per person as a bus seat. The excellent microbus services of Velotax have been recommended. If you entrust your luggage to the bus companies' luggage rooms, remember to load it on to the bus yourself; it will not automatically be done. Never leave your possessions unattended on buses—you may never see them again.

Documents A passport is always necessary. Visas are not usually required for residents of Western European countries, the USA, Israel, Japan, and some Latin American countries, but a tourist card must be filled in in advance at the airline or Colombian consulate. Two photographs are needed. Visas are required for residents of Chile, Cuba, Guatemala, Mexico, Nicaragua, Paraguay, Uruguay and Venezuela. Canadian citizens must have a tourist card. A new regulation forbids foreigners who have spent 40 consecutive days in Colombia from returning for one year. For a longer stay a 90-day visa should be obtained from the Colombian embassy in your country. Visitors must have certificates of vaccination against smallpox. It is almost impossible to enter the country without an onward ticket though, apparently, consular exemption can be obtained from Colombian consulates. Visitors must also prove that they have US$20 for each day of their stay (US$10 for students). Note that to leave Colombia you must normally get an exit stamp from the DAS (security police). They often do not have offices at the small frontier towns, so try to get your stamp in a main city, and save time. It is possible to get a Venezuelan visa in Bogotá, Cartagena, Barranquilla and Bucaramanga. However, you may find that your onward ticket, which you must show before you can obtain a visa, is stamped "non-refundable". The Brazilian embassy only grants visas to Colombian residents but visas are necessary for Australians and New Zealanders and you must push for one; though better to get it at home before you leave.

Duty-free admission is granted for portable typewriters, radios, binoculars, personal and cine cameras, but all must show use; 200 cigarettes or 50 cigars or 250 grams of tobacco or up to 250 grams of manufactured tobacco in any form, 3 litres of alcoholic beverages per person.

Tourist Information The Corporación Nacional de Turismo (CNT), with its headquarters at Bogotá, has branches in several other towns. The Coordinadora de Turismo de Bogotá (Carrera 13, No. 27-95) has daily tours of the city with interpreters. The Automobile Club in Bogotá has offices on Avenida Caracas, No. 46-64 (Tel.: 451534 and 452684). Branches are at Manizales, Medellín, Cali, Barranquilla and Cartagena. It supplies Esso, Texaco and Mobil maps: good, but not quite up-to-date. The Texaco map has plans of the major towns. Even the Shell series lacks detail. A good road map is obtainable from Instituto Geográfico Codazzi, Carrera 3a, Bogotá. Drivers' route maps are available from the CNT. The Colombian Tourist Board in New York is at 608 Fifth Avenue.

The **best time for a visit** is December, January and February: the driest months. But pleasure—it happens sometimes—is in conflict with duty, because most businessmen are then on holiday. There is heavy rain in many places from June to September.

Warnings Visitors are warned that Colombia is very well known for pickpockets and thieves. In large cities, especially, watch your pockets, handbag, camera, watch and luggage closely and it is better not to wear a watch, eyeglasses or jewellery. Documents and high-value notes should be pinned to inside pocket, or carried in special pouch tied under shirt, or round waist under skirt (for women), or kept in trouser pocket inside waistband. When travelling by bus keep your luggage close to you, or else get out at each stop to check that no one else takes it from the luggage compartment. Travelling by car, always keep an eye on your petrol cap at filling stations; otherwise it too might vanish! Caution cannot be urged too strongly, as thieves, who tend to be particularly active in and around bus and railway stations, are not even above cutting the straps of a backpack which is being worn. Gangs of up to six men armed with knives and other weapons have frequently attacked single or couples of tourists and they do not hesitate to use their knives. Avoid money changers on the street who offer favourable rates of exchange. They often short change you or run off with your dollars and pesos, pretending that the police are coming.

Colombia is also part of a major drug smuggling route. Police and customs activities have greatly intensified since 1974 and smugglers increasingly try to use innocent carriers. Travellers are warned against carrying packages for other people without checking the contents. Penalties run up to 12 years in none too comfortable jails, and the police sometimes behave very roughly towards those they choose for a spot check at airports; complaints have been made in this connection to the Colombian authorities, whom we ourselves urge to behave more temperately. All young travellers are suspect, regardless of hair length, so be very polite if approached by policemen. Colombians who offer you drugs may well be setting you up for the police, who are very active on the north coast and San Andrés island, and other tourist resorts such as Popayán. Again, this warning cannot be stressed too emphatically.

Working hours   Monday to Friday, commercial firms work from 0800 to mid-day and from 1400 to 1730 or 1800. Certain firms in the warmer towns such as Cali start at 0700 and finish earlier. Government offices follow the same hours as a whole as the commercial firms, but generally prefer to do business with the public in the afternoon only. Embassy hours for the public are from 0900 to noon and from 1400 to 1700 (Mondays to Fridays). Bank hours in Bogotá are 0900 to 1500 Mondays to Thursdays, 0900 to 1530 on Fridays except the last Friday in the month when they close at 1200; banks in Medellín, Cali, Barranquilla, Bucaramanga, Cartagena and Manizales open from 0800 to 1130 and 1400 to 1600 on Mondays to Thursdays; on Fridays they are open until 1630 but shut at 1130 on the last Friday in the month; banks in Pasto, Popayán, Cúcuta, Neiva, Tunja, Ibagué and Santa Marta open from 0800 to 1130 and 1400 to 1530 on Mondays to Fridays and 0800 to 1100 on Saturdays and the last day of the month. Shopping hours are 0900 to 1230 and 1430 to 1830, including Saturdays.

British Businessmen should consult "Hints to Businessmen Visiting Colombia", free from Room CO7, Export Services Branch, Department of Trade, Export House, 50 Ludgate Hill, London EC4M 7HU. Similar U.S. publications may be obtained from the Government Printing Office, Washington, D.C.

Climate and Clothing   Climate is entirely a matter of altitude: there are no seasons to speak of, though some periods are wetter than others. Tropical clothing is necessary in the hot and humid climate of the coastal fringe and the eastern Llanos. In Bogotá frosts occur and winter-weight clothing is needed all the year round, but no overcoat is necessary during the daytime. Between these two extremes there is every type of intermediate climate. Medellín requires light clothing; Manizales very similar to Bogotá. A dual-purpose raincoat and overcoat is useful in the uplands.

Health   The larger cities have well organised sanitary services, and the water may be safely drunk. Take Halazone with you, or boil the water, or use the excellent mineral waters, in the smaller towns of the tropical coast and the interior. Choose your food and eating place with care everywhere. Hepatitis is common; have a gamma-globulin injection before arriving. Mosquito nets are useful in the coastal swampy regions. There is some risk of malaria in the coastal areas and the eastern Llanos/jungle regions; prophylaxis is advised.

The **Cost of Living** varies considerably from place to place. It rose 20% in 1975, 25% in 1976 and 30% in 1977. In 1977 Bogotá had one of the lowest rates of inflation (22%).

Hotels There is a tourist tax of 5% on rooms, but no service charge, and tipping is at discretion: 10% is generous. Prices are not high in modest hotels. Food is not expensive. A good lunch costs about US$2.50. A restaurant meal that a businessman might give to a prospective customer would cost from US$3.50 to US$6 p.p. In many hotels outside the main cities you can only stay (very cheaply) at *en pension* rates and no allowance is made for missing a meal. The Colombian tourist office has lists of authorized prices for all hotels. If you are overcharged the tourist office will arrange a refund. Most hotels in Colombia charge US$1 to US$1.50 for extra beds (for children) up to a maximum (usually) of 4 beds per room.

Camping Some camping sites in Colombia are: Camping del Sol, Melgar (Cundinamarca), with services; Camping del Sol, Tolú (Sucre), with services; *Motel Osoguaico* and *Hotel Yalconia* at San Agustín, with services; Camping de Coveñas (Sucre), without services; Camping El Diamante, Villeta, 2 km. on the road to Guaduas; Parque del Sopó (Cundinamarca), without services; Parque Tayrona (Magdalena), without services; Sierra de la Marcarena (Llanos Orientales), without services.

Tipping Hotels and restaurants 10%. Porters, cloakroom attendants, hairdressers and barbers, US$0.05-0.25. Taxi-drivers are not tipped.

Weights and Measures are metric, and weights should always be quoted in kilogrammes. Litres are used for liquid measures but US gallons and quarts are standard for the petroleum industry. Linear measures are usually metric, but the inch is quite commonly used by engineers and the yard on golf courses. For land measurement the hectare and cubic metre are officially employed but the traditional measures "vara" (80 centimetres) and "fanegada" (1,000 square varas) are still in common use. As in many other republics food, etc. is often sold in libras (pounds).

Postage There are separate post offices for surface mail and airmail. Send both internal and external letters by airmail, for surface mail is very unreliable. Correspondence with U.K. is reported to be good. It costs US$0.20 to send a letter to the U.S.

International Telecommunications Empresa Nacional de Telecomunicaciones has offices in Bogotá, Barranquilla, Cali, Medellín and other main cities.

Cable rates to the U.K. are now US$0.65 per word (US$7 for 22 words LT) and to the U.S. US$0.42 per word (LT US$4.50). Phone rates to the U.S. US$8.15 for 3 minutes, and US$2.70 for every subsequent minute. To the U.K. US$14, and US$4.50 respectively.

Telephone systems have been automated; the larger towns are inter-connected. From the larger towns it is possible to telephone to Canada, the U.S.A., the U.K., and to several of the Latin American republics. Collect, or reversed-charge, telephone calls are not very common, so make sure the operator understands what is involved or you may be billed in any case.

Difference in Time GMT minus 5 hours.

Currency The monetary unit is the peso, divided into 100 centavos. There are coins of 5, 10, 20 and 50 centavos and of 1 and 2 pesos; there are notes of 1, 2, 5, 10, 20, 50, 100, 200 and 500 pesos. The new red 500-peso note has only recently been issued; the previous one was taken out of circulation in 1973 and is no longer legal tender. The present rate is about 38 per US dollar but there is a discount when you change foreign currency into pesos. In February 1978 this was 7%, but was expected to be reduced or even abolished during the year. There is no limit on imports of pesos; up to the equivalent of US$60 in pesos may be changed back into foreign currencies when leaving. Travellers' cheques are not always easy to change in smaller towns and hotels normally only cash travellers' cheques if you are a resident. As it is unwise to carry large quantities of cash, credit cards are widely used, especially the Diners' Club, American Express and Bankamericard (Visa) (Barclaycard in UK). The Master Charge card (Access in UK) is beginning to be accepted.

The **public holidays** are on the following days:

January 1: Circumcision of our Lord.	July 20: Independence Day.
January 6: Epiphany.	August 7: Battle of Boyacá.
March 19: St. Joseph.	August 15: Assumption.
Maundy Thursday.	October 12: Discovery of America.
Good Friday, Holy Saturday.	November 1: All Saints' day.
May 1: Labour Day.	November 11: Independence of
Ascension Day.	Cartagena.
Corpus Christi.	December 8: Immaculate Conception.
Sacred Heart.	December 25: Christmas Day.
June 29: SS. Peter and Paul.	

On election day, once every two years, road and rail transport is suspended.

Best Buys Emeralds in Bogotá; handworked silver (excellent); Indian pottery and textiles. The state-run Artesanías de Colombia for craft work (see under Bogotá). In Antioquia buy the handbag—*carriel antioqueño*—traditionally made from otter skin, but nowadays from calf skin and plastic trimmed at that. At Cartagena crude rubber is moulded into little dyed figurines: odd but attractive. Clothing and shoes are cheap. The Colombian *ruana* (poncho), conveniently open in front (for ladies), is cheap, chic and warm in any cool climate, and comes in an incredible variety of colours. Silver and gold work is cheaper than in Peru. Good duty-free shop at Bogotá airport. Leatherwork is generally good and not expensive.

Other shopping tips Colombia is one of the few countries which sell "white gas" for camping stoves etc., so stock up here. Camera film is cheap in San Andrés island.

Colombian Food The food served in restaurants is more varied than in other countries. Colombia's dishes are very regional; it is quite difficult to buy in Medellín, say, a dish you particularly liked in Bogotá.

Locro de choclos is a potato and maize soup so rich and nourishing that, with salad and coffee, it would make a meal in itself, but be moderate: there are some five more courses to come. Colombia has its own variant of the inevitable *arroz con pollo* (chicken and rice) which is excellent. For a change *pollo en salsa de mostaza* (chicken in mustard sauce—fried chicken in wine baked en casserole with a hot sauce) is recommended. *Ajiaco de pollo* is a delicious chicken, maize, manioc, cabbage and potato stew served with cream and capers, and lumps of avocado pear; it is a Bogotá speciality (*El Zaguán de las Aguas* and the *Casa Vieja* restaurants in Bogotá are recommended for these dishes). *Bandeja Antioqueña* costs as little as US$0.30 and consists of meat grilled and served with rice, beans, potato, manioc and a green salad. Cartagena's rice with coconut can be compared with rice *a la Valenciana*. *Tamales* are meat pies made by folding a maize dough round chopped pork mixed with rice, peas, onions, eggs and olives seasoned with garlic, cloves and paprika, and steaming the whole in banana leaves. A baked dish of squash, beaten eggs and seafood covered with sauce is known as the *souffle de calabaza*. *Magras* is a typical Colombian dish of eggs and chicken baked together and served with a tomato sauce. *Sancocho* is a filling combination of all the tuberous vegetables, including the tropical cassava and yam, with chopped fresh fish or any kind of meat, possibly chicken; made with shad, it compares with the best bouillabaisse. On the Caribbean coast, eat an egg empanada, which consists of two layers of corn (maize) dough that open like an oyster-shell, fried with eggs in the middle, and try the *patacón,* a cake of mashed and baked plantain (green banana). *Huevos pericos,* eggs scrambled with onions and tomatoes, are a popular, cheap and nourishing snack for the impecunious—available almost anywhere. A good local sweet is the *canastas de coco:* pastry containing coconut custard made tasty with wine and surmounted with meringue. There is, indeed, quite an assortment of little fruit pasties and preserves. Then there are the most of the usual fruits: bananas, oranges, mangoes, avocado pears, and (at least in the tropical zones) chirimoyas, papayas, guavas, and the delicious pitahaya, taken either as an appetizer or dessert and, for the wise, in moderation, because even a little of it has a laxative effect. Other fruits such as the *guayaba* (guava), *guanábana* (soursop), *maracuyá* (passion fruit), *lulo* (naranjilla), *mora* (blackberry) and *curuba* makes delicious juices, sometimes with milk added to make a "sorbete". *Tinto,* the national small cup of black coffee, is taken ritually at all hours. Colombian coffee is always mild. On Tuesdays and Fridays beef consumption in restaurants was prohibited, but this is now being relaxed in some places.

Drink   Many acceptable brands of beer are produced. The local rum is good and cheap; ask for "ron", not "aguardiente", because in Colombia the latter word refers to a popular drink containing aniseed. Try canelazo—cold or hot rum with water, sugar, lime and cinnamon. The wines are imported.

Warning   Great care should be exercised when buying imported spirits in shops. It has been reported that bottles bearing well-known labels have often been "recycled" and contain a cheap, and poor, imitation of the original contents. This can be dangerous to the health, and travellers are warned to stick to beer and rum.

Sport   The only native sport, *tejo,* a form of quoits, is still played in Cundinamarca, Boyacá and Tolima. There has been a remarkable growth of the cult of the open air, though golf, tennis, and riding for pleasure are still the privilege of the wealthy. There are bullrings at Bogotá, Cali, Manizales, Medellín, Sincelejo and Cerete. Polo is played at Medellín and Bogotá. Most of the larger towns have stadiums. Association football is the most popular game. Basketball has a singular attraction for men as well as for women. American baseball is played at Cartagena and Barranquilla. Cockfights are popular. So is boxing.

Fishing is particularly good at Girardot. Santa Marta, and Barranquilla; marlin is fished off Barranquilla. There is good trout fishing, in season, in the lakes in the Bogotá area, particularly at Lake Tota (235 km.), in the mountains.

Great Britain is represented in Colombia by an Ambassador and Consul at Bogotá (Calle 38, 13-35, Tel.: 69-81-00). Airmail to Apartado Aéreo 4508. Consular offices at Cali, Medellín and Barranquilla.

The **United States** is represented in Colombia by an Ambassador and Consul at Bogotá (Calle 37, No. 8-40, Tel.: 32-91-00), Consuls at Medellín, Cali, and Cúcuta, a Vice-Consul at Cartagena, and a Consular Agent at Buenaventura.

American Express Agents   Barranquilla: Tierra Mar Aire, Calle 35, No. 43-43, Tel.: 17083, 19333. Bogotá: Tierra Mar Aire, Edf. Bavaria, Torre B, locales 1-25, Carrera 10, No. 27-91, Tel.: 436363, 832955. Cali: Tierra Mar Aire, Carrera 3a, No. 8-13, Tel.: 731333. Cartagena: Tierra Mar Aire, Calle del Colegio 34-28, Tel.: 13442. Medellín: Tierra Mar Aire, Calle 53 (Maracaibo) No. 49-8.

(This section has been revised with the very welcome help of Sarah Cameron, of CBI Economics Department, Patricia Amaya de Crane, Lands of Colombia (Bogotá), Joe Hiss and Kenneth E. Shirley, of the US Peace Corps, Tolima, Sarita Kendall and Tim Ross (Bogotá), and the following travellers: Roselyn van Benschoten and Johanna Noordhoek (Netherlands), Ingela Björck and Per

Andersson (Sweden), James K. Bock (Mexico City), Dan Bodo and Martin Filiponis (USA), the Boyce family (Cambridge, Mass.), Andrew Brown and Ken Trainer (USA), Ken Catlin (San Diego, Calif.), Olivier Chaudouet (Voiteur, France), P. F. Cheesewright, Cliff Cordy (USA), Christine Czajkowski, Michael Davison, John Eames and Maggie Harvey, Ben Fawcett, Peter Ford and Sally Wilson, Tim and Arlene Frost (Hamilton, New Zealand), Anton Fuchs (Innsbruck), Bob Gebken (USA), Helen J. Glover, Mary Goodykoontz and Ken Scarlett (Woodlands, Calif.), Ucky Hamilton (New Zealand), Hans Hartung (Ludwigshafen), Robert Hertzig (New York City), Etienne Istasse (Belgium), Detlef Körner (Hamburg), Jerry Leon (Havertown, Penn.), Cornelius Lindenburg and Marieke van der Ploeg (Amersfoort, Netherlands), Andreas Lutz (Switzerland), Rolf Maag (Caracas), Daniel and Jan McAleese (Belfast), Ian MacDonell, Nikolaus Müller (Cologne), Larry O'Brien, Karin Östman (Spanga, Sweden), Thomas Pensler (Benediktbeuern, W. Germany), Ingrid Pitzer (W. Berlin), Henri van Rooy (Roosendaal, Netherlands), John Roper-Lindsay, Jerry Rowe (El Cerrito, Calif.), Wendy Sarsby (Port Credit, Ontario), André Schepens (Brussels), Helga Schmidt-Frank and Herbert Schmidt (W. Germany), Michael Scott, Ross Smith (Camberwell, Australia), Chris Sharpe (Mullewa, W. Australia), David Gaddis Smith (USA), E. Spieth (Frankfurt), Ken and Judy Stevenson (Ottawa), John Streather, Margaret Symons (New Zealand), Erich and Angelica Uteregelsbacker (Canada), René Werren (Köniz, Switzerland), Terry and Rosaura West (USA), Nicholas Westwood and Julia Amies, Anne Williams, and Dr. Henry M. Wilson (Madison, Wis.).

ECUADOR

ECUADOR has Colombia to the north, Peru to the east and south and the Pacific Ocean to the west. Its area is about 283,520 square km. which makes it the second smallest republic in South America. About 40% of its 6,521,710 people are Indians, 40% mestizo, 10% European; the remainder are black or Asian.

The Andes, running from the Colombian border in the north to the borders of Peru in the south, form a mountainous backbone to the country. There are two main ranges, the Eastern Cordillera and the Western Cordillera, separated by a 400-km. long trough, the Central Valley, whose rims are from 40 to 65 km. apart. The rims are joined together, like the two sides of a ladder, by hilly rungs, and between each rung lies an intermont basin with a dense cluster of population. These basins, which vary in altitude between 1,800 and 3,000 metres, are drained by rivers which cut through the rims to run either west to the Pacific or east to join the Amazon. The whole mountain area is known as the Sierra.

Both rims of the Central Valley are lined with the cones of more than thirty volcanos. Most of them have long been extinct, for example, Chimborazo, the highest (6,270 metres), Antisana (5,704 metres), Illiniza (5,305 metres) and Altar (5,270 metres). Three, however, are still active; Cotopaxi, the world's highest active volcano (5,896 metres), which had several violent eruptions in the nineteeth century; Tungurahua (5,033 metres), which had a major eruption early this century, and Sangay (5,332 metres) one of the world's most active volcanos, continuously emitting fumes and ash. Humboldt nearly climbed Chimborazo in 1802, and Bolivar tried later. Cotopaxi was conquered in 1872 by Wilhelm Reiss and A. M. Escobar. Edward Whymper climbed most of them in 1880, and nowadays all the main peaks except for Altar and Sangay, which are less accessible, are climbed fairly regularly by Ecuadorean and foreign climbers.

East of the Eastern Cordillera the forest-clad mountains fall sharply to the plains—the Oriente—through which meander the tributaries of the Amazon. Ecuador lost much of this eastern lowland territory to Peru after the disastrous war of 1941, but a large area still remains, making up 36% of Ecuador's total territory. In spite of its size, the Oriente is only sparsely populated by native Indians and mestizo agricultural colonists from the highlands. In total, the region has only 3.5% of the national population, but colonization is now proceeding rapidly in the wake of an oil boom. Oil companies have discovered substantial oil reserves in the northern Oriente near the Colombian border, and exports began in August, 1972. The Oriente is Ecuador's great hope for a change from the status of a poverty-stricken banana republic to a wealthy oil-exporter. Exploration is now moving very slowly in both the Oriente and the Gulf of Guayaquil, where there are substantial gas reserves, and Ecuador is planning to allow foreign companies to operate under risk contracts, in order to attract investors.

Between the Western Cordillera and the Pacific lies the Costa, 685 km. from north to south and some 100 km. wide, which is part swampy plain and lowland, part low hilly land, particularly towards the coast. It is from this area that Ecuador draws the majority of its agricultural products for export. Guayaquil, the commercial capital of this region, is 464 km. from the political capital, Quito, which lies high in a northern intermont basin. Since the people, the climate, and the economies of the two areas in which these capitals lie are sharply different, each will be considered separately.

The Central Valley   There are altogether ten intermont basins strung along the Sierra from north to south. There is little variation by day or by season in the temperature in any particular basin: temperature depends on altitude. The basins lie at an elevation of between 2,130 and 2,750 metres, and the range of temperature is from 7°C to 20°C. There is one rainy season, from November to May, when the average fall in Quito is 1,270 mm. This is enough moisture to support forest, but the soil, which is porous volcanic ash, will only permit the growth of brush, and most of that has been burnt during the long human habitation of the valley. Over half the area is now grassy páramo on which cattle and sheep are raised and subsistence crops grown. What crops are grown is determined by altitude, but the hardiest of them, the potato, cannot thrive above 3,800 metres or so. The intermont basins produce livestock, poultry, wheat, barley, oats, maize, quinoa, fruit and vegetables, some of which find their way down to the coastal plain.

The headwaters of the rivers which drain the basins have cut deep, sharp valleys in the soft volcanic ash which lies thick upon the basin floors. The general level of the Ibarra basin floor is 2,300 metres, but just to the N is the Chota valley bottom in which cotton and sugar are grown at only 1,500 metres above sea-level. Because of these deep river dissections of the basin floors and the presence of the surrounding mountains the scenery has sometimes been compared to that of North Wales.

Some 45% of the people of Ecuador live in the central trough of the Andes, and the majority of the valley people, again, are pure Indians. The two biggest areas of rural mestizo population are in the extreme north and south of the Sierra: the Province of Carchi, and Loja town and the area south of it are all mestizo. Most of the land is held in large private estates worked by the Indians, but some of it is held by Indian communities. With the limited application of an agrarian-reform programme, the "huasipungo" system whereby Indians were virtual slaves on the big highland haciendas is now disappearing, and co-operatives are proliferating. Though many Indian communities live at subsistence level and remain isolated from national centres, others have developed good

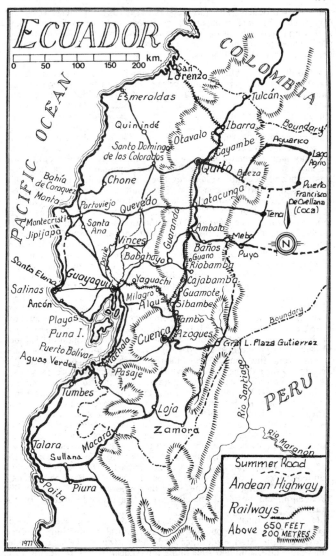

ROUGH SKETCH

markets for products using traditional skills such as embroidery, weaving, carving etc. There are strong moves to improve the lot of the Indian, from both within and without the communities, and several organizations are now struggling to bring them a better standard of living without destroying their cultural values.

West of the Andes   Most of the Costa region is lowland at an altitude of less than 300 metres, apart from a belt of hilly land which runs west from Guayaquil to the coast and trends northwards. These hills never reach a height of more than 750 metres. The climate and vegetation vary somewhat. In the extreme north there are two rainy seasons, as in Colombia, and a typical tropical rain forest. But the two rainy seasons soon merge into one, running from December to June. The further south we go, the later the rains begin and the sooner they end: at Guayaquil the rains normally fall between January and April. The forests thin out too as we move south, and give way to thorn and savannah. The Santa Elena Peninsula and the south-western coast near Peru have little or no rainfall.

Along the northern coast, in Esmeraldas Province, blacks predominate, some of them descendants of shipwrecked slaves. Further south a more Indian strain is noticeable. Coastal fishermen in particular look very Indian. The main areas of population are at Esmeraldas, along the highways inland, in the irrigated lands of northern Manabí, and near Manta, Montecristi, and Jipijapa: in the last two towns Panama hats are woven, using the shredded fibre of a cloud forest plant. It is from this area, too, that tagua nuts, the fruits of a palm fern, come to Guayaquil for export, but appreciable quantities of castor seed, tagua nuts and coffee are exported through the port of Manta. From the dry Santa Elena Peninsula in the SW comes a comparatively small and declining volume of oil; the Government has encouraged further exploration in this area.

But the main agricultural exports come from a small area of lowland to the SE and N of Guayaquil. It lies between the hills and the Andes; rains are heavy, the temperature and the humidity high: ideal conditions for the growth of tropical crops. One part of this Guayas lowland is subject to floods from the four rivers which traverse it: bananas, normally accounting for half the exports of the lowland, are grown here, as well as rice. Cacao too is farmed on the natural levees of this flood plain, but the main crop comes from the alluvial fans at the foot of the mountains rising out of the plain. High on these same alluvial fans excellent coffee is also grown; cacao, bananas, coffee and sugar are almost 40% of the exports by value. Cotton is developing. Add to this that the Guayas lowland is a great cattle-fattening area in the dry season, and its importance in the national economy becomes obvious. Produce was once floated in barges down the Guayas and its tributaries, the Babahoyo, Vinces and Daule, to the port of Guayaquil, but now the greater part is transported in gaily-painted trucks. A good network of paved roads has been constructed since 1960, linking Guayaquil with the major zones of agricultural production, and the once thriving river-ports have now declined almost to nothing.

Over the last thirty years, two areas of the coastlands have experienced spectacular rises in population and agricultural production: El Oro Province in the extreme south, centred on the town of Machala, and the Quevedo-Santo Domingo zone along the Andean fringe to the north of Guayaquil. In both areas, highland settlers have mixed with coastal entrepreneurs to produce a particularly progressive agriculture. El Oro was devastated in the 1941 war with Peru, but now irrigation developments have produced a thriving zone of very intensive banana plantations. In the Quevedo-Santo Domingo area, large areas of forest have been cleared; bananas used to be the main crop, but are now being replaced by African palm. Further north, in Esmeraldas Province, there still remain large areas of land which could be cleared and developed for farming, although the fertility of this zone is reputedly much lower than that of the Quevedo, Guayaquil and Machala areas.

Population   About 52% of Ecuador's inhabitants live in the Costa region west of the Andes, and 45% in the Andean Sierra. Migration is occurring from the rural zones of both the coast and the highlands to the towns and cities, particularly Guayaquil and Quito, and agricultural colonization by highlanders is occurring in parts of the coastal lowlands and the Oriente. About 30% of the inhabitants over 10 years of age are illiterate and less than half the children between the ages of 6 and 15 actually attend school. 41% of the population is urban (living in a cantonal or provincial capital), and 59% is rural. The population is growing by 3.3% per annum, so that, if this rate continues, it will double every 23 years. Birth rate 45 per thousand inhabitants per annum; death rate 12 per thousand per annum. National average population density is 25 per square kilometre, the highest in South America. Average per capita income has risen fast in recent years to match other oil-exporting countries, but the distribution has not improved and a few citizens are spectacularly wealthy.

History   The Incas of Peru, with their capital at Cuzco, began to conquer the Central Valley of Ecuador, already densely populated, towards the middle of the 15th century. A wide road was built between Cuzco and Quito, ruled respectively during the early 16th century by two brothers, Huáscar at Cuzco, Atahualpa at Quito. In 1526/27 Pizarro's men had already touched at Esmeraldas, the Gulf of Guayaquil, and Santa Elena, but Pizarro's main Peruvian expedition did not take place until 1532, when there was civil war between the two brothers. Atahualpa, who had won the war, was put to death by Pizarro in 1533, and the Inca empire was over.

Pizarro claimed the northern kingdom of Quito, but another of the conquistadores, Pedro de Alvarado, suddenly marched south to occupy it. Pizarro's lieutenants Benalcázar and Diego de Almagro moved north to forestall him, and won the race by a narrow margin. Pizarro founded Lima in 1535 as capital of the whole region, and four years later replaced Benalcázar at Quito with his own brother, Gonzalo. Gonzalo, lusting for gold, set out on the exploration of the Oriente. He moved down the Napo river, and sent forward Francisco de Orellana to prospect. Orellana did not return: he drifted down the river and finally reached the mouth of the Amazon: the first white man to cross the continent in this way.

Furious dissension amongst the conquistadores, the execution of Almagro followed by the assassination of Pizarro, led to an attempt by the Spanish king to supersede them. Núñez Vela was sent to Lima to take charge, but he was soon overthrown by Gonzalo. On his way home he collected a small company, was joined by the disgruntled Benalcázar, and moved on Quito, where Gonzalo defeated them. The home government next sent out an astute priest, Pedro de la Gasca. He succeeded in executing Gonzalo after his men had deserted him.

Quito became an audiencia under the Viceroy of Peru. For 280 years Ecuador was more or less peacefully absorbing the new ways brought by the conqueror. Gonzalo had already introduced pigs and cattle; wheat was now added. The Indians were christianized, colonial laws and customs and ideas introduced. The marriage of the arts of mediaeval Spain to those of the Incas led to a remarkable efflorescence of painting and carving and building at Quito. During the 18th century black slave labour was brought in to work the plantations near the coast.

There was an abortive attempt at independence in the strongly garrisoned capital in 1809, but it was not until 1822 that Sucre, moving north from Guayaquil at the head of a force of Venezuelans and Colombians, defeated the Spanish at Pichincha and occupied Quito. Soon afterwards Bolívar arrived, and Ecuador was induced to join the Venezuelan and Colombian confederation, the Gran Colombia of Bolivar's dream. On July 26 and 27, 1822, Bolívar met San Martín, fresh from liberating Peru, at Guayaquil. What happened at that famous encounter is not known, but San Martín left it silently for a self-imposed exile in France. Venezuela separated itself from Gran Colombia in 1829, and Ecuador decided on complete independence in August, 1830, under the presidency of Juan Flores. The Indian parts of southern Colombia wished to join with Ecuador, but Colombian forces moved south, and after a brief struggle, Ecuador agreed on the present day boundary: a boundary which actually dissects a cluster of population in the intermont basin of Tulcán, a rarity in Latin America. Colombia and Ecuador are now co-operating in developing the Tulcán basin.

Its later history for many generations was troubled, but during the last twenty years the standard of living has been rising steadily.

Government

There are 20 provinces, including the Galápagos Islands, which were given provincial status in 1973. They are divided into cantons and parishes for administration.

The governors of the provinces are appointed by the President. The President is popularly elected for four years, and cannot be re-elected until four years after his retirement. Executive power is in the President's hands; he appoints his own cabinet. The legislative power is the National Congress, which consists of a Senate, 33 of whose members are elected and 12 "functional"; and a Chamber of Deputies of one deputy for each 50,000 people. All people over 18 have votes, and voting is compulsory for men, optional for women.

In 1963 a military junta took over the government, ending a 15-year period of political stability and constitutional rule and returning Ecuador to its more typical political pattern of coups, counter-coups and continual instability. The junta finally fled in March, 1966, and in 1968, Dr. José María Velasco Ibarra was elected President democratically for the fifth time in his life. He took over at a time of economic crisis, and assumed dictatorial powers in June 1970. He was finally overthrown by another military coup in February 1972, when General Guillermo Rodríguez Lara assumed the Presidency at the head of a military junta. Gen. Rodríguez was in turn removed from the Presidency in January 1976, since when another military junta has ruled the country. It is making preparations for a return to civilian rule in 1978, and elections were scheduled for 16th July. A new Constitution, approved in January 1978, was to come into effect after the July elections.

Guayaquil and the Lowland Towns

Approach by Sea   Entering the Gulf of Guayaquil from the open sea, the visitor sees the large Isla de Puná at its mouth. The Gulf is 160 km. long. At the neck of the Gulf the ship enters the Guayas river, here some 5 km. wide. Thick jungle runs down to the water's edge in places, with canoes running between the settlements. Some 58 km. from the Gulf, and 10 km. from the centre of Guayaquil, is Puerto Marítimo, the new port opened in 1962. Ocean-going vessels now load and unload there.

The port is ultra-modern. The Custom House and Port Authority buildings are decorated by paintings and sculptures. The dual carriage way to the city is excellent. Buses run quite often.

Guayaquil, the chief seaport and commercial city, stands on the west bank of the Guayas river, some 56 km. from its outflow into the Gulf of Guayaquil. Its population of about a million makes it the largest city in the Republic. The climate is at its best from May to December with little or no rain and cool nights, though the sky is overcast more often than not. The heat during the rainy season, January to April, is oppressive. The city handles about 95% of the country's imports, and 50% of its exports.

The city is dotted with small parks and pleasant gardens. A water-front drive, known as the Malecón, runs along the shores of the Guayas river. Here are the splendid Palacio Municipal and the severe Government Palace. From the landing pier of the Yacht Club the drive is known as the Paseo de las Colonias. From the last pier, due north, runs the main street: the Avenida 9 de Octubre. About half-way along it is the Plaza Centenario, the main and central square of the city. Here is the large liberation monument set up in 1920. Many of the squares and gardens have statuary, little of it of intrinsic value, but most of it interesting to those who know the history of Ecuador. At La Rotonda, on the waterfront near the beginning of Av. 9 de Octubre, is a statue depicting the famous and very mysterious meeting of Bolívar and José de San Martín during the wars of independence. In the grounds of the University is a small bust of Darwin. The dazzling white cemetery, north of the city at the foot of a hill, is worth seeing. The snow-capped peak of Chimborazo can sometimes be glimpsed from Guayaquil, as it can from Quito.

Along the Malecón waterfront there are several piers suitable only for small river craft. The town is bustling and prosperous, with modern steam sawmills, foundries, machine-shops, breweries and two of the most modern flour mills in South America. But a few metres across the Plaza to the inside of the Cathedral church of San Francisco (now being restored and truly beautiful), carry the traveller back to Colonial repose. There are many cinemas and several clubs, including the Club de la Unión, Country, Metropolitano, Nacional, Lion's, and Rotary. The British and American colonies frequent the Phoenix Club. There is a golf club, a tennis club, a yachting club, and a race track set in delightful surroundings some 5 km. outside the city: a football stadium has now been added and an enclosed coliseum for boxing, basketball, etc. The

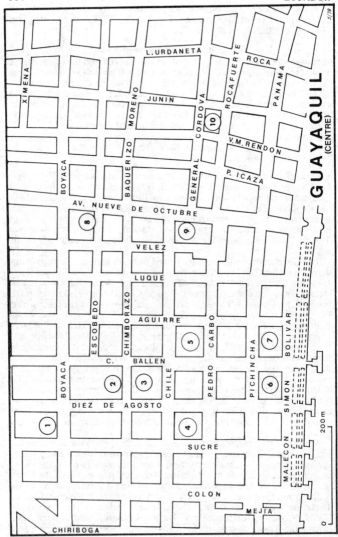

Key to Map of Guayaquil   *ROUGH SKETCH*
1. El Telégrafo building ; 2. Cathedral ; 3. Parque Simón Bolívar ; 4. Municipal
Library ; 5. Post Office ; 6. and 7. Government buildings ; 8. El Universo building ;
9. San Francisco church ; La Merced church.

pleasant suburb of Urdesa, NW of the city, contains some of the best restaurants.

One of the oldest and most interesting districts is Las Peñas, at the foot of Cerro Santa Ana, by the river. Here is the city's first church, Santo Domingo (1548). Nearby is an open-air theatre, the Bogotá. Then, as you start up the hill, you stop at a plateau where two cannon point riverward, a memento of the days when pirates sailed up the Guayas to sack the city. Here begins a curving, narrow street, Numa Pompilio Llona, that dates back to the Colonial era. Paved with huge stone slabs, this is a picturesque but somewhat neglected street. To reach Las Peñas, turn left at end of Av. 9 de Octubre.

The museum which was formerly in the Palacio Municipal (Jívaro Indian shrunken heads and much else of interest) is now housed in a new building, one block away on Pedro Carbo where there is also a good newspaper library—both are recommended. The museum is open Tues.-Sat. 0900-1200 and 1500-1900; Sun. 0900-1200. Another museum is at the Casa de Cultura on Plaza Centenario (see the room of gold objects; also closed Mons.). At the Museo de Guayas are gold and archaeological collections. At Valdivia, a nearby port, is the site of the supposed Japanese Jomón culture contact—via fishermen—c. 3000 B.C. Philatelic museum on 2nd floor of post office.

Warning Guayaquil is notorious for thieves and pickpockets, often working in pairs. Guard valuables and luggage closely. The cost of living is much higher in Guayaquil than in Quito.

The pride of Guayaquil is the enormous River Guayas Bridge linking the city with **Durán,** the rail terminal on the east bank of the Guayas River. Vehicles must pay a US$1.35 toll to cross the bridge, but about half an hour is saved in comparison with the ferry journey, which costs US$0.04 (and leaves every 15 minutes). From Durán, paved highways fan out to Babahoyo, Milagro, Riobamba, Cuenca (only the first half is paved), and Machala.

Local Holidays October 9 and 12.

Festival 24 July to celebrate foundation of city, not recommended as a tourist attraction.

Hotels Hotel prices in Guayaquil are set by Tourist Board and should be posted inside hotel. Most hotels charge over the approved price, however. Rooms are much in demand in better hotels, the cheap ones being pretty basic. All tend to be heavily booked in the week before July 24, the fiesta.

Name	Address	Single	Double	Category
		(Price US$)		
Gran Hotel Guayaquil*	Boyacáy 10 de Agosto ..	15	20	Lux.
Continental	Chile y 10 de Agosto ..	27	32	Lux.
Suites "El Ejecutivo" ..	Escobedo 1409 y Luque	22	30	Lux.
Atahualpa	Av. P. Ycaza	14.30	28.50	Lux.
Humboldt*	Malecón 2309	13	18	Lux.
Palace*	Chile 216	20	27	Lux.
Rizzo	Ballén 319 y Chile ..	14	17	1
Italia	Av. 10 de Agosto 115 ..	9	12	1
Alexander	Luque 1107	11	13	1
Sanders*	P. Moncayo 1100 y Luque	7	10	1

*Recommended by travellers.

Also there are: *Metropolitan,* Rendón 120, US$10.30 s; *Cima's,* US$11.20 s, on Quito road, excellent food; *Tourist,* Baquerizo Moreno y Junín, 903, US$6 d; *Residencial Londres,* 9 de Octubre 709, US$5 d; *Apartamentos Boulevard,* 9 de

Octubre 432, US$7 d; *Residencial Equinnorial Vélez,* near Plaza Centenario, US$5 d, reasonable; *Residencial Embajador,* Chimborazo 1106, US$2.10 p.p.; *Imperial,* Urdaneta 705, US$7 d, clean; *Crillón,* US$4.40 d, clean but noisy, cheap food; *Pensión Pauker,* Baquerizo Moreno 402, US$5 p.p., excellent rooms, good food; *Residencial Helbig,* Luque y Chile, US$2.50; *Residencial Francisco de Orellana,* Villamil 106, US$7 d, good breakfast; *Boston,* Chimborazo 711, US$3 p.p., central, clean; *Residencial Cervera,* Córdoba 1036, US$5.20 p.p.; *Residencial Roma,* Ayacucho 415, US$2.30 p.p.; *Residencial Filadelfia,* Villamil 119, US$1.20 p.p., noisy; *Santa María,* Villamil 102, central, adequate, restaurant US$8 d; *Residencial Medellín,* Rumichaca 1502 y Sucre, US$1 p.p.; opposite, *Ecuatoriana,* US$2 p.p. with private bath; *Pensión Babahoyo,* Sucre 109, US$1.25 s; *Delicia,* Ballén 1105, US$2.20 d; *Ecuador,* Moncayo 1117, US$7 d; *Guayaquil,* Aguirre 1003, US$4 d; *Marco Polo,* 6 de Marzo 948, US$7 d; *Residencial Viena,* Montúfar 534, US$2 d; *Residencial Horizontales,* Rumichaca 828, US$2 d. Sra. Gretna Portugal at Imbabura 214 y Rocafuerte, Aptdo 4-2, lets rooms for US$12-14 d, US$10-12 s, recommended. A tax of 10% on all hotel rates, plus 3% for local Red Cross.

Motel   *Monzón,* secure parking at least.

Restaurants   *Melba,* General Córdova 1036, excellent, not dear; *Flamingo, Rex* (lunch or dinner, US$1.20-US$2); *Club de la Unión* (private club); excellent restaurant service for members and friends. First class food at *Hotel Continental; Olmos,* Av. P. Ycaza (steaks); *Mamma Rosina,* on road to Urdesa (Italian); *Castillo Suizo,* Los Rios y Piedrahita (general European); and three good Chinese: *El Dragón Dorado,* Av. C. J. Arosemena; *Joug Yep,* Los Ceibos; *Chifa China,* on road to airport. Outdoor restaurant at corner of Chimborazo and Huancavilca, serves chusos—kebabs—US$0.55. *Moby Dick,* for seafood, on road to Urdesa. *Los Estribos,* on road to airport, pleasant, good food. *Canton,* on 9 de Octubre, very good, menu for US$1. *Mesón Español,* US$1.50 a meal. *Que Buena Gente,* good meal for US$0.80; *Acapulco,* Calle Chimborazo, US$1 meal. *Pizzería Don Camilo, Restaurante Rei-Sar. Restaurante Roma,* 9 de Octubre 720. *Nandu,* Av. 9 de Octubre 828. Many, especially fish restaurants, in Urdesa district.

Shopping   Beware of newly manufactured "Inca Relics" sold in souvenir shops. Artesanías del Ecuador (Ocepa), Urdesa, good and reliable. There are souvenir shops in front of, or next to, the hotels *Gran Guayaquil, Atahualpa* and *Continental.* Stands in street near Post Office, and a small market in Calle Chile, between 9 de Octubre and Vélez, next to San Francisco church, open daily.

Tipping   Hotels and restaurants, 10% usually in the bill. Taxi, nil. Airport railway porters, US$0.08-0.20, according to number of suitcases; cloakroom attendants, US$0.04; hairdressers, 20%.

Electric Current   110 volts, 60 cycles, A.C. throughout Ecuador.

Tourist Bureau   Dituris, Malecón 2321 y Av. Olmedo; Tel.: 510445 and 515183. Helpful, English spoken, closed 1200-1500. A Policía de Turismo man can be hired for a guided tour of Guayaquil. Cost will be about US$3 per hour for taxi (2 hours will do) and US$2 to the Policía de Turismo.

Travel Agents   Servitours, next to *Hotel Atahualpa,* helpful, English spoken, Galápagos tours arranged. Darwin Tours, near Malecón, also arrange Galápagos tours. Transnave, Malecón 905 and Junin, for boats to Galápagos, telephone 304 724 or 304 780 (P.O. Box 4706).

Conveyances   Buses and colectivos about US$0.07 (most visitors dare not try them, but they are not lethal). Minibuses or "bus" colectivos. Taxis: Short runs, US$0.50; by the hour, US$1.20; US$2.30 to and from airport. To Durán, across bridge, US$6. Taxis are notorious for overcharging; check on fare before entering.

Rail   To Quito (464 km.—see page 513), US$3.20. Travellers arriving in Durán and ferrying to Guayaquil land about 8 blocks still from the main city area, Avda. 9 de Octubre. Train to Riobamba, daily 0645, US$1.50

Bus Services   To Cuenca, US$2, Manta 3 hours, Esmeraldas 7 hours, Riobamba 5 hours, Santo Domingo de los Colorados, 5½ hours, US$1.20. Machala (for Peru) 4½ hours, US$1.40, frequent. Huaquillas, avoiding Machala, by Ecuatoriano, US$2, 5 hours; *via* Machala, several companies, best Transportes Ecuador, US$1.80,

6 hours. To Ambato, US$2, 6 hours. Zarumilla (0200 daily). Excellent service by Viatur Bus to Quito *via* Santo Domingo; snack/steward service, book day in advance; US$3.20 for air-conditioned luxury; US$2.80 for ordinary bus (Carchi). For Lima direct, Tepsa leaves Tues. and Fri. at 0800, US$35.50 single; (Lima to Guayaquil, Wed. and Sat., at 0830). Cheaper to go to Lima as follows: Guayaquil-Huaquillas, US$3.20 (Ecuatoriano) to Tumbes, US$0.50 colectivo, to Lima, US$12 (Tepsa or Roggero) for total US$15.70. **Trucks** carry freight and passengers, slower, bumpy, cheaper than buses, and you see better. Inquire at 1104 Sucre. Regular and frequent buses to Playas and to Salinas (2½ hours, US$0.60). Trans Esmeraldas has new buses for the run to Esmeraldas.

Simón Bolívar Airport, near the centre. US$2.30 for cab to city. US$0.22 for bus.

Air Services Two flights a day except Sunday to Quito by CEA and Tame, US$20, 40—50 minutes. There are flights to Cuenca, Manta, Machala, Esmeraldas, Portviejo, Tulcán and Loja. Twice a week to Galápagos (see page 542). Andes Airlines will ship vehicles to Panama (US$680 for VW microbus).

Weekly Steamer to the ports of Manta and Esmeraldas. Steamer service to Puerto Bolivar (for Machala and Peru) was suspended in 1973.

P.S.N.C. Agents Anglo-Ecuatoriana (Agencias), C. Ltda., Casilla 410, Junín 105. Cable address: "Scael"; Tel.: 305-700.

Cable Instituto Ecuatoriano de Telecomuncaciones (Itel) public telex booth.

Horse-Racing Hipódromo Santa Cecilia. Parimutuel betting. Amazingly low standard.

Bank of London and South America, Calle Pichincha 108/110 and Mercado Central and Urdesa agencies; Banco Holandés Unido, 9 de Octubre 419; Citibank Pichincha 412; Bank of America, Elizalde 100. Open 0900-1330. Closed Saturday.

Exchange Houses There are several on Av. 9 de Octubre, one on corner with Panamá; several on Av. Panamá, where you can get reasonable rate for soles depending on market conditions.

British Hon. Consul S.A. Comercial Anglo-Ecuatoriana, Junín 105 y Malecón. Correspondence: Casilla 410, Guayaquil. Tel.: 305-700.

Books Librería Científica, for English and US books, Luque 225. Librería Cervantes, Aguirre 606; Su Librería, Chimborazo 416. Librerías ABC, Cento Comercial Urdesa.

Medical Dr. Evén Alfago, Tel.: 302 540 and 404 480, bilingual and very helpful, Dr. Angel Serrano Sáenz, Av. Boyacá 821, Tel.: 301785.

Churches Episcopalian Church of U.S.A.; Lutheran Church; Anglican Church, Luis Urdaneta y Malecón del Salado, Urdesa.

Schools US and German. School year, May—mid-January.

The Northern Lowlands

The three tropical river towns of the Guayas Lowland, **Vinces, Babahoyo,** and **Daule,** can be reached along good roads from Guayaquil. Another way is by river boat up the respective rivers on which they lie. There are nightly boats to Babahoyo (193 km. 7 hrs.), a sizable town of 28,345 inhabitants. Little can be said for the towns themselves, but the trips give a good idea of tropical Ecuador, with its exotic bird life and jungle and plantations of cacao, sugar, bananas, oranges, tropical fruits and rice. The main road to Quito, paved and improved, passes through dry lands north of Guayaquil into marshy ricelands near Daule, and then into fertile banana lands further north. The road is busy, and heavily-laden lorries travelling at speed and dodging potholes make driving at least exciting.

Quevedo (51,000 people), the main focus of this agricultural area, is known as the "Chinatown" of Ecuador, for it has a fair-sized Chinese colony and several Chinese restaurants. It is a bustling town which has grown exceptionally rapidly over the last 20 years. The town itself is unattractive, but it functions as an important route centre, being connected with Guayaquil not only by the paved highway through Balzar and Daule, but also by a better-quality and less frequented highway through Babahoyo. To the north another busy paved highway connects it with Santo Domingo de los Colorados (see page 530), and from there good roads continue to Quito and Esmeraldas. The old paved highway from Latacunga in the highlands to Portoviejo and Manta in the lowlands passes through Quevedo. It carries very little trafic, but for a leisurely traveller it is the most beautiful of the routes connecting the highlands with the coast. (Bus, Quevedo-Latacunga, "Cotopaxi" line, 6 hours, US$1.) On this road is the *Selva Negra* hotel, basic accommodation, but excellent food.

Quevedo is very noisy, and none of its hotels offers a quiet night. (*Hotel Guayaquil,* 7 de Octubre, US$1.10 p.p., near bus station.) The town's water supply is notoriously inadequate, but you can swim in the river!

Popular weekend trips from Guayaquil are usually to the west along a good paved highway (toll). The road divides at Progreso. One branch leads to Villamil, normally known as **Playas**, the nearest seaside resort to Guayaquil (2 hours by frequent bus—US$0.40—and lorry services). Playas is now a busy bathing and fun centre. Its old charm as a fishing village has almost gone, although every day between noon and 1500 dozens of single-sailed balsa rafts return laden with fish. These rafts are unique, highly ingenious and very simple.

Hotels *Humboldt,* expensive (US$15 d, meals US$1.50—2., on beach) *Residencial Cattan* (US$3.20 daily and good food); *Miraglia* (US$5 d with bath); *Hotel Guayaquil,* US$2.20, not good value. Camping at S end of beach. Beware of thieves.

West of Progreso the road runs through a vast area of arid thorn-scrub land whose occupants look very Indian and produce little besides charcoal. At Santa Elena the road forks. To the left, south, we pass a petroleum refinery and enter the port and regional market centre of **La Libertad**, busy and unattractive. A few miles further on is **Salinas**, the self-styled best resort in Ecuador. The beaches are good and the town has 2 large hotels, a casino and many elegant villas, but it is very quiet outside the holiday season. The flat-topped hill at Punta Santa Elena dominates the landscape. Good deep-sea fishing. Bus from Guayaquil, US$1.15, 3½ hours.

Hotels *Salinas,* US$8.50 d, new, modern, off Malecón; *Miramar,* with casino; single room with bath and telephone, US$3.20 to US$16; *Samarina,* US$3.20, acceptable; *Cantábrico* and *Samarina Tivoli,* US$2.30-US$2.75 p.p., meals US$4 a day; *Yulee,* clean, US$4 p.p., with own bath (but try bargaining), excellent food; *Herminia,* basic, US$1.40 and closer to beaches.
Cables Ietel public telex booth at Radio Internacional.

Punta Carnero is on the S shore of the Santa Elena Peninsula. Magnificent 15-km. beach with wild surf and heavy undertow.

Carnero Inn, famous luxury hotel with all amenities, perched over beach. Single, US$10 upwards. Food excellent. Total cost US$20-25 a day, but still good value.

To the E of Punta Carnero, along the coast, lies Anconcito, a picturesque fishing port at the foot of steep cliffs; further on is Ancón, centre of the declining local oilfield.

The northward fork of the road at Santa Elena leads us along the coast as far north, in the wet season, as La Entrada. During dry periods Manta can be reached. For the most part the road is a low-tide beach road and therefore fast, but caution should be taken as the tide rises fast and suddenly: La Entrada can be reached in less than 5 hours from Guayaquil, and because of this a number of attractive fishing villages along this stretch of coast contain the modern bungalows of Guayaquileños. Almost all the villages have good beaches, and there is particularly good swimming near the attractive fishing villages of Palmar and Ayangue (latter crowded at week-ends). **Manglaralto,** the main centre of the region north of Santa Elena, is reached by a daily bus from Guayaquil as well as by numerous lorries.

Hotels: *Manglaralto* (N. of town and newish), *Hotel del Mar* (US$3 daily and v. fair).

North of Manglaralto the rainfall increases and at La Entrada the road peters out in the wet season (Dec-Feb.; July-Sept.)

The road from Guayaquil to Manta is fairly good. From dry land, with rice cultivation in the valleys, north of Guayaquil it climbs into the humid hills of S. Manabí, then descends to the dry savannah scrub around **Jipijapa** (16,000 inhabitants), an important centre for the region's farmers, trading cotton, fruit, kapok (from the fat-trunked ceiba tree) and the straw hats for which the town is famous. The market is full of them. Thirty-two km. across dusty hills is **Montecristi** (19,000 people), below an imposing hill, high enough to be watered by low cloud which gives the region its only source of drinking water. The town is famous for its 'Panama' hats, which along with cane-work products, are much cheaper than in Quito.

Soon after we reach **Manta** (45,000 people), the main commercial centre of western Ecuador, with vegetable oil plants and cotton ginning factories and a fishing fleet which supplies its modern cannery with tunny. It is a dry and dusty town—steep streets and a fine wooden church—and economically very active. With its twin town, Tarqui, it has the largest population W of Guayaquil. The Tarqui beaches are fine for sunbathing, but the water is dirty; it is interesting to see fishing boats being built on the beach. The beach at the Manta end is clean and fairly quiet, with moderate surf. There is a new mole and coffee exports are growing. Italia Line passenger ships sometimes call. Eloy Alfaro airport is nearby.

Hotels *Manabí Hotel* (best), beside the beach in Tarqui; *Hotel Riviera* (both at US$2.80 daily); *Hotel Paris,* in central Manta, US$2.80; *Manta Imperial,* US$10 s, helpful, beach in front of hotel is clean. *Panorama Inn.*

Motel *Tojalli,* with swimming pool, 10 minutes outside Manta, but watch the bill.

Restaurants *Manabí Hotel* and *Hotel Lun Fun* (Chinese).

Air Service to Quito and Guayaquil.

Buses To Guayaquil, every 3 hours on weekdays, twice on Sundays.

Portoviejo (60,000 inhabitants) is another major commercial centre with agricultural processing plants and connections by road and air with Quito and Guayaquil. **Bahía de Caráquez** (12,000 people) is another coastal port of some importance, to the north of Manta. The town has an attractive setting on the seaward southern end of an inlet and the river front is attractively laid out. In general, the town has a pleasant ambience. Smart new homes fringe the seaward side of the town, which is a centre of banana and other agricultural exports and a considerable contraband trade, despite its shallow harbour entrance. There is a paved road to

Chone (22,000 people—80 km.) and thence E to Santo Domingo de los Colorados or S to Portoviejo and Guayaquil; there is another road to El Rodeo, where it meets the Quevedo road. Air to Quito, Guayaquil (TAME).

Hotels at Bahía de Caráquez   *Hotel Herradura,* excellent, buy a lobster in the market (US$1) and the hotel will prepare it for US$0.40; *Italia,* at a pinch; *Don Antonio,* US$1, and others in centre. *Americano,* US$3 p.p.; *Manabí,* US$1.40 s, clean and friendly.

Those interested in exploring the coast further north may take the ferry (US$0.10) to **San Vicente,** on the far side of the inlet, a thriving market (about 3 km. from San Vicente, *Motel La Playa,* US$16 for beach chalet sleeping 5, good food in restaurant), and on by bus, lorry or car north along the beach to Canoa, thence inland, cutting across Cape San Lorenzo through the more humid pasturelands to the small market centre of **Jama** (small pensión). From there the road runs parallel to the beach past coconut groves, inland across some low hills and across the Equator to **Pedernales,** another small market town half a mile inland. Northwards we follow the beach past dead palm trees (killed by disease) to the end of the road at **Cojimíes** (*Hotel España* US$1). Cojimíes was a major pre-conquest centre but little of this is noticeable now. It is reached on alternate days by a bus or truck from San Vicente (about 8 hours, US$2), and often by small plane which flies shrimps to Guayaquil.

North of Cojimíes is a rich banana-growing region, and **Muisne,** reached only by various boats from Esmeraldas (US$1, about 7 hours), or by the small plane which visits Cojimíes, is the centre and main outlet of this area; through it some 50,000 stems of bananas a month are exported *via* Esmeraldas. On the Río Sucio, inland from Muisne and Cojimíes, is an isolated group of Cayapa Indians, some of whom visit the towns on Sundays. Muisne is an attractive little town (*Pensión Reiba,* US$0.80); another, without a name, US$0.75, with fine deserted beaches nearby. It can be reached from Cojimíes by canoe to Bolívar, walk to Portete, canoe to beach, walk to Las Manchas village, canoe across river, then walk to Muisne.

Esmeraldas (60,000 people) is rapidly improving. It has one of Ecuador's best water supplies, a good 24-hour electricity service, and many streets are paved. Modern mercury vapour lights shine on the nightly *paseos,* best at week-ends: the main street is closed to traffic from 1930 to 2130 nightly. The town is lucky not to suffer the oppressive heat of Guayaquil during the rainy season, January to April. Banana exports are falling but more tourists are coming in by the much improved paved road from Quito. (Bus to Quito, US$2.20, 7 hours.) Gold mines nearby, tobacco and cacao grown inland, cattle ranching along the coast, timber exported, and an oil pipeline from the rich oil finds in the Oriente to an ocean terminal at nearby Balao; an oil refinery has been built nearby. Ships anchor some distance from the town. Canoes bring passengers ashore, US$0.40 after bargaining, Harbour to town centre is a long walk; taxis, buses. Esmeraldas still has spectacular sea-front slums. General Rivadeneira airport. Last bus to Sua and Atacames (see below) is at 1600, ½ hours, US$0.60.

Hotels   *Diana* (meals at restaurant next door); *El Tirol,* food is excellent; *Hotel Colón* is rough and cheap (US$1). *Bolívar,* US$3.50 d.

Atacames, a beach resort 25 km. S of Esmeraldas, is very attractive. *Hotel Tahiti,* US$5.50 p.p. (negotiable) serves breakfasts, full meals in holiday periods, very good restaurant; *Hotel Atacames,* US$2.80 d, basic. Tents or beach bungalows can be hired at under US$1 a night; no facilities but can arrange with hotels. Beach huts at El Chavalito, US$1.10 p.p. Restaurants on beach are reasonable; try Dorde Jacobo for seafood. Bus to Esmeraldas, US$0.50, departs from the main plaza.

Motels   Several, US$4 s.

Sua, another beach resort a little S of Atacames (20 min. walk at low tide), is quiet and pleasant. Several hotels and pensiones at US$1.20 s; *Residencial España* and

Hotel Turista. **M**otel *Chaguaramas,* on beach, US$1.60 s, with good restaurant. Insect repellent is useful along this coast. Bus to Esmeraldas US$0.60.

The mangrove coastlands north of La Tola stretch into Colombia, and have only two towns of note:

Limones, the main commercial centre, largely a saw-milling town. It is the focus of traffic down-river from much of northern Esmeraldas Province where bananas from the Río Santiago are sent to Esmeraldas for export. The Cayapa Indians live up the Río Cayapa and can often be seen in Limones, especially during the crowded Sunday morning social jamboree. Two hotels, both execrable. Boat from Esmeraldas, Thurs. a.m. and Sat., US$2, 6½ hours. Return trip Thurs. p.m. and Sun. a.m. Bunks on the boat are reportedly "buggy". Daily launch to San Lorenzo US$1.10. Information on boat journeys from the Capitania del Puerto, Las Palmas, reached by bus No. 1 from the main square in Esmeraldas. Better to stay at San Lorenzo.

San Lorenzo is relatively more attractive than Limones, but is of less importance. Despite its expensively constructed railway to Ibarra and its seaward channel it remains commercially dead. Its sawmill and fish-packing plant are its main activities.

Hotels *Pailón* (satisfactory at US$1.20 a night); *Imperial* US$1.10 p.p., not recommended. Eat at the *Salón Ibarra.* There is new residencia, reported to be good, charging US$1.60 p.p. Insect repellent is a "must" in San Lorenzo. Be sure to check your bedding for scorpions.

Train Autocarro (a decrepit motor rail-coach) leaves the town daily from the sheds at 0545, but stops for passengers at the new station, hopefully located where they want the new town to be. Main snag: no new town. The train journey to or from San Lorenzo gives an excellent transect of Ecuador. (see page 533). Buy tickets the day before.

Buses To Ibarra, US$1.20, 8 hours.

Boats Dugouts, with motors, to Limones, US$1.10. Boat to Esmeraldas, Wed. and Sun.

The Southern Lowlands

On the southern shore of the Gulf of Guayaquil is **Puerto Bolívar,** built above a swamp and backed by jungle. A quarter of the banana exports pass through this port. It serves (6½ km.) **Machala,** a growing agricultural town of 69,000 with an annual banana fair in September. The area is an unattractive but prosperous irrigated banana zone. From Machala paved roads run inland to Pasaje (26 km.), and Arenillas (76 km.). An all-weather road (183 km.) runs NE from Puerto Bolívar *via* Pasaje and Girón to Cuenca. Another good all-weather road runs SE through Arenillas to Loja (161 km., bus US$1.25).

Various bus companies run from Guayaquil to Machala (4½ hours, US$1.40) on a new paved road.

The regular boat service between Guayaquil and Puerto Bolívar was suspended after a serious accident took place at the end of 1973. There are occasional freight services, carrying passengers, advertised in *El Universo* the morning they leave. Buses run every ten minutes from Puerto Bolívar to Machala, and taxis are available. Bus to Cuenca US$1.40; to Huaquillas US$0.50 (2 hours). The town has the nearest bank to the border.

Machala Hotels *Rizzo* (luxury), Guayas y Bolivar, US$15 d, *Gran Hotel Machala,* US$9 p.p., clean; *Residencial La Internacional,* new, US$2 p.p., recommended; *Machala Motor Hotel,* good but expensive; *Residencial El Oro,* US$2.40 d;

Residencial León, US$2 p.p.; *Residencial Almacha,* US$1.60 d, near Azuay bus station; *Residencial Pichincha,* clean, central, US$2.50 d; *Residencial Ecuador.*A mosquito net may be needed for sleeping.

Restaurants *Café Colón,* run by an Italian priestly sociologist, very interesting. *Te Kaybara.*

Crossing the border into Peru The normal route overland to Peru is *via* Machala. Buses run every half-hour (US$0.50, 2 hours) to **Huaquillas,** the Ecuadorean border town. Travellers who haven't obtained their Peruvian tourist cards in Guayaquil or Quito can get them at the border. There is also the Ecuadorean exit tax of US$2 (unless your entry stamp is a "T-3"), payable in Machala or Huaquillas (the Huaquillas office is closed 1200-1400). From Huaquillas (*Hotel Continental,* US$1.50 p.p.; *Residencial Huaquillas,* US$1.15 s, basic, clean; *Hotel Guayaquil,* expensive, dirty; *Pensión Internacional,* US$1; *Residencial Cuenca,* US$1.85 d; *Pensión Turista,* 100 metres from bridge, US$1), you walk across the border to the Peruvian side (rubber stamp procedure on both sides) and take a colectivo to the Peruvian border town of Zarumilla, or to Tumbes (US$0.50) which is a better place to stay than Huaquillas. Colectivo from Zarumilla to Tumbes (US$0.50), the first large Peruvian town further south, and from there, fast long-distance buses run to Lima, though you may have to wait a day or so to get a seat. Panamericana, Tepsa and Roggero organise through bus services from Quito to Lima twice a week *via* Machala(see page 512). Coming from Peru into Ecuador the reverse applies; take a bus to Tumbes and a colectivo from there. Some travellers crossing border from Peru to Ecuador at Huaquillas report being required to show an exit ticket (a bus ticket will do) by the Ecuadorean authorities. Border practices tend to vary, so check to make sure what the authorities require. There are several direct buses from Huaquillas to Quito each day, 12 hours, US$4.40; a good idea to go by Panamericana who travel *via* Riobamba and Ambato, showing you all the great volcanoes, also to Guayaquil about 6 hours, US$1.50. To Cuenca several daily, 9 to 11 hours. US$3.

An alterative point for crossing the Peruvian border is Macará in Loja Province (see page 538), but the trip *via* Macará is much more difficult than *via* Huaquillas. All borders open 0800-1800, but some travellers have reported that the border closes for lunch 1200-1400.

Warning You must have a ticket out of Peru before you will be allowed in. This can be bought at the border (but not at Macará) but may cost up to twice what it should and it is much better to buy a ticket in Guayaquil or Quito. If intending to travel from Puno to La Paz *via* boat and rail obtain a letter from the Peruvian consulate in Quito. Beware of buying a round-ticket to Lima with Tepsa or a Puno-La Paz ticket, as neither is refundable. A Tepsa ticket from Lima to Tacna costs US$11 and is one of the cheapest ways of satisfying this requirement. An air ticket or Miscellaneous Charges Voucher (MCV) is the best thing to have, as it can always be changed or cashed in.

One must fill out a money declaration card at the Peruvian border; any undeclared dollars are likely to be confiscated if discovered by the Peruvian authorities. All travellers entering Peru should buy Peruvian money on the Ecuadorean side of the border from street money changers (recognisable by their black brief cases) or from shops in Huaquillas, but be sure to try a good many changers to get a better idea of the current rate.

The Peruvian sol has been greatly devalued recently, so verify the rate. A good rate of exchange can also be had in Guayaquil. At the border, the best rate will be had if offering cash dollars. Be sure to count your change carefully; the money changers are not always totally honest. Only 5,000 soles may be taken into Peru. Travellers leaving Peru should get rid of their soles inside Peru, and buy sucres on the Ecuadorean side. Exchange only what is needed to get to Guayaquil, where a better rate can normally be had.

From Guayaquil to Quito

Note to Motorists   There is a 3¼-km. bridge from Guayaquil across the river to Durán, where the train starts, but railway passengers normally use the ferry; it's cheaper than taxis across the bridge. A good paved road from there connects with the Andean Highway at Cajabamba, near Riobamba (see page 515).

The railway line (1.067 metre gauge) passes through 87 km. of delta lands and then, in 80 km., climbs to 3,238 metres. At the summit 3,609 metres is reached; it then rises and falls between 2,450 metres and 3,350 metres before debouching on the Quito plateau at 2,857 metres. The line is a most interesting piece of railway engineering, with a maximum gradient of 5.5 per cent. Its greatest triumphs, the Alausí Loop and the Devil's Nose double zigzag (including a V switchback), are between Sibambe and Alausí. Before 1908, when the line was opened, the journey between Guayaquil and Quito took a fortnight. Despite the time taken, the journey is well worth the effort, though the track is rather rough.

Altitude in metres	Stations	Km. from Guayaquil	Altitude in metres	Stations	Km. from Guayaquil
4	Durán (Guayaquil)	0	3,163	Luisa	228
6	Yaguachi	22	2,749	Riobamba	241
13	Milagro	34	3,609	Urbina	274
30	Naranjito	50	3,154	Mocha	287
91	Barraganeta	69	2,774	Cevallos	299
297	Bucay	87	2,571	Ambato	315
1,219	Huigra	116	2,135	San Miguel	354
1,485	Chanchán	122	2,760	Latacunga	365
1,806	Sibambe	130	3,162	Lasso	384
2,607	Alausí	143	3,561	Cotopaxi	402
2,804	Tixán	153	3,084	Machachi	419
3,238	Palmira	166	2,770	Aloag	428
3,048	Guamote	180	3,014	Tambil	440
3,166	Cajabamba	212	2,857	Quito	464

There are two types of passenger services from Durán, reached by the Guayas River bridge or by ferry from Guayaquil: the train ticket covers the ferry. One is by "autoferro" which leaves Durán at 0640 (ferry at 0600) Mon., Wed., Fri.; and Quito at 0620 for Guayaquil on Tues., Thurs., and Sat. The journey takes 12 hours; one class (a converted bus), seats are reserved, so book in advance. The fare is about US$5. Carry your own lunch if you wish, but the food offered to travellers is generally reliable; also the fruit (if peelable) at many lowland stations. Keep a close eye on your luggage and handbags. Give your luggage only to porters with official tags in exchange for your luggage tickets—many others will try and grab it. The second type of service is a combined goods and passenger train, "tren mixto", which stops at all stations but only goes as far as Riobamba. It leaves each weekday at 0620 and arrives at Riobamba at

1600. Travellers who aren't in a hurry to get to Quito and don't mind unexpected delays (e.g. derailments) should take the second train (US$1.50, first class including ferry). Whilst the "autoferro" (which stops 20 minutes for lunch at Riobamba, incidentally) speeds through many stations, the "tren mixto" takes its time and gives marvellous opportunities for photography and the enjoyment of a train ride which has hardly changed since 1908, although it is now far more crowded today. (Return train leaves Riobamba 0630, arrives Durán 1600, stopping for breakfast at Guamote and lunch at Huigra). There are, incidentally, advantages in leaving the train at Riobamba for a bus to Quito; the road is generally at a higher level than the railway and gives better views of the noble chain of volcanoes—and the buses are modern and comfortable.

Tickets for autoferro bought in Guayaquil at Loja y Malecón, on the river-front.

Leaving the river the train strikes out across the broad, fertile Guayas Valley. It rolls through fields of sugar cane, or rice, past split cane houses built on high stilts, past sugar mills with their owners' fine homes. Everywhere there are waterways, with thousands of water-birds, and down them ply the big dugouts piled high with produce bound for Guayaquil.

The first station is **Yaguachi.** On August 15 and 16 more than 15,000 visitors pour into this little town to attend the feast day celebrations at the church of San Jacinto, who is famous in the region as having put an end to many epidemics.

The first stop of importance is **Milagro** *(Hotel Viker,* US$3.60 d, good. *Restaurant Topo-Gigio,* nearby, good, cheap food). Women swarm about the train selling pineapples which are particularly sweet and juicy. About 87 km. from Durán the train stops at **Bucay,** at the base of the Andes, where a more powerful engine is attached for the steep Andean ascent. Now the landscape spreads before you in every shade of green; row on row of coffee and cacao trees, with occasional groves of mango and breadfruit trees, lush banana plantations, fields of sugar cane, tobacco, and pineapple. The train follows the gorge of the River Chanchán until it reaches **Huigra,** at 1,219 metres, where the fragrant smell of empanadas (little meat pies) reminds you it is time for a bite. The food here seems to be quite reliable.

After leaving Huigra the train crosses and recrosses the River Chanchán, and then creeps along a narrow ledge between the mountain and the canyon. Here begins the most exciting part of the trip. The first mountain town reached is Chanchán, where the gorge is so narrow that the train has to pass through a series of tunnels and over many bridges in its zigzag course. Next is **Sibambe,** the junction for trains to Cuenca, 0600 and 1200. (There are also buses to Cuenca, which are quicker, and a little dearer (5½ hours, US$1.75), and miss some of the stunning scenery.) Shortly after leaving Sibambe the train starts climbing the famous Nariz del Diablo (Devil's Nose), a perpendicular ridge rising in the gorge of the Chanchán to a height of 305 metres. This almost insurmountable engineering obstacle was finally conquered when a series of switch-backs was built on a 5½ per cent grade. First one way and then the other the train zigzags higher and higher, while Sibambe directly below grows smaller and smaller. The air is chilly and stimulating. Next comes **Alausí** (2,607 metres), a mountain resort popular with Guayaquileños. *(Residencia Tequendama,* US$1.20; *Hotel Gampala,* US$2 s, good). The passenger can go on to Quito from Alausí by the Pan-American Highway, if he wants to. After crossing the 120 metre long Shucos Bridge, the train pulls into Palmira, on the crest of the first range of the Andes crossed by the railway. The train has climbed nearly 3,350 metres in less than 160 km. Precipitous mountain slopes covered with temperate-climate crops such as wheat and alfalfa gradually change to a bleak, desolate *páramo* (moor) where nothing grows except stiff clumps of grass. Now and then the drab, depressing landscape is brightened by the red poncho of an Indian shepherd watching his sheep. One by one the great snow-capped volcanoes appear: Chimborazo, Altar, Tungurahua, Carihuairazo, and the burning head of Sangay, the world's most active and inaccessible volcano. They all seem very close because of the clear atmosphere.

Guamote (180 km.) is another point where passengers may transfer to a car, if they like, and travel along the Pan-American Highway to the capital in five hours. The train skirts the shores of a shimmering little lake, Colta, before reaching the fertile Cajabamba Valley. Here, the Indian men wear the usual poncho and some the woolly chaps traditional among American cowboys.

Cajabamba is a small, rather poor town. In 1534 the original Riobamba was founded on this site and, over the years, it developed into a prosperous moderate-sized city. Then, in 1797, a disastrous earthquake caused a large section of the hill on the north side of the town to collapse as a great landslide, which can still be seen. It killed several thousand of the original inhabitants of Riobamba and the town was moved almost twenty kilometres north-east to its present site. The new Riobamba has prospered and grown into one of Ecuador's largest cities, but Cajabamba, where a few of the inhabitants of the original Riobamba remained after the earthquake, has stagnated. Indian market on Sundays.

Cajabamba is connected to Riobamba by a good paved highway, and there is another paved highway from Cajabamba to Bucay, in the lowlands, and on to Guayaquil. An old dirt road leaves the Pan-American Highway soon after Cajabamba to the west; it is one of the oldest of the coast-sierra routes and links Riobamba and Cajabamba with Guaranda and Babahoyo.

Riobamba (2,750 metres) is the capital of Chimborazo Province. Passengers on the autoferro have 20 minutes for lunch here. The town, which now has 68,000 inhabitants, was founded after the 1797 earthquake which destroyed most of the old Riobamba. It is built on a large, almost flat plain and has wide streets and many ageing, rather impressive buildings. Altogether, it seems a quiet, dignified place, with the nickname "Sultan of the Andes". The Ecuadoreans of the Sierra are excellent stonemasons, and throughout the Andean towns public buildings and churches reflect the finer points of their craftsmanship. Riobamba has many fine churches and public buildings and magnificent views of three of the great highland peaks, Chimborazo, Altar and Tungurahua. A new road between Riobamba and Baños affords excellent views of Tungurahua.

The Saturday and Sunday fair of Riobamba is worth seeing. It is carried on in nine separate plazas according to the type of product sold. The sleepy streets come to life in a surge of bright red figures that half trot and half walk. Open-air restaurants do a flourishing business in that

Andean delicacy, baked guinea pig. There are fine ponchos, rope sandals, peculiarly shaped hats, embroidered belts, hand-tooled leather articles, baskets, and innumerable other objects for sale. Hotel prices rise during independence fiestas in April.

Both at the station and at the hotel there are vendors of tagua-nut carvings, an art which has been highly perfected in the valley. The work offered for sale consists of a great variety of bright novelty rings, hollow fruit which contain minute reproductions of cups, pitchers, candlesticks, etc., and some very well sculptured busts about 5 cm. high.

Hotels A new and very good hotel with a recommended restaurant is the *Galpón*, US$12 p.p.; also new is the *Liribamba*, (US$20 d) and only serves breakfast; *Humboldt*, (out of town), new, clean, good (US$7 s); order breakfast night before); *Residencial Segovia*, Primer Constituyente 2228, modern, friendly, US$3.50 p.p., hot water; *Central* (formerly *Granada*), near railway station, US$2 each, pleasant, cheap food; *Guayaquil*, also near railway station, US$1 p.p.; *Venecia*, US$1.25; *Metro*, near station, US$6 d, a pleasant, central traditional hotel, with good cheap food, but noisy at back because of nearby rail shunting; *Ecuador*, opposite station, US$2.30 d (negotiable), clean, pleasant, but noisy; *Residencial Colonial*, US$1.60 s; *Residencial Chimborazo*, Guayaquil 30-17, also opposite the station, US$1 s, fairly clean, no hot water, beds OK; *Hotel Turismo*, US$2 s; *Juan Montalvo*, clean, friendly, US$2 d; *Americano*, US$1, very basic, *Residencias Villa Esther*, US$3 d, good value.

Restaurants *Candilejas*, expensive and not very good; *Oriente*, good meal for US$1; *Chifa Chang*, near railway station (does not serve Chinese food); *Puruhá* and *El Rincón de Chimborazo*; *Monaco*, near *Candilejas*, cheap, good food; *Europeo*, German food; *El Botecito*, also cheap; *Pato Juan*, near main square, new, pleasant. For US$1.20 you can also eat well at the *Metro Hotel* restaurant.

Transport Train to Guayaquil, US$1.40 first class, not available Sundays, US$1, second, leaves at 0630, but get there early, 12 hours. To Cuenca, 0620 (4 hours to Sibambe, 2½ in Sibambe, 6 to Cuenca), US$1.90, takes time, but enjoyable and scenic. Bus to Quito, US$1.20 5 hours (one leaves every hour or so). Bus to Cuenca, 0530, reservations may be advised, 9 hours US$2.20. (Transportes Riobamba not recommended.) Bus to Latacunga, US$0.80, 2½ hours, to Baños, US$0.55, also 2½ hours (a bit rough, trip to Baños *via* Ambato is easier). (Trip to Ambato recommended *via* Guaranda; mountain sunsets are spectacular). There is a through bus to Huaquillas every evening, which avoids Guayaquil. Bus to Guayaquil US$1.40, 5½ hours.

Industries Liquors, woollen and cotton goods, cement, and ceramics.

Excursions Two are of great interest: the first, to **Guano**, a hemp-working and carpet-making town of 2,000 inhabitants 10 km. to the north; and the second, a 2½ hour trip by bus (US$0.40), to **Baños** (see page 518).

Climbing To climb Chimborazo contact Enrique Vélez C., Presidente de la Asociación de Andinismo de Chimborazo, Chile 3321, Riobamba (Tel. 60916). He charges US$40 a day to act as guide and will provide all necessary equipment. (See also under Ambato.)

From Riobamba to Quito the road is paved. Between Riobamba and Cevallos the railway reaches its highest point at Urbina Pass (3,609 metres). At the pass, there are fine views in the dry season (June is probably the first safe month) of Chimborazo and its smaller sister mountain, Carihuairazo. Then the railway and the Pan-American Highway wind down towards the Ambato basin. Fine views of the valley and its patchwork of fields give an impression of greater fertility and prosperity than the Riobamba zone. The houses seem larger and better built, and almost universally, a small crucifix crowns the roof where figurines of domestic animals are also found. Large areas of apple orchards and onion fields are passed before Ambato is finally reached.

Ambato (2,570 metres, population 80,000) is the fourth largest city in Ecuador after Guayaquil, Quito and Cuenca. It is known as the garden city of Ecuador, but it is difficult to see how it got that reputation. Ambato was almost completely destroyed in the great 1949 earthquake which devastated much of Tungurahua Province. Reconstruction was rapid, and the city and its surrounding area are prosperous and go-ahead. The cathedral faces an attractive plaza where there is a statue of the writer Juan Montalvo (1833-1889) who is buried in a memorial built in his honour in a neighbouring street. Out along the River Ambato (a pleasant walk) is the fashionable suburb of Miraflores, the home of most of Ambato's wealthy families and a popular area for the summer homes of rich Guayaquilenos. Ambato has a famous festival in February, the "Fiesta de frutas y flores". It is an important centre for the manufacture of rugs and has some excellent tourist shops in the centre. On a clear day Tungurahua and Chimborazo can be seen from the town.

The main market, held on Mondays, has by all accounts become rather disappointing recently. There are smaller markets on Wednesdays and Fridays.

Hotels The best are the *Florida* (US$8 s, with bath and breakfast) and the *Villa Hilda*, US$9 s, with bath, US$6 without, in Avenida Miraflores, somewhat out of town but recommended. (Camping is allowed, free of charge, in the grounds of the *Villa Hilda*. You are, however, "invited" to eat breakfast in the hotel); *Residencial Americana*, basic, friendly, Plaza 12 de Noviembre, US$3.50 d, hot showers extra, on main plaza; *Hotel Asia*, US$3.50 d, hot water, central; *Hotel Nacional*, US$2 s; *Europa*, US$1.40 s; *Residencial La Unión*, US$3 d, reasonable; *Hotel Vivero*, no bath, US$4 s, US$6 with full board. There are a host of cheap "pensiones" and hotels charging US$1-1.50 p.p. A new luxury hotel, the *Miraflores* on the Av. Miraflores, was opened in 1975. The manager speaks English. Prices are about US$10 s, US$18 d, and a swimming pool is to be built.

Restaurants Good, but expensive meals at the *Villa Hildu* and the *Florida*. An excellent, clean restaurant in the centre is *El Alamo* (about US$1 the meal, without drinks). The *Chozón Azul* is recommended. *Café Los Monjes* also recommended; so is the restaurant opposite the Anglo service station (with old car on roof) on Pan-American Highway going south; *Hotel Nacional* serves a 4-course meal US$1 excellent value. For rock-bottom prices with rather dubious hygiene, try the markets or the *Rondador* restaurant near the Mercado Central; also *Chifa Chang*, Mariano Eguez.

Buses To Quito, 2 hours 40 minutes, US$2.20. To Guayaquil, 6 hours, US$4. To Cuenca, US$4, 9-10 hours. To Baños, paved road, 45 mins., US$1. To Huaquillas US$3, involves changes. To Latacunga, 1 hour, US$1. To Santo Domingo de los Colorados, 4 hours, US$4.80. Main bus station is 2 km. N from centre, near the railway station.

Ambato is connected by the excellent paved Pan-American Highway south to Riobamba and north to Latacunga and Quito. To the west, a narrow, winding road leads up the valley of the Ambato river, over a high area of desert called the "Grande Arenal", past Carihuairazo and Chimborazo, and down into the Chimbo valley to Guaranda. This spectacular journey takes about three hours on Santa or Flota Bolívar buses.

Chimborazo To climb the mountain, take bus to Pogyo (or Poggios) (5 straw huts) on road to Guaranda, at 4,000 metres. Ingo Pauler, from Vienna, writes: "For those driving a car it is important to know that Pogyo (or Poggios) is exactly 50 km. from the police station outside Ambato on the road to Guaranda (otherwise one may easily overlook the "village"). There is a house with metal roofing close to the road, which may be used by mountaineers. Next to this house lives Sr. Angel Chico, who rents mules for US$2 to carry luggage to the Chimborazo hut. From Poggios it is 3 hours to the hut, which is a bright orange wooden octagon with stone floors, offering no facilities or furniture whatsoever. It is essential to carry either enough water or stove to melt snow. Although the ascent to the summit presents no technical problems it is very steep and partly exposed (falling could be fatal!) No one without mountaineering experience should attempt the climb, and the use of rope, ice-axe and crampons is a must!''

Guaranda (12,000 inhabitants) is the capital of Bolívar Province. It is a quiet, rather dismal town which, because it is built on seven hills, proudly calls itself ''the Rome of Ecuador''. Market day is Saturday. Guaranda is connected by very poor roads to Ambato Riobamba and Babahoyo. It is the main centre for the wheat and maize-growing Chimbo valley, but has long stagnated in isolation since newer, faster routes replaced the old Guayaquil-Quito trail through Babahoyo and Guaranda.

To the east of Ambato, an important road leads to Salasaca, Pelileo, and Baños (paved to Baños) and then on along the Pastaza valley to Mera, Shell Mera, Puyo and Tena in the Oriente (see page 540).

Salasaca is a small modernised village 14 km.(½ hour) from Ambato, at the centre of the Salasaca Indian zone, reached by bus. The Salasacas are a group of about 2,000 Indians who wear distinctive black ponchos with white shirts, trousers and broad white hats. Most of them are farmers, but they are best known for weaving ''tapices'', strips of cloth with remarkable bird and animal shapes in the centre. These tapices can also be seen at the Otavalo market at a lower price, but all are made in Salasaca. A co-operative has fixed the prices on the tapices it sells in its store near the church. (The main co-operative store is in Ambato.) Throughout the village the prices are the same, and not cheaper than in Quito.

Pelileo, 5 km. beyond Salasaca, is a small market town which has been almost completely rebuilt on a new site since the older town was destroyed in the 1949 earthquake. In all Pelileo has been destroyed by four earthquakes during its 400-years history. The new town is dull and rather ugly, although it springs to life on Saturday, the main market day. The ruins of Pelileo Viejo can be seen about 2 km. east of the present site on the north side of the road to Baños.

From Pelileo, the road gradually descends to Las Juntas, the meeting point of the Patate and Chambo rivers to form the Pastaza river, and then goes on along the lower slopes of the volcano Tungurahua to Baños (25 km. from Pelileo). The road gives spectacularly good views of the Pastaza gorge and the volcano.

Baños (1,800 metres) is a holiday resort with a supposedly miraculous Virgin and very pleasant hot springs. The central church is the focus for religious devotions and attracts many pilgrims; the paintings of miracles performed by Nuestra Señora de Santa Agua are worth seeing. Interesting walks can be taken on the lower slopes of Tungurahua or along the side of the gorge of the Pastaza river, which rushes past Baños to the magnificent Agoyán Falls 10 km. further down the valley. The whole area between Pelileo and Baños has a delightful sub-tropical climate (the rainy season is from May to October) and large areas are devoted to growing sugar cane, mandarin oranges, tomatoes and even peaches and grapes. It is from here that Ecuador's best aguardiente comes. One set of thermal baths is in the town; the other, Salado, is 1½ km. out of town on the Ambato road; walk W out of the town, turn up a path which is just after crossing the bridge and just before joining the new road. One traveller suggests walking out of town along main street till it joins the Ambato road (beyond bridge) turn left on the first main street (cobbled) leading uphill (entrance US$0.12). Interesting side trips are possible from the main Pelileo-Baños highway across the main valley, north to Patate, or up the Chambo valley to Penipe and Riobamba, or take taxi to Puente Vendas, 2 hours, US$3.20, beautiful ride. From Baños it is possible to walk up (at least part of) Tungurahua; follow road opposite police control on Ambato side of town, then first mule track to right of store, where sketch-map of route can be obtained. Allow 2 days for return journey, take plenty of food. Horses can be hired for US$0.80 an hour, and mules can be hired at Pondua, a village on the lower slopes, to carry luggage up to a cabin. Here you can camp (also possible near Agoyán Falls). The climb takes 6-8 hours and it is another 2 hours to the snow line. You will get a guide for the price of the mule.

Hotels Many, of all types, but they fill up quickly during the day. Government-controlled prices, per room, of US$1.50 for hotels, US$1 for residencias and US$0.75 for pensiones. *Sangay,* best, English owner, US$3.50 without or US$5 with bath, US$11.20 full board s, US$10 d, tennis court, the owner may let you have a shower if you are non-resident; he will also change money, and provides afternoon tea for US$o.50. Guides for climbing can be arranged at the hotel. *Villa Gertrudis* also good; *Hotel Paraíso* (formerly *Humboldt*), near bus station, US$5 s plus board or US$2 without food, not as good as *Sangay* and noisy from buses; *Hotel Palace,* good facilities clean, US$6 s; *Residencial Teresita,* on main square, hot water, recommended, about US$3 d; *Hotel Acapulco,* US$1.60 d; *Americano,* US$2.30 d, basic but friendly, with good "gringo" food, cooking facilities available; *Hotel Paisano,* US$1.50 d; *Hotel Delicia,* on main square, good, clean, friendly, hot showers, US$2.50 d; *Residencial Altamira,* US$2.50 d, friendly, food available; *Residencial Olguita,* US$1 each, front rooms best, very clean, good value; Cheap: *Hotel Santa Clara,* US$1 s, use of kitchen possible; *Residencial Puerto de Dorado,* US$1.80 s, clean. Also, houses for rent on a monthly basis, US$4-8.

Restaurants *Puerta del Dorado,* good meal but expensive; *Luis P. Martínez,* opposite hospital; *Mercedes,* Eloy Alfaro 420, superb home cooking; near market, good food; vegetarian food at the *Hotel Americano. Oriental; Cordillera; El Paisano,* also recommended, *Pan de Casa* for breakfast.

Entertainment Cockfighting, Coliseo, Sat. and Sun. p.m.

Buses To Quito, *via* Ambato, 4½ hours, US$1.25; to Ambato, ¾ hour, US$0.40; to Riobamba, 2½ hours, US$0.60 (only one direct bus a day); to Puyo in Oriente, 2½ hours, US$1.60; to Misahualli, 7½ hours, US$1.20, Amazonia Bus Company reportedly unreliable.

North from Ambato the railway and Pan-American Highway pass through Salcedo (good Thursday and Sunday markets) to Latacunga, the capital of Cotopaxi Province.

Latacunga, with 27,000 inhabitants. Here the abundance of light grey lava rock has been artfully employed to build many a home and public building. Cotopaxi (5,896 metres) is much in evidence, though it is 29 km. away. Provided they are not hidden in the clouds, which unfortunately is all too often, as many as nine volcanic cones can be seen from Latacunga. The central park is worth a visit. The town has a Saturday market (and a smaller one on Tuesdays). A fine paved road leads west to **Pujilí** (good Sunday market but beware local illicit liquor and pickpockets), 12 km. away, and then on over the Western Cordillera to Zumbahua, Macuchi and Quevedo. **Zumbahua,** a cluster of 40 rustic houses by an old hacienda, has a fine Saturday market with a lot of llamas on view, and is the point to turn off for a visit to **Quilotoa.** Quilotoa is an old volcanic crater filled by a beautiful emerald lake about 3½ hours' walk, ½ hour's

drive up a rough and dusty road which runs north from Zumbahua to
Quilotoa and on to Chugchilán (this last stretch is the worst) a very poor
village set in one of the most scenic areas of Ecuador. The volcanic lake
can be reached by taking a truck to Zumbahua from Latacunga (2 hours),
the walk to Quilotoa is a good day's hike; llama herds may be seen en
route. The Saturday trip to Zumbahua market and the Quilotoa crater is
one of the best excursions in Ecuador, but there is no accommodation in
Zumbahua (but ask Don Alejandro Correa for sleeping-bag space in his
barn) or Quilotoa. The 0600 from Latacunga to Cotopaxi/Quevedo bus
passes Zumbahua at 0900. Except on Saturday, there are no buses to
Quilotoa: however Hugo Rengifo (contact through *Hotel Interandino*)
has a 4-wheel drive vehicle and for the trip to Pujilí, Zumbahua, Quilotoa
and Chugchilán, charges US$40. Alternatively, hitch a truck, you will be
dropped close to the volcano. One traveller suggests the trip to Quilotoa
be made Saturday morning, returning to Pujilí for the Sunday market
there. (Hotel on market square.) Macuchi, on the main road to Quevedo
some way beyond Zumbahua, is a mining centre for gold and various
other non-ferrous metals. The mines were developed in the thirties and
forties by an American company, and now they are almost abandoned.

Buses to Quevedo, about 6 hours, US$2; to Quito, 2 hours, US$2.20; to Zumbahua,
2 hours, US$2; to Ambato, 1 hour, US$0.50; to Riobamba, US$0.50.

Hotels   *Hotel Interandino* (US$6 p.p., near central square, good and friendly). The
Fogón, on the southern exit (the Ambato road) is a superb restaurant, offering better
food and much better value than the best hotels in Quito (closed Sunday). *Hotel
Estambul,* good, but no private bath, US$5 d. Cheap and central is the *Pensión
Imperial,* US$2.50 d, dilapidated but clean, next to *Restaurante Humboldt* and near
Restaurante Familiar. Also, *Costas Azules,* US$2 each, very basic; *Hotel Turismo,*
next door, US$1.80 d, also good restaurant; *Residencial Boyacá.* Accommodation is
not abundant and travellers to the Thursday Saquisilí market are advised to arrive
early Wednesday.

About 20 minutes drive north-west of Latacunga is the small, but very
important market town of **Saquisilí.** Its Thursday (0700-1100) market is
famous throughout Ecuador for the way in which all eight of its plazas
and most of its streets become jam-packed with people, the great majority
of them local Indians with red ponchos and little white felt hats, The best
time to visit the market is between 0900 and 1000; be sure to bargain,
prices may be inflated. (Rated the best market in Ecuador by one who has
visited them all. There is a basic residencial on main plaza—no sign; also
Hotel Pichincha, basic, US$1 p.p.) The Saquisilí bus company has
frequent services between Latacunga and Saquisilí (US$0.30) and several
buses a day run from Saquisilí to Quito (catch them in Quito on the
Avenida 24 de Mayo in the old centre, US$1, 2½ hours). The *Hotel
Interncontinental Quito* and the *Hotel Colón Internacional* in Quito both
organise efficient but expensive taxis for a 2-hour visit to Saquisilí market
on Thursdays.

North from Latacunga, the railway and the Pan-American Highway
cross one another at Lasso, a small village with a milk bottling plant. Just
north of Lasso, on the east side of the highway, is the San Agustín hill,
thought to be a prehistoric pyramid.

The area around San Agustín is owned by the Plaza family, which includes Galo
Plaza, a former President of Ecuador and later a Secretary-General of the Organization of American States. The Plazas have two large haciendas and breed splendid
bulls for the big bull-fights in Quito in December. One of the two haciendas is

actually at the base of the San Agustín hill and includes some converted Inca buildings.

A little beyond San Agustín, a poor road leads off towards the Cotopaxi volcano, at Parque Nacional de Cotopaxi sign. Following this it is possible to climb up to an altitude of over 4,600 metres in an ordinary car, and on the north side of the mountain a jeep can reach the permanent snow-line near the newly constructed mountaineering hut. National Park authorities are breeding a fine llama herd on the lower slopes. (See Excursions from Quito, page 530.)

Thirty-seven km. beyond, at Cotopaxi, the line begins to dip into the basin in which Quito lies. In a valley below the bleak *páramo* the train has crossed, lies the town of **Machachi,** famous for its mineral water springs and swimming pool. The water—"Agua Güitig"—is bottled and sold throughout the country. Machachi is much frequented by the people of Quito, only 40 km. away. It produces a very good cheese. Cock-fights on Sundays. *Pensión El Tiempo,* US$2.50 double, clean.

And so the train arrives at the capital, Quito, an exceptionally beautiful city set in a hollow at the foot of the volcano Pichincha (4,776 metres). It was an Inca city, refounded by Sebastián de Benalcázar, Pizarro's lieutenant, in 1534, and the old part still retains much of its Colonial flavour.

Quito (2,850 metres), with a population of 600,000, is within 25 km. of the equator, but it stands high enough to make its climate much like that of spring in England, the days warm and the nights cool. Because of the height, visitors may initially feel some discomfort and should slow their pace for the first 24 hours. Mean temperature, 13°C, rainfall, 1,473 mm.; rainy season: Feb.-May and Oct-Nov., raining sometimes for days but usually only for a few hours in the afternoon, when it is very chilly; other seasons normally have little rain though heavy storms in July are not unknown. Night and day are of almost equal length; sunset is at 1814 hours, but is not really dark until about 1900.

Few cities have a setting to match Quito's. Although nearly 3 km. high—it is the second highest capital in Latin America—the mountains which circle it are higher still. Their slopes are covered with a rumpled patchwork-quilt pattern of grain fields. The slumbering volcano of Pichincha overshadows the city.

Modern Quito extends northwards into a luxuriant plain; it has wide avenues, fine private residences, parks, embassies and villas. But Quito's charm lies in the old south-western section where cobbled streets are steep and winding, dipping to deep ravines which have either been filled in or have stone viaducts built over them. Through this section hurries the Machángara river, now too polluted to wash clothes in, as was done traditionally. The houses in the old part are mostly Indian-made adobe brick, with low red roof tiles, or of whitened stone. Westwards the valley is closed by Cerro Panecillo (Bread Roll Hill); from its top (183 metres above the city level), scattered with picnic parties, there is a fine view of the city below and the encircling cones of volcanoes and mountains, as from the excellent Panecillo restaurant, just below the summit. A bus marked "Mitad del Mundo-Panecillo" goes right to the top from the equator mark—see page 530. Inca temple near summit, which has observation tower in poor repair; new one being built.

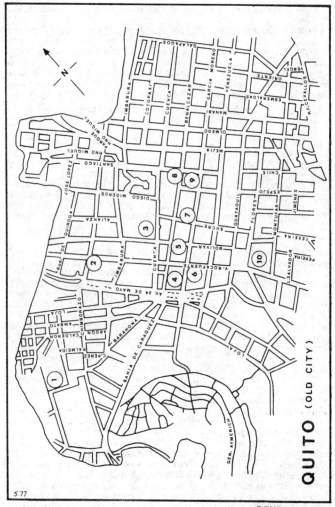

ROUGH SKETCH

Key to Map of Quito
1. San Diego church and convent; 2. San Roque church; 3. San Francisco church and monastery; 4. El Carmen Alto convent; 5. Railway station; 6. San Juan de Dios hospital; 7. La Compañia church; 8. Post Office; 9. Government Palace (Cathedral nearby); 10. Santo Domingo church.

The heart of the city is Plaza Independencia, dominated by a somewhat grim Cathedral with grey stone porticos and green tile cupolas. On its outer walls are plaques listing the names of the founding fathers of Quito, and inside are the tomb of Sucre and a famous Descent from the Cross by the Indian painter Caspicara. Facing the Cathedral is the Archbishop's Palace, and on the northeast corner is the Municipal Palace whose street floor, built in a series of graceful arcades, has small shops which sell a great variety of things. A new concrete municipal palace is being built. The low colonial Palacio de Gobierno (Government Palace), on the northwest side of the Plaza, is silhouetted against the great flank of Mount Pichincha. On the first floor is a gigantic mosaic mural of Orellana discovering the Amazon. The President's offices are on the second floor.

The best way to see old Quito is to walk its narrow streets. Wander down the Calle Ronda (or Morales), one of the oldest streets in the City, past Plaza Santo Domingo to Carrera Guayaquil, the main shopping district, and on to shady Parque Alameda, which has the oldest astronomical observatory in South America and the Escuela de Bellas Artes (School of Fine Arts). There is also a splendid monument to Simón Bolívar, the Liberator, and a coloured relief map of Ecuador. The traditional old Colonial area is being carefully preserved, with the buildings painted white and blue, but other parts of the city are being radically altered as a result of road improvements.

From Plaza Independencia two main streets, Carrera Venezuela and Calle García Moreno, lead straight towards the Panecillo to the wide Avda. 24 de Mayo, where the Indian market is held on Wednesdays and Saturdays. (Beware of thieves in the market.) Try roast guinea pig on Wednesdays. This area has many cheap lodgings, but very dirty.

Plaza San Francisco or Bolívar is west of Plaza Independencia; on the north-western side of this plaza is the great church and monastery of San Francisco, the earliest religious foundation in South America (1535); a modest statue of the founder, Fray Jodoco Ricke, a Flemish Franciscan who sowed the first wheat in Ecuador, stands at the foot of the stairs to the church portal. The glorious church of La Compania is in Calle García Moreno, one block from Plaza Independencia, and not far away to the north-east is the church of La Merced. In the Monastery of La Merced is Quito's oldest clock (twin-brother of London's Big Ben), built in 1817 by the firm of Handley, Moore, of Clerkenwell, London. Women are not allowed into this monastery. La Merced church, recently renovated, contains many splendidly elaborate styles.

Plaza Santo Domingo or Sucre, to the south-east of Plaza San Francisco, has to the SE the church and monastery of Santo Domingo, with its rich wood-carvings and a remarkable Chapel of the Rosary to the right of the main altar. In the centre of the square is a statue to Sucre, pointing with justifiable pride to the slopes of Pichincha where he won his battle with the Royalists and created the new Ecuador. The rather striking University City is on the NW side of the city, on the lower slopes of Pichincha by the Avenida de las Américas. Notice also the curious new basilica under construction on a hill in the centre of the town. (You go up Carrera Venezuela to see it, puffing all the way.)

There are altogether 86 churches in Quito. La Compañía has the most ornate and richly sculptured façade and interior. See its gorgeously coloured columns, its ten side altars plated with gold, the high altar of solid gold and the gilded balconies. Several of its most precious treasures, including a painting of the Virgen Dolorosa, framed in emeralds and gold and worth US$10 million, are kept in the vaults of the Banco Central del Ecuador and appear only at special festivals.

The church of San Francisco (1535), Quito's largest, is rich in art treasures. The two towers were shaken down by earthquake in 1868 and rebuilt. See the fine wood-carvings in the choir, a magnificent high altar of gold and an exquisite carved ceiling. There are some paintings in the aisles by Miguel de Santiago, the colonial mestizo painter. His paintings of the life of Saint Francis decorate the monastery of San Francisco close by. In the atrium of San Francisco is the Cantona Chapel with sculptures.

Many of the heroes of Ecuador's struggle for independence are buried in the Monastery of San Agustín, where the treaty of independence from Spain was signed. The Church of El Carmen Moderno has a fine collection of Quito ceramics. In the Monastery of San Diego are some unique paintings with figures dressed in fabrics sewn to the canvas—a curious instance of our present-day "collage". Also, the Sagrario, next to the Cathedral, ornate, gilded entrance portal; San Agustín, Flores and Mejía, paintings; La Concepción, Mejía and García Moreno; San Blas, Guayaquil and 10 de Agosto. The church of La Merced is also worth a visit.

Museums Quito prides itself on its painting. The Casa de la Cultura Ecutoriana, at the west side of Parque de Mayo, has good murals, a picture gallery, an exhibition of Ecuadorean books, and a unique museum of musical instruments (now closed for alterations). There is a good collection of Ecuadorean sculptures and painting at the Museum of Colonial Art, on the corner of Calle Cuenca and Calle Mejía, and of religious art at the Franciscan Museum and the Museum of the Monastery of Santo Domingo. The Museo Jijón y Caamaño, now housed in the Catholic University, has a private collection of archaeological objects, historical documents, portraits, uniforms, etc., housed in an 18th century mansion. Open by appointment through the University 1000 to 1300. Admission: US$1.10. Interesting. There are two first class museums in the Banco Central del Ecuador (Av. 10 de Agosto), the Archaeological Museum on the fifth floor with beautiful pre-Colombian ceramics, and the Museo Colonial y de Arte Religioso on the 6th. Open 0900-2000; closed Mondays. There are guided tours in English, French and German. Students are allowed in free, for others the charge is US$0.20. There is also an excellent library (for academics) but this is difficult to get into. Natural history museum in Eloy Alfaro military college, open to public Sat. and Sun., 1500-1700, and to scholars (possibly) on application to Professor Pérez of the military college. Other museums: National Museum of Popular Arts and Crafts, Mejía and García Moreno, 0900-1200 and 1500-1800; Municipal Museum of Art and History, Espejo 1147, near main square, Tues. to Sun.; Museum of Ethnology, Dr Antonio Santiana, Teatro Universitario, Tues. to Fri. 0900-1230, Wed. and Fri. 1500-1700, Tues. and Thurs. 1500-1830.

Airport Mariscal Sucre Airport. Taxi to centre of Quito, US$3. From airport catch bus No. 1 or 16 to go to Plaza de Santo Domingo. The Iñaquito, Aeropuerto, and Panecillo buses all go to the airport (US$0.05), look for a sign "*Aeropuerto*" in the windscreen. The tourist desk at the airport is helpful; they may be prepared to ring around for a hotel. There is a US$7 departure tax.

Hotels *Intercontinental Quito,* with casino and pool (US$24) s, US$30 d, plus 20% service and tax. Meals dear), popular, advance bookings recommended; *Colón Internacional* (US$22 s, US$28 d), excellent food, cheaper in café alongside than in restaurant, good discotheque; *Auca Continental,* corner of Venezuela and Sucre, US$15 s, bath, television, excellent food in restaurant; *Coral Internacional,* Manuel Larrea 90, recommended, US$10 s; US$15 d; *Rapa-Nui,* Av. 6 de Diciembre 4454; *Zumac,* Av. 10 de Agosto y Mariana de Jesús; *Waldorf,* Tamayo 233; *Carolina,* Leonidas Plaza 150, US$6 p.p. (US$7.20 with private bath), inc. breakfast, strongly recommended but often full; under same management *Residencial Santa Clara,* Veintimilla and 10 de Agosto, equally good and full board available; *Humboldt,* now refurbished, central, US$12 s, US$15 d; *Hotel Alcron* (American plan only, US$8 s, US$12 d, Buenos Aires 200, special terms for Peace Corps), slightly seedy but friendly and helpful; *Embajador,* Av. Colón US$4 p.p. (US$8 full board), good food and service; the new *Hotel Inca Imperial* (US$15 s, US$21 d), Calle Bogatá 239; *Hostel Imperio,* good for modern area, Luis Cordero and 10 de Agosto, US$7 p.p.; *Hotel Quirimba,* nice rooms, US$3.50 s, US$5.50 d; *Hotel Plaza,* central (US$9, not all the rooms have windows, English spoken); *Pensión Florida* (single and full board, US$13), excellent. Students can try *Hotel La Buena Esperanza,* Calle Ronda 755 (name changed from Calle Morales), intersection Guayaquil (US$3.50 d, US$1.70 p.p., basic), if all else fails, there are other places, same price, same street; *Residencia Dapsilia,* Calle Caldas 718, near Basilica (US$6.60 full board); or the *Hotel Toral,* Venezuela 976; *Residencia Lutecia,* Av. Jorge Washington 909 y Páez, in a restored Colonial house (single and full board US$13.50, US$15 s, with bath); *Residencia* by the Santa Clara market, single and full board, US$9.50, excellent; *Hotel Colonial,* Maldonado 3035 (US$4.40 p.p., with shower, US$3.50 without), helpful, quiet room, clean and secure for luggage, recommended (US$7.50 d with private bathroom, cheaper rooms in annex); *Santa María,* US$5, en route to airport; *Hotel Interamericano* US$7 d; *Europa* (US$2.60 per head, Guayaquil, near Olmedo, basic, close to Plaza Teatro; *Viena,* Flores 562 and Chile, pleasant rooms, (US$3 p.p.), without hot water; *Ecuador,* Flores 650, top floor, US$2, with hot water; *Pensión Minerva,* Calle Loja, very hospitable, US$1.50 s, US$2.50 d. Near *Viena* and *Ecuador* is *Occidental,* US$1.75; *Residencial Los Olivos,* good, restaurant downstairs (US$3 s), corner of Plaza Santo Domingo, hot water; *Residencial Mesón Colonial,* Maldonado (US$1.80 s); *Atahualpa,* Riofrío 75's and Manuel Larrea; *Residencial Cumbes,* Calle Baquedano 164, US$15 d, recommended, friendly; *Residencias Bolívar,* Calle Espejo 832 (US$3 s), cold water, clean. Many cheap hotels in old city. *Hotel Hogar,* Montúfar 208, US$3.50 s, very good. *Residencial Martinique,* on Calle Amazonas by the La Favorita supermarket (US$3 a night, food extra). The *Quito, Colón,* and *Florida* are well away from the centre. *Hotel Astoria,* Loja 630, US$2.35 s, noisy, open all night; *Hotel Minerva,* Loja 656, US$2 s, hot water; *Residencial Dorado,* US$5 d, reasonable; *Hotel Monasterio,* Calle 24 de Mayo, US$2.50; *Los Andes,* US$1.75 s; *Huasi Continental,* Calle Flores, US$4 s.

Guayaquil No. 1, Maldonado 3248, near Plaza San Domingo, where Guayaquil bus leaves (US$4 d, with bath); basic; to make sure of room ring early in morning, it's popular with foreigners; the *Gran Casino,* García Moreno and Ambato, US$2.50 d, hot water, good meals, is popular with "gringos", but is sometimes raided for drugs.

Note Those travelling by car may have difficulty parking in the centre of Quito and are therefore advised to choose less central hotels.

Restaurants Excellent food at *Hotel Colón Internacional* for non-residents. Restaurants *Normandie* (French food); *España Cani; La Cholita; Le Toucan,* expensive; *Los Faroles,* Amazonas with Luis Cordero for Spanish food; Italian food at *Rincón de Sicilia* and at *Vieja Europa,* Calle Calama, native food at *Atahualpa.* At lunchtimes the *Epicur* sometimes serves local specialities, though the normal fare

is Chinese. Good seafood at *Flandes* (music at weekends) and *La Jaiba. Chalet
Suisse,* dear but excellent steaks. *Restaurant Tokyo; La Choza,* Bello Horizonte 404,
good native food. The *Imperador,* on García Moreno, is reasonable; so is *Viña del
Mar,* near central post office. Simple food at *Chifa Chang* (not only Chinese), at
Chile 1102-1110, near Flores, it also has good pastries, but the service doesn't merit
any awards. Good Chinese food at *Restaurant Pekin* on Bella Horizonte and *Chifa
China* on Versalles. Fish at *Delfin Dorado* on Caloma and American barbecued
food. *Restaurant Helvetia,* good, quite expensive; *Fondue Bar,* Calle Baquerizo
Moreno, Swiss food; *Bauhaus,* on Amazonas, German food; *Manolo's Churrería,*
Río Amazonas, very reasonable for snacks; on same street *El Coyote Flaco,* Av.
Amazonas 547, inexpensive for Mexican dishes; also *Marco Antonio's* snack bar,
more expensive than *Manolo's. Casa de los Steaks,* on 6 de Diciembre. Seafood at *El
Tartaro* and at *Los Picapiedras* is recommended and reasonably priced. *Restaurant
Manila,* nearby, is good. Good place to eat cheaply is *Salón Italia,* Olmedo 651, by
Hotel Ecuador, plentiful, good, cheap, or *Cafeteria Mil y Una Noches,* Espejo 824;
Restaurante La Española, good value. A good breakfast can be had at *Café Niza,* on
Venezuela, near *Hotel Metropolitan. La Soga,* Venezuela 10-70, reasonably priced.
Good pastries at *Cyrano,* on Av. 6 de Diciembre. *Café Madrilón* recommended.
Tierra Buena, now at Calle Tamayo, 1295, vegetarian restaurant and shop, plus craft
store, recommended, especially for its ice cream. Recommended is *Chifa Ling Yu
Tang,* Calle Mejia between García Moreno and Venezuela, cheap and good;
Alpuerco, US$0.60; excellent food at *Restaurante Viena; Hojas de Hierba,* 6 de
Diciembre, between Veintimilla and Carrión, falafel, salads, teas self-selected, nice
atmosphere, Indian music at night, recommended, doubles as a bookstore
(English/Spanish). A new recommendation is *Le Bistro,* excellent but expensive,
opposite *Hotel Quito.* There is an English Pub, *El Pub,* also opposite *Hotel Quito,*
with an English menu including Cornish pasties and fish and chips; also *McDonalds,*
near Avda. Amazonas, and *London Pub,* new, Quiteño Libre 683. **N.B.** Many of the
restaurants in the old town close at about 2100 every evening. Also, prices listed on
menus may not be true prices; is worth asking.

Clubs Country Club (15 minutes; golf, tennis, and indoor swimming pool); Polo
Club; Pichincha; Rotary; Lions.

Night Clubs Licorne, at *Hotel Colón Internacional*; Bagatelle; Pigalle (outside).
Night Club and Casino at *Hotel Humboldt*; Pianoteca; Rolls Royce; *Plaza Hotel*
café, with international pop records, recommended for cheap and interesting
evenings. Good Latin American music at Bar Salu and Jatari Tambo, groups play
weekends after 2100.

Tipping See under Guayaquil, page 503.

Transport Standard fare on local buses of 1 sucre (about US$0.04). For trips
outside Quito taxi tariffs should be agreed beforehand. Outside main hotels drivers
have a list of agreed excursion prices. Standard tariff in the city is US$0.60 to US$2
and not more than double by night; no increase for extra passengers; by the hour,
US$4 up. (**N.B.** Beware, however, of taxi drivers who offer to take you to "good,
cheap" hotels—they will be neither good nor cheap, and you will have to lengthen
your journey to find a satisfactory one).

Buses going N leave from various depots in N of town; those going S leave from
Calle 24 de Mayo in old city. The Colón-Camal No. 2 bus connects the northern
terminals with the southern ones (in the Plaza San Francisco). Buses to Esmeraldas,
US$7, 10 hours. Buses to Otavalo, 2½ hours, US$0.75 (Bus to the Otavalo Saturday
fair at 0600, Flota Imbabura, from N bus station. Also minibuses; to Ibarra, 3½
hours, US$3; to Tulcán, 5½-6½ hours, US$4; frequent buses to Guayaquil, 8 hours,
several companies do the trip, which costs about US$6 on an ordinary bus or
US$7.50 on a pullman coach. Ambato, US$0.90; Cuenca, US$2. To Santo Domingo
de los Colorados, 3 hours, US$1.50, lovely scenery; to Quevedo *via* Santo Domingo,
US$2.50, 5 hours; to Cuenca, 12 hours, US$7; to Latacunga, 2 hours, US$1.10. To
Machala, US$7 first class, 10 hours. Panamericana runs an "international" bus to
Bogotá, but this involves many changes and greater expense; again, it is better to
take a bus to the border and change. Flota Imbabura goes to the Colombian border
for US$3.

The times of departure of buses plying from Plazoleta del Cumandá are given in page 2 of Quito's "El Comercio". (Information office, Tel.: 570040.)

By bus to Lima 2,124 km., is crowded and tiring, but very interesting. The Ecuadorean company Panamericana and the Peruvian Tepsa (*via* Guayaquil) and Roggero organize through connections for a 48-hour journey (US$27.50), the latter being the better bet, but it is more convenient and less expensive (US$15) to arrange your own buses to Machala, the last major Ecuadorean town before the border, cross the border (see border crossing details on page 512) and catch one of the Peruvian long-distance buses from Tumbes on to Piura, Truijilo and Lima. You can reach Machala *via* Santo Domingo and Guayaquil from Quito, or *via* Riobamba and Guayaquil, or *via* Riobamba and Cuenca. The alternative route for crossing the Peruvian border *via* Loja and Macará takes much longer than the Machala route and is no more interesting (see page 538).

Railway to Guayaquil: booking office (Ferrocarriles del Estado) at Calle Bolívar, half a block lower than Plaza San Francisco. Station is one km. from centre, along continuation of Calle Maldonado, reached by buses along that street (e.g. Colón Camal No.2) Fare to Guayaquil, US$5, train leaves at 0600, stopping at Lasso for breakfast and Riobamba for lunch. Services also on Cuenca and Ibarra-San Lorenzo lines.

Car Rentals International Rent-a-Car, Av. 10 de Agosto.

Bank of London & South America, Av. Carrión y Amazonas, with Torres de Colón and San Agustín agencies; Citibank; Banco Holandés Unido. Open 0900-1330. Closed Saturday. Banco Central del Ecuador has superb museums on 5th and 6th floors.

Exchange Houses Calle Venezuela, near Plaza. Rodrigo Paz, Venezuela 659 and Av. Amazonas close to Supermarket, and at Jarmillo Arteaga, Calle Colombia, recommended. Also branches in La Favorita supermarkets.

Sport Horse racing on Sundays at La Carolina track; pari mutuel betting. A local game, Pelota de Guante (stone ball), is played, Saturday afternoon and Sunday, at Estadio Mejía. Soccer is played Saturday afternoons and Sunday mornings at Atahualpa stadium, and basket-ball in the Coliseo. There are bullfights.

Festivals A New Year fiesta, the *Inocentes,* from Dec. 28 to Jan. 6, fills the streets with people; clowns, some disguised as husky old women, and others, armed with long clubs stuffed with rags, indulging in bitter satire on the politicians. Another festival, for week ending Dec. 5, celebrates foundation of city. Hotels allowed to charge extra. Bullfights and music in streets.

Carnival at Shrovetide is celebrated, as elsewhere in the Andes, by throwing plastic bags of water at passers-by. So you need a raincoat and umbrella at that season! The Good Friday processions are most impressive and moving.

Theatre Teatro Sucre, redecorated and now most elegant; plays in Spanish.

Tourist Office Dituris, Calle Reina Victoria 514 and Roca, gives maps and other information, friendly and helpful. Information on visiting Galápagos Islands (Tel.: 23904). Quito has special tourist police with recognizable shirt-sleeve badge. There is also an information desk at the airport, in the international arrivals building. Maps may also be obtained from the Ministry of Public Works.

Tourist Agencies Ecuadorian Tours, American Express agent, on Av. Amazonas. Metropolitan Touring; Interturis, Av. Colón y 6 de Diciembre, new; Turismundia, friendly, on Av. Venezuela 736, near the Plaza Independencia (reservations to Galápagos). Offices also at Guayaquil. Anyone seriously interested in genuine archaeological (and botanical, ornithological and zoological) expeditions in Ecuador should contact: Educational Programmes in Archaeology and the Natural Sciences (E.P.A.N.S.), 4 Av. 8-72, Zona 1, Guatemala City. EPANS organizes tours to well-known and almost unknown areas of archaeological (etc.) importance. Transnave office (for booking Galápagos tours on a government ship) at Benalcázar 1000.

Medical Clínica de Especialidades for amoebic dysentery test, US$4. All-night chemist, Calle Venezuela 664.

Immigration Office Av. Caracas, just off Av. 10 de Agosto.

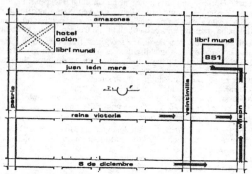

Laundramat Lavanderías Modernas, coin-op., Av. 6 de Diciembre 24-00 y Orellana, opposite Fiat office. Can be reached from Plaza Santo Domingo by No. 2 bus, walking left for 6 blocks after alighting at Av. 6 de Diciembre. Others are Martinaicing, Av. Colón, and La Química, 6 de Diciembre y Orellana.

Climbing Nuevos Horizontes Club, Venezuela 659, on Pasaje Amador near Plaza Independencia, open Tues. and Fri. p.m., will advise on climbing Chimborazo and Cotopaxi, including purchase or hire of crampons, ice axes etc., but does not hire them (best to have with you). Non-members may go on the club's trips if these are not fully-booked. Cóndores, Padre José Ribas of Colegio San Gabriel is helpful. Sr. Enrique Vélez of Riobamba arranges trips to Chimborazo (see page 518). Other clubs for climbers: Sadday Manabi 621, near Plaza Independencia, and Yanasacha, near Avda. Amazonas. The International Andean Mountaineers' Club is open to visitors and residents of Ecuador; equipment rented, call G. Rae at 230070. The best time for climbing is between November and February.

Rugby Sunday 1000 at Colegio Militar. Inquire at *El Pub*.

P.S.N.C. Agents Anglo Ecuatoriana (Agencias) C, Ltda., Av. 10 de Agosto 2604. Cables: "Scael"; Tel.: 30015.

Bookshops Libri Mundi, Juan León Mera 851 y Veintimilla, English, French and German books; Librería Central, García Moreno 750; Su Librería; Librería Científica; Hojas de Hierbas, 6 de Diciembre, Spanish/English, coffee shop as well.

Shopping Articles typical of Ecuador can be bought in the main shopping district on and near curving Avenida Guayaquil or at the three main markets. There are carved figures, plates and other items of native wood, balsa wood boxes, silver of all types, Indian textiles, buttons, toys and other things fashioned from tagua, hand-painted tiles, hand-woven rugs and a variety of antiques dating back to Colonial days. Panama hats are a good buy; Eljuri, Chile 1062. Indian garments (for Indians rather than tourists) can be seen and bought on the north end of the Plaza Sucre and along the nearest stretch of the nearby Calle General Flores. Akios, a large shop, sells almost all types of handicraft; Gorivar 250, Coma Grande, Barrio Obrero, an easy walk from Santo Domingo down Rocafuerte, friendly and cheaper. Ocepa, at Carrión 1336, near 10 de Agosto, good selection, government run; branches also in Guayaquil and Cuenca. Also Cooperativo de Tejidos de Otavalo, 10 de Agosto 442, near the Ejido Park, and nearby Cooperativa Atahualpa at No. 523, and shops near British Embassy and under Palacio de Gobierno. Near *Hotel Quito* at Av. Colón 260, is Folklore, the store of Olga Fisch, a most attractive array of handicrafts and famous rugs, but distinctly expensive, as accords with the designer's international reputation. Excellent museum. Productos Andinos, an artisans' co-operative, has opened in north Quito at Calle Urbina 111, good quality, reasonably priced. After it in quality is Artes, Av. 6 de Diciembre 1118 and Veintimilla. La Bodega, Juan León Mera 614 and Carrión, is recommended for antiques and artisan goods. On Avda. Amazonas, NE of *Hotel Colón*, are a number of handicraft shops. Rugs can be bought from a workshop in a courtyard off the Calle Ronda. Casa de los Regallos, Calle Mañosca 456, for souvenirs and antiquities. Bargaining is customary in small shops and at street stalls. Offices and stores are open 0830-1200 and 1400-1800. "Typical" articles tend to be cheaper outside Quito. Tailor and shirt-marker, warmly recommended, is Miguel Mafla, Ronda 764 (near Buena Esperanza). Recommended watchmaker, Sr. Torres, Relojeria Patek Phillipe, Mejía 329. Food is cheap at La Favorita supermarkets. See H. Stern's jewelry store at *Hotel Intercontinental*. Casa Americana, on Venezuela, inexpensive department store. For sports equipment, Yanasacha, Almagro y República.

Warnings Visitors should know—for their own good—that a thriving industry in Quito is the production of religious paintings of a medieval type. And another is the stealthy sale by dubious chaps of shrunken heads (*tsantsa*), war trophies of the Jivaro head-hunters. Nowadays they are fakes made out of goat skin, their long black hair making them look very like the real thing.

Cables Ietel, Carrera Venezuela 961 and 969, also at *Hotel Quito* and in Av. Colón.

Excursions   23 km. N of Quito (½ hour by taxi or 1 by bus, US$0.16), is the Equatorial Line Monument. On overcast days it is chilly, for the Monument stands at an altitude of 2,374 metres. The exact equatorial line here was determined by Charles de la Condamine and his French expedition in 1735. The T-shaped Solar Museum a short distance SE, in village of San Antonio, is open Sats. 1400-1800 and Sun. 0700-1800. The two entrances to the building are marked Northern Hemisphere and Southern Hemisphere. There are displays about the cult of the sun, worshipped in these highlands before the Spanish came. A paved road runs from Quito to the Monument, which you can reach by a "Mitad del Mundo" bus from Callas Sucre and García Moreno or 6 de Diciembre and Patria. It seems that this trip is only of interest to those who want to say they've been to the equator. Two minutes walk before the Monument, there is a restaurant *Equinoctio*, excellent food, inexpensive. A few km. beyond the Monument is the Pululagua crater, well worth visiting, though a jeep is advisable as the road is very rough in parts. The footpath to the top of the crater starts 14 km. off road to Calacalí. Also beyond the Monument, 5 km. after San Antonio on the road to Atahualpa, is the ruined Inca fortress of Rumicucho. Restoration poor, but situation magnificent.

It is only fair to tell tourists that the Equator line as determined by a precise survey is a few hundred metres away from the monument. The Equator line also crosses the Pan-American Highway 8 km. south of Cayambe, where there is a concrete globe beside the road. Midday by the sun, incidentally, is at 1214. Take Cayambe bus from Estación Norte (2 hours, US$0.80) and ask for Mitad del Mundo. From Panecillo, US$0.20, 1¾ hours.

Another favourite Saturday trip is to Otavalo's Indian fair (see page 542). In the valley of Chillos (1 hour by car) are the thermal pools of Alaugasí and Tingo María. A few km. from Tingo María is La Merced, which has thermal baths. Camping is allowed in the vicinity.

A scenic bus trip can be taken to (129 km. US$1.50, 3 hrs.) **Santo Domingo de los Colorados,** in the W lowlands (pop. about 25,000). There is a large Sunday market which used to be favoured by the Colorado Indians; recent travellers tell us that Indians at the market are now comparatively few, and that the market itself is an unexciting "tourist trap". Santo Domingo, now the hub of roads radiating to Quito, Guayaquil (by bus 5 hrs, US$1.60), Esmeraldas (bus, 4 hours, US$1.20) and Manta, has the boom town air of the American west a century ago: wooden houses, mud streets, a number of cabarets and houses of pleasure and music blaring nightly in the byways.

Hotels   *Hotel Caleta,* noisy, US$2.20 s, US$3.60 d; *Hotel Europa;* the motel-type *Miraflores,* and *Zaracay,* 2 km. out of town on the road to Quito, with restaurant, attractive gardens and swimming pool; excellent, but advisable to book, especially if planning to stay over a weekend. Next to it is the *Hotel del Toachi.* On the same road, some 20 mins drive from Santo Domingo, is *Tinalandia,* with its own golf course, and excellent food. Nearer the town centre, still on the Quito road, is the *Hotel La Siesta,* German-run, superb value at US$2.50 a night p.p. *Hotel Victoria,* US$1.25 s, basic, restaurant. *Residencial Dormicentro,* central plaza, US$3 d. Many cheap pensions. Café *Humboldt.*

N.B.   Visitors to Santo Domingo should, if interested in the Indians, try to meet their "gobernador" and medicine-man, Sr. Abraham Calazacón.

Cotopaxi   Ingo Pauler tells us it is best reached by turning left (very robust vehicle needed) off Pan-American Highway at the *Parque Nacional de Cotopaxi* sign. It is possible to drive about 30 km. up the road to about 4,600 metres. From here it is 30 min. to a hut (very basic) with beds (take your own sleeping bag) and a kitchen. The ascent from the hut (4,800 metres) to the summit takes about 6 hours. (The hut holds 80 people; US$0.75 per night.) It is very steep; equipment and experience are required. (Be sure to keep the right of the path and follow the crest of the ridge.) Snowline at 5,000 metres. Stupendous views in good weather. If you are out of condition do not try to go too fast at this height.

Day tours *via* Cotopaxi to Indian fair (Thursday 0700-1100) at Saquisilí about 93 km. each way. (Tapices are cheaper here than at Salasaca.) Much cheaper than organized tour is taxi from Quito (US$12 per car), with 2 hour wait at fair. Cheaper still, of course, are buses; US$1.20 return, the journey taking 1½-2 hours each way. Corpus Christi processions are particularly colourful at Saquisilí, and also at Calderón, just north of Quito. Direct buses from Quito or change at Lasso for Saquisilí; wear your old clothes. (See also page 520.)

Another interesting trip is to Sangolquí, about 20 minutes away by bus. There is a colourful Sunday market and there are thermal baths nearby.

By taking a bus on Friday afternoon to Riobamba (4 hrs.) you can see the colourful market next morning before catching the down train (or a bus) to Guayaquil at 1130.

Calderón, 30 km. N of Quito, is the place where dolls are made of bread; you can see them being made, and of course their prices are much lower than in Quito.

North of Quito

Both the railway and the Pan-American Highway run north-east from Quito by different routes to Otavalo (121 km.) and Ibarra (145 km.). The highway is now paved and, compared with its winding, cobbled predecessor, in splended condition. The rail journey to Ibarra takes over twice as long as the road journey and cannot be recommended for comfort or scenic beauty. At Ibarra, the railway and Pan-American Highway separate. The railway goes north-west to the Pacific port of San Lorenzo, a very spectacular and worthwhile trip, and the highway runs north for another 108 km. to Tulcán and on to Ipiales in Colombia. From Ibarra to Tulcán the Pan-American Highway is now paved.

The road for north leaves Quito through the Indian area around Calderón, descends the spectacular Guayllabamba gorge and climbs out again to the fertile oasis of Guayllabamba village, noted for its avocado pears. Further north the road runs for many kilometres through some of the driest, dustiest, most barren land in the Andes before irrigated land is reached again at Cayambe. This area of rich dairy farms produces a fine range of European-style cheeses. Cayambe is the Agrarian Reform Institute's showplace; its only major project. The road forks north of Cayambe: to the right a cobbled road runs through Olmedo, a short cut to Ibarra; to the left, the main paved road crosses a *páramo* and suddenly a panorama of lake, mountain and farmland lies below: the Province of Imbabura. (Just outside Olmedo, *El Coche Rojo* restaurant is reasonable and serves excellent seafood). The road descends and we enter the land of the Otavalo Indians, a singularly lively and fairly prosperous group who have been making commercial woollens for well over forty years. The men are recognizable by their white, bell-bottomed, mild-calf-length trousers, long braided hair and blue ponchos. Although some work on haciendas between San Pablo and Ibarra, most of the scattered homes in the fields belong to Indians.

Otavalo (2,530 metres, population 8,000) is notable for its colourful Indian fair on Saturday. It begins at 0700 in the morning, and the earlier you get there, the better. Here the Indians bring their woollen fabrics and beautiful shawls to market; ponchos, bags and sweaters are especially good value. Cockfights are held in the afternoon. From June 24 to 29 there are bullfights in the plaza and regattas on the beautiful Laguna de San Pablo, 8 km. away, and there is the "Fiesta del Yamor" in early September. En route to the Laguna de San Pablo is the Club de Tiro, Casa y Pesca where one can rent canoes. It is worth hiking to Laguna de San Pablo for the views. The newly built 6-roomed *Hotel Chicapán* is on the lakeshore. There are several picturesque lakes in the mountains around, such as Lago Cuichocha, a splendid crater lake, which has an island where a band plays on Sundays (take bus to Cotocochi, US$2, and then walk, hitch or take taxi); paved road to Pan-American Highway. Also Lagunas Mojanda consisting of 4 lakes, with a simple hostel (take food).

Hotels   May be full on Friday nights, before fair, when prices go up. *Otavalo,* very good, US$5.50-9.50 p.p. en pension; similar charges for double room without pension, must reserve in advance, clean, recommended; *Pensión Residencial; Mariscal,* US$1.20, not safe; *Central; Riviera,* US$3 d, comfortable; *Pensión Otavalo,* US$1.25 s; *Residencias Colón,* US$1.60 p.p., hot water; *Residencias Sami Huasi,* US$1.50, near market, friendly, clean; *Pensión Los Andes,* US$2 d, very grimy; the old "duena" seems to be almost blind. (The landlady's brother will show you his small museum of archaeological and anthropological artefacts.) *Pensión Los Angels,* US$1.20 p.p., clean, friendly; *Pensión Vaca No. 2* US$1.50 p.p., without bath or hot water, clean, friendly; *Hospedaje San Agustín,* US$1.50 s, friendly.

Restaurants   *Herradura,* best; *Camba Huasy* (with enclosed parking); *San Crystal,* clean, merienda, US$0.65. *Ari Micui,* vegetarian food and cheeseburgers, also on Plaza de los Ponchos, not particularly cheap but good value. *Casa de Corea,* opposite *Hotel Riviera,* Korean and Ecuadorean food. *Casa Utopia,* English owner and his wife are generous with meals and information, vegetarian, recommended; *Pinky's,* American owner, reasonable price, excellent views; *María Rosita's,* cheap food.

The fair is a "must" for tourists, but the organized tour sold by hotels is extremely expensive. It is far cheaper (and more interesting) to go by rail car (leave Quito 1300 Friday; arrive Otavalo 1730). The vehicle is second class, but passable, and seats are booked ahead. From Quito by taxi takes 1½ hours (US$12); by minibus (Transportes Andina) from 18 de Septiembre (and Av. Guerrero), 1½ hours, US$1.30; by bus (Flota Imbabura or Expreso Turismo) 2½ hours (US$0.75). The Tourist Office in Quito will help with reservations. There are 3 markets in different places: (a) woollen fabrics and shawls, 0600-1200; (b) animal auction, 0400-0800 (the most picturesque according to one traveller); (c) produce, 0800-1300. The market is rated highly for woollen goods, though it is now rather highly organized and touristy and prices are not especially low; very little of the traditional weaving is now to be seen and many of the ponchos are made of orlon. All the same, Otavalo is the best place in Ecuador to buy a man's woollen poncho. Apart from the market, there is a reliable selection of goods at Artesanías de Norte, at corner of Modesto Jaramillo and Salinas. There is also a small market on Wednesdays.

The Otavalo Indian weavers come from the villages of Peguche, Iluman and Quinchuqui, close to Otavalo. Their clean, painted homes are remarkable. They are most friendly and will indicate where you can buy their products—from the loom as it were. Nice embroidered clothes can be bought cheaply at nearby village of Esperanza. **Note:** If planning a spending spree, bring plenty of cash. There are no facilities for cashing travellers' cheques.

Bus to Tulcán, US$1, 4 hours.

Off the road between Otavalo and Ibarra are **Cotacachi,** where leather goods are made and sold, and **San Antonio de Ibarra,** famous for its wood carvings though the part near the main road is rather touristy. Buses can be taken there from Ibarra. If you walk uphill, away from the main square, you will find cheaper carvings and a better selection. Visit the workshop of Moreo Santacruz, and the exhibiton of Oswaldo Garrido in the Palacio de Arte.

Ibarra stands at 2,225 metres, population 41,500. It is a pleasant colonial town with a good hotel. A unique form of paddle ball is played on Saturdays and Sundays near the railway station. The players have huge spiked paddles for striking the 4 lb. ball! Take your camera. The town also has a picturesque market, and a local industry produces delicious candies made from walnuts and local fruits. Local festival, September 22-25. Some interesting paintings are to be seen in the Church of Santo Domingo.

A 293 km. railway runs to the port of San Lorenzo, N of Esmeraldas. An autoferro runs daily from Ibarra, leaving about 0700, and taking about 6 hours. Steam trains run less frequently and take from 12 to 15 hours. Direct Quito-San Lorenzo autoferro thrice weekly.

N.B. In mid-1976 a railway bridge was damaged and the first stage of the trip to Tercer Paso, near Carolina, is made by bus convoy, leaving Ibarra not later than 0700, arriving 1000. Train arrives 1800 in San Lorenzo.

Leaving Ibarra, the train descends past Salinas into the narrow gorge of the Río Mira (called Chota upstream) inhabited first by the blacks growing fruit and sugar cane, of origin similar to those further upstream. They sell fruit at the station. After three hours the valley widens near Collapi (730 metres) and the land becomes better watered and has been more recently colonized. Lita (460 metres) is reached after four hours and a stop is made for refreshment. The foaming Río Blanco enters the Mira beside the station. Through the lowlands cultivated land becomes commoner until 6 hours after leaving Ibarra we reach San Lorenzo. The trip costs US$1.60.

Hotels at Ibarra S on Quito road; *Hostería San Agustín, Hostería Chorlavi,* off highway 2 km. S of Ibarra, US$8 p.p., elegant surroundings of converted hacienda; nearer town, *Hotel Ajavi,* US$7 s, very good restaurant; *Hotel Hong Kong,* main plaza, US$2.65 p.p., clean, quiet. *Residencial Los Ceibos,* Calle Oviedo 9-51, friendly, English spoken, US$3.80 d, hot water, warmly recommended; *Residencial Vaca,* US$3.50 s, clean, hot water; *Residencial Imbabura,* ½ block W of main plaza, US$1 p.p.; *Hotel Imbabura,* 1 block S of main plaza, US$2.20 p.p., clean, hot showers downstairs in public baths (US$0.10); *Residencial Familial,* Calle 9, Carrera 7, US$3 p.p., clean and good; *Residencial Imperial,* US$4, recommended; *Residencial Astorias,* 1 block from railway station, US$1.10 p.p., hot water, recommended; *Pensión Descanso,* US$80 p.p., one block from main plaza, reasonable; *Residencial Atahualpa,* US$0.80 p.p.; *Yaguarcocha,* clean, US$1.50 p.p.; *Tulcán,* about US$0.80 p.p.; *Residencial Colón,* US$2 p.p., clean; *Pensión Varsovia,* US$2 s, unfriendly; *Pensión San Lorenzo,* US$1.50 p.p., basic. At edge of Lago Yaguarcocha is *Hotel del Lago,* no accommodation, only refreshments.

Restaurant *Gaucho,* not recommended, next to Hotel Imbabura. Good breakfast at *Café Pushkin,* nearby. Local specialities are blackberry sweets and nougat. *El Caribe,* Calle 7, Carrera 7, excellent three-course *merienda* for US$0.60. *Rojo*

Oriente, Chinese. *El Molino Viejo*, recommended. *Sergio's*, good and cheap food (near *Hotel Imbabura*).

Shopping Artesanías del Norte, Olmedo 551, good for embroidery; local Ibarra products cheaper than in Otavalo market or Quito.

Bus to Quito, 3½ hours, US$0.80. Colectivo taxis for about double. Minibus, US$2.40. To Yaguarcocha, US$1.20. Bus to Tulcán, US$0.80, 3½ hours. To Otavalo, US$0.25, ½ hr.

North of Ibarra the Pan-American Highway goes past Lake Yaguarcocha, the "Lake of Blood", and descends to cross the Chota Valley. The Highway divides in the valley, and you can go to Tulcán either *via* El Angel over a long stretch of *páramo* or, like most of the lorries and buses, further east over a paved road over eroded hill sides and through farmland *via* San Gabriel. On the El Angel road at the village of Chota and on the San Gabriel road at El Juncal, the highway has descended to a mere 1,520 metres; in the tropical Chota valley you can buy excellent fruit from the local blacks, descendants of slaves brought from Africa in the 17th century by Jesuits to farm their estates. The El Angel route is still heavy going; the San Gabriel route should be fine now. (though it was reported closed due to a damaged bridge in mid-1976—check).

N of San Gabriel, on a side road from La Paz, you reach the Gruta de La Paz, a grotto through which runs a river. There are stalactites and a shrine.

Tulcán is a chilly small town of 25,000 people at an altitude of 3,000 metres; it is the centre of a rich farming area and is famous for its dairy products. It is not particularly interesting for the tourist except for the famous cemetery, where the topiarist's art reaches its apogee; bushes are trimmed into fantastic figures of animals, plants, geometrical shapes etc. Camera essential. Automobile carnets and passports are checked at the Aduna office (hard to find, at a corner of a large plaza) and at the migration office in the Edificio Portuario in the centre is a side street off the main plaza where entry and exit stamps are also obtained (may be closed Sat. and Sun.), and tourist cards are examined at the border; however, practices may vary. Both Edificio Portuario and border are closed from 1800 to 0800 hours (check to be sure), and for lunch between 1130 and 1430 (though sometimes the border is open at lunch-time). Americans and Canadians need visas to enter Colombia, which can be obtained at the Colombian Consulate in Tulcán. Car drivers must complete formalities at the migration office, and then return to the border for a transit stamp. On Sat. and Sun. papers are checked at the police station between Tulcán and the border. (Sometimes it seems that all formalities are in fact carried out at the border itself. Reports—and possibly practices—differ.) There is a US$2 exit stamp for those who have stayed in Ecuador more than 36 hours, unless your entry stamp is a "T-3" (see page 548). Due to the high volume of local traffic, border crossing is fairly relaxed. The highway descends tortuously for 6½ km. through the mountains to the river Carchi, on the border, which is crossed by the natural bridge of Rumichaca. Ipiales is 4 km. beyond the bridge.

Hotels and Restaurants *Tulcán,* hot water, US$1.50; *Quito,* US$2.50, clean, central; *Residencial España,* US$2.40 p.p., hot water, clean, recommended, opposite bus station; *Residencial Oasis,* US$1; *Residencial Guaya,* US$0.80. *Hotel Ali y Huasi,* reasonable prices, quiet. If all are full, try police station! Right at the border is the *Hotel Rumichaca,* with a government tourist office down by the swimming pool—also excellent restaurant, with bowling alley. Hot public showers next to the Edificio Portuario. Restaurant at the bus stop not recommended.

Camping Possible at the sports field next to the cemetery.

Air Service by TAME to Quito and Ibarra.

Taxi to border, US$0.25; to Ipiales, US$2, however many people share it. Bus, if you can get one, is cheaper, US$0.50. Bus to Quito, 6½-8 hours, US$3; minibus 5 hours, US$2; Velotax 4 hours, US$2.40; to Ibarra, 3-4 hours, US$1. To Otavalo, US$1, 4 hours. Better choice of buses a.m. Plenty of colectivos also; to Quito, 4 hours, US$2.40. Bus terminal for Quito is long uphill walk from centre; best to take taxi or little blue bus. Colectivo to Ipiales, stopping at border for passport checks. US$0.80 a head; just to the border, US$0.10. Taxi stops at migration office in Tulcán to get Ecuadorean exit stamp. At the frontier one then goes straight to the Colombian side for entrance stamp, and on to Ipiales.

Those travelling from Ecuador into Colombia should change all their sucres before they reach the frontier, making sure they bargain for a good rate; this is better at Tulcán, where you can buy US dollars easily, than at Ipiales, where you can get only Colombian pesos. Try Almacén Rosa, next Banco de Colombia, for travellers' cheques. For those arriving in Ecuador, change only what you need to get to Quito.

N.B. Travellers may be asked to prove that they have US$20 for each day they intend to spend in Colombia or Ecuador, when passing this frontier.

The Southern Sierra

The Southern Sierra is much less visited than the rest of the country but nonetheless has many features worth seeing. The road and railway S of Sibambe (where we leave the Quito-Guayaquil railway) run through mountainous country and high above the valleys of the west-bound rivers. The countryside is poor, dry, chilly and wind-swept, and the Indians small, withdrawn and wrapped-up. Near Gun and Cañar, more Indians, dressed in black, are seen. At Gun an all-weather road runs to Cochancay in the coastal lowlands, from where there are paved roads to Guayaquil and Machala. Towards Cuenca the road, which is paved from Biblián onwards, loses height and the land is more intensively farmed. Between Biblián and Cuenca there are signs of the straw hat industry; **Azogues** (11,500) has a large Saturday market. Both Azogues and Biblián have attractive churches overlooking the towns from neighbouring hillsides.

Cuenca (2,595 metres), with 105,000 people, is the third largest city in Ecuador. It was founded by the Spaniards in 1557. A 146 km. railway runs from the Guayaquil-Quito line to Cuenca. The climate is spring-like, but the nights are chilly. The city has preserved its colonial air, with its cobblestone streets and quaint old buildings, many of them built of the marble quarried nearby. A fine new cathedral, which contains a famous crowned image of the Virgin, has now been built in the central square, Parque Calderón, where the old Government House, the old cathedral and the Courthouse (once the University) are. The University is now on the other side of the Tomebamba river. The fair is on Thursdays; there is a smaller one on Sunday. The Municipal Museum has a magnificent stock of Indian artefacts. The Salesian Museum in Colegio Salesiano is a private museum run by Padre Crespi (make an appointment) in which he displays exhibits to substantiate his theory that the Phoenicians reached Cuenca *via* the Amazon. Humboldt was a guest in 1802 at the old Casa de Gobierno (Government House). A pleasant walk is upstream along the river.

The churches which deserve a visit are: the old Cathedral, which has a fine organ; La Concepción (convent founded 1599), Las Carmelitas

Descalzas (1682), San Blas, San Francisco, Santo Cenáculo, and Santo Domingo. Inca ruins have been found in Cuenca on the banks of the river, and some houses are now undergoing restoration.

Cuenca has the best drinking water in Ecuador and visitors are welcomed at the attractively built and sited water plant, with its beautiful gardens. There are sulphur baths at Baños, with a beautiful church in a delightful landscape, 5 km. S of Cuenca. Two separate warm baths, of which the lower one is better (the main unit is US$0.20, private bathroom is US$0.30). Buses from Cuenca US$0.05).

There is a market on Thursday when pottery, clothes and local produce are sold in the 9 de Octubre and San Francisco areas.

Shopping Productos Andinos, Calle Gran Colombia, entre Luis Cordero y Benigno Malo. Run by a cooperative; very reasonable—no middleman. Many craftware shops along Gran Colombia, near *El Dorado* hotel. Good souvenirs are carvings, leather, basketwork, painted wood, onyx, woven stuffs (cheapest in Ecuador) embroidered shirts, etc. Jewellery, moderate prices, at Bolívar 420. Interesting market behind new cathedral. Ocepa shop at airport is good.

Taxis US$0.32 for short journey; US$1 per hour. There are buses.

Hotels *El Dorado,* Gran Colombia y Luis Cordero, night club, US$20 d, very good; *Crespo,* Calle Larga 793, US$13 d; *El Conquistador,* Gran Colombia 665, US$16 d, with breakfast, sauna; *Cuenca,* Borrero 861, US$8 d (French), good restaurant, recommended; *Internacional,* Benigna Malo 1015, US$7 d; *Majestic,* Luis Cordero 1129, US$5 d; *Pichincha,* Gral. Torres y Bolívar, US$2 s; *Hilton,* Pres. Córdova 985 y Aguirre, US$3.20 d, lovely view from balcony; *Paris,* Gral. Torres 770, US$3.20 d; *Niza,* Gral. Lamar, US$5.70 d, clean; *Residencial El Gaucho,* Luis Cordero 940, US$4.90 d; *Londres,* Bolívar 344, US$1.80 s; *Cantábrica,* Pres. Córdova, US$2.60 d no hot water; *Residencial Atenas,* US$4 d, clean; *Pensión Azuay,* Padre Aguirre 775, US$2.90 d; *Pensión Granada,* Sucre 1074, US$1.40 s; *Pensión El Oro,* Gabriel Ullavri 509, US$15; Pensión El Inca, Gral. Torres 842, US$1 s, good value; *Pensión Norte,* Mariano Cueva 1163, US$0.80 s; *Residencial Colombia,* Mariano Cueva 1161, US$1.30 s, recommended; *Residencial Tito,* Sangurima 149, US$1.40 s, clean, recommended; *Pensión Andaluz,* Mariano Cueva 1221, US$0.70 s; *Residencial España,* Sangurima 117, US$3.70 d, hot water; *Pensión San Francisco,* Padre Aguirre 622, US$0.70 s; *Pensión Sucre,* Presidente Córdova, US$1 s.

Restaurants *El Fogón,* airport road, superb steaks; *El Portón,* on main square, pleasant; *Fiesta, Bolívar* and *Gen Torres,* cheap; *Gran Torre,* good view, reasonable Chinese food; *Mariscal,* cheap; *El Scorpio,* good food; *Rancho Chileño,* near airport, good steak and seafood; *Salón Turista,* Vega Muñoz 3-53, US$0.75 for a meal; *Cafeteria Roma,* Luis Cordero, try the lasagna; *El Gaucho,* near main plaza, 3-course meal US$1-2; *El Mesón Rojo; La Carreta, Salón España* (next to *Residencia Tito*), good, cheap; *Comedor Hiltons,* highly recommended meal for US$0.60; *Restaurante San Francisco,* good, next door to *Pensión España;* good *helados* on Calle Simón Bolívar, near San Blas Church; *El Bodegón de Fraile,* on main plaza, good food, medium priced; *Reismipampa,* on main plaza, US$1-2.

Banks Citibank and local banks.

Buses To Loja, 5 a day (not between 1000 and 1700), 8 hours, US$1.50; Ambato, 0645, 9 hours, US$2.80 (travel during day because scenery is magnificent); Quito, 12 hours, US$3; Machala, 6 hours, US$2.10 (try to sit on left side of bus for best scenery). To Huaquillas, 8 hours, with Buenos Hermanos bus company, US$2.40. To Riobamba, 12 hours, US$2; the direct road to Riobamba is very poor.

Air Service Two daily connections with Quito and Guayaquil.

Tourist Office at Edificio Carmela, corner of Calles Mariscal Sucre and Benigno Malo 725, 4th floor.

Excursions Cañar, 1½ hours N from Cuenca, is famous for its double weaving. One hour by bus every ½ hour, US$0.40 (Coop. Santo Bárbara) E to **Gualaceo** (Sunday market), pretty town in beautiful landscape, with charming plaza and fine new church with spendid modern glass; embroidered goods sold from private home above general store on main square; good, cheap restaurant off main square; a recommended trip. The town is the centre of ikat dyeing and weaving in Ecuador. To **Chordeleg** by colectivo (plenty), or by local bus, US$0.08 from Gualaceo market square (every ½ hour), a village famous for its crafts in wood, silver and gold filigree and pottery (most shops etc. closed Sunday and Monday). Chordeleg is a very pleasant hour's walk from Gualaceo. *La Hualeca* recommended; very reasonable.

Ecuador's sole major Inca ruin, **Ingapirca**, a fortress complex, can be visited from Cuenca by taking (0430, 2 hours, US$0.50, not necessarily daily) the autoferro to Ingapirca station (returning time is 1530) and walking up (40 minutes or so). Purchase ticket night before from Ferrocarril office corner of Mariscal le Mar and Padre Guirres. Alternatively you can take a taxi for US$20 for the 5-hour round trip. There are also buses, depart 0100, return 0300 and occasional trucks along the new road (16 km.) E from the Pan-American Highway at Cañar, which passes San Pedro railway station, 11 km. from Cañar. On Fridays there is an Indian market at Ingapirca. The stonework is very fine, and camping at the site is possible. A "tourist hostel" may be open soon near the ruins; ask at the Regional Tourist Office in Cuenca.

From Cuenca, the Pan-American Highway runs S to La "Y", about 20 km. away near the village of Cumbe. Here the road divides into two all-weather gravel roads: one continuing the Pan-American to Loja (very bad) and the other running to Paseje and Machala in El Oro province. The right fork (to Machala) carries more traffic and is the best route to follow to reach Peru, *via* Huaquillas, see page 512. Between La "Y" and Machala, the road gradually descends the northern flank of the valley of the Jubones River, a scenic area producing large quantities of sugar cane. (One traveller reports that on a night trip on this route, the bus driver stopped before beginning the descent, made a collection from the passengers and having made the sign of the Cross, tossed the money over the edge of the cliff.) Santa Isabel and Pasaje, the main towns along the route, have little to recommend them.

The Pan American Highway climbs S from La "Y" and rises eventually to the 3,500 metres high Tinajilas Pass. The highest points give magnificent views W and E, where the edge of the mountains is marked by huge cloud banks. The road descends sharply into the warm upper Jubones valley past cane fields and rises again near the small town of Oña. From there it weaves through highland *páramo* pastures and then descends towards **Saraguro**. Here we meet Indians once more, the most southerly Andean group in Ecuador, dressed all in black. They wear very broad flat-brimmed hard felt hats: the men are notable for their black shorts (sometimes covered by a whitish kind of divided apron) and a particular kind of double bag, the *alforja*, used for purchases, and the women for their pleated black skirts, necklaces of coloured beads and silver *topos*, ornate pins fastening their shawls. They have made a greater success of life than most Andean Indians; many now take cattle across the mountains east to the tropical pastures above the Amazonian jungle.

The road runs through Saraguro town (picturesque Sunday Indian market), over the mountain and then a long, very tortuous, descent towards Loja. Although the direct Cuenca-Loja road is not particularly recommended for its quality, the alternative route *via* Arenillas is not much better, and is further.

Loja (2,225 metres, 48,000 inhabitants), lies near the Oriente. There are crude but original paintings on the patio walls of many of the old houses. There are two universities, with a well-known law school. The town, circled by hills, can be reached by air from Guayaquil to La Toma and then a short way by paved road. There is a market on Sats. and Suns.

Hotels *Rio Amazonas* (closed for repairs in 1976); *Hostería Casablanca*, US$5 s, best but often full; *París*, new, clean with hot showers, US$2.30 s, recommended; *Amencuna*, US$0.80; *Internacional*, US$1; *Residencial Cooperativa Loja*, US$0.80 a bed; *México*, US$2 s, good; *Residencial Caribe*, US$1.25 s.

Excursions A bus ride from Loja is **Vilcabamba**, where people were reputed to live to over 100 as often as not; recent research has exploded this belief, but it's still a very pleasant and healthy valley!

A beautiful hour-long bus trip from Loja takes one to the town of Jirón, whose beauty is spoiled only by a modern concrete church. From there trucks take passengers up a winding road to the hamlets of San Gregorio and Chumblín. Friendly inhabitants will act as guides to three lakes high in the *páramo* where excellent trout-fishing is to be had. Take camping gear.

Buses Cuenca, 8 hours, US$1.20; Machala, 8 hours, US$1.25.

Most road travellers enter and leave Loja *via* Machala (see page 512), the capital of El Oro Province in the coastal lowlands near the Peruvian border. A fairly good dirt road with occasional paved stretches links Loja with Machala, and from there buses run to Guayaquil and to the Peruvian border. Nearly everyone who crosses from Ecuador into Peru now goes *via* Machala; it can be avoided, however, if you take a Machala bus to the Huaquillas crossroads and there catch another one straight to Huaquillas, the border town. There is also a road into the Oriente, at Zamora. The Portovelo gold mines at Zaruma, between Loja and Machala, are well worth a visit.

An alternative route to Peru is, however, available from Loja *via* Macará, a small town on the border in Loja Province with road connections to Sullana near the Peruvian coast. Leaving Loja on the main paved highway going westward, the airport at La Toma is reached after about half an hour's drive. At La Toma, the Pan-American Highway divides into two branches, one going to Macará *via* Cariamanga and the other *via* Catacocha. The Catacocha branch is faster and the whole journey from Loja to Macará takes from 6 to 8 hours. All money should be changed in Macará and, if one hasn't been obtained in Quito or Guayaquil, a Peruvian tourist card can be obtained at the border. Having dealt with money and tourist cards, there is a 2½ km. walk or taxi ride to the international bridge over the Río Macará. Border crossing formalities usually last about ¾ hour. There are no regular buses from La Tina on the Peruvian side to Sullana (4 hours' drive away on the main Peruvian coastal highway), so that travellers need to take a taxi, or wait a few hours before getting a ride on a cattle truck. The border is hot, dusty and unpleasant, although a swim in the river can make waiting a little more bearable. Altogether, the Machala route to Peru is more enjoyable and quicker than the Macará route.

The Oriente

Ecuador's eastern tropical lowlands can now be reached by four separate road routes:

Quito-Papallacta-Baeza-Lago Agrio-Coca; Ambato-Pelileo-Baños-Mera-Shell-Mera-Puyo-Napo-Tena; Cuenca-El Descanso-Gualaceo-Limón-Méndez-Sucua-Macas; Loja-Zamora-Yanzaza-Gualaquiza.

These roads are narrow and tortuous, but all have regular bus services and all can be attempted in a jeep or, with luck, in an ordinary car. Their construction has led to a considerable amount of colonization by highlanders in the lowland areas and a journey on any one of them takes you into a land of pioneer opportunism in luscious tropical jungle zones. Several of the towns and villages on the roads can be reached by air services from Quito, Cuenca and Guayaquil, and places further into the immense Amazonian forests are generally accessible by river canoe or small aircraft. The country is particularly beautiful, and some of the disadvantages of other parts of Amazonia, such as the inadvisability of swimming in the rivers, are here absent. Anti-malaria tablets are recommended, however, and be sure to take a mosquito net.

Most visitors to the Oriente use either the Quito-Coca route or the Ambato-Tena route, although the trips from Cuenca and Loja are most certainly worthwhile. Metropolitan Tours of Quito do trips to the Oriente for about US$600; going by bus etc. you can do a round trip for about US$30. The Oriente also has an unpredictable air service provided by army planes. Passengers pay insurance, US$1-2; apart from that, fares are low.

From Quito   The road into the Oriente from Quito was built in 1969-71 by various contracting firms working for the Texaco-Gulf consortium that had discovered large oil deposits in the area between Lago Agrio and Coca. From Quito as far as Pifo the road is paved and in excellent condition, but then it gradually worsens until it becomes a narrow, muddy, gravel-covered track. It crosses the Eastern Cordillera at an altitude of 4,064 metres at a pass just north of the extinct volcano Antisana (5,704 metres), and then descends *via* the small villages of Papallacta and Cuyuja, to the old mission settlements of Baeza and Borja. It then follows the Coca river past the village of El Chaco to the slopes of the volcano Reventador. Reventador is still active, and potential heroes armed with machetes can try hacking their way through the thick forests which cover its slopes to reach the crater at 3,485 metres. The road winds around the lower slopes of Reventador along the north side of the river, past the immensely impressive San Rafael Falls (145 metres high and discharging an average of 325 cubic metres of water per second), until it crosses the watershed between the Coca and Aguarico rivers . A large steel bridge has been completed across the Aguarico and the road then runs along the north bank of the river to the oil camps and developing towns of **Santa Cecilia** and **Lago Agrio,** where there are hotels. (*Oro Negro,* US$1.25 s.) At Lago Agrio, the road heads south across the Aguarico River to **Coca,** a sleepy river port at the junction of the Coca and Napo rivers, now called Puerto Francisco de Orellana. (Hotels: *Auco* US$3 p.p., pleasant; a couple of pensions.) Canoes (beware mosquitoes) pass Coca carrying passengers and cargo down-river to the mission settlement of Limón Cocha and the border post of Nueva Rocafuerte (US$4 for 2-day trip). In Limón Cocha it is possible to stay cheaply (US$7 d) with the mission, and interesting side trips may be made to see wild life; be sure to take plenty of mosquito repellent. The mission also organizes visits to more remote Indian villages. Fishing, boating and swimming are also available. Reservations and information are available from the Instituto de Verano, Casilla 5080, Quito, tel. 245308. There are twice weekly flights to Coca and Iquitos. At Nueva Rocafuerte is the immigration office for those going on to Peru; on Sats. a small boat from the military post at Pantoja (Peru) collects supplies and will take passengers as well. From Pantoja there are flights every weekend to Iquitos (US$15). In Nueva Rocafuerte, Sra. Jesús lets rooms. From Coca there are also boats going upstream to Misahuallí (see page 541), from which a bus can be caught to Puerto Napo (officially known as Puerto Nuevo), and then another to Puyo (Coca to Misahuallí *via* motorized canoe, US$5). The canoe trip upstream to Misahuallí takes about 14 hours; if it is not reached before nightfall, the party will camp beside the river. For the less hardy the return trip downstream is advised, 5 to 6 hours. For a price, of course, the willing traveller can hire his own canoe with owner and outboard motor to take him anywhere along the Napo. (To Misahuallí the charge is about US$60.)

James Bock, of Mexico City, writes:

"Getting to Iquitos *via* the Río Napo is not easy, but it can be done. The first step, getting to Coca on the Napo, is not a problem. There are outboard canoes from Misahuallí, as well as a bus service through Lago Agrio. Getting from Coca to Nueva Rocafuerte on the Ecuador-Peru border (no roads) is tougher. A few launches, all carrying cargo, make the trip, Richard Bolaños, a guide in Misahuallí, should know if a canoe is going. The port captain's offices, where you get your passport stamped, may also help, although they tend to discourage river travel to Peru. Once in Nueva Rocafuerte, Don Bolívar, owner of the store, can help one find a canoe to Pantoja, Peru. Pantoja is a forlorn military outpost and tiny settlement. There one gets permission from the military authorities to await a 16-seat TANS (Peruvian Air Force) seaplane that arrives Saturday morning from Iquitos. The Peruvians prohibit river travel to Iquitos, so the plane (fare about 1,900 soles) is the only hope. If seats are not available, one must return to Nueva Rocafuerte and either wait another week or catch the next canoe back up the Río Napo (such canoes are not plentiful)."

The Centinela del Norte, Pastaza and Interoceánica bus companies run from Quito to Lago Agrio (10 hours), Coca and Puerto Napo. The Amazonas and Baños bus companies have buses from Quito to Tena (*via* Baños) each day, (US$3). Another company, Quito-Baeza-Lago Agrio-Coca, US$4. Hotels are now becoming much more plentiful, but anti-mosquito precautions are very necessary.

Remember to get your passport stamped in Nueva Rocafuerte if going on to Peru.

From Ambato   Beyond Baños (see page 518), the road eastward winds along the north side of the Pastaza river until eventually, after a long descent, the broad extent of the Amazonian plains becomes visible. The road between Ambato and Baños is newly paved, and from Baños to Puyo it is under reconstruction, which is likely to take until 1978 to complete. For this reason the road is not always open. **Shell-Mera** (50 km. from Baños) is the first major stop. Here there is a checkpoint run by the army (special permits are not now needed to visit the Oriente) and an important airfield used by Ecuadorean military and commercial services and by the oil companies. Shell-Mera can be reached by military flight, from Quito, US$2, ½ hour. Accommodation is available in the mission opposite the Hospital in Shell-Mera, US$0.75 per person with hot water and comfortable beds. Military flights from Shell-Mera to Montalvo (US$2), Tiputini (US$4). A few km. on is the larger and busier town of **Puyo,** the most important centre in the whole Oriente. The pioneer fringe has now left Puyo far behind, but the town still retains a certain Wild West atmosphere with its wooden buildings, board-walks and swinging saloon doors.

Acommodation in *Hotel Turingia,* on the Ambato side, US$7, American owned (Joe Brenner, the owner, raises orchids which he shows to interested visitors); *Hotel Europa,* US$3 s, very good, good restaurant; *Pensión Ecuador,* US$1.20 s, clean. Many pensions. Many cheap restaurants, e.g. *La Canasta.*

From Puyo, a short road goes east to Vera Cruz, but the main highway runs northward to Puerto Napo and Tena. The whole area is a large-scale producer of sugar cane, yuca and naranjillas (an orange fruit related to the tomato used for making a delightfully refreshing traditional Ecuadorean fruit drink), and tea has recently been introduced around Shell-Mera by two foreign companies. Puerto Napo, 72 km. north of Puyo, has a bridge across the Napo River. There are downriver canoe services with anything from 10 to 25 people in the vessel. On the north bank, a road leads eastwards to **Misahuallí**, a small river port about 17 km. down stream with several hotels. From Misahuallí, the canoe services to the downriver ports of Coca, Limón Cocha and Nueva Rocafuerte have been reduced since the road was built. By dugout to Coca (Monday, Thursday and Saturday mornings returning the following day) costs US$5 p.p. for the 6-12 hour trip (boats often crowded, best to be early); there is also a mail boat in both directions twice a month. During and after heavy rainfall there are obviously no services. An excursion taking 3 to 4 days to visit an Auca tribe can be arranged by contacting "Hector", US$20 p.p. Recommended only for the hardy. (Fluvial River Tours, of Misahuallí, will arrange visits to various Indian villages and other jungle locations. An excursion of 4-5 days costs US$20. Also trips to Coca and longer ones into the jungle.) A short canoe trip to El Ahuano (US$1) gives a good idea of the jungle river life. The main road from Puerto Napo, however, runs 10 km. north to **Tena,** the capital of Napo Province, and then on to Archidona, a small mission settlement about 10 km. further on. Tena is a quiet, rather dignified town with several small hotels, whilst **Archidona** is a village (with hotel, US$1.25 s) centred around its mission and an extraordinary church. Both settlements have good views of Sumaco, an extinct volcano to the north (3,807 metres), and both have a large lowland Quechua Indian population living in the vicinity. These docile Indians are dependent on the local Catholic missions and are very unlike the wild Indian groups further into Oriente forests. From Tena or Archidona, a visit can be made to the famous Jumbandi caves by the Río Latas. (You need your own light.)

Alastair Morrison, of Bearsden, Glasgow, writes: *"Anaconda Hotel,* on Anaconda Island in the Río Napo, about 1 hour by canoe downstream from Puerto Misahuallí, deserves to be mentioned. It consists of three bungalows of bamboo and thatch, with space for about 12 guests. There are no electric lights, but there are flush toilets and cold showers, with water available most of the time. The meals are good. The staff do their best to ensure that the guests see as much as possible in a limited time. Villages of Indian shifting cultivators, complete with witch doctor, can be reached by canoe, but a full day's hike is needed to reach Indians only partly affected by civilisation. Cost was US$15 p.p. per night including 3 meals, plus US$16 per party for canoe, plus US$16 per party for guide, plus US$16 per party "commission", plus US$2 p.p. for canoe from Misahuallí. Travellers' cheques accepted but at a poor rate. With a party of five this works out at US$27 p.p. for 24 hours from Misahuallí and back, which seemed to compare favourably with the more widely advertised jungle lodges near Iquitos and Leticia."

Buses Puyo-Puerto Napo, US$0.60. Napo-Misahuallí, US$0.20. Ambato-Puyo, 5 hours, US$0.70; Baños-Puyo-Misahuallí, 7½ hours, US$1.20; Misahuallí-Baños, US$2.

Hotels   Puerto Napo: *Hotel Acapulco*, at bridge, US$1.25 s; *Residencia*, US$0.60.
Misahuallí: better accommodation than at Tena or Puyo; *Anconda; Jaguar* (slightly
downstream), US$12 s, full board; *Francisco de Orellana* (a boat!); *Balcón del
Napo*, US$1.25 s, meals available; *Residencia*, US$0.60, but you need to bargain. *La
Posada*, US$1 s. Tena: better accommodation than Puerto Napo, *Hotel Tena*,
US$1.20-1.60 p.p., noisy at night, due to restaurant below; *Hotel Danubio*,
US$1.20, good merienda served.

From Cuenca   The journey into the Oriente is longer and less spectacular
than from Quito or Ambato, but there are several beautiful stretches.
Sucua (8-hour bus trip from Cuenca US$2.90 Hotel Cuhanda US$2) is of
particular interest at the centre of the now-civilized branch of the ex-head-
hunting Jívaro Indians; their crafts can be seen and bought but it is
tactless to ask them about head-hunting and shrinking! There is still a
wild group, the "Jívaros bravos" in the forest; they and the Ecuadorean
Government have an arrangement to leave each other alone. **Macas**, the
last major settlement on the road, is very beautiful and the surrounding
hills give excellent views of the volcano Sangay (2 buses a day from
Cuenca by Turismo Oriental). The road into Macas can be made
impassable by rain, causing a delay of several hours. You can cross the
River Upano there by Jívaro dugout canoe-ferry and visit the Salesian
Sevilla-Don Bosco mission, and various Indian villages. Good swimming.
Flight to Puyo, for round trip back to Quito (instead of returning to
Cuenca), US$10. The whole colonization zone has been developed for
beef production.

Between Cuenca and Sucua is the attractive town of Gualaceo (see page 536).

From Loja   The road to the Oriente crosses a low pass and descends
rapidly to Zamora, an old mission settlement about 2 hours' drive away.
From there on, the road follows the Zamora river to Gualaquiza. The
valley produces large quantities of naranjillas and some sugar cane,
maize, bananas and yuca. Regular bus services from Loja to Zamora and
beyond on Cenepa-Pacífico and other companies. Cheap, basic hotels are
available in Zamora and Gualaquiza.

The Galápagos Islands

Lying on the Equator, 970 km. west of the Ecuadorean coast, the
Galápagos consist of 6 main islands, San Cristóbal, Santa Cruz, Isabela,
Floreana, Santiago and Fernandina. The last two are uninhabited. There
are also 12 smaller islands: Baltra, with an air base, and the uninhabited
islands of Santa Fe, Pinzón, Española, Rábida, Daphne, Seymour,
Genovesa, Marchena, Pinta, Darwin and Wolf; and over 40 small islets.
The islands, which were once the refuge of buccaneers and whalers, used
to bear English names but these have now been largely replaced. The
largest island, Isabela (formerly Albemarle), is 120 km. long and forms
half the total land area of the archipelago. Its terrible convict colony was
closed in 1958; some 500 people live there now. San Cristóbal (Chatham)
has a population of nearly 2,000 and is the administrative centre of the
archipelago. San Cruz (Indefatigable) has about 1,000; and Floreana
(Charles) fewer than 50. The group is quite widely scattered; by boat,
Santa Cruz and San Cristóbal are 6 hours apart, and the airport at Baltra
is about 5 hours from Santa Cruz and 7 from San Cristóbal.

The islands are the peaks of gigantic volcanoes, composed almost
exclusively of basalt. Most of them rise from 2,000 to 3,000 metres above

the seabed. Eruptions have taken place in historical times on Fernandina, Isabela, Pinta, Marchena, Santiago and Floreana. The most active today are Fernandina, Isabela, Pinta and Marchena, and fumarolic activity may be seen intermittently on each of these islands. There have been recent eruptions on Volcán, Sierra Negra, Isabela (April 1963) and on Fernandina (June 1968).

The Galápagos have almost certainly never been connected with the continent. Gradually, over many hundreds of thousands of years, animals and plants from over the sea developed there and as time went by they adapted themselves to Galápagos conditions and came to differ more and more from their continental ancestors. Thus many of them are unique: a quarter of the species of shore fish, half of the plants and almost all the reptiles are found nowhere else. In many cases different forms have evolved on the different islands. Charles Darwin recognized this speciation within the archipelago when he visited the Galápagos on the *Beagle* in 1835 and his observations played a substantial part in his formulation of the theory of evolution. Darwin's visit to the Galápagos Islands is one of the landmarks in the history of science. Since no large land mammals reached the islands, reptiles became dominant just as they were all over the world in the very distant past. Another of the extraordinary features of the islands is the tameness of the animals. The islands were uninhabited when they were discovered in 1535 and the animals have still little instinctive fear of man.

The most spectacular species to be seen by the visitor are the giant tortoise (in many cases these are rare and confined to the less accessible areas, but species still survive in 6 or 7 of the islands); marine iguana (the only seagoing lizard in the world and found throughout most of the archipelago); land iguana (on Fernandina, Santa Cruz, Santa Fe, Isbela, Seymour and Plaza); Galápagos albatross (which nests only on the island of Española); Galápagos hawk, red-footed, blue-footed and masked boobies, red-billed tropic-bird, frigate birds, swallow-tailed and dusky lava gulls (both endemic species), mockingbirds, 13 species of Darwin's finches (all endemic and the classic examples of speciation quoted by Darwin); Galápagos sea-lion (common in many areas) and the Galápagos fur-seal (on the more remote and rocky coasts). Santiago and Plaza islands are particularly interesting for students of these species.

In 1959, the centenary of the publication of Darwin's *Origin of Species,* the Government of Ecuador and the international Charles Darwin Foundation established, with the support of Unesco, a biological research station at Academy Bay on Santa Cruz, the most central of the Galápagos islands. Collections of several of the rare races of giant toroise are maintained on the station as breeding nuclei and, together with a tortoise-rearing house incorporating incubators and pens for the young, may be seen by visitors between the hours of 0900 and 1600 from Mondays to Fridays. The Darwin Foundation staff will help bona fide students of the fauna to plan an itinerary, if they stay some time and hire a boat.

Travel to the Islands There is a scheduled flight every Fri. (0730 from Quito and 0945 from Guayaquil with TAME. For reservations write to TAME, Av. 10 de Agosto 239, Quito; one-way tickets can be obtained in Galápagos; the round trip is US$175 from Quito, US$150 from Guayaquil. Metropolitan Touring charters TAME aircraft, write to Metropolitan Touring or Galápagos Cruises (address below), week-long excursions Tues. to Tues., luxury. Fri. to Fri., US$450 inclusive; 5-day excursions 1st class, US$570, 2nd class US$350, 3rd class US$270, all inclusive.

M.V. Iguana leaves every 22 days from Guayaquil from US$335 to 580 for 5 to 7 days; write Metropolitan Touring, Casilla 2542, Quito, or Galápagos Cruises, Casilla 7132, Guayaquil. There are 2 yachts, the *Cathcar* and *Laura María*, which take up to 14 people on private charter or 32 on group tours which include a stay ashore. Prices US$380-480, including airfare to and from the islands. The Ecuadorean navy-owned *Culicuchima* also operates from Guayaquil and charges US$320-400 (first class), US$250-280 (tourist class) for the 11-day round trip; this may be the cheapest tour available, but several travellers have made complaints about the boat. Itinerary includes visit to San Cristóbal, Santa Cruz, Plaza, Baltra, Bartolomé, Santiago (James), Floreana, Española. (Travel pills recommended.) It is possible to break the trip, staying on one of the islands. Guides and lectures are provided. Boat leaves every three weeks. Advise to reserve, Primera Zona Naval, Departamento Logístico, Guayaquil. The schooner *Golden Cachalot* (US$100 a day for a 2-week trip round 10 islands) can be booked at Discover Galapagos Ltd., Oare Windmill, Faversham, Kent, England, or 55 West 42 Street, New York 10036, USA. The same firm also organises tours on the *Iguana*. Apparently boats can be hired at US$80 per day for 8 people. Other operators are the Galápagos Tourist Corporation, P.O. Box 5284, Guayaquil; Galápagos Cruises or Metropolitan Touring, P.O. Box 2542, Quito; Turismundial, Quito and Serviturs. There are usually 1 or 2 cargo ships making the trip, but dates are irregular; check with the naval port authorities on the Malecón in Guayaquil. Inclusive tours from Britain start at £1,100 and can be booked through Twickenham Travel, 22 Church Street, Twickenham, TW1 3NW, England, or through Peregrine Holidays at Oxford. The cheapest way of getting to the islands is by Air Force planes, known as "logísticos", which fly to Baltra on Sundays from Quito (0530, US$60, one way) and Guayaquil (0700, US$50). For this you should be an Ecuadorean national, but unfilled seats are given to tourists. Go on Friday to the Ministry of Defence in Quito. These flights are not easy to get on. There is a long waiting list, and to get a flight now one must have a scientific reason for going. If you get there with the Air Force, it does not mean they will bring you back. It is easier to get a logístico for the return journey than for the outward journey. From the airport,

one takes a combination of bus (US$0.50), ferry (US$1) and taxi (US$2) to Puerto Ayora, Santa Cruz. Hotel may make prior arrangements. There is a US$6 National Park Tax. We have been told that since Galapageans take their holidays in September it is difficult in that month for non-nationals to get places on the military planes and boats which serve the islands.

N.B. All prices likely to have risen 10 per cent on those quoted above.

Accommodation and the cost of living in the Galápagos are not particularly cheap. Most foods have to be imported although certain meats, fish, vegetables and fruit are available locally.

At present there are only about 80-90 beds available in the various hotels and other types of lodging found at Puerto Ayora, Santa Cruz. Their availability without prior reservation is becoming increasingly difficult; write to the owners (names below); Isla Santa Cruz, Galápagos, Ecuador.

Cabinas de Gusch Angermeyer: about 20 beds; prices US$1.25-2 per bed; no meals offered. Write to Mr. Angermeyer, or contact him upon arrival. Mr. Angermeyer is an excellent source of information on the islands.

Hotel Galápagos: 26 beds (double and triples) in cabins; US$14/person/day, without meals; US$30/person/day, including 3 meals; reservations exclusively made through Metropolitan Touring, or the owner, Forrest Nelson.

Hotel/Sol y Mar: 20 beds (double, triples and quadruples) in cabins; US$9.60/person/day without meals; US$21.60/person/day for room and 3 meals; 10% discount for stays of 2 weeks or more; children under 12 one-half price. Reservations can be made by writing to the owner (Sr. Jimmy Pérez), or Macchiavello Tours, Casilla 318, Guayaquil.

Hotel Colón: 22 beds (doubles) in third class rooms; US$4/person/day, without food; US$7.60/person/day, including 3 meals. Write to Sra. Piedad Moya.

There are also small hotels on San Cristóbal (Sr. Raúl Jerias) and Floreana (Mrs. M. Wittmer, *Wittmer Inn*, c/o Diego Trujillo 185, Quito).

A Frenchman, Max Christian, offers room, board (his own magnificent cooking) and his professional services as guide and under-water explorer for US$15 a day. He also charters boats to tour the islands, US$20 a day for a party.

There are 3-4 small restaurants each at Puerto Ayora, Santa Cruz, and Puerto Baquerizo Moreno, San Cristóbal, and one at port of Floreana where all meals can be taken.

For boat charters and camping trips most basic foodstuffs generally can be purchased in the islands, although occasionally there are shortages. However, no special items (dehydrated or freezedried foods) are available other than a few common ones such as oatmeal and dried soups.

Medicines, sun lotions, film, pipe tobacco, and certain similar items are usually not available in the islands.

Some of the prices charged are exorbitant. There are now certain areas where camping is permitted but permission must be obtained from the National Parks Office; tents are necessary because of damp and mosquitos. If you have a tent, you can obtain permission from the Darwin Research Station to camp in the Giant Tortoise reserve on Santa Cruz.

Excursions on Santa Cruz   Hike to Tortuga Bay. Round trip, including 3 to 4 hours at the beach, may be done in one day. Total distance is approximately 14 km. Arduous trek, but a beautiful bay.

Hike to the higher parts of the island called Media Luna, Puntudo and Mt. Crocker. Trail starts at Bellavista (which can be reached by car), 7 km. from Puerto Ayora. Round trip from Bellavista is 4 to 8 hours, depending upon distance hiked, 10-18 km. (permit and guide required).

Hike to the Tortoise Reserve; trail starts at Santa Rosa, 22 km. from Puerto Ayora; vehicle must be obtained to arrive at trail head; round trip takes one day. From Santa Rosa, distance to different sites within the reserve is 6-8 km. (permit and guide required).

Visit the giant Galápagos tortoises in pens at the Darwin Station, a short distance from the centre of Puerto Ayora. Small tortoises in tortoise rearing pens may be observed as well.

Travel within the Islands The best centre from which to visit the Islands is Santa Cruz. Here you can hire boats which take 6-8 people for about US$80-120 a day, extra for food, though you can keep the cost down by providing your own. Write to Mr. David Balfour, Metropolitan Touring, Isla Santa Cruz, Galápagos. Reservations are strongly recommended for June-August and December-January. Other trips (from plush to basic) available through Metropolitan Touring. Cargo and mail boats available on very irregular basis (cheap, US$4-6 between ports). Sr. Tobias Escarabay, Mr. Carl Angermeyer and Mr. Fritz Angermeyer have boats for hire; the latter two reported to be most comfortable. These boats provide an excellent way of seeing the wildlife.

The climate can be divided into a hot season (January to April), when there is a possibility of heavy showers, and the cool or *garía* season (May to December), when the days generally are more cloudy. Daytime clothing should be lightweight. At night, however, particularly at sea and at higher altitudes, temperatures fall below 15°C and warm clothing is required. Boots and shoes soon wear out on the lava terrain and there is need for protection against rain and sun. There are no beaches on Santa Cruz, but several on San Cristóbal.

Currency It is advisable to take as much cash as you think you will want; there are few facilities for cashing cheques, and high commissions are charged.

Guide Book The Galápagos Guide can be bought in Guayaquil or at the Charles Darwin station for US$7. National Park Office, Puerto Ayora, Santa Cruz, Mon-Fri. 0800-1200, 1400-1800, Sat. 0800-1000. For more information write to the Director of the Charles Darwin Research Station or the Superintendent of the Galápagos National Park Service, Isla Santa Cruz, Galápagos. (Correspondence in English.)

(With acknowledgements to the Charles Darwin Foundation and the Galápagos National Park Service.)

The Economy

Until 1972, Ecuador's main source of wealth was agriculture; it accounted for 90% of export earnings. However, the discovery of oil in the Oriente region has provided a new source of wealth, and with estimated reserves of some 5-6,000m. barrels, Ecuador has become the second largest oil exporting country in South America. A 504 km. pipeline was built from Lago Agrio to Esmeraldas on the northern coast, and its initial capacity of 250,000 barrels per day was reached early in 1973. This level of throughput has not, however, been sustained. Exports of petroleum began in August 1972, and in 1973 it replaced bananas as the most important export commodity. Following a recommendation by the Organization of Petroleum-Exporting Countries (Opec) in which Ecuador was granted membership in November 1973, the State oil agency, Cepe, took a 25% share in the operations of the Texaco-Gulf consortium, the largest operator in the country. It subsequently bought out Gulf and now has 62.5% ownership in the consortium. The high world price of petroleum, brought about by the world energy shortage has done much to enhance Ecuador's balance of payments, though oil income fell from US$615m. in 1974 and US$565.1m. in 1976 to US$484m. in 1977 because of problems with transport, marketing, storage, the pipeline, the Esmeraldas refinery and the Gulf take-over. The opening of the Esmeraldas refinery, capable of processing 55,600 barrels per day of crude oil, in early 1978 should help to reduce the amount of Ecuador's imported petroleum derivatives. Large deposits of natural gas have been discovered in the Oriente and in the Gulf of Guayaquil. The new source of wealth, however, is exerting inflationary pressures (14-15% in 1977) on the economy because development expenditure has not yet been sufficient to absorb it into productive uses. The situation has been aggravated by falling agricultural production.

Ecuador's agricultural wealth remains largely undeveloped. Out of a total of 30 million hectares only 5% is cultivated; another 4% yields "natural" products and 72% of the land is covered with forest. Over 47% of active labour is engaged in agriculture. Land ownership is unevenly distributed: 1% of the proprietors hold 40% of the land by value: 92% hold only 32% by value. Primitive methods tend to keep prices high, and the country has been becoming more reliant on importing basic foodstuffs. In an attempt to remedy the situation the Government introduced an agrarian reform programme towards the end of 1973, providing for the expropriation of inefficiently used agricultural land, but this is being implemented very slowly. The chief crops are bananas, coffee, cocoa and sugar, all of which are exported. Recently, exports of fish products have replaced sugar in importance in the list of exported goods. Small quantities of pyrethrum (flower and extract for insecticides), of scopolamine (the extract of guanto leaves), edible oils, balsa and plywood, Panama hats, tagua and rice are also exported. Increasing quantities of agricultural products are however being exported in processed form.

Although the old mines for gold and other non-ferrous metals at Portovelo in El Oro province and at Macuchi in Cotopaxi province seem almost exhausted, two new deposits of gold and silver were recently discovered in the Province of Loja. A large deposit of low-grade copper ore has also been discovered west of Cuenca in the Chaucha-Molleturo zone, inland from Naranjal. A little sulphur is mined at Tixán in Chimborazo province, and very low-grade coal deposits are found at Biblián, near Cuenca. Feasibility studies are also underway on reported deposits of lead, zinc, copper, gold, tungsten, quartz, marble, molybdenum and silver in Loja and Azuay province. Ecuador's limited industrial activities are mostly concentrated in Guayaquil and Quito, principally textiles (a third of the total), cement, pharmaceuticals, sugar and cocoa-processing and cheap ceramics. There is as yet no heavy industry, but some lines are being developed as a result of the activities of the Andean Group, which is aiming to establish a Common Market among the five Andean countries by 1985. Andean Group regulations also control the nature of foreign investment in Ecuador.

International Trade (US$ m.)

	1972	1973	1974	1975	1976	1977
Exports (f.o.b.)...	301.5	550.7	1,050.3	897.1	1,127.3	1,187.6
Imports (c.i.f.) ...	249.3	345.7	958.5	943.2	860.7	1,276.8

Information for Visitors

By Air No direct flights from U.K., but British Airways flies several times a week to Miami and British Caledonian to Bogotá where there are connections to Quito and Guayaquil. Air France and Avianca between them fly 3 times a week from Paris to Quito. Some Aero Perú flights stop in Guayaquil en route to Miami. Iberia flies from Madrid to Quito and Guayaquil and KLM weekly from Amsterdam to Guayaquil. There are flights from New York by Braniff International Airways and Lufthansa. Equatoriana, the national company, has some Boeing 707s on international runs; you can't miss their psychedelic colour scheme! There is a 10 per cent tax on international air tickets bought in Ecuador, and a tax of US$7 on all passengers departing on international flights.

The **best time for a visit** is from June to October, during the dry season. The coastal area is extremely hot and wet from December to May.

By Sea   The cargo (no passengers) route from England to Ecuador is by the Pacific Steam Navigation Company *via* the Panama Canal to La Libertad or Guayaquil. A faster but more expensive route is from England to New York and thence to Guayaquil *via* the Panama Canal by direct cargo ships of the Grace Line. Gran Colombiana ships sail from New York, Baltimore and New Orleans. New York to Guayaquil takes 10 days with 20 days from a U.K. port to Guayaquil by a cargo-passenger vessel. Serving the Continent of Europe are the Hamburg American Line and the North German Line jointly; Knutsen Line (from Copenhagen, Oslo, Stockholm, Göteborg, Hamburg, Bremen, Antwerp and Lisbon), and the Italian Line (from Naples, Genoa, Cannes and Barcelona).

Documents   Passport, smallpox vaccination certificate and a tourist card (reported not necessary in 1978) valid for 90 days (tourists are now allowed only 90 days in any one calendar year). These are obtainable at airline or steamship offices, travel agencies or Ecuadorean Consulates or even on arrival. You are required to say how many days you intend to stay and the card will be stamped accordingly; some travellers report being given 30-day stamps irrespective of their requests (at Tulcán), and travellers arriving by air may be given a stamp valid for only 10 days unless they request otherwise. It is therefore better to overestimate as you can be fined on leaving the country for staying too long. An extension can be obtained at the Department of Immigration in Quito; evidence of sufficient funds (US$20 per day of stay intended) will be required. A visa is required only for business people who stay longer than 90 days, and they must get an exit permit. All tourist passport holders need the tourist card; this normally needs a US$2 exit stamp when one leaves the country, unless one has received a "T-3" entry stamp in passport. In any case it can be obtained at Quito, Guayaquil or at the border town; the stamp is not always available at frontier posts. Tourists crossing from Colombia or Peru should visit Ecuadorean immigration at the border; they may be asked for evidence that they possess US$20 per person for each day they propose to spend in Ecuador. Theoretically you must have an onward ticket out of Ecuador. Consulates can insist on this.

Personal effects, 200 grammes of pipe tobacco, or 300 cigarettes, or 50 cigars, and a litre of spirits and a reasonable amount of perfume are admitted free of duty.

Clothing   Spring clothing for Quito. In Guayaquil tropical or light-weight suits for men, light cotton dresses or separates for women. A raincoat and umbrella are useful in both cities. Laundering is excellent, but dry-cleaning is expensive.

Local Time is 5 hours behind Greenwich Mean Time. (Galápagos, 6 hours behind.)

Health   Amoebic dysentery is a danger. When outside the larger cities visitors should drink Güitig water and not eat uncooked vegetables or salads. Travellers should be vaccinated against smallpox and inoculated against typhoid and take a good remedy against stomach upsets. Hepatitis (jaundice) is a very real risk and should be inoculated against with gamma globulin; this can be got from chemists, and hospitals will give the injection. Travellers in the Oriente are advised to take anti-malaria tablets. There are several excellent hospitals both in Quito and Guayaquil.

Warning   Beware of thieves and pickpockets, especially in Guayaquil.

Entertaining   There are few places of entertainment. Theatrical performances are rare and only cinema-shows are permanently available. Entertaining is therefore chiefly confined to social intercourse, dinners, dances and picnics.

Food   Well worth trying are *humitas* (tamales made of sweet maize), *llapingachos* (fried mashed potatoes with cheese), and *locro* (a soup of stewed potatoes and cheese topped with an avocado). Highly spiced native fish dishes served, with a beer, at bars, are *ceviche de corvina* and *ceviche de langostinos* or *cocktail de camarones*. Native food is highly spiced only when *ají* (red pepper) sauce is added, and then it is very hot, but the food is often unspiced. *Tamales de morocho* (not unlike Venezuelan *Hallaca*) and *empanadas de morocho* are delicious (same insides, breadcrust outside). A typical food (but a matter of taste) is roast *Cuy* (guinea pig). *Mondongo* is a filling soup made from peanuts and sweetcorn among other things. *Cacho*, a croissant-like pastry, is cheap and filling. If economizing at restaurants ask for the standard meal, *merienda*—very cheap; it costs between US\$0.50 and US\$1.

Drink Wine is expensive if imported; the local wine, Vino Nuestro is very sweet and not very good. The best fruit drinks are *naranjilla, taxo* and *mora* (blackberries). Pilsener, Chopp and Victoria beers excellent. International drinks, when they can be had, are costly. Good *pisco, aguardiente, paico* and *trago de caña*. The usual soft drinks, known as *colas,* are available. Afternoon tea is common.

Gambling Casinos in Guayaquil, at the beach resorts of Playas and Salinas, near Guayaquil, and at *Hotel Quito* and *Hotel Colón,* in Quito. There is a national weekly lottery.

Accommodation outside the main towns; almost standard prices are charged of US\$1-US\$1.25 for a bedroom (without bath) in a pensión, residencial, or hotel (where this is the minimum charge). One can bargain at cheaper pensiónes and residenciales. Outside the provincial capitals and the resorts of Salinas and Playas, there are few of what the well-to-do tourist would call good hotels. Service of 10% and tax of 10% added to 1st and 2nd class hotel and restaurant bills. In the main cities, however, inflation has increased hotel prices quite considerably.

Internal Air Travel The local airline Saeta and the air force (TAME) operate internal flights between the main cities. (Quito-Guayaquil, US\$11.)

Railway Travel The railways are not too comfortable or reliable. The total track length is 1,043 km., divided between three lines. The line from Guayaquil to Quito is described in detail in the text.

Road Travel Bus travel has improved greatly. Half the 17,700 km. of road are open the year round. The length of paved highway is developing rapidly, including Quito-Guayaquil, Quito-Riobamba, Quito-Tulcán, Guayaquil-Machala. When touring by car, beware the bus drivers, they often drive very fast and rather recklessly. The lack of road signs can be a nuisance. Hitch-hiking on the main roads is not difficult, but it can be very cold in the mountains in the back of a truck. In the arid S the unpaved roads are dusty; use a wet cotton handkerchief to filter the air you breathe. Gasoline costs US\$0.23 Imp/gallon for extra and US\$0.21 for regular.

The best road map of Ecuador may be obtained quite cheaply from the Departamento de Obras Públicas, 16 de Diciembre 11-84, Quito, near the tourist office in Quito. It is also available from the Libri Mundi bookstore in Quito.

Roads to Peru From Quito through Santo Domingo-Quevedo-Guayaquil to Machala. More interesting, Ambato-Riobamba-Guayaquil-Machala. The least good road is the one through Cuenca, Loja and Macará. A ticket out of Peru is a prerequisite of being allowed in. Buy this before reaching the border as prices there are extremely high.

Sport The Sierra country is excellent for riding, and good horses can be hired. Quito, Guayaquil and Riobamba have polo clubs. There are golf clubs at Guayaquil and Quito and on the Santa Elena Peninsula. There is excellent big-game fishing for bonito and marlin off Playas (launch with crew and 4 lines at least US\$28 a day) Salinas, or Manta. Bull fighting is rarely seen at Guayaquil, but there is a well-known bullfight festival on Dec. 6 at Quito. A favourite sport is cock fighting; every town has its pits, but association football is fast taking over as the national sport. Baseball, volley ball and basket-ball are also popular. There is Sunday horse-racing at Quito and Guayaquil.

Wild Life includes the jaguar, puma, tapir, several kinds of monkeys, the armadillo, ant-bear, squirrel, porcupine, peccary, various kinds of deer, and many rodents, including the guinea pig. There are also tortoises, lizards, and iguanas. Among the snakes are the boa-constrictor and the anaconda. The alligator is also met with. The most striking of the birds are the condor of the Andes, falcons, kites, macaws, owls, flamingoes, parrots, ibises, cranes, and storks. Unhappily, every type of insect is found in the coastal towns and the Oriente.

Public Holidays New Year's Day; Epiphany; Monday and Tuesday before Lent: Carnival; Holy Thursday; Good Friday; Holy Saturday; May 1: Labour Day; May 24: Battle of Pichincha; July 24: Birthday of Bolívar; August 10: Independence of Quito, Opening of Congress; October 9: Independence of Guayaquil; October 12: Discovery of America; November 1: All Saints' Day; November 2: All Souls' Day; November 3: Independence of Cuenca; December 6: Foundation of Quito; Christmas Day.

Postal All the principal towns have telephone exchanges, and there is a public long distance telephone service between Guayaquil and Quito. Ietel, the state tele-communications agency, has offices at Guayaquil, Quito and Salinas. There are radio telegraph and telephone services to most South American republics.

Telephone call to Britain is about US$12 for each 3 minutes. Unreliable. Telegrams, ordinary, S12.16 and Night letter S6.08 per word. There are public telex booths in the Humboldt Hotels in Quito and Guayaquil (US$10.50 for 3 minutes), and at Cuenca. The charge for air mail letter to Britain is S6.30, to USA, S4.

Many post offices away from Quito may not know the foreign rates and give incorrect ones. Postal service is extremely unreliable, with frequent thefts and losses.

Currency The Sucre, divided into 100 centavos, is the unit of currency. Bank notes of the Banco Central de Ecuador are for 5, 10, 20, 50, 100, 500, and 1,000 sucres; there are nickel coins of one sucre, 50, 20 and 10 centavos. Units of 10 centavos are commonly known as *reales,* so 50 c. is *cinco reales.* The one sucre coin is also sometimes called an *ayora.* Free market rate about S27 for US$.

There is no restriction on the amount of foreign money or sucres you can take into or out of Ecuador. Visitors will find it difficult to change travellers' cheques made out in sterling, so have them in US dollars, but even these can be difficult to exchange outside the main cities. Tariff barriers have led to smuggling on a large scale. In smaller towns banks do not change money. It is very easy to change US$ cheques into US$ notes at the *cambios,* with at most only 1% commission. This means that Ecuador, together with Panama, is the best place in South America to have money sent to. Note that Diners Club and Master Charge and Bankamericard systems' credit cards are widely accepted.

Weights and Measures The metric system is legal. It is generally used in foreign trade and must be used in legal documents. English measures are understood in the hardware and textile trades. Spanish measures are often used in the retail trade.

Electric Current 110 volts, 60 cycles, A.C.

Newspapers The main newspapers are "El Comercio" and "Ultimas Noticias", at Quito; "El Telégrafo", "El Universo", "La Prensa", "La Razón", at Guayaquil; "El Mercurio", at Cuenca; and "La Opinión de Sur", at Loja.

Information for businessmen is given (1) in "Hints to Business Men Visiting Ecuador", supplied free from Room CO7, Export Services Branch, Department of Trade, Export House, 50 Ludgate Hill, London EC4 7HU; (2) the Ecuadorean-American Association, Inc. (55 Liberty St., New York, NY 10005) issues monthly bulletins about developments in the republic and a free sample copy may be requested.

Representation Britain is represented by an Ambassador in Quito and an Honorary Consul at Guayaquil. The British Embassy is at Calle González Suárez 111, opposite the Hotel Quito (correspondence to Casilla 314, Tel.: 230070/3).

The United States is represented by an Embassy and Consulate at Quito and a consulate-general in Guayaquil.

There is an Ecuadorean Embassy and Consulate at 3 Hans Crescent, Knightsbridge, London, SW1. Tel.: Embassy, 01-584 1367; Consulate, 01-584 2648.

American Express Agents Guayaquil: Ecuadorian Tours, Pedro Carbo 427, Tel.: 306111. Quito: Ecuadorian Tours, Ave. Amazonas 399, Tel.: 219000.

For extensive improvements to this chapter, we are most grateful to Monique Merriam, of LBI Economics Department; to Sarita Kendall and Tim Ross, and Kevin and K. C. Kierst, resident in Ecuador; and to the following travellers: Willem and Jack de Beaufort (Wassenaar, Netherlands), Ingela Björck and Per Andersson (Sweden), James K. Bock (Mexico City), Dan Bodo and Martin Filiponis (USA), Rick Carder (Windsor, Ontario), Ken Catlin (San Diego, Calif.), Olivier Chaudöuet (Voiteur, France), Christine Czajkowski, Michael Davidson, John Eames and Maggie Harvey, Rand Fay (Gunnison, Colorado), Peter Ford and Sally Wilson, Gabriel Foscal-Mella (Longueuil, Québec), Tim and Arlene Frost (Hamilton, N.Z.), Helen Glover, Mary Goodykoontz and Ken Scarlett (Woodland, Calif.), Schelte de Graaf (Netherlands), Olive Green (Peru), Hans Hartung (Ludwigshafen), Joe Hiss (US-PCV, Tolima), Detlef Körner (Hamburg), Jerry Leon (Havertown, Penn.), Cornelio Lindenburg and Marieke van der Ploeg (Amersfoort, Netherlands), Rolf Maag (Caracas), Daniel and Jan McAleese (Belfast), Ian MacDonell, Bernard Mallet (Paris), Moira O'Grady (New York), Karim Östman (Spanga, Sweden), Jenny Owen, Thomas Pensler (Benediktbeuern, W. Germany), Andrew Radclyffe, John Roper-Lindsay, Helga Schmidt-Frank and Herbert Schmidt (W. Germany), Ross Scott (Camberwell, W. Australia), Chris Sharpe Mullewa, W. Australia), Kenneth E. Shirley (US-PCV, Tolima), Ken and Judy Stevenson (Ottawa), John Streather, Margaret Symons (New Zealand), Ralf and Angela Trosiner (Hamburg), Erich and Angelica Unteregelsbacher (Canada), R. F. Vandersteen and Anne M. Walley (Peru), René Werren (Köniz, Switzerland), Terry and Rosaura West (USA), Nicholas Westwood and Julia Amies, Tim Williams and Elizabeth Young, and Dr. Henry M. Wilson (Madison, Wis.).

PARAGUAY

PARAGUAY is entirely encircled and land-locked by Argentina, Bolivia and Brazil. Its total land area is put at 406,750 square km., cleft into two quite distinct parts by a great river. It has 2,800,000 people, nearly all of whom live on one side of that river. It has not as yet developed its potential, largely because it was deeply involved in two out of the three major wars staged in Latin America since independence.

Paraguay is one of two inland countries of South America, with fair access by river, road and rail to the sea, 1,450 km. away. Its southern boundary with Argentina from just N of the Argentine town of Corrientes to Encarnación, a distance of 320 km., is the Alto Paraná river. This river course, which sweeps northwards, remains the border with Argentina as far as the Iguazú river, a distance of 346 km. From that point to the Guairá Falls (193 km.), that Alto Paraná is the eastern border with Brazil; from the Falls the northern boundary with Brazil runs north-westwards across the land mass to the confluence between the Apa and Paraguay rivers.

The Alto Paraná is joined near Corrientes by the southward flowing Paraguay river. From Corrientes as far N as Asunción (354 km.), it is the western boundary with Argentina. From Asunción as far N as the confluence with the Apa (603 km.), the river divides Paraguay into two: Paraguay proper to the E, and the Chaco to the W. For some distance N of the entry of the Apa, the Paraguay river is the Chaco's eastern boundary with Brazil.

The Paraguayan lands divided by the Paraguay river are in extreme contrast: the Chaco (246,950 square km.), a sparsely inhabited tract of cattle and scrub forest country and Paraguay proper (159,800 square km.), a rich land in which almost all the population is concentrated. But Paraguay proper is itself divided into two contrasting areas by a high cliffed formation which runs almost due N from the Alto Paraná river, W of Encarnación, to the Brazilian border. E of this cliff lies the Paraná plateau; W of it, as far as the Paraguay river, lie gently rolling hills and flat plains.

The Paraná Plateau, ranging from 300 to 600 metres in height, has comparatively heavy falls of rain and is one vast forest. It is in this forest that most of the yerba maté is gathered for export. Across the plateau runs the Paraná river. At the point where the northern boundary of Paraguay reaches the river are the great Guairá (or Sete Quedas) Falls.

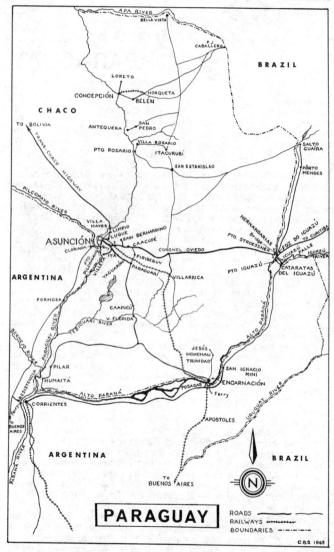

PARAGUAY

ROADS ———
RAILWAYS ++++++++
BOUNDARIES — · — · —

C.B.S. 1965

ROUGH SKETCH

From the Falls to Encarnación (539 km.), the river runs through a canyon incised into the deep lava floor of the plateau, which dips into the plains just W of Encarnación.

West of the high cliff which rims the western edge of the plateau lies a fertile plain stretching to the Paraguay river. This plain is diversified by rolling, well wooded hills: one range runs from the cliff to the Paraguay river N of Concepción; another, broad based on the plateau, reaches the river at Asunción. Most of Paraguay's population is concentrated in these last hilly lands, stretching eastwards from Asunción to Encarnación.

Much of the flat plain is flooded once a year; it is wet savannah, treeless, but covered with coarse grasses. On this plain, rice, sugar, tobacco, grains and cotton are grown. Several heavily forested rivers drain the plain and hill lands into the Paraguay.

The Chaco, lying W of the Paraguay river, is mostly cattle country or scrub forest. Along the river there are grassy plains and clumps of palms, but westwards the land grows drier and more and more bleak. Much of the north-western area is almost waterless. The marshy, unnavigable Pilcomayo river, one of the few draining the Chaco, represents the boundary between the Paraguayan and Argentine Chacos. Apart from Mennonite colonies, small settlements on the river banks, and a number of estancias in the SW, only a few nomadic Indian tribes live in the vast region. (The average density is less than 1 person to the square km.). The quebracho (axe-breaker) tree, the world's principal source (with mimosa) of tannin, comes from the scrub forests of the Chaco and of the Paraná river.

Some 54% of the country is covered with forest, 40% is pastoral, 4% is agricultural but only 1% is cultivated. Even eastern Paraguay supports only 11 people to the square km.

Communications The only practicable water route is by the Paraná to the Plate estuary, and Buenos Aires is 1,450 km. from Asunción. The river winds excessively; it constantly changes its bed and the locus of its sandbanks. Large ocean-going vessels can ascend as far as Rosario with safety, but meet with many difficulties between Rosario and Santa Fe. So difficult is the river that communication with Buenos Aires was mainly by road before the railway from Asunción to Buenos Aires, via the Posadas-Encarnación ferry, was opened in 1913. The high cost of transport allows only those products which can bear that cost competitively to flow out into world markets. The greatly improved roads to Buenos Aires are now used for freight, and so is the new road, paved throughout, to Curitiba and São Paulo, in Brazil.

The external communications by air, and the internal communications by air, railway, road and river are given under "Information for Visitors". The importance of the railways is explained by these facts: it takes 4 days by river from Buenos Aires to Asunción, 54 hours by rail, 24 hours by road, 1½ to 3 hours by air; it is over 4,830 km. by land to La Paz and takes nearly 6 days by train and 3-4 by road, but by air it is 1,770 km. and takes 3 hours only.

History The original inhabitants of Paraguay were the Guaraní Indians; they had spread by the 16th century to the foothills of the Andes, along the coast of Brazil, and even into the basin of the Amazon. They were a singularly peaceful people who did not contest the coming of the Spaniards, the first of whom, under the navigator Diego de Solís, arrived at the River Paraguay in 1524. The main body, led by Juan de Ayolas, came from Buenos Aires, where the earliest Spanish settlement was made in 1536. Finding no gold, and pestered by the hostile Indians of the Pampa, they pushed north along the river, seeking a short route to the gold and silver of Peru. They reached the friendly Guaranís in 1537 and a member of the party, Juan de Salazar de Espinosa, is generally credited with founding Asunción on August 15th. The shifting sands and treacherous channel of the Paraná river made it almost impossible for further forces to be brought that way: what little reinforcement there was came overland across Brazil. Because the garrison at Asunción remained small, the Paraguayan mestizo has a far higher proportion of Indian blood than any other in Latin America. The result is singularly fortunate: the Paraguayan is both good-looking (to our Western eyes) and, for all his obduracy in war, kindly and peaceable.

Asunción became the nucleus of Spanish settlement in southeastern South America, and it was from Asunción that this part of the world was colonized. Spaniards pushed NW across the Chaco to found Santa Cruz, in Bolivia, eastwards to occupy the rest of Paraguay, and southwards along the river to re-found Buenos Aires in 1580, 43 years after they had abandoned it.

During the Colonial era one of the world's most interesting experiments in dealing with a native population was carried out, not by the conquerors, but by their missionaries, over whom the civil power had little or no control. In 1609 the Society of Jesus sent a number of missionaries to Paraguay to civilize the Indians. The Jesuits were in the country until they were expelled in 1767: a period of 158 years. During that time they formed 30 "reductions", or settlements, run along paternal-socialist lines. They induced the Indians to leave the forests and settle in townships, where they built magnificent churches, employing unsuspected native skills in masonry, stone and wood carving, and painting. Selected natives were even given a sound classical education. The first reductions were in the north, but they were forced to abandon these because of constant attacks from Brazil. They settled finally in Misiones; part of the area of settlement is now in Argentina. At the expulsion, the reductions fell to pieces: the Indians left, and were reduced to peonage under other masters. Most of the great churches have fallen into ruin, or been destroyed, but a few that remain are dealt with in the text.

Paraguay got its independence from Spain, without bloodshed, on May 14, 1811. Gaspar Rodríguez de Francia, the dictator known as "El Supremo", took power in 1814 and held it until 1840. His policy was the simple one of complete isolation: no one might leave the country, no one might enter it, and trade was not permitted. He was followed as dictator by his nephew, Carlos Antonio López, who ruled until his death in 1862. He reversed Francia's policy of isolation and it was he who began in 1854 the building of the Central Paraguayan Railway from Asunción to Encarnación. He was followed by a third dictator: his son, Francisco Solano López, who is today the most venerated of Paraguay's heroes. He aspired to be the Napoleon of South America and, with the encouragement of his Irish mistress, Madame Eliza Lynch, he became involved in 1865 in a disastrous war against Brazil, Argentina and Uruguay—The War of the Triple Alliance. The courageous Paraguayan nation, led by Marshal López, fought and held out against overwhelming odds until he was killed at Cerro Corá in 1870, when the war ended. Out of a population of 525,000, only 221,000 were left alive after the war, and of these, only 28,000 were male. Paraguay was occupied for eight years. After 1870 a certain number of European immigrants arrived; their descendants are powerful in the social life of Paraguay. Various religious and ideological communities were among them; the Mennonites, mostly of German descent, are the most notable and in the 1890s a party of Australians left Sydney to form a Utopian Socialist Colony in Paraguay, under the leadership of William Lane. Mary Gilmour the poet was among them. The colony lasted for a few years, then broke up, many of the colonists returning to Australia, some remaining in Paraguay. Their descendants are still there.

The country's history since 1870 has been the story of a recovery from disaster, but this process received a severe setback in the wars with Bolivia which broke out intermittently between 1929 and 1935 over the Chaco. The Paraguayans, fighting with their customary courage and tenacity, triumphed, and were given a large area of the Chaco in the final settlement. Bolivia was given an outlet, of little use, to the Paraguay river. Paraguay is now justifying its victory by opening up and colonizing the Chaco, which is believed to contain huge deposits of natural gas, but this is necessarily a slow process.

At the end of the 2nd World War President Morínigo allowed political exiles to return. Civil war broke out, the President fled, and some years of disorder were capped by the seizure of power in 1954 by General Alfredo Stroessner, soon appointed President. He is still in power.

The People of Paraguay Because the proportion of Spanish blood is smaller than elsewhere, the people of Paraguay today are bilingual, speaking both the Spanish of the conqueror and the Guaraní of the conquered. Outside Asunción, most people speak Guaraní by preference. There is a Guaraní theatre, and books and periodicals are published in that tongue, which has official status as the second national language. There are about 40,000 pure-bred Indians left: most of them are in the Chaco.

Population: 2.8m. Urban growth: 3.8%; annual growth: 3.5%. Life expectancy at birth: 61.9 years. Infant mortality: 84 per thousand. Some 30% live in towns. Over 65% work on the land, nearly 20% in industry. 25% of all Paraguayans live abroad.

Government There was a new Constitution in 1967. Executive power rests in the President, elected for five years. A Senate has been added to the existing Chamber of Deputies. Voting is secret and obligatory on all citizens over 18, including women, who voted for the first time in the general elections on February 10, 1963.

PRESIDENT: General Alfredo Stroessner (1954-date)

Main Towns

Asunción, the capital and only large town in Paraguay, is built on the shores of a bay cutting into the eastern bank of the Paraguay river, almost opposite its confluence with the Pilcomayo. Its urban population is 440,000, a sixth of the country's total; the district population is about 450,000. The city, built on a low hill crowned by the large modern church of La Encarnación, is laid out in the Colonial Spanish rectangular manner; a few of its avenues are lined with trees. The oldest part is down by the water's edge, but none of the public buildings is earlier than the last half of the 19th century. The city has spread into the hilly land beyond.

Dwelling houses are in a variety of styles; new villas in every kind of taste have replaced the old one-storey pastel-hued Spanish-Moorish type of house with its iron grill work and flower-filled patio, except in the poorer quarters. The three busiest streets are Estrella, Oliva, and Palma, but even these have no storm drains yet (they are being installed), and cars and pedestrians have to cope with much water flowing through the main streets. In general, though, the streets and markets are kept clean. The antique trams are back in use. There is a good selection of cheap English books at Librería Universal, Palma 519.

You see most public buildings by following Calle El Paraguayo Independiente from the Custom House. The first is the Government Palace, built during the Triple Alliance War in the style of the Louvre. In Plaza Constitución stands the big Congressional Palace (debates can be attended during session from April-December, on Thursdays and Fridays), with the Cathedral at the corner of the square. Two blocks SW, along Calle Chile, is Plaza de los Héroes, with a building based on the Invalides in Paris. This is the Pantheon of Heroes, begun during the Triple Alliance War and finished in 1937. It now contains the tombs of Carlos and Francisco López, of two unknown Paraguayan soldiers, and of Marshal Estigarribia, the victor of the Chaco War in the 1930s.

The best of several parks are Parque Carlos Antonio López, set high and with a grand view but unfortunately not well maintained; Parque Caballero, laid out along a stream (swimming pool and water-falls and plantations); and Parque Gaspar Rodriguez de Francia. The not-too-well maintained Botanical Gardens are 6½ km. out, at Trinidad, quickly reached by rail or bus (US$0.10, about 45 minutes). They lie along the Paraguay river, on the former estate of the López family, and have an enormous range of plants, a nine-hole golf course, and a rather depressing little zoo. The López residence is near Trinidad; a typical Paraguayan country house with verandahs, which has become a natural history museum. The beautiful pink church of Santísima Trinidad, dating from 1856 with paintings inside, is well worth a visit. From the Botanical Gardens (several town buses), it is about 3 km. to the bank of the river, across which is the island reservation of the Maca tribe, brought from the Chaco, who live by peddling their handicrafts to tourists. To cross, tourists now have to take a special launch, so collect several people for the trip as the cost is quite high (US$1), it can go as high as US$3 per person for the trip and the services of a guide. Fee to enter reservation, which is often crowded with tourists: US$0.50. If you want to photograph the Indians, bargain with them first! Many people feel the reservation is very commercialized.

Hotels   *Hotel Guaraní,* at the centre, very modern, 13 floors, air conditioned, swimming pool and night club; from US$37 d, without meals. *Gran del Paraguay,* out of town, in a park, with swimming pool and a night club on Fridays, decent but old; was the palace in which López lived. The dining-room, with floral murals, was the private theatre of his mistress, Madame Lynch; an air conditioned annex has been built in the gardens; from US$21, without meals. The *Hotel y Casino Itá Enramada,* 7 km. S. of Asunción, from US$24; *Paraná* (25 de Mayo y Caballero) from US$15; *Premier* (Curupayty y 25 de Mayo), from US$12; *Plaza* (Eligio Ayala y Paraguari), US$13 d, breakfast only, no taxes; *Hotel Terraza,* Caballero 1, quiet but central, lovely view overlooking the "bay", US$10 d, with shower and breakfast, an old house, converted, not as clean as it used to be. *Sahara,* Oliva near Montevideo, good clean, air conditioning, small pool, US$11 s. *Hotel Chaco,* Caballero y Mariscal Estigarribia, US$28 d, new. Not to be confused with

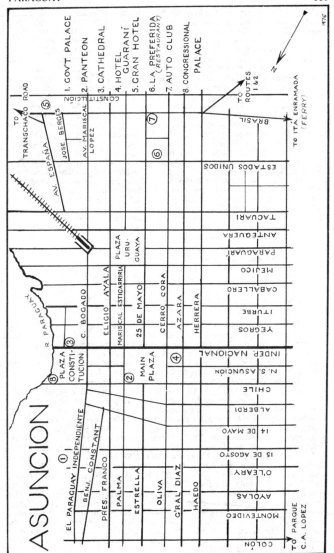

ASUNCION

1. GOV'T PALACE
2. PANTEON
3. CATHEDRAL
4. HOTEL GUARANÍ
5. GRAN HOTEL
6. LA PREFERIDA (RESTAURANT)
7. AUTO CLUB
8. CONGRESSIONAL PALACE

ROUGH SKETCH

Residencial Chaco, Yegros y Eligio Ayala, which has rooms for about US$4, is clean but there are mosquitoes. *Imperial,* Oliva y Colón, about US$10 d, clean and friendly. *Hotel Presidente,* Azara e Independencia Nacional, US$11 d. *Grand Hotel Armele,* Palma y Colón, very modern, a/c, US$15 s. *Montserrat,* from US$7.80; *International,* from US$10.70; *La Estancia,* Caballero y Abay, from US$4, clean and friendly; *Ipiranga,* on Iturbe, US$6 d, with bath and breakfast. *Senorial,* Colonial style (Mcal. López y Perú), swimming pool, US$16 d, a/c. *India,* Gral. Diaz y Montevideo, US$10 d, in season (US$6-7 d and US$3.30 s out of season), very good, quiet and clean. *Asunción Palace* (Colón y Estrella), US$12.20 d, with breakfast; *Española,* US$12 with meals, friendly; *City Hotel,* just off Nuestra Sra. de la Asunción, US$8 s. *Residencial Asunción,* Oliva 476 US$4 d, *Hotel Lord,* Tacuari y Azara, US$10.60 for two, a/c, incl. private shower and large breakfast. *Hotel Azara,* Azara, 860, recommended by Auto club. Most rooms face a shady patio and pool. *Residencial Alvear,* opposite Banco Exterior de España, US$5.50 d, with breakfast. *Residencial del Turista,* Hernandarias 772, clean, friendly, hot water, shower, US$5 d; *Hotel Stella d'Italia,* near Estados Unidos and Tacuari (cheap); *Residencia* (also Restaurant) *Japón de Kikoyo Uchiyamada,* Constitución 763 (Tel.: 22038), US$3 s, good meals; *Hotel Carlitos,* Montevideo 453, US$14 d, a/c and pool; *Pensión Santa Rosa,* Azara 664, US$2.25 s; *Residencial Brasil House,* suits Peace Corps, US$3 d. *Pensión Asunción,* Eligio Ayala 376, US$3 d, basic, meals for about US$0.70; *Residencial Nanduti,* Presidente Franco, US$3.50 with bath and breakfast. *Hotel de Mayo,* 25 de Mayo 336, and Caballero, dirty, US$6 d, in pleasant annex. *Hoopedar Voajero,* Antequera, clean and friendly, US$2.50. Many cheap places near railway station, e.g. *Hotel Savoy,* US$7 d. with breakfast; *Hotel América,* near terminal for Itá Enramada buses, US$1.80 p.p., clean, hot water, mosquito nets.

Hotels in Paraguay are generally more expensive than in the rest of South America. It has been suggested that Brazilian tourists forced up prices. Beware: hotels tend to lack table water, toilet paper, towels and soap.

The hotel bill does not usually contain a service charge, but it pays to tip when you arrive as well as when you go, say US$1 to the table waiter at both ends of a week's visit. A tip of 10% is enough for non-residents, at hotels and in restaurants.

Restaurants   At the hotels *Guaraní* (Parque Independencia), *Gran del Paraguay* (Mazzini y Sarmiento); *Preferida,* Estados Unidos y 25 de Mayo, recommended; *Germania,* Cerro Corá 180, near *Guarani Hotel,* recommended; *La Pergola del Bolsi,* Estrella 389, recommended; *El Dragón de Oro* (Chinese), Independencia Nacional y Azara, good but expensive; *Kung Fu* also does good Chinese; a cheaper Chinese restaurant, Casa China, is on 25 de Mayo, two blocks from the Plaza de Independencia; *Suki Yaki,* for reasonably-priced Japanese food; *La Carrela,* serves local dishes; *Hermitage* (15 de Agosto), folk dances and music at night with a Paraguayan harp/guitar conjunto, food is moderately expensive, there is a cover charge, US$4 food is almost all international; *Bar Munich,* Eligio Ayala 163, good food but slow service; *Hostería de Caballito Blanco,* Alberti 631, Austrian-run, good food and service. *Jardín de la Cerveza,* Ave. Rep. Argentina y Castillo, good food and good entertainment; a meal with drinks costs about US$3. Good place is the *Lido,* a lunch counter in Plaza de los Héroes, open until midnight, will suit P.C.V.'s and students. For good roast chicken for about US$1 try *Rotisería,* known as Nick's Restaurant, on Azara near Iturbe. For local food and folk-music, try *Paraguay-Chóferes del Chaco,* away from centre. The Paraguayan harp can also be heard at *Café Rosendal,* Estados Unidos y Figueroa; also at the beer-garden opposite the Hospital Bautista. Music, folk show and good food and service at *Yguazú,* US$30 for two, but some distance from centre. About 20 minutes out of town on bus route 26 or 27 is the *Nandutí Parrillada* (Tel.: 24643), an open-air restaurant with good atmosphere. Highly recommended. Good ice cream at *Confitería Vertua.* Good cafeteria in same block as *Guaraní Hotel.* Good Paraguayan harp/guitar conjunto at *Churrasquería Sajón,* Av. Carlos A. López, bus 26 from centre. *Restaurant Exótica,* best and cheapest food in town.

For music and "local colour" try the bars along Benjamín Constant.

Night Clubs La Calandria, an open air show; Playboy, 14 de Mayo y Oliva; Aztec, Mcal. López y Pitiantuta; Le Carusel, Independencia Nacional y Azara (next to *Hotel Guaraní*). Safari's (discotheque).

Clubs Centenario; Unión; Golf.

Airport Presidente Gral. Stroessner, 15 km. NE of centre. Taxi to centre, US$9; buses from airport to Asunción (number 139) and Luque, US$0.35. Reported that buses to Luque (130, 139) do not go *via* the airport but only within 1 km. Ask to be set down at road fork. Buses only recommended outside rush-hours, with light luggage. LAP has its own colectivo which collects from hotels, US$3.10 p.p. Enquire at offices.

A new airport terminal is being built 1 km. from the old building.

Rail Presidente Carlos Antonio López Railway to Encarnación and Buenos Aires (1,510 km.) Leaves Asunción Mon., Wed. and Fri., at 1630, journey of 54 hours.

Sleeper between B.A. and Posadas in both directions. Fares to Buenos Aires, 1st class, about US$19; 2nd class, US$13.85; sleeper, US$5.50. Quite tolerable 2nd class. To Encarnación, 1st class, US$3.70 (strongly recommended); 2nd class US$2.80, basic. To Posadas US$3.70 in 2nd class Argentine coach. In dry weather dust, and in wet weather rain, gets into 2nd-class carriages. (Trains may be cancelled on public holidays such as Christmas).

River Steamers To Concepción (24 hours) with Flota Mercantil del Estado, Estrella 672-682. Weekly (every Tuesday—returns on Wednesday), US$15 without food, but there is a restaurant on board. Boats are modern, elegant and comfortable. The 2nd class fare is about a third of the 1st class but accommodation and food are adequate and you can use the swimming pool, lounges, etc. Corumbá can be reached by bargaining for a trip on a cargo boat; alternatively take monthly boat to Bahía Negra (on border with Bolivia and Brazil) but get off at Porto Murtinho, take daily bus to Campo Grande and from there to Corumbá.

N.B. The river passenger link with Buenos Aires is often suspended, especially in summer.

Roads There is a 10 km. road S from Asunción to Itá Enramada, on the Río Paraguay, where a ferry links with the Argentine town of Clorinda (US$2) and the Pan-American Highway to Buenos Aires. (The *Hotel y Casino Itá Enramada,* recently built, offers 150 rooms and suites in a 7-hectare park with swimming pools, tennis courts, a sauna, a night-club, mini-golf and water-skiing, from US$24, without meals. (reservations worldwide through KLM or LAP. Tel.: 70-014). Good fishing facilities on the River Paraguay nearby.) The bus fare to and from Asunción is about US$0.12. (Alternatively, to reach Clorinda, you can cross the river at Asunción on the Chaco E ferry, and then cross the border at Puente Pilcomayo.) There is a good bus service to Resistencia and Buenos Aires from the Argentine side, by Empresa Godoy. There is a 32 km. road NW to Villa Hayes (ferry) and on through the Chaco (Route 9) to Filadelfia and Bolivia, 805 km. (an account of a direct journey from Sucre, Bolivia, using this road will be found in the Bolivian section). Route 8 runs N from Coronel Oviedo, 100 km. to San Estanislao (see also under Coronel Oviedo, page 565), where it becomes successively Routes 3 and 5 and runs 305 km. N and then NE, to Pedro Juan Caballero on the Brazilian frontier. The only paved long-distance roads are Route 1 to Encarnación (372 km.); and Route 2 to Coronel Oviedo, which leads to Route 7 to Puerto Stroessner and the Iguazú falls (362 km.). They are described in the text.

Buses To Puerto Pte. Stroessner, US$3.50 with Flota San Agustín (Plaza Uruguaya) or US$4.50 with the Rápido Yguazú company (also Plaza Uruguaya), or with Nuestra Sra. de Asunción (Plaza Uruguaya), US$5, recommended as the best and quickest, or Pluma companies. All three companies go on to Foz do Iguaçu, total cost US$5.50 (about US$6.50 on a Pluma bus, which is luxury Pullman), 5-7 hours, according to company. It is cheaper to get local bus from Foz to the falls than to go straight through. Passengers who want to go straight through to Foz and have paid to do so from Asunción, must make absolutly sure that the bus they book does go straight through. Bus to Encarnación (ferry to Posadas in Argentina) US$6, 8 hours, frequent.

Routes 2 and 7 have buses to Curitiba and São Paulo; bus leaves daily at 1000. Don't buy a through ticket to Sao Paulo with stopover in Iguazú; buy one to Iguazú and there buy another to Sao Paulo; otherwise you will have to return to the border and re-enter Brazil to conform with police regulations.

Other international bus routes: Asunción-Buenos Aires, daily 0630 and 1500, 24 hours, US$15 with Rio Paraná company, or US$21.40 with Pluma. Asunción-Santa Fe, 15 hours, US$13. Asunción-Montevideo, Mon., Thurs., 26 hours, US$17.

Buses for anywhere within about 80 km. (incl. San Bernardino, Itauguá and Yagurón) leave from the Litorina bus station at Constitución y Herrera. San Bernardino, US$0.60; Itauguá, US$0.50; Caapucú (on Encarnación road) US$1.25.

Tourist Office   Alberdi y Oliva.

Tourist Agencies (all very helpful)   Inter-Express, Nuestra Sra. de Asunción 588; Menno Tour, Azara 532 (English spoken); Continental, Independencia Nacional 225; Iguazú, in Calle Palma next to *Hotel Colonial*.

Banks   Bank of London and South America, Ltd., Palma and O'Leary, and 6 agencies; Banco de la Nación Argentina; Banco do Brazil; Citibank, Calle Chile; Banco Exterior de España; Bank of America; Banco Transatlántico Alemán, 14 de Mayo y Estrella; Banco Holandés Unido, Palma y Na. Sra. Asunción; Banco Francés e Italiano, Herrera esq. Independencia Nacional. Open 0700 to 1030 Oct-March, 0730 to 1130 April-Sept. And national banks. Several casas de cambio on Palma; rates for neighbouring countries' currencies usually good, and better than at the various frontiers. Be careful to count money received from street exchange-sellers.

General Post Office   Alberdi, Benjamin Constant y El Paraguayo Independiente. Tel.: 48891. There is a sub-office in *Hotel Guaraní*.

Museums   Natural History Museum, at the former López residence, 6½ km. out, entrance US$0.30; National Museum of Fine Arts, and the Asunción Seminary Museum, both showing some "mission" art. At the Museum of Fine Arts (in Calle Mariscal Estigarribia, off Plaza Uruguay), the paintings are very badly displayed; it has a Murillo and a Tintoretto. (In 1976 it was reported to be closed for an indefinite period.) A museum in the Botanical Gardens has Indian and historical exhibitions well worth seeing, and the house is lovely. In the Casa de la Independencia (14 de Mayo and Presidente Franco) is an interesting historical collection; entry free.

Addresses   British Embassy and Consulate: 25 de Mayo y Yegros (Banco Exterior de España building); U.S. Embassy and Consulate: Av. Mariscal López esq. Kubitschek; Compania Marítima, on Benjamin Constant, for all shipping enquiries. Anglican Church: St. Andrew, on España with Uruguay; Peace Corps, Brasil 365.

Electricity   Domestic and industrial: 220 volts A.C., 50 cycles.

Shopping   Calle Colón, starting at the port, is lined with good tourist shops, Casa Arnoldo, Calle Palma 640, is a good place for hand-embroidered blouse lengths. La Asunceña, Palma 766, leatherware. Calle Franco for handmade furniture. For wooden articles and carvings go to the shop in Calle Independencia Nacional, behind the Guaraní Hotel, which used to be owned by the Society of Brothers. See H. Stern's jewelry store at Hotel Guaraní. Paraguayan leatherwork is cheap and very good. The markets are worth a visit, especially the Petti Rossi.

Taxis   Minimum fare in Asunción is US$0.16 plus US$0.02 for every 133 metres. The average journey costs under US$1. Hire by the hour: about US$2.50. Tip 10%.

Trams   These venerable, charming, single-deck vehicles, which are understood to be under the personal protection of President Stroessner, were taken out of service in 1973; however, the increased cost of oil fuel has led to their partial reinstatement (US$0.18).

Buses   Journeys within city, US$0.15.

Excursions The travel agencies listed above offer car tours, with or without guides, round the City and to the Botanical Gardens; to the old "mission" towns in the area; and further afield, by road or by Brazilian Varig Airline to the Iguazú Falls (see page 105), 75 minutes. The three-day package trips to the Falls cost about US$300 all in. Near La Colmena are the Salto Cristal falls, which are worth a visit. There are day river trips by launch S to **Villeta** (27 km. 10,000 people), a cotton and tobacco town on the E bank; or up the Pilcomayo to see the Chaco and its wild life.

A bus ride to **Filadelfia**, in the Chaco, from Asunción costs US$10 with the Nueva Asunción company. The town is the centre of a Mennonite colony; having refused to take part in wars, the Mennonites, mostly of German origin, arrived in the area between 1927 and 1947 and today make a significant contribution to the country's economy. (*Hotel Florida*, US$4).

The most popular trip is east to **San Bernardino**, on Lake Ypacaraí, by road (56 km.) or partly by rail. The lake is 24 km. by 5, and its shores are covered with tropical trees and plants. Many Asunción families live at this resort, crowded from December through February. It has facilities for swimming, sunbathing and water sports. Aregua, on the far shore, is also a resort. The President has a week-end house on the lake.

Hotels *Hotel del Lago; Santa Rita.* It is possible to find rooms in private houses, which are cheaper than hotel rooms.

Clubs *Náutico San Bernardino.*

A trip up the Paraguay to Concepción, about 312 km. N of Asunción, is one of the easiest ways of seeing more of the country. The countryside is alternately reported as flat and dull, and as interesting with thick vegetation and palm groves. Take your choice! The winding river is 400 metres wide, with shoals of vicious caribe fish. There is a lot of traffic, for in the absence of a direct road this is the trade route for all the products of northern Paraguay: cattle, hides, yerba maté, tobacco, timber and quebracho.

Concepción (34,000 inhabitants), a free port for Brazil, lies on the E bank. It is not in itself, apart from the life of the streets, particularly notable, but it is the trade centre of the N, doing a considerable business with Brazil. There is an interesting market.

Concepción Hotels *Francés,* double, without bath, US$4 in season and US$2 out of season; some dearer rooms have baths; US$7 full board if in annex. There is a hotel above *Bar Victoria. Hotel Paraguay.*

A metre gauge railway runs from Concepción to Horqueta, 56 km. to the E, a cattle and lumbering town of 10,000 people. There is now a dry-season road from Concepción W across the Chaco, to Pozo Colorado on the Trans-Chaco highway. The Concepción—Pozo Colorado bus takes 2 hours, US$3, but it is difficult to get onward connections. Once a week the "Camioneta Cristo Rey", a jeep belonging to the Anglican Church, goes across to the Trans-Chaco highway.

There is a bad 114 km. road (Route 5) to the border town of **Pedro Juan Caballero**, opposite Ponta Pora, Brazil, which has a road and railway to São Paulo and the Atlantic coast. The two towns are divided only by a road and the locals come and go as they please. To cross into Brazil officially visit Delegación de Gobierno and Brazilian consul in P. J. Caballero, and then report to Brazilian federal police in P. Pora. From P.

J. Caballero there are Thursday flights to Concepción and daily to Asunción; buses to both.

Buses Concepción-Pedro Juan Caballero, two daily, US$4, 6 hours. Asunción-Pedro Juan Caballero, two daily, US$8.75, 12 hours.

From the river port of Puerto Casado, about 210 km. N of Concepción, a 200 km. railway runs W into the heart of the Chaco. It is used mostly by the Mennonite settlers and soldiers stationed in the Chaco.

Another trip, this time down the river, can be made to **Pilar,** (10,000 inhabitants), 306 km. S of Asunción, opposite the confluence of the Paraguay and the Bermejo, coming in from the Argentine Chaco. A road (Route 4) is open E to San Ignacio Guazú, on the Asunción-Encarnación highway; in the other direction, it continues to the extreme SW tip of Paraguay, near Humaitá, the site of an heroic siege during the War of the Triple Alliance. Flights from Pilar to Asunción and Resistencia, Argentina, on Mon. and Thurs. by LAP.

Hotels *Gardel; Prinquelli.*

Industries Cotton ginning; distilleries; sawmills. Products: hides, cotton, timber, oranges.

Other excursions can be made along the two paved main roads from Asunción: Route 2 runs E for 134 km. to Coronel Oviedo and is continued another 196 km. by Route 7 to Puerto Stroessner, opposite Foz do Iguaçu, a pleasant 4-5-hour trip by car or 5-7 hours by bus; or Route 1, which runs SE to Encarnación. All along Route 2 are extensive plantations of palm trees—the hearts of palm are canned and exported.

Route Two The Mariscal Estigarribia Highway leaves Asunción past typical markets where Guaraní-speaking women, colourfully dressed and smoking big cigars, offer the local merchandise. These markets can be reached by 26 bus from Asunción: ask for Mercado No. 4. At km. 12 is San Lorenzo, an industrial town with the National School of Agriculture. At km. 20 is **Capiatá,** where there is a fine cathedral with remarkable 17th century sculpture made by Indians under the tutelage of the Jesuit Fathers.

Km. 30, **Itauguá,** founded in 1728, not on the railway from Asunción, is where the famous nandutí, or spiderweb lace, a harmonious blending of geometry and design, is made. Some of the items take 5 years to complete. The blocks of uniform dwellings in the broad plaza, with their reddish tile roofs projecting over the side-walk and their lines of pillars, are (according to Mr. Paul Dony) very close to the descriptions we have of Guaraní Jesuit settlements. The church and the market are worth seeing, and the town looks most attractive with the nandutí work spread or hanging outside the houses. (It's cheaper here than in Asunción). There is a 3-day festival in mid-July, including processions and the crowning of Miss Nandutí. Accommodation poor (there is only one pensión, US$2 double), but Itauguá is only one hour by bus from Asunción, US$0.20. At km. 40 a branch road, 5 km. long, leads off to San Bernardino (see page 563).

Approaching Caacupé we see from the top of a large hill the cattle plains spread out below. They are dotted with small farms. In the distance is Lake Ypacaraí. One of the farms is run by the Inter-American Service of Agricultural Co-operation. On the far side of the hill, at km. 54, is **Caacupé,** a popular resort and a Paraguayan religious centre with 19,500 inhabitants. Its sights include the beautiful Church of the Blue Virgin of the Miracles. Her day is December 8, when pilgrims come to the town from far and wide. There are swimming pools in the streams nearby.

Thousands of people from Paraguay, Brazil and Argentina flock to the shrine. Besides fireworks and candle-lit processions pilgrims watch the agile gyrations of Paraguayan bottle-dancers; they weave in intricate measures whilst balancing one or more bottles pyramided on their heads. The top bottle carries a spray of flowers and the more expert dancers never let drop a single petal.

Hotels *Gran Hotel Victoria; Hotel Uruguayo,* with good restaurant, US$3 s, meal US$2-3.

Excursions Poor roads lead to several interesting churches. One is at Tobati, a tobacco centre 16 km. to the N. At km. 64 beyond Caacupé a paved road runs 13 km. SE to **Piribebuy,** founded in 1640 and noted for its strong native drink, cana. In the central plaza is the church (1640), with fine sculptures, high altar and pulpit. Near the town are the attractive small falls of Piraretá. The road goes on to Chololo (grand views from a hill), and reaches Route 1 at Paraguarí, 22 km. from Piribebuy (see next page).

The land unrolls itself: green hills, tobacco, cotton and rice fields, woodland and running streams. At km. 134, **Coronel Oviedo**, the road branches: one branch, Route 8, is paved for 42 km. S to Villarrica and continues S (unpaved) through Caazapá to Boquerón; another, the paved 189-km. Route 7 through bush forest land and across the Caaguazú mountain, runs to the spectacular 500 metre single span international bridge across the Paraná at **Puerto Presidente Stroessner,** where there is an airport. This is the fastest growing city in the country. It is now the centre of operations for the construction of the Itaipú dam (projected to be the largest hydroelectric plant in the world, with over 12m kw capacity) and has been described as the biggest late-night shopping centre in Latin America. The nearby town of Hernandarias and Puerto Franco have also had a tremendous increase in population and the activity in the whole area is hectic. The road links with the Brazilian road system at Foz do Iguaçu across the bridge, from where another 32-km. road leads to the Iguazú Falls (see page 105) in the Argentine section).

Hotels (incl. breakfast) *(Acaraí Casino,* a/c, with swimming pool and casino, US$16 d; *Catedial,* a/c, with swimming pool, from US$9 s and US$14 d; *Munich,* US$13; *Hanga Roa* chalet, US$14; *Itaipu,* US$ 12; *Motel Mi Abuela* US$8, including breakfast; cheaper ones on main street and near market.

Restaurants *Mburucuyá,* with music, at Alejo García y A. Jara; *Hostelería del Lago* at the same address; *Rosa de Lago* at B. Caballero (opposite the park); *Cary-Bar* at Nanawa y Monsenor Rodriquez; *Guaranía,* at Pto Piribebuy; *Tripolis* for good moderately-priced meal. Cheaper ones in market.

Another road from Coronel Oviedo (dry-weather, but wide and smooth) runs N to San Estanislao, then (Route 10) NE for 323 km. to the Guairá falls, past numerous "colonies" where the jungle is being cleared. There are daily buses from Asunción (14 hours). The falls are best visited from the Brazilian side; walk or take taxi along the W bank of the Paraná to the first Brazilian village, then take boat (US$1.10) across river to town of Guairá, in the Brazilian state of Paraná (see also page 271).

Villarrica, 177 km. by road or rail from Asunción and 219 from Encarnación, with 30, 700 people, is delightfully set on a hill rich with orange trees. It has a splendid Cathedral. Products of the region are tobacco, cotton, sugar, yerba maté, hides, meat and wine produced by German settlers.

Hotel *Internacional.*

Route One   The other main road from Asunción runs through some of the old mission towns to Encarnación, 372 km. away, on the Alto Paraná.

Fast, comfortable colectivos run by Halcones, Calle Antequera 215, do the trip to Encarnación in 7 hours.

Km. 35.5, **Itá,** an old village turning out crude rustic pottery.

Km. 48, **Yaguarón,** set on a river at the foot of a hill in an orange growing district. It has a famous church—one of the most exciting in Latin America—begun by the Franciscans in 1640 and finished in 1720, and reconstructed in 1885. (Sometimes locked on weekdays.) The tints, made by the Indians from local plants, are still bright on the woodcarvings. Most of Paraguay's petit-grain comes from the area. For the by-road to Caacupé see Excursions from Caacupé, previous page. Buses every 15 minutes or so from Asunción (US$0.40).

"The corridor, or outside walk under a projecting roof supported by pillars, is a typical feature of Paraguayan churches. It is an agreeable meeting place for the parishioners. Generally it runs all the way round the church, forming an entrance portico in front. An excellent example is the church at Yaguarón. It is the prototype of the mission sanctuaries of the early 18th century, when the structure was built with a sturdy wooden skeleton and the walls—simple screens of adobe or brick—had no function of support. The front portico is nothing but an outside continuation of the nave. The belfry is a modest little wooden tower somewhat apart from the church; in the missions it also served as a *mangrullo,* or watch tower."—Paul Dony.

Museum   Museo Doctor Francia, 700 metres from church, with relics of Paraguay's first dictator, "El Supremo". Open Tues., Thurs., Sat. 1500-1700; Sun. and holidays 0930-1130; 1500-1700.

Km. 63, **Paraguarí,** founded 1775, the N entrance to the mission area.

Paraguarí, on the railway (10,000 people), is set among hills and encircled by streams. Its church, though cruder, is reminiscent of the famous church at Yaguarón. It has a curious bell tower.

Hotels   Paraguarí; Domínguez.

Just before km. 160 where the Tebicuary river is crossed by bridge (toll) is Caapucú *(Hotel Misiones,* US$0.75 p.p.). Km. 226, San Ignacio Guazú; there is a museum of Guaraní carvings in the old Jesuits' home. About 16 km. to the NE is the new church of Santa María de Fe, with some 60 to 70 Guaraní sculptures in the chapel. From San Ignacio Guazú a road, 156 km., runs W to Pilar. A famous church at km.248, Santa Rosa, was destroyed by fire in 1883, and little remains. Coronel Bogado, km. 288, is the southern limit to the mission area. The road reaches the Alto Paraná at Carmen del Paraná, km. 331, 40 km. W of Encarnación, the terminus of the railway from Asunción. The road goes on 28 km. to Trinidad, and beyond to the thriving German colonies of Obligado and Bella Vista (another, Colonia Hohenau, is due E of Trinidad on the Alto Paraná); this road is being continued N as Route 6, paralleling the Alto Paraná, to meet Route 7 near Puerto Stroessner. Beyond again, 71 km. from Encarnación, is the Japanese Colonia Pirapo. At **Trinidad** there is a great Jesuit church, once utterly in ruins but now being carefully restored. Ten km. N of Trinidad, at Jesús, there is another ruined church, which is also being restored.

Next to the ruined church at Trinidad is a small modern church; it contains a large carved wooden statue of the Deity, so hollowed at the back that a priest in hiding could simulate the resounding voice of the Eternal Father to impress the Indians of the mission.

"The ruins at Trinidad are easily reached by colectivo from Encarnación. They are set in a beautiful, peaceful, rolling green country that might be England except for the orange trees and weird birds. All the area is heavily colonized by Germans and Japanese (more recent comers). The farms are neat and well kept, with pretty houses in tidy gardens surrounded by orchards of oranges, tung and yerba maté. There are quite a few Japanese shops in Encarnación, and some colectivos even have the name in Japanese as well as Spanish."—Miss Caroline Whitehead.

Sixteen km. from Encarnación on the road to Trinidad is *Tirol del Paraguay,* a nice hotel with 2 swimming pools, chalets for 40 people and a landing strip; European-run, with good food.

Encarnación (pop. 35,000), a busy port on the Alto Paraná, is opposite the Argentine town of Posadas, from which there is a road and air service for the Iguazú Falls. The town is now the centre for the construction of the "Yacyretá-Apipé" dam to be shared by Paraguay and Argentina. It is also undergoing rapid economic growth because of the great increase in soya bean exports. The Jesuit ruins of San Ignacio Miní (see page 104) are on this road. Encarnación exports the products of a rich area: timber, maté, tobacco, cotton, and hides. Trains from Buenos Aires are ferried across to Posadas. Encarnación appears very old and very rural: horses and chickens on the water-front, bullock carts and gauchos in the wide sandy streets, some fine old houses and delightfully sleepy atmosphere. Numerous passenger ferries daily to Posadas; they run 0700-1100, 1400-1800, carry vehicles, charge US$2 for a car. A bus service to Asunción Rápido Yguazú, excellent new Brazilian buses. (8 hrs., US$6). Train to Asunción, three times a week, 18 hours; US$2.25 second, US$3 first.

Hotels *Retka*, a small pink house in pretty garden, private baths, very good home cooking, bed and breakfast, US$3.80. *Central*, US$8 includes private bath and meals; *Viena*, a/c, good location, US$9, private bath, without food. *Suizo; Colón;* others near railway station, mostly around US$1 p.p., such as *Hospedaje Comercio*.
Taxis Horsedrawn (about US$0.25), but some motor driven ones for those in a hurry.
Bank of London and South America, agency at Villarrica y Mariscal Estigarribia, open Mon.-Fri. 0730-1100.
Nearby is the village of Quindy where "anillas de coca"—wooden rings inlaid with mother-of-pearl designs—are made.

The Economy

Paraguay is essentially an agricultural country; conditions for many small farmers are still almost feudal. Estates covering some 27 million hectares are owned by fewer than 2,000 landowners; over 110,000 small farmers occupy 1.9 million hectares, but 85% of them have no title to their land. Agriculture employs 60% of the labour force, but accounts for only a third of production. Income per head (US$620 in 1976) is one of the lowest in Latin America, but it is rising.

Despite the importance of agriculture, of the 40.7 million hectares in the country (or 16 million hectares excluding the Chaco), less than 3% can be cultivated. Agriculture is confined to forest clearings, where the soil is remarkably fertile. Nevertheless, some food has to be imported; mainly wheat, of which 50,000 tons are produced annually to meet a consumption of over 110,000 tons. There are 5m. head of cattle in Paraguay, occupying 15m. hectares, and the economy is based mainly on cattle raising and on forest products. Meat production has fallen sharply, principally because of the EEC's ban on meat imports, which was lifted in

April 1977; in 1976 it contributed only 12% of total export earnings compared with over 33% in 1973. The blow has been more than compensated by increases in sugar, tobacco, soyabean, timber, coffee and cotton production and exports. There are also exports of tung and coconut oil, cotton fibre, hearts of palm, hides and skins and quebracho extract.

Until recently, industry was confined to small units, mainly in meat and timber processing, textiles, sugar, and extraction plants for quebracho, petit grain and vegetable oils. The country is now industrializing fast, and manufacturing now accounts for 30-40% of total production. The expansion is largely due to the activity generated by large hydro-electric plants on the Paraná river system, particularly in cement for the civil works and in high energy-consumption industries such as steel, aluminium and metal fabrication. Most projects have received financing from Paraguay's larger neighbours, and from Japan and the USA.

The economic position is already receiving a substantial boost from a massive hydroelectric scheme currently being undertaken jointly by Brazil and Paraguay. The project, at Itaipú on the river Paraná, is reported to be the largest of its kind in the world. Both the total cost, of about US$7,600m., and the final capacity, of 12.6m. kilowatts, will be shared equally between the two countries. Paraguay's share will easily exceed domestic requirements and the surplus energy will be sold to Brazil. By the time the complex comes into full operation, Paraguay is expected to earn over US$300m. a year from exports of energy alone: this is over three times the value of traditional exports in 1972. Moreover in December 1973 agreement was reached with Argentina for the joint development of the hydroelectric resources of Yacyretá-Apipé, also on the river Paraná, at an estimated cost of US$2,500m., to produce a capacity of 4.0m. kilowatts; and planning is underway for another joint Paraná river project at Corpus, with a projected capacity of 5.0m. kilowatts. These projects will further enlarge Paraguay's foreign exchange earnings and thus contribute to an accelerated rate of development.

Foreign Trade (US$ m.)

	1972	1973	1974	1975	1976	1977*
Exports (f.o.b.)	86.2	126.9	169.8	176.7	181.8	278.9
Imports (c.i.f.)	82.5	122.3	174.0	205.6	220.2	301.7

*Provisional

Information for Visitors

How to get to Paraguay by air:

From Europe Iberia has a weekly service to Asunción from Madrid, *via* Rio and São Paulo. Lufthansa operate Frankfurt-Dakar (Senegal)-Rio-São Paulo-Asunción, also once a week. From other points in Europe, connections can be made *via* Rio or São Paulo.

From North America Braniff operate 4 times per week to Asunción from Miami, Washington and/or New York, *via* La Paz and one or two other points. Alternatively, from New York, good connections every day *via* Rio. From California, connections most days *via* Lima.

Within South America From Montevideo (5 flights a week) by LAP or Pluna; from Buenos Aires (19 a week) by Aerolineas Argentinas (*via* Resistencia or Corrientes), LAP, Braniff or Iberia; from Santiago (once a week) by LAN-Chile; from Lima (5 a week) by LAP or Braniff; from Guayaquil (twice a week) by Braniff; from La Paz (4 non-stop per week) by Braniff, or *via* Santa Cruz (2 a week) by LAP or LAB; from Rio, São Paulo and Iguazú Falls (daily) by Varig; also from São Paulo (3 a week) by LAP.

Airport tax is now US$5.50, or US$4 if travelling to Argentina, Bolivia, Brazil or Uruguay.

From Britain By sea or air to Rio de Janeiro, Montevideo, or Buenos Aires, and on to Paraguay by one of the routes given above. The Rotterdam-Zuid Amerika Lyn has a direct service from N.W. Europe to Asunción, about every 5 weeks, calling on demand at London to pick up cargo (though this is not very often).

From the U.S.A. By boat from New York to Buenos Aires and on to Asunción by one of the routes given above. The Netherlands-owned Holland Pan-American Line has a direct service between New York and Asunción.

From Argentina: By River River steamers of the Argentine line, Compañía de Navegación Fluvial Argentina, Av. Corrientes 389, Buenos Aires. There is a passenger boat service between Buenos Aires and Asunción, every other week, journey takes five days and costs US$90, but may be suspended in the dry season.

By Land The international rail route from Buenos Aires to Posadas is given on page 100. At Posadas the train is ferried across the Alto Paraná to Encarnación, from which there is a line to Asunción. The 1,510 km. are done by through trains in 54 hours. Adding the cost of meals, the fare works out at much more than by road. Travellers who want to see as much of Paraguay and Argentina as possible are advised to go to Asunción by train and return by bus. There is a paved road from Buenos Aires *via* Santa Fe to Clorinda, for the ferry crossing to Itá Enramada, 8 km. from Asunción: 1,450 km. about 23 hours. Good bus services on this route.

From Brazil The headwaters of both the Paraguay and the Alto Paraná are in Brazil. There are unscheduled boat services from Asunción northward along the Paraguay river to Porto Esperança, Brazil (from which there is a railway to SãoPaulo), and to Corumbá (1,220 km.), which is connected by rail and air with Bolivian and Brazilian cities.

International Bus Services Daily bus service from Buenos Aires to Asunción by Brújala S.R. L., 23 hours if roads are in good state. From São Paulo to Asunción: Rapido Yguazú S.R.L. buses leave São Paulo on Sun., Wed., and Fri.; Empresa Sudamericana on Tues., and Sat., and Empresa Nuestra Señora de la Asunción on Tues. and Sat. About 25 hours.

Travel in Paraguay: By Rail There are 497 km. of public railways, and 732 km. of private industrial lines, mostly forest lines of metre gauge or narrower, operated by companies trading in forest produce. The only important line is the standard gauge railway, 440 km. long, between Asunción and Encarnación, and passing through Villarrica.

By Air There are scheduled services to most parts of the country by the Paraguayan Transportes Aéreos Militares (TAM) and Lineas Aéreas de Transporte Nacional (LATN). Planes can be chartered.

By Road Buses ply on the main roads. Good new buses, some with stewardesses and bar on board, are now connecting Asunción with the most important cities of Brazil, Uruguay and Argentina. For motorists, there are few petrol stations in Paraguay, especially in the Chaco area. Volkswagen and Landrover have representatives in Paraguay, parts are easily available—(Volkswagen, 14 de Mayo y 15 de Agosto, Asunción). When travelling from Argentina, fill up with petrol there, as petrol is much dearer in Paraguay. Motor fuel and oil is sold in Paraguay by the litre (gasoline costing about US$0.45 a litre). The documents needed in Paraguay for private cars are *carnet de passages en douanes,* international car registration and driver's licence. For entry into Brazil the only document necessary is the title to the car (or other proof of ownership). There are Esso and Shell road maps of Paraguay.

Tourist Information   There is a Dirección Nacional de Turismo at the corner of Alberdi and Oliva, Asunción. Other fruitful sources of information, particularly about weather and roads, are the Touring & Automobile Club of Paraguay at 25 de Mayo y Brasil, and the office of the traffic police in Asunción. The USAID office has a good booklet on Paraguay.

Interpreters are supplied by the Federación de la Producción, la Industria y el Comercio (Feprinco), Palma y 15 de Agosto (Altos), Asunción. (Tel: 4-6638), main tourist agencies, and the Commercial Department of the British Embassy.

Passport   The entry requirements are a passport, and an international certificate of vaccination against smallpox, preferably in Spanish. Visitors are registered at the port or airport by the immigration authorities and get their documents back immediately. Visas are normally not required for a stay of up to 90 days, by visitors who hold tourist cards (see below). This concession does not apply to citizens of the communist countries who need visas. (We are also told that New Zealanders need visas.)

Tourist Card   Law 152 of 1969 requires the purchase, for US$1, of a tourist card when entering the country (no photos required); cards are supplied by airlines and are also available from main hotels and the Tourist Office. The exit half of the card must be kept until handed in at the point of exit. Tourists who enter Paraguay without a card may be charged a US$1 exit tax and a US$4 exit tax if their stay exceeds 24 hours.

Customs   "Reasonable quantities" of tobacco products, alcoholic drinks and perfume are admitted free of duty.

Warning   The prejudice against "hippie-looking" people carrying rucksacks seems to have diminished of late. The proverbial "official-looking" letter is, however, still useful. Any public criticism of the Government is unwise and can result in a brief stay in prison.

Currency   The Guaraní (plural Guaraníes) is the unit of currency, symbolised by the letter G (crossed). There are paper notes for 1, 5, 10, 50, 100, 500, 1,000, 5,000 and 10,000 guaraníes and coins for 1, 5 and 10 guaraníes. The free rate of exchange at the time of going to press was G140 to the US dollar. Travellers going to Brazil and Argentina (and indeed to other countries) are advised to buy currency in Asunción, where the rates tend to favour the holder of dollars (the currencies may be cheaper on black markets in Brazil and Argentina, but this cannot be relied on in advance). There are no restrictions on the sale and purchase of foreign currencies. Get rid of all your guaraníes before leaving Paraguay; there is no market for them elsewhere. Banks will not cash travellers' cheques, only Casas de Cambio, where it is also possible to obtain US$ banknotes (2.5% commission) and travellers' cheques. Most of them are situated along Palma, near the crossing with Alberdi, in Asunción. Street touts will not necessarily give better rates than the cambios.

Sports   Football was introduced some 60 years ago, and has become remarkably popular. Almost every town and village has one or more clubs. In the capital the League has about 30 clubs, some with seating for 8,000 to 15,000 people. Tennis and horse-racing are popular. There are two rowing and swimming clubs of some 2,000 members, and a motor-boat club with 150 members. Golf is played in the Botanical Garden, and there is a Paraguayan Aviation Club. There are two boxing rings. Fishing, basketball and rugby football are popular.

Business Visitors   Nearly all foreign business is transacted at Asunción; business-men do not generally find it worth while to visit other parts of the country. From May to October is the best time for a visit. British businessmen are advised to get a copy of "Hints to Business Men Visiting Paraguay," free on application to the

Department of Trade, Export Services Branch, Room CO7, Export House, 50 Ludgate Hill, London EC4M 7HU.

Business Hours Paraguayans are up early and many shops, offices and businesses open between 0630 and 0700. Siesta (well observed during the hot season) is from 1200 to 1500. Commercial office hours are from 0730 to 1100 or 1130, and 1430 or 1500 to 1730 or 1900. Banks: from 0700 to 1030 in summer and 0700 to 1130 in winter, closed on Saturday. Government offices are open 0630 to 1130 in summer, 0730 to noon, in winter. Open on Saturday.

Weights and Measures The metric system is used except by carpenters, who use inches.

Electricity 220 volts and 50 cycles.

Postal and Telegraph Services The telephone service links Asunción with Villarrica, Encarnación, Montevideo and Buenos Aires. There is a radio-telegraph service between Asunción and Buenos Aires, Montevideo, Rio, La Paz, and Hamburg, besides several internal radio-telegraph services. International long-distance telephone calls are all routed through Buenos Aires, and are very unreliable. There is a telephone service with New York, London, Rio de Janeiro and São Paulo, and a teletype service between Asunción and New York. Branch post office in lobby of Guaraní Hotel. Time is 3-4 hours behind GMT (clocks go on one hour in the local summer).

A phone call to Britain is G2,025 for 3 minutes, plus G675 for each minute more. A telegram costs G108 a word, minimum 7. Night letter is G54 a word, minimum of 22. A telex message to Britain is G1,652 for 3 minutes plus G562 for each minute more.

Climate and What to Wear The climate is sub-tropical, with a marked difference between summer and winter. Summer (Dec. 21-March 21), is hot. Temperatures range from 25 to 43°C: tropical clothing, cotton underwear for men, light cotton or linen dresses or suits and cotton underwear for women. Shorts are never worn. Sunglasses and an umbrella are useful. The autumn (March 21 until June 21) is mild, but nights are cold. Light sweaters, coats and raincoats are needed. During winter (June 21-Sep 21) the temperature can be as low as 5°C, though it can equally well be much higher. Temperatures below freezing are rare, occur only at night, and it never snows. This season demands medium weight suits and a light overcoat for men, woollens and a top coat for women. The best time for a visit is from May to September; at other times the heat is often oppressive. The heaviest rains are from October to April, but some rain falls each month.

Cost of Living This rose rapidly in 1974 (22%), but the rise was then reduced to 8.7% in 1975 and only 3.4% in 1976. The 1977 rate rose again, to 9.4%. Cheap and comfortable hotels are hard to find—a fact that will be most noticeable to those who arrive from the Andean countries.

Tipping Hotels, restaurants, 10%. Hotel waiters, US$1.20 at beginning and end of a week's stay. Railway and airport porters US$0.15 a suitcase. Porters at docks US$0.40 a suitcase. Cinema usherettes are not tipped.

What to Buy The famous ñandutí lace, made exclusively by the women of Itauguá (see page 564). The local jewellery is also attractive. Handmade "Aho-Poí" (fine cloth) is suitable for shirts and blouses, and there are cotton thread belts for men and women in all colours. The best place to buy these items is in Villarrica. Tourists are often attracted by the leather articles, the pottery and small wooden articles made from Paraguayan woods. Some of these are exhibited, and sold, at the Inter-Express Travel Agency's shop, Galería del Turista. See also "Shopping", under Asunción (see page 562). Some 30,000 tourists visit Paraguay each year.

Health Tuberculosis creates the greatest ravages, and there are minor epidemics of malaria, typhoid, dysentery, and occasionally hepatitis. Hookworm is the most common disease in the country, and there is a considerable amount of venereal disease, goitre and leprosy. Visitors should certainly be vaccinated against smallpox, inoculated against tetanus, typhoid, and para-typhoid take anti-malaria tablets if visiting the interior, and take extreme care over such things as salad and drinking water. The tap water in Asunción is safe to drink. Medical fees are high.

Newspapers "La Tribuna"; "A.B.C. Color".

Official Holidays Jan. 1, Feb. 3, March 1, Maundy Thursday, Good Friday, May 1, 14, 15, Corpus Christi, June 12, Aug. 15, 25, Sep. 29, Oct. 12, Nov. 1, Dec. 8, 25.

The British Embassy and Consulate are in Asunción, with offices at Calle 25 de Mayo 271. Casilla de Correo 404 for correspondence. Telephone 4-9146. Telex: 139 a/b Prodrome ASN.

The United States is represented by an Embassy and Consulate on Avenida Mariscal López, at the corner of Kubitschek.

Food and Drink Typical local foods include *chipas* (maize bread flavoured with egg and cheese) and *sopa paraguaya* (a kind of dumpling of ground maize and onion). *Soyo* is a soup of different meats and vegetables, (or sometimes just soya), really delicious; *albondiga* a soup of meat balls; *bori bori* another type of soup with diced meat, vegetables, and small balls of maize mixed with cheese; *empanada* a kind of meat pastry. *Palmitos* (palm hearts) should not be missed; the beef is, of course, excellent. *Surubí,* a Paraná river fish, is worth trying. Sugar-cane juice, greatly beloved, is known as *mosto*. Fruit is magnificent.

(The two maps are from sketches drawn by Mr. and Mrs. Richard G. Pohl.)

American Express Agents Asunción: Inter-Express S.R.L., Ntra. Sra. de la Asunción 588, Tel. 48-888.

(This section has been revised with the most welcome help of Prudence Judd, late of LBI Economic Department, of Mr. C. D. Sykes, BOLSA manager in Asunción, of Rosalind and Stuart Read, resident in Asunción, and of the following travellers: Williem and Jack de Beaufort (Wassenaar, Netherlands), Diana Birkbeck and Nicholas Davies, James K. Bock (Mexico City), Andrew Cox, D. Cox (Saarenkyta, Finland), Johan P. Dahl and Ulla R. Hoyna (Sweden), Dieter E. Jungblut (W. Berlin), Paul and Theresa Legare (Ottawa), Dr. Terry McCarthy (Singapore), Klaus Matzka (Perchtoldsdorf, (Austria), Phoebe Meyer (USA), Dr. Patrick von zur Mühlen (Bonn), Dr. Margaret Peil, Inés and Joggi Riedtmann (Basel), Helga Schmidt-Frank and Herbert Schmidt (W. Germany), Lothar Springer (Münster), and Margaret Thoms and Neil Duncan (Australia).

PERU

PERU, the third largest South American country, is over twice the size of France. It is a country which presents formidable difficulties to human habitation. The whole of its western seaboard with the Pacific is desert on which rain seldom falls. From this coastal shelf the Andes rise steeply to a high Sierra which is studded with massive groups of soaring mountains and gouged with deep canyons. The highland slopes eastwards; the mountains in its eastern zone are deeply forested and ravined. At the foot of these mountains and eastwards lie the vast jungle lands of the Amazonian basin.

The coastal area, a narrow ribbon of desert, 2,250 km. long, takes up 11% of the country and holds 43% of the population. Fifty-two rivers flow from the mountains to the Pacific, but only ten have water in their beds the year round. When irrigated, the valleys are extremely fertile; almost 600,000 hectares are watered today, creating 40 oases which grow cotton throughout the country, sugar-cane and rice in the N; and grapes, fruit and olives in the S. Petroleum comes from the N and Amazonia, and guano from Pacific islands. The coastal zone is the economic heart of Peru, containing its two largest urban areas: Lima/Callao and Trujillo; it consumes most of the imports and supplies most of the exports. Climate is determined by cold sea-water adjoining deserts. Prevailing inshore winds pick up so little moisture over the cold Peruvian currrent that only for five months, from June to October, does it condense. The resultant blanket of cloud and sea-mist extends from the S to about 200 km. N of Lima. This *garúa* dampens isolated coastal zones of vegetation (called *lomas*) and they are grazed by livestock driven down from the mountains. The Peruvian coastal currrent teems with fish, and Peru normally has the largest catch in the world. The 10-12 cm. *anchoveta,* ground into fish meal for animal food and fertilizer, are an important foreign exchange earner. An astounding number of sea birds feed on them and their excrement provides guano to fertilize the oases. At rare intervals during summer a current of warm water, known as "El Niño", is blown S from the equator over the cold off-shore waters and the surface temperature rises. Evaporation is so great that the desert is deluged with rain which creates havoc; the fish migrate and the birds die in large numbers.

In the Sierra, at an average altitude of 3,000 metres, which covers 26% of the country, live 49% of the people, an excessive density on such poor land. This high-level land of gentle slopes is surrounded by towering groups and ranges of high peaks. Ten are over 6,000 metres; the highest, Huascarán, is 6,768 metres. There are many volcanoes in the S. The continental divide is the western rim of mountains looking down on the Pacific. Rivers which rise in these mountains and flow towards the Amazon criss-cross the cold and freezing surface of the plateau with canyons, sometimes 1,500 metres deep, in which the climate is tropical. Pastoral farming is possible on about 13 million hectares of the plateau; the deeper valley basins alone are suitable for arable farming.

The plateau and the mountains and canyons are inhabited mostly by Indians. There are 5,000 Indian communities but few densely populated settlements. Their literacy rate is the lowest of any comparable group in S. America. Their diet is 40% below acceptable levels. Nearly 99% of the rural population and 60% of the town dwellers have no running water or drainage. About 1,700,000 Indians speak no Spanish, though their main tongue, Quechua (the language of the Incas), now has official status; they are virtually outside the money economy.

A mostly Indian labour force of over 80,000 is engaged in mining, and mineral exports from the Sierra represents half of total exports. Minerals are mined up to 5,200 metres. Some of the sheep-farming areas are at altitudes ranging from 2,750 to 4,250 metres. Only the Andean Indian can work the mineral and agricultural wealth of these uplands, for he has become not only physically but psychologically adapted to the great altitudes.

Climate The climate of the highlands is varied: the W side is dry, but the northern and eastern half get very heavy rains from October to April, and are heavily forested up to a limit of 3,350 metres: in this area the grasslands are between the forest line and the snowline, which rises from 5,000 metres in the latitude of Lima to 5,800 metres in the S. Most of the Sierra is covered with grasses and shrubs, with Puna vegetation (bunch grass mixed with low, hairy-leaved plants) from N of Huarás to the S.

The wide areas of high and wind-swept Altiplano in S Peru are above the limit of agriculture—though some potatoes and cereals (quinoa and cañihua) are grown—but the Indians use it for grazing llamas and alpacas and sheep. It cannot support cattle. The pastoral Indians of the area, living off their flocks, are large producers of alpaca and llama and sheep wools for the local market and for export. They weave their clothes from the wools, eat the meat of their flocks, use their dried dung for fuel and the llamas for transport. They are, in short, almost entirely self-supporting.

The further away from the equator, the higher the annual range of temperature. There is a range of 4°C at Cuzco, a wider range between day and night, and a startling difference between sun and shade. It freezes in the higher altitudes all the year round.

The **Montaña,** or Selva, the forested eastern half of the Andes and the land beyond covered with tropical forest and jungle, is 62% of the country's area but holds only 8% of the population. Its inhabitants are crowded on the river banks in the cultivable land—a tiny part of the area. The few roads which have penetrated the region from the Sierra (they are given in the text) have to cope with dense forest, deep stream valleys, and sharp eastern slopes ranging from 2,150 metres in the N to 5,800 metres E of Lake Titicaca. Rivers are the main highways, though navigation is hazardous and the draught of the vessels small. The area's potential is enormous: immense reserves of timber, excellent lands for the production of rubber, jute, rice, tropical fruits and coffee and the breeding of cattle. Oilfields have been discovered southwards from the Ecuadorean border E of Iquitos down as far as Pucallpa. Few of these products come out by road to the W; most of them converge by river on Iquitos, which is 11,250 km. from Callao *via* the Panama Canal but only 1,010 km. as the condor flies.

Peru is now beginning to develop the area. Army engineers and private contractors are pushing penetration roads into the zone, and an intensive oil search is going on. The Nor Peruano oil pipeline to link the Amazon area with the coast has now been completed and Occidental Oil has discovered a large oil deposit; Peru was again self-sufficient in oil, with a small surplus for export, by the end of 1978.

Communications are all-important in integrating three such diverse areas. Much has already been done for the coastlands and the Sierra. Several roads and two railways run up the slopes of the Andes to reach the Sierra. These railways, once British owned, run from Lima in the centre and the ports of Matarani and Mollendo in the S. There are in all 2,740 km. of railway. There are three main paved roads: the Pan-American Highway runs N-S through the coastal desert and sends a spur NE into the Sierra to Arequipa, with an unpaved continuation to Puno on Lake Titicaca which then skirts the lake to Desaguadero, on the Bolivian frontier, a total of 3,418 km.; the Central Highway from Lima to Huancayo, which continues (unpaved) to Pucallpa in the Amazon basin, and the direct road from Lima N to Huarás, with the branch from Huarás W to the coast at Casma. Both roads and railways are given in the text and shown on sketch maps.

History Tom Lynch, of Cornell University, has written an interesting critique of early hunter sites in South America. There is no doubt at all that man had settled the length of the Andes by 10,500 years ago, which would mean that he arrived *via* the Bering Straits shortly after the retreat of the ice-age. Two Harvard archaeologists, Michael Moseley and Robert Feldman, have come to the conclusion based on excavations at coastal sites at Ancón, Supe, etc., that an early civilization sprang up on the coast on the basis of a fishing economy and was well developed by 2100 B.C. (This is in complete contradiction of one of archaeology's basic tenets that development of agriculture must invariably precede civilization.) The key site is Aspero near Supe, where an unprepossessing collection of low mounds facing the shore revealed stone walls, plaster clap-board shaped friezes, wall niches, a trapezoidal doorway (predating the Incas by 3,500 years) and unbaked clay figurines. One of the mounds is bisected by a gigantic looters' pit which gives an interesting cross-section across the mound, showing at least fifteen different occupation levels defined by floors and bands of ash and burnt rocks (heated and dropped into gourds or tightly-woven baskets to cook fish before the days of cooking pots).

This early start on the coast developed into a Huaca (mound)-building culture of whose works the best and easiest to visit is Garagay, within sight of Lima Airport and identified easily by an electricity pylon built on top. It is a U-shaped complex of three mounds with magnificent adobe friezes (not open to the public as there is no way of preserving them) half way up the main mound, dated by Dr. Roggero Ravines to 1000 B.C. In the huge plaza enclosed by the mounds a circular subterranean plaza has been found with symmetrical staircases. This is an important find, as a similar circular plaza was found recently at Chavín. The one at Garagay is assumed to be older as Garagay is an older site. Indeed it is now held by experts on the Chavín, such as Dr. Rosa Fung of the University of San Marcos (where there is an interesting museum including a collection of Chavín pottery) that the Chavín culture began on the coast and later spread up to Chavín de Huantar, which was a cross-roads of trade between coast, Sierra and jungle. The first readily definable culture, the Chavín, flourished mainly in the highlands near the coast from Piura S to Pisco, from about 800 to 200 BC. From this was derived the Paracas culture of the S at about 200 BC to 200 AD (see under Nazca), the high Nazca culture (400-800 AD) the more primitive culture around Lima in the centre, and the Mochica culture in the N (400-800 AD), characterized by realistic moulded pottery, sculptured wood and worked metals and by the huge adobe pyramids of the Moche valley (see under Trujillo). The southern, artistically a more abstract culture, seems to have spread into the Sierra and there given rise to the classical Tiahuanaco culture, whose great monument is the ruins of Tiahuanaco, E of Lake Titicaca in Bolivia. This culture seems to have dominated the coast from the 10th to the 13th century, but neither the Tiahuanaco culture in the S nor the Chimú culture in the N (apart from their gold work) were as effective artistically as their predecessors had been in the same areas from the 7th to the 9th centuries. In the meantime, possibly towards the end of the 11th century, the Incas had begun to rise in the Cuzco basin; their conquest of Peru and Ecuador was only completed around 1450. (Their civilization is briefly described under Cuzco.) A short time before the Spaniards arrived Peru was being ruled from Cuzco by the Sapa Inca Huáscar and from Quito by his half-brother Atahualpa, who was victorious in the civil war between the two. When Francisco Pizarro and Diego de Almagro landed a tiny force in Peru in 1532 Atahualpa, no doubt anxious for allies, allowed them to reach the Sierra. Pizarro's only chance against the formidable imperial army he encountered at Cajamarca was a bold stroke. He drew Atahualpa into an ambush, slaughtered his guards, promised him liberty if a certain room were filled with treasure, and finally killed him after receiving news that another Inca army was on its way to free him. Pushing on to Cuzco, he was at first hailed as the executioner of a traitor; Atahualpa had killed Huáscar after the battle of Huancavelica two years previously. Panic followed when the conquistadores set about sacking the city, and they fought off with difficulty an attempt by Manco Inca to recapture Cuzco in 1538. (For the whole period of the Conquest John Hemming's "The Conquest of the Incas" is invaluable.)

A mountain capital was useless to the sea-going Spaniards, and in 1535 Pizarro founded Lima, near the ocean. The same year Almagro set out to conquer Chile. Disillusioned, he returned to Peru, quarrelled with Pizarro, and in 1538 fought a pitched battle with Pizarro's men at the Salt Pits, near Cuzco. He was defeated and put to death. Pizarro, who had not been present, was assasinated in his palace at Lima by Almagro's son three years later.

For the next 27 years each succeeding representative of the Kingdom of Spain, some of whom died violent deaths, sought to subdue the Inca successor state of Vilcabamba, N of Cuzco, and to placate the fierce Spanish factions. Francisco de Toledo (appointed 1568) solved both problems during his 14 years in office; Vilcabamba was crushed in 1572 and the last reigning Inca, Túpac Amaru, put to death. For the next 200 years the Viceroys followed closely Toledo's system, if not his methods. The Major Government—the Viceroy, the High Court (Audiencia), and corregidores (administrators)—ruled through the Minor Government—Indian chiefs put in charge of large groups of natives: a rough approximation of the original Incal system. The Indians rose in 1780, under leadership of an Inca noble who called himself Túpac Amaru II. He and many of his lieutenants were captured and put to death under torture at Cuzco. Another Indian leader in revolt suffered the same fate in 1814. But this last flare-up had the sympathy of a dissident group amongst the Spanish themselves: the growing body of Creoles—or Spaniards who had been born in the new world. As elsewhere in Latin America, they resented their inferior status to the Spaniards born in Spain, the refusal to give them any but the lowest office, the high taxation imposed by the home government, and the severe restrictions upon trade with any country but Spain. Help came to them from the outside world: José de San Martín's troops, convoyed from Chile under the protection of Lord Cochrane's squadron, landed in southern Peru on September 7, 1820. San Martín proclaimed Peruvian independence in Lima on July 28, 1821, though most of the country was still in the hands of the Viceroy, La Serna. Bolívar, who had already freed Venezuela, Colombia and Ecuador, sent Sucre to Ecuador where, on May 24, 1822, he gained a victory over La Serna at Pichincha. San Martín, after a meeting with Bolívar at Guayaquil, left for Argentina and a self-imposed exile in France, whilst Bolívar and Sucre completed the conquest of Peru by defeating La Serna at the battle of Junín (August 6, 1824) and the decisive battle of Ayacucho (December 9, 1824). For about a year there was a last desperate stand in the Real Felipe fortress at Callao by the Spanish troops under General Rodil before they capitulated on January 22, 1826. Bolívar was invited to stay in Peru, but left for Colombia in 1826.

Important events were a temporary confederation between Peru and Bolivia in the 1830s; the Peruvian-Spanish War (1866); and the War of the Pacific (1879-1883). A long standing legacy of this was the Tacna-Arica dispute, which was not settled until 1929 (see under Tacna).

Population At present about 15.3m., growing at an annual rate of 2.9% (1975). Birth rate, 41 per 1,000; death rate 11.9.

Constitution The present one dates from 1933, amended in 1939. Legislation is vested in a Congress composed of a Senate and a Chamber of Deputies. Men and women over 21 who can read and write are eligible to vote; registration and voting is compulsory until the age of 60. The President, to whom is entrusted the Executive Power, is elected for six years and may not be re-elected until after one Presidential term has passed. He exercises his functions through a Cabinet of 12 members. The Constitution is now suspended.

Government On July 18, 1962, a military junta deposed President Manuel Prado and took power. Sr. Fernando Belaúnde became President on July 28, 1963, but after mounting political tension he was deposed by the Army and a military junta took over control of the country in October 1968. Under its first leader, Gen. Juan Velasco Alvarado, the junta instituted a series of drastic measures to raise the personal status standard of living of the workers and the rural Indians, by land reform, worker participation in industry, and nationalization of basic industries, exhibiting and ideology perhaps best described as "military socialism". In view of his failing health Gen. Velasco was replaced in 1975 by Gen. Francisco Morales Bermúdez and policy (in view of a mounting economic crisis and the consequent need to seek financial aid from abroad) swung to the Right. It is reported that the Government intends to hold presidential elections by 1980, and elections for a constituent assembly were held in 1978.

Peru's 24 Departments are divided into 150 Provinces, and the Provinces into 1,321 districts. Each Department is administered by a Prefect and each Province by a Sub-Prefect. There are 12 judicial districts in which justice is administered by superior and minor courts. There is a Supreme Court at Lima; the judicial system is now being reorganised.

The official religion is Roman Catholicism, but the Constitution guarantees complete religious freedom. Churches and convents are protected by the State. Civil marriage is obligatory and absolute divorce was established in 1930.

Education is free and compulsory for both sexes between 6 and 14. There are public and private secondary schools and private elementary schools. Literacy rate: 40%. There are 32 State and private universities, and two Catholic universities. A new educational system is being implemented as too many children cannot complete secondary school.

Language Spanish. Quechua, the language of the Inca empire, has become the country's second official language; it is now to be taught in all schools and may be used for all official purposes. Another important Indian language is Aymará, used in the area around Lake Titicaca.

Cities and Towns

Lima, capital of Peru, was the capital of Spanish South America from its founding in 1535 until the independence of the South American republics in the early 19th century. The wide irrigated plain on which it stands slopes gently to the sea. The Andes, whose high crest is within 160 km., send their foothills almost to the city gates. Lima, built on both sides of the Río Rímac, lies at the foot of the Cerro San Cristóbal. The city was once a pure enchantment of colonial buildings and dwellings, but its population has grown from below 100,000 to over 3,500,000—it is the fifth largest city in South America—and from amongst the traditional buildings and dwellings which still survive soar many tall skyscrapers which have changed the old skyline out of recognition. The city is now surrounded by "Pueblos Jóvenes," or shanty settlements of squatters who have migrated from the Sierra; much self-help building is in progress. There are still signs of earthquake damage after the disastrous 1970 earthquakes nearby.

Half of the town-dwellers of Peru now live in Lima and Callao. Greater Lima, with 3,500,000, contains nearly 25% of the country's total population and two-thirds of its industries.

The old town was built in the shape of a triangle, and the streets run straight and intersect at right angles. In the older part the way the streets are named may confuse the visitor. Some blocks still have the names they bore during colonial days. Several blocks make up a long street—a jirón—and the jirón is named after a Department or city or famous person. The visitor is greatly helped by the corner signs which bear, above, the name of the jirón, and below, the name of the block. Many of

the old plazas, churches and convents are still there, and Spanish-style balconies still give a charm to the streets. (Beware name changes; people continue to use Colmena for Nicolás de Piérola, Carabaya for Augusto N. Wiese and Garcilaso de la Vega for Av. Wilson, and there are many others.)

Only 12° S of the equator, one would expect a tropical climate, but from June to at least October the skies are grey; it feels almost chilly, clothes take ages to dry, and a damp *garúa,* or Scotch mist, is common. The rest of the year is mild and pleasant with temperatures ranging from 10° to 27°C.

History   The University of San Marcos was founded in 1551, and a printing press in 1595: both the first of their kind in America. The first theatre opened in 1563. The Inquisition was created in 1570 and was not abolished until 1813. For some time the Viceroyalty of Peru embraced Colombia, Ecuador, Bolivia, Chile and Argentina. The rapidly growing city was made glorious by some of the best colonial building in South America. Its wealth attracted many freebooters and in 1670 a protecting wall 11 km. long, which was demolished in 1869, was built round it.

Lima's power was at its height during the 18th century. There were few cities in the old world which could rival the wealth of its men or the luxury of its women. It was rich enough and strong enough to repel outside enemies, but it had no armour against the new libertarian ideas harrowing the old world and spreading to the new, and the arrival of San Martín on July 9, 1821, put the Viceroy to flight; he was never to return. It was only comparatively recently, with the coming of industry, that Lima began to change into what it is today.

Sightseeing   The heart of the city, at least in plan, is still what it was in colonial days. A single block S of the Río Rímac lies the Plaza de Armas; the Desamparados Station of the Central Railway is quite near. Most of what the tourist wants to see is in this area. The newer parts of the City are based on Plaza San Martín, S of Jirón de la Unión, with a statue of San Martín in the centre. In this plaza are the National, Phoenix, and Círculo Militar Clubs and the *Hotel Bolívar.* One and a quarter km. W is the Plaza Dos de Mayo. About 1 km. due S of this again is the circular Plaza Bolognesi, from which many great Avenidas radiate. These four plazas are the keys to the city.

The Jirón de La Unión, the main shopping street, runs to the Plaza de Armas, usually the first objective of visitors to Lima. In the first two blocks of La Unión several shops sell souvenirs and curios: the nearer the shops are to the best hotels the dearer the souvenirs are. Around the great Plaza de Armas stand the Government Palace, the Cathedral, the Archbishop's Palace, the City Hall and the Unión Club. The Central Post Office is opposite the visitors' entrance to Government Palace. Running along two sides are arcades with shops: Portal de Escribanos and Portal de Botoneros. In the centre is a bronze fountain put there in 1650.

The **Palacio de Gobierno** (Government Palace), built 1938, on the site of and with some of the characteristics of Pizarro's palace. Visitors' entrance is on Jirón de la Unión. Tourists are shown the Salón Dorado and the Sala de Pizarro (renamed Sala Túpac Amaru by the military government) if they are not being used for official functions. The ceremonial changing of the guard is worth watching, daily 1200-1245. The **Cathedral** has been partly reconstructed several times. See the splendidly carved stalls (mid-17th century); the silver-covered altars; the small chapel, the first on the right of the entrance, in which are Pizarro's shrivelled remains (authenticity said to be dubious) in a glass coffin; and mosaic-covered walls bearing the coats of arms of Lima and Pizarro and

Key to Map.

1. Plaza de Armas.
2. Palacio de Gobierno.
3. Cathedral.
4. Union Club.
5. Plaza San Martín.
6. Torre Tagle Palace.
7. Plaza 2 de Mayo.
8. Plaza Bolognesi.
9. Plaza Grau.
10. Palacio de Justicia.
11. National Museum of Art.
12. Museum of Italian Art.
13. Panteón de los Próceres.

14. Museum of Peruvian Culture.
16. National Library.
17. Hotel Bolívar.
18. Hotel Crillon.
19. Hotel Riviera.
20. Hotel Savoy.
21. Hotel Maury.
22. Municipal Theatre.
23. Teatro Segura.
24. Hotel Continental.
25. Hotel Sheraton.
26. Civic Centre.
27. City Hall.
28. Parque Universitario.

N.B. A good map of Greater Lima may be bought at the Jorge Chávez airport and in the main shopping streets (US$1.75). It is not a bad idea to acquire one as the Limeños are totally unreliable at giving directions.

an allegory of the "Thirteen Men of Isla del Gallo". Museum of Religious Art in the cathedral, entrance US$0.90; US$0.15 is charged to see Pizarro's remains. The archbishop's Palace was rebuilt in 1924, with a superb wooden balcony.

The **Municipalidad de Lima** (City Hall), built 1945—a magnificent building—has a picture gallery.

Near San Pedro, on Jirón Ucayali, is **Torre Tagle Palace**, the city's best surviving specimen of colonial architecture: a Sevillian mansion built in 1735. Now occupied by the Foreign Ministry, but visitors are allowed to enter courtyards to inspect fine wood-carving in balconies, wrought iron work, and a 16th-century coach complete with commode. Open to visitors 1400-1600 weekdays. Tip concierge to take you round.

A short taxi ride across the Río Rímac to see Monastery of the Barefooted Brethren (Descalzos) and the Quinta de Presa (reputed to be the house of La Perricholi, but in reality the house of a colonel of the Royal Army, Pedro Carrillo de Albornoz), now the Viceregal Museum (Museo Virreynal—see page 584). La Perricholi—real name Micaela Villegas—was a beauty, wit, actress, and mistress of Viceroy Amat (1761-1776). Legend says he installed her in this mansion, but the house the Viceroy built for her was torn down last century. She has inspired plays, an opera (by Offenbach) and many books, the best known of which is "The Bridge of San Luis Rey". The Puente de Piedra, behind Presidential Palace, is a Roman-style stone bridge built 1610. Hundreds of thousands of egg whites were used in its mortar to make a better binding.

Other important mansions worth visiting are the **Casa Pilatos**, opposite the San Francisco Church at Jirón Ancash 390; **Casa de la Riva** at Jirón Ica 426; **Casa de Oquendo** at Conde de Superunda 298; **Casa Negreiros** (a restaurant), at Jirón Azángaro 532; and **Casa de las Trece Monedas** (also a restaurant), at Jirón Ancash 536. The Casa Aliaga, at Unión 224, is still inhabited by the Aliaga family and is not open to visitors.

The Lima skyline is changing very rapidly as the skyscrapers go up. (A comfortable place for the romantic to reflect on this discomforting fact is the top of the Crillón Hotel.) The tallest building used to be the Ministry of Education, at the corner of Av. Abancay, facing Parque Univeritario, with 22 storeys, but it has now been overtaken by the headquarters of the State oil agency, Petroperú, 5 km. S in the suburbs, which is 3 metres higher.

Churches

Four notable churches are quite near the Plaza de Armas: La Merced, Santo Domingo, San Francisco, and San Pedro. **La Merced** and its monastery are in Plazuela de la Merced, Jirón de la Unión, two blocks from the Plaza de Armas. The first mass in Lima was said on this site. Very fine restored colonial façade, and attractive cloister. See the choir stalls and the vestry's panelled ceiling. Patriots of the Independence gathered in the Monastery to make the Virgin of La Merced a Marshal of the Peruvian army. **Santo Domingo** is in Jirón Camaná (first block)—a lofty church of some grandeur built in 1549. In an urn in one of the altars are the remains of Santa Rosa de Lima (1586-1617), the first saint of the New World: August 30 is her day. Pope Clement presented, 1669, the alabaster statue of the Saint in front of the altar. The University of San Marcos was at the monastery for the first 20 years of its existence, from

1551 to 1571. The main hall has some interesting relics. **San Francisco,** open till 1800, in first block of Jirón Lampa, is a baroque church with Arabic influences, finished 1674. See carved "Sillería Coral" (1622), gold monstrance set with jewels made in Cuzco (1671), and Zurbarán's paintings (1672). The monastery is famous for Sevillian tilework and panelled ceilings in the cloisters (1620). Library has 20,000 volumes. Catacombs under church and part of monastery; entry charge is US$0.75; catacombs well worth seeing, but beware of the scorpions. The baroque Church of **San Pedro,** 3rd block of Jirón Ucayali, finished by Jesuits in 1638. Marvellous altars with Moorish-style balconies, rich gilded wood carvings in choir and vestry. Several Viceroys buried here; bell called La Abuelita (the little grandmother), first rung in 1590, sounded the Declaration of Independence in 1821.

Santuario de Santa Rosa (Av. Tacna, 1st block), small but graceful church. A pilgrimage centre; here are preserved the hermitage built by Santa Rosa herself, the house in which she was born, a section of the house in which she attended to the sick, her well, and other relics. Open 0800-1245 and 1530-1900.

Las Nazarenas Church (Av. Tacna, 4th block), built around an image of Christ Crucified painted by a liberated slave in 1655 on the wall of a house occupied by an old Negro Brotherhood. This, the most venerated image in Lima, and an oil copy of El Señor de los Milagros (Lord of Miracles), encased in a gold frame, are carried on a silver litter—the whole weighing nearly a ton—on the shoulders of 30 retainers of the Negro Brotherhood dressed in purple, through the streets on October 18, 19, and 28 and again on November 1 (All Saint's Day). The procession marches to slow music; the perfume of incense fills the air; flowers rain from the balconies; old ballads are sung during halts. In the streets are numerous stands selling the "Turrón de Doña Pepa", made for the occasion, and other typical Peruvian sweets.

San Agustín (Jirón Ica, 2nd block), W of the Plaza de Armas, is a much changed old church, but its piazza (1720) is a splendid example of churriguerresque architecture. See carved choir stalls and effigies, and a sculpture of Death, said to have frightened its maker into an early grave. Some 18th century paintings by a Cuzco artist. Open 0630-1200, 1530-1900.

Fine 18th century carving also in gilt altars of **Jesús María** (Jirón Moquegua; 1st block), and in **Church of Magdalena Vieja** (1557, but reconstructed in 1931). Altar pieces, of gilded and carved wood, particularly fine. Church should be seen during visit to the museum at Magdalena Vieja. Another church worth seeing for its two beautiful Colonial doors is San Marcelo, at Av. de la Emancipación, 4th block. *Note: Churches are open between 1800 and 2100 unless otherwise stated.*

Museums

Museum of the Republic, Plaza Bolívar, Pueblo Libre, in a mansion built by Viceroy Pezuela and occupied by San Martín (1821-1822) and Bolívar (1823-1826). Exhibits: colonial and early republican paintings, manuscripts, portraits, uniforms, etc. Paintings mainly of historical episodes. 0900-1800 Mon.-Fri.; 0900-1200 Sun. Admission US$0.25. Bus No. 12 from Av. Alfonso Ugarte.

The Peruvian Gold Museum (Museo Miguel Muijica Gallo), in Monterrico, near Lima (bus 71, 596 from Parque Universitario, 1 hour), is still privately owned. An underground museum contains items which have been exhibited in the world's leading museums and a remarkably complete arms collection. Well worth seeing. Open daily, 1500 to 1900; Sat., 1500-1900, but closed holidays. Admission: US$2, students half price.

National Museum of Art, Paseo Colón, in the Palacio de la Exposición, built in 1868 in Parque de la Exposición. The building is also used for exhibitions of art. More than 7,000 exhibits, giving a chronological history of Peruvian cultures and art from the 2,000-year-old Paracas civilization until today. Excellent examples of 17th and 18th century Cuzco paintings, a beautiful display of carved furniture, heavy silver and jewelled shoes. During the autumn and winter seasons, starting in April, there are guided tours, lectures and films every Friday evening (called "viernes cultural"). 0900-1900 Tues.-Thurs., 0900-2200 Fri., closed on holidays. Admission US$0.65.

Museum of the Inquisition, Plaza Bolívar, corner of Av. Abancay and Calle Junín: the main hall, with splendidly carved mahogany ceiling, remains untouched. Court of Inquisition held here 1570-1820; until 1930 used by the Senate. In the basement there is an accurate re-creation *in situ* of the tortures. A description in English is available at the desk. Open 0900-1900 Mon.-Fri.; 0900-1700 Sat.; 0900-1300 Sun.

Museum of Anthropology and Archaeology, Av. Gral. Vivanco, Pueblo Libre, a museum for exhibition and study of art and history of aboriginal races of Peru. Most interesting textiles from Paracas and ceramics of Chimú, Nazca, and Pachacámac cultures, and various Inca curiosities and works of art. Also see the Raimundi stella and the Tello obelisk from Chavín, and the marvellous Mochica pottery, and a subterranean reconstruction of one of the galleries at Chavín. An impressive model of Machu-Picchu in the Sala Inca. Easily the most interesting museum in Peru. Open Tues.-Sat. 1000-1800, Sun. and holidays 1030-1415. Admission US$0.75 (students US$0.25), Saturdays free. Bus 12 from Av. Alfonso Ugarte, also bus 21, 41 or 48 from Parque Universitario.

There is another Archaeological Museum at Puruchuco, at the base of one of the foothills of the Andes, at Km. 11 on the Central Highway (a one-km. branch road runs to it). Open 0900-1730. Closed Mondays, May 1 and July 28. Contents: ceramics, textiles, etc., from the lower Rímac or Lima valley. Near a restored pre-Incaic ruin. Entrance: US$0.50. Chosica bus, or colectivo from Parque Universitario.

In San Isidro, on Av. Rosario, are the pre-Inca ruins of **Huallamarca**, consisting of a mound of small adobe bricks. Specimens found in the tombs are in a museum. 1000-1200, 1500-1800 (closed Mon.) Admission US$0.30. Bus No. 1 from Av. Tacna.

Museum of Peruvian Culture, Av. Alfonso Ugarte, 650, showing pots and popular art, and costumes worn by Indians in various parts of Peru, includes exhibition of *maté burilado* (carved gourds); open 1000-1700, Mon.-Fri.; 0900-1700 Sat. (closed Sun.). Admission US$0.25; free Fri. and Sat.

Rafael Larco Herrera Museum, Av. Bolívar 1515, Pueblo Libre, is the famous Chiclín pottery museum brought from Truijillo. The greatest number of exhibits stem from the Mochica period (A.D. 400-800). The Cupisnique period, dating back to 1,000 B.C., as well as exhibits from the Nazca, Chimú, and Inca periods, are also well represented. Despite the extra-cultural interest of the erotica section (separate building), this is a museum for the pottery specialist rather than for the general visitor, though it also has the best collection of pre-Columbian weaving, including a sample of two-ply yarns with 398 threads to the inch. Also several mummified weavers buried with their looms. Admission US$2, 0900-1300, 1500-1800. Closed Sundays and holidays. Bus 23 from Avenida Abancay.

Museum of the Viceroyalty (Quinta de Presa), is a fine 18th century mansion worth going over. Exhibits: colonial portraits, furniture, dresses, candelabra, and so on; one of the Viceroy's carriages is shown. Open 0900-1800. Admission US$0.25. Closed Sun. a.m. and Saturdays. Bus 10B from Parque Universitario.

Museo Histórico Militar (Real Felipe Fortress, Callao), has most interesting military relics: a cannon brought by Pizarro, a cannon used in the War of Independence, the Spanish flag that flew during the last Spanish stand in the fortress, portraits of General Rodil and of Lord Cochrane, and the remains of the small Bleriot plane in which the Peruvian pilot, Jorge Chávez, made the first crossing of the Alps from Switzerland to Italy: he was killed when the plane crashed at Domodossola on Sept. 23, 1910. Open 0900-1200, 1500-1700 (closed Mon. and Fri.; also closed Wed. during summer). Entrance free. Bus No. 56 from Plaza San Martín.

Museo Naval (Av. Jorge Chávez, off Plaza Grau, Callao), open 0900-1230, 1500-1730 on Mon., Wed., Fri. and Sat. Admission free. Bus 56 from Plaza San Martín.

Museo Hospital Dos de Mayo open 0900-1800 daily, admission US$1.25.

Pinacoteca Municipal (Municipal Building, Plaza de Armas), contains a large collection of paintings by Peruvian artists. The best of the painters is Ignacio Merino (1817-1876).

Museum of Italian Art (Paseo de la República, 2nd block), is in a building, Italian renaissance style, given by the Italian colony to Peru on the centenary of its independence. Open Tues.-Fri., 1700-2100, free of charge. Large collection of Italian works of art, but most of the paintings are reproductions. Now also houses Institute of Contemporary Art, which has many exhibitions.

Museum of Natural History (Av. Arenales, 1200) belongs to University of San Marcos. Exhibits: Peruvian flora, birds, mammals, butterflies, insects, minerals and shells. Prize exhibit is a sun fish—only two other examples known, one in Japan and another in the Auckland Museum, New Zealand. Open Tues.-Sun. 0900-1900 (Fri. to 2000); admission US$0.70. Bus No. 54A or Santa Cruz microbus (white with red line along it) from Av. Tacna.

Numismatic Museum (Jirón Junín 791). Open 1000-1300 on Mon., Wed. and Fri. except holidays.

Philatelic Museum (Central Post Office, off Plaza de Armas). Open 0800-1230, 1500-1815, Mon.-Fri., except holidays. You can buy stamps here as well, and the museum also has information on the Inca postal system.

Bullfight Museum (Hualgayoc 332, Plaza de Acho, Rímac). Open 0900-1300, 1500-1800. Closed Sat., Sun. and holidays in the afternoons. Admission US$0.20.

Amano Museum (Calle Retiro 160, Miraflores). A very fine private collection of artefacts from the Chancay, Chimú and Nazca periods owned by Mr. Yoshitaro Amano—one of the most complete exhibits of Chancay weaving. Particularly interesting for pottery and pre-Columbian textiles. Open Monday-Friday. Guided tours 1400, 1500, 1600, 1700. Phone 412909 for an appointment as only 10 people allowed in at a time. Admission free. Bus No. 1 or Santa Cruz microbus from Av. Tacna.

Pedro de Osma Museum (Av. Pedro de Osma 421, Barranco). A private collection of colonial art from the Cuzco, Ayacucho and Arequipa schools. Phone 670019 for an appointment. No. 54A bus from Av. Tacna.

Parks and Gardens

Lima has many fine parks and gardens, with a profusion of flowers and trees in leaf the year round, the results of well concealed artifical irrigation. One park, the **Alameda de los Descalzos,** at the foot of the Cerro San Cristóbal, was built by a viceroy as early as 1610. This alameda is a walk shaded by ancient trees and fenced by a wrought-iron grill. It was, even into the early days of the Republic, a haunt of Lima's aristocracy, though today it is run-down. The marble statues, each representing a month of the year, and the marble seats date from 1856. Nearby is another walk, the **Paseo de Aguas,** created by the Viceroy Amat at the end of the 18th century to please his mistress, La Perricholi. The great arch with cascades was rebuilt in 1938.

Campo de Marte (Plaza Jorge Chávez and Av. Salaverry), a large open park. In the centre is a huge monument to "The Peruvian Soldier". The National Symphony Orchestra plays in the auditorium on the W side during the summer.

Parque Universitario, where the old San Carlos Jesuit church was turned into a **Pantheon of the Heroes** (Panteón de los Próceres) on the 100th anniversary of the Battle of Ayacucho. A gracious 18th century church with a circle of famous tombs under the rotunda. General Miller, the Englishman who fought in the wars of independence, and whose memoirs contain an excellent picture of the time, is buried here, and so is Admiral Guise, of Gloucestershire, who was killed at Guayaquil. Also the poet and composer who wrote the Peruvian national anthem. Next to the church is the former building of San Marcos University, which has now been restored and is used for meetings and conferences. Worthy of a visit is the beautiful patio and the small archaeological museum. In the centre is the clock tower presented by the German colony on the centenary of Peruvian independence. On the far corner of the park is the great 22-storey Ministry of Education building.

Paseo Colón is the avenue which lies between where old Lima ends and modern Lima begins. There is a monument to Columbus in the Paseo (1856). Between it and Av. 28 de Julio is **Parque de La Exposición,** a quiet place shaded by trees; several of the main avenues border it. It was opened for the 1868 International Exhibition. The great Palace of the Exhibition, facing Paseo Colón, is now the Museum of Art. North of Parque de la Exposición, across Paseo Colón, is the quiet

Parque Neptuno, shaded by trees. Within its grounds is the Museum of Italian Art (see page 584), and a fountain of Neptune.

Parque de la Reserva (Av. Arequipa, 6th block). In the middle is a statue of Sucre; of the other two statues, one is of Tangüis, who selected the famous cotton. Overlooking the park is the 14-storey rectangular glass and aluminium tower of Edificio El Pacífico-Washington (British and Israeli embassies).

Parque de las Leyendas, between Lima and Callao, one of the most interesting parks, beautifully arranged to represent the three regions of Peru: the coast, the mountainous Sierra, and the tropical jungles of the Montaña, with appropriate houses, animals and plants, recommended, children's playground. The Park, which has been described as a zoo with a difference, is open 0900-1630 (closed Mondays), entrance US$0.25. There is a handicrafts fair (Feria Artesanal) at the entrance to the park.

A look at Lima   A good deal of Lima and its environs can be seen by following this itinerary: 0930. Walk to the Plaza de Armas and visit the Cathedral. Engage a taxi for a few hours and visit San Francisco church and its catacombs, the Inquisition Building, the Torre Tagle Palace and San Pedro church, then over the River Rimac to pass by the Acho bull ring, Paseo de Aguas and Alameda de los Descalzos. Lunch at the superb Tambo de Oro restaurant. In the afternoon drive to Miraflores by the beautiful Avenida Arequipa, passing by the Olivar in San Isidro and seeing the attractive residential areas. From Miraflores drive to the Archaeological Museum just off Av. de la Marina, and if time permits, visit the two native handicraft markets on that avenue. You should arrive back in the centre of Lima by about 1700. This should cost you at the most US$30 per car, including entrance fees, but not, of course, lunch.

If travelling on a budget, you can have a lot of fun taking a tour by bus, and there is certainly nothing cheaper. Buses leave from the Plaza San Martín for Callao and La Punta. Come back to Callao in the same bus and change to a No. 48 at Plaza Grau (better than Av. 2 de Mayo as will pass Parque de las Leyendas). This bus comes back to Lima via Pueblo Libre and Jesús Maria. Get off at the Parque Universitario, cross the street and walk 3 blocks to the Plaza San Martín again. This time take the No. 2 bus on the corner of the Colón cinema. This bus will take you right down Avenida Arequipa to Miraflores. Get off at Barranco by the Parque Confraternidad and take the 54A on into Chorrillos. Take the same bus back to Lima and stay on as it goes through the centre in order to see the Rimac section. The bus will bring you back to Avenida Tacna, 4 blocks from the Plaza San Martín, where you started. This extensive tour will cost you the princely sum of US$0.80, but you are recommended to try it between 1000 and 1600, outside rush hours!

Hotels

			US$		Tax &
Name	Address	Beds	Single	Double	Service
Miraflores Cesar's	La Paz y Diez Canseco, Miraflores		35.00	45.00	21%
Lima Sheraton	Paseo de la República 170	650	35.00	40.00	21%
Gran Bolívar	Plaza San Martín	350	28.00	36.00	21%
Crillón	N. de Piérola 589	620	27.00	36.00	21%
Country Club	Av. Golf, San Isidro	150	24.00	36.00	21%
Continental	Puno 196	150	15.00	20.00	17%
Gran Maury	Ucayali 201	140	13.00	22.00	17%
Savoy	Cailloma 224	400	17.00	25.00	21%
Alcázar	Camaná 564	160	18.00	26.00	17%
Riviera	Inca G. de la Vega 981	300	27.00	39.00	21%
Columbus	Av. Arequipa 1421	150	15.00	20.00	17%
Wilson	Chancay 639	150	9.00	14.00	17%
La Granja Azul					
Country Inn	16 km. out, off Central Highway		23.00	36.00	21%

All hotel prices rose steeply in 1976 and 1977, so these lists may not be completely up-to-date.

There are many pensiones, at from US$35 a week, with meals. Two excellent ones (25 and 15 minutes respectively by bus to centre) are Mrs. Tupholme's *Hotel Residencial Miramar,* at Malecón Cisneros 1244, Miraflores, US$13.50 s per day with all meals, and the *Beach* (US$12.50 a day, including food); another guest house is run by Mr. and Mrs. E. Dawson (US$12 and large English breakfast) at Raimundo Morales de la Torre 138, San Isidro, Tel.: 224514 (must book); these well-run English pensiones are highly recommended. Also at San Isidro, *Pensión Astoria,* US$4.70 a day including breakfast and dinner; also has small apartments with kitchenette and maid service, US$8.10 a day. Another very good pensión is run by Pablo W. See at Hernán Velarde 72, moderately priced, 5 minutes by bus to centre. *Hotel Damasco,* Jirón Ucayali 199, a block from Plaza de Armas, shower, hot water, US$7.50 d; take a back room. Good middle income hotels are *Hotel del Sol,* across from the Teatro Municipal, US$11 d, and *Hotel Oriental.* Jirón Cuzco 696, US$6 s, US$11 d, a bit noisy but recommended; *Hotel Universo,* 1 block from Parque Univeritario, US$6 s, with bath; P.C. Volunteers US$2. *Pensión Antoinette,* Miraflores, US$8 s with breakfast; *Hotel Claridge,* Cailloma 437, US$14 d, being refurbished. Those who don't mind some discomfort can try the *Casa Vasca,* A. N. Wiese 1033, good full board, US$8; the *Residencial Camaná,* US$2; or *Pensión Belén,* just off San Martín, S of La Unión, US$6.50 d, good value (hot showers), full board, annex of the *Belén* is above the Y.M.C.A. annex at Augusto N. Wiese 664, US$3.30 p.p. incl. continental breakfast; *Pensión Machu-Picchu,* Jirón Cailloma 231, central, dear for what you get. *Richmond Hotel,* Jirón de la Unión, US$4 p.p. not very friendly, but central. Cheaper accommodation includes *Hotel Sandia,* US$3 s; *Hotel Carona,* off Av. Abancay near Parque Universitario, US$4 d with bath, dingy but cheap; *Hotel Europa,* Jirón Ancash 376, near Plaza San Francisco "gringo" hotel and most popular hotel for budget travellers in Lima, US$2 each in 4-6 bedded rooms, hot water at times, good, friendly; *Hotel Pacífico,* Augusto N. Wiese, near presidential palace and station, US$3.50 d, only front rooms have windows, basic, hippy, convenient; *Residencial Roma,* Ica 326, US$7 d with bath; *Hotel Amat,* Av. Cuzco 777, US$3 d, with bath. YMCA annex, Augusto N. Wiese 664, full board US$3.20 p.p., clean and friendly, with hot showers. *Hotel Gran,* Av. Avancay 546, US$5.50 d, spacious rooms, clean; *Alojamiento Hamburg,* Av. N. de Piérola 459, US$2 s. *Pensión Ibarra,* Av. Tacna 359, Apt. 162, US$5 d, including breakfast, clean, friendly, very helpful owner, full board available; *Hotel San Cristóbal,* US$1.20; *Hotel Colmena,* US$7.50 d with bath, clean and old fashioned (near Plaza San Martín); *Hotel Comercio,* next door to *Pacífico,* though not as friendly, US$3 d, hot shower US$0.30 extra; *Hotel San Carlos,* US$6.50 with bath; *Pensión Unión,* Jirón Unión, entry through bookshop (Librería Unión), US$1.50 s, US$3 d; on same street, *Pensión Lima,* recommended. Three new *pensiones* recommended are *Hostal Huaychulo,* Av. 2 de Mayo 494, Miraflores, excellent (German owner-manager); *Hostal Callacocha,* Coronel Andrés Reyes 100, *San Isidro,* very good; *Hostal Miraflores,* Av. Petit Thouars 5444, Miraflores, US$14. English and German spoken. Also try *Hotel Comansa,* Moquegua 299, new and clean, US$6.75 p.p., and *Pensión Alemana,* Av. Arequipa 4704, *Hotel Astor,* Jirón Pasura 1345; *Hotel Leticia* US$2.50 d. If arriving by air, especially at night, a visit to the tourist office at the airport (before passport control) is helpful if you want to arrange a hotel room.

China town Lima's Chinese district is centred on Calle Huallaga, south of Av. Abancay. Chinese clothing, food and souvenirs.

Camping Apparently possible near beach at Miraflores, and off beach road near lighthouse. Closer than Miraflores is the German Club at Avenida Tomás Marsano and Alfredo Benavides, SSE of Lima, US$0.30 per vehicle per day. May have to take temporary membership out, but tennis courts and swimming pool may be used. Propane gas available from Delta-Gas, Av. Benavides (former Colonial) 5425, Lima.

Electric Current 220 volts A.C., 60 cycles.

Restaurants In the past few years many new restaurants serving food of excellent quality have opened in Lima, Miraflores and San Isidro. In Lima we can recommend the restaurants at the *Crillón* and *Bolívar* hotels (see **Hotels,** above); *Roof Garden* 91, Avenida Wilson 911; *El Cortijo Steak House,* N. de Piérola 890; *Tambo de Oro,* (Unión 1066), lavish, colonial decor, excellent international and criollo cooking, music and a select handicraft market, described to us as "the most beautiful restaurant in Peru", also very expensive; *El Dorado* (Chinese); *Vista Alegre,* Av. Atocongo 1401, Surco section (Creole and Chinese); *Casa de Vasca,* good food and atmosphere; *Goyescas,* Plaza S. Martín; *Espinel* (seafood); *Giannino,* R. Torrico 899; *La Granja Azul,* (also hotel—see previous page) Carretera Central (turn off between Km. 13 and 14 of Carretera Central, buses from Parque Universitario every 15 minutes; last bus back leaves 2000 but a minibus leaves the hotel for Lima at 2200), a really high spot, specialising in exotic cocktails and chicken dishes, dancing every night; *Restaurant Kuo Wha,* Pasaje Sta. Rosa 115, just off Plaza de Armas; *Las Trece Monedas,* in an old colonial mansion off Av. Abancay (Ancash 536), but insist on an itemised bill; *Chalet Suisse,* Av. Nicolás de Piérola 560, recommended, international cuisine; *Rosita Ríos* (Av. el Altillo 100, Rimac section), for highly seasoned Peruvian food at reasonable prices, easy to get back to Lima by bus; *Mesón La Ronda,* in the Bullring, has an excellent Bullfight Museum. *Raimondo,* Miró Quesada 110, excellent throughout price range. Cheaper restaurants include: *Rincón Toni,* Nicolás de Piérola, friendly service, main dishes US$2 (German food, good); *El Torreón* (Jirón Camaná 571), good, US$1.50 p.p.; *Don Juan* (off Plaza de Armas), good and cheap; *Salón de Té Colmena* (Nicolás de Piérola 1139), excellent simple food, served quickly. Also try Rimac section of city, over Puente de Piedra, for cheaper food, e.g. the chicken restaurants on Av. Trujillo. There is a reasonable vegetarian restaurant at Augusto N. Wiese 744, where a meal costs US$1.05; another vegetarian restaurant in Calle Ica, US$0.75 lunch or dinner. For students, Comedor Universitario Cangallo, filling meal for US$0.20. An excellent coffee bar for snacks and sandwiches is *Googies* in Plaza San Martín; also Tivola bar, Nicolás de Piérola 820. Also try *Restaurante Bar Mesón del Marqués,* Calle Azángara, near the Torre Tagle Palace, dinner expensive but lunch is cheap and good, piano music; *Restaurante Balkan,* Av. Tacna 555 (German spoken); *Comedor Nacional* at Jirón Ocoña and Jirón Cailloma, nr. Garcilaso de la Vega, good and cheap. *Restaurante Populares* near Hotel Crillón on Jirón Ocoña (full course meal US$0.50); *Restaurante Cordano* near Desumparados station, reasonably priced; *Restaurante Chez Guelle,* opp. Hotel Savoy on Av. Cailloma. 3-course meal US$0.80. Near the Hotel Europa on corner of Ancash and Lampa there is a Chinese restaurant, recommended for its good quality, low prices and large portions. There are good cheap fish restaurants near Parque Universitario. For breakfast there is a good café underneath the Hotel Pacífico. Also recommended, *Restaurante Luigi* near Panteón de los Próceres, US$1.20 meal.

   In San Isidro these restaurants are recommended: *Aquarium* (at the Country Club Hotel); *La Calesa; La Caleta* and *La Barca* (both sea food); *The Key Club; Beverley Inn; Todo Fresco* (sea food); *Lung Fung* (Chinese); *Ebony* 56; *Micasa* (Japanese); *Todos* (American style); *Blue Room* at Las Begonias No. 379; *El Chalán,* Av. Limatambo 3091; *The Unicorn,* 3030 Paseo de la República; *La Chasse à Licorne,* expensive.

   In Miraflores we recommend the following: *Roxy* (quite good, Italian); *El Pacífico Chifa* (Pacífico Building); *La Pizzería* (Avenida Diagonal); *Bavaria,* Av. Diagonal (German style); *Pío Pío,* specialises in chicken; *Kuo Wha,* Paseo de la República 5046; *El Cendrillón; Firenze; La Costa Verde; Rincón Gaucho* (speciality Argentine parrilladas); *La Barca* (sea food), Av. del Ejército 2195. *Restaurante Daworís* and *El Tieber* recommended, to meet local people. Typical Peruvian restaurants serving Creole food can be found at the end of Avenida Brasil. Two vegetarian restaurants are the *Bircher Berner* and *Restaurante Samas,* excellent and inexpensive. Try also *Restaurante Carlin,* Av. de la Paz 644. In Magdalena, *Restaurante José Antonio* (Peruvian food, music after 2200), Monteagudo 210 B.

Air Lines   All the main airlines serving Peru, except Braniff and Faucett (in Unión) and Avianca (Av. Tacna 665), have their offices along Av. Nicolás de Piérola.

Tourist Offices   Enturperú, which administers the State Tourist Hotel chain, has moved to Jirón Unión 1066, open Mon.-Fri., 1000-1900, very helpful. All tourists should visit this office, where rooms in the state hotels may be booked in advance. (There is another office at the airport.) The Dirección General de Turismo, Avenida Corpac, San Isidro, in the Ministry of Industry building (behind the Ministry of the Interior) provides maps and folders on Lima, Cuzco, Puno, Iquitos, etc. A useful map of Lima can be found in telephone directories. The pink paper in the telephone directories shows the itineraries of Lima buses, or you can buy a "transit map" from news stands for US$0.50. A good map of the whole country is available free from Petroperú, Av. Corpac and Paseo de la República, Mon.-Fri. 1000-1100 and 1400-1500; must show your passport.

Bus Offices Tepsa, Roggero, Morales Moralitos are on Paseo de la República, Olmeño depot is near Parque Universitario. Colectivos leave for all parts of Peru from Parque Universitario.

The Peruvian Touring and Automobile Club, at Av. César Vallejo 699, Lince, Lima (Tel.: 403270), offers help to tourists and particularly to members of the leading associations of motorists. Letters to Casilla No. 22-19 Lima. Good maps available cheaply.

Tourist Information See the publication "Adónde Iré Hoy?" ("Where shall I go today?"). There is also a small American booklet (name not known) at ABC bookshop for US$0.60, about Lima. Best guide to archaeological sites is *Manual de Arqueología Peruana,* by Kaufmann Doig, on sale from stalls and most bookshops. Only published in Spanish. Booklet "Lima, City of Treasures and Traditions" by Frances E. Parodi (published by the American Woman's Literary Club, Lima).

Travel Agents Sudex S.A., Sudamérica building (Plaza San Martín), of. 311-314, Tel.: 28-6054; Lima Tours, Ocoña 160, Tel.: 27-6624, Exprinter, N. de Piérola 805; Coltur S.A., Jr. Camaná 868; Melitur, Av. Emancipación 328; Wagons Lits/Cook, Jr. Ocoña 170; Universal Travels, R. Torrico 965; Dasatour S.A., Jr. A. N. Wiese 671; Turamérica S.A. Jirón Ocoña 164; Receptur S.A. Rufino Torrico 889; Laser Tours, Av. Nicolás de Piérola 757; Casupia Express Tours S.A., Tel.: 289-551, Av. N. de Piérola 661.

Peruvian travel agents offer a wide and varied series of package tours to all places likely to interest a tourist in Peru.

Taxis No taxis have metres, so try to fix rates first. Official fares: on entering US$0.12; each 300 metres US$0.02, say about US$0.50 for short journeys and US$1 from the centre to the suburbs. After 2200, 50% surcharge. Be careful of "pirate" taxis; they usually charge 50% more.

Drivers don't expect tips; give them small change from the fare. If hiring a taxi for over 1 hour agree on price per hour beforehand. To Callao, La Punta, San Miguel, Magdalena, Miraflores, Barranco, Chorrillos, by agreement, basis US$5 per hour. Colectivos are fine, with legally fixed prices, e.g. US$0.05 from Miraflores to Lima centre. Taxi to or from airport, US$5, but the colectivos from Av. Nicolás de Piérola charge only US$0.20 p.p. and per item of luggage. However they run only during the daytime.

Self-drive cars from US$10 a day plus US$0.10 per km. depending on size, plus US$2 a day for insurance. Local petrol is US$0.80 a gallon, more for high octane. Cars can be hired from Hertz Rent-a-Car, 262 Ocoña (beside *Hotel Bolívar*), Tel.: 289477; Graf Automóviles Seleccionados, S.A. (Avis); Av. Petit Thouars 915, Tel., 233486; Turamérica, 164, Ocoña (beside *Hotel Bolívar*), Tel.: 276413-5, or 590 Nicolás de Piérola (opp. *Hotel Crillón*), Tel.: 278970. Beware of deep street potholes.

Motor Parts International Motors S.A. in Lima is only Land Rover agent in Peru; 100% tax on all imported parts!

Night Clubs International cabaret—"Sky Room" at the *Crillón Hotel,* "Embassy" in the Plaza San Martín and "Yorkas" on Av. Nicolás de Piérola. "Charlie's Night Club", Le Popol", "Peppermint Club", Latin American cabaret—"El Tumi" in San Isidro and "El Palermo" in *Residencial San Felipe.* "Creole" or Peruvian cabaret, very lively and great fun; "El Chalán in San Isidro, US$4 admission, a very good typical show; "La Peña de Pocho Ugarte" (ex-Huerto de mi Amada) in Miraflores.

Bars (with music) *Ed's Bar, Charlie's Peppermint Bar,* Av. Corpac, *Percy's Candlelight Room,* at Todos shopping centre, all in San Isidro. *Johann Sebastian Bar* in Miraflores. Those on a tight budget might enjoy the indulgence of having a 'pisco sour' in the Bar Bolívar of the *Gran Hotel Bolívar.* It costs only US$1 and is served in luxurious surroundings.

Discotheques Unicorn, Jumbo, Ebony 56 and Bonnie and Clyde in San Isidro. Unicorn del Mar at Herradura beach in summer.

Theatre Most professional plays are put on at the Teatro Segura, Teatro Municipal (Jirón Ica, 300 block—also orchestral and ballet performances); Teatro Arequipa and Sala Alzedo. Others are produced by amateur and University groups. See the newspapers for announcements. Teatro Cabaña in the Parque de la Exposición puts on strong programme of progressive theatre. Theatre Workshop, Jirón Ica 323.

Folklore Every Sunday at the Coliseo Cerrado, Av. Alfonso Ugarte. For the more sophisticated, the Sky Room of the Hotel Crillón every evening. Good to visit Lima during Fiesta de la Patria, July 24th to 30th.

Bridge Clubs Av. Santa María 125, Miraflores (Hall of the Church of the Good Shepherd) duplicate games for pairs open to all bridge players every Thursday at 1945 sharp. For further information call Mrs. Lola Bonner, Tel.: 222252.

Club de Bridge del Perú, Máximo Abril 596, Lima, Tel.: 246041. Duplicate games every Tuesday and Friday at 1945. For ladies: every Monday, 1545.

Best Buys Silver and gold handicrafts of all kinds, often very beautiful; Indian hand-loomed and hand-spun textiles; manufactured textiles in unusual Indian designs; an infinity of llama and alpaca wool products such as ponchos, rugs, hats, blankets, slippers, coats, sweaters, etc.; fine leather products mostly hand made. Silvania prints, found at N. de Piérola 727, are modern silk-screen prints with pre-Columbian designs. Huancayano, Unión 1041—native handicrafts. Plaza México—jewellery in pre-Columbian designs. On Av. Nicolás de Piérola vendors sell oil paintings of Andean scenes, bargains abound. The *maté burilado,* or carved gourd found in every tourist shop, is cheap, interesting, lends itself to modern decor, and is a genuine expression of folk art (cheaper in Huancayo). One of the best selections of folk art, but not the cheapest, will be found at the Artesanías del Perú shops in Lima, Cuzco, Arequipa and Iquitos. Native handicrafts are sold at the Mercado Artesanal in Pueblo Libre on Avenida de la Marina 790, about 6 km. from the centre; take bus 48 on Av. Abancay but watch your possessions closely as thieves are abundant. Also in Pueblo Libre, Artesanía El Inca, junction of Av. de la Marina with Av. Sucre, great variety of handicrafts, cheap. Artesanía Huancayana, Belén 1041 between Hotels *Sheraton* and *Bolívar,* the best store for high-quality weavings, specializes in Indian weavings from San Pedro de Cajas. Next door is a permanent exhibition incl. a century-old loom. EPPA (Empresa Peruana de Promoción Artesana) Belén 1066, government store for Peruvian handicrafts; stores also in San Isidro and Cuzco. Art-Andina, Belén 1045, good selection of Indian weaving and rugs. Pre-Columbian textiles can be bought from a nameless shop in an alley off Jirón de la Unión, on right between Plaza San Martín and Plaza de Armas, past Merced church. On Unión itself is Casa Mas, with a wonderful display of gold and silver handicrafts. In Miraflores, lovely shopping arcade called El Suche at La Paz 646 (excellent restaurant there, *El Carlín*). Most Indian textiles, alpaca and llama products are cheaper in Cuzco, Puno, Arequipa and Bolivia. Vicuña is unobtainable for the time being in Peru and Bolivia alike. Souvenirs are much dearer in Lima than elsewhere. See H. Stern's jewellery stores at Hotels Bolívar and Sheraton. (Note: It is better to buy pullovers in the Sierra. However, although Lima is more expensive, it is often impossible to find the same quality of goods elsewhere.)

Shops are open from 0930 to 1245 and from 1615 to 1900 in summer time (January to March). From 0900 to 1245 and 1515 to 1900 from April to December. Some shops close on Saturday afternoon.

Bookshop ABC Bookstores S.A., Edificio Hotel Bolívar, Plaza San Martín; also at N. de Piérola 689, Todos shopping area, Galax commercial centre, Miraflores and Jorge Chávez airport. Books and magazines in English, French and German.

Supermarkets Todos, Super Epsa, Galax, Scala Gigante, Monterrey.

Department Stores Sears Roebuck, Oechsle (good book department), Santa Catalina, Monterrey, Tía and Scala, all down town in or near Jirón de la Unión, the best shopping area, and also in surburbs.

Launderette Rápido, Augusto N. Wiese 1027-1029, off Plaza San Martín.

Sports There are two bull-fight seasons, one in October-November and a short one in March. They are held in the afternoons on Sundays and holidays. Tickets at 2nd block of Calle Huancavelica, or at the Plaza de Acho bullring early on the day of the corrida. Famous toreros practise in the Lima ring, the oldest in the Americas, and fighting bulls are of Spanish stock. Cockfights are frequently organised and advertised: the Plaza de Gallos at Calle Sandía 150, near Parque Universitario, is recommended, US$2 for best seats. Horse racing on Tuesday and Thursday evenings and Saturday and Sunday afternoons in summer, and in winter on Tuesday evening and Saturday and Sunday afternoons. Colectivos on race days leave from the Plaza San Martín. Fare US$0.10. The popular stand is not recommended. Pelouse and Primera stands US$0.60. Tourists may enter the members' stand on production of their passports. The Lima, Inca, Granja Azul and La Planicie golf clubs and the Country Club de Villa all have 18-hole courses. The Santa Rosa, Cruz de Hueso and Huampani golf clubs have 9-hole courses. (Contact Mr. Astruck of Sudex S.A., telephone 28-6054, for particulars.) Polo and tennis are also played. Boxing or "All-in" wrestling (Saturday night) at the Coliseo Nacional.

Association football matches and various athletic events take place at the National Stadium, seating 45,000, well placed in the centre of the city on ground given by the British community on the 100th anniversary of Peru's Declaration of Independence.

Banks Bank of London & South America, Ltd., Augusto N. Wiese 442, and branches at Avenida Arenales, San Isidro, Callao and Miraflores; Citibank, Av. N. de Piérola 1062; Bank of America, Augusto Tamayo, San Isidro. Peruvian banks. Open: Jan. 1 to March 31—0830 to 1130; April 1 to Dec. 31—0830 to 1200. Closed Saturday except Banco de la Nación in Rufino Torrico (opposite *Hotel Crillón*), which is open Sats. 0900-1300.

Post Offices The main post office is on Jirón Junín, west of the Plaza de Armas. An ordinary post office is on Av. Nicolás de Piérola, opp. Hotel Crillón. Buy stamps in Lima; post offices elsewhere hard to find.

Cables Nationalized on March 1st 1975. Offices at Jirón A. Miró Quesada 324, sub-offices at Hotels *Bolívar, Crillón* and *Country Club,* also Jirón Lampa 667 and San Isidro. Public telex booths.

Airport The Jorge Chávez airport is 16 km. from the centre of Lima. Taxi, about US$5, though double outside normal hours. Colectivos leave frequently from Av. N. de Piérola in the day-time, US$0.20 p.p. and per item of luggage. There is a duty-free shop, dearer than at Bogotá, but none at La Paz, Buenos Aires or Santiago. Airport tax of US$5 (payable in dollars) for international flights.

Rail Central Railway of Peru maintains passenger and freight service to Oroya (with an extension N to Cerro de Pasco) and S to Huancayo (with an extension to Huancavelica). The train to Huancayo leaves Desamparados station daily except Sun. at 0740, arriving about 12 hours later. The return train leaves 0700, arriving Lima 1600. Single, 1st class, US$4.50, 2nd US$3.50. You can buy your ticket from 1430 the previous day. Train Oroya-Cerro de Pasco, 2 hours, US$1.50. Guard your possessions very carefully against pickpockets and thieves at the station.

Roads The Pan-American Highway is open from Lima N along the coast to the Ecuadorean frontier, and S to Arequipa and Chile. It is mostly through desert, with occasional valley oases. The Central Highway from Lima goes through Oroya NE to Cerro de Pasco, Huánuco, Tingo María and terminates at Pucallpa on the Ucayali River. From Oroya a branch goes SE to Huancayo, Ayacucho, Cuzco, Puno on Lake Titicaca, and on into Bolivia. These two roads to Cuzco, one by the Central Andes and the other by Arequipa and Puno, make a grand circuit of 2,400 km. possible. Preferably it should be done clockwise: there would be less driving on the outsides of precipices; it would be *downhill* on the bad stretch between Puno and Arequipa, and the return to Lima would be by a good road. Another road from Lima to the Sierra deviates from the Lima-Oroya highway at Chosica; it goes along the Río Santa Eulalia and joins the road from Oroya to Cerro de Pasco just beyond Marcapomacocha. The main road is miserably bad from Huancayo to Cuzco; the Puno-Cuzco section has short paved sections at each end. Most of the high Sierra roads are dangerous, narrow, unsurfaced and liable to landslides; many accidents. Make sure you travel with a reliable company. Coastal buses are usually good (especially Roggero) although liable to delays. Tepsa and Morales-Moralitos operate in the Sierra; in view of the road surfaces, their buses often break down.

Buses   The Peruvian Turismo Expreso Pullman (Tepsa), offices opp. Sheraton hotel, Av. de la República, runs a twice weekly service to Santiago, Chile (3,500 km.) leaving Lima on Thursday and Sunday at 0830, fare US$35. Arrives on the third day at 1200. Also twice weekly services to Guayaquil and Quito leaving Lima on Wednesday and Sunday at 0845. Fare US$22.50 to Guayaquil and US$24 to Quito. The trip takes 2½ days; often long frontier delays. The Roggero bus company also covers the trip to Santiago, Chile and is recommended for it, 60 hours with an overnight stop in Arica. It also goes to Quito. Tepsa runs to Trujillo for US$5.65, 9 hours, leaving 0830, 2100 and 2200 daily.

Morales Moralitos run to La Paz *via* Arequipa and Puno three times a week, on Tuesday, Friday and Sunday, leaving Lima at 1300, taking 2½ days. Fare US$24. (Lima-Arequipa, 17-18 hrs. US$11.) Also to Tacna, US$11.50. Roggero runs to Arequipa, 19 hours, US$10 and to Tumbes, US$11. We should mention that we have received many complaints about the services of Morales; they seem to be unreliable on bookings, to the extent that only the journeys between terminal points of a service can be guaranteed to take place without some difficulties.

Warning   Luggage often snatched at terminals. Make sure your luggage is well guarded and put on the right bus.

These international trips are much cheaper if one is prepared to take buses to frontier posts only, walk across frontiers, and buy tickets as one goes along; on the other hand the extra paperwork involved, as compared with the through bus, is irritating. To enter Peru, a ticket out of the country must be produced. If you have to buy a bus ticket, be warned: they are not transferable or refundable.

British Schools   Markham College, for boys of all ages, is one of the only four Headmasters' Conference Schools outside the Commonwealth. Colegio San Andrés, for boys, run by the Free Church of Scotland. Colegio San Silvestre, a school for girls at Miraflores; it is represented in the Association of Headmistresses. Colegio Peruano-Británico, San Isidro, co-educational.

American Schools   The American School of Lima, Monterrico, co-eductional: Villa María, La Planicie (for girls); María Alvarado, Lima (girls).

Alliance Française, Avenida Garcilaso de la Vega 1850.

Addresses

British Embassy and Consulate: Edificio Pacífico-Washington, Plaza Washington, corner of Av. Arequipa (5th block) and N. Sánchez. Tel.: 283830.
U.S.A. Embassy and Consulate: Av. Wilson 1400. Tel.: 286000.
Canadian Embassy: 130 La Libertad. Tel.: 46-3890.
Australian Embassy: Plaza Washington, 5th block, Av. Arequipa. Tel.: 288315.
New Zealand Embassy: Av. Salaverry 3006, San Isidro. Tel.: 621890.
Swiss Consulate: Las Camelias 780, 2nd floor, open 0900-1200. Tel.: 227706.
South African Embassy and Consulate in Plaza Washington, 5th block Av. Arequipa. Tel.: 247949.

P.S.N.C.: Nicolás de Piérola 1002-06, Plaza San Martín (in the same building as the Phoenix Club). Tel.: 283250.

Y.M.C.A.: Jirón Augusto N. Wiese 664. New building with more facilities on Avenida Bolívar in suburb of Pueblo Libre.

Peruvian-British Cultural Association, Jirón Camaná 787, Tel.: 277927; branches at Av. Benavides, 620, Miraflores, Tel.: 454326, and at Av. Arequipa 3485, San Isidro. A two-days old *Daily Telegraph* can be read there.

British Council, Edificio Pacífico-Washington, Av. Arequipa. Tel.: 283770.

Peruvian North American Cultural Institute, Jirón Cuzco 446 (said to be good place to eat, too), branch at Av. Arequipa 4798, Miraflores.

Anglo-American Hospital, Av. Salazar, 3rd block, San Isidro. Tel.: 403570.

American Chamber of Commerce, Juan de Arona, San Isidro.

The Union Church of Lima (Interdenominational), Av. Angamos 1155, Miraflores.

Trinity Lutheran Church of Peru, Las Magnolias 495, Urb. Jardin, San Isidro.

Church of the Good Shepherd, Av. Santa Cruz 491, Miraflores (Anglican).

First Baptist Church of Lima, Av. Garcilaso de la Vega, 1734.

Christian Science Society, 1285 Mayta Capac (near Av. Salaverry) Jesús María.

Santa Fe Clinic (Av. Abancay), US$4.50 consultation fee. Doctors speak English but nurses not used to giving injections.

The American Society of Peru, Calle Retiro, Miraflores. Tel.: 20659.

Hospital de Niñas, Av. Brasil, Vaccination centre at the side.

Clubs (for golf clubs, see page 591 under **Sports**) Phoenix Club: Av. Nicolás de Piérola 1014, 3rd floor (Plaza San Martín). The Club Callao, Callao. Lima Cricket and Football Club: Sánchez Carrión (no number), Magadalena. The Peruvian Touring Club. Club Regatas. Club Samoa. National Club. Union Club. Club Cóndores. Club Esmeralda. Club de la Banca y Comercio. Club Waikiki. Club Santa María.

South American Explorers' Club Av. Portugal 146, Casilla 3714, Lima 100 (telephone 31-44-80), has recently been formed to bring together all in Peru (and by extension, all in Latin America or visiting it) who are interested in activities off the beaten track. It is producing a magazine, *The South American Explorer*. Don Montague, editor of the magazine, will provide further information. Open every day; visitors welcome.

Short Excursions Two short excursions in the neighbourhood of Lima, one to Pachacámac and one to Chosica, are well worthwhile. The road to Pachacámac passes through the southern residential extensions of Lima to the sea. The road, the Avenida Arequipa expressway from the centre of Lima, is a 4-lane highway, 10 km. long, with gardens and a double row of trees in the centre. Parallel to this, a few blocks away, is the Paseo de la República expressway where the large Sears-Todos shopping complex is located. At **San Isidro** is El Oliver, an old olive grove turned into a delightful park. Beyond this is the Lima Golf Club where the Country Club is found, primarily a hotel, which incorporates the new Real Club with swimming pools, tennis courts, etc. This is an 8 km. taxi ride from the centre of Lima. Between San Isidro and Miraflores is the Pan de Azúcar, an adobe pyramid of the Maranga culture, of about A.D. 100-500. One km. from Pan de Azúcar are Huaquerones and Catalina Huanca, sites now being restored. Nearby, at Chivateros, is a quarry said to date from 10,000 B.C.

The road reaches the sea at **Miraflores,** the largest, most important suburb of Lima, with well stocked shops and many first class restaurants. There is a handsome park in the middle of the shopping centre and at the end of Avenida Diagonal you can get the best view of the whole Lima coastline from Chorrillos to La Punta. The Mariscal Necochea clifftop park overlooks the Waikiki Club, a favourite with Lima surfers. It is possible to camp on Miraflores beach.

Buses to Miraflores No. 1 from Plaza de Armas; No. 2 from Plaza San Martín. The road passes through **Barranco,** with an attractive plaza and nearby the interesting "bajada", a steep path down to the beach, where many of Lima's young artists now live and exhibit their work. The Aviation School is at Barranco. (Take bus No. 2 to Miraflores and Barranco beaches from Plaza San Martín, for US$0.07). The next development on the coast is at **Chorrillos,** a fashionable resort with a cliff promenade, and boating. The Military School is a fine modern building. Barranco and Chorrillos damaged in October 1974 earthquake. Beyond it is **La Herradura,** another bathing resort with several restaurants. The private *Club Unicornio* is open to tourists. Some of the beaches round Lima are none too clean; La Herradura, however, is a welcome exception. A new beach road circles the entire bay; the main access to it is either at the end of the Paseo de la República on Barranco or by the Bajada de Balta, which is at the end of Av. Diagonal in Miraflores. Bathing at all points.

Pachacámac is some distance further along the coast, in the Lurín valley, 20 km. from Lima. When the Spaniards arrived, Pachacámac was the largest city on the coast. The ruins encircle the top of a low hill, the crest of which was crowned with a Temple of the Sun, a large pyramid built, in 1350, of sun-baked bricks. (There is also a reconstructed "Temple of the Virgins" and the ancient temple of the " Creator God"), Hernando Pizarro, brother of the leader, was the first European to come to Pachacámac; in 1533 he destroyed "idols", killed the priests and looted the temples. Francisco Pizarro himself spent several weeks here whilst his emissaries were seeking a site for the capital. Bus or colectivo from Lima, caught at the Plaza Santa Catalina, two blocks from Av. Abancay at the crossing of Puno with Andahuaylas. The buses (US$0.10 single) and colectivos (US$0.25) go *via* the Miraflores-Chorrillos sections, but tell the driver you are going to the "ruinas" or he will land you in Pachacámac town further on. Open every day except May 1 and July 28 from 0900 to 1700. Entrance US$0.70.

Return by Avenida Costanera (Coastal Drive) along the tops of the cliffs and with beautiful views over the bay. Beyond Miraflores it passes through a seaside resort, **Magdalena del Mar,** served by a separate road and bus route from Lima. A little inland, along this route, is **Pueblo Libre,** where the Museum of Anthropology and Archaeology, the Museum of the Republic and the Rafael Larco Herrera Museum are found (see under Museums), as well as the old church of Magdalena Vieja (1557), which was unfortunately heavily damaged in the 1970 earthquake.

The second pleasure drive is to **Chosica,** 40 km. up the Rímac valley (see also page 647). In the residential district of Chaclacayo, just before Chosica, is the *Huampani Hotel,* modern, attractive, and run by the Government's hotel chain. The meals are good and the beautiful swimming pool an additional attraction, but the hotel does go in heavily for conventions, which may not be to everyone's liking. An excellent lunch or light refreshments can be had at *San Jorge* in Chosica; or chicken meals at the *Granja Azul* and several other places on the road from Lima to Chosica. Try restaurant and campground of *Puerto del Sol,* owned by Sr. Italo de Neqzi Herreros. A delightful place for dinner and dancing is the restaurant *Fiesta,* at km. 6 on the Central Highway. At km. 33 is *El Bosque* Country Club (by invitation only) (private lake, 4 swimming pools, tennis and ball courts, riding stables, bull ring, etc.). Colectivos for

Chosica leave from just W of Parque Universitario, near the Ministry of Education building.

Just before coming into Chosica there is a large sign on the left *"Qué Buena Mesa"* which is a hotel (US$10 d, child free with own bed) with a big yard, clean pool and friendly atmosphere. Guests eat with the family.

On the way to Chosica a diversion may be made by **Puruchuco,** to see the reconstructed palace of a pre-Inca Huacho noble; with small museum and a selection of indigenous plants and animals, including hairless dogs and guinea pigs. The large adobe pre-Inca city of **Cajamarquilla** may also be visited, for which the turnoff (left, at Huachipa) is about 6 km. on from the Puruchuco turn. The site is difficult to find—you can't see it from the road—but look for a sign "Zona Arqueológica" in the middle of a brick yard. Keep on driving through the yard, and you will find Cajamarquilla at the end of an ill-kept dirt road.

The Central Highway to Oroya opens up possibilities of excursions by car with attractive stopping places like Matucana (1 hour), San Mateo and Río Blanco (2 hours). The trip to Oroya takes over 5 hours, and crosses the Andean divide at 4,843 metres. An excursion may be made to Infiernillo ("Little Hell") Canyon, beyond Matucana, which is well worth seeing.

There is bathing, tennis, a yacht club, and the luxury *Hotel Playa Hermosa* at **Ancón,** 30 km. N of Lima, reached by a double lane asphalted highway. It is the only real seaside resort in Peru. Beaches are very small. Crowded Jan-March holidays, good for fish. There are the pre-Inca ruins of a small town on the hill of San Pedro, a fortress on the hills of Loma de los Papas, and an ancient cemetery to the S. There are also Inca ruins at Maranga and Chuquitanta, nearby.

Callao Passengers coming to Peru by sea usually land at Callao (now virtually part of Lima) and make for Lima (13 km.). A new passenger terminal was inaugurated in 1973. Callao handles 75% of the nation's imports and some 25% of its exports.

Callao's maritime terminal or inner harbour covers 100 hectares, and the largest steamers go alongside. Population, 400,000, mainly workers. San Lorenzo island, a submarine and naval station, protects the roadstead from the S; inland stretches the green Rímac valley. It is a commercial place with no architectural beauty. Lima is reached by road (20 minutes by car or by omnibus). Passengers are expected to be on board half-an-hour before the vessel's departure. (Some have been attacked and robbed just outside the dock gates.) "The Club", the oldest English club on the W coast, is at Pasaje Ronald, Calle Constitución, Callao.

History Drake and others raided Callao in the 16th century. An earthquake wiped it out in 1746. On November 5, 1820, Lord Cochrane boarded and captured, after a bloody fight in which he was wounded, the Spanish frigate "Esmeralda". The Real Felipe fortress (1774), last stronghold of the Royalists in S. America, withstood a siege of a year and finally gave in after terrible sufferings in 1826. It is still a military post, and tourists are allowed to visit it. The Military Museum (see page 584) is in the old barracks. The railway to Lima, opened May 17, 1851, was one of the first in S. America.

Leading Restaurant *El Chalaquito,* Calle Constitución. There are a number of reliable bars in the Pasaje Ríos and Calle Constitución.

Fares to and from Lima Taxis have metres. The fare is about US$2 for up to 3 passengers. Colectivos charge US$0.20. There are bus services.

Taxis In Callao use taxis recommended by U.S. Embassy or port authorities—for safety's sake. About US$10 for 3 hours.

Steamers Ocean sailings to all parts and local steamers N and S every week. P.S.N.C. fast freight service N and S. Prudential Grace Line's weekly service between New York, Callao and Valparaíso. The Cía. Real Holandesa de Vapores has a fortnightly service between Cristóbal, Valparaíso, and Europe. Local coastwise services by the C. P. V. and the Compañía Sud-Americana de Vapores. Other shipping companies operating from Europe are the Knutsen Line, Cie. Générale Transatlantique, Italian Line, Westfal Larsen Line, Johnson Line, and Hapag/Lloyd from the U.S.A., the Gulf & South American Line and Gran Colombiana; from Australia, the Kawasaki Kisen Kaisha; from India, Bank Line.

Addresses British Vice-Consulate, Sáenz Peña 154. P.S.N.C.: Calle Independencia 150 (Casilla 368), Tel.: 299040.

Bank of London & South America, Av. Sáenz Peña 352. Open 0830-1130 January-March, 0830-1200 April-December.

Cables Pasaje Ronald y Constitución 258. Sáenz Peña 160; Tel.: 29-0117 (Public Telex booth).

The Naval School is at **La Punta,** just beyond Callao, served by municipal buses and colectivos through Callao from Lima. La Punta is on a spit of land stretching out to sea; a once fashionable beach, but water is cool. A new yacht club has been built on the N side.

The road from Callao to Lima is lined by factories, many of them producing fishmeal. Shipyards, miles from sea, load the fishing vessels they build on huge lorries and launch them into the ocean at Callao. San Marcos University (founded May 12, 1551) has now been transferred to a new University City, near the Naval Hospital.

On Avenida Marina between Lima and Callao, a turn-off opposite the entrance to the Pacific Fair Grounds (Feria del Pacífico) leads to the remarkable Parque de Las Leyendas. (For further details of park, see page 585).

North West of Lima

From Lima to Chimbote Between Lima and Pativilca there is a narrow belt of coastal land deposited at the mouths of the rivers, but from Pativilca to the mouth of the Río Santa, N of Chimbote, the Andes come down to the sea. Between Lima and Pativilca cotton and sugar-cane are grown, though the yield of sugar is less than it is further N, where the sunshine is not interrupted by cloud. Cotton is harvested from April to September by Indian migrants from the basins of Jauja and Huancayo. Much irrigated land grows vegetables and crops for the feeding of Lima and Callao. Cattle are driven down from the Highlands to graze the *lomas* on the mountain sides when the mists come between June and October.

There are coastal vessels from port to port along the coast, but travel is slow and irregular. The Pan-American Highway parallels the coast all the way to the far N, and feeder roads branch from it up the various valleys.

Just N of Ancón, the next port N of Callao, there is the Pasamayo sand dune stretching for 20 km., which comes right down to the sea-shore. The old road which snakes along the base beside the sea, is spectacular, but is now closed. The new toll road (US$0.20) which goes right over the top, is much safer and you get spectacular views over the surrounding coast and valleys.

The road passes through the minor port of **Huacho,** 132 km. from Lima. It is the capital of Chancay, a centre for fish-meal production, and the outlet for cotton and sugar grown in the rich Huaura Valley; a branch road runs up it to Sayán and beyond to Churín and Raura. There are cotton-seed oil and other factories. P.S.N.C. steamers and most of the big lines call regularly northbound. Port and sea are sometimes alive with monstrous jellyfish. Pop.: 35,000.

Hotels *Gran Pacífico; Italia; Grace; Hostal Maury,* US$3.40 d, basic but friendly. The journey inland from Huacho is splendid. Beyond Sayán are terrific rock formations, then road passes through subtropical vegetation around Churín, which is visited for its mineral springs. There are many coal mines. Above 4,000 metres is a chain of lakes which reflect the Cordillera Raura (up to 5,800 metres). Road ends at Raura mine.

Just across the river is **Huaura,** which was half-destroyed by an earthquake in 1967; the balcony is still preserved from which San Martín declared the country's independence from Spain. Try Guinda, the local cherry brandy. We pass from the wide valley of Mazo through the irrigated valley of San Felipe. There is more desert and then the cotton-fields of San Nicolás lead to **Supe,** a small busy port shipping fish-meal, cotton, sugar and minerals. At Aspero, near Supe, is one of the earliest prehistoric sites in Peru (see History section, page 575). After passing through the town of **Barranca** (*Hotel Chavín,* US$7, tolerable but no food, front rooms are noisy), we come to the village of **Pativilca,** (bus from Lima US$4, 2½ hours) from which a road turns off for the Callejón de Huaylas and Huarás (see page 601). 4 km. beyond the turn-off, beside the Highway, are the well preserved ruins of the Chimú temple of **Paramonga.** Set on high ground (view of the ocean), the fortress-like mound is reinforced by 8 quadrangular walls rising in tiers to the top of the hill. It overlooks the large Paramonga sugar plantation and the paper making and chemical industries now run by the State. Paramonga is a small port, 200 km. from Lima, shipping sugar.

The Pativilca-Huarás road has recently been paved; the car journey is down to 4-5 hours, truck 5-6, bus 6-8. Beware static mist area half-way. Spectacular journey so try to get a ride in a government vehicle, which can travel the route by day. Buses travel at night.

Hotel There is no hotel at Paramonga. Pativilca has *Hotel El Sol,* US$1.25 s, with restaurant, both good and clean. There are several hotels in Barranca; as bus companies have their offices there, buses will stop there rather than at Pativilca and Paramonga.

Bus from Lima to Paramonga. US$4, 3 hours. Colectivos run to Barranca (US$1.30) then you need to catch another for the 7-8 km. to Paramonga. Bus from Barranca to Casma US$0.70. Truck, Pativilca-Huarás, 5-6 hours, US$3.30.

Between Paramonga and Chimbote (225 km.) the mountains come down to the sea. The road passes by a few very small protected harbours in tiny rock-encircled bays—Puerto Huarmey (small *Tourist Hotel,* US$9.50 d, clean and good service, rebuilt and reopened after earthquake, at **Huarmey** town, not port), Puerto Casma, and Vesique. From Casma a road runs through the Callán Pass (4,224 metres) to Huarás. (Bus, US$2.10.) A hard but lovely trip.

From Casma to Chimbote and as far north as Trujillo the coast road and the towns along it were badly damaged by earthquake on May 31, 1970. Repairs have now however been carried out in all but the smallest villages in the area.

Casma The town was largely destroyed by the 1970 earthquake, but has since been rebuilt. A good new food market.

Hotels *Hotel Central,* US$3.30 d, not recommended, about 1 km. along the road. *Motel El Farol,* good, US$5.75 d, with bathroom, restaurant in hotel grounds good. *Restaurant Tumi,* recommended.

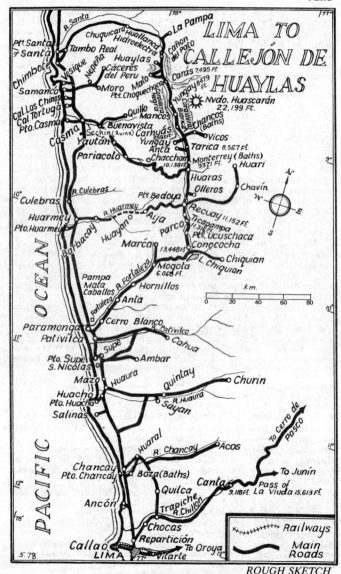

LIMA TO CALLEJÓN DE HUAYLAS

ROUGH SKETCH

Bus From Parque Universitario, Lima, colectivo to Casma, US$7. Bus to Lima leaves 1100 daily (Tepsa) US$4.10. Bus to Huarás, Empresa Soledad, US$4, leaves 0930 daily. Casma-Huarás road now paved (toll US$0.50).

Sechín At km. 370, shortly before reaching the town of Casma, watch for a large concrete sign to Sechín on the right with an arrow pointing to a side road. Follow this road for about 2 km. until you reach the ruins. The archaeologist in charge of the excavations in Sechín, Dr. Lorenzo A. Samaniego, lives in a small house next to the ruins. Three sides of the large stone temple have been excavated and restored. You cannot see the adobe buildings inside the stone walls which, according to Dr. Samaniego, belong to an earlier period. They were later covered up and used as a base for a second storey which unfortunately has been completely destroyed. Some experts think the temple and surroundings were buried on purpose. Others believe it was engulfed by natural disaster. The latter theory is supported by finds of human skeletons. Tombs have been found in front and at the same level as the temple. A wall of a large adobe building under excavation can already be seen and runs round the sides and back of the temple but only the two sides could be completely cleared as the present excavation programme money ran out in September 1974. The site is open to tourists, 0800-1700 (US$0.50, children half price), and there is an attractive, shady picnic garden. Camping is permitted. It is quite easy to walk to the ruins from Casma. One must walk about 3 km. S to a well posted sign showing a left turn, then simply follow the road for 2 km. to the ruins. (Taxi, US$3 from Casma, but they may try for more; colectivo US$0.25; easy to hitchhike from Casma to Sechín, but leave early in the morning; no buses.

John Hemming writes: "New archaeological discoveries are making Sechín the most important ruin on the Peruvian coast. It consists of a large square temple completely faced with carved stone monoliths—probably over 500 of them—which depict gruesome battle scenes: men being eviscerated, heads with blood gushing from eyes or mouths, dismembered legs, arms, torsos, ears, eyes and vertebrae. The style is unique in Peru for its naturalistic vigour. Within the stone temple is an earlier, pre-ceramic mud temple with painted walls. The temples are pre-Chavín, about 1500 BC, which makes them the oldest important monuments in South America." The site has been embellished with groves of native trees and plants.

Chimbote, 320 km. from Lima, is one of the few natural harbours on the W coast, ample in area and depth of water. Rapidly growing population of 180,000; a new port has been built to serve a steel industry started in 1958: iron ore from Marcona field is shipped from the port of San Juan, 547 km. S of Lima; anthracite comes by railway from the hinterland, and power comes from the hydroelectric station in the Cañón del Pato, 129 km. inland. Chimbote is Peru's largest fishing port; large quantities of fish-meal are exported. The bay with its precipitous islands looks interesting; but everything smells of fish-meal—water, houses, people. Bathing is forbidden on the beach near the hotel. Shanty towns have burgeoned around.

Deep drafted vessels berth alongside the pier; C.S.A.V. vessels bound for Callao call weekly. Small airport. It can be reached from Lima by daily "colectivo" car service (4½ to 5 hours, US$4); or bus to Lima, 7-8 hours, US$4; to Tumbes, by night, US$8.

Buses Since the Santa valley road *via* Huallanca to the Callejón de Huaylas and beyond has been closed for some time and was not expected to be open before the end of 1978, buses to this area have had to go S, *via* Casma, Colectivo to Casma, US$1; bus to Huarás. Transportes Soledad, 8½ hours, leave about 0800 every day, fare US$4 passing Casma at 1000. (Casma-Huarás road now paved). Buses run Chimbote to Trujillo. Colectivo to Trujillo US$2.25 (2 hours).

Hotels *Chimú,* now a State Tourist Hotel (US$14 d); there are some cheaper rooms at the back, must ask; *Presidente,* new; *Hotel San Felipe,* US$3.50 s; *Hotel María Teresa; Pacífico; Ferrocarril.* For hard-up: *Los Angeles* (US$3) across from station; *El Santa,* US$4 d, with bath, clean and good; *Hotel Venus,* US$3 d; *Hotel Huascarán,* US$1.10 s, US$2 d; *Hotel Las Vegas,* US$2.25 d; *Hotel Augusto,* Aguirre 265, US$3.75 d, modern, hot water, friendly.

Restaurants *Café El Mundo* serves good Chinese food, also on Av. Pardo; *Los Portales. Panchito,* good cheap food.

From Chimbote a road branches off to the NE and, joining another road from Santa, goes up the Santa valley following the route, including tunnels, of the old Santa Corporation Railway. (This used to run as far as Huallanca, 138 km. up the valley, but was largely destroyed by the 1970 earthquake.) At the top of the valley the road goes through the very narrow Cañon del Pato before reaching the Callejón de Huaylas and going on to Carás and Huarás. Much of the road along the Santa valley has in fact been closed for repairs for some time but should be open again by 1979.

Just before the Cañon del Pato is **Huallanca,** a quiet but friendly village with an impressive hydroelectric plant built into a mountain. This can be visited by getting a permit at the office. *Hotel Huascarán,* US$1.25, good value.

Carás This town, also badly damaged by the 1970 earthquake, is now almost totally restored, and is reported a pleasant place and a good centre for walking; splendid views of Huandoy and Huascarán. Information on mountaineering obtainable from the director of the Huascarán National Park. *Hotel La Suiza Peruana,* in main square, US$2 s, US$4 d after bargaining, quiet, secure for left-luggage; *Hotel El Cafetal,* US$3.20 d; both are friendly and clean. *Hotel Carás,* US$1.80 d. *Restaurante Carás* on main square, cheap, clean. Bus to Lima 18 hrs, direct 1500, *via* Huarás (to which the 67-km. road is now paved) 0600, US$17. Also frequent buses to and from Huarás.

From Carás a road branches off to the spectacularly beautiful Lake Parón (taxi from Carás US$15-25) nesting right under the snow-capped peak of Huandoy. It continues on to the equally magnificent valley of Callejón de Conchucos on the E side of the Cordillera Blanca. Basic accommodation in Piscobamba, where the road used to end. Local buses ply between Carás and Piscobamba. The road has been extended to connect with Huari and Chavin, and it certainly provides one of the most spectacular circuits in the country.

The main road goes on to **Yungay.** The town of Yungay was completely buried as a result of the 1970 earthquake—a hideous tragedy in which 20,000 people lost their lives. The survivors are housed just north of the old town, which is now getting into order with houses and a concrete market. A hotel without a signboard is on the left of the Carhuás road, and there is a good restaurant run by the local cooperative. The site now has a few monuments and a field of rose bushes.

For trekkers, one of the finest walks is over the path by Huascarán and Lake Llanganuco from Yungay to Piscobamba (2 buses daily, and trucks charging US$1.50, Yungay to Lake Llanganuco, enquire at Expreso

Ancash in Carás. No known buses to Piscobamba.) It is a 3-4 day hike over well-travelled route, but don't try it unless you are properly equipped. (Advice from National Park office, Av. Centenario 912, Huarás and from local Club Andino at Electropo.) Also try walk from Llanganuco to Colcabamba, Huaypampa to Punto Unión and La Cruz. The mountain flowers and humming birds at these altitudes are magnificent. The road to the lake (full of trout) continues up to the tongue of the glacier of Cerro Chopicalqui (6,354 metres)—insect repellent needed.

After Yungay, the main road goes to Mancos (at least one hotel) at the foot of Huascarán and on to **Carhuás**, with fair hotels *(Perú* and *Gran Hotel)* and very good walking in the neighbourhood. Before Huarás the road goes to Marcará, where there is a branch road 3 km. to Chancos, another thermal resort *(Hotel Chancos* closed but you can camp in the neighbourhood) and on to Tarica where there is cheap accommodation.

The valley's focus is **Huarás,** capital of the Department of Ancash, at 3,028 metres, 348 km. from Lima. It is very much the climbing centre of Peru, particularly between May and October. It is the headquarters of the Huascarán National Park, whose office (helpful) is at the Ministry of Agriculture building, Av. Centenario 912. The park includes the snowcapped Cordillera Blanca (see also pages 602-3, and above under Yungay).

One-third of Huarás was swept away by an avalanche in 1958. It was caused by ice from a glacier falling into a lake above the town and sending a surge of water down the mountainside into a second lake, which in its turn, sent a surge of water down to Huarás. It is said that the level of the lakes has since been lowered to prevent a repetition of this tragedy. The town had been totally reconstructed when it was half destroyed in the earthquake of 1970. After the collapsed buildings had been cleared away, for a time, the dome of the cathedral was left standing as a memorial of the tragedy. It has, however, since been taken down as it was considered unsafe. Reconstruction of the town is now well advanced. The life of the town is now centred on the Avenida Centenario on the other side of the river, and the place is reported to be very much alive, but it is too much to expect that the colourful ceremonies described in our 1971 and earlier editions will have yet recovered their vigour (however, Chichas—brass-bands accompanied by dancers—can be seen in the streets). The setting, with the peaks of Huascarán, Huandoy, and San Cristóbal in the background, is tremendous. Only one branch of Banco de la Nación, on the north side of the town.

Aeroperú has three services a week between Lima and Anta opposite the giant massif of Huandoy, with its four peaks. There is a bus every 1½ hours (US$1) from the new Anta airport, about 24 km. N of Huarás, to the *Hotel Monterrey* and Huarás (road now paved). Buses to and from Lima travel only at night, but Comité 14 has a car leaving at 0600. The 400 km. run takes 8 hours. Colectivo taxis to and from Lima leave about 0400 and 1900, cost about US$6 one way, and arrive about 1300. The road to the coast at Casma is also paved now (toll, US$0.50).

There is a spectacular transandine route, Huarás-Recuay-Chiquián-La Unión (Dos de Mayo)-Chavinillo-Huánuco, but avoid in rainy season.

Hotels *Hotel Termas de Monterrey,* 7 km. N, run by State Tourist Hotel chain, recommended for walking, swimming in hot springs, US$9.50 d, plus taxes; bus Huarás-Monterrey, US$0.10, leaves every few minutes, takes ½ hr.; US$0.50 swim, US$0.20 bath. Don't be too vigorous at the start; it's over 2,750 metres up. In town, new *State Tourist Hotel,* US$13 d; *Hotel Sascofón* also recently built, US$7.50 d, recommended; *Hostal Andino,* again new, US$4 s, good; *Hostal Colomba* (bungalow-type), US$11 s, US$15 d, plus 21%; *Hotel Barcelona,* Av. Raymondi 618, US$7.50 d with bath; top floor, known as *Pepe's Place,* has mattresses for budget travellers, US$0.50 each, safe for left luggage; *San Isidro,* US$1.25, recommended; *Pensión Los Queñuales,* US$2; *Hotel Raymondi,* US$4.40 s, bath, not recommended; *Hotel Gran,* US$3.30 d, clean; *Alojamiento Janett,* Av. Centenario, recommended.

Restaurants *Enriques,* Rolandi 800, reasonable. *Chifa Familiar,* good and cheap, serves local food as well; several other Chinese restaurants. Restaurant and bar at *Ebony 76,* friendly, clean and not expensive. *Café Melina* at the Monterrey, Italian proprietor, excellent food cooked to order. *Restaurante Lorgio,* Av. Centenario 809, good food and cheap. *La Cabañita* is also good and cheap.

Museum A new museum containing stone monoliths and "huacos" from the Recuay culture has been set up in the *Casa de Cultura.* Open from 0830.

Excursions Two hours' walk into mountains is Willcawain archaeological site, the ruins of a Tiahuanaco-style temple, dating from about 1000 A.D. The site is now signposted; walk down Av. Centenario and take the signed right turn 1 km. out of town. Bring torch. Don't miss the extra ruins at end of the track.

Buses Empresa Soledad, 6¼ hours to Casma (137 km.) US$4 (leaves at 1000). Bus to Chimbote US$3.50, 0900, 6½ hours, colectivo to Chimbote, daily, leave early, US$1.20, 6 hours. Colectivos take visitors to see the Cordillera, and there is also a trip to the Chavín site, Huari and Huacarán. Truck to Pativilca on coast, 5 hours, US$1.10. Buses only every second day. Buses to Lima only at night US$6, (trucks are much cheaper) to Carás, US$0.90, colectivo US$1.20, frequent, to Yungay US$0.70. Bus to Chavín.

Tourist Office Av. Centenario 130, maps and information but no English spoken.

Chavín The Chavín ruins, of a temple built over 2,500 years ago, are about 6 hours' drive (64 km.) from Huarás, reached by a bad but spectacular road branching E from Catac. (Transport is difficult from Catac except in early morning and late evening.) Entry US$0.20. There are seven underground storeys, but at present only two are open. There is a guided tour round ruins by a caretaker at fixed opening hours. Gates close at lunchtime and seem permanently closed, so shout. The main attraction is the marvellous carved stone heads and designs in relief of symbolic "gourd" figures. The carvings are unusual and charming and in excellent condition. The famous Lanzón dagger-shaped stone monolith of 800 B.C. is found inside the temple tunnel. The *Hotel Gantu* (not recommended), *Hotel El Cóndor* and *Hotel Inca* (US$0.54 s, bathrooms filthy) in Chavín village basic but friendly. A recommended restaurant is the *Comedor de Cooperativa de Chavín,* behind main church. (Better hotels in Huari, 44 km. further on.) There are hot sulphur baths about 3 km. S of Chavín. Beautiful walk from Chavín to the village of San Marcos 7 km.

Bus to Chavín "Huascarán" from Huarás, 1000 on Tues., Thurs., Sun.; returning Mon., Wed., Fri., US$3. A magnificent 7-hour scenic journey. The Huarás-Chavín road was closed in 1976 for reconstruction, and it is difficult to find trucks or buses to go on this route. Trucks US$2, 7 hours, but very cold. A new agency, Ancash Tours, is authorised to make daytime excursions to Chavín and other places of interest; the tour to Chavín leaves at 0700 and costs US$11 and is the only reliable way of getting there and back. Apparently direct buses Lima to Chavín run twice a week, US$9 by Cóndor de Chavín, main office in Lima, Montevideo 1039. Tel.: 288122. The Lima-Chavín bus goes on to Pomabamba, or Huari. From Barranca, every second day by truck, US$2.50, 17 hours, trip is very bumpy and cold. For the active, there is the possibility of a 3-day walk from Olleros, reached by bus from Huarás. Enquire at National Park Office about necessary equipment for walk.

Another way to see the Santa Valley and the Callejón de Huaylas, which contains some of the most spectacular scenery in Peru, is to take the recently paved road which branches off the coast road into the mountains just N of Pativilca, 187 km. from Lima. This route also gives a more spectacular view of the Cordillera Blanca. In 120 km. it climbs to Lake Conococha, at 4,100 metres, where the Santa River rises. After crossing the high level surface it descends gradually for 87 km. to Huarás, passes Tarica and Carhuás, and goes on to the Callejón de Huaylas, where it runs between the towering Cordillera Negra, snowless and rising to 4,600 metres and the snow-covered Cordillera Blanca, whose highest point is the 6,768 metres high Huascarán (excellent map of Callejón published by Instituto Geográfico Militar). Farms appear at about 4,000 metres, but most of the farming is around Huarás. The inhabitants grow potatoes and barley at the higher and maize and alfalfa at the lower altitudes. The valley has many picturesque villages and small towns, with narrow cobblestone streets and odd-angled house roofs, but earthquake damage in 1970 was very heavy.

The alternative route to the Callejón de Huaylas is *via* the Callán pass from Casma to Huarás (see page 597).

The Northern Oases N of the mouth of the River Santa the Andes recede, leaving a coastal desert belt of from 8 to 16 km. wide containing the three great oases of Northern Peru—the areas of Trujillo, Chiclayo and Piura. The main towns are inland, but connected by short railways and roads to their ports, little more than collections of low buildings and warehouses set in barren desert.

N of Chimbote we pass through the valleys of Chao and Virú, arriving after an 137 km. drive at the first great oasis of Northern Peru, Trujillo. Coming down from the desert we notice the abrupt line between desert and greenery; cultivation can only be carried out with irrigation ditches which take their water from far up in the mountains. The large cooperatives here and in the nearby Chicama Valley turn out about 55% of all Peruvian sugar. The area's port is **Salaverry**, exporting sugar and minerals, importing consumer goods and machinery. Two piers have berths for frieghters up to 20,000 tons. There is an 8 km. road to Trujillo. Salaverry is a modern, completely mechanised port.

The Quiruvilca copper mines are 120 km. inland by motor road from Salaverry. The concentrating plant at Shorey is connected with the mines by a 3 km. aerial cableway, and with its coal mine by a further 8 km. The ore is then taken by a 40 km. cableway to Samne, where it is sent by road to Salaverry. The concentrates contain 35% copper, 30 ounces of silver and 4 grams of gold per ton.

Trujillo, capital of the Department of La Libertad, second largest city in Peru, ranks after Lima/Callao and before Arequipa. Population 400,000. The traveller entering Trujillo is delighted with its surrounding greenness against a backcloth of brown Andean foothills and peaks. Founded by Pizarro, 1536, with ample space for small parks and plazas; Charles V ordered a wall around it. Its modern buildings have been asimilated without discord: it remains a city of old churches, graceful colonial balconies and windows overhanging its modern pavements, of homes built during the reigns of the viceroys. Besides the Cathedral it has 10 colonial churches as well as old convents and monasteries. Its University of La Libertad, second only to that of San Marcos at Lima, was founded in 1824; in its Archaeological Museum are interesting collections of Chimú and Mochica pottery; its biological museum is at San Martín 368. On one of the main streets near the Plaza de Armas is the spacious courtyard, patio and high-ceilinged rooms of the 18th century house in which General Iturregui lived when he pronounced the city's freedom from Spain in 1820. It is now the exclusive Club Central and Chamber of Commerce, at Pizarro 688 (may be visited in mornings). Two other beautiful colonial mansions on the Plaza have been taken over by the Banco Central and Banco Hipotecario, who maintain as museums the parts that are surplus to their requirements as offices (they may be visited a.m.). Certain other mansions, still in private hands, may occasionally be visited with the help of Trujillo Tours; one is the magnificent Orbegoso house at Pizarro 316.

The focal point is the spacious, well landscaped Plaza de Armas, with a somewhat unfortunate sculptured group to the heroes of the Liberation. Fronting it is the Cathedral, with the old palace of the Archbishop next door; the Tourist Hotel; the building in colonial style of the Sociedad de Beneficencia Pública de Trujillo housing the Peruvian North American Cultural Institute; and the Municipality building. Many churches damaged in the 1970 earthquake. One of the best, La Merced at Pizarro 550, with picturesque moulded figures below the dome, is being restored. El Carmen church and monastery, described as "most valuable jewel of Colonial art in Trujillo", is still closed after earthquake. The city has a golf club. Trujillo to Lima, by road, 551 km.

Fiesta At end-September—all transport and hotels booked.

How to get to Trujillo Faucett and Aeroperú daily flights from Lima, 1 hour, US$21. Faucett from Tumbes, US$18.50. From Lima, by day in "colectivo", 7-8 hours, for US$9, or by bus, 8-9 hours, US$5.65 (mostly at night). Buses from Lima quite frequent but difficult to go north as buses booked for days. Regular flights by Faucett and Aeroperú to Iquitos (2 flights a week, Saturday and Monday). Cajamarca, Chiclayo and points N and to a multitude of small jungle towns. Bus to Chimbote US$1.50 leaves 1300, Empresa Chinday-Suyo; colectivo US$3; 2-3 hrs. Bus to Cajamarca US$4 daily, 11 hrs; colectivo to Piura, 1000 daily, US$7.80; to Chiclayo, US$3, 3-4 hours. Bus from Tumbes US$7.80, 12 hours.

Taxis Town trip, US$0.15; out of town US$0.20. Chan-Chan, Huanchaco, US$0.35 and airport, US$1.50. By the hour, in town, US$1.05, outside US$1.25.

Archaeological Museum, normally open 0800-1300 in Jan.-March and 0800-1200, 1500-1800 the rest of the year, has been moved to Calle Bolívar, 446. One of the finest things to see in Trujillo is the basement of the Cassinelli garage on the fork of the Pan-American and Huanchaco roads; it contains a superb private collection of Mochica and Chimú pottery, beautifully housed and arranged. Trujillo Tours arrange visits.

Industries Sugar mills, motor-vehicle assembly, paper and cardboard factory, rum distillery, fruit and fish canning, brewery, candle factory, etc. A new industrial estate has been set up.

Hotels *Hotel Trujillo* (State Tourist Hotel), Plaza de Armas, US$12 d, adequate but antiquated; *El Golf,* swimming pool, sauna and discotheque; *San José,* US$3 s, in 5th block of Grau; *San Antonio,* in 8th block of Gamarra; *San Martín,* in 7th block of San Martín, US$4 p.p., clean, modern and good, has more than 100 rooms, bath, good restaurant. These three hotels are new, medium-priced and very comfortable. *Hotel Opt Gar* (5th block Grau) good, excellent restaurant (try sea

KEY TO
MAP SECTIONS

These maps are for interest only and
are not of political significance.

2

1 : 20,000,000

English Miles

© — John Bartholomew & Son, Ltd. 3

PANAMA
Panama
G. of Panama
Gulf of Darien
COLOMBIA
VENEZUELA
GUYANA
SURINAM
FRENCH GUIANA
ECUADOR
TRINIDAD AND TOBAGO
Port of Spain
Tobago I.
Grenada
Margarita I.
Curaçao I.
Bonaire I.
Aruba
GEORGETOWN
Paramaribo
New Amsterdam
CARACAS
Maracaibo
Barranquilla
Cartagena
Sta. Marta
Rio Hacha
BOGOTÁ
Medellin
Cali
Popayan
Pasto
QUITO
Guayaquil
Cuenca
Buenaventura
Tumaco
Esmeraldas
Valencia
Barquisimeto
Coro
Barcelona
Cumaná
Ciudad Bolivar
Manaus
Santarem
Obidos
Iquitos
Leticia
Brazilian Guiana
AMAZONAS
RORAIMA
Boa Vista
Rio Negro
R. Amazon
R. Orinoco
R. Magdalena
R. Putumayo
R. Caqueta
R. Napo
R. Branco
R. Japurá
R. Purus
R. Madeira
R. Trombetas
R. Essequibo
R. Meta
C. Corrientes
L. Maracaibo
Sª Pacaraima
Tumuc-Humac Mts

B R A Z I L

Plateau of MATO GROSSO

RONDÔNIA

Theodore Roosevelt

B O L I V I A

SUCRE

La Paz

Cochabamba

Potosí

Oruro

Santa Cruz

PARAGUAY

ASUNCION

Chaco Boreal

FORMOSA

CHACO

PERU

LIMA

Callao

AREQUIPA

MOLLENDO

Arica

Iquique

ANTOFAGASTA

Tropic of Capricorn

Callao to Valparaiso 1305

West of 75 Green.

1 : 20,000,000

English Miles
50   100   200   300

Kilometres
50   100   200   300   400

Gonzalez I.   San Felix I. (Chile)

S.Ambrosio I.

80

1:20,000,000

English Miles

Kilometres

© — John Bartholomew & So

ARGENTINA

URUGUAY

BUENOS AIRES

MONTEVIDEO

La Plata

River Plate

ENTRE RIOS

SANTA FE

CORDOBA

CORRIENTES

MENDOZA

SAN LUIS

SAN JUAN

LA RIOJA

CATAMARCA

LA PAMPA

RIO NEGRO

NEUQUEN

CHUBUT

Great Plateau of Patagonia

PATAGONIA

Valdes Peninsula

G. San Matias

G. de San Jorge (G. of St. George)

Santa Cruz

Rio Gallegos

Strait of Magellan

Tierra del Fuego

Staten I.

FALKLAND ISLANDS (ISLAS MALVINAS)

W. Falkland   E. Falkland

Stanley

Beauchène I.

Valparaiso

SANTIAGO

La Serena

Coquimbo

Copiapó

Caldera

Concepcion

Valdivia

Chiloé I.

Chonos Archipelago

Taitao Peninsula

Wellington I.

Madre de Dios Archipelago

Queen Adelaide Arch.

Desolacion

Strait of Magellan

Mar del Plata

Bahia Blanca

Comodoro Rivadavia

Deseado

These maps are for interest only are not of political significance

1 : 20,000,000

English Miles
0   50   100   200

Kilometres
0   50   100   200   300   40

food) and snack bar, US$7.50 s, US$11 d; *Hotel Granada,* US$3 d; *Hotel Palermo,* US$8 d, hot water, by market; *Hotel Premier,* recommended strongly, hot water, clean, central, US$5.50 d, with shower; *Hotel Los Incas,* Av. César Vallejo, US$1.20, not very clean; *Hotel Chan Chan,* US$3.50 d with shower; *Primavera,* US$2.45 each; *Hotel Internacional* (6th block Bolívar—US$3 d, without bathroom) not recommended; *Lima,* Calle Ayacucho and *Giralda* (9th block Gamarra—US$6.50 d) are cheap and clean. *Hotel Americano* Pizarro 758-768, is a vast old barn, comfortable, cheap, US$2.50. *Hotel Latino* (5th block Grau), not recommended, US$3.50 d; *Hotel Astro; Hotels Paris* and *Perú,* opposite each other on Ayacucho, both US$1.20 s, US$2 d; *Hostería El Sol,* recently opened by Dr. Kaufmann of Coina (see page 607), US$1, 10 mins. from centre by bus; it is at Calle Los Brillantes 224, in front of the Parque Ramón Castilla, in Urbanización Santa Inés

Restaurants *Demarco* and *Romano* (7th block Pizarro); Chinese food at *Gallo Rojo* (5th block Grau), and *Kuon Wha* (8th block Gamarra); *Chifa Oriental* on Gamarra recommended. Excellent local dishes at *Pedro Moriallas* in nearby seaside resort of Buenos Aires. Good Argentine-style food at *Parrillada El Gaucho. Bar Snack Central* (Gamarra) excellent expresso coffee. *Subterráneo* Plaza Murillo, set lunch US$1; *Marisco* (Gamarra), recommend *pescado al mashe.*

Tourist Office Independencia 509, very helpful, and at airport. Information also from Sra. Carmen Melly, Trujillo Tours, Gamarra 440 (Tel.: 3149). Maps and information also from Touring and Automobile Club, 707 Almagro.

Night Club Granja Azul—country club. Billy Bob's for drinking.

Excursions from Trujillo

About five km. by car to the crumbling adobe ruins of **Chan-Chan,** imperial city of the Chimú domains. The ruins consist of nine great citadels each of which was a compound built by one of the Chimú kings. The nine-metre high perimeter walls surrounded sacred enclosures with usually only one narrow entrance. Inside, serried rows of storerooms contained the agricultural wealth of the kingdom, which stretched 1,000 km. along the coast, from near Guayaquil to Paramonga. Most of the compounds contain a huge walk-in well which tapped the ground water, raised to a high level by irrigation higher up the valley. Each compound also included a platform mound which was the burial place of the king. On the death of each king his attendant women were sacrificed and buried in the mound together with his treasure. One of the smallest mounds recently yielded thirteen skeletons of young women in one tiny chamber; the biggest may have contained the bodies of up to a thousand sacrificial victims. The compound of the dead king was then probably maintained as a memorial. The Incas almost certainly copied this system and transported it to Cuzco where the last Incas continued building huge enclosures. Chan-Chan was taken by the Incas about A.D. 1450 but not looted; the Spaniards, however, despoiled its burial mounds of all the gold and silver statuettes and ornaments buried with the Chimú nobles. The dilapidated city walls enclose an area of 28 square km. containing the remains of palaces, temples, workshops, streets, houses, gardens and a canal. What is left of the adobe walls bear well-preserved moulded decorations in artistic patterns, and painted designs have been found on pottery unearthed from the debris of a city ravaged by floods, earthquakes, and treasure seekers. It is still one of the strangest sights in the world. The Ciudadela of Tschudi has been reconstructed (15 minute walk from the road) open 0900 to 1700 (US$0.50).

See also the restored temple, Huaca El Dragón which dates from the Mochica empire of between 800 and 100 B.C. It is also known as Huaca Arco Iris (rainbow), after shape of friezes which decorate it, on the W

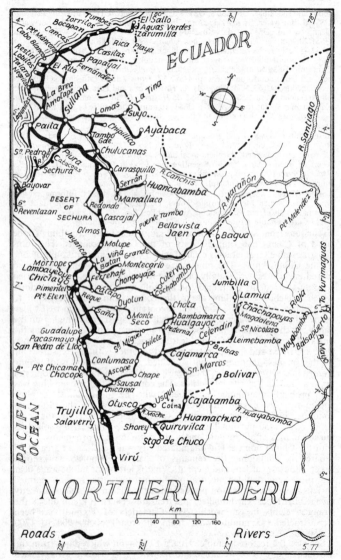

NORTHERN PERU

km.
0   40   80   120   160

Roads ～   Rivers ～

5 77

ROUGH SKETCH

side of the Pan-American Highway in the district of La Esperanza; these were damaged by the earthquake. Cheap way of getting there: by hourly bus to the resort of Huanchaco from the corner of Calle Bolívar and central market, dropping off at the ruins, US$0.20. Colectivo is US$0.30, and taxi US$1. Open 0800-1700.

Professor Pedro Puerta, the (English speaking) expert on Chan-Chan, has a gallery of original prints at Carretera Pan-Americana Norte, km. 564. His little decorated white booth is quite close to the Huaca El Dragón, and he can also be found in the State Tourist Hotel.

The small fishing village of **Huanchaco** is worth visiting to see the craft the fishermen use in the bay. (*Poseidon* is a very good fish restaurant by the pier.) They are narrow pointed rafts, known as *caballitos,* made of tortora reeds; unlike those used on Lake Titicaca, they are flat, not hollow, and ride the breakers rather like surfboards. These craft are depicted on ancient Mochica and Chimú pottery. It is possible to walk along the shore from Chan-Chan to Huanchaco in 2 hours. You can camp on the beach. There is a *pensión.*

A few km. south of Trujillo are the huge Moche pyramids, the Huaca de Sol and the Huaca de la Luna (colectivo US$0.30, taxi US$2). They consist of millions of adobe bricks and are the largest pre-Columbian structures in South America (take old clothes and a torch). An interesting feature of the site is the innumerable number of ancient pottery shards lying around on the ground. Best to visit a.m.; after noon the wind gets up, and blows the sand.

A visit should be made to one of the sugar estates, say the Hacienda Cartavio, in the Chicama Valley (43 km.); this hacienda together with the Chiclín estate now make up the Cartavio agricultural cooperative, under the agrarian reform programme. One of the biggest sugar estates in the world, also in the Chicama valley, is the Casa Grande cooperative. It covers over 6,000 hectares and employs 4,000 members. The Chiclín museum, once famous for items from Chan-Chan, now contains interesting collection of colonial religious paintings and statuary.

132 km. E from Trujillo is the village of **Coina**, at 1,500 metres in the Sierra Alto Chicama, where Dr. Kaufmann, from Germany, has opened a hospital for Indians and built the Hostería *El Sol,* with glorious views. About US$8 a night and 3 meals thrown in. Riding, swimming or walking by day, dancing in the evening. Grand place for rest; very, very friendly; English, French and German spoken. A bus runs to Coina from Trujillo every Tues. p.m. and Sat. a.m. (US$3.50). Dr. Kaufmann is adding a special centre for 150 people—showers, clothes-washers and cooking facilities, specially recommended. The profits are used to improve the hospital. Details from the office Trujillo-Primavera, Calle Héctor Villalobos 663, Trujillo. Tel.: 2869. Mail can be forwarded to its Post Box, Apartado 775, Trujillo.

To the E of Trujillo is Cajamarca, which can be reached either from Trujillo or from Pacasmayo. The main road from Trujillo is poor, taking twice the time to travel of the other route, but it is more interesting passing over the bare puna before dropping to the Huamachuco valley. Off it lies **Otusco**, an attractive Andean town with an imposing but unfinished church and narrow cobbled streets. Further on, at the mining town of Shorey, a road branches off to Santiago de Chuco, birthplace of the poet César Vallejo where there is the annual festival of Santiago El Mayor in the second half of July. The main procession is on July 25, when the image is carried through the streets. The road runs on to the colonial town of **Huamachuco**, 181 km. from Trujillo, which has a huge main plaza and a modern cathedral which is not universally popular. A 2-hour walk (take the track which goes off to the right just after crossing the bridge on the road to Trujillo) takes you to the extensive ruin of a hilltop pre-Inca fortress, Marcahuamachuco (taxi US$4 per person).

Hotels Best is *La Libertad*, US$1.25, clean. Recommended restaurants: *Creole* (on main square) and *Danubio*.

Buses Transportes Quiroz from Trujillo, US$4, travel at night so take warm clothing. There are also colectivos from Trujillo. Buses to Cajamarca, US$1.

From Huamachuco buses (Empresa Huancapata which start in Trujillo) run to Tayabamba, on the far bank of the Marañón, passing through the old gold-mining centres of Pataz province, such as Parcoy and Buldibuyo. This journey takes a good 18 hours in "normal" conditions. Also worth seeing in the Huamachuco area are Laguna Sausacocha, and haciendas Yanasara and Cochabamba, deep down in the valley of the river Chusgón, about 2-3 hours by truck east of the town. The latter hacienda has now become the sociedad Agrícola de Interés Social (SAIS) Tahuantinsuyo, under the agrarian reform programme, but Yanasara, noted for its fighting bulls, is still in the hands of its long-term owner, Francisco Pinillos Montoya, a well-known local character. There is a guest-house at Cochabamba, which used to be the Andean retreat of the owners of the Laredo sugar plantation, near Trujillo. The estate produces butter, cheese and milk, and is surrounded by lovely eucalyptus and pine woods. The climate, at about 2,300 metres, is mild and sheltered.

From Huamachuco the road runs on 48 km. through impressive eucalyptus groves to **Cajabamba,** which lies in the high part of the sugar-producing and once malaria-infested Condebamba valley. It has an attractive square. The best hotel is the *Flores* on the Plaza de Armas. Quiroz bus from Huamachuco takes 3 hours, also trucks and lorries, US$1.20

Cajabamba can also be reached in a strenuous but marvellous two-day hike from Coina (see page 607). The first day's walk brings you to Hacienda Santa Rosa where you stay overnight. The second day you cross the mountains at about 4,000 metres, coming through Arequeda to Cajabamba. It is advisable to hire a guide, and a donkey to carry the luggage. The cost for both is about US$4 a day.

The road continues from Cajabamba through San Marcos, important for its Sunday cattle market to Cajamarca. Bus to Cajamarca (124 km.) takes 4-5 hours, US$3.

Pacasmayo, port for the most southerly of the three oases, is 109 km. N of Salaverry on the Pan-American Highway running N from Trujillo to Chiclayo. Population: 11,890.

Hotel *Ferrocarril* US$6.50 d, on seafront, quiet and clean; *Perú.* Several cheap restaurants on the main street.

Pacasmayo is the best starting point for visiting Cajamarca (2,750 metres). The 180 km. road to it branches off the Pan-American Highway soon after it crosses the Jequetepeque River. 156 km. of this road are already paved. It was expected to be fully paved by 1978. A few km. to N on other side of River Jequetepeque are the ruins of Pacotnamú—ruins of pyramids, cemetery and living quarters of nobles and fishermen, seems to have been built in Chavín period. Evidence also of Moche tribes. At the mining town of Chilete, a worthwhile diversion is to take the road N to San Pablo. 3 km. before reaching the village are the stone monoliths of the Kuntur Huasi Culture which resemble those of San Agustín in Colombia.

Cajamarca, the chief town of the northern mountain area, has kept its colonial air. Here Pizarro ambushed and captured Atahualpa, the Inca emperor. The Cuarto de Rescate (Ransom Chamber—closed on Mondays) can be seen (US$0.10) but a red line purporting to be the height of Atahualpa's hand was only recently painted in. (The room's measurements are not quite the same as those given in Prescott's *Conquest of Peru* but it is now doubted whether Prescott was ever there, as the room has been closed to the public for centuries, and used by the nuns of Belén hospital). The Plaza where Atahualpa was ambushed and the stone seat set high on a hill where he reviewed his subjects are also shown. The Cathedral, San Francisco and Belén churches are well worth seeing. Many curious half-finished belfries were a protest against a Spanish king's tax levied on the completion of a church. The Cathedral, which took 350 years to build, was completed in 1960; it still has no belfry. Next to the Belén Church is an ancient hospital; the two, known as the Conjunto de Belén, are being restored as a centre for the handicraft trade. Points of interest include many old colonial houses with garden patios. See palace of the Condes de Uceda, now occupied by the Banco de Crédito; The Education Faculty of the University, near Calle Revilla, has a museum with objects of the pre-Inca Cajamarca culture, not seen in Lima; the attendant knows much about Cajamarca and the surrounding area and will be happy to tell you anything you want to know. Open 0800-1200, 1400-1700. Population: 58,000 (note, especially in the men, the rather narrow and long eyes, uncommonly bright, and white skin in contrast to the Indians of the centre and Cuzco regions. Quechua language also different from the south and most country people speak Spanish. Nearby are the naturally warm, distinctly sulphurous thermal springs known as Los Baños del Inca, now fed into proper baths. Atahualpa tried the effect of these waters on a festering war wound. Here can also be seen trout hatcheries and a farm of the Ministry of Agriculture with splendid bulls for breeding. There is a minibus service from the main square, US$0.10. The surrounding countryside is enchanting. Other excursions include Ventanillas de Otuzco, part of an old Inca sanctuary (airport road, 8 km., minibus from town, US$0.10), gallery of niches; Cumbemayo, mountain village (14 km. SW of Cajamarca but no bus service; taxi US$14), pre-Inca caves, sanctuary and canal which can be followed for several miles, very remarkable but guide necessary to find the way. Hill of Santa Apollonia—the so-called "seat of the Inca" is in fact a sacrificial altar dating to Chavín times. The hill, overlooking the town is an excellent natural vantage point. The top can easily be reached by walking up Dos de Mayo. The town is a favourite among Peruvians for holidays, and has an interesting market with some crafts.

Hotels *State Tourist Hotel* (60 rooms) in the Plaza de Armas, with its 350-year-old fountain (US$7.50 s, US$10 d with private bath). There is an annex at Los Baños del Inca but this is expensive and not very clean. *Hotel Fernandito,* US$1.25; *Sucre* US$1, noisy; *Amazonas,* modern, medium-priced. *Gran Hotel Plaza,* on Plaza, old building with handmade wood furnishings, US$2 s, US$3.90 d, private bath and balcony (no shower), with new annex (dirty); *Hotel San Francisco,* US$2 d; *Hotel Bolívar,* US$1; *Hotel Yusovi,* new, comfortable, all rooms with private baths; *Hotel Becerra* (unsigned), US$3, recommended; *Hotel Casablanca* on Plaza de Armas, US$2.50; *Hotel Cajamarca,* newly opened in colonial-style house, clean, US$1.85 each.

Restaurants *Salas,* Plaza de Armas, best; *Café Bolívar,* on Amalia Puga, for good chocolate cake; *Cabaña,* on main square, recommended; *200 Millas,* cheap fish dishes; *Restaurant del Rescate,* recommended.

Tea Room *La Florida,* in the main square with manjar blanco.

City Specialities   Queso mantecoso (full-cream cheese); manjar blanco (sweet); humitas (ground corn with cheese); cuy frito (guinea pig roast); eucalyptus honey (see below under Industries).

Festivals   Plenty. Corpus Christi is a favourite. Carnival has been revived; it is spectacular but includes much water-throwing.

Air Service   Aeroperú flights to Trujillo and Lima on Mon., Thurs. and Sat. Cheaper to pay for each stage separately. **Warning:** Delays at Cajamarca are all too frequent.

Industries   Mining; dairying (Nestlé plant at Los Baños del Inca); cloth; leather; straw hats. Cajamarca is famous for its eucalyptus-favoured honey, said to be a remedy for rheumatism, sold loose by the kilo in the market in Calle Amazonas.

Tourist Information   Dirección de Turismo, Conjunto de Belén. Kinjyo Travel Service is reputed not to be very reliable. Better to take a taxi for any trips you want to make.

Buses   Daily buses and colectivos from Lima, Trujillo (8 hours, US$4) and Chiclayo (US$3.60, 6 hours by Empresa Díaz). Tepsa leaves for Trujillo and Lima at 1800; Empresa Díaz for Trujillo at 0630 and 2000, for Lima at 1800 and for Celendín at 1530. Also daily to and from Cajabamba, US$3, 5 hours. The bus from Trujillo *via* Contumazá passes through the cane-fields and rice plantations of the Chicama valley before branching off to climb over the watershed of the Jequetepeque. From Contumazá, an attractive little town with long, straight, narrow streets lined with tile-roofed houses, lorries or vans can be taken to Cajamarca, *via* the mining centre of Chilete. From Cajamarca one can reach Cajabamba (bus US$2.50, 5 hours), a mountain town with more donkeys than cars (basic hotel), and then on to Huamachuco (US$1.20, 3 hours), stay night and then back to Trujillo (see page 607). Take 0715 bus from Cajamarca, arrives Cajabamba 1230, and then take 1400 bus to Huamachuco.

North of Cajamarca is Hualgayoc (see page 613). Trip with fantastic scenery. There is excellent trout served in restaurant on the way there; easy to find as it is the only place for miles. Order on your way there to eat on the way back.

Cajamarca is the starting point for the northern route to Iquitos. From Cajamarca there are two buses daily to Celendín—a 5 hour journey. There are several cheap hotels off the main plaza (*Hotel Jorge Girón*, US$0.70 p.p.; *Amazonas* and *Maxmar*, US$0.75, not recommended) and cock fighting every night in the local arena for the *aficionados*. The town has electricity only between 1800 and 2400. Lorries (no buses) leave Celendín every Monday at 0300 (check details at *Hotel Maxmar*) for Chachapoyas (14 hour journey). The road follows a winding course through the northern Andes, crossing the deep canyon of the River Marañón at Balsas. Balsas is reached after 4 hours and then the road climbs steeply with superb views of the mountains and the valleys below. After rain, landslides can be quite a problem. The road on to Chachapoyas is poor and the journey by bus takes over 10 hours, but the scenery is magnificent. Suitable only in dry weather. Food and warm clothing are necessary on this journey. If you want to go through to Iquitos, better to fly.

Chachapoyas   Population 5,000, is the capital of the Department of Amazonas. There is little of interest for the tourist, but it has been called, by the American explorer Gene Savoy, "the friendliest town in Peru".

Buses   Daily to Chiclayo (US$7.75) *via* Bagua and Jaén (16 hours). There are trucks to Celendín on Wed. and Thurs., US$4. On other days there may be "camionetas."

Air Service   A new airport is under construction and services are irregular.

Hotels   *Maranón*, best, and *Amazonas* in Plaza de Armas (US$1-3). A new tourist hotel is being built at Pomacocha Lagoon near Chachapoyas.

Restaurant   Various on Plaza de Armas.

The road is now open *via* Chachapoyas to Mendoza, a five-hour journey from Chachapoyas by lorry (again no buses).

Faucett flies three times weekly from Mendoza to Rioja for US$6.50. Alternative flights are from Trujillo to Rioja. "Two hours by lorry on the road to Mendoza is Molinopampa, which marks the starting point of an adventurous five-day hike to Rioja. Only experienced hikers should attempt this journey, which is very difficult. Food supplies for the whole journey should be purchased at Chachapoyas and a guide, absolutely essential, hired at Molinopampa for about US$5. The steep trail leads through waist-high unbridged rivers, over the cold, high sierra and then for three days one follows the muddy trail down to the dense and humid Peruvian jungle. Along the journey we were accompanied by exotic butterflies, and never a quiet moment with the chattering of birds and monkeys. The whole magic of the jungle—trees, birds, animals and insects—can be seen untouched in their natural surroundings." (Katrina Farrar and Andy Thornton).

From Rioja (2 hotels) there is a road to Naranjillo and Aguas Verdes, with a 5-hour walk to Venceremos, a pleasant way to see the jungle in good weather (don't attempt otherwise), and a good road with plenty of transport (colectivo, US$1.50, beautiful valley journey) *via* **Moyabamba** (915 metres, 5,000 people, *Hotel Monterrey,* US$1.50) to **Tarapoto** (colectivo US$3), a busy town with several hotels.

Hotels   *State Tourist Hotel* (US$10.50 d) non-residents can use the swimming pool for a small fee; *Hotel Juan Alfonso,* US$12 d, with shower, swimming pool, recommended as the only hotel for a sedentary relaxing holiday. *Gran Hotel,* Plaza de Armas US$4.50 d, shower. *Hotel Edinson,* near Plaza de Armas US$7 d clean and comfortable; *Hotel Tarapoto,* US$5.

Restaurants   *Chalet Venecia* and *Achín* both good; *Heladería Tip Top* for ices.

Taxis in this area are very expensive, US$1.10 p.p. taxi airport to town. An airport takes jets. Flights by Faucett and Aeroperú to Lima, Iquitos, Juinjui, and Yurimaguas. Those visiting Tarapoto and Iquitos would be advised to visit Tarapoto first, as aircraft leaving Iquitos tend to overfly Tarapoto; possible to be stuck there for days.

Between Tarapoto and Moyabamba a road leads off to Lamas (colectivo from Tarapoto, US$0.75, 35 km.), where there is a pictureque Indian community completely unspoilt by tourism. Interesting journey also from Tarapoto to Tingo María (see page 656), not advisable in the rainy season. From Tarapoto to Yurimaguas (131 km.) the road can be very bad in the wet season, taking 8 hours; there is a daily bus, also colectivo, US$3.75; take plane, US$4.50, on wet days. From Yurimaguas (see page 657), on the Huallaga River, launches ply to Iquitos.

Cuelap   By driving up the Utcubamba valley from Chachapoyas to Tingo (there is a cheap, friendly, pensión at the entrance to the village), and a 3-hour walk uphill (take waterproof, food and drink, and start early a.m.), one can reach Cuelap, a spectacular pre-Inca walled city. Its massive stone walls are the most formidable in prehistoric South America. The ruins of Cuelap and also La Congona, set on 3 hills can also be reached from Leimebamba (two cheap hotels). The whole area is full of largely unexplored remains; some of them have been studied by the American archaeologist Gene Savoy. A local man who knows the area well is Carlos Gates, a correspondent of several Lima newspapers.

Further N are two ports serving the Chiclayo area. The more southerly is **Etén,** an open roadstead 21 km. by road from Chiclayo; Panama hats are local industry. **Pimentel,** N of Etén is larger, a favourite summer bathing place, with a broad sandy beach. Reached from Chiclayo (14½ km.) by road branching off from the Pan-American Highway. Coastal steamers call at both ports. Also worth seeing is **Santa Rosa,** situated between the two; excellent *cebiche*. The 3 ports may be visited on a pleasant ½ day trip. A red bus leaves Chiclayo market place every ½ hr. for Pimental and Santa Rosa. Colectivos run frequently from Pimental to Santa Rosa, and on to Etén and back to Chiclayo.

Ten km. to the N of Chiclayo is **Lambayeque,** population 20,000, well worth a visit, for while industry and commerce have developed in Chiclayo, the 20th century seems to have by-passed this quaint colonial town. The narrow streets are lined with adobe houses, many retaining their distinctive wooden balconies and wrought iron grill-work over the windows. But the town's most interesting feature is the well-known Brunning Museum, relocated in an impressive modern building. It specialises in Cupisnique, Lambayeque and Vicus cultures, has a fine collection of Mochica and Chimú ceramics and household implements, open 0900-1200 and 1500-1700. Admission, US$0.20. An hotel is soon to be opened.

Chiclayo, on a plain near coast, capital of Lambayeque Department, which is the largest rice producer and the second largest sugar producer in Peru; wheat and cotton are also grown. Population, about 337,000. Nothing much for the tourist to see, but it is the liveliest of all the northern cities, with many parks and gardens. The most interesting spot is the new market place; the market is the best on the coast of Peru; well worth a visit. The new Cathedral, principal club, and Municipal Palace front the Plaza de Armas. Sunday is the day for horse racing.

Hotels   *State Tourist Hotel* (US$13.30 d, with bath), some distance from business centre, good, recommended, swimming pool; *Astoria,* in centre, recommended. Best cheap hotel: *Americano* (US$2.75 each, with bath) on Calle Balta, which always has water when Chiclayo is waterless; *Mediteráneo,* on Calle Balta, near Plaza, US$2 p.p., friendly, clean; *Hotel Mundial,* Calle Balta, near Plaza de Armas, basic, US$2.25 d, without bath; *Hotel Adriático,* US$4 d; *Hotel Inca*—new and good; *Hotel Madrid,* Calle Balta, near Plaza, US$2.20 p.p. Several cheap hotels on Calle Balta, near bus station.

Restaurants   First-class and very reasonable food at *Restaurant Roma,* near *Hotel Astoria; Restaurant Bristol,* good and cheap. Special dish: Alfajor King Kong (pie crust and manjarblanco). *Restaurante Nápoli,* Calle Balta, recommended.

Air Service   Coronel Ruiz airport 2 km. from town. Daily Faucett and Aeroperú jet flights from Lima US$27; flights to Iquitos and intermediate stops. Faucett flies to Chachapoyas 2nd and 4th Sat. each month, US$11.50.

Buses and Colectivos   Daily from Lima, Trujillo (US$3) and Piura. Bus from Lima, US$6. Bus from Piura, US$2.25, 7 hours. To Lambayeque, US$0.10. Direct bus to Cajamarca, Empresa Díaz, and Tepsa, US$3.60, 6 hours. Tepsa to Tumbes, 0100 daily, US$5, 11 hours. Trucks and lorries going in all directions leave from Calle Pedro Ruiz 948 and from the market.

Tourist Office   Las Acacias 305, Urb, La Victoria.

Industries   Rice mills and a jute mill; breweries, machine shops, timber mills, tanneries, shoes, furniture, glass, fruit canning, a cement plant, Nestlé products.

Excursions   Visit Macaurasi, a flat-topped table mountain about 3 km. by 3 km. at 4,500 metres near the village of San Pedro de Castro, 2 areas of extensive Inca ruins at 2 corners of the table *(mesa).* Also see gigantic stone figures, possibly created by a much more ancient people. Truck to San Pedro de Castro, 3 hours, colectivo 2 hours. Trail starts by cemetery, bending to the left. Buses available for US$1.50. Take food as no-one living on the mesa; 2 lakes; nights cold. A minor road runs to Chongayape, a quaint old town 77 km. to the E. It goes *via* Chota (two hotels) to Bambamarca which has an attractive Sunday morning market (lorry from Chota US$0.80; Empresa Diaz to Cajamarca daily at 0700, Sundays 1200, 8 hours, US$2). From there it goes on to Hualgayoc and Cajamarca; a very interesting and beautiful journey, but few buses. The stretch from Bambamarca to Cajamarca is exhilarating; the road climbs to about 4,000 metres through the Andean highlands. **Hualgayoc**, a quaint old mining town, is beautifully situated. Branching off the Pan-American Highway to Piura at Olmos (885 km. from Lima) is a poor road which runs eastwards over the Porciulla Pass (2,150 metres); at km. 257 is a restaurant, but there are better ones at Jaén and Bagua Chica. A road branching from Chamaya leads to the towns of Jaén and Bellavista. **Jaén** (population: 3,500), an old settlement, has recently been revived as a rice-growing centre. Almost life-size images in the churches may have come from Europe. They are unusually beautiful. The annual festival of the patron saint, Our Lord of Huamantanga, is on September 14. Hotel at Jaén: *Danubio*. A road has been built N from Jaén to San Ignacio (114 km.), near the frontier of Ecuador. It crosses the valley of the Chinchipe, renowned for its lost Inca gold. San Ignacio has a fiesta on August 31. A road also goes to Aramongó (280 km.), on the Marañón; it is being extended to Nazareth.

The main road has been pushed on to the Marañón, which is crossed by the July 24th Bridge, and into the Department of the Amazonas, towards Puerto Delfos, on the Lower Marañón; the Marañón is navigable from that point to Iquitos. Another branch road from Jaén has been built SE to Chachapoyas, 263 km. from Olmos. It is being pushed on another 359 km. to Yurimaguas, on the Huallaga River.

A large area of shifting sands—the Sechura Desert—separates the oases of Chiclayo from the oasis at Piura. Water for irrigation comes from the Chira and Piura rivers. The southern part of the Sechura Desert is being turned green by the vast Olmos and Tinajones irrigation projects, financed by the Russians and West Germans respectively. These operations bring water from the Amazon watershed by means of tunnels (one over 16 km. long) through the Andes to the Pacific coast. They will eventually water some 400,000 hectares of desert land. The northern river—the Chira—has usually a super-abundance of water: along its irrigated banks large crops of Tangüis cotton are grown. Irrigation works are being carried out by a Jugoslavian firm, and a massive dam has now been built at Poechos on the Chira river, to divert water to Piura valley. In its upper area the Piura—whose flow is far less dependable—is mostly used to grow subsistence food crops, but around Piura, when there is enough water, the hardy indigenous Peruvian cotton—Pima-is planted.

The Chiclayo—Piura road is now good—with only a few potholes—though there are still bad stretches between Pacasmayo and Chiclayo.

Piura, an oasis in the hot and parched desert, is a proud and historic city (264 km. from Chiclayo). Population, 284,000. Founded in 1532, three years before Lima, by the conquistadores left behind by Pizarro. It is the capital of the Department of the same name. There are well kept parks and public gardens, old buildings are kept in repair and new buildings blend with the old Spanish style of the ancient city. Its special dish is the delicious natillas, made mostly of milk and sugar.

A few blocks from the Plaza de Armas is the San Francisco church, where the city's independence from Spain was declared on January 4, 1821, nearly 8 months before Lima. The colonial church of Las Mercedes has ornately carved balconies, three-tiered archway, hand-hewn supports and massive furnishings. Birthplace of Admiral Miguel Grau, hero of the

War of the Pacific with Chile, whose house has now been opened as a museum. Interesting local craftwork is sold at the Model Market.

Cotton has been grown mainly on medium-sized properties, which have changed hands frequently in recent years and which now form communal or co-operative farms, sponsored by the Agrarian Reform programme. There was a lot of people of German and English origin in the business; most of them have now been expropriated. Worth seeing as an example of a fine old plantation is the former Hacienda Sojo, in the lower Chira valley, which was the centre of the properties of the Checa family. "Its graceful white columns and magnificent verandah overlooking a sweeping curve in the river are memorable." (Colin Harding.)

Hotels   *State Tourist Hotel* (US$13 d), bath and air conditioning, the City's social centre, facing Plaza de Armas; The following four are all located within 1 or 2 blocks of Plaza Grau: *Hotel Cristina* US$8 d, parking facilities; *Hispano* US$1.75; *La Terraza*, US$2.30 each, clean, cheerful, cheap, two blocks from Plaza Grau; *Residencial Piura*, very good, US$12 d; *San Martín*, Av. Cuzco, new; *Hotel Edén*, US$2.60 d; *San Jorge* and *Tambo*, both new; *Hotel Bolognesi*, US$7 d, with private bath; a little out of Piura but worth finding. The town suffers from water shortages. New hotels on Pan-American highway are *Hotel El Sol*, US$11.50 d and bath, snack bar; *Hotel Vicus*, US$10.80 d and bath, restaurant. Also *Hotel Ica*, basic, US$1.50 s, cheapest.

Tourist Offices   Av. La Libertad 945-951 and at airport.

Air   Faucett and Aeroperú daily jet flights from Lima, US$40; 4 flights daily to Lima, 2 Faucett, 2 Aeroperú, always in evening, always late.

Buses   Tepsa buses leave daily from Lima (Paseo de la República) *via* Piura (US$10) to Tumbes (US$13), 22 hours, 1,300 km. Roggero has a new super sultana bus leaving Lima at 1800 for Piura, very reasonable. To Trujillo, 10 hours, US$4 (Roggero). To Tumbes, US$3, 5 hours, colectivo US$4; to Chiclayo, US$3, 7 hours, leave 1400; colectivo to Chiclayo US$4.55 each, leaves from near La Terraza, 4 hours.

Restaurants and Night Clubs   *Tiburón*, 2 km. out of Piura on Panamericana South. In town: *Tres Estrellas*; *Club Grau*; *Ganso Azul* restaurant recommended, it's a group of steak houses just out of town. Two other good central restaurants are *Berlin* and *Torina*. A good ice cream shop is *Venecia* on the main square. *La Huerta*, Huancavelica 277, good for fruit juices.

Excursion   A few km, to the SW of Piura is the village of **Catacaos** (colectivos and buses over the footbridge on Av. Ramón Castilla) famous for its Chicha (maize beer), picanterias (local restaurants, some with music), tooled leather, gold filigree jewellery and the best straw hats in Peru (US$0.25 colectivo).

The port for the area is **Paita**, 50 km. from Piura (colectivos and buses near Plaza Grau, US$1), which exports cotton, cotton seed, wool and flax. Population only 50,000, but it ranks as the fifth port of Peru, for it serves by far the most important cotton-growing districts. Built on a small beach, flanked on three sides by a towering, sandy bluff, it is connected with Piura and Sullana by asphalt highways. The Paita-Piura road is notoriously dangerous (straight, narrow and potholed); better to do the journey *via* Sullana.

Fishing and whaling (at Tierra Colorada, 6½ km. S of Paita) are prosperous industries. The Russians have built a modern fishing and fish-processing complex in Paita, and the Japanese are building one alongside.

On a bluff looming over Paita is a small colonial fortress built to repel pirates. A short distance up the coast is Colán, a summer resort, reached by driving down a large, sandy bluff; near the base is a striking and oddly lonely church over 300 years old. There is a good beach, but Colán is rather derelict since the agrarian reform; it used to be a favourite resort of the hacienda-owners.

Bolívar's mistress, Manuela Sáenz, lived the last 24 years of her life in Paita, supporting herself until her death in 1856 by weaving and embroidering and making candy after refusing the fortune left her by her husband.

Shipping   Outward and homeward port of call for the P.S.N.C. cargo vessels. To Guayaquil fortnightly; weekly coastal service to Callao. Grace Line weekly sailings N to New York and S to Valparaíso each month.

The *Paita* hotel has closed down; there is a guest-house which must be booked in Lima.

Felicity and Emilio Gabbrielli write: From Piura it is possible to make an excursion to Canchaque and Huancabamba in the northern sierra. The trip to **Canchaque** *(Hostal Don Félix,* central square, good and new, approx. US$5 d; otherwise simple clean accommodation for about US$2 on right hand side of church), a delightfully-situated small centre for coffee, sugar-cane and fruit production, is easy, although the last 10 km. are usually impossible for cars in the rainy season. To Huancabamba it is a difficult and tiring road, impossible for ordinary vehicles in the wet season, which crosses the Andes over a pass of more than 3,000 metres. (Although we didn't look for it, local people told us that the Inca highway passes near the road.) The road runs among peaks, which vanish in the mist, and slopes covered with colourful and varied rich subtropical flora (e.g. wild orchids), something in between the overpowering vegetation of the tropical jungle and the predominantly barren mountains further south.

Huancabamba (several small hotels, including *Hotel El Dorado,* with restaurant, on the most attractive main square). Local specialities: Ron Popey, a rich and strong drink made of egg, spices and cañazo (sugar-cane spirit); baked cuy (guinea-pig); and local cheeses, the capital of the province of the same name and a very pretty town in a wonderful setting, has three claims to fame. First, the predominance of European features, due to the fact that it was an important Spanish settlement in colonial times. Second, it is called "the walking town" ("la ciudad que camina" as it is built on irregularly slipping strata which cause the position of houses and streets to vary continually. There are curious evidences of this fact for the tourist, such as the fall of the bridge over the Rio Huancabamba some years ago. Third, and by far the most remarkable element, it is the base for reaching Las Huaringas, a series of lakes at about 4,000 metres. Around here live the most famous witchdoctors of Peru, to whom sick people from all over the country and abroad hopefully flock. The present witchdoctors are the descendants of witches settled here from ancient times; they dress extravagantly but modernly, and their group therapies and magic ceremonies are based on old rites. There are two basic ceremonies; one in the daytime culminating with a communal bath in the curative waters of a lagoon (not obligatory for the extremely uncommon tourist!), and one lasting all through the night during which hallucinatory drugs are used. The witchdoctors are reputed to be millionaires.

Each day a guide leaves Huancabamba with a group of patients on muleback for the five-hour ride to the first witch settlement, where the night is usually spent. Food and sleeping bag, and maybe a tent, must be taken. Reputedly there is also a witch at just twenty minutes' walk from Huancabamba.

Transport from Piura   A bus to Canchaque and Huancabamba leaves daily from Castilla (just across the river from Piura) and takes a minimum of eight hours to reach its destination, the same as by car in good weather. Take the Panamerican Highway south of Piura for 66 km. where there is a signpost to Huancabamba. Canchaque is about 70 km. along this same road (good but unpaved) and then there are 50 km. more of steep and winding road to Huancabamba.

Sullana (population 147,000), 39 km. N of Piura, is built on a headland over the fertile Chira valley. Here the Pan-American Highway bifurcates. To the E it crosses the Peru-Ecuador frontier at La Tina and continues to Cuenca, but the road is poor and little used. The best route is on the W section which passes through Talara and Tumbes, crossing the border at Huaquillas and on *via* Machala to Guayaquil. This road is entirely asphalted and has excellent bus services. The main product of the area is the fine Tangüis cotton.

Hotels *Sullana* (rooms with bath), US$2 s; *Wilson,* US$2 s; *Hotel Bolívar,* US$1 s.
N of Sullana to the border of Ecuador (209 km.) lies the main area in
which Petroperú, the state petroleum agency, operates. The main centre is
Talara (135 km. from Piura, 1,177 km. from Lima), in a desert oasis,
which has a State-owned 60,000 barrel-a-day oil refinery and a new
fertilizer plant. Water is piped 40 km. from the Chira River. An asphalted
network of highways connects the town with the Negritos, Lagunitos, La
Brea and other oil fields; trucks, buses and cars run to Mancora (wayside
fish restaurants superb, including lobster), Lobitos, Zorritos (*State
Tourist Hotel,* US$8 d) and Tumbes in one direction, and to Sullana,
Piura and Paita in the other. The town is a triumph over most formidable
natural difficulties. Population 43,000. Airport with daily flights to Lima
by Faucett and Aeroperú, US$36.

When petroleum was exported, Talara was the second port in Peru. Of
historical interest are the old tarpits at La Brea, 21 km. inland from
Punta Pariñas, S of Talara, and near the foot of the Amotape Mountains.
Here the Spaniards boiled the tar to get pitch for caulking their vessels.
Near this site is the first Peruvian oil well brought into production in
1850, by digging and not by drilling. Production on land from this area is
declining, but there are hopes of offshore production.

Talara Hotels   *Hotel Talara* (no food except breakfast, but a/c in all rooms); *Royal,*
US$2 s (basic).
Restaurants   *La Colmena; Club de Golf*
La Peña beach, 2 km. from Talara, is still unspoilt.
N of Talara, 51 km. is the small port of **Cabo Blanco**, until recently famous for its
excellent sea-fishing: black marlin, striped marlin, broadbill swordfish and rooster
fish and tuna could all be caught in the same waters. The largest fish ever taken on a
rod (a black marlin weighing 707 kg.) was caught here in 1953 by Mr. Alfred
Glassell, Jr. A black marlin weighing 691 kg., caught here by Miss Kimberley Wiss in
1954, is a world record for women. Camping permitted free of charge at Cabo
Blanco, by the Fishing Club Lodge, overlooking the sea (at least in the off-season
June-December).

Tumbes, about 141 km. N of Talara, and 265 km. N of Piura, the most
northerly of Peruvian towns, belonged to Ecuador until 1941. Tumbes
has 33,000 inhabitants, and is a garrison town. There is a long promenade
along the high banks of the Tumbes River. There are some old houses in
the centre and the main square is quite attractive—trees, flowers,
pavement restaurants and the usual church. Small buses and colectivos
leave about every 20 minutes and take 30 minutes to get to Aguas Verdes
on the Peruvian side of the international bridge. On the way most of them
pass by the airport. By taxi it costs about US$2.20, colectivo fare is
US$0.55 and bus fare US$0.30. Huaquillas is the town on the Ecuadorean
side and with a pass from the authorities at the border you can spend the
day there, as long as you are back by 1800. There is nothing much to see
there, but some people hunt for bargains as prices are much lower than in
Peru. Before entry into Peru is allowed, a ticket out is a necessity.
Cheapest is Puno-La Paz, but is non-transferable and non-refundable,
and Tacna-Arica.

This is the only area in Peru where the sea is at all warm in the cooler
months of April to December, so people going S should take advantage of
this fact. Two good beaches near Tumbes, one at Caleta La Cruz about
24 km. S, where Pizarro landed, is easy to get to with regular colectivos
(US$0.50 each way), which go on to Zorritos (also a nice beach—State

Tourist Hotel), water sometimes oily. Nearby is Puerto Pizarro, a small disused port at the edge of the mangrove swamps. In spite of the mangroves, this is an extremely attractive beach (though water sometimes muddy), though difficult to get to by public transport. *Puerto Pizarro Motel* (US$9 d, no hot water, swimming pool). Plenty of fishing, swimming and water-skiing. Mosquito repellent is a must for Tumbes.

Hotels   *State Tourist Hotel,* is being refurbished and was due to be open again in mid-1978; *Toloa,* good at US$6 d; *Hotel Conquistador,* US$4 d and bath but no hot water; *Hotel Cardona,* US$4.50 d, good; *Hotel San Martín,* US$3.50 d; *Florián* and *Cosmos,* both US$5 d, US$3 s, no hot water (but who needs it in this climate?); *Hotel Gondolfo,* US$2 p.p., US$5 d, clean, recommended, near colectivos for Aguas Verdes; *Hostal Kisko,* US$4.50 d with shower; *Hotel Cristina* US$2.50; *Hotel Bolívar,* US$1.80 d, clean but noisy; *Hotel Pilsen,* US$1.50 p.p. Many other cheap hotels. One is on corner of the Plaza, unsigned, US$1.

Restaurants   *Restaurant Florián,* good value, good restaurant 40 metres down road from Roggero bus company; fish only, US$0.55. Try parihuela. Try *Restaurant Bolívar* (same street as Roggero bus company) the *Europa* and *Pez Espada* are good for fish and *Restaurant Curich* in the Plaza de Armas. A new restaurant which is good for seafood is *Tito's* Alfonso Ugarte 212, about 2 blocks from park. *El Bruto* also recommended. There are other good, inexpensive restaurants on the Plaza de Armas and near the markets.

Buses   Daily to and from Lima (US$11) by Roggero (best—leaves 0800, 1400, 1800, though not too reliable on departure times, 23 hour journey) or Sudamericano, cheaper than the others (leave 0800); Tepsa (leaves 1100, 1400 and 1700); 1,333 km., 24 hours, comfortable. Difficult to get buses other than to Lima (which are often booked well in advance) but Piura is a good place for connections. Tepsa and Roggero do take passengers for intermediate stops to Lima. To Piura, US$3, 6 hours. Colectivo, US$4.70. Several bus stations in Tumbes, some for buses to Lima, others for Piura. Guayaquil direct bus to Lima better, costs more but worth while. On the bus to Lima try to get a seat on the right hand side in order to have a good view of the coast.

Taxi to Lima US$20 per seat. Hitching slow.

Road   The Pan-American Highway from Tumbes to Cuenca (see Index) has been partly paved (along the coast) and the mountain stretch has been improved; you can drive the journey in one day. However, the Tumbes-Huaquillas-Machala link is much the best surface route between Peru and Ecuador. A branch of the Automobile Club on the main square sells maps of Peru which are adequate though details (e.g. hotels) are sometimes out of date.

Air   Auroperú flies here from Lima on Mon. and Fri., (US$50).

Tourist Office   Huáscar 381, tel.: 2719.

Warnings   The Banco de la Nación branch at Aguas Verdes will not buy back your surplus soles. Try at the Bank's larger branch in Tumbes below the bridge.

Checks for goods smuggled into Peru are carried out especially at Tepsa bus station as well as at Aguas Verdes. Checks are rigid, both of luggage and body. Checks also intermittently on road to Piura.

South-East of Lima

Lima to Ica   The group of oases in this area grow Pima cotton, sugar-cane and vegetables for Lima and Callao, but the more southern valleys specialize in vineyards—Ica in particular is well known for this and its port, Pisco, has given its name to the celebrated brandy sold all along the coast. Livestock from the sierra are grazed on the green lomas which spring up when the mists soak the mountain slopes from June to October. The Pan-American Highway runs S from Lima through all the places now

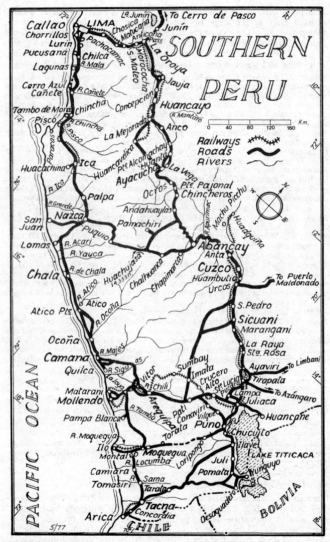

ROUGH SKETCH

to be described to Tacna and Arica. The first 60 km. from Lima are dotted with a series of seaside resort towns and clubs.

Resort town of **Santa María,** 40 km. from Lima, beautiful hotel *Santa María Hotel,* US$50 d, meals included.

Pisco, population 28,519, largest port between Callao and Mollendo, 237 km. S of Lima, serves a large agricultural hinterland. Passengers by ship going N see a green valley and bright vegetation, a welcome relief from the deserts of the coast. The town is divided into two: Pisco Pueblo, faithful to its past—colonial style homes with patios and gardens; and Pisco Puerto, which has been replaced as a port by the new deep-water Puerto General San Martín, beyond Paracas. In Pisco Pueblo, half a block W of the quiet Plaza de Armas, with its equestrian statue of San Martín under a giant ficus tree, is the Club Social Pisco, the H.Q. of San Martín after he had landed at Paracas Bay. There is an old baroque church hiding behind the new one. The Avenida San Martín goes past this building and leads, in little over a mile, to Pisco Puerto. Pisco is an alternative airport when landing is not possible at Lima. A 364 km. road has been built to Ayacucho, with a branch to Huancavelica (see Tambo Colorado, below).

Hotels *Pisco; Humberto; Grau; Hotel Jorge Chávez,* cold showers, cheap, unfortunately some rooms without windows; *Hotel Progreso,* US$2 d; *Restaurant La Rinconada* recommended.

Bank Banco de la Nación is on the main road between Pisco Pueblo and Pisco Puerto.

Industries Cotton seed oil mills, cotton textile factory, whaling factory.

Transport Colectivo to Lima, 3½ hours, US$4. Bus to Lima, Roggero, US$3.50; colectivo to Ica US$1.50. Reservations can be made here at Nazca Tours for flights over the Nazca lines for US$25 p.p.

Fifteen km. down the coast from Pisco Puerto is the bay of **Paracas,** sheltered by the Paracas peninsula, now being developed as a nature reserve. A new monument on the sands marks the spot where San Martín set foot in Peru. The area has been developed as a resort: a beautiful bay, good sands, bathing and fishing and excursions by boat to off-shore islands and to the Paracas necropolis: the burial place of a civilization which flourished here between 700 and 300 B.C. About 1½ hrs walk away is the "candelabra" traced in the hillside, 50 metres long, visible from the sea. *Hotel Paracas* (recommended as best hotel in Peru, about US$16 d) restaurant superb, facing the bay, is a good centre for excursions; it has tennis courts, and an open-air swimming pool. (Small fee for use by non-residents.) Near *Hotel Paracas* is the *Hotel Bahía,* much cheaper, good, US$8 d, good food, discotheque. Poor archaeological museum near Paracas. On the southern side of the peninsula there is a colony of sealions to which a boat can be taken for US$4 each and is worth while. On the northern side, in the bay, there are flamingoes. Condors may be seen from the (bad) road between Paracas and Laguna Grande. Taxi from Pisco to Paracas (return) US$3.50. Colectivo, one way, US$0.50 or US$0.40 if you change at San Andrés.

Up the Pisco valley, 48 km. from Pisco on the road to Huaytará and Ayacucho, is **Tambo Colorado,** one of the best-preserved pre-Inca ruins in coastal Peru (entrance US$0.30); apparently a palace with ancillary buildings; the wall paintings have survived from Inca times. Buses from Pisco, US$1 (1½ hours), by "Huaytarino" for Huaytará or "Oropesa" for Huancavelica, leaves Pisco 1100. Alight 20 minutes after stop at Humay; the road passes right through the site. Return by bus to Pisco in afternoon; for bus or truck back to Pisco wait at the caretaker's house, as the area is said to be dangerous.

From Pisco the Pan-American Highway runs 93 km. S to **Ica**, on the Ica river, a pleasant town with a charming centre; population 143,000. It has an interesting archaeological museum, well laid out and one of the best in Peru, with maps of all sites in the Department; 300 metres from the Tourist Hotel. The image of El Señor de Luren in a magnificent church in Parque Luren draws pilgrims from all Peru to the twice-yearly festivals in March and October, when there are all-night processions. Ica is famous for its tejas, a local sweet made of a fruit filled with manjarblanco; it is also Peru's chief wine centre and has a harvest festival in March.

The waters of the Choclacocha and Orococha lakes from the Amazonian side of the Andes are tunnelled into the Ica valley and irrigate 30,000 hectares of land. The lakes are at 4,570 metres. The tunnel is over 9 km. long.

Hotels *State Tourist,* large and modern, with swimming pool, US$11.50 d, with private bath; *Colón,* on main square, US$3.50 s, US$6 d, with bath, is good value and restaurant serves full-course meals for US$1; *Borjas; Imperial; Bolívar; Pensión Campos. Hotel Gran.* US$2.50, on Amazonas.

Buses To Lima (Morales) US$2.75, 6 hours. Several buses daily to Nazca, US$1.75, 2-3 hours. Colectivo to Nazca, US$3; to Pisco, US$1.50; to Marcona, US$4.50. Morales run daily buses to Cuzco leaving 2300, 36 hours, US$16.50; Ormeño go to Cuzco Wed. and Fri., leaving 1700, 30 hours, US$16.50.

Tourist Office Jirón Cajamarca 179.

Among the sand dunes 5 km. from Ica, on the shores of its much shrunken lagoon, is the summer resort of **Huacachina**. The *Hotel Mossone* (4 hours' drive from Lima), US$12 full board, is at the eastern end of the lagoon, whose vivid green water is strongly alkaline and cures many skin diseases and mitigates—more doubtfully—the pains of rheumatism and arthritis. Another good hotel is the *Salvatierra*. The Laguna de la Victoria, backing on to the dunes parallel to the highway to the N, is picturesque and pleasant, though not perfectly clean. Local bus from Ica to Huacachina costs US$0.10.

The Southern Oases, S of Ica to the Chilean frontier, produce enough to support themselves, but little more. The highlands grow increasingly arid and the coast more rugged. There are only thin ribbons of cultivable lands along valley bottoms, and most of these can be irrigated only in their upper reaches. Most of the inhabitants are Indians. But there are two exceptions: the large and well-watered oasis centring upon Arequipa, and the smaller oasis of the river Moquegua further S. Matarani and Mollendo are the ports for the first and Ilo for the second. In several places the Highway is not protected against drifting sand and calls for cautious driving.

From Ica the Pan-American Highway runs 140 km. S to **Nazca**, a small Colonial town of 20,000 people set in a green valley amongst a perimeter of mountains, 472 km. from Lima. A wide stretch of rolling desert circles the green valley. Its altitude of 619 metres puts Nazca just above any fog which may drift in from the sea: the sun blazes the year round by day and the nights are crisp. A 506 km. road cuts off through Puquío and NE to Abancay (page 653) on the Ayacucho-Cuzco road. Many buses from Lima to Cuzco take this route, which is extremely rough, but offers wild scenery; the journey may be broken at Puquío, although the town has little to recommend it. A branch off this road leads to the Government's vicuña reserve at Pampa Galera.

Buses Lima-Nazca (Tepsa), US$4, 7hrs, Wed. and Sat., leaves 0830 and 2000. Nazca-Cuzco (Morales), US$12, leaves 0500. Lima-Nazca-Cuzco takes 59 hours. Ormeño to Arequipa, US$6. Colectivo to Ica, US$3. Colectivo to Marcona, US$1.50. Colectivo from Lima US$7, reckless driving almost guaranteed!

Camping On Cuzco road, possible to camp at the rangers' camp, at National Park of Vicuñas, a forestry area 3 hours east of Nazca.

Hotels *Nazca State Tourist Hotel,* US$9.50 d, excellent, hot water, peaceful, highly recommended; swimming pool, not to be confused with *Hotel Nazca* near bus station, very clean and friendly, US$3 d; *Montecarlo,* near a Colectivo office; *Hotel Royal,* US$1.30.

The Nazcas had a highly developed civilization which reached its peak about A.D. 800. Their exquisitely decorated ceramics and their wood carvings and adornments of gold are on display in the museums of the world. The Nazca municipality's own excellent museum, on the main Plaza, has a small but fine collection. The valley is full of ruins, temples, and cemeteries; the last-named are quite difficult to find. At the edge of the town is the reservoir of Bisambra, whose water was led by Nazca engineers through underground aqueducts—many still in use—to water the land.

About 22 km. N of Nazca, along the Pan-American Highway, are the famous markings on the land, the Nazca Lines (buses, one or two a day, US$0.25, go early as the site gets very hot). Cut into the stony desert are large numbers of triangular and parallel lines, forming the shape of a dog, an enormous monkey and a bird with a wing span of over 100 metres as well as other birds, a spider and a tree. The lines are so enormous that they can only be appreciated properly from the air; it is now forbidden to walk or drive on the lines, so climb the small hillock by the main road for views. A German expert, Maria Reiche, who has studied the lines for over 25 years, maintains that they represent some sort of vast astronomical pre-Inca calendar, and has dated them at about 1000 B.C., which means that in fact they were carved out long before the Nazca era. In 1976 she had a platform put up at her own expense, from which two of the huge designs can be seen. Bus leaves Nazca at midday and will drop you there, but you have to hitch-hike back.

Small planes take 3 passengers at US$25 each to see the Nazca lines; apply at the Aerocóndor office in Lima (Paseo de la República 144, Oficina 5, Centro Cívica, Tel.: 316028) or on the ground floor of the *Hotel Montecarlo,* Nazca. Flights 45 minutes. The best time to fly is early in the morning, to benefit from the horizontal light.

From a point 40 km. beyond Nazca along the Pan-American Highway a branch road (39 km.) runs to the ports of **San Juan** and **San Nicolás,** built to ship iron ore from the Marcona field, 29 km. inland, and Acarí, 53 km. E again, where a copper deposit is also being worked. San Juan, 553 km. S of Lima, has a beautiful deep-water bay sheltered by land on three sides.

The Highway continues through many small ports: Lomas (one hotel with only 3 rooms), Chala (*State Tourist Hotel,* US$9.50 d, do not drink water even in coffee and soup), Atico, Ocoña, and Camaná (392 km. from Nazca), each at the mouth of a river. Camaná *(State Tourist Hotel,* US$9.50 d, poor), a picturesque little town with a good food market, is 5 km. inland and sends its products to the small port of Quilca, S on the Río Quilca, formerly the unloading point for all sorts of quality goods imported *via* Arequipa to Potosí. Now a seedy harbour. The village of Quilca is further along, perched on a cliff overlooking the Siquas river.

The Pan-American Highway swings inland from Camaná and runs along the top of a plateau with strange crescent-shaped dunes, named Barchans. The sudden descents into miniature "grand canyons" are interesting; two such are the canyons of the Siguas and Víctor rivers. Before Repartición a branch to the left leads to Alpao and the valley of the Majes river. From there continue past Coropina, the highest mountain in southern Peru, to Andahua, a village lying at the head of the valley of the volcanoes. This remarkable area is soon to be opened up by the Peruvian Tourist Board. At Repartición, 134 km. from Camaná, the Highway bifurcates: one branch runs through Arequipa into the highlands (near Arequipa is a new 39 km. toll road, US$0.30); another leads S to the Chilean border. From this latter road a branch leads off from La Joya to Mollendo and Matarani.

Mollendo, 14,251 people, an ill-protected open roadstead, has now been replaced as a port by **Matarani,** a new harbour 14½ km. to the NW: well sheltered but difficult to enter because the coast is very rocky and the approach is not a straight line. Port workers still live mostly in Mollendo, where the main customs agencies are. In the poorer section there is a cliff road with a sheer drop from the high bluff to the sea-pounded rocks below. S of this cliff a beautiful sandy beach stretches down the coast. Mollendo now depends partly upon the summer attraction of this beach and partly upon the 15,000 hectares of irrigated land in the nearby Tambo valley. On the coast, a few km. SE by road, is the rapidly growing fashionable summer resort of Mejía.

Hotel *Salerno,* 30 rooms, all with bath, excellent seafood.

Customs Agency Luis Calvimontes S.A., Calle Arequipa 100 (good).

Sailings Cargo/passenger lines—Prudential-Grace; Gulf & South American; Hamburg-Amerika; Johnson; Knutsen; North-German Lloyd. Cargo only—P.S.N.C.

The railway journey from Arequipa to Juliaca, Puno and Cuzco, is described later (page 600). The Pan-American Highway runs S from La Joya through Moquegua to Tacna and Arica (Chile). The Highway to Moquegua is paved all the way. **Moquegua** (200 km. from Arequipa), population of 10,178, is a small town of winding cobblestone streets at 1,370 metres in the narrow valley of the Moquegua river. The Plaza has llama-shaped hedges. The roofs are built with sugar-cane thatch and clay. Most of the valley below the city grows grapes—there are no bodegas at Moquegua—and the upper part grows avocados (*paltas*), wheat, maize, potatoes, some cotton, and fruits. Climate: semi-tropical. Its few exports—avocados and wine—go by an excellent 96-km. road to the port of **Ilo** (population 2,000). C.S.A.V. and C.P.V. coasting steamers call weekly.

Bus Moquegua-Ilo, US$0.90, leaves at 1100. Returns from Ilo at 1700.

There are three Ilos: Ilo Viejo, in ruins after the earthquake of 1868; Ilo Nuevo, the present town, dirty, with a fishmeal factory, oil tanks, and dusty and sometimes cobbled streets and "half-door" saloons; and the spick and span village built by the Southern Peru Copper Corporation (hospital, cinema, playgrounds, etc.) where the engineers and their families live.

Some 70 km. S of Moquegua a sign points to the "Minas de Toquepala" (64 km. by a good road), an impressive sight. Toquepala township, in a hollow, has a guest house (swimming pool), a church, club house and an American school, and is a pleasant place. Helio Courier planes reach it from Moquegua (12 minutes) and Ilo (26 minutes). Taxis from Ilo.

The Southern Peru Copper Corporation is exploiting its copper property at Toquepals, SE of Moquegua (177 km. NE of Ilo) at an altitude of 3,050 metres, and is developing its property at Cuajone nearby; good view of valley, which is full of cacti. All exports are through Ilo, along the 183-km. railway and road from Toquepala. The SPCC smelter is on the coast, 18 km. from the port of Ilo.

Moquegua Hotels *State Tourist Hotel*, US$12.50 d; *Moquegua; Los Limoneros*, US$11.50 d, hot showers, pretty garden, swimming pool, few foreigners.

Ilo Hotel *State Tourist Hotel*, US$14 d.

The 156-km. stretch of the Pan-American Highway between Moquegua and Tacna is paved and in good condition.

Tacna, at 550 metres, and backed by the snow-capped peak of Tacora, is 156 km. S of Moquegua by Pan-American Highway, 42 km. from the Chilean frontier, and 64 km. from the international port of Arica. The railway to Arica was the second built in South America. Above the city, on the heights, is the Campo de la Alianza, scene of the battle between Peru and Chile in 1880. Tacna is 1,400 km. from Lima by road, 987 by air.

Tacna was in Chilean hands from 1880 to 1929. In an unsuccessful attempt to Chilenize the city so many schools were built that Tacna has the highest literacy rate in Peru. The narrow, clean streets are paved; the water system is excellent; there are handsome modern schools, housing estates, a stadium to seat 10,000 people, an airport suitable for jet planes. Many military posts and one of the best hospitals in Peru. Population: 45,000.

Around the city the tawny desert is giving way to green fields as an expanding web of irrigation canals brings water. The waters of Aricota Lagoon, 80 km. N, are now being tapped for further irrigation and hydroelectric power for industry. The cathedral, designed by Eiffel and begun in 1872, has been completed; it faces the main square, Plaza de Armas, which contains huge bronze statues of Admiral Grau and Colonel Bolognesi. The road E to Bolivia—*via* Tarata (where Inca terraces are still in use) and Challapalca to Ilave—where it connects with the Puno-La Paz highway—is not too bad in the dry season, though difficult in the rains. Bus service to the copper mines at Toquepala. Buses to Arica will not take passengers who have to stop at the Chilean frontier for passport formalities, and colectivos won't take passport-holders and border-card holders in same car. There is also a train service to Arica, at 0830 and 1430. If you take this you must get your passport stamped first in Tacna. Coming into Peru from Chile, you can change pesos into soles with street money changers in Tacna. Apparently legal, but street rate is bad. Better when leaving Peru to change soles to dollars at Banco de la Nación in Tacna and then buy pesos with dollars. You probably get a better rate for pesos here than in Chile.

Hotels *State Tourist Hotel*, gardens and swimming pool, US$9.50 d; *Lima; Chiclayo*, US$3 d (adequate); *Las Vegas Internacional*, US$3.60 p.p.; *Callao,*

US$4.20 d, average; *Hotel Central; Hotel Internacional,* US$3 s with bath, no hot
water or food but adequate; cheaper hotels recommended are the *Luz* and the *Gruta.*
Restaurant   *Comedor Municipal,* in market, cheap and recommended.

Air   Faucett daily jet flights to Lima; Aeroperú on Mon., Tues., Fri. and Sat.
Cheap way to fly from Lima to Santiago, Chile: Faucett to Tacna, then colectivo to
Arica connecting with LAN Chile flight to Santiago. *Via* Tacna, US$79. Direct
US$99.

Buses   Tacna-Arequipa, US$2. Only 3 a day to Lima, generally booked up; Tepsa
at 1400, Morales Moralitos 1100, Ormeño at 1300. All take 25-27 hours, US$10. Bus
Moquegua-Tacna, US$1.40. Plenty of colectivos (Empresa Chasqui) to and from
Arica for about US$2.50.

Travel Information   Sr. Roberto Burns, San Martín 340, office No. 4, Tel.: 2602.

Tourist Office, Av. Bolognesi 2088 and Complejo Fronterizo "Santa Rosa".

Club   Unión de Tacna. There is an exclusive Casino.

From Arequipa to Cuzco

Mollendo-Arequipa-Juliaca-Cuzco   The Southern Railway no longer
carries passengers between Mollendo and Arequipa, but there is a road
following a similar course. The sea is left behind, a steady climb begins,
winding in, out and around the desert foothills. The Tambo Valley comes
into view on the right and miles of fields with alfalfa, sugar cane and
cotton contrast with the barren slopes on the left.

The ash-grey sand dunes near La Joya, about half way to Arequipa, are
unique in appearance and formation. All are crescent shaped and of
varying sizes, from 6 to 30 metres across and from 2 to 5 metres high, with
the points of the crescent on the leeward side. The sand is slowly blown up
the convex side, drifts down into the concave side, and the dunes move
about 15 metres a year.

Arequipa, 146 km. from Mollendo by road, stands at 2,380 metres in a
beautiful valley at the foot of El Misti, otherwise known as El Volcán de
Arequipa. This is a snow-capped, perfect cone, 5,843 metres high,
guarded on either side by Chachani (6,096 metres), and Pichu-Pichu
(5,669 metres). The city has quaint old Spanish buildings and many
ancient and interesting churches built of "sillar", a pearly white volcanic
material almost exclusively used in the construction of Arequipa. It was
re-founded on August 15, 1540, by an emissary of Pizarro's, but even at
that date it was an old Inca city. Its main churches are the huge, twin-
towered Cathedral on the Plaza de Armas and the nearby small Jesuit
church of La Compañía (1698), as elaborate as the Cathedral is simple,

admission US$0.10. See in particular the Royal Chapel to the left of the Sanctuary. The churches of San Francisco (an arcade to the side, displaying pictures and handicrafts, is now open), San Agustín, La Merced and Santo Domingo are all well worth seeing; they were badly damaged in the earthquakes of 1958 and 1960, but the damage has been repaired. San Francisco's fine old cloister is now open to the public. Opposite the church is a handicraft centre, housed in a beautiful former prison. Spanish wealth was early lavished on magnificent mansions also. There are a university, a theatre, a museum and several libraries.

Because of the danger of earthquakes the churches are not tall, the houses have one storey only, patios are small with no galleries. Roofs are flat and windows are small, disguised by superimposed lintels or heavy grills.

Interesting Holy Week ceremonies, culminating in burning of effigy of Judas on Easter Sunday and the reading of his "will", containing minor criticisms of the city authorities. On 14th August, eve of the city's anniversary, there is a splendid firework display in the Plaza de Armas and a decorated float parade.

Arequipa, third city of Peru, 355,000 people, is an extremely busy commercial centre which strongly dislikes its commerce, or anything else, being run from Lima, a fact which businessmen should know. The climate is delightful, with a mean temperature before sundown of 23°C, and after sundown of 14½°C. The weather is normally ideal between April and December, though freak cloud and rain is sometimes experienced in August-September. The sun shines on 360 days of the year. Annual rainfall is less than 150 mm.

Points of Interest   Cathedral, founded 1612, largely rebuilt 19th century; La Compañía Church, whose main façade (1698) and side portal (1654) are striking examples of the florid Andean mestizo style, its San Ignacio chapel has an interesting polichromed cupola; Puente Bolívar, designed by Eiffel; Hospital Goyeneche; the Orphanage; the Charcani electric plant, in a gorge between Misti and Chachani. Arequipa has several fine seignorial houses with large carved tympanums over the entrance. The Gibbs-Ricketts house (now offices), with its fine portal and puma-head waterspouts, and the Casa del Moral, or Williams house (Banco Industrial, with museum) are good examples. Colonial streets and residences are preserved within the Santa Catalina Convent, now open to visitors. One of the oldest districts is San Lázaro, a collection of tiny climbing streets and houses quite close to the Tourist Hotel at Selva Alegre; the newly opened hotel, Parador El Molino Blanco, a converted mill in a traditional San Lázaro setting, can be visited. Besides San Francisco Church the cloistered monastery has been reconstructed. Behind the cathedral there is a very attractive alley with more handicraft shops. Churches are usually open 0700-0900 and 1800-2000.

By far the most interesting visit is to Santa Catalina Convent, opened in 1970 after centuries of mystery, the most remarkable sight in Arequipa; excellently refurbished, very beautiful, period furniture, kitchen utensils, and paintings. It is a miniature town over two hectares in area in the midst of the city; about 450 nuns used to live there in total seclusion, attended by some 200 unpaid servant girls who also spent their lives within the walls. The few remaining nuns have retreated to one section of the convent, allowing visitors to see a maze of cobbled streets, flower-decked cloisters and buttressed houses. These have been well restored and painted in vivid browns and blues. Open 0900-1630 (but they're not strict about throwing you out), admission US$1.20 (US$0.90 for students), US$0.50 on Sundays. A visit lasts two hours; many tourists. The many pictures of the Arequipa and Cuzco schools are worth a look.

The flowered Plaza de Armas is faced on three sides by colonial arcaded buildings, and on the fourth by the Cathedral. Many narrow, cobbled streets lead away from this centre. The central market (San Camilo) is also worth visiting. The city's other speciality is leatherwork. At Selva Alegre (where the Tourist Hotel is), hundreds of people spend Sunday on the grass under eucalyptus trees. The Tourist Hotel is within easy walking distance of all the famous churches and main plaza. Arequipa is said to have the best-preserved colonial architecture in Peru, apart from Cuzco. A cheap tour of the city can be made in a Vallecito bus, 1½ hours for US$0.15.

Industries   Large woollen mill, textiles, leather, soap and candles, canning, flour, brewing, nylon plant, plastic products, steel plant.

Hotels   *State Tourist Hotel,* US$7.75 d, without bath, US$13.30 d, with bath; *Presidente,* first class, US$12.50 d, with shower; *Jerusalén,* US$7 s, US$11 d; *Crismar,* in Calle Moral, opposite main Post Office, modern central, civilized, US$9 d; *San Martín* and *Country Club,* US$6 d, quiet, clean, on Calle San Martín. *Hostal Centenario,* on Mercaderes—no hot water, clean; *Hotel Casa de Familia* (Av. Siglo 124), US$6.50, bed and board; *Hotel Lira,* central, US$4 d. Recommended are: *Hotel International,* 3 blocks from Plaza de Armas, located across the street from the market at Piérola 333 and can be noisy; ask for a room at the back, US$3 s, US$5 d; *Hotel Excelsior,* US$1.50 s, without shower, clean; *Hotel Rosdal,* US$2 s; *Hotel Royal,* US$2.50 d, quiet and clean, cold water only; *Hotel Comercial,* US$3 d; *Hotel Moderno,* cold shower, US$2.40 s; *Hotel Catalina,* new, US$3 s, near Convent; *Hotel Wilson,* US$5 d, hot shower, laundry facilities in annex which is more expensive and better; *Hotel Pacifico,* US$3 d; *Hotel El Emperador,* Calle Moral, US$5 d; *Residencial Rivero,* Rivero 420, US$2.25 s; *Residencial Lima,* US$2.50 s; *Residencial Salaverry,* US$3.25 s; *Residencial San Luis,* US$3 s; *Gran Hotel,* US$2, no hot water; *Parador El Molino Blanco,* old mill in San Lázaro, overlooking the River Chili, superbly furnished with antiques; room for 6 persons and only breakfast served, US$20 s, very luxurious; *Hotel Crillón Serrano,* Calle Perú 106, recommended, US$3.10 d; *Hotel Americano,* US$3.70 d, hot shower; *Hotel Vargas,* US$3.20 d, on Calle Perú, hot water, recommended. Also try *Hotel Mitre,* US$5 d; *Hotel Roma,* US$3.60 d; *Hotel Corona; San Juande Dios,* US$1.20 s. hot water, clean and friendly; *Hotel Metro,* central, US$5.50 d, clean; *Residencial Bolívar,* Calle Bolívar 202, US$3-4 each with shower, clean and friendly.

Restaurants   *Chez Nino* and *Capri* on Calle San Francisco, near the Plaza de Armas; another *Chez Niño* on Calle Jerusalén, but not as good as the one on Calle San Francisco; *Astoria,* Calle S. Domingo, recommended; *Chopería,* vaguely German, beer good, on road to airport, quite expensive; *La Taverna,* San Juan de Dios, criollo food, not very good value; Pizzeria ½ block east of cathedral, recommended; *La Estancia,* Calle San Domingo, Argentine food, good, sometimes live music. Also recommended, *Restaurant La Casona,* Calle Jerusalén; *Los Candiles,* Calle Zela 210, opp. San Francisco Church, a typical Arequipeño interior but limited menu, very good; *Bar Economía,* good local food, Calle San Francisco. *Café-Bar-Restaurant Dalmacia,* San Juan de Dios 514B, cheap good food; *Fonda del Sol,* lunch only, in open air, on road to airport, good. Recommended cafés are the *Monaco,* Calle Mercaderes and the *Astoria,* Calle Santo Domingo. A score of picanterias specialize in hot foods: try one called *El Pato; rocoto relleno* (hot stuffed peppers), *cuy chactado* (seared guinea-pig), *papas con ocopa* (boiled potatoes with a hot yellow sauce) and *adobo* (pork stew). Try them in Yanahuara suburb, or the well-known *Sol de Mayo,* just off airport road, over the Puente Grau and up Ejército, fourth road to the right, cheap, noisy and serves excellent Arequipeño lunches. A good local speciality is Mejía cheese; try also the *queso helado* (ice-cream cheese).

Tourist Office La Merced 117. Complaints and suggestions are actively welcomed, very helpful, open 0800-1330, free street plans. Police have recently opened an office at their station on 2nd block of Av. Ejército, in Yanahuara, where they offer information every day (normal office closed Sat.-Sun.).

British Consul Office now closed, but Mr. Ricketts will help unofficially, at Moral 114, next to Post Office.

Current 220 volts A.C., 50 cycles.

Clubs Club Arequipa; Golf Club; North American Cultural Institute; International Club; Club Hípico Los Leones (riding club).

Bank Banco de la Nación—branch which changes foreign money is in Mercaderes—3 blocks from Cathedral.

Shopping Casa Secchi, Mercaderes 111, sells good arts, crafts and clothing. Sr. Fernando Delange, Zela 103, repairs all kinds of electrical equipment as well as cameras.

Taxi Fares US$1.80 an hour within the town, US$0.50 for one trip; US$1.90 in the country; US$1.80 airport to city.

English library at Peruvian-North American centre, Calle Melgar 109.

Cables At central Post Office, in Moral opposite *Hotel Crismar*.

Sports Two public stadiums, a racecourse, several swimming pools, tennis courts and golf links (18 holes). The Arequipa Golf Club welcomes visitors from abroad. Riding is very popular. There are bullfights, and elaborate occasional firework displays (especially on August 14).

Roads To Lima, 1,030 km. Colectivos, very fast, take 12 to 18 hours; fare US$9.50, leave from Parque Universitario (Lima) at 0830, 1400 and 0200. Warning: need to book in advance to and from Lima in Jan.-March holiday season. Buses, de luxe Pullman, air conditioned, many daily, 17-18 hours, US$11 (recommended is Ormeño or Tepsa, 16 hours only; Morales Moralitos not the best; Sudamericana is cheapest). Trucks to Lima take 3-4 days. After Arequipa both roads and buses are very bad; a train would be better. To and from Cuzco by bus (680 km.), 24 hours, US$14. Colectivo-taxi Arequipa-Cuzco US$14 and Arequipa to Tacna (5 hours) for US$4.20. Bus to Mollendo (2 hours), US$1.25. Colectivo to Juliaca US$7; to Puno (San Cristóbal) at 1100. Bus Arequipa-Juliaca 8½-9½ hours. Bus Arequipa to Tacna, Transportes Angelitos Negros (Calle San Juan de Dios 502) leaves 1630, US$2.80, 7 hours. Arequipa-Moquegua by Angelitos Negros, leaves in the morning, US$2, interesting journey. Buses must be booked 24 hours in advance.

Air Chachani Airport 5 km. from town. To and from Lima, daily air service by Faucett and Aeroperú, about US$36; sit on left side of aeroplane Lima to Arequipa and get the stewardess to point out the Nazca lines. To Cuzco by Faucett temporarily suspended; by Aeroperú, 4 flights, Sun., Tues., Thurs., Fri. (Fokker jet), US$17.10 s, US$32.50 return. To Juliaca by Aeroperú on Wednesdays and Sundays. To and from Tacna by Faucett on Mon., Thurs. and Sat. Shared taxi to town US$1.25.

Rail To Puno, Mondays, Wednesdays and Fridays, 0845 and daily at 2200, with connections to Cuzco via Juliaca; trains arrive Puno 1900 and 0840. Fares: Buffet US$7.50, 1st US$6, 2nd US$3. Only the buffet car is heated—important in passes above 4,000 metres. Tickets for the morning train can be bought between 1800 and 1900 the night before. Connections with lake steamer to La Paz only on Wednesdays at Puno; hydrofoils now daily. Rail trip to Puno and Cuzco is spectacular.

The buffet car ticket allows you to sit there throughout the journey but the fare does not include the lunch. If you feel bad on Arequipa-Puno train ask for the oxygen mask at once; sucking coramina glucosa tablets during the journey may prove helpful. Best recommended are Effortil pills.

Warning Train tends to fill up 2 hours before departure. Beware of thieves on Arequipa station.

Excursions Many swimming pools and countryside; the nearby hillside village of **Cayma,** with delightful 18th century church (open only until 1600) and splendid views from the roof (the sexton is friendly and for a small tip takes you up; best view is in the afternoon). It also has many old buildings associated with Bolívar and Garcilaso de la Vega and is the home of contemporary Arequipeño poet, Manuel Gallegos Sanz. The Candelaria festival on 2nd February is colourful. Many local buses marked Cayma. **Yanahuara**, also virtually a suburb of the city, with a 1750 mestizo-style church, (opens 1500) with magnificent churrigueresque façade, all in sillar; the Tiabaya valley; Sabandia mill, built 1600, entrance fee US$0.50, swimming bath and countryside; then the three famous thermal baths: **Jesús** (½ hour by car, on the slopes of Pichu-Pichu); **Yura**, 29 km. from Arequipa (hourly bus, US$0.27) in a small valley on the W slopes of Chachani (*Yura Tourist Hotel,* US$11.50 d); and **Socosani** (1½ hours by rail and road, or by road), now a spa owned by a mining consortium, can only be visited by appointment; 40 km. from Arequipa, in a beautiful small valley SW of Chachani, with a modern hotel providing meals and Socosani water; sports in Socosani: tennis, bowls. **Tingo**, which has a small lake and 3 swimming pools, should be visited on Sunday (bus no. 7) for *anticuchos* and *buñuelos.*

Three hours from Arequipa, up a passable dirt road running through Cayma between Misti and Chinchanay, is the village of Chivay (regular buses) lying in the spectacular terraced valley of the Colca river. Water from this river is currently being diverted through a series of tunnels and canals to the desert between Repartición and Camaná, where it will irrigate the Siguas and Majes pampas. Further down the Colca valley on both sides, unspoilt Andean villages are to be found, overlooked by the two volcanoes, Hualca-Hualca and Ampato. Below one of these villages, Cabana Conde, the river runs through a canyon said to be the deepest in the Americas.

Mr. Tony Holley takes small private groups by Land Rover to other interesting places in the area such as the rock carvings at Toro Muerto (off the Majes Canyon), the slopes of the Misti, cave drawings at Sumbay etc. Excursions cost from US$40, irrespective of how many people (up to six) go. Mr. Holley's postal address is Casilla 77, Arequipa, and his home address is Urb. Tahuaycani F-28, Umacollo, Arequipa.

The early morning scene as the train winds its way up the valley towards Juliaca is enchanting. In the foreground are irrigated fields of alfalfa, wheat and other grains. Winding around the volcanoes Misti and Chachani the train climbs steadily past Yura, Socosani and Pampa de Arrieros; lunch is served on the train. The train climbs another 80 km. until it reaches Crucero Alto, the highest point on the line (4,500 metres). All water E of this point flows into the Atlantic. The first mountain lakes appear. The largest are Lagunillas and Saracocha. They are very pretty and both come into sight at the same time from opposite sides of the train, which winds along their margins for nearly an hour. The mountain sides and canyons are dotted with flocks of sheep, llamas, alpacas and occasional vicuñas. As the descent continues streams become more plentiful. The scene changes in a few hours from desolate mountain peaks; a fertile pampa carrying a fairly populous agricultural community. The train arrives in the evening at Juliaca and Puno. Indian women in brilliantly coloured costumes sell equally brilliant knitted garments at the station. The train stops long enough at Juliaca for you to buy woollen goods on square just outside station. Train to Cuzco daily, Mon.-Fri. 0835, Sat. 1025.

Road The fairly rough dirt road from Arequipa to Juliaca reaches its highest point at Alto de Toroya, 4,693 metres.

Juliaca, 304 km. from Arequipa, at 3,825 metrés, has a population—mostly Indian—of 35,000. It is the highland centre for wool and hides and has many tanneries. Alpaca knitted goods are cheap. On the huge Plaza Melgar, several blocks from the main part of the town, is an interesting colonial church. Large daily market in the Plaza, reported cheaper than Cuzco and Puno. A first class hospital is run by the Seventh Day Adventists. Aeroperú flies to Juliaca Wed., Fri., Sat. and Sun., *via* Arequipa.

Hotels *State Tourist Hotel,* very good, US$12 d; *Hotel Benique,* opposite station, acceptable, US$1 s; *Hotel Arce,* clean, cold water, US$4 d; *Hotel Barreros,* opposite railway station, recommended, US$4 d. Also recommended: *Hotel Victoria,* simple. *Gran Hotel,* US$1.25, not recommended; *Sur,* US$1.75 each, not really recommended; *Alojamiento San Antonio,* US$1, basic but clean.

Excursion to thermal springs at village of Putina, near Puno. Bus from Juliaca, US$0.50. Near Juliaca is the unspoiled (because inaccessible) little Colonial town of **Lampa,** with splendid church (see also page 631).Colectivos Juliaca to Puno US$1 per head; frequent buses US$0.50.

Puno, capital of its Department, altitude 3,855 metres, population 35,000 on the NW shore of Lake Titicaca, dull at first acquaintance, is really very interesting, with a fine main square and a fascinating lakeside quarter. The coldly austere Cathedral was built in 1754. Puno gets bitterly cold, especially at night.

Hotels *State Tourist Hotel* (US$11.50 d) with good food, hot-water bottle on request; the hotel is much in need of refurbishing. *Hotel Sillustani* now taken over by the Navy. The *Hotel Ferrocarril,* Av. de Torre 185, opposite station, is modern, reasonable (US$15 a day) with shower and some hot water, food fair, but good rooms, said to be better than *State Tourist Hotel;* annex (US$5 d) but no hot water. The *Hotel Torino,* near bus station, US$1.50 s, no hot water, but it is clean and quiet, unlike the *Hotel Tito* (US$5 d, hot water). *Hotel Colonial,* US$3 s. *Hotel Roma* (US$1.10) is passable. Good place is the *Motel Tambo Titikaka* (US$13 s, US$18.50 d, with half-pension), nice restaurant, at Chucuito on the lakeside; book in advance. Puno suffers from power and water shortages. *Hotel Extra,* Calle Moquegua, US$1.50 p.p., clean and hot water; *Hotel Tumi,* US$3 d; *Residencial Italia* (behind Ferrocarril), US$9 d, and breakfast; *Hotel Lima,* new, US$1.50 each in 4-bedded room, hot water 1830-2030 recommended. Many economy hotels; e.g. *Venecia* (US$1.50 s) and *Colón* both on Av. Tacna and others near the Morales bus station. *Hotel Centenario,* US$1 each, adequate; *Palermo,* US$0.60 s. *Monterrey* (US$5.50 d, with bath), not recommended; and *Ambassador,* in Calle Lima, are recommended. *Hotel Palaca Puno,* Av. Tacna 786, US$10 d. Hotel rooms are difficult to find after trains arrive as everyone else is also looking.

Restaurants *Al Lago,* no longer recommended. *La Isla,* recommended, especially for its trout. Also try *Restaurant Sala Caliente* or any of the Pollo (chicken) places: ¼ chicken and french fries, US$1. *Restaurant Ambassador,* Calle Lima, highly recommended; *Restaurant Delta,* good for snacks.

Museums Municipal, in main square; Private Museum of Sr. Dreyer, Calle Conde de Lemos 289 (by permission).

Market In the covered part there are model reed boats and attractive carved stone amulets and Ekekos (Bolivian household gods). Reported, with Juliaca, to be the best place in Peru for llama and alpaca wool articles though possibly more expensive than Juliaca.

Festival February 2-10, the very colourful Fiesta de la Virgen de la Candelaria. November 4-5, pageant on founding of Puno and arrival of Manco Capac from waters of Lake Titicaca.

Railways There is a 48-km. railway from Juliaca to Puno, and another to Cuzco (338 km.). On the Cuzco-La Paz route, all except buffet car 1st class passengers change at Juliaca and go through Puno to the wharf, where Peruvian immigration and Customs operate. There is often no room for a ticket-holder in the steamer across Lake Titicaca. From the mole the *Inca* makes the eleven-hour crossing to Guaqui at 2000 on Wednesday night, returning on Friday night. Cost for combined first-class boat and train, including dinner, US$18. You cannot book the boat train until you reach Puno. The boat awaits the train from Cuzco. There are bunk beds with mattresses and it is impeccably clean, though there are not enough bunks for all passengers. 2nd class bunks US$5 s; cannot book in advance. Puno to Guaqui by ship 2nd class, better value. A train for La Paz connects with steamers at Guaqui. From Puno to La Paz is 275 km. Puno to Cuzco train leaves 0645 Mon.-Fri. and 0920 Sat., arriving at 1735 and 1940. 1st class US$7, 2nd US$3.50, buffet US$9. Second class is usually to be recommended as new carriages with padded seats have been introduced, but travellers with an extra-sensitive sense of smell, beware!. Tickets only on sale an hour before departure. A magnificent run, with shopping possibilities at stations. Puno to Arequipa daily leaves 2030 and also on Tues. and Thurs. at 0655 and on Sat. at 0920, 1st class US$7, 2nd class US$3.50, 10 hours. Recommended travel Arequipa to Cuzco is to stay overnight at Juliaca not Puno so you do not travel Juliaca to Puno at night. Sit on east side on Puno-Cuzco train for best views and on the left-hand side going Puno-La Paz.

Tourist Information at *Tourist Hotel,* from Turismo Titicaca, and Kinjyo Travel Service, Calle Arequipa 401. Government Tourist Office at Calle Deustua 342.

Roads To Arequipa, road bad, few bridges and many streams. Several bus companies leave in the morning. Sur Peruano leaves at 0900, charges US$5.80 for door-to-door service. To Cuzco, road first 40 km. and last 45 km. paved, other 302 km. very bad, again several bus companies cover the route, Sur Peruano for US$6.10 and Transportes San Cristóbal for US$3; To Lima, 18 hours, several companies. To Bolivia either by lake-side road through Copacabana and ferry across Straits of Tiquina (US$2.25, ferry carries vehicles) or directly *via* frontier at Desaguadero (the way buses go)—shorter and faster, but a day's drive either way. Bus (Morales Moralitos) to La Paz (12 hours) leaves Puno 0900, Sat., Tues., and Thurs. (0800 Sun., arrives Desaguadero at 1630 and at La Paz at 2145), rough trip, bad road, US$10 s, colectivos US$15 per seat, more reliable in the dry season but sometimes cannot get through in rainy season; the buses break down often. Colectivo Juliaca Express Puno-La Paz, twice daily, US$12.30. Offices: Puno—Tacna 298; Arequipa—Salaverry 111; Cuzco—Ruinas 407; Juliaca—San Román 129. Transturin of La Paz runs a luxury bus Cuzco-Puno-La Paz; Puno-La Paz, US$20, including 3 meals, leaves Puno 0500, arrives La Paz 1730 on Mon., Wed., Fri. stopping at Tiahuanaco. Transturin has offices in both Puno (State tourist hotel) and Cuzco (main square) where tickets can be booked in advance. If you pay as you go, paying at Puno and Desaguadero (a miserable place—don't stay the night) it is much less. To cross the international bridge on trip Puno *via* Desaguadero there is a US$1 charge. Hydrofoil from Copacabana to Huatajata combined with private car from Puno, Tues., Thurs., Sat., US$50 p.p. Includes visit to the ruins on the Island of the Sun (see page 170, Bolivia section). There are buses to Desaguadero (about US$3), also to Tacna and Moquegua (Sur Peruano).

Puno-Yunguyo-Copacabana-La Paz by far the more beautiful journey. Bolivian authorities want proof that you have US$10 for each day in Bolivia.

The cheap way: bus Puno-Yunguyo, US$2.50, 4 hours (Colectivo US$3), several buses daily, but only one on Sunday, 0800 (*Hotel Amazonas,* US$1; *Hostal Yunguyo,* also US$1, clean). Avoid staying overnight at Yunguyo, little privacy. Passport stamped at Yunguyo, walk across bridge to Kasami—1 km., passport stamped again, then bus or 3 km. walk to Copacabana for Immigration, then Copacabana-La Paz bus, US$1.40, 5 hours. Alternatively local buses and trucks go from Yunguyo to Copacabana, stopping at the frontier, for US$0.15. On Sundays there are many trucks carrying people between the markets. Coming into Peru at this point you can get an overnight truck to Puno for about US$1, though these are cold and uncomfortable.

N.B. Delays and consequent expenses have been reported by travellers going from Puno to Bolivia by hired car. Tourists should note that Immigration, Customs and

Police offices are all at different places on both the Peruvian and Bolivian sides and that failure to check in at each usually means several hours wasted. When crossing Peru to Bolivia get an entry stamp in Copacabana (exit stamp in Peru of course). If you go *via* Desaguadero there are two Peruvian offices to visit (colectivo drivers know where they are) and only one Bolivian—at the frontier. It is understood that there is no longer any need to register arrival in La Paz. Peruvian guards will exchange soles.

Excursions Motorboats charging upwards of US$1.50 each take tourists to the "floating islands" of the Uru Indians. The most interesting island to visit is Taquile, some 24 km. from Puno, on which there are numerous pre-Inca and Inca ruins. On the N side of the island is the warmest part of Lake Titicaca and there is a waterfall where you can take a shower. Also here, and only here, you will see small green birds, like budgerigars, and butterflies. Accommodation can be found in private houses (about US$2 including meals) but best to take a sleeping bag and some extra food as the islanders' diet, based as it is on potatoes, is rather dreary. Boats to Taquile charge about US$12. Unfortunately on Taquile, as on the other islands, the Indians have become all too aware of the benefits to be reaped from tourists—the children beg and the women sell handicrafts. They also demand presents for being photographed, fresh fruit being particularly popular. Take precautions against sunburn.

Anybody interested in religious architecture should go from Puno by car or taxi (US$25) along the western shore of Lake Titicaca to the churches of **Juli, Pomata** and **Zepita**, all outstanding "mestizo". The church at Pomata has beautiful stone carving both inside and out, and has a dome which is unusual in Peru. On the road to Juli is **Ilave,** where the road for Tacna branches off; (this road is unpaved, but in good condition and a worthwhile journey, preferable not only in terms of scenery, but also because road conditions are better than on the alternative Juliaca-Arequipa route to the coast from Lake Titicaca) it is typical of a gaunt *altiplano* town; has a good Sunday market, (high prices). Many buses go there from Puno (US$0.50). You pass these places when travelling by road (unpaved) between Puno and La Paz.

For accommodation in Juli, try Talleres Centeno, Av. El Sol, 1179 to stay the night. Small charge. Alternatively there is the *Albergue* on the lake shore which charges US$4 s, has no hot water and is shabby. This hotel no longer changes travellers cheques, but there is a branch of the Banco de la Nación which will do so.

"Juli has three churches, two of them in ruins, that the visitor should see. The keys to two of these (Santa Cruz and San Juan Bautista) are kept by the American Mary-knoll Bishop and his staff in their building alongside San Pedro, which is now designated as the Cathedral. The Peruvians have established a school of picture restoration at Juli to restore its mass of paintings, and the Government plans to make it an important tourist centre. The picture restorers are housed in the former slaughterhouse at the edge of the town." (John Hemming.)

All the Juli churches are being renovated. San Pedro has been extensively restored, it contains a series of superb screens, some in ungilded mahogany and others taken from other churches; also fine paintings, and a collection of coloured objects in the sacristy. San Juan Bautista has two sets of 17th century paintings of the lives of St. John the Baptist and of St. Teresa, contained in sumptuous gilded frames. San Juan is now a state museum, open all day; it also has intricate mestizo carving in pink stone. Santa Cruz is another fine Jesuit church, partly roofless, so that it is easy to photograph the carvings of monkeys, papayas and grapes.

There is also a road along the eastern shore of Lake Titicaca; excellent until Puerto Acosta, but from then on very poor.

There are other excursions, S of Puno, to Lampa's imposing church and the "chullpas" (pre-Columbian funeral towers) of Sillustani, on a peninsula in Lake

Umano, 32 km. from Puno and 6 km. from Lampa (colectivo US$1.25 for 3 hours).
It is possible to take Puno-Juliaca bus and get off after 17 km. For the following
14 km. to ruins there is no regular transport except for expensive taxis (about US$8)
from Puno. Camera fans will find the afternoon light best (note carved lizard on
northern tower); desert country, but impressive.

On the way from Puno to Cuzco there is much to see from the train:
flocks of sheep, llamas and alpacas, herded always by Indian women. At
the stations, crowds of Indians sell food and local specialities such as
pottery bulls at Pucará; fur caps, furs and rugs at Sicuani; knitted alpaca
ponchos and pullovers and miniture llamas at Santa Rosa.

Ten km. after La Raya, the highest spot (160 km. from Julica; 4,321
metres), there is a research station for high-altitude animals, run by the
University of San Marcos, Lima. Up on the heights breathing may be a
little difficult, but the descent along the river Vilcanota is rapid. The
valley widens and the panorama of snow-capped peaks, tall mountains,
green pastures and woods is superb.

The next stop is at the little station of Aguas Calientes: to the right are
steaming pools of hot water in the middle of the green grass; a startling
sight. The temperature of the springs is 40°C, and they show beautiful
deposits of red ferro-oxide. At Marangani, the river is wider, the fields
greener, with groves of eucalyptus trees.

Sicuani, 38 km. beyond the divide, is an important agricultural centre,
and an excellent place for items of llama and alpaca wool and skins; they
sell them on the railway station.

Hotels *Manzanares, Mollendo, Vilcanota.* Also fine tourist hotel—highly
recommended, range US$5-US$12 d, private baths. Horses can be hired.

On the right, a few kilometres past the San Pedro stop, you get the first
glimpse of Inca ruins, the so-called "Templo de Viracocha", grandiose,
though almost unknown, with Inca baths 180 metres to the E.

"I had difficulty in locating them. They lie behind the pueblo of Racchi
(folklore meeting in June—see page 638—good local food), a few km.
past the village of San Pedro, some 20 km. from Sicuani towards Cuzco:
turn E before reaching Tinta. Little can be seen from road or railway."
Mr. Paul Dony.

N of Sicuani the fields are gorgeous with California golden poppies and
lupins.

The Vilcanota now plunges into a gorge, but the train winds above it
and round the side of the mountain. More small stops with strangely alien
names, and we come to Cusipata, with an Inca gate and wall and a small
forest on the hill, and Rumicolca, a large stone quarry. At Huambutio we
turn left to follow the river Huatanay—the Vilcanota here widens into the
great Urubamba canyon, flanked on both sides by high cliffs, on its way
to join the Ucayali, a tributary of the Amazon. We are now 32 km. from
Cuzco: dusk is falling. Around us is the rugged Sierra: the mountain
rocks purple and red, cacti lifting their long fingers and grey moss
hanging like a tattered veil from cliffs and shrubs. But Scotch broom trees
add a note of cheerful yellow, and we come out into the valley head with
its gnarled pepper trees and rain-swept green meadows. Cuzco is just
beyond.

Cuzco, once the capital of the Inca Empire, stands at 3,500 metres. Its
143,000 inhabitants are mostly Indian, though many old families of pure
Spanish descent live in and around the city, which is remarkable for its
many colonial churches, monasteries and convents, and for its extensive

Inca ruins. Because of the altitude, two or three hours in bed after arriving make a great difference; eat lightly don't drink alcohol, but suck glucose sweets the first day, and remember to walk slowly.

Almost every central street has remains of Incaic walls, arches and doorways. The city was once surrounded by a wall; enough remains to show its course. Many streets are lined with perfect stonework, now serving as foundations for more modern dwellings. This ancient stonework has one distinguishing feature: every wall has a perfect line of inclination towards the centre, from bottom to top. In the language of the stonemason, they are "battered", with each corner rounded. The circular stonework of the Temple of the Sun, for example, is probably unequalled in the world. Centuries of earthquakes have not disturbed it, save for one diagonal crack.

History Cuzco was the capital of the Incas—one of the greatest planned societies the world has known—from its rise towards the end of the 11th century to its death in the early 16th century. As we have seen in the History section, it was solidly based on other Peruvian civilizations which had attained great skill in the weaving of textiles, in the arts of building, of making ceramics and of working in metal. Immemorially, the political structure of the Andean Indian had been the ayllu, the village community; it had its divine ancestor, worshipped household gods, was closely knit by ties of blood to the family and by economic necessity to the land, which was held in common. Submission to the ayllu was absolute, because it was only by such discipline that food could be gained in an unsympathetic environment. All the domestic animals—the llama and the alpaca and the dog—had long been tamed, and the great staple crops—maize and potatoes—established. What the Incas did—and it was a magnificent feat—was to conquer enormous territories and impose upon the variety of ayllus, through an unchallengeable central government, a spiritual and economic submission to the state. The common religion, already developed by the classical Tiahuanaco culture, was worship of the Sun, whose vice-regent on earth was the absolute Sapa Inca. Around him, in the capital, was a religious and secular elite which never froze into a caste because it was open to talent: to distinguish them from the mass the priests and administrators and generals were allowed to wear ear pendants, and even to hold as private property those gifts of land or llamas granted, for services rendered, by the Sapa Inca. The elite was often recruited from chieftains defeated by the Incas: an effective way of mastering local opposition. The mass of the people were subjected to rigorous planning. They were allotted land to work, for their group and for the State; set various tasks—the making of textiles, pottery, arms for the armies, ropes, etc.—from primary materials supplied by the functionaries, or used in enlarging the area of cultivation by building terraces on the hill-sides. Their political organisation was simple but effective. The family, and not the individual, was the unit. Families were grouped in units of 10, 100, 500, 1,000, 10,000 and 40,000, each group with a leader responsible to the next largest group. The Sapa Inca crowned the political edifice; his four immediate counsellors were those to whom he had allotted responsibility for the northern, southern, eastern and western regions *(suyos)* of the empire.

Equilibrium between production and consumption, in the absence of a free price mechanism, must depend heavily upon statistical information.

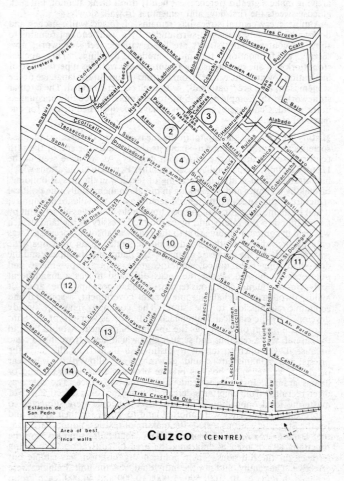

Cuzco (CENTRE)

Area of best Inca walls

Estación de San Pedro

This the Incas raised to a high degree of efficiency by means of their quipus: a decimal system of recording numbers by knots in cords. Seasonal variations were guarded against by creating a system of state barns in which provender could be stored during years of plenty, to be used in years of scarcity. Statistical efficiency alone necessitated that no one should be permitted to leave his home or his work. The loss of personal liberty was the price paid by the masses for economic security. In order to obtain information and to transmit orders quickly, the Incas built magnificent roads along which couriers sped on foot. The whole system of rigorous control was completed by the greatest of all their monarchs, Pachacutec (1400-48). He even imposed a common language, Quechua, as a further cementing force. After him nothing remained to be done save further conquest, and the Incas conquered all Bolivia, northern Argentina, northern and central Chile, and Ecuador by the end. The empire grew too large to be easily controlled from one centre, and the last of the great emperors, Huayna Capac, made the fatal mistake of dividing his realm between his two sons, Atahualpa reigning from Quito and Huáscar from Cuzco; the civil war that ended just before the Spaniards' arrival resulted in Atahualpa's victory but weakened the empire. Resistance to the Spaniards was reduced by the fact that Huáscar's faction at first looked on the invaders as allies; the struggle was in any case a most unequal one because of the Spaniards' superiority in equipment, though Manco Inca almost recaptured Cuzco in 1536 and the Inca successor state of Vilcabamba, centred in the jungle foothills N of Cuzco, only fell to the Spaniards in 1572.

The heart of the city, as in Inca days, is the **Plaza de Armas:** on feast days the Incas brought out their mummies from the Temple of the Sun and ranged them in rows beside the reigning Inca. The square has witnessed the execution of Incas in revolt, of conquistador by conquistador, and of rebels during the war of independence, but is now full of amicable tourists. Around the square are colonial arcades and four churches. To the N is the **Cathedral** (early 17th century, in renaissance style), built on the site of the Palace of Viracocha. The high altar is silvered and there is a painting of Christ attributed to Van Dyck. The elaborate pulpit, the gold monstrance with jewel-encrusted figurines, the choir and the sacristy are notable. Much venerated is the crucifix of El Señor de las Temblores, the object of many pilgrimages and viewed all over Peru as a guardian against earthquakes. (A joint ticket for the Cathedral, San Blas, and the Religious Art Museum is US$0.70.) Doors from the Cathedral open into Jesús María and El Triunfo, which has a fine granite altar and a statue of the Virgin of the Descent, reputed to have helped the Spaniards repel Manco Inca when he besieged the city in 1536.

On the E side of the plaza is the most beautiful church in Cuzco: **La Compañía de Jesús,** built on the site of the Palace of the Serpents (Amaru-cancha) in the late 17th century. Its twin-towered exterior is

---

Key to map of Cuzco

1. Church of San Cristóbal; 2. Almirante Palace; 3. Church of San Antonio; 4. Cathedral; 5. Museum; 6. Church of Santa Catalina; 7. Hotel Cuzco (Turistas); 8. Church of the Society of Jesus; 9. House of Garcilaso de la Vega; 10. Church of La Merced; 11. Church of Santo Domingo; 12. Convent of San Francisco; 13. Church of Santa Clara; 14. Church of San Pedro.

extremely graceful, and the interior rich in fine murals, paintings and carved altars. The cloister is also noteworthy.

Three outstanding churches are La Merced, San Francisco, and Belén de los Reyes. **La Merced,** in a side street to the S of Plaza de Armas; first built, 1534; rebuilt late 17th century; attached is a very fine monastery, with an exquisite cloister. Inside the church are buried Gonzalo Pizarro, half-brother of Francisco, and the two Almagros, father and son. Their tombs were discovered in 1946. The church is most famous for its jewelled monstrance, a masterpiece of goldsmith's work encrusted with jewellery, which is shown to the public at 1700 daily; also on view in the monastery's museum during normal visiting hours. **San Francisco** (3 blocks SW of the Plaza de Armas), is an austere small church reflecting many Indian influences. Its monastery is being rebuilt. Opposite the Savoy Hotel there is a statue commemorating the first expedition by raft down the Amazon. **Belén de los Reyes** (in the southern outskirts), built by an Indian in the 17th century, has a gorgeous main altar, with silver embellishments at the centre and gold-washed retablos at the sides. **Santo Domingo** (SE of the main Plaza) was built in the 17th century on the walls of the Temple of the Sun and from its stones; visit the Convent to see the ancient walls of the Temple of the Sun, now restored. Current excavation is revealing more and more of the five chambers of the Temple of the Sun, which shows the best Inca stonework to be seen in Cuzco. Santa Catalina, on the street of the same name, is a magnificent building. There are five guided tours a day around its Church, Convent and Museum. Entrance to both Santo Domingo and Santa Catalina is US$0.70, to the latter alone, US$0.15. **San Pedro** (in front of the market) was built in 1688, its two towers from stones brought from some Inca ruin. The nun's church of **Santa Clara** is unique in South America for its decoration which covers the whole of the interior. The smaller and less well-known church of **San Blas** has a magnificent "mestizo" carved cedar pulpit; entrance for San Blas US$0.70 except in the early morning when free. Market opposite station Santa Ana—for variety of goods—best Indian market. The market by San Pedro station is reported as being less self-conscious and less expensive than Pisac. There is a Mercado Ferial de Artesanías (crafts market) close to Palace of Justice on Av. Sol.

San Sebastián an interesting church with a baroque façade, is in the little village of San Sebastián, 6½ km. from Cuzco.

Much Inca stonework can be seen in the streets and more particularly in the Callejón Loreto, running SE past La Compañía de Jesús from the main plaza: the walls of the House of the Women of the Sun are on one side, and of the Palace of the Serpents on the other. There are ancient remains in Calle San Agustín, to the NE of the plaza. What is left of the Temple of the Sun and its five great halls lies beyond the Callejón Loreto: on part of its walls is Santo Domingo. The Temple of the Sun was awarded to Juan Pizarro, the younger brother of Francisco, who willed it to the Dominicans after he had been fatally wounded in the Sacsahuamán siege. The temples of the Stars and of the Moon are still more or less intact. The famous stone of 12 angles is in Calle Triunfo (Calle Hatun Rumioc) half way along 2nd block from the square beside the Cathedral, on the right-hand side going away from the Plaza. The Religious Art Museum in the old Archbishop's Palace, is nearby.

There is some magnificent walling in the ruined fortress of **Sacsahuamán,** on a hill in the northern outskirts, which is within walking distance (about ½ hour walk, very tiring because of the altitude). The Incaic stones are bigger and even more impressive than at Machu-Picchu; huge rocks weighing up to 300 tons are fitted together with absolute perfection; 3 walls run parallel for over 360 metres and there are 21 bastions. Here was the parade ground. Carved out of the solid rock is the throne on which the Inca sat whilst reviewing the troops: broad steps lead to it from either side. Zig-zags in the boulders round the throne are apparently "chicha grooves", channels down which maize beer flowed during festivals. Up the hill is an ancient rock slide for children: the Rodadero; near it are many "seats" cut perfectly into smooth rock. The Temple and Amphitheatre of Kkenkko (Quenco), with excellent examples of Inca stone carving, especially inside the large hollowed-cut stone that houses an altar, are along the road from Sacsahuamán to Pisac, past a radio station. On the same road are the Inca fortress of Puka Pukará and the spring shrine of Tambo Machay, thought to have been a resting place for the Inca. The structure is in excellent condition; water still flows by a hidden channel out of the masonry wall, straight into the Inca's bath. The admission ticket to Sacsahuamán (US$1—students US$0.50 ticket valid for 1 day) also gives admission to these 3 sites, as well as to Santo Domingo and Santa Catalina, though you can see the three sites for free before 0800, when the gates are manned. After seeing 3 sites you can catch truck back along road, 8 km., for US$0.25. Taxi to Inca sites outside Cuzco for 3 hours costs US$10. Also Gloria Hermosa Tapiá, Bazar Coquito Ruinas 431, offers a tour of the 4 ruins in her car for US$2.65 p.p. including admission; Spanish speaking only. Flocks of llamas are brought to Sacsahuamán at weekends; this makes photography more interesting.

Several notable **palaces**, most of them built upon and incorporating older Inca dwellings, suffered terribly in the 1950 earthquake. The Palacio del Almirante, just N of the Plaza de Armas, is impressive. Nearby, in a small square, is the colonial House of San Borja, where Bolívar stayed after the Battle of Ayacucho. The Concha Palace (on Calle Santa Catalina), with its finely carved balcony, is now used by a business firm. The Palace of the Marquis of Valleumbroso (3 blocks SW of the Plaza de Armas) was gutted by fire in 1973 and is now being restored. The Archbishop's Palace (two blocks NE of Plaza de Armas) was built on the site of the palace occupied in 1400 by the Inca Roca and was formerly the home of the Marqueses de Buena Vista; it has been opened to the public and contains a fine collection of colonial paintings and furniture, including the paintings of a 17th century Corpus Christi procession that used to hang in the church of Santa Ana. Well worth visiting. Those who know the great chronicles of Garcilaso de la Vega will visit Valverde House (near La Merced), where he was born and where his father lived in great magnificence with his concubine, an Inca princess who was a niece of the Inca Huayna Capac; the house is now a historical museum. Also visit the palace called Casa de los Cuatros Bustos at San Agustín 400 and the Convento de las Nazarenas, Plaza de las Nazarenas (alias Casa de la Sirena). See the Inca-colonial doorway with a mermaid motif.

Local Crafts In the Plaza San Blas and the surrounding area, authentic Cuzco crafts still survive. Wood workers may be seen in almost any street. Leading craftsmen who welcome visitors include: Hilario Mendivil, Plazoleta San Blas 634 (biblical figures from plaster, wheatflour and potatoes); Edilberta Mérida, Carmen Alto 123 (earthenware figures showing physical and mental anguish of the Indian peasant), Victor Vivero Holgado, Tandapato 172 (painter of pious subjects); Antonio Olave Palomino, Siete Angelitos 752 (reproductions of pre-hispanic ceramics and colonial sculptures). There is a shop in Plaza Santiago called Tahuantinsuyo, which sells, at reasonable prices, all the knitted and woven goods that a tourist might like.

Warning Thieves are becoming bolder and more numerous. Be especially careful in the railway stations and the market (otherwise recommended). Railway stations becoming increasingly notorious; beware 0530 local train to Machu-Picchu. Station half dark, and thieves will slit open luggage with razor blades.

Folklore June 24; dance and song and the pageant of *Inti Raymi* (Indians outnumber tourists) enacted at the fortress of Sacsahuamán. (Try to arrive in Cuzco 15 days before *Inti Raymi*, as many festivals.) On Corpus Christi day statues and silver are paraded through the streets; colourful. One week before the Inti Raymi, there is a dance festival in the village of **Racchi**. A special train leaves Cuzco early in the morning. At this festival dancers come to Racchi from all over Peru; through music and dance they illustrate everything from the ploughing of fields to bull fights, reported to be most enjoyable. Regular nightly folklore show at Av. Sol. 604, at 1830 hours, for US$2. Carnival at Cuzco most unpleasant: flour, water, cacti, bad fruit and animal manure thrown about in streets.

Hotels Prices often higher in June-August though you can often bargain, especially if you plan to stay a long time. Best are *Libertador-Marriott* (5-star); *Savoy, Marqués de Picoagua* on Calle Sta. Teresa; *Viracocha, Espinar* and *El Inca* on Calle Quera (all 4-star) and *Hostal El Dorado* (3-star) on Av. Sol. Others: 1st class, *State Tourist Hotel (Hotel Cuzco)*, US$22 d, 80 rooms (insist on 2nd floor; 3rd floor said to be much inferior), largest and best known, central, service definitely good; *Tambo Real*, US$7 d; excellent service, will store luggage safely; *Garcilaso de la Vega*, Garcilaso 233 (his former home); *Virrey*, small but attractive hotel in Plaza de Armas, US$11 d; *Conquistador*, near Plaza de Armas, US$6 s; *Ambassador*, Av. Tullumayo 440, in centre of old town, US$10.50 d with bath, clean but expensive; and *Cusi*; all modern, central (with exception of *Cusi*) and fitted with all mod. cons. *El Sol*; *Conquistador* (annex); *Ollanta*, US$12 and bath, hard beds, recommended for back sufferers; *Santa Catalina*, US$7.50 d; and *Los Marqueses*, Garcilaso 256, US$6 s, US$10 d (beautifully furnished and refurbished early Colonial house). *Hotel del Angel*, Av. Afligidos, US$8 d with bath, good service, excellent value; *Hotel Imperia*, US$6 d; *Gran Hotel Bolívar*, cheap and basic but central and friendly, though watch out for clothes on washing line (US$1), gringo hotel of drug-taking type; *Plaza*, US$2 p.p., hot water, rough, good, safe to leave luggage; *Trinitarias*, US$4.50 p.p., clean, hot water in shower, secure for left luggage; *Panamericano*, Calle San Agustín, friendly, clean; *Hotel Palermo*, US$1.50 p.p.; *El Solar*, Plaza San Francisco 162, US$4; *Gran Hotel Machu Picchu*, near station, friendly, US$1.50; *Residencial Cabildo*, Calle Garcilaso, US$5, pleasant, very close to Plaza. Other hotels in the city are *Hotel k'Ancharina*, US$12 d, quiet, clean, hot water (near market, railway station and main square), now well recommended; *Hotel Cahuide*, inside Inca walls, US$11 and shower, breakfast, transport to town, inefficient service; *Hotel San Agustín*, US$12.50 d; *Hotel Moderna*, US$7 d; *Hotel John Kennedy*, US$6.25 p.p.; *Hotel San Martín*, US$2.50 p.p.; *Hotel San Blas*, US$2.50, friendly, hot water; *Hotel Plateros*, off Plaza de Armas, US$2.20 friendly; *Hotel Europa*, US$3 d; *Hotel Central, Hotel Roma*, Espaderos y Bolívar, near Plaza de Armas, cheapest in Cuzco, US$1; boarding house of Sra. de Angulo at Tullumayo 860 near Puno station, US$3 p.p., recommended; private house of Señores Paredes, Quiskpatal 250, US$2 d, very nice people; *Hotel Alamo*, US$4.50 d; *Albergue Familiar* (Sra. Vegade Pineda), Av. de la Infancia 433, US$3.30 full board; *Bridge Hostal* (Av. Tacna 166), US$2.50 p.p.; *Hostal Málaga*, Av. Infancia 535 on airport side of town, good food and generally recommended; *Hotel los Portales*, Matará 322, Tel.: 2191, warmly recommended, new hotel though not newly built, homely, very clean, good breakfast, hot water, owners Jorge and Marta Orihuela, extremely friendly and kind, US$3 p.p.; *Hotel Mantas*, Calle Mantas 115 (near Plaza de Armas), US$10 d, recommended, can leave luggage, has laundry service; *Hostal Tipón*, Calle Tecte, US$2.70 d, friendly and secure. *Hostal La Castellana*, Av. Sol 819, Tel.: 4053, US$2 s, hot water, snack bar; *Residencia Beatriz*, Av. Pardo 987, near Puno station, US$5 s with bath, friendly, English spoken, very well recommended; *Hostal Argentina*, Calle Plateros 313, US$4 d, hot water; *Hostal Inti Raymi*, US$1.50, clean and hot water; *Hotel Casona*, many rooms overlook the Plaza de Armas, US$2.50 p.p.; *Hotel Santa Teresa,* on Calle Santa Teresa, no sign but same building as immigration office, US$1.30 p.p., hot water, may use washing machine, good value; *Hotel Richmond,* in La Unión, expensive; *Hotel América,* US$2.50 d; *Pensión Las Rejas,* entrance by Crem Rica restaurant on Plaza de Armas; *Alojamiento Procuradores* on street of same name, cheap.

Travel Agencies Book more expensive hotels well in advance through a good travel agency, for Cuzco is often very crowded, and particularly for the week or so around June 24 when the Inti Raymi celebrations take place. Exprinter and Dasatour are at the *Tourist Hotel,* Lima Tours (American Express) is opposite the main door, Cooks around the corner. Receptur and Universal Tours have offices in the *Hotel Savoy.* Kinjyo, agent for Transturin buses to La Paz, is at side of *Tourist Hotel.* Despite rumours, Lima Tours does not sell travellers cheques or forward emergency money; only possible at American Express office in Lima.

Restaurants Best are *Crem Rica* and *Victor* on Plaza de Armas, *Sumac* and *1890* on Calle Mantas and *Tumi* in Portal Belén. *Roma,* on Plaza de Armas; neat, clean, good food, not too expensive. *Cuzco* and *Paititi,* recommended, both in Plaza; *Café Cande,* Portal Corrizos in Plaza, excellent food including local specialities; *Café Milán,* at Cruz Verde, SE of Plaza. *Mini,* good cheap trout; *La Nusta,* Calle del Medio 134, good for local dishes. Excellent food and best coffee in Cuzco at *Fuente de Soda y Restaurante Viracocha,* on Plaza; clean, quick and reasonable. Adventurous visitors should try a typical Cuzco picantería, called *La Chola,* serving excellent chicha and delicious kidneys and other snacks in the inner courtyard of a colonial house on Calle Palacio up the hill from the Nazarenas; open only from 1500-1800. The *Quinta* in Choquechaca serves good, typical food. *Salón Azul,* US$1 for a churrasco, good and very cheap. *Cana de Pastas,* on Triunfo, sells meats, cheese, wines, etc. for a picnic lunch. *Bucaro* and *Cuzco* are both fair, reasonable service; *Savoy,* expensive, slow service. Other restaurants and bars recommended include *Casa Bethania,* vegetarian; *Hutun Rumiyuk,* 4 course for US$1; *Café-Bar Central,* good meal, US$0.80; *Banda,* Plaza de Armas, excellent, reasonable prices; *Nacional,* US$0.60 lunch or dinner; *Café Ayllu,* classical music, home made pasties; *San Juan de Dios,* excellent pastries and provides lunches for Machu-Picchu trip; *Bar Retabillo,* good music. Try the following new restaurants in Plaza de Armas: *Tambo de Oro,* expensive; *Mandala,* vegetarian, in the south arcade; and *Conquistador*—cafeteria style. *Piccolo* on Plaza, is meeting place for gringos. A gringo bar is *John's Bar* on Calle Procuradores (between Plaza de Armas and *Gran Hotel*). *Restaurante La Posada* good salads. Best place to eat cheaply is the market; a saltado (a mixture of meat and vegetables) costs about US$0.15. Chicha (maize beer) is sold at houses which display a small red flag.

Discotheques *El Túnel* and *El Muki* (opposite *Hotel Conquistador*) recommended.

Camping Permitted on hill above Cuzco museum, about ½ km. past museum on left; also permitted near Sacsahuamán ruins, but arrive late and leave early so as not to interfere with the sightseeing.

Archaeological Museum On Tigre, two blocks from *Tourist Hotel.* First-rate pre-Columbian collection. Contains Spanish paintings of imitation Inca royalty dating from the 18th century. Visitors should ask to see the forty miniature pre-Inca turquoise figures found at Piquillacta and the golden treasures, all kept under lock and key but reported as now on display. Open every day, 0800-1230 and 1500-1800 in winter months and 0715-1300 in summer months. Maps of Sacsahuamán, Pisac and Machu-Picchu no longer available.

Religious Art Museum New, at old Archbishop's Palace in Calle Hatun Rumioc (constructed over temple of Inca Roca), with religious paintings of the Cuzco School and Colonial furniture. Open Mon.-Sat., 0800-1200, 1500-1800, entrance US$0.30. (Good cheap restaurant right opposite, in same street.)

Regional History Museum in the house of Garcilaso de la Vega, Calle Heladeros. Open Mon.-Sat. 0700-1730, US$0.10. Contains Inca agricultural implements, colonial furniture and paintings and mementos of more recent times.

Tourist Office   At airport and Plaza de Armas, in wing of La Compañia church, at
Capilla Lourdes, with free maps of Cuzco and Inca Trail to Machu-Picchu. (For
Inca Trail, buy book called "Journey through the Clouds" in shop opposite *Tourist
Hotel.*) Motorists beware: many streets end in flights of steps not marked as such.

Banco de la Nación open until 1700.

Post Office   Principal one on Av. Sol.

Roads   To Juliaca, Puno, La Paz and Arequipa, road in fair condition but most
parts are unsurfaced; Morales Moralitos run daily to Puno, leaves 0800, 10 hours,
US$6, and also a direct bus Cuzco-La Paz, leaving Calle Belén 451 at 2000 on Mon.,
Tues. and Sat. at US$14, 22-24 hours. Luxury bus by Transturin of La Paz, office in
Plaza de Armas, US$35 including meals, 22-hour journey, leaves Cuzco 1900 on
Sun., Tues. and Thurs., breakfast 0600 following morning near Puno at Lake
Titicaca and lunch 1100 at Copacabana (Bolivia); arrive La Paz 1700. No problems
at Peruvian or Bolivian border; agent for both companies is Kinjyo Travel. To Lima
(1,180 km.), road *via* Huancayo and Ayacucho is recommended for magnificent
scenery and interesting towns, but road is appalling in places and takes from 3 to 6
days by successive buses or colectivos; bus to Ayacucho, US$9.50. A rough trip, not
recommended to pleasure-seekers; a plane is not much dearer (US$17). An
alternative road goes SW from Abancay through Puquío and Nazca to Lima though
this road too is rough. By this road the bus Cuzco-Lima takes 2½ days (Ormeño
recommended, leaves 0800 Thurs. and Sun., US$18). Cuzco-Abancay US$4. You
can sleep in the Cuzco-Lima bus when it stops for the night at Abancay. Cuzco-
Nazca, US$12, 31 hours. By bus to Lima *via* Arequipa, 1,838 km., 3 days non-stop
but the stretch Juliaca-Arequipa is very poor. Morales Moralitos bus to Lima often
breaks down.
    Cuzco-Lima *via* Abancay, Andahuaylas, Ayacucho, Huancayo and Oroya has
been recommended. Departures (Hidalgo) 0730 Mon., Wed., Fri., Sat.; 1700 Thurs.
Approx. times of journeys from Cuzco: Abancay 8 hrs.; Andahuaylas 14 hrs.;
Ayacucho 24 hrs.; Huancayo 36 hrs.; Lima 2-3 days. Those who tire of buses can
transfer to a train at Mejorada, about 3 hrs. before Huancayo. Through fare Cuzco-
Lima about US$18; Cuzco-Huancayo now US$8.50. Bus to Huancayo departs 1415,
arrives 0600 next day. Bus to Andahuaylas and Ayacucho does operate at night
(Andinos) departs 0100, arrives 1200. Not recommended, US$12. Times dependent
on weather and driver . Advisable to take own food.

Rail   To Juliaca and Puno, daily, except Sundays, at 0810, arriving at Juliaca 1735
and Puno 1900. To Puno, US$8, 1st class, US$4.50, 2nd; club car, good, is 1st class
fare plus US$2. To La Paz, US$24 1st class, US$16 2nd, which should be booked the
previous day (and be early at the station for the train); take own provisions. (Advise
take train to La Paz 0600 Wed. rather than Morales bus.) Train to Juliaca, Sicuani,
Arequipa leaves daily 2130, arrives Sicuari 0127, arrives Juliaca 0635, arrives
Arequipa 1440. 1st class to Arequipa US$13.50, 2nd class US$7. To Juliaca,
US$2.30, 2nd class. To Lima, cheaper to go *via* Arequipa but make sure that your
carriage does not detatch at Juliaca. To Anta and Ollantaitambo and Machu-Picchu.
Trains Cuzco-Machu-Picchu and Chaullay daily, leave 0530 and 1330, arriving at
Huarocondo at 0646 and 1446, Machu-Picchu at 0910 and 1720, Santa Teresa at
1005 and 1810 and Chaullay at 1051 and 1855. Return trains leave Chaullay at 0600
and 1200, arriving in Cuzco at 1200 and 1735. Also stops at Aguas Calientes. Watch
out for thieves on these trains.
    The trains to Machu-Picchu do not use the same station as the trains to Arequipa
and Puno. Machu-Picchu trains leave from Estación San Pedro, opposite the
market. The others leave from Av. Sol station (booking office in Plaza).

Air   From Lima, Faucett has three flights a day, 0810, 0930, 1110, US$38 one way.
Aeroperú also has daily flights. Cuzco-Ayacucho, US$17-25, Fridays with Aeroperú.
A new airport at Quispiquilla is in use. Book return well in advance, especially in the
busy season. Aeroperú to Arequipa on Mon., Wed., and Fri., US$17.10 s. Faucett
flies to Puerto Maldonado in the jungle.

Warning   Cuzco-Lima, high possibility of cancelled flights during wet season;
tourists sometimes stranded for 24 hrs. Possible for planes to leave early if bad

weather. Sit on right side of aircraft for best view of mountains when flying Cuzco-Lima.

Taxis Airport-town, US$1.50 (bus US$0.05); Railway-town, US$0.50; per hour in town, US$1.75, out of town, US$2.50.

Local Specialities Roast stuffed guinea pig (*cuy*). Order in advance at one of the "quintas" (inns in the suburbs). Quinta Zarate, Calle Tortera Paccha, recommended. Tel.: 2349. Also Quinta Eulalia, Choquechaca 384, Tel.: 2421. Very rich and exotically spiced. The yogurt is excellent. Try the anticuchos (stuffed beef hearts) cooked in side streets. The local drink, herb tea with caña, very warming in the cold evenings.

Excursions Cuzco is at the W end of the gently sloping Cuzco valley, which stretches 32 km. E as far as Huambutío. This valley, and the partly isolated basin of Anta, NW of Cuzco, are densely populated. Also densely populated with tenant farmers growing grains for local consumption is the Urubamba Valley, stretching from Sicuani (on the railway to Puno, at 3,960 metres) to the Gorge of Torontoi, 600 metres lower, to the NW of Cuzco. There are several ruins of Inca buildings and fortresses in the Cuzco Valley itself, especially at Piquillacta (also pre-Inca) on the road to Andahuaylillas, the monkey temple (Templo de los Monos) NW of Piquillacta, the amphitheatre at Moray, the administrative and storage centre of Colcampata, and Rumicolca, on the shores of Lake Lucre. The specialist may be interested in the following trips, recommended by John Hemming, the expert on the Incas:

Chinchero has an attractive church built on an Inca temple, and recent excavations there have revealed many Inca walls and terraces. It has become very tourist-oriented but nonetheless the Sunday market and Indian mass are more authentic than at Pisac. (*Tourist Hotel*, very comfortable, US$3, s.)

There is a permanent market and shops—varied selection of handicrafts, including weaving, pottery and alpaca goods.

Chinchero is 2 hrs from Cuzco by truck, leaving about 0500 from near the market on Sunday mornings. Watch your baggage very carefully on the truck. Many people have had bags slashed and contents stolen.

76 km. from Cuzco on the Abancay road, 2 km. before Limatambo, at Hacienda Tarahuasi a few hundred metres from the road, is a very well-preserved Inca temple platform, with 28 tall niches, and a long stretch of fine polygonal masonry.

100 km. from Cuzco along this road is the exciting descent into the Apurímac canyon, near the former Inca suspension bridge that inspired Thornton Wilder's *The Bridge of San Luis Rey*.

Also, 153 km. along the road to Abancay from Cuzco, near Carahuasi, is the rock of Sahuite, carved with animals, houses, etc., which appears to be a relief map of an Indian village.

For US$40 a taxi can be hired for a whole day (ideally Sunday) to take you to Cachimayo, Chinchero, Maras, Urubamba, Ollantaitambo, Calca, Lamay, Coya, Pisac, Tambo Machay, Kkenkko and Sacsahuamán.

The non-specialist will content himself with a visit to Machu-Picchu and possibly to Ollantaitambo. The tourist train and the ordinary train (far cheaper) start from Cuzco at 0700. They reach the heights N of the city by a series of switchbacks and then descend to the floor of the Anta basin, with its herds of cattle. The railway goes through the Anta Canyon (10 km.), and then, at a sharp angle, the Urubamba Canyon, and descends along the river valley, flanked by high cliffs and peaks. There is a tourist hotel (US$10.50 d) in Urubamba. In the high season reservations on the tourist train should be made one day in advance, at the San Pedro station in Cuzco, between 1500 and 1700. In the dry season (May-November) the "Inca Trail" walk makes a spectacular 3 or 4 day trip. It runs from Km. 88, a point immediately after the first tunnel 22 km.

beyond Ollantaitambo station, to Machu-Picchu. (Train to km. 88 is US$1.20 first, US$0.80 2nd; to avoid the crowds take the 1330 train.) The trail is rugged and steep, at one stage traversing a 4,200-metre high pass, but the magnificent views compensate for any weariness which may be felt. It is cold at night, however, and weather conditions change rapidly, so it is advisable to take not only strong footwear and warm clothing but also food, water, coverings, a good sleeping bag, a light tent and primus. All the necessary equipment can be rented from the Tourist Office in Cuzco which also sells a map of the route; this is essential. If you can't get a map at the tourist office, try for US$0.65 at the Club Andino, Calle Procuradores, or at Copias Vélez, Plaza San Francisco, Cuzco. Try to get the map prepared by the curator of Machu-Picchu Museum; it shows where to sleep, and drinking water. (Note: People have been spoiling the trail by leaving litter; do not follow their example.) A 53-km. road also goes to

Ollantaitambo, 70 km., a small town (Alt.: 2,800 metres) built on and out of the stones of an Inca town, "which is a fine example of Inca canchas or corral enclosures, almost entirely intact. The so-called Baño de la Ñusta (bath of the princess) is of grey granite, and is in a small field between the town and the temple fortress. The flights of terraces leading up above the town are superb, and so are the curving terraces following the contours of the rocks overlooking the Urubamba. These terraces were successfully defended by Manco Inca's warriors against Hernando Pizarro in 1536. Manco Inca built the defensive wall above the site and another wall closing the Yucay valley against attack from Cuzco, still visible on either side of the valley. Visitors should also note the Inca masonry channelling the river and the piers of the bridge of Ollantaitambo.

"The temple itself was started by Pachacuti, using Colla Indians from Lake Titicaca—hence the similarities of the monoliths facing the central platform with the Tiahuanaco remains. The Colla are said to have deserted half-way through the work, which explains the many unfinished blocks lying about the site"—(John Hemming). Admission to the site costs US$1, which also gives entry to Pisac.

Albergue, near the station, US$0.30 each or US$0.15 if you camp in the orchard, basic but friendly, run by two Canadians. *Alojamiento Yavar,* US$0.80 s (must ask for it); Pepe and Lisa Blas have opened a small restaurant.
Camping possible in eucalyptus grove, ½ km. from town, and along the river between the town and the railway station.

For those travelling by car, it is recommended to leave the car in Ollantaitambo (or the station previous on the road from Cuzco) for a day excursion by train to Machu-Picchu. (Park car in front of the local police station at Ollantaitambo. Much safer there than parked in Cuzco for US$1 a day. The local train starts here at 0730 for Machu-Picchu.) It is possible to get off the local train (US$0.25) returning from Machu-Picchu at Ollantaitambo, visit the ruins, and then catch a bus to Cuzco. Bus (Empresa Caparo) to the sacred valley of the Incas *via* Pisac US$0.80.

Machu-Picchu, 42 km. beyond (2,280 metres), has much more important ruins. Tourists now ride up from the station in buses (US$1.30), and are further cossetted by a *State Tourist Hotel* (US$20, and US$3.50 for meals, only 32 beds) from which they can explore. Here is a complete city, set on a saddle of a high mountain with terraced slopes falling away to the Urubamba river rushing in great hairpin bends below. It is in a comparatively good state of preservation because the Spaniards never found it. For centuries it was buried in jungle, until Hiram Bingham stumbled upon it in 1911. It was then explored by an archaeological expedition sent by Yale, and with strange results: the skeletons showed a ratio of 10 females to one male. It is possible that the Virgins of the Sun fled here after the sacking of Cuzco? But the place must have had a long history before that.

The ruins—staircases, terraces, temples, palaces, towers, fountains, the famous sun-dial and the "Museo de Sitio" below the ruins—require at least a day—some say two (take an insect-repellent). The botanist will find the giant perennial *calceolaria tormentosum* rearing its yellow flowers to a height of 6 metres. In the deep canyons around Cuzco the tree tobacco (*Nicotiana tormentosa*) grows in hundreds. A hydro-electric power plant has now been built in the canyon of the Vilcanota river below Machu-Picchu. The mountain overlooking the site, Huayna Picchu (on which there are also some ruins), has steps to the top for a superlative view of the whole site but it is not for those who get giddy; the walk up takes about 45 minutes but the steps are dangerous after bad weather. An almost equally good view can be had from the trail behind the Tourist Hotel.

The railway goes on another 37 km. to Chaullay; it is now being extended another 42 km. to the small town of **Quillabamba** (20,000 people) in the Urubamba Valley, where there is a Dominican mission. (*Hotel* on square, US$1.) There are regular buses from Cuzco; the road is spectacularly beautiful.

The most convenient way of seeing the ruins is to pay US$20 (including lunch at tourist hotel) to an agency for a 1-day guided trip to Machu-Picchu by tourist trains, which leave at 0700 each day, enabling tourists to visit the ruins and return to Cuzco (1600; journey takes 3½ hrs.) in one day. But it is several times more costly (basic fare US$8 return) than the local trains, which leave at 0530 and 1330, arrive Machu-Picchu 0910 and 1720. US$2.70 return first class, US$1 return second, though this class is very crowded. The local trains return at 0730 and 1340; the journey takes ½ hour longer each way. For the local train, pay up to 12 hours in advance. You must buy train tickets in advance; you cannot pay on the train. Arrive early at station, and you will have to fight if you want a seat, particularly one on the left-hand side which gives a better view. Beware of thieves. Microbuses start at 0800 and meet both local and tourist trains, and charge US$1.10 return for the trip to the ruins. There are now enough seats on the microbuses for all the train passengers. Last bus down to station goes at about 1700. You can walk up in 1 to 1½ hours, and down again in 40 minutes, if you have no luggage. Luggage can be deposited safely at the museum (on opposite side of river from station, open Tues.-Sun. 1030-1530) for a small fee. Cost of entry to the ruins, US$2, students US$0.75; they are open 0630-1730. Tickets are valid for the following day (before the tourist train invasion arrives at 1100), if you have them stamped accordingly when purchasing. For the student reduction for groups, apply at Casa de Cultura. **Note:** In the rainy season trains are often delayed by landslides.

The excursion can be taken without a guide, paying each item separately, for much less. Monday and Friday are bad days for this because there is usually a crowd of people on the guided tour who are going or have been to Pisac market on Sunday, and too many people all want lunch at the same time. Food is available at the houses around the station.

Camping Not permitted on the site, nor on Huayna-Picchu; may be possible at Aguas Calientes.

A good idea, travelling by either of the trains, is to take lunch with you and stay at the *Tourist Hotel* at the ruins. It is heavily booked during the week; try Sunday night as other tourists find Pisac market a greater attraction. Book well in advance, through a reliable agency, or at the Aeroperú office in Lima (Enturperú desk); in this way you can spend 24 hours at the site. At the *Tourist Hotel* there is no electricity or water between 1400 and 1800 and between 2200 and 0700, the food is not very good and the staff are not helpful. However, as they state in the English version of the rules card: "The grandeur of nature is such, that the conniving of man is overcome." The cheapest and best way to visit the site is to take the "Indian train" from Cuzco at 1330, stay overnight at one of the hotels (*Hospedaje Los Caminantes* and *Municipal* US$1 each; *Machu-Picchu*, US$1.25 each, clean. Also three cheap restaurants. The thermal baths are particularly welcome to those who have walked the "Inca Trail") offering basic accommodation at Aguas Calientes, 3 km. back along the railway (the *Hospedajes* and the *Machu Picchu* are both better than the *Municipal*; there are thermal baths and food available) climb up to Machu-Picchu in time for the opening of the gate at 0630, or take a workers truck (up to US$0.30).

For those who choose to stay at the Urubamba Tourist Hotel in pleasant country surroundings, the Machu-Picchu tourist train can be caught at Pachar, about 20 minutes' drive away, at the more civilized hour of 0830; no fare reduction. The more active visitors can leave the train at Km. 88 and walk the "Inca Trail" to Machu-Picchu (see page 641).

From Machu-Picchu one can take the trail that climbs up behind the Tourist Hotel to (3 hours' walk) the Inca settlement of Huiñay-Huayna, a village of roofless but otherwise well-preserved Inca houses. About 30 mins. along the trail is the famous Inca bridge. The walk itself gives spectacular views of the Urubamba River and the thickly wooded mountains, and the butterflies and flowers are beautiful. Half way between Huiñay-Huayna and Machu-Picchu the new tourist hotel is being built at Km. 106, 1,000 metres above the river and the railway line. Visitors will be taken up by cable car, and there is talk of opening a tunnel between the new hotel and Machu-Picchu. What all this will do to one of the most beautiful and magnificent archaeological sites in the world can only be imagined.

A recommended walk from Aguas Calientes is to go back along the railway to Km. 106 and cross the bridge, going up by the pylons to the Inca trail. Go back half km. to see Huiñay-Huayna and then walk to Machu-Picchu.

Note Advisable to purchase paperback edition of "Lost City of the Incas" by Hiram Bingham, in Lima. Choice of guide books in Cuzco much improved.

Pisac, 32 km. N of Cuzco, is at the bottom of the Urubamba valley; high above it, on the mountainside, is a superb Inca fortress (entrance US$1, also gives admission to Ollantaitambo (see page 642). The masonry is better than at Machu-Picchu, the terraces more extensive and better preserved. When you climb it (a must), remember that there are 3 hill fortifications, but the third is the fortress proper: so go on to it and get the glorious view from the top. The climb is best done on a weekday, in the morning, when there are fewer visitors. Allow yourself plenty of time. John Hemming tells us that the best view is obtained from a point on the Inca road 20 minutes' walk beyond the ruins. The famous agricultural terraces can be reached in 2 hours. (*Hotel Albergue Chongo Chico;* 200-yr.-old hacienda at foot of the Pisac ruins, 45 mins. climb, US$12-20 p.p., half board and bath. (Some cheaper rooms.) No electricity; candles only; recommended. There is also a cheap place to stay just by the bridge;

no name, basic but only US$0.75 each.) Pisac has a Sunday morning market, described as very touristy and expensive; it starts at 0900 and is usually over by midday. There are picturesque Indian processions to Mass, during which, and afterwards, there is music—a brief honking of conch shells. The Chinchero market (see page 641) is much smaller and almost entirely typical. Pisac has another market on Thursday morning. A good thing to do is to continue the Sunday morning tour to Pisac along the Urumbamba to Ollantaitambo, with lunch at the *Tourist Hotel* in Urubamba. Not cheap, but cheaper than two separate tours, especially if there is a car-full of people. Splendid scenery. Apart from Sunday, there are very few tourists.

Buses The road to Pisac is in poor condition but passable. Early morning buses on Sunday, every ten minutes, from 0540 to 0700, (queue early) to Pisac from Cuzco; they return all afternoon until 1715. Return buses to Cuzco always full on Sundays. Fare US$0.50; try and book the previous day if possible. On weekdays buses leave at 0615, 1000, 1100, return from Pisac at 1530 and 1715. Taxi fare (return) from Cuzco to the fortress costs US$8 and includes a visit to the market.

Andahuayllillas, village 32 km. S of Cuzco, with early 17th century church; remarkable and a visit highly recommended; beautiful frescoes and a gilded main altar. The road from Cuzco passes the Piquillacta ruin. Taxis and buses go there.

Paucartambo, on E slope of Andes, reached from Cuzco by a good road (one way on alternate days). In this remote though now popular tourist town is held the Fiesta of Carmen usually on July 16, 17, 18, with some primitive dances. (Fiesta dates should be checked in Cuzco.) A family will usually provide lunch and with luck a bed for the night; to be certain of accommodation, camping is probably the best alternative. Private car hire for round trip on July 16: US$25, or the Tourist Office in Cuzco arranges an overnight trip (you sleep in the bus) for US$10.

From Paucartambo you can go 44 km. to Tres Cruces, along the Pilcopata road, turning left after 25 km. Tres Cruces gives a wonderful view of the sunrise and many private cars leave Paucartambo between 0100 and 0200 to see it; they may give you a lift.

North of Cuzco (We are indebted for the following information on the southern jungle region to Robert and Ana Cook, of Lima.)

From Urcos, near Cuzco, a spectacular 484-km road has been constructed over the Eastern cordillera of the Andes to Puerto Maldonado in the heart of the jungle. Traffic is one way into Quincemil (240 km.) on Mon., Wed., Fri., and out to Urcos on Tues., Thurs., Sat. 47 km. after passing the snow-line Hualla-Hualla Pass (4,820 metres) the super-hot thermal baths (US$9.05) of Marcapata provide a relaxing break. From here the road continues its descent through a tropical rain forest well stocked with orchids. Faucett provides air service from Cuzco and Puerto Maldonado to Quincemil (*Hotel Areza,* US$0.70 p.p. restaurant is good). This marks the half-way point and the end to the all-weather road. Even during the dry season (May to October) trucks and high-clearance vehicles have difficulty beyond here. Gas is scarce because most road vehicles continue on 70 km. to Masuco where they fill up with the cheaper gas of the jungle region. Thirty more km. of sloshing mud and cascading waterfalls brings one out of the mountainous jungle and into the flat plains, for the fast but boring 141 km. straight shot to Puerto Maldonado.

Puerto Maldonado is capital of the jungle Department of Madre de Dios. (Altitude, 250 metres; population, 7,000.) Overlooking the confluence of the rivers Tambopata and Madre de Dios, this frontier town is the centre for development of Peru's southern jungle. An international airport is under construction and a dry-weather road should reach the Brazilian border and the Trans-Amazon Highway in 1979. This will make it possible for a suitable vehicle to drive from the Pacific Ocean to the Atlantic Ocean across the Amazon Basin. Although the temperature normally hovers around 37°-40°C during the dry season, a "friaje" (freezing wind from the snow-capped Andes) will send the temperature plummeting to zero. Insects and reptiles are almost completely wiped out; warm-blooded animals, while suffering considerably, do survive. Because of this climate phenomenon, the fauna of the Madre de Dios include many unusual species not found in other jungle areas. Also unique to this area is the *Rayo Blanco* (white rainbow) that can be seen at sunset on the Madre de Dios River.

Excursions   A very worthwhile one- or two-day excursion by motorcycle (US$12 per day) is to boat across the Madre de Dios River and follow the trail towards Iberia (*Hotel Aquino,* US$1.50 p.p.). Along the trail are picturesque *caserios* (settlements) that serve as collecting and processing centres for the Brazil nut. Approximately 70% of the inhabitants in the Madre de Dios are involved in the collection of this prized nut. The beautiful and tranquil Lake Sandoval is a 45-minute walk or 20-minute boat ride (US$1.10) along the Madre de Dios River and then a 2-km. walk into the jungle. For hunting and fishing Lake Valencia, 60 km. away near the Bolivian border, is unsurpassed (2 days, US$30). Many excellent beaches and islands are located within an hour's boat ride; however, make sure you have a ride back at the end of the day. For the adventurous a one- or two-day trip can be planned to visit Indians still relatively unaffected by civilization; the Indians living nearer Puerto Maldonado, like those near Iquitos and Manaus, are strictly tourist Indians.

Transport   Faucett and Aeroperú to and from Cuzco, Mon., Wed., Fri., and Sat., US$22. Faucett and Grupo 8 to Iberia, US$3.30. Regular service by Faucett to Rio Branco, Brazil, is scheduled to begin 1977-78, thus making direct travel between Brazil and Southern Peru, a reality. Private boats can be contracted for travel into Bolivia; to Puerto Heath, at the border (US$28, one day); to Riberalta (US$90-120, 4 days). The only land transport to Cuzco is by truck, since cars and buses cannot negotiate the muddy and tortuous section near Qincemil (see page 645).

Hotels   Cuzco Amazonic Lodge (*Albergue Cuzco Amazónico*), 45 minutes by boat down the Madre de Dios River, excellent jungle tours and good accommodation, US$24 p.p., includes all meals. *Explorers Inn* (Casilla 48) located in middle of Tambopata wild-life reserve: an authentic jungle experience. *State Tourist Hotel,* on the bank of the Tambopata River, US$9.50 d, with private bath. *Hotel Wilson* (well run), US$2 p.p. *Hotel Oriental,* on the Plaza, *Hotel Chávez, Hotel Central* and *Hotel Moderno* (very clean and friendly), all US$1 p.p.

Restaurants   Apart from restaurants in the *Tourist Hotel* (fair food, expensive), there are no formal restaurants. Look for "Pensiones" where meals are served at fixed times (lunch is at 1300).

Typical Foods   *Castañas* (Brazil nut), try them chocolate- or sugar-coated. *Patarashca,* fish barbecued in banana leaves. *Sopa de motelo,* turtle soup cooked and served in its own shell. *Mazato,* an alcoholic drink prepared from yuca and drunk by the Indians at their festivals. *Sangre de Grado,* a thick deep-red sap collected from trees deep in the jungle which is a highly prized "cure-all" throughout Peru.

North-East of Lima

Lima-Oroya-Huancayo Daily, except Sunday, by train (see page 591) from Desamparados station, behind Presidential Palace: 0740, arriving Huancayo 1640. Return journey: Huancayo 0700, Lima 1600, arrival times optimistic, can take 14 hours. The second class is quite comfortable. Buy ticket the day before, as not on sale before trains leave, and arrive at the station early. Seat reservation is US$0.20. Best value is 2nd class Lima-Oroya, but 1st for Oroya onwards because 2nd gets very crowded then. 1st class US$5.50 single, US$10.35 return. The best views are to be had from the right-hand side of the train. Connection at Oroya for Cerro de Pasco.

Huancayo can also be reached by ordinary buses and by colectivo services (5 passengers) several times a day. The bus goes through the same valley as the train. One Lima colectivo service is run by "Comité No. 12 de Automóviles", Calle Montevideo 736 (Tel.: 271283) in Lima and at Loreto 425 in Huancayo. This firm has colectivo services to Huanta and Ayacucho also. The road on both sides of the Anticona Pass is now paved except for a short stretch (about 6½ km.) on the W side; between Oroya and Huancayo the road is good. Lima-Huancayo bus takes 8 hours; fare US$5, 1st class, return US$10, Hidalgo, can only book ticket in Lima. Colectivo, US$6.50, will stop at Oroya for photographs.

The Central Railway from Callao to Oroya and on to Huancayo (420 km.) is one of the wonders of Latin America. It reaches its greatest altitude 4,782 metres, inside the tunnel between Ticlio and Galera, 173 km. from Callao. The ruling grade is about 4½%. Along the whole of its length it traverses 66 tunnels, 59 bridges, and 22 zig-zags where the steep mountainside permits no other way of scaling or descending it. It is by far the most important railway in the country, and the views during the ascent are beyond compare. Much of the most picturesque scenery is during the 119-km. journey between Lima and Río Blanco (3,505 metres). Galera, the highest station in the world for a standard gauge railway (4,781 metres), is 158 km. from Lima. This masterpiece was the project of the great American railway engineer, Henry Meiggs; it was built, mostly by imported Chinese labour, between 1870 and 1893. This is the original reason for the very large number of excellent Chinese restaurants to be found all over Peru, and especially in Lima.

The line crosses and re-crosses the River Rímac, whose course it follows. At Los Angeles the hills seem to close ranks to block our way, but the valley soon opens up again.

Note Be prepared for extremely cold weather if you arrive in Cerro de Pasco or Oroya during the night to await a train.

Chosica (40 km.), the real starting place for the mountains, is at 860 metres, and is a popular winter resort because it is above the cloudbank covering Lima from May to October. One train a day and frequent buses and microbuses. Beyond the town looms a precipitous range of hills almost overhanging the streets. Up picturesque Santa Eulalia valley off the Rímac valley are the Central Fruit Culture Nurseries. There is some dramatic scenery on the road up the valley, fairly good as far as the hydroelectric station at Callahuanca, but the road is afterwards quite nasty in places, narrow and rocky. Population: 30,400.

Hotels *Pensión San Jorge; La Quinta Pensión.* At Santa Eulalia, *Hotel Las Kiskas* (bungalow-type).

N.B. The Lima-Chosica-Santa Eulalia-Huanza-Casapalca trip is the best in the environs of Lima, and can be done in one day.

For a while, beyond Chosica, each successive valley seems to be greener, with a greater variety of trees and flowers. At **San Bartolomé** (1,492 metres), the platform is often crowded with local fruit sellers, the women in bright shawls, skirts, and black and white panamas. The first zig-zags begin. Then we pass through tunnels and over bridges to the next canyon, where there are more zig-zags. Sometimes the train seems airborne over the valley and the road far below: each turn brings a fresh view of the tremendous mountains.

Matucana, 27 km. beyond San Bartolomé, at 2,390 metres, is a small town set in wild scenery. Beyond it is Infiernillo (Little Hell) Canyon, to which car excursions are made from Lima. At **Tamboraque** (3,009 metres) is the first of the mountain mines, with its overhead cables and smelter down a gorge. Climbing always, we pass **San Mateo,** where the San Mateo mineral water originates. From San Mateo a spectacular and interesting side-road branches off to the Germania mine. Between Río Blanco and Chicla (a rise from 3,506 to 3,734 metres), the ancient Inca contour-terraces can be seen quite clearly.

Casapalca (4,154 metres) has mines developed by the Cerro de Pasco Corporation, now nationalized and called Centromín; its concentrators are at the foot of a deep gorge. A climb to the dizzy heights beyond ends in a glorious view of the highest peaks. Soon we see a large metal flag of Peru at the top of Mount Meiggs, not by any means the highest in the area, but through it runs Galera Tunnel, 1,175 metres long. Ticlio station, at the mouth of the tunnel, is on one side of a kind of crater in which lies a dark, still lake; the station serves the lead and zinc mines of the Volcán company. At Ticlio the line forks, one through the tunnel to Oroya; the other line goes 14½ km. to **Morococha,** where there are important mines. The highest point, 4,818 metres, is reached on this latter line at La Cima. A siding off this line reaches 4,829 metres; higher than the peak of any mountain in Europe.

Beyond the tunnel zig-zags bring us down to **Yauli** (4,142 metres). The tunnel at the next station, Mahr Tunnel, has nothing to do with the railway; it carries water drained from the mines at Morococha. Left is the ugliness inseparable from mining; right is a wide expanse of brown moors with cold, small mountain tarns and herds of grazing llamas.

Oroya, with its smelters, ugly slag heaps and black hills, is not attractive. This is the large smelting centre of Centromín. Population: 35,000. Oroya is at the fork of the Yauli and Mantaro rivers at 3,826 metres, 187 km. from Lima by a road which is paved except for 6½ km. near where it crosses the Anticona Pass at 4,843 metres.

Hotels *Junín* (by permission of the Centromin at Lima, which also arranges visits to the smelter), very satisfactory, with heat and plenty of hot water. *Hotel Wilson.*

Railway N to Tambo del Sol and Cerro de Pasco; S to Huancayo and Huancavelica; W to Lima and Callao. Train to Cerro de Pasco leaving 1430 and arriving 1815. To Lima at 1005 and Huancayo at 1400. (Local train to Huancayo on Sun.)

Roads S to Huancayo, Ayacucho, and Cuzco, paved to Huancayo save for a very stony 6½-km. stretch half-way; N to Cerro de Pasco and on to Pucallpa; E to Tarma, San Ramón, the Perené colony, and Oxapampa, US$3.20; 7 or less by colectivo). Between Oroya and Huancayo is Jauja, which has a very colourful Sunday market (see page 650).

Huancayo, an old market town and capital of Junín Department. Alt.: 3,261 metres; pop.: 260,000. The valley, which produces 40% of all Peru's wheat, is mostly Indian. Picturesque architecture and good Sunday markets: the Indians flock in from far and wide with an incredible range of food and rugs and blankets of llama and alpaca wool for sale.

The market at the bottom end of the city, called the *feria*, sells handicrafts; otherwise the Sunday markets are for food and clothing. Huancayo is a good place to buy carved gourds. The colourful annual fiesta of the Virgin of Cocharcas starts on September 8 at Sapallanga, a 20 minutes' ride from Huancayo; the feasting and dancing last a week. Costumes and dances are then at their best. In Huancayo, ponchos and various alpaca woollen goods are quite cheap, but often factory-made; most goods are reported to be cheaper than in Lima particularly silver jewellery. Beware of thieves, especially in the market. For alpaca goods go to Hualhuas, 11 km. from Huancayo; microbus from Huancayo US$0.15 from main plaza.

In Huancayo itself, on Good Friday, 15 pall-bearers carry an enormous wooden coffin with glass sides containing a more than life-size figure of Christ through the city, followed by an army band playing a haunting slow march. Ten women at the end of the procession carry a large representation of the Virgin of Sorrows. A crowd of Indians in their Sunday best follow the cavalcade into the Cathedral.

Industries Woollen mills; alpaca yarn and textiles; artificial silk factory.

Hotels *State Tourist Hotel,* US$9 s, US$12 d, for room with bath, US$3 extra for meals; service charge 10%, tax 12% on bill, expensive and not very good; *Iquitos,* Calle Pirua, US$1.30, clean, but rather cold, hot water; *Ferrocarril,* US$2.60 d, very dirty; *Hilton,* US$2 d, no longer recommended; *Comfort,* Calle Ancash 297, US$5 d, private bath; *Roma,* US$3, not recommended; *Centro,* Calle Loreto, US$1.85 s, not recommended; *Cebolla,* US$1.20, private toilet, cold shower. Other recommended hotels include *Residencia Huancayo,* near railway station, US$1.60 d, (watch for overcharging by younger staff), basic; *Residencia Baldeón* (Amazonas 543), US$1.35 s, hot water, friendly; *Kiya,* new, recommended, no restaurant, US$10 d; *Palermo,* US$1.40 s, US$1.90 d; *Mirador,* US$5.50 p.p.; *Universal,* opp. railway station, US$1.50 s, reasonable.

Restaurants *Olímpico* (recommended); *Puppos,* N of town, American drive-in style; *Mandarín* (Chinese); *Inca,* changed hands, no longer recommended; *Café Viena,* excellent cakes.

Tourist Information Sr. Oscar Alvarez, Huanamarca 270, Tel.: 2760. State tourist office, Jirón Puno 279-281.

Crafts Visit Jirón Brasilia 200, in San Carlos (20 min. walk), workshop of Sra. Francisca Mayer—workroom, museum and local weaving co-operative. For carved gourds, visit Hermanos Leoncio y Pedro Veli Alfaro, Cochas Chicas, Km. 9, Huancayo (Apartado 402), and Nicanor Sanabria Osores, Cochas Grandes, Km. 10, Huancayo. Also visit Izcuchaca, 1¾ hrs. from Huancayo by truck, where Harry Davies is building a pottery centre, in a beautiful village.

Excursions

About 15 km. W (20 min. bus ride), past Chupaca (Saturday market), is a group of buildings on the open pampa, partly surrounded by eucalyptus trees: the Geophysics Institute of Huayo, where metereological, seismic and cosmic-ray observations are made. The Institute is situated on the "Magnetic Equator", not to be confused with the geographical equator 12½° further N, in Ecuador. Six km. (standard taxi fare US$1.50) S of Huancayo the remarkable pre-Inca shrine of Wari-Willka has been reconstructed in a corner of the main plaza of the community of **Huari,** the capital of the Huari civilisation which flourished from A.D. 600 to 1100. The ruins of the city are extensive but have been virtually untouched by archaeologists (see page 653). Bus to Huari, US$0.09. Museum in the plaza, of modelled and painted pottery of successive Tiahuanaco, Huanca and Inca occupations of the shrine. Open 1000-1200 and 1500-1700, US$0.27 admission. *Hotel Central,* US$1.10, good. Take a taxi to it and walk down (45 minutes). Take a mini-bus to Cerrito de la Libertad, walk up hill to Torre Torre to see impressive eroded sandstone towers on the hillside. Another pleasant excursion is to Cochos Chicas, where gourds are carved. Buses leave Huancayo every ½ hour from Church of the Immaculate Conception, for 9 km. journey.

22 km. NW of Huancayo is the village of **Concepción**, which has a market on Sundays as well as a colourful bullfight later in the day during the season. Colectivos to Concepción from near *Hotel Turistas*, US$0.35, 30 mins. From Concepción a branch road (5 km.) leads to the Convent of Santa Rosa de Ocopa, a Franciscan monastery formed in 1724 for training missionaries for the jungle, open 1000-1200 and 1500-1700; closed Tues. Tour costs US$0.65 (students US$0.25). It contains a fine library with over 20,000 volumes. The convent has a guesthouse, US$2.50 each. There is also a good restaurant. Bus from Huancayo (change at Concepción) takes 1½ hours, US$0.27. Near Concepción is the village of San Jerónimo, renowned for the making of silver filigree jewellery; 18 km. beyond Concepción is the ancient town of **Jauja,** Pizarro's provisional capital of the territory until the founding of Lima, where there is an interesting festival on January 20 and a very colourful Sunday market. Jauji is a good area for walking, with ruins near a lake 3½ km. away (*Hotel Jauja* and *Hotel Pizarro,* both US$2 s). Nearby is the pleasant Laguna de Paca (*State Tourist Hotel,* US$6 d; *Hotel Huaychulo*), where there is a government trout farm. Follow the road past the trout farm to Satipo; spectacular scenery, snow-capped mountains in the Paso de la Tortuga, followed by a rapid drop to the Caja de Silva in Satipo. Best hotel is the *Central*—quite clean. Try *Dany's Restaurant,* surprisingly good food for such an out-of-the-way place.

Local Rail Service   Railcar leaves Huancayo 1705, arriving Oroya 2005. Connection at Oroya for Cerro de Pasco. Train leaves Huancayo, Sundays only, 1600, arriving Oroya 2054. Railcars leave Chilca station (about 1 km. from main station) to Huancavelica, 0645 and 1300 (3½ hrs.) on weekdays, 1330 on Sundays (take 5-6 hours). Train from Huancayo to Lima (US$5.50, 1st class, US$3, 2nd class), 0700 daily, execpt Sunday. **Warning:** take your luggage with you if you want to see the items offered for sale at the many intermediate stations.

Roads and Buses   To Ayacucho, 261 km. from Huancayo, the road is narrow, rough and tortuous, following a river gorge for much of the way, but the scenery is splendid. Huanto, between Huancayo and Ayacucho, *Gran Hotel,* US$1.25 p.p. Hidalgo bus Huancayo-Ayacucho (15 hours), leaves 1630, US$5.50; other lines mostly run at night also; day-time buses are difficult to get a seat on. Two roads, *via* Huancavelica or *via* Parpas; colectivos (US$20) usually go by Parpas. In rainy season go *via* Huancavelica; even so expect to move boulders and fill in the potholes. A beautiful drive, Andean flamingoes, llamas, alpacas, vicuñas, but snow and rain storms. Direct buses to Tarma (see page 654) twice daily, 0630 and 1600, US$0.90. In the river gorge between La Mejorada (77 km. S of Huancayo) and Ayacucho, there is a narrow stretch 113 km. in length, which takes 4-5 hours driving depending on hold-ups due to frequent landslides. Possible to fly Huancayo to Ayacucho on Friday afternoons, though departure times are rarely as scheduled and the airstrip is reached by taking a punt across a river. Note: Huancayo and other towns in the area have a fiesta in January when it is impossible to get a colectivo to Ayacucho and buses are fully booked.

Buses to Cuzco can be something of a problem; get a seat on a lorry if stuck. The Hidalgo line seems to be the best: buses leave for Cuzco, Mon., Wed., Fri., 48 hrs (US$8.50), lovely scenery. This road is often closed during wet season, and there have been reports of a broken bridge. Book as far ahead as possible, as buses tend to be heavily overbooked. They also frequently break down. Trucks are cheaper and offer better views—but take blankets against the cold on the mountains. The trip gives a fine view of the sierra, one passes the site of the last battle against the Spaniards, near Ayacucho; some distance before Abancay one passes a bridge built by the Spaniards. The canyon of the Río Tomás is recommended for a visit. Those who have made this journey describe it as one of the most beautiful in Peru. Bus to Lima, about US$4, depending on the line. To Nazca (Roggero or Morales Moralitos) US$4.70.

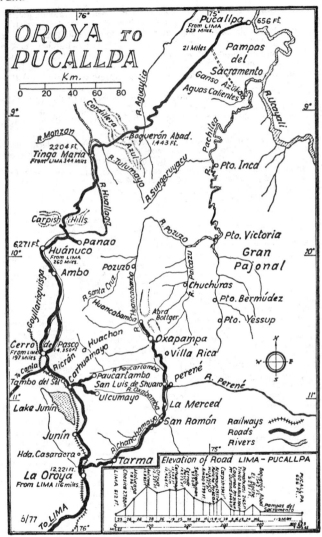

OROYA TO PUCALLPA

ROUGH SKETCH

Huancavelica, capital of its Department (altitude, 3,680 metres; population, 17,000) was founded over 400 years ago by the Spanish to exploit rich deposits of mercury and silver; the town is still a major centre for mining. Although predominantly an Indian city its churches and old buildings, are a reminder of its colonial grandeur. The cathedral, located on the Plaza de Armas, has an altar considered to be one of the finest examples of colonial art in Peru. Also very impressive are the five other churches in town.

Bisecting the town is the Huancavelica River. South of the river is the main commercial centre where fine leather and alpaca products can be purchased. North of the river on the hillside are the thermal baths (US$0.15).

Hotels *State Tourist Hotel,* US$6 s, US$8 d, with private bath and slightly warm water. *Hotel Flash,* US$1 p.p. (basic and clean), with restaurant; *Hotel San Francisco,* similar price; *Hotel América* (dirty), US$0.90 p.p.; *Hotel Savoy.*

Restaurants *Tourist Hotel,* food is expensive and only fair. *Restaurant Villa Hermosa,* typical food and reasonable prices. *Restaurant Fidel. Snake Bar Joy.*

Transport Daily to Huancayo (146 km.) are trains, autovagons, colectivos, and buses. To Pisco (267 km.) only buses. Getting to Ayacucho (257 km.) is a problem. The easiest and safest way is to head toward Huancayo, transferring at Mejorada or Izcuchaca to a bus or colectivo heading toward Ayacucho. More adventurous is the daily bus to Pisco: disembark at Santa Ines (4,020 metres) and wait, usually in the bitter cold, for a bus or colectivo from Pisco to Ayacucho.

For those accustomed to bad roads and high altitudes (a week at 3,000 metres), the drive to Ayacucho *via* Santa Ines will be an unforgetable experience (either good or bad). This is the highest continuous road in the world, rarely dropping below 4,000 metres for 150 km. Out of Huancavelica one climbs steeply on a road that switchbacks between herds of llamas grazing on rocky perches. Around Pucapampa (Km. 43) is one of the highest inhabitable altiplanos (4,500 metres), where the locals claim the finest alpaca wool is grown; the rare and highly prized ash-grey alpaca can be seen here. Eleven km. later one encounters Paso Chonta (4,850 metres) and the turnoff to Huachocolpa. By taking the turnoff and driving (it is impossible to walk) 3 km. one discovers the highest drivable pass (5,059 metres) in the world. Continuing on to Ayacucho one passes some very cold, fish-filled lakes before the road branches to Pisco at Km. 77. Seventy km. later the high (4,750 metres) but unimpressive Abra Apachenta is reached, leaving a 98-km. descent into Ayacucho.

(The preceding paragraphs on Huancavelica have been kindly contributed by Ana and Robert Cook, of Lima.)

Ayacucho, capital of its Department, was founded on January 9, 1539. This old colonial city is built round Parque Sucre with the Cathedral, City Hall and Government Palace facing on to it. Its time-worn romantic streets, no longer cobbled, radiate from the central square. The city is famous for its religious processions and its splendid market. There are no less than 33 churches—some long deserted—and a number of ruined colonial mansions. A week can be spent there and in the surroundings, which include La Quinua, site of the Battle of Ayacucho, December 9, 1824, which brought Spanish rule to an end in Peru (the nearby village is recommended for handicrafts). Ayacucho has a very active student life. Altitude: 2,440 metres, with gently rolling hills around. A 364-km. road has been built to Pisco on the coast. Population: 30,000.

Visitors are advised to see the 17th century Cathedral and churches of San Francisco de Asís, La Compañia de Jesús, Santa Clara, Santo Domingo, and Santa Teresa, all with magnificent gold leafed altars heavily brocaded and carved in the churrigueresque style. There is a small but surprising Museo Histórico (free on Fridays). The ancient University, founded 1677, closed 1886, was reopened in 1958. Local craftsmen produce filigree silver, often using Mudéjar patterns; others make little painted altars which show the manger scene, manufacture harps, or carry on the pre-Inca tradition of carving dried gourds. A charming Palm Sunday daylight procession of a multitude of palm-bearing children accompanies a statue of Christ riding on a white donkey.

Excursions Inca ruins at Vilcashuamán, to the S, and pre-Inca, Tiahuanaco-type ruins at Huari, to the N. Huari is reached by going 24 km. to Pacaycasa, then an hour's walk ESE to hill with ruins. Trips can be arranged by Ayacucho Tours at San Martín 406. They do a tour to Huari, Quinua village and battlefield for about US$3.60.

Hotels *State Tourist Hotel,* US$10 d; *Colmena,* a beautiful building warmly recommended, clean, hot showers in mornings, US$2.20 p.p., but one bathroom; *Huamanga,* Asamblea 112 (near Plaza de Armas), US$1.25 p.p. very basic and dirty; *Hostelería Santa Rosa,* with bath, US$8 d. Also recommended: *Hotel Santiago,* just up from the market, US$2.20 p.p.; *Hotel Sucre,* US$1.20 p.p.; *Hotel Puñoy Wuasi,* Garcilaso de la Vega 258, US$1.50, new and clean; *Hotel Crillón* and *Santiago,* both cheap; and a private home at 405 Libertad.

Restaurants *La Fortaleza,* 3 courses for US$0.80; *Chalán,* on same street as the *Fortaleza* and just as good; *Tirol, El Alamo,* and *El Agallo de Oro* for fish. Many good small cafés; one inside University buildings. Reserve early for Holy Week.

Tourist Information Sra. María Luisa Kajatt, Portal Constitución 2-3, Tel.: 253. State tourist office at Asamblea 138.

Air To and from Lima by Faucett or Aeroperú, 90 minutes, Faucett on Wed. and Sat., Aeroperú on Mon., Wed. and Sat., fare US$19.50; flight from Huancayo on Friday afternoons; flights Ayacucho-Cuzco, 1½ hours (40 minutes by jet), by Aeroperú, US$17.25, Mon., Wed. and Fri., leave 0730, always heavily booked but worthwhile turning up on the off-chance of a spare seat. To Andahuaylas by Aeroperú on Sun.; 25 minutes (US$9).

Roads The road to Cuzco goes through **Andahuaylas.** 10 km. from Andahuaylas is a beautiful deserted lake. Bus Ayacucho-Andahuaylas 11 hours, about US$5. The road crosses 3 mountain ranges and is very rough in places but is definitely worthwhile. **Abancay** is first glimpsed when you are 56 km. away by road, nestled between mountains in the upper reaches of a glacial valley. The town has surprisingly a paved centre, a busy petrol pump and cheap oranges. From Abancay a 274 km. road runs SW through Puquío to Nazca (page 620) on the main Lima-Arequipa road. This is on the whole an easier journey from Lima to Cuzco than going by Ayacucho, and the scenery is just as impressive. Trucks leave Andahuaylas for Abancay at 0700 take 6 hours, US$1.50. There is a bus from Ayacucho to Cuzco, three times a week; should take 24 hours but recently took 3 days because of drivers' fears of driving at night and because of the collapse of a bridge. The road is appalling in the rainy season. The bus is difficult to get on; people have been stuck in Ayacucho for days. It is impossible to book a seat on the bus (Hidalgo) from Ayacucho to Cuzco or Andahuaylas; you have to wait and see if there is a spare seat or not. Buses from Abancay to Cuzco leave early morning, US$3. Bus Ayacucho-Huancayo, 17 hours, leaves 1500 and 1800 daily. Also two colectivos (9 hours) go to Huancayo 0300, 0400. Office of bus line near tourist hotel at 9 de Diciembre 230. The other is by the square. Colectivos go also to Pucallpa.

Andahuaylas Hotels *Gran Hotel,* Plaza de Armas, US$1.10 p.p., basic, and *Restaurant Las Palmeras,* meal for US$0.25, is possible; *Hotel Chifara,* US$1 p.p.; *Hotel Delicias,* new, US$3 d, only 7 rooms. *Hotel 28 de Julio,* cheap, adequate.

Abancay Hotels *State Tourist Hotel,* US$9 d, food good; *Gran,* US$1 each, with bath, clean; *El Misti,* US$1, fair.

East of Oroya The 60-km. road to Tarma, unsurfaced but quite reasonable, follows the Cerro de Pasco road for 25 km., then branches off to rejoin the old road quite near Tarma, which is 600 metres lower than Oroya.

Tarma, population 28,933; altitude 3,050 metres, is a nice little flat-roofed town, founded in 1545, with plenty of trees. It has a very colourful Easter Sunday morning procession in main plaza; Indians come with fine flower-carpets.

Hotels *State Tourist Hotel,* US$9 d, recommended; *Plaza; Vargas; Ritz; Hotel Unión,* hot showers; *Bodega Central,* near *Unión,* has good breakfasts.

An Englishman, Mr. V. J. Barnes, an authority on the area east of Oroya, would welcome visitors seeking information at his home in Lima. His Lima telephone number is 287800.

Direct bus service, Huancayo-Tarma, twice daily 0630 and 1600, US$0.90. Passes over high limestone hills with caves. Visit the Grotos de Huagapo, 4 km. from town of Polcamoyo—bus twice daily from Tarma US$0.20. Cave guide, Modesto Castro, lives opposite caves and is a mine of information.

Beyond Tarma the road is steep and crooked but there are few places where cars cannot pass one another. In the 80 km. between Tarma and La Merced the road, passing by great overhanging cliffs, drops 2,450 metres and the vegetation changes dramatically from temperate to tropical. A really beautiful run. Eight km. from Tarma, the small hillside town of **Acobamba** has the futuristic Santuario de Muruhuay, with a venerated picture painted on the rock behind the altar. Festivities all May. Some 11 km. before La Merced is **San Ramón,** whose *Tourist Hotel* (US$7 d) is at the airport; ask at tourist hotel about journey to Pamposilva and Puerto Ubirique (see below). Try *Hotel Chanchamayo,* fairly cheap, or *Hotel Selva.* **La Merced** (*Hotels: Cristiana* (the best), *San Felipe*) lies in the fertile Chanchamayo valley. The ordinary telephone service does not go beyond La Merced. There is an "air-colectivo" service to Puerto Bermúdez on the Río Neguachi, US$9.50 a seat, 10 kg. baggage allowance, US$5 per kg. of excess luggage.

Note that San Ramón and La Merced are collectively referred to as Chanchamayo. Many buses, both from Lima and from Tarma.

From La Merced you can take the Carretera Marginal de la Selva (a grandiose edge-of-the-jungle project of the mid-1960s, of which some parts have now been built) to the jungle town of **Satipo** (Lobato or Estrella Andina buses from La Merced, many small hotels). A beautiful trip. There are buses direct from Satipo to Huancayo, so no need to return from Satipo *via* La Merced. Satipo can also be reached from Jauja, following the Santa Rosa de Ocopa road (see page 650).

About 22 km. beyond La Merced is San Luis de Shuaro, but 3 km. before it is reached a road, right, runs up the valley of the Perené river. The Perené Colony, a concession of 400,000 hectares, nine-tenths of it still unexplored, has large coffee plantations. The altitude is only 700 metres. Saturday and Sunday are colourful market days for the Indians. Beyond San Luis de Shuaro a branch road runs right to Villa Rica. It is possible to take motorised canoes from Pampasilva (on River Perené) to Puerto Ubirique; the motorized canoes are not really intended for tourists but to bring fruit and vegetables from areas not served by road. At weekends and public holidays it is possible for tourists to rent them. Take 2½ hours there and back to Puerto Ubirique; the journey is like shooting the rapids between high walls of jungle and plantations. The boatmen land you at one point to meet the local people, and you can sometimes buy a Peruvian bow and arrow or something similar. This is in no way an organized tour, like meeting the Indians at Iquitos.

The road has been extended from San Luis de Shuaro over an intervening mountain range for 56 km. to **Oxapampa,** in a fertile plain on the Huancabamba river, a tributary of the Ucayali. Population, 5,000;

altitude, 1,794 metres. Logging, coffee, cattle are local industries. A third of the inhabitants are descendants of a German-Austrian community of 70 families which settled in 1859 at Pozuzo, 60 km. downstream, and spread later to Oxapampa. There is much livestock farming and coffee is planted on land cleared by the timber trade. From Lima: 390 km. The road goes on through Huancabamba to Pozuzo, another 55 km., but it is very rough.

Oxapampa Hotel *Baumann.*

North of Oroya A railway, 130 km. runs N from Oroya to Cerro de Pasco, an important mining centre. It runs up the Mantaro river valley road through narrow canyons to the wet and mournful Junín pampa at over 4,250 metres, one of the world's largest high-altitude plains: an obelisk marks the battlefield where the Peruvians under Bolívar defeated the Spaniards in 1824. Blue peaks line the pampa in a distant wall. The wind-swept sheet of yellow grass is bitterly cold. The only signs of life are the hardy boy and girl shepherds with their sheep and llamas. The line follows the E shores of Lake Junín. The town of **Junín**, with its picturesque red-tiled roofs, stands beside its lake, whose myriads of water birds have made it famous for its shooting. At Smelter, the coal washing plant, the track branches to Goyllarisquisga, while the main line goes to **Cerro de Pasco** (population 29,000, altitude 4,330 metres), 130 km. from Oroya by road. Copper, zinc, lead, gold and silver are extracted from ores. Coal comes from the deep canyon of Goyllarisquisga, the "place where a star fell", the highest coal mine in the world, 42 km. N of Cerro de Pasco. The McCune open pit is encroaching on the old town, a mining centre since the Spanish Conquest. Recommend visit to market square early in morning. Workmen have come upon old mine galleries at a depth of 26 metres, and a cache of golden Spanish doubloons. A fine new town—San Juan de Pampa—has been built 1½ km. away.

Hotels *Gran* (the best); *América; Centromín Hotel,* emergency only; *Hotel Santa Rosa,* US$4 d, basic. *Restaurant Los Angeles* (near market) recommended.

Train Through tickets to Cerro de Pasco can be bought at the Desamparados Station in Lima for the train, leaving Lima 0740, arriving 1815. The return train for Lima leaves at 0600 from the station, which is 20 minutes out of town on foot. The churrasco served for breakfast on the train is welcome defence against the cold.

Buses Bus to Lima, departs 0830, 9 hours, US$5.50. To Huancayo, US$3. Colectivos to Huánuco, US$4.50, from the central plaza. Buses to Huánuco leave between 0800 and 0900 from Plaza de Armas.

Cerro de Pasco to Pucallpa

Three bus companies run the 847 km. from Lima to Pucallpa. Their offices in Lima are at the corner of Av. Luna Pizarro and 28 de Julio. The fare is about US$15. Buses start at around 1530 daily. Transportes Arellano looks safest.

The Central Highway There are two roads from Lima to Cerro de Pasco. One goes *via* Canta (3 buses daily to Lima, US$1.30) and the beautiful high pass of La Viuda (4,748 metres) and Bosque de Piedras to Cerro de Pasco; the other, the Central Highway, accompanies the Central Railway, more or less, and goes over the Anticona Pass (4,843 metres) to Oroya. From Oroya it crosses the Junín plateau to Cerro de Pasco (130 km.), never far from the railway. From Cerro de Pasco it is continued N another 528 km. to Pucallpa, the limit of navigation for large Amazon river boats. The western part of this road (Cerro de Pasco-Huánuco) has been rebuilt into an all-weather highway (see map, page 651, for its contour). It is 14 hours by road from Lima to Huánuco, 2½ hours from Huánuco to Tingo María, and another 11 hours to Pucallpa. Buses run daily between Lima and Pucallpa, taking 32 hours, but ask about the state of the road during the rainy season from November to March, when the trip may take a week.

The sharp descent along the nascent Huallaga River (the road drops 2,450 metres in the 100 km. from Cerro de Pasco to Huánuco, and most of it is in the first 32 km.) is a tonic to travellers suffering from Soroche, or altitude sickness. From the bleak vistas of the high ranges one drops below the tree line to vistas of great beauty. The only town of any size before Huánuco is Ambo.

Huánuco, on the Upper Huallaga, is an attractive Andean town with an interesting market and the two ancient (but much restored) churches of San Cristóbal and San Francisco (16th century paintings). There is a small but interesting natural history museum. Visit ruin 3 km. on road to La Unión; the Temple of Crossed Hands (2000 B.C.). You must ford a stream to get there and beware of the vicious black flies. The ruin has been sadly neglected since the original excavation in 1963. Main industry: sugar and rum. Altitude 1,812 metres, population 38,000.

Hotels *State Tourist Hotel* (US$9.50 d); *Inca; Nacional* (cheap but adequate); *Bella Durmiente,* near market square, cheap; *Hotel Astoria,* cheap and clean; *Hotel Imperial,* US$3.50 d, with shower, good value and clean; *Hotel Cabaña del Prado,* US$1 p.p.; *Hotel Internacional,* US$2.40, clean and cheap; *Central,* US$0.90 s.

Camping Camp by river, near stadium.

Restaurants *Las Palmeras,* good and cheap. *Tokio* and *El Iman,* off main square, both good.

Buses To Lima, US$3, 15 hours; colectivo to Lima, US$10, leaves 0400, arrives 1400; book the night before at General Prado 607, one block from the main square. Bus Huánuco-Cerro de Pasco, half bus half lorry, departs 0400, 3 hours, US$2.50; colectivo US$4.50. Frequent buses and colectivos to Tingo María, 4 hours.

From Huánuco, road leads to **La Unión,** capital of Dos de Mayo district, truck 10½ hours, leaves late morning. *Hotel Dos de Mayo,* at La Unión (US$0.90) and another for same price. Neither safe for left luggage. Near La Unión are the Inca ruins of **Huánuco Viejo:** they are a 2½ hour walk from the town and are extensive, well worth the walk. Bus to Lima daily, crowded. Also possible to get to Callejón de Huaylas by taking 1600 bus to Conococha (US$3.50, 9 hours) and waiting there for a truck (they are frequent) to Huarás (2-3 hours). The wait is very cold, at 4,100 metres.

The journey to Tingo María, 135 km., is very dusty but gives a good view of the jungle. Some 25 km. beyond Huánuco the road begins a sharp climb to the heights of Carpish (3,023 metres). A descent of 58 km. brings it ti the Huallaga river again; it continues along the river to Tingo María. Landslides along this section are frequent and construction work causes delays.

Tingo María is on the middle Huallaga, in the Ceja de Montaña, or edge of the mountains—warning; isolated for 10 days in rainy season. Climate tropical; annual rainfall 2,642 mm. Actively colonized since 1936. Population, about 20,000 and very mixed. The altitude (655 metres) prevents the climate from being oppressive. The Cordillera Azul, the front range of the Andes, covered with jungle-like vegetation to its top, separates it from the jungle lowlands to the E. The net effect of Sierra and Selva is to make the landscape extremely striking, and when the highway becomes tolerable no doubt Tingo María will draw tourists in plenty.

Bananas, sugar cane, cocoa, rubber, tea and coffee are grown. A university, with 250 students, was opened in 1968; it has a museum-cum-zoo, with animals of that zone and botanical gardens; entrance free but a small tip would help to keep things in order. About 3 km. from Tingo are fascinating caves, the Cueva de las Lachuzas (best reached by boat from by the bridge, US$0.50, to within 2 km. of the Cueva de las Lechuzas, then walk); 13 km. from Tingo is the small gorge known as Cueva de las Pavas.

The only industries are saw-mills, wood processing, and distilling. The Huallaga is wide here, but most of the produce goes by road to Lima or Pucallpa. There is an airport. Flights from Tingo María go to Lima and Pucallpa. Normally 5 to 6 flights a week to Tingo María by Faucett and Aeroperú, but times often change. Flight to Lima 1100 Thurs., US$20, 35 mins. From Tingo María on, several transport services are run; the road is narrow and stony. Landslides and mud are a problem; at least four hours are needed for the 80 km. to Aguaytía. Some construction work is going on. From Lima by road, 558 km. Many Lima-Pucallpa buses go *via* Tingo, the best is Arellano, on Avenida Raimondi whose buses leave between 0700 and 0900. Bus takes 18 hours. From Tingo to Pucallpa, US$4.50, 8 hours. (Nor-Oriente and La Perla not recommended for this journey.) Local bus Tingo María-Huánuco takes 5-6 hours. Departs 0800, US$1.15; Colectivos take 3 hours, US$2.10. León de Huánuco coach, US$1.50, 4 hours.

Hotels *State Tourist Hotel* (US$8 d), very good, swimming pool, three course menu for US$1.75, some way out of town; *Gran* (US$2.40 d); *Viena; Royal,* US$3.20 d bed and private showers; *Cabana,* good restaurant; *Cuzco* (US$1.50 d), clean and good; *Hotel Raimundo,* US$1.25 p.p.; *Hotel Palacio,* US$2 d, shower, but basic and not very clean.

Restaurants *Pensión Gonález; Café Rex,* Avenida Raimondi 500, run by a Swiss lady and an Italian; good European food, cakes and ice cream, also some accommodation; *Gran Chifa Oriental,* Chinese restaurant, on main street, cheap. Also 2 other restaurants of the same name elsewhere in the town—beware, they're not so good. *Restaurant Tingo,* on main street, recommended. Restaurant at *La Cabana Hotel,* good and cheap.

Tourist Information Jorge Maretl, Botica Leonicia Prado, Raimondi 321, Tel.: 2251.

The Huallaga river winds northwards for 930 km. dropping from high snow and tundra to the Amazon. The Upper Huallaga is a torrent, dropping 15.8 metres per kilometre between its source and Tingo María. The Lower Huallaga moves through an enervation of flatness, with its main port, Yurimaguas, below the last rapids and only 150 metres above the Atlantic ocean, yet distant from that ocean by over a month's run by launch and steamer. Between the Upper and Lower lies the Middle Huallaga: that third of the river which is downstream from Tingo María, upstream from Yurimaguas. The valleys, ridges and plateaux have been compared with Kenya, but the area is so isolated that less than 100,000 people now live where a million might flourish. The southern part of the Middle Huallaga centres upon Tingo María; down-river, beyond Bellavista, the orientation is towards **Yurimaguas**, which is connected by road with the Pacific coast, *via* Tarapoto and Moyobamba (see page 611). There is a fine church of the Passionist Fathers, based on the Cathedral of Burgos, Spain, at Yurimaguas; population 25,000. Airport.

Yurimaguas Hotels *Estrella,* US$2 s, and shower; *Florinda,* US$8 d, shower; *Florida* (no "n"), US$1.75 p.p.; *Felix,* US$8 d not recommended; *Heladería,* round corner from *Estrella,* serves good cheap lunch and dinner. Recommended restaurants, *El Aguila* and *Copacabana.*

Air   Yurimaguas, flights to Lima, Aeroperú, Thurs. and Sun.; to Tarapoto, Tues., Thurs., Sat., Sun., to Iquitos, Mon., Tues., Wed., Fri. and Sat. Flights also to Juinjui. Faucett flights to Tarapoto and Lima on Mon., Thurs. and Sat.

River Travel   Yurimaguas-Iquitos by boat, downstream, US$12.50, with food, 48 hours; upstream, US$15, six days. The Government has announced plans to develop Yurimaguas as a river port. Times of boats to Iquitos and Pucallpa very vague.

At Tulumayo, soon after leaving Tingo María, a road runs N along the Huallaga past La Morada, successfully colonized by people from Lima's slums, to Aucayacu (*Hotel Monte Carlo,* US$4 s with bath) and Tocache (emergency accommodation). Colectivos run; Tingo-Tocache about US$7. The road has been pushed N to join another built S from Tarapoto and has now been joined at Tarapoto to the Olmos-Bagua-Yurimaguas transandine highway to the coast at Chiclayo. The Juanjui-Tocache road is almost ready but awaits five necessary bridges; meanwhile passengers and freight travel by open boat on the River Huallaga between those two places (one day, US$5 p.p.); Juanjui-Tarapoto by colectivo US$4. For the river journey, start early in the morning if you do not wish to spend a night at the river village of Sión. No facilities, but night is not cold. The river runs through marvellous jungle with high cliffs. A few boats run aground in the river near Sión. Take food and water purifier. Many rafts of balsa wood.

From Tingo María to the end of the road at Pucallpa is 288 km. with one climb over the watershed—the Cordillera Azul—between the Huallaga and Ucayali rivers. When the road was being surveyed it was thought that the lowest pass over the Cordillera Azul was over 3,650 metres high, but the Director of Roads and Railways chanced across an old document stating that a Father Abad had found a pass through these mountains in 1757. After a long search it was rediscovered, and the road now goes through the pass of Father Abad, a gigantic gap 4 km. long and 2,000 metres deep. At the top of the pass is a Peruvian Customs house, exactly as if the jungle land to the E were a foreign country. Coming down from the pass the road bed is along the floor of a magnificent canyon, the Boquerón Abad: luxuriant jungle and ferns and sheer walls of bare rock punctuated by occasional waterfalls into the roaring torrent below. E of the foot of the pass the all-weather road goes over flat pampa with few curves until the village of **Aguaytía** (gasoline; 2 restaurants) is reached. On to Pucallpa (160 km.); the last half has no service stations. The whole journey from Tingo María to Pucallpa takes anything from 6 hours to 1 day in dry weather; may be 3 days in wet season.

About an hour's drive to the E we enter hilly country for a while. About 34 km. from Pucallpa a road leads right to Turnavista, a large ranch turned from jungle to grassland, and also to the Ganso Azul oilfield.

Pucallpa, an unattractive town, is on the Ucayali, navigable by vessels of 3,000 tons from Iquitos, 533 nautical miles away. Population has increased to about 55,000 (district 70,000), but the town is still in the pioneer stage, with unpaved but lit streets, and no adequate water or sewage system. However, the economy of the area is growing fast; sawmills, plywood factories, a paper mill, oil refinery and boat building are all thriving activities; timber is trucked out to the Highlands and the coast. The Ganso Azul oilfield has a 75-km. pipeline to the Pucallpa refinery. From Tingo María, 286 km.; from Lima, 847 km. Sr. Jorge

Mattos Grijalva, Jirón 28 de Julio, Puerto Callao, is a teacher of English who likes to show people around.

Hotels *State Tourist Hotel,* new, US$14 d; *Comfort, Choy Sánchez,* new and clean; *Sisley,* adequate; *Mercedes,* the best in town; *Hotel La Cabaña,* on Lake Yarinacocha, German owner, highly recommended, US$12 each, check your bill; *Hotel Roma,* US$3 (not recommended); *Hotel Perú,* US$5 d (try bargaining), dirty and not recommended, basic; *Hotel Don José,* basic but good value; *Hotel Marinhor; Hotel Amazonas,* good dining room, US$2, best place for information on boats going to Iquitos; *Hotel los Angeles,* about US$3 d, shower; *Hotel Tariri,* new, US$9 s, US$13.50 d, with air conditioning, food cheaper and better than at *Amazonas,* Calle Raimondi, near Calle Frederico Basadre; *Hotel Europa,* US$3 d.
  For longer stays, houses may be rented at US$5-10 a month at Puerto Callao, on Lake Yarinacocha (see below).

Restaurant Two "chifas" - (Chinese restaurant) downtown: *Chifa Hongkong* recommended; *Jugos Don José,* good and cheap; *Restaurant D'Onofrio* recommended. **Note:** Both restaurants and hotels in Pucallpa are expensive.

Bookshop Librería La Verdad has collection of English books on loan; a boon for stranded travellers!

Air Faucett jet flights to and from Lima daily and to and from Iquitos on Mondays, Wednesdays, Fridays and Sundays. Propeller aircraft flights on Tuesdays and Thursdays terminating at Pucallpa. Aeroperú jet flights to and from Lima (US$30) and Iquitos (Pucallpa-Iquitos, US$30) daily, and to and from Tarapoto and Tingo María on Tues. and Thurs. TANS also have a hydro plane service to Iquitos, Mon., Wed. and Fri., US$25, 8 hours with many stops at villages on the way. Airport to town, bus US$0.05; taxi US$1.25.

Buses Arellano and others from Lima to Pucallpa (US$15, 32 hrs.) *via* Huánuco (US$3.80, 18 hrs.). From Pucallpa Nor-Oriente goes to Tingo María. US$3.50, 10-11 hours. Advised to take travelling rug or blankets as the crossing of the Cordillera at night is bitterly cold and most of road is unpaved. It is also possible to get to Lima by lorry.

Inoculation against (rare) yellow-fever outbreaks in the Ucayali river basin is recommended, and so is prophylaxis against malaria. The Hospital Amazónico Albert Schweitzer, which serves the local Indians, is near Pucallpa. The Summer School of Linguistics for the study of Indian languages is on picturesque **Lake Yarinacocha,** 30 minutes by bus (*Hotel La Cabaña,* expensive but poor service; *La Brisa,* US-run, recommended, good excursions). Here is excellent bathing in clean water. It is a pleasant change after the mud of Pucallpa and the Amazon; you can camp, though it is hot and insect-ridden. Motor canoes can be hired for about US$12 a day; they are the best way of visiting the Indian tribes. Photo the Indians here if they'll let you. Taxi from airport to port on lake, US$3, then take boat to *Hotel La Cabaña,* US$0.80. The owner of the *Cabaña* organizes boat trips on River Ucayali; the shorter trips have been recommended. He also owns the houseboat *Mamuri.*

River Service To Iquitos by steamer, some better than others. Either 2-berth or 4-berth cabins. Food simple. With a little organization this can be a wonderful trip; tinned food, mosquito netting and fishing line all help. The smaller boats call often at jungle villages if you want to see them. Average time: 5 days. Boats leave very irregularly. When conditions are bad they leave in convoy: none may leave afterwards for 4 to 6 weeks. Take lots of insect repellant (try local brand, called Black Flag), water purifier and tummy pills. The fare is about US$25 a head with cabin, rice and beans. **Advice** Buy a hammock and a cheap blanket before getting on a boat on the Amazon region. It is possible to hire a small boat from Pucallpa to Iquitos for US$89. Further up the Ucayali river is Requena, from which launches sail to Iquitos every other day taking 12 hours, US$4. Roroboya, a small Shipibo Indian village about 12 hours downstream from Pucallpa, should not be missed, as most other villages down to Iquitos are metizo. You can go to Puerto La Hoyada and Puerto Italia (smaller boats) to find a boat going to Iquitos, or the Capitanía on the waterfront will give you information about sailings, but this is not always reliable.

Iquitos, the legal and financial capital of Peru's jungle region, is a fast developing city of 150,000 people on the W bank of the Amazon, with

Padre Isla island (14½ by 3 km.) facing it in midstream. It has paved streets and plenty of automobiles (including taxis) but roads out of the city go only a little way. Iquitos is completely cut off, except by air and river. Some 800 km. downstream from Pucallpa and 3,200 km. from the mouth of the Amazon, it is a surprising accomplishment in such untamed country. It serves an area of 300,000 people, and has recently taken on a new lease of life as the centre for oil exploration in Peruvian Amazonia. As one might expect from its use by the oil industry and its remoteness, it is the most expensive town in Peru.

Local tourist literature talks of an iron house in the Plaza de Armas, designed by Eiffel in Paris, and assembled in Iquitos. This may be the building on the corner of the Plaza de Armas and Calle Putumayo, but there is no clear reference as such.

Belén, the waterfront slum, is lively and colourful, and does not seem a dangerous place to visit, in daylight. Most of its huts are built on rafts to cope with the river's 10-metre change of level during floods. A short drive S of the city is beautiful Quistacocha Lake in lush jungle, with a fish hatchery at the lakeside. The aquarium has been moved to Ramírez Hurtado. See in the city the Market, at the end of the Malecón, or riverside walk, which had been slipping down the embankment for years, but has now been repaired.

The university of Loreto (1962) specializes now in engineering and agriculture. Of special interest are the older buildings, former residences, faced with azulejos (glazed tiles) of great merit. They date from the rubber boom of 1890 to 1920, when the rubber barons imported tiles from Portugal and Italy and ironwork from England to embellish their homes. Vultures still stalk the streets like turkeys. Loreto Zoo is no longer in operation.

Hotels   *Tourist Hotel* (US$18.50 d and shower), with many good air-conditioned rooms. Can be booked from Lima. The *Hotel Imperial Amazonas,* much cheaper, US$11.55, run down, no air conditioning, no restaurant, but eat at *Caravelle,* a delightful French-style café. *Hotel Isabel,* US$5.25 s, US$9 d, very good and very, very clean. *Lima,* US$5 p.p., with bath, very good. *Perú,* US$4.60 s, US$7 d, excellent. *Res. Internacional,* Calle Lima, no private bath, US$2 s, good; *Tacna,* US$2 s; *Hostal San Antonio,* US$3.30 d with bath and fan, recommended; *Europa,* very good, US$4 p.p., with shower, water if lucky; *Oriental,* US$8 d, large fan and showers, continental breakfast for under US$0.50. *Hotel Anita,* US$2.50 p.p. with shower, recommended. *Hotel Residencial,* Juan Lima, US$2 d. Other hotels include *Excelsior,* US$9 without bathroom; *Ambassador,* US$16.65 d with shower, air conditioning and snack-bar; *Loreto,* US$12.20 d, with shower, no air conditioning; *Acosta,* US$18 d, shower, air conditioning, snack bar.

Restaurants   *Río Nanay,* N of city, fried chicken in tropical atmosphere, is now dilapidated. *Chifa Central* (Chinese, good). Good ice cream at *Tregal* and *La Favorita. Cohen's* next to La Favorita, not cheap but good. *Wung Cha,* corner of San Martín and Arica, is good but expensive. Recommended restaurants include a good Swiss chalet restaurant on the Malecón, expensive. Try also *El Mesón* in Jirón Napo, and a restaurant on Calle Raimondo. Río Negro restaurants are to be avoided. Pineapples are good and cheap. Try the local drink Chuchuasi, which is supposed to have aphrodisiac qualities! You can eat cheaply, especially fish, at the market.

Current   220 volts, A.C.

Museum   Municipal Museum has a large, old collection of stuffed Amazonian fauna which is rather disappointing. Open 0900-1300, 1530-1900, US$0.50. It has a somewhat dilapidated aquarium.

Air   Taxi to the airport costs US$2; bus, US$0.15. Faucett, two daily jet flights to Lima (US$45) one direct, the other *via* Pucallpa or Tarapoto on alternating days. Faucett flight from Iquitos to Pucallpa costs US$35. Mon., Wed., Fri., Sat.; to

Tarapoto, Tues., Thurs., Sun. Aeroperú daily jet flights and extra on Tues., Thurs. and Sats. Aeroperú flies Iquitos-Trujillo on Mon., Wed., Fri. and to Lima two flights daily, one direct and the other one *via* Tarapoto, US$44. No flights Iquitos-Ecuador. TANS Catalina flying-boat to Ramón Castilla, and across Amazon by motor-boat to Leticia, Colombia, or Benjamin Constant, Brazil, for onward flights to Bogotá and Manaus, respectively. Cheap way to Bogotá by TANS flight Iquitos-Santo Tojada (Sat.), US$10, across River Putumayo, then flight Legisanio (Colombia)-Bogotá (Mon., Wed. and Fri.), US$4.20. The Brazilian airline Cruzeiro do Sul has two weekly flights on Wednesday and Saturdays, between Iquitos, Leticia and Manaus (US$45 Iquitos-Leticia and US$76 Iquitos-Manaus). It is also possible to fly from Tefé (Brazil—see page 321) to Iquotos for US$87, stopping at Tabatinga for border formalities. (Mark your luggage "Iquitos" or it will be unloaded at Tabatinga.) Flights Leticia-Iquitos on Sun., Wed., Fri., will have a connection flight to Pucallpa for US$70. (Exit tax Leticia airport US$10.) Leaves Leticia 0800. Leaves Iquitos for Pucallpa 1510; probably delayed. Iquitos flights frequently delayed. Peruvian Air Force flies Pucallpa-Iquitos, US$20, but unreliable in that plane may be requisitioned at short notice, and Iquitos-Leticia, US$12.

Tourist Office Corner of Julio C. Arana and Condomina, has town maps.

Local Tourist Agencies arrange half-day, one-day, or longer trips to places of interest with guides speaking some English; the packaged tours cost US$100-125 for three days. Launches for impromptu river trips can be hired by the hour or day; the tour operators are located near the Plaza: Explorama Tours; Wong's Amazon Tours; Amazon Lodge Safaris Tours. Good lodges with good local food, are *Yanamono* (owned by Explorama) and *Amazon Lodge* (owned by Amazon Lodge Safaris). The Yanamono lodge is highly recommended but is not the cheapest. River journey there downstream 2½ hrs., 4 hours back. Overnight tours to all the lodges cost between US$37 and US$45. An excursion with Amazon Lodge Safaris to the Río Yanayacu costs US$40 for 3 days (2 nights), including transport in motor boat, and full board. Exploraciones Amazónicas, Casilla 446, Iquitos, has a centre 80 km. from Iquitos, with rustic facilities, for trips by boat into virtually uninhabited jungle. No children under 15. It is advisable to take a waterproof coat and shoes or light boots on such trips, as well as "espirales" to ward off the mosquitoes at night—they can be bought from a drugstore in Iquitos. Paseos Amazónicos Ambassador (office opposite *Hotel Turistas* does a cheap one day tour for US$12. A bus from Jirón Lima takes you to Nanay river. Launches may do cruises to Leticia. Enquire at Jeson Travel, Wright Way Tours or at any reputable travel agency.

Clubs Club Social Iquitos, overlooking Plaza de Armas; Military Casino, for all classes; Centro Internacional.

Cinemas Many cinemas (about US$0.35) show English-language films.

Bookshops The Librería Mosqueña sells a few English books, and the Salón de Belleza Florcita in Calle Putumayo sells second-hand English books.

Industries, based on produce brought down from the Selva by river, are saw-milling, cotton-ginning the preparation of rubber, and oil refining.

Exports are mainly rubber, balatá, vegetable ivory, nuts, skins, tobacco and hardwoods.

Shipping Enasa boats occasionally to and from Belén. River boats to Pucallpa (infrequent) or Yurimaguas, 6-8 day trip, very cheap. Cabins are 4 berth and you have to buy both a first class ticket, which entitles you to food and deck space to sling your hammock, and a cabin ticket if you want the luxury of a berth. Plenty of washing and toilet facilities, but the food is rice and beans cooked in river water. There is a good cheap bar. Take plenty of prophylactic enteritis tablets; many contract dysentery on the trip. Also take insect repellent. One sold locally is called Black Flag and is quite effective. Motor vessel "Santa Rosa" (Arica 616, Iquitos) sails every 15 days for Pucallpa, US$20, cabin for 2, US$2.50. Communications with Manaus by river are most unreliable and the journey takes about 15 days; best go to Leticia first. Information on boats for Pucallpa obtained on wharves, or at Meneses (Jirón Lima), Bellavista (Malecón Tarapacá 596) Hurtado (Av. Grau 1223) and Casa Pinto (Sgto. Flores 164).

The Inca Road

We have great pleasure in incorporating an account by Christopher Portway, the explorer and author, of the Andean Inca road. Mr Portway took part recently, in company with David Taylor, in a preliminary exploration of the course of the road in Central Peru; another expedition led by Mr. Taylor left in the summer of 1978.

Roads and buried gold are probably the most universally remembered legacies of the Incas. Gold treasure, hidden since the Spanish began their conquest, is still occasionally unearthed, usually by accident, and gold fever is rampant amongst the villagers of the remote northern Andean districts of Peru. But whatever your reasons for visiting the less frequented central and northern areas of the country a very good one is to observe and marvel at sections of the Central Andean Inca road that still exists for considerable stretches.

In order to hold the Inca realm together and to convert regions of desert, mountain and jungle into the closely-knit empire it became, good communications were necessary; the result was the Inca road which Alexander von Humboldt characterized as "the most useful and stupendous work ever executed by man". The roads were also strategic and, like their 20th-century counterparts in Europe and North Africa—the *Autobahnen* and *Autostrade* of Germany, Italy and their once conquered territories—they were instrumental in the expansion of the empire.

Basically, there were two great roads in the Inca system. One was the royal road between Cuzco and Quito, progressively extended to take in northern Ecuador, southern Colombia, and southwards, Bolivia and northern Argentina. A mind-boggling 5,230 km. in length, its remains have been best preserved (more through remoteness than any preserving agency) in Peru. Much of the 4,050 km. of the other artery, the coastal road between Tumbes in the north of Peru and the River Maule in Chile, has been built over by the Pan American Highway, as have the lateral roads connecting the two. Of the 2,010 km. of royal road between Cuzco and Quito sections remain to stride across the mountains.

The standard width of the royal road varied between 5 and 6 metres (as against the 8 metres of the less-obstructed coastal road). It was unpaved, except where there was unavoidable water or when climbing steep hillsides necessitating the use of stone steps.

A good section, bordered by stone, may be seen some 13 km. east of the village of Shelby, served by the railway from La Oroya to Cerro de Pasco. Its course is marked by the lonely ruins of Bonbón, an Inca community centre only recently identified, which in turn lies close to the modern dam holding back the Mantaro River as it flows out of the northern end of Lake Junín.

But perhaps the most astounding survival of Inca roads is the long stretch displaying varied construction over differing terrain, between Yanahuanca and Huari.

Yanahuanca is situated in the river valley of the same name. An incredibly beautiful valley, its sides are flecked with a profusion of wild flowers, yellow gorse and eucalyptus trees, and chequered with a multitude of cultivated plots. Lofty mountains, evocative with snow, give an air of Swiss Alpine splendour though never could Switzerland produce so much grandeur on such a scale untrodden by tourist feet and unseen by tourist eyes. Yanahuanca itself is rarely entered by foreigners and thus a visitor has to contend with a retinue of a hundred or more curious inhabitants in his passage through the village. Its amenities include a few bars, a simple restaurant and a community social centre, but no hotel.

Two km. up the Yanahuanca Valley a lesser valley cuts northwards between the towering crags. At this point may be seen the remnants of the Inca road zigzagging down almost perpendicular gradients and burrowing through outcrops of rock on the other side of the river. A series of Inca steps can also be discerned and these are still used by villagers. The road, its paving uneven and disturbed by countless horse and donkey convoys, leads up the smaller valley, its course sometimes shared by a stream, to the village is Huarautombo, a community of some 220 people, about 4 km. distant.

This village is surrounded by many pre-Inca remains and the learned schoolmaster, Sr. Valentín Inga Castro, will be only too happy to show visitors the many ruins of the area, as well as the cave-tomb full of deformed skulls only recently discovered by him, a crop of cave paintings and numerous underground chambers. As at Yanahuanca a visitor will have to contend with a great deal of unashamed curiosity. He will also be met by the first of many enquiries as to whether his baggage includes a metel-detector, for the region is alive with rumour of hidden gold and 'gringos' alone are immune from the wrath of the gods; in addition presumably, to the more earthly jealousies of rival factions in the village.

For more than 150 km. the "Camino Incaico" is not only in almost continuous existence from the Yanahuanca Valley but is actually shown on the map issued by the Instituto Geográfico Militar. From Huarautambo, in company with lesser tracks, it winds up the head of the Huarautambo valley, often in the form of widely-spaced steps, and across rock-scattered grasslands, over escarpments, following valleys, then veering away to utilize more valleys hidden by saddles over which the road triumphs even if the weary 20th-century traveller wilts along the way. At a spot known locally as Incapoyo, superb views of the Cordillera Huayhuasma, with peaks soaring to 6,000 metres and more, are to be seen.

While the road fades from sight or has become muddled with present day tracks the route is marked by the ruins of *tampus*—or Inca rest houses—and, occasionally, larger sites. Any respectable road depends for its life and usage on two functions: one is maintenance; the other accommodation. Thus all Inca roads had a system of *tampus*. . . "these were buildings and storehouses", wrote a traveller in 1547, "at every four-six leagues (20-30 km.), with great abundance of all provisions that the surrounding districts could supply".

Tampus were official and utilitarian. Some of them consisted of a single structure, 30 by 100 metres; others had a series of smaller rooms opening on a large corral where the llamas were stabled. Each was maintained by the local *ayllu* as part of its labour tax; individual communities were expected to ensure that the parts of the road near their sections were in constant repair.

Between Yanahuanca and Huari pre-Inca *tampus* and other remains provide landmarks for the road. Andahuayla, Yanagalán, Gashapampa, Tamboccocha, nearby Baños, the great temple-fortress of Huánuco Viejo, Taparaku, Huamanín, Pomacocha, are lonely communities and ancient ruins slowly dying. Thereafter traces of the road become fainter though short sections can be identified in the hills behind San Luis, Piscobamba and Pomabamba. Information can be wrung out of local people, but then directions will be tinged with ignorance or confused by vague knowledge of earlier civilizations and their surviving relics. Behind Pomabamba, far up upon the final crest of the mountains to the west, the road is revealed by a chain of old forts older than the highway itself, but it is left to such disintegrating edifices to mark the route to Cajamarca and northwards into Ecuador.

Townships and villages along the way include the following: *Tamboccocha and Gashapampa:* One single shop with little to offer enlivens these two remote villages. *Pilcocancha:* A few km. north of the township of Baños, this village is notable only for its hot thermal pools lying a kilometre south. Otherwise a somewhat depressing Community centred round its square with three shops and not much in them. *La Unión.* A "double town" with its main residential section across the River Vizcarra in the sheer-sided valley of the same name. Two bridges, but the one in centre of town had its centre span swept away by flood waters. Several small hotels, simple but adequate at about US$1 per night but no hot water, a farce of a cinema and half a dozen restaurants. On the grass plateau—the pampa—above the town and reached by a strong and extremely steep path are the spectacular ruins of Huánuco Veijo with its plaza, temple and dwellings of an Inca administrative centre. *Pomachaca:* A small village with a couple of shops at a road and river junction. The roads lead to Huari, San Marcos and Llamellín. *Huari* (page 649). *San Luis:* A village in the shadow of the Cordillera Blanca. A few small restaurants and an occasional bus service to *Piscobamba:* A larger square than usual registers this village in the memory but, again, no hotels and only a few shops and small restaurants.

The staff of the mayor's office are helpful and from behind the town views across the valley are superb. Occasional buses to **Pomabamba:** A very pleasant town indeed, with one hotel, restaurants, a bank and a baker's shop that serves the best-value cakes in the province. Down in the valley are hot thermal springs, some of which have been channelled into stone baths open to the public at US$0.03 a time. The valley is fertile and its soil excites into growth oranges, lemons and all manner of fruits. On both sides of the valley in which Pomabamba stands are pre-Inca ruins of considerable interest. *Sihuas:* A small township clinging to a hilltop. No hotel, but a couple of restaurants. *Huamachucho* (page 607). *Cajabamba* (Peru): Lively little town with a hotel or two and a number of restaurants (not to be confused with the Ecuadorean town of the same name). *Ichocán:* Pleasant village with an interesting church and a few small restaurants. The council do not object to overnight camping in the plaza with its fountain and trees. *San Marcos:* Lively little town with a hotel or two. *Cajabamba* (page 608).

(**Warning** The Andean Inca road in the north of Peru passes through extremely remote mountain territory. Travellers are advised, therefore, to take full precautions against starvation and exposure. There is, apparently, some danger of attack by cattle rustlers whose designs on inquisitive travellers are said to be lethal).

The Economy

Peru's economic performance since 1967 has been closely related to the performance of the copper and fishmeal industries. In 1970 the country became the world's leading fishing nation in terms of both value and volume of catch, and the value of fish export earnings exceeded for the first time those of all other categories. Anchoveta fishing (from which fishmeal is derived) was prevented for most of 1972 and 1973 by the arrival of the warm niño current off the Peruvian coast; though the shoals returned in smaller numbers in 1974/75 it is now believed that the total may have been permanently reduced by disturbance of the ecological balance, following departure of seabirds from islands offshore.

1976 and 1977 were disappointing years for the Peruvian economy, with a growth rate of only 2% being recorded in 1976 and a fall of 1% in 1977. The government has had to introduce a number of strict austerity measures to combat inflation, which has been rising rapidly since 1973. These measures have dampened business confidence at a time when the balance of payments has been under a considerable strain. Exports failed to rise as fast as expected chiefly because of lower copper and zinc prices, the slump in the world sugar market and, of course, the lag in the fishmeal industry which, with the reappearance of the niño current in 1977, suffered another setback. Consequently trade deficits of US$761 m. and US$369 m. were registered for 1976 and 1977 respectively. At the same time the sol came under such pressure that since July 1976 it was progressively devalued from 65 soles per US$1 to 150 by June 1978.

The outlook for 1978 is somewhat brighter given that oil exports should start and that, with the opening of new mines, copper sales should increase. Moreover the IMF has given its support to the government's stabilisation programme with a stand-by credit of US$106 m. Inflation however is still expected to be a serious problem; the rate was reduced from 45% in 1976 to 32% in 1977, but rose steeply in 1978 because of the sharp devaluations and the Government's austerity measures.

Fishing, copper mining and export agriculture help make the coastal area (*costa*) the dominant economic region of Peru, though an ever-larger proportion of food production is now coming, from the Sierra. The chief centre is Chimbote, where most of the anchoveta catch is landed, and where several of the state-owned fishmeal processing plants have been built. A new fishing complex under construction at Paita began production late in 1975. Other government-financed complexes at Oquendo, La Puntilla, Samanco, Tacna, Iquitos and Puno opened at about the same time.

There is open-cast copper mining at Toquepala, and there are plans to mine and refine copper on a large scale at Cerro Verde, Santa Rosa and Cuajone near Arequipa, and at Michiquillay and Antamina in the north. These new sources are expected to increase significantly the volume of copper available for export from 1977 onwards.

Most of Peru's export crops are grown on the *costa*, and particularly cotton and sugar; yields of sugar here are three times the world's average.

There is, however, a shortfall in most food items and significant food imports are necessary.

The Lima-Callao conurbation houses two-thirds of all Peruvian industrial establishments and contains over half the population with incomes above subsistence levels. These industries include the preparation and packaging of chemicals, pharmaceuticals, plastics, furniture, clothing, acrylic fibres, motor vehicles and a shipbuilding industry which is rapidly becoming one of the most important in Latin America. Work has begun on expansion of the Sima shipyard at Callao; the plan includes a dry-dock for the building of ships of up to 300,000 tons. Many ships hitherto mainly fishing vessels have been exported to other Latin American countries and to France. Industrialization is becoming increasingly important in Peru's second city, Trujillo, and its third, Arequipa.

Emphasis is placed by the Government on basic industrialization and the development of the steel, cement, chemical, fertilizer and non-ferrous metals industries. Petroleum is becoming increasingly important; since 1971 new wells have been sunk in the north-eastern jungle region near the borders with Ecuador, Colombia and Brazil. A pipeline has been built across the Andes, and Peru is already self-supporting in petroleum; it is hoped that the level of exports will become significant by 1980.

The Government is still experiencing some difficulty in stimulating private investment, though this situation should be eased by the reversal of previous policies that involved the nationalization of companies in some sectors and worker participation in management.

Foreign Trade (US$m.)

		1972	1973	1974	1975	1976	1977*
Exports	..	944	1,119	1,521	1,378	1,359	1,726
Imports	..	797	1,029	1,531	2,491	2,100	2,095

*Provisional.

Information for Visitors

Air Services from Europe British Caledonian flies twice weekly to Lima *via* Caracas and Bogotá, taking 14 hours. Direct flights also from Frankfurt, Paris, Amsterdam, Madrid and Lisbon by Lufthansa, Air France, KLM, Iberia, Viasa and Avianca. Several low-price charters from Paris; apply to Jumbo (subsidiary of Air France), 60 rue Monsieur le Prince, Paris 75006 (Tel.: 325-93-75); or Uniclam-Voyages, 63 rue Monsieur le Prince, Paris 75006 (Tel.: 633-59-14); or Nouvelles Frontières, 63 av. Denfert-Rochereau, Paris 75014 (Tel.: 325-57-51); or Le Point Mulhouse, 4 rue des Orphelins, Mulhouse 68200 (Tel.:[89]42-44-61). Also Le Point flights with SATA, a Swiss company operating from Zurich to Lima twice a month US$525. Lima office for Le Point: Jirón Ica 242. Office 109. Aeroflot fly from Frankfurt *via* Cuba. 3 hour stopover in Havana including sightseeing. Tickets from Uniclam-Solmatur, La Paz 742, Miraflores, Lima.

From U.S.A. and Canada Miami is the main gateway to Peru with flights every day. Air Panamá does the cheapest flight. Other direct flights from New York, San Francisco, Los Angeles, Washington, Vancouver, Toronto and Montreal by Braniff, CP Air, Lufthansa, Avianca, Aerolíneas Argentinas, Varig, LAN Chile and Ecuatoriana.

From South America Lima is a transit stop for most South American routes and therefore there are regular flights to all South American countries; in most cases, daily. LAB (non-IATA) is usually the cheapest airline for flights out of Lima but tickets bought in Peru are more expensive; try to get Lima-La Paz ticket in Colombia, for US$73. In Lima it costs US$90.

Trans-Pacific Flights from Tokyo by Varig and CP Air. Air France also flies from Tokyo *via* Tahiti twice weekly. From Australia and New Zealand to Santiago by LAN Chile (allow for stopover in Easter Island) or Tahiti by Qantas or Air New Zealand, from where there are immediate connections.

Trans-South Atlantic From South Africa to Rio de Janeiro by South African Airlines or Varig, with immediate connections. There is a US$5 airport tax for international flight departures. It is payable in dollars.

Shipping Services The most direct sea route from the U.K. is the P.S.N.C.'s (freight only) from Liverpool. Prudential Grace Line is the most important plying between the U.S.A. and Peru. Another sea route from Europe is *via* New York, where transatlantic steamers connect with American vessels. European lines serving Peru are Norwegian Knutsen, the Swedish Johnson, the Italia Line, the French Compagnie Générale Transatlantique, the Royal Netherlands Steamship Company, the German Hamburg Amerika Line and the Norddeutscher Lloyd and the Westfal Larsen Line. The Kawasaki Kisen Kaisha serves Peru from Australia, and the Bank Line from India; the Pacific Steam Navigation Company vessel, the *Tropic,* sails every six weeks from Callao to New Zealand (16 days), US$360, taking three passengers. Further details can be obtained from the P.S.N.C. offices at Av. Nicolás de Piérola, Lima. The Booth Line runs vessels to the Peruvian reaches of the Amazon. The Chilean Cía. Sudamericana de Vapores, C.P.V., and Flota Gran Colombiana ply between Peru and Europe but carry no passengers. Italian Line has ended its passenger services.

Documents No visa is necessary for citizens of Western European countries, South American countries (except for Chileans and Venezuelans, who need them), Canada, the USA and Japan. A Tourist Card is obligatory. These may be obtained free from the immigration authorities on arrival in Peru for visits up to 90 days. The tourist card can be renewed for another 90 days. Give yourself plenty of time (and insist on getting the full 90 days at the border) because extensions cost US$8.70 and delays. The tourist card, called "Cédula C", is in duplicate, the original given up on arrival and the copy on departure. A new tourist card must be obtained for each re-entry or when an extension is given. All travellers must have an International Certificate of Vaccination with the smallpox vaccination up to date. Declaration of foreign currency no longer required. All foreigners should be able to produce on demand some recognizable means of identification, preferably a passport. At most frontier posts (particularly at Aguas Verdes) Peruvian immigration officials are insisting that travellers have in their possession an exit ticket before allowing entry into Peru, though much persistence can get you through without a ticket. If you do not have one on arrival at the border, you may be forced to pay US$11 minimum for an outgoing bus ticket, which cannot be transferred or refunded (although sometimes you may be lucky in changing the ticket). Better to get a miscellaneous charges order from an airline, which can be refunded. Immigration formalities and baggage checks at Jorge Chávez (Lima) airport are very protracted and require much patience.

British businessmen are strongly advised to get "Hints to Business Men Visiting Peru", issued free from Export Services Division, Department of Trade, Room CO7, Export House, 50 Ludgate Hill, London EC4M 7HU.

Export Ban No object of archaeological interest may be taken out of Peru.

Import Ban In February 1974 imports—even temporary—of radios, record players and tape recorders were banned. Visitors bringing in these items may have them confiscated. Check with Consulate for up-to-date information.

Duty-free Imports   400 cigarettes or 50 cigars or 500 grams of tobacco, 2 litres of alcoholic drinks, new articles for personal use or gifts up to value US$200.

Warning   Thieves are becoming increasingly active in streets, hotels, buses and trains, choosing especially tourists as their targets. Take care, especially in Cuzco.

Important   If your belongings are stolen: (1) If the value is over US$20, go to PIP International Police, if under US$20 go to the Guardia Civil. (2) Make declaration of loss as soon as possible. (3) Buy *papel sellado* (stamped paper) on which to make statement.

A *denuncia*—an annoucement of a theft signed by police—is valid in place of a student card if student card is taken.

Motoring   The Peruvian Touring and Automobile Club, Av. César Vallejo 699, Lince, Lima (Tel.: 403270), with offices in most provincial cities including Tumbes, Tacna and Puno, gives the latest news about the roads and hotels along the way. It sells a very good road map at US$2.25 and route maps covering most of Peru at US$0.40. AAA maps sold at "Lima Times" office. Buy maps separately or in packages of 8. Other maps are published by Petroperú; these are free of charge but extremely difficult to obtain from petrol stations or the head office, Petroperú, Av. Central 717, San Isidro. A free map is obtainable from the Department of Tourism, off the Paseo de la República, Lima. Gasoline per US gallon: "extra" (84 octane), US$0.70; "importada" (95 octane), US$1, found in Lima, the coastal towns and Arequipa. In Lima never trust the green light; motorists often drive through the red lights. When parking remove stealable accessories and screen wipers; there is a large black market in car parts.

Roads go to very high altitudes in Peru—make sure that the spark is properly adjusted. Avoid mountain travel between December and April. Take 2 planks of wood in case car gets stuck in soft soil when allowing other vehicles to pass.

No imported car spares available. Must have international driving licence—especially with a number. If you don't have a number on your licence, improvise.

Surface Transport   Few roads in Peru, except for the Pan American and Central Highways and the roads connecting Huarás and Carás with Pativilca and Casma, are paved. Landslides are frequent, surfaces are usually very rough, and this makes for slow travel and frequent breakdowns. Timekeeping is not very good, and most buses, especially in the mountain areas, are small, old and offer little comfort. Blankets and emergency food are a *must* in the mountains. Always possible to buy food on the roadside, as buses stop frequently. Colectivos not always much dearer; trucks not always much cheaper; they charge ¾ bus fare, but wholly unpredictable, not for long hops, and comfort depends on the load: the ideal is a half load of sugar. Colectivos go almost anywhere in Peru; more often during the day than buses. Sit in front, better views. Most colectivo firms have offices. Book one day in advance. They pick you up at your hotel or in main square. If long journey take a water bottle. **Note for Hitch-Hikers:** Hitch-hiking is not too difficult, especially on the coast. Freight traffic has to stop at the police "garitas" outside each town and hence it is quite easy to get a lift at these points. Drivers usually ask for money but don't always expect to get it. In mountain and jungle areas you usually have to pay drivers of lorries, vans and even private cars; ask the driver first how much he is going to charge, and then recheck with the locals (the Sierra Indians for whom it is normal method of travel). Private cars are very few and far between.

Bus Companies   Roggero operates only on coast; Tepsa operates on coast and to Cajamarca; Ormeño only south to Arequipa and Tacna.

Morales Moralitos south to Arequipa and Cuzco. Hidalgo only in Sierra. We have received many complaints about the services of Morales Moralitos, together with suggestions for another version of their name, and would advise readers to travel by other companies when possible.

Taxis   In most places taxi fares are fixed before the journey; therefore it is best to ask local advice on average charges before you bargain with taxi drivers.

Hotels   The *State Tourist Hotels* (commonly known as *Hotel Turistas*) are run by Enturperú. They vary considerably but generally offer the best accommodation in town in terms of cleanliness and reliable food. They provide safe garaging for cars at US$0.50 a night. Reservations can be made at Enturperú, Jirón Junín 455, Lima, Tel.: 287450. Heating in rooms often unsatisfactory. Good local maps can usually be obtained at the Tourist Hotels; in some of the smaller towns they function as tourist offices. All de luxe, 1st class and State Tourist Hotels charge a high 21% in taxes, which includes service charges; lower category hotels charge 13-19%. Most hotels have this surcharge included in their prices, but best check first. Under a new regulation all prices which have accommodation now have a plaque outside bearing the letters H (Hotel), Hs (Hostal), HR (Hotel Residencial) or P (Pensión) according to type. Previously, in many cases, there was no indication that these places did in fact offer accommodation.

In reply to our 1972 statement that some State Tourist Hotels find the proper tariff too difficult to calculate and charge a blanket 12%, the Tourist Department emphatically deny that there is any surcharge for extra blankets at any of their hotels.

Camping   Easy in Peru, especially along the coast.

Swimming   Between December and April the entire coast of Peru offers good bathing, but during the rest of the year only the northern beaches near Tumbes are pleasant for bathing.

Internal Air Services link towns which are often far apart and can only be reached otherwise with difficulty. Virtually all the air traffic is in the hands of the Cía. de Aviación Faucett and Aeroperú. They fly N from Lima to Talara with calls at Trujillo, Chiclayo and Piura and an extension to Tumbes, and S from Lima to Arequipa and Tacna. There are also scheduled flights to the interior towns of Huánuco, Tingo María, Pucallpa, Iquitos, Ayacucho, Andahuaylas, and Cuzco. There are propeller flights from Iquitos to Chiclayo and Trujillo *via* Tarapoto, Yurimaguas and Rioja, and from Cuzco to Puerto Maldonado, Quincemil and Iberia. Aeroperú flies to Anta (Callejón de Huaylas) and Juliaca (Lake Titicaca), and also has many services in the Ucayali and Huallaga areas. There is a 9% government tax on economy class air tickets in or out of Peru, if purchased in the country.

N.B.   Both companies are often criticized for frequent cancellations and poor time-keeping. We realize that the Andean area is dangerous for flying and unpredictable weather contributes to poor time-keeping, but companies are also criticized for bad passenger service, especially as regards information and overbooking. Note that flights into the mountains may well be put forward 1 hour if there are reports of bad weather. Advisable to be in plenty of time for boarding plane.

Flights should be reconfirmed 24 hours in advance. Twenty minutes before departure, the clerk is allowed by law to let waiting passengers board, taking the reserved seats of those who haven't turned up.

Climate, Clothing   The coast is at its most agreeable from December to April inclusive. Men need lightweight suits then and women cotton or linen dresses. Business is more active later, but climate does not interfere much with business. During the cooler months, June to November, there is little or no rain but Lima's humidity is from 90 to 98%—and there is little sunshine from Paramonga S to Arica.

During this period medium English summer clothing is the most suitable: the temperature rarely falls below 13°C, or rises above 27°C. For the high Sierra heavier clothing should be taken, including a winter overcoat or lightweight waterproofed overcoat—difference between day and night temperatures is great. The jungles beyond are tropical.

Health Water from the tap is safe in most cities of Peru, but if you are unused to changes of mineral content etc., you may wish to drink bottled water, which is available everywhere. Cleaning your teeth, ice, and salads washed in tap water hold few dangers and are not likely to cause "Inca Quickstep"! Fruit should be peeled when bought in the street, or take it to your hotel and have it washed. Food at better hotels and restaurants is fine, even salads, but watch out for the typical dishes seasoned with highly spiced Peruvian peppers. In cases of diarrhoea, take "Colitina", an effective local remedy. There is a chance of malaria in the jungle areas; take the normal prophylactic measures.

Altitude is often a problem in the mountain cities. Rest on arrival for at least two hours, eat, drink and smoke lightly, walk slowly and *never* exert yourself. "Micoren" (small red pills), "Efortil" pills (to strengthen the circulation), and "Coramina Glucosa" (US$0.50 for box of 10 tablets), available from any chemist, have been found helpful for short time. Try also "mate de coca", a mild herb tea made from coca leaves, the source of cocaine. Coca leaves are easily bought in markets; they appear to combat lassitude and heavy headaches caused by altitude. (See also **Health Information** at front of book.)

Cost of Living Import tariffs make imported goods extremely expensive. Women should bring what clothes they need with them, for local buying is unsatisfactory and very expensive. Men's shoes are, however, good and reasonably priced. Agfa and Kodak film very expensive. Living costs in the Provinces are from 10 to 20% below those of Lima. Peru is not too expensive for those who want comfort and reasonable food; eat table d'hôte meals when possible; they are served more quickly. The Lima cost of living index rose by 23% in 1975, 45% in 1976 and 32% in 1977.

Tips Hotel and restaurant: 10% in addition to the 10% on the bill. Taxi drivers, none. Cloakroom attendants, 5 soles. Hairdressers (very high class only), 10 soles. Railway and airport porters, 5 to 10 soles per bag, according to distance carried. Usherettes, none.

Currency The monetary unit is the sol, divided into 100 centavos. There are nickel coins for 10 and 5 soles (rare) and bronze alloy coins (2 different issues of different sizes) for 1 sol and for 50, 25, 20, 10 and 5 centavos. Bank notes are for 1,000, 500, 200, 100, 50, 10, and 5 soles. Exchange is 150 soles to the US$. Only 5,000 soles in Peruvian currency may be taken in or out. The formerly-required currency declaration has been discontinued. It is extremely difficult to change currencies other than sterling, US$, Canadian dollars, Deutsche marks, Swiss and French francs. The Banco de la Nación at Lima airport, and at large towns near the frontier, will repurchase soles from departing travellers, but don't leave it too late; you will not be able to buy dollars at the frontier itself. For repurchase, it is essential to retain Banco de la Nación exchange slips.

Warning We have been informed that a large number of forged sol notes are in circulation; check the numbers if possible.

Banco de la Nación This is the *only* institution regularly authorized to deal in foreign exchange. All its branches are open from 0800-1130 from Jan. to March; the rest of the year Lima branches open from 0900 to 1330 and provincial branches from 0830 to 1300. The branch at 830 Rufino Torrico, Lima, opens 0830-1200 and 1530-1800. All banks close Sat., Sun. and holidays, except that the Jorge Chávez Airport branch is open 24 hours every day of the year. The main hotels and other banks are now allowed to exchange currencies, as agents of the Banco de la Nación. Travel agents are *not* allowed to exchange currencies, but only to accept them in payment for their services. However, American Express state that they will sell travellers' cheques and give out emergency money, but only in Lima.

Note: Once upon a time the exchange rate for the sol was 10 to the £; 10 soles are still commonly referred to as "una libra", 50 soles as "cinco libras", and so on.

Telephones Calls to Europe cost US$13.25 for 3 minutes, US$3.25 for each extra minute. Three different kinds of public telephone boxes, each accepting different weight and size of sol coins. Local calls 5 soles (4 on Sundays). Telephone directories found in most hotel rooms have a useful map of Lima and show itineraries of the buses.

The metric system of **weights and measures** is compulsory.

Public Holidays

January 1: New Year.	August 30: S Rosa de Lima.
March or April: Maundy Thursday, Good Friday.	October 9: National Dignity Day.
	November 1: All Saints.
May 1: Labour Day.	December 8: Immaculate Conception.
June 29: SS. Peter and Paul.	December 25: Christmas.
July 28, 29: Independence.	

Hours of business *Shops:* Jan. to March, 0900-1230 and 1600-1900. Rest of year: 0900-1230, 1530-1900. Some are closed on Saturday; many close later in the evening. *Banks:* Jan. to March, 0830-1130. Rest of year: 0830-1200. Close Saturday. *Offices:* Jan. to March, 0830-1130, and 1500-1830. Rest of year: 0830-1230 and 1500-1830. Many now work a through day, 0800-1500, and most close on Sat. *Government Offices:* Jan. to March, 0930-1130, Sat. 0900-1130. Rest of year: 0930-1100, 1500-1700; on Sat. 0930-1130.

Credit Cards Diners Club is most useful.

The Press Lima has 6 morning papers, which were all expropriated by the Government in July 1974 and handed over to various interest groups—peasants, industrial workers, professional workers, etc.—to run. They are: "La Prensa", "El Comercio", "La Crónica", "Expreso", "Correo", and "Ojo". There is a weekly privately-owned paper in English, the "Lima Times". The official gazette is "El Peruano". The main provincial cities have at least one newspaper each.

Sports Association football is the most popular. Basket-ball and other sports are also played on the coast, particularly around Lima and Callao. There are many bathing resorts near Lima. Golf clubs and racecourses are mentioned in the text. Riding is a favourite recreation in the Sierra, where horses can be hired at reasonable rates. There is excellent deep-sea fishing off Ancón, N of Lima, and at the small port of Cabo Blanco, N of Talara (see text). In that part of the Andes easily reached from Oroya, the lakes and streams have been stocked with trout, and fly fishing is quite good. Bullfights and cockfights are held in Lima.

For details about the best rainbow trout fishing in Peru (near Juliaca and in Lakes Arapa and Titicaca) write to Sr. José Bernal Paredes, Casilla 874, Arequipa.

Food The high-class hotels and restaurants serve international food and, on demand, some native dishes, but it is in the taverns (*chicherías*) and the Creole restaurants (*picanterías*) that the highly seasoned native food is often at its best. Generally found that the modest cafés are best value. Soups tend to be very good, and a meal in themselves. In the Lima area the most popular fish dishes are the *cebiche de corvina*—fish seasoned with lemons, onions and red peppers; the *escabeche de corvina*—fish with onions, hot green pepper, red peppers, prawns (*camarones*), cumin, hard eggs, olives, and sprinkled with cheese; and *chupe de camarones*, a fish stew made with varying and somewhat surprising ingredients. *Yacu-chupe*, or green soup, has a basis of potato, with cheese, garlic, coriander leaves, parsley, peppers, eggs, onions, and mint. *Causa* and *carapulca* are two good potato dishes; *causa* is made

:llow potatoes, lemons, pepper, hard-boiled eggs; olives, lettuce, sweet cooked corn, sweet cooked potato, fresh cheese, and served with onion sauce. Favourite meat dishes are *ollucos con charqui* (a kind of potato with dried meat as basis), *caucau*, made with tripe, potatoes, peppers, and parsley and served with rice; *anticuchos,* hearts of beef with garlic, peppers, cumin seeds and vinegar; *estofado de carne,* a stew which often contains wine; *carne en adobe,* a cut and seasoned steak; *sancochado*, meat and all kinds of vegetables stewed together and seasoned with ground garlic; *lomo a la huancaina,* beef with egg and cheese sauce; and *sopa a la criolla* containing thin noodles, beef heart, bits of egg and vegetables and pleasantly spiced. Any dish described as *arequipeño* can be expected to be hot and spicy. There is a ban on the sale of beef in restaurants and shops on the first 15 days of each month, in all the cities on the coast; but the supply of fish is improving and there is always plenty of pork, veal and lamb. The best beef is imported from Argentina and is expensive. Duck is excellent. For snacks, Peruvian *empanadas* are good. *Palta rellena* is avocado filled with chicken salad.

Among the desserts and confections are *cocada al horno*—coconut, with yolk of egg, sesame seed, wine and butter; *picarones*—frittered cassava flour and eggs fried in fat and served with honey; *mazamorra morada*—purple maize, sweet potato starch, lemons, various dried fruits, sticks of ground cinnamon and cloves and perfumed pepper; *manjar blanco*—milk, sugar and eggs; *maná*—an almond paste with eggs, vanilla and milk; *pastellillos*—yucas with sweet potato, sugar and anise fried in fat and powdered with sugar and served hot; and *zango de pasas,* made with maize, syrup, raisins and sugar. *Turrón,* the Lima nougat, is worth trying. The various Peruvian fruits are of good quality. They include bananas, the citrus fruits, pineapples, dates, avocados (*paltas*), eggfruit (*lúcuma*), the custard apple (*chirimoya*), quince, papaya mango, guava, the passion-fruit (*maracuyá*) and the soursop (*guanábana*).

During the summer (December through February) people take 3½ hours for lunch so that they can fit in a bathe at the nearby beaches. The tea hour starts about 1800 at the good hotels. If asked to a party ask the hostess what time you are *really* expected unless the time is specified on the invitation card as *hora inglesa*—English time; Peruvians tend to ask guests for dinner at 2000, but don't expect them till at least 2130!

A normal lunch or dinner costs about US$4.50, but can go up to about US$25 in a first class restaurant, with drinks and wine included. Nevertheless there are no end of cheap and good restaurants around the centre of Lima and most offer a "businessman's lunch" called "menú fijo" for no more than US$1 for a 3-course meal. There are many Chinese restaurants in Peru which serve good food at reasonable prices. For really economically-minded people the "Comedores Nacionales" in most cities of Peru offer a standard 3-course meal for only US$0.40.

Drinks The usual international drinks with several very good local ones: *Pisco,* a brandy made in the Ica valley, from which pisco sour is made; *Chilcano,* a longer refreshing drink also made with *Guinda,* a local cherry brandy; and *Algarrobina,* a sweet cocktail made with the syrup from the bark of the carob tree. Wine is quite good, the best brands being the Ica wines Tacama and Ocucaje; both come in red, white and rosé, sweet and dry varieties. Casapalca is not recommended. Beer is best in lager and stout types, especially the Cuzco and Arequipa brands. *Chicha de Jora* is a maize beer, and *Chicha Morada* is a soft drink made with purple maize. There are many different types of herb tea, the commonest being *manzanilla* and *hierbaluisa*.

Great Britain is represented in Peru by an Embassy and Consulate at Lima; they are together in Edificio El Pacífico Washington, corner of Av. Arequipa, Casilla 854 for mail. There are also consular offices at Callao, Arequipa, Mollendo and Iquitos.

First Secretary, Commercial: Casilla 854 for mail, 5th floor Edificio República, Paseo de la República 111 for visitors. Tel.: 283830. The commercial section of the British Embassy at Natalio Sánchez 125 produces a monthly commercial bulletin. The **United States** is represented by an Embassy and Consulate at Lima. **Canada, Australia** and **New Zealand** have Embassies in Lima (mailing address for New Zealand embassy: Casilla 5587), and **South Africa** has a Consulate.

The Peruvian Embassy and Consulate-General in London is at 52 Sloane Street S.W.1, Tel.: 01-235-6867. There are consular offices in Belfast, Birmingham, Glasgow, Hull and Liverpool.

American Express Agents Arequipa: Lima Tours, S.A., Santa Catalina 120, Tel.: 24143. Cuzco: Lima Tours, S.A., Heladores 167. Tel.: 2809. Lima: Lima Tours, S.A., Ocoña 160, Tel.: 27-6624.

This chapter has been revised by Philippa Hughes, late of LBI Economics Department, with the most welcome help of Gerard and Inge Astruck and Ruth Silbermann, of Sudex Travel Bureau and Nicholas Asheshov, of "Lima Times", and Olive Green and Phoebe Meyer, resident in Peru. We also wish to thank the following travellers: Philip Allen (São Paulo), Alan Angell (Oxford), William and Jack de Beaufort (Wassenaar, Netherlands), Ingela Björck and Per Andersson (Sweden), James K. Bock (Mexico City), Niels Brouwer (Amsterdam), Bruno and Verena Bürgi Burri (Oberwil-Zug, Switz.), Rick Carder (Windsor, Ont.), Ken Catlin (San Diego, Calif.), Olivier Chaudonet (Voiteur, France), G. H. Clark (Bonnet Bay, NSW), D. Cox (Saarenkylä, Finland), Jerry Coyne (Cambridge, Mass.), Christine Czajkowski, Michael Davison (Caracas), Mrs. B. Eales, John Eames and Maggie Harvey, Peter Ford and Sally Wilson, Tim and Arlene Frost (Hamilton, N.Z.), Peter Fürst and Hakon Hegnar (Norway), Bob Gebken (USA), Helen J. Glover, Mary Goodykoontz and Ken Scarlett (Woodland, Calif.), Ucky Hamilton (N.Z.), Gerrit Jachtenberg (Gellicum, Netherlands), Monica Joseph (Australia), Dieter Jungblut (W. Berlin), Gerhard Keilbach (Stuttgart), Leslie Kent (Pretoria), Detlef Körner (Hamburg), Paul and Theresa Legare (Ottawa), Jerry Leon (Havertown, Pa.), Cornelio Lindenberg and Marieke van der Ploeg (Amersfoort, Neth.), Daniel and Jan McAleese (Belfast), Dr. Terry McCarthy (Singapore), Ian MacDonell, Bernd Morgeneyer (W. Berlin), Alexander Nemeth and Janette Roberts (Australia), Graham and Toni O'Meara (Australia), Karin Östman (Spanga, Sweden), Dr. Margaret Peil, Thomas Pensler (Benediktbeuern, W. Germany), Joni Perkins (Canada), Andrew Radclyffe, Rosalind and Stuart Read (N.Z.), Michael Reeve, Jules Salomon (Pully, Lausanne), Andre Schepens (Brussels), Helga Schmidt—Frank and Herbert Schmidt (W. Germany), Michael Scott, Chris Sharpe (Mullewa, W. Australia), P. H. Sherville, Ken and Judy Stevenson (Ottawa), Margaret Symons (N.Z.), Ralf and Angela Trosiner (Hamburg), Peter Varey, Andreas Weber (Wohlen, Switz.), René Werren (Köniz, Switz.), Terry and Rosaura West (USA), Nicholas Westwood and Julia Amies, Anne Williams, Tim Williams and Elizabeth Young, and Dr. Henry M. Wilson (Madison, Wis.).

URUGUAY

URUGUAY (area 184,335 square km.) is the smallest Hispanic country in South America, about the same size as England and Wales together, but its population, 3,100,000, is less than that of Wales alone. It has Brazil to the north, the river Uruguay between it and Argentina to the west, and the wide estuary of the Plate to the south. The Atlantic Ocean washes its shores on the east.

Apart from a narrow plain which fringes most of the coast (but not near Montevideo), and an alluvial flood plain stretching N from Colonia to Fray Bentos, the general character of the land is undulating, with little forest except on the banks of its numerous streams. The long grass slopes rise gently to far-off hills, but none of these is higher than 600 metres. To the W and N the hills are known as the Cuchilla de Haedo; to the S, where they start at Montevideo and the sea and trend north-eastwards to the Brazilian frontier, as the Cuchilla Grande. The Río Negro, which rises in Brazil, crosses Uruguay from NE to SW, where it empties, amid dense forest, into the Uruguay River. It is navigable for some distance; other rivers are short and navigable for small distances only, but altogether there are 1,250 km. of navigable waterways.

The black soil, rich in potash, produces grasses superior even to those of Argentina. About 90% of the land is suitable for agriculture. Most of it is suitable for arable farming but only 12% of it is so farmed.

The **climate** is temperate, if somewhat damp and windy, and summer heat is tempered by Atlantic breezes. But there are occasional great, if no extreme, variations. In winter (June-September), when the average temperature is 14 to 16°C, the temperature can fall now and then to well below freezing. It is generally humid, but there is little snow. Summer (December-March), with an average temperature of 22° to 26°C, has irregular dry periods. There is always some wind and for the most part the nights are relatively cool. There are normally 120 sunny days in the year. The rainfall, with prolonged wet periods in July and August, is about 1,200 mm. at Montevideo and some 250 more in the N. But there are considerable variations in the amount of rain from year to year.

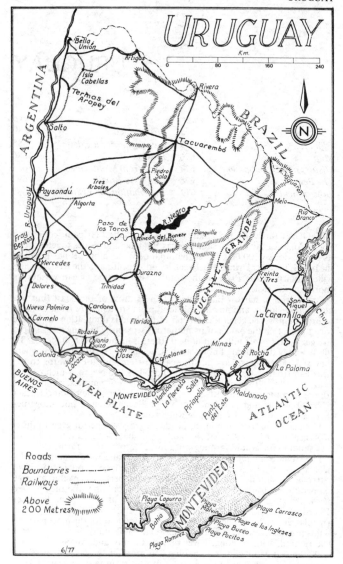

URUGUAY

Km.

0   80   160   240

N

ARGENTINA

Bella Unión
Artigas
Isla Cabellas
Termas del Arapey
Salto
Rivera
Tacuarembó

BRAZIL

Piedra Sola
Tres Arboles
Paysandú
Algorta
Paso de los Toros
R. Negro
Rincón del Bonete
Blanquilla
Melo
Río Branco

R. Uruguay

Fray Bentos
Mercedes
Dolores
Nueva Palmira
Carmelo
Rosario
Colonia Suiza
San José
Durazno
Trinidad
Cardona
Florida
Treinta y Tres
San Miguel
La Caranilla
Chuy

CUCHILLA GRANDE

Colonia
Juan Lacaze
Canelones
Minas
Rocha
San Carlos
La Paloma

BUENOS AIRES

RIVER PLATE
MONTEVIDEO
Atlántida
La Floresta
Solís
Piriápolis
Maldonado
Punta del Este

ATLANTIC OCEAN

Roads ▬▬▬
Boundaries —·—·—
Railways ·················
Above 200 Metres ᨖᨖᨖᨖ

MONTEVIDEO

Playa Capurro
Playa Malvín
Playa Carrasco
Bahía
Playa de los Ingleses
Playa Buceo
Playa Ramirez
Playa Pocitos

6/77

History and settlement The Spanish explorer, Juan Díaz de Solís, sailed up the River Plate in 1515, landed E of Montevideo, and was killed by the Charrúa Indians. There was no gold or silver in Uruguay, and it was only after Buenos Aires had been founded that the Spaniards showed much interest in it. Military expeditions against the Indians were unsuccessful, but Jesuit and Franciscan missionaries, landing in 1624, succeeded where the soldiers had failed. It is said that cattle were first introduced during an unsuccessful expedition by Hernando Arias in 1580.

By 1680, the Portuguese in Brazil had pushed S to the Plata and founded Colonia as a rival to Buenos Aires, on the opposite shore. The Argentines attacked it and indeed, until Uruguay attained independence, the rest of its story is a wearisome rivalry for possession between Buenos Aires and Rio de Janeiro. It was the Portuguese who planned, but the Spaniards who actually founded, the city of Montevideo in 1726. It changed hands several times and was actually taken by the British in 1806, but next year, after their failure to hold Buenos Aires, they withdrew altogether. This repulse of a major power led to a growing demand for complete independence from Spain in both Argentina and Uruguay. In 1808 Montevideo declared itself independent of Buenos Aires. In 1811, the Brazilians attacked from the N, but the Uruguayan patriot, Artigas, rose in arms against them. In the early stages he had some of the Argentine provinces for allies, but soon declared the independence of Uruguay from both Brazil and Argentina. The struggle continued from 1814 to 1820, but Artigas had to flee to Paraguay when Brazil took Montevideo in 1820. In 1825 Lavalleja, at the head of 33 patriots (the Treinta y Tres Orientales) crossed the river and returned to Uruguay to harass, with Argentine aid, the invaders. After the defeat of the Brazilians at Ituzaingó on February 20th, 1827, Great Britain interceded, both Argentina and Brazil relinquished all claims on the country, and independence was declared on August 25th, 1828.

The early history of the republic was wretchedly confused by civil war between two rival presidents, Rivera and his Colorados (reds), and Oribe with his Blancos (whites). Oribe, in this ten years' war, was helped by the Argentine dictator, Rosas, and Montevideo was besieged. Rosas fell from power in 1852, but the contest between Colorados and Blancos still went on. A Colorado, Flores, helped by Brazil, became president, and Uruguay was dragged into the war of the Triple Alliance against the Paraguayan dictator, López. Flores was assassinated in 1868. The country, ruined by civil war, dictatorship and intrigue, only emerged from its long agony in 1903, when a great but controversial man, José Batlle y Ordóñez, was elected president. But before we go on to consider what Uruguay has since accomplished, it is expedient to glance at the interesting history of its colonisation and economic development.

Settlement and economic development The cattle were quicker than the Spaniards to grasp the potential of this gently sloping grass land with its many clear streams and temperate climate. The Spaniards did not settle in Uruguay for 200 years after coming to the Plate, but the cattle, once introduced, multiplied exceedingly and were responsible for a long time for the social structure of Uruguay. Groups of gauchos trailed after the herds, killing them for food and selling their hides only. These gauchos were nomadic, claiming no stake in the land. Organised commerce began with the arrival of Argentine cattle buyers who found it profitable to hire herdsmen to look after cattle in defined areas around their headquarters. Slowly, almost imperceptibly, this arrangement spread. By about 1800 most of the land had been parcelled out into large estancias. The only commercial farming was around Montevideo, where small *chacras* grew vegetables, wheat and maize for the near-by town. It was only after independence in 1828 that immigration began on any scale.

Montevideo was then a small town of 20,000 inhabitants. Between 1836 and 1926 about 648,000 immigrants arrived in Uruguay. Italians and Spaniards flowed in, some into the towns, some to grow crops and vegetables round Montevideo. The traditional Uruguayans have never taken to this form of farming; they have remained pastoralists, leaving commercial farming to the immigrants. Unlike Argentina, Uruguay has remained to this day a preponderantly pastoral country. Until 1947, there was little increase in the area given over to commercial crops; that came later. The pastoral life alone changed. The up-grading of cattle, importing livestock from England, made Uruguay second only to Argentina as a meat and meat-product exporter. From the middle of the 19th century high grade wool, again the result of importing pedigree sheep from England, became an increasingly important item in the Uruguayan economy.

The **pastoral way of life** is so important in Uruguay that an intimate glimpse of it must be given. The typical *estancia* is set within a grove of high trees. At or near the gate is a small house, brick or adobe, with a roof often of thatch. This is the home of one of the *puesteros,* or pasture tenders, whose duty it is to look after one of the large potreros, or pastures, and to keep the gate. Entering the pasture and driving through one follows a cart track or an avenue of eucalypti. The pasture may be of from 50 to 2,000 hectares. The estancia headquarters gleam white through the trees. There are the *galpones,* or barns, for shearing and possibly storing the wool; stables for horses and sheds perhaps for cattle; small houses for the labourers; and last, the house of the *estanciero* himself, which may be large, but is usually a rambling, roomy, one-storey brick building, plastered on the outside and roofed with tiles. It is probably surrounded by a garden yielding oranges, peaches, apricots, figs, plums, roses, other flowers and vegetables. In ordinary weather, when there is little to do for the sheep, the men are employed in perfecting the fences, repairing the houses, assorting or culling the sheep, or in work with the cattle. The fences are inspected at short intervals and there is a rigid scrutiny of each sheep for scab. Lambing begins in April, May or June. Lambs born then get a good start during the winter and grow rapidly in August and September, when the spring comes. Other *estancieros* have all the lambs born in August and September, or sometimes as late as October. Droughts in Uruguay are possibly less severe than in Argentina. Locusts, which come at irregular intervals in swarms from the N, are a serious pest.

The legendary pastoral figure is the gaucho, or cowboy, stocky and wearing a broad brimmed black hat, tight fitting shirt, hand embroidered bolero-style jacket, knotted scarf, baggy trousers, a silver decorated belt and short leather boots. When it is cold he wears a poncho—a square of wool with a slit in the centre to slip his head through. He carries a silver handled rawhide whip, and a silver handled short knife at the belt to cut away the barbecued meat on which he lives almost exclusively. His saddle is usually hand tooled and decorated with silver; and the bridle is elegant. He carries with him his silver-edged gourd and silver tube for sipping his yerba maté. He is not easily separated from his horse, and sits astride it when talking to friends or even fishing. These men are held in great respect in Uruguay, but in fact are fast disappearing, tending to be more and more restricted to the northern and central cattle-breeding districts of the country.

Present Social Structure   With the election of José Batlle y Ordóñez as president from 1903 to 1907, and his re-election in 1911, the history of Uruguay was given a sharp new direction which was to turn it in a short space of time into the only "welfare state" in Latin America. The reforms initiated by him created a state which has nationalised electricity, railways, tramways, and the waterworks system. It controls the manufacture and distribution of such diverse products as petrol, alcohol, cement and chemicals, controls insurance; runs its own banks, theatres, hotels, casinos, and telephones; administers the port of Montevideo and provides its own tug boats; subsidises music and controls broadcasting. Its working man's charter provides for a short working week, a minimum wage, holidays with pay, liability insurance, free medical service, old age and service pensions and unemployment pay. Women have the vote and the vote is secret: divorce is legalised (women may divorce without giving a reason; a proposal to extend this to men met with vehement opposition); illegitimate children have status and the right to inherit, and the investigation of paternity is obligatory. Education is free and compulsory, capital punishment abolished, and the church disestablished.

The per capita income is the third highest in the continent. But a theoretically admirable welfare state is far from perfect in practice. The bureaucracy is large and inefficient. The living standard is only relatively high: there is still very real poverty. Wages and salaries seem to be low in relation to prices; compared with Argentina there are more beggars (including small children who come into restaurants), and street vendors who make a miserable living. The gap between social expectations and actual conditions led in the years before 1973 to disaffection and numerous strikes. The point has often been made that the main social benefits have not been extended to the country people, and over the past few years inflation has been very serious. The lack of economic progress, and (since 1973) an abrupt political change from Uruguay's traditional liberalism, have caused much emigration; the population fell by some 100,000 between 1970 and 1975.

Government by a 9-man council was abolished in 1967 and Uruguay reverted to the presidential form of government, with a bicameral parliamentary system: a Chamber of Deputies with 99 seats and a Senate of 30. General elections should be held every five years. All over 18 have the vote. The President is Dr. Aparicio Méndez, who succeeded when the Armed Forces deposed his predecessor, Sr. Juan María Bordaberry, in June 1976. From February 1973 the military have exercised great influence in the Government; in July 1973, on their advice and with their help, the Congress was closed and a period of executive rule instituted.

Population   The population, 520,000 in 1883, was 3,100,000 by mid 1976; nearly half lives in Montevideo. Only some 14% is rural, and the drift to the towns is 1.7% per year. Both the death rate and the birth rate are low. The people are almost entirely white, mostly of Spanish and Italian stock, for there are no native Indians left, and only a few light-skinned "blacks" in parts of Montevideo and near the Brazilian border. Possibly 10% are mestizos, the descendants of intermarriage between Europeans and the native Indians or immigrant blacks. About 91% are literate. The natural population increase is low for Latin America: 1.2% per annum. So is infant mortality, 48 per thousand.

Montevideo, the capital and one of the main cities of the continent, was founded in 1726. Population, in and near: 1,250,000. Originally built on a low promontory between the ocean and Horseshoe Bay (around where the port works are today), the city has spread into the flat country behind, and westwards round the Cerro, the low isolated cone to which Montevideo owes its name. The original site, though the fortifications have been destroyed, still retains a certain Colonial atmosphere, though few of its buildings are earlier than the close of the 18th or opening of the 19th centuries. The rest of the city is modern, criss-crossed with wide avenues and tree-lined streets, and laid out with large open spaces, parks, and gardens. Above the flat-roofed houses, several buildings (including the Post Office and a skyscraper in Plaza Independencia) tower above the Cathedral, 40 metres high, flanked by two side turrets and surmounted by a dome. One is the Palacio Salvo, with a main building of 12 storeys surmounted by a tower of 14 crowned by a television transmitter. (It is closed to visitors.) Another—also on Plaza Independencia—is the *Victoria Plaza Hotel,* with a fine view from the roof (1130-1530). All are visible for many km. The city not only dominates the country's commerce and culture—almost 90% of all the imports and exports pass through it—but is, in its own right, a summer resort and the point of departure for a string of seaside resorts along the coastline to the E. The area attracts 600,000 tourists a year, who normally bring in about US$100m. of foreign exchange.

There were once relatively large Italian, British, American, German, Hungarian and French communities in Montevideo, but assimilation is far advanced. The main foreign communities now are Armenian and Syrian. Registration as Uruguayan citizens of all who are born in the country is compulsory on reaching the age of 18.

The centre of city life is the Plaza Independencia, a square park surrounded with colonnaded buildings set between the old town and the new. At its centre is a statue of Artigas, atop an underground mausoleum. In this square is the splendid Solís Theatre, with the Museum of Natural History alongside. On the southern side is the Government House, and quite a short way down the Avenida 18 de Julio to the E is the Palacio Salvo. Calle Sarandí runs W from the Plaza through the old town to the port. In the old town, a short distance west of Plaza Independencia, is the oldest square in Montevideo: the Plaza Constitución. Here on one side is the Cathedral (1790-1804), with the Cabildo, or town hall (1804-1810) opposite. On the S side is the Club Uruguay. Still further west along Calle Rincón is the small Plaza Zabala, with a monument to Zabala, founder of the city. E of this plaza are three buildings well worth seeing: the Banco de la República, the Bolsa, or Stock Exchange, and the monumental Customs House.

The Avenida 18 de Julio, whose pavements are always thronged, begins at the Palacio Salvo. Along this avenue is the Plaza del Entrevero, between Julio Herrera and Río Negro, a very pleasant place to sit; and the Plaza Cagancha (or Plaza Libertad), with a statue of Liberty, the main tourist office, and the Atheneum. The next small square—the Plazuela Lorenzo Justiniano Pérez (or El Gaucho)—has a statue to the gaucho of that name and the new Municipal Palace. Up the avenue again is the Plaza Treinta y Tres (or Bomberos), with the headquarters of the fire brigade. Beyond is the University, and nearby are the National Library, the French *lycée*, and the Ministry of Health. The avenue ends at an intersection with Bulevard Artigas. Here is an obelisk commemorating the patriots of independence, and here, too, one may enter the park of Batlle y Ordóñez (see below). The immense Legislative Palace, built on a rise, almost entirely of native marble, is reached from Av. 18 de Julio along Av. Agraciada, 5 blocks E of Plaza Independencia.

At the western end of the bay is the Cerro, or hill, 118 metres high, with an old fort on the top, now a military museum (1600-2000) with arms, flags and drums. It is surmounted by the oldest lighthouse in the country (1804). From the fort there is a splendid view of the Plate estuary and the countryside. Villa del Cerro, a suburb of 50,000 people, is on the SE slopes. In the port, opposite the Port Administrative Building, the ship's bell of H.M.S. *Ajax* has been set up to commemorate the sinking of the *Graf Spee*. The anchor of the *Graf Spee* was set up at the entrance to the port area in December 1964 to commemorate the 25th anniversary of the battle; the wreck of the *Graf Spee* itself lies about 3 km. offshore and can be seen (appropriately) from Rambla Gran Bretaña. Bus from centre to Cerro: No. 125 from Mercedes, and others.

Of the many splendid parks, El Prado (about 5 km. from Av. 18 de Julio, along Av. Agraciada) is the oldest. The horse-breaking competitions are held here during Tourist Week. Among rolling lawns, trees, lakes and grottoes, a delight to wander through, is a most magnificent rose garden planted with 850 varieties; also in the Park is La Diligencia (the stage coach). The two buildings of the Municipal Museums of Fine Art and History are in the grounds. (The National Museum of History is in the old town.) The largest and most popular park is Parque Rodó, on Rambla Presidente Wilson. Here are an open air theatre, an amusement park, an artificial lake studded with islands round which motor boat, gondola and canoe ply. The National Museum of Fine Arts, with works by living artists, and a children's playground are at the eastern end. Due S and close to it is a golf course overlooking the sea. In Parque Batlle y Ordóñez (reached by a continuation eastwards of Av. 18 de Julio), are a number of statues. The most interesting group is the very well-known "La Carreta" monument showing three yoke of oxen drawing a waggon. In the grounds is the magnificent Estadio Centenario with a seating capacity of 70,000 and the pitch where international football matches are played. There is a field for athletic sports and a bicycle race-course as well. The Zoological Gardens are a few blocks E of this park (open until 2000 hrs.); in the Gardens is a planetarium, one of the best in South America, displays Tuesdays and Saturdays 1800 and 1900 and Sundays and holidays 1700, 1800 and 1900.

The Beaches Eight or nine bathing beaches extend along almost the whole of the metropolitan water front, extending from Playa Ramírez in the W to Playa Carrasco at the eastern extension of the city. Along the whole waterfront, joining up these beaches, runs the magnificent Rambla Naciones Unidas, differently named along its different stretches in honour of several nations. The beaches are sandy; the most popular, from W to E, are Playa Ramírez, Playa Pocitos (until recently the most fashionable) and Playa Malvín. They are cleaner the further E you go. Bus No. 21 from Calle San José gives a pleasant ride past all the beaches to Playa Miramar, beyond Carrasco; also No. 104 goes to Carrasco.

Among the main residential areas are Pocitos, well supplied with hotels, restaurants and night-clubs *(boites)*, with the reputation of being the "Copacabana" of Montevideo; and Carrasco, a delightful semi-rural place behind the beach of the same name. Playa Carrasco, perhaps the finest of all the beaches, is at the end of the Rambla Sur. It is backed by the town and a thick forest which has been partly turned into a national park. Carrasco has the luxurious *Casino Hotel*, and the international airport is nearby. E along the coast is a string of resorts, which are dealt with later in "East from Montevideo".

Hotels

Below are leading hotels, with their average charges per person per day, with private bath but no board during the tourist season, when they should be booked in advance. Prices are lower during other seasons. When not included, breakfast usually costs US$1-US$2.

	Single US$	Double US$	Remarks
Victoria Plaza	{ 27	35	A/c.
	(51	73	Full board)
Columbia Palace	13	17	Including breakfast
California	11	17	Including breakfast
Crillón	12	14	A/c. and including breakfast
Lancaster	10	15	A/c. and including breakfast
London Palace	10	17	
Oxford	11	15 (18 a/c)	Including breakfast
Iguazú	8	14	Including breakfast
Parque	10	13	Including breakfast
Presidente	11	16	
Ermitage	11	15	
Cottage	10	16	
Casino Carrasco	14	18	Including breakfast and 7% tax

There is a 7% tax on hotel bills in Montevideo. Tipping 20%.

There are a number of hotels in different parts of the city, most of them cheaper than the ones listed. For example, *Hotel Ateneo*, Colonia 1147, clean (US$2.80 d); the *Hotel Pyramides* (Sarandí corner Ituzaingó) in the shopping centre (US$4.40 d); the Hotels *Colón, Florida,* and the *Residencial Uruguay, Hotel los Angeles,* Av. 18 de Julio 974, modern, private bath, US$4 s, US$9 d; *Hotel Cervantes,* Soriano 868, plain but clean room with bath, US$4 s; *Hotel del Centro,* Soriano 1126, most reasonable and cheap accommodation. *Nuevo Hotel, España,* central, US$3 p.p. *Hotel Puertolas,* 3 blocks along Av. 18 de Julio from Plaza Independencia, US$4.80 d, with bath. At Pocitos are the Hotels *Exquisito* and *Bulevar*; at Carrasco, the *Bristol* and the luxurious *Casino Carrasco*; and at Playa Malvín the *Playa Malvín Hotel, Hotel Savoy,* Bartolomé Mitre, US$2.50 s. Other cheap hotels are the *Hotel Libertad,* Plaza Zabala, US$3 d, with shower; *Hotel Rex,* 18 de Julio, near Plaza Independencia, comfortable. *Hotel Río de la Plata,* US$5-6; *Hotel Central Río Negro,* near railway station, US$4 d; and *Hotel Gil,* Brandzen 2284, very clean. *Hotel Tío Tom,* corner Canelones and Paraguay, US$3.50 d, recommended; *Hotel Niza,* Calle Maldonado, basic, US$2 s; *Hotel Calabria,* Calle Washington, US$1.80, with shower; *Hotel Diagonal,* near bus station, hot water shared, US$4.50 d; *Hotel Continental,* 18 de Julio 1253, US$4 s; *Hotel Santander,* Ejido 1212, US$4 s; *Residencial Suevia,* Uruguay 1242, US$3.50 d, hot water; *Hotel Buenos Aires,* 18 de Julio 204, US$2.50 s—basic; *Pensión Matriz,* Ituzaingó 1327, US$2.90 d.

At the beaches many hotels offer only American plan terms during the season. After April 1 prices are greatly reduced and some hotel dining rooms shut down.

For Carnival week, on the other hand, prices are raised by 20%.

Youth Hostel, only US$2 a head, very central at Canelones 935.

Information on cheaper hotels from tourist office on Plaza Cagancha (Libertad) and Centro de Hoteles y Restaurantes del Uruguay (Ibicuy 1213).

Youth Hostel   Canelones 935, US$2 a night.

Electric Power   220 volts 50 cycles, A.C.

Restaurants   The dinner hour is very late, from 2100 to 2400. First class restaurants at the centre are *El Aguila,* Buenos Aires 694, next to the Solís Theatre; *Morini,* Ciudadela 1229 (excellent steak and fish: *corvina a la parrilla*); *Catarí,* Colonia 971; *Club Aleman,* Paysandú 935; *Bungalow Suizo,* Andes 1435; *La Cigarra,* Joanicó y Av. Centenario; *Victoria Plaza Hotel,* Plaza Independencia; *El Pollo Dorado,* Yi 1372.

At Pocitos are: *El Galeón,* Leyenda Patria 3096; *El Malecón,* Juan B. Blanco 1269; *La Azotea,* Rambla Perú 1063; *El Panamericano,* Luis A. de Herrera y Rambla Armenia; *Hostel Suizo,* Ellauri y Pereira; and *La Solera,* 21 de Setiembre. At Carrasco is *Bungalow Suizo,* Camino Carrasco at Km. 16.

Other quite good restaurants are: *El Balón de Oro,* 18 de Julio 1616; *La Genovesa* (Spanish), San José 1242; *El Triángulo* (sea food), Rambla Chile 4555; *Hong Kong Restaurant,* 8 de Octubre 2691; *Costa Brava* (sea food), Ejido 1427; *London Grill,* Yí 1375; *Otto,* Río Negro 1301; *El Fogón,* San José 1080. A good place for lunch is the Golf Club, good food, excellent surroundings and grand view. Typical local food is served at: *Forte di Makale,* Parque Rodó; *Tahiti,* Bulevard Artigas; *La Paloma,* Rambla Chile 4639; *Rovella,* Jackson 874, and *Las Brasas,* San José 909; *Aloha,* close to the Onda bus station. The Automóvil Club on Av. Agraciada (between Uruguay and Paysandú) serves extremely good food at reasonable prices. Other good cheap places are *La Gloria,* Calle Yaguarón, large portions; and restaurant on 6th floor of YMCA building, Calle Colonia, open for lunch and 1900-2200, cheap and plentiful with good views too. (Ask for the Asociación Cristiana de Jóvenes.) *Gran Coco* on Yí, offers a variety of good meat and vegetable dishes for about US$0.50. At the *Mercado del Puerto,* opposite the Custom House, on Calle Piedras, between Maciel and Castellanas, grills cooked on huge charcoal grates, cheap, generous and the atmosphere is friendly.

Camping   Parque Franklin D. Roosevelt, near Carrasco; get police permission at Av. Italia 5569.

Information   Dial "214" and you are through to the central bureau of information (in front of Onda bus terminal) about communications, the weather, pharmacies on night duty and anything you want to know about streets in the city. Dial "6" for exact time.

Tourist Commission   Headquarters is at Avda. Agraciada 1409, fifth floor. Information Centre is on Plaza Cagancha (Libertad), at 18 de Julio 845; gives away good maps.

Travel Agents   C.E.V.I., 18 de Julio 1121; Wagon-Lits/Cooks, Rio Negro 1356; Buemes Viajes, Colonia 997; C.O.T., Sarandi 699; Exprinter, Sarandi 700; Turisport Ltda., Bartolomé Mitre 1318; Viajes C.Y.N.S.A., 18 de Julio 1120.

Night Clubs   Centres around the *Parque Hotel* and *Casino Carrasco* in the summer. The Bar and the *Záfiro Room* at the *Victoria Plaza*; also *Lancaster Hotel.* Other night-spots giving floor shows are *El Patio, Bonanza,* and *Porto Fino.* Others are *Zum Zum, Ton Ton* (Km. 16.5 off Av. Italia), *Parador del Cerro* (on the Cerro), and *Lancelot.* Discotheques, called "boites", admit couples only.

Tea Shops, known locally as confiterías. The most popular are along 18 de Julio, including *Latino, Facal, Manchester, Lusitano, Café del Rex, La Pasiva, Soko's, Lion D'Or, Payaso, La Puerta del Sol, Hispano.* A good one is *Oro del Rhin,*

Colonia y Convención. At Pocitos are *La Goleta, Haiti, La Conaprole, Anrejo, La Castellana, El Vitral* and *Las Palmas.* At Puerto Buceo Yacht Club, where tourists are allowed in.

Shopping Try the shop at Reconquista 599 y Juan Carlos Gómez for good hand-made woollen goods. Excellent cheap leatherwork also available; for this try Casa Mario, Piedras 641. Suede clothes cheaper than in Buenos Aires. See H. Stern's jewellery store at *Hotel Victoria Plaza;* amethysts and topazes are mined in Uruguay and are good buys. For woollen wall hangings see Manos del Uruguay, Reconquista 616, near the *Colombia Palace Hotel.*

Bookshops English and American books: Librería Barreiro y Ramos, 25 de Mayo and J. C. Gómez; Librería José Wainstein, Sarandí 530.

Casinos Parque Hotel at Playa Ramírez; Carrasco at Carrasco.

Museums Historical: Casa Lavalleja, Zabala 1464, and Casa Rivera, Rincón 437. Natural History: Buenos Aires 562 (has a well-preserved, half-unwrapped mummy). Botanical: 19 de Abril 1179. Art: Museo Nacional de Bellas Artes, in Parque Rodó. Municipal: in large rooms upstairs at the Cabildo. Zoological Museum, Rambla República de Chile 4215, on beach at Puerto Buceo. No entrance fees. Museum schedules are indefinitè. Most are open Sundays and Tuesday through Friday, but at times are open only in the afternoon, so make sure.

Clubs Uruguay; Military & Naval; Jockey; Rotary; Lions; Y.M.C.A.; Y.W.C.A.; French; English; Italian; La Prensa; Catholic; Brazilian; Spanish; Alemán, Paysandú 935; Automóvil; Yacht Club; Club Nacional de Regatas; Rowing Club; Touring Club; Punta Carretas Golf Club; Montevideo Cricket Club; Carrasco Lawn Tennis; Argentine; Carrasco Polo; Cerro Golf Club; American Women's Club.

Theatres Solís, housing the national theatre company and occasional visiting companies: Café Teatro "El Reloj"; Circular; Notariado; Palacio Salvo; Stella d'Italia; Círculo; Centro. All these are more or less professional. Occasionally, small amateur or semi-professional groups put on plays in cinemas or other places. There is much interest in the drama and the cinema.

Sports The beach is more popular than the water, but there are four large swimming clubs in Montevideo, the best of them being the Neptuno; also one at Y.M.C.A. Uruguay has three important yacht clubs, the Uruguayo, the Nautilus and the Punta del Este. The Uruguayo has a good club-house at Buceo. Both the Montevideo Rowing Club and the Club Nacional de Regatas have club houses on the Bay. The German Rowing Club is on the Santa Lucia River. Fishing is becoming popular. Association football is played intensively. Rugby football is also played, and there is a yearly championship. There are two good 18-hole municipal links. There are several lawn tennis clubs, and two for polo players. Horse races are held on the "Maroñas" race track, or Hipódromo of Las Piedras, on Thursdays, Saturdays and Sundays, with parimutuels. There is a national lottery.

Schools "The British School" at Carrasco, and some 4 other British schools, 1 French, 1 German school, and the Crandon Institute, an American school for children up to 17. All have good scholastic ratings.

Churches Most Uruguayans are Roman Catholic but there is complete freedom of worship. The Roman Catholic Cathedral is known locally as the Iglesia San Juan. Holy Trinity Episcopal (British), and the Emanuel Methodist Church (American), hold regular services in English. There is a Jewish synagogue. Mormons and Jehovah's Witnesses are very active. There are Methodist and Baptist missions in most of the larger towns.

Addresses

British Embassy, Marco Bruto 1073. Tel.: 92501.
U.S. Embassy and Consulate, Rambla Wilson 1776.
British Chamber of Commerce, Av. Agraciada 1641, piso 2°. Tel.: 80936.
American Chamber of Commerce, Bartolomè Mitre 1337, esc. 108.
The English Club, Treinta y Tres 1309. Tel.: 82180.
The British Council, San José 1426, 3° piso. Tel.: 8 84 68.
The British Hospital, Av. Italia 2420. Tel.: 40 90 11.

Anglican Church, Reconquista 522. Tel.: 8 80 62.

The Apostleship of the Sea, Washington 274. Tel.: 8 30 52.

Cables All America Cables & Radio Inc., Plaza Independencia, Italcable S.A., 25 de Mayo 400; Western Telegraph Co., Ltd., Cerrito 449; Telégrafo Nacional, Sarandí 472.

Banks Bank of London & South America, Calle Zabala 1500, and 11 city agencies; Citibank, Cerrito 455 (corner Misiones); Banco Holandés Unido, 25 de Mayo 501; and Banco Comercial, Cerrito 400 and Banco Panamericano Uruguayo on Plaza Cajárí. Open: summer, 1330-1730; winter, 1300-1700, Mon.-Fri. All money-changing is done by banks, hotels and shops; there are no exchange houses.

Taxis US$0.27 for first 600 metres, and US$0.02 for each 140 metres afterwards; an additional 20% from midnight to 0600. Charge for each piece of large luggage, US$0.12; charge for each hour of waiting, US$2.60. Taxis can be hired, by agreement, by the hour within city limits. Taxis to airport, US$0.27 for first 700 metres and US$0.04 for each 110 metres afterwards. Taxi drivers expect a minimum tip of 10% of the fare.

Buses City and suburbs at a flat rate of US$0.15.

Car Hire without chauffeur, US$20 per 24 hours, plus $0.16 per kilometre. Hirer pays for petrol. A guarantee of US$100 must be deposited before taking over the car. The only firm offering this is Sudan Car Corps, Galicia 1469. With chauffeur, US$35 per 8-hour day plus US$0.12 per kilometre, and payment for a chauffeur's lunch or supper. Rogelio Martinelli, Canelones 1450; Luis Moro e Hijos, Camino Ariel 4737; Empresa Salhon, Av. 8 de Octubre 4199; F. Miramonte, Magallanes 1446.

Landing Ships go alongside. Motor launches are usually available.

Local Steamers To Buenos Aires: daily service, 2100 all year round and taking about 11 hours (about US$18.70 1st class, US$14.40 second, single). Car ferry, about US$23-38, *via* Colonia, according to size of car, see also under Colonia (page 689). To Santos and to Rio de Janeiro (various companies), several services a week.

N.B. Travel to Buenos Aires by Onda bus and plane, or hovercraft, or launch *via* Colonia costs around US$16 single, whichever way you go; by launch *via* Carmelo it is nearer US$15.

Airport The main airport is at Carrasco, 5 km. from the beach and 21 km. outside the city; 30 minutes by car to Montevideo or about 50 by bus (US$0.30) from Av. 18 de Julio. Buenos Aires-Montevideo by air, US$23 (jet) or US$20. Airport tax, 3%.

Rail Trains to Salto and Paysandú (both twice a week; to Salto US$5.50 (US$8.40 with berth), 16 hours and all parts. Restaurant cars on all long-distance trains. Best to book sleeping berths beforehand. Buses are much quicker.

Buses Within Uruguay, good services to most towns; to Paysandú, US$6.20, 6 or 7 hours, according to route. Twice-weekly bus (Tues. and Fri.) to Asunción, Paraguay (24 hours, US$23), and daily buses to São Paulo. To Porto Alegre, *via* Chuy, 10 hours, US$14.75. To Santa Fe, Argentina, daily *via* Paysandú bridge; offers easy connection to Asunción. Arco office for buses to Colonia on Plaza Libertad. Onda runs services all over the country, but the smaller competing services are just as fast and less expensive; differences in prices can be as high as 50%. Bus from Montevideo to Punta del Este, US$2.50.

East from Montevideo

Almost all the 600,000 tourists who visit Uruguay every year either stay at Montevideo and its beaches, or go eastwards to the estuary and Atlantic coast resorts. The season is from December to the middle of April. This beautiful coastline, over 320 km. long, contains an endless succession of small bays, beaches and promontories set among hills and woods.

Two roads, both paved, go to Punta del Este. The northern branch (no tolls) *via* Pando and Soca, is Route 8; at Km. 68 (42 miles) it branches off NE towards Minas (see page 692): it continues as Route 9 to San Carlos (14½ km. N of Maldonado or 19 km. N of Punta del Este) through beautiful rolling country with views of the Laguna del Sauce (Willow Lake). The southern branch, the "Interbalnearia", runs largely along the coast, with short branches to some of the resorts, and is the one described in the text. There are toll posts at Arroyo Pando and at Arroyo Solís Grande. Route 9, the road to Chuy, is now completely paved. The railway from Montevideo and a spur of the road turn S to La Paloma, and there are secondary roads to some of the resorts further along the coast. Shortly before Atlántida, in an old fortress set in pine woods, is *El Fortín de Santa Rosa* hotel and restaurant, 2 minutes from a lovely sandy beach. Small Zoo not far off.

Atlántida (*Rex* is main hotel; many good residenciales charging less than US$2 p.p. off season; some good restaurants—try the *Banzai*), 45 km. from Montevideo, is ringed by fir forest and has a good golf course and country club. A short distance beyond, in groves of eucalyptus and pine, is the small and intimate beach of Las Toscas, followed by Parque del Plata, on the Solís Chico river.

At Km. 64.5 on the Interbalnearia is Sr.Garabedian's campsite, with Youth Hostel. For bookings, telephone Sr. Garabedian at Montevideo 56 12 30.

Crossing by a (Toll) bridge we come to

La Floresta (*Oriental; del Parque*), surrounded by woods which can be explored on foot or on horseback. The chalets are pretty; the place reminds one of the villages of the Landes, near Biarritz. About 35 km. on, over a toll bridge, is **Solís** (*Solis Golf; El Chajá*), at the mouth of the River Solís. It has a very long beach, good fishing, delightful river and hill scenery.

Piriápolis, the next resort, 16 km. from Solís, 101 from Montevideo, has a fine casino hotel and some 50 others. It has a good beach, a yacht harbour, a country club, a golf course, a motor-racing track and is particularly popular with Argentines. The town, set amongst hills, is laid out prettily with an abundance of shade trees, and the district is rich in pine, eucalyptus and acacia woods. The hills, of volcanic origin, rise to over 300 metres, and there are medicinal springs. There is a good motor road which winds spirally round Cerro del Inglés or Cerro San Antonio. At the top of this hill there is a tea-room and restaurant. Sixteen km. to the N is Cerro Pan de Azúcar (Sugar Loaf), crowned by a tall cross with a circular stairway inside; there is only a path up to the cross.

Hotels   *Argentino*, with casino; *Esmeralds; Gutiérrez; Ocean; City; Genovés; Rex; Selecciones* (US$2.50 s—reported as "best value in town"); *San Sebastián* (US$3.50 s).

Restaurants   *Argentino; Parador Punta Fria; Puertito Don Anselmo* (shellfish); *El Grillo; Entrevero*, in which vermouth is offered with about 20 side dishes, described as "a meal in itself".

Youth Hostel   Close to beach, behind *Hotel Argentino*, at Simón del Pino 1136, US$2 a night.

Bus to Montevideo, US$2, 1½ hours.

Portezuelo has fine beaches with the Laguna del Sauce and the glorious Lussich woods behind. At **Punta Ballena** there is a lovely wide crescent beach, calm water and very clean sand. The *Solana del Mar Hotel*, modern, well run, is on the beach. (Full board rate: US$20-30 a day plus 26% service charges.) The place is a residential resort but is still quiet and beautiful; some Americans and Europeans prefer it to the more ostentatious places. Casa Pueblo, the house of Uruguayan artist Carlos Páez Villaro can be visited. It is built in a Spanish-Moroccan style on a cliff over the sea. There are paintings, collages and ceramics on display, and for sale. Season: Nov. 1 to April 1.

Maldonado, capital of Maldonado Department, 140 km. from Montevideo; population 6,000. This peaceful small town, sacked by the British in 1806, has many colonial remains: the parish church, El Vigia watch tower, and fortifications on Gorriti Island in the semi-circular bay. Gorriti Island, densely wooded and with superb beaches, is an ideal spot for campers. See also the Mazzoni Museum and the windmill. There is a choice of hotels (reasonably priced).

Camping Two sites: one free, in Parque El Placer; the other charges.

Punta del Este Five km. on, facing the bay on one side, and the open waters of the Atlantic on the other, lies the largest, most fashionable and internationally best known of the resorts, Punta del Este. Here, in December 1939, in full sight of the built-up point, the German pocket-battleship *Graf von Spee* was defeated by the British South Atlantic Squadron. The narrow peninsula of Punta del Este has been entirely built over; it has excellent bathing beaches, the calm *playa mansa* on the bay side, the rough *playa brava* on the ocean side. There is water ski-ing in the bay, surfing on the ocean coast, an excellent yacht marina, a yacht club, and a fishing club. There is good fishing both at sea and in three near-by lakes and the river Maldonado (which the main road crosses at Manantiales by a unique inverted-W-shaped bridge); on Isla de Lobos, which is a government reserve within sight of the town, there is a huge sea-lion colony (excursions to it every morning at 0800, return at 1115 (US$7 p.p.); ticket should be bought at the harbour the day before); also on it stands the tallest and most powerful beamed lighthouse in South America, marking the entrance to the River Plate. Direct daily planes from Buenos Aires to Punta del Este airport. On the land side, Punta del Este is flanked by large planted forests of eucalyptus, pine and mimosa; the woods are dotted with thousands of villas and chalets. A large country club (the Cantegril) lets cottages and hotel apartments at a high price. There is a golf course, and two casinos.

Hotels *Arena,* US$25 d; *Oasis,* US$26 d; *Palace,* US$75 d, with full board; *Las Delicias,* US$16 d or US$30 full board; *Peninsula, London,* and *Playa Brava,* US$20 each; *Tamoris,* very modern but only showers; *Kennedy; Santos Dumont; España; Iberia; Peninsula; Edén; Milano; Playa,* US$25-US$40 d, with breakfast; *La Cigale.* Very few moderately priced hotels but try *Colombia,* back of railway station (US$3.50 s); *Hotel Puerto* (near Onda bus station), US$12 d, clean and friendly, English spoken; *Tourbillón,* Calles 9 and 12, basic, not hot water (US3 s). Hotel rates are down by half in the winter months.

Restaurants *Bungalow Suizo; Las Tablitas; Piccolo; Picasso; Puerto del Sol; Tío Paco; Las Casitas; Marisconea; El Mastil* (behind port); *El Ciclista,* inexpensive Italian cooking; *El Cacique,* Calle 28, No. 620; *El Sargo,* on Av. Gorlero. Many enticing ice-cream parlours, such as *Confitería Gorlero.*

Buses To Montevideo, Onda or Cut buses, US$2.50; to Piriápolis, US$0.70.

Train To Montevideo, US$2, comfortable, time 2 hrs. 40 mins.

Tourist Information Liga de Fomento, Parada 1 (near railway station).

Near Punta del Este, to the E, **Playa San Rafael,** where there is an 18-hole golf course, is growing rapidly. (*Casino San Rafael,* US$82 d incl. full board, good, much used for conferences; *San Marcos,* US$26 d, incl. 2 meals; *L'Auberge,* US$37 d).

Rocha Both road and railway run on to Rocha, 211 km. from Montevideo and a few km. from the sea. Population: 20,000. Groves of palms dotted about the duneland give it an unusual beauty. The railway is continued southwards to the coast at

La Paloma *(Hotels Del Cabo; Barceló; Ocean; Viola; Trocadero; Parque),* a good port for yachts for it is protected by two islands. There is attractive scenery and good sea and lake fishing.

Hotels at Rocha: *Arrate; Roma.*

Camping Site at La Paloma.

Beyond Rocha lies the colonial fortress (reconstructed and converted into a museum) of Santa Teresa, begun by the Portuguese and finished by the Spaniards in the 1750s, when they held the land. (It was the other way round with the fortress of San Miguel—see below—neither smelt battle.) It is set in a magnificent national park, the Parque de Santa Teresa, with avenues of palms, a bird sanctuary, and beautifully arranged fresh water pools to bathe in. There are cottages to let for the summer season, beside the sea. Three km. beyond is the bathing resort of La Coronilla, with excellent ocean fishing for sharks, skate and black corvina from the rocks: some of the skate caught weigh 50 kilos. For a moderate fee a taxi will take you on a sightseeing tour from La Coronilla to the Santa Teresa fortress and the strange and gloomy Laguna Negra.

Hotels *Parador La Coronilla; El Pescador; costas del Mar.*

At **Chuy,** on the Brazilian frontier, 338 km. from Montevideo, the road branches off towards the elongated Laguna Merín; the frontier is along its middle. On the Uruguayan side, overlooking the lake, stands the rugged old fortress of **San Miguel,** also set in a magnificent park in which many curious native and foreign plants and animals are preserved. An interesting museum is attached to the fortress. There is a fair hotel, the *Parador San Miguel,* and fine bathing on the sea-shore of the near-by Barra del Chuy. The first petrol station is 80 km. from Chuy. There is a facility for tourists arriving from Uruguay, who may cross the border to the Brazilian side of the town (named Xuí), and purchase a certain amount of Brazilian manufactured goods, without formalities. Uruguayan taxis are allowed 25 km. beyond the frontier, and vice versa.

The coastal road, now excellent, goes on to Pelotas and Porto Alegre, in Brazil. Ordinary (not international) buses ply the route. The border runs down the middle of the main street in Chuy. Passengers from Montevideo are set down at the *Hotel Chuy,* good for a border town, at the last street corner in Uruguay. Next morning you get passport clearance at the Uruguayan immigration, two blocks back on the way to Montevideo. Money exchange not far from hotel, bank won't change travellers' cheques. Motorists should buy gasoline in Chuy. The office for the bus to Pelotas is across the road from the hotel, one block inside Brazil, by the *Hotel Guaraní,* US$3 d. Make sure your passport is stamped, or you may have difficulty in leaving Brazil. Getting a car into Brazil is no trouble, but gasoline is very expensive there.

West from Montevideo

There is a toll on Route No. 1 linking Colonia with the Atlantic coastal resorts, and tolls also on Routes No. 2 to Fray Bentos and No. 3 to Paysandú and Salto. The road to Colonia is paved but the surface has deteriorated in spots.

There are roads and railways to nearly all the towns which will be dealt with now, and buses run along most of the roads. The towns on the coast or on the Río Uruguay can be reached by boat, and there are air services from Montevideo to most of them.

An almost straight paved road, part of the Pan-American Highway, runs from Montevideo westwards for 177 km. to Colonia del Sacramento, where passenger boats from Buenos Aires berth. Much traffic from Argentina flows along this busy road.

About 119 km. from Montevideo, a 5 km. branch leads N to **Colonia Suiza**, a Swiss settlement of some 4,500 people, with good hotels and a Youth Hostel (three meals US$1.80), in the "Switzerland of Uruguay". It lies in a beautiful area. Quite near is Nueva Helvecia, where the tourist can buy locally made Swiss musical boxes. At 120 km. along the main road, and just S, is **Colonia Valdense**, another colony, this time of Waldensians, who still cling to some of the old manners and customs of the Piedmontese Alps.

Camping *Parador Tajes*, 34 km. W of Montevideo, has a camp site.

Hotels at Colonia Suiza *Nirvana* (good); *Suizo.*

Hotels at Colonia Valdense *Brisas del Plata; Parador los Ceibos.*

About 6½ km. further on, a paved main road branches off right to **Rosario** (5 km.), Mercedes (164 km.), and Fray Bentos (34 km. further). Rosario is a typical agricultural town given over to dairying and grain production. Its port, Juan Lacaze, reached by a branch railway, lies 22 km. SW. Population: 8,000.

Clubs Club Cyssa, a social, cultural and sporting club, with a stadium, football field and basketball ground. Two fishing clubs.

Hotels *Ricardi* and *Riviera*, from US$2 p.p., good.

Colonia (del Sacramento) is a pleasure resort on land jutting into the River Plate. It was founded by Portuguese settlers from Brazil in 1680 and contains rebuilt city walls and quite a number of Colonial buildings and narrow streets in the older part of the town; all the more interesting because few examples are left in this part of the continent. Worth seeing are the Parochial Church, the Municipal Museum in the ancient house of Almirante Brown (open Thurs., Sat. and Sun. 1300-1700), the Mansion of the Viceroy, the house of General Mitre, and the Farola. The plaza is particularly picturesque. Buenos Aires, to which there is a ferry service, is only 50 km. A "free zone" has been created here. Pop.: 10,000. At Real San Carlos, just out of town (take the blue bus from the centre) is the racecourse (Hipódromo) and bull-ring (out of use).

Hotels *Esperanza; El Mirador; Colonial; Buenos Aires*, Calle Artigas 384, good, US$2.50 p.p.; *Italiano*, US$2 s; *Español*, at Manuel de Lobos 377, cheapest, US$3 d, with shower; *Leoncia*, Rivera 216, modern, good, US$3 (owns the *Nuevo Galpón* restaurant).

Restaurant *El Nuevo Galpón*, cheap and good.

Camping Site at Colonia.

Shipping Steamers of Cía. de Navegación Fluvial Argentina to Buenos Aires, daily at 1330. Check time: some winter departures are at 1130; Single fare: US$14.

Hydrofoil 3 daily services, each way, US$15 s (hard currencies only, about US$17 if paid in Uruguayan pesos) to Buenos Aires. It is substantially cheaper to buy ticket from office (Alimar Alíscafos) than from a tourist agency.

Air Service Aerolíneas Argentinas, Colonia to Buenos Aires, 3 times a day.

Road See below, unpaved but good as far as Mercedes, paved on to Fray Bentos.

Bus to or from Montevideo, US$2, 3 hours, or US$4 (2½ hours) by luxury bus, three a day. Cheapest is Caruel Colonia, US$0.90.

The road swings N and NW to reach the resort of **Carmelo**, 74 km. away, on the shores of Las Vacas River. (There is no railway to it.) On the right, between the two towns, are the ruins of a colonial building known as Calera de las Huérfanas. Population: 15,000. The port harbours several hundred yachts during the season. There is a launch service to Tigre, across the delta, a most interesting ride past innumerable islands (leaves 1100, 4 hours, US$7.50 s). You can pay at the Onda bus station in Montevideo for both bus and launch, US$17. The ruins of a Jesuit building lie not far away. There is a "free zone" at the port.

Hotels *Casino Carmelo; Comercio; Hospedaje* on Calle Uruguay 368, US$1.50 p.p., very good value. **Youth Hostel** at Parador Zagarzazu, Km. 260.5 on Route 21, 5 km. NW from Carmelo.

Some 30 km. up the river, by car, is **Nueva Palmira** (population 3,500), a port of call for river steamers. Worth visiting in the town are the Pirámide of Solís, the Calera, the Camacho, the Capilla de la Concepción, and the Convento de la Reducción Jesuítica (1780). A "free zone" at the port.

Some 20 km. away is the historic beach of La Agraciada, famous for the landing of the Thirty-Three patriots on April 19, 1825, an event which led to Uruguayan independence. On the beach is a statue to General Lavalleja, leader of the Treinta y Tres. A patriotic festival is held on each anniversary.

The road is continued (not in very good condition), through the small river port of **Dolores** (population: 13,000), 32 km. up-river from the confluence of the Río San Salvador with the Río Uruguay to

Mercedes This livestock centre and resort is best reached, however, either by road from the main Colonia-Montevideo highway, or by railway from the capital (275 km.). It is set on the S bank of the Río Negro, 48 km. above the point where it empties into the Río Uruguay. Small vessels plying on the Río Negro connect at its mouth with large steamers plying between Salto, Montevideo, and Buenos Aires. This pleasant small town of 34,000 inhabitants is a yachting and fishing centre during the season.

The charm of the town derives from its Spanish-colonial appearance, though it is not as old as the older parts of Colonia: one- to two-storey houses are neatly set along streets laid out in chessboard fashion. There is a pleasant costañera (riverside drive).

Hotels *Brisas del Hum,* US$5 s; *Comercio; Petit Hotel,* (US$2 s); *Hotel Himalaya,* US$6 d, with bath; *Hotel Martín,* US$6 d.; *Hotel Universal,* US$2.80 p.p., recommended.

Camping Site at Mercedes.

Excursions To the islands in the Río Negro—the largest has an inn. To the small town of **Santo Domingo,** first town to be founded in Uruguay, to see a fine Colonial church and an old house.

Museums Palaeontology and Natural Sciences; the Museum of Eusebio Giménez, with a gallery of paintings.

Bus to Paysandú, 2½ hours, US$2.

The road continues westwards (34 km.) to

Fray Bentos, a port on the Uruguay River, 193 km. above Buenos Aires and 402 km. by water from Montevideo. The road from Mercedes crosses the Rio Negro by a new bridge, and an international bridge has been built across the Río Uruguay to Puerto Unzué (Argentina). Main industry: meat packing and canning; it is here that the Liebig extracts are made. The excellent port has 7.3 metres of water. Population: 14,000.

Hotel *Gran* (satisfactory); **Restaurant** *Club Armonía.*

Steamers Launch services four times a week to Gualeguaychú, in Argentina.

Paysandú, on the E bank of the Río Uruguay (navigable here by vessels of 4.2 metres draught), 122 km. by good but mostly unpaved road from Fray Bentos, and 480 by paved road *via* Trinidad from Montevideo, is one of the two provincial towns with a population of about 80,000. There is a golf club, and a rowing club which holds regattas. The cathedral is 19th century with cannon balls embedded in walls from the 1865 Brazilian siege (at the time the town was held by the Paraguayans). The attached Salesian college has an interesting museum. The cemetery on the outskirts is worth a look. A new historical museum is being opened at Florida 930. Afternoon ferry to Concepción; the international bridge to Colón (Argentina) was completed in October 1975 (US$1.40 per car for crossing). Airport.

Hotels *Gran Hotel Paysandú,* best; *Montevideo; Internacional,* clean and central, US$3.50 d; cheapest is *Bary Pensión Popular,* US$3 d, with shower; or *Hotel Lobato,* Luís Gómez 1415, US$1.80 s, good.

Youth Hostel Liga Departmental de Football, Gran Bretaña 872.

Camping Free facilities available in a municipal park by the river.

Industries Textiles, leather, sugar refining, brewing, plastics.

Tourist Bureau Plaza de Armas, 18 de Julio 1226.

Excursions To the waterfalls of the River Quequay, a few km. to the N; the Termas del Guaviyú thermal springs 8 km. away; to the Meseta de Artigas, 90 km. N of Paysandú, 13 km. off the highway to Salto. The Meseta, where General Artigas lived (statue), is 45 metres above the Uruguay river, which here narrows and forms whirlpools at the rapids of El Hervidero. A terrace commands a fine view, but the rapids are not visible from the Meseta. The statue, with the general's head topping a tall shaft, looks very peculiar.

Bus to Montevideo, US$5, 7 hours.

Train to Salto US$1.90 (2nd) and Montevideo US$5.50 (2nd).

Salto, 120 km. by paved road N of Paysandú (whence it can also be reached by rail), is the other city which has reached a population of 80,000. It is a centre for oranges and citrus fruit and now processes the latter. See the beautiful park of Solari; the municipal park with an open air theatre; the fine-arts museum in the donated mansion, French style, of a rich estanciero, Uruguay 1067; and the promenade along the River Uruguay. Across the river is Concordia, in Argentina, to which there are 5-6 ferries (15 mins.) on weekdays, three on Saturdays and two on Sundays (US$0.30 a seat if full; more if it isn't).

Hotels *Gran Hotel Salto,* best; *Los Cedros,* a/c, newest, US$10; *Uruguay,* US$5.50; *Español; Magnolias,* US$6 p.p.; *Plaza,* near bus station, simple, clean, good food, US$3 p.p.; *Rosa* and *Delma,* and *Pensión Sabarros,* US$1.80 s, are also fairly cheap.

Youth Hostel Colegio Oriental, Invernizzi 89.

Restaurants *Los Pingüinos,* Uruguay 702; *Chef Restaurant,* Uruguay 639; *Club de Remeros de Salto.*

Camping Site at Salto.

Bank of London & South America, two agencies: Uruguay 585 and Blandengues y 8 Octubre. Open 1300-1700, Mon.-Fri.

Bus to Montevideo, US$7.50; to Termas del Arapey, 2 hours, daily, US$1.90.

Air Service Daily to and from Montevideo *via* Paysandú.

Rail To Montevideo, Mon. and Thurs.

Above Salto the river runs between high banks, with many rapids, so that only small boats can ply on it. A favourite excursion from Salto is by launch to one of these rapids, the Salto Chico; another is to see the picturesque waterfall of Salto Grande, where a ranch-style guest house for fishermen is run by the Tourist Commission. A joint Argentine-Uruguayan hydroelectric plant is being built here, for completion in the 1980s. Medicinal springs at Fuente Salto, 6 km. N of the city.

The road to **Termas del Arapey** branches off the partially paved highway to Bella Unión, 61 km. N of Salto, and then runs 35 km. first E and then S. It is an interesting journey through rolling countryside, with pampa birds, ostriches and metre-long lizards much in evidence. Termas del Arapey is on the Arapey river S of Isla Cabellos (Baltazar Brum). The healing waters at these famous thermal baths contain bicarbonated salts, calcium and magnesium. There are a **Motel** (very small bungalows with kitchens, no sheets provided), a nice swimming pool and a very simple *parador* (meals only). Book ahead in Salto or Montevideo.

Both road (148 km.) and railway run N to the little town of **Bella Unión** (5,000 people), near the Brazilian frontier. From Isla Cabellos on the line to Bella Unión, a railway runs NE to **Artigas**, a frontier town in a cattle raising and agricultural area which does considerable trade with Brazil. There is a bridge across the Río Cuaraim to the Brazilian town of Quaraí opposite. Population: 14,000.

Hotels   *Concordia; Oriental.*

Camping   US$0.24 p.p. a day.

Bus service to Salto, 225 km. **Airport** at Bella Unión.

Montevideo North-east to Brazil: Route 8

The Pan-American Highway, 486 km. long, runs NE into the hills away from the coast. Route 8 is paved to about 30 km. beyond Minas, 120 km. from Montevideo; beyond it is all-weather.

Minas, with 25,000 inhabitants, is a picturesque small town set in the wooded hills, which supply granite and marble. Lavalleja, the leader of the Thirty-Three who brought independence to the country, was born here. There is an equestrian statue to him. The church's portico and towers, some caves in the neighbourhood, and the countryside around are worth seeing. The Parque Salus, on the slopes of Sierras de las Animas, is only 8 km. to the S and very attractive; take the town bus marked "Cervecería Salus" from plaza to the Salus brewery, then walk 2 km. to the mineral spring and bottling plant. (*Parador Salus,* acceptable.) Different kinds of fine confectionery are made in Minas; the largest firm, opposite *Hotel Verdun,* shows tourists round its premises.

Hotels   *Garibaldi; Verdun.*

Youth Hostel   In small village of Villa Serrana, 28 km. beyond Minas on road to Treinta y Tres; most attractive.

Air Service   Daily flight by Pluna from Montevideo.

Railway from Montevideo.

Bus   To Montevideo, US$1.50.

The next centre of any importance, 286 km. from Montevideo, is

Trienta y Tres, 15,000 people, picturesquely placed a little way from the Olimar River. Some 20 km. beyond, a dirt road, left, runs 19 km. among and over hills to a craggy region with small streams—the Quebrada de los Cuervos—now a beautiful and quite unspoilt national park.

Hotel   *Central.*

Air Service   Daily by Pluna from Montevideo.

Railway   It is on the line from Montevideo through José Batlle y Ordóñez to Río Branco.

Railway and road go on through **Melo** (111 km. from Treinta y Tres) to the border town of Río Branco, 88 km. from Melo. **Río Branco,** founded in 1914, is on the Yaguarón River. The 1½ km.-long Mauá bridge across the river leads to the Brazilian town of Jaguarão.

This is where most international traffic used to cross the frontier; now the road *via* Chuy is better. Customs officials are at the international bridge, passport officials at the police station at Jaguarão. There is a better rate of exchange at Melo than at the frontier. *Hotel Internacional* at Melo is just acceptable.

Montevideo North to Brazil

This 509 km. road (there is also a railway) from Montevideo to the border town of Rivera runs almost due north, at first over rolling hills through cattle country, rich vineyards, apple orchards, orange, lemon and olive groves. Further N, hilly cattle-range land is crossed.

Las Piedras, 24 km. from Montevideo, in vineyard country, has a Gothic Chapel of the Silesians. Meetings are held on its racecourse on Tuesday and Thursday.

Bank of London and South America, Calle General Artigas 652. Open 1200-1600, Mon.-Fri.

Canelones, 45 km. from the capital, is a typical small town of 10,000 people in a grain growing area. Travellers then pass through the pleasant country towns of Florida, Durazno, Paso de los Toros (close to the huge lake created by the Rincón del Bonete dam on the Río Negro) and Tacuarembó.

Florida   Famous for a folklore festival on Independence Day each year.

Hotel   *Español,* US$4 d.

Rivera is a town of 22,000 people, on the Brazilian frontier. It is divided by a street from the Brazilian town of Santa Ana do Livramento, which has a good golf course, and a daily bus to Porto Alegre. Rivera is built on two small hills. Points of interest are the park, where there are free camping facilities, the Plaza Internacional, and the dam of Cañapirú. Buy Brazilian currency at Rivera.

Hotels   *Casino; Nuevo.*   **Airport.**

The Economy

The Uruguayan economy is in the process of recuperation and continues to benefit from the stabilisation programme initiated in 1975 and continued in collaboration with the IMF. In 1977 GDP increased by over 2% for the third successive year. The country's agricultural base is slowly diversifying with the greater development of the industrial and service sectors, but its problems of inflation, stagnant real income per head, lack of investment and balance-of-payments deficits remain to be overcome. These problems stem partly from the pattern of Uruguay's development earlier this century. Prosperity derived from beef and wool exports gave rise to an economy where wealth is fairly evenly distributed with a large middle class and an educated work-force (the literacy rate is over 90%). The burdens of developing a welfare state, with for example retirement at about 50, became too much for an undynamic economy, primarily based on commodity exports, and the country's economic problems became increasingly apparent from the late 1950s, with consequent severe political and social repercussions.

The country's prime resources are its skilled work-force and good agricultural land, with 90% of the land surface being devoted to stockraising, 7% to crops and with only 3% unproductive. The beef-cattle sector has been considerably improved by various programmes in recent years, but currently suffers from a lack of market outlets, which has led to an increase in herd size, to 12m. head of cattle, and problems of overgrazing and feed supply. The agricultural sector has been notable for its lack of flexibility in responding to changing world markets. Generally speaking the basic requirements of a heavy industrial economy are lacking, as there are no major resources of coal, petroleum (though exploration continues), other basic minerals, timber or an internal market sufficiently large to support heavy industry. The economy has developed on the basis of beef and wool exports, with the production of consumer goods by a highly protected industrial sector and the provision of services for the small local market. An abundant hydroelectric potential still awaits full development (see below).

The distribution of the economically active population is estimated as follows: agriculture 18.1%; industry and construction 27.6%; commerce 11.1%; services and transport 35.0% and others 8.2%. These represent only 48.4% of the total population, which has been estimated at 3,100,000 at May 1976. The agricultural sector, which even now still provides two-thirds of exports by value, employs less than 20% of the work-force; a quarter are employed by the government and state corporations.

The immediate economic problems of the 1970s have been the related issues of inflation and balance-of-payments deficits. The latter is the result of fluctuating terms of trade and in particular of the closure of the EEC market to traditional beef suppliers, the increase in petroleum prices and the effect of inflation on the prices of manufactured goods imported by Uruguay. In 1977 inflation reached 60% and there was a trade deficit, on a balance-of-payments basis, of US$113.4m. In response the Government's economic programme has introduced greater liberalisation and freedom from controls in the economy, especially with regard to foreign trade, has attempted to reduce the budget deficit, and is encouraging foreign investment and utilizing financial aid from the IMF to cover the increased cost of petroleum imports (US$210m. in 1977) and the balance-of-payments deficits.

In the longer run the aim is to restructure the economic life of the country to develop a dynamic high-skill high-value industrial export-based economy. The country's long-neglected infrastructure—roads, railways, other public services—is being rehabilitated and extended with aid from international agencies. The joint Argentine-Uruguayan hydroelectric project at Salto Grande will make Uruguay a net exporter of electric energy in the mid 1980s. Smaller hydroelectric projects are also being undertaken in conjunction with Brazil, and the Chevron Overseas Petroleum Co. has been awarded a contract for oil exploration and development on part of the continental shelf; a semi-submersible platform began drilling in 1976, but has not as yet produced results. A general improvement in trading relations with the other nations of southern South America is slowly leading to greater economic integration, providing Uruguay with a larger market for its products and additional sources of finance to help develop its resources.

Foreign Trade
(US$ millions)

	1972	1973	1974	1975	1976	1977
Exports (f.o.b.) ..	214.1	321.5	382.2	375.0	541.2	607.5
Imports (c.i.f.) ..	211.6	284.8	481.3	542.0	571.4	720.9

Information for Visitors

Routes to Uruguay

From Europe   By any of the steamship lines to Buenos Aires, or by air: direct flights by Air France, Iberia, KLM, Lufthansa and SAS. Flying by other carriers, such as British Caledonian, a change must be made at Rio or Buenos Aires.

From the U.S.A.   Several shipping lines serve Montevideo from New York (13 days), Baltimore, Boston, Charleston, Norfolk, Savannah, Jacksonville, and New Orleans. Air services are run by Pan American World Airways (5 a week), Varig, and Lan-Chile, and (as far as Buenos Aires) by Braniff, Canadian Pacific Airlines, Avianca and Aerolíneas Argentinas. Braniff has 2 flights a week to the U.S. *via* Rio or Buenos Aires.

From Argentina   The Cía. de Navegación Fluvial Argentina runs a service every night between Buenos Aires and Montevideo, 12 hours for the crossing. Car ferry, twice daily, single-class service (once daily in winter) between Buenos Aires and Colonia, about 2½ hours. Hydrofoil passenger vessels (Alíscafos) ply between Buenos Aires and Colonia 3 times a day; they carry 100 passengers and cross in 50 minutes. Slightly cheaper: short crossing by launch between Carmelo and Tigre. Aerolíneas Argentinas, Austral, and Pluna have several flights a day between Aeroparque in Buenos Aires and Carrasco Airport. (Pluna flies Viscounts, for lower fares than the Argentine lines.) Arco flies between Colonia and Buenos Aires. From Colonia there is a fast bus service by Onda to Montevideo. Foreign airlines also connect Carrasco with the Buenos Aires international airport at Ezeiza. Buses are now running between Argentina and Uruguay, across the Paysandú and Fray Bentos bridges.

From Brazil   To Montevideo by sea with European and United States lines, calling at Brazilian ports *en route* for Uruguay. By Air: Direct connection between Brazil and Uruguay by all the international lines landing at Montevideo. Varig flies 3 times a week from Rio de Janeiro to Montevideo, *via* Buenos Aires. Cruzeiro do Sul has daily flights Rio de Janeiro, São Paulo, Porto Alegre and Montevideo. By Road: The Pan-American Highway runs 2,880 km. from Rio de Janeiro to Montevideo and on to Colonia. It is poorly surfaced in parts.

From Chile   All the international services from Europe fly on to Buenos Aires and Santiago de Chile. The Chilean Lan-Chile company flies between Santiago, Buenos Aires and Montevideo and from Montevideo to Lima.

From Paraguay   By Cía. de Navegación Fluvial Argentina river steamers from Asunción to Buenos Aires (frequently suspended); by air, twice weekly by Pluna, 3 times weekly by LAP airlines, and weekly by Iberia. Twice-weekly buses Asuncion-Montevideo.

Airport Tax of US$1 on all air travellers leaving Uruguay for South American republics or Mexico; US$2 for all other countries, and a tax of 3% on all tickets issued and paid for in Uruguay.

Documents   A passport is necessary for entry except for nationals of other American countries, who can get in with national identity documents. Visas are not required for passports by nationals of American and Western European countries, Israel and Japan. All visitors must have a valid international Vaccination Certificate against smallpox. Duties are not usually charged on a reasonable quantity of goods (such as tobacco and spirits), brought in obviously for the traveller's own use: 200 cigarettes or 50 cigars or 3 small packets of tobacco are admitted duty-free; so is 1 bottle of alcoholic drink, 3 little bottles of perfume and gifts up to the value of US$5.

Warning   The frequent prejudice against rucksacks (backpacks) applies here too.

Hours of Business   Most department stores generally are open 0900 to 1200, 1400 to 1900, but 0900 to 1230 on Saturdays. Business houses vary but most work from 0830 to 1200, 1430 to 1830 or 1900, according to whether they open on Saturday. Banking hours are 1300 to 1700 in Montevideo; there are special summer hours (Dec. 1-March 15) in Montevideo (1330-1730), in the interior (0730-1130) and in Punta del Este (1600-2000); banks are closed on Saturdays. Government departments, mid-March to mid-November, 1300 to 1830 from Monday to Friday; rest of the year, 0700 to 1230, but not Saturdays.

All the better hotels will find an interpreter or translator. Only translations by authorised public translators, who charge thumping fees, are accepted for offical purposes. Their names and addresses are in the local Telephone Directory, classified section, under "Traductores Públicos". An excellent bi-lingual secretarial bureau is the *E.M.E. Relaciones Públicas* in the *Hotel Victoria Plaza*.

British Businessmen are strongly advised to read "Hints to Business Men visiting Uruguay", free on application to the Department of Trade, Export Services Division, room CO7, Export House, 50 Ludgate Hill, London EC4M 7HU.

Best times for visiting Most tourists visit during the summer (December-mid March), though hotels are then full and have to be booked in advance. Business visits can be paid throughout the year, but it is best to avoid the tourist months. In June, July, and August, orders are placed for the winter season 12 months ahead.

Roads There are 45,000 km. of roads, 90% of them paved or all-weather. Main roads shown on map. The Comisión Nacional de Turismo will help to plan itineraries by car. Onda buses radiate into the interior from Montevideo, using comfortable American long-distance coaches; other companies do not run the same extensive network, but are often cheaper and just as fast. All hotels have Onda timetables. There are overland links with Argentina, across the Fray Bentos and Paysandú bridges, Brazil (frequent buses to Porto Alegre and São Paulo) and Paraguay (26-28 hours, twice weekly, leaving 0530, by COIT, Calle Paraguay 1473). Hitch-hiking can be difficult as drivers have memories of the Tupamaro urban-guerrilla movement: at that time many hitch-hikers became hi-jackers. Gasoline prices are high, but less high than in Brazil.

Motoring Carnet required. Vehicles do not stop, nor is there a right of way, at uncontrolled intersections. Montevideo is the most nerve-shattering capital in the Americas for a driver. **Automóvil Club del Uruguay**, Av. Agraciada 1532, Montevideo, publishes road maps of the city and the country at large.

The Railways also converge upon Montevideo and have a total length of 3,016 km. They were mainly built by the British from 1868 on but were all sold to Uruguay in 1948. They are all of standard (1.435 metres) gauge.

Internal Flights Pluna, a Uruguayan company, provides services between Montevideo and all important towns. Internal air transport is also provided by Tamu, an arm of the air force.

Clothing Light or tropical suits during the warm weather from December to March. (It is also very warm now and then in November and April.) Warm clothing during the cold months from June to September, particularly in Montevideo, where cold winds are frequent. There are heavy rains at all times of year, and a light raincoat and umbrella come in handy.

Youth Hostels Asociación de Alberguistas del Uruguay, Reconquista 745, Montevideo (Tel.: 981324) operates hostels at Montevideo (Canelones 935), Carmelo, Paysandú, Piriápolis, Salto, Los Titanes (Km. 64.5 on Interbalnearia) and Villa Serrana, near Minas.

Camping Several good sites in Montevideo and outside; see references in main text.

Shopping Bargains Uruguayan nutria, a highly prized fur, is the best in the world, with longer, thicker, softer hair and a better colour than elsewhere, and not dear. Inexpensive also are the excellent woollen goods; try Ovalle Taylor in 2 locations on 18 de Julio. Suede and leather bags, jackets, and belts are both good and cheap. So are amethysts, *alpargatas* (local sandals) and canvas ballerina slippers with rubber soles: gramophone records. Bargains at the street fairs on Sundays. Film processing is the cheapest in South America.

Food and Drink Beef is consumed at almost all meals when available, though it is not so good or so plentiful as in Argentina. *Asado* (barbecued beef) is popular; the main dishes are *asado de tira* (ribs) and *pulpa* (no bones). *Churrasco* (steak), *costilla* (chop) and *Milanesa* (veal cutlet) are also popular. To get a lean piece of *asado*, ask for *asado flaco*. Two other good local dishes are *puchero* (beef with vegetables, bacon, beans and sausages) and the local varieties of pizza, fast becoming a staple. Other specialities are pie, barbecued pork and grilled chicken in wine. An excellent dessert is *chajá*, a type of sponge cake in ball-shape with cream and jam inside and sprinkled with coconut. *Morcilla dulce,* a sweet black pudding, has been highly praised. The local wines are acceptable and the beers are very good. Maté is a favourite drink between meal hours. There is much difficulty in obtaining imported drinks such as whisky, and they are expensive. The local spirits are *caña* and *grappa*; some find the locally-made whisky and gin acceptable. Pastries are very good indeed, and crystallized egg-yolks, known as *yemas,* are popular sweets. Milk is often scarce. The dinner hour is late, usually from 2100 to 2400.

Health Milk and fresh water can be drunk and fresh salads eaten fairly freely throughout the country. Many of Montevideo's residents inoculate against typhoid, though cases are now extremely rare. All travellers must have a vaccination certificate against smallpox. Medical services maintain a high standard, but they and medicines are expensive.

Tipping Normally all hotel and restaurant bills include a percentage service charge, but an additional small tip is expected. In other cases give 10% of the total bill. Porters at the airfield expect about US$0.05 per piece of luggage; although there is an official rate of tips for porters at seaports, the actual charges are mostly higher. Taxi drivers are tipped 10% of the fare. Tips at cafés are about 15%. Cinema ushers get a small tip.

Local Information Centres The Comisión Nacional de Turismo central office, at 18 de Julio 845 (Plaza Cagancha), Montevideo, issues tourist literature. It has built a number of good guest houses at the various resorts and gives information about them at the Information Office. There is a good information kiosk at Montevideo's main bus station. Your hotel usually knows a good deal about what is going on.

Holidays Jan. 1, 6; Carnival (see below); Easter week; April 19; May 1, 18; June 19; July 18; August 25; October 12; November 2; December 8, 25.

Carnival Week is officially the Monday and Tuesday immediately preceding Ash Wednesday, but a great many firms close for the whole of the week. Carnival in Montevideo is no longer as lively as it was; festivities are mainly in evidence along the 18 de Julio.

Business comes to a standstill also during Tourist week, which coincides with La Semana Criolla (horse-breaking, stunt riding by cowboys, dances and song). Department stores close only from Good Friday. Banks close all week. Easter Monday is not a holiday.

The **Cost of Living** is high for manufactures (mostly imported), but low for food, lodgings and services. Inflation is again serious and prices went up by 60% in 1977, against a rise of 39% in 1976. This does not, of course, affect foreign visitors as seriously as Uruguayans; the value of the dollar rises more or less in step.

Prices The Government has fixed authorised tariffs for luggage carriers and outside porters; for tug boat excursions and launch journeys to and from vessels off-shore; charges at its own hotels, at beaches and admission to casinos. They are worth knowing.

Currency The "new peso" (Ur$), equivalent to 1,000 pesos, was introduced in July 1975. Bank notes issued are for 5, 10, and 50 centésimos and 1, 5, and 10 new pesos, and coins for 1, 2, 5, 10 and 50 centésimos and 1 and 5 new pesos. Hotels tend to give unfavourable rates. Any amount of currency can be taken in or out. Exchange rates at mid-April 1978 were about 5.625 to the US$ on the "free financial market". Many exchange houses *(casas de cambio)* will give you US$ cash for US$ travellers' cheques without commission. Dollars can be repurchased when leaving the country, as long as they were sold on the "financial market" and you have the slips to prove it. Exchange houses now closed. The currency was devalued by 46.7% against the US$ in 1976, and 35.3% in 1977 by means of 23 small adjustments.

Weights and Measures   Metric units alone are legal, but this does not apply to material sent direct from Britain. All the same, the metric system should be used in trade literature. Odd fact: the timber trade still uses inches for the cross section of lengths of timber.

Letters, telephones, and telegrams: Inflation is such that it is not considered worth while giving the rates, which are often changed. Postal services, even international ones, are rather poor, and strikes are frequent.

Cables   Western Telegraph Co. Ltd. (British), ITT Comunicaciones Mundiales S.A., and Italcable provide communication with all parts of the world through their cable stations at Montevideo.

The Government-owned Cerrito station supplies international radio-telegraph communication service. Press wireless service is provided by Press Wireless Uruguaya Ltda. Radio-telephonic conversations with the United States and Europe, etc., are routed through Buenos Aires.

British Embassy and Consulate in Uruguay   The Embassy and Consulate are at Marco Bruto 1073. Telephone number of the First Secretary (Commercial): 9-2501.

The **United States** maintains an Embassy and Consulate at Rambla Wilson 1776.

American Express Agents   Montevideo: Turisport Ltda., Bartolomé Mitre 1318, Tel.: 86300/94823.

(We are deeply grateful for help in revising this chapter from the following travellers: James K. Bock (Mexico City), Lesley and Milan Carnogursky (Inuvik, Canada), Olive Green (Peru), Hansruedi Lehmann (Bolligen, Switzerland), James N. Maas, Dr. Terry McCarthy (Singapore), Jean Marion (French Embassy, Brazil, Dr. Patrik von zur Mühlen (Bonn), Inés and Joggi Riedtmann (Basel), Barbara Singleton (USA) and Lothar Springer (Münster). We are also most grateful to Michael Wooller, of LBI Economics Department, for doing the updating, and revising the Economy section.)

VENEZUELA

WHEN the Spaniards came to Venezuela in 1499 they found a poor country thinly populated with Indians who had created no distinctive culture. Four hundred years later it was still poor, almost exclusively agrarian, exporting little, importing less. The miracle year which changed all that was 1917, when oil was discovered at Maracaibo. Today, Venezuela is said to be the richest country in Latin America and is one of the largest producers and exporters of oil in the world. Of all the countries of Latin America, Venezuela has the highest per capita income, the highest standard of living, the largest number of telephones per head, the greatest per capita consumption of electricity, and one of the lowest rates in inflation. All this is due to the vast revenues from oil which have poured into the state coffers. These have been used to rebuild Caracas and Maracaibo and other cities, and to create the best network of roads on the continent. There is only one foreseeable snag: at the present rate of extraction oil may be exhausted in eighteen years. To offset this possible calamity production has been restricted, and vast investments are now being poured into state industry and agrarian reform and into tackling the perennial Latin American problems of education, housing and unemployment.

Venezuela has 2,800 km. of coastline on the Caribbean Sea. To the east is Guyana, to the south Brazil, and to the west Colombia. Its area is 912,050 square km., and its population is 13,122,000. It was given its name—"Little Venice"—by the early Spanish navigators, who saw in the Indian pile dwellings on Lake Maracaibo a dim reminder of Venetian waterways.

The country falls into four very different regions: the Venezuelan Highlands to the west and along the north; the Maracaibo Lowlands around the fresh water lake of Maracaibo; the vast central plain of the Llanos of the Orinoco; and the Guayana Highlands, which take up over half the country.

The Highlands are an offshoot of the Andes. From the Colombian border they trend, at first, towards the NE to enfold the Maracaibo Lowlands. This section is known as the Sierra Nevada de Mérida. Beyond they swell out into the Segovia Highlands N of Barquisimeto: they then turn E in parallel ridges along the coast to form the Central Highlands,

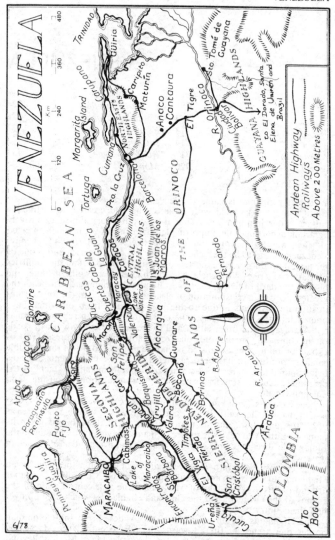

dipping into the Caribbean Sea only to rise again into the North-Eastern Highlands of the peninsulas of Paria and Araya.

Each distinctive area will be described as we travel into it by road or plane: there is only one 175-km. passenger railway line, of little importance to tourists, though a large railway-building programme is in hand. The general outline of each area we give in the text will reveal that Venezuela is a country in which natural obstacles to farming, cattle breeding, and communications are formidable. It explains why the country was poverty stricken for so long.

History   At the beginning of the 16th century, Venezuela was inhabited by various tribes of Caribs and Arawaks: better fed, healthier and more virile on the uplands, poorer and more disease-ridden in the lowlands. They could make no effective resistance against the Spaniards who landed on the Peninsula of Paria in 1499. The first permanent Spanish settlement was at Cumaná, in 1520. Soon afterwards settlers reached Coro, at the foot of the Paraguaná Peninsula. Indian slaves were used to mine and pan for gold, but the results were disappointing and the settlers turned to agriculture, forming settlements at Barquisimeto in 1552, at Valencia in 1555, and at Caracas in 1567. It was not until a hundred years of consolidation in these areas that they began to occupy the rest of the country, inter-marrying freely with the Indians and later introducing black slaves to work the sugar plantations. Centralised colonial control from Spain was as irksome here as in the rest of Latin America to the mestizos and American-born Spaniards. Three risings reflecting these discontents took place in 1749, 1775 and 1797, and there were two abortive attempts by Francisco Miranda to achieve independence in 1806 and 1811. When Miranda had been captured, the movement was led by Simón Bolívar, a Venezuelan with a touch of Indian blood, born in Caracas in 1783. He met with mixed success until his capture of Angostura, now Ciudad Bolívar, in 1817. There he was joined by a contingent of experienced Peninsular veterans recruited in London. At their head, together with the horsemen of the llanos, he undertook a dramatic march over the Andes to win the battle of Boyacá and capture Bogotá. Three months later, the revolutionary congress at Angostura—with most of Venezuela still in Royalist hands—was announcing the republic of Gran Colombia, a union of what is at present Ecuador, Colombia, Venezuela, and Panama. Six months later, on June 24, 1821, the revolutionaries routed the Spanish forces at Carabobo. The 10-year struggle for independence had reduced the population by a quarter and devastated the country. There was some desultory fighting for two more years, but the last of the Spanish forces surrendered at Puerto Cabello in 1823.

Before Bolívar's death in 1830 Páez declared Venezuela an independent republic. Other presidents of note were Guzmán Blanco, Juan Vicente Gómez (1909-1935), a brutal but efficient dictator, and Isaías Medina Angarita, who introduced the oil laws. There was considerable progress under the 6-year dictatorship of Gen. Marcos Pérez Jiménez (1952-58), but his Gómez-like methods led to his overthrow in January 1958, a month after he had been re-elected President, by an uprising in which some 600 people were killed or wounded in Caracas. A more stable democracy has been created since.

In December 1958, in the first free election in ten years, Sr. Rómulo Betancourt, of the leftist Democratic Action party, was elected President. He completed his term of office on March 13, 1964—the first constitutionally elected President of Venezuela to do so—and was succeeded by a party colleague, the late Dr. Raúl Leoni. In 1969 Dr. Rafael Caldera Rodríguez, of the Christian Democratic party (Copei), became President. Presidential elections were held in December 1973; the new President, Sr. Carlos Andrés Pérez of the Democratic-Action party, took office in March 1974 for a five-year term; the next presidential elections are due in December 1978.

Population 53% are under 18. A large number are of mixed Spanish and Indian blood. There are some pure Indians, but they are mostly in the Guayana Highlands and in the forests west of Lake Maracaibo. There are some pure-blooded Africans and a strong admixture of black blood along the coast, particularly at the ports. The arrival of 800,000 European immigrants since the war has greatly modified the racial make-up in Venezuela. Total population was 13,121,952 on 1st January 1978.

About 75% of the population is urban. Agriculture still occupies 25%. Annual growth: 3.5%; urban growth: 5.8%. Birth-rate, per 1,000: 44.2%; death-rate: 6.7; expectation of life, 66 years. One in 6 of all Venezuelans is foreign born. Peak immigration, mostly from Europe, was in the early and mid-1950s. Tourist influx—180,000 in 1972, spending US$46m.

Venezuela is the richest country in South America, but it still faces much the same problems as most other Latin American countries. About 300,000 are unemployed; about 20% are illiterate. Many rural dwellers, seduced by thoughts of an easier life, have drifted to the cities and often ended up jobless in the shanty towns, which have sprung up like mushrooms about the bigger centres. One result of this exodus is that Venezuelan farmers still do not provide all the food the nation needs; there was a serious food-supply crisis as late as 1977.

Education Elementary schools are free, and education is compulsory from the age of 7 to the completion of the primary grade. Primary school enrolment is 76%, secondary school registration 21% and university entries 3% of the total. There are now ten universities: Caracas has two state-financed universities—Universidad Central (chartered in 1721) and the new Universidad Simón Bolívar—and three private ones; the Universidad Metropolitana; Universidad Católica Andrés Bello; and the Universidad Santa María. There are also one in Mérida, one in Maracaibo, the University of Lara in Barquisimeto, and the youngest in Valencia (1958) and Eastern Venezuela (1960). In 1970 there were 68,760 students enrolled. There are teacher training centres in Caracas, Barquisimeto and Maturín.

Government The Republic of Venezuela is a federal republic of 20 states, a Federal District, and two territories. All its 26 constitutions have been singularly enlightened but often, until 1958, in abeyance. The latest is dated January 23, 1961. Voting is now compulsory for all over 18.

The Central Highlands

Of the sub-divisions of the Andes in Venezuela, the **Central Highlands** are by far the most important: they have the densest population, for they contain the capital, Caracas, and the cities of Valencia and Maracay. The mountains here rise abruptly from a lush green coast cooled by breezes to heights of from two to three thousand metres. Above an elevation of a few hundred metres there is abundant rainfall, so the slopes are covered with tropical forest. The capital, Caracas, lies in a small basin, a rift in the mountains which runs some 24 km. east and west. This historic and once serenely small Colonial town has been transformed into one of the most astonishing modern cities in Latin America: the nation's cultural and administrative centre and hub of its industry.

A hundred km. W of Caracas is the great basin in which lies the Lake of Valencia and the towns of Maracay and Valencia. After Caracas, these are two of the chief cities in Venezuela, turning out a large number of varied and sophisticated industrial products. The basin, which is only 450 metres above sea-level, receives plenty of rain and is one of the most important agricultural areas in the country; sugar, cotton, maize, beans and rice are the main crops. In the other valleys and depressions in the Central Highlands, the crops are cacao and coffee with lesser cultivation of maize, beans, rice, manioc and bananas.

Caracas, the capital, founded in 1567, has a population of 2,576,000. It lies at 960 metres, but the southern parts of the city are 120 metres lower. Although in the torrid zone, the temperatures are moderate (a maximum of 32°C in July and August, and an occasional minimum of 9°C in January and February) and it is always cool at night.

A comparatively low pass (1,040 metres) in the mountains gives Caracas access by road to its port, La Guaira. The distance down the sharp slope is only 14½ km.; a magnificently engineered road between the two is only 17½ km.—20 minutes by automobile (toll US$0.85). The hiker can still follow the old Spanish road to the sea, free for a while from the gasoline that has made Venezuela rich.

Caracas is 15 km. long. Its proportionate growth since the war has been greater than that of any other Latin American capital. Large new urban areas have been added and the look of the centre itself changed from year to year as Colonial buildings give way to modern many-storeyed edifices and new avenues are hewn across its face, and as new colleges, public buildings, great blocks of workers' flats and other improvements are added. All this new building, with the exception of the flats, is architecturally impressive. No visitor could fail to respond to such typical examples as the magnificent University City, the Centro Simón Bolívar, and the Círculo Militar.

Starting in Catia, an ugly industrial area in the W where both roads from La Guaira enter, Avenida Sucre goes past the 23 de Enero workers' flats to join Av. Urdaneta between Palacio Miraflores and the Palacio Blanco, housing government offices. Later come the Post Office and Santa Capilla Church, looking like a wedding cake by a Parisian master pastrycook. Turn right here for Plaza Bolívar and the Capitol (the National Congress), or carry straight on down the Av. Urdaneta to San Bernardino (Colonial Museum; Hotels *Potomac* and *Avila*). Here, we enter Av. Andrés Bello which passes just below the Cable Railway Station to join Av. Libertador to the Country Club and the E, or we can turn down the Av. La Salle to the eastern end of Los Caobos Park, with the fine mahoganies which give it its popular name and a fountain representing the rivers and mountains of Venezuela. From the Plaza Venezuela intersection at the eastern end of the park, the Avenida Abraham Lincoln leads E through Sabana Grande, a modern shopping and business centre, and continues as the Avenida Francisco Miranda to

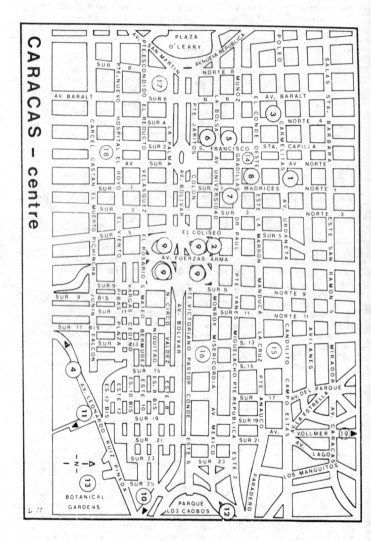

CARACAS – centre

the residential section of Altamira, with its magnificent Plaza and obelisk reflected in an artificial lake.

Alternatively, forking right out of Avenida Sucre and crossing the viaduct, we reach El Silencio, with its rowdy stallholders, and thence pass through the Centro Simón Bolívar, with its twin sky-scrapers and underground parking and shopping centre (with an interesting mosaic at the lowest level), and finally along the Avenida Bolívar past Nuevo Circo bullring and a new ice-skating rink towards University City, Sports Stadium, Lagovén offices, the *Tamanaco Hotel,* the Maravén offices (housing the British and Canadian embassies) and La Casona, residence of the President. S of the Nuevo Circo is the Helicoide, planned as a commercial centre under the Pérez Jiménez regime but left uncompleted at his fall in 1958. From the Viaduct, we can also take Av. Universidad past the National Library (former University), Capitol and San Francisco church. Two corners later, we glimpse, left, Bolívar's birthplace, before continuing to the Art Museum and on round Los Caobos Park, or by the Av. Libertador, to the east.

Another west-east route is along the new Avenida Boyacá from San Bernardino to El Marqués, which skirts the Ávila hill and gives fine views along the length of the city. Towards the E end is a monument commemorating the battle of Boyacá, and a viaduct strides majestically over the recently remodelled park in Los Chorros suburb, to which access is signposted.

To the SW from El Silencio the Avenida San Martín leads towards the factories of Antímano. This area can also be reached direct from Catia by the Planicie Tunnel. In the SW is also the older residential section of El Paraíso.

The shady Plaza Bolívar with its fine equestrian statue of the Liberator and pleasant old colonial cathedral is still the official centre of the city, though no longer geographically so. In fact, several centres (Plaza Bolívar, Plaza Venezuela, Sabana Grande, Chacaíto, La Floresta, Boleíta) are strung along the valley like so many beads with residential areas mixed in between; residential areas, in turn, change rapidly from middle to low to high class without much pattern.

National Monuments

Panteón Nacional Av. Norte: open 0800-1200 and 1400-1800 daily except Monday. This was designed as the resting place of Bolívar, the Liberator, and Miranda, the Precursor of Independence. The remains of Bolívar lie there, but the tomb of Miranda, who died in a Spanish prison, has been left open to await the return of his body.

Capitolio Nacional The Elliptical Salon has some impressive paintings and a bronze urn containing the 1811 Declaration of Independence; men must wear jackets.

Key to map on page opposite
1. Airways office; 2. Tourist information centre; 3. Central Post Office; 4. Road to airport; 5. Capitol; 6. National Library; 7. Bolívar's House and Historical Museum; 8. Cathedral; 9. Centro Simón Bolívar; 10. Road to University; 11. Road to Macuto; 12. Museo de Bellas Artes; 13. Museo de Ciencias Naturales; 14. Plaza Bolívar; 15. Plaza Candelaria; 16 Parque Carabobo; 17. Plaza Miranda; 18. Plaza La Concordia; 19. Road to Museo de Arte Colonial (Quinta Anauco).

Parks

Jardín Botánico, near Plaza Venezuela; Parque Central (futuristic, tall apartment buildings on Av. Lecuna, very impressive architecture); Parque Nacional del Este has a zoo and is a peaceful place to relax, except at weekends. The Parque Los Chorros at the foot of the mountain and the Parque Los Caobos (see page 703) are also recommended, El Calvario, west of Plaza O'Leary, is quiet and pleasant with a good view of Centro Simón Bolívar.

Museums

Museo de Bellas Artes, Plaza Morelos in Parque Los Caobos: open 0900-1200 and 1500-1730 daily except Monday; 1200-1700 on Sunday. Pictures include an El Greco.

Museo de Arte Colonial, Quinta Anauco, Av. Panteón, San Bernardino: open 0900-1200 and 1500-1700 Wed., Thurs., Sat.; 0900-1800 Sundays and national holidays. Admission US$0.20. A delightful house built in 1720. The beautiful suburb of San Bernardino glories in tropical flowers and whole avenues of forest trees, smothered in blossom in season.

Museo de Arte Contemporáneo, Parque Central, Cuadra Bolívar, six blocks south of the twin towers. Open Tues.-Fri. 1200-1900. Sat. 1100-2100, Sun. 1100-1900.

Casa Natal del Libertador   Open 0900-1200 and 1500-1800 daily except Monday; Saturday and Sunday 1000-1300. The present house is a reconstruction of the house where Bolívar was born. The first, of adobe, was destroyed by an earthquake. The second degenerated into a stable for mules and donkeys and was pulled down. The present building of stone was built by order of Gómez (whose birthday was the same as Bolívar's) in the early 1920s; it contains interesting pictures and furniture.

The Museo Bolivariano is alongside the Casa Natal and contains the Liberator's war relics.

Museo de Ciencias Naturales, Plaza Morelos in Parque Los Caobos; open 0900-1200, 1500-1730 except Mondays.

House of Arturo Michelena, in the La Pastora section, is a typical 19th century home, now a museum.

The Ministry of Foreign Relations contains pictures mostly of national heroes and history. Check museum schedules in *El Universal, El Nacional* or the *Daily Journal.*

The Concejo Municipal (City Hall) on Plaza Bolívar contains two museums: a collection of the paintings of Emilio Boggio, a Venezuelan painter, and the Raúl Santana Museum of the Creole Way of Life, a collection of miniature figures in costumes and poses characteristic of Venezuelan life, all handmade by Raúl Santana and extremely realistic. Well worth a visit.

Churches

The **Cathedral** should be seen for its beautiful façade, and pictures including an alleged Rubens and Murillo.
San Francisco should be seen for its colonial altars.
Modern Caracas   Visitors should see the Avenida de los Próceres with its twin monoliths and other monuments to the heroes of independence; the

Cuadra Bolívar, the summer residence of the liberator; the magnificent Officers' Club on the same avenue; and the University City, an enormous and coherent complex of great buildings in which paintings, sculpture and stained glass are completely integrated with the architecture (which is now showing signs of wear).

Hotels

	Daily rates (US$)	
	Single	Double
Tamanaco ..	44-60	44-60
Caracas Hilton	35-38	40-45
Holiday Inn (next to Tamanaco) ..	25-30	35-40
Ávila	20-30	30-40
Kursal	25	30
Tampa	15	21
La Floresta	11-16	14-33
Residencia El Cid ..	28	33

The new Hotel Las Américas (US$18 d), exclusive of breakfast, service and taxes: food passable but unexciting) and Hotel Cristal, both on Sabana Grande, and Hotel Capitol, a half block from the Capitol, are reasonable, decent hotels near the centre. Hotel City (US$12.50 s, US$18 d and US$21 for a suite) all rooms have private bath and TV, Sabana Grande. Also new is the Hotel Tanausú, on the south extension of Av. Las Acacias (US$9 s, a/c, US$6.25 not a/c). We can recommend the Italian-run Hotel San Carlo, in San Bernardino, Esmeralda a Brisas de Gamboa 121 (US$7 s, US$12 d, three excellent meals). Hotel Madrid, Av. Chacaíto, small (US$3 s, US$4.50 d, hot water, showers in all rooms). Hotel Everest (US$7.50 s) and Hotel Myriam (US$8 d, some baths, good value for location, very clean), both in Av. Las Acacias, near junction with Sabana Grande; Hotel Estación (US$2.50) suits the Peace Corps, and gives them a discount. Other places recommended are Hotel Savoy (US$16 s); Hotel Continental Altamira, in Av. San Juan Bosco (US$24 s), good for businessmen; Hotel Macuto (US$8-10 p.p.), not luxurious but has a good swimming pool; Hotel Caracol, Coliseo a Pincino, near bus station (US$8.50 d, with bath); Pensión Galicia, off Av. del Este (US$4), simple but clean; Hotel San Vicente (US$8.15 d), Plaza Concordia; Kings Inn (US$20 d, with bath), Calle Olimpo, near Avenida Lincoln; Hotel Pensión Restaurant Villa Verde (US$8 d, good Italian food, 4 courses, US$2.50); and Pensión Maribel (US$5 d, without food), near Esquina Carcel on Oeste 14; Hotel Bahía (US$14 d, swimming pool, good restaurant); Hotel Miami, at Candilito (US$11.50 d, with shower); Hotel Marly, Carcel a Monzón 113 (US$6 d); Pensión Sucre, a couple of blocks above Nuevo Circo (US$3). Hotel Turín, near centre, hot shower (US$8 d); Hotel Niteroy, on Av. Baratt (US$12 a/c); Hotel Bakistan, Quebrado Apescador 23 San Juan (US$4 s); Hotel Pon Pen (US$4.50 d, basic), near bus terminus Este 8; Hospedaje (US$3.25 d, reasonable), Sur 5; Hotel ABC, Av. Lecuna (US$4.75); Hotel Inter, Animas a Calero on corner of Av. Urdaneta (US$14 d), very clean, shower and toilet with each room, friendly, English spoken; Hotel K, Sur 2 and Oeste 10 (US$1.60) men only, basic, clean; Hospedaje Carballino, US$8 d, near the Nuevo Circo bus station, secure but little else. For other cheap hotels look on Calle Sur 2.

The Ávila is in San Bernardino on the higher levels of the city, set in park-like gardens and very pleasant; it serves a good lunch. The Astor is just outside the centre of the city. The Mara, Conde and Veroes are in the centre, convenient for banks and business houses, but noisy. The small, convenient Hotel Luna is on Av. Casanova, one block from Sabana Grande.

If you arrive in Caracas in doubt, ask a taxi driver to take you to Las Acacias in Sabana Grande, where you can choose a hotel from the very large number in that area. There are various grades all close together so you can walk from one to another until you find one suitable. (The weekend is not a very good time to look for a room.)

Hotel Reservations Anahovén, in Plaza Venezuela, Centro Capriles on the ground floor, charges US$1.20 to US$2.40. Telephone: 781-54 22.

Shopping   See H. Stern's jewellery stores at *Tamanaco* and *Hilton* hotels.

Restaurants   There is such a profusion of eating places in Caracas that we give the following general advice, with a mention of just a few places currently reported reliable, rather than attempt the impossible task of keeping up to date with all the changes. The cheapest foods is in *fuentes de soda* and cafés (steak, chips and salad, US$1.75). Food in bars may cost 50% more. Don't be shy about asking the price before you order in a bar as beer in one will cost three times as much as in another, and a modest portion of manchego cheese will cost more than a good steak. Food on display in a bar is free with your drink if they offer it as a *pasapalo* but will be charged for if offered as a *ración*. You can save on the service charge by eating at the bar and not at a table. Coffee in a café is at government-controlled price if taken at the counter, but not if served at a table. For dining out, there are three centres in the main body of the city. One is around Avenida Urdaneta (*El Parador* and the *Politena*). Another is around La Castellana and Plaza Altamira *(Le Grand Charolais)*. The third is Sabana Grande (*Al Vecchio Molino* in Francisco Solano). Guides to eating are published in the VAAUW Guide to Caracas and the magazine *Ve Venezuela*. Advertisements appear in the *Daily Journal* and the Yellow Pages of the telephone directory. Allow US$16 p.p. for dinner with a drink. Cheaper food at between US$2 and US$6 available at *Bar Amsterdam* (German/Dutch) in Avenida Sucre in Chacao; the *Fritz y Frantz Salchicha Grills* (German) in Los Ruices and El Rosal; *El Montañés* (Yugoslav) in El Rosal; *El Gato Pescador* (Hungarian) in Avenida Quito by Plaza Venezuela; *Urrutia* (Spanish) in Francisco Solano; *La Cita* (Spanish) by the Plaza Candelaria, south of Urdaneta; *Rincón de Baviera* (German), opposite Quinta Anauco and Museo de Arte Colonial; *Tokay* (Hungarian), Primera Calle south of Casanova; *Bar La Oficina* (Spanish), Avenida Francisco de Miranda, Chacao; *La Chuleta,* Francisco Solano, Sabana Grande, their fish is fresh and highly recommended; *El Buffet Vegetariano* in Avda. Los Jardines, La Florida; *Sorrento,* in Francisco Solano; and *El Mar* in Calle San Gerónimo in Sabana Grande. The best buy for lunch is a three-course meal called *cubierto,* which costs between US$2 and US$3; it is sometimes known as *menú ejecutivo.*

Best Night Clubs   Caracas is a swinging city by night, and there are many and varied discotheques and night clubs. Caraqueños dine at home around 2000, and in restaurants from 2100 to 2300, so night clubs don't usually come to life until after 2300, and then go on to all hours of the morning. Naiguatá *(Hotel Tamanaco),*expensive; best show in town. El Greco, Av. Principal de Macaracuay (also restaurant in same building). Hipocampo, Plaza Chacaíto. Mon Petit, Plaza Altamira Sur (there are many small clubs, restaurants and bars on Plaza Altamira Sur). The "Noches Caraqueñas" show put on by the *Hilton* each Monday evening makes a pleasant introduction to Caracas night-life.

Discotheques   Silver Ball, Centro Comercial, El Parque de Los Palos Grandes, and Blow-up, Plaza Altamira Sur, have been recommended; also Teorema, La Jungla, Eva, The Flower, and many others.

Sports and Recreations   Golf, tennis, riding, fishing, horse-racing every Saturday and Sunday at La Rinconada (a truly magnificent grandstand), motoring, bull fights (in season), baseball (October-January), football, swimming, etc. Horse-racing commences at 1300, admission price to grandstand US$1.10. Several buses go to La Rinconada. There are numerous cinemas; in those charging Bs.10 men are required to wear jackets (this may not however be the rule in all cases and it may be wise to enquire beforehand if a jacket is required) but not in the equally comfortable ones charging Bs.5. Parque del Este (Av. Fco. Miranda) has a planetarium. The recreational event of the year is the two days of Carnival. A cock-fighting tournament is held at San Juan de los Morros, 115 km. (2½ hours drive) from Caracas.

Clubs   The luxurious Country Club in the eastern part, at the foot of the mountains, has an 18-hole golf course. Other clubs are Valle Arriba, Caracas Sports Club, Altamira Tennis, Paraíso, and Caracas Theatre Club. Membership of the better clubs is by the purchase of a share, but this is only suitable for people spending several months in town because of red tape and expense. An exception is the sports club run by the *Tamanaco Hotel,* open to non-guests and suitable for people staying a short time. The Military Club (Círculo de las Fuerzas Armadas) is well worth seeing and, provided that there is no public function and that the visitors are soberly dressed, permission to view the premises, including a fine mural of the history of Venezuela, is often granted. Flying Club, at La Carlota, near *Tamanaco Hotel*.

Cultural Events There are frequent Sunday morning concerts in the Teatro Municipal, 1100, usually US$2.25. For details of these and other events, see the newspapers, *El Universal, El Nacional* and *Daily Journal*.

Addresses In the centre of Caracas, each street corner has a name, and addresses are generally given as, for example, "Santa Capilla a Mijares" (the address of Aeropostal Internacional cables office), rather than the official "Calle Norte 2, No. 26". Maps can be bought at Nuevo Circo bus station, but generally there is a shortage of good, reliable maps.

British Embassy, Consulate and British Council Edificio La Estancia, near *Tamanaco Hotel*. Also the Canadian Embassy and Consulate, the British Trade Promotion Centre, and the American Chamber of Commerce.

U.S.A. Embassy and Consulate Av. Francisco Miranda, La Floresta.

Centro Venezolano-Americano Av. Las Mercedes, good free library of books in English, and free concerts.

Anglican Church San Román section of Las Mercedes (near *Tamanaco*).

The United Christian Church, interdenominational, Av. Arboleda, El Bosque.

Instituto Cultural Venezolano-Británico, Quinta Coromoto, Av. San Gabriel, Urbanización Avila. Modest library for members.

Tourist Office Organización Nacional de Turismo. Main office in Plaza Venezuela, 7th Floor, near the *Hilton* hotel at the newly built Conference Centre. There are also smaller offices at the bus station, at Nuevo Circo and the Airport. The publication *Adónde Vamos,* free in hotels and shops, is good for information on tourist sights.

Local Tours are offered by: Agencia Candes, Edificio Roraima, Av. Francisco de Miranda; Tel.: 33-93-46. Agencia Wallis, Edificio Karam, Av. Urdaneta; Tel.: 81-56-81. Bolívar Tourism, Av. Baralt, Truco a Guanábana 1910-A; Tel.: 81-74-72. Club de Turismo Venezolano, Conde a Carmelitas No. 4; Tel.: 81-02-66. Exprinter, *Hotel Tamanaco;* Tel.: 91-45-55. Sightseeing de Venezuela, Apt. 2586; Tel.: 41-93-77; Novel Tours (Plaza Venezuela).

Passenger Services Starting from the bus station at Nuevo Circo, there are many buses, overcrowded in the rush hours (urban fare usually US$0.06). "Por Puestos", cars running on regular routes which charge US$0.12-0.23 per seat according to distance, and taxis which charge by distance from US$1-3. After midnight they charge anything they feel like, so bargain before you get into one. Tips are not necessary. Taxi fares from Maiquetía airport to Caracas are US$10-12, or US$2.25 por puesto; if you walk about 200 metres to the highway you can catch a Caracas or El Silencio por puesto for US$0.50 or a bus for US$0.35 will take you to the Nuevo Circo bus terminal (but they are often unwilling to stop if you have a suitcase). The tourist office at the airport is very helpful; hotel bookings can be made there. Buses from Nuevo Circo to the airport are marked Catia La Mar.

Self-drive cars (Hertz, Avis, Volkswagen) are available at Maiquetía Airport and in town. They are cheaper than guided excursions for less than full loads. Driver's licence from home state or country accepted. Typical rates: Avis; VW: US$10/day plus US$0.10 km. or US$14/day with unlimited mileage (VW without radio; US$12 with radio) a deposit of US$150 or so may be required. First tankful of gasoline free. The super-highway between Caracas and La Guaira costs US$0.85 toll (down only; coming up is free): the toll road to Valencia, US$1.25.

Aeropostal Cable Internacionales, Calle Norte 2, No. 26. Servicio de Tele-comunicaciones de Venezuela, Centro Simón Bolívar, Nivel Puente.

P.S.N.C. Agents Alcoa Steamship Co. Inc., Edificio Phelps (P.O. Box 226). Also agents of **Royal Mail Lines.**

Banks Banco Central; Banco de Venezuela; Banco Caracas; Banco La Guaira Internacional (in which Bank of London and Montreal is a minority shareholder); Banco Royal Venezolano; Banco Holandés Unido; Citibank; Banco Latino-americano de Venezuela; Banco Mercantil (affiliate of Chase Manhattan).

Long Distance Bus Lines operate from the Nuevo Circo bus station in the city centre. Aerobuses maintain regular services by air-conditioned coaches with reclining seats between Caracas and the main towns in eastern and western Venezuela, and also to Cúcuta, in Colombia. The fares of other good companies are a third less. Information at the Nuevo Circo. Fare to Maracaibo, US$8, 11 hours; to Cumaná, US$5.80; to Maturín, US$6, 8 hours (overnight). Buses to Mérida, Expresos Mérida, US$8, 12 hours, overnight to Mérida, US$7 *via* Panamericana or Los Llanos (12 hours) to San Cristóbal. To Ciudad Bolívar, US$7. Expresos Alianzas Caracas to Cúcuta, US$12.50, 8 hours, daily at 2100. Get passport exit stamp at San Antonio; bus will stop there. Always take identification when booking a long-distance journey.

Long-distance bus travel varies a lot in quality. Most companies are liable to run both luxury coaches and bone-shaking wrecks on the same route. However, buses from Caracas to Maracaibo, Mérida and San Cristóbal are usually in excellent condition; buses to Guayana are of poorer quality. Frequent service to Maracay, Valencia and Barquisimeto, but buses are often in bad shape; the Panamericana route is not recommended as it takes the old road where many accidents occur. The best lines are: to Maracaibo, Expresos del Lago; to Guayana, Providencial; to the eastern coast, Responsable. Buses stop frequently but there will not always be a toilet at the stop. Even when there is one, there may not always be toilet paper; take your own.

Approximate fares between towns: Valencia-Barquisimeto, US$2.75; Acarigua-Barinas, US$2.30; Barinas-Mérida, US$3.45; Mérida-Valera, US$3.45; Valera-Maracaibo, US$2.30; Maracaibo-Maicao (por puesto), US$3.45.

Excursions Up Mount Avila by cable railway for a stupendous view of the city and the coast; avoid weekends. The Caracas station, near Av. Andrés Bello, is at 995 metres; it can be reached by a bus marked "Puerta de Caracas-Simón Rodríguez". The top station is at 2,215 metres, cablecars leave every 65 minutes, journey takes 45 minutes. At the top is a restaurant and ice-rink, and from it you can walk to the 16-storey cylindrical *Hotel Humboldt,* one of the more sensational projects of the dictator Pérez Jiménez; no longer used as a hotel. Round trip fare: US$0.90. The cable railway can also be taken down to the coast at Macuto for US$2.30 (return). Tickets can be purchased at the top of the mountain, but if you buy round trip ticket (Caracas-Avila-Macuto-Avila-Caracas) you save money.

Good hiking. The three principal entrances to the Avila park are (a) 100 metres W of the restaurant *Tarzilandia* in Altamira (the easiest climb); (b) the car park on the N side of Av. Boyacá above Urbanización Los Chorros (where there is a crude map); and (c) the entrance to the Av. Boyacá from El Marqués (this route well signposted). Essential to carry your own drinking water. Serious danger of bush fires in the dry season January-April, so be careful with cigarettes, etc.

Maximum rates for excursions and transportation are published by the Ministry of Development's Tourist Dept., which solicits complaints in case of non-compliance. The official Tourist Office is situated at Centro Capriles, Plaza Venezuela, 7th floor. Typical tours for up to 5 persons: from Maiquetía Airport, *Macuto-Sheraton Hotel* or La Guaira passenger terminal to Caracas and back: full day US$20 or US$25, depending on whether a Spanish- or English-speaking guide is specified; half day (old or new Caracas) US$15 or US$18, respectively; to Maracay, US$30 or

US$35, respectively; to Valencia, US$35 or US$40. The list of published prices should be shown to the driver *before* he quotes the price. There is a bus which runs from Maiquetía Airport to the *Macuto-Sheraton* for US$0.12.

La Guaira, Venezuela's main port, is an artifical harbour which handles over a million tons of cargo a year. It has a fine passenger terminal to berth four liners simultaneously and excellent quays and warehouses with berths for about 16 cargo vessels. By the new road it is now 20 minutes to Caracas, but those with time and a car should take the narrow, winding, paved and much higher old road, which has much better scenery. Population: 20,275. Mean temperature: 29°C.

In the area are many seaside resorts and residential districts with a total population of about 70,000. There is a small museum (Museo Fundación John Boulton) in Calle Bolivar. Old La Guaira is worth visiting and a short bus ride up the hill to the lighthouse gives a fine view of the port and its surroundings. A pleasant drive can be made along the Avenida Soublette eastwards to Macuto, Laguna Beach, Caraballeda and so on to Los Caracas (45 km.), a Government holiday resort for workers. (All these places can be reached quite cheaply by bus.) Westward, on the way to Caracas, is the international airport of Maiquetía.

Restaurant Passenger Terminal.

Tourist Office At the terminal, open when ships are in.

The taxi fare, US$10 from the passenger terminal to Caracas, is strictly for the tourist. Walk to the end of the terminal and you can catch a "por puesto" to El Silencio, Caracas, at US$0.50 a seat (US$0.70 on Sundays and holidays), or a bus at US$0.37. But a taxi from El Silencio to a hotel costs about US$2-6. The prices at the International Passenger Terminal snack-bar are also strictly for the tourist.

Aeropostal Cables Internacionales Avenida Soublette 68.

P.S.N.C. and *Royal Mail Lines Agents* Alcoa Steamship Co., Inc., Apartados 138-9.

Macuto is a delightful seaside resort with a fine, tree-lined promenade, a splendid yacht marina and a "pigeon housing estate": a remarkable gesture for South America of kind intent towards the local fauna. The bus ride to Macuto from Caracas costs US$0.50 and takes 45 minutes. The taxi fare from the airport is US$3.50 and from Macuto to Caracas US$11.70.

Hotels On the coast, not too far from Maiquetía airport: *Macuto-Sheraton,* US$20-35 s, US$25-40 d, luxury. *Macuto,* at half the price, is clean, has swimming pool, and beach is only a 5 minute walk. *Hotel Riviera,* clean, good food, US$10.25 d, cookery (French), Boulevard Caraballeda. *Hotel Puerta del Sol,* US$7 d, bathless on weekdays, but friendly. Good restaurant: *Las Quince Letras,* Av. La Playa, good seafood. Recommended restaurant for paella is the *Solimar* on Urb. Caribe-Caraballeda.

Beaches Fishing (boats for hire at Macuto-Sheraton Marina) just N of La Guaira (mostly marlin) and the overnight trip to Los Roques Islands, directly N of La Guaira, is well worth it. These islands, the only atolls in the Atlantic-Caribbean, are truly beautiful, with long stretches of white beaches and mile upon mile of coral reef, perfect for underwater fishing or exploration. There is a small hotel. There are three beaches, with all facilities, along 27 km. of Caribbean seashore: one, Catia La Mar, W of La Guaira, and two—Macuto and Naiguatá—E of it. Catia La Mar is less recommended because it is rather industrial (*Hotel Bahía La Mar,* US$15, very comfortable and clean, food quite good, only problem is that it is under flight path for Maiquetía airport). New beaches are being prepared. The beaches themselves are enclosed by breakwaters as the seas and currents in the area can be very strong. From Caracas, by car, it takes 30 minutes to the 1st, 45 minutes to the 2nd, and 1 hour to the 3rd. Far lovelier beaches are three or four hours by car from Caracas: Cata (see page 714) and Ocumare de la Costa (N of Maraca, past Rancho Grande and through the lovely rain forests of Henri Pittier National Park), Chichiriviche (W of Puerto Cabello, see page 714) and several others in the Puerto Cabello area; also to the W of Macuto. These more distant beaches are recommended, but a day trip is tiring because of traffic jams particularly when returning to Caracas. A small beach closer to Caracas is Oricao, west of La Guaira, recommended as being unspoilt, nearly empty on weekdays and safe for swimming. Suitable for day trip.

Further afield, in **San Francisco de Yare**, a celebration is held on Corpus Christi day; the dance before the church of the enormously masked red devils, and of most of the villagers. It lasts the whole day. Yare is about 90 km. from Caracas; the road to it is through Petare and down the Río Guaira as far as Santa Teresa, and then up the Río Tuy. From Santa Teresa a detour may be made to the beautiful and little frequented Guatopo National Park (see below) on the road to Altagracia de Orituco, but you must return to Santa Teresa to continue your journey to Yare. A trip to Cúcuta takes 12 hours each way (US$8) while an interesting trip is the bus journey to Los Caracas via Guaira (US$0.30) for a long scenic ride.

At the Parque Guatopo two picnic places have been arranged at the far end around a river and by a lagoon, with piped drinking water. There are also various convenient places to picnic on the route through the forest, though no special arrangements have been made. Take insect repellent. To stay the night in the park a permit must be obtained.

Another good excursion is into the mountains to **Colonia Tovar** (1,890 metres), a village so isolated that its blond, blue-eyed people still speak the Black Forest German of their ancestors who settled there in 1843, bringing a printing press, a brick kiln and their tools. They now grow coffee, garlic, rhubarb and flowers for the Caracas market. See their Scandinavian-style ceramics. (We have however received several adverse comments on high prices and overcrowding from tourists.) The hour and a half drive from Caracas is delightful. Along the road are small parks where picnic lunch can be taken, but at weekends there are long traffic queues and you have to be early just to find a roadside spot to picnic.

The road to Colonia Tovar passes through **El Junquito**, a picturesque small town with roadside stands selling fruit and barbecued meat. You see Caracas from one side of the road, the Caribbean from the other. A dirt road with beautiful views winds down the mountain to the sea and back to Maiquetía. Another road, 34 km. (18 not paved), leads through glorious mountain scenery from Colonia Tovar to La Victoria on the Caracas-Valencia highway.

Taxi fare for the round trip from Caracas (driver will wait) is about US$23. A little old bus leaves Plaza Catia, Caracas, each day except Thursday at 0800 (be there early for seat), fare US$1.40 one way. Bus leaves Colonia Tovar for Caracas 1500.

Hotels *Bergland*, US$13 s; *Selva Negra*, US$15 p.p., including three tremendous meals; *Edelweiss; Freiburg; Kaiserstuhl; Alta Baviera*. All serve German-style food in good restaurants.

West from Caracas

The Pan-American Highway, which links Caracas by road with the other capitals of South America, follows closely the route of Gómez's Great Andean Highway as far as Lake Maracaibo, though many sections have been widened and straightened. On it, or by it, all the important towns in Western Venezuela can be reached. It is, therefore, proposed to follow this route in some detail.

The Pan-American Highway can be reached from the Caracas central autopista. At the start, we have the choice of a direct toll motorway to Valencia (with exit to Maracay), or the old road called, familiarly, "La Panamericana" and known for its dangerous corners. It leaves La Rinconada race course to its left, and climbs steadily but easily towards

Los Teques, capital of Miranda state (pop.: 42,000, *Hotel Los Alpes,* very good). This passes on its way the park of Las Colinas de Carrizal (aquarium of Venezuelan fish, a collection of Venezuelan birds, and pleasant paths). Twenty-four km. beyond Los Teques on the way down into the fertile valleys of Aragua, we can either join the Caracas to Valencia tollway or take the older road through several attractive little towns such as La Victoria, from which there is a hair-raising but immensely beautiful side road to Colonia Tovar (see page 712). The Quinta de Bolívar is at San Mateo, between La Victoria and Maracay. A little nearer Maracay, a good road leads off to San Juan de Los Morros where a cock-fighting tournament is held each year (new *motel*). It has natural hot springs. The road divides later: S to Guárico dam, the llanos and S. Fernando de Apure, and E to Valle de la Pascua *(Hotel Venzuela)* and El Tigre.

The old Pan-American Highway to Maracay should be taken at least once, for views and local colour, but winding up and down the mountains behind slow, smelly trucks is not excessively pleasurable. The toll road also offers good views.

The Pan-American avoids city centres, so all that is seen of Maracay, Valencia and Barquisimeto are factories plus the huge concrete Barquisimeto Fourth Centenary Monument. As far as Valencia, the countryside is speckled with factories, but is less urban from there to Barquisimeto—pleasant green hills with orange sellers. Beyond Barquisimeto there are mountains like slag heaps, peopled by goats and hawkers of cheese, guitars and hammocks, until we reach the green of the Andes. When entering Valencia, there are girls selling sweet rusks called panelas.

Maracay, capital of Aragua State, has a population of 260,000, and is at an altitude of 455 metres. In its heyday it was the playground of General Gómez after he had cornered the cattle industry, and some of his most fantastic whims are still there for all to see; the previous *Hotel Jardín* with its beautiful park and fountain, built for his revels; the unfinished opera house opposite; his modest little house for personal use, and the bull ring, an exact replica of the one at Seville. The Gómez mausoleum, built in his honour, has a huge triumphal arch. Maracay is the centre of an important agricultural zone, and the school and experimental stations of the Ministry of Agriculture are worth visiting; it is also important industrially and militarily. *Museo Aeronáutico,* open weekends only, fine collection of old aircraft.

Hotels   *Maracay; Micotti; San Luis,* off the main shopping street, US$7 d, clean, showers, friendly; *Bermúdez; Wadimis,* US$12 d. bath, friendly, good restaurant at reasonable prices.

Restaurants   *El Dragón de Plata; Paella Valenciana; Italo.* Recommended is *Pipo's* at El Castaño, located in the hills above *Hotel Maracay;* "parrillas" are a house speciality.

Industries   Textiles, sugar, paper, rayon, rubber, animal foodstuffs, and cement.

Excursions   Lake Valencia; to Las Delicias, Gómez's country house, where he died, with its adjoining zoo. The huge 100,000-hectare Rancho Grande Park stretches from 24 km. N of Maracay to the Caribbean on both sides of the Andes. A road runs from Maracay over the 1,130-metre high Portachuelo Pass, guarded by twin peaks, to three places by the sea: **Ocumare de la Costa**, 37 km. from Maracay; the naval base of Turiamo; and **Cata** (restaurant/hotel/cabins), the most beautiful beach in Venezuela. The road was built by Gómez as an escape route if things grew too hot for him. Near the pass is Rancho Grande, the uncompleted palace Gómez was building when he died; it is in the shape of a question mark and is worth visiting. It houses a natural history museum, which has been closed to the public for some time and fallen into a dilapidated state (check). A taxi can be hired at Maracay for a day's outing in the park for about US$20.

Fifty km. to the west of Maracay the road reaches, through low hills thickly planted with citrus, coffee and sugar,

Valencia (population, about 380,000), the capital of Carabobo State. It stands on the W bank of the Cabriales river, 5 km. before it empties into Lake Valencia. It is the third largest city in the republic, the centre of its most developed agricultural region, and the most industrialised. Annual mean temperature 24°C; altitude 490 metres; rainfall, 914 mm. a year. The atmosphere of the more ancient and narrower streets is that of old Spain. The interesting 18th century Cathedral is on the central Plaza Bolívar. See also the Capitol, the Municipal Theatre, the old Carabobo University building and the shapely new bull ring, which holds the world record for takings at a single corrida. Many Europeans and Americans live in Valencia, which has an International School and is famous for its oranges. There is a nice country club.

Hotels   *Excelsior; "400"* (good food); *Francia; Carabobo; Victoria; Gran Hotel; Hotel le Paris* (expensive); *Valencia Intercontinental,* new, US$3.75 s; *Oasis-Oriental,* US$5.80 d.

Restaurants   *Brahman Grill,* excellent barbecues; *El Coche* (good local food).

Excursions   To the monument on the battlefield of Carabobo, southwards, to see the battle story told in bronze: the British soldiers who helped Bolívar are particularly realistic. Buses to the battlefield leave from *La Sanidad* (Health Centre), US$0.12, one hour.

British Vice-Consul (Hon.): Corporación Mercantil Venezolana, Av. 100, 93-7.

The Caracas-Valencia motorway continues down the mountains to Puerto Cabello, past Las Trincheras, a decaying spa with radio-active mud; it reaches the sea near El Palito (refinery and pier). Here we turn right to Puerto Cabello.

Puerto Cabello, 96 km. W of La Guaira, is the natural entry by road, over a low pass, of the raw materials for Valencia's industries; it is in itself a large industrial centre turning out petrochemicals, soap, vegetable oils, assembled cars and tractors. Valencia itself is 55 km. away by modern highway. This, the second most important Venezuelan port, has an excellent harbour with a lighthouse, and a shipyard with dry dock. Average temperature, 28°C; population, 70,000. A standard-gauge 175-km. railway runs to Barquisimeto.

Hotel *Riviera,* with good restaurant. Other good restaurants are *El Parque, Mar y Sol* and *San Antonio del Mar.* Best hotels near are the *Cumboto, La Hacienda* (good German food), and the hotels of Palma Sola (see below).

Royal Mail Lines Agents Alcoa Steamship Co., Inc., Apartado 50.

About half an hour E of Puerto Cabello over a rough road is a beautiful horseshoe-shaped beach shaded by palms called La Bahía. It is well worth the drive, has a refreshment stand, changing rooms, toilet facilities and life guards, but take your own lunch. You can buy raw oysters from little boys who open them for you and douse them with lemon juice.

Puerto Cabello has another beach, Quizandal, with a coral reef, near the naval base. (Taxi fare, US$3.50, but you may find it hard to get one on the way back.) The nearby Country Club also has a beach with coral reefs within reach by boat. There are two Spanish forts at Puerto Cabello, one on the water, the other on a hill over the city. The fort on the water can be reached by a small ferry boat, but the one on the hill is in a military zone and it is difficult to get permission to enter.

N.B. The beach to the W of Puerto Cabello is not so attractive; be careful of going beyond the bathing area as the beach is notorious for armed robbery.

Twenty-four km. W of Puerto Cabello, at the junction of the Pan-American and the road to Tucacas, is **Morón,** where the giant government petrochemical plant produces fertilizers, refrigerants and ammonia sulphate.

Quite near Morón is the lovely beach of **Palma Sola,** 16 km. long and deserted save at Easter time when Venezuelans camp out there in crowds. The water is a trifle dangerous but the sands and palms are superb. There are two motels, two restaurants and changing rooms. A road has been built from Morón to Coro *via* Tucacas, an hour from Puerto Cabello. **Tucacas** is a small, dirty town of wooden shacks where bananas and other fruit are loaded for Curaçao and Aruba. But offshore are hundreds of coral reefs, palm-studded islets, small cosy beaches and calm water for water-skiing and skin diving. Venezuelan skin-diving clubs come here for their contests. This is one of the two main fishing grounds of Venezuela; the other is off Puerto La Cruz. The men of Tucacas have boats for hire at US$4.50 a day. A few km. beyond, towards Coro, is the favourite beach resort of **Chichiriviche,** which has numerous islands and coral reefs. It is possible to hire a boat to any one of the offshore islands for US$18 return; recommended for a weekend away from Caracas. Hermit crabs and lizards are found on the islands. Nearby is a vast nesting area for scarlet ibis, flamingoes and herons.

From Tucacas it is 177 km. to **Coro** (population 44,757), capital of the state of Falcón—a hot desert town, with some interesting colonial buildings, surrounded by sand dunes. There is an interesting xerophytic garden open to the public. At Punta Cumarebo, just before Coro, is a clean cheap hotel, with beach. From Coro, there is a fine but uninteresting road to Maracaibo and another paved road along the narrow strip of land leading to the Paraguaná Peninsula, along whose beaches men fish, 15 to 20 a net. Airport has a direct service to Caracas and Las Piedras. Bus from Coro to Caracas US$3.75.

Hotels at Coro *Miranda* (best); *Venecia,* US$7 s, US$10 d (recommended); *Capri* (friendly). The *Bella Napoli* is good at US$3 but the *Italia* is cheaper.

The Paraguaná Peninsula is connected by pipelines with the oilfields of Lake Maracaibo. The Maravén (ex-Shell) and Lagovén (ex-Esso) groups have refineries, the former at Cardón, and the latter at Amuay. The airport, which has services to Maracaibo (30 min.), Coro and Maiquetía, is known as Las Piedras, the town itself as Punto Fijo (Hotels: *Victoria,* 154 Garcés, friendly and reasonably priced; *del Este, Miami, Caribe).* Eventually, all four places will merge into one large town. There is a public seaport, Las Piedras-Paraguaná, between Amuay and Cardón, which are oil ports. This port also serves the town of Coro.

There is now a ferry boat service (Ferrys del Caribe) from La Vela de Coro and Punto Fijo to Aruba and Curaçao. The schedules are continually being changed, so apply to the company's offices. Buy tickets on morning of departure. The journey to both Aruba and Curaçao usually takes four hours, but the bureaucracy can lengthen this period to 8-12 hours. Fare to Curaçao US$35 return. It is necessary to have a ticket out of Curaçao before entering. No amenities at ferry terminal or on the boat. Take food and drinks with you. The tourist office can provide more information. The office for the boat is Oficina de Caderco, Calle Zamora (Tel.: 3522); there are also offices in Caracas. Por puesto between La Vela de Coro and Coro itself costs US$2 per seat.

The Segovia Highlands, lying N of Barquisimeto, suffer from droughts, and are only sparsely settled where the river valleys remain wet. From Morón the Pan-American Highway strikes up into the hills, reaching 550 metres at **San Felipe** (population 29,274), capital of Yaracuy state, which produces sugar, cacao, cotton, maize, fruits, rice and hides (Hotel: *Venezuela).*

If you do not want to go to Puerto Cabello and the coast, a newer section of the Pan-American Highway from Valencia *via* Carabobo to just beyond San Felipe is 56 km. shorter.

Barquisimeto, capital of Lara state, has a population of 340,000. Altitude 565 metres, mean temperature 25°C. It stands on one of the alluvial fans so prominent in the Andes, and deals largely in the produce of the area: sugar, coffee, cacao, cereals and cattle. It manufactures biscuits and textiles, especially sacking. The city, with one foot as it were in the llanos, is the gateway to and the collecting point of the semi-barren Segovia Highlands to the N. It is Venezuela's fourth largest city, and has the University of Lara. The Cathedral, an ultramodern structure of free-form concrete and glass, is very interesting. There is a road from Barquisimeto to Acarigua on the alternative route from Caracas to Mérida (see page 724). Railway to Puerto Cabello, and an airport. (No bus from airport, only taxis. There is a single bus terminal on the edge of the city.) Bus to Mérida, only one a day, leaves at 0315, 8 hours *via* Agua Viva and El Vigia, US$6.

Hotels *Hostería El Obelisco,* American motel-style, swimming pool, a/c rooms, best; *Hotel Barquisimeto,* good (swimming pool and disco, clean, comfortable and helpful; long way from city centre); *Gran Hotel* (US$6 s), swimming pool; *Rex; Comercio* (US$3.40 s); *Yacambú; Príncipe* (reservations advisable), Carrera 19 y Calle 23 in centre, US$10.50 s, US$16.50 d; *Hotel Miami* (US$18.80, 4-bed room) no a/c, private bath.

Eating Places Terminal Vargas and railway station restaurant, excellent.

About 24 km. SW of Barquisimeto is the small town of **Quibor.** Turn right a few km. from Quibor to get to a tiny rancho in the village of El Tintoreto where "blankets" are made from local wool. These are in bright coloured stripes or plaids and serve well as colourful rugs, but not as what we call blankets. The single blanket can be bought at Quibor for

US$9-12 and the double size for US$18-21. You won't get more than US$1 or so off by bargaining. They are well worth the price.

Quíbor has a new tourist attraction: 2,000-year-old skeletons. Locals sidle up and offer "pre-historic" bone skeletons and earthenware pots. A pot or necklace fetches US$10.

Some 75 km. past Barquisimeto the Lara-Zulia motorway to Maracaibo forks off to the right (Caracas-Maracaibo 660 km.), through Carora (*Motel* and *Restaurant Mara*, reasonable; a new hostería nearby, with a very good restaurant, offers greater comfort at higher prices).

The **Lowlands of Maracaibo,** lying in the encircling arms of the mountains, are more or less windless, extremely hot, and excessively humid. Average annual temperature is higher than anywhere else in Latin America. Rainfall steadily decreases from the foothills of the Sierra Nevada to the coast; this is expressed, in terms of vegetation, in the merging of tropical forest into semi-deciduous forest, and then into scrub forest as it nears the coast.

In these lowlands is the semi-salt Lake Maracaibo, of about 12,800 square km., 155 km. long and in places over 120 km. wide. It is joined to the sea by a waterway, 3 to 11 km. wide and 55 km. long, at the mouth of which is the bar of Maracaibo. A 12-metre channel has been cut across the Maracaibo Bar, but dry-cargo vessels, unless they first discharge to lighters, are still limited by the depth, a maximum of 7.3 metres alongside the quay in Maracaibo port.

The area was once poor enough, dependent on fishing and the carriage of coffee across the lake from the Sierra. Since the discovery there of one of the world's greatest oil fields in 1917, there has been a magical transformation, both in appearance (a forest of oil derricks covers the shore swamps and some of the lake), and in prosperity. The little town of Maracaibo, which had 18,000 people in 1918, is now a large modern city. Into it the Lara-Zulia motorway enters by the beautiful 8-km. long General Rafael Urdaneta bridge, which has the longest pre-stressed concrete span in the world.

Maracaibo, on the north-western shore of Lake Maracaibo, capital of the State of Zulia, is 582 km. by sea from La Guaira. It exports coffee from the Sierra Nevada de Mérida and the Colombian border, and shrimps to the U.S.A., but the key to its great population and importance is oil: 70% of Venezuela's output comes from the Lake area. Maracaibo, which is also becoming a very important cattle and dairy region, is 55 minutes by jet from Caracas. It is the country's second largest city. Population: 690,000. The airport is at La Chinita; there is no bus service (only taxis) into town. The bus terminal is on the edge of the city.

The climate is damp and hot, but healthy. The hottest months are July, August and September, but there is usually a sea breeze from 1500 until morning. The mean temperature of 28°C and average humidity of 78% are most felt at sea level. The new part of the city round Bella Vista and towards the University, with wide avenues and modern business and private buildings, is in vivid contrast with the old town near the docks; this, with narrow streets and colonial style adobe houses, is hardly changed from the last century. The scenery around Maracaibo is, in general, not very attractive. A trip across the lake through the oil derricks is science fiction at its most weird, but it is difficult to organise as the oilfields are a long way from Maracaibo. The zone begins at Cabimas on the E shore of the lake and you can get a good view of the oil rigs from there and from other towns further down, such as Lagunillas.

From the port you can take a ferry to Altagracia for US$0.70, 25 minutes, and either return the same way or take a microbus for US$0.50, travelling through exotic scenery for almost an hour and crossing the impressive General Urdaneta bridge.

Hotels *Hotel del Lago Intercontinental* (US$15-25 without meals, non-residents can use the pool for US$1.60); *Granada* (US$16, with meals); *Shamrock; Roma*, US$8, a/c, popular with Italians, accommodation poor but food is very good; *Kristof*, nice, on Av. Santa Rita (US$24 d); *Hotel Londres*, Calle 94, Av. 6, US$5.50 d, with bath; *Carrizal; San José; Dancoli; Falcón; Venecia; River; Vesuvio; Caribe*, US$11.60 d, a/c and shower; *Palace*, US$12.50 d, a/c.

Restaurants *El Chicote* (sea food), Av. Bellavista, corner with Calle 70; *Rincón Boricua*, Av. 23, between Calles 66 and 67 (good meat); *El Pozo* (Spanish dishes); *El Pescadito* (Av. 2, No. 76-A-209), by lakeside, with agreeable breeze; *Mi Vacita; Central Lunch*, Calle 98, Chinese run, good helpings, cheap for Maracaibo, open when other places are shut.

Communications are by air with airports of Maiquetia, Mérida, Valera, Barquisimeto, Las Piedras (for Amuay and Cardón) and other Venezuelan towns. Other air lines connect Maracaibo with Barranquilla, Curaçao, Trinidad, Miami, New York and Europe. No exchange facilities at airport, no buses, only taxis with set fare of US$5.75. There are several fast and comfortable buses daily to Valencia (US$5.75 by Expresos del Lago), and Caracas (US$7). The bus terminal is 1 km. S of the old town. Bus lines, other than Aerobuses de Venezuela, recommended are "Occidente" and "Alianza" whose fares are cheaper. Bus to Maicao, at nearest Colombian border point (US$0.60); por puesto to Mérida, 7 hours (US$11). It is often possible to find taxis both to Caracas and the Andes towns, which charge so much per person. Por puesto to Caracas costs US$15. The last bus for Caracas leaves at 2300.

Royal Mail Agents Alcoa Steamship Co., Inc., Edificio Banco Holandés Unido, Apartado 633.

Aeropostal Cables Internacionales, Calle 98, 2-32. Servicio de Telecommunicaciones de Venezuela, Calle 99, Antes Comercio Esquina, Av. 3, Edición Correos.

Banks Banco de Venezuela; Banco Comercial de Maracaibo; Banco de Maracaibo; Banco Royal Venezolano; Banco Holandés Unido; Banco Latinoamericano de Venezuela; Citibank.

British Vice-Consul (Hon.): Apartado 285, Edificio Gòmez Castro, Av. El Milagro.

On the W side of the lake, between the rivers Santa Ana and Catatumbo, a large area of swampland is crossed by the road to La Fria. The swamp is inhabited by the Motilones, who, until 1960, refused to have dealings either with white men or other Indians. The southern border of the Motilones' territory, the River Catatumbo, is famed for its almost nightly display of lightning for which there is, as yet, no accepted explanation and which caused it to be known in the old days as "The Lighthouse of Maracaibo". There are various missions you can visit, and the easiest is Los Angeles del Tocuco, 51 km. from Machiques, where they welcome visitors but it helps to take a present, such as dried milk. There is a priest at the mission who was attacked, and they now preserve the arrow head they took from his body in their museum. Machiques is on a fast road from San Cristóbal *via* La Fria to Maracaibo, and has the good *Motel Tukuko*, US$17.50 d and US$12.80 s.

The best sightseeing trip is north about 1 hour to the Río Limón (it has another local name). Take a bus (US$0.25) to El Mojàn, riding with the Guajira Indians as they return to their homes on the peninsula. Another bus or taxi (US$1.20) can be taken to the river. Alternatively, take a Sinamaica bus from the new station, US$1, then a colectivo to a small port on the lagoon called Cuervaito, US$0.20. Hire a boat (bargaining recommended as the price varies from US$6 to US$9), and go up the river for an hour to see families still living in houses made of woven reed mats built on stilts: the only place where they can be seen. By crossing the bridge over the river you come, in the north, to a paved road that leads to Riohacha, in Colombia, where border formalities are quick and informal, a recommended route, but the Colombian border town, Maicao, has a rather unsavoury reputation. best not to stop there. Along the way you see Guajira Indians, the men with bare legs, on horseback; the women with long, black, tent-shaped dresses and painted faces, wearing the sandals with big wool pom-poms which they make and sell for US$2, as against the US$7-10 in the tourist shops. The men do nothing: women do all the work, tending sheep and goats, selling slippers and raising very little on the dry, hot, scrubby Guajira Peninsula. If you fail to do the trip, you can see these Indians in the Ziruma district of Maracaibo. There is an interesting Guajira market at Los Filuos, a mile beyond Paraguaipoa.

Those who wish to go on to the Sierra Nevada de Mérida or the State of Trujillo should return over the lake and turn sharp right through Cabimas, Lagunillas, Bachaquero and Mene Grande, all unattractive petroleum towns, to rejoin the Pan-American Highway at Agua Viva. For the Colombian frontier or San Cristóbal we follow the Pan-American Highway.

The Pan-American Highway from Agua Viva is a splendid asphalt speed track, but devoid of much scenic or historic attraction. It runs along the foot of the Andes through rolling country planted with sugar or bananas, or park-like cattle land. At Sabana de Mendoza, 24 km. S of Agua Viva, is a possible stopover—*Hotel Panamérica* (good; air-conditioned). This road has plenty of restaurants, hotels and filling-stations, especially at Caja Seca and El Vigía, both rather new and raw looking towns. At El Vigía, where the road from Mérida to Santa Bárbara (Zulia) crosses it, there is a fine bridge over 1 km. long over the river Chama. Santa Bárbara (56 km. NW) is a milk, meat and plantain producing centre, with air and boat services to Maracaibo and an important annual cattle show.

From El Vigía, the road continues fairly flat until La Fría, with a large natural-gas fuelled power station, where it is joined by the road along the west side of Lake Maracaibo and begins to climb to San Cristóbal.

The **Sierra Nevada de Mérida**, running from S of Maracaibo to the Colombian frontier, is the only range in the Venezuelan Highlands where snow lies permanently on the higher peaks. Near Mérida itself there are five such snow caps of almost 5,000 metres. Several basins lying between the mountains are actively cultivated.

The inhabitants are concentrated mainly in valleys and basins at between 800 and 1,300 metres above sea level. The three towns of Mérida, Valera and San Cristóbal are in this zone. The high moorlands, or *páramos*, are almost deserted.

The Sierra is peculiar in that it has two distinct rainy and dry seasons in the year. Two crops of the staple food, maize, can be harvested up to an elevation of about 2,000 metres.

Those who wish to visit the Sierra Nevada should turn left at Agua Viva to **Valera**, the most important town in the state of Trujillo, with a population of 44,820 and an airport with connections to Barquisimeto, Caracas and Maracaibo. The bus terminal is on the edge of the town.

Hotels *Ambassador* (US$12.50 d, a/c and bath); *Motel Valera; Hotel Martini* (US$7 d); *Hotel Haack* (US$3.75, with private cold shower); *Hotel Victoria*, US$7 d, with bath, basic, noisy.

From Valera a visit can be made to the state capital, **Trujillo** (19,258 people; *Hotel Trujillo; Hotel Cabimbu*), at 805 metres; a por puesto from Valera costs US$1. This politically important town is gradually losing ground commercially to Valera. Trujillo runs up and down hill. At the top, across from the university, is a lovely park with waterfalls and paths. The Centro de Historia de Trujillo is a restored Colonial house, now a museum. Bolívar lived there and signed the "proclamation of war to the death" in the house.

From Trujillo there is a high, winding, spectacular paved road to **Boconó**, a town built on steep mountain sides with a nice German hotel, the *Steinberg*, as well as another hotel, the *Vega El Río*. From there you can continue down to Guanare in the llanos.

We are now in the Sierra Nevada de Mérida, the Western Andes of Venezuela. The people are friendly, and very colourful in their red and navy blue ruanas. Forty km. beyond Trujillo we come to **Timotes** (hotels: *Truchas, Aliso*), a mountainous little place set high in the cold grain zone. Near Timotes are La Mesa *(Hotel Tibisay)* and La Puerta (*Guadalupe,* a fine hotel), both places hill resorts for Maracaibo and district. The road now climbs steadily by tortuous loops through increasingly wild and more and more barren and rugged country, past the tree line and on through the windy pass of Pico del Aguila (4,115 metres). This is the way Bolívar went when crossing the Andes to liberate Colombia, and on the peak is the statue of an eagle. In the pass is the very pleasant little *Hotel Páramo* in chalet style. The road then dips rapidly through **Apartaderos;** over the centuries the Indians have piled up stones from the rocky mountainside into fences and houses, hence the name. They grow wheat, plough with oxen, plant and thresh by hand. On Sunday they all stand and watch the tourists; the children sell flowers and fat puppies called Mucuchíes (a variant of the Grand Pyrenée) after a near-by town. Only 3 km. from Apartaderos is Laguna Mucubají, and a 40-minute walk takes you to Laguna Negra for trout fishing. Guides can be found at Laguna Mucubají or at the hotels in Santo Domingo (its *Hotel Moruco* is very good). This quaint little hamlet lies a few km. away on the road which leads off to Barinas in the Llanos and then on to Valencia; between Santo Domingo and Laguna Mucubají is the *Hotel Los Frailes,* said to be one of the best in Venezuela. Book well ahead.

From Apartaderos the road to Mérida leads down to **Mucuchíes**, where there is a trout farm. We descend through striated zones of timber, grain, coffee and tropical products to reach level land at last and the city of Mérida. All through the mountain land we have been travelling you see a plant with curious felt-like leaves of pale grey-green. This is the *frailejón* (or great friar) which blooms with yellow flowers from October to December.

The patron saint of Mucuchíes is San Benito; his festival is on December 29 and is celebrated by participants wearing flower-decorated hats and firing blunderbusses continuously.

Mérida (173 km. from Valera and 674 km. from Caracas) founded 1558 by Captain Juan Rodríguez Suárez and named Santiago de los Caballeros de Mérida. It is the capital of Mérida State. Its white towers have long been visible from the road, and it stands at 1,640 metres (mean temperature 19°C) on an alluvial terrace 15 km. long, 2½ km. wide, surrounded by cliffs and plantations and within sight of Pico Bolívar, the highest in Venezuela (5,007 metres), crowned with a bust of Bolívar. Mérida has grace and charm, and still retains some Colonial buildings which contrast with the new wide avenues and fine modern buildings, such as those of the University of the Andes (founded 1785). The main square with rebuilt Cathedral is pleasant, but is no longer Colonial. Its fiesta is the week of December 8; hotels will only let for the whole week. It is also well known for its Feria del Sol, held on the week preceding Ash Wednesday. Population: 90,000, including 22,000 students.

The city is famous for its candied fruits, and you can buy the typical red and navy blue wool ruana worn by the Venezuelan mountain Indians. (The wool is imported, however.) Mérida is also well known for its many parks (twenty-one); the Parque de las Cinco Repúblicas has the first monument in the world to Bolívar (1842) and the park contains each of the five countries he liberated; the Parque Los Chorros de Milla has a good zoo in a beautiful hilly setting with a waterfall; the Parque La Isla is an attractive complex containing the Museum of Colonial Art, basketball and tennis courts, an amphitheatre and fountains; Jardín Acuario is an exhibition centre, with an aquarium, mainly devoted to the way of life and the crafts of the Andean peasants, admission US$0.25. There is fishing and mountaineering in the neighbouring Sierra Nevada. The world's highest cable railway now runs to Pico Espejo (4,765 metres) in four stages. The trip up and down takes 3 hours and costs US$6; Thurs. half price and therefore crowded, student cards cheaper; check beforehand that the cable railway is operating; it normally runs Wed.-Sun. and holidays, starting up at 0800, last trip up at 1200, last trip down at 1400. This is a "must", best done early in the morning, before the clouds spoil the view, and from November to June. (In the summer the top with its statue to Our Lady of the Snows, is clouded and covered with snow and there is no view.) The glacier on Pico Bolívar can be seen clearly; so can Picos Humboldt and Bonpland, forming the Corona, and to the E, on a clear day, the blue haze of the llanos. Electric storms in the mountains are not uncommon. If the peak is slightly clouded when you start, stop at the Redonda station (4,045 metres) the last station but one. From this station there is a path (3 hours' walking) to Los Nevados, highest village in Venezuela (3,830 metres), a pretty little place but no restaurant. It is possible to get a room to stay overnight. A guide charges US$2.50. There is also an ice cave with dazzling crystal ice stalactites two hours' rough walk from the last station. Only those in good heart can make this high trip. The Andean Club in Mérida organises trips to the top. The cable railway is again in service after being closed for two years; travellers should book in advance for "white" tickets as there is now a quota of 200 people per hour. In the station in Mérida one can hire warm jackets, gloves and caps. At Aguada station you can see the *frailejón* plant (see page 720).

Note The managers of the Pico Espejo cable railway will not let you walk in the mountains unless you sign a responsibility discharge. Permission is also needed from the Guardia Civil.

Air Services Airport is on the main highway, buses into town US$0.70. LAV and Avensa. To Caracas, 1¼ hours, US$25, San Antonio, US$10.

Hotels *Prado Río,* main building and individual cabins, US$18 s; *Belensate,* US$14 s; *La Sierra,* US$6 s; *Luxemburgo,* US$5 s; *Tinjaca,* US$4 s; *Chama,* US$8 s, 12 d, private bath; *Hotel Mucubají,* Av. Universidad, US$13 d, clean and pleasant, dinner US$3.50, Tel.: 25.070; *Budapest; Frailejones,* Av. Independencia 3, US$12 d, with bath; *Hotel Bologna,* near the Aeropostal office; *Gran Balcón* (US$10 s, US$13 d); *Hotel Sierra,* US$13 d (opposite old university); *Hotel Santiago de los Caballeros,* clean, central (US$14 d); *Hotel Llanero,* US$4.50 d, basic, on Avenida Obispo Lora; *Hotel Italia,* Calle 19 y Avenida 3, US$4.65 d, hot water, clean. It is difficult to get rooms during school holidays. Recommended to book in advance.

Restaurants *Casa Vieja,* decorated as 19th-century Andean home, good food and moderately priced; good food at *Chama Hotel; Chipen Restaurant,* good cheap food; *La Paellera,* good food, reasonable prices; *El Gaucho Martín,* Argentine food; *Hotel Europa* for cheap, good meals.

Museum Colonial Art Museum and Museum of Modern Art (open Tues.-Fri., 0900-1200, 1500-1800, Sat. 1500-1800, Sun. 1000-1200, 1500-1800).

Bullfights Mérida is a famous centre.

Bus To Caracas, US$7 (16 hours), por puesto US$14; daily por puesto service to Maracaibo, US$11, by Unión de Conductores, Tel.: 24.364. Buses leave Caracas for Mérida at 1800 and 2100 hours only. Por puesto from Los Charros, US$6.50; to San Cristóbal, US$7, 4 hours, leaving 0400 onwards. No buses.

Shopping Casa de las Artesanías sells local crafts, reasonable prices, recommended.

Tourist Offices On the highway at the north and south entrances to the city.

Excursions Visits to other resorts near Mérida: to Laguna de Mucubají and then with a guide to Laguna Negra for trout fishing, or to Pico del Águila (see page 720). To **San Javier del Valle,** a retreat centre, built 1952 in memory of 27 pupils who died in a plane crash in 1950. Lovely grounds, chapel with mahogany wood carving, worth a visit (open daily 1100 to 1230. Por puesto from Mérida US$0.25). To Plaza Beethoven where a different melody of Beethoven's works is chimed every hour. The Museo de Arte Moderno on the same square has a nice small collection with paintings by local artists. *Hotel Valle Grande,* good, nearby, chalets for 5 or 6 people. Through splendid scenery to dreary Lagunilla, with pleasant lakeside restaurant, but the lake is tiny and drying up. Thirty minutes beyond Lagunilla lies the little church of Estanques (seldom open except on Christmas Day) with a stupendous glittering gold Colonial altar. To Jají, by por puesto (US$1), famous for its colonial architecture. Tourists can get advice from the Club Andino (P.O. Box 66) or Casa del Turista, La Compalla; Tel.: 3391. Recommended hotel and restaurant *Posada de Jají* (US$12 s), good food.

The road passes on through the moderately fruitful Chama valley to Lagunillas. Ninety-six km. beyond Mérida comes Tovar (population 18,000; *Hotel Junín,* US$2.25 s; *Motel Sabaneta,* good and cheap, US$3.40 s), a nice little town with pleasant excursions, whence we can rejoin the Pan-American *via* Zea or tackle the old, wild and beautiful mountain road over La Negra to San Cristóbal. There is a new hotel (*Hotel de Montaña,* Tel.: 077-82401/2), recommended, 7 km. before La Grita on the road from Mérida.

San Cristóbal, on a plateau 55 km. from the Colombian border, at 830 metres. Average temperature 22°C, population 160,000. The city is on three levels, running N-S: a 1½ km. wide level zone along the Torbes river, which flows S into the Orinoco basin, and two terraces, one of them 200 metres above the river, and 5½°C cooler. This, and the La Concordia sector to the S, are the "select" suburbs. The city was founded in 1561, and the Spanish Colonial appearance—the appearance only—is preserved. The sports centre is in La Concordia. The Cathedral, finished in 1908, had its towers and façade rebuilt in Colonial style for the 400th anniversary of the foundation. San Cristóbal, the capital of Táchira state, is a pretty town with 14 plazas in all. There is a good road over the mountains, with beautiful Andean views, to San Antonio.

Airports for San Cristóbal: at San Antonio (1 hour) and La Fría (90 mins.).

Por Puesto to Mérida, US$7; to Cúcuta, Colombia, US$3.50; to San Antonio, US$0.90.

Bus To Maracaibo, one daily, fills up early and leaves at 2100. More are planned. To Caracas, US$7, about 7 hours by Llanos route.

Hotels At San Cristóbal: *Motel Torbes; El Cid; Hamburgo; Bella Vista,* US$14.10 d, private bath; *Hospedaje Luby* (2nd class); *Hotel de Ferias El Tama,* US$20 d, overlooking the town, has an Olympic-size swimming pool; *Alba,* US$14, good; *Hotel del Sur,* US$4.50, noisy, no room key provided, near bus terminal; *Horizonte,* US$7 s. There are several cheap hotels on Avenida 6A, just off the central plaza at about US$3 d.

Restaurant *Bella Nápoli,* good, cheap, near Plaza Bolívar.

San Antonio is the frontier town (not a tourist attraction), and is connected by international bridge with Colombia. Crossing this bridge the traveller reaches the Colombian town of Cúcuta, distant about 16 km. (bus US$0.60—in bolívares or pesos—to international bridge), whence he can continue by road or air to Bogotá. Thirteen km. N on the Venezuelan side lies the new spa of Ureña, with natural hot springs. *(Hotel Aguas Calientes.)* The *Moruco,* US$18.60, nearby at Santo Domingo, is recommended, as is the hotel at Santa Elena (US$6, d).

Hotels At San Antonio: *Don Jorge,* US$13 d, a/c; *Hotel Táchira,* US$13 d, with bath, recommended; *Hotel Los Andes,* US$5 d, cheap; many hotels near town centre.

Exchange, at the Banco de Venezuela on main square. Casas de Cambio near the International Bridge will not change cheques and some will only change Colombian pesos, not even US dollars cash.

Llanos of the Orinoco This area of flat grasslands, 1,000 km. long and 320 km. wide, lies between the Andes and the Orinoco River. It is veined by numerous slow running rivers, forested along their banks, running from the mountains to the Orinoco. The vast flatland is only varied here and there by *mesas,* or slight upthrusts of the land. Ever since 1548, when they were introduced by the Spaniards, cattle have ranged over this area. About 5 million of the country's 6,400,000 cattle, many of the Zebu type from Brazil and India, are in the llanos, 30% of the country's area, but holding no more than 13% of the population. The llaneros are most of them cattlemen, working against great odds. When the whole plain is periodically under water, they drive their cattle into the hills or through the flood from one mesa to another. When the plain is parched by the sun and the savannah grasses become uneatable they herd them down to the damper region of the Apure and Orinoco. Finally they drive a vast number into the valley of Valencia to be fattened before slaughter.

Parts of the area are coming under cultivation. The Guárico dam has created thousands of hectares of fertile land by controlling flood and drought. The llanos State of Portuguesa has now the largest cultivated area of any: rice and cotton are coming out of the region.

There are several roads to the llanos. Sixteen km. E of Maracay, a good road leads off to San Juan de los Morros, with natural hot springs and a new hotel. Later it divides S to the Guárico dam, the llanos and Puerto Miranda and E to Valle de la Pascua *(Hotel Venezuela)* and El Tigre. Going S, keep an eye open for the egrets, which were almost exterminated early in the century for their feathers, once a valuable export. Crossing the bridge over the River Apure at Puerto Miranda we come to San Fernando de Apure.

Alternative route from Caracas to Mérida

There is a splendid road to the western llanos of Barinas, from Valencia through San Carlos, capital of Cojedes state (uninteresting), **Acarigua**, a thriving agricultural centre (*Hotel Payara,* nice), and **Guanare**, a national place of pilgrimage with an old parish church containing the much venerated relic of the Virgin of Coromoto, Patron of Venezuela. Population 30,000. Hotels: *La Coromoto* and *Lido* (US$4 s), slightly out of town, are reasonable.

After the first appearance of the Virgin, Chief Coromoto failed to be baptised, though he did hedge by getting other members of the tribe baptised. When the Virgin reappeared he told her gruffly to be gone and made a grab at her, but she vanished leaving in his hand a likeness of herself on the inner surface of a split stone now on display in the church. For a hundred years little attention was paid to the image, and it was only in 1946 that this Virgin was declared the Patron of Venezuela.

Our asphalted road continues to **Barinas** (population 60,000), the capital of the cattle-raising and oil-rich State of Barinas. Fishing and game-watching excursions into the llanos. The rivers are full of caribes (piranha) and many kinds of fish good to eat, some weighing up to 30 kg.

Hotels   *Internacional; Motel El Cacique; Suine,* quiet (US$3.40 with shower; no hot water; restaurant).

Bus, one only, leaves at 0900 for Mérida. Por puesto costs US$5.70. The bus terminal is on the edge of the town.

Airport, with local services and to Caracas.

From Barinas there is a beautifully scenic road to Apartaderos, in the Sierra Nevada de Mérida (see page 719).

Eastern Venezuela

The eastern part of the North-eastern Highlands, with summits rising to 2,000 metres, has abundant rainfall in its tropical forest. The western part is comparatively dry; most of the inhabitants live in this region, some 130,000 of them at Cumaná, the oldest European settlement in South America, and 60,000 at Barcelona.

Eastern Venezuela, with the Highlands in the NE, the great Llanos of the Orinoco to the south, and south of the Orinoco again the range of Guayana Highlands, was until quite recently not of much account in the Venezuelan economy. Some coffee and cacao are grown on the eastern slopes of the north-eastern Highlands in the tropical forest, but the western slopes are subject to drought. Cattle roam the Llanos, and the Guayana Highlands produce gold and diamonds. The picture has now been changed, as about 30% of Venezuelan oil now comes from this area. South of the Orinoco vast iron ore deposits are now being mined.

Eastern Venezuela has little to offer the tourist except along the coast, for it is hot, dry and covered with low scrub. Skinny cattle roam around and there are plenty of pipelines and oil wells for those who are interested, but little else. The area can most conveniently be divided into three zones: the petroleum zone, the Orinoco zone, and the coastal zone.

The journey into the petroleum zone may well begin at the airport of Barcelona, or at Caracas, for it now takes only 5 hours from East Caracas to Barcelona by car along the direct road through Caucagua, from which there is a 47-km. road NE to Higuerote, which has a number of beaches, currently the focus of large-scale tourist development projects.

On all the roads mentioned taxis carry passengers on a por puesto basis, or they can be hired for exclusive use.

Barcelona, capital of Anzoátegui state, population 60,000, is on the W bank of the Neveri River, 5 km. from the ocean. You might be interested in the ruins of the Casa Fuerte, grim relic of the War of Independence. (Hotels: *Plaza; Neveri.*) Steamers from La Guaira call at Guanta, 22 km. away, now connected with the 4-lane highway which goes through Puerto La Cruz and an airport with services to Caracas.

Mean temperature: 27°C. Products: livestock, sugar, cacao, coffee, tobacco. Industry: brewery and bottling plant.

Barcelona has a few modern buildings, but has been surpassed commercially by **Puerto La Cruz,** 22 km. away by an asphalted highway skirting the pleasant residential and bathing resort of Lechería. This ex-fishing hamlet is now a thriving town of 82,000 with two oil refineries (former Mene Grande and Sinclair). Its sea port is also Guanta, with regular lines to U.S. and European ports. There is a good beach at Playa Colorada, which is situated 26 km. E of Puerto La Cruz; there are buses and it is easy to hitch to the beach.

On the highway from Puerto La Cruz to Barcelona is the Polideportivo Sports Stadium seating 10,000 people: covered gymnasium, velodrome, tennis, volleyball, and basket-ball courts and two swimming pools. A new Institute of Technology, part of the Universidad del Oriente, is near the stadium.

Hotels *Miramar; Náutico; Europa; Neptuno; Pelícano; San Remo; Italia; Regis,* US$7 d; *Hotel Meliá,* new luxury hotel.

Bank Banco Royal Venezolano.

Royal Mail Line Agents Alcoa Steamship Co., Inc., P.O. Box 412.

The Coastal Zone Starting east from Puerto La Cruz, the road passes through Guanta and Pertigalete (cement factory), and goes on through the most beautiful coastal scenery in Venezuela—a Côte d'Azur without people—to the seaport of Cumaná, 84 km. from Puerto La Cruz; por puesto costs US$9.20. On the way it passes Colorado with its red sands (restaurant). Boys sell oysters on the palm-lined beach.

Cumaná, capital of Sucre state, founded 1520, is the oldest Hispanic city in South America. It straddles both banks of the Manzanares, 1½ km. from Puerto Sucre. The castle of San Antonio is worth a visit, and there are good walks along the tree-lined Manzanares; San Luis beach, short local bus ride, recommended. Cumaná has an important sardine canning industry and exports coffee and cacao. Airport. Average temperature 27°C. Population 130,000. Car ferry to Margarita Island. Famous for its carnival. A new museum was built in 1974 to commemorate the battle of Ayacucho; mainly portraits, relics and letters of Sucre and Bolívar.

Hotels *Cumanagoto; Río; Los Bordones; Hotel Villa Mar; Hotel Regina; El Río* (basic); *América.* Good food at *El Colmao* Restaurant in the centre as well as *El Teide* (sea food); *Parrilla Vittorio, El Bucanero; Fuente de Soda Monumental.*

Royal Mail Line Agents E. Berrizbeitia y Hnos, Sucrs, C.A. Calle Paraíso, Aptdo 16.

Bus To Güiria (see page 727), US$3.50 (5 hours).

The road goes on to the port of **Carúpano,** on the Pariá Peninsula. This little place is famous throughout Venezuela for its Carnival celebrations, and becomes a focus for tourists at that time. Population 30,000; airport; exports coffee and cacao.

Hotels   *Hotel San Francisco* (try the mussels: *mejillones*). And 11 km. away the luxury seaside *Hotel El Copey; Hotel Bologna* (US$5 d, a/c), owner speaks German, recommended.

Royal Mail Line Agents   Francisco A. Pavàn Sucrs, Aptdo 517.

Margarita Island, off the N coast, is a popular holiday and weekend resort for Caracas, easily reached by air or by ferry boat from Puerto La Cruz or Cumaná to Punta de Piedras. Ferry boats leave Puerto La Cruz for the island at 0700, 1200, 1600 and 2000 and from Cumaná at 0800 and 1700; return from Punta de Piedras at 0800, 1200, 1600 and 2000 for Puerto La Cruz and at 0700 and 1700 for Cumaná. Several firms at Nuevo Circo in Caracas sell through tickets (US$9.50) from Caracas to Porlamar, arriving about midday. Properly speaking, it is one island whose two sections are linked by the spit of land which separates the sea from the Laguna Arestinga. Most of its 87,500 people live in the developed eastern part; the western one, the Peninsula de Macanao, hotter and more barren, is the roaming place of wild deer, goats, hares and the occasional huntsman. The climate is exceptionally good but rain is scanty. Water is piped from the mainland. The roads are as good as nearly all roads are in Venezuela.

Most of the hotels are near the airport at **Porlamar** (20,000 people), the largest port, with a magnificent cathedral. Not far N is the capital, **La Asunción** (5,540 people), full of Colonial buildings: the Castle of Santa Rosa, with a famous bottle dungeon, and a cathedral whose Virgin wears robes covered with pearls. Further N lie the fishing port of Puerto Fermín; the windswept beach of El Agua with a tremendously powerful surf; and Manzanillo, peaceful and charming but the water gets deep rather suddenly. The bay of Juan Griego, to the W, is a big attraction. NE is the picturesque Pedro González with its *mirador* on a sleepy little bay. To the S lies La Guardia. W of this town a long narrow dyke of broken sea-shells stretches over 20 km. to the Peninsula of Macanao: on its right a spotlessly clean long beach, on its left the lagoon. At the far end is a cluster of fishermen's huts with landing stages from which motor boats take visitors on trips through the labyrinth of canals in the heart of the lagoons. But the best thing in Margarita Island is its beaches: long white stretches of sand, white sand, bordered by palms, but rather hot, with little shade. A full-scale model of Columbus' "Santa María" is used for taking tourists on trips.

The islanders are mainly occupied in fishing and fibre work, such as hammocks and straw hats. Margarita is now a duty-free zone and goods of all kinds can be bought cheaply. The best way of getting round the island is by hiring a car, an economic proposition for any number above one!

Hotels at Porlamar   *Bahía,* US$10 s; *Bella Vista,* Av. Santiago, US$12 s; *Mariño,* US$17.50 s; *Caribbean,* Via El Morro, US$19 s; *Vista Mar, Colibri,* Av. Santiago Mariño, US$10 s.

Communications   Porlamar is linked by air with Caracas. Car ferries to Cumaná and Puerto La Cruz.

Royal Mail Line Agents   C.A. Comercial Reina Antoni, P.O. Box 19, Isla Margarita.

From Puerto La Cruz a toll road goes inland, skirting Barcelona. At Km. 52 (where there is a restaurant) a road forks left to (near) Santa Bárbara (airport) ex-Sinclair oil camp. It goes on to Jusepín, Quiriquire, and Caripito, all Lagovén oil camps. **Maturín,** capital of Monagas state, an important commercial centre, is 16 km. beyond Jusepín. Population 130,000.

Hotels *El Cacique, Monagas, Pensión El Nacional* (US$4 d) and *Latino* (US$7 d) are recommended as simple and clean. Also *Hotel Emperador* (US$17.50 d) on Av. Bolívar; *Hotel Trinidad* (US$7 d, private bathroom, with a/c) clean, English speaking; *Hotel Europa,* US$7 d, recommended as being as good as the *Trinidad* but with larger roms; *Hotel Astrolobia,* US$2.50 s, good food, near bus station; *Hotel Paris,* near airport, good food, US$4. The *Hotel Tamanaco* at US$5 d is reasonable.

Transport Air services to Caracas, and to Trinidad (US$28) on Tuesdays and Saturdays, both ways on same day. Bus to Caracas (US$6, 8 hours). Buses leave three times a day for Caracas from the central bus terminal; buses for Ciudad Guayana (US$3) and El Dorado leave from the terminus near the airport. No bus services to Puerto La Cruz or Barcelona; only por puestos at US$6. Por puestos only to Ciudad Bolívar. Leaving the country from Maturín airport you require a 3-bolivares stamp for passport stamping, which can be got at the airport. (If leaving Venezuela for some destinations tax can be 9 bolivares.) Non-tourists have to pay an exit tax of US$18.50 as well. Colectivos Nos. 1 and 6 to and from the airport (US$0.40). Bus US$0.20. Taxis from the Reponsable de Venezuela office will try to charge US$4.50 p.p.. The bus leaves from the main road outside the airport grounds when going into town.

There are no exchange facilities in the airport except at the Aeropostal desk, and they give a very bad rate.

In Santa Bárbara can be bought the native chinchorros, hammocks made by hand of woven moriche palm leaves, decorated with coloured yarn. This is the only place to find them. They "give" when you lie on them and do not absorb moisture when used on the beach. Very good for camping. You can also buy the manares and sebucans the people use when straining juice from yucca and sieving it to make their big, round, flat loaves of yucca bread which tastes like pressed sawdust. The juice is poisonous. The process is interesting, if you are lucky enough to see them at it. A chinchorro costs about US$24, a sebucan US$1.20.

Just beyond Jusepín, an unpaved 32-km. road, left, joins the Maturín-Cumaná road; 30 km. NW is San Francisco, from which a branch road runs 22½ km. NE to **Caripe,** a short distance from the remarkable **Cueva del Guáchero.** It was discovered by Humboldt, who went a little way in. Men have since penetrated 8 km. along a small, crystal-clear stream. First comes the *Cueva del Silencio* (Cave of Silence), where you can hear a pin drop. About 2 km. in is the *Pozo del Viento* (Well of the Wind). There are weird and wonderful shapes, stalactites, and sounds. Inside live a large number of *guácheros* (oil birds) with an in-built radar system for sightless flight. For two hours at dusk the shrieking birds pour out of the cave's mouth, coming back at dawn with their pouches full (naturalists say) of fruit from the Gran Sabana, 450 km. away. The cave is well worth a visit. Take a torch as guides' hurricane lamps are not always bright enough to see all the rock formations. Wear old clothes and be prepared to take off your shoes and socks (thongs provided) and wade in river and scramble over rocks. Two nice clean hotels at Caripe and a huge *samán* tree in purple glory when the orchids which cover it bloom in May.

There is an interesting journey from Maturín to **Güiria** by bus, US$5.10, 6 hours. Güiria is very hot and dress is more casual than is common elsewhere. (*Hotel Fortuna,* US$9.30 d with shower and fan; restaurant.) A boat leaves for Trinidad on Tuesdays at 0400 hours (US$13.60) if there are eight or more prospective passengers; if not, the only way to get to Trinidad seems to be by plane from Maturín.

Continuing straight on from Km. 52, the road passes W of Anaco *(Hotel Club Molino).* It has an airport, is an important centre for oil well service contracting companies, and is the headquarters of the ex-Mobil Oil Company. Beyond Anaco a branch road leads to the oilfields of San Joaquín and San Roque.

The main road passes near Cantaura, a market town, and goes on to **El Tigre** and El Tigrito (Hotels: *Arichuna; Oasis; El Rancho*), two important trading centres within 20 km. of one another. About 8 km. along the road is San Tomé (airport), the eastern headquarters of Menevén, the former Mene Grande oil company.

From El Tigre a good asphalt road leads off to Caracas; the one we are following leads, straight and flat, 120 km. over the Llanos to the new Angostura bridge over the Orinoco to Ciudad Bolívar, 282 km. from Puerto La Cruz.

This suspension bridge, opened 1967, is 1,668 metres in length, or over a mile. Clearance is 56 metres above normal water levels.

The Guayana Highlands, lying S of the Orinoco River, constitute half of Venezuela. They rise, in rounded forested hills and narrow valleys, to flat topped tablelands on the borders of Brazil. These lands are very sparsely populated; they are not even fully explored; but the savannahs (mixed with semi-deciduous forest), would make better cattle country than the llanos. So far, communications have been the main difficulty, but a road has now been driven to Santa Elena de Uairén on the Brazilian frontier (see page 730) to open up the country. This road, as yet unpaved, may be followed to Manaus, and thence, by a suitable vehicle, to Brasília and southern Brazil. The area is Venezuela's largest gold and diamond source, but its immense reserves of iron ore, manganese and bauxite are of far greater economic importance.

Ciudad Bolívar, on the S bank of the Orinoco, is 400 km. from its delta and 640 by road from Caracas. The city lies on a low hill inclined towards the river. Average temperature 29°C, but a cool and refreshing breeze usually springs up in the evening. It still has much Spanish Colonial building but is changing rapidly. Part of the University of the Oriente is here. Population 110,000.

It is the trading centre for the Guayana Highlands and the great forest lands away to the SW. River craft bring to the city the balatá, chicle, tonka beans, skins, gold and diamonds in which it trades. Only 105 km. down-river lies the Pittsburg of Venezuela, Ciudad Guayana, but so far this industrial upheaval seems to have by-passed Ciudad Bolivar, which continues its tranquil life by the narrows of the Orinoco, with its Cathedral, on a small hill, dominating the city.

The narrows, not more than 300 metres wide, gave the town its old name of Angostura (or "Narrows"), and it was here that Bolívar came after defeat to reorganise his forces, and the British Legionnaires joined him; it was at Angostura that he was declared President of that Gran Colombia which was to fragment before his death. When the town was still known as Angostura a physician invented the famous bitters there in 1824. The factory moved to Port of Spain in 1875.

It is, in many ways, a busy, romantic place, with a constant coming and going of the most varied river-craft. It has now a floating pontoon dock where ocean-going cargo boats discharge.

In C.B., as it is known locally, you can buy a sweet kind of sugar candy with nuts, baskets and items made by the Indians. It is the best place in Venezuala for anything made of gold. There are beautiful hand-made charms for charm bracelets and, most typical of all, the Venezuelan orchid, made by hand, of red, yellow and green gold. Native gold is called "cochano" gold. The gold orchid pin or ear-rings is the best souvenir of Venezuela. A feature is the netting of *sapoara,* a delicious fish 30 to 35 cm. long which pours from the inlets when the river begins to swell in late June at the start of the rainy season and swims up stream to spawn. During its short season this is the favourite dish of the town.

Hotels *Gran Hotel Bolívar,* Paseo Orinoco; *La Cumbre,* Av. 5 de Julio, good view of town but rather run down (US$8.50 d, without food); *Roma,* US$5 d; *Valentina,* Av. Maracay, far from centre, a/c, US$6 d; *La Redoma,* US$9 d, Av. Upata; *Italia,* on the riverfront, highly recommended for the budget traveller, US$5 s, food excellent, try dulce de merey for dessert; *Sicilia,* US$5 s, with shower; *Pensión Panamericana,* Calle Rocía 6, US$5 d, clean; *Pensión Boyacá,* US$4.70 d, clean and comfortable. It is often difficult to find rooms in hotels here.

Restaurants *Alfonso,* Av. Maracay; *Almanola,* Av. Cumaná; *La Cabaña,* Paseo Menerses; *Las Cibeles,* Paseo Orinoco; *La Cumbre,* Av. 5 de Julio; *La Paragua,* Av. La Mariquita; *La Playa,* Paseo Orinoco 84, seafood.

Tourist Office Edificio Bolívar, Plaza Bolívar.

Museum The Museo Soto on the outskirts of the town is a modern art museum featuring Venezuela's José Rafael Soto and other artists.

Bank Banco Royal Venezolano.

Airport Served by Avensa, and LAV which flies 4 times a week to Sta. Elena de Uairen for connections to Manaus and Brazil. Mini-buses to town centre.

Buses Several daily to Caracas 9 hours, US$7.25. Tumeremo US$4.75; Terminal at junction of Av. República and Av. Sucre.

Five days by boat (800 km.) up the Orinoco lies Puerto Ayacucho, deep in the wild (see below), but it seems to be accessible only by air—no boats carry passengers. Nowadays river traffic only becomes active beyond Caicara de Orinoco and Cabruta, from where second-class roads go north and south. These ports are almost halfway to Puerto Ayacucho from Ciudad Bolívar.

Up river from Ciudad Bolívar, boats (no passengers) ply the 800 km. to **Puerto Ayacucho** *(Hotel Amazonas),* capital of the Federal Territory of Amazonas, which has an area of 175,000 square kilometres and a population of only 15,000, of whom about 8,000 live in Puerto Ayacucho. The town has LAV air service. Beyond Puerto Ayacucho are rapids, but smaller launches on the upper Orinoco can reach the Casiquiare and the Río Negro which flows into the Amazon. In 1955/56, two Americans successfully canoed to the Argentine, continuing from the Amazon by way of the Tapajós, Paraguay and Paraná. The trip took about one year. The journey up the Amazon to the Casiquiare and Orinoco has also been successfully negotiated by a hovercraft with a British crew. Trips up the Amazon tributaries are organized in Caracas by Italcambio (Tel.: 820611) and Turismo Colorama (Tel.: 337326).

In an area rich in natural resources 105 km. down-river from Ciudad Bolívar, an entirely new metropolis, known as **Ciudad Guayana,** is now being built on about 36 square km. It will forge into one of the four centres of San Félix, Palúa, Puerto Ordaz and Matanzas. Its population is already 250,000, but it is planned for an eventual million. its location is the south bank of the Orinoco and both sides of the Caroní river before it spills into the Orinoco. East of the Caroní are the commercial port of San Félix and the Palúa iron-ore terminal of the railway from El Pao. Crossing the Caroní by the 470-metre concrete bridge we come to **Puerto Ordaz** (airport), the iron-ore loading port of the Orinoco Mining Company (now nationalized), connected by rail with the famous Cerro Bolívar open-cast iron mine. The Orinoco is dredged to permit year-round traffic of ships drawing 9 metres and the 570-metre dock can load 80,000 tons a day. The iron-tinted waterfall, which looks like a beerfall, in the pretty Parque Cachamay is worth a visit. To the west is the Government-owned Siderúrgica del Orinoco with a production of 667,000 tons a year, and an aluminium plant operated in conjunction with Reynolds Metals. Just up the Caroní is the macagua hydroelectric plant with a capacity of 370,000 kw.; there are some truly beautiful cataracts as you enter the grounds. Higher up the river is the Guri dam and hydroelectric undertaking with a capacity of 1,750,000 kw., to be raised in its final stages to 6 million kw. (The trip to Guri takes 90 minutes by taxi; conducted tours start at 0900.) About 1,000 people a month are flocking into the town. About 3 km. away, across bare savannah, is an area reserved for smaller industries; half a dozen plants are already built.

Hotels *Hotel Intercontinental, Guayana, Punta Vista; Hotel Dos Ríos,* Calle Mexico; *El Rasil,* with all comforts in Puerto Ordaz, the "planned" part of the city; *Centro Cívico; Del Río,* run down, US$6.80 d; several acceptable hotels, much cheaper, in San Félix, the historical town.

Restaurants *El Embajador* in Puerto Ordaz; also *Key Club; El Churrasco; El Minichet; La Romanina* (Italian); *Salvador* (fish); *La Bavaria* (German); *Guayana* (Dutch).

General Airport, with daily flights to Caracas. A stadium. A planning office in the outskirts of Puerto Ordaz, where young architects welcome visitors interested in problems of building a new city. The Corporación Venezolana de Guayana sells a good city map.

Round Trip from Caracas *Via* El Tigre by road to Santo Tomé, N *via* Maturín (road not good but scenery worth it) to Cumaná and along the glorious coast back to Caracas. Plenty of buses to Caracas.

Bank Banco Royal Venezolano at Puerto Ordaz.

Transport Bus from Ciudad Guayana to El Dorado US$4; to Maturín US$3.

Ana and Robert Cook write: South from Ciudad Guayana there is a 285-km. paved road to El Dorado, where stands the regional prison made famous by Papillon's stay there. Although any reliable car can ply the graded roads south of here, four-wheel drive is necessary if one wanders off the main road (particularly in the rainy season). Fill up with gasoline at each station; the next one may have run out. It is advisable to take extra cans of gasoline and water and plenty of food. At Km. 88 (food and gas) the steep climb begins up to La Escalera and the beginning of the Gran Sabana National Reserve. Characteristic to this area are the large abrupt *tapuis* (flat-topped mountains or mesas) and the hundreds of powerful but graceful waterfalls.

At Km. 120 a short trail leads to Danto Falls. Beyond the military checkpoint at Ciudadela is a bad road leading to Cavanayen (food, airport) and the beautiful falls at the headwaters of the Caroní River. For the remaining 200 km. to Santa Elena de Uairen few people or villages are seen. The falls at the Cama river should not be missed. Excellent regional food is available near the police checkpoint at San Ignacio. **Santa Elena de Uairen** (*Hotel Fronteras,* very nice and modern, US$12 s, with bath; *Hospedaje Roraima, Hotel MacKing, Hotel Kukeman,* US$2; *Hotel Brasilia,* US$3.50 s), is a rugged and growing frontier town. Passports and car documents must be stamped here if leaving or entering the country. A 2- or 3-day trip can be made to Pauji, Icabaru (food, lodging), and the diamond mines of Los Caribes. After rain in Icabaru the children search the streets for gold nuggets and diamonds washed free of the earth by the water. Buses and trucks leave from Santa Elena. Transport agency *La Reina* has irregular microbus service El Dorado to Boa Vista (Brazil).

A little-known jaunt by hired dugout canoe from San Félix or Puerto Ordaz is down the Orinoco to Los Castillos (1 hour). There is now a good track there. Candes Tours run an excursion from Puerto Ordaz but only if there are four people. There are two old forts here: one on a huge rock near the water, the other on top of a hill and both in good condition. A tiny village lies at their feet. Children will sell you cannon balls and old Spanish coins (1815, Province of Guiana), which they find in the river. It was here, probably, that Sir Walter Raleigh's son was killed in battle whilst searching for El Dorado.

Alan Rosenberg, of Homebush, Australia, writes as follows: "The most interesting excursion I was able to make in Venezuela was to **Tucupita** in the Orinoco delta. Transport from Ciudad Guayana is available, and the roads are asphalted. Tucupita is a river town, and one can bargain with the many boat operators for river trips through country of outstanding beauty. There is at least one clean, air-conditioned hotel.''

Angel Falls

Angel Falls, the highest fall in the world (979 metres) and Canaima, a nearby tourist lodge and hotel, are best reached from Caracas or from Puerto Ordaz. Avensa Airlines has inclusive charges for tours which leave twice daily from Maiquetía Airport, or a week's tour can be taken. The daily flights stop at Puerto Ordaz which can be the starting point for the trip. Trips to the falls have to be booked in advance. A five-day trip to Canaima may cost about US$470, of which half must be paid one month in advance. Reductions are available for parties, and 2-day excursion from Caracas costs US$130, each additional day US$29. At Ciudad Bolívar airport Aerotaxis Tanca arranges Cessna flights for 3 persons for a whole day at Angel Falls and Canaima; the one-day excursion includes lunch at Canaima, a boat tour of the lagoon and the falls (US$87). The return flight is usually just after sunset. Canaima, where the night is spent in quite comfortable cabins, is on the edge of a pink lagoon with soft beige beaches. Food at the camp is very good; each cabin is complete with shower and toilet; there are no hardships whatsoever. The Río Carrao tumbles over seven beautiful falls into the lagoon below. The country is very beautiful. Excursions are made into the jungle to visit diamond prospectors or Indian villages. A local guide, ''Jungle Rudy'' Truffino, takes you up to Angel Falls in an outboard launch; a week's trip. He operates from Campollcaima, above the Hacha Falls near Canaima. This route is only open in the wet season from June to December, as rivers are too shallow in the dry season. The flat-topped Auyan-Tepuy, from which spring the Angel Falls, was the setting for W. H. Hudson's *Green Mansions*. The sheer rock face of the Falls was climbed in 1971 by three Americans and an Englishman, David Nott, who recounts the ten-day adventure in his book *Angels Four* (Prentice-Hall).

In Caracas contact *Hotel Tamanaco*, Tel.: 914555, or Caribex Tours, Tel.: 728271/2, for trips to Falls. Italcambio, Tel.: 820611, organizes camping trips up the River Paragua for parties of four at a cost of US$180 for three days, or US$205 four days. Avensa has a list of tours from Canaima and for the Angel Falls trip.

Warning Take plenty of spare cash as there have been reports of these trips not being as all-inclusive as they are advertised to be. Credit cards are not accepted by the people who take you on excursions.

The Economy

In 1973 Venezuela entered the threshold of a petroleum boom that promises to be of unprecedented magnitude in its history. Cashing in handsomely on the energy crisis since January 1973, Venezuela raised its oil reference price and even though a contraction in production has since taken place, both for reasons of falling demand and of conservation, the value of sales is quite likely to remain at about US$9,000m. a year.

The Government obtains the greater part of its internal revenue and about 95% of export revenue from the petroleum sector and uses it to finance large public-works and industrial programmes. As a result the country has a well-developed infrastructure—transport, communications, public utilities etc., as well as the highest g.n.p. in the whole of South America; in 1974 this figure exceeded the US$2,300 mark, which technically meant that Venezuela was no longer a ''developing country'' in the strict sense.

Iron-ore and petroleum have been nationalized under the present Government. Regarding iron-ore, the two US companies involved have entered into agreements to supply technology and to continue their purchases of ore. The long-range plan is to cease exporting iron-ore and to develop a national steel industry capable of utilizing present ore production. From 1st January 1976 the petroleum industry has been controlled by Petróleos de Venezuela (Petrovén), a state organization set up to manage the 22 concessionary and 16 other companies nationalized on that date; Petrovén now has 4 operating companies and is responsible for general planning and supervision of the industry. Some of the big international oil companies have entered into agreements with the Government to supply technical assistance, and are to continue utilizing Venezuelan oil. Oil supply agreements have also been signed with Japan, Brazil, Peru and Argentina. An investment fund known as the Fondo de Inversiones de Venezuela (FIV) has been set up to channel petroleum profits into industrial and agricultural development projects. Emphasis is to be given to development of the interior and the further growth of Caracas will be discouraged. In line with these new developments in policy new investments will be considered in the light of the additional employment and social benefit created.

Abundant reserves of oil (about 70,000m. barrels) are estimated to exist in the so-called Orinoco Tar Belt, but most of it has a high viscosity—it is literally tar. Although the Government intends to develop this belt at a later stage, the high costs involved and the need for lighter grades of oil forced Petrovén to start exploration offshore in 1978 and postpone the Orinoco development.

One factor hindering the manufacturing sector has been the relatively small size of the home market. This particular constraint was removed in February 1973 when Venezuela joined the Andean Group, a developing customs union of five countries—the other members are Peru, Bolivia, Ecuador, and Colombia—which effectively provides a "home market" of 60 millions, compared with the 13 millions in Venezuela alone. This move should provide a stimulus to the manufacturing sector, particularly textiles, paper products, food and drink, furniture, petrochemicals and aluminium smelting, in addition to the steel already mentioned.

The unit of currency, the bolívar, is stable (it has twice been revalued against the U.S. dollar since December 1971) and well supported by the highest level of gold and dollar reserves in Latin America. In 1976 the bolívar was established as an official reserve currency, under Article 8 of the IMF Charter. The slow growth of the agricultural sector in recent years has caused shortages of both food and raw materials. The Government has, however, apart from the creation of a fund of 2,000m bolivares for the agricultural sector, approved plans for specific projects at a cost of 3,500m. bolívares to overcome the problems of agriculture; 1m. hectares of land in Apure have been expropriated for an irrigation-based feed lot experiment; long-term low interest loans are being made to small farmers to develop 450,000 hectares for groundnut, maize, and sesame production. At the same time credit will be made available for machinery purchases.

Foreign Trade (US$m.)

	1972	1973	1974	1975	1976	1977*
Exports (f.o.b.)..	3,782	5,645	15,197	11,117	9,418	9,939
Petroleum and products	3,509	5,311	14,669	10,635	8,861	9,382
Iron-ore	131	170	273	268	256	243
Imports (f.o.b.)	2,222	2,626	3,876	5,462	6,543	8,787

*Provisional

Information for Visitors

Routes to Venezuela

From U.K. and Europe The quickest route from London is to Paris, and then by Air France "Concorde". British Caledonian Airways direct flights from London to Maiquetia, the airport for Caracas. There are also services from Europe by K.L.M., Viasa, Iberia, Alitalia, Lufthansa and Avianca. The cheapest route appears to be by ABC to Port of Spain, Trinidad (British Airways or BWIA) and then by scheduled flight to Caracas.

By sea, French Line (C.G.M.) has passenger sailings to and from Southampton Italian and Spanish ports are served by Sidarma, Italia and other Italian and Spanish passenger services. Scandinavia and Belgium have direct passenger cargo-service by Johnson Line. From Holland there are passenger ships of the K.N.S.M. The Italian "C" Line (Costa) to and from Italy, calls at Miami. The Grimaldi Siosa Lines have passenger services to Venezuela from the Mediterranean and from the U.K. (Southampton). Royal Mail Lines has a cargo service only from the U.K. to Venezuelan ports. There are direct cargo sailings (no passengers) by Harrison and Blue Star Lines also.

From the U.S. By air, passengers may reach Venezuela by Delta, K.L.M., Pan American, Varig and Viasa. Jets fly from New York to Caracas in 4 hours 15 minutes. By sea, there are passenger services from New York by Grace Line and to Miami by Cía. Colonial. And there are cargo services, some with limited passenger space, from Atlantic and or Gulf ports by Alcoa, C.A.V.N., Grace, Peninsular & Occidental, Insco, K.N.S.M., Lykes & Torm, and from the Pacific by Moore-McCormack. From the Great Lakes, Grace Lines. Mitsui O.S.K. Lines call at La Guaira on outward voyages from Japan *via* Hawaii, Los Angeles, Cristóbal and Curaçao to Rio de Janeiro, Santos, and Buenos Aires.

From Colombia There are direct flights by Pan American, Viasa, Iberia, British Caledonian, Air France, Lufthansa and Avianca. Caracas can also be reached from Bogotá by road, and a new Caribbean coastal highway has been opened. By sea, there are frequent services by Italia, and some cargo vessels.

From Argentina, Brazil and Uruguay There are direct air services by Pan American and Varig. By sea, the Argentine State Line maintains a passenger liner service, every two or three weeks.

Others Lacsa flies from San José (Costa Rica), Panama and Barranquilla (Colombia) to Maracaibo and Caracas. LAV has a daily service to Port of Spain, Curaçao and Aruba. Viasa also flies to Bridgetown, Barbados (US$64). There is direct air service from Chile (Air France), Peru (Air France, Iberia, Viasa), Santo Domingo (Viasa, Dominicana de Aviación), Puerto Rico (Pan American), Curaçao (KLM, Viasa), Trinidad (LAV, Pan American). Caracas may now be reached by road from Brazil, *via* the frontier town of Santa Elena de Uairén. (Four-wheel-drive vehicle recommended; colectivos and buses have begun to run.) As yet, Venezuela has no road connexion with Guyana, except through Brazil. Ferry from Curaçao, three times a week at US$50.

Documents Entry is by passport and visa or Tourist Card (Carta de Ingreso—DIEX 2). Cards are issued by Venezuelan consulates (valid 90 days, extendable for 90 more). International airlines or shipping companies serving Venezuela may issue cards (valid 45 days, non-extendable), only to nationals of Australia, Austria, Barbados, Belgium, Brazil, British West Indies, Canada, Costa Rica, Denmark, France,

French Antilles, West Germany, Guyane, Iceland, Irish Republic, Italy, Japan, Luxembourg, Mexico, Netherlands, Netherlands Antilles, New Zealand, Norway, Surinam, Switzerland, Trinidad and Tobago, UK and USA. They may issue cards for transit entry (valid 72 hours) to nationals of the countries mentioned above and also to those of the other Latin American countries (except Chile and Haiti), Andorra, Bahamas, Bermuda, Finland, Grenada, Guyana, Jamaica, Portugal, South Africa, Spain and Uruguay. Only three Cartas de Ingreso may be provided in one year, except for nationals of Canada, Denmark, W. Germany, Sweden, Switzerland and the USA. Airlines and shipping lines can only provide Cartas de Ingreso if presented with a passport and a ticket out of the country. Difficulties have been reported in obtaining tourist cards or visas for entry overland from Colombia and it is usually easier to get a visa in your home country than applying for one en route.

A smallpox vaccination certificate is required by all. Transit passengers to another country can only stay 72 hours.

Details about other kinds of visitors, such as commercial travellers and business-men, are given in "Hints to Businessmen Visiting Venezuela", issued by the Export Services Division, Dept. of Trade, Room CO7, Export House, 50 Ludgate Hill, London EC4M 7HU. All visitors to Venezuela applying to the Consulate for a visa have to produce a letter of introduction from their bank manager. Processing normally takes three days.

Persons who intend staying much longer than a week must report within that period to the Dirección de Extranjeros, Registro de Pasaportes, 4th floor, office 13, Plaza Miranda, Caracas, or to the local office of the Extranjería. Paradoxically, it seems to be easier for tourists to enter Venezuela than for businessmen.

Taxes Business visitors applying for entry or re-entry must pay US$4.50 (Canadian, West German, Swedish, Swiss and U.S. nationals pay US$2.25) before they can withdraw their luggage, after landing. Payment must be in bolivares or US dollars.

All persons leaving the country, except nationals of Denmark, tourists, and transit passengers who stay for 7 days or less, must pay US$19 at the airport or port of embarkation. Minors under seven years of age do not pay the exit tax. This means for a business visitor from an unprivileged country who stays a couple of days a total charge of US$23.50 on entering and leaving.

Customs You may bring into Venezuela, free of duty, 25 cigars and 200 cigarettes, 2 litres of alcoholic drinks, 4 small bottles of perfume, and gifts at the inspector's discretion.

Motoring A tourist can bring in his car without paying duty, but must get a Venezuelan Consul's certification of a document identifying his car. The document gives the serial and motor number, registry, make, etc., and states if the car carries a spare. If the tourist is staying longer than 8 days, the certification should be included on his Carta de Turismo given him at the Consulate. When he gets to Venezuela the car owner should present this document to the nearest office of the Turismo Department, to arrange customs clearance. All visitors to Venezuela can drive if they are over 18 and have a valid driving licence from their own country. It is a good idea to hire a car; many of the best places are off the beaten track. If you have an accident and someone is injured, you will be detained as a matter of routine, even if you are not at fault. Be careful of motor cyclists; if you injure one, others will surround you in a threatening and dangerous manner. Motor cyclists also drive very dangerously, sometimes even on the pavements, and are responsible for many assaults on pedestrians. Do not drive at night if you can help it.

There are 3 grades of petrol: "normal", 82 octane (Bs.0.10 a litre about US$0.09 per U.S. gallon); "popular" (Bs.0.15 a litre, or US$0.12 a U.S. gallon), and "alta", 94 octane (Bs.0.35 a litre, or US$0.25 per U.S. gallon). Diesel (US$0.10 a litre). Prices are higher in remote places.

Hitch-Hiking is still quite easy as there are not too many people doing it. The Venezuelans are usually friendly and helpful if you know some Spanish.

Tourist information may be obtained from the Tourist Department, Ministry of Development, Caracas. Ask for details of the five 8-day "Golden Orchid" tours to various parts of Venezuela now available. A useful publication is the *Guía Turística y Hoteles de Venezuela,* published by the Corporación de Turismo at 20 bolívares (US$4.65), which includes not only hotel details, but also road maps and tourist attractions.

Tipping Taxi drivers and usherettes are not tipped. Hotel porters, Bs.2; airport porters Bs.2 per piece of baggage. Restaurants, between 5 and 10% of bill.

Hours of business Banks are open from 0830 to 1130 and 1400 to 1630. Mondays to Fridays, but are no longer open on Saturdays. Government office hours vary, but 0800-1200 are usual morning hours. Government officials have fixed hours, usually 0900-1000 or 1500-1600, for receiving visitors. Business firms generally start work about 0800, and some continue until about 1800 with a midday break. Shops, 0900-1300, 1500-1900, Monday to Saturday. Generally speaking, the Venezuelan begins his day early, and by seven in the morning everything is in full swing. Most firms and offices close on Saturday.

Holidays Official: January 1, 6; March, 2 days of Carnival, and 19; Wednesday-Saturday, Holy Week; April 19; May 1; Ascension Day, Corpus Christi; June 24, 29; July 5, 24; October 12 (and at Maracaibo Oct. 24): November 1 (and 18 at Maracaibo); December 8, 17, 24, 25, 31. The 2 days of Carnival have been declared "working days", but will anyone work? Businessmen should not visit during Holy Week or Carnival.

Local: (Local business closed. Only passenger ships worked). La Guaira: March 10th. Maracaibo: October 24th, November 18th.

Health conditions are good. Water in all main towns is chlorinated and is safe to drink. Medical attendance is good, but extremely expensive. Inoculation against typhoid and yellow fever, and protection against malaria, is recommended for the Orinoco and other swampy or forest regions. It is as well to carry some remedy in case of gastric upsets.

Climate is tropical, with little change between season and season. Temperature is a matter of altitude. Mean annual temperatures are given in the text. At Caracas it is 20°C, but during the dry season (December to April), there is a great difference between day and night temperatures, and during the whole year there is a burst of heat around mid-day. Rainfall in mm.: Caracas, 762; Maracaibo, 1,270; Barcelona, 660; Merida, 1,295; Amazonas and parts of Barinas state 2,540.

Clothing Tropical worsted in normal city colours is best for Caracas. In Maracaibo and the hot, humid coastal and low-lying areas, regular washable tropical clothing is used. In Western Venezuela, in the higher Andes, a light overcoat and a woollen sports jacket come in handy, as they may do even in Caracas. Khaki bush clothing is needed for a visit to the oilfields, but men wear long trousers; shorts are never worn away from the beach. For women: slacks; cotton dresses, with a wrap for cool evenings, and for air-conditioned restaurants and cinemas.

Railways The only passenger traffic of any importance is on the Barquisimeto to Puerto Cabello line, but there is a plan for a huge extension of the rail network.

Road Transport There are excellent bus services between the major cities, but the colectivo taxis, known in Venezuela as "por puesto", seem to monopolize transport to and from smaller towns and villages.

Air Services Most places of importance are served by Avensa and/or LAV. Abroad, they run a joint service called Viasa. Viasa provides a "Conozca Venezuela" internal air travel plan (US$80), which is valid for 17 days of unlimited travel. Both internal airlines offer special family discounts. Beware of overbooking during holiday time, especially at Maiquetía airport; it is recommended that you check in two hours before departure, particularly at Easter. If you travel with Viasa or any other airline for which Viasa is agent, it is possible to check in the night before at any Viasa office in town if your flight leaves before noon. Handling charge for your luggage US$0.23.

Currency The unit of currency is the bolívar, which is divided into 100 céntimos. There are nickel alloy coins for 5, 12½, 25 and 50 céntimos and 1, 2 and 5 bolívares, and notes for 5, 10, 20, 50, 100, 500 and 1,000 bolívares. Visitors can change money at Bs.4.28 per US$1. There are no restrictions on the import and export of bolívares or of foreign currency. Popular names for coins: Real, Bs.0.50; Médio, 0.25; Puya or Centavo, 0.05.

Weights and Measures are metric.

Voltage 110 volts, 60 cycles, throughout the country.

The **Cost of Living** depends largely on who you are and where you are. Income tax is low. With Bs.3,000 monthly, unmarried pay 5.2% and married 4.7% or less. Travellers normally reckon Bs.120 daily in Caracas or Maracaibo and Bs.80 in the provinces, without long distance fares. A Peace Corps volunteer tells us, however, that one can manage on Bs.45 in Caracas and Maracaibo, including hotel, food and taxis, and on Bs.25 in the interior, and one informant living in Caracas manages bed and three meals *(en pensión)*, together with lunch out, for about US$14 a day. Breakfast at a *fuente de soda* in Caracas (orange juice, ham-and-cheese roll and coffee with milk) should not cost over US$1. Many set commercial lunches *(gran cubierto* or *menú ejecutivo)* cost no more than US$3.50, and steak, chips and salad at a *fuente de soda* should not set you back more than US$2.

Goods in shops bear a label "PVP" followed by the price. This is the maximum authorized price; you may be able to negotiate a discount but should in no case pay more than the PVP price.

Pickpockets. We are advised that cameras and other valuables should not be exposed prominently, especially in shanty-town areas.

Food Both in Caracas and to a lesser extent in Maracaibo there are excellent restaurants specialising in foreign regional cuisines: French, Chinese, Arab, Austrian, Bavarian, Hungarian, Argentine, Spanish, and especially Italian. Poultry and meat, except for pheasants and lamb, are locally produced. Venezuelan beef is comparable with Argentina's and, surprisingly, portions are larger. There is excellent local fish (we recommend *pargo* or red snapper), crayfish, small oysters and prawns, though sole, trout and large oysters are imported. Sometimes there is turtle. Of true Venezuelan food there is *sancocho* (a stew of vegetables, especially yuca, with meat, chicken or fish); *arepas,* a kind of white maize bread, very bland in flavour; toasted arepas served with a wide selection of relishes or the local somewhat salty white cheese are cheap, filling and nutritious; *cachapas,* a corn pancake (soft, not hard like Mexican tortillas) wrapped around white cheese; *pabellón,* made of shredded meat, beans, rice and fried plantains; and *empanadas,* maize-flour pies containing cheese, meat or fish. At Christmas only there are *hallacas,* a maize pancake stuffed with chicken, pork, olives, etc. boiled in a plantain leaf (but don't eat the leaf). The main fruits are bananas, oranges, grapefruit, mangoes, pineapple and pawpaws. Apples, pears plums, grapes, and (sometimes) strawberries are imported. A delicious sweet is *huevos chimbos*—egg yolk boiled and bottled in sugar syrup. There is no local wine though some foreign wines are bottled locally. There are several good local beers, mineral waters, gin and excellent rum. The coffee is very good; visitors should also try a *batido,* a delicious drink made from fruit pulp, milk and sugar. Water is free in all restaurants even if no food is bought. The Caracas "Daily Journal" (in English) lists many reliable restaurants in Caracas and Maracaibo. Venezuelans dine late.

Postal Rates From Venezuela: Air mail (5 grams): To U.K. Bs.1.25; to U.S.A., Bs.0.80. Air mail should take 3 to 7 days but can take a lot longer. City mail takes 3 to 7 days.

Cables Aeropostal Cables Internacionales provides communication with all parts of the world through its cable stations at Caracas, Coro, La Guaira and Maracaibo. From Venezuela: Ordinary (per word): To U.K., Bs.2.76; to New York, Bs.1.04; to other U.S. cities, Bs.1.30. **Warning** Cables into Venezuela are very slow, sometimes taking longer to be delivered than air mail. If it's urgent, telephone or telex is far preferable.

Telephone Service to other countries is mostly routed by submarine cable to U.S.A. Most major cities are now linked by direct dialling. Calls: To U.K., Bs.60 (Sunday Bs.48) for the first 3 minutes, Bs.20 for each minute after. To New York, Bs.27 (Sunday or after 1900, Bs.22.50). Calls out of Venezuela are more expensive than calls into it.

Official Time in Venezuela is 4 hours behind G.M.T.

Press

Caracas "El Universal", "El Nacional" (both very good papers indeed), "La Religión", "Ultimas Noticias", "The Daily Journal" (very good standard), "El Mundo" (evening), "Elite" (weekly), "Momento" (weekly), "Venezuela Gráfica" (weekly), "Páginas" (weekly), "Semana" (weekly), "Ve Venezuela", tourist bi-monthly.

Maracaibo "Panorama", "La Crítica". **Puerto La Cruz:** "El Tiempo".

British Representation in Venezuela The Embassy (including the Commercial Department), the Consulate and the British Council, are at Edificio La Estancia, Apartado 1246 (for letters), 12th floor, Av. La Estancia, No. 10, Ciudad Comercial Tamanaco, Chuao, Caracas. (Tel.: 91-12-55.)

There are British Vice-Consuls at Maracaibo, Puerto La Cruz, Punto Fijo and Valencia.

The **United States of America** is represented in Venezuela by an Embassy and Consulate at Caracas, with Vice-Consuls at La Guaira, Maracaibo, Puerto La Cruz and Caripito.

American Express Agents Caracas: Turismo Maso Consolidado, *Hotel Tamanaco*, Las Mercedes. Tel.: 914308, 914555.

(Our thanks for help in revising this section go to Michael Davison, now again resident in Caracas, whose contributions have been many and invaluable; to Sarah Cameron, of LBI Economics Department, for updating the whole chapter and revising the Economy section; and to the following travellers: James K. Bock (Mexico City), W. O. Boyes, Urcel Daniel (Washington, D.C.), John Eames and Maggie Harvey, Tim and Arlene Frost (Hamilton, N.Z), Peter Fürst and Hakon Hegnar (Norway), Schelte de Graaf (Netherlands), Ucky Hamilton (N.Z.), Robert Hertzig (New York City), Dieter E. Jungblut (W. Berlin), Per Leth-Espensen (Herler, Denmark), Dr. Terry McCarthy (Singapore), Bernard Mallet (Paris), Karin Östman (Spanga, Sweden), Jenny Owen, and Henri van Rooy (Roosendaal, Netherlands) and Magaret Symons (N.Z.).

Will you help us?

We do all we can to get our facts right in *The South American Handbook*. Each chapter is thoroughly revised each year, by people living in each country. When revision is not enough, whole chapters are rewritten. But Latin America and the West Indies cover a vast area, and our eyes cannot be everywhere. A hotel, a restaurant, a cabaret dies; another, a good one, is born; a building we describe is pulled down, a street renamed. Names and addresses of good hotels and restaurants for "budget-minded" travellers are always very welcome.

Your information may be far more up-to-date than ours. If your letter reaches us early enough in the year it will be used in our next edition, but write whenever you want to, for all your letters are used sooner or later.

—Thank you

Trade & Travel Publications Ltd
THE MENDIP PRESS · PARSONAGE LANE
WESTGATE ST. · BATH BA1 1EN · ENGLAND

THE GUIANAS

LIKE the West Indians, the people of the three Guianas, Guyana (formerly British Guiana), Suriname and French Guyane, are not regarded even by their close neighbours as belonging to Latin America. This was the only part of South America, if one excludes the Falkland Islands, to have been colonized by Northern Europeans. The difference in cultural influence, and the fact that the Guianas remained colonies long after the rest of the Continent had achieved independence, established them as countries apart. Their populations are different, too; a great proportion of them are of Asian descent and there are also the differences of language and religions. Although French Guyane is largely Roman Catholic and its people mostly black, in Guyana and especially in Suriname the European element is very small and the majority is composed of people of East Indian, Indonesian and Chinese descent. Religions range from Christian to Hindu and Muslim.

The explanation of the apparent anomaly of these three Northern European possessions on the South American continent goes back to the early days of the Spanish conquest of the New World. There was go gold or any other apparent source of wealth to attract the attention of the Spanish discoverers. This part of the coast, which Columbus had first sighted in 1498, seemed to them not only barren but scantily populated and seemingly uninhabitable. The English, the French and the Dutch, anxious to establish a foothold in this part of the world, were not so fastidious. English, and particularly French and Dutch attempts to settle in other parts of the Continent had been repelled, although the Dutch came very near to holding a part of the north-eastern coast of Brazil. Furthermore, apart from the approach by sea, the Guianas were, and still are, largely isolated from the rest of the Continent by virtually uninhabited country, either mountainous or swampy. This was to discourage Spanish and Portuguese settlers.

Today, the only country which is challenging the existence of these "remnants of colonialism" is Venezuela, which has formally claimed the part of Guyana W of the River Essequibo—more than half of that country's whole territory. The other two Guianas are the Republic of Suriname, independent since November 1975, and Guyane, formerly the colony of Cayenne, now a Department of Metropolitan France.

The Dutch were the first on the scene: they settled on the banks of the Essequibo river (now in Guyana) as early as 1596. By 1613 the British had arrived in Suriname and by 1626 the French had taken possession of Cayenne. The Dutch, well practised in such work, proceeded to drain the swamps and lagoons into the sea, but both the British and the French confined themselves to narrow strips of cultivable land near the coastal margins. By the Peace of Breda in 1667, the British bartered their possession for Dutch Nieuw Amsterdam (now New York). During the wars of 1793-1814 the Dutch for a time held all three colonies, and later the British. The present division was agreed upon by the three nations between 1814 and 1817.

Guiana is an Amerindian word meaning land surrounded by water. It is an apt description, for the Guianas lie in the basins of rivers and streams which run into the Atlantic between the great river systems of the Amazon and the Orinoco.

All three countries have much the same surface: along the coast runs a belt of narrow, flat marshy land, at its widest in Suriname. This coastland carries almost all the crops and most of the population. Behind lies a belt of crystalline upland, heavily gouged and weathered. The bauxite, gold and diamonds are in this area. Behind this again is the massif of the Guiana Highlands. Rising sheer out of the sea of forest the peaks, some of them over 9,000 feet, present a fantastic wall of glowing red sandstone cliffs, broken into immense ravines and colossal monoliths of canted rock. Mountains with rounded tops reach a height of 3,000 feet in the Tumac-Humac range, the divide between French Guyane and Suriname, and Brazil, and 8,630 feet at flat-topped Mount Roraima, where Guyana, Venezuela and Brazil have a common frontier. This mountain (Conan Doyle's "Lost World") is walled around by 2,000-foot cliffs rising sheer from the forest.

The hill land and, apart from occasional dry savannahs, the mountain land, is very heavily forested. From the sandstone mountain prateau in western Guyana the rivers fall precipitously into the hills: the Potaro drops 741 feet at the Kaieteur Fall. Cascades and rapids make all the rivers unnavigable save for short distances inland from the coastal flats. Rainfall over the whole area is very heavy.

All three countries share with the northern coast of Venezuela the distinction of having the highest annual temperatures in South America. There is a 5°C range between night and day, a greater range than there is between the seasons. Humidity is very high, but is tempered by the prevailing north-eastern winds.

Very few of the inhabitants are of European origin: less than 1.4% in Guyana and 1% in Suriname. In the comparative absence of indigenous populations, the great problem has been to get enough labour to work the sugar and coffee plantations and rice fields. African slaves were brought in to begin with; these were later supplemented in Guyana and Suriname by East Indians and Javanese and even Chinese. More than half the total population of those two countries is today of Asian origin.

N.B. You need to have your own shoe-cleaning equipment; there seem to be no shoeshine boys in any of the Guianas!

GUYANA

GUYANA has an area of 83,000 square miles, nearly the size of Britain, but only about 0.5% (or 280,000 acres) is cultivated. The population is about 794,000 (1975), of whom about 80% are literate. Some 10% of the country is the upland savannah of the Rupununi and Kanaku mountains, in the remote hinterland of the SW. Here, and between the Pomeroon River and the Venezuelan border, live some 6,000 people, half of them aborigines. Little of their land is cultivated. They herd cattle, but the grass is poor. Transport to the coast is difficult.

A huge tract of thick, hilly jungle and forest—85% of the country—slopes down from this high plateau towards the sea. The soil is poor and sandy; there is little cultivation, but the bauxite, gold and diamonds are in this area. The rest of the country—3.5%—is a narrow belt, seldom 8 miles deep, running 200 miles along the coast. It contains some 90% of the total population, grows all the sugar, which accounts for 33% of the exports, and the rice which is the main subsistence crop. Much of this belt, which is 4 feet below sea-level, is intersected by great rivers and suffers from both deluge and drought; it can only be maintained by a complicated system of dykes and drains, a permanent costly burden on agriculture. Nearly all the cultivated land is in this belt.

From 80 to 100 inches of rain fall mostly in two well defined seasons: April to August and November to January. A little natural drainage is given by the rivers; the Corentyne, along the Suriname border to the E; the Berbice and Demerara, 30 and 100 miles respectively to the W; and the Essequibo, which drains most of the country and enters the sea midway along the coast. All rivers, large and small, are tidal up to the limit of the coastal plain. Falls and rapids make difficult their use as communications into the interior, but 60 miles of the Demerara river are navigable by shallow-draft ocean craft up to the Mackenzie bauxite mines.

There is a curious example of the Corentyne, the river which separates Guyana from Suriname, of the fatuous way in which one nation will cede to, or obtain from, another nation some quite senseless ruling which is bound later to cause trouble between them. There is a legal ruling that Suriname's territorial waters extend to the high-water mark on the Guyanese side of the Corentyne river. This has already led to one unpleasant incident in which some Guyanese loggers were arrested for taking timber from the Suriname side (that is, the Guyana side) of the river!

The original Dutch and English settlers at the beginning of the 17th century established posts up-river, in the hills, mostly as trading points with the Amerindian natives. Plantations laid out were worked by slaves from Africa. Poor soil defeated this venture, and the settlers retreated to the coastal area in mid-18th century: the old plantations can still be detected from the air. Coffee and cotton, with a little tobacco and sugar cane, were the main crops up to the end of the 18th century, but sugar had become the dominant crop by 1820. To grow it 110,000 slaves had been imported by 1830. In 1834 slavery was abolished. Many of the slaves scattered as small landholders, and the plantation owners had to look for another source of labour. It was found in indentured East Indians, a few Chinese, and some Portuguese labourers from the Azores and Madeira. About 240,000 had come from British India by 1914. At the end of their indentures most went home; others settled in Guyana.

Sugar and rice are largely dependent for labour on the Guyanese of Indian descent; some 80,000 live on the sugar estates alone. The Africans prefer town life, working in offices and shops or for the Government and manning the police force. They are outnumbered and will progressively be more so as the population increases. Europeans comprise about 1%, East Indians about 51%, Africans some 43%, and the others about 5%. Religious affiliation is also varied: Christian 57%, Hindu 34%, Moslem 9%.

Nearly 25% of the population lives in Georgetown or close by. Density per square mile in the coastal belt is over 1,700. Until 1920 there was little natural increase, but the suppression of malaria and other diseases has since led to a large growth of population. The country is overpopulated in relation to its readily exploitable resources and is becoming more so. Whether the interior—96% of the country—could support more people even if it were opened up is debatable.

The Amerindians, of the Arawak and Carib groups, a short, stocky, coffee-coloured race with dark hair and sensitive faces, are rapidly losing their isolation. Contact with civilisation has brought European education, clothes, drink, money, and disease. Their tribal organisation is breaking down and the sense of community and the ethical standards imposed by a primitive life will soon have disappeared.

History

The country was first partially settled between 1616 and 1621 by the Dutch West India Company, who erected a fort and depot at Fort Kyk-over-al (County of Essequibo). In 1624, a settlement was founded on the Berbice River by Van Peere, a Flushing merchant. The first English attempt at settlement was made by Captain Leigh on the Oiapoque River (now French Guyane) in 1604. The effort, though followed up by Robert Harcourt in 1613 and 1627, failed to establish a permanent settlement. Lord Willoughby, famous in the early history of Barbados, founded a settlement in 1663 at Suriname, which was captured by the Dutch in 1667 and ceded to them at the Peace of Breda in exchange for New York. The Dutch held the three colonies with more or less firmness, now yielding to England, now to France, till 1796 when, during the French Revolution, they were captured by a British fleet sailing from Barbados. The territory was restored to the Dutch in 1802, but in the following year was retaken by Great Britain, which finally gained it in 1814. In 1899 a commission arbitrating on a boundary dispute between Britain and Venezuela awarded over half the present territory of Guyana, consisting of the territory to the W of the River Essequibo, to Britain. Venezuela is claiming the land then ceded, and a Venezuelan-Guyanese commission is seeking a solution.

On May 26, 1966, Guyana was granted independence, with a Governor-General appointed by the Queen. On February 23, 1970 it became a co-operative republic within the Commonwealth, with a President as Head of State; the President is Arthur Chung. The bauxite and sugar industries have been nationalized, and the country appears firmly set on a Co-operative path. A Prime Minister and Cabinet are responsible to the National Assembly, which has 53 members elected under a single-list system of proportional representation for a maximum term of five years. Mr. Forbes Burnham, leader of the People's National Congress, is Prime Minister.

Georgetown, the chief town and port and capital, is on the right bank at the mouth of the River Demerara. It extends two miles along the river front and has a depth of about a mile. Its population is 188,000, or roughly a quarter of the total population. The climate is tropical, with a mean temperature of 80.5°F, and there are two rainy and two dry seasons in the coastal area. Georgetown, with 19th century wooden houses supported on stilts, and charming green boulevards laid along the lines of the old Dutch canals, has a character of its own.

Because Georgetown is a tidal port, vessels with draught of more than 20 ft. cannot cross the bar, which is around 12 to 15 miles from the port. The 20 ft. draught allows for pulling 1 ft. through mud when the predicted depth at the bar is 19 ft. Ships work cargo with their own gear.

The town, protected by a sea-wall and a system of dykes opened at low tide, is set on an alluvial flat below the high-water mark. All that is seen of it from the sea are the masts of the wireless station, the Lighthouse (which may be visited by arrangement with the Harbour Master), the Gothic tower of Stabroek Market, the twin dishes of the radio-telephone system, the tower of the *Pegasus Hotel* and the twin square towers of the Church of the Sacred Heart. The other main buildings come into sight when the river is entered, their clean, bright whiteness shining through the belt of trees. Most of the older buildings are of wood and some are shapely, but since the disastrous fire of 1945 many concrete buildings have been put up in the commercial centre. Some of the most impressive wooden buildings from the colonial past are: the City Hall (Avenue of the Republic) constructed in 1887 is in Gothic style; St. George's Cathedral (North Road) dates from 1892, and with a height of 143 feet is said to be the tallest wooden building in the world; the Law Courts (High Street) were finished in 1878 and have mock Tudor framing; the President's residence at Guyana House (Main Street), built in 1852; and the imposing Parliament Building (Avenue of the Republic). Other important public buildings are the Roman Catholic Cathedral (Brickdam), one of the tallest buildings in the city; the Bishops High School; St. Stanislaus College (Jesuit); Queens College; the Technical Institute; the Stabroek Market (Water Street) is a focal point of the city—a large iron structure with an imposing clock tower where anything from a hairpin to a house can be bought; the Public Free Library; the Guyana Museum (Company Path); and several churches. The Playhouse Theatre, seating 216, is in Parade Street. There is a museum opposite the post office, which has some excellent Indian exhibits. Modern architecture, by comparison, is represented by the *Pegasus Hotel;* the Bank of Guyana Building; and Telephone House. At the head of Brickdam, a main street, is an exciting aluminium arch which commemorates independence. Across the road is a new monument to the 1763 Slave Rebellion surmounted by a striking statue of Cuffy, leader of the rebellion. At night water cascades from different levels and is prettily lit. Adjacent to the Botanic Gardens on Homestretch Avenue is the new Cultural Centre. This is a magnificent theatre probably the best in the Caribbean, air-conditioned, comfortable, with a large stage and fine acoustics. All it needs now is a regular schedule of performances; for the most part it is closed.

On the outskirts are many cricket, football and hockey grounds, tennis courts, and a golf course (8 miles out). The Georgetown Cricket Club, with its pavilions and club rooms, has one of the finest cricket grounds in the tropics. Test matches are played here as well as international motor-car and motor-cycle racing (Easter and November). There are several open spaces and promenades. The old Dutch-built sea-wall (now being rebuilt) is cool in the evening. The mud makes it undesirable to swim in the sea but many locals do so, then go home and bathe! The racecourse has been closed. The international airport is at Timehri, 25 miles S of Georgetown on the first piece of solid ground in the coastlands—a hill rising to the phenomenal altitude of 40 feet. There is an airstrip for local flights at Ogle, six miles from the city.

Things to See The Botanic Gardens, covering 120 acres, have a fine collection of palms, as well as orchids and ponds of Victoria Regia and lotus lilies. There are thousands of birds in the shrubberies. Its Zoo has a fine collection of local animals including the manatee, the model for the mermaid legend. It appears that about half of the gardens are now closed to the public.

The Natural History museum has an up-to-date display of all aspects of Guyanese life and culture; admission free. Entry to Botanic Gardens free; to Zoo, adults 25 cents, children 5 cents.

The University of Guyana is at Turkeyen, near the city. The Promenade Gardens on Middle Street (entry free) have many beautiful tropical plants and flowers, including the rare Cannonball Tree *(Couroupita guianensis),* so named for the appearance of its poisonous fruit.

Shopping The East Indian shops have a fine assortment of the beaten brasswork commonly known as Benares ware. They sell gold and silver Indian jewellery and knick-knacks. Other possible buys are fragrant kus-kus grass, guava jelly, cassava cakes, many Amerindian curios such as bead aprons, bows and arrows, blowpipes, basket work and bright plumed head-dresses. Buy these in Stabroek Market, souvenir shops in Water Street, Margarita Gift Shop in Middle Street, or in the *Tower Hotel* and at the Guyana Crafts Co-operative in High Street. A more interesting way of getting curios is to go into the Bush (special permit needed) among the Amerindians.

Travel Agency Guyana Overland Tours, P.O. box 300, 38 Main Street (below *Park Hotel),* Georgetown. Tel.: 69876. Cables: Gotours. They offer a number of tours of one, two and more days in the interior, and will send details on request. They sell good maps. Cacique Travel Agency (Main and Hope St.), Neil Mendoza (the manager) is very helpful and informative.

Hotels Air-conditioned, private bathroom; prices for single or double room in G$: *Guyana Pegasus,* 70-96, swimming pool, extra; *Tower,* 60-75, swimming pool (open to respectable non-residents at G$1.50, also 3-course meals at G$10 p.p.); *Woodbine,* 20-30, recommended; *Belvedere,* Camp Street, G$40 d; *Park,* 40-60;

Palm Court, 16 p.p., with breakfast; *Le Grille,* 176 Middle Street, P.O. Box 744, Tel.: 62000, especially recommended, G$16 d, incl. good breakfast; *Demico* (opposite Staboek Market, over cafeteria) G$30 d a/c, book a month ahead. *Wagon Wheel,* G$12 p.p., a bit noisy. All in main business area. Several comfortable and central boarding houses, e.g. *Bill's Guest House,* 46 High Street, G$5 d. highly recommended, meals not available; *Ark Guesthouse,* Coral Street, G$20 d; *Elizabeth Guest House,* Wellington Street, G$7 s; *Rima Guest House,* Middle Street, G$25 d with breakfast, modernised and good.

Restaurants At *Pegasus* and *Tower* Hotels, good Anglo-American food; the *Pegasus* puts on Sunday lunch for G$8.25—there is a steel band and you can use the swimming pool for free; *Palm Court,* quite good; *Belvedere Hotel,* "The Hut", Anglo-American and French; *Qik-Serv,* good and clean self-service; *Park Hotel's* new pavement restaurant; *Kwang Chou,* Camp St. and Regent St., and *Chinese Dragon,* Robb St. and Av. of the Republic, both good Chinese; Indian/Chinese/Creole fare provided at the *Rice Bowl/Doc's Creole Corner* on Robb Street, recommended. *The Local,* on Avenue of the Republic, also recommended for casareep, a manioc dish; *Grubb Inn,* good cheap Creole food and dancing.

Tipping Hotel and restaurant staff, 10%; taxis, same; airport porters, 25 cents a bag; hairdressers, 50 cents; cloakroom attendants and cinema usherettes, no tip.

Current 110 volts.

Banks The Royal Bank of Canada (6 branches); Barclays Bank International (6 branches); Chase Manhattan Bank; Bank of Baroda Ltd. (2); Bank of Nova Scotia; Guyana Co-operative Bank (7). Open: 0800-1200, but 0800-1100 on Saturday.

Post Office Main one at North Road, open 0730-1600.

British High Commission First Secretary at 44 Main Street, P.O. Box 625. Tel.: 65881. Telex: GY221.

Motor Cars Self-drive from Sankar Bros., Main Street (Tel.: 61058), book a month in advance, G$30 a day, free for 30 miles, then G$0.30 a mile. Fuel: G$2.36 for Imperial gallon of "regular".

Bus Service In the city (15 cents) and long distance, fairly good. Main terminal at Staboek Market Square. City services run 0600-2200. Bus to New Amsterdam leaves 0700, or 0900; journey takes 3 hours, G$7 (launch across river G$7 and bus on to Springlands G$0.15).

Taxis G$2-3 per fare in city limits.

Ferries The "Makouria" and "Kurupukari" cross the Demerara River between Georgetown's Ferry Stelling and Vreed-en-Hoop every half-hour between 0530 and 1930. Single fare: 20 cents.

International Telecommunications: Telegraph, Telephone and Telex: Cable and Wireless (West Indies) Ltd., Bank of Guyana building. No "collect" telephone calls may be made.

Roads There is a good two-lane highway from Georgetown to Springlands on the Suriname border, with a ferry across the Berbice river. There is also a good road between Linden (Mackenzie) and the East Bank; it joins the road which runs from Georgetown to the airport.

Air Services Guyana Airways has many scheduled and non-scheduled passenger and freight services to airfields in Guyana, including the Kaieteur Fall (G$82 return). To Lethem on the Brazilian frontier, G$55, Mon.-Fri.; scheduled flights to Suriname, French Guiana and nearby Caribbean islands. Shared taxi (arranged by travel agent with Loy's Taxi Service on booking flight) between Georgetown and airport, G$5.50 per seat or G$18-20 per taxi; you may get a seat for less *from* airport *into* town; bus, G$1.25. British Airways office in *Tower Hotel.*

Warning Elizabeth Allen writes: Georgetown has acquired an unpleasant reputation for assaults and robberies, especially in the evening and at night. There is no need for undue alarm, but do not wear jewellery or carry handbags or wallets, etc. in easily accessible places and take particular care at night by travelling in a taxi (G$3 in town). Most people are friendly: don't offer temptation.

Linden, the bauxite town, is made up of 3 towns: Mackenzie, Wismar and Christianburg. The latter two are separated from Mackenzie by the Demerara River on whose banks they all lie, in dense jungle. The Guyana Bauxite Company (formerly an Alcan subsidiary but now nationalized) supports a community of about 35,000. There is a golf club; visitors are welcome. The forest crowds down to the edge of the russet-tinged river, but is cleared here and there for farms and logging camps. The river is navigable right up to the mine, and it is disconcerting on rounding its bends to meet large ocean-going steamers. Linden is the second largest community in Guyana, but accommodation is scarce and expensive (*Mackenzie Hotel,* G$30-50 double). There is a bridge across the river and a road to Georgetown.

Current 220 volts. Same as New Amsterdam and Bartica, below.

New Amsterdam, capital of Berbice, the most easterly county of Guyana, is on the right bank of the Berbice river near its mouth. It is 65 miles SE of Georgetown, from which there is a road to Rosignol, ferry point (20 cents) for New Amsterdam, across the river. Pop. 25,000. The foliage gives the town a picturesque air. Poor roads, water should be boiled before drinking; there is electricity.

Hotels *Embassy,* new; *Penguin,* G$25-35; *Church View Guest House.*
Banks The Royal Bank of Canada (branch also at Rose Hall); Barclays Bank International; New Bank of Baroda.
Bus To Georgetown, two a day, G$7; shared taxi to Georgetown, G$8; to Springlands, G$0.15. Taxi to Springlands, G$12.

Springlands, near the mouth of the Corentyne River, is a small port frequented by sailing vessels. There is a daily ferry (not Sundays or national holidays of either country) to and from Nieuw Nickerie (Suriname). Border formalities at Springlands are very thorough and slow; it can take as much as ten hours to cross the river. The town is officially referred to as **Corriverton,** as it has been joined with Skeldon to form the Corentyne River Town (population 17,000). The road from Springlands to New Amsterdam has been rebuilt.

Hotels *Ambassador,* close to point for ferry to Nickerie; *Arawak,* opposite ferry, G$4 d, good value; *Liberty.*
Banks Royal Bank of Canada and Barclays Bank International.
Taxi Shared taxi to Georgetown, G$10 each.
Bus To Georgetown, changing at New Amsterdam, G$8.

Morawhanna, on the Waini River (near the Venezuelan frontier) is another small port.

Bartica, at the junction of the Essequibo and Mazaruni rivers, is the "take-off" town for the gold and diamond fields, Kaieteur Fall, and the interior generally. Here an Amazonian mass of waters meet, but vastly more beautiful, for they are coloured the deep indigo purple of all Guyanese rivers and not the dull mud-brown of the Amazon. A boat takes you between Bartica and Parika (36 miles) three times a week; buses ply between Parika and Vreed-en-Hoop, connecting with the ferry for Georgetown. The m.v. *Malili* plies daily between Parika and Adventure (Essequibo Coast area)—see the book *Three Singles to Adventure,* by Gerald Durrell.

Hotels *Marin* (best); *Modern*.

Airstrip Six flights a week to and from Ogle airstrip, 6 miles from Georgetown.

The Essequibo is navigable to large boats for some miles above Bartica. The Cuyuni flows into the Mazaruni 3 miles above Bartica, and above this confluence the Marazuni is blocked for 120 miles by thousands of islands, rapids and waterfalls. To avoid this stretch of treacherous river a road has been built from Bartica to Issano, where boats can be taken up the more tranquil upper Mazaruni. For those who want to visit the diamond fields there are regular air trips by Guyana Airways to Kurupung on the Mazaruni river. From there it is just a walk (but not without a permit) to the diamond fields. Elizabeth Allen writes: The Upper Mazaruni River has been selected as the site of a large dam to provide electricity for development. Many people will have to be resettled elsewhere. The sovereignty of this area is under dispute with Venezuela. The eastern coastland, drained by four major rivers, was first settled by slave labour under the Dutch in the eighteenth century, draining the land and erecting sea defences to found sugar plantations. Twenty-one new agricultural settlements have been attempted since 1880, mainly involved in the production of rice, often on abandoned sugar plantations. Only thirteen continue to be active.

The **Kaieteur Fall**, on the Potaro River, in the heart of tropical Guyana, ranks with the Niagara, Victoria, and Iguazú Falls in majesty and beauty. This Fall, nearly five times the height of Niagara, with a sheer drop of 741 ft., pours its waters over a channel nearly 300 ft. wide. Kaieteur can be visited by air from Georgetown in one day; the scheduled service, on Sundays, costs G$85 and includes a stop at Orinduik Falls. (You must book at least 6 weeks in advance to ensure a seat.)

The overland route to the Fall takes 7 days. The first day's journey is from Georgetown to Bartica; either take the steamer round the coast and see the Island of Leguan at the mouth of the Essequibo or cross the Demerara by ferry to Vreed-en-Hoop and on by bus or motor car to Parika, there to join the steamer for Bartica at the confluence of the Essequibo and Mazaruni. The second day is a 113-mile journey *via* Garraway Stream with its fine suspension bridge across the Potaro, over a jungle road to Kangaruma where the night is spent at a government rest house. The next day a boat is taken to Tukeit with portages at the Amatuk and Waratuk Falls. There is a rest house at Tukeit and good bathing from a white sand beach. The climb to the top of the Kaieteur Fall takes at least two hours (but is worth it) to watch the blue, white and brown water tumbling into a stupendous gorge.

The Kaieteur Falls lie within the Kaieteur National Park where there is a variety of wildlife—tapirs, ocelots, monkeys, armadillos, anteaters, and jungle and river birds. The Pakaraima Mountains stretch from Kaieteur westwards to include the highest peak in Guyana, Mt. Roraima (9,094 feet), and the inspiration for Conan Doyle's "Lost World".

Precautions Book accommodation at Bartica and the Rest House and arrange for boats on the Potaro in advance. Take what tobacco, food and drink you need, a sleeping bag, a sheet and blanket, a mosquito net, and kerosene for the Tilley lamps; also anti-malarial tablets, a must in this area.

Elizabeth Allen writes: The south-western area of Guyana is known as the Rupununi Savanna. 13,000 sq. km. lie in Guyana and a further 47,000 sq. km. in Venezuela and Brazil. The Kanuku Mountains divide the Rupununi from west to east, and rise to 3,143 feet in Mt. Ilamikipang. The savanna is a dry grassland region covered with native grasses, scattered scrub, and termite hills. Since the late nineteenth century it has been settled by cattle ranchers and Jesuit missionaries. It is one of the more densely settled Amerindian areas. Special permits must be obtained to visit, from the Secretary of Home Affairs, 6 Brickdam, Georgetown. Malaria is prevalent and Paludrin (or alternative prophylactic) should be taken.

Lethem, on the Brazilian frontier in the SW, has no reliable road connection as yet with the rest of the country. Guyana Airways flies every day from Georgetown, flying *via* Kato in the Pakaraima Mountains where tomatoes are being produced. The flight takes one hour and costs G$55 single. There is no direct air connection to Boa Vista, capital of Roraima, Brazil; the 130 km. have to be travelled by road: cost G$2 p.p. s. There are tracks NE to Manari and Annai, and the Tacutu river can easily be crossed to enter Brazil (rowing boat, or ford in dry season; there is now a vehicle pontoon, G$2 p.p., one way).

Elizabeth Allen writes: Lethem is the local administrative centre for the Rupununi District, supporting 3 bars (the coldest beer is sold nearest the airstrip) a military post, telegraph office and a number of small stores. It is the centre of the ranching economy of the area and was the centre of disagreement between the Government and ranchers in the late 1960s. The first Jesuit Mission to be established in Guyana is at the village of St. Ignatius, about 1½ miles from Lethem—it was founded in 1911 by the famous Jesuit Cary Elwes. There has been an attempt to settle blacks from the coast on agricultural land near Lethem.

Hotels Mr. Arthur M. Bobb's *Tacutu Hotel,* near airfield (he organizes trips into Brazil), G$60 d, full board; *Manari Guest House and Ranch,* 10 km. from airport by jeep, G$60 d, with bath and full board, very good, riding, fishing and swimming. Elizabeth Allen writes: The creek at the rear of the ranch-house is safe for swimming, and horses may be hired for riding, and there is good fishing nearby. Day trips can be arranged to the Kanuku Mountains, about 2 hours' drive by jeep, appearing blue, clad in forest and occasional cloud in the distance. A half-day visit can be made to the Moco-Moco Falls to bathe and eat lunch by the cascading river after walking for about a mile through the rich jungle vegetation.

Border Crossing Exit stamp, customs forms and declarations and all immigration procedures must be conducted at the police station before leaving Guyana for Brazil. The Brazilian military post at Bomfim is some 3 miles inside Brazilian territory and closes at 1800 each evening. There is no public transport from the Tacutu River crossing to the village; given time and patience a vehicle can be arranged in Lethem with "Selino". (Brazilian time is one hour behind Guyanese time.)

Onward transport to Boa Vista, Roraima, needs to be arranged in Lethem, or in Bomfim at the military post, or at Masie Ward's bar in Bomfim. Approx. cost of journey Bomfim-Boa Vista, US$50 per vehicle, single journey.

The Economy

The main crops on the agricultural land of the coast are sugar and rice. The recent nationalization of the sugar industry has placed control of the Guyanese monocultural economy in the hands of the Government. Until recently Bookers McConnell owned or controlled the Guyanese sugar plantations, it was the sector which contributed 11.5% of the gross domestic product (g.d.p.) in 1973 but had, since the Second World War, shown increasing production allied with a decline in employment. Rice production (1973) represented 2.1% of g.d.p.

Reserves of timber have been estimated at 70,000 sq. metres, and include substantial stands of valuable greenheart. Forest stretches from the swampy coastal lowlands right up to the highlands and savanna of the south-western borderlands. Forestry represented 1.2% of g.d.p. in 1973.

The cattle industry is also located in the interior principally in the savanna areas, such as the Rupununi (g.d.p. 2.4% in 1973).

Food imports are 21% of the total; many could be produced locally and the strict import regulations in force are intended to try and reduce this dependence on imported foodstuffs. Most consumer goods and all machinery and fuel have to be imported.

Bauxite accounted in 1976 for 34% of all exports by value. Guyana is the second largest producer of bauxite in the world, producing 20% of world output. In 1970 the mineral accounted for 53% of all exports by value, and was the main contributor to the 15.5% g.d.p. of mining and quarrying in 1973. The largest bauxite deposits in the world are at Mackenzie, on the Demerara river. The Guyana Bauxite Company (Guybau) produces 77% of the bauxite from the Demba mines S of Mackenzie on both sides of the Demerara river, and at Ituni, 35 miles to the SE. It has, at Mackenzie, the largest bauxite calcining kiln in the world, and an alumina plant. The Reynolds Metals Company (23%), gets its bauxite at Kwakwani, 100 miles up the Berbice river from Everton, near New Amsterdam. This is a better grade than at Mackenzie, but the Berbice river has not been dredged for ocean-going vessels and the ore is taken by barge to Everton for trans-shipment. It has a calcining plant. The bauxite industry has now been nationalized.

Guyana supplies 90% of the world's calcined bauxite. There are enough reserves to keep up the present rate of extraction until 1985. The industry employs 3,000 men and women: 2% of the country's labour force.

Foreign Trade (G$m) (US$1 = G$2.55, June 1978)

	1971	1972	1973	1974	1975	1976
Exports (f.o.b.) ..	298.4	292.8	288.3	594.9	837.2	701.9
Imports (c.i.f.) ..	267.6	299.0	349.2	565.0	806.4	912.8

The main imports are food, machinery, oils, piece-goods and clothing. Guyana's main trading partners, in order of importance, are the U.S.A., the U.K. and Canada.

The only **industries** of any consequence are the sugar and rice factories, the processing of coconut oil and essential oil of limes, the saw mills and woodworking factories, and aerated water establishments. Georgetown has abundant electric power. Secondary industries have been increasing in recent years and include shipbuilding, general engineering, fruit-canning, brewing, rum-distilling, the manufacture of biscuits, edible oils, margarine, soap, underwear, building blocks, and compressed building boards. The Industrial Development Corporation is actively promoting new industries, the only way the country can possibly absorb its rapidly growing population. New items are plastic products and cosmetics.

Information for Visitors

Air Services

From Europe: 4 flights a week from London by British Airways, taking 12 hours and daily flights *via* Antigua and Barbados; connections from other points *via* Curaçao, Trinidad (Port of Spain), Guadeloupe or Martinique. Paramaribo is not very good for connections to/from Europe—a night-stop is always incurred.

From North America: by Pan Am from New York (4 flights a week), taking 7 hours; or from Miami (2 a week) *via* Caracas and Port of Spain.

Connections three times a week *via* Port of Spain by BWIA.

Regional Services: From Paramaribo (7 a week) by Air France (through-service from Cayenne), BWIA, ALM or Suriname Airways. From Port of Spain (25 a week) and other islands by BWIA, British Airways, Pan Am, Air France, ALM, Suriname Airways or Cubana. KLM's Curaçao-Georgetown-Paramaribo services are now operated by ALM (Antilles) and Suriname Airways. Note that Guyana Airways no longer fly to Suriname, and that they no longer fly between Guyana and Brazil; Cruzeiro do Sul flights terminate at Paramaribo. Connecting flights to Paramaribo and Cayenne for Belém leave weekly (Thursday). Return flights also weekly, leaving Belém on Fridays. The quickest way to Brazil is to fly *via* Caracas for Rio de Janeiro. Air France fly to Brazil once a week *via* Cayenne. Cubana fly Havana-Barbados-Trinidad-Georgetown.

Internal   Guyana Airways run scheduled flights to 22 places within the country, some from Timehri airport (25 miles from Georgetown) and some from the Ogle airstrip (6 miles out). Special charter flights can be arranged to other points in the West Indian area.

Sea Transport   Guyana is served from the Continent and Great Britain by Harrison Line, Booker Line, Royal Netherlands S.S. Coy., French Line, and Saguenay Shipping Ltd. From Canada (*via* the West Indies)—Saguenay Shipping Ltd. From the United States—Royal Netherlands Steamship Co., and Atlantic Line. From India—Nourse Line (trans-shipment at Trinidad). From British and French West Indies—Cie. Genérale Maritime. From Australia—"K" Line (Kawasaki Kisen Kaisha Ltd., Japan). From Hong Kong, Japan, Honolulu and Mexico—"K" Line N.Y.K. (Nippon Yusen Kaisha) line, and the OSK (Mitsui) Line.

Up to 12 passengers are carried by cargo vessels run by the Royal Netherlands Steamship Co. (agents: Phs. Van Ommeren, Ltd., Avenfield House, 118/121 Park Lane, London W1) and Saguenay Shipping Ltd. (agents: Stewart & Esplen Ltd., 3-6 Rangoon Street, London EC3), who ply from London, Liverpool and Southampton to Georgetown. An alternative route is from Southampton to Trinidad and on to Guyana by sea or air.

Exit Tax   Visitors pay a tax of G$20 on leaving, if they stay more than 24 hours.

Documents and Customs   All visitors must carry passports. Visas are required, except for nationals of West European and Commonwealth countries, Turkey, Uruguay and USA. Vaccination for smallpox required by all; for yellow fever by passengers arriving from most tropical countries (check). A through or return ticket to a destination outside the country is essential; a ticket out from Suriname or French Guyane is accepted. In the absence of such a ticket you may be required to pay a deposit. A permit is required from the Home Department at 6 Brickdam to visit the interior. Tourists may bring in duty free one-sixth of a gallon of spirits and of wine, 200 cigarettes or 50 cigars or half a pound of tobacco. Baggage examination is very thorough. You may be required to show you have enough money for your stay and fill in forms declaring money and jewellery that you may have with you. Foodstuffs generally may *not* be imported. Baggage checks are thorough and time-consuming.

Railways   None for passengers. Buses cover the old railway route.

Riverways   The Transport and Harbours Department operates: (1) Ferries across the Demerara, Berbice, and Essequibo; (2) Steamer services from Georgetown to Morawhanna and Mabaruma, on the Barima and Arika rivers, N.W. District; (3) Georgetown to Adventure on the Essequibo coast; (4) Georgetown to Bartica at the junction of the

Essequibo, Mazaruni, and Cuyuni rivers; (5) Georgetown to Pickersgill and other stations on the upper reaches of the Pomeroon river; (6) Parika to Adventure and Bartica; (7) New Amsterdam to Kwakwani, the bauxite town; (8) Launch service from New Amsterdam to Ikuruwa, up the Canje Creek; (9) Daily ferries up Mahaica and Mahaicony creeks.

Roads   A rebuilt 185-mile road runs along the coast from Springlands on the Corentyne to Charity on the Pomeroon; the Berbice, Demerara and Essequibo rivers are crossed by ferries. In the interior the road from Bartica to Garraway Stream on the Potaro River (102 miles) links up with the old Potaro road system, leading to the gold fields, and a branch road to Issano, Mazaruni River, gives easy access to the principal diamond areas. The new road from Georgetown to Linden will, if linked with the Ituni road, open a new route to the interior. A new road has been built from Bartica to Mahdia in the deep interior, but the "self-help" road from Mahdia to Annai is reported to be reverting to forest. A new road is being built along the Upper Mazaruni river; this will eventually link up with another road being built north along the Essequibo river, which is already open between Wismar and Rockstone. Roads and trails usable by vehicles total 1,810 miles.

Clothes   No elaborate outfit is necessary. For day wear, drill, tropical suitings, or light tweeds. A light waterproof raincoat is useful. For the interior, khaki and good boots and leggings. A permit is required to bring in a shotgun.

Women need light-weight dresses and cotton underwear. Long evening dresses are sometimes worn and stockings only now and then in the evening.

Food, Drink and Restaurants   Elizabeth Allen writes: The variety of races which constitute the population has led to the emergence of a variety of local food specialities—Indian curries, Portuguese garlic pork, African meat dishes, English food, and Creole food. Of the latter, the best known is "pepper-pot", a meat dish cooked in cassava juice with peppers and herbs. Most meals are accompanied by rice. Seafood, found in restaurants near the Stabroek Market, is good, as are the wide variety of tropical fruits such as mangoes, papayas, oranges, bananas, etc. (Guyanese hot pepper sauce is *very* hot!)

Rum is the most popular drink. Produced locally it is quite cheap (XM Gold Medal Rum G$8.50 a bottle.) Other recommended brands are XM Liquid Gold (10 years old) and Eldorado Bottle Reserve. It is used in many drinks, such as punches, mixed with ginger beer, etc. Sometimes Angostura bitters are added for flavour as it is rather a light rum. The local beer is called "Banks".

Health   There is some risk of malaria in the interior; take prophylactics and better sleep under a mosquito net, and vaccinate against typhoid too. Boil milk and drinking water outside Georgetown.

The **climate**, although hot, is not unhealthy. Mean shade temperature throughout the year is 80°F, the mean maximum is about 87°F and the mean minimum 75°F. The heat is greatly tempered by cooling breezes from the sea and is most felt from August to October. There are two wet seasons, from the middle of April to the middle of August, and from the middle of November to the end of January. Rainfall averages 91 inches a year in Georgetown.

Cost of Living   Shopping and entertainments are expensive, though you can get a good meal for G$4 in one of the cheaper restaurants. The cost of living rose by 6.8% in 1975 and 8.4% in 1976.

Hours of Business Shops and offices, 0800-1130, 1300-1600; Banks, 0800-1200 Mon. to Fri., 0800-1100 Sat., Government offices, 0800-1130, 1300-1600 Mon. to Fri., 0800-1200 Sat., British High Commission, 0800-1100, 1300-1600 Mon. to Fri., 0800-1130 Sat.

Currency The unit is the Guyana dollar (G$) divided into 100 cents. The exchange rate (June 1978) is G$2.55 to the US$. Notes: 1, 5, 10, and 20 dollars. Coins: 1, 5,10, 25, and 50 cents. Only G$15 in local currency may be taken in or out, and there are long bureaucratic procedures at the banks to exchange currency because of strict controls. The airport bank is not always open and procedures require that local currency must be changed back into foreign currency at a named bank. Banks in the city are only open in the mornings 0800-1200. There is an "open" market on which well over G$3 may be bought for US$1.

Weights and Measures Imperial weights and measures are used.

A radio telephone service connects with a number of Government and private radio telephone stations in the interior. Overseas telegrams are transmitted *via* Guyintel, formerly Cable and Wireless Ltd., at Bank of Guyana Building, Georgetown, who also operate radio telephone services to most countries throughout the world. Cable to U.K. costs G$3 per 10 words. Local calls in Georgetown cost ten cents.

There are 2 broadcasting stations, Guyana United Broadcasting Company (0530-2300), and Guyana Broadcasting Service (0600-2300). Both take commercial advertising.

Diplomatic Representatives The British High Commission is at 44 Main Street, Georgetown; the U.S. Embassy is at 31 Main Street.

Time 3 hours behind GMT.

Press Daily newspapers at Georgetown: "The Chronicle", "Guyana Graphic" and "The Mirror" (4 issues a week). There are 2 weeklies. The Georgetown Chamber of Commerce issues a monthly "Commercial Review".

Public Holidays

January 1: New Year	July 2: Caribbean Day
February: Youman-Nabbi	August 6: Freedom Day
February 23: Republic Day	October: Deepavali
Easter: Good Friday, Monday	Oct.-Nov.: Eid-ul-Azha
March: Phagwah	December 25: Christmas Day
May 1: Labour Day	December 26: Boxing Day

Precise dates for Phagwah, Eid-ul-Azha, Youman Nabbi and Deepavali depend on specific phases of the moon.

(We are again profoundly grateful to Mr. J. Dalzell of Guyana Overland Tours, to the Ministry of Information for invaluable background material, and for new information, which has made the whole chapter much more valuable, to Elizabeth Allen, who has also revised the Economy section. Acknowledgements to travellers will be found at the end of the Guyane section.)

SURINAME

SURINAME lies on the north-eastern coast of the South American continent. To the N it has a coast line on the Atlantic; it is bounded towards the W by Guyana and on the E by French Guyane; Brazil is to the S. Its area is 163,265 sq. km.

The principal rivers in the country are the Marowijne in the E, the Corantijne in the W, and the Suriname, the Commewijne (with its tributary, the Cottica), Coppename, Saramacca and Nickerie. The country is divided into topographically quite diverse natural regions: lowland, savannah, and highland.

The northern part of the country consists of lowland, with a width in the E of 25 km., and in the W of about 80 km. The soil (clay) is covered with swamps under a layer of humus under them. Marks of the old sea-shores can be seen in the shell and sand ridges, overgrown with tall trees.

There follows a region, 5-6 km. wide, of a loamy and sandy soil, then a slightly undulating region, about 30 km. wide. It is mainly savannah, mostly covered with quartz sand, and overgrown with grass and shrubs.

South of this lies the interior highland, consisting of hills and mountains, almost entirely overgrown with dense tropical forests and intersected by streams of all sizes. At the southern boundary with Brazil there are again savannahs. These, however, differ in soil and vegetation from the northern ones. A large area in the SW is in dispute between Guyana and Suriname. A less serious border dispute exists with Guyane in the SE.

Population, in 1977, was 387,000. It consisted of Creoles (Suriname-born persons of European-African and other descent), 32%; East Indians (known locally as Hindustanis), 35%; Indonesians, 16%; Chinese, 2%; Amerindians, 3%; Bush Blacks (descendants of escaped slaves), 10%; European and others 2%. The population has been declining until 1976; it is estimated that 25-30% of the total have emigrated to the Netherlands. About 90% of the existing population live in or around Paramaribo or in the coastal towns; the remainder, mostly Carib and Arawak Indians and Bush Blacks, are scattered elsewhere.

The Asian people originally entered the country as contracted estate labourers, but settled in agriculture or commerce after completion of their term. They dominate the countryside, whereas Paramaribo is a predominantly Creole city. One of Suriname's main problems is the racial tension between Creoles and East Indians; paradoxically, many Indonesians side with the Creoles.

The official **language** is Dutch. The native dialect, called negro English, originally the speech of the Creoles, is now a *lingua franca* understood by all groups, and standard English is widely spoken and understood. The Asian peoples still speak their own languages among themselves.

All **religions** are equally free before the law. They include the Netherlands Reformed, Moravian and Roman Catholic Churches, Hinduism, Islam and numerous smaller groups.

Constitution   After the amendment of the Netherlands constitution in 1948 Suriname ceased to be a colony and became part of the Kingdom of the Netherlands, consisting of the 3 territories of the Netherlands in Europe, Suriname, and the Netherlands Antilles. From December 29, 1954, Suriname's autonomous structure was symbolised by a coat of arms, a flag, and a national anthem of its own. On November 25, 1975, the country became a completely independent republic, with a new constitution and a new flag. The new republic signed a treaty with the Netherlands for massive economic aid during the next 10 years. The last Governor became the first President of the Republic. There is a cabinet of 12 ministers headed by the Minister-President; the first Minister-President is Henck Arron, of the four-party Creole-Indonesian Coalition.

The ministers are responsible to the Suriname parliament of 39 members, elected by universal suffrage.

The country is divided into 9 districts administered by commissioners.

History   Although Amsterdam merchants had been trading with the "wild coast" of Guiana as early as 1613 (the name Parmurbo-Paramaribo was already known) it was not before 1630 that 60 English settlers came to Suriname under Captain Marshall. They planted tobacco. The actual founder of the colony was Francis Willoughby, fifth Baron Willoughby of Parham, governor of Barbados, who sent an expedition to Suriname under Anthony Rowse to find a suitable place for settlement. Rowse was the first governor (1651-1654). Willoughby visited Suriname from March to May 1652, and from November 1664 to May 1665. Willoughbyland became an agricultural colony with 500 little sugar plantations, 1,000 white inhabitants and 2,000 African slaves. Jews from Holland and Italy joined them, as well as those who originally migrated from Brazil after the final expulsion of the Dutch in 1661, driven by the French out of Cayenne in 1664. On August 17, 1665, these colonists obtained a special grant from Lord Willoughby, the patron of Suriname, the first of its kind made by an English Government to the Jews. By letters patent dated June 2, 1662, Charles II granted Willoughbyland to Francis Lord Willoughby of Parham and Lawrence Hyde, second son of the High Chancellor Edward, Earl of Clarendon, and their heirs and successors. Five years after, on February 27, Admiral Crynssen conquered the colony for the states of Zeeland and Willoughbyfort became the present Fort Zeelandia. Although the English reconquered the colony on October 18, 1667, a second expedition under Crynssen regained it again for the States of Zeeland. By the Peace of Breda—July 31, 1667—it was agreed that Suriname should be restored to the Netherlands, while Nieuw Amsterdam (New York) should be given to England. In 1682 the states of Zeeland sold the colony to the West India Company, and the States General gave their sanction by granting a charter to the Company. In the following year this company sold two-thirds of the shares to the town of Amsterdam and one-third to Cornelis van Aerssen, Lord of Sommelsdyck, whose heirs in 1770 sold their share to the town of Amsterdam. The colony was conquered by the British in 1799 and remained under British rule until 1802, when it was restored to the Netherlands by the Peace of Amiens. It again became a British colony in 1804, and not until the Treaty of Paris in 1814 was it finally restored to the Netherlands. Slavery was abolished in 1863.

Paramaribo, the capital and chief port, lies on the Suriname river, 12 km. from the sea. It has a population of about 150,000, mainly Creoles.

The Presidential Palace (the old Governor's Mansion) is on Onaf-hankelijkheidsplein (formerly Oranjeplein) and many beautiful 18th and 19th century buildings in Dutch style are in the same area, including churches and synagogues. The recently restored Fort Zeelandia is nearby; it now houses the Suriname Museum, although some exhibits are still in the old museum in the residential suburb of Zorg-en-Hoop. Search out Mr. F. Lim-A-Po-straat if you wish to see what Paramaribo looked like only a comparatively short time ago. The enormous nineteenth-century Roman Catholic cathedral is built entirely of wood and is well worth a visit. Other things to see are the colourful market and the waterfront (sea-going vessels, river-boats and dugout canoes). A new harbour has been constructed about 1½ km. upstream. Two pleasant parks are the Palmentuin and the Cultuurtuin (with Zoo)—but the latter is quite a distance from the town and there are no buses to it. Native dress is normally only worn at national holidays and wedding parties, but many Javanese women still go about in sarong and klambi. A university was opened in 1968. There is an exotic Asian flavour to the market and nearby streets.

Tourist Bureau Kerkplein 10, Paramaribo, telephone 73733. Very friendly and helpful; organizes tours and bus journeys. Does Travel Service, Dominestraat, has free maps of town.

Hotels *Krasnapolsky,* newest, swimming pool and shops, US$29-33 d (cheaper annexe, formerly *Hotel Kersten,* US$18 d); *Torarica,* US$32-34 d, swimming pool, casino, nightclub, central, the largest; *Palace,* Onafhankelijkheidsplein, US$12-21 d, nightclub, casino; *Riverclub,* at Leonsberg (8 km. from city), US$15-20 d (**motel** annexe), swimming pool. All have a/c.

Cheaper hotels and boarding houses: *YMCA* and *YWCA Guesthouse* (Sf 7.50 p.p., with a/c); *Bechan Hotel* (Sf10 s); *Johnny's Hotel,* Sf10 s, good; all centrally located with optional a/c; *Blue Moon,* Sf10 d; *Windcorner* (corner of Keizerstraat and Jodebreestraat), Sf10 each.

For the hard up: *Centraal Pension* (men only), Sf10 p.p., in Heiligenweg opposite bus station. Service charge at hotels is 10-15%. *Pension "Ifs" Palace,* Keizerstraat 68, Sf 13.75-30.25, and *Fanna,* Princessestraat 31, Sf10-20, with breakfast; and *Pension Cinada,* Sf4-10, basic. One can get a cheaper hotel at Brownsberg Park.

Restaurants There are some good restaurants, mainly Indonesian and Chinese dishes for as little as Sf3. Food at *Palace Hotel,* good. Try a "rijsttafel" in an Indonesian restaurant. The *Star Restaurant,* opposite *Krasnapolsky Hotel,* recommended. The *YMCA cafeteria* has good, cheap breakfasts and lunches. Meat and noodles from stalls costs Sf0.50.

Banks Algemene Bank Nederland (Kerkplein 1), Surinaamse Bank and Hakrin Bank. 0730-1230/1300.

Current 127 volts AC, 60 cycles.

Golf Course Introduction from a member required.

Bus services on the 376 km. East-West Highway: E from Paramaribo through the bauxite town of Moengo to Albina, on the French Guyane border; and W through Coronie and Wageningen to Nickerie. Many buses of different companies leave in the morning for Albina (Sf4.80). Transport from the border on to Cayenne is more difficult (shared taxis, buses rare) and more expensive. One Suriname company runs direct buses from Paramaribo to Cayenne, but not regularly. Transport to Georgetown is easy and cheap, but takes two days (night stop at Nieuw Nickerie). Buses to Nickerie leave early in the morning (0500-0700, Sf7). Get there early for a seat. For all details enquire at Tourist Office.

The government runs a city bus service, but most people use so-called "wild buses" running on fixed routes in and around Paramaribo. Not very comfortable, but very cheap and fast. Most towns and villages are served by private buses.

Taxis generally have no meters. The price should be agreed on beforehand to avoid trouble. A trip inside the city costs about Sf4-5. Fare for one to Zanderij Airport is Sf25-30; by minibus or shared taxi Sf10. Cheap local buses (route PZB7 fairly frequent, but only run in the day, Sf.1.50.

Local Shipping The six ferries across the main rivers operate only in daytime (the Paramaribo-Meerzorg ferry until 2300). The Suriname Navigation Co. (SMS) has a daily service on the Commewijne river and infrequent services on other rivers. The coastal service to Nieuw Nickerie has been discontinued.

Self-Drive Cars "City Taxi" charges Sf27.50 a day plus Sf0.25 per km. after the first 100 km. All drivers' licences accepted, but you need a stamp from the local police and a deposit of Sf100. Gasoline costs Sf0.51 a litre for "regular" and Sf0.54 for "extra".

Airports The international airport is Zanderij, 45 km. S of Paramaribo. Internal flights leave from Zorg-en-Hoop airfield in a suburb of Paramaribo—twice daily to Nieuw Nickerie (Sf35), to Stoelmanseiland in the interior 3 times a week, and to Moengo once a week.

Shopping Amerindian goods more plentiful here than in Guyana: bauxite jewellery, batik prints, carvings, basket work.

Excursions By bus or taxi and ferry to Nieuw Amsterdam, the capital of the pre-dominantly Javanese district of Commenwijne. There is an open-air museum inside the old fortress (open only in mornings except Fridays 1700-1900), which guarded the confluence of the Suriname and Commewijne rivers. The District Commissioner lives in the Commander's original house inside the fortress. There are some old plantation mansions left in the Commewijne district which are of interest. Accommodation for 6-8 persons with own cooking facilities is available on an old citrus plantation, *De Nieuwe Grand,* which is owned by an English couple: details c/o P.O. Box 2976, Paramaribo.

By private car to **Jodensavanne** (Jews' Savannah), S of Paramaribo on the opposite bank of the Suriname river, where part of one of the oldest synagogues in the Western Hemisphere has been restored. Small museum. Interesting Amerindian villages nearby. You need permission from the Forestry Department (LBB), in Jongbawstraat, to use the ferry to Jodensavanne. There is a new guesthouse at Blakwatra, nearby. Near Zanderij Airport there is a resort called Kola Kreek, with swimming area.

By bus (Sf3) or car to Afobakka, where there is a large lake behind a hydro-electric dam on the Suriname river. There is a government guesthouse Sf17.50-25.00 (including 3 meals a day) in nearby Brokopondo. The Brownsberg National Park is one hour by car from here.

There is also a 70-year-old narrow-gauge railway, originally built for the Lawa goldfields, which leaves from the village of Onverwacht (½ hour from Paramaribo by bus, Sf1, route PBO) for Brownsweg (87 km.) and passes through savannah and jungle. The complete journey to Brownsweg is done only once a week, on Thursday, returning Friday. On Mondays a shorter journey is undertaken, to the village of Kwakoegron, returning to Onverwacht the same day. There is no hotel at Brownsweg, but transport to **Brownsberg**, where there is accommodation, can be arranged. A bus to Paramaribo leaves Brownsweg every morning. The Stinasu Organization (Foundation for Natural Preservation in Suriname), Jongbawstraat 10, arranges trips to the Brownsberg Park as well as the Raleigh Falls/Voltzberg Natural Reserve on the Coppename river, the Wia-Wia reserve on the northeast coast where giant sea-turtles nest, and the Galibi reserve on the Marowijne river, another nesting place for turtles near several Carib Indian villages. There is accommodation of sorts in all these places.

Suriname Airways (SLM) has organised tours to Stoelmanseiland (Guest House with full board, Sf25.50 a day, including meals) in the interior and to the Bush Black villages and rapids in that area.

Note It is advisable to check the weather conditions and probabilities of returning on schedule before you set out on a trip to the interior. Heavy rains can make it impossible for 'planes to land in some jungle areas; little or no provision is made for such delays and it can be a long and hungry wait for better conditions.

Nieuw Nickerie, on the S bank of the Nickerie River, 5 km. from its mouth, is the main town of the Nickerie district and is distinguished for the number and viciousness of its mosquitoes. The town has a population of more than 8,000, the district of 35,000, mostly East Indian; it can be reached by vessels of moderate draught, and there are facilities for loading and discharging cargoes. Paramaribo is 240 km. away by road. Buses leave early (about 0400, Sf7) and take a long time as there are 4 rivers to cross on not too modern ferries. SLM has two daily flights to the capital (Sf35). The coastal boat service has been discontinued.

Hotels *Blue Hawaii,* Sf8 s, clean, central, recommended; *Darien,* Sf22.50, bed and breakfast; *Hotel de Lotus* (near ferry); *Ashoko,* US4 d; *Nickerie Logeergebouw,* Sf17.50 American Plan; *Hotel Sjiem Fat,* Sf10-15, without meals; *Hotel Oasis* (men only), Sf3 s, basic. Restaurant: *Tokyo,* rather basic.

Ferry to Springlands, Guyana, Sf3. Leaves 0730; can take 10 hours including formalities! Go to police station at 1700 for exit stamp. No service on Sundays, or national holidays of either country; a passenger service only.

Banks Algemene Bank Nederland, Hakrin-Bank, Post Office Savings Bank, People's Credit Bank, De Surinaamsche Bank.

Albina, a frontier village, 140 km. from Paramaribo, 29 km. from the mouth of the Marowijne River—the boundary with French Guyane—is accessible to vessels of moderate size, and has loading and discharging facilities. Albina is the centre for trips by powered dugouts to Amerindian and Bush Black villages, on the Marowijne, Tapanahoni and Lawa rivers. It takes 1½-2 days to get to the beautiful Stoelmanseiland (Stoelman's Island—see **Excursions,** page 756). Opposite Albina, in French Guyane, is St. Laurent (see page 764), with good restaurants and the old penal settlement to see (ferry 3 francs). The French authorities will sometimes ask for yellow-fever vaccination certificates and cars must have at least "green card" insurance; this card is purchased in Paramaribo.

There is no bank in Albina, but some shops will change money.

Bus Paramaribo-Albina, Sf4.80 and Sf0.50 for 2 ferries, 3½ hours. Buses leave for Paramaribo at 0600 and 1200 daily.

Hotels *Albina Government Guesthouse,* Sf10-12.50 s; *Marowijne,* Sf7.50 s; *Happy Day Inn,* Sf17 s. If these are full, enquire at the police station; they'll let you camp in the park.

Totness is the largest village in the Coronie district, along the coast between Paramaribo and Nieuw Nickerie. There is a good government guesthouse (Sf8-12 s). The road leads through an extensive forest of coconut palms.

Wageningen is a modern little town, the centre of the Suriname rice-growing area. The road from Nickerie has recently been renewed. One of the largest fully mechanised rice farms in the world is found here. (*Hotel de Wereld,* Sf25-30 s.)

Moengo, 160 km. up the Cottica River from Paramaribo, is a mining and loading centre for the Suriname Aluminium Company (Suralco). Extensive mining is done here. (Government Guesthouse, Sf10-15 s.) Paranam, another loading centre for the Company, is on the left bank of the Suriname River. It can be reached by medium draught ships and by cars. Near Paranam is Smalkalden, where bauxite is loaded by the Billiton company on the road to Paramaribo.

The Economy

Economic Problems include the restricted opportunities for both skilled and unskilled labour (one-third of the labour force is in government service); the unwillingness of many people to work in agriculture; and problems of industrial development. Per capita income is about US$1,000 annually.

Agriculture is restricted to some districts of the alluvial coastal zone. This is largely marshy, but is locally traversed by a number of higher sandy ridges more or less parallel to the coast. The sandy soils, if properly drained, are suitable for growing tree crops, peanuts, etc. The marshes mostly have a heavy clay soil; they can only be developed agriculturally after empoldering. Since the polders depend almost exclusively on the tidal effect for adequate drainage they are found along the lower reaches of the rivers. Their clay soils are suitable for sugar cane, rice, and citrus fruits, all of which are exported to Europe, along with small quantities of coffee and bananas. Agriculture accounts for 10% of gnp and about 10% of exports, although less than 4% of area is used for farming.

Suriname grows, mainly for local consumption, sugar-cane, plantains, bananas, pulses, maize, coconuts, citrus, peanuts and coffee.

The staple food crop and most important agricultural export is rice. It is cultivated on wet, unmanured rice-fields. The heavy clay soils and the climate suit the crop, of which yields of from 3,000 to 5,500 kg. per hectare of paddy are harvested.

Sugar, citrus fruits (especially oranges) and bananas are the most important crops after rice. Coffee and cacao are grown in small quantities.

Cattlebreeding in Suriname is not sufficient for the local meat and dairy supply. There is, however, a modern slaughterhouse. Fish (fresh and dried) is more important than meat in the local diet. Frozen prawns are exported in increasing quantities. A US$150m. programme is being undertaken between 1976 and 1986 to develop rice, oil palm and cattle production.

Forestry   Suriname has great timber resources. A forestry development programme is being carried out. A plywood factory and several sawmills are in production. There are exports of plywood, sawlogs and veneer logs, sawn or planed lumber, sleepers and particle board. Production of charcoal is increasing.

Bauxite (aluminium ore) is mined near the Cottica and Para rivers. The Suriname Aluminium Company (Suralco), a subsidiary of the Aluminium Company of America, started operations in 1916 at Moengo on the Cottica river. Seagoing vessels sail up the river to Moengo, 160 km. from Paramaribo—a remarkable trip for tourists in the Alcoa ships. The ore is exported *via* Trinidad loading station to New Orleans and Mobile. Alcoa's second plant, at Paranam, is on the Suriname river, about 35 km. from Paramaribo; there is a road to Paranam and sea-going ships reach it. In 1942 a Netherlands company, the Billiton Maatschappij, started a new plant near the Para river, a tributary of the Suriname; this plant has access to the Suriname river just below the plant at Paranam. Production in 1976 was 4.6m. tons of bauxite, 1.2m. tons of alumina and 46,000 tons of aluminium.

Vast reserves of bauxite have been discovered in the Bakhuis Mountains, in the northern part of Nickerie District. A road has been built from Zanderij to the Bakhuis Mountains and on the Kabalebo River, where an enormous hydroelectric station is planned. A railway will be built from the mountains to Apoera on the Corantijne, which can be reached by sea-going vessels.

Foreign Trade

			(Sf million)		
			1972	1973	1974	1975
Exports (f.o.b.)	..	..	306	320	481	495
Imports (c.i.f.)	..	..	258	282	410	467

Information for Visitors

Air Services Zanderij airport is served by KLM (Royal Dutch Airlines) and its subsidiary ALM (Antillean Airlines), SLM (Suriname Airways), Air France and Cruzeiro do Sul. ALM and SLM fly to Curaçao *via* Guyana and Trinidad five times a week. KLM and SLM fly direct to the Netherlands three times a week (advance booking advisable, especially in the holiday season); Air France flies to Guyana, Cayenne, Trinidad, Martinique and Guadeloupe twice a week. Cruzeiro do Sul flies to and from Belém on Fridays *via* Cayenne; there is a connecting flight by BWIA to Georgetown but it involves a night spent at Zanderij airport. BWIA fly on to Trinidad. There is an exit tax of Sf5. Internal services are maintained by SLM.

Sea Services Three shipping companies have regular sailings to and from Paramaribo: Kroonvlag (former Royal Netherlands Steamship Co., KNSM), Alcoa Steamship Co. and Scheepvaart Maatschappij Suriname (SMS), all with freighters with limited passenger accommodation only. Kroonvlag has a regular service from Europe and from many ports in the Western Hemisphere. Alcoa has sailings from different ports in the USA. SMS has a service to and from New Orleans, *via* some Caribbean ports. In addition there are many freighters of different companies, which take passengers but have no regular service. Flying is generally cheaper than coming by ship.

Documents Visitors must have a passport (or a national identity document—for a stay of 40 days or less—issued by any government other than those of the communist countries), a certificate of smallpox vaccination within the previous 3 years, a through ticket to another country or a return ticket home from any of the Guianas. If travelling on a passport, visas are not normally required, except for nationals of the communist countries. If the visitor wants to stay longer than 30 days he must report to the Immigration Office in Paramaribo as soon as he arrives and take with him two passport-size photographs.

Customs Duty-free imports include (if declared) 400 cigarettes or 100 cigars or ½ kg. of tobacco, 2 litres of spirits and 4 litres of wine, 50 grams of perfume and 1 litre of toilet water, 8 rolls of still film and 60 metres of cinefilm, 100 metres of recording tape, and other goods up to a value of Sf40. Personal baggage is free of duty. Customs examination of baggage is very thorough.

Communication with the interior is by river, air, or by road. Roads are being built all over the country. Driving is on the left: today Guyana and Suriname are the only two countries on the Continent where this is so. Most settlements have an airstrip for the internal air services.

The draught of vessels entering the harbour is limited by the bars. At low water springs the clearance over the bar for the Suriname River is 3½ metres, and at high water springs some 7 metres. The Suriname River is navigable 12 km. inland to Paramaribo, and another 34 km. to Paranam. The Nickerie River is controlled by a bar of 2 metres, l.w.s., and is navigable for 100 km.; the Coppename by a bar of 2.1

metres, l.w.s., to the Wayombo; the Corantijne by a bar of 2¾ metres, l.w.s., and is navigable 110 km. inland. The Commewijne up to Casewinica, and the Cottica up to Moengo, are controlled by a bar of 3⅓ metres, l.w.s. The Morowijne river is controlled by a bar of 2.1 metres, and is navigable up to Albina.

Clothing   Except for official meetings, informal tropical clothing is worn, but not shorts. An umbrella or plastic raincoat is very useful.

Climate   Tropical and moist, but not very hot, since the north-east trade wind makes itself felt during the whole year. In the coastal area the temperature varies on an average from 23° to 31°C, during the day; the annual mean is 27°C, and the monthly mean ranges from 26° to 28°C, only. The mean annual rainfall is about 2,340 mm. for Paramaribo and 1,930 mm for the western division. The seasons are; minor rainy season, November-February; minor dry season, February-April; main rainy season, April-August; main dry season, August-November. None of these seasons is, however, usually either very dry or very wet. The degree of cloudiness is fairly high and the average humidity is 82%; The climate of the interior is similar but with higher rainfall.

Health   No special precautions except for a trip to the malarial interior; for free malaria prophylaxis contact the Public Health Department (B.O.G.). Mosquitoes are no worry during the day but mosquito nets should be used at night over beds in rooms not air-conditioned or screened. Outside Paramaribo drinking water should be boiled. In some coastal districts there is a risk of bilharzia (schistosomiasis).

Working Hours   Shops: 0800-1300, 1600-1800 on week days, 0800-1300 and 1600-1900 on Sat. (Shops in fact open between 0700 and 0800.) Business houses: 0700-1300 and 1500-1700 on Sat. Government departments: 0700-1400, but 0700-1130 on Sat. Banks are open 0730-1230 weekdays, 0730-1100 Sat.

Post, telegraph, telephone   Postal rates are those of the Postal Union. Telegrams can be sent from 0700 until 2200 and in urgent cases during closed hours. Cables are sent by wireless from the Government station in Paramaribo.

There is a new telephone and telegraph office on Vaillantplein. Calls can be made to the US and UK *via* satellite, Sf18 for 3 minutes. The office is open 0700-2000; calls booked before 2000 can be made up till midnight.

Currency   The unit of currency is the Suriname guilder (Sf) divided into 100 cents. There are notes for 1, 2½, 5, 10, 25, 100 and 1,000 guilders. Coins are for 1, 5, 10 and 25 cents (25-cent coin is usually known as a "Kwartje"). Suriname's monetary system is now quite independent of Holland's; the Suriname guilder (or florin), is now valued against the US dollar; US$1 = Sf1.785.

Currency Regulations   Visitors are allowed to keep all foreign currency, cheques and bank drafts in their possession. On leaving Suriname, up to the equivalent of Sf2,500 in foreign currency can be taken out without declaration. All amounts in foreign currency exceeding the equivalent of Sf2,500 must be covered by a declaration made for these amounts upon arrival in Suriname. It is advisable though to declare all amounts of foreign currency (even if less than Sf5,000) upon arrival. On departure visitors may change up to Sf250 into the currency of the country to which they are proceeding at one of the local banks without an exchange permit, on showing their ticket and passport.

Time is 3½ hours behind GMT.

Cost of Living   The increase was 8.4% in 1975, and 11.5% in 1976 and in 1977 was reported to be at the same rate as in 1976.

Public Holidays   January 1, New Year; Holi Phagwa (1 day in March); Good Friday; Easter (2 days); May 1 (Labour Day); July 1 (Abolition of Slavery); Id-Ul-Fitr (usually in October); November 25 (Independence Day); Christmas (2 days).

The **metric** system is in general use.

Newspapers are printed in Dutch. The principal ones are "De West"; "De Ware Tijd", "De Vrije Stem"; "De West" is an evening paper; and the others are morning papers.

Broadcasting There are several stations in Paramaribo and in the districts, broadcasting in Dutch, Hindi, Negro English and Javanese. There is also one television station called Surinaamse Televisie Stichting (STVS), transmitting on channel 8 (in Dutch).

Embassies USA, Netherlands, Brazil, France, Venezuela, South Korea, Indonesia, Guyana, India, Japan, Canada, Taiwan.

Consulates There are consuls-general, vice-consuls or consular agents for Belgium, Colombia, Denmark, Dominican Republic, Ecuador, Finland, W. Germany, Haiti, U.K., Mexico, Norway, Spain, and Sweden—all in Paramaribo.

Information about Suriname can be had from: Suriname Tourist Bureau, Suite 1408, 1 Rockefeller Plaza, New York, N.Y. 10020, and from the Suriname Embassy, Alex. Gogelweg 2, The Hague, Netherlands.

American Express Agents Paramaribo: C. Kersten & Co., *Hotel Krasnapolsky,* Tel.: 74448.

We are once again profoundly grateful to the Suriname Tourist Bureau and to Dr. K. Schaapveld, of Tamanredjo, Commewijne, for a thorough updating of the Suriname section.

GUYANE
(FRENCH GUIANA)

GUYANE, a Département of France in South America, lies N of Brazil, its eastern frontier formed partly by the River Oiapoque (Oyapoc in French) and its southern by the Tumuc-Humac mountains. The western frontier with Suriname is along the River Maroni-Itani. The northern boundary is the Atlantic coastline of 320 km. The area is estimated at 88,896 square km., or one-sixth that of France. The land rises gradually from the coastal regions to the higher slopes and plains or savannahs, about 80 km. inland. Forests cover some 8 million hectares of the hills and valleys of the interior. The total population (1975) was about 55,000.

The territory is well watered, for over twenty rivers run to the Atlantic. Besides those named above, there are the Mana, Cayenne, Sinnamarie (with its tributary the Coureibo), Maroni, Oyack, and Approuage. Smaller rivers and tributaries are the Inini, Ardoua, and Camopi.

The only mountain range of importance is the Tumuc-Humac. Among the higher peaks are Mounts Mitarka, Temorairem, Leblond, and Timotakem; this last in the extreme S on the Brazilian frontier. The mountains reach a height of 800 metres.

The discovery of important deposits of bauxite has contributed to optimism about the future, though they are not as yet developed. In recent years new building has taken place and facilities for visitors have been much improved. There are some excellent new hotels and tourism is being actively encouraged. The last (1967) census showed a total population of 44,330; of which, Cayenne 25,700; Saint-Laurent du Maroni 4,600; Kourou 3,117. The basic population consists of "Creoles", the descendants of non-indigenous blacks, Asians and whites, but it is proposed to settle 30,000 French colonists there to develop the territory's resources. The Amerindian villages in the Haut-Maroni and Haut-Oyapoc areas may only be visited if permission has been obtained from the Préfecture in Cayenne *before* departure to Guyane.

History

Awarded to France by the Peace of Breda in 1667, French Guyane was twice attacked, first by the British in 1654 and later by the Dutch in 1676, when the Governor was taken a prisoner to Holland. In the same year the French re-took possession and remained undisturbed until 1809. In that year a combined Anglo-Portuguese naval force captured the colony, which was handed over to the Portuguese (Brazilians). Though the land was restored to France by the Treaty of Paris in 1814, the Portuguese remained until 1817. Gold was discovered in 1853, and disputes arose about the frontiers of the colony with Suriname and Brazil. These were settled by arbitration in 1891, 1899, and 1915. By the law of March 19, 1946, the Colony of French Guiana became the Department of Guyane, with the same laws, regulations, and administration as a department in metropolitan France. The seat of the Prefect and of the principal courts is at Cayenne.

Cayenne, the capital and the chief port, is on the island of Cayenne at the mouth of the Cayenne River. It is 645 km. from Georgetown (Guyana's capital) and 420 km. from Paramaribo (Suriname) by sea. All along the coastal region the NE winds temper the climate (annual average temperature 27°C, 80°F, falling at night). There is an interesting Museum (open daily, except Mondays; Tuesday-Saturday 0900-1300, and Sunday 0900-1200; free admission); the Jesuit-built residence of the Prefect; the Botanical Gardens; the Place des Palmistes, with assorted palms; a swimming pool; a municipal library and 4 cinemas. There are bathing beaches (water rather muddy) around the island. Trips by motor-canoe up-river into the jungle can be arranged. Six-and-a-half km. outside Cayenne is a restaurant with paintings of prison life by an ex-convict whose work can also be seen in the Church at Iracoubo. Ten km. out, near the Ferry, is an American shrimp-packing plant. The road to Iracoubo is narrow but well surfaced. There is a road to St. Laurent (now paved) and another inland.

Hotels *Hotel du Montabo,* pleasantly situated 60 metres up on Montabo Hill, 5 km. out of town; most rooms air-conditioned; very good, booking advisable, expensive (150 francs d) (Tel.: 31-25-75). *Hotel Kimelone,* 12 Rue Lallouette (Tel.: 90), 25 francs d a night, complaints about cleanliness; *Hotel Neptima,* Rue F. Eboué 21 (15 rooms), 85 francs d, breakfast 5 francs, a/c, friendly. *Hotel Ket-Tai,* 50 francs d (now called *Central Hotel*), not recommended. *Chez Matilde,* 45 Av. de Gaulle, good, 40-75 francs d. *Clinique Saint-Paul,* S side Place des Palmistes, lets top-floor rooms at 30-35 francs p.p., including breakfast. Budget travellers may care to try *Cluniac Sisters* on east side of Place des Palmistes, or guest house of St. Paul's Hospital (25 francs).

Restaurants and Bars *Hotel du Montabo; Hotel Kimelone; La Rôtisserie,* 5 Place de Grenoble; *Gastonville,* Av. de Gaulle, good; *T-A-Hing (Huguette) La Gaité,* Av. Lt. Brassé; *Le Viet Nam; Club 106,* about 4 km. outside Cayenne; *Montjoly Bar; Beaurivage; Palmiste,* central and spacious; *Frégate,* Ave. Charles de Gaulle; *Tatou* (Creole), Ave. Pres. Monnerville; *La Baie D'Alang.*

International Airport Cayenne-Rochambeau is 16 km. from Cayenne. (See Routes to Guyane, page 764). Local air services: Soc. Guyane Air Transport. No public transport; only taxis (50 francs, but you can probably bargain). Cheaper taxi: Richard Lugret,Tel.: 31-29-89.

Car Hire R. Desmond & Cie, Hertz International Licensee, route de La Madeleine, BP 148, Cayenne. Cables: Hertzcars and Auto Guyane, BP 853. Tel.: 31-17-70.

Bus From Cayenne to St. Laurent, for Suriname, leaves 0500, 71 francs (shared taxi costs 90 francs, 8 hours). Then ferry or dugout to Albina, 3 francs or Sf0.75. Bus leaves Albina for Paramaribo 0700 and 1230, 3½ hours. No money exchange at border. To Kourou on St. Laurent bus costs 13 francs. To Paramaribo direct 84 francs. Transport John (proprietor, John Hector, speaks English), Route Baduel, Tel.: 31-16-19, runs taxis to Paramaribo, 90 francs per seat. Leaves 0200, arrives 1000. It is much cheaper to buy a bus ticket to St. Laurent and another from Albina to Paramaribo than to buy a through ticket.

Bank Banque de la Guyane, Place Schoelcher. Open 0715-1130 and 1445-1730, and Sat. a.m., but no exchange facilities on Sat. There are no exchange facilities at the airport; if in extreme need on Sat. you may be able to change money at Air France office in Place des Palmistes. Central drugstore may help when banks closed. Purchase francs before arrival if possible.

Tourist Office Pavillon du Tourisme, 23 rue Lallavette (BP 79).

Travel Agent Takari Tour, *Hotel du Montabo,* Tel.: 31-19-60 (BP 513) and Somarig Travel, very helpful.

Kourou, 56 km. W of Cayenne, where the new French space centre was built, was a village of barely 600 people in 1965. By 1970, the new town had a population of 6,000, but it is no longer increasing, with the approaching end of the space programme. It has two excellent hotels, one of them the best for many hundreds of miles, and a number of good restaurants. Tourist attractions include bathing, fishing, sporting and aeroclub, and a variety of organized excursions. There are banking facilities, tourist agencies, doctors, a dental surgeon, pharmacists, garages, a supermarket and a wide range of shops. The space centre occupies an area of about 4 km. deep along some 30 km. of coast, bisected by the Kourou river. It is open to the public on Wednesday mornings and well worth a visit. Phone 33.44.82 to reserve a place on the tour of the centre. Kourou has its own port facilities. Boats to Iles du Salut (27 francs return) depending on tide, but around 0800, returning at 1600; "Taxis Collectifs" leave for Cayenne at 0730 and 1400.

Hotels *Hotel des Roches* (restaurant); *Hotel Albia* (self service and snack bar); *Hotel Central,* 40 francs d, adequate.

Restaurants *Guinguette Pim-Pum* (dinner only); *le Saramaca; Viet Huong* (behind the Church; Vietnamese cooking) *Le Mandarin* (Chinese cuisine); *Le Cactus; Le Bretagne; L'Estrambord; Au Bon Accueil* (Creole specialities).

The Iles du Salut islands, opposite Kourou, include the Ile Royale, the Ile Saint-Joseph, and the Ile du Diable. They were the scene of the notorious convict settlement built in 1852; the last prisoners left in 1953. The Ile du Diable ("Devil's Island"), a rocky palm-covered islet almost inaccessible from the sea, was where political prisoners, including Alfred Dreyfus, were held. There is a hotel (ex-mess hall for warders, with good food) on Ile Royale.

St. Laurent du Maroni (population 6,000) is a quiet Colonial town on the River Maroni bordering Suriname. There are 3 hotels and several restaurants. *Hotel Prévost,* 30 francs s, adequate; *Hotel Toucan* from 20 francs, others 35 francs d. (Nearby is St. Jean du Maroni, an Indian village.) We are informed that the restaurants are better than Albina's on the other side of the river, and that the old Camp de Transportation (the original penal centre but now full of squatters) can be wandered round at will, though if you want to see the cells you will have to apply to the local *gendarmerie.* Change money here, there is no bank in Albina (though some shops will change money there). Ferry to Albina (every two hours), 3 francs; a dugout can be hired for a bit more. Get your passport stamped at the ferry terminals on both sides of the river. Bus to Cayenne, 71 francs, 0500 daily; "Taxis collectifs" to and from Cayenne 90 francs a head.

Natural Resources

Guyane has natural riches in its timber forests and mineral resources, but these are barely exploited at present. An estimated 42 million tons of extractable bauxite have been located in the Kaw mountains to the E of Cayenne and it is thought that other minerals may be found.

Guyane imports a substantial amount of foodstuffs and manufactured goods. The value of exports, mainly shrimps, rum, essence of rosewood, hardwoods and gold, is very low.

Information for Visitors

Routes to Guyane Air France has flights on Wed. and Thurs. the year round and on Sat. between Jan. 19 and Oct. 20 from Paris to Pointe à Pitre (Guadeloupe); thence flights on Mon., Tues. and Fri. to Cayenne. Cruzeiro do Sul flies to Belém on Fridays, US$67, Taba-Nota Aerotaxis on Tuesdays and Fridays fly to Cayenne from Belém. The cost is about

US$80. There is an airtaxi service from St. Georges to Cayenne every day except Sundays. The Suriname Navigation Company has a fortnightly service between Cayenne and Suriname. The Compagnie Générale Maritime runs a passenger service to France once a month, *via* Martinique, and a freight service every three months.

Transport There are no railways, and the 300 km. of road lead to the capital. The main road, narrow but now paved, runs for 130 km. from Pointe Macouris, on the roadstead of Cayenne, to Iracoubo. Another 117 km. takes it to Mana (where giant tortoises may be seen in March/April) and St. Laurent. One- to three-ton boats which can be hauled over the rapids are used to reach the gold-seekers, the forest workers, and the rosewood establishments. Internal air services are being increasingly used (e.g. Cayenne-St. Georges, US$12). There is a small steamship service which calls at nearly all the coastal towns of Guyane. Ferries are free except those at the frontier.

Transport to Brazil by motorized dugout from Oiapoque to St. Georges, is only for Brazilians; no customs or immigration post, and foreigners are returned to Guyane.

Travellers Passport not required by nationals of France and most French-speaking African countries carrying identity cards. No visa required for most nationalities (except for those of Guyana, the communist, Asian—not Japan—and other African countries) for a stay of up to 3 months, but an exit ticket out of the country (a ticket out of one of the other Guianas is not sufficient) is essential; a deposit is required otherwise. Inoculation against yellow-fever officially required only for those staying in Guyane longer than 2 weeks, but advisable for all. Travel to certain Amerindian villages is restricted (see page 762). Malaria prophylaxis recommended.

Climate is tropical with a very heavy rainfall. Average temperature at sea-level is 27°C, and fairly constant at that. Night and day temperatures vary more in the highlands. The rainy season is from November to July, with (sometimes) a short dry interruption in February and March. The great rains begin in May. The dry season is from July to mid-November. The best months to arrive are February and March. Tropical diseases, dysentery, malaria, etc., occur, but the country is fairly healthy.

Public Holidays In addition to the feasts of the Church: January 1, New Year's Day and July 14, Fête Nationale. Mohammedan holidays are observed, but the dates vary according to the lunar calendar.

Communications There is radio-telephone communication between Cayenne, St. Laurent, St. Georges, Régina (Approuage), the Iles du Salut, and Suriname. Two ordinary telephone lines connect Cayenne and Iracoubo *via* Macouris, Kourou, and Sinnamary, and St. Laurent and Mana. International telephone calls very difficult, and expensive. Foreign telegraph communication is *via* Paramaribo or Fort-de-France, from the TSF station at Cayenne.

Consulates British, Rue l'Alouette (B.P. 664, Cayenne 97300); Brazilian, also in Rue l'Alouette.

General Information

The language is French. The religion is predominantly Roman Catholic. Weights and measures are metric. The currency is the French franc. Guyane is much more expensive for visitors than either Guyana or Suriname; it is virtually impossible to find a hotel single room under 25 francs a night or a 3-course meal for under 30 francs. "France-Guyane-Antilles" is a weekly newspaper with a good information page for the tourist.

We are most grateful to Michael Wooller, of LBI Economics Department, for editorial help, and to the following travellers for information, on the Guianas: Peter Darrah (particularly for Guyane), Mary Goldring and Jonathan Shier (Australia), Donald Illerman (Brackenbridge, Pa.), Dr. Christopher Jeffree, Dr. Terry McCarthy (Singapore), Len Macdonald (USA), Alan Rosenberg (Los Angeles), and Anne Williams.

This publication was
Phototypeset by

DAWSON & GOODALL
LIMITED

**THE MENDIP PRESS
BATH · ENGLAND**

Tel: 0225 64156
Telex: 44600 SOWPAL G

Established in 1770, we are
specialists in the production of fine
colour work in litho and letterpress

MEXICO

CORTÉS, asked what the country looked like, crushed a piece of parchment in his fist, released it and said: "That is the map of Mexico." This crumpled land is so splendid to the eye that about 1,700,000 American tourists visit Mexico each year and spend a sum equal to 30% of Mexico's total exports.

Mexico is the second most populous country in Latin America (65m. people) and the largest Spanish-speaking one. It comprises very great variety, ranging from swamp to desert, from tropical lowland jungle to high alpine vegetation above the tree line, from thin arid soils to others so rich that they grow three crops a year. Over half the country is at an altitude of over 1,000 metres and much at over 2,000 metres; over half is arid and another 30% semi-arid, for rain is irregular in both fall and duration. Only about 30m. hectares (16% of the total land area) can be cultivated, and of these 33% are irrigable.

Mexico, properly the Estados Unidos Mexicanos (United Mexican States), the third largest country in Latin America, has an area equal to about a quarter of the United States, with which it has a frontier of 2,400 km. The southern frontier of 885 km. is with Guatemala and Belize. It has a coast line of 2,780 km. on the Mexican Gulf and the Caribbean, and of 7,360 km. on the Pacific and the Gulf of California, which penetrates the continental land mass for no less a distance than 1,190 km.

The central land mass is extremely complicated, but may be simplified (with large reservations) as a plateau flanked by an eastern and a western range of mountains set back from the coasts and roughly paralleling them. The plateau floor is at 1,100 metres at El Paso, on the Texas border. At 400 km. to the S the general elevation is much the same, with occasional block ranges rising a further 900 metres. This, the northern part of the plateau, is arid and thinly populated; it takes up 40% of the total area of Mexico but holds only 19% of its people. But from the

Bolsón de Mayrán as far S as the Balsas valley, the level rises considerably. This southern section of the central plateau is crossed, from Cape Corrientes in the W, south-eastwards through the Valley of México in the centre, to Veracruz in the E, by a volcanic range of mountains in which the intermont basins are high and separated. The basin of Guadalajara is at 1,500 metres, the basin of Mexico at 2,300 metres, and the basin of Toluca, W of Mexico City, is at 2,600 metres. Above the lakes and valley bottoms of this contorted middle-land rise the magnificent volcano cones of Orizaba (5,700 metres), Popocatépetl (5,452 metres), Ixtaccíhuatl (5,286 metres), Nevado de Toluca (4,583 metres), Matlalcueyetl or La Malinche (4,461 metres), and Cofre de Peroté (4,282 metres). This mountainous southern end of the plateau, the heart of Mexico, has ample rainfall. Though only 14% of the area of Mexico, it holds nearly half of the country's people. And here, in a small high intermont basin measuring only 50 km. square, is the nation's political, cultural and industrial centre, Mexico City, with 11 million inhabitants.

The two high ranges of mountains which rise E and W of the plateau between it and the sea are great barriers against communications: there are far easier routes N along the floor of the plateau to the United States than there are to either the east coast or the west. In the W a railway and a road have penetrated the Sierra Madre Occidental from Guadalajara to the Pacific at the port of Mazatlán; both continue northward through a coastal desert to Nogales: little rain falls on all western coasts between latitudes 20° and 30°. The Sierra Madre Oriental is more kindly; in its mountain ramparts a pass inland from Tampico gives road-rail access to Monterrey (a great industrial centre) and the Highland basins; and another from Veracruz leads by a fair gradient to the Basin of México.

South of the seven intermont basins in the south-central region the mountainland is still rugged but a little lower (between 1,800 and 2,400 metres). After some 560 km. it falls away into the low-lying Isthmus of Tehuantepec. Population is sparse in these southern mountains and is settled on the few flat places on which commercial crops can be grown—subsistence crops are sown on incredibly steep slopes. The Pacific coast here is forbidding and its few ports of little use. Very different from this area—and indeed from the rest of Mexico—are the Gulf Coast and Yucatán; half this area is classed as flat, and 75% of it gets enough rain the year round: two unusual facts, for Mexico, which have led to its becoming one of the most important agricultural and cattle raising areas in the country. What it provides at the moment is oil and sulphur. Geographically, North America may be said to come to an end in the Isthmus of Tehuantepec. South of the Isthmus the land rises again into the thinly populated highlands of Chiapas. This state chose to leave Guatemala and join the Mexican federation in 1824.

Climate and vegetation depend upon altitude. The hot, steamy, often swampy lowland—the *tierra caliente*—takes in the coastlands and plateau lands below 750 metres. In the *tierra templada,* or temperate zone (750 to 2,000 metres), the summers shed the humidity of the coastlands and the winters the cold of the highlands. The *tierra fría,* or cold zone, is from 2,000 metres upwards. The tree line is at 4,000 metres; above it, as far as the lower limit of the permanent snow line (about 4,450 metres) are high moorlands *(páramos).*

The climate of the inland highlands is mostly mild, but with sharp changes of temperature between day and night, sunshine and shade. Generally, winter is the dry season and summer the wet season, but rainfall varies greatly in different territories. There are only two areas where enough rain falls the year round: S of Tampico along the lower slopes of the Sierra Madre Oriental and across the Isthmus of Tehuantepec into Tabasco state; and along the Pacific coast of the state of Chiapas. Both areas together cover only 12% of Mexico. All the rest of the country lacks rain at some time of the year. The whole of the central plateau except its southern and south-western parts is either arid or semi-arid. These wetter parts get most of their rain between June and September, when it falls nearly every day and the skies are so full of clouds that the temperature is lowered: May is a hotter month than July. Apart from these favoured regions, the rest of the country suffers from a climate in which the rainy season hardly lives up to its name and the dry season does.

Population, the second largest in Latin America, is now about 65 millions. It is growing at the rate of 1½ millions a year, or 3.5%. Birth rate per thousand, 47; death rate, 9. Urban growth is 4.7%; 50% of the population is under 20. Mexicans range from pure Indian to pure European by hardly perceptible gradations. About 5% consider themselves pure white and about 25% pure Indian; about 60% are mestizos, a mixture in varying proportions, of Spanish and Indian bloods; some 10% are a mixture of black and white or black and Indian or mestizo. Mexico also has infusions of other European, Arab and Chinese blood. About 24% are still illiterate; 59% live in towns or cities; 41% are rural; 49% of these are peasants who receive less than 20% of the national income. Some mestizos are prejudiced in favour of their Indian rather than their white blood; some Mexicans of Spanish descent are using Indian surnames in place of their Spanish patronymics. There is hardly a single statue of Cortés in the whole of Mexico, but he does figure, pejoratively, in the frescoes of Diego Rivera and his contemporaries.

Amongst the estimated 25 million Indians there are 56 groups or sub-divisions, each with its own language. The Indians are far from evenly distributed; 36% live on the Central Plateau (mostly Puebla, Hidalgo, and México); 35% are along the southern Pacific coast (Oaxaca, Chiapas, Guerrero), and 23% along the Gulf coast (mostly Yucatán and Veracruz): 94% of them, that is, live in these three regions.

Between the Spanish conquest and the revolution of 1910—a period of nearly 400 years—the condition of the peasant was one of growing misery. His standard of living was extremely low, he owned little or no land, was often a semi-enslaved peón, wretchedly housed and always illiterate. This no doubt, explains why, until very recently, human life had so little value in Mexico. Both the Aztec emperor and the great landowner demanded human sacrifice, each in his way. The individual was of small importance to either. Death held no great terror to a peasantry whose rights and dignities had been so trespassed on by 1910 that two-thirds of the land was owned by 836 proprietors, most of them absentee landlords and the Roman Catholic Church. The hacienda system had grown monstrous: 300 of them had at least 10,000 hectares each, 51 averaged 30,000 hectares each, and 11 covered 100,000 hectares each.

The issue of access to the land has always been the country's fundamental problem, and it was a despairing landless peasantry that rose in

1910 and swept away Porifirio Díaz and the old system. Since 1927 the Partido Revolucionario Institucional, the party which incorporates the social-democratic ideal of the revolution, has been in power. What has it accomplished in 50 years? Life for the peasant is still hard. His minimum wage barely allows him a simple diet of beans, rice, and tortillas. His home is still, possibly, a shack of sun-dried bricks or a hut of sticks and thatch, no windows, no water, no sanitation, and he may still not be able to read or write. And yet his life has been transformed by a revolution that has always insisted it was purely Mexican and with its own ideology. Much has been done to redistribute the land in the so-called *ejido* system, which does give the peasant either communal or personal control of the land he cultivates. Depressed he may still be, but he is freed from his landowner and from fear. His wife has the vote, his children go to school, and his family get badly needed help from the state.

Constitution   Under the 1917 Constitution Mexico is a federal republic of 31 states and a Federal District containing the capital, Mexico City. On October 9, 1974 the former territories of Baja California Sur and Quintana Roo were granted the status of states. The President, who appoints the Ministers, is elected for 6 years and can never be re-elected. The States have the right to manage their local affairs. Congress consists of the Cámara de Senadores, elected every 6 years, and the Cámara de Diputados, elected every 3 years. Any party gaining a minimum of 2.5% of the total votes cast is allowed between 5 and 20 seats in the Cámara de Diputados—a method of creating an opposition. There is universal suffrage, and one Deputy for 60,000 inhabitants. The President (1976-82) is Lic. José López Portillo.

Local Administration   The States enjoy local autonomy but the Customs are under the Federal Administration. States can levy their own taxes, and each State has its Governor, legislature and judicature popularly elected in the same way as the Federation. The President appoints the Chief of the Federal District, but the States elect their own Governors. Roman Catholicism is the religion of the great majority, but the State is determinedly secular; because of its identification firstly with Spain, then with the Emperor Maximilian and finally with Porfirio Díaz, the Church has been severely persecuted by reform-minded administrations.

History   Of the many tribes of Indians in the vast territory of Mexico, the two most important before the Conquest were the Aztecs of Tenochtitlán (now Mexico City) and the Mayas of Yucatán. The Aztecs, a militarist, theocratic culture, had obtained absolute control over the whole valley of México and a loose control of some other regions. The Mayas (whose early history is given in the Central American chapter) were already in decline by the time the Spaniards arrived. The 34-year-old Cortés disembarked near the present Veracruz with about 500 men, some horses and cannon, on April 21, 1519. They marched into the interior; their passage was not contested; they arrived at Tenochtitlán in November and were admitted into the city as guests of the reigning monarch, Moctezuma. There they remained until June of the next year, when Pedro de Alvarado, in the absence of Cortés, murdered hundreds of Indians to quell his own fear of a rising. At this treacherous act the Indians did in fact rebel, and it was only by good luck that the Spanish troops, with heavy losses, were able to fight their way out of the city on the Noche Triste (the Night of Sorrows), of June 30.

Next year Cortés came back with reinforcements and besieged the city. It fell on August 30, 1521, and was utterly razed. Cortés then turned to the conquest of the rest of the country. The main factor in his Mexican success was his alliance with the Tlaxcalans, old rivals of the Aztecs. The fight was ruthless. On the one hand, western military tradition and discipline, steel weapons and cavalry; on the other, Indians used to individual combat and trained not so much to kill the enemy as to capture him and offer him in sacrifice. Interminable religious wars and the subordination of their whole life to the propitiation of insatiable gods had already weakened the Aztecs before the arrival of the Spaniards. They were soon mastered.

There followed 300 years of Spanish rule and the making of a new country. For this task the Spaniards had three major virtues: they believed in themselves, their God, and their culture. To serve the first they found was often happily synonymous with serving the second. In the early years all the main sources of gold and silver were discovered, and Indians hastily baptised and converted to slave in the mines. Spanish grandees stepped into the shoes of dead Aztec lords and inherited their great estates and their wealth of savable souls with little disturbance, for Aztec and Spanish ways of holding land were not unlike: the *ejido* (or agrarian community holding lands in common), the *rancho,* or small private property worked by the owner; and that usually huge area which paid tribute to its master—the Spanish *encomienda*—soon to be converted into the *hacienda,* with its absolute title to the land and its almost feudal way of life. Within the first 50 years all the Indians in the populous southern valleys of the plateau had been christianised and harnessed to Spanish wealth-getting from mine or soil. The more scattered and less profitable Indians of the north and south had to await the coming of the missionising Jesuits in 1571, a year behind the Inquisition. Too often, alas, the crowded Jesuit missions proved as fruitful a source of smallpox or measles as of salvation, with the unhappy result that large numbers of Indians died; their deserted communal lands were promptly filched by some neighbouring *encomendero*: a thieving of public lands by private interests which continued for 400 years.

Churches, monasteries, schools were built in numbers. Within 13 years of the Conquest a printing press, the first in the New World, had been set up. Two years later the first college was opened for the education of the children of the conquered; these, as often as not, were also the children of the conqueror: miscegenation was one of the Spanish habits. By the end of the 16th century the Spaniards had founded most of the towns which are still important, tapped great wealth in mining, stock raising and sugar-growing, and firmly imposed their way of life and belief. In the 286 years between 1535 and independence in 1821, some 60 viceroys succeeded greatly in maintaining the Spanish colonial pattern: government by a Spanish-born upper class based on the subordination of the Indian and mestizo populations; a strict dependence on Spain for all things, from trade to viceroy, and a cool disregard for the interests of Mexico. As in all the other Latin American states, Spain built up resistance to itself by excluding from government both Spaniards born in Mexico and the small body of educated mestizos.

The standard of revolt was raised in 1810 by the curate of Dolores, Manuel Hidalgo. The Grito de Dolores: "Perish the Spaniards", collected 80,000 armed supporters, and had it not been for Hidalgo's loss of nerve and failure to engage in battle, the capital might have been captured in the first month and a Government created not differing much from the royal Spanish government. But eleven years of fighting created bitter differences. A loyalist general, Augustín de Iturbide, joined the rebels and proclaimed an independent Mexico in 1821. His Plan of Iguala proposed an independent monarchy with a ruler from the Spanish royal family, but on second thoughts Iturbide proclaimed himself Emperor in 1822: a fantasy which lasted one year. A federal republic was created on October 4, 1824, with General Guadalupe Victoria as President. Conservatives stood for a highly centralised government; Liberals favoured federated sovereign states. The tussle of interest expressed itself in endemic insurrection. In 1836, Texas, whose cotton-growers and cattle-ranchers had been infuriated by the abolition of slavery in 1829, rebelled against the dictator, Santa Ana, and declared its independence. It was annexed by the United States in 1845. War broke out and U.S. troops occupied Mexico City in 1847. Next year, under the terms of the treaty of Guadalupe Hidalgo, the U.S. bought for a song—15 million dollars—all the land from Texas to California and from the Río Grande to Oregon. In Mexico, broken by the war, the turbulent Santa Ana once more declared himself dictator in 1853, with the ironic title of Most Serene Highness. He was soon deposed.

A period of reform, dominated by the pure-blooded Zapotec Indian, Benito Juárez, began in 1857. The church, in league with the conservatives, hotly contested by civil war his liberal programme of popular education, freedom of the press and of speech, civil marriage and the separation of church and state. Juárez won; men were free, but Mexico was ruined, and Juárez was forced to suspend payment on the national debt. Promptly, Spain, France and Britain landed a joint force at Veracruz to protect their financial rights. The British and the Spanish soon withdrew, but the French force pushed inland and occupied Mexico City in 1863. Juárez took to guerrilla warfare against the invaders. The Archduke Maximilian of Austria and his wife Carlotta became Emperor and Empress of Mexico with Napoleon III's help, but United States insistence led to the withdrawal of the French troops in 1867. Poor Maximilian, betrayed and deserted, was captured by the Juaristas at Querétaro and shot on June 19. Juárez resumed control and died in July 1872. He was the first Mexican leader of any note who had died naturally since 1810.

The distinguished scholar who followed him was soon tricked, very easily, out of office by Porfirio Díaz, who ruled Mexico as a dictator from 1876 to 1910. But Díaz's paternal, though often ruthless, central authority did introduce a period of 35 years of peace. Prosperity followed upon peace; a real civil service was created, finances put on a sound basis, banditry put down, industries started, railways built, international relations improved, and foreign capital protected. But the main mass of illiterate and half-starved peasants had never been so wretched; their lands were stolen from them, their personal liberties curtailed, and many were sold into forced labour on tobacco and henequen plantations from which death was a release.

It was this open contradiction between dazzling prosperity and hideous distress which led to the upheaval of 1910 and to Porfirio Díaz's self-exile in Paris. A new leader, Francisco Madero, who came from a landowning family in Coahuila, championed a programme of both political and social reform: control of the Presidency, and the restoration of stolen lands. The reactionaries rose and Madero was brutally murdered, but the great new cry, *Tierra y Libertad* (Land and Liberty) was not to be silenced until the revolution was made safe by the election of Alvaro Obregón to the Presidency. Later, President Lázaro Cárdenas fulfilled some of the more important economic objectives of the revolution. It was his regime (1934-40) that brought about the division of the big estates into *ejidos* (or communal lands), irrigation, the raising of wages, the spread of education, the beginnings of industrialisation, the nationalisation of the oil wells and the railways. Later presidents nationalised electric power, most of the railways, the main airlines and parts of industry. All have pursued an independent and non-aligned foreign policy. One of the remarkable things about this transformation is that—unlike in totalitarian countries—it has been able to express itself as successfully in terms of painting, poetry and architecture as it has in economic progress.

U.S.A. to Mexico City, by Road: The Gulf Route

The vast majority of visitors to Mexico, particularly of tourists, come from the United States, by air, train, road or sea. Details about plane, railway and shipping services are given in "Information for Visitors", at the end of this section. We are concerned here with the four great road routes from the U.S. border to Mexico City: the Gulf Route (by Pan American Highway), the Eagle Pass/Piedras Negras route, the Central Route from El Paso/Ciudad Juárez, and the Pacific Route, from Nogales. The first of these to be opened—and it still carries heavy traffic and is showing signs of consequent deterioration (beware of overtaking buses)—was the Gulf Route: Nuevo Laredo-Mexico City: 1,226 km. (760 miles).

Traffic from the central and eastern parts of the United States can enter north-eastern Mexico through four gateways along the Río Bravo; at Matamoros, opposite Brownsville; at Reynosa, opposite McAllen; at Ciudad Miguel Alemán, opposite Roma; and at Nuevo Laredo, opposite Laredo—by far the most important of them. A glance at the map will show how the roads from these places all converge upon Monterrey, though there are alternative roads from Reynosa and Matamoros which join the Laredo-Mexico City highway at Montemorelos and Ciudad Victoria, respectively: the latter runs along the tropical Gulf coastal plain and then climbs sharply through the Sierra Madre Oriental to Ciudad Victoria, at 333 metres.

Buses for Monterrey (US$4.50, leave at 0800), Mexico City (15 hours, US$13.50 (leave at 1400) and intermediate points may be taken from the Greyhound bus station in **Nuevo Laredo.** If pressed for time, avoid November 20 and other national holidays as there are delays at customs owing to Mexicans visiting the U.S.A. in large numbers. We have been informed that at the border crossing of Matamoros guards are known to have demanded bribes from US$5 to US$20.

Train To Mexico City from Nuevo Laredo US$7.30 1st, US$4.50 2nd class, daily at 0800 and 1820, 24 hours, no difference between classes.

Crafts Shop Centro Artesanal Nuevo Laredo, Maclovio Herrera 3030. Tel.: 2-63-99.

Matamoros (151,000 people), has a Mexican museum, bright and unforbidding, designed to let a prospective tourist know what he can expect in Mexico. It is well worth a visit. Several lines run first-class buses to Mexico City in 18 hours for US$10. Transportes del Norte to Ciudad Victoria for US$5 (4 hours). Craft shop: Centro Artesanal Matamoros, Calle 5a Hurtside and Alvaro Obregón (Tel.: 2-03-84).

There is little at any of the somewhat hybrid border towns to detain the motorist. After 130 km. of grey-green desert, the road from Nuevo Laredo climbs the Mamulique Pass, which it crosses at 700 metres, and then descends to

Monterrey, capital of Nuevo León State, third largest city and the second industrial city in Mexico. It is in a barren plain through which runs an almost dry river bed, 253 km. S of the border and at km. 915 from Mexico City. The city, which is powerfully dominated by the Cerro de la Silla from the E, has increased its population (1,200,000) by a third since 1960 and is still growing fast. In spite of its unattractive climate—too hot in summer, too cold in winter, dusty at most times—and its shortage of water, it now turns out (using cheap gas from near the Texas border), over 75% of Mexico's iron and steel, most of the lead, much glass, cement, chemicals and excellent beer, accompanied by an almost permanent industrial smog. Its people are highly skilled and educated, but its architecture is drab. There, in its social centre, Plaza Zaragoza, is a pleasant 18th century Cathedral badly damaged in the war against the U.S. in 1846-47, when it was used by Mexican troops as a powder magazine. Its famous Technological Institute has valuable collections of books on 16th century Mexican history, of rare books printed in Indian tongues, and 2,000 editions of Don Quixote in all languages. Visitors make a point of touring the Carta Blanca brewery and sampling free beer in the garden. Altitude: 538 metres, and evenings are cool.

Students of architecture should see the remarkable church of San José Obrero built in a working-class district by Sr. Enrique de la Mora and his team. Daily flights from Mexico City take 1¼ hours. The road link (915 km.) can be covered in a day.

Hotels *Holiday Inn; Ancira* (Hidalgo y Escobedo); *Ambassador* (Hidalgo y Galeana); *Colonial* (Escobedo y Hidalgo); *El Paso* (Zaragoza y R. Martínez); *Monterrey* (Morelos y Zaragoza); *Plaza* (Corregidora 633); *Hotel Nuevo Amado,* US$2 s with toilet and shower. *Reforma* (Av. Universidad Norte 11 3 2). Many hotels between Colón and Reforma, 2 blocks from the bus station.

Motels *Anfa Super* (km. 915, on edge of town), and *El Paso Autel,* both very satisfying.

Restaurant *La Cabaña,* Calle Pinto Suárez, good proper meals and snacks.

Railways To Mexico City and the port of Tampico. Day trains are slow but a night express does the trip to Mexico City in 15 or 16 hours.

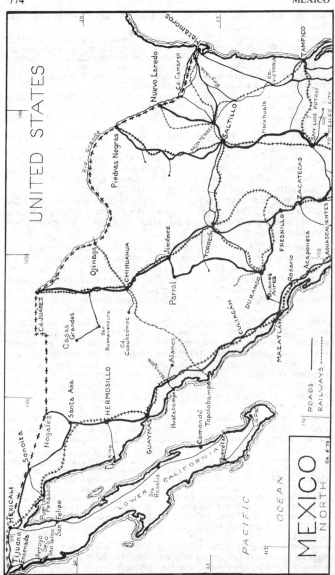

ROUGH SKETCH

Airport Aeropuerto del Norte, 24 km. from centre.

British Consulate Edificio Nacional, 310. Tel.: (91-83) 42-06-41.

In the hills around are the bathing resort of Topo Chico, 6½ km. to the NW: water from its hot springs is bottled and sold throughout Mexico; and 18 km. away Chipinque Mesa, at 1,280 metres in the Sierra Madre, with magnificent views of the Monterrey area.

Leaving Monterrey, the road threads the narrow and lovely Huajuco canyon; from Santiago village a road runs to within 2 km. of the Cola de Caballo, or Horsetail Falls. (First-class hotel on the way.) Our road drops gradually into lower and warmer regions, passing through a succession of sub-tropical valleys with orange groves, banana plantations and vegetable gardens.

At **Montemorelos,** just off the highway, 79 km. S of Monterrey, a branch road from the Matamoros-Monterrey highway comes in. On 53 km. is **Linares** (13,518 people), a charming small town.

A most picturesque 96 km. highway runs west from Linares through an attractive village: Iturbide. The road goes up the lovely Santa Rosa canyon, up and over the Sierra Madre after Iturbide, turn S on top of the Sierra Madre and drive on on good road through the unspoilt Sierra *via* La Escondida and Dr. Arroyo; at Matehuala (see page 778) join the Highway 57 route from Eagle Pass to Mexico City.

(Km. 706) **Ciudad Victoria,** capital of Tamaulipas State, a quiet, unhurried city with a shaded plaza and a tiny church perched on the top of a hill. It is often used as a stop-over. Alt.: 336 metres; pop.: 70,000 people. Hotels: *Sierra Gorda,* US$8 d, garage US$0.55 a night; *Cordesa,* US$3 s, bath. Omnibuses Blancos to Ciudad Valles (see below) for US$3.

After crossing the Tropic of Cancer the road enters the solid green jungle of the tropical lowlands: orchids in the trees, brightly coloured birds, and thatched bamboo Indian huts in the clearings.

Monterrey trains run *via* Ciudad Victoria to the Atlantic port of **Tampico,** reached by a fine road from (km. 570) El Mante, in a rich sugar-growing area, a deviation of 156 km. Tampico is on the northern bank of the Río Pánuco, not far from a large oilfield: there are oil tanks and refineries for miles along the southern bank. The summer heat, rarely above 35°C, is tempered by sea breezes, but June and July are trying. Cold northerlies blow now and again during the winter. Fishing (both sea and river) is excellent. The Playa de Miramar, a beach resort, is a tram or bus-ride from the city. Population: 260,000. A second paved road from Tampico joins the Laredo-Mexico highway further S at Ciudad Valles. Trains west to San Luis Potosí. There are direct buses to Brownsville (Texas), leaving at 2400 and 0545, US$7. Ferry to Villa Cuauhtémoc.

Hotels *Impala* (air-conditioned); *Inglaterra; Imperial; Tampico; Riviera; Mundo. Nuevo León,* US$6.40 d, air conditioned, shower, clean.

British Consul Edificio Luz, 314; Tel.: (91-121) 2-32-84. Postal Address: Apdo. 775.

(Km. 548) Antiguo Morelos. A road turns off W to San Luis Potosí, 314 km. and Guadalajara. (Km. 476) **Ciudad Valles,** on a winding river and a popular stop-over with many hotels *(Casa Grande; Valles).* Omnibus Oriente to San Luis Potosí for US$2 (4 hours). The road to Tampico (145 km.) goes through the oil camp of El Ebano.

(Km. 370) **Tamazunchale** (alt. 206 metres), with riotous tropical vegetation, and perhaps the most popular of all the overnight stops. (*San Antonio Hotel; Mirador,* US$4 s, good, but passing traffic by night is noisy; *Pemex Tourist Camp).* S of this little place begins a spectacular climb to the highland, winding with a steady grade over the extremely rugged terrain cut by the Río Moctezuma and its tributaries. The highest point on the road is 2,502 metres. From (km. 279) **Jacala** there is a dizzying view into a chasm. **Zimapán** (*Posada del Rey,* out in the highway), with a charming market place and a small old church in the plaza, is as good a place as any to stay the night. From (km. 178) **Portezuelo** a paved road runs W to Querétaro, 140 km. In an area of 23,300 sq. km. N and S of (km. 169) **Ixmiquilpan**, just off the highway, 65,000 Otomí Indians "live the bitterest and saddest life". The Patrimonio which is helping them has its H.Q. here; some of the beautifully worked Otomí belts and bags may sometimes be bought at the Monday market, and also in the Artesanía shop in the main street almost opposite the government aid offices.

See early Indian frescoes in the main church, which is one of the 16th century battlemented Augustinian monastery-churches; the monastery is open to the public. John Streather writes: "At sunset each day white egrets come to roost in the trees outside the church; it's worth going up onto the battlements to see them swoop down. The church of El Carmen is worth a visit too, lovely west façade and gilded altars inside. There is also a 16th century bridge over the river; beautiful walk along the ahuehuete-lined banks".

Near Ixmiquilpan are several warm swimming pools, both natural and man-made—San Antonio, Dios Padre, Las Humedades, and near Tephé (the only warm-water bath, clean, entry US$0.40) and Tzindejé (this is about 20 mins. from town). The Otomí villages of La Lagunita, La Pechuga and La Bonanza, in a beautiful valley, have no modern conveniences, but the people are charming and friendly.

Actopán (km. 119) has another fine 16th century Augustinian church and convent. In the church's carving, moulding and frescoes, baroque richness is already spreading over the old austere lines. From Actopán a 56 km. branch road runs to one of Mexico's more important archaeological sites:

Tula, capital of the Toltecs, very interesting, with four huge warriors in black basalt on a pyramid, the huge Atlantes anthropomorphic pillars, and extraordinary temples, whose friezes represent the emblems of the Toltec warriors. It is more easily accessible from the Mexico City-Querétaro toll highway, or a 2-hour bus service "Valle del Mesquital" (US$1.15, every 20 minutes) leaves from Terminal Central del Norte, Avenida de los Cien Metros, in Mexico City. There is also a train from Mexico City at 0800. Return journey takes twice as long, leaves early evening (see also page 820). On the way to Tula there is an interesting cooperative village **Cruz Azul.** Free concerts on Sun. mornings at 1000 in front of main market. At (km. 85) Colonia, a road runs left for 8 km. to **Pachuca**, one of the oldest silver-mining centres in Mexico and capital of Hidalgo state. Pop.: 70,000; alt.: 2,445 metres. The Aztecs mined here before the Spaniards came and the hills are honeycombed with old workings and terraced with tailings. Even today the silver output is the largest of any mine in the world. A large number of colonial buildings amongst its narrow, steep and crooked streets include the treasury for the royal tribute, La Caja, in Calle Cajas (1670), now used as offices: Las Casas Coloradas (1785), now the Courts of Justice; and a former Franciscan Convent (1596). The modern buildings include a notable theatre and the Banco de Hidalgo. An electric railway and a road run

10 km. to the large mining camp of Real del Monte, picturesque and with steep streets. The mine turns out 10% of Mexico's silver production.

British Vice-Consul, Av. de la Revolución 1209. Tel.: (91-771) 2-27-77.

Hotels *De los Baños; Grenfell; América,* US$2.80, one block from Zócalo, quiet.

Cornish miners settled at Real del Monte in the 19th century; their descendants can be recognised among the people. Farther N (34 km. from Pachuca) is **San Miguel Regla,** a mid-18th century hacienda built by the Conde de Regla, and now run as a resort. A good place. Some 190 km. E of Pachuca to **Poza Rica** (*Hotel Fénix,* basic, opposite ADO bus station; *Hotel San Roman,* Plaza Ciorca, 18 de Marzo; *Hotel Juárez*); from Poza Rica you can visit the Castillo de Teayo, a pyramid with the original sanctuary on top, frequent buses, change halfway. Sixteen km. S of Poza Rica are the Pyramids of El Tajín, with unique niches and carvings (described under Jalapa; see page 834). They can be reached from Poza Rica by bus, changing at Chupe. On the way, stay the night in Xicotepec de Juárez at *Mi Ranchito,* one of the nicest small hotels in Mexico. If going S after Tajín, stop at Teziutlán for the night; *Hotel Valdez,* with car park and hot water, US$4.40 d. Another day excursion can be made from Pachuca by going to Molango, where there is a restored convent, *via* Atotonilco, where there is a chapel and convent half-way down a beautiful canyon. A 4-lane highway now runs from Pachuca to Mexico City *via* (km. 27) Venta de Carpio, from which a road runs E to Acolman, 12 km., and San Juan Teotihuacán (The Place where the Gods Live), another 10 km. Neither of these places should be missed by a visitor, but they are usually visited from Mexico City and a day given to them. They are described on page 818.

At Santa Clara, 13 km. short of the Capital, the road forks. The right-hand fork (easy driving) goes direct to the City; the left fork goes through Villa Madero, where you can see the shrine of Guadalupe (see page 816).

Eagle Pass—Piedras Negras to Mexico City

This route, 1,328 km. (825 miles), is 103 km. longer than the Laredo route, but is very wide, very fast and much easier to drive. It is by now the most popular route, but is far from being the most interesting. The 338 km. from Saltillo to Huizache junction is an exceptionally fine stretch of road. The route runs over plains and rolling hills. There are good hotels and motels at Monclova, Saltillo, Matehuala, San Luis Potosí and Querétaro. Take in enough gasoline at Monclova to cover the 195 km. to Saltillo.

Piedras Negras, pop. 27,578, altitude 220 metres, across the Río Bravo from Eagle Pass, Texas. Beyond (137 km.) Hermanas the highway begins to climb gradually up to the plateau country. **Monclova** (243 km.) has one of the largest steel mills in Mexico (Artesanía shop—Centro Artesanal Piedras Negras, Edificio la Estrella, Puerta México, Tel.: 2-10-87). The first big town is **Saltillo** (448 km.; alt.: 1,600 metres; population: 191,900), capital of Coahuila state, a cool, dry popular resort noted for the excellence of its sarapes. Its 18th century Cathedral is the best in northern Mexico and it has a grand market. Indian dances during May 30 and August 30; picturesque ceremonies and bullfights during October fiestas. *Pastorelas,* the story of the Nativity, are performed in the neighbourhood in Christmas week. Good hotels, and good sport: golf, tennis, swimming, hunting. College students from the U.S. attend the popular Summer School. An 87-km. road runs E to Monterrey. You turn right for Mexico City.

Several good motels in this area, e.g. *Huizache,* US$8 d; *La Fuente,* US$8 or 12 d; *Camino Real,* more expensive.

(581 km.) San Roberto junction, where a 96-km. road runs E over the Sierra Madre to Linares, on the Gulf Route.

At about 720 km. we reach **Matehuala** *(Hotel Matehuala)*, an important road junction (fiesta, January 6-20). 56 km. W is one of Mexico's most interesting ghost towns, **Real de Catorce**, founded in 1772.

Tim Connell writes: Four minibuses a day go there from the agency by the *Hotel Matehuala* (US$1.50 s). A taxi can be hired nearby for US$11—economic for 4 people. Tours can be arranged with Turismos del Altiplano, Bustamante 128, Tel.: 3-40.
Route: turn left along the Zacatecas road (not signposted); road goes through Cedral, which has little to offer, apart from an agricultural college and one for training teachers. After 27 km. turn left off the paved road, onto a gravel one—which is actually due to be properly paved. The road passes through Potrero, a big centre for nopal. Some people live in the old mine workings, and old buildings. Huichol Indians are seen here occasionally. A silver mine is still being worked at Santana. Ruined buildings stretch up one side of the valley. Slurry runs down one side of the highway into a big reservoir.
Real de Catorce is approached through Ogarrio, an old mine gallery widened (only just) to allow trucks through. It is 1½ miles long, and very eerie, with the odd tunnel leading off into the gloom on either side. There is an overtaking lay-by half way through. A small chapel to the Virgen de los Dolores is by the entrance. The tunnel opens out abruptly into the old city, once a major mining centre, with its own mint, and nearly 40,000 inhabitants. Some people still live here, mainly round the Zócalo, looking for silver. The cockpit and the 16 chapels are worth seeing; the Church of San Francisco is believed to be miraculous. There is a pilgrimage here, on foot from Matehuala, overnight on October 4th. The floor of the church is made of wooden panels, which can be lifted up to see the catacombs below. In a room to one side of the main altar are *retablos*, touchingly simple paintings on tin, as votive offerings to the Saint, for his intercession. Also, in the sacristy, is a portrait of Silvestre López Portillo, a direct ancestor of today's President, who held the mining concession here, and also incidentally was head of the *cofradía* of San Francisco. President López Portillo has acknowledged this by promising to develop the town as a tourist centre, which will probably destroy the timeless peace of this remarkable city, clustering around the sides of a valley, and so quiet that you can hear the river in the canyon, 1,000 metres below. Juan Rulfo's classic "Pedro Páramo" was filmed here.

Huizache (785 km.) is the junction with the Guadalajara-Antiguo Morelos-Tampico highway. At 901 km. we come to the most interesting town of

San Luis Potosí, capital of its state and the centre of a rich mining and agricultural area, which has expanded rapidly in recent years, because of industrial development. Alt.: 1,880 metres; pop.: 380,000. Glazed, many-coloured tiles are a feature of the city: one of its shopping streets, the main plaza, and the domes of many of its churches are covered with them. The pink sandstone used for building is attractive. It became an important colonial centre after the discovery of the famous San Pedro silver mine in the 16th century, and a city in 1658. The Cathedral is on Plaza Hidalgo. See the churches of San Francisco, with its white and blue tiled dome and suspended glass boat in the transept; Carmen, in Plaza Morelos, with a grand tiled dome, an intricate façade, and a fine pulpit and altar inside (the Teatro de la Paz is next door); the Capilla de Aranzazu, behind San Francisco inside the regional museum; the Capilla de Loreto with a baroque façade; and San Agustín, with its ornate baroque tower. The Palacio de Gobierno, begun 1770, contains oil-paintings of past governors. Other points of interest are the pedestrian precinct in Calle Hidalgo and the Caja del Agua fountain (1835) in Av.

Juárez. The modern railway station has frescoes by Fernando Leal. The Teatro Alarcón is by Tresguerras (see under Celaya, page 785). Locally made rebozos (the best are from Santa María de Río) are for sale in the two markets. The University was founded in 1804. Flecha Amarilla to Querétaro for US$1.60 (3 hours). A scenic road leads to Aguascalientes. Airport.

Hotels *Posada de la Reina; Gante; Roma; Progreso.* Very cheap: *Posada España,* Calle Aldama, US$1.20 s. *Nápoles; Jardín* (Los Bravos 530); *María Cristina,* new with swimming pool on top (Juan Sarabia 110, Altos).

Motels *Santa Fe* (very good, particularly the dining room); *Cactus Motel,* US$16.

Restaurants *Panorama,* roof-garden restaurant, Plaza de la Universidad, good; *La Lonja* and *La Virreina,* both popular eating places; *Café Stamboul,* Madero 145, for excellent coffee and delicious home-made yoghurt. *Café Versalles,* near Jardin Hidalgo; good cafeteria at bus station.

Museum Museo Regional de Arte Popular, open 1000-1300, 1600-1800; Sats. 1000-1300.

Excursions Hot springs at Ojocaliente, Balneario de Lourdes and Gogorrón.

(1,021 km.) San Luis de la Paz, the junction with Highway 110 leading west to three of the most attractive towns in Mexico: Dolores Hidalgo, Guanajuato, and San Miguel de Allende. (See pages 785-786.) No one who yields to the temptation of this detour can hope to get back to the main route for three or four days.

(1,105 km.) Querétaro, pop.: 140,000; alt.: 1,865 metres; capital of Querétaro state, an antique and beautiful city captured by the conquistadores in 1531. Hidalgo's rising in 1810 was plotted in this town, and it was here that the unfortunate Emperor Maximilian yielded up his sword after defeat and was shot, on June 19th, 1867, on the Cerro de las Campanas (the Hill of Bells), outside the city.

La Corregidora (Doña Josefa Ortiz de Dominguez, wife of the Corregidor, or Mayor), a member of the group of plotters for independence masquerading as a society for the study of the fine arts, was able, in 1810, to get word to Father Hidalgo that their plans for revolt had been discovered. Hidalgo immediately gave the cry *(grito)* for independence. Today, the Corregidor gives the Grito from the balcony of the Palacio Municipal (on Plaza Independencia) every September 15 at 1100. La Corregidora's home is shown.

Buildings to see: The Santa Rosa de Viterbo church and monastery, remodelled by Tresguerras; his reconstruction of Santa Clara, one of the loveliest churches in Mexico, and that is saying much, the Church and Monastery of Santa Cruz, ancient Franciscan headquarters and also the H.Q. of Maximilian and his forces (view from the bell tower); the Church of San Felipe, now being restored for use as the Cathedral; the damaged but still glorious Federal Palace, once a monastery; the important Museum of Pío Mariano, on Plaza Obregón, and the house it is in; the aqueduct, built in 1726. Several *andadores* (pedestrian precincts) have been developed, greatly adding to the amenities of the city. There are local opals, amethysts and topazes for sale; remarkable mineral specimens are shaped into spheres, eggs, mushrooms, and then polished until they shine like jewels (US$10-30).

Hotels *Impala* (best); *Del Márques; Gran Hotel,* on Zócalo, recommended; *Plaza,* airy but primitive.

Motels *Casa Blanca; Hidalgo,* US$1.60 s, without bath, good, laundering facilities and cheap restaurant; *La Mansión,* US$10 d a night. 6½ km. S of town, excellent dining facilities. *Motel Flamingo,* on Panamericana, comfortable; *Jurica,* outside city, hacienda-style, with gardens, squash, golf-course; opulent.

Restaurants *La Marquesa,* good, in magnificent old Colonial house; *Fonda San Antonio,* Corregidora Norte 44; *Fonda del Camino,* on Highway 57; *Fonda del Refugio,* Jardín Corregidora; Pizza La Rondine.

There is now a 240 km. 4-lane motorway (US$1.20 a car) from Querétaro to Mexico City. Along it (1,152 km.), **San Juan del Río,** near where the best fighting bulls are raised; the town is also a centre for *artesanías,* and also for polishing gemstones—opals and amethysts. A branch road runs NE from San Juan to the picturesque town of *Tequesquiapán,* with thermal baths, fine climate, good and cheap hotels. (*Los Virreyes; El Reloj,* etc.). Then, at 1,167 km., Palmillas. Beyond it, the 153-km. road to Mexico City reaches a height of about 2,670 metres in two places.

The Querétaro-Mexico City road passes close to Tula and Tepozotlán (see page 819).

The Central Highway Route

Ciudad Juárez, opposite El Paso, Texas. To Mexico City: 1,852 km. Buses connect Ciudad Juárez with El Paso.

Rail Train from Ciudad Juárez to Mexico City (1,970 km.), 36 hrs, US$25 1st class. Reverse journey leaves at 1950 from Mexico City. The route is through Chihuahua, Torreón, Zacatecas, Aguascalientes, León, Siao (for Guanajuato), Celaya and Querétaro. There are daily passenger Pullman trains.

Road Pemex Travel Club, Chamber of Commerce Building, El Paso. A.A.A. office: 916 Mesa Avenue, El Paso. By bus the trip to Mexico City takes about 26 hours, US$21. To Chihuahua, 5 hours, about US$5.

This and the Nogales route serve the western states of the U.S.A. The road is wide, mostly flat, easy to drive along, but not as interesting as the Gulf and Pacific routes. From Ciudad Juárez, for some 50 km. along the Río Bravo, there is an oasis which grows cotton of an exceptionally high grade. Ciudad Juárez is at an altitude of 1,150 metres; population, 436,000; Airport.

Juárez, like Tijuana on the California border, maintains a pleasure "industry" which brings a nightly horde of tourists to be fascinated by a swarm of bead and spinach-jade peddlers, strip joints, doll shops blazing in magenta and green, dubious book stores, and "native dance" halls, mitigated by nightly bouts of that swift and beautiful ball game, jai-alai. It has a famous race course, too. A monument to Father Hidalgo, who sparked off the 1810 revolution, in the form of a giant head, surmounts a hill. See the cheerful Museum which acts as a Mexican "shop window"—well worth it for the tourist who is about to see Mexico.

The first 160 km. of the road to Mexico City are through desert sand, then we enter grazing lands and the valley of Chihuahua. This is the country of the long-haired, fleet-footed Tarahumara Indians, able, it is said, to outstrip a galloping horse and to run down birds.

About 225 km. S of Juárez, near the village of El Sueco, is the turnoff to the **Casas Grandes** ruins. Follow paved State Highway 10 W for about 105 km. then turn NW for about 55. The place is spectacular: pyramids, a large ball court, an irrigation system and a great number of large adobe-brick houses. Motel *Casa Grande* has air-conditioning, good dining room, fair accommodation.

(Km. 1,638) **Chihuahua,** capital of Chihuahua state; alt.: 1,420 metres; pop.: 375,000; centre of a mining and cattle area and not particularly attractive. Worth looking at are the Cathedral on Plaza Constitución, begun 1717, finished 72 years later; the old tower of the Capilla Real (in the modern Federal Palace on Calle Libertad) in which Hidalgo awaited his execution. Good Sunday market. The famous Santa Eulalia mining camp is 16 km. away; 8 km. from town is one of the largest smelting plants in the world. Pancho Villa operated in the country around, and once captured the city by disguising his men as peasants going to market.

His home at Calle Norte 3014 is shown. Summer temperatures often reach 40°C. Rain falls from July to September. The local hairless small dog is famous; it has a constant body temperature of 40°C (104°F)—the world's only authentic "hot dog".

Excursion to La Compañia (Jesuit church 50 km. away, by train US$2.80 s).

Hotels *Palacio-Hilton; Victoria; Del Real; Santa Rita; Plaza,* behind cathedral, clean, US$2.70 s; *Maceyra,* US$3.20 s with shower, simple but clean, despite occasional beetles; *Reforma,* US$3 d, good; *Hotel El Cobre,* US$5 with bathroom, beside bus terminal, very good. *Alojamiento Fátima,* Doblada 113 and *Cuauhtémoc,* nearby, cheap.

Motel *Mirador* (quite good).

Restaurant *Casita de Paja,* cheap and good around the corner from Hotel Plaza.

Bus To El Paso, Texas, US$4.80 first class, 7 hrs. 2nd class bus to Hidalgo del Parral, US$2.55, 5 hours.

Airport 2 km. from centre.

Railway Take bus marked C. Rosario as far as the prison (*cárcel*); the station is one block behind it. Train journey to Los Mochis, on Pacific Railway (*Autovia,* no airconditioning, one way, *vistratrén* (reclining seats) more expensive, 1st class fare US$7.90 (special) US$6.50. Book up in advance) is very spectacular and exciting. Don't reserve seats in the panoramic "Domo"; it is at the disposal of *all* passengers, free. Sit on left hand side of carriage going to Los Mochis. As the train weaves through the mountains it crosses over 30 bridges and passes through ten tunnels. It crosses the Sierra of the Tarahumara Indians. The train stops about 15 mins. at Divisadero Barrancas in the Barranca del Cobre, comparable to the Grand Canyon in the U.S.A. Local women sell their handicrafts at bargain prices. *Hotel Canon del Cobre,* US$35 (full board).

The train has a good dining car and takes about 12 hours to reach Los Mochis. Trains leave on Mon., Thurs. and Sat. arriving next day and returning on Tue., Fri. and Sun. (leaves 0820).

Hugo Pfandler writes: On the Chihuahua-Los Mochis line is **Creel,** the centre of the Tarahumara region and an upcoming tourist resort. Several hotels: *Motel Parador La Montaña,* expensive; *Hotel Nuevo,* US$4.25 s, meals overpriced; cheap, nice and clean; *Hotel Korachi,* US$2.25 s. Cheap meals at *Café El Manzano* next to railway station. A few km. out of town is *Hotel Cabaña de las Barrancas,* US$25 d with 3 meals, with minibus service to and from station. Places of interest near Creel include **Cuzarare** ("Place of the Eagles") 20 km. from Creel with Jesuit Church (1767) painted by Indians; **Norogachi,** (80 km. away) with Tarahumara school and authentic costumes worn on Sundays, typical fiestas; El Tejabán (Copper Canyon); **Basihuara** ("Sash") village, surrounded by pink and white rock formations (40 km. from Creel); Puente del Río Urique, spans the Urique Canyon, ideal camping climate. **Samachique,** where the *rari-pame* race, consisting of kicking a wooden ball in a foot-race of 150 miles without rest, often takes 2-3 days and nights. **Kirare,** on the road to La Bufa mine, offers sights of Batopilas Canyon, of great beauty. The area is inhabited by the Tarahumaras known as Gentiles. **Chomachi,** famous for its caves, some over 10 km. deep, inhabited in the past by Apaches. **Basaseachi,** with highest (over 300 metres) single-jump waterfall in North America.

(Km. 1,484) **Ciudad Camargo,** a small cattle town in a green valley, quiet save for its eight days of fiesta for Santa Rosalia beginning on Sept. 4, when there are cockfights, horse racing and dancing. Black bass fishing at the dam lake, and warm sulphur springs 5 km. away.

Hotel *Santa Rosalia Courts.*

Motel *Baca.*

(Km. 1,225) Ciudad Jiménez.
There is a route from Ciudad Jiménez through Torreón to Fresnillo and Zacatecas which is much shorter than the Central Highway we give through Durango. By Highway 49 it is 391 km. from Torreón to

Zacatecas; by Highways 40 and 45 through Durango it is 544 km. By this direct route it is about 290 km. from Ciudad Jiménez to

Torreón, the principal city of La Laguna cotton and wheat district. Population, 283,000, and shrinking. Here is the Bolsón de Mayrán (altitude 1,137 metres) an oasis of about 28,500 square km. which might be irrigated, but only about 200,000 hectares have been developed and much of that is stricken with drought. Some 3,000 desperate peasants have been moved to Yucatán. On the far side of the Nazas river running through (the bed is mostly bone dry) are the two towns of Gómez Palacio (61,000 people) and Lerdo (18,000 people). There are frequent buses to Chihuahua (10 hrs.). Bus to Tepic, US$10.80; to Ciudad Juárez, US9.80. There is also an airport.

Hotels   *Nazas,* towering high in the sky; *Elvira; Galicia; Laguna. Casa del Viajero,* Ave. Morelos 772, near *Nazas Hotel* cheap.

Restaurant   *La República,* abundant *comida corrida* at US$1.60, beside market.

From Ciudad Jiménez it is 77 km. to

(Km. 1,138) Hidalgo del Parral, an old picturesque mining town of 70,000 people with mule waggons in its steep and narrow streets. See the parochial church and one dedicated to the Lightning Virgin (Virgen del Rayo).

Buses   Each company has its own terminal.

Hotels   Near the Estrella Blanca terminal are 3 hotels; *Internacional,* US$2 s; *Pinos Alros* (basic), US$1.60 s; and *La Fe,* US$1.60 s. *Hotel Viajero,* near main square, US$2.25 s. *Café Tupinamba,* near *Restaurant España,* has good food and service at reasonable prices.

(Km. 926) Durango, capital of Durango state: alt.: 1,924 metres; pop.: 137,000; founded in 1563. It is a pleasant city, with parks, a Cathedral (1695) and a famous iron-water spring. Presa Victoria can be reached by bus from Durango; there is a new dam and one can swim there.

Hotels   *Casa Blanca; Posada Durán; Metropolitano; Campo México Courts* (good but restaurant service poor); *Gallo,* US$2.70 d with bath, good.

Durango is on the Coast-to-Coast Highway from Mazatlán to Matamoros. The 320 km. stretch of road from Durango W to Mazatlán is through splendid not-to-be-missed mountain scenery. Some 260 km. E of Durango is Torreón.

Buses   Several buses a day cross the Sierra Madre Occidental to Mazatlán (Transporte del Norte, 1st class, 7 hours, US$3.30). Second class buses for Camera buffs, stop more frequently. Second class bus to Hidalgo del Parral, 7 hours, US$3.45 with Transporte Chihuahuence.

Airport   5 km. from centre.

(Km. 636) Zacatecas, capital of Zacatecas state; alt.: 2,495 metres; pop.: 38,000; picturesque up-and-down mining city built in a ravine, houses towering above one another and sprinkled over the hills. It was founded in 1548 and, because of the immense wealth from its mines—visits can be arranged—made a city in 1588. Places to see are the Cathedral (1625), the Jesuit church of Santo Domingo, Plaza Hidalgo and its statues, the Casa Moneda, the Calderón Theatre, and the Chapel of Los Remedios (1728), on the Cerro de la Bufa which dominates the city, through which an old aqueduct runs. Zacatecas is famous for its sarapes and has two delicacies: the local cheese, and *queso de tuna,* a candy made from the fruit of the nopal cactus. Visit the small *tortilla* factories near the station, on the main road.

Hotels   *Condesa; Colón; Barranco; Posada del Parque.*

Motels   *Del Bosque* (US$10 d), *Parador Zacatecas,* excellent.

   See Chicomostoc ruins, 56 km. S.

(Km. 508) **Aguascalientes,** which was founded in 1575 and is capital of its state; alt.: 1,190 metres; pop.: 127,000; its name comes from its many hot mineral springs. An oddity is that the city is built over a network of tunnels dug out by forgotten people. It has pretty parks, a pleasant climate, delicious fruits, and specializes in drawn linen work, pottery, and leather goods. Places to see are the Government Palace (once the castle of the Marqués of Guadalupe, with colourful murals round inner court-yards), the churches of San Marcos and San Antonio (somewhat odd) and the Municipal Palace.

On items of interest in Aguascalientes, Tim Connell writes:

Museo de la Ciudad, Calle Zaragoza 505, is by Church of San Antonio. The José Guadalupe Posada museum is in a priest's house, by the Templo del Cristo Negro, close to a pleasant garden—Díaz de León (known locally as the Jardín del Enciso). A remarkable collection of prints by the lithographer Posada, best known for his "calaveras", macabre skeletal figures illustrating and satirizing the Revolution and events leading up to it. The original blocks of many of his best-known prints may be seen. Admission free, Tues.-Sun. 1000-1400, 1700-2100. Shut Mondays. Cultural events in the courtyard on Saturdays and Sundays. The Casa de las Artesanías is near main square. The Casa de la Cultura, on Venustiano Carranza and Galeana Norte is a fine Colonial building. Display of artesanía during the feria.

Hacienda de San Blas, 34 km. away, contains Museo de la Insurgencia. Murals by Alfredo Zermeño. The area is famous for viticulture—22,000 acres are under vines. The local wine is called San Marcos, and the *feria* in his honour lasts for 3 weeks, starting in the middle of April, with processions, cockfights (in Mexico's largest *palenque,* seating 4,000), bullfights, agricultural shows etc. The Plaza de Armas is lavishly decorated. The feria, covered by national TV networks, is said to be the biggest in Mexico. Accommodation can be very difficult; some hotels are booked up a year in advance, and even local railway carriages are converted into sleeping quarters.

Teatro Morelos next to Cathedral; Tel.: 5-00-97. The University is ¼ hour from the city centre. Its administrative offices are in the ex-convento de San Diego, by the attractive Jardín del Estudiante, and the Parián, a shopping centre. The market is not far away. There is carp fishing at El Jocoqui and Abelardo Rodríguez. The bull ring is on Avenida López Mateos.

Tourist Office next to the Cathedral. Tel.: 5-11-55.

Taxis There is a ticket system for taxis from the Central Camionera, with the city divided into different fare zones. There is no need to pay extra; a phone number for complaints is on the ticket.

Some 170 km. to the E is San Luis Potosí (see page 778). Aguascalientes has an airport.

Hotels *Fancia,* airy, colonial style; good restaurant *("El Fausto")* for breakfast and lunch; *Río Grande,* US$9 d; *Praga,* US$6 d with TV, Calle Zaragoza, near Centre. 5-23-57.

There are lots of cheap hotels near the bus station, like *Las Américas.*

Restaurants *Mitla* (on Av. Francisco I. Madero), cheap and clean. Good Mexican menu; *Cascada,* by the tourist office; *Bugambilia,* by *Hotel Río Grande,* on corner of main square, is quite plush, has a reasonable menu, but service can be morose.

(Km. 425) at **Lagos de Moreno,** a charming old town with fine baroque churches, a road turns off right to Guadalajara, 197 km. away; the same road leads, left, to Antiguo Morelos *via* San Luis Potosí.

After about 1,600 km. of desert or semi-arid country, we now enter, surprisingly, the Basin of Guanajuato, known as the Bajío, greener, more fertile, higher (on average over 1,800 metres), and wetter, though the rainfall is still not more than 635 to 740 mm. a year. The Bajío is the granary of central Mexico, growing maize, wheat, and fruits. The agricultural towns which we pass through, León, Irapuato, and Celaya, have grown enormously in population and importance. The last two are leading centres of cigarette manufacture.

(Km. 382) León (de los Aldamas), in the fertile plain of the Gómez river. The business centre—and León is the shoe capital of Mexico—is the Plaza de Constitución. There is a striking municipal palace, a cathedral, many shaded plazas and gardens. León is noted for its leather work, fine silver-trimmed saddles, and rebozos. Alt.: 1,885 metres; pop.: 306,000. Frequent buses to Torreón (10 hours).

Hotels *Léon; México.*

Airport San Carlos, 15 km. from centre.

(Km. 430) Silao (24,000 people). Eleven km. beyond, at Los Infantes, a short side road through the picturesque Marfil canyon leads to the enchanting small town of

Guanajuato, capital of Guanajuato state and important for its silver since 1548. Population, 70,000 in 1880, now only 45,000, altitude, 2,010 metres, and a popular tourist town. It stands in a narrow gorge amid wild and striking scenery; the Guanajuato river cutting through it has been covered over and an underground street (the "calle subterráneo") opened—a new and effective attraction. The streets, steep, twisted and narrow, follow the contour of the hills and are sometimes steps cut into the rock: one, the Street of the Kiss, is so narrow that kisses can be—and are—exchanged from opposite balconies. Over the city looms the shoulder of La Bufa mountain. A most interesting building is the massive Alhóndiga de Granadita, built as a granary, turned into a fortress, and now an attractive museum with a good section on folk art. Guanajuato contains a series of fine museums, as well as the most elegant marble-lined public lavatories in Mexico. The best of many colonial churches are San Francisco (1671); La Compañía (Jesuit, 18th century); the baroque San Diego (1663) on the Plaza de la Unión; and the exquisite church of La Valenciana, one of the most beautiful in Mexico, 5 km. out of town and built for the workers of the Valenciana silver mine, once the richest in the world. A gruesome sight shown to visitors is of mummified bodies arranged against the walls of the vaults in the cemetery. The Cathedral (Basílica) and the church of San Roque should also be visited. Local pottery can be bought at the Hidalgo market and the street the potters frequent. The University was founded in 1732. The painter Diego Rivera was born in Calle de Pocitos. The area is being industrialized.

When Father Hidalgo took the city in 1810, the Alhóndiga was last to surrender, and there was a wanton slaughter of Spanish soldiers and royalist prisoners. When Hidalgo was himself caught and executed, along with three other leaders, at Chihuahua, their heads, in revenge, were fixed at the four corners of the Alhóndiga. There is a fine view from the monument to "Pipila", the man who fired the door of the Alhóndiga so that the patriots could take it, which crowns the high hill of Hormiguera. Look for the "Al Pipila" sign. Steep climb.

Buses direct from Mexico City or from Guadalajara. Bus to San Miguel de Allende, a grand ride over mountains. Frequent buses to León.

Hotels *Posada de la Presa;* on Jardín de la Unión are *Posada Santa Fe,* and *Hotel San Diego,* good bar, dearer but better run; *Hotel Real de Minas,* large and new; *Hosteria del Frayle; Valencia; Picachos; Reforma* (bus stop, US$1.20); *Castillo de Santa Cecilia,* first class; *Orozco; Hotel Central,* unnamed, by bus station, good value, US$3.50 s with shower. *Hotel Granadería,* central, adequate, car park; *Casa de Huéspedes Martínez,* Calle Alonso 20, US$2.70 d. friendly. Next to each other on the main square between the bus terminal and market are *Posada Juárez,* US$3.40 s and *Hotel Granadita,* clean, friendly, US$1.50 on Calle Alhóndiga 7 (also the *Central* and *Reforma*); opposite this, and near the bus terminal is the *Hotel Mineral de Rayas,* US$4 s, US$6 d, with bath, spotless, warmly recommended; *Casa Smith,*

Sopena 1, US$4.50 d with bath, clean. Parallel is the main street to a street full of *Casas de huéspedes.*

Motels *Guanajuato; El Laurel; Embajadores,* where road to the dam at Pastita branches left from Paseo de la Presa, good food.

Entertainment Sketches from classical authors out of doors in lovely old plazas from April to August. Programme at Teatro Juárez (a magnificent French-type second Empire building), on Friday and Saturday nights. A band plays in Jardín de la Unión (next to the theatre) thrice weekly. At old site of La Cata mine (local bus near market), a church with a magnificent baroque façade, also the Shrine of El Señor de Villa Seca (the patron of adulterers) with retablos and crude drawings of miraculous escapes from harm, mostly due to poor shooting by husbands.

Excursion A very good round trip is through Dolores Hidalgo to San Miguel de Allende, taking in Atotonilco (see below and page 786). See also the three local silver mines of La Cata, La Raya and La Valenciana. Between the nearby villages of Silai and León are the famous swimming pools of Comanjilla, fed by hot sulphurous springs. 30 km. from Guanajato is Mount Cubilete, with a statue of Christ the King; local buses take 1½ hours, spectacular view.

Bus Guanajuato-San Miguel de Allende, 1st class, 2 hours *via* Dolores Hidalgo (most of them go on to Mexico City), US$0.80; to Guadalajara, 2nd class, US$3.20. To Mexico City, 1st class, Estrella Blanco, 5 hrs. US$3.20; frequent services.

Rail One train a day to Irapuato, at 0820.

(Km. 315) Irapuato, 176,000 people *(Hotel Rioja),* noted for delicious strawberries. (Km. 265) **Celaya,** population, 59,000; altitude, 1,800 metres; famous for its sweetmeats, especially a caramel sauce called *cajeta,* and its churches, built by Mexico's greatest architect Tresguerras (1765-1833), a native of the town. His best church is El Carmen (1807), with a glorious tower and dome; see also his fine bridge, El Puente de la Laja.

From Celaya to Querétaro there is a 56-km. limited-access toll motorway (US$0.40 a car), or the old road through Apaseo el Alto.

(Km. 220) Querétaro, where we join the route from Eagle Pass. (See page 777.)

San Miguel de Allende, a charming old town at 1,850 metres, on a steep hillside facing the broad sweep of the Laja River and the distant blue of the Guanajuato Mountains, is 50 km. N of Querétaro by paved road. Population, 15,000. It has a large number of arcaded seignorial mansions and flower-filled mudéjar patios; its people are much given to fiestas. Its twisting cobbled streets rise in terraces, each street higher than the next, to the mineral spring of El Chorro, from which the blue and yellow tiled cupolas of some 20 churches can be seen. It has been declared a national monument and all changes in the town are strictly controlled.

Social life centres around the market and the Jardín, or central plaza, an open-air living room for the whole town. Around it are the Colonial city hall, several hotels, and the parish church with a beautiful façade and a Gothic tower. The Church of St. Philip Neri, with its glorious baroque façade, is on a hill just S of the town. Notable among the baroque façades and doors rich in Churrigueresque details is the Casa del Mayorazgo de Canal, and San Francisco Church, designed by Tresguerras. One of the oldest places, the Convent of La Concepción, built in 1734, has since 1938 been transformed into an art school, the Instituto Allende (which has an English-language library), with an annual enrolment of over a thousand students. There is an American colony. Handicrafts are the traditional tin, silver, and leather work, sarape weaving and hand embroidery. The city was founded as San Miguel in 1542, and Allende added in honour of the independence patriot born there. Local American women's committees run house and garden tours for charity: ask at the hotel. (They start at noon every Sunday, and cost US$4.)

Fiestas   One every 10 days or so. Main ones are Independence Day (Sept. 15-16);
Fiesta of San Miguel (Sept. 28-Oct. 1, with Conchero dancers from many places);
Day of the Dead (Nov. 2); the Christmas Posadas, celebrated in the traditional
Colonial manner (Dec. 16-24); the pre-Lenten carnivals, Easter Week, and Corpus
Christi (June).

Hotels   *Posada de San Francisco; Instituto Allende* (connected with the art centre);
Colonial; Vista Hermosa; (first grand, last good). *San Miguel. The Rancho—Hotel
El Atascadero,* in an old Colonial hacienda, very satisfactory. *Posada de las Monjas,*
US$6.50 d with shower. Near Jardín, on Calle Vinaron, *El Fuente* has a few rooms,
good food (by arrangement). *Posada de Allende,* nice and clean, near Zócalo,
US$2.70 s with bath. Best bargain: *Quinta Loreto,* off Calle Loreto, modern rooms,
h. and c. water, swimming pool, pleasant garden, US$2.80 s, US$4 d, good cheap
food, splendid value. *Hidalgo,* US$2 d with bath, on Calle Hidalgo, also good value.
Serious students go to *Bellas Artes,* in splendid Colonial building. *Hostería del
Parque,* intimate, good Mexican folk music; *Restaurant Castillo,* near Zócalo, is
good and cheap.

Motel   *Atascadero,* edge of town, modern cabins, best food (own gardens).

Communications   The crack Aguila Azteca through train between Laredo and
Mexico City stops here. The El Paso train stops at Celaya and Querétaro, 64 km. by
bus. Frequent buses to Guanajuato (2 hours). Buses to Mexico City every 2 hrs.,
US$3, 2nd class, crowded but interesting. Buses to Morelia until 2040 daily 4 hours,
US$1.60 2nd class.

Excursions   Twenty minutes away is the small village of **Atotonilco,** where there is a
church whose inside walls and ceiling are covered with frescoes done in black, red
and grey earth: unrivalled anywhere for sheer native exuberance. There is a
radioactive spa, the Balneario Taboada between San Miguel and El Cortijo (about 20
minutes bus ride on the way to Dolores Hidalgo very near Atotonilco), a fine
swimming pool and good fishing in a nearby lake. **Dolores Hidalgo,** the home of
Father Hidalgo, is 29 km. on, another most attractive small town; celebrations are
held there on 16 September. Traditional Talavera tiles still made there.

The Western Route: Pacific Highway

From Nogales-Santa Ana (a feeder entry) to Mexico City *via* Guadalajara
is 2,043 km. (1,492 miles).

Rail   Pacific Railway as far as Guadalajara, and on by National Railways of
Mexico. Guadalajara, 1,759 km. away, is reached in 29 hours, at a speed of 60 km.
an hour, and Mexico City in 40 hours (Mexicali-Mexico City costs US$16, 2nd,
US$31, 1st class). Conditions vary in both 1st and 2nd class carriages, several
unpleasant experiences reported, e.g. lack of air conditioning, dirt, overcrowding,
etc. Sometimes 1st class trains stop at Guadalajara and 2nd class train, which is
slower, is only available as alternative.

Road Journey   It takes 18 hours, driving at an average of 65 km.p.h. to get to
Mazatlán, 1,202 km. from Nogales. The West Coast Highway—Highway 15—has a
good road—Highway 2—from Tijuana (entry from San Diego), going through
Mexicali (see page 870), Sonoita (*Desert Sun Motel;* customs inspection and
immigration check), and Caborca to Santa Ana, where it joins the Highway 15 route
to Mexico City. Between La Rumerosa and Mexicali, the road descends about 1,200
metres in fantastic, panoramic serpentines from the coastal highland to the desert.
Between Mexicali and Sonoita is **San Luis** (25,000 people), in the "free zone" and
serving cotton country: summer bullfights, small night life district like those of the
"open towns of the old west". Coming from Lukeville, Arizona, make sure you take
the road to San Luisito and not San Luis; they are both on Route 2, but 200 miles
apart in opposite directions.

   1st class bus to Mexico City, 50 hrs. by Estrella de Oro Pacífico and Norte de
Sonora, US$33.60; 2nd class (without toilet), US$31.20. There is no central bus
station in Tijuana (see page 870). Tijuana to Guadalajara, US$21.90 with Transporte
del Pacífico, leave daily at 1300, 1800 and 2200, 36 hours. Do not take Sunday bus as

it is not serviced and all sorts of problems can occur. Customs stop at Sonoita, then 18 hours on at Guaymas, then Los Mochis. Best to take food and make use of toilet facilities at stops, though they are reported filthy.

Motel   *Naranjo* (first class); *El Rey* and others.

Economy hotel   *Capra.*

Between San Luis and Sonoita is the Mexican Sahara, 200 km. with only three houses in the whole stretch. There are sand dunes and volcanic hills on the way. The desert has interesting vegetation, peculiar formations and few stopping places, but Caborca has the Motel *Posada San Cristóbal.* Sonoita is a good place for exploring the famous Kino missions, and there are recently discovered and very interesting archaeological ruins. Transportes Norte de Sonora and Tres Estrellas have first class services (the former is slightly better). Water and snacks should be carried, the tank kept full and replenished whenever possible. This feeder road can also be entered at Sonoita on the border S of Organ Pipe National Monument (Arizona). The very good highway from Tijuana to Hermosillo is patrolled by the Free Assistance Service of the Mexican Tourist Department, whose green coloured jeeps patrol most of Mexico's main roads. The drivers speak English, are trained to give first aid and to make minor auto repairs and deal with flat tyres. They carry gasoline and have radio connection. All help is completely free. Gasoline at cost price.

In summer, west coast drivers prefer the Central Route from El Paso, Texas, unless their cars are air-conditioned, or they love heat. It is dangerous to drive on retread tyres over the hot desert.

The trip down the coast to Acapulco, by-passing Guadalajara and Mexico City, is rather long and gruelling, and with many military searches in the State of Guerrero (where there has recently been guerrilla activity). The coast road goes on from Acapulco to Puerto Angel and Salina Cruz, but is not paved throughout.

Note   The amount of accommodation along the Pacific highway has increased greatly in recent years. There is a large number of motels along the whole route, so that each town of any importance has one or more. All available accommodation is listed in the American Automobile Association's *"Mexico by Motor"*.

From Nogales at 1,180 metres to Guaymas, at sea level on the Gulf, the road runs along the western slopes of the Sierra Madre, whose surprisingly high summits rise to 3,000 metres. From Guaymas on to Mazatlán it threads along the lowland, with the Sierra Madre Occidental's bold and commanding escarpment to the E. Like the W coasts of all continents between latitudes 20° and 30°, the whole area is desert, but fruitful wherever irrigated by water flowing from the mountains. Summers are very hot, sometimes rainy, but winters are mild and very dry. Within the Sierra Madre a nomadic people hunts the many wild animals; along the coasts available water determines the spots of concentrated settlements and of agriculture. Mexico gets most of its wheat from the southern part of Sonora state, and the irrigated valley bottoms (around Hermosillo) are also used for maize, cotton and beans. Farther S, in frost-free Sinaloa and Nayarit, sugar, rice, winter vegetables, tomatoes, and tobacco are grown. The three coastal states we pass through make up 21% of Mexico's area, but include only 6% of its population.

(Km. 2,403) **Nogales,** half in Mexico, half in Arizona, lies astride a mountain pass at 1,180 metres. It is a mining centre, with walnut groves around it and cattle ranches. It has the usual border night life. It is through Nogales and Mexicali that the winter vegetable crops of southern Sonora and Sinaloa are exported. Population, 38,000.

Festival   Cinco de Mayo Festival, lasting four days, celebrates the defeat of the French army at Puebla on May 5, 1862.

Hotel   *Fray Marcos de Niza.*

Restaurant   *Caverna Greca,* in a cave.

Train   Nogales to Mexico City US$96 for a double compartment with bathroom. Food on train good until Guadalajara, then becomes overpriced. If coming from the US, book seat and ticket at Nogales station by telephone, pay day you leave, much cheaper. 2nd class train to Guadalajara 48 hours, crowded.

Bus   to Mexico City 42 hrs. with Transportes de Pacifico or Norte de Sonora, US$15.50, Tres Estrellas de Oro, 36 hrs. US$16.80. To Guadalajara 1st class, US$12.70, 26 hours, very clean, fold-down seats, many food stops leaves 1600, arrives 0700.

The highway passes through the small mining towns of Imuris and Magdelena, both in the Magdalena Valley. The Cocospera mines are near Imuris and there are famous gold and silver mines near Magdalena, which has a great Indian fiesta in the first week of October. Beyond the cactus-strewn desert begins. At 120 km. from Nogales is Santa Ana.

(Km. 2,123) **Hermosillo**, capital of Sonora state, is a modern city, a winter resort town, and centre of a rich orchard area. The La Colorada copper mines are to the E. It has a colonial Cathedral, an old quarter round an old plaza, and houses the University of Sonora. Altitude, 237 metres; population, 206,600. Golf course. Airport.

Excursion   A dry-weather road, 106 km., goes W to Puerto Kino, on the Gulf. Across El Canal del Infiernillo (Little Hell Strait) from the port is the romantic and mountainous Isla del Tiburón (Shark Island), where the Indians paint their faces.

Hotels   *Bugambilia; Laval; San Alberto; Kino Hotel,* reasonable; *Hotel Lourdes,* US$8 d with bath; *Monte Carlo,* cheap; *Guaymas Inn,* 5½ km. N, air-conditioned rooms with shower, US$5 s, US$6 d. *Asa,* furnished apartments. There is a small city park where free overnight camping is permitted.

Bus   to Nogales US$4.20, 4 hrs. dull; 2nd class to Agua Prieta, 7 hours, US$3.30; to Los Mochis, 1st class, US$7.80, 2nd, US$7.40, 7½ hrs. through scrubland and wheat fields. The bus station is on the outskirts.

At km. 1,988 the road reaches the Gulf at the port of **Guaymas**, on a lovely bay backed by harsh desert mountains. Good bathing especially at Playa de Cortés, excellent deep-sea fishing, and sea-food for the gourmet. Miramar beach, on Bocochibampo bay circled by purple mountains, its blue seas sprinkled with green islets, is the resort section. Water sports on May 10. The climate is ideal in winter but unpleasant in summer. The 18th century church of San Fernando is worth a visit; so also, outside the town, is the 17th century church of San José de Guaymas. Excursions to the cactus "forests". Some 22 km. N of Guaymas is the Balúa San Carlos, where "Catch 22" was filmed; there is free camping on a good beach at the end of the runway made for the film; also good fishing. Pop.: 60,000. Airport.

Hotels   *Rubi,* US$4.80 d, with shower and w.c., in the town; *Playa de Cortés,* on Bocochibampo Bay, best and most expensive; *Miramar Beach. Casa de Huéspedes La Colimense,* very basic, US$2.70 s with fan, opp. bus station. Opposite the small prison is another *Casa de Huéspedes,* looks better, US$3.15 s. Same price applies to *Hotel Rolyat* on the main street. Those who feel like fleeing high prices at Guaymas and can make Ciudad Obregon, 129 km. S (68,000 people), will find *Costa de Oro* well kept and pleasant.

British Vice-Consul   Apartado 88 for letters. Casa 3, Av. 11 (Tel: 26).

Rail   Autovia from Guaymas to Nogales leaves at 1000, 6 hours, US$7.80, daily except Sat.; book in advance;

Buses   Transbordadores go from Guaymas to Santa Rosalia at 1200 every Sat., Sun. and Thur., and return on the same day at 2200. 2nd class bus Guaymas-Hermosillo (1½ hours, US$1.10).

From Guaymas to Mazatlán is 784 km. We pass through a number of towns, about 2 or 3 hours' driving time apart, so it is wise to have alternative stops. First comes **Ciudad Obregón** *(Motel Valle Grande, Costa de Oro)*, mainly important as the centre of an agricultural region. **Navajoa** (31,000 people) has the *Motel El Rancho* and *Motel del Río;* 52 km. E into the hills is the delightful old Colonial town of **Alamos** *(Los Portales Hotel)* now declared a national monument. It is set in a mining area fascinating for rock enthusiasts. West of Navajoa, on Huatabampo Bay, are the survivors of the Mayo Indians; their festivals are in May. **Los Mochis,** in a sugar-cane area, is a fishing resort with an American colony and an American-style layout and facilities. Km 1,636.5; 100,000 people; hotels *Santa Anita* US$16 d has own bus service to station; *Parque,* US$3.50; *Lorena* modern, air-conditioned, US$9 s; *Obregón* (Calle Obregón, E of Zaragoza), US$2 s, basic; *Heredia,* US$2.70 s reasonably clean, old, bath; *Casa de Huéspedes Carmelita,* small, basic, by bus station, US$4.50 d.

A railcar (*Autovía*) trip from Los Mochis (station reached only by taxi, US$2.70; no buses) to Chihuahua and back gives fine views of the wild Barranca de Tarahumara, lived in by the primitive Tarahumara Indians. The trip is recommended from Los Mochis because that way you can see the best part of the scenery in daylight. Several trips weekly, at 0700, (12 hrs) but you must be prepared to spend at least one night in the Cañón as trains only leave on alternate days from both places. Return, with reserved seat, US$7.90 each, or less by slower, less comfortable ordinary train, 2nd class tickets only available on overnight train Chihuahua-Los Mochis, US$4.50 (see also page 781). There are frequent daily buses to Tijuana (16 hours travel). Airport.

Bus Los Mochis-Mazatlán US$4.50, 2nd class; US$6 1st class, leaves 2100, arrives 0345. No reservations can be made for buses N or S at the terminal of Tres Estrellas de Oro and it is difficult to get on buses. Try instead Transportes del Pacífico, a few blocks away. First class bus to Guaymas 5½ hrs, US$3.20.

About half an hour's drive along a side road takes us to **Topolobampo,** on the beautiful bay-and-lagoon-indented coast. (Now that a railway—take food with you—has been opened to Ojinaga (Chihuahua), Topolobampo is being developed as a deep-sea port).

Hotels *Yacht Hotel,* modern, clean and good food; *Casa de Huéspedes* not recommended.

Ferry There is a ferry from Topolobampo to La Paz, Baja California Sur, several times a week (see also page 872).

Some 240 km. beyond Los Mochis (at km. 1,429) is the capital of Sinaloa state, **Culiacán** (358,800 people), chief centre for winter vegetables. It has a University. The Colonial town has gone. Most of North America's illegal marijuana is grown in the mountains beyond Culiacán. Hotel: *El Venado.* Romantic night clubs: *La Fogata; La Fuente; Chinacos.* Other motels: *Los Caminos; Los Tres Ríos.* The safe beaches of Altata are 30 minutes by dirt road.

Firmly rooted and extremely popular in the State of Sinaloa is a type of orchestra known as the Banda Sinaloense, which can be seen and heard at almost any time of day or night in restaurants, dance halls, bars, at family feasts or on the street. It usually has from 14 to 16 musicians, 4 saxophones, 4 trumpets, clarinets, tuba, 3-4 men on drums and other percussion instruments, including maracas, guiro, and loud, strong voices. It is unabashed, brutal music, loud and lively sometimes with very fast rhythms—a mixture of military brass band, dixieland jazz orchestra and Cuban rumba band. It has an incomparable acoustic potency and liveliness not found anywhere else.

Airport 10 km. from centre.

Another 208 km. bring us to a roadside monument marking the Tropic of Cancer; there is a time-change here (see page 879). Thirteen km. beyond is (km. 1,204) **Mazatlán**, spread along a peninsula at the foot of the lofty Sierra Madre. It is the largest Mexican port on the Pacific Ocean and the main industrial and commercial centre in the W. The beauty of its setting and its warm winters have made it a popular resort, but unfortunately with expansion it has become rather noisy and lost some of its attraction. It overlooks Olas Altas (High Waves) bay. On one side of the peninsula, the beach is fringed with groves of coconut palm; on the other a fine promenade overlooks a number of picturesque islands. There are more islands in the nearby lagoons, which teem with wild life. A great promenade lined by hotels, with a long slender beach at its foot, curves round the bay. Here people walk when the day is done and watch the famous sunsets. The local carnival is almost as good as at Veracruz. Buses go into town from the new bus station at Centro Colonia. The best beaches, 3 to 5 km. from the city, are easily reached by taxi. Boats ply between the shore and the island beaches. The crooked streets can be explored in reasonably cheap three-wheeled taxis. On top of the only hill in the city is a park. The Lighthouse, on El Faro Island, is 157 metres above sea-water. Its light is visible 50 km. away. Population, 174,000. Airport 26 km. from centre. (Taxi, fixed fare US$6.60 airport-Mazatlán).

Fishing is the big sport (sailfish, tarpon, marlin, etc.). Shrimp from the Gulf are sent, frozen, to all parts of Mexico. Its famous fishing tournament follows Acapulco's and precedes the one at Guaymas. In the mangrove swamps are egrets, flamingoes, pelicans, cranes, herons, and duck. Nearby at Camarones there is "parachute flying", drawn by motorboats.

Excursion to Isles de Piedras, 30 km. of good clean beach. Take a small boat from E of Armada (naval station near brewery) regular service, US$0.20, walk across island (10 mins.). Local *comedores* on beach provide primitive accommodation. About 100 km. N of Mazatlán is a turn-off to the town of La Cruz. You can rent small beach huts locally. Few tourists. A boat excursion on the "Yate Fiesta" cruises out at 1000 or 2000 (with dancing), from second last bus stop in the direction of Playa del Sur. Refreshments included, and you can see the wildlife in the day time; US$4.40.

Hotels *Freeman; Belmar; Siesta* (good evening entertainment); *Playa,* facing Gulf and Three Sisters' Islands; *Hacienda,* expensive; *De Cima. Posada Colonial,* on Miguel Alemán, N of the South Docks, is a well kept motel and has the best food in town; *Hotel El Dorado* on North Beach; at Playa de las Gaviotas outside town, is *Playa Mazatlán* hotel, and one block back from beach. *Hotel Playamar,* US$9 d, run by Canadian, air-conditioned, on N beach near centre of town; *Hotel Las Brisas,* Ave del Mar 900, recommended US$10.55 d with shower; swimming pool and on sea front. Air-conditioned. *Hotel del Centro,* modern, central US$8.40 d, *Hotel Alberto,* Calle Luis de Zubido, US$4.20 d with shower. *Pensión María Luisa,* central, US$1.50 s, quiet. *Posada Santa Fe* (private beach). *Hotel San Jorge,* clean, modern, near market and beach, US$3.50 s with shower. *Hotel Lerma,* Calle Simón Bolívar, near beach, US$3.35 d, friendly. *Hotel Vialta,* three blocks from market, US$3-5 d with bath. *Hotel Pescador,* recommended; *Hotel Villa del Mar,* central, nice and clean, with car park, US$5 d, with fan and private facilities. N of the city there are undeveloped beaches with free overnight camping. Night club in romantic setting: *El Corral.*

Motels *Palo Alto; Agua Marina; Las Palmas; Marley; Las Gaviotas* (also bungalows).

Restaurants *El Patio,* Avenida del Mar, particularly recommended for superb 4-course dinner at US$5.50 incl. cocktail or liqueur, with nightly entertainment. *Zaragoza* and *Guillerno Nelson,* recommended, Mexican dishes reasonable. *Doney,* 5 de Mayo and Canizales in the centre, good home cooking, US$1.30 for 3-course meal; *El Shrimp Bucket; Señor Frog* restaurant/bar (with rock music) on beach, between central Mazatlán and northern beaches, pleasant atmosphere. Behind *Hotel Alberto* is a nice small restaurant, serves duck cheaply. Seafood is very good in the restaurants.

Bus Station is on the outskirts of the town. Bus fare Mazatlán-Mexico City about US$11.40 (2nd class); train fare about US$11 (1st class). Mazatlán-Guadalajara, US$5.25 (9 hours). Mazatlán-Tepic US$3.25, (5¾ hrs.); bus to Los Mochis, (7 hrs.), US$5 2nd class, US$5.25 1st. There is a free Red Cross treatment station at Mazatlán, 9 blocks along the avenue opposite the Beach Man on the right.

Shipping   Joint fast cargo service from and to Europe of Central American Services Line. Agents: Agencias Marítimas del Pacifico S.A., Constitución y Av. del Puerto. Ferryboat to La Paz (Baja California Sur), daily at 1700; car (one way), US$30-40, plus US$15 for cabin. US$5 seat in salon. Allow plenty of time for booking and customs procedure.

Rail   Train Mazatlán-Guadalajara, departs 2000, very comfortable, Japanese built, air-conditioned. Best travel 1st class US$4.35 or pullman, US$8.50, 2nd class dirty and uncomfortable. Buy tickets at *Hotel Hacienda,* on the seafront near centre. Arrival in Guadalajara at 0700.

Twenty-four km. beyond Mazatlán, the Coast to Coast Highway to Durango Torreón, Monterrey and Matamoros turns off left at Villa Unión. Before reaching Tepic both road and railway begin that long climb from the lowland level over the Sierra Madre to the Basin of Jalisco, 1,500 metres above sea-level. Eleven km. from Tepic a road on the right descends 900 metres to a pretty South Sea-type beach. The resort of **San Blas** (possible to take a 4-hr jungle trip in a boat for US$2.80, to small resort with fresh water swimming hole), fast becoming popular with young Americans, is 33 km. from Tepic. The road is quite good and the ride is outstandingly beautiful. (Lots of blackfly.) It has an old Spanish fortress. (There are bus services between the two.) In August it becomes very hot and there are many gnats, but not on the beach. Few tourists at this time. About 5 km. from San Blas is the beach of Matanchén, good swimming. 16 km. from San Blas is the beautiful Los Cocos beach.

Hotels   *Playa Hermosa; Bucanero,* US$4.10 s, frequented by Americans, swimming pool, food good. *María's,* all-American, friendly, with cooking, washing and fridge facilities, US$2.40 each. No camping permitted on beaches but several pay campsites available. Sometimes free camping possible behind *Playa Hermosa Hotel.*

Restaurants   *Tropicana,* try its *sopa mariuera,* fish soup; turtle tacos at *MacDonald* on Zócalo.

Quaint tiny towns just off the highway between Mazatlán and Tepic are Acaponeta, Rosario, Tuxpan and Santiago.

Bus   San Blas-Tepic, 2nd class, US$0.75, 1½ hrs.

(Km. 909) **Tepic,** capital of Nayarit state, altitude 900 metres, population 111,300, founded in 1531 at the foot of the extinct volcano of Sangagüey. It still retains, after disastrous modernization, some of its colonial streets. The Huichol and Cora Indians of the Sierra come to town in very picturesque dresses; their craftwork—bags (worn only by men), scarves woven in colourful designs and necklaces (*chaquira*) of tiny beads and wall-hangings of brightly coloured wool stuck on to boards to record the artist's dream or impression—is available from 3 or 4 expensive souvenir shops, but best is to let Indians approach you when they come to town. These handicrafts are reported to be cheaper in Guadalajara, at the Casa de Artesanías. There are many little squares, all filled with trees and flowers. The Cathedral, with two fine Gothic towers, is in Plaza Principal. Worth seeing are the Municipal Palace, whose lower floor is in Doric and the upper in Ionic; the Casa de Amado Nervo (the celebrated

Mexican poet and diplomat); the Regional Museum, Av. México 91 Norte (open 1000-1400 and 1700-2000 hours, closed Monday) and the Convento de la Cruz, on the summit of a pleasant wooded hill. The landscape around Tepic is wild and mountainous. Nearby are the Ingenio and Jala waterfalls, good places for picnics. Tombs in cemetery worth seeing.

Hotels *Sierra de Alica; La Loma. Imperial,* US$4 s, basic; *San Jorge,* US$6 d, very comfortable, good value; *Avenida,* US$2.80 d; *Hotel Brandy,* US$1.60 adequate. *Hotel Ibarra,* Calle Durango 297 Norte, has luxurious noisy rooms for US$6 d with bath, and very quiet, slightly spartan, cooler rooms without bath at US$2.50 d, very clean. *Casa de Huéspedes Grijalva,* US$2.80 each, on Zócalo, hot water; *Hotel Tepic,* new, US$5 d, with bath, near bus station outside town, clean, friendly; *Hotel Mayo,* near bus station, US$5 d, clean and bright; *Hotel Corita,* modern, US$4 s, US$6 d, free parking in locked yard; good reasonable restaurant, attractive gardens; *Hotel Central,* US$1 s; *Hotel Juárez,* US$8 d, near Palacio de Gobierno.

Motels *La Lorna* (swimming pool); *Cora. Motel Apartamentos Koala,* La Laguna, Santa María del Oro, has units for up to 3 people with kitchen and bathroom, and snack bar, US$6.50 per unit. Fishing and waterskiing on nearby lagoon.

Transport Bus, Tepic-Guadalajara, US$2.60; Tepic-Mazatlán, 4½ hours, US$4 (2nd class); Tepic-Mexico City US$9; Tepic-Torreón, US$10.80. Train to Guadalajara, US$2.30 (2nd class), US$3.80 (1st) leaves at 1145, arrives at 1800, sit on left-hand side for best views. Airport.

Excursions To large Toltec ruins not far away; to various beaches along the coast, some of them off the Nogales Highway we have come along: Novillero (turn off at Acaponeta); San Blas (turn off 11 km. from Tepic) now very commercial; to the Matanchén beach, where wet, dark and menacing jungle comes down to the shore: the area teems with waterfowl. A road runs through Compostela, a pleasant small town with an old church (1539) and overlooked by a peak surmounted by a large metal cross, to **Santa Cruz,** about 37 km. from Tepic, has a rocky beach. 2½-hours ride by open-sided lorry, US$0.50, difficult to leave the town again, check for transport. Accommodation at Peter's Shop, US$0.40 (!) a night, basic but pleasant and friendly. Simple food available; all reminiscent of the South Seas.

Other beaches between Santa Cruz and Puerto Vallarta include Rincón de los Guayabitos, which is being developed as a tourist resort with holiday village and trailer park; Chacala, lined with coconut palms and reached by an unsurfaced road through jungle; and Canalán, near Las Varas, reached only on foot, isolated and beautiful.

Puerto Vallarta, now a well-known resort, is reached by plane from Tepic, Tijuana, Los Angeles and Mexico City. It offers aquatic sports, particularly fishing and hunting for sharks. The beach at Puerto Vallarta is not particularly good but there are nice ones about 8-10 km. south along the coast. There is now a paved road from Tepic to Puerto Vallarta, continuing down the coast to Barra de Navidad and Manzanillo.

Hotels *Hotel Rosita* very pleasantly situated, 5 min. bus ride to beaches on other side of town. From US$5 s; *Molino de Agua,* US$18 s; *Playa de Oro; Oceano; Río,* and a new hotel, *Posada de Roger,* B. Badillo 137, good value, near two main city beaches, US$4 d, with bath, US$2.80 s but do beware of thieves; popular with Americans; *Hotel Ocampo,* US$4 d; *Casa Siete Enanos,* US$3 d; *Hotel Lima,* clean, friendly, US$5 with bath, d. Several "casas de huéspedes" (US$4-5 d) in newer part of town, across bridge, as well as better hotels with swimming pools, US$7.50 d. In Barra de Navidad, on Calle Moreno one hotel without board.

Restaurants The *Mercado Restaurant* is good and very cheap. *Mismaloya Beach* restaurant, opposite *Moby Dick* restaurant, excellent, US$2-4 for dinner (8 km. S of Puerto Vallarta). Popular local restaurant, *Carlos O'Brians,* beautifully decorated, well worth visiting. Puerto Vallarta has an active night life, with many bars and discotheques.

Camping Free overnight camping permitted on the large sandbar of Barra de Navidad; also 8 km. S of Puerto Vallarta at Playa Mismaloya, popular with Americans and Canadians travelling by car.

Excursions from Puerto Vallarta To Yelapa, beautiful tropical village with waterfall; "Night of the Iguana" was filmed nearby. Beaches in the area include Melaque, 10 km. from Barra de Navidad; Tenatica, unspoiled, and Manzanilla close by.

Ferry To Cabo San Lucas in Baja California Sur, Sat. and Tues., 1600 hours, one way fare US$11 (reclining seat), US$20 (cabin), 17 hours.

Buses By Autobuses del Pacifico, from Mexico City, the trip takes 15 hours (US$12.40). From Puerto Vallarta to Guadalajara costs US$4.60 (7 hours). Bus by ferry, Pto. Vallarta-Cabo San Lucas, Sat. and Tue. at 1600, return Wed. and Sun. at 1600. Transbordadores, run by Caminas y Puentes Federales.

Air Travel International airport 7 km. from centre.

Tequila (58 km. from Guadalajara), in the maguey lands, is one of the places where the famous local drink named after it is distilled from maguey. In a flat basin N of Lake Chapala lies Guadalajara. The new road from Tepic to Guadalajara follows an easier course than the old railway, now closed to passenger traffic.

Tequila and Guadalajara are in the State of Jalisco, and Jalisco's cultural life has been helped by an economy based on crafts, agriculture, and livestock, with fewer pockets of abject poverty than elsewhere in Mexico. Many villages have traditional skills such as pottery, blown glass, shoemaking, and a curious and beautiful form of filigree weaving in which miniature flower baskets, fruit and religious images are shaped from *chilte* (chicle, the raw substance from which chewing-gum is made). There is an air about these hamlets of quiet, industrious good living. The State is the original home of Mexico's mariachis: roving musical groups who play standing, dressed in the gala suits and sombreros of early 19th century rural gentry. They specialize in romantic ballads (boleros), huapangos and the Son.

(Km. 686) **Guadalajara**, capital of Jalisco state; altitude 1,650 metres, and slightly warmer than at the capital; population, 2,000,000, and 686 km. from Mexico City, was founded in 1530. It is a fine, clean city, not unlike the towns of southern Spain. Graceful colonial arcades, or *portales,* flank scores of old plazas and shaded parks. The climate is mild, dry and clear all through the year. The best shops are all found in or near the Plaza Mayor and the Avenida Juárez. The Plaza Mayor is flanked by the Government Palace (1643) where in 1810 Hidalgo issued his first proclamation abolishing slavery (plaque). The main attraction here is Orozco's great murals on the central staircase. Other works by this artist can be seen at the University, the Museo Taller José Clemente Orozco, and at the massive Cabañas Orphanage, a beautiful building with 22 patios, which is floodlit at night (entry US$0.40). The contents of the former Orozco museum in Mexico City have also been transferred to Guadalajara. The Orozco frescoes have an extraordinary daring. Here, surrounded by 3 figures—man asleep, man meditating, and man creating—a man of flames rises in receding perpective to some unknown heaven. On the Plaza Mayor also is the Cathedral, begun in 1561, finished in 1618, and rather a medley of styles; excellent view from the tower. There is a reputed Murillo Virgin inside (painted 1650), and the famous La Virgen del Carmen, painted by Miguel de Cabrera, a Zapotec Indian from Oaxaca. NE of the Cathedral is the State Museum (US$0.50) in an old monastery (1700), and two blocks E is the enormous and fantastically decorated Degollado Theatre (1866), half-price for students on Saturdays.

The best churches are Santa Mónica (1718), with a richly carved façade; El Carmen, whose main altar is surrounded by newly gilded Corinthian columns and has an 18th century rococo pulpit in the middle of the central nave; and San Francisco (1550). To the S of this last church is the quite exquisite Jardín San Francisco, and to the E the old and quaint church of Our Lady of Aranzazu, with two fantastic Churrigueresque altarpieces. There are 3 universities (visit architectural faculty, 20 minutes by car from centre, overlooking Barranca de Oblatos, a huge cañyon), a theatre, a Cultural Institute, and an open-air theatre, Auditorio Gonzalo Cunel. Other sights worth seeing are the Agua Azul park in the southern suburbs (swimming pools; dances); the markets (in particular the Libertad market); the two glass factories at **Tlaquepaque** where the blue, green, amber and amthyst blown glass articles are made; and the Casa de los Telares (Calle de Hidalgo 1378), where Indian textiles are woven on hand looms. Potters can be watched at work both here and at Tlaquepaque; price-wise you may find better bargains at Tonalá, (pottery and ceramics) 15 km. SW of Guadalajara, on the road to Mexico City. Best buys: glass, leather (cheapest in Mexico), and ceramics. About 4,000 Americans live in and around the town.

Sport   Bullfights: November to March; Football throughout year; baseball, April-Sept.; 18-hole golf at airport and Country Club, which has tennis and swimming also.

Tourist Office—helpful, has maps, ask about free open-air events in courtyard of the office.

Festival   March 21, commemorates Benito Juárez's birthday and everything is closed for the day. Ceremonies around his monument at the Agua Azul park. At the end of October there is also a great fiesta with concerts, bullfights, sports and exhibitions.

Casa de Artesanías, edge of Agua Azul park, high quality display (and sale) of handicrafts. There is another shop-cum-exhibition at the Instituto de Artesanía Jaliscense, México 54, extension of the Avenida Alcalde and Avila Camacho. Look out for leather belts with sewn-on tapestry. See also the Tienda Tlaquepaque, at Av. Juárez 267-B, in Tlaquepaque, Tel.: 35-56-63.

Cultural Institutes   US at Tolsa 300; British at Tomás V. Gómez 125.

Hotels   *Guadalajara-Hilton; Camino Real; Fenix; Gran; Roma; del Parque; Tres Estrellas,* cheap and clean, all rooms with bath, a restaurant and garage, Independencia Sur 667 near bus station, recommended, (restaurant closed in January) US$3.30 s; *Hotel Rose,* bungalows; *Hotel San Carlos* US$13.65; *Occidental,* modern but noisy, corner of Huerta and Villagómez, US$3 s; *Morales, Francés,* behind the Palacio de Gobierno, serves an excellent five-course lunch for US$1.25, very good value, old-world colonial atmosphere, cheapest single room costs US$3.10, not bad for centre of town; *Reno,* Calle Independencia, US$3.75 d; *Costa Brava,* US$6 d; *Praga,* near bus station and across from San Carlos, US$6.15 d, clean, no comfort, nice people; also *Hotel Morelia* on 20 de Enero; *Hotel Nueva Galicia,* modern, on Avenida Corena; *Hotel Mendoza,* US$8.50 d with bath, old style and very pleasant; *Hotel Balderas,* Calle Balderas, near bus station, US$3 d, dirty. On same street *Pensión Jalisco* US$2.20 with bath, d, spotless, comfortable, but in horrible district. *Hotel Sevilla,* Prisciliano Sánchez 413, reasonable, clean (2 blocks from centre). Near Ave Independencia Sur, *Pensión Lidia,* US$2.25 d, and *Hotel Pacífico,* nice clean rooms US$2.70 d; *Hotel Fermoselle,* Morelos 119 in centre, 200 metres from Cathedral, clean, US$4.85 d with shower (take a back room). *Hotel Lisboa,* near Mercado Libertad, US$3.20 d with bath, friendly, clean. *Posada de la Fuente,* basic, US$2.80 d. *Hotel Américas,* Hidalgo 76, comfortable, US$5.60 d, shower. *Hotel Janiero,* by market, clean, US$3.30 d; *Hotel Central,* US$3.80 d, and *Hotel Consul,* US$8 d, both near bus terminal on 20 de Enero, clean. Plenty of good cheap *hospedajes* about 2 blocks from bus station, in direction of

centre, e.g. *Casa de Huéspedes Norteña*, Calle 28 de Enero, US$2.50 d, without
bath, clean. Room to wash clothes in patio; also *Hotel Oriental,* US$4 d, basic.
Hotel Colinino, US$1.30, by bus station; *Manzanillo,* Calle Estadio 2074, near bus
station US$2.50 d.

Motels *American; Tropicana; Chapalita* (US$3-4 s). *La Giralda,* good for families
and long stays. Many along López Mateos near the edge of town, before the
periférico road.

Restaurants *Jacques* (in Lafayette Park); *Chamberi; Takare; Cazadores; Copa de
Leche,* on Juárez; *Las Margaritas,* López Cotilla 1477, good vegetarian dishes.
Businessman's lunch at *Cadillac, Nápoles.* Cheap meals at *El Bordo,* Calle
Independencia and at the *Fonda Vieja Mexicali* at No. 391 (Sur) of the same street.
Nino's, Ave México and Manuel, reasonable and good; *Alpes,* Calle López Cotilla,
German food, inexpensive; *Fogón.*

British Vice-Consul España 280. Tel.: 3.64.01.

Rail Ticket office in town, Ave Libertad and Colonias, near the American
Consulate. Mexican Pacific to Nogales and Los Angeles; National Railways to
Mexico City, US$3.50; to Manzanillo. The train which arrives from Tepic usually
arrives after the cheap train for Mexico City has departed, leaving you with the
choice of staying in a hotel or taking the expensive but very comfortable Pullman
which also has a dining car. Mexico City-Guadalajara on this train at 2030 daily, 12
hours, US$14. The ordinary train from Mexico City to Guadalajara leaves at 0705
and 1805 daily, 14 hours, US$5 (1st class), US$3.50 (2nd class). There is a first and
special first class; only the latter is better than 2nd class. Train to Mexicali, 0900
hours (Pullman), 28 hours, US$60; (ordinary) 1200 hours, 44 hours, US$24 (1st),
US$14 (2nd). Train to Tepic, 8 hours (1st class, US$3.10, 2nd class US$2). Train to
Mazatlán (book well in advance) 1st class and Pullman at 0910, US$4.35 and
US$8.50 respectively. All classes on 1330 train, 2nd class US$2.50 (price difference
really shows).

Airport Miguel Hidalgo, 20 km. from town; taxi, fixed rate from centre US$5.30.
Eight flights daily to and from Mexico City, 50 minutes.

Bus To Uruapan, US$4.30, 1st class, 5 hours, with Estrella de Oro; with Norte de
Sonora to Mazatlán, 9½ hours, US$4.40; Ciudad Obregón, 15 hours, US$11.50;
Hermosillo, 19 hours, US$15; Mexicali, 32 hours, US$21; Tijuana, 36 hours, US$24
with Omnibus de México, Mexico City, US$9, 9 hrs, leaves at 0900, much of road
under repair; Nogales, US$12.40, 26 hours.

Entertainment Folk dances every Sunday at 1000 in the Degollado Theatre; concert
every Sunday at 1830 in the Plaza de Armas, in front of the Palacio de Gobierno,
free. Music from Latin America played by 2-5 people at La Peña on Avenida Unión.

Excursions 8 km. to the great canyon of Barranca de Oblatos, 600 metres deep,
with the Río Santiago hurling and cascading at the bottom: a stupendous sight.
Guides to the bottom. Also to Barranco de Huentitán, in the Canyon of the River
Lerma, access *via* the Mirador de Huentitán, interesting flora, tremendous natural
site. Buses going there are not marked; ask at tourist office. To the north-eastern
suburbs of Tlaquepaque and Tonalá by tram or bus to see the glass factories, the
potters at work, or just for enjoyment: much mariachi music.

Lago de Chapala, 64 km. to the south-east, is near the town of Sayula about which
D. H. Lawrence wrote "The Plumed Serpent". At El Castillo, 24 km. along the
route, turn off along a dirt road to (13 km.) the Salto de Juanacatlán, a waterfall
which drops 21 metres over a 140-metres wide horseshoe into a giant chasm. Enquire
first, it is sometimes quite dry. **Chapala** town, on the northern shore of Lake
Chapala (113 km. long, 24 to 32 wide), has thermal springs, several good hotels, and
is a popular resort. The lake is set in beautiful scenery. There are boats of all kinds
for hire, water-fowl shooting in autumn and winter, sailing, and the lake teems with
freshwater fish. Indian fishing methods are fascinating. **Ajijic,** 7 km. to the W, a
smaller and more Indian village; it has an arty-crafty American colony. *Posada
Ajijic* is a pleasant place to stay at; very cheap basic accommodation at *La Playita,*
Calle Hidalgo 12B. Try the *Teheban* bar for entertainment. Beyond Ajijic is the
Indian fishing village of **Jocotepec,** a sizeable agricultural centre (recently invaded by
more cosmopolitan types) on the lake; there is a local fiesta on January 11-18. Stay at

La Quinta, built 1828 as coaching inn, good food, US$3.20 s, with shower, or US$10 s, with full board. *Hotel Olmedo,* US$2.20, opposite police chief's house. New Casa de Huéspedes on Calle Matamoros 83 (same street as bus station), US$2.50 d, without bath, modern facilities. *Ramón's Bar,* popular drinking place. It can be reached from Ajijic or, right, from the Mexico-Guadalajara highway. The Indians make famous black-and-white sarapes. Nearby is the *Motel El Pescador.* Between Ajijic and Jocotepec lies the small town of **San Juan Cosalá,** with thermal springs at *Balnearios y Suites Cosalá,* which has private rooms for bathing with large tiled baths. Sunbathing in private rooms also possible. Also rooms to let. *Hotel Kikos,* nearby, not so good.

Chapala Hotels *Villa Montecarlo; Nido; Posada Santa María* (Hidalgo 244, excellent); *Las Palmitas,* US$2, good. Good discotheque, *Pantera Rosa.*

About 130 km. S of Guadalajara off the road to Sayula and Ciudad Guzmán, is **Tapalpa,** virtually a small twin city of Pátzcuaro (see page 798) and very pretty indeed.

To **Manzanillo,** which, since a spectacular 257-km. railway has been driven down the sharp slopes of the Sierra Madre through Colima, has become an important port on the Pacific. The road from Guadalajara is *via* Jal. 33 to Ciudad Guzmán and on to Manzanillo. Distractions at Manzanillo (population, 26,000), are deep-sea fishing, bathing, and walking in the hills. The best beach is the lovely crescent of Santiago, 8 km. N, but there are three others. Airport.

Hotels At Santiago Beach: *Playa de Santiago; Parador Marbella,* US$18 d including breakfast and dinner; *Club Las Hadas; Anita.* At the port: *Foreign Club; Colonial.* Other hotels: *Medina,* US$1.75 d; *Pacífico,* US$2.50 d, with bath; both on Calle México. Camping at Miramar and Santiago beaches. Bus to Miramar US$0.20.

Another route to Manzanillo Turn off Mexico City highway 35 km. S of Guadalajara and continue 270 km. S to Melaque Bay and the village of Barra de Navidad (commercial but still pleasant; stay at *Alice's Restaurant,* US$2 s, simple food; fish restaurants on beach), where there is a monument to the Spanish ships which set out in 1648 to conquer the Philippines. This road is paved. Pretty seaside villages near Barra de Navidad include La Manzanilla *(Posada del Cazador)* and Tenacatita, with perfect beach complete with palm huts, tropical fish among rocks. *Hotel* (no name) in village near beach, US$2.40 a night, or you can sleep on the beach under a palm shelter—but beware mosquitoes. Melaque Bay is one of the most beautiful on the Pacific coast but the place has become very commercialized. (Hotel: *Melaque,* quite satisfactory). The road, paved, goes on to Manzanillo. If not impressed by the accommodation there, move on to Colima along a particularly beautiful hilly road.

Colima, 96 km. from Manzanillo, capital of Colima state, is at an altitude of 494 metres, and has a population of 58,000. Grand views of Colima volcano (3,842 metres), which erupted with great loss of life in 1941, and of El Nevado (4,339 metres). They can be climbed from Zapotlán. Colima is a most charming and hospitable town with Gothic arcade on main square and strange rebuilt Gothic ruin on road beyond Cathedral; the museum at Colima University is well worth a visit. *Motel Costeño* on outskirts is recommended. *Hotel América,* Calle Morelos, cheap and clean, US$2 s, lunch US$1.60, light dinner US$0.80. Airport.

Continuing to Mexico City

We go round the southern shores of Lake Chapala, and after 154 km. come to Jiquilpan (a road leads off, right, to Manzanillo). There are frescoes by Orozco in the library, which was formerly a church.

We are now in the state of Michoacán, where the Tarascan Indians live. It is a romantic country of deep woods, fine rivers and great lakes. Climates run the whole gamut from tropical through temperate to cold as altitudes vary. Fruit, game, and fish are abundant. It has some of the most attractive towns and villages in the country. The Tarascans are among the more interesting Indians of Mexico. Visitors are captivated by their as yet uncorrupted customs, folklore, ways of life, craft skills (pottery, lacquer), music and dance. Some of the Tarascan potters are so devout that they will only ply their hereditary trade on the feast days of St. Ursula and St. Martin. The dance is of first importance to them. It is usually performed to the music of wooden drum, flute and occasionally, a fiddle. Masks are often worn and since the dance is part of a meaningful ritual, it is done intently and seriously. The dances which most impress outsiders are the dance of Los Viejitos (Old Men; at Janitzio, January 1); Los Sembradores (The Sowers; February 2); Los Moros (The Moors; Lake Pátzcuaro region, fiestas and carnival); Los Negritos (Black Men; fiestas at Tzintzuntzan); Los Apaches (February 4, at the churches); Las Canacuas (The Crown dance; Uruapan, on Corpus Christi). At the weddings of fisherfolk the couple dance inside a fish net. In the local fandango the women has fruits in her hand, the man has a glass of aguardiente balanced on his head, and a sword; the gyrating stops abruptly and the man slashes a great arc with his blade.

Zamora (58 km. beyond Jiquilpan), with 88,000 people, is an agricultural centre with passable hotels *(Fenix, Mendoza)*. It was founded in 1540. On 40 km. is Carapán, from which a branch road runs 72 km. S through pine woods to **Uruapan** ("Place where flowers are plentiful"), a town of 120,000 set amongst streams, orchards and waterfalls at 1,610 metres (reached by 2nd class bus from Pátzcuaro, US$0.65 each, 1½ hrs.). The most attractive of its three plazas is the Jardín de los Mártires, with the 16th century church facing it. In the portales or at the market can be bought the local lacquered bowls and trays, or the delicate woodwork of the Paracho craftsmen, Patamban green pottery and Capácuaro embroideries. Restored hospital, built by Bishop Vasco de Quiroga in 16th-century chapel now converted into a craft shop. There is also a church of the same period, and a public park full of streams and waterfalls with a good handicraft shop at the entrance, selling wooden boxes and bracelets. Airport.

Uruapan Hotels *Victoria* (best); *Mi Solar; Mirador; Progreso; Hotel Moderno,* by main square, bus station and market, US$4 d, good; *Mansión Urani,* modest, clean, good, Calle Madero 3; *San Martín, México, Alameda,* in main square; *Tivoli; Aldama, Monte Carlo,* basic; *Casa de la Maravillas,* very pretty and clean, US$6-10 d, with shower, no hot water until 0700; *Hotel Cairo,* near Occidente bus station, cheap; *Hotel Michoacán,* US$1 s; *Posada Morelos, Hotel Vergel, Paris, Santa Fé, Plaza,* basic; *Motel Mi Paraíso,* expensive, outside town.

Motel *Pie de la Sierra,* on N outskirts, US$10 d, good moderately-priced restaurant.

Restaurants One with English menu near bus depot at back of church, reasonably priced; *Restaurant Oriental,* on the Plaza, near *Hotel Moderno,* reasonable and clean. Locals eat at open-air food stalls under one roof at back of cathedral, very picturesque. Excellent *comida corrida* at *Hotel Progreso; La Brasa Fría,* Madero 3A, good local food. *Typ's Restaurant* is quite good, but expensive; recommended is *La Estrella,* near the square.

Festival Around September 16, San Juan, in nearby village, to celebrate the saving of a Christ from the San Juan church (see below) at the time of the Paricutín eruption. Endless fireworks that week in Uruapan, too.

Bus To Mexico City, 9¼ hours, 2nd class, leaves 0845 and then every hour, US$5.60 each, many stops; 1st class less frequent but quicker, US$6.70.

Excursions Through coffee groves and orchards along the Cupatizio (meaning Singing River) to the Zararacua Falls. Good camping some 300 metres below the village under the shelter on the top of a rim, with a view down into the valley to the waterfall (1 km. away) and a small lake. A bus will take you from the Galeana bus station at Uruapan to Zararacua, US$0.30, starting 0700 or 1030, bus marked "Los Reyes".

To the volcano of **Paricutín**, 64 km.; it started erupting under the eyes of a startled peasant, on February 20, 1943, became fiery and violent and rose to a height of 1,200 metres above the 2,100-metre-high region, and then died down after several years into a quiet grey mountain surrounded by a sea of cold lava. The church spires of San Juan, a buried Indian village, thrusting up through cold lava is a fantastic sight. Paracutín is best reached by taking a bus over rough track to Angahuán (unsuitable for VW bus or saloon car) and then hiring a mule. Sr. José Gómez is a guide and lives in Angahuán; he has horses for hire and is very well informed on the geology of the volcano. Two horses and guide, US$4.10, to San Juan, about 3 hours journey through Tarascan villages, unforgettable experience. Turpentine is produced locally, as well as wood carvings, by the Tarascan population.

Past Angahuán and Peribán, after the volcano, is the pretty little town of **Los Reyes**; good swim *above* the electricity generating plant in clear streams (take care not to get sucked down the feed pipe!). Hotels: *Arias,* best, US$4.50 d, clean, friendly; *Fénix,* clean, cheaper; *Plaza,* not as good as *Arias;* Restaurant: *La Fogata,* in main square. Buses from Uruapán to Los Reyes pass Angahuán, with Paricutin in the distance.

Paracho itself is a quaint, very traditional Indian village of small wooden houses; in every other one craftsmen make guitars worth from US$10 to 1,000 according to the wood used. The town is virtually traffic free.

Food Try local sweet savoury pancakes.

(Km. 400) Zacapu, 22,000 people. See Franciscan church (1548).

(Km. 357) **Quiroga,** where a road turns off right for Pátzcuaro and its lake, heart of the Tarascan Indian country. The town is named after Bishop Vasco de Quiroga, who was responsible for most of the Spanish building in the area and for teaching the natives the various crafts they still practise. We pass through **Tzintzuntzan,** the pre-conquest Tarascan capital; the fascinating ruins just above the town have now been completely restored, and are well worth visiting. In Calle Magdalena is a monastery built in 1533 but closed over 250 years ago, which has been restored. The bells of its church, now burnt down, date from the 16th century. A most interesting Passion play is given at Tzintzuntzan. Beautiful and extensive display of hand-painted pottery, very cheap but also brittle. Good bargaining opportunities.

Pátzcuaro (23 km. from Quiroga; altitude 2,110 metres; population 24,300), one of the most picturesque small towns in Mexico (now rather commercialized), with narrow cobbled streets, is built on Lake Pátzcuaro, about 50 km. in circumference, with Tarascan Indian villages on its shores and many islands. The Indians come by huge dugout canoes at 0600 on Friday for the market, held in the main plaza, shaded by great trees. There are several interesting buildings: the unfinished La Colegiata (1603), known locally as La Basílica, with its much venerated Virgin fashioned by an Indian from a paste made with cornstalk pith and said to have been found floating in a canoe (behind the Basílica there are remains of the pre-Columbian town and of a pyramid in the precincts of the Museum of Popular Art); the restored Jesuit church of La Compañia (and, almost opposite, the early 17th-century church of the Sagrario) at the top of Calle Portugal; behind this street are two more ecclesiastical buildings: the Colegio Teresiano and the restored Templo del Santuario; on Calle Lerín is the ancient monastery, with a series of small patios. (Murals by Juan O'Gorman in the Library, formerly San Agustín). On Calle Allende is the residence of the first Governor. On Calle Terán is the Church of San Francisco; nearby is San Juan de Dios, on the corner of Calle Romero. Fifteen minutes walk outside the town is the Chapel of El Calvario, on the summit of Cerro del Calvario, a hill giving wide views; good views also from the old chapel of the Humilladero, above the cemetery on the old road to Morelia. The very well arranged Museum of Popular Art is in the Colegio de San Nicolás (1540) entrance US$0.16, English speaking, friendly guide: ask there for the "Casa de los once patios", which contains the local tourist office and boutiques selling handicrafts. See also the attractive Jardín de la Revolución and, nearby, the old church of the Hospitalito in Calle Codallos. Excellent Friday market. Some stalls open daily, selling handicrafts, and there is a friendly handicraft shop on the road down to the lake, Vicky's, with very funny toys. There is a free medical clinic, English-speaking, on the outskirts of Pátzcuaro.

An excursion can be made into the hills to the village of Santa Clara del Cobre (fine old church), where all the hand-wrought copper vessels come from. (Fiesta: August 12-15.) Nearby is Lake Zirahuen, a very pretty lake, but villagers reported unfriendly. Past Santa Clara, on the La Huacana road, after Ario de Rosales, one descends into the tropics; fine views all along this road, which ends at Churumuco. The best island to visit is **Janitzio**, although it is now rather overrun by tourists (45 minutes by motorboat, US$0.80, make sure to book the return trip), most picturesque, with the charming small church of San Jerónimo containing Indian idols, but an unfortunate monument to Morelos crowning a hill. The lake water is cold. Winter is the best time for fishing in the somewhat fish-depleted lake, where Indians throw nets shaped like dragonflies. White fish from the lake is a delicacy. On a lakeside estate is the Educational Centre for Community Development in Latin America, better known as "Crefal". For a truly spectacular view of the lake, the islands and the surrounding countryside, walk to Cerro del Estribo: an ideal site for a quiet picnic.

Fiestas Nov. 1-2: Día de Muertos (All Souls' Day), ceremony at midnight, Nov. 1, on Janitzio island, but mostly a tourist event, heavily commercialized; Dec. 8, when Tarascan dances are performed, including the Dance of the Old Men; Carnival in February when the Dance of the Moors is done.

Transport From Mexico City "Tres Estrellas de Oro" and Autobuses de Occidente—ADO (which also runs once a day from Pátzcuaro to Guadalajara), 1st and 2nd class buses. Fares, US$2.50 and US$2.25 respectively. Very enjoyable and cheaper though slower 10 hrs train ride around lake and plateau to Mexico City. Train leaves daily at 0655, from Mexico City to Pázcuaro, 1st class, US$2.40; 2nd, US$1.80. Take pullover. Regular bus service from Morelia, 1½ hrs, US$0.50. Buses to Guadalajara go through Zamora, 2nd class US$2.60, 6 hours; no trains to Guadalajara. Local buses from town to lakeside.

Hotels Posada de don Vasco (halfway between lake and town) presents "*La Danza de los Viejitos*" (the Dance of the Old Folk) on Wed. and Sat. at 2100, no charge, non-residents welcome. Hotel Pátzcuaro, Calle Ramos off Plaza San Agustin, US$1.30 s, with bath, rooms without showers not recommended; Mansiin Iturbe, restored mansion on main square, US$3.20 s, good food; San Agustín, above restaurant, US$3.25 d, with shower and toilet, very clean, next to De la Rosa; Atzimba; Linda Vista; Valmen, US$5.50 d, with bath, charming Colonial building; Blanquita, US$2, on market square, hot shower; Pito Pérez, on the second main plaza, US$2.25 d, without bath, shower facilities inadequate. De la Rosa, US$1.50 s. Hotel El Artillero, nice, clean, with hot water US$2.70 s, near Zócalo. Hotel Concordia near one of the two main squares of town, cheap.

Motel Mesón del Cortijo.

(Km. 314) **Morelia**, capital of Michoacán state; population 209,500; altitude 1,882 metres; a beautifully built rose-tinted city with attractive colonial style buildings, rather quiet, founded in 1541. The Cathedral (1640), set between the two main plazas, with graceful towers and a fine façade, is the only large church in Mexico in the Plateresque style; there are paintings by Juárez in the sacristy. Other important churches are the Virgin of Guadalupe (also known as San Diego), with a most ornate Pueblan interior, the modernised Iglesia dela Cruz, and the churches in charming small Plaza de las Rosas and Plaza del Carmen. The oldest of Morelia's churches is the San Francisco. Even more interesting than its five colonial churches are the many beautiful colonial houses still standing. The revolutionary Morelos, Melchior Ocampo, and the two unfortunate Emperors of Mexico (Agustín de Iturbide and the Archduke Maximilian of Austria) are commemorated by plaques on their houses. The Colegio de San Nicolás (1540) is the oldest surviving institution of higher learning in Latin America. (It has a Summer School for foreign students.) The fine former Jesuit college, now called the Palacio Clavijero, is the cultural centre of the city, with a helpful tourist office on the ground floor. Also notable are the law school, in the former monastery of San Diego, next to the Guadalupe church; the Palacio de Gobierno (1732-70), facing the Cathedral; the Palacio Municipal; and the Palacio Federal. Visit also the churches of La Merced, with its lovely tower, and Santa María, near the post office in the main street. Thursday is market day: specialities are pottery, lacquer, woodcarving, jewellery, blankets, leather sandals; in this connection the Casa de Artesanías de Michoacán, in the former convent of San Francisco, next to the church of the same name; it is full of fine regional products for sale, expensive. Shops close early. Food and drink specialities in the *portales* (arches) round the main plaza: fruit jams *(ates),* candies, and *rompope* (a milk-egg rum). Free weekly concerts are held in the municipal theatre. On the outskirts, on the road to Mexico City, are the 224 arches of a ruined aqueduct built in 1788. There are two museums, the Museo de Michoacán and the new modern art museum on the same street as the aqueduct. Airport.

Hotels   Virrey de Mendoza, superb old-style building, good food, could be cleaner; part of the same chain, off the Zócalo and much quieter is the *Posada de la Soledad,* glorious courtyards, converted chapel as dining room, US$15 d; *Alameda; Casino; Oseguera,* Colonial building, recommended, US$3.10 d with shower, next to Cathedral on Avenida Francisco I Madero Oriente; *Casa de Huéspedes Chelita,* Morelos Norte 340, 10 minutes' walk from centre, US$2 d, without bath, very clean and pleasant, laundering facilities; *Roma,* cheap and clean, US$2.60 d, with bath. The *Félix* is good and clean. *Hotels Villa Montaña* (each room a house on its own, run by French aristocrats, very expensive but value for money), *Vista Bella* and *Villa San José* are on a hill, S of city, with glorious views.

Restaurants   *Rincón de Tarasco,* good. *Café Cola,* Av. Obregón, recommended, popular with students, cheap, delicious meals. Excellent *comidas corridas* at the *Paraíso,* US$1.40-1.55, on the main street facing the cathedral. Down Calle León Guzmán opposite the Church of la Merced there is, on the right, a market for local sweets and egg-nog!

Motel   *Los Pérez.*

Diversion   Just after Morelia there is a good road to two villages on beautiful Lake Cuitzeo. At **Cuitzeo,** the first one, there is a fine Agustinian church and convent, a lovely cloister, a huge open chapel, and grand choir stalls in the sacristy. The second village, **Yuriria,** has a large-scale Indian version of the splendid church and convent at Actopán. The road continues to Salamanca, where one turns left for Irapuato or right for Querétaro. Near Morelia is Zinapécuaro, and near this is the large swimming pool of San Miguel Taimeo.

The road soon climbs and we run through 50 km. of splendid mountain scenery: forests, waterfalls, and gorges, to the highest point at (km. 244) Mil Cumbres (2,886 metres), with a magnificent view over mountain and valley. The road descends into a tropical valley. Worth a glance are the façade of the 16th century church at **Ciudad Hidalgo** (km. 212); and the old Colonial bridge and church at **Tuxpan** (km. 193) (*Hotel Florida* US\$7.90 for three, damp rooms, garage US\$0.50 a night). At km. 183 a side road runs, right, to the spa of **San José Purúa** at 1,800 metres, in a wild setting of mountain and gorge and orchard. The radioactive thermal waters are strong. First-class hotel.

(Km. 86) A branch road, right, goes to the mountain resort of **Valle de Bravo,** a charming old town on the edge of an attractive artificial lake. This area gets the week-end crowd from Mexico City.

Hotel *Refugio del Salto; Hotel Los Arcos* (expensive but good) is several km. beyond, in pine woods.

Motel *Avándaro* (nice, but expensive).

(Km. 75) A road branches off to the volcano of Toluca and climbs to the deep blue lakes of the Sun and the Moon in its two craters, at about 4,270 metres, from which there is a wide and awe-inspiring view; this diversion has been highly recommended. The mountain (4,583 metres) is the fourth highest in Mexico.

(Km. 64) **Toluca,** population 220,200, altitude 2,639 metres, about 4¾ hrs from Morelia by bus; capital of the state of México, known mostly for its vivid Friday market where tourist-conscious Indians sell colourful woven baskets, sarapes, rebozos, pottery and embroidered goods (beware of handbag slashers). See churches of Tercer Orden and Vera Cruz, convent of Carmen and chapel of S. María de Guadalupe, all in centre of city; also Museo de Arte Popular and Casa de las Artesanías, with magnificent display of local artistic products for sale, at corner of Paseo Chamizal and Paseo Tollocan. New market building in Calle Manuel Gómez Pedraza, Oriente, open daily, good textiles.

Hotels *San Carlos* (good); *Hotel Mansión,* US\$5 d with bath; handy for those who wish to drive to Ixtapan de la Sal and Cuernavaca (see page 835) before Mexico City. *Morelia,* clean, nice; *Colonial,* clean, US\$6 d, with shower, near cheap and good *Restaurant Palenque; Hotel Bravo,* US\$3.20, near bus terminal in centre.

Bus To Mexico City, US\$0.80. New bus station, away from centre.

Excursions From near the town of Lerma (see next page), on the road to Mexico City, a side road runs S. Along the road, or reached from it, are a number of most interesting "art and craft" producing villages, all with old churches. Passenger cars (Turismos) go though them as far as Ixtapan de la Sal from Toluca and from Plaza de las Vizcaínas, 37, Mexico City. The first village is **Metepec,** the pottery-making centre of the valley, 1½ km. off the road. The clay figurines made here—painted bright fuchsia, purple, green and gold—are unique. Market is on Monday. Interesting convent. The main road descends gradually to Tenango del Valle and then (48 km. from Toluca) abruptly through gorges to **Tenancingo,** still at 1,830 metres, but with a soft, warm all-the-year-round climate. Nearby is the magnificent 18th century Carmelite Convent of El Santo Desierto, making beautiful rebozos. The town itself weaves fine rebozos and its fruit wines are delicious and cheap. Market day is on Sunday. Recommended hotels at Tenancingo are *El Jardín* and *San Carlos,* good value. About 11 km. to the E over a dirt road (buses rarely take this route now, as it is often washed out, but go back halfway to Tenancingo and take another road)—the last 2 km. descend almost vertically into the valley—is **Malinalco,** from which a path winds up 1 km. to Malinalco ruins, for the specialist certainly one of the most remarkable pre-Hispanic ruins in Mexico, now partly excavated. You can also go to Malinalco from Toluca by leaving the Toluca-Tenancingo road after San Pedro Zictepec, 13 km. S of Tenancingo, which is gravel surfaced and 28 km. long. Journey will take 45 mins. Here is a fantastic rock-cut temple in the side of a mountain which conceals in its interior sculptures of eagle and jaguar effigies. Though small, this shrine is in a grandiose and savage setting. Visit also the Augustinian Convent to see the early frescoes. Return to Toluca—unless your car has a 4-wheel drive—by a circle drive *via* Chalma (where roads are being improved), a popular pilgrimage spot, and N to the Toluca-México Highway. On 32 km. from Tenancingo is **Ixtapan de la Sal,** a forest-surrounded leisure spa with medicinal hot springs. Market day: Sunday. Fiesta: second Friday in Lent. *(Hotel Ixtapan; Bungalow Lolita.)* The road goes on to Taxco (see page 837).

Take bus (US$0.08) to pyramids and Aztec seminary of **Calixtlahuaca;** pyramids are to Quetzalcoatl (circular) and to Tlaloc. Also, take bus S to Tenango and change there for local bus to **Teotenango,** a site of the Matlazinca culture (also represented, with later Aztec additions, at Malinalco—see above), reminiscent of La Ciudadela at Teotihuacán. It has 11 ball courts; good museum at entrance.

The basin of Toluca, the highest in the central region, is the first of a series of basins drained by the Río Lerma into the Pacific. To reach Mexico City from Toluca—64 km. by road—it is necessary to climb over the intervening mountain range. The centre of the basin is swampy. (Km. 50) **Lerma,** a small city, is on the edge of the swamp, the source of the Lerma river. The road climbs through hills and woods and meadows (with backward views of the snow-capped Nevado de Toluca volcano) to the summit at Las Cruces (km. 32; 3,164 metres). There is a good Bavarian restaurant, *La Escondida,* about 100 metres to the left of the Toluca-México road at 38 km., on a beautiful site. There are occasional great panoramic views of the City and the Valley of México during the descent. (Km. 24) **Desierto de los Leones,** a beautiful pine forest made into a national park, can be reached from Mexico City by a fine scenic road through Villa Obregón. In the woods is an old Carmelite convent, around are numerous hermitages, inside are several subterranean passages and a secret hall with curious acoustic properties. Enter Mexico City by the Paseo de la Reforma and Avenida Insurgentes.

Mexico City

Mexico City, the capital, altitude 2,240 metres, population about 12,000,000, is of outstanding importance in politics, culture, commerce and industry. The city, the oldest capital in North America, is built upon the remains of Tenochtitlán, the Aztec capital, and covers some 200 square km. The Valley of México, the intermont basin in which it lies, is about 110 km. long by 30 km. wide. Rimming this valley is a sentinel-like chain of mountain peaks and extinct volcanoes of the Sierra Nevada mountains. Towards the SE tower two tall volcanoes: the warrior Popocatépetl and his beloved Ixtaccíhuatl, the Aztec princess who died rather than outlive him. Popocatépetl is 5,452 metres high, and Ixtaccíhuatl (Eestaseewatl) 5,286 metres. Both are snow-capped. To the S the crest of the cordillera is capped by the wooded volcano of Ajusco. Mexico City is said by the Mexicans to be the third largest city in the world, after London and Tokyo.

One in six of the total population lives in this city, which has over half the country's manufacturing employment, pays 82% of all wages, has some 34% of the country's retail sales, half the nation's telephones, radios and television sets, 125 cinemas, 30 radio stations, 18,000 taxis, 400,000 other vehicles and almost all the nation's industrial smog. Within a small radius there are 16 million people, a quarter of the country's total.

Mexico's architecture ranges from Spanish-Baroque to ultra-modern: it is, indeed, fast becoming a city of skyscrapers. The tallest is now the Hotel de México in Insurgentes Sur, with a restaurant; US$2 just to go up, but the ticket lets you see *son et lumière* in the Siqueiros Polyforum next door. The Polyforum includes a handicraft shop, a "museum of the evolution of man'', and huge frescoes by Siqueiros, including the largest mural in the world, inside the huge ovoid dome. Entrance frescoes, US$0.16. The city suffers from a fever of demolition and rebuilding. Of late years it has burst its ancient boundaries and spread, but the new residential suburbs are most imaginatively planned, though some of the outskirts are shabbily blatant. Like all big centres it is faced with a fearsome traffic problem, despite the building of a new inner ring road; the big modern avenues can take the car traffic but the old narrow streets create terrible congestion. The noise can be deafening; Elizabeth Allen tells us that the definition of a split second in Mexico City is the amount of time between the traffic-lights going green and the first horn sounding. A further law to restrict the use of horns has been introduced. To relieve congestion three underground railway lines are now operating.

Because of the altitude the climate is mild and exhilarating save for a few days in mid-winter. Tourists pour in between November and March, but residents like the summer months best. The normal annual rainfall is 660 mm., and all of it falls—usually in the late afternoon—between May and October. December and January are the coldest months. Even in summer the temperature at night is rarely above 13°C—evening wraps are needed—and in winter there can be sharp frosts. Despite this central heating is not common.

Hotels				Single US$	Double US$
Alameda	..	..	.. Av. Juárez 50	24.40	41.55
Aristos	..	..	.. Paseo de la Reforma 276 ..	26.00	30.00
Bamer	..	..	.. Av. Juárez 52 ..	16.00	17.35
Camino Real	..		.. Mariano Escobedo 700 ..	30.00	33.00
Continental	..		.. Paseo de la Reforma 166 ..	26.00	30.00
De Cortés	..	..	.. Av. Hidalgo 85 ..	14.20	20.00
Del Paseo	..		.. Paseo de la Reforma 208 ..	25.35	29.30
Del Prado	..		.. Av. Juárez 70 ..	20.00	23.00
Diplomático	..		.. Av. Insurgentes Sur 1105 ..	17.00	23.00
Fiesta Palace	..		.. Paseo de la Reforma 80 ..	29.00	34.00
Geneve	..		.. Londres 130	10.50	20.50
Holiday Inn Zona Rosa	..		Liverpool 155 ..	23.55	26.40
Majestic	..		.. Madero 73	12.00	14.00
María Cristina	..		.. Lerma 31	13.00	16.00
María Isobel Sheraton	..		Paseo de la Reforma 325 ..	24.00	32.00
Monte Casino	..		.. Génova 56	11.00	18.00
Palace	..		.. Ignacio Ramírez 7	9.00	16.45
Presidente	..		.. Hamburgo 135 ..	14.00.	17.50
Purúa Hidalgo	..		.. Colón 27	13.00	16.00
Reforma	..		.. Paseo de la Reforma y París	17.30	20.00
Regis	..		.. Av. Juárez 77	7.55	12.50
Ritz	..		.. Madero 30	12.00	15.00
Motels					
Holiday Inn	..	..	Blvd. Aeropuerto 502 ..	23.75	29.30
Shirley Courts	..	..	Sullivan 166 (near centre) ..	13.00 (10 summer)	
Dawn Motor Motel	..	..	Mex 57 highway	10.00	13.00
Park Villa Motel	..	..	Gómez Pedraza 68 (near Chapultepec Park)	10.00	12.00

There is an excellent hotel reservation service at the railway station. Double rooms usually much less than twice the price of single rooms. *Hotel Bristol*, Pánuco and Sena, from US$10; *Carlton*, Ignacio Mariscal 32-bis US$5.30; *Ejecutivo*, Viena 8,

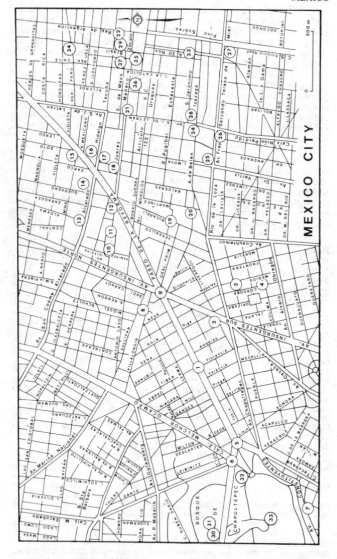

MEXICO CITY

US$12; *El Romano,* Humboldt 55, US$7.70; *Estoril,* Luis Moya 93, US$7.50; *Internacional Havre,* Havre 21, US$17.15; *Lisboa,* Av. Cuauhtémoc 273, US$9.70; *Azteca Apartments,* Hamburgo 29, US$5.30. *Comportela,* Sullivan 35, US$5.10; *Del Valle,* Independencia 35, US$5.20; *Francis,* Paseo de la Reforma 64, US$9.50; *Hotel Suites Orleans,* Hamburgo 67, US$13.20; *Marbella,* Frontera 205, US$8.35; *Metropol,* Luis Moya 39, US$12; *Pisa,* Insurgentes Centro 58, US$5.75; *Plaza Florencia,* Florencia 61, US23; *Premier,* Atenas 72, US$8.45; *Regente,* Paris 9, US$7.50; *Royal Plaza,* B. California y Medellía, US$10.55; *Stella Maris,* Sullivan 69, US$10.55; *Viena,* Marsella 28, US$8.35. Cheaper hotels are clustered together N of the Plaza República and can also be found in the oldest part of the City W of the Zócalo. Reasonable hotels we can recommend are: *Hotel Paraíso,* Ignacio Mariscal 99, US$6 d; *Hotel Ensenada,* Alvaro Obregón, US$9.50 d; *Hotel Polanco,* on Edgar Poe, near Chapultepec, dark, quiet, US$8 d; *Emporío,* Paseo de la Reforma 124, US$12.20 d; *Romfels* (now *Fleming*), on Revillagigedo, US$9 d very noisy; *Texas,* clean and respectable for US$6 d; *Sevilla,* Serapío Rendón and Sullivan, US$13.30 d, restaurant, garage; *Iberia,* Mina and Zaragoza, US$3 d, good for buses and trains; *Hotel Nueva Estación,* Zaragoza 14, US$5 d, with bath; *Mayaland,* Maestro Antonio Caso 23, US$8.80 d, with bath; *México (Tlalnepantla)* near ADO bus station, US$3.50 s, US$4 d, somewhat primitive; *Coliseo,* Bolívar near Madero, US$3.20 s. *Hotel Unión,* Bolívar y El Salvador, US$3.60-4.50 d. A room with a shower in the old *Hotel Fornos,* Revillagigedo 92, is being renovated and is still only US$5 d, with bath and phone. *Hotel Monte Carlo,* Uruguay 69 (D. H. Lawrence's hotel), US$8 d with bath (US$4.80 without bath); good about storing luggage, bit noisy at front. *Hotel Moneda,* Calle Moneda 8, just off Zócalo, good value US$3.75 s, US$4.25 d, with bath; *Hotel Yale,* Mosqueta 200 (near main railway station), US$4.80 d, recommended; or *Hotel Suiza,* Aldama in Guerrero District, near Delagación de Cuauhtémoc, (near bus and railway stations), US$4.80 d, shower, recommended. *Hotel Isabel la Católica* (street of the same name) is good, central, US$5 s, US$8.20 d luggage held; *Hotel Torreón,* next to Isabel la Católica metro station, quiet, clean, US$4.40 with bath for one or two; *Ambassador,* Humboldt 38, central, from US$11; *Las Américas,* on Magnolia, US$4, has small free enclosed parking, rates double at weekend; *Santander,* on Calle Arista, US$5.60 d with bath, good and clean. We strongly recommend *Hotel Vasco de Quiroga,* Londres 15, US$11 d with bath, very pleasant. Very cheap: *Regio Amatlán,* República Argentina 3, US$1 p.p., primitive, not recommended; and others near Plaza Mayor. Also *Hospedaje Familiar,* formerly Casa de huéspedes la Asturiana, Uruguay 115, in early 17th century house with pretty courtyard, central, US$4.50 d; cheap meals for under US$1. *Hotel Toledo,* US$5 d, without shower; *Hotel Detroit,* Calle Zaragoza 55, US$3.10 s, US$4.25 d; *Hotel Montejo,* Paseo de la Reforma 240, US$18.20 d, with bath, old style; *Hotel Zamora,* Avenida 5 de Mayo, US$2.80 d; *Hotel Gran Cosmos, Petit,* US$3 s; *Hotel Ontario,* Calle Uruguay 87, US$3.60 d, not recommended; on same street, one block away, *Hotel Roble,* US$4.50 d, with shower, recommended; *Hotel Pensylvania,* Ignacio Mariscal 15, esq. Puente Arriga, US$3 s; *Casa de los*

Key to Map of Mexico City on page 804).
1. Independence Monument; 2. Benjamin Franklin Library; 3. Institute of Mexican Art; 4. National Institute of Anthropology and History; 5. Fountain of Diana the Huntress; 6. Carranza and Bolívar Monuments; 7. Women's University; 8. "La Madre" Monument; 9. Cuauhtémoc Monument; 10. Independence Monument; 11. Department of Tourism; 12. "El Caballito" (Carlos IV) Monument; 13. National School of Plastic Arts; 14. San Fernando Church; 15. San Hipólito Church; 16. Santa Veracruz; 17. Palace of Fine Arts; 18. Vice-regal Art Gallery (San Diego); 19. Chinese Clock; 20. Morelos Monument; 21. Latin American Tower and House of Tiles; 22. Aztec Ruins; 23. Hospital of Jesus; 24. "Salto del Agua" Fountain; 25. Civil Registry Office; 26. Department of Labour; 27. Church of Tlaxcoaque; 28. College of the Vizcaínas; 29. Cathedral; 30. National Museum of Archaeology; 31. Tlaloc Monolith; 32. Museum of Modern Art; 33. Castle of Chapultepec; 34. Santo Domingo Church and Colegio Nacional; 35. Palace of the Counts of Valparaiso; 36. Iturbide Palace; 37. Monte de Piedad.

Amigos, Mariscal 132, near train and bus station, US$2.20 s, for Quakers only; *Hotel La Paz* on Mina, close to bus stations on Insurgentes, US$5.60 d, with bathrooms. Also on Calle Mina, at 186, US$3 d, without bath, very clean, good facilities and laundering possible. *Hotel Frimont,* US$10.40 d, good, Jesús Terán 35; *Hotel El Salvador,* Rep. de El Salvador 16, good value at US$6.50 s, US$8.50 d. *Hotel German-American,* Avenida Buenavista, US$3.25 d, near ADO terminal and ½-km. from railway station, clean and safe; *Hotel Royalty,* US$5.50 d; *Hotel de Carlo,* Plaza República, US$17.50 with two double beds, private bath, TV, very good; *Hotel Conde,* Pescaditos 15, off Luis Moya, 10 mins. walk from Alameda, excellent value, US$4.50 d, with bath, clean, friendly; *Hotel Prince,* close to Alameda, some rooms facing into vent shaft, US$5 d, with bath, others US$8.70, modern block, noisy; *Hotel La Fuente,* Orozco y Berra 10 (near ADO bus station and Hidalgo metro), US$4.25 d, with bath; *Hotel Congreso,* good, central, US$6.80 d, at Allende 18; *Hotel Canadá,* 5 de Mayo 47, US$7.50 d, good value; *Hotel Avenida,* San Juan de Letrán 38, US$6.40 d with shower, central but dirty. *Hotel Capitol,* Ave. Uruguay 12, US$4.80 s, with shower, noisy but clean; *Hotel Principal,* Calle Bolívar, US$6.25 d, with bath, noisy and cramped, but clean, some rooms without baths, at half this price; *Dormitorio,* B. Domínguez Palma, US$0.72, men only. *Hotel María,* opposite central telephone company, US$4 d, adequate; *Hotel Ma. Angelo,* Calle Lerma 11 from US$6 s, with private bath, weekly rates possible, quite pleasant; *Hotel Ibero,* US$3 s, US$4 d, with bath, very good. *Hotel Imperio,* Correo Mayor 94, near Zócalo, US$3 s, with bath, old fashioned with Mexican residents, sheets changed daily. Very good value and near Zócalo is the *Hotel Rioja,* Av. 5 de Mayo 45, share bath, spotless, US$3.50. *Hotel Galveston,* satisfactory, US$3. *Hotel Ambos Mundos,* Calle Bolívar, US$1.50 s. Hostel at Cozumel 57, student card required, very basic, US$1.50. *Hotel España,* Pte Alvarado 100, US$3 d; *Hotel Lafayette,* Motolinia 40 and 16 de Septiembre, US$6.50 d, with bath; *Hotel Milán,* Av. Alvaro Obregón 94, US$14 d, with bath; *Hotel Ambasad,* US$6 d, with bath, US$3.50 s, telephone, TV room, clean, very good value, beside Pino Suárez metro station. *Casa González,* Lerma y Sena (near British Embassy), US$11, full board, shower, clean and friendly; *El Porvenir,* on Bernal Diaz, 200 metres from Revolución metro station, cheap. *Lido,* Ave Brasil 208, near Zócalo. *Hotel Oxford,* Mariscal 67, US$4.50 s.

Camp sites Mexico City has two camp sites, for addresses see American Automobile Association's "Mexico by Motor".

Youth Hostels Association Asociación Mexicana de Albergues de la Juventud, Madero 6, Of. 314, México 1, D.F. Write for information. Mexico City Hostel at 57 Calle Cozumel, Colonia Roma, not far from Chapultepec Park. Breakfast US$0.50.

Restaurants All the best hotels have excellent restaurants. Others that have been recommended include:

Ambassadeurs, Paseo de la Reforma 12 (swank and high priced); *Prendes,* 16 de Septiembre 12 (good European food, moderate); *La Cava,* Insurgentes Sur 2465 (excellent French food and steaks, lavishly decorated as an old French tavern, moderate); *Restaurant del Lago,* in exciting modern building in Chapultepec Park, excellent and less dear than one would expect; *Tibet-Hamz,* Avenida Juárez 64 (Chinese restaurant specializing in Cantónese and Mexican national dishes, centrally located, nice atmosphere, moderate); *Chalet Suizo,* Niza 37 (very popular with tourists, specializes in Swiss and German food, moderate); *Shirley's Restaurant,* Villalongín 139 (real American food, moderate); *Focolare,* Hamburgo 87 (swank and high priced); *Rivoli,* Hamburgo 123 (a gourmet's delight, high priced); *Jena,* Morelos 110 (deservedly famous, á la carte, expensive); *Chanteclair,* in the *Hotel de Niza* (Spanish specialities, expensive, good); *Burges Boy,* 27 locations; *Sanborn's,* 14 locations; *Del Prado Hotel* Arcade and Paseo de la Reforma 45, Tiber and Reforma, near the new building of the United States Embassy, Madero 4 (United States dishes and Mexican, too). Other recommended restaurants are *Delmonico's,* Londres 87; *Mesón del Cid,* Calle Humboldt, offering medieval Castilian menu; *Restaurant 1-2-3,* Liverpool 123; *Chipp's,* Génova 59; *Café Konditori,* Génova 61, wholesome Mexican snacks, salads and cake, quick and quiet; *Monte Cassino,* also in Génova, loud music but spacious, good convivial spot; *Horreo,* Calle Dr. Mora (Reforma end of Parque Alameda), expensive and good; *Mesón del Castellano,* Bolívar esquina Uruguay, good, plentiful and not too dear; *Alex Cardini's,* Madrid 21, home of the famous Caesar Salad. French cuisine at *La Lorraine,* San Luís Potosí 132, and at *Laes Moustaches,* Rio Sena 88. *La Marinera,* Liverpool 183, best sea-food restaurant in Mexico City.

Reasonable in centre: *Centro Castellano,* Uruaguay 16, one flight up; *Café Rosalia,* San Juan de Letrán 46, 5-course lunch for US$2.50 and good wine. On Reforma: *Restaurant de la Reforma,* cheap and good; *Blanco y Negro* Vallarta y Plaza de la República, good lunch for US$2, excellent cheesecake; *Amicale Française de México,* 5 de Mayo 61, semi-French food, good lunch 1330-1700, US$2, no dinner, good view over Zócalo, closed Sundays. *Pensión Francesa,* 1st floor, 5 de Febrero 33, delicious, cheap abundant meals. Cheap lunches at *Pensión Española* at Isabel la Católica 10, off 5 de Mayo, 1st floor. *Anderson's,* Reforma 400, very good atmosphere, reasonable, excellent local menu. *Sírvase Vd. Mismo,* on Iturbide, near Av. Juárez, fine smorgasbord lunch with choice of 4 hot meals, plus salads and dessert, US$2. *Hoyin Restaurant,* near Estrella Blanco bus station, US$1 for a 3-course meal. *Mesón del Perro Andaluz,* Copenhague 26, very pleasant, US$4 for Spanish all-inclusive meal. Many economical restaurants in Calle 5 de Mayo: the *Cinco de Mayo, Latino, La Blanca,* and *El Popular,* also *Amicale Française* at No. 61 on 7th floor. *Rincón Gaucho,* Insurgentes Sur 1162, Argentine food; *La Pérgola,* near Siqueiros Polyforum, Italian; *La Casserole,* Insurgentes Sur near Núcleo Radio Mil building, French; *Restaurant Rhin,* Av. Juárez, cheap, good, German décor; *Lonchería la Torta,* Av. de la Independencia 16, clean, cheap and very friendly.

The British Embassy recommends two others not included in this list. They are the *Normandia,* López 16; and *Passy,* Amberes 10. *San Angel Inn,* in San Angel, is excellent and very popular, so book well in advance. The *Piccadilly Pub,* Copenhague 23, is dear but serves British food at its best; very popular with Mexicans and expatriates alike. Similar, but nicer surroundings (and dearer), is *Sir Winston Churchill,* Avila Camacho 67.

Others recommended are *Acapulco,* López 9 (excellent sea food, inexpensive); *Casa Regional Valenciana,* Calle López 60, 3rd floor; *Restaurante Ehden,* Correo Mayor 74, 1st floor, open Sundays, authentic and reasonably priced Arab food; *Centro Asturiano* (Orizaba and Puebla), both Spanish; *Napoleón,* French, and *Viena,* Viennese, in Plaza Popocatépetl; *Kineret,* Hamburgo and Génova, New York—kosher; *Sep's* good value and very popular, excellent oyster soup for US$0.90; *Pena El Comdor Pasa* is a cafetería, open 1900-0100, closed on Tues., on Rafael Checal, San Angel. It has different folk-music groups every night with music from Latin America; get there early. *Fonda del Recuerdo* for excellent *mole poblano,* Bahía de las Palmas 39A, 17DF, near Reforma, with music. Very good, *Club de Periodistas de México,* F. Mata 8, near Calle 5 de Mayo, 1DF, open to public. *Centro Republicano Español,* Calle López, 1st floor, inside arcade. More expensive but still good value, *Las Delicias* in Venezuela 41; *El Parador,* Niza 17, good local and international; *Lory's de México,* Génova 73, and *La Calesa de Londres,* Londres 102, good meat at both; *Le Gourmet,* Dakota 155, said to be most expensive restaurant in Mexico, and also said to be worth it! Good small restaurants in Uruguay, near *Monte Carlo Hotel,* 5-course comida, US$1.25. Another centre for small restaurants is Pasaje Jacarandas, off Génova: *Llave de Oro* and many others. *Restaurant Alicia,* nr. Hotel German-American, cheap. *Lady Baltimore,* good cheap and clean on F. I. Madero. *Francis Drake* on Ave Juárez, reasonable and good.

One of the best Mexican restaurants, but somewhat touristy, is *El Refugio,* in the Niza district, off Paseo de la Reforma. A very old restaurant with interesting tile décor and not touristy is the *Cafe Tacuba,* Tacuba 28; it specializes in Mexican food. *Restaurant Los Commerciales* has good Mexican food, waiters race about on roller-skates. Best Puebla-style *tacos* at *La Poblanita* (near Cine Eremita). A fine place for light refreshments and music is the *Hospedaje del Bohemio,* formerly the San Hipólito monastery on Hidalgo, near Reforma, next to the church of that name. Look hard for the entrance: no sign, poetry and music every night from 1700 to 2200. Light snacks and refreshments US$0.80. No cover charge. Cheap cafeterias in Calle Belisario Domínguez.

Bars   *Bar Jardin,* in the Hotel Reforma; *Montenegro* and *Nicte-Ha,* in Hotel del Prado; *El Colmenar,* Ejido y Eliseo; *El Parador,* on top of Latino Americano skyscraper, for sunsets and views at night.

Cabarets and Night Clubs   *Capri,* at the *Regis Hotel,* Juárez 77; *El Patio,* Atenas 9; *Passepartout, Hamburgo, Chanteclair, Hotel Reforma; Jacaranda,* Génova 54; *Señorial,* Hamburgo 188. There are night clubs at many of the smarter hotels. Night club tours include several of the more risqué—and interesting—ones.

Electric Current   125 volts, 60 cycles A.C. in Mexico City, mostly 110-120 volts elsewhere.

Telephones   Public 'phones have now been converted for new 20-centavo coins.

International Airport, 13 km. from city. Yellow VW buses go from airport to centre or to your hotel, US$1.25 per seat, under name of Setta. Taxi to airport US$4.40. There is a bus, US$0.80. See under "Metro" on how to get to it cheaply (see below), if you have no heavy luggage. Airport tax US$4.40 on leaving; US$1.80 for internal flights.

The Mexican Hotel Association desk at the airport will call any hotel and reserve a room for you, also has a collective taxi which will drop you at your hotel.

The **Mexican Tourist Board** is now on Calle Masaryk, Colonia Polanco. It gives the best tourist service in Latin America, and is genuinely anxious to investigate any complaints you may have. You may also refer your problems to the tourist police, in blue uniforms. Articles from the various craft displays can be bought. Free maps, not always available, but may be got from Department of Public Works. Office hours: 1000-1230 and 1700-1900, closed Sun., one person only on duty Sat. morning, avoid. Incidentally, museums are closed Mondays, except Chapultepec Castle, closed Tuesdays.

Travel and Tourist Agencies   Excursions y Viajes S.A. (Evisa), Reforma 76, 4th Floor; Garza López Tours, Juárez, 64; Mexamérica, S.A., Reforma 92; Turismo Mundial Iter, Reforma 104; Viajes Panamericanos, S.A., Reforma 20-103. Viajes Felgueres, Florencia 17; Viajes Meliá, Madrid 21; Viajes Mundiales, S.A., Reforma 12; Wells Fargo & Co. Express, S.A., Calle Niza 22; Wilfer Tours, Morelos 37-201. Thomas Cook, about 11 branches, main office Av. Juárez 88; American Express, Hamburgo 75, charges US$3-4 for poste restante if you do not have their travellers' cheques.

General Steamship Agencies   H. E. Bourchier Sucrs., S.A., Calle Petrarca 117, Mexico City, representatives for Cunard Line and P. & O.-Orient Lines.

Ferry Information from Caminos y Puentes Federales de Ingresos y Servicios Conexos, Av. Juárez 97.

Royal Mail Lines   Agents: Norse-Mex S.A.R.L., Calle Gante 9 (Aptdo. 1635).

Metro   Three lines are in service. 1 (Pink), from Observatorio (by Chapultepec Park) to Zaragoza in the eastern suburbs. It goes under Av. Chapultepec and not far from the lower half of Paseo de la Reforma, the Mercado Merced, and near the airport. (From subway station Aeropuerto a local bus runs to the airport.) 2 (Blue) from Tacuba in the NW to the Zócalo and then S above ground to Taxqueña, it is being extended further N from Tacuba to Azcapotzalco; 3 (Green), from Tlatelolco S to the Hospital General, being extended N from Tlatelolco to Villa Guadalupe. Trains are noiseless on rubber wheels, with no draught. Music is played quietly at the stations. Tickets 1.50 pesos (US$0.12) each, or 5 pesos (US$0.40) for five. A splendidly modern service, and virtually impossible to get lost! But beware thieves. Also beware: no heavy luggage or back-packs permitted. Map from tourist office.

Conveyances   Trams and trolley buses, fare US$0.03. Buses: US$0.03-0.09, according to distance and age of bus. "Expreso" buses, with fewer stops, are recommended for tourists; they are known as "delfines", are cream and white, and the fare is US$0.10; no standing. We are informed that thieves and pickpockets haunt the buses plying along Reforma and Juárez. Be careful of your valuables! A most useful route for tourists (fare about US$0.08, standing allowed) is the Route

100 bus from the Zócalo along Paseo de la Reforma to the Auditorio in Chapultepec Park.

Long-distance Buses Buses to destinations in N. Mexico, including US borders, leave from *Central del Norte,* Avenida Cien Metros 4907 (34 bus companies in all). City buses marked Cien Metros or Terminal del Norte go directly there, or take bus 7B or 70 from corner of Bucareli with Av. Juárez. Bus 81 from Alameda. *Central Auto-buses del Sur,* at corner of Tlalpan 2205 across from metro at Taxqueña, serves Cuernavaca, Acapulco, Zihuatanejo areas. Direct buses to centre of town from both terminals, and an express bus connects the Sur and Norte terminals. Most buses to the south leave from the companies' (ADO, Cristóbal Colón, etc.) own terminals. Cristóbal Colón's is one block from San Lorenzo metro station (pink line) on Ignacio Zaragoza 38, which operates buses to the Guatemalan border, Oaxaca and Villarhermosa, but not to Yucatán or Veracruz. ADO buses only operate a 1st class service from Buenavista 9, 10 min. walk from the Tourist Office, to the Gulf of Mexico area and Yucatán. Advance booking is recommended for all trips, and very early reservation if going to fiestas, etc. You must go and queue at the bus stations; this can involve some long waits, sometimes 2-2½ hours.

Taxis Taxis are fitted with taximeters, but they are often not used. Cabs called by radio charge from the time of the call. So-called "peso taxis" (peseros) go back and forth on Reforma and its eastern extensions as far as the Zócalo, and on Insurgentes. Number of fingers held out indicates the route travelled (e.g. on Reforma two fingers mean the Zócalo, and three La Villa. Fares 5 or 7 pesos. Wave down at special stops on kerb or even from kerb itself. Fixed routes. No tip necessary.

Agree fares in advance, on basis of time and distance, outside the City. Taxis are very cheap, but the drivers often do not know where the street you want is; try and give the name of the intersection between two streets rather than a number, because the city's numbering can be erratic. When it is raining or dark you may have to agree to pay up to twice the normal amount. There are special tourist taxis, called "Turismo", which are dearer because they have English-speaking drivers, outside the main hotels, but they have no metres: arrange the prices beforehand. VW taxis are very cheap, but make sure they put the meter on; they should be tipped. Hired cars, with or without driver, are dear.

Car Hire Agencies Budget Rent Auto; Hertz; Avis; VW and many local firms, which tend to be cheaper. Gasoline is reassuringly cheap.

Entertainments Theatres: Palacio de Bellas Artes (for ballet, songs, dances), Fábregas, Lírico, Iris, Sullivan, Alarcón, Hidalgo, Urueta and Insurgentes in town and a cluster of theatres around the Auditorio Nacional in Chapultepec Park. Spectaculars (e.g. presidential inauguration) are often staged in the Auditorio Nacional itself. Also in Chapultepec Park is the Audiorama (behind the Castle on the Constituyentes side) where one may listen to recorded classical music in a small open ampitheatre in a charming wooded glade. A request book is provided, for the following day. Rodeo shows *(charros)* most Sundays at Exército Nacional or Molino de Ray, 1100-1330, and possibly a free performace of a play in one of the parks by the Teatro Trashumante (Normadic Theatre). For mariachi bands at Plaza Garibaldi see page 814. Sunday is the best day. The parks and the churches are full of gaily dressed families. There is afternoon bull-fighting in a vast ring and morning football at the stadium. The balloon sellers are everywhere. Especially recommended, the Ballet Folklórico de México, at Palacio de Bellas Artes (see page 812).

Football Sunday midday, Aztec and Olympic stadia; also Thursday (2100) and Saturday (1700).

Horse Races Hipódromo de las Américas, every Tuesday, Thursday, Saturday and Sunday almost all the year. Pari-mutuel betting (minimum bet US$1). Races begin at 1400, and may be watched from Jockey Club restaurant. Beautiful track with infield lagoons and flamingoes, and plenty of atmosphere.

Jai-Alai Events with the foremost players in the world every day at the "Frontón México". Pari-mutuel betting. US$0.40.

Golf at Chapultepec Golf Club and Churubusco Country Club. These are private clubs, open to visitors only if accompanied by a member. Green fees are high (US$20 upwards).

Boxing Every Wednesday and Saturday at the Arena Coliseo.

Wrestling Every Thursday and Sunday.

Hiking Every weekend at the Alpino and Everest clubs.

Baseball at Parque Seguridad Social, 1900 hrs. during season

Swimming Agua Caliente, Las Termas, Balneario Olímpico, Elba, Centro Deportivo Chapultepec and others.

Tennis, golf, association football, baseball and basketball are very popular in Mexico City.

Charreadas (Cowboy displays), Rancho Grande de La Villa, at very top of Insurgentes Norte, Suns. 1200-1500, US$1.30.

Clubs

Sports Reforma Athletic Club, Hacienda de los Morales, Lomas de Chapultepec; Country Club in Churubusco suburb (golf, tennis, swimming); Club de Golf México, Tlalpan; Chapultepec Golf Club, Lomas (golf and swimming); French Club in San Ángel; British, Mexican, and Spanish boating clubs, in Xochimilco, near Mexico City; Polo Club in Chapultepec Heights.

General American Legion, Lucerna 71; American Club, Plaza Santos Degollado 10; Spanish Club, Isabel la Católica 29; Y.M.C.A., Av. Ejército Nacional 253; Y.W.C.A., corner of Humboldt 62 and Artículo 123 (US$4.80 for single room with bath, good restaurant and laundry); Lions Club, Ures 13; Rotary Club, Londres 15; Automobile Club (Associación Mexicana Automovilística-AMA), Av. Chapultepec 276; Women's International Club, Humboldt 47; University of Mexico, Paseo Reforma 150; Junior League Library, Iturbide Building, Av. Madero.

Addresses

British Embassy, Calle Río Lerma 71. Tel.: 5-11-48-80.

British Chamber of Commerce, Río Tiber 103, 6th floor, Cuauhtémoc, Tel.: 5-33-24-53.

Guatemalan Consulate, Vallarta 1-501-A; tourist card costs US$1; visa now costs US$3.50 (take 2 photos) for UK passports.

U.S.A. Embassy, Reforma 305.

American Chamber of Commerce, Lucerna 78.

Immigration Department, Bucareli 99.

Anglo-Mexican Cultural Institute (with British Council Library), Maestro Antonio Caso 127. Tel.: 5-66-61-44.

Canadian Embassy, Melchor Ocampo 463.

Australian Embassy, Paseo de la Reforma 195, 5th Floor. Tel.: 5-66-30-55.

Chief Telegraph Office for internal telegrams, Palace of Communications and Transport, Plaza Senado de la República, off Calle Tacuba. For international telegrams, see page 881.

Mountain Rescue, Socorro Alpino, San Juan de Letrán 80-305.

Instituto Mexicano Norteamericano, Hamburgo 115; 4-week intensive and painless courses in Spanish, US$80 a course, less intensive, US$40; free, excellent concerts, art exhibits, reading-room, bulletin board advertising rooms. Instituto Italiano has the same courses, but less crowded, US$95 including books. The Universidad Nacional Autónoma de México (UNAM) offers cheap 7-week courses which include history lectures.

Instituto Francés de la América Latina, Nazas 43, free films every Thursday at 2030.

Airlines British Airways: Reforma 332, 525-91-33; Braniff: Reforma 381, 1° piso, 533-02-45; Pan Am: Avila Camacho 1-702, 595-00-77; TWA: Río Marne 17-102, 566-99-44; Mexicana: Juárez y Balderas, 585-26-66.

English-Speaking Churches Protestant—Christ Church in Artículo 123/134; Roman Catholic—St. Patrick's, Calle Bondojito; Evangelical Union—Reforma 1870; Baptist—Capital City Baptist Church, Calle Sur 136; Lutheran—Church of the Good Shepherd, Palmas 1910; First Church of Christ Scientist—21 Dante, Col. Anzures.

British American Cowdray Hospital, or the A.B.C., to give it its popular name, at Observatorio and Calle Sur 136. Tel.: 577-75-00; very helpful.

English-speaking Doctor   C. German, Calle Eucker No. 16-601, Tel.: 5-45-94-34. Dr. César Calva Pellicer (who also speaks French and German), Copenhague 24, 3° piso, Tel.: 514-25-29, 525-53-71.

Vaccination Centre   Benjamín Hill 14, near Soviet Embassy. Open Mon.-Fri. 0800-1200, 1600-2000, avoid last half hour; smallpox and yellow fever vaccination free.

Banks (Mexico City)   0900-1300 (Sat. 0900-1230, head offices only): Banco de Comercio, S.A., Venustiano Carranza y Bolívar (Branch: 85 Gracechurch St., London, E.C.3); Banco Nacional de México, S.A., Av. Isabel la Católica 44 (said to give best exchange rates); Banco de Londres y México, S.A., corner of 16 de Septiembre y Bolívar; Citibank, Uruguay e Isabel la Católica; Banco del Atlántico changes Eurocheques. American Express office at Hamburgo 75, (Zona Rosa) is the only place one can change cheques on Sats. till 1300. Open Mon.-Fri. until 1800; and many others.

Shops and Stores   Mexico's ''West End'' is the Zona Rosa (Pink Zone), where most of the fashionable shops and many restaurants are found. It is bounded by the Paseo de la Reforma, Av. Chapultepec, Calle Florencia and Calle Napolés. Note that most streets in the Zone are called after foreign cities—Londres, Liverpool, Hamburgo, Niza, Amberes (Antwerp), Génova, Copenhague, etc. The handicrafts section is between Liverpool and Hamburgo.

Avenida Madero is like the Rue de la Paix in Paris. Sanborn's is famous for textiles and handicrafts; you can also change up to US$10 (not cheques) there when banks are closed. There are also good shops on 5 de Mayo, 16 de Septiembre, Insurgentes, Colonia Juárez. Mexican jewellery and hand-made silver can be bought everywhere. Among the good silver shops are Sanborn's, Calpini, Prieto, and Vendome. There are also good buys in perfumes, quality leather, and suede articles. San Juan market, Calle Ayuntamiento and Arandas, good prices for handicrafts, especially leather travel goods; some bargaining acceptable. The Ciudadela market (Plaza Ciudadela) is cheaper than San Juan. There is a market in every district selling pottery, glassware, textiles, sarapes and jewellery. Try also San Angel market, although expensive, many items are exclusive to it. Good leather belts. Open Saturday. The Balderas market is Government sponsored and very reasonable and uncrowded, Calle Balderas. The National Pawn Shop (Monte de Piedad) turns up a bargain now and then. Mexican tinware and lacquer are found everywhere. You can bargain in the markets and smaller shops. Government Artesanía shop at Versalles eusquina Atenas, opposite Turismo in Juárez. Also in basement of Siqueiros Polyforum, on Insurgentes Sur. Other sponsored shops: Art and Crafts of Guerrero, Paseo de la Reforma 8, by the Caballito (Tel.: 546-63-78) of Michoacán and Querétaro, Glorieta del Metro de Los Insurgentes, Locales 14 and 17 (Tel.: 525.01.37). New Oaxaca shop next to the *Prado Hotel* on Juárez. Try also Decorask, Pino Suárez 28; Exposición Turística Artesanal Av. Juárez 92 and at 89 Exposición Nacional de Arte Popular. On Av. Hidalgo, near corner S. Juan Dios is a huge commercial market of popular arts in the former S. Juan Dios monastery. Good selection of onyx articles at the Brunner shop, in Calle Dolores. Mercado Lagunilla near Plaza de Sta. Cecilia (formerly Garibaldi) has everything from antiques to typical Mexican tourist wares, open Sundays. For first class luxury leather goods, go to Arias, in Av. Juárez near Turismo building, and in Florencia, Antil. Luggage repairs (moderate prices) at Talabarbería Gutiérrez, Rinconada de Jesús 15-G, opposite Museum of the City of Mexico in Pino Suárez.

Bookshops   Many good ones, e.g. American Book Store, Madero 21; Librería Anglo-Americana, Serapio Rendón 125; *Librairie Française,* Reforma 250A and Madero 30; The *Injuve Bookshop* (Instituto Mexicano de la Juventud) along Serapio Rendón (San Cosmé metro station) sells *México Desconocido* by Harry Möller, only obtainable at this shop and in government museums about the country, US$1.50. This book tells you about all kinds of amazing off-the-beaten-track places which are mostly accessible by bus. Libros y Discos, Madero 1.

Excursions in and around the city may easily take up ten days. The main places of interest are listed below.

You will find, as you explore the city, that you use three thoroughfares more than any others. The most famous is Paseo de la Reforma, with a tree-shaded, wide centre section and two side lanes; it runs somewhat diagonally NE between Chapultepec Park and "El Caballito" monument. At the monument it bends eastwards and becomes Avenida Juárez, still fairly wide but without side lanes. Beyond the Palacio de Bellas Artes this becomes Av. Madero, quite narrow, with one-way traffic. The other and longer thoroughfare is Av. Insurgentes, a diagonal north-south artery about 25 km. long. The two avenues bisect in front of the Continental Hotel at a plazuela which has a figure of an Indian, spear in hand: Cuauhtémoc, the last of the Aztec emperors.

The Zócalo, the main square, or Plaza Mayor, centre of the oldest part, always alive with people, and often vivid with official ceremonies and celebrations. (The main square of most Mexican towns is called the Zócalo.) On the north side, on the site of the Great Teocalli or temple of the Aztecs, is

The Cathedral, the largest and oldest cathedral in Latin America; first built 1525; rebuilding began 1573; consecrated 1667; finished 1813. Singularly harmonious, considering the many architects employed and time taken to build it. At present only certain parts can be visited, as some restoration work is being carried out. Next to the Cathedral is the **Sagrario Metropolitano,** 1769, with exquisite Churrigueresque façade. Behind the Cathedral at the corner of Av. Guatemala and Calle Seminario are some Aztec ruins. On the W side of the Zócalo are the Portales de los Mercaderes (Arcades of the Merchants), very busy since 1524. North of them, opposite the Cathedral, is

The Monte de Piedad (National Pawnshop), a Colonial building where bargains are often found. Monthly auctions of unredeemed pledges.

Palacio Nacional (National Palace), takes up the whole eastern side of the Zócalo. Built on the site of the Palace of Moctezuma and rebuilt in 1692 in Colonial-Baroque, with its exterior faced in the red volcanic stone called *tezontle;* the top floor was added by President Calles. It houses various government departments and the Juárez museum, full of mementoes (free). Over the central door hangs the Liberty Bell, rung at 2300 on September 15 by the President, who gives the multitude the *Grito*—Viva México! The thronged frescoes around the staircase are by Diego Rivera. Open daily; guides. Other fine murals by Rivera can be seen at the Ministry of Education, four blocks N of Zócalo. In the Calle Moneda and adjoining the back of the Palace is the **Museo de las Culturas,** with interesting international archaeological and historical exhibits. Open 0930-1800; Suns. 0900-1600. Also in Moneda are the site of the first university in the New World (building now dilapidated), the Archbishop's Palace, and the site of the New World's first printing press.

Museo de Artes e Industrias Populares de Mexico (Museum of popular arts and industries) is in Av. Juárez. It has well-arranged permanent exhibitions and the articles are for sale.

Palacio de Justicia (Palace of Justice), modern, in Colonial style; see frescoes by Orozco.

Palacio de Bellas Artes (Palace of Fine Arts), a large, showy building which houses a museum and a theatre. Its domes are lavishly decorated with coloured stone. The museum has old and contemporary paintings, prints, sculptures, and handicraft articles. The fresco by Rivera is a copy of the one rubbed out in disapproval at Radio City, New York, and there are spirited Riveras in the room of oils and water-colours. Other frescoes are by Orozco, Tamayo and Siqueiros, Daily, 1000-1730; Sundays, 1000-1400. The most remarkable thing about the theatre is its glass curtain designed by Tiffany. It is solemnly raised and lowered—for a fee—on Sunday mornings between 0900 and 1000. The Palace is listing badly, for it has sunk 4 metres since it was built. Operas are performed; there are orchestral concerts and performances by the superb Mexican Folklore Ballet on Wednesdays and Sundays—one must book in advance. Tickets: US$5.20, US$4 and US$2. Cheap concerts at 1200 on Sundays, and also at Teatro Hidalgo, behind Bellas Artes on Hidalgo, at the same time.

Across the road, on the 41st floor of the Torre Latinoamericana, is a good restaurant and bar with splendid sunsets, and views of the city, especially after dark (entry fee US$1). This great glass tower dominates the **Alameda Gardens**, once the Aztec market and later the place of execution for the Spanish Inquisition. Today, the gardens and their immediate surroundings encompass all the raw vitality, the gaiety and the harsh contrasts that make up the character of Mexico City. Beneath the broken shade of eucalyptus, cypress and ragged palms, wide paths link fountains and heroic statues in these well-kept gardens.

On the northern side of the Alameda, on Av. Hidalgo, is the Jardín Morelos, flanked by two old churches: Santa Veracruz (1730) to the right and San Juan de Dios to the left. The latter has a richly carved Baroque exterior; its image of San Antonio de Padua is visited by those who are broken-hearted by love or by lack of it.

Escuela Nacional Preparatoria (National Preparatory School) built 1749 as the Jesuit School of San Ildefonso in splendid Baroque. There are some exciting frescoes by Orozco and (in the Anfiteatro Bolívar) by Diego Rivera and Fernando Leal.

Ministry of Education, built 1922, contains frescoes by a number of painters. Here are Diego Rivera's masterpieces, painted between 1923 and 1930, illustrating the lives and sufferings of the common people.

Plaza 23 de Mayo (formerly Santo Domingo), two blocks N of the Cathedral, a small, intimate little plaza surrounded by fine colonial buildings:

    (a) To the SW, a beautiful Colonial palace;

    (b) On the west side, ancient Arcades of Santo Domingo, where public scribes still carry on their business;

    (c) On the north side, the Church of Santo Domingo, in Mexican baroque, 1737. Note the carving on the doors and façade;

    (d) In the NE corner, the School of Medicine, where the tribunals of the Inquisition were held. There is a remarkable staircase in the patio, and striking Siqueiros murals above it.

The nearby streets contain some fine examples of Colonial architecture.

Two blocks E of Santo Domingo are the Church and Convent of **San Pedro y San Pablo** (1603), both massively built and now turned over to secular use. A block N of it is the public market of Abelardo L. Rodríguez, with striking mural decorations. The market is nearly always the most interesting sight in any Mexican town; in Mexico City each quarter has one.

Church of Loreto, built 1816, and now tilting badly, is on a square of the same name, surrounded by Colonial buildings.

La Santísima Trinidad (1677, remodelled 1755), to be seen for its fine towers and the rich carvings on its façade.

The Mercado Merced, said to be the largest market in all the Americas, dating back over 400 years. Its activities spread over several blocks. In the northern quarter of this market are the ruins of La Merced Monastery; the 18th century patio is almost all that survives, but this is so fine that it is worth some trouble to find. (It is on Avenida Uruguay, between Calle Talavera and Calle Jesús Maria, opposite No. 171.)

The oldest hospital in the New World, **Jesús Nazareno**, founded 1526 by Cortés, but remodelled in 1928, save for the patio and staircase.

Biblioteca Nacional (National Library), in the bulky Colonial church of San Agustín. Over 250,000 volumes, including the first books printed in Mexico.

Avenida Madero leads from Zócalo W to the Alameda. On it is **La Profesa** church, late 16th century, with a fine high altar and a leaning tower. The 18th century **Iturbide Palace**, Av. Madero 17, once the home of Emperor Iturbide (1821-23), is now a congerie of shops and offices. But to the tourist the great sight of Av. Madero, however, is the **Casa de los Azulejos** (House of Tiles) at the Alameda end of the street. Now occupied by Sanborn's Restaurant, it was built in the 16th century, and is brilliantly faced with blue and white Puebla tiles. The staircase walls are covered with Orozco frescoes. Over the way is the **Church of San Francisco**, founded in 1525 by the "Apostles of Mexico", the first 12 Franciscans to reach the country. It was by far the most important church in colonial days. Cortés was buried here for some time, so was Iturbide; all the Viceroys attended the church.

Beyond San Francisco church, Calle San Juan de Letrán leads S towards **Las Vizcaínas** (The Biscayans), at Plaza Las Vizcaínas, one block E. This huge building was put up in 1734 as a school for girls; some of it is still so used, but some of it has become slum tenements. In spite of neglect, it is still the best example of Colonial baroque in the city.

Escuela Nacional de Artes Plásticas (School of Fine Arts), at the corner of Academia and Calle Moneda (1000 to 1300), has fine Mexican Colonial painting and a first-class collection of European painting by Geertgentot Sint Jans, Titian (3), Tintoretto (3), Ingres, Poussin, Daumier, Pisarro, Delacroix, El Greco (2), Goya, Zurbarán, Ribera, the 14th century Catalan Luís Borrasa, Rubens, Breughel, and Lawrence and Opie of the English school. We are informed that these paintings have now been moved to the Museo San Carlos, a fine early 19th century palace, near the Revolución metro station in Calle Puente de Alvarado. There is another picture gallery, the **Pinacoteca Nacional de San Diego,** in the former church of San Diego in Calle Dr. Mora, at the Juárez end of the Alameda. (Cheap concerts on Thursdays at 2000 hours.)

Moving eastwards along Av. Hidalgo, before the Palace of Fine Arts, on the right is the **Post Office,** open for letters 0800-2400 Mon.-Fri., 0800-2000 Sat., and 0900-1600 Sun. For parcels open 0900-1500 Mon.-Fri. only; parcels larger than 2 kilograms not accepted (see page 881). Built in 1904, in mock-antique.

North from the west side of the Post Office leads to the Calle Santa María la Redonda, at the end of which is **Plaza Santiago de Tlalteloco,** next oldest Plaza to the Zócalo. Here was the main market of the Aztecs, and on it, in 1524, the Franciscans built a huge church and convent. This is now the Plaza of the Three Cultures: (a) the Aztec ruins have been restored; (b) the magnificent baroque church of Santiago Tlaltelolco is now the focus of (c) the massive, multi-storey Nonoalco-Tlaltelolco housing scheme with school, shops, and tall blocks of flats stretching from Reforma to the unusual triangular office building on Insurgentes, a garden city within a city, with pedestrian and wheeled traffic entirely separate. It is well worth walking through.

About 5 or 6 blocks N of the Post Office off San Juan de Letrán is **Plaza Garibaldi,** a must, especially on Saturday night, when up to 200 mariachis in their traditional costume of huge sombrero, tight silver-embroidered trousers, pistol and sarape, will play your favourite Mexican serenade for US$4. If you arrive by taxi you will be besieged. The whole square throbs with life and the packed bars are cheerful, though there is some danger from thieves and pickpockets. The Lagunilla market is held near the plaza on Sundays. Inexpensive nearby bar is *Guadalajara:* good drinks, dancing to mariachi band, not dear. If very crowded, try *Tenampa,* somewhat dearer.

Palacio de Mineria (School of Mines), Calle Tacuba 9 (1797), a glorious old building, now restored, and once more level on its foundations. (Cheap concerts on Sundays at 1700, upstairs.)

Among the S side of the Alameda runs Av. Juárez, a fine street with a mixture of old and new buildings. In the *Hotel del Prado* vestibule, facing the Alameda, Diego Rivera's "scandalous" fresco, "Sunday in the Alameda", is now exhibited. A stroll down Calle Dolores, a busy and fascinating street, leads to the market of San Juan. The Colonial church of Corpus Christi, on Av. Juárez, is now used to display and sell folk arts and crafts. The avenue ends at the small Plaza de la Reforma, on which is a magnificent equestrian statue, "El Caballito", of King Charles IV cast in 1802; it weighs 26 tons and is the second-largest bronze casting in the world. Near it is the National Lottery building. Drawings are held three times a week, at 2000: an interesting scene open to the public. Beyond "El Caballito" is the Monument to the Revolution of 1910: a great copper dome, now rather tarnished, soaring above supporting columns set on the largest triumpal arches in the world.

South of this area, on Plaza Ciudadela, is a large Colonial building, **La Ciudadela,** put up in 1700. It has been used for all kinds of purposes but is now a School for Plastic Arts (Sculpture, metal, decorative glass). Enjoyable.

Beyond El Caballito the Av. Juárez continues as the wide and handsome Paseo de la Reforma, 3 km. long, to Chapultepec Park: shops, offices, hotels, restaurants all the way. Along it are monuments to Columbus; to Cuauhtémoc, the last Aztec emperor; and a 45-metre marble column to Independence, topped by the golden-winged figure of a woman, "El Angelito" to the Mexicans. Grand view from the summit. Just before entering the park is the Salubridad (Health) Building. Rivera's frescoes of Life, Wisdom, Science, Health, Purity, and Continence, all, curiously enough, women and all nude, cannot be seen by the public, who can view only the stained-glass windows on the staircases.

Chapultepec Park, at the end of Paseo de la Reforma, with its thousands of ahuehuete trees, is one of the most beautiful in the world. It contains a maze of pathways, a large lake, a marvellous botanical garden, shaded lawns, a zoo, a large amusement park with huge roller-coasters (open Wed., Sat. and Sun., entry US$0.90, all rides free, except roller-coaster; on Sat. and Sun. only, US$0.22), bridle paths and polo grounds. Just below the castle and a little to the left is the famous Arbol de Moctezuma, known locally as ''El Sargento''. Even without its historical connotation, it is worth seeing this immense tree which has a circumference of 14 metres and is about 60 metres high. In this park too, are the Don Quixote fountain, the Frog's fountain, the Niños Monument, and Monkey Island, a replica of Cacahuamilpa Caves. At the top of a hill in the park is Chapultepec Castle, with a view over Mexico Valley from its beautiful balconies. (Visitors to the castle should take car or bus marked ''Tacubaya'', ''La Chima'', or ''Lomas de Chapultepec''.) It has now become the **National Museum of History,** open 0900-1800; closed on Tuesday. Its rooms were used by the Emperor Maximilian and the Empress Carlotta during their brief reign. There is an unfinished mural by Siqueiros and a notable mural by O'Gorman on the theme of independence. Entrance US$0.40; US$0.80 on Sunday. Halfway down the hill is the new **Gallery of Mexican History.** On Sunday mornings large numbers of people gather round the lake for open-air extension classes in a great variety of subjects (e.g. hairdressing, artificial flower-making, guitar-playing) organized by the University and open to all.

But the crowning wonder of the park is the new **Anthropological Museum** built by architect Pedro Ramírez Vásquez to house a vast collection illustrating pre-conquest Mexican culture. It has a 350-metre façade and an immense patio shaded by a gigantic concrete mushroom, 4,200 square metres—the world's largest concrete expanse supported by a single pillar. The largest exhibit (8¼ metres high, weighing 167 tons) is Tlaloc the rain god, removed—accompanied by protesting cloud bursts—from near the town of Texcoco to the museum. Open 0900-1900 except on Sunday, 1000-1800, and Monday, closed. Entrance is US$0.75 except Sunday, when all museums charge US$0.45. Free entry for students on presentation of international student card. Guides in English cost an additional US$0.80; guided tours in Spanish free. The most fanatical museum hater will enjoy this one, particularly the display of folk costumes on the first floor. There is an excellent collection of English, French, German and Spanish books. Restaurant on site is expensive. **Note** We are told that when the Museum of Anthropology closes in the evening, Chapultepec park abounds with thieves.

There are now three other museums in Chapultepec Park: the museums of Natural History, Technology and Modern Art (US$1). The latter shows Mexican art only in two buildings, pleasantly set among trees with some sculptures in the grounds. The smaller building shows temporary exhibitions. The delightfully light architecture of the larger building is spoilt by a heavy, vulgar marble staircase, with a curious acoustic effect on the central landing under a translucent dome, which must have been unplanned. At the Audiorama, on the Constituyentes side of the Castle, one may listen any day to recorded classical music in a small open amphitheatre (requests between 1300 and 1500). The Gallery of Mexican History has dioramas, with tape-recorded explanations, of Mexican history, and fantastic photographs of the 1910 Revolution.

The Museum of Technology is free; it is operated by the Federal Electricity Commission, has ''touchable'' exhibits which demonstrate electrical and energy principles.

Further places of interest to tourists are as follows:

Natural History Museum Now moved to the Bosque Nuevo de Chapultepec, reached by bus along Constituyentes. Open 1000-1300 and 1500-1700, except Saturdays and Sundays. Entry US$0.05.

Museum of the City, on Av. Pino Suárez and República de El Salvador, shows the geology of the city and has life size figures in period costumes. In the attic above the museum is the studio of Joaquín Clausell, with walls covered with impressionist miniatures. Free admittance.

Museo Nacional de las Culturas, Moneda 13, open 0900-1800, closed Friday.

Museo Arqueológico del Sitio (ruins of main pyramid of Tenochtitlán), Seminario 4 y Guatemala, open 0900-2000, Sat. and Sun. 0900-1800, closed Monday.

Museo del Convento de Carmen, Av. Revolución 4, open 1000-1700.

The Bull Ring, Plaza México, is the largest in the world, and holds 60,000 spectators. Bull fights are held every Sunday at 1600 from October through March. Buy tickets on Saturday: seat in sun US$0.32, in shade US$0.48. The Bull Ring is in the Ciudad de los Deportes (City of Sports), Plaza México, reached from Paseo de la Reforma by Av. de los Insurgentes. (A little to the W of where Los Insurgentes crosses Chapultepec, and on Av. Chapultepec itself between Calles Praga and Varsovia, are the remains of the old aqueduct built in 1779 to bring water to the city). Besides the Bull Ring, the Sports City contains a football stadium holding 50,000 people, a boxing ring, a cinema, a frontón court for jai-alai, a swimming pool, restaurants, hotels, etc.

On Avenida Insurgentes Norte itself is a remarkable new building by the architect Alejandro Prieto: the Teatro de Los Insurgentes, a theatre and opera house seating 1,300 people. The main frontage on the Avenida consists of a high curved wall without windows. This wall is entirely covered with mosaic decoration, the work of Diego Rivera: appropriate figures, scenes, and portraits composed round the central motif of a gigantic pair of hands holding a mask, an intricate and delicate design worth going a distance to see.

Sullivan Park (popularly known as Colonia Park) is reached by going up Paseo de la Reforma to the intersection with Los Insurgentes, and then W two blocks between Calles Sullivan and Villalongín. Here, each Sunday afternoon, there is a display of paintings, engravings and sculptures near the ponderous monument to Motherhood. This Garden of Art, which has been open each Sunday since 1955, is packed with sightseers and buyers, for everything is for sale.

Frontón México, on the north side of Plaza República, reached by Av. Juárez from "El Caballito", is the best place to watch Jai-Alai, played by Basque descendants. It seats 4,000. The people in red caps amongst the spectators are the "corredores" who place the bets.

The most successful and original architecture in Mexico today is to be found in the churches put up by Sres. Enrique de la Mora and Félix Candela; a good example is the chapel they built in 1957 for the Missionaries of the Holy Spirit, in a garden behind high walls. (An exquisite Candela church, and easy to get at, is the Church of Medalla Milagrosa, just to the E of Avenida Universidad at the junction of Avenida División Norte.) "All the churches and chapels built by this team have such lightness and balance that they seem scarcely to rest on their foundations." The National institute of Architects, Casa de Arquitectos, Veracruz 24, Mexico City, will be glad to give the locations of the various buildings put up by the team. See also the *objet trouvé* mural at the Diana cinema in the centre of the city. And Orozco's great thundercloud of composition, the "Apocalypse", at the Church of Jesús Nazareno. Consult Max Cetto's book on modern Mexican architecture.

The **Basilica of Guadalupe**, is the Gustavo A. Madero district, often called Villa de Guadalupe, in the outer suburbs to the NE, is the most venerated shrine in Mexico, for it was here, in December 1531, that the Virgin appeared three times, in the guise of an Indian princess, to the Indian Juan Diego and imprinted her portrait on his cloak. The cloak is preserved, set in gold and protected by a 27-ton railing of silver, at the centre of the magnificent altar. A chapel stands over the well which gushed at the spot where the virgin appeared. The great day here is December 12, the great night the night before. A new basilica has recently been opened next door, impressive and worth visiting; it holds over 20,000 people. The original basilica, now closed, is to be converted into a museum. There are, in fact, about seven churches in the immediate neighbourhood, including one on the hill above; most of them are at crazy angles to each other and to the ground, because of subsidence; the subsoil is very soft. Buses marked La Villa go close to the site.

Suburbs of Mexico City

Churubusco, 10 km. SE, reached from the Zócalo by "Coyoacán" or "Tlalpan" car or bus, or from General Anaya metro station, to see the picturesque and partly ruined convent (1762), now become a historical museum (open 1000-1700, closed Mon.). There is a golf course at the Churubusco Country Club. Churbusco has the principal Mexican film studios. The new Olympic swimming pool is here. Near enough to Coyoacán (see page 818) to walk there.

Tlalpan, 6½ km. further, or direct from Villa Obregón (see next page), a most picturesque old town on the slopes of Ajusco, an extinct volcano: Colonial houses, gardens, and near the main square an early 16th century church with a glorious altar and paintings by Cabrera. There is a cosy, small museum of *Charrería,* the national horse-riding sport, in a beautiful Colonial house. Reached by bus from the Taxqueña metro station. Two-and-a-half km. W is the village of Peña Pobre, near which, to the NE, is the Pyamid of **Cuicuilco**, believed to be the oldest in Mexico (archaeological museum on site, Insurgentes Sur Km. 16, open 0800-1800, closed Mon.). The pyramid dates from the 5th or 6th century B.C.; it is over 100 metres in diameter but only 18 high. Cuicuilco is about 15 minutes walk from the University (see below). The Olympic Village was built within sight of it. On the road from Mexico City to Cuicuilco there is a pre-classic burial area under the lava flow, at Copilco.

Xochimilco, to the SE, in the Valley of México. Take metro to Taxqueña (terminus) and catch a trolley-bus to the market. Bus service from Zócalo (Calle Mesones and Pino Suárez, US$0.06) to **Ixtapalapa** and Xochimilco (22 km.), a long ride. The first (2 good churches) is at the foot of the Cerro de Estrella, whose top is reached by a bad motor road or by a path for a good view. Xochimilco has a maze of canals which wander round fruit and flower gardens. Punts, piled with flowers, poled by Indians, can be hired for about US$7. At the canal-side restaurants there is music and dancing. The canals are busy on Sundays. Xochimilco has a fine market on Saturday; Indians come from miles around. It has a 16th century church. Only one hotel, basic, US$1. Many cheap souvenirs. One of the most spectacular of Mexican passion-plays begins at Ixtapalapa on Holy Thursday. Note that it is virtually impossible to get to the Mexico City-Cuernavaca toll road from Xochimilco. If going to Tepoztlán (see page 837) it is better to return to Cuernavaca rather than try to get on to Yautepec.

University City, world-famous, is 18 km. *via* Insurgentes Sur on the Cuernavaca highway. This magnificent group of buildings is set amongst the black boulders, green grass, trees and flowers of the Pedregal, a sea of petrified lava. Perhaps the most notable building is the 10-storied library tower, by Juan O'Gorman, its walls iridescent with mosaics telling the story of Mexican culture. The Administrative Building has a vast, mosaic-covered and semi-sculptured mural by Siqueiros. Across the highway is the Olympic Stadium, with seats for 80,000, in shape, colour, and situation a world's wonder. Diego Rivera has a sculpture-painting telling the story of Mexican sport. Pedregal is the city's newest and most original suburb. It is well worth a visit to see how the architectural problems of building homes on a tortured lava bed have been magnificently solved. The University of Mexico was founded in 1551, nearly 90 years before Harvard. Bus (marked C.U., one passes through Av. San Juan de Letrán; another to the university from Taxqueña metro station) gets you there for US$0.10.

On the same pedregal bed as the University but further out is **Anahuacalli** (usually called the Diego Rivera Museum). Here is the best collection of pre-Columbian pots (some sculpture) possible. Effectively displayed, too, in a pseudo-Mayan tomb built for it by Diego Rivera. View of southern rim of mountains from the roof. In some ways it beats the Anthropological Museum. Most remarkable. Reached by bus from the Taxqueña metro station.

Villa Obregón, 13 km. SW. It has narrow, cobble-stone streets, many old homes, huge trees, and the charm of an era now largely passed. See the triple domes of its church, covered with coloured tiles, and the former Carmen monastery, now a museum (open 1000-1700). See also the beautifully furnished and preserved old house, Casa del Risco, near the market, and the church of San Jacinto and its adjoining monastery. In **San Angel** nearby, a very pretty colonial-style suburb, there is a *bazar sábado*, a splendid Saturday folk art and curiosity market, and the Parroquia, a Dominican convent dating from 1566. Excellent restaurants. The *San Angel Inn* is first class.

Coyoacán, an old and beautiful suburb adjoining Villa Obregón, is the place from which Cortés launched his attack on Tenochtitlán. There are some fine local stories of what he did in the Casa de Cortés, now the Municipal Hall, but actually built 244 years after the Conquest. The rose-coloured house, Francisco Sosa 383, is said to have been built by Alvarado. The San Juan Bautista church and the nearby Franciscan monastery are both early 16th century. Friday market. The Frida Kahlo Museum, preserved as lived in by Diego Rivera and Frida Kahlo, is fascinating and well worth an afternoon. Drawings and paintings by both. Nearby, Trotsky's house is now open, at irregular hours (students man it), as a museum at Viena 45. The new market and the remarkable Chapel of our Lady of Solitude are by Enrique de la Mora and Félix Candela. *El Coyote Flaco* is a good restaurant; Night Club Peña Nahuatl, fine folk singing and poetry readings. For Desierto de los Leones, reached from Villa Obregón by a scenic road, see page 802.

At Tlatilco, NW of the city (just outside the city boundary on Querétaro road), pre-classic Olmec-influenced figurines can be seen.

The **Pyramid of Tenayuca,** 10 km. to the NW, is about 15 metres high and the best-preserved in Mexico. The Aztecs rebuilt this temple every 52 years; this one was built before the Spanish conquest and reconstructed about 1507. It is not in the accepted tourist round and taxi drivers and travel agents tend to ignore or deny its existence; but it is there and well worth seeing, for it is a strange pyramid surrounded with serpents in masonry. The easiest way to get there by car from Mexico City centre is to take Vallejo, 11 km. N of the intersection of Insurgentes and Rio Consulado. Admission US$0.08. By bus, catch bus to Tenayuca from the Calle Isabel La Católica; ask driver and passengers to advise you on arrival as site is not easily visible. It is not far from the old town of Tlalnepantla: see the ancient convent on the Plaza and the church (1583), which contains the first image, a Christ of Mercy, brought to the New World. Two-and-a-half km. to the N is the smaller pyramid of Santa Cecillia, interesting for its restored sanctuary.

Los Remedios, a small town 13 km. NW of Mexico City. In its famous church is an image, a foot high, adorned with jewels valued at a million pesos. See the old aqueduct, with a winding stair leading to the top. It can be reached by car or by taking the "Los Remedios" bus at Tacuba. Fiesta: September 1 to the climax September 8.

Excursions from Mexico City

San Agustín Acolman is a formidable fortress-like convent and church dating from 1539-60, with much delicate detail on the façade and some interesting murals inside. Note the dazzling portal and the carved stone cross at the entrance to the atrium. Also reached by bus from the Zócalo. It is 42 km. from the city.

Teotihuacán, 9 km. beyond San Agustín Acolman, has some of the most remarkable relics of an ancient civilization in the world. The old city is traceable over an area of 3¼ by 6½ km. The Pyramids make the largest artificial mounds on the American continent: the Pyramid of the Sun (64 metres high, 213 metres square at the base) covers almost the same space as the Great Pyramid of Cheops in Egypt. The sides are terraced, and wide stairs lead to the summit; unfortunately its surface was restored in the wrong materials to wrong specifications around 1910. The Pyramid of the Moon, 1 km. away, is only half its size. There are temples of agriculture, of Tlaloc (the Rain God), of the Plumed Serpent, of Quetzalcoatl (Lord of Air and Wind), and a broad Highway of the Dead. There are subterranean buildings with large halls and coloured decorations, and many superimposed buildings of a later epoch. The

Chinese Academy has found evidence of Chinese influence at Teotihuacán. The pyramids, buildings, courts, etc., are now completely restored and well worth a visit; but beware the fake "idol" sellers. A very fine rebuilt palace and patio is the Palace of Quetzalpapalotl, where the priests serving the sanctuaries of the Moon lived. Site open 0800-1800. Entrance, US$0.80, half price for students. US$0.40 per car. Entrance US$0.45 on Sundays. Tetitla and Atetelco, two smaller sites to the W of the perimetral road, are worth seeing; they are about 1 km. N of the main entrance from the *autovía*. There is a spectacular, though expensive, restaurant overlooking the buildings. There is a small museum below the restaurant. Easily reached by 1st class bus leaving every 20 minutes from Calle Alarcón 19, 8 blocks from Candelaria metro station (a dirty, and in the dark a dangerous, place) passing a continuum of bus depots, somewhat difficult to find, 1 hr., US$0.65, but make sure you take the bus that goes along the *autovía* (most of their buses do not). Alternative bus service from Buses Teotihuacán, near Manuel González and Prol. Héroes in Insurgentes Sur area, or from Terminal Norte (take bus from Bucareli, near Juárez to this terminal) and take bus there (from Sala 8), US$0.60, half-hourly. Buses also from Tlateloco metro station. Interesting restaurant, *La Gruta,* in cave, costume waitresses, mariachis, dancers on Sundays, reasonable prices, but takes a long time serving so take into account if you want to go to *Son et lumière*. Son-et-lumière display costs US$4 per person (good *lumière*, not so good *son*); lasts 45 mins., starts at 1900. English commentary. Shown between January and end-April; take blanket or rent one there. You can ride back to town with one of the tourist buses for about US$2. Note that the site is more generally known as "Pirámides" than as "Teotihuacán".

Tepozotlán, about 43 km. from Mexico City just off the route to Querétaro, has a splendid Jesuit church in Churrigueresque style. The church and chapels are rich in decoration and gold leaf. There are fine colonial paintings in the convent corridors. The old Jesuit monastery has been converted into a Colonial Art museum (Museo Nacional del Virreinato, open 1000-1700, closed Mon. entry US$0.40 (US$0.20 Sun.)) and tourist centre with restaurants: the *Hostería del Monasterio* has very good Mexican food and a band on Sundays; try their coffee with cinnamon. Also good food at *Brookwell's Posada*. Well worth a visit for the paintings alone. Autobuses Zacatepec operate a direct bus service (every 4 hours) from Mexico City to Tepozotlán.

Another splendid one-day excursion is to **Tula**, some 65 km., or 2 hours away by train from Buenavista station; the return fare is under a dollar. It can also be reached by bus (from Terminal de Norte, US$1) or by car from Actopán, on the Pan-American Highway (see page 776). At Tula, the most important Toltec site in Mexico, a ball court, pyramids, a frieze in colour, and remarkable sculptures over 20 metres high have been uncovered. Other discoveries have been made in the neighbourhood. The museum is well worth visiting and there is a massive fortress-style church, dating from 1553, near the market. A 2nd class bus, "Valle de Mesquital", from Terminal Central de Norte, Avenida de los Cien Metros, goes to Tula in 2 hours; US$0.72 each way, 20-minute service. Admission to site and museum, US$0.24 (free on Thursdays). All the guided tours have left by 1600; as the site is open until 1800 the best visiting time is in these 2 hours of comparative calm. The town itself is dusty, however, with poor roads and no good restaurants.

If driving from Mexico City, take the turn for Actopán before entering Tula, then look for the Zona Arqueológica sign (and the great statues) on your left.

Mexico City-Veracruz-Mexico City

By Rail Overnight Pullman train to Veracruz. Daytime trains are not a/c but are best for seeing the country. Air service, 3 flights daily, about 45 minutes, cost about US$17.

By Road A round tour by way of Cholula, Puebla, Tehuacán, Orizaba, Córdoba, Veracruz, Jalapa, Tlaxcala, and Alvarado. Paved all the way. Distance: 924 km., or 577 miles. Best bus company: ADO, from Buenavista 9, Mexico City. Book well in advance, long waits (1½-2 hrs.) at booking office in bus station possible. Bus, Mexico City-Veracruz, US$6. A new toll autopista (motorway) from Mexico City to Veracruz has been finished as far as Córdoba. From there on you take the regular highway. Autobuses Unidos to Puebla for US$1.80, 2 hours. Our description is a trip along the old road.

We go E along the Puebla road, past the airport and swimming pools. At (km. 19) Los Reyes, a road runs left into a valley containing the now almost completely drained Lake Texcoco, a valley early settled by the Conquistadores, who built some of their first schools and churches for the Indians here. Along it we come to **Chapingo,** where there is a famous agricultural college with particularly fine frescoes by Rivera in the chapel. Next comes **Texcoco,** a good centre for touring picturesque villages in the area. Near Chapingo a road runs right to the lovely village of **Huexotla** (see the Aztec wall and the old church). Another road from Texcoco runs through the very beautiful public park of Molino de las Flores. From the old hacienda buildings, now in ruin, a road (right) runs up the hill of Tetzcotingo, near the top of which are the Baths of Netzahualcoyotl, the poet-prince. All the nearby villages are charming to stroll through. Another village worth visiting is **San Miguel de Chiconcuac** (road to San Andrés and left at its church), only 4 km. away. Here Texcoco serapes are woven. Tuesday is their market day and there is a rousing fiesta in honour of their patron saint on September 29.

Bus to Texcoco from Mexico City, from Emiliano Zapata 92, near Candelaria metro station.

At km. 29, Santa Bárbara, a road on the right leads to the small town of **Amecameca** (60 km. from Mexico City), at the foot of the twin volcanoes Popocatépetl and Ixtaccíhuatl; the saddle between them, reached by car up to the Paso de Cortés, gives particularly fine views. A road reaches the sanctuary of El Sacromonte, 90 metres above the town (magnificent views), a small and very beautiful church built round a cave in which once lived Fray Martín de Valencia, a conquistador who came to Mexico in 1524. It is, next to the shrine of Guadalupe, the most sacred place in Mexico and has a much venerated full-sized image of Santo Entierro weighing 1½ kg. only. Population of Amecameca: 10,000; altitude: 2,315 metres; market day is Saturday. (On the way to Amecameca, see the restored 16th century convent and church at Chalco, and the fine church, convent and open-air chapel of the same period at Tlamanalco.) Near Amecameca there is a national park; experienced climbers (who must register at the entrance, US$0.48) may wish to climb up to the refuge at 3,800 metres, about 11 hrs climb; but beware of altitude sickness. It is also possible to take a taxi from Amecameca to Tlamacas (3,700 metres), US$9, 26 km., entrance US$0.25. There are a few houses and a Youth Hostel, US$1.50 a night; beautiful house but very cold at night; no food, only coffee available. Minibuses charge US$2.50 p.p. From Tlamacas a path goes up to a hut at 4,400 metres and the snow-area is two hours further on. Equipment hire at Amecameca. If you wish to go to the top of Popocatépetl (5,400 metres) leave at 0600, as the ground is more solid early on.

The road leads on to the semi-tropical little town of **Cuautla** (20,000 people), a popular sulphur spring (known as *aguas hediondas* or stinking waters) and bath, week-end resort for the Capital. Tourist Cuautla is divided from native Cuautla by a wide river, and the natives have the best bargain: it is worth crossing the stream.

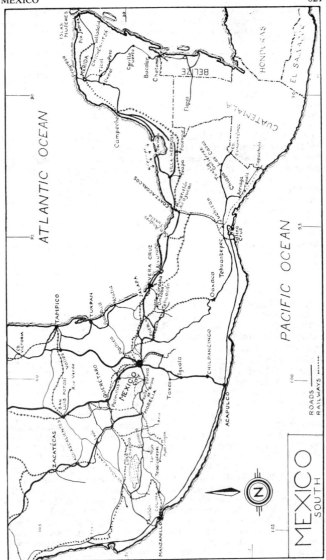

ROUGH SKETCH

From Cuautla go to Atotonilco by bus for a swim. Buses from Mexico City to Amecameca and Cuautla from Cristóbal Colón terminal, Ignacio Zaragoza 38, near San Lázaro underground station. *Hotel Colón* in Cuautla, is on the main square, good, US$7.20 d.

Beyond Santa Bárbara our road climbs through pine forests to reach 3,196 metres about 63 km. from Mexico City, and then descends in a series of sharp bends to the quiet town of San Martín Texmelucan, km 91. Market day is Tuesday. From here a side-road leads NE for 24 km. to the quaint old Indian town of **Tlaxcala**, capital of small Tlaxcala state whose wealthy ranches breed fighting bulls, but whose landless peasantry is sordidly poor. At the time of the Conquest the Tlaxcalans were Cortés' faithful allies against their enemies the Aztecs; but for their help Cortés' expedition might well have failed. To see: the Church of San Francisco (1521), from whose pulpit the first Christian sermon was preached in the New World—its severe façade conceals a most sumptuous interior; the Indian decorations in the Sanctuary of Ocotlán, on a hill outside the town, described as "the most delicious building in the world"; and the very ruinous ruins of the pyramid temple of San Esteban de Tizatlán, 5 km. outside the town. Most interesting relics are two sacrificial altars with original colour frescoes preserved under glass. The pictures tell the story of the wars with Aztec and Chichimec. Population 10,000. Altitude 2,240 metres.

The **Sanctuary of Ocotlán** (1541), on a hill, commands a view of valley and volcano. "Its two towers are of lozenge-shaped vermillion bricks set in white stucco, giving an effect of scarlet shagreen, while their upper storeys are dazzlingly white, with fretted cornices and salomonic pillars. . . . A pure-blooded Indian, Francisco Miguel, worked for 25 years on the interior, converting it into a kind of golden grotto."—Sacheverell Sitwell.

(Km. 106) **Huejotzingo**. It has the second-oldest church and monastery in Mexico, built 1529; now a museum. Market: Saturday, Tuesday. Dramatic carnival on Shrove Tuesday, portraying the story of Agustín Lorenzo, a famous local bandit.

(Km. 122) **Cholula**, is a small somnolent town, but one of the strangest-looking in all Mexico. When Cortés arrived, this was a holy centre with 100,000 inhabitants and 400 shrines, or teocallis, grouped round the great pyramid of Quetzalcoatl. In fact there were a series of pyramids built one atop another, and the site is open 1000-1700, closed Mon. When razing them, Cortés vowed to build a chapel for each of the teocallis destroyed, but in fact there are no more than about seventy. Places to see are the excavated pyramid, admission US$0.16, (it has 8 km. of tunnels and some recently discovered frescoes inside) and the Chapel of Los Remedios on top of it, for the view; the Franciscan fortress church of San Gabriel (1552), in the plaza (open 0600-1200, 1600-1900, Suns. 0600-1900); and next to it, the Capilla Real, which has 48 domes (open 1000-1200, 1530-1800, Suns. 0900-1800); the Indian statuary and stucco work, newly repainted, of the 16th century church of (Santa María de) **Tonantzintla**, outside the town; the church is one of the most beautiful in Mexico (open 1000-1300, 1500-1700 daily), and may also be reached by paved road from (San Francisco) **Acatepec** (see its 16th century church also, open 0900-1800 daily) on the highway from Puebla to Cholula. Cholula has the University of the Americas. Population 13,000. Hotels are rather basic. Second-class bus from Puebla, 13 km., US$0.08. Good views of volcanoes.

"The churches of Tonantzintla and Acatepec should on no account be missed; they are resplendent with Poblano tiles and their interiors are a riot of Indian stucco work and carving"—(John Hemming). If you have time for only one, Tonantzintla is the one to choose.

Beyond Acatepec (S of Puebla) is **Atlixco**, with 2 elaborate 16th century churches of San Francisco and a beautiful parish church in the main square; *Hotel Balmori* there, serves *comida corrida*. Nearby are the curative springs of Axocopán.

Just before Puebla one comes to the superb church of **Tlaxcalantzingo**, with an extravagantly tiled façade, domes and tower. It is worth climbing up on the roof for photographs.

(Km. 134) Puebla, "The City of the Angels", one of Mexico's oldest and most famous cities and the capital of Puebla state, at 2,060 metres. Unfortunately, its recent great growth in industry—the population has risen to 740,000—is rapidly destroying its Colonial air, and the centre, though still beautifully Colonial, is filled with noisy and air polluting traffic jams, except in those shopping streets reserved for pedestrians. On the central arcaded plaza is a fine Cathedral notable for its marble floors, onyx and marble statuary and gold leaf decoration. The bell tower gives a grand view of the city and snow-capped volcanoes. There are 60 churches in all, many of their domes shining with the glazed tiles for which the city is famous. Earthquake damage in 1973. Craft shop sponsored by the authorities: Tienda Convento Sta. Rosa Calle 3 Norte 1203, Tel.: 2-89-04. Feria in mid-April for two weeks.

In the Rosario chapel of the Church of Santo Domingo (1596-1659), the baroque displays a beauty of style and prodigality of form which served as an examplar and inspiration for all later baroque in Mexico. There is a strong Mexican note in Puebla's baroque; the hand of the Indian is evident in the variety and exuberance of the colouring and in the portrayal of human and celestial figures. This can be seen in the 16th century churches of Tonantzintla and Acatepec (see above); it is not so evident, but it is still there, in the opulent Renaissance work in the Cathedral. Beyond the church, up towards the top of the Avenida Internacional, there is a spectacular view of the volcanoes in the area. Other places well worth visiting are the churches of San Cristóbal (1687), with modern Churrigueresque towers and Tonantzintla-like plasterwork inside; San José (18th century), with attractive tiled façade and decorated walls around the main doors, as well as beautiful altar pieces inside; the Senado del Estado in Calle 5 Poniente, formerly the Consejo de Justicia, near the post office, is a converted 19th century Moorish style town house—the tiled entrance and courtyard are very attractive—it had a theatre inside (shown to visitors on request), it is now the seat of the state government; and the Museo de Santa Rosa has a priceless collection of 16th century Talavera tiles on its walls and ceilings. The Patio de los Azulejos should also be visited; it has fabulous tiled façades on the former almshouses for old retired priests of the order of San Felipe Neri; the colours and designs are beautiful; it is at 11 Poniente 110, with a tiny entrance which is hard to find unless one knows where to look. One of the most famous and oldest local churches is San Francisco, with a glorious tiled façade and a mummified saint in its side chapel. Santa Catalina, 3 Norte with 8 Poniente, has beautiful altarpieces; Nuestra Señora de la Luz, 14 Sur and 2 Oriente, has a good tiled façade and so has San Marcos at Av. Reforma and 9 Norte. The Maronite church of Belén on 7 Norte and 4 Oriente has a lovely old tiled façade and a beautifully tiled interior. Worth visiting is also the library of Bishop Palafox, by the tourist office, 5 Oriente No. 5, opposite the Cathedral. Besides the churches, the absurdly fragile and extravagantly ornamented Casa del Alfeñique (Sugar Candy House), a few blocks from the Cathedral dominating the centre of the town, is worth seeing. Nearby is Plaza Parián, with onyx souvenir shops (6 Norte and 4 Oriente). Onyx figures and chess sets are attractive and cheaper than elsewhere, but the *poblanos* are hard bargainers; another attractive buy is the very typical glass animal figures, quite incredibly tiny. A former convent is now the Museum of Santa Mónica; generations of nuns hid there after the reform laws of 1857 made the convent illegal. The Cinco de Mayo civic centre, with a monolithic statue of Benito Juárez, is, among other things, a regional centre of arts, crafts and folklore and has a nice museum of popular art. The forts of Guadalupe and Loreto have been restored. They were the scene of the Battle of Puebla, in which 2,000 Mexican troops defeated Maximilian's 6,000 European troops on May 5, 1862. May 5 is a holiday in Mexico. Near the forts is an excellent museum showing all phases of Mexican history.

Other places worth seeing are the church and monastery of El Carmen, with its strange façade and beautiful tile work; the Theatre (1550), the oldest in the Americas; the grand staircase of the 17th century Academia de las Bellas Artes and its exhibition of Mexican Colonial painting; a magnificent library, one of the oldest in the Americas, access through the Casa Cultural and the Jesuit Church of La Compañía, where a plaque in the sacristy shows where China Poblana lies buried. This mythical figure, a Chinese princess captured by pirates and abducted to Mexico, is said to have taken to Christianity and good works and evolved a penitential dress for herself which has now become the regional costume; positively dazzling with flowered reds and greens and worn with a strong sparkle of bright beads. Also worth visiting is the house of Aquiles Serdán, a leader of the Revolution, preserved as it was during his life. The tiled façade of the Casa de los Muñecos, 2 Norte No. 1 (corner of the main square) is famous for its caricatures in tiles of the enemies of the 17th century builder.

The famous Puebla tiles may be purchased from factories outside Puebla, or from Fábrica de Azulejos La Guadalupana, Ave. 4 Poniente 911, with a tile museum upstairs; D. Aguilar, 18 Poniente 106, opposite Convent of Sta. Mónica, and Casa Rugerio opposite at No. 111; Margarita Guevara, 20 Poniente 30.

Barrio del Artista The artists' studios are near to Hotel Latino and adjoining Mercado El Parián, with tourist shops. Live music and refreshments at small *Café del Artista*.

Museums Museo de Bello—the house of the collector and connoisseur Bello—has good displays of Chinese porcelain and Talavera pottery; the building is beautifully furnished. Museo Regional de Puebla, in the Centro Cívico 5 de Mayo, is open 1000-1900; Museo de Santa Mónica (convent) at 18 Poniente 103, open 1000-1800, closed Mon.; and Museo de la No Intervención, in Calzada de los Fuertes, open 1000-1700, closed Mon.

Hotels *Lastra* (Calz. de Loreto); *Royalty* (Portal Hidalgo 8); *San Miguel* (3 Poniente 721); *Palace* (3 Oriente No. 13); cheap, adequate, students' hotel; *Reforma Agua Azul* (Calzada Agua Azul); *Colonial* (Ayuntamiento y 4 Sur) old-fashioned and charming; *Imperial* (2 Norte y 2 Oriente); *Panamericana*, Reforma 2114, recommended, US$3-5 s; *Latino*, US$7 d, with bath, hot water, US$3 d without bath, next ADO bus station, clean and good value; *Teresita* (near San Agustín church), 3 Poniente, 309, from US$3, with shower; *Ritz* (2 Norte), US$2.50, without bath, friendly; *San Francisco*, US$4 s, reasonable; *Augusta* (Calle 4 Poniente), US$2.60 d: *Sononel*, one block from UA bus station, US$8 s. Best: *Mesón del Angel*, near first Puebla interchange on Mexico-Puebla motorway.

Food speciality *Mole poblana.* Cheap *mole* at *Fonda la Mexicana,* 16 Sept. 706; best *mole* at *La Poblanita,* 10 Norte 1404-B, and *Fonda Sta. Clara,* 3 Poniente 307, expensive but good for local specialities. Also on Zócalo, at *Hostería de Los Angeles.* Also good, *Iberia,* Portal Juárez No. 101, 1st floor; *La Bola Roja,* 17 Sur 1305. *Camotes* (candied sweet potatoes) and *dulces* (sweets). Also *nieves*—drinks of alcohol, fruit and milk—worth trying, and excellent empanadas bought from a lady just outside the ADO station. Also noted are *quesadillas*—fried *tortillas* with cheese and herbs inside.

Other Restaurants *Monza's* (Calle Reforma), reasonable, good food. Cheap *comidas* at *Las Cazuelas del Chato,* 2 Oriente 209. *Alianza Francesa,* 2 Poniente, 101-402. Many cheap places between ADO depot and main square. *Hostería del Virrey,* 11 Sur and 15 Poniente, live music and good atmosphere.

Excursions Interesting day-trip to **Cuetzalán** market (*via* Tetela-Huahuaztla) which is held on Sundays in the Zócalo. On October 4 each year dancers from local villages gather and "voladores" "fly" from the top of their pole. Nahua Indians sell cradles *(huacal)* for children; machetes and embroidered garments. Big clay dogs are made locally, unique stoves which hold big flat clay plates on which tortillas are baked and stews are cooked in big stew pots. Also available in nearby Huitzitlán. *Casa Elvira Mora,* Hidalgo 54, cheap, friendly place, to stay in Cuetzalán. Women decorate their hair with skeins of wool. You can also go *via* Zaragoza, Zacapoaxtla and Apulco, where one can walk along a path, left of the road, to the fine 35-metre waterfall of La Gloria.

Direct buses from Puebla (Tezinteco line at Ave. 12 Oriente and Calle 4 Norte) leaves 0830. Leaves Cuetzalán at 1520, back at Puebla at 2100. ADO has a night-bus, 1915 arrives, 2245 returns 0700, arriving 1030. There are many buses to Zacapoaxtla with frequent connections for Cuetzalán.

15 km. S of Puebla lies Lake Valsequillo, with Africam, a zoo of free-roaming *African* animals! (entry US$1).

Road A 4-lane highway, 70 minutes, to Mexico City, toll US$1.30 (half-hourly buses, seats bookable, 2 hours, US$1.04); 2-lane highway to Orizaba, toll US$1.85. For the road from Pueblo S through Oaxaca to Guatemala, see page 833. Bus from Puebla to Oaxaca costs US$3.10 (9 hours). Bus Puebla-Veracruz 1st class, US$3.70.

Rail Trains from Mexico City, US$0.40 2nd class, train to Oaxaca (1st class) US$2.40, 12 hours.

(Km. 151) Amozoc, where they make tooled leather goods and silver incrustations on steel, both mostly as outfits for the Charros, or Mexican horseriders. They also make clay toys. Beyond Amozoc lies **Tepeaca** with its late 16th century monastery, well worth a visit—its weekly market is the 2nd largest in the whole of Mexico. Beyond Tepeaca, at 57½ km. from Puebla lies **Tecamachalco** with its vast 16th century Franciscan monastery church with beautiful murals on the choir vault, in late medieval Flemish style, by a local Indian. Beyond, the road leads to **Tehuacán** (population 32,000, altitude 1,676 metres), a charming health resort with an equable climate. It has some old churches. Water from the mineral springs is bottled and sent all over the country by Garci Crespi and Peñafiel, who also have baths at the spas where people come to bathe for health reasons. The town is the largest in the zone of irrigated land drawing water from the Ríos Salado and Grande. From the small dam at Malpaso on the Río Grande an annual race is held for craft without motors as far as the village of Quiotepec. This is an arid area, producing maize, alfalfa and fruit, *pulque,* and eggs for sale in the capital. The central plaza is pleasant and shaded; the nights are cool. A paved road has just been completed to Oaxaca (1976) passing through the irrigated zone, the arid area studded by cacti called the Cañada, and up over the mountains; it takes 3½-4 hours of driving. Railway junction for Oaxaca and Veracruz. Wild maize was first identified by an archaeologist in caves nearby. There is an airport.

Hotels *Hotel-Spa Peñafiel,* with night-club, 9-hole golf course, etc.; *Garci-Crespo; México; Villa Grañadas; Ibero.*

Above Tehuacán, in the hills, is the Indian town of Huautla de Jiménez, where the local Mazateca Indians consume the hallucinogenic "magic" mushrooms made famous by Dr. Timothy Leary. A study of these Indians is being made by Dr. and Mrs. Gordon Wasson, of Harvard University, who have published several learned works from which, John Streather tells us, Carlos Castaneda culled material for his Donovan books.

Beyond, our road soon begins to climb into the mountains. At Cumbres we reach 2,300 metres and a wide view of blue and purple mountains: the silvered peak of Citlaltépetl (or Orizaba) volcano to the E, the green valley of Orizaba below. In 10 km. we drop down, through steep curves, sometimes rather misty, to Acultzingo 830 metres below. The road joins the main toll road from Puebla to Orizaba at Ciudad Mendoza, where it has emerged from the descent through the Cumbres de Maltrata which are usually misty and need to be driven with care and patience. This descent is described by Graham Greene in his railway journey in *The Lawless Roads*.

(Km. 317) **Orizaba**, the favourite resort of the Emperor Maximilian (population 81,000, altitude 1,283 metres), has in the past been compared for beauty, by some, with Córdoba (see next page), but much of its charm was destroyed by the 1973 earthquake, when the bullring, many houses and other buildings were lost. There are hills nearby and in the distance is the majestic volcanic cone of Orizaba (for access, see page 835), the highest peak in Mexico (5,700 metres). The town developed because of the natural springs emerging in the valley, some of which are used by the industries and others are dammed to form small pools for bathing beside picnic areas. Its Zócalo has been cheated of much of its area by permanent snack bars. On the N side is the market, with a wide variety of local produce and local women in traditional dress, and the many-domed San Miguel church (1690-1729). There are several other moderately good churches, and there is an Orozco mural in the Federal School on Av. Colón. The Palacio Municipal is the actual cast-iron Belgian Pavilion brought piece by piece from France after the famous 19th century Paris Exhibition—an odd sight.

Industries Railway workshops; the most importan' textile factories in the country; paper mills; breweries. It is also the main centre for industrial and machinery sales, distilling rum, food production such as biscuits, and rice milling.

Hotels *De France; Américas; Aries* (nightclub on top floor).

Cafés *Romanchu* and *Paso Real,* on the main street, have excellent cuisine.

Beyond Orizaba the scenery is magnificent. We descend to coffee and sugar-cane country and a tropical riot of flowers (roses, gardenias, orchids, camelias, lilies). It is delectable country except when a northerly blows, or in the intolerable heat and mugginess of the wet season.

(Km. 331) **Fortín de las Flores,** a village devoted to growing a multitude of flowers in its fields and exporting them. Indian women sell choice blossoms in small baskets made of banana-tree bark.

Hotel *Ruiz Galindo* (swimming pool, over-elaborate for some tastes). There are others, slightly cheaper, which also offer a tropical garden for relaxation.

Near Fortín there is a viewpoint looking out over a dramatic gorge (entry free). The autopista from Orizaba to Córdoba passes over this deep valley on a wide four-lane concrete bridge.

A road leaves Orizaba southwards, up into the mountains of Zongolica, a dry, poor and isolated region, cold and inhospitable, inhabited by various groups of Indians who speak Nahuatl, the language of the Aztecs.

Córdoba (population 60,000, altitude 923 metres), 8 km. on in the rich valley of the Río Seco, is also crazy with flowers. Some of its houses have heavily barred Moorish windows, thick old doors and little wooden balconies. Its Zócalo is spacious and leafy; three sides are arcaded; two of them are lined with tables. On the fourth is an imposing church with a chiming clock. The town hall is in German Classical style. There are hotels in the Zócalo, which is alive and relaxed at night. There is a local museum at Calle 3, 303, open 1000-1300 and 1600-2000. It is a good centre for buses into the mountains and hill towns, and to Fortín and

Orizaba. It has the highest rainfall in Mexico, but at predictable times. The area grows coffee.

Hotels *Ceballos,* half a block from the Zócalo; *Virreynal, Mansur,* both moderate; *Posada La Loma,* very attractive, moderately expensive; *Hotel Ruiz Galindo; Vigo,* US\$10 d. Near the ADO terminal is *Hotel Palacio; Hotels Marina, Iberia, Riscado* and *Casa de Huéspedes Regis* are all on Avenida 2. *Casa de Huéspedes, La Sin Rival* and *La Nueva Querétana* are at 511 and 508 of Avenida 4, respectively. *Hotel Los Reyes,* US\$3 with bath.

The direct road from Córdoba to Veracruz is not interesting, but is lined by stalls selling fruit and local honey between Yanga and Cuitláhuac. Yanga is a small village named after the leader of a group of escaped black slaves in Colonial times. A slightly longer but far more attractive road goes from Córdoba northwards through Huatusco and Totutla, then swings E to Veracruz.

(Km. 476) **Veracruz,** the principal port of entry for Mexico, lies on a low alluvial plain bordering the Gulf coast. Cortés landed here on 17 April, 1519. The town is a mixture of the very old and the new; there are still many picturesque white-walled buildings and winding side-streets, and venerable 1907 trams. In spite of the occasional chill north winds, it has become a great holiday resort, and is reported touristy, noisy and expensive. The best beach, Mocambo (very clean with beautiful and well kept public area), is S of the town, reached by bus from fish market. Villa del Mar beach is now developed (dressing room, US\$0.25). Some of the beaches in and around Veracruz are polluted from the many ships. The food is good, the fishing not bad, and the people gay: there is much marimba and guitar playing, café life and dancing. (The most famous dances, accompanied by the Conjunto Jarocho, are the Bamba and Zapateado to harp and guitar, with much stamping and lashing of feet.) At night the Malecón is very lively, and sometimes fire-eaters and other performers entertain the public. The heart of the city is Plaza Constitución; make at once for the excellent *La Parroquia* café, cool and tiled. (The newer café of the same name on the Malecón does not have the same atmosphere.) The local craft is tortoishell jewellery adorned with silver but remember that the import of tortoiseshell into the USA is prohibited under the Endangered Species Act. There are two buildings of great interest: the very fine 17th-century Palacio Municipal, on Plaza Constitución, with a splendid façade and courtyard, and the castle of San Juan de Ulúa (1565), on Gallega Island, now joined by road to the mainland; take bus marked Ulúa (30 & Mex). It failed to deter the buccaneers and later became a political prison. Mexico's "Robin Hood", Chucho el Roto, was imprisoned there, and escaped three times. There is a city history museum with good collection of photographs; traces history from Conquest to 1910. It is at Francisco Canal y Gómez Farias, open 1000-1300 and 1600-1900, Suns. and holidays, 1600-1900, closed Tuesdays. On the southern arm of the harbour breakwater there is a small aquarium, admission US\$0.10, best items outside for free though. Population 242,400; the people are called "Jarochos". There is a British Consulate at the corner of Avenida Morelos 145 with Calle Emparán. Tel.: (91-293) 2-43-23. Airport at Las Bajadas, 3 flights daily to the capital.

Dr. Robin Hoult comments: "Veracruz is the main port, and popular holiday resort (for Mexicans at least!). Scorned by the guide books, but we liked it—it made a good stopping off point on the long journey from Mexico City to Yucatán. Although there isn't really much to see in the town in the way of interesting buildings, and it is not well provided with restaurants (this means that a visit to the fruit restaurant and to one of the better fish restaurants is practically mandatory), the Zócalo redeems all this. White-paved, and with attractive cast iron lampstands and benches, and surrounded by the impressive cathedral, governor's palace and colonial-style hotels, the place comes alive in the evening at weekends. All Veracruz parades here: the combination of the crush of people, colour, marimba music in the flood-lit setting is very impressive.

"The local beach snakes along the waterfront, but is filthy and the water even worse (ever seen brown waves?), but a short bus ride takes you to the out-of-town Mocambo beach, This has all the facilities—a good swimming bath, beach restaurants, caribbean-style beach huts—and the water is quite a bit cleaner though still rather uninviting a colour. The gulf is even warmer than the Caribbean. Mocambo is not for the solitary minded, unless you get there before seven in the morning."

Sunday trip: to Mandinga for cheap fresh sea food—big prawns. Native entertainment.

Hotels *Mocambo*, 8 km. out on Mocambo Beach; *Veracruz* (new, big, air-conditioned with swimming pool and night club), on Plaza Constitución, US$11 s, US$13-US$29 d); *Emporio* (swimming pool, night club); *Villa del Mar* (blvd. M. Avila Camacho); *Diligencias; Colonial; Impala,* on Calle Orizaba, US$3.50 s, with bath and hot water, clean, near bus station; *Prendes.* Many hotels in port area, including *Hotel Royalty,* US$5 d, nice and clean, near beach, 20 min. walk from Zócalo; *Hotel México,* US$2.20 p.p., with bathroom, clean, secure; *Hotel Latino,* near bus station, US$3.20 d; *Hotel La Santilla,* pleasant, US$5.60 d, incl. fan; *La Paz,* Av. Díaz Mirón 1242, nr. bus station, US$6.40 d, with bath, highly recommended, cheap, clean and helpful; *Hotel Córdoba,* US$3 s, good value; *Hotel Cheto,* near bus station, overpriced; *Hotel Amparo,* 68 Calle A. Serdán, US$4.50 d, adequate. *Hotel Mar y Tierra,* US$6, good value, some rooms with balconies overlooking the harbour. *Hotel Central,* US$5-8 d; *Hotel Vigo,* Avenida Landero y Casa, US$3.70 d; and on same street *Hotel Santillana,* both in the port area, and reached by bus from the bus terminal. Two more on Miguel Lerdo, near the Portales: *Rías* and *Concha Dorada.*

Excursion Isla de Sacrificios, half an hour from the harbour, beautiful beach (trip US$0.80 return). Trips Sundays and holidays, every hour between 0900 and 1400. Excursion to Zempoala (see page 834), buses from ADO terminal 1½ hrs. each way, *via* Candel.

Restaurants *La Parroquia* (original), *Hotel Colonial, Prendes,* also *El Chato Moya* on the Malecón and the market for excellent fish, and *El Azteca de Cayetano* where *mondongos de fruta* are prepared (a selection of all the fruits in season on one plate!) *Torros* are the local drinks made of eggs, milk, fruit and alcohol—delicious and potent! *El Nuevo Vaso de Leche; El Azteca; La Paella,* Plaza Constitución, has its name written into the concrete of the entrance floor, no sign otherwise; *El Unico,* cheap Mexican dishes. *Restaurant Silver,* on the Malecón, good and cheap. There is a good local fish restaurant near the fish market in the street running parallel to Av. 16 de Septiembre, not far from the central square. Fruit-only restaurant in the Plazuela La Campana, with exotic fruit salads and drinks.

Transport For local buses, get accurate information from the friendly tourist office on the Zócalo, in the Palacio Municipal. Buses to the main bus station run along Av. 5 de Mayo. Bus from Mexico City, US$3.50 (6 hrs.), *via* Jalapa, misses out Orizaba, Fostía and Córdoba; from Villahermosa US$4.50. from Reynosa US$10.60 (18 hours), from Matamoros US$10 (14 hours). By car or bus S to Puerto Alvarado on the tip of a peninsula and claimed to be the most modern fishing port in the world.

Elizabeth Allen, who has worked there, writes about the Papaloapan region as follows: At Alvarado, cross the Río Papaloapan (Butterfly River) by a toll bridge (US$0.50), go along Route 180, on the coastal sand dunes past the estuary of the river and lagoons below, into the sugar-cane area around Lerdo de Tejada and Angel R. Cabada. At El Trópico a dirt road turns left to some quiet beaches such as Salinas and Roca Partida, reached by car and by bus. Only at Easter are the beaches crowded: they are normally the preserve of fishermen using hand nets from small boats. In the dry season (Dec.-May) the road is passable around the coast to Sontecomapan.

At Tula, a little further along the main road, is a spectacular waterfall—El Salto de Tula—a restaurant is set beside the falls. The road then climbs up into the mountainous volcanic area of Los Tuxtlas, known as the Switzerland of Mexico for its mountains and perennial greenness.

Santiago Tuxtla, set on a river, is a small town of Colonial origin. In the main square is the largest known Olmec head carved in solid stone, and also a recently opened museum containing modern and historical exhibits, open 0900-1500, Sat.-Sun. 0900-1200 and 1500-1800 hrs. Not only are there examples of local tools, photos, items used in witchcraft *(brujería)* but there are also the first cane press used in Mexico and another Olmec head.

The archaeological site of **Tres Zapotes** lies to the west but is reached by leaving the paved road south towards Villa Isla and taking either the dirt road at Tres Caminos (signposted) in the dry season (a quagmire from May-Dec.) or in the wet season access can be slowly achieved by turning right at about km. 40, called Tibernal, and following the dirt road north to the site of the Museum which is open 0900-1700 hrs. (If it is closed, the lady in the nearby shop has a key.) There is another Olmec head, also the largest carved stela ever found and stela fragments bearing the New World's oldest Long Count Date, equal to 31 B.C. Not far from Tres Zapotes are three other archaeological sites: Cerro de las Mesas, Laguna de los Cerros, and San Lorenzo Tenochtitlán (Olmec sites).

Overlooking Santiago Tuxtla is the hillside restaurant *El Balcón,* which, apart from the spectacular view of the town and the mountains, serves excellent langostino (crayfish) for US$4 and *horchata de coco,* a drink made from the flesh and milk of coconut.

15 km. beyond lies **San Andrés Tuxtla,** the largest town of the area, with narrow winding streets, fortunately now by-passed by a ring road, usually lined with lorries and heavy traffic. This town is also Colonial in style and has a well-stocked market with a number of foods of Oaxacan style such at *totopos, carne enchilada,* and *tamales de elote* (hard tortillas, spicy meat, and cakes of maize-flour steamed on leaves). It is the terminal for trains (daily) from Rodríguez Clara to the south and it is the centre of the cigar trade. It is said that the best tobacco in the world is produced on these rich volcanic soils; drying houses can be seen beside the road to Catemaco, and there are a number of cigar producers in the town. One factory beside the main road permits visitors to watch the process and will produce special orders of cigars *(puros),* marked with an individual's name, in ½ hour. Other producers are Flor de Oaxaca (boxes from US$8) and Ejecutivos. Near the town centre is the restaurant *La Flor de Guadalajara*; it appears small from the outside but is large and pleasant inside, well recommended. Sells *tepache,* a drink made from pineapple, similar in flavour to cider, and *agua de jamaica.* Hotels: *Colonial, Figueroa, Hotel del Parque,* Madero 5, US$9.60 d, air conditioned, very clean, good restaurant); *Casa de Huéspedes La Orizabana,* in the centre of town, US$1.75 d, without bath, clean, hot water, friendly.

At Sihuapan, 5 km. towards Catemaco, is a turning to the right onto a very bumpy dirt road which leads to the impressive waterfall of Salto de Eyipantla. Bridge toll payable at Comoapan, US$0.10, plenty of small boys offer themselves as guides at the falls to explain (most of) the details.

Catemaco, a pleasant little town (15,000 people) with large Colonial church and picturesque situation on lake, 13 km. from San Andrés Tuxtla. Beware of thieves at all times. *Hotel Catemaco,* US$7.50 d, excellent food and swimming pool (monkey meat, *chango,* a local speciality, served at the Hotel) and *Hotel Berthangel,* similar prices; both on main square of Catemaco town. *Hotel Tío Tin,* older, with views of lake, US$4 s, no food, but close to good restaurants beside lake, on which boats are for hire; *Hotel Playa Azul,* some km. away from Catemaco, US$15 d, modern, comfortable and shady, with water-skiing on lake. A number of hotels are situated at the lakeside; *Posada Komiapan* (swimming-pool and restaurant) is very comfortable,

US$10 s. On the promenade are a number of good restaurants—*La Julita* (*anguila* and *tacholgolo*), *La Ola* (*payiscadas, anguila, tegogalos, carne de chango,* and *cesina*) built almost entirely by the owner in the local natural materials, and *La Luna*, among others. At weekends there is a stall selling handicrafts from Oaxaca, and boat trips out on the lakes to see the shrine where the Virgin appeared, the spa at Coyame and the Isla de Chagos, and to make a necklace of lilies are always available (about US$5). The town is noted for its *brujos* (sorcerers) and the Monte del Cerro Blanco to the north is the site of their annual reunion. Catemaco can be reached by bus from Veracruz, changing to a local bus at San Andrés Tuxtla.

The Gulf Coast may be reached from Catemaco by car or by bus along a dirt road. It is about 10 km. to Sontecomapan, crossing over the pass at Buena Vista and looking down to the Laguna where, it is said, Francis Drake sought refuge. A large part of this area has been deforested, but part is preserved for study by the Universidad Nacional Autónoma de México and virgin jungle may still be seen from the road. The village of **Sontecomapan** (1.465 pop.) lies on an entry to the Laguna and boats may be hired for the 20-min. ride out to the Bar where the Laguna meets the sea (US$10 return). A large part of the Laguna is surrounded by mangrove swamp, but the sweep of the bright green volcanic slopes coming down to the coast is breathtaking and the sandy beaches, edged by cliffs, are almost deserted except for local fishermen and groups of pelicans. Two good restaurants in Sontecomapan. The whole of the coastal area to the west and the Laguna are to be developed as a fishing zone, but beaches are accessible to those who enjoy isolation—such as Jical, Playa Escondida (small hotel, US$5 a night and superb cooking), Montepilo, Playa Hermosa. At Easter time many people from the nearby towns camp on the beaches. Catemaco is about 120 km. NW of Minatitlán.

At Acayucán, 267 km. from Veracruz, turn right for Route 185 if you want to go across the Isthmus to Tehuantepec and Tuxtla Gutiérrez and Central America but continue on Route 180 for Minatitlán, Coatzacoalcos and Villahermosa (Tabasco). The road across the Isthmus is straight but is not always a fast road to drive because of high winds (changing air systems from Pacific to Atlantic). Gasoline and food on sale at the half-way point, Palomares (where there is a paved road to Tuxtepec, 2½ hours' drive). A few miles south of Palomares a gravelled road enters on the eastern side; this passes under an imposing gateway "La Puerta de Uxpanapa" where some 2,500 families are being settled in the jungle. An hour's drive further south the road crosses the watershed and passes across the flat coastal plain to Juchitán.

About 15 km. from Alvarado a new bridge replaces the old ferry-crossing at Buenavista over the Papaloapan River and the road heads southwards to the fishing village of **Tlacotalpan** where the Papaloapan and San Juan rivers meet. Turtles, clams, shrimps and crayfish are sold here or shipped by road to be sold at the fish market in Alvarado with their final destination in Mexico City. Tlacotalpan consists of amazing streets with one storey houses all fronted by lovely arcades and colonnades; there is a famous fiesta there on January 31st. The stuccoed Romanesque and Classical columns and arches are painted in various bright pastel colours. Two churches in the Zócalo. The *Viajero* and *Reforma* hotels are good. Excellent *sopa de mariscos* and *Jaiba a la Tlacotalpina* (crab) at the Restaurant *La Flecha*. Buses go to Veracruz *via* Alvarado, to San Andrés, Tuxtla Gutiérrez and to Villahermosa.

Cosamaloapan, some 40 km. beyond Tlacotalpan, is the local market centre with a number of hotels, and the staging point for most bus lines from Veracruz, Orizaba and Oaxaca. The largest sugar mill in Mexico is situated just outside the town—Ingenio San Cristóbal—and there is a local airstrip. From Cosamaloapan to Papaloapan the banks on either side of the river are lined with fruit trees such as mangoes (the best are produced in Chacaltianguis on the east bank of the river, reached by car ferry; like Tlacotalpan, it has houses fronted by columns), oranges, avocados, pomelos (sweet grapefruit) and sugar-cane.

40 km. beyond Cosamaloapan is a ferry point for the crossing to **Otatitlán**, also on the east bank of the river. The passenger ferry leaves whenever there are sufficient passengers (US$0.08 the ride). At the embarkation is *Restaurant-Bar Pepe*, which serves delicious food unlikely to be found in many places—turtle, lizard, crayfish, armadillo, shrimps, steaks etc.

Otatitlán, also known as El Sanctuario, is well worth a visit. The town dates back to early Colonial times, its houses with tiled roofs supported by columns, but most interesting is the church. The padre maintains that the gold-patterned dome is the largest unsupported structure of its kind in Mexico, measuring 20 metres wide and 40 high. El Sanctuario is a place of pilgrimage; it has one of the three black wooden statues of Christ brought over from Spain for the son of Hernán Cortés. Legend has it that this effigy was brought up from the coast on a raft, destined for Oaxaca, but three times the raft broke away and came to a halt at the place where Otatitlán now stands. It was installed in the church and during the anti-clerical violence of the 1930s attempts to burn it failed, although the original head was amputated and now stands in a glass case. The first weekend in May is the saint's day and fair, for which pilgrims flock in from the sierra and from the Tuxtlas, many in local dress. The *Restaurant-Bar Ipiranga III* by the ferry embarkation offers excellent cuisine and is highly recommended. The balcony there makes a suitable viewpoint for the annual motorboat race held in mid-May.

Papaloapan is on the eastern bank of the river, and despite the perseverance of the inhabitants who continue to defy harsh floods, has little of note except as a route centre. At this point the main road from Orizaba to Rodríguez Clara crosses the main road from Alvarado to Oaxaca; the railway station serves trains to Yucatán and Chiapas coming from Orizaba or Veracruz. On the west bank of the river is the bus terminal of Santa Cruz (almost under the railway bridge) where all second class buses stop and connections can be made in all directions. A passenger ferry may be taken from here to Papaloapan (US$0.08). Although Papaloapan is the route centre for the area the most convenient centre for visiting this region is Tuxtepec, 9 km. further south (see page 832).

The river basin drained by the Papaloapan and its tributaries covers some 47,000 sq. km.—about twice the size of the Netherlands—and is subject to a programme of regional development by the Comisión del Papaloapan, which includes the construction of two large dams to control the sometimes severe flooding of the lower basin. To date, one dam, the Presidente Alemán dam, has been completed at Temascal. This aims to control flooding on the River Tonto and provide hydro-electricity; another dam is to be built on the River Santo Domingo to control those waters before the two rivers merge to form the Papaloapan.

The lake formed behind the dam is scenically very attractive and boats may be hired to go to settlements on the islands or on the other side. There is also a daily ferry passing round the lake. **Soyaltepec** is the closest settlement, situated high above the water on an island, the peak crowned by a church. This island and surrounding settlements are inhabited by Mazatec Indians, and locally made handicrafts, huipiles, tablecloths, etc. may be bought. **Ixcatlan** lies on a peninsula jutting into the lake on the SE side; it has one hotel and one restaurant, as well as a large beer repository. Ixcatlan may also be reached by dirt road from Tuxtepec, but it is less nerve-racking to take a ferry! The lake is used for commercial fishing of native and imported *mojarra* (experimental fish farm in the village) which are sent for sale to Alvarado and Mexico City. The *mojarra* cooked in this region are excellent fish with good flavour and few bones.

Temascal (Sunday is the most active day) may be reached by taking Route 145 from Papaloapan through Gabino Barreda, Ciudad Alemán (no facilities, centre of the Papaloapan Commission) Novara (petrol and 3 restaurants of varying prices, 1 air-conditioned), as far as La Granja where the turn to Temascal is clearly marked. The road is paved and straight, continuing on to **Tierra Blanca** (a regional centre, railway junction, shopping centre, market, hotels, car repairs, e.g. Volkswagen agent, *Bimbis* restaurant by ADO bus station, good) and thence to join the main Orizaba-Veracruz road (Route 150) at Tinajas after passing under a sign saying "La Puerta del Papaloapan".

In this area scattered oilfields are being exploited (flares gleam at night) but it is quite dry and irrigation is often necessary. **Tinajas** is a second-class bus junction, also gasoline, and restaurants (1 air-condtioned at service station). Papaloapan to Tinajas takes about 1 hour, the road often has a lot of lorries and in the cane-cutting season great care should be taken at night for carts travelling on the road without lights. There are three railway crossings on the road, also poorly marked, two near La Granja and one near Tierra Blanca. The tarmac is often damaged in the wet season (June-Dec.).

Near to Papaloapan and beside Route 145 is the town of **Tres Valles**, now developing an industrial complex of paper mill and sugar mill, which is a railway and bus halt. There is activity and life, bustle and movement and cheap, good food of regional style can be found on the main plaza and opposite the railway station. In the evening, a street vendor on the road from the plaza to the main street sells *atole de coyol* (a local drink), stuffed bananas and *tacos* which are highly recommended. The annual fair is in mid-Nov.

From Papaloapan a paved road runs eastwards as far as Rodríguez Clara (planned to continue to Sayula on the Trans-Isthmic road). This road passes through the main pineapple-producing region of Mexico, which has encouraged the development of towns such as **Loma Bonita** (local airstrip, hotels and restaurants, pineapple-packing and canning plants—pineapples can be bought beside the railway station—gasoline) and **Villa Isla** (hotels, *La Choca* restaurant good, railway station, ADO bus terminal, and centre for the rich cattle-producing area that surrounds it).

From Villa Isla a good dirt road runs south to **Playa Vicente** (6,974 pop.), through undulating country opened in the last 25 years from jungle to grassland. This town is full of ranching life, located beside a wide river, and excellent crayfish may be eaten at the *Restaurant La Candileja*, while the café on the central plaza produces steaks which are tender and tasty. Another dirt road leaves the Villa Isla-Playa Vicente road for Abasolo del Valle (2,000 pop.), but only reaches to within 7 km. The last few kms. can be impassable by vehicle in the wet season. There are no hotels in Abasolo and no restaurants but the town is set beside a lagoon and the houses are surrounded by fruit trees. Gasoline can be bought—ask at a shop who has some to sell.

At the cross-roads of the Papaloapan-Sayula road about 80 km. from Papaloapan, where the S turn is to Villa Isla, the N turn is a paved road which in about ¼ hour will take you past two turnings to Tres Zapotes and up to Santiago Tuxtla.

The road from Papaloapan continues E to a point just N of **Rodríguez Clara**, which is reached by branching off S down a dirt road. This is a compact, thriving town, also with a railway station and providing agricultural services for the farmers in the area. There are 2 hotels, the better is in the centre of the town, *Hotel Roa* (US$2.50 p.p.); *Restaurant Mexicana* recommended for meals.

The railway line from Papaloapan follows the same general direction as the road, weaving its way between the fruit trees, pineapples and cattle pastures towards the Isthmus. It is the only all-year means of transport to visit the villages and towns E of Rodríguez Clara.

Tuxtepec is the natural centre for a stay to get to know the Papaloapan area. It lies some 9 km. south of Papaloapan (toll for Caracol bridge, US$0.40) and is a small market town at the junction between the mountains and the lowlands. Consequently the streets are alive every day with Indians who have come from surrounding villages to buy and sell, and there is a fascinating mixture of the music and exuberance of Veracruz with the food and handicrafts of Oaxaca. The town is built on a meander of the Santo Domingo River and a walk past the main shops in Calle Independencia will allow two halts at viewpoints for the river.

Hotels *El Rancho* (restaurant, bar, evening entertainment, most expensive, recommended); *Tuxtepec* (good value); *Sacre* (also good, basic); *Mirador*. Very good value is the *Casa de Huéspedes La Jarochita* in Independencia round the corner from ADO bus station at US$3.20 s—bathroom *and* ventilator. There are others.

Restaurants *El Estero* (fish dishes and local cuisine excellent), *El Mino* (near Fletes y Pasajes bus terminal), *Mandinga* for fish dishes, *Queso Fundido* in Independencia. Beer from the barrel can be bought from the bar next to the Palacio Municipal, and the best ices are found in *La Morida*.

Transport   ADO bus services to Mexico City, Veracruz and regular daily minibus (taking 5-6 hrs.) to Oaxaca leaving at 0800 and 1230, US$1.06. The Oaxaca-Tuxtepec journey is beautiful, with mountains, tropical rainforests on the way through Valle Nacional; the road is in acceptable condition. AU (Autobuses Unidos) daily to wide variety of destinations—sometimes called the "aaagh-oooh!" for the drivers' style. Fletes y Pasajes to local villages and Juchitán; Cristóbal Colón sometimes stop by the ADO office to find passengers for Chiapas or Mexico City. Two service stations adjacent to the road. The road Tuxtepec-Palomares is now open and provides a short cut to the Trans-Istmica; it passes through many newly-felled jungle areas. There are scattered villages, the main halt being at María Lombardo (some 2 hrs. from Tuxtepec where food is sold); Zócalo is attractive. Gas station being built 4 km. further on at Cihualtepec junction, a village of Indians from the area flooded by the Temascal.

Excursions   To Temascal, also a visit to the Indian villages of Ojitlán and Jalapa de Díaz is well worth the ride; easily reached by car along paved road and also by AU bus service.

The Chinatec Indians' handicrafts may be bought on enquiry; hotels non-existent and eating facilities limited but some superb scenery, luxuriant vegetation and little-visited area. Part of the area will be flooded when the Cerro de Oro dam is finished and the lake will join that of Temascal.

Tuxtepec northward to **Tierra Blanca**, 1½ hrs., US$0.50 (hotel *Casa de Huéspedes El Viajero*, US$2.65, on main street, clean and friendly). Mérida train from Tierra Blanca leaves late although scheduled for 0530 (2nd class, US$2.30, crowded) stops at Palenque, 15½ hrs. later. Train also stops at Ciudad Alemán on the way.

Industries   Fábricas de Papel Tuxtepec, drying of barbasco (for contraceptive pills), rubber processing, sugar milling.

The road from Tuxtepec south to Oaxaca (Route 175) is now well paved, and although it has many sharp curves, requiring careful driving and a car in good condition, it is a spectacular route. Best to start early in the day to make the most of daylight; it takes about 5 hours to drive. It passes the new López Mateos sugar mill and up Valle Nacional. This valley, despite its horrific reputation as the "Valley of the Dead" or "Valle de los Miserables" in the era of Porfirio Díaz, for political imprisonment and virtual slavery from which there was no escape, is astoundingly beautiful. The road follows the valley floor, often alongside the Río Valle Nacional, and the mountain slopes are generally covered with rich, green vegetation or small cultivated plots. On the valley bottom are cattle pastures, fruit trees and a chain of small villages such as Chiltepec (very good bathing in the river), Jacatepec (reached by ferry over the river, produces rich honey and abounds in all varieties of fruit, there are no cars at all), Monte Flor (where swimming and picknicking are possible beside natural springs, but *very* cold water, and an archaeological site) and finally Valle Nacional. The road crosses the river here—an attractive viewpoint—and the steep curves begin. (No hotels, but restaurants, stores, and gasoline available.) The road climbs up into the Sierra, getting cooler, and slopes more heavily vegetated with tropical forest, and there are panoramic views down into the valleys below, across to cascading waterfalls and back down into the Papaloapan Basin.

San Pedro Yolox lies some 20 minutes' drive W of this route down a dirt road; it is a peaceful Chinantec village clustered on the side of the mountain, while Llano de Flores is a huge grassy clearing in the pine forest with grazing animals and cool, scented air. Wood from these forests is cut for the paper factory in Tuxtepec. Ixtlán de Juárez is a small town, set beside the road, and acting as a market centre (gasoline). While houses in the lowlands are made of wood with palm roofs, here the houses are of adobe or brick. Guelatao is the birthplace of President Benito Juárez, the Indian who became Mexico's great national leader in the mid-19th century; there are a memorial and a museum to him built on the hillside within the village (entry US$0.16) and a pleasant, quiet lake with a statue of a shepherd and his lambs. From here it is about 1½ hours' drive, mainly downhill, to Oaxaca (see page 842), with the land becoming drier and the air warmer.

Connections with Guatemala   There are no through buses to Guatemala, but there are connecting services. Train leaves Veracruz 0915 daily for Ixtepec and Tapachula;

continues to Guatemalan border, 1st class (recommended), US$7.70, 2nd US$1.60. Take your own toiletries and food. No sleeping accommodation. Connection for Guatemala City arrives the same evening, though the Guatemalan railways are not recommended. (Mexican 1st-class railway accommodation quite good.) Local bus services run Tapachula-Tecún Omán-Guatemala City; quicker than more mountainous route to the N. Alternatively, take ADO bus from Veracruz to Oaxaca (US$6.20 1st class), departures morning and evening, then carry on to Tapachula (11½ hrs.) by bus. Further bus to frontier at Hidalgo, US$0.25. This route allows you to stop at intermediate points of your choice, but has few "comfort" stops. Buy bus tickets out in Veracruz well in advance. (See also page 842).

By the road we have followed, the driving time from Mexico City to Veracruz is about 9 hours. We can return to the Capital by a shorter route through Jalapa which takes 6 hours; this was the old Colonial route to the port, and is the way the railway goes today.

Jalapa, capital of Veracruz state, 132 km. from the port, is in the *tierra templada,* at 1,425 metres. A curious thing about Jalapa is that there seems to have been a passion for renovation in the flamboyant Gothic style during the first part of the 19th century. It is yet another "City of Flowers", with walled gardens, stone-built houses, wide avenidas in the newer town and steep cobbled crooked streets in the old. The 18th century cathedral, with its sloping floor, has been recently restored. Population 127,000. A good centre for exploring mountains, rivers, waterfalls and many interesting villages. Just outside is a splendid modern museum showing archaeological treasures of the Olmec, Totonac and Huastec coastal cultures of ancient Mexico. The three colossal heads dating from the 2nd to the 5th centuries A.D., and displayed in the grounds of the museum, are Olmec. Jalapa (spelt Xalapa locally) has a University; you can take a pleasant stroll round the grounds, known as El Dique.

Hotels New *Hotel del Pardo,* probably the best, but noisy; *María Victoria,* from US$15 s, also recommended; *Limón,* US$3.20 s, with shower; *Hotel Regis,* US$3.75 d, with hot shower, US$1.60 s, with hot shower (recommended); *México,* US$3.60 s, with shower; *Principal; Salmones; Dulcilandia,* on Revolución.

Restaurants *La Parroquia,* Zaragoza 18, recommended; *El Escorial; La Cocina Económica; Enrico,* good value; *El Mayab,* next to *Hotel Regis,* for Mexican *antojitos; El Escorial; La Tasca,* recommended.

Theatre Teatro del Estado, Av. Avila Camacho; good Ballet Folklórico Veracruzano and fair symphony orchestra.

Airport 15 km. SE, on Veracruz road.

Communications Radio-telephone available opposite *Hotel María Victoria.*

Festival Feria de Primavera, mid-April.

Excursions To ruins of **Zempoala,** the coastal city which was conquered by Cortés and whose inhabitants became his allies. The ruins are interesting because of the round stones uniquely used in construction. (Entry US$0.40, small museum on site.) Take 2nd class bus to Zempoala *via* Candel, which will let you off at the ruins, or take a taxi from the Plaza de Zempoala, US$1.20 return. You can also get there from Veracruz (see page 828).

Tim Connell writes, about excursions from Jalapa: "**Naolinco** is ½ hour ride 40 km. NE of Jalapa up a winding hilly road, rather like a tropical Devon! *Restaurant La Fuente* serves local food; has nice garden. Las Cascadas, with a mirador to admire them from, are on the way into the town: 2 waterfalls, with various pools, tumble several thousand feet over steep wooded slopes. Hordes of zopilotes (buzzards) collect late in the afternoon, soaring high up into the thermals. Baños Carrizal: 8 km. off main road, 40 km. from Veracruz. Chachalacas is a beach with swimming pool and changing facilities in *hotel* of same name, US$0.70 adults.

Thatched huts; local delicacies sold on beach, including *robalito* fish. **La Antigua:** collection of Totonac ruins, plus Colonial church, near the main coast-road toll booths for Veracruz (US$0.50 toll)''.

Easily reached by road from Mexico City and Jalapa, but a good distance to the N, is **Papantla** (which is also easily reached from Veracruz, 4 hrs., by bus, good road) and through tropical scenery, between Nautla and Poza Rica. Papantla is interesting in itself; men and women come to market in the local costume. There is one good hotel on the main square, Papantla is also the centre of the vanilla-producing zone, and small figures and animals made in vanilla are for sale, as well as the essence.

Hotels *Pulido*, new and recommended, US$3.50 s or d, with bath, parking; *Hotel Papantla*, on Zócalo; *Trujillo*, Calle 5 de Mayo; *Tajín*, Calle Dr. Núñez, with restaurant and bars.

Restaurant *Las Porisas del Golfo*, Calle Dr. Núñez, reasonable and very good.

A few km. away, in the forest, is **Tajin** (reached by taxi) the ruined capital of the Totonac culture (6th to 10th century), entry, US$0.10. At the centre of this vast complex is the Pyramid of El Tajín, whose 365 squared openings make it look like a vast beehive. Here a remarkable ceremony takes place on Corpus Christi. Totonac rain dancers erect a 30-metre mast with a rotating structure at the top. Four *voladores* (flyers) and a musician climb to the surmounting platform. There the musician dances to his own pipe and drum music, whilst the roped *voladores* throw themselves into space to make a dizzy spiral descent, sometimes head up, sometimes head down, to the ground. This colourful ceremony of the *voladores* also takes place every Saturday at 1400, cost US$0.80. Not all sizes of camera film stocked at the site shop.

Also between Nautla and Poza Rica, to the E of Papantla and on the coast is **Tecolutla,** a charming small resort on the river of that name. *Hotels Tecolutla,* and *Marsol* are on the beach. *Posada Guadalupe* and *Casa de Huéspedes Malena* are on Avenida Carlos Prieto, near the river landing stage.

Eight km. W of Jalapa, where the road begins to climb, the Lecuona family has a fine orchard and tropical flower garden, which is now overgrown and unkempt. The road continues to climb to Perote, 53 km. from Jalapa. The San Carlos fort here, now a military prison, was built in 1770-77; there is a good view of Cofre de Perote volcano. The old convent at **Acatzingo,** 93 km. beyond, is worth looking at. Another 10 km. and we join the road to Puebla and Mexico City.

Mt. Orizaba From Acatzingo one can go *via* a paved road to Tlachichuca (35 km.) and contact the Reyes family to get a jeep-type car to go up an appalling road to a hut on Mount Orizaba, one of the highest peaks in Mexico (Cizantépetl) (5,700 metres). There is no hut custodian; it's usually fairly empty, except on Sat. night. No food or light, or wood; provide your own. There is a glacier some 150 metres above the hut. Water close at hand, but no cooking facilities.

Mexico City-Cuernavaca-Taxco-Acapulco

The country behind the resort of Acapulco is so difficult that no railway has ever reached it. Now a 450-km. road, beginning as a 4-lane toll motorway, leaves Mexico City at 2,300 metres, climbs to 3,100 metres, and descends again to Acapulco. (The 4-lane ends at Iguala, 209 km. from Acapulco.) Driving time is about 6 hours. The new road by-passes Taxco, but this superb town can be reached by the old road (no toll), which is in good condition.

The highest point, La Cima, 3,016 metres, is reached at km. 42. The road spirals down through precipitous forests to

(Km. 75) **Cuernavaca,** capital of Morelos state, at 1,542 metres: 724 metres less, that is, than the altitude of Mexico City. Because of its comfortable climate, the city has always attracted visitors from the more rigorous highlands. The Spaniards captured it in 1521 and Cortés himself, following the custom of the Aztec nobility, lived in it. The outskirts are dotted with the ultra-modern walled homes of writers, film-stars and members of the international set, and the summer houses of people from Mexico City; golf links, naturally. There is much to enjoy. The Cathedral (frescoes) stands at one end of an enclosed garden. By the entrance to it stands the charming small Church of the Tercera Orden (1529), whose quaint façade carved by Indian craftsmen contains a small figure suspected to be one of the only two statues of Cortés in Mexico. (The other is a mounted statue near the entrance of the *Casino de la Selva* hotel.) The palace Cortés built in 1531 for his second wife stands near the city's central tree-shaded plaza; on the rear balcony is a Diego Rivera mural depicting the conquest of Mexico. It was the seat of the State Legislature until 1967, when the new legislative building opposite was completed; it has now become a museum, showing everything from dinosaur remains to contemporary Indian culture. The 18th century Borda Gardens, on Calle Morelos, were a favourite resort of Maximilian and Carlota (small fee), but have now more or less run rampant. The weekend retreat of the ill-fated imperial couple, in the Acapantzingo district, is being restored. Other places worth seeing are the three plazas, Calle Guerrero, and, some distance from the main plaza, the new market buildings on different levels. The very unusual Teopanzolco pyramid is to be found near the railway station. Remarkable frescoes have recently been found in the old Franciscan church of La Parroquia. On Sundays, divers perform in San Antón for small donations. Population 125,000. The temperature never exceeds 27°C nor falls below 10°C, and there is almost daily sunshine even during the rainy season. Cuernavaca is called Cuauhnahuac, the original Aztec version of its name, in Malcolm Lowry's *Under the Volcano*; it is also distinguished for an excellent Spanish-language school, Cale, and there is a new co-operative language centre, called Cuauhnahuac, with Spanish courses, at 1414 Ave. Morelos Sur. Intensive courses also at Instituto Fénix, San Jerónimo 304, which also has excursions and minor courses in politics, art and music; and at Cemanahmac Calle San Juan 4, Las Palmas, which includes weaving and pottery classes.

The Sunday morning masses at 1100 at the superbly restored Cathedral are accompanied by a special mariachi band and have a singularly free and exhilarating ritual. Go early for a seat. The bishop mingles with the congregation in the Cathedral garden after the service.

Hotels *Papagayo; Mandel; Capri; Baños; Colón; Miller's "El Buen Retiro"*, in a park. Hotel-restaurant *Las Mañanitas* (delightful), Mexican colonial style, many birds in lovely gardens. Excellent food. *Hotel Casino de la Selva*, with huge mural by Siqueiros on the future of humanity from now till A.D. 3000; *Del Parque*, moderate, on main square; *Hostería Las Quintas*, new, built in traditional Mexican style, owner has splendid collection of bonsai trees; *Hostería Peñalba*, US$7 d, beautiful courtyard setting, was once Zapata's H.Q. during the Revolution (warmly recommended); *Casa de Huéspedes*, Morelos Sur 702, good value at US$8 a day including 3 good meals; for economy, *Hotel Roma* in Calle Matamoros, US$4.25 d, clean, excellent value, with hot water and shower; *Royal Hotel*, US$2.80 s. Several cheaper hotels in Calles Aragón and León, including *El Buen Vecino, Casa La Paz, Mariló, Posada San José, Hotel Francis,* and *América,* US$3 (couples only).

Near Cuernavaca is the *Hacienda de Cocoyoc*, an old converted *hacienda* with a swimming pool backed by the mill aqueduct. Glorious gardens, 18-hole golf-course, tennis and riding, US$24 d.

Motels *Los Canarios; Jacaranda; Arocena Holiday. Suits OK Motel*, 27 rooms, bungalows, double US$60 a week, trailer park; accommodation for students with communal kitchen, US$2 a day each; swimming pool and squash courts; at entrance to Cuernavaca, Bld. Emiliano Zapata 825. Tel.: (731) 3-12-70.

Restaurants *Las Mañanitas* (see above); *Harry's Bar* (New York style); *Los Arcos,* in Zócalo, good, prices reasonable, full at weekends. *Restaurant Chispas,* excellent. *Château Renel,* Swiss-European cuisine, in woods above town. *Peña El Picaflor,* Club on Zócalo, evening from 2000, live music, refreshments, cover charge US$1, good. *Madreterra,* vegetarian, in pretty patio near Cortés Palace, Sunday lunch with live music. *Portal,* nearby, in Calle Galinea, has good cheap breakfasts.

Tourist Office At top of the Cathedral street, by the entrance of the Borda Gardens. Very helpful.

Excursions To the newly opened Chapultepec Park, just outside town, with boating facilities, small zoo, water gardens, small admission charge. To the Potters' village of San Antón, perched above a waterfall, a little W of the town. To the charming village of **Acapantzingo,** S of the town, another retreat of Maximilian. To the village of **Tepoztlán**—24 km.—isolated, picturesque steep cobbled streets, wild view, with a pyramid high up in the mountains (the climb is an hour long, and strenuous, but the view is magnificent) and a remarkable 16th century church and convent: the Virgin and Child stand upon a crescent moon above the elaborated Plateresque portal (*Posada del Tepozteco,* a very good inn with swimming pool). There is a small archaeological museum behind the church. This was the village studied by Robert Redfield and later by Oscar Lewis. Local bus from Cuernavaca Market bus terminal takes 40 mins.

Near Cuernavaca is Chalcatzingo, where there are interesting Olmec-style rock carvings.

Buses From Mexico City, frequent buses to Cuernavaca (every 15 minutes from Central del Sur, Mexico City, US$0.80, 1 hour). To Taxco, Flecha Roja, 2nd-class buses, US$0.72, 2¼ hours, fairly comfortable, or Estrella de Oro, 1st class, Calzada Tlalpan 2205. Buses to Cacahuamilpa (see below), 2 hours.

Warning There are many and notorious thieves stealing luggage from waiting buses in Cuernavaca; don't ever leave belongings unattended!

(Km. 100) **Alpuyeca,** whose church has good Indian murals. A road to the left runs to the largest sugar mill in the country, at Zacatepec, and to **Lake Tequesquitengo** and the lagoon and sulphur baths of Tehuixtla. Near the lake a popular resort—swimming, boating, water skiing and fishing—is *Hotel Vista Hermosa,* once an old ingenio (sugar mill), and several lakeside hotels. From Alpuyeca also a road runs right for 50 km. to the **Cacahuamilpa** caverns, some of the largest caves in North America, open 1000 to 1500 (well lit); strange stalactite and stalagmite formations (entry, US$0.60). They can also be reached from the old Cuernavaca-Acapulco road. Buses going to Cacahuamilpa are usually overcrowded; enquire about schedules for local buses or buses from Taxco to Toluca, which stop there. At 15 km. is the right-hand turn to the **Xochicalco** ruins, a pyramid on the top of a rocky hill, dedicated to the Plumed Serpent whose coils enfold the whole building and enclose fine carvings which represent priests. There are interesting underground buildings; Xochicalco is well worth the 5 km. walk from the bus stop; take a torch for the underground part to save employing a guide. (Flecha Roja bus to Xochicalco from terminal in Ave. Morelos, marked Las Grutas, leaves at 0930.)

(Km. 121) Amacuzac. Leave the toll road here and take the old road for Taxco, 39 km.

Taxco, population 15,000; with steep, twisty, cobbled streets and many picturesque Colonial buildings. The first silver shipped to Spain came from the mines of Taxco. A Frenchman, Borda, made and spent three immense fortunes here in the 1700's, and it was he who founded the present town and built the magnificent twin-towered, rose-coloured parish church of Santa Prisca which soars above everything but the mountains. Well worth a visit are the Casa Humboldt, where Baron von Humboldt once stayed, and the Casa Figueroa, the "House of Tears", so called because the Colonial judge who owned it forced Indian labourers to work on it to pay their fines. The town is a Colonial gem. The roof of every building is of red tile, every nook or corner in the place is a picture, and even the cobblestone streets have patterns woven in them. It is now a national monument and all modern building is forbidden. Gas stations are outside the city limits. The plaza is 1,700 metres above sea-level, but many of the houses are perched 100 metres higher up the mountain and others that much lower down. The climate is ideal, never any high winds (for it is protected by huge mountains immediately to the N); never cold and never hot, but sometimes foggy. Silverwork is a speciality and there are important lead and zinc mines. The processions during Holy Week are spectacular. The most tourist-free part is up from the main street where the taxis can't go. Wear flat rubber-soled shoes to avoid slithering over the cobbles. The two "Sligo" shops are best for silver goods in contemporary design. On the 2nd Sunday in December there is an interesting national silversmiths' competition. Platería La Azteca has good jewellery.

One of the most interesting of Mexican stone-age cultures, the Mezcala or Chontal, is based on the State of Guerrero in which Taxco lies. Its remarkable artefacts, of which there are many imitations are almost surrealist. The culture remained virtually intact into historic times.

Excursion 12 km. from Taxco to Acuitlapán waterfalls, with Flecha Roja bus; hire a horse to travel down 4 km. path to large clear pools for swimming.

Hotels New *Holiday Inn* on a hilltop 400 metres above Taxco, good restaurant, special buses to town; *Victoria; Rancho Taxco; Borda; Santa Prisca; Los Arcos; Hotel Meléndez,* US$6.25 d, good and clean, somewhat noisy as it is near market, meals available; *Hotel Aguas lo Escondidas,* near Zócalo, US$7.15 d, very good value and nice view; *Hotel Casa Grande,* only for the desperate, clean rooms with shower (hot water in mornings only), US$4.05 and US$5.40 d; *Posada Santa Anita,* US$1.75 s, near bus station, clean and very pleasant; *Posada de la Misión* is a good hotel; *Hotel Jardín,* 6 rooms, cheap, clean, view from patio.

Motel *Loma Linda* on highway is satisfactory.

Restaurants *Alarcón,* overlooking Zócalo, very good meal for US$2.80, with everything included. *Sr Costilla,* next to church on main square, good drinks and grilled ribs. Next door is *Papa's Bar,* a discotheque and a small pizza place in an arcade. *Paco's Bar,* at other end of square for drinks and people-watching. Good drinks at *Berta's Bar. Mi Oficina,* straight up hill from where buses from Cuernavaca arrive. Good food at *Los Arcos* and *Victoria* hotels. Many small restaurants just near *Hotel Meléndez,* good value.

Buses Plenty from Mexico City, e.g. Flecha Roja, 2nd class, US$1.80, 4 hrs. (by San Antonio Abad metro station, also by Taxqueña metro station, ask for Calzada Tlalpan, Estrella 26). Reported OK until Cuernavaca, then a very slow trip through back roads and letting people on and off with overcrowding. Buses to Mexico City every hour, but again, crowded up to Cuernavaca. Little 24-seaters, "Los Burritos", take you up the hill from the bus terminal on main road. Spectacular journey from Toluca.

The road descends. The heat grows. We join the main road again at Iguala, 36 km. from Taxco. Beyond the Mexcala river, the road passes for some 30 km. through the dramatic canyon of Zopilote to reach **Chilpancingo,** capital of Guerrero state, at km. 302. Population 32,000, altitude 1,250 metres. The colourful reed bags from the distant village of

Chilapa are sold in the market. Its fiesta starts on December 16 and lasts a fortnight. It has a University. Hotel: *La Posada Mélémdez.* Not far from Chilpancingo are Oxtotitlán and Juxtlahuaca, where Olmec cave paintings can be seen. The road goes down to Acapulco (about 420 km. from Mexico City), rising and dipping until a sudden view of the blue waters of the bay, ringed by green hills, breaks from the top of the ridge.

Warning Avoid travelling by car at night in the State of Guerrero, except on the Mexico City-Acapulco highway. Guerrilleros have been active in recent years.

Acapulco (population 240,000) has of late years become the most popular resort in Mexico. Americans, Europeans, Mexicans pour in, spring and winter, by plane, by fast motor road from Mexico City, and by sea. During Holy Week there is a plane from the capital to the jet airport every 3 minutes. The town stretches for 16 km. in a series of bays and cliff coves and is invading the hills. The hotels, of which there are 250, are mostly perched high to catch the breeze, for between 1130 and 1630 the heat is sizzling. They are filled to overflowing in January and February. It has all the paraphernalia of a booming resort: smart shops, night clubs, quaint red light district, golf club, touts and street vendors. There are some twenty beaches, all with fine, golden sand. The two most popular are the sickle-curved and shielded Caleta, with its smooth water, and the surf-pounded straight beach of Los Hornos. One can swim, and fish, the year round. There are numerous excursions. The lagoons can be explored by motor boats; one, Coyuca Lagoon, is over 110 km. long; strange birds, water hyacinths, tropical flowers. Daily, in the morning and after dark, amazing 40-metre dives into shallow water by boys, for money, can be watched from the Quebrada. There is a jai-alai palace. Acapulco in Colonial times was the terminal for the Manila convoy. Its main defence, Fort San Diego, still stands in the middle of the city and is worth a visit. Pleasant boat trip across beach to Puerto Marqués, US$0.80 return; one can hire small sailing boats there, US$6.50 an hour. Visit island of La Roqueta, glass-bottomed boat, US$0.24 return. Take local bus to La Pie de la Cuesta, 8 km. (*Hotel Villa Rosita*, US$3.30 per day for a bungalow) nice lagoon and big beaches (warning: the surf is dangerous), where you drink "coco loco"—fortified coconut milk—and watch the sunset from a hammock. Beware at all times of thieves.

Hotels can cost up to US$200 a night double. Expensive: *El Presidente; Elcano; Prado-Américas; Acapulco Princess,* built in pyramid-shape, huge open lobby with pools and waterfalls, on Puerto Marqués open-sea beach, many sports facilities, including golf. *Palacio Tropical; Flamingos; Majestic; El Mirador; Caleta; Club de Pesca.* Cheaper: *Bahía; Playa; Del Monte; La Riviera; Ritz; Aloha; Mallorca; La Quebreta Panamericana; Las Hamacas,* etc. The *Hilton* hotel is a resort in itself. The *Casablanca Tropical,* US$20 s, with swimming pool, is recommended; so is the *Hotel del Pacífico,* on Caleta beach, US$23 d including huge breakfast. The fabulous *Club Residencial de las Brisas* is a private club rather than a hotel proper. (It begins as sea-level and reaches up the mountain slope in a series of detached villas and public rooms to a point 300 metres above sea-level. Guests use pink jeeps to travel to the dining-room and recreation areas.) The *Acapulco Princess Country Club,* part of the *Acapulco Princess,* 20 km. away on Revolcadero Beach, is highly fashionable. Good is the *Sutter* (US$3 s a day in the high season). Nearby *Casa de Huéspedes,* closer to Zócalo, US$4.50 d, with fan and bath. *Hotel La Cima,* good position, good food, US$10 a day full board. *Hotel Marsella,* centre old area, is cheap. Other cheaper hotels recommended include *El Faro,* next to *El Mirador,* US$12 d; *Villa Rocío,* UD$7 d; *Hotel Felmar,* US$4 s, and *Hotel Acapulco,* US$3 s, with shower, on Calle Benito Juárez 28, off Zócalo, noisy, no air conditioning;

Amueblados Orozco, near Quebrada, friendly, clean, US$3.50 s, with shower; *Alta Mar,* near Caleta beach, US$4.20 s, excellent breakfast for US$1, recommended. *Hotel Añorvel,* 2 blocks off Zócalo, clean, US$7.50 d, with bath; *Hotel Colimense,* US$7.20 d, off Zócalo, pleasant; *Hotel Jungla,* Miguel Alemán, towards Caleta beach; *Hotel Morales* (behind new Artesanía buildings), cheap. Probably cheapest in town *La Casa del Río,* 1½ blocks from the 2nd class bus terminal towards Los Hornos beach. Cabins with stretchers and sheets, US$1.35 p.p., rooms US$2.25 a night. The Acapulco student organization Setei offers dormitory accommodation, US$1.25 each, if one has a valid international student card; hours, 0700-2400. For longer (1 month plus) stays, try *Amueblados Etel,* Ave. la Pinzona 92 (near Quebrada) for self-catering apartments, cheap off-season (before November). The Tourist Bureau is helpful in finding a hotel in any price range.

Motel *Impala,* on southern half of the bay, is very good.

Restaurant *Armando's,* near Zócalo, particularly recommended; it is a replica of Taj Mahal, with illuminated pools, also has lively discothèque. *Restaurante Carmons,* good 4-course meal US$1.60; *DJ's; Blackbeards; Carlos and Charlie's,* informal. Good cheap restaurant, *Evita,* opposite Flecha Roja bus station. Plenty of cheap American-style take-away food. *Sanborn's* has pleasant terrace facing the sea.

Night Clubs *Armando's; El Club; Boccaccio; Le Dome.* Superb night-life!

Taxis US$8 an hour.

Buses From Mexico City, 443 km., 9 hours; de luxe air-conditioned express buses, 6½ hours, US$5.70; ordinary bus, about US$4.70, all-day services from Estación Central de Autobuses del Sur at junction of Pino Suárez with Mesones, by the Taxqueña underground station, with Estrella de Oro; by air, 50 minutes. 1st class bus depot at Av. Cuauhtémoc 1490. Taxi to Zócalo, US$1.65. To Oaxaca by continuation of the scenic highway from the beach and naval base at Icacas, 402 km., 6 hours on paved and 264 km. of which 170 km. unpaved, 6 hours on rough dirt road through mountains by bus, change at Pinoteca; caught close to where highway from Mexico City joins the beach. One 2nd class (Flecha Roja) bus a day to Taxco at 1730; alternate journey: take bus to Iguala (4 hrs., US$2.10) and then on to Taxco with local bus (1 hr., US$0.35).

Air Services Airport, Plan de los Amales, 26 km. from Acapulco. The route Mexico City-Acapulco-Oaxaca-Mérida is operated by Aeroméxico DC9 jets. There are also direct connections with New York, Philadelphia and Toronto, with Aeroméxico. At weekends Acapulco is very popular. Book well in advance and don't forget to reconfirm your ticket. Ask for exact conditions of travel when booking or you may lose your seat.

Between Acapulco and Zihuatanejo are: Coyuca de Benítez, a lagoon with little islands 38 km. from Acapulco (*Hotel—Bungalows El Camizal,* swimming pool, access to lagoon); San Jerónimo, 83 km. from Acapulco, has 18th century parish church, you can make canoe trips up river to restaurants; Tecpan de Galeana, 108 km. from Acapulco, is a fishing village; there is a beach further on at Cayaquitos and one can also visit the lovely bay of Papanda.

Zihuatanejo is a beautiful fishing port and tourist resort 237 km. NW of Acapulco by a paved road, which continues *via* Playa Azul and Barra de Navidad along the Pacific coast to Puerto Vallarta (see page 792); 1st class bus from Acapulco US$3.15. (This road goes through coconut plantations where you can buy *tuba,* a drink made from coconut milk fermented on the tree, only slightly alcoholic.) The chief attraction, apart from beaches (one can only bathe within the natural harbour), is clam fishing; there is also a small shark-processing factory. The desert islands off the coast may be visited.

Hotels *Casa Elvira* hotel-restaurant, US$7 p.p. off-season, US$12 on, recommended. Several simple hotels along the beach, US$10-12 d: try *Del Mar;*

Playa de la Madera; Catalina; Safari (by bus station, expensive); *Casa La Playa*, similar to *Elvira*, but not as good; *Casa Arcadia*, good; *Belmar*, all rooms face sea; *Sinar-Bahagra*, very good value (formerly *Catazaja*). Expensive hotels: *Hotel Las Tres Marías; Palacios; Irma* (Plaza de la Madera), very warmly recommended; *Capricho del Rey; Sotavento*, the best. *Bungalows Gutiérrez* at far end of Playa de la Ropa, bargain to US\$8 d, beautiful situation, no fan, but shower, monthly rent possible; *Hotel Calpulli* on same beach, US\$15 d; *Playa Club* on Playa de las Gatas, thatched huts in lovely setting, boat from Zihuatanejo town pier. *Pesada Caracol*, *Bungalows Pacíficos* and *Allec* (expensive) on Playa de la Madera. Medium hotels: *Casa la Mariana*, pretty, on seafront; *Bahía*, by town pier; *Avila*, behind Belmar; *Corona*, in coconut plantation on the road to other beaches; *Casa Lulu*, at end of main beach. From Zihuatanejo one can drive to Nuevo Zihuatanejo where there is a huge luxury hotel. Take bus or drive to Ixtapa where there is a famous island a few hundred metres offshore; boats go over. Restaurants both in Ixtapa and on the island.

Restaurants On Playa de la Ropa, cheap: *Elvi* and *Gabachito*. In Zihuatanejo, cheap: *La Bocano, Centamar, Yella, La Mesa del Capitán*, owned by an Englishman.

Night Clubs *Ballena Blanca, El Chololo, El Cancán*.

Skin diving US\$15 an hour and hire of all equipment and guide from Oliverio, on Playa de las Gatas, off which is an underwater wall built by the Tarascan king Calzonzin, to keep the sharks away while he bathed; the wall is fairly massive and can be seen clearly while skin diving. Many fish too.

Buses Three direct buses a day from Mexico City, Estrella de Oro at Central Camionera del Sur (by Taxqueña underground station), leave at 0015, 0600 and 2300, a good 12 hrs.

Airport Daily service to and from Mexico City.

British Vice-Consul at Zihuatanejo: Sr. D. B. Gore, *Hotel Las Brisas*, Aptdo Postal 281. Tel.: (91-748) 4.15.80 and 4.16.50.

Puerto Escondido Highway 200, E from Acapulco along the coast, is paved all the way to Puerto Escondido, on a beautiful bay south of Oaxaca: very popular with young people, good surfing; camping, with showers US\$1 a day, also trailer facilities. *Alojamiento Las Cabañas* has dormitories with bunks, US\$1.15 each. Dr. Robin Hoult writes: "Delightful, as yet unspoilt, fishing village ideally located on the Pacific coast, far enough from Acapulco and on a bad enough road from Oaxaca (first 80 km. paved) to have lagged behind some other resorts in its development. Palm trees line the beach, which is well provided with good quality reasonably priced restaurants; ideal to intersperse bathing and sunbathing with drinks of coconut milk or freshly grilled fish such as huachinango (red snapper), or prawns fried in garlic and onion. Best value for food at small nameless restaurant opposite the trailer park.

"Miles of empty sand further round the bay, good for surfing, but dangerous cross-currents and definitely not for the non-swimmer. There are quite a few youngish tourists about, and the rumour that hippies abound appears unfounded.

"Hurry, hurry while it's all still there. But where can one go in a few years time when this spot is taken over? It seems about the last unspoilt place on the Pacific—one gathers that Acapulco and points north already cater for the jetting tourist who stays in steak and ice-water hotels. East of Puerto Angel, the coast is unexciting, and in any case crowded at the only towns, Juchitán and Salina Cruz." Served by Autobuses Gacela, 2nd class. There are 3-4 new hotels, e.g. *Hotel Las Palmas*, US\$9 d, with bath; *Hotel Paraíso Escondido*, air-conditioned, US\$12.50 d; *Ranchero El Pescador*, a/c, US\$10 d, free minibus service, good restaurant, pool. Some 13 hotels, mainly on the beach, little air-conditioning. Fishing port becoming resort. Three km. N is Zipolite beach; dangerous for bathing. 1st class bus to Puerto Escondido ("La Solteca") from Oaxaca, 5 blocks S of the central market, 9-10 hrs., US\$1.80, also Auto Transportes Oaxaca-Pacifico. Twice daily 20-seater plane from Oaxaca, 40 mins., US\$12.70 return. Bus from Acapulco, 2nd class, Flecha Roja, 5-6 hrs., US\$5.05. The 1030 bus stops for 2 hours' lunch at Pinotepa.

Pan-American Highway: Mexico City to Guatemala

The National Railway runs daily from Mexico City to Tapachula. Taxi to Talismán, on the Guatemalan border, for bus to Guatemala City (also accessible from Puebla, page 833). There is a new bridge which links Ciudad Hidalgo with Tecún-Umán (formerly Ayutla) in Guatemala. Cristóbal Colón bus Mexico City-Guatemala City, 30 hrs., US$20.50; at border change to Rutas Limas. Bus Mexico City-Tapachula, 20 hrs., US$14.20. Bus, Tecún-Umán-Guatemala City US$4.

Note Motorists who know the area well advise that anyone driving from Mexico City to Tehuantepec should go *via* Orizaba-Tinajas-Papaloapan-Tuxtepec-Palomares. The road between the last two places, opened 1975, makes this route preferable to Veracruz-Acayucán and far preferable to the route which follows, *via* Matomoros and Oaxaca, if drivers are in a hurry. The reason given is that between Oaxaca and Tehuantepec the road, although in good condition, serpentines unendingly over the Sierras and it is villainously hot, windy and dry in winter. But as the Oaxaca route is far more interesting and spectacular (and paved throughout in excellent condition) we describe it below. For the alternative journey through the Papaloapan region, see pages 828-831).

This road through southern Mexico is 1,355 km. long. It can be done in 3 or 4 days' driving time. There are bus services from Mexico City along the route through Oaxaca to Tehuantepec and on to the Guatemalan frontier through San Cristóbal de Las Casas to Ciudad Cuauhtémoc or (preferably) through Arriaga to Tapachula. A road will run from Paso Hondo near Ciudad Cuauhtémoc *via* Comalapa and Porvenir to Huixtla on the S road, and from Porvenir to Revolución Mexicana.

The Cristóbal Colón bus from Oaxaca to Tuxtla Gutiérrez invariably arrives full from Mexico City, so it's hard to get seats. Try instead the Diego de Mazariegos Line, which leaves from its own terminal. The railway journey to Guatemala is not very interesting. There is an air service from the capital to Ixtepec (Isthmus of Tehuantepec), 3 hours; to Tuxtla Gutiérrez, 3 hours 45 minutes; and from Oaxaca to Tuxtla Gutiérrez, 1 hour.

The road first runs generally eastwards to Puebla (see page 823), where it turns S to wind through wooded mountains at altitudes of between 1,500 and 1,800 metres, emerging at last into the warm, red-soiled Oaxaca valley.

Oaxaca (population 116,800, altitude 1,546 metres), 413 km. from Puebla, 531 km. from Mexico City. It is a very Indian town, of airy patios with pink arcades, famous for its colourful market, its sarapes, crafts, dances and feast days. On Saturdays Indians of the Zapotec and Mixtec tribes come to market, which starts before 0800; prices are rising because of tourists' interest. Specialities: black earthenware, tooled leather, blankets, ponchos, shawls, embroidered blouses, the drink mescal (beware pickpockets). The main plaza, the Zócalo with its arcades, is the heart of the town; its bandstand has a nice little market underneath. On the Zócalo is the 17th century Cathedral, with a fine baroque façade, but the best sight, about 4 blocks from the square, is the Church of Santo Domingo with its adjoining monastery, now the Regional Museum (see below). The church's gold leaf has to be seen to be believed; its interior is the most splendid in the country. There is an extraordinary vaulted decoration under the raised choir, right on the reverse of the facade wall: a number of crowned heads—kings and queens—appear on the branches of a tree. It is not, as sometimes supposed, a "Stem of Jesse" but a geneological tree of the family of Santo Domingo de Guzmán (died 1221), whose lineage was indirectly related to the royal dynasties of Castile and Portugal. (By making a donation (say 20 pesos) to the church you can get the lady at the bookstall on the right of the Church to light up the various features of the Church.) The Capilla del Rosario in the church has recently been restored, and no flash pictures are allowed. The massive 17th century church of La Soledad has fine Colonial ironwork and sculpture; there are elaborate altars at the green-stone church of San Felipe Neri, and Indian versions in paint of the conquest at San Juan de Dios. The church of San Agustín has a fine façade, with bas-relief of St. Augustine holding the City of God above adoring Augustinian monks. The Regional Museum (entry US$0.45, open 1000-1300 and 1600-1900, closed Mon.) has displays of regional costumes, and pottery, glass, alabaster, jewellery and other treasures from Monte Albán, whose jewellery is copied with surprising skill in several home factories near Oaxaca. Museo Rufino Tamayo, Av. Morelos 503, has a beautiful display of pre-Columbian artefacts (1000-1400, 1600-1900); entry for US$0.16. Teatro Macedonio Alcalá, 5 de Mayo with Independencia, beautifully restored theatre, from Porfirio Díaz's time. There is a grand view from the monument to Juárez on Cerro de Fortín hill. D. H. Lawrence wrote "Mornings in Mexico" here. The Zapotec language is used by over 300,000 people in the State as a first or second language. Mexico's most famous 19th-century President, Benito Juárez, was a Zapotec Indian from Guelatao, Oaxaca.

The best mescal in the region is El Minero, made in Mitla. Mescal sours are good as made at the bar of *Misión Los Angeles.* The poor man's drink is pulque. Local sarapes are more varied and cheaper than in Mexico City. Buy at the market (which will come down a third) or at Casa Cervantes. The Zapotec Indians weave fantastic toys of grass. Their dance is the *Jarabe Tlacolula Zandunga* danced by barefooted girls splendid in most becoming coifs, short, brightly coloured skirts and ribbons and long lace petticoats, while the men, all in white with gay handkerchiefs, dance opposite them with their hands behind their backs. Only women—from Tehuantepec or Juchitán—dance the slow and stately *La Zandunga,* costumes gorgeously embroidered on velvet blouse, full skirts with white pleated and starched lace ruffles and huipil.

Fiestas Los Lunes del Cerro, on the first two Mondays after July 16 (the first is the more spontaneous, when Indian groups come to a hill outside the city to present the seven regional dances of the State in a great festival, also known as La Guelaguetza). Hotels book up early. Upper seats free, getting expensive near the front; tickets from Tourist Office on Calle Independencia and Alameda (between Cathedral and Post Office): Nov. 1-2; Dec. 8, 12, 19 (Soledad), and 23 (Rabanos) with huge radishes carved in grotesque shapes sold for fake money. Buñuelos are sold and eaten in the streets on this night, and the dishes ceremonially smashed after serving. Night of Dec. 24, a parade of floats (best seen from balcony of *Merendero El Tule* on the Plaza; go for supper and select a window table). Posadas in San Felipe (5 km. N) and at Xoxo, to the S, the week before Christmas. Bands play in the Zócalo every evening except Saturday, and there are regional folk dances twice a week.

Hotels *Presidente,* 5 de Mayo 300, in a well-restored 16th century convent, wind-free swimming pool, near Sto Domingo, US$16 s, US$18 d, beautiful but service slow and interior rooms rather hot; *Marqués del Valle,* US$10, on Zócalo, noisy but very attractive; *Margarita Courts,* at N entrance to city, good and reasonable, US$11 d; *Misión Los Angeles* (formerly Oaxaca Courts) motel-style, 2 km. from centre, quiet and most attractive, with swimming pool; *Victoria,* Colonial house turned into hotel; new bedrooms with shower built round the garden, excellent; *Santo Tomás,* new, clean, private shower, some comfort, US$3.50, without meals; *Francia,* US$6.20 d, hot water, has good maps of town for guests, next to it, clean, good food (D. H. Lawrence once stayed there); *Plaza,* on Trujano, near centre, US$9 d, including breakfast and bath, recommended; *Veracruz,* next to ADO bus station, US$7.60 d, with bath, clean and quite good, 20 min. walk to centre; *La Tule,* room with bath and shower (hot water in mornings), US$3, recommended. Near centre at 5 de Mayo 208 is *Principal,* US$8 d, very clean, friendly, private shower with hot and cold water. Round a corner from *La Tule* is *Vallarta,* US$6.80 d, enclosed parking. *Mansión Imperial,* US$7.50 d, good value. Cheap: *Julita,* US$4.80 d, with own shower and toilet; *María Luisa,* US$5 with bath, good; *Rex,* Calle Las Casas 308, impeccable, US$4 d, close to market, narrow entrance; *Hotel Restaurant Vegetariano; Pombo,* Calle Morelos (US$3, with cold shower); *Donají,* Calle Hidalgo, all less than US$1.60 s, basic; *Señorial,* Portal de Flores 6, US$11 d, with bath, swimming pool, with meals US$23.60 d, on main square, so rather noisy; *Virreyes,* central, US$6; *Isabel,* US$10.20 d, with bath; *Monte Albán,* US$9.25 d, friendly, some rooms look onto a small plaza where Indians weave every day; *América,* Aldama 513, near market, US$4 d; *Central,* 20 de Noviembre 104, US$2.50 p.p. (private bathroom), very noisy; *Modelo,* Portal de los Mercaderes; *Posada Colonial,* very attractive; *Antiquera,* near Zócalo, very good value, US$9 d, with bath; also *Reforma,* US$6 s, Morelos 1004, annexe cheaper; *Fortín,* Díaz Ordaz 312, nr. south side of main market, modern, good value, US$3, with bath; *San José,* 5 mins. from Zócalo, US$2 s; *Paraíso,* near *Palestina,* by the market, US$2.75 d, without bath, clean, laundering facilities; *Yalalag,* US$3.30 s, just by market, restaurant, recommended; *Pasaje,* Calle Mina 302, near market, US$1.85 d, US$0.10 for shower, very friendly; *Chavo,* opposite market, clean, showers, cheap; *El Valle,* US$4.80 d, quite good. The cheapest accommodation is in private houses which rent rooms *(casas de huéspedes);* recommended is *Sra. Margarita de Pérez,* Labastida 115 (one block from Santo Domingo), US$1.50 s for one night, less per night for longer stays. *Hotel Veracruz,* next to ADO terminal, good but noisy, US$3.75 s, with bath; *Posada Las Palmas,* Ave. Juárez 516, US$1.55 s, without bath, restaurant, recommended.

Restaurants *Flor de Oaxaca,* Armenta y López 311; *Casa de Doña Elpidia,* M. Cabrera 413, lunch only (there is no sign; it is reputed to be so good that advertising is not necessary); *La Ilusión,* friendly and good; *Montecarlo,* good; *Guelatao; Kiko,* Independencia 504, cheap lunch US$0.75; *Las Palmas; Villahermosa,* Calle Trujano 106A; *Montebello,* good, at Trujano 307; *Colón,* Colón 111; *Café ADO,* ADO Terminal; *La Pantera Rosa,* Calle J. P. García 100, with patio, has choice of 415 set meals, US$1; *restaurant Colonial,* 20 de Noviembre, cheap *comidas corridas.* However, the best Oaxacan food is found in the *comedores familiares* such as *Clemente, Los Almendros, La Juchita.*

Camping Good campsite: *La Resolana,* 2½ km. from city centre, with good bus services, hot showers and clothes washing facilities, US$1.65 p.p.

Shops The market is full of endless temptations such as green and black pottery, baskets and bags made from cane and rushes, embroidered shirts, skirts, and blankets of all colours and designs; Saturdays are best for buying woollen sarapes cheaply. *Pepe,* Avenida Hidalgo, for jewellery; cheap local crafts. *Yalalag,* Alcalá 105, has good selection of jewellery, rugs and pottery. *Victor,* Porfirio Díaz 111; cheapest and largest selection of pottery plus a variety of fabrics and sandals at *Productos Típicos de Oaxaca,* Ave. Dr. B. Domínguez 602; city bus near ADO depot goes there. *Casa Aragón,* J. P. García 503, famous for knives and machetes. Galerías Audiffred, Avenida Independencia 508, is yet another fabulous museum-like shop. Ask for pottery on outskirts of town; fine cream and purple-black pottery (Zapotec and Mixtec designs) available at *Alfarería Jiménez,* Zaragoza 402; further along Zaragoza is a small straw market with all kinds of baskets and bags. Other potteries at Las Casas 614, makers of the Oaxacan daisy design, and Trujano 508, brash flower designs. There is another handicraft market, not always open, on the outskirts of the city. In a small square just off Calle Alcalá, between the Zócalo and Santo Domingo (opposite *Pensión Margarita),* the Indians meet to knit, weave, whittle and carve, and their products are cheaper than elsewhere.

Dr. Robin Hoult adds: "Some of the local clothing factories are worth visiting (e.g. for cloths, tablecloths and blankets), and the work is attractive, of good quality and reasonably priced. Also well worth driving out of town (or bussing) to buy unique black pottery, e.g. at San Bártolo de Coyotepec; it's quite special. Zócalo is large and interesting (though the Indians no longer weave there; see previous paragraph); their products are bought rapidly. Several good gift shops, at top end of market. Visits out of town to Mitla and Monte Albán part of the obligatory programme."

Railway from Mexico City, 563 km., ends 20 km. beyond Oaxaca, 15-20 hours, US$1.90 2nd, US$2.80 1st class, at 1730 daily. To Mexico City daily at 1930, only one sleeper, US$5.30. Tickets must be bought the same day. Seats scarce in 2nd class, quite a scramble!

Buses ADO, on outskirts of city, to Mexico City, 8 hours, US$7.50, 2nd class by Fletes y Pasajes, 9 hrs., comfortable; 1st class to Cuautla, US$5.10; Puebla (2nd class, 11 hours, US$1) to Tuxtepec (2nd class, 8½ hours, US$1.05) and other towns; to Villahermosa, US$8.15, 13½ hours, daily at 0030 hours, 1st class; Cristóbal Colón (1st class) to Mexico City, US$4.25; San Cristóbal de las Casas (US$7.20, 10 hours) and Tapachula US$7. Also Fletes y Pasajes and Diego de Mazariegos (2nd class). Book well in advance as buses often come almost full from Mexico City. 2nd class bus to Tuxtla Gutiérrez, 19 hrs., US$4.20. 2 hr. wait in Juchitán (see page 847). Oaxaca-Tehuantepec, US$2.90. If travelling S 2nd class go from new 2nd class terminal; from Oaxaca, Diego de Mazariegos goes under the name of Transportes Oaxaca-Istmo. Buses to most local villages go from this terminal, too.

Air Services from Mexico City daily by Aeroméxico in less than an hour; to Tuxtla Gutiérrez, Tapachula and Mérida.

Excursions To **Monte Albán**, about 20 minutes from Oaxaca, up a bold and steep hill outside the city to see the pyramids, walls, terraces, tombs, staircases and sculptures of a prehistoric sacred city, once capital of the Zapotec culture. The place is radiantly colourful during some sunsets. Autobuses Turisticos (Trujano 607) from Oaxaca thrice daily (1000, 1230, 1600, returns 1200, 1400, and 1730, fare US$0.75 return) allow not quite enough time to tour ruins before returning. A private museum in an old Colonial house is worth visiting. To the right, before getting to the ruins, is Tomb 7, where a fabulous treasure trove of gold artifacts, jewellery, mosaics, crystal and alabaster vessels was found in January 1932; most are in the Regional Museum in the convent of Santo Domingo. The ruins are on the flattened top of a hill. Only a small part of the old city has been partly restored. The remarkable rectangular plaza, 300 by 200 metres, is rimmed by big cememonial platforms: the Ball Court, and possibly a palace to the E, stairs rising to an unexcavated platform to the S, several platforms and temples to the W and one—Temple of the Dancers—with bas-reliefs, glyphs and calendar signs (probably 5th century B.C.). A grand wide stairway leads to a platform on the N side. Most of the ruins visible are early 10th century when the city was abandoned and became a burial place. Entry US$0.45; you need a torch. There is a footpath back to Oaxaca, ask for information. No informative literature available at the site. Just before the ruins is a swimming pool, Granja Tita; San Juanito buses take you there.

A dry-weather road leads to **Teotitlán del Valle**, where Oaxaca sarapes are woven. If you knock at any door down the street, you will get them cheaper than at the market. Buses leave every 2½ hrs. from 0800 from Miguel Cabrera nr. corner with Mina (US$0.22 return). *Juvenal Mendoza*, Buenavista 9, will make any design any size into a rug to order (daily at 1100 hrs.). Opposite the turning for Teotitlán, turn right for **Dainzu**, another important ruin recently excavated. Its pyramid contains figures, probably ball players, similar to the Monte Albán dancers. The nearby site of **Lambytieco** is also well worth visiting, to see several fine and well-preserved stucco heads. Only 72 km. from Oaxaca is **Yanhuitlán**, with a beautiful 400-year-old church, part of a monastery. NW of Yanhuitlán is **Huajuapan de León**, with *Hotel García Peral*, on the Zócalo, good restaurant.

To **Mitla**, paved road, 42 km. from Oaxaca past (1) Tlacochahuaya, 16th century church, vivid Indian murals, carpets and blouses sold in market nearby; (2) **Santa María del Tulee** which has what is reputed the world's largest tree, a sabino (*Taxodium Mucronatum*), estimated at 2,000 years old, 40 metres high, 42 metres round at base, weighing an estimated 550 tons, in churchyard, market on Wednesday; and (3) **Tlacolula**, with a good Sunday market and the renowned Capilla del Santo Cristo in the church, elaborate decorations and gruesome figures of saints;

can be reached by bus from Oaxaca, from the 2nd class bus station. Taxi costs US$4 each to Mitla for 4 sharing, with time to take photographs at Tule and Mitla and to buy souvenirs at ruins. Co-operative "Fletes y Pasajes", Trujano in the 700s block, every 30 minutes to Mitla, 75 mins., US$0.35.

From the main road a turn left leads to Mitla (whose name means "place of the dead") where there are ruins of four great palaces amongst minor ones. Entry US$0.50, no literature available on site. Wide steps lead to the angular entry doors. See in particular the magnificent bas-reliefs, the sculptured designs in the Hall of Mosaics, the Hall of the Columns, and in the depths of a palace La Columna de la Muerte (Column of Death), which people embrace and measure what they can't reach with their fingers to know how many years they have left to live. There is a private museum at the site, a soberly decorated Colonial church with three cupolas, and a rash of guides and pedlars. Beautiful traditional Indian clothes and other goods may be bought at the new permanent market. Fletes y Pasajes buses and taxis from Oaxaca go to the ruins of **Yagul** (on the way to Mitla), an outstandingly picturesque site where the ball courts and quarters of the priests are set in a landscape punctuated by candelabra cactus and agaves. Views of great beauty, tombs, skulls, temples. Yagul is a large Zapotec and Mixtec religious centre; the ball courts are perhaps the most perfect discovered to date. You will have to walk some 2 km. from the bus stop to the site.

Hotel Mitla, US$1.50 s, clean, local food, beautiful garden. The University of the Americas runs a small guest-house. Small museum in Zócalo at Mitla; none at the site.

A primitive road runs to **Puerto Angel** (240 km., 13 hours by bus), a coffee port on the Pacific, and another to Puerto Escondido (see page 841). On the way from Oaxaca to Puerto Angel stop at San José del Pacífico, for a beautiful view from an altitude of over 2,000 metres. Friday trips from Oaxaca to market at Ocotlán on the road to it. Stop in San Bartolo Coyotepec to see Doña Rosa's black pottery and don't try and bargain.

17 km. SW of Oaxaca is **Cuilapan**, where there is a vast earthquake-shattered convent with a famous nave and columns and Zapotec-Mixtec ruins on the river bank S of the village. The last Zapotec princess was buried at Cuilapan. Reached by bus from Oaxaca.

To (San Pablo de) **Guelatao** (65 km. from Oaxaca), the birthplace of Benito Juárez. The town is located in the mountains NE of Oaxaca and can be reached by bus (3 hours) along a tortuously winding albeit paved (be thankful for small favours!) road. There is a library with current US magazines and a small museum on the hillside. The beautiful road continues up to Tuxtepec (see page 832).

We are approaching a more primitive part of Mexico: Tehuantepec peninsula and the mountains of Chiapas beyond, a land inhabited by Indians less influenced than elsewhere by the Spanish conquest. They have kept intact their languages, their religions, their tribal organisations and ways of life, their dresses and dances; but ten years of the New World's juke box will do more to demolish a delicate Indian adjustment than 450 years of the Old World's culture. Chiapas, the Isthmus region and Guatemala are the home of the marimba, a large wooden xylophone played by several men at once and accompanied by drums and saxophone.

Only about 210 km. separate the Atlantic and the Pacific at the Isthmus of Tehuantepec, where the land does not rise more than 250 metres. There are a railway (to be renewed) and a Trans-Isthmian Highway between Coatzacoalcos and Salina Cruz, the terminal cities on the two oceans.

Salina Cruz This once quaint, sleepy and unspoiled small port (which has a naval base) is now booming; extensive oil-storge installations have been built. Bathing is dangerous because of the heavy swell from Pacific breakers and also sharks. Ten km. to the S is the picturesque fishing village with La Ventosa beach which, as the name says, is windy.

Warning Do not wander too far off along the beach as people have been severely attacked and robbed. Do not sleep on the beach or in your car.

Hotels *Hotel Paraíso,* US$4 d, shower, car park; *Hotel La Posada de Rustrian,* with restaurant, overlooking sea, US$3.75 s, with bath in new block, half in old block. Friendly family at the top of the dirt road coming from Salina Cruz (on the right) and 200 metres after the path that leads down to the beach, rents hammocks, US$0.20 a night, fried fish US$1.

(Km. 804) Tehuantepec (population 10,087, altitude 150 metres) is 257 km. from Oaxaca and 21 km. inland from Salina Cruz, Pacific terminal of the Tehuantepec National Railway across the narrow, heavily jungled, hot, flat peninsula to Coatzacoalcos on the Caribbean. The town of Tehuantepec is on the bend of a river around which most of its activities are centred: washing, bathing, gossiping. The plaza has arcades down one side, a market on the other, and many stands selling agua fresca, an iced fruit drink. Houses are low, in white or pastel shades. The Indians are mostly Zapotecs whose social organisation is matriarchal: women do the buying and selling, the fishing, even the governing; they are high-pressure saleswomen, quick-minded, alert, intelligent, short, stocky, with some Spanish blood; their hair is braided and brightly ribboned and they wear embroidered costumes. The dependent and far less important male (who still survives; there are some in the streets), does not dare put a foot in the market, and for the most part works humbly in the fields, or as potter or weaver. Hammocks made in this area are of the best quality. The town is divided into wards, 15 of them, and each holds a fiesta, the main one at the end of Holy Week, when the women wear their finest costumes and jewellery. There is another splendid fiesta in honour of St. John the Baptist on June 22-25. January and February are good months for the ward fiestas. Population 35,000.

Excursions To neighbouring villages for fiestas: the hotel knows about them. By bus to La Ventosa beach by dirt road. Accommodation: champas, or hammocks under thatch shelters by the beach, US$0.25-0.40 a night. The owners serve drinks and food (fish, shrimps, crabs just caught) from early morning on. Prices often extortionate.

Hotels *Tehuantepec; Oasis* (fairly primitive, but central and good atmosphere), US$2.65 s, with bath, near Zócalo; *Hotel Tehuanita,* US$1.60 s, adequate. The local *quesadillas* made of maize and cheese are delicious; sold at bus stops.

Bus from Oaxaca,US$2.90; to Salina Cruz, US$0.10.

27 km. beyond Tehuantepec on the road to Tuxtla Gutiérrez is **Juchitán** (*Hotel Don Alex,* US$1.75 s; beware of overcharging in cheap hotels), very old, Indian, with an extensive market, many fiestas and a special one on June 19 (2nd class bus Oaxaca-Juchitán, US$1.60). A road runs 16 km. N to **Ixtepec** (airport), railway junction for Guatemala (Hotels: *Pan-Americano, Colón*). At Las Cruces, a road runs right to **Arriaga** (12,000 people), (Hotels: *El Parador,* clean with swimming pool; *Juchitán,* US$5 s, with bathroom; *Restaurant Xochimilco* near bus stations), through **Tonalá** (small museum) to (Route 200) **Tapachula** (airport) and the Talismán bridge to Guatemala. It is now paved and beyond Tonalá is mostly straight, smooth and fast. (North of Arriaga a road is now open paralleling the railway and by-passing Las Cruces, so avoiding dozens of sharp curves on a steep road.) This is by far the better road for travellers seeking the quickest way from Mexico City to

Guatemala. There are frequent 2nd class buses from Tapachula including Cristóbal Colón, which leaves at noon (US$0.20), and Progreso (US$0.15) near the market (1st class leave 0900 and 1100, US$0.40) the border town (border open 24 hours a day) to the Talismán bridge (8 km.) but no through buses. (Taxi Talismán-Tapachula, US$5), exit tax US$0.25.

Guatemalan buses (Galdós) leave Talismán bridge at about 1200 and 1600 for Coatepeque, Quezaltenango and Guatemala City (fare US$5, entry tax US$0.25). It is difficult to get a bus from the Talismán bridge to Oaxaca or Mexico City (though they do exist); advisable therefore to travel to Tapachula for connection. Buses to Mexico City leave at 1400 and 2200, take 12 hrs. to reach Oaxaca, and same again to Mexico City, US$5.75. The train from Mexico City to Tapachula leaves daily at 2100, it costs only US$8.50 1st class but takes 37 hours to complete the journey, changing at Veracruz, stops to get food on the way. The bus ride to the frontier (20 minutes) costs US$0.25; no immigration services between 1200 and 1400, and the exchange facilities are not good. It is possible to get a visa for El Salvador at the Salvadorean Consulate in Tapachula (Calle 2a Sur, No. 10) without any delay. There is a Guatemalan Consulate in Tapachula.

Michael Reeve writes: If crossing from Guatemala in afternoon, you can catch a Cristóbal Colón bus from Tapachula to Arriaga (1600, 3½ hours, US$2.50), then Fletes y Pasajes (1100, 8 hours, US$3.50) to Oaxaca via Juchitán and Tehuantepec. **British Vice-Consul**, 2a Ave, Norte No. 3; Tel.: Tapachula 12-88. Postal address Apdo. 74.

Tomalá Hotel *Galilea,* US$6.50 d, with bath, air-conditioned, good, on main square. Good restaurant there; *Sta. Elena Restaurant,* nr. Cristóbal Colón bus station on outskirts, good.

Tapachula Hotels *Internacional,* good, with restaurant; *Hotel Central,* US$6.60 d, with shower, clean; just around the corner is *Hotel Tazacapec,* US$4.40 d; *Hotel Puebla,* US$8 d. Beware overcharging in cheaper hotels. *San Francisco,* good, air-conditioned, US$15 s; *Rochester,* 2a Avenida Norte Nina, US$7 d, with bath, comfortable; *Monaco,* similar. In general, shortage of accommodation. *Hotel Colonial,* reasonable, US$4.80 d; *Hotel Colón,* Central Norte Juárez, US$4.10 d, near bus station; *Hotel Tayopec,* US$3.20 d, friendly. *Motel del Bosque,* US$6.40 d, not recommended. Good restaurant next to Cristóbal Colón terminal.

Off the road between Tonalá and Tapachula are several fine and undeveloped beaches, such as **Puerto Arista** (bus from Tonalá US$0.25—one hotel or hammocks on beach, US$0.40 a night, also several guest houses, US$24 a month, 3 or 4 good restaurants with rooms to rent; *Hotel Vacacional* for cheap accommodation).

Puerto Madero, 20 km. from Tapachula (bus US$0.80), not as pleasant as Puerto Arista, because built up. (*Hotel Puerto Maderno,* accommodation in cement block room, US$2 d, also excellent Chinese-style seafood cooked by the owner, Victor Saul.) Other Puerto Maderno hotels: *Playa Bonita,* best value, US$2.50 s, *Miramar, Estrada, Margarita, Pacifico, Hermanos Riyán;* humble cheap room, US$1.50, with Sr. Echeverria by the cemetery—all one needs and half the price of others (which are fairly basic). Many fish-eateries on beach. Buses also go from Tonalá to Boca del Cillo further down the coast, which is good for bathing but has no accommodation, and similarly Cabeza del Toro. **Paredón**, on the huge lagoon Mar Muerto near Tonalá, has excellent seafood and one very basic guest house. One can take a local fishing boat out into the lagoon to swim; the shore stinks. Good place to eat though. Served by frequent buses. En route for Tapachula one passes through Pijijiapan where there is the *Hotel Pijijilton* (!) next to the C. Colón bus station.

Hitch-hikers should note that there is little through international traffic at Talismán bridge.

Just beyond Tapachula, on the way to Guatemala, is **Unión Juárez**; *Hotel Colonial,* US$2.50 s. *Restaurant Carmelita* on the square is modest with fair prices. Visit the ruins of **Izapa** (stelae, small museum) on the way to Unión Juárez; they were influenced by Teotihuacán and in turn influenced Kaminal Juyú near Guatemala City. In Unión Juárez one can have one's papers stamped and proceed on foot *via* Talquián to the Guatemalan border at Sibinal. Take a guide!

Beyond Las Cruces we enter the mountainous Chiapas state, mostly peopled by Maya Indians whose extreme isolation has now been ended by air services and our highway, which threads its way through the rift valley of Chiapas, with high mountains to right and left. Chiapas ranks first in cacao production, second in coffee, bananas and mangoes, and cattle-grazing is important. Hardwoods are floated out down the rivers which flow into the Gulf.

(Km. 1,085) **Tuxtla Gutiérrez**, capital of Chiapas; pop.: 90,000; alt.: 1,739 ft., 301 km. (183 miles) from Tehuantepec, is a hot, modern city of no great interest to the tourist except during the fair of Guadalupe, on December 12. The market is worth a look. There is a State Archaeological Museum (closed on Saturdays) and a botanical garden with a zoo, worth a visit because it contains only animals from Chiapas. Airport. Tourist office in the same building as the Archaeological Museum.

Two vast artifical lakes made by dams are worth visiting: the Presa Netzalhualcoyotl, 77 km. NW of Tuxtla, and La Angostura, S of the city. Information from the tourist office. The former can also be visited from Cárdenas (see page 855).

Excursions See under Veracruz on how to get from Veracruz to Tuxtla Cutiérrez. By paved road, which starts at zoo gates (23 km.), in excellent condition, to the rim of the tremendous El Sumiero Canyon, truly one of the world's wonders (taxi fare US$12 return; minibus daily except Sun. from *Hotel Posada del Rey,* where places can be booked, US$2.50. Indian warriors galled by the Spanish conquest hurled themselves into it rather than submit. Excursions by air to Bonampak and Yaxchilán cheaper from San Cristóbal (see page 850). There is a 1st class bus from Tuxtla to Palenque (see page 858) at US$4.80 one way, which leaves Tuxtla at 0500; 9-hour fascinating journey *via* Pichucalco and Villahermosa.

Hotels *Bonampak,* the social centre, US$7, reasonable but noisy; *Brindis,* Ave. Central, US$1.80 s, with bath; *Balum Canaan,* new, Av. Central Oriente 922, US$5.50 s, good value; *Hotel Olimpio,* US$3 s, shower; *Posada del Rey; Cano,* near Cristóbal Colón terminal; *Jardín.* Cheap: *Serrano,* US$2.35 s, with bath; *Posada México,* near bus station, US$2 p.p., not recommended. Good expensive regional restaurant, *Los Cazadores.* Reasonable *Restaurant Central,* on Zócalo.

Transport 35 km. E of Tuxtla, just past Chiapa de Corzo (see below, a road runs N, 294 km., to Villahermosa *via* Pichucalco (see page 855). It is paved all the way. There is a petrol station before Pichucalco at Bochil (130 km. from Tuxtla). Bus (2nd class) to Villahermosa daily at 0500, 0600 and 0900, 8½ hours, fare US$3.20; Cristóbal Colón (1st class) leaves at 1300, 7½ hrs. The scenery is very fine, and the road provides the best route between Guatemala and Yucatán. Buses from Tapachula to Tuxtla Gutiérrez, 2nd class, 1600, US$3.50, 8½ hours; Tuxtla to Pichucalco, 1600, 1800, 2100, US$3, 8 hours; Pichucalo Villahermosa and Villahermosa-Campeche (US$3.75, 6 hours) have frequent services; 2nd class bus to Mérida from Calle Sur Oriente; No. 712 at 1330. No changing, arrives 0600, US$9. Bus, Tuxtla-San Cristóbal, 2 hours, US$1. No direct 2nd class buses. Superb mountain journey. Other bus lines (2nd class) are cheaper than Cristóbal Colón in this area, and daily buses run between Comitán, San Cristóbal, Tuxtla and Oaxaca (US$4.90 first class at 1330 or 2100, very crowded, 10 hrs.; 2nd class, US$4.50, leaves 1730. Bus all the way to Palenque (*via* Villahermosa) leaves 0500, arrives at Palenque at 1500, US$4.40, stops often, leaves from Cooperativa at 2a Ave Sur-Oriente 712. A new road has been built from Tuxtla to Comalapa; a 4½ hour drive with a fantastic view from the top.

Chiapa de Corzo, 14½ km. on, a Colonial township of about 7,000 people on a bluff overlooking the Grijalva river, is more interesting than Tuxtla: a lovely 16th century fountain, a church whose engraved altar is of solid silver, and famous craftsmen in gold and jewellery and lacquer work who travel the fairs. The distinguishing feature of the fountain is that it is crown-shaped and said to represent the crown of Spain. Painted and lacquered vessels made of Pumpkins are a local speciality. There is a small lacquer museum. The fiestas here are outstanding: January 20-23 and another, early February, with a pageant on the river. Hotels basic, Zócalo filled with bars playing jukeboxes. The town suffered badly in an earthquake in November 1975, but buildings are being rebuilt or restored. The town has become increasingly affected by the onslaught of tourism; it is now expensive and many locals have become unfriendly.

(Km. 1,170) San Cristóbal de Las Casas (40,000 people), 83 km. beyond Tuxtla Gutiérrez, was founded in 1528 by Diego de Mazariegos and was the Colonial capital of the region. It stands in a high mountain valley at 2,110 metres. It was named after Las Casas, protector of the Indians, its second bishop. The town has arcaded palaces and typical low, red-tiled dwellings with charming patios and forbiddingly barred windows. There are many old churches; two of them cap the two hills which overlook the town. Santo Domingo, built in 1547, has a baroque façade, a gaily gilt rococo interior and a famous carved wooden pulpit (see below). Other churches include San Nicolás, with an interesting facade, El Carmen, La Merced, and La Caridad (1730), Various kinds of craftwork are sold in the new central market, open daily, and in the Sunday markets of the local Indian villages. The very best work is put into the silver-encrusted saddles. A good place to buy handicrafts is at Doña Paula, Calle Real de Guadalupe 25, just off the Zócalo (there are craft shops all along the Guadalupe; the farther along, the cheaper they are) and El Quetzal for costumes from local villages. Used clothing market on Saturdays at bottom of Santo Domingo steps. The convent of Santo Domingo has been converted into a local handicraft centre and market, and the streets are all being repaved. There is a small American colony. July 25 is fiesta day, when all bicycles and vehicles, including Unesco's malaria jeep, go uphill to be blessed by the Bishop. There is also a popular spring festival on April 18-25. The regional headquarters of the Mexican Indigenous Institute, responsible for 16,000 mountain Indians, is here. Most Indian tribes here are members of the Tzotzil race. The Tenejapans wear black knee-length tunics. the Chamulans black and white tunics and white bandanas; and the Zinacantecans multicoloured outfits, with their men exhibiting marital status by wearing ribbons on their hats; bachelors allow ribbons to flow freely.

The archaeologist Frans Blom died here in 1963. His house at Na Bolom (meaning house of the jaguar) has become a museum, open 1600-1730 (except Mondays); address: Vicente Guerrero 33, and a beautiful expensive guest house (previous reservation necessary, double room with 3 meals, US$24 a day), with good library run by his widow. It is worth visiting: beautifully displayed artefacts, pictures of Lacandón Indians, with information about their history and present way of life (in English). Also only obtainable map of Lacandón jungle. Guides take you round display, rooms of beautiful old house, and garden. Entrance US$0.40. The Na-Bolom library opens as follows: Mon., 1430-1830; Tues.-Sat., 0800-1200.

Dr. Robin Hoult writes: "The quality of the light here is astonishing—clear and crisp—especially in the morning before the clouds come over. San Cristóbal is an

Indian town of immense character, and with a definite special atmosphere—best appreciated when shopping, especially in the market. Physically, the upland Indians are different from the lowland Mayans, but have the same dignity and other-worldliness in their faces. Yet they bustle and rush more, with an extra degree of earnestness. Women wear multicoloured cloth blouses, black skirts; many men wear coarse wool sleeveless jackets, leather hats and tasselled belts with multi-coloured streamers. It is all very photogenic, and a friendly place, justifiably popular. Good shopping—leather and clothes shops; market has large food and fruit section, and a vast range of very cheap but most graceful Indian pottery (getting it home is the problem!).

"Although there aren't many buildings of special interest, San Cristóbal is very pleasing to the eye; most of the centre is old—houses have characteristic iron grilles over the windows, carved doors, elegant stone-carving over arches, and tiled roofs.

"The museum Na Bolom (15 minutes walk from the Zócalo) is well worth the modest entrance fee: there is an extraordinary collection of archaeological and anthropological artefacts, with specially interesting items from the isolated and tantalising tribe of Lacandonian Indians (now facing possible extinction in the face of declining numbers, disease and intrusion and destruction of habitat by the modern world). Blom and his widow have devoted their lives to the study of this extraordinary people, and you readily appreciate a real sense of mystery after visiting this elegant house with shady courts and patios. Flowers, plants and furniture combine to give it a very special atmosphere."

Excursions On Sunday visit (first ask permission at municipal offices on Zócalo) the villages of San Juan Chamula (horses can be hired in Na Bolom to go here for a morning, at corner of Calle Comitán and Av. Vicente Guerrero, US$3 for horse and US$3 for guide), Zinacantán and Tenejapa. You can catch a lorry ride to **Chamula** (1 hr.) from 0600 to 1000 and visit the local church; you must make a small donation and photographing is absolutely forbidden! (two tourists were killed for ignoring the warning). Pleasant walk back *via* the "milpoleta" road, some 8 km. downhill, 2 hrs., ask locals. The Sunday market at **Tenejapa** is very colourful, excellent woven items can be bought from local people in their homes. Buses leave from San Cristóbal market at 0700 and 1100. (2-2½ hr. journey.) Be discreet with cameras. Market thins out by noon. Two other excursions can be made, by car or local bus, from San Cristóbal S on the Interamerican Highway (½ hr. by car) to **Amatenango del Valle,** a Tzeltal village where the women make and fire pottery in their yards, and then W (15 min. by car) to Aguacatenango, picturesque village at the foot of a mountain, near lakes. Continue 1 hr. along road past Villa de las Rosa (hotel) to **Carranza,** women with fine costumes, extremely good view of the entire valley. Autotransportes Lacandonia run to all local accessible villages; interesting are Oxchuc, Ocosingo (market town), Yajalón (5 hrs. from San Cristóbal), centre of coffee industry of Chiapas (*Hotel López,* US$3 d, with bath, no sign) and Toniná ruins.

Shopping For purchases of local goods try *Miscellánea Betty,* Gen. Utrillo 45, good value. Leather goods purchases recommended in San Cristóbal. Good English bookshop at *El Recoveco,* Real de Guadalupe 24A. Also try *rompope,* a local egg-nog, and local sweets and confectionery.

Hotels *Hotel Español,* two blocks from the Plaza, N of the Cathedral, US$7 s, US$10 d, with fireplaces and shower. Good bar, best restaurant in town and one of best in S. Mexico; *Posada San Cristóbal,* US$2; *Posada del Marqués,* off Calle Insurgentes, US$1.65 p.p., hot shower, friendly. *Casa de Huéspedes Margarita,* 1½ blocks from Zócalo, clean, comfortable, hot water, US$1.10 s, popular among younger tourists, can do laundry, communal washing, Calle Real de Guadalupe 34; *San Francisco,* Calle Insurgentes, 3 blocks S of Plaza, clean, with bath, US$1.10 s; *Posada Colonial,* US$1.30 s; *Santa Clara,* on Plaza, US$4.20 s, with bath (restaurant fair, lunch US$2); *Hotel Fray Bartolomé de Las Casas,* US$6 s, pleasant, colonial, with plenty of good local pottery and woodwork (will open up late at night if you knock hard); *Molino de la Alborada,* opposite airport, has modern ranch house and bungalows, US$25 d, all meals; *Ciudad Real,* on Plaza, US$15 d, with bath, hot water, clean, good value, with very good restaurant. New motel with good restaurant, *El Español,* just outside town. Several unmarked guest houses, US$1.80 for 2 is typical. Even cheaper *Los Banos,* US$0.90 per head, shared quarters, cheap meals. Next door also *Los Baños Torres,* similar. For a change, ask at Tienda Santo Domingo for *La Carpintería,* small pine-built rooms round carpenter's courtyard, cheapest is US$1.10 a night, at Av. Gen. Utrillo and Calle Flavio A. Paniagua, steam baths, US$0.48, toilets filthy, sometimes fleas (avoid really filthy pensión across from *Carpintería*); *Casa de Huéspedes,* 1 block N of main square, US$2.40 d; *Casa Peta* on Benito Juárez, US$1 each, very friendly; *Casa Pola,* nr. Plaza, Calle Benito Juárez 6, US$4 d, without bath, clean, hot water; *Posada Santo Domingo,* Utrillo 10. Many others not listed.

Restaurants *Los Baños,* meals US$0.90, showers US$0.23, steam baths US$0.35, Calle 1° de Marzo 55; also *Casa Blanca,* Calle Real de Guadalupe, cheap; *Capri,* two blocks off main square, about US$1.20, clean toilets!; *Laguito Azul; Café Central.* Good pizzeria, charming atmosphere on Crescencia Rosa, US$3 for very large pizzas. Try "soya" drink at *El Asador* on Calle Juárez, good value restaurant. Several others.

Buses Direct to border 1st class, or 2nd class, in stages to Comitán, takes 2-3 hrs., US$1 (Ciudad Cuauhtémoc), leaves at 0630. There is a paved, but not very good, road to Palenque; direct bus leaves at 0430 (or 0900), US$2.70, beware of overcharging, 7 hours, later (0600) buses leave one at Ocosingo (US$0.96) 4 hours, which connects to Palenque, 4 hours, US$4.60 (with 0900 bus arrive at 1900). If the Ocosingo-Palenque bus is not running (the road is often washed out) continue on the 1st bus to Yajabón, where you can catch a little private plane to Palenque, US$8. The journey *via* Ocosingo is rather uncomfortable and is recommended only for the very brave or very broke. Autobuses Tuxtla Gutiérrez run a service that leaves at 0830 and arrives after 1600, having called at Villahermosa, US$3. Several buses a day to Tuxtla, US$0.90, crowded, 2nd class, 2 hrs. Bus to Oaxaca 12 hrs., US$8.50, 2nd class, from 2nd class bus terminal and Cristóbal Colón terminal, monotonous trip. Bus to Mexico City, US$14.20, 1st class, 20 hrs. Buses to Tehuantepec and Puebla. Bus to Tapachula US$3.75.

Get to outlying villages by bus or communal lorry (both very squashed); buses leave very early, lorries are more frequent. To Zinacantán, choose Chamula direction from market; to Tenejapa from Plaza Guadalupe. Buses from the market to Chanal, Chenalhó, Penbelhó and Larrainzar. Transportes Lacandonia go to the interior villages of Huistán, Oxchuc, Yajalán, Pujiltic, La Mesilla and Carranza.

Airport Regular daily flights, except Sundays, to Palenque, 0715, US$10. Charter flights to see Lacanjá, Bonampak and Yaxchilán, 7 hours in all, US$80 p.p. All with Aerochiapas in Calle Real de Guadalupe.

Comitán is a large and active town with a shady Zócalo.

The 170-km. road to the border at Ciudad Cuauhtémoc (no town!) is paved. A road branches off the Pan American Highway 16 km. after Comitán to the very beautiful region of vari-coloured lakes, the Lagunas de **Montebello**; in the deep forest a road is being built to connect the Lagunas with Bonampak; frequent buses from Comitán. On the road to Montebello lie the ruins of Chinkultic, with temples, ballcourt and cenote (deep round lake). Watch for the very small sign and gate where road to ruins starts, worth visiting when passing.

Buses to the Lagunas de Montebello (56 km. from Comitán), or the Lagunas de Siete Colores (so-called because the oxides in the water give varieties of colours: one leaves at 1130, arrives 1330, and the last bus back is at 1600. (Costs US$5 s.) This area is now a reserve (there are restaurants as well as picnic areas, but no shops) and there are caves.

Hotels *Hotel Internacional,* US$8 d, with shower, near Zócalo; decent restaurant; *Hotel Delfín,* good. Both in the square. Parking in inner courtyard. *Hotel Morales,* new, very comfortable, parking, restaurant and bar, US$4 s; *San Francisco,* clean, US$2.80 s. *Posada Primavera* is very close to the Cristóbal Colón bus station, basic, clean and helpful, US$2 p.p.

Restaurants *La Pantera Rosa* on the Zócalo, with flowers on the tables and big helpings. *Lupita*, just off the Zócalo, for regional food e.g. *palmita* and *queso frito con crema*, also large portions.

From Comitán the road winds down to the Guatemalan border at La Mesilla. Beyond, the "El Tapón" section, a beautiful stretch, leads to Huehuetenango, 85 km. This route is far more interesting than the one through Tapachula; the border crossing at La Mesilla is also reported as easier than that at Tapachula. A tourist card for Guatemala can be obtained at the Guatemalan Consulate in Comitán, Calle 1 Sur Poniente 42, normally available for 30 days, renewable in Guatemala City, US$1. Thirty-day visa, US$3.50.

Buses The Cristóbal Colón bus leaves Comitán at 0900 daily for the Guatemalan border at Ciudad Cuauhtémoc (not a town, despite its name: just a few buildings and a small restaurant), fare US$1. Once on the bus, fares are accepted in pesos, dollars or quetzales. Two buses come from Tuxtla at about 0800. Put name on waiting list. Connections with Rutas Lima at border for Guatemala City, which can be reached at 2000 hrs. (US$5) or El Cóndor, 2nd class, US$3.50 (7 hours). If you stop at Huehuetenango (an interesting place) there are plenty of buses on. If going to Panajachel or Chichicastenango first, better to stop overnight in Quezaltenango (US$3 from border), but there is a direct bus from the border to Los Encuentros (US$2.50), where a local bus may be caught (US$0.25) for Chichicastenango. Bus Tapachula-Comitán, US$4.80.

Airport Flights available to Lacanjá, Bonampak, Yaxchilán, contact Capitán Pérez Esquinca, Tel.: Comitán 4-91.

Yucatán Peninsula

A large and steadily increasing number of tourists come to Yucatán by road, railway, plane or cruise ship. Coatzacoalcos is the gateway to the area. The places which attract most visitors are: Villahermosa, Campeche, Mérida, the ruins of Palenque, Chichén Itza and Uxmal. A good paved road runs from Coatzacoalcos through Villahermosa, Campeche and Mérida (Route 180). All the great archaeological sites except one, Palenque, are on or just off this road and its continuation beyond Mérida. An inland road has been built from Villahermosa to Campeche to avoid 4 ferries across stretches of water around Ciudad del Carmen (this city has important fiestas at the end of July), which cause delays of several days during heavy rainstorms or *nortes*. This new road gives easy access by car to Palenque, hitherto reached only by train. There is now a train from Mexico City to Mérida which goes through Palenque; Pullman passengers can make the whole trip without leaving the car in 2 nights, US$16.50. Route 307 from Puerto Juárez to Chetumal is all paved and in very good condition; it is straight and there is very little traffic. Plane services from the U.S.A. and Mexico City are given under Mérida. Details of the direct road route from Guatemala City to Yucatán are given on page 792).

The Peninsula of Yucatán is a flat land of tangled scrub in the drier north-west, merging into exuberant jungle and tall trees in the wetter south-east. There are no surface streams. The underlying geological foundation is a horizontal bed of limestone in which rainwater has dissolved enormous caverns. Here and there their roofs have collapsed, disclosing deep holes or *cenotes* in the ground, their bottoms filled with water. Today this water is raised to surface-level by wind-pumps: a typical feature of the landscape. If there is no wind-pump, villages have to spend most of the day fetching water. It is hot during the day but cool after sunset. Humidity is often high. All round the peninsula are splendid beaches fringed with palm groves and forests of coconut palms. The best time for a visit is from October to March.

The people are divided into two groups: the pure-blooded Maya Indians, the minority, and the mestizos: the blood fusion of Spaniard and Mayan. The women wear huipiles, or white cotton tunics (silk for fiestas) which reach the ankles and are embroidered round the square neck and bottom hem. The huipiles are often worn short, disclosing an embroidered skirt flounce. Their hair is done in a tight bun, with a bow at the back. Ornaments are mostly gold. A few of the men still wear straight white cotton (occasionally silk) jackets and pants, often with gold or silver buttons, and when working protect this dress with aprons. Carnival is the year's most joyous occasion, with concerts, dances, processions. It ends with the crowning of the beauty queen and the ugly king. Yucatán's folk dance is the Jarana, the man dancing with his hands behind his back, the girl riasing her skirts a little, and with interludes when they pretend to be bullfighting. During pauses in the music the man, in a high falsetto voice, sings out *bambas* (compliments) to the girl.

The Mayas are a lovable, courteous, gentle, strictly honest and scrupulously clean people. They drink little, except on feast days, speak Mayan, and profess Christianity laced with a more ancient nature worship. Most of them live in Yucatán, Chiapas and Quintana Roo, but there is an aberrant offshoot in Veracruz which is Maya in speech but is not, it seems, ethnically allied. In Yucatán and Quintana Roo, the economy has long been dependent on the export of henequén (sisal), and chicle. There are 59,000 *ejido* henequén farmers and they are in a bad way—the trade is collapsing. A synthetic substitute has also been found for chicle, too, and the airstrips used for flying it out of the jungle are closing down.

Besides the Uxmal and Chichen-Itzá ruins of the early Maya cities described in the text, there are many others, most of them inaccessible, not yet excavated or even properly explored. They are not included here: archaeologists will know of them. The early history and accomplishments of the Maya people when they lived in Guatemala and Honduras before their mysterious trek northwards in the 10th century is given in the introductory chapter on Central America. (See page 883). They arrived in Yucatán about A.D. 600 and rebuilt their cities, but later in a different line, probably because of the arrival of Toltecs in the ninth and tenth centuries. Each city was autonomous, and in rivalry with other cities. In 1007, the League of Mayapán made a Triple Alliance between the cities of Chichén-Itzá, Uxmal, and Mayapán, with Chichén as capital. In 1194 Hunac Ceel, ruler of Mayapán, drove the Itzás out of Chichén and the league was at an end. The wars went on and the cities were weakened until they were reduced to ghosts of themselves. Before the Spaniards arrived the Mayas had developed a writing in which the hieroglyphic was somewhere between the pictograph and the letter. Bishop Landa collected their books, wrote a sinfully bad summary, the *Relación de las Cosas de Yucatán,* and with Christian but unscholarlike zeal, burnt all his priceless sources.

In 1511 some Spanish adventurers were shipwrecked on the coast. Two survived. One of them, Juan de Aguilar, taught a Maya girl Spanish. She became interpreter for Cortés after he had landed in 1519. The Spaniards found little to please them: no gold, no concentration of natives, but Mérida was founded in 1542 and the few natives handed over to the conquerors in encomiendas. The Spaniards found them difficult to exploit: even as late as 1847 there was a major revolt.

Coatzacoalcos, 60,000 people, the gateway for Yucatán, is 1½ km. from the mouth of its wide river. Built on a series of hills, it is pleasant but hot, and there is not much to do save watch the river traffic (river too polluted for fishing and swimming). Ocean-going vessels go upriver for 39 km. to Minatitlán, the petrochemical centre (35,000 people), whose huge oil refinery sends its products by pipeline to Salina Cruz. The road between the two towns carries very heavy industrial traffic. The offshore oil rigs are serviced from Coatzacoalcos. Sulphur is exported from the mines, 69 km. away.

Graham Greene landed at Coatzacoalcos and travelled to Villahermosa, Palenque, San Cristóbal de Las Casas, Mexico City and Veracruz, when he came to Mexico to obtain material for *The Power and the Glory* and the travel essays *The Lawless Roads*.

Hotels *Lemarroy; Oliden; Ritz; Tubilla; Palacio; Hotel Doce,* US$2.80 d, with shower and W.C. New hotels: *Margón; Valgrande.* Meals at Gloria Café.

Shipping Regular calls by Transportación Marítima Mexicana. Boats of many nations come and go several times a week.

Bus Regular bus service between Mexico City and Coatzacoalcos, US$9.60; Coatzacoalcos-Mérida US$11.20. To Veracruz (312 km.), Salina Cruz (US$1.60) and to near-by towns; to Minatitlán, to which taxis also ply.

Rail Train to Tehuantepec takes 13 hours (208 km.). Avoid train to Mérida.

Air Services Minatitlán airport, 30 minutes.

British Vice-Consul (also Lloyd's Agent), Lerdo 202 (Tel.: 420).

Cárdenas Elizabeth Allen writes: This town, 116 km. from Coatzacoalcos and 48 km. from Villahermosa, is expanding rapidly (headquarters of the Comisión del Grijalva, which is encouraging regional development). It has the Tikal chocolate factory which sells chocolate from stores quite cheaply. Just before Cárdenas the road passes through the area of the Chontalpa Project, which aims to bring previously unused marshy land into agricultural production by the resettlement of a scattered population into new villages. Between Cárdenas and Villahermosa are many stalls selling all varieties of bananas, a speciality of the area, and the road passes through the Samaria oilfield—the most northerly of the developing Tabascan fields. (From Chontalpa there is irregular transport to Randales on the lake formed by the Netzahualcoyotl dam.)

Villahermosa, capital of Tabasco State, is on the River Grijalva, navigable to the sea. It is very hot and rainy. There is an excellent archaeological museum (the Tabasco State museum), open 0900-1300, 1730-2000, on the very attractive main square above the river: trees, fountains and comparative coolness. There are astonishing monuments at roundabouts, etc., on the main roads around. Paved road to Coatzacoalcos and another S to the railway at Teapa, 50 km.; paved road to Tuxtla Gutiérrez (page 849). New inland road to Campeche, avoiding ferries, on which is the turnoff for Palenque. Population, over 110,000. Bus marked "Circuito 1" serves both the airport and the La Venta museum. Bus marked "C. Camionera" connects the 2nd class bus terminal on the edge of town with the ADO 1st class terminal, US$0.05. Turismo Nieves, Aldama 517, has been recommended to us and is reported to provide better information and to be more helpful than the tourist office on the Zócalo. Villahermosa is benefitting from the current oil boom, and many improvements are being carried out in the city. Perhaps this is also why it is now such an expensive place; hotels and restaurants cost twice as much as elsewhere in Mexico. Another drawback is that buses to Mexico City are often booked up well in advance, as are hotel rooms during the holiday season (May onwards).

Excursion NW of Villahermosa are the ruins of **Comalcalco,** easily reached by bus over dirt roads. The ruins are unique because the palaces and pyramids are built of bricks, long and narrow like ancient Roman bricks, and not of stone.

Airport Daily services to Mexico City, Tuxtla Gutiérrez and Mérida. Local flights to Palenque cost US$24, to Bonampak US$64.

In 1925 an expedition discovered huge sculptured animal figures, urns and altars in almost impenetrable forest at La Venta, 96 km. from Villahermosa. One puzzling fact is that the human figures are distinctly negroid, like those of some of the peoples of Oceania. About 1950 the monuments were threatened with destruction by the discovery of oil nearby. The poet Carlos Pellicer saved them by getting them hauled all the way to a woodland area near Villahermosa, now a beautiful small park with scattered lakes, next to a children's playground and almost opposite the airport entrance. There, in Parque La Venta, they may be seen today, dispersed in various small clearings. The huge heads—one of them weighs 20 tons—are Olmec, a culture which flourished about 1150-150 B.C. They are among the finest artefacts of the pre-Columbian era. Be sure to take insect-repellent for the visit. There is also a collection of lonely, dispirited and wretched live animals from the Tabasco jungle: monkeys, alligators, jaguars, deer, wild pigs and birds. Open 0830-1700, entrance US$0.17. There is an excellent swimming pool in the Ciudad Deportiva.

Hotels   *Manzur,* with restaurant, best food in town, new rooms, pleasant bar, from US$11 s, air-conditioned; *Gallardi; Tabasco,* US$8 s, not recommended; *San Diego,* US$5 s; *Hotel Pino Suárez,* near ADO bus station, not recommended; US$5.20 d; *Olmeca,* good and fairly reasonable, stocked fridge in room; meals US$2.40-3.20 (US$15 d); *Buenos Aires; Hotel María Dolores,* on Aldama and Reforma, from US$8.50 s, US$13 d, hot showers, excellent restaurant (closed Sundays); *Trébol,* Constitución 707, US$2.80 s, not recommended; *Palma de Mallorca.* Two new hotels, *Aristo* and *Maya Tabasco* on Coatzacoalcos-Campeche road; *Orient,* US$6.40 d, recommended; *Caballero,* US$5 s; *San Miguel,* US$6 s, clean, very good value, *Aurora,* Ave. 27 de Febrero, hot showers, US$2.50 s.

Motel   *Greene* (outside town, quite good, but no restaurant).

Restaurants   *El Mural,* highly recommended, 4-course lunch with drink included, US$4, dinner US$8, with band; *La Embajada,* good local food, suckling pig is the best; *Café Paris,* cheap and good; *La Rueda* serves good local specialities; the *Casino* for odd dishes like turtle steaks and dogfish; *Restaurant Los Azulejos* serves good lunch for US$2.40; avoid the bad and expensive tourist eating places on and near the river front.

If the Villahermosa-Mexico City bus is booked out, try taking the train from Teapa (buses run between Teapa and Villahermosa), 1st class pullman fare, US$20.50 p.p. (double the 1st class bus fare). The dining car is good but very expensive. Check in rainy season whether bridges are OK. (It took one passenger 56 hrs. to travel some 950 km. after being diverted.)

From Villahermosa you can fly to Campeche, or direct by a small plane carrying 3 passengers, to Palenque, in Chiapas, which can also be reached by plane from Tuxtla Gutiérrez and San Cristóbal de Las Casas, or by train from Coatzacoalcos, or by the new paved road from Villahermosa to Campeche (no gas stations until the Palenque turn-off; if you look like running out, turn left half-way for Macuspana, where there is one). This road, at 117 km. from Villahermosa, has a turning for Palenque, 26 km. away on a good paved road. (If short of time you can fly Mérida-Villahermosa early a.m., hire car at Villahermosa airport, drive to Palenque and back with 3½ hrs. at ruins, and catch 2000 flight from Villahermosa to Mexico City. The Editor did it!) Palenque can also be reached by a dirt road from San Cristóbal de Las Casas,, a rather rough ride; see also pages 849 and 851. There are fast trains daily from Mexico City at 0850 and Mérida, arrive at Campeche at 1230 and at Mérida at 0300 (1st class US$3.75, 2nd class US$2), just as good, daily at 2030. Tickets on sale from Estación de Ferrocarril Buenavista on day of departure after a certain hour, no numbered seats. Sandwiches and coke available, 12 hrs., and intolerably slow trains—freight is carried—on Tuesday, Thursday and Saturday; there is a regular bus service from the railway station of Palenque to the ruins (about 6 km.). The train return trip Palenque-Mérida (11 hrs.) at 2200 hrs. is very crowded and it may be necessary to stand all the way. Your best bet is to arrange for the "dormitorio" ahead of time (US$4-7). **N.B.** If returning from Palenque to Mérida on the night train, bear in mind that in Dec. and Jan. it is nearly impossible to make reservations. The station is 4 km. from Palenque. Beware of thieves at all times. Bus (1st class) to Mexico City, US$14.30, 15 hours, direct bus leaves 1730; to Campeche, US$4.40 (6 hrs.) daily at 1700; to Coatzacoalcos, US$1.45; to Tapachula, US$8.20, 14 hrs.; to Mérida leaves at 0920; to San Cristóbal, US$4.80, 9 hrs.; also 2nd class bus with one change at Tuxtla, leaves 0800, arrives 2100, fine scenery. Transportes Maya leave at 1230, reach Palenque at 2230.

Palenque is eminently worthwhile, with its series of hilltop temples in surprisingly good condition. The site is in a jungle clearing (with interesting wildlife, including mosquitoes) on a steep green hill overlooking the plain and crossed by a clear cascading brook (swimming no longer allowed), entry US$0.65, car park US$0.40. *Motel La Cañada*, not too clean, US$5.30 s, lovely garden, restaurant open, with dirt floor; meal US$2-2.50; the owner, Sr. Morales, is an expert on the ruins, which are located 8 km. from the village and have a museum, open 0700-1730. A restaurant by the cascades serves a limited range of food. Fresh orange juice at stalls inside ruins. *Motel Chan-Kah*, at Km. 31, between village and ruins, expensive (US$18 d) but good. The *Centro Turístico Cultural Chan-Kah* shows slides on Mayan art every evening and a drink thrown in. *Centro Turístico Tulijá*, on road to ruins, US$9-13 d, car park, satisfactory and convenient; hot water if you make them turn it on; mostly bungalows, 10 km. from ruins, 1 km. from village; pool being built. *Hotel Lacroix*, US$10.40 d; *Hotel Palenque*, US$4.20 s, with bath, a/c restaurant, poor service, has good rooms, long-distance telephone calls can be made from this hotel (sometimes "no rooms available", means "beds not made yet"; allow for this and insist). Opposite church: *Hotel León*, room and shower for US$2.80 with bath, not recommended. *Hotel Avenida,* clean, large rooms, US$8 d. Avoid *Hotel Regional,* unless on a budget, US$3 d, get an upstairs room with fan; *Hotel Mi-Sol-Ha,* new with a/c, very clean, US$10 for three. *Posada Alicia,* on the road on the left from the main road out, quiet, US$3.20 s. Eat at *Restaurant Maya,* on Zócalo, at moderately priced *Restaurant Tarde,* or rough restaurant *El Jade* in town. Water is often hard to get in the area. There is a good and friendly restaurant at the 2nd class bus station. *Comedor La Terminada,* off the main street, good value. We are told that the large influx of young "hippie-like" people has put off the locals, and visitors may be given misleading information. Visitors should respect the local customs and dress in such a way as not to offend—wear shoes and always a shirt; shorts on women are unwelcome!

First class bus goes daily from the ADO terminal (which is some way from the centre and beaches) at Villahermosa at 0800 and returns in afternoon, allowing 4½ hours (adequate) at ruins, US$4.80 return. Second class bus, US$3.20 return from the bus depot in the suburbs. One direct bus a day from Campeche to Palenque, leaves 0200, US$3.15. 9 hrs., US$1.45 (2nd), US$2.35 first class is the cost of the train from Campeche to Palenque, leaves at 2300. No regular bus service from station to town, taxi US$1.35. Daily 2nd class bus from Palenque to Mérida at 1700 (8 hrs.) and 1st class minibus to San Cristóbal de las Casas *via* Villahermosa. Bus from Palenque village to ruins leaves every hour (US$0.15), from *Hotel Léon* or at Pemex gas station at the top of the village. Some also go to Agua Azul, past ruins to beautiful waterfall. Local people rent rooms cheaply. Bus Agua Azul-Ocoringo, 4 hours, US$2, catch at 0500 to road junction (4 km.) and change to Ocosingo bus at 0600; this bus can connect to San Cristóbal de las Casas, 3 hours.

Camping *Trailer Park Mayabel,* on road to ruins 2 km. before entrance has all modern comforts for caravans and tents, hammocks permitted, US$0.70, good food. At night one can often hear the howler monkeys screaming in the jungle; quite eerie. *Agua Azul,* popular camping spot, but now littered by tourists, 63 km. from Palenque (abour 2 hrs.), on new road to San Cristóbal (2/3 km. tarmac, and Tulijá bridge under construction, temporary "hairy" bridge, direct bus twice daily, mainly morning, otherwise take bus to Ocosingo; buses stop at km. 63 where at 4 km. a dirt road to the waterfalls turns off), US$0.90. There are about 7 km. of fast-flowing river cascades near the small village of Agua Azul, aptly named for dazzling blue water swirling over petrified tree trunks that have over the ages created the cascades. Local *comedor* allows hammocks at US$0.45 a night. Good swimming at Nututún, 3 km. along Palenque-Agua Azul road (US$1.10 camping site per night, no tent rentals, no showers, restaurant; also a good hotel at Nututún, but expensive) and beautiful waterfall, Misolhá, at 22 km. Beware of ticks when camping in long grass, use kerosene to remove them. Watch out carefully for thieves; bring your own food, etc.

The ruins are impressive indeed, particularly the Pyramid of the Inscriptions, in the heart of which was discovered an intact funerary crypt with the Sarcophagus of the Sun God (illuminated 1000-1200 only), the temples around and the sculptured wall panels, undoubtedly the most exquisite achievement of the Mayas. Check time of opening of crypt. A small museum at the ruin has some excellent classical Mayan carvings. Entry to ruins, US$0.65, 0.40 per car for parking (Sundays cheaper).

Flights from Palenque to Bonampak and another site, at Yaxchilán, in light plane, for 4, US$144, to both places, whole trip 6 hrs. Prices set, list available; to Bonampak, US$108 for four; Yaxchilán more interesting. Otherwise hire a jeep at Palenque and drive there yourself; road very difficult in July-November.

Travelling from Villahermosa to Campeche one can follow either the old coastal route, Highway 180, which has 4 ferries (total cost for one car US$6.60) or the inland Highway 186, with 2 toll bridges (cost US$1.35). The coast road is good fun; **Ciudad del Carmen**, on the way, is hot, lazy and untouristy, and there are good beaches nearby. *Hotel Roma,* US$6 d, basic, but cheaper ones exist. Watch fishermen catch shrimp, or dolphins, in the harbour.

Elizabeth Allen writes: "The old coast road from Villahermosa to Campeche takes about 10 hours to drive but the views of the bright blue sea, the white sand and the palm trees are superb. You can also bathe on sandy beaches while waiting for the ferry to arrive! Ciudad del Carmen is renowned for its sea-food: giant prawns, clams, ceviche and baby hammerhead shark are all tasty. Petrol in Champotón (an attractive fishing village where the coastal and inland roads converge).

"Villahermosa-Chetumal takes about 6-7 hours to drive; service stations at the Palenque turning, just after the Candelaria turning, at Francisco Escárcega (where repairs can also be made, bank, market and road junction for Campeche) and only one gas station between there and Chetumal. Shortly after the turning to Palenque lies a newly paved road to Balancán. To the E of this village the road is unpaved and the area from San Pedro and El Triunfo to Tenosique is being opened up for a settlement scheme. Where the present railway bridge crosses the San Pedro River, Cortés and his men built a 500-metre bridge in four days. The Mayas had constructed dams or dykes in the river and it is said that these control it so that it barely flows. These dykes are decaying but can still be seen from the air and by boat. Other unexcavated ruins."

Villahermosa to Guatemala by car is *via* route 195 and 190 to Ciudad Cuauhtémoc *via* San Cristóbal de Las Casas. Highway 195 is very dangerous, narrow and winding with numerous landslides and washouts; high altitudes, beautiful scenery. Alternatively, travel back *via* route 180 to Acayucan, to 190, *via* 185 and go to Ciudad Cuauhtémoc or *via* route 200 to Tapachula.

Campeche, capital of Campeche state, population 120,000, is beautifully set on the western coast of Yucatán. It was the very first place at which the Spaniards set foot in 1517. In the 17th century it was fortified against pirates and still has the air of a fortress; seven bastions of the old walls and an ancient fort near the crumbling Cathedral remain. There are several 16th and 17th century churches within and without the city walls. The most interesting churches are San Francisquito (16th century with wooden altars painted in vermillion and white), Jesús, San Juan de Dios, Guadalupe and Cristo Negro de San Román. Its old houses are warmly coloured in pink and red and yellow. The rocky beaches are strewn with beautiful shells; nearest beaches are Playa Bonita and San Lorenzo. The people fish, trawl for shrimp, carve curios and make combs from tortoiseshell. There is a good museum and the new market building is attractive. The swimming and fishing resort of Lerma is quite near; take a rickety bus marked Lerma or Playa Bonita, 30-40 mins. (US$0.03). To the bus station, marked Gobernadores. Both these buses make a clockwise circuit around the ring road surrounding the old part of the city. Airport.

Dr. Robin Hoult writes: "Campeche still retains something of a colonial flavour, since it is a small town with an old centre of narrow streets, enclosed by an ancient rampart. This gives character to the place: this is reinforced by its inhabitants, who include many Mayans. The new market (just outside the city wall) is worth a visit, particularly to see Mayan women doing their shopping: they catch the eye with their grace and evident composure; beautifully dressed in embroidered white dresses showing long lace-trimmed petticoats. Plenty of bargains in the market here, especially Mexican and Mayan clothes, hats and shoes, fruit, vegetables; try some delicious ice-cream—though preferably from a shop rather than from a barrow. Campeche does not have its own beach, but it is a short bus ride to Playa Bonita where there is a beach with good facilities (café, beach huts and chairs), and good bathing—by Gulf standards at least. Campeche is also handy for several nearby Mayan sites."

Hotels *Baluartes,* new, good accommodation; parking for campers, who can use the hotel washrooms, US$16 d, meal US$2.40-3.20, pool; *López,* Calle 12, No. 189, US$7.40d, with bath, better food; *Señorial,* Calle 10 (comfortable, US$16 d, with bath, no restaurant); *Hotel Campeche,* US$3.20 d, with shower and w.c.; *Castelmar,* colonial style, US$4.60 d, with bath, good value; *Cuauhtémoc,* US$3.20s, with bath, in old house near the square (Calle 57); *Casa de Huéspedes Reyes,* clean, US$4 large d, and *Roma, América* and *México,* US$5.60 d, on Calle 10. A new *Hotel El Presidente* is being built near the *Baluartes* on the seafront. *Colonial,* clean, good, Calle 10, nr. Calle 57, US$7.45 d; *Hotel Central,* opp. bus terminal, clean, fan and bathroom, US$5.85 d, front rooms somewhat noisy; *Regis,* US$1.50 s. 20 km. S of Campeche is *Hotel Sel-ho,* US$11 for three, excellent, beautiful setting on Gulf coast, swimming and other facilities. It is virtually impossible to get hotel rooms around the Mexican holiday period, starting May.

Restaurants *Campeche,* good value; cafeteria next door sells good yoghurt and fruit juices; *Miramar* (good seafood, reasonable); *La Perla* (excellent fish, cheap), venison, squid; locals' haunt, sometimes erratic service, off Zócalo; *Lonchería Puga; Portales.*

Tourist Information New centre near beach, close to Palacio de Gobierno, good.

Shopping Good state Artesanía shop on top of Baluarte San Carlos; excellent cheap Panama hats. Handicrafts are generally cheaper than in Mérida.

Excursions Two km. S. of Campeche is the 18th-century fort of San Miguel, containing museums and worth visiting. One display demonstrates the repeated sackings, by pirates, of Campeche before its great walls were built.

About 40 km. beyond Campeche on the road to Uxmal, there is a deviation, right, along a white stone road for 7 km. to the pyramid of Edzná, worth a visit (entry, US$0.16); if time allows about 70 mins. by bus, US$0.35, at 0700. Return 1200. SE of Edzná are Dzibilnocac and Hochob sites, with elaborately decorated temples and palaces. For these sites you need a car as the bus returns to Campeche almost at once after arrival at Dzibilnocac, and there is nowhere to stay. About half-way to Mérida a sign, right, points to the Sayil ruins by a dry-season dirt road; 1 km. after leaving the main road, take the right-hand fork and carry on for 4 km. (bad road). Eight km. beyond Sayil is a small ruin, X-Lapak, and 8 km. further on is Labná. By the main road, right, about 5½ km. beyond the sign for Sayil, are the ruins of Kabah where there is a fascinating Palace of Masks, whose façade bears the image of Chac, repeated over and over again about six hundred times in a mesmeric way which even Stalin never quite managed. (The style is classic Puuc. Watch out for snakes and spiders.) There is no transport between Kabah and Sayil except for private jeeps. The walk between Sayil and the Palace (admission US$0.40) takes a good 2 hours. Bus: Campeche-Kabah, US$1.28. For those with a car continue from Kabah on route 261 to the very picturesque villages of Hopelchen and Bolonchen de Rejón. Kabah is also not far from Uxmal, and is often visited in the course of tours of the latter. Recommended reading for the area: *The Maya,* by D. M. Coe (Pelican Books).

For the ruins of Labná, leave the road 5 km. beyond Kabah, at Santa Elena, and take a roughish track. Labná has a most astonishing arch. Both Sayil and Labná are in deep jungle. From Labná, continue to immense galleries and caves of Bolonchén (bus from Mérida). You *must* take a guide and a powerful torch. If visiting Sayil, X-Lapak and Labná, it is cheaper to hire a jeep and driver from the village of Santa Elena, costing US$19.80 for 1-3 persons. Roads are now being built to these ruins.

Eighty km. N of Campeche is Becal, centre of the panama hat trade. The hats are made in man-made limestone caves, whose coolness and dampness facilitate the weaving.

You can go to Mérida by rail, 4 hours, or by road, 252 km. (158 miles). First class buses go by the Camino Real, which does *not* pass through Uxmal, Kabah, etc. Take a really quite comfortable 2nd class bus (US$0.08) from the same terminal, have 3 hours at the ruins, and catch the next bus to Mérida (US$0.24), but don't buy a through ticket to Mérida; you'll have to pay again when you board the bus. Check bus times, as there are fewer in the afternoon. Buses along new inland road to Villahermosa. Bus (2nd class) to Uxmal costs US$1.80; Bus Kabah-Uxmal US$0.32. Bus Campeche-Uxmal, US$1.80, 1½ hours. Train Campeche-Palenque, 2nd class, US$2.30, 9½ hours, leaves at 2310.

177 km. beyond Campeche is **Uxmal**, 74 km. from Mérida. The famous Mayan ruins at Uxmal (meaning Three Times Sacred) are on a plain circled by hills and, unlike those of Chichén-Itza, cover comparatively little ground: the ruins (entrance US$0.40), indeed, are quite unlike those at Chichen-Itzá. Uxmal, the home of the Xiu tribe, was founded in 1007. Its finest buildings seem to have been built much later, under Nahua (late Maya) influence. See El Adivino (the Sorcerer, pyramid-shaped, topped by two temples with a splendid view); the Casa de las Monjas (House of Nuns), a quadrangle with 88 much adorned rooms; the Casa de Gobernador (House of the Governor), on three terraces, with well preserved fine sculptures; the Casa de las Tortugas (Turtle House) with six rooms; the Casa de las Palomas (House of Doves), probably the oldest; and the Cemetery. Ruins close at 1700. Expensive drinks at entrance of ruins. Many iguanas (harmless) wandering about, watch out for occasional scorpions. There is a *son et lumière* display at the ruins nightly—English version at 2100 (check for times). From Mérida go with Autotransportes from the main bus station at 1715. Return ticket US$2.75. Return to Mérida after the show is only possible with tourist buses. *Son et lumière* costs US$4. For best photographs early morning arrival is essential.

Hotels *Hacienda Uxmal,* in Uxmal, is quite good but very expensive (US$43 for 2, including meals, daily). Swimming pool. It has less expensive dependency *Posada Uxmal*—US$32 for 2, including meals; dinner costs US$5 and is overpriced. Accommodation only at *Posada Uxmal* is US$11 d. *Hotel Lapalapa,* US$36 for 2, including meals. Uxmal is easily reached by 1st and 2nd class buses from Mérida. From the *Hacienda Uxmal* jeeps visit the four ruins of Kabah, Sayil, Xlapac and Labná daily, US$20 p.p., incl. box lunch. The Sayil and Labná road is only passable with a 4-wheel drive vehicle.

There is a good paved road (74 km.) from Uxmal to Mérida. Muna (15 km. from Uxmal; delightful square and old church), is the nearest station to Uxmal. There are two roads connecting Uxmal with Chetumal, on the Belize frontier. One (Highway 186) (paved) branches off to the SE from Francisco Escárcega with interesting ruins at Chicana (145 km.), Becán (watch for very small sign—146 km.), X-Puhil (153 km.), *via Francisco Villa* (217 km.) (see below). The road is in excellent condition and there is very little traffic. There are a couple of military checkpoints en route where documents must be shown. The other Uxmal-Chetumal road is through Muna, Ticul (where pottery, hats and shoes are made), **Peto** and Felipe Carrillo Puerto. All the towns between Muna and Peto have large old churches. Beyond Peto the scenery is scrub and swamp as far as the frontier.

F. Escárcega has a couple of hotels, better avoided; but if you do stop there, there is a bus to Palenque at 0430, US$4.30, 3 hrs.; the Mayan site of Hochob, with ornate palace façades reminiscent of the Chinese, is near the town. Escárcega is on the Mexico City-Palenque-Mérida railway line, Bus, Escárcega-Chetunmal, 3½ hrs., US$4.50

Chetumal, the capital of the state of Quintana Roo, is a free port with clean wide streets. Good for imported goods such as cameras and radios; also foreign foodstuffs—cheaper at covered market in outskirts than in centre (Also good to sell an imported car at advantage, in suburb of Calderitas; ask for Lorenzo.) Bad for mosquitoes though, and otherwise high prices. W of Chetumal, just before turn to Belize, a restaurant. Just N of Chetumal is Laguna de los Milagros, a beautiful lagoon, and 34 km. N of Chetumal, on the road to Tulum, is Cenote Azul, over 70 metres deep, with an expensive waterside restaurant serving good regional food. About 3 km. N is the village of **Bacalar** on the Laguna de Siete Colores; swimming and skin-diving. There is a frequent minibus service from the street alongside the bus terminal in Chetumal, US$0.35 s. There is a Spanish fort there; hotel and good restaurants on the Laguna. *Buk-Halot*, US$9.50 d, and a cheap but comfortable *casa de huéspedes* near the *fortín* on the park; gasoline is sold in a side-street. From Chetumal one can visit the fascinating Mayan ruins that lie on the way to Escárcega. Buses leave at 0600 (2nd class) from Chetumal to Francisco Villa and X-Puhil; there is no direct transport to Kohunlich, Becán and Chicana, so from X-Puhil the following journey must be done privately. Just before Francisco Villa lie the ruins of **Kohunlich** (entry US$0.40), about 7 km. S to the main road, where there are fabulous masks set on the side of the main pyramid, still bearing red colouring; they are unique of their kind. Seven km. further on from **X-Puhil** (all that remains of one large pyramid, beside the road), lies the large maya site of **Becán,** shielded by the forest with wild animals still wandering among the ruins, with vast temples and plazas and a decayed ball court. Two km. further on and 10 minutes down a dirt track lies **Chicana**, with a superb Toltec-cum-Maya temple with an ornate central door which has been formed in the shape of the open-fanged jaws of the plumed serpent. Buses return from X-Puhil at 1300 and 1700. N of Chetumal are also 3 unexcavated archaeological sites, Ichpaatun (13 km.), Oxtancah (14) and Nohochmul (20). Chetumal has an airport. There are no banks at the border.

Hotels at Chetumal: *San Jorge,* US$8 d, car parking, highly recommended; *San Francisco,* US$2.70 d, if desperate; better nearby is *Pensión Tabasco,* clean, fan, US$3.60 d, with bath; *El Dorado,* Avenida 5 de Mayo 21, US$8 d (no restaurant); *America,* US$2 s, basic; six blocks downhill from bus station on the right; *Posada Margot,* 5 de Mayo 12, basic, US$3.20 d; *Jacarandá,* not recommended; *Alcócer,* US$2.70, clean and friendly, near post-office, Av. Lázaro Cárdenas; *Luz María,* clean, friendly, US$7.20 d, owner speaks English; *Hotel Baroudi,* Obregón y Héroes, *Hotel María Dolores,* Alvaro y Obregón 206 and *Hotel Dorys,* Avenida Héroes 41a, all charge US$3.50 s, with bath. Plenty more. *Restaurant Vaticano* at back of bus station, reasonable.

Buses from Chetumal   Many buses going to the border, US$0.15. ADO to Mexico City *via* Villahermosa, 22 hours, US$20, leaves at 2100 daily; bus to Francisco Escárcega, 3½ hrs., US$2.75; Batty-Bus to Belize, 5½ hours, US$3, leaves Tues., Thurs., and Sat. at 1000; from main bus station. (Ask Mr. Batty, the owner of Batty-Buses, for his opinion, based on appearance, of whether you will be allowed to enter

Belize!) Blue Bird bus from bus terminal to Belize City on Tues., Thurs, and Sat., 1000 hrs., US$2.65 s. On entering Belize you must purchase insurance at a cost of BH$4 a week. Bus, Chetumal to Mérida, US$5.60 1st class, at 0700 and 1850, about 5½ hrs. Bus Chetumal-Felipe Carrillo Puerto, US$1.60, 2 hours, many, on excellent road.

Maps of roads in Quintana Roo are obtainable in Chetumal at Junta Local de Caminos, Secretaría de Obras Públicas. The road from Chetumal through Tulum (see page 868) to Merida (*via* Cancún) is paved.

Mérida, capital of Yucatán state, population 253,900, is one of the most interesting cities in Mexico. It was founded in 1542 on the site of the Mayan city of Tihoo. Its centre is Plaza Mayor, green and shaded by trees and bright with promenading youth in the evening; its arcades have more than a touch of the Moorish style brought by the Spanish conquerors. It is surrounded by the severe twin-towered 16th century Cathedral, the City Hall, the State Government Palace, and Montejo House, originally built in 1549 by the *conquistador* of the region and rebuilt around 1850 (open each afternoon exc. Sundays, guided tour by present owner, a Montejo descendant and a real character). Its porch and window frames are richly ornamented with Mannerist sculpture. In the basement of the Casa de los Gobernadores, on Paseo de Montejo—an impressive building in the turn-of-the-century French style of the Porfirio Díaz era—is a most interesting museum well worth a visit by scholars: the Museo de Arqueología, closed on Mondays (open 0800-1400 Sun, 0800-2000 all other days). There are several 16th and 17th century churches dotted about the city: Tercera Orden, San Francisco, San Cristóbal, and La Mejorada. The streets are narrow—a tropical downpour is liable to turn them into water courses—with antique walls, pink, green and pale blue. Along them ply horse-drawn cabs of a curious local design. All the markets, and there are several, are interesting in the early morning. One can buy traditional crafts: a basket or sombrero of sisal, a filigree necklace, also a good selection of Maya replicas. Tortoiseshell articles are also sold, but cannot be imported to the USA as sea turtles are protected by law under the Endangered Species Act of 1973. The Mérida market is also particularly good for made-to-measure sandals of deerskin and tyre-soles, panama hats, and hammocks of all sizes and qualities. One of the most typical products is the *guayabera,* a pleated and/or embroidered shirt worn universally in the town, its feminine counterpart the *guayablusa,* and beautiful Mayan blouses and *huipiles.* In the Park of the Americas is an open-air theatre giving plays and concerts. There are quite a number of monuments to Felipe Carrillo Puerto, an agrarian labour leader prominent in the 1910 revolution. Redevelopment is rapid; many of the old houses are being pulled down. Mérida is a safe city at night. The Mayas are a gentle people; (for example) the number of murders in the city in 1977 was one.

Dr. Robin Hoult writes: "A large and prosperous town, bustling with tourists; colourful, noisy, alive. Cathedral, main square, library (very musty old books!), horse-drawn carriages, some outlying churches, all have modest appeal. Lots of things to buy—well supplied with markets, tourist shops and so on.

"Tourists are mainly Americans and French, with some Germans and very few Britons. Several charter flights operate directly to Mérida, e.g. from Paris, and this explains the Common Market flavour down the Yucatán-San Cristóbal-Belize-Guatemala axis. It is worth looking into and having a drink at some of the best hotels: they cater principally for Americans, and have beautiful patios with tropical plants, often laid out and decorated in colonial style with considerable flair."

In Paseo de Montejo, together with the archaeological museum and many shops and restaurants, there are many grand late 19th century houses. The streets are laid out in rectangles, with numbers instead of names: Calle 65 is the main shopping street. Odd numbers are E and W, even numbers N and S. In Colonial times, painted or sculpted men or animals placed at intersections were used as symbols for the street: some still exist in the small towns of Yucatán. The houses are mostly of Spanish-Moorish type, painted in soft pastel tones, thick walls, flat roofs, massive doors, grilled windows, flowery patios. The water supply, once notorious, is now good. There are still horse-drawn carriages for hire. Begging and much molestation from car-washers, shoe-shiners and souvenir-peddlers. All streets are one-way. Local town maps are poor, but you can enquire very politely for a free map at the Secretaría de Obras Públicas, almost opposite airport at Mérida (cheap bus from centre). Enquire at hotels about the House and Garden Tours run by the local society women for tourists to raise money for charity. Every Thursday evening there is free local music, dancing and poetry in the Plaza Santa Lucía, two blocks from the Plaza Mayor, popular with locals and visitors. Silver items are much better and cheaper than in Mexico City, or in Peru. There is a particularly good shop next to Pan-Am offices. The Ermita, an 18th century chapel with beautiful well-laid-out grounds is full of impressive pre-Columbian sculpture; a lonely, deserted place 10-15 minutes from the centre.

In the State Government Palace, on the Plaza Mayor, there is a series of superb symbolic and historical paintings, finished 1978, by a fine local artist, Fernando Castro Pacheco. The Palace is open evenings and very well lit to display the paintings.

Fiesta Carnival on Tuesday before Ash Wednesday.

Hotels *Francia,* US$8 d; *Mérida; Colón; Grande,* US$10 d, good, fine restaurant; *Casa Bowen,* restored Colonial house, corner of Calle 66, No. 521-B, and 65, US$5 d, excellent value, as is *Posada del Angel,* Calle 67, No. 535, between Calle 66 and 68, US$6.60 d, clean, excellent value; *Reforma,* US$7.20 d; *México,* US$8.80 (good restaurant, attractive); *Caribe,* US$8.80, on Calle 62 and others, all expensive. *Hotel Milo,* Calle 63, basic but very clean and friendly, US$6 d. New: *Panamericana* (good, expensive, with elaborate courtyard in the perfect, bad "Porfirian" style, very spacious and airy, with swimming pool, and close to centre); and *Castellano,* Calle 57, No. 513, modern, clean, friendly, pool, US$27 s, US$28 d; *Montejo* (do bargain here to approx. US$4.50), recommended, as is *Hotel Cayre; Sevilla,* US$5 s, with bath; *América,* simple, private shower and toilet, clean, US$4 d. Recommended: *Posada Toledo,* central, in charming old house, US$7.50 for two, without meals; *Hotel del Maya,* US$7 d, with bath, swimming pool and car park; *Hotel Chac-mool,* a few blocks W of railway station, pool, night-club (very noisy, poor service), US$5 s; *Hotel Flamingo,* US$10 d, with private shower, swimming pool, excellent value; *Nacional,* US$8 d; *Palacio,* Calle 54/55, US$2.80; *Margarita,* Calle 63/67, US$2.80; *Del Arco,* Calle 63-452, US$3.60 s; *Princess,* cheap, good value; *Hotel Regis,* US$5 d; *Hotel San Jorge* (across from main bus terminal), new, clean, US$9 d; *Hotel San José,* cheap, US$5 d, half block from Plaza Mayor, clean; *Hotel Mucuy,* Calle 57, friendly, good, US$4.50 d, with shower; *Hotel Rodríguez,* Calle 69, near market, US$5.60 d, clean, good service, recommended; *Casa de Huéspedes,* US$3.60 d, pleasant and quiet, Calle 62, No. 507. Rooms on Calle 66 Norte No. 386 (with private bath and single rooms from US$1). New, out of town and pleasant is *El Cortijo,* Calle 54 No. 365, all a/c (mind the mosquitoes).

Restaurants Specialist dishes good. *Los Tulipanes; Itzá.* Very good ones: *Pancho Villa's Follies,* very friendly, try *abalones,* owner speaks English; and *Soberani,* Paseo de Montejo, serving delicious fish dishes. *Los Almendros,* Calle 50, for Yucatán specialities, recommended but mind the peppers!; *Tepepan, Mesón del Mestizo* (Plaza Sta. Lucía), *Pórtico del Peregrino* (Calle 57, between 60 and 62), Cafetería of *Hotel Caribe* (Parque Hidalgo, on Calle 60), *Los Portales,* Calle 60 (charming patio) and *Yanal-Luum* are medium-price; there is a vegetarian restaurant on the Paseo de Montejo; *Reforma, Eriks* and *Pancho Villa's Follies* are cheap; the *Patio Español,* inside the *Gran Hotel,* well cooked and abundant food, local and Spanish specialities, moderate prices; *Restaurant Express,* Calle 60, has good *huachinango a la Veracruzana; Filili; Louvre,* cheap; *Restaurant David,* Calle 62 No. 468A (Arab food); *Leo's,* good value for meat dishes, pleasant, Calle 60, just N of Plaza Santa Lucía; *La Sin Rival,* Calle 60, 501, great value, locals go there. Next door is *Jugos California,* good fruit juices, also in Calle 65. *Dulcería Colón,* on Zócalo, for excellent ices; *Pop,* opposite university, popular with students. A splendid open-air *pizzería,* warmly recommended (both drive-in and tables) on the big roundabout at N end of Paseo de Montejo.

Shopping *Guayaberas:* good ones at *Canul,* Calle 59, No. 496; terylene ones at *Genuina Yucatteca,* Calle 50, N. 520. At *Mayalandia* on Calle 61, before Calle 48 archway, one can bargain. *Jack* in Calle 59, near Canul, makes *guayaberas* to measure in 4 hrs., expensive.

The best hammocks are the so-called 3-ply, about US$13; also mosquito nets. Try *Mayoreo de Mérida,* Calle 65, or *La Poblana,* both near Post Office; *La Poblana* also has a shop in Calle 65.

Travel Agents Barbachano's Travel Service, very efficient but expensive; Cooks Wagon-Lits, helpful, Calle 60, No. 466; Cozumel Travel Service. Avis; Hertz; Yucatán Trails.

Train To Mexico City, US$12.80 1st class, US$36 Pullman, leaves Mérida at 1940 (36 hrs.). Possible to break journey at Palenque but not on one ticket. Sleeping car to Palenque, "Alcoba", old-fashioned but very comfortable.

Buses To Mexico City, US$17.60, 22 hrs.; to Coatzacoalcos, US$11.20. To Puerto Juárez, US$3.90 1st, US$3.40 2nd class. Excursions to Uxmal and Chichén Itzá by 1st and 2nd class buses from ADO terminal on Calle 69 and 68. To Uxmal, 2nd class buses leave every 3 hours from 0600, 1½ hrs., US$0.70; regular buses to Campeche (2nd class, US$1.70) also pass Uxmal. Last bus from Uxmal to Campeche (2¼ hrs., US$1.40) at 2315 is quite crowded. To Chichén Itza at 0900, 1030, 1300, US$1.05 (return at 1530, 1700 and 2000), and for 1st class (US$3) at 0830. Buses to Progreso and Dzibilchaltun (3 a day, 0730, 1215 and 1600), leave from the bus station on Calle 62, between Calle 65 and 67. One direct bus daily at 1300 from Mérida (*via* Villahermosa and Pichucalco) to Tuxtla Gutiérrez, arrives in the 2nd class bus station, Autotransportes del Sureste de Yucatán, at 0600. One can arrange to visit Kabah, Sayil, X-Lapak and Labná at the Mérida bus station; one goes to Muna by ordinary bus and from there by pre-arranged jeep.

Bus to Palenque from Mérida leaves 2330 from ADO terminal on Calle 69, arrives 0830. Bus to Mérida *via* Campeche from Palenque, with Líneas Unidas de Chiapas, leaves Palenque at 1700 hrs., daily.

Route 261 Mérida-Escárcega, paved and in very good condition. Buses.

Central Post Office Calle 65. Generally crowded, use branches at airport (also for quick delivery) or on Calle 58, instead.

British Vice Consul Corner Calles 58 and 53. Tel.: (91-992) 1-679-9. Postal address Apdo. 89.

To Guatemala by public transport from Yucatán, take train from Mérida to Pichucalco; it get in about 1300. Take a small bus downtown and catch the bus to Tuxtla Gutiérrez. Road is slow, so it is probably quicker to cut across from Coatzacoalcos. Alternatively travel on the Mexico-Mérida line to San Pedro (2 hrs. east of Palenque) on the San Pedro River and catch a small boat up river (ask for La Coya cheap rate) to El Martillo, the Mexican border post, then carry on to El Ceibo in Guatemala. Beautiful trip. Autotransportes del Sureste de Yucatán bus from Mérida to Tuxtla, *via* Palenque and Ocosingo to either San Cristóbal or Comitán; 2 or 3 changes of bus. Alternatively, go from Mérida direct to Tuxtla at 1330 hrs., then direct either Tuxtla-Ciudad Cuauhtémoc or to Tapachula; although the journey may not be as pretty, it saves changing. Road to Belize: paved all the way to Chetumal. (See the route given in the opposite direction, page 849.)

By Air 2½ hours from New Orleans (US$71, five days a week on Aviateca); 1¾ hours from Miami (US$77) *via* Tampa; 2 hours from Mexico City, 960 km. Pan-American World Airways flies the routes Miami-Tampa-Mérida-Mexico City and Miami-Mérida-Central America. One-day round trip from Tijuana (20 min. from San Diego, California) by Acsa airline, US$159. Vega flies every other day to Oaxaca on to Acapulco. Lufthansa flies Frankfurt-Montreal-Mérida-Mexico twice weekly. Aeroméxico flies from Mérida *via* Veracruz and Monterrey to Los Angeles, 3 times a week. A No. 79 bus marked "Aviación" will take you from and to the terminal to town for a few coppers. The airport is splendid; direct flights also to Guatemala City by Aviateca on Tues., Thurs. and Sat. The smaller airlines tend to offer cheaper flights, in older aircraft. Food and drinks at the airport are very expensive. Airport tax US$4.80.

Halfway to Progreso turn right from the Maya ruins of Dzibilchaltun. This unique city, according to carbon dating, was founded as early as 1000 B.C. The most important building is the Temple of the Seven Dolls (partly restored). The Cenote Xlaca contains very clear water and is 44 metres deep.

Progreso, the port, 39 km. away, is reached by road or railway. Population 14,000; temperatures range from 27° to 35°C. Main export: henequen. It claims to have the longest stone-bridge pier in the world. Distances, in sea miles: to Veracruz, 400; to New Orleans, 550. Hotel on the lovely beach. Pleasant bathing.

The beach front by the pier is devoted to cafés with seafood cocktails as their speciality. They also have little groups performing every weekend afternoon in summer; and the noise can be both spirited and deafening.

A short bus journey from Progreso are Puerto Yucalpetén and Chelem. Balneario Yucalpetén has a beach with lovely shells. Nearby Chelem is a small, unspoilt fishing village. Between the Balneario and Chelem there is a nice hotel of small Mayan-hut type bungalows, *Hotel Villanueva* and also *Costa Maya*, on Calle 29 Carretera Cortera, with restaurant. Fish restaurants in Chelem, *Las Palmas* and *El Cocalito,* reasonable, also other small restaurants.

Hotels in Progreso *Hotel Miramar, Posada Familiar* and *Casa de Huéspedes Bonanza*. Good restaurant and quite cheap is *El Cordobés*; expensive but good are *Soberanis* and *La Terraza*. Police permit free beach camping. Many homes, owned by Mexico City residents, available for rent; typical prices, US$50 a month (4 beds) services included. Good local market with lowest food prices in Yucatán. You can buy fresh shrimps cheaply in the mornings on the beach.

North-west of Mérida, about 52 km. (buses), is Sisal beach where one can hire a boat and go to the reef of Los Alacranes where many ancient wrecks are visible in clear water. West of Mérida regular buses serve Celestún beach with a huge lagoon with flamingoes; hire a boat. From Mérida one can get to **Loltún**, taking a bus to Oxcutzcab between Ticul and Peto (see page 839) and from there by local lorry plus guide to Loltún, fantastic caverns.

Excursions from Mérida To **Chichén-Itzá,** 120 km. by a paved road running SE from Mérida. The scrub forest has been cleared from over 5 square km. of ruins. The city was founded in 432, refounded in 987, and taken over by the militaristic Toltecs in the 10th century; the major buildings in the northern half are Toltec. Dominating them is El Castillo, its top decorated by the symbol of Quetzacoatl, and the balustrade of the 91 stairs up each of the four sides is decorated by a plumed, open-mouthed serpent. There is also an interior ascent to a chamber lit by electricity where the red-painted jaguar which probably served as the throne of the high priest burns bright, its eyes of jade, its fangs of flint; special tours to see this. There is a ball court with grandstand and towering walls each set with a projecting ring of stone high up; at eye-level is a relief showing the decapitation—death was the penalty for defeat—of the losing captain. El Castillo stands at the centre of the northern half of the site, and almost at right-angles to its northern face, runs the sacred way to the Cenote Sagrado, the Well of Sacrifice. The other cenote, the Xtoloc Well, was probably used as a water supply. It requires at least one day to see the many pyramids, temples, ballcourts and palaces, all of them adorned with astonishing sculptures, and excavation and renovation is still going on. Old Chichén, where the Mayan buildings of the earlier city are, lies about ½ km. by path from the main clearing. Chichén-Itzá is easily reached from Mérida by 1st (ADO) and 2nd class buses, about 2 hours' journey; the journey can later be continued to Puerto Juárez and Isla Mujeres, which is reached by launches (45 min. crossing), US$0.50. Entry to Chichén-Itzá, US$0.70 (Sunday morning US$0.45); check at entrance for opening times of the various buildings. Entry to see the jaguar is at 1130-1300 and 1600-1700. The badly translated guide-book of José Díaz Bolio provides some interesting background comment; the little Bloomgarden booklet is also interesting.

Into the Cenote Sagrado were thrown valuable propitiatory objects of all kinds, animals and human sacrifices. The well was first dredged by Edward H. Thompson, the U.S. Consul in Mérida, between 1904 and 1907; he accumulated a vast quantity of objects in pottery, jade, copper and gold. In 1962 the well was explored again by an expedition sponsored by the National Geographical Society and some 4,000 further artefacts were recovered, including beads, polished jade, lumps of copal resin, small bells, a statuette of rubber latex, another of wood, and a quantity of animal and human bones. The bottom of the well is paved with the ruins of a fallen temple. There are several tours daily to the Balancanchén Caves, 3 km. E, just off the highway, but bad guidance. However, worth the trip, it is very humid and you may have to go through tight apertures, so dress accordingly. Not for claustrophobics. Open 0800-1100 and 1400-1600, except Sunday afternoons.

Hotels *Mayaland Hotel,* very, very expensive; *Hacienda,* with swimming pool, etc., room US$10 s, US$14 d EP. *Pirámide Inn,* US$28 d with food, swimming pool, well run, also *Pirámide Inn Trailer Court,* camping, US$1, allows use of *Pirámide Inn* swimming pool; *Chichén-Itzá,* US$36 d with food; *Lapalapa Chichén,* US$26.25 d with breakfast and dinner, a few km. from the ruins, excellent restaurant, modern, park with animals. *Hacienda Chichén,* US$28 d, once owned by Edward Thompson, the U.S. consul in Mérida, who originally investigated the ruins. *Hotel Restaurant Carrousel,* US$7 d. But you can enquire at the village for the owner of a thatched cottage and stay there for US$0.80; Cafés and restaurants at Chichén-Itzá and the next village are dear too. *Dolores Alba,* small hotel, 2½ km. on the road to Puerto Juárez, good and comfortable, US$6.50 d, with shower; has swimming pool and serves meals. Campers welcomed. English spoken. New cheaper hotel: *Posada Novelo,* about 2 km. from ruins, US$4.40 s, in village of Pisté, reasonable restaurants nearby. *Hotel Cunanchén,* also in Pisté, prices negotiable with owner; ask to see private cenote.

On the way back, turn to the right at Kantunil (68 km. from Mérida) for a short excursion to the charming little town of **Izamal,** to see the ruins of a great mausoleum, a huge old convent, and the magnificent early Franciscan church (1553).

From Izamal one can go by the 1630 bus to **Cenotillo,** where there are several lovely cenotes within easy walking distance from the town (avoid the one *in* town), especially U-Cil, excellent for swimming, and La Unión. From Mérida, take 1530 train to Tunkas, and then bus to Cenotillo. Lovely train ride, US$0.20. Past Cenotillo is Espita and then a road forks left to Tizimín (see below).

Mayapán is a large, peaceful late Mayan site easily visited by bus from Mérida; also two large pyramids in village of Acanceh en route.

From Mérida one can also visit **Valladolid** (pop. 30,000), a Mayan town on the paved road between Mérida and Puerto Juárez.

Hotels *María de la Luz,* good, swimming pool and small night-club, restaurant, closes at 2230; *San Clemente,* US$6.80 s, US$9.80 d, with air conditioning, US$4.60 with fan, has car park, swimming pool, opposite Cathedral, in centre of town.

Mesón del Marqués, US$2.20 or US$3 s (air-conditioned), with bath. New, quiet and excellent is *Hotel María Guadalupe,* Calle 44, No. 198, US$2.50 d, with bath. *Hotel Lili,* US$3 d, without bath, clean, friendly, good; next to it is *Hotel Osorno,* US$2.70 d, hot water (but only very early a.m.), next to market, recommended. In *Casa de los Huéspedes,* 6 blocks from bus station, hammocks US$0.40 a night.

Direct buses to Chichén-Itzá, allowing 3½-hour visit, US$0.35, 1 hour ride, and to Puerto Juárez, US$1.35, from 0800.

One can swim in the electrically-lit cenote of Dzit-Nup (US$0.16) outside Valladolid. Extensive ruins at Aké, unique structure; take bus from Mérida (last bus back 1700). Also from Mérida, take bus to Tecóh, and see the caverns of Dzab-Náh; you must take a guide as there are treacherous drops into cenotes. Grottoes of Loltún (see page 865) are spectacular. Visit the big cenote of Zaci with a restaurant and lighted promenades. Road turns left from Puerto Juárez road a couple of blocks from Zócalo.

A paved road heads N (buses) from Valldolid to **Tizimín**, a very pleasant town with a 16th-century church and convent, open squares and narrow streets. There is a good restaurant, *Tres Reyes.* The road continues N over the flat landscape to **Río Lagartos**, where the Mayans extracted salt. A new hotel has been built, there are a number of small eating places, and boat-trips can be arranged to see the flocks of flamingoes feeding on the lagoon. The locals are said to catch sharks from canoes, using black beans as bait; whether true or not, swimming seems inadvisable!

110 km. from Puerto Juárez off the rough and mostly unpopulated bulge of the Yucatán coastline are several islands, once notorious for contraband. Beware of mosquitoes in the area. Both Isla Mujeres and the larger **Cozumel** have developed their tourist potentials. Their turquoise waters and glittering sands attract the overflow from Miami; they are nearer to the Florida coast than to Mexico City. A paved road runs from Mérida to the so-called port—**Puerto Juárez** (cheapest hotel starts at US$4.20; *Hotel Isabel* at ferry terminal, with restaurant, US$7.30 s or d; *Hotel Los Faroles,* US$16 d, with bath, expensive)—which serves Isla Mujeres. Passenger ferry leaves from the jetty opposite the bus terminal at Puerto Juárez at 0800, 1100, 1300, 1500, 1700 and 1900, returns at 0700, 1000, 1200, 1300 and 1600. Also small boats, US$0.45. Ferry from Punta Sam, 5 km. from Puerto Juárez (facilities to store luggage) leaves 0830, 1130, 1445, 1700; returns 0715, 1100, 1315, 1600. The bus from Mérida stops at the ferry. The boat trip across is US$4 for car, US$0.80 p.p. Ferry runs 3 times a day each way, single journey 45 mins.; or go to Cozumel, go to Playa del Carmen (68 km. from Tulum, avoid *Hotel Molcas*) ferry, US$2.50, leaves at 0600, 1200 and 1800 or Puerto Morelos. There is a small hotel and restaurant. Buses go from Puerto Juárez to Tulum (see page 868), F. Carrillo Puerto and Chetumal. All regular buses to Puerto Juárez stop at Tulum.

Dr. Robin Hoult writes: "**Isla Mujeres** (which got its name from the large number of female idols first found by the Spaniards) epitomises the Caribbean island: long silver beaches, palm trees and clean blue water (at least at the N end, away from the beach pollution of the town, and the airstrip being prepared to the SW of the town). Isla Mujeres is very expensive by Yucatán standards, and not overprovided with facilities, although there are plenty of second-grade hotels, all comparatively expensive but negotiable. Food is expensive as well: everything has to be brought here, and it's a long journey—several hours by road from Mérida and an hour's ferry crossing.

"The place will soon be overdeveloped, but at present it is fun, and most of the tourists were youngish and relatively impecunious. Worth hiring a bicycle (wonderfully rickety—no brakes!), US$1.80 a day, or a Honda 50 (expensive) at US$6.75 a day, to visit the rest of this tiny island.

"Do not miss Garrafón, where there is a tropical fish reserve (fishing forbidden) on a small coral reef. Take a snorkel (rental US$2.25 a day) and swim among an astonishing variety of multicoloured tropical fish—they aren't at all shy. Worth walking on from here up a track to the lighthouse, on a rocky headland where there is a small and very ruinous Mayan 'temple'. Fine views.'' (Taxi to the Garrafón US$2.25.)

The islands have several cheap hotels and food is generally expensive. Try, however, the *Hostel Poc-Na*, dormitory style, bunks or hammocks, very clean (check to see if it is open; was being done up), US$1.75 p.p., American-run; or hire hammock on beach for US$1.80 a night. (As ever, have plenty of mosquito repellent or pyrethrum coils.) Cheap places to stay at on Isla Mujeres are *Hotel Zorro* and *Mesón del Pescador*, not bad. More expensive, *San Luis* and *Xel-Ha*, US$8 d, with bath. *Hotel Caracol*, US$6.25 d, good value; *Hotel María de los Angeles*, US$9, with bath. *Las Hamacas*, US$1.70 p.p with hired hammock, US$1.35 with own, has lockers for hammocks and permits the use of showers for US$0.40. *Famitel*, next door, has a similar set up but is cheaper, US$0.90 a night. Best value for money on Cozumel island are the *Hotel Pepita-Bungalows* (US$5 s); *Posada Martín* (US$4 s); *Posada Cozumel*; *Hotel López*, US$12 d, clean, hot showers, recommended, only 1½ blocks from ferry landing. *Hotel Malibu*, US$9 d, with pool; *El Pirite*, US$7 d, with private bath. Restaurants: *Ciro's*, excellent; *Las Palmeras*, recommended, in front of ferry landing. *Villa del mar*, recommended, about US$2.70-3.20; *Gomar*, *Pepe's*, *La Langosta* with lovely view and *Los Arcos*, with open terrace, near the beach end of town. Try turtle steak. Boats, fishing tackle and motor cycles are for hire; paved roads; on Cozumel, snorkel 9 km. S of San Miguel de Cozumel. Rent equipment for US$1.80. Beautiful beaches on E side; on Isla Mujeres the northern beach is really spectacular, with dazzzling white sand, so wear sunglasses; you can camp there, possible to hire tent or hammock, cooking and shower facilities available. One can holiday in these islands the year round. Cycle down to the southern end of the island—there are the curious remains of a pirate's domain, called Casa de Mundaca, a nature reserve with giant turtles at El Chequero, the Garrafón fish reserve, and a little Mayan lighthouse or shrine of Ixtel.

There is no public transport on Isla Mujeres, apart from taxis. You can rent skin and scuba diving equipment, together with guide, from Divers of Mexico, on the waterfront N of the public pier. They can set up group excursions to the Cave of the Sleeping Sharks; English spoken.

There is a road from Puerto Juárez to Belize *via* Chetumal (paved all the way to Chetumal, fast). About 40 km. before Chetumal there are seven cenotes which are ideal for swimming. The much-talked about resort of **Cancún** (near the north-eastern tip of the Yucatán peninsula) can be reached by bus from Puerto Juárez, which also connects with ferry services from the islands. The Cancún tourist development project has converted a deserted 22.4 km. stretch of gleaming white beach, backed by a blue lagoon, into a thriving resort complex and town, strictly for the rich; prices are at least three times higher than in the rest of the country—although hotel charges in the town are less prohibitive than on the beaches and the latter can be reached easily by bus; at present it has 30,000 inhabitants, and is near completion. Luxury hotels: *El Presidente* and *Cancún Camino Real;* cheapest hotel, *Bohorquez,* US$15.40 d. Within easy reach of the new resort are Chichén-Itzá (bus, 3½ hrs., US$1.70), Tulum, and many lesser known Maya centres such as Cobá and Tablé. The road from Cancún to Tulum is completely paved; it starts at Mérida, goes through Chetumal. Local bus Puerto Juárez-Canún US$10.

Air Services Cancún, Cozumel and Isla Mujeres have airports; light aircraft connect the latter with Mérida, Cozumel and Cancún. Mexicana has direct flights Mexico City-Cancún-Miami; also daily flights Mexico City-Cancún-Mérida.

Cobá is also being developed (go *via* Valladolid, Chemax on Puerto Juárez road)—no buses. N of Valladolid is Holbox island. Buses to Chiquilá, for boats, 3 times a day. Totally unspoiled, take blankets and hammock. Five more uninhabited islands beyond Holbox. Beware of sharks and barracuda, though few nasty occurrences have been reported.

Tulum The Tulum ruins, Maya-Toltec, are 12th century, with city walls of white stone atop seashore cliffs (frescoes still visible on interior walls of temples). The temples were dedicated to the worship of the Falling God,

or the Setting Sun, represented as a falling character over nearly all the
West-facing doors (Cozumel was the home of the Rising Sun). The same
idea is reflected in the buildings, which are wider at the top than at the
bottom. The archaeologist in charge of excavations at Tulum is Señor
Dávila. They are on the road (paved) between Felipe Carrillo Puerto
(100 km.), where there is a junction with the Mérida-Chetumal paved
road, and Puerto Juárez (130 km.), and can also be visited by boat from
Cozumel. (Entrance to ruins, US$0.50.) There is a newly-laid road linking
Tulum with the large but little-excavated city of Cobá, which is being
extended to join the Valladolid-Puerto Juárez road (the paved road stops
5 km. before Cobá) at X-Can, thus greatly shortening the distance
between Chichén-Itzá and Tulum. Hammock space may be rented in the
village of Tulum, 5 km. from ruins (minibus to ruins at 0900, US$0.50);
Posada El Mirador hires little thatched cottages along the beach with
hammocks, US$0.90 p.p., with own hammock, US$1.20, poor food and
no cold drinks, but mosquitoes abound; quiet, lovely, unspoiled beaches
nearby. Near El Mirador is *Camping Posada Paraíso,* but it tends to
overcharge. *Pablo's house* on the beach to the road to ruins, US$0.80
each, US$0.65 for hammocks, meals; otherwise the *Hotel Carrillo Puerto*
at Felipe Carrillo Puerto has been recommended. The road from Tulum
to Felipe Carrillo Pueto is paved. Petrol stations at Tulum, Felipe Carrillo
Puerto and Puerto Juárez; make sure you have sufficient supplies. **N.B.:**
There is no gasoline between Tulum and Cancún (140 km.). Ruins of
Chumyaxche on the left-hand side of this road, worth a visit.

Parking or camping possible on beach S of lighthouse, whose keeper also rents huts
along beach for US$1.20 a day. Good swimming locally; divers bring in lobster from
a coral reef about 400 metres offshore. N of Tulum (10 km.) is a beautiful clear
lagoon (Laguna Xelhá) full of fish, but no fishing allowed as it is a national park,
entry US$0.20. Snorkelling gear can be rented at US$2 for two hours. Bungalows
being built. There is a marvellous jungle path to one of the lagoon bays. Small ruins
of Ak are near Xelhá. N of Tulum, at Tancáh, are newly-discovered bright post-
classic Maya murals.

Akumal, a luxury resort, is 20km. N of Tulum. Cove owned by Mexican Skin-Divers
Society, 110 km. S from Puerto Juárez. Bungalows US$70 d, with three meals,
excellent beach. Recommended as base for excursions to Xelhá, Tulum and Cobá.

Bus from Mérida to Tulum, 2nd class, 0900 daily *via* Puerto Morelos (both paying
and free camping here; popular with scuba divers and snorkellers; but beware of
sharks); from Tulum to Carrillo Puerto, 1 hr., US$1.10, few buses; from F.C.
Puerto to Chetumal, US$1.60; from Chetumal to Tulum, US$2; from Tulum to
Puerto Juárez, 1½ hrs., 2nd class, US$1.15; from Tulum to Valladolid, US$3.20, 4
hrs., *via* Puerto Juárez; few buses.

Baja California (Lower California)

Baja California is that long narrow arm of land which dangles
southwards from the U.S. border between the Pacific and the Gulf of
California for 1,300 km. It is divided administratively into the States of
Baja California and Baja California Sur. The average width is only
80 km. Rugged and almost uninhabited mountains split its tapering
length. Only the southern tip gets enough rain: the northern half gets its
small quota during the winter, the southern half during the summer. Most
of the land is hot, parched desert. There are some Indians still, but
without any tribal organisation. Not only the northern part, bordering the
U.S.A., but also the southern tip is attracting increasing numbers of

tourists. The U.S. dollar is preferred for all transactions in most places north of La Paz. Hitch-hiking is difficult.

Cortés paid a brief visit to La Paz, in the S, soon after the Conquest, but the land had nothing but its beauty to recommend it and it was left to the Missions to develop. The first Jesuit settlement was at Loreto in 1697. Other orders took over when the Jesuits were expelled in 1768. The results were ironic: the Indians were almost wiped out by the diseases of the Fathers. Scattered about the Sierras are the beautiful ruins of these well-meaning but lethal missions. In 1911 a band of North Americans and Mexicans invaded Baja California and tried to set up a socialist republic. They were routed by Mexican troops.

Baja California's population has increased by two-thirds in the past decade through migration from Mexico's interior and Central Pacific coast. The development of agriculture, tourism, industry, and migrant labour for California has caused a great upsurge of economic growth and consequently of prices, especially in areas favoured by tourists.

The Morelos dam on the upper reaches of the Colorado river has turned the Mexicali valley into a major agricultural area: 400,000 acres under irrigation to grow cotton, and olive groves, are also succeeding. Industries are encouraged in all border regions by handsome investment incentives.

Mexicali (pop. 390,000), capital of Baja California state, is a major agricultural service centre with cotton processing establishments, transport facilities, distribution depots for chemicals, fertilizers and insecticides. Mexicali is a combination of "Mexico" and "California". Opposite, on the U.S. side of the border, is the town of Calexico—again a compound name.

Hotels *Capri,* acceptable, in centre, US$5; *Rivera,* near railway station, US$5.50.

Train To Guadalajara from Mexicali, US$23.35 1st class. Slow train (leaves 2100) to Mexico City takes 74 hours, fast train 40 hours, little price difference. Train from Mexicali to Guadalajara twice a day, morning twice as fast as other.

The road to Tijuana leads from below-sea-level desert over endless 1,200-metre high serpentines on to the coastal ranges. At Rumorosa a breathtaking panorama of the desert is one of the most dramatic views in the continent.

Tijuana (pop. 335,000), where 15 million tourists a year (up to 130,000 on Sundays) pop across the border for a quick visit. Besides countless native bars, about 90 nightclubs and tourist bars range from the extremely stark to the respectable, with top class international entertainment. Daily horse or dog races at Caliente track; jai-alai games Sunday to Thursday. Bullfights on most Sundays from April to October. One of its two bull rings is unique in the world for being set on an ocean beach. There are more and more light industries, mostly making articles for interior decoration. N.B. There are many good and inexpensive English-speaking dentists in the town, who attract Americans with their low fees. The road from Tijuana to La Paz is all paved.

Hotels and Motels, first rate: *Country Club; León.* Economy: *Alaska;* and *Díaz,* both US$5 d; *Roma; Machado,* US$5; *Tijuana.* Avoid *Hotel Juárez,* dirty, US$7.50.

Night Clubs recommended: Flamingos, S on old Ensenada road; Chantecler.

Travel bargains from Tijuana Airport (20 mins. from San Diego, California); Mexico City and Acapulco, US$143 round trip with stopovers in La Paz, Mazatlán, Guadalajara and Puerto Vallarta, without stop-overs, 30 days, depending on day of departure, US$115-130, by Aeroméxico. ACSA airline offers a round trip to Mérida (Yucatán) for US$159. "Expreso de Lujo" round trip to Puerto Vallarta, US$117. Tijuana to Mexico City by first-class bus lines, US$33.20, about 51 hours; similar price and duration by train. Bus: Tijuana-La Paz (down peninsula) leaves twice daily, Tres Estrellas, 10 min. walk from US border (22 hours, US$18), book well in advance. Bus to Mazatlán, US$22, 28 hours, not recommended (only two rest stops and numberless customs stops). Cheap Greyhound bus to and from San Diego.

A dramatic 96-km. toll road (US$2.40) leads along cliffs overhanging the sea to **Ensenada,** whose Todos Santos Bay, a gigantic beautiful curve, underlines the austere character of a landscape reduced to water, sky and scorched brown earth. Fishing for sport and commercial fishing, canning, wineries, olive groves and agriculture. The port serves deep-sea vessels, primarily for cotton export. In general, the town is of no great interest. Several hotels, many motels, good to modest. (*Hotel Pacífico,* US$2.25 s, clean and hot shower). Handicrafts at Centro Artesanal Ensenada, Av. López Mateos 1306, Tel.: 9-15-36. Population 113,000.

La Bufadora, the largest blowhole on the Pacific Coast, is located 16 km. S of Ensenada. Take the paved road which heads W from Mancadero, and follow it to the end (12½ km.). Spectacular scene of solid rock shuddering underfoot with each wave.

Rosarito, between Tijuana and Ensenada along the old "free" road, is a fast growing, informal and drab seaside resort. *Rosarito Beach Hotel,* de luxe. Other hotels: *Hotel Ensenada; Hotel Rosita,* US$5, adequate. Many economy motels.

San Felipe, a fishing village on the Gulf, 196 km. by paved road from Mexicali, is another place which attracts visitors. It has fine beaches, good fishing, and facilities for camping, but is now becoming dirty and noisy as a result of mass tourism.

Motels *Augie's Riviera; Del mar; El Cortez.*

The new 1,556-km. road from the border, *via* Ensenada, Arroyo Seco, San Quintín and Santa Rosalía (an industrial town; difficult to find accommodation), to La Paz is now completed, and services en route are adequate. Petrol is now in ample supply, too. The road passes through a land of astonishing beauty and grotesque ugliness. Half-way down the peninsula there is a time-change; Baja California Sur is one hour ahead of Baja California (Norte). It is one of the few places in the world where you can see the cirio (candle) cactus, which grows to heights of 6 to 10 metres. Many of the peninsula's coastal villages have become popular with fishermen, such as Mulegé and Bahía de los Angeles, both on the Gulf side.

Several luxury beach hotels (US$12-20 d) at **Mulegé,** a lovely oasis N of La Paz, reached by good roads *via* Loreto where the first California mission church was founded; it is a drab town which boasts a fine museum and has a wide range of hotels: *Oasis* and *El Presidente,* US$20 d; *San Martín,* US$6.50 d, with shower. Mulegé has *Casa Nachita,* US$2, basic and pleasant, *Hotel Hacienda* with good bar; also several other less expensive hotels; e.g. *Hotel La Palma,* US$6 d, with shower, US$4.50 s, with bath, US$6 d, no food. Nearby are Bahía Coyote and Bahía Concepción, with very varied marine life. You can stay on the beach for US$1 a day; the only problem is fresh water, which is obtainable in Pemex station, near Mulegé.

Hotel at **Bahía de Los Angeles,** *Mama and Papa Díaz,* US$16 with full board, each. Lynn and Walt Sutherland from Vancouver write: "Bahía de los Angeles (600 inhab.) is worth a visit for its sea life. There are thousands of dolphins in the bay June-December. Some stay all year. In July and August you can hear the whales breathe as you stand on shore. There are large colonies of seals and many exotic seabirds. Fishing is excellent. A boat and guide can be rented for US$40 a day; try Raúl, a local fisherman, who speaks English". Camping free and safe on beach.

At San Quintín, 193 km. from Ensenada, is *Ernesto's Resort Motel.* At Guerrero Negro, there is a government-owned motel *El Presidente,* US$20 d, very clean. These motels are found at about every 150 km. along the route. Guerrero Negro is a salt-mining area. Scammon's Lagoon whale watchers have a good view of the breeding animals from December to January, 29 km. from G. Negro. As there are few gas stations on the way, fill up wherever you can. San Ignacio is a charming oasis with a well-preserved church (founded 1728). Local dates are the best in Baja California. Again, *Hotel Presidente*. At Santa Rosalia is *Hotel Francés*, bad restaurant service; *Hotel del Real*, US$3.75 s, with bath. Plenty of new hotels here.

La Paz is a peaceful town (and a free port) whose mild winter climate is attracting more and more tourists. They come in by private yacht or by air from Mazatlán, Culiacán, and Guaymas, or by ferryboat from Mazatlán, 294 km. away (US$5.20 for cheapest class), or from Guaymas. The best beaches are in the S. Its famous pearling industry, which had died, is reviving. There is a helpful tourist office at Av. 5 de Mayo, and a Centro Artesanal La Paz, on Parque Cuauhtémoc, between Bravo and Rosales. Population, 37,000. On the way to Cabo San Lucas are the wood carving centre of San Pedro and leather work at Miraflores (2 km. off road). San José del Cabo is good for everyday shopping needs.

Excursions to Cabo San Lucas (see also next page) organized by travel agency next door to *Hotel Yeneka* on Av. Madero, US$11. This includes: breakfast at the travel agency, transport by mini-bus and lunch at Cabo San Lucas, and a motor-boat excursion to see the marine life. Assembly at 0700, return 1600, good value.

Hotels   *La Perla; La Misión de la Paz; Jalisco; Yeneka*, on Francisco I. Madero, clean, some comfort, US$4 s, with bath; *Hotel Guadalajara*, US$2.50 s (opp. bus station). On Av. 16 de Septiembre, 3 to 5 blocks from sea, reasonable, *Hotel Moyron; San Carlos*; also *La Purísima*, very friendly, clean, restaurant next door, US$7 s, with bath. Trailer park near airport, US$2 a day. Most hotels here are very expensive. Cheapest accommodation probably available at the language school in Edificio Biblioteca across street from Servi-Centro food market, 4 blocks from the bus station—cots for renting. Sleep on beach if you're stuck.

Buses   Tres Estrellas de Oro (1st class) La Paz-Tijuana, US$13, 22½ hrs., 1000, 1300, 1800. Stops at Loreto (5 hours), Santa Rosalia (8), Guerrero Negro (11), San Quintín (16), Ensenada (21). La Paz-Cabo San Lucas, US$2.10, 2nd class, 3½ hours.

Air Services   Aeroméxico from Los Angeles, Tijuana and Mexico City. Hughes Air Corporation from Tucson. La Paz international airport is 10 km. from centre. Taxi from airport US$3.50, fixed rate.

Ferry Services   Book in town or at the ferry terminal for ferry to Mazatlán; allow plenty of time for this as there are long queues and there may not be room until the next day as a great many heavy trucks take produce across; the trip takes 12 hours, US$6 reclining chair, US$17.70 cabin, goes daily, at 1700 hrs. each way, except Sun. from Mazatlán and Mon. from La Paz. Customs clearance is necessary if taking a car (US$26.70), allow plenty of time, US$4.80; available in La Paz, not at ferry terminal. Ferry also available to Guaymas at 2000 (return trip, 1200) from Santa Rosalia, both on Sun., Tues. and Thurs., US$5, reclining chair (single fare), car US$17.80. Ferry to Topolobampo, Sun., Mon., Wed. and Sat. at 2000, leaves on same days to La Paz at 1000, reclining seat US$8.90; car US$26.70, 11 hours. Ferry from Cabo San Lucas to Puerto Vallarta, Sun. and Wed., 1600 hrs., returning Sat. and the same time, single fare, reclining chair, US$11, cabin US$22, car US$33.35, 17 hrs. Addresses for reservations: La Paz: Independencia 107-B; Puerto Vallarta: Muelle Marítimo (Tel.: 20476); Cabo San Lucas: Muelle Marítimo (Tel.: 30079); Guaymas: Muelle Patio (Tel.: 22324); Sta. Rosalia: Muelle de la Aduana (Tel.: 20013/14).

At extreme tip of peninsula, 201 km. S by air from La Paz, is **Cabo San Lucas**. Bus: La Paz-Cabo San Lucas, US$2.50, 3 hrs. *Hotel Mi Ranchito*, US$7.25 d, with shower, nice rooms but unfriendly. *Mar de Cortés*, US$16 d; *Sol Mar*, on the beach with beautiful view; *Hotel Finisterra*, built on rocks, US$11.25 s, superb view. *Camino Real*, very exclusive apartments but beach surrounded by repair shops and factories. All the better hotels can offer safaris in the desert, diving gear, fishing boats, etc. Entertainment only in hotel bars. Bank hours: Mon.-Fri., 0830-1300 hrs.

Only one bank, Banco de México. The rainy months are Sept.-Oct., but also occasional rain at the end of January. La Paz can also be reached from Cabo San Lucas *via* Todos Los Santos; there is a 80 km. dirt road, with the only problem that you must be careful when passing another vehicle as the shoulders are very sandy. Todos Los Santos is very dull.

The Economy

The Mexican economy is one of the most diversified in Latin America, and between 1945 and 1972 it was among the most dynamic and stable in the area. But, beginning in 1972, the economic and financial situation showed a steady deterioration, largely because of mounting public-sector deficits. In 1974 and 1975, this deterioration was aggravated by the shocks to the world economy resulting from the oil crisis of late 1973; and the growing financial imbalances, together with an unfavourable external situation, created strong pressures on domestic prices and the balance of payments. In 1975 and 1976 these adverse developments were compounded by large outflows of private short-term capital, and resulted in a sharp increase in the external debt. Faced with an untenable foreign-exchange situation, in September 1976 the authorities ended the fixed link of 12.50 pesos to the US dollar, which had been maintained since 1954, and permitted the peso to float independently; the exchange rate depreciated at once to over 20 pesos to the dollar. Thus, in 1976, Mexico experienced the most serious economic crisis since the Depression of the late 1920s and early 1930s.

The administration of President José López Portillo, which took office on 1st December 1976 for a six-year term, has done much towards restoring confidence and engendering recovery within a short space of time. It has introduced a stabilization programme, to be carried out between 1977 and 1979, designed to control inflation and improve the balance of payments, with the overall aim of permitting the resumption of the rapid economic growth necessary to absorb the growing labour force and ensure the improvement of living standards. The programme includes measures providing for strict control of public expenditure to reduce the budget deficit from about 6% of gross domestic product in 1977 to 2.5% by 1979, the expansion of exports and the replacement of imports, and the encouragement of the private sector to assume greater responsibility for investment and the creation of job opportunities; it is being carried out with the support of the International Monetary Fund, which granted an extended facility arrangement of up to US$1.200m. in late-1976.

The following results demonstrate the success of the programme. There was a growth rate of 2.8% in 1977 compared with 2.0% in 1976, with rises of 3.0% in industrial output (2.6% in 1976) and of 4% in agriculture, forestry and fishing (3.4%). The rises in the consumer- and wholesale-price indices in 1977 were 20.7% and 18.1% respectively, against 27.2% and 45.9% in 1976. In 1977, there was a deficit of US$1,780m. on the current account of the balance of payments, a 41.5% decrease from that of 1976, mainly due to a fall in the trade deficit and increased inflows from tourism and border transactions as a consequence of the devaluation of the peso. The exchange rate has stabilized at 22-23 pesos to the US dollar as confidence in the currency has been restored. Mexico's international credit rating is now high despite the fact of its large public external debt, estimated at US$20,185m. at end-1977. Although initially the response of investment and output to the improving financial situation was sluggish and hesitant, the available indicators suggest growing signs of a broadly-based uptrend in economic activity. Nevertheless this amelioration has been achieved at the cost of an increase in unemployment and underemployment and a decline in real wages. The Government is aiming at an annual growth of between 6 and 7% between 1978 and 1982, with petroleum, petrochemicals, electric energy, capital goods, steel, agriculture, forestry and fishing as the priority sectors. Observers consider that this target can be met in the light of the impressive progress being made towards stabilization and the spectacular upsurge in oil and natural gas production and exports which has already begun to appear.

Mexico was the world's leading oil producer in 1921 and the country's first oil well was drilled 95 years ago. By 1938, when the oil industry was nationalized and the state petroleum agency, Petróleos Mexicanos (Pemex), set up, output had fallen to 39m. barrels a year from 193m. barrels in 1921. The stage was set for renewed growth when discoveries in the southern states of Tabasco and Chiapas enabled the country to become self sufficient in oil output in 1974. Petroleum production and exports in 1977 were 1.1m. and 220,000 barrels a day respectively and are expected to rise to 2.24-3.2m. and 1.1m. barrels by 1982. Mexico's proved recoverable oil reserves are 17,000 m. barrels and it is thought that they might be as high as 150,000m. Pemex is investing US$40,000m. (equivalent) in the development of hydrocarbon resources between 1977 and 1982, including US$14,000m. in capital investment; an ambitious offshore prospecting programme is being undertaken, particularly in the Gulf of California. Natural gas output is anticipated to increase to 4,000m. cubic feet a day by 1982 and a large pipeline is to be laid from Tabasco to Cárdenas in the North East, and substantial exports to the USA are planned once prices have been agreed. Increased oil production is to be used as the spur for an expansion of output of basic petrochemicals which is to increase to 18m. tons by 1982. As well as oil and related products, Mexico has a considerable capacity for the growth of mineral output as it is one of the world's major producers of fluospar, antimony and silver.

The Government is spending US$9,000m. (equivalent) to increase electricity generating capacity from 12,300m. kw. at end-1976 to 20,000m. by end-1982. It is expected that Mexico will become self sufficient in all types of steel products in 1978; current installed capacity is 9m. tons against output of 6.3m. tons in 1977, and this can satisfy domestic demand until 1981. Output of capital goods is being promoted, and it is expected that between 1978 and 1987, 48% of overall requirements can be met locally. The authorities are also taking steps to develop the other important manufacturing industries, which include motor vehicles, cement, textiles, paper, beer and household durables.

Agriculture has given cause for increasing official concern in recent years; yields are still low and only 12% of the land area is suitable for cultivation; it employs 40% of the economically active population, and coffee, sugar, cotton, fruit and tomatoes account for a large proportion of primary exports. The need to develop agriculture is one of the Government's most pressing challenges as the population is expected to grow from 63m. at present to 120m. by the year 2000 with a higher proportion consuming, not producing, food. A total of 34,500m. pesos is to be invested in farming between 1978 and 1982, including 7,000m. on the rehabilitation and cleaning of existing ground. Reafforestation is to be undertaken of 30m. trees by 1982 and US$1,200m. is to be invested to increase the fish catch by 30% to 2.4m. tons a year annually by that year.

The Government is also making determined efforts to strengthen the infrastructure especially in large cities in face of the population explosion; the population of Mexico City is expected to rise from 12 at present to 25-30m. by the year 2000. Sewerage, water supply and housing projects are forecast to register increases of 13.2%, 6.7% and 5.8% respectively by 1982. In Mexico City, it is planned to develop transport facilities by extending the existing underground railway from three to six lines, at an estimated cost of US$800m. (equivalent) each and to build an ancillary suburban railway system. In public health, emphasis is being given to the development of preventive medicine and in education to secondary school teaching. Tourist facilities are being expanded to attract 7m. foreign visitors a year by 1982, and tourism is expected to provide an increase of 8% a year in new jobs by that year with a 9% increase in local tourism, a 3.4% growth of border transactions and a 12.5% rise in visitors from abroad by 1982.

The conclusion appears to be that the López Portillo administration is implementing economic policies which should lead to a solution of the temporary difficulties caused by the 1976 crisis, and which should ensure a lessening of population and agrarian problems by the end of its term in office. With its well-diversified base and immeasurable oil resources, prospects for the Mexican economy registering sustained expansion over the next decade are much more promising than for most developing countries.

		Foreign Trade (US$m.)				
		1972	1973	1974	1975	1976	1977
Imports (c.i.f.) ..	..	2,937	3,840	5,947	6,580	6,030	5,487
Exports (f.o.b.)..	..	1,812	2,084	2,755	2,858	3,263	4,012

Information for Visitors

How to get there Several air lines have regular flights from Europe to Mexico. *British Airways* from London *via* Bermuda and Jamaica to Mexico City. *Braniff* from London *via* Dallas to Mexico City. *Air France* from Paris *via* Houston to Mexico City. *Iberia* from Madrid *via* Santo Domingo to Mexico City. *Aeroméxico* from Paris and Madrid to Mexico City. *Sabena* from Brussels *via* Montreal to Mexico City. *KLM* from Amsterdam *via* Montreal and Houston to Mexico City. *Canadian Pacific* from Amsterdam *via* Montreal to Mexico City. *Lufthansa* from Frankfurt *via* Montreal to Mérida, Monterrey and Mexico City. There are many flights from New York to Mexico City. *Braniff* flies direct from Minneapolis-St. Paul *via* Kansas City, Dallas and San Antonio to Mexico City. To Mexico City from New York, under 4 hours; from Chicago, 4 hours; from Los Angeles, 4¾ hours (US$138 return with *Mexicana* "Moonlight Express"); from Houston, 3 hours; from Brownsville (Texas), *via* Tampico, 2½ hours; from St. Louis or Washington (by connecting air lines through Houston), 6¾ hours and 9 hours respectively. *Mexicana* does a US$110 round trip Los Angeles-Guadalajara ("Moonlight Express") nightly. There are direct *Pan-Am* and *Aeroméxico* (US$68) flights connecting Miami with Mérida, and direct *Aeroméxico* flights daily connecting New York with Tijuana. From Kingston, Jamaica to Mérida with *Mexicana* on Mon. and Fri. evenings, US$88, or US$137 return 3-week excursion. Many direct cheap charter flights from continental European airports to Mexico City and Mérida, for instance, try Le Point, 4 rue des Orphelins, 68200 Mulhouse, France, or Uniclam-Voyages, 63 rue Monsieur-le-Prince, 75006 Paris.

P. & O.-Orient Line ships call at Acapulco en route to and from Europe and give an excellent, fast (15 days) service to Le Havre and Southampton *via* the Caribbean. All the following are cargo services carrying a limited number of passengers unless otherwise stated.

Mexican Line, from New York to Veracruz, sailing every Friday, 7 days. Northbound ships leave Tampico every Sunday *via* Philadelphia to New York, 7 days. Commodore Cruise Lines from Miami to Cozumel, sail every Saturday night (November-Spring). Cruise continues on Mondays to Haiti, Jamaica and back to Miami. Naviera Turistica Mexicana makes 2 round trips a month between Los Angles, Mazatlán, and Acapulco.

Hamburg-American Line, joint service with North German Lloyd, Bremen, 2 to 3 sailings a month from Hamburg, Bremen, Antwerp to Veracruz and Tampico.

Royal Mail Lines and Holland America Line, joint fast cargo service (no passengers) from Europe to Mazatlán and Guaymas. Harrison Line: from Liverpool, every fortnight. Sidarma Line: monthly from Genoa to Veracruz. Spanish Line: from Spain to Veracruz. S.A. Armement Deppe: from Antwerp to Tampico and Veracruz. Italian Line: from Trieste, Venice, Naples, Leghorn, Genoa, Marseilles, Barcelona through the Panama Canal to Acapulco.

Norwegian Caribbean Lines occasionally take one-way passengers with about 2 weeks advance booking at a flat rate of US$67 a night.

Overland Toronto to Mexico City, *via* Chicago-St. Louis-Dallas-San Antonio-Laredo-Monterrey, with greyhound bus (74 hours, Can$93 one way). If coming from the US it is usually cheaper to travel to the border and buy your connecting bus ticket into Mexico from the Mexican company.

To Cuba Return flight to Cuba, US$190 with Cubana (Paseo de la Reforma), Mondays and Fridays, or Aeroméxico, Wednesdays, with stop at Mérida if plane is not fully booked.

Travel in Mexico Book ahead for buses when possible, and try to travel from the starting-point of a route; trying to get on a bus at the mid-point of its route can be frustrating.

There are three kinds of buses, first and second class, and local. Terminals for each are usually distinct, and may not be in one bus station. First-class buses assign you a seat. It is not easy to choose which seat or to change it later. No standing, and you may have to wait for the next one (next day, perhaps) if all seats are taken. You *must* book in advance for buses travelling in the Yucatán Peninsula. Be especially careful during school holidays, around August and the 15 days up to New Year when many public servants take holidays in all resorts; transport from Mexico City is booked up a long time in advance and hotels are filled, too. Beware of "scalpers" who try to sell you a seat at a higher price, which you can usually get on a stand-by basis, when somebody doesn't turn up, at the regular price. Sometimes it helps to talk to the driver, who has two places to use at his discretion. Second-class buses are often antiques (interesting) or may be brand new, but the passengers are invariably more entertaining and courteous than in other types of buses. They call at towns and villages and go up side roads the first-class buses never touch. They stop quite as often for meals and toilets as their superiors do and—unlike the first-class buses—people get on and off so often that it takes no wit or ruthlessness to get a seat by a window even if you start off standing. Seats are not bookable, except in Baja California. The rate all over Mexico is 2.70 pesos for 10 km. There is a monthly bus guide, available for US$1 (year's subscription) from Guía de Autotransportes de México, Apartado 8929, México 1, D.F.

As for trains, apart from one narrow gauge line, most of the passenger equipment in use now dates from the forties or fifties, including a number of *autovías*. In some cases they are slow, but there are now completely modern trains from Mexicali to Mexico City in 40 hours, and overnight good Pullman trains from Mexico City to Monterrey, Guadalajara, Veracruz and Mérida. The railways claim that you can see more from a train than from any other form of transport; this may well be true, but they tend to be slower (though generally cheaper if you take 2nd class and carriages are empty at non-holiday periods) than the buses except for the Mexico City-Mexicali first class train to the USA; they generally have comfortable sleeper cars. A condensed railway timetable may be obtained from the Mexican railways' office at 500 Fifth Ave. (Room 2623), New York, N.Y. 10036. (For extensive information about the Mexican railway network consult *Makens' Guide to Mexican Train Travel*, compiled by James C. Makens and published by Le Voyageur Publishing Co., 1319 Wentwood Drive, Irving, Texas 75061, at about US$3.50.)

If you should get caught during the holiday season try to book a 2nd class train but this may involve queuing 12 hrs. or more if you want a seat. First class seats—more tickets are sold than seats but passengers are allowed on first, so you may still find a 2nd class seat.

Documents A passport and a smallpox vaccination certificate not more than 3 years old are necessary, but US and Canadian citizens need only show birth certificate (or for US, a naturalization certificate). Smallpox vaccination certificate not required for those coming direct from Canada or USA who have stayed there at least 14 days. Tourists need the free tourist card, which can be obtained from any Mexican Consulate or Tourist Commission office, at the Mexican airport on entry, from the offices or on the aircraft of airlines operating into Mexico, ask for at least 30 days; if you say you are in transit you may be charged US$8. (Airlines may issue cards only to citizens of West European countries, most Latin American countries—not Cuba, Chile or Haiti—the USA, Canada, Japan and the Philippines.) Also at border offices of the American Automobile Association (AAA), which gives this service to members and non-members. There is a multiple entry card valid for all visits within 6 months for US nationals; the normal validity for other nationals is 90 days. Travellers not carrying tourist cards need visas. Tourist cards are not required for cities close to the US border, such as Tijuana, Mexicali, etc. Businessmen who want to study the Mexican market or to appoint an agent must apply for the requisite visa and permit.

At certain border crossings see that the customs people don't con you to pay a dollar for the card or visa. It is free and the man typing it out is only doing his job. We would warn travellers that there have been several cases of tourist cards not being honoured, or a charge being imposed, or the validity being changed arbitrarily to 60 days or less. In this case, complaint should be made to the authorities in Mexico City. Some border stations do not issue tourist cards; you are therefore strongly advised, if travelling by land, to obtain a card before arriving at the border. Above all, do not lose your tourist card—you cannot leave the country without it and it takes at least a week to replace. We have heard about discrimination against young men with long hair. There is an airport tax of US$5 on all international flights from Mexico and of US$1 for internal flights within the country; these taxes are not charged at Cozumel (a free zone).

At the land frontiers with Belize and Guatemala, you may be refused entry into Mexico if you have less than US$200. Persuasion, whether verbal or financial, can sometimes remedy this.

British businessmen are strongly advised to read "Hints to Businessmen Visiting Mexico", free on application to the Department of Trade, Export Services Division, Room CO7, Export House, 50 Ludgate Hill, London EC4M 7HU.

Customs Regulations The luggage of tourist-card holders is often passed unexamined provided they complete a Customs declaration that it does not contain more than a tourist is legally entitled to bring in. You can take in your own clothing and equipment without paying duty, but all valuable and non-US-made objects (diamonds, cameras, binoculars, typewriters, etc.), should be registered at the US Customs office in your port of exit so that you will not be charged duty on returning.

Radios and television sets must be registered and taken out when leaving. Tourists are allowed to take in duty-free 1 kg. of tobacco and 400 cigarettes (or 50 cigars), 2 bottles of liquor, US$80 worth of gifts and 12 rolls of film, but the US will allow them to take out only a quart of duty-free liquor. There are no restrictions on the import or export of money apart from gold but foreign gold coins are allowed into the US only if they are clearly made into jewellery (perforated or otherwise worked on). On return to the US a person may take from Mexico, free of duty, up to $100 worth of merchandise for personal use or for personal gifts, every 31 days, if acquired merely as an incident of the trip. Alcoholic drinks may not be taken across the border from Mexico to California. Archaeological relics may not be taken out of Mexico. US tourists should remember that the US Endangered Species Act, 1973, prohibits importing into the States of products from endangered species, e.g. tortoiseshell. The Department of the Interior issues a leaflet about this.

Automobiles   These may be brought into Mexico on a Tourist Permit for 180 days. No fee is charged for the permit, and the AAA always writes "free" across the preliminary application form it gives its clients because, apparently, some Mexican border officials absentmindedly forget this fact. Your US car insurance does not cover you while driving in Mexico, but agencies on both sides of the border will sell you Mexican automobile insurance, so only buy 1-day US insurance if crossing the border. Holders of 180-days tourist cards can keep their automobiles in Mexico for that time. Luggage is no longer inspected at the checkpoints along the road where tourist cards and/or car permits are examined. Gasoline—regular and medium (94°) octane (no high octane)—can be got throughout Mexico. Prices range from 2.80 to 3.07 pesos per litre. Government road patrols using green jeeps offer helpful service to motorists.

Warning   When two cars converge on a narrow bridge from opposite directions, the driver who first flashes his lights has the right of way. Don't drive fast at night; farm and wild animals roam freely and are easily injured, let alone your car. Some motorists report that it is better not to stop if you hit another car, as although Mexican insurance is proof of your ability to pay, both parties may sometimes be incarcerated until all claims are settled!

On the west coast, the Government has set up military checkpoints to look out for drug-smugglers and gun-runners, almost as far south as Puerto Angel. Papers will be checked at these points and your car searched. The degree of search is apparently linked to general appearance; young people travelling in VW vans can expect thorough searches all the way. Watch searchers carefully; sometimes they try to make off with tools, camping gear and the like, especially if there are two or more of them.

Local Information   All Mexican Government tourist agencies are now grouped in the Department of Tourism building at Juárez 92, near corner of reforma. A few cities run municipal tourist offices to help travellers. The Mexican Automobile Association (AMA) is at Chapultepec 276, México, D.F.; they sell an indispensable road guide, with good maps and very useful lists of hotels, with current prices. The ANA (Asociación Nacional Automobilistica) sells similar but not such good material; offices in Insurgentes (Metro Glorieta) and Av. Jalisco 27, Mexio 18 D.F. For road conditions consult the AMA, which is quite reliable. A calendar of fiestas is published by "Mexico This Month".

The Dirección General de Oceanografia in Calle Medellin 10, near Insurgentes underground station, sells excellent maps of the entire coastline of Mexico. Good detailed maps of states of Mexico and the country itself from Dirección General de Geografia y Metereologia, Av. Observatorio 192, Mexico 18, D.F. Tel.: 5.15.15.27 (go to Observatorio underground station and up Calle Sur 114, then turn right a short distance down Av. Observatorio). Best road maps of Mexican states, free, on polite written request, from Ing. Daniel Diaz Díaz, Director General de Programación, Xola 1755, 8° Piso, Mexico 12 D.F. Building is on the corner of Xola with Av. Universidad.

Guidebooks   Travellers wanting more information than we have space to provide, on archaeological sites for instance, would do well to use the booklets written by Richard Bloomgarden—about US$2 each—with plans and good illustrations.

Hours of Business in Mexico City are extremely variable. The banks are open from 0900 to 1300 from Monday to Friday and (head offices only) 0900 to 1230 on Saturdays. Business offices usually open at 0900 or 1000 and close at 1300 or 1400. They reopen at 1400 or 1500, but senior executives may not return until much later, although they may then stay until after 1900. Other businesses, especially those on the outskirts of the city, and many Government offices, work from 0800 to 1400 or 1500 and then close for the rest of the day. Business hours in other parts of the country vary considerably according to the climate and local custom. In Monterrey they are roughly as in Britain.

Standard Time The same as US Central Standard Time, 6 hours behind Greenwich Mean Time. In Sonora, Sinaloa, Nayarit and Baja California Sur, 7 hours behind GMT; and in Baja California (Norte) 8 hours behind GMT.

The **best season** for a business visit is from late January to May, but for pleasure between October and March, when it hardly ever rains in most of the country.

Hotel rates, in nearly all cases, are posted in the rooms. Even when not, the rates for all rooms are always posted or available in the office. English is spoken at the best hotels. Beware of "helpfuls" who try to find you a hotel, as prices quoted at the hotel desk rise to give them a commission. If backpacking, best for one of you to watch over luggage while the other goes to book a room and pay for it; some hotels are put off by backpacks.

Airport Taxis To avoid overcharging, the Government has taken control of taxi services from airports to cities and only those with government licences are allowed to carry passengers from the airport. Sometimes one does not pay the driver but purchases a ticket from a booth on leaving the airport.

Tipping 10% at hotels (unless on bill) and bars; 10-15% at restaurants; 5 pesos for cloak-room attendants, 5 pesos per bag for porters, or bell boys; 2 pesos at most for theatre usherettes, and nothing for a taxi driver unless he gives some extra service. It is not necessary to tip the drivers of hired cars. Porters usually have a fixed tariff.

Health Water in the cities is potable, but you are recommended to use bottled or mineral water for drinking. Tehuacán mineral water is sold all over Mexico; both plain and flavoured are first class. Where water is dubious avoid drinking it, and drop a "Sterotab" in the bedroom's iced water, even if you use it only for cleaning your teeth. Raw salads and vegetables, and food sold on the streets and in cheap cafés, especially in Mexico City, may be dangerous. Vaccination against smallpox is obligatory. Advisable to vaccinate against typhoid, para-typhoid and poliomyelitis if visiting the low-lying tropical zones, where there is also some risk of malaria. Heavy eating and drinking of alcohol is unwise in the capital because of its altitude; so is overdoing it physically in the first few days.

Drink The beer (best brands: Bavaria, Bohemia, XXX, Superior and Tecate) is quite good. Local wine, some of it of good quality, is very cheap (Domecq, Casa Madero, Santo Tomás, etc.). The native drinks are tequila, made mostly in Jalisco and potent, and pulque, also powerful. Mescal is another drink to be careful with. Imported whiskies and brandies are expensive. Rum is cheap and good but "drunks" are detested in Mexico. There are always plenty of non-alcoholic soft drinks, "refrescos" (mineral water). Water-purifying tablets can be bought in Mexico City; hydro-chlorozone, US$0.35 for 100 tablets, one tablet per litre of water. Tea is expensive.

Food Usual meals are a light breakfast, and a heavy lunch between 1400 and 1500. Dinner, between 2100 and 2300, is light. Many restaurants give foreigners the menu without the *comida corrida* (specials of the day), and so forcing them to order *à la carte* at double the price; watch this!

What to Eat   *Tamales* on special occasions. Turkey, chicken and pork with exotic sauces—*mole de guajolote* and *mole poblana* (chile and chocolate sauce with grated coconut) are famous. *Tacos* (without chiles) and *enchiladas* (with all too many of them!) are made of meat or chicken rolled in *tortillas* (maize pancackes) and fried in oil; they are delicious. Indian dishes are found everywhere: for instance, *tostadas* (toasted fried *tortillas* with chicken, beans and lettuce). Black kidney beans *(frijoles)* appear in various dishes. Red snapper *(huachinango),* Veracruz style, is a famous fish dish, sautéd with *pimientos* and spices. Another excellent fish is the sea bass *(robalo).* Fruits include a vast assortment of tropical types—avocados, bananas, pineapples, *zapotes,* pomegranates, guavas, limes and *mangos de Manila,* which are delicious. Don't eat fruit unless you peel it yourself, and avoid raw vegetables. Try *higos rebanados* (delicious fresh sliced figs), *guacamole* (a mashed avocado seasoned with tomatoes, onions, coriander and chile peppers) and of course, *papaya,* or papaw. In Mexico City you can get any type of food you want, and milk for the children. There is sliced and packaged bread throughout Mexico but it is not served in most restaurants. Mexico has various elaborate regional cuisines. Chinese restaurants, present in most towns, generally give clean and efficient service. Milk is only safe when in sealed containers maked "pasteurizado".

Clothing   People are usually smartly dressed in Mexico City. Women visitors should not wear shorts other than at the seaside. Cool nights and occasional cool days at the high altitudes demand a light overcoat; the rainy season calls for an umbrella and a raincoat. There is little central-heating, so warm clothing is needed in winter. It is hot in the coastal resorts: cotton frocks, pastel silks, bathing suits, sports clothes. Two musts are good walking shoes and dark glasses. Sweaters are useful. Men should take linen or seersucker jackets and suits; lightweight woollen suits for Mexico City and a light overcoat, sports shirts and slacks, swimming trunks and a bathrobe. Women are always escorted, except in the main streets of the larger cities. A light straw hat is recommended.

Currency   The monetary unit is the Mexican peso, divided into 100 centavos. There are silver and alloy coins of 10, 5 and 1 pesos, and 50 centavos, bronze coins of 50, 20, and 10 centavos and nickel coins of 20 centavos. Special 25-peso silver coins were issued in 1968 for the Olympic Games, and in 1972 for the centenary of the death of Juárez. A 100-peso coin, 72% silver, was introduced in 1977. Notes in circulation are for 10, 20, 50, 100, 500, and 1,000 pesos. Exchange is at the rate of about 22.50 pesos to the US dollar.

In the border states such as Baja California, the most-used currency is the US dollar, and the Mexican peso is often accepted by stores on the USA side of the border. Travellers' cheques from any well-known bank can be cashed in Mexico City if drawn in US dollars; travellers' cheques in terms of sterling are harder to cash, and certainly not worth carrying outside Mexico City. Beware of short-changing at all times. Few Mexicans are familiar with sterling and sterling notes are not readily negotiable.

Weights and Measures   The metric system is compulsory.

Business Holidays   Sunday is a statutory holiday. Saturday is also observed·as a holiday, except by the shops. There is no early-closing day. National holidays are as follows:

January 1: New Year.	May 5: Battle of Puebla.
February 5: Constitution Day.	September 1: President's Annual Message.
March 21: Birthday of Juárez.	September 16: Independence Day.
Maundy Thursday.	October 12: Discovery of America.
Good Friday.	November 20: Day of the Revolution.
Easter Saturday.	December 25: Christmas Day.
May 1: Labour Day.	

Nov. 2, All Souls' Day, and Dec, 12, Our Lady of Guadalupe, are not national holidays, but are widely celebrated.

Press The more important journals are in Mexico City. The most influential dailies are: "Excelsior", "Novedades", "El Día" (throughout Mexico); "The News" (in English, for the American community); "El Universal" ("El Universal Gráfico"); "La Prensa", a popular tabloid, has the largest circulation. "El Nacional" is the mouthpiece of the Government; "El Heraldo", a new paper. A number of monthly and weekly magazines have a wide circulation and outweigh the influence of the dailies. The most influential are the two weekly magazines "Siempre" and "Sucesos", both left of centre, very nationalistic and somewhat critical. The political satirical weekly is "Los Agachados". The monthly "Revista Industrial" is the leading trade journal, but there are 14 others.

Postal Services, organised on a federal basis, are slow; ordinary mail, internal or international, takes up to two weeks outside the capital. In Mexico City there is an immediate delivery *(entrega immediata)* service which is supposed to deliver in 2-3 days, but may take longer than an ordinary letter. Elsewhere, air mail is better. Air mail letters to the US take about three days, and to the UK *via* the US about four days. Weight limit from the UK to Mexico: 22 lb., and 5 kilos in the reverse direction. Charges for sending air mail parcels are high. As for most of Latin America send printed matter such as magazines registered. International parcels must be examined by the Customs Office at Dr. Andrade, nr. Río de La Loza (or main Post Office window No. 48, in Mexico City) before posting. Dr. Andrade Post Office open 0800-1300 Mon.-Fri. No more than 3 parcels may be sent at a time; registered letters received here. We have heard that the Customs Department at the airport hold up registered parcels coming in from abroad. A permit is needed from the Bellas Artes office to send paintings or drawings out of Mexico.

Telégrafos Nacionales maintains the national(see also page 814) and international telegraph systems. It is separate from the Post Office and telegrams have to be handed in at its office. There is a special office at Balderas, just near corner of Colón, in Mexico City to deal with international traffic. A telegram to Britain costs 5 pesos a word, but 55 pesos for 21 words at night letter rate. Telephone service to USA, Canada and Europe. Calls to Britain are 75 pesos per minute from 0500 to 1700, but 60 pesos per minute from 1700 to 0500 and all day on Sunday.

Cost of Living The rise in the cost of living was 27% in 1976, slowing down to 20% in 1977; a rather lower rate was expected for 1978. Manufactured goods and clothing tend to be dearer than in the USA. Film is usually expensive, e.g. Kodak 36 exposures for slides, US$9. Food is cheaper but often of an inferior quality—the meat is deficient in iron, ice-cream is produced with water and skimmed milk. Services are abundant and cheap: there are armies of waiters, waitresses, chauffeurs, maids, gardeners, night watchmen, etc. Rent for living quarters is low.

Great Britain is represented by an Embassy at Calle Río Lerma 71, Colonia Cuauhtémoc, Mexico City 5, D.F. Consul at Tampico, and Vice-Consuls at Coatzacoalcos, Guadalajara, Guaymas, Mazatlán, Mérida, Monterrey, Pachuca, Tampico, Tapachula, Torreón, and Veracruz. Telephone number of Counsellor (Commercial) is 511.48.80-85. The telegraphic address is "Britain" followed by the appropriate town or city.

The United States is represented by an Embassy and a Consulate at Mexico (Reforma 305), Consuls at Mexico City, Ciudad Juárez, Guadalajara, Guaymas, Matamoros, Mazatlán, Mexicali, Monterrey, Nogales, Nuevo Laredo, Piedras Negras, Tampico, Tijuana, San Luis Potosí, Mérida.

American Express Agents Mérida: Barbachanos Travel Svc., Loby Panamericana, Tel.: 17640. Mexico City: American Express Co., Hamburgo 75, Tel.: 533-0380. Monterrey: Industria Turistica, Pino Suárez 135 Sur, Tel.: 437170. Acapulco: American Express Co., Costera Alemán 709A, Tel.: 4-10-95. Puerto Vallarta: Viva Tours, Paseo Presidente Díaz, Tel.: 2-00-03. Guadalajara: Convisa S.A., Edf. Condominio B-1, Tel.: 4-44-14. Mazatlán: Viva Tours, Olas Atlas Sur 21-A, Tel.: 64-10.

We have pleasure in acknowledging the great assistance received in revising this chapter from Tim Connell (especially for San Luis Potosí, Aguascalientes, Querétaro, Guadalajara, Jalapa and Mexico City); from Mike Shawcross (for the State of Chiapas); from John Streather, whose wanderings again produced so much of such great interest. Then, thanks for a most difficult updating job to Barbara Wijngaard of LBI Economics Department, and also to the many travellers, whose names are listed as follows: Roselyn van Benschoten and Johanna Noordhoek (Netherlands), Ingela Björck and Per Andersson (Sweden), Andrew Brown and Ken Trainer (USA), Olivier Chaudouet (Voiteur, France), P. F. Cheesewright, Martin R. Elton, Ben Fawcett, Vittorio Ferretti (São Paulo), Gabriel Foscal-Mella (Longueuil, Québec), Tim and Arlene Frost (Hamilton, N.Z.), Hans Hartung (Ludwigshafen), Etienne Istasse (Belgium), Dr. Brian Jeffery (San Francisco, Calif.), Monica Joseph (Australia), Arnold Koiter (Weert, Netherlands), David E. López (Los Angeles, Calif.), Andreas Lutz (Switzerland), Daniel and Jan McAleese (Belfast), Miss E. M. McLeod, John Mead (Cleveland, Ohio) and Robert Bührer (Hofen, Switz.), Andy Millington (Calgary, Canada), Nikolaus Müller (Köln), Roger Pauling and Dr. C. F. Hoyle, Hugo Pfandler (W. Germany), M. G. Powell, Nick Purbeck, Michael Reeve, John Roper-Lindsay, Ornan Rotem and Naomi Stibbe, Jules Salomon (Pully, Lausanne), Helga Schmidt-Frank and Herbert Schmidt (W. Germany), Hans André Schultz (Bremen), Michael Scott, Chris Sharpe (Mullewa, W. Australia), J. Troller (Visp, Switz.), and Terry and Rosaura West (USA). Finally, John and Sylvia Brooks (the Editor and his wife), who made their first visit to Mexico in Feb.-March 1978, have added their own mite.

CENTRAL AMERICA

CENTRAL AMERICA comprises seven of the smallest countries of Latin America: Panama, Costa Rica, Nicaragua, Honduras, El Salvador, Guatemala and the self-governing colony of Belize (formerly British Honduras). Together they occupy 544,700 square km., which is less than the size of Texas. The total population of Central America in 1970 was well over 16 million and it is increasing by 3.2% each year. As in other parts of Latin America, some of these countries suffer from an over-concentration of population in relatively small areas. In Guatemala, only about half the country is populated and a sixth of the population lives in and around the capital, Guatemala City. Generally speaking, the gap between the conditions of life in the towns and in rural areas is very wide.

The degree of development in these countries differs sharply. Costa Rica has the highest standard of living and the highest rate of economic and social advancement, with one of the highest rates of literacy in all Latin America. At the other end of the scale, Honduras has one of the lowest standards of living. In Nicaragua, only about 8% of the whole land area is in economic use.

Geographically, these countries have much in common. All of them are mountainous, have a similar climate and produce much the same kind of products, mainly agricultural: bananas, cotton, sugar, coffee, cocoa and gold and silver. But there are sharp differences in the racial composition and traditions of their peoples. Costa Ricans are almost wholly white, Guatemalans are largely Amerindian or of mixed blood; Hondurans, Nicaraguans and Salvadoreans are almost entirely mestizo. Panama has perhaps the most racially varied population, with a large white group. Some of these countries also have a black element, the largest being found in Panama and Nicaragua.

The local name for mestizo in Central America and southern Mexico is "ladino" (Latin). The distinction between Ladino and Indio is as often cultural as racial; ladinos speak Spanish and wear European-style clothes but are quite likely to be pure Indian racially.

Early History

The fragmentation of Central America into such small entities had its roots in the pre-Conquest Indian populations of the area. The best known of these was the Maya civilisation which is thought to have originated in about A.D. 100 in the Pacific Highlands of Guatemala and El Salvador. After 200 years of evolution it entered what is known today as its "classic" period when the civilisation flourished in Guatemala, Belize, Honduras, Chiapas and parts of Campeche (Mexico). This period lasted until A.D. 900-1000, after which time the Mayas, forced to converge on Yucatán after a successful invasion of their lands by non-Maya Mexicans (this is only one theory: another is that they were forced to flee after a peasants' revolt against them), came under the influence of the Toltecs who also lived in the area. From that time their culture declined, though there is a theory that but for the Spanish Conquest, there might well have been a Maya renaissance for, at the time of the conquest, "Mayanised" Mexicans had begun to settle in areas where the Maya civilisation had originated and were refurbishing the old cities and building new ones along similar lines. The Mayan civilisation was one based on independent and antagonistic city states, some having suzerainty over others. Hence the construction of so many cities, including Tikal, Uaxactún, Kaminal Juyú, Iximché, Zacaleu and Quiriguá in Guatemala; Copán in Honduras; Altún Ha in Belize; Tazumal and San Andrés in El Salvador and Palenque, Bonampak (both in Chiapas) and Uxmal, Chichén Itza, Mayapán, Tulum and the Puuc hill cities of Sayil, Labná and Kabah (all on the Yucatán peninsula) in Mexico.

The cities were all meticulously dated: we know, that is, the exact interval of time between the rise of a city and the departure of its inhabitants, but we can only guess at the corresponding dates in our calendar. Mayan art is a mathematical art: each column, figure, face, animal, frieze, stairway and temple expresses a date or a time relationship. Nothing was random. each single creation in stone was a mathematical symbol. When, for example, an ornament on the ramp of the Hieroglyphic Stairway at Copán was repeated some 15 times, it was to express that number of elapsed "leap" years. The 75 steps stand for the number of elapsed intercalary days. The Mayan calendar was a nearer approximation to sidereal time than either the Julian or the Gregorian calendars of the west; it was only .000069 of a day out of true in a year. They used the zero centuries in advance of the Old World, plotted the movements of the sun, moon, Venus and other planets, conceived a cycle of more than 1,800 million days, achieved paper codices and glyphic writing, were skilled potters and weavers and traded over wide areas though they had not discovered the wheel and had no beasts of burden (Pacific Coast shells have been found in their sites in Belize territory). Their tools and weapons were flint and hard stone, obsidian and fire-hardened wood, and yet with these they grew lavish crops, hewed out and transported great monoliths over miles of difficult country, and carved them over with intricate glyphs and figures which would be difficult enough with modern chisels. They moved amazing tonnages of earth and rock, terraced hillsides, truncated and levelled hilltops and built on them high pyramids and massive stone buildings. One article of their faith was that the world was supported on the backs of two giant alligators.

The Mayan cities were principally ceremonial centres controlled by a theocratic minority of priests and nobles in whom was vested the entire cultural activity of each state; ordinary people also lived in these places. The Toltecs, who had firm control in Yucatán in the 10th century, gradually spread their empire as far as the southern borders of Guatemala. They in turn, however, were conquered by the Aztecs, one of whose revolutionary principles was the private ownership of land, but they did not penetrate into Central America. At the time of the coming of the Spaniards there were several other cultural groups of Indians dotted over the Central American area: the Pipil, in El Salvador; the Lenca, in Honduras; the Suma, on the northern border of Nicaragua; the Miskito, on the "Mosquito" coast of the Caribbean; the Guaymi, in Costa Rica; and the San Blas, in Panama. These groups were all isolated and were mostly shifting cultivators or nomadic hunters and fishermen. A few places only were occupied by sedentary agriculturists: what remained of the Maya in the highlands of Guatemala; a group on the south-western shores of Lakes Managua and Nicaragua; and another in the highlands of Costa Rica. The Spanish conquerors were attracted by two things only: precious metals, or native sedentary farmers who could be Christianized and exploited to raise commercial crops. There were little of either, and comparatively few Spaniards settled in Central America.

It was only during his fourth voyage, in 1502, that Columbus reached the mainland of Central America; he landed in Panama, which he called Veragua, and founded the town of Santa María de Belén. But Rodrigo Bastidas and Vasco Núñez de Balboa, a bankrupt planter from Haiti, had forestalled him by two years. Juan Díaz de Solís and Pinzón explored the coast again in 1506. In 1508 Alonso de Ojeda received a grant of land on the Pearl Coast east of Panama, and Diego de Nicuesa obtained a grant of land from Panama northwards. In 1509 Ojeda founded the town of San Sebastián, later moved to a new site called Santa María la Antigua del Darién. In 1513 the governor of the colony at Darién was the red-headed and energetic Balboa. Taking 190 men he crossed the isthmus in 18 days and caught the first glimpse of the Pacific; a few days later he was striding into the water, sword in hand, possessing it and all neighbouring lands in the name of the King of Spain. But from the folowing year, when Pedrarias replaced him as Governor, Balboa fell on evil days, and he was executed in 1519. That same year Pedrarias crossed the isthmus and founded the town of Panamá on the Pacific side. It was in April, 1519, too, that Cortés began his conquest of Mexico.

Central America was explored from these two nodal points of Panama and Mexico cities: Pedrarias sent expeditions northwards from Panama City and Cortés southwards from Mexico City. Cortés' lieutenant, Alvarado, had conquered as far south as San Salvador by 1523. He established himself there as an independent ruler, but Cortés, speeding south, displaced him the following year. Meanwhile Pedrarias was sending forces into Panama and Costa Rica: the latter was abandoned, for the natives were hostile, but was finally colonised from Mexico City when the rest of Central America had been taken. In 1522 and 1523 Andrés Nino and Gil Gonzales Dávila explored the Pacific coast of Nicaragua. In 1524, Dávila went from Hispaniola to Honduras. Many towns were founded by these forces from Panama: León, Granada, Trujillo, San Gil de Buenavista, Bruselas, and others. Spanish forces from the north and south sometimes met and fought bitterly. The gentle Bartolomé de Las Casas, the "apostle of the Indies", went as a Dominican missionary to Nicaragua in 1532, and to Guatemala in 1536, making a great nuisance of himself with his Christian themes of love for, and forbearance towards, the natives.

Settlement

The Spanish groups of settlers were few and distant from one another. Panama was ruled from Bogotá, but the rest of Central America was subordinate to the Viceroyalty at Mexico City, with Guatemala City as an Audencia for the area. Panama was of paramount importance for colonial Latin America for its strategic importance, and for the trade passing across the isthmus to and from the southern colonies. The other provinces were of comparatively little value.

The Spanish settlers brought their grains and animals and diseases with them. The diseases flourished, reducing enormously the population of Indians. The comparatively small number of Spaniards intermarried freely with the few survivors: it is this that accounts for the predominance of *ladinos* in Central America today. In Guatemala, where there were the most Indians and most survivors, intermarriage affected fewer of the natives, and over half the population today is pure-bred Indian. On the *meseta central* of Costa Rica, the Indians were all but wiped out by disease; intermarriage was no longer possible, and today, as one of the consequences of this great disaster, there is a buoyant community of over 1,500,000 European descendants in the highlands. Blacks predominate all along the Caribbean coasts of Central America; they were not brought in by the colonists as slaves, as in Brazil and Venezuela, but by the banana planters of the late nineteenth century and the canal cutters of the twentieth, as cheap labour.

The colonial populations of Central America were too poor and too widely scattered to make desirable or possible any very restrictive control by the mother country. On November 5, 1811, José Matías Delgado, a Creole priest and jurist born at San Salvador, in conjunction with another priest, Manuel José Arce, organised a revolt and rose in arms. After removing the Spanish officials from office, the patriots proclaimed the independence of El Salvador. But the Audencia at Guatemala City quickly suppressed the revolt, took Delgado prisoner and moved him to Guatemala, where he continued to make trouble.

Independence and Federation

It was the revolution of 1820 in Spain itself that precipitated revolt in Central America. The Creoles were divided into two groups: one, headed by Delgado, with Pedro Molina's periodical *El Editor Constitucional* as its mouthpiece, stood for an immediate declaration of independence; the other, under José Cecilio del Valle, believed the time was not yet ripe. But when on February 24, 1821, the Mexican patriot officer, Iturbide, announced his "Plan of Iguala" for an independent Mexico, the Central American Creoles decided to follow his example, and a declaration of independence, drafted by del Valle, was announced in Guatemala City. This was on September 15, 1821. A few months later, Iturbide, invited the provinces of Central America to join his empire. Most accepted, and on January 5, 1822, Central America was declared annexed to Mexico, whose Imperial Congress admitted the peoples of Central America into Mexican citizenship. Nevertheless, some parts of El Salvador (under the influence of Delgado), of Honduras, and Nicaragua, refused to accept this decree, and Iturbide, who had now assumed the title of Emperor Agustín the First, sent an army south under Vicente Filisola to enforce it. Filisola had completed his task when he heard of Iturbide's abdication, and at once convened a general congress of the Central American provinces. It met on June 24, 1823, and declared all the provinces free of Spain but bound as federates of the *Provincias Unidas del Centro de América*. The Mexican republic acknowledged their independence on August 1, 1824, and Filisola's soldiers were withdrawn.

The congress, presided over by Delgado, proceeded to discuss its constitution; one party, the *Serviles,* or Conservatives, favoured a strong central government; the *Radicales,* or Liberals, favoured a federal republic and abolition of the conservative privileges. A provisional governing junta was appointed which promulgated a constitution modelled on that of the United States on November 22, 1824. The Province of Chiapas was not included in the Federation, for it had already adhered to Mexico in 1821. No federal capital was chosen, but Guatemala City, by force of tradition, soon became its seat. Catholicism was declared the state's religion and slavery was abolished.

The Breakdown of the Federation

The first President of the first congress meeting under the new constitution was Manuel José Arce, a liberal; the chosen vice-president was del Valle, a conservative, but he declined, and Mariano Beltranea took his place. Arce was soon at loggerheads with his party and with the state authorities of Guatemala. One of his first acts was to abolish slavery and the slave trade. El Salvador, protesting that he had exceeded his power, rose in December, 1826, when Arce called an extraordinary congress to consider the political situation. Honduras, Nicaragua, and Costa Rica joined El Salvador in the revolt, and in 1828 General Francisco Morazán, in charge of the army of Honduras, defeated the federal forces and forced them to evacuate El Salvador. Morazán entered San Salvador in triumph, collected new forces, and marched against Guatemala City. After an early repulse he captured the city on April 13, 1829, and established that contradiction in terms: a Liberal dictatorship. A new congress elected a new president: Pedro Molina. Many Conservative leaders were expelled, most monasteries abolished, and church and monastic properties confiscated. Morazán himself became president of the Federation in 1830. He was a man of considerable ability. he ruled with a strong hand, encouraged education, fostered trade and industry, opened the country to immigrants, and reorganized the administration. In 1835 the capital was moved to San Salvador.

These reforms had antagonized the Conservatives and there were several risings. A canard that Morazán had caused an epidemic of cholera amongst the natives by ordering the water supplies to be poisoned led to a serious revolt amongst the Indians. It was led by Rafael Carrera, an illiterate *ladino*, but a born leader. "Long live religion and death to foreigners" was his battle cry, with its inevitable sequel of wholesale murder and depredation. When defeated by Government forces he fled to the mountains, reassembled his forces, and marched against Guatemala City, whose authorities were forced to pay a large ransom to keep him from entering. Carrera then marched against the city of Mita and entered it. His position thereafter was a fluctuation of defeats and successes, during the course of which the Federation withered away. On May 18, 1838, the federal congress committed suicide; it passed an act which allowed each province to assume what government it chose.

But the idea of a federation was not quite dead. It was Morazán who, on May 18, 1838, became President of El Salvador. Fearing his intentions, the other states made war against him. Carrera, who was in control of Guatemala, defeated Morazán in battle and forced him to leave the country. Immediately afterwards there was a general massacre of Liberals throughout Central America. But in 1842, Morazán, returning to Central America, overthrew Braulio Carrillo, then dictator of Costa Rica, and became president himself. At once he set about rebuilding the Federation, but was defeated by the united forces of the other states, and shot on September 15, 1842. With him perished any practical hope of Central American political union.

The Separate States

Costa Rica, with its mainly white population, is in a sense a republic apart, and Panama was Colombian territory until 1903. The history of the four remaining republics, from the breakdown of federation to the twenties of the present century, was tempestuous in the extreme: a story of civil war, of war against neighbours, of shifting alliances and antagonisms, and of recurrent dictatorship. Each had (and still has) its interior tensions of wealth side-by-side with poverty; in each the ruling class was divided into pro-clerical Conservatives and anti-clerical Liberals, with constant changes of power. Each was weak, and therefore suspicious of its neighbours. each tried repeatedly to buttress its weakness by alliances with others, which invariably broke up because one of the allies sought supremacy in council. The wars have rarely been over boundaries, or been carried on for hope of gain; they have been mainly ideological wars between Conservatives and Liberals, or wars motivated by the pride and sensitivities of an inflamed nationalism. Nicaragua, for instance, was riven internally for most of the period by the mutual hatreds of the Conservatives of Granada and the Liberals of León, and there were repeated conflicts between the Caribbean and interior parts of Honduras.

Of the four republics, Guatemala was certainly the strongest and in some ways the most stable. Whilst the other states were skittling their Presidents like so many ninepins, Guatemala was being ruled by a succession of strong dictators: Rafael Carrera (1838-1865), Justo Rufino Barrios (1873-1885), Manuel Cabrera (1896-1920), and the eccentric despot Jorge Ubico (1931-44). These were separated by intervals of constitutional government, anarchy, or attempts at dictatorship which failed. Even in Guatemala few presidents handed over power peacefully or voluntarily to their successors; most of them were forcibly removed or assassinated.

Through the permutations and combinations of external and civil war it is possible to detect one hopeful theme: a recurrent desire to bind the brittle sticks into one strong faggot. We have seen how the first federation broke down. In 1842, El Salvador, Honduras and Nicaragua entered into a new confederation at Chinandega. It ended two years later in an attack by the other two confederates against Nicaragua. In 1845 there was an attempt at federation between Guatemala and El Salvador, which never got beyond the planning stage. There was another abortive attempt in 1847 to federate El Salvador, Nicaragua and Honduras, and again in 1849, and 1862. War broke out between Guatemala and El Salvador in 1876 while delegates from the five republics were discussing union. President Barrios of Guatemala was killed in 1885 whilst engaged in trying to enforce union. In 1895 Nicaragua, El Salvador and Honduras entered into a partial federation under the Treaty of Ampala, but the government of El Salvador was overthrown and it came to nothing. In 1907 José Santos Zelaya, dictator of Nicaragua from 1893 to 1909, attempted to unite Central America by force; the other states resisted and intervention by Mexico and the United States brought the war to an end. But that same year delegates from the republics signed a treaty at Washington providing for the maintenance of peace and the compulsory judicial settlement of all disputes, and established a Central American Court of Justice, which functioned until 1918. On January 19, 1921, Guatemala, Honduras, El Salvador and Costa Rica agreed at San José on yet another federation. It broke down almost immediately.

Relations with UK and USA

Both Great Britain and the United States have been embroiled in disputes in Central America. As long ago as 1678 the Governor of Jamaica had set up a protectorate of the Indians along the Mosquito coast, where the British were interested in logging and, during the 19th century, in a canal across the isthmus. In 1841 the protectorate was re-affirmed but in 1856, under diplomatic pressure from the United States, Britain withdrew its claim, and in 1860 signed a treaty with Nicaragua recognising the latter's sovereignty over the Mosquito Indians. In 1894, however, when Nicaraguan troops entered the Mosquito territory and the Indians applied to Great Britain for help, the British (and sympathizing U.S.A.) landed forces at Bluefields. Later in the year a convention was signed in which the Indians were incorporated with Nicaragua, and both British and U.S. forces withdrew. Britain had already ceded the Bay Islands to Honduras in 1859. The same year, there was a settlement of disputes over boundaries between Guatemala and Belize, then known as British Honduras, but Guatemala still claims sovereignty over Belize; the dispute has led to Guatemala suspending diplomatic relations with Britain.

Friction between the Government of the United States and the Central American republics has in the main been confined to Nicaragua, and is discussed in the Nicaraguan section.

The Changing Scene

Prosperity and change are now coming to Central America. During Colonial times the area suffered from great poverty; trade with the mother country was confined to a small amount of silver and gold, a little cacao and sugar, a little cochineal and indigo. But during the present century the great banana plantations of the Caribbean, the growing coffee and cotton trades and industrialization have brought a modified prosperity and greater stability. The overwhelming power of the United States, both as trader and peacemaker, is also a potent factor. Continued peace is more and more likely, but continued disunion also seems certain. A tradition of self-sufficiency, in isolation, rooted in the original native tribes and persisting throughout the colonial period in fact if not in theory, remains too strong to be broken. Political nationalism is more rabid here than in most parts of the world, and that is saying much. But poverty, still the fate of the great majority, is forcing a closer economic integration between the five republics, which in 1960 established the Central American Common Market (CACM) to weld them into one sizeable and reasonably viable economic unit. Where each is too weak to prosper, solidarity may prove a way out of their economic distress. Surprisingly, the Common Market appeared to be a great success until 1968, when integration fostered national antagonisms, and there was a growing conviction in Honduras and Nicaragua, which were doing least well out of integration, that they were being exploited by the others. In 1969 the "Football War" broke out between El Salvador and Honduras, basically because of a dispute arising out of illicit emigration by Salvadoreans into Honduras, and there has been no trade and little other direct contact between the two since. Not surprisingly, the CACM has not recovered from this blow. The effects of world recession have brought the presidents together to consider a new form of association, the Central American Economic and Social Community, but it seems likely that nationalist feeling will continue to block attempts to re-establish economic integration.

(For revising the Central American sections, we are most grateful to Christine Mellor, of LBI Economics Department, for doing the updating; to the Instituto

Guatemalteco de Turismo; and to the following travellers: James M. Barrett (USA), Roselyn van Benschoten and Johanna Noordhoek (Netherlands), Ingela Björck and Per Andersson (Sweden), James K. Bock (Mexico City), William Brice (Jamaica), Andrew Brown and Ken Trainer (USA), Olivier Chaudouet (Voiteur, France), Martin Davidshofer (Switzerland), Martin R. Elton, Ben Fawcett, Peter Ford and Sally Wilson, Gabriel Foscal-Mella (Longueuil, Québec), Louise Lawrence Foster (Pensacola, Fla.), Anton Fuchs (Innsbruck), Ucky Hamilton (N.Z.), Hans Hartung (Ludwigshafen), Monica Joseph (Australia), A. R. Koiter (Netherlands), Detlef Körner (Hamburg), Cornelio Lindenburg and Marieke van der Ploeg (Amersfoort, Neth.), Andreas Lutz (Switzerland), B. and J. McAndrew, Len Macdonald (USA), Andy Millington (Calgary, Canada), Nikolaus Müller (Köln), Roger Pawling and Dr. C. F. Hoyle, Hugo Pfandler (W. Germany), Nick Purbeck, Michael Reeve, Jacob Rietsema (W. Hartford, Conn.), John Roper-Lindsay, Helga Schmidt-Frank and Herbert Schmidt (W. Germany), Hans-André Schultz (Bremen), Michael Scott, Chris Sharpe (Mullewa, W. Australia), E. Spieth (Frankfurt), Margaret Symons (N.Z.) and Terry and Rosaura West (USA). The names of others, whose contributions were for one country only, will be found at the end of the appropriate country section.)

GUATEMALA

GUATEMALA (109,000 square km., 6 million people), is the most populous of the Central American republics and the only one which is predominantly Indian. It still has large areas of unoccupied land, especially in the north; only about two-thirds is populated. Two-thirds of it is mountainous and 62% forested. It has coastlines on the Pacific (240 km.), and on the Caribbean (110 km.). A sixth of the total population lives in its one great city, the capital, which is more than three times as large as any other town.

A lowland ribbon, nowhere more than 50 km. wide, runs the whole length of the Pacific shore. There are two ports on this coast: San José and Champerico. Both are open and unprotected, and ships have to lie well offshore. Cotton, sugar, bananas and maize are the chief crops of this lowland, particularly in the Department of Escuintla. There is some stock raising as well. Summer rain is heavy and the lowland carries scrub forest. Numerous creeks of brackish water form outlets to the many rivers flowing to the sea.

From this plain the highlands rise sharply to heights of between 2,500 and 3,000 metres and stretch some 240 km. to the N before sinking into the northern lowlands. A string of volcanoes juts boldly above the southern highlands along the Pacific; three (Pacaya, Fuego and Santiaguito) are still active; three are above 4,000 metres. There are large and small intermont basins at from 1,500 to 2,450 metres in this volcanic area. Most of the people of Guatemala live in these basins, drained by short rivers into the Pacific and by longer rivers into the Atlantic. One basin W of the capital has no outlet and here, ringed by volcanoes, is the splendid Lake Atitlán.

The southern highlands are covered with a deep layer of lava and ash. This clears away in the central highlands, exposing the crystalline rock of the E-W running ranges. This area is lower but more rugged, with sharp-faced ridges and deep ravines modifying into gentle slopes and occasional valley lowlands as it loses height and approaches the Caribbean coastal levels and the flatlands of El Petén.

The lower slopes of these highlands, from about 600 to 1,500 metres, are planted with coffee which is some 60% by value of the total exports. Coffee plantations make almost a complete belt around them. Above 1,500 metres is given over to wheat and the great subsistence crops of maize and beans. The highlands, which receive much rain, are forested: pine at the heights, oak and other broadleaf species lower down and tropical evergreens in the valleys. Deforestation is, however, becoming a serious problem. Where rainfall is low there are savannas; the middle Motagua valley is so parched that it can only bear xerophytic plants like cactus, but abundant water for irrigation is now drawn from wells and the area is being reclaimed for pasture and fruit growing.

Two large valleys thrust down to the Caribbean Gulf of Honduras from the highlands: one is the valley of the Motagua, 400 km. long, rising

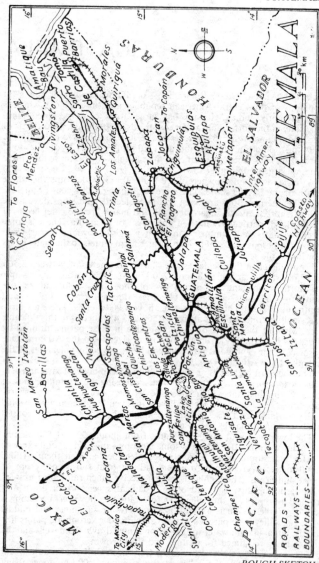

ROUGH SKETCH

amongst the southern volcanoes; the other, further N, is the Río Polochic, 298 km. long, which drains into large Lake Izabal and the Bay of Amatique. The Motagua is navigable for small craft to within 144 km. of Guatemala City. There are large areas of lowland in the lower reaches of both rivers; this was, and may be again, the great banana zone.

To the NW, bordering on Belize and Mexico, in the Peninsula of Yucatán, lies the low, undulating tableland of Petén, 36,300 square km. of almost inaccessible wilderness covered with dense hardwood forest. Deep in this tangled rain-forest lie the ruins of Maya cities such as Tikal and Uaxactún. This plateau is drained E into the Gulf by the Río Sarstún, and W into the Río Usumacinta by the Río Cancuén. On Lake Petén, in the N, is one small town, Flores, living on the chicle-bleeding in the area. In the Department of Petén, almost one-third of the national territory, there are only 40,000 people. In some parts there is natural grassland with woods and streams suitable for cattle. There is much smuggling along the Belize border.

Settlement When the Spaniards arrived from Mexico City in 1523 they found little precious metal: only some silver at Huehuetenango. Those who stayed settled in the intermont basins of the south-eastern parts of the southern highlands around Antigua and Guatemala City and intermarried with the groups of subsistence native farmers living there. This early pattern has now developed into the present "ladino" (mestizo) population slowly acquiring Western culture and living in the cities and towns as well as in all parts of the southern highlands and in the flatlands along the Pacific coast; the indigenous population—more than half the total—is still at its most dense in the western highlands and Alta Verapaz. They form two distinct cultures: the almost self-supporting system of production, distribution and consumption of goods in the highlands, and the commercial economy represented by the importing and exporting houses and banks of Guatemala City. At first sight the two seem to have much in common, for the Indian regional economy is also monetary. Money comes from the sale of chickens, meat, fruit, vegetables, flowers, charcoal and firewood to the cities and from the wages received for agricultural work. This money circulates within the regional economy and a little of it goes to buying a few manufacturing articles. Nearly all Indian communities specialize in making something and interchange their goods at fairs. Family industry is important to them, and they are industrious. But a gulf opens between the two systems when it is realised that an Indian will take an article a hundred km. and ask no more for it than he would at home. To him, trade seems to be a social act, not done out of need, and certainly from no impulse to make a profit and grow rich.

Cochineal and indigo were the great exports until 1857, when both were wiped out by synthetic dyes. The vacuum was filled by cacao, followed by two commercial crops, coffee and bananas—both introductions from the outside world—and essential oils. The upland soil and climate are particularly favourable to coffee. Since harvesting is slow and done exclusively by hand it needs a large labour force, and it is here that the self-contained regional economy makes its vital contribution to the international economy: it is the Indian who does the picking.

Only coffee of the Bourbon variety is planted below 600 metres, and until 1906, when bananas were first planted there, the low-lying *tierra caliente* had been used mostly for cane and cattle raising. The first plantations of the United Fruit Company were at the mouth of the Motagua, near Puerto Barrios, then little more than a village. Blacks from Jamaica were brought in to work them. The plantations expanded until they covered most of the *tierra caliente* in the NE—along the lower Motagua and around Lake Izabal. Puerto Barrios was developed as a modern port to handle these crops and also the country's imports, and railways were built, not only in to the plantations, but all the way to the capital. The port is now connected to Guatemala City by a paved highway.

In the thirties, however, the plantations were struck by disease and the Company began planting bananas in the Pacific lowlands, in the Tiquisate region half-way between the ports of San José and Champerico. The bananas are railed across country to the Caribbean ports, but there are substantial plantations still at Bananera, 58 km. from Puerto Barrios, though some of the old banana land is used for cotton and *abacá*. Most of the workers on the Pacific side are not blacks, but Indians and *ladinos*. Exports of bananas have fallen a lot since 1947, however, overall exports have increased greatly, because of the growth of other export lines such as coffee, cotton and sugar. As a result of the increase in cotton-growing, many Indians are now moving from the highlands to the hot mosquito-ridden *ladino* cotton areas; a new factor which will hasten the coalescence of the two cultures.

The equitable distribution of occupied land is a pressing problem. The Agrarian Census of 1950 disclosed that 70% of the cultivable land was in the hands of 2% of the landowners, 20% in the hands of 22%, and 10% in the hands of 76%—these figures corresponding to the large, medium and small landowners. A quarter of the land held by the small owners was sub-let to peasants who owned none at all. There were over 417,000 farms according to the 1964 census, and 10,000 land titles have been given to landless peasants since 1970; this means that there has been some spread of landownership since the 1950s.

Communications by rail and road are being developed. The only **railway** (apart from the Government's Verapaz Railway of 46 km. and a few private branch lines on the United Brands estates) is the Guatemalan Railways, bought by the State from U.S. company, International Railways of Central America, in 1968. This railway links the Caribbean seaboard with the Pacific littoral, running from Puerto Barrios up the Motagua valley to Guatemala City and on to the port of San José. From Santa María a branch line runs W through Mazatenango to the ports of Champerico and Ocós and the Mexican frontier, where northbound passengers change trains at Tecún Umán. From Zacapa, half-way from Puerto Barrios to the Capital, a branch line runs S to San Salvador. There are 867 km. of public service railways and 290 km. of plantation lines.

The 1976 earthquake caused heavy damage to roads and railways; much has now been repaired. The main road and railway between Guatemala City and Puerto Barrios are again open to traffic.

Roads   There are now 13,632 km. of roads, 2,638 of which are paved. They are shown in the map. Volcanic ash makes the unpaved roads dusty in the dry, and muddy in the wet season.

Population   Birth rate: 44.0 per 1,000 (60% born to unmarried mothers); infant mortality, 75 (1974); population growth: 3.1%; urban growth: 8%.

About 51% are literate. Malaria and intestinal parasites reduce the labourer's health. His diet is mostly maize (served as *tortillas* and a variety of other ways), black beans and rice. Skilled workers are comparatively few, but the Indians have an innate capacity which, properly organized, could turn Guatemala into a great food-producing country and the Government is currently trying to promote co-operatives, so as to improve productivity. Some 65% of the people live at elevations above 1,000 metres in 30% of the total territory; only 35% live at lower elevations in 70% of the total territory.

Government

Guatemala is administratively divided into 22 Departments. The Governor of each is appointed by the President, whose term is for 4 years. The latest constitution was dated May, 1966.

Recent History   For early history see the Introductory Chapter to Central America. President Ubico, an efficient dictator who came to power in 1931, was deposed in 1944 when rioting broke out in the capital. After some confusion, Juan José Arévalo, a teacher, was elected President. He set out to accomplish a social (and somewhat radical) revolution, paying particular attention to education and labour problems. He survived several conspiracies and finished his term of six years. Jacobo Arbenz became President in 1950, and the pace of reform was quickened. His Agrarian Reform Law, dividing large estates expropriated without adequate compensation amongst the numerous landless peasantry, aroused opposition from landowners. In June, 1954, Colonel Carlos Castillo Armas, backed by interested parties and with the encouragement of the United States, led a successful insurrection. Arbenz was overthrown and Castillo Armas became President. He was assassinated in July, 1957. General Miguel Ydígoras Fuentes was elected President, but he was deposed by the army in March, 1963. The army retired from direct rule in 1966 and allowed Dr. Julio César Méndez Montenegro to be elected, though it retained a large measure of indirect control. In July 1970 General Carlos Arana Osorio became President. The ruthless struggle between left and right has continued, with great violence, but there are now signs of a return to greater order. Another army leader, Gen. Kjell Laugerud García, was President 1974-78; the new President is Gen. Romeo Lucas García.

Cities and Towns

Note: *The capital (to a somewhat lesser extent) and many other towns and villages sustained severe damage as a result of an earthquake in February 1976 when 23,000 people died. Guatemala lost some of its most beautiful tourist attractions. The text has been revised accordingly, but inevitably there will be some instances where we have failed to delete reference to a destroyed church, hotel or some other building.*

Guatemala City, at 1,500 metres, was founded by decree of Charles III of Spain in 1776 to serve as capital after earthquake damage to the earlier capital, Antigua, in 1773. The city lies on a plateau, a gash through the high Sierra Madre. The lofty ranges of these green mountains almost overhang the capital. To the S looms a group of volcanoes. Population, 1,127,845.

The climate is mildly temperate, with little variation around the year. The average annual temperature is about 18°C, with a monthly average high of 20° in May and a low of 16° in December-January. Daily temperatures range from a low of 10°C at night to a high of about 29° when the sun is at its most glaring point at midday. The rainy season is from May to October but rainfall is not heavy; it averages about 1,270 mm. a year, and sunshine is plentiful.

It was almost completely destroyed by earthquakes in 1917-18 and rebuilt in modern fashion or in copied Colonial. Houses are mostly of one storey, but several high multi-storey buildings have now been put up. A plaza called Parque Central lies at its heart: the Plaza is intersected by the N-S running Avenida 6, the main shopping centre. The E half has a floodlit fountain; on the W side is Parque Centenario, with an acoustic shell in cement used for open-air concerts and public meetings. To the E of the Plaza is the Cathedral; the Central Market in the block behind it has been levelled to enable construction of a new building. To the W are the National Library and the Banco del Ejército; to the N the large Palacio Nacional. Behind the Palacio Nacional, built of light green stone, is the Presidential Mansion. Apart from the Mercado Terminal, in Zona 4, where buses leave for everywhere except Cobán, Flores, the Pacific Coast and the Mexican frontier (these leave from Zona 1), there is the Mercado del Sur, 6 Av. 19-21, Zona 1. The latter is primarily a food market though a section for popular handicrafts was set up in 1976. There is also a new *artesanía* market in Parque Aurora, near the airport, where marimba music is played, and which is strictly for tourists, and on Fridays there is a market at San Francisco El Alto; during Advent there is yet another market in the Parque Colón. The Mercado Central was destroyed by the earthquake, but its "artesanía" stalls, particularly good for silver, are now operating in temporary quarters on Calle 18, Zona 1, between 9 and 10 Avenidas.

Readers should note, incidentally, that Guatemala City is quite a large city. Any address not in Zona 1—and it is absolutely essential to quote Zone numbers in addresses—is probably some way from the centre.

Many of the hotels and boarding houses are in the main shopping quarter in 6, 7, and 8 Avenidas leading S of Parque Central as far as the intersecting 13 Calle. The railway station is in the central part of the city, facing Plaza Justo Rufino Barrios, to whom there is a fine bronze statue on Av. de las Américas, Zona 13, in the southern part of the city. To see the finest residential district go S down 7 Avenida to Plaza 11 de Marzo. Beyond it, to the left, Av. 11 de Marzo runs diagonally into the wide tree-lined Avenida de la Reforma, with the splendid Botanical Gardens (open every day, 0800-1200, except Sun.) just opposite. The boulevard is lined with trees and fine residences and is dotted with statues. Parque de los Próceres, with a monolith to Guatemalan independence, is towards the S of the boulevard. La Aurora Airport, the Zoo, the Observatory, the Archaeological Museum and racetrack are in Parque Aurora, in the southern part of the city.

The National Museum of Archaeology and Ethnology, which contains stelae from Piedras Negras and typical Guatemalan costumes, has been closed for repairs for some time, but is tentatively scheduled for reopening in 1978. There is a temporary exhibit at the National Palace, including a good model of Tikal and other Mayan items, open Mon.-Fri., 0900-1700; Sat. and Sun., 1000-1200 and 1500-1700.

The National Museum of History and Fine Arts in Parque Aurora has 17th, 18th and 19th century Guatemalan paintings as well as a complete collection of Guatemalan coins. Open 1000-1730, Tues.-Fri.; 1000-1200, 1500-1730 Sat. and Sun.

National Museum of Arts and Popular Crafts, 10 Av. 10-72, Zona 1, small exhibition of popular ceramics, textiles, silversmiths' work etc. Hours as History and Fine Arts.

Museo Ixchel del Traje Indígena, 4 Av. 16-27, Zona 10, is recently reopened and has good display of regional Indian textiles and costumes. Open 1000-1800 daily, entrance US$0.50; Buses from city centre.

Fuerte de San José museum, opposite Banco de Guatemala on 22 C. and 7 Av., Zona 1, has collection of guns and other weaponry.

On Avenida de las Américas, near the airport, is a very nice new plaza with a statue of Columbus standing on a globe.

In the northern part are two fine parks: Parque Morazán and the Hipódromo del Norte. The fiesta of Jocotenango is held on August 14-16 in the latter, where there is a huge and most instructive relief map of the country made in 1905 by Francisco Vela, an engineer, to a horizontal scale of 1 in 10,000 and a vertical scale of 1 in 2,000. Bus No. 18 runs to the park, where there is a swimming pool. The Hipódromo has tennis, basket-ball and baseball courts, two swimming pools and a children's playground.

The most notable public buildings built 1920-44 after the first earthquake are the National Palace, the Police Headquarters, the Chamber of Deputies and the Post Office. The modern civic centre includes the City Hall, the Supreme Court, the Ministry of Finance, the Banco de Guatemala, the mortgage bank, the social-security commission and the tourist board. There are five particularly beautiful churches: the Cathedral, the Cerro del Carmen, La Merced, San Francisco, and the strikingly yellow-coloured Santo Domingo. The University was founded in 1676; it has archaeological and natural history museums.

On the W outskirts (easily reached by local bus) are the Mayan ruins of Kaminal Juyú (Valley of Death). About 200 mounds have been examined by the Archaeological Museum and the Carnegie Institute. There are also conducted tours.

Damage to Guatemala City's principal churches in the earthquake was less heavy than had been feared; apart from those marked by an asterisk, they are still open to the public.

Cathedral Begun 1782, finished 1815; towers and main domes new though the whole building has been damaged by the earthquake. Paintings and statues from ruined Antigua. Solid silver and sacramental reliquary in the E. side chapel of Sagrario. Next to the Cathedral is the colonial mansion of the Archbishop.

Cerro del Carmen a copy of a hermitage destroyed in 1917-18, containing a famous image of the Virgen del Carmen, situated on a hill with views of the city, has in its turn been almost completely ruined.

La Merced (11 Av. and 5 C), which has housed beautiful altars, organ and pulpit from Antigua as well as jewellery, art treasures and fine statues, has also been damaged.*

Santo Domingo church (12 Av. and 10 C), 1782-1807, reconstructed after 1917, Image of Our Lady of the Rosary and sculptures.

Templo de la Expiación (26 C and 7 Av., Zona 1), modern, holding 3,000 people; colourful, exciting architecture by a young Salvadorean architect who had not qualified when he built it in the shape of a fish.

Las Capuchinas (10 Av. and 10 C, Zona 1) was another victim of the earthquake. It has a very fine St. Anthony altarpiece, and other pieces from Antigua.*

Santa Rosa (12 Av. and 9 C, Zona 1) was used for 26 years as the cathedral until the present building was ready. Altarpieces again from Antigua (except above the main altar). Now damaged.

San Francisco (6 Av. and 13 C, Zona 1) has a sculpture of the Sacred Head, originally from Extremadura.

Capilla de Yurrita (Calle Mariscal Cruz and 10 Av., Zona 4), built on the lines of a Russian orthodox church as a private chapel. It has been described as a place of "opulent 19th century bizarreness and over-ripe extravagance."

Carmen El Bajo (8 Av. and 10 C, Zona 1) built in the late 18th century.

Hotels (all in Zona 1 unless otherwise stated; Av. = Avenida; C. = Calle). Expensive: *El Conquistador Sheraton,* Vía 5, 4-68, Zona 4, US$26-40 d, the newest and most luxurious; *Ritz Continental,* 6a Av. "A" 10-13, US$24-40 d, more convenient to centre; *Pan American,* 9a C. 5-63, US$18-26 d, central and recommended as quiet and comfortable with good and reasonable food; *Maya Excelsior,* 7a Av. 12-46, US$25-30 d, crowded, noisy and commercial; *El Camino Real-Biltmore,* Av. Reforma and 14 C., Zona 10, US$31-32 d; *Guatemala Internacional,* 6a Av. 12-21, US$18-40 s, US$22-45 d; *Cortijo Reforma,* Av. Reforma 2-18, Zona 9, US$25-35 s, US$30-40 d; *Guatamala Fiesta,* 1a Av. 13-22, Zona 10, US$28 s, 34 d; *Hotel del Centro,* 13 C., 4-55, US$20 s, US$26 d.

Motel *Plaza*, Vía 7, 6-16, Zona 4, US$17-27 d, satisfactory.

Medium-price range: *Hotel Centenario*, 6a C. 5-33, US$14 d, US$8 s, with breakfast, commercial, but recommended, excellent facilities; *Casa Sanchinelli*, 13 C. "A", 10-30, US$10 s, US$14 d, with bath, in a colonial-style house. (The owners, an anthropologist and his wife, in conjunction with a tourist agency, offer a 1 week tour of Guatemala, including 2 nights in their hotel, for US$260-380 p.p.). *Hogar del Turista* (ex-*Pensión Alemana*), 11 C. 10-43, US$6.50 s, US$12 d, US$9.50 full board for one, clean, friendly; *Brasilia*, 2 Av. 4-20, US$11 s, US$15 d (both with bath), 20% discount if staying a week or more; *Pensión Patricia*, 13 C. 2-30, about US$5 p.p., own shower, friendly; *Pensión Asturias*, 9C 6-13 (third floor), US$8 full board; *Mansión San Francisco*, 6 Av. 12-62, US$5-15 s, 8-20 d; *Colonial*, 7 Av. 14-19, US$6-8 s, 9-14 d (though more may be asked), reasonable restaurant, quiet and recommended; *Hotel Rivera*, 9C. 1-80, US$5.50 s, with own bathroom; *Hotel Centroamérica*, 9 Av. 16-38, US$7, full board with bathroom, US$6 without; *Fénix*, 7 Av. 15-81, US$3 p.p., with bath; *Montecarlo*, about US$7 s; *Venecia*, 4a Av. "A" 6-90. Zona 4, very comfortable, US$7 d, with bath, reasonable meals; *Guatemala Inn*, 13 C. 8-30, US$8 d, with bath, includes 3 meals; *Casa Familiar Orellana*, 14 C. 3-68, next to Tica bus terminal, US$6 d, with shower, US$4 without, meals US$1.50; *Casa Shaw*, 8a Av. 12-75, Zona 2, US$8.50 s, with bath, recommended; *La Posada*, 7 Av. 5-41, US$5 all-in, s, US$2.50 s room, less good value than *Fénix*; *Nuevo Hotel Florida*, 4 Av. 3-25, US$4 s, US$7 d, friendly and pleasant. *Mansión Española*, 6 Av. "A" 14-61, US$3 s. not recommended. *Chalet Suizo*, 14 C. 6-82, US$2.50 s, good meals and recommended, but don't trust reservations, often crowded. *Pensión Pérez*, 7 Av. 15-46, US$5 for room with own shower, including three meals; *Spring Hotel*, 8 Av. 12-65, US$3.30-5 s, US$6-9 d; *Royal Home*, 13a C. 2-52, US$7.50 s, US$10.50 d, with bath; *Ritz*, 6 Av. 9-28, US$5.50 s, US$9 d, with shower.

Less expensive: *Mansión Mundial*, 16 C. 6-75, US$1.25 p.p., meals US$0.50, friendly and good value; *Hotel Mundial*, 16 C. 6-23, US$1.50 and meals at US$0.50 each, again good value; *La Catorce*, 14 C. 9-53, US$2 p.p., not recommended; *La Tranquilidad*, 14 C. 9-59, US$2.50 per room; *Posada Guatemala*, 8 Av. 13-30, US$4 s, including 3 meals, excellent value and very friendly; *La Luna*, 6 Av. 15-50, US$2 p.p.; *Astoria*, 6 Av. 15-48, US$1-1.50 p.p.; *Belmont*, 9 Av. 15-30 and 46 (there are two houses), US$2.50 p.p., clean, or US$3.50 in the second house, with bath; *Gran Central*, 9 Av. 15-31, US$1.75 p.p., without bath, US$2.50 with; *Hotel España*, 9 Av. 15-59, US$1.75 p.p., without private bath, US$3 with; *San Antonio*, 8 C. 3-11, US$2.50 p.p.; *Hotel Atitlán*, 3 Av. 7-35, US$2.50 p.p., friendly; *Pensión Alzamora*, 9 Av. 10-46, US$1.85 p.p.; *Hotel San Salvador*, 8 Av. 15-30, US$1.25 each in shared room or US$2.50 s, with bath, cheap meals; *Pensión Meza*, 10 C. and 10 Av., US$2.50 p.p., including 3 meals, friendly, inhabited mainly by travellers, basic, beware of petty theft; *Casa Real*, 11 C., 10-57 (Tel.: 21142), US$3 p.p., hot water, very clean, good meals; *Quiriguá*, 9a Av. corner of 17 C, US$1.50 p.p.; *Nuevo Mundo*, 17 C. 9-49, US$2.50 p.p.; *Pensión Tropical*, 9a Av. 5-19, US$1.50 p.p., quiet; Pensión at 12 C. 2-47 (no name), US$2 s, good, cheap meals; *Nuevo Hotel León*, 13 C. between 9 and 10 Av., basic, but good value at US$1.50 each; *Casa Pinto*, 12 C. 2-47, charges the same; *Atenas*, *7a Av. 20 C., US$1.50 d, friendly*; *Capri*, 9 Av. 16 C., US$4 s, clean, hot water, recommended; *Albergue*, 13 C. 9-49, US$2 d; *Bristol*, 15 C. 7-36, US$5 d. All in Zona 1 unless otherwise stated. The water supply in hotels tends to be spasmodic and water for showering is often unobtainable between 1000 and 1800. **N.B.** At the cheaper hotels it is not always possible to get single rooms. There is a 10% tax on hotel rates. it may be noted that due to inflation prices are often higher than those mentioned.

Electric Current　110 volts A.C., 60 cycles.

Restaurants at hotels. Food prices vary less than quality. *Ranchón Antigueno*, 13 C. 3-50, good local food; *Costa Brava*, 11 C. 7-44, Zona 1; *Restaurant Cantón*, 6a Av. 14-29, Zona 1, is Chinese but has some vegetarian dishes; *Vittorio*, 7a Av. 14-68, Zona 9; *Las Vegas*, 12 C. 6-31, Zona 1(pizzas); *Mediterráneo*, 7a Av. 3-31, Zona 9; *Petit Suisse*, Av. La Reforma 6-67, Zona 10; *La Mesa Larga*, 7a Av. 15-55, Zona 9; *Giovanni Canessa*, 7 Av. and C. 12, Italian food; *El Alicante*, 7 Av. 7-46, Zona 4, good Spanish food; *La Barraca*, 13 C. 2-28, Zona 1, best Spanish restaurant; *La*

Puerta, Av. Reforma 14-34, Zona 9; *La Tablita,* Av. Reforma 12-74, Zona 10: *La Parrillita,* Plazuela Espana, Zona 9; *Altuna,* 12 C. 5-47, Zona 1, Spanish cuisine and sea-food; *Il Foco Lare,* 6 Av. 11-43, Zona 1, Italian; *El Bodegón,* Plazuela Espana, Zona 9; *El Encanto* (Chinese), 7 Av. 8-81, Zona 4; *Delicias del Mar,* Ruta 4, 4-33, Zona 9; *La Estancia,* Av. la Reforma 6-89 (Zona 9), Argentine-style restaurant; *Puerto Chico,* Edif. Real Reforma, 14 C. y Av. La Reforma, Zona 9; *El Gran Pescador,* 6 Av. 10-07, Zona 9; *Katok,* 15 C. 1-59, Zona 10; *Alemana,* 7 Av. 9-58, and *Francesca, 6 C. 3-63, both Zona 1, good; Martin's,* Ruta 5, 7-69, Zona 4; *La Tertulia,* 6 Av. 8-25, Zona 4; *Sorrento,* 6 Av. 18-59, Zona 1; *Nuria,* 6 Av. 6-98, Zona 9; *Auto Mariscos, Vía 9, 5-04, Zona 4; a German restaurant, Delicadeza Hamburgo,* is at 15 C. 5-34, Zona 1;*Ruby,* 11 C. and 6 Av., excellent 4-course meals; La Chicharronera, 6 Av. y Ruta 7, Zona 4; *Pollo Campero,* 7a Av., Zona 1, chicken and chips with beer, US$1.50. *Baviera,* 11 C. 6-55, Zona 1, very good German food, US$1.75 for special lunches. *Bremen,* 3a C. 6-39 (Zona 9) also German; *El Paso,* quite good, medium prices. In same area *McDonald's* and *Dairy Queen* for cheap, American food; the latter is the cheaper. In Zona 10 is the *Jolly Roger* where you can get an American meal for about US$3. Many acceptable cafeterias, such as *Cafeteria Vascongada,* 10 C. 8-68, lunch for US$0.60.

Local food at *Siguan Quiché,* to the S, near the Trocadero; parties are served in individual huts; *El Parador* (12 C. 4-69, Zona 9); sea food at *Hawai;* other good Chinese restaurants are *Chung King* and *Fu Lu Shu,* 6 Av. and 12 C, Zona 1 (good value). *Los Tilos,* 11 C, 6-54, Zona 1, is an excellent tea room; another is *Jensen,* 10 C. 6-66, Zona 1. All these are in town. *El Intimo* is further out. Snacks at *Pecos Bill's,* the cafeterias *Lutecia, Simmons* and *Plaza.* Lunch for US$0.60 at 4 Av. 9-58, Zona 1. *La Gran Pasteleria Palace, 12 C. 4-37, Zona 1,* Swiss pastry shop and tea room—delicious. *Café L'Avenue,* 7 Av. 13-70, Zona 9, coffee house. *Feo Karril,* Ave. Las Américas 2-50, Zona 13, bar and restaurant in railway carriages; expensive. *The Greenhouse,* 12 C. 6-70, excellent fruit and vegetable juices, fresh yoghurt and all kinds of herbs and spices for sale. (There is a vegetarian restaurant at 6a Av. 15-64, which is also a centre for yoga, eastern culture, astrology, etc.).

Night Clubs La Flamme, Blvd. Liberación 4-43, Zona 9; La Quebrada, 6a Av. 4-60, Zona 4; Plaza Inn, Motel Plaza, Vía 7, 6-16, Zona 4; Moulin Rouge, Plazuela España, Ed. Etisa 12-49, Zona 9; Brasilia in *Hotel Ritz Continental.* Discothèques: Andromeda, Feocarril, Jaguar, La Petite Discothéque, La Manzana, After Dark, Toucan.

Guatemala is the home of "marimba" music. It can be heard nightly at "El Gallito" club. The marimba is a gigantic xylophone played with large drum sticks by from 4 to 9 players. Aldous Huxley didn't like the instrument but plenty of people (including the Editor) do! Up country the sounding boxes are differently sized gourds, the *marimbas de tecomates.* The city ones are marvels of fine cabinet work and cost up to a thousand dollars.

Airport At La Aurora, 8 km. S. Taxi to town, US$5-6. No. 2 and no. 6 buses also run (US$0.15); ½ hour's journey between airport and centre. Domestic flights, e.g. to Tikal, leave from the other side of town.

Taxis from US$1 for a short run to US$5 for a long run inside the city. Hourly rates are from US$8 to US$10. Taxis of the Azules, Concordia and Palace companies recommended. Agree fares in advance; no meters.

Swimming Pools Apart from those at the Hipódromo(page 810) there are pools at Ciudad Olimpica, 7 C, 12 Av., Zona 5; Piscina Ciudad Vieja, Zona 15. Try the hotels too.

Rent a Car Hertz, 7a Av. y 19 C., Tel.: 80202; Avis, *Hotel Camino Real,* Tel.: 680107; Tabarini, Tel.: 61228: Jerry's Tours, Tel.: 85623; Tilden International, Tel.: 65373. Thrifty Rent-A-Car, 7a Ave. 10-34, Zona 1, good service, reasonable. Budget has recently opened and has reasonable rates. Car hire can be arranged by the hotels. Tabarini claims cheapest rates, at US$15.55 a day with unlimited mileage. Insurance rate, if separate, is some US1.50 a day.

Local Buses in town, US$0.05 per journey. Not many before 0600. Fares are higher on holidays.

Theatres   The best plays are at weekends in the theatre of Edificio del Centro. Also Teatro Gadem, Teatro el Puente, and Antiguo Paraninfo de la Universidad, 2 Av. 12-13, Zona 1. Occasional plays in English at theatre of Instituto Guatemalteco Americano (IGA).

Cinemas are numerous and often show films in English with Spanish subtitles. Prices are US$0.50-1.

Bookshops   Arnel, Edificio El Centro No. 308, 9 C., 7 Av., Zona 1; Tuncho, 10 C. 6-56, Zona 1, very expensive; Geminis, 6 Av. 7-24, Zona 9 and La Plazuela, 12 C. 6-14, Zona 9; all have French, English and German books. Asociación Tikal bookshop, 2 C. 7-58, Zona 9, has books on pre-Colombian art, crafts and natural history.

Laundromat   Ruta 6, 7-53, Zona 4.

Consulates   British, Edificio Maya, Av. 7, 4-13, Zona 9, (Tel.: 63-302). Mexican: 14C. 6-12, Zona 1 (5th floor).

Concerts   During the rainy season at the Conservatorio Nacional and occasionally in the Banco de Guatemala. Also, baroque concerts are sometimes given in the Casa de la Música in Calle Sta. Lucia.

Shopping   The Central Market was destroyed in the earthquake and the stalls have been moved to three different places: Plaza Barrios, in Zona 1 between Calle 18 and 19, Av. 8, is likely to be of most tourist interest; La Placita by the Church of Guadalupe at the end of Av. 6 is good for conventional clothes, leather suitcases, etc.; Plaza Colón for vegetables etc., though some pottery is sold. Silverware is cheaper at the market than anywhere else in Guatemala City, but we are told that a **better place for silverware is Cobán (see page 906). The Market is, however,** recommended for all local products. Also, Ahau, 11 c. 3-76, Zona 1, very good for *huipiles* and other textiles; hand-woven textiles from Miranda factory, 8a Av. 30-90, Zona 8; La Tinaja, 12 c. 6-21, Zona 1, El Patio, 11 c. 3-57. Zona 1, Rodas and Barrientos, have high quality (and priced) silver and antiques. La Momosteca has a stall in Plaza Barrios and a shop in Av. 8 near Calle 14 and sells both textiles and silver. Roberto de León Galin at Passaje Rubio No. 24, off 9 C. near 6 Av. is good for antique silver charms and coins.

Cables   Empresa Guatemalteca de Telecommunicaciones (Guatel), 7a Av. 12-39, Zona 1.

Bank of London and Montreal, Ltd. (8a Av. 10-67, Zona 1); agencies at Plazuela 11 de Marzo, 7a Av. 4-87, Zona 4; Autovia Mixco 4-39, Zona 11 and C. Marti 14-57, Zona 6. Bank of America (5a Av. y 11 C., Zona 1). and national banks. Open weekdays, 0900-1500 (special cash facilities 1500-2000, Sat., 0900-1200). Banco de Guatemala (7 Av., C. 22, Zona 1) will cash travellers cheques. There is a bank open 7 days a week at the airport, 0900-1100, 1400-1800 weekdays, 1500-1700 Sundays. It is claimed that the Banco Industrial is open right through until 2030.

Clubs   Guatemala Club; the American Club (introductions can be arranged for temporary membership). There is an 18 hole golf course at the Guatemala Country Club, 8 km. from the city, and a 9 hole course at the Mayan Club. The Guatemala Lawn Tennis Club and the Mayan Club are the chief centres for tennis. Lions Club. Rotary Club. Von Humboldt (German). Italian Club. Club Caza, Tiro & Pesca, 23-30 and Juniors. Alianza Francesa, 4 Av. between 12 and 13 C., free film shows on Mondays at 1900.

Travel Agents   Clarke Tours, Hayter Travel, Eca Tours, Agencia Liang, Ney's and Jerry's Tours and many others arrange visits by car to all parts of the country. (If going to Tikal with Jerry's Tours be warned that you will not get private washing facilities unless you ask for them.) Jerry's Tours US$10 trip to Chichicastenango and Lake Atitlán is recommended. English-speaking guides are provided free of cost. Fixed prices.

Archaeological Tours   Anyone interested in genuine archaeological (or botanical, ornithological and zoological) expeditions should contact: Educational Programmes in Archaeology and the Natural Sciences (EPANS), Ltda., Edificio El Prado, 9 Calle 4-69, Av. 8-72, Zona 1. This organization runs trips to the well-known and almost unknown areas of interest. Slide lectures on Mayan civilization and ruins are given every night by E.P.A.N.S. (not Sats.) for which a donation is requested (US$1-3).

E.P.A.N.S. has published "Maya Archaeology Travel Guide", by Nicholas Hellmuth, on all the Mayan sites in Guatemala, El Salvador and Honduras. It costs US$6 and gives useful tips on how to get to each of the sites. Turismo Kim Arrin, Edificio Maya Office No. 103, Via 5, 4-50, Zona 4, arranges similar tours. These two agencies, plus a third in Flores (page 927), will arrange visits to the newly discovered Mayan sites described in the Tikal section.

Royal Mail Lines Agent   E. G. Cizon, Representaciones, Apto 230.

Airline Agents   International Air Bahama and Icelandic Airlines (Loftleidir) have an agency at Edif. El Triángulo (segundo nivel), 7 Av. and Ruta 6, Zona 4. Both have cheap flights from the Caribbean islands to Luxembourg. Agencia de Viajes Mundial, 5 Av. 12-44, Zona 1, is also useful.

Tourist Bureau   6a Av. 5-34, Zona 1; Tel.: 24015, 24118, 85262, 85311. Hotel lists, bus timetables and a basic roadmap. Closes 1700; open 0800-1200 Sats. Check its information carefully. New tourist office, 7 Av. 1-17, Zona 4, good information, but no maps.

Maps   Good maps of all sorts can be bought from the Instituto Geográfico Nacional, Av. las Américas 5-76, Zona 13, open until 1500 Monday to Friday, closed Saturdays and Sundays. Texaco also publishes a good map of the country, obtainable from Texaco stations for US$0.25.

Protestant Churches   Episcopalian Church of St. James, Av. Castellana, Zona 8, and the Union Church of Guatemala (Plazuela España). Sunday morning service in English at the first: 0930; at the second: 1100.

Synagogue   7a Av. 3-30, Zona 9.

Traffic   Traffic lights only operate between 0800 and 2000; at all other times Avenidas have priority over Calles.

Rail   Guatemalan Railways to Puerto Barrios on Tues., Thurs. and Sat. at 0630, 12½ hours. Return service on Wed., Fri. and Sun., at 0700, 10½ hours (US$2).San Salvador via Zacapa, on Mon., Wed. and Fri. (2-day journey with overnight stay at Zacapa); connection is made at Tecún Umán (290 km.) with the National Railways of Mexico. Trains to Tecún Umán on Tues., Thurs. and Sat., leaving at 0715. Return Wed., Fri. and Sun., US$1.80. No meals are served in trains, although sandwiches and light refreshments, iced beer and soft drinks can be bought. Station at Av. 9, C. 18, Zona 1. All earthquake damage to railways now repaired.

Buses   To San Salvador, Tegucigalpa, Managua, San José and Panamá by Tica-Bus (14 C. and 4 Av., Zona 1), costs US$5, US$10, US$17, US$23 and US$35.50.

Note   Although Tica-Bus offers the facility of through-travel, you still have to book your seat at each stage of the journey and there is no guarantee that you may not have to wait a couple of days at any point for a seat. Also some travellers have complained that border crossings take much longer with Tica-Bus than with other lines. The facilities offered by Tica-Bus, such as loos and air-conditioning, are more often than not out of order, so be warned on that score too. Other national lines are cheaper. To San Salvador Transportes Pezzarossi and Transportes Melva, US$2 (both from Zona 4). Autopullmans Galgos, one bus on Mon., Wed. and Fri., US$3, comfortable buses. (It has been recently noted, however, that Pezzarossi and Galgos no longer seem to go direct to Mexico or the other Central American countries, although this has to be substantiated.) Mermex, daily except Suns., US$4; Ramírez, US$2; Futuro-Express Internacional, 8a Av. 15-69, Zona 1, more expensive at US$4 (or US$5 if picked up at hotel); Transportes Internacionales, 10 A. 10-40, Zona 1, US$5. To Mexico City Galgos is cheapest (US$20) but there is not always a connecting bus at Talisman Bridge; Rutas Lima, Transportes Cóndor, US$3.50 to La Mesilla. Unión Pacifica to El Carmen, US$4. To Flores (for Tikal and Belize) Fuente de Norte 17 C., 9-08, Zona 1, US$8. La Higuera, 17 C. 6-25, for Panajachel and Quezaltenango. Galgos to Quezaltenango, several daily, US$2.50. The Zona 1 bus terminal is at Plaza Barrios, the railway station square on 19 C., beyond 13 Av.

Warning   Do not park on the street at night, or your car may well be broken into. There are plenty of lock-up garages.

Near-by Excursions To **Antigua,** the shortest route is 45 km. *via* San Lucas by asphalted road passing (24 km. out) El Mirador (1,830 metres), overlooking Guatemala City; fine view of the capital. Restaurant *Miralvalle* in vicinity. Road then rises to 2,130 metres and gradually drops to 1,520 metres at Antigua, the capital until it was seriously damaged by earthquake in 1773. Population today: 50,000. Good hotels for visitors who wish to inspect the impressive ruins, each alone in a built-up area. Founded in 1543, after destruction of a still earlier capital, Ciudad Vieja. Grew to be the most splendid city and cultural centre in Central America, with a population of 60,000, numerous great churches, a University, a printing press (founded 1660)*, famous sculptors, painters, writers and craftsmen. Centre of the city is Plaza de Armas, the old Plaza Real, where bullfights and markets were held. The Cathedral (1534) is to the E, the Palace of the Captains-General to the S, the Municipal Palace to the N, and an arcade of small shops to the W. Alvarado was buried in the Cathedral, partly rebuilt, but where is not known. All the ruined buildings, though built over a period of three centuries, are difficult to date by eye, partly because of the massive, almost Norman architecture against earthquakes: cloisters of the Convent of Capuchinas, for example, built 18th century, look 12th century, with immensely thick round pillars. The most interesting ruins (apart from those mentioned) are of the Monastery of San Francisco, the Convent of Santa Clara*, El Carmen, La Companía, Santo Domingo*, Santa Cruz, Escuela de Cristo Church, La Recolección (off the road in a coffee plantation), La Merced, the Hospital, Cabildo, the Museum*, and Casa de los Leones. John Streather tells us that other churches, such as Santa Isabel, San Cristóbal, El Calvario and San Gaspar, are well worth visiting. Many sculptures and paintings and altars have been removed to Guatemala City.

N.B. Buildings marked * were badly damaged by the 1976 earthquake, and some are closed.

Many of the restored Colonial houses can be visited, though one of the best, Casa Popenoe, was damaged by the earthquake and is closed for repairs. In Antigua lived Bernal Díaz de Castillo, *Conquistador* and historian, who summed up the motives of the Conquest as follows: "por servir a Dios y a Su Majestad, y dar luz a los que estaban en tinieblas, y también por haber riquezas" (to serve God and His Majesty, and to bring light to those who were in darkness, and also to become rich). Admirably honest and succinct!

Antigua is so restored that only convents and churches are in ruins, and San Francisco Church has been rebuilt. Many churches and other old buildings were damaged by the 1976 earthquake; most are now open to the public again, but should be entered with caution. The old cobblestones are being replaced in the original pattern. Indian women sit in their colourful costumes amid the ruins and sell handicrafts. Most picturesque, and the goods are not expensive. A good textile shop is Gwendolyn Ritz, Casa de Artes, 9 Av. Sur, No. 11.

Tourist Office, at 5 Calle Poniente, No. 2, is very helpful.

Warning Watch out for would-be guides in Antigua who engage you in friendly conversation and then charge you US$3 for the privilege.

Buses Excellent buses half-hourly from Guatemala City from 15 C., Zona 1, between 3a and 4a Av. with Preciosa company, US$0.50; 75 minutes.

Hotels *Antigua* (best), US$27 d, non-residents may use the pool for a fee; *Posada de Don Rodrigo,* US$15 s, US$22 d; very agreeable, food only fair, in Colonial house; *Hotel Aurora,* US$8 s, US$9-12 d; *Casa del Patio,* by Merced church, new, US$9 p.p.; *Posada Colonial,* picturesque, US$5 p.p., with bath; *Convento Las*

Catalinas, US$5-15 s, US$8-18 d. *El Rosario* is good, a pleasant apartment-lodge motel complex on the S edge of town in a coffee and orange farm round the corner from the *Antigua*: hot water, swimming pool, US$8 s, 10 d, proprietress speaks English and will tell you all about Antigua and the area; *La Casa de Santa Lucía,* on Alameda Santa Lucía, is near the bus terminal, new and highly recommended, US$6.70 d, with bath; *Hotel Contreras,* US$3.50 p.p., good restaurant; *Posada San Francisco,* US$3.50-4 s, new and recommended; *Pensión El Arco,* US$2 p.p., clean and friendly, meals (also for non-residents) for about US$0.75; *Pensión Barrera,* new, US$2.25 s; *Hospedaje El Marne,* US$1.50 p.p.; *Posada del Emperador,* US$7 p.p., with bath and breakfast. During Holy Week hotel prices are much higher.

Restaurants *El Arco* (international, moderate prices); *Gran Tasca* (Spanish); *Gran Muralla* (Chinese); *Fonda de la Calle Real,* 5a Av. Norte, No. 5, highly recommended, speciality is cheese fondue. *Nimbar,* 4 Calle Poniente; *Emilio Chang; La Mananera,* comida corrida, very good value; *El Portón,* expensive but good; *Emilio,* Chinese, reasonable; *El Paso,* sandwiches and chicken, very moderate. Near the theatre a teashop serves a good home-style dinner. A sandwich shop near *El Rosario* motel serves breakfast, lunch and sells fine ice-cream. Also a restaurant opposite the *Pensión del Arco* sells sandwiches and soup.

Museum, in old University of San Carlos Borromeo (1670), includes colonial sculptures and paintings, printing press (the third in the Americas after Mexico and Lima) old documents and representations of the colonial way of life.

Shopping Casa de los Gigantes for handicrafts. Fábrica de Tejidos Maya, 1 Av. Norte, makes and sells good, cheap textiles, wall-hangings, etc. Cereria del Pinal, 6 Av. and 5 C., decorative candles. The Cooperativa in Calle Sta. Catalina sells good quality *huipiles.* and the Artext Store sells native handicrafts from all over the country at fixed prices, though it is not cheap. There is an extensive market on Wednesdays, now in the bus depot. Good hand-made silver articles. Timms. on Plaza de Armas, sells English language books. Hand painted pottery can be obtained from private houses in the road opposite Calle San Sebastián in Calle Ancha; the craftsmen work down near Church of Santa Lucía.

Market Mon., Thurs. and Sat., near monument to Rafael Landívar in the Horta Popular Santa Lucía. Picturesque, with good handmade textiles, pottery and silver.

Industries Pottery; ironwork; weaving of native cloth; colonial furniture and woodwork. On the outskirts of the town is an excellent silver factory.

Fiestas Holy Week, particularly in Church of San Felipe de Jesùs, in the suburbs. Processions begin at 0800, may last all day, pass through all the streets, and sometimes visit other towns. Gay carpets, made of dyed sawdust and flowers, are laid on the route. The litter bearers wear purple until 1500 on Good Friday afternoon (the hour of Christ's death), and black afterwards. Only the litter bearing Christ and His Cross passes over the carpets, which are thereby destroyed.

Buses Frequent buses to Chimaltenango (¾ hour, US$0.25) for connections to Chichicastenango and Panajachel (2 hours, US$0.75).

Bank of London & Montreal, 4a Calle Oriente No. 2, Antigua. Open 0830-1200, 1400-1600 (Fridays until 1630). Banco de Guatemala and Banco del Agro, on central Plaza.

Spanish Language School Proyecto Lingüístico Francisco Marroquín, Apartado 237, Antigua. This school, like its sisters in Huehuetanango and Quezaltenango, provides 7 hrs. individual tuition a day and places students with local families. The fee for one month (incl. board and lodging is US$300. Another school with similar charges is the Estela Maya, at 7 Av. Norte, No. 47.

Discothèque in cinema building, off main square. Reasonable prices for drinks. Open every night except Sunday.

Excursions To **Ciudad Vieja,** 5½ km. SE at the foot of Agua Volcano. In 1541, after days of torrential rain, an immense mud-slide came down the mountain and overwhelmed the city. Alvarado's widow, newly elected Governor after his death, was among the drowned; you can see the ruins of the first town hall. Today it is a mere village *(Hotel Cortijo de las Flores,* in restored Colonial mansion, closed for repairs after the earthquake, and another (cheap) hotel at the other end of the village), but with a handsome pink and red church, founded 1534, one of the oldest in Central America. There is a fine vegetable market early in the morning. At San Juan Obispo, not far, is the restored palace of Francisco Marroquín, first bishop of Guatemala, now a convent, though visits are allowed. The parish church has some fine 16th century images. Behind San Juan Obispo, on side of Agua volcano, is village of **Santa María de Jesús**, where horses can be hired for a trip to the summit. It is a charming village, with a beautiful view of Antigua. Beautiful *huipiles* are made and sold in the houses. Bus from Antigua, US$0.20 though the service is infrequent. Six-and-a-half km. E. of Antigua (bus service) is San Antonio de las Aguas Calientes, which is now a village of lean-to shacks as a result of the 1976 earthquake. Fiestas: first Sunday in January; June 13; November 1. **San José Nacahuil** is 27 km. from Antigua and can be reached by bus from the town. With permission from Sr. Cornelio Suyoz you can stay the night at the Casa Comunal (take a sleeping bag). From San José you can walk to San Pedro Ayampuc (1½ hours) which has a basic *pensión*. Both villages produce fine *huipiles*. Acatenango volcano is approachable from San José and it is possible to see Fuego erupting from here. Near Ciudad Vieja is El Cubo which has a swimming pool fed by springs; open at weekends. Buses to most of the outlying villages leave from La Parroquia, by the market in Antigua. A trip to San Felipe is said to be interesting because of the silversmiths working there.

Three Indian villages N of Guatemala City are easily reached by bus. At Chinautla (9½ km.), the village women turn out hand-made pottery. Five miles beyond is another small village, San Antonio las Flores: good walking to a small lake (70 minutes) for bathing. Santo Domingo Xenacoj can be reached by bus from the Zona 4 terminal. It has a fine old church and produces good *huipiles*.

A most interesting short trip by car or bus from the capital is to **San Pedro Sacatepéquez**, 22½ km. NW. Good view over Guatemala valley and mountains to the N. The village itself was almost totally destroyed by the 1976 earthqake. Its inhabitants are now more concerned with rebuilding than with the weaving for which the village was renowned before the disaster. Bus from Guatemala, US$0.20, 1 hour. No hotels functioning at present, though *Pensión El Valle* (US$2 p.p.) may again be open. Fiestas: Carnival before Lent; June 29 (a trifle rough, much drinking) and great ceremony on March 15 when processing the Image of Christ from one officeholder to the next, and in honour of the same image in May.

6½ km. beyond, through flower-growing area, is **San Juan Sacatepé-quez,** where textiles were also made before this village too became a casualty of the earthquake.

Near San Juan is **Mixco Viejo**, the excavated site of a post-classic Mayan fortress, which spans several hilltops, but has been almost ruined by the earthquake. It was the 16th century capital of the Pokoman Maja; there are a few buses a day from the capital (Transporto Alborez). Also visit **San Lucas Sacatepéquez** where the Fábrica de Alfombras Típicas Kakchikel at Km. 29½, Carretera Roosevelt, will make rugs for you. Restaurants: *La Parrilla, La Cabaña, Nim-Guaa, La Diligencia* and *El Ganadero,* all good for steaks; *Delicias del Mar* for seafood.

San Raimundo beyond is a friendly town. Buses go N through Rabinal to Cobán (see page 907).

The village of **Rabinal** was founded in 1537 by Las Casas as the first of his "peaceful conquest" demonstrations to Charles V. It has a handsome 16th century church which was unfortunately badly damaged in the 1976 earthquake. Sunday market interesting; brightly lacquered gourds, beautiful *huipiles* and embroidered napkins, all very cheap. The local pottery is exceptional, for the most part. The road up from San Juan Sacatepéquez has spectacular views.

Another excursion is to the still active Pacaya volcano. Tours are available for US$16. Alternatively take a bus from the central bus station in Zona 4 at 1300 to San Vicente de Pacaya (US$0.50) or San Francisco and walk up the mountain from either place (1-2 hours and a hard climb). There is no bus back until the next day, however, so take camping equipment, and warm clothing. It is well worth staying overnight as you get the full, visual benefit of the incandescent ashes and lava from the volcano's eruptions. The best view is to be had from the top of the old cone of the volcano which is above the new one. There is also a bus from Palín (see page 910), US$0.20.

The town of **Salamá** can be reached from the capital direct, or from San Juan Sacatepéquez *via* San Miguel Chicaj along another road which offers stunning views. Its church, also damaged by the 1976 earthquake, contains very fine carved gilt altarpieces. Market day is Monday; worth a visit. *Pensión Juárez,* US$2 s, not recommended; *Hotel Tezulutlán,* US$3 s, better.

The Caribbean to Guatemala City

Santo Tomás de Castilla is a few km. S of Puerto Barrios on Santo Tomás bay. Its port works have been completed, and it is now not only the H.Q. of the Guatemalan navy, but the country's largest and most efficient port on the Caribbean, connected with the capital by rail, a paved road, and air. It handles 77% of the exports and half the imports as well as 20% of El Salvador's imports and 10% of its exports. Cruise ships are also beginning to put in to Santo Tomás and before long the town will become more expensive. However, at present, it is still being built. Apart from *Hotel Puerto Libre* (see below), no good hotel or eating place as yet, and nothing to do save sea bathing and swimming (along with fishes) in a natural pool in the park. The buses leave for Guatemala City about half-an-hour before the times listed for Puerto Barrios below. Bus terminal is by beach beyond the Naval Station.

Hotel *Puerto Libre,* 8 rooms, at highway fork for Santo Tomás and Puerto Barrios, US$5-8 s, 8-12 d.

Steamers Weekly to New Orleans and New York. Flomerca Line to Montreal and New York, and to Europe. A motor-boat service is maintained with Livingston and Puerto Cortés and a "ferry-boat" service to Miami. A weekly car and trunk ferry (10 passengers) to Port Everglades, Florida. Fast cargo service of Royal Mail Lines, with transhipment at Kingston (Jamaica).

Railway To Guatemala City, 0725, arrive 1800. Also night service, 12 hours, but best avoided unless there is a semi-Pullman car. Fare: US$5.90. Return from Guatemala to Puerto Barrios: depart 0720, arrive 1830.

Puerto Barrios, also on the Caribbean (population 23,000), 320 km. from the capital by air (1 hour) and with rail and road connections also, has now been largely superseded as a port by Santo Tomás. It is the capital of the Department of Izabal. The beach of Escabas on the northern peninsula, is recommended. Toll, US$0.25.

Hotels *Del Norte,* on sea front, US$5-12 s, US$8-18 d; *San Marcos,* US$2.75 p.p., with bath, nice and clean; *El Dorado,* clean, US$2.50 p.p. (with bath), *not* air-conditioned as the sign claims; fans only; has restaurant which is open to non-residents. *Tivoli,* also on sea front, US$1 p.p., basic; *Hospedaje los Arbolites,* US$1.50, basic; *Gran Hotel Quinto,* US$8 d, with bath; *Español,* US$2.50-6 p.p.; *Xelajú,* near bus terminal, US$1.50 s, noisy; *Restaurant Belleza,* near landing stage for Livingston ferry, very cheap and good.

Bank of London and Montreal, Ltd., 7a Calle y 2a Avenida. Open 0800-1200, 1400-1600 (Fridays to 1630).

Cables Guatel, United Brands building.

Buses to Capital, 0730 and 1600. Greyhound Pullman, 5½ hours, return same times from Capital, fare US$3.50; Once a day a semi-Pullman, luggage on top, to Pacific coast. There are good road connections to the Honduran and Salvadorean frontiers. In April 1977, however, it was reported that there was no way of getting directly to Honduras, without going as far south as Copán.

Puerto Barrios to Cobán Launch to **Livingston** (22½ km.), on left bank of Río Dulce, leaves at 1030 and 1700, cost US$0.50. (Launch returns at

0500 and 1400.) Very quiet, now little trade save some export of famous Verapaz coffee from Cobán. Population: 3,026, mostly blacks of Jamaican origin, many English-speaking.

Hotel Del Mar, US$15 d, including private bath and 3 meals; *La Casa Rosada,* 5 bungalows for 10 people on the beach, US$6 s, US$8 d, light meals and bar, boat trips to Río Dulce or just for swimming can be arranged, American owner; *Pensión Río Dulce,* US$2.50-3 d, basic, popular but not very safe. There is another, cheap *pensión* towards the harbour. Camping is said to be good. Once a week (Friday) a motorized dugout boat links Livingston with Punta Gorda, Belize, US$6.

Airport with services to tourist resorts of Rio Dulce, San Felipe and Lake Izabal.

At **Rio Dulce** is *Turicentro Marimonte* (US$15 or 25 for bungalow), with restaurant, and a camping site. *Castillo San Felipe,* alongside fort, US$12 d (not recommended: in ruinous state, apparently no electricity or running water!); *Del Río,* US$9-17 s, US$15-30 d, upstream from ferry (it is not recommended to hire a boat to Livingstone from here as very high prices are charged); *Hospedaje Río Dulce,* US$1.50-2.50 s, near ferry on S side of river, good food, mosquito repellant advisable. The U.S.-owned *Catamaran,* US$16-18 d, pool, meals about US$4 is reached by outboard canoe from Río Dulce; it is about 30 minutes downstream. Recently opened Cayuco trailer park, US$0.50 p.p. and per car. French owners serve meals at the "coffee shop". The ferry at Río Dulce operates between 0700 and 2400.

There is no regular, cheap, boat service from Río Dulce up the river to Lake Izabal, though you can rent a boat for about US$30, hitch a ride from the Texaco station for US$3 or take a bus. On Lake Izabal is the old Spanish fort of San Felipe in an attractive setting. It is officially closed for repairs, but with a bit of persistence you can see round it. Lake Izabal is the only fresh-water lake in the world in which manatees (see cows) are to be found. On the NW shore is El Estor—its name dates back to the days when the British living in the Atlantic area got their provisions from a *store* situated at this spot—where nickel-mining has now begun. *Hospedaje El Milagro* and *Santa Clara* (friendly) both US$1.25 s, others at similar prices. Also restaurants. A ferry leaves El Estor at 0530 for Mariscos (US$1.50, 2¼ hours) from where there are buses to Barrios and Bananera; from Bananera there are buses to Río Dulce and the Petén; At Mariscos *Pensión Dalya,* US$1 each, good food; *Pensión Fernández,* less good. From El Estor there is a road through Panzós (guest house) to

Tactic, which is famous for beautiful *huipiles* and for its "living well", in which the water becomes agitated as one approaches. (Ask for the Pozo Vivo; it is along a path which starts opposite the petrol station on the main road.) Colonial church with Byzantine-influenced paintings, well worth a visit. *(Pensión Central* and *Hospedaje Pocompchi,* both US$1 s.) Doña Rogelia sells *huipiles* made in the surrounding area, and the silversmith near her shop will make silver buttons etc. to order. The town suffered some earthquake damage in 1976; so did the church. To the W of Tactic is San Cristóbal Verapaz, which has a large colonial church with interesting altar silver and statue of San Joaquín, and is famous for coffee, candles and food colorants *(Pensión Central,* US$1). The lake is popular for fishing and swimming. Markets: Tuesday and Sunday. From Tactic the road runs on, *via* Santa Cruz Verapaz, which has a fine old 16th century church, to

Cobán, capital of Alta Verapaz Department and centre of a rich coffee district. Population 11,000, altitude 1,320 metres, climate semi-tropical. Road S to El Rancho (buses), on Guatemalan Railway and the highway to Guatemala City. Founded by Apostle of the Indies, Las Casas, in 1544.

See Church of El Calvario (1559), now completely renovated, original facade still intact. Daily market. Fiestas: Holy Week (which is said to be fascinating) and August 4. Note women's dress, especially their *huipiles*. Aerolíneas air service. Cabán is best reached by road from the capital; the road is now asphalted. Buses from Guatemala City, US$2.50, leave from Calle 14, Zona 1, between Avs. 8 and 9. The trip takes about 5 hours. The bus from El Estor takes 8 hours, 3 services a day. Return buses leave at 0400 and 0800. The trip from the capital *via* Rabinal, along an old dirt road, takes about 12 hours. Cobán can also be reached from Sacapulas and Quiché (page 918) and from Huehuetenango (page 922). From Cobán it is possible to get to the Mayan sites of the Petén. For the route, see page 928.

Hotels at Cobán: *La Posada*, US$12 p.p., incl. 3 meals; *San Juan Acalá*, US$7 p.p., incl. 3 meals; *Hotel Central*, US$4.50 p.p., with meals; *Pensión Norte*, US$1.50; *Hotel Chipi Chipi*, US$3-4 s; *Hotel Oxib Peck*, US$3 p.p., with bath; *Pensión Minerva*, US$2.50 s, friendly, but a little far from the centre; *Pensión El Portillo*, new and very good, US$3 s; *Valenciana*, US$1.25 each, basic; *El Carmen*, on main square, US$2 s, clean; *Pensión Apolo*, 3 blocks from main square, US$1.25 each; *Pensión Internacional*, US$1.50 d; *Hotel Viajero*, US$1 each, dirty; *La Paz*, US$4 p.p.; *Pensión Familiar*, US$2 p.p., hot water, good; *Pensión Continental*, US$1 each, basic but clean; *Hotel Central* has a good restaurant but mealtimes are rigidly fixed; *Comedores Chinita* and *Las Delicias* serve meals for less than US$1.

Excursions Near Cobán is the old Colonial church of San Juan Chamelco, well worth a visit. Also worth visiting is Senahú though it takes at least 5 hours by bus to get there. (*Pension González*, and another, more friendly, at bus terminal, both serve meals.) Climb to the cemetery for good views: at dusk one can see *quetzales* flying home. Senahú *huipiles* are particularly sought after. Tucurú, with its fine *huipiles*, would also involve more than a day trip. Market days Thurs. and Sat. Interesting images in church. Tanahú is another village worth visiting which also produces some fine *huipiles*. San Pedro Carchá (5 km. east of Cobán) is famous for its pottery, textiles and wooden masks, and silver which is cheaper than in Cobán. The Tuesday market in San Pedro is also said to be better than Cobán's. Good swimming and walks at Balneario Las Islas, just outside the village, well signposted.

From Cobán a rough road runs to **Lanquin Caves**, a large underground grotto through which the Lanquin river runs. If you want to visit the caves ask at the police station to turn the lights on; the entrance fee is US$0.50. The caves are very slippery so wear appropriate shoes and take a torch or candles for additional lighting. Outside the caves are clear pools in which you can swim. From Lanquin there is a well-marked but mountainous path (4-5 hours hard walk); 10-km. trail (3 hours) to the natural bridge of Semuc Champey stretching 60 metres across the Cahabón gorge. The bridge has water on top of it as well as below, and the falls are spectacular. There is a ferry (canoe) at this point but it is not always manned and you may have to swim across. At all events, cross the river as soon as you reach it, for it is too dangerous further up; after crossing, turn right and walk another km. or two to get to the bridge. At Semuc Champey is a shelter where you can camp. At Lanquin there are two *pensiónes* and restaurants. The church has fine images and some lovely silver. Bus from Cobán at 0530, 1½ hours, US$1; returns at 0800.

To the W of Cobán is Nebaj (page 919) which can be reached by taking the Huehuetenango bus to San Andrés Sajcabala and either hitching from there or waiting for the bus from Quiché.

Puerto Barrios to Guatemala City, 320 km. The ordinary first-class train accommodation is not crowded and is comfortable, for most people do the journey by air or by road. There are only sandwiches and cold drinks on the train, but a meal can usually be taken at the station hotel at Zacapa during a 35-minute halt. Average speed from Puerto Barrios to Guatemala City is 32 km. an hour, with 50 km. an hour on the return (downhill) trip.

The railway goes through deep jungle and occasional banana plantations to (96 km.) **Quiriguá**, about 4 km. from some remarkable Mayan Old Empire remains: temple, carved stelae, etc. In 1975 a sun-god stone statue was unearthed here, and Pennsylvania University is now carrying out further excavations. Walk or hire a taxi as there are no buses, and try to visit the ruins in the morning as the afternoon sun casts shadows on many of the stelae. The tallest stone is over 8 metres high. *Hotel Royal* recently opened, US$2 s. Reached by road from Guatemala City to Los Amates, then a 3½-km. dirt road (ask to be put down at the "ruinas de Quiriguá" before you reach Los Amates; that village is some way past the turning for the ruins). Take insect-repellant as Quiriguá is a hotbed of mosquitoes. The best reference book is S. G. Morley's "Guide Book to Ruins of Quiriguá", which must be obtained before going to the ruins. At (161 km.) **Zacapa**, half-way to the capital, the train halts—for a meal. Fare to capital US$0.75. Population 11,173, altitude 187 metres, very heavy earthquake damage in 1976. Sulphur springs for rheumatic sufferers at Banos de Agua Caliente, well worth a visit (closed on Mondays); tobacco grown. It is an attractive town with a colourful market, reached from Guatemala City by the new paved road to Honduras *via* Esquipulas. Zacapa is the junction for the railway to San Salvador (train early morning, three times a week). Climate hot and dry: strange Indian rain-making rites on April 30, May 1, at city, 3 km. from the station. Fiestas: June 29, Dec. 1-9. Just outside the town is Estanzuela, a village whose museum houses a complete skeleton of a prehistoric monster.

Hotels *Wong*, US$3 s, without bath; US$7.50 d, with bath; *De León*, US$2 p.p.; *Pensión Central*, US$1.50 p.p., very good; *Motel Langarone*, W of Zacapa on road to the capital, US$7-15 s, US$10-20 d (higher prices for a/c); swimming pool, delightful setting.

Excursion Road S to Chiquimula and Esquipulas. **Chiquimula** (21 km.) is capital of its Department. Population 42,000; It is on the branch railway leading to El Salvador, and has a colonial character. See church ruined by 1765 earthquake. Bus from Zacapa US$0.25, and from Cobán *via* El Rancho (where a change must be made) US$3.25. Daily market. Fiesta, January 6. The town has a historic ceiba tree. A road, 203 km., runs W through splendid scenery to the capital (see page 926).

Hotels *Pensión Hernández*, US$1.50 or 3 p.p.; *Hotel Chiquimula*, US$9 d, with bath; *Darío*, US$3 s, US$5.50 d, without bath.

At Vado Hondo (10 km.) on road to Esquipulas, 51 km. from Chiquimula, a road branches E to the great Mayan ruins of Copán (see Honduras section, page 976). It goes through the small town of **Jocotán** (*Pensión Ramírez*, basic, US$1 p.p.), which has hot springs, and on the border at El Florido, where there is now a good bridge. To Copán there is a 14-km. dirt road, which has become less strenuous thanks to recent improvements, but fording the many streams after heavy rain can still be hazardous. The drive to Copán takes 6 hours from Guatemala City, or 3 from Vado Hondo, including the frontier crossing.

There is a through bus from Chiquimula to El Florido at 1100 (Transportes Vásquez, US$1); by catching a Transportes Guerra or Transportes Rutas Orientales bus from 19 C. and 8 Av., Guatemala City, to Chiquimula at 0700 (US$1.50) you should be able to make this connection. Alternatively there are pick-up trucks which meet the morning bus from Zacapa in Jocotán and run to the border for US$1 each; They also do the return trip; the last bus from Jocotán to Zacapa is at 1400. From the border to Copán there are minibuses, US$1. The road is really too rough to walk. Those travelling by bus will find that it is impossible to do the trip to Copán and return to Guatemala in one day. Instead you can spend the night at El Florido and catch the 0500 bus from there to Chiquimula (although there may be delays in Honduras) or spend the night in Copán village, catching a minibus back to the border next morning and from there taking a colectivo to Chiquimula, US$1.50; It appears that there may now also be a bus at 0800 from the border to Chiquimula, but check before making your overnight plans as there is no minibus service from Copán until 0630. It is not clear whether buses and minibuses operate on Sundays. An alternative route into Guatemala is described on page 913. If you are coming in to Guatemala at this point you must have a visa or tourist card as there are absolutely no facilities for obtaining one. If returning to Guatemala remember that you must have a new visa or tourist card, or else a multi-entry tourist card. The customs officials are difficult and will try all kinds of excuses to get money out of you. One that has been tried is to claim that you must have a tourist card and not a visa; we are not aware that this is the case, and if you do have undue difficulties at this crossing, ask to speak to the "delegado". Make sure that the customs official stamps your papers. There is a US$1.50 charge to leave Guatemala and a US$1.50 entry charge for Honduras. Unfortunately the border officials of the two countries do not keep the same hours: Guatemalan hours are 0800-1200, 1400-1800; Honduran hours 0800-1530. You can sometimes get a lift to Guatemala City with tourist agency guides whose minibuses are not full—cost about US$2; Travel agents do a one-day tour from Guatemala City to Copán and back, for about US$35 p.p. though there is one which has cheaper rates (see page 901).

To visit the Mayan ruins of El Petén, take a bus from Chiquimula to Río Hondo (US$0.50, 1 hour) to connect with the 0730 bus from Guatemala City to Flores which leaves Río Hondo at 1030. cost US$5 (see page 922).

Esquipulas is a typical market town in semi-lowland, but at the end of its 1½-km. shabby street is a magnificent white sepulchre, one of the finest colonial churches in the Americas. In it is a black Christ carved by Quirio Catano in 1594 which draws pilgrims from all Central America, especially on January 15 and during Lent and Holy Week. The image was first placed in a local church in 1595, but was moved in 1758 to the present many towered and domed sanctuary built by the Archbishop of Guatemala.

The Benedictine monks who look after the shrine are from Louisiana and therefore speak English. They show visitors over their lovely garden.

Buses from the capital (US$2.50) for celebrations, which are also festivities. The road goes on to Atulapa, on the Honduran border, and continues to the Honduran town of Nueva Ocotepeque and S to San Salvador. Population of Esquipulas: 7,500.

Since the border between Honduras and El Salvador is closed at this point (see page 976), the only way to get from one to another is *via* Guatemala. Coming from Nueva Ocotepeque drive towards Esquipulas but before reaching it take the road to Chiquimula. About 10 km. before the town there is an army checkpoint where the road divides: take the left fork to Concepción Las Minas and go on to the Salvadorean border at Anguiatú. From there a good road goes to Metapán.

Hotels *Payaqui,* US$10 s; US$18 d. Others: cost p.p.: *Los Angeles,* US$3-4; *Montecristo,* US$2.50-4; *Rosas,* US$3; *Zacapa,* US$1; *Pensión Modelo,* US$1.50; *Hotel San Carlos,* US$0.75; *Pensión Lemus,* US$0.75; *Pensión Mi Hotelito,* US1.50; *Pensión La Favorita,* US$0.75.

Restaurants There are plenty of cheap restaurants, but as the town is a tourist centre, they do not post price lists and tend to charge foreigners more than the locals. By being friendly and courteous you will get a less exaggerated bill!

The route just described is for sightseeing. It is much quicker to follow the Atlantic Highway if one just wants to get to Guatemala City; it passes through very few towns, and there is a US$0.90 toll between Guatemala and Río Hondo. Keep your receipt; it is checked along the route. Since the earthquake there have been some delays on this route because of damage to the Aguas Calientes bridge. This will take some time to repair; a temporary bridge is in use.

A road and a railway run from Zacapa to the capital; the road, N of the line, goes through the Indian villages of Usumatlán, Acasaguastlán, and San Agustín, which were all badly hit by the earthquake, to El Rancho, on the railway. These villages have ancient churches, which were unfortunately damaged in the earthquake. From El Rancho there is a road N to Cobán (see under Puerto Barrios). The green luxuriance of the coastal belt gives way up the valley of the Motagua to drought and dust and parched hills. The train begins to climb. At El Progreso, a dismal place, a large Greek temple of Minerva made of cement and corrugated iron dominates the landscape; Guatemala has many of them, decreed by President Cabrera (1896-1920). The railway climbs steadily until, all of a sudden, three volcano cones and the capital come in sight.

Guatemala City to San José

Amatitlán is 37 km. by rail and 27 by road SW of the capital, on attractive Lake Amatitlán, 12 by 4 km. Fishing and boating; swimming actually in the lake is not advisable, as the water has become seriously contaminated and can harm the skin. The thermal springs on the lake side, with groves of trees and coffee plantations, feed pools which *are* safe to bathe in. Lake surrounded by picturesque chalets with lawns to the water's edge. (It is not easy to reach that water's edge unless you own one!) Altitude 1,240 metres, population 12,225. Grand view from the United Nations Park, 2½ km. N, above Amatitlán. A road goes round the lake; a branch runs to the slopes of Pacaya Volcano; the summit, 2,542 metres, can be reached on horseback from Lake Calderas or from village of San Vicente, 18 km. from the main road (see page 904). The town has two famous ceiba trees, one dating from the 16th century and one in Morazán Park. (A ceiba may have a gigantic spread of as much as 1,600 square metres.) Buses from Guatemala City (every ½-hour) go right to the lakeside.

Hotel   *Los Arcos,* US$7-10 d.

Fiesta   Santa Cruz, May 2-3

Camping   The by-road to the U.N. Park (turning at 19½ km. from Guatemala City) ends at camping sites and shelters; it is rather steep and narrow for caravans. View, US$0.25 entrance fee. Another camping site (with accommodation) is the Monkey River Ranch (km. 27.5 on C.A. 9 highway). A third is La Red, which has swimming pools fed by hot, volcanic springs. Yet another is Las Hamacas, with swimming pool and good café; charge is US$1 each.

Road and rail continue S to the Pacific port of San José through

Palín, 14½ km. from Amatitlán, which has a Sunday Indian market in a square under an enormous 400-year-old ceiba tree. Grand views to E of Pacaya, to NW of Agua Volcano, to W of Pacific lowland. Power plant at Michatoya Falls below town. Road runs NW to Antigua through Santa María de Jesús, an Indian village on slope of Agua volcano (see page 903), with great view of Pacaya. See old Franciscan church (1560). Fiestas: December 8, first Sunday January , June 3, and movable Holy Trinity and Sacred Heart of Jesus. Textiles here are exceptional, but are becoming hard to find. *Pensión Senorial,* US$1, basic.

A motor road leading off the Palín-Antigua road leads to within a trip on foot to the summit of **Agua Volcano**, 3,750 metres, though a jeep might go further. The crater is open on one side. It is a bit tricky but well worth climbing to the summit and returning by the other side. Splendid views. (See also page 903).

Escuintla, 18 km. from Palín on the road to San José, a market town in a rich tropical valley at 335 metres. Population 62,500. Famous for its medicinal baths and fruits. Airport at Concepción, 3 km. Agua volcano looms to the N. Road N to Antigua. Beyond Escuintla a railway branches W at the station of Santa María to Mexico. The Coastal Slope Highway to the Mexican border at Tecún Umán and E to Salvador runs through it; however, it is more often blocked and less good as a route to Mexico than the alternative El Tapón route to the N. There is a meat packing plant. Fiesta: December 8 (holiday) to 12. Many buses from the capital.

Hotels (each with good restaurant)   *Metropol; Tahormina; Motel Sarita,* US$8 s, US$12 d; *Motel Texas,* US$6 s, US$10 d.

The Department of Escuintla, between the Pacific and the chain of volcanoes, is the richest in the country, producing 80% of the sugar, 20% of the coffee, 85% of the cotton, and 70% of the cattle of the whole country.

Bank of London & Montreal (agency) 7a Calle 3-09, Zona 1. Open 0830-1200, 1400-1600 (Fridays until 1630).

Between Escuintla and **Santa Lucía Cotzumalhuapa** is **La Democracia,** where sculptures found in the Monte Alto and Costa Brava estates *(fincas)* are displayed. These are not, as some suggest, influenced by the early Olmec style, but are a purely local development, dating, according to some experts, from between 800 and 400 B.C. Visit the Museo del Pueblo on the main square. At Santa Lucía proper is the 9th century site of Bilbao (or Cotzumalhuapa), which shows Teotihuacán and Veracruz influences. Nearby is El Baúl, a pre-Classic monument which dates back to Izapán. From this early art, the classic Mayan art developed. El Castillo, between Bilbao and El Baúl, has some small sculptures dating back to Mayan times. On the Las Ilusiones and Finca Pantaleón estates are ruined temples, pyramids and sculptures, and indeed there are other stelae to be found in the area. More detailed information and a map can be obtained from EPANS in Guatemala (page 901). N. Hellmuth's "Maya Archaeology Travel Guide" and M. Coe's "The Maya" are the best books on the Santa Lucía and La Democracia remains. Hotel at Santa Lucía: *Caminotel Santiaguito,* US$8 s; Buses from the Zona 4 terminal in the capital run to Santa Lucía and La Democracia.

San José, 52 km. beyond Escuintla, 109 km. by road and 121 by rail from the capital, is the country's second largest port; it handles nearly half the imports. Open roadstead with long wharf (10½ metres depth at pier head) and large coffee warehouses. Chief exports: coffee, cotton, honey, sugar, timber, essence of lemongrass. Population 8,000. Heavy surf and ships, anchoring 1½ km. offshore, transport passengers and cargo by lighter. Hot climate. Fishing, swimming, though beware the strong undercurrent. Fiesta: March 19 when town is crowded and hotel accommodation difficult to get. Interesting trip can be taken through Chiquimulilla Canal by launch from the old Spanish port of **Iztapa,** now a bathing resort with huts, a short distance to the E. At Iztapa rooms can be found for US$1 or you can camp on the beach.

Hotels   *Club Chulamar,* US$15-20 s, 20-25 d; *Balneario Chulamar,* bungalows, US$16 upwards; *Casetas San Jorge,* US$5 p.p.; *Casetas Chaluita,* from US$5 p.p.; *Hotel Viñas del Mar,* US$7 p.p.; *Hotel Pacífico,* US$2 s, dirty; new, *Turicentro El Coquito,* US$8-10 s, 12-15 d; *Motel La Roca,* US$2 s, 8-10 d.

Rail   To Guatemala City and Puerto Barrios; also to Champerico *via* Retalhuleu and to the Mexican border. Train for the capital leaves at 0500, arriving at 1200. Fare, US$1.50.

Steamers Regular two-weekly service between Champerico and Puntarenas, Costa Rica and Ecuadorean, Peruvian and Chilean ports; also with Seattle, Vancouver, and French, German, Belgian, Scandinavian and Mediterranean ports. Fortnightly fast joint cargo service (no passengers) of Central America Services to and from Europe. Passenger accommodation is difficult to get, though for those who want to "miss out" the rest of Central America, a passage to Guayaquil can be obtained for US$60.

Beyond San José is the smart, expensive resort of **Likin,** which fronts on both the Chiquimulilla Canal and the Pacific. (Hotel: *Turicentro Likin,* US$15-21 d, or US$25-40 per bungalow.) Further on is the less expensive resort of Monterrico.

West from Guatemala City

The Pacific Highway goes W from Guatemala City to Tapachula and Arriaga in Mexico. The Inter-American Highway cuts off NW at San Cristóbal and goes into Chiapas by the El Tapón, or Selegua, canyon. This is a better and far more interesting route, with breathtaking scenery.

The highway to Tapachula will be followed first. It and its many offshoots to N and S lead to a large number of highland towns and villages of great interest.

A railway also runs through south-western Guatemala from Guatemala City to Mexico. It runs parallel with the new Pacific Highway through the coastal plain to Tecún Umán on the border, with spurs S to Champerico and Ocós.

Most tourists to Guatemala City visit both Lake Atitlán and Chichicastenango. All the agencies offer a two-day (one-night) trip by taxi, with an English-speaking driver-guide, at an inclusive price of about US$100 for two persons; or a 1-day tour, with a good lunch at lake, costs about US$20 a person. There are also organized trips by bus. But the tourist with a little Spanish can do it for much less. Rutas Lima (8 Calle No. 3-63, Zona 1) run a reserved-seat Pullman type bus daily in each direction between Guatemala and Chichicastenango. Fare, US$2.50 one way; time, 5 hours. Crowded, cheaper and more entertaining local buses do the same route, passing through Los Encuentros; other local buses run to Panajachel, on Lake Atitlán. The charge to Los Encuentros is US$1; from there to Chichicastenango, US$0.25. Local buses travel by daylight only. Hitching on these roads is easy, not least because many Americans live around Lake Atitlán.

The mountain, lake and valley scenery is generally superb and full of colour. In the towns and villages are a number of Colonial churches, some half ruined by earthquakes but often with splendid interiors. Tourists are usually most interested in the Indians. They speak some 20 languages and 100 or more dialects. The coming of the Spaniards certainly transformed their outer lives: they sing old Spanish songs, wear 17th and 18th century types of dresses, and their religion is a compound of image-worshipping paganism and the outward forms of Catholicism, but their inner natures remain largely untouched. The Indian has his own environment, materials and techniques, his social, political and religious organization, his way of thinking, believing and looking at the world.

Their markets and fiestas are of outstanding interest. The often crowded markets are quiet and restrained: no voice raised, no gesture made, no anxiety to buy or sell; but the fiestas are a riot of noise, a confusion of processions, usually carrying saints, and the whole punctuated by grand firework displays and masked dancers—all part of a strict schedule not usually comprehensive to the onlooker but orderly and significant for the participants. Each municipality has its patron saint, honoured above all other saints revered. The chief fiesta is always to the patron saint, but all the main Catholic festivals and Christmas are more or less celebrated everywhere.

Indian dress, not easily described, is unique and attractive: the colourful head-dresses, *huipiles* (blouses) and skirts of the women, the often richly patterned sashes and kerchiefs, the hatbands and tassels of the men. It varies greatly, often from village to near-by village. Unfortunately a new outfit is costly, the Indians are poor, and denims are cheap.

A large number of Indians is met on the road: peripatetic merchants laden with goods, or villagers driving pigs to market, or women carrying babies and cockerels and fruits. Your driver can usually tell from their costumes where they come from. The merchant will often do a round of 200 km. and make no more than a dollar or two, but he likes wandering, the contacts with strange people and the novel sights. He pleases himself, pleases his customers and (like a good tourist) is not much concerned whether he can make pleasure pay. Supported by the *mecapal,* a wide band round the forehead which takes the strain of the burden, the Indian's pack may be bigger than he is, made up of rustic wooden furniture, a plethora of pots of all sizes and shapes, or piled high with lengths of cloth. Women do not use the *mecapal*; they carry their waterpots and coloured bundles on a ring of twisted cloth haloing their heads.

Some 6½ km. W of the capital a road (right) leads to San Pedro Sacatepéquez (see page 904) and Cobán. Our road twists upwards steeply, giving grand views, with a branch to (14½ km.) Mixco. The climb continues. About 6 km. beyond, a road to Antigua turns sharp left. **Sumpango,** which is a little over 19 km. beyond this turn-off, has a Sunday market, but *huipiles* can be bought from private houses. The *huipiles* are of all colours but preponderantly red, as it is believed to ward off the evil eye. Good font in church. Both Mixco and Sumpango were damaged by the 1976 earthquake. At **Chimaltenango,** similarly affected by the earthquake, another road runs left, 20 km. to Antigua; this road is served by a shuttle-bus (25 cents), so Antigua can be included in the Guatemala-Chichicastenango circuit. Chimaltenango is the capital of its Department *(Pensión La Predilecta,* US$1.50 p.p., rebuilt since the earthquake). Excellent views and an undistinguished fountain at 1,790 metres, from which water flows one side to the Atlantic, the other side to the Pacific.

In the Behrhorst Clinic, run by an American doctor, many of the nurses are Indian girls wearing native dress.

This clinic is interesting in that members of patients' families are encouraged to cook for them; everything is done to make the Indians feel at home. There is also a scheme to train medical orderlies to serve remote areas where there are no doctors.

A side-road runs 21 km. N to **San Martín Jilotepeque** over deep *barrancas*; markets on Sundays, Thursdays—again badly damaged. Fiesta: November 11. Fine weaving. Striking *huipiles* worn by the women. Buses run to famous nearby park and swimming pool of Los Aposentos—about 2 km. Ten km. beyond Chimaltenango is Zaragoza, former Spanish penal settlement, and beyond that (right) a road (13 km.) leads N to the interesting village of **Comalapa:** afternoon markets Monday, Wednesday, Friday, bright with Indian costumes. Glorious old church of San Juan Bautista (1564), severely damaged in the earthquake. Fiestas: June 24, Dec. 8, 12.

There are several Indian artists working in Comalapa; no studios, so best to ask where you can see their works. There is a *pensión* here for US$1 per night.

Six km. beyond Zaragoza the road divides. The S branch—the old Inter-American Highway—goes to Lake Atitlán and then N to Los Encuentros.

The northern branch, much faster, goes over the Chichoy Pass, by-passing Lake Atitlán, also to Los Encuentros. Since the earthquake only this road has been used by buses, *via* Los Encuentros and Sololá, to reach Lake Atitlán. From Los Encuentros there is only the one road W to San Cristóbal, where the new road swings NW to El Tapón, Ciudad Cuauhtémoc, or El Ocotal, as it is sometimes called, and La Mesilla into Mexico, and the old route goes W through Quezaltenango and San Marcos to Tapachula, in Mexico. Chichicastenango is 17½ km. NE from Los Encuentros.

The southern road to Los Encuentros goes through **Patzicía**, a small Indian village founded 1545 and heavily damaged by the 1976 earthquake. Market on Wednesdays and Saturdays. Fiesta for the patron, Saint James, on July 23-26. The famous church, which had a fine altar and beautiful silver, was destroyed by the earthquake; some of the silver is now in the temporary church. Fourteen km. beyond is the small township of **Patzún**, which was also affected by the earthquake. Its famous church, dating from 1570, was severely damaged; it is still standing, but is not open to the public. Sunday market, which is famous for the silk (and wool) embroidered napkins worn by the women to church, and for woven *fajas* and striped red cotton cloth. Fiesta: May 20. Road climbs, then descends to Godínez, 19 km. W of Patzún, where there is a good place for meals. A branch road runs S to village of San Lucas Tolimán and continues to Santiago de Atitlán; both can be reached by a lake boat. The high plateau, with vast wheat and maize fields, now breaks away suddenly as though pared by a knife. From a view-point here, there is an incomparable view of Lake Atitlán, 600 metres below; beyond it tower three 3,350 metres high volcano cones, Tolimán and Atitlán in line, San Pedro to the W. The very picturesque village of San Antonio Palopó is right underneath, on slopes leading to the water. At the bottom of the hill, in pinewoods, is Tzanjuyu, at the edge of the lake.

Lake Atitlán, 100 km. from the capital, 1,500 metres above sea-level, about 27 km. across, between 110 and 130 km. in circumference, is one of the most beautiful and colourful lakes in the world. The lake ("more beautiful than Lake Como"—Aldous Huxley) changes colour constantly— lapis lazuli, emerald, azure— and is shut in by purple highlands and olive green mountains. Over a dozen villages on its shores, some named after the Apostles, house three tribes with distinct languages, costumes and cultures. The lake is the only place in the world where the "poc", a large flightless water grebe, may be seen.

Three hotels are actually on the lake: *Atitlán, Monterrey* and *Tzanjuyu.* Apart from them, visitors to the lake stay at **Panajachel,** but it is 1 km. from the lake; the main attraction is the scenery. (Visitors planning to travel round the lake should be warned that the only bank is here.) There are few Indians to be seen now, as the town is a popular tourist resort and inhabited by quite a few "gringos". Hot springs feed directly to the lake shore. There is water-skiing, private boating and swimming in fresh clear water. Good market on Sundays; you are expected to bargain. Visit Nan Cuz (who lives in the same road as the *Rancho Grande* hotel), an Indian woman painter whose pictures evoke the spirit of village life. The village church, originally built in 1567, was restored, only to be badly damaged by the earthquake.

Hotels (Prices will tend to be higher during Easter week.) *El Aguacatal* has bungalows for US$30 for Sat. and Sun., US$20 on other days. *Rancho Grande,* cottages in charming setting, 4 blocks from beach, popular for long stay; good, simple food, US$9.50-12.50 d, including breakfast. Recommended. *Hotel Tzanjuyu,* a somewhat large lakeside hotel with good and varied food, US$20 d; it has balconies overlooking the lake and a private beach for guests. *Hotel Regis,* US$16 d, new. Opposite entrance to *Regis* is *Casa Cakchiquel,* new, US$3 s, or US$2.50 to share, staff not reliable; *Hotel Cross,* American-run, good value at US$1.50 s. *Monterrey Hotel* has opened a new building (reported that all its bedroom windows face away from lake) and the 80-year-old wooden hotel has been pulled down, US$9 s, US$14 d; restaurant menu is dull and service in general poor, not recommended. *Maya Azteca,* good guest house, US$5; *Hotel Panajachel* is simple, US$2-3 p.p., hot water sometimes, clean, lots of other travellers; other places are *Cacique Inn,* US$14 d; *Minimotel Riva Bella,* US$5 s; *Visión Azul,* US$12 d, both overpriced; *Casa Suiza* (same owners as hotel of same name in Quezaltenango), US$4 s, US$7 d, hot water, clean and friendly, near Texaco service station. *Fonda del Sol,* on main street, US$4 each, not recommended. *Las Casitas,* US$2.50 p.p. *Playa Linda,* US$9-10 s, US$15-16 d, by the lake. Further on is *Casa Loma,* US$2.50 p.p. *Maya Palace,* US$11 d. *Maya Kanek,* on main square, has new annex, US$5 each, some rooms better than others, be careful of valuables, very good food. *Casa de Viajero* has rooms to rent very cheaply, at US$2 per head. *Hospedaje Posada,* central, quiet, US$1 each. One km. beyond town, by lake, is new *Hotel Atitlán,* in old hacienda, US$20 d. *Chico's,* also near beach, US$1.50 s, with breakfast, has laundry service. *Pensión Rosita,* US$1.50 p.p. Several houses on road to beach rent clean rooms; one such in Santa Isabel at US$3 each; others are cheaper. For long stay, ask around for houses to rent; available at all prices from US$20-150 a month, but almost impossible to find in November and December. Camping on the lakeshore is not allowed (there is a US$10 fine for doing so) but there is a campsite at some distance from the beach which has cabins to let at US$1 p.p.; it also has a laundry.

Entertainment Entertainment at *Roger's Pub* and *Discothèque Jaguar.*

Restaurants *Bodega,* 2 blocks from *Rancho Grande; Mama Ramírez,* on road to Santa Catarina, 2nd block after log footbridge; another branch near *Hotel Regis;* good meals for about US$1, sometimes close at 2100; *Nuestra Casa,* US$0.75 for a good meal (also sells yoghurt and second-hand books!); the *Pie Shop* (called Casa de Pays) very popular, good square meals for about US$1.25; *Hsieng* has vegetarian food; *Cisne,* fairly cheap; *Charrasco,* near *Hamburguesa,* good food but expensive, bills sometimes wrong; *La Librería* (near *Hsieng*) has good, cheap restaurant at the back. Cheap American food also at *Hamburguesa,* near Texaco service station; *Iximché,* very good meals; *Restaurant Cakchiquel* (nothing to do with hotel) delicious food at reasonable prices. Go to *La Tienda* at 1500 for fresh brown and banana bread. *Comedor Estrella* for cheap food; *Asia Restaurant* in main street, modest prices; very good food at *Hotel Maya Kanek.*

Shops La Librería has (second-hand) books and woodcuts; Mario Creations has root carvings; on road to San Andrés Semetebaj is the Idol's House, an antique shop where you must bargain.

"Gringo" Market One of the offshoots of Panajachel having become a tourist resort is that there is now a market at 1400 every Saturday where tourists sell goods they no longer want, such as old clothes, camping equipment etc.

Health There is a good clinic at Santiago de Atitlán and also one at San Lucas, which specialize in treating dysentery.

Buses Frequent buses to Guatemala City US$1.25, 3-4 hours, by Rebuli and Higueros. To Quezaltenango, US$1.25; to Santiago de Atitlán (change at Godinez), US$0.50, 3 hours. Direct service to Chichicastenango, US$2; changing at Los Encuentros cheaper at US$1.75; changing at both Sololá and Los Encuentros cheaper still at US$0.75. Bus from Los Encuentros US$0.75. Sololá US$0.25, frequent departures. Rutas Limas apparently overcharge on some routes. In case of complaint go to the tourist office on the main street.

Excursions To **Santiago de Atitlán** by boat at 0900 from the *Hotel Tzanjuyu,* US$2.50 one way (returns at 1200) or by public boat (or bus) to San Lucas Tolimán, and from there by bus. The women wear fine costumes, but of late, the Indians have become only too aware of the tourist trade. There is a market on Tuesdays and Saturdays (better). Fiesta July 25. The Franciscan church dates back to 1568. Nearby are the ruins of the fortified Tzutuhil capital on the Cerro de Chuirinamit. *Pensión Rosita,* near the church, US$1.50 each, US$0.50 for a vegetarian evening meal. *Hospedaje Chi-Nim-Ya,* US$1.50 each, clean and provides good meals. There are other pensións, and the *Santa Rita* restaurant which is good and cheap.) Bus to Guatemala City, US$1.50, 4 hours. Buses back to Panajachel at 1200 and 1500 with one change. The boat to **San Lucas Tolimán** leaves the public beach at Panajachel at 0700 every day except Sundays (US$0.50) and will stop at San Antonio Palopó either going or returning; a bus leaves San Lucas for Santiago at 0900, 1200 and 1500 (US$0.25). It returns at the same times. It is difficult to return to Panajachel the same day, unless one gets the tourist boat at 1200 or the bus at 1230. There is a market on Thursdays and Sundays. From San Lucas (which can also be reached by road from Godinez) the cones of Atitlán, 3,503 metres, and Tolimán, 3,276 metres, can be climbed. Warm clothing and sleeping gear are essential, as the climb takes 2 days. There is a good, cheap restaurant off the main square. Between Santiago and San Lucas is Cerro de Oro, a small village on the lake. At 0600 on Tues., Fri. and Sun., ferries leave the public beach at Panajachel for **San Pedro La Laguna,** San Juan and San Pablo; they return the next morning. (There is also a ferry at 0600 from the Tzanjuyu pier, but this is more expensive.) There is a ferry from Santiago to San Pedro at 1300 (US$0.35). Alternatively, there is a canoe at 0800, US$0.25, or less if you help paddle! San Pedro is at the foot of the San Pedro volcano and is surrounded by coffee plantations. Canoes are made here and a visit to the rug-making cooperative on the beach is of interest. Market days Thurs. and Sun. (better). As yet the village is unspoilt by tourism. There are many *pensións,* including two on the public beach, at US$1 p.p., all are basic; houses can be rented quite cheaply on a weekly basis. Pizzas and fresh wholemeal bread can be obtained from Panadería El Buen Gusto. A boat returns to Panajachel at 1600. If you disembark at San Pablo (on the way to San Pedro) and walk to San Marcos and Santa Cruz (a difficult track), where there is a 16th century church, you can get beautiful views of the lake and volcanoes in the early morning light. Sisal bags and hammocks are made at San Pablo.

Santa Catarina Palopó is within walking distance of Panajachel (about 2 hours). The town has an attractive adobe church. Reed mats are made here, and you can buy *huipiles* and men's shirts. *(Posada Camino Real Atitlán,* US$15 s, US$20 d, de luxe.)

San Antonio Palopó has another splendid church; it lies at the head of the lake in an amphitheatre formed by the mountains behind. The village is noted for the costumes and headdress of the men, and *huipiles* and shirts are cheaper than in Santa Catarina *(Hotel Casa de don Félix* (or Casa del Lago), superb views and good bathing, US$10 d, only a few rooms but gradually being expanded.)

San Andrés Semetebaj, about 6½ km. from Panajachel, has a beautiful ruined early 17th-century church. Market on Tues.

Warning   Long-haired men should know that the Panajachel police are biased against them. Heavy fines are sometimes imposed for wearing shorts. Also identification checks are often made.

From Panajachel the Inter-American Highway climbs 790 metres in 6 km. to Sololá: grand views on the way. Take the bus up, but quite easy to walk down, either direct by the road or *via* San Jorge La Laguna. You can return to Panajachel from San Jorge along the lake, if you take the southern road from the plaza, go through the woods and down to the flats. Ask permission at the house on the lake shore to follow the trail; a 3-hour walk.

Sololá, at 2,135 metres, has superb views across the lake. Population 4,000. Fine Tuesday and Friday market, though crowded with tourists.

Note costumes of men. Great fiesta: August 15. Hot baths for US$0.25 a few blocks N of the plaza; no sign, but ask. Bus from Chichicastenango US$0.50, 2 hrs.

Tightly woven woollen bags are sold here: far superior to the usual type of widely-sold tourist bags. Prices are high due to proximity of tourist centres of Panajachel and Chichicastenango.

Hotels *Hotel Letona* recently reopened, US$5.50 d; *Pensión Salas,* very basic, US$1 s, meals US$0.50.

Los Encuentros, 11 km. from Sololá, is the meeting place of the old and the new Inter-American Highways and the road to Chichicastenango (see page 917). Altitude 2,450 metres.

The northern road to Los Encuentros. From the fork the road runs 19 km. to near **Tecpán,** which is slightly off the road, at 2,316 metres. It has a particularly fine church: silver altars, carved wooden pillars, odd images, a wonderful ceiling which was severely damaged by the earthquake. The women wear most striking costumes. Market: Thursdays. Fiestas: May 3 (Santa Cruz), October 1-8, and December 8. Nowhere to stay at present; both *Hotel Iximché* and *Hostelería de la Montaña* completely destroyed by earthquake.

Near Tecpán are the very important Mayan ruins of **Iximché,** once capital and court of the Cakchiqueles, 3 km. of unpaved road from Tecpán. Iximché was also the first capital of Guatemala after its conquest by the Spaniards: there have been four in all as it was followed by Ciudad Vieja, Antigua and Guatemala City.

Beyond Tecpán the road swings up a spectacular 900 metres to the summit of the Chichoy Pass at 3,048 metres. The pass is often covered in fog or rain but on clear days there are striking views of the volcanoes S of Antigua and of Lake Atitlán and its volcano cones. Some 50 km. from the fork the new northern road joins the old southern one at Los Encuentros.

A road, 18 km., goes NE from Los Encuentros to **Chichicastenango,** popular with tourists. It is the hub of the Maya-Quiché highlands, to which tours are arranged, with guides, from the *Mayan Inn,* one of the best hotels in the country. Stay of several days recommended. Altitude 2,130 metres, and nights cold, but fires at *Mayan Inn.* About 1,000 ladinos in the town, but 20,000 Indians live in the hills near-by and flood the town, almost empty on other days, for the Thursday and Sunday markets, now very commercialized because of mass tourism. Town is built around large square plaza of 180 metres a side, once planted with eucalyptus and jacaranda trees though these remain no longer. Two churches face one another across the square, Santo Tomás parish church and Calvario. Santo Tomás is at present out of action as a result of the 1976 earthquake, and is shored up with beams. In normal times, however, both its steps and platform are of great importance in Indian ritual. Groups burn incense and light candles on steps and platform before entering. Inside, from door to high altar, stretch rows of glimmering candles, Indians kneeling beside them. Later they offer copal candles and flower-petals to the black image of Pascual Abaj, a Mayan god, on a hilltop behind. (This "Idolo" too has unfortunately been damaged by the earthquake.) "There are no better Catholics and probably no better pagans in Guatemala."—Aldous Huxley. For many years visitors were not allowed across the threshold of either church, but recently (before the earthquake) guides have been showing tourists round both Santo Tomás and Calvario, and cameras have been allowed. Next to church are the

Cloisters of the Dominican Monastery (1542) where the famous Popol
Vuh manuscript of Mayan mythology was found in 1690; Father
Rossbach's jade collection can be seen (US$0.25); his museum of Mayan
relics is well worth a visit, and so is the house of a mask-maker on the way
up to the "Idolo", who rents masks and costumes to the dancers and will
show visitors the path to the idol. This is a little difficult to find even then,
and clear instructions should be obtained before setting out.

Rutas Lima bus leaves Guatemala City 0730, arriving 1100. For return, take local bus
(US$0.25) to Los Encuentros where you can pick up another for the capital. The
price is the same, US$2.50, whether one gets off at Atitlán, Chichicastenango, or
goes all the way to Quezaltenango. The slower Rebuli bus from the capital, leaving at
0800, costs only US$0.75, and there is also a cheap bus from Panajachel to Los
Encuentros. Tourist agencies offer one day trips to Chichicastenango for US$10-15.
   Derivation of town's name: *chichicaste*—a prickly purple plant like a nettle that
grows profusely—and *nango*, place of. The town itself, usually called Santo Tomás
by natives, is charming: winding streets of white houses roofed with bright red tiles
wandering over a little knoll in the centre of a cup-shaped valley surrounded by high
mountains. Fine views from every street corner. The costumes are particularly
splendid. Men wear a short-waisted embroidered jacket and knee breeches of black
cloth, a gay woven sash and an embroidered kerchief round the head. The cost of
this outfit, over US$100, means that fewer and fewer men are in fact wearing it.
Women wear *huipiles* with red embroidery against black or brown and skirts with
dark blue stripes. The Sunday market is more colourful than the one on Thursday:
more Indians and brighter costumes, but it certainly becomes very touristy after the
buses arrive from Guatemala City. We are told that in fact the market begins on Sat.
p.m. Sololá and Panajachel shirts are cheaper, and better, here than in their own
markets. Otherwise, textiles, pottery etc. are very expensive as the market has
become so commercialized. You must bargain hard.

Hotels   *Mayan Inn* (US$16-18 s, 21-25 d); very good, with beautiful Colonial
furnishings: a museum in itself. *Mayan Inn Annexe*, slightly cheaper; both oriented
to the tourist trade. *Maya Lodge, US$14 d, good; Pensión Chigüilá*, clean, good,
US$7 p.p., with bath, or US$6 d without, meals another US$4 (some rooms have
fireplaces, wood costs US$0.90 a day extra). *Cantina Claveles*, US$1.50 each plus
US$0.75 for a good meal. There is a bakery attached. *Pensión Girón*, US$2 p.p.
Local boys will show you other cheap lodgings at US$1.50 p.p. Marimba musicians
sometimes play in the patio of *Mayan Inn* and to non-guests at night, no charge: a
typical piece of local goodwill.

Restaurants   *Tziguantinamit; Pensión-Restaurant Katokok* serves good lunches;
Las Marimbitas; El Samaritano (reasonable).

Fiestas   Santo Tomás, December 17-21: processions, dances, marimba music; Holy
Week; November 1; January 20; March 19; June 24 (shepherds). There is also a
fiesta at the end of May.

Excursions   Nineteen km. N by road to (Santa Cruz del) **Quiché**, a
quaint town at 2,000 metres, colourful market on Sunday and Thursday.
Bus from Chichicastenango, US$0.25. Quiché's speciality is palm hats,
which are made and worn in the area. Population 7,750. Remains of
palaces of former Quiché capital, Gumarcaj, or as Alvarado's soldiers
called it, Utatlán, destroyed by Spaniards 5 km. away; the ruins consist of
adobe mounds, their chief attraction being the setting. They can be
reached on foot. Mineral baths. Fiestas: August 16-20, May 3. Serious
eathquake damage.

Pensións   *La Providencia*, US$1.50 s, clean and pleasant; *Hospedaje San Pascual*,
US$2.50 s; *Pensión San Carlos*, US$1.50 s, plus US$0.50 for good meals; *Tropical*.
Restaurant: *Café Luisito*. Thermal baths at Pachitac, 4 km. away and in the town's
main square.

There is a road E from Quiché to (8 km.) Santo Tomás Chiche, a picturesque village with a fine Saturday market; fiesta, December 21-28, which suffered badly in the 1976 earthquake. (There is also a road to this village from Chichicastenango. Although it is a short-cut, it is rough and should be attempted in dry weather only and even then only in a sturdy vehicle.)

On 32 km. is **Zacualpa**, where beautiful woollen bags are woven. There is an unnamed *pensión* near the square; on the square itself is a private house which has rooms for US$0.50 and meals for US$0.60. (Mosquito coils are a must.) Market: Sunday, Thursday. Church with remarkably fine façade. On another 11 km. is **Joyabaj**, where women weave fascinating *huipiles*; there is nowhere to stay, but the mayor may have some ideas. This was a stopping place on the old route from Mexico to Antigua. During fiesta week (the second in August) Joyabaj has a "Palo Volador"—the two men dangle from a 60-ft. pole while the ropes they are attached to unravel to the ground. Both Zacualpa and Joyabaj were severely affected by the 1976 earthquake. The villages of San Pedro and San Juan Sacatepéquez (see page 904) can be reached from Joyabaj by a dry-season road suitable only for strong vehicles. The scenery en route is spectacular.

Road N from Quiché, 48 km., to **Sacapulas**, 1,220 metres, at foot of Cuchumatanes mountains, highest in the country. (Bus from Quiché, US$0.75, 2½ hours for rough journey.) Remains of bridge over Río Negro built by Las Casas. Primitive salt extraction. Market under large ceiba tree on Thursdays and Sundays (better). There is a *pensión* which is clean and friendly and charges US$1.50 d. Colonial church with surprising treasures inside, built 1554, and there are hot springs. The road E to Cobán is one of the most beautiful, if rough, mountain roads in all Guatemala, with magnificent views in the narrow valleys. (Bus at 0500 and 1600, takes 7½ hours, cost US$2. The morning bus starts at 0200 in Quiché.) Branching off this road, about 5 km. N of Sacapulas, is a road to the Indian villages of Nebaj, Chajul and San Juan Cotzal. It is easy enough to get by lorry to Nebaj and it seems that there is a bus in the late afternoon from Sacapulas as well as one from Quiché. It is not so easy to Chajul and Cotzal, although there *is* a lorry on Sundays to Cotzal from Nebaj and Quiché. **Nebaj** has two *pensiones*, the *Arduin*, and *Tres Hermanas*, both US$1 each, food available for about US$0.60. Alternatively you can get a room in a private house for slightly less. In Chajul and Cotzal it is possible to stay in the monastery. In all three places there are very fine *huipiles*—in Nebaj buy them at the pensión or private houses. This village has a magnificent Sunday market. The local Ixil Indians are somewhat hostile towards foreigners as recently some images have been stolen from their churches. Although the weather is not very good at this altitude, the views of the Cuchumatanes mountains are spectacular. The views are also fine on the road which runs W from Sacapulas to (32 km.) Aguacatán at 1,670 metres, where the market has finely embroidered belts; the road goes on to Huehuetenango (another 26 km.—see page 922). There are buses from Huehuetenango at 0430 and 1200 every day except Mon. and Thurs., US$0.90.

The stretch of Inter-American Highway between Los Encuentros and San Cristóbal runs through **Nahualá**, at 1,930 metres, a most interesting

Indian village where *metates,* or stones on which maize is ground to make *tortillas,* are made. The inhabitants wear distinctive costumes, and are considered by other Indians to be somewhat hostile. Good stone church worth going into. Market on Thursdays and Sundays, at which finely embroidered cuffs and collars are sold. Fiesta (St. Catherine) on November 25. Population 1,369.

There is another all-weather road a little to the N and 16 km. longer, from Los Encuentros to San Cristóbal. In 40 km. it reaches Totonicapán.

Totonicapán, 14½ km. E of San Cristóbal, is the capital of its Department, at 2,500 metres. Population 52,000, almost all Indian. This thriving industrial town makes pottery for sale throughout the country. There are sulphur baths, but they are dirty and crowded. Market considered by Guatemalans to be one of the cheapest, and certainly very colourful, on Tuesday and Saturday; annual fair September 26-30; fiestas on September 29 and July 25. The School of Handicrafts in the centre of town is well worth a visit. There is a beautiful cemetery. Frequent buses to Quezaltenango along a paved road, US$1.50, and there are buses from Quiché at 0400 and 0500 daily on a little-travelled but spectacular route. Name often abbreviated to "Toto" on bus destination boards.

Hotels   *Casa de Huéspedes Doris,* sign on main street, clean, pleasant, US$5 per bed; good meals available for US$1. *Pensión Rosario,* more basic than *Doris,* US$1 s.

San Cristóbal has a huge church, built by Franciscan friars, which has recently been renovated. The silver lamps, altars and screens, all hand-hammered, and Venetian glass altars are worth seeing. Noted for textiles (and *huipiles* in particular) sold all over Guatemala; they are cheap here because the town is off the main tourist circuit. Market, Sunday, on banks of river. Annual fair, July 20-26. Altitude 2,380 metres, population 3,186.

Excursion   A road runs N to San Francisco el Alto (5 km.) and Momostenango (21 km.). **San Francisco el Alto,** at 2,640 metres, stands in the mountain cold, above the great valley in which are Totonicapán San Cristóbal and Quezaltenango. Church of metropolitan magnificence. Crammed market on Friday: Indians buying woollen blankets for resale throughout country. An excellent place for buying woven and embroidered textiles of good quality. There is a bus from Totonicapán at 0800 on Fridays. Fiesta, October 4.

Hotel   *Pensión San Francisco* on main street near market, US$1.50, clean and friendly.

Momostenango, at 2,220 metres, is the chief blanket weaving centre. Indians can be seen beating the blankets on stones to shrink them. The Feast of the Uajxaquip Vats (pronounced washakip) is celebrated by 30,000 Indians every 260 days by the ancient Mayan calendar. Frequent masked dances also. Momostenango means "place of the altars", and there are many on the outskirts but they are not worth looking for; there is, however, a hilltop image of a Mayan god, similar to the one outside Chichicastenango. There are said to be 300 medicine-men or sorcerers, "half priesthood, half Medical Association", practising in the town. Insignia of office is a little bag containing beans and quartz crystals In the neighbourhood are three sets of "riscos": fantastic eroded columns of sandstone with embedded quartz particles which are worth visiting. the most beautiful are the least accessible, in the hills to the N of the town.

The town is quiet except on Wednesday and Sunday, the market days. It has a spring-fed swimming pool; also a mineral water pool at Pala Chiquita, just outside the town. Bus service (poor road) from Quezaltenango, US$0.50.

Accommodation Rooms at *Cantina Paclom*, US$2 d, basic. There is another *pensión*, one block from main square, which charges US$1.25 each.

At San Cristóbal the old and the new routes of the Inter-American Highway, which joined at Los Encuentros, part again. The new route to the Mexican border at Ciudad Cuauhtémoc (not a town, despite its name: just a few buildings) goes NW, by-passing Huehuetenango before entering the stretch known as El Tapón, now in very good condition. The old route, running W to Tapachula, in Mexico, reaches 5 km. from San Cristóbal the small ladino town of

Salcajá, well worth a visit. Jaspé skirt material has been woven here since 1861. Yarn is tied and dyed, then untied and warps stretched around telephone poles along the road or along the riverside. (Those interested in Central American textiles should read "Indian Crafts of Guatemala and El Salvador" by Lilly de Jongh Osborn.) Many small home weavers will sell the lengths—5 or 8 varas—depending on whether the skirt is to be wrapped or pleated. The finest, of imported English yarn, cost US$30. Market, Tuesday; it is early, as in all country towns. The church of San Jacinto behind the market is 16th century and also worth a visit. The taxi rate is US$5-6 per hour. Several minibuses a day from new commercial centre of Quezaltenango en route to Totonicapán.

Quezaltenango, 4½ km. SW of San Cristóbal, 268,000 people, is the most important city in western Guatemala. Altitude 2,335 metres, and climate decidedly cool. Set amongst a group of high mountains and volcanoes one of which, Santa María, destroyed the city in 1902 and is still active sometimes. A modern city, but with narrow colonial looking streets, broad avenues, fine public buildings, a magnificent plaza, and a most varied market to which Indians from the entire western highlands bring their handiwork. It is four-fifths Indian. Especially interesting is the stately but quaint Municipal Theatre; there is also a small museum. There is a modern gothic-style church, the Sagrada Corazón on the Parque Juárez; other churches include San Juan de Dios and La Transfiguración, from which there is a good view. The cathedral is modern with a 17th-century façade. A place to stay several days for excursions, as Quezaltenango is a centre for buses to all parts of the Indian highlands. The Tourist Board on the main plaza (helpful) has a leaflet on the nearby villages and markets. Airport. Tourist cards (free) for Mexico can be obtained from the Mexican consulate at the Pensión Bonifaz.

Hotels *Pensión Bonifaz* (the best, US$11-14 s, 20 d, with bath and hot water, also good and expensive restaurant; really not a *pensión* but an excellent Hotel!); *Quetzalcoatl Inn*, US$5-15 s, 9-25 d; *Canadá*, corner of main square, US$2.25 p.p., room with cold shower, food is an extra, US$2, not very good value; *Capri*, behind museum, new, US$2 p.p., with bath, clean; *Casa Suiza*, US$2 p.p., 3 with bath, constant hot water, clean, good meals, US$1.50; *Modelo*, US$8 s, 14 d. with good restaurant, good; *Hotel Exito* and *Casa de H.*, on Av. 9a, the Almolonga road, charge US$3 d, adequate; *Hospedaje Central*, US$1.25; *Del Campo*, US$9 s, 12 d; *Pensión Altense*, on road out of town to S, US$1.25 each, good and clean, hot water extra. *Casa del Viajero*, US$2 p.p., recommended. *El Quijote*, US$1 s, basic; *Pensión Andina*, US$1.50; *Hotel Volga*, US$1.50 s; *Hotel Radar 99*, US$1.25 s, 2.25 d, best of poor bunch near main square, can use kitchen, popular with travellers; *Marquense*, near market, US$1.50 d; *Rabanales; El Aguila; Victoria*, US$4 d, clean, hot water, good cheap meals; *San Nicolás*, US$1; *Enriquez; Casa Kaehler*, US$4 p.p. with bath; *Pensión Mesa*, US$2.50 p.p.

Restaurants Restaurant and Discothèque *Ram*, 14a Avenida 1-40, Zona 1, hot dogs *con guacamole* (avocado salad) for US$0.25. *Bikini*, central, economical, recommended. *Shanghai*, good Chinese restaurant in the same building as the *Hotel Canadá*. *Pájaro Azul* in main park is good. *Taberna de don Rodrigo*, hamburgers and beer, coffee and cakes. *Salchichonería Alemana*, next to *Hotel Modelo*, sells delicious sausage and other delicacies. *Bonanza*, good steaks, somewhat expensive. *Restaurant Capri* (next to hotel), meals from US$1.

Shopping   The Cooperativa in the new Centro Comercial, Artexco, has textiles, but prices are fixed and quite high; better to try the markets. In the same area you can have clothes made up very cheaply. Curiosidades La Chivita makes up locally produced woollen blankets into jackets. The old market in Zona 2 is big, cheap and clean.

Excursions   Many places of interest around on roads N to Huehuetenango, W to San Marcos and Mexico, S to Ocós and Champerico. 1½ km. SE is **Almolonga**, which is noted for its fine 16th-century church and beautiful costumes, especially skirts which are hard to buy. There is also an interesting vegetable market. Fiesta June 29. About 1 km. further on are the thermal baths of Cirilo Flores and El Recreo (entrance, US$0.30). There are also hot springs at Fuentes Georginas (4 km. from Quezaltenango in direction of Zunil, see page 925) which are in very attractive surroundings (entrance US$0.50; rooms for night with individual hot spring baths, US$7 s, 12 d). They can be reached by bus from Quezaltenango; from Zunil you must walk the 8 km. or hire a truck (about US$5). Take picnic or barbecue equipment, but it might be best to avoid Sundays when the Guatemalans descend on the springs. There are also hot steam baths at Los Vahos; a taxi will take you there and back with a one-hour wait for US$3. To reach the Santa María volcano you can take a bus from the market in Quezaltenango to Llano de Piñal, from where it takes 4 hours to walk up the volcano to watch the still active cone on the Pacific side.

Bus   to Los Encuentros for Chichicastenango at 0800 (2 hours). Daily bus for Mexican frontier at Talismán bridge or Ciudad Cuauhtémoc at 0500 with Rutas Lima, US$4. Also daily bus for border at La Mesilla *via* Huehuetenango. Also second class buses to border. La Higuera runs twice daily to Guatemala City *via* Panajachel; last bus is at 1600 (about US$1.75 to Panajachel, wonderful scenery), Ramírez and Velásquez lines also go to the capital. As normally there are two routes to the capital (highland and lowland) check you take the highland one if you want to stop off at Lake Atitlán. Bus to Los Encuentros for Panajachel, US$1.50. To Totonicapán, US$0.40, about 1 hour. To Zunil, about US$0.20.

Spanish Language School   Proyecto Lingüístico Francisco Marroquín, 12 Av. 8-31 (Aptdo 23).

Warning   Local people often call the town by its old name of Xelajú. On some local bus destination boards this is abbreviated to "Xela".

Road North to Huehuetenango   This road goes into the region of the Mam branch of the Mayas. The scenery is wild and awe-inspiring and the road has been improved.

According to folklore, at Olintepeque, an Indian town 6 km. from Quezaltenango, the greatest battle of the conquest was fought, and Alvarado slew King Tecún Umán, in single combat. Its river is still known as Xequizel, the river of blood. Market, Tuesday; fiestas, June 24, August 29. Road climbs 18 km. to Sija, at 3,200 metres, with wide views. The Spanish strain is still noticeable amongst the inhabitants, most of whom are tall and fair. A climb through conifers for another 10 km. to Cumbre del Aire, with grand views behind of volcanoes, and forward of Cuchumatanes mountains. Another 45 km. to ladino town of Malacatancito where the Inter-American Highway swings NW through the Selegua (El Tapón) Gap to Mexico.

A 6½ km. spur from this road leads to **Huehuetenango**, a lead and copper mining centre. A beautiful town in beautiful surroundings, with Indians from remote mountain fastnesses coming in for the daily market, and particularly Thursday and Sunday, though this has now become more tourist-oriented. Fair, July 12-18. Racecourse. Population, 14,000; altitude, 1,905 metres. Ruins of Zaculeu Pyramid, old capital of the Mam tribe, 5 km. W on top of a hill ringed by river and *barrancas*. Yellow Alex Bus runs to the ruins from near 5 Calle at 1030, 1330 and 1530; the return bus gives you an hour at the ruins. Fare US$0.20 return. The Honorary Mexican Consul at the Farmacia El Cid will provide you with the Mexican tourist card for US$1; Huehuetenango is the last town before the La Mesilla border post, on the Inter-American Highway into Mexico.

Hotels *Zaculeu*, best, with good restaurant, US$4-7 s, 6-13 d; *Gran Hotel Shinula*, US$8 d; *Palacio*, US$1-1.50 p.p.; *Pensión Astoria*, US$1.50-2 p.p., good meals for about US$1.25; *Hotel Central*, opposite *Zaculeu*, US$1.50 p.p., excellent meals for about US$1; *Posada Española*, US$1.50; *Pensión Tikal*, by market, US$0.60 s; next door is *Pensión San Antonio*, US$0.75 each, clean. *Nueva Posada Familiar*, US$3 d, clean and good; *Hospedaje Viajero*, US$1 s, clean, recommended.

Restaurants *Plombier; Buen Samaritano*; breakfast at *Posada Española; Comedor Ideal*, near market, US$0.60 for a meal, friendly.

Spanish Language School Proyecto Lingüístico Francisco Marroquín, 2a Calle, 6-09 (Aptdo 41).

Bus Los Halcones from Guatemala City, Calle 25 7-66, Zona 1, US$3, 6 hours. To border, US$1, or US$2 with Rutas Lima. To Cuatro Caminos, the junction with road to Quezaltenango, Momostenango and Totonicapán, US$0.75. To Todos Santos (see page 923), US$1.

Chiantla, 5 km. N of Huehuetenango, has a great pilgrimage to the silver Virgin of La Candelaria on February 2. Another fiesta on September 8. Daily market, largest on Sunday. There are lead mines at Torlón, some distance from Chiantla, which may date back to Spanish times. Road runs N 71 km. to **San Mateo Ixtatán**, at 2,530 metres, in the Cuchumatanes Mountains; there is a bus from Huehuetenango at 0500 (El Cóndor). The *huipiles* made there are unlike any others produced in Guatemala, and are much cheaper than in Huehuetenango. The road passes through San Juan Ixcoy, Soloma *(Mansión Katty* recommended; *Hospedaje San Ignacio),* and Santa Eulalia. San Mateo itself is a colourful town, with an interesting old church and black salt mines nearby. The bus returns to Huehuetenango at 1330, giving you an hour in San Mateo.

After San Mateo the road runs 27 km. E to Barillas: a magnificent scenic route. Some 13 km. N of Chiantla is a view-point with magnificent views over mountain and valley.

The village of **Todos Santos** *(Hospedaje Lucy*, US$1 p.p., meals US$0.50; *Hotel Rex*, US$1; *Hotel Paz*, US$0.50, recommended; *Pensión San Lucas*, US$0.40; three cheap *comedores*) has been recommended as interesting; some of Guatemala's best weaving is done there, and fine *huipiles* may be inspected—and bought—in the makers' huts. There are also embroidered cuffs and collars for men's shirts. The best selection of old woven items can be bought from a small house behind the church. The Saturday market is fascinating. There are buses from Huehuetenango at 0500 and 1200, US$1. The drive is spectacular. Near the village are the ruins of Ixcán. Also interesting: Nebaj, Chajul and Cotzal (see page 919).

The Inter-American Highway runs W through the Selegua Canyon, sometimes called El Tapón, to La Mesilla and Mexico, a very good and interesting route. Air service from Guatemala City to Ciudad Cuauhtémoc (or El Ocotal, as it is often called), which is the Mexican border point. (Its name is deceptive; there is no city or town there, and therefore no accommodation.) From there Autobuses Tuxtla Gutiérrez run into Chiapas. Ciudad Cuauhtémoc is about 4 km. from the Guatemalan border point at La Mesilla. There are taxis and buses between the two during the day. La Mesilla has rooms in its café. The Guatemalan authorities charge US$1.50 exit and entry. Bus from La Mesilla to Huehuetenango, US$1; to Quezaltenango, US$4. If arriving by bus at the border avoid being made to wait by the bus company until the lunch hour so that you have to pay extra to the guards for "off-hours".

For the 130-km. route from Huehuetenango by way of Sacapulas to Chichicastenango, see under excursions from Chichicastenango, pages 917/918).

Quezaltenango W to Mexico   Eighteen km. to San Juan Ostuncalco, at
2,530 metres, noted for good Sunday market and beautiful sashes worn
by men. Fiesta, Candlemas. See later for road S to Pacific town of Ocós.
The road, which is paved, switchbacks 60 km. down valleys and over
pine-clad mountains to a plateau looking over the valley in which are San
Pedro and San Marcos, also known as La Unión. Interesting town hall,
known as the Maya Palace. **San Marcos,** at 2,350 metres, is 2 km. or so
beyond **San Pedro.** San Pedro has a huge market every Thursday. Its
Sunday market is less interesting. The Indian women wear golden-purple
skirts. Fiesta, with fair, April 22-30; radio station. Tajumulco volcano,
4,200 metres, can be climbed from the junction of the Tacana and
Tajumulco village roads; at about 5 hours' climb. About 15 km. W of
San Marcos the road begins its descent from 2,500 metres to the lowlands.
In 53 km. to **Malacatán** it drops to 366 metres, one of the toughest
stretches in Central America—even for 4-wheel drive vehicles. It is a
disagreeable ride with continuous bends, but the scenery is attractive.

Hotels   At San Marcos: *Pérez,* with good dining room, US$1.75-2.25 p.p., meals
US$1; *Pensión Minerva,* US$1, basic. At San Pedro: *Hotel El Valle,* US$1.50-2 p.p.,
said to be good. *Bagod,* US$1.50 p.p. At Malacatán: *Hotel América,* US$2 p.p.,
good; *Pensión Santa Lucía,* US$1.25 p.p.; *Hospedaje La Predilecta,* US$1 p.p.

The international bridge over the Suchiate River at Talismán into Mexico
is 18 km. W of Malacatán. Beyond the bridge the road goes on *via*
Tapachula and Tonolá to Arriaga and Las Cruces (195 km.), where it
joins the Pan-American Highway to Mexico City; 95% of the motor
traffic from Mexico comes down this road. Aerolíneas flies Guatemala
City-Tapachula direct. Entering from Mexico you may be charged US$2
by the Guatemalan customs and immigration officers.

There is a Mexican consular service at Malacatán (closed after 1300), and another at
Pensión Bonifaz, Quezaltenango. Travelling by bus to Mexico is quicker from
Quezaltenango than from San Marcos. Most traffic seems to go *via* Coatepeque and
Quezaltenango and not *via* San Marcos; the former is longer but is reported a very
good road. There is one direct bus from the border to Quezaltenango in the early
morning (Rutas Lima, US$4). Otherwise you must make your way to Malacatán
(only one bus a day, at 1500) from where there are 3 buses a day to Quezaltenango.

Quezaltenango to Ocós   W 18 km. to Ostuncalco (*huipiles* from the
whole highland area, and embroidered sashes, are sold at the twice-
weekly market); then S for 5 km. to **Concepción Chiquirichapa,** an
attractive village, one of the wealthiest in the country. It has a small
market early every Thursday morning where some of the most beautiful
huipiles in Guatemala are to be seen. 5½ km. to **San Martín** (sometimes
known as Chile Verde; this village appears in Miguel Angel Asturias'
"The Mulatta and the Fly"), in a windy, cold gash in the mountains.
Huipiles and shirts from the cottage up behind the church.
Accommodation next door to the Centro de Salud (ask at the Centro),
US$1. Food in *comedor* opposite church, US$0.40. Indians speak a
dialect of Mam not understood by other Maya tribes, having been
separated from them during the Quiché invasion of the Guatemalan
highlands. The men wear very striking costumes. Fiesta, November 11.
Primitive ceremonies of witchdoctor initiation held on May 2 at nearby
Lake Chicabal, in crater of volcano. The walk to the lake from San
Martín takes about 2 hours. There are two paths. Ask the way to the
"Laguna", not Chicabal which the Indians do not understand. Also do
not attempt to ask the women the way; they will only run away. The last

bus to Quezaltenango leaves at 1900. Road descends to lowlands. From Colomba a road branches S (28 km.) to Retalhuleu: the road to Ocós runs 21 km. W from Colomba to **Coatepeque**, at 700 metres, with a population of 13,657; one of the richest coffee zones in the country; also maize, sugar-cane and bananas, and cattle. Fair, March 10-15.

Hotels at Coatepeque *Europa*, US$2.50-5 s, 4-8 d; *Virginia*, US$5-6 s, 8-10 d; and *Baechli*, US$3 p.p.; *Pensión Montecarlo*, US$1 p.p. Bus from Quezaltenango, US$0.75.

Both railway and paved Pacific Highway to

Tecún Umán (Ayutla), W 34 km., terminus of Guatemalan Railways, on the Mexican frontier, separated by Suchiate river from Mexican town of Suchiate: the two railway stations are 5 km. apart. This is an alternative crossing point to the Talismán bridge and many buses run to it from Guatemala. (Be warned, however, that you have to walk across a very long bridge (toll, US$0.20) over the river between the two border posts.) The bus to the capital costs US$4. Colectivo from Coatepeque, US$1. Road N to Malacatán for international road bridge into Mexico. Population 4,250. Hotels: *La Perla; Pensión Rosita*. **Ocós**, a small port now closed to shipping, is served by a 22-km. road S from Tecún Umán. Across the river from Ocós is **Tilapa**, a small resort; buses from Coatepeque and ferries from Ocós. *Pensión Teddy*, US$2 d, friendly, but said to have deteriorated in standards. The swimming is good, but both here and at Ocós there are sharks, so stay close to the shore.

Quezaltenango to Champerico, *via* Retalhuleu: a 53-km. link between the old Inter-American Highway and Pacific Highway, paved all the way. A toll (Quezaltenango-Retalhuleu, US$0.25) is collected. The first town (15 minutes) is **Cantel**, which has the largest textile factory in the country: it uses Indian labour. Market, Sunday; *fiestas*, August 15 and a passion play at Easter. Nine km. S is **Zunil**, picturesquely located in canyon of Samalá river. Market, Monday; fiesta, November 25, and a very colourful procession on Palm Sunday. Striking church, inside and out. The local idol is San Simón, described by one traveller as a plastic tailor's dummy, dressed in suit, shoes and hat, but fervently worshipped by the Indians who bring him drinks, cigarettes and other gifts; the statue is lodged in a greenhouse on the far side of the river. Behind the church is a co-operative which sells beautiful *huipiles*, and shirt and skirt materials. Zunil volcano to E, Thermal baths of Fuentes Georginas are nearby (see page 922). Our road descends through Santa Maria de Jesús (large hydro-electric station) to San Felipe, at 760 metres, 35 km. from Zunil. Tropical jungle fruits. Spur line to Mulua, on Guatemalan Railway. Beyond, 3 km., is San Martín, with a branch road to Mazatenango. On this latter road are the thermal baths of Aguas Amargas. **N.B.** San Felipe has a one way road system, and you can wait up to 1½ hrs. to go through the town.

Mazatenango, 18 km. from San Martín, on the railway, is chief city of the Costa Grande zone. Products: coffee, sugar, cacao, tropical fruits. Altitude 380 metres, population 21,000. Chitalón airfield 3 km. away. The Pacific Highway (see map) passes through.

Hotels *Jumay*, US$2 p.p.; *Alba*, US$5 s, 9 d; *La Gran Tasca*, US$2.50 p.p.; *Roma*, US$4 p.p.; *Costa Rica*, US$2 p.p.; *Pensión Mejía*, US$1 p.p., without bath. **Motel** *Texas*.

SW 11 km. from San Martín is *Retalhuleu*, at 240 metres, a town of 42,000 people on the Pacific Highway and on the Guatemalan Railway to

Champerico. It serves a large number of coffee and sugar estates. Fair, December 6-12.

Hotels *Astor*, US$2.50-3.50 p.p.; *Modeloo*, US$4 p.p.; *Pacifico*, US$1.50 each, next to new market; *Posada de Don José*, US$6 s, US$9 d.

Motel *La Colonia* (swimming pool), 1½ km. to the N, is good (US$9 d).

Champerico, 43 km. SW of Retalhuleu by an asphalted road, is the third most important port in the country, with the best facilities on the Pacific side. Population 4,500. Good beach, though the sand is black and there is a strong undercurrent; good fishing.

Hotels *Martita*, US$4 d, without private bath; *Miramar*, US$1.75-2 p.p.

Trains 2 a day to and from the capital.

Shipping Frequent calls by steamers to Europe *via* Panama Canal and by steamers plying between Puget Sound, San Francisco, and the ports of Ecuador, Peru and Chile. Joint fast cargo service of Royal Mail Lines and Holland-America Line to Europe. Port now nationalized.

Guatemala City to San Salvador The paved Inter-American Highway through Fraijanes, Barberena and Cuilapa keeps to the crest of the ridges most of the way to the border, 166 km. Beyond Cuilapa it crosses the Río de los Esclavos by a bridge first built in the 16th century. Fifty km. on is Jutiapa (population 9,200). Beyond, it goes through the villages of Progreso and Asunción Mita, where another road runs to Lake Güija. Before reaching the border at Cristóbal it dips and skirts the shores (right) of Lake Atescatempa, an irregular sheet of water with several islands and set in heavy forest. From the border to San Salvador, where all the main highways are paved, is 100 km.

The quickest way of getting to San Salvador is to take a paved highway which cuts off right from this route at Molino, beyond the Esclavos Bridge. This cut-off goes through El Oratorio and Valle Nuevo to Ahuachapán and San Salvador. (Try *Motel Martha*, 15 km. from frontier on Guatemalan side, US$2 p.p., excellent breakfast, swimming pool.) A third paved road, in less good condition, runs from Guatemala City through Escuintla and Guazacapán to the border bridge over the Río Paz at La Hachadura, then through the coastal plain to Sonsonate and on to San Salvador, 290 km in all; this road gives excellent views of the volcanoes. If travelling direct from San Salvador into Mexico, this road is recommended; at Escuintla you take the coastal highway to Mazatenango and thence to Tapachula, Mexico.

If stuck at La Hachadura (the last bus for Sonsonate leaves at 1800), you can get food at the service station restaurant and there is a very basic *hospedaje* for US$1.20 nearby—not recommended for women.

Guatemala City E to Chiquimula This gravel road, 203 km. long, goes up-hill and down-dale through fine scenery. It runs E by way of San José Pinula, Mataquescuintla, Jalapa, San Pedro, Pinula, Jilotepeque, and Ipala to Chiquimula (see page 908). It was the route to the great shrine at Esquipulas, but visitors now use the Atlantic Highway to Río Hondo and the new road to Honduras past Zacapa and Chiquimula.

Jalapa, capital of Jalapa Department, 114 km. from Guatemala City, is particularly attractive. It is set in a lovely valley at 1,380 metres; average temperature 20°C, but falls in December and January to as low as 5°C. Valley of Monjas, near city, is one of the most fertile in Guatemala. Bus service daily to capital, which can also be reached by bus on road NW to

Jalapa station on Guatemalan Railway and thence by train, but this route takes longer. Population 42,000.

Hotel   *Pensión Casa del Viajero,* US$3 p.p.

El Petén: the Maya Centres and the Jungle

One other area must be noted: El Petén Department in the far N, which was so impenetrable that its inhabitants, the Itzás, were not conquered by the Spaniards until 1697—185 years after they arrived in Guatemala. The local products are chicle and timber—and mosquitos; take plenty of repellent, and re-apply frequently.

Flores, the Department's capital, lies in the heart of the Petén forests, and is built on an island in the middle of the beautiful Lake Petén Itzá. It is linked by a causeway with Santa Elena (airport). Its population is 5,000. From Flores the ruins of Tikal and other Mayan cities can be reached. (For description of Maya culture see pages 883-4).

Hotels In Flores: *Yum Kax,* US$8 p.p., new and nice; *El Itzá,* US$6-8 p.p. (the owner is a good doctor); *Petén,* US$3-3.50 p.p., good meals, US$2, comfortable; *Guayacán,* US$2 p.p.; *Pensión Universal,* US$1.50 p.p., very clean; *Casa Blanca,* US$1 p.p. (US$0.25 on the balcony), poor food, but good view and swimming (although there are recent reports of petty theft and noise from the bar); *Santana,* new, US$2 p.p. At Santa Elena: *Maya Internacional,* US$10 s, 16 d, pool, recommended; *Monja Blanca,* US$3 p.p.; *Ahauna-Ula,* US$2 p.p., good restaurant. *Santa Ana,* US$1.50; *Hospedaje Esquipulas,* US$1 p.p.

Restaurants   *Comedor Isabelita* on Calle Centroamérica, hard to find, but the food is good and plentiful. Restaurant of *Ahauna-Ula Hotel* recommended. *Santa Bárbara* restaurant on "Radio Petén" island, excellent meals for about US$2. Also *Palacio Maya* and *Restaurant Santana.*
  Dugouts can be hired to paddle yourself around the lake.
  San Benito, a US$0.10 ride across the lake, has a better selection of fruit and vegetables and some small restaurants, which are cheaper but less inviting than those in Flores. It also has *pensiones: Hospedaje Hernández,* US$2, *Hospedaje Favorito,* US$1, and *Palermo.* A dirty village.

Airport   Daily flights to Santa Elena from Guatemala City (*not* Sundays), US$25 one way; return at 0930. A new international airport is being built at Santa Elena.

Buses   Daily (Fuente del Norte, 17 C. 9-68, Zona 1, and Rápido del Sur, 9 Av., 19 and 20 C.) leave Guatemala City at 0200, 0400, 0500 and 0730 for the 14-hour (at least) run *via* Morales-San Felipe-Puerto Modesto Méndez to Flores (US$8 one way, take lunch). In the rainy season the trip can take as much as 28 hours, and in all weathers it is very uncomfortable. Those who wish to break the journey could get off the bus and spend a night in Morales, Río Dulce, San Luis (basic pensión) or Poptún. Poptún is 125 km. from Flores and has a good *pensión* in the centre of town, US$1, and a camping area called "Finca Poptún, Camping IX". Also at certain times of the year delicious mangoes are on sale in this area.
  Buses leave Flores daily at 0600 and 1230 for Tikal, US$2 (70 km.—at least 4 hours on a bad road) they return at 0530 and 1330. A sum of US$1 has to be paid at the police checkpoint before the village, which serves as an entrance fee to the ruins and museum. Alternatively, take minibus from *Hotel Casa Blanca,* leaving at 0600 and returning at 1500. (No service on Mondays.) Driving from Guatemala City or from Puerto Barrios, take the Atlantic Highway, which is paved, to Morales (bus from Puerto Barrios, US$0.50); 30 km. after turnoff, ferry over Río Dulce (where a side trip can be made to the San Felipe fortress on Lake Izabal—see page 906), US$2, then 260 km.along narrow, winding, dusty or muddy potholed road (bus from Morales, US$4). Bus between Flores and Quiriguá (see page 907), US$5.50, 11 hours. Return buses to Guatemala City leave from Santa Elena rather than Flores; check times at bus company offices.
  For Belize there is a bus from Flores to **Melchor de Mencos** (US$3) on the border.

This can be caught at El Cruce if coming from Tikal. The 0530 bus from Tikal gives you a 20-min. wait at El Cruce for the Flores bus. (Cost Tikal-Melchor de Mencos, US$2, journey takes about 4½ hours.) There is a later connection too. From Melchor de Mencos there are taxis to take you over the border to Benque Viejo. US$0.70. From there you can catch a bus to Belize City. Hitching is not easy as there is little traffic on these roads, and the political situation is not always favourable to easy movement over this frontier.

Hotels at Melchor de Mencos: *Hotel Maya*, US$2.50 s; *Pensión Central*, US$1.25, dirty; *Hotel Esquipulas*, US$1.50, all basic though will sometimes change Belizean dollars for quetzales and vice versa.

Mayan ruins fans wishing to economize can travel to Copán by bus from Flores (La Pinata 0500) to Río Hondo, then from Río Hondo to Chiquimula, then from Chiquimula to El Florido (see page 908) or La Entrada, and finally from either of these places to Copán.

N.B.   Take your passport and tourist card to Tikal or you will not be allowed to visit the ruins.

Tikal   The great Mayan ruins of vast temples and public buildings are reached by plane, US$75 return from Guatemala City, but flights tend to be booked up especially at holiday periods; however it sometimes happens that the late morning flight to Flores goes on to Tikal, although you have to buy a ticket on to Tikal at Flores (which works out more expensive than the direct ticket). You can get there also by bus from Flores. Tikal lasted from the 4th century A.D. until the tenth. An overall impression of the ruins may be gained in 4-5 hours, but you need two days to see everything, and detailed study needs much longer. The jungle setting of the ruins also has its attractions for botanists and zoologists. Guides are available at the airstrip. An entrance fee of US$1 per day is charged and US$5 is charged for a Land Rover trip through the ruins. Camping is free with a daily water allowance of 1 gallon p.p.

Hotels   (Note: It is advisable to book a hotel room or camping space as soon as you arrive as there are many other tourists.) *Jaguar Inn* (US$16 d, all in, with best food and will provide picnic lunch at US$1); *Tikal Inn*, US$4-8 s, 7-14 d, meals expensive, but said to be poor. *Posada de la Selva* (Jungle Lodge), US$2.50 p.p., or US$6 p.p. for bungalow, meals also expensive. Visitors should be warned that there is a proposal to remove all hotels from Tikal and concentrate them at Santa Elena, operating a shuttle-bus service to Tikal. Economical travellers are best to bring their own food, and especially drink.

Wear light cotton clothes and a broad-brimmed hat. The nights can be cold, however; at least one warm garment is advisable. Free palm-thatch shelters are available, where you can sling your own hammock. There is a campsite near the airstrip where hammocks can be hired (US$0.50). At the site is a *comedor*, good meals for about US$0.60. Bathing in the camp reservoir is not advised and take care to bring water with you as there is no supply for campers other than between 1600 and 1700 near the museum. There are no fresh fruit or vegetables available either. There are 3 other *comedores* and the *Jaguar Inn* restaurant is open to non-residents; relatively inexpensive and good. Both ruins (open 0600-1730) and museum at Tikal are free. Recommended guide book is "Tikal", by W. R. Coe, price US$4.50 in the capital or at the Tikal Museum; either a guide book or a guide is essential, as outlying structures can otherwise easily be missed. Not possible to go by bus from Flores to Tikal and back within one day, unless one is content to spend only an hour or so at the ruins.

Sayaxche is a good centre for visiting the Petén, whether your interest is in the wild life or the Mayan ruins. There are buses to and from Flores and it is also possible to reach the town from Sebol, N of Cobán. There is a bus at 0500 from Cobán to Sebol. From there cargo boats sail to various points on the Río de la Pasión, including Sayaxche. It appears that it is easier to get a lift on one towards the end of the week. With a good knowledge of Spanish you can make your way up the river in stages.

The trip takes anything from 2-12 days, depending on how long you have to wait at each stage for another boat. Each day's boat trip should not cost more than US$1. There are places to stay overnight if you have a hammock (insect repellent is also advisable). At Sayaxche is *Hotel Guayacán,* known locally as *Hotel de Godoy* after the owner, US$2 s, meals US$0.75, excellent value; or *Hotel Sayaxche,* US$1.50 p.p., not clean, but food not bad.

Downriver from Sayaxche is **Seibal,** where the ruins were excavated by Peabody Museum and Harvard. There is now a road linking Sayaxche with Seibal so the trip can be made either by road or by river. From Sayaxche the altar of sacrifice at the mouth of the Usumacinta river can also be reached. Further down the Usumacinta river is Yaxchilán, just over the border in Mexico (temples still standing, with sculptures and carved lintels). The Río de la Pasión is a good route to follow to visit other, more recently discovered Maya ruins. From Laguna Petex Batun, which can be reached by outboard canoe from Sayaxche (US$12 for 6 people and luggage) excursions can be made to unexcavated ruins **Dos Pilas** (many well-preserved stelae), **Aguateca** (excursion over only known Mayan bridge and down into huge chasm) and **Itzán**—discovered only in 1968. Lagoon fishing includes 150-lb. tarpon, snoek and local varieties. Many interesting birds, including toucan and guacamaya.

(On the foregoing information, Mr. John Streather comments that the ruins are spread over a large area and that the prices of launches and guides have risen very substantially. Mr. Streather says further that the non-specialist could well content himself with seeing **Seibal** and, possibly, **Dos Pilas.**)

About 30 km. from Flores, on the road towards the Belize border, is Lake Yaxhá. On the northern shore is the site of **Yaxhá,** the third-largest known classic Maya site in the country, although this status has now possibly been taken over by a new find at Zotz. In the lake is the site of Topoxte. (The island is accessible by boat.) The site is unique since it flourished between the 12th and 14th century, long after the abandonment of all other classic centres. Twenty km. further north lies **Nakum,** with standing Mayan buildings. It is possible to drive part of the way, or else to walk, but since there are numerous forks in the track, it is essential to hire a guide. The largest Maya site in the country is at the more or less inaccessible **El Mirador,** 80 km. by jungle track from Flores or 25 from the airstrip at Carmelita (a 2-4 day trek). In the same direction as El Mirador, though much nearer Tikal, is **Uaxactún,** which has a stuccoed temple with serpent head decoration. Uaxactún is one of the longest-occupied Maya sites. Flights from Flores, Tues., Thurs. and Sat., returning 24 hours later US$15 per round trip). The hardy might consider walking the 32 km. through the jungle from Tikal, as the dirt road is impassable to vehicles from June to February and at other times a four-wheel drive vehicle is essential. No *pensiónes,* but the signalman at the airfield will let you sling your hammock in his home for US$0.50. All the sites are accessible by jeep or 'plane. In the extreme western part of the Péten department is **Piedras Negras,** which can be reached by boat, at some considerable expense.

The Economy

The economy of Guatemala is growing at a steady rate: over the past five years it has grown by an average of 6%, no mean achievement since the world recession and earthquake damage have not been without effect. Inflation became serious for the first time in 1973, and has since continued to be a problem, not least because soaring coffee revenues and the influx of foreign funds for reconstruction have given rise to an accelerated money-supply expansion. In 1976 the rate of inflation was 18%, but it moderated to 7% in 1977.

In international trade the accent is still heavily on agriculture which accounts for some 65% of total exports. Coffee and cotton account for a large proportion of foreign trade, but bananas and sugar are also important crops. There has been an attempt to diversify agricultural exports with tobacco, other vegetables and fruit, and beef exports are increasing.

The industrial sector is growing steadily; the main activities, apart from food and drink production, include the rubber, textile, paper and pharmaceuticals industries. Chemicals, furniture, petroleum products, tobacco and building materials are also produced. Local industries, encouraged by tax remissions and tariff barriers, are gradually eliminating the need for imported products. Guatemala's exports to the other Central American countries account for some 27% of its total exports.

After many years of preparatory work, production has begun from the nickel-mining project at Lake Izabal in eastern Guatemala. This project will make Guatemala the area's largest producer and is set to become the country's second most important export after coffee. A Canadian company is responsible for the project. Lead and zinc, silver, antimony and tungsten are mined in small quantities, and there are known reserves of sulphur, uranium and copper. Marble is exported to Mexico and the rest of Central America.

Petroleum has been discovered at Las Tortugas and Rubelsanto in the Department of Alta Verapaz. The Rubelsanto find is estimated to have proven and probable reserves of 27.3 m barrels, with production in mid-1977 running at 3,200 bpd. It is hoped that work on a pipeline linking Rubelsanto and Livingston will begin as soon as government approval is given and this will have a capacity of 15,000 bpd. Exploration is continuing in both the Rubelsanto area and in the nearby department of El Petén. Offshore exploration has so far been unsuccessful.

Foreign Trade (US$m)

	1971	1972	1973	1974	1975	1976
Exports (f.o.b.)	290.0	338.4	444.8	582.2	640.9	782.1
Imports (c.i.f.)	303.3	324.0	431.0	700.5	732.7	838.9

Information for Visitors

By Air   There are direct daily air services to Guatemala from New York, Houston, San Francisco, Los Angeles, New Orleans, Miami, Washington, Panama, Mexico City and the capitals of other Central American republics. Airlines serving Guatemala are Pan American Airways, Sabena, Iberia, Air Panama, Taca, and Sahsa. Aerolíneas de Guatemala flies daily (except Sunday) to the Petén, and also to and from San Salvador. It also flies to Miami (connecting with British Airways from London), New Orleans, Mérida and Mexico City. The Mexico City services connect with flights to Europe. Iberia provides direct links with Dominican Republic and to Madrid *via* Panama. SAM flies to Bogotá from Guatemala (US$129).

By Sea   There are passenger steamship services between Antwerp, Göteborg and Stockholm and San José, and between Rotterdam, New York (6½ days) and New Orleans (4 days) and Santo Tomás. Central America Services have a fast cargo service from European ports to the Pacific ports of San José and Champerico. The Italia Line has a service from Mediterranean ports to San José. The Mamenic, Tica, and Grancolombia Lines sail bi-monthly to Santo Tomás from New York, New Orleans and Galveston. KNSM, Hapag Lloyd and the French Line from Europe call at Santo Tomás. Seven direct lines link Guatemala with the Orient.

There is a 10% ticket tax, single or return, on all international tickets sold in Guatemala. A stamp tax of 1.5% is payable on single, return, baggage tickets and exchange vouchers issued in Guatemala and paid for in or out of the country. A US$5 tourism tax is levied on all tickets sold in Guatemala to Guatemalan residents for travel abroad. There is also a US$5 airport departure tax and a tax of US$1.50 for arrival and departure by road or rail.

British Businessmen and commercial travellers should read "Hints to Business Men Visiting Guatemala", free from Room CO7, Export House, 50 Ludgate Hill, London, EC4M 7HU.

Business and commercial offices are open from 0800-1200, and 1400-1800 except Saturdays. Shops: 0800-1200, 1400-1800, but 0800-1200 on Saturday. Banks in Guatemala City: 0900-1200, 1400-1630, but 0900-1200. 1400-1700 on Friday and closed on Saturday. In the interior banks tend to open earlier in the morning and close earlier in the afternoon. Government offices open 0700-1530.

Documents Necessary, a passport (except for tourists from USA and Canada who can offer proof of citizenship) and visa, or tourist card. Visas, for which there is a charge of US$3-5 in some places, allow a stay of 30 days (extendable in Guatemala City) and are valid for 2 years. Tourist cards cost only US$1. though sometimes more is charged, and are valid for only 3 months; they may no longer be applied for on arrival at Guatemala City airport or at the border, but must be obtained beforehand. Those wishing to make more than òne visit to Guatemala (or even just to cross the border to Copán and return) should make sure they get a multiple entry visa or tourist card. Tourist cards are not issued to nationals of communist countries, nor to black people unless they are citizens of the USA. All must have a valid international smallpox vaccination certificate. (Since Guatemala has suspended its consular services in Britain tourist cards or visas must be obtained from the Guatemalan Embassy, 73 Rue de Courcelles, Paris (8e), from consulates in New York or Miami, or from any Latin American country on the way; in Mexico City the consulate is at Vallarta 1; visas cost US$3.50 but, in San José they cost US$4 and in Belize, US$5. Visitors staying less than 30 days, and holders of tourist cards, do not need an exit permit, which costs US$2.50. It appears, however, that whatever the length of stay, you will be charged US$5 travel tax upon leaving the country. The authorities at borders may show hostility to long-haired "hippie" visitors, and may refuse them entry. Entry is refused to all passengers whose passports show evidence of their having been in a communist country. United Kingdom nationals need visas, but citizens of other West European countries and Israel do not.

Tourists can get permission from the customs to take their cars into Guatemala for 30 days, renewable for up to 180 days at the Ministry of Finance. There is an exit and entry tax for cars (the amount seems to vary but is about US$1.50-US$2). There is also a charge for tyre fumigation on entry. Tyres without rims are confiscated and burnt.

You are allowed to take in, free of duty, personal effects and articles for your own use, 2 bottles of spirit and 80 cigarettes or 100 grams of tobacco. Once every 6 months you can take in, free, dutiable items worth US$100. Temporary visitors can take in, or out, any amount of quetzales or foreign currencies; there are now no currency restrictions.

Official border crossing hours are 0800-1200, 1400-1800, weekdays. Crossing at any other time involves a service charge.

Information The Centro Guatemalteco de Turismo, 6 Av., 5-34, Zona 1, Guatemala, provides bus timetables, hotel lists and good road maps, but is otherwise not very helpful.

Internal Travel The paved roads are excellent, but the dirt roads are often very bad. There are army checkpoints in many places along the main roads; stopping is compulsory, so if driving your own vehicle, watch out for the "ALTO" sign. Second-class buses are not always mechanically sound, and are often overloaded. Hitchhiking is comparatively easy.

Note Petrol stations in Guatemala often have clean lavatories and sometimes showers.

The railways operate from Atlantic to Pacific and to San Salvador and Mexican border. Service is neither luxurious nor reliable. Much earthquake damage in February 1976.

Warning When travelling on second-class buses, resist overcharging. The correct fare should be posted up; if not, ask your neighbours.

Clothing In the hot coastal regions—for men: tropical suits and light cotton underwear; for women: cotton or linen dresses and light cotton underwear. In Guatemala City and the uplands—men: light woollens may be needed for evening wear; medium weight suits and a light overcoat for December and January. Women: woollens for the evenings and a light topcoat in December and January. Men and women should wear dark clothes in the evening. Extremes of fashion should be avoided, as should very long hair for men; in fact, scissors are provided at the border. A raincoat is needed during the rainy season.

Shopping Woven goods are normally cheapest bought in the town of origin. Try to avoid middlemen and buy direct from the weaver or from a cooperative like Artexco with branches in Quezaltenango and Huehuetenango, or the Zunil weavers' cooperative. Tourism has had the unfortunate effect of inflating prices, so much so that even the women who make the costumes cannot afford to keep one for themselves.

Health Guatemala is healthy enough if precautions are taken about drinking-water, milk, uncooked vegetables and peeled fruits; carelessness on this point is likely to lead to amoebic dysentery, which is endemic. In Guatemala City the American, Bella Aurora, and Centro Médico hospitals are good. Herrera Llerandi is a good private hospital. There is an immunization centre at Centro de Salud, No. 1, 1 Av. between 11 and 12 C, Zona 1, Guatemala City. In the high places avoid excessive exertion. If going to the Maya sites and the jungle areas, prophylaxis against malaria is strongly advised; there may also be a yellow fever risk.

Hotels Tourist office in Guatemala City will deal with complaints about overcharging if you can produce bills etc.

Tipping Hotels, about 10%; hotel staff: bell boys, $0.25 for light luggage, $0.50 for heavy. Chamber maids at discretion. Restaurants: 10%, minimum $0.25. Taxi drivers: $0.25 to $0.50, according to time and distance. Airport porters: $0.25 per piece of luggage. Cloakroom attendants and cinema usherettes are not tipped.

Climate, which depends upon altitude, varies greatly. Most of the population lives at between 900 and 2,500 metres, where the climate is healthy and of an even springlike warmth—warm days and cool nights. The temperature in this temperate region ranges between 7°C in December and January to 29°C in March and April. The coast lands and northern region, low-lying, hot, humid and tropical, are covered with dense vegetation. The mean annual temperature in this "tierra caliente" is about 27°C. The winter months are 3-7°C cooler than the hot months of March and April. The pronounced rainy season in the highlands is from May to October; the dry from November to April.

Currency The unit is the "quetzal", divided into 100 centavos, at par with the U.S. dollar. There are coins of 25, 10, 5 and 1 centavos. The paper currency is for 50 centavos, and 1, 5, 10, 20, 50 and 100 quetzales. U.S. dollars are readily accepted as currency in some places. Inflation comes in spasms: after high rates in 1973-74 it declined to only 0.6% in 1975, then shot up to 17.6% in 1976, followed by a moderate rise of 7.4% in 1977. **Warning:** Torn notes are not always accepted, so avoid accepting them yourself if possible.

The quetzal, an almost extinct bird of the Trogon family, is the national emblem. A real, stuffed quetzal is perched on the national coat of arms in the Presidential Palace's ceremonial hall and another one is at the Archaeological Museum in Aurora Park.

Weights and Measures The metric system is obligatory on all Customs documents: specific duties are levied on the basis of weight, usually gross kilogrammes. United States measures are widely used in commerce. The metric ton of 1,000 kg. is generally used; so is the U.S. gallon. Old Spanish measures are often used; e.g., vara

(32.9 inches), caballería (111.51 acres), Manzana (1.727 acres) arroba (25 lbs.), and quintal (101.43 lbs.).

Public Holidays

January 1.
January 6: Epiphany.
Holy Week (4 days).
May 1: Labour Day.
June 30.
August 15: (Guatemala City only).
September 15: Independence Day.

October 12: Discovery of America.
October 20: Revolution Day.
November 1: All Saints.
Dec. 24: Christmas Eve; from noon.
Dec. 25: Christmas Day.
Dec. 31 (from noon).

June 30, October 12 and Christmas Eve are not business holidays.

Although specific dates are given for *fiestas* they often involve about a week of jollification beforehand.

Postal Information Urgent telegrams are charged double the ordinary rate. The cable companies are given under the towns. Sea mail from Europe takes about 40 days. Airmail from Great Britain takes from 4 to 6 days. Telephone calls to other countries can be made any day at any time. The international service is in the hands of Guatel, 7a Av. and 8a C. Zona 1. Guatemalan time is 6 hours behind G.M.T. **N.B.** The Lista de Correos charge US$0.06 per letter received. Correos y Telégrafos, 7a Av. 12 C Zona 1.

Guatemala has suspended its consular services in Britain.

The **British** Consulate-General is at Vía 5, 4-50, Zona 4 (8th floor, above *Hotel Conquistador*). (Tel.: 61-329, 64-375). There is a Consular office at Bananera, the United Brands H.Q. on the Atlantic coast.

Other consulates and embassies' addresses are as follows: Canada, Vía 5, 4-50. Zona 4, Maya Building (same as British); France, 14 C. 5-52, Zona 9; Spain, 6 C. 6-48, Zona 9; Italy, 20 C. 6-51, Zona 10; West Germany, Avenida La Reforma 14-70, Zona 9 (13th floor); U.S.A., Avenida La Reforma 1-01, Zona 10: Mexico, 14 C. 6-12, Zona 1 (5th floor Valenzuela Building); El Salvador, 3 C. 6-09, Zona 9; Honduras, 12 C. 6-14, Zona 9; Nicaragua, 5 C. 4-24, Zona 9; Costa Rica, 24 C. 16-09, Zona 10; Panama, 8 C. 11-13, Zona 1; Colombia, 7 Av. 15-13, Zona 1 (5th floor Ejecutivo Building); South Africa, Consul-General, 10 Av. 30-57, Zona 5.

American Express Agents Guatemala City: Clark Tours, Edf. El Triángulo, Calle Mariscal Cruz and Avenida 7, Zona 4. Tel.: 60213/6.

(We are particularly grateful to the Instituto Guatemalteco de Turismo, to the indefatigable John Streather, and to many travellers, including Sally Boggs and friends (USA), Alan Caplan (Bala Cynwyd, Pennsylvania), and others whose names will be found at the end of the general Central America section.

BELIZE

The name Belize was adopted in June 1973 for the territory previously known as British Honduras.

BELIZE is unique as the last remaining British territory on the American mainland. It borders Mexico and Guatemala, and has an area of about 8,900 square miles, including numerous small islands. Its greatest length (N-S) is 174 miles and its greatest width (E-W) is 68 miles. Forests occupy some 65% of the area and a further substantial proportion is coastal swamp.

The coast lands are low and swampy with much mangrove in evidence, many salt and fresh water lagoons and some sandy beaches. In the north the land is low and flat, but in the south-west there is a heavily forested mountain massif with a general elevation of between 2,000 and 3,000 ft. In the eastern part are the Maya Mountains, not yet wholly explored, and the Cockscomb Range which rises to a height of 3,681 ft. at Victoria Peak. To the west are some 250 square miles of the Mountain Pine Ridge, with large open spaces and some of the best scenery in the country.

Off the coast the sea is generally shallow, access for shipping is difficult, and vessels of any size are obliged to anchor a mile or so offshore. From 10 to 40 miles off the coast an almost continuous line of reefs and "cays" (meaning islands, pronounced "keys") provides shelter from the Caribbean and forms the longest coral reef in the Western Hemisphere. Most of the cays are quite tiny, and only a few are inhabited, but some have been developed as tourist resorts. Many have beautiful sandy beaches with clear, clean water, where swimming and diving are excellent.

The most fertile areas of the country are in the northern foothills of the Maya Mountains: citrus fruit is grown in the Stann Creek valley, while in the valley of the Mopan, or upper Belize river, cattle raising and mixed farming are successful. The northern area of the country has long proved suitable for sugar cane production. In the south bananas and mangoes are cultivated; the lower valley of the Belize river is a rice-growing area as well as being used for mixed farming and citrus cultivation.

Climate Belize is fortunate in this respect. For part of the year, trade winds blowing inshore off the Caribbean keep the temperatures down to a tolerable level. Shade temperature is not often over 90°F even in the hotter months of February to May. Inland, in the W, day temperatures are higher than 100°F, but the nights are cooler. Between November and February there are cold spells during which the temperature at Belize City may fall to 55°F.

There are sharp annual variations of rainfall—there is even an occasional drought—but the average at Belize City is 65″, with about 50″

in the N and a great increase to 170″ in the S. An abundant rainfall, coupled with high temperatures, accounts for the fact that 90% of the land is forested. Hurricanes can threaten the country from June to November, but do not occur frequently; there have been only three in the past quarter-century. An efficient warning system has been established and there are hurrican shelters in most towns and large villages.

The **population** is estimated at 140,000. Half of it is of mixed ancestry, the so-called "Creoles", a term widely used in the Caribbean. They predominate in Belize City and along the coast, and on the navigable rivers. About 17% of the population are Indians, mostly Mayas, who predominate in the north between the Hondo and New rivers and in the extreme south and west. About 10% of the population are Black Caribs, an indigenous people with a distinct language, found in the villages and towns along the southern coast. Another 10% are of unmixed European ancestry (the majority Mennonites) and a rapidly growing group of North Americans. The rest are Arabs (mostly Lebanese), Chinese (Cantonese), the descendants of indentured labourers from India, and political and economic refugees from the neighbouring republics and their descendants. Birth rate (1964), 44.3 per 1,000; death rate, 7.1; annual population growth, 2.8%; adult literacy 90%. Free elementary education is available to all, and all the towns have secondary schools.
About 75% speak fluent but mostly "Creole" English. Many speak fluent Spanish, though it is the mother tongue for only 15%. About 30% are bilingual, and 10% trilingual. Spanish is widely spoken in the northern and western areas.

The most striking thing about the country is its emptiness: the population density is about 15 people per square mile, but since half the population live in the towns rural population density is very low. It is only in relation to the territory's history that this phenomenon becomes understandable.

Deep in the forests of the centre and S are many ruins of the Old Mayan empire which flourished here and in neighbouring Guatemala from the 4th to the 9th century and then somewhat mysteriously emigrated to Yucatán. It has been estimated that the population then was ten times what it is now, but this is guesswork.
The first settlers were Englishmen and their black slaves from Jamaica who came about 1640 to cut logwood, then the source of textile dyes. These wood-cutters were raided from time to time by the Spaniards and driven out, but they returned after each raid. The British Government made no claim to the territory but tried to secure the protection of the wood-cutters by treaties with Spain. Even after 1798, when a strong Spanish force was decisively beaten off at St. George's Cay, the British Government still failed to claim the territory, though the settlers maintained that it had now become British by conquest.
When they achieved independence from Spain in 1821, both Guatemala and Mexico laid claim to sovereignty over Belize as successors to Spain, but these claims were rejected by Britain. Long before 1821, in defiance of Spain, the British settlers had established themselves as far south as the river Sarstoon, the present southern boundary. Independent Guatemala claimed that these settlers were trespassing and that Belize was no more than a province of the new republic. Protests and counter-protests led to no decision, but by the middle of the 19th century Guatemalan fears of aggression by the United States led to a *rapprochement* with Britain. In 1859, an Anglo-Guatemalan Convention was signed by which Guatemala recognised the boundaries of Belize while, by Article 7, the United Kingdon undertook to contribute to the cost of a road from Guatemala City to the sea "near the settlement of Belize".
Heartened by what is considered a final solution of the dispute, Great Britain declared Belize, still officially a settlement, a Colony in 1862, and a Crown Colony nine years later. Mexico, by treaty, renounced any claims it had on Belize in 1893.
But Guatemala, which in fact never ratified the 1859 agreement, renews its claims sporadically. The issue was complicated further by the granting of full internal self-government to Belize in 1964. The British Government is prepared to grant full independence to Belize, but Guatemala's claim to the territory and Belize's

dependence on the United Kingdom for defence make this rather difficult to bring about. The Belizean government has sought and received support from other Commonwealth countries as well as from the United Nations for its bid for untroubled independence. Talks between the U.K. and Guatemala were resumed in 1976 without apparent result.

But the emptiness of the land is due to economic rather than political reasons. The dyewood trade of the early days was killed by the synthetic dyes of the 19th century, but by that time, fortunately, the Victorian desire to "have one's feet under the mahogany" had opened out a fruitful new enterprise. The mahogany trade was at its height in the twenties. Since then there has been a sharp decline.

For some three centuries the only major activity had been forestry: timber felling and chicle bleeding, both of them seasonal and both of them wasting assets. Trade was mostly with the United States and since 1894 the currency had been linked by law with the dollar. There was very little agriculture. Food was mostly bought from the States. When trade with the States fell away this was no longer possible. Belize became much more dependent on Britain. The monetary link with the States was broken in 1949; when sterling was devalued, the local dollar was also devalued and linked to sterling at 4 to the £1; the Belizean dollar has now been re-linked to the US$ at B$2—US$1.

The central problem is how, in the face of tradition, to become self-sufficient in food: imports of food are still some 25% of the total imports. Necessity is forcing the people to grow food for themselves and this is gathering pace. One difficulty is that the territory is seriously under-populated, but three immigrant Mennonite communities have already increased farm production, and new legislation provides for the development of lands not utilized by private landowners.

Communications Formerly the only means of inland communication were the rivers, with sea links between the coastal towns and settlements. The Belize river can be navigated by light motor boats, with enclosed propellers, to near the Guatemalan border in most seasons of the year, but this route is no longer used commercially and is difficult because of the many rapids. The Honda river and the New river are both navigable for 100 miles or so, and small boats ply on them. Although boats continue to serve the sugar industry in the north, and to provide a tenuous coastwise link (motorized canoe) with Livingston and Santo Tomás in Guatemala, the use of water-borne transport is much diminished. Domestic coastwise traffic, except to the largest cays, is so much reduced that it is now insufficient to support regular scheduled services.

Some 400 miles of all-weather roads, with bus and passenger-and-goods truck services, connect the eight towns in the territory. There are road links with Chetumal, the Mexican border town, and the Guatemalan border town of Melchor de Mencos.

Heavy rain can often play havoc with the road system, making roads impassable, bridges unsafe and ferries unmanageable. Efforts are being made to improve the roads which are, taken as a whole, probably the worst in Central America, but external help is necessary and progress is slow. There are also some 33 miles of secondary roads, but these are not always open to the public, or even passable, and it is extremely difficult to get reliable information about them.

There are no railways in Belize.

Government

The territory is a British Crown Colony with internal self-government granted by the new constitution which came into effect on January 13, 1964. There is a ministerial system and Cabinet responsibility, Belize has a two-chamber National Assembly, a House of Representatives of 18 members elected by universal adult suffrage, and a

Senate of 8; 5 appointed by the advice of the Premier, 2 on the advice of the Leader of the opposition, 1 by the governor after consultation. The Cabinet consists of the Premier and other Ministers. The Governor retains some reserve powers for defence, foreign affairs, internal security and finance. General elections are held at intervals of not more than 5 years.

Premier: Mr. George Price (re-elected October 1974).

Belmopan is the new capital since the seat of Government was moved there from Belize City in August 1970. It is 50 miles inland to the west, near the junction of the Western Highway and the Hummingbird Highway to Stann Creek Town. It has a National Assembly building (which is open to the public), two blocks of government offices, police headquarters, a public works department, over 700 houses for civil servants and a market. Recent additions have been a cinema and a civic centre, but no non-civil-service residential area as yet. The Western Highway from Belize City is now good (one hour's drive), and an airfield has been completed. Hotel: *Circle A Lodgings,* Half Moon Street, B$15 s, with bath. There are two restaurants; economy-minded travellers can eat in the market, which is very clean. No cafés open Sundays.

Bank Barclays Bank International; Royal Bank of Canada.

Excursion 13 miles from Belmopan along a good road is the Blue Hole. This is a natural pool which lies about 100 ft. below the road. It can be reached by steps and swimming is possible.

Belize City Most people reach Belize City, the old capital and chief town, by air. One flies in over the Cays, and sees a somewhat small town, compact and surrounded by mangrove swamp. Most of the houses are built of wood, with galvanized iron roofs; they stand for the most part on piles about seven feet above the ground, which is often swampy and flooded. Ground-floor rooms are used as kitchens, or for storage. There is no sewerage except by septic tank and drainage to the sea; the drains are open and very smelly. Water is laid on for the hospitals and for *Fort George Hotel,* but most people get theirs by catchment. In hotels there is usually water only at night. For the tropics the climate is both cool and healthy. Humidity is high, but the summer heat is tempered by the NE trades. The population—42,000—is about a third of the total population. The African strain predominates. The Anglican Cathedral and Government House nearby are interesting; both were built in the early 19th century. In the days before the foundation of the Crown Colony the kings of the Mosquito Coast were crowned in the Cathedral.

Coming in by sea, after passing the barrier reef, Belize City is approached by a narrow tortuous channel. This and the chain of mangrove cays give shelter to what would otherwise be an open roadstead. Vessels anchor from one to four miles off-shore according to their draught.

Belize is the nearest adequate port to the State of Quintana Roo (Mexico), and re-exports mahogany from that area.

Note Hurricane Hattie swept a 10-ft. tidal wave into the town on October 31, 1961, and caused much damage and loss of life. Hattieville, 16 miles from Belize City on the road to Cayo, originally a temporary settlement for the homeless after the hurricane, still has from 2,000 to 3,000 people.

Hotels *Fort George Hotel,* has much the same tariff as luxury Caribbean hotels, but the amenities are less good; rooms are air-conditioned, B$66 s. Non-residents may use the swimming pool for B$1. Other hotels: *Bellevue,* B$78 for two, including

2 meals, a/c, and private bath; *Bliss,* B$35 d, also a/c and private bath; *Hilltown,* B$13 d, good value and friendly, recommended; *Vinat's,* B$5 each, pleasant; *Belcove,* 9 Regent Street, recommended, B$10 s, B$14 d, private bathrooms available at extra cost; *Handyside,* B$25 d, with bar and restaurant; *El Centro,* Bishop St., B$12-18 s; *Mallorca,* Albert St., B$12 s; *Nu Lodge Inn,* West St., B$12 s; *Windsor,* Handyside St., B$18 s; *Fendes Inn,* in same street, B$9 s; *Jane's,* Barrack Rd., B$12 s; *Plaza House,* B$16 d; *Mopan,* in historic house, B$12 s, B$16 d, very clean; *Golden Dragon,* B$18 s, with bath and a/c; *Crossroads,* B$20 d; *Mississippi Lodge,* new, just outside town, B$15 s; *Riverview,* basic, B$5 s; *Palms Motel* (2 miles along Western Highway), B$15 s; *Sunshine Home,* B$4 s, no electricity; *Posada Tropicana,* 55 Eve St., B$5-11 s, or B$3.70 each in dormitory, safe and recommended, not least for its cuisine, also you can leave luggage there but it tends to be rather crowded; *Minerva,* B$6.50 s; *Hotel Havana,* B$5 s, basic, rather noisy. A good boarding house is owned by the Misses Gabourel (B$16 and no food). *Mrs. Haylock's Boarding House,* 57 Eve Street, B$5 s, has been recommended, very friendly. *Mrs. Griffiths' Guest House,* also recommended, B$12 d; *Anita's,* near bus station for Corozal, B$5 s; *Clarke's,* Eve Street, B$6 s; *Freddie's,* also on Eve St., B$5 s; *Visitor's Home,* N. Front St., B$4 s; *Posada Mexicana,* Freetown Rd., B$3 s, in a dubious area, but friendly; *Trade Winds,* Douglas Jones St., B$5 s, restaurant. Many private houses let rooms for about B$10 d.

Restaurants   *Golden Dragon; Mom's Triangle,* US and Creole food, next to *Bliss Hotel; Hong Kong,* near police station, good, Chinese; *El Patio,* by bridge, for local food; *Caribbean,* also Chinese; *Katy's,* good and cheap, supper B$1; *Belicean Roast Chicken,* S end of swing bridge, cheap; *Sandy's,* cheap and popular. Lots of bars, some with juke boxes and poolrooms; worth a visit are *Chad's* and the *Bamboo Bay,* near the bridge. Try the local drink, anise and peppermint, known as "A and P"; also the powerful "Old Belizeno" rum.

Electricity   110/220 volts single phase, 60 cycles for domestic supply. There are frequent power cuts.

Airport   There is a 9-mile tarmac road to the Belize International Airport; collective taxi B$7 or hitchhike. There are flights to the Central American capitals, to Jamaica, Miami and New Orleans. Note that there is a municipal airstrip near the racecourse for local flights.

Banks   The Royal Bank of Canada; Barclays Bank International, both with some country branches. Atlantic Bank; Bank of Nova Scotia; Canadian Bank of Commerce. The *Bellevue Hotel* will change travellers' cheques. Difficulty sometimes experienced in changing Mexican pesos.

Baron Bliss Institute   Interesting Maya remains, and public library with UK newspapers.

Churches   There are a Methodist and a Presbyterian church.

Cinemas   Four cinemas with a daily change of film, B$0.40.

Consulates of the U.S.A., Guatemala, Mexico, Honduras (20 Park St.), El Salvador (13 Eve St.), Norway and the Netherlands.

Transport   There are bus services to the main towns (see their names in text) and to Chetumal, Mexico (see page 861), on Mon., Wed. and Fri. Within the city the fare is B$0.25. Trucks are a cheaper mode of transport; enquire about them near the market.

Taxis within Belize, B$1 for one person; additional charge for each extra passenger. No meters. No tips necessary. Charges by arrangement beyond the town.

Warning   Take good care of your possessions or they will be stolen. Cars should only be left in guarded carparks (such as Majarrez in N Front St., B$10 a night). The city is not at all safe at night.

Car Hire   Land Rovers at about B$60 a day, at Belize.

Shipping   "Suyapa" plies to Puerto Cortés, Honduras (US$20 p.p.), from Belize with crowded accommodation and poor food. A cement-carrying vessel, the "Mirtha", does the same journey twice a week and takes a few passengers for US$10 each. "Maya Prince" (Mr. Westby, Tel.: 2034) plies to Punta Gorda (20 hours) at irregular intervals. Livingston (Guatemala) is reached from Punta Gorda in the extreme S of the territory, by chartered dories or by sailing boat.

International Telecommunications Telegraph, telephone, telex services, Cable & Wireless Ltd., Albert Cattouse Building, Regent Street.

Tourist Information Belize Government Tourist Board (old Government building, next to Court House), Regent Street, Belize, P.O. Box 325, Tel.: 3013, provides complete bus schedule as well as list of hotels and their prices. Good maps of the country can be obtained from the second floor of the post office building. Closes 1230 on Sat.

Shopping Handicrafts, woodcarvings, straw and tortoiseshell items are all good buys,. Try Vogue (Front and Queen Streets); National Craft Centre, 13 Vernon Street; Cottage Industries, 26 Albert Street. There are two good English-language bookshops.

Fishing The rivers abound with tarpon and snoek. The sea provides game fish such as sailfish, marlin, wahoo, barracuda and tuna. On the flats, the most exciting fish for light tackle—the bone fish—are found in great abundance.

Skin Diving The shores are protected by the world's second largest barrier reef. Old wrecks and other underwater treasures are protected by law and cannot be removed. Spear fishing, as a sport, is discouraged as a means of conservation. The beautiful coral formation is a great attraction for scuba diving. Fishing boats (no motor) can be rented at flat rate of B$30 a day, for boat and crew, for trips to reef.

The Cays off the coast are most attractive. They are used by holiday campers from February to May and in August. From many of the holiday villas extend pens or "crawls" to protect the bather from sharks or barracudas, and to keep the water clean.

There are 212 square miles of Cays. St. George's Cay, 9 miles NE of Belize, was once the capital and was the scene of the battle in 1798 which established British possession. The larger ones are Turneffe Island and Ambergris, Caulker, and English Cays. Some have such picturesque names as Hut Cay, Blackadore Cay, Hen and Chicken, the Triangles, and Laughing Cay. Fishermen live on some; coconuts are grown on others, but many are uninhabited swamps. The smaller cays do not have much shade, so be careful if you go bathing on them. On Big Cay Bockel, at the southern end of the Turneffe group, are 3 "Caribbean Lodges" for fishermen and skin-divers, each holding 12 guests. Cay Chapel has a large hotel and an airstrip, and Cay Caulker several guest rooms and hotels. The "Mermaid" runs regular trips from the Customs Pier to Cay Caulker and Cay Chapel on Saturday and Monday, returning Friday and Sunday (B$5 s). Boats also leave from fishing co-operative up Belize river a few blocks from bridge (B$5 p.p.). "Elsa P." runs to San Pedro, Ambergris Cay. Connexions between Ambergris, Caulker and Chapel Cays are quite frequent though it may be harder to "hop" between the other cays, making it necessary to return to Belize City first. For cheap boats to the Cays ask around the market pier, or at Poppy's Bar on North Front St.

Ambergris Cay This island, with its village of San Pedro, is being rapidly developed as a tourist resort and is expensive. Hotels: *San Pedro Holiday Hotel*, B$50 including meals; *Coral Beach Hotel*, B$30 incl. meals; *Ambergris Lodge*, B$54 s; *Casa Solana*, B$45; *San Pedrano*, B$35; *El Pescador*, on Punta Arena beach, B$72 s, a/c; facilities for sailing, diving etc. There are several basic hotels for about B$4 each. At Coral Beach, the Forman, Gómez, González and Paz families provide rooms and meals for B$18 each. At Sea Breeze, the Paz and Núñez families offer the same accommodation at the same price. It is possible to camp on the beach. Two flights daily to and from Belize City, US$24 return.

Cay Caulker A lobster-fishing island, which is relatively unspoilt by tourism though there are always quite a number of tourists on the island. The *Don Pedro* sails daily from Belize and there are several other boats. (Ask at Poppy's Bar, on North Front St.)

Hotels: *Lone Jib Lodge*, B$10 s; *Favorite Inn*, B$5 s; *Shirley's Guest House*, B$10 s; *Hotel Martínez*, B$12 d, basic; *Hotel Edits*, B$10 d, good. Miss Riva has rooms for B$3, meals for B$2.50 (also for non-residents if booked in advance), highly recommended. Frank Bazzell and Tony Vega rent rooms, the latter for B$3; he also has space for camping, B$1, and can rent out camping gear. (Mr. Vega is an expert on the reef and arranges snorkelling trips.) Beach houses can also be rented for B$40-50 a week. Camping on the beach is made difficult by sandflies.

Restaurant *Birds Isle Club;* several bars.

Reef trips, B$4 each for 3 hours as long as there are 3 or more in a group. Ask for Crispin if you are interested in snorkelling. Lobster fishing and diving for conch is also possible.

Other Excursions Bargain with local drivers for a visit to Tikal ruins, in Guatemala (page 928). Mr. Richard Smith has his own station waggon. Flights to Tikal can be arranged through Maya Corporation, although there may be problems due to border difficulties. There is a bus from Belize to the Guatemalan border at 1000; this connects with one to Flores, though an hour's wait is necessary (see page 941 under Benque Viejo).

The Mayan remains of **Altun Ha,** 30 miles N of Belize City and 3 miles off the main road, are worth a visit (insect repellent necessary). You can hitch from Belize. Tourist Board provides a good booklet on the ruins for B$1.25, and a guide book for B$12. Entry B$5. The largest piece of worked Mayan jade ever found, a head of the Sun God weighing 9¾ pounds, was found here in 1968. It is now in the vaults of the Royal Bank of Canada in Belize City.

Camping There is a caravan site trailer park about 20 miles from Belize on the road to Orange Walk, B$2 per vehicle, regardless of number of passengers. In the city itself is the Caribbean Trailer Park, on Barracks Road. Camping on the beach is not allowed.

Two roads penetrate the country from Belize City: one to the N and another to the SW. The northern road (very rough) runs to (70 miles) the Orange Walk district, where about 17,000 Creoles, Mennonites and Mayan Indians get their living from timber, sugar planting, general agriculture and chicle bleeding. A district trade is done with Mexico. In the Orange Walk District is a large Old Mayan ceremonial site, **Nohochtunich;** enormous masonry slabs were used in a stairway up one of the pyramids. The population of **Orange Walk Town,** a bustling agricultural centre, is 5,500. A toll bridge (B$0.75) now spans the New River.

Hotels *Mi Amor,* B$10 s; *Tropical; La Favorita,* B$5 s; *Orbell Inn,* B$9 s; *Nuevo,* B$8 s; *Belize,* B$6 s. *Rocky's Restaurant,* only one, rather dear.

Banks Barclays Bank International; Royal Bank of Canada. Open on Sat. mornings.

For bus services on this northern road, see under Corozal, below. The road runs another 28 miles to Corozal (96 miles from Belize), and on for 8 miles to the Mexican frontier, where a bridge across the Río Hondo connects with a road from Chetumal in Quintana Roo, Mexico. Although paved, the road is fairly rough going. Travellers are warned that the border crossing into Mexico at Chetumal can take a lot of time; there are lengthy formalities both there and further into Mexico because Chetumal is a free port. It appears to be easier to cross the border if you do so in a Belizean taxi—if you wait on Chetumal's main street long enough, you'll find one. Driving time, Belize-frontier, 3½-4 hours. (Taxi, B$8 Corozal-border, B$17 Corozal-Chetumal.)

Corozal, with a population of over 5,000, is the second most important town in the Colony. It is open to the sea.

Hotels *Royal Caribbean,* B$15 s, a/c; *Hotel Capri,* B$5 p.p. Two motels: *Caribbean,* rooms B$15 d; *Tony's,* B$15 s. Both have restaurants. *Mom's Triangle* restaurant.

Banks Barclays Bank International; Bank of Nova Scotia; Royal Bank of Canada. There is now a bus service every day from Belize to Corozal by Venus Bus, leaving

1100, 4 hrs., B$3; and Mon., Wed. and Fri. to Chetumal, Mexico, by Batty-Bus, leaving 1000, arriving 1600 (B$4), and returning the next day. It is also possible to cross Belize from San Ignacio Town (see below) to Corozal by bus, US$6, 8 hours. Collectivo to Mexican border from Corozal, B$5; to Chetumal bus station, B$12.

The south-western road runs through savannah, pine ridge and high canopied forest to **San Ignacio Town** (capital of El Cayo District, 72 miles) and the Guatemalan frontier. About 60 miles along this road is Ontario Village and *Lili's Restaurant,* where you can get one of the best meals outside the capital, cooked by a European couple, the Schultzes. There is camping space and a trailer to rent. San Ignacio Town, known locally as Cayo, has a population of about 4,000. It stands at 200-250 feet and is a good base for excursions into the Mountain Pine Ridge, some 120 square miles of well-watered, undulating country rising to 3,000 feet.

Hotels *Golden Orange,* B$25 s, with private bath; *Central* and *Belmoral,* both US$7 s; *Pensión Farías,* B$3 s.

Bank Royal Bank of Canada.

The British Army's Holdfast camp is about 12 miles from the border; the soldiers are friendly and like to see a new face, so stop and say hello.

San Ignacio Town is on the eastern branch of the Old, or Belize river, known as the Macal, navigable almost to the Guatemalan frontier. The river journey, 121 miles from Belize and broken by many rapids, is done by light motor-boats with specially enclosed propellers in from 2 to 7 days, according to the season. It needs considerable ingenuity to negotiate the numerous "runs".

Blancaneaux Lodge, in the Mountain Pine Ridge reserve at 1,600 ft., has accommodation for 28 guests at B$70 s, AP. Airstrip and a campsite. Trips are organized for sightseeing, bird-watching, cave exploring (Mayan remains) and visiting the Xunantunich ruins and the Hidden Valley waterfall, among the world's highest—1,665 ft. (For bookings, write P.O. Box 652, Belize.)

Nine miles up-river from San Ignacio is **Benque Viejo,** near the Guatemalan frontier. A road connects the two towns. Population, 1,900. If you need a visa or a tourist card, there is a Guatemalan consul in Benque Viejo, though it is easier to get it in Belize City.

Hotels *Border,* B$3 each; *Roxi,* B$2.50 d, unsavoury; *Popular,* B$4 s. Meals at *Riverside Restaurant,* on main square, or at one of picturesque huts.

Four miles away, at **Xunantunich,** now free of heavy bush, there are Mayan remains, particularly a fine carved astronomical frieze from the roof façade of the spectacular main temple. Xunantunich is the eastern outpost of the group of Mayan ceremonial centres which flourished in the Petén district of Guatemala from the fourth to the ninth century or thereabouts. (A booklet on the area is available from the Tourist Board for B$0.65.) Xunantunich can be reached by walking along the Cayo road for about 10 minutes until you reach the landing stage for a dory; this will take you across the river (B$0.50 return). On the far side turn right for Xunantunich. If you take food you can stay at a palm hut at the ruins.

There are three buses from Belize to San Ignacio Town and Benque Viejo (BS$3, 4 hours), every day leaving at 0600, 1000 and 1300 and collectivos (shared taxis) from San Ignacio to Benque Viejo at B$1.50 a seat. To reach Guatemalan frontier (2½ miles, or 4 km.) walk or take a taxi, B$1.50. Free passage of border only weekdays, 0800-1200 and 1400-1700; at other times a fee is charged. (The bridge over the Río Mopán has been rebuilt.) On far side someone will carry the luggage to Melchor de Mencos (hotels, and money change possible—see page 927), where there is a landing strip with flights, for example, to Flores. There is also a road (very rough) on to Flores (buses from Melchor de Mencos at 0600 and 1500, 3½ hours, US$1.50). By catching an early bus it is possible to go to Tikal without first going to Flores; change at El Cruce (see page 927). Charge to El Cruce, US$1.25. It has been reported that direct Guatemala City-Belize City buses are operating; enquire in Belize.

Along the south-western road, at Belmopan. some 48 miles from Belize City, the 52-mile Hummingbird Highway branches off SE through beautiful jungle scenery to **Stann Creek**, some 105 miles from Belize City. Road surface bad: 2-2½ hours' drive from Belmopan. Stann Creek's population is over 7,000. In this, the most fertile area in the country, are grown citrus fruits, bananas, cassava, and general food crops. The town is on the seashore, and has an airstrip. Houses built of wood, on piles. Mosquitoes and sand flies are a nuisance.

Hotels   *Riverside* (B$10 d); *Pelican Beach,* new, outside town, on the beach, B$25 s, with private bath and a/c, has restaurant; *Gateway Motel,* B$16 s. Cheaper lodgings in *Hotel Catalina* (B$4 each) and in private homes (basic). *Riverside* has best restaurant. Unfurnished houses are rented out for B$40-60 a month.

Banks   Royal Bank of Canada; Barclays Bank International.

Local Holiday   Nov. 19 (Stann Creek and Toledo Districts only).

Bus from Belize City, at 1400 and 1500, B$2.80, or truck, B$2.

Placencia, a quiet little resort S of Stann Creek, reached by truck to Mango Creek (B$2), and a boat from there (B$4). It has a pleasant hotel (B$6 d).

Eighty miles down the coast by road from Stann Creek is **Punta Gorda**, port of the Toledo District. Its population of 2,500 is mostly Carib. Rainfall is exceptionally heavy: over 170 inches. The coast, which is some 10 feet above sea-level, is fringed with coconut palms. The main products are beans, rice, cattle and pigs.

Hotels   *Foster's Hotel,* B$4 s; *Mira Mar,* B$12 s, with private bath and a/c, has restaurant; *Isabel,* B$12 d, basic. The town has a cinema.

Bus from Belize, 14 hours, B$7.50, on Tuesday and Friday at 0700; returns on same days.

Boat   Connection (irregular) with Belize by motor vessel "Maya Prince" (about 20 hours). A motorized dory (canoe) leaves Punta Gorda on Wednesdays, returning Fridays (US$5) for Livingston (Guatemala) where there is a ferry to Puerto Barrios (US$0.50). There is no other regular transport of any kind between Punta Gorda and Guatemala, but a dory may be chartered for the trip at US$25.

There is a road inland to two villages in the foothills of the Maya mountains; **San Antonio** (21 miles), with Maya ruins of mainly scientific interest, from which a 6-mile branch runs to **San Pedro Columbia**, a Kekchi village. (Kekchi is a sub-tribe of Maya speaking a distinct language.) San Antonio is mostly Maya, has also some Kekchi. These villages are by far the most colourful and interesting places in Belize.The Maya and Kekchi women wear picturesque costumes. There are many religious celebrations, at their most intense (mixed with general gaiety) on San Luis Rey Day (August 5). No bus; contact Mr. Wagner for hire of pick-up van in Stann Creek, or get a ride in a truck from the market or rice co-operative's mill in Punta Gorda. There is no accommodation in San Antonio, but the police station might help.

Turn left, just after crossing the new bridge at San Pedro Columbia, for one mile to reach the Mayan remains of **Lubantum**, excavated by Cambridge University in 1970 and found to date from the 8th to 9th centuries A.D., late in the Mayan culture and therefore unique; according to latest reports, however, the site is fast reverting to jungle. Local food at a hut and swimming in a river nearby.

The Economy

Agriculture is by far the most important sector of the Belizean economy, employing more than half the population, and bringing in 75% of the country's total foreign-exchange earnings. In 1976 production of sugar, the main export commodity, stood at 65,000 tons. Citrus fruits are also a main export crop. The banana industry has recently been revived, and although it suffered a slight setback when Hurrican Fifi destroyed some of the plantations in 1974, this fruit is nevertheless expected to become a major export, perhaps even vying with sugar for first place. Maize, beans and rice are grown, and attempts are also being made to increase the cattle herd. The basic aim of the Government's agricultural policy is self-sufficiency, and it offers some price subsidies to encourage production of certain crops. Foreign funds and technical assistance are helping the country develop its hitherto untapped agricultural potential.

Forests cover about 65% of the country, and timber is extracted during the first six months of the year. Most of the forest workers are blacks, Creoles, or immigrant Waika Indians. Forest products were for a long time the country's most important export, but have now been superseded by sugar and citrus fruit.

Fish is the third largest export item, though some of the traditional grounds have been overfished and restrictions necessary for conservation are enforced.

The Government is encouraging the development of tourist facilities: in 1974 52,000 people visited the country. There is also some light industry.

Income per head is about US$500 year.

Foreign Trade (US$m)

			1971	1972	1973	1974	1975
Exports	..	..	15.8	15.2	26.2	49.1	64.8
Imports	..	..	29.3	34.6	36.2	54.5	92.8

Information for Visitors

How to get there   Belize is 5,700 miles from England, 660 miles W of Jamaica.

There is no regular sea passenger service (but see under Belize City). To get into the Territory from Guatemala without flying, the best way is by daily bus from Guatemala City *via* Flores and Tikal to Benque Viejo and Belize—the cost is about US$12—or by small boat from Livingston to Punta Gorda, about 3 hours, for US$5 per head. Avoid the trip if the sea is choppy. There is, however, a first-class airport, 9 miles from Belize, served by TAN Airlines, Taca International and Sahsa; there are daily flights from Miami and New Orleans. Also flights to Mexico City, Jamaica and Honduras and bus communication from Chetumal, Mexico.

Documents and Customs   British and US visitors who begin their journeys in their own countries and stay for not over 6 months do not need passports. Other nationalities do, but visas are not required from nationals of the Commonwealth, Western European countries, Mexico, Turkey, Tunisia and Uruguay. Citizens of other countries may find that even though they have bought an entry visa from a British Consulate elsewhere (US$2.50) it may be ignored! Those going to other countries after leaving Belize should get any necessary visas in their home country. Travellers should note that the border guards seem to have complete power to refuse entry to people whose looks they do not like, and recently there have been reports of "scruffy" people being refused entry; there seems to be a prejudice against backpacks. There have also been reports that tourists with less than US$500 on them have been refused entry. (These difficulties seem to be experienced particularly on the border with Mexico, and by men. Politeness will help iron them out.) Visas may be extended in Belize, though once again a show of funds may be requested. Drivers must report to a police station soon after entry to get a "circulation permit"—they must also have a B$10 a week insurance policy, which can be obtained at the Mexican border. A valid smallpox vaccination certificate is mandatory.

Clothing and articles for personal use are allowed in without payment of duty, but a deposit may be required to cover the amount of duty on typewriters, dictaphones, cameras and radios. The duty, if claimed, is refunded when the visitor leaves the country. Visitors can take in up to £10 in sterling notes and any amount of other currencies.

Departure tax of B$8 on leaving, but not for transit passengers who have spent less than 48 hours in the Territory, nor for children of under 12.

Language   English is the official language, but Spanish is also spoken, particularly in the north and west. Radio Belize devotes about 40 per cent of its air-time to the Spanish language. German is spoken by the Mennonite settlers.

Internal Transport   Traffic drives on the right. Hitch-hiking (without payment) is reported to be easy. The Belize stretch of the road to Mexico is in bad shape, although some improvements are being made, but the Belize-Belmopan road is good. Petrol costs about B$1.30 a gallon. In Belize there is a B$10 per week compulsory road insurance.

Maya Corporation flies three times daily from the municipal airstrip, Belize City to Ambergris Cay (B$12 s). It also has scheduled flights daily to each of the main towns and offers charter rates to all local airstrips of which there are 25. Chemicals Ltd. also have charters from Belize City to outlying districts.

Passenger transport between the main towns is by motor-car or bus, and goods are carried by motor trucks, which also carry passengers to many isolated destinations. Enquire at market place in Belize City. Coastwise transport is by motor vessels and sailing boats.

Health   Europeans leading a normal life and taking common precautions find the climate pleasant and healthy. Malaria is almost extinct, but cases do occur; prophylaxis is advisable. Inoculation against yellow fever and tetanus is advisable but not obligatory.

Climate   The NE trades blow throughout the summer, with heavy SE winds in October, and N winds which sometimes reduce the depth of water along the coast by 2 feet from November to February. The average temperature at Belize ranges from 76°F. in January, the coolest month, to 83°F. in August. The dry season is due about the end of February and the wet season about the end of May.

Official time is 6 hours behind G.M.T.

Clothing   The business dress for men is a plain cotton or poplin shirt with tie and trousers of some tropical weight material. Jackets are seldom worn except in the evening. Underwear should be lightweight cotton. A black or white dinner jacket is suitable for formal occasions. For women, cotton frocks or skirts and blouses, preferably washable, during the day, and hats and gloves for the most formal daytime occasions only. Evening wear is usually a cocktail dress or short evening dress. There are only limited laundry and dry-cleaning facilities.

The **monetary unit** is the Belizean dollar, stabilized at B$2 = US$1. Currency notes are issued in the denominations of 20, 10, 5, 2 and 1 dollars, and coinage of 50, 25, 10, 5 and 1 cent is in use. The American expressions Quarter (25c.), Dime (10c.) and Nickel (5c.) are common, although 25c. are sometimes referred to as a shilling. There is a B$0.50 charge for cashing travellers' cheques.

Shopping   Zinicote (a type of tree found only in Belize) wood carvings can be bought in Belize City.

Weights and measures   Imperial and U.S. standard weights and measures. The U.S. gallon is used for gasoline and motor oil.

UNIFORM WITH THIS VOLUME:

THE GULF HANDBOOK

Public Holidays

January 1: New Year's Day.	Sept. 10: National Day.
March 9: Baron Bliss Day.	Oct. 12: Pan American Day (celebrated
Good Friday and Saturday.	in Corozal and Orange Walk).
Easter Monday.	Nov. 14: Prince Charles' Birthday.
April 21: Queen's Birthday.	Nov. 19: Carib Settlement Day.
May 1: Labour Day.	(Stann Creek and Toledo.)
May 24: Commonwealth Day.	December 25 and 26.

Warning The whole territory seems to close down completely during Easter Week.

Telephone and Cable There is a direct-dialling system between the major towns and this should be extended to Mérida, Mexico City and Chetumal in the near future. Cable and Wireless, open 0730-2100 Mon.-Sat., 0800-1800 Suns. and holidays, has an international telephone, telegraph and telex service. To make an international call from Belize costs far less than from neighbouring countries.

Press Belize: "Belize Times"; "Amandala", "Beacon", "Reporter" (weekly). "The Belizean Tourister" (monthly) offers useful information for tourists.

The **Cost of Living** is high. There is an acute shortage of houses. A moderate unfurnished house in the capital rents from B$250 to B$400 a month, if it can be found. Moderate sized houses sell at B$25,000/35,000. Inclusive wages for a cook and maid run to B$40 a week, plus food. There are no free social, medical or other health services.

Retail shops are open from 0730-1130 and 1300-1600 Mondays to Saturdays with a half day from 1200 on Wednesdays.

Government and commercial office hours are 0800-1200 and 1300-1600 Mondays to Fridays and 0800-1230 on Saturdays.

Banks are open from 0800-1230 and 1300-1400, but 0830-1130 on Wednesdays and Saturdays.

EL SALVADOR

EL SALVADOR is the smallest, most densely populated, most industrialized and most integrated of the Central American republics. In El Salvador and Uruguay alone of the Latin American countries is the whole of the national territory occupied and developed, despite the fact that most of El Salvador is volcanic upland: the prolongation eastwards of the southern highlands of Guatemala. But its intermont basins are a good deal lower than those of Guatemala, rising to little more than 600 metres at the capital, San Salvador. Across this upland and surmounting it run two more or less parallel rows of volcanoes, 14 of which are over 900 metres. The highest are San Miguel (2,164 metres), San Vicente (2,209), Santa Ana (2,347), and San Salvador (1,943). One important result of this volcanic activity is that the highlands are covered with a deep layer of ash and lava which forms a porous soil ideal for coffee planting.

The total area of El Salvador is 21,200 square km. Guatemala is to the W, Honduras to the N and E, and the Pacific coastline to the S is 260 km. or so.

Lowlands lie to the N and S of the high backbone. S, on the 260 km. of Pacific coast, the lowlands of Guatemala are continued to a little E. of Acajutla; beyond are lava promontories till we reach another 30-km. belt of lowlands where the Río Lempa flows into the sea. The northern lowlands are in the wide depression along the course of the Río Lempa, buttressed S by the highlands of El Salvador, and N by the basalt cliffs edging the highlands of Honduras. After 160 km. the Lempa cuts through the southern uplands to reach the Pacific; the depression is prolonged SE till it reaches the Gulf of Fonseca.

The population of 4 million is far more homogenous than that of Guatemala. There is a reason for this: for a very long while El Salvador was neglected by the Spanish conquerors. It lay comparatively isolated from the main stream of conquest, midway between the offshoots sent S into Guatemala from Mexico City and N into Nicaragua from Panama, and it had neither the precious metals nor the agriculturally active Indians which acted as a magnet for the Spaniards. The small number of Spanish settlers intermarried with the Indians to form a group of mestizos herding cattle in the valley of the Lempa and growing subsistence crops in the highlands. Even when El Salvador seceded from Guatemala in 1841 to set up as an independent republic, the population was only a few hundred thousand. There were only about half a million people as late as 1879. But soon afterwards coffee was planted in the highlands; easy access to the coast made this crop competitively profitable. The population grew quickly and the prosperity of the coffee planters fertilized the whole economy. By 1930 the population had risen to 1,500,000, and it was 3,000,000 by 1966. The internal pressure of population has led to the occupation of all the available land. Coffee land is limited: the crop can

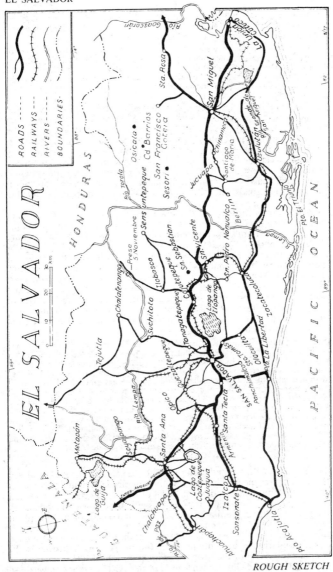

EL SALVADOR

ROADS
RAILWAYS
RIVERS
BOUNDARIES

ROUGH SKETCH

scarcely be grown below 600 metres, but cultivation has climbed the cones of volcanoes up to 1,200 metres and beyond. Several hundred thousand Salvadoreans have emigrated to neighbouring republics.

Of the total population only some 10% are purely Indian. Less than 10% are of unmixed white ancestry. The rest are mestizos. Birth rate: 46.1 per 1,000; death rate, 11.4; infant mortality, 78.7 per 1,000 live births. Annual growth factor, 3.5%; urban growth: 4.8%; and 50% live in the towns. Expectation of life at birth, 56 years. The 1971 census states that 26% of the population lives in concubinage and 68% of births are illegitimate.

Coffee is the basis of prosperity. It created the fine capital city of San Salvador, with a population today of over 500,000. It created the system of roads and railways. And it created the port works at La Unión/Cutuco, in the Gulf of Fonseca. Along the short Pacific coast line there are two other ports: La Libertad and Acajutla: all three have easy access by road, or by road and railway, to the interior. The roads are better than in most other Central American republics; the main system is paved and nearly all towns and villages can be reached by motor transport. The roads and railways are shown on the map and detailed in the text.

El Salvador is fortunate in one other respect: its temperatures are not excessively high. Climate depends on altitude. Along the coast and in the lowlands it is certainly hot and humid, but in the uplands the temperature varies from about 10° to 36°C in the shade: the average for San Salvador is 23°C with a range of only about 3°. March, April, May are the hottest months; December, January, February the coolest. There is one rainy season, from May to August, with only light rains for the rest of the year: the average is about 1,830 mm. Occasionally, during June and September, and, less often, in December and March, there is a spell of continuously rainy weather, the *temporal,* which may last from two or three days to as many weeks. The most pleasant months are those from November to January.

The Constitution in force is that of 1962. The Government is republican and composed of three separate and independent powers, but the military is very powerful. Legislation is by a Congress of 52 Deputies, one for each 25,000 citizens. The National Assembly meets ordinarily between June 1 and December 1 of each year, and extraordinarily when called by the Executive in Council of Ministers or by the Permanent Commission of the Assembly that functions when the latter is in recess. Executive power is vested in the President of the Republic, the Ministers and Under-Secretaries. The President is elected for a term of five years; no extension is permitted and he may not be elected for the following term. Voting is secret and women have the franchise. Extremist political parties are outlawed. The prevailing religion is Roman Catholicism. There is an archbishop in San Salvador and episcopal sees at Santa Ana, San Miguel, San Vicente and Santiago de María.

President: Gen. Carlos Humberto Romero (1977-82).

The People   With a population of 157 to the square km., El Salvador is the most densely peopled country on the American mainland. It is not yet very prosperous; the standard of living of the artisan class has risen but that of the agricultural labourer remains low, though with a tendency to improve. Health and sanitation outside the capital and some of the towns leave much to be desired, but a great effort is now being made to improve the water and sewage systems and to provide the basic necessities for good health. Malaria has been dominated. Housing is being improved in the capital and several of the towns. The illiteracy rate is 50%. Education is free if given by the Government, and obligatory. There are 2 universities,

one national and the other Catholic, and a National School for
Agriculture.

Cities and Towns

San Salvador, the capital, 37 km. from the port of La Libertad, is in an
intermont basin at 680 metres, on the Río Acelhuate in the Valle de las
Hamacas and with a ring of mountains round it. The population is about
500,000. it was founded by Pedro de Alvarado in 1525, but not in the
valley where it now stands. The area is volcanic; the city was destroyed by
earthquake in 1854, and that explains why no trace of its colonial days
can now be found. It is a modern city, its architecture conditioned by its
liability to seismic shocks. The climate is semi-tropical and healthy, the
water supply pure and abundant. (Average temperature, 23°C; average
rainfall, 1,830 mm.) Days are often hot, but the temperature drops in the
late afternoon and nights are always pleasantly mild. Since it is in a
hollow, the city has a smog problem, caused mainly by traffic pollution.

Four broad streets meet at the centre: the Av. Cuscatlán and its
continuation the Av. España run S to N, Calle Delgado and its
continuation Calle Arce from E to W. The city is laid out like a chess
board and this pattern is kept throughout: the avenidas, that is, running
N to S and the calles E to W. The even-numbered avenidas are E of the
central avenidas, odd numbers W; N of the central calles they are dubbed
Norte; S of the central calles Sur. The even-numbered calles are S of the
two central calles, the odd numbers N. E of the central avenidas they are
dubbed Oriente, W of the central avenidas Poniente. It takes a little time
to get used to this.

Nearly all the more important buildings are near the intersection. On
the E side of Av. Cuscatlán, back before the intersection, is Plaza
Barrios, the heart of the city. A fine equestrian statue looks W towards
the Renaissance-style National Palace, where the National Assembly
meets. To the N is the new, modern cathedral; to the W is a small park.
To the E of Plaza Barrios, on Calle Delgado, is the National Theatre
(which early in 1977 was closed for repairs). If we walk along 2a Calle
Oriente we come, on the right to the Parque Libertad; in its centre is a
flamboyant monument to Liberty looking E towards the rebuilt Church
of El Rosario where José Matías Delgado, father of the independence
movement, lies buried. The Archbishop's Palace is next door. The big
building on the S side of the square is the Municipal Palace. Not far away
to the SE (on 10a Av. Sur) is another rebuilt church, La Merced, from
whose bell-tower went out Father Delgado's tocsin call to independence in
1811.

Opposite the Cathedral, across Calle Delgado, is the General Post
Office; across Calle Delgado, opposite the theatre, is Plaza Morazán,
with a monument to General Morazán, and beyond it the Nuevo Mundo
hotel. Calle Arce runs W to the Hospital Rosales, in its own gardens. (SW
of the Hospital, along Av. Roosevelt, is the National Stadium.) On the
way to the Hospital, if you turn S opposite the great church of El Sagrado
Corazón de Jesús, you come after one block to Parque Bolívar, with the
Jail to the W of it, the National Printing Works to the S, and the
Department of Health to the N.

At the edge of the city (to the N along Avenida España and W along 9a Calle
Poniente) is the Campo de Marte, ı large and popular park with tennis courts.

During Holy Week and the fortnight preceding August 6, is held the Fiesta of the Saviour, ranging from religious ceremonies to gay festivities which attract people from all over the country and from neighbouring republics. As a climax colourful floats wind up the Campo de Marte. On August 5, an ancient image of the Saviour is borne before a large procession; there are church services on the 6th, Feast of the Transfiguration. On Dec. 12, Day of the Indian, there are processions of children and young people honouring the Virgin of Guadalupe in El Salvador.

Hotels *El Salvador Sheraton,* 89 Av. Norte on the slopes of a volcano on the outskirts, US$12-18 s, US$16-28 d; suites US$28-36; outdoor swimming pool. *Grand Hotel,* air-conditioned, corner Av. España and 1a Calle Oriente, US$10 s, US$13 d. *Escalón Apartments,* Paseo Escalón at Calle 71, highly recommended, US$8 full board or US$5 room only, very friendly. *Hotel Fénix,* Calle 45 Norte and La Poniente, US$10 d, free parking. The following 3 charge US$6 s, US$10 d: *Nuevo Mundo,* 1a Calle Oriente 217; *Morazán,* 1a Calle Oriente 17 (US$6 d for some rooms, comfortable, friendly), and *Internacional,* 8a Av.Sur 108. The last has rooms without bath for about US$2 each. Opposite the *Internacional* is the *Panamericano,* which has rooms for US$2, meals for US$1 and parking space. *Motel El Patio,* close to *Hotel El Salvador,* charges US$6 d, but has no hot water. *Hotel Terraza,* just off Paseo Escalón, near Calle 85, good and dear (US$18 d). *Hotel León,* Calle Delgado, US$2 each; *Hotel Anguilla,* Paseo Independencia, opposite cinema, US$1.20 d for room without window (US$2 with); *La Libertad,* US$5 d, Calle Castillo, nr. station. Boarding houses are: *Parker House,* 17a Calle Oriente 217 (US$12 s, with meals, US$10 d, without meals); *Casa Clark,* 7a Calle Oriente 144 (without bath and with meals, US$8 s); *American Guest House,* US$5 s, without bath, US$6 with; and *Austria Guest House,* in front of *El Salvador Sheraton,* small and quiet with family atmosphere, US$14 d; *Family Guest House,* US$3 s, US$5, with bath. *Oberholzer Guest House,* 9 Av. Norte and 5 Calle Poniente, US$5 or US$6 with bath; *Hospedaje Sonsonate,* US$1.60 each; *Imperial,* Calle Concepción 659, friendly, serves good meals and has car park, US$2 s, US$4 with bath. The hard up can try *Colonial* boarding house, next to Ramírez bus station, 6a Av. Sur, US$1.20 s, after bargaining; or *Barletta* boarding house, 8 Av. Sur 129, US$1.80 s, clean and quiet; *Bruno Hotel* (1 Calle Oriente, between 8 and 10 Av.) at Tica bus terminal, is US$2 s or US$3 s, with private bath; its annexe is US$1.60 each, good value though noisy; *Hotel Custodio,* 10a Av. Sur 109, also near Tica bus terminal, US$3.20 d, clean and friendly but noisy; *Hotel San Carlos,* again near Tica terminal, US$2 p.p., good; in same area: *Casa de Huéspedes Moderno,* 8a Av. Sur 125, US$1 after bargaining, basic. *Hotel Roosevelt,* US$2 p.p., without meals, US$4 with; *Hotel Lita,* US$1 s; *Lucedencia,* Calle Arce and 9 Av. Norte, US$2 d, basic; *Hotel Prat,* near market, US$0.75; *Hospedaje Yucatán,* US$1 s, excellent restaurant downstairs. Prices are without meals unless otherwise stated. Hotel tax: 10%.

Motel *Boulevard,* US$3 p.p. with shower, very clean, with parking, 2 km. from centre, but good bus service.

Restaurants At hotels. *Siete Mares,* Bvd. Hipódromo, Colonia San Benito; *La Fonda,* Paseo Escalón y 85 Av. Norte; *El Greco,* Paseo General Escalón, Colonia Escalón; *Romano,* Av. Roosevelt, 45 y 47 Av. Norte. *Chez Balta,* Av. Roosevelt 3104; *China Palace,* Av. Roosevelt 2605; *Monterrey,* Planes de Renderos (7 km. outside); *La Carreta,* 45 Av. Sur 116; *El Coche Rojo,* Calle Santa Tecla km. 4: *Royal,* 8a Av. Norte 342. Others are *La Parrilla; El Deportivo; El Casino; Rudi's El Café Don Pedro* (drive-in in Av. Roosevelt); *El Chalet suizo,* Av. Roosevelt with 53 Av.; *Hardees Hamburgers* on Bvd. las Héroes; also a branch of MacDonalds; *Cuatro por Uno; La Escondida; El Tucán; El Perico Camelón. Hamburger House; Malibú; La Chusita. Comedor Izalqueño,* corner of 6 Av. Norte and 7 Calle Oriente, good, cheap meals. *Cafeteria Florida,* 5a Calle Poniente 149, good cheap vegetarian meals. Try some of the delicious and very popular *Pupusas,* native food of El Salvador. They are particularly good at a cave restaurant in Puerta del Diablo. The food market, one of the biggest and cleanest in Latin America, has many stalls selling cheap food. *Pops,* near *Bruno Hotel* on 1 Calle Poniente, is a good ice-cream parlour.

Tips at hotels and restaurants: 10%, but 15% for small bills. Nothing for taximen except when hired for the day; airport/railway porters US$0.20 a bag; haircut, US$0.20.

Electric Current 110 volts, 60 cycles, A.C. Special transformer plugs not needed.

Clubs Club Salvadoreño, admits foreigners, owns a fine Country Club on Ilopango Lake called Corinto (with a golf course), and has a seaside branch near La Libertad, much frequented during the dry season, November to May. The Automobile Club of El Salvador has a chalet for bathing at La Libertad. International Rotary; Lions; British Club (7a Calle Poniente 3804, Colonia Escalón. Tel.: 234273), for the British colony of about 200. (Temporary visitors' cards if you apply to the Bank of London and South America.) Club Deportivo Internacional (Calle Santa Tecla), The Country Club Campestre (Paseo Escalón), admits foreigners with cards only. Club Náutico, at the Estero of Jaltepeque, famous for its mud boat races.

Night Clubs The Club Salvadore no (for members and guests only). Gran Mirador, in the hills; dinner and dance, Friday and Saturday, Chalo's, in the hills; Deportivo (members and guests only); Cocktail Lounge; El Cisne; La Llave.

Complaints Director General of Police, 6a Calle Oriente. Tel.: 216605.

Amusements many cinemas, with Cinerama at the Grand Majestic. Or ballet and plays at the National Theatre of Fine Arts, and music or plays at the Cámara Theatre. There are three juke box dance halls: El Hipopótamo, El Sapo, and La Rana, and more dancing at the night-clubs and Juke Boxes á Go-Go. There's bowling at Bolerama Jardín and Club Salvadoreño, and mini-golfing at *Hotel El Salvador Sheraton*. Kermesses are held pretty nearly every Sunday. Football is played at the Stadium on Sunday and some week nights. There's basketball, tennis, international swimming, fishing, target shooting, wrestling, boxing and boat and sailing boat races, but in private clubs only. Good free entertainment takes place between 2200 and 0200 on 2 Av. N. and 3 Calle O. where professional mariachis sing and play for prospective customers. Some excellent performers!

Museum Museo Nacional David J. Guzmán, on the outskirts of the city, has a small but good archaeological exhibition.

Airport At Ilopango, 13 km. away. There is a sales tax of 10% on all air tickets bought in or outside El Salvador for all journeys beginning in that country. No internal air lines but charter flights are easily arranged. Bus No. 29 goes to the airport, US$0.10; Taxi, US$1.60.

Rail Salvador Railway Co.: W to Santa Ana, Sonsonate and Acajutla. A steam train to Sonsonate runs for special tourist groups. International Railway of C.A.: E to Cojutepeque, San Vicente, Usulután, Zacatecoluca, San Miguel, and La Unión (US$1.60); W to Santa Ana (*via* Lemoa Valley) and to Ahuachapán, Guatemala and Puerto Barrios. Trains are very slow (it takes 2 days to get to Guatemala City, stopping overnight in Zacapa) and passenger accommodation is primitive, but the scenery is rewarding.

Long Distance Buses Central bus terminal, down an alleyway off Boulevard Venezuela, opposite No. 2963. Most international buses pass through if not start from here. About 5 buses a day (various companies) to Guatemala City (5 hours). Leave at 0800. Single, US$5; return, US$8. By car to Guatemala City takes 4 hours. Ticabus (1 Calle Oriente 531) also provides international services between the five Central American capitals and to David and Panama City; the cost of tickets is US$5 to Guatemala City and Tegucigalpa, US$12 to Managua direct, US$14 to Managua *via* Tegucigalpa, US$18 to San José, and US$30.50 to Panama City. The service to Tegucigalpa leaves at 0600. Mermex (6 Av. Sur 333), Sirca and Futuro-Express (13 Av. Sur 409) also go to Guatemala and are generally thought to be better than Tica-bus. The latter will collect you from your hotel. One bus a day to Puerto Barrios (Guatemala) with Rutas del Atlántico from central terminal. For those prepared to put up with inconvenience, the cost of the trip to Managua can be halved by taking a local bus to the Honduran border, another one across to the Nicaraguan border and a third from there to Managua. Good bus services to other main cities: to San Miguel every half hour and to La Unión five times a day (for ferry to Nicaragua).

Local Buses Flat fare of US$0.10.

Taxis Plenty, but no meters. Fares: from Ilopango Airport, US$1.60; from centre to outskirts or *Hotel El Salvador Sheraton,* US$1.20; central runs, US$0.60; by the hour, US$1.60; half-day, US$6, per day, US$12. Double fare after dark. Taxis from Taxis Atayco (Tels.: 218870 and 216644) and Taxis Santa Fe (Tel.: 217500 and 215044). Self-drive cars cost US$6 to US$16 per day or US$40 to US$80 per week according to size of car plus a rate per km. of US$0.08.

Bank of London and South America Ltd., 2a Calle Oriente 215 and 2 agencies; Citibank, 1a Calle Poniente 609, and national banks. Open 0830-1130, 1430-1600; Sat. 0830-1100. Banks charge 1 colón for changing money and cheques; cashing travellers' cheques involves lengthy paperwork.

Tropical Radio Telegraph Co., Primera Calle Poniente No. 114. Tel.: 214821, 214822 and 216620.

Tourist Agents El Salvador Travel Service, 23 Av. Sur No. 201. Ibalaca Tours, Edificio La Reforma, 4a Calle Oriente.

National Tourist Committee Calle Rubén Darío 619. Tel.: 217445/214845. They give away a map of the country and city, but the Texaco and Esso maps (obtainable from their respective petrol stations) are more accurate. The office is very helpful. Also "Advice to Tour Guides", a recommended booklet. The best map of the country is obtainable from the Instituto Nacional de Geografía, Av. Juan Bertis, No. 59.

Immigration Department 25a Av. Norte 11-57. Tel.: 218387.

Bookshop Librería Cultural Salvadorena (owner, Kurt Wahn), Calle Delgado 117.

Churches American Episcopal Church of St. John, 43 Av. Norte 123 (Sunday morning at 0930, in English); American Union Church, Calle Lorena 4 (Sunday at 10.30, in English). Jewish Synagogue, 23a Av. Norte 215.

International Industrial Fair, held in November, every two years (even dates), in Calle Santa Tecla, near the Monument of the Revolution.

A good **sightseeing tour** of from 2 to 3 hours by car is along Av. Cuscutlán, past the Zoo (which though small, is quiet and attractive) and the Casa Presidencial and up to the new residential district in the mountain range of **Planes de Renderos**. This place, reached by bus 12 from the centre, is crowned by the beautiful Balboa Park. From the park a scenic road runs to the summit of Mount Chulul, from which the view, seen through the **Puerta del Diablo** (Devil's Door), is even better. The "Door" consists of two enormous vertical rocks which frame a magnificent view of the city. At the foot of Cerro Chulul is Panchimalco (see below). There are local buses (Nos. 12 and 17) to Puerta del Diablo about every hour.

Excursions can be made by road to Panchimalco and Lake Ilopango; to the crater of San Salvador volcano; and to the volcano of Izalco and the near-by Park of Atecosol, and Cerro Verde (see Sonsonate, page 958); to the garden park of Ichanmichen (see Zacatecoluca, page 957); to Lake Coatepeque (lunch at *Hotel del Lago*) and to Cerro Verde in 90 minutes. Another interesting trip is to the excavated site of San Andrés, on the estate of the same name, 32 km. west of San Salvador (see page 957). Any bus going W from the Terminal del Occidente will take you there. Buses from here also go to Costa del Sol, Sihuatehucán and Los Chorros (see page 892) where there are swimming pools. Buses from the Oriente terminal go to Quetzaltepeque, near which is La Toma, a popular inland resort which has a spring-fed swimming pool, to Amapulapa, where there are gardens and a swimming pool, and to Lake Apastepeque.

Panchimalco is 14½ km. S by a passable road. Around it live the Pancho Indians, pure-blooded descendants of the original Pipil tribes; they have retained more or less their old traditions and dress. Streets of low adobe houses thread their way amongst huge boulders at the foot of Cerro Chulul (rolled down the hill to terrify the Spaniards, according to local legend). A very fine Baroque colonial church with splendid woodcarvings in the interior and a bell incised with the cypher and titles of the Holy Roman Emperor Charles V. An ancient ceiba tree shades the market place. Bus No. 17 from San Salvador, every 45 minutes, US$0.20, 1½ hrs.

Lake Ilopango A 4-lane highway, the Ilopango Boulevard, runs E for 14½ km. from San Salvador to Ilopango Airport, quite near Lake Ilopango, 15 km. by 8, in the crater of an old volcano, 150 metres below the level of the capital and well worth a visit for its extraordinarily effective scenery. Pre-Conquest Indians used to propitiate the harvest gods by drowning four virgins here each year. A geological disturbance caused an island to rear out of the waters in 1880 and the water-level fell greatly, but the channel draining the lake has now become blocked and the waters have risen considerably. There are a number of other lakeside cafés and bathing clubs, some of which hire dug-outs by the hour. A bus, No. 15, marked Apulo, which leaves from Av. Cuscatlán, runs to the lake (*via* the airport), 70 minutes, US$0.14. The "Turicentro" camping site costs US$0.18 and is highly recommended. Showers and swimming facilities.

Santa Tecla, 13 km. W of the capital by the Inter-American Highway, is 240 metres higher and much cooler; a coffee-growing district. Population, 52,563. The huge crater of San Salvador volcano—1½ km. wide and 1 km. deep—can be reached from Santa Tecla or from Boquerón. Buses leave 3 Av. Norte, near the junction with Calle Rubén Darío, San Salvador, every ten minutes for Santa Tecla (US$0.12). There is a bus from there to Boquerón (US$0.30) and from there you must walk the last 1½ km. to the crater's peak. It is possible to walk round the crater, but is rather rough going and it can take 3-4 hours. The views are magnificent. The volcano is 1,930 metres high. The inner slopes of the crater are covered with trees. At the bottom is a smaller cone left by the eruption of 1917. Santa Tecla, also known as Nueva San Salvador, has a training school for factory technicians, set up with British funds and technical help. Bus No. 101 from San Salvador, US$0.12.

The National Museum, with Indian relics, is now in a new building off the road to Santa Tecla. The road to San Salvador volcano can be taken farther N, descending through extensive coffee plantations. Return to San Salvador *via* Nejapa, Apopa and Villa Delgado. At **Los Chorros,** in a natural gorge 6 km. W of Santa Tecla, there is a beautiful landscaping of 4 pools below some waterfalls. The first pool is shallow, and bathers can stand under the cascades, but there is glorious swimming in the other three. Visit at night for the unusual artificial lighting effects. Car park fee: US$0.40. Camping is allowed, US$1 for two people. Any bus to Santa Ana or Sonsonate will take you to Los Chorros, e.g. Durán buses leave from 4 Calle Poniente, near 11 Av. Sur—timetable rather erratic. Bus from Santa Tecla, US$0.08.

Just before Santa Tecla is reached, a branch road turns S for another 24 km. to

La Libertad, the second largest port of the Republic. Discharge is by lighter. Population 14,500. It is also a popular sea-side resort during the dry season, with good fishing and surf bathing, but watch out for undercurrents and sharks. The beaches are black volcanic sand, but the surf is reported to be magnificent. Those interested should go to the Restaurant Punta Roca. (The Automobile Club and the Club Salvadoreño have beach chalets.) Bus from San Salvador leaves from 4 Calle Poniente, 17 Av. Sur, US$0.30.

The Costa del Bálsamo (the Balsam Coast), with thick forests of tall balsam trees tapped for the gum, stretches between La Libertad and Acajutla. The balsam tree *(Myroxylon pereirue)*, a giant of the tropical forest, stands erect like a mast. It takes 25 years to mature and then yields about 4 kg. when tapped, usually between December and June. Vertical incisions are made in the bark; a torch is applied to the wound to encourage the flow of resin into bandages which, when saturated, are boiled. The extract is slowly cooked to eliminate water. The balsam tapper—usually an Indian of the Tunalá tribe—works on a sharing arrangement, getting half of what he gathers. The local Indians venerate the tree. The pain-relieving balsam was once a large export, avidly sought by pirates, but has now almost disappeared.

Shipping   Passenger: Italia. Cargo-passenger: French, Hamburg-Amerika, Holland America, Johnson, North German Lloyd, Marina Mercante Nicaraguense. Fortnightly fast cargo service (no passengers) of Central America Services to and from Europe.

Hotels   *El Faro,* US$4.80-6, basic; *Roca Linda,* US$6, primitive, but splendid position above sea and good meals (US$2.40 each); *Hospedaje Atlántida,* US$1.60 each. **Motel**   *Siboney,* nearby, good. *Bar Gringo* on the beach front lets rooms for US$2; so does the *Miramar* restaurant (US$2.40 negotiable); *pensión San Miguel,* US$2 s.

Excursions   To the large village of Jicalapa, on high rockland above the sea, for its magnificent festival on St. Ursula's day (October 21).

Eastern El Salvador

E to La Unión/Cutuco   There are three ways of reaching the port of La Unión/Cutuco on the Gulf of Fonseca from the capital: (i) by International Railways of Central America, 251 km. by a somewhat roundabout way through Cojutepeque, San Vicente, Zacatecoluca, Usulután and San Miguel (this is a slow journey but passes through spectacular countryside); (ii) by the fine paved Inter-American Highway, 185 km., through Cojutepeque, San Vicente, Cuscutlán Bridge and San Miguel; (iii) by a paved road, partly over the coastal highway, running through Santo Tomás de Aquino, Olocuilta, Zacatecoluca, and Usulután.
By Inter-American Highway, 185 km. Some 5 km. from the capital a dry-weather highway branches off N to Tonocatepeque, Suchitoto, and Chalatenango.

Tonocatepeque, 13 km. from the capital, is an attractive small town on the high plateau, in an agricultural setting but with a small weaving industry. A large ceiba tree stands in the main plaza. There has been some archaeological exploration of the town's original site, 5 km. away. The image of the old town's saint, Nicolas, often disappeared from his church and was always found under the ceiba tree: a preference finally shared by the townspeople.

Suchitoto is quite near the Lempa River, and **Chalatenango,** capital of its Department, some km. beyond. Chalatenango, 55 km. from San Salvador, is a quaint small town with an annual fair and fiesta on June 24. Population, 15,137. A track goes on into Honduras (now closed at frontier).

Continuing along the Inter-American Highway: beyond the railway crossing a short branch road leads off right to the W shores of Lake Ilopango. The first town is **Cojutepeque,** capital of Cuscatlán Department, 34 km. from San Salvador. Population 18,347. Lake Ilopango is to the SW. Good weekly market. The volcano of Cojutepeque is nearby. The town is famous for cigars, smoked sausages and tongues, and its annual fair on August 29 has fruits and sweets, saddlery, coloured saddle bags, leather goods, pottery and headwear on sale from neighbouring villages, and sisal hammocks, ropes, bags and hats from the small factories of Cacaopera (Dept. of Morazán).

Motel *Eden,* US$1.40 s. Bus No. 113 from the Oriente terminal in San Salvador runs to Cojutepeque.

Cerro de la Virgen, a conical hill near Cojutepeque, dominates Lake Ilopango and gives splendid views of wide valleys and tall mountains. Its shrine of Our Lady of Fátima draws many pilgrims. Lake Apastepeque, near the Inter-American Highway, is small but very picturesque. The Tourist Board has built a pier and bathing cabins. Hotel: *París.*

Excursion   From San Rafael Cedros, 6 km. E of Cojutepeque, a 16-km. paved road N to Ilobasco, has a branch road E to Sensuntepeque at about Km. 13. **Ilobasco** has 26,703 people, many of them workers in clay; its pottery is now mass-produced and has lost much of its charm. The area around, devoted to cattle, coffee, sugar and indigo, is exceptionally beautiful. Annual fair: September 29. An all-weather road leads from Ilobasco to the great dam and hydroelectric station of Cinco de Noviembre at the Chorrera del Guayabo, on the Lempa River. Bus to Cojutepeque.

Four km. further S along the Pan-American Highway at San Domingo (km. 44 from San Salvador) an unpaved road leads in 5 km. to **San Sebastián** where people prepare and weave cotton yarn into colourfully patterned hammocks and bedspreads. You can watch them weaving on astonishingly complex looms of wood and string, and can buy from the loom. The No. 110 bus from the Oriente terminal runs from San Salvador to San Sebastián. There are also buses from Cojutepeque.

Sensuntepeque, 35 km. E of Ilobasco, is an attractive small town at 900 metres, in the hills S of the Lempa valley. It is the capital of Cabañas Department, once a great source of indigo. Pottery and distilling are now the major industries. There are some amusing processions during its fair on December 4, the day of its patroness, Santa Bárbara. It can be reached from the Inter-American Highway from near San Vicente. Population: 30,000.

San Vicente, 61 km. from the capital (bus no. 116 from Oriente terminal) is a little SE of the Highway on the Río Alcahuapa, at the foot of Chinchontepec volcano, with very fine views of the Jiboa valley as it is approached. Population: 48,000. Its pride and gem is El Pilar, most original church in the country. It was here that the Indian chief, Anastasio Aquino, took the crown from the statue of San José and crowned himself King of the Nonualcos during the Indian rebellion of 1833. In its main square is the tempesque tree under which the city's foundation charter was drawn up. Carnival day: November 1.

Hotels   *Pensión Vicentina,* US$4. Better is *Casa Romero,* which is near the bridge but has no sign, so ask for directions; US$4 d; good meals for US$0.80.

Two km. E of the town is the Balneario Amapulapa, one of a number of recreational centres developed by the National Tourist Board. There are three pools at different levels in a wooded setting. Small entry and parking charges.

The Highway crosses the Río Lempa by the 411-metre-long Cuscatlán suspension bridge and goes on to

San Miguel, 142 km. from San Salvador, capital of its Department, founded in 1530 at the foot of the extinct volcanoes of San Miguel and Chinameca. It has some very good parks, a bare 18th century Cathedral, and the charming church of Chinameca with statues and fountains in its gardens. Some silver and gold are mined. It is an important distributing centre. Population, 112,600. Carnival day: November 27.

Hotels *Hispano-Americano,* US$4 s, with bath, air-conditioned; *Motel Milián* (pool), US$5 s, US$8 d. *Central,* US$1.60. English spoken. *San Luis,* US$1.20, clean and quiet. *Hospedaje Primavera,* US$1.20, clean.

Clubs International Rotary; Lions.

Products Coffee, sisal, cotton, cattle, cereals, milk products.

Bank of London & South America Ltd., 1a Av. Norte y 4a Calle Poniente. Open: 0830-1200, 1430-1800; Sat. 0830-1130.

From San Miguel a good paved road runs S to the Pacific Highway. Go S along it for 12 km., where a dirt road leads to Playa El Cuco, a pleasant long beach, a small motel 1 km. from the village. A climate that doesn't let you down. Another interesting excursion is to Sabanetas (10 km.) on the Honduran border (though the border is closed here). The road from San Miguel runs to Jocaitique (there is a bus) from where an unpaved road climbs into the mountains through pine forests. Accommodation at both Jocaitique and Sabanetas. Accessible only by private car from San Miguel are two places worth a visit: **Laguna de Alegría** which is in a crater of an extinct volcano and is fed by both hot and cold springs. Good swimming. To the N are the Indian ruins of **Quelapa.**

It is another 42 km. to the port of La Unión/Cutuco. Before it gets there the Inter-American Highway turns N for the Goascarán Bridge to Honduras.

To save time take the good Ruta Militar NE through (34 km.) Santa Rosa de Lima (15,770 people, gold and silver mines), to the Goascarán Bridge on the border with Honduras, 56 km. International buses go through, but a Salvadorean-registered car would probably not be allowed to cross the frontier though cars of any other registration can. Relations between El Salvador and Honduras have been severely restricted since the war of 1969.

La Unión/Cutuco, on the Gulf of Fonseca, is the only port in El Salvador except Acajutla at which ships can berth. Steamers drawing 8½ metres go alongside at Cutuco. Population, 22,500. The port handles half the country's trade. There is good fishing and swimming, but much mud during the rains. It is a holiday resort during the dry season.

Shipping Passenger line: Italia. Cargo-passenger: Hamburg-Amerika, Johnson, Marina Mercante Nicaragüense, North German Lloyd. Joint fast cargo vessels (no passengers) of Central America Services to and from Europe.

Ferry Motor-boat and barge services across the Gulf to Puerto Morazán, Corinto and particularly Potosí (Nicaragua). There is one ferry a day to Potosí, departure time depending on the tide. This ferry traffic is the only regular means of communication for Salvadorean citizens and goods with Nicaragua and Costa Rica since the Honduran frontier was closed to Salvadoreans in 1969. The ferry, 6 hours' passage—sometimes much longer if the tide is out—costs US$3 p.p., US$100 per car. If crossing by ferry, get your passport stamped at the migration office first.

Industry Flour mill; objects made from the shell of tortoises caught in the Gulf (but remember you can't bring them into the USA). Large export of cotton-seed cake.

Hotels *Centroamérica,* US$1.20 p.p., US$2.40 with fan, US$4 with a/c; *Hotel Miramar,* US$2 d, good; *Hospedaje Santa Marta,* basic, but friendly; *Hotel San Carlos,* opposite railway station, US$3 d, good meals available.

Restaurant *La Patia—fish.*

Rail To San Salvador. Through trains take 8-11 hours.

Bus to San Salvador, US$1.60, 9 hours. Bus to Honduran border leaves at 0700, US$1.

Excursion To El Tamarindo (bus US$0.25), a small but attractive fishing village with beautiful white beaches and good breakers. No accommodation, but you can rent a grass hut to sling your hammock for US$2.50 a week each. Also from La Unión the ruins of Los Llanitos can be visited.

The second road route, running through the southern cotton lands, is the Coastal Highway. The first place of any importance after leaving the capital is (13 km.) Santo Tomás de Aquino. The Indian ruins of Cushululitán, a short distance to N, are moderately interesting.

Beyond, a new road to the E runs S of Lake Ilopango to join the Inter-American Highway beyond Cojutepeque. The road rises to 1,000 metres.

Ten km. on from Santo Tomás is **Olocuilta,** an old city with a colourful market on Sunday under a great tree. Good church. (Both Santo Tomás and Olocuilta can be reached by bus no. 21 from San Salvador.) When our road joins the coastal highway, we go E across the Río Jiboa to

Zacatecoluca, capital of La Paz Department, 56 km. from San Salvador by road, 19 km. S of San Vicente by road or rail. José Simeón Cañas, who abolished slavery in Central America, was born here. Population, 56,400. Quite near are the small towns of San Pedro Nonualco and Santa María Ostuma (with a famous fiesta on February 2).

Near the town is the garden park of Ichanmichen ("the place of the little fish"). It is crossed by canals and decorated with pools: there is, in fact, an attractive swimming pool. It is very hot but there is plenty of shade.

Hotel   *América,* US$4.

Industries   Cigar factories, hand looms.

Both road and railway cross the wide Lempa River by the Puente de Oro (Golden Bridge) at San Marcos. A branch road (right) leads to tiny Puerto El Triunfo on the Bay of Jiquilisco, with a large shrimp-freezing plant. About 110 km. from the capital is

Usulután, capital of its Department, also on the railway. Population, 40,350.

Hotels   *Motel Usulután,* US$8 d; *Central,* US$3.

Road and rail continue some 45 km. to San Miguel (see page 955) where the road joins the Inter-American Highway to La Unión/Cutuco, but the coastal highway goes direct to La Unión/Cutuco.

Western El Salvador

The route from the capital S to the port of La Libertad has already been given. Both a paved road and the Salvador Railway connect San Salvador with Sonsonate and the port of Acajutla. The road goes W through Santa Tecla (see page 953) to Sonsonate, and then S to the port; 6 km. W of Santa Tecla on the main road is Los Chorros (see under Santa Tecla); 3½ km. beyond, the Inter-American Highway runs NW past Lake Coatepeque to Santa Ana. The railway from the capital, which has made a loop to the N of the road, also bifurcates: one branch paralleling the road, one going NW past the lake to Santa Ana.

Acajutla, Salvador's main port, serving the western and central areas, is 85 km. from San Salvador, 58 km. from Santa Ana. It handles about 40% of the coffee exports and is a popular sea-side resort (good surf riding) during the summer. Population: 15,635.

The old town has been rebuilt inland to make room for the new port, where vessels of 9-metres draught can dock at the mole. There is a modern cement factory, 2 oil refineries and a fertilizer and sulphuric acid plant. The Coastal Highway is 8 km. to the N.

Shipping Grace Line; joint service of Hamburg-Amerika Line and Nord-Deutscher Lloyd; fortnightly fast cargo service, no passengers, of the Central America Services to and from Europe.

Hotels *Miramar; California,* US$5. Good, cheap pensión at back of La Campana store.

The nearby beaches at El Espino, El Cuco, Jaltepeque and Barra de Santiago are recommended.

Sonsonate, 19 km. N on both road and railway to the capital (64 km.) produces sugar, tobacco, rice, tropical fruits, hides and balsam from the coast lands between Acajutla and La Libertad. An important market is held each Sunday. Sonsonate is in the chief cattle-raising region and is famous for its cream cheeses, milk and butter. Population: 48,200. It was founded in 1552. The beautiful El Pilar church is strongly reminiscent of the church of El Pilar in San Vicente. The Cathedral has many of the cupolas (the largest covered with white porcelain) which serve as a protection against earthquakes. The old church of San Antonio del Monte, just outside the city, draws pilgrims from afar. Capital to Sonsonate by bus, 90 minutes; by train, 4 hours.

Roads N to Santa Ana, 39 km.; NW to Ahuachapán, 40 km., and on to Guatemala (this is a poor road, at least as far as Ahuachapán, but passes through some spectacular scenery); S and W to the Guatemalan frontier points of La Hachadura and Ciudad Pedro de Alvarado at the bridge over the Río Paz: this is the fastest road link between San Salvador and Guatemala City. Many buses ply between La Hachadura and Sonsonate, US$0.60 to Ahuachapán, US$0.50, 4 hours.

Industries Cotton cloth; cigars; baskets.

Hotels *Sonsonate,* 6 Av. Norte with Calle Obispo Marroquín, US$3 s, with a/c, meals available, but seems a bit overpriced; *Hospedaje Taplán,* near bus station, US$1.20 d, basic; *Hotel del Viajero,* opposite bus station, US$2.40 d, very clean.

Restaurant Milkbar.

Clubs Casino Sonsonateco; International Rotary; Lions.

At the foot of Izalco volcano, close together, 8 km. from Sonsonate, are the ladino village of Dolores Izalco and the Indian village of **Asunción Izalco.** The latter has a notable church facing a large plaza at which splendid Indian ceremonies are held from August 8 to 15 and during the Feast of St. John the Baptist from June 17 to 24; the latter a strange mixture of devout Catholicism and certain distressing native rituals. (Horsemen gallop under a branch from which four live cocks are suspended, try to shear off their heads, and then use the dead cocks as weapons to unseat one another.) The strange community and solo dances in the plaza on Christmas Eve are particularly colourful. Near Izalco, on the slopes, is the spacious swimming pool of Atecozol, in the middle of a beautiful park with a restaurant. The park is shaded by huge mahogany trees, palms, aromatic balsam trees and "amates". There is a battlemented tower; a monument to Tlaloc, god of the rain; another to Atonatl, the Indian who, on this spot, shot the arrow which lamed the *Conquistador* Pedro de Alvarado; and a statue to the toad found jumping on the spot where water was found. Asunción Izalco and Izalco volcano are not directly connected by road. A paved road branches from the highway 14 km. from the turning for Asunción Izalco (about 22 km. from Sonsonate) and goes up towards Lake Coatepeque (see below); when you reach the summit, an all-weather road branches right for **Cerro Verde** with its fine views down into the Izalco crater. A camping ground and car park at 1,980 metres overlooks the crater. The main paved road goes on to the lakeshore. The magnificent (now open) *Hotel Montaña* (US$14 d) at the top of Cerro Verde was originally built so that the international set could watch Izalco in eruption; unfortunately, the eruptions stopped just as the hotel was completed and it was empty for years. Good food is provided at fairly reasonable prices. There is a US$0.25 charge for parking, but none for camping. There is a bus twice daily from Santa Ana to the top of Cerro Verde (US$2). The bus from Sonsonate to the turn-off for Cerro Verde costs US$0.30; from there it is a long walk though you may be lucky enough to hitch a lift.

Both the Inter-American Highway through Santa Tecla and the San Salvador Railway through Quezaltepeque run to Santa Ana.

There is an archaeological site at San Andrés, half-way between Santa Tecla and Coatepeque. Exhibits from it and from Tazumal are at the National Museum.

Some 13 km. short of Santa Ana a short branch road leads (left) to **Lake Coatepeque,** a favourite week-end resort with good sailing, swimming, and fishing near the foot of Santa Ana volcano. There are good hotels, restaurants, and lodging houses. The surroundings are exceptionally beautiful. (Local buses from Santa Ana; from the junction with the Inter-American Highway the bus costs US$0.16. Bus 201 from the capital.) Cerro Verde is easily reached in 90 minutes by good roads through impressive scenery.

Tourists are put up free in cabins with mattresses and showers at Balneario Los Obreros (a resort for workers). When you reach the lake shore from the rim of the crater follow the road a little. Permission to stay must be obtained from Sra. Avelar, Departmento de Bienestar, Ministerio de Trabajo, 2a Av. Norte, San Salvador. Restaurant and supervised swimming. Otherwise, water difficult to reach because of the number of weekend homes.

Hotels   *Hotel del Lago* (try the crab soup), US$10 d; *Casa Blanca,* US$1.20 s; *Lido,* US$4; *Costa Azul,* near telegraph office, US$2 s., pleasant, meals available.

Santa Ana, 55 km. from San Salvador and capital of its Department, is the second largest town in the country. The intermont basin in which it lies at 656 metres on the NE slopes of Santa Ana volcano is exceptionally fertile. Coffee is the great crop, with sugar-cane a good second. The city is the business centre of western El Salvador. There are some quite splendid buildings, particularly the classical Theatre, the neo-gothic cathedral, and several other churches, especially El Calvario, in Colonial style. It is famous for a delicious confection. Population: 170,300.

The border with Guatemala is 30 km. by paved road from Santa Ana. Buses leave from the *Pensión Lux* on the main square for Guatemala City, US$2, 4½ hours. Alternatively there are local buses to the border for US$0.30; they leave from the market. Bus 201 from the capital.

Hotels   *Casa Familiar Leiva,* near cathedral, US$2.40 each, good meals for about US$1-1.20; *Roosevelt,* US$2.50 p.p., good meals for US$1.60; *Florida,* room with bath, US$4, serves excellent meals for US$2; *Pensión Monterrey,* US$2.40 d, near bus station. Nearby, *Pensión Lux,* on main square.

Clubs   International Rotary; Lions.

Bank of London & South America, Ltd., Avenida Independencia. Open 0830-1200, 1430-1700; Sat. 0830-11.30.

Excursions   To Lake Coatepeque, 19 km. (bus to *Hotel del Lago*). A branch of the International Railways of Central America reaches Santa Ana from Soyapango junction and goes W through Chalchuapa to Ahuachapán. (Also a road to both.) **Chalchuapa,** 16 km. from Santa Ana, population 34,865, is at 640 metres. It was here that President Barrios of Guatemala was killed in battle. There is some good Colonial-style domestic building; the church of Santiago is particularly striking. See the small but picturesque lake; the very interesting church, almost the only one in El Salvador which shows strong indigenous influences, and the **Tazumal** ruin just E of Chalchuapa, built about A.D. 980 by the Pipil Indians but with its 14-step pyramid now, alas, restored in concrete. The site has been occupied since 5000 B.C. and in the simple museum are the artefacts found in the mud under the lake. There are very interesting bowls used for burning incense, intricately decorated with animal designs. The ruin, which is open 0900-1200 and 1300-1730, is free and only 5 minutes' walk from the main road. Minibuses from Santa Ana, 20 minutes, US$0.10.

Hotel at Chalchuapa   *Gloria*, US$5.

Ahuachapán, capital of its Department, is 35 km. from Santa Ana, at 753 metres. Population, 53,260. It is a quiet, small town with low and simple houses, but quite an important distribution centre. Coffee is the great product. Like many places in the area, it draws the mineral water for its bath-house from some hot springs near the falls of Malacatiupán, near-by. Power is from the falls of Atehuezián on the Río Molino, which cascades prettily down the mountain-side. (It is very difficult to find either set of falls as the locals do not know where they are and cannot give you directions.) See also the "ausoles"—geysers of boiling mud with plumes of steam and strong whiffs of sulphur, which are now being harnessed to produce electric power. A road runs NW through the treeless Llano del Espino, with its popular small lake, and across the Río Paz into Guatemala. There are two other small lakes amongst pines and cypresses in the high Apaneca mountain S of the city which are popular with tourists: Laguna Verde and Apaneca. Local buses run quite near both, leaving only a short but pleasant walk. Ahuachapán is 116 km. from the capital by rail, or you can take bus 202 from San Salvador.

The "ausoles" are truly interesting—an acre of ground which is warm to the touch. They pop up anywhere, in the road and in the middle of the football field. Women have not been slow in using hot water from a little stream to wash their clothes. A geothermal plant, depending on electricity generation from the ausoles, came into operation in July 1975 and further plants are being built; the geysers are being covered by drums and pipes and only the smallest will soon remain untouched. Take a taxi; it would be a long walk.

Hotel   *Astoria*, US$3.20 s; *La Ahuachapaneca* guest house, US$2.40; *Hospedaje San Juan*, US$0.80 each.

The North-West   The International Railways of Central America run due N from San Salvador to the Lempa River and then curve W to **Soyapango,** junction for the branch S to Santa Ana. From Soyapango the line continues N past Lake Güija to Metapán, and then W into Guatemala, where it connects with the Guatemalan trans-isthmus line at Zacapa.

Lake Güija, on the Guatemalan border, 16 km. by 8, is the most beautiful sheet of water in El Salvador, dotted with small islands, but it is not easy to reach. A new dam at the lake's outlet generates electricity for the western part of the country. **Metapán** (32 km. N of Santa Ana) is about 10 km. NE of the lake. Its baroque Cathedral is almost the only Colonial church which has survived in the country. The altarpieces have some very good silver work (the silver is from local mines) and the façade is splendid. There are many lime kilns and a huge cement plant.

Pensións   *Gallo de Oro*, US$2; *Ferrocarril*, US$1.60.

Economy

Agriculture is the dominant sector of the economy, accounting for 75% of export earnings as well as employing some 30% of the population. Coffee and cotton are the most important crops, but attempts have been made at diversification and now sugar and maize are becoming increasingly important as foreign exchange earners. Land ownership is unevenly distributed with a few wealthy families owning most of the land, while the majority of agricultural workers merely live at subsistence level. Inflation steepened sharply in 1974 to 21% as a result of the oil crisis, easing only slightly to 15.1% in 1975, falling to 5.3% in 1976, but rising sharply again by 14.8% in 1977.

With the expansion of the industrial sector in recent years, there has been a rapid growth in the middle and industrial working classes. El Salvador is probably the most highly industrialized of the Central American states; manufacturing industries account for about 17% of g.d.p. The most important industry is textiles; others include shoes, furniture, chemicals and fertilizers, pharmaceuticals, cosmetics, construction materials, cement (and asbestos cement), food and drink processing, rubber goods. A small quantity of petroleum products, including asphalt, is also produced. Exports of manufactured goods, mostly to other Central American countries, account for some 24% of foreign exchange earnings.

There are small deposits of various minerals: gold, silver, copper, iron ore, sulphur, mercury, lead, zinc, salt and lime. There is a gold and silver mine at San Cristóbal in the Department of Morazán. In July 1975 a geothermal power plant came into operation at Ahuachapán, with capacity of 30 Mw; it should save some US$7.5m. a year in fuel costs. The plant will be expanded by 60 Mw by 1978. Hydraulic resources are also being exploited as a means of generating power. In 1977 a new 270 Mw plant came into operation at Cerrón Grande and work is expected to start on a further plant at San Lorenzo; this has meant that thermal plants can be shut down, thus affording an even greater saving in oil import costs. Production of electrical energy is growing at 10% a year.

After the war of 1969, El Salvador not only lost the Honduran market, but also was cut off from Costa Rica and Nicaragua (except by sea) by Honduras' decision to close its section of the Inter-American Highway to Salvadorean goods. El Salvador therefore attempted to increase its exports to the rest of the world; to this end a new export development law was published in 1974 which offers generous incentives to exporters. The main importers of Salvadorean goods are the U.S.A., Western Germany, Guatemala and Japan.

Foreign Trade (US$m.)

		1972	1973	1974	1975	1976	1977
Exports f.o.b. ...	..	301.7	358.4	464.4	514.7	720.7	959.4
Imports c.i.f. ...	..	278.1	373.8	563.4	598.0	717.9	949.9

Information for Visitors

Warning Prices in El Salvador are sometimes quoted in U.S. dollars. You should make sure which currency is being used, for if you unwittingly pay in dollars instead of colones you will be paying two-and-a-half times too much.

How to get there The quickest route from England is by British Airways to Panama or Miami, and on by air to San Salvador by Taca or Pan Am. There is a Pan American service from New Orleans *via* Mérida and Guatemala (6 hours); from Houston and Dallas, *via* New Orleans or Mexico City; and from Los Angeles *via* Guatemala or Mexico City (10½ hours). From Mexico City 4 hours.

Taca (cargo and passengers) runs direct services between San Salvador and New Orleans daily (4 hours). Taca and Pan Am also have a daily service direct to all the capitals of Central America and a flight to Mexico City. American Airlines connect at Mexico City with both Pan American and Taca and so does the KLM London-Amsterdam-Montreal-Houston-Mexico service, leaving London at 1610, and reaching San Salvador at 1125 next day. Iberia has two flights a week between Madrid and El Salvador, stopping at Puerto Rico and San José.

Lacsa flies tri-weekly the route San José (Costa Rica)-San Salvador-Mexico City. There are services also by Lanica (Nicaraguan) airline.

A good sea route from England is by Royal Mail Lines or the PSNC (no passengers) to Cristóbal. (Agent for these lines at San Salvador: Messrs. Pierre Wolff, 6a Calle Oriente 233 (Altos), Apartado 933). Royal Netherlands Line, the Johnson Line, Royal Mail Lines, Hamburg America Line, N.G. Lloyd, and Marina Mercante Nicaragüense operate cargo/passenger services between North Sea ports and El Salvador.

Alternatively, and more cheaply, trains can be taken from New York to New Orleans, and a United Brands cargo boat on to Santo Tomás (Guatemala). Guatemalan Railways takes the passenger to San Salvador in 20 hours. This company also plies from New York and Philadelphia to Puerto Barrios; it also has a service from New Orleans to the Panama Canal, where trans-shipment is made to the ports of El Salvador. The Grace Line runs freighters (with limited passenger accommodation) from San Francisco and Los Angeles to El Salvador. From Nicaragua it is cheaper and quicker, if you don't want to see Honduras, to get to El Salvador on the Potosí-La Unión ferry.

N.B. There is a 10% tax on international air tickets bought in El Salvador.

Documents Necessary: a passport (not necessary for US citizens with proof of identity, nor for citizens of any country who have been issued with 90-day tourist cards, costing US$2, by airlines or Salvadorean consulates) and an international smallpox vaccination certificate less than 3 years old, or you may be vaccinated when you land. At the border a visa for 30 days is obligatory for many countries (cost US$0.80), but not for citizens of Western European, Latin American (but see below) or Commonwealth countries, or of Ethiopia, Egypt, Israel, Japan, Jordan, Lebanon, Malagasy, Morocco, Philippines, South Africa and Turkey. Businessmen doing business directly in the country must get an ordinary (non-immigrant) visa at a cost of US$1.60, and visit the Immigration Bureau (25a Av. Norte 11-57) within 48 hours of arrival and get a permit to stay for 30 days. It costs US$4. They must get an exit permit from the same place, at the same price, before they leave the country. Businessmen are sometimes assessed for income tax during their stay. Border officials are reported to be particularly friendly and helpful though border formalities tend to take a long time. There is an exit tax of US$0.40 and an airport tax of US$3. There are restrictions on entry by citizens of Belize, Cuba and Honduras.

Up to 200 kilogrammes of personal luggage is allowed in free of duty. Also allowed in free: 1 kg. of tobacco products, or 100 cigars or 400 cigarettes, and 2 bottles of liqueur. There are no restrictions on export or import of any currency.

"Hints to Business Men visiting El Salvador" can be got, free, by British businessmen from Room CO7, Export House, Dept. of Trade, 50 Ludgate Hill, London EC4M 7HU.

Motoring At the border, after producing a driving licence, log book and proof of ownership, you are given a permit to stay for 15 days. This can be extended at the National Tourist Board, Calle Rubén Darío 519, San Salvador (Tel.: 217445 and 214845) or you can simply cross the border, turn round and get another permit to stay another 15 days. In any case the formalities for bringing in a car involve considerable paperwork. There is a US$0.50 charge for compulsory tyre fumigation. There is also a US$0.40 departure tax for cars. Insurance is not compulsory in El Salvador, but you should arrange cover. A good map, both of republic and of capital, can be obtained from Texaco or Esso, or from the Tourist Board.

Local Information can be got by tourists from the National Tourist Board, Calle Rubén Darío 519, San Salvador (branch office at Ilopango Airport), or from the capital's two big hotels, *El Salvador Sheraton* and *Gran Hotel San Salvador*. The hotels arrange excursions by car for up to 6 people, with maps and lunch boxes. The Tourist Board provides a small map of the country with at least ten camp sites or "Turicentros" marked on it.

The **best months** for a commercial visit are from February to May, when there is least rainfall and most business. August is the holiday season. Business is centralized at the capital, but it is as well to visit Santa Ana, Sonsonate and San Miguel.

Language Spanish, but English is widely understood. Spanish should be used for letters, catalogues, etc.

Clothing Light-weight unlined or half-lined suits, which can be worn by day and at night. White suits and white dinner jackets are not worn. A plastic raincoat is useful in the rainy season. Coats and ties are worn in the streets and when visiting. Hats are not used except as protection against the sun. Women wear light dresses of cotton or like material during the day, and more formal evening dresses.

Food Try *pupusas*, cheese or bacon in a little savoury pancake, cheap and tasty. They are sold at many street stalls and in fact are better there than in restaurants. On Saturday and Sunday nights many local people congregate in "pupuserías".

Health The gastro-enteric diseases are the most common. Visitors should take care over what they eat during the first few weeks and should drink Agua Cristal (bottled water). Specifics against malaria should be taken if a night is spent on the coast. The San Salvador milk supply is good.

Internal Transport Buses are excellent (if sometimes crowded) and usually faster than trains. San Salvador has plenty of taxis. Hitchhiking is comparatively easy.

Currency The unit is the colón, divided into 100 centavos. Banknotes of 1, 2, 5, 10, 25 and 100 colones are used, and there are nickel coins for the fractional amounts. The colón is often called a peso. The legal rate is 2.5025/2.5075 colones to the U.S. dollar, buying and selling.

The **metric system** of weights and measures is used alongside certain local units such as the *vara* (836 millimetres, 32.9 inches), *manzana* (7,000 square metres, or 1.67 acres), the *libra* (0.454 kilogramme, about 1 English pound), and the *quintal* of 100 libras. Some U.S. weights and measures are also used. U.S. gallons are used for gasoline and quarts for oil.

Posts and Telegraphs Sea-mail to and from Britain takes from 3 to 5 weeks; air mail takes 4 days. Because there are 12 other San Salvadors in Latin America, the correct address for any letter to the capital is "San Salvador, El Salvador, Central America". Lista de Correos is at new post office building on Av. 11a Norte, 300 yards past the British Embassy.

The charge for a local telephone call is C0.10 for 3 minutes. A telephone call to Britain on weekdays is C37.50 for 3 minutes, C12.50 for each extra minute. On Sunday, between 0800 and 2200 it is C30 for the minimum 3 minutes and C10 for each extra minute. Time in El Salvador is 6 hours behind G.M.T.

All America Cables and Radio Inc., communicates with all parts of the world through local stations. Public telex at Antel, the Government's telecommunications office. British businessmen can use the telex system at the Embassy. Minimum rate for a call to Britain is C36 for 3 minutes.

Hours of Business 0800-1200 and 1400-1800 Monday to Friday; 0800-1200 Saturday. Banks in San Salvador 0830-1130, 1430-1600 Monday to Friday; 0900-1130 Saturday; different hours for other towns given in text. Government offices: 0730-1230 and 1500-1730 Monday to Friday. Department of Migration also open on Saturday from 0900-1200. British Embassy: 0800-1200 and 1500-1730 Monday to Friday.

Public Holidays The usual ones are January 1, Holy Week (3 days), April 14, 17, May 1, 10, Corpus Christi (half day), August 3-7, September 15, October 12,

November 2 and 5 (half-day), December 24 (half-day), and Christmas Day. Government offices are also often closed on religious holidays. Little business in weeks ending Easter week, the first week of August, and the Christmas-New Year period. Banks are closed for balance June 29, 30, and December 30, 31.

Press

San Salvador "Diario de Hoy", "La Prensa Gráfica", every day, including Sunday. "Diario Latino" and "El Mundo", afternoon papers, but not on Sunday. There are provincial newspapers in Santa Ana, San Miguel and elsewhere, with small circulations.

There are 39 radio stations, at least 4 of which cover the whole country, and all but one accept advertisements. There are 2 commercial television stations, one of which has a national coverage.

The **British Consulate** is at San Salvador (13a Av. Norte (Continuación) 611, Colonia Dueñas, Tel.: 219667. Letters to Consulado Británica, Apartado 601, San Salvador, El Salvador, Central America). There is a Vice-Consul (c/o La Agencia Salvadoreña, Tel.: 2 de La Libertad) at the port of La Libertad. (Shipping matters only.) The Embassy for all Central America is in San José, Costa Rica.

The United States Embassy and Consulate-General are at 25 Av. Norte, 1230, in front of Fuente Luminosa, Tel.: 257100.

American Express Agents San Salvador: El Salvador Travel Service, Centro Comercial La Mascota, Carretera a Sta. Tecla, Tel.: 23-0177. They will not, however, cash travellers' cheques; this must be done at a bank.

We are particularly grateful for updating material to Joyce Howe (from Nicaragua), and to John Streather; also to other travellers listed under the general Central America section.

HONDURAS

HONDURAS is larger than all the other Central American republics except Nicaragua, but has a smaller population than El Salvador, less than a fifth its size. Bordered by Nicaragua, Guatemala, and El Salvador, it has an area of 112,088 square km.—rather less than England. It has a narrow Pacific coastal strip, 124 km. long, on the Gulf of Fonseca, but its northern coast on the Caribbean is some 640 km. long. Most of its 2,660,000 inhabitants live in the western half of the country.

Much of the country is mountainous: a rough plateau covered with volcanic ash and lava in the S, rising to peaks such as Cerro de las Minas in the Celaque range (2,849 metres), but with some intermont basins at between 900 and 1,400 metres. The volcanic detritus disappears to the N, revealing saw-toothed ranges which approach the coast at an angle; the one in the extreme NW, along the border with Guatemala, disappears under the sea and shows itself again in the Bay Islands. At most places in the N there is only a narrow shelf of lowland between the sea and the sharp upthrust of the mountains, but along two rivers—the Aguán in the NE, and the Ulúa in the NW, long fingers of marshy lowland stretch inland between the ranges. The great banana plantations are all in these hot and humid northern lowlands, with their lush green vegetation and a multitude of palm trees. The Ulúa lowland is particularly important; it is about 40 km. wide and stretches southwards for 100 km. From its southern limit a deep gash continues across the highland to the Gulf of Fonseca, on the Pacific. The distance between the Caribbean and the Pacific along this trough is 280 km.; the altitude at the divide between the Río Comayagua, running into the Ulúa and the Caribbean, and the streams flowing into the Pacific, is only 950 metres. In this trough, where it narrows to a mere 16 km., lies Comayagua, the old colonial capital. The lowlands along the Gulf of Fonseca are narrower than they are along the Caribbean; there is no major thrust inland as along the Ulúa.

The prevailing winds are from the E, and the Caribbean coast has a high rainfall and is covered with deep tropical forest. The forest also mantles the eastern-facing slopes of the mountains, none of which rises above the forest zone. The intermont basins, the valleys, and the slopes sheltered from the prevailing winds bear oak and pine down to as low as 600 metres. Timber is almost the only fuel available. There is a little coal near the capital but no oil has been found. In the drier areas, as to the N and E of Tegucigalpa, there are extensive treeless savannahs.

The Spaniards, arriving in the early 16th century, found groups of Indians of the Mayan culture (Chortis, Hicaques and Lenchas) and from other cultures (Payas and Chorotegas). Pushing E from Guatemala City they came upon silver in the SE, and in 1524 founded Tegucigalpa near the mines. The yield was comparatively poor, but enough to attract a thin stream of immigrants. Settlement during the ensuing century was mostly

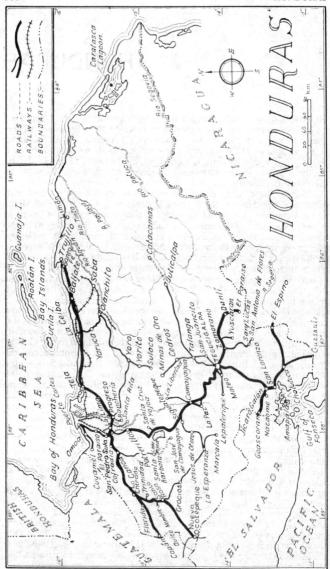

ROUGH SKETCH

along the trail from Guatemala City: at Santa Rosa de Copán, La Esperanza and Comayagua. Gradually these settlements spread over the S and W, and this, with the N coast, is where the bulk of the population lives today. The Spaniards and their descendants ignored the northern littoral and the Ulúa lowlands, but during the 19th century American companies, depending partly upon black workers from the British West Indies and Belize, developed the northern lowlands as a great banana-growing area. Today the second largest concentration of population per square mile is in the Department of Cortés, which extends northwards from Lake Yojoa towards the Caribbean; it includes the major portion of the river basins of Ulúa and Chamelecón, also known as the Sula Valley: the most important agricultural area in the country, with San Pedro Sula as its commercial centre and Puerto Cortés as its seaport. The Atlantic littoral consumes two-thirds of the country's imports, and ships the bananas which are half the country's exports.

Even today, land under some form of cultivation is only 22.4% of the total; 45% of Honduras is forest. Rugged country makes large areas unsuitable for any kind of agriculture. Nevertheless, there are undeveloped agricultural potentials in the vast, flat, almost unpopulated lands of the coastal plain E of Tela to Trujillo and Puerto Castilla, in the Aguán Valley southward and in the region NE of Juticalpa. The area further to the NE known as the Mosquitia Plain, is mostly unexplored and little is known of its potential.

Population There are very few pure blooded Indians, and fewer (less than 1%) of pure Spanish ancestry. The largest proportion of Indian blood is found from Santa Rosa de Copán westwards to the border with Guatemala. The population is 90% mestizo. Along the northern coast there is a large black element. The population was 2,656,948 in 1974; death rate 12.4%; birth, 49.3%; annual population growth: 2.7%; urban growth, 5.1%, but only 31.4% is urban; 47.5% are illiterate. Some 68.6% are peasants or agricultural labourers, with a relatively low standard of living. Education is compulsory, but half the rural children have no school to go to. The middle class is small, and the purchasing power of the people low.

Communications There are no railways at all where most of the people live, in the W; even the capital has the rare distinction of not being served by a railway. All the lines are in the N, and since 1975 the 1,268 km. in operation belong to the Ferrocarril Nacional de Honduras.

A light aeroplane is the only way of getting to large areas of the country, but the road system has improved rapidly in recent years. Total road length is now 6,136 km. of which 2,155 are paved. The paved roads are the Northern Highway linking Tegucigalpa, San Pedro Sula and Puerto Cortés; the "Emergency" (Inter-American) Highway in the SW between El Salvador and Nicaragua, and the Southern Highway which runs to it from Tegucigalpa (both this and part of the northern Highway are in poor shape at present); the North Coast Highway joining San Pedro Sula with Progreso, Tela and La Ceiba; the Western Highway linking San Pedro Sula with Santa Rosa de Copán, Nuevo Ocotepeque and the Guatemalan and Salvadorean frontiers; and the Eastern Highway linking Tegucigalpa, Danlí, El Paraíso and Las Manos (Nicaraguan frontier). Travel is still by oxcart and mule in many areas. Tegucigalpa, La Ceiba and San Pedro Sula all have international airports.

The **Legislature** consists of a single Chamber. Congress assembles annually on May 26 and the sessions last till October 26. Deputies are elected by a proportional vote. Executive authority rests with a President, elected for 6 years and assisted by a Cabinet of 10 Secretaries of State. No President may serve two terms in succession. The Constitution is at present largely suspended.

There is a Supreme Court with 7 judges and 5 substitute judges, elected by Congress for 6 years. There are also Courts of Appeal and various lesser tribunals.

The Constitution of December 1957 gave the vote to all over 18; the death penalty is abolished; it recognises the right of Habeas Corpus, civil marriage, and divorce; and grants to workers a 48-hour week and protection against unemployment. Primary education is compulsory. Military service is obligatory.

The National University is centred in Tegucigalpa though it also has departments in San Pedro Sula and La Ceiba.

In 1957 free and authentic popular elections brought a Liberal Government into power with Ramón Villeda Morales as President. He was deposed in October 1963, and a military junta took over. A constituent assembly was elected in February 1965 to draw up the nation's 12th constitution since independence in 1838. It elected Gen. Osvaldo López Arellano (head of the junta), as President. A civilian, Ramón Ernesto Cruz, was elected President in June 1971 at the head of a coalition government; he was ousted by the military in December 1972, and Gen. López Arellano resumed the presidency, which he retained until April 1975 when he was, in turn, ousted by another military man, Gen. Juan Melgar Castro. There are plans for a return to constitutional rule by 1980.

Cities and Towns

Tegucigalpa, the capital, a city of 275,000 inhabitants, stands in an intermont basin at an altitude of 975 metres. No railway serves it. Its only communications are by road and air: 100 km. by air from Amapala, on the Pacific Gulf of Fonseca, 346 km. from Puerto Cortés on the Atlantic. It was founded as a mining camp in about 1524: the miners found their first gold where the N end of the Soberanía bridge now is. The name means "silver hill" in the original Indian tongue. On three sides it is surrounded by sharp, high peaks. It is an amalgam of two towns: the almost flat Comayagüela, and the hilly Tegucigalpa built at the foot and up the slopes of Mount Picacho. A steeply banked river, the Choluteca, runs between the two towns, now united administratively as the Distrito Central. Four bridges cross the river: the old Colonial bridge of Mallol, and the modern bridges of Carías, Soberanía and Juan Ramón Molina. Tegucigalpa has not been subjected to any disaster by fire or earthquake and remains much as it always has been, apart from recent adaptations of road surface to motor traffic. Many of the stuccoed houses, with a single heavily barred entrance leading to a central patio, are attractively coloured. Differences of levels are sometimes spanned by picturesque stepped streets. But the old low skyline of the city has now been punctured by several modern buildings of from 6 to 8 storeys. The new congressional building, the Central Bank of Honduras, and an American insurance block are good examples.

Its altitude gives it a reliable climate: temperate during the rainy season from May to November; torrid, with cool nights, in March and April, and cool and dry, with very cool nights, in December to February. The annual mean temperature is about 74°F (23°C).

The Carretera del Sur (Southern Highway), which brings in passengers from the S and from Toncontín Airport, 6½ km. outside the city, runs through Comayagüela into Tegucigalpa. It goes past the huge obelisk set up to commemorate a hundred years of Central American independence; the ancient town hall of Comayagüela (on the left) and, near the river, the

School of Arts and Crafts, with a decorated Mayan corridor and a collection of contemporary paintings and crafts.

The market in Comayagüela is perhaps the most interesting place in the whole city. Nearby, Artesanía Hondureña offers an outstanding display of native handicrafts. You can get a fine view of the city by walking or driving to the Peace Monument on Juana Laínez hill, near the football stadium.

We cross the river by the Puente Mallol. Immediately on the left is the Presidential Palace, a massive structure with a beautiful interior courtyard which, unfortunately, is no longer open to the public. The barracks housing the President's guard of honour is at the back of it. If we go by Calle Bolívar we pass through the area in which are the Congress building and the former site of the University, founded in 1847. Calle Bolívar leads to the main square, Plaza Morazán (commonly known as Parque Central), with a statue to General Francisco Morazán. (For an account of Morazán, see the introduction to Central America.) The southern side of the square takes us by the City Hall, the eastern by the domed and double-towered Cathedral built in the late 18th century. (See the beautiful silver altar, the fine examples of Spanish colonial art, the cloisters and, in Holy Week, the magnificent ceremony of the Descent from the Cross.)

On Avenida La Paz, on the long hill across the bridge, is the large, imposing fortress-like U.S. embassy. The University has moved to a new campus E of the city, on the road to Suyapa.

Av. Paz Barahona, running through the northern side of the square, is a key avenue containing most of the best shops. On it is the rebuilt church of San Francisco, with its clangorous bells, and (on Av. Cervantes) the Palace of Justice.

If, from Plaza Morazán, we go along Av. Paz Barahona westwards towards the river, by turning right along Calle 4a we come to the market of Dolores opposite the 18th century church of Virgen de los Dolores: the streets around the market are a babel of country folk—one of the more interesting sights of Tegucigalpa. Pottery and baskets and carvings are for sale. Av. Paz Barahona is closed to traffic in the city centre, being reserved for pedestrians.

Two blocks N and 2 blocks W of the Church is Parque Concordia. In the Jardín Maya are copies of Mayan Sculpture.

Back on Av. Paz Barahona and further W are the Ministerial Palace, the Post Office (stamps of all issues on sale), the National Theatre and, across the square, the beautiful old church of El Calvario. If we cross the bridge of Carías (quite near the theatre) we can visit Comayagüela's market of San Isidro (burnt in 1972, but now reconstructed).

One is always conscious, at Tegucigalpa, of the summit of El Pichacho looming up to the N. From Plaxa Morazán go up Calle 7a and the Calle de la Leona to Parque Leona, where there is a handsome small park with a railed walk overlooking the city. Higher still is the reservoir in the United Nations Park, from which the city draws its water. The park, which can be reached by bus from the city, has various reproductions of Mayan objects.

Hotels *Honduras Maya,* newest, about US$30 d; *Hotel La Ronda,* 4 blocks from cathedral, a/c, recommended, US$20 d; *Hotel Lincoln,* about US$9 s, US$15 d; *Hotel Prado,* from US$12.50 s, US$18 d, with bath, meals extra *à la carte* in restaurant, guests allowed to use *Honduras Maya* swimming pool, somewhat noisy nightclub at weekends; *Hotel Boston,* US$6-7 s, with bath; *Hotel Palace Marichal,*

US$5 s, with private bath (US$4.50 without), clean, hot water,cafeteria, centrally located. *Hotel MacArthur,* US$5 s, with bath, US$3 without, US$8 d, with bath, US$5 without; *Granada,* 6a Calle 1330, US$6 d, very clean, recommended by Peace Corps; *Hotel Ritz,* 4a Calle 4 and 5 Av., Comayagüela, from US$3.50 to 6 s, cold shower, clean but noisy; *Eden House,* on winding road to Parque La Leona, about US$3 with food, poor value. *Hotel Rimak,* close to *Hotel Boston,* US$2.50 s. Lots of cheap *pensiones* and rooms in Comayagüela but most are not suitable for travellers; *Hotel Bristol,* 5a Calle between 4 and 5 Av., Comayagüela, US$4 p.p., no hot water, recommended; *Hotel San Pedro,* Calle 9, Av. 6, US$2 , clean; *Hotel Jupiter,* 6a Av., 5 and 6 Calles 509, Comayagüela, US$8 d, clean and comfortable; *Hotel Richard No. 1,* 4a Calle, 6 and 7 Av., Comayagüela, US$2 each, recommended; *Hotel Richard Nos. 2* and *3,* at 5a Calle, 6 and 7 Av., Comayagüela, same prices, fewer facilities. A 3% sales tax is added to hotel bills.

Electric Current Generally 110 volts, 60 cycles A.C. in hotels and most houses, though some houses receive 220.

Restaurants *El Chico Club,* very good; *Villa Real, El Asador, La Pagoda de Oro, La Parrilla, Roma,* good. Advisable to order in advance. Prices are *à la carte* and run to US$6 for a good meal. Others are *Dinos* (good); *El Fogón,* near *Honduras Maya Hotel,* very good; *La Barbacoa* (barbecues); *Riviera Drive-in* (close to airport, good food); *Panamerican Grill* (by Plaza Libertad, Comayagüela, bar and grills). *El Torino,* for Italian food; *Quijote,* Spanish food, recommended; *El Patio,* near town centre, good shish and kebabs; *China Palace, Lung Fung.* Good pizzeria: *Tito, Coliseo. Hotel Honduras Maya* has a 24-hr. cafeteria. *La Olla,* good local dishes: *Nankin,* below *Granada Hotel,* also good; *Brik Brak,* off main square, serves nice breakfasts. *Jardín de Italia,* cheap, snacks only. Tegucigalpa now also has a MacDonalds hamburger restaurant. Solmans, branches throughout the city, excellent bread and ice cream. *Hotel La Ronda* serves good international food, and very good seafood is obtainable at *The Hungry Fisherman.*

Clubs Country Club (golf, tennis, swimming); Club Fontana, near airport (swimming pool, restaurant, bar, dancing, occasional floor shows); Rotary Lions, Junior Chamber of Commerce.

Night Clubs and Discothèques *Hotel Prado* has bar facilities (only in the so-called Terraza Club); Belle Epoque in *Hotel Honduras Maya;* Jaque Club in *Hotel La Ronda;* Boccaccio 3000; La Naranja Mecánica; Aeropuerto; Boccaccio 2000; Watergate. For the dissolute there is the Casine, near Parque Leona and German Embassy—a lovely view of the city lights below and other beautiful if expensive sights. Belén, sprawling untidily on the hillside above Comayagüela, is the centre of this city's "low" night life and is generally uncouth, sometimes dangerous and always entertaining.

Bookshop The Bookstore, Arcade Midence Soto Bldg.

Tourist Office Bank of London and Montreal building (see below). Very helpful; maps and brochures. Provides lists of hotels and sells posters. The best map of the country is produced by the Instituto Nacional de Geografia and may be bought from the Institute on production of passport. Open weekday mornings only.

Taxis Flat rate, US$0.50 p.p. (no reduction for sharing); more after 2000 hours.

Local buses Cost US$0.08, no fixed stops.

Airport Toncontín, 6½ km. from the centre. Minibuses into town, US$0.10, 20 minutes; taxis, US$5-8.

Bank of London & Montreal Ltd., Cruce 5a Av. y 4a Calle, and agencies at San Isidro (Comayagüela) and Barrio Abajo. Open 0900-1500; closed Sat. Banco Atlántida; Banco de Ahorro Hondureño; Banco de Honduras (Citibank); Bank of America. All cash travellers' cheques.

Cables Tropical Radio Telegraph Co., Av. Cervantes 808. Public telex office in TRT office in Tegucigalpa.

Fair at Comayagüela December 7 to 24.

School American and Elvel School, on US lines with US staff.

Museum Museo Nacional Villa Roy, in home of former Chief of State, has an exhibition of archaeological finds.

Protestant Churches Anglican and Union Churches, with services in English.

Buses (or hired cars) to San Pedro Sula on mostly good Northern Highway; 4 hours, for US$4. To Choluteca, 3 hours, US$2.50. The international Tica bus service, with Greyhound-style buses to all the Central American capitals, has offices on Calle Real, opp. Parque La Libertad, Comayagüela; it now has a fleet of new buses running from Guatemala to Panama (including Honduras), but minibuses are sometimes used between Tegucigalpa and Jícaro-Galán. To Panama, US$27.50; to San José, US$15; to Managua, US$9; to San Salvador, US$5 and Guatemala, US$10.

Excursions Eight km. NE to the Church at Suyapa, which attracts pilgrims to its wooden figure of the virgin, a tiny image about 8 cm. high set into the altar. Excursions to Copán (1 hour by air, US$295 for a plane taking 5 passengers), the Agricultural School at Zamorano and elsewhere, and sight-seeing tours of Tegucigalpa and Comayagüela are arranged by several tour operators. About 50 km. to the N is Parque Aurora, which has a nice zoo. It is about an hour's drive to Valle de Angeles (old mines and native handcraft) and on to San Juancito (mines). On the way to Valle de Angeles take a right turn off to visit the quaint old mining village of **Santa Lucía**, perched precariously on a steep mountainside overlooking the wide valley with Tegucigalpa below. Delightful walk down old mule trail across pine-clad ridges to the city. Charming legend of the local statue of the Virgin considered by outsiders too good for Santa Lucía and carried off by them. At each step it grew heavier and heavier, but became light as a feather once they had decided to return it to its church at Santa Lucía.

There are bracing climbs to the heights of Picacho; don't take left fork at summit; take right fork to El Hatillo and on 24 km. to visit the rain forest. Jeeps and 4-wheel drive vehicles can go on in dry weather to San Juancito.

Over an hour's drive past President's residence and through rugged, forested terrain to Colonial village of Lapaterique. Distant view of Pacific on fine days from heights above village. A half-hour drive from Tegucigalpa to **Ojojona**, another quaint old village; turn right 24 km. down southern highway. The village's pottery is interesting. Fiesta Jan. 18-20.

Swimming at thermal springs of Balneario de Francisco Támara; 32 km., along road to San Pedro Sula turn off right 8 km. N of Támara.

At km. 17 on Zamorano road (at summit of range overlooking Suyapa church) take dirt road left to T.V. tower. From here a delightful 2-hour walk over forested ridges leads to Santa Lucía. At km. 24 on Zamorano road, climb the highest peak through the Uyuca rain forest, but get written permission to do so from Panamerican Agricultural School at Zamorano from their office in the Banco Atlántida building in capital. The school has rooms for visitors.

The North Coast

The routes from the three Atlantic ports of Cortés, Tela and La Ceiba to Potrerillos, on which they converge, and on by road to the capital, Tegucigalpa, are now described; then the route running S from the capital to the Pacific port of Amapala, and others to the NE, E, and W of the capital. Tegucigalpa is the commercial centre of the Pacific littoral, San Pedro Sula of the Atlantic.

Puerto Cortés, the Republic's principal port, at the mouth of the Ulúa river, is 58 km. by road and rail from San Pedro Sula, 333 from Tegucigalpa, and only two days' steam from New Orleans. About half of Honduran trade passes through it. The climate is torrid, modified by sea breezes; many beautiful palm-fringed beaches nearby; rainfall, 2,921 mm. It has a small oil refinery, and a free zone is due to open in 1978. Population 44,000.

The town is changing rapidly: new buildings and factories, completely new port facilities, new bus services, local and long distance with new modern buses, but dreadful roads in the town which are dangerous after rain: a puddle is often a foot deep.

Rail Daily train to San Pedro Sula and Potrerillos, 95 km., 1.067 metres gauge. Two daily trains to Tela.

Road To San Pedro Sula and Potrerillos and on to the capital. Road mostly good. Bus service several times an hour to San Pedro Sula, US$0.75, 1½ hours. Citul and Impala lines.

Hotels *Craniotis,* US$11 d, only 2 rooms are a/c; *Cosenza; Colón,* clean, cheap, no hot water. *Formosa,* US$1.25, clean but dusty from the road.

Restaurants *La Playa,* on outskirts, fish dishes excellent, others O.K. *Hotel Craniotis. Restaurant-Cafe Kalua* in centre of town. *Restaurant Formosa,* expensive, but good.

Protestant Church Anglican.

Bank of London & Montreal, Ltd. (agency), 2a Av. y 3a Calle; Banco Atlántida and other local banks. Open 0800-1130, 1330-1600; Sats. 0800-1100.

Excursions W to Tulián, along the bay, for picnics and freshwater bathing. New microbuses (US$0.25 each way) make the delightful drive along the tropical shoreline past Tulián W to Omoa, with its splendidly preserved 17th century castle, which is well worth a visit. Other buses go E to tropical beaches of coconut palms and white sands at Travesía, Baja Mar, etc. From November to May, because of tourist ships arriving two or three times a week, there are tours to La Lima to visit the banana plantations, trips to Copán to visit the Mayan ruins and tourist parties at the Ustaris Hacienda.

Shipping Hapag-Lloyd, C.C.T., Hamburg-America, Kawasaki Lines (all cargo only). Continental Line (Miami-Panama) operates passenger cruises. No regular passenger sailings to New Orleans, Belize or Santo Tomás.

Shops There are two souvenir shops in the customs house at the entrance to the National Port Authority, which sell hand-embroidered clothes. A shop on the main street sells mahogany wood carvings and the market in the town centre is quite interesting.

Tela, another important banana port some 50 km. to the E, is reached from Puerto Cortés by sea, rail, road or plane, or from San Pedro Sula by rail and by bus service *via* Progreso. It is a clean, pleasantly laid out town with a good sandy beach. A paved road runs to the wooden buildings and wide streets of Tela Vieja. Population 17,500.

Hotels *Miramar; Tela La Playa,* US$4 s; *Balderach,* US$4; *Motel Paradise,* a few km. E with chalets to let, US$12.50 s. Good beach.

Restaurant *César's,* on the beach, serves good seafood.

Protestant Church Anglican.

Bank Banco Atlántida.

Buses Cati or Tupsa lines from San Pedro Sula to Progreso (US$1.20) where you must change to go on to Tela and La Ceiba. Or there is an express bus through from San Pedro Sula which costs an extra US$1.

Rail The National Railways 1.067-metre gauge line W to Puerto Cortés; a branch of this line runs south along the eastern bank of the Ulúa River to Progreso and Potrerillos. There is no longer a rail link with La Ceiba but frequent buses run from San Pedro Sula or Tela (US$1.75) on paved roads.

Excursion It is interesting to go, by rail or road, to the tropical experimental farm at Lancetilla, a few km. inland.

El Progreso, on the Río Ulúa, an important agricultural and commerical centre (no longer just a banana town) is on the road and railway route between Tela and San Pedro Sula. Population, about 40,000.

La Ceiba, the country's busiest port for the export of bananas and pineapples, is 64 km. E of Tela, from which it is reached by air, boat, road or rail (85 km.). The capital of Atlántida Department, it lies in a green valley at the foot of Pico Bonito (2,580 metres) and is both clean and attractive. The climate is hot, but tempered by sea winds. There are some fine beaches nearby, though some are dirty. Beyond La Ceiba is the old Colonial village of Jutiapa. The Bay Islands are usually visited from La Ceiba, although Roatán is more easily reached from Puerto Cortes. Population 55,000. Regular bus service to San Pedro Sula, US$4.

Hotels   *Gran Hotel París,* US$13-17 s, a/c, with good cafeteria, swimming pool and small night club; *Ceiba,* US$8-13 s, a/c, restaurant and bar; *Los Angeles,* US$3.75 s; *Royal,* US$3.50 s; *Casino,* US$3; *San Carlos,* good, US$3 d, with shower; *Hotel Figeros; Hotelito Lis,* near the docks, US$1.50-2.50 d, with shower, clean; the owner has a restaurant near the railway and can give you plenty of information about the surrounding area.

Restaurants   *Atlantic, Partenón, Montmartre (Gran Hotel París), Lido, Maxims, La Piraña, Rex's.*

Night Clubs   Emperador, Rex, Pigalle, Flamingo.

Casino   Open in *Gran Hotel París.*

Protestant Churches   Anglican, Methodist, Mennonite, Evangelist and Jehovah's Witnesses, among others.

Banks   Bank of London & Montreal, Av. San Isidro y 10a Calle; Banco Atlántida and other local banks. Open 0830-1130, 1330-1600; Sats. 0800-1200.

Airport   Golosón, with direct jet services to Miami and New Orleans as well as Mexican and internal destinations.

Festival   Carnival in May, especially on the 15th, honours San Isidro, the patron saint; it attracts many visitors.

Travel Agencies   Pasajes y Viajes Lafitte, Viajes Transmundo.

Rent a Car   Molinari.

The **Bay Islands** (Islas de Bahía) lie in an arc which curves NE away from a point some 30 km. N of La Ceiba. The three main ones are Utila, Roatán, and Guanaja. At the eastern end of Roatán are three small ones: Morat, Santa Elena, and Barbareta. Their total population, trading mostly in coconuts, bananas and plantains, with boat-building as the only and dying industry, is 8,863. About half are blacks and Black Caribs; the other half are fair-skinned people originally of British stock and still English-speaking. Columbus anchored here in 1502, on his fourth voyage. In the 18th century they were bases for English, French and Dutch buccaneers. They were in British hands for over a century but were finally ceded to Honduras in 1859. The Government schools teach in Spanish, and the population is bi-lingual. **Utila** (population 1,500) is only 32 km. by launch (US$6) or daily Sansa air service from La Ceiba (US$7.50 each way). Utila, the main town, known locally as East Harbour, is a 40-minute boat ride from the Cays, a chain of small islands off the S coast. It is the cheapest of the islands to visit.

Hotels on Utila   *Sonny's Villa,* US$5 s; *Captain Spencer,* similar price; *Trudy's,* US$3 s; *Bahia Lodge,* US$10 s, full board; *Villa Utila,* US$2.50-5 s, full board; *Pensión Las Palmas.*

It is a few hours' sail to **Roatán,** the largest of the islands. The capital of the department, Roatán (locally known as Coxen's Hole), is on the south-western shore. It was from here that William Walker set sail in 1860 to conquer Honduras and met his death at Trujillo. Port Royal, towards the eastern end of the island, and famous in the annals of buccaneering, is now almost deserted. Archaeologists have been busy on the islands but their findings are too confused to make sense. Take a plane to Coxen's Hole and launch up coast to French Harbour and Oak Ridge.

Boats go irregularly from Puerto Cortés to Roatán, US$5 plus US$0.50 dock charge for tourists. There is a regular ferry from La Ceiba to the three main islands. Jeeps across island to Sandy Bay (US$0.50). Beaches excellent but Roatán is expensive, half as much again as on the mainland.

Hotels on Roatán: *Lost Paradise of the West End,* US$20 s, full board; at Sandy bay: *Anthony's Key Resort,* US$50 s, 80 d, full board; *Pirate's Den,* US$20 s, full board; at French Harbour: *Coral Reef Inn,* US$2.50 s; *Caribinn,* US$15-25 s, with meals; at Oak Ridge, *Reef House Resort,* US$35 s, with meals; *Roatán Lodge,* same prices, accommodation in cabins; *Miss Merlee's guest house.* There are other, cheaper, places to stay and houses to let.

Columbus called Guanaja, the easternmost of the group, the Island of Pines, and the tree is still abundant, though much damage was done by a serious fire in February 1978. The locals call the island Bonacca. Much of Bonacca town, covering a small Cay off the coast, is built on stilts above sea water: hence its nick-name, the "Venice of Honduras". An airport. Bathing is made somewhat unpleasant by the many sandfleas. The "Suyapa" sails between Guanaja and La Ceiba and Puerto Cortés. The "Miss Sheila" also does the same run and goes on to George Town (Grand Cayman). There are plenty of places to stay on all the islands. Also boats to the islands from Trujillo.

Hotels on Guanaja *Miller,* US$3.50 s; *Boatel Playa,* US$12 s; *Hally Carter,* US$6 s.

A roundabout railway and a direct road run from La Ceiba to **Olanchito,** in the hills to the SE. It was founded, according to tradition, by a few stragglers who escaped from the destruction of Olancho el Viejo, between Juticalpa and Catacamas, then a wealthy town. They brought with them the crown made of hides which the Virgin still wears in the church of Olanchito. Population: 3,256.

Bank Banco Atlántida.

Trujillo, 90 km. to the east again, was once a dead port but has recently become revitalised. It was near here that William Walker (see under Nicaragua) was shot in 1860. To the S, and E to the Río Segovia, lies a huge territory of jungled swamps and mountains lived in by a few Indians and timber men (see page 981). Flying in is best—Sahsa and Lansa have several flights a week. The town can be reached by bus from San Pedro Sula, Tela and La Ceiba, now that a road has been built from La Ceiba.

Hotel *Central,* US$3.50 s, with bath, not for lone women.

There are interesting villages of Black Caribs at Santa Fe, 10 km. W of Trujillo, and eastwards at Limón. At Puerto Castilla (where Columbus landed), near Trujillo, is a meat-packing station and active shrimping. There are some pleasant beaches near Trujillo.

San Pedro Sula and Western Honduras

San Pedro Sula, 58 km. S of Puerto Cortés on the road and railway to Potrerillos, is the second largest city in Honduras and one of the most rapidly growing cities in Latin America. It is a centre for the banana, coffee, sugar and timber trades, a focal distributing point for northern and western Honduras, and the most highly industrialised centre in the country. Industries include a small steel rolling mill, textiles and shirt making, margarine, furniture (wooden and metal), zinc roofing, cement and concrete blocks, and all forms of plastic ware. Its merchants are mainly of foreign extraction: Arab, North American, German and Jewish. The population is about 200,000

The city was founded by Pedro de Alvarado in 1536 but nothing remains of the old city and there are no old buildings of interest. The fine colonial-style cathedral has been under construction since 1949 and is still unfinished. San Pedro Sula is situated in the lush and fertile valley of the Ulúa (Sula) river and though pleasant in the cooler season from October to March, reaches high temperatures in the summer months with considerable humidity levels.

The high and cooler suburb of Bella Vista with its fine views over the city affords relief from the intense heat of the town centre.

Hotels *Gran Hotel Sula* (the best), US$22 s, US$34 d, all a/c, pool, restaurant and café, large carpark; *Hotel Bolívar* (second best), US$15 s, with a/c, US$10 with fans, US$21 d, with a/c, US$15 with fans, pool and restaurant, enclosed carpark; *Motel Vitanza* (third best), on northern outskirts of city, about same prices as *Bolívar*, also has pool and restaurant; *Hotel San Pedro*, US$8 s, with a/c, US$5 without, US$15 d with a/c, US$10 without; *Hotel Palmira*, US$8 s with a/c, US$6 without, US$15 d with a/c, US$10 without, large carpark in front; *Hotel Manhattan* (new and clean but no a/c), US$5 s, US$6 d; *Hotel Terraza*, US$8 s with a/c, US$6 without, US$14 d with a/c, US$10 without; *Hotel Colombia*, US$8 s with a/c, US$5 without, US$14 d with a/c, US$8 without; *Hotel Castillo*, US$5-15 d.

Other hotels of lower category and cheaper prices are the *Continental, París, Ritz, Roosevelt, San Juan, Copán, Nueva España*. Prices range from US$2.50 to US$5.

Restaurants *Granada (Gran Hotel Sula)*, good food and service; *Touché*, good food, but expensive and slow service; *Pat's Steak House*, good food and service; *Motel Vitanza* and *Mesón Español*, good, typical dishes available; *Vicente* and *Nápoli* restaurants, centre of town, Italian food available at reasonable prices; others include *El Rincón Gaucho, Westphalia* and the 24-hour-service café *Skandia*, in *Gran Hotel Sula.*

Clubs The nearest club, the La Lima Club, in the town of La Lima about 15 km. from San Pedro Sula, belongs to the banana agency but other people are allowed membership. It has a good golf course, swimming pool, and tennis courts. The private Casino Club in the centre of town also has a swimming pool and tennis courts and a dance hall.

Theatre The Círculo Teatral Sampedrano puts on plays at the Centro Cultural Sampedrano, 3 Calle N-O, No. 20, which also has an art gallery and an English and Spanish library. There are three air-conditioned cinemas.

Shopping Excellent wood and leather products are sold at C.C.T.I., in the old U.S. Consulate building.

School La Escuela Internacional. On U.S. lines with U.S. and some British staff. The Escuela Bilingüal also has some expatriate teachers.

Bank of London & Montreal, Ltd. at 4a Av. S.O. 26, between 3a and 4a Calle; Banco Atlántida; Bank of America, 3a Av.; Banco de Honduras (Citibank); Banco de Ahorro Hondureño. Open 0830-1500, closed Sat.

Cables Tropical Radio Telegraph Co.

Airport Ramón Villeda Morales, 13 km. from city centre, US$4 p.p. by taxi. Buses do not go to the airport terminal itself; you have to walk the final 2 km. from the La Lima road. Flights to Tegucigalpa (35 minutes) twice daily. Once daily to La Ceiba and to Belize. Direct flights three times a week to Guatemala, New Orleans and Miami. Irregular internal flights to other Honduran cities and to the Copán ruins.

Buses To Tegucigalpa 3½-4 hours by paved road. Main bus services with comfortable coaches and terminals in the town centre are Hedman Alas (US$6), which is the best, and Transportes Sáenz (US$5.50). Other services operate with less comfortable buses and cheaper prices. To Puerto Cortés, many buses each hour, US$0.75. The road is paved and takes about an hour; a pleasant journey down the lush green river valley. Train journey takes two hours at least to cover the same distance and there are two or three trains a day. Buses run N to Puerto Cortés, E to La Lima, El Progreso, Tela and La Ceiba, S to Lake Yojoa and Tegucigalpa, and SW to Santa Rosa and then through the Department of Ocotepeque with its magnificent mountain scenery to the Guatemalan border. Road well paved all the way.

Excursions The H.Q. of the former United Brands subsidiary is at **La Lima** (4,000 inhabitants), 15 km. to the E by road (bus frequent, US$0.25), where the banana estate and processing plants can be seeen. There is a club for golf and other games which takes members from outside. A little to the E, near the Ulúa river, are the Mayan ruins of Travesía (not the Travesía near Puerto Cortés). Buses run E to Progreso and on N to Tela on the coast, and to La Ceiba.

From San Pedro Sula there are regular buses *via* Santa Rosa south to Nueva Ocotepeque; road is well paved. There are splendid mountain views. The Salvadorean border S of Nueva Ocotepeque is normally closed, but apparently open on occasion (check this at the immigration office near the main square) and you can cross into Guatemala at Atulapa, just after Agua Caliente. There are several buses a day from San Pedro Sula to Agua Caliente. You can get into El Salvador *via* Esquipulas, Guatemala (see page 908). Before you reach Nueva Ocotepeque there is a police checkpoint, where Guatemalan currency can be bought as well as at the border (though probably cheaper to buy at banks in the cities) and an army checkpoint on the continental divide at 2,130 metres. Make sure all documents are in order and to hand. There are Guatemalan consuls in San Pedro Sula and Nueva Ocotepeque from whom visas or tourist cards may be obtained. There are also, of course, excursions to Copán (see below), and to the beautiful Lake Yojoa (page 977) on the Tegucigalpa road (1½ hours).

The Western Highway (171 km.) runs from San Pedro Sula SW along the Río Chamelecón to Canoa (from which there is a road S to Santa Bárbara) and Santa Rosa de Copán; it goes on to San Salvador. **Santa Bárbara** (6,000 inhabitants) is 32 km. W of Lake Yojoa, in hot lowlands. In the vicinity the ruined colonial city of Tencoa has recently been rediscovered. The road goes on to join the Northern Highway S of Lake Yojoa.

Santa Rosa de Copán, 153 km. by road from San Pedro Sula, is the centre of a rich agricultural and cattle-raising area. Altitude 1,040 metres, population mostly Indian, 16,000. Much maize and tobacco are grown in the area. Excellent *sombreros de junco* (Panama hats) are made here and at Santa Bárbara. Santa Rosa is an old Colonial town with most attractive narrow cobbled streets. It holds a festval in the last 10 days of August.

Bank Banco de Occidente.

Hotels *Elvir* (the best), all rooms have own bath, good, cheap meals in cafeteria or restaurant, about US$5 s; *Hospedaje Victoria,* cheap and clean; *Hotel Maya* and *Hotel Eric,* both comparable to U.S. motels, charge US$2.50 and US$3 s, with bath respectively; *Hotel Rosario; Hospedaje Las Américas,* US$1 s, rough.

The magnificent Mayan ruins of **Copán** are 225 km. by air from Tegucigalpa or 186 by air or paved road from San Pedro Sula, and 1 km. from the village of the same name. The road runs SW for 125 km. to La Entrada, where it forks left for Santa Rosa and right for Copán, 60 km. away. Copán can also be reached by road from Guatemala City. The Honduran immigration office is actually in Copán. For one route from Guatemala (see page 909).

To enter (or return to) Guatemala an alternative route is *via* Nueva Ocotepeque (see above); at 0600 a bus leaves Copán for La Entrada (US$1.75, 2¼ hours). From there, there are several buses a day to Santa Rosa (US$0.50, 1 hour). Minibuses run from Santa Rosa to Nueva Ocotepeque (US$1.50, 2½ hours). Trucks take you across the Agua Caliente border into Guatemala (US$1) and minibuses run on to Esquipulas (US$0.50, ½ hour) from where there is a regular bus service to Chiquimula (US$0.50, 1½ hours).

If you are leaving Honduras make sure to get your exit stamp at the police check point just outside Copán on the road to the border.

How to get there Sahsa have a flight on Sundays from San Pedro Sula. Alternatively there are charter flights from Tegucigalpa and Guatemala City. There are also buses (Copanecos, Impala or Torito lines) from San Pedro Sula to La Entrada, US$2; from La Entrada to Copán, US$2.50 by minibus. Some direct. Jerry's Tours in Guatemala City run a one-day tour from there to Copán and back.

A few km. on from La Entrada (*Hospedaje María*, US$0.50, clean, good food also) is the small town of Florida (primitive accommodation). The owner of the gas station here will advise archaeologists about the many Maya ruins between Florida and Copán. The road from La Entrada to Copán is very rough and takes 2 hrs. by bus, although there are now definite plans to pave this route.

In Copán there are two comfortable hotels (*Maya Inn*, US$4-6 d; US$8 including meals; and *Marina* (better, US$6-8 d, meals US$1.50; cheaper annexe US$1.50, excellent value). There is also a cheaper hotel, *Hospedaje Hernández*, US$1, food available. *Mini-restaurant Paty*, under the same ownership as one of the mini-bus companies, has good meals for US$0.75 and four rooms which are sometimes available at US$1 p.p. There is a small museum in the plaza, which is worth seeing.

N.B. It is best to get to the ruins as early as possible; this way you will miss the guided tours; the walk takes only 15 minutes. There is a cafeteria by the entrance to the ruins, and also a shop which sells a guide to Copán, written by Jesús Núñez Chinchilla.

When Stephens and Catherwood examined the ruins in 1839, they were engulfed in jungle. In the 1930s the Carnegie Institute cleared the ground and rebuilt the Great Stairway, and since then they have been maintained by the Government. Ruins and museum cost US$1 for foreigners. They close at 1630. (Do not part with your ticket at the ruins if you have not been to the museum.)

The principal archaeological remains and the reconstructed buildings lie beside the airport and alongside the Río Copán, 1 km. E of the small town of Copán. The ruins represent the whole complex of buildings upon which life in this region must have been focused. Some of the most complex carvings are found on the 21 stelae, or 3-metre columns of stones on which the passage of time was originally believed to be recorded, and which are still in their original sites among the buildings. Under each stela is a vault; some have been excavated. The stelae are deeply incised and carved with faces and figures and animals. One is of a woman; another has a beard. (John Streather tells us that the stelae are not chronologies but in fact "are royal portraits with inscriptions recording deeds and lineage of those portrayed as well as dates of birth, marriage(s) and death".) One frieze shows fantastically adorned astronomer priests in scientific conference. (Some of the finest examples of sculpture in the round from Copán are now in the British Museum or at Boston.) Ball courts were revealed during excavation, and one of them, with the stone seats of its amphitheatre, has been fully restored. The Hieroglyphic Stairway leads from the lower level to an upper, which looks over the river. A temple, approached by more steps and guarded by heraldic beasts, was on the upper level.

The last stela was set up in Copán between A.D. 800 and 820, after less than five centuries of civilised existence. That no further developments took place is attributed to an invasion by other nations from the north. (See general account of Maya history on pages 883-4.)

Potrerillos *(Hotel Alvarez)*, the railhead, is 37 km. from San Pedro Sula. From Potrerillos the paved Northern Highway (288 km.) climbs some 37 km. from the hot lowlands to **Lake Yojoa**, 600 metres high, 22½ km. long and 10 km. wide, gloriously beautiful in a setting of mountains. To the E rise the Jicaque mountains; to the W some lower hills, with Los Naranjos and other villages along the shores or set back towards the hills. Pumas, bears and jaguars range the forests and pine-clad slopes. There are two islands in the lake. The road follows the eastern margin to the lake's southern tip at Pito Solo, where sailing boats and motor boats can be hired. The road is mostly out of sight of the lake: the side-road to the lake itself is not signposted and can be easily overlooked.

Accommodation *Hotel Los Remos* has cabins at US$10 each; *Motel Agua Azul*, US$12 s, good meals for non-residents. A large hydro-electric scheme is being planned. Accommodation can be booked at El Mochito mine of the Honduras Rosario Mining Company (U.S.-owned), near Lake Yojoa.

Thirty-two km. beyond Pito Solo is **Siguatepeque**, near Siguatepeque mountain—a little town with a cool climate (several hotels all charging about US$1.50 s). There is a midday bus from Comayagua which goes to Siguatepeque and on 98 km. through lovely forested mountainous country SW to **La Esperanza**, capital of Intibucá Department, at 1,485 metres. This old, Colonial town set in a pleasant valley has simple but attractive *pensiónes* (e.g. *Pensión Mina*, US$1 s, adequate; *Pensión Mejía Paz*, US$2.50 s, without bath). The townsmen are mostly Indians who handweave blankets and cloth from the wool of the sheep they tend in the hills. A rough road runs from La Esperanza E to **Marcala**, Department of La Paz, along which there are buses. The Marcala region is one of the finest coffee-producing areas of Honduras, and this road gives access to markets.

NW from La Esperanza a very bad road runs to **Gracias** (a minibus leaves at 0800 and rides can be bought on pick-up trucks for US$2; a plane trip costs US$8). It is one of the oldest and most historic settlements in the country. There are 3 Colonial churches and a restored ancient fort on a hill in the outskirts. Some 8 km. from Gracias there is swimming in a hot thermal pool. There is a frequent service of small buses south to Nueva Ocotepeque (fair *pensiónes*), a few km. from the border with El Salvador (though the crossing is closed) and Guatemala (see page 975). Along those few km. is the old Colonial church of La Vieja (or La Antigua), well worth seeing. There is also a bus service from Gracias to the old Colonial town of Santa Rosa de Copán, US$1.25 (see page 976).

Gracias was the centre from which Montejo, thrice Governor of Honduras, put down the great Indian revolt of 1537-38. Cáceres, his lieutenant, besieging Lempira the Indian leader in his impregnable mountain-top fortress, finally lured him out in all his finery under a false flag of truce, ambushed him and treacherously killed him. The revolt died with him. When the Audiencia de los Confines was formed in 1544 Gracias became for a time the administrative centre of Central America.

Thirty-two km. beyond Siguatepeque the road dips into the rich Comayagua plain, part of the gap in the mountains which stretches N from Ulúa lowlands to the Gulf of Fonseca. In this plain lies

Comayagua, a small town of 13,500 people. It was the capital for 357 years until Tegucigalpa, 120 km. away, displaced it in 1880. It was founded about 1523, and there is a number of old colonial buildings: the former University, the first in Central America, founded in 1632; the Cathedral, of the early 18th century; the churches of La Merced and La Caridad, both built in 1550; San Francisco (built in 1575 but badly damaged by earthquake in 1976 and now being renovated); San Sebastián (1585); and San Juan de Dios (1590), the church where the Inquisition sat. El Carmen was built in 1785. The most interesting building is the Cathedral, with its square plain tower and its decorated front, which contains some of the finest examples of colonial art in Honduras. From the tower there is a grand view of the Comayagua valley. The army still uses a quaint old fortress built when Comayagua was the capital.

There are two museums nearby: the ecclesiastical museum (a small contribution is expected) and the anthropological museum with Indian artefacts. Both quite interesting.

The cobbled streets, the whitewashed one-storied houses, and the inhabitants themselves—of less-mixed blood than usual—have a curious other-worldly air. It seems paradoxical that these sedate, puritanical people, who ceased to be citizens of a capital because they would not tolerate the Governor's mistress, manufacture the fireworks which rejoice the people of Honduras on fiesta nights.

Hotels *Libertad*, on Parque Central, good, US$1.50; *Hospedaje Primavera*, US$1, basic. *Las Palmeras*, adequate; *Boarding House San Francisco*, in old-fashioned house near main square, US$2 s, simple cheap meals.

Motel *Quan*, US$3.50 s with private bath.

Bank Banco Atlántida.

A dirt road runs (with bus service) S of Comayagua to **La Paz**, capital of its Department in the western part of the Comayagua valley. Population: 4,000. A short road runs E from La Paz to Villa San Antonio on the highway to Tegucigalpa.

Hotels in La Paz: *Córdoba*, *Pensión San Francisco* (cheaper).

A new dry-weather road now runs SW from La Paz to Marcala (see page 978). Along this road lies **Tutule**, one of the relatively few pure Indian communities in Honduras. Market: Thurs. and Sun. The Mayor, Don Miguel Torres, is a mine of information about the area. There are two minibus services a day from Marcala (US$1) and Don Miguel will put you up.

There are periodic daily bus services between Comayagua and Tegucigalpa and La Paz and Tegucigalpa. The road is paved and the journey (about 2 hours) is fast. About half way we cross the Continental Divide at 1,676 metres.

From Tegucigalpa to the Pacific

A paved road runs S from the Capital through fine scenery. Just off the highway is Sabanagrande, with an interesting old Colonial church. Further S is **Pespire**, a picturesque colonial village with a beautiful silver-domed church; at **Jícaro Galán** (92 km.) our road joins the Inter-American Highway. This highway—now known in Honduras as the Emergency Military Highway—enters Honduras from El Salvador over the Santa Clara bridge at Goascarán and runs through Nacaome, where there is a 16th-century Colonial church, to Jícaro Galán (40 km.). The two roads have a common bed as far as San Lorenzo, on the shores of the Gulf of Fonseca. The climate on the Pacific littoral is very hot, but healthy. Launch to Amapala.

Hotels The only good modern hotel is the *Miramar* at San Lorenzo, 26 rooms, 4 air-conditioned, US$5-8 d. There are hotels of a sort at Goascorán (pop.: 2,190), Nacaome (pop. 4,474) and Jícaro Galán (pop.: 3,007). Restaurants at all: *Oasis*, modern and clean, but not cheap, at Jícaro Galán.

Frequent service of small busitos from Tegucigalpa to San Lorenzo (US$1) and to Choluteca (US$1.50).

The only Pacific port with a good anchorage is **Amapala**, on Tigre Island, not well equipped, but being improved. Vessels lie offshore and small boats land passengers. Fishermen will take you—but not by motor launch—to San Lorenzo (9,300 people) at a low charge: the trip takes half a day. There is an airport, and a plane for the capital (35 minutes) can always be chartered. The deep-sea fishing in the gulf is good. There is a passable bathing beach. Population of Amapala: 5,600. Hotel: *Morazán*.

The San Lorenzo river is now navigable as far as San Lorenzo for steamers drawing up to 6 metres; anchor can safely be dropped near the large timber mill at San Lorenzo, whose roads are bad and mostly under water at high tide. Large export of pitch pine.

Steamship Services besides coastal vessels, there are regular calls by the freighters of Grace Line from North America, Hapag/Lloyd and K.N.S.M. from Europe, the K. Line and N.Y.K. from Japan, Mamenic, the joint service of Hamburg-Amerika Line and Nord-Deutscher Lloyd from Europe, and the joint fast cargo service (no passengers) of Central America Services to and from Europe. All imports which arrive by the Pacific Ocean must now clear through the Amapala Customs.

Royal Mail Agents Tegucigalpa & Amapala, Casa Uhler, S.A., Aptdo. 95, Tegucigalpa.

The Inter-American Highway runs SE from Jícaro Galán past Choluteca to the Nicaraguan border at El Espino, on the Río Negro, 111 km. (Bus from El Espino to Tegucigalpa about midday, US$2.50.) A shorter and quicker way to Managua, however, is to take the new paved road from Choluteca to Chinandega *via* El Triunfo and Guasaule, which runs mainly over the coastal plain.

Choluteca, 34 km. from San Lorenzo in the plain of Choluteca, has a population of 49,000, expanding rapidly. Coffee and cattle are the local industries; a visit to the sawmill is interesting. The town was one of the earliest foundations in Honduras and is still a fascinating old Colonial centre. The climate is very hot.

Hotels *La Fuente,* US$10 s, with bath, swimming pool, a/c; *Imperia Maya,* US$6-11 s, similar facilities; *Camina Real,* US$5-10 s; *Lisboa,* US$1.50-2.50 s, good, has restaurant; *San Carlos,* US$1 s; *Hibueras,* US$1.25 s; *Motel Fraternidad,* US$2.50-5 s.

Banco de Honduras and Banco Atlántida. The Texaco service station, which is known as Gringo Jim's as it is run by a retired American, is very helpful in case of car trouble. Camping is also possible.

An hour's drive from Choluteca over an excellent road leads to Cedeño beach, primitive accommodation and meals. A lovely spot, but avoid public holiday crowds. Turning for Cedeño is 13 km. W of Choluteca.

Beyond Choluteca is a long climb to San Marcos de Colón, 915 metres in the hills (hotel), with beautiful views of the Gulf of Fonseca. Fourteen-and-a-half km. beyond San Marcos the road enters Nicaragua at El Espino (altitude 890 metres). The Inter-American Highway from the border of El Salvador to the border of Nicaragua is 151 km. Border formalities tedious, both at El Espino and Guasaule. Changing of currency sometimes uncertain.

East of Tegucigalpa

A good road runs E from the Capital to Danlí, about 121 km. away, in the department of El Paraíso: good walking country. Some 40 km. along, in the Zamorano valley (see page 971), is the Pan-American Agricultural School run for all students of the Americas with U.S. help: it has a fine collection of tropical flowers. At Zamorano turn off up a narrow winding road for about 5 km. to the picturesque centuries-old mining village of **San Antonio de Oriente**, much favoured by celebrated Honduran painters like Velásquez. A little further along our road branches S to **Yuscarán**, in rolling pine-land country at 1,070 metres. The climate here is semi-tropical. Yuscarán was an important mining centre in Colonial days and is a picturesque, typically Spanish Colonial village, with cobbled streets and ancient houses on a steep hillside. The disued Agua Fría mines are 10 km. to the SE by a steep, narrow, twisting and very picturesque road. Population, 1,250.

Danlí (11,400 people) uses the sugar it grows for making *aguardiente* and is a centre of the tobacco industry, making powerful cigars. There are regular buses which take 2 hours (US$2) between Tegucigalpa and Danlí. One road continues from Dalí to Santa María, crossing a mountain range with panoramic views. Another, now paved, goes S to El Paraíso (124 km. from the capital; 2,805 people), not far from the Nicaraguan frontier, from which a connecting paved road has now been built, linking with the Nicaraguan road network at Ocotal. A taxi to the Nicaraguan border from El Paraíso costs US$1.

Hotels at Danlí *La Esperanza,* US$2.50 s; *Danlí,* US$1.25 s; *Apolo,* US$2 s; *Maya Ejecutivo,* US$5 s, with bath; *Regis,* US$3 s, with bath, basic.

North-east of Tegucigalpa

The Carretera de Olancho runs from the capital to the Río Guayape, 143 km., and continues, in a very rough state (to be paved soon), another 50 km. to **Juticalpa,** at 820 metres above sea-level in a rich agricultural area herding cattle and growing cereals and sugar-cane. There are gravel roads N to Olanchito and NE through the cattle land of Catacamas to the coast of Cabo Camarón. Population 11,000. Airfield.

Hotels at Juticalpa *Antúñez,* US$2-4 s; *Las Vegas,* US$2.50 s.

Mosquitia is the name given to the region in the far NE of the country, which is forested, swampy and almost uninhabited. C. J. Tyrrell writes: Apart from the one road that stretches 100 km. from Puerto Lempira to Leymus and a further 100 km. to Ausbila, both on the Río Coco, there are no roads in the Honduran Mosquitia. The Government expect to start on the last stage of the Tegucigalpa-Puerto Lempira road, between Catacamas and Mokoron, in 1977. It would then be a two-day rough ride to Puerto Lempira. In this area, near the border of the Departments of Francisca Díaz and Colón, are the ruins of the Ciudad Blanca, believed to be an important Mayan ruin, which has so far been seen only from the air. Communications are by plane: Sahsa flies from Tegucigalpa weekly, and Lansa from La Ceiba twice weekly, to Ahuas, Brus Laguna and Puerto Lempira for US$28 one way; or by boat: coastal steamers leave infrequently from La Ceiba to Brus Laguna and Puerto Lempira, carrying passengers and cargo. The Missionary Aviation Fellowship, based in Ahuas, flies mission and medical trips to many remote villages, and may offer spare seats cheaply to the traveller. Within the area, transport is by dugout canoe with outboard motor—Don Juan, an Italian, has a few huts for tourists at Río Plátano reached by an hour's boat journey from Brus Laguna (US$7 for a charter canoe one-way), plus one hour's walk. The beautiful village of Cocabila is two hours' walk or horse ride further along the coast.

Accommodation in the Mosquitia is sometimes a problem as there are few facilities for the tourist. In villages, and as a last resort in the towns, the Baptist, Moravian and Catholic US missionaries and local clergy are very helpful to stranded travellers. In fact, the only reliable means of communication in both the Honduran and Nicaraguan Mosquitia are the two radio netweorks maintained by the Catholic and Moravian churches.

The adventurous might like to try to cross into Nicaragua *via* Leymus on the Río Coco, by getting a ride on one of the government jeeps from Puerto Lempira, or with a local trader, who makes the trip occasionally (US$5, or US$40 for a charter). There is sometimes a light plane at Puerto Lempira which will fly you there at US$20 a passenger. The Honduran immigration and customs at Leymus are very helpful. (For notes on Nicaraguan Mosquitia see page 913).

Economy

Honduras has the poorest economy in Central America and one of the lowest income rates per head in all Latin America. The damage done by Hurricane Fifi and the ensuing floods in September 1974 did little to improve the outlook for the economy, which grew by less than 2% in 1975, though it improved later to 6% in 1976 and to an estimated 8% in 1977. About 75% of the population live by the land, coffee and bananas are the main export crops. Cotton, once important, is now far less so. Tobacco, maize, beans, rice and sugar are grown mostly for domestic use but small quantities are sometimes exported. Cattle raising is becoming important and exports of both meat and livestock are growing. Some 45% of the land is forested and timber is the third leading export; it is to become more important as the development of forestry reserves in the Department of Olancho is carried out. This project includes the installation of a vast paper and pulp complex and is expected to have a considerable impact on the whole economy, once implemented.

Honduras' hopes of bettering itself through the Central American Common Market (CACM) were dashed by a 6-day war with El Salvador in July 1969. The CACM itself has been jeopardised by it but the signing of bilateral agreements with Guatemala, Nicaragua, Costa Rica, and also Panama, has offered wider trading possibilities.

Honduras has considerable reserves of silver, gold, lead, zinc, tin, iron, copper, coal and antimony, but only silver, gold, lead and zinc are mined and exported. Considerable offshore exploration for petroleum is in progress. There is an oil refinery at Puerto Cortés and exports of petroleum derivatives are becoming significant. An industrial free trade zone is to open here to encourage small industries to produce for export.

Local industries are small, turning out a wide range of consumer goods, besides being engaged in the processing of timber and agricultural products. The more important products are furniture, textiles, footwear, chemicals, cement and rubber.

Lead, zinc and silver are mined at El Mochito, W side of Lake Yojoa, by the New York and Honduras Rosario Mining Co.

Foreign Trade (US$m.)

	1971	1972	1973	1974	1975	1976
Exports (f.o.b.) ..	194.4	210.0	261.8	295.4	293.2	391.8
Imports (c.i.f.) ..	193.4	192.8	262.3	391.7	400.0	453.1

Information for Visitors

How to get there   The French Line sails regularly from London, the Hamburg-America Line, the Royal Netherlands Steamship Co. and others run regular cargo vessels with limited passenger space from North Sea ports to the Atlantic ports of Honduras; 3 or 4 weeks. The Hamburg-America Line, N.G. Lloyd and Johnson Line have cargo/passenger services from North Sea ports to Amapala, on the Pacific coast of Honduras. The Grace Line, United Fruit Line and the Standard Fruit Co. have services from continental and U.S. ports.

The best way is by air from the United States or from neighbouring countries. There are direct services by Taca, Sahsa, TAN and many others from Belize, Guatemala City, Mexico City, Miami, New Orleans, Panama City/Balboa, and San José (Costa Rica).

There are airstrips in the larger and smaller towns. Sahsa, Aero Servicios and Lansa have daily services between Tegucigalpa, San Pedro and La Ceiba.

There is an airport tax and hospital tax of 2.5% on all tickets sold for domestic journeys. There is an exit charge of US$2.50 for holiday makers. Note that the border offices close at 1700, not 1800 as in most other countries; there is an extra fee charged after that time.

Documents   Visitors must have a passport and visa. A valid International Certificate of Vaccination against smallpox is required only from visitors coming from the Indian subcontinent, Indonesia and the countries of southern Africa. Passport not needed by holders of tourist card (issued for 90 days to nationals of every country except Cuba), bought from Honduran consulates for US$2-3. Holders of the card must show proof of nationality. Visa not required, nor tourist card, for 90-day stay by nationals of West European countries (except Denmark, Ireland and Portugal), Japan and Costa Rica. Tourists can extend their visas or cards allowing a stay of 3 months for another 90 days if they have registered within 48 hours, and if towards the end of their permitted stay they present, either in person or through a representative, an application to stay on for not more than another 90 days. Address this to the Ministry of Foreign Affairs (Passport Section), enclosing a good conduct certificate issued by the Identification Dept. of the Directorate General of Public Security. Sometimes an entry or exit tax is charged ranging between US$0.40 to US$1. Some motorists have been charged an exit fee of US$2.50. There are no Customs duties on personal effects; 200 cigarettes or 100 cigars, or ½ kg. of tobacco and 2 quarts of spirit are allowed in free. No fresh food is allowed to cross the border and the interiors of cars are fumigated.

British business men planning a visit should get a copy of "Hints to Business Men Visiting Honduras", free on application to Dept. of Trade, Export Services Division, Export House, 50 Ludgate Hill, London, EC4M 7HU.

Hours of Business Monday to Friday: 0800-1200; 1330 or 1400-1700. Saturday: 0800-1100, and some open in the afternoon. Banks in Tegucigalpa 0900-1500; 0800-1100 only along the N coast on Saturday. In San Pedro Sula and along the N coast most places open and close half an hour earlier in the morning and afternoon than in Tegucigalpa.

Language Spanish, but English is spoken in the N, in the Bay Islands, by West Indian settlers on the coast, and is understood in most of the big business houses. Trade literature and correspondence should be in Spanish.

Tipping Normally 10% of bill.

Internal Transport Hitch-hiking is easy. The best map of the country is produced by the Instituto Nacional de Geografía, open weekday mornings. Take your passport when you go to buy one. Another map is issued by Texaco; after some persistence the tourist office may provide one.

Cost of Living Inflation has dealt less severely with Honduras than with some other Central American countries, but the cost of living rose in 1974 by 13.4%, in the wake of the oil crisis, compared with 4.7% in 1973; it moderated to 6.5% in 1975, 5.6% in 1976 and 7.4% in 1977.

Climate Temperature is a matter of altitude. It is hot in the coastal regions but not unpleasant in Tegucigalpa and other districts at about 1,000 metres. Rain is frequent on the Atlantic littoral during the whole year; the heaviest occurs from September to February inclusive. In Tegucigalpa the dry season is normally from December to mid-May inclusive. The coolest months are December and January but if a traveller visits the Atlantic littoral he should avoid these months because heavy rains impede travel; the best months for this area are April and May, though very hot.

Clothing Men wear dark light-weight suits in the capital most of the year and slightly heavier worsteds from November to February. When it is very hot light coloured tropical-weight suits can be worn. Black dinner jackets for formal wear. On the north coast, which is much hotter and damper, dress is more informal.

Women wear light cotton dresses from March to October and light woollen garments from November to February. Cocktail or dinner dresses are worn in the evening for social occasions and a fur or stole is necessary. Shorts and scanty attire are not worn in public by anybody, except on the beach. Laundering is undertaken by most hotels.

Health Dysentery and stomach parasites are prevalent and malaria is endemic in coastal regions, where mosquito nets should be carried. Inoculate against typhoid and tetanus. Drinking water is definitely not safe; drink bottled water. Salads and raw vegetables must be sterilized under personal supervision. There are hospitals at Tegucigalpa and all the bigger towns. Leotards, a Danish formula, is excellent when suffering from intestinal parasites. Excellent ointments for curing the all-too-prevalent tropical skin complaints are Scabisan (Mexican) and Betnovate (Glaxo).

Currency The unit is a lempira, also known as a peso. It is divided into 100 centavos and its par value is half the United States dollar. There are copper coins of 1 and 2 centavos and nickel coins of 5 (cinquinto), 10 (búfalo), 20 (daime), and 50 (tostón) centavos. U.S. visitors will find that the coins are exactly the same size and material as U.S. coins of equivalent value; hence the 20 centavos is a "dime". A "real" is 12½ centavos (there are no coins of this value, but the term is much used). Bank notes are for 1, 5, 10, 20 and 100 lempiras. Any amount of any currency can be taken in or out.

The metric system of weights is official and should be used. Land is measured in varas (838 mm.) and manzanas (0.7 hectate).

Shopping Leather is cheaper than in El Salvador and Nicaragua, but not as cheap as in Colombia.

Sea-Mails from London to Tegucigalpa take 1 to 3 months. Parcels from the United States for Tegucigalpa arrive *via* Puerto Cortés.

Air Mail takes 4 to 7 days to Europe and the same for New York. Airmail to Britain 40 centavos; aerograms, 30.

Telephones are installed in most of the main towns. ITT Comunicaciones and the Tropical Radio Telegraph Company provide international radio telephone and radio telegraph services from their stations at Puerto Cortés, Tela, La Lima and Tegucigalpa, and other interior points.

Telephone service between Honduras and Britain is available on weekdays between 1500 and 2130 (G.M.T.). The cost of a 3-minute call is about L35.85. Local Standard Time is 6 hours behind G.M.T.

The principal **newspapers** in Tegucigalpa are "El Dia", "El Cronista", "La Tribuna", and "La Noticia". In San Pedro Sula: "El Tiempo" and "La Prensa" (circulation about 45,000). None is of very high quality.

Public Holidays Most of the feast days of the Roman Catholic religion and also

January 1: New Year's Day.	September 15: Independence Day.
April 14: Day of the Americas.	October 3: Francisco Morazán.
Holy Week: Thurs., Fri., and Sat.	October 12: Discovery of America.
before Easter Sunday.	October 21: Army Day.
May 1: Labour Day.	December 25.

Great Britain has a Consulate-General at Tegucigalpa (Edif. Palic, 4F, Av. República de Chile; P.O. Box 290; Tel.: 2-0479), and is re-establishing its Embassy there.

The **United States of America** has an Embassy and Consulate in Tegucigalpa.

Honduras Consul, 48 George Street, London W1. Tel.: 01-486-4880.

American Express Agents Tegucigalpa: Mundirama Travel Service, Edif. Fiallos, Planta Baja 123. Tel.: 2-6979, 2-6111.

We are deeply grateful to John C. Moran (Nashville, Tennessee) and John Streather for invaluable assistance in updating this section; also to other travellers whose names are listed in the general Central American section.

NICARAGUA

NICARAGUA (148,000 square km.), the same size as England and Wales, is the largest Central American republic. It has 541 km. of coast on the Caribbean and 352 km. on the Pacific. Costa Rica is to the S, Honduras to the N. Only 8% of the whole country, out of a possible 28%, is in economic use and population density is low: 12.2 persons to the square km., as compared with El Salvador's 157.3. Nine-tenths of its 2.5m. people live in the west. An odd feature for a country so sketchily industrialized is that 42% of its people live in towns. One in six lived in the capital, Managua, now being rebuilt after it was largely destroyed by an earthquake in December 1972.

There are three well-marked regions: (1) a large triangular-shaped central mountain land whose apex rests almost on the southern border with Costa Rica; the prevailing moisture-laden NE winds drench its eastern slopes, which are deeply forested with oak and pine on the drier, cooler heights. (2) A wide belt of eastern lowland through which a number of rivers flow from the mountains into the Atlantic. (3) The belt of lowland which runs from the Gulf of Fonseca, on the Pacific, diagonally across the isthmus, through two great lakes, to the Caribbean: the proposed route of a canal which was finally built in Panama. All the large towns and nine-tenths of the people are in this lowland. Out of it, to the E, rise the lava cliffs of the mountains to a height of from 1,500 to 2,100 metres. Peninsulas of high land jut out here and there into the lowland, which is from 65 to 80 km. wide along the Pacific.

In this diagonal plain are two large sheets of water. The capital, Managua, is on the shores of Lake Managua, 52 km. long, 15 to 25 wide, and 39 metres above sea-level. The river Tipitapa drains it into Lake Nicaragua, 148 km. long, about 55 km. at its widest, and 32 metres above the sea. Granada is on its shores. It is navigable, and launches ply on the Rio San Juan which drains it into the Caribbean.

There has been great volcanic activity at the north-western end of the lowland, from Lake Nicaragua to the Gulf of Fonseca. Three volcano cones rise to 1,500 metres or so in Lake Nicaragua itself, and one, the famous Momotombo, on the northern shore of Lake Managua. From Momotombo north-westwards to the truncated cone of Cosegüina, overlooking the Gulf of Fonseca, there is a row of over 20 volcanoes, some of them active. Their ash makes a rich soil for crops. The wet, warm winds of the Caribbean pour heavy rain on the basin of the San Juan river, which is forested as far as Lake Nicaragua. But rains are moderate in the rest of the lowlands running NW to the Gulf of Fonseca.

A finger of narrow highland stretches N along the Pacific coast from Costa Rica through the lowlands; with one interruption at Rivas, it reaches as far as Managua.

Settlement The Spanish *conquistadores* reached the lowland from Panama as early as 1519. On the south-western shores of Lake Nicaragua they found an area comparatively densely settled by peaceful Indians, who lavished gold ornaments on them. Five years later another expedition

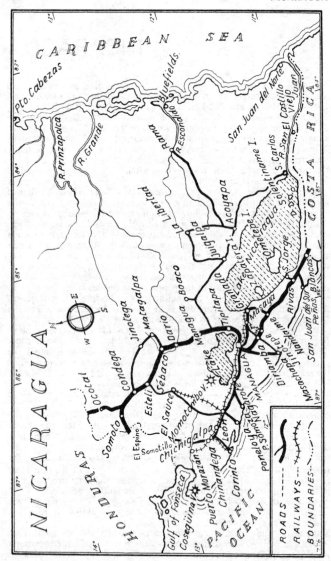

ROUGH SKETCH

founded colonies at Granada and León, but the flow of gold soon stopped and most of the Spaniards moved elsewhere. In 1570, both colonies were put under the jurisdiction of Guatemala. The local administrative centre was not rich Granada, with its profitable crops of sugar, cocoa, and indigo, but impoverished León, then barely able to subsist on its crops of maize, beans, rice, and bananas. This reversal of the Spanish policy of choosing the most successful settlement as administrative centre was due to the ease with which León could be reached from the Pacific. In 1858 Managua was chosen as a new capital.

Nine in ten of the people of Nicaragua live and work between the Pacific and the western shores of Lake Nicaragua, the south-western shore of Lake Managua, and the south-western sides of the row of volcanoes. It is only of late years that settlers have taken to coffee-growing and cattle-rearing in the highlands at Matagalpa and Jinotega. Elsewhere the highlands, save for an occasional mining camp, are almost empty.

The densely forested eastern lowlands fronting the Caribbean were neglected, partly because of the heavy rainfall, partly on account of their unhealthiness, until the British settled several colonies of Jamaicans in the 18th century at Bluefields and San Juan del Norte (Greytown). But early this century the United Fruit Company of America opened banana plantations inland from Puerto Cabezas, worked by blacks from Jamaica. Other companies followed suit along the coast, but the bananas were later attacked by Panama disease and exports today are small. Along the Mosquito coast there are still English-speaking communities in which African, or mixed African and indigenous, blood predominates.

This area, together with about half the coastal area of Honduras, was a British Protectorate from 1780 to 1885, and was known as the Miskito kingdom. It was populated then, as now, by Misquito Indians, but today there is a predominance of African blood. They still speak English and in spite of Spanish influence at school and elsewhere, they maintain their special way of life. They are different even in religion. (Protestant missions played a most important role in the making of Bluefields and are still significant in the social organisation of the town, where there is a protestant cathedral.) Spanish-speaking Nicaraguans, and some Europeans, Americans and Chinese also live in the area.

Ports and Communications The main Pacific ports are Corinto, San Juan del Sur, and Puerto Somoza. The two most-used Atlantic ports are Puerto Cabezas and Bluefields. The **roads** have been greatly extended and improved. The Inter-American Highway from the Honduran border to the borders of Costa Rica (384 km.), is paved the whole way and so is the shorter international road to Honduras *via* Choluteca from Chinandega; the new road between Managua and Rama (for Bluefields) is almost all paved and in good condition. There are now 2,060 km. of road, 900 paved and 1,300 km. all-weather. There is only one **railway**, the Ferrocarril del Pacífico, 349 km. long, single track, and with a gauge of 1.067 metres. (The map makes its course clear.) A diesel service has increased both speed and comfort. The **air services** are given in "Information for Visitors".

The People Besides the Mestizo intermixtures of Spanish and Indian blood (77%), there are pure blacks (9%), pure Indians (4%), and mixtures of the two (mostly along the Atlantic coast). A small proportion is of pure Spanish and European blood. Death rate is 8.37 per 1,000; birth rate, 41.24; infant mortality, 65; life expectancy, 50 years. Annual population growth: 3.5%; urban growth: 6.1%; illiteracy, 50%.

Administration The republic is divided into 16 departments and one Comarca, each under a civil Governor who supervises finance, education and other matters. Judicial power is vested in a Supreme Court of Justice at Managua, five Chambers of Second Instance (León, Masaya, Granada, Matagalpa, and Bluefields), and 153 judges of lower tribunals. National Defence is the responsibility of the national Guard, represented in each locality by the respective Military Commandant.

Roman Catholicism is the prevailing religion, but there are Episcopal, Baptist, Methodist and other Protestant churches. There is an archbishop, with his seat at Managua, and 7 bishoprics. Education at the Universidad Nacional Autónoma de Nicaragua at León, with 3 faculties at Managua, and the private Jesuit Universidad Centroamericana at Managua is of the highest, but only 0.5% get to a university; 58% of school-age children do not attend school.

The **Constitution** of November 6, 1950, provides for a Congress of two houses, consisting of 42 Deputies and 16 Senators elected every 5 years. The executive power is vested in a President, who is elected for 6 years and many not be re-elected for a consecutive second term. The first secret ballot was in the 1963 elections.

On May 1, 1972, power was vested in a provisional Junta composed of members of the two traditional parties: Liberal and Conservative. General elections were held in September 1974, and Gen. Anastasio Somoza Debayle (see next page) was again elected President.

History For Nicaragua's early history, see the introductory chapter to Central America. It became an independent state in 1838.

The famous (or infamous) filibustering expedition of William Walker is often referred to in the text. William Walker (1824-1860) was born in Nashville, U.S.A., graduated at the University in 1838, studied medicine at Edinburgh and Heidelberg, was granted his M.D. in 1843, and then studied law and was called to the bar. On October 5, 1853, he sailed with a filibustering force to conquer Mexican territory, declared Lower California and Sonora an independent republic and was then driven out. In May, 1855, with 56 followers armed with a new type of rifle, he sailed for Nicaragua, where a belligerent faction had invited him to come to its aid. In October he seized a steamer on Lake Nicaragua belonging to the Accessory Transit Company, an American corporation controlled by Cornelius Vanderbilt engaged in carrying passengers and freight across the Isthmus. He was then able to surprise and capture Granada and make himself master of Nicaragua. Rivas was made President, with Walker in real control as Commander of the Forces. Two officials decided to use him to get control of the Transit Company, advanced him funds and brought him recruits, free of charge, from the U.S. The Company was seized and handed over to his friends. A new Government was formed in 1855 and in June 1856 Walker was elected President. On September 22, from alleged economic necessity and to gain support from the slave states in America he suspended the Nicaraguan laws against slavery. The government was formally recognised by the U.S. that year. A coalition of Central American states, backed by Cornelius Vanderbilt, fought against him, but he was able to hold his own until May 1857, when he surrendered to the U.S. Navy to avoid capture. In November, 1857, he sailed from Mobile with another expedition, but soon after landing near Greytown, Nicaragua, he was arrested by a naval commander and returned to the U.S. In 1860 he sailed again from Mobile and landed in Honduras. There he was taken prisoner by Captain Salmon, of the British Navy, and handed over to the Honduran authorities, who tried and executed him on September 12, 1860. Walker's own book, *The War in Nicaragua,* is a fascinating document.

In 1911 the United States pledged help in securing a loan to be guaranteed through the control of Nicaraguan customs by an American board. In 1912 the United States sent marines into Nicaragua to enforce the control. Apart from short intervals, they stayed there until 1933. During the last five years of occupation, nationalists under General César Augusto Sandino waged relentless guerrilla war against the U.S. Marines, who failed to suppress it. In November 1932 the American high command appointed Anastasio Somoza supreme commander of the Nicaraguan National

Guard—the beginning of a complete domination of Nicaragua by the Somoza family which has lasted to this day. General Sandino was killed by Somoza's men in February 1933. American forces were finally withdrawn in 1933, when President Franklin Roosevelt announced the "Good Neighbour" policy, pledging non-intervention.

From 1932, with brief intervals, Nicaraguan affairs were dominated by General Anastasio Somoza until he was assassinated in 1956. His two sons have both served a presidential term, and President Anastasio Somoza (junior) began his second term of office as President on December 1, 1974; the length of the term is six years.

Cities and Towns

Managua, the nation's capital and commercial centre since 1858, is on the southern shores of Lake Managua, at an altitude of 55 metres. It is 45 km. from the Pacific, but 140 km. from its port, Corinto, though a new port, Puerto Somoza, built by the late President, is only 70 km. away. Managua was destroyed by earthquake in March 1931, and part of it swept by fire five years later; it was completely rebuilt as an up-to-date capital and commercial city (population 300,000) but the centre was again completely destroyed, apart from a few modern buildings, by another earthquake in December 1972.

The Government has now decided that it will rebuild the old centre, adding parks and recreational facilities, although it is anticipated that this project will take years to complete. Present-day Managua has no centre as such, but rather consists of a series of commercial developments which have been built in what used to be the outskirts of the old city.

The principal commercial areas of Managua are now situated on the Masaya Road and the two bypass roads S of the city. These centres contain a wide variety of shops, modern cinemas and discothèques.

In the old centre of Managua, one can still see examples of colonial architecture in the Presidential Palace and the Cathedral. These buildings are situated on the Parque Central and provide a striking contrast with the modern Ruben Dario theatre on the lake shore and the Banco de América building in the background.

Points of Interest There are several volcanic-crater lagoons in the environs of Managua, some of which have become centres of residential development and also have swimming, boating, fishing and picnicking facilities for the public. Among the more attractive of these lagoons is Laguna de Jiloa, situated about 10 km. from Managua just off the new road to León. At Jiloa a new private aquatic club (El Náutico) has recently opened; here boats can be rented. Other lagoons within a ¼ hour drive of Managua are the Laguna de Apoyo and Laguna de Masaya, situated respectively at Kms. 35 and 15 of the Masaya road.

The Huellas de Acahualinca are Managua's only site of archaeological interest. These are prehistoric animal footprints which have been preserved in solidified lava, and are assumed to have come into existence as animals fled from a volcanic eruption about 3,000 years ago. The Huellas are located close to the old centre of town, near the lakeshore at the end of the South Highway.

On this site there is also a small museum which exhibits a variety of prehistoric artefacts.

A 10-km. drive down Carretera Sur—this is the Inter-American Highway—through the residential section of Las Piedrecitas takes us by the U.S. Ambassador's residence to Laguna de Asososca, another small lake (the city's reservoir) in the wooded crater of an old volcano.

Piedrecitas Park is to one side of the lagoon: there is a beautiful 3½-km. ride, playgrounds for children, a café, and splendid views of Lake Managua, two lagoons—Asososca and Jiloa—and on Momotombo. Beyond again is little Nejapa Lagoon (medicinal waters). The Inter-American Highway to Costa Rica passes through Casa Colorada (hotel), 26 km. from Managua, at 900 metres, with commanding views of both the Pacific and of Lake Managua, and a delightful climate.

Boats can be hired on the shores of Lake Managua for visiting the still-smoking Momotombo and the shore villages (see also page 993). At its foot lies León Viejo, which was destroyed in 1609 and is now being excavated. It was in the Cathedral here that Pedrarias and his wife were buried. Near the large volcano is a smaller one, Momotombito. A fine drive skirts the shores of the lake. Volcano fans can also visit the Santiago volcano (page 995). The Las Mercedes international airport is near the lake, 9 km. E of the city, reached by bus No. 4 and others.

Coffee and cotton are the great crops of the country around. A third of Nicaragua's industry is concentrated in or near Managua, where there is an Esso refinery.

Beaches   For those who are interested in less energetic activities there are several beaches on the Pacific coast, about an hour's drive from the city. The nearest are Pochomil, Masachapa and Casares. Because of their proximity to the capital, these are very popular during the season (Jan.-April) and tend to be somewhat crowded. A visit to the El Velero beach (turn off at Km. 60 on the old road to León and then follow signs) is recommended despite the US$3.50 entrance charge. Here, a broad expanse of sand leads down to the rolling waves of the Pacific. There is a motel (US$30 for a double room) and a restaurant (food adequate but expensive). However, the beach itself is beautiful, and the sea is ideal for both body surfing and swimming.

Fiesta   Santo Domingo is the patron saint of Managua. His festival is held at El Malecón from August 1 to 10: church ceremonies, horse racing, bull-fights, cock-fights, a lively carnival; proceeds to the General Hospital. August 1 (half day) and August 10 are local holidays.

Voltage   110 A.C., 60 cycles.

Hotels   New hotels are gradually being opened in Managua. Several have been built along the highway that bypasses the old part of the city, but there is still a shortage: *Intercontinental,* US$35 d; *Camino Real,* US$35 d; *Carlos V,* US$25 d; *Aeropuerto Las Mercedes,* US$20 d; *Hotel Siete Mares* (one block E of *Intercontinental*), has good Chinese restaurant; also a block away from the *Intercontinental* is *Embassy,* US$25 d, German-run, good, relatively cheap meals; *Ticomo* at Km. 8½, Carretera Sur, has parking facilities, rents apartments, a/c, with maid service and kitchenette, US$20 per night, good for longer stay; *Española,* 3 blocks NE of *Intercontinental,* US$13 d, restaurant; *Estrella,* US$16.50 d with breakfast; *Casa de Fiedler,* 8a Calle Sur-Oeste 1320, *Colonia Residencial Pereira,* small and quiet, US$7-10 s, meals US$2.50; *Palace,* 3 blocks from Ticabus terminal, US$11 d, with bath, comfortable, quiet, good value; nearby *El Dorado,* new and expensive at US$14 d (try and bargain for a lower rate); *residencias* at US$15 d are *Casa Skandia, Bolonia Inn, Pataky Residence; Colón,* US$5 s, good meals; *Sultana* at the Ticabus terminal (basic) at US$3; *Pensión Cerna,* one block away from the Ticabus terminal, US$1.50 p.p.; *Su Hospedaje,* US$1.50 p.p. *Comedor Internacional,* also near Ticabus terminal, has rooms for US$1.50 d. or s, noisy; *Hospedaje Oriental,* near eastern market, US$1.40 each, clean. *Pensión Molinito* (no sign), one block from the Ticabus Station, basic but clean, US$1.50 p.p. It is possible to camp on the wasteland in front of the *Intercontinental Hotel.*

Restaurants   *The Lobster Inn* (Km. 5½ South Highway), good for guess what; *Los Ranchos* (Km. 3 South Highway), *El Corral* (Km. 8½ North Highway), and *Los Gauchos* (Km. 3 Masaya Highway), for steaks; *El Coliseo* (Km. 8 Masaya Highway), Italian; *El Rincón Español* (old Managua), Spanish; *Peppers* (Drefus Centre), pizzas; *Pizza Deli* (Km. 6 Masaya Highway); *Antojitos* (opposite *Intercontinental Hotel*), Mexican; *La Marseillaise* (Colonia los Robles), excellent French food, and *Zummen Cafetería* (Bypass South) for cheap eating; *El Rubi* (Chinese, good food, bad service); *Gambrinus; Chips* (snack bar at Cine Dorado). However, for a good overall selection of international cuisine, it is best to eat in the restaurants of the principal hotels.

Discothèques   Lobo Jack, La Nueva Managua, Frisco Disco, Casa Blanca, Pantera Rosa. Live music is offered at La Vista, Torre Blanca, Tiffany's Saloon and El Arroyito.

Tourist Board   Located 1 block from the *Intercontinental Hotel*. Hours: 0900 to 1500. Standard information available, including a good map of Managua. The best map of the capital and country can be bought from the Instituto Nacional Geográfico. The Esso map is also good.

Clubs   Terraza, Nejapa Country Club, Cuesta Club, Club Náutico, Lions, Rotary.

Shopping   Some handicrafts (goldwork, embroidery, etc.) are available in the Centro Comercial de Managua. Worth a visit is the Casa del Lagarto, where alligator handbags and shoes are sold at reasonable prices but US visitors had better make sure first whether they may be imported; the Endangered Species Act is very stringent. Also, a visit to the handicrafts market in Masay (30 km. away) is worthwhile.

Local Transport   Bus service in Managua is poor but cheap. Taxis can be flagged down along the street. Prices vary from US$0.80 to US$1.50 within Managua, depending on the distance involved. Be sure to agree price before entering taxi. Taxis stationed at the *Intercontinental Hotel* and the airport are relatively more expensive. US$3 for a short trip, US$6 from the airport to downtown.

Car Hire   There are three rental firms in Managua, Hertz, Avis and Budget. Rates start at US17 per day. Given the poor public transportation and the decentralized layout of Managua, renting a car is often the best way to get around. Daily rate for a rented Volkswagen: US$17 plus 5 cents a km. Weekly rate: US$50, plus 5 cents a km. Gasoline is US$0.85 the U.S. gallon.

Buses   Bus to Granada, Ruta 4, US$0.70, 1½ hrs. To Masaya, US$0.30. To Peñas Blancas, on border with Costa Rica, US$2, 2 hours. To León, US$1, 2 hours.

Banks   Bank of London & South America, Plaza de Compras, Colonia Centro América, with agencies on the North Highway (Blvd. Kennedy), Centro Comercial Nejapa and Montoya., Banco Caley Dagnall, Banco de América, Citibank, Bank of America, Banco Nacional de Nicaragua, Banco Nicaragüense. Open Monday-Friday 0900-1500, Saturday 0830-1130.

Cables   Telcor, Radio Nacional.

Airlines   Telephone numbers: Pan American, 3521/3; Lanica, 23341/2; Taca International, 25482; Copa, 25808; Sahsa, 3624/9.

Rail   Pacific Railway to port of Corinto *via* León (branch to El Sauce) and Chinandega; to Granada, Masaya, Masatepe, San Marcos, Diriamba, Jinotepe.

Roads   to León and Chinandega and then to Choluteca in Honduras; to Masaya and Granada; Inter-American Highway N to Honduras (to Tegucigalpa is 444 km.), and SE to Costa Rica. Good paved roads from Casa Colorada to Masachapa, Managua to Granada and Nandaime.

International Buses   Tica bus to Central American capitals daily. To Panama US$18.50, to San José US$6, to Tegucigalpa US$9, to San Salvador US$12 and to Guatemala US$17. Make sure that the driver does not overcharge for border crossing dues. Ticabus can also be caught in León or Granada subject to previous arrangement in Managua. Sirca Express (cheaper than Tica) leaves 0500 for Honduras, Salvador, Guatemala and Mexico; 0600 for Costa Rica and Panama.

Tours of city by private car, 1 or 3 persons, about US$10. All-day tour to Granada and León, US$30. A 2-day round trip by motor bus and riverboat from Managua to Bluefields costs US$20.

Sport   Baseball (the national game), basketball, cockfighting and bullfighting (but no kill), swimming, hunting, sailing, tennis, golf.

Camping   A few km. W of Managua on Ruta 12 is the Nica Trailer Park.

Warning   Managua is full of thieves; even in daylight it is not safe to walk in some areas.

Inter-American Highway from Managua to Honduras: 214 km., and paved the whole way. Comfortable bus services. Also paved are the branch roads to Matagalpa and Jinotega. The first stretch of 21 km. to Tipitapa is along the southern edge of Lake Managua. **Tipitapa**, on the SE shore of the lake, is a tourist resort with hot sulphur baths, an hotel, a casino, a colourful market, and a Fiesta of El Señor de Esquipulas on January 13-16. (Honduras can also be reached further east by a road from Ocotal *via* Las Manos to Danlí, and further west by the Chinandega-Río Gusaule-Choluteca link.)

Hotel   *Baños Termales* has closed, though its swimming pool still functions.

Restaurant   *Salón Silva,* unpretentious, but excellent lake fish.

Bus from Managua (minibus), US$0.20.

From San Benito, near Tipitapa, the Atlantic Highway runs E through Juigalpa (3,989 people; 109 km. from Managua) and La Libertad, a goldmining town at 600 metres, to Cara de Mono, on the Río Mico, and finally to Rama, on the Río Escondido or Bluefields River, 290 km. from Managua. River boats ply from Rama 100 km. down stream to Bluefields (see page 998).

The Inter-American Highway goes N through Tipitapa to Sébaco, 105 km. The road has been newly paved, is wide and very good. Fourteen km. before reaching Sébaco is Ciudad Darío, where the poet Rubén Darío was born; you can see the house, which is maintained as a museum. From Sébaco a 24-km. branch road leads (right) to **Matagalpa** at 678 metres; population 40,000. Buses every half hour to Managua, 127 km., take 2½ hours (US$1.45). Matagalpa has an old church, but it is about the only Colonial style building left; the town has developed rapidly in recent years. There are gold mines in the area, but they are exhausted; the main occupation is coffee planting and there are cattle ranges; the chief industry is the Nestlé powdered-milk plant. A 32-km. road runs from Matagalpa to the Tuma valley. September 24, Día de La Merced, is a local holiday.

Hotels   *Ideal,* now the best; *Bermúdez, Monteleón; Plaza.* **Motel**   *Las Marías,* 3 km. out on El Tuma road.

Restaurants   *Corona de Oro, Monte Sol, Oriental, Cantón, Royal Bar, El Establo.*

Bank of London and South America, Edificio Delaney, Av. Central y Calle de Paraíso, and four national banks.

There is a fine 34-km. highway from Matagalpa to **Jinotega,** and on another 80 km., *via* the picturesque villages of San Rafael del Norte and Yalí, to join the main highway at Condega, 51 km. from the Honduras border. Jinotega (altitude 1,004 metres) is served by buses from Managua and Matagalpa. Population 20,000; famous images in church. The coffee grown here and in Matagalpa is so excellent that a premium is usually paid for it. Road (18 km.) to El Tuma power station; another to Estelí.

Hotel Santa María de Ostuma is a fine mountain inn, at over 1,200 metres, 10 km. along the scenic paved road from Matagalpa to Jinotega; good food, superb scenery. At Jinotega is the *Moderno Hotel.*

Beyond Sébaco the Inter-American Highway goes through **Estelí**, a rapidly developing departmental capital of about 20,000 people, and Condega (2,000 people) to Somoto, near Honduran border, centre of pitch-pine industry. (Local holiday: Nov. 11.) Just before reaching Somoto a road leads off from Yalagüina right (18 km.) to **Ocotal**, an attractive, but surprisingly expensive, small town of 3,863 people at 600 metres on a sandy plain near the Honduras border, to which a road runs N. Close by, at San Albino, there are many gold mines and gold is washed in the river Coco.

Hotels at Ocotal   *Hotel Central*, on main plaza, recommended; *El Portal*, nice and clean, US$3.60 d; *Pensión Centroamericana; Hospedaje Central.* For eating, *Restaurant La Cabaña.*

The 134-km. section from Sébaco to the border at El Espino is through sharp hills with steep climbs and descents, but reasonably well banked and smooth.

Hotels on Inter-American Highway   At Esteli, 839 metres (site of prehistoric carved stone figures and a recommended overnight stop) there is the *Motel Estelí*, excellent, with *El Bramadero* restaurant and good parking lot; *Motel El Chico*, similar facilities, US$5.50 d; *Alpino; Hotel Adeli*, US$1.50 d, good cheap food; *El Chalet.* At Somoto: *Panaméricano* and *Internacional*, both only fair, at US$1.30 s. At Ciudad Dario: *Grande.*

A fine new highway leads off the Inter-American Highway near San Isidro, about 20 km. SE of Estelí, to join the Pacific Highway near León. This is an attractive alternative route to Managua through the Chinandega cotton growing area, past the spectacular chain of volcanoes running W from Lake Managua, and through León.

Managua to Corinto: 140 km. the first city of any note along the railway is León, 88 km. from Managua, reached in 2¼ hours. There is also a road (the Pacific Highway) between the two cities; it goes on to Chinandega and has been continued to Corinto and the Honduran border; it joins the Inter-American Highway at Choluteca, Honduras, and now offers the quickest route between Managua and the countries to the N.

About 60 km. down the new road to León lies the village of La Paz Centro. It is from here that one can gain access to the volcano Momotombo (see page 993), which dominates the Managua skyline from the West. Although it is possible to drive half way up the volcano, access to the crater itself involves a further 2-3 hour hike. Proper preparations should be made if this expedition is undertaken as the terrain is rough and dry and there are poisonous snakes in the area. During the ascent of the mountain, it is possible to observe geysers being tapped for thermal energy. Another interesting active volcano, easier to visit, is Santiago (see page 995).

León, with a population of 63,000, was founded by Hernández de Córdoba in 1524 at León Viejo, 32 km. from its present site, at the foot of Momotombo. It was destroyed by earthquake on December 31, 1609 (the ruins are best reached by boat from Managua), and the city moved to its present site the next year. It was the capital from its foundation until Managua took over in 1858; it is still the "intellectual" capital, with a university (founded 1804), religious colleges, the largest cathedral in Central America, and at least a dozen Colonial churches. It is said that Managua became the capital, although at the time it was only an Indian settlement, because it was half-way between violently Liberal León and equally violently Conservative Granada. Be that as it may, the "Liberals" are now as dominant in Managua as they ever were in León.

The city has an ancient air: tortuous streets, roofs tiled in red, low adobe houses and time-worn buildings everywhere. The old Plaza de Armas, in front of the Cathedral, is now Parque Jérez; it contains a statue of General Jérez, a mid-19th century Liberal leader. Four bronze lions stand at the four entrances.

The Cathedral, begun in 1746 and not completed for 100 years, is an enormous building. It has a famous shrine, 145 cm. high, covered by white topazes from India given by Philip II of Spain, which is kept in a safe in the vestry, and the bishop holds the key; a very fine ivory Christ; the consecrated Altar of Sacrifices and the Choir of Córdoba; the Great Christ of Esquipulas, a Colonial work in bronze whose cross is of very fine silver; and statues of the 12 Apostles. At the foot of one of these statues is the tomb of Rubén Darío, the 19th-century Nicaraguan poet, guarded by a sorrowing lion.

The western end of the city is the oldest, and here is the most ancient of all the churches: the parish church of Subtiava (1530) where Las Casas, the "Apostle of the Indies", preached on several occasions. It has the best Colonial altar in the country and a very remarkable representation of the sun ("El Sol") revered by the Indians. The house of Rubén Darío, one of the greatest Latin American poets, the famous "Four Corners" in Calle Rubén Darío, is now the Museo-Archivo Rubén Darío; in 1916 he died in another house in the NW sector marked with a plaque. The Holy Week ceremonies are outstanding. There is a good road (20 km.) to the sandy Pacific beach at Poneloya (Hotel Lacayo, basic); the local bus from León is a converted truck. A branch railway runs to (64 km.) El Sauce, where there is an old church, and a riotous fair in February.

Local Holidays September 24, November 1 (All Saints' Day).

Hotels at León Europa, best, US$7-10 s, good meals US$2 each; América, Av. Santiago Argüello; Pensión Carmen, US$1.70 p.p., stay there only if desperate. La Libertad, US$5 per room with bath, no hot water, new, clean and comfortable. Hospedaje La Primavera, US$1.20. Several cheap pensiones near the railway station.

Bank of London and South America (agency), 1a Calle Norte, between Av. Este and Av. Central. Agencies of Banco Nacional de Nicaragua, Banco de América, and Banco Nicaragüense.

Industries Cotton mills, sawmills, fertilizers, manufacture of barrels, salt, soft drinks, insecticides and sterilized milk plant. Centre of León Valley Irrigation Project.

Bus Managua-León, Route 12, 1¼ hours, US$1. Colectivo, US$1.50.

Train Managua-León, US$0.80, 2 hours. Trip gives good views of lakes and volcanoes.

Chinandega is about 35 km. beyond León. Population 37,000. This is one of the big cotton-growing districts, and also grows bananas and sugar cane. Not far away, at Chichigalpa, is Ingenio San Antonio, the largest sugar mill in Nicaragua, with its own private railway to its own port on the Pacific. From Managua, by road, 2½ hours; by train, 4 hours. Hourly buses to Managua from 0500. From León, 1 hour by bus, US$0.50. To the Honduran border, US$1.40. Local holiday: July 26.

Hotels Salón Carlos, US$3 p.p. with breakfast, share shower; Pensión Cortés, US$1.40 s, basic. Pensión Urbina, US1.10, basic. On the road to Honduras border, Hotel Cosigüina, 50 rooms, 2 restaurants, shops, cinema and discothèque.

Industries Cotton mills, cottonseed oil plant, sawmills, flour mill, sugar refinery.

Bank of London and South America, Av. Central y Calle Central.

A road runs NE to Puerto Morazán. This passes through the village of El Viejo, where there is an ancient church. Puerto Morazán (hotel), 26 km. from Chinandega, is a modern town on a navigable river running into the Gulf of Fonseca. There are only very rare boat services between it and La Unión (El Salvador), across the Gulf, but there is a daily vehicle ferry from nearby Potosí to La Unión. The charge is US$3 p.p., US$100 per car. (Coming into Nicaragua customs and immigration formalities can take time.) Colectivo, Chinandega-Potosí, US$2, 2½ hours. A few km. to the W is the cone of Cosigüina volcano. On January 23, 1835, one of the biggest eruptions in history blew off most of the cone, reducing it from 3,000 metres to its present height of 870 metres. From Chinandega a paved road goes to the Honduran border at Somotillo where it is continued by an equally good road to Choluteca, Honduras.

Corinto, 21 km. from Chinandega, is the main port of entry. It is the only port at which vessels of any considerable size can berth and the only port joined by railway to the three largest cities in the country: Managua, León, and Granada. About 60% of the country's commerce passes through it, notably coffee, cotton, sugar, timber and hides as exports. The town itself is on a sandy island, Punto Icaco, connected with the mainland by long railway and road bridges. Population: 10,000.

Hotels *Costa Azul; Restaurant Imperial* on Calle Mario Izaguarre has double rooms for US$2.
Steamers Passenger: Italia Line. Cargo: French Line; Hamburg-Amerika; Holland-America; Johnson; Mamenic; North German Lloyd. Fortnighly joint fast cargo service (no passengers) of Central America Services to and from Europe.
Royal Mail Agents at Managua and Corinto: J. L. Griffith (Sucs) Ltd., P.O. Box 3513, Managua.

Managua to Granada There are two routes, one by rail and one by a very good 61 km. paved road with a fast and comfortable bus service; both run through Masaya.
Santiago Volcano Turn right on the Masaya road at—or take bus US$0.30 from Managua to—Piedras Quemadas (km. 18) just before Masaya (any bus to Masaya or Granada will leave you there—ask the driver), into a narrow, steep road (1½ hours' walk; leave luggage at restaurant by turning) across the western side of the lava flow. Taxi from Managua to top of volcano US$13. There is another road up to the crater, some 200 metres on; it also has a restaurant at the turning and follows much the same route. A 4-wheel-drive vehicle can get right to the crater. A VW will go to within a 20-minute walk of the top. The volcano is double-crested, but half is dormant. The other crater is spectacular and best seen at dawn or twilight: colourful rock dropping 60 metres to the lava plug with steaming red hot vents and encrustations of multi-coloured sulphur. Many squawking green parakeets dive and wheel in and out of the sulphurous clouds emitted by the crater. The lava-flow vegetation and the view across Lake Managua to Momotombo are of the greatest interest. The best view of the crater itself is from the far side, opposite the approach road. Do not walk on the lava cinders or go down the crater, unless you have strong boots and climbing experience.

Masaya (population 38,000), 30 km. SE of Managua, is the centre of a rich agricultural area growing tobacco. Small Laguna de Masaya (at the foot of Masaya volcano), and Santiago volcano are near the town. Interesting Indian handicrafts and a gorgeous *fiesta* on September 30, to its patron, San Jerónimo. (Indian dances and local costumes.) The best place for Indian craft work is Monimbo, and 15 minutes from Masaya is Villa Nindirí, which has a rich museum and an old church with some even older images. A branch railway runs SW to Jinotepe and Diriamba in the small highland between the two lakes.

Hotel *Victoria; Josefina,* US$1.50-2 s (you must haggle), basic rooms but good meals for US$0.60; *Rex,* cheap, near the church.

Restaurant   *Tip Top,* outside town.

From Managua   By train, 1 hour; by car, ½ hour.

Bank of London and South America agency.

Excursions to El Campamiento de Los Igloos, a village of polystyrene huts, experimental structures designed to provide shelter for the homeless. The inhabitants have lived in them for over 15 years. A track opposite the turnoff to Masaya on the Inter-American Highway goes to the village (about 1 km.).

Just outside Masaya, on the road from Managua, is an old fortress, La Fortillera. Apart from its fame as an erstwhile torture place, the fortress (entrance US$0.15) offers a good view of the lakes, volcanoes and plain.

Another 18 km. by road (bus, US$0.50) and rail is

Granada, on Lake Nicaragua, the terminus of the railway from the port of Corinto (190 km.). It is the third city of the republic, with a population of 45,200. It was founded by Hernández de Córdoba in 1524 at the foot of Mombacho volcano. The rich city was three times invaded by British and French pirates coming up the San Juan and Escalante rivers, and much of old Granada was burnt by filibuster William Walker in 1856. But it still has many beautiful buildings and has faithfully preserved its Castilian traditions. Both the Cathedral and La Merced church have been rebuilt in Colonial style. More or less built by the *conquistadores* are the church of Jalteva, in the outskirts, and the fortress-church of San Francisco: its Chapel of María Auxiliadora, where Las Casas, Apostle of the Indies, often preached, is hung with Indian lace and needlework. Granada, more traditional than León, has a delightful old-fashioned peaceful atmosphere: horse-drawn cabs for hire, many oxcarts and a fine cemetery. Roads to Managua (61 km.), Diriamba and Nandaime, and a new 24-km. autopista through Masaya joins it with Managua. Launches to the islands on the lake leave from a pier about 2 km. from the city centre (taxi, US$0.50). Take the road along the lake shore from Guadalupe church. Launches cost US$10 for 30 mins., but that is for the launch, which can carry 15 or 20 people, so find a group. The island vegetation is unusual and different, so are the Indian idols found there on display in the Instituto Nacional del Oriente, next door to the San Francisco church. (The key is available from the municipal offices.) Worth visiting.

Fiestas   Holy Week: Assumption of the Virgin, August 14-30; and Christmas (masked and costumed mummers).

Hotels   *Alhambra,* good; *Pensión Cabrera,* US$2.15 p.p., meals US$0.80 each, pleasant; *La Cigarra,* near wharf, US$1.60; *Pensión Vargas,* similar. *Pensión Esfinge,* opposite entrance to main market, US$2.20 d; *Hotel Imperial,* on main square, US$2.10 p.p.

Restaurants   *El Gran Restaurant Asia,* good steaks, and Chinese food for US$2. Meals at *Casino* on main square and at *Alhambra. La Cabana Amarilla,* on lakeshore, sometimes has shark on the menu. *Chupi's Ice Cream Parlour.*

Bus   Many fast minibuses from Managua, US$0.60, 1 hour. Bus to Nandaime, US$0.40.

Industries   Furniture, soap, clothing, distilling, cotton, oil, rum.

Lake Nicaragua, the "Gran Lago", 148 km. long by 55 at its widest, is a fresh-water lake abounding in salt-water fish, including sharks, which swim up the San Juan river from the sea and later return. Terrapins can be seen sunning themselves on the rocks and there are many interesting birds. There are about 310 small islands of great beauty, "Las Isletas", one of the greatest tourist attractions in the country. These can be visited either by hired boats or motor launches. People live on most of them. Most of the Indian idols in the Instituto Nacional del Oriente come from one of them; the Isla Zapatera (Cobbler's Island). The largest, Isla Omtepe, has two volcano cones, one of them a perfect cone rising to 1,610 metres. There are two villages on the island—Moyogalpa and Alta Garcia. The boat fare from Granada is US$1; alternatively, launches can be hired for about US$20 an hour from the Cabana Amarilla, about 2 km. along the beach from Granada. *Pensión Salón Jade,* US$0.85 each, three meals, another US$0.75. There is one boat a day (US$0.70) to **San Jorge** on the lake's SW shore. From here a short road runs through Rivas to the port of San Juan del Sur. The Rio San Juan, running through deep jungles, drains the lake from the eastern end into the Caribbean at San Juan del Norte; because of the migratory sharks, swimming in the river is dangerous. Launches ply down the river irregularly from the lakeside town of **San Carlos** (1,500 people) at the SE corner of the Lake. There is a regular service from Granada to San Carlos; boats leave every Monday and Thursday afternoon at 1400, 1500 and 1600, US$3, takes 15 hours, returning Tuesdays and Fridays leaving San Carlos at roughly the same times. Take your own food and a hammock if you want to get some sleep. At San Carlos (hotel) are the ruins of a fortress built for defence against pirates. Some three hours down the river are the ruins of another Spanish fort, Castillo Viejo *(pensión).* About 40 km. S of San Carlos, on the river, is Los Chiles, over the border in Costa Rica (see also page 1014). It can be reached by motorised dugout (US$0.50). Interesting trip, especially if you already know something about the birds and animals of the region and are good at spotting alligators. Allow 2 hours to get an exit permit at the Comandatura in San Carlos. Los Chiles has a couple of small hotels which are clean and comfortable, about US$2.50 each. There is a bank open until 1500 which takes travellers' cheques, but seems reluctant to take córdobas which can, however, be changed at stores. From Los Chiles, John Streather tells us, "one can continue down the Rio San Juan to **San Juan del Norte** (Greytown), a curious little backwater inhabited by friendly black people. Occasionally a boat goes up to Bluefields" (see page 998). If you want to cross the lagoon into Costa Rica, get your passport stamped in San Juan (see also page 1014).

Fishing Seven-day fishing safaris on the lake, men only, cost some US$340 each all in. They start with a 55-minute light plane flight from Managua to San Carlos, at the opposite end of the lake, and continue down San Juan river to Tarpon Camp where there are clean, comfortable cabins. Tarpon strikes the year round.

By Inter-American Highway from Managua to Costa Rica: 148 km.; comfortable bus services all the way to San José de Costa Rica. The road, in good condition, runs into the Sierra de Managua, reaching 900 metres at Casa Colorada, 26 km. from Managua. Further on, at El Crucero, a paved branch road goes through the Sierra S to the Pacific bathing beaches of Masachapa, a popular playground of Managuans. Our road continues through the beautiful scenery of the Sierras to

Diriamba, 42 km. from Managua, at 760 metres, in a coffee-growing district. Population 26,500. It is a picturesque town with a hotel, the *Majestic.* Its great *fiesta* is on January 20. There is a 32-km. road direct to Masachapa, and another NE to Masaya, on the Managua-Granada highway. Five km. beyond Diriamba we pass through

Jinotepe, capital of the coffee-growing district of Carazo. It is joined by railway with Diriamba and Masaya. Its *fiesta* in honour of St. James the Greater is on July 24-26. Altitude 760 metres; population 17,600; hotel, *Imperial*; local holiday, July 25.

From Nadaime, 21 km. from Jinotepe, altitude 130 metres, a paved road runs N to Granada (bus US$0.30). About 45 km. beyond Nandaime is

Rivas, a town with 21,000 people. (Hotel: *Centro Americano.*) The Costa Rican Juan Santamaría sacrificed his life here in 1856 when setting fire to a building captured by the filibuster William Walker and his men. The town has a lovely old church. The road from the lake port of San Jorge joins this road at Rivas; 11 km. beyond Rivas, at La Virgen on the shore of Lake Nicaragua, it branches S to San Juan del Sur. Buses to the frontier are irregular.

These 2 roads were part of the famous Vanderbilt Road, the old overland link between Lake Nicaragua and the Pacific along which many "forty-niners" trooped on their way to the Californian gold rush.

San Juan del Sur, 34 km. from Rivas, 93 from Granada. Cargo at the port is still handled by little old lighters. There is a large bathing-beach on the horseshoe-shaped bay. There are roads from Managua (a 2½-hour drive) and Granada. A slower route for goods and passengers from Managua is by rail or road to Granada, lake steamer to San Jorge, and on by road *via* Rivas. Population 4,750. It is a beautiful bay with a sandy beach and some rocky caves reached by walking round the point past the harbour. Check tides with officials at the Customs Office, who will give permission to park motor-caravans and trailers on the wharves if you ask them nicely first.

These vehicles can also be parked on Marsella beach, about 5 km. from San Juan; coming S, turn right on entering San Juan, by shrimp-packing plant.

Main Exports   Coffee, timber, cocoa, sugar, balsam.

Shipping   Cargo/passenger: Mamenic; Hamburg-Amerika; Holland-America; Johnson; North German Lloyd. Fast fortnightly joint cargo service (no passengers) of Central America Services to and from Europe. Loading and unloading is by lighter.

Royal Mail Agents   E. and F. Kelly & Co. Ltd.

Hotels   *Barlovento,* on a hill overlooking the bay, good; *Estrella,* on Pacific, US$4 d.

Restaurant   *Salón Siria,* good.

Our road reaches the Costa Rican boundary at Peñas Blancas, 37 km. beyond Rivas. There is a duty-free shop on the Nicaraguan side of the border.

The Caribbean Coast has more rain than the Pacific coast (for its history see page 987). Its economy is based on the export of bananas, cocoa, mahogany, black walnut, rose-wood, and other high-class timbers. There are gold mines in the interior.

There are three small ports: San Juan del Norte (Greytown), at the mouth of the San Juan river (see above), Bluefields, further N; and Puerto Cabezas, further N still. There is little incoming cargo, but the bulk of the timber and banana exports passes through them.

Bluefields, the most important, 1,200 nautical miles S of New Orleans, gets its name from the Dutch pirate Bleuwveldt. It stands behind the Bluff at the mouth of the Bluefields river (Río Escondido), which is navigable as far as Rama (96 km.). From Rama an improved highway runs through Santo Tomás (*Hotel Rosaura* and two others charging about US$1, good food at *Rosaura*) and Juigalpa to Managua, 290 km. away; a 40 km. stretch of the road W of Santo Tomás is still rough, however. Bananas, cabinet woods, frozen fish, shrimps and lobsters are main exports. Population 17,700. Small steamers ply to Tampa (Florida) 4 times a week. Lanica flies to Managua (1 hour) on Mon., Wed. and Fri., US$20 (double-check bookings made in Managua for this flight). It used to be possible to get to San Andrés, a Colombian island in the Caribbean (see page 481) but boats there are now very infrequent, there are no air services, and the customs officials are not always willing to give an exit stamp.

From Managua to Bluefields Take a bus from Managua to Rama along the now-completed road. Microbus, several companies (e.g. Cotran, on Carretera Norte), US$3.50, 6 hours. They leave from Km. 5. (There is an express bus to Rama which leaves at 0630 and gets to Rama in time for you to catch the boat to Bluefields.) Or take your car and park it in the compound at the Chinaman's store (opposite *Hotel Amy*) for US$0.50 a day. Buses back to Managua leave Rama from 0300 onwards. *Hotel Amy* (US$1.40 p.p. and good, inexpensive food), near main jetty. *Pensión Rama* charges US$1 each, no water or electricity but very good food for US$0.50. There are several boats down the Escondido river to Bluefields, the only way of getting there. The express, or "rápido" costs US$3.60 (tickets can be bought at *Hotel Amy*); others US$2.10, taking 6-8 hours; take your own food and drink. At night, watch alligators picked out by bright torches used to warn river-dwellers of your coming. "Cena", the typical supper, is served and you can sling a hammock and sleep in your cabin. By day you see the *finca* owners along the banks. Barges carry sacks of cocoa and beans to ship them for market, cartage paid in part by gifts of oranges, coconuts, cheese. Mail is delivered, people pop on and off to visit neighbours. The intimate community atmosphere of Bluefields starts right at Rama.

Hotels at Bluefields: *Hueto; Hollywood* (no sign), US$2.10 d, basic; *Darío; Pensión Sylvia G.,* unsavoury. There is a *pensión* next to *Darío,* above shoe shop, US$3 d; *Hospedaje Cristóbal,* US$1 each.

Cables Tropical Radio; Radio Nacional.

The Corn Islands, in the Caribbean opposite Bluefields, are two small beautiful islands fringed with white coral sand and slender coconut trees. The larger is a popular Nicaraguan holiday resort; its surfing and bathing facilities make the island ideal for tourists. Regular air services by Lanica. Local industries: coconut oil, lobsters, and shrimp-freezing plants. Spanish name: Islas del Maiz. Hotels and food are expensive. *Lundy's Island Inn* has beach huts with hot water, dining room and bar, US$25 s, US$45 d.

From El Bluff, on the headland opposite Bluefields, you can hitch a lift on a fishing boat to Monkey Point and from there another to Cocal. From Cocal it is a 3½-km. walk to San Juan de Norte, to which there is the occasional direct boat from Bluefields. From San Juan you can go up the river of the same name to Lake Nicaragua or cross lagoons to a sandbar in Costa Rica. From this bar it is a 2-hour walk to Barra del Colorado, Costa Rica (see page 1014). Don't forget to get your passport stamped in both San Juan and Barra.

Puerto Cabezas (Bragman's Bluff), is N of the Río Grande. Population: 11,850. There are Lanica air-services 6 days a week to Managua. It has a modest hotel, and the Standard Fruit Company and Nipco have guest-houses for business visitors.

C. J. Tyrell writes: From Leymus (Honduras) one can hitch a lift to Tronquera, a lumber town, on one of the frequent lorries taking pine roots out from Leymust. From Tronquera buses run 3-4 times daily to Waspam (¾ hour, US$1) and in the other direction to Puerto Cabezas (2½ hours, US$2). There is a Moravian Church hospital in Bilwaskarma (½ hour, US$0.50 by pickup from Waspam). From Waspam, launches go twice weekly visiting Miskito Indian communities from the mouth of the Río Coco to San Carlos (Ahuasbila). In Waspam there is a hotel, and the *Comedor Morava* does cheap food. In Puerto Cabezas, one can stay at a number of hotels and hospedajes. *Hospedaje Carutón* is US$3 per night—not cheap but clean—one block away from the bus stop and Anglican Church. There are at least three Chinese restaurants.

Lanica has daily flights connecting Waspam and Puerto Cabezas with Managua. For notes on Honduran Mosquitia, see page 981).

Accommodation in the Mosquitia is sometimes a problem as there are few facilities for the tourist. In villages, and as a last resort in the town, the Baptist, Moravian and Catholic US missionaries and local clergy are very helpful to stranded travellers. In fact, the only reliable means of communication in both the Honduran and Nicaraguan Mosquitia are the two radio networks maintained by the Catholic and Moravian churches.

The Economy

Nicaragua's economy has been able to show a fairly stable annual growth rate over the past two decades, although sharp fluctuations occur from year to year as agricultural production and world commodity prices vary. The economy is based on agriculture, which employs about 50% of the labour force. The principal export items are cotton, coffee, sugar and beef. The Government is encouraging a diversification of exports, and exports of shellfish, tobacco, bananas and other agricultural products are gaining in importance. Nicaragua's extensive agricultural resources should permit a continued growth of agricultural production in the future.

Real gdp grew by 5% in 1977, due to continuing favourable prices for coffee and cotton, although this was lower than the 6% achieved in 1976. This compared with only a 2% increase in real terms in 1975. Nicaragua achieved one of its highest growth rates, over 11%, due to the post-earthquake construction boom which reinforced above-average export earnings.

Inflation, which has been traditionally low, has been a problem since the 1972 earthquake; prices rose 27% in 1973 and 17% in 1974. However, more recently rates have decreased somewhat, with a rate of 6.2% in 1976, but with a rise of 10.1 for 1977.

Manufacturing and mining are relatively less important to the Nicaraguan economy than agriculture. At present agriculture constitutes 24% of gdp but employs 48% of the economically active population and is responsible for by far the largest proportion of exports. Recently, however, a substantial amount of industrializatiion has developed, mainly due to foreign investment. There are few mineral resources in Nicaragua, and although gold, copper and silver are mined, they are of little importance to the overall economy.

Foreign Trade (US$m)

	1972	1973	1974	1975	1976	1977
Exports (f.o.b.) ..	249.7	284.3	381.6	376.6	541.8	629.6
Imports (c.i.f.) ..	218.5	318.6	562.9	518.7	497.7	747.6

Information for Visitors

Air Services Daily to Managua from Miami, Mexico City, Panama (connection with British Airways London-Panama flight on Thurs. and Sun.), and Central American capitals. Lanica, the local airline, flies 5 days a week from Managua to Puerto Cabezas, 4 days a week to Bluefields and 5 days a week to the gold-mining centres of Siuna and Bonanza; also to the Corn Islands.

All passengers have to pay a sales tax of 8% on all tickets issued in and paid for in Nicaragua; a transportation tax of 1% on all tickets issued in Nicaragua to any destination; a consular fee of US$1.50 from all passengers who arrive, and an airport tax of US$5 on all departing passengers.

By Sea   There are good steamship services from the United Kingdom to Cristóbal (14 to 16 days), including those of the P.S.N.C. and Royal Mail Lines (no passengers). The port of Corinto, on the Pacific Coast, is served by Grace Line vessels from Cristóbal, and also from San Francisco and Los Angeles.

Both the Royal Netherland Steamship Company and the local Mamenic Line run monthly services from Europe to San Juan del Sur or Corinto or Puerto Somoza: the former from Amsterdam and the latter from Antwerp. The Mamenic Line also serves most other central and north American ports. There is a ferry between La Unión (El Salvador) and Potosí, which can save both time and money for those not wishing to go to Honduras.

Documents   Visitors must have a passport and a valid international certificate of smallpox vaccination. Tourist cards are available for US nationals, who do not then require passports if they have other proof of identification. No visa is required by nationals of Belgium, Denmark, Liechtenstein, Luxembourg, Netherlands, Norway, Spain, Sweden, Switzerland or the United Kingdom for a 90-day stay. Commercial travellers should carry a document from their firm accrediting them as such. Only those visitors who have no tourist cards and require visas for entry need an exit permit, but salesmen must produce a *Boleta* to show they have paid their taxes on sales. Motorists pay US$1.50 for a customs clearance. Anyone arriving at Managua airport without a valid international certificate of vaccination is vaccinated on the spot. A ticket out of the country is sometimes required as a condition for entering. An air ticket can be cashed if not used, especially if issued by a large company, but bus tickets are sometimes difficult to encash. It is reported, however, that the Nicaraguan Embassy in a neighbouring country is empowered to authorize entry without the outward ticket, if the traveller has enough money to buy the ticket. Sometimes a border charge of US$2 is imposed. On Sundays there is an additional charge of US$0.70. Difficulties upon entry have been encountered by people who have communist countries' stamps in their passports, and entry is forbidden to nationals of communist countries, including Yugoslavia, and to people whose passports contain visas for Cuba.

Customs   Duty-free import of ½ kg. of tobacco products, 3 litres of alcoholic drinks and 1 large bottle (or 3 small bottles) of perfume is permitted.

Much detailed commercial information is given in "Hints to Business Men visiting Nicaragua", free on application to the Dept. of Trade, Export Services Division, Room CO7, Export House, 50 Ludgate Hill, London EC4M 7HU.

Motoring   Low octane gasoline costs US$1.05 a US gallon.

Clothing should be of the lightest possible: linen or lightweight suiting. These can be used all the year round, except at higher altitudes. There is a wide range of climates, but there are no extremes of heat or cold. According to altitude, average annual temperatures vary between 15°C and 35°C. Mid-day temperatures at Managua range from 30° to 36°C, but readings of 38° are not uncommon from March to May. Maximum daily humidity ranges from 90% to 100%. Dress is informal; business men often shed jackets and wear sports shirts, but shorts are never worn. Light cotton or silk dresses and lightweight underwear for women. The dry season runs from December to May, and the wet season covers the remaining months. The wettest are usually June and October. A light raincoat comes in useful. Best time for a business visit: from March to June, but December and January are the pleasantest months.

Warning   Border officials do not like army-type clothing on travellers, and may confiscate green or khaki rucksacks (backpacks).

Internal Transport   Hitchhiking is easy.

Health   The usual tropical precautions about food and drink. Tap water is reasonably safe but avoid uncooked vegetables and peeled fruit. A T.A.B. inoculation is strongly recommended. Meningitis is endemic and many visitors choose to be immunized against it. Some malaria risk; take regular prophylaxis.

Tipping in Nicaragua: 10% of bill in hotels and restaurants; C$1 per bag for porters; no tip for taxi drivers.

Hours of Business   0800-1200, 1430-1730 or 1800. Banks: 0830-1200, 1400-1600, but 0830-1130 on Saturday. Government offices are not normally open in the afternoon.

Standard Time   Six hours behind G.M.T.

Cost of living   Imported goods tend to be expensive. Nicaragua is in general more expensive than its neighbours.

Currency   The unit is the córdoba (C$), divided into 100 centavos. There are notes for 1,000, 500, 100, 50, 20, 10, 5, and 1 córdobas and coins of 5, 10, 25 and 50 centavos. Some notes and coins have popular names: the córdoba is often known as a peso, 25 centavos as a chollina or peseta and 10 centavos as a real. Currency restrictions are non-existent. Legal parity is C$7 to the US$. Dollar notes and travellers' cheques get slightly better terms on the free market. Branches of foreign banks tend to give better rates of exchange than the national ones.

Weights and Measures   The metric system is official, but in domestic trade local terms are in use; for example, the medio, which equals a peck, and the fanega, of 24 medios. These are not used in foreign trade. The principal local weight is the arroba = 25 lb. and the quintal of 101.417 English lb. Random variety of other measures in use include U.S. gallon for petrol, U.S. quart and pint for liquids; vara (33 ins.) for short distances and the lb. for certain weights.

Mails from the United Kingdom to Nicaragua are sent *via* Panama, and take 4 to 5 weeks. There are delays in forwarding between the western ports and the interior due to poor communications. Air-mail from London takes 4 to 6 days. Airmail letters: C$2.20 per 5 gms.

Telegraph and Telephone lines are owned by the Government. Rather unreliable automatic telephone services between Managua, León, Chinandega and Corinto. No public telephones except at the airport. The cable and telegraph companies are given under the towns. There are wireless transmitting stations at Managua, Bluefields and Cabo Gracias a Dios, and private stations at Puerto Cabezas, El Gallo, and Río Grande.

Telephone calls from Managua to Britain: 0700-2100 weekdays, 0800-1100 and 1700-1900 on Sundays. Rates: weekdays, C$127.30 per 3 minutes; Sundays, C$101.85.

Telex   A 3-minute call to Britain costs C$100.80.

Public Holidays

January 1: New Year's Day.
March or April: Holy Week.
May 1: Labour Day.
June 30: Banks only.
September 14: Battle of San Jacinto.
September 15: Independence Day.

October 12: Discovery of America.
November 2: All Saints' Day.
December 8: Immaculate Conception.
December 24: (From noon).
December 25: Christmas Day.
December 31: Banks only.

Business is at a standstill the whole of Holy Week; many companies also close down during the Christmas-New Year period. Holidays which fall on a Sunday are given the following Monday. Local holidays are given under the towns.

Press   Managua: "La Prensa", circ. 50,000; "Novedades", circ. 30,000. León: "El Centroamericano". "La Gaceta" is the official gazette. "Revista Conservadora" is the best monthly magazine. "El Pez y la Serpiente" is a monthly magazine devoted to the arts, poetry and literature.

Great Britain is represented by a Consulate at 208 Av. Roosevelt (Tel.: 25301/2), 3rd floor of the old Bank of London and South America building. Letters to Apartado 13, Managua.

The **United States** is represented by an Embassy and Consulate at Managua (Km. 4½, Carretera del Sur, Tel.: 23881) and a Vice-Consul at Puerto Cabezas.

The **Nicaraguan Embassy** is at 8 Gloucester Road, London S.W.7. Tel.: 01-584-3231.

American Express Agents Managua: Agencias Vassalli S.A., Lomas de Guadalupe, Apto. 609. Tel.: 27674 and 24207.

We are deeply grateful to Monique Merriam for help in updating the Managua section; to John Streather, and to other travellers listed in the general Central America section.

COSTA RICA

COSTA RICA is the smallest but one—El Salvador—of the Central American republics, and only Panama has fewer inhabitants, but its population is altogether remarkable in Central America: it is very largely white. There are, it is true, small clusters of mestizos, blacks and indigenous Indians in various parts of the Republic, but the whole population is integrated into one democratic body. The Army was abolished in 1948, though it should be stressed that there is a very efficient-looking khaki-clad National Guard. Costa Rica has the highest standard of living in Central America, the least illiteracy, the fastest population growth and the greatest degree of economic and social advance. Area, 51,100 square km. Population (beginning of 1976) 1,993,784—a density of 39 to the square kilometre.

The highland basin in which most of the people live has one of the greatest densities of rural population in Latin America. Most remarkable of all, this population is expanding without creating an enfeebled centre—a rare occurrence in Latin America.

Costa Rica lies between Nicaragua and Panama, with coast-lines upon both the Caribbean (212 km.) and the Pacific (1,016 km.). The distance between sea and sea is from 119 to 282 km. A low, thin line of hills between Lake Nicaragua and the Pacific is prolonged into northern Costa Rica, broadening and rising into high and rugged mountains in the centre and S. The highest peak, Chiripó Grande, SE of the capital, reaches 3,819 metres. Within these highlands are certain structural depressions, one of them, the Meseta Central, of paramount importance. To the SW this basin is rimmed by the comb of the *cordillera*; at the foot of its slopes, inside the basin, are the present capital, San José, and the old capital, Cartago. To the NE of these cities and parallel with the comb of the mountain, but 32 km. away, four volcano cones soar from a massive common pedestal. From NW to SE these are Poás (2,704 metres), Barba (2,906 metres), Irazú (3,432 metres), and Turrialba (3,339 metres). Irazú and Poás are intermittently active. Between the sharp cascading slopes of the *cordillera* and the gentle lower slopes of the volcanoes is the rolling, ash-covered depression known as the Meseta Central: an area of 5,200 square km. at an altitude of between 900 and 1800 metres, an average of 1,200 metres. Two-thirds of the population live here. The north-eastern part of the basin is drained by the Reventazón through turbulent gorges into the Caribbean; the Río Grande drains the western part of it into the Pacific.

There are lowlands on both oceans. The Nicaraguan lowland along the Río San Juan is continued into Costa Rica, wide and sparsely inhabited as far as Puerto Limón. A great deal of this land, particularly near the coast, is swampy; below Puerto Limón the swamps are continued as far as Panama in a narrow belt of lowland between sea and mountain.

The Gulf of Nicoya, on the Pacific side, thrusts some 65 km. inland; its waters separate the mountains of the mainland from the 900-metre high

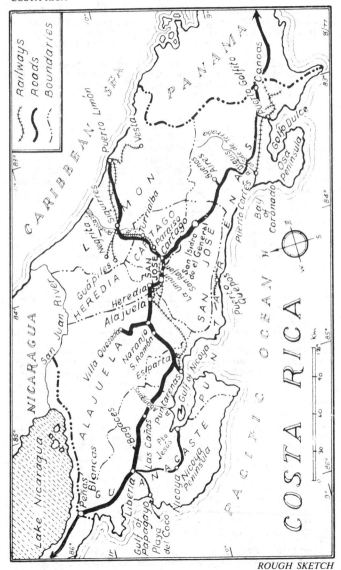

ROUGH SKETCH

mountains of the narrow Nicoya Peninsula. From a little to the S of the mouth of the Río Grande de Tárcoles, a lowland savanna stretches past the port of Puntarenas and along the whole north-eastern shore of the Gulf, and it is prolonged, with a width of about 50 km., for another 80 km., towards Nicaragua.

Below the Río Grande the savanna is pinched out by mountains, but there are other lowlands between mountain and sea to the S. From Puerto Quepos, built by the United Fruit Company, 188 km. of railway run NW to beyond the Río Pirris and SW to the Río Savegre through banana-growing lowlands, which are not now as productive as they were. Small quantities of African palm and cacao are now being grown in these lowlands. In the far S there are swampy lowlands again at the base of the Peninsula of Osa and between the Golfo Dulce and the borders of Panama. Here there are 12,000 hectares planted to bananas; 317 km. of railway run to the United Brands banana port of Golfito. The Río General, a tributary of the Río Diquis or Grande de Térraba (which cuts through the mountains to reach the Pacific N of the Peninsula of Osa), runs through a southern structural depression almost as large as the Meseta Central; this is now being occupied.

Altitude, as elsewhere in Central America, determines the climate, but the *tierra templada* and the *tierra fría* start at nearly a thousand feet lower on the Pacific than on the Atlantic side. The Pacific side is the drier, with patches of savanna among the deciduous forest; the Atlantic side has heavy rainfall—300 days a year of it—and is covered far up the slopes with tropical forest: about two-fifths of Costa Rica is forested.

Settlements The Spaniards discovered the Nicoya Peninsula in 1522, and returned soon after. They settled in the Meseta Central, where there were some thousands of sedentary Indian farmers. The settlers, as usual, adopted the *hacienda* system, and soon began to intermarry with the Indians. Cartago was founded in 1563 by Juan Vásquez de Coronado, but there was no sign of expansion in this central nucleus until 145 years later, when a small number left Cartago for the valleys of Aserrí and Escazú in that area which is drained into the Pacific by the Río Grande. They founded Heredia in 1717, and San José in 1737. Alajuela, not far from San José, was founded in 1782. The settlers were growing in numbers but were still poor and raising subsistence crops only. Independence from Spain was declared in 1821 whereupon Costa Rica, with the rest of Central America, immediately became part of Mexico. This led to a civil war, during which, two years later, the capital was moved from Cartago to San José. After independence, the government sought anxiously for some product which could be exported and taxed for revenue. It was found in coffee, introduced from Cuba in 1808, which Costa Rica was the first of the Central American countries to grow. The Government offered free land to coffee growers, thus building up a peasant landowning class. In 1825 there was a trickle of exports, carried on mule-back to the ports. Great Britain received a few bags in 1845. By 1846 there were ox-cart roads to Puntarenas. By 1850 there was a large flow of coffee to overseas markets: it was greatly increased by the opening of a railway from San José and Cartago to Puerto Limón along the valley of the Reventazón in 1890.

From 1850, coffee prosperity began to affect the country profoundly: the birth rate grew, land for coffee was free, and the peasant settlements started spreading, first down the Río Reventazón as far as Turrialba, standing at 600 metres; then up the slopes of the volcanoes to the limit for coffee and beyond to pasture cattle and grow potatoes; then down the new railway from San José to the Pacific port of Puntarenas. The internal immigration map shows that the people of the Meseta Central, whilst increasing in absolute population, are now spreading out into the area around the Gulf of Nicoya, along the whole Pacific coast, into the eastern parts of the country, and down the valley of the Reventazón. Roads have always followed expansion, to make access to the highland markets easy.

Much of the Caribbean coastland, more especially in the N, is still unoccupied. Bananas were first introduced in 1878 to provide revenue for the railway line which was being built from Puerto Limón to San José. Costa Rica was the first Central American republic to grow bananas. Labour was brought in from Jamaica to clear the forest and work the plantations. The industry grew and in 1913, the peak year, the Caribbean coastlands provided 11 million bunches for export. But the spread of disease lowered the exports progressively. The United Fruit Company then turned its attentions to the Pacific littoral and for a time this area produced more bananas than the Caribbean plantations. However, although some of the Caribbean plantations were turned over to cacao, *abacá* (Manilla hemp) and African palm, the region has regained its ascendancy over the Pacific littoral as a banana producer.

On the Pacific coastlands tenure is more like that in Nicaragua than in the Meseta Central: here a minority of pure-blooded whites own and work the land on the *hacienda* system rejected by the uplands. About 46% of the people are mestizos. In the S, inland from the port of Golfito, there are huge banana plantations. To the N, most of the country's cattle come from the large estates of the savannas, and timber is exploited along the northern coast. The mountainous Peninsula of Nicoya is an important source of coffee, maize, rice and beans. Its population has risen sharply. Rainfall is moderate: 1,000 to 2,000 mm. a year, but there is a long dry season which makes irrigation important.

Population In all provinces save Limón and Puntarenas over 99.5% are whites and mestizos; in Puntarenas they are 98.2%, but in Limón 33.2% are blacks and 3.1% indigenous Indians, of whom only 5,000 survive in the whole country. But even in Limón the percentage of blacks is falling: it was 57.1 in 1927. Many of them speak Jamaican dialect as their native tongue. Some 33.5% are urban. Illiteracy, at 5%, is among the lowest in Latin America.

Roads Costa Rica has a total of 22,530 km. of roads. Details are given in the text, and the route of the Inter-American Highway (now almost all paved) is described below.

The Inter-American Highway to the Panama border runs 351 km. from San José. First to Cartago, and southwards over the mountains between Cartago and San Isidro del General (115 km.). At Cartago begins the ascent of Cerro Buena Vista, a climb of 1,830 metres to the Continental Divide at 3,490 metres; this is the highest spot on the Highway. For 16 km. it follows the crest of the Talamanca Ridge, with views, on clear days, of the Pacific, 50 km. away, and even of the Atlantic, over 80 km. away. The road then drops down into **San Isidro de El General**, 760 metres above sea-level in a fertile valley in the centre of a coffee and cattle district. The town is growing fast and now has several hotels: *Hotel Balboa* in the centre; *Hotel San Isidro*, US$0.75 each; *Hotel Comodoro*, US$2.20 each, simple but clean. The road goes on to Paso Canoas on the Panama border, where it connects with the Panama section of the Highway. Thirty-two km. N of the general a road (26 km.) branches S to **Golfito**, the banana port. It may interest some travellers to see the growing, harvesting and loading operations. Golfito is really two towns: the banana company community and the town itself—about 2½ km. apart. (There are two hotels charging US$3, also *Pensión Minerva*, US$1.25.) About 10 km. from Golfito is the Playa de Cacao and Captain Tom's place, where you can sling your hammock or camp for US$0.35 a day, but take your own food as local shopping is poor. A taxi boat from Golfito will take you there for US$0.50, or you can drive (if you have four-wheel drive) along a beach track if the tide is far enough out. There is a train from Golfito on Mon., Wed., Fri. and Sat. at 0830 to the Panama border. Also near the border is the town of San Vito, built by Italian immigrants among hills. It has hotels (as does the nearby village of Cañas Gordas), and a botanical garden is being established. At Palmar Sur, 98 km. from the border, a banana plantation has stone spheres, 1½ metres in diameter and accurate within ½ cm., which can also be seen in various places in Costa Rica. They are of pre-Columbian Indian manufacture, but their use is a matter of conjecture; the most recent theory is that they were made to represent the planets of the solar system. About 70 km. from the border is the *Motel Tico-Alemán*. At Villa Neilly, about 18 km. from the border, is the *Hotel Albufer* (noisy) and 6 km. from the border is the *Camino Real* where it is possible to camp. Here and there on the road *cantinas* sell local food. Those motoring N can get insurance cover at the border ensuring public liability and property damage for US$5. At the highest point is *Hotel Georgina*, clean, hot shower, good food, US$1; before you get there a side road leads off to the peaceful mountain villages of Santa María and San Marcos, each with a hotel. No fruit or vegetables can be taken into Panama.

The Inter-American Highway to the Nicaraguan border, 332 km. almost completely paved. From San José it leads past El Coco airport, Heredia and Alajuela, on a new two-carriageway section, to San Ramón (79 km.) in the middle of a coffee area, where there are good hotels. From San Ramón to Cañas, now resurfaced, is 98 km.; this stretch includes the sharp fall of 800 metres from the Meseta Central between San Ramón and Esparza (34 km.). Beyond Esparza there is a left turn for Puntarenas. From Esparza through Cañas to the frontier (198 km.) the road runs through the low forest-covered hills of northern Guanacaste Province, a region of large cattle estates and coffee and banana plantations. The largest town, and possible stopover, is Liberia (see page 1019), 119 km. from Esparza and 79 from Peñas Blancas on the Nicaraguan border. The northern section of the Inter-American Highway has been poorly maintained near the Nicaraguan frontier, but a complete rebuilding has been completed between San José and San Ramón. At Peñas Blancas is a duty-free shop.

Railways There are 1,286 km., all of 1.067-metre gauge; 967 are plantation lines—336 km. of the Northern Railway and 631 km. of the United Brands Company. The formerly British-owned Northern Railway has 525 km.: its main line is between Puerto Limón and San José (166 km.), and it has a branch line (21 km.) between San José and Alajuela. The government-owned Ferrocarril Eléctrico al Pacífica between San José and Puntarenas has 132 km. of track.

Constitution and Government

Legislative power is vested in a Legislative Assembly, made up of 57 deputies. They are elected for four years. Executive authority is in the hands of the president, elected for the same term by popular vote. Men and women over 20 have the right to vote. Voting is secret, direct and free, and the country is one of Latin America's few genuine democracies. The President (1978-82) is Lic. Rodrigo Carazo Odio.

Main Towns

NOTE: The vara, 11/12 of a yard, is used almost exclusively in giving directions. Instead of saying "go 6 blocks", most Costa Ricans will tell you to go 600 varas.

San José, population 228,302, stands in a broad, fertile valley producing coffee, sugar-cane and some of the most attractive women in the world—the abundance of pretty girls in San José is truly remarkable.

Some of our correspondents disagree with this judgement, but the Editor, having visited San José himself and been entranced, is exercising his right to agree with his predecessors. This may be a matter of the generation gap, or just of taste, but the opinion stands. Janna Brooks (no relation to the Editor) has asked us to point out that the attractiveness of San José men is no less remarkable than that of the women.

It was founded in 1737 and its architecture is a medley of traditional Spanish and modern. Some wide avenues are flanked by spacious green parks and flower gardens at every turn; other streets are narrow with wooden houses and one-way traffic. The climate is excellent, but the evenings can be chilly. The lowest and highest temperatures run from 15° to 26°C. Slight earthquake shocks are frequent. Rainy season: May to November. Other months are dry.

Streets cross one another at right-angles. Avenidas run E-W; the Calles N-S. The three main ones are Av. Central and Av. 2 and the intersecting Calle Central: the business centres are along these three. The best shops are along Av.Central, much of which is closed to traffic; it is continued W by the Paseo Colón to the old airport and National Stadium at La Sabana, near which is a large natural history collection in La Salle museum.

Avenidas to the N of Av. Central are given odd numbers; those to the S even numbers. Calles to the W of Calle Central are even-numbered; those to the E odd-numbered. The Instituto Costarricense de Turismo has an excellent map of the city, marking all the important sights and business houses. With its aid, finding one's way about is easy.

Local Holiday December 28 to 31.

Hotels

	Telephone	Rooms	US$ Single	Double
Ambassador	21-81-55	20	17-35	25-50
Balmoral	22-56-22	76	10-20	18-30
Gran Hotel Costa Rica	21-40-00	96	14-20	19-25
Pensión Niza	21-22-30	17	18	33
Central	22-03-00	52	12	24
(annex)	21-24-24	40	12	24
Royal Dutch*	22-14-14	59	14-19	16-24
Tennis Club	22-15-88	26	13-18	16-24
Pensión Americana	21-41-71	21	14	24
Chorotega tower	25-25-55	60	15-18	18-24
Holland House*†‡	25-14-74	21	10-14	14-24
Apartotel San José	22-04-55	14	16-20	22-24
Europa†	22-12-22	68	20	25
Crystal‡	22-34-76	37	17	24
President	22-30-22	42	14	19-23
"Sheraton"'**	21-30-45	56	12-16	18-20
Motel Bemo‡	21-67-44	23	10-15	14-20
Apartotel El Conquistador	25-30-22	27	16	20
Fortuna	23-53-44	25	12	15-18
Apartamentos Lamm	21-47-20	21	15	18
Amstel*	22-46-22	47	13	17
Diplomat	21-83-77	27	9-12	12-15
Residencial Florida	23-43-44	21	9	17

*Food recommended   †Swimming pool   ‡Out of town
**Not a member of the Sheraton group; said to be a "hot pillow" establishment.

These rates are per day, without food. *Hotel Príncipe,* central, new, US$8 d; *Gran Vía,* US$14-18 s.

Amongst other possible hotels are the *Pan-American* (US$3-5 s, 6.50-9 d); *Park* US$5-6 s, 8-10 d); *Plaza* (US$4-7 s, 7-9 d); *Metropoli; Ritz* (US$5 s, US$8.25 d, manager helpful) and *Terminal. Apartotel Los Yoses,* US$5 s, 7.50 d. *Hotel Galilea,* Av. Central, US$6 s, new and comfortable; *Hotel Canadá,* 5 Av. and Calle 6, US$1.40 s, hot showers (but in the red light district); *Hotel-Pensión Canadá,* US$19.50 d, full board· only; *Hotel Boston,* central location, US$7 d, with bathroom, good; *Centroamericano,* Av. 2, US$2.25-4 s, 4-6.50 d, very clean, hot water, very noisy; *Johnson,* highly recommended, US$8 d; *Hotel Regis,* Calle 8 y Av. 4, US$5 s, without bath, clean and friendly, has dining room; *Hotel Ruiz,* US$6 d, private shower. *Pensiones* are: *Costa Rica Inn,* best, US$5 s, with breakfast; *Morazán; Tala Inn,* US$5-6 s, 8-10 d; *Alhambra Inn* and many others. *Hotel Astoria,* Av. 7, No. 344, US$3 d, clean, hot water; annex is US$4.50, popular with travellers, has good restaurant, but some evidence of petty theft, so be careful; nearby on Av. 7 between Calles 2 and 4 is *Villa Blanca,* about US$2 each, quiet and friendly: *Hotel Covadonga,* US$1.50, Av. 3 and Calle 6, clean. *Hotel Illimani,* US$3 p.p., spasmodic hot water, friendly; *Pensión Americana,* half a block from main square, US$2.25 each, good, but noisy, meals available; *Hotel Prado,* Calle 8, Av. 1-3, US$0.90 each, basic; *hotel Musoc,* Calle 16, Av. 1-3, US$3 s, with private bath, very clean, hot water, near to (and somewhat noisy because of) bus stations, but recommended; *Hotel Rialto,* Av. 5 and Calle 2, US$2 each, clean, hot water, good value; *Anexo Hotel Rialto,* Av. 8, Calles 8 and 9, near Tica bus terminal, recommended, and *Araica,* also near terminal, both charge about US$2 each; *Pensión El Progreso,* in same area, US$2; *Moderno,* Calle 8, Avs. 1 and 3, opposite market, US$1.50; *Hotel de Jardín,* US$1.50 d, clean and pleasant but noisy. *Hotel Lincoln,* US$1.50, clean, friendly, with hot water, on Calle Central between Avs. 14 and 16. Students are taken in as guests in private houses at low rates. *El Faro,* Calle 8, No. 153, is central and cheap: US$0.90 s, but is dirty and noisy, the food is reasonable. *Pensión Salamanca,* US$2.90 s. There are several new hotels near the various markets, such as the *Managua, Comericante* Annex and *Valencia* which charge US$2 each and are quite clean. *Pensión Tracopa,* near bus terminal, US$1.30 each.

Electric Current   110/220 volts, 60 cycles, A.C.

Restaurants   Apart from the hotels, the best ones are the *Bastille,* French type, on Paseo Colón, *L'Escargot,* also French, on Av. 5; *Asana Tokyo,* Calle 3, Avs. 7/9, Japanese; *Los Anonos,* in Escazú area, grills; *Irazú; La Cascade; Bonanza; El Chicote; El Chalet Suizo,* recommended, meals from US$3. Others are: *Le Gourmet; Ana* (Italian food), recommended; *Vesuvio;* and *Soda Palace. Café Mallorquina,* Calle 9, is good and cheap; so is *El Caudil.* A good Chinese restaurant is *Kuang Chaou* on Calle 11 between Av. Central and Av. 2; another is *Fortuna,* Av. 6, Calle 2/4; yet another is *Lung Mun* on Av. 1, between Calles 5 and 7, reasonably priced. *Morazán,* near park of same name, cheap.

The *Van Gogh,* strongly recommended; *Winner Inn; El Balcón de Europa; Americano; Trixie's; Los Yoses,* drive in. *Dos Pinos Auto Soda* drive in (Calle 21 and Av. 12) has gigantic banana splits made from pasteurized ice-cream, and large hamburgers; *Finisterre,* Av. Central, good, cheap food; *Malé,* on same street, hamburgers and chiles, popular; *MacDonald's,* near Banco Central, also for hamburgers; *Kentucky Fried Chicken,* opposite British Embassy; *Antojitas,* on Paseo Colón and on road to suburb of San Pedro, serves excellent Mexican food at moderate prices; *La Fanega,* in San Pedro, for excellent hamburgers, folk music some nights; *Orléans,* also in San Pedro, serves crèpes; *Arturo's,* Calle 5 between Av. 1 and Central, American-style bar; *Mr. Pizza,* Av. 1, Calles 7/9, *Billy Boy,* Av. Central, snacks; *Pops,* near Banco Central; *Soda Central* on Calle Central, good local dishes; *La Tranquera* (parking space) on the highway to Cartago at Curribadat, 6-8 km. E of San José, serves good steaks and other foods (orchestra for dancing at weekends). On N side of La Sabana airport on Av. 3 and approximately Calle 50 are two good restaurants, *El Chicote,* see above (country-style; good grills) and *El Molino,* and *The Pub*—almost a genuine English pub! The food is good even in modest places such as *Restaurant Magnolia. La Selecta* bakeries recommended; *Casey's Donuts,* Calle Central, between Av. 7 and 9 (also deals in paperbacks). Restaurants are decidedly expensive in San José; the budget traveller is advised to stick to those W of Calle 8, *i.e.* in even-numbered Calles with a number larger than 8.

Night Clubs, very mild, are: Boite Europa; and one at the *Hotel Balmoral,* Grill la Orquidea; La Tranquera. Interesting night life in dance casinos at Av. 2, corner of Calle 8. "Aquarius" discothèque recommended for the young; Le Club is considered to be the liveliest night spot; Discothèque Casáblanca, behind *Van Gogh* restaurant, is expensive.

Clubs Colegio de Abogados, Club Alemán de Costa Rica, Club Amateur de Pesca, Cariari International Country Club, Casa España, Casa Italia, Centro Israelita de Costa Rica, Cooperativa Las Cabañas, Costa Rica Country Club, Costa Rica Tennis Club, Costa Rica Yacht Club, Club Los Leones, A.C.E.A., Club El Contador, El Castillo Country Club, Club Hípico La Caraña Río Oro de Santa Ana, Club Kiwanism Club La Guaria, Club Los Angeles, Club Médico Deportivo, Club Rotario de San José, Club Social, Club Union, Club Campestre del Río, Club Campestre Español, Club Campestre Valle del Sol, Club de Jardines de San José, Club Deportivo Aéreo Costarricense, Club Punta Leona S.A., San José Indoor Club (with many sports facilities).

Airports The Juan Santamaría international airport is at El Coco, 16 km. from San José by motorway. Taxi US$7, or minibus from outside San Juan de Dios hospital or by Alajuela bus (US$0.25) *via* the motorway. Taxis Unidos run a colectivo for US$1-2 each. Light aircraft use the Tobias Bolaños airport at Pavas, about 5 km. W of San José. The old La Sabana airport is not used.

Protestant Churches the Good Shepherd (Anglican), Union Church (Non-conformist). Services in English.

Libraries Centro Cultural Costarricense-Norteamericano (Calle Negritos—good films, plays, art exhibitions and English-language library), University of Costa Rica (in San Pedro suburb), and National Library (near Northern Railway station), all entry free.

Banks Opening times: Mon.-Fri. 0800-1100, 1330-1500. Note that it is sometimes difficult to change your surplus colones at the frontiers. Only take out of San José what you are sure you will need.

Bookshops The Bookstore, Av. 1, Calle 1 and 3, good selection of English language books; Universal, Av. Central for Spanish books.

Language School Conversa, Calle 38 (Tel.: 21-76-49).

Laundromat Av. 2, opposite Parque Carrillo.

Taxis Plenty of taxis; an average journey in town costs about US$0.80.

Car Rentals Self-drive cars can be hired for US$10 a day or US$50 a week plus US$0.09 a kilometre, petrol inclusive. Avis, *Hotel President,* Av. Central, Calle 7/9 (Tel.: 21-65-69); National, Calle Central, Av. 1a (Tel.: 22-95-69); Rent-a-Jeep, Calle 24, Av. 7 (Tel.: 21-22-31); Hertz.

Swimming Pools The best is at Ojo de Agua, 5 minutes from the airport, 15 minutes from San José. It is open up to 1700 hours; take bus to Alajuela *via* San Antonio de Belén. On Sundays there is a direct bus service from Parque la Merced in San José to the pool. There is also a completely new pool outside the Ministry of Transport, about 2 km. from the city centre.

Inoculations Clínica Bíblica (Tel.: 21-39-22) has been recommended; also said to be good for medical attention.

Tourist Office On Calle Central between Avs. 4 and 6, off main square (Apt. 777), very helpful, good maps. The Instituto Geográfico supplies very good topographical maps for walkers. The national park service can provide very interesting material on the flora and fauna of the parks. Esso maps, free at petrol stations, are also good.

Shopping Market on Av. Central, Calles 6-8, open 0600-1800, good leather suitcases, hammocks. Mercado Borbón, Avs. 3-5, Calles 8-10, fruit and vegetables in abundance.

Sightseeing Many of the most interesting public buildings are near the intersection of Av. Central and Calle Central. The Teatro Nacional—marble staircases, statuary, frescoes and foyer decorated in gold with Venetian plate mirrors—is just off Av. Central, on Calle 3. Go below stage to see how it is elevated. The Palacio Nacional (Av. Central, Calle 15), where the Legislative Assembly meets, is a simple building. Any visitor can attend the debates. Along Calle Central is Parque Central, with a bandstand in the middle among tropical trees. To the E of the park is the Cathedral; to the N are the Raventros and Palace theatres, interesting; to the S are the Rex Theatre and a branch of the Banco Nacional. N of Av. Central, on Calle 2, is the Unión Club, the principal social centre of the country. Opposite it is the General Post and Telegraph Office, a fine building put up in 1916. The National Museum, with a good collection of pre-Columbian antiquities, is the reconstructed Vista Buena barracks, E along Av. Central. Two blocks N of it is Parque Nacional, with a grandiloquent bronze monument representing the five central American republics ousting the filibuster William Walker (see Nicaraguan chapter) and the abolition of slavery in Central America.

Still further N is Parque Bolívar, now turned into a playground, with zoo, for children. Along Av. 3, to the W of Parque Nacional, are the four gardens of Parque Morazán, with another bandstand at the centre. There is a statue of Bolívar in one of the gardens. A little to the NE, Parque España—cool, quiet, and intimate—has for neighbours the National Liquor Factory (try a glass of Crema de Nance—the factory is open to visitors between 1300 and 1430 on weekdays), the Casa Amarilla (Yellow House), seat of the Ministry of Foreign Affairs, and the Edificio Metálico (Metal Building), which houses several of the main schools.

The attractive Paseo Colón continues Av. Central W to the old La Sabana airport (now being developed as a sports centre) with a Colonial-style building with frescoes of Costa Rican life in the Salón Dorado, on the upper floor. To the W of the airport is the National Stadium, seating 20,000 spectators at (mainly) football matches. There is a polo field nearby.

Museums Museo Nacional, very interesting, open Tues.-Sun., 0830-1100, 1300-1730; replicas of pre-Columbian jewellery may be bought at reasonable prices. Banco Central de Costa Rica has a gold museum, open Wed. and Sat., 0900-1130, free. Castle on Calle 19, between Avs. Central and 2, now converted into museum, open 0900-1100, 1400-1700; closed Mon.

Railway Services On the NE side of Parque Nacional is the main station of the Northern Railway to the Atlantic port of Limón and to Heredia and Alajuela in the Meseta Central. The main station of the Ferrocarril Eléctrico al Pacifico to the Pacific port of Puntarenas is in the extreme S of the city (take bus marked Paso Ancho). The two 1.067-metre gauge lines are connected. The trains are slow, but clean and comfortable; recommended also for beautiful views.

There is one train a day each way between San José and Puerto Limón; from Limón to San José leaving 0600; from San José to Limón leaving 0730. Journey takes about 7 hours to Limón and 9 back. Fare: US$3.25. Baggage 20 kilos free, excess US$0.03 per kilo. Light refreshments are served on all trains except the local service, which operates once a day between San José, Heredia and Alajuela on the Northern Railway.

Between San José and Puntarenas there are five trains daily; from Puntarenas to San José leaving at 0600, 0800, 1200, 1500 and 1800 and from San José to Puntarenas leaving at 0300 (summer Sundays only), 0600, 0815, 1200 (1245 on Sats.), 1500 and 1800. Journey takes about 4 hours. Fastest trains 3 hours. Fares US$1.40, or US$2.35 return. Passengers can buy light refreshments at wayside stations and stops.

Buses There are services to all the nearby towns and to Turrialba and Puntarenas. Cartago and Turrialba buses start from behind service station at corner of Av. Central and Calle 13. Those for Puntarenas (8 a day) leave from the corner of Av. 7 and Calle 12; journey takes 1½ hours, US$2.20. It is possible to get to Limón by bus, changing two or three times, in 3½-4 hours.

Fares Bus fares in San José: US$0.05 from the centre outwards. Hand baggage in reasonable quantities is not charged, but no trunks of any kind are taken.

Cables All America Cables & Radio, Inc., Calle 1,658. Radiográfica Compañía Internacional de Costa Rica, Calle 3, between Av. Central and Av. 1.

Excursions San José is a good centre for excursions into the beautiful Meseta Central, to its coffee plantations and towns and volcanoes. The excursions to the Orosí valley and volcano of Irazú are given under Cartago; tourist minibuses organized by the travel agencies run to Irazú on Mon., Thurs. and Sat. (An organized trip is said to cost US$30.50; *Restaurant Palomo* recommended for fish, though service "lively".) Public buses to Poás run from Estanción Terminal Raventos, Av. 3, Calles 10 and 12, on Sundays only. To reach Barba take a bus to San José de las Montañas and walk to the village of Sacramento and on from there up the volcano. A road runs NE of San José to (11 km.) San Isidro de Coronado, a popular summer resort (bus from La Coca station); its *fiesta* is on February 15. Those interested in medical research can visit the Instituto Clodomiro Picado snake farm, open Mon.-Fri. 0800-1400 and Sat. 0900-1100. The road goes on through a fine countryside of (32 km.) Las Nubes, a country village which commands a great view of Irazú. A paved road and a railway run from the capital to the two other main towns of the Meseta: Heredia and Alajuela (see pages 1016/7).

International Buses Ecatra (Expreso Centroamericano, Av. Central, Calle 11-15) and Sirca (Av. 5-7, Calle Central) run a scheduled daily service along the Inter-American Highway from San José to Peñas Blancas, on the Nicaraguan frontier, and on to Managua; Sirca now connects all the Central American capitals. Tica buses run from Panama City over the Inter-American Highway all the way to Guatemala City, serving every Central American capital; but the line does have its defects, as explained on page 901. The terminal is at Calle 9 and Av. 2b. It is to this office that all refund claims have to be made (take 10 days and have to be collected in person). The Ticabus journey from San José to Panama City now takes 15 hours, US$13.20, two trips a day, 0845 and 2400. To Managua the trip takes 10 hours and costs US$6. To Tegucigalpa US$15; to San Salvador US$18; to Guatemala US$23. Panaica, Av. Central and Calle 13b-15, runs to Panama and Managua; Tracopa, Av. 5 and Calle 14, goes as far as David, and now also runs to Managua. *Warning:* The Panaica office has been known to sell tickets for buses from Colombia to Ecuador; these seem not to be valid for any known bus line and moreover are not refundable as Panaica does not have, as it claims it does, offices in major S. American cities.

Campsites At San Antonio de Belén, 8 km. from San José, Belén Trailer Park, US$2.50, very good facilities. In San José, a small space behind *Hal Restaurant,* San Pedro district. Also at Tres Ríos, a few km. S on Inter-American Highway, 1 km. S of Tres Ríos.

Puerto Limón is on a palm-fringed shore backed by mountains and is the country's most important port. It was built on the site of an ancient Indian village, Cariari, where Columbus landed on his fourth and last voyage. The bulk of the population is black. The town itself is laid out in square, well-paved blocks. Visitors should see the palm promenade and tropical flowers of Vargas Park (where sloths live in the trees) and the open-air swimming pool of the Club Miramar. There are several daily flights to San José (US$7) besides the railway and the new road, which has been greatly improved. Population 49,600. Some 2.8 million bunches of bananas are exported each year. The town is quite expensive.

Hotels *Puerto* and *Acón,* both fairly new, US$12-17; *Lincoln; Caribe* (US$5 s); *Park,* US$3.50 s, with bath (cold water), comfortable, dining room; *Gran Hotel Los Angeles,* new, US$8 d, with bath; *Miami,* US$4.25 s, with bath, recommended; *Palace; Limón; Venus; Oriental. Hotel Wong,* US$1.45 each, basic, but friendly. Many *pensiones,* e.g. *Vicky,* by waterfront, US$2.20 d; *Niza,* near railway station, US$3.60 d. First four have some a/c rooms. Several Chinese restaurants. Also *Restaurant La Chucheca* serves good *comidas* for US$1 and breakfast US$0.75. *Milk Bar La Negra Mendoza* at the central market has good milk shakes and snacks.

Cables All America Cables and Radio, Inc., Calle 2a, entre Avenidas B. & C. Tropical Radio Company.

Shipping Cargo/passenger lines: Royal Netherlands; Hamburg Amerika; Horn Line. Royal Mail Lines fast cargo service with transhipment at Cristóbal. The mechanical process of banana-loading is fascinating; well worth watching.

Protestant Church Anglican, with services in English.

Buses Frequent service to San José; leave from in front of the post office, US$2.25, 3½ hours. It is not clear whether you have to change.

Warning There have apparently been some incidents when young people have had drugs planted on them only to be searched by the police who have demanded large sums of money in fines. Be very careful.

The Atlantic Coast Apart from the area near Limón, the Atlantic coastal region, rugged and deeply jungled, is very little visited, though it has recently been declared a national park and the tourist inflow will soon begin. The enterprising might care to travel by motorized dugout canoe along the Río Frío between San Carlos, on Lake Nicaragua (in Nicaragua) and Los Chiles (Costa Rica), from which a plane flies daily (except Sun.) to San José for US$11; also occasional flights to Alajuela. The river trip, between thickly wooded banks, offers absorbing interest. **Los Chiles** itself is an interesting town, if only because there is no traffic other than boats. Cheap accommodation (US$2.50 a night) and restaurants are available. English is spoken widely along the coast. Southward from Limón, travellers can catch a train to Penshurst or can drive, though the road is not paved. From Penshurst it is a 11½-km. walk to **Cahuita** to which there is also an excellent road and bus service direct from Puerto Limón. Cahuita, which is on the coast, has a unique coral reef and an ancient Spanish wrecked ship may be seen. The beaches (one with white sand, the other black) are reported to be excellent, as is the skin-diving, though there is a strong undercurrent. *Hotel Lamm,* US$2.35 s, adequate, *Hotel Kee,* US$2.40 each. There are also empty rooms to let, so take a hammock or sleeping bag. On public holidays Cahuita is very crowded; the remainder of the year it is a favourite resort of backpackers. The beaches at Puerto Viejo, 13 km. from Cahuita, are also worth a visit. There is a spectacular waterfall on the route through Puerto Viejo and the local bus drivers will stop to let you off. Continuing S from Cahuita is Guabito, on the border with Panama (Miss Rachel rents rooms for US$0.60). A narrow-gauge railway runs to Almirante from Guabito.

Northward from Limón, past Siquirres (several hotels), trains run to Guápiles, centre of the new Río Frío banana region. There is also a good new road (toll) to Siquirres. Standard Fruit have built about 75 km. of new railway lines on from Guápiles (three hotels). On the coast N of Limón, there is good fishing at Tortuguero and Barra del Colorado. Philippe Delahaut, from Belgium, reached Barra del Colorado by bus from Limón to Moín and by boat from Moín to Barra (112 km.). On the boat trip he passed through beautiful jungle surroundings, stopping at Parismina where there is one hotel. Barra del Colorado also has an hotel, and an airstrip. There is an annual tarpon fishing competition. Tortuguero, as its name suggests, is frequented by sea turtles to lay their eggs.

It is 166 km. by Northern Railway to San José. There is one train in either direction each day; "up" takes 9 and "down" 7 hours. The narrow-gauge railway skirts the coast for 16 km., giving an almost continuous view of the surf of breakers, often through groves of graceful coconut palms. When Minor C. Keith was building this line in the 1870s—it took 19 years to complete—the first 40 km. cost the lives of 4,000 men (most of them Chinese labourers but also including three of Minor Keith's brothers and his uncle, Henry Meiggs) from yellow fever. The Río Matina is crossed by bridge, and next the Pacuare. From Siquirres (60 km. from Limón) on to **Turrialba** (27,620 people), where the Inter-American Institute of Agricultural Sciences (rooms for visitors) and the first coffee farms are, the railway runs on a narrow ledge poised between mountain and river. On the left are the rushing waters of the Reventazón, and on the right the high forested mountains. In the 101 km. from Limón to Turrialba the train has climbed 640 metres; in the next 50 km. it has to climb a further

900 metres. The view throughout this section is gorgeous; ride in the observation car at the rear of the train if there is one. The whole valley of the Reventazón can be seen at one sweep, the river itself appearing as a narrow ribbon of foam 300 metres below. At this altitude there is a cool snap in the air as the tropics are left behind and the train reaches the Meseta Central, where the climate is more or less constant the year round.

From Turrialba you can get to the village of Moravia del Chiripó, where guides and horses can be hired for an excursion into the jungled, trackless area of the Talamanca Indians, where there are legends of lost goldfields. About 30 km. E of Turrialba, near Guayabo, an Indian ceremonial centre has been excavated and there are clear signs of its paved streets and stone-lined water-channels. There are buses from Turrialba (US$0.35) to Guayabo from where it is a 1½ hour walk to the site.

Cartago, 145 km. from Limón, 22½ from San José, stands at 1,439 metres at the foot of the Irazú volcanic peak and is encircled by mountains. It was founded in 1563 and was the capital until 1823. It is a small city, with a population of only 25,000, though the neighbourhood is densely populated. Earthquakes destroyed it in 1841 and 1910, and it has been severely shaken on other occasions. That is why there are no old buildings, though some have been rebuilt in Colonial style.

The most interesting church is the Basilica, built in Byzantine style, of Nuestra Señora de Los Angeles, the Patroness of Costa Rica; it houses La Negrita, under 15 cm. high, a famous Indian Virgin who draws pilgrims from all over Central America because of great healing powers attributed to her image. Her feast day is August 2, when her image is carried in procession to other churches in Cartago and there are celebrations thoughout Costa Rica. In her shrine is a bubbling spring surrounded by the gifts of her devotees.

The image first appeared on August 2, 1635. It was stolen on August 2, 1824—it was then at the Parish Church (ruined in the earthquake of 1910)—and reappeared two days later behind the atrium of the triforium. On November 22, 1866, the valuable crown and "resplandor" (a circle of golden rays) were stolen, but not the stone image. The jewellery was replaced by subscription. On the night of May 12-13, 1950, robbers killed a watchman and stole the image, its jewels and votive offerings to the value of several million colones. On May 20, it was discovered inside the Basilica.

Worth seeing is the old parish church (La Parroquia), ruined by the 1910 earthquake and now converted into a delightful garden retreat with flowers, fish and humming birds.

Hotels *Majestic,* Avenida Central, moderate; *Tarsis,* US$4 p.p.; *Venecia,* US$1.20 p.p., adequate; *Hospedaje Familial,* at railway station, US$2 s.

Restaurants *Café San Remo* for the best value in town. Restaurants, among other things, are closed on the Thursday and Friday of Holy Week, so take your own food.

Excursions Best is by a road (paved, but still poor) to the crater of Irazú (2,906 metres)—*(Hotel Robert).* Cartago buses to Irazú at 0600 and 1300, giving a 20-minute stop at the volcano, US$1.40 return; taxi is US$3.50 return. (The 0600 bus is preferable as the clouds come down early obscuring the view.) Alternatively you can take a bus from Cartago to San Antonio. Ask the driver at the crossroads just outside the village. From there you walk to the summit. Tourist minibuses go to Irazú from San José, about US$10.

Mike Marlowe, of Blacksburg, Virginia, writes as follows: "In the afternoon (Irazú's) mountain top is buried in fog and mist or drizzle. But the ride up in the mist can be half magical, for the mountainside is half-displaced in time. There are new jeeps and tractors, but the herds of cattle are small, the fields are quilt-work, handcarts and oxcarts are to be seen under the fretworked porches of well-kept frame houses. The land is fertile, the pace is slow, the air is clean, there is no (great) poverty. It is a very attractive mixture of old and new. Many of the people are surprisingly pale-skinned, even freckled. Irazú is a strange mountain, well worth the two-plus hours' bus ride up. What would be even better would be a long, slow walk."

Aguas Calientes is 4 km. SE of Cartago and 90 metres lower. Its *balneario* (warm water swimming pool) is a good place for picnics. **Ujarrás** (ruins of a Colonial church and village) is 6½ km. E of Cartago by a road which goes from Paraíso through a beautiful valley to the small town of **Orosi**, in the enchanting Orosi valley, down which flows the tumultuous Reventazón (*Motel* and *Restaurant Río Palomo*). Here are magnificent views of the valley, a beautiful 18th century church with museum alongside, a 17th century mission with Colonial treasures, a pretty waterfall tumbling 90 metres from the heights, and just outside the town 2 *balnearios* and restaurants serving good meals at fair prices. The *miradores* of Ujarrás and Orosí both offer excellent views of the Reventazón valley. There are buses from Cartago to all these places.

The Turrialba volcano may be visited from Cartago by a bus to the village of Pacayas, where horses may be hired to take you to the top (where there is a fine view and a guesthouse). Alternatively there are buses from Turrialba town to Santa Cruz, which is perhaps a closer starting point.

From Cartago the railway (and a road) follow the coffee-planted Reventazón valley to the Continental Divide, which is crossed at 1,566 metres. From this highest point, there is a gentle decline to the capital, which stands at 1,160 metres.

Heredia, capital of its province, 10 km. from San José, is a great coffee and cattle centre. It looks a little like the towns of southern Spain: church towers above red-tiled roofs, iron grilles at the windows, and bright gardens set among whitewashed adobe and stone walls. There is a statue to the poet Aquileo Echeverría (1866-1909). The Tourist Institute will arrange a visit to a coffee *finca*. Altitude 1,137 metres, population 23,600.

From Heredia a paved road runs to 2,704-metre volcano Poás (37 km. by road from San José). The crater is 1½ km. across. Within one area of its sharp-sided walls is a lake of crystal-clear water. In another area geysers throw steam 600 metres or so occasionally. One km. away is a still, forest-fringed water lake in another crater. There is a wide view from the summit of Poás; the whole Meseta Central is laid out at one's feet. The volcano can be reached by car or bus; take a bus from Alajuela to Poasito from behind the market. From Poasito hitch a lift as it is a long walk. (Buses marked "Poás" are no use as they are going to San Pedro de Poás.)

Excursion Beautiful views from road across mountains to town of Puerto Viejo de Sarapiquí (3 small hotels) on river with good fishing. There is an express minibus service from San José (*via* Heredia), US$3, as well as ordinary buses 3 times a day from Heredia. The river flows into the San Juan, which forms the northern border of Costa Rica.

Alajuela, 13 km. beyond Heredia, capital of its province, stands at 952 metres, and is a mid-summer resort for people from the capital. It is famous for its flowers and its market days; an interesting craft cooperative produces pictures in relief metalwork; the interesting church of La Agonía in the E part of town has murals done from life. Juan Santamaría, the peasant drummer who fired the building at Rivas (Nicaragua) in which Walker's filibusters were entrenched in 1856, is commemorated by a monument. Just outside the town is the Ojo de Agua swimming pool (good restaurant) in beautiful surroundings: a popular bathing resort where boating also takes place. Entrance, US$1.20 p.p., plus US$0.80 per vehicle. The gushing spring which feeds the pool also supplies water for Puntarenas. Population 28,700.

Campsites Two trailer parks nearby, with hookups: the Yaluca and the Inca.

Villa Quesada lies some 25 km. from the Inter-American highway and can be reached by a road which branches off the highway near Naranjo. There are frequent buses from San José. From Quesada there are buses to towns on the San Carlos and Sarapiquí rivers (incl. Puerto Viejo) where launches can be taken down to the San Juan river and either up to Lake Nicaragua, or down, *via* the Colorado river, to the Canales de Tortuguero and Moín, about 10 km. by road and rail from Puerto Limón. (Agencies in Puerto Limón run tours on the canals.)

Beyond Alajuela the Inter-American Highway divides into a toll road and a "vía libre", which is the old road. Though it is rough, it passes through attractive countryside and the towns of Naranjo, Sarchí and Grecia. At **Sarchí** one may visit the factory that produces the traditional painted ox-carts, which are almost a national emblem. Also, hand-made cow-hide rocking chairs and wooden products may be purchased at Fábricas de Carretas. Grecia is the centre for the pineapple-growing area.

Puntarenas (population 30,829) is on a 5-km. spit of land thrusting out into Nicoya Gulf and enclosing the Estero lagoon. It is hot (mean temperature 27°C), but from January to March the town is much frequented by visitors from the Central Valley for sea-bathing and shark and tuna fishing off the coast. The beaches are, however, said to be dirty. There is a new public swimming pool on the end of the point (US$0.35 entrance). Good surfing off the headland. Across the gulf are the mountains of the Nicoya Peninsula. In the gulf are several islands, the Islas Negritos, to which there are passenger launches. The chief products around Puntarenas are bananas, rice, cattle, and coconuts. Puntarenas is connected with San José by a road, a railway (116 km.; 4 hours, see page 1008), and an air service.

Air Service from San José, US$4.50, in 15 minutes against 4 hours by train. Flight (US$15) and bus also from San José to new, still isolated Playa del Jacó (*Hotel Austral,* US$11 full board), south of Puntarenas.

Hotels *Tioga,* near beach (US$13.50 d, including continental breakfast), very good indeed. Next best is *Cayuga,* with a/c. Others are *Las Hamacas; Imperial; Marbella; Los Banos; La Riviera; Arenas; Chanita; Mata de Limón Verano,* US$2.40 each; *San Luis,* US$3.50 d, clean; *Prado,* US$1.50 s; *Arca de Noél; Castalias* (US$1 p.p.). *Viking,* new, on the beach, US$5-7 s, US$10-12 d; *Hotel Río,* near Market, US$1.40 s, without shower, basic and noisy, but clean and friendly; *Paris,* US$13.50 d; *Colonial,* US$16 d with breakfast, recommended. Numerous *pensiones.* Accommodation difficult January to March, especially at weekends. Next to the *Tioga* is *Aloha Restaurant* (good). A number of Chinese restaurants on the main street. There is a lively night life in the cheaper bars.

Ferry to Playa Naranjo US$0.80 p.p., US$0.35-20.50 per car, depending on length, 1¼ hours, 4 crossings a day, 5 on Sundays.

Cables All America Cables & Radio Inc., Casa Blanca.

Warning Thieves abound on the beach.

Shipping Passenger Line: Italia. Cargo/passenger: North German Lloyd; Hamburg Amerika; Holland America; Johnson; Marina Mercante Nicaragüense. Fortnightly fast cargo vessels of Central America Services. There are passenger launches to various islands and ports of the Gulf, as well as to Puerto Cortés and Bahía Draque on the Osa peninsula.

San Lucas island is open to the public on Sundays (only) and can be reached by a launch which sets off from Puntarenas every half hour between 0830 and 1000, returning up to 1800 (round trip US$1.20). Its magnificent beach, El Coro, is far superior to any at Puntarenas and there are beautiful rolling hills, but the island's great interest lies in its unique experimental penal colony. The "interns", after a short trial period in the dormitories, get their own place to live in and its key. They are free to study, to earn a modest income from work, to have wife or friend visit them for 5 days each month, during which they are free and enjoy complete privacy. English-speaking prisoners take visitors around. Various tourist items made by them are for sale, but take your own food as hardly any is available. San Lucas is also a favourite with Costa Rican tourists.

Also S of San José one can visit Aserrí, a village with a beautiful white church; further along the same road is the *Mirador Ram Luna,* a restaurant with a fine panoramic view. At the end of the road is San Ignacio de Acosta, again with a good church containing life-size Nativity figures for use in Christmas processions.

SW of San José is the Santa Ana valley, which includes the popular weekend centre of Lagos de Lindora. The road goes on through lovely scenery to Puriscal and Puerto Quepos (see next paragraph).

Some 55 km. S of San José, in Puntarenas province, is **Puerto Quepos,** built by United Fruit as a banana exporting port, but now rather run down. There is a frequent bus service from the capital, 5 hours, about US$2, and there are daily flights, US$5, 25 mins. (*Hotel América,* US$2 each; others). A few km. E of Quepos lie the beautiful beaches of Manuel Antonio which have been declared a national park. They can be reached by jeep from Quepos, and one of the beaches has a hotel with cabins to let at US$3 p.p. and meals for about US$2. A road (difficult in the rainy season) runs from Quepos to other pleasant beaches at Dominical, Esterillos and Jacó (all these beaches have simple cabins for rent) then to Puerto Cortés and on to Palmar Norte on the Inter-American Highway.

Cocos Island, 24 square km. of barren, rugged, uninhabited rock, lies 320 km. off the Peninsula of Osa, in the S. Arrangements for reaching it by chartered boat can be made in Puntarenas, after a permit has been got from the Government. It was at one time a refuge for pirates, who are supposed to have buried great treasure there, though none has been found by the 500 expeditions which have sought it. Treasure seekers make an initial cash payment, agree to share any treasure found with the Government, and are supervised by Costa Rican police. The offshore waters are a fisherman's paradise, for they abound in fish of all kinds.

Guanacaste Province includes the Peninsula of Nicoya and the lowlands at the head of the gulf. The Province, whose capital is Liberia (see next page) has a distinctive people, way of life, flora and fauna. The smallholdings of the highlands give way here to large *haciendas* and great cattle estates. Maize, rice, cotton, beans and fruit are other products, and there is manganese at Playa Real. The rivers teem with fish; there are all kinds of wildlife in the uplands.

The people are open-handed, hospitable, fond of the pleasures of life: music, which they play on odd instruments; dancing (the Punto Guanacasteco has been officially declared the typical national dance); and merry-making (cattle and jollity seem to go together). There are no hotels worthy of the name, and the lowlands are deep in mud during the rainy season. Buses ply along the road from Playa Naranjo (due W across the Gulf from Puntarenas) to Nicoya (40 km. unpaved, 30 km. paved road), US$1.50, 2¼ hours. At Nicoya there are connections for Liberia (US$1.10, 2 hours) on the Inter-American Highway.

From Puntarenas a road runs to the Inter-American Highway at Las Cañas. From there are buses *via* Tilarán (change) to Arenal (both are busy towns because of the construction of the Arenal Dam which will eventually flood the latter). From Arenal there are buses to the villages of the Guatuso Indians near the Nicaraguan border, US$1.90, 3 hours, Upala and Caño Negro. (In Upala are the *Hotel Rigo, Pensión Isabela, Pensión Buena Vista,* basic, US$2.30 d, food available.) 5 km. N of Las Cañas is a very good campsite, La Pacifica, run by a Swiss family, with restaurant, cottages, cabins, small zoo, medical service, workshop, spare parts, etc.; camping US$1 per day, cabins US$5.80 p.p. There is free camping along the river. Good camping is also reported at a beach 2 km. north of Brasilito.

Nicoya, on the Peninsula, is a pleasant little town distinguished by possessing the country's second-oldest church.

Hotels *Chorotega,* US$1.90 each, very good; *Pensión Venecia,* US$1.50 each; *Pensión Eureka,* basic.

Liberia (pop.: 13,700) is a neat, clean, cattle town with a church in the most modern style and a small meticulous market. There is a tourist office at the junction of the Inter-American Highway and the road leading to the town. There are air connections with the capital. A well paved branch road leads SW into the Nicoya Peninsula, a pleasant and increasingly developed agricultural region which is well served by buses. A number of beaches are reached by unpaved roads. One of the most pleasant and frequented is **Playa del Coco** in an attractive islet-scattered bay hemmed in by rocky headlands, to reach which one should leave the bus at Comunidad. There are bars, restaurants and one or two motels along the sandy beach: *Casino Playa del Coco,* US$4.70-US$7 d; *Luna Tica* has a dormitory, US$1.80 p.p. Bus to San José, US$2.75, 4 hours. Another good beach is Playa Tamarindo, though it has few facilities. Samara is also recommended.

Hotels at Liberia: *Bramadero Hotel,* US$4.50 s, without bath or a/c, US$6 with, good, fair restaurant and bar but somewhat noisy. *Playa Hermosa,* cabins run by an American couple, US$9 d, clean, good reasonably priced food; *Hotel Liberia,* US$4 d, good and clean; *Casa del Ganadero Hotel; Hotel Rivas,* US$1.20, basic. *Motel Delfín,* 5 km. N of Liberia on the Inter-American Highway, with excellent campsite and large swimming pool. On the coast, *Motel Tamarindo Diria,* recommended.

The Economy

The per capita income of Costa Rica in 1976 was estimated at US$1,161 (at current prices), which is the highest in Central America. The country's economy is based on the export of coffee, bananas, meat, sugar and cocoa. The Meseta Central with its volcanic soil is the coffee-growing area: here too are grown the staple crops: beans, maize, potatoes and sugar cane, and the dairy farming is both efficient and lucrative. Some 22% of the land area is planted to crops, 36% to pasture and 40% is forested. The country's timber industry is very small and its resources have yet to be commercially utilised.

Mining and manufacturing together account for about 18% of g.d.p. Industry is largely concerned with food processing but there is also some production of chemicals (including fertilizers—also exported), plastics, tyres, etc.

There are small deposits of manganese, mercury, gold and silver, but only the last two are worked. Deposits of iron ore are estimated at 400m. tons and sulphur deposits at 11m. tons. Considerable bauxite deposits have been found, and if these were developed Costa Rica's export earnings would increase considerably. The Government is presently interested in developing a hydroelectricity programme as well as improving the port of Coldera on the Pacific coast and encouraging manufacturing *via* the state agency Codesa. Oil companies are interested in offshore concessions in the Pacific. The State has recently taken over the oil refinery at Puerto Limón.

		Foreign Trade (USm.)					
		1972	1973	1974	1975	1976	1977*
Exports (f.o.b.)	..	278.8	344.8	440.7	488.6	586.9	815.0
Imports (c.i.f.)	..	337.1	412.1	626.3	628.2	695.6	909.0

Information for Visitors

How to get there:

By Air From London: British Airways to Panama (Thurs. and Sun.) or Miami (or U.S. airlines to Miami) and then by Lacsa, Taca or Pan Am to San José. Lacsa flies directly to Costa Rica from New Orleans, Miami and Mexico City; Copa flies from Panama City, and Pan Am and Taca from Miami, Mexico City and the Central American capitals. There are also flights to Colombia *via* San Andrés island with SAM—this is the cheapest way of getting to Colombia, US$54. Iberia, Viasa and Sahsa also fly to Costa Rica. There is an airport tax of US$7, and a 5% tax on airline tickets purchased in the country. Tickets bought in San Andrés carry no tax.

By Sea The quickest and cheapest sea route from the United Kingdom is by steamers of the Pacific Steam Navigation Co., with trans-shipment at Cristóbal: thence by local service through the Canal to Puntarenas. Hamburg-Amerika Line and the Horn Line have services from European ports to Puntarenas and Puerto Limón. R.M. Lines and P.S.N.C. carry no passengers.

Royal Mail Lines Agents F. J. Alvarado & Cía. Sucrs. S.A. San José: Casilla 474. Puntarenas: Casilla 25. Limón: Casilla 112.

Documents Passports are required, except for holders of tourist cards, who must also hold proof of identity. Visas are not required for visits of up to 30 days by nationals of Western European countries, Argentina, Canada, Chile, Colombia, other Central American countries, Israel, Japan, Panama, Romania and Yugoslavia. Tourist cards can be got from Costa Rican consular officers or from tourist agencies; they are valid for 30 days but may be extended to 6 months, and cost US$2. Sometimes it is difficult to get an extension, which costs US$1.20 and involves a lot of "red tape". Those who stay for more than 30 days have to get exit permits before they can leave the country, and pay a 20-colones (US$2.25) emigration tax. All visitors must have a valid smallpox vaccination certificate and an onward ticket (a bus ticket will do) before being allowed into the country. There is an exit tax which seems to vary but is normally US$2.35 for overland departures and US$5 for international flights. Half a kilo of manufactured tobacco and 3 litres of liquor are allowed in duty-free. Any amount of foreign or local currency can be taken in or out.

Warning The immigration authorities do not like men with a "hippy" appearance, i.e. who have long hair and/or beards and who carry rucksacks (this last also applies to girls), and may refuse them entry. Those arriving by air at the international airport who have however vague a resemblance to a "hippy" will have their persons and baggage carefully searched, especially if they have arrived from Colombia, because of the rampant drug traffic in the area.

The information offices of the **Instituto Costarricense de Turismo** are in Calle Central, Avenidas 4/6, San José (Postal address: Apartado 777; Tel.: 23-17-33). There is a branch office at Cartago. All tourist information is given here. Various tourist agencies arrange trips. **Note:** Whereas in most South American countries a "cuadra" means a block (of buildings), in Costa Rica it means 100 metres, or maybe 100 *varas* (yards), which is rather less.

Shopping Best buys are wooden items, ceramics and leather handicrafts.

British Businessmen and commercial travellers going to Costa Rica are strongly advised to get a copy of "Hints to Business Men Visiting Costa Rica". It is supplied free from Room CO7, Export Services Division, Dept. of Trade, Export House, 50 Ludgate Hill, London EC4M 7HU.

Business Hours 0800 or 0830 to 1100 or 1130 and 1300 to 1700 or 1730, Monday to Friday, and 0800 to 1100 on Saturday. Shops: 0800 to 1200, 1300 to 1800 Monday to Saturday.

Standard Time is 6 hours behind Greenwich Mean Time.

The climate varies from the heat and humidity of the Caribbean and Atlantic lowlands to warm temperate on the Meseta Central and chilly temperatures at the greater heights. There are dry and wet seasons: the dry runs from December to May, the wet from June to November, when the rainfall in the Meseta Central averages 1,956 mm. and roads are often bogged down. The hottest months are March, April and May. Between December and May is the best time to visit.

Clothing Linen or cotton suits for the tropical lowlands, lightweight suits of worsted or synthetic fibres for men on the plateau the year round, with a light overcoat for December through May, and a waterproof for the wet season; sweaters and overcoats for visiting the volcanoes. Cotton underclothing is best. Women wear dresses or suits of silk, nylon, cotton or silk and wool jerseys and light woollen coats for the chilly evenings of the dry season. Strapless sun-dresses are never worn in San José, nor are shorts. A light cotton raincoat, an umbrella and plastic overshoes are essential for the rainy season. Hats are needed only for weddings and official functions.

Health Drinking water outside San José should be boiled. Intestinal disorders and Chagas disease are prevalent in the lowlands although malaria has to a great extent been eradicated; malaria prophylaxis is advised for visitors to the lowlands, all the same. Uncooked foods should not be eaten.

Motoring Tourists who come by car do not pay customs duty and can keep their cars for an initial period of 30 days. This can be extended for a total period of 6 months at the Instituto Costarricense de Turismo, or at the Customs office if you take your passport, car entry permit, and a piece of "stamped paper" *(papel sellado)* obtainable at any bookshop for one colón. It is now mandatory for foreign drivers to buy insurance stamps on entry to cover the length of their stay; e.g. a LWB Landrover needs US$2.35 for two weeks' cover. If you want to travel on from Costa Rica without your car, you should leave it in the customs warehouse at the international airport at San José. For a longer period than 60 days, however, it is necessary to leave it in a private bonded warehouse. The cost is about US$30 a month, plus US$25 in customs agents' fees, plus a considerable amount of paperwork. San José is the best place to get Landrover spares. The Texaco road map, which is the best available, can be bought for US$0.10. To sell a car in Costa Rica you must pay a duty which is equivalent to four times the market value of the car. **Important Note:** Only regular-grade gasoline is available; high-compression engines need to be adjusted before entering Costa Rica. Tyres without rims are confiscated and burnt by the Customs.

Currency The unit is the Colón (plural Colones) sub-divided into 100 céntimos. Notes of 5, 10, 20, 50, 100, 500 and 1,000 colones, and coins of 5, 10, 25 and 50 céntimos, and 1, 2, 5, 10 and 20 colones circulate; also dollars. Twenty-five cents are sometimes referred to as a *peseta* and the colón itself is sometimes called a *peso*. The rate of exchange is 8.57 colones to the dollar. (It is not easy to change colones into dollars, either at the frontier or in Panama.) The cost of living is not very high; though inflation was running at about 20% a year in 1973-75, it actually fell by 2.7% in 1976 and rose by 5.3% in 1977.

Tips One colón per bag for porters; same for hairdressers. Taxis and cinema usherettes, nil; 10% at hotels, restaurants, cafés, bars; 50 céntimos for cloakroom attendants.

Mails by sea from the U.K. take from a month to 6 weeks and 3 to 5 days by airmail. Airmail letters to Britain cost 1 colón. All parcels sent out of the country by foreigners must have clearance from the Banco Central de Costa Rica (there is a branch near San José's main post office).
All America Cables & Radio Inc., have stations at San José, Puerto Limón and Puntarenas. These stations, and the long-range radio-telephone service, are run by

the Cía. Radiográfica Internacional de Costa Rica, whose H.Q. is at San José. A telephone system connects San José with the country's main centres. The Government's wireless station at San José communicates with Mexico, Guatemala and El Salvador. A telephone call to the U.K. costs US$18 for a minimum of 3 minutes, with US$6 for each extra minute. There is a public telex booth at the Central Telegraph office in San José.

For Customs the metric system of **weights and measures** is compulsory. Traders use a variety of weights and measures, including English ones and the old Spanish ones.

Public Holidays: .

January 1: New Year's Day.	August 2: Virgin of Los Angeles.
March 19: St. Joseph.	August 15: Mothers' Day.
Easter: Three Days.	September 15: Independence Day.
April 11: Battle of Rivas.	October 12: Colombus Day.
May 1: Labour Day.	December 8: Conception of the Virgin.
June: Corpus Christi.	December 25: Christmas Day.
June 29: St. Peter and St. Paul.	December 28-31: San José only.
July 25: Guanacaste Day.	

Association football is the **national sport.** There are golf courses at San José and Puerto Limón. There is sea-bathing on both Atlantic and Pacific coasts (see text). The plateau is good country for riding; horses can be hired anywhere. Most *fiestas* end with bullfighting in the squares, an innocuous but amusing set-to with no horses used. Much wildlife in the Guanacaste area. There is good sea-fishing off Puntarenas and in the mouth of the Río Chiripó, on the Caribbean side near the Nicaraguan border; inland river-fishing has been ruined by dynamiting.

Newspapers The best San José morning papers are "La Nación" and "La República" (both very good). "La Prensa Libre" is an evening paper. "Tico Times" (weekly) in English; also the "San José News" which is published twice a week. "Excelsior", a new morning paper (in Spanish) has one page of news in English.

Great Britain has an Embassy and Consulate at San José (Paseo Colón 3202, Apartado 10056, San José. Tel.: 21-58-16 and 21-56-88). The Embassy serves Nicaragua also.

The **United States** is represented by an Embassy and Consulate at San José, and Vice-Consuls at Puerto Limón, Golfito, and Quepos.

South Africa has a consulate at Paseo de los Estudiantes, Av. 9-11, San José. Postal address: Aptdo. 2515. Tel.: 22-6985. The Tourist Office will supply you with the addresses of other embassies and consulates.

The **Costa Rican** Embassy and Consular Office in London are at 1 Culross Street, W.1. Tel.: 01-493 9761 for Embassy and 01-491 4697 for Consulate. There is a consular officer at 4 Exeter Street, Holloway Head, Birmingham 1.

American Express Agents San José: TAM Travel Agency, Calle Central y 1a Av. Segunda, Tel.: 23-51-11.

We are most grateful for the assistance received from John Streather, and from the travellers listed in the general Central America section.

PANAMA

THE S-SHAPED ISTHMUS OF PANAMA, 80 km. at its narrowest and no more than 193 km. at its widest, is one of the great cross-roads of the world. Its destiny has been entirely shaped by that fact. To it Panama owes its national existence, the make-up of its 1.63 million population and its distribution: two-fifths of it are concentrated at the two cities which control the entry and exit of the canal. Panama covers 82,860 square km., including the Canal Zone, which has 1,380 square km. The Canal Zone, the strip 8 km. in width on each side of the Canal, is under U.S. military jurisdiction. Panama secured, in 1964, the right to fly its flag in the Canal Zone alongside that of the U.S.A., and the Treaty of 1903 has been revised to restore its sovereignty and other rights. The new Treaty, ratified finally in 1978, provides for Panamanian occupation of most of the Canal Zone by 1981, by stages, and for completion of this process and Panamanian operation of the Canal by 2000.

Only about a quarter of the country is inhabited and most of it is mountainous, with shelvings of lowland on both its 1,234 km. of Pacific and 767 km. of Atlantic coastlines. (The longer Pacific distance is due to the bold out-thrust of the Peninsula of Azuero.) The lowlands are traversed by hundreds of streams flowing from the mountains. The country's axis is, in general, SW to NE, but the mountain chains do not conform to this and run NW to SE. The Costa Rican mountains enter Panama from the W. At the border there are several volcanic cones, the boldest of which is the extinct Barú, in Chiriquí, 3,383 metres high. The sharp-sided Cordillera de Talamanca continues SE at a general altitude of about 900 metres, but subsides suddenly SW of Panama City. Folded in its ranges are intermont basins of great fertility. The next range, the San Blas, rises E of Colón and runs into Colombia; its highest peaks are not more than 900 metres. A third range rises from the Pacific littoral in the SE; it, too, runs into Colombia and along the Pacific as the Serranía de Baudó.

Good fortune decreed a gap between the Cordillera de Talamanca and the San Blass range in which the divide is no more than 87 metres high. It is here that the Canal runs. The end of one range and the beginning of the other are so placed that the gap runs from NW to SE. Geography stands on its head. To reach the Pacific from the Atlantic we must travel eastwards. The Pacific exit is E of the Atlantic entry by 43 km. At dawn the sun rises over the Pacific.

Rainfall is heavy along the Caribbean coast: more than 3,800 mm. a year in some places, with huge but brief downpours between April and December. Temperature in the lowland ranges from 21°C (70°F) at night to 32°C (90°F) by day. The result is deep tropical forest along the coast and far up the sides of the ranges: 76% of the whole land surface of Panama is forested. The rain begins to shade off towards the crests of the mountains (10° to 18°C), and is much less along the Pacific, though there is no scarcity of it anywhere. At Balboa it is only 1,727 mm. a year, and the tropical forest gives way to semi-deciduous trees and areas of savanna between the Pacific and the mountains.

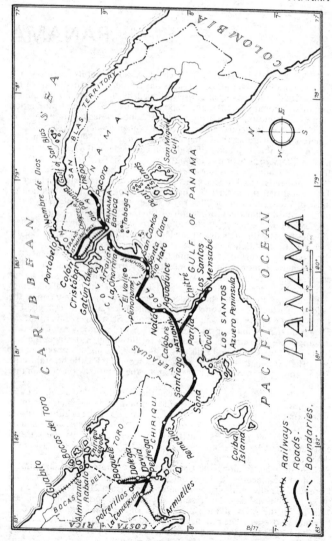

Most of the rural population live in the 6 provinces on the Pacific side, W of the canal. Only 16% of the total land area is farmed; 7.3% is pasture, nearly all of it in the 6 provinces; 3.1% only is under crops, almost all in the same provinces. There are some very large estates but the land-reform process has begun. There is only one rural population centre of any importance on the Caribbean: in Bocas del Toro, in the extreme NW.

Population The population is mostly of mixed blood but there are communities of Indians, blacks and a few Asians. About 40% live in or near Panama City and Colón, at opposite ends of the Canal. The civilian and military population of the Canal Zone is 51,000. Annual population growth is 3.2%. Of the sixty Indian tribes who inhabited the isthmus at the time of the Spanish conquest, only three have survived: the Cunas of the San Blas Islands, the Guaymíes of the western provinces and the Chocóes of Darién.

The birth-rate is 30.6 and the death-rate 4.9 per thousand, 48% are urban; in the countryside 43%, and in the towns 6% are illiterate; 65.5% of the children are born to unmarried mothers. In Bocas de Toro half the population speaks Spanish, half speaks English. Only 3% of the indigenous Indians can speak Spanish. Panama spends a quarter of its budget on education, and another quarter on public works, health and social security. An active Guardia Nacional has land, sea and air units plus a police force.

Numbers of African slaves escaped from their Spanish owners during the 16th century. They set up free communities in the Darién jungles and their chocolate coloured, Spanish-speaking descendants can still be seen there and in the Pearl Islands. But the majority of Panama's blacks are English-speaking British West Indians, descended from those brought in for the building of the railway in 1850, and later of the Canal. Most of them stayed on, and are being assimilated. There are also a number of East Indians and Chinese who tend to cling to their languages and customs. A serious social problem is that many families (perhaps a quarter of the population), are living on lands not their own and for which they pay no rent. "Good sized towns have sprung up in Panama where not one lot in the entire town was owned by any dweller nor any rent paid." The Government is now actively selling low cost houses on long term credits to these squatters.

Panama is ahead of most Latin American countries in the emancipation of women. It produced the first woman cabinet minister and the first woman ambassador in Latin America, and women have acted as provincial governors and mayors of Panama's two largest cities. They have the vote, and women in government are frequent. Education is compulsory up to the age of 14. English is the compulsory second language in the schools.

Communications Roads and railways are detailed in the text. There are now about 7,680 km. of paved roads. Road building is complicated by the extraordinary number of bridges and the large amount of grading required. The road running from Colón to Panama City is the only paved one crossing the isthmus, and the Inter-American Highway connecting Chepo and Panama City with the Costa Rican border is paved throughout.

The **Constitution** of 1972 provides for a president and vice-president, but it is the Chief of Government, Gen. Omar Torrijos, commander of the National Guard, who holds the power. The Assembly contains 505 Representatives. Panama is divided into nine provinces and three autonomous Indian reservations. Provincial governors and mayors of towns are appointed by the central authorities. Elections for the Assembly, which is expected subsequently to vote for a new President, were to be held in mid-1978.

History The history of Panama is the history of its pass-route; its fate was determined on that day in 1513 when Balboa first glimpsed the

Pacific. Since then each epoch has used what technique was available to cross the isthmus: road, then railway, then canal, then all three. Panama City was of paramount importance for the Spaniards: it was the focus of conquering expeditions northwards to Nicaragua and southwards to Ecuador, Peru, and distant Chile. All trade to and from these Pacific countries passed across the isthmus.

Panama City was founded in 1519 after a trail had been discovered between it and the Caribbean, where the Spaniards used three ports of entry: the risky open-sea anchorages of Nombre de Dios and the Bay of Portobelo, and the mouth of the Chagres river. The Camino Real (the Royal Road) ran from Panama City to Nombre de Dios until it was re-routed to Portobelo. An alternative route was used later: a road built from Panama City to Las Cruces, now swallowed up by Gatún Lake; it ran near Gamboa, the Canal town which guards the Culebra Cut, and traces of it can still be seen. Las Cruces was on the Chagres river, which was navigable to the Caribbean, particularly during the rainy season.

Intruders were early attracted by the wealth passing over the Royal Road. Sir Francis Drake attacked Nombre de Dios, and in 1573 his men penetrated inland to Cruces, captured its treasures and burnt the town. Twenty-six years later Drake attacked again. Spain countered by building strongholds and forts to protect the route: among others San Felipe at the entrances to Portobelo and San Lorenzo at the mouth of the Chagres. Spanish galleons, loaded with treasure and escorted against attack, left Portobelo once a year. They returned with valuable cargoes which were sold at great fairs held at Portobelo, Cartagena and Vera Cruz. There was feverish activity for several weeks as the galleons were loaded and unloaded. It was a favourite time for attack by enemies, especially those with political as well as pecuniary motives. Perhaps the most famous was the attack by Henry Morgan in 1671. He captured the fort of San Lorenzo, manned it, and pushed up the Chagres river. Seven days later, famished and exhausted, his men were at Cruces. From there they descended upon Panama City, which they looted and burnt. A month later Morgan returned to the Caribbean with 195 mules loaded with booty. Panama City was re-built on a new site, at the base of Ancón hill, and a costly fort built. With Britain and Spain at war, attacks reached their climax in Admiral Vernon's capture of Portobelo in 1739 and the fort of San Lorenzo the next year. Spain abandoned the route in 1746 and began trading round Cape Horn. San Lorenzo was rebuilt: it is still there, with its moat, battlements and parapets and rusty cannon, tidied up and landscaped by the U.S. Army.

A hundred years after the capture of Portobelo by Vernon, streams of men were once more moving up the fever-infested Chagres to Panama City: the forty-niners on their way to the newly discovered gold fields of California. Many perished on this "road to hell", as it was called. It was this gold rush which brought into being a railway across the isthmus. The Panama Railroad from Colón (then only two streets) to Panama City took four years to build, at great loss of life. The first train was run on November 26th, 1853. The railway was an enormous financial success until the re-routing of the Pacific Steam Navigation Company's ships round Cape Horn in 1867 and the opening of the first U.S. transcontinental railroad in 1869 reduced its traffic.

Ferdinand de Lesseps arrived in Panama in 1881 and after a preliminary survey decided on a canal along the Chagres river and the Río

Grande. A company was formed with a capital of £53,000,000. Work started in 1882. One of the diggers in 1886 and 1887 was the painter Gauguin, aged 39. Thirty km. had been dug before the Company crashed in 1893, defeated by squandermania, malaria, yellow fever, cholera and the fungoid diseases of the tropics. Eventually Colombia (of which Panama was then a Department) authorized the Company to sell all its rights and properties to the United States. The Colombian Senate later rejected the treaty, and the inhabitants of Panama, encouraged by the States, declared their independence on November 3, 1903. The United States intervened and, in spite of protests by Colombia, recognized the new republic. Colombia did not accept the severance until 1921.

Before beginning on the task of building the Canal the United States performed one of the greatest sanitary operations in history: the clearance from the area of the more malignant tropical diseases. The name of William Crawford Gorgas will always be associated with this, as will that of George Washington Goethals with the actual building of the Canal. On August 15, 1914, the first passage was made, by the ship *Ancón*.

The Canal Zone is a ribbon of territory placed under the jurisdiction of the U.S.A. for the construction, operation, maintenance and defence of the Canal in accordance with the treaty signed in 1903. It extends 8 km. on either side of the Canal and includes the cities of Cristóbal and Balboa. The price paid by the United States Government to Panama for construction rights was US$10m. The French Company received US$40m. for its rights and properties. US$25m. were given to Colombia in compensation for the transfer of the French company's rights. The total cost at completion was US$387m. Panama no longer accepts the perpetuity clause of the original Canal Treaty and is seeking to reassert full sovereignty over the Canal Zone, a process initiated in 1964 when it was decided that the Panamanian and U.S. flags should fly together in the Zone, and in April 1978 a new treaty was ratified guaranteeing the return of the Zone to Panama by the year 2000.

Landfall on the Caribbean side for the crossing of the Canal is made at the twin cities of Cristóbal and Colón, the one merging into the other almost imperceptibly and both built on Manzanillo Island at the entrance of the Canal; the island has now been connected with the mainland and looks like a peninsula. Colón was founded in 1852 as the terminus of the railway across the isthmus, and is, in fact, a Panamanian enclave within the Zone. Cristóbal came into being as the port of entry for the supplies used in building the Canal, and is in the Canal Zone.

Cristóbal   Ships usually dock at Pier No. 9 five minutes from the shops of Colón, but sometimes at No. 6, 7 or 8, No. 6 being 15 minutes from the shopping centre. Conveyances are always waiting at the docks for those who want to visit Colón and other places. P.S.N.C. vessels call at Cristóbal on both homeward and outward voyages; so do the cargo ships of Central America Services plying to and from Europe. Service from New Orleans by S.S. *Cristóbal* (cargo and canal employees only). Cristóbal Yacht Club has a good restaurant.

Colón, population 68,000, the second largest city in Panama, was originally called Aspinwall, after one of the founders of the railway. Despite its fine public buildings, hospitals, theatres and well-stocked shops, it has some of the nastiest slums in Latin America, and is generally dirty. Annual mean temperature: 26°C.

Warning   Mugging, even in daylight, is a real threat in both Colón and Cristóbal. There is a Free Zone at Colón which offers facilities for the import, free of duty, of bulk goods for re-export to neighbouring countries after packaging; it is not, however, open for retail purchases and you need a pass to get in.

There are good roads to Coco Solo, nearby; to France Field; and to Fort Davis and the Gatún Locks, some 11 km. away. The Colón Corridor gives access to the Republic without entering the Canal Zone.

The tourist should see the beautiful Cathedral between Herrera and Av. Amador Guerrero, and the statues on the promenade known as the Paseo Centenarío; a bust of de Lesseps, a monument to the builders of the railway, a group commemorating the firemen of the city, and a statue of Columbus. The historic *Hotel Washington Hyatt* is worth a view.

Other Places of Interest Front Street, famous the world over as a shopping centre for perfumes, ivory, furniture, duty-free liquor, English bone china, electronic appliances, cameras, oriental goods, etc. Main stores: French Bazaar; Maduros; Pohoomull Bros.; Novedades Atlántico; ''Slim's'' and Jhangimal. For more local products, try Isthmian Curio Shop, between Calle 10 and 11, and Sombrería Aldao for panama hats.

The Beach Drive round Colón, pleasant and cool in the evening, takes 30 minutes or longer.

Hotels *Washington Hyatt,* from US$22 s, US$25 d, there is a small casino; *Hotel Sotelo,* US$14 d, 10 s minimum, also has casino; *Andros,* US$6 s, US$8 d; *Plaza,* US$4-7 s, 6-10 d; *García,* US$6 per room; *Hotel Astor,* US$3-6. These rates are without meals, whose average price is from US$5-8. *Pensión Plaza,* Av. Central, is clean, cheap (US$6 d). *Pensión Acrópolis,* US$4 s, clean and comfortable; *Pensión Andros Annex,* US$8 d, comfortable and safe; *Pensión Kingston,* US$3 s, good. If destitute try the Salvation Army. The YMCA only caters for US servicemen.

Principal Restaurants *Alhambra,* Front Street, is best; *Cristóbal Yacht Club; La Nueva China,* Av. Central and Calle 8, a/c; *VIP Club* in Front Street; *El Trópico.*

Cafés *Tropic Bar,* Calle 10 and Av. Balboa, open day and night. Restaurant and bar; lunch US$0.75 and dinner US$2.

Cabarets Club 61, Av. Bolívar. No cover charge. Three shows nightly at 2000, 2300 and 0100. Club Florida, 3 shows nightly. Café Esquire.

Shipping a vehicle to Colombia, see page 1044.

Taxi Tariffs vary, but are generally not high and may be agreed on in advance. Most drivers speak some English.

Tour Tariffs Four persons to Fort San Lorenzo, Gatún Locks, and Margarita, US$20; US$60 for day tour of Panama City. It is possible, however, to arrange cheaper trips with individual drivers (4 persons).

Bus Service Every hour to Panama City: US$1 s, 2 hours. Express bus leaves Colón bus station at 0700, 1000, 1200, 1800 and 2200.

Trains On weekdays there are 7 trains a day, and on Sundays 6, between Panama City and Colón in both directions. First class US$1.50 s, second US$1. Colón station is at Calle 11 and Front Street, near the shopping area. The journey is interesting as the railway runs through the Canal Zone, with fine views of Canal, ships and jungle.

Air Services International flights are from Tocumen airport, outside Panama City; local ones from Panama City's Paitilla airport.

Cinemas Non-stop performances on Av. Central.

Fishing The Panama Canal Tarpon Club (entrance US$15, annual subscription US$15) has accommodation for anglers at the Gatún Spillway at a charge of US$5 per day. Live bait is provided, tackle is loaned. The sleeping cots are not furnished with bedding. The kitchen has facilities for cooking foods bought from the club attendant. The hut is a few yards only from the Spillway, a torrent teeming with large fish.

Clubs Golf (18 holes) at Brazos Brook Country Club. Rotary Club, weekly lunches.

Cables Tropical Radio Telegraph Co., Av. Roosevelt.

Post Office On corner of Av. Bolívar and Calle 9.

Banks Chase Manhattan Bank; Citibank; Banco Nacional de Panamá; Caja de Ahorros; Bank of London and South America agency in Free Zone, at Calle 15 & D. Open 0800-1300, Monday to Friday.

British Consulate P.O. Box 1108, Cristóbal, Canal Zone. Tel.: 7-3075. Also on Front Street, address: P.O. Box 448, Colón, Republic of Panama.

Royal Mail Lines & P.S.N.C. Office The Pacific Steam Navigation Company, Terminal Street (P.O. Box 5066), Cristóbal.

Trips from Colón: Portobelo is 48 km. NE of Colón by sea or by road. Colombus used the harbour in 1502 and it was a Spanish garrison town for more than two centuries. Drake died and was buried at sea off the Bay of Portobelo. Three large stone forts face the entrance to the harbour. There can be seen old Spanish cannon, and the treasure house where gold from Peru brought over the Las Cruces trail from Panama City was stored until the galleons for Spain arrived. There are ruins of various forts, a waterfall, and mountain views. In the Cathedral is a statue of the Black Christ; it was being shipped from Spain to the Viceroy of Peru, but the ship was wrecked in the bay and the statue salvaged by the natives. The image is carried through the streets at 1800 on October 21; afterwards there is feasting and dancing till dawn. Local rainfall, 4,080 mm. a year. Population 1,980.

Buses from Colón to Portobelo, frequent, leave from Calle 12. Many beaches on the way, such as Cangrejo, about 8 km. from Colón. Playa Langosta, 8 km. from Portobelo, is also recommended, though facilities there are basic. María Chiquita beach has a bathing pavilion managed by the government tourist bureau.

From Colón, visit also the Old French Canal, modern American township of Margarita, Gatún Locks (one hour). The locks are open to visitors every day until 1700; they can enter the lock area and take photographs, while guides expain the Canal operation. (Bus from Colón to Miraflores locks, US$0.20.) Visitors can cross the locks at Gatún, and also ride through virgin jungle where wild pigs, iguanas, land crabs and snakes scuttle across the road. Fort San Lorenzo, at the mouth of the Chagres River, is the most interesting historical monument on the Atlantic side. It was sacked by Henry Morgan, and by Admiral Vernon.

Fort San Lorenzo, on the other side of the Canal, is a 16th-century fort with 18th-century additions, reached from Gatún locks by road to Fort Sherman in the Canal Zone. From Fort Sherman one must drive, hitch-hike or walk to the fort; the 18th-century part, on the top of cliffs, commands a fine view of the mouth of the Chagres river and the bay below. One of Admiral Vernon's cannon with the GR monogram can be seen.

San Blas Islands   An interesting trip can be made to the San Blas archipelago, which has 365 islands ranging in size from tiny ones with a few coconut palms to islands on which hundreds of Cuna Indians live. (The coconuts of San Blas are the best in the country.) The islands, off the Caribbean coast E of Colón, vary in distance from the shore from 100 metres to several kilometres.

The Cuna are the most sophisticated and politically organized of the country's three major tribes. They run the San Blas Territory virtually on their own terms, with internal autonomy and, uniquely among Panama's Indians, send their representative to the National Assembly. The women wear gold nose- and ear-rings, and costumes suggestive of ancient Egyptians. They are outside the Panamanian tax-zone and negotiated a treaty perpetuating their long-standing trade with small craft from Colombia.

One can arrange to stay on the island of **Pidertupo** in a comfortable thatched hut for US$50 s, US$70 d a day, including 3 meals, sightseeing, boat trips, loan of equipment etc. Sasa flies to the Río Sidra airstrip, on the mainland opposite, where one is met by motor boat. The island is run by an American couple, Tom and Joan Moody, who can be contacted *via* Box 7773, Panamá 9, Rep. of Panama; bookings may also be made through Hanns Ebensten Travel, 55 W 42 Street, New York, N.Y. 10036. One can also reach Pidertupo from the neighbouring island of El Porvenir, to which Sasa also flies and from which there are boats; *Hotel Porvenir,* US$20 each incl. meals and tours; *Hotel Anai,* also US$20 each incl. meals, is on the island of Wichut Walla.

Photographers need plenty of small change, as set price for a Cuna to pose is US$0.25. Molas (decorative handsewn appliqué for blouse fronts) cost upwards of US$5 each (also obtainable in many Panama City and Colón shops). Agencies run cheap day trips, bookable at the major Panama hotels, which can be extended for a few nights at Indian hotels on the two islands nearest to Colón. These charge US$20 a day, inclusive of food and sightseeing. The airline serving the islands, Sasa (Paitilla Airport), can provide further information, and also runs trips to the Chocó Indians of the Darién jungle.

There are occasional boats to the San Blas islands from Colón, but there is no scheduled service and the trip can be rough.

Through the Canal to Panama City   As the crow flies the distance across the isthmus is 55 km. From shore to shore the Canal is 67½ km., or 82 km. (44.08 nautical miles) from deep water to deep water. It has been widened to 150 metres in most places. The trip normally takes 8 or 9 hours for the 36 ships a day passing through.

About 10 km. beyond Cristóbal, up the Chagres river, is the Gatún Dam, built to impound its waters. The dam is a long low ridge of earth, 1 km. wide at the base; it narrows to 30 metres at the top, 32 metres above sea-level. The almost circular 422 square km. Gatún Lake serves as a reservoir to hold sufficient water in the channel and for use in the locks during dry spells. A high-level reservoir, the Madden Dam, feeds the lake and maintains its level, 26 metres above the sea. A ship ascends into Lake Gatún in three steps or lockages. Each of the twin chambers in each flight of locks has a usable length of 305 metres, a width of 33½ metres, and is about 21 metres deep. The flights are in duplicate to allow ships to be passed in opposite directions simultaneously. Passage of the Gatún Locks takes about an hour. (The locks are open to the public from 0800-1700 daily.)

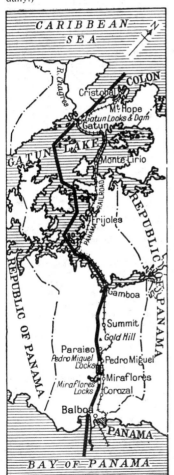

The largest section of the Canal is in Gatún Lake. In the lake is Barro Colorado Island, to which the animals fled as the basin slowly filled. It is now a biological reserve for scientific research. (Visits can be arranged with the Smithsonian Institute in Ancón, US$6 including boat and lunch.) We steam through the lake for 37 km. and then along the narrow rock defile of the Gaillard or Culebra Cut for 13 km. to Pedro Miguel Locks, where the descent to sea-level is begun. The first stage is a descent into Miraflores Lake, 16½ metres above sea-level. The process is completed at the Miraflores Locks, 1½ km. further on. The Canal channel takes us on to Balboa and the Pacific. An odd fact is that the mean level of the Pacific is some 20 cm. higher than the Atlantic, but the disparity is not constant throughout the year. On the Atlantic side there is a normal variation of 30 cm. between high and low tides, and on the Pacific of about 3.8 metres, rising sometimes to 6.4 metres.

Most people are utterly surprised by the Canal. Few foresee that scenery is so beautiful or that the mechanics of the passage are so absorbing. Travellers not wishing to spend the time on the Canal passage can see large sections of the Canal from the railway between Panama City and Colón. Otherwise take a bus to the Miraflores Locks, where there is a film and guide commentary. (These are open 0800-1700 daily.)

Balboa   The ship usually berths at Pier 18, though other berths may be used. Panama City is about 3¼ km. from the docks, an average of 10 minutes, that is, by taxi.

Balboa stands attractively between the Canal quays and Ancón Hill, which lies between it and Panama City. It is in the Canal Zone, an efficient, planned, sterilized town, a typical American answer to the wilfulness and riot of the tropics.

The Canal Zone Administration Building and a few official residences are on Balboa Heights. Inside the building are murals showing the construction of the Canal. At the foot of Balboa Heights is Balboa. It has a small park, a reflecting pool and marble shaft commemorating Goethals, and a long parkway flanked with royal palms known as the Prado. At its eastern end is a theatre, a service centre building, post office and bank. Farther along Balboa Road are a large Y.M.C.A. (where only employees of the Canal Company can stay, but where all comers may eat), various churches, a Scottish Rite Masonic temple, and an employee-operated C.Z. Credit Union. Balboa also has a civic centre, including an English-language library with periodicals as well as books. It also houses a Canal museum.

Banks   Citibank; Chase Manhattan Bank.

Telegrams   ITT Communicaciones Mundiales S.A., Gavilán Road; Tropical Radio & Telegraph Co. Public Telex booth in TRT office.

Ancón   curves round the hill N and E and merges into Panama City. It has picturesque views of the palm-fringed shore. Among trees and flowers is the famous Gorgas Hospital for tropical diseases. In the Civil Affairs Building, on Gaillard Highway near the Panama Canal Zone boundary at Ancón, is the interesting U.S. Government Canal Museum, with exhibits of pre-Columbian art and ceramics as well as an illuminated model of the canal and locks.

Shipping   P.S.N.C. have frequent sailings homeward and outward (no passengers); Balboa is also a port of call for several other European, U.S., and Far Eastern lines.

Excursions   There is a launch service to **Taboga Island**, about 20 km. offshore (return fare US$3). Taboga is reached in about an hour from Pier 18 in Balboa. There are two or three services daily during the week (depending on the day), 6 on Saturdays and 7 on Sundays. The island is a favourite year-round resort. The islands pineapples and mangoes have a high reputation. Its church is the second oldest in the western hemisphere.

Hotels   *Taboga* (US$15.23 s, 18.90 d, a/c) and *Chu* (US$5 s, 8 d, beautiful views, restaurant, own beach and bar).

The trip out to Taboga is very interesting, passing the naval installations of the Pacific end of the Canal, the great bridge linking the Americas (see page 1040), tuna boats and shrimp fishers in for supplies, visiting yachts from all over the world at the Balboa Yacht Club, and the 5-km. causeway connecting the mainland with three islands in the bay. Part of the route follows the channel of the Canal, with its busy traffic of liners, warships, tankers and freighters. Taboga itself, with a promontory rising to 488 metres, is carpeted with flowers at certain seasons and looks like "a multi-coloured bouquet laid on a giant green leaf floating in a sea of tropic blue". There are no horses, no cows, no animals, and no cars in the meandering, helter-skelter streets, and only one footpath as a road.

Swimming is not advised as the water is badly polluted by shipping.

The first Spanish settlement was in 1515, two years after Balboa had discovered the Pacific. It was from here that Pizzaro set out for Peru in 1524. For two centuries it was a stronghold of the pirates who preyed on the traffic to Panama. Because it has a deep-water, sheltered anchorage, it was during Colonial times the terminal point for ships coming up the W coast of South America. El Morro, at low tide joined to Taboga, is at high tide an island; it was once owned by the Pacific Steam Navigation Company, whose ships sailed from there.

It is a longer trip by launch—some 75 km.—to the **Pearl Islands**, visited mostly by sea-anglers for the Spanish mackerel, red snapper, corvina, sailfish, marlin, and other species which teem in the waters around. High mountains rise from the sea, but there is a little village on a shelf of land at the water's edge; here the native fishers live in bamboo huts. There was much pearl fishing in colonial days. **Contadora**, one of the smallest Pearl Islands, has become quite famous since talks on the Panama Canal were held there between US and Panamanian officials; it has *El Galeón Hotel*, US$30 d , and the very luxurious chalet complex known as *Hotel-Casino Contadora*. Return air ticket from Paitilla, US$12.75 by Aerolineas Islas de las Perlas, Tel.: 64-2906. Good skin-diving and sailing, 3-hour boat trip. Beware the sharks.

Argonaut Steamship Agency, Calle 55 No. 7-82, Panama City, Tel.: 64-3459, runs launch cruises.

Panama City, capital of the Republic, has a population of 456,000. It was founded on its present site in 1673 after Morgan had sacked the old town, now known as Panamá Viejo, 6½ km. away by road. Most of Panama City is modern; the old quarter of the city—the part that Spain fortified so effectively that it was never successfully attacked—lies at the tip of the peninsula; both it and Panamá Viejo are due for extensive restoration.

Note Some of the street names have recently been changed, which may make finding your way around a little difficult. The locals are likely still to refer to the streets by their old names so, if in doubt, ask.

Panama City is a curious blend of old Spain, American progress, and the bazaar atmosphere of the East. It is a city of beautiful homes, squalid slums now gradually disappearing, modern buildings, tawdry honkey-tonks, priceless treasures, and a polyglot population unrivalled in any other Latin American city. For the sober minded, the palm-shaded beaches, the islands of the Bay, and the encircling hills, constitute a large part of its charm. The cabarets and night life (very enterprising) are an attraction to those so inclined.

Most of the interesting sights are in the old part of the city and can easily be reached by foot, taxi, or bus. A good starting place is the Plaza de Francia, in the extreme S. In this picturesque little Plaza, with its red poinciana trees, is an obelisk (topped by a cock) to the French pioneers in building the Canal, and monuments to a former President, Pablo Arosemena, and to Finlay, the Cuban who discovered the cause of yellow fever. Facing the Plaza are several colonial buildings and the Palace of Justice, where the Supreme Court meets. Behind it runs part of the old sea wall—Las Bóvedas (The Dungeons)—built around the city to protect it from pirates. There are steps up this ancient wall to the beautiful promenade—the Paseo de las Bóvedas—along its top, from which there is a glorious view of the Bay of Panama and the fortified islands of Flamenco, Naos, and Perico. Beyond are Taboga and Taboguilla, tinged with blue or violet. Just beyond the end of the promenade is the Club de Clases de la Guardia Nacional, previously the Club Unión, the city's leading club, which is now housed in a new building in the residential area. (Visitors may use the Club's restaurant which serves good, cheap, meals.)

Flush under the wall, at the side of the Palace of Justice, are the old dungeons, with thick walls, arched ceilings and tiny barred windows looking on to the Bay. Behind the French monument, in a recess in the walls, is a series of large tablets recording, in Spanish, the early attempts to build the Canal. The French Embassy faces the Plaza.

A little way from the Club de Clases, along Av. A, and to the right, are the ruins of Santo Domingo church. Its flat arch, made entirely of bricks and mortar, with no internal support, has stood for three centuries. When the great debate as to where the Canal should be built was going on, a Nicaraguan stamp showing a volcano, with all its connotations of earthquake, and the stability of this arch—a proof of no earthquakes—are said to have played a large part in determining the choice in Panama's favour. At the Santo Domingo site is the interesting Museum of Colonial Religious Art.

Panama City's main street, the Av. Central, runs W from the old city and sweeps right and almost parallel with the shore through the whole town. On the right, at the intersection with Calle 3a, is the National Theatre, built in 1907, and recently restored. Up Calle 3a on the right is San Francisco Church (colonial, but modernized), and the Instituto Bolívar, where the Liberator proposed a United States of South America during the Bolivarian Congress of 1826. On Av. Norte, running along the Bay, is the President's Palace (La Presidencia), the most impressive building in the city. It is locally known as Palacio de las Garzas, or herons, which are kept in a fountain area there. It was the residence of the Spanish Governor during Colonial days, and is well worth visiting to see its patio with a fountain and strolling birds and a fine yellow salon. Av. Norte goes on to the colourful Public Market, on the waterfront. On Av. Norte are the wharves where coastal boats anchor and fishermen land their catches.

Av. Central runs on to the Plaza Independencia, or Plaza Catedral. This Plaza, with busts of the Republic's founders, is the heart of the Colonial city. Facing it are the Cathedral, the old Cabildo (which has now become the Central Post Office), the venerable *Hotel Central* and the Archbishop's Palace. The Cathedral has twin towers and domes encased in mother-of-pearl. The Post Office was the headquarters of the French during their attempt to build the Canal. Beyond the Cathedral, Calle 8a runs S to the church of San José. Its golden baroque altar is a magnificent sight. It was originally installed at a church in Panamá Viejo and resourcefully painted black by a monk to camouflage it during Morgan's famous raid. San José has a famous organ, too.

On Av. Central, to the right, in the second block beyond the Cathedral, is the church of La Merced, burnt in 1963 and now completely restored. It was near here that the landward gate of the fortified city stood. Further along the now curving Av. Central is the small Plaza Santa Ana, a favourite place for political meetings. Its church is Colonial. Not far is the section Sal si Puedes, "Get out if you can", a knot of narrow streets swarming with vendors.

Some blocks W is the Caledonia district, where lived the Protestant descendants of the British West-Indian blacks brought in ·to build the railway and the Canal. Caledonia is the Harlem of Panama City, exotic and unassimilated; whites are said to be unwelcome there.

Much farther along Av. Central, on Plaza 5 de Mayo, is the old railway station, now the Museo Nacional de Hombre (National Anthropological Museum), and almost opposite is the Plaza De Lesseps. The National

Museum is on the corner of Av. Cuba (which branches off right from the Av. Central), and Calle 30 Este. This part of the city is known as La Exposición because of the International Fair held here in 1916 to celebrate the building of the Canal. Calle 30 Este leads down to the Av. Balboa along the waterfront. The Santo Tomás hospital is here and on a promontary jutting out from this popular promenade is a great monument to Balboa, who stands on a marble globe poised on the shoulders of a supporting group, representing the four races of man.

A visit is usually paid to **Panamá Viejo** and its ruins, 6½ km. away. A concrete highway to it runs parallel to the sea. On the way you can visit a small zoo at the Justo Arosemena Institute in the Paitilla district. Panamá Viejo, founded in 1519 by Pedrarias the Cruel, was the point where gold from Peru was unloaded and kept in the King's storehouse. There it was loaded on to mules and transported across the Isthmus to Nombre de Dios and Portobelo for shipment to Spain. In January, 1671, Henry Morgan looted and destroyed the city. Because the old site was hard to defend, the city was refounded on its present site.

Today the visitor can wander among the ruins of the Cathedral, its plaza with moss-covered stone pillars and what remains of old government buildings. The King's Bridge, the starting point of the three trails across the Isthmus, still stands. Past the Plaza and near the sea is what remains of San José, where the golden altar was. At one side are the dungeons where prisoners were drowned by the rising tide. The whole area is attractively landscaped and floodlit: a pleasure to visit. Taxi from the centre, US$1.50; bus US$0.10 from Vía España.

In Panamá Viejo is the Artesanía Nacional shop, for handicrafts.

On the way back to Panama City the tourist can see the beautiful outlying residential districts, which include Bella Vista, La Cresta, Golf Heights,

Campo Alegre and El Cangrejo. There is a glorious view of the sea and bay from the summit at La Cresta. There is an excellent drive along the beach past the United States Embassy, the Santo Tomás Hospital, and the monument to Balboa.

At the foot of Ancón Hill the Instituto Nacional stands on the 6-lane Fourth of July (Tivoli) Avenue separating Panama from the Canal Zone. The gleaming University City is on the Trans-Isthmian Highway. Opposite the campus is the Social Security Hospital.

Industries Panama manufactures clothes, shoes, leather goods, furniture, matches, confectionery, biscuits, ceramics, tiles, cement, cigarettes, dairy products, alcoholic drinks, soft drinks, canned juices, flour, refined sugar, refined oil products, aluminium and plastic products.

Climate The Isthmus is only 9°N of the equator, but prevailing winds reduce the discomfort, especially in the cool evenings of the dry season, though the humidity is high. The mean temperature in the City is 26°C with a maximum temperature record of 36°C and a minimum of 17°. The average rainfall in the area is 1,524 mm. a year.

| | | | US$ | |
Hotels	Address	Telephone	Single	Double
Holiday Inn	Winston Churchill y Via Italia, Punta Paitilla	25-9541	37	42
El Panamá	Via España, 111	23-1660	24-37	28-42
El Continental	Via España	23-0123	24-28	28-32
El Ejecutivo*	Calle Aquilino de la Guardia	64-3333	22-24	22-28
La Siesta	Near Tocumen airport	66-1400	22-26	28-32
Granada	Av. Eusebio Morales	64-4900	18-22	22-26
Internacional*	Plaza 5 de Mayo	62-1000	13-17	16-21
Caribe*	Av. Perú y Calle 28	25-0404	12-16	16-20
Monteserín	Calle Monteserín	62-5133	12-16	16-20
Roma	Av. Justo Arosemena	25-3845	12-15	16-18
Gran Hotel Lux*	Av. Perú	25-1950	12-15	15-18
Branca Plaza	(not available)	27-3777	18.50	22.50

*Close to business area.

No meals are included in the prices. Average price of meals is from US$6-8. Note also a 10% tax on all hotel prices. All hotels are air-conditioned and, except the *Gran Lux*, include private baths or showers. The *Siesta* allows camping for US$5 per vehicle per day. The *Holiday Inn* is reputed to be the best hotel in town, has an excellent night club. The *Caribe* and the *Internacional* are the modern hotels most conveniently situated for the commercial centre. *Castellana Inn*, US$10-17 s, 17-20 d, good; *Hotel Centroamericana*, US$15 d; *El Conquistador*, US$30 d, new, luxurious; *Colón*, Calle 12, Oeste and Calle "B", US$4.20-7.35 s, 7.50-12.60 d; *Hotel Central*, US$6 s, 10 d, uncomfortable, but good cheap meals in restaurant; better than nearby *Hotel Colonial*, Plaza Bolívar, US$3-6 s, 4-10 d; good value for money and wonderful old building; *Hotel Premier*, Av. Central 18-105, US$10-12 s, US$14-16 d; *Bella Vista*, Via España, US$12.60 s, 14.70 d; *Ideal*, above Ticabus terminal, US$5-11 s, 8-13 d, with a/c and private bath, good meals for US$1; *Hotel Ideal* annexe, cheaper at US$4 s, but not recommended for women travelling alone, some rebate for Ticabus travellers. *Hotel Riazor*, near *Ideal*, US$6-8 s, 8-10 d, a/c with bath, good value, cheap restaurant downstairs.

Pensiones Cheaper accommodation can be found in *pensiones*: *Alfaro*, Calle 8, 3-23, US$3 s; *América*, Av. Justo Arosemena, US$4 s, 8 d, clean and pleasant; *Catedral*, Calle 6, 3-48, US$3 p.p.; *Chiriquí*, Santa Ana district, US$3 s, US$4 d; *Darling*, US$4 p.p., Calle 6, 3-22; *David*, Av. 7, 13-63, US$3 p.p.; *Foyo*, Calle 6, US$4 s, 5.50 d, very good; *Herrera*, Calle J. Obadaldía and Calle 9, Santa Ana, US$4.70 s; *Las Tablas*, Av. Perú 28-30, US$4 s, 5 d; *Lila*, Vía Brasil, US$3 s; *Mi Posada*, Calle Este 5-31, US$3 s, 4 d; *México*, Av. México 3-69, between Calles 41E and 42E, US$8 d, near sea, owner speaks English; many others (unlisted here) on same street; *Nacional*, Av. Central 22-19, near Plaza 5 de Mayo, US$3 s; *Panamá*,

Calle 6, 8-40, US$4 s, 5.50 d., "interesting and ramshackle, but friendly and clean"; *Panamericana,* Av. A, 8-15 with Calle 10, Santa Ana, US$3 s, 4 d; *Pacífico,* Calle Carlos Mendoza, US$3 s; *Riviera,* Vía España, US$8 s, 14 d; *Residencias Sevilla,* Av. Justo Arosemena, US$7 s, 10 d; *Santa Ana,* Calle 12, 7B-45, US$3 s, 4 d; *Tiza,* Av. B, 13A-18, US$3 s, 4 d; *Tropical,* Calle 8, 8-31, US$3 s, 4 d; *Universal,* Av. 7 Central, 8-16 (between Calles 9 and 10), US$4 p.p.; *Vásquez,* Av. A, 2-47, US$3 s, 4 d.

N.B. It may not be easy to find accomodation just before Christmas, as Central Americans tend to invade the city to do their shopping.

Electricity In modern homes and hotels, 220 volts. Otherwise 110 volt 3 phase, 60 cycles A.C.

Water Supply Water can be drunk freely from taps anywhere in the city.

Restaurants (apart from hotels). The best are: *Pana China* (Chinese and international food), Vía España; *Sarti's* (Italian food), Calle Ricardo Arias; *Panamá Señorial,* Calle 50, corner of Calle Ricardo Arias; *Panamar,* end of Calle 50, specializes in seafood; *Pez de Oro* (Peruvian), Vía Argentina; *Las Rejas,* Av. Justo Arosemena; *Las Américas,* Calle San Miguel, Obarrio.

La Casa del Marisco (sea food) and *La Pampa* (steak), both on Av. Balboa, are open-air restaurants.

Other restaurants include: *Gallo de Oro,* Vía Brasil off Vía España, reasonable, local food; *Piscolabis,* Transisthmian Highway, Vista Hermosa district, local food, reasonable; *El Jorrón,* Vía Fernandez de Córdoba, Vista Hermosa district, local food, reasonable and good; *La Tablita,* Transisthmian Highway, Los Angeles district, reasonable; *Dragón de Oro* (Chinese), Vía España, reasonable; *Nápoli,* Av. 13, No. 24, corner of Calle 1, Italian, good and cheap; *Gran China,* Av. Balboa, between Calles 26 and 27, Chinese, good value; *Madrid,* Vía España near UK Consulate, Spanish and local food, *corrida* daily for US$2.60; *Marbella,* Av. Balboa y Calle 39, Spanish, small, good value; *Nueva Oriente,* near Plaza Catedral, good, cheap Chinese food; *El Dorado,* Calle 52 y Vía España, good service, excellent seafood, recommended; *El Patio Andaluz,* Calle Elvira Méndez, in El Panamá sector, flamenco dancing. There are good pavement cafés along Av. Balboa. *Yate de Angelo,* dinner (US$5) and dance, Final de la Vía Porras, San Francisco district. Many other good Chinese and Italian places; also the *Kyoto* (Japanese)' on Vía España and the *Azteca* (Mexican) on the Transisthmian Highway at Las Cumbres. *Krispy, Macdonalds* and *Kentucky Fried Chicken* all have their branches. A good cheap meal can be got at the Y.M.C.A. in the Canal Zone (you can only stay at the Y.M.C.A., if you work for the U.S.).

Tourist Bureau. Information office of the Instituto Pañameno de Turismo, Vía España, near *Hotel El Panamá,* issues a list of hotels, *pensiones,* motels and restaurants. It shows whether rooms are air-conditioned and what prices are charged. One list is for "Chiriqui", and the other for "Provincias Centrales". Worth getting. Good maps from Instituto Nacional Geográfico.

National Museum, on Av. Cuba between Calles 29 and 30. Well worth a visit to see Inca and Spanish treasures. Instituto Pañameno de Arte, Av. Perú y Calle 38, art gallery. Open 0900-1200, 1500-1800 except Sunday.

Cabarets and Discothèques Hotels *El Panamá, Holiday Inn* and *El Continental; Maxims,* Calle 48 Sur; *Playboy de Panamá,* Calle 55, El Cangrejo; *Zebra,* Vía España; *Bunny Club,* Jerónimo de la Ossa; *Zebra* Vía España; *Oasis,* Vía Brasil; *Los Cuatro Ases,* Calle L; *Las Molas,* entrance to Chase Manhattan Bank, Vía España, Los Angeles district, small band, rural decor, drinks US$1.50; *Unicornio,* Calle 50 y R. Arias 23, is night club with discothèque and gambling; reasonable prices, will admit foreigners for US$3 a week. El Bon Ton and Camelot, Río Abajo. Caballo de Hierro, Av. 11 de Octubre in Hato Pintado district, is a restaurant in a railway carriage with a discothèque in a neighbouring carriage! Discothèque also at Fiesta Yatch on Av. Balboa.

Photographic Equipment Camera Center, on Tivoli at 4 de Julío (P.O. Box 7279); Foto Internacional, on main street. Panafoto, Av. Central by Plaza 5 de Mayo. Movifoto on Plaza 5 de Mayo guarantees to match or even beat any other duty-free shops' prices. Prices in the city are much cheaper than at the airport. Some deliver goods to airport, or to transit passengers staying 30 mins., at 5% less than Panama City price. Parcels can be collected in customs shed. If you have a contact in the U.S. forces, get your film in the Canal Zone PX! Panama is a good place to get film developed. Shortwave radios can also be bought cheaply at the airport.

Taxis have no meters; charges are according to how many "zones" are traversed. The adventurous will board one of the numerous small buses nick-named "chivas", (goats). These charge from 5 c. to 20 c. p.p., according to distance, are not very comfortable but take you anywhere. Note that there are large taxis *(grandes)* and small ones *(chicos)*; the latter are cheaper.

Bathing Piscina Patria (the Olympic pool), take San Pedro or Juan Díaz bus, US$0.15. Piscina Adán Gordon, between Av. Cuba and Av. Justo Arosemena, near Calle 31, 0600-1145, 1400-2100 (except weekends to 1700 only). Admission US$0.25, but beards and long hair frowned on. *Hotel El Continental, Ejecutivo, Holiday Inn, El Panamá, Granada* and *La Siesta* have pools. Many beaches within 1½ hours' drive of the city. Santa Clara beach is 120 km. away. Vera Cruz beach is not recommended as it is both dirty and dangerous.

Warning Thieves abound, and muggings are frequent. It is not safe to walk on side streets after dark.

Theatres There are occasional performances at the National Theatre. The usual air-conditioned cinemas. Foreign films must, legally, have Spanish sub-titles.

Casinos In the main hotels, at Unicornio on Calle 50, and at airport.

Clubs Unión (admittance by members' introduction only); Rotary; Lions Club, Miuras Club; Cámara Internacional de Jóvenes, Panama Chapter of the Junior Chamber of Commerce; Panama Rod and Reel Club; Club de Equitación (riding club); American Public Relations Association; Soroptimist Club; Club Continental (plush executives' club, top floor *El Continental Hotel)*; Club Panamá, excellent food, especially seafood. Rotary luncheons at *Hotel El Continental.*

Golf Panama Golf Club; Coronado Beach Golf Club (open to tourists who get guest cards at Coronado office on Calle 50).

Fishing Mackerel, red snapper, sail fish and other species. Boats for charter at *Hotel El Panamá.*

Horse races (pari-mutuel betting) are held Thurs., Sat., Sun. and holidays at the President Remón track. Cockfights are held on Vía España, near the road that leads to Panamá Viejo; fights are usually in progress Saturdays, Sundays and holidays.

Hospitals Gorgas Hospital, Balboa, but normally visitors are treated at either the Clínica San Fernando, Clínica Paitilla (both have hospital annexes) or the Hospital Santo Tomás (free inoculations).

British Embassy Residence Avenida Balboa, Exposition Grounds. First Secretary and Consul, Vía España 120, P.O. Box 889. Tel.: 23-0451. The British Pan-American Trade Centre, S.A. has its head office at P.O. Box 4595, Panamá 5. The Casa Británica Warehouse is at P.O. Box No. 2092, Colón Free Zone, Panama.

American Embassy Av. Balboa and Calle 37; P.O. Box 1099. Tel.: 5.3600.

Banks The Chase Manhattan Bank; Citibank; Bank of London and South America, Av. Justo Arosemena 32 (with El Cangrejo agency); Bank of America; Banco de Colombia; Swiss Bank Corporation. Panamanian banks. Open 0800-1300. Closed Sat., except for Banco General which takes Bank of America travellers' cheques. About 70 other banks have "offshore" operating licences.

Exchange Change currency at the "filatería" on corner of Av. Central and Calle 22E. Free market for almost all currencies, and good rates for all South American currencies. Canal Cambios, at *Hotel El Panamá,* has been recommended.

Distinctive Merchandise Duty-free imported luxuries of all kinds from all nations. Panamanian items include "molas" (embroidered blouse fronts made by Cuna Indians); straw, leather, wooden and ceramic items; the "pollera" circular dress, the "montuno" shirts (embroidered) and hats, and jewellery; good selection at Artesanías Nacionales, in Panamá Viejo.

Shopping *Casa Salih,* Av. Central 125, try local perfume Kantule from San Blas islands; *Casa Fastlich,* Av. Central at Plaza 5 de Mayo, good local jewellery; *Nat.*

Méndez, Calle Jota 13, near Av. Tivoli, for Colombian emeralds and pearls; *Curiosidades Típicas de Panamá,* Av. 4 de Julio y Calle J. B. Sosa, for local craft work; *Curiosidades Panameñas,* Calle 55 near *Hotel El Panamá,* local crafts; *Panamá Típico,* Via España y Calle La Perejil, same again; *Inovación* is a gift shop in the *Hotel El Panamá* complex on Via España, has wide selection of new and used "molas"; *Crossroads,* Calle E. A. Morales, by *Granada Hotel,* more "typical" goods; *Joyería La Huaca,* Av. Central y Calle 21, genuine pre-Colombian objects for sale upstairs. Good selections also in main hotels. Food is expensive in Panama City. Gago supermarkets are said to be the best.

Bookshop   English books at Gran Morrison; shops, Via España, Av. 4 de Julio, Transisthmian Highway, El Dorado.

Cables   All America Cables & Radio, Inc., Calle 228, No. 12-17; Tropical Radio Telegraph Co., Calle Samuel Lewis. Tel.: 3-7474. Intel, Edificio Aresa, Via España. Public Telex booth available TRT office. Excellent long-distance telephone by Intel and Tropical Radio.

Buses   Tica Bus, with office on ground floor of *Hotel Ideal,* run air-conditioned buses to the Central American capitals daily; the Tica fare to Guatemala is US$35.50; to San José US$12.50; to Managua US$18.50; to Tegucigalpa US$27.50; to San Salvador US$30.50. Sirca also runs buses to all Central American capitals. Panaica runs between Panama City and San José, US$12.50; buses also air-conditioned, office in Calle Monteserin. Buses going north tend to be well booked up, so make sure you reserve a seat in advance, and never later than the night before you leave. A good service to David is by Transportes Unidos Transchiri, from Plaza Herrera, US$6, 7 hours.

Rail   Seven trains daily, except six on Sun., to Colón from Panamá. Station now on Frangipani St., just inside the border of C.Z. Comfortable steel-car trains run roughly parallel to the Canal, of which there are excellent views, especially of Gatún Lake, crossed by a causeway. Round trip costs US$3, 1st class (a/c), US$2 on 2nd.

Airport (civilian) at Tocumen, 27 km. Taxi fares about US$10 per car, or US$3 a seat in a "cooperativa". For a little extra driver takes you by Panamá Viejo, just off the main airport road. Travellers whiling away desperate hours at the airport should visit the delightful nearby village of Pacora, a few km. off the Inter-American Highway. Bus marked Tocumen, every 15 minutes, from Plaza 5 de Mayo, US$0.50, one hour's journey, run every 30-45 mins. The new Belisario Porras airport at Tocumen was due to open in 1977; there is a small airport at La Paitilla, nearer Panama City, for domestic and private flights.

Royal Mail Lines & P.S.N.C. Office Pacific-Ford (Agencia de Transportes S.A.), P.O. Box 8151, Av. Cuba 34-44. Tel.: 5.0260.

Worship   Bahai temple, 11 km. N of Panama City on Trans-Isthmian Highway, in the Ojo de Agua district. Modern; worth seeing for its architecture. Taxi round trip for US$5, with an hour to see the temple, should be possible to arrange.

Camping   There are no official sites but it is possible to camp on some beaches in the Canal Zone and in the Balboa Yacht Club car park. It is also possible to camp in the Hipódromo grounds (on Avenida España) where you can use the swimming pool showers; this is allowed if you are waiting to ship your vehicle out of the country. Also possible, by previous arrangement, at La Patria swimming pool nearby, and at the Chorrera (La Herradura) and La Siesta beaches on the Inter-American Highway. When leaving Panama it is only possible to stay in the "Zone" for 24 hours, when camping is allowed near the race track, so alternative accommodation should be found.

Other Excursions   See Balboa (page 1032) for trips to Taboga Island and Pearl Islands. A good excursion—a 2-hour drive through picturesque jungle—is to Madden Dam. The drive runs from Balboa along the Gaillard Highway and near the Canal. Beyond Fort Clayton there is a fine view of the Pedro Miguel and Miraflores locks. Beyond Pedro Miguel town a road branches off to Summit, where there are experimental gardens containing tropical plants from all over the world, and a small zoo containing native wild life. (The trip may be made by buses marked

Gamboa, Paraíso or Pedro Miguel, from near Plaza 5 de Mayo (US$0.15); the Paraíso bus will also take you to the Miraflores and San Pedro Miguel locks.) The road to Madden Dam crosses the Las Cruces trail (old cannon mark the spot), and beyond is deep jungle. Madden Dam itself, controlling the turbulent Chagres and forming a reserve of water to maintain lake levels, is 37 km. from Panama City.

The dam is used to generate electricity. A short trip through part of the Canal by the launch "Las Cruces" cost US$4 for adults and US$2 for children, and lasts about 2 hours.

The return from Madden Dam to Panama City can be made by the Trans-Isthmian Highway. In Las Cumbres the restaurant *La Hacienda* serves native dishes, and *La Azteca,* Mexican food.

The Inter-American Highway penetrates E 50 km. to the sizeable town of **Chepo,** full of friendly blacks. From Chepo work is in progress on the construction of a further stretch of the highway which will eventually link Panama with Colombia. This task will take many years as the road is being built through the difficult Darién Gap territory.

West from Panama City

The Inter-American Highway now penetrates from Panama City west through Concepción to the Costa Rican border (493 km.), and is well graded and completely paved. The Highway begins at the Puente de las Américas across the Canal at the Pacific entrance. The bridge, 1,653 metres long and high enough to allow all ships to pass under it, has 3 lanes, and a 4-lane approach from Panama City and a pedestrian pavement all the way (muggings have occurred on the bridge in broad daylight, so be careful!).

Where the road W crosses the savannas, there are open pastures and fields where clumps of beautiful trees—bushy, intensely green mangoes, and parasol-shaped palm groves—alternate with grass. Double strips of forest form living corridors along the river banks, so that rivers can be anticipated from far away. One passes through the humble rural villages with their thatched huts, and the towns, so reminiscent of Andalusia and Estremadura. The village of Las Tablas has a picturesque and famous *fiesta* at Carnival time, just before Lent. Tourist agencies in Panama City can arrange trips to La Arena, which is the centre of Panamanian native pottery.

Near the border of the Canal Zone, 23 km. from Panama City, is the small town of Arraiján (2,200 people). On 21 km. is **La Chorrera** (26,317 people); an interesting store, "Artes de las Américas", has items in wood, etc. A branch road (right) leads 1½ km. to a waterfall. On 20 km., amongst hills, is the old town of Capira (12,744 people). We pass through the orange groves of Campana (where a 10-km. road climbs to Cerro Campana and the 6-room *Hotel Sulin,* about US$25 d, full board), and then twist down to Rio Sajalises (bathing) and the low-level plains. On through Bejuco and Chame to the town of **San Carlos** (7,289 people); (Hotels: *Río Mar,* from US$12 d; *El Palmar,* US$20 d), near the sea; good river and sea-bathing. Near San Carlos are the Nueva Gorgona (*Cabañas Ocean Blue,* US$13.50 d) and Coronado (*Golf Club* villas, US$35 d) beaches, both with restaurants. Beyond San Carlos is the Rio Mar beach, with a good seafood restaurant. Five km. on a road (right) leads after a few km. to a climb through fine scenery to the summit of Los Llanitos (792 metres), and then down 200 metres to a mountain-rimmed plateau (7 by 5½ km.) on which is comparatively cool **El Valle**, a small summer resort for people from the towns. (*Club Turístico*, US$16 d; *El Greco Motel*, US$10 d.) Soapstone carvings of animals, and straw birds, for sale. The town's Sunday market, though small, is renowned throughout Panama—the basketwork is very fine—and the town itself is a good example of what life away from the Canal and the cities is like.

We leave Panamá Province at La Ermita and enter Coclé, whose large tracts of semi-arid land are used for cattle raising.

Santa Clara, with its famous beach, 120 km. from Panama City, is the usual target for motorists: fishing, launches for hire, and riding (Hotels: *Muu Muu*, US$20 per cabin; *Vista Bella*, US$30-40 per cabin per weekend). About 13 km. beyond is Antón (20,561 people): it has a special local type of *manjar blanco*. (*Hotel Rivera*, US$6 s, 10 d.) On 20 km. is the capital of Coclé: **Penonomé** (30,913 people), an old town even when the Spaniards arrived. An advanced culture here, revealed by archaeologists (things found are in National Museum, Panama City), was overwhelmed by volcanic eruption (*Hotel Dos Continentes*, US$6-8 s, 8-10 d; *Pensión Motel*; both new). In another 18 km., passing a number of anthills, 1½-2 metres high and as hard as cement, we come to **Natá** (9,318 people), an important place in colonial days; old church and other colonial buildings. A few km. beyond we enter the sugar area and come to (10 km.) **Aguadulce** (15,076 people); its port is 5 km. from the town; native pottery for sale; large salt-beds nearby. Hotel: *El Interamericano* (US$4-6 s, US$6-8 d, air-conditioned). On the way to (22½ km.) Divisa, just beyond the large Santa Rosa sugar plantation, a road leads off right to the mountain spa of Calobre, 37 km. from Aguadulce; the hot springs are, however, a good hour's drive away, on a very rough road; grand mountain scenery. From Divisa a road leads (left) into the Azuero Peninsula through Parita (6,554 people; colonial church); Chitré (14,635 people), capital of Herrera Province (bus from Panama City, US$3.50, 4 hours) (Hotels: *El Prado*, US$4-7 s, 7-12 d; *Hong Kong*, US$3 p.p.; *Rex*, US$4-7 s, 7-10 d; *Santa Rita*, US$4 s, 7 d; *Versalles*, US$4-6 s, 10 d; *Toledo*, US$4.20-7.35 s, 7.35-12.60 d). **Los Santos** (13,999 people), an old and charming town of cobbled streets in Los Santos Province with a fine church containing many images. (Hotel: *La Villa de las Santos*, US$9 s, 15 d, a/c caravans, with swimming pool and good restaurant); and **Las Tablas** (19,323 people), capital of Los Santos (Hotels: *Oria*, US$10 d; *Juliana*, US$5 d; *Afú*, US$4 d). From Divisa to Las Tablas is 67 km.; the road runs on nearly 13 km. to the port of Mensabé. **N.B.** This Las Tablas is not to be confused with the village of the same name near the capital, which has a famous carnival.

About 32 km. W. of Chitré by road into the mountains, is **Ocú** (12,722 people), an old colonial town whose inhabitants wear traditional dress during the fiesta to its patron saint, San Sebastián, January 19-24.

Travel Ocú can be reached from David (see below) by taking a bus to the Ocú turning at Chitré on the Inter-American Highway (US$4) and a colectivo from there (US$0.50). One bus a day to Chitré, and several minibuses from Chitré to Panama City, US$3.50.

Hotels At Ocú: *Posada San Sebastián*.

Our road from Divisa to Santiago, the next town, 37 km., is uphill part of the way. It runs across the Province of Veraguas, the only one which lies across the whole isthmus and has seaboards on both oceans. **Santiago** (28,866 people), capital of the Province, is well inland; one of the oldest towns in the country, in a grain-growing area. Nearby is **San Francisco;** it has a wonderful old church with wooden images, altar pieces and pulpit.

Hotels in Santiago: *Motel Sanson,* US$12-25 d; *Continental* and *Magnolia,* US$4 d; *Santiago,* US$3 p.p.

The bad road through Soná (19,372 people) in a deep fertile valley to Guabalá, near Remedios (4,809 people), the country's largest stock-raising centre, has now been replaced by a direct paved highway from Santiago to Guabalá. This saves a couple of hours. From Guabalá to David is 92 km.

17 km. W of Guabalá, on the highway, is a hotel just outside Las Lajas, US$4 d, with restaurant. No hotels in Las Lajas itself.

David, 39,717 people, capital of Chiriquí Province, rich in timber, coffee, cacao, sugar, rice, bananas and cattle. The third city in the Republic, it was founded in colonial times and has kept its traditions intact whilst modernizing itself. Farmers from the countryside sell a wide variety of things in its colourful market. The town has a fine park and beautiful precincts. Pedregal, its port, is 8 km. away. Las Lajas, a small town close to David, has very nice beaches. There is an airport. International fair and *fiesta,* March 19.

Hotels   *Nacional,* US$12 s, US$18 d; *Palacio Imperial,* US$8.50 s, 10.50 d; *Saval,* US$4-7 s, 8-13 d; *El Camino Real,* US$6 s, 8 d; *Pensión Fanita,* a/c rooms with bath, US$4.50 p.p., others US$4.20 d, basic, food fair. *Hotel Iris* in central square, US$8 d, recommended. *Pensión Chiriquí,* Av. 4 Este, W of Calle Central, clean, US$2 p.p. *Pensión Costa Rica,* near Ticabus terminal, US$4 d; *Hotel Valle de la Luna,* US$3 s; reasonable food; *David* and *Madrid* also charge US$3 s.

Restaurants   *Oriente; Mesa España* on the square, has good, reasonably priced Spanish food.

Clubs   David; Lions; Rotary; Soroptimist.

Bus from Panama City: apart from the international lines, try Transchiri, Calle 8, 7A-23, US$4. From Cartago (Costa Rica) with Panaica, US$8, 7 hours.

Note: If driving S, stock up with food in David: it is much cheaper than in Panama City.

Inland from David are the deeply forested highlands of Chiriquí, rising to 3,383 metres at the extinct Barú volcano. The region favours coffee, fruit and flowers and is very beautiful, with delightful mountain streams for bathing and fishing. A great variety of wildlife flourishes in the area. There is some camping. There is a road from David to the mountain village of **Boquete,** at 900 metres, on the slopes of Chiriquí. It enjoys a spring-like climate the year round and has many attractions for the holiday-maker: good lodging and board, excellent river bathing, fishing, riding, and mountain climbing. Around is a beautiful panorama of coffee plantations, orange groves, and gardens which grow the best flowers in the country. There are frequent minibuses from David, US$1.

Hotels   *Panamonte,* US$12-20 s, US$16-34 d, full board, in very attractive surroundings, recommended. Cheaper hotels: *Fundadores* and *Los Quetzales,* both from US$11 d; *Pensión Marilos,* US$3 p.p., English spoken, very clean and well run with good, cheap food; *Pensión Wing,* US$4.50 d; *Pensión Virginia,* US$7.35 d for cheapest rooms, clean, friendly, English spoken, restaurant downstairs.

The road (and a railway) goes on from David to **Concepción** (24 km.; 6,532 people), a point of departure for those who wish to visit the beautiful Highlands to the N (US$4.50 bus fare—Transchiri—from Panama City). A road runs 29 km. N to the settlement of **El Hato del Volcán** (Hotels: *Dos Ríos,* US$10 p.p.; *California,* US$7 p.p.) and on to Río Sereno (no hotel) or to Cerro Punta (inns). It passes through fertile pasture land and offers excellent views of the Pacific. (At Bambito there is a hotel which serves good but expensive meals.) From Volcán to Cerro Punta the road follows the Chiriquí Viejo river valley. Of interest to birdwatchers is that just beyond Cerro Punta lies the Finca Fernández (only a 4-wheel drive vehicle can get to it). At the Finca Sr. José will show you the haunts of the quetzal. Concepción is 30 km. from the Costa Rican border at Rio Sereno by road. The railway goes on to

Puerto Armuelles (10,712 people), the port through which all the bananas grown in the area are exported. Puerto Armuelles and Bocas del Toro are the only ports in the republic proper at which ocean-going vessels habitually call and anchor in deep water close inshore.

Chiriquí railway, S from Concepción to Puerto Armuelles, with passenger trains leaving Concepción at 0730 and 1430, arriving 1145 and 1730. Leaving Armuelles 0645 and 1400, arriving in Concepción at 1145 and 1900. Freight service only in David and to Pedregal.

Across the Cordillera from David, on the Caribbean side, are the once thriving but now depressed banana ports of **Bocas del Toro,** on Colón Island, and Almirante, on the SW side of Almirante Bay, the H.Q. of United Brands company. Some of the plantations, destroyed by disease, have been converted to *abacá* and cacao, but are now being planted again, especially near **Changuinola** (airfield). No tourist ever goes there, but Bocas del Toro and Changuinola can be reached by Copa both from Tocument Airport and David Airport, and from Colón (257 km.) with luck, by local coasters or by weekly motor-launch.

Hotels At Concepción: *Rocio,* new, some a/c rooms and a/c bar and dining rooms, very reasonable; *Pensión Caribe.* At Bocas del Toro; *Copa* and *Bahía* (US$6 s, 10 d). At Changuinola: *Changuinola* (US$6-8 s, 10 d). At Almirante: *Hong Kong,* US$3-6 s, 6-8 d.

Railways The banana railways provide links between Guabito on the Costa Rican frontier and Changuinola and Almirante.

How to get to Colombia

Darién East of Chepo (see page 1040) is Darién, almost half the area of Panama and completely undeveloped. The few villages are accessible only by air or river and on foot. At Bahía Piñas is the *Tropic Star Lodge,* where a luxury fishing holiday may be enjoyed on the sea and in the jungle for over US$1,000 a week. (Information from *Hotel El Panamá.*)

The Darién Gap will not be open for some years, so the usual way of getting to Colombia is by sea or air. It is possible to go overland: the journey is in fact more expensive than going by air, but it is a worthwhile and challenging adventure for those so inclined. Maps of the Darién area can be purchased from the Ministro de Obras Públicas, Instituto Geográfico Nacional, "Tommy Guardia" in Panama City. The best time to go is in the dry months (Jan.-mid April). The journey as described below takes about 10 days.

One way is to take a boat (or drive) from Panamá to Yaviza (US$5); walk Yaviza-Pinogana (guide); motor dugout, Pinogana-Boca de Cupe (US$2). Or you can take a boat from Panamá to El Real (US$6) and from there a motor dugout to Boca de Cupe (US$3 after bargaining). In Boca de Cupe get your exit stamp and keep your eye on your luggage. From Boca de Cupe to Pucuro, dugout US$4. Pucuro is a Cuna Indian village and it is customary to ask the chief's permission to stay. From Pucuro, an 8½-hr. walk through lush jungle to Paya (guide costs US$1) which was the capital of the Cuna Empire. Walk from Paya to El Esfuerzo on bank of river Cacarica (Colombia) *via* Palo de las Letras (very rugged); El Esfuerzo-Vijado, dugout US$18. Occasionally there are motor dugouts from El Esfuerzo or Vijado to Turbo. It is probably quicker, however, to take a dugout from Vijado (even though you may have to wait a day or two for one) to Travesia (about US$4) and from there catch a banana boat to Turbo (US$1.50). Again, you may have to wait in Travesia. Get your Colombian entry stamp at the D.A.S. office in Turbo.

You can get some food along the way, but take enough for at least 5 days. Malaria pills, mosquito netting, salt tablets and insect repellents are a must as are water sterilization tablets—you cannot be too careful about the water. In all other respects travel as light as possible because the heat and humidity can make the going difficult.

There are about two boats a week from Colón for San Andrés Island (see page 437, from which there are connections with Cartagena; the ''Johnny Walker'' takes 30 hours, costs US$20, including food. Boats also leave the Fox River Dock in Colón for Puerto Obaldía, via the San Blas Islands. There are boats or planes from Puerto Obaldía (after clearing Customs) to Turbo, on the Gulf of Urabá (see page 466), from which Medellín can be reached by road; this route, however, should only be considered by the hardy. There are also (contraband) boats from Dock 5, Colón, to Barranquilla. 3 day journey, US$25, uncomfortable, and entirely at your own risk. You have to bargain for your fare on these boats. Accommodation is a little primitive. These are the cheapest routes. Alternatively one can get from Puerto Obaldía to Acandí on the Colombian side of the border, either by walking seven hours or by hiring a dugout or a launch (about 2-3 hours). From Acandí every other day a small boat or plane goes to Turbo.

It is not easy to get a passage to any of the larger Colombian ports as the main shipping lines rarely take passengers. Those that do are booked up well in advance. The only easy way of getting to Colombia is to fly. Copa, SAM and Avianca fly to Medellín, Cartagena and Barranquilla for US$50-60.

Colombia demands an exit ticket from the country. These tickets should be bought outside Panama and Columbia, which have taxes on all international air tickets. If you buy air tickets from IATA companies, they can be refunded. (So do not buy, for instance, a Copa return ticket Panamá-Medellín-Panamá; there are no Copa offices in Colombia or Ecuador and Copa is not a member of IATA.) Those who do not want to go to Panama can fly from San José (Costa Rica) to San Andrés and on to Cartagena for US$43. (In many cases it is cheaper to fly from Costa Rica to Colombia than from Panama, because Costa Rican taxes are less.)

Shipping a Vehicle either from Colón to Barranquilla or Cartagena, or from Balboa or Cristóbal to Buenaventura, is not easy or cheap. The following gives an idea of the charges for a 1.6-ton Land Rover; Agencia Motonaves (Colón) US$425; Prudential Line US$450; Litres US$442; Pacific Ford US$612; French Line US$500; Lauro Line US$406. The Italian Line takes vehicles (about US$500) but tends to be booked well in advance. It has an office opposite the Post Office in Cristóbal, Canal Zone, or you can book through a travel agent. Cheaper than the Italian line is the Unif. Trading Company in Colón (contact Captain Gilberto Pavis, Tel.: 47-3867). The charge for an LWB Land Rover ranges from US$450-600 depending on the line. (For the return journey contact the Remar Agency in Buenaventura.) With a great deal of luck you might get one of the sugar vehicles bringing cargo to Aguadulce (page 1041) to ship you and your car to Colombia. One traveller was lucky and it cost him only US$100. Sometimes, if enough vehicles are collected together, it is possible to charter a boat to Buenaventura from the Zócalo (Nuevo Panamá). In addition to freight charges there are, of course, handling charges of about US$25. Very few lines take passengers; if you do succeed in getting a passage it may cost as much as US$180. Otherwise you must make other arrangements to get yourself to Colombia. A cheaper alternative to the above-named lines is the Rodson Shipping Line, run by a Mr. George Brown who uses tugs and even fishing boats for the crossing from Colón to Cartagena. Obviously there is a considerable element of risk involved though the financial cost is far lower; e.g. a VW bus and two people can make the crossing for about US$450. In Balboa shipping arrangements can be made at the Port Captain's Building on Pier 18 where the Fenton Company's representative is based. Alternatively the Panama Agencies can help you arrange shipment. Once you have a bill of lading, have it stamped by a Colombian consulate; the charge is US$10, though the Colón consulate may charge US$20. (The consulate also provides tourist cards. They require proof, in the form of a letter from your Embassy (or the Embassy representing your country in Panama) that you do not intend to sell the car in Colombia, though this requirement can sometimes be dispensed with.) Then go to the customs office in Panama City (Calle 80 and 55) to have the vehicle cleared for export. After that the vehicle must be removed from your passport at the customs office at the port of departure. In Colón the customs office is behind the post office. The utmost patience is needed for this operation as regulations change frequently, so do not expect it to be the work of a few minutes.

The same is true of formalities at the Colombian end. It will take at least a full day to clear (customs officials do not work at weekends) even if you have a *Carnet de Passages*. Clearance from the Colombian consul at the Panamanian port of embarkation may reduce the bureaucracy when you arrive in Colombia, but it will cost you US$10. In Colombia you can pay an agent US$15 to deal with the paperwork for you, which can reduce the aggravation if not the waiting time! It is understood that Cartagena is much more efficient (and therefore less expensive) as far as paperwork is concerned. The Colombian government has recently introduced a tax on vehicles coming into the country, which is reported to be quite steep.

Warning The contents of your vehicle are shipped at your own risk—generally considered to be a high one!

Sometimes Aerocosta, Calle 40 entre Av. Justo Arosemena y Av. Perú, will charter DC-3s and DC-6s to fly vehicles and their passengers from Panama City to Medellín; the price has however soared and it now costs US$800 for the car without passengers. One disadvantage here is that Medellín airport customs do not normally work Saturday or Sunday.

The Instituto Panameño de Turismo has informed us of the following rates for shipping vehicles, at January 1977 (in US dollars per cubic metre):

Company	Telephone No. in Panama City	Destination			
		Cartagena	Buenaventura	Guayaquil	Callao
Agencias Motonaves	47-8886	—	38.00	—	—
Prudential Lines	64-6366	38.50	38.00	—	—
Gran Colombiana	64-3453	—	40.50	42.90	46.00
Pacific Ford	25-0260	—	37.50	—	—
Norton & Lilly	52-5746	38.50	40.50	—	—
C. B. Fenton & Co.	43-2754	37.50	41.50	—	—
Panaco Panamá	52-2150	—	31.00	—	—

The Economy

Panama's economy has traditionally been founded on income derived from services rendered to incoming visitors, taking advantage of its geographical position, and Canal Zone employees and U.S. military personnel of the Zone spending money in the Republic. However, this contribution is lessening as the country is developing new sources of income: tourism, industry, copper, etc.

The other traditional mainstay of the Panamanian economy is agriculture. It contributes about 16% of the g.d.p., but its growth over the last decade has been sluggish. 38.6% of the population works in agriculture, which is a high proportion in relation to the share of the g.d.p. Agrarian reform has begun, and has brought the present Government much support from tenant-farmers and squatters. Most of the land is forested, and development here could also bring added wealth into the country, at the same time helping to reduce the country's dependence on the Canal. Industry accounts also for 16% of g.d.p. Recently the Government has taken a more significant role in this sector and now owns sugar mills and cement plants. The main industry is food processing and there are textile and clothing concerns and chemicals, plastics and other light industries. Petroleum products are the only industrial export.

Mining should also help to lessen the Republic's dependence on the Canal. Vast deposits of copper have been found at Cerro Colorado and if fully developed the mine could be the largest in the world. There is also copper at Petaquilla, Cerro Chorcha and Río Pinto. Large coal deposits have been found at Rio Indio. The country also has gold and silver deposits. So far no oil has been discovered, but exploration is taking place.

One of the most dynamic sectors of the economy is banking. Since 1970 offshore banks have increased from 20 to over 100 in number. It is hoped that as well as becoming an important financial centre, Panama will also attract international reinsurance business. In 1976 tourism earned US$89.5m.; considerable efforts are being made to expand the country's tourist facilities.

On the strength of its future prospects, which in the long term even include the possibility of a new sea-level canal and a transisthmian oil pipeline, Panama has been able to borrow abroad more heavily than formerly, but real social advance can only be achieved through proper long-term planned exploitation of the country's resources, which needs the help of foreign capital if they are to be exploited quickly on a big enough scale.

Foreign Trade (US$m.)

		1972	1973	1974	1975	1976
Exports (f.o.b.)	..	122.6	137.8	210.2	285.0	232.8
Imports (c.i.f.)	..	440.5	502.2	822.4	870.0	840.3

Information for Visitors

Air Services Airlines flying to Panama from North America include: from New York City, Pan American, Air Panamá, Braniff; from Washington, PanAm, Braniff; from Miami, Air Panamá, Braniff, PanAm, LAN-Chile, Ecuatoriana; from Los Angeles and San Francisco, PanAm and Air Panamá; from Dallas, Braniff; from New Orleans, Braniff, Taca; from Houston, Braniff, PanAm. From Mexico, PanAm, Air Panamá, Aeroméxico, Lanica. From Central America, Taca, PanAm, Iberia, Copa, Lacsa, Lanica, Sahsa. From South America, Air Panamá, Lacsa, Copa, LAN-Chile, Aeroméxico, Braniff, Avianca, Ecuatoriana, Varig, Viasa, Lloyd Aéreo Boliviano, KLM, PanAm, SAM. From Europe, British Airways (Thurs. and Sun.), Iberia, KLM, Viasa.

There are local flights to most parts of Panama by the national airlines Copa and Adsa. There is a service between Paitilla airport (Panama City) and the Comarca de San Blas by Sasa. Chitreana, Isla de las Perlas and Aviones de Panamá also fly on domestic routes.

An airport tax of US$5 has to be paid by all passengers, even those in transit (unless for under 3 hours). There is a 4% tax on air tickets purchased in Panama. Similarly, motorists have to pay a US$2.05 tax on leaving.

Shipping Services From Panama there are frequent steamship services with the principal European and North American ports; with the Far East, New Zealand, and Australia, with both the E and W coast ports of South America and Central America, regularly with some, irregularly with others. Direct steamship services with the U.K. are provided by the P.S.N.C. (no passengers), R.M.L. Ltd. (no passengers); Holland America Line; Port Line, Ltd.; Furness (Pacific) Ltd.; the New Zealand Shipping Co., and Shaw, Savill & Albion. Chandris Lines have ships going from New Zealand and Australia to Europe, stopping in Panama. A youth fare is available for those under 25. New York and the East Coast U.S.A. are served by Prudential Line, United Brands, and Panama Line (between New Orleans and Cristóbal and restricted to cargo and Canal employees). Gulf ports served by Lykes Line, and United Brands. The West Coast U.S.A. and Canada are served by a number of European as well as American lines. Freighters carrying a limited number of passengers operate in all trades. The Italian Line serves Cristóbal from

Mediterranean ports. Cargo boats of Central America Services ply to and from Europe.

Documents Visitors must have a passport, together with a tourist card (issued for 30 days and renewable for another 60) or a visa (issued for 90 days), and an International Certificate of Vaccination less than 3 years old. Holders of visas require exit permits unless they stay in Panama less than 48 hours; holders of tourist cards (US$2 from Panamanian consulates or airlines, valid 30 days) do not need exit permits. Neither visas nor tourist cards are required by nationals of Costa Rica, the Dominican Republic, El Salvador, Western Germany, Honduras, Spain, Switzerland and the UK. Tourist cards may not be issued to citizens of Communist countries, India and Pakistan, who must have visas. The Canal Zone may be entered by visitors to Panama without further documentation.

Customs Even if you only change 'planes in Panama you must have the necessary papers for the airport officials. Cameras, binoculars, etc., 500 cigarettes or 500 grams of tobacco and 3 bottles of alcoholic drinks for personal use are taken in free. The Panamanian Customs are strict; drugs without a doctor's prescription and books deemed "subversive" are confiscated. In the latter case, a student's or teacher's card helps. **Note:** Passengers leaving Panama by land are *not* entitled to any duty-free goods, which are delivered only to ships and aircraft. **Another Note:** Travellers must have an outward ticket; a Ticabus ticket back to San José is allowed, but you can only get a refund from Ticabus (if you do not intend to travel back) if you obtain written permission from the Panamanian immigration officials. This costs US$10. You may be asked to show that you have at least US$150, or US$10 for each day of intended stay if that exceeds 15 days, before being allowed in. There is a prejudice against long hair for young men.

Motoring Coming in by car visit Customs and Immigration in the same building for a 20-day visa, entry documents for your car (initially only for 3 days; check in at Panama City customs office for extension) and specify your point of exit from Panama. The need to get the entry permit for your car extended in Panama City does limit the time you can spend in western Panama. Exit calls for 4 papers which cost US$3.50. Entering Panama by sea with a car is time-wasting—at least at Colón, where papers have to be presented at both Panamanian and Canal Zone Customs. Low octane gasoline costs US$1.13 per gallon. For motorcyclists, note that Panama is the only place in Latin America where a crash helmet must be worn. **Note** that you may not take dogs into Panama by car, though they may be flown or shipped in if they have rabies and general health certificates; dogs and cats now have to spend 40 days in quarantine after entry.

Warning It is virtually impossible for a tourist to sell his car in Panama unless he can show (with help from his Consulate) that he needs the money for his fare home. He will in this case have to pay import duty on the sale. The only alternative is to sell the car in Costa Rica, but the level of tax incurred is very high. It is also impossible to leave a vehicle in Panama while travelling on.

British businessmen are advised to get "Hints to Business Men Visiting Panama", free on application to the Export Services Division of the Dept. of Trade, Room CO7, Export House, 50 Ludgate Hill, London EC4M 7HU.

Hours of Business Government departments, 0800-1200, 1230-1630 (Monday to Friday). Banks: open and close at different times, but are usually open all morning, but not on Saturdays. British Embassy: 0800-1330 and 1430-1630 Monday to Friday. Shops and most private enterprises: 0700 or 0800-1200 and 1400-1800 or 1900 every day, including Saturdays.

Business interests are concentrated in Panama City and Colón.

Clothing Light weight tropical type suits, light cotton shirts and underwear for men, light cotton or linen dresses for women. Take a raincoat and umbrella. The dry season, January-April, is the pleasantest time. Heavy rainfall sometimes in October and November.

Health No particular precautions are necessary. Water in Panama City and Colón is safe to drink.

Language Spanish, but English is widely understood.

Living is costly. U.S. Canal Zone employees live in houses provided by the Government, and buy what they want at the commissary stores run by the Government or the Government-owned Panama Canal Company; they eat at clubs and go to cinemas run by the Government. The armed forces are equally privileged. These facilities are not available to tourists, of course, but checks on users' status are said to be few and far between! These privileges will of course be reduced as the Zone is gradually handed back to Panama under the new Treaties. Inflation is again very low; the cost of living rose by 16.7% in 1974, but the rise was reduced to 1.8% in 1975; in 1976 the figure was 3.3% and in 1977 almost zero.

Festivals The fiestas in the towns are well worth seeing. That of Panama City at Carnival time, held on the four days before Ash Wednesday, is the best. During carnival the women wear the *pollera* dress, with its "infinity of diminutive gathers and its sweeping skirt finely embroidered", a shawl folded across the shoulders, satin slippers, tinkling pearl hair ornaments in spirited shapes and colours, and the *chácara,* or small purse. The men wear a *montuño* outfit: native straw hats, embroidered blouses and trousers sometimes to below the knee only. There is also a splendid local Carnival at the village of Las Tablas, near Panama City.

The Holy Week ceremonies, however, are at their most spectacular in the interior. The peasants, some of them Indian, come down from the mountains dressed in their regional costumes. Images of the Saviour and the Virgin and the saints are borne aloft, with processions of little children, with angel wings on their shoulders, scattering flowers before them. On Holy Saturday, Judas is carried through the streets; early on Sunday morning, after Christ risen has met Mary and the Beloved Disciple, Judas' last testament is read in the main Plaza: a merrily pungent document aimed at the sins and follies of local residents. The effigy is then burnt. At Villa de los Santos the farces and acrobatics of the big devils—with their debates and trials in which the main devil accuses and an angel defends the soul—the dance of the "dirty little devils" and the dancing drama of the Montezumas are all notable.

There are, too, the folk-tunes and dances. The music is cheerful, optimistic, frank: the contagious rhythms of the African blended with the melodic tones and dance-steps of Andalusia to which certain characteristics of the Indian pentatonic scale have been added. The *tamborito* is the national dance. Couples dance separately and the song—which is sung by the women only, just as the song part of the *mejorana* or *socavón* is exclusively for male voices—is accompanied by the clapping of the audience in time with the music and three kinds of regional drums. The *mejorana* is danced to the music of native guitars and in the interior is often heard the laments known as the *gallo* (rooster), *gallina* (hen), *zapatero* (shoemaker), or *mesano.* Two other dances commonly seen at fiestas are the *punto,* with its promenades and foot tapping, and the *cumbia,* of African origin, in which the dancers carry lighted candles and strut high.

The Guaymí Indians of Chiriquí province meet around February 12 to transact tribal business, hold feasts and choose mates by tossing balsa logs at one another; those unhurt in this contest, known as "Las Balserías", are allowed to select the most desirable women.

What to eat Best hors d'oeuvre is *carimañola,* cooked mashed yucca wrapped round a savoury filling of chopped seasoned fried pork and fried a golden brown. The traditional stew, *sancocho,* made from stewing chicken, plus yucca, dasheen, cut-up corn on the cob, plantain, potatoes, onions, flavoured with salt, pepper and coriander. *Ropa vieja,* meat dish of shredded beef mixed with fried onions, garlic, tomatoes and green peppers and served with white rice, baked plantain or fried yucca. *Sopa borracha,* a rich sponge cake soaked in rum and garnished with raisins and prunes marinated in sherry. Panama is famous for its seafood: lobsters, corvina, shrimp, tuna, etc. Piquant *seviche* is usually corvina or white fish seasoned with tiny red and yellow peppers, thin slices of onion and marinated in lemon juice; it is served very cold and has a bite. A luscious preparation, *arroz con coco y titi,* is rice with coconut and tiny dried shrimp. Plain coconut rice is also delicious. Corn is eaten in various forms, depending on season, e.g. *tamales,* made of corn meal mash filled with cooked chicken or pork, olives and prunes; or *empanadas,* toothsome meat tarts fried crisp. Plantain, used as a vegetable, appears in various forms. A fine dessert is made from green plantain flour served with coconut cream. Other desserts are *arroz con cacao*, chocolate rice pudding; *buñuelos de viento*, a puffy fried fritter served with syrup; *sopa de gloria*, sponge cake soaked in cooked cream mixture with rum added; *guanábana* ice cream is made from sweet ripe soursop.

Tipping at hotels, restaurants: 10% of bill. Porters, 15 cents per item. Cloakroom, 25 cents. Hairdressers, 25 cents. Cinema usherettes, nothing. Taxi drivers don't expect tips; rates should be arranged before the trip.

Currency Panama is one of the few countries in the world which issues no paper money; U.S. banknotes are used exclusively, being called balboas instead of dollars. It has silver coins of 50c, 25c, 10c, nickel of 5c and copper of 1c. All the silver money is used interchangeably with U.S. currency; each coin is the same size and material as the U.S. coin of equivalent value. You can take in or out any amount of foreign or Panamanian currency.

Both metric and the U.S. system of weights and measures are used.

Foreign Postage All outgoing mail posted in the Republic must bear a special 1 cent tax stamp. The Canal Zone posts are reported as more reliable in general than those of the Republic.

Great care should be taken to address all mail for towns outside the Canal Zone as "Republic of Panama", otherwise they are returned to sender. Air mail takes 3-5 days, sea mail 3-5 weeks from Britain. Rates in the Republic (examples) for air mail (up to 15 grams) are as follows: Central America, 23c; North and South America and Caribbean, 26c; Spain, 57c, other countries in Europe, 40c.

Inland letters Canal Zone, 5 cents per ounce; Panama Republic 4 cents. The U.S. Government has a **wireless station** at Gatún which is open to commercial traffic; such messages are handled through the Government telegraph offices. The telegraph and cable companies are given under the towns in which they operate.

Telex is available at the airport, the cable companies and many hotels. Rate for a 3-minute call to Britain is US$14.40, and US$4.80 for each minute more.

Telephone calls can be made between the U.K. and Panama any time, day or night. Minimum charge for 3 minute call: US$15 on weekdays, $12 on Sundays plus tax of $1 on each call. Difference in time: GMT minus 5 hours.

Inter-continental contact by satellite is laid on by the Panamerican Earth Satellite Station. The local company is *Intercomsa S.A.*

Public Holidays

Jan. 1: New Year's Day.
Jan. 9: National Mourning.
Shrove Tuesday: Carnival.
Good Friday.
May 1: Labour Day (Republic).
Aug. 15: (Panama City only) (O).
Oct. 11: National Revolution Day.
Nov. 1: National Anthem Day (O).

Nov.2 : All Souls (O).
Nov. 3: Independence Day.
Nov. 4: Flag Day (O).
Nov. 5: Independence Day (Colón only).
Nov. 10: First Call of Independence.
Nov. 28: Independence from Spain.
Dec. 8: Mothers' Day.
Dec. 25: Christmas Day.

O = Official holiday, when banks and government offices close. On the rest—national holidays—business offices close too. Many others are added at short notice. U.S. national holidays are observed in the Canal Zone.

Press The "Star and Herald" and the "Panama-American" (English) and "La Estrella de Panamá", "La República" (Spanish) are the largest daily newspapers. Other papers are: "Crítica", and "Matutino" (daily Spanish); "Colón News" (weekly—Spanish and English).

British and U.S. Representation in Panama There is a British Embassy in Panama City above the Chase Manhattan Bank facing the *El Panamá Hotel.*

First Secretary and Consul, British Embassy, Via España 120, Box B, Balboa Post Office, Canal Zone, Panama (Tel.: 23-0451). Postal address: P.O. Box 889, Panamá 1, R.P. Consul at P.O. Box 1108, Cristóbal, Canal Zone (Tel.: 7-3075). Also P.O. Box 448, Colón, R.P.

The United States of America is represented in Panama by an Ambassador and Consul at Panama City, and Consuls at Colón and David.

South Africa is represented by an Honorary Consul General at Edificio Las Vegas, Panama City. Postal address: P.O. Box 7010 (Tel.: 23-1834).

American Express Agents   Panama City: Boyd Brothers Inc., Calle 50, Edif. San Miguel 58, Tel.: 64-7433.

(We are deeply grateful to the travellers listed in the general Central American section for vital assistance in revising this section.)

CUBA

THE ISLAND OF CUBA, 1,050 km. long, 160 km. at its widest point, is the largest of the Caribbean islands and only 145 km. S of Florida. Gifted with a moderate climate broken only occasionally by hurricanes, not cursed by frosts, blessed by an ample and well distributed rainfall and excellent soils for tropical crops, it has become the second largest source of cane sugar in the world. The population is about 9.6 million.

About a quarter of Cuba is fairly mountainous. To the W of Havana is the narrow Sierra de los Órganos, rising to 750 metres and containing, in the extreme W, the strange scenery of the Guaniguánicos hill country. S of these Sierras, in a strip 145 km. long and 16 km. wide along the piedmont, is the Vuelta Abajo area which grows the finest of all Cuban tobaccos. Towards the centre of the island are the Trinidad mountains, rising to 1,100 metres, and in the E, encircling the port of Santiago, are the most rugged mountains of all, the Sierra Maestra, in which Pico Turquino reaches 1,980 metres. In the rough and stony headland E of Guantánamo Bay are copper, manganese, chromium and iron mines. About a fourth of the land surface is covered with mountain forests of pine and mahogany. The coastline, with a remarkable number of fine ports and anchorages, is about 3,540 km. long.

History Cuba was discovered by Columbus during his first voyage on October 27, 1492, and he paid a brief visit two years later on his way to the discovery of Jamaica. Columbus did not realise it was an island; it was first circumnavigated by Sebastián de Ocampo in 1508. Diego Velásquez conquered it in 1511 and founded several towns, including Havana. The first African slaves were imported in 1526. Sugar was introduced soon after but was not important until the last decade of the 16th century. When the British took Jamaica in 1655 a number of Spanish settlers fled to Cuba, already famous for its cigars, made a strict monopoly of Spain in 1717. The coffee tree was introduced in 1748. The British, under Lord Albemarle and Admiral Pocock, held the island in 1762-63, but it was returned to Spain in exchange for Florida. In 1763 the Sociedad Patriótica established schools and the press. Cuba was all but autonomous during the Napoleonic Wars.

The tobacco monopoly was abolished in 1816 and Cuba was given the right to trade with the world in 1818. Virtual autonomy, however, had bred ambitions, and a strong movement for independence was quelled by Vives, the Captain General, in 1823. He was given absolute powers and the first martyrs to independence were executed in 1826. By this time the blacks outnumbered the whites in the island; there were several slave rebellions and little by little the Creoles (or Spaniards born in Cuba) made common cause with them. A slave rising in 1837 was savagely repressed and the poet Gabriel de la Concepción Valdés was shot. The leaders of an

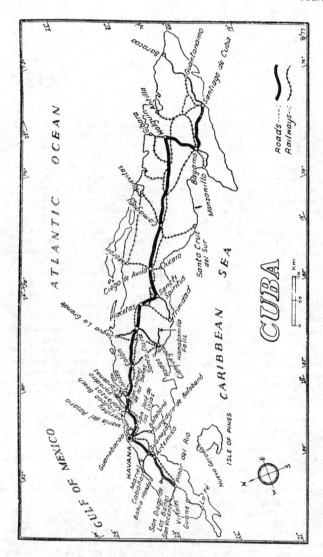

abortive movement for independence in 1851 were also shot. There was a ten-year rebellion against Spain between 1868 and 1878, but it gained little save the effective abolition of slavery, which had been officially forbidden since 1847. From 1895 to 1898 rebellion flared up again under Jose Martí and Máximo Gómez. The United States was now in sympathy with the rebels, and when the U.S. battleship, the *Maine*, was blown up in Havana harbour on February 15, 1898, it was made a pretext for declaring war on Spain. American forces (which included Colonel Theodore Roosevelt) were landed, a squadron blockaded Havana and defeated the Spanish fleet at Santiago de Cuba. In December peace was signed and Spain's long struggle to hold the island was over. The Government of Cuba was handed over to its first president, Tomás Estrada Palma, on May 20, 1902, but the U.S. retained naval bases at Río Hondo and Guantánamo Bay, reserved the right of intervention in Cuban domestic affairs, but granted the island a handsome import preference for its sugar. The U.S.A. chose to intervene several times, but relinquished this right in 1934. From 1925 to 1933 the "strong man" Machado ruled Cuba as a dictator. His downfall was brought about by General Batista, then a sergeant, whose increasingly corrupt dictatorship was brought to an end by Fidel Castro in January 1959, after a three years' campaign. Castro was later to lead Cuba into communism. All farms of over 67 hectares have been taken over by the state. Rationing is still fierce, though less so than formerly; milk, fruit, fish and some articles of clothing became more widely available in 1972. There are great shortages of consumer goods. However, education, housing and health services are said to have been greatly improved; for instance, at the end of 1973 there were 33,380 schools and colleges, compared with 7,565 in 1959, just after the Revolution.

The American treaty with Cuba was the turning point in its history. During the whole of the Spanish regime the island had been badly neglected. By 1898 only about 3% of it was cultivated. Over the rest roamed semi-nomadic cattle. Highways were few and poor. The right to intervene brought an immense inflow of American investment; roads and railways were built, the capital modernized, and new technical equipment quartered the cost of the rapidly increasing sugar production.

Before the revolution of 1959 the United States had investments in Cuba worth about 1,000 million dollars, covering nearly every activity from agriculture and mining to oil installations. Of the gross national product before 1959 salaries and wages paid by American enterprises accounted for no less than 7.1%. Before the revolution the U.S. took 66.8% of Cuba's exports and supplied 69.8% of the imports. Today all American businesses, including banks, have been nationalized; the U.S. has cut off sugar imports from Cuba, placed an embargo on exports to Cuba, and broken off diplomatic relations with it. Some 80% of Cuba's exports were sugar, most of it sold to the U.S.; it is now sold largely to Communist countries, which are now granting Cuba over US$500m. in aid each year. Of recent years, though, sugar sales to countries outside the Communist group, for instance Japan, have increased appreciably, and it is hoped that relations with the U.S.A. may soon be normalized.

Government Early in 1976 a new constitution was approved by 97.7% of the voters, setting up municipal, provincial and national assemblies to govern the country. As a result of the decisions of the First Congress of the Communist Party of Cuba in December 1975, the number of provinces was increased from six to fourteen, which was seen as a necessity for the establishment of "Popular Power". Delegates were elected to the municipal assemblies in October 1976, and the National Assembly was convoked on December 2, 1976. Dr. Fidel Castro was elected President of the Council of State by the 481 deputies. His brother, Major Raúl Castro, was similarly elected First Vice-President of the Council, and the former president, Dr. Osvaldo Dorticós, became a non-ranking member.

The People Some 73% of Cubans firmly register themselves as whites: they are mostly the descendants of Spanish colonial settlers and immigrants; 26% are blacks and mulattoes, now living mostly along the coasts and in certain provinces, Oriente in particular; about 1% are Chinese. The indigenous Indians disappeared long ago. Some 50% live in the towns, of which there are 9 with over 50,000 inhabitants each. The population is estimated at 9,600,000; a third lives in Havana province, a fifth in Havana itself, though recent population movements have swelled the rural population at the expense of the urban. It is claimed that illiteracy has been wiped out.

Communications Cuba has 18,115 km. of railway and over 20,000 km. of roads. They are shown on the map. An 8-lane highway along the length of the island, between Pinar del Río and Santiago, is being built.

Havana, the capital, was (before the Revolution) the largest, most beautiful and the most sumptuous city in the Caribbean. Today it is rather run-down, but thanks to the Government's policy of developing the countryside, it does not have the shantytowns that so many other Latin American capitals show. With its suburbs it has 1,800,000 people. Some of it is very old—the city was founded in 1515—but the ancient palaces, plazas, colonnades, churches and monasteries merge agreeably with the new.

The best approach is by sea, a memorable experience. A short channel leads to a large and beautiful harbour, 3½ km. long, 1½ km. wide, and safely protected against storms. As we approach the channel we see, to the left, the time-worn walls of Morro Castle. To the right is the fortress of La Punta, and beyond it the many-coloured city. From the harbour one looks E towards high hills, but westwards is the more or less level land, backed by low hills, on which much of the city is built. The residential sections of Marianao and Vedado are in the low hills.

The oldest part of the city, around the Plaza de Armas, is quite near the docks. Here are the former palace of the Captains-General, the temple of El Templete, and La Fuerza, the oldest of all the forts. From Plaza de Armas two narrow and picturesque streets, Calles Obispo and O'Reilly, go W to the heart of the City: Parque Central, with its laurels, poncianas, almonds, palms, shrubs and gorgeous flowers. Round this busy square are hotels, clubs, and cafes. To the SW rises the golden dome of the Capitol. From the NW corner of Parque Central, the Paseo del Prado runs to the fortress of La Punta. It is a wide, tree-shaded avenue lined by hotels, clubs, theatres, restaurants, bars and stores once crowded at night. At its northern sea-side end is the Malecón, a splendid highway along the coast to the western residential sections of Vedado and Marianao. Calle San Lázaro leads directly from the monument to Gen. Antonio Maceo on the Malecón to the magnificent central stairway of Havana University. This was the scene of many student demonstrations in the Batista period. A new monument to Julio Antonio Mella, founder of the original Cuban Communist Party, stands across from the stairway. Further out, past El

Príncipe Castle, is Plaza Revolucionaria, with the impressive monument to José Martí at its centre. The large buildings surrounding the square were mostly built in the 50's and house the principal government ministries. The long grey building behind the monument is the former Justice Ministry (1958), now the H.Q. of the Central Committee of the Communist Party, where Fidel Castro has his office. The Square is the scene of massive parades and speeches marking important events. From near the fortress of La Punta a tunnel runs eastwards under the mouth of the harbour; it emerges in the rocky ground between the Castillo del Morro and the fort of La Cabaña, some 550 metres away and a 5-km. highway connects with the Havana-Matanzas road.

The project for housing 3,000 families in Havana East is worth seeing. The houses are functional, economic, and pleasant. An even larger and more impressive project is underway, further east past Cojimar, at Alamar.

The Cuban pavilion, a large building on Calle 23, Vedado, is a combination of a tropical glade and a museum of social history. It tells the nation's story by a brilliant combination of objects, photography and the architectural manipulation of space.

The new Arts Centre, a series of buildings in Marianao to house schools for different arts, was designed by Ricardo Porro. Architects will be interested in this "new spatial sensation".

The street map of Havana given here is marked with numerals showing the places of most interest to visitors.

1. Castillo del Morro (El Morro Castle), built, like all the fortresses, by Spain, to repel the buccaneers. Drake appeared before Havana in 1585. El Morro was built between 1587 and 1597, with a 20-metre moat, but has been much altered. It stands on a bold headland; the flash of its light tower, built in 1844, is visible 30 km. out to sea. The Castle is no longer open to the public, since it is now a prison, but the Government hopes eventually to convert it into a museum. On the harbour side, down by the water, is the Battery of the 12 Apostles, each gun named after an Apostle. It can be reached by bus through the tunnel to the former toll gates.

An amphibious attack by the British captured Havana in 1762. The expeditionary force, under Admiral Sir George Pocock, was drawn from England, North America, and the West Indies. It appeared before Havana on June 6. Whilst Pocock made a feint attack on the city and on Morro Castle, Lord Albermarle, in charge of the land forces, deployed his sailors and marines on the open beaches near Cojimar: a complete surprise. Albemarle then marched his men over goat tracks and broken ground covered with thorn, scrub and prickly pear to where Cabaña fort now stands, a distance of 8 km. From Cabaña ridge he could bombard both the city and Morro Castle. Pocock meanwhile established a naval base at the mouth of the Chorrera river (where Vedado is today), blockaded the harbour, and bombarded the Morro. On July 30 Albemarle sprang a mine under the north-east bastion of the Morro and his men stormed the Castle "like people going to see a show at fair time". The Morro gone, British troops attacked the city from the west. Havana capitulated on August 12, and with it the strong Spanish naval squadron in the harbour. The cost to the British was heavy. Unknown to them, a merchant ship from Veracruz had, in the autumn of 1761, brought the *vómito negro*, or yellow fever, to Cuba. Only 646 men were killed, but 6,008 men died of this disease. There are no monuments to the campaign, but the little castle at the mouth of the Chorrera which Pocock captured is still there, though now surrounded and dwarfed by gleaming white blocks of flats.

2. Fortaleza De La Cabaña (La Cabaña Fortress) reached by harbour boat from near the Fuerza Castle. Steep ascent on foot from the shore. Built 1763-1774, after the British had left. Fronting the harbour is a high wall; the ditch on the landward side, 12 metres deep, has a drawbridge to the main entrance. Inside are Los Fosos de los Laureles (Laurel Ditch) where political prisoners were shot during the Cuban fight for independence. Visitors are no longer allowed inside La Cabaña as it is now a barracks.

HAVANA

N

GULF OF MEXICO

CHANNEL

MALECON

C. CARCEL

C. GENIOS

C. REFUGIOS

C. COLON

C. ANIMAS

C. VIRTUDES

C. NEPTUNO

EL PRADO

C. ZULUETA

DE BELGICA

AV.

C. PEÑA POBRE

C. CUARTELES

C. CHACON

C. TEJADILLO

C. EMPEDRADO

S. JUAN DE DIOS

O'REILLY

OBISPO

OBRAPIA

C. LAMPARILLA

C. AMARGURA

C. TENIENTE REY

C. MURALLA

C. DRAGONES

C. REINA

C. MONTE

C. CORRALES

C. APODACA

C. GLORIA

C. MISION

C. ARSENAL

C. BERNAZA

C. VILLEGAS

C. AGUAR

C. CUBA

C. SAN IGNACIO

C. MERCADERES

C. SOL

C. LUZ

HABANA

C. ACOSTA

C. JESUS MARIA

C. MERCED

C. PAULA

C. SAN ISIDRO

C. COMPOSTELA

C. ZULUETA (EGIDO)

AVE. DE BELGICA

BAY

The National Observatory and the railway terminus are on the same side of the Channel as these two forts.

3. La Punta Fortress (Castilla de la Punta), built at the end of the 16th century, a squat building with 2½-metre thick walls, is now used by the Cuban Navy. Opposite the fortress, across the Malecón, is the Máximo Gómez monument; he led the Cubans to victory and independence.

4. Castillo de la Fuerza (The Fortress), Cuba's oldest building and the second oldest fort in the New World. Built, 1538-1544, after the city had been sacked by buccaneers. It is a low, long building with a picturesque tower from which there is a grand view. Hernando de Soto set out from here in 1539 to discover the Mississippi. Legend says that his wife, Isabela de Bobadilla, used to climb the tower to watch for his return; that the strain on her eyes made her blind; and that she died of sorrow when she heard of her husband's death. In 1762 the occupying British stole from the tower a statue of La Habana, the Indian girl who first greeted the Spaniards; a replica now serves as a weathervane. The moat has been turned into a sunken garden. *Note* There are two other old forts in Havana: Atarés, finished in 1763, on a hill overlooking the south-west end of the harbour; and El Príncipe, on a hill at the far end of Av. Independencia. Built 1774-94. Now the city gaol. Finest view in Havana from this hill.

5. The Cathedral, a picturesque building in Hispano-American style, massively built of native limestone, which is much weathered. Built in 1704 by the Jesuits, who were expelled in 1767. Belltowers flank the Tuscan façade; there is a grand view from the E tower, which has two musical bells, a small one, cast in Matanzas, bearing the date 1664, and the larger one, cast in Spain, bearing the date 1698. The church is officially dedicated to the Virgin of the Immaculate Conception, but is better known as the church of Havana's patron saint, San Cristóbal, and as the Columbus cathedral. The bones of Christopher Columbus were sent to this cathedral when Santo Domingo was ceded by Spain to France in 1795, and were not removed until the Spanish-American war. The bones were in fact those of another Columbus. The Cathedral is open Mon-Fri. 0900-1130 and Sat. 1530-1730.

6. Plaza de Armas (now known as Plaza Carlos Manuel Céspedes), has been restored to very much what it once was. The statue in the centre is of Céspedes. In the NE corner of the square is the temple of El Tamplete; a column in front of it marks the spot where the first mass was said in 1519 under a ceiba tree. A sapling of the same tree, blown down by hurricane in 1753, was planted on the same spot, and under its branches the supposed bones of Columbus reposed in state before being taken to the cathedral. This tree was cut down in 1828, the present tree planted, and the Doric temple opened. There are paintings by Vermay, a pupil of David, inside.

7. On the W side of Plaza de Armas is the former palace of the Captains General, built in 1780, a charming example of the colonial period. The Spanish Governors and the Presidents lived here until 1917, when it became the City Hall. It is now the Historical Museum of the city of Havana. Open Tues.-Sat., 1430-1800, 1900-2200; Sun. 1500-1900. The arcaded and balconied patio is well worth a visit. The former Supreme Court on the N side of the Plaza is another colonial building, but not such a good example. It has a large patio.

8. The Church and convent of San Francisco, built 1608, reconstructed 1737; a massive, sombre edifice suggesting defence rather than worship. The three-storeyed tower was both a landmark for returning voyagers and a look-out for pirates. The convent now houses the government antique market (open Mon.-Fri. 0800-1130 and 1300-1630, Sat. 0800-1130) and the church is a warehouse for vegetables.

9. The Corinthian white marble building on Calle Oficinas S of the Post Office was once the legislative building where the House of Representatives met before the Capitol was built.

10. The Santa Clare Convent was built in 1635 for the Clarisan nuns. The quaint old patio has been carefully preserved; in it are the city's first slaughter house, first public fountain and public baths, and a house built by a sailor for his love-lorn daughter. You can still see the nuns' cemetery and their cells.

11. La Merced church, built in 1746, rebuilt 1792. It has a beautiful exterior and a redecorated lavish interior.

12. The Palacio de Bellas Artes now houses the contents of the National Museum. It also has a large collection of relics of the struggle for independence, sculptures, classical paintings (most of them copies), and a fine array of modern paintings by native and other artists. Open Tues.-Sat. 1300-2030, Sun. 0900-1230.

13. Parque Fraternidad, landscaped to show off the Capitol, N of it, to the best effect. At its centre is a ceiba tree growing in soil provided by each of the American republics. In the park also is a famous statue of an Indian woman: La Noble Habana, sculpted in 1837. From the SW corner the handsome Avenida Allende runs due W to the high hill to which stands Príncipe Castle (now the City Gaol). On this Avenue, at the foot of the hill, are the Botanical Gardens (collection of flora, bird houses, fish-ponds, etc.) N, along Calle Universidad, on a hill which gives a good view, is the University.

14. The Capitol, opened May 1929, has a large dome over a rotunda; at the centre of its floor is set a 24-carat diamond, zero for all distance measurements in Cuba. The interior has large halls and stately staircases, all most sumptuously decorated. Entrance for visitors is to the left of the stairway. The Capitol now houses the Museum of Natural Science, which is open Tues. to Sat. 1400-2130, and Sun. 1400-1800.

15. Parque Central. See the introduction to this chapter.

16. The National Theatre.

17. Presidential Palace (1922), a huge, costly, ornate building topped by a dome, facing Av. de la Misiones Park; now contains the Museum of the Revolution. Open Tues.-Sat. 1300-1930, Sun. 0900-1300. A bit of the old city wall is preserved in front of the front entrance. The yacht *Granma*, from which Dr Castro disembarked with his companions in 1956 to initiate the Revolution, has been installed in the park facing the S entrance.

18. The Church of El Santo Angel Custodio was built by the Jesuits in 1672 on the slight elevation of Peña Pobre Hill (the street of that name is the narrowest in the City). It has white, laced Gothic towers and 10 chapels, the best of which is back of the high altar. A tragic scene in the famous novel, *Cecilia Valdés*, was set on the steps of this church.

Other Museums   Colonial Museum, Plaza de la Catedral (Tues.-Sat. 1300-2100, Sun. 0900-1300); Medical Science Museum, Calle Cuba 460 (Mon.-Fri. 0900-1200, 1300-1700); Birthplace of José Martí, opposite central railway station (Tues.-Sun. 0900-1645); Napoleonic Museum, Calle Ronda (Tues.-Sat. 1300-2100; Sun. 0900-1300); Decorative Arts Museum, 17th and E Streets, Vedado (Tues.-Sat. 1300-2100; Sun. 0900-1300). Admission to all museums, galleries etc. free.

Transport   Taxis tend to be scarce. The newer taxis have meters, but in the older ones there are no meters and there is normally a fixed charge between points in or near the city. The fare should be fixed before setting out on a journey. Town buses are frequent and cheap (5 centavos flat rate fare), though crowded, and run hourly through the night as well. Bus to Santiago, US$12 second class, US$30 first (a/c) 17-22 hours.

Shopping   Local cigars, cigarettes and rum are excellent. Original lithographs and other works of art can be purchased directly from the artists at the Galería del Grabado, Plaza de la Catedral (Mon.-Fri. 1400-2100, Sat. 1400-1900). There is a special boutique in the old mansion at Calle Cuba 64 where the largest selection of Cuban handicrafts is available; the artisans have their workshops in the back of the same building (Open, Mon.-Fri. 0800-1200, 1300-1700, Sat. 0800-1200). All the larger hotels have boutiques where visitors can make purchases on presentation of their white currency-exchange papers. The best boutiques are those located in the *Riviera*, *Habana Libre*, *Nacional* and *Deauville* hotels.

UNIFORM WITH THIS VOLUME:
THE GULF HANDBOOK

Leading Hotels

	Address	No. of rooms	Telephone	Rates (Cuban pesos)* Single	Double
Capri	21 y N, Vedado	220	32-0511	25	31
Riviera	Paseo y Malecón, Vedado	360	30-5051	25	31
Nacional	21 y O, Vedado	525	7-8981	19	24
Habana Libre	L y 23, Vedado	568	30-5011	19	24
Victoria	19 y M, Vedado	32	32-0531	12	16
Sevilla	Trocadero y Zulueta	196	6-9961	11	14
Deauville	Galiano y Malecón	140	61-6901	11	14
Bristol	San Rafael y Amistad	124	61-9944	6	11
Lincoln	Galiano y Virtudes	140	61-7961	5	7
Alamac	Galiano 308	50	61-6971	3	5

*Official rate: 1 peso = US$1.20; free rate closer to US$0.25.

The first five (the best) are away from the centre; the last five reasonably close to it. Other economy hotels are the *New York, Presidente,* and *Plaza* hotels. The cheaper hotels are usually hard to get into; often full. Theoretically foreign tourists must obtain a reservation from Cubatur, the government tourist agency, before proceeding to the hotels (all government-owned) although this rule is not always followed, especially at night. A Cubatur hostess is always on duty in the immigration area at José Marti International Airport to receive incoming flights, and visitors arriving on their own would be best to have her book them a room at one of the hotels at that time. The main Cubatur office is at Calle 23, No. 156 between N y O, La Rampa, Vedado (open Mon.-Fri. 0800-1700, Sat. 0800-1200), and reservations for all Cuban hotels, restaurants, and night clubs can be made here.

Tipping Visitors are not allowed to tip in hotels and restaurants. Porters, cloakroom attendants, etc. get 25-50 centavos. Taxi drivers are not tipped.

Restaurants are not cheap. The choice of food is very restricted by rationing. Book a table between 2200 and midnight the evening before, if you can, in the main ones, where meals are from US$5-10. The *Bodeguita del Medio,* near the Cathedral, made famous by Hemingway, and *The Patio,* nearby, are recommended for national dishes; so is *Rincón Criollo,* on outskirts of town. *Las Ruinas* in Lenin Park is Cuba's most exclusive restaurant. *El Floridito,* near the Parque Central, is reputedly the original home of the *daiquiri.* The *Sevilla Hotel* has the best hotel restaurant.

Night Club Tropicana. Admission is free, but the drinks are expensive: minimum charge is US$10 a head. All the main hotels have their own cabarets. Best to reserve through Cubatur.

Zoo 26th Av. Vedado (open Tues.-Sun. 0900-1800).

Airport José Marti, 18 km. from Havana.

Electric Current 110-230 V. 3 phase 60 cycles, A.C.

Banks Banco Nacional and its branches. Banco Internacional, Aguiar 411, is the only bank that handles personal cheques.

Cables Western Union, Calle Obispo 351. Tel.: 6-9901/5. Cuba Transatlantic Radio Corpn. (RCA), Obispo y Aguiar.

Suburbs The western sections of the old city merge imperceptibly into **El Vedado.** W of it, and reached by a tunnel under the Almandores river, lies **Marianao,** Havana's main suburb, some 16 km. W of the Capital, and easily reached by bus. Population: 235,492.

Guanabacoa is 5 km. to the E and is reached by a road turning off the Central Highway, or by the Hershey Railway, or by launch from Muelle Luz (not far from No. 9 on the map) to the suburb of Regla, then by bus direct to Guanabacoa. Excellent views of the harbour from the launch (fare 5 centavos). It is a well preserved small colonial town with an old parochial church which has a splendid altar: the monastery of San Francisco; the Carral Theatre; and some attractive mansions. The Historical Museum of Guanabacoa, a former estate mansion, has an unusual voodoo collection in the former slave quarters at the back of the building. Open: Tues.-Sat., 1600-2200; Sun., 1200-1800. Closed on rainy days.

A delightful old colonial town, **Santa María del Rosario**, founded in 1732, is 16 km. E of Havana. It is reached from Cotorro, on the Central Highway, or by 97 bus from Guanabacoa, and was carefully restored and preserved before the revolution. The village church is particularly good. See the paintings, one by Veronese. There are curative springs nearby.

West from Havana along the northern coast road is some beautiful countryside: sugar and tobacco plantations. Near Vinales are several caves in the limestone which are open to the public.

Hemingway fans may wish to visit the house in San Francisco de Paula where he lived from 1939 to 1960. Bus No. 7 from the Capitolio. Open Tues.-Sat. (closed Mon.) 0900-1200 and 1300-1700, Sun. 0900-1300. There is a bust of the author in the village of Cojimar.

The old provincial town of **Matanzas** lies 104 km. E of Havana along the Vía Blanca, which links the capital with Varadero Beach, 79 km. further E. There are frequent buses but the journey *via* the Hershey Railway is much more memorable (eight trains daily from the Casablanca station, which is reached by public launch from near La Fuerza Castle). Those who wish to make it a day trip from Havana can easily do so, or one can continue on to Varadero and use that tourist centre as a base from which to explore the interesting town of **Cárdenas**. It was there that the present Cuban flag was raised for the first time back in 1850.

In Matanzas one should visit the Pharmaceutical Museum (Mon.-Sat. 1400-1800, 1900-2100), the Matanzas Museum (Tues.-Sun. 1500-1800, 1900-2200), and the cathedral, all near Parque La Libertad. There is a wonderful view of the surrounding countryside from the Iglesia de Montserrat.

Trinidad, 133 km. south of Santa Clara, further E, is a perfect relic of the early days of the Spanish colony, with many fine palaces and churches. The Museo Ignacio Agramonte in the large city of **Camagüey** is one of the biggest and most impressive museums in the country. Adequate food and lodging at the *Gran Hotel*.

Santiago, near the E end of the island, is Cuba's second city and the focal point of much of its colonial and contemporary history. Excellent excursions can be made to the Gran Piedra and along the Ruta Turística to the Morro Castle. In the city there are a number of museums, the best of which are the Colonial Museum located in Diego Velázquez' house and the Moncada barracks museum. *Motel Versailles,* near airport; *Hotel Casa Grande* opposite the cathedral.

Economy

The Cuban State controls all branches of the economy, which is kept going largely by aid from the Communist bloc. Russia has extended large credits since 1960. Statistical data are at last improving: the rate of economic growth in 1976 was 4%, following an average annual increase of 10% in 1971-75.

Sugar dominates the economy. Cuba produces 14% of the world's sugar. By-products are black-strap and high test molasses, anhydrous alcohol, brandy and rum. Most of the exports are to Russia; the rest goes to other Communist countries and to Japan, Canada, Ceylon, Morocco and Egypt. The 1970 crop, a record, was over 8½m. tons, but despite continued efforts this figure has not been repeated. Sugar accounts for about 80% by value of the total exports.

Tobacco is the second largest export crop, planted in early November and harvested in early January.

After sugar, meat production is the most important agricultural activity. The 4,500,000 head of cattle fend for themselves in the savannas of central and eastern Cuba, putting on weight during the wet season but generally lean of flesh—a local preference. Dairy cattle are being introduced on a large scale and citrus fruits are of increasing importance. Cuba grows enough coffee for itself. Cacao, like coffee, is grown on small inaccessible farms in Oriente Province. Much rice is imported. Farm production showed marked increases in 1976.

Cuba is potentially one of the world's most important sources of nickel and iron. Deposits of copper, manganese and chrome are substantial, and there is some petroleum. Non-ferrous ores and concentrates are exported.

Foreign Trade (million Cuban pesos)

					1972	1973	1974
Exports	..	..	..	..	1,189.8	1,467.0	2,225.9
Imports	..	..	..	..	770.9	1,153.0	2,222.2

Information for Visitors

No passenger ships call regularly but see Germany (East) in the Shipping Section.

Eastern European and Russian airlines fly direct from East Berlin, Frankfurt, Moscow, Prague and Rabat (Morocco), and anyone thinking of going that way should contact the Czechoslovak National Airlines, Cubana de Aviación, Interflug or Aeroflot for further information.

Cubana, the Cuban national airline, also operates a twice weekly service in both directions Havana-Mexico City, normally on Mon. and Fri. but often subject to delay. Cubana and Aeroflot fly to Havana from Lima and Georgetown. Cubana also flies weekly to Barbados, Trinidad and Jamaica. Iberia, the Spanish airline, and Cubana both fly twice a week between Madrid and Havana. This is probably the most convenient route from Western Europe. Cubana also has flights to Montreal; Air Canada fly between Toronto and Montreal and Havana. British Airways runs a weekly service from London to Mexico and Mexicana de Aviación flies from Mexico to Cuba calling at Mérida (Yucatán). There are non-stop scheduled flights linking Havana with Lima, Montreal, Panama City, San José (Costa Rica) and Toronto. Some Latin American countries will not admit anyone carrying a passport stamped by the Cuban authorities. Outward flights from Havana are often fully booked and a booking is imperative before entering Cuba. Unitours (Canada) run package tours to Cuba for all nationalities.

From Cuba to Mexico Travellers from Cuba to Mexico are allowed to stay in Mexico for 5 days only. Transit cards for this can be got only from the Mexican Consulate in Havana. Present three photographs. (Mexican visas got by travellers before going to Cuba don't count for this journey.) A confirmed onward booking leaving Mexico within 5 days is a must, or you may not be allowed to board your aircraft at Havana. Mexican Immigration stamps the passports of everyone coming from Cuba to show they have been there. This, of course, may make it difficult to visit other Latin American countries.

Documents Citizens of Austria, Canada, Denmark, France, Italy, Norway, Sweden, Switzerland, Yugoslavia and most East European countries only need a valid passport, but a visa is required by British subjects of the United Kingdom and the Channel Isles, travelling in Cuba in transit for a period of 30 days, or as tourists or temporary visitors for up to 6 months (renewable for a like period). In the USA, the Czechoslovak Embassy in Washington, D.C. will process applications for visas for US$5. Visas can take several weeks to be granted, and are apparently difficult to obtain for people other than businessmen, guests of the Cuban Government or Embassy officials, or those going on package tours. When the applicant is too far from a Cuban consulate to be able to apply conveniently for a visa, he may apply direct to the Cuban Foreign Ministry for a visa waiver.

Visitors must go in person to the Immigration Office for registration within 72 hours after arrival. The office is in Marianao; take bus 132 to end of line and walk from there. Ask for directions. When you register you will be given a tourist card. Tell the officials if you wish to visit the provinces. Application for an exit visa should be made 72 hours before the date of departure. Unless an authorized group tourist, you will be required to show US$10 in foreign currency for each day you intend to spend in Cuba. Exit permits are normally not needed by tourists or business visitors who stay in Cuba for less than 15 days.

To get into Cuba you need an international certificate against smallpox. T.A.B. vaccination in advisable. Those coming from or going through infected areas must have certificates of vaccination against cholera and yellow fever.

British businessmen should get "Hints to Business Men visiting Cuba", free on application to the Dept. of Trade, Export Services Division, Room CO7, Export House, 50 Ludgate Hill, London EC4M 7HU.

Customs   Personal baggage and articles for personal use are allowed in free of duty; so are 200 cigarettes, or 25 cigars, or 1 lb. of tobacco, and 2 bottles of alcoholic drinks. Many things are scarce or unobtainable in Cuba: take in everything you are likely to need other than food (say razor blades, medicines and pills, reading and writing material and photographic supplies).

Currency Control   The visitor should be careful to retain the white exchange paper every time he changes money; this will enable all Cuban pesos remaining at the end of the stay to be changed back into foreign currency.

Travellers' cheques expressed in U.S. or Canadian dollars or sterling are valid in Cuba. Don't enter the place or date when signing cheques, or they may be refused.

Hotel Reservations anywhere in the country can be made through the national tourist office in Havana.

Language is Spanish, with local variants in pronunciation and vocabulary. Some English is spoken.

Hours of Business   Government offices: 0830-1230 and 1330-1730 Mon. to Fri. Offices open on Sat. morning. Banks: 0800-1200, 1415-1615 Mon. to Fri., 0930-1200 Sat. The National Bank of Cuba is open on Sat. p.m. from 1300-1500. Shops: 1230-1930 Mon. to Sat.

Internal Transport   Cubana de Aviación services between most of the main towns. (Camagüey, Cienfuegos, Holguín, Baracoa, Guantánamo, Manzanillo, Moa, Nueva Gerona and Santiago all have airports.) There are bus and rail services too, but these tend to be rather uncomfortable. The Havana town bus services, on the other hand, are excellent and cheap (5 centavos flat fare).

Health   Sanitary reforms have transformed Cuba into a healthy country. The venomous Havana mosquito is not malarial, though malaria is known outside the towns. Vigilance is necessary in the choice of foodstuffs, especially uncooked green vegetables. All fresh fruit should be peeled. Tap water is not safe to drink and bottled water and mineral water are recommended. Medical service is free to all but prescription drugs must be purchased.

Climate   NE Trade winds temper the heat. Average summer shade temperatures rise to 30°C (86°F) in Havana, and higher elsewhere. In winter, day temperatures drop to 19°C (66°F). Average rainfall is from 860 mm. in Oriente to 1,730 mm. in Havana; it falls mostly in the summer and autumn, but there can be torrential rains at any time. Hurricanes come in the autumn. The best time for a visit is during the cooler dry season (November to April). Walking is uncomfortable in summer but most offices, hotels, leading restaurants and cinemas are air-conditioned. Humidity varies between 75 and 95%

Dress is much less formal since the Revolution. Summer calls for the very lightest clothing, such as cotton or cotton-terylene mixture. Cuban men mostly wear the *guayabera* (a light pleated shirt worn outside white trousers). Formal wear is not often needed nowadays. Hats are rarely worn.

Women wear lightweight cotton dresses during the day and cocktail dresses for formal evenings.

Currency The monetary unit is the peso, officially equal to US$1.20, though it fetches less than 25 U.S. cents in the free market. There are notes for 1, 5, 10, 20, and 50 pesos, and coins for 1, 5, 20, and 40 centavos. Essentials—rent and most food—are cheap, but non-essentials tend to be very expensive. US dollars are accepted by hotels and other official institutions.

Post, telegraph and telephone Where possible correspondence should be addressed to post office boxes (Apartados), where delivery is more certain. Telegraphic services are adequate. So are telephone facilities. Telegrams to Britain cost 35 centavos a word. The night letter rate is 3 pesos 85 centavos for 22 words. Local telephone calls can be made from public telephones for free. A telephone call to Britain costs 15 pesos for the first 3 minutes. Air mail rates to Britain are 31 centavos for half an ounce and 13 centavos to Canada. All postal services, national and international, have been described as appalling. Cuban time is 5 hours behind Greenwich Mean Time.

Internal Telecommunications Western Union maintain an office in Havana and the Cuba Transatlantic Radio Corpn (RCA) have offices in Havana, Camagüey, Cienfuegos and Santiago de Cuba.

Weights and Measures The metric system is compulsory, but exists side by side with American and old Spanish systems.

Newspapers "Granma", mornings except Sunday; and "Juvantud Rebelede", evening paper. No foreign newspapers are for sale, but "Granma" has a weekly English edition.

Holidays

January 1: Liberation Day.	July 26: Revolution Day.
January 2: Victory of Armed Forces.	December 7: Day of Mourning.
May 1: Labour Day.	

The British Embassy is on the 8th floor, Edificio Bolívar, Capdevila 101-103, Havana. Telegraphic address: Prodrome, Havana. Tel.: 61-5681/4.

The Canadian Embassy, Calle 30 (No. 518) and Av. 7 in Miramar.

HISPANIOLA

One might expect that a relatively small island such as Hispaniola (from Spanish "Isla Española"—the Spanish island) lying in the heart of the Caribbean would be occupied by one nation, or at least that its people should be without great ethnic and cultural differences. This is not so. Hispaniola, which has an area of just over 76,900 square km. not much more than half the size of Cuba, is in fact shared by two countries, the Dominican Republic and Haiti. There are very marked differences between the two, both as regards the people and their cultural and economic development, and there is not much love lost between them either; indeed, we are informed that the Haitians will not let visitors travel by land to the Dominican Republic, and a special permit is required for land travel in the other direction.

The Haitians are almost wholly black, with a culture which is a strange mixture of African and French influences. Haiti was a French colony until 1804 when, fired by the example of the French Revolution, the black slaves revolted, massacred the French land-owners and proclaimed the first black republic in the world. Throughout the 19th century the Haitians reverted to a primitive way of life, indulging in a succession of bloody, almost tribal wars. Even today, nowhere else in the Caribbean do African cults, particularly voodoo, play such a part in everyday life. The standard of living is one of the lowest in the New World.

The Dominicans are a mixture of black, Amerindian and white, and with a far greater European strain. Their culture and language are Spanish and their religion Roman Catholic. Economically, the country is much more developed, despite a stormy political past and unsavoury periods of corruption and dictatorship, particularly under Generalissimo Trujillo, whose notorious rule began in 1930 and lasted for 31 years until he was assassinated in 1961. Nevertheless, in a material sense the country did prosper during what became known as the Trujillo Era and today, although there is a good deal of poverty, the standard of living generally is much higher than it is in Haiti.

Both countries have been occupied by the United States: Haiti in 1915-1934 and the Dominican Republic in 1916-1924. Despite bitterness and protests over this, both countries, especially Haiti, benefited materially because the Americans were able not only to introduce some measures of law and order, but they also began the first development projects that Haiti, for example, had ever known. The Spanish-speaking part was also ruled by France from 1795 to 1808 and, unbelievable as it might seem today, by Haiti between 1822 and 1844, after just one year, 1821-22, of what the Dominicans call their "Independencia Efímera" under José Núñez de Cáceres. In 1844, the Haitians were driven out by a national movement led by the writer Duarte, the lawyer Sánchez and the soldier Mella and the Republic of Santo Domingo was proclaimed. In 1861, however, following various tribulations, the country reannexed itself to Spain for four years; finally dissatisfied with this, in 1865 it applied unsuccessfully to join the USA. It was, therefore, as a kind of third best that the Republic settled for independence for the third time. The country must be one of the very few where a Roman Catholic archbishop has served as head of state: Archbishop Merño was President from 1880 to 1883.

Unlike the West Indians or the Puerto Ricans, the Haitians and the Dominicans are fully accepted by Latin Americans as members of the family in the same way as Cubans are accepted.

Hispaniola is mountainous and forested, with plains and plateaux. The land is well watered and fertile. The climate is tropical but tempered by sea breezes. The cooler months are between December and March.

Haiti, with 27,750 square km., has a population of 5.3 millions increasing at an annual rate of 4%. The Dominican Republic is larger—about 49,200 square km.—but its population is slightly smaller at 5 millions, growing at 3.3% a year.

HAITI

The Republic of Haiti forms the western third of the island. French is the official language, though the common speech of all classes is a Creole patois. Nine-tenths of the people are African, and the remainder are mulattoes, the descendants of French settlers.

Government The constitution provides for a U.S.-style presidential régime, with separation of powers. In practice, however, Haiti has been ruled by a series of dictatorships; the President for Life, M. Jean-François Duvalier, still in his twenties and known colloquially as Baby Doc, is the son and successor of the long-time dictator and president for life, the late Dr. François Duvalier (Papa Doc). No criticism of the régime is tolerated though there has been some liberalization since Papa Doc's time.

Haiti is interesting for the visitor. It is now tourist conscious, and the tourist is certainly splendidly handled by an extremely pleasant people eager to give good service and guidance (in English). It is especially fascinating for the tourist who is avid for out-of-the-way experience. Prophylaxis against malaria is essential.

N.B. *Tourists wishing to visit the interior must have a (free) laissez-passer from the Tourist Office. Map may be obtained from the Arco office, or from the Tourist office, at the corner of Rues Marie-Jeanne and Roux, near the GPO. Street naming in Port-au-Prince is chaotic; keep asking.*

Port-au-Prince, capital and chief port of Haiti, population 500,000, has an excellent natural harbour with 9 metres of water alongside the wharf. It is set at the further end of a beautiful deep horseshoe bay, with high mountains behind and a small island across the bay protecting it from high seas and tidal waves. The town is built in the form of an amphitheatre. In the lower part, at sea-level, is concentrated the business section, with a very pleasant palm-shaded sea-front known as the Exposition; on the heights are the private houses, generally surrounded by shady gardens. The heat is some degrees less at several summer resorts easily reached from the city. Buses marked "St.-Marc" pass the more distant beaches.

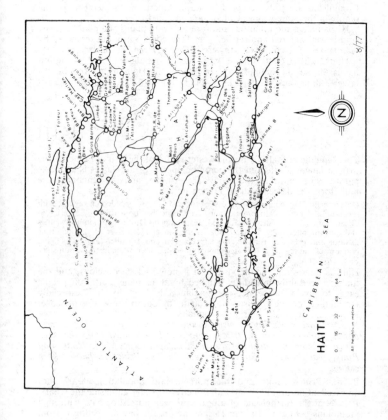

HAITI

0   16   32   48   64 km

All heights in metres

8/77

There are several clubs—the Turgeau Club; society clubs such as the Bellevue and the Port-au-Princien; the American Colony Club at Bourdon, and sports clubs. One of the "sights" is the Iron Market, a wild, roaring African scene. Small boys offer their services as guides as soon as you step outside your hotel.

Hotels in Port-au-Prince *Castel d'Haiti* (most rooms air-conditioned, swimming pool), US$28-32 s; *Beau Rivage* (swimming pool), US$18-24 s; *Sans Souci* (best for businessmen, good cuisine, swimming pool), US$32 s; *Oloffson* (swimming pool), from US$38, in interesting Victorian house, very good food; *Splendid* (swimming pool), US$25-30 s; *Plaza*, US$26-32 s; *Park*, US$15-20 s; *Chatelet*, US$18-20 s; *Coconut Villa*, US$18 s; *El Dorado*, US$18; *Excelsior*, US$15; *Palace*, US$18; *Paloma*, US$24; *Simbic*, US$24-30; *Royal Haitian Club*, US$35-45 s; *Central*, rue du Centre 78, central, US$8 s, fairly basic; good cheap restaurant below. Others across the street.

Guest Houses *Hillside*, rue Bazelais, off Pétionville road and on way to museum, US$8 with 2 meals, US$12 air-conditioned. *Carl Bjenson's*, nearby, similar. *Holiday*, on main street, US$6-9 s; *Haiti Chérie*, near drive-in cinema en route for airport, run by Haitian/American couple, US$10 s; *Hérvia, G, Jean-Charles, La Gaité* and *Rocourt*. Two other guest houses recommended as both cheap and good, the *Santos Guest House*, rue Pacot, US$18 d including 2 meals; *La Griffone* in Canape Vert (Zone Jean-Baptiste), US$10-15 s, US$20-28 d., including 2 meals. *May's Guest House*, Debussy District, US$10 including 2 meals, swimming pool and panoramic view of the city. There are a number of other guest houses whose prices vary from US$5 to 16 for a single room.

Restaurants *Aux Cosaques* (local food); *Au Rond Point* (local food); *Le Carillon* (local food); *Chandler*, opposite Banque d'Haiti, has US$1 lunch (several restaurants on both sides of Grand rue to S have meals for US$0.50); *Le Perchoir*, 17 km. from Port-au-Prince, overlooking the town and bay (Continental food); *Château Caprice*, at Mousseau (Continental and American food).

Night Club *La Lambie*, just S of Port-au-Prince (take a taxi, there are no buses), good national food and music, open to the ocean.

Art Centres Musée Nationale, now outside town in former presidential mansion; Musée Archéologique is in old Musée Nationale building on southern side of Place de l'Independance; there is a new modern art museum across from the French Embassy, near the Place de l'Independance. Art Centre (Centre d'Art), on Rue de la Révolution. Commercial galleries include the Néhémy, Nader's and Issa's (17 rue Chile), very good quality for buyers. Local art can be seen at the Cathedral of S. Trinité, the Airport, and Exposition buildings, and in the principal hotels. There are many craft shops and stalls, and many of the products are of high quality. Many good bargains to be had at Iron Market.

Shopping There are a large number of tourist shops in Port-au-Prince, but be warned that they charge high prices for items which can be bought for far less in the market. Good quality local crafts can be purchased in the Anglican Cathedral craftshop and at the Kenscoff Baptist Church.

Banks Royal Bank of Canada, and others. Banque d'Haiti reported to have best rate for £.

ITT Communicaciones Mundiales SA, 364 Jean-Jacques Dessalines.

RCA Communications, Inc., Place Geffrard, rues Férou et Courbe.

Library Alliance Française, opposite Pan-Am., open 0830-1200, 1430-1900 except Mon. and Sat. p.m. Book: *You can learn Creole*, from Caravelle bookshop (US$1.25)

Airport Aérport François Duvalier, 13 km. out of town. Taxi into town, US$5, or walk down the main road to Port-au-Prince and hail a "tap-tap" (pick-up truck) for much less. Tourist bureau at the airport, of little use.

Taxis "Publiques", shared taxis, charge US$0.20-0.40 a trip. They are identified by a red cloth in the window. "Camionettes" charge the same for a trip to Pétion-ville.

Excursions An asphalt road leads to (10 km.) **Pétionville**. Hotels and guest houses include: *Choucoune, Montana, Majestie Dambala, Villa Creole, Ibo Lele, Villa Quisqueya, Marabou, El Rancho,* and *Doux Séjours,* cheaper and delightfully eccentric, 460 metres above sea-level. An excellent sea food restaurant is *La Recife* in Rte Delmas; also good is *Le Picardie* (French). A good asphalt road, 16 km. long, runs from Pétionville to the holiday resort of **Kenscoff** (*Hotels Dereix, Florville,* collective taxi from Pétionville market, US$0.30), 1,370 metres above sea-level, where climatic conditions are excellent all the year round. If you have time, a drive through the fertile Cul-de-Sac plain, about 30 km. each way, is well worth while for those interested in agriculture and local life.

Excursions At Pétionville visit the Jane Barbancourt Castle. One can sample an unlimited quantity of the company's 17 differently-flavoured rums, which include coffee, mango, coconut, orange. Rum is sold at US$3 a bottle. From the castle one can visit the Bouteilliers and get an excellent view of Port-au-Prince. A Peristyle Voodoo show open every evening at 2200 on road west of Pétionville.

At **Gonaives**, on the road to Cap Haitien, there is a motel, *Chez Franz* (on the Cap side); *Bon Acceuil,* opposite barracks, US$3 s, with breakfast. The restaurant in town lets rooms above. Bus from Port-au-Prince, US$2, no fixed schedule. Most leave between 0700 and 1200. Buses Gonaives to Cap Haitien also leave mornings only.

Cap Haitien, 274 km. from the capital, is the second city. Population 30,000. It is on the N coast 10 hours by bus (known as *camion*) from the capital; this costs US$5 and is a rough trip. Buses leave in front of Texaco station in Port-au-Prince between 0700 and 0730. Usually leave 4-5 in a convoy. However, Turks and Caicos Airways have flights from the capital, US$32 return, inc. tax. Cap Haitien, known locally as Le Cap, has been described as "perhaps the most harmonious architectural ensemble in the hemisphere, as yet almost untouched by modern building"—(Michael Garthwaite). There is a beach 5 km. away (along rue 21) and others beyond, but no transport except taxis. You can camp on Ibo beach (good snorkelling), but take all the supplies you will need; there are no facilities there. Cruise ship visits Monday and Thursday. Tourist bureau at rue 24, Esplanade. Banque Union Haitien changestravellers' cheques. Open until 1800.

Hotels at Cap *Beck,* US$20 s; *Mont Joli,* US$24 s; *Roi Christophe,* US$20 s. Cheaper: *Pension Colon* on seafront opposite Post Office, US$4s, without food (not recommended); *Dupuy,* US$5.50 s, US$11.50 s, including 2 meals. At W end of town, on beach, *Brise de Mer,* US$10 p.p., with 2 meals, excellent food, private bathroom, hot water. Recommended, Mme. Merioin who runs an unmarked *pension* in a rambling old colonial house on Av. E between rues 24 and 25, US$6.50 including 2 meals. Also serves free ice-cold grapefruit.

Restaurants *Sacade,* rues 18 et B, near *Pension Dupuy; San Raison,* near market, cheaper. A good plate of food is available at US$0.50. Fresh and cold fruit juices served on Av. A, between rues 23 and 24.

Excursion Citadelle du Roi Christophe, a great ruined fortress built in the early 1800's, also known as La Ferrière. Take collective taxi to Milot (US$0.40, every two hours); horse and "boy" (an adult man) are provided there by the police for US$1.50 and US$1 respectively (otherwise it is an interesting but rugged two-hour walk uphill to the fortress); admission to the fortress costs an extra US$1. (The "boy" will appreciate 2 gourdes—US$0.40—tip.) At the bottom of the hill where the Citadelle stands is the palace of Sans-Souci, named by Christophe after Frederick the Great's palace; it is also well worth a visit. Avoid visiting on Mondays and Thursdays, when up to 4 cruise ships call at Cap Haitien.

Jacmel, a port on the S coast, is 6 hours by *tap-tap* (leaves 0600) from Port-au-Prince—seat by driver US$2, in back US$1 after bargaining; they will start by asking US$5. A new road has recently been built from Port-au-Prince. Only one hotel, *Pension Craft,* quaint and clean, room with meals US$10 s—but try bargaining. No restaurants. No public transport for beaches but a horse may be hired for Bassin Bleu and other places of interest. The University of Calgary, Canada, is opening an art school in Jacmel. No bus connection for Les Cayes, other main town in S. Haiti, but timber trucks pass.

Jeremie, reached by overnight boat from Port-au-Prince, US$2 passage, plus US$3 for bunk in bridge-house. Take food and drink. *Pension Frankel,* US$8 with food. Road to Les Cayes.

How to get to Haiti:

Shipping Port-au-Prince is served by Grace Lines from New York and by Royal Mail Lines cargo vessels from the U.K. by transhipment. R.M.L. Agent: O. J. Brandt, M.B.E., Rue de Quai (P.O. Box B65).

Air Services From USA: Pan Am., Air France, Eastern Airlines, American Airlines and ALM all fly direct from New York or Miami, or San Juan, Puerto Rico. ALM also flies from Curaçao, Kingston and Aruba; PanAm flies from Santo Domingo. British Airways flies to Kingston; enquire about connecting flights. Haiti can often be reached by making a stop-over between Miami and S. America. No extra charge depending on the routing of the ticket. There are also flights from Grand Turk and Bahamas to Cap Haitien and Port-au-Prince on Mon., Wed. and Fri. Internal flights are provided by Cohata, a branch of the Haitian Air Force, in old C-46s from an airfield on the Route de Delmas and from François Duvalier International Airport. They are very often full. In addition, Turks and Caicos Airways have a franchise for internal flights; they fly every weekday from Port-au-Prince to Jacmel, Cap Haitien, Jeremie and Les Cayes and back. They also fly to Port de Paix. Fares are low.

Buses Public transport services between towns are mainly operated by collective taxis known as *publiques* (they have a "P" on registration plate) and by open-backed pick-up trucks, known as "tap-tap". Buses between Port-au-Prince and Cap Haitien.

Tip (!) Though there are an increasing number of tours vising Haiti, budget travellers, particularly outside Port-au-Prince, are a rarity. Expect to be the subject of much friendly curiosity, and keep a pocketful of small change to conform with the local custom of tipping on every conceivable occasion!

Documents U.S. and Canadian citizens do not need a passport or a visa for a stay of up to 30 days—just some proof of citizenship, e.g. birth certificate. All other passengers need passports, and visas are required for all except nationals of Austria, Belgium, Denmark, France, Western Germany, Israel, Luxembourg, Netherlands, Switzerland and the U.K. All visitors must have a ticket for leaving Haiti. All visitors except those from USA and Canada must have current smallpox vaccination certificate. If going to the Dominican Republic next door, all visitors must call at the Dominican consulate.

Tax There is a "head tax", payable when leaving Haiti, of US$2 for non-residents. It is not payable by those who stay in Haiti less than 72 hours.

Clothing The climate is generally warm, but the cool on- and off-shore winds of morning and evening make the heat bearable: the cool hill resorts (Haiti is the most mountainous country in the Caribbean) can be reached in 15 minutes. Men wear tropical clothing the year round—seersucker, palm beach, or linen—but seldom wear hats. Women wear cotton dresses.

Currency The unit is the Gourde, divided into 100 centimes (kob); it is exchangeable on demand and without charge at the fixed rate of 5 gourdes to the U.S. dollar. U.S. notes and coins co-circulate with local currency; the U.S. cent is known as a "centimeor". There is no exchange control. Weights and measures are computed on the metric system. The **cost of living** rose by 7.4% in 1976, compared with 16.8% in 1975, 14.9% in 1974, and 22.7% in 1973.

The economy is based upon coffee (40% of exports), bauxite, sugar, sisal and tourism. Cement, textiles, soap, and rum are produced.
Exports in 1975 were about US$73.9m. and imports (c.i.f.) US$109.1m., against US$79.7m. and US$141.9m. in 1974.

Tourist Office The one in Port-au-Prince gives information on hotels and guest-houses (very helpful and sells maps of Haiti for US$0.25). In New York: 30 Rockefeller Plaza, NY 10020.

American Express Agents Port-au-Prince: Southerland Tours, 45 Ave. Marie Jeanne, Tel.: 3989/3591.

Federico Bertaccini, of Litchfield, Conn., who last year virtually rewrote the Dominican Republic section, has this year given us much useful information on Haiti, for which we are most grateful.

DOMINICAN REPUBLIC

As in Haiti, agriculture is the mainstay of the Dominican economy and provides employment for the bulk of the working population. A large proportion of the people, however, are still engaged on little more than subsistence farming.

Government The Republic has the conventional type of presidential system, with separation of powers, but in practice for many years anarchy alternated with dictatorship. Though President Trujillo (see page 1064) was killed in 1961, his associates have retained power ever since, except for a few months in 1963. President (1966-78): Dr. Joaquín Balaguer. President elected for 1978-82: Sr. Antonio Guzmán.

Sugar is the main crop (often 50% of exports), and U.S. interests have a big stake; in this respect the Republic has profited greatly from the conversion of the U.S.'s previous main sugar supplier, Cuba, to communism. Although Dominican capital has also helped to modernize the sugar industry, in latter years the Government has become increasingly anxious to break this dependence on the crop, so much at the mercy of fluctuating prices and foreign-imposed quota system. Efforts are being made to diversify production and to encourage mining and light industry. Coffee, cocoa, bauxite and tobacco are quite substantial exports now, and ferro-nickel exports began in 1973. The rate of economic growth in 1973 and 1974 was 8.9%, one of the highest in the hemisphere; in 1975 it was 4.7% and in 1976 5.0%.
Exports (f.o.b.) in 1976 totalled US$708.6m. and imports (c.i.f.) US$932.8m. compared with US$893.8m. and US$888.6m. in 1975.
The Dominican Republic is also trying to build up its tourist trade, and has much to offer in the way of natural beauty and old colonial architecture, which is disappearing so fast in so many other parts of the New World. The climate is tropical. The rainy months are May and June, September to November. The temperature does not vary much during the year and is usually about 24°-30°C.

Santo Domingo, the capital and chief seaport, population now about 1 million, has many fine Colonial buildings, including a fine Isabeline

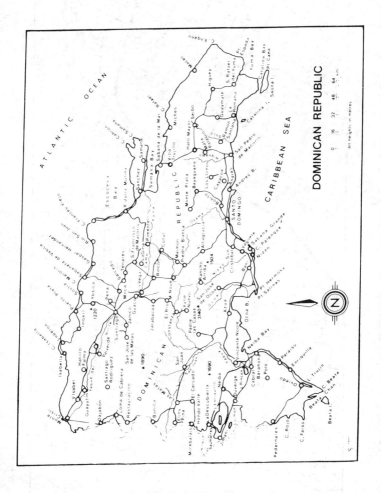

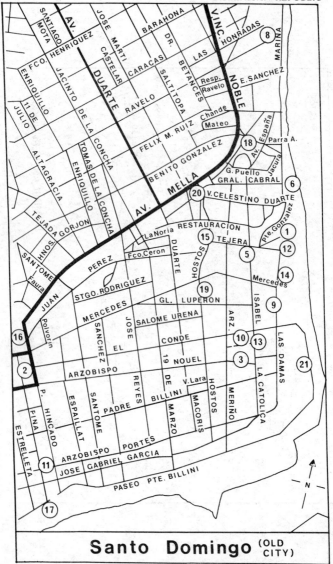

Santo Domingo (OLD CITY)

Gothic cathedral, the first to be founded in the New World, the splendid administrative buildings (Casas Reales), now a museum, and several churches, detailed below. There are, besides, several splendid ruins, such as San Nicolás, the first stone-built hospital in the Americas, and San Francisco, both on Calle Hostos. The 16th century castle, Alcázar de Colón, has been reconstructed and splendidly furnished with period furniture. The 16th century Jesuit Convent has been turned into a National Pantheon. The Government, with Spanish help, has instituted a comprehensive restoration programme for Colonial buildings. The city was the first capital of Spanish America; the restored early 16th century buildings and ruins in the old part, on the W bank of the River Ozama, are of the greatest interest. The principal ones are as follows:

Cathedral Basílica Menor de Santa María, Primada de América, Isabel La Católica esq. Nouel. First stone laid by Diego Colón, son of Cristóbal, in 1514. Architect: Alonzo Rodríguez. Finished 1540. First bishop to serve, Alessandro Geraldini. Remains of Christóbal Colón found in 1877 during restoration work. In 1892, Government of Spain donated tomb in which remains now rest, behind the high altar.

Torre del Homenaje inside Fortaleza Ozama, reached through the mansion of Rodrigo Bastidas (later the founder of Santa Marta in Colombia) on Calle Las Damas, which is now completely restored. Construction 1505-07. Oldest fortress in America, constructed by Nicolás de Ovando, whose house, further along the street has been restored and turned into a splendid hotel.

Museo de Las Casas Reales up Calle Las Damas on left, in a reconstructed early 16th-century building, which was the legal and administrative centre for the country until recent times; in colonial days it was the Palace of the Governors and Captains-General, and of the *Real Audiencia* and Chancery of the Indies. It is an excellent museum dealing with the colonial period of the island (often has special exhibits); entry US$0.50; open 0900-1200, 1430-1730.

Alcázar de Colón at the end of Las Damas, constructed by Diego Colón 1510-14. For six decades it was the seat of the Spanish Crown in the New World. Sacked by Drake in 1586. Now completely restored; entry US$0.75, also gets you into the Viceregal Museum (Museo Virreinal) just across the park; interesting. Open 0900-1200, 1430-1730.

Casa del Cordón, Isabel La Católica esq. Emiliano Tejera, built in 1503 by Francisco de Garay who accompanied Colón on his first voyage to Hispaniola. Named for the cord of the Fraciscan Order, sculpted above the entrance.

Monasterio de San Francisco, Hostos esq. E. Tejera, first monastery in America, constructed in the first decade of the 16th century, now in ruins. Sacked by Drake and suffered destruction by earthquakes in 1673 and 1751.

Reloj de Sol (sundial) built 1753, near end of Las Damas, under order of General Francisco de Rubio y Penaranda; by its side is,

Capilla de Nuestra Senora de Los Remedios.

La Ataranza, near the Alcázar, a 16th-century building which served as a warehouse. Presently restored and contains shops, bars and restaurants.

Hospital-Iglesia de San Nicolás de Bari (ruins), Hostos between Mercedes and Luperón, began in 1509 by Nicolás de Ovando, completed 1552. Sacked by Drake. Probably one of the best constructed buildings of the period, it survived many

Key to Map of Santo Domingo

1. Castle of Columbus (Alcázar de Colón); 2. Independence Arch (Altar de la Patria); 3. Cathedral (with tomb of Columbus); 5. House of the Cord (Casa del Cordón); 6. Columbus' ceiba tree; 8. Fountain of Columbus; 9. Pantheon (Convento de San Ignacio); 10. Plaza Colón; 11. Puerta de la Misericordia; 12. Puerta de San Diego; 13. Borgella Palace; 14. Sundial; 15. Church and Monastery of S. Francisco (ruins); 16. Fort of La Concepción (ruins); 17. Fort of San Gil (ruins); 18. Fort of Santa Bárbara (ruins); 19. Hospital of San Nicolás de Bari (ruins); 20. Church of San Antón (ruins); 21. Tower of Homage (Torre del Homenaje).

earthquakes and hurricanes. In 1911 some of its walls were knocked down because they posed a hazard to passers-by; also the last of its valuable wood was taken.

Convento de San Ignacio de Loyola (Pantheon), Las Damas between Mercedes and El Conde. Finished in 1743. Restored 1955 and contains memorials to many of the country's heroes and patriots. It also contains an ornate tomb built before his death for the dictator Trujillo, the "Benefactor of the Fatherland", but his remains do not lie there.

Iglesia de Santa Bárbara and the ruins of its fort. Off Mella to left near Calle J. Parra, near end of Isabel La Católica. Built in 1574. Sacked by Drake in 1586, destroyed by a hurricane in 1591. Reconstructed at the beginning of the 17th century. Behind the church are the ruins of the fort, where one can get a view of the harbour and the surrounding neighbourhoods of the city.

Convento de los Dominicanos, built in 1510. Here in 1538 the first university in the Americas was founded, named for Santo Tomás de Aquino, now bearing the title of the Universidad Autónoma de Santo Domingo. It has a unique ceiling which shows the medieval concept that identified the elements of the universe, the classical gods and the Christian icons in one system. The Sun is God, the 4 evangelists are the planetary symbols Mars, Mercury, Jupiter and Saturn. The University has moved to a site in the suburbs.

Iglesia de la Regina Angelorum, built 1537, contains a wall of silver near one of its altars.

Iglesia del Carmen, built in 1564 at side of Capilla de San Andrés, contains interesting sculpture in wood of Christ.

Puerta del Conde (Baluarte de 27 de Febrero), at the end of El Conde in the Parque Independencia. Named for the Conde de Peñalva, who helped defend the city against William Penn in 1655. Restored in 1976, now under it lie the remains of Sánchez, Mella and Duarte, the 1844 independence leaders.

Puerta de la Misericordia, Palo Hincado con Arzobispo Portes. So named because people fled under it for protection during earthquakes and hurricanes. It forms part of the wall that used to surround the colonial city. It is interesting to note that the wall now forms a part of many of the houses and shops of Ciudad Nueva. It was here on Feb. 27, 1844 that Mella fired the first shot in the struggle for independence from Haiti.

Capilla de La Virgen del Rosario, on the other side of the Río Ozama near the Molinos Dominicanos at the end of Av. Olegario Vargas. It was the first church constructed in America, restored in 1943.

Museo Duartiano, Isabel La Católica 138. Contains items linked with the Independence struggle and Duarte the national hero.

Iglesia de las Mercedes, dating from 1555.

Puerta de San Diego, near Alcázar.

Palacio de Borgella, Isabel la Católica, near Plaza Colón.

Ruins of Fuerte de la Concepción, corner Mella and Palo Hincado.

Ruins of Fuerte de San Gil, Paseo de Pte. Billini, near end of Calle Pina.

Ruins of Iglesia de San Antón, off Mella, near V. Celestino Duarte.

There are fine avenues in the outer city, especially Av. George Washington, Av. Independencia, Av. Bolívar and Av. Abraham Lincoln. The ancient gate at Calle Pina and Arzobispo Portes lends itself to photography. Among the attractive parks are Parque Independencia and Parque Eugenio M. de Hostos. A trip to the new Botanical Gardens and Zoo N of the city is well worth while; the old gardens and zoo off Av. Bolívar are now a children's amusement park. The 1955/56 World's Fair grounds, which once served as a magnificent showcase for national achievements in art and architecture, are now run-down government offices and law courts. The national museum collection has been moved to the Museo del Hombre Dominicano, which forms part of a new cultural centre also including the ultra-modern national theatre and national library; there is also an art gallery. There is duty-free shopping in the freeport zone. The city has the oldest university (Universidad Autónoma de Santo Domingo, now on a new site in the SW of the city) in the hemisphere; it was founded in 1538. The new pink stone National Capitol is worth seeing. Many beaches E of city: Boca Chica, Caribe, Guayacanes. Boca Chica is a shallow lagoon with a shale beach which, despite its reputation, has no facilities, and is poor for swimming. Guayacanes and Embassy beaches are much better, but tend to be overcrowded at the weekends. Buses to San Pedro de Macorís and beyond will drop you, and pick you up again, at the turn-off to the beaches. On the road to the airport are Los Tres Ojos de Agua, three impressive water-filled caves which are worth a visit. There is excellent scuba diving at La Caleta, a small beach near the turn-off to the airport, on the Autopista de las Américas.

Hotels

	Address	Rooms	Single	Double
Loew's Dominicano†	Av. Anacaona	316	22-32	27-36
Santo Domingo†	Av. Independencia y Av. Abraham Lincoln	220	25-35	35-40
El Embajador†	Av. Sarasota	320	21-27	25-33
Hispaniola†	Av. Independencia y Av. Abraham Lincoln	165	24-30	31-36
Jaragua	Av. Independencia	253	22	26
Comercial*	Calle Hostos, near Calle El Conde	75	11.50	16
Continental*†	Calle Máximo Gómez, near Av. Independencia	100	22	28
Nautilus	Av. Las Américas, near Tres Ojos	45	10	14-18
Hostal Nicolás de Ovando*†	Calle Las Damas	60	20	25
Villas Las Américas	Av. Las Américas 96	36	10	13

*Convenient to centre.   †Swimming pool and fully air-conditioned

Other hotels include *Holiday Inn,* near the *Jaragua; Naco,* US$18 s, 23 d; *San Gerónimo,* US$18 s, 22 d; *Comodoro,* US$18 s, 22 d; *Napolitano,* US$20 s, 25 d; *Neptuno Inn,* Av. Jorge Washington, US$11 s, 14 d; and *Cervantes,* US$14s, 17 d. The *Sheraton* on Av. Independencia opened early in 1978. *Lina,* reputedly the best hotel in Santo Domingo, also recommended, US$22 s, 28 d, good restaurant, swimming pool and air-conditioning. *Hostal Nicolás de Ovando,* a restored Colonial mansion, in the oldest part of the city, is warmly recommended for comfort, quiet, food and atmosphere.

Three cheaper hotels, the *Victoria,* Calle 19 de Marzo, US$3.85 s, with shower; *Aida,* El Conde and Santome, and *La Fama,* Av. Mella 141, US$7 a room, have been recommended. *Pensión Ana,* Av. Mella 139, 2nd floor, US$2.25 each in shared room, shower; *Estrella,* on Isabel La Católica near cathedral, looks basic but is central for old city; *Hotel Princess,* near corner of Calle Caracas and Av. Duarte, US$3.50 s, near terminal for airport bus, noisy; also *Colón,* Emiliano Tejera 17, US$6 per bed, clean, honest.

Restaurants In hotels: *Marios,* on Av. Mella, near Párque Independencia; *El Restaurant Lina,* Av. Máximo Gómez, very good, but better during the week than at weekends when crowded and service is not as good; *Pizzeria El Vesuvio,* Av. George Washington and also in Av. Tiradientes; *Chantilly,* Av. Máximo Gómez; *Restaurant Italia,* Calle Juan Isidro Jiménez; *El Cantábrico,* for splendid seafood. Others are: *Napolitano,* same street; *El Dragón,* Av. Independencia; *Bar-Restaurant Pan-Americano,* Calle El Conde (excellent meal, US$1.50; *Cari Mar,* Av. George Washington (good sea food); *Paco's Café,* Plaza Independencia, recommended. Many good ones along the Malecón (Av. George Washington) on the seafront. Also try *Via Veneta* on Av. Independencia near the *Hotel Jaragua* (Italian cuisine); and *La Fromagerie* on Av. Pasteur, four blocks up from the Malecón (French cuisine, cheese dishes and fondue). *La Plaza Rendezvous,* alongside the Cathedral on Isabel La Católica, is a good place for snacks and drinks in the old part of the city.

Airport 23 km. out of town. Departure tax US$3.50. Taxi to town US$10 (max. 5 people) or less if you bargain with drivers in the car park. Bus to town from Restaurante La Caleta; turn right out of airport compound along main road; walk to end of road (25 minutes), turn left and walk to La Caleta. Bus passes every ½ hour, until 2200. Buses back leave from Calles Caracas and José Martí, US$0.30. Ask driver to drop you at nearest point to airport. Agencia de Viajes Vallentín (Tel.: 682-6376) runs a minibus to the airport, US$3, which will pick you up at your hotel.

Clubs Español, Naco, Arroyo Hondo, Santo Domingo Country Club.

All America Cables and Radio, Inc. *Hotel El Embajador.*

Royal Mail Lines Agency Frederick Schad, C. por A. José Gabriel Garcia 26, P.O. Box 941.

Library Instituto Cultural Domínico-Americano, corner of Av. Abraham Lincoln and Calle Antonio de la Maza. English and Spanish books.

Night Clubs at *Hotel Embajador* and *Hispaniola;* La Voz de Santo Domingo; La Fuente, next to *Hotel Jaragua,* is the most classy; Morocco, in the new Cinema Centro which has six cinemas and a wine bar; Sui Genaris on the Malecón; Teatro Agua; Luz (Jockey Club); Chantilly. **Bars:** La Pipa; Moulin Rouge.

Casinos in *Hotel El Embajador, Jaragua* and *Naco.*

Buses City bus fares are US$0.15, but the service is limited.

Taxis *Carreras* are private taxis, can be expensive; settle price before getting in. *Carros públicos* are shared taxis usually operating on set routes; fare is US$0.25 each, though can be more for longer routes. Fares are higher at Christmas time. Públicos also run on long-distance routes; ask around to find the cheapest.

Car Rentals Avis, Hertz, Via, Neily, El Mundo, National, Dial.

Tourist Office Dirección General de Turismo, César Nicolás Penson 59, at corner of Calle Rosa Duarte, Tel.: 688-5537. Useful information but no street map (obtainable from Esso). Also in arrival area at airport.

Travel Agents Viajes Internacionales, El Conde 15; Servicios Turísticos, Av. George Washington 67; Metro Tours, Ataranza 3, Sector Colonial; Santoni, José Joaquín Pérez 6.

Shopping Duty-free Cento de los Héroes (items bought here will be delivered to your 'plane or ship); Enbajador hotel shop; departure lounge at airport; all purchases must be in US dollars. Mercado Modelo, on Av. Mella esq. Santome, include gift shops.

Main Post Office Calle Tejera, opp. Alcázar de Colón. Open 0700-1200, 1400-1800, Mon.-Fri.

Sports *Golf:* Country Club, Santo Domingo; Casa de Campo Hotel in La Romana; some hotels can arrange guest passes. Polo matches at weekends at Sierra Prieta, Santo Domingo. Baseball at Quisqueya stadium, water skiing/deep-sea fishing at Náutico Club, Boca Chica beach. Basketball, boxing and wrestling matches can also be seen in Santo Domingo.

Health Specialists in most branches of medicine can be found at 22 Av. Independencia. Fees are high but care is good. Dr. Yunen's Clinic, at same address, recommended for those needing hospitalization.

Other cities easily reached by visitors are Santiago de Los Caballeros, capital of the Cibao valley in the north-central part of the country; San Francisco de Macorís, La Vega and Moca, also important towns of the Cibao; Puerto Plata, chief Atlantic port: San Juan de la Maguana in the west-central part of the Republic; San Pedro de Macorís, La Romana, and Barahona, three interesting towns along the Caribbean coast. Sosúa, near Puerto Plata on the N coast, has a superb bathing beach and is popular with the well-to-do and the diplomatic set.

Santiago de Los Caballeros is the second largest city in the Republic. It is much smaller, quieter, cleaner, cooler and "slower" than the capital and can be easily reached by bus (US$2.50). Places worth visiting are the

Universidad Católica Madre y Maestra (founded 1962), and the Monumento a Los Héroes de la Restauración, which was originally constructed by Trujillo as a monument to himself. From this hill of the monument there is an excellent view of the city and the Cordillera Septentrional. There is an Instituto Superior de Agricultura in the Herradura on the other side of the Río Yaque del Norte (km. 6). A carriage around the city should not be passed up. Price depends upon the length of the ride and how well one can bargain.

Hotels: *Don Diego,* on outskirts, US$14 s, 20 d, has restaurant and night club, very good; *Matum,* US$16 s, 23 d, luxury, with night club; *Mercedes,* US$5 per room; *Corona,* away from centre, US$7 s, 10 d; *Mercedes,* US$6 s, 10 d. A new hotel is under construction on the corner of Del Sol and Mella. It will be 1st class but completion date is unknown. Some good *pensiones* are the *Roma* (Del Sol 60), *Diri* (las Carreras and Juan Pablo Duarte), and *Alaska* (Benito Monción and 16 de Agosto; there is no sign, just go up to the 2nd floor).

Restaurants The best are the *Pez Dorado* (Chinese and Dominican, the restaurant of the *Hotel Don Diego.* Excellent sandwich and pizza places are *Olé* (Av. Juan Pablo Duarte, esq., Independencia), *El Edén* (Av. Sadhala), *Dinós* (formerly *Capri,* Del Sol). Others include *Las Antillas* (Parque Duarte), *El Mexicano* (Ensanche El Ensueño), *Yaque* (Restauración), and *La Suiza.*

Buses in Santiago US$0.10. Públicos charge US$0.15 in the city. There is a Tourist office on the 2nd floor of the Town Hall (Ayuntamiento) on Av. Juan Pablo Duarte. The markets are located at Del Sol and España, Av. J. Armado Bernúdez and near the lower part of 16 de Agosto.

About half-way from the capital to Santiago is **Bonao** (Hotel: *Yaraví Rooms,* US$6 s, 9 d).

Puerto Plata, the chief town on the Atlantic coast, is reached by bus from Santo Domingo (US$3.50), or by taxi (US$5). Bus to Long Beach. A visit to the colonial fortress, La Fortaleza San Felipe, at the end of The Malécon, and a ride in the "teleférico" are recommended. The latter goes some 1,000 metres up behind the town to the summit of Isabel de Torres, with a statue of Christ, craft shops, café and some fine gardens with a view of the coast and mountains. (Cost US$1 for cable-car round trip; from town to *teleférico* station is US$2 by taxi, US$1 by colectivo. (The cable-car does not run on Tues. or Wed.).

Hotels *Hotel Montemar,* on beach, all facilities, US$14 s, 21 d; *Hotel Castilla,* in centre of town, US$5, splendid atmosphere. *Hotel Caracol,* on sea front, modern, US$10 s, 17.50 d. In town, *Lira* and *Colonial,* US$10 s. The modern *Hotel Miramar,* US$11 s, is not recommended. At nearby Cofresi beach, a holiday centre with cabins, US$10 p.p., 25% more at weekends.

To the east of Puerto Plata is **Sosúa,** which has an excellent beach in a small bay. There are many cabins and houses for rent here. Farther to the east is **Río San Juan,** which has a beautiful lagoon called Gri-Gri and a nice beach. Between Río San Juan and Samaná, on the coast, is Nagua *(Hotel-Restaurant China).* A new airport is being built to serve Puerto Plata and Sosúa.

On the peninsula of **Samaná** is the city of the same name. Recently the entire city was reconstructed. Many new restaurants and hotels have been built, but as of yet many of the new installations are not functioning. A new airport for the peninsula was recently inaugurated and the city should be fully functional soon. There are several beautiful offshore islands here too. In fact, the whole peninsula is beautiful but many beaches are accessible only by boat (the sailors in Samaná charge the earth to take visitors out).

Communications with the capital rather difficult: either Santo Domingo-Nagua (taxi US$3.50), new road Nagua-Sánchez-Samaná (taxi US$1); or Santo Domingo-Sabana (taxi US$3, Plas Batista, Tel.: 688-7419) and boat Sabana-Samaná, US$1 (better). (Alas del Caribe now has flights to the airport from Santo Domingo). Road Puerto Plata-Samaná excellent, bus US$4, 3½ hours. Road to Hato Mayor is bad, and from Hato Mayor to San Pedro de Macorio unpaved.

To the west of Puerto Plata is the resort of Cofresu. Punta Rucia farther to the west has a beautiful beach, but it is not well developed for tourists. If one plans to go from Santiago to Puerto Plata or Sosúa it is much more scenic and interesting to go by the old road, than the new one; the road is worse, but the scenery is well worth it. At one point the road passes La Cumbre, which used to be a Trujillo mansion, but is now the property of the Secretary of Agriculture. Between Santiago and Montecristi, in the Yaque del Norte valley, is **Mao** (*Hotel Caoba,* US$7.50 d, 15.50 a/c).

Monte Cristi is a dusty little town in the northwest corner of the country. One can visit the house of Máximo Gómez, a Dominican patriot who played an important role in the struggle for Cuban independence and in the Dominican Restoration. Very near Monte Cristi is the peak named El Moro which has a beach (very rocky) on its east side and from the top there is a good view of the surrounding area. There are a couple of decent hotels there (*Montechico,* on Bolaños beach, US$5.50 a room).

To the north of Santo Domingo, along the Carretera Duarte, is the city of **La Vega,** a quiet place in the heart of the Cibao Valley, the main agricultural region of the country. The town itself does not have much to offer for sights to see. (*Hotel Guaricano,* US$7.) Further along the road from La Vega on the right is the turn for Santo Cerro. From there one can get a fantastic view of the valley of La Vega Real. There is a small church one can visit. If one continues along the road to the other side of the hill and into the valley the ruins of La Vega Vieja can be seen. It was founded by Columbus but destroyed by an earthquake in 1564 and abandoned; it is presently undergoing restoration.

Further along the highway on the left is the turn for **Jarabacoa,** a beautiful town in the Cordillera Central which is becoming better developed for tourism every year. It is cooler here. It now has several hotels including *La Montaña,* US$9 s, and *Pinar Dorado,* US$16 s, US$18 d, new swimming pool; *Nacional,* in town, US$5 s, US$6.60 d. Also there are several clubs offering diversions such as golf, tennis and horseback riding. Further along the same road which goes to Jarabacoa is **Constanza,** situated in the Constanza Valley. The scenery is better here than in Jarabacoa, with many rivers, forests, waterfalls, etc. The valley is famous for its strawberries, mushrooms and ornamental flowers. (*Hotel Mi Caboña,* in valley outside, US$6.50 s, US$7.50 d.)

In the Cordillera Central near both of these towns is Pico Duarte, the highest in the Caribbean, measuring 3,075 metres in altitude. Before climbing it one must secure the permission of the army in Jarabacoa. (When doing this you will be told that mules are necessary for the ascent and they will try to hire them to you. But this is not true and if they are not wanted, they should be politely refused.)

To the west of Santo Domingo, one can visit **San Cristóbal** in the interior; it is interesting as the birthplace of the dictator Trujillo. A mansion, El Cerro, built for him by his admirers but never used by him, is open to visitors 0800-1700; it may become a casino (longish walk up hill). Trujillo's home, the Casa de Caoba (open 0900-1700) may be reached by a Land-Rover bus from behind the market though you may have to walk the last km., uphill. Nearby are La Toma pools for scenery and swimming. *Hotel San Cristóbal,* US$8.80 s, US$10.50 d. *Hotel Constitución,* US$5 s, US$6 d.

Haina, between S. Domingo and S. Cristóbal, is the main port of the country and has the world's largest sugar cane mill *(ingenio).* A good beach is Las Salinas to the west of Bani near Punta Salina. Azúa and Barahona have beautiful beaches also.

Further west near the Haitian border is the salt-water, below-sea-level Lago Enriquillo which also boasts crocodiles. Along the southern coast are many white sand beaches which offer the best snorkling and scuba diving in the Republic. Behind some of these beaches are cool fresh-water lagoons. One must explore for oneself, as this area is still underdeveloped for tourism.

San Juan de la Maguana is towards the Haitian border *(Hotel Maguana,* US$8 per room). Visit the "Corral de Los Indios" an ancient Indian meeting ground several km. north of the town. On the border is Jimani *(Hotel Jimani.* US$8 per room). Also visit **San José de las Matas,** a beautiful town to the SW of Santiago. A new hotel is presently under construction there. A new hotel is also planned for El Seibo in the east.

San Pedro de Macorís, a quiet town on the Caribbean coast now being developed for tourism *(Hotel Macorís,* US$9 s, 14 d). On nearby Juan Dolio beach are *Palmas de Mar* and *Punta Garza* bungalows (US$20 s, 30 d) and *Villas de Mar,* US$14 s, 17 d, near Boca Chica. E of San Pedro is **La Romana** *(Casa del Campo* and *Hotel La Romana),* both good but expensive at US$40 a room; *Roma,* much cheaper at US$6 s, 10 d. Further E still is **Punta Cana,** a newly opened resort with beautiful beaches to the N. Can be reached by air from Santo Domingo. Bungalows US$26 s, 38 d.

Barahona, on the coast near the Haitian border (US$3 by *público).* No public transport to the beautiful but rather distant beaches *(Hotel Guarocuya,* US$5 s, US$9 d, with shower, drinks and food dear, reported not well run).

In **Higüey** in the SE the main item to see is the Basilica de Nuestra Señora de la Altagracia. It is a very impressive modern building to which every year there is a pilgrimage on Jan. 20; the old 16th-century church is still standing.

There is a beautiful resort at Punta Cana on the east coast, but it is best to fly there from Santo Domingo (Alas del Caribe).

Boca de Yuma is an interesting little fishing village which is the scene of a deep-sea fishing tournament every year. It can be reached easily on a recently repaved road from Higüey.

Information for Visitors

How to get there There are cargo and passenger steamer services with Europe, New York, New Orleans, Puerto Rico, Jamaica, Curaçao, and connections with Aruba and all the Americas. There is no passenger service from the U.K. Air services are operated by Iberia, American, Eastern, Pan Am, Viasa, Aerocóndor, Prinair, and ALM. Dominicana flies between the U.S., Puerto Rico, Venezuela and the Dominican Republic; another local airline is Aerovías Quisqueyanas.

Documents No passport—only proof of identity—required for nationals of Canada, Jamaica, Mexico, USA (including Puerto Rico) and Venezuela. Citizens of Austria, Belgium, Denmark, France, West Germany, Israel, Italy, Japan,

Luxembourg, Netherlands, Panama, Spain, Switzerland and the U.K. need passports, but not visas, for stays of up to 90 days. All others need visas; entry may be refused to nationals of communist countries. Allow at least 15 days for visas to be granted. There is a US$2 charge for tourist cards, needed by all tourists; they may be bought in transit or on arrival.

All visitors should have an outward ticket. The airport police are on the lookout for illegal drugs. Backpackers especially can expect a thorough search of person and property.

Currency The official rate of exchange of RD$ to US dollars is one for one. But one can obtain between 15 and 20% more (depending on the quantity one wants to change and the amount of dollars in the country) for US bills and between 14 and 17% for travellers' cheques or money orders. There are many money changers along Isabel La Católica in Santo Domingo. Also many travel agencies change money. In Santiago the changers are near the Correo (post office), but good rates can be obtained at the Colmado El Parque (Del Sol esq. 30 de Marzo). Dominican currency may not be imported nor exported. Remember that if you use the free market you will not be able to change back into US$: that can only be done if you produce bank exchange slips.

Internal Travel Hitchhiking is perfectly possible, though bus and público services are fairly good. The transportation situation in the Republic is improving. In Santo Domingo and Santiago there are cars called *públicos* or *conchos* which travel certain routes. They are distinguished from private cars by different coloured licence plates. The fare is the same for any stop on the route (US$0.25 in Santo Domingo, 0.15 in Santiago). Certain longer routes cost more in Santo Domingo. One can also obtain a "carrera" from a público, i.e. one hires the público to go outside its normal route.

Between cities *públicos* also operate. There are usually fixed rates between cities, so inquire first before travelling. Bargaining can be important also. Travellers should also be warned that many drivers pack a truly incredible number of passengers in their cars, so the ride is often not that comfortable.

Buses There are more and more buses travelling between cities. In Santo Domingo two of the main companies are Expresos Dominicanos and Autobuses Metro. The former has its station on Av. Independencia near the Parque Independencia, and the latter at Estación La Ruta (Shell), Av. San Martín 154. They have buses to Bonao (1.25), La Vega (1.75), Santiago (2.50), Puerto Plata (3.50), San Pedro de Macorís (1.00) and the airport (2.00). La Romana, US$1.00; Jarabacoa, US$2.25; San Cristóbal, US$0.25. In the capital many buses leave from Parque Enriquillo (Av. Duarte and Ravelo) for various points, like Higüey, Nagua, San Francisco de Macorís, Miches, etc. In Santiago the stations of the Expresos Dominicanos are at the corner of San Luis and Beller and of the Metro at the corner of Av. Colón and Metropolitana.

Cost of Living This is rather high. The increase in 1975 was 16.6%, against 17.2% and 10.5% in 1973 and 1974 respectively. For tourists however, it is one of the cheapest countries in the Caribbean. The 1976 inflation rate was much reduced, to 7%.

Customs Duty-free import of 200 cigarettes or one box of cigars, plus one opened bottle of alcoholic liquor, is permitted.

Health It is not advisable to drink tap water. The better hotels will have bottled water.

Electricity 110 volts, 60 cycles A.C. current.

Tipping No need to tip hotel employees. Porters receive US$0.25 per bag; taxi drivers, no tip.

Food and Drink A truly excellent beer is made here, "Presidente". There are also many rums of varying qualities from good to excellent. Local dishes include *sancocho* (a type of stew made of local meats and vegetables, often including *plátanos, ñame* and *yautia*), *mondongo* (a tripe soup), *codida* (a soup of garbanzos, meat and vegetables), *chivo* (goat), the salads are often good, another good side dish is *tostones* (fried and flattened *plátanos), Quipes* (made of wheat and meat) and *pastelitos* (fried dough with meat or cheese inside) can be bought from street vendors. Also try *pipián*, goats' offal served as a stew. The traveller should be warned that Dominican food is rather on the greasy side, with most of the foods being fried. Another dish is *moro*, which is rice cooked with beans.

Folklore The national music and dance is called the *merengue*. The most popular dances are the *merengue* and the *salsa*. The truly typical and traditional merengue is played by a 3-man group called a "perico ripiao" which consist of a *tambora* (small drum), a *guirra* (a percussion instrument scraped by a metal rod) and an accordion.

Banks Royal Bank of Canada at Santo Domingo, La Romana, Puerto Plata, San Pedro de Macoris, Santiago de los Caballeros, and Valverde; Bank of Nova Scotia at Santo Domingo and Santiago. The Chase Manhattan Bank, Santo Domingo.Citibank, Santo Domingo; Bank of America, Santo Domingo; Banco de Santo Domingo.

Business Hours Shops: 0800-1200, 1300-1700 Mon.-Fri.; 0800-1200 Sat. Banks: 0800-1200 Mon.-Fri.

Newspapers The best daily papers are *Listín Diario, El Caribe, Ahora Nacional* and *Ultima Hora.*

Maps Arco (Tel.: 565-7756) has map of Hispaniola; Esso (Tel.: 565-6641) Santo Domingo and Dominican Republic. Texaco also produce a good map of the country, though neither theirs nor the Esso map is available at the Tourist Office.

British Ambassador and Consul-General at Santo Domingo (Av. Independencia 506, Santo Domingo, P.O. Box 1352).

U.S. Embassy and Consulate, César Nicolás Penson; Tel.: (embassy) 682-2171; (consulate) 689-2111.

American Express Agents Santo Domingo: Vimenca, Av. Abraham Lincoln 72-A, Tel.: 533-1303.

Holidays

Jan. 1: New Year's Day
Jan. 6: Epiphany
Jan. 21: Our Lady of Altagracia
Jan. 26: Duarte Day
Feb. 27: Independence Day
April 14: Panamerican Day
May 1: Labour Day
July 16: Founding of Sociedad La Trinitaria
Aug. 16: Restoration Day
Sep. 24: Our Lady of Las Mercedes
Oct. 12: Columbus Day
Oct. 24: United Nations Day
Nov. 1: All Saints
Dec. 25: Christmas Day

Our most profound thanks again to Federico Bertaccini, recently of the Universidad Católica Madre y Maestra, Santiago, for adding immeasurably to the value of this section. Following a four-day visit in March 1978, the Editor has himself been able to make a modest contribution to expanding the Dominican section. Thanks also to Mary Cann and Simon Pearson.

PUERTO RICO

THE COMMONWEALTH OF PUERTO RICO, the smallest and most easterly island of the Greater Antilles, is the first Overseas Commonwealth Territory (defined as a "free and associated State") of the U.S.A. Spanish is the first language but the citizenship is U.S. and English is widely spoken. Puerto Rico lies at the north of the Caribbean sea about a thousand miles south-east of Miami between the island of Hispaniola and the Virgin Islands, which give it some shelter from the open Atlantic, and is between longitudes 66° and 67° west and latitudes 18° and 18°30′ north.

Almost rectangular in shape, slightly smaller than Jamaica, it measures 153 km. in length (east to west), 58 km. in width, and has a total land area of some 8,768 square km.

Old volcanic mountains, long inactive, occupy a large part of the interior of the island, with the highest peak, Cerro de Punta, at 1,325 metres in the Cordillera Central. N of the Cordillera is the Karst country where the limestone has been acted upon by water to produce a series of small steep hills and deep holes, both conical in shape. The mountains are surrounded by a coastal plain with the Atlantic shore beaches cooled all the year round by trade winds which make the temperatures of 28-30°C bearable in the summer. Temperatures in the winter drop to the range 21-26°C and the climate all the year round is very agreeable.

History Puerto Rico was discovered by Columbus, accompanied by a young nobleman, Juan Ponce de León, on November 19, 1493. Attracted by tales of gold, Ponce obtained permission to colonize Borinquén, as it was called by the natives. In 1508 he established the first settlement at Caparra, a small village not far from the harbour of San Juan. A year later the Spanish Crown appointed him the first Governor. In 1521, however, the village was moved to the present site of Old San Juan as the former site was declared unhealthy and not advantageous to commercial enterprise. In that year Ponce de León was mortally wounded in the conquest of Florida.

Because of Puerto Rico's excellent location at the gateway to Latin America, it played an important part in defending the Spanish empire against attacks from French, English and Dutch invaders until the Spanish-American war, when Spain ceded the island to the United States in 1898. The inhabitants became U.S. citizens in 1917, with their own Senate and House of Delegates, and in 1948 they elected their own Governor, who was authorized to appoint his own Cabinet and members of the Supreme Court. In 1952 Puerto Rico became a Commonwealth voluntarily associated with the United States.

Government The Governor (1976-80) is Sr. Carlos Romero Barceló, of the New Progressive Party, which favours Puerto Rico's full accession to the USA as the 51st State. The other main party is the Popular Democratic Party, which held office

1948-68 and 1972-76 and favours the island's existing Commonwealth status. Pro-independence groups receive little support. Puerto Ricans do not vote in US federal elections; nor do they pay federal taxes when resident on the island.

There is a population of about 3.2 million in Puerto Rico, of whom all speak Spanish and a large majority English; half of them live in urban areas. The country is a strange mixture of very new and very old, exhibiting the frank, open American way of life yet retaining the sheltered and more formal Spanish influences. The economy depends on tourism (in the 1976/77 fiscal year there were 1.8m. visitors altogether) and sugar.

Social Statistics Income per head is well over US$2,000 a year, among the highest in Latin America. Life expectancy is now 71 years, and illiteracy has been reduced to about 10%. Great economic progress has been made in the past thirty years, as a result of the "Operation Bootstrap" industrialization programme supported by the US and Puerto Rican governments.

San Juan Founded in 1510, San Juan, the capital (population about 850,000) spreads several miles along the N coast and also inland. The nucleus is Old San Juan, the old walled city on a tongue of land between the Atlantic and San Juan bay. It has a great deal of charm and character; the Institute of Culture restores and renovates old buildings, museums and places of particular beauty. The narrow streets of Old San Juan, some paved with small grey-blue blocks which were cast from the residues of iron furnaces in Spain and brought over as ships' ballast, are lined with colonial-style churches, houses and mansions, in a much better state of repair than is usual elsewhere in Latin America.

Some of the restored and interesting buildings to visit include La Fortaleza, the Governor's Palace, built between 1533 and 1540 as a fortress but greatly expanded in the 19th century (open 0900-1100, 1330-1615 Mon.-Fri.); the Cathedral built in the 16th century but extensively restored in the 19th and 20th, in which the body of Juan Ponce de León rests in a marble tomb; the tiny Cristo Chapel with its silver altar, built after a young man competing in 1753 in the horse-race that was part of the San Juan festival celebrations plunged with his horse over the precipice at that very spot; El Morro, built in 1591 to defend the entrance to the harbour (open daily 0800-1700, entry for adults US$0.50, for children free); the 11-hectare Fort San Cristóbal, completed in 1772 to support El Morro and to defend the landward side of the city, with its five independent units connected by tunnels and dry moats, rising 46 metres above the ocean (open daily 0800-1700, entry for adults US$0.50, for children free); the Dominican Convent built in the early 16th century, later used as a headquarters by the US Army and now the office of the Institute of Culture; the 16th-century San José church, now being restored; the early 18th century Casa de los Contrafuertes, now containing specialized museums (open 0900-1700); the Casa Blanca, built in 1523 by the family of Ponce de León, who lived in it for 250 years until it became the residence for the Spanish and then the US military commanders-in-chief, and is now a historical museum (open 0900-1700, except Mon.); the Alcaldía, or City Hall, built 1604-1789 (open Mon.-Fri. 0800-1615 except holidays); the Intendencia, formerly the Spanish colonial exchequer; the naval arsenal, now closed for restoration, which was the last place in Puerto Rico to be evacuated by the Spanish in 1898; and the Casa del Callejón, a restored 18th-century house containing two colonial museums, the architectural (open 0900-1700) and the Puerto

Rican Family (open 0900-1200, 1300-1630, entry for adults US$0.25, for children free).

Old San Juan is also the central shopping area for goods from all over the world and particularly popular with visitors from Latin America and the United States, as in comparison with those countries the prices are very reasonable. Old San Juan is also the centre for the night life unless one visits the hotels. Discotheques and dance clubs abound and Spanish flamenco dancing is a great attraction.

Excursions Of the many excursions around metropolitan San Juan a visit to the Bacardi rum plant is very pleasant. A 10-cent ferry ride crosses every 15 minutes to Cataño where mini-buses (25 cents) go direct to the gates of the plant. (Do not take a taxi inside the plant as it is expensive and the walk from the main gate to the pavilion is very short, along a tree-lined drive.) Young girls conduct tours around the plant every hour, travelling from one building to the next by a little open motor "train".

The University of Puerto Rico at Río Piedras is in a lovely area. (Bus from Río Piedras to Fajardo for the little train, US$1—see next page.) The University Museum has archaeological and historic exhibitions, and also monthly art exhibitions.

On Sundays and holidays at 1430 and 1630 there are trips around the bay lasting 1½ hours. The boat passes the City Wall, the San Juan Gate and La Fortaleza. Another boat trip is around the Torrecilla Lagoon, which takes two hours and shows passengers the mangrove forests and the beautiful birds in the bird sanctuary. This runs daily, except Monday, at 1430.

Museums Apart from those in historic buildings listed above, there are the Children's Museum in an 18th-century powder-house in El Morro grounds (Tues.-Sun. 0900-1200. 1300-1700); the Pablo Casals Museum beside San José church, with Casals' cello and other memorabilia (Tues.-Sat. 0900-1200. 1300-1600. Sun; 1200-1700); the Museum of Puerto Rican Art (daily 0900-1700); the Casa del Libro (Mon.-Sat. 1100-1700); and the Museum of the Sea on Pier One (daily 0900-1700).

Other museums include a military museum at Fort San Jerónimo (open from 0900-1700 25 cents, free Sat.); the Ponce de León Museum at Caparra, Puerto Rico's first Spanish settlement, which has many exhibits from the period when the Taino Indians inhabited the township (open 0900-1700, closed Sunday); and the Adolfo de Hostos archaeological museum behind the Tapia theatre on Plaza Colón (in the old public baths, open Tues.-Sat. 1000-1700, Sun. 1200-1900).

The Interior Out of the metropolitan area "on the island" are a variety of excursions; as it is a small island it is possible to see forested mountains and desert-like areas in only a short time.

An interesting round trip through the eastern half of the island, starting E from San Juan, is as follows: San Juan-Río Piedras-Fajardo-El-Yunque-Vieques-Culebra-Humacao-Yabucoa-Guayama-Cayey-Aibonito-Barranquitas-Bayamón-San Juan.

El Yunque is a tropical forest of 11,200 hectares with some 240 varieties of different trees. The complete area is a bird sanctuary. Trails (very stony) to the various peaks: El Yungue itself, Mount Britton, Los Picachos. As more than 100,000 million gallons of rain fall in a year, another name for the forest is Rain Forest. Visitors need not worry unduly as storms are usually brief and plenty of shelter is provided. (No buses through the national forests, unfortunately; El Yunque is reached *via* Route 3 from San Juan towards Fajardo, and then right on Route 191; a superb and cheap typical restaurant on Route 191 in the forest.) A narrow-gauge steam railway offers a novel method of travel for Fajardo to El Yunque on Sundays, taking an hour for the return journey. Adults US$1.75 and children US$1.25. From Fajardo beach launches ply (US$2) to the comparatively unspoilt islands of Vieques and Culebra. One of the prettiest parts of Puerto Rico, which should be visited, lies S of Humacao, between Yabucoa and Guayama.

A round trip through the western half of the island would take in Ponce, the second city (reached by motorway from San Juan *via* Caguas), Guayanilla, San Germán, Parguera, Boquerón, Mayaguez (the third city), Aguadila, Quebradillas and Arecibo, with side trips to the Maricao State Forest and fish hatchery, the Río Abajo State Forest and Lake Dos Bocas (launch trips all day), the pre-Columbian ceremonial ball-park near Utuado (open 0900-1700, free), and the Arecibo observatory (open Sun. p.m.).

Ponce has a very fine art museum, donated by a Foundation established by Luis A. Ferré, Governor 1968-72. on a modern building now famous. It contains a representative collection of European and American art of the last five centuries. (Open 1000-12000, 1300-1600, Mon. and Wed.-Fri., 100-1600 Sat., 1000-1700 Sun. and holidays, closed Tues.; entry US$1 for adults, US$0.25 for children under 12.) The cathedral is also worth a look, and so is the polychromatic fire-station, built for a fair in 1883 and now used by the information office.

Near Parguera fishing village on the west part of the south coast is an area of phosphorescent water, occurring through a permanent population of minescent dinoflagellates, a tiny form of marine life, which produce sparks of chemical light when disturbed. A launch leaves Villa Parguera pier nightly at 1930 at a cost of US$1.50 p.p. A nearby fine beach, Playa Boquerón, has cabins to stay at.

San Germán is a town of some Colonial-type charm; it was the second town to be founded on the island and has preserved its traditional atmosphere. The beautiful little Porta Coeli chapel on the plaza contains a small museum of religious art. (Normally open 0900-1200, 1400-1600 but reported closed for restoration.)

As there is a large forest area, there are several excursions to various countryside resorts. The Maricao State Forest (Monte del Estado) is open from 0600 to 1800, and is a beautiful forest with magnificent views. Also the views are marvellous at the Toro Negro State Forest, open from 0800 to 1700, and at Río Abajo State Forest (open 0600-1800) where there is a swimming pool and various picnic spots. It is approached through breathtaking views of the karst hills and the Dos Bocas Lake. Free launch trips are offered on this lake at 0700, 1000, 1400 and 1700. The trips last two hours and are provided by the Public Works Department.

Sports The main attractions are water sports. All the hotels provide instruction and equipment for water skiing, snorkeling, boating and day trips to areas of aquatic interest. Fishing-boat charters are available.

Swimming from most beaches is safe, but the best beaches nearest to San Juan are those at Isla Verde in front of the main hotels; there are twelve "balneario" beaches round the island where lockers, showers and parking places are provided; there are also deserted beaches "out on the island".

Boating Puerto Rico's coastline is protected in many places by coral reefs and cays and they are fun to visit and explore. Sloops can be hired at US$35 a day, with crew, and hold six passengers.

There are three marinas at Fajardo, one small one at Miramar (San Juan) and one near Humacao.

Deep-sea fishing is popular and more than 30 world records have been broken in Puerto Rican waters, where blue and white marlin, sailfish, wahoo, dolphin, mackerel and tarpon, to mention a few, are a challenge to the angler.

Surfing   The most popular beaches for surfing are the Pine Beach Grove in Isla Verde (San Juan) and Punta Higuero, Route 413 between Aguadilla and Rincón on the west coast, where several international surfing competions have been held.

Golf   The Cerromar and Dorado Beach hotels in Dorado have excellent 36-hole championship golf courses, there are several 18-hole courses, and in Ponce the hotel *International Ponce* makes arrangements for guests to play at a nearby country club's 9-hole course.

Cockfighting   The season is from November 1 to August 31. This sport, peculiar to Latin America, is held at the new, air-conditioned Coliseo Gallistico in Isla Verde, near the Holiday Inn. Wed. and Fri. 2030; Sat. and Sun. 1400. Admission from US$4 to US$10.

Racing   El Comandante, Route 3, Km. 5.5, is one of the hemisphere's most beautiful race courses. Races are held all the year round (Wednesday, Friday and Sunday). First race is at 1415. Wednesday is Ladies' Day. Children under 12 not admitted at any time.

Riding   Rancho Borinquén, at Carolina, near San Juan, rents horses at US$7 an hour, or US$15 for half-day.

Taxis   Hertz Rent-A-Car System, Isla Verde International Airport; Lease Division Caribe Motors, 519 Fernández Juncos; Metro Taxicabs, Inc., Km. 3.3 Route 3, Isla Verde; Metropolitan Taxi Cabs Inc., 165 Quisquella; National Car Rental System, 1102 Magdalena Ave.; University Taxi, Río Piedras. A small car may be hired for US$24 for 24 hours, unlimited mileage (national driving licence preferred to international licence). All taxis are metered and charge 40 cents for initial charge and 10 cents for every additional ⅓ km.; 25 cents is charged for a taxi called from home or business. Taxis may be hired at US$6 an hour unmetered.

Buses   *San Juan*: There is a frequent city bus ("guagua") service with a fixed charge of 15 cents for ordinary buses and 25 cents for air-conditioned buses. They have special routes against the normal direction of traffic and the bus lanes are marked by yellow and white lines. Bus stops are marked by yellow posts or signs marked "Parada de Guaguas". The centre terminal is at Plaza Colón and there is another at the San Juan main post office. No. 10 passes near all the main hotels: No. 17 goes to the airport (US$0.25; does not allow passengers with luggage however) and No. 1 to the University of Puerto Rico. (No change given; make sure you have right money.) *Interurban*: Puerto Rico Motor Coach company has daily scheduled services between San Juan, Ponce (US$3, one per day), and Mayaguez (US$3, 8 per day) through Caguas and Cayey or through Salinas.

Airlines   *International*: BWIA (Tel.: 791.1190); Iberia (Tel.: 725.5630); Avianca (Tel.: 724.6900); Liat (Tel.: 791.1190); Mexicana (Tel.: 725.5450); Dominicana (Tel.: 725,9393); Air France (Tel.: 724.0500); ALM (Tel.: 724.3013). *Domestic*: American Airlines (Tel.: 725.8484); Delta (Tel.: 724.5221); Eastern (Tel.: 725.3131); Pan American (Tel.: 767.5447). Several local airlines operate services within Puerto Rico and between the islands, including Antilles Air Boats, Caribair, Air Best, Culebra Aviation, Dorado Wings, Air Indies and Vieques Air Link, and they all have offices at the International Airport. Antilles Air Boats use Grumman Goose flying boats, which land in the harbours and thus save taxi fares. There is a cheap Pan-Am night flight between New York and San Juan.

Hotels   Most of the large hotels are situated on Ocean Front in Condado or Isla Verde and are new establishments built on modern lines, overlooking the sea, with swimming pools, night clubs, restaurants, shops and bars. The summer season runs from April 18 to December 15 and is somewhat cheaper than the winter season, for which we give rates. A 15% tax is payable on rooms costing more than US$5 a day. A full list is given in the monthly tourist guide, "Que Pasa", published by the Tourism Development Company, but listed here is a selection. *Caribbean Beach Club*, Loiza and Jupiter, Isla Verde, US$50 p.p.; *Borinquén*, Fernández Juncos 725, Miramar, US$32-38 d; *Howard Johnson's Nabori Lodge*, 1369 Ashford, US$53 d; *Caribe Hilton*, Ocean Front, Puerta de Tierra, US$88 d; *Castilla*, Calle Cruz, in the old city, small and new (US$8-10 s); *Dutch Inn*, 55 Condado Ave., Condado, US$68 d; *El San Juan*, Ocean Front, Isla Verde, US$78 d; *Puerto Rico Sheraton*, 1309

Ashford Ave., Condado, US$79 d; *San Cristóbal*, opposite the fort (US$8 s, with shower); *Condado Holiday Inn*, 999 Ashford Ave., Condado, US$75 d; *The Duffy's*, 9 Isla Verde Road, popular for its pub-like bar, US$24 d; *El Palmar*, Pte. 187, km. 0.3, Isla Verde, US$25-30 d, swimming pool. In Old San Juan: *El Convento* is a charming hotel with a Spanish atmosphere and the dining room is in the former chapel (US$65-70 d). Also in Old San Juan is *La Fortaleza*, US$18.90 d. *Villa Firenze*, Avenida Miramar, US$7 d, basic but good value, American-run. In Ponce, *El Coche* and *Hotel Meliá* can be recommended (US$18 d and 34 d respectively), also the *Holiday Inn Ponce*, US$46 d, where there are tennis courts, pools, and golf arrangements made. Cheaper hotels round main square. At Barranquitas the *Barranquitas Resort Hotel*, 700 metres above sea level, offers a quiet mountain setting with golf, tennis, horse-riding and swimming in a heated pool, US$32 d. In Santurce, *Hotel Colonial*, Av. Fernández Juncos, from US$20 a week, s. In San Germán, *Oasis Hotel*, US$10.50 s; US$4 for room on top of Giuseppi's shop on main plaza. In Parguera, several hotels at US$12 s, upwards. At Vieques, *Sportsman's House*, near Esperanza, US$15-22 s; *Carmen*, US$5 s with hot shower. At Culebra, *Hotel Puerto Rico*; *Seafarer's Inn*, US$10-15 s. At Guayama, *Hotel Carite*, US$4 s, clean, with hot public shower. There are seven of the new Paradores Puertorriqueños to put you up while touring (US$21-36 d, various prices).

Restaurants   All major hotels. *Galería, Fortaleza*; for Puerto Rican cuisine, *La Fonda del Callejón*, 319 Fortaleza; *La Mallorquina*, 207 San Justo; *La Posada de San Luis Rey*, 317 Fortaleza; *La Danza*, corner of Cristo and Fortaleza (all these are in Old San Juan). *Cecilia's Place*, Rosa St., Isla Verde. *Atena*, on corner of Luna and San Justo.

Tourist Information can be obtained from the Puerto Rico Tourist Bureau, P.O. Box 3968, San Juan (and at international airport—very helpful); the Puerto Rico Tourism Company, Banco de Ponce Building, Hato Rey, San Juan (GPO Box BN, San Juan PR 00936), with offices in New York, Chicago, Los Angeles, Washington D.C., Atlanta, Toronto and Frankfurt/Main.

"Qué Pasa", a monthly guide for tourists published by the Tourism Company, can be obtained free from the tourist office. It is very helpful, and we wish here to acknowledge our debt to it for some new information.

Food   Two good local dishes are the mixed stew, *asopao*, and a splendid risotto known as *yuquiyú*, a mixture of rice, sausage, turtlemeat, pineapple, peppers, etc., cooked in a pineapple husk.

Currency   United States currency.

Public Holidays

New Year's Day
Jan. 6: Three King's Day
Jan. 11: De Hostos' Birthday
Feb. 22: Washington's Birthday
March 22: Emancipation Day
Good Friday
April 16: José de Diego's Birthday
May 30: Memorial Day
July 4: Independence Day

July 17: Muñoz Rivera's Birthday
July 25: Constitution Day
July 27: Dr. José Celso Barbosa's Birthday
Sept. 1: Labour Day
Oct. 12: Columbus Day
Nov. 11: Veterans' Day
Nov. 19: Discovery of Puerto Rico
Nov. 25: Thanksgiving Day
Christmas Day

Newspapers and Periodicals   *San Juan Star* is the only daily English paper. There are three Spanish daily papers of note, *El Mundo, El Impacial* and *El Día*.

Churches   Roman Catholic, Episcopal, Baptist, Seventh Day Adventist, Presbyterian, Lutheran, Christian Science and Union Church. There is also a Jewish community.

British Consulate   Room 1014, Banco Popular Center (10th Floor), Hato Rey, Puerto Rico. Tel.: (809)767-4435.

Medical Services There are a number of Government and private hospitals. Hospital charges are high.

Banks Banco Crédito y Ahorro Ponceño, Degatau Plaza, Ponce; Banco de Ponce; Banco de San Juan; Banco Mercentil de Puerto Rico; and branches of foreign banks.

Postal Service The United States Post Office Department operates the postal service. Inside the new Post Office building in Old San Juan there is a separate counter for sales of special tourist stamps.

Telephone Operated by ITT; said not to be good.

External Communications Puerto Rico has direct cable and wireless services including satelite routing to all points in the world.

Broadcasting Two radio stations have English programmes.

Tipping Fixed service charges are not included in bills and it is recommended that 15% is given to waiters, taxi drivers, etc.

American Express Agents San Juan: Agencia Solar, Inc., 1226 Ashford Avenue, Tel.: (802) 722-1479.

During a four-day visit to the island in February 1978, the Editor was able to gather information to update this section; thanks also to Ucky Hamilton, of New Zealand, for a most useful letter.

THE WEST INDIES

A West Indian holiday is not now such an unattainable dream for so many as it was a few years ago. Larger and faster aircraft and cheaper fares have brought these islands, from the point of view of time as well as cost, within the reach of a growing number of people. For the greater part of the year the weather is near-perfect; sunshine, superb beaches, picturesque and splendid scenery.

Broadly speaking these islands can be grouped into three categories. There are the Americanized, luxurious and sophisticated resorts, such as in parts of the Bahamas and of the older resorts, which will give you exactly what you want, at a price.

The larger and older holiday islands such as Jamaica, Barbados and Trinidad are in the second category. Here, prices can be high. This does not mean that you cannot get good value here as elsewhere in the West Indies—if you choose the right area. And if you are not staying longer than 21 days, you can book a British Airways Earlybird return ticket from London to the main islands for not much more than one-third of the normal fare or half of the 15-day excursion return fare. (Laker Airways now have a London-Barbados weekly flight for £196-£258 return, according to season.)

The third category covers what could be described as the unspoilt West Indies. It comprises a scatter of small islands, some of them quite new as resorts, others still undiscovered by tourists and with few facilities in the way of accommodation. Many of them are to be found in the Leewards, the Windwards and in the Netherlands Antilles. The place you stay at is simple. The food is nothing to write home about. Hot water may be missing. But the service is warm hearted, and you live cheaply.

Antigua is the air terminal for the Leewards and St. Lucia for the Windwards; they are served by many of the major world airlines,· and there are usually good local air services to the surrounding islands. Some of the smaller islands do not have adequate airstrips and getting there can be quite an adventure. Most of the larger islands are on direct air routes from Europe, the U.S.A. and Canada.

Most of the main West Indian Islands can be reached by sea and not merely by cruise ships. (See Shipping Services.) The "Nomad" a mainly cargo boat, sails once a month from Jamaica to Grenada *via* Dominica, Martinique, St. Lucia, St. Vincent and Barbados. Deck passage is US$100 one way if you can get a berth. You can sometimes get a passage on other cargo boats travelling between the islands, though apparently a local law prevents cargo boats from carrying passengers when sailing from Port of Spain, Trinidad. If you do choose to travel by cargo boats, you must have flexible travel plans as far as dates and times are concerned.

We wish to express our gratitude to Federico Bertaccini (Litchfield, Conn.), James K. Bock (Mexico City), W. O. Boyes, Cliff Cordy (USA), Richard Drysdale, John Eames and Maggie Harvey, Vittorio Ferretti (São Paulo), Ucky Hamilton (N.Z.), Len Macdonald (USA), Nick Purbeck, A. Rooke, Margaret Symons (N.Z.), R. F. Vandersteen and Anne M. Walley (Peru), and Anne Williams, for most useful updating material on the various British and ex-British West Indian islands.

JAMAICA

JAMAICA lies some 90 miles south of Cuba and 4,500 miles from England. With an area of only 4,411 square miles, it is nevertheless the third largest island in the Antilles group. It has a population of just under 2 million. After three centuries of British rule, Jamaica became independent as a member of the Commonwealth on August 6, 1962.

This narrow island, only 146 miles from E to W and not much more than 51 miles from N to S at its widest, is bounded by the Caribbean. Like other West Indian Islands, it is one of the peaks of a submerged mountain range. It is crossed by a range of mountains reaching 7,402 ft. in the E and descending towards the W, with a series of spurs and forested gullies running N and S.

Jamaica has magnificent scenery and a remarkably fine climate freshened by sea breezes. The nights are warm, though not oppressive, flower-scented and often lit by clouds of flickering fireflies. The easily accessible hill and mountain resorts provide a more temperate climate, sunny but invigorating. Inland, in the mountains, the temperature can fall to as low as 7°C during the winter season. Temperatures on the coast average 27°C, rising occasionally to 32° in July and August and never falling below 20°. The humidity is fairly high. The best months are December to April. Rain falls intermittently from about May, with daily short tropical showers in September, October and November. Light summer clothing is needed all the year round, with a stole or sweater for cooler evenings.

The main products are sugar and rum, tobacco, bauxite, bananas, coffee, coconuts, and palm products. The island is fertile and green; there is excellent grazing and good beef cattle are raised. All kinds of vegetables and fruit are grown: sweet potatoes, yams, plantains, avocado pears, melons, bananas, pineapples, oranges, guavas and grapefruit; also exotic fruits such as uglifruit and ortaniques. Peaches and strawberries are grown in the Blue Mountains. There is plenty of coarse fish and delicious crayfish. Understandably, tourism is a major source of income.

It would be hard to find, in so small an area, a greater variety of tropical and sub-tropical natural beauty. Jamaica has been called "The Island of Springs" and the luxuriance of the vegetation is striking. Everywhere there are trees, shrubs, bushes and ferns, brilliant with flowers or vividly green. There are the silk cotton trees, the ceiba, huge banyans, yacca and cedar, ebony and mahogany, satin-wood, tamarind, calabash and cashew; annato, with its rose-coloured flowers, and golden cassias; the yellow spikes of the corato, the crimson hibiscus and orange-red poinciana; pink and purple bougainvillea and blue jacaranda. The scent of frangipani, oleander and jasmin in the long warm nights is not easily forgotten. It is not only tropical flowers and orchids that flourish in Jamaica; as well as many varieties of cactus, roses, carnations, lilies, geraniums and forget-me-nots are grown. This is also a land of humming-birds and butterflies, and around the harbour the huge frigate birds fly, with a wing-span of 10 feet. Sea-cows and the Pedro seal are found in the island's waters. There are crocodiles, a variety of lizards, frogs, toads and non-poisonous snakes, but no wild mammals apart from the mongoose and, in the mountains, wild pig.

The climate and the natural beauty of the island are the greatest tourist attractions, but there are also good sporting facilities. They include, golf, fishing, polo and horse-racing. The major tourist centres, however, are very expensive. A large part of the island can be visited by railway and all of it by scenic roads.

History Jamaica was discovered by Columbus in 1494; in 1505 it was occupied by Spain. Under Spanish rule the original inhabitants, the peaceful Arawaks, virtually disappeared and African slaves were brought in. In 1655, an English expeditionary force sent out by Cromwell attacked the island, and three years later, the Spanish settlers abandoned Jamaica. After a short period of military rule, the colony was organised with an English type of constitution and a legislative council. The great sugar plantations flourished and the island became the haunt of buccaneers and slave traders. The Declaration of 1833 freed the slaves and gave birth to the Jamaica of today.

Most of the earlier historical landmarks have been destroyed by hurricanes and earthquakes. In 1692 one destroyed the grave of Morgan, the pirate who dominated the Spanish Main, raised the Black Flag at Port Royal itself, and later received a knighthood for his service as Governor. The old Port Royal was built on a shelving bank of sand and most of it slid into the sea in the disastrous earthquake of 1692. More recent historic buildings, including 18th century churches at Port Royal, St. Ann's Bay and Montego Bay, are now in the care of the National Trust Commission. Very little trace, except for place names, remains of the Spanish occupation. The great sugar estates which form such an important part of the island's wealth date back to the days of the early British settlers.

The People Over 75% of Jamaicans are of West African descent and Ashanti words still figure very largely in their dialect. There are also Chinese, East Indians, British and other European minorities. The population is around 2,000,000 and the annual rate of growth is 1.2%. Their religion is predominantly Protestant: Baptist and Methodist, as well as Anglican. There are also a large Roman Catholic community and Hindu and Rastafarian minorities. Jamaicans tend to take their religion seriously and there are over 1,000 churches and chapels on the island. It should be stressed that great poverty coexists on the island with great (largely tourist) wealth; this has contributed to racial problems.

Administration Prime Minister, Cabinet, House of Representatives and Senate. All citizens over 18 are eligible for the vote. The judicial system is on English lines. There is a functioning two-party system; the Prime Minister is Mr. Michael Manley, of the People's National Party.

Kingston, the capital since 1870 and the island's commercial centre has a most beautiful harbour which is deep enough to take most ocean going liners. Kingston has a population of 180,000; together with Port Royal and St. Andrew it has over half a million people. Among its many attractions are the free port concessions available to visitors. Jamaica rum, J$1.70 a bottle; English and American cigarettes from J$0.46 for 20. Local cigarettes are very strong. Jamaican cigars cost from US$1.50 a box. There is interesting shopping of all kinds; the Jamaica Crafts Market on Harbour Street, at W end of Port Royal Street, Things Jamaican, Hanover Street, and Hill's Art Galleries, Harbour Street, have local crafts; the style is derived from Haiti and the quality is said to be better there. Shopping hours in Kingston are: downtown—0930-1700 except Sat. (0930-1730) and Wed. (0930-1300); uptown—0900-1700 except Thurs. (0900-1300). There is a wide range of hotels and restaurants. All the better places serve European and Jamaican food. Local dishes, fragrant and spicy, are usually served with rice. There are many unusual and delicious vegetables and fruits.

Amusements in Kingston include cinemas (the Carib is the most luxurious), and concerts and plays at the Ward Theatre and Little Theatre (St. Andrew) where the local Repertory Company performs regularly. Next door is a good library with overseas newspapers available in the reading room. At the Institute of Jamaica, in East Street, visitors can see Arawak carvings, old almanacs, natural history and art sections and many other historical relics. Another museum is now at Devon House, a former "great house" at the corner of Trafalgar and Hope Roads, with an open-air restaurant next door. Among buildings of note are Gordon House, dating from the mid-18th century, and the early 18th century parish church where Admiral Benbow is buried. The Parish Church at St. Andrew dates from 1700; here, too, is King's House, the official residence of the Governor-General.

Kingston is a convenient centre for excursions. A little over five miles away, at the foot of the mountains at Hope, are the Royal Botanical Gardens with a splendid collection of orchids and tropical trees and plants. Not very far away, threequarters of a mile above sea level, is the Blue Mountain military station of Newcastle. Spanish Town, the old capital, is 14 miles away. The airport for Kingston is the Norman Manley (with good tourist office, offering much information, maps and up-to-date hotel and guest-house lists), 11 miles away, about 30 minutes' drive.

Bus No. X97 leaves West Parade every half hour for the airport, US$0.45; the service is infrequent, however, so allow for "waiting" time. Taxis generally charge between US$9-12 for the same trip. In town taxis are hard to find. There is no sales tax on air tickets purchased in Jamaica, but tourists arriving by air are not allowed, generally, to visit the Island unless they have an onward ticket. New arrivals are always besieged by hustlers, so make a speedy exit. There is a US$3 airport tax.

For the athletic, a walk (or muleback ride) to the Blue Mountain Peak is recommended. A bus goes from Kingston to Mount Charles, from where it is a steep 6 km. walk to the Whitfield Hall Hostel, where you spend the night (US$3, but no charge for camping). Then start early a.m. for the peak, which will show you most of the E half of the island on a good day. You will need your own food, torch, sweater and rainproof. There are two huts on the peak which are quite adequate for overnight shelter though it is easily possible to walk down again in a day. The next day walk down to Mavis Bank and catch a bus back to Kingston. For information (and transport if needed) write to Mr. John Allgrove, Whitfield Hall P.O., Portland, Jamaica. For the less ambitious, a car trip into the Blue Mountains, to Newcastle, Hollywell or Clydesdale, is an interesting experience, as is the bus trip to Mount Charles.

Kingston Hotels (All for double room, EP—without meals—unless specified): *The Stony Hill,* US$28.40; *Sheraton-Kingston,* US$42-46; *Casa Monte* (Hills of St. Andrew), US$22.50-26.50; *Jamaica Pegasus,* US$46-50 ; *Courtleigh Manor,* US$33.40-39.50; *Terra Nova,* US$27.50; *Adventure Inn,* Port Henderson, US$30; *Clevedon Court,* US$16.70; *Four Seasons,* US$14-16; *Intercontinental,* rates on application; *Morgan's Harbour,* Port Royal, US$30-34; *Mountain Valley,* US$16 CP; *Sandhurst,* US$19-23. In the foothills (9 miles from Kingston) is the very good

Blue Mountain Inn. Ferry Inn is 7 miles from Kingston. *Strawberry Hill Guest House,* 14 miles away up hairpin bends at 2,800 ft., has a fine view. Cheaper: *Indies Hotel,* Holborn Road, US\$16-18 d, good value; *Rosneath Hotel,* Eureka Road, US\$18-25, CP; *Olympia,* University Crescent, US\$20; *Olive's Guest House,* downtown Kingston, US\$18 d, friendly; *Mayfair,* US\$13.50-20, attractive setting; *Beverly Cliff Guest House,* 200 Mount View Ave., US\$15 d, friendly, swimming pool; at 46 Luke Lane, near Victoria Park, is a cheap hotel charging US\$3.30 s (after bargaining); *Maryfields Apartments,* 60 Hope Road, US\$6 s; *YMCA,* 21 Hope Road, US\$5.50; *Mrs. Hewitt,* 22 Lady Musgrove Road, US\$6. *Danesbury,* 5 Ivy Grn. Cresc. Kgn. 5, US\$13-16 d; *Marvista,* 11 Seashore Place, Kgn. 17, US\$10 p.p.; *Retreat,* 19 Seaview Ave., Kgn. 10, US\$16 d; *Wyncliffe,* 222 Mtn. View Ave., US\$18 d.

(AP, 3 meals, EP, without meals; CP, breakfast only; MAP, breakfast and dinner.)

Restaurants Nine miles from Kingston is the *Blue Mountain Inn,* has an excellent night club and restaurant; *Casa Monte* is reported to have the most imaginative and varied cuisine in Kingston; *Herb's Steak House; Mill; Victoria Grill; Trafalgar Square; Dynasty* (Chinese); *Bistro, Manor Park Plaza; Jamaica Arms; Paul's 104,* 104 Harbour Street; *Cathay* (Chinese). In Half Way Tree area: *La France Continental; Bird-in-Hand; Oriental, House of Chen,* and *Golden Dragon* (Chinese); *Tip Top* (German), and *Swiss Chalet.* At the Palisadoes Airport is the *Horizon Room,* where meals are served until midnight. At Liguanea, *Golden Dragon* (also Chinese) in Hope Road. For the Impecunious, meat patties may be had at US\$0.20 each. Out of town there are the *Rodney Arms; Port Henderson;* and *Morgan's Harbour Hotel.*

Night Life Most hotels have dancing at weekends, and there is a good discotheque, Epiphany, at Spanish Court, New Kingston. Tourists are strongly advised not to try, unless they have Jamaican friends, to probe deeply into real Jamaican night life, at least in towns. For genuine local dances and songs, try to see Olive Lewin's "Jamaican Folksinger", or a performance by Louise Bennett.

Warning There are many thieves and pickpockets. Don't wander around on your own after dark. There is also a regrettable atmosphere of racial tension in the capital.

Tipping Hotel staff, waiters at restaurants, barmen, taxi drivers, cloakroom attendants, hairdressers get 10% of the bill. A 5% government hotel accommodation tax is added to room charges.

Electric Current 110 volt, 50 cycle A.C.

Horse Racing at Caymanas Park (10 miles); cup and stake races are held on Saturdays and public holidays.

Golf at Liguanea (2½ miles; 9 holes), Caymanas and Constant Spring golf clubs (10 miles). A 9-hole course is also attached to the Manchester Club in Mandeville.

Yachting at the Jamaican Yacht Club and Morgan Harbour Club.

Fishing Boats can be hired from almost any hotel to fish for marlin, sailfish, wahoo, dolphin, tuna and barracuda.

Clubs Rotary International; Kiwanis; Lions Club.

Buses A free map of Kingston bus routes is available from Jamaica Omnibus Services Ltd., 80 King Street. Travelling by bus is not too safe after dark.

Cable International Cable, Telephone and Telex services. Cable and Wireless (West Indies) Ltd., 9 East Parade, Kingston.

Banks The Royal Bank of Jamaica at Kingston (8 branches), Montego Bay and Mandeville. Bank of Montreal (Jamaica) 111-113 Harbour St. and Halfway Tree branch; Barclays Bank International main office in Kingston and branches all over the island. The same applies to the Bank of Nova Scotia Jamaica, Ltd. The Canadian Imperial Bank of Commerce (main office at 121 Harbour St., Kingston) has branches in the main towns. Citibank, 4½ King Street, Kingston. First National Bank of Chicago, 32½ Duke Street, Kingston.

Jamaica Chamber of Commerce and Merchants Exchange, 7/8 East Parade, Kingston. U.K. Trade Commissioner: Barclays Bank Building, King Street.

Royal Mail Lines Agency Grace Kennedy & Co. (Shipping) Ltd., 8 Port Royal Street, New Port West, P.O. Box 86.

Internal Transport There are a number of flights each day from Kingston to Montego Bay, US$17.50. Rutair rents Cessna planes and provides sightseeing flights. Domestic flights leave from Tinson Pen airfield, 2 miles from the centre of Kingston on Marcus Garvey Drive. They are operated by Trans-Jamaica Airlines. Airfields at Montego Bay, Negril, Ocho Rios, Port Antonio and Mandeville. Trains between same places are picturesque and safe. There is a daily train (called "The Diesel") from Kingston to Montego Bay, US$2.20. There is also a train service between Kingston and Port Antonio. Local buses are slow and sometimes dangerous, but are a cheap mode of transport. There are also minibuses which ply all the main routes and operate on a "collectivo" basis, leaving only when full. They leave from the Parade in Kingston. To Mandeville costs about US$2.25. Transfer service on Martins minibus from Montego Bay to Kingston takes 5 hours, costs US$25. The buses are invaded by touts as they approach the bus station. Best way of exploring interior: hire a car; the interior is well worth it. The Jamaica Car Rentals company rents cars for US$100 a week which is cheaper than other companies; Martins charge from US$140 to US$255 a week according to type. Inspect the car carefully before you take it.

Port Royal, the old naval base, lies across the harbour from Kingston, beyond the international airport, some 15 miles by excellent road; it can also be reached by boat from near the Craft Centre, W of new Kingston Mall. They leave every 2 hours, take 20 mins. and cost US$0.15. Nelson served here as a post-captain from 1779 to 1780 and commanded Fort Charles, key battery in the island's fortifications. Part of the ramparts, known as Nelson's Quarterdeck, still stands. St. Peter's Church, though the restoration is unfortunate, is of historic interest. *Morgan's Harbour Hotel* at Port Royal (US$30-34 d, EP, 54-58 MAP) is a favourite holiday centre, with water ski-ing, a salt water swimming pool, beach cabins, a good sea-food restaurant, and dancing to calypso bands. The beach and water, however, are dirtied by the adjacent harbour, and the sea is shark-infested. Boats may be hired for a picnic bathing lunch at Lime Cay or Port Henderson. Bus X20 also runs from Victoria Square to Port Henderson (*Adventure Inn,* US$30 d EP, 56 MAP).

N.B. Most of the best beaches are on the NE and W coasts. The only acceptable S-coast beach is Treasure Beach (*Treasure Beach Hotel,* no telephone).

Spanish Town, the former capital, some 14 miles W of Kingston by road or train, is historically the most interesting of Jamaica's towns. Its English-style architecture dates from the 18th century. Well worth seeing are the Cathedral; the fine Georgian main square with, of special note, the ruins of the King's House built in 1762; a colonade and statue commemorating Rodney's victory at the Battle of the Saints; the House of Assembly and the Court House. There is a museum with interesting relics of Jamaican history and accurate portrayal of life of the country people.

Mandeville About 40 miles further W again, high in the heart of the island, lies Mandeville, a beautiful, peaceful mountain resort with perhaps the best climate in the island. It looks very English with its village green on either side of which stand a Georgian court house and the Church. Riding and walking are the best ways of enjoying the magnificent scenery and sparkling mountain air. (*Hotel Mandeville,* US$20 d; *Hotel Astra,* 62 Ward Avenue, US$13.50 p.p., good.) There are interesting excursions to Christiana (about 2,800 ft., *Villa Bella*, US$17.60 per room); Alligator Pond on the south coast; the Santa Cruz Mountains and the Bamboo Avenue at Lacovia, which is rather like the roof of a Gothic cathedral. Beyond, past Black River, is the only sandy beach for miles. The coast road takes you on to Negril.

Mandeville is reported very expensive because of the nearby U.S.-owned bauxite industry. It is cheaper to drive on to Savannah-la-Mar and stay at *Hendon House* (a nice old "great house"), or further to Bluefields, about 15 miles W of Savannah, and stay at *Bluefields Great House*. Negril is only 1-1½ hours' drive W from Bluefields.

Negril, on a seven-mile stretch of pure white sand (on the western side of the Island), can still claim to be relatively cheap and unspoilt, though it is becoming less so. Accommodation: the *Sundowner, Charella* and *Coconut Cove* hotels are expensive at US$65 d, MAP, but the *Negril Beach Village* has beach cottages at US$319 a week, AP. A room can be rented at *Sunrise* for US$6 d and in other houses for about the same. There are also rooms at the *Yacht Club*, US$7 p.p. The cheaper hotels tend to be at the W end of the village. The *New Providence Guest House* has huts for US$3,85-5. Grandma, who is known by everybody, has rooms for US$3 a night each. Houses can be rented for about US$22-44 a month. Locals living along the beach will often let you camp on their property. *The Yacht Club* and *Wharf Club* both have restaurants, the latter being cheaper. For entertainment try the *White Swan*, where the locals go. *The Dolphin*, next to *New Providence Guest House*, is good. *Peewee's Restaurant*, in the West End of Negril, has excellent seafood and other dishes at reasonable prices.

Bus from Montego Bay (50 miles), US$1. 1½ miles from Negril are the Cliffs, where swimming and snorkelling are particularly good. Huts to rent at US$7 a night. Money can be changed at Savannah-la-Mar, 45 mins. by bus from Negril, US$1.10; about the same by bus from Montego Bay.

Still further on is Lucea, a charming spot on the north coast. (Bus Montego Bay-Lucea US$0.88.) Tamarind Lodge serves excellent Jamaican food. At Tryall there is the best golf course on the island.

Montego Bay (international airport only 3 miles). About 120 miles from Kingston by road or rail, situated on the NW coast, is Montego Bay, which rivals Kingston as a tourist centre. It has superb natural features, sunshine most of the year round, a beautiful coastline with miles of white sand and deep blue water never too cold for bathing (20°-26°C average temperature) and gentle winds which make sailing a favourite sport. There are underwater coral gardens in a sea so clear that they can be seen without effort from glass-bottomed boats at the Doctor's Cave, which is also the social centre of beach life. Montego Bay caters also for the rich and sophisticated. Some of its hotels and restaurants offer complete luxury and are very expensive. Others are less lavish but very comfortable. In the hills around the bay one can stay in well-equipped resort cottages or excellent guest houses. Visitors enjoy the same duty-free concessions as in Kingston and there are excellent shops and hairdressers (early closing Thurs.). For amusement there are open-air cinemas and nightclubs with floor shows and calypso bands. The variety of sports is probably as great as could be found in any one place: tennis, golf, badminton, polo, sailing, water ski-ing, skin-diving, spear-fishing and **deep-sea fishing for tuna, barracuda and marlin. Two days' instruction for** scuba diving costs US$33. Cricket is the most popular spectator sport.

(Test matches in the West Indian series are played at Kingston.) Other spectator sports at Montego Bay and Kingston include horse-racing, soccer, netball, athletics, professional cycle-racing, boxing and motor-racing. Of interest to the sightseer are an old British fort and an 18th century church in Montego Bay, and the Arawak rock carving at Kempshot.

From Montego Bay the so-called "Cockpit Country" can be visited. It was here that runaway slaves hid, out of reach of the British whose authority did not extend so far. To this day each village has a "head man". The tourist office in Montego Bay will recommend the best villages to visit. They recommend you to take a bottle of rum for the local head man, to guarantee your visit is welcomed.

On the Gold Coast strip of beach are some of the hotels much frequented by the international set, such as *Half Moon, Round Hill, Royal Caribbean* and *Montego Beach*. Quite near the *Doctor's Cave Beach Club* is *Doctor's Cave Beach Hotel*, quieter but excellent. In the same area, facing the sea at about 500 ft. and with splendid views, are very good hotels, including *Beach View, Casa Montego, Hacton House* and *Harmony House Hotel*. The *Half Moon* is 4 miles away along the coast, and the pleasant *Royal Caribbean* is on the lovely Mahoe Bay. *Bay Roc, Chatham,* and *Colony* are other good places to stay at. The general hotel rate is from US$20-30 p.p. per day, without meals, and from 40-50 MAP, all meals included. There are several night clubs in Montego Bay: the *Rum Barrel*, the *Cellar*, and the *Reef Club*. Ten miles W of Montego Bay is the very exclusive *Round Hill Hotel*.

Cheaper hotels and restaurants *Pelican Inn* (US$15 d), and *Pelican Grill*, US$2.50 for meal, near Doctor's Cave Beach. Also near Doctor's Cave Beach, on Gloucester Avenue, are *Chiltern Apartments and Rooms*, US$10 s, peak rate. Next door *Wexford Court Apartments*, also good, same ownership; *Chiltern* residents may use its pool (US$30-40 d, EP). *Harvey Beach Hotel*, E of Montego Bay, US$16.25 d, very quiet. *Ocean View Guesthouse*, near airport. At 34 Church Street a room is US$5.50. Recommended is the *Montenegro Restaurant*, on beach, very quiet, and less expensive than most.

Train to Kingston at 0645 and 1530, getting there in 4 hours. Return at 0700 and 1530. Highly recommended, scenic journey, costing about US$2.20 second class.

Falmouth, a charming small town, is about 20 miles E of Montego Bay. It has a fine Colonial court house (restored inside), a church, some 18th century houses, and Antonio's claimed to be the world's best shop for beach shirts. There is a fine fishing (tarpon and kingfish) at the mouth of the Martha Brae, near Falmouth, and no licence is required. Rafting on Martha Brae river. Jamaica Swamp Safaris (a crocodile farm). Some 10 miles inland is the 18th century plantation guest-house of Good Hope amongst coconut palms: horses for hire and its own beach on the coast. No accommodation at beach.

Ocho Rios On a bay sheltered by reefs and surrounded by coconut groves, sugar cane and fruit plantations, is Ocho Rios, the newest and one of the cheaper resorts, which has become increasingly popular. It is 64 miles E of Montego Bay and 7 miles E of St. Ann's Bay. The coastline is historic and, as elsewhere on the island, offers all-the-year-round sun and sea bathing. The scenery is an added attraction. Most spectacular are the beauty spots of Fern Gulley, a marvel of unspoilt tropical vegetation, Roaring River Falls and Dunn's River Falls tumbling into the Caribbean with invigorating salt and fresh water bathing at its foot. Discovery Bay has historic associations, for Columbus landed here.

At Runaway Bay, an attractive and friendly spot near Ocho Rios, is the *Runaway Bay Hotel* and *Country Club* (US$100-200 d, MAP), and *Eaton House*, both of which have excellent facilities. *Silver Spray Club* is splendid for a family or small group (US$60-70 d, MAP). Beautifully sited, near Ocho Rios, is the *Upton Country Club*: golf links, tennis, riding and swimming. The local night club is *The Ruin*. Next door is the *Chela Bay Hotel* which is really for young people, US$40 d with two meals.

In the Ocho Rios area, along the shore, are *Jamaica Inn* (luxurious, US$230-250 d, AP); the *Shaw Park Beach Club* (US$27-33 d, EP); the cottage *Sans Souci* (apartments from US$60 to US$170 a night, EP); and the *Tower Isle Hotel* (a big, popular, self-contained resort), (US$55-75 d, EP). The *Plantation Inn,* set back above the sea, looks like a plantation house and is delightful (US$98-108 d, MAP). The *Pineapple Penthouse* is very good value. The *Inn on the beach* (US$36 d, EP) serves good, cheap hamburgers. At Mamee Bay, between Ocho Rios and St. Ann's Bay, is the air-conditioned *Jamaica Hilton Hotel* (US$58-73 d, EP). At Port Maria, 12 miles E of Ocho Rios, where many celebrities have their summer homes, the small but excellent *Casa Maria* (US$54-60 d, MAP) is set on a hill above the bay (swimming pool and private beach).

Port Antonio One of the older touring resorts, Port Antonio lies on the NE coast at the foot of the island's highest mountains. It has a splendid yachting harbour and excellent fishing. This part of the island is particularly rich in tropical plant life. Boston Beach and San San Bay and the Blue Lagoon are notable beauty spots. The mountains which lie inland are a great attraction. Expert guides take tourists on bamboo rafts down the rapids of the Rio Grande, an exhilarating but safe experience. Each raft carries two passengers and the trip takes over 2 hours through wonderfully luxuriant vegetation. A driver will take your car from the point of departure to the point of arrival.

Hotels (US$ d rates, EP unless otherwise stated): *Bonnie View* (23-32), *Dragon Bay* (95-120 for suite), *Goblin Hill* (50 for 1-bedroom villa), *Trident Villas* (90-120 MAP), the luxurious *Frenchmen's Cove,* and the *De Montevin's Lodge* (good front rooms and first class Jamaican food, 16 p.p., MAP). Also, *Scotia Guest House*. The annual International Marlin Tournament, which is held in October, attracts anglers from all over the world.

The aquamarine waters of the Blue Hole, 7 miles E, are worth a visit; nearby are other picturesque small beach resorts.

The railway journey between Port Antonio and Kingston is an interesting experience.

Economy Jamaica was until recently one of the more prosperous islands in the West Indies. The island is the world's second largest producer of bauxite and alumina, but the decline in world demand for aluminium from 1975 onwards has adversely affected the economy. At the same time, political tension has deterred tourists from visiting Jamaica and hence its second most important foreign exchange earner has also been hit. The slump in the world sugar market and reduced citrus fruit production due to drought have been additional factors contributing to a drop in foreign exchange earnings, poor economic growth and high unemployment in the past two years.

Foreign Trade—J$million

		1973	1974	1975	1976
Exports (f.o.b.)	..	354.7	652.9	740.6	575.7
Imports (c.i.f.)	..	604.5	850.8	1,021.4	829.8

Jamaica Tourist Board 80 Harbour Street, P.O. Box 284, Kingston. *New York:* 866 Second Avenue, 10th Floor (2 Dag Hammarskjold Plaza), New York, N.Y. 10017; *Chicago:* Suite 1210, 36 South Wabash Avenue, Chicago, Illinois 60603; *Detroit:* 107 Northland Towers West, Southfield, Michigan 48075; *Philadelphia:* Suite 1604, 2 Penn Center Plaza, Philadelphia, Pa.; *Dallas:* 1140 Empire & Central, Suite 100, Dallas, Texas 75247; *Miami:* 702 Security Trust Bldg., 700 Brickell Ave., Miami, Fla. 33131; *Atlanta:* 2311 Cain Tower, 229 Beachtree St. N.E., Atlanta, Ga. 30303; *Toronto:* 2221 Yonge Street, Suite 507, Toronto, Ontario M4S 2B4; *Mexico:*

c/o Mexicana Airlines, 36 Balderas, Mexico D.F.; *London:* 6-10 Bruton Street, London W1X 8HN; *Frankfurt:* 6000 Frankfurt/Main 1, Friedenstrasse 7. Many brochures and hotel lists available.

Air Services Many flights from London and US and Canadian cities. There is a weekly flight from Belize City.

Documents Canadian and U.S. citizens do not need passports or visas for a stay of up to six months, if they reside in their own countries and have some form of identification e.g. a driver's licence. Residents of Commonwealth countries need only a birth certificate for entry. Other nationalities require passports; but people of West European countries, Bangladesh, Israel, Mexico, Pakistan, and Turkey do not need visas. All visitors need an onward ticket. Passengers arriving from Canada, the USA, Curaçao and British and ex-British Caribbean territories do not need a smallpox vaccination certificate. All visitors must pay a US$3.50 airport tax when leaving Jamaica.

Currency Jamaican dollar. J$1 = US$1.25. Some banks charge commission on changing cheques, some do not. Local currency cannot be imported or exported.

American Express Agents Kingston: Martins Jamaica, Harbour and East Streets, Tel.: 922-1440. Port Antonio: Martins Jamaica, Center Shopping Plaza, Tel.: 993-2625. Montego Bay: Martins Jamaica, 45 St. James Street, Tel.: 952-4350. Ocho Rios: Martins Jamaica, Pineapple Place, Main Street, Tel.: 974-2594/5. Mandeville: Martins Jamaica, Willogate Shopping Center, Tel.: 962-2203.

(We are grateful to Federico Bertaccini, of Litchfield, Conn., for providing us with invaluable updating information.)

BARBADOS

THIS, the most easterly of the islands, has the healthiest and pleasantest climate in the West Indies. It has a peculiarly English air, so much so that Barbados is known in the Caribbean as "Little England". Although only slightly larger than the Isle of Wight and about three times the size of Staten Island, its charm and natural attractions have made it one of the most popular holiday resorts in the world. Barbados is 1,200 miles from Miami, 2,100 from New York, and 3,456 from London. It has only 166 square miles and lies 100 miles off-course from the main curve of the West Indies, which perhaps explains why it was missed by Columbus on his second voyage of discovery. Its name is thought to derive from the Portuguese word *barbudos,* the name they gave to the bearded fig trees they found when they landed here briefly in 1536. It was the British who colonized the island and it remained under the British Crown from 1625 until, after a period of internal self government, Barbados achieved independence within the Commonwealth in November 1966. It has also retained institutional links with Britain as, for example, its legal system.

Although the island is so small (its greatest length is 21 miles and its extreme width only 14) there are nearly 140 hotels and guest houses, many with dancing and first-class floor shows. Tourism is a major industry and one of increasing importance. The Grantley Adams airport, at Seawell, 11 miles from Bridgetown (about 25 minutes' drive) is on direct jet routes to London, the USA, Canada, Luxemburg, Zurich and Caracas. Not surprisingly, since it is the home of film stars and wealthy expatriates, the visitor will find excellent shops and boutiques and sophisticated entertainment.

Over three centuries of British influence have imparted a special character to Barbados, this exotic island of donkey carts and twisting narrow lanes paved, incredibly, with coral. Along the neat hedgerows vivid tropical flowers, hibiscus, croton and bougainvillea bloom in profusion and scarlet flame trees shade smooth, well-tended lawns. Unlike the luxuriant natural grandeur of Jamaica and Trinidad, the island is neat and flat with pale green fields of sugar cane and colour-washed houses standing behind coral walls. The clear, brilliant light, the spectacularly coloured sea and the pervading air of peacefulness contribute to a charm that is hard to forget. Some of the places well worth a visit are St. John's Church, built 1836, from where there is a magnificent view of the E coast; Farley Hill, a now deserted plantation mansion; Cherry Tree Hill where, in the evenings, monkeys can be seen playing in the mahogany trees; Hackleton's Cliff, looking over the lovely beaches of Bathsheba; the Morgan Lewis Windmill; Welchman Hall Gulley, an old plantation house with its tropical gardens, and Christchurch Parish Church, with its eerie "Chase vault".

One of the charms of the island is the wide variety of flowering trees and shrubs, and the air is filled with the scent of oleander, frangipani, jessamine, poinsettia, flamboyant, cassia, cassica, japonica, bougainvillea, hibiscus and lady-of-the-night. Wild life still survives, and there are monkeys, raccoons, hares and mongooses. A familiar sound at night is the chorus of whistling tree frogs. There are about 20 species of native birds; the humming birds are perhaps the most beautiful. The "sugar-bird", the yellow breasted finch, is a common sight darting among the tables, picking up tit-bits.

The People The population is about 238,000, of whom over 90% are black. Europeans account for about 5%. Annual rate of growth 2%. There is little illiteracy. Barbadians (known locally as "Bajans") are predominantly Anglican.

Bridgetown, the capital, with a population of over 95,000, is on Carlisle Bay, an open roadstead exposed to the wind from the S and the W, but there is an inner harbour protected by the Mole Head. Larger ships land passengers and discharge and load cargo in the new deep-water harbour to the NW of Carlisle Bay and immediately W of Bridgetown.

Bridgetown is rather like an English market town on a hot summer day, but there are donkeys in the High Street and a colourful and fascinating waterfront. The main street is Broad Street, which leads into Trafalgar Square, where are found the chief public buildings, Nelson's statue, 50 years older than the one in London, and nearby, the Cathedral. Government House and the house once occupied by George Washington are interesting but not open to the public. The straw market is well worth a visit. Buses run at frequent intervals from Fairchild Street and Lower Green to the out-districts. The information Bureaux at the Deepwater Harbour and at Grantley Adams Airport are helpful about places of interest, hotels, taxi fares, etc. The yellow pages of the telephone directory are a fund of classified information. The local daily newspaper, the *Advocate-News,* also published on Sundays, and a free news sheet called the *Barbados News,* published by Carib Publicity Company, contain useful information on current entertainment.

Buses are useful for excursions. Transport Board bus No. 1c goes to Connell Town for Animal Flower Cave (admission B$1) and the Sam Lord's Castle (beautiful garden and beach), bus passes the airport. "The open Rocklyn Motor Omnibus No. 4 leaves Pelican Village near deep-water dock for Morgan Lewis (sugar windmill belonging to Barbados National Trust) *via* Welchman's Hall Gully (tropical jungle garden, admission charge) through Scotland and the island's finest scenery. Elite Co. No. 7 & No. 9 go to Codington College, whence one may walk up the E coast, along the abandoned railway track to the Atlantis Hotel beneath the Andromeda Gardens (admission B$1), before which passes a bus coming from Powell Spring Hotel (surfing), a little further N up the coast" (Michael Garthwaite). To visit the ruined plantation at Farley's Hill, change buses in Speightstown.

Motor-cars can be taken to Hackleton's Cliff (997 ft.), where there is a view of the eastern hills; or to St. John's Church (824 ft.), to see the windward coast and other points. Codrington College (affiliated to the University of The West Indies) is interesting.

Visitors can see the manufacture of sugar at the larger factories, such as Searles, Foursquare, Bulkeley, or Corrington. The noted Barbadian rum is made at Mount Gay, parish of St. Lucy, and at two distilleries near Bridgetown.

At about 1600 hrs. the fishermen return to Bridgetown with their catch, which they sell in the harbour.

Climate and what to wear Temperatures average 24° to 30°C. They rarely exceed 32° or drop below 20°. The island is cooled by NE trade winds which are strongest on the Atlantic coast. June to November is the rainy season, with heavy, short downfalls which soon drain away in the porous coral. Cottons and washable summer clothes, cocktail wear, light-weight suitings and a wrap for cooler evenings are suitable.

Sports and Entertainment Water sports, as well as swimming, surfing (on the E coast, though the sea can be dangerous), water skiing, skin-diving and snorkelling, fishing for tuna, marlin, wahoo, dolphin, tarpon and sailfish, and sailing. Sea life among the coral reefs can be viewed from glass bottomed boats. Camping on the beaches is *not* allowed, and in some places the sea can be dangerous.

Golf: The Rocklay Golf and Country Club has an excellent 18-hole course and a splendid club house, to which visitors are cordially invited. Special subscription rates per day or per week. The Sandy Lane Golf Club, 7 miles from Bridgetown on the west coast, has a splendidly landscaped 9-hole course of 3,400 yards. There is a golf course at Durrants Golf and Country Club, Christ Church.

There are good tennis courts at the Yacht Club, Sandy Lane, Sam Lord's, Garrison Savannah, Sunset Crest and the Government Courts, Deepwater Harbour. Riding can be arranged through the hotels.

First class cricket matches are played at Kingston Oval throughout the season (June to November). There is horse racing and polo at the Garrison Savannah.

Cinemas include 2 drive-ins near Bridgetown. The night life is colourful and lively. The leading hotels provide a variety of first class entertainment with steelbands, calypsos, flaming limbo dancers and floorshows. Each hotel has its special night, e.g. *Island Inn,* Monday night, floorshow and dancing; *Riviera Beach,* Tuesday night, steelband and floorshow; *Paradise Beach,* Wednesday, barbecue, floorshow and dancing; *Coral Reef,* Thursday, barbecue, floorshow and dancing; *Holiday Inn,* Friday, barbecue, floorshow and dancing; *Hilton,* Saturday, International buffet and dancing. Among several good night clubs and discothèques are the *Caribbean Pepperpot, Alexandra's* (until 0400 every night, admission B$7), *Talk of the Town* and *Hippo.*

There are excellent independently-run restaurants, as well as good eating places at the leading hotels. As well as evening barbecues, many hotels offer sumptuous luncheon buffets: *Sam Lord's Castle, Sandy Lane, Paradise Beach, Atlantis* and the *Edgewater* are well known for their Sunday buffets. Visitors can sample local dishes, tropical fruits, vegetables and seafoods at many restaurants. Good places include: *La Bonne Auberge* (French specialities), *Bagatelle Great House* (international cusine), *Dolly's* (many local dishes including flying fish, good atmosphere), *Luigi's* (Italian food), the *Steak House,* the *Pelican,* in Pelican Village (lunch from US$1.50).

There is a wide variety of fresh fruit drinks and delicious concoctions laced with rum. The local beer is good. Cold water from the tap is perfectly safe.

Roads throughout the island are good and self-drive cars are available at B$140-160 per week with unlimited mileage. (Petrol costs about US$1.20 a gallon.) Drive on the left. Most driving licences are valid in Barbados, but you must also acquire a Barbados permit, cost B$10. Taxis are plentiful and charge about 90c per mile. There is a speed limit in Bridgetown and Speightstown (on the west coast) of 20 mph; elsewhere 30 mph (not, apparently, that buses pay much heed to it!). Bus fares vary between 30c and 65c. To Accra beach or Bridgetown from the road past the airport, 30c; to Oistins 40c.

Shops are excellent with duty-free concessions for visitors. Best buys are British-made fine leather goods, cashmeres and luxury knitwear, high quality tweeds and porcelain. A very useful facility offered by several shops is made-to-measure clothing. One can order dresses, beachwear, shirts and suits in a variety of materials, from Sea Island cotton to imported tweeds. At the West Indies Handicraft Centre, Women's Self-Help, Pelican Village and other stores one can find an attractive variety of locally produced articles, including decorative straw-work, combs, boxes and dressing-table sets of turtleshell, ornamental candles and the attractive Christopher Russell pottery made in Bridgetown. Most chemists stock photographic materials. English and American cigarettes are reasonable; local cigarettes and Jamaican cigars are cheap. Shopping hours 0800 to 1600 weekdays, 0800 to 1200 Sats. Banking hours 0800 to 1200 Mon.-Thurs., 0800-1200 and 1500-1800 Fri. Some banks charge a fee for cashing travellers' cheques.

Economy   Tourism is very important for Barbados having increased its earnings from US$7 million in 1960 to US$82 million in 1976. Sugar has traditionally been the mainstay of the economy, with rum and molasses being produced as by-products, but especially with the fall in world prices, there has been a tendency to diversify into other crops. Manufacturing is also being encouraged in order to reduce the island's dependence on tourism and agriculture. Barbados has a considerable transit trade, being in some respects the central exchange market for all the Windward Islands.

Foreign Trade (B$ million)

	1973	1974	1975	1976	1977
Exports (f.o.b.) ..	102.6	172.3	217.1	207.4	190.9
Imports (c.i.f.) ..	299.2	418.3	437.2	474.7	550.8

Information for Visitors   Barbados Board of Tourism Marine House, Hastings, Christ Church; 6 Upper Belgrave Street, London, S.W.1; 11 King Street West, Suite 1108, Toronto 105; Münchenerstrasse 48, Postfach 3009, 6000 Frankfurt/Main 1; Apartado 1706, Zona Postal 101, Chacao, Caracas; 801 Second Avenue, New York 10017. Immigration authorities now require a ticket (and *not* a miscellaneous charges order) out of the country before allowing entry.

Shipping   Information about cargo boats going to Trinidad or the mainland of South America can be obtained from the customs house, shipping agents and harbour staff. However, it is not easy to get a berth on one and if you succeed you may have to pay more than it costs to fly.

Air   To Trinidad US$92 return.

Currency   The Barbados dollar is now at a fixed parity with the US dollar, of B$2 = US$1. Barbados began to issue its own currency in September 1973. Export of local and foreign currencies limited up to the amounts declared on arrival.

Cruise-Ship passengers are refreshed and entertained at an establishment set up at Holetown, St. James: local drinks and food, changing-rooms, water sports, steel bands and calypso singers.

Hotels   Barbados has a wide range of luxury, first-class and moderately priced hotels, guest houses and furnished apartments. The peak tourist season is from 16 December to 15 April, when rates are much higher than the rest of the year. Electric current is 110 volts AC.

UNIFORM WITH THIS VOLUME:

THE GULF HANDBOOK

Per day—Winter
Dec. 16-April 15
US$

Hotels	Address				
Hilton	..	..	..	St. Michael ..	..	..	78-88 (EP)
Windsor Hotel	..	..	Hastings ..	..	..	35-40 (EP)
Regency Cove Hotel	..	..	Hastings ..	..	..	38-65 (EP)
Holiday Inn	..	..	..	Aquatic Gap ..	..	70 (EP)
Silver Beach	..	..	Rockley	..	..	40 (MAP)
Ocean View	..	..	Hastings ..	..	..	52-62 (MAP)
Accra Beach Hotel	..	..	Rockley	..	..	58-84 (MAP)
Torrington	..	..	..	Rockley	..	..	28-32 (MAP)
Sam Lord's Castle	..	..	..	St. Philip	..	..	63-88 (EP)
Sandy Lane Hotel	..	..	St. James	..	..	180 (MAP)
Miramar Beach Hotel	..	..	St. James	..	..	62-112 (CP)
Coral Reef Club	..	..	St. James	..	..	130-170 (AP)
Colony Club	..	..	..	St. James ·	..	..	99-135 (MAP)
Paradise Beach	..	..	St. Michael ..	..	..	105-170 (MAP)
Super Mare	..	..	Worthing	..	..	28-40 (MAP)

Rates are for a double room. AP = all meals included; CP = breakfast included;
EP = without meals; MAP = breakfast and dinner included.

Guesthouses (Peak rates are quoted where possible.) *Altrio,* Rendezvous Gardens,
US$26 d (MAP); *Carib Guest House,* Worthing, US$20 d (MAP); *Berwyn on Sea,*
Rockley, US$12-18 d (CP); *Crystal Waters,* Worthing, US$18 d (CP); *Summer
Place,* Worthing, US$10 s (EP); *Coral House,* Silver Sands, has apartments and also
lets room for US$3 p.p. (out of season); *Broome's Vacation Homes,* Pine Gardens,
just outside Bridgetown, US$20 (MAP), clean and friendly, has restaurant; *Tropical
Guest House,* Fontabelle (another suburb), does not accept unmarried couples.
YMCA in Bridgetown has occasional vacancies; US$10.50 for full board or US$5
for bed and breakfast, not very clean. *Brigade House,* Garrison Savannah (about 1½
miles from Bridgetown on airport road), US$15 s (EP). *Salvation Army Men's
Hostel,* Bridgetown, US$1 per night. *Roman's Apartments,* just outside Oistins, on
S coast, on the beach, US$10-20 s; each double room has a kitchen and there are
separate laundry facilities; maid service is provided at extra cost; highly
recommended. The *Youth Hostel,* Worthing, has dormitories and charges US$3 a
bed or US$1.50 to sleep on the floor. It is on the bus route from the airport to
Bridgetown. (The hostel incorporates a health food restaurant and yoga centre.)

Beaches The Sandy Lane Hotel beach at St. James is good. Small sailing boats can
be hired for US$7 an hour and glass-bottomed boats for about US$3.50 p.p. per
hour.

Documents You must have an onward ticket, or make a deposit of B$100-1,500.
Sometimes people with backpacks have trouble with customs officials.
Passports are not required by nationals of Canada and the USA who have proof of
identity, nor by residents of other British and ex-British Caribbean islands holding
permits to travel. Passports, but not visas, are required by nationals of West
European countries, Commonwealth countries, Bangladesh, Israel, Peru, Suriname,
Turkey and Venezuela.

Customs Duty-free import: 200 cigarettes or ½ lb. of other tobacco products, one
quart of alcoholic drinks and 150 grams of perfume.

Travel Agents Safari Tours, on corner of St. George and Prince Alfred Street,
Bridgetown, arrange tours to other Caribbean islands.

International Telecommunications Telegraph, telephone and telex services. Cable
and Wireless (W.I.) Ltd., Gardiner Austin Building, Lower Broad St., Bridgetown.
(Tel.: 63178) and St. Lawrence Gap, Christ Church (Tel.: 87187—acceptance of
telegrams 24 hours a day) and Wilder, St. Michael (Tel.: 75200). Cables can also be
handed in at hotel desks.

Banks Barclays Bank International, Royal Bank of Canada, Canadian Imperial
Bank of Commerce, Bank of Nova Scotia, Bank of America, Chase Manhattan
Bank, Citibank. Hours are 0800-1300 Mon.-Fri., and 1500-1730 on Fri.

Air Services   *From Europe:* British Airways (5 a week) and BWIA (weekly) from London; SAS (weekly) from Zürich and Copenhagen; cheap flights by Caribbean Airways (from about US$235 s) from London and Luxembourg up to four times a week; weekly from London for £196-258 return with Laker Airways. *From North America.* From New York (twice daily) by American Airlines or BWIA; from Miami (daily) by BWIA; from Toronto and Montreal by Air Canada or BWIA (up to 12 weekly). *Within Caribbean:* Links with many points by LIAT, BWIA, British Airways, Eastern Airlines (San Juan-St. Maarten-Port-of-Spain, daily), Cubana (Havana-Kingston-Port-of-Spain-Georgetown, weekly), and Viasa (Caracas and Port of Spain, four times weekly, US$190 and US$98 return respectively).

There is an airport tax of B$5 on flights within the West Indies and of B$10 to other places. There are taxis from the airport to Bridgetown (B$14), but it is much cheaper to walk to the main road and catch a bus from there. Many hotels are situated on this road.

Shipping   Geest Industries have a weekly service of banana boats between Barry, Wales, or Preston, Lancs. and Barbados. The boats call at the Windward Islands and carry between 8 and 16 passengers.

British High Commission, Barclays Bank Building, Roebuck Street, Bridgetown.

Embassy of the U.S.A., Canadian Imperial Bank of Commerce Building, Broad Street, Bridgetown.

American Express Agents   Bridgetown: Johnson's Stables and Garage Ltd., Coleridge Street, Tel.: 4205/6655.

TRINIDAD AND TOBAGO

Trinidad, the most southerly of the Caribbean islands, lying only seven miles off the Venezuelan coast, is one of the better known and one of the more colourful of the West Indian islands. It is an island of 1,864 square miles, traversed by two mountain ranges, the northern and southern ranges, running roughly east and west, and a third, the central range, running diagonally across the island. Apart from small areas in the northern range, of which the main peaks are Cerro del Aripo (3,083 feet) and El Tucuche (3,072 feet), and in the central range, of which Mount Tamana (1,009 feet) is the principal peak, all the land is below 1,000 feet.

Tobago (116 square miles) is only 21 miles by sea to the North-East. It is 32 miles long and only 11 miles wide, shaped like a cigar with a central 18-mile ridge of hills in the North (highest point 1,890 feet) running parallel with the coast. The coast itself is pitted with any number of inlets and sheltered beaches. These north-eastern hills are of volcanic origin; the South West is flat or undulating and coralline, but at this end lies the fascinating undersea garden of Buccoo Reef. On an ebbing tide small boats push out into the sea for the Reef, where the visitor steps overboard into waist-high water to peer through goggles "walk-snorkling" to see an enchanted life with under-water plants and anemones; myriads of painted fish slipping through coral: a still world of breathless beauty.

The climate on the islands is tropical, but, thanks to the trade winds, rarely excessively hot. Temperatures vary between 18° and 34°C, the coolest time being from December to April. There is a dry season from January to mid-May and a wet season from June to December, with a short break in September, but the rain falls in heavy showers and is rarely prolonged. Humidity is fairly high, however.

History   The aboriginal name for the island of Trinidad was Iere (Land of the Humming Bird). Columbus landed there on his third voyage in 1498 and, taking possession on behalf of the Crown of Spain, named the island Trinidad, supposedly after a "trinity" of prominent hilltops. The first Spanish settlement was established under Don Antonio Sedeno in 1532 but even then, and for many years afterwards, the Spanish colonists had the greatest difficulty in maintaining a footing on the island. In 1595 Sir Walter Raleigh arrived at Trinidad to caulk his ships in Pitch Lake before destroying the newly-founded Spanish town of San José (now St. Joseph). In 1640 it was raided by the Dutch, and in 1677 and 1690 by the French. In 1797, during the Revolutionary War between England and Spain, a British expedition sailed into the Gulf of Paria. The force was commanded by Sir Ralph Abercromby and Rear Admiral Henry Harvey and appeared so aggressive that Spanish resistance was purely nominal, resulting in the surrender of the island. In 1802 Trinidad was ceded to the British Crown by the Treaty of Amiens.

Tobago was discovered by Columbus in 1498, at which time it was occupied by Caribs. In 1641 James, Duke of Courland, obtained a grant of the island from Charles I and in 1642 two vessels arrived with a number of Courlanders who settled on the north side. In 1658 the Courlanders were overpowered by the Dutch, who remained in possession of the island until 1662 when the Dutch company resigned their right to it. In this year Cornelius Lampsius procured Letters Patent from Louis XIV creating him the Baron of Tobago and proprietor of the island under the crown of France. After being occupied for short periods by the Dutch and the French, Tobago was ceded by France to Britain in 1763 by the Treaty of Paris. But it was not until 1804, after further invasions by the French and subsequent recapture by the British, that it was ceded in perpetuity to the British Crown, becoming a Crown Colony in 1877. In 1888 Tobago was amalgamated politically with Trinidad. The Federation of the West Indies was formed in 1958 with a membership including Trinidad and Tobago; after the breakup of the Federation, Trinidad and Tobago was granted independence on August 31, 1962; it became a republic within the Commonwealth on August 1, 1976.

Government   The People's National Movement has provided the Government since independence; it largely represents the black majority whereas the Opposition groups derive most of their support from the East Indian minority. President: Sir Ellis Clark. Prime Minister: Dr. Eric Williams.

The People   Trinidad has one of the world's most cosmopolitan populations. The emancipation of the slaves in 1834 and the adoption of free trade by Britain in 1846 resulted in far-reaching social and economic changes. To meet labour shortages over 150,000 immigrants were encouraged to settle from India, China and Madeira. Of to-day's population of approximately 1,300,000, about 45% are black and 35% East Indian. French and Spanish influences dominated for a long time—the main religion is still Roman Catholicism—but gradually the English language and institutions prevailed and to-day the great variety of peoples has become a fairly harmonious entity, despite some tension between blacks and those of East Indian descent. Spanish is still spoken in small pockets in the northern mountains and French patois here and there. Tobago's population, mainly black, numbers about 50,000.

It should be stressed that, even in Port-of-Spain, the people are extremely friendly and helpful to visitors—unlike the situation in other parts of the Caribbean.

What to do   Tourism is a growing industry. The islands have, indeed, many attractions for visitors. There is water-skiing, deep-sea fishing, surfing, bathing, snorkelling, scuba-diving, glass-bottom boat tours and moonlight cruises. In the northern mountains visitors can walk and do some not-over-strenuous climbing. Sports include golf (on a magnificent 18-hole championship golf course), tennis, horse-racing, sailing, football and hockey and of course that English eccentricity, cricket.

Three planes on weekdays, four at weekends between Trinidad and Tobago; the crossing takes 20 minutes and costs TT$15. Departures, however, are often subject to long delays. There are regular steamers for those who would rather go by sea. They leave every other day from each place at 2100: TT$6 (deck class) or TT$13 (tourist class) return. The trip takes 6-9 hours and can be rough. "Little Tobago", a near-by inlet of the NE coast, was a sanctuary for birds-of-paradise imported from New Guinea in 1909, but it seems that there are none left.

To see the interior of Tobago, the bus ride from Scarborough (the capital) to Charlotteville is recommended at TT$1. From Scarborough to Buccoo by bus is TT$0.20.

The main attraction of Trinidad and Tobago is the natural wonders to admire. The scenery shows some of the most lovely flowering trees and shrubs in the world— bougainvillea, the clear, clean beauty of the yellow and pink poui, the red and yellow balisier, the blue petrea, the tall immortelle, and, in the forests, an unbelievable variety of orchids in their wild state.

The islands are a delight for the bird-watcher, who can see flocks of scarlet ibis at the Caroni Bird Sanctuary, herons, egrets, kingfishers, humming-birds and brightly coloured parrots, to mention but few.

The whole Atlantic coast from Matura to Mayaro is divided into three huge sweeping bays, while all around are palm trees, some growing as high as 200 feet.

Festivals Trinidad is the birthplace of the calypso; and here, too, the steel band was born, and it is of fairly recent origin. Towards the end of the last war, the local inhabitants discovered that the empty oil drums left behind by the Forces could be transformed into musical instruments. A crude musical drum, or "pan", was first played, so it is claimed, on Lady Day 1945. Since then it has become perfected and almost sophisticated. To tune a "pan" is a complicated business entailing heating and cooling and hours of pounding. The whole process can take anything from days to weeks. Today, some leading steel bands will bravely tackle the classics, and in fact, the test piece for steel bands in the annual music festival is classical.

Carnival takes place each year on the two days before Ash Wednesday. The happy participants, good-humoured and colourful, dance to the rhythmic throbbing of the steel band, all converging from parts of the island on Port of Spain. The festivities start with "J'ouvert" at about 0400 on the Monday. This is followed by "Ole Mas" which lasts until 0900. In the afternoon is "Lil Mas" when the bands start moving, followed by their lively and gaily dressed supporters. Tuesday is the more important day, however, when the bands all have their own troops of followers, there is a procession of floats and everyone is "jumping up" in the street. (Beware of pickpockets!) Rather different is the Hosein Festival, commemorating the cruel murder of two Moslem princes. It starts ten days after the first appearance of the new moon in the Moharrun month of the Moslem calendar. Colourful processions, hauling 10- to 30-ft.-high miniature wooden temples, start the next day, heralded by moon dancers and accompanied by drum-beating.

On August 29 in Arima the feast of St. Rose of Lima is celebrated; the parish church is dedicated to her. Descendants of the original Amerindians come from all over the island to walk in solemn procession round it. However, these holidays are special occasions, but day-to-day life on the islands is an attraction to visitors—see the great variety of peoples and ways of living, the Moslem mosques, Hindu temples and gingerbread Victorian mansions, the colourful dresses of African street vendors counterpointed by Hindu women in saris; to hear the calypso singing, the strident steel bands, the ritual music of the East Indians, and the odd but attractive English spoken.

Port of Spain, with a population of 350,000, is on a gently sloping plain between the Gulf of Paria and the foothills of the Northern Range. A background of mountains would give a lovely setting if it were not for the outcrop of shanty towns. The city has a pleasant atmosphere but unfortunately it has become very dirty; the streets and buildings are not at all well maintained. The streets are mostly at right-angles to one another and the buildings of fretwork wooden architecture, interspersed with modern office towers. Within easy reach of the port (King's Wharf and its extension) are some of the main buildings of interest—the Red House, which contains the House of Representatives, the Senate and other government departments; the General Post Office; the beautifully designed Anglican Cathedral Church of the Holy Trinity, with a fine and elaborate hammer-beam roof festooned with carvings. These buildings are around Woodford Square, named after Sir Ralph Woodford; the Cathedral was built during his Governorship (1813-28) and contains a very fine monument to him. On the opposite side of the Square to the Cathedral is the Town Hall, with a fine relief sculpture on the front. Woodford Square itself is planted with trees and shrubs and has a quiet, tropical peace as if time had stood still. However, people if they wish may make speeches, and often the Square resembles Speaker's Corner in London's Hyde Park. Woodford Square, in fact, played an important part in Trinidad's path to independence, as it was here that Dr. Eric Williams, now Prime Minister, gave a series of open-air lectures teaching the people to prepare for the future; it became known as "The University of Woodford Square".

In Independence Square is the Roman Catholic Cathedral, built in 1832, and the modern Textel and Salvatori buildings. Behind the Cathedral is Columbus Square, with a statue of the island's discoverer.

To the north of the city are the truly remarkable Botanic Gardens, founded in 1818 by Sir Ralph Woodford. There is an amazing variety of tropical and sub-tropical plants from India, Burma, Java, Malaya and South America, as well as Trinidad's own indigenous trees and shrubs.

Adjoining the Gardens is the small Emperor Valley Zoo, sited in a natural park. It specializes in animals living wild on the island. Also next to the Gardens is the Presidential residence—a colonial style building in a "L" shape in honour of Governor James Robert Longden. There are several other Victorian-colonial mansions along the seaward side of Queen's Park Savannah, north of the city.

Before leaving this area, pay a visit to the Lookout. It is 300 feet high and gives superb views across the town to the Gulf of Paria. Continuing on towards the mountains of the northern range lies the Queen's Park Savannah, a pleasure ground with many playing fields and a racecourse with grandstands. Just off the Savannah is Queen's Hall, a modern building where concerts and other entertainments are given.

There are pleasant drives in the hills around, with attractive views of city, sea, and mountain: to Mount St. Benedict, 11 miles, at 800 ft., and a good guest house; by Lady Chancellor Road to a look-out 600 ft. above sea-level; to the Laventile Hills to see the view from the tower of a chapel; to Fort George, an ex-signal station at 1,100 ft: along the Western Main Road to St. Peter's (a remarkable little church on the waterside) and on to Carenage, with many pretty views, especially of the Five Islands; or by the enchanting Morne Coco circular run; or the longer and even better "Saddle" circular run, with its most varied views, with an offshoot road to Maracas Bay, one of the best beaches on the island. There is a round-the-island trip which includes jungle, coconut grove, lovely valleys and tall mountains and picturesque villages, and there are boat trips to the Caroni Bird Sanctuary (admission TT$6), the home of vast flocks of scarlet ibis. Driving S you see dhoti-clad Indians in the rice fields, herds of water buffalo, Hindu temples and Moslem mosques.

Inland from Port of Spain lies Arima and on the way is St. Joseph, once the seat of the Government. At St. Joseph is the imposing Jinnah Memorial Mosque and nearby, high on a hill, is Mount St. Benedict monastery, which has a guest house. There are marvellous views over the Caroni Plain to the sea.

San Fernando on the SW coast is a busy little town, as yet not spoilt by tourism. In its neighbourhood are the principal industrial-development area of Point Lisas and the Pointe-a-Pierre oil refinery.

A scenic phenomenon to visit on the south-west coast near San Fernando is **Pitch Lake**. It is about 110 acres of smooth surface resembling caked mud but which in fact is hot black tar. (In fact, it has been described by disappointed tourists, expecting something more dramatic, as looking like a parking lot!) If care is taken it is possible to walk on it, watching out for air holes bubbling up from the pressure under the ooze. The legend is that long ago the gods interred an entire tribe of Chayma Indians for daring to eat sacred humming-birds containing the souls of their ancestors. In the place where the entire Carib village sank into the ground there erupted a sluggish flow of black pitch gradually becoming an ever-refilling large pool. It has supplied Trinidad and Tobago and many lands all over the globe with asphalt for hundreds of years and still has uncountable supplies, as, although it drops six inches a year, the centre is several hundred feet deep. It provides a healthy, though recently decreasing, item in Trinidad's export figures. It can be reached by taking a bus from Port of Spain to San Fernando (TT$0.75) and then another from there to La Brea (TT$0.40).

Beaches The nearest beach to Port of Spain is Carenage, but it is badly polluted. Maracas Bay on the north coast over the hills, 10 miles from the capital, has a sheltered sandy beach fringed with coconut palms. There are buses to Maracas Bay on Sats., Suns. and holidays only, from the bus terminal. At other times a taxi from Port of Spain costs US$9 or there is a pick-up "collectivo" service from the centre of town, US$0.62. (Alternatively it is quite easy to hitch a lift from the Queen's Park Savannah roundabout.) Blanchisseuse and Balendra, near Toco, have lovely beaches but are more difficult to reach. Mayaro and Manzanilla to the east have beautiful sandy bays and there are one or two pleasant swimming places at Chaguaramas, though the beach is owned by a hotel and you have to pay TT$1.70 to use it. Maqueripe Bay has a sheltered beach. In general the beaches are difficult to get to except by taxi or hired car and there are no hotels on the beaches.

Economy The economy is firmly based on the petroleum industry and the natural gas reserves, though consumer-goods industries are multiplying. Trinidad not only refines its own crude oil but imports about 115 million barrels a year, about half of it from Venezuela. Visitors can be shown the refinery at Pointe-a-Pierre by arrangement. Production of natural gas now runs to about 121m. cubic feet a year. Asphalt is another important by-product of the oil industry; in 1975 79,443 tons were produced.

Although the soil is remarkably rich and Trinidad has a large sugar production it still has to import a good deal of food. Besides coffee, sugar, rum and molasses, main agricultural exports are cocoa, citrus fruits, bananas and coconut oil. Tourism is growing.

Foreign Trade (TT$m.)

	1973	1974	1975	1976	1977
Exports (f.o.b.) ..	1,375	4,098	3,884	5,393	5,216
Imports (c.i.f.) ..	1,557	3,814	3,244	4,827	4,252

Where to Stay There are a great many hotels on the islands and the better known ones are expensive, but there are very good guest houses and smaller hotels which are reasonable. There is also a YWCA (TT$12 bed and breakfast). Information about accommodation can be obtained from: Trinidad and Tobago Tourist Board, 56 Frederick Street, Port of Spain (there is also an office at the international airport—both are helpful). The High Commissioner for Trinidad and Tobago, 42 Belgrave Square, London S.W.1. In the U.S.A.: Suite 712-14, 400 Madison Avenue, New York, 10017. In Canada: Suite 1006, 110 Yonge Street, Toronto, 105. The following are some of the better known hotels and guest houses—prices quoted in TT dollars for summer rates (mid-April-mid-December). Winter rates tend to be dearer. Rates quoted are for single room per day. If you intend to stay in Trinidad for Carnival you must book a hotel well in advance. Some are booked a year ahead. Hotels and restaurants in Trinidad are on the expensive side.

Hotels   Trinidad—*Port of Spain*

Trinidad Hilton, Belmont Hill (Tel.: 62.43211), EP from 58, beautifully spread all over a hilltop, but a long way from the centre. *Queen's Park,* Queen's Park West (Tel.: 62.51061): EP from 24. *Normandie Hotel,* 2 & 4 Nook Avenue, St. Anns (Tel.: 62.42486) EP from 28; MAP from 42. *Holiday Inn* (Tel.: 62.53361) EP 65 (non-residents can use the swimming pool for TT$7), very convenient to centre for businessmen; *Parillon* (Tel.: 62.42973) CP from 15; *Bagshot House* (Tel.: 62.26828) EP 20; *Chaconia Inn* (Tel.: 62.25474) EP from 36; *Errol Lau* (Tel.: 62.54381) CP from 16; *Tropical* (Tel.: 62.22603) EP 22. *Bretton Hall,* 16 Victoria Avenue (Tel.: 62.52751): CP from 22. *Kapok Hotel,* 16-18 Cotton Hill (Tel.: 62.26441): EP from 25. *Avenue House,* 80 Ariapita Avenue (Tel.: 62.26618): CP from 14.

Guest Houses—*Port of Spain:*

Hillcrest Haven, Hillcrest Avenue, Cascade (Tel.: 62.41344): from 8, each room has cooking facilities, within walking distance of city centre (or TT$0.40 by route Taxi), recommended. *Stone's,* CP from 6.30. *Alcazar's* (Tel.: 62.26920) CP from 14; *Briar House* (Tel.: 62.21013), CP from 11; *Mrs. Williams'* (no sign), 103a St. Vincent Street, 12 d; *Royal,* Charlotte Street, EP about 6; *Monique's,* Maraval, CP 16.50, very friendly and extremely helpful. *Fabienne's,* 13 Stanmore Av., EP 24 d; *Central Guest House,* 45 Murray St., Woodbrook, CP 24 d, friendly, Guyanese proprietor, clean.

Outside Port of Spain:

Bel Air Hotel, Piarco Airport (Tel.: 664.4771) EP from 30. *Pan American Guesthouse,* Piarco Airport (Tel.: 664.4731) EP 24, very helpful. *Gulf Coast,* Clifton Hill, Point Fortin (Tel.: 648.3374) CP 11.

The Pelican Inn, 2-4 Coblentz Avenue, Cascade, CP from 12, has an "authentic British pub", which does bar meals for reasonable prices. At Chaguaramas, *Chagacabana,* EP 26. Olivers Metal Works in Junapuna has a guesthouse attached, MAP 20.

Note: Some guest houses may try to charge you more than the price listed by the tourist office. Ask the office to help, if in doubt.

Tobago hotels

Mt. Irvine Bay, Mount Irvine (Tel.: 639.8871): MAP from 59. *Radisson Crown,* Store Bay, Scarborough (Tel.: 639.8571): MAP from 110. *Arnos Vale,* Plymouth (Tel.: 639.2881): MAP from 60. *Tabo,* Bacolet, Scarborough (Tel.: 639.2731): CP from 26. *Buccoo Reef Guest House,* Buccoo Reef, 20. s, full board, basic. *Coral Reef Guest House,* Milford Road (Tel.: 639.2536): MAP from 18. *Della Mira,* Scarborough: MAP from 21; *Robinson Crusoe,* Milford Road: MAP from 32; *Sunstar Haven,* Scarborough: MAP from 15; *Treasure Isle,* Bacolet EP 30. *Mrs. Davies' Guest House,* at Hope Cottage, Scarborough, highly recommended at TT$16 a day, including three excellent meals.

MAP—Modified American Plan (Room, breakfast, dinner)
EP—European Plan (Room only)
CP—Continental Plan (Room and breakfast)

Nightclub *Penthouse,* cover charge TT$5, drinks not too expensive.

Taxis are not marked. Look for cars with first letter H on licence plates. Agree on a price before the journey and determine whether the price is in TT or US dollars. Taxis are expensive, although route taxis (similar to collectivos) are very cheap. These cannot be distinguished from ordinary taxis, so ask the driver. They travel along fixed routes, like buses, but have no set stops, so you can hail them and be dropped anywhere along the route. During rush hour it is not easy to hail them, however. They usually set off from Independence Square. Fares in town TT$0.50-1. (Be warned that route taxis are not covered by insurance so you cannot claim against the driver if you are involved in an accident.) There are also "pirate" taxis with the P registration of a private car, which cost the same as the ordinary taxis, although you can sometimes bargain with the drivers. Taxis to airport: the charge is supposed to be fixed but seems in fact to range from TT$15-25; TT$1.75 by route taxi. Catch one on the Aruca road, outside the airport, and change at Aruca (or take a bus) for Port of Spain. Taxi from Scarborough Airport to Buccoo Reef costs about TT$11.

Car Rentals Medium-sized cars can be rented for TT$35 daily with a mileage allowance of 75 a day, 500 a week and 18c excess mileage per mile. Driving is on the left and the roads are narrow and winding, similar to many English country minor roads. Insurance costs TT$6-7. Taxi and car rental firms include Battoo Bros. and Hub Travel Ltd. Most companies, however, only rent for a minimum of 3 days.

Scooter Rentals Tragarete Road, TT$15 for 24 hours, and 69 Mucurapo Road, St. James's, TT$16 a day for one person, TT$20 for two. Mr. Mackenzie, at Scarborough bus station, can arrange scooter hire in Tobago for TT$20 a day. Bicycles can be hired at the Mount Irvine Bay hotel on Tobago.

Buses The bus service has been somewhat improved by the acquisition of new buses though there are still not enough to meet demand and buses and bus stops are therefore very crowded. Buses are cheap, however.

Camping is easy, as people are helpful. At Pitch Lake (see page 1109) there are no facilities for camping but if you contact a Mr. Byron you may be able to sleep in the school at La Brea.

Airport Piarco International (runway length 9,500 ft.), 16 miles SE of Port of Spain. There is a TT$3 exit tax. There are occasional buses to the airport (check at transport terminal on Charlotte Street); otherwise it is quite easy to hitchhike. Taxis cost TT$15-25; even 30 at dead of night! TT$1.75 by route taxi.

Information for Visitors

Air Services BWIA links Trinidad with Tobago (daily flights).

U.S.A.: Pan American; British Airways; KLM; BWIA; Air France.

Canada: Air Canada, BWIA from Montreal and Toronto.

Europe: British Airways; Air France; KLM; Pan American; Caribbean Airways (*via* Luxembourg and Barbados); Jetsave.

Venezuela: Local air lines. To Maturin US$57 return, Mon. and Sat. by Aeropostal. Book well in advance. LAV office at 21 Chacon Street. To Caracas is about US$52.

Guyana: Twice weekly flights to Georgetown.

Inter-Island Leeward Islands Air Transport (Liat) and Cubana airlines connect Trinidad and Tobago with other Caribbean islands.

Shipping All shipping lines are reducing their services unfortunately, owing to the docking and handling charges being the highest in the Caribbean. Passages can occasionally be arranged on cruise ships (mainly Italian lines). Cargo ships are not allowed to carry passengers when leaving Port of Spain.

To Venezuela There is a boat to Güiria (Venezuela) from Port of Spain, TT$115 return; departure times are uncertain as they depend on when the boat has arrived, check at Casa Mauricio on Henny St.; there are 3 boats a week from Güiria (US$23). In Güiria the office is at Oficina Petrocinil. There are also first class (only) berths on the Alcoa steamship cargo boats to Venezuela. Offices at Carenage, Port of Spain. (It is also possible for a lone traveller to get a passage to Georgetown, Guyana, on one of the bauxite boats.) The shrimp boats will not take passengers.

Banks Barclays Bank International, Royal Bank of Canada, Canadian Imperial Bank of Commerce, Bank of Nova Scotia, Trinidad Co-operative Bank, the Chase Manhattan Bank, Citibank, National Bank of Trinidad and Tobago. Open from 1000 to 1700, weekdays only. All banks charge a fee for cashing travellers' cheques, some more than others. So check first.

Useful Addresses (Port of Spain) Canadian High Commission, Colonial Bldg., 72 South Quay; US Embassy, 15 Queen's Park West; British High Commission, 3rd floor, Furness House, 90 Independence Square (P.O. Box 778). Tel.: 52861-6; New Zealand High Commission, same building; Brazilian Consulate, 6 Elizabeth St., St. Clair; Argentine Consulate 2nd floor, 3a Queen's Park West. Tourist Board, 56 Frederick Street (not very helpful).

Travel Agents Wong and Kahn Travel Service, Woodford Street, Newtown, Port of Spain. (Tel.: 62-25603.)

Airline Offices British Airways and Air France both have offices in Independence Square; BWIA on St. Vincent St. and the Jetsave representative on Edward St.

Currency The Trinidad and Tobago dollar is the local currency. Notes are for $1, 5, 10 and 20. In 1976 the Trinidad and Tobago dollar was fixed at TT$2.40 to the US dollar. Metal coins are for 1, 5, 10, 25 and 50 cents. Not more than £50 in sterling notes can be brought in by visitors from the U.K., or TT$48 by visitors from other countries. The Bureau de Change, King's Wharf Passenger Centre, changes dollars and pounds into Trinidad and Tobago currency, *using a distinctive envelope*. What remains unspent can be changed back at the bureau if the original envelope is produced and if there is no more money taken out than was brought in.

Documents Passports are required by all visitors. Visas are not normally required by nationals of Commonwealth countries (New Zealanders do need them), West European countries (except Portugal), Brazil, Colombia, Israel, Suriname and Turkey for visits of up to 3 months; for US citizens for visits up to 6 months; and for Venezuelans for stays of up to 14 days. Entry permits for one month are given on arrival; they can be extended at the immigration office in Port of Spain (Wrightson Road). All travellers need onward or return tickets, proof that they can support themselves during their stay, an address at which they will be staying in Trinidad (the tourist office at the airport can help in this respect), and must pay the embarkation tax (if staying over 48 hours) and the airport service charge of TT$1 each. Visitors from Europe and those arriving from Venezuela need a smallpox vaccination certificate. Only those coming from an infected area need a yellow fever inoculation certificate. **Warning:** The immigration officials do not take too kindly to those with a "hippy"-type appearance and may refuse them entry.

Customs Duty-free imports. 200 cigarettes or 50 cigars or ½ lb. tobacco, and 1 quart wine or spirits. Perfume may not be imported free of duty, but may be deposited with Customs until departure.

Entertainment Trinidad abounds in evening entertainment, with calypso dancing, limbo shows and international cabaret acts. For those wishing to visit the places where the local, rather than tourist population go, anyone in the street will give directions. Though the atmosphere will be natural and hospitality generous, it will not be luxurious and the local rum is likely to flow.

Several places have "calypso" evenings and tourist demonstrations. They include *The Penthouse* (Wed.), *Holiday Inn* (Sun 1400) and the *Hilton* (Sat.).

Food A wide variety of European, American and traditional West Indian dishes (these include pork souse, black pudding, roast sucking pig, salcoche and callaloo stews, and many others) is served at hotels and guest houses. Some also specialize in Creole cooking. There is also, of course, a strong East Indian influence in the local cuisine. Seafood, particularly local oysters and crab, is excellent. The many tropical fruits and vegetables grown locally include grapefruit, mangoes, bananas, paw-paws, sapodillas, avocado pears, oranges, pineapples, sweet potatoes, aubergines, eddoes and yam tanias. The variety of juices and ice creams made from the fruit is endless. For those economizing, the *Roti*, a pancake which comes in various forms, filled with peppery stew for about TT$1.50, is very good. So is *Pilau*, savoury rice and meat, but when offered pepper, refuse! Too hot for non-tropical palates. A good restaurant outside Port of Spain is *Marsang's* in central San Fernando. Well worth trying. There is also a good Chinese restaurant there, called *New City*. Many good Chinese restaurants in Port of Spain offer 2-course meals for TT$3. A local drink is mauby, like ginger beer, and the rum punches are recommended. Fresh lime juice is also recommended; it is sometimes served with a dash of Angostura bitters.

As Sir Edward Beetham, a former Governor, advises, the tourist should not leave without trying the local dishes: "they are excellent and not too rich for the European and, wonder of wonders, very few visitors suffer from the 'tummy upset' which so often spoils a holiday in other parts of the world. Trinidad even grows small oysters on mangrove trees".

Tipping   If no service charge on bill, 10-15% for hotel staff and restaurant waiters; taxi drivers, 10% of fare, minimum of 25 cents; dock-side and airport porters, say 25 cents for each piece carried; hairdressers (in all leading hotels), 50 cents.

Tobago is not as lively as Trinidad, but offers dancing in its hotels and a variety of places to dine. The Buccoo Folk Theatre offers a lively show of dancing and calypso every Thursday at 2100, admission TT$3.

Buccoo Reef   Glass-bottomed boats for visiting the reef tend to be cheaper if rented at Buccoo village rather than Scarborough or Pigeon Point: the charge is TT$10 (including use of snorkel equipment) for 2½ hours. The *Mount Irvine Bay Hotel's* beach is good and so is Pigeon Point.

Holidays and special events   Carnival Sunday, Monday, (Shrove) Tuesday, before Ash Wednesday, Good Friday; Easter Monday; Butler's Day (June 19); Corpus Christi; Whit Monday; Independence Day (August 31); Divali, Hindu Light Festival in October-November; All Souls' Day (November 2); Christmas Day; Boxing Day.

Shopping   Shops are open from 0800 to 1700. The main Port of Spain shopping area is in Frederick Street. Nothing is open on Sunday. Purchases can be made at in-bond prices at duty-free shops at the airport. Markets offer wide varieties of fruit—mangoes, lemons, limes, oranges, watermelons, pumpkins. Handicrafts can also be purchased at markets. A new market on the Beetham Highway has replaced the Central Market.

American Express Agents   Port of Spain: Hub Travel Ltd., 44 New Street, Tel.: 62-54086.

LEEWARD AND WINDWARD ISLANDS

This scatter of islands clustered in two main groups, together with the Virgin Islands, form the Lesser Antilles. The Leewards, to the NE of the Caribbean, comprise Antigua, Barbuda, Redonda, St. Christopher (now commonly known as St. Kitts), Nevis, Anguilla and Montserrat. The Windwards (Dominica, St. Lucia, St. Vincent, the Grenadines and Grenada) spread southwards across the path of the cooling trade winds which sweep over this area. (The French and Dutch islands in these groups are dealt with under French and Netherlands Antilles, and the Virgin Islands, both US and British, are also discussed separately.) These small islands, like so many others in the West Indies, depend heavily on holiday makers and they are doing all they can to build up their tourist industry. The best months are from January to May, January and February being the peak season. Summer is from April to December; winter from January to March (hotel seasons). At any time between June and October the weather can be blustery and unpredictable. The climate is best in the Leewards. There is little humidity and summer temperatures are around 28-29°C, falling to 24°C in winter.

Currency East Caribbean dollar (EC$), 4.80 to the £; about 2.60 to the US$ in June 1978. (Also known as a BWI (pronounced "bee-wee") dollar.) **Note:** When shopping make sure you establish which type of dollars you are dealing in.

LEEWARD ISLANDS

ANTIGUA

Although only about 108 square miles, this is the largest of the Leewards. It has a population of around 72,000, most of them of African origin although a fairly large proportion are of English descent. It is also the most popular and the most developed of the Leewards. This is largely thanks to its airport—Coolidge, some 4½ miles from St. John's, the capital—which is a centre for air traffic in the area. The big jet aircraft can land here and Coolidge is, in fact, served by several of the major international air lines such as British Airways, Eastern Airlines, Air Canada and Air France. There are direct jet flights to Antigua from London, the U.S.A. and Canada, and frequent air services to neighbouring islands operated by Leeward Islands Air Transport (Liat).

Antigua (pronounced Anteega) was discovered by Columbus on his second voyage in 1493. It was occupied for brief periods by the Spanish and the French and finally by the British in 1667. Today the island is an associated state of the United Kingdom, which by agreement is responsible for its external affairs and defence. Otherwise it is completely independent.

The island is low-lying and volcanic in origin; its highest point is 1,330 feet and there is nothing spectacular about its landscape, but its coast line, curving into coves and graceful harbours, once the craters of now dead volcanoes, with soft, white sand beaches fringed with palm trees, is among the loveliest in the West Indies.

St. John's Built around the largest of these natural harbours is St. John's, the capital, with an estimated population of about 25,000. It is a charming but run-down town with historical associations which still retains an air of the past. In the 18th century it was an important depot in the Royal Navy's West Indies Station. Nelson served here as a young man for almost three years. In 1805, during his long chase of Villeneuve which was to end with the Battle of Trafalgar, Nelson put into English Harbour. "Nelson's Dockyard" has been restored and this old haven is one of the more interesting historical monuments in the West Indies. The anchorage of English Harbour has become one of the world's most attractive yachting centres. There are a number of historical buildings on the island; near the Dockyard, Clarence House still stands where Prince William, Duke of Clarence, later to become William IV, stayed when he served as a midshipman here.

At Shirley Heights, overlooking English Harbour, are the ruins of fortifications built in the 18th century to protect Antigua during the French wars. Great George Fort, on Mon's Hill, above Falmouth Harbour (a 30-minute walk from the village of Liberta) has been less well preserved than that of Goat Hill which also gives excellent views across Deep Bay. There is an archaeological museum in the Dow Hill tracking station building (formerly used in connection with the U.S. "Apollo" space programme). On Thursday afternoons a talk is given at the museum (check the details at Nicholson's travel agency).

Carnival Antigua's carnival, second only to Trinidad's in the Caribbean, is at the end of July and lasts into August. Hotels and airlines tend to be booked up well in advance.

Sport and Entertainment Like all other major West Indian resorts, Antigua offers a variety of both: sailing, water-skiing, snorkelling, deep-sea fishing, golf, tennis, and of course cricket. The largest hotels provide such night-time entertainments as dancing, calypso, steel bands, limbo dancers and moonlight barbecues. There are cinemas and a casino.

Hotels in St. John's: *Silver Dollar*, Otto's Main Road, US$9 s, US$14-17 d; *Palm View*, St. Mary's St., US$6 s, US$12 d; *Main Road Guesthouse*, Otto's Main Road, US$3.50 s, US$7 d, pleasant; *Open View*, Edward St., US$3.50 s; *Barrymore*, Fort Road, US$30 s incl. 2 meals; *Cortsland*, Upper Gambles, US$20 s (inc. 2 meals); *Stephendale*, Fort Road, US$20-25 s (incl. 2 meals); *Beachcomber; Sugar Mill*, near the airport; *Skyline*, on airport road, US$12 s; *Castle Harbour*, US$18-26 s incl. 2 meals. At Dickerson Bay: *Halcyon Cove*, US$53-76 s (incl. 2 meals). At English Harbour: *Admiral's Inn*, US$42-56 (incl. 2 meals). At Marmora Bay: *Holiday Inn*, US$55-85 s with 2 meals. At Falmouth Harbour: *Catamaran*, on beach, clean, friendly, good food, US$32 with two meals.

Note There is a 10% service charge and 5% government tax at all hotels.

Restaurants *Admiral's Inn*, expensive. *Mark's Restaurant*, Market St., local food. *Mill's Restaurant and Hotel*, Camacho Ave., good but rather pricey. *Darcy's* Kensington Court, steel band at noon. *Spanish Main*, East St., *Roots*, Upper St. George's St., *Golden Peanut Lounge*, old Parham Road, are all recommended. *Brother B's* and *Golden Peanut* are good for local food and hamburgers. *Castle Harbour*, Indian curries. *Barrymore's Restaurant* and the *Spaniard's* are recommended. Antigua Yacht Club provides a moderately priced dinner on Thursdays and more expensive *à la carte* meals on Saturdays.

Night Clubs Maurice's, Market St.; *Roots*, Upper St. George's St.; *Third World*, First Road.

Transport Minivans (shared taxis) go to all parts of the island from the West End bus terminal in St. John's. Frequent services to English Harbour, EC$0.70. There are also buses from the E terminal to Willikies, whence a 20 min. walk to Long Bay beach. Taxis between St. John's and Coolidge airport are EC$7; between English Harbour and Coolidge, EC$20. There are no buses to the airport but hitch-hiking is quite easy. The same applies to Dickerson Bay which is the nearest beach to St. John's and is very good.

Car Hire (all in St. John's and some at airport) Antigua Car Rentals (*Barrymore Hotel*); Carib Car Rentals (*Michaels Mount Hotel*); Lapp's Rent-a-Car (Long and Cross Streets); Alexander Parris (St. Mary's St.); Prince's Rent-a-Car (Fort Road); E. J. Wolfe Ltd. (Long St.). Rates are US$12-14 a day (no mileage charge, petrol is EC$1.60 a gallon). A local driver's licence, US$5, must be purchased.

Tourist Office Antigua Tourist Office on the corner of High Street and Corn Alley. Postal address: P.O. Box 363, St. John's, Antigua. Tel.: 20029. Open 0830-1600 (Mon-Fri.) and 0830-1200 (Sat.). Gives list of official taxi charges. Also has an office at airport.

Food In addition to a wide selection of imported delicacies served in the larger hotels, local specialities, often very reasonable, should never be missed: lobster, freshly caught fish, charcoal grills, sucking pig, free-range chickens, pilaffs and curries. There is a wide variety of fruit and salads. Imported wines and spirits are reasonably priced but here again local drinks (fruit and sugar cane juice, coconut milk, and Antiguan rum punches and swizzles, ice cold) must be experienced. There are no licensing restrictions. Tap water is safe in St. John's but heavily chlorinated. Most luxury hotels will provide rain water.

Shopping The island has good buys in cotton, handicrafts, pottery, Antigua rum, English wollens and linen, bone china, silk screened fabric and a local game called "warri". Gift shops include the Anastasia Gift Shop in both St. John's and English Harbour, Coco Shop, Madeira Shop, Pink Mongoose and Treasure Cove, all in St. John's. There is a fruit and vegetable market (0600-1800 Mon.-Sat.) opp. West End bus terminal in St. John's.

Banks Bank of Nova Scotia, Barclays Bank International, Canadian Imperial Bank of Commerce, Royal Bank of Canada, Antigua Commercial Bank.

Hours of Business Banks: 0800-1200 Mon.-Thurs.; 0800-1200 and 1500-1700 Fri. Shops: 0800-1200, 1300-1600 Mon.-Sat. Thursday is early closing day for most non-tourist shops.

Documents A valid onward ticket is necessary. American, Canadian and British nationals only need proof of citizenship. Passports but not visas are required by nationals of other Commonwealth countries, West European countries (except Austria and Portugal), Tunisia, Turkey, Uruguay and Venezuela. Nationals of almost all other countries may stay for up to 14 days without visa if travelling to a third country; this concession does not apply to citizens of Communist countries and of Haiti. Valid smallpox inoculations are required for all nationalities except U.S.

Cables Cable and Wireless Ltd., St. Mary's St., St. John's. Tel.: 20078.

Overseas Information Eastern Caribbean Tourist Association, 200E 42nd St., New York; Editorial Services Ltd., 980 Yonge St., 6th floor, Toronto; Eastern Caribbean Tourist Association, Rooms 238-250, 200 Buckingham Palace Road, London S.W.1.

American Express Agents St. John's: V. E. B. Nicholson and Son Travel Service, Long and Thames Streets, Tel.: 20106.

Airline Offices Air Canada, St. Mary's St.; Air France, High St.; British Airways, High St.; BWIA, Long and Thames Streets; International Caribbean Airways, St. Mary's St.; Pan Am, High St.; Liat, Coolidge Airport. There is an airport tax of EC$8 for flights to destinations other than Montserrat, St. Kitts, Dominica, St. Lucia, St. Vincent and Grenada, for which a EC$5 tax applies.

Barbuda Some 30 miles to the North and easily reached by air, or by freight or fishing boat from St. John's, is the small island of Barbuda, one of the two island dependencies of Antigua. The population is only about 1,000 and most of them live in the only village on the island, Codrington, which stands on the edge of the lagoon. Barbuda, too, has some enchanting beaches. This is one of the few islands in the area where there is still a good deal of wild life; duck, guinea fowl, wild deer, pigeon and wild pig. Wild donkeys also roam the island. Barbuda is to be developed as a tourist resort with such attractions for snorkellers and skin-divers as exploring old wrecks. The only hotel is *Coco Point Lodge,* which is expensive.

Redonda This is Antigua's second dependency, little more than a rocky islet. It is uninhabited.

We are most grateful to A. Rooke, for two years a resident of Antigua, for sending us some excellent updating material.

ST. KITTS—NEVIS—ANGUILLA
These three islands were supposed to form a unit, with the centre of government in St. Kitts. Anguilla first openly rebelled against this association in 1967 and more spectacularly (and so far permanently) in 1969. Nevisians also complain that the Government neglects their island.

St. Kitts was the scene of the first British settlement in the West Indies back in 1623. For over 150 years it was a pawn in the swashbuckling encounters between the British, the French and the Spanish. For a time it was shared by France and England but it finally became a British colony in 1783. Reminders of those stormy days can still be found in the old fortifications (the most famous is the Citadel on Brimstone Hill) and in the tombs of early settlers and the dead of long-forgotten battles. Sir Thomas Warner, the founder of the British West Indian colonies, is buried here. There are also Carib and Amerindian remains.

Only about 68 square miles, St. Kitts is scenically one of the more spectacular of the Leeward Islands, with the forested slopes of its volcanic hills, rushing streams and jagged cliffs rising from the foaming breakers. There are sheltered beaches, especially at Salt Ponds, some of them of black volcanic sand. Inland, the valleys are ablaze with flowering shrubs and there are the green and white fields of sugar cane and cotton. The sugar mill is now owned by the Government.

The small port of **Basseterre** is the capital and chief town, with a population of about 16,000. The population of the island is about 49,000. St. Kitts has good main roads (cars can be hired) and shops in Basseterre are well stocked with imported goods and luxuries. Local Sea Island cotton-wear and cane and basket work are attractive and fairly reasonable. Food on the whole is good: apart from almost every kind of imported food and drink, there is a wide variety of local fish, pork, poultry and fruit and vegetables. Local rum is excellent; it is also the cheapest drink available.

On the whole, St. Kitts is a quiet resort. Apart from swimming, there is tennis, riding, sailing, skin-diving and fishing. There are a few first class hotels and also modest guest houses. Cottages can also be rented. It is advisable to book accommodation well in advance. Information from St. Kitts Tourist Board, P.O. Box 132, Basseterre, St. Kitts, W. Indies. The tourist office by the landing stage in Basseterre has useful information.

Accommodation   Cheaper in Basseterre, *Parkview,* EC$36 s (MAP); *Blakeney,* central, from EC$45 s (MAP); *Fort Thomas* and *Ocean Terrace Inn,* both near the University centre on the edge of town and both EC$50-60 s (EP); *Martin's Guest House,* College and Cayon Streets, EC$8 s with breakfast; *Morton,* Cayon and Market Streets; *Liburd's; Caine's; Roseate.* Buses on St. Kitts are 5 cents a mile. The airport is at Golden Rock, two miles from Basseterre. There is an EC$5 departure tax.

The climate is pleasant all the year round, but the best time is during the dry months from December to April.

Nevis   Across a 3-mile channel—The Narrows—from St. Kitts lies Nevis. Smaller, and with less than half the population of St. Kitts, in other respects it is very similar, although more rocky and less fertile. It has superb beaches and a treasure of historical relics. Here Nelson met and married Frances Nesbit; the Nesbit plantation still exists today and is a guest house open all the year round (US$40 s, MAP). Here, too, was born Alexander Hamilton, who helped to draft the American constitution. The former capital, Jamestown, was drowned by a tidal wave in 1680. The submerged town can still be visited by snorkellers and skindivers and, according to the locals, the tolling of its church bells can still be heard.

The main town and port is Charlestown. It was once famous for its thermal springs. Nevis (pronounced Neevis) is reached by boat daily from St. Kitts, except Thursday and Sunday, or in a few minutes by airbus. There are few but pleasant hotels. The whole population is only 12,770. For further information consult the St. Kitts Tourist Board (see St. Kitts).

Accommodation   In Charlestown, *Austin Hotel,* EC$10 s with shower; *Lyndale,* EC$12 s; *Pinney's Beach Hotel,* EC$80 s AP. The best beaches are in the N, at Newcastle. Some collective taxis run (EC$6 from Charlestown to airport at Newcastle).

Anguilla   Until it seceded from the association with St. Kitts and Nevis, this small island, only about 35 square miles and with a population of about 8,000, was almost unknown outside the area. It is low lying and unlike its larger sisters it is not volcanic but of coral formation. It has excellent beaches and good game fishing. The Valley, the administrative centre and principal village on the island, is near Wall Blake airport. The island's name derives from the Spanish word *anguilla* (eel)—a reference to its long, narrow shape.

Government   Since its secession from St. Kitts-Nevis in 1969, Anguilla has been governed by a Commissioner, directly responsible to London, assisted by an elected Council. There is no income tax; the U.K. meets 60 per cent of the normal budget and all capital needs.

Transport   Weekday ferry from Marigot, Saint-Martin, and daily air service from Juliana, Saint Maarten, and St. Thomas, U.S. Virgin Is.

Accommodation   *Rendezvous Bay Hotel,* US$35 d MAP; *Lloyds,* US$24 d AP; *Rosemary's Villa,* US$18 d MAP, other hotels, and various guest houses in The Valley and Sandy Ground villages, such as *Florencia Guest House* in the former.

Documents   See under Antigua.

MONTSERRAT

This volcanic island has a peculiar beauty of its own, with its black and golden beaches and forested mountains. There are three main volcanic mountains on the island. The crater of Galway, with its sulphur welling over its sides, can be reached by road. For the more energetic there is the charm and challenge of climbing to see the hot springs and to swim in high mountain pools. The Great Alps Waterfall is one of the more spectacular sights in the West Indies but it is not an easy climb to reach it.

Montserrat is sometimes called the Emerald Isle, not only because of its greenness; some of its early settlers in the 17th century were Irish. The island is about the size of Anguilla but with a population of around 15,000. It is a self-governing British colony. Montserrat's economy is growing as tourism becomes more developed. It is also becoming a popular home for retired US citizens, Canadians and Britons, which has a positive effect on its economy. Cotton, fruit and vegetables are grown and exported to neighbouring islands, as are cattle. There are two flights a day from Antigua (US$25 return), BWIA also flies to Barbados. The capital and only town is Plymouth, with a population of 2,500. The people are friendly and relaxed and seem pleasantly averse from rushing about. A walk N along the beach will bring you to a hot pond and, further on, to the mangrove where the island's cattle egrets come in to roost at dusk.

Hotels All rates are for a double room and MAP. *Caribella Inn,* US$55; *Coconut Hill,* US$35, very good value; *Hideaway,* US$30; *Letts Guest House,* US$28; *Olveston House,* US$58; *Sea Haven,* US$25; *Vue Pointe,* US$54; *Wade Inn,* US$25.

Restaurants *The Anchorage,* where lunch can be obtained for about EC$5 and dinner for EC$10. Night life is found at *The Cellar* bar/restaurant and at *Jerry's Drive-in Disco.*

Transport Taxi to airport from Plymouth (9 miles), EC$12, LIAT has a bus service to town, but there are no public buses to the airport. Airport departure tax EC$2.50.

Tourist Information from Tourist Board, Plymouth, Montserrat, W.I., or West India Committee, 40 Norfork St., London, W.C.2.

Documents See under Antigua.

THE WINDWARD ISLANDS

The four main ex-British islands of the Windward group together cover an area of some 820 square miles with a total population of about 400,000. Lying between Dominica and St. Lucia is the French island of Martinique, and N of Dominica is Guadeloupe. The dry season, which lasts from December to May, is the best time for tourists.

DOMINICA
This is the largest of the Windward Islands and also one of the most mountainous, its main heights rising to 5,000 feet. It has a savage beauty of volcanic peaks, raging mountain streams and rivers, over 350 of them; in fact; deep forests, quiet lakes, waterfalls (the Trafagar Falls in the Roseau Valley—5 miles from the capital—are particularly beautiful), geysers and boiling pools, against a background of black and blood red rocks stained with yellow and saffron. Here, too, there are beaches of black and golden sands but these, at least so far, are not Dominica's main attraction. This, in a sense, is a mountain and nature resort with a Boiling Lake, reached after a three-hour climb with a guide from the village of Laudat, and a Freshwater Lake which can be reached by road. It is a botanist's paradise, too, for in the valleys there are orchids and a wild garden of strange plant life.

In Dominica, one can also meet what are virtually the last remnants of the original inhabitants of the Caribbean, the once war-like Caribs. There are about 1,500 of them left, although perhaps fewer than 100 are pure blooded. They live in the Carib Reserve, a 3,000-acre reservation near the airport. The total population of Dominica is around 107,000, of whom about 25% live in and around **Roseau**, the capital, situated on the Caribbean coast, 35 miles from the airport. A deepwater harbour is being built from which the island's main export, bananas, will be loaded weekly on to a Geest boat for England. The once-famous Botanical Garden has been reduced in size and lost its collection of exotic plants, but is an idyllic setting for cricket, the island's main sport. The new market in Roseau on Saturday mornings is a fascinating sight. The second town is Portsmouth in the north-west with a natural yacht harbour, near the ruins of an 18th-century fort on the Cabrits. Accommodation ranges from beach hotel to village guest-house, with *Fort Young Hotel* in Roseau being among the best-value small hotels in the Eastern Caribbean. Like St. Lucia, Dominica was once a French possession and there is still a fair amount of French influence including the local patois, although English is the official tongue.

Note There is unfortunately a certain amount of anti-European feeling on this island.

Accommodation In Roseau, *Asta*, EC$40 s with 2 meals; *Fort Young*, from about EC$35 s; *Overnighter*, EC$10.40 s; *Kent Anthony*, EC$8.40 s (EC$19.80 including 3 meals); *Travel Lodge*, EC$11 with breakfast; *Cherry Lodge*, EC$20 with 2 meals. Guest houses in Portsmouth and main villages. All hotels charge 5% tax and some add 10% service charge. All visitors must be in possession of a ticket out of Dominica.

Transport Seat in taxi from airport to Roseau is EC$36; there is only one bus a day to Roseau from the airport which leaves early in the morning. The 35 miles between the two places is difficult to hitch as there is little traffic; budget-minded travellers might consider walking to Marigot from the airport (about 2 miles), spending the night there and taking a bus next day to Roseau (EC$3.50). A collectivo-taxi from Roseau (leaves early in the morning) to Marigot costs EC$10; fix this price before undertaking the trip. There is an airport tax of EC$3. Passenger trucks depart from villages at dawn for Roseau, returning at noon.

ST. LUCIA

This is another island with plans to become an international holiday centre. Its total population is around 113,000. The area is about 238 square miles.

St. Lucia (pronounced "Loosha") has all the attractions one has come to expect of these islands; plenty of sport, splendid beaches, a clear, warm sea (which can be dangerous) and golden sunshine. It also has some of the finest mountain scenery in the West Indies, with the splashes of colour of jasmine, scarlet chenile and wild orchids on the green slopes. (The island was the scene of the film "Dr Doolittle".) The highest peak is Mt. Gimie (3,145 feet); the most spectacular are the Gros Piton (2,619 feet) and the Petit Piton (2,461 feet) which are old volcanic forest-clad cones rising sheer out of the sea near the town of Soufriere on the W coast. A few miles away is one of the world's most accessible volcanoes. Here you can see *soufrières:* vents in the volcano which exude hydrogen sulphide, steam and other gases and deposit sulphur and other compounds. There are also pools of boiling water. The mountains are intersected by numerous short rivers; in places, these rivers debouch into broad, fertile and well-cultivated valleys. The scenery is of outstanding beauty, even when compared with other Caribbean islands, and in the neigbourhood of the Pitons it has the less common element of grandeur.

There is a dry season roughly from January to April, and a rainy season from May to August, with an Indian summer in September-October. Towards the end of the year it is usually wet. The island lies in latitudes where the north-east trade winds are an almost constant influence. The mean annual temperature is about 26°C. Rainfall varies (according to altitude) in different parts of the island from 60 to 138 inches.

Neither the date of discovery nor the discoverer of St. Lucia is known, for according to the evidence of Columbus's voyage, he appears to have missed the island. As early as 1605, 67 Englishmen en route to Guiana touched at St. Lucia and made an unsuccessful effort to settle. The island at the time was peopled by Caribs and continued in their possession till 1635, when it was granted by the King of France to MM. de L'Olive and Duplessis. In 1638 the first recorded settlement was made by English from Bermuda and St. Kitts, but the colonists were murdered by the Caribs about three years later.

In 1642 the King of France, still claiming sovereignty over the island, ceded it to the French West India Company, who in 1650 sold it to MM. Honel and Du Parquet. After repeated attempts by the Caribs to expel the French, the latter concluded a treaty of peace with them in 1660. In all, St. Lucia changed hands fourteen times before it became a British Crown Colony in 1814 by the Treaty of Paris.

St. Lucia now enjoys the status of association with the United Kingdom. It is fully self-governing in all its internal affairs, with the United Kingdom responsible for defence and external affairs. There is still a good deal of French influence. Many of the islanders speak a French patois. There is still a French provincal style of architecture and a large proportion of the population are Roman Catholics.

The capital, **Castries,** rebuilt after being destroyed by fire in 1948, is splendidly set on a natural harbour against a background of mountains. It has a covered market. From the old Morne fortress, above the town, you get an excellent view of the town, coast-line and mountains. Soufriere, the other main town, also has an attractive setting. You can walk (though it is fairly strenuous) to the volcano or to the mineral baths. There are two beaches.

Airports St. Lucia has two airports—Vigie Airport (near Castries, taxi for EC$2 or walk across runway) and Hewanorra International Airport (formerly Beane Field). The runway at Hewanorra, in the Vieux Fort District, was recently lengthened from 5,000 to 9,000 feet. Air services are maintained by British West Indian Airways (BWIA) and Leeward Islands Air Transport (LIAT), Caribbean Atlantic Airlines (Caribair), Dutch Antillean Airlines (ALM), and British Airways. There is an exit tax of EC$5 at Vigie and EC$10 at Hewanorra. Taxi from Hewanorra to Vieux Fort, EC$5.

Shipping The island is served by the following shipping lines: Harrison Lines—cargo vessels only; Geest Industries—cargo and passenger vessels; French Lines—passenger vessels.

Documents Regulations for St. Lucia and the other Windward Islands are similar to those for the Leewards, given under Antigua (page 1114).

There is a commerial radio station, Radio Caribbean International St. Lucia, which broadcasts daily in French and English, and a Government-owned station, Radio St. Lucia. A commercial television service is also in operation.

Accommodation Although the island is a relatively new resort, tourism is developing. There is a fairly wide variety of accommodation ranging from first-class hotels to cottages, yacht marinas and more modest small hotels. It is advisable to book well in advance.

Hotels *Halayon Sands; Hurricane Hole* (Marigot Bay), where much of the Dr. Doolittle film was made, is recommended; *La Toc*, from US$70 EP; *Villa* (Castries), US$16 EP; *Steigenberger Cariblue Hotel* (Cap Estate), from US$64 EP; *Holiday Inn* (Reduit Beach), from US$45 EP; *East Winds Inn* (La Brelotte Bay), US$20 EP; *Malabar Beach* (Vigie Beach) from US$45 EP; *Halcyon Beach Club* (Choc Beach), US$18 EP; *Mornie Fortune Apartments,* from US$14 for 2; *Villa Beach Cottages* (Choc Beach), US$14 s; *Marigot des Roseaux,* US$20 MAP; *Anse Chastenet Hotel* (Soufriere), from US$16 EP; *Home Hotel* (Soufriere), US$12.50 AP; *Allain's Guest House* (Soufriere), US$10 MAP; *Halcyon Beach Hotel* (Vieux Fort), US$15 MAP; *Kimatri Hotel* (Vieux Fort), US$15 MAP; *Cloud's Nest Hotel* (Vieux Fort), from US$20 MAP. All prices quoted are single rates for peak periods. They do not include hotel tax. *Ann's Guest House,* 36 Micoud Street, Main Sq., Castries; *William's,* Chausee Road; *Matthew's* EC17.50 s MAP. *La Luna* and *St. Martin,* both in Clarke St., Vieux Fort, both about EC$12; *La Luna* also provides an evening meal for EC$7. AP = All meals; MAP = breakfast and dinner; EP = no meals; CP = breakfast.

Restaurants include the *Flamingo Restaurant, Seven Seas Club, Margot, Diamond Slipper; Rains* (expensive); the *Green Parrot* (recommended) and the *Pizza House.*

Tourist Information Cars and mini-mokes can be rented at reasonable daily rates, but at 25 cents a mile they become expensive. Taxis are reasonable and a tour of the capital costs about a dollar. For longer trips, i.e. to other points on the island, it is advisable to bargain with a number of taxi drivers to get the best price. Alternatively—and much cheaper—go by bus. St. Lucia's buses are pick-ups with benches; they leave for various destinations from behind the market in Castries. Water taxis and speedboats can be rented and there is also a ferry service. As some of the best views are from the sea, it is recommended to take at least one boat trip. A trip along the rugged east coast road to Vieux Fort is also recommended. By bus it costs EC$3.

Other attractions for visitors include a trip to Pigeon Island, which has recently been connected to the mainland by a causeway. A yacht basin is being built there. A day can be spent beachcombing and treasure hunting among the wrecks offshore; there is crab racing; a visit to a coconut oil factory; skin-diving; deepsea fishing; sailing and shopping for local handicrafts.

The address of the Office of the British Government Representative is: George Gordon Building (P.O. Box 227), Castries. Tel.: 2484/5/6.

Banks Bank of Nova Scotia, Barclays Bank International, Royal Bank of Canada and the St. Lucia Co-operative Bank.

American Express Agents Castries: Carib Travel Agency, 5 Jeremie Street, Tel.: 597.

Cable and Wireless (West Indies) Ltd., George Gordon Building.

The largest car rental firm is Freddy's Rent-a-car Service, 6 Manoel St. (Tel.: 2177).

Tourist information is available from St. Lucia Tourist Board, Castries, St. Lucia, W. Indies.

ST. VINCENT

Until fairly recently this island was almost unknown to tourists. Its popularity began when certain prominent people chose it as a site for their holiday homes. It is like all the Windwards, volcanic, mountainous and with luxuriant scenery. It is one of the more picturesque islands of the Windwards, with its fishing villages on palm-fringed coves, its coconut groves and fields of arrowroot, of which the island is the world's main supplier. St. Vincent is a British "associated state", with full internal self-government. Unfortunately there is a certain amount of political (racial) tension.

About 133 square miles, it has a population of some 90,000 mostly African and East Indian. Here, too, there is a small community of descendants of the Caribs, although it is believed that there are no pure-bloods left as there are in Dominica. The capital, **Kingstown,** stands on a sheltered bay where scores of schooners, banana boats and island craft laden with fruit and vegetables add their touch of colour and noisy gaiety to the town. The highest peak on the island, the Soufriere, rises to about 4,000 feet; some 2,000 feet down in the crater is still, glossy lake. In 1970 an island reared itself up out of the lake. The island smokes and the water round it is very warm. It takes about 2 hours of rough walking to reach the crater edge from the end of the jeep track. There are good roads; cars, including self-drive (about EC$8 a day) can be hired and most of the beauty spots are accessible by road. The Botanical Gardens just below Government House are well worth a visit. Here there still stands a bread-fruit tree planted by Captain Bligh of the *Bounty*, who brought the first bread-fruit here from the Pacific; it became a staple diet of the West Indies. St. Vincent also has splendid beaches, mostly volcanic "black" beaches. There is excellent sailing, boats can be hired from the Aquatic Club; deep-sea fishing, tennis and golf. There are first-class hotels and more modest guest houses charging around EC$8-12 a day s with meals. Best months are December to May. There is an airport tax of EC$5. There are regular boat services to Granada and the Grenadines (see page 1125).

Accommodation   All prices are for a double room, MAP, unless otherwise stated: *Blue Lagoon,* US$35; *Cobblestone Inn,* US$48; *Grand View,* US$42; *Haddon,* US$23; *Heron,* US$27; *Indian Bay,* US$20 for a double self-catering flat, recommended; *Mariner's Inn,* US$45; *New Haven* CP, US$17; *Olives,* US$7, but not at all safe; *Rawacou,* US$52; *Sugar Mill Inn,* US$35; *Sunset Shores,* US$40; *Treasure Island,* EP, US$35; *Tropic Breeze,* EP, US$35; *Valley Inn,* US$45; *Villa Lodge,* US$45; *Young Island,* AP, US$98; *Yvonette Beach,* EP, US$220. At the *Bounty Café,* where local artists' paintings are exhibited, you can have a good, light meal.

Buses from Kingstown to Arnos Vale airport, 40 cents; to Mesopotamia (Mespo) 40 cents; frequent service to Indian Bay, the main hotel area, it stops on demand rather than at bus-stops. Also to Layon in the N, but hard to return the same day. Buses in fact are not a particularly good form of transport for the sightseer; if you do want to travel round St. Vincent, it is better to hire a car for about EC$30 a day, but sometimes none is available.

GRENADA

This, the most southerly of the Windwards, can be described, among other things, as a spice island, for it produces large quantities of cloves and mace and about a third of the world's nutmeg. It also grows cacao and sugar. Some of its beaches, specially Grand Anse, a dazzling two-mile stretch of white sand, are considered to be among the finest in the world. The island's capital, **St. George's,** with its terraces of pale, colour-washed houses and gay red roofs, is thought by many travellers to be the most picturesque town in the West Indies. St. George's was established in 1705 by French settlers, who called it Fort Royal; and much of its present-day charm comes from the blend of two colonial cultures, typical 18th century French provincial houses intermingle with fine examples of English Georgian architecture. It stands on an almost land-locked sparkling blue harbour against a background of green and hazy blue hills. Inland, the scenery is just as enchanting; wooded hills, wild flowers, rivers, waterfalls and quiet crater pools and lakes.

Grenada (pronounced "Gren*ay*da") is about the same size as St. Vincent but with a population of some 110,000. There is a good variety of accommodation. First-class hotels are expensive but there are smaller hotels and guest houses. Grenada was the site of the 1969 Caribbean Free Trade Association Fair, Expo 69, and this inspired the building of new hotels including a 50-room, American-financed motel. Average temperature is 18°F. The weather is sunny and hot from December to May. The tourist season is at its height between Jan. and March. The rainy season runs from June to November. For information write to Grenada Tourist Board, St. George's, Grenada, W. Indies, or 64 Bury Walk, London, S.W.3: or 20 E 46th St., New York.

Unlike the other ex-British Windward and Leeward Islands, Grenada did not opt for associated-state status, and became independent in 1974. Prime Minister: Sir Eric Gairy.

Hotels (all prices for double room) St. George's: *Cinnamon Hill*, EC$160 EP; *Crescent Inn*, EC$100 MAP; *Ross Point Inn*, EC$110 MAP; Grand Anse Beach; *Spice Island Inn*, EC$176-220 AP; *Holiday Inn*, EC$100-156 EP; *Blue Horizon*, EC$68 EP. Lance aux Epines: *Secret Harbour*, EC$190 MAP and *Horseshoe Bay*, EC$160 MAP.

Guesthouses St. George's: *Tita's Guest House*, EC$30 EP; *Adam's Guest House*, EC$21 MAP; *Winter Rest Guest House*, EC$30 AP; *Mitchell's Guest House* EC$30 AP; *St. Ann's Guest House*, beyond Botanic Gardens, EC10 s EP, clean and friendly; *Lakeside*, Belmont, run by Mrs. Haynes, EC$11 each MAP, pleasant guesthouse, excellent meals; also in Belmont, *Skyline*, EC$8 s, recommended. Grenville: *St. Andrew's Guest House*, EC$24 EP. You might be able to get a room in a private house if you ask around.

Restaurants *Nutmeg; The Pebble; Snug Corner; Pitch Pine Bar; Portofino.* Be sure to try the local sea-moss drink.

Airport The airport, Pearls, is just N of Grenville, the second most important town, and 18 miles from St. George's. Buses from market in St. George's run to Grenville and sometimes on to the airport for EC$3. (The driver can sometimes be persuaded to go on to the airport.) Airport departure tax is EC$3.

Transport Buses run to all parts of the island from the market place. They are colourful but basic. The last buses tend to be in the mid-afternoon and there are very few on Sundays. Within St. George's and Grenville fares are EC$0.25-0.30. The official maximum rate for taxis is EC$20; the drivers will ask for more but you can bargain with them for less. A trip to the airport from St. George's should cost about EC$20-25. A shared taxi is about EC$7. You can take a bus from St. George's to Grenville, EC$1.50, and hitchhike or walk from there. There are infrequent buses from Grenville to the airport, EC$0.50. Hitchhiking is quite easy.

Warning St. George's has had an unfortunate upsurge of armed robberies of late, so don't walk around the streets after dark or camp near St. George's or on the Grand Anse beach.

Tourist Office Carenage, St. George's. Open 0800-1600 and is helpful. Has information on the two Grenadines which are dependencies of Grenada: Carriacou and Petit Martinique (see below).

Travel Agents (all in St. George's) Grenada International Travel Service, of Church St. (American Express representative), Huggins Travel Service, McIntyre Brothers, George Otway.

Banks Barclays Bank International, Royal Bank of Canada, Chase Manhattan, Canadian Imperial Bank of Commerce, Bank of Nova Scotia.

Business Hours Banks: 0800-1200 Mon.-Thurs; 0800-1200, 1500-1800 Fri. Shops: 0800-1145, 1300-1600 Mon.-Fri., 0800-1200 Sat. Government offices: 0800-1145, 1300-1600 Mon.-Fri.

Holidays
January 1: New Year's Day
February 7: Independence Day
Good Friday and Easter Monday

May 1: Labour Day
First Mon. in August
December 25 and 26

Sports Tennis, golf (9 hole course), swimming, snorkelling, scuba diving and water-skiing.

Food Lambi (a sea shellfish), sea-moss drink, callaloo soup, soue (a sauce made from pig's feet), wild meat e.g. tattoo (armadillo) and manacou (opossum).

Cables Cable and Wireless Ltd., Carenage, St. George's. Open 0700-1900 Mon.-Sat.; 1600-1800 Sun.

Electricity 220/240 volts, 50 cycles A.C.

International Transport Liat flies to Grenada from Barbados, Trinidad and St. Vincent. There are also flights to Maturin (Venezuela). There is a EC$5 tax on airline tickets purchased in Grenada. Chandris American Line, Royal Caribbean Cruise Line call at the island. There is a schooner to Trinidad every Tuesday, EC$15, as well as other unscheduled services. Also regular sailings to St. Vincent and the Grenadines (see page 1054).

THE GRENADINES

These islands are dependencies of St. Vincent and Grenada, a string of tiny, rocky islands stretching across some 35 miles of sea between the two. With a population of around 18,000 they are still very much off the beaten track as far as tourists are concerned. **Carriacou** (pronounced *Carr*-yacoo) and **Petit Martinique** are dependencies of Grenada. Carriacou's sandy island has interesting underwater reefs. Visitors should see the oyster beds where "tree-oysters" grow. Big drum dances take place around Easter. The Tombstone Feasts are unique. An annual regatta takes place in early August which is a good time to visit. Out of season the island is quiet, even depressed, and not all the hotels are open. Barclay's Bank International has a branch on Carriacou.

Hotels on Carriacou: *Silver Beach Cottages,* from EC$25 s; *Mermaid Tavern* from EC$58 in season, AP; *Silver Beach Hotel,* EC$42 s in season, MAP; *Amigo Guest House,* EC$21, AP; *Modern Guest House,* EC$13 s AP. Mr. Prescott Simon, at Hillsborough, takes guests at EC$7.50 each a night, quiet and pleasant. (Plus 10% service and 5% government tax).

Bequia (pronounced Bek-*wee*) and **Mustique** are the largest of the St. Vincent dependencies. Hotels in Bequia include: *Always Spring,* US$40 s MAP; *Frangipani,* US$25 s, MAP; *Mitchells,* US$8´s, EP; *Sunny Caribee* from US$17 MAP. On Mustique: *Cotton House,* US$75 s. Other islands are Union Island, Prune Island and Petit St. Vincent.

Two mail boats sail to the islands. The "Seimstrand" sails from St. Vincent at 0900 on Mon., Thurs. and Sun. to Bequia (EC$5) and Mustique (EC$10). On Mon. and Thurs. it goes on to Union (EC$10), Carriacou (EC$20) and Grenada (EC$30); it also calls at Canouan and Mayreuth if weather conditions permit. The "Seimstrand" sails from Grenada at 0900 on Tues. and Fri., calling at all the same ports, though it stops at Mustique only on request. On Sun. it sails from Mustique to St. Vincent at 1530, going *via* Bequia. Every Tues. and Sat. the "Emmanuel C" sails from Grenada to Carriacou (EC$10). There are daily Liat flights (heavily booked) from Grenada to St. Vincent, *via* Carriacou and Union Island, EC$61. (The airline is sometimes forgetful where luggage is concerned, so make sure yours is loaded on and off the 'plane.) Twice a week a trading schooner sails from Grenada to Carriacou, EC$3. There are also unscheduled schooner services between these islands; by asking around you might be able to get a passage on one.

BAHAMAS

ALTHOUGH GEOGRAPHICALLY these islands belong to the West Indies, the people dislike this association. Admittedly there are a number of differences between them, the most important, perhaps, being the fact that they were always British until they became independent in July 1973, and have never experienced any other cultural influence.

The Bahamas consist of some 3,000 low-lying islands, most of them nothing more than islets and rocks. Grand Bahama Island is only 60 miles from Florida. Nassau, the capital, on New Providence Island, is 184 miles by air from Miami.

There are some 30 main islands with a total population of about 175,000; 101,000 live in New Providence and 36,000 in Grand Bahama. Thanks partly to the Gulf Stream, the climate is one of the finest in the world; the seas are turquoise and a dozen other colours, and so clear that fish can be seen from the air. It is a paradise for tourists, mostly American, Canadian and English, and they get what they want: good hotels, good shops, picturesque buildings and a round of sport and entertainment. The "Family Islands" (the new name for the Out Islands) include Grand Bahama, Bimini, Abaco, Harbour Island, the Exumas, Andros and Eleuthera. The last two are particularly lovely. They are all being transformed now; there are already no less than 23 Family Island landing strips, and those which have none are served by amphibian aircraft as well as the normal inter-island surface vessels.

The total area of the islands is about 5,400 square miles, roughly the same as Jamaica. The whole archipelago extends for about 600 miles south eastward from the Mantanilla shoal off the coast of Florida to 50 miles north of Cuba. The tiny islets, of which there are about 670, are known as "cays" (pronounced "keys"). Some of these are privately owned but most of them are uninhabited and some possibly have never even been visited.

Perhaps the greatest beauty of the Bahamas is the coastline of the islands. The vast submarine plateau on which most of the larger ones rest falls away so steeply on the eastern shores that ocean depths of 15,000 feet are reached within a mile of the coast. On the west and south western shores, in the shallows of the Grand Bahama Bank, the sea is rarely deeper than 25 feet. The colour ranges from deep blue to purple near the reefs and lightens to turquoise and green near the pale golden sand of the beaches.

The soil is thin but in some places fertile. On the more developed islands careful cultivation produces a wealth of flowering tropical and sub-tropical shrubs, vivid pink and purple bougainvillea, red poinsettias and passion-flowers, casuarinas, silk-cotton trees and many others. The sunny climate favours the cultivation of an exotic variety of fruit: pineapples, mangoes, guavas, sapodillas, soursop, grapefruit and sea-grapes. On the less developed islands there are large areas of pine forest, rocky and barren land, and swamp, as well as countless tiny harbours and unspoilt beaches. It is this variety which gives the Bahamas a unique place among holiday resorts, for these enchanting spots are within easy reach of some of the most sophisticated and luxurious hotels in the world.

Throughout their long history the people of the Bahamas have experienced bursts of prosperity and periods of slump. Since 1945, however, the economy seems to have become firmly established, based mainly on tourism and real estate. Thanks to the sunny climate (the Bahamas have been called "The Isles of June") visitors are attracted throughout the year. Recently, the most striking development has taken place in Grand Bahama Island and Freeport has become an important trade, industrial and shipping centre. It is a tax-free area providing a base from which international companies can operate with as few restrictions as possible. The Family Islands are now beginning to share this prosperity and tourist facilities are being developed and agriculture extended. Some steps have been taken to encourage light industries, notably timber and salt production.

History Columbus discovered the Bahamas in 1492. The island of Guanahani (renamed by him San Salvador) is generally accredited as his first landfall in the New World. In 1513 Ponce de León set sail in search of the island of Bimini and its legendary Fountain of Youth. He sailed past the eastern shores of the Bahamas to discover Florida. John Rut and John Hawkins were among English navigators who explored the area in the 16th century, and Francis Drake anchored off Bimini in 1586. It was after founding their first colonies in Virginia that the English realised the strategic importance of the Bahamas, and in 1629 the islands received their first constitution as part of the Carolinas. This was under dispute for some years and it was not until some twenty years later that the first European settlers arrived. In fact, the first settlers came from Bermuda with the aim of founding a colony free from the religious and constitutional troubles surrounding Charles I. Then William Sayle, who had been Governor of Bermuda, published in London in 1647 *A Broadside Advertising Eleutheria and the Bahama Islands.* As a result of this publicity, a company of Eleutherian Adventurers was formed and a party of about 70, led by Sayle himself, set out for Eleuthera. Their ship was wrecked on the reefs. The party managed to land but most of the stores were lost and the settlers barely managed to survive by trading ambergris.

From this time on, the life of the Bahamas was largely influenced by their proximity to the American mainland and their place on the sea routes. Piracy, buccaneering and the slave trade were features of the next two centuries. After the American Civil War, the Bahamas lost their strategic importance, but in 1919, with the advent of Prohibition in the United States, Nassau became a bootleggers' paradise and the money poured in. With the repeal of prohibition, this source of wealth dried up and the islands had little to fall back on. The thirties, a time of severe depression, ended in disaster in 1939 when disease killed off the sponges which had provided some means of livelihood. Once again, it was war which brought prosperity back. This time, however, foundations were laid for more stable conditions in the future and the two bases of prosperity, tourism and the real estate business, with all their attendant economic activity, became firmly established. In 1969 new gambling laws were introduced to exclude "undesirable" interests from the casinos.

Political After three centuries of rule by the merchant classes of Nassau, an administration supported by the black majority came to power in 1967, led by Mr. Lynden Pindling. The Bahamas became independent, within the Commonwealth, in July 1973; Mr. Pindling is still Prime Minister.

Nassau (population: 110,000), on New Providence Island, is the capital. It looks comfortably old-fashioned with its white and pink houses: shrewd by-laws forbid the shattering of a dream by skyscrapers and there are few neon lights. Many of the hotels are designed for Americans who have come south for the sun and the sea, and are expensive. Gambling at Paradise Island Hotel (US$40 a day d, European plan) in a casino as big as a large railway station, and at 2 casinos in Freeport. There is a seaquarium at Nassau; it costs US$2 to see a show there; this includes the return bus fare from the town centre.

Nassau has plenty to interest the tourist: spear fishing, deep-sea fishing, skin diving, golf, ski-ing, tennis, bowling, a visit to the flamingo gardens, a trip on a glass-bottomed boat, a sight-seeing tour of the ancient fort and churches, and attractive examples of early local architecture: houses built of limestone, with wide wooden verandas. There is a *son-et-lumière* show every night at Fort Charlotte; visit too the Versailles Gardens and Cloisters on Paradise Island, Straw Market, the Queen's Staircase and Woodes Rogers Walk. In the night-clubs you can hear the haunting beat of the Goombay drums, the strumming of guitars and the Calypso singers. And five minutes across Nassau harbour is the famous Paradise Island, reached by an extremely ugly steel toll bridge ($2), entitling you to eat in the Café Martinique or to gamble in the Casino. Shopping is also one of Nassau's attractions: low import duties make many goods relatively cheap. Rum costs under US$3 a bottle and cigarettes are 33c. for 20. Beer is, however, more expensive.

Warning to young women. Beware the "beach bums" who earn a living picking up girl tourists!

Hotels There is a great variety of accommodation in the Bahamas, ranging from small guest houses offering only rooms to luxury hotels complete with swimming pools, private beaches, sailboats and skin-diving equipment, restaurant, dancing and entertainment. Many of the large hotels offer a choice of Modified American Plan (room, breakfast and dinner) or European Plan (room only). Prices vary considerably. As a general guide, an hotel room is from about US$20 MAP s a day. The hotels to the W of Nassau and on Paradise Island have the most amenities, but are also the most expensive. Those in the centre are the cheapest but have least to offer; to the E are the medium-priced hotels with many facilities. A limited amount of less expensive accommodation exists in some of the Family Islands. Most hotels offer lower rates in summer (May to November). *Flagler Inn*, Paradise Island, US$34-43 s, US$37-47 d with breakfast, water taxi connects hotel with Nassau shopping centre; also on Paradise Island, *Holiday Inn*, charging from US$40 d; *Graycliff*, formerly the winter home of the Countess of Dudley, comfortable surroundings and good cooking; *Hotel Cable Beach Manor*, apartments (US$36 for 3 per day) with well-equipped kitchens, recommended; *Buena Vista*, Delancy St., US$19.70 s EP; *Beachcomber*, East Bay St., US$18.50 s EP; *Grand Central*, Charlotte St., US$18.50 s EP; *Columbus*, Bay St., US$14.50 s EP; *Delancy Heights Guest House*, US$8 s, some self-catering facilities, recommended; *Kemp's Guest House*, US$10, recommended; *Pearl Cox's Guest House*, 30 Augusta St., US$7 s, friendly, close to beach and about 10 mins. walk from centre; *Mignon Guest House*, Market St., US$10 s; *Providence Guest House*, US$8 s, clean and central; *Salvation Army Men's Hostel*, Grantstown, US$3 each. For families wanting private garden or pool try *Little Orchard Cottages*, near Fort Montague beach. For further information, write to Bahamas Ministry of Tourism, Nassau Court, Nassau,

BAHAMAS

Bahamas, or at 23 Old Bond Street, London, W.1 (Tel.: 629-5238); 30 Rockefeller Plaza, New York, N.Y. 10020; 85 Richmond Street W, Toronto 1, Ont.

Restaurants At Nassau: *El Toro*; *Dirty Dick's*; *Pilot House*; the *Poop Deck* at the Nassau Yacht Haven serves lunch and dinner; *Green Shutters*, Parliament Street, good bar and restaurant; *Buena Vista Hotel*, restaurant recommended; *Grand Central Restaurant*; *Blackbeard's Tavern*; *Riviera*, Bay Street, near Charlotte Street, good for breakfast and quick lunches, cheap; *Sandpiper* and *Skan Cafeterias* for quick, relatively cheap meals. Also *Kentucky Fried Chicken*, *Macdonalds*, *Lums*, *Lofthouse* and *Mermaid Tavern*. To the W of Nassau, at Gambier, is *Travellers' Rest*. At Freeport: *The Fishing Hole*; *Island House*; *The Pub on the Mall*; *Paul Mack's Recreation and Lounge*; *Village Inn*. Restaurant meals are very expensive. Near the Pearl Cox Guest House, on the beach, fish is cooked and makes a cheap meal.

Night-life Most of the large hotels have night clubs. Other night spots include King Eric's (good floor show), Peanut Taylor's (expensive), Dirty Dick's and Pino's. Some clubs have a cover charge or a two-drink minimum.

Clubs East Hill Club and Lyford Key Club at W end of island, with fine golf course.

Diving Equipment Boats and diving equipment can be hired at shops by the Paradise Island bridge. The cost of hire for a morning's dive is about US$22. Scuba-diving with an instructor costs about US$28 a day.

Swimming Non-residents can swim in the Sheraton-Colonial hotel's swimming pool and use its beach.

Camping is illegal on Nassau beach.

Tourist Office, Rawson Square. Ask for "What to Do" pamphlet. Another, "Best-Buys", is in your hotel or at the airport. There is also an office at the airport which will help you find accommodation. The Ministry of Tourism is at Nassau Court. The tourist office has a list of churches (and church services) by denomination.

Tourist Agencies Majestic Tours (Tel.: 2-2606) arranges day trips to "deserted" islands or cays. The cost is US$25 each which includes lunch.

Shipping A cargo service (no passengers) from Liverpool (Pacific Steam Navigation Co., Liverpool), New York, Miami and Florida to Nassau. Home Lines (Nassau to New York); Eastern Steamship Corporation (Nassau to Miami).

Royal Mail Lines Agency R. H. Curry & Co., Ltd., 303 Bay Street, P.O. Box 168 (freight only).

Banks Royal Bank of Canada at Nassau, Bimini, Harbour Island, Hatchet Bay (Eleuthera Island), Lyford Key, and Spanish Wells. Bank of London & Montreal; Barclays Bank International; Bank of Nova Scotia; Canadian Imperial Bank of Commerce; Chase Manhattan Bank; Bank of America; Citibank.

Hours of Business Banks 0930-1500 Mon.-Fri.; Shops 0900-1700 Mon.-Sat. Govt. offices 0900-1730 Mon.-Fri.

Airport Windsor Field, about 14 miles from Nassau. Taxi to Nassau, US$10. There is no public bus service to or from the airport, though some hotels have buses. If you ask politely and discreetly you might be able to get a lift on the bus which takes the luggage men to town. Otherwise you can try getting a lift in the car park. For the return journey there is a bus from Nassau to Clifton (US$0.75); it leaves on the hour from Bay and Frederick Streets (Western Transportation Company) and will drop you 1½ miles from the airport. The airport departure tax is US$3. During the day immigration and customs formalities for those going to the U.S. are carried out at Nassau.

Transport Taxis are abundant and expensive: the minimum charge is US$0.90, plus US$0.50 p.p. per mile. There are very few public buses, but minibuses called "jitneys" go all over New Providence Island from Woodes Rogers Walk.

Car Hire Avis, W. Bay St.; Hertz, Sheraton-Colonial hotel; National, Bay St.; S. J. Humes, W. Bay St. All these have offices at the airport. Their rates start from

US$27 a day. Motor scooters can be hired from US$14 a day and bicycles from US$4 a day.

Communications Main post office is at East Hill. Air mail to U.K. and Europe, US$0.21 per ½ oz.; to U.S.A. and Canada, US$0.18 per ½ oz. Telephone calls and cables can be made from Bahamas Telecommunications Corp., East St. Open 24 hours. There is now direct telephone dialing to North American cities.

Electricity 110 volts, 60 cycle A.C.

U.S. Embassy Mosmar Building, Queen St. Tel.: 2-4733.

British High Commission Bitco Building, East St. Tel.: 5-7471.

Grand Bahama Island, the nearest to the U.S.A. and, with Great Abaco, the most northerly of the Bahamas, is where the most spectacular development has taken place. The island has several natural advantages over others in the group. It has miles of south-facing beaches sheltered from northerly winds and enjoys the full benefit of the Gulf Stream. Thanks to a fresh water table under the island it has no water problem. The pinewoods which this natural irrigation supports were, indirectly, the beginning of the present prosperity. Early in the 1940s, an American financier bought a small timber company and developed it into an enterprise employing 2,000 people. In 1955, the Bahamas Government entered into an agreement with him as president of the Grand Bahama Port Authority Ltd., granting to the specific area, called **Freeport,** owned by the Port Authority, certain rights and privileges which apply to that area only and to no other sections of the Colony. The aim of the Agreement (to which amendments giving greater breadth were added in 1960 and 1966) was to create an economic climate to encourage the establishment of factories and commerial enterprises for the benefit of the Colony and the exploitation of its raw material and natural resources.

So successful was this that the population of the island grew from 9,500 in 1963 to 35,250 in 1967. In the same period, the total investment rose from US$150m. to US$577m. and the tonnage of cargo handled increased ten times to 1¼ m. tons. In 1969, however, the Government decided to introduce controls on the expansion of Freeport, and the vertiginous growth process has since slowed down.

International Shopping Centre at Freeport is an integrated shopping-complex with streets built in Hong Kong, Spanish, Scandinavian and Indian style; the English street is a Tudor-style courtyard.

Hotels in Freeport: *Oceanus Beach,* US$28 s; *Palm Court,* US$27 s; *Freeport Inn,* from US$23; *Lucayan Harbour Inn,* from US$20.

On Bimini: *Brown's Hotel,* N. Bimini, US$19 s.

On Abaco: *Elbow Cay Club,* Hopetown, US$18 s; *Running Light Inn,* Marsh Harbour, US$14 s; *Paradise Hill Hotel,* Cooper's Town, US$17.25 s.

On Andros: *Chickcharnie Hotel,* Fresh Creek, Andros Town, US$20 s; *King's Guest House,* Mangrove Cay, US$17 s.

Long Island has been recommended to us as the "least-spoiled, habitable Family Island. *Stella Maris,* a German establishment, is not cheap, but best value. Generally speaking accommodation on all the Family Islands is expensive, US$30 being an average price for a hotel room and meals for one person a day.

Air Services to the mainland: Pan American, Air-Canada, British Airways, Bahamas Air, Flamingo Airlines, Mackey, Shawnee, Delta, and Eastern Air Lines. To and from the U.K., Bermuda and Kingston: British Airways; and for other European cities, Sabena and Lufthansa. Air and sea services to the Bahamas are continually increased: for Panama by British Airways, for Haiti by Flamingo Airlines and Bahamas Air, for Jamaica by Air Jamaica, for Mérida, Mexico, by Lufthansa. Icelandic Airways flies daily from Nassau to Luxembourg, except Wednesday;

special youth fares apply throughout the year. International Air Bahamas also flies between Nassau and Luxembourg, for about US$235 s. There is also a flying-boat service between Nassau and Miami.

Information for Visitors U.S. and Canadian citizens do not need passports or visas but must carry some form of identification. British subjects: no passport or visa required if in transit or for stays of up to three weeks; for longer, a valid passport is required. Visitors who have sufficient funds for their stay and a ticket to a country for which they have a valid visa may remain in the Bahamas for up to eight months. Passports are required by all other nationalities, but visas are not needed by nationals of Commonwealth and West European countries, nor by most Latin American nationals if staying no longer than 14 days. To enter the Bahamas for business purposes the permission of the Immigration Officer, Nassau, must be obtained. It is advisable to apply in writing to: Chief Immigration Officer, Immigration Office, P.O. Box 831, Nassau.

Visitors are permitted to drive on a valid British licence or International Permit for up to 3 months. Beyond that they need a local licence issued by the Road Traffic Department in Nassau. Traffic keeps left. Strict speed limits: Nassau and Freeport 20 m.p.h.; elsewhere 30 m.p.h. Bahamas time is 5 hours behind G.M.T. A number of publications of interest to tourists can be obtained free from hotels.

Currency The unit of currency is the Bahamian Dollar (B$) which is at par with the U.S. dollar. There is no restriction on foreign currency taken in or out; Bahamian currency may be exported up to B$70 p.p.; imports of Bahamian currency only by permission of the Central Bank. Notes of B$100, 50, 20, 10, 5, 3, 1 and 50c; coins of B$5, 2, 1, 50c, 25c, 15c, 10c, 5c and 1c.

Foreign Trade Exports, mostly refined oil products, reached US$1,439m. in 1976, and imports US$1,780m.

Local Travel Outisland Airways and Flamingo Airlines operate scheduled flights between Nassau and 14 of the main Family Islands, including several flights daily to Freeport. Bahamas Air has a daily service to nearly all the Family Islands. Also regular services between Miami and Nassau, Miami and Freeport, and West Palm Beach-Freeport-Abaco-Nassau. Charter flights and excursions available through them and several private companies. The Family Islands can also be reached by regular ferry boat services timed to connect with arrivals by air in Nassau. A colourful way of travelling to the islands is on the mail boats which also carry merchandise. They leave from Potters Cay and Woodes Rogers Walk; their drawback is that they are slow and accommodation on board is very basic. The Bahamas Family Islands Association has a helpful brochure listing fares and schedules. On New Providence Island the main out-of-town hotels provide frequent free bus transport for their guests to and from Rawson Square, Nassau Harbour. Taxis are usually available from ranks in the towns. For radio cabs in Nassau Tel.: 3-5111; Freeport 6666. British and American cars are available for hire, the former more suited to the relatively narrow roads $20-30 a day, unlimited mileage according to type. Freeport: Five Wheels Car Hire, Tel.: 7001; Hertz, Tel.: 6288; National, Tel.: 7251. On some other islands cars can be hired through your hotel but in many of the Family Islands bicycles and mopeds are appropriate. These can be hired in Nassau, Tel.: 2-2374 or 2-3788; in Freeport, Tel.: 6090; in many other places through hotels. Approx. rates: bicycles US$4 per day, 15 per week; mopeds: US$5 per day, 25 per week. Scooters and light motorcycles can be hired from about US$14 per day. A drive in a "Surrey" horse-drawn carriage is a pleasant way of seeing Nassau; about US$5 per hour. The number of minibuses, or "jitneys" on the main islands is expanding fast: fare about US$0.50.

Sightseeing Tours The many organised excursions offer the visitor an easy way of getting about. As well as drives to places of interest, tours include visits to beaches on the Family Islands and trips aboard a catamaran with stops for swimming and sunbathing. Details from hotels or Playtours, Tel.: 2-4018; Nassau Tours, Tel.: 2-2881; Mauras Tourist Services, Tel.: 2-8262; Triangle Tours, Tel.: 5-9603; Tropical Travel Tours, Tel.: 2-3802.

Climate   The sunshine and warm seas attract visitors throughout the year but winter, from December to April, is the high season. Temperatures are around 21°-23°C. Summer temperatures average about 30°-32°C. Humidity is fairly high but is tempered by sea breezes and is not oppressive. Light rain showers occur throughout the year but heavy thunderstorms take place mainly in June, July and October.

What to Wear   During the daytime women use lightweight casual wear, but brief shorts and suntops are not worn in town. The temperature drops at night and a sweater or stole is needed. In the winter season, particularly, more formal clothing is worn at night in the hotels. A light raincoat is useful throughout the year.

Sport   *Yachting* There are now 30 official ports of entry for private boats; a continuous series of competitions is organized ranging from the Family Island Regatta to the Bahamas 500, a gruelling 500-mile race for high-powered craft from Miami to Nassau to Freeport. *Private Flying* The Annual Flying Treasure Hunt, started in 1963, has attracted increasing number of private aircraft. There are 24 official ports of entry for sea or land aircraft. Light aircraft can be hired by licensed pilots. *Golf* Splendid championship courses, most of them built since 1964. The main golfing centre is Grand Bahama, followed by Nassau. A notable course is the Cotton Bay Club on Eleuthera. *Auto Races* Grand Prix in Freeport and other events during winter season. *Water Sports* The Bahamas have hundreds of miles of sunny beaches and comprise an area of about 100,000 square miles of warm, clear Atlantic ocean. Every conceivable type of water sport is available and the variety of deep-sea fishing is famous.

Food   Conch, a shellfish meal, baked crab, grouper cutlets, red snapper fillets. The Bahamas have some good fruit: sapodilla, mango, breadfruit, sugar apple and papaya.

American Express Agents   Nassau: Playtours/R. H. Curry & Co., Bay Street, Tel.: 32286. Freeport: Freeport/Lucaya Tours, Intl. Credit Bank Blg. Tel.: 352-708.

We are deeply indebted to Richard Drysdale and Vittorio Farretto for some most useful updating information.

TURKS AND CAICOS ISLANDS

THE TURKS AND CAICOS ISLANDS lie 550 miles SE of Miami, Florida, directly east of the Bahamas and north of Haiti and the Dominican Republic, in the Atlantic Ocean. They consist of some thirty islands covering 166 square miles, only seven of which are inhabited. About 6,000 local people and another 2,000 or so Canadians, Americans, and Europeans—mostly British—make their home on these islands. Since 1973, the Turks and Caicos have been a British Crown Colony, whose main income derives from tourism, which is nonetheless still low-keyed.

History Christopher Columbus may have made his first landfall here on October 12, 1492, off the eastern cliffs of the Grand Turk Island, and his logs are said to describe the Turks and Caicos with remarkable accuracy. Officially though, these islands were not discovered until Ponce de León arrived in 1512. The native Arawak Indians, a peaceful people, were almost entirely wiped out in succeeding years by Spanish and French invasions. In 1766, Britain planted its roots, hoisted its flag, and set up a proper administration under Andrew Summer. Shortly thereafter, during the American War for Independence, pirates and British loyalists fleeing the colonies found refuge on the Turks and Caicos. Many set up cotton plantations with the help of their slaves, whom they brought from the U.S.A. With hurricanes repeatedly destroying their crops every twenty years or so, many of the plantation owners returned to England defeated, leaving behind their workers who today still own the bulk of island property and often still bear the names of their ancestors' owners. Hurricanes again at the beginning of this century created havoc with the British-managed agricultural and shellfish industries, and by the 1950s even the thriving salt-harvesting trade had been all but completely abandoned. Finally, given the disastrous economic situation, the government decided in the 1960s to turn to tourism, and tried to encourage developers to retain the quiet charm of the islands—so far, with success.

The Turks Islands comprise Grand Turk, which has the seat of government, and tiny Salt Cay.

Grand Turk has four small hotels, of which three face westward over the coral sand beach: *Turks Head Inn*, built over a hundred years ago, was once a government guest house and is still a favourite haunt of government officials, US$32 d, US$15-20 s EP. *Kittina* is the newest and has air-conditioning; US$24-30 d, US$17-22 s. *Salt Raker Inn*, US$24 d, US$16 s, has a friendly bar which is open late. In town is the *Windjammer Guest House*, the least expensive: US$12 s.

Salt Cay offers accommodations at the *Mt. Pleasant Guest House* and at *The Brown House*.

The Caicos Islands lie 22 miles from the Turks across the Turks Island Passage (a diver's paradise, particularly its spectacular "edge-of-the-deep" drop-off). Lying in a semi-circle, with a 25- to 50-foot-high ridge along the northern and eastern exposures which protects them from storms blowing in off the South Atlantic, are the South, East, Middle, West and North Caicos, and Providenciales. Low hills slope down from the ridge to the shallow waters of the Caicos Bank, which have a healthy shellfish population.

South Caicos has low, scrub-covered hills and not much to offer the tourist. There is, however, accommodation available at the *Admiral's Arms,* which has a sea-water pool (US$46 d, US$31 s, MAP).

North Caicos has a five-mile-long beach called Sandy Point and a hotel called *Prospect of Whitby,* US$55 d, US$40 s, all meals included.

Providenciales, or "Provo" as the locals call it, is the westernmost inhabited island of the Caicos and is being developed wholesale; plans are under way for a condominium development intended to attract thousands of visitors to the island. At the moment, there are two inns: the *Third Turtle Inn,* US$48 d, US$30 s, all meals included; and the *Erebus,* which is newer and overlooks the former, with air-conditioning and a seawater pool, US$32 d EP. The *Leeward-Going-Through,* overlooking the deep-water channel of the same name at the eastern end of the island, rents houses at US$2,000 a month including maid and cook.

Pine Cay, one of six tiny islands between North Caicos and Provo, measures only 700 acres, but has an airstrip 4,000 feet long which can land a DC-3. It is a prively-owned vacation resort with the exclusive *Meridian Club,* US$50 d, US$40 s, EP, a full-service deep-water marina, fishing and diving gear, and French cuisine—no minor attraction in this area.

Practical Information   The official currency is the U.S. dollar. Hotels and Barclays Bank International, which has offices, will accept travellers' cheques, and the main hotels now take credit cards. For diving equipment: Pepcor, Ltd. on Grand Turk; the Meridian Club on Pine Cay.

Holidays   Carnival is a week-long celebration in September. Each island enters a float in the parade on Grand Turk, and a queen is elected. There is also an annual regatta on May 24, drawing boats from as far away as Jamaica, Miami, and islands dotting the area.

Transport   Mackey Airways (MI) runs flights thrice-weekly from Miami, Florida, to the Bahamas, Provo, and Grand Turk. The local inter-island Turks and Caicos Airways (TCA) flies to Haiti, and runs four daily island-hopping flights connecting Grand Turk, South Caicos, North Caicos, Pine Cay and Provo. The fare from Grand Turk to North Caicos, for example, is US$19.

Further Information   Write Caribbean Travel Association, 2 West 46th St., New York, N.Y. 1003.

CAYMAN ISLANDS

THE BRITISH CROWN COLONY of the Cayman Islands consists of three small islands set in the Caribbean Sea. **George Town,** the capital and financial and administrative centre, with a population of about 10,000, is located on **Grand Cayman,** the largest of the three islands lying about 180 miles NW of Jamaica and 480 miles S of Miami. Cayman Brac and Little Cayman lie respectively 89 and 74 miles ENE of the larger island of Grand Cayman. The Cayman Islands are peaks of a subterranean mountain range extending from Cuba's Sierra Maestra westward across the Misteriosa Bank towards the Gulf of Honduras. Between the Cayman Islands and Jamaica lies the famous Cayman Trench, which exceeds 24,500 ft. in depth and is the deepest part of the Caribbean.

The Beaches and The Sea. The beaches of the Cayman Islands are said to be the best in the Caribbean. On Grand Cayman, West Bay Beach, now known as Seven Mile Beach, stretches out endlessly with dazzling white sand. Tall Australian pines line the beach. Small coral reefs just offshore provide superb snorkelling grounds for both novice and veteran. Beaches on the E and N coasts are equally good, and are protected by an offshore barrier reef.

The waters surrounding the three islands abound with fish of all kinds. Bottom fishing along the reefs will produce an almost unlimited assortment of colourful fish, with grouper and snapper among the most plentiful. Trolling in slightly deeper water almost always produces results, with bonito, jack and barracuda providing much of the excitement. On Little Cayman the flats offer what may claim to be the best bone fishing in the world and farther out are the big ones, marlin, tuna, wahoo, in such quantities and size that they attract sportmen from all over the world. Experienced guides and charter boats are available at very reasonable rates. Many of the hotels in the Cayman Islands have sailing boats for the use of their guest. The waters are usually calm enough for good water skiing; hotels have all necessary equipment and can provide power boats and experienced boatmen. The water and beach provide incomparable swimming conditions.

The Cayman Islands are world-famous for their underwater scenery. Skin divers the world over have come to regard the Cayman Islands as a Mecca for clear water (200 feet submarine visibility), multitudes of fish, impressive coral formations and interesting wrecks. Many of the better reefs and several wrecks are found in water shallow enough to require only mask, snorkel and fins. A complete selection of diving equipment and reliable supplies of air are offered at several locations and there are a number of highly-qualified instructor guides.

History The Cayman Islands were first sighted by Columbus in May 1503. At that time he named the islands "Las Tortugas" which means "The Turtles". The Islands were ceded to the English Crown under the Treaty of Madrid in 1670; early inhabitants were mixed groups of shipwrecked sailors, debtors, buccaneers and beachcombers, and no serious settlement took place until the early part of the 18th century. Cayman Brac and Little Cayman were permanently settled as recently as 1833, when several families from Grand Cayman established themselves and lived in isolation until 1850. The Cayman Islands were relatively isolated from the world until the 1940s when modern transport began to develop.

Political and Economic   A Governor appointed by the British Crown is the head of Government. Major policies are studied and proposed by the Executive Council comprised of three official and four elected members, and laws are enacted by the Legislative Assembly which is mostly elective. The standard of living is one of the highest in the Caribbean. Apart from a certain amount of meat, turtle, fish and a few local fruits and vegetables, almost all foodstuffs and other necessities are imported.

Speech   Dialect and vocal intonations used by Caymanians have puzzled linguists, but you'll have no difficulty communicating with them. Their speech is a mixture of American Southern drawl, and the English slur, with a Scottish lilt to end the statement, all combined to fall charmingly on the ears. V's are pronounced as W's, as in Dickens; "prewailing" and "warying wind" are classic examples used by these seafaring people, and nautical terms are used unconsciously.

Cayman Brac   Cayman Brac (Gaelic for "bluff") gets its name from the high bluff rising from sea level to a height of 140 feet. The island is 89 miles ENE of Grand Cayman, about 12 miles long and a little more than a mile wide. Here are beaches, lapped by calm waters, ideal for swimming, sunning and diving. Those who may find Grand Cayman (population about 12,000) a little too "citified" will enjoy lingering on Cayman Brac, where the population is less than 2,000. Closely united, they are a warm and friendly people.

In the reefs and flats the grouper and wahoo run thick. This is the best bonefishing territory in the Cayman Islands, and also offers excellent skindiving and paradise for beachcombers; there are many stories of undiscovered treasure hoards. The sands are covered with souvenirs cast from the sea for the collector. There are caves for exploring, and a climb to the top of the bluff for the physically fit. Top it all off with the traditional Saturday night swinging dances. Cayman Airways offer reasonably priced excursion trips to the Brac.

Hotel accommodation can be found on the Brac at *Buccaneer's Inn* and cottages, offering good food and calm waters.

Little Cayman   The oft-repeated legend that many Cayman Islanders have lived to the age of 115 or so can readily be accepted after a visit to Little Cayman, which is 74 miles ENE of Grand Cayman. It is peaceful, but not dull, for here is exhilarating excitement for the dedicated pursuer of the bonefish and wahoo. Perhaps no greater fishing grounds in the world exist than these, where it has been said the fishing line cannot penetrate the throngs of giant grouper.

No doubt it was the unparalled fishing that lured a distinguished group of wealthy businessmen to establish their exclusive sport-fishing organization here. Blossom Village and the Southern Cross Club are the only signs of settled life on this, one of the few nearly undeveloped islands remaining in the hemisphere.

Ten miles long, two at its widest, with an area of approximately ten square miles, Little Cayman numbers only a few dozen in population. It is said that each one of these few counts for a hundred, a multiplication of friendliness and hospitality. Cayman Airways operates excursions flights.

Nature lovers will see multitudes of iguana and wild birds, and the history lover will find plenty of interest: Little Cayman is said to have been the site of a bloody battle when British troops waylaid a gang of desperate pirates trapped on the island.

Information for Visitors

Documents No passports are required for U.S., British or Canadian citizens. However, proof of citizenship such as voter registration or "British Visitors' Passport" is required, as well as a return ticket. Passports but not visas are required for citizens of West European and Commonwealth countries, Israel, Japan and South Africa. A visitor from any of these countries may be admitted to the Cayman Islands for a period of up to six months providing he has proof of citizenship, sufficient resources to maintain himself during his stay, and a return ticket to his country of origin or another country in which he will be accepted. Visitors from other countries may enter without visa if staying only 14 days; this concession does not apply to nationals of communist countries—other than Yugoslavia.

Climate The Cayman Islands lie in the trade-wind belt and the prevailing NE winds moderate the temperatures, making the climate delightful all year round. Average winter temperatures are approximately 24°C and average summer temperatures are around 26°-29°C. The winter season, running from December to April, is the peak tourist season. Visitors intending to come to the island during this period are advised to make hotel and travel arrangements well in advance.

What to Wear Dress in the Cayman Islands is very informal, and light summer clothing is worn the year round. Ladies will wear mainly informal tropical attire, but casual (semi-dressy) cottons would be in order for hotel dining. A light wrap or sweater may be needed on the occasional breezy winter evening. The men will need casual clothes. During dinner hours sports jackets are seen at some hotels, but a tie is seldom needed.

How to Get There Air communications are good, with a number of airlines serving the islands. Grand Cayman is served from Miami by Cayman Airways, Lacsa and Southern Airways. Cayman Airways also provides inter-island services from Grand Cayman to Cayman Brac and Little Cayman and return, and between Grand Cayman and Kingston, Jamaica. Lacsa operates between San José, Costa Rica, and Grand Cayman. Owen Roberts International Airport is situated less than 2 miles from the centre of George Town and only ten minutes drive from most of the hotels on Seven Mile Beach. The average taxi fare from the airport to a Seven Mile Beach hotel will be about US$6.25. There is a departure tax of CI$2.40 (US$3) payable either in Cayman or US currency when you leave the Islands.

Where to Stay Accommodations are many and varied, ranging from resort hotels on the beach to small out-of-the-way family-run guest houses. There is also a wide variety of cottages, apartments and villas available for daily, weekly or monthly rental. A full list of tourist accommodation and prices, including hotels, cottages, apartments and villas is available from the Cayman Islands Department of Tourism at the addresses shown at the end of this section. As a guide to the visitor, daily rates for rooms in hotels on Seven Mile Beach range from about US$24 to US$100 d during the summer and about US$38 to US$185 during the winter season. In addition a government tax of 5% is added to the room charge and most hotels also add a 10 to 15% service charge to the bill in lieu of tipping.

Currency The legal currency is the Cayman Islands dollar (CI$). At current exchange rates, CI$1 equals US$1.25, or CI$0.80 to US$1. It is suggested that you check exchange rates upon arrival on the island. U.S. currency is readily acceptable throughout the Islands, and Canadian and British currencies can be exchanged at all banks.

Banks Most of the major international banks are represented in George Town, Grand Cayman. These include Bank of America, Bank of Montreal, Bank of Nova Scotia, Barclays Bank International, Canadian Imperial Bank of Commerce, Citibank, Lloyds Bank International (by a wholly-owned subidiary, LBI Bank & Trust Co. (Cayman Ltd.) and Royal Bank of Canada. Commercial banking hours are 0830 to 1300 Monday to Thursday, and 0830 to 1300 and 1630 to 1800 on Friday.

Sightseeing Some of the many things of interest to visit in Grand Cayman includes a tour round Turtle Land, which houses giant green turtles. Located at North West Point, this is the only commercial turtle farm in the world. A trip to Gun Bay at the east end of the island will show you the scene of the famous "Wreck of the Ten Sails", which took place in 1788. On this trip you will pass the blow-holes—waterspouts that rise above the coral rock in unusual patterns as a result of water being funnelled along passages in the rock as the waves come rolling in. Hell, situated near West Bay, is an unusual rock formation worth visiting. Have your cards and letters postmarked "Hell Grand Cayman" at the little sub-post-office situated there. For a pleasurable day's outing, arrange a boat trip to North Sound. This will include snorkelling, fishing and a good look at marine life on a barrier reef. Your guide will cook fish and lobster for you by wrapping them in foil and roasting them in hot coals.

Local Travel There is a regular bus and jitney service between West Bay and George Town that stops at all the hotels on Seven Mile Beach. The fare from the hotels to town is approx. 50c each way. Taxis are readily obtainable at hotels and restaurants, and fares are moderate, based on a fixed place to place tariff rather than a meter charge. For car hire, National, Avis and Hertz are represented and there are a number of good local companies as well. For small European cars daily rentals start at about US$15, or US$90 per week. Rental firms are able to issue visitors driving permits on production of a valid driving licence from the visitor's country of residence. Island tours can be arranged at about US$40 for a taxi, or US$6 p.p. on a bus with a minimum of 20 persons. Check with your hotel for full details.

What to Buy Bargains of merchandise from many parts of the world are found in the many free-port shops. China, crystal and silver are priced below many U.S. stores. British woollens, fine Irish linen, French perfume and bottled in-bond liquors are other bargain items. Native crafts of turtle jewellery, thatch-woven baskets and purses, and tortoise-shell creations are intriguing. Some artists have captured the scenery and have prints on sale at waterfront shops.

Time Eastern Standard time (USA) for the whole year.

Department of Tourism Further information may be obtained from the Cayman Islands Department of Tourism at: 250 Catalonia Ave., Suite 604, Coral Gables, Florida 33134, Tel.: (305) 444-6551; 2711 W. 183 Street, Homewood, Illinois 60430, Tel.: (312) 957-9750; 270 Madison Ave., New York, N.Y. 10016, Tel.: (212) 689-7750; 18 Grosvenor Street, London W1X 0HP, Tel.: 01-629 6353; P.O. Box 67, George Town, Grand Cayman, B.W.I., Tel.: 9-4844 Ext. 175.

BERMUDA

THIS GROUP of coralstone islands and tiny islets, of which only 20 are inhabited, lies in the western Atlantic, about 800 miles SE of New York and 750 miles NW from the Turks and Caicos Islands. Planes direct from England reach Bermuda in 7 hours and from New York in 1¾ hours.

The islands are believed to have been discovered by the Spaniard Juan Bermúdez in 1503 and they are the oldest British colony. Only the Parliament at Westminster is older than that at Hamilton, the capital. Bermuda was first inhabited by the company of a British ship, the *Sea Venture*; bound for Virginia, she ran into a storm near the Islands and foundered on a reef in 1609. The ship's company, headed by Admiral Sir George Somers, remained there for nearly a year before resuming their voyage. A replica of the ship *Honey* built to carry on the voyage is moored in St. George harbour. In 1612, a charter was granted by King James I to the Virginia Company to include the Bermudas as part of its dominion and the first party of settlers arrived from England. Shortly afterwards the Virginia Company sold the islands to the Governor and Company of the City of London "for the plantation of the Somers Islands". But in 1684 the Company's charter was annulled and the colony passed to the Crown.

Today, the islands have one of the highest densities of population in the world. The score of them that are inhabited have a total area of slightly more than 22 square miles and a civilian population of about 53,000, of whom about two thirds are black; the remainder are mainly of English or Portuguese stock. The ten largest islands, which comprise 21 square miles, form a narrow chain, linked by causeways and bridges. Some 2.3 sq. miles are leased to the United States Government for naval and military purposes. The Bermudas are hilly but lack rivers and streams. The water supply is derived from rainfall and the conversion of sea water into fresh water.

Bermuda's chief source of income, and one which is growing, is the tourist industry. In 1966, 256,772 tourists, including those on cruise ships, visited the islands. By 1974 the total had reached 531,568, of whom only 110,347 were from cruise ships. There is a certain amount of small-scale industry, notably ship repairing and small boat building; cedar woodwork and the manufacture of handicraft souvenirs, perfume, pharmaceuticals, mineral water extracts and essential oils all help to support the population and in recent years the cultivation of Bermuda lilies, for export by air, assumed importance. The time to see these is at Easter, when a Lily Queen is chosen. Easter is a favourite time for American student visitors.

Bermuda offers sunshine, coral islands and white surf, and a vivid blue-green sea breaking on small bays of fine, pale sand. It is less sophisticated than some other resorts in the area and is not exclusively a rich man's playground, although the cost of living is geared to the North American standard. There is residential accommodation and guest houses offering terms which young people can afford. The season is a long one, from mid-March to autumn. Even in February the coolest month, temperatures rarely fall below 15°C. The peak temperatures of July and August, about 30°C, are tempered by trade winds. In September, strong winds can reach hurricane force.

There are many picturesque and interesting places to visit, reached by roads and lanes bordered with vivid, flowering sub-tropical shrubs. The scent from the neatly cultivated fields of Bermuda lilies mingles with that of the oleanders lining the road. Speed limits are strictly controlled and a drive in a horse-drawn carriage is one of the pleasantest ways of enjoying the peaceful beauties of the rural landscape, with the sparkling coastline never far distant and the colour-washed cottages and white-lined roofs of the houses glowing in the sun. There are some interesting old forts and a number of attractive 17th century churches in the nine parishes into which Bermuda is divided, notably St. Peter's in St. George's Parish. The old town of **St. George** (pop. 1,800), the capital until 1815, is a delightful old place with its ancient houses and walled gardens and picturesque alleyways leading to the harbour. The islands are said to be the scene of Shakespeare's *Tempest* (though they could hardly have been well known in London by the time the play was written) and Ariel's Cave is one of many beauty spots. The lighthouse at Gibb's Hill, in Southampton Parish, is one of the oldest in the world. For a superb view of the islands and lagoons and of the entire Colony, visit the gallery. A famous drive along the North Shore is past the Governor's Residence, with its 200-acre estate, while at Sandys Parish you can see the world's smallest drawbridge. Ferry boats ply to Ireland Island and to Somerset, Paget and Warwick.

Hamilton, the capital (pop. 3,700) is a charming small town, laid out geometrically on rising ground. Most of the public buildings are built around a square near the wharf. Here is the seat of the second oldest British parliament, the Sessions House. Bermuda Cathedral is in Hamilton, and the Library and the Historical Museum are also well worth visiting. There is a fine aquarium at Flatts, with a fascinating collection of rainbow-coloured fish. The Crystal and Leamington Caves and the Devil's Hole are all well worth visiting.

Motor cars were not admitted until 1947 and they are limited as to size. The maximum speed limit is 20 m.p.h., and 15 m.p.h. in built-up areas (traffic keeps left). International driving licences are not valid. Visitors wishing to drive must hold a Bermudian licence, not issued until after a minimum stay of 30 days. There are no car hire facilities. The island is well served by bus routes and ferryboat connections to the main shoreline points, but the most popular form of transport is the bicycle, usually with a motor. These can be hired for about US$7 a day from shops on the waterfront. Pedal cycles can also be hired. (Approx. US$2 per day or 10 a week.) Taxis are available and can also be hired by the day or week. There is a 25% surcharge between midnight and 0600. Horse-drawn carriages (single for 2 people, double for 4) charge about US$12 or 15 an hour.

Best Buys   The main shopping centre is at Hamilton. Here, in department stores, such as Smith's, A. S. Cooper, Calypso and Triminghams, British and European luxury goods are offered at prices which are very attractive by North American standards: sterling silver, English bone china and crystal, Liberty silks, cashmere sweaters, Irish linen, British wollens, luxury fabrics and tailormade clothes; German cameras, Swiss watches, French perfume and gloves. Bermuda specialities can be bought at the Old Cellar and Bermuda Handicraft in Hamilton, at John Davies'

Cedar Shop in Somerset, and at a number of places throughout the islands. They include all kinds of carved cedarwood ornaments; shell and copper enamel jewellery; baskets, straw hats and dolls made of palmetto and banana leaves; ceramic tiles and trays; angel fish buttons and seahorse lapel pins. There is one Chinese shop on the island (Fong's, in Hamilton) which sells ivory, jade, lacquerwork, teak and camphorwood chests. Sports clothes and men's Madras cotton jackets and shorts can be bought at many smaller shops outside the capital.

U.S. citizens may buy one quart of liquor duty-free. Leading brands of tobacco and cigarettes and all leading makes of film are on sale. (Cameras need frequent cleaning because of the salt atmosphere.) Shopping hours 0900 to 1700. Early closing Thurs. (1200); open all day Sat. Hairdressing is excellent but expensive for women.

What to Wear During the summer season, cool, informal clothing is suitable and Bermuda shorts are worn by both sexes. For evenings, men can wear Bermuda shorts with a white or black dinner jacket for dining and dancing. Women usually wear skirts after 1800 in hotels. Formal wear, with hat and gloves for women, is customary for calls at Government House. During the cooler months warmer clothing, with raincoats and cardigans, is needed.

Food, much of it imported, is excellent. There is good fresh milk, plenty of fruit and vegetables, and Canadian type bread. Tap-water is safe, though sometimes brakish, but on no account drink water from wells. Hotel cooking is usually international, but Bermuda specialities are sometimes served, especially in restaurants. Lobster and fish chowder are favourites, and mussel pie, conch stew, shark and other fish delicacies are popular. Local desserts include sweet potato pudding, bay grape jelly and a syllabub of guava jelly, cream and sherry. All kinds of rum punches and cocktails are served. (A particularly good planter's punch is served at the *Robin Hood* pub.) Of the many good, restaurants, some of the better-known are: *Tom Moore's, Little Venice, Plantation, The Waterfront, Breaker's Club, Hog Penny,* the *Waterlot Inn, Henry VIII, Parakeet* (medium price), *Lobster Pot,* and *Harbour Front.* Restaurant charges are in line with American prices. There are many smaller, less expensive restaurants (e.g. *Richardson's, North Shore, Pembroke*) and snack bars throughout the islands where packed lunch-boxes can usually be obtained. Many night-clubs and discotheques.

Where to stay Probably no place of comparable size has so many hotels, guest houses, pensions and private homes taking in a few visitors. Most hotels are in the luxury class, but the very wide range of accommodation available makes it possible for tourists on a lower budget to stay in Bermuda. It is advisable to book accommodation well in advance. Be warned that it is not easy to find accommodation for less than US$12 a night. For a full list (indeed, so full and so readily available that it does not seem worth while for a book of this type to go into details), including board and lodging in private houses, write to the Bermuda Department of Tourism, at Old Town Hall, Front Street, Hamilton 5-23; or at 58 Grosvenor Street, London W1X 0JD (Tel.: 01-499 1777); 610 Fifth Avenue, New York 10020; 85 Richmond Street W., Toronto M5H 2C9. Alternatively, the information airport desk will help you find a hotel.

Sport and Entertainment Fishing is at its best between mid-April and mid-October. No fishing licence is required and all tackle can be hired. Bonefish, grey snapper, amberjack, porgy and bream are caught off-shore; yellowtail, bonito, amberjack and others off the reefs. Boats can be hired for ocean fishing (wahoo, white marlin, blackfin and yellowfin tuna, sometimes blue marlin and mako). Visitors can take part in fishing tournaments.

Nine golf courses (6 of 18 holes) provide an interesting and challenging variety of play. An introduction can be arranged through the visitor's hotel or guest house. Green fees: US$7-12. Sailing dinghies (about 16 foot) can be hired by the day or half day. There are races twice a week. Swimming at beach clubs and hotel pools as well as public beaches. (Horse Shoe Bay is recommended.) The islands provide ideal conditions for underwater sports: helmet tours US$15 for 4 hours; skin-diving on reefs US$20 per hour. Spear-fishing is prohibited within one mile of the coast and spear guns are banned. Water ski-ing from US$6 per lesson. Equipment for aqua-planing can also be hired. Tennis can be played at all-weather courts throughout the islands. Approximate fees at Bermuda Tennis Stadium US$2 an hour; at Southampton, Princess Hotel and Elbow Beach Surf Club US$5 an hour. Rackets can be hired.

Cinemas show up-to-date British and American films and there is a theatre in the City Hall at Hamilton, but a main attraction for the visitor is the night life at night clubs and in hotels. Here, as elsewhere in the area, limbo dancers are a feature of floorshows, and the audience are invited to try it themselves. All the big hotels and many smaller ones have dancing and a floor show. Other night clubs are: The Jungle Room; Harmony Hall (with the African witch-doctor Gombey Dancers); the Forty Thieves Club and the Four Aces, all of which have dancing and floor shows every night of the week. The Guinea Discotheque, mainly for dancing, is open every night except Sunday. Most night clubs close at 0300. There are two commercial radio and TV companies.

Currency A new currency unit, the Bermuda dollar, valued at par with the US$, has replaced the Bermuda pound. U.S. and Canadian currencies are accepted everywhere. Sterling notes and travellers' cheques are no longer normally accepted, so should be changed into Bermudian currency at the banks. The import and export of Bermudian currency is prohibited. There is no limit to the amount of foreign currency which may be taken into Bermuda, but the amount taken out must not exceed that declared on entry. There are now restrictions on the movement of private sterling funds between Bermuda and Britain or vice versa. There is no income tax in Bermuda.

Banks Hours are 0930-1500 Mon.-Fri. and 1630-1730 Fri. only. Four banks operate: Bank of Bermuda, Front Street, Hamilton 5-31, with branches in Church Street, Hamilton, and in Somerset and St. George's; Bank of N.T. Butterfield, Front Street, Hamilton 5-24, with branches in Somerset and St. George's; Bermuda National Bank, Church Street, Hamilton 5-24, with branches in St. George's and Southampton Princess Hotel; and Bermuda Provident Bank, Church Street, Hamilton 5-24. Only the Bank of Bermuda (up to $100) and the Provident Bank (Barclays group cheques only) will normally cash foreign personal cheques.

Road Travel Bus services run to all parts along 150 miles of road. Bus from Hamilton to airport US$0.25; from Hamilton to St. George's US$0.30. Taxi from Hamilton to airport US$5. Taxis have metres and cost $1 for the first mile and 50 cents each mile beyond. From midnight until 0600 they cost 25% more.

How to get to Bermuda

The international airport, at Kindley Field, is some 12 miles from Hamilton, about 35 minutes drive across the causeway. It belongs to one of the U.S. bases and is used by military and civil aircraft. British Airways operate direct services from London, New York and points in the Caribbean. Pan American Airways, Delta Airlines and Eastern Airlines also provide frequent services from New York and other cities in the U.S.A. Air Canada operates flights from Toronto and Montreal and between Canada, Barbados, Antigua and Trinidad. Qantas calls at Bermuda on its flights from Sydney to London.

By Sea The Pacific Steam Navigation Co. have no passenger accommodation on their cargo ships calling at Bermuda. Holland America Home Lines operate a weekly cruise service between New York and Bermuda from April to October. Accommodation can sometimes be obtained via New York (Cunard) and then to Bermuda. Ships of the P. & O. occasionally call at Bermuda.

Cables International Cables, Telephones and Telex services. Cable and Wireless (West Indies) Ltd., Church Street, Hamilton.

Newspapers "The Royal Gazette" is the only daily (not Sun.) newspaper.

American Express Agents Hamilton: L. P. Gutteridge, Harold Hayes Frith Bldg., Tel.: 2-8500.

VIRGIN ISLANDS

THE VIRGIN ISLANDS are a group of small islands situated between Puerto Rico and the Leeward Islands; the total population is upward of 100,000. Politically they are divided into two groups: the larger eastern group, with a population of about 90,000, were purchased from Denmark by the U.S.A. in 1917 and remain a U.S. territory; the smaller western group constitutes a British Crown Colony, with a population of only about 10,000.

The **U.S. Virgin Islands** (USVI), in which the legacies of Danish ownership are very apparent, contain three main islands—St. Thomas, St. John and St. Croix. They have long been developed as holiday centres for U.S. citizens, and the population, mainly black, has always been English-speaking, despite the nearness of Puerto Rico and the long period of Danish control.

Government The USVI are an unincorporated Territory under the U.S. Department of Interior with a non-voting Delegate in the House of Representatives. The government is made up of three branches: Executive, Legislative and Judicial. The Governor is elected every four years; there are 15 Senators; judicial power is vested in local courts. All persons born in the USVI are citizens of the United States.

History Columbus discovered the Virgin Islands on his second voyage to the New World in 1493. He first came upon St. Croix (Santa Cruz) and then moved on to St. Thomas and St. John. The islands remained almost forgotten for more than a century, and then on St. Croix in 1625, both English and French colonists were engaged in agriculture. By 1650, only the English remained.

In that very year, the English were ejected by the Spanish on St. Croix; later that year the Spanish were usurped by the French. In 1653, St. Croix was willed to the Knights of Malta, but the Knights were unaccustomed to the rigours of the Caribbean and sold St. Croix to the French West India Company.

The Danes took possession of St. Thomas in 1666 and of St. John shortly thereafter. They divided St. Thomas into 125-acre plantations, which at their peak numbered more than 170. But the terrain was not especially suited for agriculture, and by the middle 1700s commerce was the backbone of St. Thomas' economy. It was part of the triangular trade route that brought slaves from Africa and sent molasses and rum to Europe.

Because St. Thomas was a free port, it was a haven for pirates who attacked Spanish, French and Dutch ships. Names of notoriety included Blackbeard and Bluebeard, Sir Francis Drake and Captain Kidd, and you will find on St. Thomas both remnants and stories of their days there.

In 1733, St. Croix was purchased by Denmark, and the USVI stayed under Danish rule for almost 200 years. St. Croix was more suitable for agriculture, and today there are the ruins of numerous sugar plantations with their proud Great Houses and windmills. (Judith's Fancy is the best preserved from the time of the French; Whim Estate is restored to the way it was under Danish rule in the 1700s.)

From 1900 on, the sugar market declined, and Denmark became eager to sell the islands. As a protection for the mainland in World War I, they were purchased on March 31, 1917 by the USA for US$25m.

The three US islands are connected by bomber chargers and sea planes which charge about US$12 a trip. On the islands camping is easy and fruit and vegetables are cheap; other food is expensive, however.

St. Thomas lies about 75 miles east of Puerto Rico at 18°N, 40 miles north of St. Croix. It is one of nearly 1,600 Virgin Islands, only a few of which are large enough to support habitation. The rest are small cays, or islets. Thirteen miles long and less than three miles wide, with area of 32 square miles, St. Thomas rises out of the sea to a peak of 1,500 feet and a mountain range that runs down its spine. It was once a sugar island, but has now been planted out to a great variety of trees and shrubs.

History The harbour at **Charlotte Amalie**, capital of St. Thomas and also of the entire USVI, still bustles with the colour and excitement that have been its daily fare for hundreds of years. The city was built by the Danes, who named it after their King's consort, but to most visitors it remains "St. Thomas". At one time the island had nearly 200 sugar plantations, but now only restored Great Houses remain as reflection of a style of life that could only exist on a plantation. The island's principal source of income today is tourism.

Population 42,000.

Commerce The island is a major distiller and exporter of rum, and is also a free port, in common with the other USVI.

Transportation Harry S. Truman international airport. Charter flights. Buses between Charlotte Amalie and Red Hook and Bordeaux. All types of wheels are available with rental firms plentiful. One popular idea, especially given the hilly nature of St. Thomas, is to get about by motor bike. There are also group tours by surrey, bus or taxi. There are a number of ferry boats to various destinations, including one from Red Hook to nearby St. John (every hour from 0700 to 1900).

Shopping St. Thomas ranks with Hong Kong as an international shopping stop for travellers. With its status as a free port, St. Thomas offers duty-free merchandise from all over the world. Most of the major shops are represented on both St. Croix and St. Thomas. U.S. Customs has done its bit to make the shopping attractive, imposing a US$200 duty-free limit on goods brought back, twice the normal amount.

Festivals Carnival in last week of April. Most spectacular.

Nightlife St. Thomas offers the greatest variety of nightlife to be found in the Virgin Islands. Bands and combos play nightly at most hotels. Several of the hotels offer limbo dancing three or four nights a week and the ubiquitous steel bands remain a great favourite with both visitors and inhabitants.

Sports Magens Bay is considered by those who have been there (including National Geographic) to be one of the most beautiful beaches in the world. There is deep sea fishing with the next world record in *every* weight class lurking just under the boat; sailing of all types and cruises are available. The waters around the islands are so clear that snorkelling is extremely popular. Equipment and instruction for underwater photography are available. Ashore, tennis, golf, riding, and on nearby St. John, camping.

St. John is about 5 miles east of St. Thomas (ferry every hour between Red Hook and Cruz Bay, 20 minutes, US$1) and 35 miles north of St. Croix. The population is only 3,000, mainly concentrated in the little town of Cruz Bay and the village of Coral Bay. Two-thirds of the island is a US National Park, but there are still plenty of places to eat and enjoy yourself. At Cinnamon Bay (four buses a day from Cruz Bay, US$1) there is a campground and chalet site run by the National Park Service (charges very reasonable); a private-enterprise campground has recently opened at Maho Bay, NE of Cinnamon Bay. Off Trunk Bay, called by many the most beautiful beach in the world, there is an underwater snorkelling trail maintained by the National Parks Service.

St. Croix is some 75 miles east of Puerto Rico and 40 miles south of St. Thomas. The Virgin Islands form the beginning of a necklace of islands stretching from Hispaniola down to the coast of South America and the Spanish Main. Columbus thought that St. Croix looked like a lush garden when he first saw it during his second voyage in 1493. It had been cultivated by the Carib Indians and the land still lies green and fertile between the rolling hills.

History Agriculture has been a staple of the economy ever since, joined in later years by cattle raising, rum distillation, tourism, and just recently, by petrochemicals. St. Croix is dotted with vacant sugar mills (many of them restored as part of private homes) that were once parts of vast sugar estates. Some 80 per cent of the population is black, the majority of them descendants of slaves brought to the island from Africa to work the plantations.

Population 45,000.

Education St. Croix is the home of the College of the Virgin Islands, a four-year school offering degrees in business and liberal arts.

Christiansted The old town square and waterfront area of Christiansted, the old Danish capital, still retain the colourful character of the early days when wealthy sugar planters and merchants dominated the island. Overhanging second-floor balconies designed by the Danes to shade the streets serve as cool arcades for shoppers scouting for duty-free bargains. Red-roofed pastel houses built by early settlers climb the hills overlooking Kings Wharf and in the old outdoor market can be heard the musical lilt of the Crucian dialect spoken by descendants of the African slaves who worked the sugar fields.

Old Christiansted is compact and easy to stroll. The best place to start is the Visitors' Bureau, housed in a building near the Wharf which served a century ago as the Customs Scale House for weighing imports and exports. Here you can pick up a number of helpful brochures.

Across the way is Fort Christiansvaern, which the Danes erected in 1774 on the foundations of a fort the French built in 1645. Admission is free. See the punishment cells, dungeons, barracks room, officers' kitchen, powder magazine, an exhibit of how to fire a cannon, and the battery—the best vantage point for photographing the old town and harbour.

The Steeple Building is a minute's walk away. Built as a church by the Danes in 1734, then converted into a military bakery, storehouse and later a hospital, it is now a museum of the island's early history. There are displays of Indian ceremonial bowls and cooking vessels, a diorama of Christiansted as it was in 1800, and a layout of an early sugar plantation which shows the various steps of producing sugar, molasses and rum.

The area here is a treasury of old Danish architecture, and many of the original buildings are still in use. The West India and Guinea Co., which bought St. Croix from the French and settled the island, built a warehouse on the corner of Church and Company Streets in 1749 which now serves as a post office.

Across the way from Government House on King St. is the building where the young Alexander Hamilton, who was to become one of the founding fathers of the

U.S.A., served as a clerk in Nicolas Cruger's countinghouse. Today the building houses the Little Switzerland shop and Hong Kong Restaurant.

Government House has all the hallmarks of the elegant and luxurious life of the merchants and planters in the days when "sugar was king". The centre section, built in 1747 as a merchant's residence, was bought by the Secret Council of St. Croix in 1771 to serve as a government office. It was later joined to another merchant's town house on the corner of Queen Cross St. and a handsome ballroom was added, which helped to pull it all together. Visitors are welcome to view the ballroom, stroll through the gardens and watch the proceedings in the Court of Justice.

Queen Cross St. leads into Strand and the fascinating maze of arcades and alleys lined with boutiques, handicrafts and jewellery shops. Along the waterfront there are bars and restaurant pavilions where weary strollers can revive themselves with Crucian cool-aids, fresh-caught shell fish and other local specialities.

Transportation Alexander Hamilton international airport. Regular buses between Christiansted and Frederiksted (where the mahogany forest is worth a visit). Boat, cycle, plane or car, the scenery is consistently beautiful and all methods of getting to see all of it are easy to arrange. Cruises under sail around St. Croix or to Buck Island (the only underwater U.S. National Park is here) are available through hotels or in either Christiansted or Frederiksted. The major car rental agencies are represented at the airport, in hotels and in both cities. Driving is on the left hand side; however, the steering wheel remains on the left, or U.S. side.

Shopping Legendary. Christiansted is a beautiful bit of 18th century Danish West Indian pastry, which seems to have been made to draw shoppers down its narrow cobbled streets to yet another discovery. Biggest bargain in the islands is still in the liquid variety, duty-free: rum, naturally, is both cheap and good.

Nightlife Most hotels provide evening entertainment on a rotating basis, the custom of many of the Caribbean islands, so it is sometimes best to stay put and let the world of West Indian music and dance come to you. Restaurant life on St. Croix is rich but basic; charcoal-boiled steaks and lobsters, West Indian creole dishes and Danish and French specialities. Do not miss the open-air Crucian picnics.

Sports St. Croix has it all—swimming, sailing, tennis, horse racing and riding, plus the only 18-hole golf course in the Virgins, at Fountain Valley. Certainly the most beautiful and rewarding sport is at Buck Island, with guided tours on under-water snorkelling trails.

The **British Virgin Islands** (BVI) are much less developed than the U.S. group, and number some 60 islands, islets, rocks, and cays, of which only 16 or so are inhabited. They are all of volcanic origin except one, Anegada, which is coral and limestone. The two major islands, Tortola and Virgin Gorda, along with the groups of Anegada and Jost Van Dykes, contain most of the total population of over 10,000. A nearly self-contained community, the islands comprise a Crown Colony with a Governor appointed by London, although to a large extent they are internally self-governing. Clean, crystal clear waters are ideal for snorkelling and diving, but for the most part the beaches tend to be rather inaccessible, rough for safe swimming, or swampy.

Tortola is the main island, with a population of nearly 9,000. **Roadtown,** on the S shore, is the capital and business centre of the territory, with about 1,500 inhabitants. There are also communities at East End and West End (reached by bus from Roadtown for US$1). From West End, regular "Bomba" launches provide a link to Virgin Gorda and the U.S. islands. Mount Sage, the highest point in the archipelago, rises to 1,780 ft., and traces of a primeval rain forest can still be found on its slopes. The Caribbean (S) coast, which looks over the Sir Francis Drake Channel with views of several other islands, is mainly swampy and still; the

Atlantic (N) coast is largely inaccessible except for a few somewhat rough beaches on the W side.

Hotels *Fort Burt*, near Roadtown, pool, d room with half board, US$70; *Treasure Isle*, pool, tennis, d, half board, US$70; *Colonial Manor Hotel* pool, gardens, d, US$47.50; *Sebastian's on the Beach*, pleasant, beach bar, U.S. management, d rooms from US$25 to 35; *Sugar Mill Estate*, a restored West Indian cottage, U.S. management, gardens, pool, beach, US$38 daily, US$225 weekly; *Smugglers Cove*, beach, d, US$28, also cottages; *Long Bay Hotel*, beach, pool, d, US$28; *Christopher's Guest House*, US$8 s.

Virgin Gorda was, over a century ago, the centre of population and commerce. It is now better known as the home of *Little Dix Bay*, BVI's largest and most exclusive hotel, as well as the site of the geological curiosity called "The Baths" where enormous boulders form a natural swimming pool and underwater caves. The isle is 7 miles long and has a population of about 1,000. The northern half is mountainous, with a peak 1,370 ft. high, while the southern half is relatively flat. There are some 20 secluded beaches; the most frequented are Devil's Bay, Spring Bay, and Trunk Bay. North of the island is the Sound, formed to the S and E by Virgin Gorda, to the N by Prickly Pear Island, and to the W by Mosquito Island. On the SE tip is Copper Mine Point, where the Spaniards mined copper, gold and silver some 400 years ago, the remains of which can be seen. The rocky façade here is reminiscent of the Cornish coast of England. There is a 3,000 ft. airstrip. The amateur geologist will find stones such as malachite and crystals embedded in quartz. All land on Virgin Gorda over 1,000 ft. high has been made into a National Park, where trails have been blazed for walking.

Hotels *Little Dix Bay*, Rockefeller's Rockresort hotel, has been operating since 1964, pool, beach, d, full board US$145; under same management is the *Virgin Gorda Yacht Harbour*, a large marina offering convenient facilities. *Biras Creek Hotel*, at North Sound, luxurious also, with Scandinavian architecture, pool, tennis, d with full board, US$112. *Ocean View Hotel*, only 12 rooms, d with half board, US$37.50. *Guavaberry Spring Bay*, cottages, d, US$45 daily, US$280 weekly. *Bitter End*, at North Sound, cottages and rooms, d, about US$75 full board. *Tony Mack's Lord Nelson Inn*, in The Valley, 5 rooms, bar with darts, croquet course, putting green, d, US$25. *Fischer's Cove Beach Hotel*, cottages at St. Thomas Bay, d, US$45 daily, $260 weekly. *Olde Yard Inn*, The Valley, d, half board $50.

Beef Island was famed as a hunting ground for beef cattle during the buccaneering days (a possible explanation of its name). The island is linked to Tortola by the Queen Elizabeth bridge. The main airport of the BVI is here. Long Bay beach is on the northern shore.

Salt Island is the location of the salt ponds, which attract tourists during the gathering season (April-May). There is a small settlement on the N side as well as a reef-protected lagoon on the E shore. The population numbers about 290.

Marina Cay is a tiny island of six acres just N of Beef Island. Robb White brought his bride some years ago and wrote his book *Our Virgin Isle*, which was made into a film starring Sidney Poitier and John Cassavetes. A charming cottage hotel, *Marina Cay Hotel*, comprises most of the island, which is encircled by a reef (d with half board, high-season US$75).

Norman Island is uninhabited, but reputed to be the "Treasure Island" of Robert Louis Stevenson fame. On its rocky west coast are caves where treasures are said to have been discovered many years ago.

Anegada is unique among this group of islands because of its coral and limestone formation. The highest point is only 28 ft. above sea level. There is an airstrip 2,500 ft. long and 60 ft. wide, which can handle light aircraft. There are still a few large iguanas which are indigenous to the island. The waters abound with fish, and the extensive reefs are popular with scuba divers who also explore wrecks of ships which foundered in years past. Some were said to hold treasures, but to date only a few dubloons have been discovered. There are beaches on the N and W ends. Its population numbers about 290.

Jost Van Dyke is mountainous, with beaches at White Bay and Great Harbour Bay on the S coast. It is surrounded by some smaller islands, one of which is Little Jost Van Dyke, where Dr. John Lettsom, one of the founders of the English Medical Society, was born. Population about 130.

Peter Island has a tiny population and offers isolated beaches and picnic spots. Dead Man's Bay has a palm-fringed beach and good anchorage. The *Peter Island Yacht Club* is built on reclaimed land jutting out into Sir Francis Drake Channel, forming a sheltered harbour with marine facilities. Built by Norwegians, there are 8 chalet-type cottages, a pool, tennis; d with full board US$145 daily.

Great Dog Island features marvellous views of frigate birds nesting.

Great Thatch, just of West End, Tortola, has a pleasant guest house.

How to get there   Pan-Am, Eastern, American and Delta airlines run services from Miami and other U.S. cities to San Juan, Puerto Rico or St. Thomas. Air Canada and BWIA provide a link with Canada. From San Juan the Antilles Air Boats have a Grumman Goose flying-boat service to St. Thomas, St. Croix, Tortola and St. Martin. From St. Croix the Air Boats go to Beef Island. (As the Goose lands in the main harbours, it saves airport taxi-fares.)

The British Virgin Islands are served by Beef Island airfield, with shuttle flights to and from St. Thomas. Prinair and BVI also fly between San Juan and Beef Island. Liat flies to Beef Island from St. Croix and Antigua (to connect with British Airways flights). A departure tax of US$1.50 for those leaving by air, US$1 by sea. Launch services run between the main islands.

Climate   Annual average temperature of 26°C, with no more than 4° between the coolest month (December) and the hottest (July and August).

Self-Drive Cars   Minimokes and jeeps can be hired on Tortola and Virgin Gorda. Jeeps may be more useful for exploring secluded beach areas.

Documents   U.S. citizens do not of course require passports for visits to the U.S. Virgin Islands, but do for the British Islands. British visitors to the U.S. islands need passport and U.S. visa. Visitors of other nationalities will need passports and visas.

Currency   The U.S. dollar circulates as the official medium of exchange in U.S. and British islands alike.

Tourist Information   For USVI, there are offices of the USVI Division of Tourism in Chicago, Miami, New York and Washington D.C., also in San Juan (Puerto Rico) and in Charlotte Amalie, Christiansted and Frederiksted. Hotel and restaurant lists and descriptive leaflets available. Texaco issue a map of the U.S. islands. Addresses: 535 N Michigan Ave., Chicago, 60611; 100 Biscayne Boulevard, Miami, 33132; 16 W 49th St., New York, 10020; 1150 17th St. NW, Washington D.C., 20036; 1300 Ashford Ave., Condado, Puerto Rico 00902. For BVI, Tortola Travel Services, Main Street, Roadtown, have brochures on all the islands. There is a Tourist Board at Roadtown.

NETHERLANDS ANTILLES

THE NETHERLANDS ANTILLES consists of the islands of Aruba, Bonaire, and Curaçao (popularly known as the ABCs) off the coast of Venezuela; and Sint Eustatius (Statia), Saba, and the southern part of Sint Maarten (St. Martin) in what are generally known as the Leeward Islands. There is some confusion regarding which islands are Leeward and which Windward: the Dutch West Indians refer to the ABC's as "Leeward Islands", and the other three as "Windward", a distinction adopted from the Spaniards, who still speak of the *Islas de Sotovento* and *de Barlovento* with reference to the trade winds.

The Netherlands Antilles is an autonomous part of the Kingdom of the Netherlands. Its administration is a parliamentary democracy, the seat of which is in Willemstad, Curaçao. A Governor, appointed by the Queen of the Netherlands, represents the Crown, and each island has its own Legislative and Executive Council.

CURAÇAO

Curaçao, the largest of the six islands comprising the Netherlands Antilles, lies in the Caribbean Sea 100 km. off the Venezuelan coast at a latitude of 12°N, outside the hurricane belt. It is 65 km. long and 11 km. at its widest, with an area of 173 square miles.

The landscape is barren—due to low rainfall (560 mm. a year) and sparse vegetation (consisting mostly of cactus thickets)—and mostly flat, except in the northwest where hills rise to 375 metres. Deep bays indent the southern coast, the largest of which, Schottegat, provides Willemstad with one of the finest harbours in the Caribbean.

Coral reefs surrounding the island, constant sunshine, a mean temperature of 81°F (27°C), and refreshing trade winds lure visitors the year round, making tourism the second industry; the first is the oil refinery dating back to 1918, now one of the largest in the world, to which the island owes its prosperity. It refines crude petroleum from Venezuela. Bunkering has also become an important segment of the economy, and Curaçao is one of the largest bunkering ports of the world. Besides oil, other exports include phosphate and the famous Curaçao liqueur, made from the peel of the native orange. The island's extensive trade makes it a port of call for a great many steamship lines and large ocean-going ships are regularly seen steaming up St. Anna Bay.

Roughly half of the cosmopolitan population of 156,000 (representing 79 nationalities, of whom 16% were born outside the Netherlands Antilles) lives in Willemstad. Dutch is the official language, and many islanders also speak English or Spanish. But the *lingua franca* of the ABCs is Papiamento, which has its roots in Dutch, Spanish, Portuguese, English, and some African and Indian dialects. Papiamento has been in existence since at least the early 18th century, but to this day has no fixed spelling, though it is more and more becoming a written language.

Religious and racial tolerance have created a multi-racial, multi-lingual, multi-cultural community. Anti-tourist sentiment is almost impossible to find.

History   The first known settlers of Curaçao were the Caiquetios, a tribe of peaceful Arawak Indians. One of the clans of the Caiquetios were called "Curaçaos", seafarers who conducted a lively traffic with Venezuelan Indians in their log canoes. In 1499, Curaçao was discovered by Alonso de Ojeda, a lieutenant of Christopher Columbus, accompanied by Amerigo Vespucci. The Spaniards settled on the island in 1527 and, there being no gold, mainly raised livestock for hides. In 1634, the Dutch occupied and fortified Curaçao, which became the base for a rich *entrepôt* trade flourishing through the 18th century. Other Spaniards and Portuguese, particularly Jews, fleeing the Inquisition, sought shelter here among the tolerant Dutch, and became important businessmen. Peter Stuyvesant as Governor in 1642 before going off to become the governor of New York, at that time New Amsterdam. Following various slave uprisings, and attempts by the English and the French to take the island, it became a British Protectorate in 1800. It was returned to the Dutch in 1802, was again captured by the British in 1807, and was returned to the Netherlands definitively by the Treaty of Paris in 1815. Slavery was finally abolished in 1863. The 19th century was a time of economic decline—alleviated only by ventures such as the cultivation of aloes for pharmaceutical products and oranges for Curaçao Liqueur—until the discovery of oil in Venezuela in 1914 and the consequent building of the Royal Dutch Shell refinery in 1916.

Willemstad, capital of the Netherland Antilles and of the island of Curaçao (population about 80,000), is full of charm and colour. The architecture is a joyous tropical adaptation of 17th-century Dutch, painted in storybook colours. Pastel shades of purples and pinks, yellows and greens, indigo, magenta, turquoise, and sun-washed ochre splash homes, shops, and government buildings alike. Rococo gables, arcades, and bulging columns evoke the jovial yet curiously solid spirit of the Dutch colonial burghers.

The earliest buildings in Willemstad were exact copies of Dutch buildings of the mid-17th century—high-rise and close together to save money and space. Not until the first quarter of the 18th century did the Dutch adapt their northern architectural ways to the tropical climate and begin building galleries on to the façades of their houses, to give shade and more living space. The chromatic explosion is attributed to a Governor-General of the islands, the eccentric Vice-Admiral Albert Kikkert ("Froggie" to his friends), who blamed his headaches on the glare of white houses and decreed in 1817 that only soft colours be used. The effect is sheer gingerbread.

Unfortunately, much of this old part of the city, called Punda, was burned down in the riots of May 1969, during the strike of oil-refinery workers. Yet enough remains, or has been rebuilt, to attract and delight visitors to Willemstad.

Almost every point of interest in the city is in or within walking distance of the shopping centre in Punda, which covers about five blocks. Some of the streets here are only five metres wide, but attract many tourists—especially Venezuelans who hop over for a day or weekend—with their myriad of shops offering international goods at near duty-free prices. Shops are open Monday to Saturday 0800-1200, 1400-1800.

The "Floating Market", a picturesque string of visiting Venezuelan, Colombian and other island schooners, lines the small canal leading to the Waaigat, a small yacht basin. Fresh fish, tropical fruit, vegetables and handicrafts are sold with much haggling. The sails of the merchant schooners are used as awnings to protect the goods from the sun and rain.

In the new ugly public market building nearby there are also some straw hats and bags, spices, butcheries, and a couple of modest restaurants upstairs offering a lunchtime view of the city (as out of a concrete tower) and genuine local food and live music.

Nearby is one of the most important historical sites on Curaçao, the Mikve Israel synagogue, which dates back to 1732, making it possibly the oldest in the Western Hemisphere. Worth seeing for its big brass chandeliers (replicas of those in the Portuguese synagogue in Amsterdam), ritual furnishings of richly carved mahogany with silver ornamentation, blue windows and stark white walls. The traditional sand on the floor is sprinkled there daily, some say, to symbolize the wandering of the Israelites in the Egyptian desert during the Exodus. Others say it is meant to muffle the sound of the feet of those who had to worship secretly during the Inquisition.

In the courtyard is the Jewish Museum, occupying two restored 18th century houses, which harbours a permanent exhibition of old Jewish religious objects. The Museum is open Monday-Friday and sometimes on Sunday if there are cruise ships in port; entrance fee is US$0.75.

The 18th century Protestant Church, located at the back of the square behind the Governor's palace, still has a British cannonball embedded in its walls.

The swinging Queen Emma Bridge *(Koningin Emma Brug)* spans St. Anna Bay, linking the two parts of the city, Punda and Otrabanda (the latter means "the other side"). Built on sixteen great pontoons, it is swung aside some thirty times a day to let ships pass in and out of the harbour. While the bridge is open, pedestrians are shuttled back and forth free by small ferry boats.

The new fixed bridge vaults about 50 metres over the bay and connects Punda and Otrabanda by a four-lane highway. Only six ships in the world are too large to pass beneath it.

Willemstad's is one of the finest harbours in the Caribbean, with its long channel, enormous bay, and very deep water. There are modern wharves for docking a great number of large vessels simultaneously. Caracas Bay harbour and Bullenbay, which can take the largest vessels, are used mainly for loading tankers and for bunkering vessels.

In Otrabanda is the Curaçao Museum—housed in an old Dutch quarantine station built in 1853—with an interesting collection of artefacts of the Caiquetios Indian culture, as well as paintings, furniture, and other antiques from the colonial era.

West of the city is the Jewish cemetery, consecrated in 1659, the oldest Caucasian burial place still in use in the New World. There are more than 1,700 tombstones from the 17th and 18th centuries, many still legible.

The countryside of Curaçao invites some exploring. The cactus plants grow up to 6 metres high, and the characteristic wind-distorted dividivi trees reach 3 metres, with another 3 metres or so of branches jutting out away from the wind at right angles to the trunk.

The occasional thatched huts and adobe homes are in striking contrast to the restored country estate houses, or *landhuisen*, which emerge here and there in the parched countryside. It is now believed that these houses were influenced by the Portuguese Jewish settlers and not the Spanish as was previously thought (because of the extroverted style of living around the perimeter of the house, a Portuguese characteristic rather than the introverted Spanish system of building round an enclosed patio). Worth visiting are the Jan Kok, built in 1654, and the Santa Martha and fortified Brievamgat dating from the 18th century.

There are many fine beaches on Curaçao, several quite isolated and uncrowded. The northeastern coast is rugged and rough for swimming, but the southwestern coast offers sheltered bays and beaches with excellent swimming, snorkelling, scuba diving, water-skiing, boating, and fishing. They are all rather difficult to get to by public transport, and it is advisable to hire a car.

Southeast of Willemstad is Jan Thiel Bay, which has coral reefs and open sea (good snorkelling and scuba diving), as well as a snack bar with hot and cold food, changing facilities, and inexpensive apartments for rent; and Santa Barbara, located at the mouth of Spanish Water Bay on the Mining Company property, which has no facilities, but refreshments on Sundays—a favourite with locals who bring picnics. Across the bay is the Curaçao Yacht Club, with a pleasant bar.

A good road leads northwest from Willemstad direct to West Point (Westpunt) beach at the northwestern tip of the island, about 45 minutes by car. Here there is a large beach, not quite as attractive to snorkellers or divers, but with a nice snack bar—restaurant offering local specialities, as well as hamburgers and drinks, overlooking the sea. Smaller and more isolated beaches nearby include Knip, Knipklein, Jeremi Bay, Port Marie and Daaibooi; the water is not as clear at Boca St. Cruz or at Blauwbaai, and the latter has changing facilities, showers, and food and drinks at weekends.

Among the hotels, the *Curaçao Hilton, Arthur Frommer, Holiday Inn,* and *Princess Isles* have beaches and pools. The *Avila* is on a lovely beach but has no pool, while the *Plaza, Airport Hotel Bianca,* and *Hotel Madeira* have pools but no beaches. Most tourists agree that the clear warm waters of the Caribbean are far more appealing here than swimming pools, particularly for anyone interested in observing marine life—so rich on the coral reefs—while snorkelling or scuba diving.

Tourism brochures warn visitors to beware of a tree with small green apples that borders some beaches. This is the *manzanilla* and its sap causes burns on exposed skin.

Scuba diving gear can be hired, as can deep-sea fishing boats. There are also glass-bottom boats for the less sporty who wish to catch a glimpse of the fascinating underwater life surrounding Curaçao. Two ranches offer horses for hire by the hour, and there are tennis courts, a golf course, a squash court, and a bowling alley on the island. For "night-owls", there are four casinos as well.

Hotels High-season rates (Dec. 16 to Apr. 15) are roughly double the low-season rates. The following are minimal high-season rates for a double room without meals, to which a 5% government tax and 10% service charge must be added; deduct 20% for single room. Rates for Modified American Plan (MAP—breakfast and one meal), per day p.p., are indicated where available: *Curaçao Hilton,* US$66 (MAP add $18 p.p. per day); *Holiday Inn,* $56 (MAP $18); *Princess Isles* (similar to *Holiday Inn* rates); *Curaçao Plaza,* $50 (MAP $17); *Arthur Frommer,* $44, villa $65 (MAP $16). On a smaller scale: *Avila Beach* (charming, Dutch colonial style, rates similar to *Arthur Frommer*); *Country Inn,* $27 (MAP $8.50); *Hotel Madeira,* $19 (MAP $7.85); *San Marco,* $18.90 (MAP $5.75). Economy: *San Marco,* central but no swimming pool, $15-17; *Park Hotel,* $12; *Curaçao Airport Hotel,* $14 with breakfast; *Hotel Paris,* Breedestraat, $19; *Begonia Apartments,* $17, one bedroom; *Motel Logement Creola,* Penstraat 61, $14 with private kitchen. Cheaper hotels (prices for one person) include: *Venezuela, Altamira* and *Caracas,* all on Van der Porandhofstraat, all charge about $20 with food; *Central,* Scharlooweg 12; *Pensión Ida,* same street, $20; *Pensión Estoril,* Breedestraat; *Madeira,* Tritonstraat 15-21, $12.50; *Carlos,* $6, good value. Cheaper hotels are often full, but taxi drivers will often be helpful in trying to find you one. Check with Tourist Board for availability and latest prices.

Restaurants and Food International food at the major hotels. Historical *Fort Nassau* (view over town and harbour) is good, but expensive; *La Bastille,* on a pier at Caracas Bay, is French, good, also expensive; *Fort Waakzaamheid Tavern,* newly restored, international food, dancing; *Bistro La Hacienda,* near *Princess Isles Hotel,* country house, features some local dishes; *Holland Club Seafood Restaurant,* Dutch-run, is above *Restaurant Indonesia* which serves only Indonesian food and is under same management; *La Parrillada Steakhouse,* strictly steaks or frozen fish; *La Bistroelle* behind shopping centre; *Golden Star* offers local food in unpretentious surroundings at modest prices (try *carco stoba* or conch stew; *bestia chiki* or goat stew; local fish with *funchi* which is the local staple made of corn meal; or *locrio,* a chicken rice dish); *San Marco,* rather staid in the heart of town; *The Wine Cellar,* informal eating and drinking; even a *McDonald's* and *Kentucky Fried Chicken.* Cheap Chinese restaurants available: *Chung-King, Sun-Sing, Kowloon* and *Bow Bon* for US$3; *Gun Kook Yuen* for US$4.

While in the Netherlands Antilles, most visitors enjoy trying a *rijsttafel* (rice table), a sort of Asian *smörgasbørd* adopted from Indonesia. Because *rijsttafel* consists of anywhere from 15 to 40 separate dishes, it is usually prepared for groups of diners, although some Curaçao restaurants will do a modified version of 10 or 15 dishes for smaller parties of two or three couples. Using white rice as a base of operations, you pile your plate high with broiled, stewed, and fried delicacies made with port, beef, chicken, shrimp, fish, and vegetables, as well as varied relishes (watch out for the *sambals*, various combinations of hot peppers to be used sparingly by the uninitiated!). *Goreng* are the fried foods, *atjar* the pickles, *sate* the kebab of tiny pork cubes often served with a peanut-butter sauce. *Kroepoek* resemble potato chips but are made of shrimp juice and cassava roots, dried, sliced, and deep-fried to serve as bread or crackers, or as a replacement for nuts or olives with cocktails. Other Indonesian dishes worth trying are *nassi rames, nassi goreng,* and *bahmi goreng*.

A limited selection of European and Californian wines is usually available in restaurants, although local waiters have little familiarity with them and it is advisable to examine your bottle well before allowing it to be opened. Curaçao's gold-medal-winning Amstel beer—the only beer in the world brewed from distilled sea water—is very good indeed and available throughout the Netherlands Antilles. Some Dutch and other European beers can also be found. Curaçao's tap water is also good; also distilled from the sea.

Clothing Summer-weight clothes (as in the USA or the Mediterranean) are in order. Women will need nothing heavier than cotton dresses, with occasionally a shawl or a light cardigan for the evening. Comfortable walking shoes, sandals, or espadrilles are suggested. For men, tropical-weight trousers and cotton or drip-dry shirts are the rule almost everywhere. A few restaurants, and the casinos, insist on jackets and ties. Wraps for the women, and jackets for the men are desirable if the evening is to be spent in an air-conditioned establishment, though hardly necessary outdoors as the night temperature varies little from the ideal daytime temperature (average 27°C), tempered by the refreshing trade winds. Bikinis are accepted on all beaches, but there is little topless or nude sunning in the ABC islands. Suitable clothes, including some top brands of French *prêt-à-porter* fashions, can be purchased in Willemstad.

Health The climate is healthy and non-malarial; epidemic incidence is slight. Rooms without air-conditioning or window and door screens may need mosquito nets during the wetter months of November and December and sometimes May and June, although some spraying is done in tourist areas. Mosquitoes don't like draughts, and it is often enough to leave two windows (or doors) open to discourage them with cross-ventilation.

Tourist Office Located on Plaza Piar, next to the *Curaçao Plaza Hotel,* as well as in the arrival and transit halls at the airport, offering helpful information, assistance in finding a hotel, brochures, maps, etc. Multi-lingual guides wearing white uniforms offer assistance.

Self-drive Cars Hertz, Avis and Budget available in town, at airport, and major hotels. Also National, Lucky, Caribe Automotive, Curaçao U-Drive (at Intercontinental), Dijs, Drive Yourself N.V., Rent a Bug, Ric, and several other local agencies. Inquire at your hotel. Prices start at about US$14 daily, $84 weekly, unlimited mileage, including insurance with $150 deductible. Cost of full collision protection is about $2.50 daily, $15 weekly.

Ferry Service Car ferry service three times weekly to La Vela de Coro, Venezuela. Taxi, ferry terminal-centre, US$3 (see page 1086).

Cable Offices All American Cables & Radio Inc., Keukenstraat; Kuyperstraat; Radio Holland N.V., De Ruyterkade 51; Sita, Curaçao Airport.

Banks Algemene Bank Nederland, Banco Popular Antilliano, Banco Venezolano Antillano, Bank of America, Maduro & Curiel's Bank, Pierson Heldring & Co. The airport bank has a reputation for giving poor rates of exchange, so avoid changing money there, especially when leaving the country.

American Express Agents Willemstad: S. E. L. Maduro and Sons, Schouwburgweg, N/N. Tel.: 37900. Their other address at Heerenstraat 21, Muskus Bldg., is the one used for mail collection.

Taxis Taxis are easily identified by the signs on their roof and TX after the licence number. There are taxi stands at all hotels and at the airport, as well as in principal locations in Willemstad. Fares for sightseeing trips should be established at beginning of trip. Tipping is not strictly obligatory.

Buses Buses are infrequent but serve outlying areas of Curaçao. Taxi-buses, which are more regular, do not tend to go further than about 16 km. from Willemstad. Buses run airport-Willemstad hourly on the hour, return hourly on the half-hour, fare US$0.35. Otrabanda-Westpoint two-hourly on the odd hour, return on the even hour, US$0.75.

ARUBA

Aruba, smallest and most westerly of the ABC group, lies 25 km. north of Venezuela and 68 km. west of Curaçao, at 12° 30′ N, outside the hurricane belt. It is 31.5 km. long, 10 km. at its widest, with an area of 184 sq. km. The average yearly temperature is 27.5°C, constantly cooled by northeasterly trade winds, with the warmest months being August and September, the coolest January and February. Average annual rainfall is less than 510 mm., and the humidity averages 76%.

Like Curaçao and Bonaire, Aruba has scant vegetation, its interior or *cunucu* a dramatic landscape of scruffy bits of foliage—mostly cacti, the weird, wind-bent dividivi trees, and tiny bright red flowers called *fioritas*—plus huge boulders and lots of dust. For centuries, it was dismissed as *waardeloos* (worthless) by the Dutch, unfit for agriculture.

Nevertheless, Aruba is the boom holiday island of the Netherlands Antilles, thanks to its glistening white coral beach north of the capital of Oranjestad—11 km. long and 180 metres wide—flanked by the turquoise waters of the Caribbean.

Mass travel to Aruba began with the opening of the first luxury hotel, the *Aruba Caribbean,* in 1959, and was sealed by KLM with the first jumbo landing in 1971. Over 200,000 tourists visited Aruba in 1977, mainly East Coast Americans, and a recently completed (1978) Venezuelan-run hotel is luring many South Americans on week-end or week-long shopping and gambling sprees. A cluster of glittering luxury hotels has sprung up in the past two decades along the northern part of Eagle and Palm beaches, with smaller and less pretentious hotels more reasonably spaced further south.

Tourism has given lifeblood to this island, where the only other major employer, the Lago oil refinery, has gradually computerized and cut its labour force. Still, most of Aruba's income is generated by the oil refineries—located at the eastern end of the island and out of the way of tourists—which distil crude from Venezuela. Prices here are generally higher than on the other two ABC islands.

Aruba is said to be the only Caribbean island on which the Indian population was not exterminated. The Aruban today is a descendant of the indigenous Arawak Indians, with a mixture of Spanish and Dutch blood from the early colonizers. Of the total population of 62,000, including some 40 different nationalities, only about 42,000 were actually born on the island. The official language here, as in the other Netherlands

Antilles, is Dutch, but Spanish predominates, and Papiamento is the colloquial tongue. English is widely spoken.

Scholars attribute Aruba's name to the Indian word *oruba,* meaning well-placed, convenient to the mainland. Other theories include *oro hubo* (there was gold), from the Spanish *conquistadores,* and *ora* (shell) and *oubao* (island) which are again Indian words.

No written historical record of Aruba's discovery exists, though the island appears on maps dating back to 1494. In 1499 Alonzo de Ojeda claimed Aruba for Spain, but because the Spanish—even before the Dutch—found the island worthless, the Indians were saved from extermination. Charles V decreed that foreign colonists should not settle on Aruba. In 1636, the Dutch came in, near the culmination of the 80-year war between Spain and Holland. The English settled in 1805 during the Napoleonic wars, but in 1816 the Dutch returned to stay. Gold was discovered in 1825, but the mine ceased to be economic in 1916. In 1929, black gold brought real prosperity to Aruba when Lago Oil and Transport Co., now a subsidiary of Exxon, built a refinery at San Nicolás at the eastern end of the island. At that time it was the largest refinery in the world, employing over 8,000 people. Within three decades Aruba became the island with possibly the highest standard of living in the West Indies: the illiteracy rate, for example, is below that of the United States.

Aruba has three ports. The port of San Nicolás is used for the import and trans-shipment of crude oil and materials for the refinery and for the export of oil products. There are also two sea-berths at San Nicolás capable of handling the largest tankers in the world; nearly 1,700 ships call there yearly. The port of Oranjestad is the commercial port of Aruba, and it is open for day and night navigation. In 1962 the port of Barcadera was built to facilitate shipment of products from Aruba's new industrial zone on the leeward coast. Aruba Chemical Industries, the first company to establish there, produces ammonia for export. A small industry, Aruba Aloe Balm, was the first company to use the island's natural resources, the aloe plant (the extract of which is used in the preparation of cosmetic products, particularly for the cure of sunburns).

Oranjestad, the capital of Aruba, population about 17,000, is a bustling little freeport town where "duty-free" generally implies a discount rather than a bargain. Liquor rates are good, but prices for jewellery, silverware and crystal are only slightly lower than US or UK prices. The main shopping street is the 6-block Nassaustraat. There's not much else of interest in Oranjestad and in fact not much sightseeing to do generally on the island.

Inland, huge boulders and enormous dioritic monoliths—seemingly tossed about in random piles—are puzzling to geologists. A recent survey explains that these great grey stones are remnants of an ancient volcanic batholith which is the core of the island. Since their formation, the land has been repeatedly submerged. In early Pleistocene times, Aruba was completely covered by a cap of reef limestone. See the strange formations of Casibari and Ayo, surrounded by hills composed of ancient limestone reefs raised up from the sea.

While the north coast is too rough for most swimmers—and can indeed be dangerous—for those who like the surf there are two picturesque yet accessible coves, Andicouri and Dos Playa. Near the former is the natural bridge which has been carved by the waves out of the coral rock. At the site is a small souvenir shop and a snack bar. Further north are the abandoned gold mines at the Pirate's Castle, as well as the site where the island's garbage is dumped daily to the hungry jaws of local sharks. It is said that by so feeding them, the sharks are kept away from the calmer waters of the heavily touristed western coast. To date, there have been no incidents of losing visitors to the sharks.

There are ancient Indian drawings on the walls and ceilings of the caves of Fontain and Canashito, and on the rocks of Arikok and Ayo. Frenchmen's Pass, near Spanish Lagoon on the south coast, is where the Indians fought the French to protect the island from foreign invaders. Nearby is a breeding place for Aruba's parakeets. The village of Noord is known for St. Ann's Church with its 17th-century Dutch hand-carved oak altar.

All around the countryside are cactus fences, and the Aruban cottages, colourfully surrounded by bougainvillea, oleanders, flamboyant, hibiscus and other tropical plants, are often protected from "evil spirits" by interesting "hex" signs carved in cement around the doorways.

There is also a 175-year-old windmill which was shipped in parts from Holland and then assembled, now a restaurant, *De Olde Molen,* and a gigantic stone oven, the Rancho Kalk Kiln, which was employed in the 1900s to produce the lime or *kalk* used to plaster the walls of Aruban homes.

Some 10,000 people a year take the guided tour of the refinery, conducted twice weekly on Tuesdays and Thursdays. Make reservations at your hotel. There is also a tour of the Government Water and Electricity Plant—the world's largest sea-water conversion plant, producing 6½ million gallons of fresh water daily and 114,000 kilowatts of electricity.

Water Sports   For water-sports enthusiasts, facilities are available for snorkelling and scuba diving, and visibility in Aruban waters is about 30 metres in favourable conditions. Organized boat trips regularly visit the two wrecks worth exploring for the fascinating marine life which surrounds them. One is a German freighter, the "Antilia" which went down just after World War II was declared and is found in 20 metres of water off the western coast between Playa Hadikurari and Malmok (where there is a good coral reef also). The other is nearby in 10 metres of water, the "Pedernales", a flat-bottomed oil tanker which was hit in a submarine attack in May 1941, while ferrying crude oil from Venezuela to Aruba. For the less sporty, a glimpse of the marine life and wrecks can be had from glass-bottom boats which cruise the same area.

Equipment is also available for water-skiing, water-bike paddling, sailing, and fishing (best sport fish here is sailfish, plus wahoo and blue and white marlin).

Near Spanish Lagoon is the Aruba Nautical Club complex, with pier facilities offering safe, all-weather mooring for almost any size yacht, plus gasoline, diesel fuel, electricity and water. For information, write P.O. Box 161. A short sail downwind from there is the Bucuti Yacht Club with clubhouse and storm-proofed pier providing docking, electricity, water, and other facilities. Write P.O. Box 743. For water sports equipment and instruction, contact also L. L. & S. Sports at the *Holiday Inn* and *Hotel Americana.*

Other Sports   There is a 9-hole golf course near San Nicolás, as well as an 18-hole mini-golf course at the *Holiday Inn,* tennis courts at most major hotels, and horses for hire as well as riding instructions at Kiki's Ranch inland from Palm Beach. Arrangements for most sports can be made through your hotel or De Palm Tours.

Hotels   High season rates (Dec. 16 to Apr. 15) are roughly double the low season rates. The following are minimal high season rates for a double room without meals, to which a 5% government tax and 10% service charge must be added. Rates for Modified American Plan (MAP—breakfast and one meal), per day p.p., are indicated where available:

At Palm Beach (calmest sea): *Aruba Caribbean Hotel & Casino,* US$60 to $100 (MAP, add $21 p.p. daily); *Aruba Sheraton Hotel & Casino,* $62 to $92 (MAP add $21); *Holiday Inn & Casino,* $60 to $74 (MAP $20); *Americana Aruba Hotel & Casino,* $92 to $112 (MAP $22); *Concorde Hotel* (further south on slightly rougher beach), $92 to $102 (MAP $22). On Manchebo Beach (between Oranjestad and Palm Beach): *Manchebo Beach Hotel,* $67 to $72 (MAP $20), all facilities interchangeable with *Talk of the Town Hotel* under same management. On Druif Beach: *Aruba Beach Club,* $60 to $150 (residential), (MAP $20); *Divi Divi Beach Hotel,* $57 to $87 (MAP $20), all facilities interchangeable with *Tamarijn Beach Hotel* just down the beach with same management; *Tamarijn Beach,* $57 to $67 (MAP $18), facilities interchangeable with *Divi Divi.* In or near Oranjestad: *Talk of the Town* (overlooking the sea, with pool), $57 to $62 (MAP $20, facilities interchangeable with *Manchebo Beach;* in town: *Victoria,* $30 (service slow); *Central,* $22; *Caribana,* $20; *Bow Bini,* $16, excellent. In San Nicolás: *Astoria,* $16. On Palm Beach, the once charming *Basi Ruti Hotel* is undergoing changes, no price available at time of writing. A list of apartments, guest houses, and rooms is available from the Tourist Office.

Restaurants   With few exceptions, meals on Aruba are expensive and generally of the beef-and-seafood variety, thus not very interesting. Most tourists are on MAP at the hotels, many of which have more than one restaurant (so you have a choice of formal or informal), and this is highly advisable in view of the lack of variety elsewhere. Best of the formal restaurants at the major hotels are the *Talk of the Town Restaurant* at the hotel of the same name, *Le Petit Bistro* at the *Aruba Caribbean* (which has a rather expensive fixed price dinner at $23), and the *French Steak House* at the *Manchebo Beach.* For outdoor informal dining at the hotels, we might recommend the *Surfside* at the *Talk of the Town* for fish or steaks, *Fisherman's Terrace* at the *Aruba Caribbean Hotel* for seafood, and the *Pelican Terrace* of the *Divi Divi Beach Hotel.* For local dishes, particularly seafood, the *Trocadero Restaurant* on Nassaustraat in Oranjestad is highly recommended: try an exotic turtle steak, or the "Pirate's Platter" which includes fish soup, scallops, lobster, shrimps, and fish balls. A full meal with wine and service comes to about $15 p.p. At the *Bali Floating Restaurant,* moored to the oldest pier in Oranjestad's harbour, you can savour an Indonesian *rijsttafel* (see page 1153). There are several Chinese restaurants, including the highly recommendable *Kowloon* (offering a five-course meal for $8), the *Dragon-Phoenix,* the *Beep-Beep,* the *Hong Kong* in Oranjestad, and the *Astoria Hotel* in San Nicolás. The new *El Gaucho* offers Argentine fare, and *De Olde Molen* has international food in an authetic windmill dating from 1804. For wine and beer, see page 1154.

Clothing and Health   See page 1154.

Tourist Office   Arnold Shuttestraat 2, Oranjestad, just off L. G. Smith Boulevard near the harbour.

Taxis   Telephone the dispatcher at Dakota Shopping Paradise, Tel.: 2116/1604. Drivers speak English, and individual tours can be arranged. Ask for flat rate tariffs (Oranjestad to Palm Beach is $6 at time of writing).

Buses   Roughly one every hour until 1800 between town and the hotels on Eagle and Palm Beach (schedules available at the hotels and the Tourist Office). One way fare is $0.40.

Self-drive Cars   Hertz, Avis, Budget, Jansen, National, and Rentcar have offices in Oranjestad. Prices begin at $16 daily (some cars available at $14), $96 weekly, with unlimited mileage, including insurance with $150 deductible. Cost of full collision protection is about $2.50 daily, $15 weekly. Some motorcycles and scooters available from Marco's (Tel.: 2743/4971), from $9.

Ferry Service   Car ferry between Aruba and Punta Fija, Venezuela, three times a week (see page 1166).

Banks   Hours from 0800-1200 and 1330-1600. Mon. to Fri.

BONAIRE

Bonaire, second largest of the six islands comprising the Netherlands Antilles, is 38 km. long and 6½-11½ km. wide. It lies 80 km. north of

Venezuela, 50 km. east of Curaçao, 140 km. east of Aruba, at 12° 5′ N and 86° 25′ W, outside the hurricane belt.

The least developed and least populated of the ABC islands, Bonaire has a special appeal. While Curaçao bustles with Venezuelan shoppers and Aruba attracts East Coast gamblers, Bonaire basks in seclusion, appealing mostly to devotees of the sea—whose treasures are unsurpassed in the Caribbean.

Surrounding the island's gently sloping beaches and beneath its calm waters—with submarine visibility up to 60′ metres—are coral reefs harbouring over a thousand different species of marine creatures.

Ranked as one of the three top dive spots in the world, and number one in the Caribbean (followed by Grand Cayman Island and Cozumal—both of which are being seriously fished out), Bonaire is a leader in the movement for preservation of underwater resources. Stringent laws passed in 1971 ban spearfishing and the removal of any marine life from Bonaire's waters. It is a serious offence to molest, pollute, or in any way disturb the natural life of the coral reefs, and the two local diving schools have set up permanent anchors in their dive spots to avoid doing any unwarranted damage.

When Amerigo Vespucci discovered Bonaire in 1499, he found a tribe of Arawak Indians, the Caiquetios, who were still living in the Stone Age. But by 1515, not one was left—some were brought to Spain and sold, the rest were all deported to Hispaniola where they were put to work in the copper mines. Some trickled back over the years, but by the early 19th century none remained. Indian inscriptions in several caves around the island can still be seen, particularly at Boca Onima, but their significance has never been understood.

The Spaniards eventually colonized Bonaire for a little over a century, but it was under the Dutch occupation that the salt industry was first developed and slaves brought in to work the salt pans. The slaves' lot was hard. Though they lived in the north in Rincón, the first Spanish settlement on the island, they spent their work week in the south—a seven hour walk from Rincón—where they slept in tiny huts lining the beach next to the great salt piles and flanked by three 10-metre obelisks that guided the early salt ships to their moorings. These can still be seen. When slavery was finally abolished in 1863 the salt industry became unprofitable and the island was parcelled up and sold.

The Antilles International Salt Company recently reactivated this long dormant industry. Bonaire's constant sunshine (with air temperatures averaging 27°C and water 26°C), scant rainfall (less than 560 mm. a year), and refreshing trade winds so inviting for tourists are also ideal for the solar manufacture of salt—a method used by the Chinese more than 2,000 years ago.

But the old salt pans of Pekelmeer, needed by the Salt Company, posed a problem: Bonaire has one of the largest flamingo colonies in the western hemisphere, and these birds had built hundreds of their conical mud nests in the salt pans. Pleas from wildlife conservationists in the Antilles, the Netherlands, and the USA convinced the company that it should set aside an area of 56 hectares fpr a flamingo sanctuary. The birds, initially rather startled by the sudden activity, have settled into a peaceful coexistence, so peaceful in fact that they have actually doubled their output and are now laying two eggs a year instead of their previous one!

There are said to be over 6,000 flamingos on the island, and they can also be seen wading in Gotomeer Bay in the northwest, in the salt lake near Playa Grandi northeast, and in Lac Bay on the southeast coast of Bonaire, feeding on algae which give them their striking rose-pink colour.

Yet another ecological problem presented itself recently when an oil terminal was built on the coast. But the terminal is far enough from the four existing hotels for most tourists never to notice its presence, and the waters and sandy beaches have not been polluted at all.

Today, Bonaire's industry is limited to the salt company, the oil terminal, and a textile factory. Tourism, according to a government brochure, is kept "low-keyed and cool, rather than swinging and frantic".

The inhabitants of Bonaire, who number around 9,000, are a very friendly and hospitable people, undisturbed as yet by mass tourism. As in Curaçao and Aruba, Dutch is the official language, Papiamento the colloquial tongue, and Spanish and English are both widely spoken.

Kralendijk, the capital of Bonaire, is a small, sleepy town with little to offer. Tourists generally stick to the beaches or concentrate on water-sports, especially scuba diving. The interior has scant vegetation but the enormous cacti provide perching places for yellow-winged parrots and food for the island's wild goats. Flamingos can be seen around the island (see above) and a sense of peace predominates.

It might be worth hiring a car for one day—as long as anyone would need to see the island. In the morning, take the drive north past the Water Distillation Plant along the "scenic" road, which offers several descents to the sea and some excellent spots for snorkelling or diving. See the Bonaire Petroleum Company where the road turns inland to Gotomeer Bay, with some flamingos, en route to Rincón, Bonaire's oldest village. Past Rincón is a side road to the Boca Onima caves with their Arawak Indian inscriptions. The road leading north from Rincón takes you to Washington National Park, which occupies the northern portion of the island and contains more than 130 species of birds. The park is open to the public daily (entrance fee US$1, children up to 15 free) from 0800 to 1700, except Wednesdays. No hunting, fishing, or camping is permitted, but an early morning drive along the 27-km. route through cactus forests and coral rock formations is a poetic experience—as long as you're not driving your own car. The road is at least as rugged as one would expect in such a wilderness sanctuary. The return to Kralendijk is inland through the villages of Noord Salinja and Antriol.

The tour south passes the airport and Trans World Radio's towering 213-metre antenna which transmits 3 million watts, making it the hemisphere's most powerful radio station. Its shortwave broadcasts can be picked up in almost any part of the world. Further on are the snow white salt piles and the three 30-foot obelisks—blue, white, and orange—dating from 1838, with the huts which sheltered the slaves who worked the saltpans. If you see the flamingos, remember they are easily startled, so move quietly. At the southern tip of the island is Willemstoren, Bonaire's lighthouse, which dates from 1837. Pass Sorobon Beach and the mangrove swamps to Boca Cai at landlocked Lac Bay, with its clear water excellent for underwater exploration. What seems to be snow-capped hills from a distance are great piles of empty conch shells left by the local fishermen at Boca Cai. Take the road back to Kralendijk through the village of Nikiboko.

Whether you dive, snorkel, or simply gaze from a glass-bottom boat, you are certain to find the underwater world of Bonaire a fascinating adventure. Most visitors are tempted to take at least the one-day "resort" or crash diving course (about US$50).

This enables you to decide whether you'd like to continue, but one day will not make a diver of anyone.

Both diving schools have highly qualified instructors and strict regulations to safeguard the divers as well as the reefs. Many programs are available, but the 6- or 10-dive packages seem to be the most popular. There are over forty different dive spots to choose from, with many entries right from the beach, shallow and deep dives, wreck and reef dives, and even a course in underwater photography.

The two schools are Aquaventure and Dive Bonaire. The first is the creation of "Captain" Don Stewart, a Californian who's made his home on Bonaire for over 15 years. Aquaventure has a base at the *Hotel Bonaire* and runs Habitat, a diving community (see Hotels).

Dive Bonaire is run by Peter Hughes, also an experienced instructor with 20 years of diving in the Caribbean, and his American wife Alice who teaches underwater photography. Their base is the *Flamingo Beach Hotel*. Prices at the two schools are competitive.

Hotels   High-season rates (Dec. 16 to Apr. 30) are roughly double low-season rates. The following are minimal high-season rates for a double room without meals, to which a 5% government tax and 10% service charge must be added. Rates for Modified American Plan (MAP—breakfast and one meal), per day p.p., are indicated where available: *Arthur Frommer's Hotel Bonaire,* US$46 and $50 (MAP add $15), is rambling yet low-keyed on its own artificial beach, with pool; dining is indoors and air-conditioned, with snack bar on the beach; small casino open until late nightly. *Flamingo Beach Hotel,* $35 to $50 (MAP add $15), is quiet, on a somewhat smaller artificial beach (but snorkelling or diving just off the beach is excellent and includes a wreck); no pool but little need for one; dining is outdoors, under a thatched roof and surrounded by tropical plants. *Habitat,* Aquaventure's diving community, offers single rooms (called "monks' cells") starting at $7, and bungalows for 2 to 6 persons ($60 sleeps 4). Inexpensive hot meals and sandwiches available in self-service style, seaside bar open until late. Informal and functional, aimed at sportsmen and sportswomen, children discouraged. *Hotel Rochaline,* $22 for doubles with bath, is in the centre of Kralendijk; new, functional, with bar facing sea and air-conditioned restaurant serving local specialities.

Check with Tourist Board on prices.

Restaurants   International food at the two major hotels, varies on different nights of the week with Bar-B-Q's or Indonesian nights, etc. Again, MAP may be advisable, as the island really has little of anything more exciting to offer on this subject. There are a few good Chinese restaurants in town, the best of which is probably the *China Garden* in an old restored mansion which is open all day. Also in town is the tiny *Beefeater,* English-run, with Franglais cuisine and slow service. Local cooking (try goat or conch stew) under neon lights at the very simple *Black and White Bar-Restaurant* near Tera Cora, southeast of Kralendijk. There are snack bars in Kralendijk and Rincón.

Tourist Office   Across from *Beefeater Restaurant* on Breedestraat, Kralendijk.

Cable and Phone   J. A. Abraham Blvd., Kralendijk.

Banks   Open 0930-1200, 1400-1600, Mon.-Fri.

Shops   Open 0800-1200 and 1400-1800, Mon.-Sat.

Taxis   Tel.: 8100. Drivers carry list of officially approved rates, including touring and waiting time.

Self-drive Cars   Hertz and Avis at airport and in town. Check for current rates.

Tennis   Courts on outskirts of Kralendijk.

Klein Bonaire ("little Bonaire"), a small (1,500 acres), flat, rocky and uninhabited islet one km. off Bonaire's shores, is frequented by snorkellers and divers.

Currency   US$1 = NA*f* (Antillean guilder) 1.77. Dollars are accepted everywhere; Dutch guilders, sterling, and other currencies must be changed in the banks.

SINT MAARTEN

Sint Maarten (Dutch) or St. Martin (French—see French Antilles, page 1174) lies 260 km. N of Guadeloupe and 310 km. E of Puerto Rico. The island is amicably shared by the Dutch, who have 41 square km., and the French, with 54 square km. The population of 14,000 depends largely on tourism for a living, which they have found easier than the traditional occupation of extracting salt from the sea.

The advent of tourism in recent years has changed St. Maarten from a sleepy provincial island to a more worldly one, particularly in the Dutch part where cruise ships are continually emptying passengers into Philipsburg for duty-free shopping and a quick meal or swim. In spite of this new boom, the island retains its natural charm, as there are no high-rise hotels and the deluxe resorts are springing up unnoticed, each tucked away on its own beach far from the others.

Dutch, French, and English are all widely spoken, as well as Papiamento on the Dutch side, and the melodious French Creole on the other. Netherlands Antillean guilders and French francs are used interchangeably, but the most common currency is the American dollar, which one need never change at all. Many wealthy Americans, among them Benny Goodman and Sen. Edward Brooke of Massachusetts, have been building homes, particularly in the Lowlands.

The Dutch side has the main airport and seaport and most of the tourists, and its capital, Philipsburg, is a veritable hub of activity. The French side is generally quieter and somewhat greener, and often preferred for its restaurants which are notably Gallic. There are no border formalities between the two parts, only a modest monument erected in 1948 which commemorates the division of the island three centuries earlier.

Originally settled by the cannibalistic Carib Indians, the island was discovered by Columbus during his second voyage on Nov. 11, 1493, and named after the saint of the day, St. Martin of Tours. The Spanish never settled and the Indians, who had called it "Sualouiga" meaning land of salt, had abandoned the island by the time the natural salt ponds attracted the first Dutch settlers in 1631. Spain reconsidered and occupied St. Maarten from 1633 to 1648, fending off an attack by Peter Stuyvesant in 1644 which cost him his leg. In 1648 the island was divided between France and the Netherlands with the signing of the Treaty of Mount Concordia. Since then, St. Maarten has changed hands 16 times, including a brief occupation by the British, but the accord has been peaceably honoured at least since it was revised in 1839.

Philipsburg, the capital of Dutch St. Maarten, is a romantic town built on a narrow strip of sandy land between the sea and the shallow lake which was once a salt pond. It has two main streets, Front and Back, which run parallel to Great Bay Beach, perhaps the safest and cleanest city beach anywhere. Front Street is lined with old wooden buildings, most of which house quaint shops offering duty-free goods such as crystal, china, Swiss watches and Japanese cameras at 10% less than the other islands. The historic Townhouse (court-house and post office) on Ruyter Square faces the Pier, which is lively with traffic from cruise ships, inter-island schooners, and fishing boats.

Hotels in St. Maarten   (For hotels in French St. Martin, see page 1175.) *Mullet Bay* (casino), Mullet Beach, 34, EP; *Great Bay*, Philipsburg, 73, MAP; *Little Bay* (casino), Little Bay, 84, MAP; *Concord* (casino), Maho Bay, 73, EP; *Oyster Pond Yacht Club*, Oyster Pond, 65; *Caravanserai*, Maho Beach, 30, EP; *Pasangrahan*, Philipsburg 40, MAP; *Captain Hodge's Inn*, Philipsburg, 25, EP; *Summit*, Simpson Bay, 34, EP; *Mary's Boon*, Simpson Bay, 40, EP; *Sea View*, Philipsburg, 44, EP;

Prince's Quarter, Philipsburg, 25, CP; *Caribbean,* Philipsburg, 15, EP; *China Night Guesthouse,* Philipsburg, 8.50, EP; *Marcus Guesthouse,* Philipsburg, 10 d, EP; *Tamarinde Guesthouse,* Pointe Blanche, 18, CP; *Sea Side Guesthouse,* Philipsburg, 10, EP; *Aambeeld Guesthouse,* Simpson Bay, 28 d, EP; *Seagrape Guesthouse,* Philipsburg, 20, EP; *Nina's Guesthouse,* Pointe Blanche, 12, EP; *Beco's Guesthouse,* Philipsburg, 9, EP.

Prices are the minimum rate for a single room in the winter (high) season and are quoted in US dollars. There is a 5% government tax on all hotel bills.

Villas: Town House Apartments, Great Bay; *Lagoon Inn,* Cole Bay; *Beachcomber Villas,* Burgeaux Bay; *Naked Boy Apartments,* Philipsburg; *Blue Waves Apartments,* Pointe Blanche; also private homes leased through various agencies, contact St. Maarten Tourist Bureau.

Restaurants All the major hotels have restaurants with international cuisine. The *Frigate,* the best of Mullet Bay's five restaurants, serves excellent charcoal broiled steaks and lobster. Highly recommended in Philipsburg for terrace dining overlooking the sea is *La Grenouille,* French and expensive, but with a reasonably priced *plat du jour.* The *West Indian Tavern* occupies the ruins of the 250-year-old synagogue. The *Rusty Pelican,* at the far end of Great Bay beach in town, serves unpretentious American food and good drinks, making it a popular, informal meeting place. *Le Panoramique,* at *Oceanside Hotel,* new, French, must book. The *Dutch Flour Mill* is an old windmill outside Philipsburg. *Nina's Cantina,* on road to Pointe Blanche, serves American food all night (also few rooms from US$12.20, EP). *Sea Grape Arbor,* West Indian food, reasonable prices. *Soerabaja* is a restaurant/night club near airport, also has some rooms. *Sam's,* E end of Front Street, good for breakfast and snacks. Indonesian *Rijsttafel* at the hotels or at the *Bilboquet* in Pointe Blanche. Pizzas at *Portofino.* Chinese fare at the *Mandarin* and *Majesty.* Americanized French at *L'Escargot.* (See page 1175.)

Taxis Rather high fixed prices to airport and the French side. Sightseeing tours can be arranged.

Buses Fairly regular service until 2000 hrs. to Marigot and Grand Case. Pick up along Front Street.

Self-drive Cars Shortage in high season: advisable to request from hotel when booking room. Largest is Risdon. Others include Avis-Holidays, Hertz-Fleming, Carnegie, Lucky, Vlaun's, Carioca, and in Marigot, Babi Richardson. Many meet flights at Juliana Airport and have offices in the major hotels. Motor-bikes at Carter's on Bush Road, Cul-de-Sac.

Telephones At cable office in Back Street. It is easier to call New York than the French side of the island.

Excursions Island day tours by air to St. Eustatius, Saba, and St. Barthélémy. Charters available to St. Barthélémy, St. Eustatius, Saba, and Anguilla aboard *La Esperanza,* and day trips to St. Barthélémy as well as diving expeditions aboard the *Maho.* (Contact Maho Bay Watersports, Mullet Bay Beach Hotel.)

Transport to St. Maarten KLM and Eastern from New York, Air France from Miami. From Europe *via* San Juan, Puerto Rico, with Pan Am, *via* Curaçao with KLM, or Guadeloupe with Air France. Direct connections also from the Virgin Islands and Antigua. By cruise ship from N.Y., Florida, New Orleans, and San Juan. Embarkation tax at Juliana Airport, 5.30 Antillean guilders.

Tourist Bureau De Ruyterplein, behind the Little Pier. Tel.: 2337. Well supplied with brochures and guides to St. Maarten, St. Eustatius, Saba and St. Barthélémy, and the monthly "St. Maarten Holiday!". Sightseeing tours available by bus or by car.

SINT EUSTATIUS (STATIA)

St. Eustatius, or Statia, 61 km. from St. Maarten, is historically the most important island of the Netherlands Antilles. As in the nearby islands, Statia was originally settled by the fierce Carib Indians, and its name is probably a sound-imitation of an Indian word. Only during the last century was the little-known saint of the same name proclaimed patron of the island.

Only 166 square kilometres, Statia was sighted by Columbus on his second voyage but never settled by the Spanish. The Dutch first colonized it in 1636 and soon built Fort Oranje which is still standing. Like St. Maarten and Saba, Statia changed flag many times—22—before becoming definitively Dutch in 1816.

During the 18th century the island became so prosperous as a market and port of transit that it was nicknamed the Golden Rock. A vital link in the supply line from Europe to the American rebels during the War of Independence, Statia was the first to salute the rebel flag after the Declaration of Independence in 1776 (a ship of the new Continental navy, the *Andrew Doria,* was saluted from Fort Oranje). A plaque commemorating the event was presented to the island by President Roosevelt in 1939.

Along with Curaçao and Jamaica, Statia was an active centre of slave trading until slavery was abolished in 1863, at which time the important sugar industry also began to disappear.

Besides Fort Oranje, which now serves as the seat of the island government, historical sites worth visiting are the Jewish synagogue, built in 1738 and restored after it was severely damaged by a hurricane in 1772, and the ruins of the Reformed Church which dates from 1776.

The island's principal town, Oranjestad, is situated on a cliff overlooking the long beach below. Lower Town, on the beach, is now mostly in ruins. It was the site of warehouses full of sugar, tobacco, rum, and slaves awaiting shipment to other points in the Caribbean.

Statia is quiet and friendly, with a population of about 1,300 given to farming and fishing. It is dominated by the long-dead volcanic mountain called the "Quill", inside which is a lush rain forest where young men hunt land crabs at night. Visitors are advised, however, to visit there only during the day.

Hotels Although deluxe hotels are under construction with U.S. financing, for the moment an economic holiday can still be had for under US$20 a day: *The Guesthouse,* a former government guest house, and the *Golden Rock Beach Hotel* are American-owned and operated. There is also the *Almond Tree Inn* in town and the *Antillean View* on the outskirts.

Transport to St. Eustatius By small aircraft, especially constructed for short landing and take-off, from St. Maarten. Occasional cruise ships stop here. Boat charters available in the larger nearby islands.

SABA

Saba, pronounced "say-bah", a mere 13 square km. and the smallest of this group of islands, 50 km. from Sint Maarten, was also inhabited originally by the Carib Indians, relics of whom have been found here. Saba was sighted by Columbus in 1493 but not settled until around 1640 by the Dutch. It became for a time a dependency of St. Eustatius and changed hands 12 times until becoming definitively Dutch in 1816; despite this, English is the predominantly-used tongue. The population numbers about 1,000, half of them white (descendants of Dutch, English, and Scots settlers) and half black, who live in separate social circles. The island is a superannuated volcano which seems to shoot out of the sea, green with lush vegetation from bougainvillea to orange and lemon groves, but without beaches. It has, however, a particular charm of its own and is completely unspoiled to date: until 1947, with the advent of the jeep, the only "roads" were steps which were cut into the rock by the first colonists (three are 800 from Fort Bay to Windwardside) in a marvel of engineering.

The Bottom, the main village and seat of Government, probably is not "the bottom" of the crater, as often believed. Its name is no doubt a derivation of the Dutch Zeeland word *botte* meaning bowl-shaped. Windwardside is a storybook village lying at 1,804 feet above sea level. Two other villages are called St. Johns and Zions Hill (which is also known as Hellsgate).

The volcanic crater, no trace of which has existed for 5000 years now, was probably near or at the top of Mount Scenery (2,854 feet above sea level). The airstrip is constructed on a solidified lava stream running into the sea.

The typical local drawn-thread work (also known as "Spanish Work" because it was learned by a Saban lady in a Spanish boarding school at the end of the last century) is sold at several shops on the island.

Hotels Windwardside: *Captain's Quarters,* best known and largest with 13 rooms and some cottages, is a handsomely decorated restored sea captain's house with a pool, about US$60 for two with all meals; *Scout's Place,* only 5 rooms, is the former government guesthouse, US$35 for two full board; another guesthouse should be ready with 10 rooms on Booby Hill by time of publication. The Bottom: *The Bottom Guesthouse,* under US$30 for two full board; also *Caribe Guesthouse,* and several smaller pensions with cheap rooms.

Transport to Saba By small aircraft from St. Maarten. The only places to get ashore are at Ladder Bay and Fort Bay.

Transport on Saba Hire jeep or car for tour; take guide if hiking to top of Mount Scenery.

Climate Curaçao, Aruba and Bonaire. Despite their tropical position, humidity is low and the climate is pleasant all the year round. January is the coolest month with an average temperature of 28.5°C. The hottest month is September with temperatures at around 30°C. There is little rain; what there is falls mostly in November and December.

Sint Maarten, Saba and Sint Eustatius. Though tropical the climate is cool, thanks to the North-East Trade winds. January and February are the coolest months with temperatures around 24.5°C. August and September are the hottest months, temperatures are around 27.5°C. The rainy season is between May and December.

Travel and Entry Regulations

Air There are direct air connections from New York or Miami to Curaçao and Aruba (KLM; ALM; U.S. airlines; Viasa) and to Sint Maarten by Pan American Carib Air. ALM operates a full schedule between all six islands. From Europe, any flight through U.S.A. or South America. Aerocóndor flies three times a week to Colombia. At Curaçao, Dr. Albert Plesman Airport has a good restaurant and is about 16 km. from Willemstad. International airports also on Aruba and St. Maarten. Airport tax in the Netherlands Antilles is US$3.

Sea From New York: Grace Line; KNSM (Royal Netherlands Steamship Company) Home Lines. From New Orleans: KNSM; Delta Line; Aldoa Steamship Co. From West Coast Ports: Italia Line; Interocean Line; French Line; Fred Oslen Line; Hanseatic Vaaxa Line; Mitsui O.S.K. Line. From Europe: KNSM from Rotterdam weekly; also some cruise ships. (Royal Mail Lines Agency: Firma C. S. Gorsira, J. P. Ez., Kerskstraat 9, Helfrichplein, P.O. Box 161).

Car ferries   Three times weekly (Mon., Wed., and Thurs.) between La Vela de Coro (Venezuela) and Curaçao, and (Fri., Sat., and Sun.), between Punto Fijo (Venezuela) and Aruba. Times: Punta Fijo, depart Tuesday 0900, arrive Curaçao 1500. Depart Curaçao 1700, arrive Aruba 2400. Depart Aruba 1000 Wednesday, arrive Punta Fijo 1500. Depart Punta Fijo 0900 Thursday, arrive Aruba 1400. Depart Aruba 1700, arrive Curaçao 2400. Depart Curaçao 1000 Friday, arrive Punta Fijo 1600. One-way fare without car, US$20.

All visitors require a through or return ticket to a destination outside the Netherlands Antilles and a valid smallpox vaccination certificate. U.S. citizens and those of the EEC countries require only documentary proof of identity, for others a valid passport is necessary. Visas are not required by nationals of most countries (except Cuba), in case of a stay of less than 14 days.

Currency   The Antillean Guilder (NA*f*) is divided into 100 cents with 1, 2½, 5 10, 25 cent coins. Banknotes in denominations of 1, 2½, 5, 10, 25, 50, 100, 250 and 500 guilders. Rate of exchange: NA*f*1.79 per US$ travellers' cheques; 1.77 per US$ cash; NA*f*1 = 1.40 Netherlands guilders. Venezuelan bolivares are accepted everywhere in Curaçao and Aruba; US dollars are accepted everywhere; sterling, Dutch guilders and other currencies must be changed in the banks.

For information write to: Information Department, Office of the Minister Plenipotentiary of the Netherlands Antilles, 175 Badhuisweg, The Hague, The Netherlands.

American Express Agents   Oranjestad: S. E. L. Maduro & Sons, Lloyd G. Smith Blvd, 106. Tel.: 3888. Bonaire: Kralendijk: Bonaire Trading Co., Kerkweg No. 6A and 9. Tel.: 8358. Sint Maarten: Philipsburg: S. E. L. Maduro & Sons, Front Street. Tel.: 2202.

We are profoundly grateful to Susan Pierres for a new revision of the sections on Curaçao, Aruba and Bonaire. Many thanks also to Cliff Cordy (USA), Schelte de Graaf (Netherlands) and Larry O'Brien for useful updating information.

FRENCH ANTILLES

THE FRENCH CARIBBEAN ISLANDS form two Départements d'Outremer: one comprises Martinique, and the other Guadeloupe with its offshore group—Marie-Galante, Les Saintes, La Désirade—and two more distant islands—Saint-Barthélémy and the French part of Saint-Martin (the Dutch have part of the island; see page 1161).

Geographically, the main islands form the N group of the Windward Islands, with the British island of Dominica in the centre of them. Saint-Barthélémy and Saint-Martin are in the Leeward group.

As the islands are politically Departments of France they have the same status as any Department in European France, such as Seine-et-Marne or Pas-de-Calais. There is a Prefect at the head of the local government of each Department, which also sends two senators and three deputies to the National Assembly in Paris. The inhabitants are French citizens. The currency is the French franc. The direct connexion with France confers many advantages on the islands which enjoy French standards of social legislation etc., but it also drives up the cost of living, which is said to be rather higher than elsewhere in the Caribbean.

Both the main islands were discovered by Columbus on his second voyage in 1493, but no colonies were established by the Spaniards because the islands were inhabited by the fierce Carib Indians (who are now virtually extinct); it was not until 1635 that the French settlers arrived.

Because of their wealth from sugar, the islands became a bone of contention between Britain and France; other French islands—Dominica, St.Lucia, Tobago—were lost by France in the Napoleonic wars. The important dates in the later history of the islands are 1848, when the slaves were freed under the influence of the French Wilberforce, Victor Schoelcher, and 1946, when the islands ceased to be colonies and became Departments of France.

Climate The dry season, which is rather cooler, is December-May, with virtually no rain in February; the wet, warmer season is June-November. The average temperature is 26°C. Low season in the hotels is April 15-December 16.

One feature in common to the two main islands is the Carnival, said to be more spontaneous and less touristy than most. There are also picturesque Ash Wednesday ceremonies, especially in Martinique, where the population dresses in black and white, and processions take place that combine the seriousness of the first day of the Christian Lent with the funeral of the Carnival King. Another common feature is the African dances—the *calinda, laghia, bel-air, haut-taille* and *gragé*—still performed in remote villages. The famous beguine, *pace* Cole Porter, is a more sophisticated dance from these islands.

The present-day economy of the main islands is based on sugar (from which a delicious, individual rum is distilled), bananas and pineapple. Tourism is gaining ground fast.

Creole Cuisine is worth mentioning for its originality and interesting combination of French, Indian, and African traditions, seasoned with the exotic spices of the Antilles. Some typical dishes are: *Calalou,* savoury soup made of local vegetables and herbs, served with *Chiquetaille,* grilled cod, or with *Feroce,* a mixture of avocado, sweet peppers, and manioc flour; *Colombo,* an East Indian curry of seeds and beef, pork, kid, or fish, cooked with rice; *Blaff,* a sort of *court-bouillon* made of *Lambis* (conch), clams, or sea urchins, with onions, limes, and spices; *Lambis* or *Chatrous* (small octopus) stewed in tomatoes and onions and accompanied by red beans and rice; *Accras,* an appetizer of African-style seafood fritters. The abundant seafood such as *Langouste* (rock lobster) and *Ouassous* (a crayfish almost as big as a lobster), as well as fresh-water *Crabes* are most often served grilled or cold with mayonnaise; *Tortue,* sea turtle, is eaten in curry, marinaded, or grilled; local fruit such as avocado, mango, pawpaw, and plantain bananas, as well as bread-fruit, are particularly exotic for foreign palates.

MARTINIQUE

Martinique (1,060 sq. km.) is an island 65 km. long and 31 km. wide situated at about 14° 40′ N and 63° 30′ W. To the W is the Caribbean and to the E, the Atlantic. To the S lies St. Lucia and to the N Dominica, with channels of about 40 km. between them and Martinique. The island is mountainous and volcanic; in the NW is the volcano Mont Pelée (1,384 metres), and in the centre, Les Pitons du Carbet (368 metres at the highest point). The inland part is covered with exotic flowers, shrubs and trees. The population is about 400,000.

Martinique was discovered in 1493 by Christopher Columbus, but not visited and named until his fourth voyage in 1502, when he gave it the name of Martinica in honour of St. Martin. The natives called it *Madinina,* the island of flowers. Because of the hostility of the Indian tribes of Cibonney, Arawak and Carib, it was only in 1635 that the French, led by Chevalier Belain d'Esnambuc, were able to settle there. Apart from two brief periods, the Seven Years' War and the French Revolution, when the island was occupied by the British, Martinique has always remained French. It enjoys the unique privilege, for an island in the New World, of having given six crowned heads to Europe. Today, with its four-lane highways, it seems more like France than a Caribbean island.

The island's capital is **Fort-de-France** (population: 100,000) which lies on the north side of the largest bay. Originally called Fort Royal, its name was changed after the French Revolution. It is a popular port of call for cruise ships and its streets are reminiscent of old New Orleans.

Among places of interest are Fort Saint-Louis, a military structure in Vauban style; La Savane square, a favourite promenade site, dominated by a marble statue of the island's most celebrated crowned head, Empress Joséphine; Schoelcher library in typical late 19th-century style; the old part of town and the artisan centre near the Tourist Office (rue Ernest Deproge); Saint-Louis Cathedral, which was built in 1895; the Martinique museum at 9 rue de la Liberté, where can be found documents, crafts and old furniture of the Arawak and Carib period. (It is open every day except Sunday from 0900 to 1200 and from 1500 to 1800); the artisan centre near the Tourist Office (rue Ernest Deproge); the colourful market places with their vast array of tropical fruit and spices; and the residential areas of Bellevue and Plateau Didier.

Shopping is a pleasant pastime in Martinique; many of the goods for sale are imported from France. There are also local handicrafts, including a doll souvenir dressed in the traditional Creole costume with a madras turban and full skirt with petticoats. There are wickerwork, jewellery, coral clusters, shells, leather goods, silk scarves etc. All French spirits can of course be purchased and the locally-produced rum is an excellent buy. Paris fashions are offered at continental prices in the many boutiques dotted about Fort-de-France. Purchases are exempt from tax when payment is made in foreign currency. Rue de la Liberté is good for shopping, and the colourful markets and handicrafts are to be found in shops mainly located on the rue Victor Hugo and near the Cathedral, in Fort-de-France.

The Tourist Office suggests four tours by car to see the island. These can equally well be combined to make two trips, which eliminates the necessity of returning to Fort-de-France each time.

1. The coastal road *via* Carbet to Saint-Pierre (24 km. N of Fort-de-France). Carbet is on a calm bay where Columbus paused in 1502 and the first French settlers landed in 1635. Saint-Pierre, the first town founded by the French in 1635, was destroyed in 1902 by one of the worst volcanic disasters in history, with the last eruption of Mt. Pelée. Only one of its 30,000 inhabitants survived—a criminal who was safely imprisoned in a solitary vault deep beneath the ground. Once called the "little Paris of the West Indies", St.-Pierre was an intellectual centre and its society was brilliant. A splendid theatre hosted the best operatic and dramatic companies on tour—now only its wide stone steps and a few vine-covered columns remain. Explore the city's ruins. Also, visit the Musée Vulcanologique (open 0900 to 1200 and 1500 to 1700) for graphic documentation. North of St.-Pierre is Le Prêcheur, ex-residence of Mme. de Maintenon, morganatic wife of King Louis XIV. Near the old city is the restored early 18th-century sugar plantation, now a hideaway resort hotel, *Plantation de Leyritz*. It was visited in December 1974 by Presidents Ford and Giscard d'Estaing during their summit conference on the island. The main building is a manor-house full of antiques. Sleeping accommodation is in two other buildings which were once slaves' quarters, with magazine-papered walls and a curious cooling system operated by turning a tap which sends spring water cascading down the bamboo roofs. The hotel is part of the *Relais de la Martinique* chain (see *Hotels*). Return by the Trace Road *via* Morne Rouge (where a guide can be hired for climbing the brooding Mont Pelée, 1,430 metres), then south through the lush rain forest. Bus Morne Rouge to Mont Pelée, US$2. Turn-off for the trail to the summit is 2 km. outside Morne Rouge on the road to Ajoupa-Bouillon (a 2-hour climb to the summit).

2. The second route cuts across the island to Trinité on the Atlantic coast and the picturesque Caravelle Peninsula, dominating Galleon Bay and Treasure Bay. Good beaches at Tartane. See the ruins of Château du Buc (once equipped with a torture chamber) and the Caravelle lighthouse.

3. To Trois-Ilets (35 km.), birthplace (in 1763) of Joséphine Rose Tascher de la Pagerie, the Creole beauty who was to reign five years as Napoleon's Empress Joséphine. (Napoleon once said: "I hold Martinique dear for more reasons than one".) Visit her house, "La Pagerie", which was destroyed by a hurricane and partially restored, also the church where she was christened and a small museum with relics of the Napoleonic period. On Anse à l'Ane is the Courbaril campsite (which also has bungalows to let at reasonable prices). Anse-Mitan, nearby, has been developed as a tourist centre with a few hotels and small restaurants with tables along the beach—15 minutes by launch to Fort-de-France across the bay. Continue to Diamant and its beach (with a heavy undertow) facing the "HMS Diamond Rock". The rock, jutting out of the sea just off the coast, was commissioned as a sloop of war by the British Navy in 1804, and held for 18 months during bombardments by the French coastal artillery. Reachable by boat. Continue west to the fishing village of Anses d'Arlets, from where there are also motor boats to the capital.

4. The fourth tour suggested is to Vauclin, a colourful fishing village on the SE coast. The palm-fringed beach becomes alive with sombrely dressed women

bargaining in patois for the fish when the boats come in. See the church in Marin and the magnificent palm-backed beach at Sainte-Luce, also the charming village of Sainte-Anne and its coral beach lined with sea grapes. You can reach the Anse Macabout through the Macabout camping site. Nearby are the salt marshes and the "Savane des Pétrifications", an eerie field in a dry, desert-like region, where the veins of a lava flow have been filled in with a crystalline substance which has given it the appearance of petrified wood.

There are also rum distilleries, sugar fields, and other historic mansions to visit. Archaeology enthusiasts may seek out recently discovered remnants from the Carib Indian days, and an ancient Arawak village. Volcanic eruptions are presumed to have buried two pre-Columbian villages on the NE coast.

Hotels Deluxe: *Bakoua,* Trois-Ilets, boat service to Fort-de-France (named after local fishermen's hats, and with a bar sheltered by a roof of the same shape), small beach, pool, animated weekly floor show, recommended; *Méridien,* Pointe du Bout (Trois-Ilets), new, enormous complex, beach, pool, casino; *Lido,* **Schoelcher,** traditional bungalows on lavishly landscaped hill overlooking dark sand beach and wharf, pool; *Martinique,* Schoelcher, actually a hotel school, but permitted to take guests when other hotels are full, 15 rooms only. Medium-priced: *Latitude,* near Carbet, new, in lush green setting, Polynesian style, young crowd, pool, nightclub; *Cap Est,* on Atlantic coast at Pointe de la Prairie (between Vauclin and François), tiny beach with shallow water, pool; *Auberge de L'Anse Mitan,* Trois-Ilets, family-run French inn, near the beach, private launch to Fort-de-France. Medium- to low-priced chain of hotels *Relais de la Martinique* offer an intimate, usually colonial atmosphere and Creole cuisine; *Plantation de Leyritz,* Basse-Pointe (see tour no. 1, previous page); *Le Manoir de Beauregard,* Ste-Anne, 1 km. from the beach, 18th century elegance, pool; *La Vallée Heureuse,* on the Ravine Vilaine just outside Fort-de-France, authentic colonial manor-house, Creole cuisine, pool; *L'Impératrice,* Fort-de-France, in city centre on La Savane; *Le Bristol, Victoria,* and *Le Gommier* near centre of Fort-de-France; *Le Montemar,* Schoelcher, Creole cuisine, pool; *Les Brisants,* François, facing the Atlantic, Creole cuisine. Other hotels in Fort-de-France: *Grillardin,* new, left bank atmosphere, friendly bar; *Malmaison,* La Savane, good; *Lafayette; L'Europe; Studio Laroc; Gallia,* on La Savane, with a good view of the harbour, US$5.50 d; *Bambou,* Trois-Ilets (Anse-Mitan Beach), 10 rooms only, pleasant outdoor dining on the beach; *Calalou,* Anse à l'Ane; *Chez André,* Trois-Islets; *Caridad Paradis,* Trois-Ilets: *Diamant les Bains,* Diamant; *Délices de la Mer,* Sainte-Luce; *Le Vieux Chalet* and *Mont Pelée Hotel* at Morne-Rouge (the latter is not recommended); *Auberge de L'Atlantique* and *Les Alizés* at Vauclin; *Tourist Hotel,* St.-Pierre (poor value); *Madras,* Tartane Beach. (Almost no accommodation in St. Pierre: stay at Morne Rouge, for Mont Pelée, or Fort-de-France and commute.) Check with Tourist Office for current hotel rates. *Chez Anna,* Fort-de-France, near the Palais de Justice, about US$12 after bargaining. *Pension de Famille,* rue Robespierre, Fort-de-France, for girls only, US$7 bed and breakfast. *Club Méditérranée,* hotel-village also called *Les Boucaniers,* at Sainte-Anne (petrified forest nearby). For information, write Club Méditérranée, 516 Fifth Ave., N.Y., N.Y. 10036; 5 South Molton Street, London W.1.

Restaurants There are more restaurants than hotels, many are excellent, most are good. For most current listing, check with the Tourist Office. Some traditional favourites: *Le Foyal,* behind La Savane in Fort-de-France, said to be best restaurant in the Caribbean; *Maxim's* tradition, elegant, intimate dining room, French and Creole cuisine, a favourite meeting spot for resident and visiting yachtsmen; *La Louisiane,* Didier, fashionable, elegant; *Chez Gérard,* rue Victor Sévère, tiny, friendly, French specialities; *L'Europe,* in hotel off La Savane, quiet, rustic atmosphere; *Baalbeck,* blvd. de Gaulle, Lebanese specialities; at least 4 restaurants specialize in Vietnamese cuisine—one is the *Mandarin,* which is excellent; the *Bambou,* on Anse-Mitan beach at Trois-Ilets has budget-priced fixed menu, fine fish fare, outdoor dining in a gay ambience; *Aux Filets Bleus* offers bikini'ed lunches and romantic dinners on the white sandy beach at Ste.-Anne; *La Dunette* is a small

Creole inn and restaurant also at Ste.-Anne; *La Guinguette,* on the beach near St.-Pierre; *Diamant Plage,* Diamant Beach; *Chez Sidonie,* Schoelcher. Another Creole restaurant is *L'Escalier,* on rue de Liberté; try the crab sauce and the octopus in red bean sauce.

Useful Addresses   *Tourist Office:* Blvd. Alfassa and rue de la Liberté (near the Savane), open 0730 to 1200 and 1500 to 1730, Saturdays from 0800 to 1200, Tel.: 71-79-60. *U.S. Consulate:* 10 rue Schoelcher, Tel.: 71-93-01. *British and Canadian Honorary Consulate:* Quartier Vieux Moulin, Didier (P.O. Box 465) 97205 Fort-de-France, Tel.: 71-25-44.

Transport on Martinque   *Taxis* have offical fixed prices, example: Lamentin Airport to Fort-de-France, 30-35 francs, to Trois-Ilets, 53 F. Buses no longer run between the airport and Fort-de-France. Colectivo 2.50 F. For current list of prices, check the Tourist Board's monthly publication, "Points Chauds". Taxis collectives congregate in a parking lot near the Yacht Club and run to most parts of the island. To St. Pierre costs 6 francs. For *Bus Tours* of the island; check with Carib Tour, rue Ernest Deproge, Tel.: 71-25-56. For *Boat Tours:* Le Sider, Tel.: 71-70-28; Martinique Charter Services, Tel.: 71-80-80; Agence de Voyages Roger Albert, Tel.: 71-71-71; Agence de Voyages Marsan, Tel.: 71-19-21. *Self-drive hire cars* available at Lamentin Airport and in Fort-de-France. Martinique also has a system of Peugeot station-wagons. They leave from near the Tourist Bureau on the Quai. Fare to St. Anne's, near Club Méditéranée Les Boucaniers, 11 F.

Entertainment   Check with Tourist Board's monthly publications, "Points Chauds", for current schedules. The Ballets Martiniquais, a local group of young people, perform Martinique's folk dances (beguine, mazurka, etc.) on cruise ships and in the major hotels. Cock fights, as well as mongoose vs. *fer-de-lance* snake fights, are held in specified arenas or *pitts* generally from December to May, accompanied by heavy betting. There are several night clubs and cinemas, as well as equestrian and shooting clubs.

GUADELOUPE

Guadeloupe is surrounded by the small islands La Désirade, Marie-Galante and Les Saintes, all of which can easily be visited from the main island, with each one offering something different. Including the two more distant islands of St.-Barthélémy and St.-Martin in the Leewards, the total area of the Department is 1,720 sq. km.

Guadeloupe (1,510 sq. km.) is rather less sophisticated and less historical than Martinique; it has a leisurely atmosphere and the forests and nature parks add to the feeling of timelessness. The island is really two small ones, separated by the narrow bridged strait of the Rivière Salée. To the west is mountainous Basse-Terre, which includes the administrative capital of the same name, with a population of 20,000. There can be found in the city some very pretty and authentic old buildings of the colonial period. Egg-shaped Basse-Terre, with the volcano Grande Soufrière (1,484 metres) at its centre, has an area of 777 sq. km. and a total of 130,000 inhabitants. The commercial capital of Guadeloupe is Point-à-Pitre, with 60,000 inhabitants, situated in the flat half of the island, in Grande-Terre; it is a lively and picturesque centre with a beautiful natural harbour. Grande-Terre, triangular in shape and slightly smaller than Basse-Terre, has a total population of 160,000 inhabitants. The names of the two parts show a most un-Gallic disregard of logic as Basse-Terre is the higher and Grande-Terre is the smaller; it may be that they were named by sailors, who found the winds lower on the Basse-Terre and greater on the Grande-Terre side. Christopher Columbus discovered Guadeloupe in 1493 and named it after the Virgin of Guadalupe, of Estremadura, Spain. The Carib Indians, who had inhabited the island, called it *Karukera,* meaning "island of beautiful waters". As in most of the Caribbean, the Spanish never settled, and Guadeloupe's history closely follows that of Martinique, beginning with French colonization in 1635. Other important dates are 1763, when Louis XV handed over Canada to Britain to secure his hold on these West Indian islands with the Treaty of Paris, and 1848, when slaves were freed by Victor Schoelcher, now a local hero.

Guadaloupe is in some ways reminiscent of Normandy or Poitou, especially the farms, built in those regional styles. The island's Natural Park covers 30,000 hectares of forest land in the centre of Basse-Terre, which is by far the more scenic part. As the island is volcanic there are a number of related places to visit, including the fumaroles, the cauldrons and the sulphur fields of the Col de l'Echelle (Ladder Pass), the hot springs and waterfalls of the Carbet river, and the towering peaks of extinct volcanoes. A spectacular view of Guadeloupe and the neighbouring islands can be seen from the summit of the Grande Soufrière volcano. The green plains below are decoratively covered with giant ferns. There are brightly coloured flowers such as bougainvillea and orchids, and tropical fruits, such as pawpaw, guava and banana. The pretty fishing villages with palm-fringed beaches are surrounded by plantations of sugar-cane.

Pointe-à-Pitre, at the S end of the Rivière Salée, is the chief port and commercial centre. A bustling town whose early colonial structures were largely destroyed in an earthquake in 1845, Pointe-à-Pitre has a lively and picturesque harbour with a colourful central market place. The tree-shaded Place de la Victoire was once the site of a guillotine, and the dock nearby is lined with inter-island schooners. Local handicrafts, particularly Madras cotton (from which the traditional costumes of the *doudous,* or local ladies, are made), are good buys, and French wines and perfumes are available at normal French domestic prices.

On Grande-Terre, the following are worth seeing: the ruins of the 18th-century fortress, Fort Fleur d'Epée, off the main road to Gosier; Gosier, the holiday centre of Guadeloupe, with its hotels, restaurants and night clubs; Sainte-Anne and its lovely beaches; and Pointe-des-Châteaux at the easternmost tip of the island, where the sea flings itself dramatically onto a mass of rugged rocks covered with sea grapes. From here there is a quiet view fo the flat island of Désirade. Also visit the eerie Beach of Skulls and Bones at Moule, which was once the main harbour of the island until it was destroyed in 1928 by a tidal wave (sea-quake). The beach is so named for the relics of Carib, English, and French warriors which have been exposed by the surging surf tearing away part of the cemetery in the rocks facing the sea. A pre-Columbian Arawak Indian village, called Morel, has been recently uncovered on the beautiful sandy beaches N of Moule.

Basse-Terre, on the other wing of the island, is the administrative capital of Guadeloupe and the entire Department. It is a charming banana-loading port town of narrow streets and well laid-out squares with palm and tamarind trees, in a lovely setting between the sea and the great volcano La Soufrière. There is an interesting 17th-century cathedral, and nearby are the ruins of Fort Richepance, a remnant of colonial days. St.-Claude, a wealthy suburb and summer resort 8 km. into the hills, is surrounded by coffee trees and tropical gardens.

On Basse-Terre, the greener of the two islands comprising Guadeloupe, the main sights are: the primeval rain forest leading to the crater of La Soufrière (the last 300 metres must be climbed on foot: take a guide or a compass as mist can sometimes make you lose sight of the coloured bollards which guide you to the top). From the top there is a spectacular view over the island and the rest of the Caribbean (if you are not enveloped in clouds, which is usually the case), above the lush jungle foliage and sulphurous fumes spurting over yellow and orange rock. Also visit the ancient Carib rock carvings near Trois Rivières. The most important of these is a drawing of the head of a Carib chief inside a cave where he is presumably buried; one can be led there for a few francs by one of the local boys. Also see Sainte-Marie where a statue commemorates the site of Columbus' landing in 1493, the calm clean beaches at Ferry and Grand-Anse and the rougher ones at Deshaies, as well as the Natural Park which one can cross from Pigeon by the Traversée Road: an unspoiled tropical forest full of gurgling waterfalls, picnic grounds, and trails for hiking. Les Saintes can be reached from Trois Rivières for about US$2.50 by boat. Les Saintes is still unspoiled. Also visit Fort Napoleon and Marigot Bay, with its shipyard accessible only by a scenic path. Matouba is an East Indian village in lovely surroundings with a good restaurant. On the SE side of Basse-Terre, along a forest path, are the Chutes de Carbet waterfalls. You can walk the Trace Victor Hugo, along the main ridge of Basse-Terre; it is a 29 km. hike.

Hotels Deluxe: *Auberge de la Vieille Tour,* Gosier, named after an 18th-century sugar tower incorporated into the main building, is on a bluff over the sea, beach, pool, tennis; *Méridien,* St.-François, Air France's new modern and conventional seaside complex, beach, pool, golf, tennis, flying school, dock, discothèque, and casino; *Caraïbe-Copatel,* Moule, brand new, 2 private beaches, pool, tennis, port, night club. Medium-priced: At Gosier: *P.L.M. Arawak* is of the Rothschilds' PLM group, beach, pool; *Callinago* is slightly smaller, beach, pool; *Le Montauban,* motel-style, 10 minutes from beach, pool; *Au Grand Corsaire,* a few cottages, private beach, good restaurant. At Pointe-à-Pitre: *le Bougainvillée, Studiotel,* and *Grand Hotel.* At Saint-Claude: *Relais de la Grande Soufrière,* an elegant old plantation mansion, now a government-sponsored hotel school. At Moule: *Les Alizés,* Canadian-owned, good horseshoe-shaped beach, pool, golf. At Ste.-Anne: *Au Grand large,* neither grand nor large, but friendly and with good restaurant on the beach; and *Mini Beach,* also on the beach. At Vieux-Habitants: *Rocroy Hotel.* Lower-priced: In Pointe-à-Pitre: *Schoelcher, Luna Park* and *Normandie,* on place de la Victoire, US$8.50 with breakfast, US$11 with breakfast and dinner, US$15 d, good value. Also *Karukera.* In Basse-Terre: *Relaxe* (reasonable) and *Basse-Terre.* Check with Tourist Board for current price lists (they run an information desk at Raizet airport). Club Mediteérranée has two hotel-villages on the island (membership is required—see Matinique Hotels, page 1170): *La Caravelle* at Ste.-Anne is on a spectacular white sand beach, perhaps the best on Guadeloupe, surrounded by a 33-acre preserve. Atmosphere strictly informal (few bikini tops seen on beach), all sports equipment available, gourmet dining unlimited. Also at Ste.-Anne, *La Villa Créole,* cheaper but friendly and clean. *Fort Royal* at Deshaies is a slightly run-down old luxurious hotel, more family-style than *La Caravelle* (which is mostly young and many singles), dramatically situated on a promontory between two beautiful but rather rough beaches. It is possible to book into the Club Méditérranée either in Bora Bora or in Moorea. The Club Méditérranée La Caravelle is US$45 per day; bus Pointe-à-Pitre to La Caravelle, US$1.

Restaurants Pointe-à-Pitre: *Oasis; Normandie; Relais des Antilles* (cheaper, but good Creole cooking). Raizet airport: *Oiseau des Iles; Le Madras.* Gosier: *La Pergola* (Hotel *Au Grand Corsaire*); *Datcha; La Créole; Chez Rosette; Le Boukarou; Pavillon de Jade* (Vietnamese). Ste.-Anne: *Hotel au Grand Large* and

Chez Yvette (budget-priced). Matouba: *Chez Paul* (Creole and East Indian cuisine). St.-François: *Madame Jerco* (good food in small creaking house).

Transport on Guadeloupe Taxis are rather expensive, but there is a network of ancient Mercedes public transport mini-buses. Organized bus tours and boat excursions available. Check with Tourist Office and Petrelluzzi Travel Agency (American Express Agents), 2 rue Henri IV, Pointe-à-Pitre. The Tourist Office at Pointe-à-Pitre has excellent guidebooks with maps of various trails. Frequent buses between Pointe-à-Pitre and airport, 1 franc. Taxis, airport to Pointe-à-Pitre, US$4. Bus Pointe-à-Pitre to Basse Terre, US$2. From there take a bus to St. Claude, US$0.50 and then walk to the excellent Natural Park and climb Mt. Soufrière. Hot springs nearby.

The French Tourist Office addresses are: *London:* 178 Piccadilly, London W1V 0AL. Tel.: 01-493 3171. *New York:* 610 Fifth Avenue, New York, N.Y. 10020. Tel.: (212) 757-1125. *Paris:* 127 Av. Champs-Elysées, 75008 Paris. Tel.: 225-12-80. *Guadeloupe:* Place de la Victoire, 97159 Pointe-à-Pitre (Antilles Françaises). Tel.: 82-09-30.

OTHER ISLANDS

The outer islands of Guadeloupe are among the most beautiful and least visited of the West Indian islands; they can easily be reached by air or boat from Guadeloupe. One can still get on a trading schooner between the islands if patient. A typical passage is Guadeloupe to Dominica for US$15.

At **Les Saintes** (whose eight small islands include Terre-de-Haut, Terre-de-Bas and the Îlet-à-Cabrit) the people are the greatest attraction, especially in Terre-de-Haut where they are descendants of Breton fishermen who have survived among themselves with little intermarriage with the dominant West Indian races. They even wear the same round hats that Breton fisherfolk wore until about twenty years ago. There is a daily boat from Trois-Rivières on Guadeloupe to Terre-de-Haut. On the Îlet-à-Cabrit is the *Hotel du Fort Joséphine.* On Terre-de-Haut is *Hôtel Bois Joli.* Rooms also at La Saintoise and La Colline.

Marie-Galante, a small round island and once an almost private rum-making empire, is absolutely delightful—simple and old-fashioned but surprisingly sophisticated when it comes to food and drink. Its beaches, so far almost completely untouched by the tourist flood, are superb. The shore road is particularly picturesque. This island was named by Chistopher Columbus after his own ship. Rooms at Le Salut and Le Belvédère.

La Désirade is an enchanting but rather arid island of simplicity and serenity of life for the 1,600 inhabitants who occupy themselves in fishing, sheep-rearing and cultivating cotton and maize. A road 10 km. long runs along the south coast to the E end of the island, where a giant cactus plantation can be seen. There are three boats weekly (2 hours, 10 francs) from St.-Francois, Guadeloupe, to La Désirade, on which is found the *Hotel La Guitourne,* 40 francs a night.

SAINT-MARTIN

St.-Martin, the largest of Guadeloupe's outer islands, is divided between France and the Netherlands. See Netherlands Antilles, page 1161, for general description and information.

Marigot, the capital of French St.-Martin, is a sleepy town between Simpson's Bay Lagoon and the sea. ("Marigot" is a French West Indian word meaning a spot from which rain water does not drain off, and forms marshy pools.) A modest waterfront marketplace offers local limes and vegetables, while mini-supermarkets abound in French delectables such as tins of *choucroute* and *cassoulet,* as well as cheeses and wines. Boutiques offer French *prêt-à-porter* fashions and St. Barts batiks, and gift shops sell liqueurs, perfumes, and cosmetics at better duty-free prices than the Dutch side. A string of restaurants and small hotels line the beach along a narrow thread of land just outside Marigot.

Grand Case, 13 km. from the capital, is anything but grand: a quaint town between an old salt pond (which has been partially filled in to provide the airstrip appropriately called L'Espérance) and a long sandy and secluded beach lined with sea grapes which are interrupted by a small pier and a smattering of guest houses and shops. At the far NE end is another beach, Petite Plage, delightfully *petite* in a calm bay. On the Atlantic, Orient Bay is beautiful but rough: beware of its undertow.

Excursions From Marigot to Anguilla by ferry boat or with the "Hon-Me" ("paradise isle" in Vietnamese), a 49-foot ketch skippered by René Peyronnet, expert diver and chef (owner of *Restaurant Chez René*), who crossed the Atlantic with it: US$30 includes day cruise and lobster-fish lunch with wine. Ferryboats go from Marigot to the Virgin Islands.

Hotels in French St. Martin *La Samanna,* rooms for US$95 without meals, apartments from US$150, villas (three bedrooms) US$360 daily in high season, making this one of the most exclusive resorts in the Caribbean. *Le Galion Beach Hotel et Club* is new and offers a private beach on the northeast side of the island near Orient, US$40-60 d. *Le Grand Saint-Martin,* with discothèque, US$60 to US$80 d; *St.-Tropez,* pool and discothèque, US$62 d, with half board; *Le Pirate,* a favourite with island-hoppers, US$60 d, with half board; *Yacht Club Résidence,* US$30; *Moulin Rouge* and *Beau Séjour,* in centre of Marigot, about US$25. At Grand Case: *Tackling's Beach Apartments; Hodge's Guest House,* US$35; *Goetz Guest House,* about US$165 weekly; *Cagan's Guest House* and *Le Fish Spot* have a few reasonably-priced rooms; *Petite Plage,* housekeeping units on beach at US$30 daily, weekly rates available. On a lonely point opposite Marigot, the multimillion dollar disaster, La Belle Créole, is an eerie ghost of a hotel left in ruins when its developers went broke before its opening: antique furniture imported from Spain is weathering away in the sea mist.

Restaurants French cuisine in all hotel restaurants on the French side is quite good, particularly *Le Pirate,* which has become a popular hangout. Picturesque gourmet dining on the seashore are the islanders' favourites: the *Mini-Club* with its bar and dining arbour and *Le Boucanier* for seafood specialities. Newest and very popular for its Créole specialities is *Chez Lolotte,* medium-priced with garden dining. Traditional French in centre of Marigot is *La Calanque,* and a new Vietnamese restaurant is *Le Santal. Chez René* at the Lagoon Bridge promises really gourmet fare if given ample warning. *La Coupole* is French fare in 1930s ambience. *Le Radeau* is a floating bar and restaurant on the outskirts of Marigot with few but tasty French dishes. At Grand Case is *Fish Pot,* with only 8 tables overlooking the sea, exquisite fish fare. Across the street is *Rosemary's* for Créole cooking. *Coralita* offers French/Creole fare. In the Tackling Building is the *New China Restaurant.*

SAINT-BARTHÉLÉMY

Saint-Barthélémy (St. Barts or St. Barth's), also in the Leewards, is 230 km. N of Guadeloupe, 240 km. E of the Virgin Islands, and 35 km. SE of St.-Martin. Its 21 sq. km. are inhabited by a population of 2,500, mostly blue-eyed blond Celts of Breton, Norman, and Poitevin descent who live in quiet harmony with the small percentage of blacks. Thiry-two splendid white sandy beaches, most of which are protected by both cliff and reef, are surrounded by lush volcanic hillsides reminiscent of Normandy and Brittany. The Norman dialect is still largely spoken while, as in the other non-British Leewards, most of the islanders also speak English. Elderly women still wear traditional costumes (with their characteristic starched white bonnets called *kichnottes*) and busy themselves cultivating sweet potato patches and weaving palm fronds into hats and purses which they sell in the village of Corosol. The men traditionally smuggled rum among neighbouring islands and now import liqueurs and perfumes, raise cattle, and fish for lobsters offshore. Unspoiled as yet by mass tourism, the people are generally known for their courtesy and honesty. Although the Rockefellers, Fords, and Rothschilds own property on the island, there is little glitter of traffic, no bill-boards, casinos, or steel bands. The small crowd of *habitués* is mostly young, chic, and French. The food, wine, and aromas are equally Gallic.

Named after Christopher Columbus' brother, St.-Barthélémy was first settled by French colonists from Dieppe in 1645. After a brief possession by the Order of the Knights of Malta, and a ravaging by the fierce Caribs, it was bought by the Compagnie des Îles and added to the French royal domain in 1672. In 1784, France ceded the island to Sweden in exchange for trading rights in the port of Göteborg. The harbour of Carénage was renamed Gustavia after the Swedish king, and became a free port, marking the beginning of the island's greatest prosperity. In 1801, St. Barts was attacked by the British, and in 1852 a fire severely damaged the capital, although the Swedish influence is still evidenced in the city hall and the trim stone houses which ring the superb hurricane-proof harbour. The island was handed back to the French after a referendum in 1878.

Hotels   At St.-Jean Beach (the best): *Eden Rock,* most picturesque, designed and owned by mayor of St. Barts, US$60 d, with full board; *Village St.-Jean,* modern bungalows, with kitchen facilities from US$40 for two, single rooms for US$27, special weekly rates available; *Emeraude Plage,* similar at US$30. At Lorient Beach: *Autour du Rocher,* good buy at US$40-45 d, including all meals and wine. At Flamands Beach: *Hotel Baie des Flamands,* modern, near Anse Rockefeller, US$55 d, US$44 s, with half board. Most expensive: *Les Castelets,* high in the hills, under new U.S. management, at US$60 d, minimum, without meals. Least expensive: *La Presqu' Ile,* US$25 d, with half board, and *Villas Prosper-Berry,* US$25 apartment for two with car included. Cars for hire are few: if desired, it is advisable to request from one's hotel when booking room.

Restaurants   *Eden Rock,* good, terrace dining, average US$10 each, with wine. *Autour de Rocher,* good lobster salad lunch for $7, indoors only. *Le Beach Club* (Village St.-Jean), reasonable lunches on the superb white sandy beach, water-sports equipment available here. *Club Estaminet* (Hotel *Les Castelets*), overpriced, in Alpine atmosphere. *La New Vielle France,* beachside with dancing at Corosol. In Gustavia: *L'Entrepont* for exquisite French cuisine; *Au Port,* with balcony overlooking the harbour, offers few but well-prepared French dishes (also has a few rooms to let); *Auberge du Fort Oscar* specializes in Créole cooking, reserve first with Mme Jacque (Tel.: 208); *La Taverne* occupies an old warehouse and is open quite late. *Bar Le Select* is a central meeting spot and sort of general store, with few tables in a small garden.

Transport to St.-Barts   Scheduled flights from St. Martin ($12.50), Guadeloupe ($25), and St. Thomas ($30). Charters available locally. Day trips from Sint Maarten aboard *La Esperanza* (US$20 p.p.) and the *Maho* (twice weekly, US$35 p.p., including lunch). Full docking facilities are available at the Yacht Club in Gustavia, and anchor-place for yachts up to 10 ft. draft at St.-Jean Bay.

How to get to the French Antilles

By Air Air France has direct flights from Paris to the international airports of Fort-de-France and Pointe-à-Pitre. Connexions *via* New York, Miami, San Juan (Puerto Rico), Curaçao. Inter-island services with Winair, Liat, Caribair, A.L.M., Air Antilles, S.A.T.A., Prinair.

By Sea The only companies offering passenger transport are the Compagnie Fabre at Marseille and the Compagnie Générale Transatlantique at Le Havre. There are, however, numerous cruises departing from U.S. and French ports, among which the Italian Linea C and Siosa lines.

Local Transport On the islands transport is convenient, in hired cars, taxis and buses.

Documents All travellers must be in possession of an outward ticket. Identity papers are required for U.S. and Canadian citizens staying less than 21 days. A passport, but no visa, is needed by citizens of EEC member-countries. No vaccination is necessary but an anti-smallpox vaccination certificate is recommended when travelling in the Caribbean zone.

What to Wear On the beach, bathing costumes, shorts. In town, lightweight clothing. Take a raincoat and woollens for evening outings and excursions into the mountains.

Currency Exchange The banks are open from 0800 to 1200 and from 1430 to 1600, Monday to Friday. There are money-changing offices in the big hotels and at airports. It is wise to use French francs, as French coins and banknotes are accepted everywhere. There is no limit to travellers' cheques and letters of credit being imported, but a declaration of foreign banknotes in excess of 3,500 F must be made. 500 F in French banknotes may be exported and 3,500 F in foreign banknotes.

Tourists on arriving at Guadeloupe would be advised to obtain a copy of a weekly booklet called "I Semaine de Loisirs" and those in Martinique, a booklet called "Choubouleoute" both published by the Tourist Board. They give current information about entertainment, hotels, tours, prices etc. For commercial visitors the "Hints to Businessmen" published by the U.K. Department of Trade has an interesting section on Martinique. The French Tourist Office (addresses under Guadeloupe) are most helpful.

American Express Agents Pointe-à-Pitre; Petrelluzzi Travel Agcy, 2 Rue Henri IV, Tel.: 341/3.

Many thanks to Peter Klika (Hawaii), and R. F. Vandersteen and Anne M. Walley (Peru) for some useful updating material.

WHERE TO BUY
THE HANDBOOK
Bookshops in Latin America and the Caribbean

This list of bookshops where the Handbook may be in stock is by no means exhaustive. It is compiled from orders received by the publishers and therefore takes no account of bookshops that order through wholesalers. We shall, however, be very pleased to expand the list in future editions, if booksellers and wholesalers—and travellers—will kindly keep us informed.

Argentina
Carlos Hirsch S.R.L. (wholesale), Florida 165, Buenos Aires.
Pigmalion Bookstore (books, records, slides), Corrientes 513, Buenos Aires.
Librería ABC, Florida 725, Buenos Aires.
Librería Rodríguez S.A., Sarmiento 835, Buenos Aires.
Mackern's English Bookstore, Sarmiento 525, Buenos Aires.

Falkland Islands
Falkland Island Trading Co. Ltd., Stanley.

Bolivia
Los Amigos del Libro (wholesale and retail), Casilla 450, Cochabamba (branches in La Paz and Santa Cruz).

Brazil
Claron (wholesale and retail), Av. São João, 324-7°, São Paulo.
Livraria Cristã Unida Ltda., Caixa Postal 1013, Campinas (SP).
Livraria Kosmos Editora, (wholesale and retail), Rua do Rosário 135-137, Caixa Postal 3481-ZC-00, Rio de Janeiro (branches in São Paulo and Porto Alegre).
Livraria Interciência, Av. Presidente Vargas 435, Rio de Janeiro.
Livraria Nova Galeria de Arte, Av. Copacabana, 291-D, Rio de Janeiro.
Padrão, Livraria Editora Ltda., Rua Miguel Couto 40, Rio de Janeiro.

Chile
Librería El Sembrador, Pasaje Matte 342, Santiago.

Colombia
Librería Aldina, Carrera 7 No. 70-80, Bogotá.
Librería Buchholz, Apartado Aéreo 22250, Bogotá.
Librería Central, Calle 16, No. 6-34, Bogotá.
Librería Continental, Junín 52-11, Medellín.
Librería Aguirre, Calle 53, No. 49-123, Medellín.
Librería Nacional Ltda., Carrera 5A, No. 11-50, Cali.
Also at Bogotá airport.

Ecuador
Librería Universitaria (formerly Librería Central), Calle García Moreno 739, Apartado 2982, Quito.
Librería SU Cía., Ltda., Apartado 2556, Quito.
Libri Mundi, Juan León Mera 851 y Veintimilla, Casilla 3029, Quito.
Librería Científica S.A., Casilla 362, Guayaquil.
Librería Española, Venezuela 961 y Mejía, Casilla 356, Quito.

Paraguay
Librería Universal, Palma 519, Asunción.

Peru
Herman Jesson's Trading Post, Jessonia, on the River Amazon.
Librería ABC, Edificio Hotel Bolívar, Avda. Nicolás de Piérola, Lima (and branches).
Librería Epoca, Belén 1042, Lima.
Also at Lima airport.

Venezuela
The American Bookshop, Av. San Juan Bosco, Altamira, Ed. Belveder, Loc. 2, Caracas.
The English Bookshop, Congresa 315 (Apartado 62243), Prados del Este, Chacao, Caracas 106.
Distribuidora Santiago C.A., Apartado 2589, Caracas.
Illustra Bookstore, Hotel Caracas Hilton, Caracas.
Librería Del Este, Av. Miranda 52, Edificio Galipán, El Rosal, Caracas.
Librería Las Mercedes C.A., Edificio Automercado, Las Mercedes, Caracas.
Librería Lectura, Centro Comercial Chacaíto, Local 129, Av. Fco. de Miranda, Chacaíto, Caracas.
Librería Unica, Apartado 3956, Caracas.

Guyana
William Fogarty Ltd., Georgetown.
S.P.C.K. Bookshop, 78 Church & Carmichael Streets, Georgetown 2.

Suriname
E. K. Friedland, P.O. Box 932, Paramaribo.
Varekamp en Co N.V., Domineestraat 26, Paramaribo.

Mexico
American Bookshop, Calle Madero (near Zócalo), México 1, DF.
The Anglo-American Bookstore, Serapio Rendón 125, México 4, DF.

Costa Rica
Libr. Imprenta y Litografía Lehmann S.A., Apartado 10011, San José.
The Bookshop, Apartado 7-1420, San José.

El Salvador
Librería Cultural Salvadoreña S.A., Calle Delgado 117, San Salvador.

Guatemala
Arnel Books, 9a Calle 6-65, Zona 1, Guatemala City.
Libros Timms Ltda., Apartado Postal 286, Antigua.

Belize
Belize Bookshop, 14 Albert Street, P.O.B. 147, Belize City.

Panama
Lewis Service Inc., Apartado 1634, Panamá 1, R.P.

Jamaica
Sangster's Bookstores Ltd., 97 Harbour Street, Kingston.
The Bolivar Bookshop, P.O. Box 413, Kingston 10.

Trinidad and Tobago
Abercromby Bookshop (formerly S.P.C.K.), 22 Abercromby Street, Port-of-Spain, Trinidad.

Barbados
Cloister Bookstore, Hincks St., Bridgetown.

Bermuda
The Bermuda Book Store, P.O. Box 486, Hamilton.

Netherlands Antilles
Firma C. S. Gorsira J.P. Ez., P.O. Box 161, Curaçao.

BOOK AND
PERIODICAL LIST

Another Guide Book

Latin American Travel Guide and Pan American Highway Guide, 6th edition, 1976. Compsco Publishing Co., 663 Fifth Avenue, New York, N.Y. 10022. Price US$9.95 plus US$1 surface-mail postage or US$4 air-mail. Recommended for the traveller for whom one guide book is not enough!

LATIN AMERICA IN GENERAL

The standard one-volume history and geography, both entitled Latin America, are both American, by Hubert Herring and Preston James, respectively.

Latin America, a catalogue of old and new available books about Latin America, by Heffers, 20 Trinity Street, Cambridge CB2 3NG.

Latin America; Essays in Continuity and Change, Ed. by Harold Blakemore. BBC, London, 1974.

Latin America; Geographical Perspectives, ed. by Harold Blakemore and Clifford T. Smith. Methuen, London, 1971.

From Cortés to Castro; an introduction to the history of Latin America 1492-1973, by Simon Collier. Secker & Warburg, London, 1974.

Economies and Societies in Latin America; a geographical interpretation, by Peter R . Odell and David A. Preston. Wiley, London, 1973.

Latin America; an economic and social geography, by J. P. Cole. Butterworth, London, 2nd edition 1975.

Latin America; the Search for a New International Role, ed. by Ronald Hellman and H. Jon Rosenbaum. Sage Publications, London, 1975.

Latin America: New World, Third World, by Stephen Clissold. Pall Mall Press, London, 1972.

A History of Latin America, by George Pendle. Penguin. Revised reprint, 1975.

History of Latin American Civilization, edited by Lewis Hanke. Vol. I: The Colonial Experience. Vol. II: The Modern Age. Methuen, 1969.

Latin America, by Harold Blakemore. Oxford University Press. London, 1966.

Latin America, the Cold War and the world powers, 1945-73; a study in diplomatic history, by F. Parkinson. Sage Publications, London, 1974.

Latin America; a Cultural Outline, by Stephen Clissold. Hutchinson. London, 1965.

The Modern Culture of Latin America, by Jean Franco. Pall Mall Press, 1967.

A Concise History of Latin American Culture, by P. Henríquez Ureña. Pall Mall Press, 1966.

The Conquistadors, by Hammond Innes. Collins, London, 1969.

South America, ed. by Alice Taylor. David and Charles, Newton Abbot, 1973. (Papers discussing the interaction of environment and economic, social and political forces.)

The Golden Man; a Quest for El Dorado, by Victor W. von Hagen. Saxon House, Farnborough (Hants), 1974.

COUNTRIES

Argentina

An Introduction to Argentina, by Robert J. Alexander. Pall Mall Press, London, 1969.

Argentina in the 20th Century, ed. by David Rock, Duckworth, London, 1975.

Bolivia

Bolivia: a Land Divided, by Harold Osborne. Revised edition. Oxford University Press for the RIIA. London, 1965.

Gate of the Sun: A prospect of Bolivia, by Margaret Joan Anstee. Longman. London, 1970.

Bolivia: Land, Location and Politics since 1825, by J. Valerie Fifer. Cambridge University Press, 1972.

Brazil

The Last Horizon—a Brazilian Journey, by Gilbert Phelps. Charles Knight & Co. 2nd edition. London, 1971.

Brazil Struggles for Development, by Gordon H. Campbell. Charles Knight & Co. London, 1972.

An Introduction to Brazil, by Charles Wagley. Revised edition. Columbia University Press. New York and London, 1971.

Brazil, by Andrew Marshall. Thames and Hudson, London, and Walker & Co., New York, 1966.

Contemporary Brazil; Issues in Economic and Political Development, ed. by H. Jon Rosenbaum and William G. Tyler. Praeger, New York, 1973.

Assault on the Amazon, by Richard Bourne. Gollancz, London, 1978.

Chile

Image of Chile, by Graeme Parrish. Charles Knight. London, 1972.

The Growth and Structure of the Chilean Economy, by M. J. Mamalakis. Yale U.P., 1976.

Colombia

Colombia: a general survey, by W. O. Galbraith. 2nd edition. Oxford University Press for the RIIA. London, 1966.

Ecuador

Ecuador: Country of Contrasts, by Lilo Linke. 3rd edition. Oxford University Press for the RIIA, 1960.

Paraguay

Paraguay: a Riverside Nation, by George Pendle. 3rd edition. Oxford University Press for the RIIA, 1967.

Land of Lace and Legend, distributed by Friends of Paraguay in Asunción.

Peru

Peru, by R. J. Owens. Oxford University Press for the RIIA, 1963.

Peru, by Robert Marett. London, 1969.

The Conquest of the Incas, by John Hemming. Macmillan, London, 1970.

Peru under the Incas, by C. A. Burland. Evans Brothers, London, 1967.

The Men of Cajamarca (a social and biographical study of the first conquerors of Peru), by James Lockhart. University of Texas Press, London, 1972.

Uruguay

Uruguay: a Contemporary Survey, by Marvin Alisky. Praeger, New York and London, 1969.

Venezuela

Venezuela, by Edwin Lieuwen. Oxford University Press for the RIIA. 2nd Edition. London, 1965.

A History of Venezuela, by Guillermo Morón. Allen & Unwin, London, 1964.

Mexico

Mexico, by Robert Marett. Thames and Hudson, London, 1971.

Mexico, by Peter Calvert, Benn, London, 1973.

The Aztecs: a History, by Nigel Davies. Macmillan, London, 1973.

New Spain: the Birth of Modern Mexico, by Nicolas Cheetham. Gollancz, London, 1974.

Central America
The Central American Republics, by R. D. Parker. Oxford University Press for the RIIA. London, 1964.
El Salvador
El Salvador, by Alistair White. Benn, London, 1973.
Guatemala
Guatemala Guide, by Paul Glassman. Passport Press, Dallas (Texas).
Dominican Republic
The Dominican Republic—a Nation in Transition, by Howard J. Wiarda. Pall Mall Press. London, 1969.
West Indies and Caribbean
A Short History of the West Indies, by J. H. Parry and P. M. Sherlock. Third edition. Macmillan, London, 1971.
A History of the British West Indies, by Alan Burns. Allen & Unwin. 2nd Edition. London, 1965.
Caribbean Patterns, Harold Mitchell. Chambers, 1967.
A History of Barbados, by Ronald Tree. Hart-Davis, London, 1972.

Periodicals
Apart from the academic journals, of which there are several, the most informative sources are:
Bank of London & South America Review, a monthly review published by Lloyds Bank International Ltd. Distributed to interested institutions and libraries, but not normally to individuals.
Latin American Political Report (weekly), published by Latin American Newsletters Ltd., 90-93 Cowcross Street, London EC1M 6BL. Annual subscription by airmail £55 (US$100). Joint subscription with *Economic Report* and *Commodities Report,* £140 (US$250); Subscription for any two of these, £100 (US$180).

A weekly newspaper, *The Times of the Americas,* is published in Miami. Among daily newspapers in English the most informative are the London *Times,* the *Financial Times,* the *Daily Telegraph, The Guardian* and the *International Herald Tribune;* and in the U.S.A. the *Journal of Commerce* (New York), the *New York Times* and the *Miami Herald.* If you read French, *Le Monde.* If German, *Neue Zürcher Zeitung.*

BRITISH-LATIN AMERICAN ORGANIZATIONS

The Hispanic and Luso-Brazilian Council, and **The Canning House Economic Affairs Council Ltd.,** Canning House, 2 Belgrave Square, SW1X 8PJ. Tel.: 01-235 2303.

Publication: *"British Bulletin of Publications on Latin America, the West Indies, Portugal and Spain."* Price £3.50 per annum.

Canning House is the Focus in Britain of the commercial and cultural interests of the Spanish and Portuguese speaking nations, and spreads knowledge throughout the United Kingdom of the culture, languages and economies of these countries.

Anglo-Argentine Society, 2 Belgrave Square, SW1X 8PJ. Tel.: 01-235 9505. Hon. Sec.: Mr. G. P. Ritchie. Sec.: Mrs. S. Williams.

Argentine Information Bureau at the Aerolíneas Argentinas office, 18 New Bond Street, London, W.1. Tel.: 01-493 6941.

Brazilian Chamber of Commerce & Economic Affairs in Great Britain, 35 Dover Street, London, W1X 3RA. Publication, monthly: *"Brazil Journal"*. Tel.: 01-499 0186. Sec.: Mr. Eric Quick. The **Brazilian Tourist Office** is in the same building.

Anglo-Brazilian Society, 2 Belgrave Square, SW1X 8PJ. Tel.: 01-235 3751. Sec.: Mrs. M. Fyfe.

Anglo-Chilean Society, 12 Devonshire St., W.1. Hon. Sec.: Mr. W. R. Smithson.

Anglo-Colombian Society, 5 Belgrave Square, London, S.W.1. Tel.: 01-235 3601. Hon. Sec.: Mr. A. Cutts-Watson.

British-Cuba Association, 101 Clarence Gate Gardens, Glentworth Street, London, NW1 6QP. Tel.: 01-723 5439. Hon. Sec.: Dr. A. M. Young.

British-Mexican Society, 52 Grosvenor Gardens, S.W.1. Tel.: 01-730 0128. Hon. Sec.: Mr. R. A. C. Du Vivier.

Mexican National Tourist Council, 52 Grosvenor Gardens, London, SW1. Tel.: 01-730 0128. Delegate: Miss Mona King.

Anglo-Peruvian Society, 52 Sloane Street, S.W.1. Tel.: 01-235 3601. Hon. Sec.: Mr. A. Cutts-Watson.

British-Uruguayan Society, Shreelane, 222 Brooklands Road, Weybridge, Surrey. Tel.: Weybridge (from London dial 97) 47455. Sec.: Miss Jill Quaife.

Anglo-Venezuelan Society, 10 Belgrave Square, London S.W.1. Tel.: 01-235 3601. Executive Sec.: Mr. A. Cutts-Watson.

London Chamber of Commerce (Incorporated), 69 Cannon Street, E.C.4. Tel.: 01-248 4444. Sections specialize in Latin America.

The Canning Club, c/o The Naval & Military Club, 94 Piccadilly, W.1. Tel.: 01-499. Membership includes South Americans and Anglo-South Americans in London. Sec.: Mr. R. B. Baker.

AVAILABILITY

One complaint we often receive from would-be readers is that they have searched bookshop after bookshop for our Handbook in vain. We should like to take this opportunity of asking all booksellers who regularly order the Handbook through wholesalers to let us have their names for listing in the next edition; we have already made a start by including, on pages 1178 and 1179, a list of booksellers, in Latin America and the Caribbean who order direct from us. Meanwhile we should like to remind would-be readers anywhere in the world that if they have any difficulty in obtaining our book through the trade, it may be ordered direct from us at the normal U.K. price plus appropriate postage and handling charges.

WEIGHTS AND MEASURES

Metric	British and U.S.

Weight:

1 kilogram (kg.) = 2,205 pounds

1 metric ton = 1.102 short tons
= 0.984 long ton

1 pound (lb.) = 0.454 kilogram

1 short ton (2,000 lb.) = 0.097 metric ton

1 long ton (2,240 lb.) = 1.016 metric tons

Length:

1 millimetre (mm.) = 0.03937 inch

1 metre = 3.281 feet

1 kilometre (km.) = 0.621 mile

1 inch = 25.417 millimetres

1 foot (ft.) = 0.305 metre

1 mile = 1.609 kilometres

Area:

1 hectare = 2.471 acres

1 square km. (km^2) = 0.386 sq. mile

1 acre = 0.405 hectare

1 square mile (sq. mile) = 2,590 km^2

Capacity:

1 litre = 0.220 Imperial gallon
= 0.264 U.S. gallon

1 Imperial gallon = 4.546 litres

1 U.S. gallon = 3.785 litres

(5 Imperial gallons are approximately equal to 6 U.S. gallons)

Volume:

1 cubic metre (m^3) = 35.31 cubic feet
= 1.31 cubic yards

1 cubic foot (cu. ft.) = 0.028 m^3

1 cubic yard (cu. yd.) = 0.765 m^3

N.B. The *manzana*, used in Central America, is about 0.7 hectare (1.73 acres).

(With acknowledgements to *Bank of London & South America Review*.)

LATEST EXCHANGE AND INFLATION RATES

This information supplements that given in the "Information for Visitors" sections of the country chapters.

	Exchange for tourists: Units per US dollar (Unofficial market rate shown in parenthesis where known)		Inflation: % increase in cost of living for period shown		
			Period	1977	1978
Argentina	June 1978	800	Jan.-April	40.7	46.4
Bolivia	July 1978	20.00 (23.00)	Jan.-March	0.5	0.4
Brazil	July 1978	18.00 (20.70)	Jan.-April	16.7	11.3
Chile	June 1978	32.06	Jan.-April	24.5	10.1
Colombia	June 1978	36.00 (39.00)	Jan.-March	10.7	5.6
Ecuador	June 1978	26.50	Jan.-March	0.9	3.6
Paraguay	June 1978	134.00 (147.00)	Jan.-March	8.3	2.8
Peru	June 1978	155.00 (180.00)	Jan.-Feb.	5.1	12.8
Uruguay	July 1978	6.025	Jan.-March	15.0	6.5
Venezuela	July 1978	4.28	Jan.-April	2.1	0.5
Mexico	June 1978	22.63	Jan.-April	8.9	5.6

We regret that we have no Central American or Caribbean countries' inflation figures more recent than those in the country sections. Their currencies have remained stable in relation to the US dollar for many years.

(With acknowledgements to *Bank of London & South America Review*.)

CLIMATIC TABLES

The following tables have been very kindly furnished by Mr. R. K. Headland. Each weather station is given with its altitude in metres (m.) Temperatures (Centigrade) are given as averages for each month; the first line is the maximum and the second the minimum. The third line is the average number of wet days encountered in each month.

MEXICO, CENTRAL AMERICA & CARIBBEAN

	Jan.	Feb.	Mar.	Apr.	May	June	July	Aug.	Sept.	Oct.	Nov.	Dec.
Acapulco 3m.	29	31	31	31	32	32	32	32	31	31	31	31
	21	21	21	22	23	24	24	24	24	23	22	21
		0	0	0	2	9	7	7	12	6	1	0
Guatemala City 1490m.	23	25	27	28	29	27	26	26	26	24	23	22
	11	12	14	14	16	16	16	16	16	15	14	13
	2	2	2	5	8	20	17	16	17	13	6	2
Havana 49m.	26	27	28	29	30	31	31	32	31	29	27	26
	18	18	19	21	22	23	24	24	24	23	21	19
	6	4	4	4	7	10	9	10	11	11	7	6
Kingston 7m.	30	29	30	30	31	31	32	32	32	31	31	30
	22	22	23	24	25	25	26	26	25	25	24	23
	3	2	2	3	5	6	3	6	6	12	5	3
Managua 46m.	30	30	30	32	32	31	31	31	32	31	30	30
	23	24	26	28	27	26	26	25	26	24	24	24
	0	0	0	0	6	12	11	12	15	16	4	1
Mérida 22m.	28	29	32	33	34	33	33	33	32	31	29	28
	17	17	19	21	22	23	23	23	23	22	19	18
	4	2	1	1	5	10	11	12	13	7	3	3
Mexico City 2309m.	19	21	24	25	26	24	23	23	23	21	20	19
	6	6	8	11	12	13	12	12	13	10	8	6
	2	1	2	6	9	14	19	18	17	8	3	2
Monterrey 538m.	20	22	24	29	31	33	32	33	30	27	22	18
	9	11	14	17	20	22	22	22	21	18	13	10
	3	3	3	4	4	4	4	3	8	5	4	4
Nassau 10m.	25	25	27	28	29	31	31	32	31	29	28	26
	17	17	18	20	22	23	24	24	24	22	20	18
	6	5	5	6	9	12	14	14	15	13	9	8
Panama City 36m.	31	31	32	32	31	30	30	31	30	30	29	30
	21	21	22	23	23	23	23	23	23	22	22	23
	4	2	1	6	15	16	15	15	15	16	18	12

	Jan.	Feb.	Mar.	Apr.	May	June	July	Aug.	Sept.	Oct.	Nov.	Dec.
Port-au-Prince 41m.	31 23 3	31 22 5	32 22 7	33 23 11	33 23 13	35 24 8	35 25 7	35 24 11	34 24 12	33 24 12	32 23 7	31 22 3
Port of Spain 12m.	30 20 11	32 21 8	31 21 2	32 21 8	32 23 9	31 23 19	31 23 23	31 23 17	32 23 16	31 22 13	31 22 17	30 21 16
San José 1172m.	24 14 1	24 14 0	26 15 1	27 16 4	27 16 17	27 16 20	26 16 18	26 16 19	27 16 20	26 15 22	25 15 14	24 15 4
San Juan 14m.	27 21 13	27 21 7	27 22 8	28 22 10	29 23 15	29 24 14	29 24 18	29 24 15	30 24 14	30 24 12	28 23 13	27 22 14
San Salvador 700m.	30 16 0	31 16 3	32 17 2	32 19 5	31 19 12	30 19 20	30 18 21	30 18 20	29 19 18	29 18 14	29 17 4	29 16 1
Santo Domingo 14m.	28 20 7	28 19 6	29 20 5	29 21 7	30 22 11	30 23 12	31 23 11	31 23 11	31 23 11	31 23 11	30 22 10	29 21 8
Tegucigalpa 935m.	25 14 4	27 14 2	29 15 1	30 16 3	30 18 14	28 19 18	28 17 10	28 17 10	29 17 17	27 17 16	26 16 8	25 15 4
Willemstad 23m.	28 24 14	29 23 8	29 23 7	30 24 4	30 25 4	31 26 7	31 25 9	31 26 8	32 26 6	31 26 9	30 24 15	29 24 16

SOUTH AMERICA

	Jan.	Feb.	Mar.	Apr.	May	June	July	Aug.	Sept.	Oct.	Nov.	Dec.
Arica 29m.	26 18 0	26 18 0	25 17 0	23 16 0	21 14 0	19 14 0	19 12 0	18 13 0	19 13 0	21 14 0	22 16 0	24 17 0
Asunción 64m.	34 22 7	34 22 6	33 21 9	28 18 7	25 14 5	22 13 4	24 14 4	25 14 4	27 16 6	29 17 6	31 19 6	33 21 7
Bariloche 825m.	21 8 2	21 8 3	18 6 5	14 4 7	10 2 11	7 1 13	6 0 11	8 0 11	10 1 8	11 3 6	16 5 4	18 6 4

CLIMATIC TABLES (Cont.)

SOUTH AMERICA (Cont.)

	Jan.	Feb.	Mar.	Apr.	May	June	July	Aug.	Sept.	Oct.	Nov.	Dec.
Barranquilla 12m.	31	30	32	33	34	33	33	33	33	32	32	30
	22	22	23	24	25	25	25	25	25	24	24	23
	0	0	0	1	4	8	5	6	8	11	6	4
Belém 24m.	31	30	30	31	31	32	32	32	32	32	32	32
	23	23	23	23	23	23	22	22	22	22	22	22
	24	26	25	22	24	15	14	15	13	10	11	4
Belo Horizonte 857m.	27	27	27	27	25	24	24	25	27	27	27	26
	18	18	17	16	12	10	10	12	14	16	17	18
	15	13	9	4	4	2	1	1	2	10	12	14
Bogotá 2560m.	21	21	21	20	20	19	19	19	20	20	20	21
	7	7	9	10	10	9	8	8	8	9	8	7
	9	7	10	18	16	10	8	10	13	18	16	13
Brasília 912m.	27	28	28	28	27	26	26	28	30	29	27	27
	18	18	18	17	15	13	13	14	16	18	18	18
	19	16	15	9	3	1	0	2	4	11	15	20
Buenos Aires 25m.	30	29	26	22	18	15	15	16	18	21	25	29
	18	17	15	12	9	6	6	6	8	11	13	16
	5	5	6	6	4	4	6	6	5	7	7	
Caracas 1035m.	26	26	28	28	28	27	26	27	28	27	27	26
	15	15	16	17	18	18	17	17	17	17	17	16
	4	3	2	4	8	13	13	11	11	11	8	6
Córdoba 425m.	32	31	28	25	21	19	19	20	23	26	28	31
	17	16	14	11	7	4	4	5	8	11	13	16
	8	9	9	6	4	2	2	1	3	7	9	10
Cuzco 3310m.	20	21	21	22	21	21	21	21	22	22	23	22
	7	7	7	4	2	1	−1	1	4	6	6	7
	18	13	11	8	3	2	2	2	7	8	12	16
Guayaquil 6m.	31	31	32	31	31	29	28	29	30	29	30	31
	22	22	23	23	23	21	20	20	20	21	21	22
	12	13	15	10	4	2	0	0	0	1	0	2
La Paz 3632m.	18	18	18	19	17	17	17	17	18	19	19	19
	6	6	6	5	3	2	1	2	3	5	6	6
	21	18	16	9	5	2	2	4	9	9	11	18

	Jan.	Feb.	Mar.	Apr.	May	June	July	Aug.	Sept.	Oct.	Nov.	Dec.
Lima 137m.	25	26	26	24	21	19	17	17	17	19	20	23
	19	20	19	18	16	15	14	13	13	14	16	17
	1	0	0	0	1	1	1	2	1	0	0	0
Manaus 48m.	30	30	30	30	31	31	32	33	33	33	32	31
	23	23	23	23	24	23	23	24	24	24	24	24
	20	18	21	20	18	12	12	5	7	8	12	16
Montevideo 22m.	28	28	26	22	18	15	14	15	17	20	23	26
	17	16	15	12	9	6	6	6	8	9	12	15
	6	5	6	6	6	5	6	7	8	6	6	7
Porto Alegre 10m.	31	30	29	25	22	20	20	21	22	24	27	29
	20	20	19	16	13	11	10	11	13	15	17	18
	9	10	10	6	6	8	8	8	11	10	8	8
Punta Arenas 28m.	15	14	13	9	6	4	3	4	7	10	12	14
	7	7	6	4	2	1	1	1	2	3	4	6
	6	5	7	9	6	8	6	5	5	5	5	8
Quito 2818m.	21	21	20	21	21	21	21	22	22	21	21	21
	8	8	8	8	8	7	7	7	7	8	8	8
	9	11	11	15	10	9	3	3	8	13	13	7
Recife 56m.	30	30	30	30	29	28	27	27	28	29	30	30
	24	25	24	23	23	22	21	21	22	23	24	24
	7	8	10	11	17	16	17	14	7	3	4	4
Rio de Janeiro 30m.	30	30	29	27	26	25	25	25	25	26	28	28
	23	23	23	21	20	18	18	18	19	20	20	22
	13	11	9	9	6	5	5	4	5	11	10	12
Salvador 8m.	29	29	29	28	27	26	26	26	27	28	28	29
	23	23	24	23	22	21	21	21	21	22	23	23
	6	9	17	19	22	23	18	15	10	8	11	11
Santa Cruz de la Sierra 437m.	30	31	30	28	25	23	24	28	29	30	31	31
	21	21	20	19	16	15	15	16	19	20	20	21
	14	10	12	9	11	8	5	4	5	7	8	11
Santiago de Chile 520m.	29	29	27	23	18	14	15	17	19	22	26	28
	12	11	9	7	5	3	3	4	6	7	9	11
	0	0	1	3	5	6	6	5	3	3	1	0
São Paulo 792m.	28	28	27	25	23	22	21	23	25	25	25	26
	18	18	17	15	13	11	10	11	13	14	15	16
	15	13	12	6	3	4	4	3	5	12	11	14

Sources :- H.M.S.O. Meteorological Reports
K.L.M. Climatic Data Publication

STANDARD TIME ZONES

(Expressed as hours behind Greenwich Mean Time)

Argentina	3	Nicaragua	6
Falkland Islands	4	Costa Rica	6
Bolivia	4	Panama	5
Brazil	3*	Cuba	5
Chile	3 (4†)	Haiti	5
Colombia	5	Dominican Republic	4
Ecuador	5	Puerto Rico	4
Paraguay	4 (3†)	Jamaica	5
Peru	5	Barbados	4
Uruguay	3	Trinidad & Tobago	4
Venezuela	4	Leeward Islands	4
Guyana	3¾	Windward Islands	4
Suriname	3½	Bahamas	5 (4**)
Guyane	3	Turks & Caicos Islands	5
Mexico	6‡	Cayman Islands	5
Guatemala	6	Bermuda	4
Belize	6	Virgin Islands	4
El Salvador	6	Netherlands Antilles	4
Honduras	6	French Antilles	4

*Standard time, except for Fernando de Noronha (2); Amazonia W of the Jari and Xingu rivers and E of the Tabatinga-Porto Acre line, and the States of Mato Grosso and Mato Grosso do Sul (4); and Amazonia W of the Tabatinga-Porto Acre line (5).

†Summer time, October-March.

‡Standard time, except for Baja California Sur, Sonora, Sinaloa and Nayarit (7); and Baja California (8).

**Summer time, May-October.

DINERS' CLUB OFFICES

Country	Address	Telephone
Argentina	Sarmiento 667, Buenos Aires	49-2853
Brazil	Rua do Ouvidor 61, Rio de Janeiro	224-1177
Colombia	Calle 31, No. 6-41, Piso 18, Bogotá	32-50-28
Costa Rica	Av. 1a entre Calle 5a y 7a, San José	22-4619
Curaçao	Ahrend-Antilliana N.V. Schottegatweg Oost 134, Willemstad	36058-59
Ecuador	Av. Amazonas 353 (2° piso), Quito	525-354
El Salvador	Alameda Roosevelt y 57 Av. Nte. 3006, San Salvador	23-72-30
Guatemala	Vía 5, 4-50, Local 4-20, Edificio Maya, Zona 4, Guatemala City	60-693
Honduras	3a, Av. No. 527, Tegucigalpa, D.C.	22-64-44
Mexico	Insurgentes Sur 724-2, México 12, D.F.	543.70-20
Nicaragua	Av. Roosevelt 302, Managua	98659
Panama	Edif. Crédito y Servicios 9, Calle 45, Panamá 5, R.P.	64-8422
Peru	Plaza San Martín 930, Lima	287670
Uruguay	Cerrito 461, Piso 1°, Montevideo	85824
Venezuela	Edificio General de Seguros, Av. La Estancia, Chuao, Caracas 101	92-91-11

SHIPPING SERVICES
TO AND FROM LATIN AMERICA

The only passenger vessels plying between Europe and Argentina/Brazil are the Italian Linea C (Costa) ships *Eugenio C* and *Enrico C*.

The following shipping lines operate passenger-carrying (up to 12 people) freighters between Latin America and Europe:

Calmedia Line (agencia Maritima Mundial, Av. Córdoba 653, Buenos Aires), one sailing a month Bs. As.-Genoa, about US$500 p.p. in cabins for 2.

Johnson Line, said to be expensive.

United Yugoslav Lines, takes passengers, but primarily on round-the-world cruise trips.

Cie Générale Maritime/French Line, sailings to Caribbean and Pacific, relatively cheap.

Armement Deppe, sailings to Caribbean, relatively cheap.

Jamaica Line (P.O. Box 167, Kingston).

Blue Star Line.

Greek South-America Line.

Lamport & Holt Line, takes passengers UK-Buenos Aires, about US$470 p.p.

Norwegian South-America Line.

Polish Ocean Line.

Royal Netherlands Line, said to be expensive.

Lloyd Triestino.

The following well-known lines do not take passengers; Shaw Savill, Thos. & Jas. Harrison, F. Laeisz, Hapag-Lloyd, Houlder Line, Saguenay Shipping, Booth Line, Messageries Maritimes, Italian Line.

For information on passenger-carrying freighters consult:

Around the World by Passenger-Carrying Freighter,
Travel Routes around the World,
Harian Publications,
Greenlawn, N.Y. 11740, U.S.A.

Trav-L-Tips,
Freighter Bulletin (US$1 monthly).
163-09 Depot Road,
Flushing, N.Y. 11358, U.S.A.

Freighter Travel News (US$8),
Freighter Club of America,
P.O. Box 504,
Newport, Oregon 97365, U.S.A.

ARGENTINA

Argentine Lines: Empresa Lineas Marítimas Argentinas S.A.

Head Office: Corrientes 389, Buenos Aires, Argentina. Cablegraphic address: "Elma Baires". Telex: 012 2363, 012 2317, 012 2807, 012 2389.

Passenger and Freight Agents: South American Purchasing Agency, Cap House, 9-12 Long Lane (4th Floor), London EC1A 9EP. Tel.: 01-6062 423-28. Telex: 8811925 Deleu.

Regular service of general, liquid, in-bulk and refrigerated loads and containers. Passenger transportation to Europe.

U.S.A. Atlantic Coast and Canada; Gulf of Mexico and Brasil; Caribbean; Cuba; Mediterranean; North of Europe, United Kingdom, Scandinavian and Baltic; West African; Pacific; Japan and Asia.

BELGIUM

Compagnie Maritime Belge (CMB) s.a.

Tel.: 34.05.05. Cables: "Comarbel". Telex: 31366. 61 St. Katelijnevest, Antwerp.
Brazil: Agência Maritima Dickinson, S.A., Rua 15 de de Novembre, 161/3, Santos.
Argentina: Algência Maritima "Marinter" S.R.L., Lavalle 348, Buenos Aires.

South American Line (East Coast): Antwerp, Rotterdam, Bremen and Hamburg to Brazil, Argentina, Uruguay, Paraguay and return.

Armement Deppe s.a. (Group CMB)

Tel.: 34.05.05. Cable: Deppe an. Telex: 31275.

Puerto Rico-Florida-U.S. Gulf Lines: Antwerp, Rotterdam, Bremen, Hamburg and Le Havre to San Juan (Puerto Rico), Jacksonville, Port Everglades, Miami, Tampa, Houston and return.

Line to Mexico and the U.S. Ports of the Gulf of Mexico: Antwerp, Rotterdam, Bremen, Hamburg and Le Havre to Veracruz, Tampico, Coatzacoalcos ("Unimex" Service, Deppe & O/S Lines) and return traffic from the U.S. Ports of the Gulf of Mexico to the European Continent, within the "Unigul" Service (Deppe and O/S Lines).

Line to the Pacific Coast of South America (Eurandino Service: Deppe-CGM-CNP Lines): Antwerp, Rotterdam, Bremen, Hamburg, Le Havre and La Rochelle-La Pallice to Cristobal (Panama), Buenaventura (Colombia), Guayaquil (Ecuador), Callao, Matarani, Paita, Chimbote, Salaverry (Peru), Arica, Tocopilla, Mejilones, Antofagasta, Talcahuano, San Antonio, Valparaiso (Chile)-La Paz (Bolivia) via Chile and/or Peru and return.

Line from Antwerp to Bridgetown (Barbados), Port of Spain (Trinidad) and Georgetown (Guyana)—Saquenay Shipping Ltd.

BRAZIL

Cia. de Navegação Lloyd Brasileiro

Head Office: Rio de Janeiro.

U.K. General Agents: Kersten, Hunik & Co., Ltd., Ibex House, Minories, London EC3N 1EU. Telephone: 01-481 2552. Telex: 886946.

The company operates cargo services between Brazil and the U.S.A., main European, African, Persian Gulf and Far East ports.

CANADA

Saguenay Shipping Limited

1060 University St., Montreal, P.Q., H3B 3A3, Canada.

Services: United Kingdom and Continent to Caribbean—Regular freighter service to Trinidad, Barbados and Guyana. No passengers.

Eastern Canada to Caribbean—Regular freighter service to Barbados, Bermuda, Guyana, Dominican Republic, Jamaica, Leeward and Windward Islands, Haiti, Trinidad and Venezuela.

FRANCE

Compagnie Générale Maritime

Takes the occasional passenger from La Pallice (Marseille).

GERMANY (EAST)

DSR Lines

(VEB Deutfracht Seereederei Rostock), 25 Rostock—Uberseehafen G.D.R. U.K. Agents, Cory Brothers, World Trade Centre, London E1 9AB. Tel.: 01-480 6321.

Services: From, Continent to Rio de Janeiro, Santos, Buenos Aires and Montevideo, with regular monthly sailings. Not all vessels carry passengers, those that do have accommodation for 4 passengers in all 2-berth cabins. All are one class vessels. Normally there is at least one sailing a month from Hamburg or Rotterdam and Antwerp, but the waiting list, particularly for Cuba, is usually long. Fares on application.

GERMANY (WEST)

Reederei W. Bruns & Co.

United Kingdom Passenger Agents: Wainwright Bros. & Co. Ltd., 20 Moorfield High Walk, London EC2Y 9DN.

Ecuador Service: Weekly sailings from Hamburg *via* Jacksonville or Puerto Rico or Curaçao to Cristóbal and Guayaquil. On return voyage vessels proceed direct from Panama Canal to Hamburg. Fully air-conditioned passenger-carrying vessels.

Hamburg-Sud Line

Ost-West Strasse 59, Hamburg, and Rua Frei Gaspar, Santos, Brazil. Regular freight service (every 7-10 days) between Hamburg, Bremen and Rotterdam, and Brazil, Montevideo and Buenos Aires. Accommodation for 12 passengers on the Cap-San-Vessels. One way DM 2,930; round trip DM 5,265.

GREECE

The Greek South America Line

Regular service from Black Sea ports, Piraeus, Adriatic, Genoa, Marseilles and Spanish ports to Rio de Janeiro, Santos, Montevideo and Buenos Aires, returning from Buenos Aires, Montevideo, Rio Grande, Santos, Rio de Janeiro, Bahia and Recife to the ports they set out from. Some passengers taken.

ITALY

Italian Line

Italia di Navigazione S.p.A.—Genova, Italy.
U.K. & Eire Owner's Representative and Booking Office: Italian General Shipping Ltd., 158 Fenchurch Street, London EC3M 6AE. Tel: 01-626 6961. Telex: 886816.
The most comprehensive freight service from Mediterranean to ports of East and West of South America and to Central America.

Linea "C" (Costa Line)

Linea Costa S.p.A.—Genova, Italy.
Passenger-cargo liners calling at Barcelona, Lisbon, Rio de Janeiro, Santos, Buenos Aires. Fares highly competitive with cargo boats; vehicles carried at prices lower than the cargo boats. Accommodation and food etc. highly recommended.

NETHERLANDS

Royal Netherlands Steamship Company
(Koninklijke Nederlandsche Stoomboot-Maatschappij B.V.)

Head Office: "Het Scheepvaarthuis", Prins Hendrikkade 108-114, Amsterdam, The Netherlands. P.O. Box 209. Tel.: 5239111. Telex No. 12202. Tel. Address: "Royal". Agents: Phs. Van Ommeren (London) Ltd., 150 High Street, Southampton SO9 4DN. Tel.: 0703 29051. Telex: 47513.
The Company operates passenger-carrying cargo services from the Continent to the West Coast of South America, with accommodation for 12 passengers.

Nedlloyd Lines

London Agents: Keller, Bryant & Co. Limited, Cereal House, 58 Mark Lane, London EC3R 7LB.

Regular fast cargo sailings from Malaysia, Hong Kong and Japan to Mexico, Central America, Caribbean, West Coast and East Coast South America.

Also South Africa to East Coast South America and V.V.

NORWAY

Den Norske Syd-Amerika Linje

Head Office: Tollbugt. 26 (P.O. Box 316), Oslo 1. (Tel.: 41-14-60.) Regular cargo-passenger service between Norway, Denmark, Canary Is., Brazil, Uruguay and Argentina (sometimes Portugal).

Lauritzen Line

3 or 4 banana boats a year sail between Ecuador (Puerto Bolivar) and New Zealand; will probably take an occasional passenger.

POLAND

Polish Ocean Line

London Agents: Stelp and Leighton Ltd., 238 City Road, London EC1V 2ND.

SWEDEN

Johnson Line

Rederiaktiebolaget Nordstjernan

Head Office: Stureplan 3, Stockholm.

London Agents: A. Johnson & Co. (London) Ltd., Villiers House, Strand, London W.C.2. Tel.: 839/1541.

(Passenger Agency): Villiers House, Strand, W.C.2. Tel.: 930-1384.

Regular services of cargo/passenger ships:

North Pacific: Car Carrier Service, Sweden, Germany, U.K. to Los Angeles, San Francisco, Portland, Seattle and Vancouver.

UNITED KINGDOM

The Bank Line Limited

Head Office: 21 Bury Street, London EC3A 5AU.

Brazil and River Plate Service: Calcutta, Chalna, Chittagong, Trincomalee or Colombo to Rio de Janeiro, Santos, Montevideo and Buenos Aires.

West Coast South American Line: Calcutta, Chalna, Chittagong, Trincomalee or Colombo, Maputo and Durban to Chilean, Peruvian, Ecuadorian and Colombian ports.

Agents: Wilson Sons S.A., Rio de Janeiro. Wilson Sons S.A., Santos. Chadwick Weir Navegación S.A., Montevideo, Chadwick Weir (Navegación) S.R.L., Buenos Aires. Kenric & Cia. Ltda., Valparaiso. Marítima Portena S.A., Callao. S.A. Comercial Anglo Ectoriana, Guayaquil. Eduardo L. Gerlein & Co., S.A., (temporary agency), Bogotá.

Blue Star Line

Head Office: Albion House, 34/35 Leadenhall Street, London EC3A 1AR.

Chief Passenger Agent: Blue Star Travel, 34 Leadenhall Street, London EC3A 1AR.

Irregular departures by "Buenos Aires Star" with accommodation for six passengers only between London, Rio de Janeiro, Santos (occasionally Montevideo) and Buenos Aires. Departures only known about two or three weeks in advance.

Brazil Agencies: Rio de Janeiro: Cia Expresso Mercantil, Agente & Comissaria de Transportes, Av. Rio Branco 25, Caixa Postal 969-ZC-00, Rio de Janeiro. Santos: Companhia Expresso Mercantil, Praça da República 62-14° Caixa Postal 445.

Uruguayan Agents: Montevideo: S.A. Financiera y Comercial, J. R. Williams (Montevideo), Solís 1533. P.O. Box 248.

Argentine Agents: Buenos Aires: Agencia Maritima Mundial S.A., Avenida Córdoba 653, Buenos Aires.

The Booth Steamship Company, Ltd.

Head Office: Albion House, 30 James Street, Liverpool L2 7SX.

Services: Freight only: (1) Liverpool and Dublin to Lisbon, Barbados, Trinidad (Tobago and Leeward and Windward Isles with transhipment), Belém (Pará), Manaus, Itaqui (São Luis), Tutoia Bay for Parnaiba, Fortaleza and to Iquitos (Peru) and Leticia (Colombia).

Fyffes Group Ltd.

Head Office: 1 Queensway, Southampton (A United Brands subsidiary).

Freight services (bananas), and also carry passengers, between USA and Honduras, Costa Rica, Puerto Rico, Dominican Republic, Panama, Colombia, Ecuador and Philippines.

Thos. & Jas. Harrison Ltd.

Head Office: Mersey Chambers, Liverpool L2 8UF.

15 Devonshire Square, London EC2M 4HA.

(a) Fully containerised regular two way services between Bremerhaven, Hamburg, Amsterdam, Zeebrugge, London, Le Havre, Liverpool to Barbados, Curaçao, Aruba, San Juan and Ponce (Puerto Rico), Rio Haina (Sto. Domingo), Port au Prince (Haiti), Kingston (Jamaica), Santo Tomas de Castilla (Guatemala) and Puerto Cortes (Honduras); also St. Martin, St. Croix and St. Thomas *via* Puerto Rico, Grand Cayman *via* Kingston and Liverpool and London to Antigua, St. Kitts, Dominica, St. Lucia, St. Vincent and Montserrat *via* Puerto Rico and Guyana *via* Barbados.

(b) A direct express regular two way fully containerised service from Hamburg, Amsterdam, Tilbury and Liverpool to Port of Spain (Trinidad).

(c) Regular services to and from U.S. Gulf, Mexico, Venezuela, Colombia and Belize.

Lamport & Holt Line Ltd.

Head Office: Albion House, 30 James Street, Liverpool L2 7SY.

Regular services from Liverpool and other U.K. ports, to and from Brazil and River Plate. Takes a few passengers.

Agents: London—Liner Shipping Agencies Ltd., Albion House, Leadenhall Street, E.C.3. Manchester—Liner Shipping Agencies Limited, 567/571 Royal Exchange, Manchester M2 7FF. Rio de Janeiro—Companhia Expresso Mercantil, Avenida Rio Branco 25. Buenos Aires—Agencia Maritima Mundial, S.A., Av. Córdoba 653.

There are agents at all the principal ports of Argentina, Uruguay and Brazil.

The Pacific Steam Navigation Company
(Incorporated by Royal Charter, 1840)

Head Office: Wheelwright House, 157 Regent Road, Liverpool L5 9YF.

Telegrams: Pacific, Liverpool; Telex: 629230; Tel.: 051-922 7222.

Directors: John J. Gawne (Chairman), D. Revel Dick, C.B.E. (Deputy) Chairman), B. P. Shaw, H. Suffield (Managing Director), Capt. O. O. Thomas, S. B. Jones.

Member of Furness Withy Group.

Freight only

United Kingdom to Bermuda, Bahamas, Colombia, Ecuador, Peru and Chile *via* Panama Canal.

Houlder Line
Member of Furness Withy Group

Address: 52 Leadenhall Street, London EC3A 2BJ.
Telegrams: Shawsavill London. Telex: 888487. Tel.: 01-481 2020.

Freight
London, Liverpool, Glasgow, Swansea, Middlesbrough to principal ports in Brazil, Uruguay, Argentia and Paraguay.
Agents in Brazilian ports: Wilson Sons SA.
Agents in Uruguay and Argentina: Houlder Brothers & Co. (Argentina) Ltd.
Agents in Paraguay: Paramar SRL.

Royal Mail Lines Limited
(Incorporated 1929)

Address: Wheelwright House, 157 Regent Road, Liverpool L5 9YF.
Telegrams: Pacific, Liverpool. Telex: 629230. Tel.: 051-922 7222.
Directors: John J. Gawne (Chairman), H. Suffield, B. P. Shaw, D. R. Dick, E. M. Rose, O. O. Thomas.
Member of Furness Withy Group.

Freight only
Managed from Liverpool: United Kingdom to Kingston (Jamaica), Cartagena, Cristóbal, Panama and Pacific ports of Costa Rica, Nicaragua, Honduras, El Salvador and Guatemala.

Managed from London: Address: 52 Leadenhall Street, London EC3A 2BJ. London, Liverpool, Glasgow, Swansea, Middlesbrough to principal ports in Brazil, Uruguay, Argentina and Paraguay.

UNITED STATES

Transportes Interoceanos Centroamericanos. S.A.

TICA Line, has bi-weekly runs between New York, Cristóbal, Puerto Limón, Puerto Barrios, and Puerto Cortés.

Lykes Bros. Steamship Co., Inc.

Lykes Center, New Orleans, La. 70130.
Modern, air-conditioned cargo liners with accommodation for 12 passengers in 6 double rooms or for 4 in 2 double rooms, each with private bath: New Orleans, Canal Zone, Buenaventura, Guayaquil, Callao, Matarani, Arica, Antofagasta, Valparaíso, and possibly others. One way passage to Valparaíso, about 20 days; round trip, about 40 days.

AIRLINES SERVING LATIN AMERICA AND THE CARIBBEAN

FROM EUROPE

Prefix

AR	Areolíneas Argentinas
AM	Areoméxico
IW	Air Bahamas
AF	Air France
JM	Air Jamaica
AZ	Alitalia
AV	Avianca (Colombia)
BA	British Airways
BR	British Caledonian Airways
BW	British West Indian Airways (BWIA)
IQ	International Caribbean Airways
IB	Iberia
KL	K.L.M.
LA	Lan-Chile
LH	Lufthansa
PA	Pan American Airways
QF	Qantas
SN	Sabena
SK	Scandinavian Airlines (S.A.S.)
SR	Swissair
TP	T.A.P. (Portugal)
RG	Varig (Brazil)
VA	Viasa (Venezuela)

Flights between Europe and Cuba

SU	Aeroflot
CU	Cubana
OK	C.S.A. (Ceskoslovenske Aerolinie)

(We are most grateful to Monty Geduld for supplying this list)

FROM NORTH AMERICA

Prefix

OD	Aerocóndor (Colombia)
AR	Aerolíneas Argentinas
AM	Aeroméxico
AC	Air Canada
AF	Air France
JM	Air Jamaica
OP	Air Panamá Internacional
LM	A.L.M. (Netherlands Antilles)
AA	American Airlines
AV	Avianca (Colombia)
GU	Aerolíneas de Guatemala
UP	Bahamas Air (formerly Out Island Airways, Flamingo Airlines)
BN	Braniff International Airways
BA	British Airways
BW	British West Indian Airways (BWIA)
CP	Canadian Pacific-Air
CB	Caribair
DL	Delta Airlines
DO	Dominicana de Aviación
EA	Eastern Airlines
EU	Ecuatoriana de Aviación
RW	Hughes Airwest
KL	K.L.M.
LR	Lasca (Costa Rica)
LA	Lan-Chile
NI	Lanica (Nicaragua)
LH	Lufthansa
MI	Mackey International Air Lines
MX	Mexicana de Aviación
PA	Pan American Airways
SH	Sahsa (Honduras)
SA	South African Airways
TA	Taca International Airlines
TX	Tan Airlines
TT	Texas International Airlines
RG	Varig (Brazil)
VA	Viasa (Venezuela)
WA	Western Airlines

Uniform with this volume: completely revised and augmented

The Gulf Handbook
A Guide for Businessmen and Visitors
3rd Edition—1979

Joint Editors: PETER KILNER and JONATHAN WALLACE

This hard-back annual guide to the Gulf States was first
published in the autumn of 1976. The editorial preparation of
THE GULF HANDBOOK is backed by the experience and
information resources of the 'Middle East Economic Digest' and
'Arab Report & Record'. Great interest has been expressed by
various ministries, government offices, trade associations and
businessmen who again have promised full support on this
important publication. Businessmen and tourists who intend
visiting the Gulf cannot afford to be without THE GULF
HANDBOOK. Write for prospectus.

ISBN 0 900751 07 X

Joint Publishers:

Trade & Travel Publications Ltd.
The Mendip Press, Parsonage Lane,
Bath BA1 1EN, England

and

The Middle East Economic Digest Ltd.
21 John Street, London WC2A 1DL

INDEX TO ADVERTISERS

INDEX TO PLACES

1202

NOTES

THOMAS COOK TRAVELLERS CHEQUES
EMERGENCY ASSISTANCE POINTS

City	Agent	Address	Phone
SOUTH AMERICA			
Argentina			
Buenos Aires	Wagon-Lits	Avenida Còrdoba 746	392-5054
Rosario	Wagon-Lits	Calle Còrdoba 1307 (local 12)	63778
Bolivia			
La Paz	Wagon-Lits	Av. Mariscal Santa Cruz esq. Colon	58499
Brazil			
Aracaju	Banco do Brasil	Praça Gen, Valadão 341	222-0234
Belém	Banco do Brasil	Av. Pres. Vargas 248	223-5291
Belo Horizonte	Banco Europeu	Av. Augusto de Lima 158	222-7979
Blumenau	Banco do Brasil	Rua XV de Novembro 1525	22-3144
Brasilia	Banco Europeu	Edif. JK, loja 3, SCS	226-7763
Campinas	Banco Itaú	Rua Dr. Costa Aguia 616	2-4611
Curitiba	Banco Itaú	Rua Mal. Deodoro 235	24-0869
Florianôpolis	Banco do Brasil	Praça XV de Novembro 20	22-7000
Fortaleza	Banco do Brasil	Rua Barão do Rio Branco 1515	226-7710
Foz do Iguaçu	Banco do Brasil	Avenida Brasil 1365	72-3344
Ilheus	Banco do Brasil	Rua Marques de Paranagua 112	231-1218
Itabuna	Banco do Brasil	Praça Olintho Leoni	211-5321
Itajaí	Banco do Brasil	Rua Felipe Schmitt 454	44-2602
João Pessoa	Banco Itaú	Praça 1817, 129	221-2203
Joinville	Banco Itaú	Rua do Principe 367	22-3571
Maceió	Banco do Brasil	Rua Senador Mendonça 120	223-2489
Manaus	Banco do Estado do Amazonas	Av. 7 de Setembro 867	234-2287
Natal	Banco do Brasil	Avenida Rio Branco 510	222-5411
Pelotas	Banco do Brasil	Rua Lobo da Costa 1315	22-7240
Porto Alegre	Banco Europeu	Rua Jose Montauri 155	24-4147
Recife	Banco do Brasil	Avenida Rio Branco 240	224-5487
Rio de Janeiro	Banco Bozano Simonsen	Av. Rio Branco 138	224-4164
Rio Grande	Banco do Brasil	Rua Benjamin Constant 72	2-1001
Salvador	Banco Cidade	Rua Conselheiro Dantas 7	242-1675
Santana do Livramento	Banco do Brasil	Rua das Andradas 525	242-2156
Santos	Banco do Brasil	Rua XV de Novembro 195	34-4496
São José dos Campos	Banco do Brasil	Agência Central	21-3644
São Paulo			
Centre	Banco Francês e Brasileiro	Rua XV de Novembro 268	239-2811
Paulista	Midland Bank Group	Rua Bela Cintra 940—10th	259-3022
Teresina	Banco do Brasil	Rua Alvaro Mendes 1313	—
Vitória	Banco do Brasil	Praça Pio XII, 30	223-4763
Chile			
Santiago	Steinsapir y Cia.	Agustinas 1028	89257
Colombia			
Bogotá	Wagons-Lits	Carrera 5, 15-89	41-9250
Cali	Banco Royal	—	—
Medellin	Wagons-Lits	Calle 52, 47-48, Local 108	31-8332
Ecuador			
Guayaquil	Banco Holandes	9 de Octubre 419 y Chile	51-1120
Quito	Banco Holandes	10 de Agosto 911 y Buenos Aires	52-4200
Falkland Islands			
Stanley	Falkland Islands Company		—
Guyana			
Georgetown	Royal Bank of Canada	38-39 Water Street	64091
Peru			
Callao	Ricardo Segale S.A.	Pasaje Rios 125-139	90316
Cuzco	Wagons-Lits	Calle Heladeros 157	2152
Lima	Banco de Lima	Esq. Carabaya y Puno	27-5860

City	Agent	Address	Phone
Uruguay			
Montevideo	Wagons-Lits	Calle Rio Negro 1356	91-1426
Venezuela			
Caracas	Wagons-Lits	Av. Urdaneta 33/2	561-2473
Maracaibo	Banco de Maracaibo	Av. 5 de Julio Esq. Av. 12	75427
Valencia	Wagons-Lits	Edif. Hotel de Paris, local 7, Av. Bolivar	21-3965

CENTRAL AMERICA

City	Agent	Address	Phone
Costa Rica			
San José	Chase SA	—	—
Guatemala			
Guatemala	Wagons-Lits	Av. Reforma 12-81 Zona 10	31-5364
Panama			
Panama	Banco Sudameris	Via España y Calle Colombia	64-9222
Mexico			
Acapulco	Wagons-Lits	Avenida Costera Miguel Alemán 239	22864
Mexico City	Wagon-Lits	Avenida Juarez 88	518-1180

WEST INDIES

City	Agent	Address	Phone
Bahamas			
Nassau	Royal Bank of Canada	323 Bay Street	322-8700
Barbados			
Bridgetown	Royal Bank of Canada	Broad Street	65-200
Cayman Islands			
George Town	Cayman National Bank	—	—
Dominican Republic			
Puerto Plata	Royal Bank of Canada		
Santo Domingo	Royal Bank of Canada	Isabela La Catolica 50A	689-7111
Grenada			
St. George's	Royal Bank of Canada	Yonge Street	2196
Guadeloupe			
Pointe-a-Pitre	Royal Bank of Canada (France)	—	—
Haiti			
Port-au-Prince	Royal Bank of Canada	Rue Abraham Lincoln and Rue des Miracles No. 18	2-2123
Jamaica			
Kingston	Royal Bank Jamaica	37 Duke Street	932-6710
Montego Bay	Royal Bank Jamaica	—	—
Martinique			
Fort-de-France	Credit Martiniquais	Rue de la Liberté	71-1240
Netherlands Antilles			
Curaçao	Algemene Bank Nederland	Pietermaaiweg 17	11488
Puerto Rico			
San Juan	Travel Services Inc.	—	—
St. Lucia			
Castries	St. Lucia Coop Bank	21 Bridge Street	—
St Vincent			
Kingstown	Royal Bank of Canada	—	61-502
Trinidad & Tobago			
Arima	National Commercial Bank	Ridgewood Plaza	—
Port of Spain	National Commercial Bank	60 Independence Square	—
San Fernando	National Commercial Bank	—	—

IMPORTANT NOTE In most of these cities there are many other banks which handle Thomas Cook Travellers Cheques which would also be pleased to assist. For direct assistance from Thomas Cook Bankers, contact Jacques Arnold, Regional Manager for Latin America, P.O. Box 36, Peterborough, England (telephone 0733-502863, telex 32581, telegrams COOKBANKER, PETERBOROUGH, U.K.).

e